ISBN 978-0-332-10082-1
PIBN 11018012

CHRISTOPHER COLUMBUS.

APPLETONS'

ANNUAL CYCLOPÆDIA

AND

REGISTER OF IMPORTANT EVENTS

OF THE YEAR

1892.

EMBRACING POLITICAL, MILITARY, AND ECCLESIASTICAL AFFAIRS; PUBLIC
DOCUMENTS; BIOGRAPHY, STATISTICS, COMMERCE, LITERA-
TURE, SCIENCE, AGRICULTURE, AND MECHANICAL INDUSTRY.

NEW SERIES, VOL. XVII.

WHOLE SERIES, VOL. XXXII.

NEW YORK:
D. APPLETON AND COMPANY,
1, 3, AND 5 BOND STREET.
1893.

CHRISTOPHER COLUMBUS.

APPLETONS'

ANNUAL CYCLOPÆDIA

AND

REGISTER OF IMPORTANT EVENTS

OF THE YEAR

1892.

EMBRACING POLITICAL, MILITARY, AND ECCLESIASTICAL, AFFAIRS; PUBLIC
DOCUMENTS; BIOGRAPHY, STATISTICS, COMMERCE, FINANCE, LITERA-
TURE, SCIENCE, AGRICULTURE, AND MECHANICAL INDUSTRY.

NEW SERIES, VOL. XVII.

WHOLE SERIES, VOL. XXXII.

NEW YORK:
D. APPLETON AND COMPANY,
I, 3, AND 5 BOND STREET.
1893.

PREFACE.

THE great topic of the year, the World's Columbian Exposition, is treated in this volume in an article of liberal proportions, with half a dozen tinted illustrations showing the more important buildings. This, together with the illustrated article in the last volume of the "Annual Cyclopædia," will perhaps give as good an idea of the great fair as can be had without a visit to Chicago. The sums appropriated for State displays, buildings, etc., may be found generally in the articles on the several States. The census articles in the volumes for 1890 and 1891 are supplemented in the present volume, which gives the latest results reached by the compilers at the Census Office on the most important subjects. The interesting story of the building of a great Navy for the United States is here brought down to time in a brief article contributed by a naval officer. Other particulars of the growth of our country may be read not only in the article "United States," but in the articles "Commerce and Navigation," "Financial Review of 1892," and "United States Finances," and in a peculiar manner in the article "Shipping on the Great Lakes." What we are likely soon to acquire by way of annexation may be read in the article "Hawaiian Islands," which is illustrated with a new colored map. Many items indicating industrial growth are to be found also in the articles on the States and Territories.

Our Canadian articles, written, as usual, by residents of Canada, are illustrated this year by a new colored map of the Province of Quebec. This, together with the maps in volumes immediately preceding, makes a complete cartography of the Dominion of Canada, of the most recent date. Newfoundland is treated by the eminent historian of that island, the Rev. Moses Harvey, and the article includes an account of the great fire in St. John's, and is illustrated with a full-page view of that city and its harbor.

The articles on the great sciences are full and brought down to time, as usual. Dr. Swift, of Warner Observatory, treats the subject "Astronomy"; Dr. Youmans, of "The Popular Science Monthly," treats "Chemistry," "Metallurgy," "Meteorology," and "Physiology"; Arthur E. Bostwick, Ph. D., treats "Physics"; and much may be learned as to the general progress of the sciences from a perusal of the article "Associations for the Advancement of Science." The geographical progress of the year is treated in the article under that title.

The necessarily rapid survey of the year's work in the production of books may be found, as usual, in the articles on American, British, and Continental literature; while more particular discussion of specific literary work is contained in articles on famous authors who have passed away during the year.

The States articles, which are always important, are especially interesting this year because of the peculiar movements in politics, which are set forth with more particularity there than elsewhere. The subjects of educational progress and penal reform may also be studied through these records.

Among South American articles the greatest interest attaches to Venezuela, and we have given liberal space to an account of the revolution in that country.

The articles on the great religious denominations are full and carefully prepared as usual, many of them by writers belonging to the particular communion treated. The Rev. Solomon E. Ochsenford furnishes the article on the Lutherans; Dr. Abram S. Isaacs, editor of the "Jewish Messenger," that on the Jews; Austin E. Ford, editor of the "Freeman's Journal," that on the "Roman Catholic Church"; William H. Larrabee, that on "Methodists"; and Jesse A. Spencer, D. D., that on the "Protestant Episcopal Church."

The work of Congress during the year, with the significant portions of the debates on all important bills, is recorded, as usual, under the title of "Congress." The peculiar value of this article lies in the fact that it is arranged topically, and conveniently subheaded, so that all the information on any given subject may be found at once and read continuously without break or cross-reference.

The special articles in the present volume include one on "Christopher Columbus," in which the whole story of his life and voyages is briefly but interestingly told. This article forms a valuable introduction to the account of the great fair. The subject of "Cholera in 1892" is treated by an expert, Dr. Morris S. French, of Philadelphia, who also writes of "Diphtheria." Another special article on a subject important at this time is that on "Sugar," furnished by James B. T. Tupper, Chief of Sugar Bounty Division, Office of Internal Revenue. There is also an article on "Pipe Lines," illustrated with a map. The special articles include, furthermore, one on the "American Society of Church History," one on the "Free Evangelical Congress," one on the "Industrial Legion," one on the "Knights of Industry," and one on "Profit-Sharing," besides that on "American Cities," which this year treats of thirty-seven.

Among the eminent dead of the year, whose lives are sketched in this volume, with portraits and other illustrations, are Tennyson, the Poet Laureate of England; John Greenleaf Whittier, perhaps the most distinctively American of our poets; Walt Whitman, one of the most peculiar of all poets; George William Curtis, the graceful writer and orator; Cyrus W. Field, originator of the Atlantic telegraph; Caroline Scott Harrison, mistress of the White House; Ernest Renan, the French scholar and author; Cardinal Henry E. Manning; Charles H. Spurgeon, the most popular of all preachers; and a long array of less noted names which will be found among the "Obituaries, American and Foreign."

The illustrations, besides the colored maps and tinted views, include three full-page portraits—Columbus, Tennyson, and Whittier—many fine vignette portraits in the text, and the usual number of miscellaneous engravings.

An excellent index, covering not only the present volume but also the four that precede it, closes the book.

NEW YORK, *April 15, 1893*.

CONTRIBUTORS.

Among the Contributors to this Volume of the "Annual Cyclopædia" are the following:

Oscar Fay Adams,
Author of "Life of Jane Austen."
FREEMAN, EDWARD A.,
LONGFELLOW, SAMUEL,
MANNING, HENRY E.,
PARSONS, THOMAS W.,
and other articles.

George N. Babbitt.
NEW BRUNSWICK.

Marcus Benjamin, Ph. D.
NEWBERRY, JOHN S.,
NEW YORK STATE,
PHARMACY,
and other articles.

J. H. A. Bone,
Of Cleveland Plaindealer.
OHIO.

Arthur E. Bostwick, Ph. D.
PHYSICS.

Rev. James M. Bruce.
CHARLES H. SPURGEON.

Thomas Campbell-Copeland.
UNITED STATES CENSUS,
WORLD'S COLUMBIAN EXPOSITION.

James P. Carey,
Financial Editor of Journal of Commerce.
FINANCIAL REVIEW OF 1892.

Hon. Benjamin F. Clayton.
FARMERS' CONGRESS.

Mrs. Bessie Nicholls Croffut.
LITERATURE, AMERICAN,
LITERATURE, BRITISH.
and articles in "Cities, American."

Austin E. Ford,
Editor of Freeman's Journal.
ROMAN CATHOLIC CHURCH.

Miss Lillie Hamilton French.
IDAHO,
IOWA,
MARYLAND,
MISSOURI,
and other articles.

Morris S. French, M. D.
CHOLERA IN 1892.
DIPHTHERIA.

Mrs. Fredericka B. Gilchrist.
VIRGINIA,
WISCONSIN.

Rev. William E. Griffis, D. D.,
Author of "The Mikado's Empire."
JAPAN.

George J. Hagar,
Of New Jersey Historical Society.
OBITUARIES, AMERICAN.

Col. Pierce S. Hamilton,
Late of Canadian Census Office.
BRITISH COLUMBIA,
DOMINION OF CANADA,
MANITOBA,
NOVA SCOTIA,
ONTARIO,
QUEBEC.

Rev. Moses Harvey,
Author of "Text-Book of Newfoundland History."
NEWFOUNDLAND.

Frank Huntington.
AFGHANISTAN,
AUSTRIA-HUNGARY,
BOLIVIA,
BULGARIA,
CHILI,
COSTA RICA,
DENMARK,
EGYPT,
GREAT BRITAIN,
RENAN, ERNEST,
SPAIN,
and other articles.

Abram S. Isaacs, Ph. D.,
Editor of Jewish Messenger.
JEWS.

Mrs. Helen Kendrick Johnson.
COLUMBUS, CHRISTOPHER,
CURTIS, GEORGE WILLIAM,
HARRISON, CAROLINE SCOTT,
TENNYSON, ALFRED,
and other articles.

William H. Larrabee.
ANGLICAN CHURCHES,
CONGREGATIONALISTS,
CHRISTIAN ENDEAVOR,
CHURCH HISTORY, AMERICAN SOCIETY OF,
DISCIPLES OF CHRIST,
FREE EVANGELICAL CONGRESS,
FRIENDS,
METHODISTS,
PRESBYTERIANS,
REUNION OF CHURCHES,
  and other articles.

Frederic G. Mather.
INDUSTRIAL LEGION,
KNIGHTS OF INDUSTRY,
PIPE LINES,
PROFIT SHARING,
RECEIVER,
SHIPPING ON THE GREAT LAKES,
UPSON, ANSON J.,
WOOD PULP,
  and other articles.

Col. Charles L. Norton,
  Author of "Political Americanisms."
ENGINEERING,
PATENTS,
  and other articles.

Rev. Solomon E. Ochsenford.
LUTHERANS,
MANN, WILLIAM JULIUS.

Mrs. Evangeline M. O'Connor.
COLORADO,
DELAWARE,
GEOGRAPHICAL PROGRESS,
INDIANA,
KENTUCKY,
MICHIGAN,
OREGON,
TENNESSEE,
  and other articles.

Thomas B. Preston.
STEVENSON, ADLAI E.

Mrs. Mary J. Reid.
SWINTON, WILLIAM.

J. E. Robinson.
ROBINSON, WILLIAM E.

William Christopher Smith.
ARIZONA,
ARKANSAS,
CONNECTICUT,
KANSAS,
MASSACHUSETTS,
MISSISSIPPI,
MONTANA,
NEVADA,
NORTH DAKOTA,
OKLAHOMA,
RHODE ISLAND,
TEXAS,
VERMONT,
  and other articles.

Rev. Jesse A. Spencer, D. D.
PROTESTANT EPISCOPAL CHURCH.

Arthur Stedman,
  Editor of "Selections from Whitman."
WALT WHITMAN.

Lewis Swift, LL. D.,
  Director of Warner Observatory.
ASTRONOMY, PROGRESS OF, IN 1892.

James B. T. Tupper,
  Chief of Sugar Bounty Division, Internal Revenue
    Office.
SUGAR.

J. Kendrick Upton,
  Of United States Census Office.
UNITED STATES, FINANCES OF THE.

Lewis S. Van Duzer, U. S. N.
NAVY OF THE UNITED STATES.

Frank Weitenkampf,
  Of the Astor Library.
LITERATURE, CONTINENTAL.

William J. Youmans, M. D.,
  Editor of Popular Science Monthly.
CHEMISTRY,
METALLURGY,
METEOROLOGY,
PHYSIOLOGY.

ILLUSTRATIONS.

FULL-PAGE PORTRAITS.

PORTRAITS IN THE TEXT.

DRAWN BY JACQUES REICH.

FULL-PAGE ILLUSTRATIONS.

ILLUSTRATIONS IN THE TEXT.

THE
ANNUAL CYCLOPÆDIA.

A

ABYSSINIA, an empire in eastern Africa. The Emperor, called the Negus Negusti, is Menelek II, who assumed the sovereignty when the Negus Johannis II was killed in a battle with the dervishes of the Soudan in 1889. The system of government is feudalistic. Justice is administered by the governors of provinces and local chiefs. The Abyssinians have been Christians since the fourth century. They worship according to the rites of the Alexandrian Church. The *abuna*, or ecclesiastical head, is a Copt, who is nominated and consecrated by the Patriarch of Alexandria. The *echeghegh,* a native dignitary, shares his power and influence. Education is mostly confined to religious exercises, and is imparted gratuitously by the clergy to a limited number of persons, whose attainments secure them a considerable degree of consequence. The monks, who number about 12,000, are under the spiritual rule of the *echeghegh.* Besides the feudal levies the Emperor has an army of *wotloader,* or mercenaries, who are armed with modern firearms. The people raise large numbers of cattle, but give little attention to agriculture. The empire is made up of the kingdoms of Tigre, with Lasta; Amhara. which includes Gojam; Shoa; and the territories of the Bogos, Shoho, Mensa, Berea, Kunama, Habab, Beni Amer, Shankalla, Afar, and Adal. The area of the empire proper is estimated at 190,000 square miles, and the population at 5,000,000. The outlying tributary territories have an area of about 120,000 square miles, and probably 600,000 inhabitants. The country produces indigo, coffee, cotton, sugar, dates, and grapes, and the forests abound in useful timber and other products. Massowah is the only seaport. The chief exports are ivory, skins, gums, butter, and mules. The metallic currency consists of Maria Theresa dollars, besides which salt and cloth are used as money. There are many towns, though none have more than 5,000 inhabitants, except Ankober, the ancient capital Aksum, and Gondar.

The Italian Protectorate.—By international agreement, the Empire of Abyssinia or Ethiopia and the outlying territories are conceded to Italy, and form the Italian sphere of influence in Africa. The Anglo-Italian arrangement gives Italy a coast-line on the Red Sea of about 670 miles, extending from Cape Kasar, in 18° 2' of north latitude, to the southern limit of the sultanate of Raheita, in 12° 30' of north latitude. In Somaliland and Gallaland, about 70,000 square miles, with an estimated population of 210,000, comprise the Italian sphere south and southeast of Abyssinia proper. On the flat seaboard fronting the Abyssinian plateau the territory of Affar or Danakil, with the sultanate of Aussa, embraces 34,000 square miles, with about 200,000 inhabitants. In the north the Italian protectorate extends over 18,000 square miles, peopled by 200,000 natives belonging to the Beni Amer, Bogos, and Habab tribes. Menelek, who accepted Italian aid when he was fighting for the throne, and who signed a treaty acknowledging Italian protection, has since repudiated this engagement. In Somaliland and Gallaland the Italians have done nothing to make the protectorate effective, except in one or two of the coast stations formerly administered by the Sultan of Zanzibar and formally ceded by him to the Italian Government. The possessions actually held and garrisoned by Italy consist of the port of Massowah. with 3,100 square miles of country, including Keren and Asmara, formerly claimed by the Emperor of Abyssinia, having a population of 250,000; the Dahlak archipelago embracing 420 square miles, with 2,000 inhabitants; and the territory on Assab bay, opposite the British colony of Aden, with an area of 580 square miles and 6,800 inhabitants. From Massowah, which is the only seaport accessible to Abyssinia, a certain degree of influence is exercised not only over the Habab, Beni Amer, and other neighboring independent tribes, but into the northern parts of Abyssinia. The Italian possessions are organized into a colony, to which the name of Evitrea has been given, having an autonomous administration and the management of its own revenues. The town of Massowah contains 16,000 civil inhabitants, of whom 500 are Italians. 50 other Europeans, 700 Greeks, and 100 Indian Banian merchants. The revenue of the colony was estimated for 1890-'91 at 1,313,300 lire or francs, of which 1,056,000 was derived from customs and the remainder from taxes. The expenditure was estimated at 2,960,000 lire, the deficit falling as a burden on the Italian treasury. Little land is cultivated in the Italian colony. The people raise camels, cattle, sheep, and goats, and meat, hides, and butter are exported. At Massowah and in the Dahlak archipelago pearls are raised of the value of from 400,000 to 600,000 lire a year, and about 200,000 lire worth of mother-of-pearl is exported. The total imports of Massowah for 1890 were 14,981,041 lire. In 1889 the number of vessels entered was 2,242, of 215,955 tons, and the number cleared was 2,519, of 219,712 tons. There were 1,535 Italian ships entered and 1,585 cleared.

AFGHANISTAN, a monarchy in central Asia. The ruling prince, called the Ameer, is Abdurrahman Khan, a son of Afzul Khan and grandson of Dost Mohammed. He was recognized as Ameer by the British in July, 1880, after their invasion and temporary occupation of the country and the expulsion of Shere Ali. The Oxus is recognized in an international arrangement between Great Britain and Russia as the northern boundary of Afghanistan from the place where it rises in the Pamir to Kamiab, and thence a boundary line has been surveyed and marked by an Anglo-Russian delimitation commission westward to Zulfikar, on the Persian frontier. The country is about 600 miles long and 500 broad at the widest part. The military system is feudal; but besides the tribal levies the Ameer has a regular army formed on the European pattern. The number of active troops in 1890 was 50.000. Afghanistan exports fruits and nuts and large quantities of asafœtida to India, and manufactures silk, felts, and carpets.

Tension between the Ameer and Great Britain.—While the Indian Government has constantly warned the Ameer against attempting to annex the districts between India and Afghanistan which he claims, and has supported the independent tribes in their determination to resist him, and thus encouraged them in their raids on the Afghan territory, the hill tribes on the side toward India are being steadily subjugated and swallowed up by the British, who have refused the Ameer's request for a delimitation of the frontier, in order that they may thus possess themselves gradually of the territories over which the Afghan rulers are unable to exercise effective dominion. The terminus of the railroad from Quetta to the Afghan frontier was placed beyond the fortified post at Chaman on land that Abdurrahman claimed was on his side of the boundary. For this reason, when the Indian Government treated his remonstrances with indifference, he refused to allow connections to be established between Afghanistan and the railroad, and, as his people sustained him in his position, the trade fell off, and a decided coolness arose in his relations with the Indian Government. He was aroused to a determination to rectify the indeterminate frontier, and thus prevent his country from being eaten up piecemeal. Gholam Hyder, his principal general. was sent, in December, 1891, to occupy the Mohmund town and state of Asmar, on the frontier of Kafiristan. The town lies halfway between Jelalabad and Chitral, about sixty-five miles northeast of the former. The late chief of Asmar, Shah Tahmasp Khan, being dissatisfied with his reception at a durbar given by Lord Dufferin at Peshawur in 1887, accepted the protection of Abdurrahman. After his murder a year later,

Umra Khan, of the neighboring state of Jandol, was encouraged to attempt the conquest of Asmar. In order to support the son of the late ruler, Gholam Hyder marched with an army against Umra Khan. At the same time Abdurrahman dispatched some of his tribal levies against the Turis of the Kuram valley, who had received a promise of protection from the British for the assistance they had rendered in the last Afghan war. The Afghan general was successful in his first engagement with Umra Khan, but afterward lost a battle, and was hard pressed and forced to send to Jelalabad for re-enforcements. At this juncture the Indian Government intervened diplomatically, and warned the Ameer not to molest Umra Khan further. Nevertheless Gholam attacked him again and made himself master of Asmar, and thus of the Dora Pass, which leads through the Pamir into Chitral. British troops were then sent to the frontier to prevent further extension of the Afghan power. A formidable rebellion in the center of Afghanistan prevented the Ameer from consolidating his position and compelling a delimitation of the Indo-Afghan frontier.

The Hazara Rebellion.—The numerous and warlike Hazara tribes, which occupy the central and most inaccessible parts of Afghanistan, as well as some districts in the north, have chafed more than other tribes under Abdurrahman's iron system of taxation and military levies, to which the people of Afghanistan have never been accustomed, but which the British subsidy and gifts of arms have enabled him to establish through a great part of northern and central Afghanistan. The Hazaras are of different origin from the Afghans, and their racial antipathy is heightened by religious differences, since they are mostly Shiites, while the pure Afghans are fanatical Sunnites.

ALABAMA, a Southern State, admitted to the Union Dec. 14, 1819; area, 52,250 square miles. The population, according to each decennial census since admission, was 127,901 in 1820; 309.527 in 1830; 590,756 in 1840; 771,623 in 1850; 964,-201 in 1860; 996,992 in 1870; 1,262,505 in 1880; and 1,513,017 in 1890. Capital, Montgomery.

Government.—The following were the State officers during the year: Governor, Thomas G. Jones, Democrat; Secretary of State, J. D. Barron; Treasurer, John L. Cobbs; Auditor, Cyrus D. Hogue; Attorney-General, William L. Martin; Superintendent of Public Instruction, John B. Harris; Commissioner of Agriculture, Hector D. Lane; Railroad Commissioners, Henry R. Shorter, Levi W. Lawler, who died early in September, and Wiley C. Tunstall; Chief Justice of the Supreme Court, George W. Stone; Associate Justices, David Clopton. who died on Feb. 5, and was succeeded by William S. Thorington, Thomas N. McClellan, Thomas W. Coleman, and R. W. Walker.

Finances.—For the fiscal year ending Sept. 30, 1891, the total receipts of the State treasury, including a balance of $332,561.17 on hand at the beginning of the year, were $1,949,945.74, and the total disbursements were $1,773,906.34, leaving a balance of $176,039.40 at the close of the year. Of this balance only the sum of $37,-358.17 is available for general State expenses. Included in the receipts were $968,112.27 from general State taxes. $150,929.37 from poll taxes, $158,784.74 from licenses, $116,942.33 from hire of convicts, $52,492.33 from the Agricultural Commissioner, $30,159.55 from solicitors' fees, and $48,000 from the United States for agricultural colleges. Among the expenditures were $623,405.27 for educational purposes, $376,356 for interest on the debt, $122,557.50 for the Hospital for the Insane, $76,503.70 for feeding prisoners, $23,484.32 for military expenses, and $18,375 for public printing.

The total bonded State debt on Sept. 30, 1891, was $9,293,400, on which the annual interest is $377,516. The tax rate is 4 mills for general State expenses, and ½ mill for Confederate pensions.

The total assessed valuation of property in 1891 was $271,953,321, of which $160,685,753 represents real estate, and $111,267,568 personal estate, including railroad property. The increase over the valuation of 1890 is $12,973,746. The valuation of railroad property alone was $46,-797,928.26, an increase of $3,459,146.79 over 1890.

Lumber.—Nearly all the large product of the south Alabama forests passes through Mobile. The total exports of lumber and timber from this place for the year ending Aug. 30 were as follow: Lumber—shipped coastwise in vessels, 22,780,789 feet; shipped foreign in vessels, 38,-318,106 feet; railroad shipments, 8,200,000 feet; towed to the islands in the harbor, 38,000 feet; total, 69,338,895 feet. Timber—shipped in vessels, 60,865,056 feet; towed to the islands, 4,091,478 feet; total. 64,956,534 feet. About 175,000,000 shingles were exported during the same year, and 147,000 staves. These figures show an increase over previous years. During the year the harbor of Mobile has been deepened and improved by dredging, so that it is nearly capable of receiving vessels of 1,500 tons when loaded to their full capacity.

Freshet.—Early in July owing to heavy rains, the Bigbee and Noxubee rivers overflowed their banks, and many people in Sumter County were driven from their homes, their crops were destroyed, and their means of subsistence were taken away. Nearly 2,000 people were affected by the flood, which exceeded anything theretofore known in that region. On learning these facts, Gov. Jones issued a proclamation on July 12, calling for contributions from the people of the State. The money so obtained was applied by the county authorities.

The Colored Race.—At a conference of colored people residing in the "black belt," so called, held at Tuskegee, on Feb. 23, the subject of the condition of the race was discussed at length, and an address or statement of their condition and purposes was issued, from which the following is an extract:

Industrially considered, most of our people are dependent upon agriculture. The majority of them live on rented lands, mortgage their crops for food on which to live from year to year, and usually at the beginning of each year are more or less in debt for the supplies of the previous year.

In a moral and religious sense, while we admit that there is much laxness in morals and superstition in religion, yet we feel that much progress has been made, that there is a growing public sentiment in favor of purity, and that the people are fast coming to make their religion less of superstition and emotion and more a matter of daily living.

As to our educational condition, it is to be noted that our country schools are in session an average of only three and a half months each year; that the Gulf States are as yet unable to provide schoolhouses, and as a result the schools are held almost out of doors, or, at best, in such rude quarters as the poverty of the people is able to provide; that the teachers are poorly paid and often very poorly fitted for their work, and, as a result of these things, both parents and scholars take but little interest in the schools, often but few children attend, and these with great irregularity.

We appreciate the spirit of friendliness and fairness shown us by the Southern white people in matters of business and in all lines of material development.

We believe that we can become prosperous, intelligent, and independent where we are, and we discourage any efforts at wholesale emigration; and, recognizing that our home is to be in the South, we urge that all strive in every way to cultivate the good feeling and friendship of those about us in all that relates to our material elevation.

Education.—The census of children of school age, taken in August, 1891, shows 309,628 white children and 241,893 colored children in the State, a total of 550,721. This is an increase of 26,823 in two years. The statement of receipts and expenses for schools in the several counties for the year ending Sept. 30, 1891, is as follows: Balance from previous years, $48,207.39; received from poll tax, $148,671 79; received from State apportionment and sixteenth-section fund, $411,-638.59; total receipts, $608,517.77; amount paid white teachers, $330,895.54; amount paid colored teachers, $208,994.95; county superintendence, $16,128.88; total expenses, $556,019.37; balance at the close of the year, $52,498.40.

For the school year 1890–'91 there were enrolled at the State University 220 students (30 being in the department of law), and at the Agricultural and Mechanical College 284 students. In the Normal College at Florence there were 263 pupils during the year; in the Normal College for Girls at Livingston, 129 pupils: in the Jacksonville Normal School, 204; in the Selma Normal School for Colored Pupils, 838: and in the Tuskegee Normal and Industrial Institute, 511.

On Dec. 1, 1891, the State Institute for the Deaf contained 85 pupils, and the Academy for the Blind 60 pupils. A State school for the colored blind and deaf was opened in January, 1892. The buildings therefor cost $12,000.

Confederate Pensions.—There were 4,955 applications for pensions this year from soldiers and widows, and each applicant received $26.50 from the fund, amounting this year to $131,-362.02, raised by the special State tax for pensions. Thirty-eight blind applicants received $31.57 each out of the fund of $1,200 set aside for them.

Political.—When the year opened, a warm political contest was in progress between Gov. Jones and ex-Commissioner of Agriculture Reuben F. Kolb, rival candidates for the gubernatorial nomination to be made by the Democratic State Convention. Primary meetings for the election of delegates to the convention had already been held in Jefferson County, in which Jones obtained a slight advantage. Early in January the Madison County primaries were held, and Jones was again successful. From this time until late in May one county after another registered its decision, until the full number of delegates were chosen. During this period the two candidates were continually on the stump, canvassing each county prior to the holding of its primaries. The conservative and hitherto dominant element of the party generally supported Gov. Jones, while Kolb drew to his support the Farmers' Alliance and other factions. As the contest progressed, and Jones continued to lead in the number of delegates secured, the Kolb managers began to claim that the delegates from several counties where the party organization was entirely in the hands of Jones men had been secured for Jones by fraud and unfair devices. After the last primaries had been held, Kolb claimed to be fairly entitled to about 270 delegates, or a majority of the convention, while the Jones faction conceded to him only about 130. Believing that he would not receive fair treatment in the convention, Kolb called a meeting of his followers, to be held on the evening of June 7. It was then decided not to enter the regular convention, but to form a separate organization, and, unless concessions were made by their opponents, to nominate a separate State ticket. Two conventions therefore assembled at Montgomery on June 8, one composed of the Jones delegates and a few Kolb delegates, who believed it their duty to enter the regular convention; the other composed of Kolb delegates and followers, both claiming to represent the true Democracy of the State. The Jones convention renominated Gov. Jones by a vote of 372 to 67 for Kolb, and selected the following candidates for the other State offices: for Secretary of State, Joseph D. Barron; for Auditor, John Purifoy; for Treasurer, Craig Smith; for Attorney-General, William L. Martin; for Superintendent of Public Instruction, John G. Harris; for Commissioner of Agriculture, Hector D. Lane; for Chief Justice of the Supreme Court, George W. Stone; for Associate Justices, Thomas W. Coleman, Thomas N. McClellan, J. B. Head, and Jon. Haralson. Democratic presidential electors were also nominated. A platform was adopted, favoring a tariff for revenue only, the coinage of silver, and the repeal of the tax on State banks, denouncing the bill for Federal control of Federal elections, praising the State administration, and containing the following paragraphs:

We demand that Congress repeal all laws authorizing national banks to issue notes to circulate as money based upon the credit of the Government.

We demand that all moneys appropriated by the Federal Government for the payment of pensions shall be raised by a graduated income tax.

We are opposed to the ownership of railroads and telegraph lines by the Federal Government, and to the multiplication of offices, but we favor the control and regulation of lines of transportation and communication so that only a fair and reasonable rate shall be exacted of the people.

We demand that free labor shall be relieved of competition with convicts, and all necessary laws shall be enacted to forever prevent such competition.

We favor the passage of such election laws as will better secure the government of the State in the hands of the intelligent and the virtuous, and will enable every elector to cast his ballot secretly and without fear or constraint.

We favor the election of railroad commissioners by the people.

The Kolb convention, after fruitless negotiations with its rival, nominated by acclamation a State ticket headed by Kolb for Governor, and containing the following names: For Secretary of State, L. C. Ramsey; for Auditor, W. L. B. Lynch; for Treasurer, T. K. Jones; for Commissioner of Agriculture, S. M. Adams; for Attorney-General, B. K. Collier; for Superintendent of Public Instruction, John O. Turner. An executive committee was chosen and authorized to nominate candidates for the Supreme Court, and to fill vacancies. The ticket was subsequently changed by the withdrawal of Ramsey and Turner, and the substitution of J. C. Fonville for the former and J. P. Olliver for the latter. A long platform was adopted, containing an attack upon the State administration and the following declarations of principles:

We hold above all other considerations the protection of life, the enjoyment of property, the peace and quiet of society, the sacredness of homes, and the social purities of communities, and we hold the present convict system is inimical to all these considerations. Therefore we favor the repeal of the same as it now exists by the Legislature of Alabama, and we favor such prompt and efficient action upon the part of the chief executive of the State as will bring about these results.

We favor just and equitable taxation, with relative exemptions as now provided, so that all property shall be equally liable for taxation; and we demand a change in the present system of listing property so that every item of property shall be disclosed and valued, and proper penalties shall be imposed so as to prevent the escape of any property liable to taxation from being listed and taxed as to its value like all other property.

We are opposed to placing convict labor in competition with free labor in this State.

We are opposed to the national bank system, and demand its repeal.

We favor an expansion of the currency to not less than fifty dollars *per capita*, with every dollar reissued a legal tender for all public and private dues and demands, and that all shall be based on a substantial foundation of value, with the National Government in control of its issue and management.

We favor the free and unlimited coinage of silver.

We favor the protection of the colored race in their legal rights, and should afford them encouragement and aid in the attainment of a higher civilization and citizenship, so that through the means of kindness, fair treatment, and just regard for them, a better understanding and more satisfactory condition may exist between the races.

We demand that the State Railroad Commission shall be elected by the people.

We demand a graduated income tax by the National Government.

During the two months remaining between the date of these conventions and the August election the contest was renewed with increased vigor. No nominations were made by the Republicans, a majority of whom probably gave their support to Kolb. The latter claimed the legal right to have at every polling place one inspector of election favorable to his candidacy, and intimated that in the counties where the county officials were supporters of Jones they intended to appoint only Jones Democrats as inspectors. The State law requires that two of the three inspectors shall be " of opposing political parties," and, as Kolb and his supporters still claimed to be Democrats, there was a plausible, if not valid, reason for ignoring his rights.

Late in June he addressed an open letter to the Governor, asking the latter to join with him in publicly advising the county officials in all cases to appoint two inspectors favorable to the Governor and one favorable to Kolb. The Governor declined to do this, alleging that the county officials knew the terms of the law, and it must be presumed that they would obey it, until there should be some evidence to the contrary. The Kolb executive committee then issued elaborate instructions to his followers to assist them in preventing or detecting fraud. The election took place on Aug. 1, and on the face of the returns resulted in the election of Jones by a majority of about 11,000, and of the remainder of his ticket by larger majorities. An analysis of the vote showed that Kolb had carried a majority of the so-called "white" counties—that is, counties where the whites outnumbered the negroes, and that he had a majority of the total vote in those counties. To overcome this majority, it appeared that Jones had received large majorities in the "black" counties, where the negroes largely outnumbered the whites. It was claimed that the negroes had voted there almost as a body for Jones. On the other hand, Kolb claimed that in those counties he had been denied inspectors at the polls to protect his interests; that it was notorious that the negroes had not voted in such large numbers as the returns indicated; that the Jones managers, who were in complete control of the election machinery in those counties, had altered the returns to suit themselves, and had defrauded him out of the election. His charges were fortified by specific facts and figures, making a strong *prima facie* case. He claimed to have carried the State by over 40,000 majority, and announced that he should contest the election before the incoming Legislature in November. Unfortunately, there existed no State law providing in what manner such a contest should be conducted; Kolb therefore publicly requested Gov. Jones to call a special legislative session to frame such a law, in order that the Legislature in November might act at once under it, but the Governor refused.

The followers of Kolb styled themselves Jeffersonian Democrats, but refused to support Grover Cleveland for President, on account of his expressed friendliness toward the Jones faction. Their State committee accordingly issued a call on Aug. 16 for a convention at Birmingham on Sept. 15 to nominate independent candidates for presidential electors, and also candidates for Congress favorable to the Kolb organization. A similar convention of the People's party, which was organized in the State at Birmingham, on May 30 of this year, was called to meet at the same time and place. A coalition was there formed, and an electoral and congressional ticket was nominated containing representatives of each organization. Resolutions were passed denouncing Mr. Cleveland, and condemning the frauds practiced at the August election. The platform contained the following demands:

A fair vote and a fair count.

That free and unlimited coinage of silver shall be authorized by law, and enforced at the earliest date possible.

That the amount of circulation shall be increased to not less than fifty dollars *per capita*, each dollar to be made the equal in value of every other dollar.

That a graduated income tax be authorized by law, and enforced at the earliest date possible.

That Americans should own the land of the country, and alien ownership should be gradually extirpated, so that every citizen should have a chance to own a home free from extortion and unjust exactions of alien or home monopolists.

That the tariff should be reduced to the lowest possible amount consistent with an economical administration of the Government, with such incidental protection as can be accorded to our industries by a wise levy of the same.

That charters of the national banks shall be repealed, and a means be provided by which money shall be issued direct to the people with safety in the security and full indemnity to the Government.

As in the August election, there were, as a rule, no regular Republican candidates in the field. The contest was between the Birmingham nominees and the candidates of the regular or Cleveland Democracy. The same alleged difficulty of securing a fair and legal representation on the board of inspectors of election in many of the counties again confronted the opponents of the regular Democratic ticket. In their efforts to secure their rights they caused the arrest of the probate judge and the clerk of Bullock County, on Oct. 10, who were brought before the Federal court at Montgomery to answer the charge of violating the law by appointing only Cleveland inspectors in certain election districts.

ANGLICAN CHURCHES. Statistics of Confirmations.—It appears by the annual report on confirmation statistics given in the "Ecclesiastical Chronicle" that 214,531 candidates were confirmed in 1891; that the annual average for the triennial period, 1889–91 was: For England and Wales, 212,335; for the province of Canterbury, 152,669; for the province of York, 59,666. Comparing this triennial period with the previous six years, there was a slight increase, but not amounting to 1 per cent. for the southern province: an increase of 2½ per cent. for the northern province; and, comparing the periods 1884–87, with 1888–91, 10 per cent. for Wales. The southern province during 1889–91 presented 9 candidates per 1,000 population, the northern province 7, and Wales 6. The six dioceses presenting the greatest number annually in proportion to population were: Oxford, 14; Chichester, 13; and Salisbury, Hereford, Winchester, and Canterbury, each 12 per 1,000.

Convocation of Canterbury.—The two houses of the Convocation of Canterbury met, Feb. 16, for the dispatch of business. Suitable notice was taken of the death of the Duke of Clarence and Avondale. The upper house, concurring in a resolution of the lower house, appointed a committee on the subject of obtaining license from the Crown to amend the canons in the matter of discipline of the clergy. The Bishop of London spoke of the impossibility of proceeding in such matters by canon alone, because of the complication of property interests, which could not be dealt with without the consent of Parliament. There were two sides to the question, the ecclesiastical and the temporal side, and it was well that in adjusting them the authorities of the Church and the authorities of the state should proceed *pari passu*. At the meeting of the convocation in May, a draft canon agreed upon by committees of the convocations of both provinces, and already approved by the Convocation of York, in anticipation of the passage of the Clergy Discipline bill then pending in Parliament, was recommended for adoption in the following language: " If any beneficed priest shall by reason of any crime or immorality proved against him become legally disqualified from holding preferment, it shall be the duty of the bishop of the diocese wherein his benefice is situate to declare without further trial the benefice with cure of souls (if any) vacant, and if it should not be so declared vacant within twenty-one days, it shall be declared vacant by the archbishop of the province, or under his authority." The Archbishop of Canterbury was requested to make application to the Crown for license to enact, promulgate, and put in use a canon in these words. The subject of the marginal references in the revised version of the Bible was considered in both houses. The archbishop said that they had got into a confused condition, and showed traces of several schools of thought. The opinion of the upper house was expressed that the question whether the new list should supersede the old one should be decided by the comparative merits of the two series. At the second meeting of convocation, May 10, a gravamen, numerously signed, was presented in the upper house, reciting that fasting previous to the communion was not authorized in the Scriptures or prescribed in any of the formularies of the Church of England, and requesting their lordships to take such steps as should disabuse the mind of the Church of the influence of the teaching of certain priests that it is a sin to communicate otherwise than fasting. A petition from the Sunday Society, presented at the meeting in February, in favor of the opening of public libraries, museums, and art galleries on Sundays was supported in the upper house by the Bishop of Rochester, and was referred to a committee of both houses. The House of Laymen, in February, expressed the opinion that the interest of the Church required that the law as to the patronage of advowsons should be wisely and temperately reformed. The ceremony of formally opening the convocation in connection with the assembling of a new Parliament took place Aug. 6. The Bishop of Guildford was unanimously elected prolocutor of the lower house.

Convocation of York.—The Convocation of York met Feb. 23. Minutes were passed concerning the deaths of Prince Albert Victor, Archbishop Magee, and the Bishop of Carlisle. Both houses acted in favor of the appointment of joint committees to consider the provisions of the Clergy Discipline bill which had been introduced into Parliament, and to suggest the principles on which future ecclesiastical legislation could best be effected, and of inviting the co-operation of the Convocation of Canterbury in both cases. The upper house declined to grant a request of the lower house that a royal commission on the subject of betting and gambling be sought. The lower house adopted a resolution representing the great importance of all ecclesiastical bills being submitted for discussion in convocation before second reading in Parliament.

The House of Laymen of the convocation assembled for the first time in York Minster, April 20. The archbishop delivered an opening address dealing with the Clergy Discipline bill, Church trusts, and the spiritual provision for inmates of workhouses; after which the house organized by the election of its officers. A resolution was adopted approving of the principle of the Clergy Discipline (immorality) bill then before Parliament, and also of the archbishop's intention to apply for license to amend the canons so as to bring them into conformity with the bill.

The convocation again met for business April 26, when the bishop reported concerning the meeting of the House of Laymen that it had been extremely successful. He said it would be a matter for the consideration of the houses how they could best bring the deliberations of that house into contact with theirs. The provisions of the Clergy Discipline bill were discussed, and a draft canon was approved by both houses corresponding with the one which has been cited already as passed by the Convocation of Canterbury. The royal assent having been given to the new canon framed to bring the rule of the Church into conformity with the Clergy Discipline bill, the Convocation of Canterbury met June 14, and the Convocation of York June 16, to promulgate and execute it. The canon (as quoted above) now goes out with the formal approval of both convocations as well as of the sovereign.

Church Missionary Society.—The annual meeting of the Church Missionary Society was held in London, May 3. Sir John Kennaway, M. P., presided. The ordinary income of the society for the year had been £231,204, and the expenditure £243,444. The gross expenditure, including that from the application of special funds, had been £251,374; and the gross receipts, in which was included a special contribution of nearly £21,000 for North American work, had been £269,377. From the mission fields were returned 316 stations, with 329 ordained, 69 lay, and 101 woman European missionaries; 2,847 native and Eurasian clergy; 4,232 lay teachers; 196,983 native Christian adherents; 50,710 native communicants; and 1,759 schools, with 70,731 pupils. The number of baptisms during the year was 10,173. Fifty-eight candidates to be missionaries had been accepted for training, and 66 for immediate service; 54 Cambridge men had offered themselves as missionaries. A medical mission auxiliary committee had formed. Still, more missionaries were wanted; from 3 alone out of 18 of the society's missions came requests for 300 additional men. The committee claimed in the report that the result of the inquiry into the Palestine mission by five prelates was a vindication of the aims and methods of the society's work among Moslems in juxtaposition with the corrupt churches of the East. The report related that the difficulties with which the work in Uganda had been attended at times arose from dissensions between Roman Catholic and Protestant adherents. In the spring of 1891 there were in Uganda about 200 baptized Christians connected with the society, a large number of those baptized since the mission started having died; about 2,000 adherents were under instruction; the native communicants numbered 60; and the adult baptisms of the year exceeded 50 in number. The congregations at the daily services were affected from time to time by the excited state of the people's minds, caused by the disputes with their Roman Catholic fellow-countrymen. Of the translated Scriptures, only the Gospel of St. Matthew, in Luganda, had been printed and circulated in the country; but translations had been prepared in manuscript of the other Gospels, the Acts, the Epistles to the Romans, Galatians, Ephesians, Philippians, and Colossians, and the Book of Revelation.

The annual meeting of the Zenana Bible and Medical Mission, which co-operates with the Church and seven other Protestant missionary societies in India, was held in London. April 27. Lord Reay presided. The receipts of the society had been £16,687, and the expenditure had been £850 more. The society had 47 woman missionaries and 26 assistants, with 203 native teachers and Bible women; 65 schools, with 2,554 pupils; and 3 medical missions, with hospitals connected with 2 of them, under the charge of 5 woman doctors. A new hospital had been opened in Lucknow, and a new medical mission in Patna. Eight thousand nine hundred and four patients had been treated at Lucknow, Benares, and Patna; 24,387 patients had visited the dispensaries; and 1,931 visits had been paid to the homes of patients.

Society for the Propagation of the Gospel.—The Society for the Propagation of the Gospel in Foreign Parts was intrusted during the year 1891 with the administration of £116,-520, which was expended chiefly in the form of block grants placed at the disposal of the respective bishops and synods throughout the world. The number of ordained missionaries on its list, including six bishops, is 672, viz., 225 in Asia, 153 in Africa, 16 in Australia and the Pacific, 211 in North America, 36 in the West Indies, and 31 in Europe. Of these, 127 were natives laboring in Asia and 35 in Africa. There were also in the various missions about 2,300 lay teachers, 2,000 students in the society's colleges, and 38,000 children in the mission schools in Asia and Africa. Among the more prominent features of the society's work in 1891 were the departure of a community of five missionaries to minister to the "peasant church" of the diocese of Chota, Nagpore; the formation of the diocese of Mashonaland, where Bishop Bruce in 1888 had planted mission stations and left teachers at many places; the mission in Corea, where a bishop and a body of clergy and teachers are supported in living a common life, without personal salaries; and the penetration into a district of the Betsiriry Sakalava, in Madagascar, by two missionaries, the first Europeans ever seen by the people. The work of the mission in Madagascar was temporarily arrested on account of the death of the Rev. A. A. Maclaren. During the one hundred and ninety years of this society's activity. it has planted missions in every colony of the British Empire except the Falkland Islands; entering the several colonies successively as they have been organized or added to the list, it has taken care of its churches till they have reached a condition of independence and self-support. It is now working and maintaining missionaries in 50 dioceses. With the growth of the colonies in wealth and power, its resources are gradually set free to meet the claims of the heathen and Mohammedan

subjects of the empire. A little more than one fourth of its funds is all that is now spent on Christian colonists; five eighths are spent on the conversion of the heathen and building up the native churches within the empire; and the remainder is spent in foreign countries—China, Japan, Borneo, Madagasear, the Sandwich Islands (Honolulu), and Corea.

The Universities' Mission.—The income of the Universities' Mission to Central Africa for 1891 was £18,782, showing a falling off of £2,281 as compared with the preceding year, while the total expenditure was £18,822, a slight increase on that of 1890. The missionary staff consisted of 64 persons. The report of work in the field narrated the advance that had been made in the enrollment of members, baptisms, schools, and attendance upon them in the several stations in Nyassaland, the Rovuma district, the Usambara country. and Zanzibar. Several translations of standard works into Suahili had been issued from the mission press. With the assistance of the British and Foreign Bible Society the third volume of the tentative edition of the Old Testament in Suahili had been printed and sent out to Zanzibar, completing the issue of the whole Bible by the society.

Other Societies.—The annual meeting of the Church House Corporation was held in London, June 30. An anonymous donor had conditionally offered at the annual meeting to give £1,000 to the fund of the House, provided £20,000 were subscribed. The challenge was generously responded to, but £8,000 was still wanting to complete this amount. The library contained more than 10,000 volumes. It was intended, the report said. that the Church House should be as much for the use of the Church abroad as of the Church at home, and it was the desire of the council that all members of the Church of England and of the churches in communion with it should make the fullest possible use of it.

The annual meetings in connection with the Church Army spiritual and social movement were held in London during the first week in May, under the presidency of the Bishop of Rochester. From the report of the treasurer it appeared that the Church Army had 170 colporteurs and 50 nurses at work, with 12,000 communicant working members. A sum of £15,000 had been received to aid the work during the year. There were now 14 labor homes open, 7 of them in London. It was proposed to establish a colporteur's van, to travel in the country and distribute Christian literature and to aid in open-air preaching.

The annual general meeting of the Church Defense Association was held in London, May 17. The Bishop of London presided. The report, after reviewing the year's work of the association, concluded with a testimonial to the vigor, spiritual growth, and loyalty of the Established Church in Wales. Resolutions were adopted declaring it the duty of Churchmen, irrespective of political party, to meet all attempts to effect the separation of the Church from the state with increased determination, and to refuse their support to any parliamentary candidate who declares himself in favor of the disestablishment of the Church, whether in England or in Wales; and expressing the opinion that every effort should be made to support and to maintain the efficiency of the Church schools and the hope that the Government might see its way to lighten the burden now pressing on the voluntary schools in the matter of rates.

The thirty-third annual meeting of the English Church Union, which numbers 33,800 members, was held June 14. The meeting resolved that a memorial be addressed in its name to the members of the episcopate and to the synods of the provinces, begging them to take steps to insure that the holy eucharist be celebrated at least on every Sunday and saint's day in every parochial church or chapel having a cure of souls attached to it: to secure an earlier hour than 11 on Sundays for divine service, and to discourage all arrangements which have the effect of substituting matins for the great act of Christian worship; to provide, in all places where it is practicable, for two celebrations of the holy communion on Sunday—one to be said not later than 8 A.M., the second to be sung not later than 10.30 or 11 after matins have been previously said or sung, in order that opportunity may be given to all to attend public worship on Sundays; to make provision that in all cathedral and collegiate churches there be a daily celebration of the holy eucharist; and to provide, as far as possible, in all parochial churches and chapels having cure of souls attached to them, where the holy eucharist can only be celebrated once on Sundays and saints' days, that such celebration be not later than 9 or 9.30, in order to facilitate the observance of the universal custom of the Church that holy communion be received fasting.

The Church Union, April 26, adopted a resolution in which, "recognizing the great injury to family life and the morals of the country which has resulted from the various divorce acts passed within the last thirty-five years in violation of the law of God as to the indissolubility of the marriage bond—declared in Holy Scripture and set forth in the Book of Common Prayer"—it called upon the members and associates of the union to make a vigorous and united effort to arouse the conscience of the country on the subject; and to use their influence to procure the repeal of at least those clauses in the divorce acts which require the parochial clergy either to perform the service themselves or to allow the churches to be used for the marriage (so called) of a divorced person whose real husband or wife is still living; and to resist the passage of a certain pending bill for extending still further the grounds for divorce.

The income of the Curates' Augmentation Fund, as returned at the annual meeting, June 15, was £9,048, showing an increase of £324 over the funds of the society during the previous year, and being the largest income for several years. A large number of new applications had been received. Three fourths of the vacancies had occurred through preferment; which showed that the fund had been helping deserving curates.

An organization called the Clergy Fees Reform Association has been set on foot, having for its objects to obtain a reduction in the scale of fees at present payable upon institution, induction, dispensation, and sequestration, and for letters of orders and curates' license, and to allow the clergy when fees in excess of those allowed by statute or order in council are demanded of them.

The receipts of the Church Pastoral Aid Society for the year ending March 31, 1892, were £58,463, exceeding the gross receipts of the previous year by £2,149. Of the whole amount, £9,000 were given to be invested for special purposes, leaving £49,463 as ordinary income. The expenditure for the year had been £51,927. The whole number of grants was 808, or 54 more than during the previous year.

Liberation Society.—The triennial conference of the Society for the Liberation of Religion from State Patronage and Control was held in London, May 3 and 4. Mr. R. Spence Watson presided. In opening the conference, he said that the work during the last three busy political years in which the society was especially interested, had shown decided progress. There were many indications of the fact. The report of the executive committee spoke of the past three years as a period during which the progress of opinion and events had been favorable to religious equality. Detailing the work of the society, it recognized the fact that it would not be possible, without a severe struggle, to establish completely the principle of religious equality in connection with national education. Decisive progress was making on the question of disestablishment in Wales, but it was recognized that the real ground of objection to Welsh disestablishment was the certainty that it must be followed by disestablishment in England. The question of Scottish disestablishment occupied substantially the same position. In regard to the approaching general election the committee called attention to the enthusiasm with which the idea of disestablishment was accepted by all advanced reformers. The financial statement showed that the receipts of the society for the past year had amounted to £5,350, that a balance of £302 was left in bank, and that there were accounts outstanding to the amount of £1,900. Resolutions were adopted congratulating the supporters of the society on the advanced position of the question of disestablishment in Wales and Scotland, as it was shown by the debates in Parliament during the past three years, by the declarations and pledges of politicians, and the attitude of the public press; expressing satisfaction that so large a number of candidates had declared in favor of religious equality; urging the importance of strenuous exertions to secure the return of such candidates and to elicit an expression of public opinion which will exert a powerful impression on the action of the new Parliament and of the next Liberal administration; citing the meager results of recent parliamentary efforts to remove abuses and anomalies in the Established Church as further proofs of the impossibility of satisfactorily regulating its affairs by parliamentary enactment, but objecting to the removal of parliamentary control from the Church as long as it remains a national institution; demanding education wholly free from sectarian influence; expressing the opinion that disestablishment would greatly facilitate the management of local affairs in rural parishes, would diminish persecution for conscience' sake, and by more fully extending religious liberty would promote not only the spiritual but also the social interests of village populations; and urging the enactment of a broader burials act.

The Case of the Bishop of Lincoln.—The Court of Privy Council rendered a decision in August in the matter of the appeal of the members of the Church Association from the decision of the Archbishop of Canterbury in the case of the proceedings against the Bishop of Lincoln for offenses in ritual, dismissing the appeal. An abstract of the decision of the Archbishop, which is thus sustained, is given in the Annual Cyclopedia for 1891.

The Church in Ireland.—The General Synod of the Anglican Church in Ireland met April 26. The Archbishop of Dublin presided, and having represented the present condition and prospects of the Church as, in his mind, full of hope, proceeded to speak in opposition to the granting of "home rule" to Ireland.

Anglicanism and Nonconformity in Wales.—An assertion made by the Bishop of St. Asaph, in 1891, that 16 nonconformist ministers in Wales had applied for ordination in the Church of England, has excited much discussion and been sturdily denied by the nonconformists of the principality, and particularly by the representatives of the Welsh Calvinistic Methodist Church. It has been confirmed by Prof. Lias, chaplain to the Bishop of Llandaff, who said publicly at a meeting in Cambridge in June, 1892, that he had seen and read a great pile of letters from dissenting ministers in Wales, and in the preceding year had examined 16 of the writers.

Church Congress.—The thirty-second annual Church Congress met at Folkestone, Oct. 4, under the presidency of the Archbishop of Canterbury. The principal subjects discussed were: "The Attitude of the Church toward Labor Combinations in Respect to their Aims and their Methods," "The Work of the Church of England on the Continent," "The Result of the Neglect of Religious Education in Elementary Schools," "The Duty of the Church to the Agricultural Population in View of their Spiritual and Social Needs, and their Increased Responsibilities as Citizens," "The Temperance Movement," "The Church in Wales," "Canon Law in Connection with the Government and Discipline of the Church of England," "Christian Ethics, Individual and Social," "The Permanent Value of the Old Testament for the Christian Church in its Educational, Evidential, and Devotional Aspects," "Do the Interests of Mankind require Experiments on Living Animals, and if so, up to what Point are they Justifiable?," "Foreign Missions," "Thrift and the Poor Law," "The Preparation for Deacons' and Priests' Orders, and the Preparation of Laymen for Evangelistic Work," "The Duty of the Church toward Soldiers," "Preaching in the Church of England," and "Church Work at the Seaside, among Residents and Visitors." A special meeting for women was held, at which the subjects of "Training of Workers," "The Industrial Condition of Women," "Co-operation," "Temperance," and "Physical Recreation" were discussed wholly by women.

ARGENTINE REPUBLIC, a federal republic in South America. The executive authority is vested in a President, elected for six years by representatives of the federated provinces, each of which chooses twice as many presidential electors as it has representatives in both branches of Congress. The Senate has 30 members, 2 from each province and 2 from the Federal District. The House of Deputies consists of 86 members, elected directly by the people for four years, the moiety being renewed every two years. The Vice-President acts as Chairman of the Senate. Dr. Carlos Pellegrini, who was elected Vice-President for the presidential term ending Oct. 12, 1892, succeeded to the presidential office. Dr. Juarez Celman resigned on Aug. 6, 1890. Luis Saenz Peña was elected President, and Z. S. Uriharru Vice-President, for the term beginning Oct. 12, 1892, in the election of April, 1892.

Finance.—The ordinary revenue of the Government in 1887 was $58,135,000, and the expenditure $54,098,227. In 1888 the receipts were $57,051,711, and the disbursements $50,801,638. In 1889 the receipts increased to $74,676,706, and the expenses were still only $50,687,544. In 1890 the revenue was $73,407,670, while the expenditures, owing to special appropriations not set down in the budget, leaped up to $92,853,846. For 1891 the revenue was estimated at $73,150,855, of which $47,546,785 represent customs duties on imports, $4,246,266 direct taxes, $4,010,240 stamp duties, $2,185,809 postal revenue, and $15,161,755 other receipts. The ordinary expenditure was originally reckoned at $67,881,884, of which $25,989,893 were allocated to the Finance Department, $16,237,406 to the Interior, $9,517,026 to Public Instruction, $9,507,839 to the Ministry of War, $4,029,440 to the Navy, and $2,600,280 to Foreign Affairs. Subsequently the total estimate of expenditure was cut down to $58,252,362. These estimates are in paper dollars. The value of the currency dollar declined from 80 cents on the gold dollar in 1886, when $70,000,000 of currency were in circulation, to 40 cents in 1890, when there were $200,000,000 out, and 27½ cents in 1891, when the amount issued was $300,000,000. The national debt is said to have grown from $117,200,000 in 1886 to $355,800,000 in 1890, and $475,000,000 in 1891. According to an official statement, the funded liabilities consisted of $157,100,000 of foreign debt, $161,766,600 of 4½-per-cent. bonds owned by national banks and deposited in the treasury to secure circulation, and $1,225,631 of internal bonds. A proposition to fund the interest on the foreign debt in 6-per-cent. gold bonds was approved by Congress in May, 1891. The floating debt was stated to be $700,961 in gold and $10,174,548 in currency. An inventory of property belonging to the National Government makes the valuation $703,793,172.

The Army and Navy.—The regular army numbers 5,585 men, including 11 generals, 1,118 officers, 2,331 infantry, 2,227 cavalry, 789 artillery, and 238 engineers. The militia numbers 236,000 men.

The naval force consists of 1 ironclad war vessel of 4,200 tons, 2 ironclad monitors, 2 deck-protected cruisers, 7 gunboats, 2 transports, 7 avisos, 1 torpedo school-ship, 4 torpedo boats, and 4 spar torpedo boats. The sea-going fighting ship is the "Almirante Brown," built in England in 1880. She is plated with 9 inches of steel-faced armor, and carries 6 11½-ton Armstrong breechloaders in a central battery, and 2 more in the bow and stern, and is fitted with Whitehead torpedoes and search lights.

Production and Commerce.—The chief industry of the country is raising cattle. Sheep breeding is also carried on extensively. There is not much agriculture, although many districts are very fertile. Only about a hundredth part of the soil is under cultivation. The chief crops are corn, wheat, and alfalfa. Flax, grapes, and cane sugar are also produced. There were 22,779,491 cattle, 70,461,665 sheep, and 4,387,280 horses in 1888, having a value of $370,061,717.

The total value of the imports of merchandise in 1890 was $142,241,000. The exports were valued at $100,819,000 in gold. The imports of gold coin and bullion were $6,946,812, and of silver $204,439, making a total of $7,151,251. The exports of gold were $5,009,358, and of silver $274,542, giving a total of $5,283,900. The values, in currency, of the principal imports in 1890 were as follow: Textiles and wearing apparel, $30,024,966; railroad and telegraph plant, etc., $36,273,503; food substances, $16,411,458; articles of drink, $12,790,340; iron and steel manufactures, $9,566,752; wood and wood manufactures, $7,399,412; coal, oil, etc., $6,290,011; china and glass ware, $4,135,523; chemicals, $3,875,542. The values of the various classes of exports, in gold dollars, were as follow: Animals and animal produce, $61,306,597; agricultural products, $25,591,401; manufactures, $8,999,236; forest products, $1,413,324; mineral products, $673,690; miscellaneous, $2,834,745. The exports of wool fell off from 141,774,435 kilos in 1889 to 118,405,604 kilos in 1890, valued at $35,521,681. The number of hides was 4,647,085, as compared with 3,638,467 in 1889, and the quantity of skins decreased from 37,896,100 to 29,542,450 kilos. The value of the hides and skins exported in 1890 was $20,097,656 in gold; of the wheat exports, $9,836,824, compared with $1,596,446 in the previous year; of the maize, $14,145,639, compared with $12,977,721. The bulk of the external trade in 1890 was divided among trading countries as follows:

COUNTRIES.	Imports.	Exports.
Great Britain	$57,816,510	$19,299,095
France	19,875,877	26,683,319
Germany	12,301,472	11,566,431
Belgium	10,986,710	12,003,086
United States	9,801,541	6,066,959
Italy	8,668,027	8,194,802
Brazil	8,354,566	8,442,563
Uruguay	5,885,758	5,506,675
Spain	4,802,284	2,088,817
Chili	51,114	2,188,951
Paraguay	1,724,050	836,566

Navigation.—During 1890 there were entered at the ports of the Argentine Republic 6,070 sailing vessels, of 1,238,066 tons, and 3,966 steamers, of 3,431,436 tons, with cargoes, and 756 sailing vessels, of 50,174 tons, and 3,081 steamers, of 1,621,279 tons, in ballast; cleared were 1,588 sailing vessels, of 402,675 tons, and 3,171 steamers, of 2,801,500 tons, taking cargoes, and 2,088 sailing vessels, of 576,148 tons, and 2,862 steamers, of 1,726,146 tons, in ballast. About 37½ per cent. of the tonnage was British, 30 per cent. Argentine, 9 per cent. French, 8 per cent. Italian, and 6 per cent. German.

Communications.—There were 6,855 completed miles of railroad in 1891, and 4,840 miles were building. The capital expended in construction up to the close of 1890 was $346,493,054. During 1890 the receipts amounted to $41,157,486, and expenses to $23,310,000. The net receipts were equal to a return of 1·7 per cent. on the capital, against 2·2 per cent. in 1889, and the Government paid about $3,100,000 of guaranteed interest.

The length of the telegraph lines in 1890 was about 19,000 miles, of which 12,000 miles belong to the Government. The length of wire in 1888 was 28,550 miles. The number of dispatches sent during 1889 was 3,511,420. A contract was made in 1889 for a direct cable to Europe, which was to have been laid before June, 1892. The Central and South American Telegraph Company in May, 1892, established a new connection between the Argentine cities and the United States and Europe vía Galveston, Texas. The post-office in 1890 forwarded 60,844,963 letters, 800,716 postal cards, and 43,974,107 newspapers and other matter.

Presidential Election.—In the struggle between the capital and the provinces, or between the Federalist and the National party, in 1886, the latter carried the day, and, with the support of ex-President Gen. Roca, elected Juarez Celman to the presidency. During his administration the provincial and national borrowings and the emission of paper money culminated in a financial crash and the revolution of July, 1890, in which he was turned out by the efforts of the Union Civica, headed by the Radicals of the country, who had with them a great part of the army and navy. The revolt, led by the Radical chiefs, Drs. Alem and Aristobulo del Valle, was suppressed after four days of fighting; but after Dr. Roque Saenz Peña and Dr. Garcia had resigned from the Cabinet, and the President lost the support of Congress and was confronted with the prospect of impeachment and the danger of a general insurrection, he resigned the executive power into the hands of the Vice-President, Dr. Pellegrini, who by his reforms stemmed the tide of national bankruptcy. Dr. Pellegrini refused to be a candidate to succeed himself. The Union Civica continued in existence, but, having been organized to meet a crisis and carry out reforms, lacked the essentials of a political party. The Nationals were led by Gen. Roca, who declined to put himself forward as a candidate. The Union Civica and the Nationalists were anxious to unite on a candidate who would carry more weight than Dr. Pellegrini, and by his reputation and character would command the confidence of foreign countries and the creditors of the Government, and encourage the nation in efforts to attain a solid financial footing. Such a man was believed to have been discovered in Gen. Mitre, a distinguished statesman and publicist, who had already filled the presidential chair with honor. His candidature, however, met with opposition in the provinces, and after a few months he formally withdrew. Dr. Roque Saenz Peña then came forward, but was not entirely acceptable to the Acuerdista or coalition party. A joint convention was held, in which his father, Dr. Luis Saenz Peña, was fixed upon as the candidate who would harmonize the party. The Radical element was not disposed to fall in with the Roca-Mitre coalition. A cry was raised against their financial conservatism and their desire to please the foreign creditors and the English investors and speculators, or perhaps to join with them in drawing profits out of the land. Dr. Alem was the head of the new patriotic movement, and Dr. Yrigoyen was put up as the Radical candidate for President. The contest was carried on with bitterness for some months, and, just as before, a considerable section of the military were on the side of the Radicals, who were unable to cope with the political organization of their opponents, and placed their hopes in popular demonstrations, or, as the last resort, in insurrection. Dr. Saenz Peña was placed in nomination on March 6, 1892. In his speech of acceptance he promised to give the minority a fair representation in the Administration; to propose a reform of the electoral laws, and to punish electoral frauds; to preserve the autonomy of the provinces; to foster desirable immigration and concede land to colonists, while putting an end to the purchase of tracts in the country by speculators; to create a Council of State to assist the Executive, like that in Chili; to advocate the establishment of the right of *habeas corpus;* to reorganize the army and navy, and to cultivate international friendships, especially with the United States and other American nations. The reciprocity proposals of the United States Government were rejected about this time by the Argentine Government. The Radicals, as soon as they began to agitate against the coalition candidate, were met by repressive measures. Their meetings were broken up, and some active men were arrested. They prepared for a violent conflict such as had occurred many times in the past electoral contests in Argentina. On April 2, the eve of the day set for a great Radical mass meeting in Buenos Ayres, the authorities scented, or pretended to have discovered, a gigantic conspiracy not only to start an insurrection, but to murder the President and Gens. Roca and Mitre, and proclaim Dr. Alem Dictator. All the troops were gathered in the central part of the city.

A state of siege was proclaimed, the troops were confined to the camps of Zarate and Maldonado, the sentinels were doubled, the officers were forbidden to pass the lines, the guns were kept ready horsed, and for two successive nights the Minister of War slept in camp. In the early morning of April 3 Dr. Alem, Gen. Garcia, and the rest of the Radical leaders, civil and military, were arrested and taken on board a man-of-war. The Government issued a proclamation charging them with plotting the wholesale destruction of the chief of the republic, the leaders of the army, and prominent citizens, by means of dynamite, and claiming to have discovered a great number of explosive bombs in a Radical club, as well as cloaks and canes by which the conspirators were to recognize each other, and documents implicating Dr. Alem and others, and unfolding the details of the plot. Many Radical chiefs who escaped arrest fled to Montevideo, and others were banished to that city by order of a court of justice. The prisoners were held in custody till after the popular election of the

presidential electors on April 10. The Radicals abstained generally from voting, and consequently Dr. Saenz Peña was declared the choice of the people by a great majority. Most of the prisoners were then released, yet Dr. Alem was still held, in spite of an order for his release that was obtained from the Federal court. In the provinces, likewise, Radical clubs were shut up, some arrests were made, and on election day no opposition was made to the return of the coalition candidate, who had the united support of the Catholic conservative element, the Nationalist party, and the greater part of the Union Civica. On the meeting of Congress President Pellegrini received an act of immunity justifying his proceedings. Dr. Alem was finally released without a trial, after many weeks of detention. The casting of the electoral votes took place on June 12. By an almost unanimous vote Luis Saenz Peña was elected President and Señor Uriburu Vice-President for the term beginning Oct. 12, 1892. The banished Radicals refused to return from Montevideo unless the state of siege was terminated, and in the beginning of July it was ended by proclamation. Riotous demonstrations against Peña took place in August in the streets of Buenos Ayres, and the tumults recurred until after his inauguration.

ARCHÆOLOGY. American. Civilization of the Ohio Mound-Builders.—Warren K. Moorehead, in his book on "Primitive Man in Ohio," presents the results of four seasons' exploration of ancient remains in that State. He draws the conclusions that the tribes did not occupy the northern parts of the State for any considerable length of time, but were settled chiefly in the larger river valleys; that both the brachycephalic and the dolicocephalic races mingled largely in all the valleys save the Muskingum; and that nothing more than the upper status of savagery was attained by any race or tribe living in the present State of Ohio. If the field testimony alone is considered, primitive man can be accredited with high attainments in only a few things, "and these indicating neither civilization nor an approach to it. First, he excelled in building fortifications and in the interment of his dead; second, he made surprisingly long journeys for mica, copper, lead, shells, and other foreign substances, to be used as tools and ornaments; third, he was an adept in the chase and in war; fourth, he chipped flint and made carvings on bone, stone, and slate exceedingly well when we consider the primitive tools he employed; fifth, a few of the more skillful men of his tribe made fairly good representations of animals, birds, and human figures in stone. . . . On the other hand, he failed to grasp the idea of communication by written characters, the use of metal (except in the cold state), the cutting of stone, or the making of brick for building purposes, and the construction of permanent homes. Ideas of transportation other than upon his own back or in frail canoes, or the use of coal, which was so abundant about him, and which he frequently made into pendants and ornaments, and a thousand other things which civilized beings enjoy, were utterly beyond his comprehension."

Age of the Central American Monuments. —From his studies of the monuments of Central

America, Mr. Alfred P. Maudsley has drawn the conclusion that the southern ruins, including Palenque, Copan, and Quirigua, are much more ancient than those of Yucatan, and were probably in full decay before the Spaniards entered the country; while in Yucatan some of the ruined structures now to be seen were inhabited by the natives at the time of the conquest. At the time of the Spanish conquest the people had abandoned their towns and religious centers south of Yucatan, while in Yucatan, where they probably still occupied some of the buildings, they were in a state of decadence and many of the large centers of population had been abandoned. The early Spanish writers speak of large numbers of books written and preserved by the natives of Yucatan. They were written in the Maya language, and in characters called hieroglyphical. The Spaniards destroyed all of these books they could, thinking them the work of the devil, but copies of them escaped, and are preserved in European museums. The characters in which they are written are similar to those of the inscriptions on the monuments; and both are believed to be in a language that is still living and spoken in the region, although it has probably been much changed in the course of years.

The Maya Inscriptions.—Dr. Cyrus Thomas believes that he has discovered the key to the reading of the Maya codices and probably of the Central American inscriptions. He has already determined the signification of some dozens of characters, and has in several instances ascertained the general sense of a group forming a sentence.

Oriental. Connections between East and West.—In his presidential address before the International Oriental Congress in London, Prof. Max Müller recognized it as among the greatest achievements of Oriental scholarship during the present century that it had proved that the break in the relations between Eastern and Western peoples which has existed during most of the period of written history did not exist from the beginning; but that in the times called prehistoric "language formed really a bond of union between the ancestors of many of the Eastern and Western nations, while more recent discoveries have proved that in historic times also language, which seemed to separate the great nations of antiquity, never separated the most important among them so completely as to make all intellectual commerce and exchange between them impossible." This is proved by the tablets found at Tel-el-Amarna, in Egypt, already described in the " Annual Cyclopædia " and by the examination of documents recovered from the ruins in Palestine and Syria.

Among the fragments of cuneiform tablets found at Tel-el-Amarna Prof. A. H. Sayce has identified a comparative dictionary of three (or five) different languages, compiled by order of the King of Egypt, and a dictionary of Babylonian and Accadian, in which the Accadian words are phonetically written.

An inscription in a strange writing upon the bandages of a mummy in the museum at Agram is regarded by eminent authorities as Etruscan, and is, if the supposition is correct, the longest Etruscan document in existence, containing more than 1,200 words.

A hieroglyphic inscription on the bronze pedestal of a bronze statue of the goddess Neith, discovered at Sais, bears a line of Karian characters, recording that the statue was dedicated to Neith and Horus by Si-Qarr, son of Kapat Qarr, born of the house of Neith-mert-ha-uah-ab-ra. Si-Qarr is construed by Danninos Pasha as meaning the son of a Karian, and Kapat Qarr as Kapat, the Karian.

A cuneiform fragment relating to a person named Adapa is supplemented by one of the cuneiform documents found at Tel-el-Amarna, of which Dr. Zimmern has published a translation. This text records the adventures of a certain Adapa, the son of the sea-god Ea, and is discussed by Dr. Zimmern as parallel both to the Greek myth of Prometheus and to the biblical accounts of the fall of man.

Among the discoveries made by Mr. F. J. Bliss at Tell-el-Hesy, the spot identified by Major Conder and Dr. W. M. Flinders Petrie as the site of the ancient city of Lachish, is a tablet containing a letter written about 1400 B. C., in the same hand-writing as that of the Tel-el-Amarna tablets which were sent from the south of Palestine to Egypt about the same time. It is a letter to Zimrida, who is mentioned in the Tel-el-Amarna tablets, and was Governor of Lachish, and was murdered there by some of his own people. A number of Babylonian cylinders and imitations and forgeries of such found at the same place are adduced by Prof. Sayce as further evidences of "the long and deep influence and authority of Babylon in western Asia."

A paper by Prof. Hommel, of Munich, on "The Babylonian Origin of Egyptian Culture," dwells on the parallelism between the names of Eridu, one of the oldest towns in Babylonia, and Memphis (Men nofer) in Egypt—both names meaning " the good city " or " city of the good (god) "—and on comparisons with the deities of the two countries.'

Archæological Survey of Egypt. — The general object of the archæological survey of Egypt carried on by Mr. Newberry and his assistants, under the direction of the Egypt Exploration fund, is to catalogue, measure, and copy all the monuments that exist above ground in Egypt. The work was begun in November, 1890, at Beni Hassan, where about 2,000 square feet of painting were traced. From Beni Hassan the surveyors went to El Bersheh, where only two inscribed tombs were previously known. These were the tomb of Tahutihotep, containing the paintings of a colossal statue on a sledge being drawn by 125 men, and the tomb of Ahanekt. Ten more inscribed tombs were found here, all of the twelfth dynasty, and containing many lines of inscriptions. Among the inscriptions was the name of one of Tahutihotep's daughters, previously unknown. Among the chief results of the work of the past two seasons are the acquisition of plans of the tombs, water-color facsimiles of many of the most interesting scenes, and copies of the inscriptions and outline tracings of all the wall paintings in the tombs at Beni Hassan and El Bersheh ; and a genealogy—the longest and fullest genealogy of any ancient Egyptian family that has been made out—showing that the two princely families buried at these two stations were related to one another, and tracing that of Beni Hassan through five and that of El Bersheh through seven generations. Mr. Newberry also made superficial explorations over a region in the Nile valley forty miles long, comprising the ancient Oryx and Hermopolite nomes, noting the mounds, place names, and objects of archæological interest. Among the discoveries of peculiar interest was that of the alabaster quarry of Hat-Nul—the quarry to which Una went to cut out the alabaster altar for his sovereign of the sixth dynasty, and the most famous quarry of the ancient kingdom.

The Palace of Khuenaten. — Dr. W. M. Flinders Petrie spent much of the season of 1891-'92 in excavating at Tel-el-Amarna, the capital of Khuenaten. His more important explorations were carried on in the palace, in which several rooms with portions of painted

old conventional grouping constrained the design—a fact which is used to show that the work was done by Egyptian artists. The absence of any geometrical ornament shows that Babylonian influence was not active. "Some small fragments of sculptured columns show that this flowing naturalism was as freely carried out in relief as in color." Of the architecture there remain only small pieces flaked off the columns. By comparing these the style can be recovered; and both the small columns in the palace and the larger ones in the river frontage appear to have been in imitation of bundles of reeds, with inscribed bands and with leafage on the base and on the capital, and groups of ducks around the neck. A roof over a well was supported by columns of a geometrical pattern, with spirals and chevrons. In the palace front

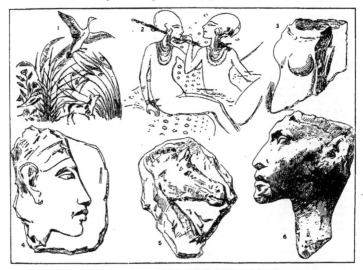

ARTICLES FOUND IN DR. FLINDERS PETRIE'S EGYPTIAN EXCAVATIONS.

1. Copy of wall-painting. 2, Makt-Aten and Merit-Aten, daughters of Khuenaten (from a painting.) 3. Fragment of statue of Netert-iti, queen of Khuenaten. 4, Khuenaten, profile portrait. 5, Rough sculpture of horse's head (on back of stone with profile of Khuenaten.) 6, Cast of head of Khuenaten, taken after death.

fresco pavements were found. One room nearly entire and two others more injured have been fully exposed to view, and protected by a convenient house. With the exception of a pavement said to exist at Thebes, these are the only examples of a branch of art which must have been familiar in Egypt. The subjects of the floors are tanks with fish, birds, and insects, and a border of bouquets and dishes. The main value of the designs, according to Dr. Petrie, lies in the new style of art displayed. "The action of the animals and the naturalistic grace of the plants are unlike any other Egyptian work, and are unparalleled even in classical frescoes." But where the lotus occurred, the

were plainer columns inscribed with scenes, and with capitals imitating gigantic jewelry.

The artistic results of the discoveries in the palace, as represented by Mr. Petrie to the International Oriental Congress, are that the direct aim of the artists was as exact an imitation of nature as possible. In sculpture, the work of the best hands equals the finest work of other countries or ages. In painting, nature is closely followed with much memory work, apart from models; the plants are superior to those in most classical work, and the animals are free and vigorous. The only ancient parallels to the character of this work are the bull fresco of Tiryns and the gold cups of Vaphio. The origin of this new departure can not have been any national movement, or it would not have been annihilated so soon after; it must have been individual, and due to the personality of Khuenaten. By an astonishing chance, we have left to us a cast from the actual face of the king, Khuenaten, who led this change. We see in it strong idealism and obstinacy allied with a curious humanism and humor. These traits of the art of Khuenaten's period are illustrated on page 13, which represents objects found at the palace as they were exhibited at the Oxford Mansions, London.

The tomb of Khuenaten was explored by M. Alexandre, who has described its passages in chambers in detail. It was never finished, and everything about it indicates that the "heretic king's reign ended in a revolution."

Lake Mœris.—The results of his studies of the supposed site of Lake Mœris were communicated by Herr H. Brugsch Bey in a paper read before the Société de Geographie Khediviale, April 8. The author maintained that there was abundant monumental evidence to show that an immense basin of water existed at a very early period near the plateau of Hawara, and gave its name to the Fayûm, or lake district. This district appears not to have been included in the forty-two divisions or nomes of Egypt, but to have formed an isolated part of the kingdom, with its own subordinate divisions. Save in the necropolis at Hawara it was given over to the worship of Sebak, the crocodile god. It was known in hieroglyphics as *To She*, the lake district, which in Coptic became *P-ium*, the maritime district, and survives to-day in the Arabic *Fayûm*. It is evident from the Fayûm papyrus, of which there are two copies, that the term *Meruer*, the great water or lake, was also applied to it; and perhaps herein lies the origin of the name *Mœris*.

Certain of the tombs of Siut are regarded by Prof. Maspero as belonging to the period of the tenth dynasty. Prof. Sayce has discovered inscriptions giving the names of some of the kings of that dynasty, one of them previously unknown, and showing that its rule was recognized as far south as the first cataract, or on the frontiers of Nubia, as well as indicating that the government passed from the tenth to the eleventh dynasty peacefully and regularly.

The American Expedition to Babylonia.— A verbal report was made by Prof. John P. Peters, at the meeting of the American Oriental Society in Washington, D. C., in April, of the chief results obtained by the expedition which had been sent out to Babylonia by the University of Pennsylvania. Excavations were made in the mounds of Niffer, where, in the old temple of Bel, tablets were found which go back to the earliest Babylonian dynasties, or four thousand years before Christ. While the expedition had been unsuccessful in the search for the clay cylinders which were placed in the corners of the building and are of great value as historical material, the orientation of the buildings had been tested and found in most cases not accurate or mathematical, but vague and often incorrect. A study of the meaning of the inscription that appeared on the wall of the banqueting chamber of Belshazzar was presented by Mr. John D. Prince, of Johns Hopkins University. Following

a hint given by M. Clermont Ganneau, he translated the words *Mene, mene, tekel upharsin*—"there have been counted a mina, a shekel, and half minas." According to Talmudic usage, an unworthy son of a worthy father is metaphorically called a "half mina, son of a mina." In this way the author of Daniel wished to draw a parallel between Nebuchadnezzar, the father, and Belshazzar, the son. The mina was the largest Babylonian weight. The shekel was one sixtieth of the mina, and would represent Belshazzar as the unworthy successor of the founder of the Babylonian empire. The two half minas point to the division of the kingdom of Nebuchadnezzar between the Medes and the Persians.

An Ancient LXX Manuscript.—A recently found papyrus manuscript of the Septuagint version of the Old Testament has been translated and described by Prof. Hechler, of the British Embassy at Vienna. The style of the writing places its date well before A. D. 300. It consists of 16 sheets written on both sides, or 32 pages, each about 16 inches by 7 inches, and contains the greater part of the Book of Zeebariah from about the fourth chapter and parts of the prophet Malachi. The readings indicate that the original scribe had an excellent copy of the LXX before him, and was himself an accurate writer.

An Accadian Creation Tablet.—A second Babylonian story of the creation has been translated and published by Mr. Theodore G. Pinches, which exhibits several variations from the biblical account and from the version translated by Mr. George Smith. It is in the Accadian or Sumerian language, and is inscribed on a small tablet of baked clay in such a way that each line is divided into two parts, between which the Semitic-Babylonian version is written. Mr. Pinches gave a full account of the new version, with explanations of the differences between it and the other versions, at the meeting of the International Oriental Congress in London.

Interpretation of the Hittite Inscriptions.—An attempt to interpret the Hittite inscriptions has been made by Prof. A. H. Sayce from data afforded by the discoveries of Messrs. Ramsay, Hogarth, and Headlam in Asia Minor. Reading in the light of the discovery he supposes he has made, he concludes that the inscriptions of Hamath and those known as the first and third inscriptions of Jerablus are records of building; while the second inscription of Jerablus is little more than a list of royal or high-priestly titles. He remarks upon a close similarity between the titles assumed by the Hittite princes and those of the Egyptian pharaohs of the eighteenth and nineteenth dynasties, and finds other evidence of likeness between the graphic systems of the Hittites and the Egyptians. Some of Prof. Sayce's conclusions respecting the ideographic character of the texts, the character and affinities of the language, and the reading of the Jerablus inscriptions, are questioned by Major C. R. Conder, who has also studied the Hittite inscriptions and proposed a reading of them, and who claims priority in comparing the Hittite and the Egyptian emblems. Mr. Conder further finds similarities between some of the Hittite emblems and some of the oldest-known Chinese characters.

Another essay in the interpretation of the Hittite inscriptions has been published in Berlin by Herr F. E. Peiser, who has sought the key to their decipherment by comparing the Hittite seals found by Mr. Layard at Koyunjik in 1851 with an Egyptian seal which was found with them. In this way the author claims that he was enabled to assign syllabic values to seven Hittite characters. Comparing these data with other seals, he gained two other signs, with which further steps could be taken. At the time of the publication of his book, " Die Hetitischen Inschriften," he had advanced to the interpretation of an inscription of twenty lines found at Jerablus. Attempts to interpret the Hittite inscriptions by regarding the characters as phonetic signs are rejected by Mr. T. Tyler, who maintains that the pictorial nature of the characters is hardly to be doubted by any observer, and that the inscriptions are in the main ideographic.

Grecian.—At the annual meeting of the Hellenic Society, in June, especial mention was made of the continuation of the explorations at Megalopolis, of which a full report was shortly to be published, and of the excavations of the American school on the site of the temple of Hera at Argos. which had been very fruitful. Among the objects recovered were three heads in the best style of the fifth century B. C., which Dr. Waldstein was disposed to ascribe to Polykleitos. Other discoveries by the various institutions engaged in the excavation of Grecian antiquities include many interesting statues of women, of Athena, and of Amazons found by the German school at Magnesia and Melandrum; additional inscriptions at Gortyna, in Crete; remains of temples at Vachlia and Voutza, in Arcadia; an ancient private house at the Piræus; emblematic designs in relief at Athens and at Laurium; an altar of sacrifice at Epidaurus; and three metopes, additional to the two found at Silenus, Sicily, adorned respectively with representations of Hercules subduing the bull, Europa and the bull, and a winged Sphinx.

A study of "The Phœnician Element in the Homeric Poems" was presented to the International Oriental Congress in London by the Hon. W. E. Gladstone. The immediate purpose of the paper was to trace the derivation and meaning of the term ἄναξ ἀνδρῶν: it brought forward many analogies illustrating the influence of Oriental thought and customs upon the Grecian life described by Homer.

Zimbabye.—Mr. Bent and Mrs. Bent, who so ably helps him in this work, spent two months at Zimbabye with satisfactory results. They then went on to the Sabi river, along the course of which they found four more sets of ruins, one of which is nearly equal to the circular building at Zimbabye. This trip led them through some very wild and deserted country. From Fort Salisbury they visited the Mazoo valley, where they examined the old workings, and found a little ruined fortress of the best Zimbabye work. The party then went on into Matoko's country, which was interesting mainly from an anthropological point of view, and on account of the connection of the present savages with the religion and customs of the people of the old Monomotapa "empire." They then visited Mangwendie's, Chipinza's, Makoni's, and Umtasa's countries, in

each of which they found either ruins or other objects of interest. Finally, the party came down to the coast by the Pungné route, and reached Cape Town on Dec. 8.

The excavations were carried on at Zimbabye during June, July, and a part of August. The first attempt was made on the large circular building at the foot of the hill, which is a perfect specimen of an ancient phallic temple; there was the solid round tower with its symbol marked in stone, the encircling wall, and "the discus," also with its appurtenant symbols. Parallels to this temple may be found in the round temples of the Cabiri at Malta, the temples on Samothrace and elsewhere, and the Phœnician coin of Byblos gives a curiously apt illustration of this temple. The excavations yielded but little beyond the interior plan of the building and traces of the Kafir habitation up to a recent date, a few decorated phalli and small fragments of soapstone bowls being the only yield belonging to the earlier periods. The results of the work on the fortress were more satisfactory as regards actual finds. The narrow approach from the plain was laid bare through two tortuous walls, protected by traverses, ambuscades, and other forms of defense. It led up to a narrow gully between the parts of a split granite bowlder, up which a set of steps led on to a parapet above the precipice of granite. On this summit an elaborate system of fortification had been erected. A wall 18 feet thick and 30 feet high runs along the edge of a sheer precipice, itself 90 feet high. This wall is surmounted by monoliths alternating with small round towers, and is again protected by an inner wall, allowing of only a narrow passage through a redundancy of defense. A fine barbed, copper spearhead and several implements of war were found here. The upper part of this fortress was adorned with huge monoliths and decorated beams of soapstone, one of which was 13 feet high, and bore patterns chiefly of a geometrical character. Flights of steps led up to the little plateau from either side, and on clearing away, a most curious plan of intricate labyrinthine confusion was disclosed. The principal finds were in the ancient temple of the fortress, which is now used as a cattle kraal. It was supported by an elaborately constructed system of under walls, and was approached by a narrow passage and a staircase of considerable architectural merit. The semicircular outer wall of this temple had been decorated by 5 carved birds on the top of soapstone pedestals from 5 to 6 feet in height, all which were found. They were all different, and archaic in design. One bore on its pedestal and wings a well-known phallic symbol. The only one that had its beak intact presented a resemblance to a vulture or raven, which was curiously emphasized by the similar appearance of the living vultures of the neighborhood when perched on monoliths. Several iron bells were found, an altar built of small granite blocks, and 40 or more soapstone phalli of different forms and shapes, some of them very realistic. In two caves and in depressions between the bowlders were found numerous fragments of soapstone bowls adorned with hunting scenes, figures of animals, a procession, etc., and some of them plain; fragments of pottery of excellent glaze and work-

manship, with geometric patterns correctly executed ; implements of war, including a gilt spearhead ; circular whorls of pottery ; fragments of
Persian and Celadon coins ; a smelting furnace,
tools, etc., connected with the working of gold.
Of other ruins near Zimbabye, and between the
Lundi and the Zambezi, the author speaks especially of those of Mattindaila, 64 miles northeast of Zimbabye. It was apparently the center
of a line of forts extending over many miles.
The area inclosed by the walls is almost as large
as that of the circular building at Zimbabye, and
somewhat resembles it. The patterns outside
the wall are more elaborate than those of Zimbabye. The interior is divided into chambers
by cross walls, and is full of large baobab trees.
The entrances are all triple and squared at the
corners, and are all walled up. Outside this
fortress are a few minor buildings and numerous
circular foundations of regularly constructed
granite blocks.

In a paper subsequently presented to the
Anthropological Institute (March or April, 1892)
Mr. Bent expressed the conclusions that the
ruins and the things in them are not connected
with any known African race. The object of
art and of special cult are foreign to the country,
where the only recognized form of religion is
and has been for centuries that of ancestor
worship. The cult, too, is distinctly pertaining
to a pre-Mohammedan period, while the ruins
presumptively date back to a period more remote
than is even implied in that term. A second
point is obvious, that the ruins formed a garrison for the protection of a gold-producing race
in remote antiquity. Forts of a similar structure
are found all the way through the gold-producing country, and were erected to protect the mines.
The cumulative evidence in favor of the race's
being one of the many tribes of Arabia is very
strong, the special cult, the monolithic decorations, and the later evidence of Arabian intercourse with the country, when their power was
reduced to the coast line.

The area covered by the ruins is very considerable, and all that Mr. Bent's party could do in
the space of time and with the money at their
command was to clear the ground of the vegetation that covered it, and excavate in some of the
most likely places. There is, therefore, a vast
area of ground still untouched, which may in
course of time yield further evidences as to the
origin of the builders of these ruins.

ARIZONA, a Territory of the United States,
organized Feb. 24, 1863; area, 113,020 square
miles. The population, according to each decennial census, was 9,658 in 1870; 40,440 in
1880; and 59,620 in 1890. Capital, Phenix.

Government.—The following were the Territorial officers during the year: Governor, John
N. Irwin, Republican, who resigned on April
20 and was succeeded by Nathan O. Murphy,
Republican; Secretary, Nathan O. Murphy, appointed Governor on April 21 and succeeded by
N. A. Morford; Treasurer, William Christy;
Auditor, Thomas Hughes; Attorney-General,
William Herring; Superintendent of Public Instruction, George W. Cheyney; Railroad Commissioners, H. B. Lighthizer, E. B. Gage, G. W.
Beecher, J. S. O'Brien; Chief Justice of the Supreme Court, Henry C. Gooding; Associate Jus-

tices, Joseph H. Kibbey, Richard E. Sloan, and
Edward W. Wells.

Finances.—The Territorial debt on Sept. 1,
1892, was as follows: Bonds issued, $581,000;
floating debt, $229,240.93; interest on bonds, $24,-
562; interest on floating debt, $26,026.92; total,
$860,829.85. At the same time the several coun-
ties owed debts, bonded and floating, with interest, amounting to $2,305,084.50, and the several
cities were indebted in the sum of $188,811.46.

The Territorial funding law, which was passed
by Congress in June, 1890, and which provided
for funding all the Territorial, county, municipal,
and school indebtedness of the Territory into
bonds, bearing 5 per cent. interest, was first made
available this year. It was amended by Congress
in July so as to provide for semiannual payments
of interest, and was changed in certain other respects so as to be satisfactory to investors, after
which the entire issue of bonds was sold to a
single New York company.

Valuations.—The total assessed valuation of
property in the Territory for 1892 was $27,923,-
162.55, being a slight decrease from the valuation
of 1891. This decrease was caused chiefly by the
reduction in value and number of cattle on the
ranges. Included in the assessment are the following items: 3,368,743 acres of land, $4,748,-
962.43; improvements thereon, $1,679,013.20;
city and town lots, $2,266,883.50; improvements
thereon, $2,453,068.20; 48,428 horses, $1,158,912,-
46; 2,013 mules, $59,937; 644.209 cattle, $5,038,-
207; 4,022 goats, $4,424; 6,670 hogs, $26,680;
1,313 asses, $13,817.75; 384,338 sheep, $768,917;
1,074 miles of railroad, $6,038,893.41; all other
property, $3,665,446.60; total, $27,923,162.55.
The rate of taxation for Territorial purposes in
1892 was 80 cents on $100.

Education.—A school month in the Territory
consists of four weeks of five days each, and, although in the cities and towns schools are maintained for nine and frequently ten months, the
average for the Territory is between six and
seven months. Districts must maintain a school
for five months in order to secure the proportion
of county moneys to which they are entitled.
In round numbers, one third of the children are
at school, while the proportion of those who attend a portion of the year is nearly half.

The Territorial Normal School at Tempe, Mari-
copa County, is thorough in all its appointments
for educational purposes, and will compare
favorably with like institutions in the States.
The average number of pupils in attendance
during 1892 was 52.

Militia.—The Arizona National Guard consists of 1 regiment of infantry, of 3 battalions, of 3
companies each. The sixteenth Legislature, in
the act authorizing the Territorial militia, provided for an allowance of $30 a month to each
company for current expenses. Several companies
had been organized prior to the passage of this
act, and had been partially equipped from funds
allotted to the militia by the General Government. Arizona's proportion of which is about
$2,000 a year.

Mining Discovery.—Late in June the discovery was announced of valuable silver deposits in the Cerbat mountains, about 50 miles
north of Kingman. The news spread rapidly,
and within a month 3,000 people visited the lo-

cality. A new town, called White Hills, sprang up. The ore is rich in silver and gold, but its distance from railroads will retard the development of the region.

Irrigation.—For 1892 the Governor reports the following statistics respecting irrigation in the Territory:

NAME OF COUNTY.	Miles of irrigating canals not including laterals.	Acres reclaimed.	Acres capable of reclamation under present water development.
Apache................	20	10,000	300,000
Cochise...............	8	4,000	40,000
Coconino.....	..	* 2,000	50,000
Gila..................	16	5,000	50,000
Graham...............	60	15,000	100,000
Mohave..............	3	1,000	10,000
Maricopa	250	240,000	600,000
Pima.................	20	10,000	100,000
Pinal................	75	20,000	150,000
Yavapai.....	10	6,000	30,000
Yuma................	50	30,000	300,000
Total..............	512	343,000	1,730,000

* Subirrigation.

It is believed that fully one third of the area of the Territory, or about 24,000,000 acres, could be reclaimed if the maximum water-storage facilities possible by a proper investment of capital could be made available.

Indians.—There was no trouble during the year with any of the Indian tribes in the Territory, with the exception of the Navajos. Between them and the white settlers there has been friction for a long period, and several persons have been killed on both sides within the past year or two. The whole matter seems to hinge upon the question what rights, if any, the Indians have on the public domain off their reservation, and what the distinction is between the rights of white and red men in this connection. The Indians contend that they have as much right on untitled land for grazing or other purposes as white men, and that their agents so advise them, while the white men of the neighborhood owning cattle and sheep insist that the Indians have no rights whatever on the public lands beyond the limits of their reservation, which seems to be the popular idea among the settlers. An investigation has been made by the Indian Bureau, and a report was published in August, which makes some recommendations but does not attempt a final settlement. The Navajos can muster over 5,000 well-armed men, and in case of war could terrorize nearly all of northern Arizona.

Penitentiary.—At the Yuma Penitentiary there were 176 prisoners in July. The prison buildings are intended for the accommodation of about half that number.

Statehood. — The proposed State Constitution, which was framed by a Territorial convention at Phenix in September, 1891, a synopsis of which appeared in the "Annual Cyclopædia" for that year, was submitted to the people of the Territory for adoption or rejection on Dec. 1 following its framing. It encountered considerable opposition in some quarters, on account of its provisions respecting water rights and irrigation, but as a whole it received the popular approval. The vote at the election was 5,440 in favor of its adoption and 2,282 against it, only

one county, and that a small one, giving an adverse majority. A bill providing for the admission of the Territory to the Union under this Constitution was immediately presented to Congress, and on June 6 of this year was passed in the House of Representatives. No action had been taken by the Senate before the adjournment of the session, but the people are confidently expecting statehood at an early day.

Development.—The growth of the Territory has been heretofore seriously retarded by lack of sufficient railroad facilities. Two transcontinental lines, the Atlantic and Pacific and the Southern Pacific, cross its limits from east to west, one in the northern and one in the southern portion, but there has been no north-and-south line connecting these parallel roads. After a long agitation the construction of such a line was undertaken in 1892, connecting the cities of Prescott in the north and Phenix in the south. The road is called the Santa Fé, Prescott and Phenix Railroad, and will be about 210 miles long. Heretofore grain, vegetables, and fruit have been imported at large expense into the northern half of the Territory from Kansas and California, while in southern Arizona those products were very cheap, because no market was easily accessible.

Political.—Early in April a Territorial Republican convention met at Phenix and elected two delegates to the national convention at Minneapolis. A few weeks later a Democratic Territorial convention selected delegates to the Chicago National Convention. Neither of these bodies named the candidates for Territorial offices. On Sept. 8, however, another Republican Territorial convention met at Prescott and nominated William G. Stewart for Delegate to Congress, and George Clough for Councilman-at-Large. The platform adopted approves the national and Territorial administration, and contains the following declarations:

We favor the free and unlimited coinage of silver as being demanded by the best interests of our nation.

We point with pride to the general close observance of all laws, both Federal and Territorial, and challenge the comparison with any State in the Union, and we earnestly urge the admission of Arizona into full Statehood.

We charge the leaders of the Democratic party of Arizona with debasing the honest labor of the Territory by arraying against it the competition of convicted criminals, by passing a law authorizing the leasing of the convict labor of the Territorial prison, and we ask from every laboring man a comparison between this action of the Democratic Legislature and the action of the Republican Governor in vetoing the measure.

We believe and urge as a public necessity that the ownership of all railroad and telegraph lines be vested in the General Government.

Large bodies of land in this Territory are held by various corporations, under congressional land grants, on which no taxes are paid, owing to their not being surveyed and patented. We pledge our Representative to urge upon Congress immediate action to have these grants and other unsurveyed land surveyed, and thus increase the taxable property by many thousands of dollars. We urge upon Congress the ceding to the different States and Territories of all arid lands now held by the Federal Government.

Two weeks later a Democratic Territorial convention met at Tombstone and renominated

Marcus A. Smith for Delegate to Congress. Thomas Norris was selected as Councilman-at-Large. At the November election the Democratic ticket was successful by a majority of 899.

ARKANSAS, a Southern State, admitted to the Union June 15, 1836; area, 53,850 square miles. The population, according to each decennial census since admission, was 97,574 in 1840; 209,897 in 1850; 435,450 in 1860; 484.471 in 1870; 802,525 in 1880; and 1,128,179 in 1890. Capital, Little Rock.

Government.—The following were the State officers during the year: Governor, James P. Eagle, Democrat; Secretary of State, B. B. Chism; Auditor, W. S. Dunlop; Treasurer, Richard B. Morrow; Attorney-General, William E. Atkinson; Superintendent of Public Instruction, Josiah H. Shinn; Commissioner of Mines, Manufactures, and Agriculture, M. F. Locke; State Land Commissioner, Charles B. Myers; Chief Justice of the Supreme Court, Sterling R. Cockrill; Associate Justices, Burrill B. Battle, Simon P. Hughes, William E. Hemingway, and W. W. Mansfield. From Aug. 11 to Oct. 16 Gov. Eagle was absent from the State, being compelled to seek medical treatment in Kentucky for a serious disease which attacked him early in June. During his absence Christopher C. Hamby, President of the State Senate, was the acting Governor.

Finances.—The State Treasurer reports the following balances on hand, July 1, 1892, the figures covering all the State funds:

In United States currency	$241,836 67
In State scrip	180,426 87
In bond scrip	56,258 38
In county scrip	20,890 99
In city scrip	105 67
Six-per-cent. funded bonds	585,000 00
Six-per-cent. funded coupons	388,580 00
Six-per-cent. funded interest	1,214 90
Loughborough bonds. 1875	1,571,000 00
R. M. Morrow notes	50,342 35
Treasury swamp-land scrip	558 25
Auditor's swamp-land warrants	70 00
Refunding certificates	766 15
Total	**$3,092,845 28**

The Woodruff Defalcation.—The first trial of ex-State Treasurer William E. Woodruff for embezzlement of State funds during his official term having resulted, in October, 1891, in a disagreement of the jury, he was put upon trial a second time on April 5, 1892. After a hearing that lasted over a week the jury found the prisoner not guilty, and he was released. When the shortage in his accounts was discovered in January, 1891, his bondsmen at once made up an acknowledged cash deficiency of $63,740.57; but subsequent investigation showed that a further deficiency existed by reason of a large amount of State securities which were missing. In order to fix the responsibility for the loss of these, a suit was begun on Feb. 25, 1892, in the Pulaski Chancery Court, against the sureties on his several bonds as Treasurer. The complaint alleged the following amounts to be due the State: State scrip, $122,286.58; uncanceled interest-bearing State scrip, $12,966.41; 6-per-cent. funding bonds, principal, $43.53; 6-per-cent. funding bonds, coupons, $11,132.53; Arkansas City scrip, $10; excess due various counties, $2,244.82; total, $148,863.87. This suit was pending at the close of the year.

Penitentiary.—On May 1, 1892, there were about 740 prisoners in the State Penitentiary, an increase of about 50 since Jan. 1, 1891. The present convict lease, which has yielded the State about $30,000 annually in the past nine years, will expire in 1893. The lessees refuse to make any bid for its renewal, and the State will probably be obliged to provide employment for its convicts on public works.

Arkansas River.—Up to June 30, 1891, the total appropriations for the improvement of Arkansas river had reached the sum of $485,251.37, nearly all of which had been expended. With this money several surveys of the river have been completed and boats have been employed in removing snags, thereby rendering navigation yearly less and less dangerous. One iron-hulled snag boat and one wooden light-draft snag boat are now employed upon the river. The removal of snags is the only work that can be profitably pursued until by some permanent improvement the banks are protected from caving and the annual supply of snags is no longer furnished.

About the middle of May, on account of heavy rains, the river began to rise, and in a few days had reached a point far above the usual flood mark. The surrounding country was overflowed, growing crops were destroyed, and people were driven from their homes and reduced to destitution. In Little Rock and other cities of the State relief funds were raised by popular subscription. From Little Rock a vessel was dispatched down the river, laden with provisions and supplies of seed corn, cotton, oats, wheat, etc., for those who were unable to buy for replanting. Early in June the river began to recede and the overflowed lands were soon restored to cultivation.

State Road Convention.—At the call of State Commissioner of Agriculture M. F. Locke, a convention of delegates from the several counties met at Little Rock on Oct. 20 to discuss the question of improving the public roads of the State. After considerable discussion, the opinion of the convention was embodied in the following resolutions:

That the General Assembly be requested to submit an amendment to the Constitution of the State allowing each or any county in the State to levy an additional tax upon the property of said counties not to exceed three mills on the dollar for building and improving the public highways.

That a committee of seven be appointed, to be known as the committee on road legislation and agitation, to urge and secure the enactment of such laws as may be proper and necessary for the improvement of our roads and highways.

That this convention favors a State equalization of assessment of taxes relatively between the counties, if the same may legally be done by legislative enactment.

That it is the sense of this convention that the State of Arkansas should connect each city of the first class, together with the county seat of each county in the State, with a State road, and that to this end the State should, by and through competent engineers, locate, construct, and maintain such roads; that in the construction and maintenance of said State roads the State should provide the means and use to the best advantage the convict labor of the State.

After the appointment of the committee the convention adjourned subject to the call of the chairman.

Negro Exodus.—About the middle of March 300 or more negroes, incited by stories of the resources of Oklahoma, emigrated in a body from Jefferson County to that Territory, going by vessel up Arkansas river. Late in the same month a company of 115 negroes set out overland from Crittenden County for the same Territory; and from various other parts of the State there was a considerable exodus of negroes during the spring of this year, in the same direction.

Political.—On April 7 a State convention of Republicans met at Little Rock and selected delegates to the National Republican Convention, who were instructed to vote for the renomination of President Harrison. The resolutions adopted included the following:

We view with alarm the increased prevalence of lynch law and mob rule in this State.

The present Democratic State administration seems to be inefficient and powerless in this regard. Mobs successfully defy the officers of the law. Citizens charged with crime and awaiting trial are wrested from sheriffs and other alleged peace officers and dragged to a speedy death, sometimes by shooting, sometimes by hanging, and in one recent instance by burning at the stake. No rewards have been offered or other adequate steps taken to secure the arrest and punishment of the perpetrators of these murders.

We appeal to the people to give us a State administration that will enforce the laws.

It remains a conceded fact, by foe as well as friend, that the Hon. Henry Pape, Republican State Treasurer, 1868-'74, was the only State Treasurer since the war and prior to the present administration who retired from office without charge of embezzlement or suspicion of peculation.

We condemn the election law passed by the last Legislature as an infamous measure, intended to deprive the citizens of the free and unrestricted exercise of the right of suffrage as guaranteed by the Constitution of the State.

The concentration of the power to appoint commissioners of election for the respective counties in a board of State officials at Little Rock is a tyrannical destruction of the right of home rule, so dear to the heart of every freeman.

We are opposed to the proposed amendment to the Constitution which tends to restrict free manhood suffrage by making the payment of a tax a condition precedent to the exercise of that right which the founders of our Government have declared to be the inalienable right of every citizen.

The convention then adjourned, to meet on July 6 for the purpose of nominating a State ticket.

On May 4 the Prohibitionist State Convention was held at Little Rock. Delegates to the National Convention of the party were chosen, and a candidate for Governor was found in the person of William J. Nelson. The question of nominating other candidates was left to a committee. The platform adopted contains the usual declarations against the liquor traffic, denounces trusts, favors arbitration in labor disputes and Government control of railroad and telegraph lines, approves woman suffrage, and demands that

The land should be controlled and possessed for the benefit of the producer, and limited in quantity to each possessor to such a degree as to insure the people against monopoly and speculation and for the possession of absolute settlement of American citizens.

The Democratic State Convention met at Little Rock on June 14, and on the first ballot nominated William M. Fishback for Governor. State Treasurer Morrow, Superintendent of Public Instruction Shinn, Land Commissioner Myers, and Associate-Justice Hemingway were renominated. For Secretary of State the nominee was H. B. Armistead; for Auditor, C. B. Mills; for Attorney-General, James P. Clarke; for Commissioner of Mines, Manufactures, and Agriculture, John D. Adams. Delegates to the National Democratic Convention and candidates for presidential electors were also chosen. The platform contains a long arraignment of the Republican party, and concludes with the following declarations:

We favor a safe and sufficient currency, composed of gold and silver and legal-tender paper, convertible into coin on demand, and maintained at par with each other.

We declare it to be the duty of the Democratic party to preserve the parity in value of gold and silver, and to provide the means by the equal and fair treatment of both metals.

We denounce the Sherman Silver bill as an obstruction to the fair treatment of silver, and as a sham and a pretense, intended to postpone honest legislation and to appease the silver producers while giving no relief to the people.

We declare it to be the sense of this convention that the Penitentiary lease system should be abolished and a system adopted for the treatment of convicts more consistent with the better instincts and more improved methods of the age, and that the next General Assembly should not adjourn without appropriate legislation on this important subject.

We declare for free and fair elections, removed from intimidation and corruption of all kinds, and to that end we will give the modified Australian ballot law, enacted by the last Democratic Legislature, a fair and full trial in the interest of good government.

We indignantly hurl back upon the Republican party the oft-repeated false accusation that elections in Arkansas are controlled by intimidation and fraud.

On June 21 the following ticket was nominated by the People's party in State Convention at Little Rock: For Governor, Jacob P. Carnahan; for Secretary of State, Paul T. Davidson; for Auditor, Abner A. Steele; for Treasurer, Warren H. Wight; for Attorney-General, William P. Parks; for State Land Commissioner, James M. L. Thomasson; for Commissioner of Mines, etc., William Manning; for Superintendent of Public Instruction, George W. Crosby; for Associate Justice of the Supreme Court, Wilbur F. Hill. Delegates to the national convention of the party and candidates for presidential electors were also chosen. The platform demands free and unlimited coinage of silver at the present ratio, an increase of the circulating medium to $50 *per capita*, a graduated income tax, the establishment of postal savings banks, and Government control of railroads, telegraphs, and telephones. Upon State issues the following declarations were made:

We condemn the Democratic administration in Arkansas for its high crimes against justice and law. Its disregard of justice and law in the furtherance of party ends has engendered a spirit of mob law, which is undermining the courts of justice, disgracing our State, and endangering life and liberty.

We condemn amendment No. 2 as a partisan effort to strengthen a corrupt party in their hold on power by limiting the right of suffrage, and as not being an honest measure for the purpose of raising revenue.

We believe that the system of paying public officers by fees is injurious to the public service.

We believe in a free-school system, and the furnishing of school-books by the State to the citizens at cost.

We condemn the present barbarous convict lease law, instituted by the Republican party and continued by its servile imitators, the Democratic party, and demand its immediate repeal.

We suggest that in lieu of the present system a penitentiary farm be provided, upon which a sufficient number of the convicts be employed to make a support for the whole body, and that all surplus labor above the farm needs be used in building State roads.

We demand a State reformatory institution for young convicts, who under the present system come out of prison worse than they enter.

We condemn the present unjust road law, under which those least able have to bear all the burden, and demand in its stead a just and equitable system of taxation for road purposes.

We demand an amendment to the State Constitution, making our elections for four-year terms, and forbidding a re-election on the part of any officer to two consecutive terms, and in this connection we demand consolidation of State and national elections.

In the present impoverished condition of our tax payers we think it would be nothing less than a crime for our Legislature to appropriate moneys for luxuries like the World's Fair at Chicago, but we approve the course of those citizens who out of their abundance contribute to that exposition.

We condemn in unmeasured terms the looting of the State treasury by Democratic officials, who now go unwhipped of justice.

We deny that the Democratic party in Arkansas has given us fair elections or believes in them, and we assert that their boasted election law is but a servile imitation of the Lodge force bill, and was devised to enable them to perpetuate their wicked lease of power, despite the will of the electors.

Upon reassembling on July 6, the Republican State Convention nominated candidates for presidential electors and the following State ticket: For Governor, William G. Whipple; for Secretary of State, James Oates; for Auditor, Samuel A. Williams; for Treasurer, Charles N. Rix; for Attorney-General, E. H. Vance; for State Land Commissioner, Jacob H. Donahoo; for Commissioner of Mines, etc., D. C. Gordon; for Superintendent of Public Instruction, Zadock P. Freeman; for Associate Justice of the Supreme Court, Wilbur F. Hill. The canvass following these nominations was uneventful. At the election on Sept. 5 the entire Democratic State ticket was elected. For Governor, Fishback received 90,115 votes, Whipple 33,644, Carnahan 31,177, and Nelson 1,310. Half of the State Senate and all the members of the House of Representatives were chosen at the same time. The Legislature of 1893 will be divided politically as follows: Senate—Democrats 29, People's Party 2, Republicans 1; House—Democrats 88, People's Party 7, Republicans 5. A proposed amendment to the State Constitution requiring payment of a poll tax as a prerequisite for voting was submitted to the people at this election, and received 75,848 affirmative and 56,589 negative votes. As it failed to receive the approval of a majority of the total number of persons voting at the election, it seems not to have been adopted.

At the November election the Democrats were again successful, electing their candidates for Congress in every district and their presidential electors. The vote on the electoral ticket was: Cleveland, 87,057; Harrison, 46,359; Weaver, 11,831. Cleveland's plurality, 40,698.

ASSOCIATIONS FOR THE ADVANCEMENT OF SCIENCE. American.—The forty-first meeting of the American Association was held in Rochester, N. Y., Aug. 17-23, 1892. The officers of the meeting were: President, Joseph Le Conte, of Berkeley, Cal.; Vice-presidents of sections: A, John R. Eastman, Washington, D. C.; B, Benjamin F. Thomas, Columbus, Ohio; C, Alfred Springer, Cincinnati, Ohio; D, John B. Johnson, St. Louis, Mo.; E, Henry S. Williams, Ithaca, N. Y.; F, Simon H. Gage, Ithaca, N. Y.; H, William H. Holmes, Washington, D. C.; I, Lester F. Ward, Washington, D. C. Per-

JOSEPH LE CONTE.

manent Secretary, Frederick W. Putnam, Cambridge (office, Salem), Mass. General Secretary, Amos W. Butler, Brookville, Ind. Secretary of the Council, Thomas H. Norton, Cincinnati, Ohio. Secretaries of the sections: A, Winslow Upton, Providence, R. I.; B, Brown Ayres, New Orleans, La.; C, James Lewis Howe, Louisville, Ky.; D, Olin H. Landreth, Nashville, Tenn.; E, Rollin D. Salisbury, Madison, Wis.; F, Byron D. Halsted, New Brunswick, N. J.; H, William M. Beauchamp, Baldwinsville, N. Y.; I, Henry Farquhar, Washington, D. C. Treasurer, William Lilly, Mauch Chunk, Pa.

Opening Proceedings.—The meeting began at noon on Aug. 16 with a preliminary meeting of the council, at which the names of 69 new members were passed. These, with the 33 elected on April 20, made 102 new members elected since the meeting a year ago. The first general session was held at 10 A. M. in the chapel of the University of Rochester, where the gathered scientists were called to order by the retiring president, Prof. Albert B. Prescott, who briefly introduced his successor, Prof. Joseph Le Conte, with a fitting tribute to the latter's eminence in geologica lscience. In taking the chair President Le Conte expressed his appreciation of the kind and courteous way in which the mantle had been transferred to him, and thanked the society for the honor conferred upon him. He said:

There were three, and only three, things which passed beyond the material and entered the spiritual. They were fine art, religion, science. Art perfected the ideal of beauty in the mind. Religion perfected it in the heart and conduct. Science strove to perfect the same image in the realm of abstract truth. Was he not right in saying that it was a great honor to take a leading place in an association which embraced all branches of science that come nearer to the people than any other scientific association?

After an invocation by the Rev. Corliss B. Gardiner, addresses of welcome were made by Dr. Edward M. Moore, President of the Local Committee, Hon. Richard Curran, Mayor of the city, and Dr. David J. Hill, President of the University of Rochester; to which a suitable reply was made by President Le Conte, who, in the course of his remarks, said:

I will not dwell too long on the utilitarian feature of the subject. We must love science for its own sake. Truth is its own chief reward. It has been mercifully ordered for our encouragement that every step in the higher walks of life shall be attended with material benefit. While astronomy opens the doors of heaven, it also directs our commerce and guides our ships; geology, besides opening the gates of infinite time, also discovers beds of coal and veins of metals; streams, rushing down mountains or reflecting the blue skies on their placid bosoms, also turn our mills and float our vessels. Science—truth—is its own exceeding great reward. There is an indissoluble connection between truth and good, between truth and utility. It may not be to-day, it may not be in this decade, this century, this millennium, but sooner or later it must bless mankind. Every community honors itself in honoring science.

The permanent secretary, Prof. Frederick W. Putnam, then made his annual report, in which he announced the decease of some twenty members, including Edward Burgess, Henry I. Bowditch, William Ferrell, T. Sterry Hunt, and Joseph Lovering.

A statement of the funds of the association was read. The Research fund contains $5,657.22, and the general fund $2,394.53, making a total of $7.932.85.

Address of the Retiring President.—The subject of President Prescott's retiring address was "The Immediate Work in Chemical Science." and in the course of it he said:

"It is well known that chemical labor has not been barren of returns. The products of chemical action, numbering thousands of thousands, have been sifted and measured and weighed. If you ask what happens in a common chemical change, you can obtain direct answers. When coal burns in the air, how much oxygen is used up can be stated with a degree of exactness true to the first decimal of mass, perhaps to the second, but questionable in the third. How much carbonic acid is made can be told in weight and in volume with approaching exactness. How much heat this chemical action is worth, how much light, how much electro-motive force, what train-load of cars it can carry, how long it can make certain wheels go round—for these questions chemists and physicists are ready.

"Chemists are concerned mainly with what can be made out of atoms, not with what atoms can be made of. Whatever they are, and by whatever force or motion it is that they unite with each other, we define them by their effects. Through their effects they are classified in the rank and file of the periodic system.

"Knowledge of molecular structure makes chemistry a science, nourishing to the reason, giving dominion over matter, for beneficence to

life. Studies of structure were never before so inviting. In this direction and in that especial opportunities appear. Moreover, the actual worker here and there breaks into unexpected paths of promise. Certainly the sugar group is presenting to the chemist an open way from simple alcohols on through to the cell substances of the vegetable world.

"I have spoken of the century of beginning chemical labor, and have referred to the divisions and specialties of chemical study. What can I say of the means of uniting the earlier and later years of the past, as well as the separated pursuits of the present, in one mobile working force? Societies of science are among these means, and it becomes us to magnify their office. Most necessary of all the means of unification in science is the use of its literature. To every solitary investigator I should desire to say: Get to a library of your subject, learn how to use its literature, and possess yourself of what there is on the theme of your choice, or else determine to give it up altogether.

"A great deal of indexing is wanted. Systematic bibliography, both of previous and of current literature, would add a third to the productive power of a large number of workers. Topical bibliographies are of great service.

"Allied to the much needed service in bibliography is the service in compilation of the constants of nature."

In closing, he made an appeal for an endowment fund, as follows:

"There are men and women who have been so far rewarded that great means of progress are in their hands. It is inevitable to wealth that it shall be put to some sort of use, for without investment it dies. The American Association, in the conservative interests of learning, proposes certain effective investments in science. If it be not given to every plodding worker to be a promoter of discovery, such, at all events, is the privilege of wealth, under the authority of this association. If it be not the good fortune of every investigator to reach knowledge that is new, there are in every section of this body workers of whom it is clear that they would reach some discovery of merit if only the means of work could be granted them. Whosoever supplies the means fairly deserves and will receive a share in the results."

Proceedings of the Sections.—There are eight sections, over each of which a vice-president presides. Subsequent to the first general session the sections are called to order by their officers and proceed to effect their organization by the election of a sectional committee, whose duty it is to arrange the business for the subsequent meetings of the section. Also, each section elects a member of the nominating committee who shall later meet to select officers for the future meeting; and each section likewise elects a sub-committee to nominate officers of the section for the future meeting. Subsequent to these duties, the section adjoins to hear its vice-presidential address, after which papers are taken up and read.

Sections.—A. *Mathematics and Astronomy.*—The presiding officer of this section was Prof. John R. Eastman, of the United States Naval Observatory in Washington, D. C. The subject of the vice-presidential address was concerning "The Neglected Field of Fundamental Astronomy," in which he called attention to certain branches of astronomy that had not been worked up, and dwelt with special emphasis on the importance of fundamental work in determining star places—a line of routine work that had been passed over in the struggle after more brilliant results in astronomical research.

The following-named papers were then read before the section :

"On the Conflict of Observation with Theory as to the Earth's Rotation," by Seth C. Chandler; "Meteorological Observations made in April, 1890, 1891, 1892, in the Totality Path of the Eclipse of 1893, April 16," by David P. Todd; "List of Thirty New Proper Motion Stars" and "Latitude of the Sayre Observatory," by C. L. Doolittle; "The Secular Motion of a Free Magnetic Needle," by Louis A. Bauer; "On the Discriminators of the Discriminant of an Algebraic Equation," by Mansfield Merriman ; "Forms of Solar Faculæ" and "The Spectroheliograph of the Kenwood Astro-physical Observatory, Chicago, and Results obtained in the Study of the Sun," by George E. Hale; "Models and Machines for showing Curves of the Third Degree," by Andrew W. Phillips; "Least Square Fallacies" and "Differential Formulæ for Orbit Corrections," by Truman H. Safford ; "On the Imaginary of Algebra," by Alexander Macfarlane; "The Iced-bar Base Apparatus of the United States Coast and Geodetic Survey," by R. S. Woodward; "On the Construction of a Prime Vertical Transit Instrument for the Determination of the Latitude of Harvard College Observatory," by William A. Rogers; "Lineo-linear Vector Functions," by Arthur S. Hathaway; "Thermal Absorption in the Solar Atmosphere," by Edwin B. Frost; "Electric Lights for Astronomical Instruments," by Jefferson E. Kershner; "European Observations," by John A. Brashear; "Proper Motions of Eighty-nine Stars within 10° of the North Pole, with Remarks on the Present State of the Problem of the Solar Motion," by Truman H. Safford ; "Concerning a Congruence Group of Order 360 contained in the Group of Linear Fractional Substitutions," by E. Hastings Moore ; "On the Intersection of an Equilateral Hyperbola and the Sides of a Plane Triangle—a Question in Trilinears," by William Hoover; "Practical Rules for testing whether a Number is divisible by Seven, or any other Small Prime, and if not divisible, to ascertain the Remainder," and "Increase in Constant for Addition in testing for Integral Values in the Equation of Quarter Squares," by James D. Warner; and "On the General Problem of Least Squares," by R. S. Woodward.

B. *Physics.*—This section was presided over by Prof. Benjamin F. Thomas, who holds the chair of Physics in the Ohio State University, in Columbus, Ohio. His address had to do with "Technical Education in High Schools and Universities." After reviewing the present very creditable position attained and occupied by the schools along technical lines, he suggested some improvements which he considered might be made, by eliminating certain of the less important branches now pursued and inserting others. After insisting on certain important modifications, he dwelt on the literary branches and reviewed them also, as subjects which have a practical bearing on the life of the engineer. Training in political science and history was considered of great importance, and the production of good citizens deemed equally important with the training of good engineers.

The following-named papers were then presented before the section :

"A Photographic Method of Mapping the Magnetic Field," by Charles B. Thwing; "Constancy of Vol-

ume of Iron in Strong Magnetic Fields" and "Note on Magnetic Disturbances caused by Electric Railways," by Frank P. Whitman; "Persistence of Vision," by Ervin S. Ferry; "Experiments on the Ocular Spectrum of the Eye and the Image presented to the Brain," by George W. Holley; "Description of a Contrivance intended for the Study of Perception at Definite Distances," by Charles A. Oliver; "Note on the Photography of the Manometric Flame and the Analysis of Vowel Sounds," by Ernest Merritt; "On the Sensitiveness of Photographic Plates," by George W. Hough; "E. M. F. between Normal and Strained Metals in Voltaic Cells," by William S. Franklin; "Influence of the Moon on the Rainfall," by Mansfield Merriman; "On the Mechanical and Physical Means of Aërial Transit without a Propeller," by David P. Todd; "Further Experiments on the Specific Inductive Capacity of Electrolytes," by Edward B. Rosa; "A Mechanical Model of Electro-magnetic Relations," by Amos E. Dolbear; "An Experimental Comparison of Formulæ for Total Radiation between 15° C. and 110° C.," by W. Le Conte Stevens; "On the Dispersion of Radiations of Great Wave Lengths in Rock Salt, Silvite, and Fluorspar," by H. Rubens and Benjamin W. Snow; "The Distribution of Energy in the Spectrum of the Glow-lamp," and "Absorption Spectra of Certain Substances in the Infra-red," by Edward L. Nichols; "On the Distribution of Energy in the Arc" and "On the Infra-red Spectra of the Alkalies," by Benjamin W. Snow; and "On the Mechanics of the Three States of Aggregation," by Gustavus Hinrichs.

C. *Chemistry.*—The vice-president in charge of this section was Dr. Alfred Springer, of Cincinnati, Ohio. He chose as the subject of his remarks "The Micro-organisms of the Soil." After a brief *résumé* of the advances and discoveries made in chemistry during the year, he took up the special topic of his address, and discussed the investigations in England and this country concerning the working of micro-organisms and as to the possibility of nitrogen starvation, which was the essential element in his address. He argued that it was an impossibility.

The following papers were subsequently read and discussed before the section :

The report of Committee on indexing Chemical Literature; "A Select Bibliography of Chemistry," by H. Carrington Bolton; "Notes on a Bibliography of Mineral Waters," by Alfred Tuckerman; "Copper Sulfate as a Material for standardizing Solutions," by Edward Hart; "An Effective Condenser for Volatile Liquids and for Water Analysis" and "Di-ethylcarbinamin and its Conduct toward Nitrous Acid," by William A. Noyes ; "The Iodomercurates of Organic Bases," by Albert B. Prescott; "Tri-methylxanthin and its Derivatives," by Moses Gomberg; "Some Points in connection with the Composition of Honey" and "A Method of Polarimetric Observation at Low Temperatures," by Harvey W. Wiley; "Note on the Effect of Fertilizers upon the Juice of the Sugar-cane," by Clinton P. Townsend ; "The Enzyms or Soluble Ferments of the Hog-cholera Germ," by Emil A. de Schweinitz; "Catalytic Influence of Ammonia on Amorphous Substances to induce Crystallization," by Edward Goldsmith ; "Post-mortem Imbibition of Arsenic," "Effect of Sedimentation upon Self-purification of Running Streams," and "The Value of a Water Analysis," by William P. Mason ; "Presentation of Samples from the Salt Mines of New York," by S. A. Lattimore; "On the Mechanical Determination of the Stereographic Constitution of Organic Compounds," by Gustavus Hinrichs; "On the Decomposition of Acetone with Concentrated Sulfuric Acid," by William R. Orndorf; "Itacolumite from North Carolina," by Laura Osborne Talbott; and "The Albuminoids of Maize," by George Archbold. Also a discussion upon the practical adoption of the report of Committee on Spelling and Pronunciation of Chemical Terms.

D. *Mechanical Science and Engineering.*—This section was presided over by Prof. John B. Johnson, who is connected with Washington University, St. Louis, Mo. His address was entitled "The Applied Scientist." The distinction between the theoretical scientist and the practical scientist was somewhat fully discussed and the sphere of each clearly defined, after which Prof. Johnson very fully elaborated the value of the practical scientist, especially in the application of mechanical engineering to every-day experiences.

The following-named papers were read and discussed before the section:

"Exhibition and Description of Combined Yard and Meter Standard Bar" and "Investigation of a 21-feet Precision Screw," by William A. Rogers; "On the Use of Long Steel Tapes in measuring Base Line," by R. S. Woodward; "Results of Municipal Ownership of Gas Works in the United States during 1891," by Edward W. Bemis; "Description of a Transmission Dynamometer," by George W. Hough; "Measurements of Total Heats of Combustion" and "Use of Anemometers for measuring Velocity of Air in Mines," by David S. Jacobus; "Negative Specific Heats," by DeVolson Wood; "Bending Tests of Timber," by J. Burkitt Webb; "Method of measuring Loss of Power and Drop of Pressure between Cylinders in Multiple-cylinder Engine," by James E. Denton; "Steam Economy of the Engines of the Screw Ferryboat ' Bremen,' " by James E. Denton and David S. Jacobus; "Peculiar Visible Strain in Steel when tested in Tension, Compression, and Cross-breaking," and "Extensometer for measuring Distortion of Specimens under Test," by John B. Johnson; "Relative Economy of the Single Cylinder Air-compressor with Cooling by a Spray of Water and the Present Economy of the Compound Compressors at Qua de la Gare, Paris," by Fred. T. Gause; "A New Window-ventilating Appliance," by A. M. Rosebrough.

Also, a meeting of the Association of Mechanical Engineering Teachers was held with this section.

E. *Geology and Geography.*—This section was presided over by Prof. Henry S. Williams, who has recently been called to succeed the venerable James D. Dana in the charge of the geology at Yale University. His address had to do with "The Scope of Palæontology, and its Value to Geologists." He said: "The scientific study of fossils is scarcely a century old. It was not until 1796 that Cuvier ventured to say that certain fossil bones found in the Paris basin represented an extinct elephant. In 1819 William Smith became famous by his assertions that rock strata could be traced across the country by their fossils. Up to that time fossils had only been regarded as curiosities. Deshayes, and later William Lonsdale, were the first to demonstrate the wide scope of the palæontology and its interpretation of the problems of geology. The old law under which fossils were studied considers the significance of fossils as marks indicating the strata to which they belong. The higher or comparative palæontology of Deshayes, Lyell, and Lonsdale considers the relationship which fossils bear to each other. It deals with the history of organisms, and is able to find in fossils the evidence of the order of sequence of rocks containing them. To the comparative palæon-

tologist, fossils are hieroglyphics which tell of the habits, customs, migrations, and environments of the successive races from the beginning of the world. The stratigraphic order is important, but the fossils are much more important than stratigraphy to the correct interpretation of geology. We owe to comparative palæontology, and not to stratigraphy or lithology, the primary classification of the geological scale and the means of distinguishing the chronological position of each formation."

The following-named papers were read before the section:

"Terminal Moraines in New England," by Charles H. Hitchcock; "A Passage in the History of the Cuyahoga River," by Edward W. Claypole; "Notes bearing upon the Changes of the Preglacial Drainage of Western Illinois and Eastern Iowa," by Frank Leverett; "Extra-morainic Drift in New Jersey," by Albert A. Wright; "The Volcanic Craters of the United States," "The Homotoxic Relations of the North American Lower Cretaceous," and "Recent Geological Explorations in Mexico," by Robert T. Hill; "Palæobotany of the Yellow Gravel at Bridgeton, N. J.," by Arthur Hollick; "Presentation of Samples from the Salt Mines of New York," by S. A. Lattimore; "The Mining, Metallurgical, Geological, and Mineralogical Exhibits to be shown at the World's Columbian Exposition," by George F. Kunz; "Cerro-Viejo and its Cones of Volcanic Ejecta and Extrusion in Nicaragua," by John Crawford; "Pleistocene Geography" and "Distributions of the LaFayette Formation," by W J McGee; "Submarine Valleys on Continental Slopes," by Warren Upham; "Cenozoic Beds of the Staked Plains of Texas," by Edward D. Cope; "Exhibitions of Guelph Fossils found in Rochester, N. Y.," by Albert L. Arey; "The American Mastodon in Florida," by John Kost; "Some Problems of the Mesabi Iron Ore," by N. H. Winchell; and "The Mathematics of Mountain Sculpture," by Verplanck Colvin.

F. *Biology.*—The presiding officer of this section was Prof. Simon H. Gage, of Cornell University, who discussed the "Comparative Physiology of Respiration." In the course of his address he said: "While the fundamental idea is probably true that respiration is in its essential process a kind of combustion or oxidation, yet the seat of this action is not the lungs or blood. The microscopic forms have no lungs, no blood, and many of them even no organs; they are, as has been well said, organless organisms; and yet every investigation since the time of Von Helmont has rendered it more and more certain that every living thing must in some way be supplied with the vital air or oxygen, and that this is in some way deteriorated by use; and the nearer investigation approaches to the real life stuff or protoplasm it alone is found to be the true breather, the true respirer; and, further, as was shown long ago, if a frog is decapitated and some of its tissue exposed in a moist place, it will continue to take up oxygen and give out carbon dioxide, thus apparently showing that the tissues of the highly organized frog may, under favorable conditions, absorb oxygen directly from the surrounding medium and return to it directly the waste carbon dioxide. This shows conclusively that it is the living substance that breathes, and the elaborate machinery of lungs, heart, and blood-vessels are only to make sure that the living matter, far removed from the external air, shall not be suffocated. Also, it has been found that if some of the living tissue is placed in an atmosphere of hydrogen or nitrogen, entirely devoid of oxygen, it will give off carbon dioxide as in the ordinary air. If it is asked, 'How can these things be?' the answer is: 'The living matter takes the oxygen and makes it an integral part of itself, as it does the carbon and nitrogen and other elements; and when, finally, energy is liberated, the oxidation occurs and the carbon dioxide appears as a waste product.'"

The question of dividing this section into one of zoölogy and one of botany was discussed, and the association thereafter adopted a resolution dividing the section into Section F, on zoölogy, and Section G, on botany.

"Notes on Ranunculus Repens and its Eastern North American Allies" and "Notes on a Monograph of the North American Species of Leopedeza," by Nathaniel L. Britton; "Contribution on the Digestive Tract of Some North American Ganoids," by Grant S. Hopkins; "Adaptation of Seeds to Facilitate Germination" and "The Root System of Mikania Scandens L." by W. W. Rowlee; "The 'Maxillary Tentacles' of Pronuba." by John B. Smith; "Preliminary Comparison of the Hepatic Flora of Boreal and Sub-boreal Regions," by L. M. Underwood; "On the Value of Wood Ashes in the Treatment of Peach Yellows" and "On the Value of Superphosphates and Muriate of Potash in the Treatment of Peach Yellows," by Edgar F. Smith; "Notes on Maize," by George Macloski; "Spikes of Wheat bearing Abnormal Spikelets" and "A Study of the Relative Lengths of the Sheaths and Internodes of Grasses for the Purpose of determining to what Extent this is a Reliable Specific Character," by William J. Beal; "Report of Biological Section of the Committee on the Naples Table," by Charles W. Stiles; "Bacteriological Investigations of Marine Waters and the Sea Floor" and "Non-parasitic Bacteria in Vegetable Tissue," by H. L. Russell; "Sketch of the Flora of Death Valley, California," by Frederick V. Coville; "Notes on Yellow Pitch-pine—Pinis rigida Mill. var. Lutea Kell. n. v." and "Germination at Intervals of Seed treated with Fungicides," by William A. Kellerman; "The Fertilization of Pear Flowers," by M. B. Waite; "On the Adult Cestodes of Cattle and Sheep," by Charles W. Stiles; "The Fertilization of the Fig, and Caprification," by C. V. Riley; "On a New Form of Marsupialia from the Laramie Formation," by Edward D. Cope; "The Proposed Columbus Biological Stations in Jamaica" and "An Interesting Case of Parasitism," by Albert H. Tuttle; "A Comparative Study of the Roots of Ranunculaciæ," by F. B. Maxwell; "Do Termites cultivate Fungi?" by Orator F. Cook; "Note on the Appearance of two Embryo Chicks in a Single Blastoderm," by Robert O. Moody; "Notes on some Fresh-water Mollusks," by William M. Beauchamp; "The Conditions which determine the Distribution of Bacteria in the Water of Rivers," by J. H. Stoller; "Adaptation of Plants to External Environment," by William P. Wilson; "Notes on Self-pollination of the Grape," by Spencer A. Beach; "The Comparative Influence of Odor and Color in attracting Insects," by George B. Sudworth; "Biological Notes on Fauna of Cold Spring Harbor" and "Notes on Daucus Carota," by Charles W. Hargitt; "A Preliminary Account of the Brain of Diemyctylus Viridescens based upon Sections made through the Entire Head," by Simon P. Gage; "Geographic Relationship of the Flora of the High Sierra Nevada-California," by Frederick V. Coville; "Variation in Native Ferns," by William M. Beauchamp; "Live-forever eradicated by a Fungous Disease," by David G. Fairchild; "Otto Kunze's Changes in Nomenclature of North American Grasses," by George Vasey; "Revised Nomenclature of the Arborescent Flora of the United States," by Bernhard E. Fernow and George B. Sudworth; "On Carpboxera Ptelearia, the New Herbarium Pest," by C. V. Riley; "The Insect Fauna of the Mississippi Bottoms," by Howard E.

Weed; "Characteristics and Adaptations of Desert Vegetation," by Frederick V. Coville; "Shrinkage of Wood as observed under the Microscope," by Filibert Roth; "Peziza Sclerotium" and "Temperature and Some of its Relations to Plant Life," by L. H. Pammel; "Pleospora of Tropæolum Majus," "Secondary Spores of Anthracnoses" and "A Bacterium of Phaseolus," by Byron D. Halsted; "The Significance of Cleislogamy," by T. Meehan; "The Animal Parasites of Dogs," by E. W. Doran; "A Preliminary Note on the Anatomy of the Urodela Brain as Exemplified by Desmognothus Fusca," by Pierre A. Fish; "How the Application of Hot Water to Seed increases the Yield," by John C. Arthur; "Heredity of Acquired Characters," by Manly Miles; "The Production of Immunity in Guinea Pigs from Hog Cholera by the Use of Blood Serum from Immunized Animals," by Emil A. de Schweinitz; "On the Supposed Correlation of Quality in Fruits—a Study in Evolution," by Liberty H. Bailey; and "The Descent of the Lepidoptera, an Application of the Theory of Natural Selection to Toxonomy," by John H. Comstock.

H. *Anthropology.*—The presiding officer of this section was William H. Holmes, of the Bureau of Ethnology, Washington, D. C., who delivered his vice-presidential address on "Evolution of the Æsthetic." Turning from the more substantial if not more practical elements of human life, he glanced into the study of the polite arts of man, a comparatively new field, turning "to the flowers of thought, to the realm of the æsthetic, to that strange land of the imagination where nothing is seen but for the pleasure of seeing, where nothing is heard but for the pleasure of hearing, and where nothing is thought but for the pleasure of thinking." After drawing a dreary picture of what life would be without perceptions of the beautiful, the speaker showed that creations of art are growths as are the products of nature, and are subject to the same inexorable laws of genesis and evolution. The several branches of æsthetic art were considered, painting, architecture, sculpture, music, poetry, drama, and romance being reviewed in the order named, their growth and evolution in relation to the development of man being illustrated by large diagrams.

"River Pebbles chipped by Modern Indians, as an Aid to the Study of the Trenton Gravel Implements," by H. C. Mercer; "A Few Psychological Inquiries," by Laura Osborne Talbott; "On Some Remains from the Oldest River Gravels along the White Water River," "On the Earthworks near Anderson, Ind.," "Some Indian Camping Sites near Brookville, Ind.," and "On Some Prehistoric Objects from the White Water Valley," by Amos W. Butler; "The Early Religion of the Iroquois" and "Early Indian Forts in New York," by William M. Beauchamp; "Ancient Earthworks in Ontario" and "Evidences of Prehistoric Trade in Ontario," by Charles A. Hirschfelder; "Explorations on the Main Structure of Copan, Honduras" and "Vandalism among the Antiquities of Yucatan and Central America," by Marshall H. Saville; "The Department of Ethnology of the World's Columbian Exposition," and "Exhibition of a Large Model of the Serpent Mound of Adams County, Ohio," by Frederick W. Putnam; "Involuntary Movements," by Joseph Jastrow; "Tusayan Legends of the Snake and Flute People," by Matilda C. Stevenson; "A Skull of a Pig having a Flint Arrow Head imbedded in the Bone," by Edward W. Claypole; "Primitive Number System," by Levi L. Conant; "Comparative Chronology," by W J McGee; "Brief Remarks upon the Alphabet of Landa," by Hilborne T. Cresson; "The Peabody Museum Honduras Expedition," by Frederick W. Putnam; "Aboriginal Quarries of Flakable Stone, and their bearing upon the Question of Palæolithic Man," "The Sacred Pipestone Quarry of Minnesota, and the Ancient Copper Mines of Lake Superior," and "On the So-called Palæolithic Implements of the Upper Mississippi," by William H. Holmes; "Cañon and Mesa Ruins in Utah " and "Singular Copper Implements and Ornaments from the Hopewell Group, Ross County, Ohio," by Warren K. Moorehead; "Proposed Classification and International Nomenclature of the Anthropological Sciences " and " Anvil-shaped Stones from Pennsylvania," by Daniel G. Brinton; "Prehistoric Earthworks of Henry County, Ind.," by T. B. Redding; "A Definition of Anthropology," by Otis T. Mason; "Pueblo Myth and Ceremonial Dances," by Frank H. Cushing; "Demonstration of a recently Discovered Cerebral Porta," by Charles P. Hart; "Ruins of Tiahuanaco," by A. E. Douglas; "Points concerning Fort Ancient," by Selden S. Scoville; and "Exhibition of a Suite of Prehistoric Pottery from a Mound on the Illinois River, between Peoria and Havana," by John Kost.

I. *Economic Science and Statistics.*—The vice-president elected to preside over this section at the Washington meeting was S. Dana Horton, but owing to his absence in Europe, Prof. Lester F. Ward, of the United States Geological Survey, Washington, D. C., was nominated by the council to the vacancy, and elected in general session. His own place as secretary of the section was filled by the election of Henry Farquhar, of Washington, D. C., to that office. Prof. Ward delivered an address on "The Psychologic Basis of Social Economics," in which he took opposite views to the generally accepted beliefs of those of the Adam Smith school.

The following-named papers were read before the section:

"The Labor Problem in America," by Robert H. Craft; "Some Statistics of the Salvation Army," by Charles W. Smiley; " Economic Conditions antagonistic to a Conservative Forest Policy,' by Bernhard E. Fernow; "Outline Plan for a Governmental Department of Beneficence," by Richard T. Colburn; "Competition and Combination in Nature " and "Movement of Duties and Prices in the United States since 1889," by Henry Farquhar; and "The Standard of Deferred Payments," by Edward A. Ross.

Popular Features of the Proceedings.— On the evening of Aug. 18 a formal reception was tendered to the association by the Woman's Reception Committee of the General Local Committee, in the Powers Art Gallery. A public address complimentary to the citizens of Rochester, on "Hypnotism and its Antecedents," was delivered on the evening of Aug. 19, by Prof. Joseph Jastrow, of the University of Wisconsin, and on the evening of Aug. 22 a similar complimentary address was delivered by Grove K. Gilbert, of the United States Geological Survey, on . "Coon Butte and the Theories of its Origin." For Saturday, Aug. 20, four excursions were provided for the members of the association by the local committee.

Affiliated Organizations.—Throughout the meeting of the association the Entomological Club met under the presidency of E. A. Schwarz, and the Botanical Club likewise held regular meetings under the presidency of Henry H. Rushy, who temporarily succeeded Volney M. Spaulding. Besides the foregoing, the American Microscopical Society held sessions on Aug. 9, 10, 11, and 12. Of this body, M. E. Sewall, of Chicago. Ill., was president, and W. H. Seaman, of Washington, D. C., was secretary. The Geo-

logical Society of America held its fourth annual meeting on Aug. 15 and 16, with Grove K. Gilbert as president, and Herman L. Fairchild as secretary. On Aug. 15 and 16 the Society for the Promotion of Agricultural Science held meetings, with Isaac P. Roberts as president, and Leland O. Howard as secretary. The Association of Economic Entomologists held their meeting on Aug. 15 and 16, with J. A. Lintner as president, and F. M. Webster as secretary. On Aug. 16 and 17 the American Chemical Society held its fifth general meeting, with vice-president Breneman as its presiding officer, and Durand Woodman as secretary. Finally, the Association of State Weather Services came into existence, holding meetings on Aug. 15 and 16, under the presidency of H. H. C. Dunwoody, and with R. E. Kerkam as secretary.

Final Sessions.—The final general meeting was held on the evening of Aug. 23, when the officers named below were elected and the place of the next meeting decided upon. With regard to the corporation of the World's Fair Auxiliary Council, it was decided that a committee of five be appointed to act with the corresponding committee of the World's Congress of the Columbian Exposition. The committee appointed at the Washington meeting last year to consider and report upon a proposed investigation of possible secular changes of terrestrial latitudes, submitted a report which recommended the appointment of a committee to confer with the International Geodetic Association for the purpose of securing simultaneous latitude determinations by similar methods upon the same parallel of latitude in Europe and America. The report further recommended that this committee be ' instructed to secure if possible a redetermination of the latitudes of certain named points. In view of the high prices of scientific instruments and books occasioned by the tariff levied upon them, it was voted to petition Congress to repeal or at least reduce these taxes. Also, it was decided to change the time of meeting, so that the association might begin its work on Monday instead of Tuesday. The meeting was a fairly successful one. More than 200 papers were read, and the registry showed 456 persons in attendance at the sessions. Besides the 102 members elected prior to the opening meeting, there were subsequently 73 additional names favorably acted on, making a total of 175 new members. The membership of the association on July 8 showed a total of 2,055 persons which, with the 175 elected at the Rochester meeting, brings the grand total number of names up to 2,230.

Next Meeting.—In 1893 the association will meet in Madison, Wis., in August. The following officers were chosen : President, William Harkness, Washington, D. C. Vice-presidents : A. C. L. Doolittle, South Bethlehem, Pa.: B, Edward L. Nichols, Ithaca, N. Y.: C, Edward Hart, Easton, Pa. ; D. S. W. Robinson, Columbus, Ohio: E. Charles D. Wolcott, Washington, D. C.; F, Henry F. Osborn, New York City,; G, Charles E. Bessey, Lincoln, Neb.; H. J. Owen Dorsey, Tacoma Park, D. C. ; I, William H. Brauner, Palo Alto, Cal. Permanent Secretary, Frederick W. Putnam, Cambridge, Mass. General Secretary, Thomas H. Norton, Cincinnati, Ohio. Secretary of the Council, Herman L. Fairchild,

Rochester, N. Y. Secretaries of the Sections, A, Andrew W. Phillips, New Haven, Conn.; B, W. Le Conte Stevens, Troy, N. Y.; C, J. U. Nef, Chicago, Ill.; D, David S. Jacobus, Hoboken, N. J.; E, Robert T. Hill, Washington, D. C.; F, L. O. Howard, Washington, D. C.; G, F. V. Coville, Washington, D. C.; H, Warren K. Moorehead, Xenia, Ohio; I, Nellie S. Kedzie, Manhattan, Kansas. Treasurer, William Lilly, Mauch Chunk, Pa. At the final session 65 members were raised to the grade of Fellow.

British.—The sixty-second annual meeting of the British Association for the Advancement of Science was held in Edinburgh during the week beginning Aug. 3. The officers of the association were: President, Sir Archibald Geikie. Section Presidents: A, Mathematics and Physics, Dr. Arthur Schuster; B, Chemistry, Prof. Herbert McLeod; C, Geology, Prof. C. Lapworth;

SIR ARCHIBALD GEIKIE.

D, Biology, Prof. William Rutherford; E, Geography, Prof. James Geikie; F, Economic Science and Statistics, Sir Charles W. Freemantle; G, Mechanical Science, W. Cawthorne Unwin; H, Anthropology, Dr. Alexander Macalister. General Secretaries, Sir Douglas Dalton and Vernon Harcourt. General Treasurer, Arthur W. Rücker.

General Meeting.—A preliminary meeting of the general committee was held on Aug. 3, when the report of the council was received and approved. It included action on the following resolutions, which were passed by the Australasian Association for the Advancement of Science at the meeting held in 1891: (1) That it is desirable to secure greater uniformity in biological nomenclature, especially in the department of morphology. (2) That in order to secure such uniformity the following steps be taken: (a) The appointment of an international committee to define terms of general importance—e. g., terms common to botany and zoölogy, terms relating to position, etc.; (b) the preparation of an authoritative historical glossary of biological terms; (c) the systematic record of new terms in the various recording publications. (3) That copies of these resolutions be transmitted to the British and American associations and to the Anatomische Gesellschaft. A committee of the council re-

ported: "After considering the resolutions submitted by the Australasian Association for the Advancement of Science, we think from the context that by the word 'nomenclature' in the first resolution is meant 'terminology.' Assuming this to be the case, we quite agree that it would be desirable to secure greater uniformity in the biological terminology, but we doubt whether the appointment of an international committee would tend to secure that object. As regards the recommendation (b) in the second resolution, we also quite agree that the preparation of a good glossary of biological terms would be of great advantage, if a qualified person could be induced to undertake the task of editorship. We also agree that the glossary ought to be supplemented from time to time by records to be kept up in the various recording publications." This report was ordered transmitted to the Australasian Association.

The names of the new members of the council were proposed and submitted to the association. The first general meeting of the association was held in the hall of the United Presbyterian Synod. The retiring president, Dr. William Huggins, opened the proceedings by introducing his successor, who then delivered the usual address.

The President's Address.—In beginning his address Sir Archibald Geikie referred to Edinburgh as a scientific center, and said: "We shall find a peculiar appropriateness in the time of this renewed visit of the association to Edinburgh. A hundred years ago a remarkable group of men was discussing here the great problem of the history of the earth. James Hutton, after many years of travel and reflection, had communicated to the Royal Society of this city, in the year 1785, the first outlines of his famous ' Theory of the Earth.' In choosing from among the many subjects which might properly engage your attention on the present occasion, I have thought that it would not be inappropriate nor uninteresting to consider the more salient features of that 'Theory,' and to mark how much in certain departments of inquiry has sprung from the fruitful teaching of its author and his associates. A theory of the earth so simple in outline, so bold in conception, so full of suggestion, and resting on so broad a base of observation and reflection, ought, we might think, to have commanded at once the attention of men of science, even if it did not immediately awaken the interest of the outside world."

After a somewhat elaborate discussion of the views of Hutton and those of Werner, he passed to the second part of his address, and said: "Thus a hundred years ago, by the brilliant theory of Hutton and the fruitful generalization of Smith, the study of the earth received in our country the impetus which has given birth to the modern science of geology. To review the marvelous progress which this science has made during the first century of its existence would require not one but many hours for adequate treatment. The march of discovery has advanced along a multitude of different paths, and the domains of Nature which have been included within the growing territories of human knowledge have been many and ample. Nevertheless, there are certain departments of investigation to which we may profitably restrict our attention on the present occasion, and wherein we may see how the leading principles that were proclaimed in this city a hundred years ago have germinated and borne fruit all over the world."

It is impossible to give the various points discussed by him, but the following is of special interest: "There is no reason to think that the rate of organic evolution has ever seriously varied; at least no proof has been adduced of such variation. Taken in connection with the testimony of the sedimentary rocks, the inferences deducible from fossils entirely bear out the opinion that the building up of the stratified crust of the earth has been extremely gradual. If the many thousands of years which have elapsed since the Ice Age have produced no appreciable modification of surviving plants and animals, how vast a period must have been required for that marvelous scheme of organic development which is chronicled in the rocks! After careful reflection on the subject, I affirm that the geological record furnishes a mass of evidence which no arguments drawn from other departments of Nature can explain away, and which, it seems to me, can not be satisfactorily interpreted save with an allowance of time much beyond the narrow limits which recent physical speculation would concede."

He closed with: "In this marvelous increase of knowledge regarding the transformation of the earth's surface, one of the most impressive features is the power of perceiving the many striking contrasts between the present and former aspects of topography and scenery. What is seen by the bodily eye—mountain, valley, or plain—serves but as a veil, beyond which, as we raise it, visions of long-lost lands and seas rise before us in a far-retreating vista. Pictures of the most diverse and opposite character are beheld, as it were, through each other, their lineaments subtly interwoven and even their most vivid contrasts subdued into one blended harmony. On every side of us rise the most convincing proofs of the reality and potency of that ceaseless sculpture by which the elements of landscape have been carved into their present shapes. Turn where we may, our eyes rest on hills that project above the lowland, not because they have been upheaved into these positions, but because their stubborn materials have enabled them better to withstand the degradation which has worn down the softer strata into the plains around them. Inch by inch the surface of the land has been lowered, and each hard rock successively laid bare has communicated its own characteristics of form and color to the scenery."

A. *Mathematics and Physics.*—The presiding officer of this section, Prof. Arthur Schuster, Ph. D., F. R. S., F. R. A. S., opened his address with a brief review of the progress of physical science, in the course of which he said: "No event has ever happened so striking as that which took place on Jan. 1, when the mantle of Sir William Thomson fell on the infant Lord Kelvin. Those who have attended these meetings will feel with me that the honor done to our foremost representative — an honor which has been a source of pride and satisfaction to every student of science—could not altogether remain

unnoticed in the section which owes him so much."

He discussed somewhat fully the subjects of moving matter and electrical action, and the sun spots and the atmosphere. In closing, he said: "The statement of a problem occasionally helps to clear it up, and I may be allowed, therefore, to put before you some questions the solution of which seems not beyond the reach of our powers: 1. Is every large rotating mass a magnet? If it is, the sun must be a powerful magnet. The effect of a magnet on the discharge is known, and careful investigations of the streamers of the solar corona ought to give an answer to the question which I have put. 2. Is there sufficient matter in interplanetary space to make it a conductor of electricity? Its conductivity can only be small, for otherwise the earth would gradually set itself to revolve about its magnetic pole. Suppose the electric resistance of interplanetary space to be so great that no appreciable change in the earth's axis of rotation could have taken place within historical times, is it not possible that the currents induced in planetary space by the earth's revolution may, by their electro-magnetic action, cause the secular variation of terrestrial magnetism? 3. What is a sun spot? The general appearance of a sun spot does not show any marked cyclonic motion, though what we see is really determined by the distribution of temperature, and not by the lines of flow. But a number of cyclones clustering together like the sun spots in a group should move round each other in a definite way, and it seems to me that the close study of the relative positions of a group of spots should give decisive evidence for or against the cyclone theory. 4. If the spot is not due to cyclonic motion, is it not possible that electric discharges setting out from the sun and accelerating artificially evaporation at the sun's surface might cool those parts from which the discharge starts, and thus produce a sun spot? 5. May not the periodicity of sun spots and the connection between two such dissimilar phenomena as spots on the sun and magnetic disturbances on the earth be due to a periodically recurring increase in the electric conductivity of the parts of space surrounding the sun? 6. What causes the anomalous law of rotation of the solar photosphere?"

Several very important subjects were discussed before this section, including one "On a National Physical Laboratory," in which several distinguished German physicists took part, among whom was Hermann L. F. von Helmholtz, of the University of Berlin. Another discussion was "On Nomenclature of Units," and reports "On Underground Temperature." "On the Discharge of Electricity from Points," and "On Electrical Standards" were discussed. The important papers included "Wire Standards of Electrical Resistance," by Dr. Lindeck; "On the Clark Cell," by Dr. Kahle; "Preliminary Accounts of Oceanic Circulation, based on the Challenger Observations," by Dr. A. Buchan; "Physical Condition of the Waters of the English Channel," by H. V. Dickson; "On Primary and Secondary Cells in which the Electrolyte is a Gas," by Dr. Arthur Schuster; "On Leaky Magnetic Circuits," by Dr. DuBois; "Experiments on the Electrical Resistance of Metallic Powders," by Dr. Dawson Turner; "On the Stability of Periodic Motions," by Lord Kelvin; "On the Specific Conductivity of Thin Films," by Profs. Reinold and Rücker; "A Contribution to the Theory of the Perfect Influence Machines," by J. Gray: "Experiments with a Ruhmkorff Coil," by Mr. Magnus and A. Galt; "The Application of Interference Methods to Spectroscopic Measurement," by Prof. Albert A. Michelson, formerly of Clark University, Worcester, Mass.; "On Graphic Solutions of Dynamical Problems" and "Reduction of every Problem of Two Freedoms in Conservative Dynamics to the Drawings of Geodetic Lines on a Surface of Given Specific Curvature," by Lord Kelvin; "A Magnetic Curve Trace," by Prof. Ewing; "The Volume of Magnetism," by Dr. C. G. Knott; and "On the Dielectric of Condensers," by W. H. Preece.

B. *Chemical Science.*—This section was presided over by Prof. Herbert McLeod, F. R. S., F. C. S., who in his opening address considered the desirability of a uniform nomenclature in chemistry. After treating the subject historically he closed this portion of his address with: "I fear we are driven to the conclusion that, notwithstanding all the progress that has been made in chemical science during the last fifty-eight years, we have not yet reached a method of notation that would have satisfied Dr. Dalton in 1834. But since that time we have learned that our formulæ ought to show even more than the number and position of the atoms of a compound; we should like them to indicate the amount of potential energy residing in a body, and our equations ought to indicate the amount of heat generated by a chemical change. Let us hope that before the next meeting of the British Association in Edinburgh these desirable developments will have been accomplished. Happily, catalytic actions are being explained one after another, so that soon the name itself may become obsolete." He then discussed the teaching of chemistry, and said: "In this city the first public chemical laboratory was started in 1823 by Dr. Anderson, the assistant of Prof. Hope." The concluding portion of the address dealt with microbes as chemical agents, in which he urged some of the younger chemists to work at the chemical aspects of bacteriology. His final remarks had to do with the great loss experienced by chemistry in the death of Prof. A. W. von Hofmann, closing with: "This seems to me the true spirit of the scientific investigator. In many cases the reward consists solely in the consciousness that the investigator has done his duty. In some cases the reward may take a more substantial form, and I have just been informed that Prof. von Hofmann has left a large fortune, the result of the applications of his discoveries in technical chemistry."

The following papers were read before the chemical section: "Electrolytic Synthesis," by Prof. Crum Brown; "Impurities in Chloroform," by Prof. Ramsey; "Luminosity of Hydrocarbon Flames," by Prof. V. B. Lewes; "Experiments on Flame," by Prof. A. Smithells; "The Reaction of Hydrogen with Mixtures of Hydrogen and Chlorine," by J. A. Harker; "Molecular Refraction and Dispersion of Metallic Carbonyls and of Indium, Gallium, and Sulphur," by Dr. J. H. Gladstone; and "Impurities of Town Air," by Dr. G. H. Bailey. An arrangement was made for a joint meeting between this section and Section G, *Mechanical Science*, to discuss the "Effects of Small Quantities of Foreign Matter on the Properties of Metals," by Prof. Roberts-Austen, but Section G failed to attend the meeting. Also a discussion to consider the "Chemical Aspects of Bacteriology" with Section D, *Biology*, was equally unsuccessful.

C. *Geology.*—The president of this section was Prof. C. Lapworth, LL. D., F. R. S., F. G. S., who reviewed the discoveries that had raised geology to a science. "Geology," he said, "is yet in her merest youth, and to justify even her very existence there can be no rest until the whole earth crust and all its phenomena, past, present, and to come, have been subjected to the domain of human thought and comprehension. There can be no more finality in geology than in any other science; the discovery of to-day is merely the stepping-stone to the discovery of to-morrow; the living theory of to-morrow is nourished by the relics of its parent theory of to-day." He then inquired into the formations which constitute the study of the geologist.

A large portion of his address was devoted to the special objects of study of the stratigraphical geologist. He illustrated the formation stratigraphy of rocks as follows: "Many of the movements which take place in a rock sheet which is being folded, or, in other words, those produced by the bending of a compound sheet composed of many leaves, can be fairly well studied in a very simple experiment. Take an ordinary large note-book, say an inch in thickness, with flexible covers, rule carefully a series of parallel lines across the edges of the leaves at the top of the book about one eighth of an inch apart and exactly at right angles to the plane of the cover; then, holding the front edges loosely, press the book slowly from back and front into an S-like form until it can be pressed no further. As the wave grows it will be noticed that the cross lines which have been drawn on the upper edge of the book remain fairly parallel throughout the whole of the folding process, except in the central third of the book, where they arrange themselves into a beautiful sheaf-like form, showing how much the leaves of the book have sheared or slidden over each other in this central portion. It will also be seen when the S is complete that the book has been forced into a third of its former breadth. It is clear that the wave the book now forms must be regarded as made up of three sections—viz., a section forming the outside of the trough on the one side, and a section forming the outside of the arch on the other, and a central or common section, which may be regarded either as uniting or dividing the other two." He concluded by illustrating his remarks by reference to the continent of America and the shores of Japan.

Nearly fifty papers were presented before this section, among which were: "The Cause of the Ice Age," by J. W. Gray and P. F. Kendall; "The Devon and Cornish Granites," by W. A. E. Ussher; "On a Bone Cave in the Limestone of Assyut," by B. N. Peach and J. Horne: "A Granite Junction in Mull" and "The St. Bees Sandstone and its Associated Rocks," by J. G. Goodchild; "Grampian Series (Pre-Cambrian Rocks) of the Central Highlands," by Henry Hicks;

"Alleged Proofs of Submergence in Scotland during the Glacial Epoch," by Dugald Bell; "A Widespread Radiolarian Chert Formation of Arenig Age in the Southern Uplands of Scotland," by B. N. Peach; and "Physical Geology of Sinai and Palestine," by Prof. E. Hull.

The third report of the committee to arrange for the collection, preservation, and systematic registration of photographs of geological interest in the United Kingdom, also the report of the committee on erratic blocks, and the report of the underground water committee, were read and discussed.

D, *Biology.*—The presiding officer of this section was Prof. William Rutherford, who holds the chair of the Institutes of Medicine in Edinburgh University, and who chose for his subject "Color Sense." He said:

"The subject I propose to discuss on this occasion is not the cause of the different kinds of sensation proper to the different sense organs, but the cause of some qualities of sensation producible through one and the same sense organ." After dealing with different theories of hearing and smell, he proceeded: "The sensory mechanism concerned in sight consists of the retina, the optic nerve, and the center for visual sensation in the occipital lobe of the brain. In the vertebrate eye the fibers of the optic nerve spread out in the inner part of the retina, and are connected with several layers of ganglionic cells placed external to them. When a beam of white light is dispersed by a prism or diffraction grating, the ether waves are spread out in the order of their frequency of undulation. The undulations of radiant energy extend through a range of many octaves, but those able to stimulate the retina are comprised within a range of rather less than one octave, extending from a frequency of about 395,000,000,000 a second at the extreme red to about 757,000,000,000 at the extreme violet end of the visible spectrum. The ultra-violet waves in the spectrum of sunlight extend through rather more than half an octave. Although mainly revealed by their chemical effects, they are not altogether invisible; their color is bluish gray. The only optical—that is, strictly physical—difference between the several ether waves in the visible or invisible spectrum is frequency of undulation, or, otherwise expressed, a difference in wave length. The chromatic—that is, the color-producing—effects of the ether waves depend on their power of exciting sensations of color, which vary with their frequency of undulation. Colors are commonly defined by three qualities or constants—hue, purity, and brightness. Their hue depends upon the chromatic effect of frequency of undulation or wave length. Their purity or saturation depends on freedom from admixture with sensations produced by other colors or by white light. Their brightness or luminosity depends on the degree to which the sensory mechanism is stimulated." Prof. Rutherford then discussed the theories of color sense propounded by Sir Isaac Newton, Clerk Maxwell, Young, and Von Helmholtz, and then proceeded to deal with the important question of color blindness.

So many important and interesting papers were submitted to the organizing committee of Section D this year that it was found necessary to divide it into the three departments of Zoölogy, Botany, and Physiology.

The following reports by committees appointed at the Cardiff meeting were submitted: (1) The Zoölogy and Botany of the West India Islands; (2) the Naples Zoölogical Station; (3) Zoölogy of the Sandwich Islands; (4) Botanical Laboratory at Ceylon; (5) Migration of Birds; (6) Plymouth Laboratory; (7) Deep-sea Tow-net; (8) Protection of Wild Birds' Eggs. All these committees were reappointed with or without grants.

Among the papers were the following: "On Secondary Tissues in Monocotyledons," by D. H. Schott and G. Brebener; "Vital Absorption," by E. Waymouth Reid; "The Social Habits of Spiders," by H. C. McCook; "The Method of Comparative Psychology," by Prof. Lloyd Morgan.

In the botanical department James Britten proposed a reform in botanical nomenclature. After commenting on the number of confusing and unnecessary changes introduced of late years into botanical nomenclature, many of them by the younger portion of American naturalists, he proposed an adherence to the resolutions of the Berlin botanists—viz., that the starting point of priority in the names both of genera and species is the year 1752; that *nomina, nuda*, and *seminuda* are to be rejected, and that similar names are to be conserved; and that the names of certain larger or universally known genera are also to be conserved. Also, Prof. John C. Arthur, of Lafayette, Ind., brought forward the subject of a proposed World's Congress of Botanists at Chicago in 1893. The American committee wished to have on this proposal the views of British botanists. A special excursion was projected, which was to take in the Yellowstone Park and include a tour of from 3,000 to 4,000 miles, it was to be hoped, at little more than nominal expense.

E. *Geography.*—The presiding officer of this section was Prof. James Geikie, LL. D., D. C. L., F. G. S., brother of the president of the association. He chose as the subject of his address "The Geographical Development of Coast Lines," in which he considered the causes which determined the general trend of the world's coast lines, and then discussed the particular development of those of the Atlantic, the Pacific, and other oceans. The more striking contrasts between the coast lines of these regions and the origin of such contrasts were considered. It was shown that the coast lines of the globe are of very unequal age; that some long ago reached a stage of comparative stability, while others were younger and had not as yet attained a relatively stable condition. He suggested that the accepted doctrine of great regional elevations was insufficient to account for the development of continental areas. His final remarks were: "I ought perhaps to apologize for having trespassed so much upon the domains of geology; but in doing so I have only followed the example of geologists themselves, whose divagations in territories adjoining their own are naturally not infrequent. From much that I have said it will be gathered that with regard to the causes of many coastal changes we are still groping in the dark. It seems not unlikely, however, that as light increases we may be compelled to modify the view that all oscillations of the sea-level are due to movements of the lithosphere alone. That is a very heretical suggestion; but that a great deal can be said for it any one will admit after a candid perusal of Suess's monumental work, 'Das Antlitz der Erde.'"

Among the papers presented before this section were: "The First Ascent of Oraefa Jökull," by F. W. W. Howell; "Place Names," by J. Burgess; "Effects of Rainfall in Formosa," by John Thompson; "The Windings of Rivers," by J. Y. Buchanan; "Lesser Tibet," by Mrs. Bishop; "The North Atlantic," by the Prince of Monaco; "Detailed Oceanography and Meteorology," by J. Y. Buchanan; "The Desert of Atacama," by Mrs. Lilly Grove; "Photography and Surveying," by Col. Tanner; "Determination of Longitude by Photography," by Dr. H. Schlichter; and "A Proposed New Map of the Globe," by E. G. Ravenstein. The whole of one day was devoted to the reading of papers bearing on Africa, almost all of which had reference to South Africa. A joint meeting of Sections B and E was held, under the presidency of J. Y. Buchanan, in order to listen to and discuss a number of papers on oceanography.

F. *Economic Science and Statistics.*—This section was presided over by Sir Charles Freemantle, Deputy Master of the Mint and also chairman of the Charity Organization Society. His address dealt with two topics with which he had been largely associated. The first of these was the restoration of the gold coinage, a question which had for many years past exercised the minds of successive chancellors of the exchequer and had been a stumbling-block to bankers and the commercial world. After discussing this subject in its different aspects he took up the main topic of his address—old-age pensions. He concluded with: "Children and other relations, who under a loose system of poor relief are too apt to consider that in one shape or other their parents and aged kinsfolk may naturally be left to the tender mercies of the Poor Law. are brought together and induced to contribute to their support; and pension societies, such as the Tower Hamlets Pension Committee, the local pension committees of the Charity Organization Society, and the like, are willing and anxious to come to the rescue. Nor is this organized assistance to those whom the late Duke of Albany called the 'aristocracy of the poor' of use to the recipients only. In hundreds of cases which have come under my own knowledge in East London, for instance, it has been the means of inspiring in men and women a holy zeal for charity which, without any hateful feeling of patronage on the one side or of cringing dependence on the other, gives a scope, such as none other can supply, for a true friendship between rich and poor, and blesses both the giver and the receiver. I have endeavored to show, in these few and necessarily brief remarks about one of the great social questions which occupy men's minds to-day, that for the promotion of the best interests of our aged poor there may be a 'more excellent way' than a vast organization of state-aided pensions. May we work out this and other similar problems, as Englishmen do, calmly, wisely, and to good effect."

Among the papers read before this section were: "Methods of Social Inquiry," by P. Geddes; "La Science Sociale et sa Methode," by M. Demolins; "Some Notes on the Compilation of Monographs on the Statistics of Large Cities," by James Mavor; "The Slums of Manchester,' by C. W. Smiley; "Parliamentary Returns on Social and Economic Subjects," by C. S. Loch; "The Relations of Ethics to Economics," by J. S. Mackenzie; "Old-Age Pensions," by W. Moore Ede; "The Poor-Law and the Friendly Societies," by T. W. Fowle; "Old-Age Pensions and Friendly Societies," by W. Frome Wilkinson; "Adam Smith and his Relations to Modern Economics," by L. L. Price; "The Effects of Consumption of Wealth on Distribution," by William Smart; "Copyright and Patents," by Robert A. Macfil; "A Plea for the Study of Railway Economics," by W. M. Acworth; "Legislation on Behalf of Destitute Children," by Miss Rosa M. Barratt; "Illegitimacy in Banffshire," by W. Cramond; "On the Taxation of Building Land," by Mark Davidson; and "The Continuance of the Supply of Wheat from the United States with Profit to the Western Farmers," by Edward Atkinson, of Boston.

G. *Mechanical Science.*—This section was presided over by Prof. W. Cawthorne Unwin, of the Central Technical Institute at South Kensington. He said: "The year just passed is not one unmemorable in the annals of engineering. By an effort remarkable for its rapidity, and as an example of organization of labor, the broad-gauge system has been extinguished. It has disappeared like some prehistoric mammoth, a large-limbed organism, perfect for its purpose and created in a generous mood, but conquered in the struggle for existence by smaller but more active rivals. If we recognize that the great controversy of fifty years ago has at last been decided against Brunel, at least we ought to remember that the broad-gauge system was one only of many original experiments due to his genius and courage—experiments in every field of engineering, in bridge building, in locomotive design, in ship construction, the successes and failures of which have alike enlarged the knowledge of engineers and helped the progress of engineering."

He described various engineering projects under construction, and in reference to American enterprises he said: "Few persons can have seen Niagara Falls without reflecting on the enormous energy which is there continuously expended, and for any useful purpose wasted. The exceptional constancy of the volume of flow, the invariability of the levels, the depth of the plunge over the escarpment, the solid character of the rocks, all mark Niagara as an ideally perfect water-power station; while, on the other hand, the remarkable facilities of transport, both by steam navigation on the lakes and by four systems of railway, afford commercial advantages of the highest importance. From a catchment basin of 240,000 square miles, an area greater than that of France, a volume of water amounting to 265,000 cubic feet per second descends from Lake Erie to Lake Ontario, a vertical distance of 326 feet in 37¼ miles." Also "supposing the whole stream could be utilized, it would supply 7,000,000 horse power. This is more than double the total steam and water power at present employed in manufacturing industry in the United States."

Of the project, he said: "The present plans contemplate the utilization of 100,000 effective horse power. The principal work of construction is a great tunnel 7,260 feet long, which is to form a tail-race to the turbines, starting from lands belonging to the company, and discharging into the lower river. The tunnel is 19 by 21 feet, or 386 square feet in area, inside a brick-work lining 16 inches thick." And closing with: "Niagara is likely to become not only a seat of large manufacturing operations of familiar types, but also the home of important new industries."

The following-named papers were read before this section: "The World's Columbian Exposition of 1893," by James Dredge and Robert S. McCormack; "The Use of Furnaces for burning Ash-bin Refuse," by G. Forbes; "The Connection of the East and West Coast of Scotland by a Waterway," by D. A. Stevenson; "A New Danger in the Destruction of Lightning Protectors by Recent Municipal Legislation," by W. H. Preece; and "London Sewage Problems," by Crawford Barlow.

H. *Anthropology.*—The president of this section, Dr. Alexander Macalister, F. R. S., Professor of Anatomy in the University of Cambridge, delivered the address. In his opening remarks he justified the separate existence of the section in that its members were honestly endeavoring to lay a definite and stable foundation upon which, in the future, a scientific anthropology might be based. The past year had not been fertile in discoveries. No new light had been shed on the darkness that enshrouded the origin of man; but in this connection Dr. Louis Robinson had, from a series of observations on the prehensile power of the hands of children at birth, arrived at the same conclusion which Mr. Robert Louis Stevenson deduced from the study of his grandfather—namely, that there still survived in the human structure and habit traces of our probably arboreal ancestry. A more perfect nomenclature, to prevent confusion in the use of such words as tribe, type, race, Celtic, etc., was wanted to bring anthropology into range with the true sciences, a broader basis of ascertained fact for inductive reasoning, and men trained in exact method, who should patiently work at facts and refrain from rushing prematurely into theory. The present position of anthropology was critical and peculiar; for while, on the one hand, the facilities for research were daily growing greater in some directions, the material was diminishing in quantity and accessibility—treasures both of the structure and the works of man were accumulating in our museums, but at the same time some of the most interesting tribes had vanished and others were rapidly disappearing or being absorbed in other races. He reviewed the physical side of the subject, or anatomical anthropology. Among civilized peoples whose feet were from infancy subjected to conditions of restraint, the little toe had become an imperfect organ. A more important branch of anthropology than the physical was the study of man's intellectual nature, and "to disentangle, out of the complex network of religion, my-

thology, and ritual, those elements which were real truths, either discovered by the exercise of man's reason or learned by him in ways whereof science took no account, from those adventitious and invented products of human fear and fancy which obscured the view of the central realities." If, however, he concluded, we should ever rise to the possession of a true appreciation of the influences which had affected mankind in the past, with such a knowledge we should be able to advance in that practical branch of anthropology, the science of education, and make progress in sociology, a study which did for the community what the science of education did for the individual.

The papers read before this section included "The Indo-Europeans' Conception of a Future Life and its Bearing upon their Religions," by G. Hartwell Jones; "The Discovery of the Common Occurrence of Palæolithic Weapons in Scotland," by Rev. Frederick Smith; "On a Fronto-Limbic Formation of the Human Cerebrum," by L. Manouvrier; "The Present Inhabitants of Mashonaland and their Origin," by J. Theodore Bent; "The Value of Art in Ethnology," by A. C. Haddon; "Similarity of Certain Ancient Necropoleis in the Pyrenees and in North Britain," by G. S. Phene; "A Contribution to the Ethnology of Jersey," by Andrew Dunlop; "Notes on the Past and Present Condition of the Natives of the Friendly Islands, or Tonga," by R. B. Leefe; "Damma Island and its Natives," by F. Bassett Smith; "On Skulls from Mobanga, Upper Congo" and "On Some Facial Characters of the Ancient Egyptians," by A. Macalister.

A plan for an ethnographical survey of the United Kingdom was explained. The reason of its proposal was the necessity of bringing together the results of the investigation which were being made into monuments of antiquity, records of custom and tradition, and physical characters. The report of the Anthropometric Laboratory Committee was presented. It was reported that at Cardiff last year 103 members of the association had been examined. Of these, 73 were males, and the mean stature of the whole was 68 inches, being one inch above the average stature of the British Isles. Also, a discussion on anthropometric identification was opened by Dr. Manouvrier, who described the system of measurements introduced by M. A. Bertillon into the French Criminal Department, and showed the manner in which they were made. He said that by its means the identification of criminals was made absolutely certain. Dr. Benedikt, of Vienna, also bore testimony to the efficiency of M. Bertillon's system and strongly advocated its introduction into Great Britain. Dr. Garson referred to Mr. Galton's method of identification by means of finger-marks. As a result of this discussion the council have been requested to draw the attention of Her Majesty's Government to the subject.

Final Sessions.—The last meeting of the General Committee was held on Aug. 10, when the report of the Committee of Recommendations was presented. The Research fund is dependent upon the number of membership tickets sold, and at Edinburgh £2,070 were received, showing that the total number of tickets sold was 2,070. Grants were made as follow: To members for researches on mathematics and physics, £235; chemistry and mineralogy, £60; geology, £60; biology, £350; geography, £110; economic science and statistics, £3; and anthropology, £170; making a total of £988. The following resolutions were adopted:

"That the council be requested to draw the attention of the Local Government Board to the desirability of the publication of the report on the examination into deviations from the normal among fifty thousand children in various schools, which has been presented to the board by the British Medical Association.

"That the council be requested to draw the attention of Her Majesty's Government to the anthropometric method of the measurement of criminals which is successfully in operation in France, Austria, and other Continental countries, and which has been found effective in the identification of habitual criminals, and consequently in the prevention and repression of crime."

Subsequently the committee adjourned to meet at Nottingham, under the presidency of Dr. Burdon Sanderson, on Sept. 13, 1893. In 1894 the association will meet in Oxford, in accordance with the invitation extended by the Mayor and the President of the Ashmolean Society.

Treasurer's Report.—The general treasurer, Arthur W. Rücker, reported that the investments amounted to £12,600—viz., £8,500 new consols, £3,600 India 3-per-cents., and £500 in the treasurer's hands as a floating balance. There was a deficit of £517, which, however, was more apparent than real, as the accounts only extended from Aug. 1, 1891, to June 30, 1892. With the addition of dividends since accrued the amount would be reduced to about £430. It was thought desirable to have a regular financial year ending June 30. Some expense in furniture and removal had been incurred in the transfer of their offices from Albemarle Street to Burlington House, but in future years the change would effect a saving of £100 a year.

Australasian.—The fourth annual meeting of the Australasian Association was held in Hobart, Tasmania, during the week beginning Jan. 7, 1892. The officers were as follow: President, Sir Robert G. C. Hamilton. Section Presidents: A, Astronomy, Mathematics, Physics, and Mechanics, W. H. Bragg; B, Chemistry and Mineralogy, W. M. Hamlet; C, Geology and Palæontology, T. W. E. David; D, Biology, W. Baldwin-Spencer; E, Geography, Crawford Pasco; F, Economic and Social Science and Statistics, Richard Teece; G, Anthropology, Lorimer Fison; H, Sanitary Science and Hygiene, W. H. Warren; I. Literature and Fine Arts, Edward E. Morris; J, Architecture and Engineering, C. Napier Bell. General Secretaries, Archibald Liversidge and Alexander Morton; General Treasurer, James B. Walker.

Opening Session.—On Jan. 7, the meeting began with a session of the general council in the rooms of the Royal Society, when the election of the sectional officers was confirmed and officers for the next meeting nominated. The first general session was held in the evening at the Town Hall, when, owing to the illness of the

retiring president, Sir James Hector, the association was called to order by its past president, Baron Ferdinand Von Mueller. who inducted the president-elect, Sir Robert G. C. Hamilton, K. C. B., Governor of Tasmania, to the chair. Various addresses of welcome were made, including one by Sir Henry Wyllie Norman, Governor of Queensland, and appropriately responded to, after which the usual presidential address was delivered.

President's Address.—In opening his address the president expressed his satisfaction, as Her Majesty's representative in Tasmania and in behalf of the colony, in extending a welcome to the association. As evidence of his desires to make the meeting valuable, he described his efforts in trying to persuade some of the eminent scientists of the Old World to attend it. He was successful in securing the presence of Robert Giffen, but unable to procure the presence of William H. Huxley, Sir Robert Ball, and Sir Lyon Playfair. He closed with a special plea for the study of science, and said:

Science directly tends to the elucidation of truth, which is its groundwork: and what can be more noble or ennobling than the pursuit of truth when accompanied by a fearless acceptance of its consequences? The love of truth is the greatest force in the moral elevation of the human race, and it is directly generated and fostered by the pursuit of science. The more the scientific habit of mind is cultivated, the more will a habit of absolute truthfulness be established in all relations of life. We are scarcely conscious of the extent to which misrepresentation or concealment of truth permeates society in all matters political, commercial, and social. I do not now refer so much to that sort of misrepresentation which would lead a man to be regarded as a liar as to the conventional want of truthfulness, or the communication of half truths only, of which society generally is so tolerant. Nor is it easy to conceive what the world would become if falsehood and deceit were as rare as robbery or murder, and the intentional conveying of a wrong impression or the permitting of a wrong impression to be received were regarded as utterly base and criminal. A scientific training of the mind must work in this direction, for it is based on truth, and is incompatible with any connivance. at or toleration of conscious misrepresentation in any shape or form.

A. Astronomy, Mathematics, Physics, and Mechanics. — The presiding officer of this section was Prof. W. H. Bragg, who fills the chair of Mathematics at the University in Adelaide, South Australia. His address was on "Mathematical Analogies between Various Branches of Science." Subsequent to the reading of the report of the Seismological Committee the following papers were read: "The Astronomical Explanation of a Glacial Period," by Sir Robert Ball; "On the Conductivity of a Salt Solution," by W. H. Steele; "Quaternions as an Instrument of Physical Research," by A. McAulay; "The 'Dodging Tide' of South Australia," by R. W. Chapman; "Solar Phenomena," by Archbishop Murphy; "Grouping of Stars in the Southern Part of the Milky Way, illustrated by Photographs," by H. C. Russell; "On Some of the Difficulties occurring in the Photographic Charting of the Heavens" and "Remarks on the Desirability of establishing Tidal Observations in Tasmania," by R. L. J. Ellery; "Unification of Standards of Weights and Measures," by R. B. Lucas; "A Graphic Method of Showing the Relations between the Temperature of the Dew Point and the Temperature of the Air for any Given Climate," by C. W. Adams; "Determining Longitude at Sea," by Capt. Shortt; "Our Tasmanian Earth Tremors," by A. B. Biggs; and "The Science of the Unseen," by Archdeacon Hales.

B. *Chemistry and Mineralogy.*—This section was presided over by W. M. Hamlet, Government Analyst of Tasmania, whose presidential address had to do with "The Progress of Chemistry in Australasia." The following-named papers were read: "Note on the Electrolysis of Fused Salts of Organic Bases," "Occurrence of the New Element Gallium and Indium in a Blende from Peelwood, New South Wales," "Note on the Volatility of Magnesium" and "Lecture Experimental on Gaseous Diffusion," by J. B. Kirkland; "The Analysis of the Cavendish Banana (*Musa Cavendishii*) in Relation to its Value as a Food," by W. M. Doherty; "On the Use of the Oleorefractometer in Organic Analysis," by W. M. Hamlet; "On Some Mineral Waters of New South Wales," by J. C. Mingaye; "Analysis of Storage-battery Plates," by A. H. Jackson; "The Jarvisfield Mineral Waters of Picton, New South Wales," by A. J. Sachs; "Minerals of East Gippsland," by Donald Clark; "The Rusting of Iron" and "The Occurrence of Magnetite in Certain Minerals," by Archibald Liversidge; "Notes on the Exudations Yielded by Some Australian Species of Pittosporum," by J. H. Maiden; "Note on a Natural Bone Ash from Narracoorte," by N. T. M. Wilsmore; and "Note on an Analysis of Water from Lake Corangamite," by A. W. Craig and N. T. M. Wilsmore.

C. *Geology and Palæontology.*—This section was presided over by Prof. T. W. E. David, who holds the chair of Geology in the University of Sydney, New South Wales. His address treated of the "Volcanic Action in Eastern Australia and Tasmania," with special reference to the relation of volcanic activity to oscillations of the earth's crust and to heavy sedimentation. The following-named papers were read: "On Occurrences of *Lepidodendron*, near Bathurst, New South Wales" and "Remarks on the Theory of Coral Reefs," by W. J. C. Ross; "An Inquiry into Supposed Indications of Catastrophe," by J. C. Corlette; "On the Age of Mammaliferous Deposits in Australia," by Ralph Tate; "Notes on the Application of Photography to Geological Work," by J. H. Harvey; "Notes on the Late Land Slips in the Dandenong Ranges, Victoria," by F. Danvers Power; "On a Sample of Cone in Cone Structure," by A. J. Sachs; "Description of Mount Bischoff and its Workings," by H. W. F. Kayser; "Fossils from the Tertiary Beds around Bairnsdale," by Donald Clark; "Notes on the Permo-Carboniferous Rocks of New South Wales," by T. W. E. David; and "Notes on the Advantages of a Federal School of Mines for Australasia," by F. Provis.

D. *Biology.*—The presiding officer of this section was W. Baldwin-Spencer, who is Professor of Biology at Melbourne University. His address consisted of a discussion on "The Fauna of Tasmania." Subsequent to a "Report of Committee on the Fertilization of the Fig," the following papers were read: "On the Systematic Posi-

tion of Bithinia Huonensis" and "On the Affinities of the Florulas of Lord Howe and Norfolk Islands," by Ralph Tate; "On the Origin of Struthion's Birds of Australasia," by F. W. Hutton; "Notes on Some Land Planarians from Tasmania and South Australia" and "Further Observations on the Eggs of Peripatus," by A. Dendy; "The Markings of Fish with Relation to their Hereditary or Phylogenetic Import," by W. Saville Kent; "Zoölogical Exploration of Timor" and "The Geographical Distribution of Australian Limicolæ," by W. V. Legge; "On a Trematode with Ciliated Integument," by W. A. Haswell; "Queensland Fungus Blights," by F. M. Bailey; "On the Preservation of our Native Plants and Animals," by A. F. Robin; "Preliminary Note on the Vesiculæ Seminales and the Spermatophores of Callorhyncus Antarcticus," by Jeffrey Parker; "Notes and Description of a Young Echidna," by Alexander Morton; "On the Habits of Ceratodus, the Lung Fish of Queensland," by W. Baldwin-Spencer; "Review of Queensland Lichens," by J. Shirley; and "List of Tasmanian Mosses," by W. A. Weymouth.

E. *Geography.* — This section was presided over by Commander Crawford Pasco, R. N., who, in his presidential address, discussed the explorations of Australia and referred to the large area of the globe yet to be explored within the Antarctic circle. Subsequently the following-named papers were read: "Report of the Antarctic Committee," "Notes on a Magnetic Shoal near Cossack, W. A.," by W. Osborne Moore; "Explorations and Discoveries in British New Guinea since the Proclamation of Sovereignty," by J. P. Thomson; "Icelandic Notes," by J. B. W. Woollnough; "A Draft of the Great South Land," by A. Mault; "The Influence of Spanish and Portuguese Discoveries on the Theory of a Southern Continent," by J. R. McClymont; "Dispatches from the Elder Exploring Expedition," by D. Murray; "Volcanic Phenomena in Samoa in 1866," by John Fraser; and "Life and Work of Sir John Franklin," by A. C. Macdonald.

F. *Economic and Social Science and Statistics.*—The presiding officer of this section was Richard Teece, the actuary of the Australian Mutual Provident Society, Sydney, whose address had to do with a "New Theory of the Relation of Profit and Wages." The following papers were read: "On International Statistical Comparisons," by Robert Giffen; "The Organization of Industry," by Alfred De Lissa; "The Obligations of a Civil Government," by J. W. Cotton; "The Effects of Protection on the Imports of Australia," by A. Sutherland; "The Incidence of Taxation," by N. J. Brown; "Is Capital the Result of Abstinence?" by A. J. Ogilvy; "Disturbance of the Population Estimates by Defective Records," by H. H. Hayter; "The Evolution of Hostility between Capital and Labor," by Mrs. A. Morton; "The Wealth of Australasia," by T. Coghlan; "The Luneral, or a Table for discovering Week-day Dates," by W. E. Stopford; "A Layman's Criticism of Current Theories of Population," by S. Ciemes; "Insanity and Crime," by E. Pariss-Nesbit; and "Australian Currencies," by A. F. Basset Hull.

G. *Anthropology.*—This section was presided over by Rev. Lorimer Fison, of Queen's College, Melbourne, who discussed the subject of "Anthropology" as his address, advocating its study and commenting on the advantages offered by British New Guinea and its outlying groups of islands for its pursuit. The following papers were then read: "Bibliographical Report"; "Story of Tu and Rei" and "Women's Omens," by Rev. Dr. Gill; "New Britain and its People," by Rev. B. Danks; "Sydney-Natives Fifty Years Ago," by Rev. W. B. Clarke; "Samoa and the Loyalty Islands," by Rev. S. Ella; "Notes on the Tannese," by Rev. W. Gray; "The Loyalty Islands," by Rev. S. M. Creagh; "Malekula Custom," by Rev. W. Legatt; "Aneityum Custom," by Rev. J. Lawrie: "Group Marriage and Relationship" and "The Nair Polyandry and the Diere Piraruru," by Rev. L. Fison; "The New Hebrides," by Rev. D. Macdonald; and "The Origin of the Sense of Duty," by A. Sutherland.

H. *Sanitary Science and Hygiene.*—The presiding officer of this section was Prof. W. H. Warren, who holds the chair of Engineering in the University of Sydney. His address dealt with the development of sanitary science and its application to present experiences both in cities and towns and in dwellings. The following papers were read: "Cremation," by T. James; "House Ventilation," by P. Hurst Seager; "The Etiology of Typhoid," by E. O. Giblin; "Physical Education in Schools," by Miss Violet Mackenzie; "Notes on a Grease Interceptor," by W. S. Cook; "Sewerage of a Seaside City," by A. Mault; "On Some Matters relating to Public Health," by C. E. Barnard; "Diseases communicable from Animals to Man, illustrated by Microscopic Slides," by A. Park; and "On the Modes of Infection in Tuberculosis," by E. Hirschfeld.

I. *Literature and Fine Arts.*—Prof. Edward E. Morris, who has the chair of English, French, and German Languages and Literatures in the University of Melbourne, was the president of this section. His address had to do with education, and he advocated fewer universities but increased teaching facilities. The following papers were read: "The Heralds of Australian Literature," by T. A. Browne; "Some Aspects of Australian Literature," by Alexander Sutherland; "Among the Western Highlands of Tasmania," by W. C. Piguenit; "Popular Errors about Art and Artists," by J. R. Ashton; "The Province of the Amateur in Art," by C. H. Dicker; "The Authorship of Shakespeare's Plays," by F. J. Young; "Shakespeare and Bacon," by C. M. Tenison; "Secondary Education in Australia," by P. A. Robin; "Elementary Science in Primary Schools," by J. Rule; "The Scientific Method of studying Languages," by R. T. Elliott; "The Rationale of Examinations," by F. J. Young; "The Modern Lyric from a Musical Standpoint," by Miss E. Mills; "Tennyson's Poetic Rhythms," by H. R. Webb; "The Australian Decorative Arts," by J. R. Tranthim-Fryer; and "Formation of Home Reading Union," by the Bishop of Tasmania.

J. *Architecture and Engineering.*—This section was presided over by C. Napier Bell, of Greymouth, New Zealand. His address was general, and described the more prominent of the recent developments in engineering science with their special suggestiveness to Australia. Papers

with the following titles were read: "Building and Architecture; a Definition and a Vindicator," by Alan C. Walker; "The Truthful Treatment of Brickwork," by A. North; "On the Making of Hydraulic Lime and Mortar," by A. O. Sachse; "Primitive Construction of Houses," by Edward Dobson: "Railway Extension and Break of Gauge," by A. Stuart; "Water Supply of Rural Towns of Tasmania," by C. W. James; "City Surveys," by D. M. Maitland; and "Fronts of Buildings in Brickwork v. Portland Cement," by W. W. Eldridge.

Entertainments.—During the meeting the following evening lectures were delivered: On Jan. 8, "The Rise and Growth of the British Empire," by Dr. Robert Giffen; on Jan. 11, "The Great Sutherland Waterfall," by C. W. Adams; and on Jan. 13, "Early Hobart," by J. B. Walker. On Jan. 12, a concert was given by the Musical Union; also garden parties were given, on Jan 7, by Sir Robert G. C. Hamilton; on Jan. 9, by Henry Dobson; on Jan. 13, by the Bishop of Tasmania; and on Jan. 15, by R. C. Read. On Sunday, Jan. 16, a science sermon, "From Man to Nature and from Man to God," was delivered by Rev. George Clarke, Vice-Chancellor of the Tasmanian University.

Next Meeting.—The fifth annual meeting of the association will be held in Adelaide, South Australia, in 1893, at a time which was left to be fixed by the officers and committee in Adelaide. For that occasion the following officers were chosen: President, Prof. Ralph Tate; Vice-Presidents, Sir Robert G. C. Hamilton, Baron Ferdinand Von Mueller, Sir James Hector, Albert Norton, and H. C. Russell; General Secretaries, E. H. Rennie and W. H. Bragg; and Local Treasurer. F. Wright.

ASTRONOMY, PROGRESS OF, IN 1892. The astronomical discoveries of the past year have been numerous and important, as the following *résumé* will show:

The Sun.—Although the present is only the second or third year of the sun-spot maximum cycle, yet the number and enormous dimensions of some of the groups and isolated spots, often visible to the naked eye, have excited much popular as well scientific interest in solar physics. Astronomers were greatly surprised at the immense size of a sun spot which appeared in September, 1891, though it was but a pygmy in extent when compared with that of February, 1892. The latter was for several days conspicuously visible to the naked eye. To record its history from its inception to its final disappearance after five axial rotations of the sun would occupy more space than this limited article will allow. Though called a sun spot, it was, in reality, an aggregation of fifty or more separate but contiguous spots, which seemed to have been thrown out from the center in wild profusion as if by an explosion. At its maximum, on Feb. 8, it is doubtful if there ever has been seen so grand a spectacle on the sun's face. As 450 miles at the sun's distance subtends an angle of but 1″, and as the spot was 5′ 30″ = 148,500 miles in length, and 3′ 15″ = 87,750 miles in breadth, it follows that it must have covered an area equal, in round numbers, to 10,000,000,000 square miles, concealing $\frac{1}{330}$ of the sun's visible hemisphere. During its visibility it drifted in latitude from 17° S. to 80° S. It was not seen at the sixth rotation of the sun upon its axis.

The diminution of light by an obscuration so extensive would equal the loss of 5,000 full moons. Whether this, when seen from a star,

THE SUN-SPOT OF FEBRUARY, 1892.
Feb. 5, 10.35 A. M.

would be sufficiently noticeable to rank our sun as a variable star, as many suppose, is exceedingly doubtful. No diminution of either the sun's heat or light upon the earth is shown by delicate tests when the orb is so largely covered, but remains the same in these particulars as when it is spotless.

Solar Prominences.—Solar activity has not been less marked in regard to the prominences than in its sun spots. M. Trouvelot, of Janssen's Observatory, at Meudon, France, makes a report of those observed during March, April, and May. He says that out of 40 observed, 23 belong to the eruptive type. April was especially rich in extraordinary outbursts. The base of one seen on April 6 extended 12° along the solar circumference, and had a length of 90,050 miles, and a height of 57,570 miles. On the 8th, one, appearing like a candle flame in shape, rose to a height of 71,970 miles at 10ʰ 54ᵐ, and a half-hour later had attained a height of 105,-550 miles.

M. Jules Fenyi, on May 5, at Kalocsa, observed a small one at 10ʰ 25ᵐ, which at 12ʰ 11ᵐ began a very rapid upper movement, and in eight minutes rose to a height of 140,000 miles, having ascended at the rate of 228 miles per second. Later, the lower portion faded, but the upper part continued to rise until an elevation of 237,-000 miles was reached. No spot or facula was

visibly connected with the outburst, and a sun spot near was undisturbed. The observer adds that a velocity so great carried the matter into space beyond the sun's attraction, and so, of course, beyond return. May not such eruptions of matter be the source of the sun's corona, and the zodiacal light and of the Gegenshein?

Sun Spots and Terrestrial Magnetism.—It is rather generally conceded, though disputed by some eminent authorities, that during the prevalence of sun spots the earth's magnetism is intensified, and auroral phenomena are more numerous. The number of auroras and magnetic disturbances, both of the earth and its atmosphere during the present year, especially on the apparition of the great sun spot of February last, seem to be proof of its truth. Numerous instances through many years may be cited confirmatory of the relationship. On the other hand, it is noteworthy that auroral and terrestrial magnetic disturbances often occur during solar quiescence, but the Astronomer Royal, Mr. Christie, argues that, seeing but one side of the sun at such a time, there may have been a spot on the other side. He further says: "There are now three or four marked cases on record of large spots on the sun being coincident with these disturbances on the scale experienced last February, but there are no cases of a large spot being seen without magnetic disturbances."

Solar Spectrum.—Lines in the invisible ultra-violet portion of the solar spectrum have, for the first time, been photographed by H. Deslandres using a Foucault siderostat with an eight-inch Rowland grating. The lines due to hydrogen in this part of the spectrum, first observed by Huggins, have also been photographed in the spectra of the protuberances, eight of the ten belonging to the series having been seen. It is believed that from a mountain elevation the other two could be detected. Photographs of the spectra

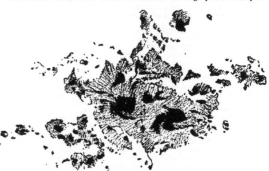

THE SUN-SPOT OF FEBRUARY, 1892.
Feb. 11, 1 P. M.

of faculæ and sun spots show the H and K lines of calcium more intense than those of hydrogen.

Spectroheliographic observations of the sun have been made by Prof. George E. Hale, of Kenwood Observatory, Chicago. In a paper read before the meeting of the American Association for the Advancement of Science, at Rochester, in August, he described the ingenious apparatus which he had invented and perfected for photographing the spots, the faculæ, and the prominences. This device records faculæ which the eye can not detect. He secures on one plate, with one exposure, the spots, faculæ, chromosphere, and the protuberances, and exhibited before the association, by the aid of the optical lantern, the first complete picture of the sun ever taken. The reader will find a description of the spectroheliograph in "Astronomy and Astro-physics" (late "Sidereal Messenger") for May, 1892, published at Northfield, Minn.

Prof. Hale's achievement in photographing ten bright lines heretofore unknown in the ultra-violet spectrum of the prominences and the chromosphere is an unrivaled one, and excites great interest among astronomers and spectroscopists. By the aid of a new objective by Brashear, which by its color correction is well adapted to this kind of work, he has photographed nineteen lines in the ultra-violet.

A photograph of importance was taken on July 15, showing simply a large spot. A few minutes later another was secured in which a bright band had developed. Twenty-seven minutes after the last named, another plate showed bright faculæ covering nearly the entire spot, which, however, soon disappeared, and the spot at the final exposure presented the same appearance as on the first plate. The accurate photographic delineation of such sudden changes is justly regarded as greatly important. On the day following these observations, a magnetic disturbance and brilliant aurora were noted. Prof. Hale estimated the size of the spot to have been 4,000,-000,000 square miles.

The Sun's Diameter.—In *Astronomische Nachrichten*, No. 3,066, Dr. Auwers gives the results for solar parallax from the German transit-of-Venus expeditions in 1874 and 1882. That of the transit of 1874 is 8·877″ ± 0·043, and that of 1882 equals 8·879″ ± 0·037.

In the same journal, No. 3,068, the same writer has a paper on the diameter of the sun as determined by the heliometric measures made in connection with the above-named expeditions by 31 observers with 4 instruments. He finds the mean results for the sun's mean diameter to be 1,919·3″, which differs considerably from that at present adopted by the various nautical almanacs, the German being 1,922·4″, the French and English 1,923·6″, and the American 1,924·0″. Dr. Auwers remarks that, if the value he finds is influenced by irradiation effects, it can only be too large, and thus the errors of the adopted diameters must be greater still. He urges that an immediate change in these values be made, and announces for the "German Almanac" that the alteration will occur in the volume for 1895.

The observations are discussed for possible ellipticity of the sun's disk, with the result that the polar diameter is found to exceed the equatorial by 0·032. Had the personalities of the observers, in both perpendicular and horizontal observations, been taken into consideration, the value for the polar diameter, it is believed, would have been less, as indeed it ought to be, considering the sun as a rotating body. But an ellip-

ticity of so small an amount as ± 0·038″ is immeasurable, and indicates that a deviation from an exact sphere has not been and can not be proved.

The Cause of Solar Heat.—In the recently issued volume of "Transactions of the Astronomical and Physical Society of Toronto," Dr. Joseph Morrison, of the "American Nautical Almanac" office, has a paper treating of the two most generally received theories of the source and maintenance of the enormous heat of the sun. One hypothesis is that it is due to the energy developed by the falling of meteoric matter on the sun. The other asserts that it is produced and kept up by slow contraction of the sun's bulk. He calculates that a pound of matter falling from infinity would develop 82,340,000 units of heat, and, therefore, that a quantity of matter equaling one one hundredth of the earth's mass falling annually on the sun would maintain an amount of heat equal to that observed.

As to the contraction theory, he says, taking the solar constant at 25 calories per square metre per minute, the linear contraction of the sun's radius requisite to keep up the present radiation is 156·9 feet in a year, or nearly 30 miles in a thousand years. As 450 miles of the sun's diameter subtends, at the earth's distance, an angle of only one second of arc, it would, therefore, require 7,575 years for the sun's angular diameter to be reduced by one second of arc, the smallest angle measurable on the sun's disk.

Direction of the Sun's Motion.—A little more than a hundred years ago Sir William Herschel, noticing that the stars in the constellation Hercules were slightly farther apart, and that those in the opposite direction were nearer together than as determined prior to his day, came to the conclusion, and so announced, that our sun, with the entire solar system, had a progressive motion in the direction of Hercules. This theory has never, from subsequent observation, been disputed, save as to the exact direction of its motion.

Prof. Lewis Boss, Director of the Dudley Observatory, has exhausted the refinements of mathematical and observational astronomy only to establish its truth. He, however, places, as the result of his calculations, the "apex of the sun's way" in R. A. 289°; Dec. + 51°, or in Cygnus instead of Hercules.

McStumpe has likewise made thorough investigation of the complex problem, but his results differ somewhat from those of Prof. Boss. His mean of four determinations gives R. A. 285°; Dec. north 36°, or between Cygnus and Hercules.

The Moon.—*Lunar Radiant Heat.*—The second series of Vol. IV of the Scientific Transactions of Royal Dublin Society contains a memoir on the moon's radiant heat as determined by Dr. Boeddicker at the observatory of Lord Rosse, Birr Castle, Ireland, during the total lunar eclipse of Jan. 28, 1888. His conclusion was that the moon's heat has much lower refrangibility than the sun's, and that the maximum of heat falls rather before than after the time of full. The results of this eclipse fully confirmed those of that of 1884, the radiation falling considerably below the commencement of the eclipse and not returning to its standard value until 1ʰ 40ᵐ after last contact with the penumbra. He considers the fact established that the decrease of heat had begun quite three minutes before first contact with the penumbra, a conclusion implying that the earth's atmosphere is capable of exercising a distinct heat absorption at a height of 100 miles.   Prof. Frank W. Very, of the Allegheny Observatory, sought the solution of this problem in a different manner, and, instead of choosing an eclipse, observed the moon in different phases, using a bolometer in conjunction with a siderostat for that purpose. The apparatus was so constructed as to enable him to view the entire moon or but a portion of it. He adopted the latter method, and, the lunar image having been projected on a white card in which a small hole had been pierced, the image of the region whose heat was to be measured was brought over this hole through which the rays passed to the sensitive surface of the bolometer. The results thus obtained are given in a series of eight charts on which are marked the different spots whose heat had been observed ; corresponding tables give the measures, and isothermal lines inferred from these measures are drawn on these charts. On the portion of the moon to which the sun is setting the heat gradient was found to be more steep than on that part to which the sun is rising. The following are the main conclusions :

1. The existence of a small heat-storing action by which an excess of heat (not more than 10 per cent.) is accumulated after many days of isolation seems to be established.

2. The circumferential zone of the full moon radiates about 20 per cent. less than its center.

3. Bright regions radiate only a little more than the dark, though they reflect nearly twice as much.

4. There is a somewhat larger proportion of reflected rays from the full moon than from the moon at first quarter.

5. The result obtained by Dr. Boeddicker as to the different law followed by the diminution of heat from that followed by the decrease of light during an eclipse, seems to be confirmed.

Prof. Very, for his paper, was awarded the prize offered by the Utrecht Society of Arts and Sciences.

Active Lunar Volcanoes.—In the June number of "Observatory," 1892, Prof.William H. Pickering has an interesting article from Arequipa, Peru, March 28, 1892, entitled "Are there at Present Active Volcanoes on the Moon?" After describing the atmospheric conditions at the observatory some 8,000 feet above tide, where a magnifying power of from 800 to 1,200 may be used to advantage, he discusses the question of active volcanoes on the moon. Comparing his own observations with the chart of the moon published by Neisen, he says : "Of a total of 67 craters, 32 were found common to both charts, 24 were given by Neisen and not found by myself. while 11 were found that were not given by Neisen. Using the 13-inch Clark telescope, all of Neisen's craters were found save two, which could not be found with a power of 800. The 11 other craters found by myself were all confirmed and a great number of other smaller ones were also seen."

A committee's report to the British Association, some twenty years ago, on the conspicuous crater Plato, mentions 36 luminous points or crater cones, No. 4 of which has entirely disappeared, only a whitish stain at present occupying its place. Nos. 7 and 31 are also missing,

but eight miles southeast is a large crater not reported by the committee. In class three as to size, out of the six recorded only one (No. 16) is now visible. These facts, taken in consideration with the falling in of the walls and the filling up of the well-known crater Linné, may well suggest the question heading this paragraph.

It may be added that No. 4, alluded to above, was seen as a conspicuous crater in 1880, 1882, 1887, and 1888.

Comets.—Since Oct. 2, 1891, the date of the latest discovery of a comet given in our last volume, the following comets have been discovered, named in the order of their finding rather than their perihelion passages :

Comet *a* (Swift) was discovered by Dr. Lewis Swift, at the Warner Observatory, in the early morning of March 6, in the constellation Sagittarius. Though detected with a telescope, it was visible (knowing its place) to the naked eye. It is still (Oct. 14) visible telescopically, and has proved a most remarkable body. As photographed on March 10 by Prof. H. C. Russell at the Sydney Observatory, Australia, it showed eight tails, two of which extended beyond the plate. On the sides of these two long rays three new streamers appear. All of these rays or actinic tails are easily seen on the photographic plates, though none were visible to the eye with the 11¼-inch telescope.

Prof. Barnard's photographs of the comet, made at the Lick Observatory with an hour's exposure, reveal, spreading out from the head, a complicated system of a dozen tails, some of which show remarkable curvatures. In less than twenty-four hours the third tail had formed to the extent of 10,000,000 miles, while the northern one had entirely disappeared. His camera was made to follow the comet, so that the stars in the field are represented by lines instead of dots. A picture secured on April 8 shows interesting changes in the tails, a large protuberant mass or semi-tail being seen on the southern side of the principal branch, which developed into a number of thin wisps not before noticed. On one occasion the tail was twenty degrees long, as seen by the naked eye. The following elliptic elements have been computed for it by Dr. A. Berberich, of Berlin :

Time of perihelion passage, 1892, April 6·69025, Berlin mean time:

From node to perihelion	= 24° 31′ 11·1″
Longitude of node	= 246° 54′ 15·4″
Inclination	= 85° 42′ 20·6″
Perihelion distance	= 1·02606
Eccentricity	= 0·998611

While its eccentricity is indicative that it is a periodic, yet its so near approach to a parabola must give it a period of several thousand years. Much uncertainty exists regarding the periodicity of a comet whose eccentricity is so nearly equal to 1.

Comet *b* (Denning) was discovered by W. F. Denning at Bristol, England, in the constellation Cepheus, on March 18, 1892. It was excessively faint, and has so remained. The following parabolic elements have been calculated by Dr. Berberich :

Perihelion passage, 1892, May 11·22042, Berlin mean time :

Node to perihelion	= 129° 18′ 34·4″
Longitude of node	= 258° 25′ 41·6″
Inclination	= 89° 42′ 4·3″
Perihelion distance	= 1·97064

Comet *c* (Pons-Winnecke) was detected on March 18, 1892, by Spitaler. It has been unusually bright at this apparition, but, unfortunately, when brightest it was badly situated, setting soon after the sun and observable only in strong twilight.

Comet *d* (Brooks) was found by W. R. Brooks, Director of the Smith Observatory, at Geneva, N. Y., on Aug. 28. Its elements have been computed by Dr. Berberich as follows:

Perihelion passage, 1892, Dec. 19·69:
    Node to perihelion = 269° 24'
    Longitude of node   = 261° 3'
    Inclination   = 27° 57'
    Perihelion distance = 0 6991

This comet promises to be much brighter before arriving at perihelion.

Comet *e* (Barnard).—On the evening of Oct. 12, Prof. E. E. Barnard, of the Lick Observatory staff, while engaged in a systematic, photographic study of the Milky Way, secured several plates. The next day, in developing the negatives, he was surprised to find depicted on one of them the impress or trail of a comet, which was visually observed that evening, Oct. 13, in right ascension $19^h 34^m$; declination north 12° 30'. Its daily motion is 1° 40' southeasterly. This is the first instance of a photographically discovered comet.

From observations of Oct. 15, 16, and 17, Prof. Campbell, of the Lick Observatory, has computed the following elements:

Perihelion passage, 1892, Aug. 26·14, Greenwich mean time:
    Node to perihelion = 114° 2'
    Longitude of node   = 184° 13'
    Inclination   = 48° 7'
    Perihelion distance = 1·9904

Neither Tempel's comet (1867, II), nor Brooks's (1886, IV), both periodic, and for which finding ephemerides were published, have been observed.

Spectrum of Swift's Comet.—Prof. W. W. Campbell, of the Lick Observatory, who on April 6 made spectroscopic observation of this comet with the 36-inch equatorial, says in "Astronomical Journal" of April 16: "The spectrum is of the usual type. That of the nucleus is apparently continuous and visible from about C to G. The three well-known yellow, green, and blue bands were present, their intensities being, approximately, in the ratio 1 : 6 : 2. Their lower edges were quite sharply defined. When the slit was narrowed to 0·004 inches the bright line on the lower edge of the green band became exceedingly sharp, and could be bisected with the micrometer thread with extreme accuracy. A 60° prism was used." He gives the wave lengths of the three bands as 5,630, 5,170·4, and 4,723 respectively.

Dr. Konkoly, of O'Gyalla, also observed the spectrum and found five bright lines.

Long Visibility of a Comet.—Until recently the great comet of 1811 had the longest period of visibility of any known, previous or subsequent—viz., eighteen months—but Barnard's comet (1889, I), discovered on Sept. 2, 1888, was still to be seen by the mammoth telescope of the Lick Observatory, with its great light-gathering power, on Aug. 18, 1890, seven hundred and fifteen days after its finding, and when its distance from the sun was 6·25 times that of the earth,

or about 580,000,000 miles, exceeding that of some of the short-period comets at their aphelia.

A Fifth Satellite to Jupiter.—The announcement recently telegraphed from the Lick Observatory of the finding of a new and fifth moon to the giant planet, which was at first received with incredulity, has been confirmed. Prof. E. E. Barnard has given in "Astronomical Journal" of Oct. 4, 1892, a complete account of the discovery supplemented with micrometrical measurements. Having the use of the great telescope on one night in each week, he says: "Nothing of special importance was encountered until the night of Sept. 9, when, in carefully examining the immediate region of the planet Jupiter, I detected an exceedingly small star close to the planet and near the third satellite. I at once measured the position angle of the object with reference to Satellite III." This being the only measurement made on that evening, he did not think the proof sufficient to warrant the publication of the discovery, which was not done until Sept. 10. As to the diameter of the satellite he declares it quite impossible to tell, but estimates it as being of the thirteenth magnitude, which would imply that it ought to be seen with a 16-inch telescope, and yet he asserts that it would require one of 26 inches aperture to observe it. As he considers it a more difficult object than the satellites of Mars, its previous nondiscovery is not at all surprising.

From a mean of three observations for distance made on Sept. 10, 12, and 14, he deduces its distance from the center of Jupiter to be about 112,450 miles or 70,000 miles from his surface. The mean period determined from the above observations is $11^h 49·63^m$, its hourly orbital velocity being about 60,000 miles. Prof. Young has also observed it, and makes the period of revolution a little greater. The discovery of this satellite is one of the most wonderful astronomical events of the nineteenth century.

New Star in Auriga.—On Feb. 1, 1892, Dr. Ralph Copeland, Astronomer Royal of Scotland, received an anonymous postal card with the following legend: "Nova in Auriga; in Milky Way about 2° south of Chi Auriga, preceding 26 Auriga; fifth magnitude; slightly brighter than Chi." This star was easily found with an opera glass by Dr. Copeland and examined by him with a prism, and found to present a spectrum very like the new star of 1866. When cabled to this country, Prof. Pickering examined his photographic plates of that region, and found depicted on one of them a star with a unique spectrum, whereupon he sent the following cablegram to Dr. Copeland: "Nova bright in photograph Dec. 10th, faint on Dec. 1st, maximum Dec. 20th." This, it appears, is the extent of our knowledge of its first appearance, an astronomical phenomenon that has attracted great and world-wide attention. Subsequently a letter was received by Dr. Copeland from Rev. Thomas D. Anderson, the writer of the anonymous card, who therein declared himself its author. The telescope used by the reverend amateur astronomer is a small spyglass of 1¼-inch aperture, magnifying ten times. It shows in a striking manner how sometimes an important discovery may be achieved with small means if combined with energy and enthusiasm.

Dr. Huggins, who with Mrs. Huggins made spectroscopic examination of the Nova on Feb. 2, says, in *Astronomische Nachrichten*, No. 3079: "The most noticeable feature to the eye of the star's spectrum was the great brilliancy of the hydrogen lines at C, F, and G, with three lines on the left side F, but the point of greatest interest was obviously that each bright hydrogen line was accompanied by a strong absorption (dark) line toward the blue. Comparison with the lines of terrestrial hydrogen showed at once a large motion of recession of the bright lines, and a motion of approach of the hydrogen which produced the absorption.

"A photograph which we have taken since gives the star's spectrum as far as the ultraviolet, or about wave length 3,200. Besides the hydrogen series there are other lines doubled in a similar manner, including the sodium lines at D. The whole visible and photographic regions from below C to about wave length 3,200 are full of dark and bright lines. There is a bright line a little more refrangible than D, which may be D_3, and there are bright lines near C."

Prof. Pickering says of eighteen photographs of this region taken with the 8-inch photographic telescope, from Nov. 3, 1885, to Nov. 2, 1891, that on none was the star visible, nor on plates obtained on thirteen nights from Oct. 21 to Dec. 1, 1891, although Chi Auriga was always clearly shown. On twelve nights, beginning Dec. 10, 1891, and ending Jan. 20, 1892, similar plates were obtained, on all of which the new star was plainly seen. He further adds: "It appears that the star was fainter than the eleventh magnitude on Nov. 2, and fainter than the sixth magnitude on Dec. 10. Its brightness increased rapidly until Dec. 18, attaining its maximum about Dec. 20, when its magnitude was 4·4. It then began to decrease slowly until Jan. 20, when it was somewhat below the fifth magnitude." All these changes occurred before its discovery by Mr. Anderson.

The doubling of the lines of the spectrum is a fact of great interest and indicates that the star is a close spectroscopic double, and that this doubling is caused by the coincidence of the approach of one with the recession of the other. Dr. Vogel, of Potsdam, asserts that both the bright and dark lines are double, and advances the hypothesis that there are three bodies, two of them circling around the third. He estimates the star with the bright-line spectrum to be receding from the earth at the rate of 300 miles per second.

The cause of the sudden increase in brightness of stars, eighteen instances of which have been recorded during the last eighteen hundred years, is unknown. Great interest is excited among astronomers by their effulgence, and the literature on the subject, especially on the Auriga Nova, is abundant; but for want of space only a few of the most interesting facts can be alluded to. All the theories advanced for the appearance of temporary stars seem to be set at naught by an announcement from Prof. Barnard that, seen with the 36-inch telescope, the Nova has changed into a nebula with a stellar nucleus of about the tenth magnitude. The nebulosity was 3" in diameter, surrounded by a fainter glow of half a minute in diameter.

Variation of Latitude.—In Nos. 251, 271, and 272 of Gould's "Astronomical Journal" Prof. S. C. Chandler has published a series of papers on the variation of latitude which he has detected, and presents apparently invulnerable proofs of the correctness of his conclusions. He finds the variation to point to a revolution of the earth's axis of inertia about that of rotation from west to east, in a period of four hundred and twenty-seven days, with a radius of 30 feet measured at the earth's surface. Though at first sight his deductions seem unwarranted, yet he has fortified them with facts which meet the approbation of such mathematical astronomers as Dr. B. A. Gould, Prof. Simon Newcomb, and others. Dr. Gould, to confirm, if possible, the truth of the theory, has examined the Cordoba (Argentine Republic) observations, and finds them corroboratory of Chandler's theory, though he admits that the manifestations fluctuated irregularly. This admission has a tendency to weaken the testimony, but it would be rash to condemn a theory having two such distinguished adherents until the arguments on which it rests are proved erroneous or insufficient.

While the present period of revolution of the pole of the earth's figure is supposed to be revolving around that of rotation in four hundred and twenty-seven days, its period, about A. D. 1770, was less than a year, and since then has been increasing. The evidence in support of these conclusions is of so extensive a character that not even an abstract can be given here. The reader is referred to the original articles, which will be found interesting reading.

Rotation of Venus and Mercury.—It is well known that Schiaparelli, from observations continued through many years, has arrived at the conclusion that, like our moon, both Mercury and Venus rotate on their axes in the same time in which they revolve around the sun, or Mercury in eighty-eight, and Venus in two hundred and twenty-five days. These ideas of the distinguished Italian astronomer do not meet with general acceptance. M. Trouvelot, who has for sixteen years studied these planets, thinks that the original period of rotation of Venus, as determined by the early astronomers, of not far from twenty-four hours, is the correct one. The equator is inclined only some 10° or 12° to the plane of its orbit, and the longitude of the ascending node is 2°. The poles are, as others have supposed, crowned with lofty mountains which rise above the dense and deep atmosphere of the planet. He decides that the irregularities noticed by so many skillful observers at the two extremities of the terminator are real, and are due to the great elevation of the polar mountains.

M. Niesten, of the Brussels Observatory, as the result of a long series of observations and drawings, coincides with the views of Trouvelot and sharply challenges those of Schiaparelli. The observations necessary for the settlement of this question are exceedingly difficult to make, and hence it may require years of careful work and many accurate drawings to decide the true rotation periods of these planets.

Opposition of Mars.—The recent favorable opposition of Mars was, as those for ages to come will be, unfortunate for northern observers, from his (on these occasions) great southern declination. The astronomers of the Lick Observatory, with its great elevation above the sea and its lower latitude, have observed this planet under more favorable auspices than those at any northern observatory, but published unofficial accounts from this point are conflicting as to the success in verifying the duplication of Schiaparelli's network of canals. The snow-cap surrounding the south pole has been conspicuously visible even in small telescopes. At the Warner Observatory both satellites have been seen frequently. On several occasions a small, circular, black spot has been noticed partly on the following edge of the snow-cap, resembling in appearance the shadow cast on Jupiter by one of his satellites. At the Lick Observatory the satellites were seen to disappear in eclipse on reaching the line of shadow in two tenths of a second, consequently, as the extent of their orbits is known, and their orbital motions cover a space equal to their diameters in two tenths of a second of time, Prof. Edward S. Holden, the director, has computed their diameters as follows: That of Phobos, the inner satellite, about eight miles; that of Deimos, the outer, about twenty miles. These values differ from those of many authorities. M. Perrotin has announced that with the great equatorial telescope at Mont Gros the luminous projections seen at the Lick Observatory have been observed since June 10. The shifting of the southern snow-cap has also been noticed, and some of the canals are apparent enough to convince the most prejudiced observer. In a letter to the New York "Herald" of Sept. 1, Prof. W. H. Pickering, of Arequipa, Peru, claims the discovery of two mountain ranges on Mars, north of the green patch near the planet's south pole. In the equatorial mountain regions snow fell on Aug. 5, covering two mountains. On Aug. 7 the snow had melted. He says in a later letter: " I have seen forty lakes varying in size. They branched out in dark lines, connecting them with two large, dark areas like seas, though not blue. Many of the canals mentioned by Schiaparelli were also seen, but they were found to be single and not double."

Algol and Other Variables.—Prof. S. C. Chandler, an authority on variable stars, has made thorough investigation of the complex changes in the variability of the light of Algol, and he declares the star to be not only a double but a triple; that it has a dark spectro-photographic companion, unseen by any eye, which revolves round its primary, partly occulting it, thus producing the long known variability of its light in 2^d 20^h 8^m, and contends that it is subject to still another orbital motion of a very different kind. Both have a revolution about a third body—a large, distant, dark companion —in a period of about one hundred and thirty years. He thinks the size of its orbit around the common center of gravity is about equal to that of Uranus around the sun. The plane of the orbit is inclined about 20° to our line of vision. Algol transited the plane, passing through the center of gravity perpendicular to this line of vision in 1804, going outward, and in 1869 coming inward. Mr. Chandler's paper on the subject will be found in "Astronomical Journal," No. 15, Vol. XI.

Mr. A. W. Roberts, of Alice, South Africa, announced the discovery of a short-period variable in Argo Navis which changes from magnitude 7·5 to 8·5 in a period of 4·6 days, increasing in brilliancy for 1·8 day, and decreasing for 2·8 days. It is in R. A. 8^h 33^m 37^s, Dec. south 46° 55'·4' (1875·0).

Mr. Espin, of Wolsingham, during 1891, discovered 120 new third-type stars, 1 fourth-type, and 5 variable stars, bringing the total number of the latter class up to 627.

Examination by Mrs. M. Fleming of photographs of stellar spectra taken at Arequipa has resulted in the detection of five new variable stars. Two are within 4° of the south pole.

Asteroids.—Since Vol. XVI went to press, 15, perhaps 16, of these small planets have been discovered visually and several photographically. The number now recognized as belonging to this group is uncertain, but is probably 340. The names given them since last report are:

305. Gordonia.	311 Claudia.	323. Brucia.
307. Nike.	312. Pierretta.	325. Heidelberga.
308. Polyxo.	315. Constancia.	330. Almatar.
310. Margarita.	322 Phaeo.	332. Columbia.

The names of the discoverers are:

322. Borelly.	328. Wolf	A. Wolf.
323. Wolf.	329. Wolf.	B is No. 163 = Erigone.
324. Palisa.	330. Wolf.	C. Staus
325. Wolf.	331. Charlois.	D. Charlois.
326. Palisa.	342. Charlois.	E. Charlois.
327. Charlois.	333. Charlois.	F. Charlois.
		G. Wolf.
		J. Wolf.

The numbers and their discoverers are so confusing that it has been decided, until all doubts are removed, to number them A, B, C, etc., giving the year of discovery.

Discovery of Nebulæ.—In *Astronomische Nachrichten*, No. 3094, Dr. Lewis Swift has chronicled a list of 60 new nebulæ found at the Warner Observatory during 1891. This catalogue is in continuation of the series of 9 previous ones of 100 each discovered at the Warner Observatory and published in the same journal. Owing to adverse conditions in the surroundings of the observatory introduced within the year, and to sky illumination from electric street lights, the quest has ceased, and the observatory is to be moved to Colorado.

In "Monthly Notices" for April, 1892, Mr. Burnham gives a list of nebulæ covering 21 pages of those discovered by himself, by Barnard, and others, and of many additional ones selected from Dreyer's New General Catalogue of Nebulæ, because of some uncertainty in description or doubt concerning place or actual existence. He has settled many disputed points, and the notes appended to the nebulæ are very interesting and valuable. His discoveries and observations were made with the 36-inch telescope during September and October, 1891.

Catalogues.—In the "Astronomical Journal." No. 268, Prof. J. C. Porter, of the Cincinnati Observatory, has a catalogue of 301 stars having a proper motion of a half-second and over. He hopes soon to publish a more extensive record of stellar proper motions.

The second installment of the Paris Catalogue has recently been issued. This volume contains the reduction of 7,538 stars within the limits of

R. A. 6ʰ to 12ʰ, made at the Paris Observatory in the years 1837 to 1881. From these comparisons the proper motions of 350 stars have been deduced.

The Draper Catalogue of Stellar Spcetra has been completed and forms Vol. XXVII of the "Annals of Harvard College Observatory." This catalogue contains details of the spectra of 10,351 stars, deduced from the measurement of 28,266 spectra.

The second Munich Catalogue of 13,200 stars has been published. The stars whose places are given are situated within about 25° of the equator both north and south.

The Pulkowa Catalogue of 5,634 stars for the epoch of 1875·0, deduced from observations with the Pulkowa Meridian Circle during the years 1874–'80, is now out.

Prof. Weiss has recently published a work of great value to practical astronomers—viz., a new edition of Oeltzen's "Catalogues of Argelander's Zones," extending from 15° to 31° of south declination. The total number of stars whose places are given is 18,276, reduced to epoch 1850·0.

Burnham's eighteenth catalogue of new double stars was recently made public in Nos. 3113 and 3114 of *Astronomische Nachrichten*. They were found with the 36-inch glass of the Lick Observatory in the year 1891. An interesting but brief description is given of each. It includes also micrometrical measures of 400 double stars previously discovered by himself and others. It is a valuable acquisition to our literature of double stars.

Mr. F. E. Espin's catalogue of 627 stars with remarkable spectra may be found in *Astronomische Nachrichten*, Nos. 3023 and 3090. "Washington Observations" for 1888, Appendix I, contains Prof. Asaph Hall's measures of 950 double stars made with the 26-inch equatorial during the years 1880–'91, and occupies 184 pages. The list is made up mostly of close and difficult pairs, and is an important addition to our double-star literature.

Medals.—The gold medal of the Royal Astronomical Society of England was awarded to Prof. G. H. Darwin for his work on "Tides and their Influence on the Figures and Motions of the Heavenly Bodies."

The Donohoe bronze comet medal of the Astronomical Society of the Pacific has been bestowed on Profs. Swift, Denning. and Barnard, for the discovery of comets (*a*, *b*, *c*, and *d*) of 1892.

AUSTRALASIA, a division of the globe which includes the continent of Australia and the other colonial possessions of Great Britain in the Pacific. The following table gives the area and population of the British Australasian colonies at the census of April 5, 1891:

COLONIES.	Square miles.	Males.	Females.	Total.
New South Wales....	310,700	616,008	518,199	1,134,207
Victoria..............	87,884	599,174	541,287	1,140,411
Queensland.........	668,497	223,779	169,939	393,718
South Australia......	903,690	161,759	153,289	315,048
Western Australia ...	1,060,000	......	......	49,782
Tasmania...........	26,215	77,560	69,107	146,667
New Zealand........	104,471	338,175	298,655	626,580
Fiji.................	7,740	......	......	121,180

In the principal colonies the movement of population was as follows in 1890:

COLONIES.	Marriages.	Births.	Deaths.	Excess of births.	Immigration.
New South Wales.....	7,876	38,964	14,217	24,747	12,992
Victoria..............	9,187	37,578	18,012	19,566	15,957
Queensland..........	8,195	15,407	5,688	9,769	6,349
South Australia.......	2,235	10,364	8,923	6,441	3,372
Western Australia.....	......	1,561	540	1,021	1,271
Tasmania.............	954	4,813	2,118	2,695	2,447
New Zealand	3,797	18,278	5,994	12,284	* 1,782

* Net emigration.

The population of Sydney, New South Wales, in 1891 was 386,400, including suburbs. Melbourne, the capital of Victoria, had 494,378 inhabitants, and the total town population of this colony was 684,260, about three fifths of the people in the colony. Adelaide, the capital of South Australia, has a population of about 133,-220. Queensland's capital, Brisbane, had 25,889 inhabitants in the north and 22,849 in the south town, and within a radius of five miles 93,657. In Wellington, the capital of New Zealand, there were 33,224 inhabitants at the time of the census. Perth, the capital of Western Australia, had 9,617.

Finances.—The following table gives the budgets of income and expenditure for each colony and the public debt of each for the financial year 1890, which ended on June 30 in Victoria, South Australia, and Queensland; on Dec. 31 in New Zealand and Fiji; and in New South Wales, Tasmania, and Western Australia on March 31.

COLONIES.	Revenue.	Expenditure.	Debt.
New South Wales..	£9,498,620	£9,558,502	£48,425,838
Victoria...........	* 8,340,813	* 9,228,693	* 43,610,265
Queensland........	* 3,850,228	* 3,684,655	28,105,684
South Australia....	* 2,782,222	* 2,603,498	20,401,500
Western Australia..	414,313	401,737	1,367,444
Tasmania	758,100	722,746	6,482,800
New Zealand	4,208,028	4,081,565	37,848,928
Fiji...............	66,817	60,826	248,969

* For 1891.

Australian Loans.—Since the commercial depression which overtook the Australian colonies one after another, their credit in the London money market has greatly declined, and the period of extravagant borrowing, accompanied by political jobbery, waste, and corruption, has come to a stop, because British investors decline to put more money in the funds of the Australian colonies, of which South Australia alone has been able to raise money at home to carry out improvements. The total debt of the seven Australian colonies amounts to nearly £190,000,-000, about £60 per head of population, which is three and a half times the proportion in the United Kingdom and almost 75 per cent. more than in France. The Australian statesmen professed satisfaction at the close of the period of borrowing, but made anxious attempts nevertheless to negotiate new loans, and predicted distressing consequences if the flow of English money ceased suddenly before the railroads that were planned were completed. Money was raised in London with much difficulty in 1891, and in 1892 it was refused altogether. The Victorian 3½ per cents., which a short time before stood at par, were quoted at 93, and the stock of the other colonies showed a like depreciation. In the summer Sir George Dibbs, the Premier of New South Wales, went to London to speak in behalf of all the colonies, but was unable to overcome the prejudices of British investors. A loan that the Queensland Government sought to place in the London market in the spring of 1891 proved an utter failure. The Bank of England having promised to subscribe £500,000 of the £1,870,000 that it was desired to raise, of which £1,170,000 were needed to take up debentures that fell due on July 1, 1891, other backers were found, and through the efforts of the brokers of the Bank of England the entire loan was placed, the bank taking the last £170,000 needed to cover the loan (amounting nominally to £2,500,000). in addition to the £500,000 with which it headed the subscription. As the bank's interest had been disposed of before the list of holders reached Australia, Sir Thomas McIlwraith, the colonial Treasurer, in his speeches in the Legislature accused the Bank of England of a breach of faith, and boasted that the colony had succeeded in spite of the treacherous desertion of that great financial institution. Sir S. W. Griffith, instead of giving the retraction and apology that was demanded, defended Sir Thomas McIlwraith's accusation against the good faith of the managers of the Bank of England, while admitting errors regarding some of the facts. On receiving his reply, William Lidderdale, governor of the bank, wrote to Sir James Garrick, Agent-General for Queensland, breaking off all financial relations with Queensland.

Commerce.—The foreign and intercolonial trade of the several colonies for 1890 is shown in the following table:

COLONIES.	Imports.	Exports.
New South Wales	£22,615,000	£22,045,937
Victoria	22,954,015	18,266,229
Queensland	5,066,700	8,554,512
South Australia	8,262,673	8,927,378
Western Australia	874,447	671,818
Tasmania	1,897,512	1,486,992
New Zealand *	6,360,525	9,811,720
Fiji	206,757	864,533

* For 1891.

The domestic exports of New South Wales were £17,232,725 in value. The export of wool was 243,738,266 pounds, valued at £9,232,672. On Jan. 1, 1891, there were in the colony 55,986,431 sheep, 1,909,009 cattle, and 444,163 horses. The average annual product of gold for the five years ending with 1890 was £388,156. The silver, silver ore, and galena raised in 1890 was valued at £2,762,554; the copper, £84,107; the tin, £179,052; the coal, £1,279,089. The wheat crop in 1891 was 3,649,216 bushels; maize, 5,713,205 bushels. The imports by sea amounted to £17,907,663, of which £8,628,007 came from Great Britain, £6,274,380 from Australasian colonies, £663,325 from other British possessions, £359,162 from the United States, and £1,482,849 from other foreign countries. The sea-borne exports were £14,019,561 in total value, and of these £6,623,431 went to the United Kingdom, £3,258,364 to Australian colonies, £674,201 to other British colonies, £1,300,375 to the United States, and £2,163,190 to other countries. The import duties collected in 1890

amounted to £1,888,321, which was 8·35 per cent. of the total value of imports.

In Victoria the customs revenue for 1890 was £2,704,380, which was about 12 per cent. of the total value of the imports. The external trade of Victoria in 1890 was divided as follows: Imports from Great Britain, £9,607,193; from Australasian colonies, £8,525,759; from India, £404,288; from Ceylon, £100,838; from Canada, £55,740; from other British possessions, £760,053; from the United States, £1,069,297; from other countries, £2,430,847. Exports to Great Britain, £6,850,014; to Australian colonies, £4,064,106; to India, £519,043; to other British possessions, £298,661; to Belgium, £654,748; to France, £452,807; to Germany, £240,088; to the United States, £155,872; to other countries, £30,883. The principal imports were wool of the value of £3,190,298, live animals of the value of £1,997,051, timber of the value of £1,288,982, sugar, iron and steel, cottons, woolens, coal, and tea. The principal exports were wool for £5,933,699, gold for £2,739,503, breadstuffs, live stock, tea re-exported, leather and leather goods, apparel, and tallow. The quantity of wool exported was 132,149,027 pounds, of which less than half was grown in the colony. There were 3,305 factories in the colony in 1890. The value of the gold raised in 1890 was about £2,354,244. There were 12,736,143 sheep, 1,780,978 cattle, and 436,459 horses in Victoria when the census was taken in 1890. The wheat crop of 1891 was 13,003,000 bushels; oats, 4,894,000 bushels; barley, 1,575,000 bushels.

The chief exports of Queensland in 1890 were: Wool, of the value of £2,524,742; gold, £2,265,408; sugar, £699,532; tin, £199,084; preserved meat, £122,566; and hides and skins, £116,714. The chief imports are textiles, metal goods, liquors, provisions, and cereals. The customs revenue in 1890 was £1,243,046, nearly 25 per cent. of the total value of the imports.

The principal exports of South Australia in 1890 were: Wool, of the value of £1,871,277; wheat, £1,382,418; wheat flour, £613,823; and copper ore, £71,575.

Western Australia in 1890 exported wool of the value of £360,934; pearl shells of the value of £88,555; gold worth £86,664; timber worth £82,052; sandalwood worth £51,355; and pearls worth £40,000.

The principal exports of Tasmania were: Wool for £419,173; tin, £296,761; fruit, both fresh and preserved, £136,502; timber and bark, £125,439; gold, £87,085; and hops, £31,348. About half the imports are articles of food and drink. The duties average about 17 per cent. of the import value.

The export of wool from New Zealand in 1890 was 102,817,077 pounds, valued at £4,150,599. Frozen meat was exported to the amount of £1,087,617; Kauri gum for £378,563; grain and flour, £1,074,354; hides, skins, and leather, £226,662; gold, £751,360; butter and cheese, £207,687; preserved meat, £136,182; timber, £162,471; and tallow, £189,694. Of the total imports in 1890 Great Britain furnished £4,221,270; Australia, £1,087,593; the United States, £355,395; and the Pacific Islands, India, China, and Mauritius most of the remainder. Of the exports, £7,401,350 went to Great Britain, £1,-

634,248 to Australia, £583,134 to the United States, and £143,767 to the islands of the Pacific.

The chief exports of Fiji in 1890 were: Sugar, of the value of £244,655; copra, £42,901; and bananas, £57,563.

Navigation.—The number of vessels and the tonnage entered and cleared at the ports of the several colonies in 1890 are given in the following table:

COLONIES.	Number entered.	Tonnage.	Number cleared.	Tonnage.
New South Wales....	2,889	2,413,247	2,777	2,848,625
Victoria............	2,474	2,178,551	2,459	2,184,790
Queensland.........	616	465,607	606	442,172
South Australia......	1,041	1,075,183	1,081	1,115,909
Western Australia ...	281	484,534	267	420,327
Tasmania...........	746	475,618	763	475,629
New Zealand	744	662,769	745	649,705
Fiji	79	56,711	....	....

Communications. — At the close of 1890 there were 2,182 miles of railroad in operation in New South Wales. The capital expenditure up to June 30, 1891, was £31,768,617. The receipts were £2,974,421 in 1890 and the expenses £1,831,371, being 61·57 per cent. of the gross earnings. The telegraphs of the colony had 23,098 miles of wire, put up at a cost of £743,698. The number of telegrams in 1890 was 3,592,519. The receipts were £222,307 and the net earnings £193,707. The receipts of the post-office were £427,330, and the expenses £435,545. The number of letters was 57,707,900: of newspapers, 40,597,200; of packets, etc., 8,939,600.

The railroads of Victoria at the close of 1890 had a length of 2,688 miles, not including 215 miles still unfinished. The capital cost up to the middle of 1890 was £34,370,031. The gross receipts for the preceding twelve months were £3,131,866, and the working expenses £2,132,158, which was 68·08 per cent. of the gross earnings. The net profits averaged 3·18 per cent. of the borrowed capital, on which the average interest is 4·14 per cent., and were only 2·91 per cent. of the capital invested. The colony had 6,958 miles of telegraph lines, with 13,490 miles of wire. The number of dispatches during the year 1890 was 3,114,783. The net receipts were £138,969. The post-office forwarded 62,526,448 letters, 7,491,316 packets, and 22,729,005 newspapers. The postal receipts were £526,400, and expenditure £637,784.

The railroads of Queensland had a total length of 2,142 miles, to which 601 miles under construction were soon to be added. The cost up to the middle of 1890 was £14,226,070. The receipts for the previous year were £821,226, and expenses of working £631,749. There were 9,830 miles of telegraph and 17,437 miles of wire. The number of messages was 1,329,925. The receipts were £91,780, and working expenses £120,556. The number of letters carried in 1890 was 14,700,504; of newspapers, 14,463,726; of packets, 2,047,446; postal receipts, £130,984; expenses, £203,046.

South Australia had 1,756 miles of railroad completed on Dec. 31, 1890, and 54 miles in course of construction. In this colony the railroads pay an average profit of 5 per cent. The telegraph lines had a length of 5,623 miles, with 12,178 miles of wire. The post-office forwarded

10,794,679 letters, 1,251,414 packets, and 9,460,975 newspapers.

In Western Australia there were 589 miles of railroad open for traffic and 12 miles under construction, besides 295 miles that were begun and 369 miles being surveyed. The telegraphs had a length of 2,921 miles, with 3,469 miles of wire, and 516 miles more were nearly ready. There were 196,536 messages sent during 1890, which brought in a net revenue of £10,890. The number of letters and postal cards that passed through the post-office was 3,175,651.

Tasmania's completed railroads had a length of 399 miles, to which 74 miles were soon to be added. There were 2,004 miles of telegraph, with 2,701 miles of wire. During 1890, 353,548 messages were sent at a cost of £18,783, while the receipts were £19,075. The number of letters carried in the mails was 5,535,667; the number of newspapers, 4,941,571. The post-office receipts were £41,759, and the expenses were £46,137.

New Zealand on March 31, 1891, had 699 miles of railroads on the North Island and 1,143 miles on the Middle Island, the total length being 1,958 miles, including 114 miles of private lines. The revenue of the Government lines for the year was £1,121,701, and the expenditure was £700,703, or 62·47 per cent. of the gross earnings. The total expenditure up to that date was £15,344,223. The telegraphs had a length of 5,060 miles, with 12,771 miles of wire. The number of dispatches in 1890 was 1,961,161. The receipts amounted to £110,697, and the expenses to £104,391. The number of letters and postal cards mailed was 48,069,051; of packets. 7,546,966: of newspapers, 18,684,242. The receipts were £109,735, and expenses £85,006.

New South Wales.—The members of the Legislative Assembly in New South Wales, as in most of the colonies, are now paid a salary, which was fixed by the act of Sept. 21, 1889, at £300 per annum. The Legislative Council, the members of which are nominated by the Government, numbered 67 in 1891, and the Legislative Assembly, which now monopolizes most of the legislative functions, numbered 141. The Governor of New South Wales is the Earl of Jersey, who received his appointment in October, 1890. The Premier and Colonial Secretary of the Ministry constituted in December, 1891, is George E. Dibbs, who was knighted during an official visit to England in 1892. The Colonial Treasurer is John Lee; the Attorney-General, E. Burton; Secretary for Lands. H. Copeland; Secretary for Public Works. W. J. Lyne; Minister of Public Instruction. F. B. Sutter; Minister of Justice. R. E. O'Connor; Postmaster-General, John Kidd; Secretary for Mines and Agriculture. T. M. Slattery: Vice-President of the Legislative Council and Government Representative in the Legislative Council, J. E. Salomons.

Victoria.—The Legislative Assembly is elected by universal manhood suffrage. It is composed of 95 members, who are elected for three years. The Legislative Council consists of 48 members, elected under a low property qualification, one third of whom retire every two years. The Governor is the Earl of Hopetoun, who entered on the active discharge of the office on Feb. 13, 1892, though appointed more than a year previously. The ministers at the beginning of

1892 were as follow: Premier and Colonial Treasurer, William Shiels: Chief Secretary, President of the Board of Land and Public Works, and Commissioner of Crown Lands and Survey, Allan McLean; Minister of Mines and of Education, A. R. Outtrim; Minister of Instruction, Lieut.-Col. Sir F. T. Sargood; Minister of Customs and Justice, George Turner; Minister of Railroads, James Wheeler; Minister of Defense and Representative of the Legislative Council, George Davis; Attorney-General and Postmaster-General, J. Gavan Duffy; Minister of Agriculture and Water Supply, George Graham; Commissioner of Public Works, A. Peacock; ministers without office, Simon Fraser, C. J. Ham, and A. J. Peacock.

The financial condition of Victoria is as bad as that of any of the colonies. The railroads are run at a loss, and 1 per cent. of the interest money has to be paid out of the other revenues. The exhibition at Melbourne cost the Government a large amount. In 1889–'90 and 1890–'91 occurred deficits of £1,000,000, and 1891–'92 closed with a deficiency of £1,500,000. The extravagances that had brought about this condition gave place to economical shifts of a humiliating kind, in spite of which Sir Graham Berry looked forward to a deficit of £1,000,000 at the end of 1892–'93. The salaries of officials and the school appropriations were cut down, the inland postage was doubled, and the customs duties on a large number of articles were raised 10 or 15 per cent. A financial panic which began in Melbourne in December, 1891, being caused by the failure of some of the numerous building societies and the suspension of 2 or 3 banks that were involved, was stopped by a bill that was hurried through the Legislature which provides that no bank or other corporation or individual can be forced into liquidation except on the demand of one third of the creditors.

In the general election which took place on April 20, 1892, the Labor party failed to gain the position which would enable them, as in New South Wales, to hold the balance of power. Out of 36 candidates only a dozen were elected, and of these not more than half were thoroughgoing working-class representatives. The principle of one man one vote, on account of which Mr. Monro resigned the premiership in the beginning of the year, taking the post of Agent-General in England, while his colleague, Mr. Shiels, succeeded him as Premier, seemed also to have lost its force. A bill to establish this principle was passed by the lower house, but was nullified by an amendment of the Legislative Council which preserved the dual vote. Mr. Monro resigned, and the Cabinet was reconstructed with the chief advocate of the measure at its head. The bill was made the principal platform of the Government party, but, as the result of the election, its supporters in the Assembly declined, and the majority of 9 members in favor of the principle in the new House were insufficient to overcome the opposition of the Legislative Council. Other measures advocated by the ministry, which was again reconstructed in consequence of the result of the election, were an increase of the stock tax—a protectionist measure demanded by the agricultural interest for the exclusion of the competition of other colonies. The new Assembly was composed of 46 Ministerialists, 25 Conservatives, 12 Independents or Radicals of the old type, and 12 Labor members. The old Radicals were divided into two antagonistic factions, one being in favor of giving public money for Catholic schools and the other acting with the Conservatives in opposition to denominational education. The financial crisis made it impossible for the ministry which had come into power as advocates of the interests of labor to continue to provide employment for workingmen at the expense of the Government. A measure for the relief of the unemployed was the village settlements bill, introduced by the Government in July, the object of which was to settle poor families who were unable to obtain a living in Melbourne on good agricultural land in the rural districts. Owing to the enormous patronage of the Government, which not only manages all the railroads but various other works that are left to private enterprise in most countries, and to the consequent high wages paid by Government and individual employers who must compete with the Government, the population of Melbourne and its suburbs is three times as great, in proportion to the total population of the country, as that of London, constituting two fifths of the population of the colony, while another fifth live in the other large towns. This congestion of the cities, and especially of the capital, is the cause of much chronic misery and idleness, which is aggravated in times of stagnation like the present period.

Queensland.—The Legislative Assembly is composed of 72 members, who have hitherto been elected for five years, but for the future the term has been reduced to three years. The members of the Legislative Council are appointed by the Crown for life, and consequently the influence of that body on the policy of the Government is less than in colonies where it is elective. The Governor is Gen. Sir Henry Wylie Norman, who received his appointment in December, 1888. The Executive Council in 1892 was composed of the following members: Premier, Chief Secretary, Attorney-General, and Vice-President of the Council, Sir Samuel W. Griffith; Minister for Lands and Agriculture, S. Cowley; Minister of Railway and Postmaster-General, T. Unmaek; Minister of Public Instruction and Minister for Mines, W. O. Hodgkinson; Colonial Secretary and Secretary for Public Works, H. Tozer; Solicitor-General, T. J. Byrnes; Colonial Treasurer, Sir Thomas McIlwraith; Minister without portfolio, W. H. Wilson.

The bill introduced into the colonial Parliament in 1891 by representatives of Northern and Central Queensland was defeated by their southern colleagues. The separation leagues of the two northern districts continued to push the matter, and in 1892 sent delegations to England to urge compulsory separation upon Lord Knutsford, Secretary of State for the Colonies, who expressed approval of the ultimate division of the colony. Sir Samuel Griffith, who had carried through the bill to revive the traffic in Polynesian laborers to please the Northern Queenslanders, framed a separation bill himself and introduced it into Parliament in order to forestall the plan of erecting the northern sections into independent colonies, like Queensland itself when it was divided from New South Wales. His proposal was that Queensland should be divided into three provinces—the northern, central, and southern, with separate executives and legislatures. There would be a central government of the united provinces similar to that which at present exists, with a legislature of two houses —one elected by the legislatures of the separate provinces, and the other by the electors of the provinces in proportion to the European population in each. In contrast to the bill of last year, the present bill reserves to the Central Government the sole right of levying customs duties, thus securing uniformity of tariff throughout the colony. With this exception, so far as the information to hand goes, the connection between the provinces and the central legislature would be extremely slender. The three provinces would have local self-government to a very full extent. The three parts have little now in common, since there is no land connection, the railroads all running east and west, and their climate and productions are dissimilar. The Premier estimated that his federation project would add £25,000 a year to the expenses of the Central Government. The bulk of the population of the colony lives in the south, which has about 269,000 inhabitants, while the central district has 47,000 and the northern 78,000. These figures do not include the aborigines, estimated at 12,000.

Kanaka Labor.—A few years after the introduction of the system of importing Pacific islanders for the cultivation of sugar plantations in Northern Queensland, the abuses accompanying the traffic led Earl Granville as Colonial Minister to issue stringent resolutions, and declare that it must be suppressed if these should not prove efficacious. In 1872 the British Parliament passed an act against kidnaping. In 1875, when a High Commissioner for the Western Pacific was created, he was empowered to deal with the Polynesian labor traffic. The regulations and restrictions proved so useless that a royal commission which looked into the subject in 1885 was compelled to report that all the efforts of the Imperial Government had failed to prevent "the continuance of a system of fraud, outrage, and murder." Constant attacks on British subjects in the South Sea Islands had no other motive than revenge for the murders and man-stealing committed by the slave ships. The condition of the islanders on the sugar plantations was practical slavery of the most brutal description. The mortality among them was fearful, and the terms of their indentures, by which they were to receive wages and be returned to their villages at the expiration of the contract period, were constantly disregarded. The Queensland Government at last stepped in and had a law passed to stop the forcible impressment of Kanakas, requiring the contract to be entered into voluntarily by each man after its terms had been explained by an interpreter, and requiring masters and owners of labor ships to give bonds to return the laborers to their homes. The act contained regulations regarding the treatment of the laborers on the plantations which provided that they should be properly housed and fed and cared for when sick. Agents were appointed to inspect the plantations and see that the regulations were carried out, and these were clothed with the powers of police magistrates. The condition of the laborers was considerably ameliorated, but the slave raids and massacres by which the labor was supplied did not cease. The acts of the officers and agent of the "Hopeful," which had led to the investigation of the British Government commission, gave a special turn to the labor agitation against Chinese, coolie, black, and all colored labor in Queensland, which was as strong in Southern Queensland as in other parts of Australia where the workingmen are a political power of prime importance. The Queensland Parliament, bowing to this movement, passed an act in 1885 to discontinue licenses to recruit Kanaka labor after 1890. There was an expectation that some other system of labor would be found for working the sugar plantations, or that the objections of white laborers, who could not work themselves under the tropical sun, to the employment of Kanakas, as all Polynesian islanders are called indiscriminately in Queensland, would abate as soon as the consequences of the loss of the sugar industry came home to the people. The Premier, Sir Samuel Griffith, who had been instrumental in carrying through the prohibition law, counted on the latter contingency when he issued a manifesto on Feb. 13, 1892, declaring that the sugar mills and plantations would soon have to stop operations unless the privilege of recruiting colored labor was renewed. In spite of the indignation excited in England at the revival of the slave trade in the Pacific and the protests of the Queensland Labor party, the Parliament of the colony passed an act to renew the importation of Kanaka labor for ten years longer. No ships are allowed to engage in recruiting laborers without a Government license, and each ship must carry a Government agent charged with seeing that no islander enters into a contract without a full knowledge of its full meaning. This is a fictitious safeguard, for none of the agents are acquainted with the twenty languages spoken on the islands. The same provisions were in force under the old law and still did not put an end to the "deceit, cruel treachery, deliberate kidnaping, and cold-blooded murder" denounced in the report of the Royal Commission in 1885.

South Australia.—The Legislative Council, consisting of 24 members, is renewed by the replacement triennially of 2 members from each of the 4 districts. The House of Assembly has 54 members, all of whom go out at the end of the electoral period, or sooner if dissolved by the Executive. The Governor is the Earl of Kintore, who assumed office on April 11, 1889. The ministry in 1892 consisted of the following members: Premier and Commissioner of Crown Lands: T. Playford; Chief Secretary, C. C. Kingston; Attorney-General, R. Homburg; Treasurer, W. B. Rounsevell; Commissioner of Public Works, J. G. Jenkins; Minister of Agriculture and Education, W. Copley.

Tasmania.—The Parliament consists of the Legislative Council of 18 members, elected by restricted suffrage for six years, and the House of Assembly of twice as many members, elected for half that term, under a slightly limited franchise, the electors for the former body in 1891 constituting 4·6 per cent. and for the other 21 per cent. of the total population. The Governor, in the beginning of 1892, was Sir Robert G. C.

Hamilton, who had filled the office since January, 1887. The Premier and Chief Secretary was Philip Oakley Fysh; the Treasurer, Bolton Stafford Bird; the Attorney-General, Andrew Inglis Clark; the Minister of Public Lands and Works, Alfred Pillinger. Like the other colonies, Tasmania has been compelled to adopt a policy of retrenchment in order to put an end to deficits that can no longer be covered out of borrowed funds.

Western Australia.—This colony was endowed with responsible government by an act of the Imperial Parliament passed in 1890, which vested the powers of government, previously exercised by a governor, assisted by a legislative council, partly composed of elective members, in the Governor and a Legislative Council and Legislative Assembly. This latter consists of 30 members, elected for four years by possessors of freehold or leasehold property, or licenses for pasturing. mining, or cultivation of the value of £10 per annum. The Governor, who was partly instrumental in securing to the colony the right of self-government, was Sir William C. F. Robinson, who assumed office in 1889. The responsible ministry is composed of the following : Premier and Treasurer, Sir John Forrest; Chief Secretary, Mr. Shenton; Attorney-General, Mr. Butt; Commissioner of Lands, Mr. Marmion; Minister of Public Works, Mr. Venn.

New Zealand.—The colony was divided before 1875 into 9 administrative provinces, each of which has a superintendent and a provincial council elected by household suffrage. The provincial system in that year gave way to a central government. in which the legislative powers are vested in a General Assembly, consisting of a Legislative Council and a House of Representatives. The former is composed of 41 members, who are appointed for life by the Executive. The popular chamber was reduced by the act of 1887 to 74 members, of whom 4 are representatives of the Maori community. They are elected by universal suffrage for three years. The Governor is the Earl of Onslow. appointed in November, 1888. The ministry, formed on Jan. 24, 1891, was composed of the following members: Premier, Colonial Treasurer, Commissioner of Trade and Customs, and Commissioner of Stamps, J. Ballance; Attorney-General and Colonial Secretary, P. A. Buckley; Minister of Agriculture and of Lands and Immigration, J. Mackenzie; Minister of Mines and Defense and Minister for Public Works, R. J. Seddon: Minister of Education and Justice, W. P. Reeves; Minister of Native Affairs, A. J. Cadman; Postmaster-General and Commissioner of Telegraphs, J. G. Ward; Speaker of the House of Representatives. Maj. W. J. Steward. New Zealand was plunged into financial straits years earlier than the Australian colonies, and has not yet emerged from the difficulties resulting from a period of speculation. inflation, and borrowing, though its position has been steadily improving, while that of the others has been growing worse. An increase of taxation has been found necessary here also to meet the demands of increased expenses and pay the interest on the enormous Government debt. An income tax like that of Great Britain has lately been decreed, and in addition to that a tax, likewise variable, on the capital value of

land. These heavy taxes on rent and capital have been accompanied by a remission of certain taxes on stock, implements, and improvements. The land tax is a graded one, levied on properties valued at £5,000 and over, which are estimated to amount in the aggregate to £45,000,-000. The aim of this is to shift the incidence upon the unearned increment in accordance with the single-tax theory. although the experiment is not an extensive one. On estates valued at less than £5,000 the burden is less than formerly, and on properties of that value the reduction of taxes on farm stock and buildings may reduce the amount of taxes paid, but on unimproved property the incidence is heavy. The taxes collected on land have amounted to about £350,000, while £1,500,000 have been raised annually through customs duties, which have not been changed. The new tax bill imposes a tax on business and professional men. The income tax is not graded, nor are any of the new taxes except that on land.

AUSTRIA-HUNGARY, a dual monarchy in central Europe. The reigning sovereign is the King and Emperor Franz Josef I, born Aug. 30, 1830, the son of the Archduke Franz Karl, son of Franz I. He was proclaimed Emperor of Austria when his uncle, Ferdinand I, resigned the throne on Dec. 2, 1848, and was crowned King of Hungary on the restoration of the Hungarian Constitution, June 8, 1867. The heir presumptive is the Archduke Franz, born Dec. 18, 1863, son of the Emperor's brother, the Archduke Karl Ludwig. The two monarchies are united in the person of the sovereign, and have a common diplomacy and the same army and navy, though each legislates independently on military affairs. They also form a customs union, and in the decennial Ausgleich financial adjustment they agree on interstate railroad tariffs and regulations. The ministers for the whole monarchy are selected by the Emperor, subject to the approval of the Delegations sent from the two Parliaments to legislate annually on common affairs and pass the budget. The Delegations consist of 60 members each, 20 being delegated from the Austrian Herrenhaus, 20 from the Hungarian Magnatentafel, 40 from the Austrian Abgeordnetenhaus or House of Deputies, and 40 from the Hungarian House of Representatives. The Delegations come together in Vienna and Buda-Pesth in alternate years. They deliberate apart, communicating to each other their decisions, but when these disagree they form a joint assembly and vote on the matter without discussion. The common ministry was composed at the beginning of 1892 of the following members: Minister of Foreign Affairs and of the Imperial House. Graf G. Kalnoky de Korospatak, born in Moravia, Dec. 29, 1832, who was appointed on the resignation of Graf Andrassy, Nov. 21, 1881; Minister of War for the Whole Monarchy, Field-Marshal Baron Ferdinand Bauer, who was appointed March 16, 1888; Minister of Finance, Benjamin de Kallay.

The Common Budget.—Of the expenses of the whole monarchy in excess of the surplus receipts from customs. Hungary pays 2 per cent. and 30 per cent. of the remainder, and Austria the remaining 40 per cent. The budget of expenditure for 1891 was 135,634,000 florins (1 florin

= 41 cents). The estimated receipts from customs were 40,492,000 florins, leaving 63,410,000 florins to be made up by Austria's contribution and 29,024,000 florins as the share of Hungary. For 1892 the budget estimate of expenditure was 139,143,000 florins, and the estimated receipts from customs were 40,155,000 florins, leaving a balance of 96,315,000 florins, of which Austria pays 66,072,000 and Hungary 30,243,000 florins. The ordinary expenditure amounts to 122,308,- 705 florins, of which 3,579,700 florins are for the diplomatic service, 107,093,247 florins for the army, 9,484,614 florins for the navy, 2,022,884 florins for the financial administration, and 128,- 260 for the board of control. The extraordinary expenditures amount to 16,834,181 florins, including 14,627,243 florins for the army, 2,143,100 florins for the navy, and 63,838 florins for other purposes. The revenue from Bosnia and Herzegovina for 1892 was estimated at 10,187,450 florins, and the expenditure at 10,136,149 florins, not including an extraordinary expenditure of 4,335,- 000 florins for military purposes. The general debt of the monarchy in 1891 amounted to 2,776,129,000 florins, Austria's special debt to 1,109,871,000 florins, and the special debt of Hungary to 1,734,185,000 florins, making a total of 5,620,185,000 florins, not including the common floating debt amounting to 351,- 945,099 florins.

Area and Population.—The area and population of the Austrian provinces on Dec. 31, 1890, when the last census was taken, were as follow:

PROVINCES.	Square miles.	Male.	Female.	Total.
Lower Austria...	7,654	1,307,918	1,353,886	2,661,799
Upper Austria...	4,631	388,762	397,069	785,831
Salzburg......	2,767	85,948	87,562	173,510
Styria, ...	8,670	685,967	646,741	1,282,708
Carinthia........	4,005	176,473	184,585	361,008
Carniola.........	3,856	238,011	260,947	498,958
Coast lands.....	3,064	351,844	343,540	695,384
Tyrol and Vorarl-				
berg..........	11,324	454,769	474,000	928,769
Bohemia	20,060	2,821,989	3,021,105	5,843,094
Moravia.........	8,583	1,087,340	1,189,530	2,276,870
Silesia..........	1,987	288,908	316,741	605,649
Galicia..........	30,307	3,260,438	3,847,383	6,607,816
Bukovina........	4,035	324,469	322,122	646,591
Dalmatia........	4,940	266,303	261,123	527,426
Total........	115,903	11,689,129	12,206,284	23,895,413

Since the census of 1880 there was an increase of 1,913,803, which was at a rate of 0·76 per cent. per annum, the same average rate as in the preceding ten years. The number of births in Austria in 1890 was 894,356; of deaths, 696,342: natural increment, 171,593. The number of marriages was 178,906; the number of illegitimate births, 128,702.

For Hungary the census of 1890 gave the following returns:

DIVISIONS.	Square miles.	Total population.
Hungary and Transylvania..........	108,258	15,122,514
Croatia and Slavonia.	16,778	2,184,414
The town of Fiume..................	8	29,001
Total.........................	125,089	17,335,929

This makes the total population of the Austro-Hungarian dominions, exclusive of Bosnia and Herzegovina, which still form nominally a part of Turkey, 41,231,342, on an area of 240,942 square miles, showing a density of 171 per square mile, 206 for Austria, and 139 for Hungary. The increase of population in Hungary during the ten years was 1,603,827, being at the rate of 1·08 per cent. per annum. The number of marriages in Hungary in 1889 was 140,524; of births, 767,- 884; of deaths, 512,852; increase of births over deaths, 255,032. The number of illegitimate births was 61,468, which was at the rate of 8 per cent., little more than half that of the Austrian dominions.

The number of emigrants from the Austro-Hungarian Empire in 1889 was 55,794. Of these, 26,424 were bound for the United States and 4,225 for the Argentine Republic. According to United States returns, that number of immigrants arrived from Austria alone, besides 15,746 from Hungary.

The principal cities of the empire had the following population in 1890 : Vienna, the Austrian capital, 1,364,548; Buda-Pesth, the Hungarian capital, 506,384; Prague, once capital of the kingdom of Bohemia, 184,109; Trieste, the Austrian seaport, 158,344; Lemberg, the principal city of Austrian Poland, 128,419; Gratz, 113,- 540; Brünn, 95,342.

The Roman Catholics comprised, according to the census, 79·2 per cent. of the population of Austria; the Greek Catholics, 11·8 per cent.; Jews, 4·8 per cent.; Greek Orientals, 2·4 per cent.; and Evangelicals, 1·8 per cent. in 1890. In Hungary in 1880 50·1 per cent. of the population was Roman Catholic, 15·6 per cent. Greek Oriental, 20·1 per cent. Protestant Evangelical, 9·5 per cent. Greek Catholic, 4·3 per cent. Israelitish, and 0·4 per cent. Unitarian. The educational laws of both Austria and Hungary require attendance in school from the age of seven. In Istria, Dalmatia, Bukovina, and Galicia compulsory attendance ends with the twelfth year, as also in Hungary. In other provinces of Austria the period extends to the completion of the fourteenth year. The number of persons able to read and write increased in Austria between 1880 and 1890 from 10,930,090 to 13,258,452.

The Army.—The term of service in the active army is three years, and when they are completed the soldiers belong for seven years in the Ersatz reserve. Those who are not drawn for active service may be enrolled at once in the Ersatz reserve. The Landwehr, which is organized independently of the common army and separately in the two halves of the monarchy, has also its Ersatz or supplementary reserve. Those who are not enrolled in the regular army must serve twelve years in the Landwehr, including all who are capable of bearing arms but fall short of the physical requirements for the regular service. Soldiers who have completed their ten years of service in the regular army enter the Landwehr for the term of two years. On passing out of the Landwehr they become members of the Landsturm for ten years. Young men who reach a certain educational standard are required to serve for one year only, either in the army or the Landwehr. The troops of the Landwehr are called out only for instruction and exercise in time of peace. Every man who is not enrolled in the army or navy or in the Landwehr from the age of nineteen to the age of forty-three is a member of the Landsturm, from which men may be drafted to fill up the army or Landwehr in time of war. The annual recruit of the regular army is 103,000 men, of whom Austria furnishes 60,389 and Hungary 42,711, besides which there is an annual contingent of 27,400 for the Ersatz reserve, 10,000 for the Austrian Landwehr, and 12,500 for the Honved or Hungarian Landwehr. Each of the 102 regiments of infantry has its recruiting district. Tyrol and Vorarlberg form a separate district, which furnishes the regiment of Tyrolese Jägers, a privileged body which remains in its province to guard the mountain marches. The marine troops are recruited in 3 districts on the Adriatic seaboard. Bosnia and Herzegovina are organized on the Austrian military system, and are required to furnish a quota of troops, which are raised in 4 recruiting districts. Each regiment has 5 battalions, except the Tyrolese Jägers, which consist of 12. There are 30 battalions of regular Jägers, 42 regiments of cavalry, 14 regiments of field artillery, 72 companies of fortress artillery, 2 regiments of engineers, 1 regiment of pioneers, and 1 regiment of railroad and telegraph troops. The peace strength of the Austro-Hungarian army in 1892 was 337,419, including 28,472 Landwehr troops under arms. The infantry numbered 204,235; cavalry, 61,-738; artillery, 33,132; technical troops, 10,148; train, 3,851; sanitary troops, 4,698; general and field officers, etc., 4,116; special formations and military establishments, 15,501. In time of war the strength of the army could be more than trebled, and nearly as many more men already trained and equipped could be called into the field from the Landwehr and Landsturm. The war strength of the army as officially given is 996,727; of the Landwehr, 434.329; of the Landsturm, 441,122. The number of men who could be called to serve in the Landsturm in case of war and who would be available to fill gaps in the army and Landwehr is over 4.000,000. The number of field guns in peace is 912 and in war 1,864. There are 56.930 horses in peace and for war 279,886 are ready.

The Navy.—The Austrian navy consists of 2 turret ships, the "Stephanie" and "Kronprinz Rudolf," protected with 9 and 12 inches of armor respectively, and carrying one, 2, and the other 3 48-ton guns, besides 16 other breechloaders and 22 machine guns between them. Eight other battle ships of from 3,550 to 7,390 tons, with armor over their vital parts from 6¼ to 14 inches thick, mount 68 heavy guns, weighing from 10 to 27 tons, in casemated central batteries, and carry 56 smaller guns and 88 machine guns. The plated wooden frigate "Habsburg" carries 5 14-ton guns. There are 2 ram cruisers. 7 torpedo cruisers, 5 torpedo vessels, 3 avisos, 2 river monitors, 4 training ships, 57 torpedo boats, 19 station and service ships, 9 school and barrack ships, 6 vessels for harbor and coast service, and 4 stationary vessels. The navy is manned in peace time by 623 officers, 7.500 sailors, and 617 surgeons, chaplains, etc. The term of service is the same as the term in the army. A Seewehr, or naval reserve or militia, corresponding to the Landwehr, has been organized since 1888.

Commerce.—The general commerce of the Austro-Hungarian customs union, which includes Bosnia and Herzegovina, amounted in 1890 to 610,700,000 florins of imports and 771,400,000 florins of exports. The values of the principal imports were as follow : Cotton, 63,500,000 florins; wool, 39,700,000 florins; coffee, 38,000,000 florins; coal, 25,700,000 florins; silk, 21,100,000 florins; machinery, 18,100,000 florins; woolen yarn, 17,900,000 florins; leaf tobacco, 15,600,000 florins; cotton yarn, 15,200,000 florins; leather, 12,600,000 florins; books and periodicals, 12,400,-000 florins; silk goods, 12,200,000 florins; cattle, 11,600,000 florins; hardware and clocks, 11,400,-000 florins; colors and tanning material, 11,-400,000 florins; grain, 11,200,000 florins; hides, skins, and fur skins, 10,100,000 florins; woolen goods, 9,600,000 florins; manufactured tobacco, 8,400,000 florins. The largest exports were of the following values : Cereals, 79,900,000 florins; sugar, 65,400,000 florins; timber, 61,700,006 florins; cattle, 35,800,000 florins; coal, 32,500,000 florins; hardware, 27.500,000 florins; woolen goods, 22,500,000 florins; flour. 21,600,000 florins; iron and manufactures of iron, 20,600,000 florins; wool, 20,000,000 florins; wood manufactures, 18,000,000 florins; eggs, 16,200,000 florins; wine, 15,500,000 florins; glass and glassware, 15,400,000 florins; minerals, 14,300,000 florins; paper manufactures, 14,300,000 florins; gloves, 14,000,000 florins; feathers, 12,400,000 florins; leather goods, 8,200,000 florins; linen yarn, 6,400,000 florins; silk goods. 6,100,000 florins. The amount of coin and bullion exported in 1890 was 4,303,000 florins, while 43,472,000 florins were imported.

Navigation.—During 1890 there were 66,271 vessels, of 8,773,713 tons, entered, and 66,527. of 8,759,632 tons, cleared at Austro-Hungarian ports. The commercial navy, including coasters and fishing boats, comprised 10,380 vessels, of 250,716 tons, on Jan. 1, 1891. Of these, 71, of 83,371 tons, were sea-going steamers; 102. of 14,481 tons, were coasting steamers; and 10,207, of 152,716 tons, were sailing vessels of all kinds. Of the vessels that visited the ports of the monarchy in 1890 about 83 per cent. were national, and of the tonnage about 82 per cent. belonged to Austria-Hungary.

Railroads.—On Jan. 1, 1891, there were 15.-193 kilometres, or 9,496 miles, of railroads in operation in Austria, and 11.541 kilometres, or 7.216 miles, in Hungary. Of the Austrian roads, 6.021 kilometres were owned and operated by the Government, 1,555 kilometres belonging to companies were leased by the state. and 7,617 kilometres were worked by companies. including 7.533 kilometres of their own and 84 kilometres owned by the Government. In Hungary the Government worked 5,756 kilometres that were owned by the state and 3,909 kilometres belonging to companies, while private corporations operated only 1,876 kilometres. The capital expenditure on the 15,172 miles of railroad that were in existence in 1888 was 3,660,501,000 florins. The receipts in that year amounted to 269,285.-000 florins, and the expenses were 124,730,000 florins. The railroads of Bosnia and Herzegovina had a length of 342 miles in 1889.

Posts and Telegraphs.—The number of letters and postal cards that passed through the post office in Austria during 1890 was 444,134,-380 ; of samples and printed inclosures, 60,198,-500 ; of newspapers, 68,985,020. The receipts were 29,530,836, and the expenses 25,187,836 florins. In Hungary the number of letters and post cards sent in 1889 was 168,801,000, and the number of printed packets and samples was 14,-762,000. The receipts were 12,268,000 florins, and expenses 9,297,000 florins. The telegraph lines of Austria had a total length in 1890 of 27,674 miles, with 71,376 miles of wire. In Hungary there were 12,340 miles of line, with 45,581 miles of wire. The lines of Bosnia and Herzegovina had a length of 1,732 miles, with 3,457 miles of wire. The number of messages sent in Austria in 1890 was 8,776,048; in Hungary, 4,211,-131; in Bosnia and Herzegovina, 22,277.

Austria.—The Empire of Austria, the Cisleithan monarchy, is a federal state in which the Provincial Diets or Landtage are competent to legislate on all matters not reserved to the Reichsrath or Central Legislature or to the Crown. The Reichsrath must give its consent to all measures relating to the army or to military duty, and its co-operation is necessary for legislation dealing with customs, commerce, banking, the postal service, telegraphs, and railroads. The Reichsrath has also to examine the accounts of revenue and expenditure, and all projects of law having to do with taxation, operations of public credit, and the national debt. There are two chambers, both of which have the right of initiating legislation. The Herrenhaus or House of Lords in 1892 was composed of 19 princes of the blood royal, 68 hereditary lords, 10 archbishops, 7 prince bishops, and 125 life members nominated by the Emperor. The Abgeordnetenhaus or House of Deputies had 353 members, of whom 85 represented the land-owning class, 21 represented boards of trade and commerce, 118 were elected by the people of the towns, and 129 were elected by the rural population. The peasant constituencies choose their members indirectly. Among them and in the towns the franchise is restricted to men twenty-four years of age who pay five florins in direct taxes. In the class of landed proprietors women who own estates have the right to vote.

The Austrian Cabinet ministers in 1892 were as follow: President of the Council and Minister of the Interior, Graf Eduard Taaffe, appointed Aug. 19, 1879 ; Minister of Finance, Dr. E. Steinbach ; Mininter of Public Instruction and Ecclesiastical Affairs, Dr. Paul Gautsch, Baron von Frankenthurn; Minister of Agriculture, Graf Julius Falkenhayn ; Minister of Commerce and National Economy, Marquis von Bacquehem ; Minister of National Vertheidigung or National Defense, Field-Marshal Graf Zeno von Welsersheimb ; Minister of Justice, Graf Friedrich von Schönborn: without portfolios. Baron von Prazak, Ritter von Zaleski, and Graf Gandolf von Khünberg.

Finance.—The financial estimates as approved by the Reichsrath for 1892 make the total revenue 585,954,126 florins, of which 741,-800 florins are the receipts of the Council of State, 1,026,168 florins of the Ministry of the Interior, 312,497 florins of the Ministry of Defense, 5,947,659 florins of the Minister of Instruction

and Worship, and 3,268,194 florins of the Ministry of Finance ; 105,834,000 florins come from direct taxes—viz., 36,052,000 florins from the land tax, 32,056,000 florins from the house tax, 11,284,000 from the tax on industries, 26,442,000 florins from the income tax ; 283,448,846 florins are raised by indirect taxation—viz., 100,935,980 florins from excise, 20,909,706 florins from salt, 84,151,300 florins from tobacco, 19,350,000 florins from stamps, 35,300,000 florins from judicial fees, 19,401,000 florins from the state lottery, and 3,400,000 florins from other sources ; 37,943,800 florins represent the receipts of the custom house, 2,753,892 florins the profits from state property, 32,674,000 florins the income from the post office and telegraphs, 76,325,450 florins that from railroads, 2,776,670 florins that from other enterprises, 4,370,020 florins from the yield of the forests and domains, 8,181,975 florins that from mines, 602,592 florins that from other real estate, 1,009,448 florins the receipts of the Ministry of Justice, and 657,142 receipts from various sources. These are the receipts from ordinary sources, making in all 567,874,153 florins, to which must be added 18,079,973 florins of extraordinary revenue.

The total expenditure for the year is estimated at 583,947,553 florins, including 40,295,-738 florins of extraordinary expenditure. Of the ordinary expenditure, amounting to 543,-651,815 florins, 4,650,000 florins are appropriated for the imperial household. 73,097 florins for the Cabinet Chancery, 726,054 florins for the Reichsrath, 23,000 florins for the Supreme Court, 1,064,-318 florins for the Council of Ministers, 17,183,-355 florins for the Ministry of the Interior, 15,-054,756 florins for the Ministry of Defense, 1,625,735 florins for the support of the Ministry of Instruction, 6,999,500 florins for Public Worship, 13,168,990 florins for Education, 13.305.227 florins for the Ministry of Agriculture, 83,823,-553 florins for administration of the Ministry of Finance and collection of revenues, 20,664,000 florins for the Ministry of Justice, 93,939,400 florins for the Ministry of Commerce, 171,300 florins for the Board of Control, 144,257,560 florins for the interest and sinking fund of the public debt, 962,790 florins for management of the debt, 17,877,240 florins for pensions and grants, 6,581,400 florins for subventions, and 101,500,540 florins for the common expenditure of the whole monarchy, being the Cisleithan quota.

Reform of the Currency.—Active steps were taken in the beginning of the year to reform and regulate the entangled currency of the dual monarchy. Committees of experts were called upon by the Ministers of Finance. Dr. Steinbach and Dr. Wekerle, for Austria and Hungary respectively, to give opinions regarding the proposed reform. The ministers finally agreed upon a measure based on the replies obtained from the experts. The measure was brought before the Austrian Reichsrath and the Hungarian Parliament, and passed in the former by a good majority and in the latter unanimously. The full amount of gold to be raised for the redemption of the Government paper currency was 312,000,000 florins, of which Austria had to procure 218,000,000 florins and Hungary 93,000,000 florins, according to the relative proportion of 70 per cent. for Austria and 30 per cent. for Hungary. Hungary possessed already 53,000,000 florins, so that she would only have to raise about 38,000,000 florins in gold. A time was not set for the redemption in gold of the Government paper currency, except the one-florin bills, which were to be redeemed after the passing of this act in any existing legal tender except the old paper currency. The new currency is established on a gold basis, and the unit will be the krone, worth 1 franc 5 centimes in French money, 85 pfennige in German, and in American money 20·3 cents. One kilo of gold, 900 fine coins, 2,952 kronen or 3,280 kronen if of pure gold. Twenty- and ten-kronen gold pieces are to be coined. Austria will only coin 20-kronen pieces for private account, while Hungary will coin both 20- and 10-kronen pieces. The mints will be free for gold only in either country. Ducats will continue to be coined for commercial purposes. The gold currency will be supplemented with silver 1-krone pieces, 835 fine, nickel pieces of 20 and 10 heller, and bronze coins of 2 and 1 heller, 100 heller making a krone. Alongside of the gold coins, the silver coins of the country will remain in use. The silver florin of Austrian coinage will be equal to 2 kronen. The coinage treaty with Hungary provides that 200,000,000 florins of silver, 60,000,000 florins of nickel, and 26,000,000 florins of bronze coin shall be coined, according to the proportion of 70 and 30 per cent. respectively. Agreements as to the continued circulation of the paper money and its redemption will be made at the proper time. The treaty will be in force until the end of 1910. In payment of obligations 42 Austrian gold florins are equal to 100 kronen. The Minister of Finance is empowered to negotiate a gold loan of 183,456,000 florins bearing 4 per cent. interest. The gold obtained shall immediately be coined and held as a special deposit, only to be disposed of by act of legislature.

The Bohemian Compromise.—The Ausgleich of 1890, made to settle the language question between the Germans and the Czechs of Bohemia, was virtually defeated by the action of the Czechs and the Feudal Conservatives, who, being in the majority, refused to accept any further alteration of the proposed arrangement to meet the views of the Government. Count Taaffe's attitude was ambiguous, and the German Left, who have been his principal supporters, and who still insisted on the carrying out of the Ausgleich, became very much embittered against him. The Government finally decided to carry out a part of the arrangement, and accordingly created a circuit court in Wekelsdorf, thereby inaugurating the division of the different courts and administrative districts according to the nationality of the inhabitants. This was really one of the most important clauses of the Ausgleich, and the decree of the Minister of Justice was hailed with satisfaction by the Germans, while the Czechs denounced him in their meetings, and introduced into the Reichsrath a bill to indict him for violating the laws of 1868, which provide that the Government has the right to create new courts, but has to take the sense of the respective Landtag first, whereas the last Bohemian Landtag had

refused to give any opinion on the Ausgleich question. The Minister of Justice proved that the Bohemian Landtag had in former years expressed an opinion favorable to the creation of the court in question, and the bill was lost.

Session of the Reichsrath.—One of the chief acts of the session of 1891–'92 was to ratify the new commercial treaties. Most of the commercial treaties with other nations lapsed on Feb. 1, 1892, and new ones had to be made. Foremost stand the new treaties with Germany and Italy, which were made for the space of twelve years. These reduce the tariff on manufactured goods from Germany in return for a reduction of duties on wheat, and effect a reduction of duties on Italian wine against a lower tariff on Austrian manufactured goods. The treaties contain the most-favored-nation clause, by which all concessions made to other nations must be made to the contracting party on demand. The treaty with Switzerland, containing similar conditions, was approved later. Other important bills passed were the Vienna city railroads bill, the currency reforms bill, a personal income tax bill, which latter is intended to affect incomes in their entirety without regard to their origin. A bill taxing the transactions of the stock exchange was passed, which will virtually amount to a taxation on all trade in active stocks. Not only the transactions on the exchange are to be taxed, but also all business done in banks and in brokers' offices. This tax is identical with the one put upon a change of possession of real property. Care was taken to arrange the tax so that it would not interfere with the methods hitherto employed in carrying on this business. Most of the transactions are in blocks of 5,000 florins, and therefore this amount was taken as a unit and a tax of 10 kreuzern put upon it, and proportionately more on larger amounts. Exempt from this taxation are all transactions in money and exchange, for as long as the currency of the country has not been regulated even the soundest merchant trading with foreign countries has to buy foreign coins and drafts in order to protect himself in proper time against a loss by exchange.

The Socialists.—The Socialistic convention, held on June 5, presented a picture of utter disorganization. It is remarkable that the so-called International Socialistic party of Austria has to contend with the very same difficulties that prevent the organization of a great Liberal or Clerical party. The Czechish workingmen stand aloof, hold their own Socialistic conventions, and build up their own organizations. The Socialistic party in Austria is divided according to nationality, and can not manage to keep peace between its sections. The workingmen's clubs numbered 331 in 1892 against 218 the year before, and 53 new workingmen's associations were organized.

A parliamentary commission, presided over by Dr. Barnreither, made an inquiry regarding the establishment and recognition of official workingmen's committees for the protection of the moral and material interests of the working people. Such committees would be composed of delegates freely elected by the workmen, and masters would treat with them regarding the regulation of wages, the disposition of the funds for sickness, pensions, and accident insurance, as well as other matters that might form the subject of disputes between the employer and the employed. The majority of the employers of labor expressed approval of the establishment of permanent committees of this character wherever the workingmen chose to appoint such representatives, but did not approve making the formation of the committees compulsory or lending them an official character.

Hungary.—The Hungarian Parliament has two branches with equal and concurrent powers. The Magnatentafel or Chamber of Magnates is composed of hereditary peers who pay a land tax of 3,000 florins a year, 286 in number; 82 life peers, of whom 50 were elected by the house after the reform act of 1885 changed its constitution, and all others are appointed by the King; 40 dignitaries of the Roman and Greek Churches and 11 representatives of Protestant confessions; 3 delegates of Croatia and Slavonia; 19 archdukes; and 17 judges and high officials who are peers *ex officio*. The Representantentafel or Chamber of Representatives contains 453 members, including 40 from Croatia-Slavonia. They are elected directly by the male citizens who are twenty years of age and possess a low property qualification. The entire house is renewed by a general election every five years.

The Hungarian ministry in the beginning of 1892 was composed of the following members: President of the Council and Minister of the Interior, Count Julius Szapary; Minister of Finance, Dr. Alexander Wekerle; Minister of Education and Ecclesiastical Affairs, Count Albin Csaky; Minister of the Honved or National Defense, Baron Geza Fejervary; Minister of Justice, Desiderius de Szilagyi; Minister *ad latus* or at the King's side, Ladislaus de Szogenyi-Marich. Count Szapary became Prime Minister on March 7, 1890. Minister of Commerce Gabriel Carops de Bellus died on May 9, and Bela Lukacs was appointed in his stead.

Finances.—The total revenue for 1892, as given in the budget estimates, is 395,353,936 florins, including 5,824,955 florins of transitory revenue. Of the ordinary receipts, amounting to 389,-528.981 florins, 3,811,573 florins are credited to state debts, 1,895 florins to the Accountant-General's office, 700 florins to the Ministry *ad latus*, 1,145.970 florins to the Ministry of the Interior, 276.865,468 florins to the Ministry of Finance, 91,872,417 florins to the Ministry of Commerce, 13,835,125 florins to the Ministry of Agriculture, 1,080,014 florins to the Minister of Public Worship, 578,358 florins to the Ministry of Justice, and 337.461 florins to the Ministry of Defense. The ordinary expenditures are estimated at 368,-100,562 florins, transitory expenditure at 7,275,-728 florins, investments at 13,317,528 florins, and extraordinary common expenditure falling to the Transleithan half of the monarchy at 6,647,123 florins, making the total for the year 395,340,941 florins. Of the ordinary expenditure, 4,650,000 florins are allocated to the civil list, 73,097 florins to the Cabinet Chancery, 1,246,931 florins to the Parliament, 24,956,725 florins to common expenses of the whole monarchy, 46,132 florins to the common pension list, 7,095,799 florins to Hungarian pensions, 118,632,863 florins to the national debt, 20,083,710 florins to debts of guaranteed railroads acquired by the Government, 1,029,976 florins to other guaranteed railroad debts, 6,923,116 florins to the administration of Croatia, 110,900 florins to the Accountant-General, 337,580 florins to the President of the Council, 58,990 florins to the Minister *ad latus*, 36,080 florins to the Minister for Croatia, 12,074,528 florins to the Minister of the Interior, 62,172,152 florins to the Minister of Finance, 61,373,740 florins to the Minister of Commerce, 13,832,395 florins to the Minister of Agriculture, 7,607,204 florins to the Minister of Worship and Instruction, 13,167,933 florins to the Minister of Justice, and 11,990,711 to the Minister of National Defense.

The Elections.—The first Hungarian Parliament of five years' duration was closed on Jan. 5, and the general elections began on Feb. 3. The strength of the different parties was not materially changed. The Liberals carried 251, the Independents 78, the Nationalists 67, and the Ugron party 17 seats. These, together with 40 delegates from Croatia and Slavonia, form the new House of Representatives. A feature of the elections was that the Liberals turned all their attention to defeating the Nationalists under the leadership of Count Apponyi, whose principles are confined to opposition and legislative obstruction, while their usual antagonists, the Independents, stand on a pronounced platform. Another important innovation was the influence that the Clericals exercised in behalf of their religious plans. This is the first time that the Clericals in Hungary have tried to influence the elections systematically, and it was principally by their aid that the Nationalists gained a few seats; but they also supported candidates of other parties, who pledged themselves to further their aims in religious matters.

Session of the Parliament.—The newly elected Parliament was opened on Feb. 22 by a speech of the King, Franz Josef, which contained an all-round programme of work and reform. Most of the session was taken up in discussing the budget, which gave rise to a good deal of parliamentary filibustering in voting the different items, and the Opposition managed to retard its acceptance until June 23. Two bills, one securing equal religious rights to all creeds, the other adopting the currency reform, were passed, and Parliament adjourned on July 20.

Particularist Movements.—The tendencies which the various races of Austria have shown toward a revival and cultivation of national languages, customs, and institutions, threatening to convert the monarchy into a loosely cemented federation of states, the latest development of which is seen in an Italian nationalist movement in the Tyrol, have manifested themselves in the Transleithan monarchy also, chiefly in the movement for the union of Croatia and Slavonia and their erection into a self-governing south Slav state. Also the Roumanian population in Hungary, which inhabits more particularly the western portion of that country and Transylvania, has for a long time past maintained a hostile attitude toward the Hungarian Government, claiming for the Roumanian element the same rights that are possessed by the Magyars. But being in a considerable minority, they have hitherto confined themselves to passive resistance, exhibited in their refraining from sending Deputies to the Parliament at Buda-Pesth. Suddenly they changed their tactics, and in May, 1892, sent to Vienna a deputation, consisting of 237 members, for the purpose of putting their grievances

before the Emperor. The Emperor, as might have been expected, refused to receive them, but from the Anti-Semites and Particularists of the Municipal Council of Vienna they received demonstrations of sympathy.

B

BAPTISTS. I. Regular Baptists in the United States.—According to the statistical tables published in the "American Baptist Year Book" for 1892, the Baptist churches in the United States include 35,890 churches, 23,800 ministers, and 3,269,806 members, and reported 160,247 baptisms during the year; and in all North America—including also Canada and the Maritime Provinces, Mexico, Cuba, Hayti, Jamaica, and other West Indian islands—there are 36,956 churches, 24,241 ministers, 3,393,118 members, and 167,459 baptisms during the y . The tables further show in Europe—including Great Britain. etc., Austria-Hungary, Denmark, Finland, France, Germany, Holland, Italy, Norway, Roumania and Bulgaria, Russia and Poland, Spain, Sweden, and Switzerland—3,870 churches, 3,041 ministers, 414,321 members, and 6,587 baptisms; in Asia, 740 churches, 488 ministers, 85,-950 members, and 8,951 baptisms; in Africa, 42 churches, 81 ministers, 2,860 members, and 28 baptisms; and in Australia, 193 churches, 131 ministers, 16,050 members, and 711 baptisms. In all, 41,808 churches, 27,933 ministers, 3,003,881 members, and 183,819 baptisms—showing an increase from the previous year's enumeration of 1,177 churches, 832 ministers, 110,803 members, and 27,325 baptisms. The churches in Asia and Africa are mainly fruits of missionary work.

The 7 Baptist theological institutions in the United States had in 1891 61 instructors and 776 students preparing for the ministry; the 36 universities and colleges, 487 instructors and 8,186 students, 889 of whom were preparing for the ministry; the 38 institutions for the instruction of young women, 422 instructors and 4,834 pupils; the 51 institutions for the education of young men and of young men and young women, 294 instructors and 6,298 pupils, 370 of whom were preparing for the ministry; and the 25 institutions for the colored race and Indians, 219 instructors and 5,193 pupils, 372 of whom were preparing for the ministry. In all, there were 157 institutions, with 813 men and 670 women as instructors. 25,287 pupils, 2,407 of whom were preparing for the ministry; having grounds and buildings valued at $11,419,379, endowment funds, so far as reported, of $14,-159,140, and libraries and apparatus at $1,147,-696; amount of gifts received in 1891, $2,547,-557; number of volumes in libraries, 903,181.

American Baptist Missionary Union.—The seventy-eighth annual meeting of the American Baptist Missionary Union was held in Philadelphia, Pa., May 19 and 20. The Rev. G. W. Northrop, D.D., presided. The Treasurer's report showed that the receipts for the year had been $569,173, indicating an increase of $96,999. It was regarded as a sign of healthy activity that the expenses of the society had increased by $221,417 in the last three years, and had more

than doubled in the last nine years. The two Women's Missionary Societies had contributed $118,191 to the funds of the society. Four hundred and seventeen missionaries and 947 native preachers had been under appointment during the year, while 1,083 preachers were engaged in European countries. Connected with the missions were 1,439 churches, with 163,881 members, of whom 83,597 were in heathen lands; and 18,549 persons, of whom 10,971 were from among the heathen, had been baptized. Thirty-nine missionaries and 207 preachers had been added to the force. Seventy-three stations and 900 out-stations are occupied in heathen lands. The pupils in Sunday schools numbered 78,187, and those in other schools 22,284, all of both classes in heathen lands. The year had been one of more than usual prosperity in nearly all the missions. Among the events especially referred to in the report were the revival in the Telugu missions in India, which had resulted in 7,905 accessions; the progress of the work in France, and the conversion of more than 60 persons at Bolengi station, near Equatorville, in the Upper Congo Valley. The work of Bible translation, printing, and distribution had been carried on as rapidly as possible. A new and cheaper edition of Judson's translation of the Bible into the Burmese language had been printed from photo-engraved plates of a reduced size. Efforts were making on the Congo for the translation of the Scriptures. The missions had been extended in the unoccupied fields of upper Burmah, closer to the Naga Hills. The Ongole Mission High School (Telugu) had been raised to a second-grade college, according to the standards of the Government of India. Two special funds of $50,000 each had been raised in this country, one for the enlargement of this mission, and the other for the endowment of the high school.

The meeting declared by resolution that while fully recognizing the right of the United States to restrict immigration, and especially the right and duty to raise the requirements of citizenship, it protested against the recent Chinese exclusion legislation as unjust and oppressive : as discriminating inequitably and cruelly against an industrious class; as violating our treaty obligations; and as threatening to imperil missionary work and workers in China.

Publication Society.—At the annual meeting of the American Baptist Publication Society Mr. Samuel Croser presided. The total receipts of all the departments had been $673,481, of which $21,412 had been in the Bible department and $118,415 in the missionary department. The Scriptures—27,064 copies—had been distributed in many languages, and to every part of the United States, as well as in Cuba, Mexico, Canada, and South America. The final revision of the New Testament by Drs. Weston, Hovey, and Broadus, had been published. The total sales of the year in the publication department amounted to $553,656. One hundred and twenty-four new publications had been issued, and 35,103,500 copies of books, tracts, pamphlets, and periodicals had been printed. The chapel car "Evangel" had been successfully used on the Pacific coast and east of the Rocky Mountains. Ten Baptist churches and 9 Sunday schools had been organized in Oregon and Washington ; 60 towns had been visited ; and 500 persons had professed conversion. One hundred and thirty-eight colporteurs had been employed, under whose labors 695 persons had been baptized, 58 churches constituted, and 376 Sunday schools organized.

Home Mission Society.—The total receipts for the year of the American Baptist Home Mission Society were reported at its annual meeting in Philadelphia, Pa., May 27, the Hon. E. N. Blake presiding, to have been $500,390 ; the expenditures had been $448,038, of which $207,467 had been for missionaries' salaries and $82,684 for teachers' salaries. The society had supported, in whole or in part, 1,053 laborers, in 49 States and Territories, Ontario, Manitoba, Northwest Territory, British Columbia, Alaska, and six States of Mexico. About 75 churches had become self-supporting, 80 more had asked for smaller appropriations than in the previous year, and 145 new stations had been taken up ; 221 of the missionaries had been laboring among the foreign population, 326 missionaries and teachers among the colored people, Indians, and Mexicans, and 505 among Americans. The missionaries represented 14 nationalities or peoples. The society aided in the maintenance of 27 established schools for the colored people, the Indians, and the Mexicans ; 9 day schools for the Chinese in California, 3 in Oregon, and 1 in Montana ; besides which 2 day schools were maintained in Utah, 2 in the Indian Territory, and 3 in Mexico. One hundred and fifty-seven teachers were employed and 4,716 students were enrolled in the schools for the colored people ; 4 teachers and 247 pupils in Mexico ; and 19 teachers and 392 students in the Indian schools. Wichita Mission School had been added to the number in the Indian Territory, making 5 in all there. The number of students for the ministry was 412. Manual training had become a prominent feature in most of the schools. The training schools for nurses at Spelman Seminary was regarded with much favor. One hundred and twenty-one churches had been aided by gifts and loans during the year. A resolution was adopted insisting, "as American Christians and as Baptists," upon the entire separation of Church and state, and "steadily and sturdily protesting against any such subtle assault upon our public-school system as that known as the Faribault and Stillwater plan" (a plan under which the priests of the Roman Catholic Church are permitted to give religious instruction after school hours in the school rooms hired from them).

Education Society.—The annual meeting of the American Baptist Education Society was held in Philadelphia, Pa., May 28. Dr. S. W. Duncan presided. The Executive Board reported

that more than $4,000,000 had been presented to Baptist institutions of learning during the last twelve months. The gifts had been distributed substantially as follows :

To 11 institutions for the colored people and the Indians	$40,000
To 6 institutions for women	100,000
To 20 academies and secondary schools	400,000
To 5 theological seminaries	250,000
To 29 colleges and universities	3,500,000
To 71 institutions an aggregate of	$4,290,000

The sum includes $1,000,000 contributed to Colgate University and more than a million contributed to the University of Chicago. Since the active work of this society began in 1889, the aggregate of Baptist educational property in the United States has increased from about $19,500,000 to $29,000,000 ; and the number of students in Baptist institutions from about 17,000 to more than 25,000.

Women's Missionary Societies.—The Woman's Baptist Home Mission Society received during the year, for its general work, $44,431, and returned a balance of $4,628. The receipts for the current expenses of the training school had been $6,331. The deficit on the training-school building fund had been reduced to $3,466. While not auxiliary to the American Baptist Home Mission Society, a plan of co-operation was in force in some of its branches, which had contributed some $5,508 to the fund of that society. The training school had made greater progress than at any time during the eleven years of its history. The society employed 84 missionaries, under whose labors 85 Sunday schools had been organized, 1,629 young people's meetings conducted, 1,621 women's meetings attended, and 19 temperance societies organized.

At the twenty-first annual meeting of the Woman's Baptist Foreign Missionary Society of the West, held at Racine, Wis., April 12, the receipts for the year were returned at $44,605, and the expenditures at $49,290. Forty-one missionaries had been in the service of the society during the year, and it had work for 13 more. Thirty schools were returned from the mission fields, with 82 native teachers and 2,234 pupils. Fifty-three Bible women had been employed, and 49 other Christian women were under training for work. Ninety-two baptisms were returned.

The receipts of the Woman's Baptist Foreign Missionary Society, according to reports made at its twenty-first annual meeting in Boston, Mass., April 20, had been $97,611 ; the expenditures had been $97,953, of which $88,476 were applied to foreign fields in Burmah, Assam, the Telugu country, China, Japan, Africa, and Europe. Among the papers read at the meeting was one on "What a Century of Christianity has done for Woman." The society undertook to raise $200,-000 during the ensuing year, half of the sum to be used as a special offering.

American Baptist Historical Society.—The library of the American Baptist Historical Society was increased during the year ending with April, 1892, by the addition of 236 bound volumes and 6,000 pamphlets. It now contains 7,477 bound volumes and thousands of minutes, college catalogues, translations, works of missionaries, manuscripts, photographs, etc. The receipts for the year were $3,500, and the ex-

54   BAPTISTS.

penditures $3,764. The invested funds amounted
to about $4.000.

Southern Baptist Convention.—The Southern Baptist Convention met in its forty-eighth
annual session at Atlanta, Ga., May 6. The
Hon. Jonathan Haralson was re-elected president.
The report of the Board of Home Missions
showed that its total receipts had been $227,281,
of which $84,871 were receipts from the States
and miscellaneous receipts; $68,683 raised by
co-operative bodies and expended in joint mission work; and $64,065 for houses of worship in
mission fields. Three hundred and sixty-five
missionaries had been employed, serving 1,324
churches and stations. They returned as the
results of their year's labors 5,274 baptisms, 342
Sunday schools organized, with 17,185 teachers
and pupils, 179 churches constituted, and 80
houses of worship built. During the past ten
years 2,692 missionaries had been employed, 2,-
290 churches constituted, 2,117 Sunday schools
organized, 630 houses of worship built, 67,166
members added to the churches, and $1,320,000
raised and expended. Forty of the missionaries
had been laboring during the year among the
Indians and in Oklahoma. The missions among
the Indians were becoming year by year more
assimilated with those among the whites, and
the necessity of preaching in the native languages was diminishing. The work of evangelization was accomplished, and the demand for
Christian development and education had arisen.
The mission in Cuba was acquiring a stronger
hold, to which the purchase of a valuable property for a church in the heart of the city of
Havana, and the establishment of a high school
for girls, had contributed much. The work
among the colored people had not increased so
rapidly as was desired.

The receipts of the Foreign Mission Board had
been $114,325. The Women's Missionary Socie-
ties had raised $25,040. Twenty-one new mis-
sionaries had gone out during the year. The
missions were in China, where 130 baptisms were
returned; West Africa, 31 baptisms; Italy, 40
baptisms; Brazil, 80 baptisms; Japan, 16 baptisms; and Mexico, 127 baptisms. The mission
in Japan was a new one. The Sunday School
Board presented its first report, and represented
the results of the year's work as encouraging.
Preparations were making for the publication of
several books and periodicals. Returns were
presented from 8,862 Sunday schools in a constituency of 1,129,942 members, with 52,513
teachers and officers and 440,262 pupils.

The committee on the celebration of the one
hundredth anniversary of the establishment of
Baptist missions reported that the subject had
been brought before the district associations and
State conventions, and that special meetings had
been held. Missionary maps had been issued,
and much literature circulated. It had been
agreed to undertake to raise money to send 100
new missionaries to the foreign field. The committee recommended in addition that $250,000
be raised as a fund for building churches. Four
general centennial meetings were arranged for;
one to be held in Atlanta, at once; one in Louisville, Ky., in October, 1892; one in Richmond,
Va., in March, 1893; and the last at the next
session of the convention.

The Woman's Missionary Union, auxiliary to
the Southern Baptist Convention, received in
1890–'91 gifts of $15,229 for home and $23,761
for foreign missions.

Societies of Colored Baptists.—The American Baptist Missionary Convention of the Western States and Territories sustains three missionaries on the foreign field, giving particular
attention to the Congo Free State.

The Baptist Foreign Missionary Convention
of the United States returned its receipts in
1891 for missionary work at $2,900, and was sup-
porting two missionaries.

The New England Baptist Missionary Convention, organized in 1875, returned in 1891 an
income of $728, and had a widow's fund of $377.
Four missionary pastors had served at four stations, in which there had been 22 conversions
and 15 baptisms, and $521 had been contributed
in support of pastoral labor. Aid was given
by the society to a seminary that is located at
Lynchburg, Va. A woman's auxiliary society
was organized in 1891.

German and Swedish Baptist Churches.—
The tenth triennial General Conference of the
German Baptists in America met in Chicago,
Ill., and transacted business of a routine character. This body represents five conferences, with
1,700 members and 200 pastors. It has an academy and a theological seminary in Rochester,
N. Y., a publication house in Cleveland, Ohio,
and an orphan's home and an old people's home
in Louisville, Ky.

The General Conference of Swedish Baptists
met in Oakland, Neb., late in September. Preparations were made for the extension of missionary
work among Swedish settlers in Texas, Manitoba, Wyoming, Dakota, and Idaho; the Divinity School at Morgan Park, Ill., where the Swedish preachers are taught, was requested to admit
no student who is wholly without experience in
the field; and the Education Society was asked
to help brethren who are well known, have experience in evangelical work, and are efficient.
The Swedish churches returned in 1890, 12,172
members of the church, 781 teachers and 6,689
pupils in Sunday schools, 129 meeting houses,
with church property valued at $392,500, and
contributed for all purposes $158,115.

Young People's Union.—The Baptist Young
People's Union of America was organized at a
Convention held in Chicago, Ill., in July, 1891,
which was attended by 1,621 delegates repre-
senting 28 States, the District of Columbia, and
Canada. Its resolutions affirmed the distinctive
principles of the Baptists, and attachment to the
American Sabbath.

Baptist Congress.—The tenth annual Bap-
tist Congress met in Philadelphia, Pa., May 18.
Col. Charles H. Banes presided. Prearranged
topics were discussed by appointed speakers as
follow: "The Christian Year: How far is its
Recognition advisable?" by President H. G.
Weston, of Crozer Theological Seminary, the
Rev. W. H. P. Faunce. and the Rev. R. S. Mac-
Arthur, D. D.; "Is a Union of the Various Bap-
tist Bodies feasible?" by the Rev. B. B. Tyler,
D. D., of the Disciples of Christ, Rev. A. H.
Lewis, D. D., of the Seventh-Day Baptist Church,
Prof. J. A. Howe, D. D., of the Free-Will Bap-
tist Church, and Prof. W. H. Whitsitt, D. D., of

the Southern Baptist Theological Seminary, Louisville, Ky.; "The Inerrancy of the Scriptures," by the Rev. T. A. T. Hanna, Prof. D. G. Lyon, Ph. D., the Rev. J. B. G. Pidge, D. D., and Prof. Howard Osgood, D. D.; "The Pulpit in Relation to Political and Social Reform," by the Rev. H. H. Peabody, D. D., Rev. C. R. Henderson, D. D., and Rev. Thomas Dixon, Jr.; "Christianity in Relation to Heathen Religions," by the Rev. Edward Braislin, D. D., Prof. Nathaniel Schmidt, and the Rev. F. M. Ellis, D. D.; and "The Relative Authority of Scripture and Reason," by Pres. David J. Hill, LL. D., Prof. W. N. Clarke, D. D., the Rev. E. G. Robinson, D. D., and Prof. A. T. Robinson. The appointed speakers were all followed in the discussion of the several topics by volunteer speakers.

II. Free-Will Baptist Church. General Conference.—An act of incorporation having been sought and obtained by the Free-Will Baptist General Conference from the State of Maine, the board of incorporators met, by direction of the statute, at Ocean Park, Old Orchard, Maine, Oct. 3, for formal organization as the Free Baptist General Conference, the name given the body in the charter. The board then adjourned, to meet with the original General Conference, with which it was to be merged. The twenty-eighth session of this body met at Lowell, Mass., Oct. 4. Prof. J. A. Howe was chosen moderator. The object sought in obtaining the act of incorporation was to bring the benevolent boards and societies of the Church into unity with the General Conference. The competency of the General Conference to consummate this measure was disputed; for the old constitution of the General Conference required the approval of three fourths of the yearly meetings and associations to any amendment. Final action on the subject was therefore delayed, and it was referred to the yearly meetings and associations, to be voted on by them. The secretary of the benevolent societies reported concerning his labors in holding conventions in behalf of the causes committed to his care. Concerning the special objects of the societies, the educational work was in good condition, and the mission in India was prospering so far as the means of the society permitted its extension. In the United States, the Church had to face the fact that it was numerically decreasing. Action was taken concerning the acceptance of an act of incorporation from the State of Maine, a draft for a constitution and by-laws, the Correspondence School of Theology, the Ministerial Relief Bureau, and the proposed denominational exhibit at the World's Columbian Fair.

III. Baptists in Canada.—"The Year-Book of the Baptist Convention of the Maritime Provinces and Canada" for 1892 enumerates 392 churches, with 42.777 members. Of these, 204 churches, with 25,855 members, are in Nova Scotia: 762 churches, with 15,007 members, in New Brunswick; and 26 churches, with 1,855 members, in Prince Edward Island. The number of baptisms during the past year had been 864 in Nova Scotia, 813 in New Brunswick, and 95 in Prince Edward Island—in all, 1,772. Five hundred and twenty-two Sunday schools had 28,829 enrolled pupils. The Baptist Convention of Ontario and Quebec met in Brantford, Oct. 14, the Rev. J. B. Thomas, D. D., presiding. The

receipts for foreign missions had been $31,845, of which $1,839 had been contributed through the Sunday schools, $7,757 through the Women's Societies of Ontario and the eastern provinces, and $3,962 through the Casey fund. The disbursements included $24,212 to the mission in India. The subjects of foreign missions and home missions were discussed; reports were made of the Superannuated Ministers' Society, the Church Edifice Board, and the Educational Board and fund; a conference of the Young People's Baptist Union was held; and a meeting was given to the celebration of the centennial of foreign missions.

IV. Baptists in Great Britain and Ireland.—"The Baptist Handbook" for 1892 gives the following statistics of the Baptist churches of Great Britain and Ireland: Number of churches, 2,812; of houses of worship, 3,798, with a seating capacity of 1,225,097; of members, 334,163; of teachers in Sunday schools, 47,784; of pupils in Sunday schools, 483,921; local preachers or licentiates, 4,155: of pastors in charge, 1,841. As compared with the previous year, these figures show an increase of 10 churches, 17 church edifices or chapels, 1,571 in seating capacity, 4,000 members, 155 local preachers, and 1,029 pupils in Sunday schools; and a decrease of 348 teachers in Sunday schools and 33 pastors. As compared with the statistics of 1888, they show a gain in three years of 42 churches, 53 chapels, 3,274 sittings, 9,665 members, 1,754 pupils in Sunday schools, and 17 local preachers: and a loss of 1,193 teachers and 24 pastors.

British Baptist Union.—The Baptist Union of Great Britain and Ireland met in London, April 25. The Rev. B. Henry Roberts presided, and delivered an inaugural address on "The Witness of the Bible to Belief." The report of the Council showed a slight advance in most of the items of denominational progress, the number of members having increased from 330,163 to 334,163, while the number of pastors had declined from 1,874 to 1,841, and the number of local preachers had increased by 155. The following sums had passed through the hands of the Council during the year: General expense fund, £1,112; Home Mission fund, £3,053; annuity fund, £8,870: the total cost of investments being £129,756; augmentation fund, £2,888: and education fund, £131. The action of a minister connected with the Union in exchanging pulpits with a Unitarian minister had been much discussed in the denomination. A resolution was adopted with reference to it, declaring that—

While fully and gladly recognizing the duty of cherishing good-will toward men of all creeds, and co-operating with them in works of piety and mercy when this can be done without disloyalty to conviction or to the Lord, the Union deprecates and disapproves any and every association with those who deny the above essential truths, which would weaken the force of our testimony or produce the impression that, in our judgment, it is a matter of secondary importance what "men think of Christ"; and that the Union, therefore, urges all the churches and pastors in connection with it jealously to "guard the trust which is committed to them," and especially to secure in the public ministry of the gospel clear and consistent and constant witness-bearing to the Deity of the "one Lord" and only Saviour, Christ.

The Rev. C. F. Aked, the minister whose conduct had given occasion for this resolution, supported it, and explained that he had invited the Unitarian as an active social reformer to speak on questions of reform, while it was understood that doctrinal questions should be avoided, and while he went into the Unitarian pulpit with full liberty. In view of complaints of lack of efficiency in the theological instruction given in the denominational colleges, a resolution was adopted suggesting that, considering the excellence of the general education facilities in the country, the colleges might be relieved of classical and preparatory work and entirely devoted to the theological and related studies: that pupils should be required to come sufficiently advanced to enter at once on these studies; that the course should include, as far as possible, Hebrew and Biblical Aramaic, New Testament Greek and Syriac, textual criticism, exegesis, systematic theology, apologetics, Christian history and literature, social economics, pastoral theology, and homiletics; and that the question of federating or uniting two or more of the colleges should be considered, each to undertake some separate department in a complete curriculum. A series of proposals for Church extension was approved, which include the formation of local societies in large towns to secure sites for prospective churches, make grants for building, and support a pastors' sustentation fund for a term of years; the establishment of a "Baptist Union Church Extension fund," by which the formation of churches shall be undertaken in towns where the local effort is inadequate; and the contribution to this fund of one fourth of the sums raised by the local societies; the better distribution of Baptist churches in town areas, the existence of other Nonconformist churches being regarded; carefulness in building churches which shall be suitable in size and architecture to the neighborhood in which they are placed; and the election of the first pastor of any church that is formed under this movement by the local Church Extension Committee and the Council of the Baptist Union.

The autumnal assembly of the Union was held in London, beginning Oct. 3. Committees appointed at previous meetings to prepare a manual for the instruction of young people in nonconformist principles, and to present a practical scheme of college reform, reported progress, and were continued. A delegate from Jamaica described the condition of the Baptist churches in that island, where out of a population of 610,000 fully 100,000 are Baptists. The principal feature of the assembly consisted in the meetings in commemoration of the centennial of Baptist missions, which included a centennial sermon, a thanksgiving, a "breakfast" meeting, and other exercises. A report of the progress of the contemplated thanksgiving fund of £100,-000 showed that £92,000 had been promised, of which the Sunday schools had given £16,000. It was desired to raise the permanent income of the society to £100,000. An offer was received from Mr. Robert Arthington, of Leeds, to expend at least £30,000 in equipping and supporting missionaries if the different missionary societies would agree on a wise distribution of the heathen world among themselves.

Baptist Missionary Society.—The one hundredth annual meeting of the Baptist Missionary Society was held in London, April 28. The total year's income of the society for general purposes had been £69,125, and the total expenditure £74,935. The contributions to the Special Centenary fund, up to the close of March, amounted to £65,707, besides £11,000 raised by special collections in the Sunday schools and Young People's Societies. Encouraging reports were received from the missions in India, where the churches were represented as gaining on the population at the rate of 10 per cent. per decade, and the Congo, concerning which a resolution of thanksgiving for success was adopted. This mission, founded in 1878, has a chain of stations reaching 1,000 miles inland, with many believers, and a large and flourishing church at San Salvador. The language of the Lower Congo has been reduced to writing by the missionaries, and a dictionary has been compiled; while other missionaries are engaged in similar work on the Upper Congo.

The report of the work shows that the number of missionaries employed is 136, eight of whom are superannuated; of evangelists, 778, more than half of whom are in Jamaica, which has for many years been independent of the mission; of stations, including Jamaica, 795; of baptisms during the year, 4,015; of members, 50,875; of teachers—in day schools 411, in Sunday schools 2,276; and of pupils—in day schools 18,069, in Sunday schools 26,849. The missions are in India, Ceylon, China, Japan, Africa, the West Indies, and parts of Europe.

The receipts for the Baptist Home Missions had been £3,129, while the expenditure had been £3,843. The Home Mission fund aided 105 mission churches and 36 mission stations, served by 64 mission pastors, and having 5,227 communicants, 8,652 in the Sunday schools, and 1,003 members of Bible classes. The mission churches had raised £7,700 for various purposes.

The Baptist Building fund made loans in aid of the building of new churches to the amount of nearly £10,000.

The Baptist Zenana Mission returns 22 stations in India, with 54 zenana visitors and more than a hundred Bible women and teachers, 64 girls' schools, with 2,200 pupils, and 1,400 pupils in the zenanas, while many hundred women are visited for Bible instruction only. The income of the mission for the year ending with March, 1892, had been £7,547, and the expenditure £7,541.

Confederation of Baptist Churches in Germany and Surrounding Countries.—This body includes five associations in Germany, with the Hungarian, Roumano-Bulgarian, Holland Union, and South African Associations, and returns for the year 1891 the following members: Of churches, including those in Denmark, 167; of stations, 1,011; of pastors or "preaching elders" (not including those in Denmark), 205; of colporteurs, 117; of members, 29,767; of persons baptized during the year, 2,556; net year's gain in members, 1,350.

BELGIUM, a constitutional monarchy in western Europe, organized as an independent state in 1830, and declared neutral and inviolable by the Treaty of London, concluded between

Austria, Great Britain, Prussia, and Russia, on Nov. 15, 1831. The reigning sovereign is Leopold II. born April 9, 1835, who succeeded his father, Leopold I, the first King, on Dec. 10, 1865. The order of succession is in the direct male line. The heir-presumptive is Prince Albert, born April 8, 1875, the sole surviving son of the King's only brother Philippe, Count of Flanders. The legislative power is vested in the Senate and Chamber of Representatives, both elective bodies. The Chambers meet annually in November, and must sit at least forty days. The King may dissolve one or both; in such case elections must be held within forty days, and the new Parliament assemble within sixty days. The members of the Senate and of the Chamber of Representatives, according to the law in force at the beginning of 1892, were chosen by the direct suffrage of all male citizens twenty-one years of age who paid 40 francs a year in direct taxes. The number of voters on the registers in 1890 was 133,039, being about 1 to 45 legal citizens. The Chamber in 1891 had 138 members. The Representatives are elected for four years, half going out every two years. The Senators are half as many, and their term is eight years, half being renewed every four years.

The Ministry, constituted on Oct. 26, 1884, which was still in office in 1892, was composed of the following members: President of the Council and Minister of Finance, A. Beernaert; Minister of Justice, J. Lejeune; Minister of the Interior and of Public Instruction, J. de Burlet; Minister of War, Gen. C. Pontus; Minister of Railroads, Posts, and Telegraphs, J. H. P. Vandenpeereboom; Minister of Foreign Affairs, Prince de Chimay; Minister of Agriculture, Industry, and Public Works, L. Debruyn.

Area and Population.—The area of Belgium is 29,455 square kilometres, equal to 11,373 square miles. The area and population of the nine provinces at the census of Dec. 31, 1890, and the density of population, were as follows:

PROVINCES.	Square miles.	Population.	Per square mile.
Antwerp	1,098	699,571	640
Brabant	1,268	1,128,728	890
West Flanders	1,249	746,928	598
East Flanders	1,158	955,752	827
Hainaut	1,437	1,068,815	743
Liége	1,117	762,196	682
Limbourg	931	224,604	241
Luxembourg	1,706	216,380	126
Namur	1,414	341,072	241
Total	11,373	6,147,041	540

There were 3,062,656 males and 3,084,385 females. Of the total population, 226,759 males and 17,549 females (244,308 in all) were employed in mining and metallurgical industries; 199,333 males and 37,411 females in agriculture and gardening, 1,236,744 altogether; 40,401 males and 24,595 females in the raising of animals, 64,996 altogether; 227,553 males and 179,346 females, 406,899 altogether. in miscellaneous industrial occupations; 143,229 males and 101,018 females, 244,247 altogether. in commercial pursuits; 457,042 males and 192,114 females in professional and official occupations, 649,156 in all; 504,584 males and 409,257 females were in various other

occupations, or independent, 913,841 in all; and 1,010,072 males and 1,824,913 females were without profession or status.

The number of marriages in 1890 was 44,596; the number of births, 176,595, not including stillborn; the number of deaths, 126,545; excess of births over deaths, 50,050. The number of emigrants in 1890 was 21,675, which was 217 more than the number of immigrants.

The Army.—The standing army is raised partly by conscription, substitution being permitted, and partly by enlistment. The annual recruit is 13,300 men. The nominal term of service is eight years, but the actual period is less than three years. The strength of the army on the peace footing is as follows: Infantry, 1,880 officers and 25,515 men; cavalry, 348 officers and 5,309 men; artillery, 447 officers and 7,507 men; engineers, 96 officers and 1,449 men; gendarmerie, 61 officers and 2,385 men; staff, train, administrative services, etc., 556 officers and 2,158 men; total, 3,388 officers and 44,323 men. The number of guns in peace is 200, and the number of horses is 7,200, besides 1,623 for the gendarmerie. The war strength is 154,780 men, with 240 guns and 14,000 horses. In addition to the regular army a garde civique is organized, which numbered 44,339 men in 1890. Gen. Brialmont in June, 1892, was succeeded as head of the engineers by Gen. Lienart, and Gen. Heurard was appointed inspector of artillery, in place of Gen. Nicaisse. The two military circumscriptions were converted into four, with headquarters at Ghent, Antwerp, Liége, and Brussels. A special general staff was appointed to put the fortifications of Liége, Namur, and Antwerp in a state of defense.

Finances.—The total ordinary revenue of the Government is set down in the budget for 1892 as 342,546,190 francs, of which 24,496,000 francs are derived from property taxes, 18,915,000 francs from personal taxes, 6,680,000 francs from trade licences, 1,600,000 francs from mines, 23,483,056 francs from customs, 41,420,235 francs from internal revenue duties, 24,400,000 francs from succession duties, 18,510,000 francs from registration duties, 6,000,000 francs from stamps, 1,481,000 francs from other indirect taxes, 138,000,000 francs from railroads, 4,100,000 francs from telegraphs, 10,620,200 francs from the post office, 2,605,000 francs from navigation dues and pilotage, 1,280,000 francs from domains and forests, 15,415,200 francs from the amortization fund and securities and from the National Bank, and 3,540,000 francs from repayments.

The total ordinary expenditure is estimated at 339,502,685 francs, divided as follows: Interest on the debt and sinking-fund charge, 103,221,797 francs; civil list and dotations, 4,576,100 francs; Ministry of Justice, 17,293,135 francs; Ministry of Foreign Affairs, 2,496,363 francs; Ministry of the Interior and Public Instruction, 23,216,997 francs; Ministry of Public Works, 17,088,428 francs; Ministry of Railroads, Posts, and Telegraphs, 103,317,028 francs; Ministry of War, 46,960,582 francs; Ministry of Finance, 15,539,255 francs; gendarmerie, 4,264,500 francs; repayments, 1,528,500 francs.

The funded debt in 1892 amounted to 2,053,560,000 francs, and the floating liabilities to 20,000,000 francs, besides which there were annuities to be paid of a capitalized value of about 30,000,000 francs. The largest part of the debt bears interest at $3\frac{1}{2}$ per cent., and the rest pays 3 and $2\frac{1}{2}$ per cent. The debt was raised for railroads and other useful works, and is being extinguished by a sinking fund, with the exception of the $2\frac{1}{2}$ per cent. debt of 208,615,792 francs, which was a part of the old debt of the Netherlands, contracted before the secession of Belgium in 1830.

Commerce.—The general imports in 1890 were 3,189,160,016 francs in value, and the general exports 2,948,151,841 francs. Of the imports, 1,504,775,060 francs were imported through the seaports and 1,684,384,956 francs by land or river; and of the general exports, 1,288,151,012 francs went by sea and 1,660,000,829 francs by way of the land frontiers. The transit trade was 1,511,100,000 francs. The special imports amounted in 1890 to 1,672,100,000, and the special exports to 1,437,000,000 francs. In the sum of the imports for domestic consumption 302,698,000 francs represent cereals, 204,524,000 francs textile materials, 93,372,000 francs vegetable substances, 76,415,000 francs various minerals, 70,363,000 francs timber, 69,259,000 francs hides and skins, 61,086,000 francs metals, 59,895,000 francs resinous and bituminous substances, 59,641.000 francs chemicals, 57,339,000 francs textile fabrics, 54,713,000 francs live animals, 52,534,000 francs coffee, 41,780,000 francs butter and eggs, 37,458,000 francs various other animal products, 30,127,000 francs coal, 28,506,000 francs yarns, 28,506,000 francs meat, 26,764,000 francs fertilizers, 26,252,000 francs vegetable oils, 24,406,000 francs wine, 17,664,000 francs rice, and 13,287,000 francs fish. In the total exports yarns were represented by 135,119,000 francs, coal and coke by 113,706,000 francs, machinery, etc., by 104,601,000 francs, textile materials by 95,090.000 francs, cereals by 90,014,000 francs, textile fabrics by 69,370,000 francs, iron by 67,925,000 francs, hides and skins by 60,386,000 francs, sugar by 53,197,000 francs, glass by 45,134,000 francs, various vegetable products by 43,523,000 francs, various animal products by 36,451,000 francs, chemicals by 35,179,000 francs, various mineral substances by 32,698,000 francs, zinc by 31,841,000 francs, meat by 30,694,000 francs, steel by 29,056,000 francs, live animals by 23,415,000 francs, stone by 22,781,000 francs, arms by 16,537,000 francs, and paper by 14,441,000 francs.

The various foreign countries participated in the import trade in the following proportions: France, 316,389,000 francs; Great Britain, 212,942,000 francs; Netherlands, 206,389,000 francs; Germany, 182,189,000 francs; United States, 157,022,000 francs; Russia, 114,334,000 francs; Roumania, 101,629,000 francs; British India, 76,615,000 francs; Argentine Republic, 74.558,000 francs; Sweden and Norway, 46,393.000 francs; Brazil, 30,503,000 francs; Spain, 21,319,000 francs; Peru, 20,965,000 francs; Italy, 19,904,000 francs; Australia, 16,923,000 francs; Chili, 14,360,000 francs; Uruguay, 12,200,000 francs.

The exports of domestic merchandise were distributed as follows: France, 358,691,000 francs; Great Britain, 267,840.000 francs; Germany, 265,116,000 francs; Netherlands, 208,336,-

000 francs; United States, 50,684,000 francs; Spain, 38,749,000 francs; Italy, 34,860,000 francs; Switzerland, 28,642,000 francs; Portugal, 16,044,000 francs; Brazil, 15,626,000 francs; Turkey, 14,033.000 francs; Sweden and Norway, 11,190,000 francs; Russia, 9,664,000 francs; British India, 9,564,000 francs; China, 8,507,000 francs; Chili, 8,186,000 francs; Australia, 5,577,000 francs.

Navigation.—The number of ships that put in at Belgian ports in the course of 1890 was 7,357; the tonnage entered, 5,785,980. The number that sailed was 7,381, and their tonnage 5.803,168. Of the total number entered, 3,984, of 2,269,105 tons, were from England, and of those cleared 1,159, of 630,987 tons, were bound for English ports. The United States stood next on the list, with 297 vessels, of 562,392 tons, entered, and 109, of 313,400 tons, cleared.

The merchant marine on Jan. 1, 1892, consisted of 10 sailing vessels, of 4,393 tons, and 46 steam vessels, of 71,553 tons.

Railroads, Posts, and Telegraphs.—On Jan. 1, 1890, there were 3,250 kilometres of railroads operated by the Government and 1,276 kilometres operated by corporations, making 4,526 kilometres, or 2,830 miles. The receipts for 1890 amounted to 141,251,314 francs on the state lines and 40,966,925 francs on the companies' lines. The working expenses of the Government lines were 83,657,947 francs, and of the others 21,054,885 francs.

The post office during 1890 carried 95,484,491 private letters, 16,567,905 official letters, 36,865,077 postal cards, 73,599,461 printed inclosures, and 94,639,558 newspapers. The post office receipts were 16,455,630, and expenditures 9,527,694 francs.

The telegraphs transmitted 8,062,837 messages, The length of the state telegraph lines in the beginning of 1891 was 4,265 miles, and the length of wires was 20,315 miles. The receipts for 1890 were 3,465,089 francs, and the expenses 4,169,222 francs.

Commercial Treaty with Germany.—The treaty that unites Belgium with the commercial league formed by the Central European Alliance under the lead of Germany encountered opposition because it seemed to many that the Belgian Government had failed to obtain as favorable terms as had been granted to Switzerland, for example. The members of the mercantile community complained that after questioning them very carefully the Government had agreed to an arrangement in which no account was taken of the views they had put forward. The treaty was approved by the Chamber on Jan. 28, by 77 votes against 16. This result was, however, not a brilliant success for the Government, since 45 members refrained from voting because they did not like the treaty. Unsatisfactory as it was, it was concluded for twelve years, and joins Belgium to the commercial combination formed by Germany, Austria-Hungary, Italy, and Switzerland, which will probably include Servia also.

Revision of the Constitution.—The agitation of the Radicals and workingmen for universal suffrage fell in with the desires of that section of the Conservative party that dominated the Government, the Clerical element, which had swept away the system of secular education elaborated by the Liberals. The Flemish peasant vote would strengthen that section even more than the labor vote would benefit the Radicals in Brussels and the industrial and mining districts. The old political chiefs and the moderate sections of both the Liberal and the Conservative parties have consistently upheld the system of a bourgeois aristocracy, perpetuated by the narrowest franchise in Europe. The Conservatives have hitherto opposed any extension of the franchise; while the Liberals, who have discussed the subject for twenty years, have not been able to unite on a plan. The opposition of Frère-Orban, the aged leader of the once powerful Liberal party, to any electoral reform going beyond a moderate diminution of the property restriction and the recognition of a certain educational qualification, has disrupted the party and converted most of his old followers into Radicals. The Constitution of 1830 established as a sole condition of the franchise a property qualification, the cense being based on the payment of direct taxes varying, according to locality, from 13 to 150 guilders. The proposition to confer the right of suffrage on university graduates was rejected, as well as the plan of having the Senators nominated by the King. The Senate was made a select edition of the Chamber, with a higher property qualification for electors and for members, and thus a purely plutocratic principle was made the foundation of the whole system of government. The persons who have a stake in the country having been constituted the only source of political power, the liberty of conscience, of instruction, of the press, and of association were guaranteed in a fuller measure than in any other country. In 1848 the differential impost was done away with, and an amendment made in the Constitution making the payment of 20 guilders of annual taxes the uniform condition of the electoral franchise.

The organized and violent agitation of the workingmen, culminating in the general strike of 1890, and the stoppage of production and commerce as a demonstration in favor of universal suffrage, convinced the Government of the danger of longer withholding the reform, and subjecting the country to the risk of revolution. The Conservatives, from a party standpoint, were not afraid of granting universal suffrage; for with the rural vote they expected to be able to retain their present two-third majority. The strike was brought to an end only when the Government gave pledges that the question of revision would be taken up. The motion of Janson, the Radical leader, in favor of revision, was supported by the ministers, who acted at the King's request, and was carried in November, 1890, by a large majority. The committee of the Chamber discussed methods of reform for many months with no tangible result, and when the Chamber took up the matter in February, 1892, M. Janson's proposal was made the basis of the discussion and was followed by other proposals emanating from the Government. M. Janson had proposed only a revision of Articles XLVII, LIII, and LVI of the Constitution, which deal with the franchise. The Constitution forbids action to be taken by the constituent Chambers on any articles not specially submitted to it by the Parliament which decides that revision shall

take place. The King and his ministers found anomalies and discrepancies to be removed in order to bring the Constitution into harmony with actual conditions. A clause in Article I makes a reserve in regard to the relations between the Belgian part of Luxembourg and the Germanic Confederation, which have ceased because that Confederation no longer exists. While correcting this point, it was thought desirable that the constituent Assembly should make provision also for the regulation of the status of the native population of the Congo Free State, which is to become Belgian territory if present plans and arrangements are carried out. The provision contained in Article LII, which allows a remuneration of 200 florins a month to members of the Chamber who live outside the limits of the town where Parliament meets, while those living in Brussels receive none, is a relic of the times when there were no railroads. The Government suggested, as a natural concomitant of a democratic extension of the franchise, that not only the Deputies but the Senators should receive a sufficient remuneration. The law which makes each house the judge of the credentials of members, contained in Article XXXIV, has given rise to abuses and contentions which would be avoided by having questions of contested seats passed upon by a legal tribunal. Articles XLVIII, LI, and LVIII bear upon the organization and powers of the Chambers. The Belgian Senate has been a useless and superfluous body, and the legislative functions have been monopolized by the Chamber of Deputies. When M. A. Demeur in 1870 made a stirring appeal which opened the battle for electoral reform, he showed that there were only 480 men in Belgium who paid 1,000 guilders in direct taxes, and were therefore qualified to sit in the Senate; that the 20-guilder limitation for voters conferred the right of suffrage upon only 110,000, while it shut out 1,400,000 adult male Belgians. The Government advocated turning the Senate into a Chamber representing diverse interests, like the upper House in Austria, except that in Austria the representatives are either hereditary proprietors, bishops, princes, etc., or are selected by the Government; whereas in Belgium all but a very few would be elected by the interests to be represented. The King desired to have Article LVIII altered, so as to allow all the princes of the royal house to enjoy the privilege accorded by the old Constitution to the heir-presumptive, of sitting in the Senate from the age of eighteen, and of voting as Senators when they reach the age of twenty-five. He asked also that the wording of Articles LX and LXI should be altered, so as to grant him the right that was conferred on the first Leopold, his father, of naming, in default of male heirs in the regular succession, the successor to the throne, subject to the approval of the Chambers, and also the power to prevent the heir-presumptive and other princes in the line of possible succession from making unsuitable marriages. An important proposition to secure the representation of minorities in the Chamber was also submitted. The most novel and the most momentous proposal of the King, and that which excited the strongest opposition, was the introduction of the referendum. The ministers yielded reluctantly when he insisted on making that a part of the Government proposals. In Switzerland, where the referendum or popular vote on legislative measures exists, it is invoked only on the demand of a certain number of electors. In the proposed amendment to Article LXVII, the right of calling for a *plébiscite* is granted to the King alone, who is empowered on his own motion to lay before the people for approval or rejection, by a general vote, any bill that has been passed by Parliament, or any legislative proposal on which Parliament has not yet taken action. The King has under the Constitution the right of naming and dismissing ministers; of dissolving the Chambers; and of withholding his signature and refusing to sanction bills that have been passed. Beyond a certain discretion in the selection of the politician whom he thinks able to command a majority in the Chamber in situations when party politics is in a confused state, he has no prerogative. The ministers determine on a dissolution only in case of a parliamentary defeat. The royal veto on legislation is a dead letter. It has never been exercised. The popular veto invited at the discretion of the King, by the advice of his responsible ministers—for the counter-signature of the ministers would be necessary to an appeal to the referendum—was strongly opposed by Frère-Orban and the rest of the old *doctrinaire* school, who declared that it would destroy the value and efficiency of a Chamber composed of the selected and trained political guides of the people to have its decisions reversed by the ignorant masses; and that for the King to descend into the arena of party politics and contend with the parliamentary majority, appealing to the support of a popular majority, would extinguish the principle of the irresponsibility of the sovereign and lower the dignity and prestige of the throne. M. de Laveleye, on the other hand, defended the referendum in a remarkable series of articles written just before his death. His principal argument in its favor is as follows:

The referendum is the only means left to the King to exercise his right of veto. Take any treatise upon public legislation. There is not one which fails to recognize that the royal veto is a necessary prerogative of the crown in a constitutional Government. But under the present system of parliamentary representation it is a dead letter; thus, a principle which science declares indispensable to constitutional royalty has, in point of fact, ceased to exist.

In England, where we look for our model of a parliamentary *régime*, the veto has not been employed since 1707 under Queen Anne. In his well-known work, " The English Constitution," Bagehot says that it is not imagined in England that the Queen could withhold her consent from a law voted by Parliament. And it is the same everywhere. The veto as a weapon is as completely out of date as the silex of prehistoric times.

Should we desire, however, in accordance with the teaching of science, that the veto should be an effectual instrument in the hands of the King, a real power and not the phantom of a right, we must allow him the means, before using it, of consulting the nation. If the result be unfavorable to the law, the King may, in all security, withhold his sanction. If, on the contrary, the people approve, the King can yield to their will clearly expressed.

The President of the United States may make use of the veto without misgiving, because his office is temporary. For a hereditary monarch the case is different. An unpopular veto carried into effect in opposition to the wishes of the majority of the nation may weigh upon an entire reign and even compromise the future of a dynasty. It was the employment of the veto by Louis XVI which gave the first blow to the French monarchy in 1790 before any one, Robespierre included, had thought of proclaiming a republic.

The King accedes to the throne in virtue of the law of succession. He has no means of bringing himself in touch with his people. If he has recourse to the veto he may appear to be actuated by motives of personal or dynastic interests, though he may have nothing else in view than the pure advancement of the nation. For this reason he abstains from using it.

While Paul Janson was as earnest an advocate of the referendum as M. Beernaert, the Prime Minister, M. Woeste, leader of the Extreme Right, was as strongly opposed to it as M. Frère-Orban. The friends of the project did not expect that the procedure would be resorted to except very rarely, but believed that it would prove a safeguard against unpopular measures which have many times been thrust upon the country against its manifest desire. Dissolution of the Chambers is a measure which is not often resorted to in Belgium, and when it occurs the legislative question that precipitated it is liable to be swamped by the multifarious interests of party politics. Often the King has been besieged with petitions praying him to veto unpopular measures. With the referendum at his disposal he could lay the question before the people, who could ratify or reject a particular law, such as the sudden reversal of the Liberal educational policy by the Conservatives when they came into power, without plunging the country into an electoral contest.

The debate on revision was opened on April 26. The Chamber agreed to submit most of the proposed articles to revision. For the revision of Article XLVII, which opens up the question of universal suffrage, the vote was almost unanimous. As an alternative to an unrestricted franchise M. Janson had declared his willingness to accept household suffrage rather than endanger revision. The submission of Article XXVI to amendment—that is, the consideration of the referendum—was approved by a vote of 78 to 48. The proposals for the proportional representation of minorities and the adjudication of contested elections by the courts were, however, defeated, and M. Beernaert contemplated resigning because a section of the Catholic party had deserted him. He declared that he and his colleagues would resign before the elections if the Right persisted in preventing the question of the referendum from being laid before the electors, and on March 24 the Right signified their submission by passing a vote of confidence. After the decision of the Chambers in favor of revision they were dissolved in accordance with the Constitution, and new elections had to be held in time to have the new Parliament meet within forty days after the dissolution. It was the first dissolution in the history of the country that fell at the regular biennial period when half the Chamber had in any case to be renewed. The new Chambers constituted a Constituent Assembly in which two thirds of the members were required to be present for the discussion of any amendment to the Constitution, and a two-third majority was necessary to carry an amendment. Parliament was dissolved on May 24, and June 14 was appointed for the elections.

In the elections the Liberals won several seats from the Clerical-Conservatives, thereby reducing their majority considerably. In the old Chamber there were 138 members altogether, and of these 44 were Liberals and 94 Clericals, while in the Senate 50 out of 69 were Clericals and 19 were Liberals. The members of the lower house were increased in proportion to the growth of population to 152 and the Senators to 76. The reduction in the strength of the Clericals was chiefly owing to the consolidation of the divided Liberals of Brussels in favor of universal suffrage, which gave them an overwhelming majority in the capital, where the Conservatives have been in the ascendency for eight years, and increased their representation in the Chamber from 3 to 18 and in the Senate won for them 8 seats. The old Liberal party virtually retired, leaving the field to the Radicals. The Moderate Conservatives, on the other hand, were pushed aside by the Clerical extremists. The election was therefore a victory for universal suffrage, which M. Woeste avowed his intention of using for the purpose of establishing a thoroughly religious system of elementary education. The ballotings on June 21 for 8 contested seats in the Chamber and 4 in the Senate decided the final proportion of the parties in the Constituent Chambers. The Clericals had 90 seats in the Chamber against 60 obtained by the Liberals, and thus the majority of 50 commanded by the Ministry in the last Parliament was reduced to 32. In the Senate the Clericals won 46 and their opponents 30 seats, reducing the Conservative majority from 31 to 16.

The Constituent Chambers were opened on July 11. The expected trial of strength between the Prime Minister and M. Woeste was avoided by the declaration of M. Beernaert that the Cabinet would not stake its fate on the referendum or household suffrage or any part of the revision scheme, but would let the Government proposals be dealt with by a committee which should endeavor, before the reassembling of the Parliament in November, so to amend them as to secure the requisite two-third majority.

Anarchist Terrorism.—On July 26 a jury at Liége brought in a verdict against 9 out of 16 Anarchists who were tried for plotting dynamite explosions. The culprits were sentenced to long terms of imprisonment, Moineau, the most deeply incriminated, being doomed to twenty-five years' hard labor and twenty years more of police supervision; Wolffs and Beaujean to twenty years of penal servitude ; Mateyssen, Marcotty, Lacroix, and Nossent to fifteen years; and Hansen and Guilmot to ten and three years of simple imprisonment. The outrages for which they were convicted were committed in Liége on May 1 and 2, and during the two months preceding the May-day labor celebration. Moineau, who was a traveling salesman, while the others were workmen and miners, was charged with having taken a prominent part with Nossent, Wolffs, and Charles Berré, who was acquitted, in the actual commission of the crimes, while Jacques Berré, who escaped conviction with his brother, was believed to have been concerned

with Beaujean in the making of the bombs and infernal machines.

On March 16 the criminal court at Liége had found three men, named Hansen, Bustin, and Langendorf, guilty of the theft of 500 pounds of dynamite from a powder mill in the neighboring village of Ombret, and of an attempt to blow up the mill for the purpose of concealing the robbery. Hansen was sentenced to imprisonment for fifteen years and his companions for twelve years. The presiding judge received letters of intimidation, and two days after the conclusion of the trial a dynamite cartridge was found on the doorstep of the house of the commissioner of police, M. Mignon. On the evening of May 1 a dynamite bomb was exploded at the residence of Senator de Selys, and another before that of his son; a third one went off in the church of St. Martin with a tremendous detonation, shattering beautiful mediæval stained-glass windows; and a fourth was found with an extinguished fuse. The consternation produced by these attempts was redoubled when, on the following night, a cartridge burst with terrific force, doing great damage to the house of Count Minette, which is in the same street in which the first outrages occurred. On May 4 Beaujean was arrested, and in his house were found dynamite and materials for manufacturing bombs. One of his accomplices, Lacroix, on being arrested, was induced to turn state's evidence, and, from information obtained from him, the rest of the gang were caught. The explosives used were forcite, stolen from the Baneux powder mills, and dynamite mixed with coarse gunpowder, stolen a year before from a factory at Flemalle. On the evening of the day on which Beaujean and Lacroix were arrested, a cartridge with a burning fuse attached was discovered in one of the suburbs.

BOLIVIA, a republic in South America. The Constitution of Oct. 28, 1880, vests the legislative power in a Senate and House of Representatives, and the executive power in a President, who is elected for four years by direct universal suffrage. There are 18 Senators and 68 Representatives. Aniceto Arce became President on Aug. 6, 1888.

Finances.—The revenue for 1891 was estimated at 3,321,280 bolivianos or silver dollars, and the expenditure at 3,613,698 bolivianos. The internal debt in 1890 amounted to $4,450,000, and the foreign debt, which is being rapidly extinguished, to $622,121.

Defense.—The regular army numbers only 140 officers and 1,112 men. The military strength of the republic consists in a well-organized militia of 20,000 men, which can be doubled in case of war.

Commerce and Production.—Bolivia is a country of great natural wealth. Wool-bearing animals, such as the vicuña, alpaca, guanaco, llama, and hairy goat, and the chinchilla, nutria, and other fur-bearing animals, and an abundance of horses, mules, and cattle are found in the cold and temperate regions. The African dromedary is bred in the south. The woods produce cabinet and dye woods, caoutchouc in inexhaustible quantity, cork, cinchona, jalap, sarsaparilla, copaiba, ipecac, camphor, balsams, etc. Cotton of three varieties of color, quillay or vegetable soap, agave, hemp, tobacco, vanilla, coffee that vics with Mocha, coca, the best cacao grown in South America, sugar-cane, and the fruits, grains, and vegetables of the temperate and torrid zones do not complete the list. Among the mineral products, besides gold and silver, are copper, tin, mercury, zinc, lead, alum, platinum, magnetic iron ore, coal, white alabaster and the clear kind called berenguela, marbles of many kinds, syenite, lapis lazuli, jasper, porphyry, agate, emeralds, opals, and other precious stones, pumice, saltpeter, borax, chalk, and magnesia.

The commerce can only be roughly estimated. The exports amount probably to $20,000,000 a year and the imports to $15,000,000. There is scarcely any direct trade with the United States, but American cottons and dry goods, hardware, machinery, and kerosene are imported through the Peruvian port of Arica and sold by the British, French, and German merchants, who have the foreign trade in their hands. A large proportion of the exports consists of silver ore, which is shipped down the La Plata to Buenos Ayres and thence to Europe.

Communications.—The seacoast territory formerly belonging to Bolivia was taken from her by Chili at the end of the war of 1879-'80. The commerce of the country has been greatly hampered for the lack of external communications. This has been partially supplied by the railroad connecting some of the richest districts with the Chilian port of Antofagasta. The line from Antofagasta to Ascotan on the Bolivian frontier has been in existence for two or three years. It was carried to Uyumi and thence to the rich silver-mining district of which Huanchaca is the center, and on May 15, 1892, the mining district of Ururo was also brought into communication with the sea by the continuation of the branch line from Huanchaca which was opened on that date.

Presidential Election.—The election of a successor to Aniceto Arce in the presidential chair took place on May 3, 1892. The candidates were ex-President Pacheco and Gen. Camacho, known from his services in the war with Chili, who were put forward by the Liberal and Democratic parties, and ex-Minister Mariano Baptista, the representative of the Conservative or Clerical party, who was the Government nominee. The Opposition hoped that the voting would be so close that the decision as to the President-elect would have to be rendered by Congress, and therefore they made strenuous efforts to elect their candidates to the national Legislature. The campaign was so heated that violent collisions took place between the rival factions. The Government was accused of using the military to coerce electors and of arresting politicians of the Opposition without cause, and the priests were charged with interfering to the extent of excommunicating political adversaries. When the election resulted in the triumph of Baptista the defeated parties were not inclined to acquiesce, but showed a disposition to unite for the purpose of contesting with arms the result of the ballot. At the first sign of a rebellion several prominent Liberals were banished. A state of siege was proclaimed, which was continued after the inauguration of the new President on Aug. 6. An attempt to prevent the installation of the new President by an in-

surrectionary rising starting from Oruro was suspected, and just before the inauguration Gen. Camacho and 16 Deputies and others were conducted across the frontier. Dr. Mariano Baptista before his candidature was Minister of Bolivia at Buenos Ayres, where he concluded a delimitation treaty with the Argentine Government which was denounced as unpatriotic by his political enemies. In his final message to Congress the retiring President recommended the lowering of the export duties in view of the fall in the price of silver, and the levying of higher imposts on imports, especially on alcoholic liquors. In the new Congress there were only 29 Liberals against 49 Conservatives in both houses. The Liberal Deputies refused to attend until the Government should explain its action in deporting some of their number. In order to get Gen. Camacho out of the way the President offered him the post of Minister to Peru, which was declined. The Cabinet was made up with Luis Pas at the head as Minister of Foreign Affairs and Worship, with Señores Lisi-Mano, Gutierez, Fernandez, Alonzo Joaquin Ichaso, and Bishop Coronados for his colleagues.

Indian Revolt.—The Bolivian Government in 1892 had to contend with the most serious uprising of the aborigines that has occurred in many years. The semicivilized Indians in the settled districts of the north, around Lake Titicaca, who are reduced to a kind of peonage and have had to suffer more or less oppression, goaded by real or fancied wrongs, banded together to the number of about 3,000, partly armed with firearms, and menaced the white settlements and missions. They killed a number of people and committed depredations, but were quieted without much display of force.

In the southeastern part of the country, on the borders of Brazil and the Argentine Republic, where there are only Indian missions and scattered haciendas of Bolivian, Chilian, and Argentine pioneers and a small agricultural population of Christian half-breeds, a rebellion that had been planned, for the insurgents were supplied with French and American rifles, spread like wildfire among the savage tribes, who were exasperated at the encroachments of the whites on their lands. A crafty old Indian of Cururuyuqui is said to have worked upon the fanaticism of the wild Indians, or *barbaros*, as they are called, by prophesying that the time had arrived for the overthrow of the *carays* or Christians, and the restoration to the Indians of the country of which they had been robbed. He represented a certain young man who went about with him as the son of their heathen deity who had been sent to be their king. At the time set by the prophet the Indians rose simultaneously through the eastern part of Bolivia. The Chaco Indians on the Brazilian and Argentinian side of the line joined their brethren in Bolivia. The Chiriguanos of the Andes distriet, who were accustomed to work for the whites, joined the wild Tobas. The missions of Santa Rosa and Cuevo and the village of Garandaiti were demolished and every person was killed. Wherever a Christian family was found, whether of Spanish or of Indian descent, old and young were brutally murdered. Houses, crops, and herds of cattle and llamas were destroyed. The Tobas were joined by the Itaquizi, Tatapeyua, Membiray, Yuti, and Gamire Indians. The towns of Yuti and Numbiti were burned to the ground. The inmates of the Nunavi mission and the people who had taken refuge there were massacred. Trading parties between Tanja and Vera Cruz were waylaid and butchered. Some of the Indians were armed with rifles, but the majority carried bows, hide shields bound on their left arms, and the stout, sharp *machetes* which serve both as weapons and utensils in the woods of South America. Whoever was struck by their poisoned arrows died. The revolt spread through the republic, and the Bolivian troops, badly armed and badly officered, were able to do little more than guard the towns. In the fights that occurred between Bolivian soldiers, like their savage adversaries, spared neither age nor sex. The first engagement occurred on Jan. 28, when Gen. Ramon Gonzalez led 200 Government troops armed with Remingtons and carbines and 1,000 Indian auxiliaries against the strongly intrenched Tobas and Chiriguanos, said to be 8,000 strong, at Cururuyuqui and put them to flight, killing 900. The Indians in former wars had never been known to throw up breastworks, nor had they ever fought so steadily and effectively. The Bolivians were unable to follow up their victory for lack of ammunition. The routed Indians retired to the mountain fastnesses of Aguaraygua, and after a few skirmishes the other bands in the Cordillera province were broken up and the district in which the rebellion began was temporarily cleared of hostiles. Yet the heathen tribes in the forests of the east and the mountains of the south were inflamed, and for months outbreaks occurred intermittently in various parts of the country. The Itaqnize, Camiri, and Huraca Indians committed horrible outrages. The few skirmishes that the Bolivian forces had with the insurgents made little impression on them. But in the early part of the summer they ceased their attacks and retired for a time to their homes, waiting till they could provide themselves with better arms.

Settlement with Chili.—Bolivia was the only State that, during their conflict with Balmaceda's Government, recognized the Congressists of Chili as a belligerent power. They were compelled to do so because the Congressists had the ports of Antofagasta and Tacna, and were the custodians of the revenues collected on imports for Bolivia. Nevertheless, the act was an important service to the Chilian insurgent party and a risky business for Bolivia, because it exposed her to the vengeance of the Balmacedists in case they won. Before the civil war broke out Balmaceda presented an ultimatum to the Bolivian Government, in which he demanded the complete cession of the territory taken from Bolivia in the war, fixing as the boundaries of the surrendered tract the Loa river in the north, the twenty-third parallel in the south, and in the east the line occupied at the time of the cessation of hostilities. The commercial arrangements agreed on at the armistice were to be embodied in the treaty. Chili was to build a narrow-gauge railroad from Arica to La Paz, and the section built on Bolivian soil was to be paid for by the Bolivian Government in fifty years by means of a sinking fund of one per cent. per annum; but in case the popular vote of the districts should restore Tacna and Arica to Peru in 1893, then Bolivia

should assume the entire railroad debt and pay an interest of five per cent. a year and one per cent. amortization. Bolivia was to engage to build no railroad that did not terminate at some point between Arica and Antofagasta, and should make no alliance at any time that was not approved by Chili. The Bolivian tariff system, so far as it affected Chilian interests, was to be regulated by mutual agreement.

These conditions would have reduced Bolivia to economical and political dependence upon Chili. From the new Government of Chili, bound as it was by gratitude to the Bolivians, much better terms could be obtained. In 1892 a treaty was arranged, of which the following are the principal provisions: (1) Bolivia makes a final cession of its coast territory within the limits of the actual Chilian occupation. (2) Chili will pay Bolivia's external debt, amounting to 6,604,000 bolivianos, of which 1,200,000 bolivianos represent the war indemnity due to the Huanchaca Silver-mining Company; 1,600,000 bolivianos the like claim of the Corocoro copper mine; 252,-000 bolivianos the damages due to the Chilian company of Oruro; 850,000 bolivianos a debt owed to Lopez Garcia; 788,000 bolivianos one due the Guarantee Bank of Chili; 250,000 bolivianos an indemnity for the Mejillones Railroad concession; 50,000 bolivianos money advanced by Garcia; and 1,614,000 bolivianos arrears of interest. (3) The importation of Chilian articles into Bolivia is subject to the regular rates of duty prescribed in the Bolivian tariff, while Chili grants to Bolivia free transit to and from the ports in direct communication with the frontier, and acknowledges the complete independence of Bolivia in tariff matters. (4) Chilian alcohol pays the same duties as foreign kinds.

BRAZIL, a republic occupying nearly half of South America. Each of the old provinces of the empire and the Federal District, which is to be reserved in the center of Brazil, forms a State governing itself and safe from the interference of the Federal Government except for the defense of the frontiers, the preservation of order, and the execution of the Federal laws. Customs, stamps, postage rates, and paper currency come within the province of the National Legislature, which consists of two houses. Members of the House of Representatives are elected for three years by the people of the Federal District and of the several States, in the proportion of 1 to every 70,000 inhabitants. Each State sends 3 Senators, whose term is nine years, one third retiring every three years. The President is elected, like the Senators, by electoral colleges in the States and the district. His term is six years, and he can not succeed himself. His powers are much the same as those of the President of the United States. Gen. Floriano Peixotto, who was the Vice-President and constitutional successor to the presidency, succeeded Marshal Deodoro da Fonseca when the latter resigned on Nov. 23, 1891.

(For area and population, see "Annual Cyclopædia" for 1891.)

Finances.—The actual revenue in 1888 was 144,969,654 milreis, and the expenditure was 146,-047,490 milreis. For 1889 a revenue of 160,060.744 milreis was expected, while the appropriations amounted to 184,565,947 milreis. The estimates for 1890 were 139,340,000 milreis of income and 153,147,844 milreis of expenditure, and those for 1891 showed 142,989.500 milreis of receipts and 151,219,720 milreis of expenditure. The budget proposed for 1892 brought the receipts up to 180,444,000 milreis, of which 98,820,000 milreis were set down to import duties, 25,020,000 milreis to export duties, 51,984,000 milreis to internal duties, 500,000 milreis to port dues, and 4,120,000 milreis to extraordinary receipts. The proposed expenditure was 240,724,558 milreis, of which 99,100,875 milreis were assigned to public works, 62,661.315 milreis to financial administration, 33,231,478 milreis to military affairs, 15,-131,351 milreis to the navy, 15,968,545 milreis to education, 7.790,072 milreis to internal affairs, 5,031,197 milreis to justice, and 1.809,725 milreis to foreign affairs. These estimates were revised and proposals submitted later which equalized the budget by bringing up the receipts from ordinary sources to 207,992,000 milreis and cut down the expenditure to 205,948,000 milreis. (The milreis has a par value of 56 cents. The exchange value corresponded with this in January, 1890, but it has fluctuated greatly since, going down in September, 1891, below 30 cents.)

The national debt in December, 1889, was officially stated to be 1,072,062,138 milreis, which is equal to $585,345,927. The foreign debt then amounted to $148,036,500. The bonds or *apolices* representing the bulk of the domestic loans bear 5 per cent. interest. On May 31, 1891, the foreign debt was reported officially to be 267,-097,778 milreis, and the internal debt to be 536,-844,800 milreis, not including a floating debt of 138,415,128 milreis, which made the total 942,-357,706 milreis. There is a sinking fund of 1 per cent. per annum for the redemption of the foreign debt, and when the bonds are above par they are called in by lot to be paid off, but when below par they are bought in the open market.

The Army and Navy.—The active army in 1891 numbered 1,600 officers and 28,877 men, not including a gendarmerie of about 15,000 men. Men serve six years in the active army and three in the reserve, and they are conscripted into the service by lot, no substitution being allowed. There are 36 battalions of infantry, 12 regiments of cavalry, 5 regiments of field artillery, 5 battalions of fortress artillery, and two battalions of engineers.

The navy in 1891 consisted of 4 sea-going ironclads, 6 armored vessels for coast defense, 5 first-class, 6 second-class, and 3 third-class torpedo boats, 1 torpedo school-ship, 5 unarmored cruisers, 2 corvettes, 17 unprotected gunboats, and 15 other vessels. The "Riachuelo," of 5,700 tons displacement, and the "Aquidaban," somewhat smaller, are English steel vessels built between 1883 and 1885, both protected by a belt of 11-inch steel-faced armor, with double turrets plated with 10-inch armor, each mounting 4 20-ton breech-loading guns.

On May 21 the "Salimões," which had been dispatched with other vessels to aid in suppressing the rebellion in the State of Matto Grosso, was wrecked off Cape Polonio on the Uruguayan coast and went down with Captain Castro and 125 of the crew, only 5 being saved. These said that they had been sent ashore for assistance after the steamer struck a sunken reef, and after

they put off a great explosion was heard, when she sank immediately in deep water.

Commerce and Production.—Only a small part of the cultivable soil is utilized and none of the valuable mines and forests have yet been exploited to any extent. Coffee, which is the chief product, is grown only in three provinces, in which the crop in 1887 amounted to $65,000,-000. Sugar is the next most important commercial product. Cotton also is grown, and is manufactured in subsidized mills. Cattle, of which there are 27,000,000 head in the country, are raised on a commercial scale in the south, and there is a considerable export of hides. From the northern ports large quantities of rubber are exported. Tobacco is also raised for export. The total value of the exports was 212,-592,000 milreis in 1888, 309,000,000 milreis in 1889, and 317,822,000 milreis in 1890. There were 4,526,906 bags of coffee, weighing 60 kilos each, shipped from Rio, Santos, and Victoria in 1890, 104,536 tons of sugar from Pernambuco, 18,682 tons of rubber from Para and Manaos, and 749,301 hides from Rio Grande do Sul. The United States take a third of the exports, Great Britain nearly the same proportion, and France and Germany about one tenth each. Export duties are levied on the principal products in addition to heavy duties on all imports. The value of the imports was 260,999,000 milreis in 1888, 221,621,000 milreis in 1889, and 260,100,000 milreis in 1890. Of the imports, 45 per cent. come from Great Britain, 17 per cent. from France, 12 per cent. from Germany, and 10 per cent. from the United States. The imports from the United States in 1889 amounted to $9,276,-908, consisting of wheat, flour, and other bread stuffs, mineral oil, iron and steel manufactures, cotton and woolen goods, timber, and lard.

Railroads, Posts, and Telegraphs.—There were 5,900 miles of completed railroads in 1890 and 984 miles under way, while 4,938 miles of new railroads and extensions were projected. The Government owns 14 lines with a length of 2,091 miles. Of the companies' lines 1,748 miles are guaranteed by the National and 1,754 miles by the State governments. The capital expenditure on all the railroads up to 1888 was 448,-148,327 milreis, of which 195,636,000 milreis were spent on State lines. The gross earnings of the State railroads in 1890 were 15,834,931 milreis, and the expenses 12,760,331 milreis. The guaranteed interest on the private lines is for the most part 6 or 7 per cent. The total guaranteed capital in 1888 amounted to 220,475,-850 milreis.

The telegraphs belong to the Government. In 1890 there were 7,765 miles of lines, with 12,467 miles of wires. The number of messages in 1890 was 750,621. The receipts amounted to 2,042,755 milreis, and the expenses, including extensions, to 2,883,950 milreis.

The post office during 1890 forwarded 18,822,-148 letters and 19,280,135 newspapers and circulars.

Extraordinary Session of Congress.—An extraordinary session of Congress, called in December, 1891, was closed on Feb. 22. The budget was voted hurriedly in pretty nearly the shape in which it was left on Nov. 3, when Congress adjourned. The bills vetoed by President Fonseca on incompatibility and on the crimes for which the President is subject to impeachment, which the Constitution had left to be defined by Congress, as also the rules of procedure for the trial of the President and the ministers of state, were passed over the veto. The most important work of the session was the enactment of a new electoral law. In the past every ministry has been able to carry the elections, no matter how unpopular its acts had been. Only a few members of the Congress that passed the measure had obtained their seats independently of official influence. One provision of the new law was that, in case the presidency or vice-presidency should become vacant within two years from the beginning of the term, a new election should be held within three months after the vacancy occurs. This required an election to be held before Feb. 23, 1892, for a President to take the place of Gen. Fonseca, who was deposed on Nov. 23, 1891; yet no preparations were made to carry out the law. The reciprocity treaty concluded with the United States by the Balmaceda Government affected injuriously the interests of Europeans who have controlled the trade of Brazil, and was therefore an object of attack for the party that brought about Balmaceda's fall. The Minister of Finance made inquiries regarding the results of reciprocity for the purpose of gathering data that should guide the Government in negotiations for the revision of the treaty, especially in reference to the Brazilian products that suffer from competition with those of the United States, and the extension of exemption of duty to grades of sugar above No. 16, Dutch standard. The Director General of Customs suggested that American lard, butter, cheese, cotton goods, canned food, and timber should pay the same duties as like articles from other countries, and that American beans, pork, cotton-seed oil, and tools should be taken off the free list. Dr. Ruy Barbosa, the Minister of Finance in the Provisional Government, declared that Dr. Salvador de Mendonça, the Brazilian minister in Washington, was instructed to negotiate a treaty of reciprocity only on condition that the United States should not make similar treaties with Spain and England.

The Administration of Peixotto. — The vices of the personal government and military dictatorship which Marshal Deodoro da Fonseca had established with the co-operation of corrupt military officers and politicians and dishonest speculators could not be extirpated at once when Marshal Floriano Peixotto assumed the presidency, whatever will the latter may have had to reorganize the government of the country on a democratic basis. Fonseca's creatures still held the places of power and influence, and the new President dared not attempt to dissolve Congress for fear of following Gen. Deodoro in his fall. The posts in the civil and military services, in the judiciary, and even in the scientific institutes, were still largely occupied by the favorites of the deposed Dictator. The first undertaking to which President Peixotto turned his attention was the removal of the adherents of Fonseca who had not been deposed from the governorships of States at the time of his overthrow. He sent war vessels and marines to Dr. Thaumaturgo de Azvedo, Governor of Amazonas,

with a demand that he should hand over the administration, but the latter replied that he held his office not from Rio Janeiro, but from the provincial Congress. The commander was not inclined to carry out the wishes of the President by force, and therefore the force was withdrawn on, before which the Governor retired because he possessed no artillery. In Goyaz Vice-Governor Mara was forcibly removed by Lieut.-Col. Abrantes, who arrived on Feb. 15, 1892, with a battalion of infantry. In this way a military dictatorship was introduced in these two States. In Ceará the military academy was employed in carrying out the designs of Peixotto. The officers sided with the cadets in various quarrels that they had with civilians and with the civil guard, though some turbulent students were placed under arrest and the battalion of infantry in Fortaleza that protected the Governor from the attacks of the students was relieved, and the gunboat that lay in the harbor had orders to protect the students from their enemies. By the aid of the Government vessel the police and the small armed force at the disposal of the Governor were finally worsted.

On Jan. 19, 1892, the prisoners confined in Fort Santa Cruz, at Rio Janeiro, 160 in number, overpowered their guards, and with the weapons thus obtained overcame the soldiers on duty in the forts of Pico and Lago, gained possession of these forts with the munitions of war that they contained, and proceeded to make them ready to receive the forces that the Government would send against them, demanding the restoration of Gen. da Fonseca to the presidency. The Government troops invested the forts on the land side, while the war ships took up their position in the harbor. While they were making their preparations for the attack the rebels kept up a desultory fire without doing much damage. On the following morning the guns of the war vessels opened fire on the forts, while the troops moved upon Fort Pico, which was carried by assault. The defenders of the other fort were forced to surrender by the bombardment. The leader of the rebels took his own life.

On April 11 the Government proclaimed a state of siege in Rio Janeiro in order to suppress a public manifestation to celebrate Marshal Deodoro da Fonseca's restoration to health, and in order to deprive of their immunities the members of Congress who were involved in the demonstration.

According to the Constitution, President Peixotto had not the right to remove or appoint governors, and in several cases changes were effected through political revolts fomented by him without his direct interference. In other parts of the country military rule superseded the civil authorities. The murmurs occasioned by the continuance of this irregular situation led about a fifth of the members of Congress to resign their seats. The general discontent emboldened the friends of the deposed President da Fonseca on April 6 to issue a *pronunciamiento* signed by 13 generals, which condemned in plain terms the methods of the new Dictator and the intervention of the military forces for the removal of governors, and called upon the Vice-President to put an end to the gradual disruption of the Government and prevent the work of Nov. 15, 1889, from lapsing into general anarchy by ordering a speedy election of a President in accordance with the requirements of the Constitution and the last electoral law, free from all military pressure. This declaration was treated by the Government as evidence of a military conspiracy, and the signers, excepting two who recanted, were banished to Amazonas. A number of other military men were imprisoned. In Minas Geraes a movement for the division of the State was fostered and encouraged from Rio Janeiro, and on this account Gen. Cesario Alvim, the Governor, resigned.

Revolt of Matto Grosso.—The vast State of Matto Grosso, covered with great forests and very rich in agricultural, forest, and mineral resources, having gold in every part of the province, abundant deposits of iron, and diamond mines in successful operation, stretches along the borders of Bolivia, and is separated by many hundred miles of impracticable country from the seaboard States, with which it has few commercial or economical interests in common. The most valuable products are medicinal plants, fine woods, cinchona bark, India-rubber, hides, and meat extract. The State has an area of 532,708 square miles, one seventh of the total area of Brazil. The Paraguay river, which is navigable for steamers, affords communication with the outside world. The population does not exceed 90,-000, but the people were strongly imbued with the State-rights doctrine, which caused many conflicts in the time of the empire, and has gained in force since the revolution. In the beginning of April Matto Grosso, by the action of the State Legislature, proclaimed itself an independent nation under the name of Republica Transatlantica. A force of 1,200 men under the command of Col. Barbosa was raised to defend the independence of the new State, which raised its standard of blue and green with a yellow star in the center. The cause of the revolt was an attempt of the central authorities in Rio Janeiro to remove the Governor and to put a man named Eubank in his place. Ever since the overthrow of Fonseca there had been constant interferences in the politics of the State, and one governor after another had been deposed. The revolutionists were well supplied with food, money, small arms, and torpedoes, but their improvised army lacked training and discipline. With the exception of one battalion the troops that manned the Brazilian river squadron were in their favor. The Central Government took active steps immediately to re-establish its authority. A flotilla of six war ships accompanied by a transport carrying a strong body of troops was sent out to suppress the uprising. The "Salimões," which was ordered to convoy the flotilla, was wrecked on a dangerous shoal off the Uruguayan coast. While the boats ascended the Paraguay river a land force was sent by rail to the end of the existing line, whence it was to march into Matto Grosso and form a junction with the troops sent by water, after which the combined forces were to attack Cuyaba, the capital. On May 7 the Government troops, under Col. Ponce, invested Cuyaba. On May 13 the garrison surrendered. In the bombardment much damage was done to the town. The commanders of the battalions of

infantry and artillery that had joined the rebellion were killed after they had surrendered. The gunboat "Iniciadora," which floated the flag of the new republic and had gone to Asuncion to carry dispatches, one of which was addressed to the Brazilian minister to Paraguay, there surrendered to the Brazilian authorities. The minister had gone aboard and asked the commander to return to his allegiance to the Federal Government. He was disposed to comply, but the second in command spoke against it, and ordered the crew to fire. Instead of that they cheered the Federal Government, and the commander and lieutenant were arrested. Col. Barbosa and Major Hannibal, the revolutionary leaders, kept up the struggle, having to contend not only against the better organization and greater resources of the military forces of the Government, but against the numerous hostile faction among the people of Matto Grosso which extended aid to the Federal troops. When people were caught in the act of furnishing supplies to the troops they were barbarously maltreated. In consequence of the civil war, food became scarce and dear. One position after another fell into the hands of the Government party, led by Eubank and the forces of Col. Ponce. About July 1 they captured Corumba, and afterward the two forces joined and swept the rebels from their remaining positions. Most of the insurgent leaders escaped into Bolivia, orders having gone forth to kill them when caught.

Conflict in Rio Grande.—In Rio Grande do Sul the contest between rival factions led to the revival of the movement for the secession of the southern provinces and the organization of a new republic. The first republican Governor of Rio Grande was Gen. Camara, Visconde de Pelotas, one of the commanders in the Paraguayan war and one of the leaders of the Liberal party. The chief of the Liberals, Silveira Martins, had been called to Rio Janeiro with the object of making him Minister-President, and there he was arrested at the instance of Minister Bocayuva. This greatly increased his popularity in Rio Grande. On his release he went to Europe, and meanwhile Julio de Castilhos, who was secretary to the Governor, came to the front in the southern province. He was one of the old Republicans and Comtists, and was the author of the Constitution adopted on July 14, 1891, an impracticable instrument that conferred the legislative as well as the executive powers upon the President of the State and gave him the right to nominate the Vice-President, while the Assembly had little left to it to do besides voting the appropriations. This opened the door to corruption and converted the officials of the state, even the school teachers, into an army of electioneering retainers for the chief of the state and his clique. On July 15, 1891, the Constituent Assembly elected Castilhos for the first President of the State. He remained in the office till on Nov. 12 a revolution, prepared long beforehand, but precipitated by the *coup d'état* of Marshal Fonseca, drove him out and at the same time swept away his Constitution. Gen. Barreto Leite succeeded him as chief executive, but the leaders of the revolution were Dr. Silva Tavares, his brother, Gen. João Nuñez da Silva Tavares, Gen. Pereira da Costa, Lieut.-Col. Onofre dos Santos, and Gen. Ozorio. The revolutionists captured Santa Anna do Livramento and many prisoners without bloodshed, and Gen. Tavares moved upon Porto Alegre ; but Castilhos issued a manifesto and then vacated the presidency without striking a blow, as more than half the troops had gone over to the revolutionists. The aged Gen. Barreto Leite was made Provisional President by acclamation, while a junta was formed consisting of Dr. Joaquim Francisco de Assis Brazil, Dr. João de Barros Cassal, and Gen. Luiz da Rocha Ozorio. In February, 1892, Dr. Barros Cassal was elected President. The old Federalist party split up into irreconcilable factions of Parliamentarists and Positivists, and the strife between the parties, which Silveira Martins endeavored fruitlessly to allay, created revolutionary conditions, which the new Governor only aggravated by issuing despotic edicts, one of which, prohibiting the publication of any article without the signature of the author, caused nearly every newspaper on March 23 to discontinue its issue. The election, which was to take place on March 21, was postponed till May 13 because the Governor and his party were rapidly losing ground. On March 21, while Silveira Martins was addressing an open-air meeting gathered to greet him on his return, as he fearlessly depicted the disorganized conditions of the country and the degradation of the judiciary and the schools, and then dwelt on the insubordination in the army, the soldiery suddenly attacked the listeners. When the Governor in April expressed the intention of putting off for a third time the elections for a Constituent Assembly that should frame a new Constitution and give the state a regular President, the Federalist party organization declared against it, and in consequence he resigned and Gen. Barreto Leite again became Provisional Governor, being assured of the support of the Central Government. When the day for the elections came round they were nevertheless postponed till June 21 in the interest of the constantly dwindling Government party. This action caused such dissatisfaction that the new Governor resigned and Visconde Pelotas became Provisional Governor. A few days later he also laid down the office, selecting as his successor Gen. Tavares. The Opposition, led by Dr. Castilhos, who still claimed to be the rightful Governor and whose adherents were also partisans of Marshal da Fonseca, would not accept his choice, and Castilhos, aided by the police, seized the Government buildings and installed Dr. Victorino Monteiros as Vice-Governor.

Gen. Tavares, the rival Vice-Governor, who was at Bage, prepared to fight, and called on the Federal authorities for aid. The Government forces in Rio Grande were at first directed to take no part in the conflict, according to a statement published in the official gazette at Rio Janeiro. A Government gunboat, the " Marajo." opened fire on Porto Alegre, but was repelled. Near Bage several skirmishes took place, in which the forces of Castilhos were generally successful. The people supported Castilhos generally. An army of over 6,000 men was raised, and after several fights near Bage and elsewhere the antirevolutionary Conservative party had to succumb. The civil strife was the outcome of the differences

of opinion regarding the organization of the National Government, represented by Castilhos and Silveira Martins, of whom the one desired a federation free from parliamentarism, with a chief of the executive responsible for the acts of the secretaries of state, while the other advocated a centralized republic having an irresponsible chief with ministers who should represent the opinions prevailing in the Parliament. The ideas of Martins prevailed, and he was made Provisional Governor. The Sebastianistas, or advocates of the restoration of the empire with Dom Pedro's grandson on the throne, were encouraged in Rio Grande and other States by the triumph of the centralist idea in the greatest State of the federation.

Italian Riot in Santos.—In consequence of an altercation between the captain of a sailing vessel and the collector of customs at Santos, in which the police intervened, the Italian colony of the city of São Paulo, on July 2, assembled to protest against the treatment of a fellow-countryman, and in the course of the meeting the excitement rose to such a pitch that the more hot-headed of them assumed a menacing attitude, tearing down a Brazilian flag and beating the police who attempted to stop them. The Brazilian populace rose after the troops had dispersed the Italian rioters, seized the Italian flags wherever they were displayed, and wrecked the office of the Italian newspaper. Santos is the port which gives access to the State of São Paulo, in which many thousand Italians have settled. In the fight, which lasted through the night, several persons were killed on both sides. An inquiry was made, and for the satisfaction of the Italian Government, the collector of customs at Santos was dismissed and the troops concerned in the fight were sent elsewhere. The explanations of the Brazilian Government were regarded as satisfactory, and the incident was closed after an interchange of diplomatic notes.

The Regular Session.—When the time came for the opening of Congress, on May 3, a quorum could not be obtained because many of the Opposition members refused to attend, as a demonstration against the interference of the Government in the affairs of the individual States and its neglect to provide for the election of a new President. At last the session was opened on May 12.

An amnesty bill for the pardon and release of persons imprisoned and banished in virtue of the Government decree of April 12 was carried in the Senate. Congress approved a proposition to postpone the election of a President till the end of the year. The Supreme Court refused to order the release of prisoners held in virtue of the decrees of military tribunals, but in the mean time the President proclaimed the amnesty of the conspirators of Santa Cruz and of others who had been engaged in similar enterprises in São Paulo and other places. The committee of the Chamber advised conforming with the wish of the Senators regarding amnesty, providing the latter left the initiative to the Chamber of Deputies and agreed to an act of indemnity, approving all the measures taken by the Government in regard to the seditious movement of April 10. On July 22 the Chamber passed an

amnesty bill for all political exiles. A commission appointed by the Minister of Finance to
study the means of putting an end to the financial crisis recommended amplifying the powers
granted by a law of 1875 to come to the aid of
great enterprises in extraordinary circumstances
by making advances to the banks out of the
funds of the treasury, and also the issue of bonds
of the character of the five-twenties of the United
States. On June 8 the minister, Rodrigues
Alves, made an arrangement with the two principal banks of issue whereby they renounced
the privilege that they had of putting into ciren-
lation about 16½ contos of new paper money, and
were allowed one of them to substitute Government bonds for its gold reserve and the other
to receive treasury notes with which to replace
its outstanding circulation of 4,000 contos. In
order to terminate the long-standing boundary
dispute with the Argentine Republic regarding
the territory of the Missions, the Brazilian Government has agreed to refer the question to the
arbitration of the President of the United States,
and sent Baron Aguilar de Andrada as envoy
extraordinary, with Capt. Guillobel and Col.
Cerqueire, in June, to lay the Brazilian case
before Mr. Harrison.

The Senate approved a bill putting limitations
on the declaration of martial law in the future.
It provided that a state of siege can only be
proclaimed when there are 10,000 men in arms
against the Government and that after the cessation of martial law all prisoners who have been
arrested must be handed over to be tried by the
ordinary courts; also that Congress must meet
at once on the proclamation of martial law, in
order to hear the explanations which the President must render, accompanied by proofs. Dr.
Victorino Monteiros, the retiring Vice-President
of Rio Grande, in September was appointed
Federal Minister of Foreign Affairs.

BRITISH COLUMBIA. The opening of the
Canadian Pacific Railroad has begun a revolution in the affairs of the Pacific province. By the
census of 1891, the population of British Columbia had increased, during the preceding decade,
at the rate of 87·56¹ per cent., exceeding in this
respect all other provinces of the Dominion except Manitoba and the Northwest Territories.

Government and Legislature.—The second
session of the Sixth Legislative Assembly was
opened at Victoria, on Jan. 8, 1892. The Lieutenant-Governor, in his opening speech, congratulated the House upon the solid prosperity
of the past year. The public revenue had far
exceeded expectations, with the prospect of a still
more satisfactory increase during the current
year; and the principal industries were, for the
most part, in a thriving condition. Especially
was this the case with respect to the mining industries and to railway extension. The Kootenay
and Columbia Railway had been completed and
in operation for some time, and the practical
completion of the Shuswap and Okanagan Railway is announced. Surveys had been vigorously prosecuted in different parts of the province during the previous season, and thereby
much valuable information had been obtained,
and a continuation of the work was recommended. The Lieutenant-Governor announced
that one of his ministers had gone to London,

where he was successful in floating a 3-per-
cent. inscribed stock loan on terms highly favorable to the province, and this, it was believed,
would enable the public debt to be consolidated
on a most advantageous basis. A further advance
was made during the session in extremely desirable legislation, "with a view to discouraging
speculation in public lands suitable for agricultural purposes," and to the preservation of the
same for actual settlers. The usual amendment
to the mining law, which has become perennial
in British Columbia, was passed as of course;
and amendments were also made in the general
municipal act and in the public-school act.
During the recess the province met with a severe loss in the sudden decease of Hon. John
Robson, the provincial Premier, which took
place in England on June 9, 1892. Mr. Robson
had been leader of the administration since
1883. He was immediately succeeded as Premier
by Hon. Theodore Davie, previously Attorney-
General in the Robson administration.

Trade.—The total exports of British Columbia during the year ending June 30, 1892,
amounted in value to $6,574,989. This exceeds
any previous year's export, the nearest approach
to it, that for the year ending June 30, 1891,
amounting to $6,257,158. This export is made
up as follows: Mining products, $2,979,470;
fisheries, $2,351,083; forest, $425,278; animals
and their produce, $390,854; agricultural prod-
ucts, $25,018; miscellaneous, $31,976; manufactures, $117,942; net product of British Colum-
bia, $253,368; total, $6,574,989.

The total imports for the same year amounted
to $6,495,589. This, too, exceeded the import
of every previous year, that of 1891, the nearest
in amount, showing a return of $5,478,883. Of
the whole amount there was, of dutiable goods,
$4,671,888; free goods, $1,803,105; leaf tobacco,
$20,596; total, $6,495,589.

The duty collected amounted to $1,412,878,
against $1,346,059 in the year ending June 30,
1891.

Railways.—That portion of the Kootenay
river which extends from the great Kootenay
lake to the junction of that river with the Columbia, is unnavigable for craft of any description, owing to rapids and cataracts. This difficulty has been overcome by the recent construction of the Kootenay and Columbia Railway,
26 miles long, the terminal stations being Robson, on the Columbia, and Nelson, on the west
arm of Kootenay lake. The opening of this
short line has had the effect of opening up for
traffic the whole Kootenay district, comprising
an immense tract of the southeastern portion of
the province, recently found to be exceedingly
rich in mineral wealth, but which was all but
inaccessible. On Columbia and Arrow lakes, a
line of steamers now plies between Revelstoke
Station, on the Canadian Pacific Railway, and
Robson. Other steamers run from the head of
Kootenay lake to the international boundary
line. Besides those already mentioned, Ainsworth and Kaslo, on Kootenay lake, and other
new towns are springing up in that vicinity
with rapidity. Another railway line is projected
from the Kootenay, via Slocan river and lake,
through a supposed rich mineral tract, to Na-
kusp, on upper Arrow lake. Another line just

completed is the Shuswap and Okanagan Railroad. This line is about sixty miles long, and extends from Sicamoose station, on the Canadian Pacific Railroad and Shuswap lake, *via* the Spalluma-chaen river to Okanagan lake. This railway opens up what is probably the most fertile and attractive agricultural country in the province.

Mines.—In former years mining for the precious metals in British Columbia was practically restricted to placer digging and washing. Until very recently no other process was really practicable, although gold and silver, in their native matrix, *in situ*, were known to abound. This was owing to the very rugged character of the country. Thus, in some instances, districts that were really rich had to be abandoned, owing to the enormous expense in transporting even the plainest and most condensed of human food to the sites of operations. As for transporting heavy machinery to those sites, that was found to be quite impracticable. The opening up of the Canadian Pacific Railway has very much reduced the expense and difficulty of the miner in these respects, especially in the midland and southern sections of the province. Then, even so short a line as the Kootenay and Columbia Railway has given easy access to an immense tract of rich mining country, comprising the whole of the Kootenay district proper, the Slocan and Salmon river valleys, and other tracts in the vicinity. Nelson, Ainsworth, Pilot Bay, Kaslo, and Slocan are centers of mining operations. For the most part, the ore consists of a native alloy of gold, silver, and copper, in varying proportions, and sometimes one or other of these metals is found wanting. These ores are found in a stratified schistose rock, which is said to be always surrounded by granite. These ores, of which argentiferous galena seems to be most abundant, vary widely in value; but we are assured that those of lower grade are most easily accessible, and are usually found in comparatively large veins. The product of gold for the whole province in 1891 amounted to $429,811 in value, being slightly less than that of the preceding year. But, owing to the heavy duty imposed by the McKinley bill, added to the cost and difficulty of transportation, no shipments of silver ore were made in 1891, although ore to the value of several hundred thousand dollars has been mined and is still lying upon the dumps. Heretofore it was necessary to send this argentiferous galena out of the country, if only to be smelted; but a smelter, with all the necessary requirements, is now about completed at Pilot Bay, on great Kootenay lake. Extensive preparations for quartz mining have been made at West Kootenay, and also large hydraulic works, in the Cariboo country, in anticipation of the succeeding year's mining operations.

The coal deposits of British Columbia that have been opened and worked are all on the east side of Vancouver Island, in the vicinity of Nannimo and Comox. The total output of coal in 1891 was 1,029,097 tons, against 678,140 tons in 1890. The total output for the past year was produced by the several collieries as follows: Nanaimo colliery, 527,457 tons; Wellington, 345,182 tons; East Wellington, 41,666 tons; Union (Comox), 114,792 tons; total, 1,029,097 tons. Of this total, 806,479 tons were exported,

and, for the most part, to California; the remainder represents the home consumption. The progress of the coal-mining industry of the province is shown by the following statistics:

	Output, tons.	Export, tons.
1888	459,300	365,714
1889	579,580	442,675
1890	678,142	508,270
1891	1,029,097	806,479

Preparations have been made for the opening of a coal mine on Tumbo island. This island is almost directly in the route of the Japan steamers and all other vessels passing to and from Burrard inlet.

The yield of platinum for 1891 is estimated at $10,000 in value.

BULGARIA, a principality in eastern Europe, tributary to Turkey, created a self-governing state by the Treaty of Berlin in 1878, which ordered that the Prince of Bulgaria should be elected by the population and confirmed by the Sublime Porte, with the consent of the powers. Ferdinand, Duke of Saxony, born Feb. 26, 1861, the youngest son of Prince August, Duke of Saxony, and Princess Clementine, daughter of Louis Philippe, King of the French, was elected Prince of Bulgaria by the unanimous vote of the Great Sobranje on July 7, 1887, and on Aug. 14, 1887, he assumed the government without the sanction of the great powers or the confirmation of the Porte, which were withheld because the objection of the Russian Government precluded a unanimous agreement among the powers. The Treaty of Berlin provides that Bulgaria shall have a Christian government and a national militia. The legislative authority, by the Constitution of 1879, is vested in a single elective representative chamber, the Sobranje or National Assembly, elected by universal suffrage in the proportion of one member to every 10,-000 inhabitants. Its duration is three years, unless dissolved by the Prince, in which case new elections must be held within four months. The executive authority is vested in a council of ministers responsible to the Prince and to the Sobranje. Eastern Roumelia or South Bulgaria was created an autonomous province of Turkey by the Berlin Treaty, to be administered by a governor-general appointed by the Sublime Porte for five years. On Sept. 17, 1885, it was annexed to Bulgaria by a revolution, and as the result of a conference of the signatory powers the Sultan issued a firman, on April 6, 1886, recognizing the *fait accompli* by appointing Prince Alexander, then Prince of Bulgaria, Governor-General of Roumelia. A commission was appointed to amend the organic statute in order to make it conform to the changed circumstances, and although it never concluded its labors, the province has been practically incorporated in the principality.

Area and Population.—The area of Bulgaria proper is estimated at 24,360 square miles and that of South Bulgaria at 13,500 square miles. The census of Jan. 1, 1888, made the total population 3,154,375, of which number 960,441 lived in South Bulgaria. There were 1,605,389 males and 1,548,986 females. Of the total population, 2,326,250 were Bulgars, 607,-

319 were Turks, and the rest were Greeks, Jews, gypsies, Russians, Servians, and other Slaves, Germans, etc. Sofia, the capital, had 30,428 inhabitants. Bulgaria had 3,844 elementary schools in 1890, in which 129,777 boys and 42,-206 girls were taught. The state subvention for education is 2,000,000 lei or francs per annum. Education is free and obligatory, and the school period is four years. There is a university at Sofia, and a gymnasium in every town of importance.

The Army.—The system of obligatory military service is in force. The army consists of 24 infantry regiments, of 2 battalions each, with a depot battalion for each regiment, 4 cavalry regiments, and 6 regiments of artillery, consisting of 4 batteries of 4 guns each, the battery numbering 120 men, besides 2 artillery depots and 1 battery of siege artillery. The field batteries have 8 guns in time of war. There is 1 company of engineers of 2 battalions and 1 of disciplinary troops. The army is organized in 3 divisions of 2 brigades. The total strength on the peace footing is about 125,000 There is a fleet of 3 war ships, 10 gun sloops, and 2 torpedo boats, manned by 12 officers and 334 men. Bulgaria is guarded on the northern frontier by the fortresses of Vidin, Rustchuk, and Silistria. Varna is a fortified port on the Black Sea, and Shumla is a strong place in the interior.

Finances.—The budget for 1891 makes the total revenue 80,478,700 lei, and the expenditure 80,208,233 lei. The army required 20,617,435 lei; the public debt, 13,078,618 lei; financial administration, 13,720,732 lei; the interior department, 8,385,430 lei; public works, 7,722,243 lei; education, 5,140,985 lei. Of the revenue, 39,-952,000 lei were derived from direct taxes and 15,893,500 lei from customs and excise duties.

The public debt is made up of the remainder of the Russian occupation debt, which is to be extinguished in 1896, and which amounts to 21,-700,000 lei and of loans of 50,000,000 and 30,-000,000 contracted lei in 1887 and 1889. Bulgaria has agreed to pay the contribution of 118,-000 Turkish liras a year to the Porte for Eastern Roumelia, and 21,000 liras that are in arrears. The tribute to be paid to Turkey by Bulgaria on her own account has never been fixed by the powers, and the obligation has thus been suffered virtually to lapse.

Commerce.—Bulgaria is a large producer of wheat, of which great quantities are exported, and also raises wine, silk, tobacco, and considerable quantities of live stock, particularly sheep, goats. and swine. The total value of the exports in 1890 was 71,051,123 lei. The exports of wheat amounted to 54,348,570 lei. Other exports are wool, tallow, attar of roses, butter, cheese, hides, flax, and timber.

The total imports were valued at 84,530,497 lei, of which 26,806,000 lei represent textile manufactures, 19,243,000 lei articles of food and drink, 10,296,000 lei chemical products, 8,363,000 lei metals and metal manufactures, and 5,025,000 lei machinery. Of the total imports, 20,020,397 lei came from Great Britain, 33,005,757 lei from Austria, 10,393,425 lei from Turkey, 5,201,724 lei from Russia, and the rest from France, Germany, Roumania, Belgium, Switzerland, Italy, Servia, Greece, the United States, and other countries.

The United States furnished only 40,652 lei of the imports and received direct none of the exports of Bulgaria. Of the total exports, Turkey received 21,928,218, France 19,496,331, Great Britain 14,936,811, and Austria 5,750,589 lei.

Communications.—The Bulgarian and Eastern Roumelian Railroads had in 1891 a total length of 507 miles. The Oriental Railroad, bringing Constantinople into communication with the European Continental system, passes through the length of Bulgaria, connecting Sofia with Constantinople and with Belgrade.

A railroad is projected to connect Sofia with Salonica and the Mediterranean. The Turkish Government has already granted a concession for the construction of a line that is to traverse Southern Macedonia, running from Salonica, *via* Drama, to Dedeagatch. The proposed railway would descend directly southward from Sofia by the towns of Radomir and Dupnitza, enter Macedonia by the Struma valley, and follow the course of that river to Seres, where it would form a junction with the South Macedonian Railway already mentioned.

The state telegraph lines, including those of Eastern Roumelia, have a total length of 2,800 miles. The number of messages sent in 1890 was 765.295. The post-office traffic in 1890 comprised 8,070,000 pieces, including letters, cards, and newspapers.

Franco-Bulgarian Incident.—Serious complications arose between France and Bulgaria about the expulsion of the French newspaper correspondent Chadourne from Sofia. Chadourne appealed to the French Government, whose *chargé d'affaires* protested against the exulsion as constituting a flagrant violation of treaties, and demanded that the decree should be rescinded and that the Government of the principality should pledge itself in writing not to molest the correspondent in the event of his return to Bulgaria. The Bulgarian Government, in its reply, reminded the acting French diplomatic agent of the repeated representations made by the Government to him regarding the correspondent in question, who, for some time past, had systematically given currency to false and calumnious reports in the European and especially the French press regarding Bulgaria and its Government, and that twice before the Government had decided to expel him, but had refrained from doing so in hopes that, owing to the representations made to the agency and the warnings given to the correspondent, the latter would change his attitude toward the Government. The Bulgarian Government were of the opinion that they had not violated any treaty, and persisted in carrying out the expulsion. Upon receipt of this note the French Government broke off diplomatic relations with Bulgaria, insisting that the French agency should have been advised of the charges against the correspondent, and the request to leave the country should have been conveyed to him through the French agent. His summary apprehension and forcible expulsion before he had any order of expulsion served upon him, and before he could make any arrangements for his departure was a violation of the capitulations. They submitted the whole matter to the Porte. The Porte, after due consideration, decided that the expulsion had been made contrary to the capitulations. Then the Bulgarian Government, through the Ottoman commissioner, communicated to the Porte an apology to be forwarded to the French Government, expressing its regret at not having complied with the capitulations, and declaring that in future it would communicate in writing to the French consular authority any decree of expulsion which might be issued against a French citizen; but should any such person not leave Bulgarian territory within the time fixed in the decree, the princely authorities would then proceed to expel him. The French Government accepted this note as satisfactory. It establishes the right of the Bulgarian Government to give effect to a decree of expulsion against a French subject. The incident was regarded as closed, and diplomatic relations were resumed.

The Vulkovitch Murder.—The Bulgarian diplomatic agent at Constantinople, Dr. Vulkovitch, was murdered on Feb. 24, 1892. In December, 1891, the Bulgarian Government forwarded a letter to the Porte which had been intercepted by the Servian authorities at Belgrade. This letter revealed a conspiracy to kill Dr. Vulkovitch, and was written by Nicholas Tufektchieff in Odessa, one of the supposed murderers of Beltcheff, was addressed to Georghieff, and implicated several others. After the murder the authorities at Constantinople proceeded at once to arrest the persons named in the letter, and succeeded in apprehending a certain Christo, who at his examination revealed the names of Merdjau, Nicholas and Naum Tufektchieff, and Shishmanoff as his confederates. Merdjan and Shishmanoff were put into prison; the latter, however, was released on demand of the Russian embassy, and was conveyed to Odessa, where the Tufektchieffs were also staying. The release of Shishmanoff and the refusal of the Porte to request the extradition of the Tufektchieffs from Russia, created a bitter feeling among the Bulgarians until the Government finally saw itself forced to address a note to the Porte, which, however, bore more the stamp of an appeal to the civilized world against the actions and interference of the Russian Government. The note, dated April 12, recapitulates the facts of the murder of Beltcheff, and characterizes that crime as the result of revolutionary schemes against the Government of the principality conducted by committees abroad having Bulgarian refugees in their pay, and reminds the Porte of the assurances given to proceed against all guilty persons who were found plotting against the Bulgarian Government on Ottoman territory. Coming to the case of Dr. Vulkovitch, it refers to the letter intercepted at Belgrade, and the deposition of Christo, that this murder was also the work of Bulgarian refugees supported by the Panslavist committee at Odessa, and the testimony elicited from the persons arrested in Constantinople going to prove the complicity of Shishmanoff in the crime. It expresses the surprise of the Princely Government at the liberation of Shishmanoff and the protection afforded him by the Russian embassy at Constantinople. The note denies that Shishmanoff was a naturalized Russian subject, but points out that, under the capitulations, foreign subjects implicated in crime are answerable to the Ottoman tribunals. It then adverts to a letter addressed to Stambuloff by Bulgarian refugees holding commissions in the Russian army, who informed the Premier that the murder of Beltcheff having been accomplished, they intended to prepare new attacks against the ministers; that the Russian Government had been advised of this letter, but instead of taking action, kept these men in the army, and that one of them, Stantcheff, although his extradition had been granted by the Porte for his complicity in the Beltcheff murder, was actually received in audience by M. de Giers, the Russian Minister for Foreign Affairs. The note next points out that Bulgarian refugees are furnished with Russian passports, although not Russian subjects. The note then concludes in the following terms:

After having preserved order and tranquillity, and after having fulfilled its duties to all foreign states, the Bulgarian Government considers that it has deserved the confidence of the Porte and gained sufficient title to the solicitude of the suzerain power to induce the latter to take into its own hands the defense of the interests of Bulgaria. The Bulgarian Government can not doubt that the Porte will demand the extradition of the men who devised the murder of Dr. Vulkovitch—namely, Nicholas and Naum Tufektchieff and Shishmanoff. Further, it begs the Porte to prohibit the stay of Bulgarian refugees in the vilayets of Turkey in Europe, and appeals to the Ottoman Government to recognize the rights of the principality by giving, from the international standpoint, its sanction, in conformity with Article III of the Treaty of Berlin, to the lawful order of things existing in Bulgaria.

No formal acknowledgment or reply to the note was given to the Bulgarian Government. The two prisoners Merdjau and Christo and the two Tufektchieffs were put on trial at Constantinople. The two former were found guilty of the willful murder of Dr. Vulkovitch and condemned to death. Nicholas and Naum Tufektchieff were convicted of instigating the crime, and were sentenced in their absence to fifteen years' penal servitude. M. Dimitroff was appointed Bulgarian agent at Constantinople in place of Dr. Vulkovitch.

The Political Trial at Sofia.—A court-martial was held at Sofia from June 30 to July 19, to try eighteen prisoners concerned in different plots, which culminated last year in the murder of the Bulgarian Minister Beltcheff. The more conspicuous among them were Petko Karaveloff, ex-Prime Minister and ex-Regent of Bulgaria; Maloff, also a former Cabinet minister; Milaroff, who was concerned in the kidnapping of Prince Alexander; and Toma Georgieff. It was shown that at the time of the Beltcheff murder plots existed to overthrow the Government, and plans to murder Prince Ferdinand and Stambuloff.

The prisoner Milaroff was convicted of having conspired with a hostile government—namely, that of Russia—with having laid a plot for the murder of Prince Ferdinand, and with arming Bulgarian subjects with a view to sedition and murder, and was condemned to death. Toma Georgieff and another prisoner named Alexander Karaguloff were convicted of participating in a plot to overthrow the Government, the first act of which was the attempt to murder Stambuloff; they were both sentenced to death.

Karaveloff, who was accused of being the

leader of this last conspiracy, was sentenced to five years' imprisonment, the evidence against him not being very strong—in fact, hardly strong enough to warrant any punishment. Another prisoner, Constantin Popoff, was sentenced to death for joining the hostile band of the Russian Captain Nabokoff, in 1886. Of the six prisoners acquitted, only one was declared absolutely "not guilty"; the others were released for want of proof. The seven remaining prisoners were sentenced to terms of imprisonment ranging from sixteen months to fifteen years. The four condemned to death were executed July 27.

During the trial, some Russian secret dispatches were published by the Bulgarian Government which tended to compromise the Government of Russia. These had been bought, together with the Russian telegraph cipher, from a man named Jacobsohn, who had been a dragoman at the Russian legation in Bucharest, and embraced the correspondence between the Russian Asiatic Department of the Ministry of Foreign Affairs with the legation at Bucharest. Some of the documents date from the autumn of 1887, and go to show that the Russian Government has sought incessantly to compass the removal of Prince Ferdinand. The Asiatic Department urged the Russian representatives at Bucharest to encourage conspiracies against the Prince, and gave orders as to the arrangements with Panitza, who offered his services as early as 1887. Nabokow's gang, armed by the aid of the Slav committee, was represented to have been directed by M. v. Nelidaw. In case of the successful removal of Prince Ferdinand, the Bulgarian army was to be doubled, each company to be half composed of Russian soldiers. The Sobranje was to elect a Russian candidate for the throne. The administration of Bulgaria by a Russian governor receiving instructions direct from the Russian Emperor was also spoken of. The Russian Government declared that the documents were spurious.

Stambuloff's Visit to Constantinople.—The Bulgarian Prime Minister visited Constantinople in compliance with an invitation from the Porte. The Sultan received him in audience, and Stambuloff broached the question of the recognition of Prince Ferdinand, to which the Sultan replied that the time was probably not far off, but that under the present circumstances nothing could be done in that respect.

C

CALIFORNIA, a Pacific coast State, admitted to the Union Sept. 9, 1850; area, 158,-360 square miles. The population, according to each decennial census since admission, was 92,-597 in 1850; 379,994 in 1860; 560,247 in 1870; 864,694 in 1880; and 1,208,130 in 1890. Capital, Sacramento.

Government.—The following were the State officers during the year: Governor, H. H. Markham, Republican: Lieutenant-Governor, J. B. Reddick; Secretary of State, Edward G. Waite; Treasurer, J. R. McDonald; Comptroller, Edwin P. Colgan; Attorney-General, W. H. H. Hart; Surveyor-General, Theodore Reichert; Superintendent of Public Instruction, James W. Anderson; Railroad Commissioners, William Beckman, J. M. Litchfield, and James W. Rea; Chief Justice of the Supreme Court, W. H. Beatty; Associate Justices, J. R. Sharpstein. T. B. McFarland, A. Van R. Paterson, C. H. Garoutte, Ralph C. Harrison, and J. J. De Haven.

Finances.—The bonded State debt amounts to $2,528,500, of which $751,000 is held by the University fund, $1,526,500 by the Common-school fund, and $251,000 by individuals. The rate of interest is 6 per cent., and the whole sum falls due in January, 1893. By an act of the Legislature of 1891 a proposition to refund the debt into new bonds bearing 4 per cent. interest was submitted to the people at the November election.

The total assessed valuation of property in the State for 1892 was $1.275,832,510, against $1.241,-966,274 for 1891. These figures include railroad property, which was valued at $41,956,000 in 1892. The valuation of San Francisco County was $412,047,076. The rate of taxation for State purposes was fixed by the State Board of Equalization at 44·6 cents on each $100 for 1891, and at 43·4 cents for 1892.

Banks.—The total resources of all banks in the State in 1891 were $283,846,270, and the total deposits therein $186,471,036. This is an increase in deposits of $15,241,505 over the report of 1890. The deposits in savings banks alone were $114,164,523, an increase of $15,722,-000 over 1890.

Tin Mine.—For many years a large deposit of tin ore has been known to exist in San Bernardino County, but prolonged litigation over the title to the land has prevented the development of the property until recently. On April 25, 1891, the first pig tin was produced, and since that time there has been a constant increase in the facilities for production. More than 150 men are now employed, and a ready market is found for the output.

Petroleum.—California is the third petroleum-producing State in the Union, ranking only after Pennsylvania and New York. Petroleum is known to exist in many widely separated sections, though confined to the Coast range of mountains. In this range it is found all the way from Orange County to Mendocino, including Los Angeles, Ventura, San Bernardino, Santa Barbara, Kern, San Luis Obispo, Monterey, Fresno, San Benito, Santa Clara, San Mateo, Alameda, Colusa, Humboldt, and Mendocino. The principal center of production is in the south, the wells of Ventura and Los Angeles Counties turning out a constantly increasing quantity of oil. At Puente, 30 miles east of Los Angeles, are extensive oil deposits, whose development only dates back to 1882. There are 16 wells, and they produce about 3,000 barrels monthly. Most of it is used for fuel and lubricating. These deposits continue into Orange County, where 2 wells have been sunk near Fullerton, which yield small quantities of oil, utilized for fuel. Oil in small amounts is found in other parts of Los

Angeles County. The district that yields the largest amount of oil is in Ventura County. Three large companies operate here, and there are wells in Torrey cañon, the Ojai valley, and Sespe, Santa Paula, Adams, Wheeler, and Aliso cañons. The wells already in existence supply 800 barrels daily, and new ones are being sunk. There is an extensive system of pipe lines in this territory, and a large refinery at Santa Paula. Besides the large companies in operation there are many small wells owned by private parties, and their product is all sold to the large concerns. The crude oil is worth about $1.00 at the well.

Agriculture.—Two States in the Union produce half of the entire barley crop of the country, and of these two California takes the lead, New York being second. While the California crop is reported to average something like 16,000,000 bushels annually, those figures are far from representing the actual amount. One of the peculiarities of California is the prominent place occupied by this grain in farm economy. The pioneer American agriculturists found the Spaniards in the habit of feeding barley to their horses, that grain taking the place occupied by oats at the East. The spirit of imitation being strong upon the newcomers, they undertook the cultivation of barley, and adopted the practice of utilizing it for food for their horses and mules, to the exclusion of other grain. That habit has become firmly fixed throughout the State. The largest barley-producing county is San Joaquin, while San Bernardino comes second, Merced third, and Contra Costa fourth. The bay counties and those adjacent to the ocean are large barley producers. The moist atmosphere of those sections, so detrimental to wheat in the production of rust, is positively beneficial to the growth of barley.

California consumes more corn than she produces. The bulk of the crop is produced in the southern counties, there being an extensive region in San Luis Obispo, Santa Barbara, Ventura, Los Angeles, Orange, and San Bernardino Counties, where this cereal is produced without the aid of irrigation, and without rainfall from seed time to harvest. In the San Joaquin valley there is considerable corn production through the agency of irrigation, but in the counties mentioned sole dependence is placed upon the natural moisture of the soil and the influence of the fogs driven inland from the ocean. Under favorable conditions crops of 60 to 125 bushels to the acre are not infrequent.

The wheat crop of 1891 proved to be nearly an average one in quantity, about 1,000,000 tons being harvested. In quality it was the best that has been raised for several years. About one fourth of it was produced north of a line drawn through San Francisco and Stockton, and the remainder south of that line.

The wool product for 1891 is estimated at 32,416,250 pounds, against 34,917,320 pounds for 1890, 33,591,720 pounds for 1889, and 32,569,972 pounds for 1888. Although there was a decrease in the product, the prices for it in 1891 were very satisfactory, and its total value is estimated at $5,500,000.

The vintage of 1891 is estimated at 16,550,000 gallons, against 17,500,000 gallons in 1890. About 1.250,000 gallons of brandy were also produced. The estimate of the raisin product is 2,500,000 twenty-pound boxes; of fresh fruit dried, 445,-800,000 pounds; of fresh fruit canned, 50,000,000 pounds; of potatoes, 125,000,000 pounds; of beans, 50,000,000 pounds; of prunes, 25,000,000 pounds; of sugar, 9,000,000 pounds; of petroleum, 474,500 barrels; of lumber, 500,000,000 feet.

Earthquakes.—In the central portion of the State, several distinct shocks of earthquake were felt on April 19 and 21, but none were severe enough to cause widespread damage. A few buildings were thrown down, ceilings cracked, plastering detached, and fragile movables broken. At Sacramento the ceiling of the State Capitol was slightly damaged. No loss of life was reported. San Francisco suffered only slight damage. The only large place reporting heavy loss was Woodland, where the damage to buildings was estimated at $50,000.

Hydraulic Mining.—On Jan. 20, a State mining convention met at San Francisco for the purpose of hastening the resumption of hydraulic mining in the State. There have always been two conflicting interests in this industry, that of the miner and that of the riparian farmer, whose lands and the stream adjoining thereto were injured by the *débris* caused by such mining operations. At this convention both parties were fully represented, and they co-operated in seeking an adjustment of their difficulties. Resolutions were passed, and the following memorial to Congress was adopted unanimously:

Your memorialists, representing the people of the State of California in convention assembled at San Francisco, for the purpose of considering the question of hydraulic mining and the improvement of water ways of the State, respectfully represent:

That for many years there has been a conflict between the farming and hydraulic mining interests of California by reason of the *débris* from said mines injuring the navigable rivers and lands bordering thereon. By decisions of the Federal courts injunctions were issued against these mines, and they were closed down, throwing many persons out of employment and causing great loss of capital invested in mines, ditches, and a great industry paralyzed. The Legislature of the State of California, realizing that a rehabilitation of this mining industry would benefit the people of the whole State and nation if it could be accomplished, by joint resolution brought the matter to the attention of Congress.

In accordance with this resolution Congress passed an act appointing a commission of engineers for the purpose of ascertaining if some plan could be devised to adjust the conflict between the mining and farming sections; and for examining the navigable rivers and their tributaries, with a view to improvement and rectification of the rivers. That this board of engineers, officers constituted under the provisions of the act of Congress entitled "An Act for the investigation of the mining *débris* question in the State of California," approved Oct. 1, 1888, have made an examination and investigation of the mining *débris* question in the State of California. and have made an examination of the injured navigable river channels, their tributaries, and lands adjacent thereto, with a view to the improvement and rectification of said rivers.

That it appears from said report that there are many hundred million dollars of gold in the auriferous gravel deposits of California which can be extracted by the hydraulic process, filling the arteries of commerce and stimulating to increased energy all the industries of this State and of the nation, and that wise statesmanship demands that this vast amount of gold should be added to the wealth of the country if it can be done without injury to the navigable rivers of the State and the adjacent lands.

That it appears by said report that dams and other restraining works may be erected in many of the cañons which will not only restrain the material producing the damage complained of in the past, but will also restrain the *débris* now dislodged but still remaining in the cañons.

We respectfully ask that your honorable body accept and adopt the report of the commission appointed by you for the purpose stated, and that Congress at once take steps to put into practical and effective operation the means suggested by the engineers, in order that mining may be again resumed in the manner indicated without the injury complained of in the past.

Your memorialists further suggest that Congress, having appointed this commission to determine the question, should accept and act upon its conclusions, which are of a nature to be acceptable to both parties to the controversy, in that they provide that mining can be again carried on under the conditions named, and also that the *débris* will be restrained from the rivers and farming lands.

It is proper to represent also that at four different sessions of the Legislature of the State of California resolutions have been adopted calling the attention of Congress to this hydraulic-mining question in California. At the last session the Governor, in his inaugural address, brought the matter again to the attention of the representatives of the people, and on Dec. 29, 1890, the Legislature again passed resolutions, which were forwarded to Congress, setting forth the facts and asking for relief.

We recognize the fact that until Congress takes proper action for the erection of suitable works for the restraining of mining *débris*, hydraulic mining is absolutely restrained by the courts, and as law-abiding citizens we recognize that the laws must be obeyed and the decrees of the courts respected ; and inasmuch as the complete cessation of hydraulic mining, until congressional action is had, will be a great hardship in the mining regions, and may result in their depopulation, we earnestly request you to take immediate action, in order that there may be an end of conflict and that no complaint may exist of enjoined mines refusing to observe the orders of court.

We earnestly request you to make sufficient appropriations for the erection of dams or other restraining works in accordance with the report of said commission, under such restrictions as to locality, size, and extent of dams as may by law be provided for that purpose, in order that the *débris* resulting from hydraulic mining may be restrained, as contemplated in said reports, and that said restraining dams shall be built in such rivers and streams, and at such places therein as the needs of the mining industries and the protection and preservation of farming and other resources of the State may require, as may be recommended by Government engineers, and that all such dams shall be built and maintained by Government appropriation.

We also recommend the appropriation of the sums recommended by the Government engineers for the improvement of the Sacramento, San Joaquin, and Feather rivers, and Petaluma creek. The commercial interests of the State of California and of the whole nation imperatively demand that these appropriations should be made.

Your memorialists above respectfully represent that the miners of the United States are dissatisfied with many of the rulings of the departments which put unnecessary burdens upon them and prevent them from readily obtaining title to mineral lands, to the great detriment of the mining interest, and we respectfully ask that prompt congressional action be taken upon the resolutions on this subject of the mining laws and department rulings which were adopted at the California State Mining Convention held in San Francisco, Jan. 20, 1892.

A State miner's association was formed, and committees were appointed to present the memorial to Congress and to aid in securing the legislation demanded.

Political.—On May 3 a Republican State convention met at Stockton, and selected delegates to the Minneapolis National Convention. Resolutions were passed approving the administration of President Harrison, demanding the passage of laws securing the free and unlimited coinage of the silver product of the United States, urging Congress to take action to insure the early completion of the Nicaragua Canal and to secure its control by the United States Government, and insisting upon legislation prohibiting Chinese immigration. The convention also expressed itself in favor of carrying out the principles of civil-service reform to the fullest extent.

On May 17 the Democratic State Convention met at Fresno and nominated delegates to the Chicago National Convention. The platform condemns the demonetization of silver, demands an increase of the currency, denounces the Republican apportionment of 1891 and the railroad commission, and demands that the next Legislature introduce an amendment to the State Constitution fixing maximum rates on railroads, and abolishing the railroad commission.

On July 26 another Republican State convention met at Sacramento for the purpose of nominating two electors at large for the State. Thomas R. Bard and Joseph C. Campbell were selected. The platform adopted reaffirms the principle of the Stockton convention of May 4, adopts the Minneapolis platform, and concludes as follows :

That the Republican party of California has always stood for the material development of the State, and, believing that increased facilities of transportation by water and by rail will conduce to that end, it demands from the General Government the early completion, under Government control, of the Nicaragua Canal and the liberal expenditure of money to improve our harbors and internal water ways, and it invites capital to build into the State other competing transcontinental lines of railway, pledging protection and support to all instrumentalities existing and to exist that may promote the general welfare and give the people the benefit of the law of competition.

That the secretary of this convention be instructed to telegraph our representatives in the Senate of the United States urging the immediate passage of the mining bill now pending in that body.

The convention then divided into seven district conventions, for the purpose of choosing district electors and congressmen.

During July the People's party held a State convention and placed an electoral and Congressional ticket in the field. A similar ticket was nominated by the Prohibitionists.

At the November election the Democratic national ticket was successful (except as to one elector) by 124 purality, and the Democrats gained two congressmen.

CANADA, DOMINION OF. See DOMINION OF CANADA.

CAPE COLONY AND SOUTH AFRICA. The Cape of Good Hope is a British colony in South Africa. The Governor is Sir Henry Loch, the Premier Sir Cecil Rhodes.

Area and Population.—The area of the colony and its dependencies is 221,311 square miles, and the population, according to the census of April 5, 1891, 1,527,224, of which 376,987 are white (195,956 males and 181,031 females) and 1,150,237(571,377 males and 578,868 females) colored. Cape Colony proper has an area of 191,416 square miles and a population of 956,485, of which 336,938 are white and 619,547 colored; Griqualand West, now incorporated in the Cape, has 15,197 square miles and a population of 83,375, of whom 29,670 are white and 53,705 colored; East Griqualand, 7,594 square miles, and a population of 152,618, of whom 4,150 are white and 148,468 colored; Tembuland, 4,122 square miles and a population of 180,415, of whom 5,179 are white and 175,236 colored; Transkei 2,552 square miles and a population of 153,563, of whom 1,019 are white and 152,544 colored; Walfisch Bay, 430 square miles and a population of 768, of whom 31 are white and 737 colored. The population of the colony proper in 1875 was 720,984, of whom 236,783 were white. The bulk of the white inhabitants is of Dutch, German, and French extraction.

Finance.—The colonial revenue in 1890 was £5,571,907, of which £1,774,352 were derived from taxation, £2,291,375 from railroad and other services, £319,198 from public lands, £45,125 from fines, etc., and £1,141,587 were raised by loans. The total expenditure was £5,327,496, of which £1,062,780 represented the service of the public debt, £1,018,065 were for railways, £142,774 for defense, £215,809 for police, £128,624 for the civil establishment, and £1,048,571 under act of Parliament. The revenue for 1892 is estimated at £4,285,650, and the expenditure at £4,216,883. The public debt in the beginning of 1891 was £22,114,159.

Production and Commerce.—The imports for 1891 were £7,518,437, of which nearly £6,-000,000 were from the United Kingdom, and the exports, mainly diamonds and wool, amounted to £10,994,970, against £9,653,982 in the preceding year. There were in the colony in 1891 1,241,000 horned cattle, 430,000 horses, 16,000,000 sheep, 3,000,000 Angora goats, and 3,000,000 other goats. In 1890 828 vessels, of 1,455,560 tons, entered, of which 601, of 1,281,169 tons, were British; and 868, of 1,501,817 tons, cleared, of which 620, of 1,317,958 tons, were British. Coastwise there entered 1,421, of 2,551,450 tons, and cleared 1,407, of 2,511,088 tons.

Communications.—There were 8,000 miles of railway in the colony at the end of 1890, of which 1,890 belonged to the Government. The Eastern Railway junction, connecting Cape Colony with the Orange Free State, was opened by the Governor on March 10, 1892. The mail matter handled in 1890 included 16,703,308 letters, 6,898,460 newspapers. 267,878 post cards, 3,431,220 books, samples, and packets, and 609,-973 parcels.

There were 4,640 miles of telegraph lines, all of which were erected by the Government, and 1,291,984 messages were sent in 1890. The receipts were £72,746, the expenditure £80,068. The telegraph line from Cape Town to Fort Salisbury, in Mashonaland, extending over 1,646 miles, was completed on Feb. 17, 1892.

Political.—The most important political event of the year was the raising of the electoral qualification from a £25 to a £75 occupation.

Persons who are unable to write their name, address, and occupation are disqualified for voting, but all persons already registered retain their right to vote as long as they remain resident in the same electoral division. It also provides for election by ballot throughout the colony after July, 1894. It is believed to be the precursor of a more harmonious sentiment between the Dutch and English population of the colony. The colored coolie population originated a movement to petition the Imperial Government to withhold its assent, but received no support from the Caffres, who seem to acquiesce in the situation, though large numbers of them will be disfranchised.

Natal, a British colony, was separated from Cape Colony in 1856. The Governor is Sir Charles B. H. Mitchell. The area is estimated at 20,460 square miles, and the population, according to the census of 1891, was 543,913, of whom 46,788 were white, 41,142 Indians, and 455,983 Caffres. The revenue in 1890 was £1,422,-688, the expenditure £1,328,468. The revenue was derived mainly from the following sources: Railways, £686,119; customs, £336,821; excise, £21,935; land sales, £41,777; posts, £45,957; telegraphs, £17,572; stamps and licenses, £25,-965; native-hut tax, £76,610. The expenditure was mainly for the following purposes: Railways, £622,173; education, £40,952; public works, £86,274; defense, £53,801. The loan expenditure was £1,166,315, and the debt at the end of 1890 was £5,060,354. The imports in 1890 were £4,417,085, and the exports £1,379,-657, including the trade with the neighboring Dutch republics. The main exports were: Wool, £725,118; gold, £358,661; hides, £59,956; and sugar, £18,491. The whites owned 575,655 sheep, 141,615 horned cattle, 65,801 Angora goats, and 27,784 horses; the natives, 543,084 horned cattle, 268,369 goats, 33,292 sheep, and 32,142 horses. The Government operates 3,39½ miles of railway. There entered 538 vessels, of 514,252 tons, and cleared 551, of 521,747 tons.

Negotiations on the subject of responsible government, the movement for which began in 1879, were continued in 1892 between the home and colonial governments, the former still awaiting a decided manifestation of public opinion on the question before giving a final decision. A clause has been inserted in the proposed Constitution, after much debate, giving the Governor authority to act as paramount native chief, responsible only to the Imperial Government, and not to the colonial, for the administration of native affairs. This removes an objection which has heretofore been made by the home Government. Provision is also made for an upper chamber, to be nominated for ten years, and a reserve of £10,000 per annum for the promotion of the welfare and education of the natives. The opposition to responsible government is based largely on the onus of defense which will fall upon the colony after the withdrawal of the imperial troops and the lack of men competent for ministerial positions.

Basutoland.—Basutoland is a British territory, governed by a resident commissioner, Sir Marshall James Clarke, under the direction of the High Commissioner for South Africa, who exercises the legislative function. The area is estimated at 9,720 square miles, and the white population in 1891 was 578 and the native 218,324. European settlement is prohibited. The live stock consisted of 302,934 cattle and 81,104 horses. The territory, which was formerly the scene of perennial warfare between the native chiefs, is now peaceful and prosperous. The exports in 1891 amounted to about £250,000, and consisted chiefly of grain, cattle, and wool. In 1891 Basutoland entered the Customs Union, and in 1892 was connected by telegraph with the Orange Free State. The revenue in 1891 was £41,784 and the expenditure £40,825, and there is no public debt.

Bechuanaland.—The Crown colony of Bechuanaland, which is under the direct administration of the Governor of Cape Colony, as High Commissioner for South Africa, who is represented by an administrator, Sir Sydney G. A. Shippard, has an area of 51,000 square miles, with a white population of 12,726 and a native population estimated at 60,000. There is in addition a protectorate of 119,000 square miles. Maize, wool, hides, cattle, and wood are exported. The revenue in 1891, including a parliamentary grant of £115,991, was £161,303, the expenditure £159,545.

British Zambesia.—The charter of the British South Africa Company was extended in the early part of 1891, so as to include all the territory under British influence north of the Zambesi river except Nyassaland, which was proclaimed under the protectorate of Great Britain on May 14, 1891, and Mr. H. H. Johnson was appointed imperial commissioner and was permitted to act, in addition, as representative of the company in its territory north of the Zambesi. The area of the company may be estimated at over 500,000 square miles.

CHEMISTRY. Chemical Theory.—The theory and properties of the metallic carbonyls have been discussed by Ludwig Mond in a lecture before the Royal Institution. Carbonyl proper is carbonic oxide, CO, but the name is also applied to the peculiar compounds which that substance forms with metals. The first of these substances discovered was a compound of carbonic oxide and potassium, which Liebig described in 1834, and from his experiments with which he concluded that carbonic oxide was a radical, or a compound having the characteristics of a simple body, and capable of combining with, replacing, and being replaced by other simple bodies; and he predicted that remarkable results would attend the further pursuit of his idea. His prediction has been verified. Carbonyl differs from other compound radicals in that it is the only one that exists in the free state as a single atom, while all the others only exist as molecules composed of two atoms the free valences of which neutralize each other. Later experiments with potassium carbonyl show it to be a compound of the benzole series, in which all the hydrogen is replaced by potassium. By treatment with an acid it can be converted into hexhydroxylbenzole, and from this substance it is possible to produce the whole wide range of the benzole compounds. While it had been found that sodium did not combine with carbonic oxide, and lithium and calcium acted similarly with potassium, systematic ex-

periments to obtain carbonyls with the other metals have only been made within a few years. The liquid nickel-carbonyl, already mentioned in the "Annual Cyclopædia," was the first of the new substances of this class to be produced. It acts chemically in an entirely different manner from potassium carbonyl, and does not lead, as the other does, by easy methods to complicated organic compounds. It is, in fact, unlike all other substances in chemical properties. It has also remarkable physical qualities, which are fully described in Prof. Mond's paper. The compound with iron—ferro-carbonyl, also liquid—bears much resemblance in properties to the nickel compound, but has a different structural composition. The red deposit which sometimes forms in ordinary steatite gas burners is supposed by Sir Henry Roscoe to be due to the presence of this substance in illuminating gas; and it has been observed by Dr. Thorne in compressed gas used for lime lights. While carbonyl acts so readily upon nickel, it is inert with respect to some of the metals, such as cobalt, which are usually associated with it; and this peculiarity has been utilized by Prof. Mond with success in experiments for the complete separation of nickel from cobalt, and by means of an apparatus constructed by Dr. Langer he has succeeded in extracting the nickel from a variety of ores. The process is adapted to the production and deposition of pure nickel immediately in any definite form. The idea of the possibilities dormant in carbonyl, enunciated by Liebig fifty-eight years ago, has thus been elaborated and developed, till it has led to results of the highest scientific importance and probably of great practical utility.

An exposition of a theory that the chemical elements have been evolved from hydrogen by a process of nebular condensation, and that their evolution follows an order corresponding with that of Bode's law in the planetary system, has been published in London by Henry Wilde. The exposition encounters the difficulty hitherto insuperable, that the atomic weights of only a very few elements appear to be multiples of that of hydrogen. This he meets by admitting, as Prout did, that hydrogen may itself " have been evolved from an ethereal substance of much greater tenuity." The author proposes a new system of classification of the elements, under seven stages of condensation, comprised from H_a to H_{7a}, and arranges them in a tabular form, with gaps left for unknown elements, and correcting the atomic weights where necessary, so as to make them accord with the hypothesis. He rejects the periodic system as having "no more relation to chemical science than the law of increase of population, or the laws of variation and inheritance in organic species."

In his vice-presidential address before the chemical section of the British Association, Prof. Herbert McLeod spoke of the many instances known of the influence which small quantities of substances have upon chemical reactions. These influences may be more common than is generally supposed. The presence of a third body is frequently helpful in the combination of elements with one another. Thus dry chlorine will not attack melted sodium or finely divided copper; an electric spark will not cause a dry mixture of carbonic oxide and oxygen to explode; carbon, phosphorus, and sulphur will not unite with dry oxygen; and as chemical science progresses we may find that many well-known actions are conditioned by the presence of minute traces of other matter which have hitherto escaped detection. We all know the profound alterations of the properties of substances by minute traces of impurities; less than one tenth per cent. of phosphorus will render steel unfit for certain purposes. The sapphire and ruby differ from colorless alumina only by the presence of traces of impurities hardly recognizable by chemical analysis.

The solutions of colloid substances, such as albumen, silicic acid, tungstic acid, etc., are supposed to differ in their nature from solutions of crystalloid substances. Graham, in his paper on that subject, defines the differences between crystalloid and colloid substances—solutions of the latter not passing through the pores of certain animal membranes and parchment paper, while solutions of crystalloids pass freely through them—and suggested that the basis of the colloid state might lie in the complex character of the molecule. The facts that the solutions of colloid substances do not have an appreciably higher boiling point than water, or a lower freezing point, and that in dissolving a colloid no change of temperature takes place, or at least only a very slight change, are regarded by C. E. Linebarger as indicating that a colloid solution is not a solution in the ordinary sense of the term, but rather a mechanical mixture, an emulsion, the colloid being held in a state of suspension in the water. The same opinion has been reached by other authors. Selecting from among the simplest and stablest colloids, Mr. Linebarger, in order to obtain results that may throw light upon the nature of colloid substances in solution, has made some determinations of the osmotic pressure of solutions of colloid tungstic acid. The results of the experiment gave a pressure corresponding to a molecular mass for colloidal tungstic acid of about 1,700, or nearly seven times 250, showing the colloidal molecule to consist of seven simple molecules. All the phenomena exhibited by colloids may be easily explained on the assumption that the colloid molecule is very large. A solution of a colloid does not seem to lower the freezing point or raise the boiling point, because the molecular mass is so great that it has but little influence. A colloid solution might be regarded as a step between a true solution and a true emulsion. The colloid molecule is so much larger than the water molecule that it stands to reason that the properties of colloid substances must differ in a marked degree from solutions of substances that possess a molecule much less heavy than water. The ease with which colloidal substances are coagulated, or pass into the solid state, indicate that there exist in the solution molecular groupings similar to those existing in a solid.

In an address on Recent Advances in "Physical Chemistry," Prof. W Ostwald mentions it as remarkable that the efforts of the investigators who have been trying to determine the value of the fundamental constant of the relation of the atomic weight of oxygen to that of hydrogen to within one part per thousand have not yet met with a generally accepted success. The question of the significance and numerical values of the atomic weights has made no progress of importance since the fundamental researches of Lothar Meyer and Mendeleeff. Speculations do not cease in the direction given by the assumption of the compound nature of the elements, but there are none of which growth and development can be prophesied. No new elements of importance have recently come to light. In the theory of gases, the investigations continue according to the general equation of condition, in that the recognition is steadily breaking its way that the nearest entrance to the theory of liquids leads necessarily over the critical point. The kinetic hypothesis is showing itself here essentially unfruitful. The stoichiometry of the liquid organic compounds, founded by Hermann Kopp, has enjoyed a steady development. While the question of the boiling point seems to be essentially postponed until the general theory of liquids becomes known, that of the molecular volumes has reached a stage which already assures the prospect of a successful period of development. The additive scheme, according to which the molecular volume is the sum of the atomic volumes, determines only the roughest outlines of the phenomena; other factors make themselves everywhere felt; and we must, more than ever before, recognize the molecular volume as a constituent property. In relation to the connection between the different properties of substances, a fruitful line of thought has been carried out by Philippe-Guye, who has verified the existence of a close connection between the critical constants and the molecular refraction. Spectrum analysis has recently taken a promising start in the stoichiometric direction. The view now held as "an undoubted dogma," that at the highest temperatures all compounds must be dissociated into their elements, is regarded as "not justified." "What we do know about the stability of compounds is . . . that all compounds which are formed with absorption of heat become more stable with rising temperature, and the reverse." Because the majority of the compounds known to us are formed from the elements with evolution of heat, and consequently become more unstable with rising temperature, the conclusion has been drawn that this is in general the case. From certain facts we may infer that the spectra occurring at high temperatures may, under proper conditions, belong to compounds which, formed with great absorption of energy, may have a fleeting existence confined to those temperatures. From this point of view many difficult facts of spectroscopy and spectrometry would have some prospect of a proper interpretation. But little is known as yet about the connection between color and constitution. The investigations of Krüss, Liebermann, and Vogel indicate that the property is in great measure constitutive, becoming additive only within the narrowest limits of closely related compounds. The constitutive character of the rotation of the plane of polarization has been always known and recognized. Since Van 't Hoff and Le Bel pointed out the connection between this property and the presence of an "asymmetrical" carbon atom, this idea has had an important development. The presence of optical activity is now held as proof of the presenee of asymmetrical carbon, and Le Bel has recently prepared optically active nitrogen compounds containing an asymmetrical nitrogen atom. Van 't Hoff's discovery of the identity of the laws of gases with those of dissolved substances is to be characterized as the greatest step forward which has been made in this direction. If we reflect that the development of the molcular idea is most decidedly based upon the laws of the gases in their simple form, we recognize at once that all the important relations which have here been found can be directly transferred to the domain of solution. The latter has, however, at the same time, far more varied possibilities in the form of its phenomena. This discovery has been of great value in the study and enlargement of the theory of molecular weight. Another aid to investigation, " of unexampled sweep and value," has been found in the theory of electrolytic dissociation of Arrhenius. In this theory, in the aqueous solutions of the electrolytes, the salts, acids, and bases, a greater or less proportion of the dissolved molecules are regarded as split up into electrically charged constituents or ions, which exist in the solution independently of one another in the same manner as the partial molecules of a dissociated gas. If in the field covered by Arrhenius the question be one of dissociation, and the laws of gases do, according to Van 't Hoff, hold for dissolved substances, it follows that the entire theory of the chemical affinity of electrolytes must be yielded by the application of those laws of dissociation. "This means nothing less," says Prof. Ostwald, "than that the problem of chemical affinity is in reality solved."

Chemical Physics.—According to the researches of P. Mylius and F. Foerster, supported by the observations of Pfeiffer and Kohlrausch, the solution of glass in water depends on a decomposition in which, first, free alkali appears. The silica of the glass is secondarily dissolved by the free alkali, the constituents of the solution varying according to the conditions of digestion. The susceptibility of glass to attack under given conditions is measured by the quantity of alkali which passes into solution from a given surface under those conditions. It increases with a rising temperature, is decreased by a previous treatment with water, and is modified by " weathering." Different sorts of glass display a different persistence of the solution. From glasses of equal susceptibility to attack unequal weights may pass into the solution. After treatment with water, surfaces of glass have the property of taking up alkali from the solutions which have been formed and of giving it up again on renewed treatment with water. Potash glasses are much more soluble than soda glasses, but the differences disappear in proportion as the glass is richer in lime. In the substance of glass vessels which are not readily attacked by cold and hot water, the lime, alkalies, and silica must bear a certain proportion to each other. Among the best-known glasses plumbiferous flint glass is least soluble in water, but it is corroded at the surface and easily decomposed by acids.

An experiment by W. Spring indicates the possibility of certain metals existing in the gaseous state at temperatures below their melting point. Leaflets of silver, platinum, and gold were heated to 150° C. with concentrated hydro-

chloric acid in sealed tubes. The metals were dissolved and the chlorides formed were reduced by the hydrogen evolved from the metals and the hydrochloric acid. They were deposited on the sides of the tubes in microscopic crystals. It may be assumed that in this experiment even the platinum existed for some time as a liquid before taking a crystalline form.

The theory of Berzelius that the spontaneous ignition of coal is promoted by the gradual oxidation of the pyrites it contains is disputed by Prof. Vivian B. Lewes, who, comparing the ignition temperatures—from 698° F. to 870·5° F.—of different kinds of coal, assumes that such degrees of heat could not be produced by that process in the small trace of pyrites scattered through a large mass of coal. The author believes that the true cause of combustion is found in the power of coal to attract and condense gases upon its surface—a power which increases in proportion to the fineness with which the coal is broken up and the total area of surface expanded. Freshly powdered charcoal ignites readily. The readiness of coal to ignite increases also with the temperature of the storage room. The tendency or power of the coal to absorb oxygen is therefore to be taken as the true index of the danger of ignition. This may be roughly gauged by the amount of moisture which the coal can absorb from the air; for if much moisture is found in an air-dried sample of coal it stamps it at once as a highly absorbent form, which must on that account be stored with special precautions, while if little moisture be present the sample is probably unable to take up enough oxygen to lead to serious mischief. When once a coal has taken up oxygen and the early stages of heating are passed and the temperature has again fallen, all danger of ignition is over, and the coal may be stored in any quantity with safety; so that if it were practicable to keep newly mined coal for a month in moderate-sized heaps, and then to avoid much breakage in afterward loading it, spontaneous ignition would be almost unknown.

The point at which sulphur ignites has not been satisfactorily determined and has been considered variable. Some authors suppose, from the ease with which sulphur has been observed sometimes to take fire, that it is low; some that allotropic conditions influence it. Prof. W. R. Hodgkinson believes that allotropic conditions have little or no effect, and that sulphur ignites only after it has reached the gaseous state. From the fact that the vapor of boiling sulphur at 448° C. may escape into the air without ignition, and from other circumstances, he is of the opinion that the element does not ignite at a lower temperature than 300° C. An experiment by Bertram Blount led him to a similar conclusion, but he has revised his opinion in the light of a more accurate experiment by J. Rutherford Hill, which gives the igniting point of sulphur as 248° C.

A study of the effect of minute percentages of foreign elements on the mechanical properties of gold disclosed to Prof. W. C. Roberts-Austen a relation between the results obtained and the position in the periodic table of the introduced elements, and he predicted a similar phenomenon in the case of iron. The prediction has been verified by the researches of M. F. Osmond, from which it appears that foreign bodies of small atomic volume tend to cause iron to assume or remain in that one of its forms which has the smallest atomic volume. Bodies of great atomic volume produce the opposite effect.

It was found in the experiments of Profs. Liveing and Dewar on the explosion of gases under high pressure that the luminosity of the flame steadily increased with increase of pressure. When hydrogen was exploded with excess of oxygen, large quantities of nitrogen peroxide were formed from the nitrogen present as impurity in the oxygen. The water formed contained 3 per cent. of nitric acid. With excess of hydrogen small quantities of ammonia were formed. It was difficult to maintain the oxyhydrogen flame in an atmosphere of carbon dioxide if the pressure exceeded two atmospheres. Experiments were also made with ethylene and cyanogen exploded with oxygen.

The experiments of the committee of the British Association on the properties of solutions have been completed as to the solubility of a salt in a solution of another salt of known strength. In general, a salt is less soluble in a salt solution than in pure water. But KNO_3 in solution of $NaNO_3$ offers an exception.

In a paper on electromotive force, Prof. C. L. Speyers referred, in the American Association, to the absence of a satisfactory explanation of the relation between chemical and electrical energies, and gave reasons for thinking that a connection exists between the electromotive force developed in a cell and the dissociation of the salt in solution.

New Substances.—Chlorofluoride of phosphorus, PF_3Cl_2, is a new gaseous compound produced by M. Poulenc by adding chlorine to phosphorus trifluoride. The combination is attended by a contraction of one half. Phosphorus chlorofluoride is a colorless, incombustible gas, possessing a powerfully irritating odor. It is instantly absorbed and decomposed by water and by solutions of alkaline or alkaline earthy hydrates. It liquefies under ordinary pressures at $-8°$ C., and is dissociated at 250° C., or by the induction spark into gaseous pentafluoride and solid pentachloride of phosphorus. It is absorbed by absolute alcohol with production of a compound possessing a penetrating odor, which burns with a bright flame bordered with green, and leaves a white residue of phosphoric acid.

A phosphorous oxide supposed to exist in addition to the pentoxide formed when phosphorus is burned in air or oxygen has been described as a white, amorphous powder of the composition P_2O_3, very voluminous, somewhat more readily fusible than the pentoxide, and instantly dissolved with great rise of temperature by water, with formation of phosphorous acid. Studies pursued during three years by Prof. T. B. Thorpe and A. E. Tutton show that as obtained by them it is, at temperatures not exceeding 22° C., a pure-white crystalline solid, compact and heavy, firm and wax-like in character. Its most striking property is the ease with which it melts, the warmth of the hand which holds the vessel containing it being more than enough to convert it into a liquid. Its melting point is 22·5° C., and when placed in that temperature it becomes a

clear, colorless liquid, very mobile, but somewhat heavy. It is best preserved in sealed glass tubes, the air in which has been replaced by carbon dioxide or nitrogen. When cooled in such a tube the oxide rapidly resolidifies, with large crystals shooting out in all directions till the whole is one compact mass of interlacing crystals. The vapor of phosphorous oxide possesses a characteristic odor, which appears to be the same as that noticeable about a lucifer-match factory. But the solid and the liquid are constantly vaporizing, and hence the odor is strongly marked. Instead of reacting with violence with water, phosphorous oxide is indifferent to it, and dissolves very slowly in it. Warmed with water nearly to the boiling point, it evolves spontaneously inflammable phosphoretted hydrogen with a loud explosion and the formation of red phosphorus and phosphoric acid. It is believed that the disease of the lower jaw suffered by persons engaged in lucifer-match making is caused by the vapor of this substance.

During the preparation of specimens of crystalline and other forms of silicon, H. N. Warren obtained a most curious form of that substance, which appears, when tested analytically, to be composed of graphitoidal silicon, constituted so as to give perfect and well-developed oblique octahedral crystals. The peculiar form first appeared on subjecting potassium silicofluoride to a most intense heat in contact with impure aluminum. A method, though uncertain, was found of obtaining it in larger quantities, the product of which was pure silicon, insoluble in all acids except hydrofluoric, and infusible. The crystals look like the crystals of cast iron which are sometimes met with on breaking a pig of that substance. The largest measured more than half an inch across the faces, and were as perfect as a crystal of alum.

A series of double compounds of phenanthraquinone with metallic salts have been described by Prof. F. R. Japp and A. E. Turner. Among them are those with $ZnCl_2$, which crystallizes in dark, reddish-brown needles; with $HgCl_2$, crystallizing in red, obliquely truncated prisms; and with $Hg(CN)_2$, crystallizing also in red forms. A similar compound was obtained from mercuric chloride and β-naphthaquinone; but double compounds could not be obtained from certain paraquinones or α-diketones, whence it was inferred that they are derivable only from orthoquinones. The intense color of the double compounds indicates that in them the quinone preserves its distinctive character.

A new acid, chromosulphuric, $H_2Cr_2(SO_4)_4$, or its salt, described by Mr. Recoure, appears to be formed by the direct combination of a previously described isometric form of chromic sulphate with one equivalent of sulphuric acid, or of a metallic sulphate. The acid has been obtained in the solid state, combined with 11 molecules of water. It is a green powder, which is very hygroscopic and deliquesces rapidly in moist air, but is permanent in a dry atmosphere. Its solution is bright green when freshly prepared, but changes to blue on standing, and after a few days passes into a violet-colored solution of ordinary chromic sulphate mixed with free sulphuric acid. The potassium salt has been obtained in the solid state, combined with 4 molecules of water, as a green powder. This salt is also formed when chrome alum is dehydrated first for some time at 90°, and finally at 110°. The sodium and ammonium salts have been obtained, and resemble the potassium salt.

A curious compound of lead, sodium, and ammonia, Pb_4Na2NH_3, is described by M. Joannis. It is obtained when a rod of pure lead is placed in a saturated solution of sodammonium in water. The reddish-brown liquid becomes rapidly blue, and at last assumes a deep-green tint. A small quantity of hydrogen is evolved by the decomposition of a part of the sodammonium with sodamide. The lead gradually disappears, and a solid substance of an indigo-blue color is deposited. It is the compound Pb_4Na2NH_3, and appears to be a sodammonium, in which a part of the sodium is replaced by lead. It dissolves readily in liquefied ammonia, with formation of a solution having a bottle-green tint. It is not very stable, and dissociates spontaneously on standing, with production of a gray substance resembling spongy platinum, which becomes warmer by oxidation on exposure to the air. When introduced in small quantities at a time into water the first portions dissolve. This is caused by the oxidation of the lead and the solution of the litharge dissolving in the alkalinized water. As soon as the oxygen in the water is used up, further additions of the substance result in the precipitation of black flocculi of metallic lead.

The yellow coloration produced by the action of hydrogen peroxide upon molybdates and tungstates has been found by Péchard to be probably due to the formation of higher oxygen compounds of those metals. The yellow crystals formed after treating potassium trimolybdate with hydrogen peroxide have the composition $K_2Mo_2O_8(H_2O)_4$, and heated gently in a vacuum lose water and oxygen, and leave a residue of acid potassium molybdate. Both this salt and the ammonium salt, which is similarly prepared, are decomposed by alkalies with evolution of oxygen, evolve chlorine when treated with hydrochloric acid, and set free iodine from potassium iodide. A similar tungsten salt is formed when sodium paratungstate is similarly treated. These results are regarded by the author as establishing the existence of permolybdic and pertungstic oxides, Mo_2O_7 and W_2O_7, and of the corresponding acids, $H_2Mo_2O_8$ and $H_2W_2O_8$.

A new variety of carbon has been observed by Luzi in the deposit that is made on a piece of porcelain heated in a blast furnace to the highest temperature that can be reached. When the access of air is cut off, the porcelain is surrounded by a smoky flame, which is allowed to act upon it for a few minutes. On removing the porcelain from the furnace it appears covered with a deposit of carbon, which on unglazed porcelain resembles graphite, but on glazed is bright and silvery, with a metallic luster, and resembles a silvered mirror. Parts of the deposit adhere firmly, while others separate, and loose portions may be pulled off. This form of carbon is opaque, is free from ash, does not contain hydrogen, and does not give the nitric-acid reaction for graphite.

A compound of carbon with barium, C_2Ba, described by M. Maquenne, was formed by the direct action of barium, in the form of an amalgam, upon powdered retort charcoal. Since, when brought in contact with water, it evolves acetylene gas rapidly, it is regarded as perhaps an acetylide of barium or a compound formed by the replacement of the hydrogen of acetylene, C_2H_2, with metallic barium. It appears as a gray, friable mass, which remains unaltered when heated to bright redness. The direct formation of the new substance from barium and carbon, together with its reaction with water, afford another mode of synthesizing acetylene, which M. Maquenne considers to be of interest from the point of view of the formation of the natural hydrocarbons. Other metals may possess the same property of forming acetylides under the influence of high temperatures. If, then, as M. Berthelot has attempted to show, acetylene is the primary material or starting point for the formation of other hydrocarbons, it is possible that such compounds of metals with carbon, upon coming in contact with water under conditions of more or less pressure, may give rise to the production of the immense stores of natural hydrocarbons represented by petroleum.

A new amine, methyl-ethylamine, $C_2H_5(CH_3)NH$, has been obtained by Drs. Skraup and Wiegmann by the action of alcoholic potash upon morphine. Besides its preparation being of importance as completing a series of isomers of the formula C_3H_9N, the fact of its derivation from morphine throws light on the constitution of that alkaloid. The four possible isomers of the formula C_3H_9N, which have now all been prepared, are trimethylamine, propylamine, isopropylamine, and the present substance. The accuracy of the analysis was tested by preparing methyl-ethylamine synthetically. The oxalate, hydrochloride, platinochloride, and gold chloride were also prepared, and in every instance the products were identical with those prepared from the base of morphine.

Two series of salts of two new platinum bases containing organic radicals have been prepared by Blomstrand and his assistants at Lund. The first series is compounded with ethyl sulphide, and of it the chloride, bromide, iodide, nitrite, sulphate, and nitrate have been obtained. The halogen salts of this group are readily transformed into the more stable platinic compounds, and these are more difficult of solution. The salts of the second series are analogous, but contain the radical methyl instead of ethyl.

A new series of well-crystallizing salts of iridium-ammonium have been prepared by Dr. Palmaer, of Upsala. They are pentammonium salts corresponding to the *purpureo* compounds, of cobalt, chromium, and rhodium. The chloride, $I_2(NH_3)_5Cl_3$, is readily obtained by the action of ammonia on the trichlorides and tetrachlorides of iridium, and crystallizes in rhombic pyramids, isomorphous with the *purpureo* cobalt and rhombic chlorides. Other salts include a chlorobromide, a chloriodide, the tribromide, sulphuric acid salts, and the hydrate.

Acetyl fluoride, CH_3COF, has been prepared and is described by M. Moissan. It is obtained by causing various inorganic fluorides to react upon acetyl chloride, the best being zinc fluoride. It is colorless, both in the liquid and the gaseous condition, is considerably more volatile than acetyl chloride, while it is also much more stable and has an odor somewhat resembling that of carbonyl chloride. Water dissolves about 20 times its volume of the gas, but the liquid does not mix with water. Alcohol, ether, benzine, and chloroform dissolve it in all proportions.

A complex nitrosilicate salt of silver, containing silica, nitric acid, and silver oxide, is described by G. Rousseau and O. Tite. It is obtained by heating for sixty hours silver nitrate with water in the presence of fragments of marble and appears in ruby-red crystals.

An interesting account has been published by Dr. Merz, of Zürich, of a compound of nitrogen and magnesium known as magnesium nitride, Mg_3N_2. Magnesium, like boron, appears to possess a considerable affinity for nitrogen. The nitride had been obtained by Deville and Caron during their distillations of magnesium for obtaining the pure metal, and by Briegleb and Genther by heating magnesium filings in the presence of a stream of nitrogen. Dr. Merz describes two simple methods of obtaining it. Magnesium nitride is described by him as a light, voluminous, friable, and yellowish-gray substance when cold, but reddish-brown while hot. When exposed to the air it smells strongly of ammonia, owing to its decomposition by the moisture present. Heat is developed, with hissing, increase of volume, and escape of steam, just as when quicklime is slaked when water is poured upon it. Ammonia is also evolved in large quantities and white magnesium hydrate remains.

The probable existence of a new element is reported by H. D. Richmond and Hussein Off, of the khedivial laboratory, in Cairo. It is found in a new Egyptian mineral called masrite, which was discovered in 1890 in one of the dried-up river beds of Upper Egypt. Suspicion that the mineral contained some hitherto unknown constituent was first aroused by the fact that when it was dissolved in water and exposed to sulphureted hydrogen and acetic acid, instead of the black sulphide of cobalt, which from its supposed composition should have been first precipitated, a white insoluble substance was thrown down, and not till this was exhausted did the black cobalt precipitate appear. The chloride, hydrate, and oxalate of the new element were obtained, and from the analysis of them it appeared to be a divalent element having an atomic weight of 228. An element of atomic weight about 225 is required to occupy a vacant place in the periodic system in the beryllium-calcium group, and this may be the substance. Metallic masrium has not yet been obtained. The name given to the new element and its mineral is derived from the Arabic name of Egypt, Masr.

New Processes.—An apparatus is described by T. B. Thorpe by which the phenomena of a coal-dust explosion, resulting either from a local explosion of fire damp or by the direct action of a blown-out shot, may be illustrated. For class-room demonstration he recommends the substitution of lycopodium powder for the coal dust, on account of the greater ease and certainty of the experiment, and also because its use allows the observance of certain phenomena, such as

the mode in which the dust that escapes is thrown on projecting objects, and the fact that the explosion gathers strength as it progresses, which is made evident by the gradually increasing area of clear space before such objects as the dust is swept away by the force of the explosive flame. By observations made by means of a List manometer with this apparatus, the author finds that there is no evidence of a diminution of pressure along the sides of the space through which the flame rushes; and he is of the opinion that there is no experimental proof of the validity of the "suction theory" held by certain colliery managers, which assumes that in consequence of this alleged diminution of pressure occluded fire damp is drawn out from the coal, and contributes to the violence of the explosion.

The Parkinson oxygen process is a modification of the method patented by Tessie du Motay many years ago for preparing oxygen by blowing steam over potassium manganate, in which the permanganic acid loses part of its oxygen and is converted into a lower oxide of manganese with formation of caustic potash. On reheating this mixture in contact with air the lower oxides of manganese absorb oxygen from the air and become converted into potassium manganate, and thus by alternate heating in presence of air and blowing steam over the mixture a constant supply of oxygen is produced. The process, after having been employed for some time with bases, was disused, mainly because of the little use that was found at the time for pure oxygen. Parkinson's process differs from Du Motay's in that Parkinson brings air in contact with his heated manganates under pressure, and removes the oxygen which has been absorbed by the manganates under a vacuum. He does not, however, by his present appliances remove all the oxygen from the air, and can not therefore prepare directly by his process pure nitrogen. The novelties in his process lie in the mechanical appliances for heating the manganates; in the use of pumps, etc., for supplying air to the retorts and withdrawing oxygen from them; and in his method for bringing the manganates into a porous condition, so that the air may act upon them more easily, which is done by mixing into a plastic mass or paste the ground permanganates with china clay or similar inert material.

Cyanide of potassium was formed by Bunsen and Playfair by heating charcoal and potassium carbonate to redness in an atmosphere of nitrogen. Since then Marguerite and Sourdeval have shown that barium carbonate may be used in place of the potash, and that the barium cyanide produced may be again decomposed by steam into ammonia and barium carbonate. These reactions afforded a theoretically continuous process for the conversion of atmospheric nitrogen into ammonia, which, if it could be worked on a large scale, might be of great value. A series of experiments by Prof. Hempel were intended to show a way of obtaining a more abundant yield of the cyanide from the mutual action of the charcoal, nitrogen, and base by the use of greatly increased pressure. A largely increased amount of barium cyanide was formed.

A. Villon's method for obtaining colorless tannius from tanning drugs includes the three chief operations of lixiviation of the tanning matters, precipitation of the tannin in the state of an insoluble tannate, and the separation of the tannin. The insoluble tannate of zinc is formed in the lixiviated liquid by acting with ammonia on zinc sulphate. This is then decomposed with dilute sulphuric acid, and tannin is set free. The zinc sulphide is separated from the liquid by adding barium sulphide, when the insoluble zinc sulphide and barium sulphate are formed. In this manner are obtained directly extracts containing from 20 to 30 per cent. of tannin free from extractive matter and almost colorless.

Three chlorobromides of silicon are described by M. Besson, all being derived from silicon tetrachloride, $SiCl_4$. The first two, $SiCl_3Br$ and $SiCl_2Br_2$, had already been prepared by M. Friedel, by the action of bromine upon silicon chloroform at 100° C. in sealed tubes. M. Besson obtains all three compounds, including the hitherto unisolated $SiClBr_3$, by the action of hydrobromic-acid gas upon silicon tetrachloride. The first-named compound is comparatively easy to separate by fractional distillation, and when obtained in a fairly pure state serves for the preparation of the second and third chlorobromides by passing its vapor, instead of the tetrachloride, through the hot porcelain tube used in the original process. The second-named product boils, according to M. Besson, at from 102° to 105° C. It was found impossible to separate the third compound from this second one by fractional distillation, but taking advantage of the fact that the second chlorobromide can not be solidified at -60° C., while the third compound solidifies at -39° C., and afterward distilling the solid obtained, the third compound, $SiClBr_3$, has been isolated as a liquid boiling at from 126° to 128° C. All three chlorobromides combine directly with gaseous ammonia to form additive compounds, white amorphous solid bodies decomposed by water.

In the determination of nitrates in water Allen Hazen and H. W. Clarke have found the phenosulphonic-acid process of Grand Val and Lajoux, with proper precautions, giving results usually too low, and often much too low, so that, while it may be useful in some cases, they have not been able to obtain results of the desired accuracy. In the aluminum process, while the action of the caustic soda and aluminum decomposes a portion of the organic matter with formation of ammonia, this error is not found to exceed from 2 to 4 per cent. of the albuminoid ammonia. With almost all ground waters, and with most surface waters, it is insignificant. It is only in the presence of large amounts of decomposing organic matter that the result becomes uncertain. With potassium-nitrite solutions in distilled water the results are satisfactory, and are as accurate as the strength of ammonia solutions can be determined at a single trial by direct Nesslerization ; and the authors believe that their results upon waters, with the exception noticed, are equally accurate.

A method for the determination of barium in the presence of calcium and magnesium, described by F. W. Mar as rapid and accurate, depends upon the fact that while barium chloride is soluble to an extent not exceeding 1 part in 20,000 in pure concentrated hydrochloric acid, the solubility increases very rapidly as the strength of the acid is diminished. In concentrated hydrochloric acid containing ether it is soluble to an amount not exceeding 1 part in about 120,000. In the separation of barium from calcium and magnesium the chlorides of the earths are dissolved in the least possible amount of boiling water and are precipitated with 25 c. c. of hydrochloric acid, with the addition of 5 c. c. of absolute ether after cooling. After standing a few minutes the precipitate is filtered, washed with hydrochloric acid containing about 10 per cent. of ether, and dried at a temperature of from 150° to 200° C.

Prof. Ramsay recommends as the best method of preparing pure nitrogen peroxide the addition of the blue-green liquid, supposed to be a mixture of this oxide with nitrous anhydride, which is obtained by condensing the products of the interaction of arsenious oxide and nitric acid to a solution of nitric anhydride in nitric acid and phosphoric acids, prepared by adding phosphoric anhydride to well-cooled nitric acid. After agitating the mixture the upper layer is decanted and distilled.

For lecture experiments showing the dissociation of soap by water, A. A. Breneman recommends pouring an alcoholic solution of soap into a glass cylinder half filled with distilled water, which also contains phenolphthalein. The line of contact of the liquid is colored bright red, and on carefully stirring with a long rod a pink flush is diffused through the mixed liquids. As both are free from color before contact, the liberation of alkali by the water is plainly shown, and the theory of the action of soap is thus illustrated.

Silicon bromoform, $SiHBr_3$, which had been observed in an impure state by Buff and Wöhler, has been obtained pure by M. Besson by repeated fractional distillation of the product obtained by passing a stream of dry hydrochloric-acid gas over crystals of silicon heated to a temperature just below redness. It is a colorless liquid, which fumes vigorously at the first contact with air and in a few minutes spontaneously inflames. The vapor forms highly explosive mixtures with air, which occasionally detonate with great violence. It remains liquid at temperatures as low as -60° C. Water at once decomposes it, and with solutions of alkalies the decomposition is violent.

Trisulphide of boron, B_2S_3, was first obtained by Berzelius, and is also prepared by the modified processes of Deville and Wöhler and of Frémy. Of these, the process of Deville and Wöhler, by massing dry sulphureted hydrogen gas over red-hot amorphous boron, is regarded as best. The deposit of boron trisulphide appears in the cooler parts of the tube, first opaline, then in a porcelainlike form, and further along in brilliant acicular crystals. These are violently decomposed by water, yielding a clear solution of boric acid, with evolution of sulphureted hydrogen. A subsulphide of boron is described by M. Sabbatier, which is left as a more volatile black substance in the porcelain boat in which the boron was placed in the first experiment, and is also formed when the trisulphide of boron is heated in a current of hydrogen. Two selenides of boron, B_2Se_3 and B_4Se, corresponding with the sulphides, are described by M. Sabbatier; also silicon selenide, $SiSe_2$, which is obtained by heating crystalline silicon to redness in a current of hydrogen selenide. It has the appearance of a fused hard metallic mass incapable of volatilization. Water reacts vigorously with it, producing silicic acid, and liberating hydrogen selenide. It emits a very irritating odor of hydrogen selenide.

Sodium amide, NH_2Na, has been prepared by Mr. Joannis in apparently a purer form than the olive-green fusible substance that was obtained by Gay-Lussac and Thénard. Mr. Joannis obtains it in well-defined colorless crystals from the sodammonium of Weyl, which decomposes spontaneously at the ordinary temperature into hydrogen and sodamide. It is, however, prepared in larger quantities and less time by allowing saturated water solutions of sodammonium and sodium chloride to react upon each other at the temperature of melting ice. When sodamide is thrown into water a lively action occurs, just as if the crystals had consisted of globules of red-hot metal, with a violent hissing and the evolution of water vapor, but of no other gas.

Herr Jannasch, in collaboration with Herr Vogtherr, has successfully applied to a large number of minerals a process of decomposing silicates in a special p̱ apparatus by strong hydrochloric acid ḻṉḏẖṟ̱pressure. In addition to silicates he succeeded in decomposing black amphibole or hornblende, cerite, etc. Chrome-iron ore was perfectly decomposed by hydrochloric acid at about 250° C.

By adding the special ferments obtained from the wines of Ay, Beaune, Chablis, and Barsac, M. G. Jacquenin has obtained fermented liquors having the special bouquet of the wines in question from malt and from pure solutions. He has also by a similar process produced cider from barley.

H. N. Warren's improved process for the manufacture of potassium cyanide depends upon the formation of potassium sulphocyanate, the conversion of that substance into potassium cyanate, and of that into potassium cyanide.

Experiments have been made in the laboratory of Siemens and Halske, in Berlin. in the commercial production of ozone. The original Siemens ozonizing tube consisted of two concentric glass cylinders, the inner one coated interiorly and the outer one exteriorly with metal. These two coatings were supplied with an alternating current of high potential, while oxygen was made to traverse the annular space between them. It now appears that only one dielectric is necessary, mica, celluloid, porcelain. and the like being available as well as glass, and the ozone tube having either a metal tube within and a metal-coated nonconducting tube without, or a metal tube without, while the inner tube is made of the nonconducting material and lined with metal. Metals not attacked by ozone should be used. Cold water flows through the inner tube and air through the ring space.

Atomic Weights.—A memoir by the late Prof. Stas has been left, almost complete, describing the results of several stoichiometrical investigations, particularly respecting silver. The validity of the author's former determination of the atomic weight of silver, by which that of oxygen would be made 15·96 instead of 16, as the advocates of Prout's hypothesis would like to have it, was doubted by Prof. Dumas, on the ground that the silver employed was not free from occluded atmospheric gases. Prof. Stas then prepared silver of perfect purity, with which, repeating his experiments, he obtained a result identical with his former one. In addition to this important memoir, Prof. Stas has left the data of a series of twelve separate determinations of the stoichiometric relation of silver to potassium chloride, the materials for which were the pure silver just mentioned, and a specimen of potassium chloride prepared with equal care : and also a third memoir relating to the spectra of several metals which he has obtained in the purest state in which they were ever probably seen.

The atomic weight of copper has been redetermined by Dr. T. W. Richards, both by investigating the methods by which the old number (63·3) was obtained, and by a new series of determinations, in which corrections for former errors were applied. The final mean value obtained was 63·604 (oxygen = 16); the maximum and minimum values were 63·609 and 63·6 respectively. If the value of oxygen is taken as 15·96, that of copper becomes 63·44.

The atomic weight of palladium has been redetermined by H. F. Keller and E. F. Smith, who find as the mean value resulting from their most exact experiments, Pd = 106·914.

The determination of the atomic weight of lanthanum by Bohuslav Brunner at 138·21 (O = 16) is identical with the results obtained by Cleve and Bettendorff.

Chemical Analysis.—What has been heretofore called amorphous boron has been shown to be a mixture of that substance with large quantities of impurities, formed by the combination of the boron at the moment of its liberation with a portion of the metal used to replace it, and with the substance of the vessel in which the action is performed. Boron has now been obtained by M. Moissan in almost perfect purity by the action of metallic magnesium on boric aubydride. This reaction had been previously studied by Prof. Winkler, who employed the magnesium in the quantity calculated to remove all the oxygen from its state of combination with the boron. M. Moissan shows that with only one third this quantity of magnesium the yield of free boron is much enhanced, and the impurities are only such as can be removed. Two borides of magnesium may be formed, one of which is dissolved by water with evolution of a mixture of hydrogen and boron hydride, while the other is permanent in the presence of both water and acids. It is this stable boride, which the author has obtained in good crystals, which is so difficult to remove from the substance hitherto considered amorphous boron.

In the estimation of unsaponifiable matter in fats, Mr. William Mansbridge uses benzoline boiling at 110° F. as a solvent instead of the usual ether. Except in the case of pure wool fat he finds a tolerably close agreement between the results obtained by this process and those arrived at by titration; hence it is indicated that for practical purposes simple titration, even with unknown greases of low quality, gives a near approximation to the real content of unsaponifiable matter. The author's experience in the case of pure wool fats has shown that there is a tolerably constant relation between the results obtained by extraction with benzoline and the titration values, such relation depending on the amount of cholesterin and similar bodies in the grease. The connection is sufficiently constant to allow of its use for determining the presence of mineral oil or resin oil in wool fat, and thus to give a valuable indication as to the purity or otherwise of the sample.

Free hydroxylamine, NH_2OH, has been isolated by M. Lobry de Bruyn. From the preliminary account which the author has published of his method, it appears to have been obtained by the successive treatment of hydroxylamine hydrochloride with methyl alcohol, sodium, and ether. It is a very hygroscopic crystalline substance, rapidly liquefying from the absorption of water when exposed to the air, melting at 33° C., and in the liquid state having the capability of rapidly dissolving metallic salts; is without odor, heavier than water; decomposes violently when rapidly heated upon platinum foil, with production of a large sheet of bright-yellow flame, and is very slightly soluble in liquid carbon compounds. The vapor attacks corks, so that the solid requires to be preserved in glass-stoppered bottles. It appears also to act upon cellulose. The pure crystals are very stable, but the solution is less so, it appearing to be affected by the alkalinity of the glass of the vessel, for when free from dissolved alkali it is perfectly stable. When warmed to a temperature of from 80° to 100° C. it is dangerously explosive.

Diethylene diamine has been obtained by Dr. J. Sieber, of Breslau, by the action of ethylene dibromide upon ethylene diamine, a liquid boiling at 123° C. Upon treating the product of this reaction with caustic potash, an oily liquid separated, consisting of a mixture of bases. The separated liquid was dehydrated and then submitted to fractional distillation, when the portion boiling between 168° and 175° C. was found to consist of diethylene diamine admixed with a little water. The affinity of the base for water is so great that it was found impossible to remove the last traces of moisture. Diethylene diamine, however, forms salts which can be isolated in a state of purity, the analyses of which prove the composition of the base. The hydrochloride crystallizes in beautiful white needles, very soluble in water, but insoluble in alcohol. The platino-chloride forms fine needle-shaped crystals, readily soluble in hot water, but soluble with difficulty in boiling alcohol. A beautiful salt is also formed with mercuric chloride. It consists of starlike aggregates of acicular crystals, soluble in hot water, but reprecipitated by the addition of alcohol.

When ammoniacal solutions of vanadates are treated with sulphureted hydrogen a beautiful purple coloration is obtained, which has been presumed to be due to the formation of sulphosalts. It has not been found possible, however, to obtain such salts by crystallization in vacuum. Ammonium sulphovanadate $((NH_4)_3VS_4)$ has been isolated in large crystals by Drs. Krüss and Ohumais, whose account of their work also covers the preparation of several other sulpho-salts of vanadium. The process is by the action of sulphureted hydrogen on solution of ammonium metavanadate (NH_4VO_3) in the strongest ammonia. The crystals consist of opaque rhombic prisms resembling those of potassium permanganate. Their faces are brilliant, and reflect a steel bluish-violet color with a greenish tint when the reflection is received at a certain angle. The mother liquors from the first crystallizations deposit magnificent crystals on being allowed to stand in dry air. The substance is obtained more quickly and in large quantity by substituting potassium or sodium vanadate for the ammonium vanadate used in the original process; but it is remarkable that no potassium or sodium sulphovanadate is found in the product. The crystals of ammonium sulphovanadate are permanent in dry air but are slowly decomposed with evolution of sulphureted hydrogen in moist air. They are readily soluble in water, forming a solution that is colored intensely violet even when very dilute.

For the detection of the higher alcohols in ethylic alcohol, M. C. Bardy first ascertains, by treatment with sodium chloride, whether the sample is rich in the higher alcohols or not. Two cases may occur: First, the salt water retains the whole of the original liquid in solution; or, second, an oily layer collects at the upper part of the tube. The procedure is the same in both cases, only the quantity of alcohol to be operated upon varies. The butylic and amylic alcohols are extracted by treatment with carbon disulphide, washing with sulphuric acid, and etherification with acetic acid. If the alcohol in question contains higher alcohols there will be formed upon the surface of the liquid an oily layer of acetic ethers more or less abundant. These ethers are then estimated, and the percentage of butylic and amylic alcohols is calculated. If the mixture contains propylic alcohol, it must be sought for in the salty alcoholic liquid which has been exhausted with carbon disulphide, by redistilling it.

Palladium and platinum being precipitated by the electric current from their solutions in the presence of an excess of an alkaline phosphate and free phosphoric acid, while metallic iridium under similar conditions is not precipitated, Edgar F. Smith describes experiments that show that the separation of palladium and platinum from iridium can be effected in this way without difficulty.

The fact that strontium, as demonstrated by his previous experiments, can be separated quantitatively from calcium by boiling the nitrates with amyl alcohol, suggested to Mr. P. E. Browning a separation of barium from calcium by the same general treatment. The process proved in the experiments to be so rapid in execution and so satisfactory in its results that the author believes it may be placed among good analytical methods.

Analyses of boiler incrustations made by Prof. V. B. Lewes three years ago indicated that the incrustations derived from fresh water consist of impure carbonate of lime, those from sea water of sulphate of lime, and those from brackish water of a mixture of the two. These differences in the deposits are important, because they enable the shipowner to come to a conclusion respecting the treatment his boilers have received during the voyage by examination and analysis of the scale in them. With the introduction of high-pressure steam, a new and very dangerous form of deposit has appeared in boilers. It is derived from the oil that distills into the boiler from the lubricants used in the cylinder, the formation of which on the plates permits them to get superheated and in a condition to collapse. Experiments and analyses are recorded in the author's paper showing how this distillation takes place, even in mineral oils, when in contact with steam, at temperatures considerably below their estimated boiling points. The distilled oil forms a scum on the top of the water, which remains there until the particles of lime salts present, coming in contact in the course of the circulation with the greasy particles, gradually acquire the gravity of the water, and then, going along with the convection currents, stick to any surface with which they come in contact. Such a deposit is more likely to be produced with boilers containing fresh or distilled water. The great points to be sought in a good lubricating oil are that it shall be a pure mineral oil, and that its boiling point shall be well above any temperature likely to be attained in the cylinder. For the prevention of the oily deposits, the author recommends, therefore, filtration of the condenser water through a coke column for the removal of traces of oil, free use of the scum cocks, the use of water of considerable density rather than of fresh water, and the use of pure mineral-oil lubricants in the smallest possible quantity.

Chemical Synthesis.—A new and simple method of synthesizing tartaric acid is described by M. Genvresse. It is by the action of nascent hydrogen on glycoxylic acid. A mixture of glycoxylic and acetic acids is treated in small quantities at a time with zinc dust. After removal of the zinc and treatment with calcium-chloride solution, a white crystalline precipitate separates, which yields all the reactions of a tartrate and proves to be tartrate of lime. The tartaric acid obtained by this synthesis is the optically inactive variety known as racemic acid.

The synthesis of the minerals crocoite and phœnicochroite may be accomplished, according to C. Ludeking, by exposing for several months to the air a solution of lead chromate in caustic potash, in a flat dish or plate. It is possible thus to obtain a mixture of the crystals of the two, from which individual crystals may be easily picked out. The author also obtained each of the minerals alone. By using a large excess of very strong solution of potash, phœnico-croite was formed, with only a very little crocoite; when, on the contrary, much $PbCrO_4$ was dissolved, and in addition K_2CrO_4 was added to the potash solution, crocoite alone was formed. The $PbCrO_4$ crystals are oblique rhombic prisms with many modifications. The fracture is uncertain, luster adamantine, color hyacinth-red. They are stable in the air. The phœnicochroite crystals are tabular, of resinous luster, of cochineal color, and appear to be orthorhombic. They, like the natural crystals, have little stability, and soon change, on exposure, to a light-yellow powder.

In a paper at the British Association, Prof.

Crum Brown showed how, by an extension of the electrolytic methods which had been already fully worked out in relation to potassium acetate, the higher fatty acids of other series could be synthesized. Thus, starting from the ethyl potassium malonate, the ether of succinic acid was obtained in considerable quantity and with great readiness. Similarly adipic, sebacic, and other ethers had been obtained. Secondary prodnets were formed which in the higher members of the series accumulated in inconveniently large quantities.

A synthesis of troilite, the crystallized monosulphide of iron, FeS, which is frequently found in meteorites and never in terrestrial rocks, has been effected by Richard Lorenz, of Göttingen. The crystals were obtained when a stream of dry sulphureted hydrogen gas was led over a bundle of iron wire contained in a combustion tube heated in a furnace. At a dull-red heat the wire became covered with brilliant little crystals that presented a bright, silver-white luster when first obtained, but after a time reflected a pale-green light. After some days they further changed to blue, and then to brown, without changing form. Wurtzite, sulphide of zinc, ZnS, may be readily artificially obtained in a similar manner by passing sulphureted hydrogen over zinc heated to whiteness.

The syntheses of azoamide (N_2H) hitherto effected, have all depended upon the introduction of an organic substance at some stage of the process. Prof. Wislicenus has now obtained it by means of a simple reaction involving only inorganic substances, or by the interaction of ammonia gas and nitrous oxide in the presence of heated metallic sodium.

Agricultural Chemistry.—From a special study of the process of the passage of granite rock into fertile soil, Alexander Johnstone finds that the agents concerned in the work are mechanical, chemical, and vital. The mechanical agencies produce the largest results in bulk, and the principal of them is frost. The first chemical change coming over the rock is the peroxidation of some of the iron that is always present in its mass, which increases to the greatest extent where air and water can most readily enter. The surface of the rock becomes browned with the hydrated ferric oxide formed, and brown skins, of a deeper color than the surface generally, coat the walls of the original rock joints. There are in the mass of the rock, away from these primary fissures, areas more permeable than others from the surface, and through these streaks of ferric oxide are produced. These lines of rust are the beginnings of a new set of joints, which the author calls weather joints, to distinguish them from the primary joints of consolidation and rock movements. Very soon the work of carbonation is seen to be progressing along with the oxidation of the iron, but at a slower rate. The carbonic-acid gas of moist air, dissolved in the penetrating water, attacks the feldspars, the biotite, and the hornblende. Two processes of decomposition have been noticed—that which occurs when the carbonic acid is in excess or can obtain free access to the mineral, and that which takes place when either of the opposite conditions prevails. In the first case, the feldspar, supposing it to be orthoclase, has the molecules of its body, which are affected, completely broken up into clay, solid secondary or colloid silica, and carbonate of potash. In the second case, when a sufficient supply of carbonic acid can not get within "chemical" distance of the feldspar molecules, clay is produced as before, only more slowly, but the potash of the molecule is carried off, a part as a carbonate and part as a soluble silicate. From the plagioclase feldspar the same conditions produce similar results, except that the soluble silica which would be produced here is of course in combination with sodium. The author has found the soluble silica of soils always in the form either of silicate of potassium or of sodium, and very frequently of both mixed. Biotite, by the continued action of carbonic acid, oxygen, and water, loses magnesia and iron, and becomes eventually the white or yellow muscovite variety, which undergoes no further chemical change. Hornblende, by carbonation, oxidation, and hydration, yields lime as a carbonate until the whole of that base is taken out. The pyrites of the rock is slow to change, but it is also eventually acted on by water and oxygen particularly, the latter combining with its substance here and there to form a sulphate, which has a great mission in the physiology of the soil. These chemical changes begin on the exposed surfaces of the rock and along the faces of the primary joints Then oxidation begins in streaks and bands through the rock mass, and around those areas carbonation is most active. In fact, oxidation opens up the rock for further change. The chemical changes are followed by a new element in the making of soil, in the action of organic matter, first living as it finds footing in the already disintegrated parts of the rock, and then dead. This in its turn reacts to enforce the chemical changes, bringing about reciprocal actions which make the changes ever greater and more rapid; or, as the author summarizes the operation, "humus is formed by lichens, and then higher plants; following this, fungoid germs capable of assimilating aërial nitrogen become abundant; finally, all three processes—mechanical, chemical, and organic—go merrily on together and contribute all in their shares to the formation of an ever-deepening soil, capable of supporting the life of the highest plants. The humic acid, which is formed by the inorganic decay of humus, has a certain decomposing action, but it gradually changes to carbonic acid, with the action of which in this connection we have already dealt."

The power of micro-organisms to effect chemical action was first studied by Pasteur in his researches on fermentation. Our knowledge of the work of bacteria in other industries has been greatly advanced in the last few years, and through the study of them some of the most important phenomena in agriculture have recently received remarkable elucidation. One of the most important plant foods in the soil is nitric acid; yet it occurs there already existent in only the most minute proportions, being carried away by rain or absorbed by vegetation as rapidly as it is formed; and it has been found that the soil, under ordinary circumstances, continuously generates nitric acid from the various nitrogenous manures that are applied to it. The researches of Schloesing and Müntz have shown that the power of soils to convert the nitrogen of nitrogenous substances into nitric acid is due to micro-organisms or bacteria; and these results have been confirmed and greatly extended by other experimenters. Prof. Frankland proved in 1885 that some micro-organisms could grow in distilled water, or in the absence of organic matter. By suitable cultures he separated the nitrifying organisms from the others; but it afterward appeared that these organisms possessed the property of converting ammonia into nitrous but not into nitric acid. Further experiments showed that the process of conversion into nitric acid was a double one, and the work of two organisms succeeding one another, and producing, the first nitrous and the second nitric acid. The second organism, or nitric ferment, resembles potassium permanganate in its activity, in that it has no effect on ammonia, but readily converts nitrous into nitric acid. The fact of the multiplication of micro-organisms in distilled water, and the further fact that the nitrification process may be continued for four years in purely mineral solutions, are strong presumptive evidence in favor of their being able to gain a livelihood in the entire absence of organic food stuffs. This supposition is supported by the experiments of M. Winogradsky, who has found that the nitrifying organisms flourish, multiply, and actually build up living protoplasm in a solution from which organic matter has been most thoroughly excluded. "Now," says Prof. Frankland, "this living protoplasm in the experiments in question must have been elaborated by these bacteria from carbonic acid as the source of the protoplasmic carbon, and from ammonia and nitrous or nitric acids as the source of the protoplasmic nitrogen. If these experiments are correct . . . they are subversive of one of the fundamental principles of vegetable physiology, which denies to all living structures, save those of green plants alone, the power of building up protoplasm from such simple materials." The question whether plants are capable of assimilating or utilizing as food the free nitrogen of the atmosphere, which has been a very difficult one, has been answered in the case of leguminous plants by the researches of Prof. Hellriegel. Dr. Wilfarth, Dr. Gilbert, and Sir John Lawes. These authors find that plants of this class are inhabited by microbes whose presence is shown by peculiar swellings or tuberosities on their roots, through the agency of which a fixation of free atmospheric nitrogen is accomplished. The researches of Prof. Frankland, from whose paper before the Royal Institution these facts are derived, have further led to interesting results concerning the selective action of micro-organisms, their relations to the optical properties of certain substances, and their individuality; and, as a whole, they lead the author to the conclusions that there may be around us numerous forms of micro-organisms of the potentiality of which we are still ignorant; and he has high anticipations of the metamorphoses which it may be possible to bring about through their agency.

It had been shown by H. T. Brown and G. H. Morris that during germination of grass seeds the cell membrane of the endosperm is broken down and destroyed by a specific cellulose-dissolving enzyme, or cytohydrolyst, such disintegration of the cell wall being necessary to bring the cell contents under the influence of the starch and proteid-dissolving enzymes secreted by a certain layer of cells in the embryo. The authors investigated whether grain-feeding animals did not possess some provision in their economy for removing, during digestion, the walls of the starch cells of the interior of the grain, in order that the cell contents may be accessible to the digestive enzymes of the alimentary canal, and found that they did not. The cell wall is completely dissolved before the grain food enters the small intestine, though the enzyme effecting the dissolution is not secreted by any part of the animal economy, but is pre-existent in the germ before ingestion. The comparative abundance of the cytohydrolyst in the various grain foods given to stock is of great importance, bearing as it does on the relative speed of digestion. Thus oats contain a particularly large proportion of the cytohydrolyst—a fact that throws considerable light on the cause of the high estimation in which oats are held as a food stuff.

The odor emitted by certain garden and other soils after a heavy shower of rain in summer is ascribed by Dr. Phipson to the presence of organic substances related to the essential oils of plants, which they absorb from the fragrance of plants during the dry season and give up again when the rain penetrates its pores. The author extracted a substance of this kind by means of a solution of bromine, and found it yellowish, soluble in water, having a strong odor of cedar wood, and similar in chemical properties, if not identical with it, to bromo-cedar, which is derived from essence of cedar.

Chemistry of Foods.—Experiments in the laboratory of the Department of Agriculture, reported by Ervin E. Ewell, show that cane sugar is the principal carbohydrate contained in the coffee berry that is soluble in water. The water-insoluble portion of coffee yields an abundance of furfuraldehyde when distilled with hydrochloric acid, which indicates the presence of a pentose-yielding carbohydrate. A gummy substance is obtained when a 5-per-cent. sodium hydroxide extract is precipitated with alcohol. When this gum is washed with alcoholic hydrochloric acid, alcohol, and finally with ether, and is dried over sulphuric acid, a slightly grayish, translucent, hard, and brittle mass is obtained, which is readily reduced to powder in a mortar. The properties of this substance were determined as far as the limited amount of material permitted; and the results obtained suggest a compound containing one galactose group and one pentose group. From a separate portion of the water-insoluble material, hydrolyzed with dilute sulphuric acid, a sirup was obtained that yielded an abundance of furfuraldehyde and mucic acid. The residue from the sucrose determination was heated for five hours with 5-per-cent. sulphuric acid, when it yielded reducing sugars, mucic acid, and furfuraldehyde.

Analyses by R. H. Chittenden and T. B. Osborne show that the maize kernel contains several distinct proteids, well characterized in reactions and composition. Of them, are three globulins, one or more albumins, and an alcohol-soluble proteid. A globulin obtained by extraction with solution of chloride of sodium is a mixture of two or more dissimilar globulins which differ from each other in composition and in coagulation points. These two globulins are a myosinlike and a vitellinlike body. They exist as distinct substances in the corn or maize kernel, and are not products of a cleavage of the "mixed" globulin. Direct extraction of finely powdered corn meal with water leaves a dilute salt solution, which dissolves the myosinlike globulin and leaves the bulk of the vitellinlike substance undissolved. The myosin can be separated from the solution in a fair degree of purity. Extraction of corn meal with 10-per-cent. salt solution, after previous extraction with water, dissolves the vitellinlike globulin, which can be separated by the customary methods. So prepared, it agrees exactly with the vitellin separated by heat coagulation from the mixed globulin. The third globulin present in the maize kernel is characterized by extreme solubility in very dilute salt solutions, especially phosphates and sulphates. It separates from such solutions only by a prolonged dialysis. It coagulates in the neighborhood of $62°$ C., and contains 15·2 per cent. of nitrogen and 1·26 per cent. of sulphur. Through the long-continued action of water or of strong solutions of salt, the myosinlike globulin and the globulin with a still lower content of nitrogen are changed into insoluble modifications, soluble, however, in 0·5-per-cent. sodium-carbonate solution, from which they are precipitated on neutralization, apparently as albuminates. So prepared, these insoluble modifications are characterized by a relatively high content of carbon. The aqueous extract of corn meal and the sodium-chloride extract contain, in addition to the globulins, apparently two albuminlike bodies, more or less coagulable by heat, but, as prepared, unlike in chemical composition. A certain amount of proteose can be detected in the extracts of corn meal after the globulins and albumins have been entirely removed, but this appears to be mainly an artificial product resulting from the hydrolysis of one or more of the preceding bodies. Especially noteworthy is the presence in the maize kernel of a peculiar proteid body known as maize fibrin, or better as zein, soluble in warm dilute alcohol, but insoluble in water. Zein is characterized by a high content of carbon, by its resistance to the action of dilute alkalies (that is, non-convertibility into alkali-albuminate), and by the ease with which it is converted into an insoluble modification on being warmed with water or with very weak alcohol. Soluble zein and the insoluble modification have the same chemical composition. Both respond to the ordinary proteid reactions.

The assertion having been made in a German pharmaceutical journal that aluminum was so affected by certain liquids as to impair its utility for purposes in which such substances may come in contact with the human body, Prof. Lunge made experiments from which he drew the conclusions that the action of coffee, tea, both of which had been poured in hot, and beer, is zero, or practically insignificant; that of brandy is also slight, and that of acids and acid liquids (wine, sour milk, fruit juices, etc.), is more pronounced, but still so slight as to give no cause for alarm. In the worst case observed—that of acetic acid—the maximum attack was less than 5 milligrammes per 100 square centimetres in six days. Now, a canteen holding a litre (or nearly a quart) has an inner surface of about 600 square centimetres, and an aluminum weight of about 200 grammes. Such a canteen would in the very worst case lose 5 milligrammes in a day, even if it was always full, or 1 gramme in two hundred days, and would require fifty-five years to be reduced to half its weight. This is certainly too trifling an action to be considered. Nor is there the slightest danger of any injurious action upon the human body by such traces of aluminum compounds, seeing that our food contains very much more of these. Moreover, aluminum compounds are not poisonous in the ordinary sense, or as compared with compounds of arsenic, mercury, lead, copper, etc.; and they can not act injuriously unless quantities a hundred times larger than those found were regularly entering the stomach. It follows that aluminum may be employed without fear for canteens or any other vessels for holding articles of food, at least at the ordinary temperature.

Industrial Chemistry. — The industrial preparation of carbonic acid, according to M. Troost, has been promoted by the consumption of beer, the quality of which is improved by the pressure of carbonic acid, while it is spoiled by compressed air; in France it has been stimulated by the demand for salicylic acid in medical treatment—a substance which is largely produced by the action of liquid carbonic acid on sodium-phenol. At the works of the Company General for the Production of Antiseptics, near Hermes, pure carbonic acid is produced very economically by the combustion of coke; is collected in a gasometer, from which it is drawn, to be dried and compressed with pressures of 5, 25, and 70 atmospheres, and stored in iron bottles. At present 300 kilogrammes are produced daily; but as other applications occur than that for the manufacture of salicylic acid, M. Gall, the director of the work, is increasing the power of manufacture, and it will soon be possible to produce 1,000 kilogrammes a day. The applications of the liquid include the manufacture of aërated waters, the filtering of wine, cooling by virtue of the great absorption of heat in vaporizing, and solidification of fused metals under high pressure.

In view of the probable eventual exhaustion of the coal supplies of Great Britain, the question of the modern developments of fuels and their use was considered by Dr. J. Emerson Reynolds in his presidential address before the Society of Chemical Industry. As a means of saving coal and obviating other difficulties attendant upon its use, the author advises the substitution, for heating purposes, of gaseous fuel, either in the form of Siemens's "producer" gas of low illuminating but high heating power or in that of water gas. Already, "the use of such gaseous fuel is so steadily extending that we may expect in the near future to reach the maximum practicable economy of coal in our greater industries, and of smoke abatement as well"; while electric lighting promises to supply the place of gas for illumination. The general use of ordinary peat is attended by the disadvantages

of its requiring much greater storage room than coal, of its producing a light and troublesome ash, and of its requiring more than thirteen times the bulk of coal to produce the same thermal effect. Even when it is compressed, peat does only 45 per cent. of the work of the same weight of coal, and can not compete with it when the same values of both substances are taken. The best chance for economically applying peat for most manufacturing purposes lies in gasifying it. If this is done, the production of ammonia from peat along with gas will, as Ludwig Mond has shown, probably pay for gasifying the fuel and materially facilitate its utilization. A superior source of fuel to either coal or peat is afforded in petroleum, a substance composed of hydrocarbides. The hydrocarbides are different in American and in Russian petroleum, but petroleum from both sources affords some of the lower homologues of marsh gas; hence, in the process of refining crude petroleum by distillation, the first products consist largely of butane, pentane, and hexane, which are separated and condensed by pressure, the product being used for refrigerating purposes by virtue of its high volatility. At the successively higher degrees of distillation a spirit and the illuminating oils are produced, while the residue which is not vaporized at 300° includes the heavier lubricating oils, which are also admirably suited for use as fuel, and are cheaper than those generally used for lighting purposes. During this process of refining by simple distillation there is always more or less decomposition in progress, hydrocarbides of high molecular weight being resolved into simpler ones at a comparatively high temperature; and when crude petroleum or its constituents are rapidly heated, this resolution can be carried so far as to convert a large proportion of the oil into permanent gas, valuable alike, for illuminating and heating purposes. Several methods are employed for the conversion of oil into rich gas and storing the latter for distribution through tubes in the ordinary way. The proofs are cited in the author's paper that petroleum is the most concentrated, and, on the whole, the most portable, of all the natural fuels met in considerable quantities.

CHILI, a republic in South America. The legislative power is exercised by the National Congress, consisting of a Senate and a Chamber of Deputies. The Deputies are elected for three years directly by the citizens who can read and write in the proportion of 1 to every 30,000 of population in each of the 68 departments. The Senators are elected for six years by direct suffrage in each of the 23 provinces, 1 Senator to every 3 Deputies. The President of the republic is elected indirectly for five years, and can not be re-elected while in office. He is assisted by a Cabinet of 6 ministers and by a Council of State, in which he nominates 5 members, while 6 are chosen by Congress. Jorge Montt was inaugurated as President, succeeding José Manuel Balmaceda, on Dec. 18, 1891.

Area and Population.—The area of the republic is 293,970 square miles, including 75,292 square miles in the territory of Magallanes and Tierra del Fuego, and 60,968 square miles forming the province of Antofagasta, which was taken from Peru in the war between the two republics.

The estimated population on **Jan. 1, 1891**, was 2,766,747, being 9·4 per square mile. The estimate is based upon the incomplete census of 1885, and is believed to fall below the real number by at least 400,000. Santiago, the capital, had 200,000 inhabitants in 1885, and Valparaiso, the chief seaport, 100,000.

The Army and Navy.—The military law of Dec. 30, 1887, limits the army to 8 regiments of infantry, 3 of cavalry, 2 of field artillery, 1 battalion of coast artillery, and 1 of engineers, and fixes the maximum strength at 5,835 men. The National Guard numbered 51,090 in 1891.

The naval forces comprise 2 ironclads, 4 deck-protected cruisers, 10 first-class and 2 second-class torpedo boats, 2 torpedo gunboats, 2 corvettes, 3 rams, 2 dispatch boats, 2 transports, 4 gunboats, and 4 sailing vessels.

Finances.—The revenue in 1889 amounted to 90,645,735 pesos or dollars, of which 41,102,402 pesos were derived from customs. The expenditure was 59,387,200 pesos. The revenue for 1890 was estimated at 58,000,000 pesos, not including the surplus of 31,257,526 pesos brought over from the preceding year. The expenditure was estimated at 67,069,809 pesos. In 1891, the year of the war, the expenditure is supposed to have been 100,000,000 pesos, in paper currency.

The public debt on Jan. 1, 1890, amounted to 93,617,955 pesos, including an external debt of 47,116,460 pesos, an internal debt of 24,013,579 pesos, and 22,487,916 pesos of paper currency. The Government proposed to raise an internal loan of 30,000,000 pesos in 1892.

Congress.—The session of Congress that closed on Jan. 30, 1892, was remarkable for the amount of work done. The most important bill passed at the close of the session was an act authorizing the President to borrow $25,000,000, in order to withdraw the notes of the dictatorship.

The regular session of Congress was opened on June 1 by President Montt. He referred to the restoration of order since he took office, and passed over the "Baltimore" affair in a few words, lamenting the attack and expressing regret at the circumstances, which at one time threatened a rupture of friendly relations between Chili and the United States, and said that a settlement would be arrived at through diplomatic channels in accord with international justice. The treaty with Bolivia, made by the Junta at Iquique in 1891, would be modified after being submitted to the Congresses of Chili and Bolivia. The diplomatic service would be reduced on grounds of economy. An amnesty law would be presented to Congress in favor of Balmacedists, excluding those officials against whom accusations were pending before Congress. Immigration would be favored, and a rural police organized. The army would be augmented to a peace footing of 6,000. The navy would not be increased during the present year. Reciprocity treaties with all the South American republics were recommended.

A bill was passed by Congress authorizing the President to issue bonds amounting to $8,750,-000, for sale in Chili and Europe, interest not to exceed 5 per cent. per annum, and a sinking fund amounting to 2 per cent. was to be provided. Interest on the loan would be payable in Santiago, London, Paris, or Berlin, at the option of the holders, and the bonds are to be secured on the export duties of nitrates and iodine. The President is authorized to increase the amount to be applied in the payments from the nitrate funds, if that should become necessary. Should the bonds not be taken up, the President is authorized to arrange for a loan, with the maximum of 6 per cent. interest, the sum realized to be devoted to extinguishing the present floating debt of $8,750,000. A bill was passed fixing the rates of duties on nitrates and iodine: the duty on nitrates equal to $1.42 per metric quintal, and that on iodine 46 cents per kilo, payments to be made as often as the Government requires them. The revenue thus raised is to be applied to the payment of interest of the coupon debt, which now amounts to $600,000 annually.

President Montt sent a message to Congress in September, calling an extra session of that body for the consideration, among other questions, of the Franco-Chilian treaty, colonization, the sales of nitrate, and the estimates for 1893. Other objects were to establish a money standard and arrange for a sufficient volume of currency, to consider an increase of pay for the army and navy, and to reorganize the civil service.

Cabinet Crises.—In forming his Cabinet, President Montt had been governed by a desire to reconcile the different parties, and it consisted of Liberals, Radicals, and Conservatives. It was evident, however, that this coalition ministry could not attain any solidity under the Liberal *régime*, and dissatisfaction with the proposals of Finance Minister Valdes Vergara to rehabilitate Chili's finances led to the resignation of the Conservative members. A new Cabinet was formed on March 13, 1892, without the Conservatives, which was composed of the following men: Premier and Minister of the Interior, Edouardo Matte; Minister for Foreign Affairs, Gaspar Toro; Minister of Justice and of Public Instruction, Señor Castello; Minister of Finance, Augustino Edwards; Minister of War and of Marine, Luis Barros Borgagno; Minister of Public Works, Jorge Riesco. The new Cabinet set out with an elaborate programme of reform; it pledged itself to adopt a course of moderation and to act in concord. Vacancies should be filled by competent men, irrespective of politics, and expenditures should be minimized. But it soon appeared that this Cabinet would not be of long duration, as the strife between the Liberals and the Conservatives was becoming bitter. The Cabinet demanded the removal of five of the railroad directors, who were held responsible for the loose and demoralizing methods prevailing in the Government railway service. The directors, expecting his support, appealed to the President, who refused to give a decision, and allowed an appeal to be made to the Commission Conservadore, the body that supervises the acts of the Government during the recess of Congress. The Cabinet was sustained, and a crisis was narrowly averted. The dissatisfaction with the Cabinet grew daily. This was due largely to its neglect to present any measures of economy, and the ministers finally saw themselves forced to resign. A new Cabinet was constituted June 11, and was composed as follows: Minister of the Interior, Barros Luco; Minister for Foreign Affairs, Isidoro Errazuriz; Minister of Fi-

nance, Enrique McIver; Minister of Justice and
Public Instruction, Maximo del Campo; Minister of Public Works, Vicente Davila; Minister
of War, Gen. Rodriguez Rosas.

Difficulties with the United States.—The
strained relations between Chili and the United
States were much intensified by a note sent by
the Chilian Minister of Foreign Affairs, Matta,
to the Chilian ministers at foreign courts and to
Minister Pedro Montt at Washington, giving the
latter authority to give it the widest publicity.
The note was a sort of vindication of the Chilian
Government, and was meant to counteract the
charges made in President Harrison's annual
message to the United States Congress. In this
document the minister alleges that the information upon which Secretary Tracy's report and
President Harrison's message to Congress were
based was erroneous or deliberately incorrect;
that the refugees in the American legation were
never threatened with cruelty, nor their removal
ever contemplated, nor had the house or person
of any of the foreign ministers been molested;
that there was a want of frankness and exactness
in the statements made in Washington relative
to the "Baltimore" affair, which occurred in a
bad quarter of the city; that, despite the fact
that interested parties might try to make their
conduct appear honest, they dodged the issue by
erroneous accounts; that Secretary Tracy and
President Harrison had been led into error concerning the Chilian people and Government;
and that their instructions to the United States
representatives, that impartiality and amity
should be observed, were not complied with.

Mr. Egan, United States minister at Santiago,
complained to the Chilian Government that the
legation was constantly being watched by the
police and private detectives; that persons passing in and out were insulted, and several Americans had been arrested on leaving the legation,
among them members of Mr. Egan's family.
The reply sent to this complaint stated that, inasmuch as the refugees at the legation had relatives and connections in the city, the maintenance of the watch was deemed necessary to protect the Chilian Government against conspiracies
which might be carried on from the legation.
Mr. Egan called the attention of the Argentine
minister to this surveillance, who, as *doyen* of
the diplomatic corps, protested against the breach
of diplomatic courtesy.

The investigation of the "Baltimore" affair
before the court of inquiry at Valparaiso lasted
nearly three months, and the evidence was then
submitted to the Procurator-Fiscal, who arrived
at the following conclusions:

1. That the unfortunate incident of Oct. 16, 1891,
originated in a brawl between intoxicated sailors of
both nations, and that the riot was aggravated on account of the special ward in which it occurred being
full of houses of bad reputation.
2. That the policemen from the first did all that
they were directed to do to suppress the riot; that the
correctness of the course adopted by the police had
been acknowledged by every one of the witnesses,
and all American sailors except two.
3. That the isolated shot wound was caused by a
revolver, whereas the police carried carbines.

The Procurator-Fiscal found further that
Rodriguez, Gomez, and Azumada, three of the

rioters, were guilty of stabbing American sailors,
but that the evidence was not strong enough to
show that the wounds inflicted by the prisoners
caused the death of the men Riggin and Turnbull. He further found that Davidson, a sailor
of the "Baltimore," was guilty of assaulting a
Chilian sailor, and declared that it was impossible to determine the person who fired the shot
that killed Riggin. He then directed Judge
Foster, at Valparaiso, to sentence the three above-
named Chilian rioters to penal servitude for
using knives.

This report was communicated to the United
States Government on Jan. 8 by Gen. Pereira,
Chilian Minister of Foreign Affairs, who had
succeeded Señor Matta. The United States Government was by no means satisfied with the
communication, as there was not a word of apology or regret in the note. On Jan. 20 the Chilian minister at Washington, Pedro Montt, presented a note from his Government to the effect
that Mr. Egan, minister of the United States in
Santiago, was not *persona grata* to his Government, which would have much pleasure in receiving another representative of the United
States, and that the motive for taking this step
was the desire of the Chilian Government to
draw closer its relations with the Government of
the United States.

No further action having been reported in regard to the punishment of the three men on
trial, and no apology or expressions of regret
having been received, President Harrison presented to the Chilian Government a note which
declared that the United States Government,
after a full consideration of all the evidence and
every suggestion affecting this matter, adhered
to the following conclusions:

1 The assault was not relieved of the aspect which
the early information concerning the event gave it,
namely, that of an attack upon the uniform of the
United States navy, having its origin and motive in a
feeling of hostility to the Government of the United
States, and not in any act of the sailors.
2. The public authorities of Valparaiso flagrantly
failed in their duty to protect the men; even some
police and some Chilian soldiers and sailors were
themselves guilty of unprovoked assaults upon the
United States sailors before and after the arrest; and
the preponderance of evidence and the inherent prob-
abilities led him to the conclusion that the man
Riggin was killed by the police or the soldiers.
3. He was compelled to bring the case back to the
position taken by the United States Government in
the note of Mr. Wharton of Oct. 23, 1891, and to ask
for suitable apologies and some adequate reparation
for the injury done to the Government of the United
States. He called the attention of the Chilian Government to the offensive character of the note addressed
by Señor Matta, its Minister of Foreign Affairs, to
Señor Montt, its minister at Washington, on Dec. 11.
This dispatch was not officially communicated to the
United States Government; but as Minister Montt
was directed to translate it and give it to the press of
this country it could not pass without official notice.
The Chilian Government was notified that, unless
this note was at once withdrawn and an apology
tendered as public as the offense, diplomatic relations would be terminated. The request for the recall
of Mr. Egan, on the ground that he is not *persona
grata*, was unaccompanied by any suggestion that
could properly be used in support of it. It must be
inferred that the request was based upon the official
acts of Mr. Egan, which had the approval of the
United States Government; but, however that might

be, he could not consent to consider such a question until it had first been settled whether correspondence with Chili could be conducted upon a basis of mutual respect.

No reply having been received, President Harrison sent a message to Congress on Jan. 25, laying before that body the whole correspondence with Chili since the breaking out of the revolution against Balmaceda. Mr. Egan's conduct was commented upon and approved by the President.

His right to give shelter in the American legation to adherents of the Balmaceda Government had not been denied by the Chilian Government, but Mr. Egan's request for a safe conduct out of the country for the refugees was denied, and not until about Jan. 16 were they placed on board the United States steamship "Yorktown," without a formal safe conduct, and merely by the acquiescence of the Chilian Government. They were subsequently conveyed to Callao, Peru. The disrespect manifested toward the United States Government by the close and offensive surveillance of the legation premises formed another ground of complaint. The correspondence with the Chilian Government relating to the "Baltimore" affair did not in any manner take the form of a manly and satisfactory expression of regret, much less of apology, and the event was so serious that if the injuries sustained by the men had been wholly the result of an accident in a Chilian port the incident would have been grave enough to have called for some public expression of sympathy and regret from the local authorities. It was not enough to say that the affair was lamentable, for humanity would require that expression even if the beating and killing of the sailors had been justifiable. It was not enough to say that the incident was regretted, coupled with the remark that the affair was not unusual in its character in ports where foreign sailors were accustomed to meet. It was not for a generous and sincere Government to seek for words of small or equivocal meaning in which to convey to a friendly power an apology for an offense so atrocious.

After a similar affair in New Orleans, in 1851, Mr. Webster immediately sent an apology to the Spanish Government, and expressed the regrets of the President at such disgraceful and flagrant breach of duty and propriety. Such treatment would have been more creditable to the Chilian authorities. In the note of Oct. 23 sent by the United States Government after the receipt of the report of the board of officers appointed by Capt. Schley to investigate the affair, the Chilian Government was called upon for any facts in its possession which might have tended to modify the unfavorable impressions which the report had created; and although the investigation was regarded by the police authorities as closed, it was reopened and protracted through a period of nearly three months. Although the United States Government might justly have complained of this unreasonable delay, yet, in view of the fact that the Government of Chili was provisional, and with a disposition to be forbearing, and hopeful of a friendly termination, the President awaited the report which had been recently made. The President's opinion was, that the demand made by the United States Government should be adhered to and enforced if the dignity as well as the prestige and the influence of the United States were not to be wholly sacrificed; that those who display in foreign ports the flag or wear the colors of the United States must be protected against insult, brutality, and death inflicted in resentment of acts of their Government, and not for any faults of their own. The prevailing feeling in the United States was that the President must be sustained in his demands, and a war with Chili was feared unless a satisfactory reply to the note should be received shortly. The reply came on the following day, and, with the answer of the United States Government, it was presented to Congress in a second message on Jan. 28.

In his response to the note of Jan. 21, Señor Pereira, the Chilian Minister of Foreign Affairs, withdrew, with expressions of regret, the offensive note of Señor Matta of Dec. 11, and also the request for the recall of Mr. Egan. He expressed the regret of the Chilian Government over the "Baltimore" affair, and offered to leave the matter to arbitration or to the decision of the United States Supreme Court at Washington, if the United States Government should not be willing to await the decision of the examining judge at Valparaiso. President Harrison declared himself satisfied with this note; and as regarded the question of arbitration of the "Baltimore" affair, he left it with the Chilian Government to finish the trial of the case. The accused were sentenced to imprisonment for participating in the riot. Chili paid the United States Government $75,000 in gold, to be distributed among the heirs of the two sailors killed and among those wounded in the riot of Oct. 16, 1891. The body of Riggin, the man who was shot in the riot, was brought home to the United States and buried in American soil in July, 1892.

CHINA, an empire in eastern Asia. The Emperor is an absolute monarch, but is governed by the traditions and laws of the empire as laid down in the "Book of Regulations of the Tsing Dynasty" and other documents. He acts on the advice of various consultative bodies, of which the chief are the Chun Chi Chu or Grand Council, the Tuchayuen or Board of Censors, the Neiko or Cabinet of two Chinese and two Manchu members, and the Hanlin or university. Under the direction of the Cabinet ministers are seven boards of administration, which deal respectively with the civil service, revenue and finance, rites and ceremonies, military affairs, public works, criminal law, and naval affairs. The Emperor Kwangsu, born in 1871, succeeded the Emperor Tungchi on Jan. 22, 1875, and nominally assumed the government in March, 1887, when he reached his majority, but the Empress Regent still remained the virtual ruler until he married, in February, 1889.

Finances.—The annual revenue of the Government at Pekin is supposed to amount to about $125,000,000. Only the receipts from foreign customs are made public. These amounted in 1890 to 21,996,226 haikwan taels, equal to $25,662,260. The yield of the land tax payable in silver is estimated at 20,000,000 taels, the value of the rice tribute at 2,800,000 taels, that of the salt tax at 9,600,000 taels, the receipts from native maritime and inland duties at 6,000,000 taels, the transit duty on foreign and native opium and miscellaneous wares at 11,000,000 taels, and license dues at 2,000,000 taels. The sale of offices, formerly a source of considerable revenue, was abolished by an imperial decree in 1878, although honorary titles are still sold sometimes, and when the Government is in need of money forced contributions are exacted from the rich officials. In the returns of the maritime customs is included the commuted *likin* tax on foreign opium, which produced 6,129,071 taels in 1890. The chief expense of the Government is for the maintenance of the army, which is supposed to cost about $75,000,000 a year. The foreign debt includes an 8-per-cent. loan of £627,625 raised in 1874 and secured on the customs, one of £1,604,276 raised in 1878, a silver loan of $7,525,000 contracted in 1884, others amounting to $11,250,000 contracted in 1886, a loan of $1,250,000 contracted in Germany in 1887, and temporary loans floated by provincial Governors in Shanghai and Hong-Kong.

The only Chinese coin was the copper cash, of which twelve are equal to a cent, until the Imperial Government in 1890 declared the new silver dollar coined at the Canton mint, current throughout the empire. It has the same value as the United States trade dollar, the Japanese yen, and the Mexican dollar. Hitherto all large payments have been in silver bullion by weight. The haikwan or customs tael was the usual standard, a tael weight of pure silver being worth, at the average rate of exchange for 1890, about $1.25. Foreign silver coins are taken by weight as bullion, except in the treaty ports.

The Army.—The Army of the Eight Banners, or old imperial army, comprising Manchus, Mongols, and Chinese of the class that joined the invaders in the seventeenth century, is officially reported as numbering 323,000 men. Of these, 100,000 are supposed to be reviewed by the Emperor every year. The guard maintained in the capital numbers only 717 men. all of whom have the grade of officers. The Ying Ping or Chinese army is returned at 6,459 officers and 650,000 soldiers. The army of Manchuria is estimated to number 70,000 men, partly armed with Mauser rifles. The army of the center, or of the capital province, of which 50,000 men are constantly under arms, is supplied with Remingtons, and is well drilled and under good discipline. The territorial militia has 200,000 men, and could be trebled in case of war.

The Navy.—The north coast squadron has 2 barbette ironclads of 7,280 tons, 1 of 9,850 tons, and 1 of 2,320 tons, 1 turret ship of 2,320 tons, 5 deck-protected cruisers of about 2,200 tons each, 4 torpedo cruisers, 23 first-class and 4 small torpedo boats, and 11 gunboats. In the Foochow squadron there are 9 cruisers ranging from 1,300 to 2,840 tons, 3 gunboats, 9 dispatch boats, and 3 revenue cruisers. · The Shanghai flotilla consists of 1 armored frigate, of 2.630 tons, 1 gunboat, 6 floating batteries, and 3 transports. The Canton flotilla has 13 river gunboats.

Commerce and Production. — China is mainly an agricultural country. Rice is the chief food crop in the south. In the north millet, beans, wheat, corn, and barley are raised. The production of opium has increased rapidly.

Sugar-cane is cultivated in the southern provinces and in the island of Formosa. Tea is raised in Fukien and Formosa, Hupeh, Hunan, Che-Kiang, Kiangsi, Anhui, Kwangtung, and Szechuen. Silk is produced in all parts of the country, but the main part of the silk exported and the best grades come from Szechuen, Che-kiang, and Kwangtung. Coal is found in immense deposits all over the empire. Mines are worked at Kaiping, north of Pekin, at Keelung in Formosa, and at Hankow. Copper is mined in Yunnan, where expert Japanese engineers have lately been employed by the Government to instruct the people in scientific methods.

The value of the imports in 1890 was reported by the customs bureau at 127,093,481 haikwan taels, that of the exports at 87,144,480 taels. Deducting from the value of imports the costs of landing, storing, and selling and the import duties, and adding to the figure given for exports the price of packing and shipping, commissions, etc., the corrected figure for the imports would be 109,547,087 taels, and that for exports 100,190,682 taels. The official figures for the principal imports were as follow : Cotton goods, 45,020,302 taels; opium, 28,956,329 taels; metals and metal wares, 6,872,084 taels; kerosene oil, 4,092,874 taels; seaweed and fishery products, 4,857,452 taels; woolens, 3,642,782 taels; coal, 1,973,173 taels; raw cotton, 1,577,-018 taels. The values of the largest exports were as follow: Silk, raw and manufactured, 30,255,905 taels; tea, 26,663,450 taels; sugar, 2,664,864 taels; straw braid, 2,088,775 taels; paper, 1,359,915 taels; clothing, 1,428,210 taels; chinaware and pottery, 617,491 taels; cow and buffalo hides, 714,967 taels. Of the imports, 72,057,314 taels came from Hong-Kong, 24,607,-989 taels from Great Britain, 10,300,101 taels from India, 7,388,685 taels from Japan, 3,676,057 taels from the United States, 2,471,075 taels from Europe apart from Great Britain and Russia, and 897,826 taels from Russia in Europe and Asia. Of the total exports, 32,930,551 taels went to Hong-Kong, to be forwarded thence to Great Britain, America, Australia, France, Germany, the Straits Settlements, India, and other countries; 37,703,273 taels were shipped direct to England, 14,100,961 went to the ports of the European Continent, 12,221,122 taels to Japan, 11,840,805 taels to the United States, 11.355,978 taels to India, and 9,754,408 taels to Russia. Of the tea exported in 1890, Great Britain took 433,964 piculs, of 133⅓ pounds, the United States 268,141 piculs, Russia 585,349 piculs, Australia 109,155 piculs, and 135,470 piculs were shipped to Hong-Kong, the total export being 1,665,396 piculs. The imports of kerosene oil rose from 8,256,000 gallons in 1882 to 49,348,000 gallons in 1891. In 1889 the exports of American oil were 14,989.942 gallons ; in 1890, 23,591,113 gallons ; in 1891, 39,348,477 gallons. Of Russian oil, 5,666,471 gallons were consumed in 1889; in 1890, 7,237,611 gallons; in 1891, 10,000,902 gallons. There are few manufacturing establishments in China besides the Government arsenals. The graving and repair docks and the rope factories, where manilla hemp is made into cordage are owned by foreigners, and so are most of the cotton mills, breweries, glass works, and other factories organized on a considerable scale. There are match factories managed by Chinamen, but most of their manufacturing enterprises are small shops employing 15 or 20 hands and using few and simple machines in the processes of making bamboo articles, silver and amber articles, fruit preserves, glassware, paper, etc. Europeans who have established factories with the object of taking advantage of the cheap labor of the country have deceived themselves, because Chinese laborers refuse to work in factories for four times their ordinary wages, and demand the full pay of Western workingmen. The import of machinery in 1890 amounted to about $5,000,000, an increase of 18 per cent. over the previous year. The bulk of it consisted of sewing machines and cotton gins, mainly from the United States.

Navigation.—The number of vessels entered and cleared at Chinese ports in 1890 was 31.133, of 24,876,459 tons. Of these, 25.838, of 23,928,-557 tons, were steamers. In respect to nationality, 16,897 vessels, of 16,087,895 tons, were British; 10,003, of 6,334,906 tons, were Chinese; 2,140, of 1,343,964 tons. German; 629, of 505,181 tons, Japanese; 174, of 239,700 tons, French; and 155, of 82,946 tons, American.

Communications. — An enormous internal traffic is carried on by means of the canals and navigable rivers and in part over the roads that traverse China in all directions. The Kaiping Railroad. which was recently extended from Petung to Tientsin, is being continued to Shanghai. In 1889 the Emperor ordered a railroad to be built from Pekin to Hankow, on the Yangtse-Kiang. and he transferred the Viceroy Chang-Chi-Tung from Canton to Hankow. in order that the latter might co-operate with Li-Hung-Chang, viceroy of the imperial province, in carrying out the project. Through lack of financial means and owing to the popular prejudice against railroads, they have not yet been able to begin the work, which is important in a commercial way, and still more so from a strategic point of view. There is a short railroad in Formosa. The telegraph lines already connect the principal cities of the coast and of the interior with the capital, and they are being extended rapidly. The delivery by a German house of rails in 1892 for another short coal road in Hunan aroused expectations among Europeans that the long-awaited era of railroad building had at last opened. The difficulties in the way of constructing railroads are little understood. The ethical repugnance of the Chinese, with whom ancestor worship takes the place of religion, to having the graves disturbed that are scattered everywhere about the country, is known but not appreciated. The engineering difficulties in the way of bridging the rivers and building a high viaduct over the intricate interlacing network of canals has been little considered. Then there are the economic obstacles arising from the fact that a large proportion of the population are dependent for their living on the occupation of carrying merchandise by the roads and canals, and the mandarins derive a large part of their revenues from the tolls.

The Disturbances in Mongolia.—The rebellion of the Chinese settlers in Mongolia and Manchuria, in which towns were sacked and many native Christians were murdered, was due, according to a report made by Gen. Li-Hung-Chang, to the cruel exactions of the Mongol prince, continued for many years, and to the barbarities committed by the Chaoyang tribesmen, who oppressed and plundered the Chinese emigrants who leased their lands. The Chinese, when redress was denied them, rose at last and killed the prince's family and every Mongol who fell into their power. They attacked the Christians at Je-Ho because the latter, who were a strong and compact community, treated them haughtily, and the authorities were either helpless or connived at their outrages. Contrary to the first reports, no foreigner was killed. The Belgian Government demanded 100,000 taels damages of the Chinese Government for the destruction of the Je-Ho mission. The disturbances were suppressed by an army from Pekin, led by Li-Hung-Chang. which returned from the expedition in February, 1892, having suffered greatly from cold and privations.

In a battle at Chihli the imperial troops lost 300 killed and 1,500 wounded, besides many prisoners. This reverse was ascribed to the lack of light guns, and on his return the viceroy ordered a large number of mounted Krupp howitzers. During the expedition 8,000 of the insurgents are said to have been put to the sword. In the district of Ching-Chang out of 1,300 rebels who fell into the hands of the imperial troops, 500 were burned, while the rest were cut down.

The Audience Question.—After the foreign ministers had so far overborne the barriers that divide them from the imperial court as to obtain an audience with the Emperor in 1891, they discovered that the building was not comportable with their dignity. It was the hall of audience in which the envoys of tributary states, like Nepaul and Tibet, were received. As this was emblematic in the eyes of the Chinese of the superiority of China, the European ministers had always refused to be received in this building, and they had consented this time on the understanding that a new hall should be built for them. They demanded that the next reception, on the Chinese New Year of 1892, should be held in the palace. Prince Tching suggested that they should present a memorial to the Emperor. Observing that there was no chance of their gaining their point, the German *doyen* of the diplomatic corps was in favor of having the audience under any conditions, and in this he was supported by the rest of the envoys except those of Russia and France, who made the question of saluting the Emperor in the palace or not at all an occasion to break with their colleagues. The British minister suggested as a compromise that they should go where they were asked this year on condition that in the following year they should have their audience in the palace. All accepted the suggestion, and a memorandum was presented to the Prince President of the Tsungli-Yamen, who when he had read the first words of the preamble, " Whereas the sovereigns of the Western states are the equals of his Imperial Majesty,'' threw aside the document and refused to hold any further discussion. The Austrian minister, Herr von Biegeleben, on Oct. 27. 1891, had presented his credentials to the Emperor in the Chen-Quan temple, having declined to be received in the building used for audiences that imply homage, and therefore the foreign ministers believed that the exclusive principle had been abandoned by the new Emperor until their memorandum was disdainfully rejected by the President of the Tsungli-Yamen.

Difficulties with the United States.—The Chinese Government, on learning that Henry W. Blair, the newly appointed minister of the United States to Pekin, had spoken in Congress in favor of the exclusion of Chinese from the United States, and in denunciation of the Mongolian race, immediately notified the Government at Washington that he was *persona non grata*, giving its reason for requesting the selection of some other person to represent the United States at Pekin. President Harrison refused to accede to this request, just as President Cleveland had done when the Austrian Government objected to receiving Mr. Keiley as minister, because the latter's wife, being of Jewish birth, was not presentable at court under the rules of court etiquette established in Vienna.

Following on this controversy came a protest communicated by Toni Kwo Yin, Chinese minister at Washington in the beginning of May, against the Chinese exclusion bill that had just been enacted by Congress. The Chinese Government objected to the act because it contained the same provisions as the Scott law of 1888, because it denied the right of *habeas corpus* to Chinamen, and because it required a registration of Chinese laborers which it is practically impossible for them to comply with, in that every Chinaman is obliged to produce before the collector of internal revenue a white witness who knew him previous to 1882, when the first exclusion act was passed. The issuance of the certificate is left to the discretion of the revenue officer. A Chinaman who has been in the United States ten years is ordinarily not able to prove it by an American citizen, because the white witnesses are not likely to be where he resides. The law is held by the Chinese Government to contravene the treaty of 1880, which guarantees to Chinese laborers the treatment of the subjects of the most favored nation.

Anti-foreign Demonstrations.—The sentiment against Europeans showed itself too general and violent among high and low to be attributed solely to the machinations of secret societies plotting revolution and seeking the overthrow of the Manchu dynasty. Foreign gunboats—English, French, American, and others—took their station in the Yangtse river and the waters near by after the riots and massacres in Hunan and the neighboring provinces in 1891. The English customhouse official, Mason, who was detected in the act of smuggling arms into Ching-Kiang to be used in a revolution against the dynasty, and was said to have been connected with the Kolao-Whei secret society, was tried in the English consular court and sentenced to a long term of imprisonment. Three Chinese whom he had employed in his fantastic criminal enterprise, probably without their guilty knowledge, for they were employees in the customhouse under his orders, were arrested and taken to Shanghai, where they were tortured almost to death by a Chinese magistrate without his being able to extract from them the confessions that he sought. Many hundreds of people were arrested and barbarously punished for their supposed connection with the secret societies, and yet high officials who were known to have connived in or to have instigated the disturbances were not molested. One of the principal authors and disseminators of the scurrilous placards and pasquinades directed against foreigners and Christians, which were distributed by the trunkful all over the Yangtse valley, was a mandarin celebrated for his learning, named Chauhan, a resident of Changsha, the capital of Hunan. In the hall of the benevolent society of that city, which is composed of the higher officials of the province, officials of other provinces who were natives of the place and were absent on leave, and the many mandarins who had not yet received official appointments, the movement for the expulsion of the foreign devils was concocted. They entered into a solemn compact, and set about to accomplish their purpose by inflaming the minds of the common people. The richer members of this aristocratic club, which has its counterpart in all the chief towns, gave liberal sums to print and publish the lampoons that their poorer associates wrote and illustrated. Eight of them, for instance, paid for the printing and distribution of 800,000 copies of a single pamphlet. The abusive and obscene literature was sent out from the pawnshops, which are the property of officials. Chanhan, who was a high official, openly signed his name to some of the placards, and avowed his object of stirring up the people to violence and outrage in letters that he wrote to the Governor of Hupeh and to various political magnates in other provinces. When a relative was arrested for distributing placards he boldly demanded his release, threatening to denounce the official who arrested him in Pekin. In consequence of the incendiary incitements of this literary clique, the people of the rich and populous provinces along the Yangtse-Kiang for 800 miles wreaked their blind vengeance on the Christian missionaries and other Europeans at every point except at Hankow, where the British consul and the Rev. Griffith John were able to frustrate the movement and also to lay bare the machinery of the gigantic conspiracy. The foreign ministers at Pekin, following the lead of Sir John Walsham, the British representative, brought the strongest pressure to bear on the Imperial Government, which had begun independently to act, but not with the effective display of authority demanded by the European diplomatists, who never will admit the irresponsibility of the Government at Pekin for the laches of the authorities in the distant, decentralized, semi-independent provinces. Printers of the incendiary placards and tracts, participants in the riots, and many other insignificant actors in the movement were caught and beheaded or otherwise punished; yet the high mandarins known to be implicated, and against whom the British minister lodged information, were allowed to go scot-free. Yielding at last to diplomatic pressure, the Imperial Government in March ordered the Governor of Hunan to arrest Chauhan, and the Viceroy Chang-Chintung sent a deputy from Shanghai, to see that his command was executed. Yet the viceroy's messenger returned with the report that the arrest had not been made. In his letter to the Governor of Hupeh, which was intercepted by the British consul at Hankow, Chauhan had alluded to the viceroy as a person with whom he was in some degree intimate. The "antiheresy publications" which had caused the outrages on Christians, he declared, had been disseminated by him in concert with the officials and gentry, both civil and military, who manage the affairs of the benevolent halls.

Soon after this fiasco, antichristian tumults broke out afresh in the Yangtse valley. In Chingho the house of two ladies, who were missionaries of the Church of England, was attacked and the ladies insulted. In Kienning the hospital of Dr. Riggs was wrecked, and he was pelted and maltreated by the mob. The woman missionaries might have escaped, it was claimed, and were actually urged to go by the native magistrate, who sent sedan chairs and an escort of soldiers, which they declined. A new Catholic mission at Tanyang was threatened, and on the demand of the French consul at Shanghai a military guard was sent to protect it. Another body of soldiers was dispatched to Soochow to guard the missions there. The soldiers recruited in Hunan were all disbanded after the riots of 1891 and were replaced by troops drawn from Canton. The large claims made by foreign governments of compensation for property destroyed and citizens maltreated were referred to the provincial governments by the authorities at Pekin. In the provinces ruled by the Viceroy of Nanking, which enjoyed great prosperity, the demands were complied with; but from Hunan and Hupeh, where the crops had failed and where the feeling against foreigners still smoldered, payment could not be obtained.

CHOLERA IN 1892. To Garcia del Huerto, a celebrated physician of Goa, we are indebted for the first accurate description of cholera. Previous to 1560 we had no record of such a disease, the literature on the subject beginning with Huerto's writings at that period. Much has been written since by eminent medical men of all countries, and to-day we have the investigations and writings of many experts upon the subject. The time is probably not far distant when we shall not only be able to treat it successfully, but literally confine the dread affection to its home, and put an end to its travels. Of all the zymotic diseases there is none that promises as easy management as does cholera. India is the country where cholera, endemic and epidemic, is always to be found. Authorities agree upon the statement that there is a certain area, with somewhat indefinite limits, where cholera is always in existence. It is between the base of the Himalayas on the north, northern Burmah on the east, the Bay of Bengal on the south, and the Northwestern and Central Provinces on the west. In this district the Ganges and the Brahmaputra continually breed and distribute cholera germs, and here an effort to kill the germ could best be made.

The three pathways of the disease start from the above-described area—that is, as far as Europe is concerned. The first pathway is the valley of the Ganges. This leads into Afghanistan, Bokhara, Turkestan and Russia. The second road is by vessels through the Persian Bay, and by this route into Europe. The third starts again at Hindostan, thence to the Arabian Sea, on to the Red Sea, thence into Egypt, and on to Europe by way of the Mediterranean. Before the Suez Canal was completed, in 1869, cholera was seldom known to take this third pathway.

When cholera assumes an epidemic form it spreads westward, its journeys being made by short stages, following lines of commerce and spreading by actual contact. The routes of the plague have been most accurately described in several epidemics, and it has been noted that, as yet, it has never been shipped aboard vessels that have doubled the Cape of Good Hope. In 1774 cholera assumed a severe epidemic form in India; again in 1817 a virulent form. This outbreak marked the beginning of a march that went steadily on, until almost every portion of the world was reached. Russia suffered in 1830, Germany in 1831, England in 1832. The first case on this continent occurred in Quebec early in June, 1832. The end of the same month found the disease in New York city, from which place it traveled westward along the Ohio river until the Mississippi was reached, where it turned southward and journeyed to New Orleans. This diversion of its usual westward course was due to the fact that the population was greater along the river's course than westward. In 1846 another epidemic appeared, spreading over Europe and reaching America in 1849. Cholera has since visited us in 1852, 1866, and 1873, and a few cases reached New York harbor in the autumn of 1886. Some writers make the bold assertion that the figures showing the number of deaths from the disease, from 1774 to 1891, are over a million. The accuracy of such a statement is open to question, as is, indeed, any compilation of the kind, on account of the inaccurate statements. But the writer of this article has collected statistics that show more than 800,000 deaths up to 1891. Considering the ratio of deaths to cases, this would show over a million and a half of cases, and it is very probable that this is below the actual number. When we stop to consider the densely populated countries of Europe and Asia, and the meager records we possess of diseases and deaths in the past, it is but fair to infer that the devastation this destroyer has wrought upon the human race has not been overestimated.

The outbreaks of cholera are generally sudden, large numbers of people being attacked in a short period. Each outbreak seems to spend itself in some one particular direction, making prominent some one special symptom. The specific cause of cholera is now recognized as a living organism, which is capable of vast multiplication and rapid propagation. Its discovery is claimed by Koch, who found it to be a specific micro-organism belonging to the vegetable kingdom. It has its own special features, which are not found to be possessed by any other plant. Koch claims that a specific germ is always found in the intestinal contents of persons suffering from cholera; that this germ is found in the intestinal contents in no other disease; that it has certain features distinguishable from the germ of all other diseases; and that it alone can produce true cholera. The truth of Koch's views has not been entirely proved, but they stand the trial of experience, and find many more supporters to-day than in 1885.

Dr. Emmerich, of Munich, has laid claim to the discovery of a straight bacillus, which he says is always present in Asiatic cholera, and without which the disease can not exist. This bacillus Emmerich has termed the Naples bacterium. Without entering upon a discussion of the subject, it can safely be asserted that the presence of the curved bacillus of Koch is a much more valuable diagnostic feature than is the Naples bacillus. Asiatic cholera is now acknowledged to be a specific disease, due to the agency of a specific cause, which attacks the human being always by way of the alimentary canal. The cause of the disease acts primarily upon the epithelial lining of the mucous membrane of the small intestines, which it has a tendency to destroy, and, secondarily, upon the blood and nervous system. Whatever this cause may be, it is essentially of a living organic nature, and, under favorable conditions, possesses the power of multiplication and propagation within the intestinal canal of the human being. It is also known that it passes in a living, active state by means of water, milk, food, or other substances into the alimentary canal. That the power of multiplication and propagation of this specific cause is limited and destroyed by certain not yet well-known, unfavorable conditions is now a recognized fact. We find these unfavorable conditions existing over the entire world, except, perhaps, in the very home of the disease. Investigations have discovered and pointed out the means by which an attack or an epidemic of cholera may be avoided, and if the proper course be pursued we shall cease hearing of the travels of this fatal disease.

Cholera is not contagious, attacks persons of any age or either sex, and claims most victims among the intemperate, those careless as to personal cleanliness, and among those living in close quarters. It is most severe in hot, moist climates and low altitudes, in the warmer rather than in the colder seasons of the year. In those localities where a great difference exists between the summer and winter temperature the disease is prone to disappear during the winter season and break out afresh during the period of greatest heat. We have an exception to this rule in an epidemic that once visited Russia, Sweden, and Norway. Here we have records of one of the most severe epidemics the world has ever seen, and in the midst of a. most severe winter. Such instances show that even now, with all the experience of the past, the exact nature of the malady is not entirely understood. Although poverty, filth, and intemperance favor the spread of cholera, it is quite certain that these agencies can not generate the disease.

This peculiar cause of the disease finds its most ready vehicle in clothing, bedclothes, carpets, and other things soiled by the excreta and vomit from the sick, also through privies, sewers, and streams that have been contaminated by discharges from those suffering from the disease. Nothing can carry and spread cholera so quickly as water. When an epidemic appears suddenly and spreads quickly in a city or town, it is through the medium of the water supply. When the disease is introduced in other ways, it spreads slowly. Fear, excesses of any kind, marked changes of temperature, crowding, anything deranging digestion, recent arrival in an infected district, predispose an individual to an attack of cholera. Attention should be paid to diet, but most important of all is attention to the water and milk consumed. These articles should always be recently boiled. In cities and towns the streets should be cleaned, cellars whitewashed and well aired, sewers flushed daily, privies disinfected with chloride of lime, or carbolic-acid solution. Everything that has been near one suffering from cholera should be thoroughly disinfected, or, better still, burned. The physician and the nurse only should come in contact with the sick, and the hands always should be washed in a weak solution of carbolic acid, or corrosive sublimate, after approaching a cholera patient. The patient should have his own knife, fork, spoon, and drinking cup, and the nurse should never partake of food in the sick room.

The first symptoms of cholera are feelings of weariness, a diarrhœa, soon followed by vomiting and cramps in the abdomen, extending down the limbs. The character of the discharges soon change. They become more numerous, very copious, often involuntary, colorless, and assume the characteristic " rice-water " appearance. Marked thirst is always associated with rice-water stools, and this is an important diagnostic sign. The secondary or algid symptoms are marked by collapse. During the intervals between the cramps the patient will lie absolutely motionless. The body temperature falls below normal, sometimes going as low as 94° F. The pulse becomes small, or very compressible, the voice is husky and hollow, the breath is icy cold. The features assume a dark hue, and the nose becomes drawn and the cheeks hollow. The eyeballs are congested, sunken, and quite hidden by the half-closed lids. The legs and feet assume a bluish tint, the skin becomes wrinkled and wet with a cold sweat. A person who has once seen a case of cholera at this stage recognizes it at a glance. Cholera is a disease not of days but of hours, and when this stage is reached we can predict with almost certainty the prognosis of the case. If the mind becomes inactive and stupor appears, death is apt to follow.

This second or algid stage may last from ten to thirty hours; in some cases only two to three hours; but after six to twenty-four hours the third train of symptoms should appear, and a stage of reaction be looked for. The body temperature gradually rises, the breathing becomes natural, the pulse increases in volume, the sweat is not clammy, the breath becomes warmer, the secretions are re-established, and the patient sleeps. At first the respirations are sighing, but very soon perfectly natural. This is the critical stage of the illness. Great care must be exercised or we have a relapse in cholera cases. Complications, such as suppression of urine, high fever, congestion of the lungs, abscesses in various parts of the body, or severe and fatal hæmorrhage from the bowels, may ensue.

The mortality of cholera varies much, being influenced as to seasons, localities, and conditions of the people attacked. At times the mortality of cholera has been frightful; and, notwithstanding better hygiene, more perfect knowledge of the modes of prevention, and more rational methods of treatment, the percentage of deaths to attacks is very little smaller now than it was many years ago. It may safely be said that the average mortality is from 30 to 40 per cent. In some epidemics it has not been over 15 per cent., while in others it has almost reached 90. It has been noted that the ratio of fatal cases depends much upon the rapidity of the spread of the disease. Where it travels rapidly the number of deaths is great; when it makes easy journeys the havoc is not so frightful. Records of the epidemic of 1885 show an average mortality of almost 30 per cent., but those of 1892 were much higher.

Concerning this epidemic there are several remarkable features, new departures from the hitherto usual course of epidemics, the meaning of which is yet to be explained. The disease has marched westward with wonderful rapidity, and its virulence is greater than that of most other epidemics of the past. Heretofore it has taken two years to travel the distance covered by the epidemic of 1892 in six months. This may be accounted for, to some extent, by the increased facilities of travel and speed, but it is more probably due to the increased virulence of the poison.

It has usually been held that one attack of cholera does not confer immunity from another; but within the past few years several eminent authorities have expressed the view that one attack does confer an immunity, but not of very long duration. A careful analysis of the epidemic of 1885 led Koch to place cholera in the class of general infectious diseases with variola and scarlatina, as concerns immunity, although it was much shorter and markedly less absolute. Griesinger recently wrote "that, next to perfect health and good hygienic surroundings, nothing affords greater protection than recovery from an attack of cholera." He also showed that when a body of troops has suffered from cholera it enjoys, for some time, an insusceptibility. Pettenkofer also has expressed the opinion that one attack of the disease protects against a second. The few American writers on the subject, within the past ten years, incline to the opinion that no immunity follows a first attack. But this view is not based upon the extensive personal experience afforded observers abroad. Inquiries have been started concerning this question, and a tabulated record of cases showing a second attack will be compiled.

The beginning of the epidemic of 1892 was about April 10, and its origin was in the Punjab, India. It seems that at Hurdwar, a place of pilgrimage, where, in spring, the largest fair in India is held, more than 200,000 annually gather, and every twelfth year from 1,000,000 to 2,000,000. This was the twelfth year. Cholera suddenly appeared about April 10, and increased with a singular rapidity, the outbreak being so virulent that the Punjab pilgrims were forced to disband, thereby carrying the seeds of the disease to various localities. By the end of the month cholera was in Afghanistan and Persia, and cases were reported in the southern parts of France, but were termed cholerine. When May closed the epidemic existed also in Harrar, Meshed, and Serinagur, where

the deaths were over 500 a day. Early in June the disease had made such frightful headway that business was completely suspended. The Persian Government ordered a military cordon placed around Teheran, the Russian Government took active measures to prevent the spread of cholera into Russia, English camps were removed, and the movements of all pilgrims were prevented by cordons. These stringent cautions failed to check the disease, and by July 1, Tiflis, Baku, the west coast of the Caspian Sea, and Asiatic Turkey were invaded. Shortly afterward it was in the suburbs of Paris, and was advancing toward Moscow. During July the disease spread in various directions throughout Russia, no fewer than 9,000 deaths being reported. In some localities the ratio of deaths to cases was more than half. So many towns were visited by the plague that on July 27 all the schools under control of the Holy Synod were ordered to be closed, not to reopen until cold weather set in. In Paris 67 deaths from the disease were reported during the month. At Argenteuil, a suburb, there were over 40 deaths from what was termed "choleraic diarrhœa." The French authorities seem to have made a systematic effort to deceive the inhabitants of Paris, as well as those outside their confines. From the first the term "cholerine" was applied to cases that were unmistakably true Asiatic cholera. At no time had any such affection producing so many deaths existed about Paris and its environs. Prof. Peter, of the Necker Hospital, in the early part of the month, declared emphatically that the prevailing malady was true Asiatic cholera. On the other hand, several high medical authorities were equally positive it was not. The same policy seems to have been pursued at Hamburg when the first suspicious cases were reported, and also by the surgeons of a line of steamers sailing for the United States from that port. Subsequent events proved that what was called "cholerine" was true Asiatic cholera, and should have been recognized as such by any honest and competent physician.

With the beginning of August came the announcement that cholera had appeared in western Siberia, ten cases existing in the prison at Tomsk. At Moscow there were over 60 deaths in a few days, while in Russian Caucasus there were over 4,000 deaths during the first week. So rapidly was the disease spreading that the Ministry of Education, on Aug. 3, published an official order that all schools be closed, and requested that medical schools suspend lectures, so that the students might assist in combating the scourge in infected districts. Long before any official announcement was made, quite a number of fatal cases of cholera were known to have occurred in St. Petersburg. Official announcement was not made until Aug. 15. At that time 154 cases, with 81 deaths, were reported.

Toward the end of the month the disease was announced in Austria, and the authorities of Hamburg about this time admitted that what they had regarded as a harmless choleraic diarrhœa was true Asiatic cholera. The disease was chiefly prevalent in the Altstadt, or old portion of the city, few cases occurring in the Neustadt, or new portion. All precautions, it was claimed, were taken, yet within a few days over 300 cases and 120 deaths were reported. Official admission was made to the American consul of the existence of true cholera in Hamburg, Aug. 23. This was the beginning of one of the most virulent epidemics that have attacked any single city in Europe.

During August much havoc was wrought in Austria by the disease, while in Russian domains 51,709 cases and 25,984 deaths were reported. Cases also occurred in Berlin and its surroundings, but of a mild type.

On Aug. 26 announcement was made that the disease had entered England. The new cases had arrived at Gravesend, upon a steamer from Hamburg.

So serious had the situation abroad become that the Government authorities of the United States at last recognized the necessity of stringent measures to prevent the introduction of cholera, and a national quarantine was established. This not being considered adequate, the President, on Sept. 1, instructed the supervising surgeon-general to issue an order declaring a twenty days' quarantine. All foreign immigrant ships were to be refused entry for at least that period.

The first cases of cholera were brought into New York harbor by the Hamburg-American Company's steamer "Moravia," which arrived on Aug. 31. This ship sailed from Hamburg Aug. 18, with 286 steerage passengers, and on the following day cholera broke out, the first death occurring within twenty-four hours. Children seemed to suffer most, and by Aug. 29 the number of deaths had reached 22. The ship's surgeon had recorded these deaths as due to "cholerine." From all that can be gathered concerning the history of cholera on board this vessel, it seems clear that the disease made its first appearance the day after she sailed from an infected port, and yet she continued on her voyage and brought the germs of the scourge into an uninfected country. The quarantine officers of New York immediately recognized the true character of the illness on board the "Moravia," and detained her at the quarantine station. On Sept. 3 the Hamburg-American liner "Normannia" entered New York harbor with cholera on board. This vessel sailed from Hamburg Aug. 26; her cabin passengers, officers, and crew numbered 666, and her steerage contained 520 souls. During the voyage 5 deaths from cholera occurred, 1 in the second cabin and 4 in the steerage. These deaths were entered upon the log as due to "cholerine." On board were 4 sick. The steamer "Rugia" left Hamburg Aug. 23, and passed into the port of New York Sept. 3. Four deaths occurred from cholera during the voyage, and at the time of her arrival 5 were ill of the same disease. This vessel brought 426 emigrants direct from a district that was afflicted with an epidemic of cholera. Every precaution known to science was said to have been adopted by those in charge of the quarantine at New York to disinfect their baggage. The emigrants coming in both steamers were kept under surveillance for some time, and were then allowed to scatter, going to various points in our country.

About a week after the arrival of the "Normannia," 8 of her crew were attacked with cholera, and within the same time 2 of the steerage passengers of the "Rugia." By Sept. 7 there were 31 new cases and 8 deaths from the plague in New York harbor. In order to remove the cabin passengers from the infected vessels to a place of safety, where they could be detained until such time as the danger of an outbreak of the pest should be passed, President Harrison, on Sept. 7, gave orders to occupy part of Sandy Hook and to forward a large number of tents to that place for their use. The epidemic in New York harbor was quite severe, and for a time was a great menace to the United States. Those in charge of the quarantine are entitled to commendation for so ably handling the epidemic and preventing its spread. Several suspicious deaths were reported in New York city, 1 in Brooklyn, 1 in New Jersey, and 1 in Chicago during September; but, with the exception of 2 in New York, these could not have been due to true cholera. The 2 spoken of as having occurred in New York city were no doubt due to Asiatic cholera.

On Sept. 10 the steamer "Scandia" entered New York Bay. This vessel left Hamburg Aug. 27, with 1,086 people on board. A few days after she sailed cholera was raging in her steerage. Forty-seven cases occurred during the voyage, 32 terminating fatally.

Toward the end of September cholera cases in Russia, France, and Hamburg showed a marked decrease. During that month the disease was really much worse in Paris and its suburbs than was supposed. Between false reports and the controversy as to the exact nature of the disease that attacked people so suddenly and ended so fatally the real condition of affairs was not widely known. During the first twenty days of September there were 357 deaths from cholera in Paris, and 342 in the suburbs. From reliable authority it is said that between May 1 and Oct. 1 there was a total of 1,461 deaths from Asiatic cholera in and around that city.

The disease made no headway in England, the few cases occurring having been imported from the Continent. In Russia, over 12,000 new cases were reported, nearly 40 per cent. of which ended fatally. This high rate of mortality is no doubt due to poverty, filth, and isolation of the people in many localities where the disease prevailed.

Reports from Hamburg show a terrible rate of mortality and a large number of cases during September. But these reports have been so manipulated that no accurate statement can be made as to the exact number. The Elbe had become so contaminated that fresh cases were discovered due to drinking its water upon every side, and it was not until this danger had been emphatically made known and the inhabitants generally used boiled water that the epidemic began to decline. The population of Hamburg and its suburbs, according to the latest figures of the Income Office, is 640,400. The official returns given out by the commissioners of the Cholera Commission of the Senate, to Oct. 1, show 18,757 cases of the disease and 7,839 deaths, a very high mortality. The death ratio in hospital practice amounted to 35 per cent., and in private practice to almost 45 per cent. The highest death ratio occurred among the working classes, those who were careless in their eating and drinking, and who were sufferers from chronic bronchitis and indigestion. In Belgium there were 1,135 cases of cholera and 563 deaths from the disease between the appearance of the first case, July 22, and Oct. 1. The majority of cholera cases, if taken in the earliest stages and properly treated, would undoubtedly recover. In the later stages, treatment is not so promising in its results, and there are certain acute, violent cases that do not yield to any form of treatment. Observations made in Hamburg during this epidemic show a tendency to lengthen in the duration of the cases, and, after the algid or secondary stage abates, a tendency to typhoidal conditions and sympathetic inflammation of the kidneys. Some practitioners in that city have expressed the view that, as a rule, all cases that lasted longer than five days manifested kidney complications. It was also noted that some patients passed through the acute stages in a favorable manner and then expired suddenly from heart failure.

In the early stage of cholera the indications demand prompt and decisive treatment of the diarrhœa. For this, warmth must be applied to the abdomen and extremities, and a full dose of morphine must be given hypodermically. The condition of the patient is such that little reliance can be placed on the prompt action of medicines when administered by the mouth. It is here that valuable time is lost. An injection of one-fourth to one-half grain of morphine should be given, and it has been found that more prompt results follow when the injection is made under the skin covering the abdomen. In quite a number of cases this treatment may be all that is required. In severe cases, where no response follows the injection it should be repeated within two hours. Cholera calls for heroic treatment.

The second indication is to destroy the germ, and for this mercury has been widely recommended. Large doses of calomel, corrosive sublimate, and carbolic acid have been administered for this purpose, but antibacterial agents do not yield very gratifying results. Sufficient quantities to destroy the bacteria can not be administered to the individual with safety. We must place greatest reliance in remedies the action of which will control the diarrhœa of the early stage; in stimulants, such as alcohol, camphor, ether, and capsicum; in friction, warmth, and mustard applied to the abdomen and to the extremities.

During the epidemic of 1885 a treatment highly recommended in Spain was the rectal injection of ether; but this does not seem to have been resorted to during the epidemic of 1892. Enteroclysis and hypodermoclysis promise the best results in the later stages of cholera. The temperature of the water should be at least 101° F., and should contain a large quantity of common salt. This should be injected into the lower bowel after each operation, at least a quart of the solution being used. When collapse occurs, the solution should be boldly injected into the breast or under the arms, a fountain syringe armed with a cannula being used for the purpose. Upon the withdrawal of the cannula, the tumor arising should be well rubbed until absorption has taken place. It is said that this is facilitated by plunging the patient into a hot bath. During the recent epidemic in Hamburg a new method of treatment by means of chlorine water was tried and was reported to be very effective. The effect of the treatment was to produce perspiration in cases that were most unpromising. During the epidemic of 1892 no attempt seems to have been made to follow the practice of Ferran as to vaccination as a means of prevention. Dr. Ferran recommended and tried this procedure in Spain during the severe epidemic of cholera in 1885, and some astonishing claims were made for it. In 22 cities and villages, with an aggregate population of 136,000, Ferran vaccinated 30,500. Of these, only 12 in 1,000 were attacked, and 3 in 1,000 died, thus reducing the mortality to 25 per cent. Of the unvaccinated, 77 per 1,000 were attacked and the deaths were 33 per 1,000. These experiments showed that the liability of those who had submitted to the vaccination was at least seven times less than that of those who had not been vaccinated. The cholera commissioners appointed by England, Belgium, Germany, and France investigated this claim made by Ferran after the epidemic had subsided, and did not extol his claims or recommend the adoption of his practice. Shortly afterward the cholera commissioner from the United States investigated the subject and thought the method worthy of a trial.

The most reliable method of security against cholera in the United States is to be found in a proper system of quarantine, and this can be the most effectually established and maintained by a system of National Quarantine. Instead of the various States having a seaboard or port of entry, maintaining a separate service, the General Government should have the absolute control and responsibility of inspection. Until such is the case a perfect cordon can not be maintained. The question of an international quarantine service has been under consideration during the present year, and several countries have already appointed commissioners to represent them at a meeting to be held in 1893. As the cholera concerns all civilized nations alike, it is but proper that all of them should take part in the proper quarantining of the source of the plague. This is the only feasible plan for the prevention of epidemics. International action means that the civilized world will contribute scientists and funds to aid in the extermination of the disease in its home.

The importance of International action is illustrated in the record of cholera in 1892. Nearly three fourths of all the cases of cholera in southern Russia, or in that vast region lying between the Caspian and the Black Seas, have proved fatal. In St. Petersburg, where a better sanitary condition prevails, over 50 per cent. of the cases have had a fatal termination. In Hamburg the ratio of deaths in cholera cases has been nearly half, while in northern Germany, in Belgium, and in France, it has been about 33 per cent. In Persia the appalling record of 85 per cent. in mortality is given. It is said that a quarter of a million Persians perished by the Asiatic cholera in 1892. In addition to the great loss of life, is the monetary loss occasioned by the interruption to commerce.

Since the outbreak of cholera in the Russian dominions, there have been in the lieutenancy of the Caucasus 125,000 cases of the disease and 65,000 deaths. In Sartaff there have been 31,000 cases and more than 11,000 deaths, and in St. Petersburg 3,500 cases and 1,250 deaths, making in these districts a total of over 160,000 cases and 77,000 deaths.

CHRISTIAN ENDEAVOR, YOUNG PEO-PLE'S SOCIETIES OF. The eleventh International Convention of the Young People's Societies of Christian Endeavor met in the city of New York, July 7. Between 20,000 and 30,000 delegates were present, so that the Madison Square Garden—the largest audience room in America—could not hold all at once the actual members of the body. The Rev. Francis E. Clark, founder of the original society, presided. The secretary reported concerning the growth and present condition of the societies: In 1881 there were 2 societies; in 1882, 7; In 1883, 56; in 1884, 156; in 1885, 253; in 1886, 850; in 1887, 2,314; in 1888, 4,879; in 1889, 7,672; in 1890, 11,013; in 1891, 16,274; in 1892, 21,080; while societies known to exist, but which had not been recorded, would swell the total up to 22,000. Thirty evangelical denominations were represented in these bodies, of which the Presbyterians stood first, with 4,806 societies; the Congregationalists next, with 4,495; then the Baptists, with 2,736; the Methodists, with 2,335;* the Disciples of Christ, with 1,557; and other denominations with smaller numbers. All the evangelical denominations were showing increasing friendliness to the societies, and the general courts and various local assemblies of many of them had formally approved of the organization. The largest number of societies in a single State was in New York, 2,532; after which followed Pennsylvania, with 1,829; Illinois, with 1,477; Ohio, with 1,363; Massachusetts, with 1,055; and Iowa, with 1,024. The greatest proportionate increase in the number of societies during the year had been made in Manitoba; the greatest absolute increase in Ontario. The first organization of a junior society was made in Tabor, Iowa, in 1884. There were now 2,574 of these bodies, of which 1,719 had been enrolled during the past year. In other countries than the United States there were: 1,377 societies in Canada, 300 in England, 232 in Australia, 32 in India, 20 in Turkey, 19 in Mexico, 12 in the West Indies, 9 in Samoa, 9 in Africa, 9 in China, 6 in Japan, and others in Bermuda, Brazil, Chili, Norway, Spain, and the Hawaiian Islands—in all, 648 societies in foreign and missionary lands. The constitution of the organization had been translated, and was printed in the German, Swedish, Norwegian, French, Danish, Dutch, Spanish, Tamil, Chinese, and Japanese languages. A tendency was remarked in the societies to become active in the promotion of missions. The Fulton pledge plan of giving two cents per week individually was in extensive operation; and many members had signed a pledge to give a proportionate part of their income, not less than one tenth, to benevolent and religious purposes. Many local unions of socie-

ties had been formed in the larger towns and cities, and were doing practical work through their missionary, executive, correspondence, lookout, press, and visiting committees; as in Philadelphia, where 280 societies were thus united and co-operating; Chicago, 244; New York, 124; Cleveland, 96; Brooklyn, 95; St. Louis, 94; Minneapolis, 91; and Baltimore, 81. During the year, 120,000 members of the societies had become church members. The meetings of the convention were continued through four days, with discussions and conversations at the regular meetings and at overflow meetings of subjects relating to religious life and work and the welfare of the societies and their members. President Merril E. Gates spoke on "The Secret of Successful Endeavor"; President Francis E. Clark, on the Christian Endeavor as "More than a Society—as a Providential Movement"; the Rev. Joseph Cook, on "Watchwords for the Twentieth Century"; the Rev. Dr. Russell H. Conwell, on "The Christian Endeavor Society's Place in Modern Religious Life"; The Rev. Dr. Josiah Strong, on "Christian Endeavor and Home Missions"; Mr. R. S. Murphy, on "Proportionate Giving to God"; the Rev. L. S. Bean, on "Systematic Giving"; the Rev. Dr. H. C. Mabie, on "The Whole World for Christ"; Mr. I. D. Sankey, on "The Advance of Christian Endeavor in England"; Mr. J. G. Woolley, on "Temperance"; the Rev. Dr. Barrows, of Chicago, on "The Religious Possibilities of the World's Fair"; the Rev. S. P. Rose, on "Self or Others?" Meetings were held for pastors, in behalf of the junior societies, in behalf of the closing of the World's Fair on Sundays, and in the interest of other special objects. A meeting to consider the relation between the Christian Endeavor and the Epworth League resulted in the appointment of a committee of Methodist pastors as a "Christian Endeavor Advisory Board." The platform of principles, carefully restated, was adopted in accordance with the annual custom, not with any change of principles, but for the sake of constantly repeating them, "that the Christian world may understand the Christian Endeavor movement." Among them is a resolution asserting "strenuous loyalty to the local church or denomination with which each society is connected. . . . The Society of Christian Endeavor is as loyal a denominational society as any in existence, as well as a broad and fraternal interdenominational society." Another resolution reaffirms "increasing confidence in the interdenominational, spiritual fellowship, through which we hope not for organic unity, but to fulfill our Lord's prayer, 'that they all may be made one.' This fellowship already extends to all evangelical denominations, and we should greatly deplore any movement that would interrupt or imperil it."

CHURCH HISTORY, AMERICAN SOCI-ETY OF. The fourth annual meeting of the American Society of Church History was held in Washington, D. C., beginning Dec. 29, 1891. The secretary reported an enrollment of 132 active and 8 honorary members. The gain in membership had been constant from the first, and the future of the society was regarded as assured. An important enterprise had been started a year previously for preparing a series of denominational

---

* In addition to these the Methodist Protestants reported 422 societies.

histories of American churches which should give a clear, succinct, and unbiased story of the rise and growth of the more important denominations in the land. The names of 13 scholars, representing as many church organizations, were given who had been engaged to write the histories of their several denominations; and arrangements were making for securing historians of other denominations. Papers were read on "The Religious Motives of Columbus," by Prof. W. K. Gillett; "The Heads of Agreement, and the Union of Congregationalists and Presbyterians based on them in London, 1691," by Prof. Williston Walker; "Christian Unity and the Kingdom of Heaven," by Mr. Thomas Davidson; "Papal Bulls distributing America," by Prof. John Gordon; "The Confessional History of the Lutheran Church in America" by the Rev. John Nicum; "Recent Researches Concerning Mediæval Sects," by Prof. A. H. Newman (read by the secretary); "Calvin and Melanchthon," by the Rev. Dr. Philip Schaff; and "Christian Thought in Architecture," by Mr. Barr Ferree. The Rev. Dr. Philip Schaff was re-elected president of the society.

CITIES, AMERICAN, RECENT GROWTH OF. This subject has been treated in every volume of the "Annual Cyclopædia" since 1886, the total number of cities described in the six volumes preceding the present one being 360. Those that are here set forth increase the number to 397.

Altoona, a city of Pennsylvania, in Blair County, on the Pennsylvania Railroad, at the eastern base of the Alleghany mountains, 117 miles from Pittsburg, 132 from Harrisburg, and 237 from Philadelphia; latitude 40° 30', longitude 78° 25'. So steep is the ascent of the mountain at this point that two locomotives are attached to each train, and the famous "horseshoe curve" is one of the marvels of engineering achievement. At the top of the mountain is a tunnel 3,500 feet long, through which the railroad passes. A branch railroad runs south to Henrietta. The city was laid out in 1849, had 2,000 inhabitants in 1854, 10,610 in 1870, 19,710 in 1880, and 30,337 by the census of 1890. As supplied by the city post office, there were 40,000 in 1892. Altoona, originally built in a valley, has extended over the eastern and western slopes of the surrounding hills, and has an elevation of 1,192 feet above sea level. The surrounding scenery is grand. In 1854 the first incorporation as a borough took place, and in 1868 it received its city charter. The assessed valuation of property in 1888-'89 was $11,500,000. Two thirds of the 7,000 homes in the city are owned by workingmen, and there are 37 building associations, capitalized at $36,400,000. Two electric-light companies, with capital of $106,000, are equipped for running 5,750 incandescent and 400 arc lights. In addition there is a gas plant, valued at $150,000. Six miles of electric street railway are in operation, with a capital of $180,000. Six miles of streets have been paved, at a cost of $302,000. Much work in the way of paving, new sewers, etc., is going on, and an investment of $220,000 to increase the water supply is contemplated. There are 9 volunteer fire companies. The bonded debt of the city is $404,000. The value of school property increased from $234,000 in 1887 to $420,485 in 1892. There are 15 public-school buildings; 125 teachers are employed, and there are 4,530 pupils. Four Catholic parochial institutions have a total attendance of 3,000. The church property is estimated at $1,040,000. Of the 39 churches, 8 are Methodist, 6 Lutheran, 5 Baptist, 4 Catholic, 4 Presbyterian, 2 Reformed, 2 United Brethren, and 1 Episcopalian. Ten newspapers are published, of which 5 are daily and 1 German. There are 2 theatres, and 2 public libraries, that of the Mechanics' having 16,000 volumes. The hospital, built from equal contributions of the State and city ($15,000 each) on ground given by the railroad company, is valued at $40,000, and received during 1891 $27,500. Including the shops of the Pennsylvania Railroad, which employ 6,500 men, the industries of Altoona aggregate $15,000,000, and pay out yearly $4,000,000 in wages. These shops were in fact the origin of the city, and remain its leading feature. There is also a machine and car manufactory, employing 200 men, an iron rolling mill employing 160, with annual capacity of 15,000 tons; 2 brick works, turning out 5,000,000 bricks yearly, and 1 fire-clay works, with output of 4,000,000 bricks. A silk mill employs 200 girls, and there is an ice plant with capacity of 22,000 tons. Other establishments include 13 planing mills, 10 wagon and carriage factories, 5 breweries, 2 bottling works, 4 marble yards, and 2 candy factories, and $500,000 are invested in shipping and mining coal. The receipts at the post office in 1891 were $34,000, and the expenditures $20,500; the profits were $13,500.

Annapolis, a city and the capital of Maryland, county seat of Anne Arundel County, on its south bank of Severn river, two miles above the entrance into Chesapeake Bay, 37 miles from Washington, and 30 miles from Baltimore. It is the terminus of the Annapolis, Washington and Baltimore, and the Annapolis and Baltimore Short Line Railroads, and has a fine harbor. In 1870 the population was 5,744; in 1880, 6,642; and in 1890, 7,604. The first settlement, known as Providence, was made by Puritans fleeing from the Commonwealth of Virginia on account of persecution, who were at first welcomed by the Governor of Maryland, whose appointment to office depended upon his bringing 500 settlers into the province. Later, on account of their independence, an attempt was made to subdue them and capture their women for wives, and a battle was fought on the present site of the city, March 25, 1655, resulting in the victory of the Puritans, who, however, were merged subsequently in the Catholic colony of Lord Baltimore. In 1694 the place was given a town government as Anne Arundel town (in honor of Lady Baltimore), and the capital was removed thither from St. Mary's. A year later its name was changed to Annapolis, in honor of Queen Anne, who in 1708 bestowed its city charter, the original of which is still preserved, conveying all the privileges of an English city. As chief port of the province it exported its large tobacco crop, and prior to the Revolution was known as the "Social Athens," its clubs drawing to their midst the wit and wealth of the day, and numbering historical characters among their members.

In October, 1774, the owner and consignees of the ship "Peggy Stewart," loaded with tea, were forced by the citizens to burn her in the harbor, and throughout the War of Independence Annapolis bore an honorable part. At the close it became for a time the national seat of government, but as a city it was rapidly eclipsed later by Baltimore, which, founded in 1739, had in 1850 169,054 inhabitants, while the population of Annapolis was but 3,011. In 1845 the United States Naval Academy was located here, which removed to Newport, R. I., during the civil war, but was restored in 1865. In 1888 the Academy wall inclosed 50 acres, the original grounds having been Fort Severn, an army post from 1809 to the founding of the institute. The several rows of barracks, etc., have been built at intervals since, the library being one of the oldest in the grounds, originally the residence of the Governors of Maryland from 1753 to 1866. In the United States Naval Institute building is one of the largest collections of captured British flags. The Tripoli monument, removed from Washington, D. C., where it was mutilated by the British in 1814, the Midshipmen's monument, and the monument to Commander Herndon are worthy of note, as are the brass guns of French manufacture captured at Vera Cruz, March 27, 1847. The course of instruction at the Academy covers six years, two of which are at sea. The Naval Ordnance Proving Grounds lie on the opposite bank of the river, on the site of Fort Madison, which was erected during the war of 1812. The Naval Hospital, erected in 1868–'69, is in a neglected condition. During the civil war earthworks were thrown up for the defense of Annapolis, and soldiers' hospitals and a parole camp for the exchange of prisoners were established. A national cemetery was located here in 1862, and the naval cemetery occupies a portion of the Government hospital grounds. The plan of Annapolis, with streets radiating from its two central points, the State House and St. Anne's Church, is said to have been that of Sir Christopher Wren for the rebuilding of London after the great fire in 1666, and by request of Washington to have been followed in laying out the capital city. Many of the streets have historic names, and, indeed, outside of the Naval Academy, the principal interest of Annapolis lies in its historic memorials, it being in other respects the "finished city" it was pronounced by De Tocqueville in 1776. The State House, a domed structure, the foundation of which was laid in 1772, has a total height of 200 feet, a frontage of 120, and a depth of 175 feet. The Senate Chamber, in which Washington surrendered his commission, in which the peace with Great Britain was ratified in 1784, and where the Annapolis Convention of 1786 was held, has been materially altered. The State library, which is contained in the building, consists of 70,000 volumes, 50,-000 of which are law-books. The State Treasury dates from colonial times. The executive mansion is modern, and cost $150,000. The courthouse dates from 1820 and contains records from 1634. Several specimens remain of colonial mansions, and the city boasts a newspaper published since 1745. In all there are 2 daily and 4 weekly papers. St. Anne's Church (Episcopal), which has been twice rebuilt since its foundation in 1694, owns a communion service presented by William III of England, engraved with the royal arms. There are also Methodist, Catholic, Presbyterian, and German Lutheran churches, and some belonging to colored people. St. John's College, chartered in 1784, has 148 students, and 11 professors and instructors. The average attendance of children at the four public schools is 400 white and 300 colored. Teachers for the whites are 20 in number, and for the colored 6. In addition there are 5 private and 3 parochial schools. Novitiates for the Catholic priesthood, of the Redemptorist order, are educated in the old Carroll mansion, given for the purpose by the granddaughters of Charles Carroll. Five priests are resident instructors, with an average attendance of 25 students. The assessed valuation of property in Annapolis is $2,500,000, and the tax rate is 80 cents on the $100. Fire protection is ample, and water is supplied by a company with a capital of $61,450, from a reservoir four miles distant, with pressure of 30 opunds in the mains. Gas is in use for illumination. There are two banks, one national. The leading industry is oyster shipping. There is also a glass factory and a marine railway in the suburbs.

Ann Arbor, a city of Michigan, county seat of Washtenaw County, on Huron river, in the southeastern part of the State, 38 miles from Detroit. In 1870 the population was 7,363; in 1880, 7,849; in 1890, 9,431. The first settlement was made in February, 1824, by pioneers from Genesee County, N. Y., and in 1828 the village contained 150 inhabitants. In 1834 it was incorporated, in 1837 was made the seat of the University of Michigan, and in 1851 received its city charter. It stands upon several long, sloping hills, 824 feet above sea-level, and from 50 to 70 feet above the river, a pretty winding stream, which enters from the north and leaves at the southeast. The soil is a drift of sand overlying a gravel-bed 50 to 70 feet thick, which with the descent to the river renders drainage easy. The average annual temperature is about 47°; the average rainfall something over 31 inches. The climate is equable, the summers being cooler and the winters warmer than in many other places having the same latitude. The streets are broad, terraces abound, and shade trees of hard maple, elm, and oak add much to the beauty of the city. The avenues surrounding the university campus are over 100 feet wide, with trees in the middle. Ingalls Street and Washtenaw Avenue, lined with handsome residences, deserve especial mention, and Cedar Bend Avenue is the most noted among many picturesque drives. There are three principal parks, and numerous neighboring resorts on small lakes. The assessed valuation in 1890 was $4,771,000, and the total of all taxes 1·35 per cent. The city debt is about $21,000, bonds having been issued to aid in building the University Hospital. Disbursements for the year ending Feb. 1, 1891, were $45,823.37, of which $9,425.40 were for streets, $5,858.17 for the fire department, $1,-957.79 for police, and $5,119.25 for public lighting; $535,945 were spent in improvements, including a new electric street railway costing $70,000. The water works are owned by a private company, the supply being drawn from springs and wells and collected in 2 reservoirs 2 miles west of the city, from which it is pumped to a storage reservoir, 175 feet above, with storage capacity of 3,000,000 gallons. Constant pressure of from 60 to 95 pounds is maintained. There are 26 miles of mains. The value of property of the paid fire department, which has 41 alarms, is $25,000. The loss by fire in the year ending April 1, 1891, was $1,844.74. Two lines of electric railway cover 4 miles, tho total property being valued at $100,000. The Thompson-Houston system of electric lighting is in use in addition to gas, 80 lamps of 2,000 candle power each being suspended at intervals in the center of the streets; 35 arc and 885 incandescent lights are used. The Michigan Central Railroad reached Ann Arbor in 1839. Seven trains are run daily by it each way: the depot, built of bowlder stones, cost $35,000. The Toledo, Ann Arbor and North Michigan Railroad passes also through the city, doing an annual business here of $100,000. Free delivery is being extended over tho entire city, and the post-office receipts for the year ending June 30, 1891, were $25,641.38, an increase of $1,704.47 over the preceding year. The post office is a three-story structure, and there is an opera house, with seating capacity of 1,200. The hotels number 3, and there are 1 daily and 7 weekly newspapers (2 in the German langnage), exclusive of college papers. The usual telegraph and express facilities are afforded, and there is a telephone system. There are 3 banks (1 national and 1 savings) with a capital of $335,000. The deposits reach $1,250,000 yearly. The court house, covering an entire square, was finished in 1878, and cost, exclusive of furniture, $70,000. The county jail cost $20,000. Ann Arbor is frequently termed the Athens of the West, owing to the location here of the State University, having the largest number of students (1,885) and the largest total income ($274,272) of any institution of its kind in the United States. The sum of $500,000 was realized from sales of lands granted by the General Government at an early date, and the present value of the grounds and buildings is placed at $740,000; that of the scientific apparatus is $450,000; $156,272 were received from State appropriation in 1889-'90. Six departments are comprised, of which the medical at one time was the largest in the country. In 1890 its enrollment was 375 regulars and 71 homœopathic. Two large hospital structures have been lately completed at a cost of $80,000. The building containing the law department is so crowded that it has been decided to build an addition to cost $30,000. Of the 581 students enrolled in 1890, only 165 were from the State proper. The law library contains 10,208 volumes. Exclusive of professional works, the general library contains 59,735 volumes, and an important part is made up of presentations—the Parsons library, the McMillan Shakespeare, the Hagerman collection of history and political science, the German-American Goethe, and the Dorsch libraries. The course of study at the university covers four years, admission being gained by the presentation of diplomas from the high schools or examination. Women and men are admitted under the same conditions and pursue the same studies. Instruction is almost free. In the museum is to be seen the Chinese exhibit, brought over to tho New Orleans Exposition and presented to tho university, valued at $250,000. For a gymnasium $20,000 have been given, and a like amount raised by subscription. Educational advantages are afforded, in addition, by six primary and grammar schools, in fine buildings, and one high school, the total value of school property being $205,000. The total enrollment in 1890 was 2,036, and 51 teachers were employed. The enrollment in the high school was 695. The school expenditure for 1890 was $37.746.38. There are 3 parochial schools also—1 Catholic, 1 German Evangelical, and 1 Lutheran. The Ladies' Library Association has a building costing $3,000. Church property, divided among 13 denominations, is valued at $365.500. A capital of $526,000 is invested in manufacturing interests, employing 590 men. These include agricultural works with capital of $75,000, employing 100 men; furniture factories employing 125; 3 flouring mills, with an annual output of $800,000; 4 factories of carriages and road-carts; 3 planing mills; a factory turning out pianos and organs to the amount of $75,000 yearly; 1 foundry and boiler factory, a dried-fruit and vinegar factory with evaporating capacity of 525,000 bushels of fruit yearly, and several smaller establishments.

Appleton, a city of Wisconsin, the county seat of Outagamie County, 185 miles north of Chicago and 100 miles northwest of Milwaukee, on the Grand Chute of Lower Fox river. It is a thriving place, the population in 1880 having been 8,005, and in 1890, 11,869. The Chicago and Northwestern, the Chicago, Milwaukee and St. Paul, and the Milwaukee, Lake Shore and Western railways all connect with the city, giving outlets for its large manufactured output. Situated on a large plateau overlooking the river, it possesses many natural beauties and is noted for picturesque scenery. Its altitude is 723 feet above sea-level. Lake Winnebago, with its 350 square miles of area, fed by Wolf and Upper Fox rivers and numerous smaller streams, furnishes the Lower Fox with an inexhaustible supply of water at all seasons, and this river, in its flow of 150 miles from the lake to Green Bay, has a fall of 150 feet. 50 of which lie within the city limits. This body of water is said to furnish over 16,000 horse power, and it has been utilized by the construction of a system of dams and canals embracing all the rapids on the river. The canal is under the control of the United States Government. and large steamers and barges can pass from the lake to Green Bay. An electric street railway is in operation, and the city is lighted with electric lamps in addition to gas. The paid fire department has an electric fire-alarm system. The streets are broad and well paved, and there are several miles of sewers. Water works of the Holly system are in use. Two daily and six weekly newspapers are published, four of the latter in German. Two national banks have aggregate capital of $450,000 and surplus of $50,000. The assessed valuation of property in 1888-'89 was $3,145,000, (actual value, $7,862,500). The total expenditure for school purposes in the same year was $38,106. The total value of public property used for school purposes was $176,500, and the enrollment

PAPER AND PULP MILLS, APPLETON, WISCONSIN.

in six ward schools was 2,119, with 48 teachers. There are also a high school, and two Roman Catholic parochial schools. Lawrence University, founded by Hon. Amos Lawrence, of Boston, Mass., was chartered in 1847, and in 1888-'89 had 284 students, of whom 94 were women, and 11 professors and instructors. The observatory has been completed recently. The churches number 11, including a Jewish synagogue. Appleton is known as the "Paper City," $2,500,000 being invested in paper mills, which turn out 250,000 pounds of paper, valued at $7,500, every twenty-four hours. A sulphite pulp manufacturing company has a capital of $350,000, employs 150 men, with an annual pay roll of $75,000, and has an output of 30 tons a day. In all, 130 tons of wood pulp are manufactured every day, and 120,000 cords of spruce and poplar are consumed yearly in the mills of this kind along the river. Appleton has also 2 agricultural-implement works, a woolen mill, carding, hub, and spoke mills, linen, flax, and Turkish-towel factories, 2 planing mills, 4 flouring mills, two large breweries, 2 factories for paper-mill machinery, factories of boots and shoes, sash, door and blinds, chairs, toys, furniture, and cigars, a wood-veneering plant, screen plate works, lime kilns, a grain elevator, and foundries and machine shops.

Argentine, a city of Kansas, in Wyandotte County, in the eastern part of the State, on the south bank of Kansas river and adjacent to Kansas City, Kan., had a population in 1890 of 4,732. It is connected with Kansas City, Kan., by a cable line of street railway, and is supplied from its water works. It has also good sewers, a fire department, electric street cars, a library, a new city hall, 2 State banks, an opera house, 4 large school buildings, and 10 churches. The assessed valuation of property is $599,665.80, of which $76,120.80 is in railroads. The shops of the Santa Fé Railroad Company here employ between 600 and 700 men the year round; they embrace a roundhouse and extensive yards. To accommodate the great quantities of grain coming over this railroad 2 elevators have been erected, one having a capacity of 60,000 bushels. The leading industry is an immense smelting and refining works, erected in 1881, the grounds of which contain 18 acres, one third of which are covered with buildings. The works have a capacity for handling 23,000 tons of ore a month, and a total refining capacity of 50,000 tons of lead and 20,000,000 ounces of silver. Gold-separating and copper-refining plants have been completed recently. The output of the smelter for the year ending Dec. 31, 1891, was 15 per cent. larger than that of the previous year, and was, approximately, 25,000 ounces of gold, 8,750,000 ounces of silver, and 50,000,000 pounds of lead. The smelter is claimed to produce one fifth of all the silver and lead smelted in the United States. It employs more than 900 men. There is also a factory of radiators, employing, in 1889, 100 hands, and reporting a capital of $200,000. A corrugated-iron factory, with capital of $100,000, employed 40 men.

Bangor, a city and port of entry of Maine, county seat of Penobscot County, at the head of ship navigation on the west bank of the Penobscot, the largest river in the State, 25 miles above its entrance into Penobscot Bay, and 60 miles from the ocean. By railroad it is 73 miles from Augusta, 138 from Portland, 246 from Boston, and a little more than 200 from St. John, N. B., with which place and with Halifax and other Canadian cities there is connection by 3 trains daily. By the census of 1890 it is the third city in population in the State, having increased to 19,103 from 16,856 in 1880. Latitude 44° 45' N., longitude 68° W. The first settlement, known as Kenduskeag Plantation, from the small stream of that name which here flows into the Penobscot, was made in 1770, on the ancient camping ground of the Tarratines. one of the most famous and intelligent of the Indian tribes of northern New England. The pioneers, who came from Massachusetts, had no title to the soil, and after the Revolution, in which the small hamlet suffered while the British held control of the river, the General Court of Massachusetts provided (in 1801) that each settler prior to 1784 for $5, and each settler between 1784 and 1798 for $100, should have a deed of 100 acres. In 1791 it was incorporated as a town of 169 inhabitants under its present name, and in 1834 as a city with a population of about 8,000. It is connected with Brewer on the opposite bank of the river by steam ferry and a bridge 1,300 feet long. The harbor, exceptionally fine for a river port, has a deep-water frontage of 3 miles. The number of vessels of all classes registered, enrolled, and licensed in 1891 was 135, with a total tonnage of 20,569 tons. The imports for the year were $1,256,371, and the exports $219,315. Steamship lines connect with Boston, New York, Bar Harbor and the river towns, and there is a line of steam tugs. The first iron steamship built in America (in 1845) ran between Bangor and Boston, and one of the first railroads in the country was built from the city to Oldtown, 12 miles distant, in 1836. The Maine Central Railroad radiates in five directions from the city, the European and North American to the New Brunswick border, the Maine Shore line to Bar Harbor and other resorts on Mount Desert Island, and the Bangor and Piscataquis to the foot of Moosehead Lake. Surveys of the Bangor and Aroostook, incorporated in 1891, are under way. The assessed valuation of property in 1888–'89 was $9,955,102, and the bonded debt $680,000, $500,000 of which were for water works. These are of the Holly system, and were erected in 1876. The supply is drawn from the river, a dam being built across just above the city, which affords water power for mills also. Six reciprocating pumps and 1 rotary have a drawing capacity of 10,000,000 gallons daily, with reserve force for fire emergency. In addition to the 25 miles of street mains, there are 5 miles in Brewer also supplied from the pumping station. The paid fire department has the Gamewell system of alarm. In addition to excellent natural drainage, 20 miles of sewers had been constructed in 1888, and the city had 130 miles of streets opened and surveyed. The paving of the principal business streets with square granite blocks was begun the same year. Seven miles of electric street railway are in operation, the road having been chartered in 1887 and opened in 1889. It connects the city with Brewer. Gas and electric lighting are employed. Five national banks

have an aggregate capital of $900,000; there are 2 savings banks with deposits aggregating $3,600,000, 3 private banks, 3 local insurance companies, and a building and loan association. The Board of Trade, organized in 1872, has a membership of 200. Two daily and 3 weekly newspapers and a literary monthly are published. In 1888–'89 the public schools of Bangor numbered 68, including 13 suburban (ungraded), in 36 schoolhouses. The value of school property was placed at $125,000; 91 teachers were employed, and the total attendance was 3,040. The expenditures for school purposes were $41,198. Private and parochial schools had an attendance of 300, and the high school an enrollment of 128. Bangor Theological Seminary (Congregational) has been in operation since 1817; the value of grounds and buildings is $65,000; the number of students varies from 40 to 60. The library contains 16,000 volumes. The religious societies and places of worship number 18, of 10 different denominations. A legacy to the city of $100,000 has been applied to the maintenance of a public library containing 25,000 volumes, and other funds are held in trust for various institutions, including a Children's Home, homes for aged and indigent women, and a Mechanics' Association. The city has a fine opera house, and the Eastern Maine State Fair Association has its grounds and driving parks on an eminence 1 mile from the business center, overlooking the city and the harbor. The granite customhouse cost $201,755. The industries of Bangor include 300 manufacturing establishments, employing about 2,500 hands, and turning out a product valued at more than $8,000,000. Next to Chicago it is the largest lumber market in the United States, and the city supplies not only the large mills in its immediate vicinity but also logging camps of from 2,500 to 3,000 men and 2,000 horses during the winter months in the woods, and on the drives in spring and early summer. The annual shipments reach 200,000,000 feet, and from 1832 to 1888 the amount surveyed was estimated at 8,537,628,202 feet. Four steam and 1 water saw mill and 3 large steam planing mills lie on the water front, and another mill on the Kenduskeag in the center of the city; the majority, however, are without the limits. The product of 1887 in long and short manufactured lumber was $2,304,000, and of boxes and box boards $210,000. This item is of considerable importance, 1,500,000 packing boxes of pine and spruce being the record of 1887, while 700,000 orange and lemon boxes, valued at $50,000, were shipped in shooks to the Mediterranean, and 365,000 to Florida and the West Indies, and 125,000 onion and tomato boxes to Bermuda. The molding and planing-mill products of 4 mills reached $250,000, and the cooperages turned out 80,000 fish barrels, supplied to fishing villages of Massachusetts. Spool wood, last blocks, and excelsior were manufactured to the amount of $216,000, 5,500,000 feet of spool bars having been shipped to Scotland. There is 1 furniture and 1 sash, door, and blind factory, and 1 establishment making brush handles and backs. The ship timber realized $100,000. Wood and sawdust for pulp was shipped to the amount of $55,000. Lumbermen's driving tools are the product of 3 firms, and there are 1 saw, 2 edge-tool factories, and 2 factories of hand-made files. Shipbuilding and repairing, carried on by 3 firms, realized in 1887 $75,000. Next to lumber, the largest industry is the manufacture of boots, shoes, and slippers, the product in 1887 being $1,000,000. Five slipper factories employ 600 hands during the busy season, with a weekly pay roll of nearly $5,000, and 1 five-story factory of men's boots produces more than $350,000 yearly. Five tanneries have an aggregate product of $160,000, and there are 3 paper-box factories. Among other establishments are 2 iron foundries and machine shops, steam-boiler works, 2 large stove foundries, 1 shoddy and wool-carding mill, grist mills, salt and plaster works, 5 cigar factories, 5 bottling works, factories of clothing with annual production of $300,000, 5 carriage factories, and 1 of carriage trimmings, a wholesale coffin and casket factory, brickyards, 3 granite-working and 4 marble yards, and potteries. The permanent ice houses on the river and in the city have a storage capacity of 230,000 tons. The total value of wool, skins, furs, etc., shipped was $200,000, and of hay and country produce $100,000.

Barre, the fifth town of Vermont, in Washington County, 6 miles southeast of Montpelier, on a branch of Winooski river. It increased in population from 2,060 in 1880 to 6,812 in 1890. It is principally known for its granite industries, the granite deposit being found in a range of hills, and extending 3 miles with a width of half a mile. The quarries are 3 or 4 miles from the village, which was incorporated in November, 1886, and there is a railroad connecting with the shops where the granite is worked. Quarrying of any sized block is allowed by the nature of the deposit, which is in layers of varying thickness. Blocks 10 feet square and upward are obtained, and shafts of any length. Barre granite is of two varieties, light and dark, remarkably clear and even in texture, and susceptible of the highest polish, while the contrast afforded by the polished and hammered surfaces makes 'lettering and designs stand out in bold relief. One of the 6 quarrying companies owns quarries covering 230 acres. About 1,500 men were employed in 1890 in connection with the business, which is carried on by 19 firms, turning out vast quantities of monuments and monumental work, shipped to all parts of the United States. There is also a factory of hay forks, rakes, diggers, etc. One national bank has a capital of $100,000, and there is a savings bank and a trust company, with total resources of $500,000. The town has a fine system of water works, a graded school system, a seminary, and a town hall which cost $30,000. Its altitude is 515 feet above sea level.

Bennington, a town of Vermont, one of the county seats of Bennington County, in the southwestern part of the State, 55 miles south by west of Rutland, and 35 miles northeast of Albany, N. Y. By the census of 1890 it had a population of 6,391. It has an altitude of 641 feet above sea level, and the surrounding scenery is magnificent. From Mount Anthony, on which there is an observatory, the Adirondacks, 100 miles away, can be seen on a clear day; and in ascending the mountains the Bennington and Glastonbury Railroad makes a deviation of 8 miles to attain a height of 1,600 feet. Other railroads are the Fitchburg to Troy, the

Bennington and Rutland, and the Lebanon Springs. The town is the site of the State Soldiers' Home, which with its grounds and buildings covers about 200 acres. It was a gift to the State from the heirs of Trenor W. Park. It has a fine fountain which obtains its supply from springs on Bald mountain and throws a stream 187 feet high. The water for the town is obtained from mountain springs 3 miles distant, and there are 33 fire hydrants. The various religious denominations are represented, and there is a large, fine hotel. The Bennington graded-school district was organized and chartered in 1870, and there is, in addition to a high school, a fine public-school house, which with its grounds covers 3 acres. Two national banks have a capital of $200,000, and there is a savings bank. Two weekly newspapers are published. The town is essentially a manufacturing place, and about one third of the inhabitants are engaged in the mills and shops. It lies also in a fine farming district. The manufactures include woolen mills turning out fine dress fabrics, cloakings, and cassimeres, 6 knitting companies, one of which employs 200 persons, and two others 150 each; factories of knitting machinery, light hardware, powder-mill, pulp and paper-making machinery; yellow ochre, crystallized quartz, and mineral soaps; steam governors and water wheels; wooden specialties, knitting-needles, and other minor industries. There are also fulling mills, marble and granite works, and a planing mill and sash, door, and blind factory.

Brainerd, a city of Minnesota, county seat of Crow Wing County, near the geographical center of the State, on Mississippi river, 115 miles from Duluth, 138 from Minneapolis, and the same distance from Fargo, N. D. In 1880 the population was 1,865; in 1890 it was 5,703. It is one of the most important stations on the Northern Pacific Railroad between Duluth and the Red River of the North, and has shops of that road employing 800 men, with a monthly pay roll of $60,000, the entire plant being valued at more than $2,000,000. The Brainerd and Northern Railroad, partially built and constructing to the international boundary line, completed 100 miles in the season of 1892. The city has an altitude of 1,209 feet above the sea, and is built on a level plateau 55 feet above the river. A dam across the Mississippi, just north of the city, gives 25,000 horse power at low water, the back water covering 2,500 acres, while the overflowage covers the bottom lands of a large lake and gives boomage for 1,000,000.000 feet of logs. There is a sewerage system furnishing thorough drainage; and water works of the Holly system, drawing from the river, have 15 miles of mains and 72 fire hydrants. The volunteer fire department consists of 5 companies, and has an electric alarm system. Contracts were let for 4 miles of electric street railway in 1892, to be in running order by Dec. 1 of that year, and the city is lighted by electricity. The paving with cedar blocks and granite curbs of one of the principal streets was undertaken in 1892, and numerous brick blocks were built. There are 6 school buildings, a high school which cost $50,000, a large Catholic parochial school, 15 churches, an opera house with a seating capacity of 1,000, a county courthouse of brick and fire proof, a jail, a sanitarium belonging to the Northern Pacific Railroad. and a Young Men's Christian Association building, owned by the association, which cost $12,000. The city supplies about 10,000 men, who are employed in the woods lumbering within a radius of 50 miles. There are 2 banks. One large saw mill employs 200 men, and the Northern Mill Company's plant was added in the summer of 1892, employing 1,000. Two smaller mills have an annual capacity of 4,000,-000 feet of lumber. There are steam brickyards, which make both red and cream brick. The city has a board of trade.

Brattleboro, a town of Vermont, in Windham County, in the southeastern part of the State, on the right bank of Connecticut river, 1 mile below the mouth of West river, 77 miles from Rutland, 110 from Montpelier, and 119 from Boston. A bridge across the river connects it with New Hampshire. Its population was 5,880 in 1880, and 6,862 in 1890. The first settlement in the State was made here, at Fort Dummer, now in the southeast corner of the town, and the charter for the village was granted by George II in 1753. It has an altitude of 228 feet above sea level, and is at the junction of the Vermont Valley, New London, Northern and Brattleboro and Whitehall Railroads. In 1888–'89 the assessed valuation of property was $3,-460,000. The streets are regularly laid out, paved with concrete, and beautifully shaded. Electricity is largely used in illumination. Water from mountain springs is supplied by numerous aqueduct companies, in addition to a reservoir with a capacity of 7,000,000 gallons. The common, on the most elevated of the terraces at the north end, is contiguous to the State Asylum for the Insane, founded in 1834. Highland Park, a gift to the town, opened in 1884, contains 30 acres of woodland. The surrounding scenery is fine. The enrollment in the public schools in 1888–'89 was 735, and expenditures for the school year reached $16,565. Public-school property was valued at $69,550, and there were 7 public-school buildings and a high school. At West Brattleboro there is a classical seminary for both sexes, dating from 1831. There are 2 national banks, with joint capital of $250,000, and 2 savings banks. Three weekly newspapers are published, 1 semimonthly, and 1 monthly. The principal hotel cost $150,000. The works of the Estey Organ Company cover 100 acres and occupy 14 buildings, isolated from each other as a protection against fire, and have 7 brick dry houses for lumber; 500 persons are employed. There is also another reed-organ company, occupying a large six-story building, and turning out 2,500 organs yearly. Other industries include planing mills, carriage factories, a foundry, a factory of children's carriages and toys, 1 of knitting-machine needles, 1 of paper-mill and special machinery, 1 of overalls and frocks, 3 marble and granite monumental works, bottling works, a cigar factory, and a jelly company.

Bridgeton, a city and port of entry of New Jersey, county seat of Cumberland County, on both sides of Cohansey river, 20 miles above its entrance into Delaware Bay, and 38 miles south of Philadelphia. The population in 1870 was 6,830; in 1880, 8,722; in 1890, 11,424. Prior

to the Revolution Bridgeton was a hamlet of 200 inhabitants, dating from about 1745, and known as Cohansey Bridge. In 1765 the name was changed to Bridgetown, and in 1816 to Bridgeton. In 1749 it was made the county seat, and the first courthouse was built. That at present in use was occupied in 1845. In 1865 the city charter was obtained. The 4 wards cover a territory about 3 miles in breadth and more than 4 miles from the northern to the southern boundary. From a valley in the heart of the city there is a gradual elevation on the east and west, the greatest height reached being 51 feet above sea level. It is surrounded by a fine agricultural and fruit-growing region, and the vicinity is rich in natural scenery. The river is navigable by steamboats and spanned by 3 handsome bridges. Railroad facilities are afforded by the West Jersey and the New Jersey Central lines, 7 trains leaving the city daily, and by the Cumberland and Maurice River Railroad to the famous oyster cove, where 300 vessels and 1,500 men are employed in planting and catching oysters. During the oyster season the captains and business men of the industry have nearly $1,000,000 on deposit in the city. The gas plant at Bridgeton is capitalized at $31,000, and an electric-light company has been in operation since 1886, with a capital of $50,000. The system is the Thomson-Houston, and 80 arc and 1,200 incandescent lamps were in use in 1889. The water works, erected in 1877, have cost nearly $100,000. They draw their supply from East Lake, which has a storage capacity of 90,000,000 gallons. From a retaining reservoir near the dam it is pumped by a Worthington engine with a capacity of 1,000,000 gallons daily, supplemented by a Blake pump, to a distributing reservoir, from which there were in 1889 16 miles of pipe. The fire department has 28 members. Four daily and 4 weekly newspapers are published. The churches number 15, of which 4 are Methodist Episcopal, 3 Presbyterian, 3 Baptist, 1 Episcopal, 1 Lutheran, 1 Catholic, 2 Methodist Protestant. The 5 public schools have an enrollment of 1,584 pupils. By law these schools receive yearly $10,000 from the surplus in the State school fund. Four academic schools are respectively the South Jersey Institute (erected in 1869 at a cost of $45,000, a brick building 5 stories high, beautifully located). West Jersey Academy, Ivy Hall Seminary, and Seven Gables Boarding School, the two last for young ladies. Two national banks have an aggregate capital of $250,000, and there are 2 building associations. All capital employed in manufacturing in Bridgeton to the amount of $10,000 and upward is exempt from city tax for ten years. The manufacturing establishments in 1889 numbered 60, with a capital of $2,143,000, employing 3,718 persons, with yearly wages of $1,043,000. The value of the manufactured product was $2,759,000. The leading industry is that of the Cumberland Nail and Iron Works, dating from 1815; 400 men and boys are employed, and 4,000,000 feet of pipe and 140,000 kegs of nails, of 220 different kinds, are turned out yearly. The first of 20 glass factories was founded in 1836. Its works now cover 6 acres and consist of 3 window-glass and 2 hollow-ware factories. When it is in full operation, 500 men and boys are employed, and the yearly product is $300,000. Window glass was first manufactured here in 1879. In addition to the great output of this article and of all sorts of hollow ware, 2 potteries are also in operation; 2 machine works, 1 with plant valued at $80,000; funnel works valued at $30,000, with product of 3,000 funnels daily; a bottle-mold factory; a paper mill, valuing its plant at $50,000; a woolen mill with capital of $300,000, and employing 100 hands; a factory of enameled and rubber cloth and carriage goods; knitting mills; 4 large lumber yards with saw and planing mills; a foundry; a tannery; brickyards; 3 carriage factories; 1 shipyard; 2 flour mills. Factories of shirts, boots and shoes, soap, fertilizers, and cigars, with 2 limekilns, and an oil refinery complete the list of manufacturing establishments, with the exception of 6 canning factories, an industry which has grown rapidly within the past few years. A million boxes of strawberries are shipped during the season from the region surrounding Bridgeton, which is also a fine peach country. The Bridgeton Opera House is a four-story brick edifice, costing $40,000, and its Young Men's Christian Association is the oldest in the State. The customhouse was erected when the city was made a port of entry immediately after the adoption of the Federal Constitution. The total number of vessels enrolled at the port in 1889 was 460, with a tonnage of 15,000 tons. Nearly half the boats enrolled are coasting vessels, the others being engaged in the oyster business.

Burlington, the fifth city in size of Iowa, county seat of Des Moines County, on the right bank of the Mississippi, in the southeastern part of the State, 45 miles above Keokuk and 82 miles below Davenport, 206 miles southwest of Chicago, 300 from Omaha, and 200 from St. Louis. In 1870 it was the third city of the State in population and commercial importance, having 14,930 inhabitants; in 1880 it had 19,450, and in 1890 22,565. The city was laid out in 1834, and in 1837-'40 was the capital of the State. It has an elevation of from 435 to 533 feet above sea level, and the view of the river, here broad and beautiful, is fine. The residence portion stands on limestone bluffs, the streets are regularly laid out, and there are 10 miles of brick, granite, and macadam paving. Ninety per cent. of the houses are owned by the people. Water works of the Holly system are in use, with 18 miles of mains; the fire department has an electric-alarm system; 4 lines of electric street railway, with 12 miles of track, operate a ten-minute service, and there are 2 electric-light plants in addition to gas. In 1888-'89, the assessed valuation of property was $5,000,000, on a basis of $16,-666,670. In 1890 the internal-revenue receipts were $292,417.85, and the post-office receipts $45,340.69; 3,776,572 pieces of mail matter were handled. The Board of Trade, recently changed to a Citizens' Association, has 260 members. Ten lines of railroad afford transportation facilities in addition to the river, and the principal shops of the Chicago, Burlington and Quincy Railroad are here. The river traffic has nearly doubled since 1888, and in 1892 it exceeded that of any other town between St. Louis and St. Paul. The wharves are commodious and substantially paved, and deep-dredged waters afford room and easy

landing to all sizes of craft. A new railroad and wagon bridge has been chartered, and a company is organized to build it. The boathouse of the Boating Association of the city is a handsome building abutting on the river, and two hunting and fishing clubs own more than 3,000 acres opposite the city. The cascades, one mile south of the city, are a summer resort. The public-school property is valued at $150,000, and in addition to the 16 public-school buildings there are 7 denominational schools, 2 especially for Germans, and a business college. The churches number 30, belonging to 26 religious organizations. There is a fine opera house, a free public library, a Young Men's Christian Association building with commodious rooms and gymnasium, a hospital, a Masonic temple and an Odd-Fellows' building, while $125,000 have been appropriated by Congress for a Federal building. Five banks, 3 of which are national and 2 savings, have yearly aggregate deposits of nearly $3,500,000; and there is a safe-deposit company as well as a loan association. Three daily and 4 weekly newspapers are published. The customary telephone and express facilities are afforded, the last by 4 companies. There are 400 coal mines near the city. An electric-power company also supplies factories, and there is a steam-heating works. The manufacturing establishments number 194, and include the largest iron works and machine shops in the State, employing 200 men; 3 large carriage and 2 large wagon factories, also roadgrader works; 3 furniture factories, one making a specialty of office desks and employing 150 men, another of school furniture, employing 175: 1 nail and 1 wire mill; 1 barb-wire and 1 carriage-wheel factory; the only rolling mill in the State, with works covering 22 acres, and a monthly pay roll of $6,000, turning out 120 tons daily; 1 paving-brick and 3 brick works; 2 wire-mattress, 1 broom. 1 boot and shoe, 1 box and basket, 1 wooden ware, 1 bookcase, 1 cigar-box, 1 overall, 1 egg-case, 1 soap, 1 axle-grease, 1 cracker, and 3 candy factories; 1 flouring mill, 3 grain elevators, a stove foundry, boiler works, a chemical company, linseed-oil, canning, and vinegar and pickle works, 3 leather and harness manufactories, 3 saw mills employing 200 men, and other smaller industries.

Burlington, the largest city in Vermont, county seat of Chittenden County, on Lake Champlain, 40 miles from Montpelier and 80 from Whitehall. Winooski river forms the northern boundary. In 1880 the population was 11,365, and in 1890 14,590. The site is remarkably beautiful. The hill on whose gentle slope the town is situated rises gradually from the lake front until its highest point is reached, 268 feet above sea level. From this eminence a magnificent view is obtained of the lake and of the Adirondack mountains. Burlington is a port of entry, and has a fine harbor protected by a breakwater built by the United States Government. There are several miles of excellent dockage. On Juniper island, in the lake, there is a lighthouse. The original charter of the town was granted on June 7, 1763. In 1791 it had 332 inhabitants, and in 1800 was the eighty-third town in size in the State. In 1830 it was second only to Bennington, and two years later it attained the place it has since retained in size and commercial importance. In 1865 it was incorporated as a city, an area 13 miles square being within its limits. The Transportation facilities are afforded by the Vermont Central, the Burlington and Lamoille, and the Rutland and Burlington Railroads, and by a line of lake steamers having its offices here and connecting by the Delaware and Hudson Railroad with the Hudson river and Lake George steamers for summer travel as well as the carriage of large amounts of freight. Boats connect also with the Delaware and Hudson Canal opposite. The streets are regularly laid out, and a considerable part of the 50 miles in all are paved and macadamized. The residence portion is beautifully shaded, and there are 6 public parks. It is thoroughly lighted by gas and electricity. Three lines of street railway aggregate 6 miles. The water supply, derived from the lake, is pumped to reservoirs 300 feet above its level, having a capacity of 6,000,000 gallons. There are 30 miles of mains, also 200 fire hydrants. The volunteer fire department has a system of electric alarm, and consists of 6 companies. Nine public schools (buildings valued at $130,000) employ 45 teachers and have an attendance of about 1800. The high school is a fine building, and there is also a business college. The Catholics maintain a college for boys, an academy for girls, and 2 parochial schools. The Vermont Episcopal Institute was founded in 1854 by the first bishop of the State, whose name was given to Bishop Hopkins Hall, a school for girls, worth $80,000. The attendance in parochial schools in 1890 was 1,322. The University of Vermont, chartered by the Legislature in 1791 and rechartered in 1865 as the University of Vermont and State Agricultural College, is valued, estimating cost and fund, at $500,000. In 1888-'89 the total number of students in all departments was 468. The medical department, organized in 1821, has a building given by John P. Howard worth $50,-000. The Billings Library building, the gift to the university of Hon. Frederick Billings, cost $130,000; it contains the college library of more than 36,000 volumes. In the park in front of the university stands a bronze statue of Lafayette which cost $25,000, and commemorates the laying of the corner stone of the university by him in 1825. In Green Mount Cemetery there is a monument to Ethan Allen, who is buried near the site. The shaft, of Barre granite, rises 42 feet above the pedestal, and is surmounted by a statue of the hero 8 feet 4 inches high. It was completed in 1873. Mary Fletcher Hospital, valued at $450,000, was a gift to the city, and received its charter in 1876. It is supplemented by various private retreats and sanitariums. The Fletcher Free Library, another gift, contains 20,000 volumes. Other charities are a Home for Destitute Children, worth $200,-000, to which John P. Howard gave the opera house, built by him at a cost of $100,000; the Howard Relief Association, worth $60,000, dating from 1888, as does also the Home for Aged Women; and 2 orphan asylums worth $100,000 each. The Young Men's Christian Association has a building worth $50,000. Ten churches are valued at $475,000. One is a Roman Catholic cathedral and one a Jewish synagogue. The city is the center of the yachting on Lake Cham-

plain, and has a yacht club house. Ice yachting in winter is a favorite amusement. The public buildings are the county courthouse, the Federal court, post office and customhouse, and the City Hall. One daily and 4 weekly newspapers are published; also a college monthly. The aggregate capital of 2 national banks is $800,000, and there are also a savings bank and a trust company. The city has a board of trade. Lumber is the most important industry. In 1890, 5 large lumber firms had an aggregate capital of $4,000,000 and handled 150,000,000 feet of lumber yearly, employing 1,000 men. Their yards cover a large area on the lake front, with miles of dockage, and they operate extensive saw and planing mills. The manufactures require a capital of $1,667,000, employ 1,689 persons with monthly wages of $52,750, and turn out an annual product of $3,237,500. They include cotton mills employing 300 persons and turning out 30,000 yards daily, a factory of hydraulic and other machinery, woolen mills, sash, door, and blind factories, wood-working establishments, Venetian-blind, shade-roller, and screen companies, machine shops, marble and granite works, iron works, car-repair shops, brush, box, cigar, carriage, candy, and various specialty factories. Ample power is furnished by Winooski river, but steam is largely employed. On the lake shore a large cold-storage building has been erected.

Chillicothe, a city of Ohio, county seat of Ross County, in the southwestern part of the State, on the right bank of Scioto river and the north bank of Paint creek, 3 miles above the mouth of the latter stream, 50 miles from Columbus, and 96 from Cincinnati. In 1880 the population was 10,938; in 1890, 11,288. Transportation is afforded by the Baltimore and Ohio, the Southwestern, the Norfolk and Western, the Chicago, Hamilton and Dayton Railroads, and the Ohio Canal. The city was founded in 1796, and settled from Kentucky and Virginia. It was the capital of the State from 1800 to 1810 and from 1813 to 1816. It is in a fertile valley, surrounded by hills, and has an elevation of 635 feet above sea level. The streets are wide and well graded, crossing each other at right angles, and many are shaded with handsome trees. The original cost of the water works was $75,000. There are efficient police and fire departments; an electric-light plant in addition to gas; a telephone exchange; 4 banks, 3 of which are national and 1 a savings bank; 1 daily and 7 weekly newspapers. One of the latter, dating from 1800, has been published longer continually than any other paper west of the Ohio. In addition to 5 public-school buildings, with an enrollment of 1,842 pupils, there are a high school, 1 free mission, and 2 Catholic schools. The assessed valuation of property in 1888-'89 was $5,698,666, and the value of public property used for school purposes was $150,000. A public library, an opera house, a fine city-hall building, and a courthouse costing $100,000 are supplemented by handsome business blocks, 12 churches, and 10 hotels. About 4,000 hands are employed in the manufacturing establishments, which include 1 paper, 2 planing, and 3 flouring mills; 2 grain elevators; 2 lumber yards; 2 breweries; 1 novelty and 1 specialty works; 7 carriage and 4 wagon factories; 1 furniture factory, which removed thither from Wheeling, W. Va., three years ago, and employs 100 hands; 2 spoke factories; 2 of fertilizers; 3 of boots and shoes; 5 of cigars; 1 each of hosiery, paper boxes, brooms, baking powder, organs, banks and furniture, combination bar and beer coolers, harness and artificial ice; 4 machine shops; 4 marble and granite works; 3 tanneries; 1 canning and 2 bottling establishments; 1 book-bindery; and 1 foundry and machine shop.

Clinton, a city of Iowa, on the Mississippi river, midway between St. Louis and St. Paul, 138 miles west of Chicago, 60 from Dubuque, and 81 from Cedar Rapids. It is the tenth city of the State, having a population in 1890 of 13,-619, an increase of 4,567 over 9,004 in 1880, or 50·5 per cent. Its location on the river, from 566 to 586 feet above sea level, is picturesque, and on the north and west it is sheltered by hills and forests. Two fine steel bridges span the river, one recently completed, three quarters of a mile in length, exclusive of the approaches, and 150 feet above the water. It is a wagon bridge, while the other, 4,000 feet long, is a draw rail. In 1890, 3,034 steamboats, 662 barges, and 538 rafts passed this bridge—an increase of 442 steamers and 131 barges over 1889. The railroads entering the city are the Chicago and Northwestern, the Chicago, Milwaukee and St. Paul, the Burlington, Cedar Rapids and Northern, the Chicago, Burlington and Quincy, and the Chicago, Burlington and Northern, all having their terminus or division endings here. During 1891 the aggregate of improvements reached $1,826,700, and $145,000 were expended on brick paving for the city streets. Fifth Avenue, 100 feet wide, and extending from the river to the bluffs on the west, is paved throughout and shaded by massive elms. Shade trees are a feature of the place. The water works, which also supply the city of Lyons, 2 miles distant, draw their supply from three artesian wells, respectively 1,050, 1,235, and 1,665 feet in depth. The receiving basin has a capacity of 1,400,000 gallons; and the pumping apparatus, with a capacity of 7,000,000 gallons in twenty-four hours, is so arranged as to be able to draw from the river in case of fire. In 1891, $30,000 were expended on improvements of the works, which had 22 miles of mains in Clinton and 7 miles in Lyons. The available pressure for fire was sufficient to throw 8 streams 80 feet high at one time. An efficient paid fire department is supplemented by 3 volunteer companies. In 1891 the gas company substituted water gas for coal gas, erecting a new reservoir and putting in 6 miles of mains, expending $60,000 in its improvements. It also operates an electric-light plant, with a capacity of 140 arc and 1,000 incandescent lamps. The Thomson-Houston system of electric street railway is in use, extending to the factory sites and to the city of Lyons. The city has 10 public-school buildings, employing 57 teachers, and the attendance for the year ending in June, 1891, was 2,808. Three daily and 5 weekly newspapers are published, one of the last in German; also 1 monthly. The various religious denominations are represented, and the Young Men's Christian Association has a

newly completed building. There is a public hospital, built by subscription. Three national banks have an aggregate capital of $310,000, and there are 1 private and 2 savings banks. Lumber is the leading industry of Clinton; 7 saw mills, employing 2,000 men, at wages of $510,000, in 1891, turned out 151,346,813 feet of lumber, and 55,367,000 shingles, also 25,097,600 laths—a decrease from 179,686,000 feet of lumber and 56,558,000 shingles in 1890, caused by low water and difficulty in rafting. A large bridge and iron works has a capacity of 500 tons of iron a month; one of the oldest establishments is a paper mill, which has been extended and improved recently; there are a sash, door, and blind factory, employing 325 men and boys, with a yearly pay roll of $150,000; a saddlery company, boiler works, 3 large furniture factories established in 1891, a wagon works which removed here the same year from Sterling, Ill., a wire-bottom-lounge company, flouring mills, brickyards, a box factory, and one of carriages, wagons, and buggies. Shops of the Chicago and Northwestern Railroad are located here.

Easton, a city of Pennsylvania, county seat of Northampton County, in the eastern part of the State, at the confluence of the Lehigh with the Delaware river, 67 miles north of Philadelphia by rail, 75 from New York, and 17 from Allentown. It is connected with Phillipsburg, N. J., by a bridge erected in 1807, and with South Easton by a suspension bridge across the Lehigh, built in 1885. The population increased from 11,924 in 1880 to 14,481 in 1890. The first settlement was made by the Dutch as early as 1654. In 1748 the town was laid out, and in 1763 there were 11 houses, and a courthouse was erected. The borough was incorporated in 1789, and again in 1828. The city charter is of recent date. Easton early acquired importance as a commercial center, receiving grain from points along Bushkill creek and the interior of the State prior to the completion of the Lehigh, Delaware, and Morris canals, which unite here, and by which large quantities of coal, iron, grain, stone, and lumber are received and shipped. In 1811 a chain bridge was substituted for the triple-arch bridge across the Lehigh, and in 1833 the stone bridge across Bushkill creek, still in use, was built. Railroad facilities are now afforded by the Central Railroad of New Jersey, the Morris and Essex, and others. It has an altitude of from 215 to 357 feet above sea level, being built partly on the sides of hills. The streets are regularly laid out, and cross each other at right angles. In the center is a public square. The electric-light plant is owned by the city, and the gas company supplies Phillipsburg and South Easton also. Water is supplied by 2 steam-pump works from the two rivers, with head sufficient in the lower part of the city to dispense with fire engines. There is a paid fire department, with 12 miles of fire-alarm wire. There are 2 lines of horse cars, connecting with Phillipsburg and South Easton, and an electric street railway to College Hill. Three daily, 1 semi-weekly, and 6 weekly newspapers are published; also a college periodical. Lafayette College (Presbyterian), established in 1832, has 26 instructors and 309 students. Easton enjoyed public educational privileges as early as 1755.

It now has a high school and 12 public-school buildings, with an enrollment, in 1888-'89, of 2,425. The total value of public-school property is placed at $275,000. There are also a business college and an academy. The Memorial Gateway in honor of the founder of the Pennsylvania public-school system, was erected by subscriptions from school children. It was completed and dedicated in 1891. Three national banks have a joint capital of $1,034,000, and there are 2 private banks. A trust company has a capital of $125,000. The city has a board of trade, an opera house and a theatre, a children's home, society halls and lodge rooms, a public library, 17 hotels, 20 churches, and the usual telegraph, telephone, and express facilities. The manufactures of the city include 1 brass foundry, 2 iron foundries and machine shops, 1 factory of grinding mills, 2 rolling mills, 6 lumber, 2 saw, and 1 planing mills, 3 breweries and 2 bottling works, spice mills, a silk mill and factory, 2 tanneries, marble, slate, and granite works, 2 furniture, 1 cordage, 4 carriage, 2 cigar-box, 3 harness, 1 organ, 1 refrigerator, 1 brush, 1 boot and shoe, 1 felting, and 2 shirt factories. New industries are rock-drill, switch and signal, and car seat and spring companies.

Elkhart, a city of Indiana, in Elkhart County, on St. Joseph river, where the Elkhart and Christiana discharge their waters, and at the intersection of the Lake Shore and Michigan Southern and the Cincinnati, Wabash and Michigan Railroads, 101 miles from Chicago, 15 from South Bend, and 10 from Goshen, the county seat. It is the tenth city in size in Indiana, having a population of 11,360 in 1890, showing an increase of 4,407 over 1880. It has an elevation of 754 feet above sea level, the river banks upon which a part of it is built being almost bluffs. The air is pure, and the views of the surrounding scenery are fine. The building review for the year ending Dec. 31, 1890, showed £118,700 expended on business blocks, and $136,950 on private dwellings, making a total, with additions, of $296,620. A fine system of water works has 12 miles of pipe and 125 hydrants. An electric fire-alarm system covers the whole city. There are 17 miles of gas mains, in addition to arc and incandescent electric lights. A belt line 4 miles long has been rebuilt recently, and there are 7 miles of electric street railway track, also 15 miles of permanent cement walks. Two daily, 3 weekly, and 5 monthly papers are published. In 1888-'89 the assessed valuation of property was $2,367,245, on a basis of $7,101,735. The total amount used for school purposes was $150,000, and there are 8 public schools, having an enrollment of 3,149, an average daily attendance of 2,101; 46 teachers were employed, and received salaries amounting to $18,865. The high school is a fine building, costing $50,000. The churches number 20. The Young Men's Christian Association owns its own brick building. There are 2 national banks, 1 State bank, 5 loan associations, 3 insurance companies, and an opera house. A new hotel opened in 1891 cost $30,000. Three water powers of the city have been developed. The principal shops of the Lake Shore and Michigan Southern Railroad were located at Elkhart about 1871, and disburse $70,000 monthly to employees. They comprise a large T-rail rolling mill, a machine shop with capacity of one new engine a week, in addition to repair works; and a roundhouse holding 62 engines. The other industries include 3 print-paper, 1 building-paper, and 2 tissue-paper mills, 2 starch factories, 2 large flouring and 2 knitting mills, 2 large carriage works, a band-instrument factory, carriage-supply works, several wood-working establishments, second largest gun factory but one in the United States, 3 medicine laboratories, and a box factory. The aggregate annual output is about $3,000,000. Highland Park and Riverside are suburban additions.

Fort Smith, the second city of Arkansas, county seat of Sebastian County, on the south bank of Arkansas river, at the mouth of the Poteau, in the western part of the State. The corporate line on the west is also the boundary of Indian Territory. It is 169 miles from Little Rock, 175 from Texarkana, and 300 from Memphis. The population increased from 3,099 in 1880 to 11,311 in 1890. A Government military post, known as Fort Smith, established here in 1817, became important during the Mexican War, and by the time the garrison was removed, in 1871, the town was in existence, with overland stages to the far West, and steamboats to Cincinnati, St. Louis, and New Orleans. The first railway, the Little Rock and Fort Smith, was completed in 1876. In addition, the city now has the Kansas and Arkansas Valley, operated by the Missouri Pacific, and the St. Louis and San Francisco, controlled by the Atchison, Topeka and Santa Fé, giving wide and important connections. The Fort Smith and Mansfield runs through the great coal fields of the county. Four other roads are partially built. The large railroad, foot, and wagon bridge across the Arkansas has 13 spans, and is 2,880 feet long. The river business, which is now confined to local trade, is carried on by three packets. The altitude of the city is 418 feet above sea level; the lowest part is 20 feet above high-water mark of the river, and the highest from 50 to 75 feet. Good natural drainage is supplemented by a sewerage system, completed in 1889, which has 26 miles of sewers. Water is pumped through sponge filters from Poteau river to an iron tower capable of holding 500,000 gallons, and the pressure is sufficient for protection without fire engines. There are 20 miles of pipe. Gas and electric lighting are in use, and there are 11 miles of street railway. Two complete systems of telephone exchange are in operation. In 1887, $987,500 were expended in building, and in 1888 $1,600,000. To 1889, $1,750,000 had been expended on the streets, many of which are paved with brick, and on the street railway. The assessed valuation of property is $4,000,000, on a basis of $8,000,000. Two daily and 3 weekly newspapers are published, one of the last in German; and 4 banks, two of which are national, have an aggregate capital of $352,000. The city has a fine opera house, a high school, and 5 public-school buildings, valued, with the grounds, at $400,000. In May, 1884, Congress gave to the city the abandoned military reservation, with the exception of the ground covered by the Federal courthouse and jail, to be sold for the benefit of the public schools, and a permanent school fund of $750,000 has been thus established. There are in addition a commercial college, 2 convent, 1 Lutheran, and several private schools. The church property in 1890 was valued at $110,000, and there were 15 churches—2 Catholic, 5 Methodist Episcopal (1 African), 3 Baptist, 1 Christian, 2 Presbyterian, 1 Episcopal, and 1 Lutheran. The Young Men's Christian Association is also flourishing. The United States district court held here has criminal jurisdiction over Indian Territory. The city has a chamber of commerce. It lies in a fine agricultural and mineral region, and mining for coal is carried on at a distance of from 10 to 50 miles. The wholesale and jobbing trade is large, extending into Indian Territory. In 1889 there were 28 manufacturing establishments, with a capital of $267,000, and employing 300 persons. They include a large cotton compress, cotton-seed-oil mills, 3 furniture factories, 3 planing mills. 2 foundries and machine shops, 1 large roller flour mill, 1 harness and saddle, 1 boot and shoe, 1 broom, 1 wood-package, 1 ice, 1 candy, and 3 cigar factories, 1 canning establishment, and 2 large paving-brick plants. The last industry is increasing, the quality of shale clay found near the city being rare in the country. Brick made from it stood a test at the School of Mines, Columbia College, New York city, of 170 tons, or more than 5,500 pounds to the cubic inch, very nearly as much as the hardest granite can endure. The average rainfall for the past ten years was 43·83 inches.

Freeport, a city of Illinois, county seat of Stephenson County, on Pecatonica river, in the northern part of the State, 110 miles northwest of Chicago and 28 from Rockford. In 1880 the population was 8,516, and in 1890 10,189. It is an important railroad center, being on four divisions of the Illinois Central Railroad, of three of which it is the headquarters, on the Chicago, Milwaukee and St. Paul, and the Chicago and Northwestern systems, all having extensive yards, shops, and roundhouses here, while the Chicago, St. Paul and Kansas City passes through South Freeport, which is becoming an important shipping point. Forty trains arrive and depart daily, and a union depot has been completed recently at a cost of $20,000. The Chicago, Milwaukee and St. Paul has also a handsome brick depot. The city has an altitude of 457 feet above sea level. The streets are well paved, and lighted by gas and electricity; street-car service extends over a large part of the place; and water from 18 artesian wells is piped for domestic purposes and for fire protection. The assessed valuation of property in 1888–'89 was $1,679,680, on a basis of $5,878,880, and the public-school property was valued at $87,226. Five public schools had an enrollment of 1,611, and the expenditure for school purposes was $30,084. The high school had an enrollment of 142, and more than 500 pupils attended private schools and the business college. St. Joseph's Church (German Catholic), one of the finest buildings, has a parochial school and a hospital, the latter erected in 1889, and valued at $30,000. There are also another Catholic, 3 Presbyterian, 1 Episcopal, 1 Reformed, 3 Evangelical, 1 English Lutheran, 1 German Evangelical Lutheran, 3 Evangelical, and 4 Methodist churches. Of the 17 church buildings, 6 are owned by Germans. Three daily and 5 weekly newspapers, two of the latter in German, are published; and there are 4 banks (2 national), with aggregate capital of $250,000. An opera house and a courthouse represent the public buildings, and there are more than 60 manufacturing establishments, employing about 1,500 persons, with a yearly pay roll of $750,000 and an annual product of $3,000,000. One of the leading interests of the city is the manufacture of bicycles, of which there are 3 factories, 1 capitalized at $100,000, employing 115 men, and with annual capacity of 5,000 wheels. There are also a large foundry and machine shops, covering 7 acres and employing 350 men, turning out, among other articles, windmills. Other industries include a heater company, with capital of $100,000, a factory of coffee mills, 4 extensive breweries, 3 flouring mills. a cooperage, hardware and hardware-novelty factories, vinegar works, and a canning factory, large buggy works, 2 tanneries, a factory of piano stools, 1 of gloves and mittens, 1 of churns, 1 cracker, 1 corn-cob-pipe, and 1 latch company, a creamery, carriage factories, brickyards, limekilns, marble and granite works, and 2 planing mills.

Kansas City, the largest city of Kansas, county seat of Wyandotte County, on the right bank of the Missouri at the mouth of Kansas river, adjacent to Kansas City, Mo., 458 miles from Chicago, 277 from St. Louis, and 213 from Omaha. In 1880 the population was 3,200. In 1886 the towns of Wyandotte (the original county seat), Armourdale, and Armstrong were consolidated with it, giving a population of 21,229. In 1887 there were 25,060 inhabitants; in 1888, 33,110; in 1889, 36,279; and in 1890, 38,316. It has an elevation of 750 feet above sea level. In 1891 the assessed valuation of property was $9,338,000, the bonded debt was $1,236,041, and the net debt $568,700.45. In the four years 1887–'91, $2,246,992.75 were expended on the thoroughfares of the city, which on Dec. 31, 1891, had 50 miles of graded and 25 miles of paved and curbed streets, 20 miles of curbing, and 58 miles of sidewalk; 17·22 miles of sewers had been laid at a cost of $251,793, and bridge work amounting to $153,138. The expenditures for general improvements in 1891 reached $375,633.79; 446 building permits were issued during the year, at a cost of $724,850. The transfers of real estate for the year ending June 30, 1891, aggregated $5,229,575. The capacity of the water works (which represent a capital of $900,000) is 2,500,000 gallons daily; there are 10 miles of mains and 44 fire hydrants. Four companies, 4 hose-carts, and 1 hook-and-ladder crew constitute the fire department, the annual expense of which is $18,000. In addition to gas, there were 2 public and 5 private electric plants supplying 508 arc and 5,205 incandescent lamps. During 1891 8½ miles of double-track street railway were constructed, making a total mileage of 26¼ miles. Of this, 11 miles are elevated road, connecting with Kansas City, Mo., steam motor and electric; the rest, with the exception of 3¼ cable and 2 miles steam motor, being electric. The value of school property is $291,224, with 21 schoolhouses, and 112 teachers are employed. The enrollment for the ward schools in 1891 was 6,536, and of the high school 179. In addition there were 5 parochial schools, with 845 pupils, and 1 commercial college. The value of church property is placed at $478,800, and the 45 churches are divided as follow: 13 Baptist, 5 Catholic, 4 Christian, 2 Congregational, 1 German Evangelical, 11 Methodist (2 German and 2 African), 1 Latter-Day Saints, 4 Presbyterian, 2 Episcopal, 1 Tabernacle, and 1 People's. St. Margaret's Hospital, valued at $50,-000, accommodates 120 patients. The city's Board of Trade dates from 1884, and there is a Chamber of Commerce. The Exchange building stands on Central Avenue, the principal business thoroughfare. Other notable buildings along it are the Simpson Block, the market house, and the Produce Exchange. Hourly local mails have been established with Kansas City, Mo., and free mail delivery is extended over the whole city. During the year ending June 30, 1891, 3,320,749 pieces of mail matter were handled at the post office, an increase of 23 per cent. over the previous year. Every important system of railway lines in the West but one connects with the city, and of the 15 great systems centering here 8 have terminals in the city and its suburbs, while the 7 others, having terminals in Kansas City, Mo., do an extensive business here also, through the belt lines and switch arrangements with other roads. There are 4 railway shops in Kansas City proper, and 1 in Kansas City, Mo. The first railroad of Kansas City was opened to Lawrence in 1864. In 1890 the two Kansas Cities united to form the Missouri River Transportation Company, which owns 3 large steamers. The stockyards of Kansas City cover more than 100 acres and are penetrated by railroad switches that enable the unloading of 4,000 cattle an hour. During 1891 4,405,331 animals were marketed, valued at $66,504,031. Of these, 1,280,-839 were cattle, 83,500 calves, 2,616,749 hogs, 338,034 sheep, and 32,209 horses and mules; 92,488 cars were required. In the city there are 4 grain elevators, with a storage capacity of 1,690,000 bushels. Beef and pork packing is the leading industry. Of the 7 large packing houses in the two Kansas Cities, 6 belong to the Kansas side, 2 for beef and 4 for pork. Together they have an area of 143 square acres, the real estate being valued at $1,500,000, and the plants at $5,701,394, while the amount of capital required to run them is $12,380,000. The value of the product in 1891 was $40,656,134; 4,433 hands were employed, with wages to the amount of $2,483,915; and 2,000,000 brick were ordered during the year for an addition to one of the plants. Packing had its beginning in 1868. In 1891 the output of the houses was 551,653 cattle, 2,071,813 hogs, and 112,057 sheep. In 1860 the total amount of capital invested in manufactures at Kansas City was $40,100, and 46 hands were employed. In 1891 $12,797,500 were invested, independent of the value of the plants, with a yearly product of $58,466,405. The establishments numbered 74. These, exclusive of the packing houses, have an annual product of $17,810,271, and include 5 foundries, 5 cooperages, 3 brickworks, 3 planing mills, 4 ice factories, desiccating works, 4 carriage and wagon, 3 harness and saddlery, 4 soap, and 3 cigar factories, and others of boxes and baskets, oilcloth, wall plaster, brooms, scales, glue, wire, furniture, steel ranges, and cement. There are also

several flouring mills and canning and evaporating factories.

Lansing, a city, the capital of Michigan, in Ingham County, on both sides of Grand river at the mouth of Cedar river, south of the center of the State, 85 miles from Detroit, 72 from Grand Rapids, and 208 from Chicago. The population by the census of 1890 was 13,102. In 1847 it was selected as the site of the capital, while still covered with a vast forest, and in 1859 it was incorporated as a city. The limits extend 2 miles from east to west, and 3 miles from north to south, embracing an area of 3,840 acres. It has four large railroads—the Chicago and Grand Trunk, the Detroit, Lansing and Northern, the Michigan Central, and the Lake Shore and Michigan Southern. The elevation above sea level is 836 feet. Latitude 42° 40', longitude 84° 32'. The assessed valuation of property in 1890 was $6,500,000, and in 1891 $6,750,000. In 1890 the sum expended for general improvements was $700,940, and in 1891 $764,950; 230 dwellings were erected during the last year, and 19 stores, aggregating an expenditure of $514,-950. The total length of the sewerage and drainage system is 20 miles, and has cost $75,-000. Street improvements for the year 1891 cost $16,000. Two systems of electric lighting, costing $40,000, are in operation, with 104 lights. The water works are owned by the city, which has derived from them a net revenue of $12,000 yearly. Their total cost equals $175,000, including 31 miles of mains. The paid fire department has a membership of 21. Eight bridges span the river. The post-office receipts for 1891 were $38,126.73, and the expenses $16,616.55, leaving a balance of $21,510 18, an excess over the previous year of $4,170.97. Free delivery has been established for eleven years. The school property, including the high school, is valued at $120,000, and 51 teachers are employed; 2,717 pupils are enrolled. The expenditure for school purposes in 1891 reached $73,242.86, of which $15,407 was for new buildings and repairs. There is also a business college. The church property is estimated at $320,000; including branches, there are 24 buildings. Two national and 3 saving banks and 3 building and loan associations facilitate business. Nine printing offices issue 13 newspapers and magazines. The street railway is of the Westinghouse (electric) system, and has a capital of $150,000. Its extension to the agricultural college, 3½ miles from the city, is contemplated. There are 2 parks, 14 hotels, and an opera house, with seating capacity of 1,300, which cost $70,000. Three State institutions are at Lansing. The Reform School, established in 1855, embraces in connection with its 32 buildings, 360 acres of land. The total value of grounds, buildings, library, apparatus, etc., is $255,000. For the year 1890 the legislative appropriations amounted to $53,-000, and the receipts from all sources aggregated $62,012. In 1891 268 inmates were received and 200 discharged. The School for the Blind, established in 1880, has 77 inmates. The value of buildings, grounds, etc., is $176,375. The buildings of the Agricultural College number 58, and cost $283,000. They are beautifully located in a park of 50 acres, and the college farm contains 676 acres. The appropriations of the State for the institution, from the time of its establishment, in 1855, to 1891, amount to $861,-966. The faculty numbers 96, and the yearly running expense is $90,000. There are more than 360 students. The Capitol, begun in 1871 and occupied in 1878, cost $1,500,000, and covers 4 blocks. The State library contains over 40,000 volumes. The manufacturing establishments of Lansing employ upward of 3,000 persons. They include a factory of farming implements, sleds, and stoves, with capital of $300,-000, having an output in 1891 of $650,000, and employing 400 men; iron and engine works; factories of carriages, roads carts, cutters, wheelbarrows, trucks, etc.; a pressed-stone company; lumber yards; a condensed-milk company, with capital of $100,000, the output of which for 1891 was placed at $300,000; a knitting factory; 3 flour mills; and a factory of gasoline and other engines, pulleys, shafting, and machinery.

Lyons, a city of Iowa, in Clinton County, on Mississippi river, opposite Fulton, Ill., 2 miles from Clinton, the county seat, 78 miles below Dubuque by river, and 58 miles by rail, 140 miles west of Chicago. It has a population of 5,799 by the census of 1890, an increase of 1,704 over 4,095 in 1880. It is finely situated where the great cliffs of the river descend to more moderate bluffs and rolling upland, and possesses beautiful scenery. Its railroads are the Chicago and Northwestern and the Chicago, Milwaukee and St. Paul. During 1891, $332,600 were expended in improvements, $90,000 of which were for the high wagon bridge of iron and steel opened on July 4 of that year, 2,652 feet long, of which 1,552 were the bridge proper. On street improvements, including a sewerage system, $6,000 were spent. $15,000 for water, which is supplied by the water works of Clinton drawing from artesian wells, and $20,000 for gas, also supplied from Clinton. There are also 40 electric street lamps. The city is connected with Clinton by an electric street railway. The old water works of the city are kept in operation for fire protection, and there are 5 volunteer fire companies. The customary telegraph, telephone, and express facilities are afforded, and there is a transfer company operating between the city and Fulton, Ill. More than 1,000 pupils attend the 4 public schools, and in addition there are a high school, a Catholic seminary, and several private schools. Two of the 8 churches are Catholic. A triweekly and a weekly newspaper are published. The public library contains 5,000 volumes. Two national banks have a joint capital of $200,000, and there is also a savings bank. Three large saw mills constitute the leading industry, and in 1891 these turned out 62,625,000 feet of lumber, 15,328,000 laths, and 13,826,000 shingles. There are also a sash, door, and blind factory, galvanized-iron cornice works, a paper mill on which $20,000 were expended in 1891, a pressed-brick and paving-brick company, machine shops, and brickyards.

Manistee, a city and port of Michigan, county seat of Manistee County, on the eastern shore of Lake Michigan, at the mouth of Manistee river, and along the west shore of Manistee lake, 72 miles north of Muskegon, 30 from Ludington, and 45 from Traverse City. By the census of 1890 it had a population of 12,812, an in-

crease of 5,880 over 1880. In 1751 a Jesuit mission was established here, but the first actual white settlement took place in 1841, when a saw mill was built. In 1855 the county was organized, and in 1866 the village contained 1,100 inhabitants. In 1869 it was incorporated as a city, and in 1871 was destroyed by fire, $1,000,000 representing the loss of property. It has an altitude of 604 feet above sea level, and is built upon hills, the residence portion commanding a prospect of great extent and rare beauty. The railroads entering the city are the Flint and Père Marquette, the Manistee and Northeastern, the Manistee and Grand Rapids, and the Manistee and Luther, the last connecting with the Grand Rapids and Indiana. The harbor is excellent, and there are 5 lines of steamboats. Of the total tonnage of the port for 1890, 634,600 tons, 28,135 tons were receipts and 606,465 shipments, the largest item of the latter being lumber; 133,123 tons were salt. The school property in Manistee is valued at $84,000. During the year 1888-'89 the school expenditure reached $38,883. There are 5 public-school buildings, including the high school, and 39 teachers are employed. The school enrollment was 2,665, and the average daily attendance 1,445. In addition, there are 1 German, 1 Lutheran, and 3 Catholic parochial schools. Of the 14 churches, 3 are Catholic, 2 German Lutheran, 2 Congregational, 3 Methodist, 2 Baptist, 1 Scandinavian Lutheran, and 1 Episcopal. One daily and 4 weekly newspapers are published, one of the latter in the German language. Two of the 3 banks are national, the other being a savings bank. The supply of water is abundant, and there are gas and electric lights, telegraph and telephone companies, free mail delivery, and an efficient fire department. A hospital has been completed recently, at a cost of $85,000, and presented to the Sisters of Charity by one of the pioneers of the city: there is a county infirmary, and an industrial home. The grounds of the Driving Park Association contain 23 acres. There are 8 firms manufacturing lumber, lath, shingles, and salt, the output of one of the largest being 12,000,000 feet of lumber, 33,000,000 shingles, 8,000,000 laths, and 500 barrels of salt a day. Other industries include iron works manufacturing in addition to stationary and marine boilers and engines, twin engine, steam feed, saw-mill machinery, and salt-well outfits; a factory of saws and tools; boiler works; a foundry and machine shops; two furniture factories, and one of cigars, the last employing 25 men.

Montpelier, the capital of Vermont and county seat of Washington County, on Winooski or Onion river, 200 miles from Boston and 40 miles from Burlington. Its population was 3,219 in 1880, and 4,160 in 1890. It has an altitude of 484 feet above sea level. It is an important railroad center, having the Vermont Central, the Boston and Montreal, with a branch to Barre and Williamstown, and the Montpelier and Wells River Railroad, connecting at Wells river with the Boston and Lowell system for all points in the White mountains. It became the capital of the State in 1805, and the Statehouse, of granite, has a frontage of 177 feet, with a dome and cupola 56 feet high. The crowning statue of Agriculture is 120 feet above the ground. The architecture is Grecian. The State Library, of 26,000 volumes, the Supreme Court, and the Historical Society occupy an annex. It is surrounded by a handsome park, which descends to the street by rounded terraces. There are also a courthouse, a fine post office, 2 national banks with a capital of $400,000, 2 savings banks, 6 churches, a fine hotel, good schools, and the Vermont Methodist Seminary, chartered in 1833, which has over 300 students. Three weekly newspapers are published, and 3 monthlies. Electric lighting is in use, and the water supply is pure and ample. There are efficient fire and police departments. There are factories of sawmill machinery, organ and piano springs, and patent candy machines, clothes wringers and washing machines, leather, clothespins, and special machinery, in addition to 4 granite companies working the celebrated Barre granite, one of which has a capital of $100,000 and employs from 75 to 100 men. There are also 2 planing mills, and a paper-box factory. A stone bridge crosses the river.

Mt. Vernon, a city of Westchester County, N. Y., incorporated March 22, 1892, as the thirty-fourth city of the State in order of incorporation, each city being required to have a population of at least 10,000 before a charter is granted. Mt. Vernon is on the main lines of the New York, New Haven and Hartford Railroad and of the New York and Harlem. A new railroad is projected from Yonkers, through Mt. Vernon, to Pelham, New Rochelle, and Glen Island, to Long Island Sound; and another, the Union, from Mt. Vernon to the Grand Central depot, in New York city, with a 5-cent fare. The city has an area of about 1 square mile, including the former village of Mt. Vernon, the suburb of Chester Hill, and a part of the town of Eastchester, but excluding South Mt. Vernon. The southerly and westerly lines run to the boundary of the "Greater New York," in which it is proposed to include the metropolis, Brooklyn, and much adjacent territory. The discussion of this scheme and the threat of annexation to New York hastened the granting of a charter to Mt. Vernon. This charter is a model of its kind, the elective officers being those usually allowed to the smaller cities of the State. The first settlement of Mt. Vernon was made about 1853, when the Home Industrial Association No. 1, of New York city, obtained a charter allowing it to purchase not less than 250 acres of land in one location, and to divide it equally among its 1,000 members, each member being required to improve his own land. The association was composed of mechanics and laboring men residing in New York city. Horace Greeley was one of the trustees. The association at once purchased 375 acres in the town of Eastchester, and at first the settlement was named Monticello, then Monticello City, and finally, in 1851, Mt. Vernon. In 1852 there had been erected 400 houses, and the settlement was incorporated as the Village of Mt. Vernon in 1853, when it contained a population of 1,400. The population of the city in 1892 was about 16,000. The surface is diversified by many small streams, the chief of which is Bronx river. From the higher portions, about 200 feet above tide water, extensive views can be had of Long Island Sound. The drainage and the system of sewerage are perfect. The broad streets are well paved or macadamized, and electric cars make communication easy. The streets are lighted with electricity. Gas and water are furnished by private corporations. There are 4 private schools, including a military institute, and 5 public schools, but the school system has not yet been organized to fit the new conditions. The churches include 2 Episcopalian, 2 Catholic, 2 Methodist, 1 Reformed, 1 Presbyterian, 1 Congregational, 1 Lutheran, 1 Universalist, and 1 Baptist. Several of the church buildings, and the building of the Young Men's Christian Association, are of modern construction. A feature of the city is the Fairfax Opera House, with seating accommodations for 1,000. It is built in the modern colonial style. The city has also 3 banks, 2 newspapers, and several small factories, the largest being that for rubber goods.

Natchez, a city of Mississippi, county seat of Adams County, in the southwestern part of the State, on a perpendicular bluff 200 feet above Mississippi river, 280 miles from New Orleans, 130 from Vicksburg, and 100 from Jackson. It is one of the oldest towns in Mississippi. In 1870 it was the second city of the State, having a population of 9,057; in 1890 the population was 10,101. At present it is the third city. It is the western terminus of the Natchez, Jackson and Columbus Railroad, and has ten trains daily. There are 4 lines of steamers, from St. Louis, Cincinnati, and New Orleans, in addition to local packets, and the river business in 1890 amounted to 50,000 tons. The streets are wide and regularly laid out, crossing each other at right angles, and beautifully shaded. Many of the residences are surrounded by spacious grounds filled with flowers at all seasons, and from its elevation it commands an unobstructed view of 10 to 15 miles over the lowlands of Louisiana. In 1888–'89 the assessed valuation of property was $3,000,000, on a basis of $4,500,000, and the value of public-school property was $41,000. In addition to the 2 public schools and the high school, with an enrollment of 1,205, there are numerous private schools and a college. The city has all modern improvements, gas and electric lighting, street railway, excellent water works and sewerage systems, a telephone exchange, public parks, 4 banks with aggregate capital of $290,000, 4 building and loan associations, an opera house, a Masonic temple, a public hospital, several orphan asylums, churches, including a Catholic cathedral and a Jewish synagogue, and 2 daily newspapers. A national cemetery is located here. The industries of the city include 2 large cotton mills, 1 of which employs over 200 persons. There are also 2 cotton-seed-oil mills, a batting mill, an ice factory, saw mills, foundries and machine shops, and candy and mineral-water factories. The cotton-compress receipts reach 50,000 bales yearly. Truck farming is carried on profitably in the county, which abounds also in kaolin, potter's clay, glass sand, timber, and plants supplying material for paper.

Nebraska City, a city of Nebraska, county seat of Otoe County, on the right bank of Missouri river, in the southeastern portion of the State, 44 miles south of Omaha by railroad, 57 from Lincoln, and 160 from Kansas City, Mo. In 1870 it was the second city in population

in the State. In 1880 it had 4,183 inhabitants, and in 1890 11,494, an increase of 7,311, or
174·78 per cent. The elevation varies from 907
to 972 feet above sea level, and overflows of the
river are unknown. Railroad facilities are afforded by the Missouri Pacific, the Kansas City,
St. Joseph and Council Bluffs, and the Burlington and Missouri River lines, the last having 14
passenger trains daily, arriving and leaving, 12
of which are fast mail express. The steel railway and wagon bridge across the Missouri cost
$1,000,000. The streets are paved with cedar
blocks and vitrified brick: a good sewerage system supplements natural drainage, and gas and
electric lights are in use; there are street cars,
water works, a fire department with all the latest
apparatus, and 4 banks with a capital of $250,-
000, 3 of which are national and 1 a farmers'
bank. Three daily and 3 weekly newspapers
are published. The Federal post-office building
cost $100,000, and there is free mail delivery.
In 1888-'89 the total of taxable property was
$1,048,677, while the amount used for school
purposes was $82,000. The expenditures for
schools were $27,661. Ten school buildings, 6
of which are fine structures, had an enrollment
of 1,354, and 27 teachers were employed, while
200 pupils attended parochial and private
schools. There is a high school. The State
School for the Blind is here. It is a brick structure, one of the finest in the State, and was
opened in 1875. There are 45 pupils. Two parks
add to the beauty of the city—one of 25 acres—
and there is a city hospital and a board of trade.
The churches number 17. There are 2 large
packing houses in Nebraska City, one of which
has a main building 5 stories high, 224 by 112
feet, and 2 large expansion ice machines, with
storage capacity of 12,000,000 pounds in the
cooling rooms; 250 men are employed, and $3,-
000,000 are disbursed yearly for hogs. The firm
owns also 150 refrigerator cars. Next to South
Omaha the city claims the largest stock yards in
the State. A large distillery company, with
capital of $300,000, manufactures 10,000 gallons
daily of cologne spirits and alcohol; 2,500 bushels of grain are consumed daily, and the firm
has its own cooper shops. The cereal mills, with
a capacity of 6,000 bushels of grain a day, have
an iron grain elevator, with capacity of 125,000
bushels; a starch company, incorporated in
1891 with a capital stock of $100,000, went into
operation in February, 1892. It has a capacity
of 2,000 bushels of corn daily. A vitrified-brick
company, established in 1889 with a capital of
$50,000, uses 40 tons of coal daily, and turns out
50,000 bricks. There are also novelty works, 2
extensive breweries, boiler works, planing mills,
lumbar yards, foundries and machine shops,
plow and wagon works, bottling establishments,
marble yards, a canning company, a creamery,
and a broom factory. About $1,000,000 are in-
vested in manufacturing. There are many handsome residences, and the business portion of the
city has fine brick and stone buildings.

Niagara Falls, a city of Niagara County, N.
Y,. incorporated March 17, 1892, as the thirty-
third city of the State in order of incorporation.
It lies 20 miles north of Buffalo. The city was
formed from the village of the same name together with the village of Suspension Bridge.

The population is estimated at 14,000. The new
city is on the following trunk lines of railroads:
New York Central and Hudson River, West
Shore, New York, Lake Erie and Western,
Michigan Central, Grand Trunk, Lehigh Valley, New York, Lackawanna and Western, and
Rome, Watertown and Ogdensburg. The gorge
of Niagara river is crossed by two railroad
bridges—the original suspension and the cantilever—and a third is projected. A carriage and
foot bridge spans the river just below the falls.
The area of the city is about 6 square miles, the
plan being that of an irregular quadrilateral.
The first side is bounded by Niagara river for
more than a mile above the falls; the second, by
the same river for two miles below the falls; the
third and fourth, by surveyed lines on the land.
The greatest length of the city is from north to
south, the two villages formerly composing it
having been about two miles from one center of
population to the other. At the southwestern
angle are the famous falls of Niagara, now under the control of the State of New York. The
State Reservation extends from just below the
falls to a point nearly a mile above, the river
boundary being the middle of the river. In
1879 Gov. Robinson. of New York, and Lord
Dufferin, Governor-General of Canada, conferred
as to the inclosure of "a suitable space on
each side of the river from which annoyances
and exactions should be excluded." On Gov.
Robinson's recommending the matter to the
Legislature, a commission was appointed to have
the lands surveyed and appraised. The survey
included Goat Island. the Three Sisters, Bird
Island, Luna Island, Chapin Island, the smaller
islands adjacent, and a strip of land from Port
Day to and including the private property
known as Prospect Park. The strip along the
shore was from 100 to 200 feet wide, and the
area of the whole tract was 118 acres. In 1885
the Legislature appropriated $1,433,429.50 for
the purchase of the tract. and the Reservation
was formally opened on July 15 of that year.
Since that time much progress has been made
in restoring the falls to a state of nature. The
Reservation is absolutely free to visitors, save
that small fees are charged for the inclined railway, the Cave of the Winds, and the steamer
at the foot of the falls   Victoria Park. on the
Canadian side, was opened on May 24, 1888, but
an admission fee is charged. Although the
project of a ship canal around the falls has been
often suggested, no practical steps have been
taken to build a water way on American soil
similar to the Welland Canal in Canada; but
the using of a part of the immense power of the
falls has become almost an accomplished fact.
The earlier efforts in this line were impractical
(see the "Annual Cyclopædia" for 1887, page
561), but in 1886 the Legislature of New York
granted a charter to a corporation with ample
capital to build a tunnel through the solid rock.
This tunnel will be opened in 1893. It will
take the water from the river a mile above the
falls and convey it through a short surface canal to the mouth of the tunnel, where it drops
to the level of the deep tunnel through a series
of wheel-pits, thus generating several hundred
thousand horse power. The power will not only
be used on the spot,. but will be conveyed to

Buffalo and other places by compressed air and electricity. The hydraulic canal, which has been doing a similar but smaller service for many years, has been enlarged recently to double its former capacity. These notable improvements have given a great impetus to the new city of Niagara Falls, and it bids fair to become one of the most important manufacturing centers in the country. One of the first ventures to take advantage of the newly developed water power is that of the Niagara Falls Paper Company, covering 11 acres. The old water power is used by about 20 factories, all of them large. This number includes the Oneida Community Plating Works, 3 pulp and paper mills, and 3 flouring mills, one of which has a capacity of 1,600 barrels daily. The broad streets of the city are well lighted with electricity and well served by electric cars. The most complete system of sewerage in the country is now in process of construction. and when this is completed the streets will be paved with stone or asphalt. There are 3 banks, 10 churches, and 4 schoolhouses, not including De Veaux College, which has been richly endowed by the Episcopalians. There are nearly 50 hotels, 2 of them being very large, and 20 of a medium size.

Owensboro, a city of Kentucky, county seat of Daviess County, in the northwestern part of the State, on Ohio river, 40 miles above Evansville, Ind., and 150 below Louisville. The population in 1890 was 9,837, an increase of 3,606 over 6,231 in 1880. The Owensboro and Nashville Railroad extends to the Tennessee border, connecting with the Louisville and Nashville and the Newport News and Mississippi Valley systems, and the Louisville, St. Louis and Texas gives outlets to the East, South, and West. A line of packets gives daily connection with Louisville, Henderson, and Evansville. Owensboro has an elevation above sea level of from 386 to 497 feet. It was made the county seat in 1815. It has now a courthouse, a customhouse, a city hall, a fire department with telegraph alarm, a county jail, a new theatre, water works, gas works. electric lighting, a street railway. 125 miles of telephone wire connecting with Henderson, Evansville, and other neighboring cities and towns, 2 daily and 5 weekly newspapers, transfer companies, 9 banks (7 national and 2 State), a trust company, and 18 churches, (3 Catholic, 2 white, and 2 colored Baptist, 1 Christian, 2 German Evangelical, 1 Hebrew, 2 Methodist Episcopal wh.te and 1 African, 3 Presbyterian, and 1 Episcopal). The assessed valuation of property in 1888-'89 was $2,752,-152. The school property is valued at $71,000, and there are 4 large ward schools, 3 for white and 1 for colored pupils. also a high school. The public-school enrollment is 1,284 white and 404 colored. Further educational advantages are afforded by a female college, 2 academies (one a Catholic institution), and private schools. The principal hotel was built at a cost of $50,000, and during 1891 $400,000 were expended in improvements. The principal business interests are tobacco and whisky. Twenty-three factories and stemmeries have a capacity for handling 18,000,000 pounds of tobacco yearly, and employ 2,000 persons. In the city and county are 14 distilleries, manufacturing

sour-mash whisky to the amount of $5,500,000 yearly, with capital invested to the amount of $1,500,000, and employing 200 persons. Other establishments include a wagon factory, in operation since 1883, turning out more than 6,000 wagons yearly, a carriage factory with output of from 4,000 to 5,000 vehicles a year, a wheel company, 2 woolen mills (one with capital of $50,000, employing 175 persons, and the other with authorized capital of $250,000, organized in 1892, which will employ from 225 to 250 persons), a cotton mill with capital of $100,000, employing 150 persons, a canning establishment, factories of vitrified brick and sewer pipe, chairs, cigars. and ice, 2 brickyards, cooper shops, 2 foundries and machine shops, 4 planing, 1 steam shingle, and 3 flouring mills. As the city lies in the center of the great Kentucky and Indiana coal fields, coal is had for the cost of hauling. Abundant timber, building stone, and material for brick are found in the county. which produces large crops of tobacco and cereals. The county fair grounds and race course are here.

Paducah, a city of Kentucky, county seat of McCracken County, on the south bank of Ohio river at the mouth of the Tennessee, 12 miles below the mouth of the Cumberland, and 50 miles from Cairo where the Ohio flows into the Mississippi. By rail it is 225 miles from Louisville, 167 from Memphis, and 165 from St. Louis. The population increased from 8,036 in 1880 to 12,797 in 1890, or 59 per cent. It has an altitude of 486 feet above sea level, with its frontage on two rivers, and has a chute a short distance above the city connecting both and giving ample steamboat channel at any season. The Ohio is navigable to Pittsburg, Pa.—1,500 miles—most of the year, and the Tennessee to Florence, Ala., all the year round. In addition, there are three railroad systems, the Newport News and Mississippi Valley. the St. Louis and Paducah, and the Paducah, Tennessee and Alabama, the first having shops here in which more than 80 per cent. of all the work done for and by the road is performed. The expenditure of the company in the city is upward of $700,000 yearly. Paducah was laid out in 1827, and incorporated as a city in 1856. In 1851, 1862, and 1890 it was visited by tornadoes, and during the civil war it suffered severely. In 1891 the value of taxable property, real and personal, was $5,009,910, and the tax levied was $1.50 on the $100, including 35 cents for schools. Water is supplied from the Ohio river by a company organized in 1888. The standpipe is 22 feet in diameter and 175 feet high. Two pumping engines have a daily capacity of 4,000,000 gallons, and there are fifteen miles of mains. Electric indicators are connected with the fire-alarm system, enabling an instantaneous increase of pressure. In addition to the regular water works there are 13 500-barrel cisterns distributed about the city. The fire department is well equipped, with 2 engines, 1 hook-and-ladder truck, 2 carriages, and 2,500 feet of hose. But this is only a reserve force, the pressure from the water works sufficing to throw 8 streams at once to a distance of 165 feet. In connection with the gas works there is an electric-light plant. An electric street railway, with 9 miles of track. has supplemented the horse cars since 1890. There are 36 miles of graveled streets with brick sidewalks, 3 parks, an opera house, 6 hotels, 3 express companies, 5) miles of telephone wire, 2 hospitals, a city hall that cost $20,000, and a Federal building and post office valued at $150,000. Two daily newspapers are published. The total value of public-school property is $96,600; there are 7 buildings, that for the colored children being nearly as large as the high school. The enrollment in 1890-'91 was 2,182, an increase of 253 over the preceding year, and the total expenditure for schools was $20,795.60. There are also a business college and a Catholic academy. In addition to a Jewish synagogue, 1 Episcopal, 1 Christian, 1 Baptist, 2 Presbyterian, 1 Cumberland Presbyterian, 1 German Lutheran. 1 German Evangelical, 1 Roman Catholic, and 2 Methodist Episcopal churches; there are 7 belonging to the colored people. Two national banks have a joint capital of $430,000, there is a private bank capitalized at $100,000, a savings bank in operation since 1888, and a building and loan association. The building contracts for the year 1891 aggregated $460,870. Paducah lies in the center of vast coal and iron-ore deposits, and has a large hard-wood territory tributary. The product of manufacturing in 1891 reached $2,927,-556; lumber, rough and dressed, constituted the largest item ($627,473), including sash, doors, and blinds; tobacco packing, including plug manufacture, realized $299,438; saddles and harness, collars and leather, $280,835; hickory woodwork and hubs, $109,360. There are furniture, boot and shoe, broom, ice, and cigar factories, brickworks, foundries and machine shops, flouring mills, vinegar works, marble yards, cooper shops, and bottling works, as well as minor industries. The city is the second largest dark-tobacco market in the world. It has 5 wholesale tobacco warehouses.

Passaic, a city of New Jersey, in Passaic County, at the head of tide water and navigation on Passaic river, 11 miles northwest of New York city, and 4 miles southeast of Paterson. In 1880 it had a population of 6,532, and in 1890 of 13,-028. During the Revolution it was known as Acquackanonk, and at the beginning of the present century was the headquarters of a large trade with the West India islands. In 1867 it was a small hamlet. The greater portion is built upon table-land, from 50 to 150 feet above tide water, and there are fine views from the upper portions of the Palisades of the Hudson, and other beautiful scenery. It contains the homes of many business men of New York, which city can be reached in 30 minutes by rail. There are 60 trains daily by the Erie Railroad, 15 by the Delaware, Lackawanna and Western, and 12 by the New York, Susquehanna and Western. In summer a steamer plies regularly between the city and Newark. The natural drainage is excellent. The streets, from 60 to 80 feet wide, are at right angles, and are curbed, guttered, crosswalked, and sidewalked with bluestone flagging, the use of no other material being permitted. In 1889 there were 50 miles of this flagging. Many of the streets are macadamized, and the majority of them are well shaded. Gas and electric lighting are in use. Handsome residences are numerous, and there are many beautiful drives in the neighborhood of the city. A few miles above are the Great Falls, where the river has a descent of nearly 90 feet. Dundee lake, 2 miles distant, from which the water supply of the city is drawn, is caused by a dam across the river, which affords power for manufacturing purposes also. The fire department consists of 3 engines, 2 hook and ladder, and 3 hose companies. Two daily and 2 weekly newspapers are published. There is telephone communication with New York, and with all the surrounding cities and villages. Ten mails arrive and depart daily. The assessed valuation of property in 1889 was $3,875,690, and the bonded debt $173,000. There are 4 ward public schools and a central building, several private and parochial institutions, a free public library, and 14 churches. One national bank, 1 bank and trust company, and 1 trust and safe-deposit company have a joint capital of $225,000. The manufacturing establishments include 2 dye and print works, 2 factories of woolen goods, worsted mills, 2 bleacheries, a whip factory, rubber works, 2 planing mills, a sash, door. and blind factory, 1 of air brakes, another of fishing tackle, 2 brick-yards, chemical works, a wine company, and a new mill, built in 1888, for satinets.

Rome, a city of New York, county seat of Oneida County, near the geographical center of the State. on the Mohawk river and the Erie Canal, at the entrance of the Black River Canal, 110 miles from Albany, 189 from Buffalo, and 255 from New York. The population in 1890 was 14,991. The elevation above sea level is 445 feet. It has 28 passenger trains daily arriving or leaving on the New York Central and Hudson River, the Rome, Watertown and Ogdensburg, and the New York, Ontario and Western Railroads, in addition to the transportation by canal. Two other railroads to Carthage and Oneida lake are projected. The water works owned by the city draw their supply from the river two miles above; the streets are lighted with electricity, and both gas and electric lighting are employed in residences and business blocks. There are 8 graded public schools, with an enrollment of 1,983, and an average daily attendance of 1,339. The high school has an enrollment of 160. Forty-three teachers are employed, and the total expenditure for 1888-'89 for school purposes was $26,832. The amount of school property was placed at $74,000. In addition, there is an academy for young ladies and a parochial school for boys. Fourteen churches are supplemented by a Young Men's Christian Association, owning a building valued at $15,000. The street railway reaches all parts of the city and extends to the county fair grounds. There are competing lines of telegraph and telephone, and a free mail-delivery system. A hospital has been completed recently at a cost of $20,000. and the Central New York Institution for Deaf Mutes, valued at $150,000, is here. The public buildings include a courthouse and jail, a surrogate's office, and a county house with a farm of 350 acres. One daily. 1 weekly, and 2 semi-weekly newspapers are issued. There are 4 national banks and 2 savings banks; 2 opera houses, one just completed; a paid fire department; and a board of trade. The city is practically out of debt. Among the industries may be noted the New York Locomotive Works, employing about 800 men, the Rome Brass and Copper Mills, the Rome Merchant Iron Mill, foundries, knitting mills, malleable iron works, brickyards, stone quarries, canning factories, breweries, and factories of saddlery, carriage goods, wagons, sleighs, lumber, furniture, doors, sashes, and fishing tackle.

Rutland, a town of Vermont, county seat of Rutland County, 68 miles south of Burlington and 55 miles from Montpelier, advantageously situated in the Otter valley, at the meeting of East and Otter creeks. It is the most important railway center, and, next to Burlington, the largest place in Vermont, having a population of 11,760 in 1890. It was incorporated in 1847, the township containing, until 1886, 26,000 acres, and embracing the famous marble quarries, which in that year were set off to the town of West Rutland. It is surrounded by mountains, Killington Peak, one of the highest of the Green mountains, being only 6 miles distant, and has an altitude of from 519 to 623 feet above sea-level. The section of country of which it is the center is rich in minerals, and besides marble and slate iron and manganese are also found. The railroads, which converge at a Union depot, are the Central Vermont, the Bennington and Rutland, the Delaware and Hudson, and the Clarendon and Pittsford. In 1890 the expenditures of the city were $36,577, of which $8,382 were for streets and sewers; 6 miles of gravel and 2 of concrete sidewalks were laid. There are two electric-light plants, in addition to gas; a volunteer fire department, valued at $17,500, with electric alarm; a telephone system, district messenger service. a public library, free mail delivery, 9 miles of horse railway, and water works which draw their supply from a tributary of East creek, about 3 miles northeast of the town. After percolating through a cobble-stone filter, the water is conducted by an aqueduct to a reservoir. The works have a head of 180 feet, with normal pressure of 75 pounds to the square inch. Six public-school buildings employ 28 teachers and have an attendance of 1,054. There are also a high school, two convents, and a military institute. The total value of public-school property is $74.000. In addition to 5 national banks, with joint capital of $1,000,000, there are 2 savings banks and 2 trust companies. Two daily papers are published. The public buildings include a town hall, a courthouse, a handsome post office, an opera house, a memorial hall that cost $50,000, 3 large hotels, and a Y. M. C. A. building. From 1784 to 1804 the town was one of the capitals of the State, and the old Statehouse, erected in 1784, is the oldest public building, save one, in Vermont. The works of the Howe Scale Company are here, and employ 400 men. They consume 25 tons of iron daily, and 2,000,000 feet of lumber a year. The town is a great marble center, and in its immediate vicinity, it is claimed, nearly half of the entire marble product of the United States is obtained. At West Rutland 3 companies are engaged in quarrying. The manufacturing establishments turn out machinery, including stone and marble quarrying and working machinery; dairy and cheese-factory apparatus; evaporators for sugar; engines and boilers; chairs, sewer-pipe, and monumental and ceme-

tery work. There are 3 sash, door, and blind factories, and 1 of children's wagons, carts, and wheelbarrows, employing 70 men. An artistic and unique industry is that of onyx decorative work, the material for which is brought from California and Mexico; 21 skilled artisans are employed, and it is, with a single exception, the only establishment of its kind in the United States. It has been in operation since 1888.

St. Albans, the third town in size of Vermont, county seat of Franklin County, in the northwestern part of the State, 3 miles from Lake Champlain, 30 from Burlington, and 59 from Montpelier. It had a population of 7,771 in 1890. It was incorporated as a village in 1859. The first settlement was made in 1763, under a charter from Benning Wentworth, Governor of the Province of New Hampshire. It is built on an elevated plain 390 feet above sea level and 375 feet above the lake, and has a park of four acres in the center. The headquarters of the Vermont Central Railroad Company are here, with car and machine-shops, and two roundhouses with compartments for 40 engines. The yard embraces nearly 70 acres, and has 12 miles of track. In addition to the passenger depot, there is a general office, 3 stories high, of brick with stone trimmings. The town is also on the Missisquoi Valley Railroad, and has 3 stage lines. There are excellent water works, a handsome academy building, and all school accommodations, the enrollment in the public schools being about 900: an opera house, a hospital, a courthouse, a large five-story hotel, a public library, 1 Congregational, 1 Methodist Episcopal, 1 Baptist, 1 Universalist, 1 Episcopal, and 2 Catholic churches, one of the latter French; 2 convents, a national bank with a capital of $100,000, and a trust company capitalized at $50,000. One daily and 2 weekly newspapers are published. There is a board of trade. Gas and electric lighting are in use. The county is noted for its stock-raising and dairy products, and the town is a butter center and has a creamery association. The manufactures include a construction company (of iron and steel bridges, viaducts, turntables, iron roofs, etc.); a foundry and machine shops which turned out 150 car wheels weekly in 1890, in addition to railroad and other castings and varied machinery; a factory of lumber-drying apparatus; 1 of overalls and clothing; and marble and granite monumental works. There is also a cold-storage company.

Selma, a city of Alabama, county seat of Dallas County, on the right bank of the Alabama river, a little south of the center of the State, 50 miles west of Montgomery, and the same distance from Demopolis, 160 from Mobile, and 85 from Birmingham. It is the sixth city of the State in population, having 7,622 inhabitants; in 1880 it was the third, with 7,529. Its limits have been extended since the war. It has an elevation of from 135 to 147 feet above sea level, being built on a high bluff overlooking the river. It is the Alabama center of the East Tennessee, Virginia and Georgia Railroad system, and has seven other lines—the Selma, Rome and Dalton; the Western; the Briarfield, Blockton and Birmingham; the Mobile and Birmingham; the Selma and Akron; the Selma and Gulf; the Birmingham, Selma and New Orleans—while the Selma and Atlanta Air Line has been surveyed. Navigation is open to the Gulf of Mexico all the year. The streets are broad and picturesque, many of them macadamized with gravel, while the two principal ones were paved in 1892 with chert from the neighboring mineral regions. They are shaded with evergreen water oaks. The river is spanned by an iron bridge; there is a complete sewerage system, and water works that draw their supply from artesian wells, with 15 miles of mains. Gas and electric lighting are in use. The street railway running through the principal business streets connects with the residence portion and with the union depot. The public buildings include a courthouse, a charity hospital, a public-school building, and another auxiliary building to accommodate the enrollment of 891 pupils in the public schools, a colored university dating from 1878, which in 1888–'89 had 382 students, and a colored academy. A large four-story brick hotel was completed in 1892. The opera house has a seating capacity of 1,500, and the Young Men's Christian Association has a handsome building. There are also club rooms, lodges, armories, and public halls, and several of the 16 churches are fine edifices. One of the 3 banks is national. Two daily and 2 weekly newspapers are published, and 1 monthly by the orphans in the Presbyterian asylum. Manufacturing is facilitated by the existence within 40 miles of the city of rich coal and iron deposits. One cotton mill has 14,000 spindles, with a capacity of 17,000 yards daily. There are 2 large cotton compresses, and a cotton-seed-oil mill which in 1885 had capital invested to the amount of $100,000 and employed 100 men; its product, valued at from $200,000 to $250,-000, was, by report of the United States Treasury Bureau of Statistics, consumed in Europe. Two iron works turn out castings, steam engines, and mining cars; the shops of the East Tennessee, Virginia and Georgia Railroad cover 10 acres and employ 300 men, and among the other industries are 1 wagon, 1 sash, door, and blind, 1 saddle and harness, 1 wagon and furniture, and 2 ice factories, ice and grist mills, a ginnery, bottling and mineral-water works, candy and cigar factories, and 2 steam laundries. The city is one of the large interior cotton markets of the South, its receipts being from 125,000 to 130,000 bales yearly.

Vicksburg, the largest city of Mississippi, county seat of Warren County, on Mississippi river, 1 mile below the mouth of the Yazoo, 400 miles above New Orleans, and 45 west of Jackson. In 1880 the population was 11,814, and in 1890 13,373. The site is very uneven, varying in elevation from 43 to 244 feet above sea level. Prior to 1876 Vicksburg was on a long bend of the river, the bed of which was over 50 feet deep at low water; but in the spring of that year the peninsula in front of the city washed in two, the new channel forming what is now De Soto Island and Centennial Lake. Engineering operations, carried on by the United States Government, checked further erosion on the Louisiana bank and insured a permanent channel for the river, and in 1883 dredging of the canal with a view to restoring navigable water to the city front was begun, but it was discontinued until 1888.

From that time it has been continuous, and by November, 1891, more than a million cubic yards had been excavated. The river traffic is carried on by 10 lines of packets, 3 of them triweekly, between the city and St. Louis, Natchez, and New Orleans, and the others weekly and semiweekly to Cincinnati and ports on the Mississippi, Yazoo, Tallahatchie, and Sunflower. The total tonnage by river in 1891 was 64,035 tons shipped and 94,102 received, while the shipments by rail were 103,019, and the receipts 125,492 tons. The total of freight handled was 391,648 tons. The railroads which intersect are the Alabama and Vicksburg and the Louisville, New Orleans and Texas. The shops and yards of the latter here cover 20 acres, with 5 large brick buildings, and employ 500 men, with a monthly pay roll of $50,-000. The plant represents an investment of $225,000. It was completed in 1891. The cotton receipts of Vicksburg in 1890–'91 were 70,784 bales. The assessed valuation of property increased from $4,500,000 in 1890 to $4,800,000 in 1891, and the municipal tax rate was 20 mills on the dollar. The revenues from all sources are placed at $140,000, and the city debt is $500,000. Bonds to the amount of $100,000 have been authorized for a sewerage system. There are paid fire and police departments, gas and electric lights, good water works, and a street railway. The real-estate transfers for 1891 aggregated $618,495, and expenditures on streets the same year were $29,238. There are 3 public schools, which have an enrollment of 1,600 p . The city is a separate school district, and upin addition to its allotment from the State its schools receive one fifth of the city tax. The total revenue for 1891 was $19,000. There are also a commercial college, a Catholic academy for young ladies, and several private schools. There are 6 churches for whites—1 Roman Catholic, 2 Episcopalian, 1 Presbyterian, 1 Baptist, and 1 Methodist—also a Jewish synagogue and buildings belonging to the colored people. A new hotel cost, inclusive of its site, $120,000; the Federal post office and customhouse building more than $100,000. The courthouse has been altered and improved recently. There is a city hospital, and also an opera house. A national cemetery is located here, in which 17,000 national soldiers are buried. Two of the 5 banks are national, and 1 is a savings bank. The total resources of the 5 are $1,985,292. There is also a building and loan association. Two daily and 2 weekly newspapers are published. The industries of the city include 3 cotton-seed-oil mills, the product of which is mainly shipped to New Orleans and thence to Europe; 3 lumber mills, cutting cypress in addition to hard wood, 1 with an output of 4,000,000 feet in 1891, and the same year 2 of the mills enlarged their plants: 2 planing mills, 2 sash, door, and blind factories, brickyards employing 250 hands, foundries, a carriage and wagon factory, 2 ice companies, marble yards, bottling works, and establishments turning out ready-made clothing, boots and shoes, and saddlery and harness. The location of a large brewery, representing an investment of $250,000, was secured in 1891. Between the city and the national cemetery there is a stone quarry.

Vincennes, a city of Indiana, county seat of Knox County, on the left bank of Wabash river, in the southwestern part of the State. 52 miles from Evansville, 117 from Indianapolis, 149 from St. Louis, and 235 from Chicago. The population in 1880 was 7,680; in 1890, 8,853. The first settlement was made in 1702 by the French, and a fort was built for protection against the Indians. The city is named from François Morgan de Vincennes, who took command of the fort in 1732. In 1763 it was taken by the English, and in the War of Independence it surrendered to Col. Clark, Feb. 26, 1779, after that officer and his army had endured the severest hardships. From 1800 to 1816 it was the capital of Indiana Territory, Gen. William Henry Harrison being the first governor. His house is still standing in good preservation. The city has an altitude of 431 feet above sea level, and the plateau upon which it is built affords excellent natural drainage. The mean annual temperature is 56°. It is surrounded by a rich agricultural country, with inexhaustible coal fields and valuable timber. Two coal mines have been recently opened within the city limits. There is daily packet service on the river, and the city has 4 lines of railroad, the Ohio and Mississippi intersecting with the Evansville and Terre Haute, and the Cairo and Vincennes, which here connects with the Indianapolis and Vincennes. Another road has been surveyed. The valuation for taxable purposes is about $6,000,-000, and the tax rate $1.15 per $100. Water works have been erected recently at a cost of $200,000. There are gas and electric-light plants, 4 miles of electric street railway, efficient fire and police departments, a telephone exchange, and telegraph and express facilities. The city is underlaid with gravel, which insures good streets, and these are beautifully shaded in the residence portion. A free bridge crosses the river. The courthouse cost $400,000, the City Hall $75,-000, and the opera house $30,000. The value of church property is $247,000, and the buildings are respectively as follow: Three Presbyterian, 2 Methodist, 2 Baptist, 2 Catholic, 1 Christian, 1 Episcopal, 1 Lutheran, and 1 German Reformed. There are 2 high schools, a central, and 4 ward public-school buildings, costing $95,000, as well as a fine building for colored children. Vincennes University, chartered in 1806, had 9 instructors and 225 male and female students in 1888–'89, and a military department with a West Point instructor has been added recently. The building cost $40,000. There is also a Catholic academy, which cost $35,000, and Catholics and Germans maintain parochial schools. Three national banks have an aggregate capital of $300,-000, and there are 7 building and loan associations. The city has a board of trade. Two daily and 2 weekly newspapers are published. Four large flouring mills have a capacity of 200,000 barrels yearly. There are also 3 saw mills in the city proper, 3 factories of staves and barrel headings, 2 foundries, agricultural-implement works, carriage and wagon factories, a paper mill, a stove company, 1 hub and spoke, 1 shoe, 1 box, 1 hoop, 1 axle-grease, 1 furniture, 2 cigar, and 2 pop factories, brickyards doing an extensive business, marble works, 2 hominy mills, 2 breweries, a butter-dish factory, machine shops, shops of the Ohio and Mississippi Railroad, and a railway river switch of the

Evansville and Terre Haute. It is the second largest chicken packing and distributing point in the United States.

COLOMBIA, a republic in South America. By the Constitution of Aug. 4, 1886, the United States of Colombia were consolidated into the centralized republic of Colombia. The term of the President was prolonged from two to six years, and the Presidents of the former States are reduced to Governors, appointed by the President. The Senate is composed of 27 members, 3 from each department, and the House of Representatives has 66 members, who are elected in the departments by universal suffrage in the proportion of 1 to 50,000 inhabitants.

Gen. Rafael Nuñez was first elected President in 1880, and was re-elected for the next two biennial terms. When the term was altered to six years he was re-elected once more, and on June 4, 1887, was inaugurated as President for the first long term. During most of it he was kept by sickness from performing the duties in person, his place being filled by Carlos Holguin. Nevertheless he was elected for the fifth time on Feb. 2, 1892, Señor Caro being chosen Vice-President, but not acting President, for Holguin was again appointed by the President as his representative, and the arrangement was unanimously approved by the Senate.

Area and Population.—The area of Colombia is estimated at 504,773 square miles, and the population at 3,878,000, including 220,000 uncivilized Indians and 80,000 people in the territories. Bogotá, the capital, which is 8,564 feet above sea-level, has about 100,000 inhabitants.

Finances.—The revenue, which is mostly derived from customs, was estimated at 20,351,100 pesos for 1891–'92, and expenditure at 23,911,515 pesos. The internal debt is 29,005,551 pesos, in addition to which 7,500,000 pesos are owing from the last war, and 11,932,780 pesos of paper currency were out in 1892. The foreign debt, held mainly in Great Britain, amounted to $14,571,-318, including unpaid interest accrued during eleven years. In June, 1891, negotiations were opened with the bondholders for a readjustment of the foreign debt.

The Army.—The strength of the army in peace time is fixed by act of Congress, and is kept at 5,500 men. In war the President can raise the forces to any strength that the exigences seem to require, and can press every able-bodied citizen into the service.

Commerce and Production.—The chief imports are food and textile fabrics. The value of imports in 1890 was 13,345,792 pesos, and of exports 20,457,855 pesos. The leading exports are coffee, cinchona bark, the export of which has greatly diminished, peanuts, corn, silver ore, cacao, dye stuffs, hides, live animals, and tobacco. Of the imports, Great Britain supplied 4,990,198 pesos; France, 2,713,046 pesos; Germany, 1,636,019 pesos; and the United States, 1,218,466 pesos. Of the exports, 4,789,918 pesos went to Great Britain, 4,384,867 pesos to the United States, 2,474,188 pesos to Germany, and 1,365,709 pesos to France. The export of coffee was 4,262,030 pesos; of gold bars and dust, 2,259,726 pesos; of other mine products, 2,205,-024 pesos; of hides, 1,023,231 pesos.

During 1890 there were 1,022 vessels, of 801,-

858 tons, entered at the ports of Colombia, of which 626, of 775,783 tons, were steamers. Of the total tonnage, 51 per cent. was British, 18 per cent. French, 13 per cent. Spanish, and 12 per cent. German. At the port of Barranquilla 365,509 tons were entered, and at Cartagena 309,-622 tons. There are 7 lines of steamers that touch monthly at the Colombian ports, of which 4 are English, and the others German, French, and Spanish.

Communications.—The length of railroad in operation in 1890 was 218 miles. There were 3 railroads completed and 5 others partly built. A contract for the construction of a railroad to Antioquia, which will open a large and productive country, was signed in September, 1892, with a firm of English engineers.

There were 5,000 miles of telegraph in 1890. The number of dispatches in 1889 was 504,720. There were sent through the post office in that year 1,044,486 letters and postal cards, 397,134 samples and printed inclosures, and 10,379 packets and registered letters.

Political Condition.—The era of peace enjoyed under the administration of President Nuñez has improved the economical and financial condition of the republic. In 1892 the Government took steps to restore the metallic currency. Formerly the silver coins, soon after they entered into the circulation, were shipped abroad wholesale for the settlement of foreign balances. In the spring of 1892 silver coins of various denominations, 835 fine, were struck in Birmingham, England, and placed in circulation to the amount of 1,000,000 pesos by the National Bank at Bogotá. In the Congress which was opened on July 21 the Government commanded a large majority, and carried through some important measures without opposition.

The Panama Canal.—The company formed by Ferdinand de Lesseps to build a canal, 46 miles long, across the Isthmus of Panama, went into liquidation on March 15, 1889, and provisional administrators were appointed by the Civil Tribunal of the Department of the Seine. Operations on the canal were suspended, and since then various plans for the reorganization of the company and the completion of the enterprise have been discussed. The French Government has been urged to come to the rescue of the undertaking, which has swallowed up about 1,300,000,000 francs of the savings of 700,000 or 800,000 French people. The terms of the concession, as extended by the Colombian Government, required that work should be resumed before March 1, 1893; otherwise the concession is forfeited, and the Colombian authorities can take possession of the works. The canal as far as it was dug was used by the people of the country for the transportation of lumber and other produce until the company placed a barrier across the entrance. This was removed by the Colombian authorities, whereupon the canal people extended a chain across the canal itself. The canal is navigable for 12 miles, and affords communication with the upper Chagres and Rio Trinidad.

COLORADO, a Western State, admitted to the Union Aug. 1, 1876; area, 103,925 square miles. The population, according to the decennial census, was 194,327 in 1880, and 412,198 in 1890. Capital, Denver.

Government.—The following were the State officers during the year: Governor, John L. Routt; Lieutenant-Governor, William W. Story; Secretary of State, Edwin J. Eaton: Treasurer, James N. Carlile; Auditor, John M. Henderson; Attorney-General, Joseph H. Maupin; Superintendent of Public Instruction, Nathan B. Coy; Railroad Commissioner, William A. Hamill; Chief Justice of the Supreme Court, Joseph C. Helm; Associate Justices, Charles D. Hoyt and Victor A. Elliot; Court of Appeals, Presiding Judge, George Q. Richmond; Judges, Gilbert B. Reed and Julius B. Bissell. All the State officials were Republicans except the Treasurer, Attorney-General, and Superintendent of Public Instruction. In September Judge Helm resigned from the bench, in order to accept the nomination for Governor of the State, and Governor Routt appointed Judge G. W. Allen, of the district court of Arapahoe Co., to the vacancy.

Finances.—The amount in the State treasury at the beginning of 1891 was $2,052,955.45; the receipts during the year were $1,371,192.64, and the disbursements $1,571,338.88. The interest received on deposits and turned into the treasury was $33,562.84.

Following is the report of the mint at Denver for the year ending June 30, 1892:

	Gold.	Silver.	Total.
Domestic.			
Arizona	$1,269 34	$39 94	$1,309 28
California	84 50	99	85 49
Colorado	1,039,650 29	20,760 50	1,060,410 79
Idaho	1,607 37	7 21	1,614 58
Montana	1,099 16	88 60	1,182 76
Nevada	1,217 84	16 06	1,233 90
New Mexico	250,584 14	1,932 40	252,466 54
Oregon	16,060 71	2 27	16,062 98
South Dakota	275 08	60	275 68
Wyoming	8,718 46	26 87	8,745 33
Total	$1,315,516 89	$22,820 44	$1,338,337 33
Foreign.			
United States coin	$4,571 22	....	$4,571 22
Foreign bullion	4,472 80	357 74	4,880 54
Foreign coin	230 14	....	230 14
Jewelers' bars, etc.	11,646 16	232 45	11,878 61
Redeposits	2,038 18	56 12	2,094 30
Grand total	$1,338,475 89	$23,466 75	$1,361,942 14

Valuations.—The aggregate of assessed valuations of the counties for 1892 was $217,824,-342.98, showing a falling off from the assessment of 1891, which was $231,405,296.04. Five of the counties refused to levy taxes for the payment of the Ute-war debt and for the Capitol-building bonds; two others made the levy, but deducted the amount from the general-revenue levy; and still another refused the Ute-war-debt levy, and deducted that for Capitol-building bonds from the general revenue.

The tax levy for State purposes was fixed as follows: For general revenue, $2\frac{4}{10}$ mill; mute and blind, $\frac{1}{4}$ mill; university, $\frac{1}{5}$ mill; agricultural college, $\frac{1}{5}$ mill; School of Mines, $\frac{1}{5}$ mill; insane asylum, $\frac{1}{4}$ mill; stock inspection, $\frac{1}{10}$ mill; Capitol building, $\frac{1}{4}$ mill; military poll, $1 each male inhabitant not exempt by law; for normal school, $\frac{1}{4}$ mill.

It was further ordered that $\frac{3}{10}$ of 1 mill, in excess of the general levy, be levied upon and collected out of and from each and every dollar of the taxable property of the State for the year

1892, to raise a fund sufficient to discharge the half-yearly interest accrued and accruing on the Capitol-building bonds.

Land Offices.—The Government report for 1891 gives the following totals for the State: Earnings of registers and receivers, $63.414.63; amount paid registers and receivers, 54.261.74; net revenue to the United States, $9,152.89; total Government fees, $24,735; total revenue to United States, $33,887.89.

Mineral Product.—The following figures show the principal items of the mineral output for 1891, the total value of which was $33,548,-934 : Copper (pounds) 5,537,001, value $733,653; lead (pounds) 126,257,345, value $5.473.225; silver (ounces) 23,102,355, value $22,767,370; gold (ounces) 217,652, value $4,498,866.

The smelters of the State for 1891 produced the unequaled product of $44,919,193, divided among the smelters as follows: Denver plants, $24.485,135; Pueblo plants, $11,241,289 : Leadville plants, $6,778,013; Durango smelter, $1,114,-756; Denver mint deposits, $1,300,000; total, $44,919,193.

The figures show that, out of the total mineral production of $33,548,934, the home smelters have treated all but $377,991, and have also smelted ores shipped in from outside States and Territories amounting to $11,748,250.

Manufactures.—The figures given out by the State Bureau of Labor Statistics show that in 1891 there were 640 industrial and manufacturing plants of all kinds in Colorado, including 85 brickyards where a superior quality of brick is made. The railroad shops of the State are not included in these statistics. The classification of industries consists of smelters, mills, factories, bottling works, foundries, steel works, brick manufacturing. Bakeries, merchant tailoring, etc., are not included in this category. The total amount of capital invested in the industries of the State is $23,347,806. There are 19,624 persons who earn their livelihood in the various industries, of whom 19,023 are males and 601 females. The total amount of wages paid was $12,951,763.55. The average earnings of male employees were from $9 to $20, exclusive of foremen. Only 53 of the women employed receive over $15 a week for their services, and this is due to a knowledge of office work, such as bookkeeping, stenography, etc. The majority of the women and girls employed receive less than $11 a week. The average earnings of a factory girl are from $4.50 to $6 a week, while some do not earn more than $3 a week in some of the smaller factories.

The total value, annually, of the manufactured product of Colorado's industries is $70,-027.854.50.

In the milling industries throughout the State there are 103 saw mills, 42 flouring mills, and 24 planing mills. There are 10 smelters in operation in Colorado.

The sandstone quarries of the State consist of 73 good producing properties, and $2,010,540 in capital is invested therein. The number of men employed in the sandstone industry in this State is 1,521. Colorado ranks third in production of sandstone, compared to other States. The output for 1891 will exceed 6,950,000 cubic feet, and yield $1,326,095 from all returns for ten months

of the current year. These figures are not included in the totals of manufacturing and industrial plants.

The oil refineries of Fremont County have an annual production of 300,000 barrels of crude oil, 140,000 barrels of refined oil, and 160,000 barrels of greases. The highest yield of a single well in one day is 201 barrels. Of the total production, 80,000 barrels of oil and 53,000 barrels of greases are shipped to other markets. The balance is consumed by local trade.

The steel works at Bessemer have a capacity for an annual production of 25,000 tons of pig iron, 16,000 tons of steel rails, 1,300 tons of iron castings, 1,200 tons of cast-iron pipe, 4,700 tons of merchant bar, 2,500 tons of spikes, and 45,000 (100-pound) kegs of nails.

The annual production of brick in the State averages 188,500,000.

The cigar factories of the State have received encouragement by the passage of the Union label bill, and there is now a larger demand for Colorado-made cigars than heretofore. The annual production of the cigar factories of the State was 15,264,000 cigars in 1890. The figures of 1891 will show an increase of at least 1,980.000 cigars over those of 1890. In 1890 the general consumption in the State was 76,323,000 cigars, including local and foreign manufactured goods.

Agriculture.—It is estimated that from 11,-000 to 15,000 men are employed in agricultural pursuits. The number of men, or "cowboys," employed on the stock ranches is about 114 in the eastern and 992 in the western part of the State. Their average wages are $20 a month, with board. The value of farming lands ranges from $5 to $50 an acre.

According to the statistics of the department of agriculture, Colorado ranks first in the yield of wheat per acre, which is 19.5 bushels, and sixth in value, which is $16.22 an acre. In rye it stands first both in the yield, which is 17.1 bushels, and in the value, which is $12.78. It is in the first of the five classes into which the States are divided in the yield and value of oats and barley, and in the second class in corn, potatoes, and hay, though in the value of hay it is in the first class with $15.76 an acre.

The value of the farm product in 1891 was $53,900,000.

Following is an extract from a report by the director of the Government experiment station at the Agricultural College:

At the date of the last report there were 4,811 ditches actually constructed, aggregating the wonderful total length of 11,052·9 miles. The area found actually irrigated in 1890 reached the enormous sum of 1,544,585 acres; while the area in acres under ditch and capable of being irrigated amounted to 4,082,738. By actual count we find the number of ditches for which decrees have been issued and statements filed to Dec. 1, 1891, to be 524. If we approximate the average length of these new ditches and the average area they subject to irrigation to be the same as that of those given in the fifth biennial report, their aggregate length will be 1,343·54 miles, placing under irrigation 496,128 acres. This gives the State of Colorado the grand total of 12,396·44 miles of irrigating canals, finished and being constructed, and a total area capable of being irrigated, when completed, of 4,578,866 acres. There were 2,538,153 acres more subject to irrigation in 1890 than were irrigated.

Agricultural lands are more appreciated than formerly. There are 4,853,496 acres in the State, ranging from $5 to $100 an acre. Their increased value in 1891 over 1890 is $2,966,513.56. The total valuation of agricultural lands, as per State Auditor's recapitulation of abstracts of assessment for the past year, is $28,733,567.62. The valuation of the less productive grazing lands has decreased about $750,000. I have been supplied by the State engineer with a table showing the number of acres of grasses irrigated in different water divisions:

SECTIONS.	Alfalfa.	Tame grass.	Natural grass.
Platte....................	117,974	38,619	201,758
Arkansas.................	24,674	8,753	19,944
Rio Grande...............	1,909	2,292	156,582
Grand River..............	17,002	2,619	7,551
White River	255	809	4,195
Total...............	161,854	42,592	889,480

The great profusion of flowers in the State makes the bee industry especially important. The secretary of the State Bee Association reports that there are 6,000 colonies of bees, producing annually 300,000 pounds of honey.

Sugar Convention. — A State convention was held in Denver, March 23-25, for the purpose of promoting the production of beet sugar. A large part of the agricultural portion of Colorado lies in the area found to be most favorable to the production of the sugar beet, as will be seen by the following extract from the report of the chemist of the Agricultural Department:

As a result of many years of careful experimentation, it may be said that, as far as temperature alone is concerned, the sugar beet attains its greatest perfection in a zone of varying width through the center of which passes the isothermal line of 70° F. for the months of June, July, and August. This isothermal line, for the United States, begins at the city of New York and passes up the Hudson river to Albany; thence, turning westward, it runs through Syracuse, and passes in a southwesterly direction, touching the shore of Lake Erie near Sandusky, Ohio; turning then in a northwesterly direction, it passes into Michigan, and reaches its highest point in that State near Lansing; then, passing in a southwesterly direction, it enters the State of Indiana near South Bend and passes through Michigan City; then in a northwesterly course continues through the cities of Chicago and Madison, reaching its highest point near St. Paul, Minn.; thence it passes in a southwesterly direction until it enters the State of South Dakota; thence it turns again northwest, and reaches its highest point in Dakota just above the forty-fifth parallel of latitude, where it crosses the Missouri river. This isothermal line then turns almost due south, following very closely the one hundred and first degree of longitude, until it leaves the State of Nebraska near the northeast corner of Colorado. Passing in a southwesterly direction through Colorado, it reaches, at Pueblo, almost to the one hundred and fifth degree of west longitude, whence it passes in a slightly southeasterly direction into New Mexico, turns to the west and crosses the one hundred and fifth degree of longitude at about the thirty-second degree of latitude; thence, turning westward, it passes in a very irregular line through the States of California, Oregon, and Washington. Extending a distance of 100 miles on each side of this isothermal line is a belt which, for the present, may be regarded as the beet-sugar area of the United States. There are doubtless many localities lying outside of this belt, both north and south, in which the sugar beet will be found to thrive, but this will be due to some exceptional qualities of the climate or soil, and not to any favorable influence of the higher or lower temperature. A

mean temperature of 70° F. in summer, however, must not be regarded as the only element of temperature which is to be taken into consideration. In those localities where winters come early and are of unusual severity, will be found greater difficulties in the production of sugar from the sugar beet than in those localities where the winters are light and mild, although the mean summer temperature of both localities will be represented by 70° F.

The convention continued three days. Resolutions were adopted favoring free coinage and the cession of the arid lands to the States and Territories. On the question as to whether the State and Federal bounties should be given to the farmer that raises the beets or the manufacturer that makes the sugar, there were two reports, the majority report being:

Resolved, That we favor a State bounty of 1 cent a pound to be paid for the manufacture of beet sugar within this State, to be divided between the farmer and the manufacturer.

The minority report was the following:

Resolved, That we favor a State bounty of half a cent per pound for ten years to be paid manufacturers of beet sugar in this State; provided any manufacturer receiving such bounty shall not raise more than one tenth of the beets used by him, and shall pay not less than $4 per ton for beets containing 12 per cent. of sugar and having a coefficient of 80 per cent., and shall further pay 25 cents per ton for each additional per cent. of sugar.

The result of the discussion on the two reports was the adoption of a compromise resolution favoring a State bounty upon the production of sugar beets and their manufacture.

A permanent association was formed, to be composed of two representatives from each county, and to meet annually, beginning in January, 1893.

The Arid Lands.—The sentiment in favor of the cession of the arid lands by the Federal Government to the States and Territories in which they lie is very strong. The argument is, that the Government can not expend upon them the amount necessary for irrigating and making them productive on account of opposition from Eastern States, where it is objected that the Government would thereby be using the money of Eastern farmers to promote competition against them in the West. But if the lands were ceded to the States the reclamation could be undertaken by them; and all danger that the land might fall into the hands of speculators and corporations could be averted by the passage of laws similar to the homestead laws of the United States.

Much has been said of a project for a State ditch in Mesa County. The Legislature passed an act providing for its construction, and for the employment of convict labor on the work. The constitutionality of the measure was questioned. A tunnel nine miles long, connecting with Grand river, will be necessary. It is estimated that 75,000 acres would be open to productiveness by the building of the ditch.

Following are the facts, in reference to the State, given out by the irrigation survey as the results of the third year's observations:

The area surveyed lies in the drainage basin of the Arkansas river, and entirely within the limits of Colorado.

The sources of the Arkansas river are among

mountains rising to an altitude of 14,000 feet. At Cañon City, where it leaves the mountain region, its bed has descended to an altitude of 4,400 feet. Its upper course is in a narrow valley, lying, except at its lower extremity, at too great an altitude for cultivation. Its lower course is through close cañons, having walls sometimes rising nearly 3,000 feet above the water's edge. The whole mountain region is one of great precipitation, and is the principal, almost the only, source of the water which the river bears to the plains.

The area of forest growth containing merchantable timber or that fit for lumber is found entirely within the mountain region, and occurs in bodies of considerable extent on the slopes of all the higher range. These areas have all been carefully noted, and comprise about 25 per cent. of the whole. The forest growth is principally of pines and spruces, not covering the ground densely, as in a more humid region, but scattered. Considerable areas of forest growth, largely composed of cedar and piñon pine, and available only for pine wood, fencing, and other farming purposes, occur throughout the mountain region, usually at lower altitudes than the merchantable timber, and extend partly over the area embraced by the Pueblo, Walsenburg, and El Moro sheets. About 20 per cent. of the area is thus covered. The immediate valleys of the streams in both mountain and plain areas often have a scattered growth of cottonwoods.

One hundred and ten possible reservoir sites are reported by the topographers of this division. Six of them are existing lakes.

In area these reservoirs range from forty acres to several square miles, and are situated at elevations varying from 4,500 to 11,000 feet. They are usually situated in the valleys of the streams by which they would be filled, and would be formed by dams built at eligible locations across the channels.

Quite a number of cases are reported where settling reservoirs might be first constructed, and the waters conducted to other reservoirs having smaller drainage area, and where the danger of silting up would be less.

Few reservoirs have been constructed throughout this region, the waters of the streams used for irrigation having simply been turned from their channels by diverting dams.

In the plains regions quite a number of sites have been reported which would be filled by storm waters only.

Classifying these reservoir sites by the drainage basins in which they are situated, and counting all the small creeks having but one site each and flowing directly into the Arkansas, and also reservoirs which would be filled by canals from the Arkansas, as of the Arkansas drainage, these are:

South Platte basin, 4; Grand River basin, 2; Arkansas basin, 39; Fountain basin, 2; St. Charles basin, 3; Huerfano basin, 6; Sangre de Cristo basin, 2; Cachara basin, 3; Greenhorn basin, 3; Purgatoire basin, 28; Apishapa basin, 9; filled by storm waters, 9; making a total of 110.

No considerable bodies of lands susceptible of successful cultivation were noted in the mountain region except in the immediate neighborhood of streams in the lower portion of the Arkansas basin.

In the plains area large bodies are reported, the amount being far in excess of the water supply.

Railroads.—The figures of the State Bureau of Labor Statistics give the number of miles of railway, including projected lines partly finished, at 4,546·61, and the assessed valuation at $30,035,215.64. The number of persons employed in railway service is 13,252, and the annual amount of wages paid $10,528,869.61. Clerical labor is the poorest paid branch of the railway service. The cause of this state of affairs is due to a surplus of young men seeking office work, particularly those from the East, who come to Colorado to benefit their health, and offer their services at low figures. A tour of inquiry revealed the fact that there is a total of 2,177 applications for places on file in all railroad offices combined at Denver, Pueblo, Trinidad, Leadville, and Colorado Springs.

The annual report of the Denver and Rio Grande for the year ending June 30, 1892, shows net earnings of $3,709,353.20, an excess of $368,736.32 over those of the previous year. During the year the Del Norte branch was extended nearly 10 miles. to Creede, at a cost of about $87,000. For this purpose the Rio Grande Gunnison Railroad Company was incorporated in the interest of the Denver and Rio Grande, and its 6-per-cent. bond was taken by the company at 87.

The completion last December of the Rio Grande Southern Railroad between Durango and Ridgeway (a station on the Ouray branch), a distance of 162 miles, with its branch to Telluride, 10 miles, has afforded direct communication by rail with productive portions of southwestern Colorado, heretofore inaccessible except by trail and wagon road.

The current resources, June 30, 1892, were $3,163,355.96. The current liabilities were $2,719,422.35, showing an increase in the current resources of $443,933.61.

The principal freight sources of revenue were precious ore, $1,375,509.62; merchandise, $1,363,586.57; bituminous coal, $1,068,920.91.

A company has been incorporated for building a road from Trinidad to El Paso, Texas.

Education.—At the close of the school year in 1891 the school population was 103,020, which included all children between the ages of six and twenty-one. Of this number, 73.391, or 72·9 per cent. of the population, were enrolled. Eighty-six and six-tenths per cent. of the population under sixteen were enrolled. The total number of teachers in the State was 2,534. There were 1,285 schoolhouses, valued at $5,079,770. Wages paid to teachers were $894,409.64. There were 2,112 pupils in high schools.

The School of Mines is at Golden, 16 miles from Denver on the lines of two railroads. It is devoted to instruction in applied sciences. There are four courses—civil engineering, mining engineering, metallurgy, and electric engineering—of four years each, besides providing for several special courses. The institution is beautifully housed, and is in charge of a president and eight members of the faculty. A museum and gymnasium are connected with the school. In 1890 there were 68 students in attendance. The State has spent $300,000 on the school, and appropriates $35,000 yearly for its maintenance.

During the year three new departments have been added to the university at Boulder—medical, law, and divinity schools. These will all be at Boulder, except the second and third years of the medical school, which circumstances require to be in Denver. Nineteen physicians compose the faculty of the medical school, while the faculty of the law school is made up of 13 instructors. Both are under the superintendence of the president of the university. The divinity school is designed to be strictly unsectarian, and is supported by subscription from the churches of the State in general.

The attendance at the university in September was about 225, a large increase over that of 1891.

A new building has been erected for the Denver University at University Park, and the college proper was removed to it in February. The preparatory departments remain in their former location, but will eventually be provided for at the Park.

The State Agricultural College at Fort Collins has also been improved by the addition of new buildings. The agricultural hall contains an experimental workroom, a museum, a room for small seeds and garden tools, and a large lecture room. The hall of mechanic arts contains a machine shop, office, and tool room, a wood shop and wood-carving room, engine room, forge room, and foundry. The college has under its control 240 acres of land, and receives from $15,000 to $20,000 yearly from the Federal Government.

The Colorado College at Colorado Springs is reported in an unprecedentedly prosperous condition. A new dormitory has been built, and the faculty increased to 14 members. The college has an endowment of $150,000, and property valued at $350,000.

The attendance at the State Normal School at Greeley for the term ending March 31 was 165 normal and 40 model students.

A table of the public libraries gives the number as 66, of which 26 are in Denver. The whole number of volumes is 108,157. The State Library has 11,450 volumes, and the Denver Public Library 11,400.

The total amount of money distributed among the counties from the State school funds for 1892 amounted to $57,731.12.

Charities.—The Insane Asylum at Pueblo cost the State, in 1891, $51,573, the number of inmates averaging about 282. The number in the asylum at the beginning of 1892 was 290, of whom 194 are men and 96 women.

A soldiers' home was dedicated at Monte Vista, Nov. 4, 1891.

The State Mute, Deaf and Blind Institute, at Colorado Springs, has an enrollment of 140. They are in charge of a superintendent and 22 teachers.

Penitentiary.—The number of convicts in the State Penitentiary in 1891 was 524. The report of the State Labor Commissioner, a part of whose duty it is to investigate the number, condition, and nature of employment of the inmates of the State prison, and ascertain to what extent their employment comes in competition with mechanics, artisans, and laborers outside of prison walls, shows by his report that the only manner in which the Colorado Penitentiary inmates compete with outside labor is in the production of lime, brick, and stone.

The cost of maintenance *per capita* of convicts in Colorado, including subsistence and all expenses, has been materially decreased in recent years. In 1886 the cost *per capita* annually was $433.33. In 1887 it was $347.34. During 1889–'90 the price was reduced to $174.10. The total expenses of the State Penitentiary for 1889–'90 were $166,098.44.

During 1889–'90 the output of the prison limekilns was 304,609 bushels, which yielded $31,-196.11. The expenses of maintaining the kilns was $16,510.52. There are 15 kilns in all. The brick output for a similar period was 2,405,314 brick, and 74,900 casings. The sales aggregate $12,465.91. The expense of production was $5,922. The stone quarries yielded $5,532.86. At the State Industrial School, about one mile from Golden, 225 boys were reported in 1892.

Timber Reserve.—Opposition to the proposed Grand Mesa timber reserve, with the boundary lines as laid out, has been developed, on the ground that the country, or at least a part of it, is rich in coal, silver, and lead, and also contains vast beds of valuable marble. Large amounts of coal lands have been entered, many mines have been located, and many more will be if the lands are left open to public occupation. A railroad is now being built into the proposed reservation, and if it is established as now proposed it will prevent the further appropriation of coal, mineral, and marble lands under the laws of the United States, and give to those who have perfected their claims a monopoly of the coal and marble production.

New Mining Towns.—According to the census of 1890, there were 50 cities in the State having a population above 1,000. Since that time the mining towns of Creede and Cripple Creek have sprung into existence. The camp at Creede, which claims a population of not fewer than 6,000, and an increase of 100 a day, had its beginning in 1889, when N. C. Creede located the Holy Moses mine. The Phoenix and the Cliff were located the same year by him and Charles F. Nelson, and the first cabins built. The following year they located the Ethel, the Solomon, the Ridge, and the Mammoth. They sold the Holy Moses in September for $70,000; the purchasers put in a large force, and the fame of the rich discoveries of silver in the Bachelor Mountains began to spread throughout the West. An extension of the Denver and Rio Grande Railroad was begun in September, 1891, and finished in December. The land had been leased to M. V. B. Wason for agricultural and grazing purposes at the rate of $12 for 100 acres. The State Board of Land Commissioners declared the lease forfeited, the lessee having let the lands out for commercial and town purposes. Mr. Wason brought suit, but the board was sustained, and the lands were sold as school lands. Sixty-six acres brought $183,662.

Soon after the discoveries at Creede gold was discovered at Cripple creek. The two principal towns there, Fremont and Moreland, are practically one, and have a combined population of 4,000 or 5,000. Other town sites have been laid out and named Beaver Park and Lawrence.

Another discovery that promises to be of great importance is that of gold at Copper Rock, in Boulder County. It is on Four Mile creek, 13 miles from Boulder. The altitude at the site of the new town is about 7,600 feet, with the surrounding country rising from the sedimentary bed of the gulch until an additional height of 8,100 feet is attained.

Many other discoveries have been reported during the year.

Park Reservation.—A movement to set apart a tract within the old Ute reservation, comprising parts of Rio Blanco, Routt, Eagle, and Garfield Counties, for a national park, was begun with a bill prepared for the State Legislature, and was favored by the Society for the Preservation of Forests. Under the act of Congress authorizing the reservation of sources of water supply, the President made a proclamation to that effect, Oct. 16, 1891. The White river plateau is described as an undulating table-land, 9,000 to 11,000 feet high, one of the principal sources of water supply for the Grand, White, and Yampa rivers. Considerable opposition has been developed among the people in the region, on the ground that there are both mineral and agricultural lands within the reservation; that there are already many settlers and claims located in it; that the timber lands of the Rio Blanco are all within its boundaries; and that the United States is under contract with the Utes to sell the land at $1.25 an acre and turn the proceeds over to the tribes interested. On the other hand, it is asserted that the land is too high for farming; that there are no valuable mineral claims within it; that the rights of settlers, of whom there are but few, are well secured by the terms of the proclamation; that the preservation of the timber lands is necessary for the water supply; and that without the park all the large game in the State will disappear within twenty years. With regard to the Utes, it appears that the treaty made with them in 1881 stipulated that as fast as the land on this reservation should be sold the amounts realized from it should be placed to their credit to pay for the land to which they were removed, so that if the land is taken for national purposes the present reservation could be turned over to the Utes in payment.

The proposed park has an area of 1,184,480 acres. In winter it is mostly covered with a great depth of snow, but "in summer it is a vast natural garden of luxuriant grass and flowers, groves, parks, crystal lakes and streams, interspersed with odd-shaped peaks and rugged cañons."

The land comprising Lost Park has also been withdrawn from settlement and entry, with a view to its being ultimately set apart as a national park and timber reservation. Lost Park is in Jefferson and Park Counties, and contains approximately 720,000 acres.

The Capitol.—The new Capitol has been more than three years in building. It has employed 500 men, at average wages of $4 for eight hours' labor. The basement, without the storage rooms below, reaches from the outside bottom to the flooring of the first story, a height of 16 feet. The first story is 21 feet, the second 20 feet 4 inches, the third 18 feet 4 inches high. Thirty-two steps, covering a width of 97 feet, with beautiful ornaments on both the sides, lead from the bottom to the flooring of the first floor. The portico has a length of 106 feet and a width of 20 feet 5 inches. Stones were used which have a length of 17 feet, a width of 3 feet 9 inches, and a height of 2 feet 9 inches. They weigh 30,000 pounds. For the building were used 250,000 cubic feet of granite, 160,000,000 bricks, and 450,000 cubic feet of building stone.

Western Congress.—The third session of the Congress of the Western Counties began at Ouray, June 14. The principal subject of discussion was railroad transportation. The rates, it was asserted, are so high as to interfere seriously with the growth of the section. An anti-pool resolution was passed, and also one appropriat-

ing $500 for the purpose of enforcing the inter-state commerce law in Colorado.

Political.—On April 26 a State convention of free-coinage clubs was held at Denver. Delegates were appointed to the National Silver Convention, to meet at Washington in May. The resolutions below express the aims of the convention:

Whereas, Silver was demonetized in 1873 by fraud and in the interest of the money power of the country; and

Whereas, The circulating medium is not sufficient for the transaction of the ordinary business without the unnecessary payment of gain to the millionaires that have grown up under our system of government; and

Whereas, The time has come that, in behalf of the laborers of all classes—the farmer, the mechanic, and the miner—a firm stand must be taken in behalf of honest money; and

Whereas, Silver is the money of the people, and the continued demonetization of it will cause a financial panic more direful in its results than is found in history; therefore, be it

Resolved, That we are in favor of the free and unlimited coinage of silver, first, last, and all the time, as paramount to all other national issues.

Resolved, That the time has come when no longer the division of party should be made upon any party political differences, and that we send greetings to the silver men of the South and all other States and Territories, asking them to meet us upon this proposition for their and our coming good.

Resolved, That it is the sentiment of this convention that the Colorado State conventions of all parties should instruct their delegates to the national conventions held for the purpose of nominating candidates for President and Vice-President to withdraw from said convention if they do not succeed in getting free-coinage planks in their party platforms, with nominees who are unquestionably in favor of the full remonetization of silver.

On Nov. 8 a Governor and other State officers and two Representatives in Congress were elected, as well as a successor to Chief-Justice Helm, of the Supreme Court, who resigned in September to become a candidate for the office of Governor. At that time also the following proposed amendments to the Constitution of the State were submitted to the electors:

Section 3 of Article X of the Constitution of the State of Colorado shall be amended so as to read as follows: Section 3. All taxes shall be uniform upon the same class of subjects within the territorial limits of the authority levying the tax, and shall be levied and collected under general laws, which shall prescribe such regulations as shall secure a just valuation for the taxation of all property, real and personal: *Provided,* that the household goods of every person being the head of a family, to the value of $200, shall be exempt from taxation. Ditches, canals, and flumes owned and used by individuals or corporations for irrigating lands owned by such individuals or corporations, or the individual members thereof, shall not be separately taxed so long as they shall be owned and used exclusively for such purpose; and *Provided,* further, that the provisions of this section shall not affect such special assessments for benefits and municipal improvements as the corporate authorities of cities, towns, or improvement districts may assess and collect under provisions to be prescribed by law.

SEC. 2. Section 11 of said article shall be amended so as to read as follows: Section 11. The rate of taxation on property for State purposes shall not exceed 4 mills on each dollar of valuation.

The Prohibition party met in May and nominated an entire State ticket. There was some discussion on a proposition to place the words

" recognizing Almighty God " in the preamble of the platform, and the words were finally inserted. The platform contains the following propositions :

The abolition of the saloon; the free and unlimited coinage of silver; abolition of the national banks; Government ownership of railroad, telegraph, and telephone lines; the election of United States Senators by a popular vote; opposition to State convict labor working in the interest of ditch corporations; and a " modification of the Australian ballot system, so that a fair and equal consideration shall be bestowed upon both old and new parties."

Delegates were appointed to the national convention at Omaha, and a preference was recorded for John P. St. John as candidate for President, and Gilbert De la Matyr for Vice-President. The following was the State ticket: Governor, John Hipp; Lieutenant-Governor, D. W. Barkly; Secretary of State, R. A. Rice; Treasurer, Fred White; State Auditor, L. C. Aley; Attorney-General, J. C. Horne; Superintendent of Schools, A. B. Hyde; Regents of the University, H. H. Bell, Edwin Hungerford. Frank I. Wilson was the nominee for Justice of the Supreme Court.

The Republican Convention, which met Sept. 8, declared for free silver, and condemned President Harrison for his opposition to free coinage. Joseph C. Helm was nominated for Governor, J. M. Downing for Lieutenant-Governor. E. J. Eaton for Secretary, Harry Mulnix for Treasurer, Harry Tarbell for Auditor, C. S. Libby for Attorney-General, G. B. Timberlake for Superintendent of Public Instruction, George W. Allen for Justice of the Supreme Court, and for Regents of the University, J. Semple and Warren E. Knapp.

The Democratic Convention met at Pueblo in September. The fusionists having gained control in the organization, the "straight" Democrats bolted and held another convention. Following is the ticket of the People's party and the fusionists : For Governor, David H. Waite; for Lieutenant-Governor, D. H. Nichols; for Secretary of State, N. O. McClees; for Treasurer, Albert Nance; for Auditor, F. M. Goodykoontz; for Attorney-General, Eugene Engley; for Regents of the University, D. M. Richards, W. E. Anderson; for Superintendent of Public Instruction, John F. Murray; for Justice of the Supreme Court, Luther M. Goddard.

The bolting Democrats nominated the following ticket: For Governor, Joseph H. Maupin; for Lieutenant-Governor, W. M. McMechen; for Secretary of State, C. B. Noland ; for Treasurer, W. E. Hamilton; for Auditor, John H. Fox; for Attorney-General, W. P. Skelton: for Superintendent of Public Instruction, Nathan B. Coy; for Regents of the University, Henry Johnson, Lee Champion: for Justice of the Supreme Court, Luther M. Goddard.

The platform approved the platform and ticket of the Chicago convention, favored the free and unlimited coinage of silver, denounced the employment of detectives to coerce labor, and urged legislation as follows: First, to prevent combinations and monopolies designed to raise the price of coal and other articles of necessity; second, to make eight hours a legal day's work; third, to secure to mechanics, miners, and laborers an effective lien law; fourth, to secure an

equitable employers' liability act; fifth, to prohibit the employment of child labor in mines and factories; sixth, to secure from railway companies fair rates for transportation, and to prevent unjust discrimination.

Earl B. Coe and H. H. Eddy were the nominees of the Republicans for members of Congress, Lafe Pence and John C. Bell of the united People's party and Democrats, John G. Taylor and John D. Bell of Democrats, and N. G. Sprague and I. J. Keator of the Prohibitionists.

At the election in November the entire People's party, or fusion ticket, was elected.

The Rev. Myron W. Reed, of Denver, was nominated for Congress from the First District by the People's party and both conventions of Democrats. He declined, and Lafe Pence was nominated on the fusion ticket, and John G. Taylor by the straight Democrats. Later in the canvass the names of the Cleveland electors were removed from the State Democratic ticket.

At the election, Nov. 8, the total vote for electors was 93,275, of which the Populists received 52,982, the Republicans 38,614, and the Prohibitionists 1,677. The People's party elected their entire State ticket. Following is the vote for Governor: Helm, 38,812; Maupin, 8,938; Waite, 41,344; Hipp, 1,742. The Republicans will have a small majority in the Legislature.

COLUMBUS, CHRISTOPHER, discoverer, born in Genoa, Italy, about 1446; died in Valladolid, Spain, May 20, 1506. The undisputed statements in the undisputed will of Columbus read: "I also pray the King and Queen, our sovereigns, and their eldest born, Prince Don Juan, our lord, and their successors, for the sake of the services I have done them, and because it is just, that it may please them not to permit this my will and constitution of my entailed estate to be in any way altered, but to leave it in the form and manner which I have ordained forever, for the greater glory of the Almighty, and that it may be the root and basis of my lineage, and a memento of the services I have rendered their highnesses, that, being born in Genoa, I came over to serve them in Castile. . . . I also enjoin Diego, or any one that may inherit the estate, to have and maintain in the city of Genoa one person of our lineage to reside there with his wife, . . . from which great good may accrue to him, inasmuch as I was born there, and came from thence. . . . I command the said Diego, or whoever may possess the said estate, to labor and strive for the honor, welfare, and aggrandizement of the city of Genoa, and to make use of all his power and means in defending and enhancing the good and credit of that republic in all things not contrary to the service of the Church of God, or the high dignity of the King and Queen, our lords, and their successors."

In view of these words, it seems amazing that the long and involved disputes in regard to the birthplace of Columbus could have arisen. That claims should have been made by other cities was natural, and they had some show of probability, as, for instance, in the case of Placentia, where the family of Columbus owned a small property in the village of Pradello, which was originally held by Bartolino Colombo, great-grandfather of Columbus, and the rental of which descended to Columbus and his brother. Piedmont was a persistent claimant. One Domenico Colombo (identical in name with the father of Columbus) was lord of Cucorro, in Montferrat, at the time of the birth of the discoverer. A claim in law to the estates of Columbus, put forth by a descendant of the lord, only brought forth proof that the father of Columbus was resident in Genoa both before and for many years after the death of the nobleman of the same name. The family of Columbus also possessed a small property at a hamlet called Terra Rosa (or Terras Rubra, in Latin), near the towns of Nervi and Quinto, which have therefore claimed him. A tower at Terra Rosa bore recently the name Torre dei Colombi; and Bartholomew, brother of Christopher, signed himself "of Terra Rubra," in a Latin inscription on a map that he presented to Henry VII of England—a subscription which his nephew says, in the life of his father, his uncle was accustomed to use. Cogoletto claimed Columbus, because two admirals of that name (Colombo), uncle and nephew, were native there. They were probably of distant kindred, for Christopher, in one of his letters, says: "I am not the first admiral of my family." Savona also claimed him, which was natural enough, as Domenico Colombo, father of Christopher, removed to that city, and lived there two or three years. One of her citizens, writing of the claim, says emphatically: "Genoa, most noble city, was the birthplace of Columbus." At the time of Christopher's birth the family were wool carders, which humble business they had followed for generations. From a notary's register, in 1311, it appears that Giacomo Colombo, wool carder, lived outside the gate of St. Andrea. In 1489 Domenico Colombo is recorded as possessing a house and shop, and a garden with a well, in the street of St. Andrew's gate, anciently without the walls, which Irving says was believed to be the same dwelling formerly owned by Giacomo. Signor Staglieno has identified and pictured one of these little rickety houses in the wool-carder's quarter of the modern city of Genoa as the home and probable birthplace of the discoverer. Domenico rented another house, from the monks of St. Stephen, his name being found several times between 1456 and 1459, the last recorded payment being in 1489. He is there called a son of Giovanni Colombo, husband of Susanna Fontanarossa, father of Christopher, Bartholomew, and Diego, a particularity in description that would lead us to conclude that others of the family were on the rent roll of the monks. We know that there were uncles and cousins from whom the fortunes of his life separated the explorer, although his memory recurred to them when, in his will, he laid injunction upon his son to "appoint two persons of conscience and authority, and most nearly related to the family, who are to examine the revenue and cause the said tenth to be paid to the most necessitated members of my family that may be found here or elsewhere."

Whether the noble Colombos and the nautical Colombos and the weaver Colombos were originally one stock, broken asunder by the early feuds of Italy, is of the less consequence, as Columbus in his early struggle certainly never had a helping hand from a rich or powerful relative, never mentions them even when, amid

the taunts of the Spanish lords on the obscurity of his birth, to have proclaimed to them his descent from titled men might have saved the long years of agonized appeal at court or quieted a mutiny in perilous conditions of the New World. If there ever was a self-made man on earth, that man was Christopher Columbus.

The only other members of the family were a brother, who probably died young, and a sister, who married Giacomo Baverello, a cheese merchant. It would be very interesting to know something of the two women who especially influenced his early life. Was it an unhappy memory of them, or the long suit he had paid to Queen Isabella, that caused him to say in his will: "This entailed estate shall in no wise be inherited by a woman, except in case that no male is to be found, either in this or any other quarter of the world, of my real lineage. In such an event (which may God forefend), then the female of legitimate birth most nearly related to the preceding possessor of the estate shall succeed to it."

HOUSE IN WHICH COLUMBUS LIVED, AS IT IS AT PRESENT.

The weavers of Genoa had established schools for themselves outside the city, and at one of these Columbus learned to read and write, becoming proficient in the latter accomplishment. In arithmetic, drawing, and painting he acquired great skill. Somehow the artisan parent managed to send his son for a little while to the then celebrated University of Pavia, where he studied grammar, Latin, geometry, geography, astronomy, and navigation. The writings of Ptolemy had been translated into Latin, while Pliny, Pomponius, Mela, and Strabo had been revived, and the great Arabian astrologers were beginning to be eagerly sought for. Columbus could have had hardly more than time to acquire a love for such studies, for he says that at fourteen years of age he began to navigate. Of his early nautical experiences little is known. The first voyage was that in the armament which Genoa fitted out to help the Duke of Calabria, John of Anjou, in an attack upon Naples to recover that kingdom for his father. Many private ships or galleys joined the expedition.

Among them was that of an admiral of Columbus's own name, with whom he sailed. This man and his nephew, also named Colombo, were well-known seamen, and he was with one or the other of them in many adventures for commerce or conquest. Genoa had then appealed to Louis XI of France, and was under his jurisdiction. Additional proof that Columbus was engaged in naval enterprises at that time—enterprises that sometimes led to conflicts with Spanish ships—lies in the fact that Ferdinand calls Columbus a subject of Louis, and Isabella rebukes him for having injured Spanish interests.

In a letter to the King and Queen, later in life, he says incidentally of this period:

It happened to me that King Reinel (whom God has taken to himself) sent me to Tunis to capture the galley "Fernandina," and when I arrived off the Island of St. Pedro, in Sardinia, I was informed that there were two ships and a carrack with the galley; by which intelligence my crew were so troubled that they determined to proceed no further, but to return to Marseilles for another vessel and more people. As I could not by any means compel them, I assented apparently to their wishes, altering the point of the compass, and spreading all sail. It was then evening, and next morning we were within the Cape of Carthagena, while all were firmly of opinion that they were sailing toward Marseilles.

Not a glimpse is shown us of the result of this bold method of dealing with a mutinous crew on the part of a captain who must have been young for such command, and as skillful and confident in navigation as he was resolute in spirit. In another letter he mentions the fact that he had been at the island of Scio, and had witnessed the process of getting mastic.

Meantime, in the intervals of his maritime expeditions, Columbus was a bookseller and chartmaker in Genoa. In 1470 he signed a contract to pay a wine merchant $60 for wine that he would take on his vessel to sell. About 1471, when Columbus was twenty-five years old, Domenico Colombo, the father, removed his business and his family to Savona. In a will left two years after that time, by Nicolo Monelone, the 6 witnesses were 3 tailors, 1 bootmaker, 1 cloth dresser, and Christoforo Colombo, weaver, of Genoa. A little later he, with his father, signed an agreement to pay for wool in cloth. These two last transactions must have taken place when Columbus was at his father's house on visits during his naval expeditions; for Oviedo says that when on shore he made maps and charts for the support of his family. He was poor, but gave what he could to his father to educate his brothers. In 1470 Columbus went to Portugal and joined his brother Bartholomew, who was earning a living in Lisbon as a chart draughtsman for the adventurous navigators of that capital. Bartholomew Columbus was an extraordinary man, overshadowed by the more remarkable brother to whom he lent great assistance from the beginning to the close of his life. Prince Henry, the navigator, was pushing his explorations far and near, especially along the coast of Africa. Columbus sailed in many of these expeditions, and afterward said in one of his letters that during this time he sailed east, west, north and south. According to the descriptions given of Columbus, he must have been, at this time, tall, well-formed and muscular. He had a long face, neither lean

nor full, fair and freckled complexion, somewhat ruddy, aquiline nose, rather high cheek bones, light-gray eyes, and light hair, turned white at thirty. His carriage was dignified and lofty, his temper quick, his eyes full of fire and enthusiasm. He was moderate and simple in diet and apparel, eloquent in conversation, and very affable. He was always devoutly religious, and on coming to Lisbon attended services frequently at the chapel of the Convent of All Saints. Here he met Doña Felipa Moñis de Perestrello, who, with other young women of rank, was received as a boarder at the convent. Columbus formed an attachment for her and married her. Her father, Bartolomeo Moñis de Perestrello, was an Italian captain in the service of Prince Henry, to whom the Prince had given the governorship of the island of Porto Santo, of the Madeira group.

On the death of the captain soon after their marriage, Columbus and his wife took up their residence with his mother-in-law on the little property bequeathed to her in Porto Santo. Here, in 1474, his son Diego was born, and here Columbus studied the maps and charts of Perestrello, and gleaned from his widow many anecdotes and incidents of his voyages. His wife's sister was married to a noted navigator, Pedro Correo. Columbus had been speculating on these matters, when it was reported to him that Paulo Toscanelli, a savant of Florence, had sent to Fernando Martinez, a learned canon of Lisbon, a letter telling him that by sailing westward he could reach India much quicker than by his proposed route around Africa. He wrote to inquire of Toscanelli, and in reply received a copy of the letter and a map that represented India as lying not far west from the coast of Spain.

In the life of his father, Fernando Columbus gives, as a summary from his father's notes and papers, what he considers to be the causes that acted upon Columbus, and led to his determination: 1, the nature of things; 2, the authority of learned writers; 3, the reports of navigators. Under the first he mentions his father's belief that the earth was a terraqueous globe, which might be traveled round from east to west, and that, when opposite, men stood foot to foot. He divided the circumference from east to west at the equator into twenty-four hours, of 15° each. Of these he thought 15° were known to the ancients. Portugal had advanced the western frontier equal to one hour more. There remained, therefore, 8° unexplored. This space might be nearly filled up with the eastern portion of Asia. Thus, by sailing westward, a navigator would find Asia and any intervening land. Under the second head he mentions Aristotle, Seneca, Pliny, Strabo, the travels of Marco Polo and John Mandeville, as believing that the space was not great between the land washed by the other extremity of the one known ocean. Under the last head he mentions signs of land, and even of civilization, that had been washed upon islands, or upon the mainland of Europe. He had a memorandum of these latter trophies—reeds, such as he believed to be described by Eastern travelers, trunks of foreign trees, carved wood, a strange iron instrument, bodies of two men of unknown race, reports of mariners of land seen at the westward, as well as the rumors of fancied islands—islands, indeed, which Toscanelli sprinkled liberally in his map as being convenient stopping places on the comparatively short route to Asia.

The riches of the Orient, dwelt upon by the travelers, were also pictured afresh in the letters of Toscanelli. It was a time of wild rumor and fantastic faith in regard to the unknown lands supposed to be hidden by the sea. The Antilla, the Seven Cities, and many other islands, lived firmly in fancy, while the unseen "Island of St. Brandon " was not only set down on the maps, but estates on it were given by princes to subjects who set out to take possession of a home that forever retreated with the margin of the sea. Columbus noted all these; but he said, especially in regard to St. Brandon, which the people of the Canary islands described as being often distinctly visible, that the mirage might have come from rocks lying in the ocean, or floating islands of twisted roots and light, porous stone, often with trees upon them, driven about the ocean by winds. Visionary in regard to mental phenomena, Columbus, though imaginative, as all genius must be, was sternly practical in regard to physical phenomena. One of the points of deepest interest in his career is the fact that his was no random or accidental discovery. It was founded on carefully considered knowledge, and carried out according to the most advanced scientific methods. That the knowledge was incorrect, and the science in part deceptive, does not in the least militate against the value to human progress of that element in the undertaking. It was better for the cause of the human intellect that savage America should have been discovered in that way than that the wealth of the Indies should have been hit upon by accident. Meantime he was gaining practical experience as a navigator. Of one of his voyages at this time he afterward writes to his son:

In the year 1477, in February, I navigated 100 leagues beyond Thule, the southern part of which is 73° distant from the equator, and not 63°, as some pretend; neither is it situated within the line which includes the west of Ptolemy, but is much more westerly. The English, principally those of Bristol, go with their merchandise to this island, which is as large as England. When I was there the sea was not frozen, and the tides were so great as to rise and fall 26 fathoms.

It was about the year 1474 that Columbus formed his conclusion that the land at the east could be reached by sailing westward. While that was a startling step in advance of those who still hooted at the idea that the earth was round, the attempt to reach it was far from feasible even to the adventurous navigator's fancy. Although the compass was in use, sailors had navigated far enough toward the equator to know that the north star was seen in a different quarter while a guide in the southern heavens had not been sought and was not known. Land in easy reach had been thus far the only safety for the mariner. A hint of the difficulties through which Columbus had worked his own way to his conclusion may be gained if we pause to remember that in all his calculations this earth was the center of the solar system. Although Copernicus was born, the most daring students of geography and astronomy had not yet got far beyond the opinion of the old Arabian writer Xerif al Edrisi: "The ocean encircles the ultimate bounds of the inhabited earth, and all beyond it is unknown. There is no mariner who dares to enter into its deep waters; or, if any have done so, they have merely kept along its coasts, fearful of departing from them. The waves of this ocean, although they roll as high as mountains, yet maintain themselves without breaking; for if they broke, it would be impossible for ship to plow them."

Meantime, while Columbus was nursing his secret project and strengthening his conclusions by every means in his power, King John II of Portugal was endeavoring to further the great scheme that Prince Henry had bequeathed to him and to the Portuguese people, to find a route to China round the shores of Africa. In furtherance of this, he called a council of the most learned scientific men of the kingdom, and as a result of this conference the astrolabe was applied to navigation, and henceforth the sailor was able, from the altitude of the sun, to ascertain his distance from the equator. This discovery allowed the mariner to forget the land, and by the sun and stars to map his course on the hitherto hopelessly wide waste of waters. To Columbus this was the final fact, and without the least hesitation he offered himself and his great enterprise at the court of Portugal.

King John received his proposition, that, if the King would furnish him with ships and men, he would sail by a shorter route, cross the Atlantic to the island of Cipango (Japan), at which he should expect first to arrive; and the reasons for this belief were fully set forth to the monarch. John called a council, in which were two able cosmographers, and the council agreed that the project was visionary and absurd. The Bishop of Ceuta took occasion to say that the whole business of discovery was detrimental to the interests of the country, and that Christian wars against the infidel Moors would be much more profitable. This drew from a distinguished courtier, Count of Villa Real, not of the council, a reply, from which the following is an abstract: Portugal is not in its infancy, nor are its princes so poor as to lack means to engage in discoveries. Even granting that those proposed by Columbus are conjectural, why should they abandon those begun by the late Prince Henry? It would be the greatest laud for Portuguese valor to penetrate into the secrets and horrors of the ocean sea, so formidable to the other nations of the world. Great souls were born for great enterprises. He wondered much that a prelate so religious as the Bishop of Ceuta should oppose this undertaking, the ultimate object of which was to augment the Catholic faith and spread it from pole to pole. He ended by saying that, although a soldier, he dared to prognosticate with a voice and spirit as if from heaven, to whatever prince should achieve this enterprise, more happy success and durable renown than had ever been obtained by sovereign the most valorous and fortunate.

His words were echoed with enthusiasm, and the King showed to his confessor such an evident desire to try the wondrous plan set forth by Columbus, that the bishop suggested its trial in a way that would secure the advantage if successful, and not injure the dignity of the Crown if it failed. In accordance with it, Columbus was required to give a detailed plan of his intended voyage with all his charts and maps, ostensibly to be examined by the council, whose decision he was to await. Having thus quieted him, the King fitted out a caravel, said to be laden with provisions for the Cape de Verde islands, but with secret instructions to sail westward in search of land, following the course laid down by Columbus. After a stormy voyage of several days the vessel returned to Lisbon, and the ridicule heaped on Columbus by the travelers was his first intimation of the deceit practiced upon him. He was deeply incensed, and immediately left a land that had proved so treacherous. This was in the latter part of 1484. His wife having died, he took with him his little son Diego, and set out secretly. Three years later King John wrote to him, addressing "Christopher Colon, our especial friend," invited him to return, and promised him immunity from any civil or criminal suit that might be pending against him. It is needless to say that the offer met with no response. There is pretty good authority for believing that, before the negotiations with King John, Columbus had, by letter, offered his services to his native and beloved Genoa. The government had declined them, but on leaving Portugal he seems to have renewed the offer in person, with a like result, and to have lived some time with his father, making maps and charts for a livelihood. It is believed that at this time also he laid his plan before the little kingdom of Venice. That he did so at some time, is shown by a letter written by Columbus two days before he sailed from Saltes, addressed to Agostino Barbarigo, Doge of Venice. It runs:

MAGNIFICENT SIR: Since your republic has not deemed it convenient to accept my offers, and all the spite of my many enemies has been brought in force to oppose my petition, I have thrown myself into the arms of God, my Maker, and he, by the intercession of the saints, has caused the most clement King of Castile not to refuse generously to assist my project toward the discovery of a new world. And praising thereby the g o God, I obtained the placing under my command of men and ships, and am about to set out on a voyage to that famous land, close to which intent God has been pleased to bestow upon me.

In 1485 Columbus set out to lay his plans before the Spanish sovereigns, Ferdinand and Isabella. On his way he stopped at the Convent of La Rabida, which was about a mile from the Andalusian seaport of Palos. He was traveling on foot, in poor clothing, accompanied by his little son Diego. As he paused to ask a morsel of bread and a drink of water for the child, the prior of the convent, Juan Perez de Marchina, happened to pass the entrance. Struck by the appearance of Columbus, and noticing his foreign accent, he questioned him, and as a result of the interview sent for a friend of his, Garcia Fernandez, the physician of Palos, who was equally impressed. Several conferences were held in the cloisters, in which some of the ancient mariners of Palos felt a deep interest, and added to the excitement if not to the information that was filling the fervid mind of Columbus. One old tar, Pedro de Velasco, said that thirty years before he was carried by stress of weather so far to the northwest that Cape Clear,

in Ireland, lay eastward of him. There, in a strong west wind, the sea was perfectly smooth, which he fancied must be caused by land that lay in that direction.

In that shelter Columbus and his boy remained all winter. In the spring of 1486 the King and Queen established their court in Cordova, in order to raise an army for the coming campaign against the Moors. Furnished with a letter from Juan Perez to his intimate friend Fernando de Talavera, confessor to the Queen, Columbus left his boy in the prior's hands and went to court.

So far from taking the view of the prior of La Rabida, Talavera pronounced the scheme absurd and impossible, and would not even secure a hearing for the applicant. Oviedo says: "Because he was a stranger and went but in simple apparel, not otherwise credited than by the letter of a gray friar, they believed him not, neither gave ear to his words, whereby he was greatly tormented in his imagination."

The war against the Moors in their last stronghold of Granada was in full tide. Not only was Ferdinand busy with the unrelaxing energy that characterized him, but the Queen took up her residence in camp. The court moved with the shifting fortunes of the war. City after city fell, triumph after triumph followed with absorbing excitement. During the summer and autumn Columbus remained in Cordova, supporting himself in the familiar way, with map and chart making, meantime trying to make friends of influential persons. Among these was Alonzo de Quintanilla, controller of the finances of Castile, who took him into his house and became a warm supporter of his theories. Antonio Geraldinus, nuncio from the Pope, and his brother, Alexander Geraldinus, preceptor of the King's younger children, warmly espoused his cause. They introduced him to Pedro Gonzales de Mendoza, Archbishop of Toledo and Grand Cardinal of Spain, who was called by Peter Martyr "the third King of Spain." He opposed the suggestions at first as heterodox, and it is infinitely to the credit both of Columbus and of this prelate, who knew more dogma than science, that he gave first an incredulous but respectful hearing, then earnest study, and finally the interest born of conviction. He obtained Columbus an interview with the sovereigns, and the result was that Talavera was ordered to convene a council of learned men to listen and report.

In the Dominican Convent of St. Stephen, Salamanca, where Columbus was maintained meanwhile, was held the conference of worldwide renown. Few in it but came with deepseated prejudice against the man they were to hear. In fact, at first a few scientific friars were all who paid any attention to him. When they finally listened it was to pour forth on him a torrent of contradiction. The Old Testament and the New Testament, the ancient fathers and the modern Popes, were cited to prove the impossibility and absurdity of his conclusions. From Lactantius was the following: "Is there any one so foolish as to believe that there are antipodes with their feet opposite to ours—people who walk with their heels upward and their heads hanging down? that there is a part of the world in which all things are topsy-turvy, and where it rains, hails, and snows upward?

The idea of the roundness of the earth was the cause of inventing this fable of the antipodes, with their heels in the air; for these philosophers, having once erred, go on in their absurdities defending one another." That the earth was flat, they proved from a hundred passages of Scripture, as where the Psalmist and St. Paul both describe the heavens as spread out like a canopy. Columbus, the devout, was in danger of the Inquisition for heresy, when some of the more enlightened prelates came to his relief. They admitted that the earth might be round, but said that the heat of the torrid zone would be insupportable; that it was only habitable in the northern hemisphere; that if a ship could reach India it could never get back, for the roundness of the earth would present a kind of mountain up which it would be impossible to sail.

To these objections Columbus answered, with profound reverence for the Scripture, held as sacred by him as by them, that the inspired writers were not speaking as cosmographers, using the language of science, but figuratively, as appeared to the eye and could be understood by all. When he came to the men who did profess so to write he took another tone. There he stood upon surer ground than they. He told them how he had himself proved the half truths of the ancients and had disproved their mistakes; that he had sailed the coast of Guinea, almost under the equator, and found abundant life and beauty. His eloquence, his fervor, his learning, his piety, his commanding presence and dignity of thought, silenced if it did not persuade, and some few were thoroughly convinced. Conference after conference followed, dragged out by counsel darkened by words without knowledge. The time wore on, now with faint hope to Columbus that he was on the eve of a decisive interview at court, again with such evident forgetfulness of his cause and wishes that he became the laughing stock of the very children in the street.

The wandering and warlike sovereigns now and then called him to attend their suite and forwarded the money for his proper presentment, but the hoped-for interview never came. Among the memorandums of these years by which Columbus may be traced is a record of Diego Ortiz de Zuñiga, of Seville, which says that, in response to a command of the sovereigns, the city furnished entertainment for Christopher Columbus, who came to the city on matters of importance, and he adds: " The same Columbus was found fighting, giving proofs of the distinguished valor which accompanied his wisdom and his lofty desires." He repaired there with renewed hope, only to be told by them that they must decline to listen further until a more convenient season.

Five years had passed between the time when Columbus entered Cordova and the time when,

in despair, he once more left the Spanish court, resolving never to return.

Meantime, in Cordova he had formed an alliance with a lady of high lineage, Beatrix Enriquez, by whom he had a son Fernando. Of her he says in the will that was executed the day before he died : " And I direct him [his son Diego] that he shall have special care for Beatrix Enriquez, the mother of Don Ferdinand, my son ; that he shall provide for her so that she may live comfortably, as a person should for whom I have so much regard. And this shall be done for the ease of my conscience, because this has weighed heavily on my soul. The reason therefor it is not proper to mention here." The son Ferdinand he took legal measures to have acknowledged, and in every way possible made him equal to his legitimate child.

Thus in 1491 Columbus left the royal presence, but so great was the interest he had awakened that he was loath to relinquish it by leaving Spain. There were noblemen of maritime enterprise, scientific attainment, and vast resources. To one of these, the Duke of Medina Sidonia, he now applied. At first he was listened to with eagerness, but Gomera persuaded him not to be dazzled by

CONVENT OF LA RÁBIDA.

the dream of an Italian visionary. It seemed indeed that in the next nobleman to whom he appealed, the Duke of Medina Cœli, he had found the needed friend; but just as he was actually on the point of dispatching Columbus with four caravels, he withdrew from the undertaking as one too great to be accomplished by a subject, and urged Columbus again to appeal to Ferdinand and Isabella. But Columbus had not only had enough of hanging upon the uncertain favor of a court that was a camp, but had meantime received a kindly letter from the King of France, and to that country he determined to repair. Before going he visited the Convent of La Rábida for the purpose of bringing his son Diego to Cordova, to be left with Ferdinand. His old friend the friar welcomed him after the seven years of absence, but as he looked sadly at his humble, dust-stained garments and mournful countenance he was deeply moved, and begged him to relate his adventures. When Columbus told him that he was on the point of leaving Spain to offer to France his great project, the prior begged him to delay until they could call some counsel. He sent again for the physician Garcia Fernandez, and for Martin Alonzo Pinzon, the head of a distinguished family of navigators. Pinzon was so earnest in his faith and interest that he offered to pay Columbus's expenses if he would once more apply at court. This so strengthened the views of the prior that he wrote a letter to Isabella, and obtained the promise of Columbus to await its answer at the convent. The answer invited the former father confessor to attend her at Santa Fé, the camp city that had been built in the Vega before Granada, which capital they were then besieging, and the friar lost not a moment in complying with the request. The result of the visit was that Columbus, furnished with money by the Queen, once more set out to seek an audience at court. He reached his destination in time to witness the surrender of the last of the Moorish kings, and amid the ceremonies and revelry of rejoicing he was forgotten. A Spanish writer gives us the picture: "A man obscure and but little known followed at this time the court. Confounded in the crowd of importunate applicants, feeding his imagination in the corners of antechambers with the pompous project of discovering a world, melancholy and dejected amid the general rejoicing, he beheld with indifference, and almost with contempt, the conclusion of a conquest which swelled all bosoms with jubilee, and seemed to have reached the utmost bounds of desire. That man was Christopher Columbus."

When the festivities were at an end, Talavera, now Archbishop of Granada, was appointed to negotiate with Columbus the terms on which he should be sent forth. What was his amazement to hear the needy adventurer claim that, as the first step, he should be made admiral and viceroy of the countries he should discover, and be given one tenth of all gains whether by trade or conquest. To the torrent of ridicule at his pretensions, and the sneer that he would at least gain a title and lose nothing, he replied that he would furnish one eighth of the cost on receiving promise of one eighth of the profits. His terms were promptly rejected by Talavera, and the powerful prelate had no difficulty in convincing the Queen that to bestow such honor on a nameless stranger would make him too powerful if successful, and render the sovereigns absurd in case of his failure. Terms deemed more suitable were offered to Columbus, but he refused them with equal determination. He mounted his horse and in February, 1492, once more set out for France. intending to make a brief stay at Cordova. No sooner did the news go out that Columbus had departed. than the men of influence and intelligence who had early espoused his cause and longed for its accomplishment, came to court and begged for his recall. Luis de Sant-angel, receiver of the ecclesiastical revenues of Arragon, especially pleaded his cause with eloquence, warmly seconded by the Marchioness of Moya.

Although the so-called calm judgment of history has professed to set aside as untrue the incident of Isabella's warm-hearted offer of her jewels to pay the cost of the expedition, when for the first time she realized the greatness of the enterprise and the cold attitude of Ferdinand regarding it, it remains undenied that she assumed the charges for her own Kingdom of Castile, and her private coffers if necessary,

which Sant-angel immediately assured her would not be needed. She sent a swift messenger to recall Columbus, and it was well that she sent an eloquent one, for Columbus at first refused to go back, and was only persuaded on learning that the Queen had given positive assurance. On his return he was well received, and in due time articles containing the following agreements were signed by both parties:

1. That Columbus was to have, for himself during his life, and his heirs and successors forever, the office of admiral in all the lands and continents which he might discover or acquire in the ocean sea, with similar honors and prerogatives to those enjoyed by the High Admiral of Castile in his district.

2. That he should be viceroy and governor-general over all the said lands and continents, with the privilege of nominating 3 candidates for the government of each island or province, one of whom should be selected by the sovereigns.

3. That he should be entitled to reserve for himself one tenth of all pearls, precious stones, gold, silver, spices, and all other articles and merchandises, in whatever manner found, bought, bartered, or gained within his admiralty, the costs being first deducted.

4. That he, or his lieutenant, should be the sole judge in all causes and disputes arising out of traffic between those countries and Spain, provided the High Admiral of Castile had similar jurisdiction in his district.

5. That he might then, and at all after times, contribute an eighth part of the expense in fitting out vessels to sail on this enterprise, and receive an eighth part of the profits.

Later, on April 30, 1492, Columbus was also given a letter of privilege, in which the dignities and prerogatives of viceroy and governor were made hereditary in his family, and he and his heirs were allowed to entitle themselves Don.

The seaport city of Palos, as punishment for some offense, had been ordered to furnish the Crown with 2 armed caravels. These ships the town was required to furnish within ten days, and to place them, with their crews, at the service of Columbus. He also set about procuring his vessel. All were to obey him implicitly, the only condition being that neither he nor they should go to St. George la Unia, nor any other Portuguese possession. All were commanded to furnish supplies at reasonable prices, and to any criminal willing to embark suspension of sentence was granted during the voyage and for two months after his return. At the same time the Queen appointed Diego Columbus page to her son Juan, the heir-apparent.

A third time Columbus appeared before the convent gate of La Rabida, and thence the prior accompanied him to Palos. Here a new discouragement awaited Columbus. Such dread of the unknown ocean prevailed among seafaring men that not one could be induced to volunteer, even though it should be an escape from prison. Weeks passed, in which the utmost influence of Columbus produced no result toward getting vessels or men for the expedition. Then came a royal mandate ordering the magistrates to press into service the vessels of any Spanish subject they might think most available, and compelling their officers and crews to sail under the new admiral. The executor of this command was to receive 200 maravedis a day while carrying it out, payment to come from those who refused to obey it. This order produced as little effect as the other. After eighteen years of effort to prevail upon governments to allow him to collect men and vessels, Columbus was likely to fail utterly because not a man was willing to risk life or treasure. He had hoped to borrow the eighth part which he had assumed to bear in the expense from Martin Alonzo Pinzon, the rich mariner who had espoused his cause so warmly in the convent. Finally, this man came forward with an offer to add to the loan Columbus asked a second vessel and his personal service as its commander. This put a somewhat new face on the matter. Two vessels were fitted out, one by Columbus and a second by Pinzon. A third was impressed by the authorities, under the royal mandate. But the trouble was not ended. The calkers, on being compelled to do over again work which they had purposely slighted, ran away, seamen deserted and hid, and ingenuity was taxed to evade the law and hinder the expedition. It was August before 3 little vessels, the size of river steamers of our day, only one of them decked, were ready to set sail, with 120 persons on board, all told.

When they crossed the bar of Saltes, Columbus was upon his flagship, the decked vessel he had fitted out, which he named the "Santa Maria," Martin Alonzo Pinzon commanded the "Pinta," the impressed vessel, while his brother, Francisco Martin, acted as pilot. The third vessel, the "Niña," furnished by the Pinzons, was commanded by a third brother, Vicente Yañez Pinzon.

On the first day out, Columbus began a description of the journey, in the following manner:

In the name of our Lord Jesus Christ. Whereas, Most Christian, High, Excellent, and Powerful Princes, King and Queen of Spain and of the Islands of the Sea, our Sovereigns, this present year, 1492, after your highnesses had terminated the war with the Moors reigning in Europe, the same having been brought to an end in the great city of Granada, where, on the second day of January, this present year, I saw the royal banners upon the towers of the Alhambra, which is the fortress of that city, and saw the Moorish king come out at the gate of the city and kiss the hand of your highnesses, and of the Prince, my sovereign; and in the present month, in consequence of

THE SANTA MARIA.

the information which I had given your highnesses respecting the countries of India and of a prince called Great Khan, which in our language signifies King of Kings; how, at many times, he and his predecessors had sent to Rome soliciting instructors who might teach him our holy faith, and the Holy Father had never granted his request, whereby great numbers of people were lost, believing in idolatry and doctrines of perdition. Your highnesses, as Catholic Christians and princes who love and promote the holy Christian faith, and are enemies of the doctrine of Mahomet and of all idolatry and heresy, determined to send me, Christopher Columbus, to the above-mentioned countries of India, to see the said princes, people, and territories, and to learn their disposition and the proper method of converting them to our holy faith; and, furthermore, directed that I should not proceed by land to the east, as is customary, but by a westerly route, in which direction we have hitherto no certain evidence that any one has gone. So, after having expelled the Jews from your dominions, your highnesses, in the same month of January, ordered me to proceed with a sufficient armament to the said regions of India, and for that purpose granted me great favors, and ennobled me that thenceforth I might call myself Don, and be high admiral of the sea, and perpetual viceroy and governor in all the islands and continents which I might discover and acquire, or which may hereafter be discovered and acquired in the ocean; and that this dignity should be inherited by my eldest son, and thus descend from degree to degree forever. Hereupon I left the city of Granada, on Saturday, the twelfth day of May, 1492, and proceeded to Palos, a seaport, where I armed 3 vessels, very fit for such an enterprise, and having provided myself with abundance of stores and seamen, I set sail from the port on Friday, the 3d of August, half an hour before sunrise, and steered for the Canary islands of your highnesses, which are in the said ocean, thence to take my departure and proceed till I arrived at the Indies, and perform the embassy of your highnesses to the princes there, and discharge the orders given me. For this purpose I determined to keep an account of the voyage, and to write down punctually everything we performed or saw from day to day, as will hereafter appear. Moreover, Sovereign Princes, besides describing every night the occurrences of the day, and every day those of the preceding night, I intend to draw up a nautical chart, which shall contain the several parts of the ocean and land in their proper situations; and also to compose a book to represent the whole by picture, with latitudes and longitudes, on all which accounts it behooves me to abstain from my sleep and make many trials in navigation, which things will demand much labor.

On the third day out the "Pinta" made a signal of distress, and reported that her rudder had been found broken and unshipped. The wind was blowing too hard to allow of the other vessels rendering any assistance to Pinzon, who had been put into this difficulty by the evident intention of the owners to unfit their caravel for the voyage, and thus secure their return before she had gone too far for their experience to be of avail in navigating her to Palos. But Pinzon had the broken rudder mended so that they could manage the vessel. The next day his device gave way, and the other ships were compelled to shorten sail while he secured the rudder firmly. Meantime, she had been found to be in such a leaky condition that Columbus resolved to leave her at the Canary islands and procure another caravel, and he announced that they were near those islands, from which opinion all the pilots dissented. On the morning of Aug. 9 they were sighted. For three weeks Columbus tried in vain to secure a ship; then a new rudder was made for the "Pinta," the lateen sails of the "Niña" were changed to square sails, and the little squadron again hoisted its canvas. While they were at the Canaries two events troubled Columbus. In sailing among the islands the crews came in sight of Teneriffe in active eruption, and were so filled with terror and gloomy predictions that it required the utmost effort to keep them from desertion. Columbus explained to them the supposed cause, and recalled descriptions of Mount Etna and other volcanoes. A far more serious danger presented itself in the report that reached him of Portuguese vessels that were waiting to attack his ships. He set out once more, on Sept. 6, but for three days his canvas fluttered idly. On Sept. 9 a breeze sprang up at sunrise, and soon the only enemy he had to fear was the one with whom he was embarked. After land was really lost to sight the hardiest among the crew shed tears like children, and filled the air with wailing. Their commander drew for their comfort the pictures that had so long warmed his own imagination—of vast splendor, gold, gems, and

precious stones—to be found in the islands of the Indian sea. He sent orders to the Pinzons that, in case any accident should separate the vessels, they were to sail due westward for 700 leagues and then lie by from midnight until daylight, as at that distance they might look for land. At the same time, in order to guard against the effect of disappointment if his hopes failed of realization, he began to keep two reckonings, one giving the real distance traveled, the other making each day's journey shorter by some leagues, that the minds of his men might be less appalled as darkness fell and they realized each night the spaces that lay between them and home. On Sept. 11,

COLUMBUS'S ARMOR.

the sight of the floating mast of a wrecked vessel alarmed them, and on the 13th Columbus himself was agitated on seeing that there was a variation in the needle; at nightfall it varied half a point from the north star, and still more on the following morning. For three days he watched the increasing change with wondering silence before the pilots of the other vessels observed it. Their terror was extreme; they had lost the one guide in the trackless waste. Tasking his utmost grasp of science for an explanation, he told them that the direction of the needle was not to the north star, which really had its revolutions and changes, going daily in a circle round the pole. They had such faith in his knowledge, that this description of the phenomenon quieted them, and he seems himself to have permanently accepted it. On the 14th a heron and a water wagtail hung about the ships, to the great delight of the sailors, who thought that neither of these birds ventured far out to sea. On the night of the 15th a meteor, which Columbus describes as a great flame of fire that seemed to fall from the sky into the sea a few leagues distant, startled and frightened the sailors.

They were now come to the region of the trade winds, and were carried swiftly and steadily on, without changing sail for many days. They began to see great fields of weeds of various colors, drifting westward. From one patch Columbus captured a live crab. They saw white birds and tunny fish, and Columbus called to mind Aristotle's description of the weedy sea from which mariners had turned back. On Sept. 18 the soft breeze from the east was filling every sail, and the crews, who had believed that the weeds indicated land, were more cheerful, when a hail from the "Pinto" brought news that Pinzon felt sure, from the bird flights, that there was land to the north. At sunset the clouds lay like islands, and there was a general clamor that the course be changed to that direction. But westward, the admiral had told them, the land should lie, and westward he must sail, or be at the mercy of every conjecture of the pilots. The following day there were showers, and two pelicans came on board. It was thought that these birds would keep close to land, but the line at 200 fathoms showed no bottom. As the days passed and all signs failed, the uneasy men began to grow louder in their murmurs. The favorable wind, they said, always blew from the east, and they could not return. On the 20th the wind veered to the southwest, and it blew from that quarter gently for many days; then they said that the calm sea in which they moved would never be disturbed, and they should perish amid stagnant and shoreless water. This fear took such hold upon them that Columbus was about to despair, when on the 25th came a heavy, windless swelling of the sea, and he confides to his journal the fact that the strange sight dispelled the fear of calm. Meantime discontent had grown almost to mutiny, and Columbus was aware that a project had been broached to fling him into the sea and persuade the other commanders to return. One calm night, when they were driven once more by a gentle wind from the east and were sailing close together, Martin Alonzo Pinzon cried from his lookout, "Land! land!" and the glad news was confirmed by many eyes when they gazed into the southwest. Columbus threw himself upon his knees, and Pinzon repeated the "Gloria in Excelsis," in which he was joined by all the crews. So sure were the lookouts, that Columbus ordered the vessels' heads turned in that direction; but the vision faded with the light. Columbus sailed once more to the west, and deeper gloom fell on the disappointed mariners.

By Oct. 1 the murmurs had again grown to menaces, but the next day there were so many signs of land that they changed their feeling to eagerness. A pension of thirty crowns was to be given by the Crown to the man who first sighted land. The false alarms became so frequent, and were so serious in their effects, that Columbus ordered that should any one make such declaration and land not be discovered within three days he should forfeit all claim to reward in future. On Oct. 6 Pinzon was so eager for the admiral to alter his course again that, fearing he might leave the company, Columbus issued an order directing the vessels to keep near him at sunrise and sunset. The next day, so certain was a sailor on board the "Niña" that he saw land that the flag was hoisted and the gun fired, and the crews were again filled with joyous excitement, only to be once more disappointed. The next day Columbus thought he saw sufficient indication that land lay in that direction, from the sunset flights of birds, that he determined to steer southwest for at least two days. At the end of that time his hope increased. Birds, fish, herbage, began to fly or float about them. But the impatient crew had lost faith completely, and they became clamorous. When gentle words failed, Columbus sternly told them that to the Indies he was bound at the Queen's command, and to the Indies they must

go. His situation was now desperate, his crew being in open mutiny; but the signs of land were increasing also. A freshly broken branch with thorn berries floated by, a carved staff, a small board, and a reed; and all thoughts were turned to dreams of land once more. After the evening singing of the "Salve Regina," Columbus addressed the company. He reminded them that when they left the Canaries he had promised that after sailing westward seven hundred leagues they should lie to before midnight each night. He added that he felt so certain of coming to land that night that a strict lookout must be kept, and he promised to add to the offer of the sovereigns a doublet of velvet to the man who first beheld land. As Columbus stood in the gathering twilight he saw a light at a distance. Fearful of trusting his hope, he called one of his company, who distinctly saw it. Then he summoned another, and from that time many on board saw the fitful gleam, but thought little of it. To Columbus it was proof not only of land, but of inhabitants. At two o'clock in the morning a gun from the "Pinta" gave tidings of the discovery of land by Rodrigo de Triana. It was then dimly seen by all, lying about two leagues distant. Sail was taken in to await the morning.

On Friday, Oct. 12, Columbus landed and took possession of the new-found country in the name of Ferdinand and Isabella, and named it San Salvador. This ceremony concluded, he called upon all present to take the oath of allegiance to him as admiral and viceroy of their majesties. Not a man but rendered hearty obedience, and the most mutinous were among the first to crave pardon. Columbus had clothed himself in scarlet and bore a sword in sign of his office. He supposed himself to have landed on the extremity of India, and he gave to the natives the name of Indians. San Salvador, it is now believed, was the present Watling Island. Thence their course would be drawn to Rum Cay (his Santa Maria de la Concepcion), to Clarence Harbor, on Long Island (his Fernandina), to Cape Verd (his Isabella, also on Long Island), to Fortune Island (his Islas de Arena), to Cuba (his Juan), and to Santo Domingo (his Hispaniola). This, in outline, is the route last traced out; in the course of its windings he touched at many points, and wrote in detail of them all. (See article on his first landfall, in "Annual Cyclopædia" for 1891, page 181.)

Of Isabella he wrote: "It seems as if one would desire never to depart from hence. I know not where first to go, nor are my eyes ever weary of gazing on the beautiful verdure." Of Cuba he said: "It is the most beautiful island that eyes ever beheld, full of excellent ports and profound rivers." Had Columbus come in search of tropical luxuriance and beauty, of a gentle and kindly though savage race, and a place in which industry might found a colony and build its home, there could have been no happier spot. But he had promised himself and the waiting sovereigns to find gold, pearls, spices, an ancient civilization, and a land where Spain could make an easy conquest, gaining thereby wealth and honor. He was always looking for signs of Eastern splendor, for news of the great Kublai Khan. At one time he sent Hebrew and Chaldaic scholars as interpreters to the Oriental prince whom he imagined to be described as their chief by the simple Indians, and they returned disgusted from the hut of a naked savage. In November, while coasting along Cuba, which to the day of his death he believed to be the mainland of Asia, he was deserted by Pinzon, who in the night steered the "Pinta" toward an island which the Indians had described to him as full of gold. While sailing on one of the rivers, he wrote to their majesties: "The amenity of this river, and the clearness of the water, through which the sand at the bottom may be seen; the multitude of palm trees of various forms, the highest and most beautiful that I have met with, and an infinity of other great

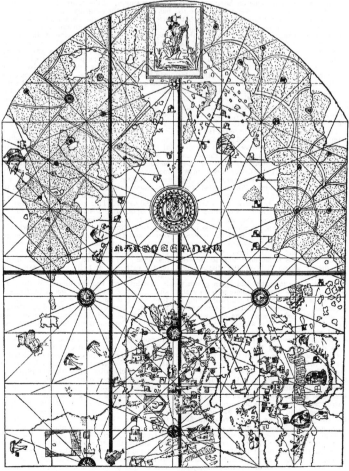

CHART DRAWN IN 1500 BY JUAN DE LA CÁSA, COLUMBUS'S PILOT.

and green trees; the birds in rich plumage, and the verdure of the fields, render this country, most serene princes, of such marvelous beauty that it surpasses all others in charms and graces as the day doth the night in luster."

Meantime the Indians were always talking of the riches of an island which they pointed out, and, sailing in search of it, on Dec. 12 Columbus arrived at Santo Domingo, and, finding a good harbor, he took possession with the usual ceremonies, including the planting of a cross. He coasted around the shores of Hispaniola, as he had done about those of Cuba, trading with the natives for food, but seeking especially for knowledge of the country and of its resources, and every now and then being rewarded by gold.

On Christmas eve Columbus set sail from Port Concepcion, in Santo Domingo, to visit a friendly chieftain, for by this time he had had much intercourse with the natives. The sea was calm as glass, the wind just filling the sails gently, and an exploring party had reported no rocks or shoals. Columbus, worn out with several nights of vigilance, left the steersman at the helm. No sooner were the admiral's eyes closed than the watch, including the steersman, who gave the helm in charge of a boy, were also wrapped in slumber. They were waked by the boy's cry for help, and Columbus was the first on deck. The current had swept the vessel among breakers, and she was soon a wreck.

After this accident the seamen pointed out to Columbus the distress and danger that would attend the voyage if the company of two vessels attempted to return in one, and many of them begged to be left in Hispaniola. This caused Columbus to conceive the idea of establishing a colony. Wood from the wrecked vessel furnished material for a fortress, which they immediately set about building. This was in Columbus's mind more as a means of maintaining discipline among the Spaniards than as defense against the natives, who had shown themselves so gentle. Already the license felt among the men since the shipwreck to wander about and plunder had shown itself. When the fort of the Nativity was finished, there were many volunteers to remain in it until Columbus should return from a visit to Spain, where he was anxious to carry the great news, in which he thought that already the deserting commander might have preceded him. Arrangements were made for the care of the colony, and men of various trades, a ship's boat, seeds of many kinds, and an ample supply of trinkets for Indian traffic, were left with them. all being placed in charge of men whom the admiral deemed most suitable. They were to collect gold, precious stones, and cotton from the natives.

On Jan. 4, 1493, Columbus set sail for the return voyage, and on the following day the "Pinta" was seen from their masthead. As Columbus was then beating against adverse wind, he turned and, signaling the "Pinta" to follow, sought safe anchorage. Pinzon's excuse that the absence was unintentional was accepted, although not believed. The vessel was his own. Many of the mariners on both ships were his relatives or retainers, and Columbus was not in a position to rebuke the conduct as he thought

it merited, although he learned later that Pinzon had gone in search of an island described by Indians as full of gold, had failed to find it, but for three weeks had been trading with the Indians for a large quantity of gold, half of which he kept, and the other half he divided among his men. He had stolen four Indian men and two girls, to sell as slaves in Spain. Columbus also learned that Pinzon had been on Santo Domingo when the wreck occurred, news of which he had received from Indians. The gold gathered on this expedition Columbus did not interfere with; but he compelled the return of the six natives, a move which evoked much contemptuous conduct from the angry commander.

Before passing out to sea Columbus landed on another island, where he found a much more warlike race. The trade winds that had proved so friendly to his outward voyage were, as the sailors feared, hard enemies to fight on the return. The expedition made little progress, and the "Pinta," which Pinzon had neglected to repair while in port, sailed so badly, even in a favorable wind, that many delays were caused by waiting on its movements. A whole month was spent in beating about before they passed out of the influence of the trades. Columbus then took a straight course for Spain. Great disputes arose among the pilots as to their whereabouts. Columbus kept his own counsel, entirely willing to be the only one whose clear vision and careful study had taught him the true path to the New World. By referring to his minute notes, he believed himself to be off the Azores when the pilots were looking for the Madeiras. On Feb. 12 a tempest of terrific violence burst upon the vessels. Columbus kept as much as possible to the northeast, arid signaled that course to the "Pinta"; but her weak foremast made her unmanageable, and she was soon lost to sight, scudding before the gale. Despair fell upon the almost helpless crew. Their leaking and crazy vessel was the plaything of waves such as they had never seen. Columbus ordered as many beans as there were persons on board to be put into a cup, one of them having a cross cut upon it, and every man vowed that, should he draw the marked bean, he would make a pilgrimage to Santa Maria de Guadalupe, bearing a wax taper of 5 pounds weight. The first to put in his hand was Columbus, and the lot fell upon him. Another lot was prepared, in which Heaven was propitiated by the promise of a pilgrimage to Our Lady of Loretto, and the bean was drawn by a seaman, whose expenses the admiral assured him he would pay. A third lot, cast for a pilgrimage to Santa Clara de Moguer, to perform solemn mass, and to watch all night in the chapel, fell again to Columbus. The tempest continued to rage, and the men made a solemn vow that, should they reach land, they would go in procession, barefooted and in their shirts, to offer up prayers and thanksgivings in some church at the shrine of Mary. Besides these, each man bound himself separately to offer to his favorite saint. They still tossed helpless in the storm; and at length Columbus caused the casks, which were now emptied of the drinking water taken for the voyage, to be filled with sea water, which gave a measure of relief by steadying the vessel somewhat. Of his feeling at this period Columbus wrote in the following words to the King and Queen:

I could have supported this evil fortune with less grief had my person alone been in jeopardy, since I am debtor for my life to the Supreme Creator, and have at other times been within a step of death. But it was a cause of infinite sorrow and trouble to think that, after having been illuminated from on high with faith and certainty to undertake this enterprise, after having victoriously achieved it, and when on the point of convincing my opponents, and securing to your highnesses great glory and vast increase of dominion, it should please the Divine Majesty to defeat all by my death. It would have been more supportable also had I not been accompanied by others who had been drawn on by my persuasions, and who in their distress cursed not only the hour of their coming, but the fear inspired by my words, which prevented their turning back as they had at various times determined. Above all, my grief was doubled when I thought of my two sons, whom I had left at school in Cordova, destitute, in a strange land, without any testimony of the services rendered by their father, which, if known, might have inclined your highnesses to befriend them. And, although, on the one hand, I was comforted by a faith that the Deity would not permit a work of such great exaltation to his Church, wrought through so many troubles and contradictions, to remain imperfect; yet, on the other hand, I reflected on my sins, for which he might intend as a punishment that I should be deprived of the glory which would redound to me in this world.

During this anxious time Columbus wrote on parchment two short accounts of his voyage and discoveries, and of his having taken possession in the name of the King and Queen of Spain, and offering 1,000 ducats to the person who would convey the paper to them. One of these he put into a waxed cloth, in the middle of a cake of wax, which he put into a barrel and threw into the sea. The other one he rolled up in a similar fashion, placing the barrel on the poop of the vessel. On the 14th the storm abated somewhat, and on the 15th a sailor on the maintop shouted "Land!" amid the mad demonstrations of the crew. It proved, as Columbus had believed, to be one of the Azores. They were making for it, when the wind changed, and for two days they were tossed about by tempestuous waves. It was not until the 18th that they were able to anchor. The day that land was seen Columbus made this entry in a letter, afterward sent to Luis de Santangel.

On board the caravel, off the Azores, Feb. 15, 1493. This is ever certain, that God grants to those that walk in his ways the performance of things that seem impossible, and this enterprise might in a signal manner have been considered so, for although many have talked of these countries, yet it has been nothing more than conjecture. Our Saviour having vouchsafed this victory to our most illustrious King and Queen, and their kingdoms, famous for so eminent a deed, all Christendom should rejoice and give solemn thanks to the Holy Trinity for the addition of as many people to our holy faith, and also for the temporal profit accruing not only to Spain but to all Christians.

The inhabitants of St. Mary's, the island to which they were come, were amazed that they had outlived a storm which had raged for fifteen days, and still more so at the news they brought. The men from the "Niña" were kept on shore, while the governor sent out provisions for the

starving voyagers. The next morning Columbus sent half the company ashore, to perform their vow at a chapel not far inland. He and the other half were to await their return. But the barefooted and half-clad procession were no sooner occupied with their devotions than they were surrounded and made prisoners. As time passed and they did not return, Columbus began to fear mischief from the Portuguese authorities. He changed his position to one that commanded the chapel, and saw a body of armed men, who immediately entered a boat and went to the caravel. Columbus armed his men, but kept them out of sight. They were principally landsmen and Indians, as the seamen had gone first to perform the vow. After an angry colloquy between the governor and Columbus, during which the latter showed his letters patent and threatened vengeance by his Government, and the Portuguese said haughtily that he was acting under orders from the King, they parted. Tempests again drove the ships to sea, and for two days they were in more deadly peril than before. When the storm abated the governor retreated from his position and released the prisoners, the truth being that his orders were to detain Columbus, whom he now found to be in high office and on his guard.

Still in an angry sea, but with a favoring wind, on the 24th they set sail for Spain. Storm followed storm, until, at midnight on March 2, the caravel was struck by a squall which tore her sail to ribbons and threatened to ingulf her. In the blackness a vow was again made and a lot cast. One of the company was to perform a pilgrimage to Santa Maria de la Ceuta, at Huelva. The lot fell upon Columbus. The whole crew vowed to fast on bread and water the following Saturday should they come to land. But the storm continued with unabated fury, and when, on the night of March 3, a seaman cried "Land!" it terrified them still more. All night they expected to be dashed helpless on the rocks. Morning found them off the rock of Cintra, and of the two perils the ocean seemed so much more formidable than the Portuguese that Columbus gave the order to run into the mouth of the Tagus for shelter. There they told him that they had watched the caravel with intense anxiety; that the oldest mariner had no memory of such a stormy winter; that few vessels had left the port, and that wreckage had been strewed along the coast. There seemed small hope for Pinzon and the disabled "Pinta." As soon as the caravel was safe, Columbus wrote to the King and Queen, and added this postscript to his letter to Santangel:

Being at sea near Castile, the wind rose with such fury from the south and southeast that I was obliged to bear away and run into the port of Lisbon, where I escaped by the greatest miracle in the world. From this place I shall write to their highnesses. Throughout the Indies I always found the weather like May. I made the passage thither in seventy-one days, and back in forty-eight, during thirteen of which number I was driven about by storms. The seamen here inform me that there was never known a winter in which so many ships were lost.

He also wrote to ask permission to take his vessel to Lisbon, the mouth of the Tagus being sparsely settled by adventurers, and rumors that he had on board great quantities of gold being spread broadcast at once.

When the news of the arrival reached the court King John sent for Columbus. As the discoverer unfolded his enterprise the King was filled with wrath that he had turned a deaf ear to Columbus, and he intimated that he thought it quite possible that these so-called new lands were countries appertaining to Portugal.

The weather having moderated, on March 13 Columbus put to sea, and two days later he crossed the bar of Saltes and dropped anchor once more in the harbor of Palos. When the news was known in the town the bells were rung, shops closed, business suspended, and a procession was formed to march to the church and give public thanks. While the rejoicings were in progress a battered little vessel entered the harbor. It was the "Pinta," and its commander, Pinzon, on learning the cause of the town's commotion, sailed away and landed privately. Believing that Columbus had perished, he had written to the sovereigns, claiming for himself the discovery, and asking permission to go to court to report it. When the deserved and severe rebuke came in answer, Pinzon's chagrin and shame added severity to his illness, and he died.

The triumphant arrival of Columbus at the Spanish court at Barcelona exceeded in magnificence all the triumphs of that grand court; and when, sitting at their request in presence of Ferdinand and Isabella, he recounted the wonders of the new land, the hour for which he had lived seemed to have arrived. The report that he gave may be found in part in a letter which he had been writing to Luis de Santangel, and part of which is copied below:

The first of these islands I named San Salvador, in commemoration of our Holy Saviour, who has in a wonderful manner granted all our success. The Indians call it Guanahani. To the second I gave the name of Santa Maria de Concepcion, to the third that of Fernandina, to the fourth that of Isabella, to the fifth that of Juana, thus giving each island a new name. I coasted along the island of Juana to the west, and found it of such extent that I took it for a continent, and imagined it must be the country of Cathay. Villages were seen near the seacoast, but as I discovered no large cities, and could not obtain any communication with the inhabitants, who all fled at our approach, I continued on west, thinking I should not fail in the end to meet with great towns and cities; but having gone many leagues without such success, and finding that the coast carried me to the north, whither I disliked to proceed on account of the impending winter, I resolved to return to the south,

and accordingly put about and arrived at an excellent harbor in the island, where I dispatched two men into the country to ascertain whether the king or any large cities were in the neighborhood. They traveled three days and met with innumerable small settlements of the natives, but did not succeed in finding any sover-

OLD ENGRAVING (1500) SHOWING COLUMBUS LANDING, AND THE KING OF SPAIN SENDING SHIPS TO AMERICA.

eign of the territory, and so returned. I made out to learn from some Indians, whom I had before taken, that this was an island, and proceeded along the coast to the east 107 leagues, till I reached the extremity. I then discovered another island east of this, 18 leagues distant, which I named Española, and followed its northern coast, as I did that of Juana, for the space of 178 leagues to the east. All these countries are of surpassing excellence, and in particular Juana, which contains abundance of fine harbors, excelling any in Christendom, as also many large and beautiful rivers. The land is high, and exhibits chains of tall mountains, which seem to reach to the skies, and surpass beyond comparison the isle of Cetrefrey. These display themselves in all manner of beautiful shapes. They are accessible in every part, and covered with a vast variety of lofty trees, which it appears to me never lose their foliage, as we found them fair and verdant as in May in Spain. Some were covered with blossoms, some with fruit, and others in different stages, according to their nature. The nightingale and a thousand other sorts of birds were singing in the month of November wherever I went. There are palm trees in these countries of 6 or 8 sorts, which are surprising to see on account of their diversity from ours; but, indeed, this is the case with respect to the other trees, as well as the fruits and weeds. Beautiful forests of pines are likewise found, and fields of vast extent. Here are also honey, and fruits of a thousand sorts, and birds of every variety. The lands contain mines of metals, and inhabitants without number. The island of Española is pre-eminent in beauty and excellence, offering to the sight the most enchanting view of mountains, plains, rich fields for cultivation, and pastures for flocks of all sorts, with situations for towns and settlements. Its harbors are of such excellence that their description would not gain belief; and the like may be said of its abundance of large and fine rivers, most of which abound in gold. The trees, fruits, and plants of this island differ considerably from those of Juana, and the place contains a great deal of spicery, and extensive mines of gold and other metals. The people of this island, and of all the others which I have become acquainted with, go naked as they were born, although some of the women wear at the loins a leaf or bit of cotton cloth, which they prepare for that purpose. They do not possess iron, steel, or weapons, and seem to have no inclination for the latter, being timorous to the last degree. They have an instrument consisting of a cane, taken while in seed, and headed with a sharp stick, but they never venture to use it. Many times I have sent 2 or 3 men to one of their villages, when whole multitudes have taken to flight at the sight of them, and this was not by reason of any injury we ever wrought them, for at every place where I have made any stay and obtained communication with them I have made them presents of cloth and such other things as I possessed, without demanding anything in return. After they have shaken off their fear of us they display a frankness and liberality in their behavior which no one would believe without witnessing it. No request of anything from them is ever refused, but they rather invite acceptance of what they possess, and manifest such a generosity that they would give away their own hearts. Let the article be of great or small value, they offer it readily, and receive anything which is tendered in return with perfect content. I forbade my men to purchase their goods with such worthless things as bits of platters and broken glass, or thongs of leather, although when they got possession of one of these they estimated it as highly as the greatest jewel in the world. The sailors would buy of them for a scrap of leather pieces of gold weighing two castellanos and a half, and even more of this metal for something still less in value. The whole of an Indian's property might be purchased of him for a few blancas. This would amount to 2 or 3 castellanos' value of gold, or the same of cotton thread. Even the pieces of broken hoops from the casks they would receive in barter for their articles, with the greatest simplicity. I thought such traffic unjust, and therefore forbade it. I presented them with a variety of things, in order to secure their affection, and that they may become Christians, and enter into the services of their highnesses and the Castilian nation, and also aid us in procuring such things as they possess and we stand in need of. They are not idolaters, nor have they any sort of religion, except believing that power and goodness are in heaven, from which place they entertained a firm persuasion that I had come with my ships and men. On this account wherever we met them they showed us the greatest reverence after they had overcome their fear. Such conduct can not be ascribed to their want of understanding, for they are a people of much ingenuity, and navigate all those seas, giving a remarkably good account of every part, but do not say they have met with people in clothes, or ships like ours. On my arrival at the Indies I took by force from the first island I came to a few of the inhabitants, in order that they might learn our language and assist us in our discoveries. We succeeded ere long in understanding one another by signs and words, and I have them now with me, still thinking we have come from heaven, as I learn by much conversation which I have had with them. This they were the first to proclaim wherever we went, and the other natives would run from house to house and from village to village, crying out, "Come and see the men from heaven!" so that all the inhabitants, both men and women, having gathered confidence, hastened toward us, bringing food and drink, which they presented to us with a surprising good will. In all the islands they possess a vast number of canoes, which are of various sizes, each one constructed of a single log and shaped like a fusta. Some of these are as large as fustas of 18 oars, although narrow, on account of the material. I have seen 60 or 80 men in one of these canoes, and each man with his paddle. They are rowed with a swiftness which no boat can equal, and serve the purpose of transporting goods among these innumerable islands. I did not observe any great diversity in the appearance of the inhabitants in the different parts of these countries, nor in their customs or language, for, singularly enough, in this last respect they all understand one another, on which account I hope their highnesses will exert themselves for the conversion of these people to our holy faith, in which undertaking they will be found very tractable. I have already related that I proceeded along the coast of Juana for 107 leagues from west to east, from which I dare affirm this island to be larger than England and Scotland together; for, besides the extent of which I coasted, there are 2 unexplored provinces to the west, in one of which, called Cibao, are people with tails. These districts can not be less than 50 or sixty leagues in extent, according as I learn from my Indians, who are acquainted with all these islands. The other island, called Española, is more extensive than the division of Spain from Coruña to Fontarabia, as I traversed one side of it for the distance of 138 leagues from west to east. This is a most beautiful and, although I have taken possession of them all in the name of their highnesses, and even one remains in their power, and as much at their disposal as the kingdoms of Castile, and although they are all furnished with every thing that can be desired, yet the preference must be given to Española, on account of the mines of gold which it possesses, and the facilities it offers for trade with continents and countries both on this side and beyond that of the Great Khan, which traffic will be great and profitable. I have accordingly taken possession of a place which I named Villa de Navidad, and built there a fortress, which is at present complete and furnished with a sufficient number of men for the enterprise. With these I have left arms, ammunition, and provisions for more than a year, a boat, and expert men in all necessary arts. The king of the country has shown great friendship toward us, and held himself a brother to me. Even should their friendly inclinations change and become hostile, yet nothing can be feared from them, as they are totally ignorant in the world. The small number of men whom I have left there would be sufficient to ravage the whole territory, and they may remain there with perfect safety, taking proper care of themselves. In all the islands, as far as I could observe, the men are content with a single wife each, except that a chief or king has as many as 20. The women appear to do more work than the men, and as to their property, I have been unable to learn that they have any private possessions, but apparently all things are in common among them, especially provisions. In none of the islands hitherto visited have I found any people of monstrous appearance, according to the expectation of some, but the inhabitants are all of very pleasing aspect, not resembling the blacks of Guinea, as their hair is straight and their color lighter. The rays of the sun are here very powerful, although the latitude is 26°, but in the islands where there are high mountains the winter is cold, which the inhabitants endure from habit and the use of hot spices with their food. An island in the second strait at the entrance to the Indies, is peopled with inhabitants who eat live flesh, and are esteemed very ferocious in all the other parts. They possess many canoes, with which they scour all the islands of India, robbing and capturing all they meet. They are not of a more deformed appearance than the others, except that they wear their hair long like women, and use bows and arrows, which last are made of cane and pointed with a stick for want of iron, which they do not possess. They exchange their wives, and although these are esteemed a fierce people among the neighboring islands, yet I do not regard them more than the others, as most of the inhabitants of these regions are great cowards. One of these islands is peopled solely by women, who practice no feminine occupations, but exercise the bow and arrow, and cover themselves with plates of copper, which metal they have in abundance. There is another island, as I am assured, larger than Española, in which the inhabitants are without hair, and which contains a great abundance of gold. In confirmation of these and other accounts, I have brought the Indians along with me for testimonies. In conclusion, and to speak only of what I have performed, this voyage so hastily dispatched will, as their highnesses may see, enable any desirable quantity of gold to be obtained by a very small assistance afforded me on their part. At present there are within reach: spices and cotton to as great an amount as they can desire, aloe in a great abundance, and equal store of mastic, a production nowhere else found except in Greece and the island of Scio, where it is sold at such a price as the possessors choose. To these may be added slaves, as numerous as may be wished for. Besides, I have, as I think, discovered rhubarb and cinnamon, and expect countless other things of value will be found by the men whom I left there, as I made it a point not to stay in any one place while the wind enabled me to proceed upon the voyage, except at Villa de Navidad, where I left them well established.

Honors fell thick and fast about the head of the discoverer. Telling of a ceremonious banquet that was given him, the Italian historian Benzoni relates the well-known anecdote of the egg. Recent historians ignore the story, thinking it trivial, probably, if not untrue. It seems to be authentic, and its value is matter of opinion. How the moral, which needs to be so often repeated, that what is accomplished seems easy, could be more succinctly put, it is hard to fancy. Perhaps it was a relative of Pinzon's who asked Columbus whether he thought, in case he had not made the discovery, there were not other men who could. Taking an egg, he asked the company to make it stand on end. Each in turn gave it up as impossible. Striking it gently on the table, Columbus broke the shell just enough to enable it to stand. Any one could make it stand, but no one had done so.

Meantime Columbus was urged to hasten his return, and he was none the less eager. The Court applied for a Papal bull announcing Spain's right to the new territory and defining the Portuguese possessions. Without further ado, the Pope drew an imaginary line through the middle of the Atlantic, from north to south, and gave all discovered to the east of it to Portugal and all to the west of it to Spain.

Isabella manifested the greatest desire for the conversion of the Indians, and for that purpose she sent 12 priests, among whom was Bernardo Boil, a Benedictine monk. The natives brought by Columbus were baptized with great ceremony, the King, the Queen, and young Prince Juan acting as sponsors. They were to return to assist in the work of conversion, and Isabella charged that all natives be treated with the utmost kindness, and that severe punishment be inflicted on any Spaniard who should be guilty of treating them wrongfully in any way. Before Columbus left the court the former provisional agreement was confirmed, and he was granted every right and title he had ever claimed, with power to invest another with the same authority in his absence.

Men were as eager now to go as before they had been reluctant, and many were re-

fused. Finally, there were collected three large ships and 14 caravels filled with a joyous company, many of them from the highest families in Spain. Among them was Don Alonzo de Ojeda, son of the Grand Inquisitor of Spain. They were supplied with husbandmen, miners, carpenters, and various other mechanics, animals, grain, seeds, plants, vines, sugar-cane, grafts, saplings, and everything necessary for trading with the Indians. Some days before setting sail Columbus drew up a paper which runs as follows:

Most high and mighty Sovereigns: In obedience to your highnesses' commands, and with submission to superior judgment, I will say whatever occurs to me in reference to the colonization and commerce of the island of Española, and of the other islands, both those already discovered and those that may be discovered hereafter.

In the first place, as regards the island of Española, inasmuch as the number of colonists who desire to go thither amounts to 2,000, owing to the land being safer and better for farming and trading, and because it will serve as a place to which they can return and from which they can carry on trade with the neighboring islands:

Item. That in the said island there shall be founded 3 or 4 towns, situated in the most convenient places, and that the settlers who are there be assigned to the aforesaid places and towns.

Item. That, for the better and more speedy colonization of the said island, no one shall have liberty to collect gold in it except those who have taken out colonists' papers and have built houses for their abode in the town in which they are, that they may live united and in greater safety.

Item. That each town shall have its alcalde or alcaldes, and its notary public, as is the use and custom in Castile.

Item. That there shall be a church and parish priests or friars to administer the sacraments, to perform divine worship, and for the conversion of the Indians.

Item. That none of the colonists shall go to seek gold without a license from the governor or alcalde of the town where he lives; and that he must first take oath to return to the place whence he sets out, for the purpose of registering faithfully all the gold he may have found, and to return once a month or once a week, as the time may have been set for him, to render account and show the quantity of said gold; and that this shall be written, done by the notary before the alcalde, or, if it seems better, that a friar or priest, deputed for the purpose, shall also be present.

Item. That the gold thus brought in shall be smelted immediately and stamped with some mark that shall distinguish each town; and that the portion which belongs to your highnesses shall be weighed, and given and consigned to each alcalde in his own town, and registered by the above-mentioned priest or friar, so that it shall not pass through the hands of one person alone, and there shall be no opportunity to conceal the truth.

Item. That all gold that may be found without the mark of one of the said towns, in the possession of any one who has once registered in accordance with the above order, shall be taken as forfeited, and that the accuser shall have one portion of it and your highnesses the other.

Item. That 1 per centum of all the gold that may be found shall be set aside for building churches and adorning the same, and for the support of the priests or friars belonging to them; and if it should be thought proper to pay anything to the alcaldes or notaries for their services or for insuring the faithful performance of their duties, that this amount shall be sent to the governor or treasurer who may be appointed there by your highnesses.

Item. As regards the division of the gold and the

share that ought to be reserved for your highnesses, this, in my opinion, must be left to the aforesaid governor and treasurer, because it will have to be greater or less, according to the quantity of gold that may be found. Or, should it seem preferable, your highnesses might, for the space of one year, take one half and the collector the other, and a better arrangement for the division be made afterward.

Item. That if the said alcaldes or notaries shall commit or be privy to any fraud, punishment shall be provided; and the same for the colonists who shall not have declared all the gold they have.

Item. That in the said island there shall be a treasurer, with a clerk to assist him, who shall receive all the gold belonging to your highnesses; and the alcaldes and notaries of the town shall each keep a record of what they deliver to the said treasurer.

Item. As in the eagerness to get gold every one will wish naturally to engage in its search in preference to any other employment, it seems to me that the privilege of going to look for gold ought to be withheld during some portion of each year, that there may be opportunity to have the other business necessary for the island performed.

Item. In regard to the discovery of new countries, I think permission should be granted to all that wish to go, and more liberality used in the matter of the fifth, making the tax easier in order that many may be disposed to go on voyage.

I will now give my opinion about ships going to the said island of Española and the order that should be maintained; and that is, that the said ships should only be allowed to discharge in one or two ports designated for the purpose, and should register there whatever cargo they bring or unload; and when the time for their departure comes, that they should sail from these same ports and register all the cargo they take in, that nothing may be concealed.

Item. In reference to the transportation of gold from the island to Castile, that all of it should be taken on board the ship, both that belonging to your highnesses and the property of every one else; that it should all be placed in one chest with two locks, with their keys, and that the master of the vessel keep one key and some person selected by the governor and treasurer the other; that there should come with the gold, for a testimony, a list of all that has been put into the said chest, properly marked, so that each owner may receive his own; and that for the faithful performance of this duty, if any gold whatsoever is found outside of the said chest in any way, be it little or much, it shall be forfeited to your highnesses.

Item. That all the ships that come from the said island shall be obliged to make their proper discharge in the port of Cadiz, and that no person shall debark or other person be permitted to go on board until the ship has been visited by the person or persons deputed for that purpose in the said city by your highnesses, to whom the master shall show all that he carries and exhibit the manifest of all the cargo, that it may be seen and examined if the said ship brings anything hidden and not known at the time of lading.

Item. That the chest in which the said gold has been carried shall be opened in the presence of the magistrates of the said city of Cadiz and of the person deputed for that purpose by y ur highnesses, and his own property be given to each owner. I beg your highnesses to hold me in your protection; and I remain, praying our Lord God for your highnesses' lives and the increase of much greater states,

S.

S. A. S.
X M Y
Xpo FERENS.

On Sept. 25, 1493, the second expedition sailed from the port of Cadiz, and on Nov. 2 Columbus announced that they might soon look for land.

On the following day they sighted a lofty island, which he named Dominica, the day being Sunday. As he could find no good anchorage at Dominica, Columbus coasted about among the Antilles, stopping at an island which he named Guadeloupe. Although there were a few evidences of greater advance in skill among the natives of this island, he became convinced that they were cannibals, and felt no small alarm on finding that the captain and 8 men from one of the caravels were missing from the fleet. For days, impatient as he was to reach the colony, Columbus waited, firing guns and sending out searching parties to find the men. At length, when they were given up for lost, to the joy of all they appeared. To pass so decided a breach of discipline would be fatal to future order, and Columbus put the captain under arrest and reduced the rations of the men.

With the most eager anticipations they drew near La Navidad. It was too dark to attempt its dangerous entrance, but guns were fired and every eye and ear strained to catch sight or sound of answering signal. The stillness was unbroken. About midnight a canoe came out to the vessels and its occupant asked for the admiral. Columbus came to his vessel's side and in the darkness recognized the friendly Indian chief, Guacanigari, who had brought him a present of 2 masks ornamented with gold. In answer to Columbus's eager inquiry for the Spaniards, he replied that some had died of sickness, others had quarreled and killed one another, others had gone off to another part of the island, where they had Indian wives. He said that Caonabo had burned his village and ravaged the country. The fort was in ruins, and garments and utensils and several dead bodies were found, but not a trace of life.

Columbus immediately looked for a site for a new colony, and finding one near Monti Christi, he called the place Isabella, and began the work of building. Streets and squares were laid out, and a church and storehouse were built of stone. Wood, plaster, and reeds formed the material of the houses, and for a time all endeavored to work diligently. But few of those colonists had ever been on the sea; there had been much illness, their provisions were half spoiled, and they knew nothing about the kind of care necessary in a new soil teeming with moisture. The work was too hard for the weakened men, and the prospect was not what was fancied by the romantic and greedy noblemen. Columbus was stricken with illness, and lay for weeks unable to rise; but he arranged plans for the new city, and gave a thousand directions for the general welfare. One thing weighed heavily on him: the vessels which he must send back to Spain were awaited with high expectations by the Court and people. They looked for shiploads of gold, and it would be hard to tell the tale of disaster. He resolved to send Ojeda to the golden mountain of Cibao, in hopes of finding the coveted treasure, and he dispatched another cavalier in another direction. Both returned with accounts of evidences of mines of great richness that only needed to be opened, and with specimens of gold and of the fruits and plants of the country. Then he dispatched 12 ships, with enough good tidings to temper the disappointment. . .

There were a thousand persons in the growing city, and Columbus begged for supplies of food, additional workmen, and especially for horses. In return he proposed to send natives of the Caribbee islands who should serve the Spaniards as slaves, and should be taught the Spanish language and the Christian faith.

When the ships had sailed for Spain there was great discontent among those whose term of service bound them to remain. A ringleader was soon found in Bernal Diaz, who proposed that they should seize the ships in the harbor and return, where the influence of Diaz at court would secure them a hearing in their complaints of the misrepresentations of Columbus. The mutiny was discovered, the leaders were arrested, and a memorial full of libelous accusations, in Diaz's handwriting, was found in the buoy of one of the ships. Columbus confined Diaz on board a vessel, intending to send him, with the memorial, to Spain for trial. The other mutineers were punished lightly, and all arms and powder were put into the largest ship under the charge of a trusty officer.

Having regained his health, Columbus, taking with him 400 of the strongest men in the settlement, set out for the golden mountains, where he intended to build a fort. Everywhere he treated the natives with the same kindness which had always won them. He saw such evidence of valuable mines that he ordered a fort to be built, to which he gave the name of St. Thomas, and left it in charge of Pedro Margarite, a cavalier for whom he had a high regard. On his return Columbus found the little settlement a garden of familiar growths. The plants and seeds brought from the Old World had sprung up wonderfully in the new; but he was distressed to find that sickness and discontent prevailed. There were not well or willing men enough to care for the growing crops, and the stock brought by them had begun to fail. Columbus set every man at work, the gentle as well as the common. The curses of the *hidalgos* were long and deep, but he was unrelenting.

He received news that the Indians had shown hostility toward the men left at St. Thomas, and sent twenty men to their assistance.

The next plan for the good of the colony was to rouse interest by sending an army to St. Thomas, whence they were to separate into exploring parties. Ojeda was to command at St. Thomas, and relieve Margarite, who was to have general charge of the explorers. Accompanying them was a letter of instructions urging strong measures for regulating the army, and gentle but firm methods with the Indians. Then, leaving his brother Diego in command of Isabella, Columbus set out with three caravels to continue his explorations. He sailed to the island of Jamaica, of which he took possession in the name of the Crown, calling it Santiago. He then sailed to Cuba, intending to skirt its shores until he had satisfied himself whether it was the mainland. Many weeks were spent in pursuing his investigations, and he came at last to the conclusion that he had already passed the boundaries of Asia as seen on the map of Ptolemy; that in his path lay Aurea Chersonesus (Malacca); and that by doubling that and crossing the Gulf of the

VOL. XXXII.—10 A

Ganges, he might pass Trapoban, and through the straits of Bab-el-mandeb and the Red Sea, then by land to Jerusalem, when, reaching the Mediterranean through Joppa, he could sail for Spain, having circumnavigated the earth.

But while Columbus was sustaining his hope with such far-reaching visions, the men who sailed with him were again almost in mutiny. This time they were not common seamen alone; there were skillful navigators and men learned in the geography of the day. They felt assured that they were skirting along the coast of Asia, and that somewhere beyond lay the ancient civilization; but they were hungry and overtasked, and opposed to proceeding any farther. For four days after the remonstrance had become almost command, Columbus kept on his course. At the end of that time, being thoroughly satisfied that he had found the mainland, he reluctantly yielded to entreaty, and turned about. Before doing so he sent to each vessel a public notary with four witnesses demanding that everybody on board should say whether he believed this was the mainland, and further demanding any reason that any one might have for believing the contrary. If a doubt existed in any mind that the land before him was the extremity of India, whence it was possible to return overland to Spain, also that traveling inland they would soon come to civilized peoples, that doubt was to be made known at once. On each of the vessels charts and maps were spread, log books consulted, and the conclusion arrived at was, that such was the deliberate opinion of his fellow-sailors. It could not be, they said, that the 335 leagues of their journey could be the circuit of a mere island, as one of that extent had never been heard of; and furthermore, the land stretched limitlessly, trending toward the south, agreeably to the maps of India. They were then required to take an oath that such was their opinion. It was proclaimed by the notary that if anybody should in future contradict this solemnly stated belief of his, he would be punished by a fine of 10,000 maravedis, if he were an officer; if a ship's boy or common seaman, by receiving 100 lashes and having his tongue cut out.

On June 13 Columbus abandoned his cherished project and began making his way backward, with many pauses to take possession of new islands, and to give the mariners time for rest and change; being delayed and almost wrecked by tempests, and finally, when he was nearly in sight of Isabella, his giant strength gave way, he sank into a lethargy resembling death, and was carried unconscious to his home in the new colony early in September.

The first person whom he saw on returning to consciousness was his brother Bartholomew, who had been sent to England to lay the project before Henry VII. There had been many delays in accomplishing this, but when Bartholomew obtained audience of the King he received an eager response, and had reached Paris on his return with Henry's agreement when he heard of Christopher's arrival in Spain. When he reached Seville Columbus had set out on his second voyage. Bartholomew went to the court, and, as a result of his conference, was furnished with three ships laden with supplies, and was sent to aid his brother. Before leaving Spain he placed his nephews Diego and Fernando in the Queen's household as pages to Prince Juan.

Columbus caused Bartholomew to take command of Isabella under the title of adelantado. He had the greatest need of this timely help. The armies that had been sent to explore and amass treasure had settled down in the richest of the Indian dominions, indulging every caprice and excess, incurring the hostility of different tribes, and being in constant quarrels. Don Diego had in vain remonstrated in his gentle fashion. Margarite had a powerful following, among whom was Father Boil, who had incited his adherents in Isabella.

On the arrival of Bartholomew, Margarite and Boil had taken possession of the ships, and, paying no regard to the protests of the authorities, set sail for Spain. Ojeda, left in command of the forces, had led them in an exterminating warfare against Caonabo, the fiercest of the native chieftains.

The first act of Columbus was to send an armed body to the relief of the Spaniards who were threatened in Fort Magdalen. He sent for his old friend the *cacique* Guarionex, and explained to him that these acts were contrary to his order. To bind him still further to the interests of the colony, he prevailed upon him to give his daughter in marriage to the Indian interpreter, Diego Colon, who had been baptized in Spain, and who remained true to Columbus till his death. The admiral then recalled Ojeda, and held consultation with him in regard to some method of ending the war by getting possession of the chieftain. Ojeda proposed a daring stratagem, which was successful, and in due time Caonabo was brought a prisoner to Isabella, where Columbus insisted upon kind treatment for him.

The old cry was going up for food, that brought by Bartholomew Columbus having been wasted in the wars, and no crops having been planted or cared for during the absence of Christopher. The half-famished colony was in danger of starvation, when 4 more ships arrived in response to the letters that Columbus had sent with the 12 vessels. The favorable reports of the returned Spaniards, added to the statements of Columbus, brought out renewed expressions of pleasure and confidence on the part of the sovereigns. A general letter in addition to those sent to Columbus called upon all who should go out on voyages of discovery to obey Columbus as they would the sovereigns themselves, under pain of high displeasure and a heavy fine for each offense.

But with these vessels also came rumors that Margarite and Boil were diligently circulating evil rumors against him, and that they found ready credence with the powerful Fonseca, who had always evinced hatred for one whom he considered a foreign upstart. Columbus sent back in the newly arrived ships his brother Don Diego to attend a conference suggested by their majesties, and 500 prisoners taken in the war, to be sold as slaves.

The capture of Caonabo caused only a cessation of hostilities, and in March, 1495, Columbus was so far recovered as to be able to set out in person with a little force. He expresses his horror at the havoc wrought by white men in the beautiful valleys of Hispaniola. He was victorious, and imposed upon each Indian above the age of fourteen the penalty of paying, every three months, half a calabash of gold or 25 pounds of cotton. Each Indian, when he paid the tribute, was to receive a copper medal which he could wear about his neck; for if found without it he might be arrested and punished. To enforce this requirement, Columbus put the fort in better condition, and built several others.

Meantime Margarite and Boil had gained the ear of royalty, to which their standing in court gave them easy access. They declared that Columbus deceived the sovereigns and the people by extravagant descriptions of the lands he had found. They said that Hispaniola was an expense instead of a profit; that the oppressions of Columbus and his brothers were causing horrible suffering; that sick men were compelled to work far beyond their strength; that food was withheld on the slightest pretexts; that the common people received cruel punishments; and that insults were heaped on the nobility. No mention was made of mutinies or disobedience, of licentiousness or idleness. The further explorations they represented as foolhardy, on account of which, in all probability, Columbus had even then lost his life, and left the colony in confusion. While deferring more definite measures, the sovereigns empowered Fonseca to send out with the caravels already provisioned a trusty person to distribute the food among the colonists, under the charge of Columbus, or whoever was in authority. He was also to collect information about the government of the island, the conduct of officials, the complaints, and the remedies. With this he was to return to Spain, and in case of the admiral's return everything was to be left subject to him. Ferdinand and Isabella also made a proclamation giving permission to any native-born subject to settle on the island of Hispaniola, and to prosecute private voyages of discovery and traffic in the New World, on condition of sailing only from Cadiz under inspection by Crown officials. All who embarked at their own expense were to have lands and provisions for one year, and a right to retain such lands and all buildings put up by them. Of all gold they might collect they could retain one third, giving the other two to the Crown. Of all island produce sold they were to pay one tenth to the Crown. Royal officers were to be present at the purchases, and the dues were to be paid to the King's receiver. The Crown officers at Cadiz were to name two persons in each ship sailing on private enterprise, and one tenth of its tonnage was to be given to the Crown free of charge. One tenth of whatever such ships should procure in the new countries was to be paid over to the Crown. For every private vessel thus fitted out, Columbus, in consideration of his privilege of an eighth of tonnage, was to have the right to freight one on his own account. Vincent Pinzon had been the most earnest applicant for this permission.

Matters were in this position when the vessels that had been taken out by Torres, containing the letters of renewed confidence and greater honor for Columbus, returned to Spain. They contained news of the admiral's return, and of the evidence that he had found the mainland. Specimens of gold from rich deposits that had been marked for future opening were shown, with many curious plants and animals. A royal mandate went forth for the sale of the Indians as slaves. This news produced an immediate effect. Instead of the man chosen by Fonseca, the sovereigns appointed Juan Aguado, of whom Columbus had spoken favorably, to go with the vessels. They wrote a letter directing the admiral to limit the persons in the settlement to 500, to deal out the rations to everybody every fifteen days, and to stop all punishment that consisted in diminishing supplies of food. They sent out an expert mineralogist, and all the needed implements for working the new mines. Isabella revoked the order for the sale of the Indians, and returned them to Hispaniola, while the pious men of the land were disputing whether their sale would be righteous or wicked. Don Diego Columbus sailed with the vessels, which reached Isabella in October, 1495, while Columbus was still absent quelling the Indian disturbances. Aguado paid no attention to the authority of Bartholomew Columbus, and lost no time in calling the officers of the admiral to account and ordering various arrests. To the demand of the adelantado that he show his authority, he at first replied by a haughty refusal, but finally he made the following proclamation to the sound of a trumpet: "Cavaliers, esquires, and other persons who by our orders are in the Indies: We send to you Juan Aguado, our groom of the chambers, who will speak to you on our part. We command you to give him faith and credit." This was followed by the clamor of every malcontent, and soon Aguado had collected a fine list of abuses. Professing to believe, or really believing, that Columbus dared not return to Isabella, he sent a body of troops in search of him. Columbus heard of these events and hurried toward the colony. Arrived there, he received Aguado with grave and ceremonious courtesy. He caused the letter of credence to be proclaimed again to the sound of the trumpet, listened with deference, and declared himself ready to consent to whatever was the pleasure of their majesties.

Aguado was disappointed, but continued, unrebuked, to interfere with matters heretofore solely in the hands of the admiral. Columbus was preparing to take the case to the Court, where he believed it might be judged justly. When the ships were ready in which Aguado was to return, Columbus announced his intention of returning also. As they were about setting out, a hurricane burst upon them, sinking three of the ships with all on board, and dashing the others to pieces on the shore. Only the unseaworthy "Niña" remained of the caravels

that were riding at anchor. Columbus ordered her repaired and another built out of the wreckage.

The adelantado brought news of the finding of another rich gold mine, from which he brought specimens, and this led Columbus to conjecture that Hispaniola might be Ophir, and these the mines from which Solomon took the gold for building the temple.

On March 10, 1496. the two caravels set sail. The admiral took with him, compliant to the

TOWER IN WHICH COLUMBUS WAS IMPRISONED.

royal order to lessen the colony, 225 passengers, and these were for the most part the sick, vicious, and worthless members. Head winds and storms caused delays that reduced the crews to the point of starvation, and a more wretched company than landed after a three months' voyage could not well be imagined. Pedro Alonzo Pinzon was about setting sail with supplies. Columbus read the dispatches he carried and wrote the adelantado how to act. So deeply did he feel that he was out of favor with the sovereigns, that he was hardly prepared for the gracious form of the summons that called him to their presence. They made no allusion to any complaints against him or to the investigation they had ordered. Columbus described the voyage around Cuba, told of the newly found gold mines, and asked for 8 ships, 2 to be sent with supplies and 6 to go with him on a grand voyage of exploration. The request was granted, but its fulfillment was delayed for two years, so that it was May, 1498. when Columbus again turned his face toward the kingdom they had solemnly sworn should be his, and of which they had not only professed not to desire to deprive him, but had distinctly reiterated the promise. During the long waiting, in 1497, Columbus had recalled the agreement by sending to them the following statement, which he considered was broken by the permission for private enterprises:

According to the capitulation entered into with their highnesses and signed with their royal names, it appears very clearly that their highnesses permit and grant to the said Admiral of the Indies all the pre-eminences and prerogatives which the Admiral of Castile holds and enjoys; to whom, in right of his privilege, it is known that the third part of whatever he shall gain belongs; and consequently the Admiral of the Indies is entitled to the third part of whatever he has acquired of the islands and mainland which he has discovered and may discover; and likewise he is to have the tenth and the eighth, as appears from the third and fifth article of the aforesaid capitulation.

And if it should be argued that the third part granted to the Admiral of Castile is to be understood as relating to movables, which he might acquire by sea; whereas, the said islands being mainland, although acquired by sea, the third part of them can not belong to the admiral, in consequence of their being immovable:

To this the said admiral replies, by saying that it is to be observed that, in the aforesaid capitulation, the said Admiral of Castile is nominated admiral of the sea; and on that account the third part of whatever he may acquire by sea is granted to him, no jurisdiction nor office being granted to him in any other part whatsoever; and it would be very improper and unreasonable to grant him a part of what is not within his jurisdiction, it being a general maxim that *propter officium datur beneficium,* because the benefit has and ought to have a connection with the office, and not out of it. But the Admiral of the Indies was constituted and nominated, according to the tenor of the aforesaid capitulation, admiral, not of the sea, but expressly of the Indies and of the mainland, which he

COLUMBUS'S CHAPEL, NEAR SANTO DOMINGO.

has acquired in executing and discharging the said office of admiral; and thus is to be understood and interpreted the privilege of the said Admiral of Castile and the article which refers to it, it being sufficiently manifest that everything is to be understood *secundum subjectam materiam, et secundum qualitatem personarum;* for by interpreting them otherwise the said privilege and article would be of no utility to the aforesaid Admiral of the Indies; for if he does not take the third of the aforesaid Indies, of which he is admiral, as he has not been constituted admiral of the sea, he ought not even to take what he might gain by the sea, on account of its being out of his jurisdiction and office, so that the said article and constitution would be of no avail to him; and such a thing is not to be asserted, for whatever expression is introduced into a contract must have its full force, and not be regarded as superfluous: how much more so in a case like this, of so much importance, utility, and glory to their highnesses, obtained at a very small expense and without any peril to their honor, persons, or property, but with considerable peril, as was well known, to the life of, and not without heavy expense to, the admiral? For which reason the tenth part only must be looked upon as very trifling (no mention being made of the eighth, because

this belongs to him as his proportion), and so very small part for so great a service would be a recompense indeed inconsiderable. And the remark of the divine laws is here very apposite, *quia beneficia Principum sunt latissime interpretanda.* And, moreover, favors conferred by pr n s ought to be understood in the most ample and complete sense, more especially by the most high and renowned princes, such as their highnesses are, from whom, more than from all other persons, the most ample favors are to be expected. And therefore the said third part, although it appears very small, belongs to the aforesaid admiral: for we observe in companies formed by merchants that the industry and foresight of one partner are looked upon and held to be upon an equal footing with the money of another, and an equal share belongs to him of the gains resulting, although obtained by the money of the other; how much more ought this to be the case of the admiral, who displayed astonishing and incredible industry, and was exposed to great labor and peril in his own person, brothers, and family? Therefore, with so much the more reason he ought to have the third of all, as was really the intention of their highnesses. And that such is truly the meaning, we see by this, that their highnesses grant to such as go to the Indies five parts out of six, and to others four parts out of five, and the administration of the land, without any peril, the road being now open, secure, and made known to everybody. And in confirmation of what I say, as is expressed in many privileges of the said Admiral of the Indies, the said admiral went by command of their highnesses to acquire not ships or vessels or any other thing of the sea, but expressly islands and the mainland, as is specifically mentioned in the privilege (which might be more properly called a grace) at the beginning, where it is thus declared: "And because you, Christopher Columbus, go by our command to discover and acquire islands and the mainland," etc. Now, if the whole acquisition was to be islands and mainland, it is a necessary consequence that the third part must be of what has been acquired; and being the third part of the acquisition, it is notorious that the third part of the islands and mainland acquired belongs to the said admiral; and certainly there is no reason to doubt that if in the beginning the aforesaid admiral had demanded a greater part it would have been granted to him, the whole of such acquisition being made by him, a thing of which nobody had any hope or expectation, and which was far beyond the knowledge and dominion of their highnesses. This, then, is a complete and distinct answer to those who assert the contrary; and the third part of the said Indies and mainland justly and clearly appears to belong to the said admiral.

That of the tenth is very clear. With respect to the eighth, although it be equally clear, I wish to observe:

If it be asserted against him that he is not to have the said eighth of the merchandise and articles conveyed and exported in the vessels which went for discovery, to those which went to the pearl fishery and to other parts of this admiralty, while he remained in the island of Española upon the service of their highnesses, because he contributed nothing toward their equipment; it is answered, that the equipment of such vessels was not notified to him, nor was he called upon or informed of it at the time of their departure; and therefore, as by law, to the ignorant, who can prove ignorance of any fact, no time elapses, but, on the contrary, such plea undoubtedly grants a legitimate excuse and even complete restitution; therefore, in the actual case it should be understood and declared that the admiral performed his part by offering to contribute his part to the present; nor can he be blamed, but rather those who did not notify to him, what it was their duty to do, etc.

In response to this they said: "It was never our intention to prejudice in any way the said Don Christobal Colon, nor to allow the conventions, privileges, and favors which we have granted him to be encroached upon or violated; but, on the contrary, in consequence of the services which he has rendered us, we intend to confer still further favors on him."

A royal letter was written conferring the office of adelantado, which Bartholomew held through his brother. Permission was granted him to take out 330 persons in royal pay, of whom 40 were to be gentlemen, 100 foot soldiers, 30 sailors, 30 ship boys, 20 miners, 50 husbandmen, 10 gardeners, 20 mechanics, and 30 women. Columbus had authority to grant lands and many other things. Another full year he waited before the first step was taken that made the rest possible—possession of the needed vessels. These were pressed into service, and then, so diligently had evil reports been doing their work in all this time of evident royal neglect, no one volunteered for the service. A general pardon was promised to criminals who would embark. Fonseca left no stone unturned to vex and delay Columbus. As they were about to set sail a last outrage offered him caused Columbus to assault a treasurer of Fonseca's. He wrote of it with bitter sorrow to Isabella, and begged that it might not prejudice their good opinion, seeing I am, he added, "absent, envied, and a stranger." Before leaving Spain on this voyage Columbus drew up a deed of entail, which is of interest as a revelation of his character, and for the pathos in its suggestion how well he knew that princes could "keep the word of promise to the ear and break it to the hope." The following are its most interesting passages:

It pleased the Lord Almighty that in the year one thousand four hundred and ninety-two I should discover the continent of the Indias and many islands, among them Española, which the Indians call Ayte and the Monicongos Cipango. I then returned to Castile to their highnesses, who approved of my undertaking a second enterprise for farther discoveries and settlements; and the Lord gave me victory over the island of Española, which extends 600 leagues, and I conquered it and made it tributary; and I discovered many islands inhabited by cannibals, and 700 to the west of Española, which is Jamaica, which we call Santiago, and 333 leagues of continent from south to west, besides 107 to the north, which I discovered in my first voyage, together with many islands, as may more clearly be seen by my letters, memorials, and maritime charts. And as we hope in God that before long a good and great revenue will be derived from the above islands and continent, of which, for the reasons aforesaid, belong to me the tenth and the eighth, with the salaries and emoluments specified above; and considering that we are mortal, and that it is proper for every one to settle his affairs and to leave declared to his heirs and successors the property he possesses or may have a right to: Wherefore I have concluded to create an entailed estate out of the said eighth of the lands, places, and revenues, in the manner which I now proceed to state:

In the first place, I am to be succeeded by Don Diego, my son, who in case of death without children is to be succeeded by my other son, Ferdinand; and should God dispose of him also without leaving children and without my having any other son, then my brother Don Bartholomew is to succeed; he shall be succeeded by his sons from one to another forever; or, in the failure of a son, to be succeeded by Don Ferdinand, after the same manner, from son to son successively; or in their place by my brothers Bartholomew and Diego. And should it please the Lord that the estate, after having continued some time in the line of any of the above successors, should stand in need of an immediate and lawful male heir, the succession shall then devolve to the nearest relation, being a man of legitimate birth and bearing the name of Columbus derived from his father and his ancestors. I pray their highnesses to order that this, my privilege and testament, be held valid and be executed summarily, and without any opposition or demur, according to the letter. I also pray the grandees of the realm, and the lords of the council, and all others having administration of justice, to be pleased not to suffer this my will and testament to be of no avail, but to cause it to be fulfilled as by me ordained; it being just that a noble who has served the King and Queen and the kingdom should be respected in the disposition of his estate by will, testament, institution of entail or inheritance, and that the same be not infringed either in whole or in part.

In the first place, my son Don Diego, and all my successors and descendants, as well as my brothers Bartholomew and Diego, shall bear my arms, such as I shall leave them after my days, without inserting anything else in them; and they shall be their seal to seal withal. Don Diego my son, or any other who may inherit this estate, on coming into possession of the inheritance, shall sign with the signature which I now make use of, which is an X with an S over it, and an M with a Roman A over it, and over that an S, and then a Greek Y, with an S over it, with its lines and points as is my custom, as may be seen by my signatures, of which there are many, and it will be seen by the present one.

He shall only write "the Admiral," whatever other titles the King may have conferred on him. This is to be understood as respects his signature, but not the enumeration of his titles, which he can make at full length if agreeable, only the signature is to be "the Admiral."

The said Don Diego, or any other inheritor of this estate, shall possess my offices of admiral of the ocean.

Item. The said Don Diego, or any other inheritor of this estate, shall distribute the revenue which it may please our Lord to grant him, in the following manner:

First—Of the whole income of this estate, now and at all times, and of whatever may be had or collected from it, he shall give the fourth part of it to my brother, Don Bartholomew Columbus, Adelantado of the Indies; and this is to continue till he shall have acquired an income of a million of maravedises * for his support, and for the services he has rendered and will continue to render to this entailed estate. . . .

Item. From the revenues of the said estate, or from any other fourth part of it (should its amount be adequate to it), shall be paid every year to my son Ferdinand 2,000,000, till such time as his revenue shall amount to 2,000,000, in the same form and manner as in the case of Bartholomew, who, as well as his heirs, are to have the million or the part that may be wanting.

Item. The said Don Diego or Don Bartholomew shall make out of the said estate, for my brother Diego, such provision as may enable him to live decently, as he is my brother, to whom I assign no particular sum, as he has attached himself to the Church, and that will be given him which is right; and this to be given him in a mass, and before anything shall have been received by Ferdinand my son, or Bartholomew my brother, or their heirs, and also according to the amount of the income of the estate. And

* Approximately $8,500, equivalent to between $10,000 and $12,000 at the present time.

in case of discord, the case is to be referred to two of our relations, or other men of honor; and should they disagree among themselves, they will choose a third person as arbitrator, being virtuous and not distrusted by either party.

Item. All this revenue which I bequeath to Bartholomew, to Ferdinand, and to Diego, shall be delivered to and received by them as prescribed under

CATHEDRAL OF SANTO DOMINGO.

the obligation of being faithful and loyal to Diego my son, or his heirs, they as well as their children; and should it appear that they, or any of them, had proceeded against him in anything touching his honor, or the prosperity of the family, or of the estate, either in word or deed, whereby might come a scandal and debasement to my family and a detriment to my estate; in that case, nothing farther shall be given to them or him, from that time forward, inasmuch as they are always to be faithful to Diego and to his successors.

Item. As it was my intention, when I first instituted this entailed estate, to dispose, or that my son Diego should dispose for me, of the tenth part of the income in favor of necessitous persons, as a tithe, and in commemoration of the almighty and eternal God; and persisting still in this opinion, and hoping that his High Majesty will assist me, and those who may inherit it, in this or the New World, I have resolved that the said tithe shall be paid in the manner following:

Item. Don Diego my son, or whoever may be the inheritor, shall appoint two persons of conscience and authority, and most nearly related to the family, who are to examine the revenue and its amount carefully, and to cause the said tenth to be paid out of the fourth from which Don Bartholomew is to receive his million, to the most necessitated members of my family that may be found here or elsewhere, whom they shall look for diligently upon their consciences; and as it might happen that said Don Diego, or others after him, for reasons which may concern their own welfare, or the credit and support of the estate, may be unwilling to make known the full amount of the income; nevertheless, I charge him on his conscience to pay the sum aforesaid; and I charge them on their souls and consciences not to denounce or make it known, except with the consent of Don Diego, or the person that may succeed him; but let the above tithe be paid in the manner I have directed. . . .

Item. The said Don Diego, or whoever shall inherit the estate, must remit in bills, or in any other way, all such sums as he may be able to save out of the revenue of the estate, and direct purchases to be made in his name, or that of his heirs, in a fund in

the Bank of St. George, which gives an interest of 6 per cent, and is secure money; and this shall be devoted to the purpose I am about to explain.

Item. As it becomes every man of rank and property to serve God, either personally or by means of his wealth; and as all moneys deposited with St. George are quite safe, and Genoa is a noble city and powerful by sea; and as at the time that I undertook to set out upon that discovery of the Indias it was with the intention of supplicating the King and Queen, our lords, that whatever moneys should be derived from the said Indias should be invested in the conquest of Jerusalem; and as I did so supplicate them, if they do this, it will be well; if not, at all events the said Diego, or such person as may succeed him in this trust, to collect together all the money he can, and accompany the King our lord, should he go to the conquest of Jerusalem, or else go there himself with all the force he can command; and in pursuing this intention, it will please the Lord to assist toward the accomplishment of the plan; and should he not be able to effect the conquest of the whole, no doubt he will achieve it in part. Let him therefore collect and make a fund of all his wealth in St. George of Genoa, and let it multiply there till such time as it may appear to him that something of consequence may be effected as respects the project on Jerusalem; for I believe that when their highnesses shall see that this is contemplated, they will wish to realize it themselves, or will afford him, as their servant and vassal, the means of doing it for them. . . .

Item. I also require of Diego, or whosoever may be in possession of the estate, that in the case of any schism taking place in the Church of God, or that any person of whatever class or condition should attempt to despoil it of its property and honors, they hasten to offer at the feet of his Holiness—that is, if they are not heretics (which God forbid)—their persons, power, and wealth, for the purpose of suppressing such schism, and preventing any spoliation of the honor and property of the Church. . . .

Item. When a suitable time shall arrive, he shall order a church to be built in the island of Española, and in the most convenient spot, to be called Santa Maria de la Concepcion; to which is to be annexed a hospital, upon the best possible plan, like those of Italy and Castile, and a chapel be erected to say mass in for the good of my soul, and those of my ancestors and successors, with great devotion, since no doubt it will please the Lord to give us a sufficient revenue for this and the aforementioned purposes.

Item. I also order Diego, my son, or whosoever may inherit after him, to spare no pains in having and maintaining in the island of Española four good professors of theology, to the end and aim of their studying and laboring to convert to our holy faith the inhabitants of the Indies; and in proportion as, by God's will, the revenue of the estate shall increase, in the same degree shall the number of teachers and devout persons increase who are to strive to make Christians of the natives; in attaining which no expense should be thought too great. And in commemoration of all that I hereby ordain, and of the foregoing, a monument of marble shall be erected in the said Church of la Concepcion, in the most conspicuous place, to serve as a record of what I here enjoin on the said Diego, as well as to other persons who may look upon it; which marble shall contain an inscription to the same effect.

Item. I also require of Diego my son, and whosoever may succeed him in the estate, that every time, and as often as he confesses, he first show his obligation, or a copy of it, to the confessor, praying him to read it through, that he may be enabled to inquire respecting its fulfillment; from which will redound great good and happiness to his soul.

SEVILLE, *February 22, 1498.*

              S.
         S   A   S
         X   M   Y
        EL ALMIRANTE.

The marvels that Columbus saw on this voyage—the variation of the needle, the stars of the southern hemisphere, the mystery of the trade winds and of the equatorial calms, the phenomena accompanying the mingling of the great river Orinoco, which he never realized to be a river, with the ocean on which he was skirting the shores of an unsuspected continent—produced so great an effect upon his imagination that his descriptive letter to the King and Queen is a blending of current events with excited speculation, and is of great interest, not only as an account of the voyage, but as revealing his character and the limits of his knowledge. The following are extracts from the letter:

I set out from San Lucar, in the name of the most holy Trinity, on Wednesday, May 30, much fatigued with my voyage, for I had hoped, when I left the Indies, to find repose in Spain; whereas, on the contrary, I experienced nothing but opposition and vexation. I sailed to the island of Madeira by a circuitous route, in order to avoid any encounter with an armed fleet from France, which was on the lookout for me off Cape St. Vincent. Thence I went to the Canaries, from which islands I sailed with but one ship and two caravels, having dispatched the other ships to Española by the direct road to the Indies; while I myself moved southward, with the view of reaching the equinoctial line, and of then proceeding westward. But having reached the Cape Verd islands (an incorrect name, for they are so barren that nothing green was to be seen there, and the people so sickly that I did not venture to remain among them), I sailed away 480 miles, which is equivalent to 120 leagues, toward the southwest, where, when it grew dark, I found the north star to be in the fifth degree. The wind then failed me, and I entered a climate where the intensity of the heat was such that I thought both ships and men would have been burned up, and everything suddenly got into such a state of confusion that no man dared go below deck to attend to the securing of the water cask and the provisions. This heat lasted eight days; on the first day the weather was fine, but on the seven other days it rained and was cloudy, yet we found no alleviation of our distress; so that I certainly believe that if the sun had shone as on the first day, we should not have been able to escape in any way.

I recollect that, in sailing toward the Indies, as soon as I passed 100 leagues to the westward of the Azores I found the temperature change: and this is so all along from north to south. At the end of these eight days it pleased our Lord to give me a favorable east wind, and I steered to the west, but did not venture to move lower down toward the south, because I discovered a very great change in the sky and the stars, although I found no alteration in the temperature. I resolved, therefore, to keep on the direct westward course, in a line from Sierra Leone. At the end of seventeen days, during which our Lord gave me a propitious wind, we saw land at noon of Tuesday, July 31. This I had expected on the Monday before, and held that route up to this point; but as the sun's strength increased, and our supply of water was failing, I resolved to make for the Caribbee islands, and set sail in that direction; when, by the mercy of God, which he has always extended to me, one of the sailors went up to the maintop, and saw to the westward a range of three mountains. Upon this we repeated the "Salve Regina," and other prayers, and all of us gave many thanks to our Lord. At the hour of complines we reached a cape, which I called Cape Galea,* having already given to the island the name of Trinidad. We saw houses and people on the spot, and the country around was very beautiful, and as

* The southeastern point of Trinidad. Here Columbus first saw the mainland of America.

fresh and green as the gardens of Valencia in the month of March. After sailing five leagues I found very good bottom, and anchored. The next day I set sail in the same direction, in search of a harbor where I might repair the vessels and take in water, as well as improve the stock of provisions which I had brought out with me. When we had taken in a pipe of water, we proceeded onward till we reached the cape, and there, finding good anchorage and protection from the east wind, I ordered the anchors to be dropped, the water cask to be repaired, a supply of water and wood to be taken in, and the people to rest themselves from the fatigues which they had endured for so long a time. I gave to this point the name of Sandy Point. On the following day a large canoe came from the eastward, containing 24 men, all in the prime of life, and well provided with arms, such as bows, arrows, and wooden shields; they were not dark black, but whiter than any other Indians that I had seen, of very graceful gesture, and handsome forms, wearing their hair long and straight, and cut in the Spanish style. I found that the island of Trinidad formed with the land of Gracia a strait of two leagues' width from east to west; and as we had to pass through it to go to the north, we found some strong currents which crossed the strait, and which made a great roaring, so that I concluded there must be a reef of sand or rocks, which would preclude our entrance; and behind this current was another and another, all making a roaring noise like the sound of breakers against the rocks. I anchored there, under the point of Arenal, outside of the strait, and found the water rushed from east to west with as much impetuosity as that of the Guadalquivir at its conflux with the sea; and this continued constantly day and night, so that it appeared to be impossible to move backward for the current or forward for the shoals. In the dead of night, while I was on deck, I heard an awful roaring that came from the south toward the ship. I stopped to observe what it might be, and I saw the sea rolling from west to east like a mountain, as high as the ship, and approaching by little and little; on the top of this rolling sea came a mighty wave roaring with a frightful noise, and with all this terrific uproar were other conflicting currents. I have a vivid recollection of the dread I then felt lest the ship might founder under the force of that tremendous sea; but it passed by, and reached the mouth of the beforementioned passage, where the uproar lasted for a considerable time. It pleased the Lord, however, to give us a favorable wind, and I passed through the middle of the strait, after which I recovered my tranquillity. The men happened at this time to draw up some water from the sea, which, strange to say, proved to be fresh. We were visited by a great number of the inhabitants, who informed us that the country was called Paria, and that farther westward it was more fully peopled. I took four of these natives and proceeded on my westward voyage, and when I had gone eight leagues farther I found on the other side of a point, which I called the Needle, one of the most lovely countries in the world, and very thickly peopled. Some of the natives soon came out to the ship in canoes to beg me, in the name of their king, to go on shore; and when they saw that I paid no attention to them, they came to the ship in their canoes in countless numbers, many of them wearing pieces of gold on their breasts, and some with bracelets of pearls on their arms; on seeing which I was much delighted, and made many inquiries, with the view of learning where they found them. They informed me that they were to be procured in their own neighborhood, and also at a spot to the northward of that place. I would have remained here, but the provisions of corn and wine and meats which I had brought out with so much care for the people whom I had left behind were nearly wasted, so that all my anxiety was to get them into a place of safety, and not to stop for anything. I wished, however, to get some of the pearls that I had seen, and with that view sent the boats on shore. My own health had been affected by long watching; and although on my former voyage, when I discovered *terra firma*, I passed thirty-three days without natural rest, and was all that time deprived of sight, yet never were my eyes so much affected or so painful as at this period. I formed the conjecture that at one time there was a continuous neck of land from the island of Trinidad and with the land of Gracia, where the two straits now are, as your

CATHEDRAL OF HAVANA.

highnesses will see by the drawing which accompanies this letter. I passed out by this northern strait, and found the fresh water came even there; and when by the aid of the wind I was enabled to proceed, I remarked, while on one of the watery billows which I have described, that in the channel the water on the inner side of the current was fresh, and on the outside salt.

I have always read that the world, comprising the land and the water, was spherical, as is testified by the investigations of Ptolemy and others, who have proved it by the eclipses of the moon, and other observations made from east to west, as well as by the elevation of the pole from north to south. But I have now seen so much irregularity, that I have come to another conclusion respecting the earth, namely, that it is not round, as they describe, but of the form of a pear, which is very round except where the stalk grows, at which part it is most prominent. Ptolemy and the others who have written upon the globe had no information respecting this part of the world, which was then unexplored; they only established their arguments with respect to their own hemisphere, which is half of a perfect sphere. And a great confirmation of this is, that when our Lord made the sun, the first light appeared in the first point of the east, where the most elevated point of

the globe is; and although it was the opinion of Aristotle that the antarctic pole, or the land which is below it, was the highest part of the world and the nearest to the heavens, other philosophers oppose him, and say that the highest part was below the arctic pole, by which reasoning it appears that they understood that one part of the world ought to be loftier and nearer the sky than the other; but it never struck them that it might be under the equinoctial, in the way that I have said, which is not to be wondered at, because they had no certain knowledge respecting this hemisphere. In the southern strait, which I named the Serpent's Mouth, I found that toward evening the polar star was nearly at 5° elevation; and in the northern, which I called the Dragon's Mouth, it was at an elevation of nearly 7° degrees. The before-mentioned Gulf of Pearls is to the west of the [words lacking in the MS.] of Ptolemy, nearly 3,900 miles, which make nearly 70 equinoctial degrees, reckoning 56⅔ to a degree. The Holy Scriptures record that our Lord made the earthly paradise and planted in it the tree of life, and thence springs a fountain from which the 4 principal rivers in the world take their source.

I do not find, nor have ever found, any account by the Romans or Greeks which fixes in a positive manner the site of the terrestrial paradise, neither have I seen it given in any mappe-monde laid down from authentic sources.

I do not suppose that the earthly paradise is in the form of a rugged mountain, as the descriptions of it have made it appear, but that it is on the summit of the spot which I have described as being in the form of the stalk of a pear: the approach of it from a distance must be by a constant and gradual ascent; but I believe that no one could ever reach the top. I think that the water I have described may proceed from it, though it be far off, and that, stopping at the place which I have just left, it forms this lake, for I have never either read or heard of fresh water coming in so large a quantity in close conjunction with the water of the sea; the idea is also corroborated by the blandness of the temperature; and if the water of which I speak does not proceed from the earthly paradise, it appears to be still more marvelous, for I do not believe that there is any river in the world so large or so deep.

Meantime affairs had continued to go ill with the colony. Don Bartholomew proved to be both an efficient and a wise commander; but too many of the colonists came for plunder and not for work, and no sagacity could foresee or correct the evils. The most serious was the conspiracy of Roldan, a man whom Columbus had raised from a menial office to be alcalde, because he believed he saw in him great natural talent and capacity. These had been turned with vigor against his benefactor. The adelantado had laid the foundations for the city desired by Columbus, first building a fort, to which he gave the name of Santo Domingo. He built several new forts, and 2 caravels. But rebellion and riot had spread, and Columbus found almost everything for which he had striven made vain through sedition. By prompt and severe measures he succeeded in restoring order, and the good effects soon began to appear in a happier condition of both white men and Indians. But at home things had been going from bad to worse. Columbus had sent thither accounts of the troubles and their causes; but enemies were numerous, and the expected riches were slow in coming. Columbus had frequently urged that a person be sent out who was learned and fair-minded, who could act as judge, though his powers should not conflict with those of the admiral. He also asked for an umpire between Roldan and himself. Ferdinand united these offices in one person, and so worded the order that the umpire in passing upon the highest acts of Columbus and his brother could supersede them. Francisco de Bobadilla, the man selected, was furnished with letters of varying import. The first mentioned the admiral's request, and said: "We order you to inform yourself of the truth of the foregoing, who and what persons they were who rose against the said admiral; .... and, the truth known, whomsoever you find culpable, take their bodies and sequestrate their effects, and, thus taken, proceed against them, and against the absent, to the greatest civil and criminal punishments that you find they merit." To this end he was to call in the assistance of the admiral, and of all persons in authority.

Another letter said: "It is our will that if the said commander should think it necessary to our service, and the purposes of justice, that any cavaliers or other persons who are at present in those islands, or may arrive there, should leave them and not return and abide in them, and that they should come and present themselves before us, he may command it in our name, and oblige them to depart." Still another letter called upon Columbus and his brothers to surrender all forts, ships, etc. And still another ordered the admiral to give faith and obedience to whatever Bobadilla might impart.

These letters were held for in Spain a year, but a rumor of their existence reached Columbus through captains who were sailing under the general orders which Columbus considered as infringing upon the rights that had been solemnly promised to him.

Bobadilla arrived during the absence of Columbus and Bartholomew, and, finding only Don Diego in charge, seized upon the office. The events that followed are told in the simple graphic style peculiar to Columbus, in a letter written to Juana de la Torres, a lady of the Queen's household. A few extracts will reveal the story of one of the most disgraceful acts ever done or allowed to be done in Christendom, better than it could be shown in any other language:

Although it is a novelty for me to complain of the ill-usage of the world, it is nevertheless no novelty for the world to practice ill-usage. I have now reached that point, that there is no man so vile but thinks it his right to insult me.

In the voyage which I made by way of Paria I found nearly half the colonists of Española in a state of revolt, and they have made war upon me until now as if I had been a Moor; while on the other side I had to contend with no less cruel Indians. Then arrived Ojeda, and he attempted to put the seal to all these disorders. He said that their highnesses had sent him, with promises of presents, of immunities, and treaties. He collected a numerous band, for in the whole island of Española there were few men who were not vagabonds, and there were none who had either wife or children. This Ojeda troubled me much, but he was obliged to retreat, and at his departure he said that he would return with more ships and men, and reported also that he had left the Queen at the point of death. In the meanwhile, Vincent Yanez came with four caravels; and there were some tumults and suspicions, but no further evil. The Indians reported many other caravels to the cannibals

and in Paria. At this time one Adrian attempted a new revolt, as he had done before. I had determined not to inflict punishment on any person, but his ingratitude obliged me, however regretfully, to abandon this resolution. I should not have acted otherwise with my own brother, if he had sought to assassinate me, and to rob me of the lordship which my sovereigns had given to my keeping.

Before my departure I often entreated their highnesses to send to these parts, at my expense, some one charged to administer justice; and since, when I found the alcalde in a state of revolt, I have besought them afresh to send at least one of their servants with letters, because I myself have had so strange a character given to me that if I were to build churches or hospitals they would call them caves for robbers. Their highnesses provided for this at last, but in a manner quite unequal to the urgency of the circumstances. However, let that point rest, since such is their good pleasure.

The commander Bobadilla arrived at Santa Domingo, at which time I was at La Vega, and the adelantado at Xaragua, where this Adrian had made his attempt; but by that time everything was quiet, the land was thriving, and the people at peace. The second day of his arrival he declared himself governor, created magistrates, ordered executions, published immunities from the collection of gold and from the paying of tithes; and, in fine, announced a general franchise for twenty years. He also gave out that he was going to pay every one, although they had not even done the service which was due up to that day; and he further proclaimed, with respect to me, that he would send me back loaded with chains, and my brother also (this he has accomplished); and that neither I, nor any of my family, should return forever to these lands. And, in addition to this, he made innumerable unjust and disgraceful charges against me. When I heard this, I thought he must be like Ojeda, or one of the other rebels; but I held my peace, when I learned for certain from the friars that he had been sent by their highnesses. I wrote to him, to salute him on his arrival, to let him know that I was ready to set out to go to court, and that I had put up to sale all that I possessed. I entreated him not to be in haste on the subject of immunities; and I assured him that I would shortly yield this, and everything else connected with the government, implicitly into his charge. I wrote the same thing to the ecclesiastics, but I received no answer either from the one or the other.

I never before heard of any one who was commissioned to make an inquiry, assembling the rebels and taking as evidence against their governor wretches without faith and who are unworthy of belief. Although I am an ignorant man, I do not imagine that any one supposed me so stupid as not to be aware that, even if the Indies had belonged to me, I could not support myself without the assistance of some prince. Since it is thus, where should I find better support, or more security against expulsion, than in the King and Queen, our sovereigns, who, from nothing, have raised me to so great an elevation, and who are the greatest princes of the world, on the land and on the sea? These princes know how I have served them, and they uphold my privileges and rewards; and if any one violates them, their highnesses augment them by ordering great favor to be shown me, and ordain me many honors, as was shown in the affair of Juan Aguado. Their highnesses have taken my son into their household, which would not have happened with another prince, because where there is no attachment all other considerations prove of little weight. If I have now spoken severely of a malicious slander, it is against my will, for it is a subject I would not willingly recall even in my dreams. I am judged in Spain as a governor who had been sent to a province, or city, under regular government. I ought to be judged as a captain, who for so many years has borne arms, never quitting them for an instant; for under any other judgment I receive great injury, because in the Indies there is neither civil law nor judgment seat.

The governor, on his arrival at Española, took up his abode in my house, and appropriated to himself all that was therein. Well and good; perhaps he was in want of it; but even a pirate does not behave in this manner toward the merchants that he plunders. That which grieved me most was the seizure of my papers, of which I have never been able to recover one; and those that would have been most useful to me in proving my innocence are precisely those which he has kept most carefully concealed. Behold the just and honest inquisitor! I am told that he does not at all confine himself to the bounds of justice, but that he acts in all things despotically. God our Saviour retains his power and wisdom as of old; and, above all things, he punishes ingratitude.

One day the gates of Columbus's prison opened, and an officer entered with a guard.

. " Villejo," said Columbus, " whither are you taking me ? "

" To the ship, your excellency, to embark."

" To embark, Villejo ! Do you speak the truth ? "

" By the life of your excellency, it is true."

Once on board the vessel and at sea, Villejo and the master of the ship proposed to remove his shackles.

" No," replied Columbus, " their majesties commanded me by letter to submit to whatever Bobadilla should order in their name. By their authority he has put upon me these chains; I will wear them until they shall order them to be taken off, and I will preserve them afterward as relics and memorials of the reward of my services."

The arrival of Columbus in chains produced in Spain a tremendous reaction in his favor. Indignation was felt through the whole country as the news swept over it. The letter given above was, through the thoughtfulness of the ship's captain, Andreas Martin, sent by swift messenger, so that it reached the court before the packet containing the statements of Bobadilla. Isabella was enraged at the liberty taken with the orders, and Ferdinand dared express nothing else, however he might have felt. Villejo and the alcalde of Cadiz, into whose hands Columbus and his brothers had been committed for safe keeping, confirmed the statements of Columbus, and the Queen ordered their instant release, and wrote a kind letter asking Columbus to come at once to the court. Happy once more in the belief that he was exonerated and trusted where he most desired to be, he hastened to the presence of the princes. Tears came into Isabella's eyes as she gazed on him, and he threw himself on his knees and could not speak for sobbing. The King and Queen expressed their wrath at Bobadilla, said he had utterly misconstrued their orders, and promised to remove him immediately. Of this Columbus was very desirous. He felt assured that their majesties, who gave him such tokens of confidence and esteem, would be eager to restore the rights and honors which were proofs of vindication to him and to the world, and for which he steadily contended. He looked for a speedy return to Santo Domingo in triumph.

But, meantime, many expeditions had been fitted out with all manner of privileges that contravened the rights given to Columbus. These had proved that the discoverer was no longer necessary as a leader to the expected wealth, and with these navigators terms could be made more advantageous to the Crown. The discontent in the colony formed a plausible excuse. Though Bobadilla was to be removed, it was represented to Columbus that the safer way for both himself and the Crown would be to send some wise person to supersede him for a time, and with this Columbus was fain to rest content. Don Nicholas de Ovando was chosen. Before he sailed several vessels had brought news of the havoc wrought throughout the new colony by the misrule of Bobadilla. Already the wretched Spaniards were looking back with regret to the firm but just severity of Columbus and Don Bartholomew. The Indians were dying under the rule of the taskmaster, and fled to mountain retreats, refusing longer to give tribute or food to the idle and worthless profligates who pursued them for gain or for revenge. In arranging for the new government, many of the suggestions which had been urged by Columbus were acted upon. Thirty vessels were fitted out, and with such aid from the Crown that on board them were 73 married men with their families, and many artisans and professional men of respectable social standing. Ovando was furnished with rich raiment in which to maintain his office, and the sick, dissolute, and worthless members of the colony were all to be returned to Spain. There was also a fresh supply of live stock, and all other things necessary for making successful this venture of a native nobleman, a prime favorite with Ferdinand.

Columbus witnessed the departure of this expedition with sorrow, but apparently not with repining. In the quiet of a monastery he pursued his studies, and prepared a manuscript volume to submit to their majesties. It concerned the accomplishment of the object that had long lain near his heart, and to which he had vowed to devote, within seven years of his discovery, at his own expense, 50,000 foot soldiers and 5,000 horse. This was a new crusade to Palestine for the recovery of the holy sepulchre. His volume was composed of prophecies from many sources, sacred and profane, which were set forth with his usual ardor.

While he was prosecuting this undertaking, news came that Vasco de Gama had reached India by rounding the Cape of Good Hope, and the wealth vainly hoped for Spain was pouring in upon Portugal. This turned Columbus's mind into the old channel, where enthusiasm was tempered by the most cogent common sense. He studied the problem of his discoveries in the light of the new knowledge gained from Portuguese navigation, and arrived at the conclusion that a more southerly route than any yet taken must lead to a shorter method of finding these same coveted countries. This idea, fully worked out, he laid before the sovereigns, his argument being that there must be a strait opening into the Indian Ocean, which, once found, would place the possessions now planted at the gate of the Orient. This strait he located near the real Isthmus of Darien. For such an expedition consent was given, and Columbus set about the preparations. In reply to a letter in regard to his rights and titles, he received a document, dated March 14,

1502, in which the King and Queen solemnly assured him that their promises to him should be fulfilled to the letter, and to his children; and that they also intended to bestow new honors upon him and his descendants. Therefore, they bade him depart in peace. This letter, with a full statement of his rights and privileges, Columbus had witnessed before the alcaldes of Seville, and caused to be copied and deposited in St. George's Bank in Genoa. He set all his affairs in order, and, so far as human foresight could, arranged for the perpetuation to his children of the rights and emoluments that were already his, or which he believed would yet accrue from his discovery, and which he might well have been convinced he alone must maintain.

On May 9, 1502, when about sixty-six years old, Columbus set sail once more from Cadiz. He had four small caravels, the largest of 70 tons burden, the smallest of 50. With these he purposed to find the Indian strait, and to circumnavigate the earth. With him were his noble and faithful brother Don Bartholomew and his younger son, Fernando. He had orders from the Crown not to stop at his own island of Hispaniola, except on his return. Extracts from a description of this voyage, in a letter to Ferdinand and Isabella, written in 1503, are given below; but they do not give Columbus due credit in many particulars. Others relate that when, from the condition of one of his ships and from stress of weather, he anchored outside Santo Domingo and asked harborage from the tempest which he foresaw, and it was denied him, he sent word to hold the fleet until it was over. There was no sign to the other mariners of such disaster, and the vessels put to sea, carrying Bobadilla and the colonists who were to be returned to Spain, and much gold. The tempest broke, and most of the ships foundered, Roldan and Bobadilla being among the lost. But one vessel, which contained 4,000 gold pieces belonging to Columbus, could proceed to Spain.

My passage from Cadiz to the Canaries occupied four days, and thence to the Indies sixteen days.

Up to the period of my reaching these shores I experienced most excellent weather, but the night of my arrival came on with a dreadful tempest. On reaching the island of Española I dispatched a packet of letters, by which I begged as a favor that a ship should be supplied me at my own cost in lieu of one of those that I had brought with me, which had become unseaworthy, and could no longer carry sail. The letters were taken, and your highnesses will know if a reply has been given to them. For my part I was forbidden to go on shore.

The tempest was terrible throughout the night, all the ships were separated, and each one driven to the last extremity, without hope of anything but death; each of them also looked upon the loss of the rest as a matter of certainty. I was in anxious fear for my own safety, and that of my son, my brother, and my friends, and yet was refused permission either to land or to put into harbor on the shores which by God's mercy I had gained for Spain with so much toil and danger.

The ship which we had the greatest fear for had put out to sea for safety, and reached the island of Gallega. The vessel in which I was, though dreadfully buffeted, was saved by our Lord's mercy from any injury whatever; my brother went in the ship that was unsound, and he under God was the cause of its being saved. With this tempest I struggled on till I reached Jamaica, and there the sea became calm, but

there was a strong current which carried me as far as the Queen's Garden without seeing land. Hence, as opportunity offered, I pushed on for *terra firma*, in spite of the wind and a fearful contrary current, against which I contended for sixty days, and during that time only made 70 leagues. All this time I was unable to get into harbor, nor was there any cessation of the tempest, which was one continuation of rain, thunder, and lightning; indeed, it seemed as if it were the end of the world. I at length reached Cape of Gracias a Dios.

I reached the land of Cariay, where I stopped to repair my vessels and take in provisions, gained information respecting the gold mines of which I was in search, in the province of Clamba; and two Indians conducted me to Carambaru, where the people (who go naked) wear golden mirrors round their necks, which they will neither sell, give, nor part with for any consideration. They named to me many places on the seacoast where there were both gold and mines. The last that they mentioned was Veragua, which was 25 leagues distant from the place where we then were.

When I discovered the Indies I said that they composed the richest lordship in the world: I spoke of gold and pearls and precious stones of spices; and the traffic that might be carried on in them; and because these things were not forthcoming at once, I was abused. This punishment causes me to refrain from relating anything but what the natives tell me. One thing I can venture upon saying, because there are so many witnesses of it, viz., that in this land of Veragua I saw more signs of gold in the first two days than I saw in Española during four years; and that there is not a more fertile or better cultivated country in all the world, nor one whose inhabitants are more timid; added to which, there is a good harbor, a beautiful river, and the whole place is capable of being easily put into a state of defense.

The people who have sailed with me have passed through incredible toil and danger, and I beseech your highnesses, since they are poor, to pay them promptly, and to be gracious to each of them according to their respective merits; for I can safely assert, that to my belief they are the bearers of the best news that ever were carried to Spain. With respect to the gold which belongs to Quibian, the cacique of Veragua, and other chiefs in the neighboring country, although it appears by the accounts we have received of it to be very abundant, I do not think it would be well or desirable, on the part of your highnesses, to take possession of it in the way of plunder. By fair dealing, scandal and disrepute will be avoided, and all the gold will thus reach your highnesses' treasury without the loss of a grain.

With one month of fair weather I shall complete my voyage. As I was deficient in ships, I did not persist in delaying my course. I think your highnesses will remember that I had intended to build some ships in a new manner, but the shortness of the time did not permit it. I think more of this opening for commerce, and of the lordship over such extensive mines, than of all that has been done in the Indies. This is not a child to be left to the care of a stepmother.

I never think of Española and Paria and other countries without shedding tears. I thought that what had occurred there would have been an example for others; on the contrary, these settlements are now in a languid state, although not dead, and the malady is incurable, or at least very extensive. Let him who brought the evil come now and cure it, if he knows the remedy or how to apply it; but when a disturbance is on foot, every one is ready to take the lead.

I am indeed in a ruined condition. Hitherto I have wept over others; may Heaven now have mercy upon me, and may the earth weep for me. With regard to temporal things, I have not even a blanca for an offering; and in spiritual things I have ceased here in the Indies from observing the prescribed forms of religion. Solitary in my trouble, sick, and in daily expectation of death, surrounded by millions of hostile savages full of cruelty, and thus separated from the blessed sacraments of our holy Church, how will my soul be forgotten if it be separated from the body in this foreign land? Weep for me whoever has charity, truth, and justice! I did not come out on this voyage to gain to myself honor or wealth; this is a certain fact, for at that time all hope of such a thing was dead. I do not lie when I say that I went to your highnesses with honest purpose of heart and sincere zeal in your cause. I humbly beseech your highnesses, that if it please God to rescue me from this place, you will graciously sanction my pilgrimage to Rome and other holy places. May the holy Trinity protect your highnesses' lives, and add to the prosperity of your exalted position!

Done in the Indies, in the island of Jamaica, on the 7th of July, in the year one thousand five hundred and three.

Columbus was now ill almost to the point of death, and with his brother and many of the company, worn out by hardships, was living in the houses built by lashing together portions of the wrecks of their vessels. In this crisis Diego Mendez returned one day from an excursion for food, in a large canoe purchased from the Indians, and a daring expedient entered the mind of Columbus. Summoning Mendez, he said: "Diego Mendez, my son, nobody of all those I have here understands the great peril in which we are placed excepting you and myself. We are few, and these savage Indians are many and of fickle and irritable natures. On the least provocation they may throw firebrands from the shore and consume us in our straw-thatched cabins. The arrangement which you have made with them for provisions, and which at present they fulfill so cheerfully, to-morrow they may break in their caprice, and may refuse to bring us anything; nor have we the means to compel them by force, but are entirely at their pleasure. I have thought of a remedy, if it meets with your views. In this canoe which you have purchased some one may pass over to Hispaniola and procure a ship, by which we may all be delivered from this great peril into which we have fallen. Tell me your opinion in the matter." "Señor," replied Mendez, "the danger in which we are placed is far greater than is easily conceived. As to passing from this island to Hispaniola in so small a vessel as a canoe, I hold it not merely as difficult, but impossible, since it is necessary to traverse a gulf of 40 leagues, and between islands where the sea is extremely impetuous and seldom in repose. I know not who there is would adventure upon a peril so notorious." The silence of Columbus showed plainly what was in his thought, and Mendez added: "Señor, I have many times put my life in peril of death to save you and all here, and God has hitherto preserved me in a miraculous manner; there are, nevertheless, murmurers, who say that your excellency intrusts to me all affairs wherein honor is to be gained, while there are others in the company who will execute them as well as I. I beg, therefore, that you would summon all the people, and propose this enterprise to them, and see if among them all there is any who will undertake it, which I doubt. If all decline it, I will then come forward and risk my life in your service, as I many times have done."

Columbus forthwith summoned the whole company, and made the proposition, and all pronounced it mad and impossible. Then Mendez stepped forward. "Señor," said he, "I have but one life to lose, yet I am willing to venture it upon your service." Columbus sent by him a request to Ovando at Santo Domingo, for a ship to be sent immediately, and also to the sovereigns the letter that has been given above. Mendez was absent so long that the crew began to despair of his return, when two of them, who had been intrusted with power, circulated the report that Columbus had been exiled from Spain and from Hispaniola, and they led a mutiny, and, seizing the canoes that Columbus had collected from the Indians for use in case the wreck was set fire to, they escaped to another part of the island. Eight months after the departure of Mendez a ship appeared in the offing, which bore a letter from Ovando expressing his sympathy and asking Columbus to accept a barrel of wine and a side of bacon. Columbus wrote a letter making renewed statements of the danger and distress of his situation, and expressing his confidence that a ship would be sent to his relief.

In June, 1504, a year after his shipwreck in Jamaica, two vessels arrived for his relief. One of them had been fitted out and provisioned at Columbus's expense by the faithful Diego Mendez, whose long journey of incredible hardship is one of the strange annals of the time. The other was ordered by Ovando from very shame to be fitted out by the agent of Columbus in Santo Domingo. The mutineers had long since returned penitent, and the whole company set sail for Santo Domingo.

Meantime, in the colony matters had gone as badly as cruelty, avarice, and ambition could make them, and when the admiral's vessels appeared in the harbor there was an ovation in his honor, in which Ovando joined. On Sept. 12 Columbus embarked for Spain, taking his company in two vessels. Many of the crew were left in Santo Domingo, the admiral paying their expenses from his own purse, and furnishing funds for those who wished to go with him. As they were leaving port, a tempest wrecked one of the ships, and, crowded into the other, he with his son and brother reached Spain after being driven and tossed by storms throughout the voyage.

Columbus found that his trials were still to be severe. He wrote to his son Diego: "I have nothing of the revenue due me. . . . I live by borrowing. . . . Little have I profited by twenty years of service, with such toils and perils, since at present I do not own a roof in Spain. If I desire to eat or sleep, I have no resort but an inn, and for the most part I have not wherewithal to pay my bill." Letter after letter he wrote to the sovereigns in behalf of the sailors who went with him, in terms like these, taken from one letter: "They are poor, and it is now nearly three years since they left their homes. They have endured infinite toils and perils, and they bring invaluable tidings, for which their majesties ought to thank God and rejoice." When he was reminded that he had brought no gold from the mines of Veragua, reported in his last journey, he answered: "I would not rob or outrage the country, since reason requires that it should be settled, and then gold may be acquired without violence.

He was very eager that public restitution should be made and his interests respected before his death. As he was unable to travel, and compelled from a disease of the eye to write only at night, Diego Mendez was pleading his cause at court. The burden of his letters was anxiety for his good name and that of his

HOUSE IN WHICH COLUMBUS DIED, VALLADOLID.

children. He wrote: "I have served their majesties with as much zeal and diligence as if it had been to gain paradise; and if I have failed in anything, it has been because my knowledge and my powers went no further."

Queen Isabella died in November, 1504, and with that event the hopes of Columbus sank completely. He went to the court to lay the matter before the King, who consented to arbitrate on the business; but Columbus saw that he referred only to the rents and revenues. What Columbus had at heart was the fulfillment of the promises to him and his. Las Casas says: "As far as actions went, the King not merely showed him no signs of favor, but, on the contrary, discountenanced him as much as possible; yet he was never wanting in complimentary expressions." Columbus wrote to entreat that Diego might be appointed to his place, saying: "This is a matter that touches my honor. As to all the rest, do as your majesty thinks proper; give or withhold, as may be most for your interest, and I shall be content. I believe it is the anxiety caused by the delay of this affair which is the principal reason of my ill health." Again he wrote: "It appears that his majesty does not think fit to fulfill that which he has promised me by word and seal, with the Queen who is now in glory. For me to contend for the contrary would be to contend with the wind. I have done all that I can do. I leave the rest to God, whom I have ever found propitious to me in my necessities."

When Columbus heard from his sick bed of the arrival of Queen Juana (daughter of Isabella) and King Philip to take possession of the vacant throne of Castile, he wrote to the young sovereigns, but with no result. He died in the city of Valladolid, May 19, 1506. His last words were: "Into thy hands, O Lord, I commend my spirit."

Columbus was buried in the Convent of St. Francisco, and a high funeral service was conducted in a church at Valladolid. In 1513 his body was removed to Seville, and in 1536 it was again transported, being carried with that of his son Diego to Santo Domingo, whence it was again removed to the cathedral in Havana in 1796. Ferdinand had caused a monument to be erected to Columbus, bearing the inscription, "For Castile and Leon Columbus found a New World."

The day before he died Columbus executed a will, which he had written nearly a year before. It is well authenticated. Its principal provisions are:

I appoint my dear son Don Diego to be my heir of all my property and offices which I hold by right and inheritance, as determined in the *mayorazgo;* and if he should have no legal male heir, that my son Don Ferdinand shall inherit in the same manner; and if he should have no legal male heir, that Don Bartholomew, my brother, shall inherit, in the same manner; and likewise if he should have no male heir, that my other brother shall inherit. Thus it is intended, from one to the other next of kin of my family, and this continually. And there shall be no female heir unless the males become extinct; and if that should happen, let it be the female nearest of kin of my family.

Because heretofore there has been no revenue received from the said Indies, so that I could separate therefrom the sums which I will mention below, and we hope that by the clemency of our sovereign it may amount to a very large sum; my intention would be and is, that Don Ferdinand, my son, should receive of it 1,500,000 each year; and Don Bartholomew, my brother, 150,000 maravedis; and Don Diego, my brother, 100,000 maravedis, because he belongs to the Church. And I say that of all the income which Don Diego shall receive by reason of the said inheritance, that he shall have 10 parts every year, and that 1 part of these 10 he shall divide among our relatives who appear to have most need of it, and poor persons, and in other pious works.

I say that this part which I direct to give to Don Ferdinand, my son, that I make of it a mayorazgo for him, and that to him shall succeed his eldest son, and in like manner from one to the other perpetually, without the power to sell or exchange or give or abuse in any way.

I say to Don Diego, my son, and I direct that as soon as he shall have income from the said mayorazgo an inheritance sufficient to maintain a chapel, that he shall cause to be appointed 3 chaplains who shall say masses every day—1 to the honor of the holy Trinity, another to the Conception of our Lady, and the other for the souls of all the faithful dead, and for my soul and that of my father and mother and wife.

As we read the story of Columbus, the personality of another great Italian, a discoverer in the realm of mind, is strongly suggested. Dante, like Columbus, believed himself to be invested with a divine mission, to be a child of destiny. Dante was noble and learned, Columbus was of humble birth and scant education; but both loved the lore they knew in the same fashion, both were called before kings and councils, and both found eloquent words for their fervid convictions. Both were tenacious of purpose and conscious of personal integrity. To both, the Hebrew prophets were familiar friends and religion the motive power of life. Both were intensely imaginative, and both lacked the quality of humor. Both were stung by the ingratitude

LEADEN CASKET SUPPOSED TO CONTAIN THE BONES OF COLUMBUS, IN SANTO DOMINGO.

of princes and of people, and the mariner who sailed the sea of darkness might well have adopted Dante's language in regard to his own career: "Truly, I have been a vessel without sail or rudder, driven to divers ports, estuaries, and shores by that hot blast. the breath of grievous poverty; and I have shown myself to the eyes of many who, perhaps through some fame of me, had imagined me in quite other guise, in whose view not only was my person debased, but every work of mine. whether done or yet to do, became of less account." Of both these prisoners of hope it may be said, in Lowell's words:

The hooting mob of yesterday with silent awe return
To glean up the scattered ashes into History's golden
  urn.

Some of the actions of Columbus are persistently criticised. As to his sending Indian prisoners to be sold to slavery: the markets of Andalusia were full of conquered Moors. and Isabella sent negroes freely as slaves to Santo Domingo. Certainly an American biographer should not be the one to cast a stone, when he remembers that three and a half centuries later the Rev. Nehemiah Adams, of Boston. Mass., in his "South-side View of Slavery," said: "Religion in the masters destroys everything in slavery that makes it obnoxious; and not only so, it converts the relation of the slave into an effectual means of happiness." In Spain in those days an infidel had no rights that a Catholic was bound to respect, and an infidel was any one who was not a Catholic. Another accusation is that cruelty and conceited bigotry in compelling the signing of the document in reference to the finding of terra firma. That point was vital to Columbus. To find not islands, but Asia, was what he had promised the sovereigns who furnished him the outfit. He was turning back under protest from a quest the results of which could only be made certain to them by the word of those who saw the land. There was no Grand Khan, no civilization, nothing but the vast extent of the country and the supposed position on the globe that could be brought to proof. Columbus was convinced, but he wanted to keep on, and, if he could not, they must at least uphold him unitedly. It has been said that he was a visionary. His words, taken as a whole, furnish the best answer to that charge. He was imaginative to a high degree, but through most of his life he was also extremely practical. When he was overwhelmed with mortification and sorrow at the treatment he received, was worn out by innumerable mental and physical trials and hardships, racked with fever. helpless, and almost blind, the gorgeons fantasy of his mingled religious and scientific imaginings is evidence of the undying nature of his love and hope.

COMMERCE AND NAVIGATION OF THE UNITED STATES. The volume of foreign commerce for 1891–'92 was the largest in the history of the country. The total value of the imports and exports of merchandise was $1,857,726,910, which was $128,329,904, or 7¼ per cent., more than in the previous year, and exceeded the total for 1889–'90 by 25 per cent. The total value of the imports was $827,391,284, which was 2 per cent. less than in the previous year. The chief items of decrease were tin plates, woolens, and tobacco, which had been largely imported in anticipation of the new tariff, and after it went into effect were imported in less quantities than they otherwise would have been in consequence of its operation. The imports of other goods on which the duties were increased likewise declined, but many articles that were placed on the free list were imported in much greater quantities. The ratio of the duty-free articles increased from 43 per cent. of the total imports in 1890–'91 to 55 per cent. in 1891–'92. They grew under the operation of the tariff changes from $366,000,000 to $458,000,000. The domestic exports in 1892 reached $1,000,-000,000 for the first time. They amounted to $1,015,789,607. There was a heavy increase in the exports of breadstuffs, owing to short crops in nearly every grain-growing district in Europe and the famine in Russia, which cut off the usual supplies from that country. In the exports of cotton there was a falling off in the value of $32,250,000, owing to a great fall in prices. The shipments of cotton were larger than ever they were before. The exports of petroleum, refined sugar, and provisions were smaller in value than in the preceding year. The other exports were normal in amount. If it had not been for the large wheat crop, the extraordinary demand in Europe for cereals, and the consequent high prices, the exports would have fallen short of the total for the previous year. The imports of free merchandise have increased from one third of the total in 1889–'90 to more than half in 1891–'92. Sugar and coffee increased enormously. The consumption of goods paying duty has shown a corresponding decrease, having shrunk greatly in the last three years. The imports of tin plate fell off from $35,746,000 in 1890–'91 to $12,315,000 in 1891–'92. The imports that took the first rank in 1891–'92 were in round numbers as follow: Coffee, $127,000,000; sugar, $107,000,000; woolen manufactures, $38,000,000; chemicals, $32,-000,000; silk manufactures, $31,000,000; cotton manufactures, $28,000,000; hides, $27,000,000; manufactures of flax, jute, and hemp, $27,000,-000; raw silk, $25,000,000. The staple exports reached the following figures: Raw cotton, $258,000,000; wheat and flour, $237,000,000; meat products, $130,000,000; Indian corn and meal, $43,000,000; mineral oil, $43,000,000; cattle, $35,000,000; iron and steel products, $29,000,000; lumber and wood manufactures, $28,000,000; tobacco, $25,000,000.

The increase in the total value of free imports was $91,758,306, and the decrease in the value of dutiable imports was $109,272,040. In the total value of the merchandise imports there was a decrease of $17,513,734. The increase in the total exports of domestic products was $143,461,728. The total exports of foreign merchandise in 1892 were $14,546,137, against $12,210,527 in 1891, showing an increase of $2,335,610.

The total value of the imports and exports carried in cars and other land vehicles in 1892 was $72,948,067, as compared with $72,856,194 in 1891, carried in American vessels, $220,173,-735, against $206,459,725; carried in foreign vessels, $1,564,558,808, against $1,450,081,087. Of the total imports of merchandise, $596,866,-819 came in foreign steamships, $23,789,821 less than in 1891; $51,669,157 in foreign sailing vessels, $4,185,966 less; $80,538,964 in American steamships, $6,327,181 more; $58,600,927 in American sailing vessels, $5,341,032 more; and $39,726,595 in cars and other land vehicles. $1,-206,160 more. Of the total exports of domestic merchandise, $810,454,897 were carried in foreign steamships, an increase of $134,917,442; $94,-909,498 in foreign sailing vessels, an increase of $5,219,165; $45,985,100 in American steamships, an increase of $3,017,902; $33,181,664 in American sailing vessels, a decrease of $776,764; and $31,200,852 in cars and other land vehicles, an increase of $1,083,983. Of the foreign exports, amounting to $14,546,137, there were $2,020,-620, an increase of $214,050, carried in land vehicles; $1,340,595, a decrease of $70,746, carried in American steam vessels; $526,485, a decrease of $70,746, carried in American sailing vessels; $10,267,275, an increase of $2,319,906, carried in foreign steam vessels; and $391,162, a decrease of $3,005, carried in foreign sailing vessels.

Of the total imports of merchandise, free and dutiable, $785,395,764 were imported direct from foreign countries in 1891–'92, against $800,737,958 in 1890–'91; $42,006,098 were imported through the exterior ports without appraisement, against $44,178,238; $734,682,160 were entered for immediate consumption, against $694,702,973; and $92,720,802 were entered for warehouse, against $150,213,223.

The total value of imported merchandise remaining in the warehouses of the various ports on June 30, 1892, was $29,575,072, compared with $26,571,261 on June 30, 1891. Of this total, $28,095,613 consisted of dutiable, and $1,479,459 of nondutiable merchandise, compared with $25,038,067 and $1,533,194 at the end of the previous year.

Of the total imports and exports in 1892 there were imported and exported at the port of New York $950,490,895, or 65·89 per cent. of the total commerce of the Atlantic coast; while Boston had $158,956,125, or 11·02 per cent.; Philadelphia. $118,548,248, or 8·22 per cent.; Baltimore, $112,268,720, or 7·78 per cent.; Savannah, $26,006,077, or 1·80 per cent.; Charleston, $17,615,067, or 1·22 per cent.; and Newport News, $14,634,481, or 1·01 per cent. Of the commerce of the Gulf ports, $150,162,426, or 70·08 per cent., was conducted through New Orleans, and $36,703,256, or 17·14 per cent., through Galveston. On the Pacific coast. 81·82 per cent. of the total commerce, or $87,872,728, passed through San Francisco. Of the total lake commerce, 21·77 per cent., $18,653,494 in value, passed through Chicago; 12·69 per cent. through Port Huron; 11·18 per cent. through Detroit, and 10·90 per cent. through Vermont. The shares of the principal customs districts in the total commerce of the country was as follows: New York, 51·18 per cent.; Boston and Charlestown, 8·56 per cent.; New Orleans, 8·09 per cent.; Philadelphia, 6·38 per cent.; Baltimore, 6·05 per cent.; San Francisco, 4·74 per cent.; Galveston, 1·98 per cent.; Savannah, 1·40 per cent.; Chicago, 1 per cent.; Charleston, 0·95 per cent.; Newport News, 0·79 per cent.; Norfolk and Portsmouth, 0·71 per cent.; Huron, 0·59 per cent.; Detroit, 0·51 per cent.; Vermont, 0·50 per cent.; Willamette, 0·43 per cent.; Puget Sound, 0·58 per cent.; Corpus Christi, 0·38 per cent.; Paso del Norte. 0·36 per cent.; Champlain, 0·34 per cent.; Richmond. 0·31 per cent.; Brunswick, Ga., 0·30 per cent.; Wilmington, 0·29 per cent.; Buffalo Creek, N. Y., 0·29 per cent.; Oswego. 0·23 per cent. Of the total external commerce of the country, $1,442,-564,718, or 77·06 per cent., passed through the Atlantic ports; $214,279,576, or 11·53 per cent., through the ports of the Gulf of Mexico; $107,-464,295, or 5·79 per cent., through the Pacific ports; $85,076,232 over the northern border and through the lake ports; and $7,695,789, or 0·42 per cent., fell to interior ports of entry.

The following table gives the values of the imports from the principal commercial countries, and the exports of domestic merchandise to each of them in 1892:

COUNTRIES.	Imports.	Domestic exports.
Europe.		
United Kingdom	$156,800,881	$493,957,868
Germany	82,907,558	164,180,782
France	68,554,793	97,896,182
Belgium	10,273,061	47,118,121
Netherlands	10,886,602	48,556,865
Italy	22,16¹,617	14,228,947
Spain	5,207,861	11,522,150
Switzerland	13,196,469	10,397
Russia	4,926,630	6,663,095
Sweden and Norway	3,774,982	6,578,857
Austria-Hungary	7,718,865	1,453,388
Denmark	228,545	8,858,881
Turkey in Europe	2,028,208	28,961
Greece	1,360,449	100,870
Gibraltar	86,931	403,165
Azores and Madeira	84,671	271,475
Greenland, Iceland, and Faroes	76,879	....
Roumania	....	25,280
Servia	17,758	....
Total Europe	$391,628,469	$841,087,022

COUNTRIES.	Imports.	Domestic exports.
North America.		
Cuba	$77,931,671	$17,622,411
British North America	85,834,547	42,580,573
Mexico	28,107,525	13,696,531
British West Indies	12,440,182	7,995,185
Hayti	3,202,729	4,963,480
Puerto Rico	3,248,007	2,808,631
Guatemala	3,152,833	1,309,577
Salvador	2,930,592	1,274,021
Santo Domingo	2,293,748	984,188
Costa Rica	2,086,046	1,122,295
Nicaragua	1,657,873	1,157,159
French West Indies	29,528	1,950,403
Honduras	962,829	473,047
Bermuda	552,315	890,952
Danish West Indies	362,673	610,843
Dutch West Indies	98,112	665,617
British Honduras	238,525	464,403
St. Pierre and Miquelon	176	957,751
Total North America	$174,054,181	$101,463,551
South America.		
Brazil	$118,088,604	$14,240,009
Venezuela	10,325,338	3,991,908
Argentine Republic	5,348,798	2,648,825
Colombia	4,116,886	3,065,466
Chili	3,487,159	3,583,342
British Guiana	4,864,204	1,885,542
Uruguay	2,480,596	907,067
Ecuador	809,831	839,466
Peru	591,300	1,002,977
Dutch Guiana	570,198	328,007
French Guiana	5,850	149,777
Bolivia	....	17,036
Total South America	$150,727,759	$32,578,922
Asia.		
British India	$24,778,107	$3,674,141
Japan	23,790,202	3,288,282
China	20,488,291	5,663,471
Dutch East Indies	6,914,743	1,372,035
Hong-Kong	784,823	4,887,850
Turkey in Asia	2,898,833	177,341
Russia, Asiatic	320,167	119,684
French East Indies	....	140,427
Corea	603	....
All other countries	188,977	258,325
Total Asia	$80,138,251	$19,581,056
Oceanica.		
British Australasia	$8,492,306	$11,246,474
Hawaiian Islands	8,075,882	3,662,018
Philippine Islands	6,308,653	60,914
French possessions	256,271	305,490
Total Oceanica	$23,133,062	$15,274,896
Africa.		
British Africa	$816,597	$3,453,700
Egypt and Tripoli	2,380,639	136,274
French Africa	680,705	806,156
Madagascar	252,650	247,923
Canary Islands	61,470	265,186
Portuguese Africa	13,580	69,389
Liberia	21,271	85,411
All other countries	1,191,140	521,124
Total Africa	$5,318,052	$5,085,162
All other countries	$2,402,688	$715,702
Grand total	$827,402,462	$1,015,732,011

The share of Great Britain in the total commerce for 1891-'92 was 35·29, in the imports 18·89, in the exports 48·46 per cent. Germany's share was 10·14 per cent. in the total, 10·02 in the imports, and 10·24 in the exports; France's was 9·03 per cent. in the total, 8·29 in the imports, and 9·62 in the exports; that of the West Indies, 7·43 per cent. in the total, 12·04 in the imports, and 3·74 in the exports; that of Brazil, 7·16 per cent. in the total, 14·34 in the imports,

and 1·39 in the exports; that of the British North American possessions, 4·32 per cent. in the total, 4·27 in the' imports, and 4·36 in the exports; Belgium's, 3·18 per cent. in the total, 1·24 in the imports, and 4·73 in the exports: that of the Netherlands, 2·95 per cent. in the total, 1·32 in the imports, and 4·26 in the exports; that of Mexico, 2·28 per cent. in the total. 3·40 in the imports, and 1·39 in the exports; that of Italy, 1·66 per cent. in the total, 2·68 in the imports, and 1·39 in the exports; that of the British East Indies, 1·53 per cent. in the total, 3 in the imports, and 0·36 in the exports; Japan's, 1·46 per cent. in the total, 2·89 in the imports, and 0·32 in the exports; China's, 1·41 per cent. in the total, 2·46 in the imports, and 0·55 in the exports; that of British Australasia, 1·07 per cent. in the total, 1·03 in the imports, and 1·11 in the exports; that of the Central American republics and British Honduras, 0·92 per cent. in the total, 1·26 in the imports, and 0·64 in the exports; that of Spain, 0·90 per cent. in the total, 0·63 in the imports, and 1·12 in the exports; that of Venezuela, 0·77 per cent. in the total, 1·25 in the imports, and 0·40 in the exports; that of Switzerland, 0·71 per cent. in the total, or 1·60 per cent. in the imports; that of the Hawaiian Islands, 0·64 per cent. of the total, 0·98 of the imports, and 0·36 of the exports; that of Sweden and Norway, 0·56 per cent. of the total, 0·45 of the imports, and 0·64 of the exports; that of Austria-Hungary, 0·50 per cent. of the total. 0·93 of the imports, and 0·15 of the exports: that of Denmark, 0·46 per cent. of the total, 0·03 of the imports, and 0·81 of the exports; that of Russia on the Baltic and the White Sea, 0·46 per cent. of the total, 0·36 of the imports, and 0·56 of the exports; that of the Dutch East Indies, 0·45 per cent. of the total, 0·84 of the imports, and 0·13 of the exports; that of the Argentine Republic, 0·45 per cent. of the total, 0·64 of the imports, and 0·28 of the exports; that of Colombia, 0·39 per cent. of the total, 0·50 of the imports, and 0·30 of the exports; that of Chili, 0·38 per cent. of the total, 0·42 of the imports, and 0·34 of the exports: that of the Philippine Islands, 0·34 per cent. of the total, 0·75 of the imports, and 0·01 of the exports; that of British Guiana, 0·34 per cent. of the total, 0·53 of the imports, and 0·19 of the exports; that of Portugal, 0·33 per cent. of the total, 0·24 of the imports, and 0·40 of the exports; that of Hong-Kong, 0·30 per cent. of the total, 0·09 of the imports, and 0·47 of the exports; that of British Africa, 0·23 per cent. of the total, 0·10 of the imports, and 0·34 of the exports; that of Uruguay, 0·18 per cent. of the total, 0·30 of the imports, and 0·09 of the exports: that of Turkey in Asia, 0·17 per cent. of the total, 0·35 of the imports, and 0·02 of the exports; that of Russia on the Black Sea, 0·16 per cent. of the total, 0·23 of the imports, and 0·10 of the exports; that of the British possessions not mentioned, 0·16 per cent. of the total, 0·28 of the imports, and 0·06 of the exports; that of Turkish provinces in Africa, or Egypt and Tripoli, 0·13 per cent. of the total, 0·28 of the imports, and 0·01 of the exports; that of Turkey in Europe, 0·11 per cent. of the total, or 0·25 per cent. of the imports; that of all other African countries, 0·09 per cent. of the total, 0·14 of the imports, and 0·05 of the exports; that of Ecuador, 0·09 per cent. of the total, 0·10 of the imports, and 0·08 of the exports; that of Peru, 0·08 per cent. of the total, 0·07 of the imports, and 0·10 of the exports; that of Bermuda, 0·08 per cent. of the total, 0·07 of the imports, and 0·09 of the exports; that of Greece, 0·08 per cent. of the total, 0·15 of the imports, and 0·01 of the exports; that of French Africa, 0·05 per cent. of the total, 0·08 of the imports, and 0·03 of the exports; that of Dutch Guiana. 0·05 per cent. of the total, 0·07 of the imports, and 0·03 of the exports: that of French islands in Oceanica. 0·03 per cent. of all three: that of all other countries, 0·20 per cent. of the total, 0·13 of the imports, and 0·24 of the exports.

Imports.—The value of the principal articles or classes of articles exempt from duty imported into the United States during the twelve months ending June 30, 1892, compared with the values for the preceding year, are shown in the following table:

FREE OF DUTY.	1891.	1892.
Animals	$2,465,110	$1,675 903
Articles, produce of U. S., returned	4,466,279	4,847,920
Art works of American artists ...	395,558	300,069
Asphaltum or bitumen...........	253,410	387,509
Bark, hemlock	274,389	256,346
Bolting cloths	290,088	279,680
Books, maps, engravings, etc	1,655,514	1,89,668
Alizarine and madder...........	667,862	1,029,148
Argol or crude tartar...........	2,197,507	2,216,525
Cinchona bark..................	301,070	301,385
Cochineal......................	55,868	19,779
Logwood and other dye woods ...	2,010,485	1,378,601
Gum shellac, gambier. etc.	6,906,914	6,080,546
Indigo.........................	1,600,680	1,772,507
Licorice root..................	896,597	1,601,028
Chloride of lime...............	1,429,509	1,889,640
Mineral waters................	862,900	436,241
Opium, crude	951,682	1,029,208
Chlorate of potash.............	238,840	358,768
Muriate of potash.............	1,178,579	1,094,122
Saltpeter.....................	277,768	435,589
Other potash..................	828,387	504,950
Sulphate of quinine, etc	833,260	572,078
Nitrate of soda................	2,9 3,374	2,976,816
Sulphur, cruds................	2,451,518	2,524,406
Vanilla beans..................	594,744	608,696
Other chemicals, drugs, and dyes.	5,444,714	4,512,950
Chicory	38,512	98,179
Cacao, crude	2,617,168	3,221,041
Coffee........................	96,123,777	126,801,607
Cork bark.....................	2,825,004	3,217,521
Diamonds and other stones, rough	804,026	1,096,587
Eggs	1,058,964	(Dutiable.)
Sago, tapioca, etc.............	543,780	257,789
Fertilizers....................	1,525,884	1,431,285
Fish, fresh....................	250,386	(Dutiable.)
Bananas......................	5,854,752	5,000,682
Cocoanuts....................	918,293	917,564
Currants......................	1,246,074	1,209,119
Dates.........................	613,845	551,629
Other fruits...................	1,730,910	1,970,634
Furs and skins, undressed	2,892,166	3,352,429
Hair..........................	2,265,714	1,665,562
Straw, and other material for hats	1,549,795	1,807,190
Goat skins....................	11,488,745	11,509,127
Other skins...................	16,497,014	15,149,006
Effects of immigrants and citizens.	2,920,050	2,921,898
India rubber and gutta-percha...	18,020,904	19,583,090
Needles.......................	285,189	387,272
Gun barrels, rough-bored	68,218	170,084
Ivory.........................	886,302	898,189
Vegetable ivory...............	76,587	114,753
Matting.......................	1,480,098	1,687,478
Oils, fixed or expressed........	1,051,265	1,872,017
Oils, volatile or essential	1,288,167	1,457,227
Ores, gold-bearing............	214,803	249,904
Ores, silver-bearing...........	8,958,608	9,656,761
Rags, other than woolen........	2,059,447	1,793,189
Other paper stock	2,960,086	3,850,124
Platinum, unmanufactured......	925,066	505,205
Plumbago.....................	500,909	796,648
Seeds.........................	880,804	1,485,044

FREE OF DUTY.	1891.	1892.
Silk cocoons..................	$62,145	$97,678
Raw silk......................	17,904,654	24,321,494
Waste silk....................	1,019,282	616,158
Nutmegs	686,019	75,818
Black and white pepper........	1,888,687	1,069,268
Other spices..................	864,495	920,006
Molasses.....................	1,9 4,987	2,877,744
Beet sugar, raw	8,870,809	8,081,170
Cane sugar, raw	84,508,507	95,761,812
Tea...........................	13,595,908	14,878,222
Istle or Tampico fiber.........	853,181	825,548
Jute and jute butts............	2,641,968	8,021,174
Manilla	6,218,254	6,672,279
Sisal..........................	4,454,578	5,157,620
Other textile grasses, etc.......	1,634,728	1,271,801
Coir yarn.....................	167,452	161,449
Tin in bars, pigs, etc..........	8,667,570	7,977,545
Wood, unmanufactured........	5,569,991	5,276,972
Articles from the Hawaiian Islands	10,749,402	267,583
Other free articles	9,401,154	9,161,149
Total free of duty	$365,241,852	$457,999,658

Of the articles imported free from the Hawaiian Islands, rice alone is given in the figures for 1892, the raw sugar being bunebed with the imports of cane sugar not above No. 16 Dutch standard of color imported from the West Indian islands and other countries that enjoy the reciprocity arrangements of the McKinley tariff bill. The ports of the United States were made free to raw sugar and molasses of those countries, and to the beet-root sugar of European countries having the footing of favored nations on April 1, 1891. The sugar imports from those countries previous to that date are included in the list of dutiable articles. The imports of unmanufactured opium, of chlorate, saltpeter, and the other compounds of potash, except the muriate, of chicory root unground, of dried currants and dates, of materials of straw, grass, chip, palm leaf, etc., for hats and bonnets, of needles for sewing by hand or darning, of unfinished shot-gun barrels, of Chinese and other straw matting, and of jute and jute butts, manilla hemp, and sisal grass for the year 1890–'91, are given only for the part of the year that came after Oct. 6, 1890, before which they were included among the dutiable articles. Eggs and fresh fish, on the other hand, were taken off the free list, and the imports of these articles are given only up to Oct. 5, 1890, from which date they are included in the returns of duty-paying imports.

The number of cattle imported free of duty declined from 2,740 in 1891 to 1,132 in 1892, sheep from 9,606 to 4,316, and horses from 6,444 to 3,312. Distilled spirits, the produce of the United States, returned free of duty, declined from 1,701,591 to 918,304 proof gallons, and in value from $2,044,925 to $1,079,385. There was a decrease of 23,858 tons, or from 84,155 to 60,-297 tons, in the imports of logwood ; of 521,832 pounds, or from 938,839 to 417,007 pounds, in gum Arabic ; of 4,951,966 pounds, or from 75,-573,414 to 70,621,448 pounds in muriate of potash ; of 478,302 ounces, or from 3,332,173 to 2,853,871 ounces in sulphate of quinine and the alkaloids or salts of cinchona bark ; of 11,385 tons in sulphur ; of 6,457 tons, or over 60 per cent., in guano, and 8,636 tons in phosphates : of 652,596 pounds in gutta-percha ; of 3,126,137 pounds, or from 121,058,212 to 117,932,075 pounds, in rags for paper stock ; of 2,204 pounds, or over a third in platinum ; of 145,402 pounds in waste silk; of nearly a third in fibrous vegetable substances other than those that were newly exempted from duty; and slight decreases in coir yarn and rice from the Hawaiian Islands. The import of the last named in 1892 was 7,489,700 pounds. Most articles showed an increase, and many a large increase. In asphaltum it was from 70,153 to 103,-157 tons; in raw cotton, from 20,908,817 to 28,-663,769 pounds; in crude cacao, including shells and leaves, from 21,539,840 to 21,955.874 pounds. The increase in the imports of coffee was 113,-413,480 pounds, or from 519,528,432 to 632,941,912 pounds. Among the chemicals, drugs, and dyes not subject to duty, natural and artificial alizarine shows an increase of 1,433,339 pounds, or from 3,404,931 to 4,838,270 pounds; cochineal, an increase of 143,640 pounds, or from 86,399 to 230,-039 pounds; argol or crude tartar, one of 3,234,-069 pounds, or from 21,579,102 to 24,813,171 pounds; mineral waters, one of 279,974 gallons, or from 1,885,100 to 2,165,074 gallons; chloride of lime or bleaching powder, an increase of 3,-272,574 pounds, or from 107,475,715 to 110,748,-289 pounds; licorice root, an increase of 43,351,-672 pounds, or from 55,307,911 to 98,659,583 pounds; indigo, one of 372,660 pounds, or from 2,089,007 to 2,461,667 pounds; crude camphor gum, one of 239,620 pounds, or from 1,716,167 to 1,955,787 pounds; and shellac, one of 56,886 pounds, or from 6,253,380 to 6,310,266 pounds; and cinchona and other barks from which quinine may be extracted, one of 533,092 pounds, or from 2,901,783 to 3,434.875 pounds. In the imports of India rubber there was an increase of 6,264,116 pounds, or from 33,712,089 to 39,976,-205 pounds. In those of ivory there was one of 28,202 pounds, or from 243,236 to 271,438 pounds, and in vegetable ivory, one of 1,374,830 pounds, or from 7,178,146 to 8,552,976 pounds. The imports of fixed and expressed oils increased from 18,816,943 to 32,532,437 pounds; and those of volatile or essential oils from 2,347,685 to 2,529,-311 pounds. Plumbago imports show an increase from 10,136 to 13,511 tons, or 3,375 tons. In silk cocoons the increase was from 82,053 to 191,221 pounds; and in raw silk or silk as reeled from the cocoon it was from 4,917,688 to 7,521,342 pounds. The imports of spices showed a considerable augmentation in the demand, the import of nutmegs increasing from 1,327,135 to 1,580,005; of black and white pepper, from 13,-564,583 to 14,799,322; and of the other kinds, from 13,732,261 to 14,511,451 pounds. The tea imports grew from 83,453,339 to 90,079,039 pounds. In the imports of tin in bars, blocks, and pigs, or grain, or granulated tin, the increase was from 39,787,622 to 43,908,652 pounds.

The values of the imports of the principal articles and classes of dutiable merchandise for 1892, and for the last preceding year, are given in the following table:

DUTIABLE.	1891.	1892.
Animals, live	$2,480,255	$2,575,513
Art works of foreign artists	2,014,510	2,080,569
Books, maps, engravings, etc	2,571,889	2,115,417
Brass, and manufactures thereof	284,848	242,564
Breadstuffs	4,484,449	4,681,408
Bristles	1,357,938	1,455,058
Brushes	863,578	797,979
Buttons and button forms	2,096,411	1,817,208
Cement	4,021,998	3,855,572
Coal-tar colors and dyes	1,673,864	1,614,226

DUTIABLE.	1891.	1892.
Glycerin	$996,686	$881,810
Logwood and other dyes	274,469	326,142
Opium, crude	220,743	(Free of duty.)
Opium, prepared for smoking	567,035	547,528
Potash, nitrate of, or saltpeter	181,816	(Free of duty.)
Caustic soda	1,874,700	1,598,908
Bicarbonate of soda	15,724	48,:22
Sal soda and soda ash	4,382,917	4,496,597
Other salts of soda	118,713	167,684
Sumac, ground	245,536	216,668
Other chemicals, drugs, and dyes	5,125,674	4,585,578
Clays or earths	437,226	523,367
Clocks, and parts of	300,492	195,590
Watches, and parts of	1,984,414	1,794,648
Coal, bituminous	3,588,278	4,374,079
Coffee (under § 3 of the tariff act)	(Free of duty.)	1,240,928
Copper ore	526,563	748,932
Bar, pig, and old copper and ingots	216,404	82,644
Copper manufactures	120,545	97,806
Cotton cloth,not bleached or colored	170,423	140,001
Cotton cloth, bleached or colored	4,237,221	4,505,666
Cotton clothing	1,201,278	1,261,848
Cotton knit goods	6,738,775	5,833,652
Cotton lace, edgings, embroideries	10,589,490	11,248,289
Thread, yarn, and warps	857,645	664,952
Other cotton manufactures	5,917,792	4,669,483
Earthen, stone, and china ware	8,881,388	8,708,598
Eggs	181,681	522,240
Feathers, natural	1,775,924	904,659
Artificial flowers and feathers	1,848,569	1,838,874
Fresh salmon	48,307	165,450
Other fresh fish	836,619	403,345
Anchovies and sardines	1,089,975	1,201,149
Dried, smoked, or pickled cod, etc.	527,113	449,567
Dried or smoked herring	101,498	66,456
Pickled or salted herring	922,099	1,178,514
Pickled or salted mackerel	1,413,875	883,423
Pickled or salted salmon	80,812	60,418
Other cured or preserved fish	274,449	287,078
Flax	1,656,779	1,964,168
Hemp, and substitutes for	1,781,396	681,809
Jute	1,217,590	(Free of duty.)
Sisal and other fibers	1,874,941	(Free of duty.)
Manufactures of flax, hemp, jute, etc	24,024,004	26,298,317
Figs	697,562	511,142
Lemons	4,351,970	4,548,263
Oranges	2,389,987	1,210,388
Plums and prunes	2,054,486	487,271
Raisins	2,016,829	1,884,809
Preserved fruits	1,289,137	1,284,898
Other fruits	762,385	588,806
Almonds	981,007	1,028,671
Other nuts	1,114,959	821,200
Furs, and manufactures of fur	7,006,688	6,844,702
Glass and glassware	8,864,812	8,758,964
Hair, and manufactures thereof	148,019	114,102
Hats, bonnets, hoods, and material	672,985	(Free of duty.)
Hay	445,461	715,131
Goat skins	(Free of duty.)	48,840
Other hides and skins	(Free of duty.)	148,245
Hops	1,797,406	883,701
India-rubber manufactures	854,645	482,856
Iron ore	2,430,159	2,592,461
Pig iron	2,018,967	1,812,675
Scrap iron and steel	815,399	548,882
Bar iron, rolled or hammered	821,613	858,297
Iron and steel rails	8,479	10,014
Hoops, ties, and bands	418,524	81,840
Hoop or band iron or steel	144,408	69,665
Steel in ingots, blooms, bars, etc	1,656,720	1,666,214
Sheet, plate, and taggers iron	789,297	840,591
Tin plates and taggers tin	25,746,920	12,815,562
Wire rods	2,124,148	1,761,776
Wire and wire rope	747,309	552,624
Anvils	184,128	110,000
Chains	86,587	60,049
Cutlery	1,458,779	1,207,020
Files, rasps, etc	144,488	81,554
Firearms	1,070,779	647,751
Machinery	2,721,580	2,891,871
Needles	78,901	(Free of duty.)
Other iron and steel manufactures	2,814,051	2,962,932
Gold and silver jewelry	1,368,892	618,518
Precious stones and imitations	12,466,976	12,854,420
Lead and lead manufactures	2,560,886	3,858,378
Leather	6,319,582	6,612,607
Gloves, kid and other leather	5,627,964	5,830,380
Other leather manufactures	736,757	6 7,934
Barley malt	78,488	6,148

DUTIABLE.	1891.	1892.
Malt liquors.....................	$1,765,702	$1,709,960
Marble and stone, and manufactures...................	1,362,718	1,385,810
Metal compositions and manufactures....................	7,222,670	6,574,488
Mineral substances...............	116,193	242,280
Musical instruments..............	1,444,755	1,031,455
Whale and fish oil...............	125,284	144,498
Other animal oils............	5,531	12,186
Mineral oils.....................	49,008	45,118
Olive oil.................	733,489	876,618
Other fixed or expressed oils.....	888,780	867,528
Volatile or essential oils.........	285,824	218,837
Paints or colors....	1,439,127	1,372,052
Paper, and manufactures thereof .	3,031.454	3,742,804
Perfumery and toilet preparations	449,964	464,855
Pipes and smokers' articles..	852,684	418,221
Meat and meat extracts..........	521,322	430,048
Other meat products............	66,385	15,386
Butter..........................	58,541	16,549
Cheese..........................	1,358,752	1,238,166
Milk............................	103,891	95,947
Rice............................	2,754,502	1,565,914
Rice flour and meal and broken rice	1,389,408	1,097,486
Sal t...........................	928,889	713,901
Linseed or flaxseed	1,667,562	319,418
Other seed	718,874	460,375
Silk wearing apparel.............	2,212,971	2,351,797
Silk dress and piece goods........	10,417,698	9,892,241
Silk laces and embroideries.......	8,181,374	4,391,257
Silk ribbons	1,834,487	1,644,769
Other manufactures of silk......	20,288,618	12,592,880
Fancy and toilet soap.	277,886	301,621
Other soap......................	301,986	310,595
Spices..........................	262,682	307,788
Brandy..........................	1,139,815	889,888
Other distilled spirits...........	1,070,421	981,227
Sponges.........................	431,873	854,416
Molasses........................	605,197	(Free of duty.)
Sugar, beet, under No. 13	9,361,968	(Free of duty.)
Sugar, cane, under No. 13.......	42,409,258	(Free of duty.)
Other sugar and confectionery....	248,094	664,072
Tobacco, leaf....................	13,284,162	10,882,423
Tobacco, manufactured...........	2,926,051	3,478,979
Vegetables......................	7,076,874	2,883,227
Champagne and sparkling wines..	5,615,872	4,571,816
Still wine in casks...............	2,641,816	2,464,484
Still wine in bottles.............	1,740,872	1,908,203
Wood, and manufactures thereof .	14,611,214	14,276,447
Wools, Class 1...................	6,919,918	9,529,773
Wools, Class 2...................	1,551,490	1,368,654
Wools, Class 3...................	9,979,969	8,795,681
Woolen manufactures........ ...	41,060,089	35,565,879
Zinc, spelter, and manufactures...	129,587	48,568
All other dutiable articles.......	7,873,646	6,457,688
Total dutiable articles........	$478,674,844	$369,402,804

The imports of live animals not for breeding purposes include 2,036 cattle, 10,762 horses, and 376,498 sheep. The average import price for horses was $106.70, compared with $78.05 in 1891. Of the cereal imports, barley decreased from 5,078,733 bushels in 1891 to 3,146,328 in 1892, while wheat increased from 545,968 to 2,-459,602 bushels. The import of cement decreased from 1.123,127,819 pounds to 1,074,768,-441 pounds. The price of crude opium fell from $2.52 to $1.75 a pound. The prices of bristles, cement, and saltpeter remained stationary. The price of logwood and other dyes decreased from 84 to 77 cents; in caustic soda there was a rise from 24 to 25 cents a pound, and in sal soda from 12 to 13 cents. There were imported 276,895 tons more of bituminous coal, the price of which declined from $3.40 to $3.28. Of copper ore there were 1,913,361 pounds more imported at a cent less a pound than in 1891, and of the metal 2,404,071 pounds more at 8·7 cents, an increase of 8¼ per cent. The average importing price of cotton piece goods remained the same, 14 cents a yard. Yarn declined from 51 to 47

cents a pound. The prices of salted and cured fish were considerably less.

The import of flax increased from 6,331 to 7,812 tons, the price declining from $261.69 to $251.43. The imports of cables, cordage, and twine increased from 759,155 pounds in 1891 to 1,007,678 in 1892, while the average price fell from 11 to 9·9 cents. The decrease in the imports of prunes and plums was from 23,411,525 pounds to 10,869,797 pounds, while the price declined from 6 to 4 cents; that of the imports of raisins was from 39,572.655 to 20,687,640, the price falling from 5·1 to 4·7 cents. The imports of unpolished cylinder and crown glass and common window glass increased from 58,932,738 pounds to 72,082,127 pounds, whereas all glass imports fell away except polished cylinder and crown glass. The importing price of hops was 35 cents, or 10 cents less than in 1891, and the import was 1,513,379 pounds, or nearly 40 per cent. less. The price of pig iron. of which the import increased from 81,916 to 82,891 tons, declined from $24.65 to $21.97. Of bar iron 45,-802,274 pounds were imported, against 42,287.-778 pounds in 1891, the price averaging the same. The import of rails was 10,014 tons, or 6,535 tons more than in the previous year; that of hoops and ties for bales, barrels, etc., declined from 26,646,549 to 1,058,657; that of steel in ingots, blooms, slabs, billets, and bars increased from 70,286,561 to 81,563,726 pounds; and that of sheet, plate, and taggers iron and steel from 25,089.455 to 32,448,322 pounds. The quantity of tin plates. terne plates, and taggers tin went down from 1,036,489,074 to 422,176.202 pounds, while the price declined from 3·4 to 2·9 cents. In wire rods there was a decrease from 112,982,740 to 97,111,641 pounds, and in wire and wire rope from 11,607,306 to 8,072,137 pounds. The malt liquors imported decreased from 3,082,-977 to 2,929,581 gallons. Of olive salad oil 706,486 gallons were imported, 100,977 gallons more than in the previous year, at an average price of $1.24, or 3 cents more. The quantity of volatile and essential oils decreased from 1,111.848 to 922,208 pounds, the price going up from 21 to 24 cents. The imports of cheese, at an average price of 15 cents for both years. were 8,305.288 pounds in 1892, a decrease of 558,352 pounds. In rice and rice flour and meal there was a decrease from 206,522.682 to 140.151.826 pounds. The quantity of toilet soaps increased from 677,-503 to 810,018 pounds. Spices of the dutiable varieties were imported to the amount of 2,381,-248 pounds, an increase of 611.622 pounds. The import of brandy fell off from 443,278 to 333,-234, and that of other distilled spirits from 1,-218,802 to 987.656 gallons, while the price increased from $2.57 to $2.67 for brandy. and from 88 to 99 cents for other liquors. The price of cigar wrappers declined from 94 to 71 cents a pound, and that of other leaf tobacco from 58 to 43 cents, but the average price of cigars, cigarettes, and cheroots increased from $3.82 to $4.30, the cheaper kinds being imported in less quantities. There were 3,073.175 pounds of tobacco for wrappers imported, 18,915,360 pounds of other leaf tobacco, and 658,169 pounds of cigars, cigarettes, and cheroots. The import of champagne and other sparkling wines decreased from 400,084 to 319,592 dozen bottles; that of

still wine in bottles increased from 348,666 to
365,140 dozen; and that of still wine in casks
decreased from 3,860,503 to 3,477,989 gallons,
the price of champagne being about 2 per cent.
and that of still wines 4 per cent. higher. The
price of boards and other sawed lumber rose
from $11.11 to $11.37, and the import declined
from 757,244 to 663,253 thousand feet; that of
shingles increased from 260,652 to 363,027 thousand, with a fall in the price of about 5 per
cent., or from $2.12 to $2.02. In wood pulp
there was a decrease of 2,197 tons, the quantity
imported being 41,118 tons. The total quantity
of raw wool imported was 148,670,652 pounds,
an increase of 19,367,004 pounds. Of this increase, 18,031,861 pounds was in the wools of
class 1, or clothing wools, of which there were
50,262,796 pounds imported, at an average price
of 19 cents, against 21 cents in 1891. The price
of combing wools, class 2 in the schedule, remained 23 cents on the average, and the imports
declined 840,449 pounds to 5,826,574 pounds. In
class 3, comprising the carpet wools and all other
of similar quality, there was an increased importation, the total quantity being 92,581,282
pounds at 9 cents, against 90,405,690 pounds
in 1891 at 11 cents. The imports of carpets
and carpeting fell off from 658,006 to 622,892
square yards. The imports of woolen cloths increased from 12,109,825 to 13,813,276 pounds,
while those of women's and children's dress
goods fell of from 86,644,096 to 78,753,033
square yards. The price of carpeting averaged
$2.06, which was 3 cents lower than in 1891;
that of cloths declined from 99 cents to 92; and
that of dress goods averaged 21 cents per yard
in both years. The imports of shoddy, mungo,
flocks, noils, rags, and woolen waste fell off from
1,185,591 to 262,992 pounds, and those of woolen
yarns, at 59 cents in both years, declined from
2,004,093 to 1,267,128 pounds. While the price
of zinc remained 5·1 cents, the imports decreased
from 1,541,836 to 494,980 pounds.

Exports.—The following table gives the values exported of the principal articles or classes
of articles, the produce of the United States, in
1892, and the values for the preceding year:

DOMESTIC EXPORTS.	1891.	1892.
Agricultural implements	$3,319,130	$3,794,988
Animals	32,935,086	36,498,221
Art works	408,874	422,238
Bark for tanning	241,352	289,708
Blacking	219,903	221,116
Bones, hoofs, and horns	335,710	218,689
Books, maps, engravings, etc.	1,920,470	1,943,223
Brass, and manufactures thereof.	296,349	526,756
Breadstuffs	128,121,656	299,368,117
Bricks	99,175	87,709
Broom corn	172,191	215,133
Brooms and brushes	150,609	181,110
Candles	149,112	165,933
Carriages and horse cars	2,015,870	1,944,170
Railroad cars	2,985,250	1,320,265
Casings for sausages	841,075	878,675
Chemicals, drugs, and dyes	6,545,354	6,693,455
Clocks and watches, and parts of.	1,530,164	1,229,616
Anthracite coal	3,796,495	3,419,660
Bituminous coal	4,594,531	5,229,498
Ground coffee, cocoa, and choco-		
late	86,986	70,651
Copper ore	7,368,898	6,086,777
Copper, manufactured	4,614,597	7,226,392
Cotton, Sea Island	3,062,968	1,591,464
Cotton, other raw	287,649,980	256,869,777
Cotton cloths, colored	2,590,934	2,484,360

DOMESTIC EXPORTS.	1891.	1892.
Cotton cloths, uncolored	$9,277,112	$8,678,608
Cotton clothing	278,169	433,102
Other cotton manufactures	1,458,642	1,685,152
Earthen, stone, and china ware.	159,526	287,481
Eggs	64,259	32,874
Fertilizers	2,182,274	2,657,120
Fish, fresh, cured, and canned..	4,996,621	4,522,763
Flax, hemp, and jute manufac-		
tures	1,504,740	1,998,663
Fruits, fresh, dried, and pre-		
served	2,484,793	6,626,145
Furs and fur skins	3,236,705	3,550,339
Glass and glassware	868,374	942,309
Glucose	1,304,131	2,272,779
Glue	110,292	66,408
Grease and soap stock	2,088,886	1,293,598
Gunpowder	68,676	108,276
Other explosives	906,570	752,079
Hair, and manufactures thereof.	394,544	370,169
Hay	470,223	582,588
Hides and skins	1,838,655	1,228,895
Honey	88,325	75,048
Hops	2,327,474	2,420,502
Ice	91,408	53,814
India-rubber manufactures	1,236,443	1,415,067
Ink, printers' and other	122,295	145,886
Instruments, scientific, electric,		
etc.	1,575,444	1,388,117
Iron and steel, and manufac-		
tures of	28,909,614	28,800,930
Jewelry	832,440	1,026,188
Lamps and lighting apparatus..	509,518	538,864
Lead, and manufactures thereof.	182,412	166,078
Leather, and manufactures		
thereof.	13,278,847	12,084,781
Lime and cement	148,938	115,205
Malt liquors	672,243	657,084
Marble and stone manufactures.	845,154	707,586
Matches	73,220	78,665
Musical instruments	1,326,349	1,164,656
Naval stores	8,191,615	7,989,983
Oil cake and oil meal	7,452,094	9,718,204
Animal oils	1,281,788	978,698
Mineral oil, crude	5,876,452	5,101,840
Mineral oil, refine'	46,150,282	39,704,152
Vegetable oils	4,802,936	5,584,905
Ore, gold and silver	84,742	80,325
Paints and colors	690,698	709,857
Paper, and manufactures thereof	1,299,169	1,892,251
Paraffin and paraffin wax	3,714,649	3,965,268
Perfumery and cosmetics	450,663	404,706
Plated ware	414,719	369,479
Provisions	139,017,471	140,362,159
Quicksilver	88,930	149,798
Seeds	2,506,899	6,252,382
Silk manufactures	92,071	152,150
Soap	1,187,263	1,062,207
Spermaceti	71,202	90,842
Spirits	1,887,481	2,401,117
Starch	475,817	612,581
Stationery, other than paper...	560,456	592,090
Stereotype and electrotype plates	25,810	47,912
Straw and palm-leaf manufac-		
tures	78,844	65,853
Sugar and molasses	7,099,788	1,985,994
Tin, manufactures of	249,886	225,113
Tobacco, unmanufactured	21,033,759	20,670,045
Tobacco, manufactured	4,186,713	4,069,860
Toys	61,186	124,869
Trunks and traveling bags	202,520	171,304
Varnish	203,285	298,059
Vegetables	1,335,975	1,809,145
Vessels sold to foreigners	96,422	257,885
Vinegar	10,489	11,690
Wax, bees'	86,027	81,998
Whalebone	717,290	427,462
Wine	371,477	489,030
Firewood	7,026	1,604
Lumber, timber, and wood		
manufactures	26,263,014	25,788,967
Wool, raw	39,423	30,864
Wool, manufactures of	519,198	367,787
Zinc ore and oxide	142,011	114,689
Zinc, manufactures of	181,732	765,567
All other manufactured articles.	2,130,331	1,852,857
All other unmanufactured arti-		
cles	535,308	1,034,243
Total domestic exports....	$872,270,283	$1,015,732,011

The export price of live cattle averaged $88.95 a head in 1892, compared with $81.26 in 1891; of hogs, $11.39, compared with $11.99; of horses, $189.45, compared with $252.38; of mules, $121.42, compared with $127.59; of sheep, $3.43, compared with $4.28. There were 394,607 cattle exported, against 374,079 in 1891; 31,963 hogs, against 95,654; 3,226 horses, against 3,110; 1,905 mules, against 2,184; and 46,960 sheep, against 60,947. The exports of wheat in 1892 amounted to 157,280,351 bushels, at an average price of $1.03, against 55,131,948 bushels in 1891, at 93 cents a bushel. The number of barrels of flour exported was 15,196,769 in 1892, and the price was $4.96 a barrel, or 14 cents higher than in 1891, when 11,334,304 barrels were shipped abroad. The corn exports rose from 30,768,213 bushels in 1891 to 75,451,849 bushels, while the price declined from an average of 57 cents to one of 55 cents. The price of rye for export rose from 64 to 95 cents, in consequence of the short crop of this grain in the Continental countries, where it is the chief food of the people. Instead of being converted into whisky, the American crop was exported to the amount of 12,041,316 bushels, compared with 332,739 bushels in the previous year. The export of oats rose from 953,010 to 9,425,078 bushels, with a decline in the average price from 43 to 41 cents, and of barley from 973,062 to 2,800,075 bushels, the price going down from 69 to 63 cents. Of oatmeal, 20,908,190 pounds were exported, an increase of 13,171,317 pounds. The only decrease in quantities in the list of breadstuffs occurred under the heads of cornmeal and of bread and biscuit. Of the latter, 14,449,655 pounds were exported, against 15,541,655 in 1891, at an average price of 5·4 cents for both years. The values of the cereal exports were as follow for the two years:

BREADSTUFFS.	1891.	1892.
Wheat	$51,420,272	$161,809,182
Wheat flour	54,705,616	75,862,288
Corn	17,652,687	41,590,460
Cornmeal	946,977	919,991
Rye	212,161	11,219,999
Rye flour	18,185	22,461
Oats	405,708	3,842,559
Oatmeal	221,316	555,957
Barley	669,208	1,751,445
Bread and biscuit	538,848	775,596
Other breadstuffs and preparations	1,030,658	1,711,103
Total	$128,121,656	$299,363,117

The export of candles increased from 1,546,079 to 1,715,130 pounds, with a decline of 6 per cent. in price. Among the chemicals, drugs, and dyes, the export of pot and pearl ashes increased from 430,582 to 1,307,634 pounds. Ginseng decreased from 283,000 pounds, valued at $959,992 to 228,916 pounds, valued at $803,529. The value of patent medicines was $1,842,889, a decrease of $37,839; of dyes and dyestuffs, $597,016, one of $63,574.

The export of anthracite coal was 808,277 tons, 116,635 less, that of bituminous coal 1,700,496 tons, 225,769 more, than in the preceding year. The export of copper in ingots, bars, etc., leaped up from 34,554,517 to 56,453,736 pounds, the average price being 12 cents, a cent lower. The export of Sea Island cotton fell

off from 37,078 bales, or 14,588,092 pounds, to 22,806 bales, or 9,074,686 pounds. The shipments of ordinary cotton were 5,868,545 bales, or 2,926,145,125 pounds, showing an increase of 85,444 bales, or 33,374,422 pounds, over the great shipments of 1891. The total figures for raw cotton are 5,820,779 bales, or 2,907,358,795 pounds, for 1891, and 5,891,411 bales, or 2,935,219,811 pounds, for 1892. Of colored cotton cloths, 40,815,450 yards, and of uncolored, 142,938,871 yards, were exported, against 39,016,682 and 135,529,590 yards. The average price of Sea Island cotton was 21 cents in 1891 and 18 cents in 1892; of other cotton, 9·9 and 8·7 cents a pound respectively; of colored cloths, 6·6 and 6·1 cents a yard; of uncolored, 6·9 and 6·6 cents. The quantity of eggs exported was 183,063 dozen, 180,053 dozen less. The export of fresh fish increased from 868,796 to 1,414,019 pounds, and that of pickled mackerel from 2,295 to 3,490 barrels; but the other fish exports showed a falling off, that of canned salmon being 18,215,025 pounds, or 4,152,200 pounds less, and that of dried codfish, haddock, hake, and pollock 14,435,878, or 2,877,292 pounds less. The export of dried apples was 26,042,063 pounds, against 6,973,168 pounds in 1891; and that of fresh apples increased from 135,207 to 938,743 barrels, the crop having been much more abundant. The export price of dried apples was 5·9 cents a pound in 1891 and 4·9 cents in 1892, that of green or ripe apples $1.41 and $1.03. The price of fertilizers advanced from $9.41 to $15.82 a ton, and the export rose from 231,915 to 251,104 tons. The export of bagging decreased from 8,092,834 to 7,603,329 pounds. The shipments of glucose increased from 149,427 to 96,486,953 pounds, at an average price of 2·4 cents throughout. There were 12,604,686 pounds of hops exported, an increase of 3,868,606 pounds, while the price fell from 27 to 19 cents. In the total for the iron and steel exports for 1892 the sum of $10,229,293 represents machinery, $3,133,992 sewing machines, $2,309,688 locks and builders' hardware, $1,900,444 saws and tools, $1,717,715 locomotive engines, $853,628 firearms, $852,659 wire, $789,546 castings, $568,485 boilers and parts of engines, $409,220 printing presses, and $325,417 scales and balances. The number of locomotive engines fell off from 275 to 197, and the export of firearms was somewhat less, but in nearly all other articles there was a larger trade, with prices considerably lower, owing to the fall in the price of iron. The average price of boots and shoes per pair advanced from $1.18 to $1.23, the export increasing from 551,733 to 745,112 pairs, while that of sole leather, of which 37,053,381 pounds were exported, remained stationary at 16 cents. The price of rosin dropped from $1.94 to $1.75 a barrel. The export of rosin was 1,950,214 barrels, and of spirits of turpentine 13,176,470 gallons, an increase of 159,963 barrels of the one and 932,849 gallons of the other. The exports of lard oil and of whale and fish oils, except sperm oil, were considerably smaller, the total for animal oils dropping from 3,072,022 to 2,150,357 gallons. The exports of illuminating mineral oils were 564,896,658, against 571,119,805 gallons; of crude oil, 103,592,767 gallons, against 91,415,095; of naphtha, 12,727,978, against 12,171,147 gallons; of lubricating and heavy paraffin oil, 33,591,076 gallons. against 33,514,730; of cotton-seed oil, 13,859,278 gallons, against 11,003,160; of oil of peppermint, 54,987 pounds, against 45,321 pounds; of paraffin and paraffin wax, 64,998,-867 pounds, against 66,366,003. The price of lard oil advanced from 52 to 55 cents; that of sperm oil fell from 75 to 73 cents; while other whale and fish oil went up to 28 cents from 25. Crude petroleum dropped from 6·4 to 4·9 cents, naphtha from 8·2 to 7·1 cents, and illuminating oil from 7 to 5·9 cents, while lubricating and heavy oils advanced from 14 to 16 cents a gallon. The price of cotton seed oil was 36 cents, remaining unchanged. The rate for bacon and hams rose from 7·6 to 8·1 cents a pound; salted beef averaged 5·7 cents for both years; fresh beef went up from 7·8 to 8·2 cents; cheese advanced from 9 to 9·4 cents; lard rose from 6·9 to 7·2 cents; pork, from 5·9 to 6 cents; and imitation butter declined from 13 to 12 cents, and oleomargarine oil kept steady at 9·8 cents, while real butter rose from 14 to 16 cents. The following table exhibits the quantities in pounds, and the values of the provision exports for 1892:

PROVISIONS.	Quantities.	Values.
Meat products :		
Canned beef..................	87,028,084	$7,878,454
Fresh beef..................	220,554,617	18,038,782
Salted or pickled beef.........	70,204,786	3,987,829
Other cured beef..............	953,712	92,524
Tallow..........	89,780,010	4,126,630
Bacon	507,919,880	39,334,983
Hams........................	76,856,509	7,757,717
Fresh pork..................	377,746	30,246
Pickled pork................	80,386,481	4,792,049
Lard........................	460,045,776	33,201,621
Mutton	101,463	9,022
Imitation butter............	1,610,837	195,587
Oleomargarine	91,581,708	9,011,889
Poultry and game..	....	18,828
All other meat products	....	1,220,205
Dairy products :		
Butter......................	15,047,246	2,445,878
Cheese......................	82,100,221	7,676,657
Milk........................	....	236,358
Total	....	$140,862,159

The export of quicksilver increased from 157,-052 to 306,047 pounds. There was a smaller export of clover seed, but an increase in cotton seed, and Timothy and linseed took a jump from 144,848 bushels to 3,613,187 bushels, valued at $3,915,547. The export of soap was 1,600,206 pounds smaller. The total exports of distilled spirits amounted to 3,350,797 proof gallons, against 1,904,972 gallons in 1891. The export of alcohol was 1,440.219 gallons, against 418,284; that of Bourbon whisky rose from 239,995 to 744,-172 gallons, and rye from 54,656 to 128,273; and that of brandy from 136,529 to 216,696 gallons; but rum declined from 1,025,226 to 773,713 gallons. The price of alcohol receded from 43 to 33 cents, that of rum was $1.20, a cent more, and whisky fell from $1.09 to 89 cents for Bourbon, and from $1.51 to $1.05 for rye. The export of refined sugar fell off from 108,228,620 pounds in 1891 to 14,604,608 pounds, while that of molasses increased from 4,495,475 to 9,343,-214 gallons. The quantity of leaf tobacco sent abroad was 255,432,077 pounds in 1892. compared with 249,232,605 pounds, the price falling

away from 8·8 to 8·4 cents. Of wine in casks, 655,-795 gallons were exported in 1892, at 64 cents, against 543,292, averaging 65 cents, in 1891. The prices of boards and planks, joists and scantling, shingles, and firewood, were higher, and those of sawed timber and other kinds of wood products lower than in the previous year. The export of boards, deals, and planks was 592,596 thousand feet, a decrease of 20,810; of sawed timber, 235,-550, an increase of 20,938 thousand feet; of hewed timber, 6,736,446 cubic feet, a decrease of 163,-627. Staves and headings, logs and other timber, and doors, sashes, and blinds showed a falling off, but in household furniture there was an increase in the value from $2,956,114 to $3,090,146, and hoops, shooks, barrels, and moldings and trimmings show a large gain.

The exports of foreign merchandise in 1891–'92 had a total value of $14,546,137, compared with $12,210,527 in 1890–'91. Of this sum, $9,990,000 consisted of dutiable merchandise, an increase of $2,942,933, and $4,556,135 of merchandise free of duty, a decrease of $607,323. Of the total, $9,972,507 was the value of merchandise exported from warehouse, and $4,573,570 that of merchandise not exported from warehouse, an increase of $3,262,095 in the former and a decrease of $926,485 in the latter.

Movement of Specie.—The total value of the gold and silver coin and bullion imported in 1891–'92 was $69.654,540, as compared with $36,-259,447 in 1890–'91, showing an increase of $33,-395,093. The gold imports were $49,699,454, against $18,232,567 in 1891, an increase of $31,-466,887. Of the gold coin, $15,432.443 were American, compared with $2,824,146 the previous year, and $22,908,493 were foreign, compared with $13,303,387. The imports of gold bullion were $11,358,518, compared with $2,195,-034. The imports of silver coin and bullion were $19,955,086 in 1892, compared with $18,-026,880 in 1891, an increase of $1,928,206. There was an increase of $3,300,046 in the imports of foreign coin, which amounted in 1892 to $14,679,709. The imports of American silver coin were $159,569, which were $165,671 less than in the preceding year, and the imports of silver bullion were $5,115,808, which was $1,206,-169 less. The imports of specie over the land frontiers were $16,446,360, compared with $10,-047,707 in 1891.

The total value of the exports of domestic gold and silver was $60,086,418 in 1892, compared with $98,973,265 in 1891, a decrease of $38,-886,847. The exports of gold amounted to $43,-321,351, against $84,939,551 in 1891, a decrease of $41,618,200. The gold exports consisted of $42,841,963 in coin, $8,260 in bars of the United States Mint or Assay Office, and $471,128 in other bullion, showing a decrease of $24,862,-937 in coin, $15,110,442 in bars, and $1,644,821 in other bullion. The silver exports of 1891–'92 amounted to $16,765,067, against $14,033,714 in 1890–'91. The exports of assayed bars were $2,-992,884, of other bullion $13,645,501, and of silver coin $126,682, showing an increase of $2,-346,815 in bars and $494,179 in other bullion, and in coin a decrease of $109,641. The exports of specie by land were $1,343,366. which was $1,333,419 more than in 1890–'91. The exports of foreign gold and silver were $22,919,-

468, against $9.980,377 in 1891, showing an increase of $12,939,091. The foreign exports of gold were $6,873,976, compared with $1,423,103 ; of silver, $16,045,492, compared with $8,557,274. The foreign exports of gold coin were $6,851,339 ; of silver coin $16,033,803 ; of gold bullion, $22,637 ; of silver bullion, $11,689. The exports of specie over the land frontiers were $137,90), compared with $64.145 in 1891.

Navigation.—The following table gives the number and tonnage of American and foreign vessels in the foreign trade entered at the ports of the United States from the various foreign countries, during the year ending June 30, 1892 :

COUNTRIES.	AMERICAN VESSELS.		FOREIGN VESSELS.	
	No.	Tonnage.	No.	Tonnage.
Austria-Hungary.............			16	27,518
Azores and Madeira......	11	6,195	30	86,758
Belgium..................	26	54,849	275	582,593
Denmark.................			18	21,175
France..................	33	57,682	854	572,404
Germany................	2	2,504	826	1,661,555
Gibraltar...............			9	13,274
Greece.................			30	40,490
Greenland and Iceland ...	6	1,456	7	3,172
Italy...................	15	12,251	408	494,687
Netherlands.............			249	463,552
Portugal................	1	472	92	55,154
Russia..................			16	16,332
Spain..................	6	4,466	259	820,975
Sweden and Norway......			57	48,610
Turkey in Europe....			1	460
United Kingdom	60	112,771	3,088	5,923,259
Bermuda................	14	6,001	64	60,067
British Honduras	4	1,685	17	5,836
British North America ...	7,658	2,286,646	12,215	2,876,480
Newfoundland...........	8	730	39	15,077
Costa Rica.............	14	1,421	79	64,449
Guatemala.............	14	6,932	14	8,006
Honduras..............	149	57,214	88	21,140
Nicaragua.............	57	33,543	72	88,162
Salvador..............	4	801	1	852
Mexico................	263	82,513	207	120,726
St. Pierre and Miquelon ...	1	106	2	1,693
British West Indies......	433	140,601	726	378,939
Danish West Indies.......	18	5,778	27	14,334
Dutch West Indies.......	26	16,851	23	8,366
French West Indies.......	33	11,458	22	12,479
Hayti..................	92	34,092	84	50,807
Santo Domingo..........	64	31,175	32	9,248
Cuba..................	1,043	739,509	983	713,163
Porto Rico.............	78	24,562	122	56,351
Argentine Republic......	27	17,477	97	69,569
Brazil.................	64	88,700	521	464,617
Chili..................	36	38,686	64	67,068
Colombia..............	121	166,266	96	48,277
British Guinna........	48	19,567	68	41,484
Dutch Guiana..........	8	2,715	9	860
French Guiana.........	1	468	1	495
Peru..................	12	11,328	11	10,174
Uruguay..............	13	7,286	72	67,762
Venezuela............	49	60,867	27	12,059
China................	10	7,629	18	24,739
British East Indies.......	18	20,900	78	115,509
Dutch East Indies......	2	1,651	28	39,746
Hong-Kong............	25	44,757	48	83,722
Japan................	12	17,489	47	76,738
Russia, Asiatic........	4	897	2	359
Turkey in Asia........			44	32 222
Australia.............	52	59,169	168	236 774
New Zealand and Tasmania	11	7,182	11	7,028
French possessions in Oceanica	14	5,055		
Hawaiian Islands........	188	116,913	21	19,980
Philippine Islands.......	16	21,678	21	28,790
British Africa..........	18	4,788	61	45,716
Canary Islands.........	1	828	80	122,916
French Africa..........	2	487	60	75,883
Madagascar...........	5	8,054	1	420
Portugese Africa........	6	875	56	68,332
Egypt...............			10	9,002
All other countries in Africa			1	848
Total..................	10,912	4,469,955	22,232	16,543,469

The number and tonnage of the vessels cleared at American ports for foreign ports in 1892 are given in the following table :

COUNTRIES.	AMERICAN VESSELS.		FOREIGN VESSELS.	
	No.	Tonnage.	No.	Tonnage.
Austria-Hungary.........			81	19,511
Azores and Madeira......			4	1,377
Belgium................	26	54,773	287	740,411
Denmark...............			86	107,494
France................	27	42,456	837	1,260,110
Germany..............	1	1,581	1,104	2,009,392
Gibraltar.............			15	20,709
Greece...............			2	2,880
Greenland and Iceland...	2	784	7	3,064
Italy.................	8	6,430	221	218,797
Netherlands...........			470	711,216
Portugal..............	5	2,358	95	84,778
Russia................	2	4,223	49	48,768
Spain................	7	4,263	189	143,918
Sweden and Norway.....			126	98,171
Turkey in Europe.......			1	448
United Kingdom........	61	96,221	3,476	6,286,842
Bermuda..............	14	6.545	56	56,655
British Honduras	7	2,775	28	10,081
British North America ...	7,760	2,804,544	12,378	2,965,408
Newfoundland.........	47	5,266	76	22,182
Costa Rica............	5	1,584	49	28,502
Guatemala............	26	10,431	11	7,026
Honduras.............	144	64,404	68	20,481
Nicaragua............	57	84,319	75	87,322
Salvador.............	3	1,251		
Mexico...............	255	93,149	169	68,850
St. Pierre and Miquelon ...	4	515	28	3,550
British West Indies.....	354	102,366	514	267,658
Danish West Indies.....	33	16,681	24	20,029
Dutch West Indies.....	11	4,675	13	4,549
French West Indies.....	108	84,757	56	35,746
Hayti................	87	33,997	110	78,135
Santo Domingo........	40	24,652	15	4,404
Cuba................	958	684,362	542	354,948
Porto Rico...........	70	23,294	52	87,687
Argentine Republic.....	58	37,734	55	55,180
Brazil...............	112	112,109	216	163,166
Chili................	32	31,819	45	54,506
Colombia............	132	183,170	73	38,087
Ecuador.............	1	90	1	1,284
British Guiana........	76	34,356	19	6,257
Dutch Guiana........	14	4,547	2	2,317
French Guiana........	11	2,389	8	1,489
Peru................	13	7,547	20	21,208
Uruguay.............	18	9,885	32	15,964
Venezuela...........	60	60,682	18	6,236
China...............	15	13,896	20	34,745
British East Indies......	9	13,246	51	84,304
Dutch East Indies......	8	3,550	40	44,814
French East Indies......	2	2,442	5	5,298
Hong-Kong..........	30	53,935	42	87,777
Japan...............	11	17,906	29	48,697
Russia, Asiatic........	5	2,268	1	547
Turkey in Asia........			1	408
All other Asiatic countries...			1	1,165
Australia.............	60	63,511	100	114,866
New Zealand and Tasmania	18	8,384	10	6,458
French possessions in Oceanica	19	6,385	4	837
Hawaiian Islands.......	167	108,473	6	7,840
Philippine Islands......	2	3,100	2	3,280
British Africa.........	87	16,187	64	81,555
Canary Islands........	6	2,146	12	5,555
French Africa.........	6	2,066	18	5,580
Madagascar..........	2	1,200	1	471
Portuguese Africa.......	6	597	12	4,718
Egypt...............			7	4,181
All other countries in Africa	5	8,788	1	1,328
All other ports and islands.	11	2,498	2	3,022
North Atlantic whale fisheries.	25	9,844		
Total.................	11,085	4,580,151	22,299	16,624,889

CONGO FREE STATE, a sovereign monarchical state created in Central Africa by the general act of the International Conference of the Congo, signed at Berlin on Feb. 26, 1885. The limits of the state were defined in that instrument, and it was declared neutral under an international guarantee, and free to the trade of all nations, together with the rest of the basin of the Congo. The International Conference which met at Brussels in 1890 authorized the Government to impose certain duties on imports in order to enable it to co-operate in the suppression of the slave trade. The King of the Belgians, who assumed the sovereignty personally and independently of the Belgian Government, by his will, dated Aug. 2, 1889, bequeathed all his rights to Belgium. The territories of the Free State were declared to be inalienable on July 31, 1890, after a convention had been concluded on July 3 between Belgium and the Free State, reserving to Belgium the right to annex the Free State at the end of ten years.

The seat of the Central Government is in Brussels. The sovereign is assisted by three heads of departments, who have charge respectively of Foreign Affairs and Justice, Finance, and the Interior.

The seat of the local government is at Boma, on the lower Congo. Under the Governor-General are a Vice Governor-General, a General Secretary, a State Inspector, a Director of Finance. a Director of Justice, and the Commander of the Forces. The armed forces consist of 4 companies, numbering 3,792 native African troops, trained in 4 camps of instruction, and commanded by 11 captains and 33 lieutenants, all of whom are Europeans.

The precise boundaries of the Congo State are defined in conventions, which were signed with Germany on Nov. 8, 1884, with England on Dec. 16, 1884, with the Netherlands on Dec. 27, 1884, with France on Feb. 5, 1885, and with Portugal on Feb. 14, 1885. The area is estimated at 900,-000 square miles, and the population at 17,000,000.

Finances.—The expenses of the Government are defrayed from a subsidy of 2,000,000 francs a year contributed by King Leopold, an advance of 2,000,000 francs voted on July 3, 1890, for ten years by the Belgian Parliament, from taxation and imposts, and from sales and leases of public land.

Commerce and Production.—The exports are palm oil, rubber, ivory, gum copal, orchilla weed, groundnuts, coffee, and camwood. The principal imports are textile fabrics, firearms, powder, spirits, and tobacco. The value of the general exports in 1888 was 7,392,348 francs; in 1889, 8,572.519 francs; in 1890, 14,109,781 francs. The values exported of the principal articles in 1890 were as follow: Ivory, 5,070,851 francs; nuts, 2,464,619 francs; rubber, 3,080,358 francs; palm oil, 1,563,766 francs; coffee, 1,085,604 francs; gum copal, 96,484 francs. The exports of the produce of the Free State in 1888 were valued at 2,609,300 francs, and in 1890 at 4,297,-544 francs.

During 1890 there were 985 vessels, of 268,408 tons, entered at the Congo ports. There is regular steamship communication with Europe, and there are 11 steamers on the upper and 7 on the lower Congo.

The Antislavery Convention.—The general act signed at the conference for the suppression of the slave trade held in 1890 at Brussels by representatives of the signatory powers, with the exception of Austria. France, the Netherlands, Portugal, Russia, Turkey, and the United States, and afterward accepted and ratified by all the powers, entered into operation on April 1, 1892. To this act a declaration was appended which empowered the Congo Free State to levy duties on imports not to exceed 10 per cent. of the value of the goods. The authorization of the powers was necessary because the general act which created the Free State in 1885 declared its territory free to the trade of all nations. Negotiations with Germany, Great Britain, and Italy resulted in an agreement made on Dec. 22, 1890. regarding a tariff for their East African possessions. Negotiations for the regulation of import duties for the west coast were carried on with France and Portugal, and on April 8, 1892, a protocol was signed at Lisbon by representatives of those powers and the independent State of the Congo fixing a uniform tariff on imports, and also regulating the export duties levied in the French and Portuguese possessions in the Congo basin. The protocol was framed in the terms that the French Government had submitted to the Chamber for approval in the previous December.

Representatives of the signatory powers of the general act of the Antislavery Conference that had not notified their adhesion before July 2, 1891, and to whom a further delay of six months had been granted, met the ministers of the other powers at the Foreign Office in Brussels, on Jan. 2, 1892, and exchanged ratifications. Austria-Hungary, Russia, and Turkey had been kept back by difficulties connected with the formalities, and France by the refusal of the French Chamber to approve the levying of import duties by the Congo State. In December the Chamber had changed its views, and thus removed this obstacle to the execution of the decisions of the Brussels conference after a delay of thirty months. The Government of the Netherlands was not yet in a position to signify its definitive adhesion, but notified its acceptance of the act subject to the confirmation of its action by the States-General a few weeks later. When that body met it ratified the convention. The Portuguese Government was unable to fulfill the formality because its action. depended for various reasons on the course that France would take, and while the question was pending before the French Parliament the Cortes refrained from discussing the treaty. The Portuguese representative at Brussels requested a further postponement of thirty days, and when this period was ended the Cortes had taken action, and he was able to signify the adhesion of Portugal to the convention, which unites all the civilized powers in a sort of league for the extirpation of the scourge of man-stealing and the slave trade in Central Africa. The United States minister obtained a similar delay, as the United States Senate had not yet approved the treaty, and on Feb. 2 he presented the ratification of the convention, and of a special treaty of commerce concluded between the Congo State and the United States on July 2, 1890. The American Senate had previously withheld its assent to the Congo act lest it might involve the United States in the position of having to take part in the decision of questions connected with territorial arrangements on the African continent. In amending its attitude the United States Senate had coupled its ratification with a declaration that the United States intended to keep aloof from any participation in a European concert of a political nature regarding Africa, and a memorandum to this effect, which had received the assent of all the signatory powers, was made a part of the ratification of the State Department at Washington presented by Mr. Terrell.

The Imposition of Import Duties. — A decree was issued on April 9, 1892, fixing the rates of duty to be raised on imports in order to enable the independent State of the Congo to support the extraordinary charges entailed by its active participation in the suppression of the Arab slave traffic. On firearms and powder the duty is 10 per cent. *ad valorem.* On spirituous liquors the duty is fixed at 15 francs per hectolitre for proof spirits; the importation and sale of alcohol in districts east of the Inkissi is prohibited. On other merchandise a duty of 6 per cent. *ad valorem* is levied, with the exception of a list of articles that are declared to be free. This includes vessels and parts and fittings of the same, steam machinery, machines and impiements for industrial and agricultural purposes, which will enjoy exemption for the period of four years. Railroad running stock is not to pay duties until it comes into actual use. Scientific instruments, the effects of travelers and settlers, educational books and apparatus, live animals, and seeds, pay no duty. Importation can only be through the customs stations.

The part of the tariff law relating to the regulation of the liquor traffic is in accordance with the provision of the Congo act signed at Brussels, which introduces a new principle and imposes international obligations regarding the liquor traffic in respect to the whole of Africa between 20° of north and 22° of south latitude, or from Egypt and the Sahara to the Transvaal. embracing nearly one fifth of the land surface of the globe. Wherever the trade has not yet penetrated, and where it has already a foothold in countries in which the religion of the people enjoins abstention from alcohol. the treaty interdicts the sale of spirits, and in all other countries the protecting powers are obliged to impose a minimum tariff, which may be increased by mutual agreement at the end of three years, and will be revised again after a further period of three years in the light of the* results. Within six months of the ratification of the Brussels convention, each power is bound to declare what parts of its possessions are already infected with the liquor traffic, and define the regions into which it has not yet penetrated. They are also bound to communicate to each other information regarding the liquor trade in their territories.

Boundary Dispute with France.—In the beginning of 1892 the French, taking umbrage at the founding of stations by explorers of the Congo State in the Ubangi region, had sent agents to the same country for the purpose of making treaties and securing annexations. The Congo State had established a prior claim two years and a half before, when Van Gele and Roget took formal possession of this same district, made treaties with the native chiefs, and organized administrative services. Ignoring the protests of the Congo Government, the French organized an expedition under Liotard in February. In order to put an end to the dispute the Congo State proposed that an international commission should meet in Paris for the purpose of adjusting the claims of the contending parties. The French Government refused to agree to this, and demanded the evacuation of the country. A conflict between the posts of the Congo State and the French expeditions was feared. In April the Congo State's Minister for Foreign Affairs, the Comte de Grelle Rogier, went to Paris to demand the arbitration of the dispute. M. Ribot suggested a direct arrangement as preferable to mediation, and M. de Grelle Rogier met two official representatives of the French Government, with whom he negotiated without coming to an agreement. The French proposal was that the boundary should follow the *Thalweg* of the Ubangi as far as Yakoma, situated at the junction of the Welle and the Mbomu, and then the lower course of this river, and the watershed of the Bili up to the twenty-fifth degree of longitude. King Leopold's representative would have accepted this settlement had it not been coupled with a demand for compensation on the lower Congo, which it was impossible to grant. Incidents occurred in the contested region that led France to increase her demands, and on July 15 the delegates separated, though not without hope of a final accord.' Soon after this a French explorer, M. de Poumayrac, was shot and killed by a native at Kotto—at the instigation of agents of the Congo State, it was assumed by the French Government—which demanded a pecuniary indemnity and the immediate evacuation of the territory that Lieut. Le Marinel had occupied. King Leopold replied with a demand that the whole matter should be submitted to an arbitrator in accordance with the provisions of the Berlin general act. To this the French Government finally agreed.

The French complained of the commercial policy of the Congo State, contending that barriers were being erected against the free exchange of commercial products in these regions. The friction between French traders and the companies chartered by the Free State was to a great extent removed by the amalgamation of Daumas et Cie., the chief French house, with the Belgian Upper Congo Association, the capital of which was raised from 3,000,000 to 5,000,000 francs, 2.000,000 francs being the valuation of the plant and business of the French firm.

Katanga.—After the English had secured Nyassaland by their treaty with Portugal the Congo authorities became anxious to establish their rights over Msiri's kingdom, a region famous for copper and gold on the borders of the British sphere, accessible from the territory of the African Lakes Company, and from that of the British South African Company, and therefore likely to fall under British influence. Msiri was much the most powerful native ruler within the limits of the Congo State. Msiri was the son of a trader from Unyanyembe who had been made the heir of an old chief whom he had helped to overcome his enemies, and after the latter's death had extended his conquests from Katanga over a great part of the Muata Yanvo kingdom. The industrious people over whom he ruled raised large crops. and exported copper and ivory and prospered until 1890, when his tyrannies, and especially his assumption of a monopoly of ivory, drove the Wasanga, the original inhabitants of the country, to revolt. The rebellion was put down with great barbarity after nine months of fighting. The country was known to contain gold as well as copper, and was supposed to be very rich in the noble metal and in quicksilver.

The Katanga Company, organized in Belgium to develop the resources of this country, received a concession from the Congo Free State authorizing it to enjoy exclusive rights to the trade and industry of Katanga, and full power to govern the country. The company sent out an expedition under Lieut. Le Marinel, who, in July, 1891, made a treaty by which Msiri recognized the sovereignty of the Congo Free State. A. Delcommune, at the head of a second expedition, arrived at the capital of Msiri in October, 1891. A third expedition, led by Capt. Stairs, consisting of 10 whites and 336 porters, went by way of Zanzibar and reached Katanga, after a journey of six months, on Dec. 14, 1891. Lieut. Le Marinel had left two Belgian officers with a small garrison to occupy a station near the King's town when he departed six months before. The King, who had received the Belgian expeditions hospitably and had welcomed English missionaries, now showed hostility toward the whites because they occupied this fortified post, from which he could not dislodge them. He met Capt. Stairs on Dec. 18, and told him that he would not raise the flag of the Free State, denying that he had acknowledged its sovereignty. When, at a second interview, Stairs said that the flag would be raised with or without his authority, he went away to a neighboring village, leaving his capital in the possession of the whites, with whom he refused to hold further intercourse. On Dec. 20 Capt. Stairs sent Capt. Bodson and the Marquis de Bouchamps with 115 armed men to bring the King if they could. Capt. Bodson boldly accompanied a messenger of the King into the stockaded village without an escort. He was led to the King, who was surrounded by 300 armed men, and when he demanded that Msiri should go with him to Capt. Stairs the despot drew his sword and advanced menacingly, whereupon Capt. Bodson shot him dead with his revolver, and was himself shot and mortally wounded by one of the chiefs. The Marquis de Bouchamps, on hearing the discharge of firearms, attacked the palisades, and after a short struggle captured the place. The people rose against the whites, who intrenched themselves effectually. After a few days he had a parley with Msiri's brothers, in consequence of which the people, who were weary of Msiri's despotism, quieted down and appeared willing to accept the disposition of the Belgian commander, who recognized Msiri's son, Mkanda Wantu, as ruler, but only of Katanga and the district immediately surrounding it. The chiefs of the other districts had the limits of their territories fixed by Capt. Stairs, who also freed a great many slaves. On Jan. 30, 1892, Capt. Bia, who came with a fourth expedition by way of the Congo, reached Katanga, and Capt. Stairs turned over the command to him, and with his own party reached the coast by way of the Zambesi on June 3, 1892. About 190 natives died from privation and fever on the road, and before he could

embark Capt. Stairs himself was attacked anew with the fever, and died at Shinde on June 8. For twenty-six days the expedition had no food except white ants and locusts.

Arab Revolt on the Upper Congo.—A Katanga trading syndicate, distinct from the Katanga Company, was formed in Belgium in 1891 for the purpose of establishing trading posts in the populous region between the Congo and the Lomami, extending from Stanley Falls to Kasongo, where large quantities of ivory were expected to be found in the hands of the natives. Arthur Hodister, who had been an efficient agent of the Free State in the negotiations with Tippoo Tib and an advocate of harmony and co-operation with the Arab traders, led the principal expedition, which reached Bena Kamba, the head of navigation on the Lomami, on April 6, 1891, where a station was established, as well as at Yanga and at Riba Riba and Nyangwe on the Congo. Parties were sent farther up both rivers to establish posts at Faki and at Kasongo, a town of 9,000 inhabitants founded by Tippoo Tib, the largest Arab settlement in Central Africa. In this whole region the Arab dealers in slaves and ivory have enjoyed hitherto a complete monopoly of trade. Five of the proposed stations were established and garrisoned, and thus the band of 19 white men and the black soldiery taken up on board the steamboat "Auguste Beernaert" were divided between posts that were separated by wide distances. Each of these posts was attacked by overwhelming Arab bands, who killed the garrisons, destroyed the stations, and carried off the trade goods as plunder. Hodister, who had lived on friendly terms with the Arab chiefs and knew every one of them from the mouth of the Lomami as far up as Nyangwe, had remained at Bena Kamba. After he fell into the hands of the Arabs he was tortured for three days before he was beheaded. Page and Doré, the only white survivors of the expedition, escaped from Bena Kamba to Stanley Falls. A supposed reason for the rising was the course taken by the commercial agents in entering into direct trading relations with the negroes. The Arabs, who consider themselves the natural masters of the blacks, will not allow the latter to sell ivory except through their instrumentality, and mercilessly put to death every one who is caught doing so. They claim a monopoly of the ivory, and exact a large profit for their services as middlemen.

As soon as the news of the Hodister disaster was brought by steamer to Leopoldville, the Congo State authorities sent all the native troops that could be spared from that place and Bangala to the upper Congo. A large force was already garrisoned at Basoko, at the mouth of the Aruwimi. This and others of the garrisons of the Congo State were largely composed of the Basoko natives, the ferocious cannibal tribe that attacked Stanley. A part of the re-enforcements were added to the garrison at Basoko, and a large force was posted at the mouth of the Lomami to observe the movements of Rachid, who was suspected of a design to join the rebellion. There were grave fears of an uprising of the Arabs of Isangi and Stanley Falls, who might have seized those stations and raided the posts established by the Congo State farther down on the banks of the river. Tippoo Tib, whose sagacious self-interest would have been effective in restraining the violent spirits, was at the time in Zanzibar; but the prompt dispatch of troops imposed a sufficient check on the insurrectionary movement.

The hostility of the Arabs toward the whites and the Congo State was not founded on trade jealousy alone, but had been excited before this by the operations of Capt. Joubert and Capt. Jacques on the west shore of Lake Tanganyika, and of the agents of the Free State on the Sankuru and Makua rivers, for the suppression of the slave trade. In fulfillment of the international engagements undertaken by the Congo State. Joubert and Jacques had for a year past carried on a war against slave raiders, and had stopped several caravans and freed many slaves. In addition to this, Capt. Joubert undertook to impose a tax on Arab caravans bringing ivory to be transported over the lake and down to the Zanzibar coast. This enraged Rumaliza, the powerful Arab chief at Ujiji, on the east side of the lake, who attacked one of Joubert's stations in April, 1892, and cut off his supplies.

At the other extremity of the territory ravaged by the Arabs of the upper Congo, south and west of the Lomami. M. Dhanis, the agent of the Congo State, was established at Lusambo, on the upper course of the Sankuru river. Shortly before the massacre of Hodister's party he had attacked a large force of Arab slave raiders, killed 10 of their chiefs, and taken 700 prisoners.

Far to the north of these regions Capt. Vandekerkhoven had for a year occupied with a strong force a station on the Makua river, the upper course of the Ubangi, better known as the Welle. After two hard-fought battles the slave raiders of that isolated and remote district were driven north of the river. The Arabs living at Isangi, at the mouth of the Lomami, and those residing at Stanley Falls, were greatly excited by these operations in a region where the Congo State had not hitherto attempted to interfere, and, headed by Rachid, the leader of the Arab rebels who seized Stanley Falls in 1886, the chiefs sent a protest to the Congo State authorities. Capt. Ponthier conducted the campaign against the Arab slavers who were devastating the regions north and south of the upper Welle. One of their strongholds was on three small islands a short distance above the mouth of the Bomokandi. This was destroyed, as well as their fortified camp on the Mokongo, and the slave raiders were completely defeated by Capt. Ponthier's force, which set 250 slaves at liberty.

Expedition to the Nile Region. — An armed expedition led by Lieut. Vandekerkhoven reached the region of the Bahr el Ghazal from the head waters of the Makua or Welle in the summer of 1892. The Congo State authorities had notified the British Government of the intended expedition, and no objections were made at first, but when Lord Salisbury learned that the aim was to find an outlet for the Congo State on the upper Nile, he intimated that the whole of the Nile provinces were in the British sphere, and that the presence of a Belgian force in that region would not be tolerated. As soon as the fact of the arrival of the expedition in the Nile region became known, the British Ministry for Foreign Affairs intimated anew that it must be withdrawn, and declined to discuss any proposition looking to the absorption of any district drained by the tributaries of the Nile into the Congo State.

CONGREGATIONALISTS. The following is a summary of the statistics of the Congregational churches in the United States as they are given in the "Congregational Year Book" for 1892: Number of churches, 4,985; of ministers, 4,886; of members, 525,097; of baptisms during the year, 14,705 of adults and 9,787 of infants; of additions during the year by confession of faith, 30,614: of families represented in the Church, 373,995; of members of Sunday schools, 625,975; average attendance in Sunday schools, 380,790; of Young People's Societies of Christian Endeavor, 2,994, with 145,100 members. Amounts of benevolent contributions, 4,180 churches reporting: For foreign missions, $423,737; for education, $156,093; for church building, $145,697; for home missions, $589,092; for the American Missionary Association, $156,830; for Sunday schools, $55,945; for the New West Education Society, $48,234; for ministers' aid, $17,830; total of benevolent contributions, $2,448,875; amount of legacies received, $861,932; of home expenditures (4,153 churches), $6,791,607; benevolent contributions of Sunday schools, $141,766. Of the churches, 3,608 are returned as supplied and 1,377 as vacant; of the ministers, 1,705 are returned as "without charge." The seven theological seminaries — Andover, Bangor, Chicago, Hartford, Oberlin, the Pacific, and Yale—returned 46 professors, 39 instructors or lecturers, 12 resident licentiates or fellows, 22 advanced or graduate students, and 562 undergraduates.

The American College and Education Society in 1891 aided 449 students, and was in its college department aiding 7 colleges.

The Congregational Sunday School and Publishing Society returned an income for 1891 of $62,055, and the expenditure of $61,690; had aided in the organization of 515 Sunday schools, and had made grants of Sunday-school literature to about 1,400 schools.

The New West Education Commission for work in Utah and adjacent States and Territories, returned, in 1890, 29 schools of all grades, with 79 teachers and 3,704 pupils, who were classed as "Mormons," "apostates," and "Mexicans," and 22 Sunday schools, with 1,900 pupils.

The Woman's Home Missionary Association, Boston, supported, in 1891, 6 teachers in Utah and 2 in New Mexico.

Congregational Church Building Society. —The thirty-ninth annual meeting of the American Congregational Union was held in New York city, Jan. 14, the Rev. William M. Taylor, D. D., presiding. The report from the board of trustees recommending a change in the corporate name to "The Congregational Church Building Society" was presented and unanimously approved, and the action thus taken was referred to the counselors of the board to secure the necessary legal confirmation. The receipts for the year from all sources had been $168,442, which, with $94,708 in the treasury at the beginning of the year, made the total available resources of the society $263,150. The disbursements had been $178,827. The society had aided during the year in the erection of 136 churches and 56 parsonages. Since in 1881 it had aided in the erection of only 48 buildings for church use, it appeared that its work had quadrupled in ten years. Of 2,172 churches that had been aided in building houses of worship, 20 had closed their accounts during the year, making 317 in all; of 326 parsonage loans made, 25 had been paid up during the year, or 83 in all since 1882. By the payment of $20,456 in aid of the building of parsonages, parsonage property valued at $64,-783 had been brought into the use of 56 pastors; and the payment of $99,884 in the church-building department had been the means of bringing in about $36,726 more from personal friends of the churches and of securing the contribution of nearly $325,997 more. In other words, gifts and loans outside of the parishes immediately interested, amounting to $136,609, had secured church-building property valued at $462,607. Adding these sums to those previously reported as having been paid out of the treasury, we foot up a total of $9,863,060 worth of church-building property brought into use by the disbursement of $1,628,-047, giving a total in the 2 departments of church and parsonage building of $10,205,217 worth of property secured for church uses by paying out less than one sixth of that amount.

American Home Missionary Society.—The sixty-sixth annual meeting of the American Home Missionary Society was held in Washington, D. C., May 25, Hon. Nelson Dingley, Jr., presiding. The receipts for the year, including a balance in the treasury at the beginning of $13,994, had been $676,783. The payments had been $504,559, besides $181,836 expended by the auxiliaries on their respective fields. Nineteen hundred and eighty-six missionaries had been employed during the year (including 49 who had labored in more than one State). 446 in the New England States, 156 in the Middle States, 85 in the Southern States, 116 in the Southwestern States, 196 on the Pacific coast, and 1,036 in the Western States and Territories, in the service of 3,389 congregations and missionary districts. Six ministers had been in commission as pastors or stated supplies of colored people, and 176 had preached in foreign languages to congregations of Welsh, Germans, Scandinavians, Bohemians, Poles, Indians, Mexicans and Spaniards, Italians, and Finns. Twenty-two hundred and ninety-eight Sunday schools and Bible classes were under the care of the missionaries, with about 159,206 pupils, while 282 new schools had been organized, 6,193 members had been received in the Church on confession of faith, 220 churches had been organized, 65 churches had assumed self-support, 174 houses of worship had been completed and 21 were in course of erection, 14 chapels had been built and 61 parsonages provided, and 137 men connected with the missionary churches were preparing for the ministry. Report was made of the extent and efficiency of the work of the women in aid of the society, and of the packages of goods and provisions forwarded to missionaries.

The American Board.—The eighty-third annual meeting of the American Board of Commissioners for Foreign Missions was held in Chicago, Ill., beginning Oct. 5, the Rev. R. S. Storrs,

D. D., presiding. The income of the society for the year had been $841,568, of which $545,097 had been derived from donations, $249,778 from legacies, $35,185 from the legacy of Asa Otis, accounted for specially, and $10,744 from interest on the general permanent fund. The expenditures had been $840,840, of which the sum of $784,856 was charged to "cost of missions." The general summary of the work in the missionary fields of the Pacific islands, the Chinese Empire, Africa, Asiatic and European Turkey, India, Japan, and Roman Catholic countries in Europe, presented the following total numbers:

Missions.

Number of missions	20
Number of stations	45
Number of out stations	1,126
Places for stated preaching	1,347
Average congregations	71,184

Laborers employed.

Number of ordained missionaries (11 being physicians)	188
Number of male physicians not ordained (besides 3 women)	18
Number of other male assistants	5
Number of women, 8 of them physicians (wives, 174; unmarried, 159)	333
Whole number of laborers sent from this country	534
Number of native pastors	200
Number of native preachers and catechists	624
Number of native school teachers	1,280
Number of other native laborers	396
Total of native laborers	2,600
Total of American and native laborers	3,184

The Churches.

Number of churches	484
Number of church members	40,333
Added during the year	3,516
Whole number from the first, as nearly as can be learned	122,023

Educational Department.

Number of theological seminaries and station classes	16
Pupils	252
Colleges and high schools	70
Number of pupils in the above	4,259
Number of boarding schools for girls	55
Number of pupils in boarding schools for girls	2,882
Number of common schools	982
Number of pupils in common schools	37,885
Whole number under instruction	47,330
Native contributions, so far as reported	$92,723

Special attention had been given by the secretaries to the training and employment of a native ministry. Work for women had widened very much, especially in the direction of evangelistic effort, and schools for the training of Bible women were being established at important stations. For want of men the care of 5 different stations had devolved on women, and the women had proved themselves equal to the emergency. Forty new missionary families and 20 single women were asked for in order that the work in hand might be maintained and properly developed—especially in Africa, India, China, and Japan. A paper concerning the fellowship of the American Board with the churches and a number of memorials from State associations of Congregational churches, requesting the board to adopt the principle of giving to the churches a voice in the election of corporate members, was referred to a committee, on the report of which the meeting resolved:

That the Committee for the Nomination of New Members, appointed at the meeting, be directed to receive from the State, Territorial, or independent organizations of Congregational churches during the coming year, nominations of persons to fill vacancies which may occur in the board, somewhat more in number being desirable than the average usually assigned to any State or Territory; and from such names, if furnished, to select and report at the next annual meeting enough to fill three fourths of the vacancies which may then exist, regard being had to a division between ministers and laymen and the apportionment of members according to the by-laws.

That inasmuch as the action recommended by this committee is in the nature of the case provisional, and it can not be foretold what will be the practical operation of the plan proposed, the committee be continued, and instructed to report at the next annual meeting such permanent scheme as shall seem most practicable and promotive of the great intents we all have at heart.

The following resolutions, offered by the minority of the committee representing the "liberal" side of thought in the board as supplementary to the report of the Home Department on the engagement of missionaries, were indefinitely postponed:

Resolved, That young men and young women of approved Christian character, possessing the needed physical and mental qualifications, who accept heartily the creeds of their respective churches and the fundamental doctrines of the Gospel as set forth in the "Burial Hill Declaration of Faith," and in the creed of the Congregational Commission of 1883, should be accepted by the Prudential Committee as suitable candidates for missionary service.

Resolved, That the missionaries of this board, while holding these fundamental truths, "shall have the same right of private judgment in the interpretation of God's Word, and the same freedom of thought and speech, as are enjoyed by their ministerial brethren in this country," whether in the pastorate or in the employ of other benevolent societies of the denomination.

A discussion concerning the right of the "liberal" minority to be represented on the Prudential Committee was terminated by the adoption of a resolution, "That the board reaffirms the rules of administration laid down by it at the annual meetings in New York and Minneapolis, and expects them to be applied in the spirit of liberty as well as of faithfulness to candidates for missionary service; and that these rules are to be interpreted liberally and faithfully in accordance with the President's letter of acceptance." (See the extract from President Storrs's letter in the "Annual Cyclopædia" for 1887.)

American Missionary Association.—The forty-sixth annual meeting of the American Missionary Association was held in Hartford, Conn., beginning Oct. 25. The Rev. F. A. Noble, D.D., presided. The receipts for the year, including the balance from the previous year, had been $430,568, and the expenditures had been $429,-585, in addition to which the income from the Daniel Hand fund had been $52,721. The death of the giver of this fund, Daniel Hand, was recorded as having taken place Dec. 17, 1891. Eighty-four schools had been maintained, classified as 6 chartered institutions, 28 normal and graded schools, and 30 common schools, which returned in all, 384 instructors and 13,062 pupils. Of the 28 normal schools in the South, 1 is in Virginia, 5 are in North Carolina, 2 in South Carolina, 5 in Georgia, 1 in Florida, 4 in Alabama, 6 in Tennessee, 2 in Kentucky, 1 in Mississippi, and 1 in Arkansas. Talladega College, in Alabama, had risen to a full college organiza-

tion. In most of the normal schools in the South and among the Indians, and in all the colleges, special instruction is given in industries. Agriculture and mechanics are taught both in their principles and in their practical applications. The Church work in the South comprised 140 churches, with 122 missionaries, 8,485 church members, and 10,884 pupils in Sunday schools, with 733 members added during the year on profession of faith. The Indian missions returned 12 churches, 461 church members, 90 missionaries and teachers, 511 pupils, and 1,047 pupils in Sunday schools. Four missionaries were laboring in Alaska, and returned nearly 200 pupils in the schools. Nearly $10,000 more had been expended on the Indian missions in the past than in the previous year. Nineteen schools were maintained among the Chinese of the Pacific coast, with 38 teachers and 1,170 pupils. Forty-five missionaries were employed, 16 of whom were Chinese, and 70 Chinese had during the year given evidence of conversion. Reports were also made concerning the "mountain work" in eastern Tennessee and Kentucky. During the past year 35 missionaries had been sustained in the field through the co-operation of the Woman's Bureau of Correspondence. Resolutions were passed declaring that

Whereas, the system known as the "contract system" in connection with Indian work is liable to very serious abuse; and *whereas*, Government schools have now reached a position, as to equipment, methods, and efficiency, where the common-school education among the Indians may be safely and advisedly intrusted to them; therefore, *Resolved*, that public money expended upon the education of Indians ought to be expended exclusively by Government officers upon Government schools; that the practice of appropriating public money for the support of sectarian schools among Indians ought henceforth to cease; and that it is wise for the American Missionary Association to join in the purpose expressed by other great ecclesiastical bodies—the Methodist General Conference, convened at Omaha, May 2, 1892; the Presbyterian General Assembly, which met at Portland, Ore., May 23, 1892; and the Episcopal Convention at Baltimore, Oct. 19, 1892—to decline to seek or accept any subsidy from the Government, and that henceforth this society act in conformity with this purpose.

Special appeals were recommended to the churches for increased contributions, to supply the place of the money taken away by the withdrawal of Government support.

National Congregational Council.—The eighth triennial National Congregational Council met in Minneapolis, Minn., Oct. 12. The Rev. A. H. Quint, D. D., was chosen moderator. It was determined that hereafter missionaries of the American Board should be recognized as honorary members of the council. A committee appointed by the previous council to consider, in connection with committees of the national benevolent societies, the subject of the relation of those societies to the churches, presented a report carefully reviewing the whole question, which, however, having been prepared previous to the action of the American Board on the same subject (see above), related to a condition of affairs which had already undergone a change. This committee presented six alternative plans for the adjustment of the relations in question, of which it specifically recommended as the most advantageous one a plan for the election of corporate members of the societies by the State societies, of 1 delegate for each body, 1 for each of 50 churches, and 1 for every certain amount ($5,000 in the foreign department and $10,000 in the home department) contributed to the treasury of the society. The subject was referred to another committee, which reported, recommending in substance that the council accept the plan proposed by the American Board, of nomination by the associations of representative members to be elected by the Society, requesting the board to consummate its measure, advising the associations to make nominations to vacancies in the board, and providing for the appointment of a new committee, to whom should be referred the subject of representation of the churches in the societies, with instructions to confer with the societies in reference to the best methods of combining stability in administration with the principle of representation of the churches. A discussion relating to the recognition of the Congregational organizations in Alabama excited interest, because it involved the question of the "color line." The council has always refused to recognize any churches or organizations which did not fellowship with Congregational bodies composed of members of the other color. There were in Alabama an association of colored churches and 10 district conferences of white churches. These conferences, seeking recognition by the missionary societies and the council, proposed to form a State convention, composed of delegates from the association and from the conferences, such as had been formed in Georgia. The churches of the association offered to unite in any way that included a recognition of membership in the State body by representation of each church by its pastor and a member, but declined to unite in forming a body of delegates from conferences. A meeting of delegates was called to consider the subject of union, the representatives in which of the association (colored) were instructed to refer any proposition to their churches for ratification. On the holding of the meeting, the delegates of the conferences proceeded to the organization of a convention, without reference to the churches, while the representatives of the association withheld their consent from such a step. Delegates appeared to claim seats in the council from the convention thus organized, from 2 of the district conferences, and from the old Alabama Association. The Committee on Credentials recommended that the delegates from the Alabama Association and from the district conferences be admitted, but that the delegates from the State convention be not admitted. The subject was referred to a special committee, on whose recommendation the delegates approved by the Committee on Credentials were admitted, and the delegate from "the body claiming to be the General Convention of Alabama," which was "not yet organized as representing all the Congregational churches of the State," was received as an honorary member. The council also, on the report of the special committee, expressed "an earnest hope that the Congregational churches of Alabama will be at an early day found in one united body, on accepted principles of Congregational fellowship," and reaffirmed "the principle which Congregationalists have

always affirmed, of equal rights of all disciples of Christ, of every race, as essential to the fellowship of Congregational churches." This meeting of the Council was marked as being the first in which a woman participated as a delegate.

Armenian Congregational Church.—The first Armenian Congregational church in America was organized in Worcester, Mass., early in January, 1892, with 19 members, while enough other persons had applied for membership to make the probable whole number of members about 40. A parish organization was formed, with special reference to persons who are unwilling to sever their connection with the churches to which they belong in Turkey, the members of which were pledged to work for the spiritual, moral, and social interest of each other and their fellow-countrymen.

II. British Congregational Churches.—The Congregational Year Book for 1892 gives as the number of Congregational churches, branch churches, and mission stations in England and Wales (including 166 mission stations supported by individuals but not embraced in county returns) as 4,652, with 1,666,867 sittings, showing an increase of 64 churches and branch churches and 19,367 sittings, and 2,747 ministers, or 15 more than were previously reported. In Great Britain and the colonies, during the year, 9 persons had left the Congregational ministry for that of other denominations, and an equal number had been received from other denominations; 27 new churches had been formed, 30 additional chapels and halls provided, 19 rebuilt or enlarged, and 28 new schoolrooms opened, while foundation stones had been laid for 7 chapels and 8 schools. There were returned in connection with the churches of the London Missionary Society 67,797 church members and 276,521 native adherents. The number of women missionaries had increased from 37 to 45.

Congregational Union of England and Wales.—The sixtieth annual meeting of the Congregational Union of England and Wales was held in London, May 9. The Rev. Dr. Herbert Evans presided. The annual report mentioned as among the events of the year the International Congregational Council, the appearance of a proposition for holding a Free Church congress, the publication of large editions of the hymn books, the sale of 7,000 copies of the chairman's address by Dr. Brown, on "The Historic Episcopate," and the collection of statistics of Congregationalism in Wales, from which it appeared that the number of Congregational churches and branch churches in the principality had increased in thirty years from 766 to 1,173 : of church members from 97,647 to 130,111 ; and of Sunday-school pupils from 88,765 to 131,418. There were in the United Kingdom 4,886 Congregational churches, branch churches, and mission stations, and 721 in the colonies. The treasurer reported that the income of the Union had been £15,813, out of which the expenses of the International Council had been paid, and a balance was left to be distributed among Mansfield College Settlement, Browning Hall, the Colonial Missionary Society, the Paris Mission, Silcoat's school, and the final settlement of the expenses of the "Tooting church case." The committee on the secretariat reported concerning the steps which it had taken to secure a suitable person for the office of secretary, in the place of the Rev. Dr. Hannay, deceased, and nominated the Rev. W. J. Woods, of Clapton, who was elected. A resolution was adopted, declaring

That, in view of the approach of a general election, the assembly expresses the earnest hope that the members of the Union will everywhere exert their influence to secure the return to Parliament of representatives who will faithfully support measures calculated to promote peace, temperance, and social purity, as well as to improve the condition of the great masses of the people. It is also impressed with the importance of efforts to strengthen the conviction, already largely prevailing in the constituencies, that the machinery of civil government should cease to be employed for ecclesiastical purposes in any part of the kingdom, and that a policy of disestablishment should be adopted for Wales and for Scotland at the earliest possible period. And the assembly is further of opinion that, while necessarily employing political means for attaining that object, the members of the Union should more generally and systematically than heretofore endeavor to advance the principles of Protestant nonconformity, and particularly among the younger members of the nonconformist communities.

The third anniversary of the Congregational Guild was held during the meeting of the Union. The autumnal assembly of the Union met in Bradford, Oct. 11. The Rev. Herbert Evans presided, and delivered an opening address on "The Living Church." During the course of the discussion of the topic of "The Church and the Labor Problem," the Rev. Dr. Charles Leach said that on the previous Sunday he had gone for the first time into a Labor church, in Bradford. He had heard a member of Parliament tell a crowded audience that "Christianity is dead, and I am glad of it"; also, that a hundred years ago the streets of Paris ran with blood, and it might come to the same in this country. Mr. Leach declared that the man who sets the man against his master, the poor against the rich, was the enemy of both, and deserved the confidence of neither. Mr. Keit Hardie, the member of Parliament and speaker whose remarks were thus condemned, was in the hall, and desired the privilege of replying to Mr. Leach and setting himself right. He was permitted to speak, and said that what he had said on Sunday was that "the Christianity *of the schools* is dead, and the Christianity of Christ is coming to the front, and I am glad of it"; and that, having described the condition of affairs at the time of the French Revolution, and the similarity of the problems existing then and now, he had said that he did not want the labor movement in England to be solved as it had been by the revolution in France, because he desired evolution—a peaceful, gradual solution of the question; because bloodshed and revolution would not settle it. He then charged the churches with neglect of the laborers and the poor, and averred that "the reason why the laboring classes turn their backs on the churches is because the churches have turned their backs on Christ." Many protests were uttered against Mr. Hardie's remarks, as unjust to the churches and their ministers. One speaker said that many ministers had been working for years for

and among the classes spoken of by Mr. Hardie. The chairman said that many men outside the churches did not really know what the churches were doing, and yet denounced the churches for doing nothing. Another speaker said that Mr. Hardie had made a strong statement, and an exaggerated statement, but it contained enough truth to give it a sting, and he fancied they were stung. "Are your churches," said another speaker, "free to the workingmen to go in when they like? and do you let them sit where they like, at least one service in the day? . . . If they are, then there has been a great change within the last two years." Mr. Leach admitted that he had found, by reference to the stenographer's notes, that Mr. Hardie's representation of what he had said was correct. By resolution the assembly invited the churches of the Congregational order in England and Wales to commemorate the martyrdoms of Henry Barrows, John Greenwood, and John Penry, who were put to death in 1593. There were especially mentioned in the call as reasons for honoring the memory of these men, "the clearness with which they saw that the will of the Lord Jesus Christ, as revealed in the New Testament, is the supreme law for the government of his Church, and that the interpretation of that will is ever to be sought in the conscience and judgment of his faithful disciples in their gatherings; the boldness with which they testified that a Christian church is an assemblage of Christian persons and no others; their unshaken loyalty to the Crown and civil government in all civil causes; their meek endurance of the penalties imposed on them for their fidelity to the truths revealed to them; and their strong abiding confidence that these truths would one day be commonly recognized." The assembly, avowing its conviction that the freedom of worship and self-government now enjoyed is largely the result of the fidelity of the sixteenth-century confessors and their fellow-separatists, recommended a careful study of their history. A discussion on college reform covered several points in which it was thought the colleges could be made stronger, but a unity of views not prevailing, further debate was postponed till the May meeting of the Union, 1893. Resolutions were adopted insisting on the introduction, at the earliest period practicable, of measures for the disestablishment of the Church of England in Wales; renewing protests against the state patronage and control of the Church of Scotland; and inviting the support by the gently required to remove disabilities from which nonconformists are still suffering; the assembly believing that "the legislation which it desires would inflict no injury on either churches or religion, while it would prove conducive to Christian union, and would otherwise promote the welfare of the community at large." Besides topics already mentioned, the subjects were discussed of "Free Church Principles," "Biblical Criticism," "Dangerous Tendencies of Modern Life," and, at a special women's conference, "Parental Responsibility" and "Women's Work among the Masses." A resolution was passed relative to the death of Lord Tennyson, recording the assembly's sense of the service which the great poet rendered during his long life to the cause of truth and purity.

London Missionary Society.—The income of the London Missionary Society was represented at its annual meeting to have been £35,000 more than it had ever been before; and the ordinary contributions were £10,000 more than in the previous year, while 20 more missionaries were in the field than then. The society having a year before decided to permit women to be chosen to the board of directors, an increase in the energy of the women in support of the missionary work promised to result from the step. There were 45 women missionaries in the field. A steady advance was reported in the amount of the subscriptions for women's work, which now reached £8,713. A larger number of women than ever before had offered for personal service. The number of girls in the mission schools had increased in ten years from 12,700 to 44,500.

Church Aid and Home Missionary Society.—The annual meeting of the Congregational Church Aid and Home Missionary Society was held in London, May 10. The society's income had been £31,859, and its expenditure £29,394. In order to avert a heavy deficit the grants had been cut down the year before by 25 per cent. The report showed 751 churches and 117 evangelistic stations aided during the year.

Colonial Missionary Society.—The report of the Colonial Missionary Society described a change of policy under which it is intended gradually to reduce or withdraw grants of some standing, and devote the entire income to new enterprises. The Canadian College would next year begin an independent career with an endowment of £10,000. The income of the society for the year had been £3,106.

Pastors' Retiring Fund.—The capital of the Congregational Pastors' Retiring fund had reached £135,669 in April, 1892. Grants had been made during the year to 158 annuitants, and to the amount of £6,174. This brought the total payments since the formation of the fund, in 1860, to upward of £121,000 to about 520 retired ministers. The supplementary fund for the widows of ministers had reached £24,400. The payments to 53 recipients during 1891 had been £1,037.

Countess' of Huntington's Connection.—The annual conference of the Countess of Huntington's Connection was held in Tunbridge Wells in July. The reports from the churches showed encouraging progress, especially in the erection of chapels and schools. A paper on " The Trust Funds of the Connection " showed how certain alterations and simplification in the management of these funds would prove of advantage in aggressive work. Papers were also read on the means of extending the work and influence of the connection, and on "the consolidation of churches."

CONGRESS OF THE UNITED STATES.
The first session of the Fifty-second Congress met on Monday, Dec. 7, 1891. The Senate was composed of the following members, the dates indicating the expiration of their terms:

Alabama.
1895. John T. Morgan. D.
1897. James L. Pugh, D.

Arkansas.
1895. James H. Berry. D.
1897. James K. Jones, D.

California.
1893. Charles N. Felton, R.
1897. Leland Stanford, R.

Colorado.
1895. Edward O. Wolcott, R.
1897. Henry M. Teller, R.

Connecticut.
1893. Joseph R. Hawley, R.
1897. Orville H. Platt, R.

Delaware.
1893. George Gray, D.
1895. Anthony Higgins, R.

Florida.
1893. Samuel Pasco, D.
1897. Wilkinson Call, D.*

Georgia.
1895. Alfred H. Colquitt, D.
1897. John B. Gordon, D.

Idaho.
1895. George L. Shoup, R.
1897. Frederick T. Dubois, R.†

Illinois.
1895. Shelby M. Cullom, R.
1897. John M. Palmer, D.

Indiana.
1893. David Turpie, D.
1897. Daniel W. Voorhees, D.

Iowa.
1895. James F. Wilson, R.
1897. William B. Allison, R.

Kansas.
1895. Bishop W. Perkins, R.
1897. William A. Peffer, F. Al.

Kentucky.
1895. John G. Carlisle, D.
1897. J. C. S. Blackburn, D.

Louisiana.
1895. Randall L. Gibson, D.
1897. Edward D. White, D.

Maine.
1893. Eugene Hale, R.
1895. William P. Frye, R.

Maryland.
1893. Arthur P. Gorman, D.
1897. Charles H. Gibson, D.

Massachusetts.
1893. Henry L. Dawes, R.
1895. George F. Hoar, R.

Michigan.
1893. F. B. Stockbridge. R.
1895. James McMillan, R.

Minnesota.
1893. Cushman K. Davis. R.
1895. Wm. D. Washburn, R.

Mississippi.
1893. James Z. George. D.
1895. E. C. Walthall, D.

Missouri.
1893. Francis M. Cockrell, D.
1897. George G. Vest, D.

Montana.
1893. Wilbur F. Sanders, R.
1895. Thomas C. Power, R.

Nebraska.
1893. A. S. Paddock, R.
1895. C. F. Manderson, R.

Nevada.
1893. William M. Stewart, R.
1897. John P. Jones, R.

New Hampshire.
1895. Wm. E. Chandler, R.
1897. Jacob H. Gallinger, R.

New Jersey.
1893. Rufus Blodgett, D.
1895. John R. McPherson, D.

New York.
1893. Frank Hiscock, R.
1897. David B. Hill, D.

North Carolina.
1895. Matt. W. Ransom, D.
1897. Zebulon B. Vance, D.

North Dakota.
1893. Lyman R. Casey, R.
1895. H. C. Hansborough, R.

Ohio.
1893. John Sherman, R.
1897. Calvin S. Brice, D.

Oregon.
1895. Joseph N. Dolph, R.
1897. John H. Mitchell, R.

Pennsylvania.
1893. Matthew S. Quay, R.
1897. J. D. Cameron, R.

Rhode Island.
1893. Nelson W. Aldrich, R.
1895. Nathan F. Dixon, R.

Sout'h Carolina.
1895. Matthew C. Butler, D.
1897. John L. M. Irby, D.

South Dakota.
1895. R. F. Pettigrew, R.
1897. James H. Kyle, F. Al.

Tennessee.
1893. William B. Bate. D.
1895. Isham G. Harris, D.

Texas.
1893. Horace Chilton, D.
1895. Richard Coke, D.

Vermont.
1893. Redfield Proctor. R.
1897. Justin S. Morrill, R.

Virginia.
1893. John W. Daniel, D.
1895. John S. Barbour, D.

Washington.
1893. John B. Allen. R.
1897. Watson C. Squire, R.

West Virginia.
1893. C. J. Faulkner, D.
1895. John E. Kenna, D.

Wisconsin.
1893. Philetus Sawyer. R.
1897. William F. Vilas, D.

Wyoming.
1893. Francis E. Warren. R.
1895. Joseph M. Carey, R.

Republicans, 47 ; Democrats, 39 ; Farmer's Alliance, 2.

* Seat contested by R. H. M. Davidson, Democrat.
† Seat contested by W. H. Claggett, Democrat.

The House of Representatives was composed of the following members:

Alabama.

Richard H. Clarke, D.
Hilary A. Herbert, D.
William C. Oates, D.
Louis W. Turpin, D.

James E. Cobb, D.
John H. Bankhead, D.
William H. Forney, D.
Joseph Wheeler, D.

Arkansas.

William H. Cate, D.
Clifton R. Breckinridge, D.
Thomas C. McRae, D.

William L. Terry, D.
Samuel W. Peel, D.

California.

Thomas J. Geary, D.
Anthony Caminetti, D.
Joseph McKenna, R.

John T. Cutting, R.
Eugene F. Loud, R.
William W. Bowers, R.

Colorado.

Hosea Townsend, R.

Connecticut.

Lewis Sperry, D.
Washington F. Willcox, D.

Charles A. Russell, R.
Robert E. DeForest, D.

Delaware.

John W. Causey, D.

Florida.

Stephen R. Mallory, D.

Robert Bullock, D.

Georgia.

Rufus E. Lester, D.
Henry G. Turner, D.
Charles F. Crisp, D.
Charles L. Moses, D.
Leonidas F. Livingston, D.

James H. Blount, D.
R. William Everett, D.
Thomas G. Lawson, D.
Thomas E. Winn, D.
Thomas E. Watson, D.

Idaho.

Willis Sweet, R.

Illinois.

Abner Taylor, R.
Lawrence E. McGann, D.
Allen C. Durborow, Jr., D.
Walter C. Newberry, D.
Albert J. Hopkins, R.
Robert R. Hitt, R.
Thomas J. Henderson, R.
Lewis Steward, D.
Herman W. Snow, D.
Philip S. Post, R.

Benjamin T. Cable, D.
Scott Wike, D.
William M. Springer, D.
Owen Scott, D.
Samuel T. Busey, D.
George W. Fithian, D.
Edward Lane, D.
William S. Forman, D.
James R. Williams, D.
George W. Smith, R.

Indiana.

William F. Parrett, D.
John L. Bretz, D.
Jason B. Brown, D.
William S. Holman, D.
George W. Cooper, D.
Henry M. Johnson, R.
William D. Bynum, D.

Elijah V. Brookshire, D.
Daniel Waugh. R.
David H. Patton, D.
Augustus N. Martin. D.
Charles A. O. McClellan. D.
Benjamin F. Shively, D.

Iowa.

John J. Seerley, D.
Walter I. Hayes, D.
David B. Henderson, R.
Walter H. Butler, D.
John T. Hamilton, D.
Frederick E. White, D.

John A. T. Hull. R.
James P. Flick, R.
Thomas Bowman, D.
Jonathan P. Dolliver, R.
George D. Perkins, R.

Kansas.

Case Broderick, R.
Edward H. Funston, R.
Benjamin H. Clover, F. Al.
John G. Otis, F. Al

John Davis, F. Al.
William Baker, F. Al.
Jeremiah Simpson, F. Al.

Kentucky.

William J. Stone, D.
William T. Ellis, D.
Isaac H. Goodnight, D.
Alexander B. Montgomery, D.
Asher G. Caruth, D.
Worth W. Dickerson, D.

Wm. C. P. Breckinridge, D
James B. McCreary, D.
Thomas H. Paynter, D.
John W. Kendall, D.
John H. Wilson, R.

Louisiana.

Adolph Meyer, D.
Matthew D. Lagan, D.
Andrew Price, D.

Newton C. Blanchard, D
Charles J. Boatner, D.
S. M. Robertson, D.

Maine.

Thomas B. Reed, R.
Nelson Dingley, Jr., R.

Seth L. Milliken, R.
Charles A. Boutelle, R.

Maryland.

Henry Page, D.
Herman Stump, D.
Harry Welles Rusk, D.

Isidor Rayner. D.
Barnes Compton, D.
William M. McKaig, D.

Massachusetts.

Charles S. Randall, R.
Elijah A. Morse, R.
John F. Andrew, D.
Joseph H. O'Neil. D.
Sherman Hoar, D.
Henry Cabot Lodge, R.

William Cogswell, R.
Moses T. Stevens, D.
George Fred. Williams, D.
Joseph H. Walker, R.
Frederic S. Coolidge, D.
John C. Crosby, D.

Michigan.

J. Logan Chipman, D.
James S. Gorman, D.
James O'Donnell, R.
Julius C. Burrows, R.
Charles E. Belknap, R.
Byron G. Stout, D.

Justin R. Whiting, D.
Henry M. Youmans, D.
Harrison H. Wheeler, D.
Thomas A. E. Weadock, D.
Samuel M. Stephenson, R.

Minnesota.

William H. Harries, D.
John Lind, R.
O. M. Hall, D.

James N. Castle, D.
Kittel Halvorsen, F. Al.

Mississippi.

John M. Allen, D.
John C. Kyle, D.
Thomas C. Catchings, D.
Clarke Lewis, D.

Joseph H. Beeman, D.
Thomas R Stockdale, D.
Charles E. Hooker, D.

Missouri.

William H. Hatch, D.
Charles H. Mansur, D.
Alexander M. Dockery, D.
Robert P. C. Wilson, D.
John C. Tarsney, D.
John T. Heard, D.
Richard H. Norton, D.

John J. O'Neil, D.
Seth W. Cobb, D.
Samuel Byrns, D.
Richard P. Bland, D.
David A. DeArmond, D.
Robert W. Fyan, D.
Marshall Arnold, D.

Montana.

William W. Dixon; D.

Nebraska.

William J. Bryan, D.
William A. McKeighan, F. Al.

Omer M. Kem, F. Al.

Nevada.

Horace F. Bartine, R.

New Hampshire.

Luther F. McKinney, D.

Warren F. Daniell, D.

New Jersey.

Christopher A. Bergen, R.
James Buchanan, R.
Jacob A. Geissenhainer, D.
Samuel Fowler, D.

Cornelius A. Cadmus, D.
Thomas Dunn English, D.
Edward F. McDonald, D.

New York.

James W. Covert, D.
Alfred C. Chapin, D.
William J. Coombs, D.
John M. Clancy, D.
Thomas F. Magner, D.
John R. Fellows, D.
Edward J. Dunphy, D.
Timothy J. Campbell, D.
Amos J. Cummings, D.
W. Bourke Cockran, D.
John DeWitt Warner, D.
Joseph J. Little, D.
Ashbel P. Fitch, D.
William G. Stahlnecker, D.
Henry Bacon, D.
John H. Ketcham, R.
Isaac N. Cox, D.

John A. Quackenbush, R.
Charles Tracey, D.
John Sanford, D.
John M. Wever, R.
W. Martin Curtis, R.
Henry W. Bentley, D.
George Van Horn, D.
James J. Belden, R.
George W. Ray, R.
Sereno E. Payne, R.
Hosea H. Rockwell, D.
John Raines, R.
Halbert S. Greenleaf, D.
James W. Wadsworth, R.
Daniel W. Lockwood, D.
Thomas L. Bunting, D.
Warren B. Hooker, R.

North Carolina.

William A. B. Branch, D.
Henry P. Cheatham. R.
Benjamin F. Grady, D.
Benjamin H. Bunn, D.
Archibald H. A. Williams, D.

Sydenham B. Alexander, D.
John S. Henderson, D.
William H. H. Cowles, D.
William T. Crawford, D.

North Dakota.

Martin N. Johnson, R.

Ohio.

Bellamy Storer, R.	William H. Enochs, R.
John A. Caldwell, R.	Irvine Dungan, D.
George W. Houk, D.	James W. Owens, D.
Martin K. Gantz, D.	Michael D. Harter, D.
Fernando C. Layton, D.	John G. Warwick, D.
Dennis D. Donovan, D.	Albert J. Pearson, D.
William E. Haynes, D.	Joseph D. Taylor, R.
Darius D. Hare, D.	Ezra B. Taylor, R.
Joseph H. Outhwaite, D.	Vincent A. Taylor, R.
Robert E. Doan, R.	Thomas L. Johnson, D.
John M. Pattison, D.	

Oregon.

Binger Hermann, R.

Pennsylvania.

Henry H. Bingham, R.	Myron B. Wright, R.
Charles O'Neill, R.	Albert C. Hopkins, R.
William McAleer, D.	Simon P. Wolverton, D.
John E. Reyburn, R.	Louis E. Atkinson. R.
Alfred C. Harmer, R.	Frank E. Beltzhoover, D.
John B. Robinson, R.	Edward Scull R.
Edwin Hallowell, D.	George F. Huff, R.
William Mutchler, D.	John Dalzell. R.
David B. Brunner, D.	William A. Stone, R.
Marlott Brosius, R.	Andrew Stewart, R.
Lemuel Amerman, D.	Eugene P. Gillespie, D.
George W. Shonk, R.	Matthew Griswold, R.
James B. Reilly, D.	Charles W. Stone, R.
John W. Rife, R.	George F. Kribbs, D.

Rhode Island.

Oscar Lapham, D.   Charles H. Page, D.

South Carolina.

William H. Brawley, D.	John T. Hemphill, D.
George D. Tillman, D.	Eli T. Stackhouse, D.
George Johnstone, D.	William Elhott, D.
George W. Shell, D.	

South Dakota.

John L. Jolley, R.

Tennessee.

Alfred A. Taylor, R.	Joseph E. Washington, D.
John C. Houk, R.	Nicholas N. Cox, D.
Henry C. Snodgrass, D.	Benjamin A. Enloe, D.
Benton McMillin, D.	Rice A. Pierce, D.
James D. Richardson, D.	Josiah Patterson, D.

Texas.

Charles Stewart, D.	William H. Crain, D.
John B. Long, D.	Littleton W. Moore, D.
C. Buckley Kilgore, D.	Roger Q. Mills, D.
David B. Culberson, D.	Joseph D. Sayers, D.
Joseph W. Bailey, D.	Samuel W. T. Lanham, D.
Jo Abbott, D.	

Vermont.

H. Henry Powers, R.   William W. Grout, R.

Virginia.

William A. Jones, D.	Paul C. Edmunds, D.
John W. Lawson, D.	Charles T. O'Ferrall, D.
George D. Wise, D.	Elisha E. Meredith, D.
James F. Epes, D.	John A. Buchanan, D.
Posey G. Lester, D.	Henry St. G. Tucker, D.

Washington.

John L. Wilson, R.

West Virginia.

John O. Pendleton, D.	John D. Alderson, D.
William L. Wilson, D.	James Capehart, D.

Wisconsin.

Clinton Babbitt, D.	Lucas M. Miller, D.
Charles Barwig, D.	Frank P. Coburn, D.
Allen R. Bushnell, D.	Nils P. Haugen, D.
John L. Mitchell, D.	Thomas Lynch, D.
George H. Brickner, D.	

Wyoming.

Clarence D. Clark, R.

Democrats, 236; Republicans, 88; Farmer's Alliance, 8.

The Territorial delegates were as follow:

Arizona—Marcus A. Smith, D.
New Mexico—Antonio Joseph, D.
Oklahoma—David A. Harvey, R.
Utah—John T. Caine, Ind.

Eppa Hunton succeeded John S. Barbour as Senator for Virginia, on the latter's death, May 14, 1892.

Roger Q. Mills succeeded Horace Chilton as Senator from Texas, the latter holding only by appointment of the Governor.

Andrew Stewart, of Pennsylvania, was unseated in favor of Alexander Craig.

Joseph McKenna, of California, resigned, and E. T. Stackhouse, of South Carolina, and J. W. Kendall, of Kentucky, died.

Dec. 8, the House of Representatives organized by choosing Charles F. Crisp, of Georgia, Speaker. There had been a lively contest among leading Democrats for the office, and the nomination was not made by the Democratic caucus until 30 ballots had been taken for a candidate. In caucus, Mr. Crisp received 119 votes to 105 for Mr. Mills, of Texas, 2 for Mr. Springer, of Illinois, and 1 for Mr. Stevens, of Massachusetts. In the House, 228 votes were cast for Mr. Crisp, 83 for Thomas B. Reed, of Maine, and 8 for Thomas E. Watson, of Georgia. There were 12 members not voting.

The Message.—On Dec. 9 the President sent in his annual message, as follows:

To the Senate and House of Representatives:

The reports of the heads of the several executive departments, required by law to be submitted to me, which are herewith transmitted, and the reports of the Secretary of the Treasury and the Attorney-General, made directly to Congress, furnish a comprehensive view of the administrative work of the last fiscal year relating to internal affairs. It would be of great advantage if these reports could have an attentive perusal by every member of Congress and by all who take an interest in public affairs. Such a perusal could not fail to excite a higher appreciation of the vast labor and conscientious effort which are given to the conduct of our civil administration.

The reports will, I believe, show that every question has been approached, considered, and decided from the standpoint of p duty and upon considerations affecting the public interests alone. Again I invite to every branch of the service the attention and scrutiny of Congress.

The work of the State Department during the last year has been characterized by an unusual number of important negotiations and by diplomatic results of a notable and highly beneficial character. Among these are the reciprocal trade arrangements which have been concluded, in the exercise of the powers conferred by section 3 of the tariff law, with the Republic of Brazil, with Spain for its West India possessions, and with Santo Domingo. Like negotiations with other countries have been much advanced, and it is hoped that before the close of the year further definitive trade arrangements of great value will be concluded.

In view of the reports which had been received as to the diminution of the seal herds in the Bering Sea I deemed it wise to propose to Her Majesty's Government in February last that an agreement for a closed season should be made, pending the negotiations for arbitration which then seemed to be approaching a favorable conclusion. After much correspondence and delays for which this Government was not responsible, an agreement was reached and signed on the 15th of June, by which Great Britain undertook, from that date and until May 1, 1892, to prohibit the killing by her subjects of seals in the Bering Sea, and the Government of the United States, during the same period, to enforce its existing prohibition against pelagic sealing and to limit the catch by the Fur Seal Company upon the islands to 7,500 skins. If this agreement could have been reached earlier, in response to the strenuous endeavors of this Government, it would have been more effective; but, coming even as late as it did, it unquestionably resulted in greatly diminishing the destruction of the seals by the Canadian sealers.

In my last annual message I stated that the basis of arbitration proposed by Her Majesty's Government for the adjustment of the long-pending controversy as to the seal fisheries was not acceptable. I am glad now to be able to announce that terms satisfactory to this Government have been agreed upon and that an agreement as to the arbitrators is all that is necessary to the completion of the convention. In view of the advanced position which this Government has taken upon the subject of international arbitration, this renewed expression of our adherence to this method for the settlement of disputes such as have arisen in the Bering Sea will, I doubt not, meet with the concurrence of Congress.

Provision should be made for a joint demarkation of the frontier line between Canada and the United States wherever required by the increasing border settlements, and especially for the exact location of the water boundary in the straits and rivers.

I should have been glad to announce some favorable disposition of the boundary dispute between Great Britain and Venezuela, touching the western frontier of British Guiana, but the friendly efforts of the United States in that direction have thus far been unavailing. This Government will continue to express its concern at any appearance of foreign encroachment on territories long under the administrative control of American states. The determination of a disputed boundary is easily attainable by amicable arbitration where the rights of the respective parties rest, as here, on historic facts, readily ascertainable.

The law of the last Congress providing a system of inspection for our meats intended for export, and clothing the President with power to exclude foreign products from our market in case the country sending them should perpetuate unjust discriminations against any product of the United States, placed this Government in a position to effectively urge the removal of such discriminations against our meats. It is gratifying to be able to state that Germany, Denmark, Italy, Austria, and France, in the order named, have opened their ports to inspected American pork products. The removal of these restrictions in every instance was asked for and given solely upon the ground that we had now provided a meat inspection that should be accepted as adequate to the complete removal of the dangers, real or fancied, which had been previously urged. The State Department, our ministers abroad, and the Secretary of Agriculture, have co-operated with unflagging and intelligent zeal for the accomplishment of this great result. The outlines of an agreement have been reached with Germany looking to equitable trade concessions in consideration of the continued free importation of her sugars, but the time has not yet arrived when this correspondence can be submitted to Congress.

The recent political disturbances in the Republic of Brazil have excited regret and solicitude. The information we possessed was too meager to enable us to form a satisfactory judgment of the causes leading to the temporary assumption of supreme power by President Fonseca; but this Government did not fail to express to him its anxious solicitude for the peace of Brazil and for the maintenance of the free political institutions which had recently been established there, nor to offer our advice that great moderation should be observed in the clash of parties and the contest for leadership. These counsels were received in the most friendly spirit, and the latest information is that constitutional government has been re-established without bloodshed.

The lynching at New Orleans in March last of eleven men of Italian nativity by a mob of citizens was a most deplorable and discreditable incident. It did not, however, have its origin in any general animosity to the Italian people, nor in any disrespect to the Government of Italy, with which our relations were of the most friendly character. The fury of the mob was directed against these men as the supposed participants or accessories in the murder of a city officer. I do not allude to this as mitigating in any degree this offense against law and humanity, but only as affecting the international questions which grew out of it. It was at once represented by the Italian minister that several of those whose lives had been taken by the mob were Italian subjects, and a demand was made for the punishment of the participants and for an indemnity to the families of those who were killed. It is to be regretted that the manner in which these claims were presented was not such as to promote a calm discussion of the questions involved; but this may well be attributed to the excitement and indignation which the crime naturally evoked. The views of this Government as to its obligations to foreigners domiciled here were fully stated in the correspondence, as well as its purpose to make an investigation of the affair with a view to determine whether there were present any circumstances that could, under such rules of duty as we had indicated, create an obligation upon the United States. The temporary absence of a minister plenipotentiary of Italy at this capital has retarded the further correspondence, but it is not doubted that a friendly conclusion is attainable.

Some suggestions growing out of this unhappy incident are worthy the attention of Congress. It would, I believe, be entirely competent for Congress to make offenses against the treaty rights of foreigners domiciled in the United States cognizable in the Federal courts. This has not, however, been done, and the Federal officers and courts have no power in such cases to intervene either for the protection of a foreign citizen or for the punishment of his slayers. It seems to me to follow, in this state of the law, that the officers of the State charged with police and judicial powers in such cases must, in the consideration of international questions growing out of such incidents, be regarded in such sense as Federal agents as to make this Government answerable for their acts in cases where it would be answerable if the United States had used its constitutional power to define and punish crimes against treaty rights.

The civil war in Chili, which began in January last, was continued, but fortunately with infrequent and not important armed collisions, until Aug. 28, when the Congressional forces landed near Valparaiso, and, after a bloody engagement, captured that city. President Balmaceda at once recognized that his cause was lost, and a provisional government was speedily established by the victorious party. Our minister was promptly directed to recognize and put himself in communication with this Government so soon as it should have established its de facto character, which was done. During the pendency of this civil contest frequent indirect appeals were made to this Government to extend belligerent rights to the insurgents and to give audience to their representatives. This was declined, and that policy was pursued throughout, which this Government, when wrenched by civil war, so strenuously insisted upon on the part of European nations. The "Itata," an armed vessel commanded by a naval officer of the insurgent fleet, manned by its sailors and with soldiers on board, was seized under process of the United States court at San Diego, California, for a violation of our neutrality laws. While in the custody of an officer of the court the vessel was forcibly wrested from his control and put to sea. It would have been inconsistent with the dignity and self-respect of this Government not to have insisted that the "Itata" should be returned to San Diego to abide the judgment of the court. This was so clear to the Junta of the Congressional party, established at Iquique, that, before the arrival of the "Itata" at that port, the Secretary of Foreign Relations of the Provisional Government addressed to

Rear-Admiral Brown, commanding the United States naval forces, a communication, from which the following is an extract :

"The Provisional Government has learned by the cablegrams of the Associated Press that the transport 'Itata,' detained in San Diego by order of the United States for taking on board munitions of war and in possession of the marshal, left the port, carrying on board this official, who was landed at a point near the coast, and then continued her voyage. . . . If this news be correct, this Government would deplore the conduct of the 'Itata,' and, as an evidence that it is not disposed to support or agree to the infraction of the laws of the United States, the undersigned takes advantage of the personal relations you have been good enough to maintain with him since your arrival in this port to declare to you that as soon as she is within reach of our orders his Government will put the 'Itata,' with the arms and munitions she took on board in San Diego, at the disposition of the United States."

A trial in the district court of the United States for the southern district of California has recently resulted in a decision holding, among other things, that inasmuch as the Congressional party had not been recognized as a belligerent, the acts done in its interest could not be a violation of our neutrality laws. From this judgment the United States has appealed, not that the condemnation of the vessel is a matter of importance, but that we may know what the present state of our law is; for, if this construction of the statute is correct, there is obvious necessity for revision and amendment.

During the progress of the war in Chili this Government tendered its good offices to bring about a peaceful adjustment, and it was at one time hoped that a good result might be reached; but in this we were disappointed.

The instructions to our naval officers and to our minister at Santiago, from the first to the last of this struggle, enjoined upon them the most impartial treatment and absolute noninterference. I am satisfied that these instructions were observed, and that our representatives were always watchful to use their influence impartially in the interest of humanity, and on more than one occasion did so effectively. We could not forget, however, that this Government was in diplomatic relations with the then established Government of Chili, as it is now in such relations with the successor of that Government. I am quite sure that President Montt, who has, under circumstances of promise for the peace of Chili, been installed as President of that republic, will not desire that, in the unfortunate event of any revolt against his authority, the policy of this Government should be other than that which we have recently observed. No official complaint of the conduct of our minister or of our naval officers during the struggle has been presented to this Government; and it is a matter of regret that so many of our own people should have given ear to unofficial charges and complaints that manifestly had their origin in rival interests and in a wish to pervert the relations of the United States with Chili.

The collapse of the Government of Balmaceda brought about a condition which is unfortunately too familiar in the history of the Central and South American States. With the overthrow of the Balmaceda Government, he, and many of his counsilors and officers, became at once fugitives for their lives and appealed to the commanding officers of the foreign naval vessels in the harbor of Valparaiso and to the resident foreign ministers at Santiago for asylum. This asylum was freely given, according to my information, by the naval vessels of several foreign powers and by several of the legations at Santiago. The American minister, as well as his colleagues, acting upon the impulses of humanity, extended asylum to political refugees whose lives were in peril. I have not been willing to direct the surrender of such of these persons as are still in the American Legation without suitable conditions.

It is believed that the Government of Chili is not in a position, in view of the precedents with which it has been connected, to broadly deny the right of asylum, and the correspondence has not thus far presented any such denial. The treatment of our minister for a time was such as to call for a decided protest, and it was very gratifying to observe that unfriendly measures, which were undoubtedly the result of the prevailing excitement, were at once rescinded or suitably relaxed.

On the 16th of October an event occurred in Valparaiso so serious and tragic in its circumstances and results as to very justly excite the indignation of our people, and to call for prompt and decided action on the part of this Government. A considerable number of the sailors of the United States steamship "Baltimore," then in the harbor of Valparaiso, being upon shore leave and unarmed, were assaulted by armed men nearly simultaneously in different localities in the city. One petty officer was killed outright and seven or eight seaman were seriously wounded, one of whom has since died. So savage and brutal was the assault that several of our sailors received more than two, and one as many as eighteen stab wounds. An investigation of the affair was promptly made by a board of officers of the "Baltimore," and their report shows that these assaults were unprovoked, that our men were conducting themselves in a peaceable and orderly manner, and that some of the police of the city took part in the assault and used their weapons with fatal effect, while a few others, with some well-disposed citizens, endeavored to protect our men. Thirty-six of our sailors were arrested, and some of them, while being taken to prison, were cruelly beaten and maltreated. The fact that they were all discharged, no criminal charge being lodged against any one of them, shows very clearly that they were innocent of any breach of the peace.

So far as I have yet been able to learn no other explanation of this bloody work has been suggested than that it had its origin in hostility to these men as sailors of the United States, wearing the uniform of their Government, and not in any individual act or personal animosity. The attention of the Chilian Government was at once called to this affair, and a statement of the facts obtained by the investigation we had conducted was submitted, accompanied by a request to be advised of any other or qualifying facts in the possession of the Chilian Government that might tend to relieve this affair of the appearance of an insult to this Government. The Chilian Government was also advised that if such qualifying facts did not exist this Government would confidently expect full and prompt reparation.

It is to be regretted that the reply of the Secretary for Foreign Affairs of the Provisional Government was couched in an offensive tone. To this no response has been made. This Government is now awaiting the result of an investigation which has been conducted by the criminal court at Valparaiso. It is reported unofficially that the investigation is about completed, and it is expected that the result will soon be communicated to this Government, together with some adequate and satisfactory response to the note by which the attention of Chili was called to this incident. If these just expectations should be disappointed or further needless delay intervene, I will, by a special message, bring this matter again to the attention of Congress for such action as may be necessary. The entire correspondence with the Government of Chili will at an early day be submitted to Congress.

I renew the recommendation of my special message, dated Jan. 16, 1890, for the adoption of the necessary legislation to enable this Government to apply in the case of Sweden and Norway the same rule in respect to the levying of tonnage dues as was claimed and secured to the shipping of the United States in 1828 under Article VIII of the treaty of 1827.

The adjournment of the Senate without action on the pending acts for the suppression of the slave traffic

In Africa and for the reform of the revenue tariff of the Independent State of the Congo left this Government unable to exchange those acts on the date fixed, July 2, 1891. A *modus vivendi* has been concluded by which the power of the Congo State to levy duties on imports is left unimpaired, and, by agreement of all the signatories to the general slave-trade act, the time for the exchange of ratifications on the part of the United States has been extended to Feb. 2, 1892.

The late outbreak against foreigners in various parts of the Chinese Empire has been a cause of deep concern in view of the numerous establishments of our citizens in the interior of that country. This Government can do no less than insist upon a continuance of the protective and punitory measures which the Chinese Government has heretofore applied. No effort will be omitted to protect our citizens peaceably sojourning in China, but recent unofficial information indicates that what was first regarded as an outbreak of mob violence against foreigners has assumed the larger form of an insurrection against public order.

The Chinese Government has declined to receive Mr. Blair as the Minister of the United States on the ground that, as a participant, while a Senator, in the enactment of the existing legislation against the introduction of Chinese laborers, he has become unfriendly and objectionable to China. I have felt constrained to point out to the Chinese Government the untenableness of this position, which seems to rest as much on the unacceptability of our legislation as on that of the person chosen, and which, if admitted, would practically debar the selection of any representative so long as the existing laws remain in force.

You will be called upon to consider the expediency of making special provision by law for the temporary admission of some Chinese artisans and laborers in connection with the exhibit of Chinese manufactures at the approaching Columbian Exposition. I regard it as desirable that the Chinese exhibit be facilitated in every proper way.

A question has arisen with the Government of Spain touching the right of American citizens in the Caroline Islands. Our citizens there, long prior to the confirmation of Spain's claim to the islands, had secured by settlement and purchase certain rights, to the recognition and maintenance of which the faith of Spain was pledged. I have had reason within the past year very strongly to protest against the failure to carry out this pledge on the part of His Majesty's ministers, which has resulted in great injustice and injury to the American residents.

The Government and people of Spain propose to celebrate the four hundredth anniversary of the discovery of America by holding an exposition at Madrid, which will open on the 12th of September and continue until the 31st of December, 1892. A cordial invitation has been extended to the United States to take part in this commemoration, and, as Spain was one of the first nations to express the intention to participate in the World's Columbian Exposition at Chicago, it would be very appropriate for this Government to give this invitation its friendly promotion.

Surveys for the connecting links of the projected Intercontinental Railway are in progress, not only in Mexico, but at various points along the course mapped out. Three surveying parties are now in the field under the direction of the commission. Nearly one thousand miles of the proposed road have been surveyed, including the most difficult part, that through Ecuador and the southern part of Colombia. The reports of the engineers are very satisfactory and show that no insurmountable obstacles have been met with.

On Nov. 12, 1884, a treaty was concluded with Mexico reaffirming the boundary between the two countries as described in the treaties of Feb. 2, 1848, and Dec. 30, 1853. March 1, 1889, a further treaty was negotiated to facilitate the carrying out of the principles of the treaty of 1884 and to avoid the difficulties occasioned by reason of the changes and altera-

tions that take place from natural causes in the Rio Grande and Colorado rivers in the portions thereof constituting the boundary line between the two republics. The International Boundary Commission, provided for by the treaty of 1889, to have exclusive jurisdiction of any question that may arise, has been named by the Mexican Government. An appropriation is necessary to enable the United States to fulfill its treaty obligation in this respect.

The death of King Kalakaua in the United States afforded occasion to testify our friendship for Hawaii by conveying the King's body to his own land in a naval vessel with all due honors. The Government of his successor, Queen Liliuokalani, is seeking to promote closer commercial relations with the United States. Surveys for the much-needed submarine cable from our Pacific Coast to Honolulu are in progress, and this enterprise should have the suitable promotion of the two governments. I strongly recommend that provision be made for improving the harbor of Pearl river and equipping it as a naval station.

The arbitration treaty formulated by the International American Conference lapsed by reason of the failure to exchange ratifications fully within the limit of time provided; but several of the governments concerned have expressed a desire to save this important result of the conference by an extension of the period. It is, in my judgment, incumbent upon the United States to conserve the influential initiative it has taken in this measure by ratifying the instrument and by advocating the proposed extension of the time for exchange. These views have been made known to the other signatories.

This Government has found occasion to express, in a friendly spirit but with much earnestness, to the Government of the Czar, its serious concern because of the harsh measures now being enforced against the Hebrews in Russia. By the revival of antisemitic laws, long in abeyance, great numbers of these unfortunate people have been constrained to abandon their homes and leave the empire by reason of the impossibility of finding subsistence within the pale to which it is sought to confine them. The immigration of these people to the United States—many other countries being closed to them—is largely increasing, and is likely to assume proportions which may make it difficult to find homes and employment for them here and to seriously affect the labor market. It is estimated that over one million will be forced from Russia within a few years. The Hebrew is never a beggar; he has always kept the law—life by toil—often under severe and oppressive civil restrictions. It is also true that no race, sect, or class has more fully cared for its own than the Hebrew race. But the sudden transfer of such a multitude, under conditions that tend to strip them of their small accumulations and to depress their energies and courage, is neither good for them nor for us.

The banishment, whether by direct decree or by not less certain indirect methods, of so large a number of men and women is not a local question. A decree to leave one country is, in the nature of things, an order to enter another—some other. This consideration, as well as the suggestions of humanity, furnishes ample ground for the remonstrances which we have presented to Russia, while our historic friendship for that Government can not fail to give the assurance that our representations are those of a sincere well-wisher.

The annual report of the Maritime Canal Company of Nicaragua shows that much costly and necessary preparatory work has been done during the year in the construction of shops, railroad tracks, and harbor piers and breakwaters, and that the work of canal construction has made some progress.

I deem it to be a matter of the highest concern to the United States that this canal, connecting the waters of the Atlantic and Pacific Oceans and giving to us a short water communication between our ports upon those two great seas, should be speedily constructed and at the smallest practicable limit of cost.

The gain in freights to the people and the direct saving to the Government of the United States in the use of its naval vessels would pay the entire cost of this work within a short series of years. The report of the Secretary of the Navy shows the saving in our naval expenditures which would result.

The Senator from Alabama (Mr. Morgan), in his argument upon this subject before the Senate at the last session, did not overestimate the importance of this work when he said that "the canal is the most important subject now connected with the commercial growth and progress of the United States."

If this work is to be promoted by the usual financial methods and without the aid of this Government, the expenditures, in its interest-bearing securities and stocks, will probably be twice the actual cost. This will necessitate higher tolls, and constitute a heavy and altogether needless burden upon our commerce and that of the world. Every dollar of the bonds and stock of the company should represent a dollar expended in the legitimate and economical prosecution of the work. This is only possible by giving to the bonds the guarantee of the United States Government. Such a guarantee would secure the ready sale at par of a 3-per-cent. bond, from time to time, as the money was needed. I do not doubt that, built upon these business methods, the canal would, when fully inaugurated, earn its fixed charges and operating expenses. But if its bonds are to be marketed at heavy discounts and every bond sold is to be accompanied by a gift of stock, as has come to be expected by investors in such enterprises, the traffic will be seriously burdened to pay interest and dividends. I am quite willing to recommend Government promotion in the prosecution of a work which, if no other means offered for securing its completion, is of such transcendent interest that the Government should, in my opinion, secure it by direct appropriations from its Treasury.

A guarantee of the bonds of the Canal Company to an amount necessary to the completion of the canal could, I think, be so given as not to involve any serious risk of ultimate loss. The things to be carefully guarded are the completion of the work within the limits of the guarantee, the subrogation of the United States to the rights of the first-mortgage bondholders for any amounts it may have to pay, and in the mean time a control of the stock of the company as a security against mismanagement and loss. I most sincerely hope that neither party nor sectional lines will be drawn upon this great American project, so full of interest to the people of all our States and so influential in its effects upon the prestige and prosperity of our common country.

The island of Navassa, in the West Indian group, has, under the provisions of Title 72 of the Revised Statutes, been recognized by the President as appertaining to the United States. It contains guano deposits, is owned by the Navassa Phosphate Company, and is occupied solely by its employees. In September, 1889, a revolt took place among these laborers, resulting in the killing of some of the agents of the company, caused, as the laborers claimed, by cruel treatment. These men were arrested and tried in the United States court at Baltimore, under section 5576 of the statute referred to, as if the offenses had been committed on board a merchant vessel of the United States on the high seas. There appeared on the trial, and otherwise came to me, such evidences of the bad treatment of the men that, in consideration of this and of the fact that the men had no access to any public officer or tribunal for protection or the redress of their wrongs, I commuted the death sentences that had been passed by the court upon three of them. In April last my attention was again called to this island, and to the unregulated condition of things there, by a letter from a colored laborer, who complained that he was wrongfully detained upon the island by the phosphate company after the expiration of his contract of service. A naval vessel was sent to examine into the case of this man and generally into the condition of things on the island. It was found that the la

borer referred to had been detained beyond the contract limit, and that a condition of revolt again existed among the laborers. A board of naval officers reported, among other things, as follows:

" We would desire to state further that the discipline maintained on the island seems to be that of a convict establishment, without its comforts and cleanliness, and that, until more attention is paid to the shipping of laborers, by placing it under Government supervision to prevent misunderstanding and misrepresentation, and until some amelioration is shown in the treatment of the laborers, these disorders will be of constant occurrence."

I recommend legislation that shall place labor contracts upon this and other islands having the relation that Navassa has to the United States under the supervision of a court commissioner, and that shall provide, at the expense of the owners, an officer to reside upon the islands with power to judge and adjust disputes and to enforce a just and humane treatment of the employees. It is inexcusable that American laborers should be left within our own jurisdiction without access to any Government officer or tribunal for their protection and the redress of their wrongs.

International copyright has been secured, in accordance with the conditions of the act of March 3, 1891, with Belgium, France, Great Britain and the British possessions, and Switzerland, the laws of those countries permitting to our citizens the benefit of copyright on substantially the same basis as to their own citizens or subjects. With Germany a special convention has been negotiated upon this subject, which will bring that country within the reciprocal benefits of our legislation.

The general interest in the operations of the Treasury Department has been much augmented during the last year by reason of the conflicting predictions, which accompanied and followed the tariff and other legislation of the last Congress affecting the revenues, as to the results of this legislation upon the Treasury and upon the country. On the one hand it was contended that imports would so fall off as to leave the Treasury bankrupt and that the prices of articles entering into the living of the people would be so enhanced as to disastrously affect their comfort and happiness, while on the other it was argued that the loss to the revenue, largely the result of placing sugar on the free list, would be a direct gain to the people; that the prices of the necessaries of life, including those most highly protected, would not be enhanced; that labor would have a larger market and the products of the farm advanced prices; while the Treasury surplus and receipts would be adequate to meet the appropriations, including those exceptional expenditures for the refunding to the States of the direct tax and the redemption of the 4½-per-cent. bonds.

It is not my purpose to enter at any length into a discussion of the effects of the legislation to which I have referred; but a brief examination of the statistics of the Treasury and a general glance at the state of business throughout the country will, I think, satisfy any impartial inquirer that its results have disappointed the evil prophecies of its opponents and in a large measure realized the hopeful predictions of its friends. Rarely, if ever before, in the history of the country has there been a time when the proceeds of one day's labor or the product of one farmed acre would purchase so large an amount of those things that enter into the living of the masses of the people. I believe that a full test will develop the fact that the tariff act of the Fifty-first Congress is very favorable in its average effect upon the prices of articles entering into common use.

During the twelve months from Oct. 1, 1890, to Sept. 30, 1891, the total value of our foreign commerce (imports and exports combined) was $1,747,806,406, which was the largest of any year in the history of the United States. The largest in any previous year was in 1890, when our commerce amounted to $1,647,139,093, and the last year exceeds this enormous aggregate by over one hundred millions. It is interesting, and to some will be surprising, to know that during the year ending Sept. 30, 1891, our imports of merchandise amounted to $824,715,270, which was an increase of more than eleven million dollars over the value of the imports of the corresponding months of the preceding year, when the imports of merchandise were unusually large in anticipation of the tariff legislation then pending. The average annual value of the imports of merchandise for the ten years from 1881 to 1890 was $692,186,522, and during the year ending Sept. 30, 1891, this annual average was exceeded by $132,528,469.

The value of free imports during the twelve months ending Sept. 30, 1891, was $118,092,387 more than the value of free imports during the corresponding twelve months of the preceding year, and there was during the same period a decrease of $106,846,508 in the value of imports of dutiable merchandise. The percentage of merchandise admitted free of duty during the year to which I have referred, the first under the new tariff, was 48·18, while during the preceding twelve months, under the old tariff, the percentage was 34·27, an increase of 13·91 per cent. If we take the six months ending Sept. 30 last, which covers the time during which sugars have been admitted free of duty, the per cent. of value of merchandise imported free of duty is found to be 55·37, which is a larger percentage of free imports than during any prior fiscal year in the history of the Government.

If we turn to exports of merchandise the statistics are full of gratification. The value of such exports of merchandise for the twelve months ending Sept. 30, 1891, was $923,091,136, while for the corresponding previous twelve months it was $860,177,115, an increase of $62,914,021, which is nearly three times the average annual increase of exports of merchandise for the preceding twenty years; this exceeds in amount and value the exports of merchandise during any year in the history of the Government. The increase in the value of exports of agricultural products during the year referred to over the corresponding twelve months of the prior year was $45,846,197, while the increase in the value of exports of manufactured products was $16,838,240.

There is certainly nothing in the condition of trade, foreign or domestic, there is certainly nothing in the condition of our people of any class, to suggest that the existing tariff and revenue legislation bears oppressively upon the people or retards the commercial development of the nation. It may be argued that our condition would be better if tariff legislation were upon a free-trade basis; but it can not be denied that all the conditions of prosperity and of general contentment are present in a larger degree than ever before in our history, and that, too, just when it was prophesied they would be in the worst state. Agitation for radical changes in tariff and financial legislation can not help but may seriously impede business, to the prosperity of which some degree of stability in legislation is essential.

I think there are condusive evidences that the new tariff has created several great industries which will, within a few years, give employment to several hundred thousand American working men and women. In view of the somewhat overcrowded condition of the labor market of the United States, every patriotic citizen should rejoice at such a result.

The report of the Secretary of the Treasury shows that the total receipts of the Government, from all sources, for the fiscal year ending June 30, 1891, were $458,544,233.03, while the expenditures for the same period were $421,304,470.46, leaving a surplus of $37,-239,762.57.

The receipts of the fiscal year ending June 30, 1892, actual and estimated, are $433,000,000, and the expenditures $409,000,000. For the fiscal year ending June 30, 1893, the estimated receipts are $455,336,356, and the expenditures $441,300,093.

Under the law of July 14, 1890, the Secretary of the Treasury has purchased (since Aug. 13) during the fiscal year 48,393,113 ounces of silver bullion at an average cost of $1.045 per ounce. The highest price paid during the year was $1.2025, and the lowest $0.9636. In exchange for this silver bullion there have been issued $50,577,498 of the Treasury notes authorized by the act. The lowest price of silver reached during the fiscal year was $0.9636 on April 22, 1891; but on Nov. 1 the market price was only $0.96, which would give to the silver dollar a bullion value of 74½ cents.

Before the influence of the prospective silver legislation was felt in the market silver was worth in New York about $0.955 per ounce. The ablest advocates of free coinage in the last Congress were most confident in their predictions that the purchases by the Government required by the law would at once bring the price of silver to $1.2929 per ounce, which would make the bullion value of a dollar 100 cents and hold it there. The prophecies of the antisilver men, of disasters to result from the coinage of $2,000,000 per month, were not wider of the mark. The friends of free silver are not agreed, I think, as to the causes that brought their hopeful predictions to naught. Some facts are known. The exports of silver from London to India during the first nine months of this calendar year fell off over 50 per cent., or $17,202,730, compared with the same months of the preceding year. The exports of domestic silver bullion from this country, which had averaged for the last ten years over $17,-000,000, fell in the last fiscal year to $13,797,391; while, for the first time in recent years, the imports of silver into this country exceeded the exports by the sum of $2,745,365. In the previous year the net exports of silver from the United States amounted to $8,545,455. The production of the United States increased from 50,000,000 ounces in 1889 to 54,500,000 in 1890. The Government is now buying and putting aside annually 54,000,000 ounces, which, allowing for 7,140,000 ounces of new bullion used in the arts, is 6,640,000 more than our domestic product available for coinage.

I hope the depression in the price of silver is temporary, and that a further trial of this legislation will more favorably affect it. That the increased volume of currency thus supplied for the use of the people was needed and that beneficial results upon trade and prices have followed this legislation I think must be very clear to every one; nor should it be forgotten that for every dollar of these notes issued a full dollar's worth of silver bullion is at the time deposited in the Treasury as a security for its redemption. Upon this subject, as upon the tariff, my recommendation is that the existing laws be given a full trial, and that our business interests be spared the distressing influences which threats of radical changes always impart. Under existing legislation it is in the power of the Treasury Department to maintain that essential condition of national finance as well as of commercial prosperity—the parity in use of the coin dollars and their paper representatives. The assurance that these powers would be freely and unhesitatingly used has done much to produce and sustain the present favorable business conditions.

I am still of the opinion that the free coinage of silver under existing conditions would disastrously affect our business interests at home and abroad. We could not hope to maintain an equality in the purchasing power of the gold and silver dollar in our own markets, and in foreign trade the stamp gives no added value to the bullion contained in coins. The producers of the country, its farmers and laborers, have the highest interest that every dollar, paper or coin, issued by the Government shall be as good as any other. If there is one less valuable than another its sure and constant errand will be to pay them for their toil and for their crops. The money-lender will protect himself by stipulating for payment in gold, but the laborer has never been able to do that. To place business upon a silver basis would mean a sudden and severe contraction of the currency, by the withdrawal of gold and gold notes, and such an unsettling of all values as would produce a commercial panic. I can not believe that a people so strong and prosperous as ours will promote such a policy.

The producers of silver are entitled to just consideration, but they should not forget that the Government is now buying and putting out of the market what is the equivalent of the entire product of our silver mines. This is more than they themselves thought of asking two years ago. I believe it is the earnest desire of a great majority of the people, as it is mine, that a full coin use shall be made of silver just as soon as the co-operation of other nations can be secured and a ratio fixed that will give circulation equally to gold and silver. The business of the world requires the use of both metals; but I do not see any prospect of gain, but much of loss, by giving up the present system, in which a full use is made of gold and a large use of silver, for one in which silver alone will circulate. Such an event would be at once fatal to the further progress of the silver movement. Bimetallism is the desired end, and the true friends of silver will be careful not to overrun the goal and bring in silver monometallism, with its necessary attendants, the loss of our gold to Europe and the relief of the pressure there for a larger currency. I have endeavored by the use of official and unofficial agencies to keep a close observation of the state of public sentiment in Europe upon this question, and have not found it to be such as to justify me in proposing an international conference. There is, however, I am sure, a growing sentiment in Europe in favor of a larger use of silver, and I know of no more effectual way of promoting this sentiment than by accumulating gold here. A scarcity of gold in the European reserves will be the most persuasive argument for the use of silver.

The exports of gold to Europe, which began in February last and continued until the close of July, aggregated over $70,000,000. The net loss of gold during the fiscal year was nearly $68,000,000. That no serious monetary disturbance resulted was most gratifying, and gave to Europe fresh evidence of the strength and stability of our financial institutions. With the movement of crops the outflow of gold was speedily stopped, and a return set in. Up to Dec. 1 we had recovered of our gold loss at the port of New York $27,854,000, and it is confidently believed that during the winter and spring this aggregate will be steadily and largely increased.

The presence of a large cash surplus in the Treasury has for many years been the subject of much unfavorable criticism, and has furnished an argument to those who have desired to place the tariff upon a purely revenue basis. It was agreed by all that the withdrawal from circulation of so large an amount of money was an embarrassment to the business of the country, and made necessary the intervention of the department at frequent intervals to relieve threatened monetary panics. The surplus on March 1, 1889, was $183,827,190.29. The policy of applying this surplus to the redemption of the interest-bearing securities of the United States was thought to be preferable to that of depositing it without interest in selected national banks. There have been redeemed since the date last mentioned of interest-bearing securities $259,079,350, resulting in a reduction of the annual interest charge of $11,684,675. The money which had been deposited in banks without interest has been gradually withdrawn and used in the redemption of bonds.

The result of this policy, of the silver legislation, and of the refunding of the 4½-per-cent. bonds has been a large increase of the money in circulation. At the date last named the circulation was $1,404,-205,896, or $23.03 per capita; while on Dec. 1, 1891, it had increased to $1,577,262,070, or $24.38 per capita. The offer of the Secretary of the Treasury to the holders of the 4½-per-cent. bonds to extend the time of redemption, at the option of the Government, at an interest of 2 per cent., was accepted by the holders of about one half the amount, and the unextended bonds are being redeemed on presentation.

The report of the Secretary of War exhibits the results of an intelligent, progressive, and business-like administration of a department which has been too much regarded as one of mere routine. The separation of Secretary Proctor from the department by reason of his appointment as a Senator from the State of Vermont is a source of great regret to me and to his colleagues in the Cabinet, as I am sure it will be to all those who have had business with the department while under his charge.

In the administration of army affairs some especially good work has been accomplished. The efforts of the Secretary to reduce the percentage of desertions by removing the causes that promoted it have been so successful as to enable him to report for the last year a lower percentage of desertion than has been before reached in the history of the army. The resulting money saving is considerable, but the improvement in the *morale* of the enlisted men is the most valuable incident of the reforms which have brought about this result.

The work of securing sites for shore batteries for harbor defense and the manufacture of mortars and guns of high power to equip them have made good progress during the year. The preliminary work of tests and plans, which so long delayed a start, is now out of the way. Some guns have been completed, and with an enlarged shop and a more complete equipment at Watervliet the army will soon be abreast of the navy in gun construction. Whatever unavoidable causes of delay may arise, there should be none from delayed or insufficient appropriations. We shall be greatly embarrassed in the proper distribution and use of naval vessels until adequate shore defenses are provided for our harbors.

I concur in the recommendation of the Secretary that the three-battalion organization be adopted for the infantry. The adoption of a smokeless powder and of a modern rifle equal in range, precision, and rapidity of fire to the best now in use will, I hope, not be longer delayed.

The project of enlisting Indians and organizing them into separate companies upon the same basis as other soldiers was made the subject of very careful study by the Secretary and received my approval. Seven companies have been completely organized and seven more are in process of organization. The results of six months' training have more than realized the highest anticipations. The men are readily brought under discipline, acquire the drill with facility, and show great pride in the right discharge of their duties and perfect loyalty to their officers, who declare that they would take them into action with confidence. The discipline, order, and cleanliness of the military posts will have a wholesome and elevating influence upon the men enlisted, and through them upon their tribes, while a more friendly feeling for the whites and a greater respect for the Government will certainly be promoted.

The great work done in the Record and Pension Division of the War Department by Major Ainsworth, of the medical corps, and the clerks under him, is entitled to honorable mention. Taking up the work with nearly 41,000 cases behind, he closed the last fiscal year without a single case left over, though the new cases had increased 52 per cent. in number over the previous year by reason of the pension legislation of the last Congress.

I concur in the recommendation of the Attorney-General that the right in felony cases to a review by the Supreme Court be limited. It would seem that personal liberty would have a safe guarantee if the right of review in cases involving only fine and imprisonment were limited to the circuit court of appeals, unless a constitutional question should in some way be involved.

The judges of the Court of Private Land Claims, provided for by the act of March 3, 1891, have been appointed and the court organized. It is now possible to give early relief to communities long repressed in their development by unsettled land titles, and to establish the possession and right of settlers whose lands have been rendered valueless by adverse and unfounded claims.

The act of July 9, 1888, provided for the incorporation and management of a reform school for girls in the District of Columbia; but it has remained inoperative for the reason that no appropriation has been made for construction or maintenance. The need of such an institution is very urgent. Many girls could be saved from depraved lives by the wholesome influences and restraints of such a school. I recommend that the necessary appropriation be made for a site and for construction.

The enforcement by the Treasury Department of the law prohibiting the coming of Chinese to the United States has been effective as to such as seek to land from vessels entering our ports. The result has been to divert the travel to vessels entering the ports of British Columbia, whence passage into the United States at obscure points along the Dominion boundary is easy. A very considerable number of Chinese laborers have, during the past year, entered the United States from Canada and Mexico.

The officers of the Treasury Department and of the Department of Justice have used every means at their command to intercept this immigration; but the impossibility of perfectly guarding our extended frontier is apparent. The Dominion Government collects a head tax of $50 from every Chinaman entering Canada, and thus derives a considerable revenue from those who only use its ports to reach a position of advantage to evade our exclusion laws. There seems to be satisfactory evidence that the business of passing Chinamen through Canada to the United States is organized and quite active. The Department of Justice has construed the laws to require the return of any Chinaman found to be unlawfully in this country from which he came, notwithstanding the fact that he came by way of Canada; but several of the district courts have, in cases brought before them, overruled this view of the law and decided that such persons must be returned to Canada. This construction robs the law of all effectiveness, even if the decrees could be executed, for the men returned can the next day recross our border. But the only appropriation made is for sending them back to China, and the Canadian officials refuse to allow them to re-enter Canada without the payment of the $50 head tax. I recommend such legislation as will remedy these defects in the law.

In previous messages I have called the attention of Congress to the necessity of so extending the jurisdiction of the United States courts as to make triable therein any felony committed while in the act of violating a law of the United States. These courts can not have that independence and effectiveness which the Constitution contemplates so long as the felonious killing of court officers, jurors, and witnesses in the discharge of their duties, or by reason of their acts as such, is only cognizable in the State courts. The work done by the Attorney-General and the officers of his department, even under the present inadequate legislation, has produced some notable results in the interest of law and order.

The Attorney-General and also the commissioners of the District of Columbia call attention to the defectiveness and inadequacy of the laws relating to crimes against chastity in the District of Columbia. A stringent code upon this subject has been provided by Congress for Utah, and it is a matter of surprise that the needs of this District should have been so long overlooked.

In the report of the Postmaster-General some very gratifying results are exhibited and many betterments of the service suggested. A perusal of the report gives abundant evidence that the supervision and direction of the postal system have been characterized by an intelligent and conscientious desire to improve the service. The revenues of the department show an increase of over $5,000,000, with a deficiency for the year 1892 of less than $4,000,000,

while the estimate for the year 1893 shows a surplus of receipts over expenditures.

Ocean mail post-offices have been established upon the steamers of the North German Lloyd and Hamburg lines, saving, by the distribution on shipboard, from two to fourteen hours' time in the delivery of mail at the port of entry, and often much more than this in the delivery at interior places. So thoroughly has this system, initiated by Germany and the United States, evidenced its usefulness that it can not be long before it is installed upon all the great ocean mail-carrying steamships.

Eight thousand miles of new postal service has been established upon railroads, the car distribution to substations in the great cities has been increased about 12 per cent., while the percentage of errors in distribution has, during the past year, been reduced over one half. An appropriation was given by the last Congress for the purpose of making some experiments in free delivery in the smaller cities and towns. The results of these experiments have been so satisfactory that the Postmaster-General recommends, and I concur in the recommendation, that the free-delivery system be at once extended to towns of 5,000 population. His discussion of the inadequate facilities extended under our present system to rural communities and his suggestions with a view to give these communities a fuller participation in the benefits of the postal service are worthy of your careful consideration. It is not just that the farmer, who receives his mail at a neighboring town, should not only be compelled to send to the post-office for it, but to pay a considerable rent for a box in which to place it or to wait his turn at a general-delivery window, while the city resident has his mail brought to his door. It is stated that over 54,000 neighborhoods are, under the present system, receiving mail at post-offices where money orders and postal notes are not issued. The extension of this system to these communities is especially desirable, as the patrons of such offices are not possessed of the other facilities offered in more populous communities for the transmission of small sums of money.

I have, in a message to the preceding Congress, expressed my views as to a modified use of the telegraph in connection with the postal service.

In pursuance of the ocean-mail law of March 3, 1891, and after a most careful study of the whole subject and frequent conferences with shipowners, boards of trade, and others, advertisements were issued by the Postmaster-General for 53 lines of ocean-mail service: 10 to Great Britain and the Continent, 27 to South America, 3 to China and Japan, 4 to Australia and the Pacific Islands, 7 to the West Indies, and 2 to Mexico. It was not, of course, expected that bids for all these lines would be received or that service upon them all would be contracted for. It was intended, in furtherance of the act, to secure as many new lines as possible, while including in the list most or all of the foreign lines now occupied by American ships. It was hoped that a line to England and perhaps one to the Continent would be secured; but the outlay required to equip such lines wholly with new ships of the first class, and the difficulty of establishing new lines in competition with those already established, deterred bidders whose interest had been enlisted. It is hoped that a way may yet be found of overcoming these difficulties. The Brazil Steamship Company, by reason of a miscalculation as to the speed of its vessels, was not able to bid under the terms of the advertisement. The policy of the department was to secure from the established lines an improved service as a condition of giving to them the benefits of the law. This in all instances has been attained. The Postmaster-General estimates that an expenditure in American ship yards of about $10,000,000 will be necessary to enable the bidders to construct the ships called for by the service which they have accepted. I do not think there is any reason for discouragement or for any turning back from the policy of this legislation. Indeed, a good beginning has been made, and, as the subject is further considered and understood by capitalists and shipping people, new lines will be ready to meet future proposals, and we may date from the passage of this law the revival of American shipping interests and the recovery of a fair share of the carrying trade of the world. We were receiving for foreign postage nearly $2,000,000 under the old system and the outlay for ocean-mail service did not exceed $600,000 per annum. It is estimated by the Postmaster-General that, if all the contracts proposed are completed, it will require $247,354 for this year, in addition to the appropriation for sea and inland postage already in the estimates, and that for the next fiscal year, ending June 30, 1893, there would probably be needed about $560,000.

The report of the Secretary of the Navy shows a gratifying increase of new naval vessels in commission. The "Newark," "Concord," "Bennington," and "Miantonomoh" have been added during the year, with an aggregate of something more than 11,000 tons. Twenty-four warships of all classes are now under construction in the navy yards and private shops, but, while the work upon them is going forward satisfactorily, the completion of the more important vessels will yet require about a year's time. Some of the vessels now under construction, it is believed, will be triumphs of naval engineering. When it is recollected that the work of building a modern navy was only initiated in the year 1883, that our naval constructors and shipbuilders were practically without experience in the construction of large iron or steel ships, that our engine shops were unfamiliar with great marine engines, and that the manufacture of steel forgings for guns and plates was almost wholly a foreign industry, the progress that has been made is not only highly satisfactory, but furnishes the assurance that the United States will before long attain, in the construction of such vessels, with their engines and armaments, the same pre-eminence which it attained when the best instrument of ocean commerce was the clipper ship and the most impressive exhibit of naval power the old wooden three-decker man-of-war. The officers of the navy and the proprietors and engineers of our great private shops have responded with wonderful intelligence and professional zeal to the confidence expressed by Congress in its liberal legislation. We have now at Washington a gun shop, organized and conducted by naval officers, that in its system, economy, and product is unexcelled. Experiments with armor plate have been conducted during the year with most important results. It is now believed that a plate of higher resisting power than any in use has been found, and that the tests have demonstrated that cheaper methods of manufacture than those heretofore thought necessary can be used.

I commend to your favorable consideration the recommendations of the Secretary, who has, I am sure, given to them the most conscientious study. There should be no hesitation in promptly completing a navy of the best modern type, large enough to enable this country to display its flag in all seas for the protection of its citizens and of its extending commerce. The world needs no assurance of the peaceful purposes of the United States, but we shall probably be in the future more largely a competitor in the commerce of the world, and it is essential to the dignity of this nation and to that peaceful influence which it should exercise on this hemisphere that its navy should be adequate, both upon the shores of the Atlantic and of the Pacific.

The report of the Secretary of the Interior shows that a very gratifying progress has been made in all of the bureaus which make up that complex and difficult department.

The work in the Bureau of Indian Affairs was perhaps never so large as now, by reason of the numerous negotiations which have been proceeding with the tribes for a reduction of the reservations, with the incident labor of making allotments, and was never more carefully conducted. The provision of adequate school facilities for Indian children and the locating of adult Indians upon farms involve the solution of the "Indian question." Everything else—rations, annuities, and tribal negotiations, with the agents, inspectors, and commissioners who distribute and conduct them—must pass away when the Indian has become a citizen, secure in the individual ownership of a farm from which he derives his subsistence by his own labor, protected by and subordinate to the laws which govern the white man, and provided by the General Government or by the local communities in which he lives with the means of educating his children. When an Indian becomes a citizen in an organized State or Territory his relation to the General Government ceases, in great measure, to be that of a ward; but the General Government ought not at once to put upon the State or Territory the burden of the education of his children. It has been my thought that the Government schools and school buildings upon the reservations would be absorbed by the school systems of the States and Territories; but, as it has been found necessary to protect the Indian against the compulsory alienation of his land by exempting him from taxation for a period of twenty-five years, it would seem to be right that the General Government, certainly where there are tribal funds in its possession, should pay to the school fund of the State what would be equivalent to the local school tax upon the property of the Indian. It will be noticed from the report of the Commissioner of Indian Affairs that already some contracts have been made with district schools for the education of Indian children. There is great advantage, I think, in bringing the Indian children into mixed schools. This process will be gradual, and in the mean time the present educational provisions and arrangements, the result of the best experience of those who have been charged with this work, should be continued. This will enable those religious bodies that have undertaken the work of Indian education with so much zeal, and with results so restraining and beneficent, to place their institutions in new and useful relations to the Indian and to his white neighbors.

The outbreak among the Sioux, which occurred in December last, is as to its causes and incidents fully reported upon by the War Department and the Department of the Interior. That these Indians had some just complaints, especially in the matter of the reduction of the appropriation for rations and in the delays attending the enactment of laws to enable the department to perform the engagements entered into with them, is probably true; but the Sioux tribes are naturally warlike and turbulent, and their warriors were excited by their medicine men and chiefs, who preached the coming of an Indian Messiah who was to give them power to destroy their enemies. In view of the alarm that prevailed among the white settlers near the reservation and of the fatal consequences that would have resulted from an Indian incursion, I placed at the disposal of Gen. Miles, commanding the Division of the Missouri, all such forces as were thought by him to be required. He is entitled to the credit of having given thorough protection to the settlers and of bringing the hostiles into subjection with the least possible loss of life.

The appropriation of $2,991,450 for the Choctaws and Chickasaws, contained in the general Indian appropriation bill of March 3, 1891, has not been expended, for the reason that I have not yet approved a release (to the Government) of the Indian claim to the lands mentioned. This matter will be made the subject of a special message, placing before Congress all the facts which have come to my knowledge.

The relation of the five civilized tribes now occupying the Indian Territory to the United States is not, I believe, that best calculated to promote the highest advancement of these Indians. That there should be within our borders five independent States, having no relations, except those growing out of treaties, with the Government of the United States, no representation in the National Legislature, its people not citizens, is a startling anomaly.

It seems to me to be inevitable that there shall be before long some organic changes in the relation of these people to the United States. What form these changes should take I do not think it desirable now to suggest, even if they were well defined in my own mind. They should certainly involve the acceptance of citizenship by the Indians and a representation in Congress. These Indians should have opportunity to present their claims and grievances upon the floor rather than, as now, in the lobby. If a commission could be appointed to visit these tribes to confer with them in a friendly spirit upon this whole subject, even if no agreement were presently reached, the feeling of the tribes upon this question would be developed and discussion would prepare the way for changes which must come sooner or later.

The good work of reducing the larger Indian reservations, by allotments in severalty to the Indians and the cession of the remaining lands to the United States for disposition under the homestead law, has been prosecuted during the year with energy and success. In September last I was enabled to open to settlement in the Territory of Oklahoma 900,000 acres of land, all of which was taken up by settlers in a single day. The rush for these lands was accompanied by a great deal of excitement, but was, happily, free from incidents of violence.

It was a source of great regret that I was not able to open at the same time the surplus lands of the Cheyenne and Arapahoe Reservation, amounting to about 3,000,000 acres, by reason of the insufficiency of the appropriation for making the allotments. Deserving and impatient settlers are waiting to occupy these lands, and I urgently recommend that a special deficiency appropriation be promptly made of the small amount needed, so that the allotments may be completed and the surplus lands opened in time to permit the settlers to get upon their homesteads in the early spring.

During the past summer the Cherokee Commission have completed arrangements with the Wichita, Kickapoo, and Tonkawa tribes, whereby, if the agreements are ratified by Congress, over 800,000 additional acres will be open to settlement in Oklahoma.

The negotiation for the release by the Cherokees of their claim to the Cherokee Strip has made no substantial progress, so far as the department is officially advised, but it is still hoped that the cession of this large and valuable tract may be secured. The price which the commission was authorized to offer—one dollar and a quarter per acre—is, in my judgment, when all the circumstances as to title and character of the lands are considered, a fair and adequate one and should have been accepted by the Indians.

Since March 4, 1889, about 23,000,000 acres have been separated from Indian reservations and added to the public domain for the use of those who desired to secure free homes under our beneficent laws. It is difficult to estimate the increase of wealth which will result from the conversion of these waste lands into farms, but it is more difficult to estimate the betterment which will result to the families that have found renewed hope and courage in the ownership of a home and the assurance of a comfortable subsistence under free and healthful conditions. It is also gratifying to be able to feel, as we may, that this work has proceeded upon lines of justice toward the Indian, and that he may now, if he will, secure to himself the good influences of a settled habitation, the fruits of industry, and the security of citizenship.

Early in this administration a special effort was begun to bring up the work of the General Land Office. By faithful work the arrearages have been rapidly reduced. At the end of the last fiscal year only 84,-172 final agricultural entries remained undisposed of, and the commissioner reports that, with the present force, the work can be fully brought up by the end of the next fiscal year..

Your attention is called to the difficulty presented by the Secretary of the Interior as to the administration of the law of March 3, 1891, establishing a Court of Private Land Claims. The small holdings intended to be protected by the law are estimated to be more than fifteen thousand in number. The claimants are a most deserving class and their titles are supported by the strongest equities. The difficulty grows out of the fact that the lands have largely been surveyed according to our methods, while the holdings, many of which have been in the same family for generations, are laid out in narrow strips a few rods wide upon a stream and running back to the hills for pasturage and timber. Provisions should be made for numbering these tracts as lots and for patenting them by such numbers, and without reference to section lines.

The administration of the Pension Bureau has been characterized during the year by great diligence. The total number of pensioners upon the roll on the 30th day of June, 1891, was 676,160. There were allowed during the fiscal year ending at that time 250,565 cases. Of this number, 102,387 were allowed under the law of June 27, 1890. The issuing of certificates has been proceeding at the rate of about 30,000 per month, about 75 per cent. of these being cases under the new law. The commissioner expresses the opinion that he will be able to carefully adjudicate and allow 350,000 claims during the present fiscal year. The appropriation for the payment of pensions for the fiscal year 1890-'91 was $127,685,793.89 and the amount expended $118,530,649.25, leaving an unexpended surplus of $9,155,144.64.

The commissioner is quite confident that there will be no call this year for a deficiency appropriation, notwithstanding the rapidity with which the work is being pushed. The mistake which has been made by many in their exaggerated estimates of the cost of pensions is in not taking account of the diminished value of first payments under the recent legislation. These payments, under the general law, have been for many years very large, as the pensions, when allowed, dated from the time of filing the claim, and most of these claims have been pending for years. The first payments under the law of June, 1890, are relatively small, and, as the per cent. of these cases increases and that of the old cases diminishes, the annual aggregate of first payments is largely reduced. The commissioner, under date of Nov. 13, furnishes me with the statement that during the last four months 113,175 certificates were issued, 27,893 under the general law and 85,282 under the act of June 27, 1890. The average first payment during these four months was $131.85, while the average first payment upon cases allowed during the year ending June 30, 1891, was $239.33, being a reduction in the average first payments during these four months of $107.48.

The estimate for pension expenditures for the fiscal year ending June 30, 1893, is $144,956,000, which, after a careful examination of the subject, the commissioner is of the opinion will be sufficient. While these disbursements to the disabled soldiers of the great civil war are large, they do not realize the exaggerated estimates of those who oppose this beneficent legislation. The Secretary of the Interior shows with great fullness the care that is taken to exclude fraudulent claims, and also the gratifying fact that the persons to whom these pensions are going are men who rendered, not slight, but substantial war service.

The report of the Commissioner of Railroads shows that the total debt of the subsidized railroads to the United States was, on Dec. 31, 1890, $112,512,613.06. A large part of this debt is now fast approaching maturity, with no adequate provision for its payment. Some policy for dealing with this debt, with a view to its ultimate collection, should be at once adopted. It is very difficult, well-nigh impossible, for so large a body as the Congress to conduct the necessary negotiations and investigations. I therefore recommend that provision be made for the appointment of a commission to agree upon and report a plan for dealing with this debt.

The work of the Census Bureau is now far in advance and the great bulk of the enormous labor involved completed. It will be more strictly a statistical exhibit and less encumbered by essays than its immediate predecessors. The methods pursued have been fair, careful, and intelligent, and have secured the approval of the statisticians, who have followed them with a scientific and non-partisan interest. The appropriations necessary to the early completion and publication of the authorized volumes should be given in time to secure against delays, which increase the cost and at the same time diminish the value of the work.

The report of the Secretary exhibits, with interesting fullness, the condition of the Territories. They have shared with the States the great increase in farm products, and are bringing yearly large areas into cultivation by extending their irrigating canals. This work is being done by individuals or local corporations, and without that system which a full preliminary survey of the water supply and of the irrigable lands would enable them to adopt. The future of the Territories of New Mexico, Arizona, and Utah, in their material growth and in the increase, independence, and happiness of their people, is very largely dependent upon wise and timely legislation, either by Congress or their own legislatures, regulating the distribution of the water supply furnished by their streams. If this matter is much longer neglected, private corporations will have unrestricted control of one of the elements of life and the patentees of the arid lands will be tenants at will of the water companies.

The United States should part with its ownership of the water sources and the sites for reservoirs, whether to the States and Territories or to individuals or corporations, only upon conditions that will insure to the settlers their proper water supply upon equal and reasonable terms. In the Territories this whole subject is under the full control of Congress, and in the States it is practically so as long as the Government holds the title to the reservoir sites and water sources and can grant them upon such conditions as it chooses to impose. The improvident granting of franchises of enormous value, without recompense to the State or municipality from which they proceed and without proper protection of the public interests, is the most noticeable and flagrant evil of modern legislation. This fault should not be committed in dealing with a subject that will, before many years, affect so vitally thousands of our people.

The legislation of Congress for the repression of polygamy has, after years of resistance on the part of the Mormons, at last brought them to the conclusion that resistance is unprofitable and unavailing. The power of Congress over this subject should not be surrendered until we have satisfactory evidence that the people of the State to be created would exercise the exclusive power of the State over this subject in the same way. The question is not whether these people now obey the laws of Congress against polygamy, but rather would they make, enforce, and maintain such laws themselves if absolutely free to regulate the subject? We can not afford to experiment with this subject, for when a State is once constituted the act is final and any mistake irretrievable. No compact in the enabling act could, in my opinion, be binding or effective.

I recommend that provision be made for the organization of a simple form of town government in Alaska, with power to regulate such matters as are usually in the States under municipal control. These local civil organizations will give better protection in some matters than the present skeleton Territorial organization. Proper restrictions as to the power to levy taxes and to create debt should be imposed.

If the establishment of the Department of Agriculture was regarded by any one as a mere concession to the unenlightened demand of a worthy class of people, that impression has been most effectually removed by the great results already attained. Its home influence has been very great in disseminating agricultural and horticultural information; in stimulating and directing a further diversification of crops; in detecting and eradicating diseases of domestic animals; and, more than all, in the close and informal contact which it has established and maintains with the farmers and stock raisers of the whole country. Every request for information has had prompt attention, and every suggestion merited consideration. The scientific corps of the department is of a high order, and is pushing its investigations with method and enthusiasm.

The inspection by this department of cattle and pork products intended for shipment abroad has been the basis of the success which has attended our efforts to secure the removal of the restrictions maintained by the European governments.

For ten years protests and petitions upon this subject from the packers and stock raisers of the United States have been directed against these restrictions, which so seriously limited our markets and curtailed the profits of the farm. It is a source of general congratulation that success has at last been attained, for the effects of an enlarged foreign market for these meats will be felt, not only by the farmer, but in our public finances and in every branch of trade. It is particularly fortunate that the increased demand for food products, resulting from the removal of the restrictions upon our meats and from the reciprocal trade arrangements to which I have referred, should have come at a time when the agricultural surplus is so large. Without the help thus derived, lower prices would have prevailed. The Secretary of Agriculture estimates that the restrictions upon the importation of our pork products into Europe lost us a market for $20,000,000 worth of these products annually.

The grain crop of this year was the largest in our history, 50 per cent. greater than that of last year, and yet the new markets that have been opened and the larger demand resulting from short crops in Europe, have sustained prices to such an extent that the enormous surplus of meats and breadstuffs will be marketed at good prices, bringing relief and prosperity to an industry that was much depressed. The value of the grain crop of the United States is estimated by the Secretary to be this year $500,000,000 more than last; of meats, $150,000,000 more, and of all products of the farm, $700,000,000 more. It is not inappropriate, I think, here to suggest that our satisfaction in the contemplation of this marvelous addition to the national wealth is unclouded by any suspicion of the currency by which it is measured, and in which the farmer is paid for the product of his fields.

The report of the Civil Service Commission should receive the careful attention of the opponents as well as the friends of this reform. The commission invites a personal inspection by Senators and Representatives of its records and methods; and every fair critic will feel that such an examination should precede a judgment of condemnation, either of the system or its administration. It is not claimed that either is perfect, but I believe that the law is being executed with impartiality, and that the system is incomparably better and fairer than that of appointments upon favor. I have during the year extended the classified service to include superintendents, teachers, matrons, and physicians in the Indian service. This branch of the service is largely related to educational and philanthropic work, and will obviously be the better for the change.

The heads of the several executive departments have been directed to establish at once an efficiency record as the basis of a comparative rating of the clerks within the classified service, with a view to placing promotions therein upon the basis of merit. I am confident that such a record, fairly kept and open to the inspection of those interested, will powerfully stimulate the work of the departments, and will be accepted by all as placing the troublesome matter of promotions upon a just basis.

I recommend that the appropriations for the Civil Service Commission be made adequate to the increased work of the next fiscal year.

I have twice before urgently called the attention of Congress to the necessity of legislation for the protection of the lives of railroad employees, but nothing has yet been done. During the year ending June 30, 1890, 369 brakemen were killed and 7,841 maimed while engaged in coupling cars. The total number of railroad employees killed during the year was 2,451, and the number injured, 22,390. This is a cruel and largely a needless sacrifice. The Government is spending nearly $1,000,000 annually to save the lives of shipwrecked seamen; every steam vessel is rigidly inspected and required to adopt the most approved safety appliances. All this is good; but how shall we excuse the lack of interest and effort in behalf of this army of brave young men who in our land commerce are being sacrificed every year by the continued use of antiquated and dangerous appliances? A law requiring of every railroad engaged in interstate commerce the equipment each year of a given per cent. of its freight cars with automatic couplers and air brakes would compel an agreement between the roads as to the kind of brakes and couplers to be used, and would very soon and very greatly reduce the present fearful death rate among railroad employees.

The method of appointment by the States of electors of President and Vice-President has recently attracted renewed interest by reason of a departure by the State of Michigan from the method which had become uniform in all the States. Prior to 1832 various methods had been used by the different States and even by the same State. In some the choice was made by the legislature; in others electors were chosen by districts, but more generally by the voters of the whole State upon a general ticket. The movement toward the adoption of the last-named method had an early beginning and went steadily forward among the States, until in 1832 there remained but a single State, South Carolina, that had not adopted it. That State, until the civil war, continued to choose its electors by a vote of the Legislature, but after the war changed its method and conformed to the practice of the other States. For nearly sixty years all the States save one have appointed their electors by a popular vote upon a general ticket, and for nearly thirty years this method was universal.

After a full test of other methods, without important division or dissent in any State and without any purpose of party advantage, as we must believe, but solely upon the considerations that uniformity was desirable and that a general election in territorial divisions not subject to change was most consistent with the popular character of our institutions, best preserved the equality of the voters, and perfectly removed the choice of President from the baneful influence of the "gerrymander," the practice of all the States was brought into harmony. That this concurrence should now be broken is, I think, an unfortunate and even a threatening episode, and one that may well suggest whether the States that still give their approval to the old and prevailing method ought not to secure, by a constitutional amendment, a practice which has had the approval of all. The recent Michigan legislation provides for choosing what are popularly known as the congressional electors for President by congressional districts, and the two senatorial electors by districts created for that purpose. This legislation was, of course, accompanied by a new congressional apportionment, and the two statutes bring the electoral vote of the State under the influence of the "gerrymander."

These gerrymanders for congressional purposes are in most cases buttressed by a gerrymander of the legislative districts, thus making it impossible for a majority of the legal voters of the State to correct the apportionment and equalize the congressional districts. A minority rule is established that only a political convulsion can overthrow. I have recently been advised that in one county of a certain State three districts for the election of members of the Legislature are constituted as follows: One has 65,000

population, one 15,000, and one 10,000; while in another county, detached, noncontiguous sections have been united to make a legislative district. These methods have already found effective application to the choice of Senators and Representatives in Congress, and now an evil start has been made in the direction of applying them to the choice by the States of electors of President and Vice-President. If this is accomplished, we shall then have the three great departments of the Government in the grasp of the "gerrymander," the legislative and executive directly and the Judiciary indirectly through the power of appointment.

An election implies a body of electors having prescribed qualifications, each one of whom has an equal value and influence in determining the result. So when the Constitution provides that "each State shall appoint" (elect), "in such manner as the legislature thereof may direct, a number of electors," etc., an unrestricted power was not given to the legislatures in the selection of the methods to be used. "A republican form of government" is guaranteed by the Constitution to each State, and the power given by the same instrument to the legislatures of the States to prescribe methods for the choice, by the State, of electors must be exercised under that limitation. The essential features of such a government are the right of the people to choose their own officers, and the nearest practicable equality of value in the suffrages given in determining that choice.

It will not be claimed that the power given to the legislature would support a law providing that the persons receiving the smallest vote should be the electors or a law that all the electors should be chosen by the voters of a single congressional district. The State is to choose, and, under the pretense of regulating methods, the legislature can neither vest the right of choice elsewhere nor adopt methods not conformable to republican institutions. It is not my purpose here to discuss the question whether a choice by the legislature or by the voters of equal single districts is a choice by the State, but only to recommend such regulation of this matter by constitutional amendment as will secure uniformity and prevent that disgraceful partisan jugglery to which such a liberty of choice, if it exists, offers a temptation.

Nothing just now is more important than to provide every guarantee for the absolutely fair and free choice by an equal suffrage, within the respective States, of all the officers of the National Government, whether that suffrage is applied directly, as in the choice of members of the House of Representatives, or indirectly, as in the choice of Senators and electors of President. Respect for public officers and obedience to law will not cease to be the characteristics of our people until our elections cease to declare the will of majorities fairly ascertained, without fraud, suppression or gerrymander. If I were called upon to declare wherein our chief national danger lies, I should say, without hesitation, in the overthrow of majority control by the suppression or perversion of the popular suffrage. That there is a real danger here all must agree, but the energies of those who see it have been chiefly expended in trying to fix responsibility upon the opposite party, rather than in efforts to make such practices impossible by either party.

Is it not possible now to adjourn that interminable and inconclusive debate while we take, by consent, one step in the direction of reform by eliminating the gerrymander, which has been denounced by all parties, as an influence in the selection of electors of President and members of Congress? All the States have, acting freely and separately, determined that the choice of electors by a general ticket is the wisest and safest method, and it would seem there could be no objection to a constitutional amendment making that method permanent. If a legislature chosen in one year upon purely local questions should, pending a presidential contest, meet, rescind the law for a choice upon a general ticket, and provide for the choice of electors by the legislature, and this trick should determine the result, it is not too much to say that the public peace might be seriously and widely endangered.

I have alluded to the "gerrymander" as affecting the method of selecting electors of President by congressional districts, but the primary intent and effect of this form of political robbery have relation to the selection of members of the House of Representatives. The power of Congress is ample to deal with this threatening and intolerable abuse. The unfailing test of sincerity in election reform will be found in a willingness to confer as to remedies, and to put into force such measures as will most effectually preserve the right of the people to free and equal representation.

An attempt was made in the last Congress to bring to bear the constitutional powers of the General Government for the correction of frauds against the suffrage. It is important to know whether the opposition to such measures is really vested in particular features supposed to be objectionable or includes any proposition to give to the election laws of the United States adequacy to the correction of grave and acknowledged evils. I must yet entertain the hope that it is possible to secure a calm, patriotic consideration of such constitutional or statutory changes as may be necessary to secure the choice of the officers of the Government to the people by fair apportionments and free elections.

I believe it would be possible to constitute a commission, non-partisan in its membership and composed of patriotic, wise, and impartial men, to whom a consideration of the question of the evils connected with our election system and methods might be committed with a good prospect of securing unanimity in some plan for removing or mitigating those evils. The Constitution would permit the selection of the commission to be vested in the Supreme Court, if that method would give the best guarantee of impartiality.

This commission should be charged with the duty of inquiring into the whole subject of the laws of elections as related to the choice of officers of the National Government, with a view to securing to every elector a free and unmolested exercise of the suffrage and as near an approach to an equality of value in each ballot cast as is attainable.

While the policies of the General Government upon the tariff, upon the restoration of our merchant marine, upon river and harbor improvements, and other such matters of grave and general concern are liable to be turned this way or that by the results of congressional elections, and administrative policies, sometimes involving issues that tend to peace or war, to be turned this way or that by the results of a presidential election, there is a rightful interest in all the States and in every congressional district that will not be deceived or silenced by the audacious pretense that the question of the right of any body of legal voters in any State or in any congressional district to give their suffrages freely upon these general questions is a matter only of local concern or control. The demand that the limitations of suffrage shall be found in the law, and only there, is a just demand, and no just man should resent or resist it. My appeal is, and must continue to be, for a consultation that shall "proceed with candor, calmness, and patience upon the lines of justice and humanity, not of prejudice and cruelty."

To the consideration of these very grave questions I invite not only the attention of Congress, but that of all patriotic citizens. We must not entertain the delusion that our people have ceased to regard a free ballot and equal representation as the price of their allegiance to laws and to civil magistrates.

I have been greatly rejoiced to notice many evidences of the increased unification of our people and of a revived national spirit. The vista that now opens to us is wider and more glorious than ever before. Gratification and amazement struggle for supremacy as we contemplate the population, wealth, and moral strength of our country. A trust, momen-

tous in its influence upon our people and upon the world, is for a brief time committed to us, and we must not be faithless to its first condition—the defense of the free and equal influence of the people in the choice of public officers and in the control of public affairs.   BENJ. HARRISON.

EXECUTIVE MANSION, *Dec.* 9, 1891.

Though several topics of great interest were discussed during the session, very few measures of importance became laws.

Shipbuilding.—The following measure "to encourage American shipbuilding" was passed by the House of Representatives, May 2, 1892:

Be it enacted, etc., That the Secretary of the Treasury is hereby authorized and directed to grant registers, as vessels of the United States, to such foreign-built steamships now engaged in freight and passenger business, and sailing in an established line from a port in the United States, as are of a tonnage of not less than 8,000 tons, and capable of a speed of not less than 20 knots per hour, according to the existing method of Government test for speed, of which not less than 90 per cent. of the shares of the capital of the foreign corporation or association owning the same was owned Jan. 1, 1890, and has continued to be owned until the passage of this act by citizens of the United States, including as such citizens corporations created under the laws of any of the States thereof, upon the American owners of such majority interest obtaining a full and complete transfer and title to such steamships from the foreign corporations owning the same: *Provided,* That such American owners shall, subsequent to the date of this law, have built, or have contracted to build, in American shipyards, steamships of an aggregate tonnage of not less in amount than that of the steamships so admitted to registry. Each steamship so built or contracted for to be of a tonnage of not less than 7,000 tons.

SEC. 2. That the Secretary of the Treasury, on being satisfied that such steamships so acquired by American citizens, or by such corporation or corporations as above set forth, are such as come within the provisions of this act, and that the American owners of such steamships, for which an American registry is to be granted under the provisions hereof, have built or contracted to build in American shipyards steamships of an aggregate tonnage as set forth in the first section hereof, shall direct the bills of sale or transfer of the foreign-built steamships so acquired to be recorded in the office of the collector of customs of the proper collection district, and cause such steamships to be registered as vessels of the United States by said collector. After which, each of such vessels shall be entitled to all the rights and privileges of a vessel of the United States, except that it shall not be employed in the coastwise trade of the United States.

SEC. 3. That no further or other inspection shall be required for the said steamship or steamships than is now required for foreign steamships carrying passengers under the existing laws of the United States, and that a special certificate of inspection may be issued for each steamship registered under this act; and that before issuing the registry to any such steamship as a vessel of the United States the collector of customs of the proper collection district shall cause such steamship to be measured and described in accordance with the laws of the United States, which measurement and description shall be recited in the certificate of registry to be issued under this act.

SEC. 4. That any steamships so registered under the provisions of this act may be taken and used by the United States as cruisers or transports upon payment to the owners of the fair actual value of the same at the time of the taking; and if there shall be a disagreement as to the fair actual value at the time of taking between the United States and the owners, then the same shall be determined by two impartial appraisers, one to be appointed by each of said parties, who, in case of disagreement, shall select a third, the award of any two of the three so chosen to be final and conclusive.

The measure passed the Senate May 9. Mr. Frye, of Maine, put the case for the act as follows:

"This bill admits two ships to an American register, and demands not an expenditure of three fourths of the value in the American shipyard, but the expenditure of the full value, and besides that $500,000 more.

"I have a right to say that a ship will be built, if this bill becomes a law, not of 10,000 tons, but of over 12,000, with a speed not of 20 knots, but of 23 knots. The Cunard Line now is building on the Clyde two vessels for the main purpose of surpassing these two, and the purpose of this company is to make one of these vessels a vessel that will be superior in every respect to the two Cunarders, so that one of these ships will be over 12,000 tons.

"I have a right to say further—I believe it fully—that another line of three of these great ships will be provided for, if this bill becomes a law, between New York and Antwerp, and with those the Government of the United States will have 7 of the finest war cruisers in the whole world. These two ships to-day are capable in two hours' time of taking on board 16 rifled cannon and going to sea and answering a necessity which war may force upon us.

"Besides, we shall have built in American shipyards five of these enormous ships, and we shall have the privilege hereafter, when we desire to go to Europe, to go under our own flag instead of under a foreign flag.

"I have been a persistent and a somewhat aggressive—I presume the Senate would say too persistent and too aggressive — friend of the American ship and the American shipyard, and in giving my adhesion to this bill I do not drop out one jot or one tittle of that devotion to those interests. It is no impulse of mine that leads me to vote for this bill. It is the result of careful, long-continued consideration. In the last Congress my hopes were exceedingly brilliant. The Senate passed two bills, one the tonnage bill and the other the postal subsidy bill. and I felt that if these two bills became laws we should be restored to our proper and rightful position upon the ocean; but, unfortunately, I say, the House of Representatives defeated the tonnage bill and crippled the postal subsidy bill, so that there was no inducement left for capital to build these first-class ships and put them on to these lines. Shortly after I spent a week in Philadelphia and New York, using all the powers of persuasion I was possessed of to induce capital to put these lines on, and it was a complete failure.

"Some six months ago a proposition was made, and I was asked if I would not assent to it, admitting these two ships, and these only, to American register, providing the company would build two equally good and equally fast vessels here in American shipyards, and thus establish an American line from New York to Liverpool. I declined to give answer. I told the gentleman who came to me that I must take that into careful consideration before I could answer. I did take it into careful consideration;

I communicated with the leading friends of the American ship and shipyard all over the United States, and I finally came to a conclusion that it was in the interest of American ships and American shipyards to enact this proposed bill into a law."

Mr. Mills, of Texas, made a protest against the passage of the bill:

"It seems to me the question presented by this bill is, Shall the owners of these vessels draw their subsidies from the treasury of Great Britain, or shall the Treasury of the people of the United States contribute to them? This measure means that we shall give out of the money placed in our Treasury by the taxpayers of the United States this subsidy, and permit the owners of these vessels to pay it back in subsidy into the coffers of Great Britain.

"I am as much in favor of free ships as any gentleman on the other side of the Chamber or any gentleman on this side of the Chamber, but I want free ships to come upon a question of principle, and I want anybody, in the exercise of his natural right as a free man, to be permitted to go anywhere in the markets of the world to buy anything, from a ship to a pin, and bring it to this country, and to display over the masts of your vessels the ensign of the republic and navigate the waters of the earth with it. I do not want to vote to permit a given company, as a favorite of the Government, to go to a foreign country and buy one or two vessels, not to enlarge the commercial marine of the United States, but to put their hands into the public Treasury and extort the revenues taken by unjust principles of taxation and placed there by the hard earnings of the people of the United States.

"Let your ship measures stand upon a principle; and if you want to enlarge the commercial marine of the United States, and you want to see the flag of the republic riding upon all the waters of the earth, then make laws that will permit all the citizens of the United States to go into foreign markets and have their ships built at foreign navy yards and bring them to the United States free of duty. If we can make ships in the United States cheaper and better than the people of other countries, there will be no necessity for the adoption of this or any other measure of this kind.

"If there is anything upon our statute books that forbids American shipbuilders from building vessels as cheap and as good here as vessels are built in foreign shipyards, then let us repeal the law and permit the American people to build their own vessels in their own shipyards, and build them without bounty contributed from the pockets of the people of the United States.

"I do not like this measure. I am sorry that the Senator has presented it so hastily, and that he demands for it such hasty and rapid consideration. There is a great question involved in this measure, which ought to receive the calm and deliberate consideration of this very deliberate body, but, instead of that, a bill is brought forward in this body without even a report, and it is demanded that it shall be rushed through, and it has nothing behind it to recommend it except the patriotic desire of the owners of these vessels that the American flag shall float above them instead of the flag of Great Britain. It is ‧the old flag and an appropriation’ again. Patriotism always comes to Congress, but it comes for dollars, and this company would not be so desirous to transfer the flag of Great Britain back to some British vessels and place upon its own vessels the Stars and Stripes, except that dollars are to be made by the transaction. If this company has the right to make these dollars, then every citizen of the United States has the same equal right, and this Senate, representing the States and the people of the United States, ought to so make the laws that they shall render equal and exact justice to all.”

The President approved of the measure May 11.

Chinese Exclusion.—On April 4, 1892, a bill reported by Mr. Geary, of California, was passed by the House, on suspension of the rules. It was designed “to absolutely prohibit the coming of Chinese persons into the United States.” Mr. Hitt, of Illinois, said in opposition to the measure :

“ Mr. Speaker, the great and fatal objection to this bill in the mind of any man of truth who regards his country’s honor is, that it deliberately violates our plighted faith as we wrote it down in a solemn treaty and proposed it to another government, they assenting to it reluctantly at our persuasion. That treaty is now in full force and binding upon the American Government. There are many considerations of interest, many great losses in business, that will follow the complete nonintercourse it would produce ; but they are of little importance compared to this proposed shame in falsifying our word as a nation in a legislative step so deliberately taken.

“ We have had many anti-Chinese bills here, each more stringent and harsher than the preceding. They come every other year with the elections, and the writer searches the dictionary for words to surpass predecessors. Heretofore they were aimed at Chinese laborers, and I will join in legislation to exclude laborers and support negotiations to exclude Chinese laborers. But this bill goes far beyond that. It does not mention them. The House has voted for severe bills to exclude them, and tried to keep within the treaty. This bill emulates barbarians, in excluding and punishing when found on our soil every man, the most exalted and the humblest, of a great nation, and does it in avowed violation of faith and truth. Never before did we, nor any other legislative body, with cold cynicism, with absolute disregard of the moral sense, violate faith and avow that we were doing it. We have now a treaty which says ‘shall not absolutely prohibit,’ and this bill selects those very words from the treaty for its title in order to make it more insulting—a bill to absolutely prohibit the coming of Chinese persons into the United States.

“ We have in that treaty a provision that ‘ Chinese subjects, whether proceeding to the United States as teachers, students, merchants, or from curiosity, together with their body and household servants, and Chinese laborers now in the United States, shall be allowed to go and

come of their own free will and accord, and shall be accorded all the rights, privileges, immunities, and exemptions which are accorded to the citizens and subjects of the most favored nations.’ This bill flagrantly violates that provision by excluding all these classes, and punishing them cruelly if found here ; but it crowns all in the last section, where it deliberately, with a cold perfidy that language can not exceed, declares that all treaties and parts of treaties that are in conflict with this act are repealed, set aside and abrogated. Mark, it proposes to save all those parts of the treaties which are of advantage to us, such as the guarantee to American citizens in China of the rights of the most favored nation, and hold China as bound by public faith to observe them. Suppose we were dealing with England and the situations were reversed, who is there here who would not vote for a declaration of nonintercourse or war ?

“ At this time we are claiming and exercising in 20 cities in China wide privileges for American citizens under this treaty.

“ To-day the missionaries are trembling amid dangers, and there are Chinese soldiers guarding American citizens in the disorders which prevail in the Chinese Empire—this upon the demand of our minister based on this treaty ; and now we propose to revoke all that part of the treaty which gives any advantage or protection to a subject of China, and then to claim that they, as honorable men, shall carry out all that they covenanted with us !

“ Nothing akin in form to the abrogation of a treaty has ever been tried in the history of this country, save once, in 1798, and then Congress solemnly declared that the French having violated their treaty obligations, carried on a war of predatory violence upon us, rejected our claims and repelled every offer of negotiation with indignity, the treaty with them was at an end. But the cold, deliberate assertion in the solemn form of law that one party will, without cause, set aside an international compact which the other party has scrupulously observed, is without precedent. Has China wronged us in anything ? She has scrupulously regarded the treaty. Has she rejected our claims ? You, sir, have taken part in legislation here to send back hundreds of thousands of dollars overpaid by China on our claims. The Chinese have been patient in a way and to a degree unknown to us, listening with calmness and dignity to our proposals of successive harsh measures ; and shall we now address them in such unchristian language as this ?

“ We are sending missionaries there with the Bible of God, and when the Chinese open its pages they read, ‘ Thou shalt not lie.’ The Christian people we represent protest against this. Here are protests from the conferences of 95,000 Methodists in New Jersey. We violate faith to do acts that would be barbarism if there were no treaty. If the late Chinese minister, who recently left here, now a private subject, and in whose house, while he was here, I have seen Representatives and Senators as guests at his entertainments, should dare now to come back to call upon his successor, or to shake hands with any of the gentlemen whom he then entertained, under this bill, if it be‘ enacted, he would go to the penitentiary for five years! Stanley found nothing in darkest Africa more barbarous. If Li-Hung-Chang, the friend of Gen. Grant, should follow Grant's example, and, leaving for a time that mighty empire of which he has been the Bismarck, should set out to visit other lands, and come here to see the widow and family of his illustrious friend, he would receive not hospitality, but a prison and a fine; and the captain that brought him here, and every man that aided in his coming, would be fined $1,000 under this inhuman bill.

" Why propose this disgrace? Why not spare us this shame? You have here in the House a bill which has passed the Senate continuing the law as it stands, lest it may expire in May. Is not that law severe enough? It excludes all laborers, and is so harsh that it recently prevented from landing and drove from San Francisco two Chinese merchants belonging to a firm known in every financial center of the world—members of a house older than this republic—and this at the very time that the great American China house of Russell had tottered to its fall. Its fall was caused by the opposition of English influence and the indifference of the Chinese Government and business world. The coldness of China was produced by the nagging, irritation, and harsh course of the United States Government, which had diverted all sympathy on the part of merchants, bankers, and government in China; and so the great house of Russell, the Barings, the Rothschilds, of the Orient—an American house that had proudly stood for eighty years—went down in ruin.

" This savage exclusion and extreme punishment of all strangers is a revival of the darkest features of the darkest ages in the history of man. It is wholly needless. It is mischievous. It increases the difficulty of making an agreement with China to help keep out laborers. It will result in nonintercourse, and break up our trade with China; but that is comparatively nothing, that is as dust in the balance, compared with the foul blot put upon the nation by placing on its rolls, on its statutes, in its laws, a deliberate declaration of our falsehood, coldly avowing that it will set aside a treaty which the other party has carefully and scrupulously observed."

Mr. Hermann, of Oregon, said in support of the bill: " Mr. Speaker, in the few minutes accorded to me I shall be only permitted to express my hearty approval of any measure which shall be presented to effectually exclude the Chinese from coming to our country. None realize so much as those of our people who live upon the Pacific shores the necessity for such repressive legislation as this. Time and time again have we invoked the aid of Congress in behalf of some such measure which should accomplish the object desired, and time and time again has all legislation upon the subject been found ineffective. Now we have approached apparently the last remedy to be applied, which we believe, if it be enacted into law, will effectually result in the exclusion of these people.

" All political parties in all of the States west of the Rocky mountains have declared themselves in favor of legislation looking to the exclusion of the Chinese. Organizations of labor,

VOL. XXXII.—13 A

almost universally, and indeed nearly all of the industrial associations of those States, have expressed themselves in favor of some such measure as this.

" These Chinese form an exception in every respect to all races of people who seek our shores. They are here simply for a temporary purpose, having none of the ambitions and none of the aspirations and none of the great objects which induce other people to come and cast their lots among us, and seek the shores of this broad land for the purpose of making a future home. Under the old provisions of law which have heretofore obtained, a cordon of soldiers would be necessary all along our border to keep these people out.

" For over a thousand miles along the entire northern line of our territory, and along the Canadian frontier, as well as along the southern borders, they have had easy means of access, and we have found it absolutely impossible to exclude them by the utmost power which the existing laws provided. Among the dense forests of British Columbia they have the most convenient means for getting off at the various little stations on the railroads, and thus they are able to find their way into our territory, with no apprehension of being prevented or obstructed in their well-worn pathways.

" We believe that they are not a part and parcel of the world's people with whom it is desirable that we should intermingle; that they can not assimilate themselves to our customs and social existence; and as a matter of fact they come here, as I have said, for mere temporary purposes, with no expectation of remaining, simply to make money and then go home to die and be buried in China. It is essential, in my judgment, that they should be absolutely excluded, and I believe this measure will accomplish that end. It is high time our gateways should be double locked and barred against the Mongolian; and the time has also arrived for turning the key against much other cheap labor which reaches us from the Old World, just as dangerous to our labor system and to our civilization as these Chinese. If we are consistent in our declarations against the admission of the pr s of cheap labor, let us begin by excluding the degraded beings who make the products. Let us now practice what we preach."

In favor of the measure, 179 votes were cast; against it, 43 votes; 107 Representatives failed to vote.

In the Senate, April 13, the Committee on Foreign Relations reported a substitute for the House bill, much milder in its provisions, and designed simply to continue existing legislation. The subject was debated at some length, and on April 25 the substitute for the House bill passed the Senate by a vote of 43 to 14.

A conference committee was then appointed, as the House nonconcurred in the Senate amendments. The report of the committee, while abandoning some of the harsh features of the original measure of the House, added several severe sections to the Senate substitute. It was adopted by the Senate May 3, and by the House May 4. The act as finally passed is as follows:

Be it enacted, etc., That all laws now in force prohibiting and regulating the coming into this country of Chinese persons and persons of Chinese descent are hereby continued in force for a period of ten years from the passage of this act.

Sec. 2.—That any Chinese person or person of Chinese descent, when convicted and adjudged under any of said laws to be not lawfully entitled to be or remain in the United States, shall be removed from the United States to China, unless he or they shall make it appear to the justice, judge, or commissioner before whom he or they are tried that he or they are subjects or citizens of some other country, in which case he or they shall be removed from the United States to such country : *Provided*, That in any case where such other country of which such Chinese person shall claim to be a citizen or subject shall demand any tax as a condition of the removal of such person to that country, he or she shall be removed to China.

Sec. 3.—That any Chinese person or person of Chinese descent arrested under the provisions of this act or the acts hereby extended shall be adjudged to be unlawfully within the United States, unless such person shall establish by affirmative proof, to the satisfaction of such justice, judge, or commissioner, his lawful right to remain in the United States.

Sec. 4.—That any such Chinese person or person of Chinese descent convicted and adjudged. to be not lawfully entitled to be or remain in the United States shall be imprisoned at hard labor for a period of not exceeding a year, and thereafter removed from the United States, as hereinbefore provided.

Sec. 5.—That after the passage of this act, on an application to any judge or court of the United States in the first instance for a writ of *habeas corpus* by a Chinese person seeking to land in the United States, to whom that privilege has been denied, no bail shall be allowed, and such application shall be heard and determined promptly, without unnecessary delay.

Sec. 6.—And it shall be the duty of all Chinese laborers within the limits of the United States at the time of the passage of this act, and who are entitled to remain in the United States, to apply to the collector of internal revenue of their respective districts, within one year after the passage of this act, for a certificate of residence; and any Chinese laborer within the limits of the United States who shall neglect, fail, or refuse to comply with the provisions of this act, or who, after one year from the passage hereof, shall be found within the jurisdiction of the United States without such certificate of residence, shall be deemed and adjudged to be unlawfully within the United States. and may be arrested by any United States customs official, collector of internal revenue or his deputies, United States marshal or his deputies, and taken before a United States judge, whose duty it shall be to order that he be deported from the United States, as hereinbefore provided, unless he shall establish clearly to the satisfaction of said judge that by reason of accident, sickness, or other unavoidable cause he has been unable to procure his certificate, and to the satisfaction of the court, and by at least one credible white witness, that he was a resident of the United States at the time of the passage of this act; and if, upon the hearing, it shall appear that he is so entitled to a certificate, it shall be granted upon his paying the costs. Should it appear that said Chinaman had procured a certificate, which has been lost or destroyed, he shall be detained and judgment suspended a reasonable time to enable him to procure a duplicate from the officer granting it, and in such cases the costs of said arrest and trial shall be in the discretion of the court. And any Chinese person other than a Chinese laborer, having a right to be and remain in the United States, desiring such certificate as evidence of such right, may apply for and receive the same without charge.

Sec. 7.—That immediately after the passage of this act the Secretary of the Treasury shall make such rules and regulations as may be necessary for the efficient execution of this act, and shall prescribe the necessary forms and furnish the necessary blanks to enable collectors of internal revenue to issue the certificates required hereby, and make such provisions that certificates may be procured in localities convenient to the applicants. Such certificates shall be issued without charge to the applicant, and shall contain the name, age, local residence, and occupation of the applicant, and such other description of the applicant as shall be prescribed by the Secretary of the Treasury, and a duplicate thereof shall be filed in the office of the collector of internal revenue for the district within which such Chinaman makes application.

Sec. 8.—That any person who shall knowingly and falsely alter or substitute any name for the name written in such certificate, or forge such certificate, or knowingly utter any forged or fraudulent certificate, or falsely personate any person named in such certificate, shall be guilty of a misdemeanor, and upon conviction thereof shall be fined in a sum not exceeding $1,000, or imprisoned in the penitentiary for a term of not more than five years.

Sec. 9.—The Secretary of the Treasury may authorize the payment of such compensation in the nature of fees to the collectors of internal revenue, for services performed under the provisions of this act, in addition to salaries now allowed by law, as he shall deem necessary, not exceeding the sum of $1 for each certificate issued.

The title of the act was changed to "An act to prohibit the coming of Chinese persons into the United States." The President approved the bill May 5.

Canal Tolls.—On July 21, 1892, the Committee on Foreign Affairs in the House introduced the following bill "to enforce reciprocal relations between the United States and Canada, and for other purposes."

Be it enacted, etc., That, with a view of securing reciprocal advantages for the citizens. ports, and vessels of the United States, on and after the 1st day of August, 1892, whenever and so often as the President shall be satisfied that the passage through any canal or lock connected with the navigation of the St. Lawrence river, the Great Lakes, or the water ways connecting the same, of any vessels of the United States, or of cargoes or passengers in transit to any port of the United States, is prohibited or is made difficult or burdensome by the imposition of tolls or otherwise, which, in view of the free passage through the St. Mary's Falls Canal, now permitted to vessels of all nations, he shall deem to be reciprocally unjust and unreasonable, he shall have the power and it shall be his duty to suspend, by proclamation to that effect, for such time and to such extent (including absolute prohibition) as he shall deem just, the right of free passage through the St. Mary's Falls Canal, so far as it relates to vessels owned by the subjects of the government so discriminating against the citizens, ports, or vessels of the United States, or to any cargoes, portions of cargoes, or passengers in transit to the ports of the government making such discrimination, whether carried in vessels of the United States or of other nations.

In such case and during such suspension tolls shall be levied, collected, and paid as follows, to wit: Upon freight of whatever kind or description, not to exceed $2 per ton; upon passengers, not to exceed $5 each, as shall be from time to time determined by the President: *Provided*, That no tolls shall be charged or collected upon freight or passengers carried to and landed at Ogdensburg, or any port west of Ogdensburg and south of a line drawn from the northern boundary of the State of New York through the St. Lawrence river, the Great Lakes, and their connecting channels to the northern boundary of the State of Minnesota.

Sec. 2.—All tolls so charged shall be. collected under such regulations as shall be prescribed by the Secretary of the Treasury, who may require the master of each vessel to furnish a sworn statement of the amount and kind of cargo, and the number of passengers carried, and the destination of the same, and such proof of the actual delivery of such cargo or passengers at some port or place within the limits above named as he shall deem satisfactory; and until such proof is furnished such freight and passengers may be considered to have been landed at some port or place outside of those limits, and the amount of tolls which would have accrued if they had been so delivered shall constitute a lien, which may be enforced against the vessel in default wherever and whenever found in the waters of the United States.

Mr. Blount, of Georgia, said in explanation of the measure: " Mr. Speaker, Article XXVII of the Treaty of Washington, concluded May 8, 1871, provides

The Government of her Britannic Majesty engages to urge upon the Government of the Dominion of Canada to secure to the citizens of the United States the use of the Welland, St. Lawrence, and other canals in the Dominion on terms of equality with the inhabitants of the Dominion; and the Government of the United States engages that the subjects of her Britannic Majesty shall enjoy the use of the St. Clair Flats canal on terms of equality with the inhabitants of the United States, and further engages to urge upon the State governments to secure to the subjects of her Britannic Majesty the use of the several State canals connected with the navigation of the lakes or rivers traversed by or contiguous to the boundary line between the possessions of the high contracting parties on terms of equality with the inhabitants of the United States.

" The President of the United States has in two messages during this session of Congress called the attention of the Congress of the United States to the condition of the rights of American citizens in the use of the Welland, St. Lawrence, and other Canadian canals. The twenty-seventh article of this treaty was intended to give our own citizens the same right to use these canals that was accorded to the citizens of Canada. It was in contemplation at the time of its ratification that the people of Canada should have from their territory north of the Great Lakes the right to transport their merchandise of various sorts through Lakes Superior, Huron, Michigan, Erie, and Ontario into Canada, east into the Atlantic Ocean, and into the marts of the world. Except by a concession on the part of the United States of the right to pass the St. Clair Flats Canal and of the right to pass the Sault St. Marie Canal, subsequently acquired by the Government of the United States, it would have been impossible for her to have carried by that route—this deep-water route—her products.

" She was enabled, through it, to have an interchange of products either way; and what was the consideration to the people of the United States? That the great Northwest should be allowed to transport through these lakes, through the Welland and St. Lawrence Canals, and through Canada, and to her own ports on the Ontario, her own products. That was the intent on the part of the Government of the United States and of the high contracting parties. It turned out, however, that the Canadian Government, with a view of affecting advantageously the interests of the St. Lawrence Canal, provides a rebate of 18 cents on such articles as shall pass the Welland Canal and the St. Lawrence Canal to Montreal. It has left

there the duties at 2 cents per ton. This was not accorded to American vessels passing through the Welland Canal and landing at ports on the Ontario and at other ports.

" By an order in council it was provided that where there was a transshipment at the Welland Canal or at Kingston, this rebate should obtain notwithstanding the transshipment. By virtue of the operation of that order of council all transshipments on the American side, even where the vessels went through the St. Lawrence canals, were deprived of the benefit of the rebate. It was claimed on the part of the Canadian Government that as the rebate applied to " vessels," and our vessels were covered by its terms provided their cargoes took the lines indicated by the order, there was absolute equality; but the language of the treaty shows that it had relation not to vessels but to citizens.

" It was intended for the benefit of the consumers in our own country; it was intended to give advantages to our ports; it was intended to give advantages to our transportation companies. The Canadians have sought, by this technical construction, to evade the spirit of the treaty. The proposition in the pending bill is to allow the President of the United States to prescribe tolls to be levied at the St. Mary's Canal on products passing through there, and also to provide that those tolls shall not operate against American vessels plying to ports within our own territory.

" The object is to apply to Canadian citizens using that canal a rule similar to that which the Canadians apply to American citizens using their canals. It is expected that in this way we shall secure a recognition of our rights under the treaty. It is believed that the result of this course on the part of our Government will be to put an end to the delay and evasion which have characterized the negotiations of the Canadian commissioners with our State Department upon this subject, and to compel on the part of Canada a recognition of our rights under the treaty.

" The President of the United States, interpreting this treaty, says:

The treaty aims to secure to the citizens of the United States the use of the Welland, St. Lawrence, and other canals in the Dominion on terms of equality with the inhabitants of the Dominion. It was intended,

says he,

to give to consumers in the United States, to our own people engaged in railroad transportation, and to those exporting from our ports, equal terms in passing their merchandise through these canals.

" If this is a correct interpretation—and I believe it is—why should we submit to a ruinous and wrongful interpretation? The suggestion comes, 'We might abrogate this treaty.' Is that the way for this great Government to meet this issue in the protection of the treaty rights of its citizens? No, sir; it should stand manfully and heroically for their rights, and meet whatever emergencies may arise as they arise.

" This bill provides simply for the application of the rule laid down by the Canadian authorities in reference to their own merchandise—nothing more, nothing less. Let them conform to the terms of the treaty, and the President has no power. But we have had first one evasion and then another; we have had delays and misunderstandings. But no Canadian is harmed thereby."

The measure passed the House without a division, passed the Senate next day in the same manner, and was approved by the President.

Columbian Exposition.—One of the perplexing questions before Congress was the grant of aid to the Columbian Exposition at Chicago. There were in the way of such a grant the doubt as to its constitutionality, the pledges made in behalf of Chicago not to ask aid if named as the city in which the exposition should be held, and these resolutions of the House in favor of strict economy passed at the opening of the session:

Resolved, That, in the judgment of this House, the granting of subsidies or bounties by Congress, in money, public lands, bonds, or by indorsement, or by pledge of the public credit, to promote special private industries or enterprises of corporations, independent of the question of the constitutional power of Congress to make such grants, is unjust and impolitic, and in manifest conflict with the spirit of our republican institutions, as it directly tends to create and foster the wealth of favored classes at the expense of the whole people who bear the burdens of government, and manifestly furnishes undue facilities for the enlargement of great private estates—a policy which a government of the people can not justly or safely encourage by any form of favoritism in legislation.

Resolved, In view of the present condition of the Treasury, and because efficient and honest government can only be assured by the frugal expenditure of the public money, while unnecessary and lavish expenditure, under any and all conditions, leads inevitably to venal and corrupt methods in public affairs, no money ought to be appropriated by Congress from the public Treasury, except such as is manifestly necessary to carry on the several departments, frugally, efficiently, and honestly administered.

An appropriation of $5,000,000 was asked; but finally a compromise measure was adopted. It was described as a bill "to aid in carrying out the act of Congress approved April 25, 1890, entitled 'An Act to provide for celebrating the four hundredth anniversary of the discovery of America by Christopher Columbus, by holding an international exposition of arts, industries, manufactures, and products of the soil, mine, and sea, in the city of Chicago, in the State of Illinois, and appropriating money therefor.'" It passed the House Aug. 5, 1892, in the following form:

Be it enacted, etc., That for the purpose of aiding in defraying the cost of completing in a suitable manner the work of preparation for inaugurating the World's Columbian Exposition, authorized by the act of Congress approved April 25, A. D. 1890, to be held at the city of Chicago, in the State of Illinois, there shall be coined at the mints of the United States silver half dollars of the legal weight and fineness, not to exceed 5,000,000 pieces, to be known as the Columbian half dollar, struck in commemoration of the World's Columbian Exposition, the devices and designs upon which shall be prescribed by the Director of the Mint, with the approval of the Secretary of the Treasury; and said silver coins shall be manufactured from uncurrent subsidiary silver coins now in the Treasury; and all provisions of law relative to the coinage, legal-tender quality, and redemption of the present subsidiary silver coins shall be applicable to the coins issued under this act, and when so recoined there is hereby appropriated from the Treasury the said 5,000,000 of souvenir half dollars; and the Secretary of the Treasury is authorized to pay the same to the World's Columbian Exposition, upon estimates and vouchers certified by the president of the World's Columbian Exposition, or, in his absence or inability to act, by the vice-president, and by the director-general of the World's Columbian Commission, or in his absence or inability to act, by the president thereof, and the Secretary of the Treasury, for labor done, materials furnished, and services performed in prosecuting said work of preparing said exposition for opening as provided by said act approved April 25, 1890; and all such estimates and vouchers shall be made in duplicate, one to be filed with the Secretary of the Treasury, the other to be retained by the World's Columbian Exposition; *Provided, however,* That before the Secretary of the Treasury shall pay to the World's Columbian Exposition any part of the said 5,000,000 silver coins, satisfactory evidence shall be furnished him showing that the sum of at least $10,000,000 has been collected and disbursed as required by said act; *And provided,* That the said World's Columbian Exposition shall furnish a satisfactory guarantee to the Secretary of the Treasury that any further sum actually necessary to complete the work of said exposition to the opening thereof has been or will be provided by said World's Columbian Exposition; but nothing herein shall be so construed as to delay or postpone the preparation of the souvenir coins hereinbefore provided for. And there is hereby appropriated, out of any moneys in the Treasury not otherwise appropriated, the sum of $50,000, or so much thereof as may be necessary, to reimburse the Treasury for loss on the recoinage herein authorized.

SEC. 2. That the appropriation provided in section 1 of this act shall be upon condition that the said World's Columbian Exposition maintain and pay all the expenses, costs, and charges of the great departments organized for the purpose of conducting the work of the exposition, said expenses, costs, and charges to be paid out of the funds of the said World's Columbian Exposition.

SEC. 3. That 50,000 bronze medals and the necessary dies therefor, with appropriate devices, emblems, and inscriptions commemorative of said exposition celebrating the four hundredth anniversary of the discovery of America by Christopher Columbus, shall be prepared under the supervision of the Secretary of the Treasury, at a cost not to exceed $60,000; and the Bureau of Engraving and Printing, under the supervision of the Secretary of the Treasury, shall prepare plates and make therefrom 50,000 vellum impressions for diplomas, at a cost not to exceed $43,000. Said medals and diplomas shall be delivered to the World's Columbian Commission, to be awarded to exhibitors in accordance with the provisions of said act of Congress approved April 25, 1890; and there is hereby appropriated, from any moneys in the Treasury not otherwise appropriated, the sum of $103,000, or so much thereof as may be necessary, to pay the expenditures authorized by this section; and authority may be granted by the Secretary of the Treasury to the holder of a medal, properly awarded to him, to have duplicates thereof made at any of the mints of the United States from gold, or silver, or bronze, at the expense of the person desiring the same.

SEC. 4. That it is hereby declared that all appropriations herein made for or pertaining to the World's Columbian Exposition are made upon the condition that the said exposition shall not be opened to the public on the first day of the week, commonly called Sunday; and if the said appropriations be accepted by the corporation of the State of Illinois, known as the World's Columbian Exposition, upon that condition it shall be, and it is hereby, made the duty of the World's Columbian Commission, created by the act of Congress of April 25, 1890, to make such rules or modification of the rules of said corporation as shall require the closing of the exposition on the said first day of the week, commonly called Sunday.

Sec. 5. That nothing contained in this act shall be construed to supersede or in any manner alter or impair the force or validity of the provisions of section 15 of the act of Congress approved April 25, A. D. 1890.

In criticism of the measure, Mr. Bailey, of Texas, said:

"Mr. Chairman, the passage of this bill fixes it as a settled and permanent policy of the Federal Government to extend aid in projecting and encouraging enterprises like the World's Columbian Exposition. Before we take that final step, sir, it may be well to review the progress of this idea, for never hereafter will it be seriously debated in the American Congress whether we have the power or whether it is wise to make appropriations like this; but hereafter it will be merely a contention over the amount—a calculation fit only for the countingroom.

"The first exposition of this kind was held in 1851, in the great city of New York. But nowhere in the records of Congress can it be found that they implored a dollar's aid from the Federal Government, and certainly it can not be found in the statutes that they received a single dollar.

"Sixteen years ago, for the first time in our history, Congress committed the Government to aid an exposition. As the one hundredth anniversary of our independence approached, patriotic men conceived the idea of its celebration. In 1871 they came to Congress and asked the enactment of a law merely authorizing the President to invite foreign nations to participate in that celebration. In 1874 they came back and asked the incorporation of the Centennial Company, and the law which incorporated it distinctly disclaimed the purpose of the Federal Government to commit itself to the appropriation of a single dollar. In 1876 they came back imploring Congress to save them from the disgrace of a failure, declaring that the law which authorized the invitations to be extended to foreign nations committed the Government by honorable engagement to make it a success. Mr. Randall, who, though a Representative from the city of Philadelphia, had stood for five years resisting the idea that the Federal Government should use the public moneys for such a purpose, finally yielded, and he yielded distinctly upon the ground that not again in one hundred years could such a demand be made.

"Eight years afterward they were here from New Orleans, and again the Congress appropriated public money for a purpose in no wise connected with the Government's service; and though they said in the beginning that not once in a hundred years could the request be repeated, yet in sixteen years we are confronted for a third time with a demand of this kind, and this time the demand is for well-nigh twice as much as ever before.

"Now, Mr. Chairman, I submit to the thoughtful consideration of members, that if they teach the people that public moneys can be used to provide entertainment for the rich and prosperous, you can not deny bread to the poor and hungry and outlive their wrath. You inculcate a lesson which the men who set the example will be the first to repent.

"And this, sir, is to be done in the name of progress. Mr. Chairman, I believe in progress; but, as I read the history of my race, man has achieved his best, his highest, his most enduring progress when the Government has made him free and left him to work out his own destiny in his own good way. I have no sympathy, sir, with this modern and dangerous tendency that subjects not only the business, but even the entertainment of our people, to legislative aid and legislative interference. It teaches a baneful lesson, and it will ultimately bring the people to believe that it is the duty of the Government to support them, instead of their duty to support the Government."

In defense of the measure, Mr. Reilly, of Pennsylvania, said:

"Let me briefly review the history of this enterprise. The propriety of celebrating the four hundredth anniversary of the discovery of America by Columbus suggested itself to the minds of American people and met with a favorable response. For several years past it has been earnestly advocated and agitated, and during the past several Congresses innumerable petitions from all parts of the country were presented to both Houses of Congress favoring such celebration in the form of a grand national and international exposition. The subject attained such magnitude, and the sentiment of the people was so pronounced and universal in favor of it, that in the Fifty-first Congress it was deemed a subject of sufficient importance to justify the appointment of a select committee, to which should be referred for consideration and action all matters touching the subject.

"The matter was considered by Congress in all its phases, and as the result of its judgment we have the act of April 25, 1890, inaugurating this great exposition. It will be borne in mind that in this respect this affair differs from any other in that it was originally inaugurated, created, established, by direct, positive action of Congress. Its action has provided for the holding, conducting, and carrying on of this exposition in all its details, and is the supreme, controlling power over it to-day. Congress determined where this exposition should be held, when it should be held, the time it should open, the time it should close, and how it should be conducted. Congress provided all the agencies and instrumentalities necessary to carry out its will.

"It seems to me, Mr. Chairman, that a mere perusal of this act is in itself sufficient to carry conviction to any fair mind upon this question. In the preamble it is declared:

Whereas, It is fitly appropriate that the four hundredth anniversary of the discovery of America be commemorated by an exhibition of the resources of the United States of America, their development, and the progress of civilization in the New World; and

Whereas, Such an exhibition should be of a national and international character, so that not only the people of our Union and this continent but those of all nations as well can participate, and should therefore have the sanction of the Congress of the United States: Therefore.

Be it enacted, etc., That an exhibition of arts, industries, manufactures, and products of the soil, mine, and sea, shall be inaugurated in the year 1892, in the city of Chicago, in the State of Illinois, as hereinafter provided.

"The act then provides that a commission, representative in its character, composed of 2 commissioners from each State and Territory, and from the District of Columbia, and 8 commissioners at large, be constituted, and designated as the World's Columbian Commission. These commissioners were duly appointed, and, under the terms of the act, clothed with full power and authority to conduct the affairs of this exposition. The commission was empowered to determine the plans and scope of the exposition, allot space for the exhibitors, prepare a classification of exhibits, appoint all judges and examiners for the exposition, award all premiums, and generally have charge of all intercourse with the exhibitors and the representatives of foreign nations. The site to be selected and plans and specifications of the buildings to be erected for such purpose were made subject to the approval of this commission ; supervision over all rules and regulations touching the management and conduct of said exposition was vested in the commission.

"So that it will be seen, Mr. Chairman, from a perusal of this law, that this work is one for which the act of Congress provides in all its details. Moreover, by the terms of the act the President of the United States was authorized to make proclamation of the time at which this exposition will open and close, the place at which it shall be held, and on behalf of the Government and people to invite foreign nations to take part in the exposition, and appoint representatives thereto. It will not do, therefore, Mr. Speaker, to assert that this is a mere local enterprise or an affair got up by a private corporation. The American people do not so understand it. They regard it as a national affair, and one in the success of which the credit and fame of our nation are involved. By the terms of the act referred to, this company were required to provide a site and the sum of $10,000,000 to be used in the erection of suitable buildings thereon for the purposes of the exposition. This site has been furnished, comprising a beautiful tract of land containing an area of 633 acres, located in Jackson Park, in the city of Chicago, fronting on Lake Michigan, and affording one of the most picturesque and beautiful pieces of landscape which can be found on the earth.

"This they have done ; and I wish to say, Mr. Speaker, that, speaking as an American citizen, I am proud that we have in our midst a community so prosperous and patriotic as to undertake the task of raising this enormous amount of money for this purpose. It may be said that they are selfish in their motives, and that their investment is for speculative purposes. I do not take such a narrow view of it, and I believe that those people are to-day animated more by sincere desire for the success and grandeur of this exposition than they are for any mere return in the way of money that they can expect from it. But be that as it may, I hope it will be a success, first, for the credit of our common country, and, second, as a reward for their enterprise and patriotism. And I, for one, should be glad to see the affair so great a success that they will get back every dollar that they invested, with a handsome return on the same.

"But again, Mr. Chairman, it is hardly consistent for any member of this House to set up the plea now that this is not a national enterprise, for by our action here we have committed ourselves on that question. On the 8th of February last this House adopted a resolution authorizing and empowering a committee of this House to inquire and report whether the requirements of the act of April 25, 1890, were being justly and properly complied with ; whether the expenditures were being judiciously made, and generally to make full investigation into all the affairs and details whatever of the exposition authorized by Congress. That resolution was adopted by a yea and nay vote of this House ; and I find by the ' Record ' that gentlemen who now oppose this appropriation upon the ground that it is in the interest of a private corporation, voted in favor of making this investigation, which, it will be borne in mind, was to be made at the public expense, and was so made. That committee made its investigation and report thereon to this House, which report was printed at the Government Printing Office at public expense, and gives to the House full particulars in the premises.

"Now, sir, if this matter is simply the affair of a private corporation, a matter in which the Government has no interest, and with which it is in no way connected, pray tell me upon what principle or authority gentlemen who voted that investigation should be made at the public expense reconcile their positions upon this question?

"So that I take it, Mr. Chairman, when we calmly reflect upon the true history of this affair, it can not be seriously asserted that there is any constitutional objection to this appropriation on the ground that it is not of a national or public character. I submit that such is its character, that it is so fully declared by law, and this being the case there can be no question about the power of Congress to legislate and appropriate money in support of it.

"Article VIII, section 1, of the Constitution, empowering Congress to legislate for the general welfare, as was clearly shown in the argument of the gentleman from Louisiana the other day, confers ample power upon Congress in this respect. But I will not take time to dilate upon the constitutional question. I take it here in this discussion there is little difference between us as to the law ; the dispute is rather as to the facts. I assert that this is not a private affair, but, on the other hand, a great national public enterprise, that is calculated to materially promote the general welfare of our people ; and gentlemen who oppose it, asserting that it is the affair of a private corporation, are, I submit, mistaken, and not borne out by the facts of the case.

"Now, Mr. Chairman, as to the necessity for this appropriation, let me say just a word. The investigating committee to which I have referred have made a scrutinizing investigation into all the affairs of this exposition, and their report is before us ; and that report shows, as the result of their own deliberate and careful judgment, that on the first day of May, 1893, the time fixed by law for the opening of the gates, there will be a deficiency of nearly $5,000,000 in the revenues of the exposition. About this there is no controversy, and the question is, under these circumstances shall the Government furnish any aid, or shall we let the management of this great exposition, to which the nations of the world have been invited, go through the money marts of Chicago, New York, London, or Paris, seeking to hypothecate their securities or receipts for the purpose of raising money to carry on the work of preparing this great exposition, which, as I have already stated, is inaugurated by act of Congress, and is being carried on under the auspices of this great Government? To my mind there ought to be no hesitation or doubt as to our duty in the premises.

"Now, as I have said, Mr. Chairman, the Columbian Exposition were to raise $10,000,000. This they have done, and, as shown by the report of the Dockery committee, nearly $8,000,000 will be expended for the construction of the buildings alone. Then, the expenses of the great departments of the exposition, organized and established by the national commission, are being paid for by the exposition, which will amount to at least $1,500,000 more by the first of May, and, taking into consideration the thousand and one other incidental expenses, which I need not stop to enumerate, it becomes readily apparent that there must be a deficiency in the revenue necessary to carry on this great work according to the plan and scope determined by the national commission.

"Again, Mr. Chairman, in response to our invitation more than 60 nations of the earth have responded in a spirit of amity, and are expending large sums of money in the preparation of exhibits to be installed at this exposition. The amount of money thus being expended by foreign nations amounts to $5,000,000. Our own States, through their Legislatures, have made liberal appropriations, my own State appropriating the sum of $300,000. The amount which will be expended by the various States and Territories will aggregate nearly $5,000,000, and all this aside from the immense amount that will be expended by individuals and private concerns in the preparation of their exhibits.

"Now, Mr. Chairman, this promises to be a grand success. The investigating committee to which I have referred so report. The management has been honest, able, and skillful. The affairs of this exposition have in all respects been managed with a degree of ability and fidelity that is highly commendable, and there is but one desire upon all sides, the management as well as the people at large, that this great event shall be a splendid success.

"Let me quote a word from the report of this committee:

In its scope and magnificence this exposition stands alone. There is nothing like it in all history. It easily surpasses all kindred enterprises, and will amply illustrate the marvelous genius of the American people in the great domains of agriculture, commerce, manufactures, and invention, which constitute the foundation upon which rests the structure of our national glory and prosperity.

"Now, Mr. Chairman, as a member of the committee on the World's Columbian Exposition I have given this subject careful thought and study. I am somewhat familiar with its origin and the legislation that has inaugurated

it. I submit there can be no question that this is and was from the beginning intended to be an affair of great national interest and character. I have no scruples whatever in giving my support to this bill, and I endeavor to be as conscientious in the discharge of my duties here as any other member upon this floor.

"This exposition will not only redound to our fame and glory, but will materially benefit our glorious republic. It will infuse new blood into the arteries of trade. It will open new channels of commerce, expand out commercial relations with the nations of the earth, elevate and advance our civilization to a still higher standard."

The bill passed the Senate the same day, but not without some serious censure. Senator Sherman said:

"Congress treated the people of Philadelphia. when they were engaged in the same kind of an enterprise, with somewhat of the grasp of a miser. When the city of Philadelphia, after going to the extreme tether to have the exposition of 1876, involved itself in debt and could go no further, it appealed to Congress for help, and how was that appeal responded to? One million five hundred thousand dollars was finally given or loaned to that exposition, upon the express condition that every dollar of that money should be refunded to the United States of America before one single cent was paid out to any person in Philadelphia who had contributed to the same purpose. It was one of those things which was regarded as harsh and unjust. Yet the people of Philadelphia were in such a condition that they could not refuse it, and they accepted the $1,500,000; and the Government of the United States collected from the people of Philadelphia every dollar of the money thus loaned before a single dollar was paid out or distributed to the shareholders who had given their money. There was an act of injustice.

"We proposed to give $5,000,000 to the people of Chicago, and to share with them the profit and loss. I would rather give $10,000,000 and share with them the profit and loss, than give them the $2,500,000 and tell them: 'Here, we throw you this bone; we will give you this $2,500,000, and we do not expect anything from it; we expect it to be all wasted and gone.' That is the way in which this enterprise is treated by the Congress of the United States.

"Sir, if this bill stood alone, without its surroundings, I should vote against it. If I were a citizen of Chicago I would not accept this money under the terms and conditions and in the way in which it is here given. The people of Chicago could raise this $2,500,000. With a little exhibition of the spirit and feeling of the people of that city they would raise it, and need not accept this appropriation."

The President approved the measure immediately before the adjournment of Congress.

Pensions.—On June 28, 1892, the House passed the following bill for pensioning army nurses:

Be it enacted, etc., That any woman who served as an army nurse in the actual personal care and nursing of the sick and wounded during the civil war, either in field or general hospitals of the United States, and who continued in such care and nursing of the sick and wounded not less than six months, and who is without other adequate means of support than her own daily labor, shall, upon making due proof of the fact, according to such rules and regulations as the Secretary of the Interior may provide, be placed upon the pension roll of the United States and be entitled to receive $12 per month; and such pension shall commence from the date of filing the application in the Pension Office after the passage of this act: *Provided*, That any pension granted under any former law to any applicant under this act shall terminate from the date of commencement of the pension under this act: *Provided further*, That no person now receiving a pension as army nurse under any special act shall be entitled to receive a pension under this act.

The report of the Committee on Pensions in favor of this measure is as follows:

From the best authorities attainable, it is ascertained that the number of persons who would become beneficiaries under this bill would not probably exceed three hundred, if, indeed, it would reach that number.

The Association of Army Nurses, with headquarters at Washington, D. C., and the Woman's Relief Corps of the United States, have both been engaged, during the past two years, in conducting a thorough correspondence throughout the entire country, with a view to secure a complete list of such women as served as army nurses during the civil war.

While their lists do not absolutely harmonize, there is sufficient in their statements, when compared, to show that together they have secured the names and addresses of approximately the entire number of such nurses, and such correspondence does not secure a list even as large as that stated—three hundred—who could possibly become beneficiaries under this act.

This small band of noble women are the sole remaining representatives of a class of patriotic women who came from every section of our land. In their service they knew no North, no South. As angels of mercy they came to care for and comfort both blue and gray. They ministered to the needs of the suffering everywhere. On field or in hospital their sweet voices were heard, and their gentle touch was given to assuage sorrow and pain.

Many of them were women of wealth, who left comfortable homes and worked without pay; many even giving of their own means to relieve the sufferings of the sick and wounded soldiers.

Others, who received small payment for their services, parted with that scanty sum of money to purchase food and medicine for the soldier boys under their charge.

Many were broken down in health, and such, if living to-day, are among the sufferers from that war.

The benefits of this bill apply only to such army nurses as "are without other adequate means of support than their own daily labor."

The measure passed the Senate and was approved by the President.

The "intermediate pension" bill also became a law. It provides for an "intermediate pension rate," $50 a month, for those incapacitated for manual labor by reason of injuries received or disease contracted in the service of the United States in the line of duty, and yet not totally helpless.

There was also a measure passed granting pensions to survivors of the Black Hawk and Seminole wars.

The Presidential Succession.—On Feb. 9, 1892, the House passed the following bill without a division:

Be it enacted, etc., That in the first section of the act of which this is amendatory there shall be inserted after the words "Secretary of the Interior" the words,

"or if there be none, or in case of his removal, death, resignation, or inability, then the Secretary of Agriculture."

It is an amendment to "An Act to provide for the performance of the duties of the office of President in case of the removal, death, resignation, or inability both of the President and Vice-President," approved Jan. 19, 1886. Mr. Powers, of Vermont, said, in explanation of the measure:

"In 1886 an act of Congress was passed providing that in case of death or inability of both the President and Vice-President, the succession to the presidential office should devolve upon the different members of the Cabinet in the order of their commissions. At that time the last official in the line of succession was the Secretary of the Interior. Since that time the Department of Agriculture has been created, the Secretary of that department being made a Cabinet official. In order, therefore, to preserve the harmony of our legislation and to avoid a seeming discrimination against the Department of Agriculture, this bill provides in reference to the succession to the presidential office that the Secretary of Agriculture shall stand after the Secretary of the Interior."

The bill passed the Senate April 22 without a division, and was approved by the President.

Other Bills that became Laws.—The following bills, among about 400 that became laws, may also be mentioned:

For the permanent preservation and custody of the records of the volunteer armies.

Increasing the maximum pay of members of life-saving crews to $65 a month.

To appropriate $50,000 for a site and pedestal for a statue of Gen. Sherman.

To establish a military board to review the findings of courts-martial.

To regulate promotions in the marine corps.

For the completion of the allotment of lands to Cheyennes and Arapahoes.

For the investigation of mining *débris* in California.

To set apart land for the use of the Lick Observatory.

To release steamers on inland waters from obligation to carry life-saving projectiles.

To protect foreign exhibitors at the World's Fair.

To permit enlisted men in the army to be examined for promotion to second lieutenancies.

Tariff Measures.—Much of the time of this Congress was taken up in the discussion of revenue measures; but no changes of the tariff law were brought about, as the Republican majority of the Senate stood in the way of the legislation adopted by the Democratic majority of the House. One important measure that passed the latter body was a bill to place wool on the free list and reduce the duties on woolen goods. It was as follows:

Be it enacted, etc., That on and after the 1st day of January, 1893, the following articles, when imported, shall be exempt from duty, namely: All wools, hair of the camel, goat, alpaca, and other like animals, and all wool and hair on the skin, all noils, top waste, slubbing waste, roving waste, ring waste, yarn waste, card waste, bur waste, rags, and flocks, including all waste or rags composed wholly or in part of wool.

SEC. 2. That on and after the 1st day of January, 1893, the articles enumerated, described, and provided for in the paragraphs hereinafter named of "An Act to reduce the revenue and equalize duties on imports, and for other purposes," approved Oct. 1, 1890, shall, when imported, be subjected to the duties hereinafter provided, and no others; that is to say:

. Upon the articles enumerated in paragraph 391 of said act the duties shall be 35 per cent. *ad valorem.*

Upon the articles enumerated in paragraph 392 the duty shall be 40 per cent. *ad valorem.*

Upon the articles enumerated in paragraph 393 the duties fixed therein at 30 per cent. *ad valorem* shall be reduced to 25 per cent. *ad valorem ;* the duties fixed at 35 per cent. *ad valorem* shall be reduced to 30 per cent. *ad valorem ;* and the duties fixed at 40 per cent. *ad valorem* shall be reduced to 35 per cent. *ad valorem ;* and no duties per pound or per square yard shall be imposed upon the articles enumerated in said paragraph.

Upon the articles enumerated in paragraph 394 the duties shall be 35 per cent. *ad valorem.*

Upon the articles enumerated in paragraphs 395 and 398 the duties shall be 40 per cent. *ad valorem.*

Upon the articles enumerated in paragraphs 396 and 397 the duties shall be 45 per cent. *ad valorem.*

Upon the articles enumerated in paragraphs 399, down to and including paragraph 408, the duty shall be 30 per cent. *ad valorem.*

And all imported articles enumerated, described, and provided for in said paragraphs, respectively, which may be in public store or in warehouse on the said 1st day of January, 1893, shall be subjected to the same duties when withdrawn for consumption, and no others, as if said articles had been imported on or after said 1st day of January; and only the *ad valorem* duties as herein provided shall thereafter be levied, collected, and paid upon the articles mentioned in said paragraphs.

SEC. 3. That the articles mentioned in paragraph 390 of said act, and likewise all mungo, shoddies, garneted or carded waste, or other waste product, any of which is composed wholly or in part of wool, and which has been improved or advanced beyond its original condition as waste by the use of machinery or the application of labor, or of both, shall, on and after the said 1st day of January, 1893, be subject to a duty of 25 per cent. *ad valorem.*

SEC. 4.—And all imported articles enumerated, described, and provided for in said paragraphs, respectively, which may be in public store or in warehouse on the said 1st day of January, 1893, shall be subjected to the same duties when withdrawn for consumption, and no others, as if said articles had been imported on or after said 1st day of January; and only the *ad valorem* duties as herein provided shall thereafter be levied, collected, and paid upon the articles mentioned in said paragraphs.

SEC. 5.—That all acts and parts of acts in conflict with the provisions of this act be and the same are hereby repealed; but this section shall not take effect until the 1st day of January, 1893.

The bill passed the House, April 7, 1892, by the following vote:

YEAS—Abbott, Alexander, Allen, Amerman, Andrew, Arnold, Bacon, Baker, Bailey, Bankhead, Barwig, Beeman, Beltzhoover, Bentley, Blanchard, Bland, Blount, Bowman, Branch, Breckinridge of Kentucky, Bretz, Brickner, Brookshire, Brown, Brunner, Bryan, Buchanan of Virginia, Bullock, Bunting, Busey, Bushnell, Butler, Bynum, Byrns, Cable, Cadmus, Caminetti, Caruth, Castle, Catchings, Cate, Causey, Chipman, Clancy, Clarke of Alabama, Clover, Cobb of Alabama, Cobb of Missouri, Coburn, Cockran, Coolidge, Coombs, Cowles, Cox of Tennessee, Craig of Pennsylvania, Crain of Texas, Crawford, Crosby, Culberson, Cummings, Davis, De Armond, De Forest, Dickerson, Dixon, Donovan, Dungan, Dunphy, Durborow, Edmunds, Elliott, Ellis, English, Enloe, Epes, Everett, Fellows, Fitch, Fithian, Forney, Fowler,

Fyan, Gantz, Geary, Geissenhainer, Goodnight, Gorman, Grady, Greenleaf, Hall, Hallowell, Halvorson, Hamilton, Hare, Harries, Harter, Hatch, Hayes of Iowa, Haynes of Ohio, Heard, Hemphill, Henderson of North Carolina, Herbert, Hoar, Holman, Hooker of Mississippi, Houk of Ohio, Johnstone of South Carolina, Kem, Kilgore, Kribbs, Kyle, Lane, Lanham, Lawson of Virginia, Lawson of Georgia, Lester of Georgia, Lewis, Little, Livingston, Lockwood, Long, Lynch, Mallory, Martin, McAleer, McClellan, McCreary, McGann, McKaig, McKeighan, McKinney, McMillin, McRae, Meredith, Meyer, Mitchell, Montgomery, Moore, Mutchler, Newberry, Norton. O'Neil of Massachusetts. O'Neill of Missouri, Outhwaite, Page of Maryland, Parrett, Patterson of Tennessee, Patton, Paynter, Pearson, Peel, Pendleton, Price, Reilly, Richardson, Robertson of Louisiana. Rockwell, Rusk, Sayers, Scott, Seerley, Shell, Shively, Simpson, Snow, Sperry, Stevens, Steward of Illinois, Stewart of Texas, Stone of Kentucky, Stout, Stump, Tarsney, Terry, Tillman, Tracey, Tucker, Turner, Van Horn, Warner, Washington, Watson, Weadock, Wheeler of Alabama, Wheeler of Michigan, White, Wike, Williams of North Carolina, Williams of Illinois, Wilson of Missouri, Wilson of West Virginia, Wise, Youmans—194.

NAYS—Babbitt, Bartine, Belden, Belknap, Bergen, Boutelle, Bowers, Brosius, Buchanan of New Jersey, Clark of Wyoming, Curtis, Cutting, Dingley, Flick, Funston, Grout, Harmer, Haugen, Henderson of Illinois, Hermann, Hitt, Hopkins of Pennsylvania, Hopkins of Illinois, Huff, Hull, Johnson of Indiana, Johnson of North Dakota, Jolley, Ketcham, Lodge, Loud, Miller, Milliken, O'Donnell, O'Neill of Pennsylvania, Otis, Perkins, Pickler, Post, Powers, Quackenbush, Ray, Reyburn, Rife, Robinson of Pennsylvania, Scull, Shonk, Smith, Stephenson, C. W. Stone, W. A. Stone, Storer, Sweet, J. D. Taylor, Townsend, Wadsworth, Walker, Wever, Wilson of Washington, Wright—60.

NOT VOTING—Alderson, Atkinson, Bingham, Boatner, Brawley, Breckinridge of Arkansas, Broderick, Bunn, Burrows, Caldwell, Campbell, Capehart, Chapin, Cheatham, Cogswell, Compton, Cooper, Covert, Cox of New York, Dalzell, Daniell, Doan, Deckery, Dolliver, Enochs, Forman, Gillespie, Griswold, Henderson of Iowa, Hooker of New York, Henk of Tennessee, Johnson of Ohio, Jones, Lagan, Lapham, Layton, Lester of Virginia, Lind, Magner, Mansur, McDonald, Morse, Moses, Oates, O'Ferrall, Owens, Page of Rhode Island, Pattison of Ohio, Payne, Pierce, Raines, Randall, Rayner, Reed, Russell, Sanford, Snodgrass, Springer, Stackhouse, Stahlnecker, Stockdale, Taylor of Illinois, Taylor of Tennessee, E. B. Taylor, V. A. Taylor, Turpin, Warwick, Waugh, Whiting, Willcox, Williams of Massachusetts, Wilson of Kentucky, Winn, Wolverton—74.

The House passed, April 9, 1892, by a vote of 167 to 46, the following bill to admit free of duty bagging for cotton, machinery for manufacturing bagging, cotton ties, and cotton gins:

Be it enacted, etc., That the following articles shall be exempt from duty, namely: Bagging for cotton, gunny cloth, and all similar material suitable for covering cotton, composed in whole or in part of flax, jute, or jute butts; cards, roving frames, winding frames, softeners, and other machinery purchased abroad and used in the manufacture of bagging for cotton, gunny cloth, and all similar materials suitable for covering cotton; cotton gins and parts thereof, and also hoop or band iron or hoop or band steel cut to length, or wholly or partially manufactured into hoops or ties for baling purposes, with or without buckles or fastenings.

On July 8, 1892, a bill "to reduce the duty on tin plate. terne plate. and taggers tin, and to repeal paragraph 209 of section 1 of an act entitled "An Act to reduce the revenues and for other purposes," was passed by the House under suspension of the rules. It is as follows :

Be it enacted, etc., That on and after Oct. 1, 1892, all iron or steel sheets or plates or taggers iron coated with pure tin, or with tin and lead, or with any mixture of which these metals are a component part, by dipping or any other process, and commercially known as tin plate, terne plate, or taggers tin, shall pay 1 cent per pound duty.

Sec. 2.—That on and after Oct. 1, 1894, tin plate, terne plate, and taggers tin shall be admitted free of duty.

Sec. 3.—That paragraph 209 of section 1 of an act entitled "An Act to reduce the revenue, and for other purposes," approved Oct. 1, 1890, together with the proviso pertaining thereto, is hereby repealed.

Sec. 4.—That on all original and unbroken packages of tin plate, terne plate, and taggers tin held by importers, dealers, or consumers at the time section 1 of this act goes into effect shall be allowed a rebate on the same of 1·2 cent per peund ; and that on all unbroken packages of tin plate, terne plate, and taggers tin held by importers, dealers, or consumers when section 2 of this act goes into effect shall be allowed a rebate or drawback of 1 cent per pound : *Provided*, That the application for such rebate or drawback shall be made within sixty days after the taking effect of sections 1 and 2, respectively, of this act, and under such regulations and in such form as shall be prescribed by the Secretary of the Treasury, who shall adopt such regulations and furnish such forms as may be necessary for the purposes of this act.

Sec. 5.—That there shall be allowed on imported tin plate used in the manufacture of cans, boxes, packages, and all articles of tinware exported, either empty or filled with domestic products, a drawback equal to the duty paid on such tin plate, terne plate, and taggers tin, less 5 per cent. of such duty, which shall be retained for the use of the Government of the United States.

Sec. 6.—That all acts or parts of acts so far as the same are inconsistent herewith are hereby repealed.

On the same day the House passed in the same way a bill " to equalize to some extent the burdens imposed upon the people by an act entitled ' An Act to reduce the revenue and equalize duties on imports, and for other purposes,' approved Oct. 1, 1890." It was as follows :

Be it enacted, etc., That the wearing apparel and other personal effects (not merchandise) in actual use of residents of the United States returning thereto from foreign countries, not exceeding $100 in value, and not intended for the use of other persons nor for sale, shall be admitted into the ports of the United States free of duty : *Provided, however*, That all the wearing apparel and other personal effects of such persons so returning as may have been by them taken out of the United States to foreign countries, and which have not been advanced in value nor improved in condition by any process of labor or manufacture in such countries, shall be admitted free of duty without regard to their value upon their identity being established, under such rules and regulations as the Secretary of the Treasury may, and is hereby authorized to, prescribe for that purpose.

Sec. 2.—That all acts and parts of acts so far as they conflict with the provisions of this act are hereby repealed.

On the same day and in the same manner the following measure was also passed :

Be it enacted, etc., That paragraph 199, Schedule C, of the act of Oct. 1, 1890, entitled "An Act to reduce the revenue and equalize duties on imports, and for other purposes," be, and the same hereby is, amended so that the same shall read as follows :

"199. Lead ore and lead dross, 1½ cent per pound : *Provided*, That all ores carrying silver and lead at the same time, except silver ores containing lead, shall pay a duty of 1½ cent per pound on the lead contained therein according to the sample and assay at the port of entry : *And provided further*, That ores containing silver and lead, in which the value of the silver contents shall be greater than the value of the lead contents according to sample and assay at the port of entry, shall be considered silver ores, and as such shall be exempt from duty."

The House, moreover, passed a bill putting binding twine on the free list.

The tariff discussion was voluminous, and many speeches valuable on account of the statistics contained in them were delivered ; but in the main the debate was on old lines.

Free Coinage.—The most important subject discussed by the Congress was free coinage. It was important not only on account of its direct relation to the finances of the country, but on account of the uncertain attitude of politicians and parties. Early in the session, Mr. Stewart, of Nevada, introduced in the Senate a bill for "the free coinage of gold and silver bullion, and for other purposes." On Jan. 6, 1892, Senator Morrill, of Vermont, made a speech in opposition to the policy which the bill embodied. In summing up his own argument he said :

"I have attempted to demonstrate : First. That the depreciation of silver is both so great and universal that unlimited coinage could not be maintained on the present standard with gold, but would suddenly wreck the country by a silver revolution.

"Second. That unlimited coinage would interdict all international silver compacts.

"Third. That there is no scarcity of money in circulation, but instead the amount is twice as great as it was in 1878, and is increasing on a canter.

"Fourth. That a silver standard would be equivalent to a horizontal reduction of the tariff of 25 per cent., if not more, and an equal reduction of all pensions.

"Fifth. That the enormous increase of silver to the extent of four times the product of 1854, coincident with a greatly lessened demand for it, has so depreciated its value that unlimited coinage by the United States must prove a disastrous national blunder.

"Sixth. That there is no magic in any law of Congress which can make the world accept an ounce of silver as worth any more in coin than in bullion.

"Seventh. That the parties to first profit by free coinage would be the corporate owners of silver mines, and the parties to finally suffer the largest losses by it would be the great mass of our people, into whose hands the depreciated coin and Treasury notes would finally pass.

"The public credit of our great republic is at stake. Shall we have the best money standard of the foremost nations of mankind, or shall we descend to the flickering and narrow gauge of silver only for the conduct of a greater home and foreign trade than that of any other people, ancient or modern ? We have paid off more than three fourths of our great war debt in gold when our resources were far less than now, and I am unwilling to forfeit our well-earned reputation and lose public confidence and all the ancestral prestige of our history by paying the sorry remnant of this debt in a legal tender of much less value."

On the same day Mr. Teller, of Colorado, put the case against an exclusive use of gold as money:

"While I am on my feet, I should like to call the attention of those who are to debate this question to the real issue. I have never met a gold man who would discuss the issue. The issue is, Have we gold enough for use as money; and, if we have not, what are we going to do about it?

"There are two kinds of circulating medium: one is credit money, and the other is money requiring no redemption. Eighteen years ago, according to the estimates of statisticians, there was in the world about $7,500,000,000 of gold and silver coin, which, in the language of the royal commission, was one money. Upon it rested the credit of the circulation of the world. To-day, according to the estimates of the Director of the Mint, there is less than $3,750,000,000 of that kind of money.

"The Senator from Vermont and all gold men say that silver must be discarded as real money; that it shall be used only as subsidiary coin; that it shall depend upon redemption in gold to give it circulating power. It is credit money. Now, the reduction of the world's money one half—that is, the reduction of the money of the world by one half in eighteen years—has brought calamity everywhere, has reduced prices everywhere, and it is not going to stop. There has been no material increase in the gold coin of the world since silver was demonetized. It is all absorbed for nonmonetary purposes.

"It is used much more largely than formerly for ornaments; it is used in dentistry; it is used in photography; it is used in ornamentation; it is hoarded in Asia, whence it never comes, because their exports exceed their imports; and the fact is that our stock of gold here is not increasing, but must diminish in the future, and the Secretary of the Treasury and others say there is not gold enough in use as money. Now, how will you increase it? You can not increase it with paper, because that has to be redeemed; you can not increase it with silver, for that has to be redeemed also, if your standard is based upon this narrow foundation of gold alone. I have not heard a gold man who would meet the question and say how he was going to supplement the gold of the world, how he was to increase it; he simply makes war on silver, talks against that, but proposes no remedy.

"There must be a remedy for this shrinking basis of circulation. The distinction between the circulation and the basis of circulation is wide. You can have circulation: you can have credit. I suppose that on the $3,727,000,000 of money used for reserve is based a credit and credit circulation of from $125,000,000,000 to $150,000,000,000. There is not of real money 3 per cent. of the credit in the world. The failure of the Barings has disclosed the fact that the world is bankrupt on a gold basis. The proposition now is to accumulate gold. Austria is going to try it and bankrupt herself. We will try it, and we shall be bankrupt.

"It is said that we will hoard gold here. What will that do for your cotton planter? If you take the gold away from Europe, where your market is, by selling bonds here and paying large interest and accumulating it, gold will become scarcer here, and they can not buy your products, and cotton will be cheaper and cheaper, and all your products will be cheaper. What we want is a proper basis, and there is no way to have it except to recognize silver as real money.

"Why are 25.8 grains of standard gold always worth $1? Because it can be exchanged at the mint for $1. Why were 412½ grains of standard silver always worth a dollar during the whole history of the country and for all time previous to 1873? Because it could be exchanged at the mint for $1. The only way to put silver on a parity with gold is to give it the same privileges. If it is treated as a commodity, it will be speculated in as a commodity and can not be a measure of value.

"I want some gold advocate to show that there is gold enough. I believe they have all admitted that there is not. Then I want to have him show out of what material we can make any real money—money that does not have to be redeemed, money that is not a promise to pay—without the use of silver as money. There is no relief from this but in the use of silver. No one has suggested it. The buying of silver and treating it as a commodity does not do it. There can be no increase in the volume of money, but it must shrink continually without the free coinage of silver; for if that metal is not to be used, and you adhere to gold, there is no prospect in the world but continued contraction. I make the statement that there is not a farm in England or in the United States where it has not been affected by immigration that will sell for 50 cents on the dollar for what it would have brought eighteen years ago, and that corresponds precisely with the shrinkage of the volume.

"There is only half as much real money of ultimate redemption as there was eighteen years ago. You circulate paper and you circulate silver; but when you come to your reserves, in which all credits must be ultimately paid, you have only half as much as you had eighteen years ago, and that is the trouble. How are you going to increase those reserves? One nation may make sacrifices, and buy gold and impoverish its people; another nation will do the same; but the people suffer.

"Since the failure of the Barings it has been the business of every great financial institution to increase its reserves at all hazards and reduce its credits; and that is why the national and state bonds of the world have shrunk $800,000,-000. It is because the moneyed institutions must have gold at all hazards; they must sacrifice everything: they must sacrifice their securities and have gold or go into bankruptcy; and thousands of them must fail, for there is no gold to give them all reserves; and business must shrink under the withering grasp of contraction, which is inevitable.

"No gold man has ever suggested a remedy. No gold man has ever suggested how we can enlarge the basis of credit, the basis of circulation. In private conversation every one admits that we are on the downward grade toward bankruptcy; that prices are shrinking every-where and enterprises are being crushed and de-stroyed. Bonds that are out are now down. We thought the bonds would be paid, but now States and nations are afraid of bankruptcy. They see that it is impossible for them to de-liver.

"Suppose the United States with all its pow-er should undertake to deliver a thousand buffa-loes; could it do it? You talk about its credit; but could it do it? No, because they do not ex-ist. And if the United States should undertake to deliver more gold than it can get or than ex-ists, more than it can obtain, then its credit is good for nothing, an utter impossibility is un-dertaken. It is impossible to find gold enough to sustain all the financial institutions that now exist, to maintain the vast fabric of credit that has been built up on this narrow foundation. There is not enough gold. The supply must be increased or bankruptcy must follow."

Discussion of the topic was renewed on May 26. Mr. Morgan, of Alabama, maintained that it was the subject nearest to the popular heart.

"This is not a temporary or an ephemeral agitation or inquiry. It has been going on since 1873 or about 1875, when the people and the President of the United States and the members of the two Houses of Congress first discovered the fatal blow which had been struck in secret against the free coinage of the silver dollar, the blow of absolute destruction to the life of silver coinage, and every year that resolution has gained strength. There is no question to-day before the people of the United States which comes as near to their hearts and as near to their pockets as the question of the free coinage of silver.

"We are informed by strategists in politics that the reformation of the tariff is the great question which is agitating the country. The House of Representatives, with a strong Demo-cratic majority committed to the reformation of the tariff, have sent to us already bill after bill for that purpose, and these bills have gone into the quiet retreat of the Committee on Finance, and the country has not bothered itself to know what they are doing with the bills, whether they are investigating their merits, whether they are being discussed in committee, or whether any report is to be made after all. The country is not agitated about that. ·I think the country ought to be; I think the country ought to hold the Finance Committee of the Senate up to the most rigid accountability if they fail to act upon these bills and present them here for considera-tion; and yet I know—every Senator here knows, and all discern—that the people of the United States are not greatly agitated about that matter.

"I am speaking of those questions which come nearest to the hearts of the people of this land. I am speaking, when I refer to the finances, of those questions which they feel to be most directly impressive upon their personal interests and welfare. I am now gauging public sentiment in the remarks I am making, and I am trying to ascertain and to convince the Sen-ate of what it knows, just as well as I do, that the great question in the minds of the people of this country at this time is the question of finance, money, some relief from their miserable condi-tion, some means of providing that the agricul-tural and other industries of this country shall have a reasonable enjoyment of the fruits of their labors—labors which have produced in every department of industry excessive abun-dance during the last twelve or fourteen months.

"With a very large crop of cotton on hand, being a second large crop; with a very large crop of wheat on hand, quite an exaggerated crop I might call it; a still larger crop of corn, and, as a consequence, a large production of provisions, far in excess of the demands of the people of the United States, the condition of our people in the agricultural regions and in the mining and other industrial regions, the forests, and elsewhere, is absolutely deplorable. No people in the United States to-day have the slightest prosperity except those who have the grasp upon the money power of this country and can contract it. or expand it to suit their ends. They are the only men in this country who are prosperous and who are satisfied with existing conditions."

On May 30 and May 31 Mr. Sherman, of Ohio, spoke against the policy of free coinage of silver. Touching the general issue, he said:

"I do not regard the bill for the free coinage of silver as a party measure or a political meas-ure upon which parties are likely to divide. It is in many respects a local measure, not exactly in the sense in which Gen. Hancock said in re-gard to the tariff that that was a local question. but it is largely a local question; yet at the same time it is a question of vast importance. No question before the Senate of the United States at this session is at all to be com-pared with it in the importance of its effects upon the business interests of the country. It affects every man, woman, and child in our broad land, the rich with his investments, the poor with his labor. Everybody is deeply inter-ested in the standard of value by which we measure all the productions of the labor and all the wealth of mankind.

"Five States largely interested in the produc-tion of silver are very ably and zealously repre-sented on this floor. They are united by their delegations, all Senators, in favor of the free coinage of silver. The South seems also to have caught something of the spirit which actuates the mining States, because they desire not ex-actly the free coinage of silver, but they desire an expansion of the currency, cheaper money, and broader credit, and they are also largely represented on this floor in support of the propo-sition in favor of the free coinage of silver. So in other parts of the country, those who have been taught to believe that great good can come to our country by an unlimited expansion of paper credit, with money more abundant than it is now, also believe in the free coinage of silver.

"I, representing a State nearly central in population, have tested the sense of the people of Ohio, and they, I believe, are by a great ma-jority not only of the party to which I belong but of the Democratic party, opposed to the free coinage of silver. They believe that that will degrade the money of our country, reduce its purchasing power fully one third, destroy the bimetallic system which we have maintained for a long period of time, and reduce us to a single monometallic standard of silver measured by the value of 371¼ grains to the dollar."

He reviewed briefly the financial history of the country, and, among other things, in explanation of the law of 1873 demonetizing silver, he said:

"Mr. President, when that law of 1873 was passed the only trouble about it was that we were not as wise as the Almighty Ruler of the universe. We could not see ahead. I have no doubt, however, that if it had been known that silver was going to fall as much as it did after that, it might have made a change. But I know myself—and I speak for myself only—that while I did not know it, did not dream of the fall in the price of silver following that law, yet I do now say, in the light of all the circumstances that surrounded us, that if I had known it I would have kept the silver dollar there and put it on the same footing as the fractional silver dollar and no better.

"Now, Mr. President, let us go a little further. A rapid change occurred in the coinage of Germany from a silver basis to a gold basis. The change in Germany necessarily suspended the coinage under the agreement of the Latin Union, which was an agreement by which each nation entering into it provided for the issue of so much silver coin of a certain character, agreeing among themselves that the balances that should be due to any nation or to the people of any nation at the end of the term should be paid in gold coin. Just about that time also the discovery of silver in the West, and other discoveries in Australia and elsewhere, together with the increased production of silver—and I will hereafter furnish a table giving the exact figures—combined with other causes, led to the gradual fall of silver.

"It was said, therefore, that we who had the law passed were unfriendly to silver. Let me answer, and state the exact facts as a denial of that.

"Why, sir, under the resumption act—and I suppose I may fairly be held responsible for that —under the resumption act we bought more of silver and issued more silver coin, fourfold, than we issued of the old silver dollars. Under the Allison act, as it was called, of 1878, together with the act of 1890, there were issued 388,000,-000 silver dollars, forty-five times as much as was issued of the old silver dollars; and of the trade dollars, which superseded the old silver dollars, we issued 36,000,000, being more than four times the amount of all the 'dollars of the daddies' that were coined prior to 1873."

In explanation of recent measures for limited silver coinage, Mr. Sherman said:

"All our money is at par with gold. How is that maintained? We have a careful series of guards and laws which practically make now in the United States gold the standard of value, not the legal standard in the sense that the Senator speaks of as the ratio, because whenever that ratio diverges from the market value the ratio ought to be changed always. It has been so for two thousand years. How, then, is this money that we now have all good in every part of the United States of America and in all the countries of the world? You may take any

form of our paper money and travel in Europe, and it is eagerly taken and sometimes chosen in preference to their own money.

"How is our silver maintained at par with gold? By carefully limiting the amount purchased and buying it at its market value. In the Allison bill it was limited to $4,000,000, with an option on the part of the Secretary of the Treasury only to buy $2,000,000. That was the limitation, $2,000,000 a month. That limitation prevented any undue thrusting of idle silver on the market. Then, by the law of 1890, which the Senator from Nevada and I are responsible for, we did the same. We carefully limited the amount. We take in respect to that money additional precautions, because we buy the silver at its market value, at 86 to 98 cents an ounce instead of $1.29. We put the whole of that bullion in our Treasury, and we only issue paper money for the actual cost of the bullion and not for legal ratio. So, behind all the money which is issued under the law of 1890, there was at the time it was purchased silver enough at its market value to be equal to gold, and that is maintained all the way through.

"Then there are other provisions in the law of 1890 which give additional guarantees. We there expressly declare that it is the public policy of the United States to maintain the parity of these two metals, and we know they can only be maintained at this parity by the redemption of one with the other. You can maintain the lower up to the standard of the higher by making it equal to that of the higher and treating it so. So, behind all this money we have not only the promise of the United States, the declared policy of the United States, but we have enough silver behind all this money to be equal to its cost at the time—even the silver that was bought under the law of 1878, a portion of which we called profit. That is a piece of folly; it is no profit at all.

"If it had been seigniorage levied upon the people, it would have been the most outrageous seigniorage ever inflicted upon a people by any government in the world; but it was not in the nature of seigniorage, but bought at its market value, and we issued money for it at its coinage value. We have behind it all the silver we bought, and we have that very surplus of silver called the profit fund in our Treasury now, which amounts to $75,000,000. We have treated it as an ordinary income, but that is not the proper way it should be treated. If the time shall come when it will be necessary, the people of the United States can without loss restore this large sum of $75,000,000 for the redemption of the silver coin or for the maintenance of it at the standard of gold.

"We maintain our United States notes at par by our ample reserve in gold and silver of $100,-000,000 of gold and the surplus in the Treasury. We maintain our gold certificates and we have behind them dollar for dollar in gold. Our silver certificates have behind them a coin dollar, what is miscalled the profit fund, and our declared policy to maintain the parity of the two metals. Our bank notes are secured by United States bonds; our fractional minor coin are received and redeemed whenever presented. But few silver dollars will circulate, but they are represented by certificates supported by bullion bought at the market price. There is the difference. That is bimetallism, the two metals maintained at parity by the power of the Government and by the credit of the Government even at a ratio far from the market value, and that is the theory and the basis of our whole system of coinage.

"But this scheme is quite' different. Here the holder of bullion has the option. He brings his bullion and demands either coin or notes, whichever he thinks he can use to the best advantage. He can present those notes the next day and demand gold. and it involves at once the question of the surrender of the bimetallic system. If we refuse to pay in gold we acknowledge that these notes are worth less than gold, and they will soon be worth only the value of the silver in the dollar. There is the difference.

"I contend for the present system. They think I am opposed to silver. I am no more opposed to silver than any other commodity. Why should we pay more for silver than the market price? We buy everything else in the open market. We are trying to prevent our servants from paying more than the market value; we make close contracts for every kind of services which are demanded. But they tell us that silver is something sacred, that silver is a money metal. Well. it is not a money metal which the people want to handle much, except for mere change. But even if it was a money metal. is that any reason why it should be favored? It must be tested as we test diamonds, silks, satins, muslins, everything we buy; we must test it by its market value; and if that market value of silver is only two thirds of its coinage value in gold, how can the parity be maintained?"

When questioned as to the possibility of maintaining the parity of gold, silver, and paper money under the existing statute, should the price of silver continue low and the mass of it in the Treasury continue to accumulate, Mr. Sherman said of the law now in force, which he thinks misnamed as the Sherman act:

"I can say myself that there are possibilities in the future in respect to that law which would make me as anxious to repeal it as I was reluctant to vote for it. The provision pointed out by the Senator from New Jersey has been constantly in my mind, that we made no provision in that law for the sale of the silver bullion in case it became necessary; that we have gone partly on trust that the law would operate as we hoped it would, to prevent the further decline of silver; but if that decline should go on, and we are called upon year by year to buy 54,000,000 ounces of silver at a depreciating price, I should feel bound, in consideration of my duty to my constituents, to arrest the purchase, if I could, by my vote."

The measure was debated at great length in the Senate, and on July 1 the following substitute was adopted and passed that body:

Be it enacted, etc., That the c wner of silver bullion may deposit the same at any mint of the United States to be coined for his benefit, and it shall be the duty of the proper officers, upon the terms and conditions which are provided by law for the deposit and coinage of gold, to coin such silver bullion into the

standard dollars authorized by the act of Feb. 28, 1878, entitled "An Act to authorize the coinage of the standard silver dollar and to restore its legal-tender character," and such coins shall be a legal tender for all debts and dues, public and private. The act of July 14, 1890, entitled "An Act directing the purchase of silver bullion and the issue of Treasury notes thereon, and for other purposes," is hereby repealed. *Provided,* That the Secretary of the Treasury shall proceed to have coined all the silver bullion in the Treasury purchased with silver or coin certificates.

The final vote on the passage of the bill was as follows :

YEAS—Allen, Bate, Berry, Blackburn, Blodgett. Butler, Cameron, Cockrell, Dubois, Faulkner, George, Harris, Hill, Jones of Nevada, Kenna, Kyle, Mills, Mitchell, Morgan, Peffer, Ransom, Sanders, Shoup, Squire, Stewart, Teller, Turpie, Vest, Wolcott—29.

NAYS—Allison, Brice, Carey, Carlisle, Cullom, Davis, Dawes, Dixon, Dolph, Felton, Gallinger, Gorman, Gray, Hale, Hawley, McPherson, Manderson, Palmer, Perkins, Proctor, Sawyer, Stockbridge, Warren, Washburn, White—25.

NOT VOTING—Aldrich, Call, Casey, Chandler, Coke, Colquitt, Daniel, Frye, Gibson of Louisiana, Gibson of Maryland, Gordon, Hansbrough, Higgins, Hiscock, Hoar, Hunton, Irby, Jones of Arkansas, McMillan, Morrill, Paddock, Pasco, Pettigrew, Platt, Power, Pugh, Quay, Sherman, Stanford, Vance, Vilas, Voorhees, Walthall, Wilson—34.

In the House, action on the silver question was difficult, not only because of a difference among Democrats as to the best policy, but because of the possible effect of the course of the Democratic majority on the choice of a presidential candidate. But on Feb. 10, 1892, the Committee on Coinage, Weights, and Measures determined to introduce a bill for the free coinage of gold and silver; and on March 7 the Committee on Rules made a report setting apart March 22, 23, and 24 for debate on that measure. The report was adopted, after a sharp contest, by the following vote:

YEAS—Abbott, Alderson, Alexander, Allen, Arnold, Babbitt, Bailey, Baker, Bankhead, Bartine. Beeman, Belden, Belknap, Bergen, Blanchard, Bland, Blount, Boatner, Boutelle, Bowers, Bowman, Branch, Bretz, Broderick, Brookshire. Bryan, Bullock, Burrows, Busey, Butler, Bynum, Byrns, Caminetti, Capehart, Caruth, Catchings, Cate, Clark of Wyoming, Clarke of Alabama, Clover, Cobb, Cobb of Alabama, Cogswell, Cooper, Cowles, Cox of Tennessee, Crain of Texas, Crawford, Culberson. Cutting, Dalzell, Davis, De Armond, Dixon, Doan, Dockery, Dolliver, Dungan. Edmunds, Ellis, Enloe, Enochs, Epes, Everett, Fithian, Flick, Forman, Forney, Fowler, Fyan, Gantz, Geary, Goodnight, Gorman, Grady, Griswold, Halvorsen, Hamilton, Hare, Harries, Hatch, Haugen, Haynes of Ohio, Heard, Hemphill, Henderson of Iowa, Henderson of North Carolina, Hermann, Hitt, Hooker of Mississippi, Hooker of New York, Hopkins of Illinois, Huff, Hull, Hooker of Indiana, Johnson of North Dakota. Johnstone of South Carolina, Jolley, Jones, Kem, Kilgore, Kyle, Lanham, Lawson of Virginia, Lawson of Georgia, Layton, Lester of Georgia, Lewis. Lind, Livingston, Long, Loud, Mallory, Mansur, Martin, McClellan, McCreary, McKeighan, McMillin, McRae, Meredith, Milliken, Montgomery, Moore, Moses, Norton, Oates, O'Donnell, O'Ferrall, O'Neill of Missouri, Otis, Owens, Parrett, Patterson of Tennessee, Patton, Paynter, Pendleton, Perkins, Pickler, Pierce, Post, Price. Raines, Randall, Richardson, Rife, Robertson of Louisiana, Sayers, Scott, Seerley, Shively, Simpson, Smith, Snodgrass, Snow, Stackhouse, Stephenson, Steward of Illinois, Stewart of Texas, Stockdale, W. A. Stone, Stone of Kentucky, Sweet, Tarsney, E. B. Taylor, J. D. Taylor, V. A.

Taylor, Terry, Tillman, Townsend. Tucker, Turner, Walker, Warwick, Washington, Watson, Waugh, Weadock, Wheeler of Alabama, White, Whiting, Wike, Williams of North Carolina, Williams of Illinois, Wilson of Washington, Wilson of Missouri, Wilson of West Virginia, Winn, Wise, Wright, Youmans —190.

NAYS—Amerman, Andrew, Barwig, Beltzhoover, Bentley, Brickner, Buchanan of New Jersey, Buntin , Bushnell, Cable, Campbell, Castle, Causey, Chapin, Chipman, Clancy, Cobb of Missouri, Coburn, Cockran, Coolidge, Coombs, Covert, Cox of New York, Crosby, Curtis, Daniell, De Forest, Dunphy, Durborow, Elliott, English, Fitch, Funston, Geissenhainer, Greenleaf, Grout, Hall, Hallowell, Harmer, Harter, Hayes of Iowa, Herbert, Hoar, Hopkins of Pennsylvania, Henk of Ohio, Johnson of Ohio, Ketcham, Kribbs, Lapham, Little, Lockwood, Lynch, McAleer, McDonald, McKinney, Miller, Mitchell, Newberry, O'Neil of Massachusetts, O'Neill of Pennsylvania, Outhwaite, Page of Rhode Island, Page of Maryland, Payne, Pearson, Powers, Ray, Rayner, Reyburn, Rusk, Sperry, Stahlnecker, Stevens, C. W. Stone, Storer, Stump, Taylor of Illinois, Taylor of Tennessee, Tracey, Van Horn, Wadsworth, Warner, Wheeler of Michigan, Williams of Massachusetts, Wilson of Kentucky—85.

NOT VOTING—Atkinson, Bacon, Bingham, Brawley, Breckinridge of Arkansas, Breckinridge of Kentucky, Brosius, Brown, Brunner, Buchanan of Virginia, Bunn, Cadmus, Caldwell, Cheatham, Compton, Craig of Pennsylvania, Cummings, Dickerson, Dingley, Donovan, Fellows, Gillespie, Henderson of Illinois, Holman, Houk of Tennessee, Kendall, Lagan, Lane, Lester of Virginia, Lodge, Magner, McGann, McKaig, McKenna, Meyer, Mills, Morse, Mutchler, Pattison of Ohio, Peel, Quackenbush, Reed, Reilly, Robinson of Pennsylvania, Rockwell, Russell, Sanford, Scull, Shell, Shonk, Springer, Stout, Turpin, Wever, Willcox, Wolverton—56.

The bill was brought up on March 22 for discussion. It was reported as follows:

Be it enacted, etc., That the unit of value in the United States shall be the standard silver dollar as now coined, consisting of 412½ grains standard silver, or the gold dollar of 25·8 grains standard gold ; that the standard gold and silver coins of the United States shall be a legal tender in p   of all debts, public and private. Any holder of gold or silver bullion of the value of $100 or more, of standard fineness, shall be entitled to have the same struck into any authorized standard coins of the United States free of charge at the mints of the United States, or the owner of the bullion may deposit the same at such mints and receive therefor coin notes equal in amount to the coinage value of the bullion deposited, and the bullion thereupon shall become the property of the Government. That the coin notes so issued shall be in denominations not less than $1 nor more than $500, and shall be legal tender in like manner and invested with the same monetary uses as the standard gold and silver coins of the United States.

SEC. 2. That after the passage of this act it shall not be lawful to issue or reissue gold or silver certificates or Treasury notes provided for in the act of July 14, 1890, entitled " An Act directing the purchase of silver bullion and the issue of Treasury notes thereon, and for other purposes." That all such certificates and Treasury notes when received in the Treasury shall be canceled and destroyed, and coin notes provided for in the first section of this act shall be issued in lieu of the certificates and Treasury notes so canceled and destroyed. *Provided,* That nothing herein shall be construed to change, modify, or alter the legal-tender character of such certificates or notes now issued.

SEC. 3. That the coin notes herein authorized may be reissued, but the amount at any time outstanding shall not be greater or less than the value of the coin and the bullion at coining value held in the Treasury.

That the said coin notes shall be redeemed in coin on demand at the Treasury or any subtreasury of the United States ; and the bullion deposited shall be coined as fast as may be necessary for such redemption.

SEC. 4. That any holder of full legal-tender gold or silver coins of the United States to the amount of $10 or more may deposit the same at the Treasury or any subtreasury of the United States and receive therefor coin notes herein authorized.

SEC. 5. That the act of July 14, 1890, hereinbefore cited, be, and the same is hereby, repealed.

SEC. 6. That so soon as France shall reopen her mints to the free and unrestricted coinage of silver at her present ratio, namely, 15½ pounds of silver to be worth one pound of gold, troy, it shall be the duty of the President of the United States to immediately make public proclamation of that fact, whereupon the said ratio shall be the legal ratio in the United States, and thereafter the standard silver dollar shall consist of 400 grains of standard silver, and the laws relating to the standard silver dollars of 412½ grains standard silver shall be applicable to the new dollar of 400 grains standard silver. That the silver dollars of 412½ grains then in the Treasury or thereafter coming into the Treasury shall immediately and as fast as practicable be coined into dollars of 400 grains standard silver. Any gain or seigniorage arising therefrom shall be accounted for and paid into the Treasury.

SEC. 7. That the Secretary of the Treasury is hereby authorized and required to make such rules and regulations as may be necessary to carry into effect the provisions of this act.

There was an interesting discussion of the measure during the three days set apart for its consideration. On March 24 came the test of its strength, when Mr. Burrows, of Michigan, moved to lay the bill on the table. That motion was lost, the vote of the Speaker making a tie. The yeas and nays were as follows:

YEAS—Amerman, Andrew, Atkinson, Bacon, Barwig, Belden, Belknap, Beltzhoover, Bentley, Bergen, Bingham, Boutelle, Bowman, Brawley, Brickner, Brosius, Brunner, Buchanan of New Jersey, Bunting, Burrows, Bushnell, Cable, Cadmus, Caldwell, Castle, Causey, Chapin, Chipman, Clancy, Cobb of Missouri, Coburn, Cockran, Cogswell, Coolidge, Coombs, Covert, Cox of New York, Craig of Pennsylvania, Crosby, Cummings, Curtis, Cutting, Dalzell, Daniell, De Forest, Dingley, Doan, Dolliver, Dunphy, English, Fellows, Fitch, Flick, Geary, Geissenhainer, Gillespie, Greenleaf, Griswold, Grout, Hall, Hallowell, Hamilton, Harmer, Harter, Haugen, Hayes of Iowa, Haynes of Ohio, Henderson of Iowa, Hitt, Hoar, Hooker of New York, Hopkins of Pennsylvania, Hopkins of Illinois, Houk of Tennessee, Huff, Hull, Johnson of Indiana, Johnson of North Dakota, Ketcham, Kribbs, Lagan, Lapham, Lind, Little, Lockwood, Lodge, Loud, Lynch, Magner, McAleer, McDonald, McGann, McKaig, McKenna, McKinney, Meyer, Miller, Milliken, Mitchell, Mutchler, Newberry, O'Donnell, O'Neil of Massachusetts, O'Neill of Pennsylvania, Outhwaite, Page of Rhode Island, Page of Maryland, Pattison of Ohio, Payne, Perkins, Post, Powers, Quackenbush, Raines, Randall, Ray, Rayner, Reed, Reyburn, Rife, Robinson of Pennsylvania, Russell, Scull, Seerley, Shonk, Smith, Sperry, Stephenson, Stevens, C. W. Stone, Storer, Stout, Stump, Taylor of Illinois, J. D. Taylor, Tracey, Walker, Warner, Waugh, Wever, Wheeler of Michigan, Willcox, Williams of Massachusetts, Wilson of Kentucky, Wilson of Washington, Wilson of West Virginia, Wolverton, Wright—148.

NAYS—Abbott, Alderson, Alexander, Allen, Arnold, Babbitt, Bailey, Baker, Bankhead, Bartine, Beeman, Blanchard, Bland, Blount, Bowers, Branch, Breckinridge of Arkansas, Breckinridge of Kentucky, Bretz, Broderick, Brookshire, Bryan, Buchanan of Virginia, Bullock, Bunn, Busey, Butler, Bynum, Byrns, Caminetti, Capehart, Caruth, Cate, Clark of Wyoming, Clarke of Alabama, Cobb of Alabama, Cowles, Cox of Tennessee, Crain of Texas, Crawford, Culberson, Davis, De Armond, Dickerson, Dixon, Dockery, Dungan, Edmunds, Ellis, Epes, Everett, Fithian, Forney, Fowler, Funston, Fyan, Gantz, Goodnight, Gorman, Grady, Halvorsen, Hare, Harries, Hatch, Heard, Hemphill, Henderson of North Carolina, Hermann, Holman, Houk of Ohio, Johnson of Ohio, Jolley, Kem, Kilgore, Kyle, Lane, Lanham, Lawson of Georgia, Lawson of Virginia, Layton, Lester of Georgia, Lewis, Livingston, Long, Mallory, Mansur, Martin, McClellan, McCreary, McKeighan, McMillin, McRae, Meredith, Mills, Montgomery, Moore, Moses, Norton, O'Ferrall, O'Neill of Missouri, Otis, Owens, Parrett, Patterson of Tennessee, Patton, Paynter, Pearson, Pendleton, Pickler, Pierce, Price, Reilly, Richardson, Robertson of Louisiana, Rockwell, Sayers, Scott, Shively, Simpson, Snodgrass, Snow, Stackhouse, Steward of Illinois, Stewart of Texas, Stockdale, Stone of Kentucky, Sweet, V. A. Taylor, Terry, Tillman, Townsend, Tucker Turner, Turpin, Warwick, Washington, Watson, Weadock, Wheeler of Alabama, White, Whiting, Williams of North Carolina, Williams of Illinois, Wilson of Missouri, Winn, Wise, Youmans, the Speaker—148.

Not Voting—Boatner, Brown, Campbell, Catchings, Cheatham, Clover, Compton, Cooper, Donovan, Durborow, Elliott, Enloe, Enochs, Forman, Henderson of Illinois, Herbert, Hooker of Mississippi, Johnstone of South Carolina, Jones, Lester of Virginia, Morse, Oates, Peel, Rusk, Sanford, Shell, Springer, Stahlnecker, W. A. Stone, Tarsney, Taylor of Tennessee, E. B. Taylor, Van Horn, Wadsworth, Wike —35.

Much fruitless skirmishing over the measure followed, and it was not until after midnight that the House adjourned, without having taken any final action. The above list shows that 67 Republicans and 81 Democrats voted against the bill, and 11 Republicans, 130 Democrats, and 7 members of the Farmers' Alliance voted in favor of it. The subject could not be brought up for consideration again, except through a report from the Committee on Rules, setting apart a day for its disposal; and that course of procedure was not adopted by the Committee on Rules until July 13, when Mr. Catchings, of Mississippi, introduced a resolution from that body providing for immediate consideration of the free-coinage measure passed by the Senate, and continuing its discussion until finally disposed of. The resolution was defeated by the following vote:

Yeas—Abbott, Alexander, Arnold, Babbitt, Bailey, Baker, Bankhead, Bartine, Beeman, Blanchard, Bland, Blount, Bowers, Bowman, Branch, Bretz, Brookshire, Brown, Bryan, Buchanan of Virginia, Bullock, Bunn, Butler, Byrns, Caminetti, Capehart, Catchings, Cate, Cheatham, Clark of Wyoming, Clover, Cobb of Alabama, Cox of Tennessee, Crain of Texas, Crawford, Crisp, Culberson, Davis, De Armond, Dixon, Dockery, Donovan, Dungan, Edmunds, Ellis, Enloe, Epes, Everett, Fithian, Forney, Fyan, Gantz, Goodnight, Gorman, Grady, Halvorsen, Hare, Harries, Hatch, Heard, Hemphill, Henderson of North Carolina, Holman, Hooker of Mississippi, Johnson of Indiana, Johnstone of South Carolina, Jolley, Jones, Kem, Kendall, Kilgore, Kyle, Lane, Lanham, Lawson of Virginia, Lawson of Georgia, Layton, Lester of Virginia, Lester of Georgia, Lewis, Livingston, Long, Mallory, Mansur, Martin, McCreary, McKeighan, McMillin, McRae, Montgomery, Moore, Moses, O'Ferrall, O'Neill of Missouri, Otis, Owens, Parrett, Patton, Paynter, Pearson, Pendleton, Pierce, Post, Price, Robertson of Louisiana,

Sayers, Seerley, Shell, Shively, Simpson, Snodgrass, Stewart of Texas, Stone of Kentucky, Sweet, Tarsney, Terry, Tillman, Townsend, Tucker, Turner, Turpin, Warwick, Washington, Watson, Weadock, Wheeler of Alabama, White, Whiting, Williams of North Carolina, Williams of Illinois, Wilson of Missouri, Winn, Wise, Youmans—136.

Nays—Amerman, Andrew, Atkinson, Barwig, Belden, Beltzhoover, Bentley, Bergen, Bingham, Brawley, Breckinridge of Arkansas, Breckinridge of Kentucky, Brickner, Brosius, Brunner, Buchanan of New Jersey, Bunting, Burrows, Busey, Bushnell, Cable, Cadmus, Caldwell, Campbell, Caruth, Castle, Causey, Chapin, Chipman, Clancy, Clarke of Alabama, Cobb of Missouri, Coburn, Cockran, Cogswell, Compton, Coolidge, Coombs, Covert, Cox of New York, Crosby, Cummings, Curtis, Cutting, Dalzell, Daniell, De Forest, Dickerson, Dingley, Doan, Dolliver, Dunphy, Durborow, English, Enochs, Fellows, Fitch, Flick, Forman, Fowler, Funston, Geissenhainer, Gillespie, Greenleaf, Grout, Hall, Hallowell, Hamilton, Harmer, Harter, Hayes of Iowa, Haynes of Ohio, Henderson of Iowa, Henderson of Illinois, Herbert, Hitt, Hoar, Hooker of New York, Hopkins of Illinois, Houk of Ohio, Houk of Tennessee, Huff, Hull, Johnson of North Dakota, Ketcham, Kribbs, Lagan, Lapham, Little, Lockwood, Lodge, Loud, Lynch, McAleer, McClellan, McDonald, McGann, McKinney, Meyer, Miller, Mitchell, Mutchler, O'Neil of Massachusetts, O'Neill of Pennsylvania, Outhwaite, Page of Rhode Island, Page of Maryland, Patterson of Tennessee, Payne, Perkins, Powers, Quackenbush, Raines, Randall, Ray, Rayner, Reed, Reilly, Reyburn, Rife, Robinson of Pennsylvania, Rusk, Russell, Scott, Scull, Shonk, Smith, Snow, Sperry, Stephenson, Stevens, Steward of Illinois, C. W. Stone. W. A. Stone, Storer, Stout, Stump, Taylor of Illinois, Taylor of Tennessee, J. D. Taylor, Tracey, Van Horn, Wadsworth, Walker, Warner, Waugh, Wheeler of Michigan, Wike, Willcox, Williams of Massachusetts, Wilson of Washington, Wilson of West Virginia, Wolverton, Wright—154.

Not Voting—Alderson, Allen, Bacon, Belknap, Boatner, Boutelle, Broderick, Bynum, Craig of Pennsylvania, Elliott, Geary, Griswold, Haugen, Hermann, Hopkins of Pennsylvania, Johnson of Ohio, Lind, Magner, McKaig, Meredith, Milliken, Morse, Newberry, Norton, Oates, O'Donnell, Pattison of Ohio, Peel, Pickler, Richardson, Rockwell, Sanford, Springer, Stahlnecker, Stockdale, E. B. Taylor, V. A. Taylor, Wever, Wilson of Kentucky—39.

And so the free-coinage question was set aside for the session.

The Pinkertons.—One of the liveliest discussions of the session arose out of the Homestead riot. The House had passed, May 12, 1892, the following resolution in regard to the Pinkerton detectives:

Whereas, It has been alleged that a certain organization known as the Pinkerton Detectives has been employed unlawfully and to the detriment of the public by railroad corporations engaged in the transportation of the United States mails and interstate commerce: Therefore,

Be it resolved, That the Committee on the Judiciary be, and it is hereby, directed to investigate the said Pinkerton Detectives, to wit: The character of their employment by corporations engaged in the transportation of interstate commerce or the United States mails, the number so employed, and whether such employment has provoked breaches of the peace or caused the destruction of property, and all the material facts connected with their alleged employment, and to report the same to this House by bill or otherwise at any time; and to this end the said Committee on the Judiciary is hereby authorized and empowered to issue and cause to be served processes for the production of papers, and to procure the attendance of witnesses, to administer oaths, and to employ a clerk and stenographer if necessary; and any subcommittee of said Judiciary Committee is hereby invested with like powers for the purposes aforesaid, and may sit wherever deemed necessary and during the sessions of the House. All the expenses of such investigation shall be paid out of the contingent fund of the House upon proper vouchers certified as correct by the chairman of the said committee or subcommittee, not to exceed the aggregate sum of $2,000, which the clerk of the House of Representatives is hereby directed to turn over to the chairman of such subcommittee, not exceeding $1,000 at a time, taking his receipt therefor, and which shall be accounted for by him to said clerk in the manner aforesaid, the same to be immediately available.

The riot at Homestead, July 6, gave a new interest to this subject, and various resolutions in regard to it were introduced in the Senate and made the occasion of heated discussion. The Democrats were disposed to throw the whole blame for the labor disturbances on the protective policy of the Republicans, and the latter were eager not to be outdone by their opponents in an appearance of devotion to the cause of labor. Beyond the mere skirmishing for advantage in the presidential election, the speech of Mr. Palmer, of Illinois, July 7, was the most significant contribution to the debate. He said:

"I understand that the Carnegie Company have determined that there shall be changes in their methods; that there shall be a different rate of compensation paid hereafter for certain kinds of labor, and that the contracts shall end at another time of the year, and that they make those conditions peremptory and absolute—the reduction of wages and the difference in the termination of the period of the contracts. It is also true that they have, in the exercise of what they claim to be their clear right, attempted to bring a large military force to their establishment—a military force which has a known and recognized existence in this country. The army raised and commanded by the Pinkertons is as distinctly known in this country as is the regular army of the United States. It is not a new thing. I am astonished to find that it excites surprise now. For years that force has existed. Its number is not always the same. The commander in chief of this army, like the barons of the Middle Ages, has a force to be increased at pleasure for the service of those who would pay him or them, and they have been employed in many places, in many of the States of the Union. They have been employed in New York, and have shed the blood of citizens of that State. They have been employed in Illinois, and have shed the blood of citizens of Illinois. At other points in the United States they have been employed.

"This company claim not only the right to regulate their own business in their own way, but they claim the right to fortify their position, and the right to introduce this armed force within their fortified lines. They claim the right to a free passage for their armed boats on the Monongahela river into their fortifications; and hence this struggle, this battle; because battles are not necessarily conflicts between armed men organized by proper authority, and there was a battle between the men who supposed they had a right and this armed force of

VOL. XXXII.—14 A

mercenaries raised and organized by the owners of this establishment.

"Mr. President, in making this statement I confess I have given no information to the Senate. We know what the facts are. It is claimed on one hand that the citizens fired on the mercenaries, and it is claimed on the other hand that the mercenaries fired first upon the citizens. It is not very material, to my mind, who fired the first shot. These are men who were taken there for the purpose of battle—a contingent purpose, I confess, but for the purpose of shedding the blood of these people if they stood in their pathway. Their boats, I understand, were lined so as to be impervious to the pistols and muskets that were supposed to be in the hands of these people.

"But even when that statement is made I have done but little toward reaching a solution of this question. What I desire from any committee of the Senate will be not to tell us the story of this outrage, nor is it material whether the blame for the present condition is cast upon the Carnegie Company or not. It is simply because they are but representatives of new conditions of society. It might have happened at any one of a hundred places in the United States where large numbers of men are employed in the service of these enormous manufacturing establishments. It may happen anywhere. It may occur in Illinois, or in New York, or in Pennsylvania, or in Ohio. Anywhere it may happen, because in the nature of things these interests oppose each other up to the extent that I shall describe.

"I speak of the Carnegie Company merely because it happens for the time being to be an actor in these things. It is claimed for them and by them that they have an absolute right to the management of their own property; that they are not bound to listen to the suggestions or the wishes of any third person; that the men who have toiled with them and for them for years have no voice whatever, have no interest in the establishment, have no right, and only speak by the permission of those who employ them. That is the broad statement of property rights in the Carnegie Company.

"The men who resist claim that they have some rights, because if it is true as a matter of law, and if it is to be regarded as true in a political sense, that these 4,500 men were simply trespassers there, then, of course, it must be very difficult to condemn the Carnegie Company, except as to the manner in which they assert their rights. It may be said that it was menacing and insulting that they should organize this force in contempt of public authority, because for a private citizen to attempt to enforce his own rights, however clear they may be, in disregard of the agents of the law, is a contempt of the law; and this attempt to maintain their rights by the aid of this organized force was a contempt of the authority of the State of Pennsylvania. The manner was menacing and insulting. To advance upon a peaceful, quiet city in the manner I have described was an insult to the people who were there. Mr. President, it is difficult for American citizens, whether they are in the right or in the wrong, to submit to be driven by an armed force. I confess that every impulse of my mind tempts me to feel that I should dislike being driven, even though I might be in the wrong, by a person who might happen to be in the right.

"I will not discuss that question. Something more, however, must be claimed for these men. I maintain—and I ask the attention of the Committee on Education and Labor, if that committee shall be instructed to inquire into this subject—that these citizens were right. I maintain, according to the law of the land, not as the law is generally understood, but according to the principles of the law which must hereafter be applied to the solution of these troubles, that those men had the right to be there. That makes it necessary for me to assert that these men had a right to employment there; they had earned the right to live there, and these large manufacturing establishments—and there is no other road out of this question—must hereafter be understood to be public establishments in the modified sense, which I will explain in a moment, in which the public is deeply interested; and the owners of these properties must hereafter be regarded as holding their property subject to the correlative rights of those without whose services the property would be utterly valueless. That concession which I make only concedes to them a right to a reasonable profit on the capital invested in their enterprises.

"I maintain, furthermore, that these laborers, having been in that service, having been engaged there, having spent their lives in this peculiar line of service, have the right to insist upon the permanency of their employment; and they have the right to insist, too, upon a reasonable compensation for their services.

"We talk about the civil-service law as applicable to Government employment. I assert that there is a law wider and broader than that, which gives to these men who have been bred in these special pursuits, as, for example, in the service of railroads or of these vast manufacturing establishments, a right to demand employment—a right which can only be defeated by misconduct on their part.

"I maintain, therefore, that at the time of the assault upon these people at Homestead they were where they had a right to be; they were upon ground they had a right to defend. Do you ask me if these men may by force take possession of the property of another? No. They were conducting themselves in the line of their rights, as I understand them. Business was suspended, and these men were simply awaiting the settlement of the disputed questions between them and their employers.

"Mark me, I maintain the right of the owners of property to operate it at their will; I maintain the right of the operatives to assist in its operation; I maintain the right of both parties to reasonable compensation for their services; I maintain the right of these laborers to continuous employment, dependent not upon the will alone of the employer, but dependent upon the good conduct of the employees.

"Mr. President, this is the only road out of the difficulty. You may call out the militia of the State of Pennsylvania, and you may exterminate all the inhabitants of that beautiful and thrifty village, and what is done? Human life

has again been sacrificed in one of these struggles for human rights. Do you establish the right of these large establishments to control their business? On the contrary, the laboring men of the country, so conscious of the existence of this right which I assert, the right to continue in employment during good behavior, will continue to resist, and this social war will be upon you, and it becomes the duty of Christian statesmen, republican statesmen, to find some road out of this difficulty.

"Within my lifetime I have seen marvelous changes. There was a time when individualism was the universal rule, and men lived alone almost, because they could support themselves; but matters have changed. To-day the world is practically divided between the employers and the employees. I do not take into account those neglected agricultural districts, those farm laborers, for whom nobody seems to care, for, in all the discussions of tariff policy we have, nobody ever speaks of the toiler upon the farm. We speak of organized labor and skilled labor, but when we come to talk about the white or the black men who toil upon the farm from the rising of the sun to the going down thereof, and speak of the influence of legislation upon these men, we do not regard them. If we pray for them, we pray for them very much as Brougham said the Queen was prayed for—for the desolate and the oppressed; if we legislate, they are not regarded. But this organized labor is a power in the state. You must regard it; you must adjust it.

"How can you adjust it? You can not do it by asserting, what I admit to be true, that every man has a right to the control of his own property in his own way; if he does not like to go to work for the Carnegies, he may go to work for somebody else. You can not settle it in that way. You can not settle it by saying that Mr. Carnegie has a right to employ whomsoever he pleases. Those are old truisms which have no application in this changed condition, when organized capital furnishes us all that we have; it furnishes all our food; it furnishes all our clothing; it furnishes our physicians; I believe it is now furnishing our lawyers; and it is said that it has furnished us our legislators sometimes, although that is a slander which I am not disposed to indorse. That being the case, you have got to find some road out. You can not admit the absolute right of capital; you can not admit the absolute right of labor; you have got to adjust their rights upon some basis. What is it? That the manufacturing establishment is a public institution, as the railroads are held to be—public because they work for the public, public because they employ the public, public because men in their service become unfit for other services, and public because there are thousands dependent upon them for food and nurture.

"Thus we have recognized the right of the capitalist to the control of his property, subject to his right to a reasonable reward for his investment; and we claim for the laborer the right to permanent employment during good behavior, though he is certainly compelled to submit to the changes of business. Where the profits are small, the parties must divide the losses; where the profits are large the profits may be divided.

That is the exact condition; that is the law to-day, as I maintain, because the law is the perfection of reason, and we have seen the law built up step after step.

"I recollect in 1839 I was compelled to hold that the Legislature of Illinois had no right arbitrarily to fix the rates for the carriage of passengers by railways, and was compelled to hold that the railroad companies had no arbitrary right to fix them, but that it was a question of reasonableness on both sides. It was then claimed by the railroad corporations that their rights were absolutely uncontrollable. The same principle must now be applied to the solution of these troubles. These parties are now confronted on the banks of the Monongahela river. Whether the battle is going on to-day or not I do not know, but we have heard the report that the lives of American citizens have been lost in the battle. It will go on.

"I invoke this committee, I invoke the Senate, if it shall appoint the committee at all, to let the committee have such powers as will allow them to look into the very heart of this question. It is a reproach to our civilization that this Senate and country—perhaps the Senate has no control over it beyond investigation—stand here now witnessing these two armed forces in battle array, and we confess we have no power except to inquire. Why inquire? What is the use of asking the bloody story to be recited if there is nothing to be done? If this war is to go on forever, why meddle with it? Let it be solved as it may, you must find some principle by which this thing can be done. You can not ask these laborers to become slaves, because if it is true, as claimed by some, that capitalists have a right to hold over the heads of their employees the rod of dismissal at their pleasure, American freedom is gone, and the vote will be cast by the master who holds the bread of the voter. You must give to the voter, if you mean that he shall be independent, a fixity of employment, so that he may defy the employer, and say to him: 'My tenure depends not on my vote, but my tenure depends upon my good behavior, upon my fidelity, my honesty, my industry, and not upon my vote.'

"If some solution is not found in that direction, this army of employees will be controlled by the employers, and there will be established an aristocracy more terrible than exists in any free country, and this nobility of wealth will become our governors."

On Aug. 2 the Senate passed the following resolution:

That a select committee of seven Senators be appointed by the President of the Senate, whose duty it shall be to investigate and report to the Senate the facts in relation to the employment for private purposes of armed bodies of men or detectives in connection with differences between workmen and employers, such investigation to include the facts in relation to the existence and employment generally of such or similar armed bodies of men or detectives in the United States since their first organization or appearance therein.

The investigation shall extend to and embrace the reasons for the creation of such organized bodies of armed men, their character and uses; also as to where, when, how, and by whom such men have been employed and paid for any services they may have rendered, and under what authority of law, if any, they have been so employed and paid.

In addition to the testimony and conclusions of fact, the committee will consider and report, by bill or otherwise, what legislation, if any, is necessary to prevent further unlawful use or employment of such armed bodies of men or other similar armed bodies for private purposes, and also for the more effective organization and employment of the *posse comitatus* in the District of Columbia and the Territories of the United States for the maintenance and execution of the laws.

Said committee, either as a full committee or through subcommittees thereof, shall have authority to send for persons and papers, administer oaths to witnesses, and take testimony in Washington or elsewhere, according to its discretion, during the present session or the approaching recess of Congress, and to employ a clerk, messenger, and stenographer; the expenses of the investigation to be paid from the contingent fund of the Senate.

Appropriations.—The table below is a summary of the appropriations made at the first session of the Fifty-second Congress.

Miscellaneous.—Among the measures that passed both Houses and were delayed in conference were the following:

To promote the safety of national banks by forbidding loans to bank employees.
To establish lineal promotions in the army.
To give claimants the right to sue the United States to obtain land patents.
To exclude beer and malt liquors from the Indian country.

OBJECT.	Passed House.	Passed Senate.	Law.
Agricultural	$3,210,495 50	$3,260,495 50	$3,282,995 50
Army	24,226,899 82	24,511,409 82	24,808,499 82
Diplomatic and consular	1,478,245 00	1,713,845 00	1,604,045 00
District of Columbia	4,987,580 27	5,906,984 27	5,823,414 27
Fortification	2,412,876 00	2,959,276 00	2,734,276 00
Indian	7,437,269 44	8,209,441 68	7,664,047 84
Legislative, executive, and judicial	21,683,752 05	22,052,412 97	21,899,252 97
Military Academy	396,665 18	484,527 83	428,917 83
Navy	23,476,773 00	24,813,885 00	23,543,855 00
Pensions	142,499,398 00	154,461,682 00	154,411,682 00
Post office	76,586,832 92	81,018,926 73	80,831,876 73
River and harbor	21,346,975 00	21,874,868 00	21,153,618 00
Sundry civil	25,292,982 27	87,437,458 70	27,537,228 93
Deficiencies	6,766,789 22	8,459,228 90	8,211,261 18
Miscellaneous			8,153,000 00
Total regular	$363,783,088 67	$396,140,881 90	$385,837,500 57
Permanent appropriations			121,868,880 00
Grand total			$507,701,880 57

Among the measures that passed the House but not the Senate were the following:

To prevent dealings in options.

To define the crimes of murder in the first and second degrees.

To forbid discrimination as to evidence in pension cases on account of the official rank of witnesses.

To ameliorate certain punishments for violation of the internal-revenue laws.

To dispense with proof of loyalty during the civil war as a prerequisite for admission to the pension roll.

To protect the title of settlers on unsurveyed Government lands when found to be within the area of railroad land grants.

To give pension claimants the right to examine papers on file in their case.

Among the measures that passed the Senate and not the House are the following:

To increase pension for deafness and also for loss of limb.

To provide for the erection of public buildings in cities where the postal receipts for three years preceding have reached $3,000 annually.

To reclassify postal railway clerks.

To reorganize various branches of the army with a view of hastening promotions.

To provide for free delivery of mail in small towns.

To revise the system of public printing.

To provide additional life-saving stations.

To provide for the improvement of the Mississippi river.

To declare lands containing phosphates to be mineral lands, and subject to entry as such.

To direct the Interstate Commerce Commission to report the action of railroad companies in regard to automatic couplers.

Adjournment.—The Congress adjourned on Aug. 5, 1892.

CONNECTICUT, a New England State, one of the original thirteen; ratified the national Constitution Jan. 9, 1788; area, 4,990 square miles. The population, according to each decennial census, was 237,946 in 1790; 251,002 in 1800; 261,942 in 1810; 275,148 in 1820; 297,675 in 1830; 309,978 in 1840; 370,792 in 1850; 460,147 in 1860; 537,454 in 1870; 622,700 in 1880; and 746,258 in 1890. Capital, Hartford.

Government.—The following were the State officers during the year: Governor, Morgan G. Bulkeley, Republican, holding over after the expiration of the term for which he was elected, in consequence of the failure of the General Assembly to declare the result of the election of November, 1890; Lieutenant-Governor, Samuel E. Merwin, Republican; Secretary of State. R. Jay Walsh, Republican; Treasurer, E. Stevens Henry, Republican (the last-mentioned three officials held over under the same tenure as the Governor); Comptroller, Nicholas Staub, Democrat; Secretary of State Board of Education, Charles D. Hine; Insurance Commissioner, Orsamus R. Fyler; Railroad Commissioners, George M. Woodruff, William H. Haywood, William O. Seymour; Chief Justice of the Supreme Court, Charles B. Andrews; Associate Justices, Elisha Carpenter, Edward W. Seymour, who died on Oct. 16, and David Torrence. There is one vacancy. During the year Judge Augustus H. Fenn, of the Superior Court, acted as one of the justices of the Supreme Court, having been designated for that service by the members of the latter court until the vacancy caused by the

failure of the General Assembly to confirm the renomination of Justice Dwight Loomis should be filled.

Valuations.—The following table shows the assessed valuation of property in each county for 1891, compared with the valuation for 1890:

COUNTIES.	1891.	1890.
Hartford	$92,133,946	$90,811,864
New Haven	100,484,983	99,122,806
New London	37,357,897	36,372,014
Fairfield	70,608,018	68,699,354
Windham	18,005,013	18,053,566
Litchfield	27,137,069	26,686,667
Middlesex	19,609,877	19,414,581
Tolland	8,537,642	8,484,950
Total	$372,874,445	$368,150,802

Legislative Session and Election Contest.—On Jan. 6 both Houses of the General Assembly of 1891 reassembled at Hartford and again attempted to settle the long-standing controversy respecting the election of State officers. (For the origin of this controversy, and the action of the General Assembly therein during 1891, see the "Annual Cyclopædia" for 1891, page 234.) Shortly before reassembling the legislators were apprised of the decision of the State Supreme Court in the case of Morris vs. Bulkeley, declaring Gov. Bulkeley to be the legal Governor until his successor should be legally qualified. In this decision all parties acquiesced, but it failed to cover the main points of difference between the two Houses. Its only effect was to compel the Democratic Senate to recognize and receive the messages of Gov. Bulkeley, which before it had declined to consider. Hitherto the Republican House of Representatives had refused to join with the Senate in declaring the election of any of the Democratic candidates for State offices, except the Comptroller, claiming that there should first be an investigation of the returns. In order to induce the House to recede from this position, so far as the office of Secretary of State was concerned, the Senate, on Jan. 7, passed a resolution declaring John J. Phelan, the Democratic candidate, to be elected to that office, and transmitted it to the House with a request that a conference committee be appointed. The House appointed such a committee, and both branches then adjourned for one week. They reassembled on Jan. 13, and adjourned to Jan. 20 without action. On the latter date only 5 Republicans and 118 Democrats were present at the roll call of the House, and as there was no quorum an adjournment of one week was declared, at the end of which time another adjournment was made to Feb. 2. The Senate met on Jan. 20 in full numbers, but after fruitless discussion adjourned to Feb. 3. When the House convened again on Feb. 2, nearly every Republican again being absent, the Democrats adopted a new line of policy. Immediately after Speaker Paige had declared an adjournment to the next day because no quorum was present, Representative Walker called the Democrats together, claiming that the House was still in session, and that Speaker Paige had no authority by law to declare such an adjournment. They then proceeded to elect a new speaker, clerk, and sergeant-at-arms, and the last-mentioned officer was instructed to compel the attendance of absent members. For the next two days the few Republicans forming the regular House met at one hour, and the Democratic House, under the leadership of Representative Walker, at another hour. On the second day the latter body passed a resolution declaring the salaries of all the absent Republicans forfeited. On Friday, Feb. 5, both factions met together, and the Democrats soon gave up their attempt to maintain their rival organization. The House adjourned from day to day till Feb. 9, when nearly all the Republican members were again in their seats. On that day the rules were amended so as to give the Speaker authority, in the absence of a quorum, to adjourn the House for not more than two months at a time. The conference committee above mentioned reported at this time against concurrence with the Senate in its resolution declaring the election of John J. Phelan. The report, after reviewing the investigations of the committee, declared that it was apparent, all things considered, that Mr. Phelan lacked 77 votes of a majority, and that the declaration of his election would be against reason, justice, and precedent. The House accordingly voted to reject the Senate resolution, and also rejected Senate resolutions declaring the election of Luzon B. Morris, Joseph W. Alsop, and Marvin H. Sanger. After passing a bill appropriating $50,000 for the World's Columbian Exposition at Chicago, the House then adjourned to May 3.

Meanwhile the Senate, after meeting on Feb. 3, adjourned from day to day till Feb. 11, its most important action being the passage of the above-mentioned resolutions declaring the election of Morris, Alsop, and Sanger. On the latter day it adjourned to May 2. Successive adjournments were then made from May 3 to June 27, from June 27 to Sept. 27, and from Sept. 27 till after the November election. The House adjourned from May 3 to Sept. 27, and from the latter date till November.

As the House, on Feb. 9, had definitely refused to declare the election of Mr. Phelan to the office of Secretary of State, the latter again turned to the courts for a determination of his rights. His counsel, on Feb. 12, filed an amended complaint in the case of Phelan vs. Walsh, begun in the preceding year, in which it was claimed that each House of the General Assembly had now declared its position, that neither could now legally take any further action, and that the court must determine the questions at issue. On Feb. 18 a similar amended complaint was filed in the case of Marvin H. Sanger vs. E. Stevens Henry, in which title to the office of State Treasurer was at issue.

A demurrer was filed by the defendant in the case of Phelan vs. Walsh, which was overruled on April 7, and the trial of the case on its merits began early in May. In the course of the hearing it became necessary to summon and hear the testimony of the town clerk and election officers of every town in the State. Nearly a month was consumed in this work, and not until late in July was Judge Hall, of the Superior Court, who heard the case, able to report his findings. He reported that Mr. Phelan had received a majority of 420 votes over all candidates, provided he had decided correctly certain legal questions raised at the trial, all of which he reported to the State

Supreme Court for final decision. Arguments were heard by the latter tribunal on Sept. 1, and a decision was rendered late in that month. The court, in the course of a long opinion, said:

We propose to consider first those questions involving the construction of the act of 1889, relating to elections, known as the "Secret-ballot act." Two considerations have had weight with us in adopting this course: First, the construction of that act is of immediate practical importance in view of the approaching elections; and there is a general desire that those questions should be authoritatively determined at an early day; and if the court should hold that it has no jurisdiction of these cases there might be some impropriety in proceeding to discuss and determine minor questions involved; secondly, if the views taken of those questions shall lead to the conclusion that it is not shown that any one has a majority of all the votes legally cast at the election in 1890 for either of the office in dispute both cases will be practically disposed of by the facts, and must necessarily be dismissed, and we shall be relieved of the necessity of considering and determining some grave questions of constitutional law. In taking this course we assume for the purposes of these cases that the court has jurisdiction, at least to the extent of inquiring into and determining the facts of the cases, whatever may be said as to the power of the court, in a certain contingency, and in the present state of things, to apply a remedy. We therefore pass by, without discussion, the questions: 1, Whether the General Assembly lost its power to declare the result of the election on the second day of its session; 2, if not, whether, since that day, from any cause whatever, it has lost that power; and, 3, whether in any event the courts have, or can have, under the Constitution any jurisdiction over that matter. We purposely refrain from expressing any opinion upon any one of these questions, and wish to have it distinctly understood that they remain open questions.

The first step in ascertaining whether the relator received a majority is to ascertain the whole number of votes cast. The returns, as made to the board of canvassers, show the whole number of votes counted. With these returns, which for convenience' sake we will call the constitutional returns, the statute requires certain other returns to be made, which we will call the statutory returns.

It appears from the statutory returns that there were eleven ballots in the town of Branford and one ballot in each of the towns of Hartford and Middletown which were rejected, and the reason for such rejection does not appear in the returns of the presiding officers, and did not appear in the evidence before the court. The court therefore held that such ballots could not be considered for the purpose of affecting the count of the votes for Secretary.

If by this is meant that those votes could not be counted for either candidate, the course taken was manifestly correct. But if we are to understand, as we think we must, that those votes were not regarded in making up the whole number of votes cast, it is not so clear that it was right.

Under a plurality rule, it is material only to count the votes of the two highest candidates; all scattering votes are practically disregarded. Under the majority rule, all scattering votes are important and must be counted.

There were in the State 500 ballots rejected "for being double." The respondent claimed that, under the act of 1889, that was not a legal cause for their rejection. Previous to that act, the statute provided "that no double ballot for the same office . . . shall be counted"; Section 238. By the act of 1889, section 9, it is provided: "if more than one ballot for the same office shall be found in any envelope, and such ballots shall be for the same person, only one shall be counted. And if such ballots shall be for different persons for the same office, neither of such ballots shall be counted." That act also contains a repealing clause, as follows: "Section 16. All acts or parts of acts inconsistent herewith are hereby repealed." Thus the law was at the last election that no ballot could be lawfully rejected for being double unless it appeared that the several ballots in the same envelope were for different candidates for the same office. That fact, if it exists, being essential to a legal cause for rejection, must be "stated specifically in the certificate." On the face of the certificates, therefore, these ballots seem to have been illegally rejected.

Discussing the effect of marks upon the ballots, the court said:

There are two classes of marks: one is where a plausible reason is or may be suggested for their existence consistent with honesty and good faith; the other, where no such reason can be suggested. The former will rarely be allowed to invalidate a ballot unless it appears that it was in fact used for corrupt purposes; the latter, unexplained, will generally be presumed to be for corrupt purposes.

The legality of those ballots printed with the word "For" p   to the name of the office, in the absence of aayxadding that they were so printed for the purpose of identification, etc., has been affirmed by this court. Such of these votes as were counted were properly counted. Those that were rejected should now be counted.

The folded or creased ballots in the town of East Lyme were each folded precisely alike, and in a strikingly unusual manner. It is difficult to imagine any legitimate purpose for which these ballots could have been so folbed. They should be rejected.

In New Haven there were nineteen Republican ballots, with each of which were found in the envelope a printed circular from the Republican town committee advising the voter to vote early, and giving the location of the voting place, etc. There are so many of these votes as to preclude the idea that they were the result of ignorance, accident, or mistake. That leaves the presumption pretty strong that the circulars were there by design. If by design, it is difficult to conceive of any honest motive for it. We think these votes should be rejected.

Of the 126 ballots rejected in the town of Bridgeport, for the reason that they had thereon marks, which were supposed to have been for the purpose of identifying them, 124 should be counted, as it now appears that the supposed marks were accidentally caused in printing.

With these and other instructions of less importance set forth at length in the opinion, the case was remanded to the Superior Court. A minority of two judges dissented from so much of the decision as relates to the "so-called" double ballots. Under the majority opinion, the Superior Court, in the absence of further evidence, will be compelled to declare that Mr. Phelan had not received a majority of the votes cast, thereby justifying the Republicans of the House in refusing to declare his election. The case of Sanger vs. Henry followed the same course as that of Phelan vs. Walsh, and the above-quoted opinion in terms covered both cases.

Decision.—Early in the year an action was brought by the State Attorney of Hartford County against Comptroller Staub, to compel the latter to distribute to the several towns the money coming into his hands for school purposes. As the General Assembly of 1891 had refused to make a special appropriation authorizing such distribution, the Comptroller was advised that he could not safely draw his warrant for the money; but the State Supreme Court, late in March, rendered a decision in the above-mentioned case, which in effect legalizes such distribution. The court found that there was a direct conflict between section 2,228 of the General Statutes, which orders the annual distribution to the towns of the income of the school fund and of $1.50 for each child of school age, and other provisions of law which require the General Assembly to make specific appropriations for all purposes authorized by law, and forbid expenditures by any department beyond the limit of such specific appropriations. The court says:

One law says to the Comptroller: "You shall settle all demands against the State for the expense of carrying on its government." The other law says: "You shall draw no order upon the Treasury." Obedience to one law involves a violation of the other. Acting is unlawful. Refusing to act is unlawful. If this is the real condition, if the conflicting laws can not be reconciled by a reasonable construction, then the paramount law must control. One law can not be said to repeal the other, for both were passed at the same time; both are contained in the General Statutes, and took effect at the same moment. The paramount must control. The command to provide for the essential operations of government must prevail against a rule of procedure in applying the funds raised by taxation for the support of the government.

If, notwithstanding what has been so well said, there should be some lingering suspicion that the prohibitory parts of the act under consideration were still in force, there is another view which is wholly conclusive. The omission by the General Assembly to pass any special appropriations has been so long continued that it must be regarded as intentional. The General Assembly is always presumed to know all the existing statutes, and the effect that its action or nonaction will have upon any one of them; and it is always presumed to have intended that effect which its action or nonaction produces. The neglect of the Assembly of 1891 to observe the mandatory provisions of the special appropriation act may be construed in one of two ways. It may be held to be equivalent to an affirmative enactment suspending the prohibitory parts of the act, or it may be construed as a design by the General Assembly to prevent the carrying on of the State government. The latter is something altogether too extravagant to be admitted. We think the former is the proper meaning; and that the omission by the General Assembly to pass any appropriation bills, being intentional, operates, and was intended to operate, as a legislative construction that all the prohibitions contained in the act were suspended.

We conclude, therefore, that there is nothing in the special appropriation act to prevent the respondent from obeying the command of the alternative writ. With the apparent prohibition contained in that act removed, the command in the said section 2,228 applies to him in full force. In observing that command the respondent will strictly obey a grant and order of the General Assembly.

Pursuant to this decision, the Comptroller, in a circular letter of May 17, modified the rule which, under legal advice, he had adopted in July, 1891, and announced his course in drawing future warrants as follows:

Believing that the opinion of the court was intended as advice to now adjust all claims heretofore covered by the usual appropriation acts in the same manner as if the laws establishing a system of special appropriation had been repealed, and that such advice will be held to protect him in now adjusting claims classed in the circular of July 15 as "demands that can not be lawfully adjusted and settled until further action of the Legislature," the Comptroller has decided to adjust and settle all such claims.

Militia.—The State militia for the year ending Nov. 30, 1891, consisted of 173 officers and 2,503 men. With the Governor's guards, there were 194 officers and 2,786 men, making a total of 2,980. The expenses for the year ending June 30, 1891, were $120,460.25.

Railroads.—Of the total amount of capital stock ($70,286,430.88) issued by Connecticut railroad companies, as shown in the thirty-ninth annual report of the commissioners, $19,269,350 is owned in Connecticut. The total indebtedness is $45,803,458.31, an increase of a little over $4,000,-000 in one year. The funded debt is $36,010,-935.88, an increase of half a million; and the current liabilities are $9,792,522.43, an increase of a little over $3,700,000. The gross earnings, $23,-401,771.25, show a gain of $1,102,949.30, or 5·21 per cent. The total reported operating expenses amounted to $16,091,932.97, an increase of $1,268,143.62, or 8·55 per cent. The net earnings amounted to $7,375,414.52, or 1·45 per cent. decrease, owing to the large increase in operating expenses. There were 31,087,344 passengers carried, an increase of 2,315,896, or 8·05 per cent. The whole number of miles of road operated is 1,688 miles. The operating expenses averaged $9,533.30 per mile, an increase of $586.87, or 6·56 per cent. Therefore, the net earnings, which averaged $4,369.40 per mile, show a falling off of $147.26, or 3·26 per mile.

Abandoned Farms.—Inquiries made this year by the Secretary of the State Board of Agriculture developed the fact that very few farms in the State are actually abandoned. But in many cases the owners of farms reported that they were desirous of selling at a low price. The number and area of the farms so offered for sale are shown in the following table:

COUNTIES.	Number of farms.	Acres for sale.	Total acres.
Hartford	49	3,868	480,640
New Haven	64	5,958	408,320
New London	18	1,470	428,800
Fairfield	94	1,770	432,000
Windham	18	1,961	354,560
Litchfield	71	8,222	584,960
Middlesex	28	2,606	243,840
Tolland	51	5,172	260,480
Total	309	30,522	3,193,600

World's Fair.—The dispute over the election of State officers having resulted in the refusal of the State Senate to consider any business sent to it from the House, it became evident early in the year that no appropriation in aid of the State exhibit at the World's Columbian Exposition could be expected from the General Assembly this year. Accordingly, on Feb. 8, at the request of the Connecticut members of the commission having charge of the Exposition, Gov. Bulkeley called a convention of persons interested to meet at Hartford on Feb. 22 to appoint a State committee and to raise funds for its use in providing and superintending a suitable exhibit for the State. This convention was entirely successful. The committee was appointed, and the sum of $50,000 was pledged in the convention for its use. It is expected that the subscribers will be reimbursed whenever the wheels of legislation are again put in motion.

Political.—Early in the year State conventions of the different parties were held to select delegates to their respective national conventions. The Republican State convention, held at Hartford on May 4, defined the position of the party in the State election contest by the following resolutions:

We heartily approve of the position of the House of Representatives of Connecticut, that the constitutional duty of the General Assembly is to declare the election only of such candidates for State officers as the Assembly shall find to be legally chosen; and we dispute the claim of the Democratic Senate that the incorrect returns of moderators are final and binding upon the Legislature.

We cordially commend the firm, united, and patriotic course of the House of Representatives in seeking, by every honorable means, to bring to a solution the existing differences between the two Houses concerning the last State election; and denounce the constant refusal of the Senate to join with the House, according to the unbroken practice of seventy years, in any reference of such differences to a joint committee, or to the Supreme Court, or to a special nonpartisan tribunal, or to join with the House in any investigation to determine the number of votes legally cast and the persons for whom they should have been counted.

We indorse the action of the House in passing the usual and necessary appropriation bills and other important public and private measures brought before it; and we condemn the Democratic Senate for its stubborn refusal to unite with the House in the legislation imperatively needed to prevent similar complications in future elections, or in any legislation whatever, by which refusal the State has been subjected to great financial loss.

We denounce the outrage upon the State Constitution perpetrated by the same Democratic Senate, without the concurrence of the House, to put in possession of State offices persons whose election was in dispute, and was at the time under investigation by a House committee.

We indorse the administration of State affairs by Gov. Morgan G. Bulkeley and the Republican State officers associated with him, for its courage, ability, and economy; and we especially commend the firmness which has successfully resisted the unlawful attempt of the Democratic party to seize the State government in defiance of the State Constitution as interpreted by our highest court.

We further extend the thanks of the Republican party to Gov. Bulkeley for his successful efforts to provide for the prompt payment of every obligation of the State.

On the same subject the Democratic convention at New Haven, on May 10, passed the following resolutions:

We enthusiastically commend the attitude of the Democratic members of the General Assembly in insisting, first of all, upon a declaration of the result of the State election and in subordinating everything else to that first and most imperative duty of the servants of the people.

We condemn the public acts of Morgan G. Bulkeley since Jan. 7, 1891, in not promptly surrendering the office of Governor of Connecticut to Luzon B. Morris, as the choice of 67,658 electors of this State as against 63,975 for his chief competitor, Samuel E. Merwin, and none for himself; we condemn him for unlawfully directing the acts of the Republican majority of the House of Representatives to nullify the election, to establish and perpetuate a deadlock, and for attempting to justify his holding office for the entire term intended by the Constitution for his successor by the flimsy excuse that a deadlock exists which he himself made.

We condemn the Republican members of the House

for their part in this plot, for their fictitious claims of doubt about the election of a Governor, for attempting to repeat in this State the injustices of an electoral commission, for their delay to declare the election of officers whose election they themselves admitted, and for refusing to make the investigation of the election which they themselves held to be needful, in order that no result might be reached.

We condemn the acts of R. Jay Walsh in keeping John J. Phelan out of the office of Secretary of State, and in permitting the case at law, begun for the purpose of inducting Mr. Phelan into the office to which he was elected, to be defended in his name, when George P. McLean, the unsuccessful candidate against Mr. Phelan, does not contest the election. We condemn him for resorting to the technicalities of the law for purposes of delay, with the result that, although the case was begun almost a year ago, a trial on their merits in the lower court is only reached today, and may outlast the term of office.

We point to Article II of the Constitution of the State, which holds that the powers of government shall be divided into three distinct departments, and each of them confided to a separate magistracy, to wit: Those which are legislative to one, those which are executive to another, and those which are judicial to another, for the purpose of criticising his flagrant disregard of the requirements in still holding the executive office of Secretary of State at all, by any title however good, while he is at the same time holding an important judicial office in this State.

We condemn the acts of E. Stevens Henry in excluding Marvin H. Sanger from the office of Treasurer, to which he was elected. We regard all these acts as a political crime, to be resisted at every point by all the resources available to freemen, and to be resented at the polls.

We commend and applaud Nicholas Staub in his conduct of the office of Comptroller in times of uncertainty and trial, and we pledge him our hearty assistance and support.

Finally, we express our disapproval of the Constitution of this State and its incoherent amendments, as a system wanting in adaptation to present conditions. Its election machinery has broken down, its representation is unjust, its provisions are cunningly devised to bring minorities into power, and are filled with distrust of the electors as the legitimate sovereign ruling power of the Commonwealth. We therefore demand its revision as a whole by a constitutional convention, to be called by the General Assembly.

On Aug. 30 the Prohibitionists at Hartford nominated presidential electors and the following State ticket: For Governor, Edwin P. Augur; for Lieutenant-Governor, Alexander M. Bancroft; for Secretary of State, Henry R. Palmer; for Treasurer, Watson M. Hurlburt; for Comptroller, Eliakim E. Wildman. In addition to the usual antilicense declarations, the convention adopted resolutions favoring protection, an increase of the circulating medium, woman suffrage, arbitration of labor disputes, restriction of immigration, the election of the President and United States Senators by direct vote of the people, and greater discrimination in the granting of pensions. Other declarations were as follow:

We stand unequivocally for the American public school and opposed to any appropriation of public moneys for sectarian schools. We declare that only by united support of such common schools, taught in the English language, can we hope to become and remain a homogeneous and harmonious people.

We favor the enactment of stringent laws to protect the dairy interests of the State against impure food products. The Storrs Agricultural School should be made the agricultural and mechanical college of this State.

We demand the Australian ballot law and a plurality of votes to elect all State officers.

We demand a reform of our criminal code, to put an end to the iniquitous farce of fines and rounders in our municipal courts, and insure equal punishment for equal crimes to both rich and poor.

The Republican State Convention for the nomination of presidential electors and candidates for State offices was held at New Haven on Sept, 7. Samuel E. Merwin, the candidate in 1890, was again nominated for Governor; Frank W. Cheney was the nominee for Lieutenant-Governor; Stiles Judson, Jr., for Secretary of State; Henry Gay for Treasurer; and George M. Clark for Comptroller. The platform contained the following:

We believe in the principle of protection to American industries and American labor.

We recognize the truth that the general prosperity of the whole land is essential to the prosperity of every part, and that a fatal blow struck at the tobacco industry, cutlery, hat making, or any one established industry, must react upon every other established industry.

We believe that the interests of the laboring men of this country demand that the tariff upon the productions of cheap foreign labor should be supplemented by the stringent prohibition of the importation of foreign paupers, criminals, and contract laborers; and that, if necessary, existing laws, regulating immigration, should be so amended as to further protect the American wage earner against degrading competition with imported cheap labor, as well as the imported products of such labor.

We hold, in the language of President Harrison, "that every dollar, paper or coin, issued or authorized by the Government, should at all times, and in all its uses, be the exact equivalent of every other dollar, not only in debt paying, but in purchasing power."

We denounce the Democratic proposition to repeal the law enacted by a Republican Congress which replaced the system of "wildcat" State bank notes by a sound national banking system.

We believe in the right of every qualified voter to cast one free ballot, and to have that ballot counted as cast. The disfranchisement of a legal elector is an offense too grave to be ignored. The attempt of the Democratic party of Connecticut to secure partisan gain through the disfranchisement of over 1,200 legal voters in the election of 1890, and the determination of the Democratic Senate to block all public business and thus take advantage of the public necessities in order to force compliance with their illegal schemes, should receive emphatic popular condemnation. The thanks of every patriotic citizen are due to the Republican executive officers and members of the House of Representatives and Senate, who so sturdily and successfully resisted the revolutionary attempt.

We pledge ourselves to maintain the plan of town representation, which for two hundred and fifty years has served Connecticut so well. Its attempted overthrow by the Democratic party would result in the partial disfranchisement of the country town, and prove detrimental to the best interests of the whole State.

On Sept. 13 the Democratic State Convention at Hartford renominated all but one of the candidates that were on the State ticket of 1890. Dr. Alsop, the candidate for Lieutenant-Governor in that year, having died in 1891. The nominees were as follow: For Governor, Luzon B. Morris; for Lieutenant-Governor, Ernest Cady; for Secretary of State, John J. Phelan; for Treasurer, Marvin H. Sanger; for Comptroller, Nicholas Staub. Presidential electors were also nominated. The platform demands a tariff for revenue only, favors the removal of taxes on raw material, and contains the following declarations:

While legislation should not be for combines and trusts, our commercial and agricultural interests, as well as those of our deserving industries, should be favorably considered when necessary legislation is adopted. Connecticut farmers are compelled to compete with the rich prairie farms of the West, and their products are restricted. They are entitled to all the favorable legislation which has been or may be adopted, whether it refers to the tobacco leaf or to their other products.

We favor the enactment of stringent laws to protect the dairy interests of the State against impure food products.

In scornfully trampling upon the decision of the people of Connecticut, the Republican House of Representatives violated the mandate of the Constitution to secure in office for a term of two years their party adherents who had been overwhelmingly defeated at the polls, or had not been voted for at all. Fitting words can hardly be found to express righteous condemnation of this outrage. Unless the people express their condemnation of it at the polls next November, a precedent will be set, involving future deadlocks and broils over election results, which the plainest provisions of the Constitution, if sustained by the people, would prevent.

County commissioners, whose powers are great, and whose duties are delicate, should be elected by the popular vote; and there should be minority representation in each board, as in the boards of selectmen, assessors, of relief, and school visitors. The public interests are not well served by packed partisan boards, appointed for the special benefit of a party.

We demand a safe currency, redeemable in gold, the standard money of the world; and protest against any issue of bank bills for circulation unless they are as safely secured as are the national-bank bills.

We uphold our secret-ballot law. It protects the dependent voter, and it is to a great extent a bar against corruption.

A plurality of votes should elect over five State officers, as it elects over 700 other representatives and municipal officers of this State.

We declare for a constitutional convention initiated by an act of the General Assembly, first submitting to the electors the question whether a convention should be held or should not be held, and finally again submitting to the electors for their approval or disapproval the form of a constitution prepared by the convention; and we pledge ourselves to revise the State Constitution to provide for the election of State officers by the greatest number of votes; for the election of county commissioners by the people; for a just system of representation in the General Assembly, and for such further reforms as will restore self-government to Connecticut.

On Sept. 24, representatives of the People's party met at Meriden, and nominated presidential electors and the following State ticket: For Governor, E. M. Ripley; for Lieutenant-Governor, Peter Lynch; for Secretary of State, C. F. Raymond; for Treasurer, G. W. Saunders; for Comptroller, Paul A. G. Schultz.

The platform approves the national ticket and platform of the People's party; invites the co-operation of all citizens of Connecticut, irrespective of sex; condemns the massing of wealth in the hands of a few; denounces the burdening of the people with taxation which fosters monopolies; demands its abolition on the comforts and necessaries of life; declares for the single tax; demands State ownership of railroads of all kinds; protection for State dairy interests against impure food products; declares for shorter hours of labor; demands the abolishment of the saloon, and declares for woman suffrage.

At the election in November the Democratic State ticket was successful by a plurality of 6,151. The vote for presidential electors was: Cleveland, 82,380; Harrison, 77,013; Bidwell, 3,999.

COSTA RICA, a republic in Central America. The executive power is vested in a President elected for four years and not re-eligible for the next succeeding term. The members of the House of Representatives are elected, like the President, by an electoral assembly. The franchise is restricted to citizens who are able to live respectably. In 1889 there were 340 electors. There are 26 representatives elected for four years, one half every two years. The President is José Joaquin Rodriguez, who was elected on May 8, 1890. The standing army numbers only 600 men, but for war 31,824 can be called out.

Area and Population.—The area is 23,233 square miles. In 1892 a census was taken which showed the population to be 243,205. San José, the capital, has 25,000 inhabitants. The Roman Catholic Church receives a subsidy of $15,540 for worship and $12,000 for education. All creeds are tolerated, and the *concordat* with the Holy See was abrogated by Congress in 1884. Education is obligatory for children of both sexes. In 1890 there were 300 schools, with 15,000 pupils, besides 90 private schools, with 2,500 pupils. In 1886 normal and model schools were established. The sum appropriated for public instruction in 1891 was 495,224 pesos. The number of marriages in 1889 were 1,228; of births, 9,151; of deaths, 5,238; excess of births, 3,913. In that year 6,330 persons arrived in the country and 3,706 went away.

Finances.—The revenue for 1890–'91 was 5,100,929 pesos, and the expenditure 5,483,430 pesos. The receipts from customs were 2,154,308 pesos, and from spirits and tobacco 2,143,088 pesos. The chief items of expenditure were as follow: Public works, 590,250 pesos; education, 495,224 pesos; interior, 376,853 pesos; finance and trade, 364,747 pesos; army, 475,729 pesos; police, 214,662 pesos.

A loan of the nominal amount of £1,000,000, bearing 6 per cent. interest, was raised in 1871, and one of £2,400,000, paying 7 per cent., was issued in 1882. The whole amount outstanding was £2,119,512 in 1887, when by arrangement with the creditors it was converted into a 5-per cent. loan of £2,000,000, which was assumed by the Costa Rican Railroad Company. The external debt in 1891 amounted to 18,864,541 pesos, and the total debt to 21,774,649 pesos.

Commerce and Production.—The chief products are coffee and bananas for export, and corn, rice, sugar-cane, beans, wheat, and potatoes for domestic consumption. The value of the agricultural products in 1888 was 16,523,014 pesos. Gold and silver are mined to a small extent. The total value of the imports in 1890 was 6,337,500 pesos, and of the exports 10,290,760 pesos. Of coffee, 334,666 quintals were exported, of the value of 9,196,202 pesos. The export of bananas was valued at 622,671 pesos: of hides and skins, 95,188 pesos; of wood, 77,572 pesos; of coin and bullion, 256,726 pesos; of rubber, 8,044 pesos; of cacao, 13,267 pesos. Of the coffee, one fifth went to the United States and three fifths to Great Britain. Of the total imports, 2,255,138 pesos came from the United States,

1,426,317 pesos from England, and 1,255,572 pesos from Germany. The principal imports are textiles, machinery and agricultural implements, tools, furniture, glass, tinware, hardware, fancy articles, wines and liquors, flour, sugar, and canned goods.

The number of vessels entered in 1889 at Port Limon and Punta Arenas was 309, of 367,052 tons, of which 136, of 149,062 tons, were British. In 1890 there were 319, of 344,695 tons, entered, and 319, of 341,883 tons, cleared. American steamers visit the ports regularly, and French and German vessels call occasionally.

Communications.—There were 180 miles of railroad in 1890, consisting of a line from Limon to Carillo, 70 miles in length, which was extended in 1891 to Cartago, 51 miles farther, and of branches of this line and a road, 14 miles long, between Punta Arenas and Esparta. In August, 1888, Minor C. Keith, an American citizen, obtained a concession for a railroad from the Jiminez to the Frio river, on the frontier of Nicaragua. In June, 1881, a contract was made for the construction of a railroad from the Pacific port Punta Arenas to San José, which has communication with the Atlantic coast by means of the Limon Railroad.

There are 600 miles of telegraph. In 1890 the number of messages sent was 163,967, which yielded a profit of $49,458. The number of letters, etc., sent through the post office in that year was 684,091.

Political Crisis.—A conflict arose in the summer of 1892 between the Legislature and President Rodriguez. In June, Ricardo Fernandez Guardia presented to the Assembly a formal accusation against the President, charging him with abuse of power and violation of the laws. The President declared himself ready to meet the charges without relying on any immunity or privilege. The chief cause of dissension was a dispute over the old question of religious instruction in the public schools. The President favored the clerical view, and in taking a stand for religious methods of education he was supported by the bulk of the lower classes and by an influential part of the intelligent people, who possess the franchise, as well as by the bishop and all the clergy. The majority of Congress and of the electors were determined to have the schools, of which the Costa Ricans are justly proud, kept entirely secular. Public feeling ran high, and deputations waited on the President to urge him to stand out for Christianity in the schools. As Congress was equally determined, he dissolved that body on Sept. 13, and, in a proclamation defending his action, declared all constitutional rights suspended. Under the military *régime* thus inaugurated many civilians and officers of the army were arrested. The official announcement of the dictatorship telegraphed abroad declared that peace was perfect and no trouble was feared.

CUBA AND PUERTO RICO, two islands constituting the only remaining Spanish colonies in America.

Cuba is administered, under the direction of the Minister of the Colonies in Madrid, by a Governor-General, who has large discretionary powers, and under him a civil governor presides over each of the six provinces. The colony sends to the Spanish Cortes 30 Deputies and 2 Senators from each province, besides 1 chosen by the University of Havana and 1 representing the Royal Society of Friends of the Country. The Governor-General is assisted by an Administrative Council appointed by the Government, but is not obliged to follow its advice.

Finances.—The revenue for 1890-'91 was estimated at $25,699,102, and expenditure at $25,622,656. The public debt in 1889 was said unofficially to amount to $186,000,000, requiring $9,000,000 a year to pay the interest.

The Army.—The armed forces are restricted by law to 20,414 men in peace. This limit was exceeded in 1891, when there were 22,454 troops stationed in Cuba and 3,857 in Puerto Rico. The militia, including a black battalion, numbered 63,115 men.

Commerce.—The chief imports are rice, flour, and dried beef. The export of sugar is about 650,000 tons a year. There are 1,000 miles of railroads and 2,810 miles of telegraphs. The forests, which abound in valuable woods, cover 4 per cent. of the surface of the island. There are large tracts that have never been explored. Since the suppression in 1878 of the disastrous rebellion which had wasted the resources and energies of Cuba for ten years, the sugar and tobacco crops have increased and improved in quality constantly, and the trade with the United States has almost doubled. The reciprocity treaty between the United States and Spain in respect to Cuba and Puerto Rico went into effect on Sept. 1, 1891. For the twelve months ending Aug. 31, 1891, the imports into the United States from Cuba amounted to $66,-057,287, and the exports of merchandise from the United States to Cuba to $11,920,214. For the fiscal year 1889-'90 the imports of the United States from Cuba had been $53,801,591, and the exports to Cuba $12,669,509 in value. For the first twelve months of the operation of the treaty, ending Aug. 31, 1892, the imports from Cuba into the United States were $80,106,459, and the exports to Cuba $19,684,729.

Puerto Rico.—The island of Puerto Rico is, next to Cuba, Hayti, and Jamaica, the largest of the Antilles. The estimated revenue for 1890-'91 was 3,683,100 pesos, of which 2,466,000 pesos were customs receipts, and 737,490 pesos the product of direct and indirect taxes. The estimate of expenditure was 3,633,583 pesos, of which 1,048,538 pesos were for military purposes, and 615,863 pesos for financial administration.

There are 470 miles of railroad, and the principal towns are connected by telegraph. The exports of the United States to Puerto Rico in 1890 amounted to $2,247,700, and the imports from Puerto Rico to the United States to $4,-053,626. For the twelve months ending Aug. 31, 1891, the imports of the United States from the island were $3,360,780, and in the succeeding twelve months were $3,446,385, while American exports to Puerto Rico increased from $2,217,672 to $2,676,596 under the reciprocity treaty.

Political Situation.—The great majority of Cubans, inclusive of the colored people, adhere to the Autonomist or home-rule party, the aim of which is to secure the same degree of independence and self-government that the Canadians or the Australians enjoy. Since the suppression of the war for independence in 1878 the Cubans have been able always, in spite of official pressure in elections, to send their best orators to the Spanish Cortes, but the plan of self-government has found acceptance there with no party except a section of the Republicans. They have nevertheless compelled the Conservative minority, which has held continued possession of the offices in Cuba, to modify its policy in important regards, as in the completion of negro emancipation. In pressing the Government to conclude the reciprocity treaty with the United States the Autonomists were joined by the Economist party. The former Conservative leader, Count Salarza, was forced to resign by dissensions in the party, and was succeeded by Marquis Azpeiteguca, a native Cuban. A part of the Conservatives are disposed to act with the Cuban home rulers on economic questions. In the last election the Autonomists or Liberals abstained from voting, in accordance with their threat that they would not enter Parliament again until the obnoxious electoral law, which disfranchises the Cuban rural population and insures a Conservative majority, is amended. The Economist party, led by Prudencio Rabeil, a Spaniard, is striving to unite the masses in order to obtain from the Spanish Government economic reforms. An important factor in the situation is the revolutionary Republican party, which has influential adherents in the island, but derives its main strength from the Cuban clubs in Key West, New York, Tampa, New Orleans, Philadelphia, and other cities of the United States and in Jamaica and Spanish American countries. Its chief is José Marti.

The Spanish ministry, in July, 1892, approved a project for farming out the Cuban customs revenue. The contract. which is to go into effect on Jan. 1, 1893, is let to the highest bidder, but not for less than $15,000,000 a year, the average amount of the customs receipts.

CURTIS, GEORGE WILLIAM, author, born in Providence, R. I., Feb. 24, 1824; died on Staten Island, N. Y., Aug. 31, 1892. Mr. Curtis's mother was a daughter of James Burrill, Chief Justice of Rhode Island. His father, George Curtis, was a business man, and wished his son to continue in his footsteps. The boy was sent to school in Jamaica Plain, Mass., but when he was fifteen years old his father, who had removed to New York, placed him in an importing house in that city. A year later he threw off the restraints of an uncongenial life, and with his elder brother joined the community at Brook Farm, Mass., being the youngest member of that distinguished company. In his preface to "The Blithedale Romance," Hawthorne says: "Even the brilliant Howadji might find as rich a theme in his youthful reminiscences of Brook Farm, and a more novel one, than those which he has since made so distant a pilgrimage to seek—in Syria and along the current of the Nile." Mr. Curtis remained four years at Brook Farm, going thence with his brother to Concord, Mass., where they lived for two years with a farmer, keeping up the admiring friendship he had formed with Emerson, Hawthorne, Lowell, and others of that community of religio-social reformers.

In August, 1846, Mr. Curtis went to Europe, where he spent four years. He visited England, Germany, Switzerland, Holland, Italy, Egypt, Palestine, and Syria. The longest stays were made in Rome and Berlin, where he witnessed the revolutionary scenes that marked those years. During his travels he contributed letters to the "New York Tribune," and on his return, in 1851, he became connected editorial-

GEORGE WILLIAM CURTIS.

ly with that paper. In the same year he published "Nile Notes of a Howadji," and in 1852 "The Howadji in Syria." He spent a summer at the famous American watering places, and wrote a series of letters, which were afterward collected into a volume entitled "Lotus-Eating." In 1852 he became associated with Parke Godwin and Charles F. Briggs in the establishment of "Putnam's Monthly Magazine," on which he worked editorially, contributing occasionally also to "Harper's Magazine." In 1853 Mr. Curtis began a career as a lyceum lecturer, and soon became one of the most popular upon a list that comprised some of the best-known men of his generation. The elegance and dignity of his manner, the beauty and refinement of his features, the melody and sympathetic quality of his voice, combined with the grace and easy flow of his language, made him an ideal platform orator. If he had not the nervous force of Emerson, the grandeur and depth of thought of Lowell, the keen penetration of Whipple, the splendor and fire of Wendell Phillips, the magnetic personality of Beecher, he yet had a genuine and tender charm that gave him an honorable place among those great lecturers.

In 1855 the original firm that published "Putnam's Monthly" was dissolved, and Mr. Curtis became a special partner in a reorganization under the name of Dix, Edwards & Co. He continued as editor, but had no share in the business management. During the continuance of the Brook Farm experiment, one of the interested spectators. who removed from Boston to West Roxbury to be near his friends who were conducting it, was Francis George Shaw, the philanthropist. Mr. Curtis's acquaintance, begun during that time. with Miss Anna. daughter of Mr. Shaw, had been continued, and in 1856 they were married. The family was one of strong antislavery proclivities (the son, Robert G. Shaw, being later the distinguished leader of the black troops, who fell at Fort Wagner), and

Mr. Curtis used his pen and his voice in the cause.

A year after his marriage the publishing firm of which he was a member failed disastrously, and Mr. Curtis had put all he had into the venture. He now became permanently associated with the Harpers, as editor of the "Easy Chair," and as "The Lounger" in "Harper's Weekly," established in 1857. In 1859, in the same periodical, appeared his novel "Trumps." Mr. Curtis led a busy life as a lecturer abroad and at home. The proceeds of all this work went to settle the claims of creditors of the bankrupt firm, and he had the satisfaction of completely paying off its indebtedness.

Meantime, he had become interested in local politics; and on Staten Island, which was his home as well as that of his father-in-law, he promoted the interests of the Republican party, of which he was an ardent adherent. In 1860 Mr. Curtis was a delegate to the convention that nominated Mr. Lincoln for the presidency. He had now become the chief editorial writer for "Harper's Weekly," and in its columns and on the platform he enthusiastically advocated the cause of the Union and emancipation.

In 1862 Mr. Curtis declined the offer of the consul-generalship of Egypt. In 1864 he was again delegate to the National Republican Convention, and was candidate for Congress in the First New York District, but was defeated. In 1867 he was delegate to the convention for revising the Constitution of New York State, and was also appointed one of the regents of the University. In 1868 he was a presidential elector on the Republican ticket. In 1869, on the death of Henry J. Raymond, the post of editor of the "New York Times" was offered to Mr. Curtis, but was declined. In 1871 Gen. Grant appointed him one of the commissioners to draw up rules to regulate the civil service. For several years Mr. Curtis had been interested in that subject, having adopted the views of Thomas A. Jenckes, of Rhode Island, and he was elected chairman of the commission and of the advisory board into which it was merged. The views of Mr. Curtis differed from those of the President, and he resigned his office, but he supported Grant's renomination in 1872.

In 1876 Mr. Curtis opposed the renomination of President Grant for a third term and favored the successful candidate, Mr. Hayes. In that year a civil-service league had been formed in New York State, and in 1880 it was revived, and Mr. Curtis became its president. This was superseded a year later by the National Civil Service

Reform League, which was essentially of his organization. In the same year Mr. Curtis supported Gen. Garfield's candidacy for President, being again a delegate to the National Republican Convention, and in 1884 he again held a seat in that body, making there his famous speech beginning, "The Democratic party is very hungry and very thirsty." After working earnestly against the nomination of Mr. Blaine, and retaining his seat to the last with no hint of his intention, he returned to New York and bolted the nomination, and worked against the Republican party. In 1888 he again supported Mr. Cleveland, but his interest in politics steadily declined.

Mr. Curtis was President of the Metropolitan Museum of Art Association, and of the National Conference of Unitarian Churches. He always manifested great interest in the denominational religious life of his home on Staten Island, and for several years, although not ordained, conducted the service of the Unitarian church, reading a sermon every Sunday. He pronounced eulogies upon Robert Burns, Sumner, Phillips, Bryant, and his life-long friend Lowell. Of his published works, "Prue and I" seems most likely to live. It belongs on the same shelf with Alexander Smith's "Dreamthorpe," Lamb's "Essays of Elia," Ik Marvel's "Reveries of a Bachelor," and Willis's "Letters from under a Bridge." As to his personal character, we may well accept the verdict of Lowell:

Dear friend, if any man I wished to please,
'Twere surely you, whose humor's honeyed ease
Flows flecked with gold of thought, whose generous
    mind
Sees paradise regained by all mankind,
Whose brave example still to vanward shines,
Checks the retreat, and spurs our lagging lines.

Mr. Curtis seemed to be in public life more by circumstance than by nature. He was essentially a home-keeping, friend-loving man. He was happiest in his country house in Ashfield, Mass., and was genial, appreciative, and kindly, in the simple, unstudied fashion of an American gentleman. His funeral was unostentatious, and he was buried in the old Moravian Cemetery on Staten Island. The complete list of his publications, besides pamphlet speeches and addresses, is as follows: "Nile Notes of a Howadji" (1851); "The Howadji in Syria" (1852); "Lotus Eating" (1852); "The Potiphar Papers" (1853); "Prue and I" (1856); "Trumps," a novel (1862); "From the Easy Chair" (1891); and "Washington Irving" (1891).

D

DAHOMEY, a native African kingdom in Upper Guinea, on the Slave Coast. It has an area of about 4,000 square miles and a population of 250,000 souls, having been much reduced in extent and power by unsuccessful wars with Abeokuta and other Yoruba tribes on the eastern frontier. On the west the river Volta divides it from Ashantee. Northward it extends to the territory of the Wangera. On the coast of the Bight of Benin it possesses the port of Whydah. The

treaty of delimitation between the West African possessions of Great Britain and France leaves Dahomey within the French sphere of influence as the Hinterland of Porto Novo.

The King of Dahomey has unlimited power, and is the religious as well as the temporal ruler. He maintains a large army, and his soldiers are noted for desperate courage, but most of all his body guard of Amazons or female warriors. The people belong to the Fon branch of the Ewe family of the negro stock. The country has been known as Dauma or Dahomey from the time when the kingdom was founded, early in the seventeenth century. The natives are industrious, raising cattle and Indian corn, and collecting ivory and rubber for export. They also produce the best palm oil obtained in Upper Guinea. The first relations of Dahomey with European countries began in the slave trade. The military power of the King is still employed in *razzias* on the neighboring peoples. Human sacrifices play an important part in the religious rites of the Dahomeyans, who are fetich worshipers. Abomey, the capital, is seventy miles north of Whydah. About ten miles nearer the coast is Cana, the King's residence, is held sacred because it contains the royal burying ground.

French Settlements.—King Toffa, of Porto Novo, placed his country under French protection in 1863, in order to save it from being absorbed by the British, who had occupied Lagos. In 1868 the French negotiated with King Gedzo, of Dahomey, for a seaport for their new possession, and obtained leave to occupy Kotonu. Gelele, the next King of Dahomey, and afterward Behanzin, the latter's successor, confirmed this cession, and yet they treated the French territory as though it were still a part of their kingdom, and oppressed the European traders settled there. The French, who took effective possession of Porto Novo in 1884, were compelled to take retaliatory measures, but recoiled from active warfare until 1890, when Gelele attempted to drive them from Porto Novo. In two battles before Porto Novo the Amazons were badly beaten, and Behanzin, who had succeeded to the throne, drew off his forces, and in October, 1890, concluded a peace with the French, who shrank from a costly campaign in the interior, such as the English war in Ashantee, and were content with obtaining a new confirmation of their right to hold the coast districts, including Kotonu, which had not been effectively occupied before. As an indemnity for the right of the black King to collect taxes, the French Government agreed to pay him an annual rental of 20,000 francs. This settlement, in the eyes of the ignorant monarch, placed the French in a position of vassalage toward him. The payment of what he considered tribute money, punctually rendered every year, made him believe that they stood in awe of his disciplined force, and, with the inflated pride that is natural to savage despots, he felt confident that he could hold his own against a country so disorganized that it had no king.

Raids of the Amazons.—After the campaign of 1890 the French were allowed to build up their settlements, and the business of the Marseilles houses and of German and other merchants trading in that region flourished until the close of 1891. Then the Amazons appeared in French territory, pillaging and destroying the native villages, and carrying off the people by hundreds to Abomey. Victims were supposed to be wanted for the annual human sacrifices. Yet it was not to this alone, nor principally to this, that the French attributed raids of such magnitude. German factors at Whydah were said to have agreed to furnish the contractors building the Congo railroad with laborers, and Dahomey was the source from which the supply was drawn.

To fulfill his engagements, and thus earn large sums of money, King Behanzin raided the populous villages of Porto Novo, at the same time sending presents to the factories on the coast with the object of inducing the French to wink at his depredations. Gangs of laborers were believed to have been taken from Whydah to the Congo on German steamers. They were not sent as slaves, but were formally emancipated by Behanzin as he turned them over to the German agents. Hundreds of laborers furnished at Boma by other West African chieftains were likewise supposed to have been procured by the customary slave raids. Belgian officers were said to have been in Dahomey in 1888 and 1890 to negotiate for laborers, and a Belgian agent is reported to have conducted to the Congo several hundreds of them in 1891 in two trips of a German steamer. After several incursions of Behanzin's warriors, in one of which the chief town of Uantechif, containing three times as many inhabitants as Porto Novo, was plundered, the French governor sent messengers to Abomey, demanding the release of the prisoners that had been carried off and the payment of an indemnity. The King, by way of an answer, sent the heads of the French messengers borne in a basket by a Dahomeyan warrior. Behanzin followed up this defiance by pouring his forces into French territory. One body advanced on Kotonu, while three others, resting on Whydah as a base, menaced Kotonu. The French garrisons were augmented as soon as possible from Senegal, and were strong enough to hold the fortifications by the end of March, when the Dahomeyans appeared before Kotonu and Porto Novo, defended by 350 and 400 troops respectively. While 6,000 Dahomeyans were encamped within four hours' march of Porto Novo, Behanzin sent a message to Lieut.-Gov. Ballot, as follows:

I have never gone to France to make war, and am pained to see that France is preventing me from making war against an African country. It is none of her business. If you are not pleased, do what you like. I am prepared.

On April 3, Ketome, containing 30,000 inhabitants, was burned. More native Senegalese troops were immediately dispatched, but the French commanders were directed not to attempt any offensive movement. All the villages in the neighborhood of Porto Novo were destroyed, and the entire population of the lower Uemi took refuge on the islands. Several gunboats were already in Benin, and others of light draft for operating in the lagoons were bought and ordered in England.

War with France.—The French Government determined on a regular campaign, and M. de Cavaignac, Minister of Marine, took charge of the arrangements. For commander-in-chief, Col. Dodds, who was in command of a regiment of marine infantry at Toulon, was selected. Col. Dodds was a mulatto, born in Senegal, who had been in command of the military forces in that colony, and had raised native troops there for the last campaign in Dahomey, and drawn up most of the plan of operations. The Dahomeyans were armed in the beginning with worthless old muzzle-loading muskets. But while the French were making ready for an aggressive campaign in a deliberate and thorough fashion, English and Belgian, and especially German traders, had time to supply Behanzin with thousands of Snyder, Winchester, and Mauser rifles, and even with Krupp guns. When the news arrived in France that the Dahomeyans had destroyed many villages in the neighborhood of Porto Novo and crossed the Uemi with 6,000 warriors, the Government asked for a credit of 2,925,000 francs, in voting which, on April 11, the Chamber authorized the intended expedition. Behanzin, through his European helpers, had telegraphic communication with Europe: for a few days after the Chambers had approved the warlike preparations, he sent his troops again across the Uemi and sent a defiant note to the lieutenant-governor of Porto Novo, in which he said:

The King is informed that the French Government has declared war on Dahomey, and that the Chambers have voted several millions to recommence operations. He holds himself quite ready, and declares that if the French touch his villages he will destroy Porto Novo and all other French ports.

The Dahomeyans did not attack Kotonu, which was protected by gunboats, but they established themselves, 4,000 strong, in the vicinity, and leveled roads for manœuvring. They had 4 cannon. There were large forces also between Godomey and Abomey - Kalavy, holding the route from Kotonu to Whydah. Their total strength was estimated at 14,000 men, armed with 4,000 breech-loading and repeating rifles, 8,000 old rifles, and 6 revolving cannon.

Col. Dodds left France on May 6, and arrived in Porto Novo on May 21. His first work was to construct shelter for the Senegal riflemen who arrived, being replaced in Senegal by soldiers of the Algerian Foreign Legion. Behanzin recalled most of his troops from the left bank of the Uemi, except 600 who held Dekame, and was in an intrenched camp at Cana. On June 16 the French Minister of Foreign Affairs notified England and Germany of a blockade of the coast, which was intended to prevent Behanzin from obtaining further supplies of modern weapons through the traders at Whydah. The English Government showed a willingness to join in any arrangement for stricter international safeguards against the importation of breech-loading rifles into Africa to be used against Europeans, and Germany was prepared to co-operate. Baron von Puttkamer, the German Imperial Commissary in Togoland, on April 11 issued a decree prohibiting the exportation of materials of war into Dahomey under severe penalties. The French force was gradually raised from 500 to 2,000. This force included a company of marine infantry and a battery of artillery. Two gunboats were placed on the Uemi. The blockading cruisers were not placed under the command of Col. Dodds. This division of authority was criticised. When, on March 4, an attack of the Dahomeyans had been repelled by the guns of the "Sane" and the land force commanded by Capt. Terrillon, Gov. Bayot requested Capt. Fournier to land a party of marines, but the latter refused, following telegraphic orders. This incident was made the basis of an interpellation, and on July 11 the policy of a dual command was condemned by a vote of 287 against 150 in the Chamber, in consequence

of which M. Cavaignac resigned the Ministry of Marine, being succeeded by M. Burdeau. The only aggressive operation undertaken by Col. Dodds before the arrival of the main body of re-enforcements was the bombardment on July 5 of the Dekames, who had attacked the village of Gome.

French Conquest.—Early in August Col. Dodds took the offensive all along the line, his first object being to drive the Dahomeyans from French territory. He had sent a demand to Behanzin that he should withdraw his troops, and the King had replied by strengthening his forces. Operations began with the bombardment of Whydah and of Abomey-Kalavy, on Lake Denham. One column, advancing from Kotonu, burned several villages, took Zobo, and had a sharp engagement with the Dahomeyans, who were finally driven into the woods. Another column set out from Porto Novo toward Dekame. The guides treacherously sought to lead the French troops into an ambush. In spite of this the operations succeeded, and the Senegalese soldiers gave an excellent account of themselves, holding their ground against a superior force for ten hours. On Aug. 17 Col. Dodds and Gov. Ballot set out from Porto Novo with 1,300 fighting men and 2,000 porters for Sakele. They were joined on the march by 2,000 native auxiliaries. They bombarded and captured a fortified place in Dekame called Taku with slight losses, and on Aug. 22 had another encounter with the Dahomeyans. The natives received the French troops hospitably, the Dahomeyans having evacuated the country, abandoning their intrenched camp at Bekanja. Two transports arrived at Kotonu on Aug. 23, bringing 1,000 men, which increased the regular French to about 3,000, including 1,000 men of the Foreign Legion. On Aug. 21 the column entered Sakele, which was not defended. On the way thence to Katugu they were attacked in a forest, and a number of Europeans were wounded. Several times the enemy fired on the officers from ambuscades in the woody region that had to be traversed. On Aug. 24 Katugu was captured, and, after two days of resting, they broke camp and advanced to the Uemi, concentrating at Kesunu. Col. Dodds returned to Porto Novo to organize the recently arrived troops and the auxiliaries that had been recruited before advancing into Dahomey. His forces consisted of 1 battalion of Legionaries, 1 company of marine infantry, 4 companies of Senegal sharpshooters, 2 of Haussa riflemen, 3 of Senegalese auxiliaries, 2 squadrons of Spahis, 1 battery of mountain artillery equipped with melinite guns, and the auxiliaries furnished by King Toffa of Porto Novo.

The column at Kesunu scoured the country, driving the Dahomeyans out of the Kingdom of Porto Novo and receiving the submission of all the native chiefs on the Uemi. The Dahomeyans fell back on Allada, south of Dahomey, where they took up a strong position. The river rose sufficiently to make transport and revictualing easy, but away from the Uemi new roads had to be broken and unfordable streams bridged. The advanced guard, consisting of cavalry and Senegalese sharpshooters, took up a position at Fanvi, on the Uemi. While the French were making ready for an advance on

Abomey a revolution broke out there, and Behanzin returned to his capital to deal with his enemies, chief among whom were his uncle and elder brother. Those adverse to the King were called the Party of the Nobles, which was nearly as numerous, but not so powerful and influential, as the Fetichmen, who were the King's supporters. The revolt was quickly quelled, and the leaders fled. A road was made from Kesunu to Dogba by the native allies, but the cavalry had to be transported in specially constructed barges on account of the sudden rise of the streams. The expedition was accompanied by 4,000 porters and 100 large pirogues, some of them large enough to carry 100 soldiers with their baggage. When the French, marching in three columns, set out from Dogba, they were surprised and attacked on unfavorable ground, on Sept. 19, by 4,000 Dahomeyans skillfully manœuvred by Gobbo, a brother of Behanzin. Col. Dodds kept his men well together, and the Senegal *tirailleurs*, who composed the first column, withstood an impetuous attack with admirable coolness. The marines and Legionaries, as soon as daylight came, broke the first impetuous assault with a rain of Lebel bullets. The Dahomeyans made repeated and desperate onsets, and left about 1,300 corpses on the field. Their loss was so heavy because, in attempting to carry off their dead, they exposed themselves recklessly to the fire of the French. The battle lasted from 5 till 9 o'clock in the morning. Terrible execution was done with the 19 field guns of the Foreign Legion. A large number of modern rifles were picked up on the battle-field. On the French side 4 were killed and 15 wounded. The killed included Lieut. Badair and a sergeant. Major Faurax died afterward from the effects of his wounds. The expeditionary force after the battle continued the march up the river to Oboa. The boats were attacked from both banks of the river on Sept. 28, but the Dahomeyans soon fled from the murderous fire of the Legionaries and the mitrailleuses on the gunboats. On Sept. 30 the French gunboat "Opale," which was returning to Porto Novo, was suddenly attacked by 600 Dahomeyans, who killed 3 soldiers and wounded several. For this the inhabitants were punished by having their villages shelled, and 200 riflemen landed and routed the Dahomeyans at Donkole, and there left the river and pressed on steadily toward Cana, where Behanzin was intrenched. Within 10 miles of Cana, between Uebomedi and Katapu, Col. Dodds halted and intrenched himself sufficiently to let his column rest safely. From the river to this point a road had been cut for the entire distance, the horses and guns were got through with the greatest difficulty, and great skill and vigilance were required to keep the host of porters from straggling off with their burdens, and to protect them and the artillery from the incessant attacks that the Dahomeyans made on them in the bush. The savages, when repelled, were not beaten, but returned to the attack as soon as they could form again. When the French crossed to the right bank of the Uemi, the Dahomeyans contested their progress at the beginning of the march through the forest from Oboa in a desperate battle that was fought on Oct. 4. The enemy occupied a strong position, but the French

were enabled by means of a road cut through the wood to execute a flank movement, and under the protection of a thick bush that surrounded the Dahomeyan camp to deploy their forces before they were attacked. The battle lasted three hours, at the end of which the Dahomeyans fled in disorder, leaving 200 dead on the plain, including 20 Amazons, who fell within 10 yards of the French line. On the French side 5 Legionaries and 3 Senegalese were killed, and 23 Europeans and 13 natives wounded. On the field were picked up 200 repeating rifles. It was thought such rifles were still supplied to Behanzin through the German colony of Togo after the blockade had stopped importations by way of Whydah. On the battle-field at Oboa shells marked with Krupp's name were found, and two German ships that arrived at Little Popo were supposed to have unloaded ammunition, which was conveyed along the French frontier to Tado, and thence to Abomey. The Dahomeyans had 6 breech-loading guns at Oboa. They were commanded by Behanzin in person, and 6,000 warriors were engaged. The blacks on both sides fought bravely, the Amazons with fury and astonishing contempt of death. Undismayed by the punishment they had received on the 4th, the Dahomeyans sharply attacked a scouting party on Oct. 6. In a skirmish that took place on Oct. 15, Capt. Marmet, Col. Dodds's orderly officer, fell fighting.

Many of the French troops fell ill and had to be taken down to the hospital at Porto Novo. To supply their places, re-enforcements were sent on from Senegal. On Oct. 20 the French camp at Akas was attacked by the whole strength of the Dahomeyans, who continued their assaults for two days. After they had been repelled with heavy losses Behanzin proposed to come to terms, but refused the preliminary condition of an evacuation of the fortifications on the river Koto. The French force having been strengthened meanwhile by re-enforcements, on Oct. 26 Col. Dodds advanced upon the enemy's fortified positions. Two lines of intrenchments were carried between Akas and the Koto, and on Oct. 27 the important line of fortifications on the river at Kotopa was taken by assault, and the main body of Behanzin's army was flung back in confusion on Cana, within 2 kilometres of which the French ceased their pursuit and pitched their camp. On the French side 10 were killed and 73 wounded.

In the different encounters that had taken place till now Behanzin had lost fully one half of his army, and his remaining force was badly demoralized. After resting his men, Col. Dodds, on Nov. 2, attacked the fort at Muaco, near Cana, and took it after a desperate resistance of the natives. On Nov. 3 the Dahomeyan forces attacked the French column before daybreak, and were beaten off after four hours of hard fighting, in which the French lost 1 officer and 6 men killed and 4 officers and 56 men wounded. On Nov. 4 Cana was taken after a fierce resistance. In the attack 11 were killed and 42 of whom 5 were French officers, were wounded. The Senegalese and Spahis fought with great steadiness. The porters, who had been drilled and armed, proved worthless as combatants, giving their attention chiefly to plunder. The march from Cana to the capital, which was not adapted for defense, was not disputed. Behanzin with his followers abandoned Abomey, sending notice of its desertion, and Col. Dodds marched in without meeting further resistance. The King fled to an inaccessible part of the country, whence he made overtures of peace, offering to pay an indemnity of 10,000,000 or 20,000,000 francs, to cede various towns to France, and to abolish the slave trade. The French commander, unmoved by his entreaties and promises, continued to occupy Abomey, where the sanitary conditions were favorable, and from there proceeded to reinstate chiefs and headmen who made their submission, and redeem the country as well as he could from the anarchy into which it had fallen, The people suffered greatly from famine caused by the war. Whydah, which had been taken early in the campaign, was fortified, and put in a condition for permanent occupatiou. Col. Dodds was promoted to general, and given a free hand in adopting measures for the permanent pacification of the country. The French Government approved his determination not to allow Behanzin, who was still a fugitive, to regain possession of the throne. Gen. Dodds proposed that all the coast places and the lagoons should be taken under direct French administration, and that Dahomey should be divided into three protected territories, ruled by native chiefs under the control of a French resident at Porto Novo. Leaving 7 companies in Abomey, Gen. Dodds withdrew the rest of his forces to the coast towns.

DELAWARE, a Middle Atlantic State, one of the original thirteen; ratified the Federal Constitution Dec. 7, 1787; area, 2,050 square miles. The population, according to each decennial census, was 59,096 in 1790: 64,273 in 1800; 72,674 in 1810; 72,749 in 1820; 76,748 in 1830: 78,085 in 1840; 91,532 in 1850; 112,216, in 1860; 125,015 in 1870; 146,608 in 1880; and 168,493 in 1890. Capital, Dover.

Government.—The following were the State officers during the year: Governor, Robert J. Reynolds (Democrat); Secretary of State, David T. Marvel; Treasurer, Wilbur H. Burnite; Auditor, John P. Dulaney; Attorney-General, John Biggs, who retired, and was succeeded in April by John R. Nicholson; Insurance Commissioner, Isaac N. Fooks; Chief Justice of the Supreme Court, Joseph P. Comegys; Associate Justices, Ignatius C. Grubb, John W. Houston, and Charles M. Cullen. Chancellor. Willard Saulsbury, who died April 6, and James L. Walcott, who was appointed to the office May 3.

Distribution of Population.—A census bulletin gives the following classification of the total population, 168,493: Males, 85,573; females. 82,920; native born, 155,332; foreign born, 13,-161; aggregate white population, 140,066; native whites, 126,970; native parents, 109,355; foreign parents, 17,615; foreign whites, 13,096; total colored (Africans, Chinese, Japanese, etc.), 28,427. The decline of the colored element in Delaware has been steady since 1850, when it was 22·25 per cent., to 1890, when it was only 16·87. The increase of whites between 1880 and 1890 was 16·57 per cent.; of colored, 7·48.

Finances.—The balance in the State treasury, Dec. 31, 1890, was $97,759.20. Of this amount,

$65,171.68 was in the general fund, $20,410.45 in the school fund, and $12,177.07 in the oyster fund. The total receipts for the general fund during the year ensuing were $534,644.30, and the total expenditures $570,812.66, leaving a balance in the general fund, Dec. 31, 1891, of $29,-003.32. The total receipts for the school fund were $159,402.02, and the disbursements $146,-244.97, leaving a balance of $33,567.50. The receipts for the oyster fund were $6,600.12, and the disbursements $18,376.84, leaving a balance of $400.35. The whole amount in the treasury, Dec. 31, 1891, was $62,971.17. The total indebtedness of the State amounts to $684,750, to meet which it has securities in bank stock and mortgages to the amount of $1,013,385, besides the balances in the treasury to the credit of the several funds.

Valuations.—A comparison of valuations by the last two census reports gives: Total assessed valuation in 1890, $74,134,401; in 1880, $59,951,-643; increase of assessed valuation, $14,182,758; assessed valuation *per capita* in 1890, $439.99; in 1880, $408.92; increase per cent. of assessed valuation, 23·66; increase per cent. of population, 14·93; assessed value of real estate in 1890, $59,-307,521; in 1880, $50,302,739; assessed value of personal property in 1890, $14,826,880; in 1880, $9,648,904; estimated true valuation for 1880, $136,000,000; estimated *per capita*, $928.

Charities.—The balance in the current fund of the State hospital, Dec. 31, 1891, was $8,730.41. The General Assembly appropriated $30,000 on March 27, 1891, for the purpose of extending the ground, erecting new buildings, and repairing and refitting the old buildings; and $16,577.59 of the appropriation was expended, leaving a balance in the improvement fund of $13,422.41. The total population of the hospital was 186, of which number 81 were white males, 21 colored males, 50 white females, and 19 colored females. At the time of the superintendent's report in June the number of patients had increased to 197. Plans have been adopted for the proposed Dr. L. P. Bush Surgical Ward.

Education.—The amount of the State school fund for the year was $148,292.98, from which was paid for beneficiaries in institutions outside of the State as follows: Blind, Deaf and Dumb, and Feeble-minded, $3,326.86; Teachers' Institute, $300; free text-books, $22,985.18; leaving a balance of $121,680.94 to be divided between the three counties; $25,000 of this sum is the State appropriation, of which $10,000 went to New Castle and $7,500 each to Kent and Sussex.

The surplus revenue fund, which amounted to $18,705, was to be divided equally between the three counties. The remainder from the general fund and other sources—except school dividends forfeited, which are returned to the counties —amounted to $103,853.61, to be divided between the three counties, as follows: New Castle County, $23,223; Kent County, $13,655; Sussex County, $20,727. The general result gave New Castle County $58,316.32, Kent $38,355.56, Sussex $51,621.20, from which amounts were to be deducted the sums paid for free text-books, as follow: New Castle County, $6,349.58; Kent, $6,378.88; Sussex, $10,256.72. The dividend is by far the heaviest ever paid by the State.

Nine students were graduated at Delaware College, Newark, on June 15. A new recitation hall has been added to the college buildings. The most important matter to come up at the annual meeting of the board of trustees was the question of discipline in the military department, and the following resolutions were adopted:

Resolved, That instruction in military science and tactics, under the direction of a competent officer of the United States army, is recognized as a valuable part of college work, and the president is requested to recommend this course to all students on entering college, but its adoption shall be optional with the student, or his parent or guardian.

Resolved, That students who have elected to take military instruction be requested to appear at drill in the prescribed uniform of cadets, and be also at such times subject to the rules adopted by the faculty for proper discipline under the officer in charge of the department.

The existing law in respect to entering the military department was stronger than this, and compelled students who were physically able and qualified, and who were not conscientiously opposed to military duty, to enter the cadet corps unless excused by the faculty.

The annual report showed a total enrollment of 97 students during the year, divided as follows: 9 seniors, 23 juniors, 21 sophomores, 41 freshmen. and 2 post-graduates.

Railroads.—Following is a synopsis of the fifteenth annual report of the directors of the Wilmington and Northern: Gross earnings, $444,-627.96; operating expenses, $375,495.12; taxes, $3,798.72. Receipts, less operating expenses, taxes, and interest on bonds, $40,287.73. Compared with the previous year, there was an increase in gross earnings of $5,436.75, or 1·24 per cent., and an increase in operating expenses of $17,168.38, or 4·79 per cent. The bonded indebtedness has been increased by the sale of $16,000 first mortgage bonds at 101 and accrued interest. The whole funded indebtedness now consists of first-mortgage 5-per-cent. bonds, $516,-000. The total mileage of the road is as follows: First track, 92·30; sidings, 25·27. The number of passengers carried was 438,820. The number the preceding year was 410,344.

At a meeting of stockholders, July. 21, 1892, resolutions were adopted "for the purpose of effecting the cancellation of all bonds of the company that remain unissued, and for the purpose of providing for the discharge of all of its existing liabilities, and for other obligations in the judgment of the directors to promote the interest of the company, an issuance of bonds of this company to the amount of $1,000,000 was authorized, the aforesaid bonds to be in sums of $1,000, payable in forty years in gold coin of the United States of the present weight and fineness or its equivalent in value, and bearing interest at the rate of 5 per centum per annum, quarterly, in like gold coin or its equivalent in value, without deduction by reason of any tax or assessment."

Wool Manufacture.—Delaware in 1890 reported 4 woolen manufactories, with land, buildings, and machinery valued at $313,000, live assets amounting to $193,974, and miscellaneous expenses amounting to $27,404. In 1880 it reported 5 factories, with a total valuation of $352,559. · In 1890 there were employed 297 persons, of whom 146 were males above sixteen

years of age, 112 were females above fifteen years, and 39 were children. In 1880 there were employed 201 persons, of whom 171 were males above sixteen years of age, 59 were females above fifteen years, and 31 were children. In 1890, $103,395 was paid in wages. $295,605 for the cost of materials used, and $482,022 was the value of products. In 1880, $108,504 was paid in wages, $448,285 for the cost of materials used, and $665,253 was the value of products. In 1890 the Delaware mills had 15 sets of cards, and in 1880 they had 13. In 1890 they had 7,306 spindles, and in 1880 they had 4,306. In 1890 they had 229 looms and in 1880 they had 126.

The Chesapeake and Delaware Canal.—It is probable that this canal will very soon be enlarged for use as a ship canal. It is 13¾ miles long, and extends from Chesapeake City. on Back creek, an arm of Elk river, in Cecil County, Md., to Delaware City, on Delaware river. It crosses the narrowest point of the Maryland-Delaware peninsula, and for the greater part of its length is a natural water way, a number of long stretches being from 200 to 300 feet wide. The land on both sides of the canal for the greater part of its length is low and swampy, and would afford unusual facilities for dumping matter excavated from the canal. The canal has 3 locks, each 24 feet wide and 224 feet long. It is proposed to enlarge the canal to 130 feet at the top, to 50 feet at the bottom, and to give it a mean depth of 27 feet, thus making it one of the largest ship canals in the world. It is also proposed to make it a tide-level canal at Delaware City, 600 feet long, 70 feet wide, and 27 feet deep.

Surveys and estimates were made in 1879 and 1883 with a view to making a ship canal across the peninsula. For such a canal, 100 feet wide at the bottom, the estimated cost varied, according to the routes surveyed, from something over $4,000,000 to $41,000,000. The canal so improved would give a route from Baltimore to Philadelphia 112 miles long, the route around the peninsula now being 422 miles.

The annual report of the canal company shows that the net revenue was $118,525.55, which fell short of meeting all fixed charges by the sum of $11,621.95. The preceding year's net revenue was $120,124.06.

Harbor Improvement.—The work of filling the gap between the ice breaker and the breakwater at Lewes has been continued for several seasons, so far as small appropriations would allow, and mattresses of brush were sunk as a foundation for the stone. The length of line to be filled is 950 feet, with the wall 40 feet wide, and rising with sloping superstructure seaward 20 feet wide at the top and about 20 feet above high-water mark. The depth of water before any stone was placed ranged from 30 feet at the ice-breaker end to about 65 feet at the breakwater.

The State Boundary.—A survey to determine and mark the line between Delaware and Pennsylvania was begun in 1891 and resumed in 1892. The marks of the original survey, made nearly two hundred years ago. are nearly all obliterated. Many difficulties have been encountered in the course of the work. It was found that the arc of the 12-mile circle with its center at New Castle would make an entirely new boundary, and one much at variance with all local traditions as to where the original boundary was really located. It would have been an upsetting of all preconceptions as to the boundary, because the original line never followed a true 12-mile circle, owing to inaccuracy in the work of Taylor and Pierson, who first surveyed it in 1701, by order of William Penn, to whom had been deeded by the Duke of York, in 1690, the "three lower counties of Pennsylvania." As the survey was undertaken some years later merely to ascertain approximately the extent of Penn's new territory, and as it was not dreamed that it would ever become the boundary between the two States, it is not surprising that it was inaccurately done.

It is the desire of the interstate commission that the new line shall largely conform to popular traditions, so as to change the State allegiance of as few as possible of the residents on the border. This will necessitate a little deviation, in that, instead of following a true 12-mile circle, the surveyors will have to make a compound curve, made up of the arcs of two different circles.

In the matter of the long-disputed flatiron or triangular territory, containing about 700 acres, the joint commission has decided to cede this to Delaware, which has long exercised jurisdiction over it, notwithstanding the dictum of Col. Graham, a Government engineer, who, after the survey of 1849, officially declared it Pennsylvania territory. At other points on the line Delaware will make considerable gain in territory. The new line will be marked by stone posts at each half mile.

The World's Fair.—The contract for the State building at the Columbian Exposition was let in June for $7,441. The agricultural exhibit promises to be large; it is to include more than one hundred exhibits of wheat, hay, and grasses. There will be a full exhibit of the timber of the State and of the fisheries. The latter will include models of boats and implements used in the oyster business. The commission has been seriously embarrassed by the small appropriation with which it had to work.

Fire and Flood.—A severe storm in June caused great damage in Wilmington. During one hour and ten minutes of the most violent rainfall on June 27, the rain gauge at the city engineering department registered a precipitation of 3 45/100 inches, by far the heaviest on record. What incidentally aided in causing the great damage in the lower part of the city was the fact that 2.42 o'clock was the hour of high tide.

On Aug. 16 the little town of Delmar was completely destroyed by fire. It was 6 miles south of Laurel and 7 miles north of Salisbury. About 1,100 people lived there, according to the last census, and during the past year it had been growing faster than any other town in lower Delaware or upper Maryland. For many years it has been a great fruit-shipping point. Seven persons were missing, and were supposed to have perished in the flames.

Court Disagreement.—An important question of law came up in April on the trial of a man who had been arrested for alleged burglary, for an assault with intent to kill the constable who made the arrest. The jury were charged by Judge Grubb, who said, in reference to the claim of the defense that the arrest was unlawful.

This ground of defense, in view of the facts disclosed by the evidence in this case, directly raises the question whether or not a county constable can, alone or with the aid of such persons—whether peace officers or private individuals—as he may call to his assistance for the purpose, lawfully arrest without a warrant any one within his county, in order to deliver him where there is probable cause to believe the party has recently committed a crime, and that without such arrest he would escape justice. This is a question of very grave importance; for if a constable may not lawfully arrest, under such circumstances, without a warrant, then a total failure of justice must inevitably result in very many cases, especially in a State of small territory. . . . Our wise system of law does not require the absurd, but the reasonable, nor the impossible, but the practicable, to be done. On one hand it makes reasonable provision for the protection of the liberty of the private citizen, and on the other for the due support of the conservators of the public peace and security; hence, when a warrant of arrest is reasonable it is required, but where it would be impracticable and unsafe to require it before making an arrest it may be dispensed with. This conclusion is founded upon reason and maintained by authority, as shown by the adjudications of courts and the treatises of text writers of the highest repute. By these it is held and declared that a peace officer, such as a county constable, etc., has authority at common law to arrest without a warrant any one he has reasonable ground to suspect to be guilty of felony, whether he acts upon his own knowledge or upon facts communicated by others.

Judge Cullen, the only other justice on the bench, arose at the close of Judge Grubb's charge, and said that the constable had no right to arrest the supposed burglars without a warrant; and that, if the suspected men had killed the constable or any of his companions, they could not have been convicted of murder in the first degree. The jury, presumably in consequence of this conflict of authorities, failed to agree upon a verdict.

Payment of Poll Taxes.—The courts have decided that in the design of the law an elector must pay his poll tax with his own money. This is in consequence of a movement to stop the payment of poll taxes by political committees, who have been in the habit of buying the receipts and distributing them gratuitously among voters since the tax law of 1873, which was decided to be constitutional by the courts in a test case two years ago, disfranchises delinquent poll-tax payers for twelve months.

Political.—A Representative in Congress was to be chosen at the November election, and a State Legislature which will elect a United States Senator in place of Hon. George Gray.

The Republican State Convention met at Dover, May 5. The platform expressed approval of the administration of President Harrison, commended the McKinley tariff act, favored American shipbuilding and a strong navy, and contained also the following declarations:

We are unreservedly in favor of the free coinage of silver whenever, but not until, by a proper agreement between the nations we are assured of a restoration of the parity of silver with gold; and we commend the efforts of President Harrison by an international conference to secure this end so much desired.

We are in favor of just and liberal pensions for the soldiers and sailors who fought for the preservation of the Union.

We again denounce the conspiracy which, under the name of the Democratic party, continues to misgovern this State, which confines to odious officials the power to deny our citizens the equal opportunity to qualify to vote, and has, by an act of unparalleled centralization, given to the Governor the power to appoint everywhere his partisans as registrars; that turned out of office in New Castle County the collectors of taxes appointed according to law, and put in the hands of one man the power over the payment of taxes and the qualification of voters, and by an act of gerrymander endeavored to place the control of that county in a levy court to be elected by a minority and not by a majority of its people.

We call the attention of the people of the State to the fact that this prolonged and hitherto successful undertaking to control our State government by the disfranchisement of its citizens has brought its legitimate fruit in a crop of defalcations of officials, and to an extent hitherto happily without precedent in our history; and that the only remedy is to let all public officials know that they hold their offices under a responsibility to the people, untrammeled and free by their votes to pass judgment upon their public servants.

We declare with emphasis all the more forcible because of recent events, that a convention should be promptly called to revise the Constitution of this State, and we believe that the vote last had should be taken as sufficient for that purpose; and we denounce the bad faith that has characterized every pretended step hitherto taken by the Democratic party in that direction.

The Congressional Convention was held at Dover, Aug. 18, when a platform substantially the same was adopted. Rev. Jonathan S. Willis was nominated for member of Congress.

The Democrats met in State Convention May 17, chose delegates to the Chicago Convention, declared in favor of Mr. Cleveland, and adopted, among other resolutions, the following:

That the principle of the McKinley tariff and its cognate laws of customs administration are fatal to commercial welfare and freedom, to the interests of labor in every department, and violate every principle of equality in the law and before the law which our Constitution was intended to secure.

That the Democracy of Delaware are opposed to any plan which will deprive them of their present standard of value. That the business of the country requires stable money, and no monetary system can be justified that admits a fluctuating measure and substitutes fictitious for real payment. Therefore we insist that every dollar authorized by the Government shall be intrinsically worth its nominal value, or be convertible at the will of the holder into a dollar capable of sustaining its own full nominal value anywhere in the civilized world.

The August convention renominated John W. Causey for member of Congress.

The Prohibition party met in State Convention at Dover, Sept. 22. The platform condemned all license laws as wrong in principle and powerless for good, recommended an educational qualification for the franchise and the removal of all restrictions on voting by reason of sex, declared in favor of restricted emigration, a new State Constitution, an elective judiciary, and local representation. Lewis M. Price was made the nominee for member of Congress.

The People's party held its State Convention at Dover, Oct. 11. The platform approved that of the National Convention of the party, demanded the equal taxation of all property, including bonds and mortgages, the abolition of

all unnecessary offices, the reduction of all salaries to a basis corresponding with the reduced prices of the products of labor, the filling of all offices by the people at elections, and the abolition of poll tax and license charges; declared that the oyster beds of the State should not be monopolized by any corporation, but should be held for the benefit of the whole people; that the "extortionate charges made by the railroads of the State in comparison with the charges made from Cape Charles " are in defiance of the interstate commerce law: and that "existing political parties are responsible for all the legislation of which we complain, and the very conditions to which they have brought us call a new party into existence to secure us any reforms in behalf of the people." E. P. Harnish was nominated for member of Congress.

Still another candidate was Henry Hubert, nominated for Congress on the ticket of the Independent Colored Republicans.

At the November election the Cleveland electors received 18,529 votes, and the Harrison electors 17,951 votes, giving Cleveland a plurality of 578. Congressman Causey was re-elected by about the same vote.

DENMARK, a kingdom in northern Europe. The Constitution of June 5, 1849, which was altered in 1855, but restored in its main features on July 28, 1866, vests the executive authority in the King, acting on the advice of responsible ministers, and the law-making power in the Rigsdag, acting in conjunction with the King. The Upper House of the Rigsdag is the Landsthing, consisting of 66 members, of whom 12 are nominated by the King and 54 are elected under a restricted franchise by an indirect vote. The Folkething, or popular chamber, contains 102 members, who are elected for three years directly by the universal suffrage of male Danes over twenty-nine years old. Members of both houses are paid at the same rate. The Rigsdag meets annually on the first Monday in October. All taxation and appropriation bills must be presented first in the Folkething.

The reigning sovereign is Christian IX, born April 8, 1818, who succeeded to the throne on the death of Frederik VII, Nov. 15, 1863. The heir-apparent is Prince Frederik, born May 26, 1842. The State Council, constituted June 11, 1875, consists of the following members: President of the Council and Minister of Finance, Jacob B. S. Estrup; Minister of the Interior, H. G. Ingerslev, appointed Aug. 7, 1885; Minister of Justice and for Iceland, J. M. V. Nellemann; Minister of Foreign Affairs, Otto Ditlev, Baron Rosencørn-Lehn; Minister of War, Col. J. J. Bahnsen, appointed Sept. 13, 1884; Minister of Marine, Commander N. F. Ravn, appointed Jan. 4, 1879; Minister of Public Instruction and Ecclesiastical Affairs, A. H. Goes, appointed July 11, 1891.

Baron Rosencørn-Lehn, Minister of Foreign Affairs, died, and his place was filled by Baron Reedtz-thott, who was appointed June 10, 1892.

Finance.—The revenue in 1890 was 57,392,986 kroner, and the expenditure 62,329,181 kroner (1 krone equals 27 cents). For 1892-'93 the budget estimate of revenue was 54,683,727 kroner, of which 35,981,000 kroner represent customs, excise, and other indirect taxes,

9,671,200 kroner the yield of the direct taxes, 4,305,470 kroner interest on assets of the Government, 1,352,680 kroner receipts from property and sinking fund, 1,025,000 kroner profits of public lotteries, 856,400 kroner profits of domains, 63,556 kroner revenue from the Faroe Islands, and 660,791 kroner various other receipts. The total expenditure was estimated at 58,578,- 341 kroner, of which 10,767,167 kroner are set down for the Ministry of War, 6,802,809 kroner for the Ministry of Marine, 6,795,680 kroner for interest and expenses of the state debt, 4,681,- 578 kroner for the Ministry of the Interior, 3,874,794 kroner for the Ministry of Justice, 3,463,464 kroner for the Ministry of Public Instruction and Ecclesiastical Affairs, 3,414,390 kroner for pensions and the military invalid fund, 3,339,895 kroner for the Ministry of Finance, 1,155,200 kroner for the civil list and appanages, 393,364 kroner for the Ministry of Foreign Affairs, 306,616 kroner for the Rigsdag and Council of State, 92,164 kroner for Iceland, 3,- 876,116 kroner for improvement of the state property and reduction of the debt, and 9,615,- 602 kroner for extraordinary state expenditure. The reserve fund, which is kept to enable the Government to meet any emergency, amounted on March 31, 1890, to 17,828,139 kroner.

The public debt, which is in part the result of large annual deficits that occurred previous to the establishment of the parliamentary system, and in part consists of borrowings for the construction of railroads, docks, lighthouses, etc., amounted on March 31, 1890, to 188,148,541 kroner. The foreign debt, which pays 4 per cent., was only 10,605,700 kroner. On the internal debt the rate of interest is 3½ per cent. The expense of the debt in 1889-'90 was 9,696,- 158 kroner. The net interest charge *per capita* is only about 68 cents a year. The assets of the state, including the reserve fund, amount to 60,- 000,000 kroner.

The Army.—All able-bodied young men are liable for service in the regular army and the reserve from the age of twenty-two to the age of thirty, and for the following eight years in the extra reserve. The recruits are trained for six months in the infantry, five months in the field artillery and engineers, nine and a half months in the cavalry, and four months in the fortress artillery and technical branches. Those who fall below a certain standard of proficiency are compelled to drill for a second and longer period, which for the infantry is nine months. Besides the preliminary training there is an annual drill lasting from a month to six weeks. The army consists of 2 divisions, one of 2 and the other of 3 brigades, each brigade containing 2 battalions. The whole army comprises 31 battalions of infantry; 5 regiments of cavalry, each with 3 active squadrons; 2 regiments of artillery, consisting of 12 batteries, with 4 more in reserve; 2 battalions of foot artillery, consisting of 6 companies, with 5 in reserve; and 1 regiment of engineers. The strength of the army on the war footing was 1,200 officers and 41,750 men in 1891. There is, also, the Citizen Corps, bringing the fighting strength up to nearly 60,000, besides an extra reserve of 16,500 officers and men available for great emergencies. When, some years ago, the Radicals refused to allow

any expenditure for the fortification of Copenhagen, the Government sanctioned an appeal to public generosity, and large sums were subscribed and expended upon the construction of a fort on the Gardenhoehe, commanding the approaches to the harbor of the capital. This fort, completed early in the summer of 1892, was handed over to Col. Bahnsen, the Minister of War, on Aug. 27, 1892.

The Navy.—The Danish naval forces in 1891 comprised 1 ironclad battle ship, 8 armored vessels for coast defense, 3 deck-protected cruisers, 1 torpedo ship, 4 seagoing torpedo boats, 5 first-class and 10 second-class torpedo boats, 20 unarmored vessels of various kinds, and 20 transports. The most powerful vessel is the "Helgoland," having a belt of 12-inch armor, displacing 5,300 tons of water, and carrying a 36-ton gun in a central battery, besides 4 22-ton guns. The turret ship "Iver Hvitfeldt," built in 1886, has 11½ inches of armor, and carries 2 28-ton guns. The "Valkyrie," a cruiser having a speed of 17¼ knots, is protected by 2¼ inches of steel on the sloping deck, and armed with 2 13¼-ton and 6 4½-ton guns.

Commerce and Production.—The land laws of Denmark encourage the division of large estates into single farms, and positively forbid the consolidation of small properties to form large estates. Tenant farmers have full control and permanent tenure of the land so long as they pay the rent. Four fifths of the area of the country is productive, and one sixth of the remainder consists of peat bogs. The value of the agricultural produce in 1889 was 274,396,459 kroner. During 1890 there were exported 16,217 horses, 139,522 cattle, 72,171 sheep and goats, and 111,028 pigs. The distilleries in 1890 produced 6,544,780 gallons of spirits, and the beet-sugar factories turned out 22,282 tons of sugar. The value of the imports in 1890 was 307,031,- 194 kroner, against 304,327,851 kroner in 1889; the value of the exports was 233,837,937 kroner, against 209,319,456. The imports of articles of food in 1890 were 110,300,000 kroner; of manufactured articles, 68,400,000 kroner; of raw materials, 106,200,000 kroner; of machinery and other means of production, 22,100,000 kroner. Of the total value of exports, 179,500,000 kroner stand for foods, 12,000,000 kroner for manufactures, 28,400,000 kroner for raw materials, and 13,900,000 kroner for means of production. The imports of colonial goods in 1890 were 25,570,- 582 kroner, against 28,897,203 in 1889 ; of drinks, 4,224,100 kroner, against 4,170,407 ; of textile manufactures, 38,483,498 kroner, against 38,116,- 178 ; of metal goods, 28,795,142 kroner, against 27,215,892 ; of timber and wood manufactures, 18,741,076 kroner, against 15,902,105 ; of coal, 22,510,725 kroner, against 23,499,138 ; of animals, 5,355,738 kroner, against 4,712,863 ; of pork, lard, butter, and eggs, 23,868,272 kroner, against 19,- 328,824 ; of cereals, 31,135,428 kroner, against 31,599,929. The exports of colonial goods were 7,103,152 kroner in 1890, against 9,227,450 in 1889 ; of drinks, 1,590,886 kroner, against 1,647,- 912 ; of textile manufactures, 4,947,643 kroner, against 4,873,426 ; of metals and hardware, 5,139,- 271 kroner, against 3,361,587 ; of wood and manufactures thereof, 2,999,187 kroner, against 3,545,- 556 ; of coal, 2,235,225 kroner, against 2,360,121 ;

of animals, 44,167,905 kroner, against 35,259,765; of butter, eggs, etc., 112,313,238 kroner, against 100,997,462; of cereals, 14,538,204 kroner, against 12,783,117.

The distribution of the commerce among the principal countries in 1890 is shown in the following table, giving the values of the imports from and the exports to each in kroner:

COUNTRIES.	Imports.	Exports.
Germany	99,509,299	58,589,578
Great Britain..................	67,561,373	129,477,205
Sweden and Norway..........	48,534,173	29,288,848
United States.................	21,845,727	2,175,566
Other American countries......	972,154	12,105
Russia.......................	27,116,367	2,734,448
Holland.......................	7,138,574	931,718
Belgium.......................	8,497,664	1,115,761
France.......................	6,949,740	2,137,204
Danish colonies...............	3,885,586	3,950,921

Navigation.—During 1890 there were 28,414 vessels, carrying 2,040,535 tons of cargo, entered, and 28,998, carrying 584,469 tons of cargo, cleared at Danish ports, besides 30,414 coasting vessels entered and 31,368 cleared.

The merchant marine in the beginning of 1891 consisted of 3,543 vessels, of 302,194 tons, of which 330, of 112,788 tons, were steamers.

Communications.—The Danish railroads in 1891 had a total length of 1,247 miles, of which 1,000 miles belonged to the Government, which, up to the beginning of the financial year 1891, had invested 164,141,474 kroner in railroads.

The post-office traffic in 1889 consisted of 49,-015,000 letters and postal cards and 4,284,000 printed inclosures and samples.

The state telegraph lines in the beginning of 1891 had a length of 2,790 miles, and the total length of the telegraphs was 3,674 miles, with 10,280 miles of wire. The state lines transmitted 1,548,493 messages during 1890, of which 567,224 were domestic, 948,399 international, and 32.870 official.

Dependencies.—Iceland has an autonomous government under a charter that went into force on Aug. 1, 1874. The legislative authority is exercised by the Althing, a single chamber containing 36 members, of whom 30 are elected by the people and 6 are appointed by the Crown. There is a governor residing at Reikjavik, who carries on the administration under the direction of the Minister for Iceland in Copenhagen. The area of the island is 39,756 square miles, and the population is 69,224.

Greenland, with an area of 46,740 square miles, had in 1888 a population of 10,221. In 1890 there were goods of the value of 490,748 kroner imported into Denmark from Greenland, while the Danish exports to Greenland amounted to 358,068 kroner.

The only other colonies are the Danish Antilles. (See WEST INDIES.)

Elections.—As the term of election for the Folkething expired in January, 1893, and the holding of elections at that time would necessitate a suspension of the work of the Rigsdag, the new elections were ordered to be held on April 20, 1892. Of 102 seats, the Right obtained 30, the Moderate Left 43, while the Radical Left only returned 29 of their candidates. The result gave the Government, for the first time since the constitutional crisis began, a ma-

jority with which it could proceed on constitutional lines with legislative business. The Moderate Left separated from their former allies, the Radical Left, and pledged themselves to vote with the ministers on all matters connected with the current administration of the Government, but retained their freedom of action in matters connected with possible demands for supplementary grants to the War Department. The reverse of the Radical Left, which ever since 1885 had been strong enough to defeat, with the help of the Moderate Left, each measure submitted by Prime-Minister Estrupp, was due principally to the rural population, which constitutes the great majority of the electorate, and which at length became alarmed by the radical and even socialistic doctrines formulated by the Extreme Left with regard to politics, religion, and social organization.

Politics.—As no understanding regarding the budget had been arrived at between the two houses of the Rigsdag before the beginning of the new financial year, April 1, 1892, after the closing of the session of the Rigsdag the King issued a decree promulgating a provisional budget for 1892-'93. An extra session of the Rigsdag, lasting from May 6 to May 11, was called for the purpose of constituting the new Folkething. The regular session was opened on Oct. 3. The Minister of Finance presented the budget for 1893-'94. The revenues are estimated at 55,-500,000 kroner, the expenses at 54,200,000 kroner, leaving a surplus of 1,300,000 kroner.

DIPHTHERIA, a specific, contagious, asthenic, constitutional disease, occurring epidemically in certain localities, endemically and, perhaps occasionally, solitarily. Its distinctive mark is first a local exudative inflammation in the throat or air passages, then the formation upon their mucous surfaces of layers of lymph or false membrane, possessing signs of bacteroid mycosis. This same membrane can show itself upon mucous surfaces other than in the throat, and also upon wounds. The disease may occur in any locality, under every condition, attacks the rich and the poor, but finds the majority of its victims among children. It has been found that a porous soil, with an understratum of clay, rather favors its development. Bad hygienic conditions increase the virulence of the poison, but good hygienic conditions offer no bar to its development. Temperature has no effect upon it, although, it is said, diphtheria prevails most during moist, cold weather. Records in large cities show the smallest number of cases during the very hot months. There seems to be a hereditary liability to diphtheria in certain families. A singular fact is that the Chinese race possess almost complete immunity. Diphtheria must have existed since early ages. A fatal affection marked by a membrane in the fauces was described by Hippocrates and Arctæus. After their time nothing is recorded of the disease for several centuries, and we are forced to the conclusion that the activity of the poison must have decreased very markedly and the disease disappeared. After this rest of centuries renewed strength must have been acquired, for the disease became so prevalent that the attention of physicians was again directed to it. The first accurate account is given by

Baillou, a French physician living at the close of the sixteenth century. Subsequently it was described by Villa Real, a Spanish physician, Alaymus, Ghisi, Home, and Cullen. The most accurate descriptions were given by Bretonneau in 1826, and by Abercromie in 1828. Since the writings of these two celebrated observers little attention seems to have been given to the subject, as not much has been added to our knowledge of the malady. There has been some advance in treatment, but the mortality still averages 30 per cent. The first positive account of an epidemic of diphtheria is that in Spain, about 1590. An epidemic appeared at Naples in 1617, in Sicily in 1625, in Italy in 1640, at Palermo in 1748, at Paris in 1750, in Sweden in 1757, at Edinburgh in 1765. The first epidemic with which America was visited occurred in New York in 1789. In 1826 the disease again appeared in epidemic form in Edinburgh, at Paris in 1853, and at Folkestone, England, in 1856. During 1858 a severe epidemic spread over most of England. In 1882 diphtheria prevailed to a very great extent in Michigan and Wisconsin. These epidemics were very fatal and very singular. The disease would appear first in one town, then in the pine forests miles distant, and no medium of communication between the cases could be discovered. Medical societies in Eastern cities sent experts to ascertain new facts concerning diphtheria, but little that of importance was learned. In the pine regions of Michigan were a vast number of immense sawdust heaps, the accumulation of years, at the saw mills; and the view that decomposition of the sawdust gave rise to the poison of diphtheria and infected surrounding localities was expressed by several investigators.

During 1892 the disease was very prevalent in Boston, New York, Philadelphia, Detroit, and Cincinnati. In Philadephia the epidemic was quite severe; the total number of cases during the year amounted to 5,051, and the deaths were 1,484. During the year the average rainfall was much below normal, consequently the sewers were dry for a considerable length of time. No effort was made to flush them, although this could easily have been done. The range of temperature during January, February, March, October, November, and December was higher than the average for the same months. During April, May, June, July, and August the range of temperature was also higher than the average for the same months, and the relative humidity was much above the usual average. Investigation shows that the greatest number of cases occurred during the cold months, and that in August, when the temperature was remarkably high and the relative humidity also, the record of new cases was lowest. When the temperature rose the disease decreased; when the temperature fell it increased. In the lower wards of Philadelphia, the old part of the city, surface drainage exists to a great extent, and in these wards the population is greatest, the poorer classes predominating. In the upper wards, the newer part of the city, the elevation is considerably higher, surface drainage does not exist, the residents are mostly of the wealthier classes, and the sewerage connections in the houses are almost universal. In these wards the number of cases

was greatest. In the district known as West Philadelphia, where the elevation is also high, the houses modern, sewer connections universal, and of the most approved pattern, the number of cases was also greater. It is also a fact that about the end of the summer months many streets were torn up in order to construct new sewers and to replace cobble stones with improved pavements. When these operations were begun the number of new cases of diphtheria increased to a marked extent, and when the work was at its height the epidemic was also. The inferences from these facts are very apparent. The rate of mortality was about what it has been from diphtheria from its earliest history.

The exciting cause of diphtheria is a specific contagium. It is exceedingly doubtful whether it ever does originate de novo. Within the past few years authorities have agreed that, in order to have what we term specific diseases, we must have the specific poison producing them. Most recent observers hold to the opinion that the poison consists of minute particles of matter which possess the power of floating in the atmosphere. Except where implanted by direct contact, this poison probably enters the human system by means of the respiratory tract. It is indeed very doubtful whether it ever enters through the digestive. That such is at times the case, has been held by several well-known writers. There is no doubt that the poison of diphtheria is influenced to a greater extent by atmospheric conditions than almost any poison of the same nature. What most affects this is dampness. Dry cold and dry heat do not favor its development. In the far north and in the tropics the disease rarely exists. Of all the contagious diseases it is the most easily contracted. Its poison seems to be more active, and remains so longer than does that of cholera, typhoid fever, or smallpox. Persons not affected can carry the poison on clothing or hands to others. Many incidents are recorded where this virus has lain dormant for more than a year.

Within the past few years the separate identity of croup and diphtheria has almost been established. Without going into a minute description of the two diseases, it can be said that the clinical history is so different that we wonder why it was that for so great a length of time they were considered identical. Diphtheria is very contagious, croup never is; diphtheria is very fatal, croup rarely is. Croup is often repeated in the same individual, while diphtheria may be, but seldom is. The membrane of croup is white, of fibrine; that of diphtheria is a dirty yellowish one, of lymph. One is capable of inoculation, the other never is. Croup appears suddenly, diphtheria has its prodromes. The period of incubation of diphtheria is short, usually from two to four days. An exposure to a severe case produces a severe case. Where we find a family predisposition, a severe case may be looked for. This disease attacks persons of all ages; yet when the victim is between one and five years of age, a severe case generally results. As a rule, after a person has passed fifteen years of age an attack of diphtheria is light, but there are many exceptions.

Diphtheria is prone to attack persons who have delicate throats; frequent sore throat seems to attract the poison. The disease is frequently a follower of measles, scarlet fever, and smallpox. At times it comes in the wake of typhoid fever and whooping cough.

As regards any protective influence of an attack of diphtheria against recurrence, there is probably a slight one, but it is not so marked as is the case in other zymotic diseases.

The symptoms of diphtheria are often so masked and slight that, until the unmistakable membrane is seen, the true character of the affection is not recognized. There are four forms of the disease, each having its special symptoms—the catarrhal, the croupous, the septicæmic, and the gangrenous. The catarrhal at first presents symptoms of catarrh. The croupous comes on more suddenly, with pain in the throat. In both these forms there is fever, headache, nausea, and debility. In certain cases the symptoms are very pronounced. The tongue is covered with a thick creamy coating, which comes to the tip, a viscid secretion covering all. The odor of the breath is peculiar, and. when the patient is old enough to know, he will complain of a bad taste continually. This is said to resemble the taste of bad eggs or of brass—children say "like cents." There is also a peculiar metallic ring to the voice. The false membrane begins to form about the second day. It may be at one point or at several. Where these points are numerous they soon run together. In the catarrhal form the patches of membrane are not so thick, come off easily, and are not so prone to reform. As the membrane comes off, the fever decreases. In the croupous form the temperature runs between 101° and 104°; above this indicates a serious case, one with much systemic infection. The septic form of the disease manifests the well-known signs of blood poisoning. The pulse is weak and rapid, the temperature below 100°, at times being below the natural rate. There is diarrhœa, the stools have the odor of the breath, the urine is small in quantity and full of albumen. The membrane forms quickly in the throat and soon becomes foul and puslike. The septic form of diphtheria is very fatal, death usually resulting about the third day; very rarely does the victim live five days. When the pulse gains in volume and force, with a rise of temperature, and we notice an improvement in the throat symptoms, recovery may be looked for. The gangrenous form is the septic intensified. Gangrene appears in the throat, the parts slough, the odor is horrible. The patient is overwhelmed with the poison, and dies quickly. At times the membrane extends into the nasal cavities, and this indicates a serious case.

Diphtheria is one of those diseases having sequelæ. Even very mild and localized cases may be followed by digestive derangement. Nervous manifestations may also arise. In the severe forms, heart troubles remain, kidney disturbance, and, what is most serious, paralyses. This may be local, or quite extensive. Recovery may usually be looked for from these results, but it is very slow, and taxes a little patient's strength to a great extent.

The treatment of diphtheria must be prompt, local, and constitutional. The patient should be at once isolated; no child should be allowed near him. It is best to have a trained nurse, and all handkerchiefs, cloths, and soiled bedclothing should be burned. All spoons, forks, glasses, and tubes should be kept in the sick-room, and washed and disinfected there. Too much care can not be taken to avoid spreading the disease. There is so much foundation for the theory of a local infection, followed by a systemic poisoning in diphtheria, that the greatest chances of success in its treatment consist in the early recognition of the disease, and the quick detection and removal, or destruction, of the first patch of false membrane. If possible, it should be carefully teased off, removed. Strong caustics do more harm than good. Most recent writers condemn their use. We should keep the throat clean, and have it frequently painted or sprayed with one of the many disinfecting solutions, hot water, a solution of the tincture chloride of iron, or, what the writer has found most serviceable, a solution of permanganate of potassium. Very recently it has been recommended to spray the throat with a very weak solution of bichloride of mercury. This has been urged by men of considerable experience, but the danger of toxic symptoms should be borne in mind. The local applications recommended have been so numerous that it is not necessary to mention them; every practitioner that has had any experience with this horrible affection has his favorites.

In treating diphtheria, the physician must personally see that all the minute directions are carried out. It is one of those diseases that require close watching on his part. The hygienic surroundings of the patient must receive careful attention. In every case of diphtheria, no matter how light, there is a tendency to marked weakness and dissolution of the blood; hence sustaining treatment is demanded. Every care must be given to sustain life for a certain number of days, as Nature makes a great curative effort. In short, like all diseases of this class, diphtheria runs a special course, and when this is done there is, except in the septic and gangrenous forms, an attempt at recovery. The diet must be very nutritious and easily digested; beef tea, beef jelly, eggs, and milk must be frequently given. If there is any specific in the treatment of diphtheria, it is alcohol. Alcoholic stimulants seem to antagonize the poison, and it is wonderful how much even a little patient will stand. It is a most excellent practice to administer strong sherry wine or brandy in beef tea. Where there is much nausea, champagne will be found valuable. If the prostration seems to increase early in the case, nothing equals brandy. Large amounts must be given, and it is well to combine it with small quantities of lime water.

The medicinal remedies that have been recommended are numerous, new ones having been thrown aside for old ones. It is necessary, however, to mention those only which the latest experience seems to approve. Emetics should rarely be given; if it is necessary to do so, one that acts quickly without producing much depression should be selected. Ipecac or sulphate of zinc is the best. It is unsafe to repeat the emetic more than twice. One of the most recent emetics suggested is apomorphia. This has an advantage in being administered hypodermically and acting very quickly. Jaborandi is one of the most recent favorites in treatment, and it has been claimed that by fair doses the false membrane may be detached. The great danger is the prostration that always follows a dose of any size. Sulphuret of potassium, chlorate of potassium, the sodic compounds, bromine compounds, cubebs, copaiba, carbolic acid, the mercurials, iron, and quinine have been successively employed, but mercury, iron, and quinine are most to be relied upon. The mercurial treatment of diphtheria is old, and, on account of the excessive doses given in the past, had fallen into disfavor, but now that we recognize the germ element in the poison of the disease and administer mercury with a better understanding of its power and action, it has risen to favor, and is beyond question a valuable agent. In the early treatment of diphtheria, calomel, in doses of 1 to 3 grains every two to four hours, until the stools are frequent and green, has received much praise. It is also a most excellent practice to blow it dry into the throat. Bichloride of mercury is the best preparation to use in treating diphtheria, and its advocates rank among the highest authorities in the profession. Within the past three years most gratifying testimony has been added to its credit. Out of 2,000 cases treated in England during the past three years, the mortality was reduced, under this treatment, to 16 per cent. In the writer's hands most favorable results have followed from this agent. It should be administered in doses of $\frac{1}{100}$ to $\frac{1}{50}$ of a grain, given every two to three hours, according to age. The remedy must be pushed, and, as in the case of alcohol, diphtheria seems to form a tolerance for mercury. In a severe case it can be given every hour. Such authorities as Dillon Brown, Huber, and O'Dyer approve the administration of even such quantities as one quarter to one half grain of bichloride of mercury within twenty-four hours. The biniodide of mercury has not proved so satisfactory in its results, and the use of the cyanide is attended with considerable risk of digestive disturbances. Inunction of the mercurial ointment or of the oleate has also been recommended, but both these preparations have many disadvantages. The hypodermic injection of bichloride of mercury is so painful, and so liable to be followed by an abscess, that it had best not be used. Within the past year bicyanide of mercury, in combination with cocaine, has been recommended for hypodermic use. Iron is a valuable agent and possesses the advantage of lessening the heart complications. It is of value both locally and internally. It must be pushed in large doses, well diluted and frequently administered. The best preparation is the tincture of the chloride of iron. After recovery this should be continued for some time. Quinine has proved of much value in the treatment of diphtheria, especially in combination with iron. In the early stages of the disease it should be given in large doses, afterward in tonic doses.

During convalescence a patient should be carefully watched. Iron, quinine, and cod-liver oil will be of great value. Change of air, especially the seashore, is of much benefit. If, as so often happens, weak and disturbed digestion follows, tonics, cold baths, and strict attention to diet must be prescribed.

The question of operation as a last resort in diphtheria is an open one. Much has been claimed for it, but experience has been most unsatisfactory. The mode of procedure has been improved, but a corresponding improvement in results is lacking. A patient suffering from diphtheria is a bad subject for an operation of any kind at best, so little can be expected from it. Some recoveries after very desperate cases have been reported; hence, as a last resort, operative procedures might be attempted. But the writer believes that almost all the cases where a recovery has followed an operation have been croup, and not true diphtheria.

DISASTERS IN 1892. The list of accidents presents no peculiar features. There is rarely a year that lacks terrible calamities, whether caused by earthquakes, storms, or other natural phenomena, and the past year is no exception in this respect. Losses of life and property by fire have been perhaps exceptionally frequent, and it will be noticed that the flames have spared neither churches nor charities nor business houses, but have consumed all alike, with seeming impartiality. The summaries of train accidents are from the tables prepared by the "Railroad Gazette," and apply to the United States alone.

January 2. Fire: warehouses burned, Nashville, Tenn., 3 killed, several hurt, loss, about $450,000. Panic in a hall, several persons badly hurt at Oella, Md., cause, an overturned lamp.

3. Shipwreck: British bark Chidwell sunk in collision, 15 drowned. Fires: grain-lifts, Brooklyn, N. Y., loss, about $100,000; stables and other buildings, Ballston, N. Y.

5. Trains wrecked in Illinois, 6 killed, several hurt; and near Asheville, N. C., 4 killed.

6. Trains wrecked near Smyrna, N. Y., 3 killed; and Fairmount, W. Va., 12 hurt. Fire: Wapello, Iowa, loss, $30,000. Tornado: Florida and Georgia, buildings destroyed and many people hurt.

7. Explosions: steam boilers burst at Bolling, Ala., 4 killed, 4 hurt; and Rankin Station, Pa., 1 killed, 12 hurt.

8. Colliery explosion, McAllister, Indian Territory, 100 killed, 115 hurt. Steam boiler bursts in Chicago, Ill., 4 killed. Fires: at Jeanette, Pa., and Syracuse, N. Y., total loss, $75,000.

9. Fires: at Jersey City, N. J.; Milwaukee, Wis.; Pittsburg, Pa.; Decatur, Ala., and Charlestown, W. Va., aggregate loss, about $375,000.

11. Trains wrecked near Nicolson Crossing, Ind., 2 killed, 29 hurt. Boiler bursts at Bridgeport, Pa., 2 killed, several hurt.

12. Fire: Worcester, Mass., mills of Pratt Manufacturing Company.

13. Fires: Cleveland, Ohio, and Topeka, Kan., losses about $210,000. Shipwreck: steamer Namchow in the China Sea, 414 lives lost.

14. Chicago, tramcar wrecked, 2 killed, 13 hurt. Fires: Waterbury, Conn., brass works, loss, $260,000; Jackson, Miss., business houses burned.

15. Train wrecked near Brainerd, Minn., 2 killed, 23 hurt. Floods in New York and New England.

16. Fires: New York, damage, $200,000, 1 life lost; Wausau, Wis., opera house, loss, $200,000; Charleston, S. C., brewery, loss, $100,000; Au Sable, Mich., loss, $75,000; unknown ship burned at sea, all hands probably lost, reported by steamer Imperial Prince.

18. Central City, W. Va., explosion of powder mill, 6 killed. Fires: Kansas City, loss, $150,000; Orleans, Neb., loss, $40,000.

19. Fires: Chicago, Ill.; Toledo, Ohio; Tarkio, Mo., and Shamokin, Pa., 2 lives lost at Chicago, damage, about $250,000. A bridge falls at Tiflis, many lives lost.

20. Train accident at grade crossing, St. Louis, Mo.,

8 killed. Fires: Roman Catholic Church and school, Fairfield, Conn., loss, $60,000; stove factory, Cleveland, Ohio, loss, $40,000.

21. Fire: business house, New York, loss, $500,000.

22. Fires: Surgical Institute, Indianapolis, Ind., 21 lives lost, 20 or more hurt; roundhouse near New Orleans, loss, $60,000; livery stable, New York, 39 horses killed, loss, $30,000; college buildings, Dueweet, N. C. Explosion: New York, 2 killed, several hurt. Russia: a church roof falls at Slobodski, 50 killed and wounded.

23. Fires: Roman Catholic Church, Connellsville, Pa., loss, $100,000; toy store, St. Louis, loss, $55,000; electric-light works, Boston, loss, $15,000. Earthquake in Rome.

24. Fires: tobacco warehouse, Pittsburg, loss, $40,000; factory, Rahway, N. J., loss, $39,000.

25. Fires: business houses, Pine Bluffs, Ark., loss, $150,000; factory, Chicago, loss, $65,000; warehouse, Providence, R. I., loss, $50,000; ice works, Danville, Va., loss, $75,000; hotel and other buildings, Beverly, W. Va., loss, $30,000.

26. Fires: opera house and business block, Columbus, Ohio, loss, $500,000; oil factory and wharves, Elizabethport, N. J., loss, $300,000; cotton works, Chester, N. C., loss, $220,000; business houses, Oakdale, Pa., loss, $30,000.

27. Fires: warehouse and workhouse, Cincinnati, loss, $250,000; railroad shops, Meridian, Miss., loss, $150,000; Roman Catholic church, Albany, N. Y.

28. Explosions: dynamite in a coal mine near Hazleton, Pa., 2 killed, 21 hurt; locomotive boiler, near St. Clair, Pa., 5 killed.

29. Explosions: dynamite, near Templeton, Ontario, 3 killed, several hurt; and near St. Louis, Mo., where no casualties were reported. Fires: dwelling at Brainerd, Minn., 4 lives lost; business houses, Jeanette, Pa., loss, $75,000; stores, Milan, Mo., loss, $60,000; marble works, West Rutland, Vt., loss, $50,000; wheel shops, La Porte, Ind., loss, $50,000.

Summary of train accidents in January: 120 collisions, 117 derailments, 12 miscellaneous; total, 249. Killed: 46 employees, 8 passengers, 7 trespassers; total, 61. Hurt: 111 employees, 147 passengers, 5 trespassers; total, 263.

February 1. Fire: Woodstock, Ill., stores burned, loss, $75,000. Shipwreck: steamer Eider, on the Isle of Wight.

2. Fire: Courthouse, Appomattox, Va., records lost. Explosion: Newark, N. J., 3 killed.

3. Slight earthquake near Portland, Ore. Fire: shoe factory, Danvers, Mass.

4. Scaffold falls at Birmingham, Ala., 2 killed, 6 hurt. Earthquake at Omaha, Neb.

5. Shipwreck: American steamer Venezuela ashore at Brigantine Shoal, N.J. Slight earthquake, San José, Cal. Fires: tobacco warehouse, Louisville, Ky., 1 life lost; flour mills, Covington, Ky., loss, $75,000; paper mills, Battle Creek. Mich., loss, $50,000; tannery, Cincinnati, loss, $55,000.

6. Shipwrecks: steamer Polynesian, ashore at Cape Henry, Va.; steamer Embricos, on the Scilly Islands, 10 lives lost. Fire: packing house, Birmingham, Ala., loss, $50,000.

7. Fires: Hotel Royal, New York, about 70 lives lost; business houses, Rochester, N. Y., loss, $125,000; houses burned, Manchester, N. H., loss, $50,000.

8. Fires: many buildings, Memphis, Tenn., loss, about $1,000,000; iron works, Indianapolis, Ind., loss, $150,000; business houses, Larned, Kan., loss, $125,000; paper mills, Springfield, Mass., loss, $70,000. Explosion: locomotive boiler, near Reading, Pa., 3 killed, 5 hurt.

9. Fire: opera house, Wilbur, Neb., loss, $50,000.

10. Fires: several houses in Cincinnati, loss, $290,000; factory, Sterling, Ill., loss, $75,000; opera house, Des Moines, Iowa, loss, $50,000.

11. Fire: hotel burned, El Paso, Texas, loss, $100,000.

12. Fires: opera house block, Monmouth, Ill., loss, $150,000; warehouses, Kingston, N. Y., loss, $75,000.

13. Fires: Murta, Ark., nearly destroyed; telephone exchange, New York city, burned, loss, $100,000; stables, Norfolk, Va., 80 horses lost; business houses, Elizabethtown, Pa., loss, $75,000; factory, Amesbury, Mass., loss, $50,000.

14. Fire: furniture factory, New York, loss, $130,000.

15. Mining accident, Aspen, Col., 3 killed.

16. Fire: asylum for the insane burned, Jackson, Miss., 1 life lost, damage, $200,000.

17. Great Britain: violent storms on the coast, many vessels lost.

18. Shipwreck: bark Tamerlane and ore off Puna, Hawaiian Islands, 18 lives lost. Fire: many buildings in New Orleans, loss, about $1,000,000. Mine caves in, Plattsburg, N. Y., 3 killed; steel converter overturned, Pittsburg, Pa., 3 killed.

20. Fire: liquor store in Ironwood, Mich., 3 lives lost; another heavy snowstorm causes much distress in Great Britain.

21. Shipwreck: steamer founders off the Cornish coast, all hands lost. Fire: stores at Malvern, Ark., loss, $100,000.

23. Fires: dwelling at McKeesport, Pa., 4 severely injured; stores, Chicago, Ill., damage, $50,000. Disastrous floods in Spain.

24. Fires: clothing house, Baltimore, 1 killed, 1 hurt, loss, $50,000; business block, Spokane Falls, Wash., loss, $56,000; Haverhill, Mass., loss, $50,000. Earthquake in California. Fall of factory chimney, Checkheaton, England, 8 girls killed.

25. Fires: several buildings, San Antonio, Texas, loss, 250,000; carriage factory, Cincinnati, loss, $40,000.

26. Fires: grain-lift, East Deerfield, Mass., loss, $100,000; oilcloth factory, Elizabeth, N. J., loss, $40,000; buildings, Newark, N. J., loss, $40,000. Shipwreck: steamers in collision in the North Sea, 1 sunk, 23 lives lost.

27. Shipwreck: ship Albano, on Hog Island, Va., crew rescued by life-saving service. Explosion of gas at East Liverpool, Ohio, 3 killed. Mine caves in, Butte, Mont., 3 killed.

28. Fire: Little Rock, Ark., ex.-Gov. Conway killed; business houses and elevated railway burned, Brooklyn, N. Y., loss, $500,000. Marble works, New York, loss, $140,000; business houses, Hot Springs, S. Dak., loss, $75,000.

29. Explosions: steam boiler, Savannah, Ga., 2 killed, 1 hurt. Fire: Hillsville, Va., town half destroyed. Anarchists explode bombs in Paris, building wrecked. Thirteen seal hunters drowned, North Pacific Coast, 100 missing.

Summary of train accidents in February: 85 collisions, 115 derailments, 12 miscellaneous; total, 212. Killed: 37 employees, 7 passengers; total, 44. Hurt: 55 employees, 40 passengers, 8 trespassers; total, 103.

March 1. Train wrecked near Milwaukee, Wis., 7 killed. Fires: goods store, Milwaukee, Wis., loss, $100,000; female reformatory, Indianapolis, loss, $100,000.

2. Train wrecked near Bridgeport, W. Va., 15 hurt. Fires: mill at Chestertown, Md., loss, $170,000; foundry, New York city, loss, $50,000. Many deaths from alleged famine in Hungary.

3. Fires: business houses, Detroit, loss, $200,000; business houses, East Liverpool, Ohio, loss, $160,000; oil works, Kansas City, Mo., loss, $75,000; shoe factory, Campbells, Mass., loss, $70,000; buildings burned, Platte Center, Neb., loss, $30,000; buildings burned, Philadelphia, 6 hurt, loss, $150,000.

4. Fires: foundry, Rouse's Point, N. Y., loss, $75,000; brewery, West St. Paul, Minn., loss, $50,000.

5. Fires: business houses and railroad station, Dexter, Mo., loss, $70,000; business house, Sioux City, Iowa, loss, $50,000.

6. Fires: apartment house, West Superior, Wis.; mills, Rock Hill, S. C.; hotels, Tybee Beach, Ga.

9. Blizzard in the Northwest: loss of life and destruction of property. Explosion in a mine near Wilkesbarre, Pa., 3 killed, 5 hurt. Fires: glassworks,

Pittsburg, Pa., loss, $250,000; factories, Chicago, loss, $125,000; Roman Catholic church, Roxbury, Mass., loss, $75,000.

10. Fires: Jackson, Tenn., business block burned, 1 life lost; art store, Milwaukee, Wis., loss, $40,000.

11. Train wrecked by malice in Illinois. Fire: business houses, Waverly, Ill., probably incendiary at the instance of "the Whisky party." Explosion: fire damp in a Belgian colliery, about 200 lives lost.

12. Explosion in Revenue Tunnel, Colorado, 2 killed, 1 hurt. Fires: Erie Railroad sheds, Jersey City, heavy loss; many buildings, Bloomfield, Ill., loss, $165,000; bolt works, Cleveland, Ohio, loss, $150,000; stores, Red Key, Ind., 1 life lost. Shipwreck: steamer Colima, on the coast of Salvador.

14. Grain-lift falls at St. Louis, Mo., 3 killed.

15. Fires: gun store, Fort Worth, Texas, loss, $150,000; warehouses, Kittanning, Pa., loss, $100,000; business houses, Danbury, Conn., loss, $75,000; hotel, Jacksonville, Fla., loss, $45,000; business houses, Mount Pleasant, Tenn.

16. Fires: tile works, Anderson, Ind., loss, $85,000; stores, Elkhart, Ind., loss, $60,000; car stables, St. Louis, loss, $45,000; stores, Louisville, Neb., and Cranesville, N. Y.

18. Shipwreck: steel clipper ship Windermere ashore at Deal Beach, N. J., crew saved by life-boat men. Severe storm in Texas, crops largely ruined. Fires: tobacco factory, St. Louis, loss, $345,000; wagon factory, Pittsburg, loss, $45,000.

19. Fires: railroad station, New Haven, Conn., loss, $150,000; station house, Cincinnati, loss, $75,000; factory, Chicago, loss, $100,000; stores, Homer, Ill., loss, $50,000.

21. Explosions: steam boiler, East Jordan, Mich., 6 killed, 4 hurt; steam boilers, Cheltenham, St. Louis, 4 killed, 2 hurt, perhaps fatally; gasoline stove in a church, Manning, Iowa, the minister killed. Fires: dwelling house, Springfield, Minn., 5 lives lost; factory, Barron Island, N. Y., loss, $100,000; stores, Corydon, Pa.

22. Fires: in the House of Representatives, Washington, D. C., loss, mainly new public documents; factory, Cambridge, Mass., loss, $145,000.

23. Fires: business section of Alto, Texas, burned, loss, $105,000; new business block, Fostoria, Ohio, loss, $40,000.

25. Explosion: steam boiler, Fidelity, Ohio, 5 killed. Fires: glass works, Braddock, Pa., loss, $100,000; courthouse, St. Charles, Mo., records lost.

26. Tornado: Piatt County, Ill., many buildings wrecked. Accident in steel converter, Homestead, Pa., 5 killed.

27. Fire: hardware works, Omaha, Neb., loss, $200,000; factory, Philadelphia, loss, $175,000.

30. Sulphur mine near Lake Charles, La., 5 men suffocated by gas. Fires: hotel in Boston, several hurt; wagon factory, Cincinnati, loss, $140,000; hotel, St. Cloud, N. J., loss, $50,000. Prairie fire: Norton County, Kan., many buildings burned, 1 life lost.

31. Tornado: Nelson, Neb., many buildings blown down. Fires: two steamboats burned at Cincinnati, loss, $100,000; factory, Milwaukee, Wis., 1 life lost, $35,000 damage; Mandalay, Burmah, several hundred houses burned.

Summary of train accidents in March: 75 collisions, 107 derailments, 12 miscellaneous; total, 194. Killed: 37 employees, 1 passenger, 2 trespassers; total, 40. Hurt: 93 employees, 95 passengers, 5 trespassers; total, 193.

April 1. Explosion: dynamite factory, near Bessemer, Ala., 4 killed. Fire: Wilkesbarre, Pa., 2 lives lost. Cyclonic storm in Kansas, extending to Chicago and vicinity, Towanda totally destroyed; altogether about 50 lives were lost and 200 people were hurt.

2. Fires: carriage works and grain elevator at Erie, Pa., loss, $200,000; 30 buildings, Greenville, Miss., loss, $100,000; warehouse, Orange, N. J.

3. Violent electric storm in West Virginia and Pennsylvania, much damage by hail, rain, and wind. Fires: cotton presses, New Orleans, loss, $2,500,000;

Milton, Ala., nearly destroyed, loss, $80,000. Tornado: Cherryville, Kan., 2 killed, many houses wrecked. Boat upset near Colerain, Mass., 6 drowned.

4. Fire: stores and other buildings, Nouma, La., loss, $50,000.

6. Explosion: locomotive bursts at Long Island City, N. Y., 2 killed, 3 hurt. Fires: 9 lives lost at Fort Madison, Iowa; furniture works, Piqua, Ohio, loss, $150,000; oil works, West St. Paul, Minn., loss, $105,000; hospital burned, Missoula, Iowa, loss, $50,000.

7. Mississippi: rain during several days causes great damage. Fires: dwelling house, St. Louis, 3 lives lost; Market Hall, Pullman, Ill., loss, $50,000.

8. Trains wrecked by collision, near Mount Vernon, Ohio, 12 hurt. Fires: distillery, Portland, Ore., loss, $50,000; coal breaker, Pittston, Pa., loss, $50,000; flour mills, Laurel, Md., loss, $40,000.

9. Fire: glass works, Beaver Falls, Pa., loss, $55,000. Boat upset, New Haven harbor, 3 drowned.

10. Fires: flour mill, Catlettsburg, Ky., 1 life lost, $50,000 damage; chemical works, Newark, N. J., loss, $50,000, 50 firemen overcome by fumes; Tokio, Japan, 6,000 houses burned, about 50 lives lost.

11. Boat upset, Boston harbor, 9 lives lost. Fires: agricultural warehouse, Newport, R. I., loss, $50,000; rubber company, New York, loss, $30,000.

12. Disastrous flood on the Tombigbee river, Alabama, great loss of life. Earthquake in western New York. Fire: iron works, Butte, Mont., loss, $250,000.

13. Explosion: powder mills near Wilkesbarre, Pa., 7 killed, 2 hurt. Boat upset near Brandon, Ore., 4 drowned. Fires: newspaper office, Washington, D. C., $25,000 damage; Clark University, Atlanta, Ga., loss, $100,000; railroad property, Long Island City, N. Y., loss, $80,000.

15. Fire: paper mill, Coltsville, Mass., loss, $125,000.

16. Destructive storms in Virginia and England. Anarchists explode a bomb in a church in Havana.

17. Earthquake in Portland, Ore.

18. Explosion: "forcite" works, near Arlington, N. J., 7 killed. Tornado: Indian Territory, 3 killed, many houses demolished. Lightning destroys a building near Charlestown, Ind., damage, $80,000. Incendiary fire, San Antonio, Texas, loss, $100,000. Fire: near Trenton, N. J., school buildings burned, loss, $40,000. Much damage by snow and frost in Great Britain. Hampstead Heath, England, 8 killed by a rush of excursionists at a railroad station.

19. Explosion: fireworks at Greenville, N. J., 2 killed, several hurt. Fire: lumber yards and factories, Kenosha, Wis., loss, $600,000; dye works, Staten Island, N. Y., loss, $100,000.

20. Earthquakes in the neighborhood of Vacaville, Sacramento, Cal., and Nevada City. Fires: synagogue at Ludwig, Pa.; brewery, Brooklyn, N. Y., damage, over $90,000 (supposed incendiary). Explosions: Anarchist bombs in three Spanish towns.

21. Colliery accident, Minersville, Pa., 10 lives lost. Earthquake shocks continue in California.

22. Train wrecked near Groton, Pa., 2 killed. Fires: the town of Slights, Mich., almost totally destroyed; six incendiary fires in San José, Cal.

23. Broken girder, Holyoke, Mass., 13 hurt. Walls fall at Chicago and Jonesborough, Tenn., 5 killed, several hurt.

24. Continued earthquake shocks in California. Fire in a Roman Catholic church, Fort Wayne, Ind., panic ensues, many hurt. Boat upset, Beaver Lake, Wis., 3 drowned.

25. Fires: stock-farm buildings, Pennington, N. J., loss, $125,000; business block, Gainesville, Texas, loss, $200,000 (supposed incendiary); stock and dairy farm buildings, Harkville, N. Y., loss, $50,000; Roman Catholic church burned, New Castle, Pa.

26. Fires: Colby Academy, New London, N. H., loss, $75,000; stores, St. Paul, Minn., loss, $60,000; 3,000 cotton bales, Savannah, Ga., loss, $50,000.

27. Fires: factory, Linwood, Ohio, loss, $35,000; Athenæum building, Chicago, loss, $60,000; theatre and "Times" building, Philadelphia, loss, $1,000,000, 6 lives lost, many hurt.

28. Unusually severe "blizzard" in Manitoba. Fires: New York city, 2 lives lost; Hudson, Ohio, loss, $80,000. Anarchist bombs exploded in France, Belgium, and Italy.

29. Storm on Lake Michigan, 12 or more lives lost. Fires: 1,000 acres of forest in New Jersey; 63 buildings in Chase, Mich., loss, $100,000; business blocks, Mount Sterling, Ill., loss, $40,000; hotels, Nantasket Beach, Mass., loss, $75,000; business houses, Browning, Mo., loss, $30,000; business houses and dwellings, Reed City, Miss., loss not stated; buildings burned, Fall River, Kan., loss, $50,000. Earthquake in California. Hurricane in Mauritius, about 1,000 lives lost, great destruction of property.

30. Train wrecked near Bonner's Ferry, Wash., 3 killed, 30 hurt. Fires: Coffeyville, Kan., business houses burned; Pittsburg, Pa., stores and factories, loss, $300,000; Corry, Pa., dwelling house burned, 2 lives lost.

Summary of train accidents in April: 47 collisions, 86 derailments, 10 miscellaneous; total, 143. Killed: 30 employees, 4 passengers, 5 trespassers; total, 39. Hurt: 107 employees, 24 passengers, 7 trespassers; total, 138.

May 1. Fires: theatre and buildings, Leadville, Col., damage, $40,000, 2 lives lost.

2. Fires: Mount Sterling, Ky., loss, $75,000; Fairlawn stables, Lexington, Ky., loss, $35,000, including valuable horses: several buildings in Ottawa, Kan.

3. Severe storms, with loss of life and property, in Kansas, Oklahoma, Illinois, and Michigan. Fires: cotton warehouse, Norfolk, Va., loss, $75,000; warehouse, Oshkosh, Wis., loss, $75,000; incendiary fire, Hillsborough, Ky., loss, $50,000.

4. Destructive floods in the Illinois, Fox, and Kankakee rivers. Tornado: DeKalb County, Mo., several killed, much damage done. Fires: photograph gallery, Ottawa, Ontario, $40,000 damage; factory, Aurora, Ill., loss, $40,000. Lightning strikes a detachment of 18 soldiers at Bourges, France, all prostrated, 1 killed.

5. Trains wrecked near Revere, Mo., 7 killed, many hurt. Fires: factories and mills, Rushville, Ind., loss, $150,000; Roman Catholic church, New York, damage, $50,000.

6. Violent and destructive gale in Pennsylvania, Delaware, and District of Columbia. Fire: packing house, New York, loss, $200,000.

8. Fires: salt works and lumber yard, Ludington, Mich., loss, about $500,000; sash and blind factory, New York; car works, Robinsdale, Minn., loss, $200,000.

9. "Cyclone-cave" falls in, Anthony, Kan., 5 killed. Fire: electrical works and other buildings, Hayward, Cal., loss, $100,000.

10. Explosion: gas in a coal mine near Roslyn, Wash., 43 killed, 250 children fatherless.

12. Fires: pottery, Trenton, N. J., loss, $175,000; foundry, Quincy, Mass., loss, $70,000.

13. Fires: dwelling house, Spades, Ind., 2 lives lost; Territorial Capitol, Santa Fé, New Mexico, loss, $205,000; dwellings, Savannah, Ga., loss, $100,000; oil storage, San Antonio, Texas, loss, $70,000; warehouse, Jefferson, Texas, loss, $70,000.

14. Mine caves in, Butte, Mont., 8 killed. Fires: Hazleton, Pa., loss, $100,000; shoe factory, Rochester, N. H., loss, $100,000; knitting mill, Cohoes, N. Y., loss, $70,000.

15. Trains wrecked, Cleves, Ohio, 7 killed, 15 hurt. Boat upset in Delaware river, 3 drowned. Crevasses along the Mississippi river.

16. Fire: buildings burned, Brooklyn, N. Y., damage, $150,000, 2 lives lost. Hurricane in New Zealand, many lives lost.

17. Cyclone: Greer County, Texas, all buildings demolished in its course. Shipwreck: steamer Alexander Wolcow, in the Caspian Sea, about 250 lives lost.

18. Floods cause widespread destruction of property and loss of life in the Mississippi and Missouri valleys. Fires: Fort McKinney, Wy., damaged; stove works, Long Island City, N. Y., loss, $50,000; Cotton block, Charleston, W. Va., loss, $30,000.

19. Tornado: Hamilton County, Ohio.

21. Train wrecked, Cotton Belt Railroad, 7 killed. Explosion: fireworks, Hartford, Conn., 5 killed, several hurt, building wrecked. Fire: opera house and buildings, Lansford, Pa.; cotton warehouse, Alexandria, Egypt, loss, $2,500,000. Church roof falls, Pittsburg, 7 hurt, 2 probably killed.

22. Shipwreck: Brazilian man-of-war of the La Plata river, 120 lives lost. Fire: Baptist church, Meridian, Miss.

23. Fires: stores, London, Ontario, loss, $30,000; stores, Bingham, Utah, loss, $100,000; Chehols, Wash., loss, $110,000; mills and factories, Spokane, Wash., loss, $230,000.

25. Fire: business houses, Wichita Falls, Texas, loss, $100,000; dwellings and stores, Bellefonte, Pa.

26. Dam breaks, Kingsman, Ohio, 6 or more drowned, buildings swept away. Fires: factory, Louisville, Ky., loss, $100,000; fire-brick works, Mexico, Mo., loss, $50,000. Tornado: Wellington, Kan., about 20 killed. Drowned at Woodville, Pa., 4 boys. Lightning: destroys Baptist church, Bordentown, N. J.; kills 2 men in Indiana.

29. Fire: tobacco warehouse, Lancaster, Pa., loss, $160,000.

30. Fire: carriage factory, Brooklyn, N. Y., loss, $150,000. Destructive floods and tornadoes in Missouri, Kansas, Arkansas, and other Western States.

Summary of train accidents in May: 61 collisions, 72 derailments, 8 miscellaneous: total, 141. Killed: 36 employees, 20 passengers, 10 trespassers; total, 66. Hurt: 109 employees, 111 passengers, 3 trespassers; total, 223.

June 1. Damage from storms in Indiana. A cloudburst wrecks buildings, including several churches, in Rushville, Mo. Fire: business houses in Coquille City, Ore.; Bohemia, fire in a silver mine, about 400 lives lost.

2. Cyclone in northern Texas, loss of life and property.

4. Heavy snow in Wyoming. Fire: carriage factory, New Haven, Conn., loss, $100,000. Tornado: the town of McCook, Neb., nearly destroyed, many hurt.

5. Floods and fire in the Pennsylvania oil regions, many lives lost, heavy damage to property. Severe snowstorm in South Dakota. Tornado: Cleborne, Texas, 42 houses demolished, 2 killed.

6. Train wrecked at South Carrolton, Ky., 4 killed, 43 hurt.

7. Destruction of Sanguir, an island in the Malay Archipelago, by volcanic eruption, several thousand lives lost. Drowned at Forest City, Mo., 4 persons. Fire: pipe works, Akron, Ohio, loss, $100,000.

9. Dangerously high floods in the Danube.

10. Fires: planing mill, Cleveland, Ohio, loss, about $250,000; hat factory, Newark, N. J., loss, $38,000; several houses, Las Vegas, New Mexico, loss, $35,000; hotel, Lake Mohican, N. Y., loss, $80,000.

11. Electric-car accidents at Andover, Mass., Benwood, W. Va., and Atlanta, Ga., 6 killed, 20 hurt. Fires: opera house and neighboring buildings, Grand Rapids, Mich., loss, $60,000; stores and dwelling houses, Cullman, Ala., loss, $60,000; store, Cleveland, Ohio, loss $50,000; mills and factories, Orono, Maine, loss, $50,000.

13. Explosion: powder in Mare Island Navy Yard, California, 12 killed, 3 hurt. Violent storm in Chicago, 1 killed. Lightning: 2 churches struck in Spain, 15 killed, many hurt.

14. Storms in the Western States, 8 killed, many hurt. Train wrecked, Lonesome Hollow, Ky., 7 killed, 6 hurt. Fire: warehouses, Baltimore, loss, $1,000,000. Lightning: steamer Petrolia struck at Blaye, France, 15 killed. Trains wrecked, London, England, 4 killed, many hurt.

15. Bridge falls, Licking river, Ky., about 40 killed. Lightning does much damage in New England. Fires: ice houses, East Hampden, Me., loss, $75,000; car shops, De Hodia, Mo.

16. Tornado in Minnesota, about 40 killed. Lightning strikes the Grant monument, Chicago, 3 killed, several hurt. Fires: factories, Elizabeth, W. Va., loss, $800,000; Elizabeth, N. J., loss, $90,000; business houses, Rich Hill, Mo., loss, $40,000; post office, customhouse, etc., New Haven, Conn., loss, $50,000.

17. Drowned near Pittsburg, 5 children.

18. Fires: Maurice, Ind., glass works, loss, $300,000.

19. Electric car wrecked, Cleveland, Ohio, several hurt. Fires: melting works, Louisville, loss, $135,000.

24. Destructive floods in Illinois. Fire lighted with kerosene, Allegheny, Pa., 3 killed, one badly burned.

25. Train wrecked near Harrisburg, Pa., 12 killed, many hurt.

26. Floods in the West, at least 7 persons drowned.

28. Fire: warehouse, Seattle, Wash., loss, $400,000.

29. Train wrecked near Little Rock, Ark., 5 killed, several hurt. Boat upset near New Orleans, 4 drowned. Tornado and lightning in New Jersey, 2 killed, several hurt. Lightning kills 4 men at Bonne Terre, Mo.

Summary of train accidents in June: 75 collisions, 88 derailments, 2 miscellaneous; total, 165. Killed: 44 employees, 21 passengers, 5 trespassers; total, 70. Hurt: 143 employees, 152 passengers, 4 trespassers; total, 299.

July 1. Providence, R. I., earthworks fall, 4 killed. Shipwreck: steamer City of Chicago ashore on the Irish coast.

2. Violent and destructive storms in several Central and Western States. Fires: warehouses burned, Providence, R. I., loss, $500,000; stores, Montgomery, Ala., loss, $250,000; furniture factory, Baltimore, loss, $150,000; barrel-stave works, St. Ignace, Mich., loss, $75,000; stores, Brooklyn, N. Y., loss, $40,000; salt works, Warsaw, N. Y., loss, $50,000.

3. Fires: many buildings, San José, Cal., loss, $500,-000; saw mill, Minneapolis, loss, $85,000; Roman Catholic church burned, Duluth.

4. Many accidents from fireworks and arms in irresponsible hands. A balloon falls into Boston harbor, 3 drowned. Tornado in Carey, Ohio, damage, $100,-000.

6. Another flood in the Mississippi. Fire: Pocomoke City, Md., loss, $200,000.

7. Fire: dwelling house, New York, 4 killed. Shipwreck: steamer Maréchal Canrobert sinks at sea, 7 lives lost.

9. Explosions: at Highland, Cal., 12 miles from San Francisco, several killed, damage, $350,000; shock felt 80 miles away. Fires: St. Johns, Newfoundland, the city nearly destroyed, estimated loss, $20,000,000; Christiansund, Norway, loss, $3,500,000; Louisville, Ky., loss, $200,000. Steamboat boiler bursts, Geneva Lake, Switzerland, 19 killed. Schooner Harry R. Tilden sunk off Sandy Hook by a projectile from the artillery proving grounds. Mount Etna, Sicily, in a state of violent eruption.

11. Destructive floods in Alabama.

12. Chicago: sidewalk caves in, 40 persons fall into a basement, many badly hurt. Fires: Leroy, Ill., loss, $68,500; coal yard and dwellings, San Francisco, loss, $65,000. Avalanche: Mont Blanc, Switzerland, village of St. Gervais les Bains destroyed, about 200 lives lost.

13. Steamboat upsets, Peoria, Ill., 16 drowned. Tornado: Springfield, Ohio, 2 killed, many buildings wrecked. Disastrous floods in the Tombigbee river. Villages destroyed by lava from Mount Etna. Fire: flouring mills, Paris, Tenn., loss, $75,000.

14. Naphtha explosion, Westport, Conn., 3 fatally hurt.

15. Violent wind storm in Cincinnati, houses unroofed, several persons hurt. Train wrecked at Evansville, Ind., 11 badly hurt. Fires: hotel and adjacent buildings, Pittsburg, Pa., loss, $70,000; flour mill, Wolcott, Iowa, loss, $40,000. Italy: Mounts Etna and Vesuvius in active eruption.

16. Four young men drowned while swimming near Princess Anne, Md.

17. Shipwreck: a tug and 4 barges, with 32 men lost, in Lake Ontario. Fires: warehouses, Independence, Iowa, loss, $50,000; stables, Monmouth Beach, N. J., loss, including 6 horses, $50,000.

18. Trains wrecked near Merritton, Ontario, 3 killed, several hurt. Fires: Montreal, Ontario, loss, $500,000; stock yards, Cleveland, Ohio, loss, $45,000; linoleum factory, Akron, Ohio, loss, $100,000; grain elevator, Richmond, Va., loss, $100,000. Lightning kills 4 persons in Richmond.

19. Fire: Atlantic Hotel, Long Branch, N. J.; warehouse, Providence, R. I., loss, $125,000. Hurricane in northern Italy, heavy loss of life and property. Storms cause loss of life in South Dakota.

20. Severe storms in Great Britain, and wrecks on the coast. Ten quarrymen buried in a slate mine, Benduff, Ireland.

21. Fires: business house, Rio Vista, Cal., loss, $150,000; railroad and other buildings, Moosup, Conn.

22. Tornado: Hiteman, Iowa, stores, a church, and some 20 buildings wrecked. Three men suffocated in a tannery in Chicago. Fires: warehouses burned, St. Louis, loss, $200,000; coal breaker, Pittston, Pa., loss, $100,000; mill, etc., Sauk Center, Minn., loss, $60,000.

23. Lightning: several persons killed and buildings fired in various parts of the country. Explosion of gas in a Pottsville colliery, 15 killed, 1 hurt. Fires in Washington, D. C., and Middleburg, Md., losses, about $130,000.

24. Shipwreck: steamer H. F. Dimmock sinks Mr. Vanderbilt's steam yacht Alva, off Pollock Rip, Mass. A mosque falls in Alexandria, Egypt, killing several hundred worshipers.

25. Fires: Bay City, Mich., 2 churches, 4 hotels, 40 stores, and some 300 dwellings burned, loss, about $1,250,000; the town of Iron River, Wis., almost destroyed; other fires at Schenectady, N. Y., and Carrolton, Mo. Forest fires in Prince Edward Island and Cape Breton. Fall of the Robber tower, Znaim, Moravia, several killed.

26. Destructive wind storms in Pennsylvania. Fires: biscuit factory, New York, loss, $500,000; oil works, Elizabeth, N. J., loss, $75,000; stores, Oakdale, Wash., loss, $50,000. Boat upset, Lake Lucerne, Switzerland, 5 drowned. Part of a theatre falls in Rueil, France, 80 or more killed.

27. Intense heat: many fatal cases of sunstroke. Four children accidentally locked in a closet at Medford, Mass., 3 died. Fires: store in Pittsburg, loss, $60,000; stable and stores, Stanford, Ky., loss, $60,-000; refinery, St. Paul, Minn., loss, about $70,000; many buildings, Bodie, Cal., loss, $50,000.

30. Lightning: several persons killed and many buildings struck. Fires: electric works, Toledo, Ohio, loss, $75,000; bank, stores, hotels, etc.. Cambridge, Md., loss, $75,000. Extensive forest fires in Cape Breton and Newfoundland.

31. Six boys drowned while bathing in Kentucky river. Lightning: several fatal strokes.

Summary of train accidents in July: 83 collisions, 104 derailments, 5 miscellaneous; total, 192. Killed: 29 employees, 5 passengers, 11 trespassers; total, 45. Hurt: 77 employees, 55 passengers, 18 trespassers; total, 150.

August 1. Fire: Wheatland, Iowa, houses burned, 1 life lost, damage, $75,000.

3. Fires: plaster works, Peoria, Ill., loss, $85,000; many buildings, New Providence, Ind.

4. Washout and flood: West St. Paul, Minn., many buildings swept away, several lives lost. Fires: courthouse, Port Tobacco, Md.; mills in Paris, Texas, loss, $250,000. Hail causes $50,000 damage in Kalamazoo, Mich.

5. Fire: lumber mills and yards burned at Stillwater, Mich., loss, $125,000.

6. Fire: lead works burned, Joplin, Mo., loss, $200,000.

7. Fires: post office and business houses, Alliance, Neb., loss, $50,000; barrel works, Ottumwa, Iowa, loss, $75,000; clothing house, New York, loss, $100,000.

8. Wind, hail, and rain cause heavy damage in Dakota, Minnesota, and Wisconsin. Fires: furniture factory and adjacent buildings, Baltimore, loss, $200,-000; druggist's warehouse, New York, loss, $100,000. Fatal fire at Kinloss, Oklahoma, 2 lives lost.

9. Boat upset near Charleston, S. C., 8 drowned. Fires: carriage works, East Buffalo, N. Y., loss, $75,-000; business houses, McKinney, Texas, loss, $60,000.

10. Excessive heat, fatal cases of sunstroke, and many destructive local thunderstorms. Fires: chemical works, Lancaster, Pa., loss, about $65,000; factory, Thomsonville, Conn., loss, $40,000; factory, Rutland, Vt., loss, $75,000.

11. Fires: planing mill, Hamilton, Ohio, loss, $80,-000; foundry, Chicago, loss, $45,000.

12. Lightning kills 2 women at Buzzard's Bay, Mass., and destroys buildings at Jamaica, Long Island, and elsewhere. Shipwreck: British men-of-war Apollo and Naiad, damaged by collision. Fires: Hotel Stratford, Washington, D. C., loss, about $25,000; grain lift, New York, loss, $150,000; factory, Farmington, Me., loss, $35,000.

13. Train wrecked near Clinton, Iowa, 14 hurt. Hand car wrecked near Schreiber, Ontario, 3 killed, 4 badly hurt. Fires: 17 buildings burned in Detroit, loss, $40,000.

14. Fires: cooperage works, New Orleans, loss, $350,000; warehouse, Norfolk, Va., loss, $30,000; the mining town of Red Mountain, Col., nearly destroyed, loss, $275,000; factories, Huntington, Pa., loss, $40,-000.

15. Shipwreck: British ship Thracian off the Isle of Man, 23 lives lost.

16. Train wrecked near Cochocton, Ohio, 6 killed, 15 badly hurt. Fires: Delmar, Del., nearly destroyed, 1 life lost; chair factory, Traverse City, Mich., loss, $55,000; dwelling, St. Paul, Minn., loss, $47,000.

17. Fires: lumber yards, MacIndoe's Falls, Vt., loss, $60,000. Several shipwrecks on the coast of New Brunswick.

18. Fires: stores, etc., Kendrick, Ida., loss, $60,-000; tannery burned at Winn, Me., loss, $75,000; stores and dwellings, South Charleston, Ohio, loss, $50,000.

19. Fires: stores, etc., Geneva, Ohio, loss, $175,-000; Delta, Ohio, loss, $200,000; refinery, Jenneretta, La., loss, $40,000.

20. Fires: pickling works, Sioux City, Iowa, loss, $75,000; mills and factories, South Royalston, Mass., loss, about $80,000; the town of Rock River, Mich., nearly destroyed.

21. Fires: pickling works, Somerville, Mass., loss, $45,000. Many deaths from sunstroke reported from Europe. Train wrecked in France, 5 killed, 18 hurt. Train wrecked in England, 50 hurt.

22. Fires: furniture warehouse, Omaha, loss, $100,-000; auction rooms, etc., St. Louis, loss, $35,000; carriage factory, Norfolk, Va., loss, $35,000.

23. Destructive rain, Roanoke, Va., 1 man drowned, loss, $100,000. Fires: railroad shops, Portsmouth, Ohio, loss, $40,000; stores, St. Paul, Minn., loss, $100,-000. Severe storms damage crops in Ireland.

24. Tornado: houses destroyed and crops damaged at Canandaigua, N. Y. Fires: buildings burned, Chenoa, Ill., loss, $40,000. Loss of life and damage to crops in Europe from excessive heat.

25. A woman aëronaut killed at Detroit. Fires: hotel at West Asheville, N. C.; stables, Columbia, Tenn., with a number of racing horses.

26. Shipwreck: steam yacht Wapiti, on Lake Huron, 7 lives lost. Colliery accident in South Wales, 110 lives lost.

27. Train wrecked near Parrott, Minn., 4 killed. Fires: Metropolitan Opera House, New York, damage, $200,000; several factories burned in New York; lumber yards, Petoskey, Mich., loss, $500,000; many buildings, Augusta, Ga., loss, $250,000; stables and business houses, Kansas City, loss, $50,000; nail works, Muncie, Ind., loss, $50,000.

29. Panic results from a fire in a Roman Catholic church at Forrestville, Mich., many hurt.

30. Shipwreck: steel steamer Western Reserve breaks in two on Lake Superior, 26 lives lost; several lake craft lost with all on board. Fires: brewery, Milwaukee, Wis., loss, $250,000; stores and workshops, Greenville, N. Y., loss, $40,000.

Summary of train accidents in August: 94 collisions, 119 derailments, 8 miscellaneous; total, 221. Killed: 35 employees, 8 passengers, 7 trespassers; total, 50. Hurt: 104 employees, 99 passengers, 10 trespassers; total, 213.

September 1. Train wrecked near New Hamburg, N. Y., 3 killed, 7 hurt. Fires: iron works, Muncie, Ind., loss, $175,000; tram-car stable, Washington, 16 horses killed. Explosion: fire damp in a Belgian mine, 56 lives lost.

3. Fires: factory, Detroit, loss, $75,000; factories, New Orleans, loss, $60,000. Explosion: 20 tons of powder on a vessel at Greenock, Scotland.

4. Fires: 9 buildings, Potoka, Ind., loss, $40,000; town of Rocky Bar, Idaho, destroyed. Naples, Italy, fall of an old palace, several persons hurt.

5. Cloud-burst, Alpine, Texas, live stock drowned, property destroyed. Fire: many buildings, Portland, Ore., loss, $100,000.

6. Fires: dwelling house, Port Deposit, Md., loss, $100,000; factory, Reading, Pa., loss, $65,000. Explosion: Sweeney's Creek, W.Va., 2 killed, 6 hurt.

7. Trains in collision at Eckenrode's Mills, Pa., 14 killed, many hurt. Fires: nearly 8,000,000 feet of lumber burned at New Boston, Ohio, also 13 loaded cars; factories burned in Philadelphia, loss, $250,000; and in Burlington, N. J., loss, $150,000.

9. Fires: many houses burned at Visalia, Cal.; dwelling house, Augusta, Me., loss, $50,000; factories and store-houses, Cincinnati, loss, $150,000; several miles of snow sheds on the Central Pacific Railroad burned, also the fire train sent to extinguish the flames.

11. Train wrecked near West Cambridge, Mass., 6 killed, 40 hurt.

12. Fire: building in Albany, N. Y., loss, $250,000.

13. Fire: hominy mills, St. Louis, Mo., loss, $110,000.

14. Fire: Indianapolis storage warehouse burned, loss, $200,000.

17. Fire: machine shop, Brooklyn Navy Yard, estimated damage, $500,000.

18. Trains wrecked near Kent, Ohio, 8 hurt. Explosion on United States steamship Philadelphia, several hurt.

19. Extended forest fire in western Colorado.

20. Fire: many buildings burned at Rockaway Beach, N. Y., loss, near $500,000.

21. Trains in collision in Ohio, 13 killed, 20 hurt. Train wrecked by brigands in Kansas, 4 killed, 25 hurt. Fires: saw mills, North Salem, N. Y., loss, $50,000; many houses, Marengo, Ill., loss, $40,000.

22. Fires: Redfield, Ark., loss, $50,000; Buctouche, New Brunswick, loss, $100,000.

23. Panic in a Hebrew synagogue, New York, 4 killed, many hurt. Fires: factory, Battle Creek, Mich., loss, $250,000; great prairie fire in North Dakota. Typhoon in Japan, 5,000 houses wrecked. Trains in collision, near New Hampshire, Iowa, 7 killed, 2 hurt.

24. Fire: shoe factory, South Braintree, Mass., loss, $60,000.

26. Wind: 6 houses blown down in Brooklyn, N. Y., 7 killed, many hurt. Mining accident: Bessemer, Mich., 4 killed. Fires: hotel, Cottage City, Mass., loss, $30,000; stables and houses, Richmond, Mo., loss, $30,000; sundry buildings in Wells River, Vt.

27. Fire: buildings burned, Howard, S. Dak., 2 women killed, loss, $100,000. Shipwreck: steamers H. M. Whitney (sunk) and Ottoman in collision off Boston; steamer Watertown burned off Boston, 1 life lost. Lightning strikes a house at Touloup, Kan., 2 killed. Train wrecked near Greenville, Ill., 3 killed, 8 hurt. Fires: at Columbus, Ohio, Warren, Mass., Elizabethport, N. J.; total loss about $600,000.

30. Freight cars and contents burned at Chicago, loss, $100,000.

Summary of train accidents in September: 113 collisions, 84 derailments, 6 miscellaneous; total, 203. Killed: 68 employees, 21 passengers, 4 trespassers; total, 93. Hurt: 110 employees, 119 passengers, 6 trespassers; total, 235.

October 1. Hailstorm, St. Paul, Minn.: 20 runaway accidents. Fires: Waco, Tex.; Austin, Minn.; losses, about $235,000.

2. Fires: Pensacola, Fla.; Pine Bluff, Ark.; losses, about $135,000.

3. Fires: Chicago (a varnish factory) and Portland, Ore., losses about $210,000.

5. Shipwreck: loss of steamer Nashua in Lake Huron, 12 lives lost. Fire: paper mills at Richmond, Ind., loss, about $100,000.

6. Fires: Mapleton, N. Y., 2 lives lost; cigarette factory, New York city; foundry and lumber yard, Jersey City; opera house and other buildings, Paragould, Ark.; Johnstown, Ohio, business houses; aggregate loss, about $675,000. Destructive storms in France and Italy.

7. Cleveland, Ohio: passenger lift breaks down, 6 hurt. Fires: Culpeper, Va., church and stores; Ballston, N. Y., factory, aggregate loss, $90,000.

8. Shipwreck: steamers Premier and Willamette in collision off Port Townsend, Puget Sound, 4 killed, 17 hurt. Fire: jail and other buildings at Clinton, N. C., loss, about $75,000.

9. Fires: factory, Clarke County, Ga.; store, New Orleans, La., losses, $180,000.

10. Prairie fire, South Dakota, 200 square miles burned over, many buildings consumed.

12. Cable car and freight train in collision near Kansas City, 4 killed. Fire: flour mills at Lockport, N. Y., loss, $150,000. Disastrous storm at the West, thousands of cattle perish; all railroads blocked in Colorado, Utah, and Wyoming.

13. Explosion: colliery, Shamokin, Pa., 5 killed, 6 hurt. Fire: hotel at Massapequa, N. Y., loss, $60,000.

14. Fire: grain works, Greenock, Pa., loss, $150,000. Trains in collision near Harrison's Landing, Va., 5 killed. Shipwrecks on the English coast. Earthquake in the Balkan mountains. Explosion of fireworks at St. Louis, 14 hurt. Disastrous storm in Great Britain.

16. Shipwrecks: steamer Bokhara in the China seas, more than 100 lives lost; steamer Stranger capsized in the Gulf of Mexico, 11 lives lost.

20. Fire: dwelling house, Claremont, S. C., 4 children locked in, parents at a religious meeting, the children perished. Shipwrecks off the coast of Spain, many lives lost.

21. Disastrous floods in Sardinia, buildings undermined, hundreds of lives lost.

22. Explosion: gas-pipe bomb, Los Angeles, Cal. 7 killed, many hurt.

24. Trains wrecked by collision near West Manayunk, Pa., 7 killed, 35 hurt.

25. Trains wrecked near Phillipsburg, Mo., 6 killed, 14 hurt.

26. Fire: dwelling houses burned in Jersey City, 35 families homeless, loss, about $500,000. Destructive gale on the British coast, several lives lost.

27. Fire: many buildings burned in Milwaukee, Wis., loss, about $5,000,000. Shipwreck: steamer Roumania on Portuguese coast, 113 lost.

28. Fire: opera house, Cleveland, Ohio, loss, $50,000. Disastrous gale on the Great Lakes.

30. Mexico: floods, 50 lives lost.

Summary of train accidents in October: 96 collisions, 94 derailments, 6 miscellaneous; total, 196. Killed: 47 employees, 11 passengers, 4 trespassers; total, 62. Hurt: 83 employees, 79 passengers; total, 162.

November 1. Violent gales on the Great Lakes, marine losses, about $450,000, 25 lives lost.

2. England: trains wrecked in Yorkshire, and near Liverpool, 13 killed, about 75 hurt. Shipwreck: British man-of-war Howe ashore off Ferrol, Spain.

10. Train wrecked in Iowa, 4 killed, many hurt.

11. Fire: Camden, Me., loss, $350,000.

12. Explosion: dynamite in Niagara Falls tunnel, 1 killed, several hurt, much damage done.

13. Earthquake: a severe shock felt throughout California.

14. Locomotive boiler bursts, Reading, Pa., 5 killed, 1 hurt.

16. Spain: fall of a building at Bejar, 9 killed.

17. Explosion of powder in Arkansas, 4 killed, 15 hurt. Tornado at Red Bud, Ill., 2 killed, many hurt; nearly 50 buildings were wrecked, including churches, schoolhouses, and other public buildings.

18. Tornadoes in different States and a blizzard in the Northwest.

19. Colliery disaster, Hazel Dell, Pa., 8 men buried, 1 killed, the rest rescued more or less hurt.

20. Fire: steamer Rosa Lee, burned at Memphis, Tenn., several lives lost. Shipwreck: two steamers ashore on Long Point, Lake Erie.

21. Explosion: blasting powder in a colliery near Steubenville, Pa., 2 killed, 10 hurt.

22. Trains wrecked near Grand Island, Neb., 7 killed. 10 hurt.

23. Floods in the Northwest cause much suffering.

26. Earthquake in San Salvador, the town of La Union destroyed, many lives lost.

30. Shipwreck: Japanese man-of-war sunk by collision.

Summary of train accidents in November: 106 collisions, 84 derailments, 9 miscellaneous; total, 199. Killed: 44 employees, 11 passengers, 6 trespassers; total, 61. Hurt: 103 employees, 92 passengers, 4 trespassers; total, 199.

December 2. Shipwreck: steamer Greystone sunk by collision in the Elbe river, about 20 lives lost.

7. Tornado in Texas. Severe snowstorm in the Northwest, several lives lost.

8. Train wrecked near Greenville, N. J., 14 hurt.

12. Fire from a broken oil tank causes much loss of property on Miller's Run, Pa.

14. Colliery explosion, Wigan, England, many lives lost.

17. Shipwreck: an American ship runs into and sinks a Spanish steamer in Manilla Bay.

18. Train wrecked near Nelson, Minn., 8 killed, several hurt.

21. Steamer Noordland breaks her shaft at sea (towed into Queenstown).

23. Steamer Umbria breaks her shaft at sea (repairs damages and reaches New York, Dec. 31).

26. Shipwreck: yacht capsized off Sydney, Australia, 10 drowned; several vessels lost on the north Atlantic coast.

27. Fire: tanneries, Milwaukee, Wis., 2 killed, loss $250,000.

28. Explosion of dynamite at Long Island City, N. Y., 5 killed.

29. Tram car wrecked by a locomotive in Chicago, 5 killed, 7 hurt.

Summary of train accidents in December: 199 collisions, 98 derailments, 10 miscellaneous; total, 307. Killed: 37 employees, 4 passengers; total, 41. Hurt: 110 employees, 115 passengers, 4 trespassers; total, 229.

Summary of train accidents for 1892: 1,062 collisions, 1,165 derailments, 100 miscellaneous; total, 2,327. Killed: 490 employees, 116 passengers, 66 trespassers; total, 672. Hurt: 1,205 employees, 1,128 passengers, 774 trespassers; total, 2,407.

DISCIPLES OF CHRIST. The General Conventions of the Disciples of Christ, including the conventions of the General, Foreign, and Woman's Missionary Societies, met in Nashville, Tenn., beginning Oct. 15. The first meeting was that of the Woman's Christian Board of Missions, Mrs. O. A. Burgess, President. Its receipts for the year ending Sept. 30, 1892, had been $52,307. It was assisted in thirty States by 1,133 auxiliary societies, with 24,276 members.

Reports were received from the mission in Jamaica, where with 18 churches the board employed 18 missionaries; Bilaspur, India, where 4 missionaries were employed, and schools, an orphanage, zenana work and medical work were sustained, and a hospital was in course of erection; and the United States, where 22 missionaries were either located in one of 15 towns or doing evangelistic work; while other workers were sustained by appropriations from the board, which passed through intermediate agencies. Mr. A. M. Atkinson presided at the forty-third annual meeting of the General Christian Missionary Convention, which met Oct. 18. Excluding the funds of the Boards of Church Extension and of Negro Evangelization and Education, the convention had received during the year $41,301. It had employed 67 missionaries and agents, by whom 165 churches had been assisted, 69 new places visited, and 27 churches organized, and who reported 1,006 conversions on their fields of labor. The reports of the work carried on by the several State organizations in co-operation with the General Convention were not complete for the present year. In 1891 these bodies had employed 338 missionaries, who had held meetings in 1,706 places, visited 352 new places, organized 172 churches and 320 Sunday schools, and returned 12,221 baptisms, $136,609 raised for evangelization and for the support of pastors, and $162,118 raised for local work. The State organizations were represented as growing in strength and efficiency. The Board of Church Extension had received $21,760; its total resources on hand, including loans, notes, pledges coming due, etc., were $134,730. Since the institution of this fund, in 1888, the receipts had shown an almost uniform increase each year of about $3,000 over the previous year. Twenty-eight loans, aggregating $11,900, had been granted and paid during the year, and 52 loans, aggregating $25,900, had been granted and were yet to be paid. The board had received during the year $6,888 in loans returned and $1,597 of interest on loans; and from the beginning, $13,-653 of loans returned, and $3,779 of interest. This showing was regarded as very favorable, and as proving that the money loaned out actually comes back to do the same work over again. The Board of Negro Evangelization reported that the Southern Christian Institute for the Education of the Negro had about 100 students, 8 of whom were preparing for the ministry. The institute possesses an estate of 800 acres in Mississippi. The meeting of the Foreign Christian Missionary Society was held Oct. 19, Mr. C. L. Loos presiding. The receipts for the year from all sources had been $74,071, of which $3,750 had been derived from the sale of interest-bearing securities, leaving the net income $70,321. The bequests had amounted to $1,751. The expenditures aggregated $75,981. Fifty-six missionaries and 48 helpers were employed in China, India, Japan, Turkey, the Scandinavian countries, and England. There were returned from the several mission fields 252 members in Japan, 85 in India, 679 in Turkey, 653 in Denmark, Norway, and Sweden, and 1,103 in 5 out of 8 stations in England, with 30 boys in the school at Nankin, China. Independent work of an evangelistic character had also been undertaken by disciples among nonchristian peoples beyond the seas; but as no account was made of it to the society at its meeting it does not appear in the report. The report to the General Convention of the Standing Committee on Christian Union expressed gratification at the increasing interest manifested in bringing about a more intimate union among all who profess and call themselves Christians. The Christian Endeavor movement, the McAll Mission in France, the Brotherhood of Christian Unity, and the union movements and œcumenical meetings taking place among the different denominations of the same family—as the Methodists, Presbyterians, and Baptists—were mentioned as promoting or illustrating this tendency.

DOMINION OF CANADA. Parliamentary.—The annual session of Parliament opened on Feb. 25 and closed on July 9, lasting one hundred and thirty-six days, and being, as is believed, the longest on Canadian record. In his opening speech, after referring to divers matters of now obsolete interest, the Governor-General called attention to the fact that, during the recess, three of his ministers had gone to Washington and conferred with representatives of the Administration of the United States on certain named subjects, conclusions on which are still pending, and went on to say:

An amiable understanding was arrived at respecting the steps to be taken for the establishment of the boundary of Alaska, and for reciprocity of services in cases of wrecks and salvage. Arrangements were also reached for the appointment of an international commission to report on the regulations which may be adopted by the United States and Canada for the prevention of destructive methods of fishing and the pollution of streams, and for establishing uniformity of close seasons, and other means for the preservation and increase of fish. A valuable and friendly interchange of views respecting other important matters also took place.

In accordance with the promise given at the close of the last session, a commission has been issued to investigate the working of the Civil-service act, and other matters connected with the civil service generally. The report of this commission will be laid before you during the present session.

It is desirable that the fishery regulations in British Columbia should be examined and revised, so as to adapt them better to the requirements of the fisheries in that province. A commission has been issued with that object.

An important measure respecting the criminal law, which was laid before you last session, has been revised and improved, as a result of the expression of views elicited by its presentation to Parliament, and will be submitted to you. Your attention will also be directed to measures for the redistribution of seats consequent upon the census returns; the establishment of the boundaries of the territories; and the amalgamation of the Departments of Marine and Fisheries. Bills will also be presented to you for the amendment of the Civil-service act, the acts relating to real property in the territories, and of those respecting the fisheries.

The sessional business of the House of Commons began by the Speaker's informing the House that, out of 215 members elected in the spring of 1891, the judges selected for the trial of election petitions, pursuant to the Dominion Controverted Elections act, had declared the seats of 31 to be void. Consequently writs had to be issued for new elections in all these cases. He also informed the House that, in the case of 35 other members petitioned against, those petitions were by a like authority dismissed, and the members were declared duly elected.

Financial.—The Minister of Finance, in the course of his budget speech, said : "In making my financial statement last year I estimated that the revenue for 1890–'91 would amount to $38,-858,701. The revenue which actually accrued fell short of that by $279,391, and was distributed as follows : Customs, $23,399,300 ; excise, $6,914,-850 ; miscellaneous, $8,265,160 ; total, $38,579,-310. Comparing these items and total revenue with the result of 1889–'90, we find a customs decrease of $589,653, an excise decrease of $703,-263, and a decrease in miscellaneous of $27,694. The total decrease amounted to $1,320,625. The issuing of the following table, showing the per capita consumption of liquors and tobacco, has become an annual habit :

AVERAGES.	Spirits, gallons.	Beer, gallons.	Wine, gallons.	Tobacco, pounds.
Average from 1867.....	1,151	2,708	140	2,128
Average, 1889–'90......	883	3,360	104	2,143
Average, 1890–'91......	866	3,282	102	2,033

When we come to the expenditures of 1890–'91, which were estimated at $36,000,000, we find that the actual expenditure exceeded that amount by $343,562, making a total actual expenditure of $36,343,562. Although the expenditure last year shows an increase of that amount over the estimate, the expenditure itself is less than the expenditure in 1888–'89. The chief items in which there was an increase of expenditure, as compared with the preceding year, are as follow : Premium, discount, and exchange, $33,285 ; sinking fund, $50,841 ; civil government, $25,366 ; administration of justice, $16,808. A large increase took place, owing to the census, for which there was an item of $252,154. The next largest item is in the collection of revenue—railways and canals—which shows an increase of $143,316. The increase in expenditure, therefore, as compared with the preceding year, is almost entirely due to the abnormal and large expenditure incurred in taking the census. Decreases took place, principally on the interest on the public debt, care of the Indians, legislation, mounted police, public works, railways and canals, and Dominion lands. Summing up, then, we have as a revenue for the past year $38,579,310, and an expenditure of $36,-343,567, which leaves us with a surplus on consolidated-fund account of $2,235,742. If it were not for the item of capital expenditure, the surplus would remain in hand for a decrease of the debt. As the net result of the operation of the year, we have provided for the ordinary expenses and services of the country out of the consolidated fund ; we have laid up in the sinking fund, which is, of course, practically a reduction of the debt, $1,938,078 ; we have provided for capital expenditures, including railway subsidies, $4,-381,564 ; and we have been able to do that with only a new addition to the debt of $275,817." The minister estimated the revenue for the " current year "—1891–'92—at " $36,655,000, divided, probably, as follows : Customs, $20,500,000 ; excise, $7,900,000 ; miscellaneous, $8,265,000. ... I estimate a total expenditure for the current year—1891–'92—of $36,650,000, which is just

about the same as my estimate of revenue, leaving $5,000 to the good." In another part of his speech Mr. Foster stated, in reference to railroads, that " in 1875 we had 4,826 miles in operation ; in 1891 we had 14,007 miles in operation. The train mileage in the same time rose from 16,680,168 miles to 43,334,891 miles, an increase of 150 per cent. The passengers increased from 5,190,416 to 13,164,420, an increase of 160 per cent. The freight increased from 5,670,836 tons to 21,727,025 tons, or 300 per cent.; and the earnings increased from $19,470,539 to $48,139,-980, an increase of 150 per cent. Taking also the shipping, which is another branch of our carrying trade, we find that the tonnage of vessels in and out, seagoing and inland, exclusive of coasting vessels, rose from 11,646,812 tons in 1879 to 18,803,648 tons in 1891, an increase of 60 per cent. The tonnage of coasting vessels in and out rose from 12,066,683 tons in 1879 to 24,986,130 tons in 1891, an increase of 100 per cent. Looking at these indications of the increase of both our foreign and interprovincial trade, the conclusion is forced upon us that there has been a great and progressive increase in the general trade and commerce of Canada." After a protracted debate upon this budget, during which the ministerial " national policy " was fiercely but vainly assailed by the Opposition, the House entered into Committee of Supply. The alterations subsequently made in the previous year's tariff were not material.

General Legislation.—Among the more important measures passed was the act respecting criminal law. This was, in fact, a carefully revised and complete criminal code for the Dominion. The act for the redistribution of seats in the House of Commons consequent upon the census returns led to another fierce contest on strictly party lines. The Opposition protested against nearly every item in this redistribution bill, which they characterized as a gerrymandering measure. The second reading of the bill was moved on May 31, but a division was not reached until June 14, when, after a fortnight's exhausting debate, the ministers carried their measure by a large majority. As a sequel to the virtual impeachment last session of Sir Hector Langevin, and the suspension of subordinate officials, on the charge of having " an itching palm " for public money, this session produced a like instance in the case of Sir Adolphe Caron, Postmaster General, who was charged with misappropriating for electioneering purposes money that had been voted by Parliament for railway subsidies. The Opposition urged that the whole matter should be referred to a committee of the House ; but the ministers carried their point, which was, to appoint two commissioners merely to take evidence, during the recess.

The Census.—Compilation for the Dominion had not been completed at the date of issue of the last " Annual Cyclopædia," nor, indeed, is it so even yet. The outcry against the reliability of that census is so loud and so general as to be in itself a historical fact, calling for special notice. The complaint is not restricted to any one subdivision of the subject, but is general. It is not alleged that the fault was intentional ; it is believed to have been owing to the incapacity of those managers who had charge of the whole business, and to the recklessness and ignorance of a large majority of the enumerators who were intrusted to collect statistics—men for the most part said to have been appointed to that duty owing to their electioneering capacity.

Ministerial.—The only change in the ministry has been the resignation of Mr. Dewdney, of the Interior, to accept the governorship of British Columbia, and the filling of his place by J. C. Patterson, member of Parliament for North Huron. In November, Sir John Thompson and Messrs. Bowell and Chapleau met at Halifax a delegation from the Newfoundland Government, when the long-standing difficulties between that island and Canada were fully and amicably arranged.

E

EAST AFRICA, a geographical division of the African continent lying east of the Congo State dominions and the former Equatorial Provinces of Egypt, and including the Portuguese territory in the south. The whole region is now partitioned out among European powers. By arrangement, Great Britain and Germany have divided the country north of the Portuguese colony of Mozambique, as far as the Somali coast, which has been conceded to Italy. The Anglo-Portuguese agreement delimits the British and Portuguese spheres in the south.

British East Africa. — The territory acquired by the Imperial British East Africa Company under a British protectorate has been called Ibea, from the initials of the company's name. In 1888 the Sultan of Zanzibar leased to the company, which was organized under the presidency of Sir William Mackinnon, the coast lying north of the German sphere of influence, and extending from the right bank of the Umbe river, as far as the Ozi, including the coast stations of Kau and Kipini. In 1889 he ceded to the company all his stations and his territorial rights north of Kipini, including the ports of Kismayu, Brava, Merka, Magadosho, Warsheik, and Maroti and the islands of the coast and in Manda Bay. In 1889 the company arranged to transfer to the Italian Government the parts lying north of Kismayu. In 1890 the German Government ceded to the company the sultanate of Vitu and its claims on the Somali coast and in the islands of Manda and Patta. In 1891 the company obtained from the Sultan of Zanzibar, in consideration of an annual payment to him of $80,000, a perpetual grant of all his territory north of the Umbe and as far as the Juba. The coast line of the British sphere is about 400 miles. The southern boundary stretches in a northwestern direction from the mouth of the Umbe, and, leaving Mount Kilimanjaro in the German sphere, strikes the shore of Victoria Nyanza in 1° of north latitude. Crossing the lake, it follows the same parallel to the boundary of the Congo, except at Mount Mfumbiro, which is included by a loop in the British sphere. On the north the Juba divides the British from the Italian sphere. The boundary-line leaves the river in 6° of north latitude, and follows that parallel as far as 35° of east longitude. This meridian is agreed on as the line of demarcation between the English and Egyptian sphere in the Blue Nile region on the one hand, and the Italian sphere in Abyssinia and Gallaland on the other. In the south the boundary of the Congo State forms the western limit of the British sphere, but in the north no limits are set. The region of the upper Nile formerly subject to Egypt, which reluctantly evacuated the country under British compulsion, is recognized as falling within the British sphere of interest, which includes farther southward the countries of Uganda, Unyoro, Usoga, Ankori, Mpororo, Koko, and a part of Ruanda. The area is estimated at 1,000,000 square miles. The customs revenue in 1888 was $36,000; in 1889, $56,000; in 1890, $70,000. The trade is carried on mainly by native merchants of India, the Banians. The chief exports are cloves, grown on the islands, ivory, India rubber, gum, copra, coir, orchilla weed, and hides. The imports are cotton goods, copper wire, beads, and other common trade articles. Harbor works and other extensive improvements at Mombasa, the principal port, have been made by Indian workmen at the cost of the company. Telegraphs connect the other ports with Mombasa, which is connected with Zanzibar by a cable. A telegraph has been constructed to Lamu, and surveys have been made for a railroad to the Victoria Nyanza. The armed force of the company consists of 200 Soudanese, 200 Sikh soldiers, and bodies of native levies. Permanent advanced posts were established in 1891 at Machakos, situate on a healthy elevated plateau 250 miles from the coast, and at Mengo, the capital of Uganda.

Uganda.—Uganda is a large and powerful equatorial state, on the northern shore of Victoria Nyanza. The area of the kingdom proper is 20,000 square miles, while Usoga and other vassal states bring up the total to about 70,000 square miles. The official title of the King is Kabakawa Buganda (Emperor of Uganda) and Overlord of Unyoro, Usoga, Karagwe, etc. His power is restricted by the Lukiko, or Privy Council, which is composed of the Katikiro (chief judge) and the Aba-saya (great chiefs), appointed by the King. The present King, Mwanga, who succeeded his father, Mtesa, in 1884, was deposed in favor of his eldest brother, Kiwewa, who in turn was dethroned and succeeded by his youngest brother, Kalema. Mwanga was reinstated in 1889 by the aid of Christian missionaries and traders. The country during those years had been the scene of civil strife between the Christian and Mohammedan parties, and latterly between the Roman Catholics and Protestant Christians. Those, however, in 1890 combined their forces against the Mohammedans, who were threatening to take possession of the country, and expelled them. Captain F. D. Lugard, who had been dispatched thither by the British East Africa Company, arrived in December, 1890, and concluded a treaty securing for them certain rights in the administration of finance. the army. and the foreign and internal affairs of the kingdom. Captain W.

H. Williams was sent with a small force of Soudanese to re-enforce him, and arrived at Uganda
on Jan. 31. Lugard had built a strong fort, in a
commanding place at Kampala, and his influence
had been greatly increased. In February he endeavored to form a court of arbitration for the
disputes about land and slaves. The King became
more amenable, and acted as arbitrator in a burza
of the 16th. His decision was regarded as unfair
by the Protestants, and the whole country got under arms. Lugard and Williams, however, with
the Soudanese and Maxim caused them to disperse and return quietly to their homes. Further
friction occurred, and murders on both sides
were common, until, at Lugard's instigation, two
laws were passed, one providing that a chief
should not evict a man from his shamba without the order of the burza, and the other that
the dwellers on a shamba should do the work of
the chief immediately over them, and he again
of his superior, providing the customary tribute
irrespective of party or creed. The Roman
Catholic chiefs became more reconciled, and were
ready to abide by Lugard's decisions.

In March, 1891, he determined to face the
Mohammedans, who had formed an alliance with
the Wanyoro and were threatening invasion. A
native army of several thousand, in addition to
his force of two hundred, was assembled, and the
Mohammedans and their allies were met and
routed on the northwest frontier. After this
Lugard went westward to Lake Albert, and
northward to Mount Ruwenzori and the Sem-
liki, for the purpose of making treaties and
breaking the power of Kabba Rega, of Unyoro.
The natives, who were at first suspicious, afterward became friendly. On Lake Albert, mines
of salt, more valuable in this region than gold,
were found, and forts were built for their protection. As a result of the expedition, Ankole,
a territory as large as Uganda, southern Unyoro,
and Toru, were added to the company's possessions, and access was obtained to the great ivory
preserve around Lake Edward. At Kavalli, on
the southern shore of the lake, Lugard met Selim
Bey, a former lieutenant of Emin, after the latter had passed northward, and persuaded him
to assist in maintaining the authority of the
British East Africa Company in Unyoro and
Uganda pending the approval of the Khedive.
They moved out from Kavalli with a combined
force of over 1,200 men and 9,000 camp followers.
A fort was erected at Kabaregas, fifteen days'
march from Kavalli, and a garrison of four companies was left under charge of Captain Rehan.
Four other forts were also built in the neighborhood and garrisoned. Lugard and Selim, with
the remainder of their men, then arrived at
Mengo, on Dec. 31, 1891, and found the British
flag flying over Fort Kampala, of which Williams was in command.

During Lugard's absence war between the
rival parties had been narrowly averted. In the
early part of December Mwanga sent 4 Roman
Catholic chiefs with 500 rifles to kill Mulondo, a
Protestant chief in Kyagwe, but owing to the
representations of Williams they were recalled.
After the arrival of a supply of ammunition from
the company and the news that Lugard was
close at hand in the Budu country with Selim's
re-enforcements, Mwanga sent word that he de-

sired to become a Protestant. On the representations of the French priests that the English
company proposed an early withdrawal from the
country, he regained confidence and became defiant. About Jan. 5 Lugard received orders
to evacuate Uganda, but they were afterward
rescinded. After the arrival of the French bishop,
on Jan. 12, quarrels began to spring up daily
between the two parties, and on Jan. 22 a
Protestant was murdered by the Roman Catholics. The King declined to punish or surrender
the murderer, who had taken refuge in the royal
grounds, and answered the protests of Lugard by
threatening to exterminate the company's forces
at Kampala if he endeavored to see justice done.
On the night of the 23d the Roman Catholic
party, who for a few days previously had been
massing in great numbers, beat the war drums,
and the next day got under arms. Five hundred
rifles were served out to the Protestant leaders
for distribution. Another Protestant was murdered, and a man was surrendered as the murderer, who, they were certain, was not the right
man, while the King and his counselors adhered
to their determination regarding the original
criminal. Negotiations were still pending, when
a part of the Roman Catholic and Protestant
forces opened fire at the foot of Mengo, near the
ex-missionary Stokes's garden. The latter were
victorious, and drove down their enemies toward
the King's fences, burning their houses. Sem-
bera Mackay, a leading Protestant chief, was
killed. A large body of Roman Catholics came
down to attack Fort Kampala, in which the English missionaries had gathered for safety. The
two Maxims of the fort opened fire, and about
40 were killed by the first volleys. The attacking force retreated, but rallied at the top of
the hill and drove back the Katikiro and his
men toward the fort and burned his house. Lugard ordered out Williams and the Soudanese,
who soon settled matters, the Katikiro's and Po-
kino's men reforming behind him, and the Roman
Catholics were driven far away toward the lake
and took refuge on the islands. The day thus
ended in victory for the Protestants, who were
in complete possession of the city. The residence of the priests had been destroyed, and they
were brought to the fort. The King, with 300
rifles and his wives and wealth, took refuge in
the small island of Burenguge, 500 or 600 yards
from the mainland, where the Christians had so
long withstood the Mohammedans. Lugard then
made endeavors to persuade the King and his
chieftains to return, and letters were received
from the former saying that he was willing, but
could not because he was detained and guarded.
The French bishop was sent with overtures of
peace, which did not meet with a favorable response. Wadi Mafutaa, Stokes's head trader,
was then commissioned to tell Mwanga that, unless he returned at once, the Mohammedans
would be called in and their Sultan, Mbogo,
made King. A final letter was sent on the 29th,
allowing all Roman Catholics ba°k except the
two leading instigators of the war. On the
morning of the 30th the Protestants went down
to attack the island, accompanied by Williams
with the Maxim, to cover their landing. As a
result, about 33 canoes were sunk and between
300 and 400 men, women, and children were shot

or drowned, while all the property on the island was looted. The King and the Roman Catholic bishop escaped to Sesse island, a stronghold of their party. From this also they were dislodged, and took refuge in the Buddu country, and thence the King fled to Bukoba, German territory. The British party at Kampala then found themselves in a precarious position, with 1,000 mouths to feed, the Roman Catholic party threatening on the left, the Mohammedans on the front, the Fubalauji, or native heathen party, on the right, and the Protestant party daily dwindling away. Williams proceeded to the German station of Bukoba to bring up the Remington ammunition which Lieut. Langheld, the officer in charge, had offered the company, and to secure the return either of Mwanga or his two nephews, who were under the charge of a French priest on the south shore of the lake in the German sphere. His mission proved unsuccessful, and Lugard began to open negotiations for the purpose of seating the Mohammedan King, Mbogo, on the throne. On the 21st of March, however, 4 Roman Catholic chiefs arrived at Kampala with overtures of peace, which Lugard refused to consider unless the King returned. The Sekibobo and others accordingly went back to get him, and succeeded in their mission, and he arrived at Kampala on March 30. He declared that he had been detained by the Roman Catholics, who had determined to kill him rather than allow him to return, and he accused the Roman Catholic bishop of having been the instigator of war in the first instance, and also of counseling its continuance when on the island. Negotiations were immediately opened up for a division of the country between the 3 parties, and envoys from the Mohammedans arrived on the day following the return of the King. After much controversy, the Roman Catholics were located in Buddu, the Protestants in the region about Mengo, while the Mohammedans were also given a strip of Uganda on the surrender of their King. On the 1st of June the temporary treaty made by Lugard on his arrival was made perpetual. Mwanga declared himself at one with the company's officer and that religion should be free. On June 16 Lugard left Mengo for the coast with Capt. Macdonald and his surveying party, who had arrived at Kampala on the 9th.

The British East Africa Company obtained in March, 1892, a vote of £20,000 for the survey of the Mombasa and Victoria Railway, and shortly afterward, not receiving expected governmental aid, notified the Salisbury Government of their intention to withdraw from Uganda at the end of 1892. In September Lord Rosebery, in behalf of the Gladstone Government, sent a letter agreeing to the evacuation, but stipulating that the company should prolong their stay till the end of March, 1893, to avoid the dangers of an immediate withdrawal. For this purpose the sum of £12,000 was voted by the Government.

German East Africa.—The German sphere borders on the British sphere on the north and on the Free State of the Congo on the west. On the south it is bounded by a line running from the south end of Lake Tanganyika north of the Stevenson road to the north end of Lake Nyassa, and thence to the Indian Ocean by the Rovuma river. The area is estimated at 345,000 square miles, and the population at 1,760,000. The coast line was leased to the Germans for fifty years by the Sultan of Zanzibar in 1888, and in 1890 the Sultan Ali ceded his sovereign rights in return for a payment of 4,000,000 marks. Most of the stations founded by the Germans in the interior and on the coast were abandoned in 1889 in consequence of a revolt of the Arabs. On the restoration of peace commercial enterprise revived. The German Government is represented by an imperial commissioner. The value of the exports for the year ending Aug. 17, 1889, was 2,847,100 rupees, and of the imports about 2,150,000 rupees. The export of ivory was 1,197,251 rupees; of gum copal, 364,289 rupees; of caoutchouc, 306,805 rupees; of sesame, 250,679 rupees. In 1890 the exports to Germany were 489,000 marks, and the imports from Germany 320,000 marks.

After the suppression of the Arab revolt and the execution of its leader, Bushiri, the backbone of the slave trade seemed to have been broken, and the native tribes were being held under control. But after the abrogation of martial law in favor of civil government, the natives began to rebel against taxation, and insurrections occurred. The Wadigos, a powerful tribe, went on the warpath and closed the caravan route between Tanga and Kilimanjaro. Captain Kreuzler, the commandant at Tanga, marched against them, but was driven back to the station. Serious disaffection was also created among the Arabs and Hindoos owing to the inexperience and inefficiency of the young German lieutenant intrusted with judicial authority by Baron von Soden, who had dismissed the officers trained in African service by his predecessor. In June, 1892, the Germans met with a serious reverse in Moshi territory. Meli, Mandara's son and successor, a boy of fourteen, evinced a strong hatred to the Germans and lost no opportunity to bring about war. He occupied the fort called Moshi, which had been built by Herr von Zalewski, but which had been abandoned by Dr. Peters for the new Kilimanjaro station at Marongu. Meli refused to obey the command of Baron von Bülow, Peters's successor, to abandon his position. The German troops, consisting of 2 officers, 2 noncommissioned officers, and 180 native soldiers, endeavored to dislodge him. Within a short distance of the station Lieut. Wolfram was killed, and the party was attacked by about 3,000 Wadshaggas, 1,000 of whom possessed breechloaders. The Germans formed a square and fired with great rapidity, but were unable to repel their adversaries, who fought with the greatest courage, and Von Bülow, who had been twice wounded, gave orders for a retreat. He was carried off the field on a hammock, and in the retreat received a wound that proved fatal. The German loss was 32, including both officers, while the native was estimated at about 40. The 4·7-centimetre gun which the expedition took with them fell into the hands of the Wadshaggas. The German force retreated to Gonga, part taking refuge at Fort Mareny, which was afterward evacuated. A relief party was sent out under the chief Johannes, and the station at Kilimanjaro was reoccupied without fighting. About the same time the native warriors in Usagara formed themselves into bands and devastated the district, but became quiet again on the arrival at Kilossa of Lieut. Prince, one of Wissmann's ablest men.

Zanzibar.— The islands of Zanzibar and Pemba and the posts on the mainland, conquered from the Portuguese and from native chiefs, were subject to the sultans of Muscat, in Arabia, until, when two sons of a deceased sultan quarreled about the succession, the sultanate of Zanzibar was awarded to one of them, and made independent of Muscat, by the award of Lord Canning, Governor-General of India, in 1861. In 1886, when Germany and Great Britain made the first agreement delimiting their spheres of influence in East Africa, they refused to recognize the rights of the Sultan over the posts and people that had been subject to him in the interior, but conceded to him a strip 10 miles broad, extending along the coast from Cape Delgado to Kipini, on the Ozi river, and north of Kipini they recognized his authority over the points where he had garrisons, viz., Lamu, Kismayu, Brava, Merka, Magadosho, and Warsheik. In 1888 the two powers forced him to lease the shores fronting their spheres, and when the final delimitation was made, in 1890, Germany acknowledged an English protectorate over the islands remaining in the possession of the Sultan of Zanzibar. This protectorate was instituted in October, 1891, when a government was established under British direction. Hugh Robertson took charge of the revenue, Capt. Hatch of the army and police, Capt. Hardinge of the harbor and lighthouses, Bonanji of public works, and Mahomed bin Saif of the treasury.

The Sultan or Seyyid of Zanzibar is Ali bin Said bin Sultan, born in 1855, who succeeded his brother, Seyyid Khalifa, in February, 1890. The area of Zanzibar is 625 square miles, and of Pemba 360 square miles. There are about 125,-000 inhabitants on Zanzibar, and 40,000 on the other island. Under the British administration the Sultan is allowed a civil list of 3 lakhs of rupees. A British officer commands the regular army of 1,200 men and the police. The imports of cotton goods in 1883 amounted to $230,000, and of other manufactured goods to $420,000. In 1890 the exports of East Africa to Great Britain were valued at £443,185, and the imports from Great Britain at £195,850. Of 145 vessels that in 1888 put in at Zanzibar, 56 were British, 17 French, 10 German, 58 Zanzibari, and 4 American. The total tonnage entered for the year 1891 was 203,000. On Feb. 1, Gerald Portal, the British agent and consul-general, declared Zanzibar a free port, all duties being removed, except those on ammunition and spirits over 50°. On March 19, Capt. Rogers, with the company's forces, made an unsuccessful attack on the Vitu people, who were afterward brought under subjection. A revolt in Lamu was also suppressed by Mr. Portal with two companies of marines from the gun vessel "Philomel."

Nyassaland.—In 1889 certain districts in the Lake Nyassa region, where the African Lakes Company had been at work for fifteen years, were declared to be within the British sphere of influence. In May, 1891, they were proclaimed as being under the protectorate of Great Britain,

with the following boundaries: On the east and south by the Portuguese dominions, and on the west by a line which starts in the south from the intersection of the Portuguese dominions and the boundary of the conventional free-trade zone, and runs northward to the line of the geographical Congo basin, which it follows to the boundary between the German and British spheres as defined in the agreement. of July, 1890. The African Lakes Company has steamers on Lake Nyassa and on the lower Shiré between Katunga and Quilimande, on the Chinde mouth of the Zambezi, and has established 12 trading stations. Mr. H. H. Johnston was appointed by the British Government imperial commissioner over the district, and has his headquarters at Zomba, in the Shiré Highlands. He has equipped a small native police force, established postal communications, and opened up roads. He had several fights with slave dealers in October and November, 1891, and defeated the Xao, compelling their chief to pay a heavy war indemnity. In January, 1892, Capt. Maguire, of the Lakes Company's steamer "Domirad," one of Johnston's officers, was informed by a minor chief, Kasembe, that he had stopped a caravan of slaves which Makanjila, a leading chief of the lowest eastern portion of the district, was preparing to convey across the lake, and that he was ready to deliver them to any one having authority from the commissioner. Maguire received orders from his chief to bring the slaves away on his steamer and a barge. After finding the 2 dhows and setting fire to one of them, he was attacked by an overwhelming force of Makanjila's people, who had been lying in ambush. A storm sprang up on the lake and rendered the barge unnavigable, and its crew were compelled to swim to the steamer. Maguire was shot as he regained his vessel, which soon afterward grounded, and was besieged for some days before it was floated. The chief engineer, MacEwan, and the Parsee doctor, Boyce, were killed while treating with the enemy. Shortly afterward a body of Sikhs and 2 Europeans were surprised in their encampment outside Fort Johnston. The 2 Europeans, Mr. King and Dr. Watson, were wounded, 2 Sikhs and 2 Zanzibaris were killed, and the gun was captured.

ECUADOR, a republic in South America. The President is chosen for four years by an electoral assembly of 900 members. The Congress consists of a Senate and a House of Representatives, the former composed of 34 members, 2 from each province, and the latter has 1 deputy for every 30,000 of population, elected for two years, half as long as the senatorial term. Antonio Flores, who was elected President on June 30, 1888, was succeeded in June, 1892, by Luis Condero.

There is a standing army of 3,341 officers and men and a National Guard of 30,000. The navy consists of a third-class cruiser, a gunboat, 3 steamships, 2 steamboats, and a transport.

Area and Population.—The area is 118,630 square miles, and the population is 1,004,651, exclusive of a large number of uncivilized Indians. Primary education is compulsory. The Government paid $243,881 for education in 1890.

Finances.—The amount of revenue collected in 1890 was 4,182,591 sucres or dollars, of which

3,175,120 sucres came from customs. The expenditure was 3,820,600 sucres. That was the amount disbursed, but other sums were due, the payment of which was deferred.

In 1854 Ecuador recognized a foreign debt of £1,824,000 as her share of the old Colombian debt. In 1867 the Government ceased to pay the interest, and in August, 1890, a compromise was agreed to on the part of the creditors, by which the debt and unpaid interest were converted into £750,000 of bonds paying 4½ per cent. for five years, 4¾ per cent. for five years more, and 5 per cent. thereafter, with a sinking fund of ½ per cent. for five years and 1 per cent. afterward. This arrangement was not consummated, because the Ecuadorian Government would not agree to a condition reviving all the prior claims of the bondholders as soon as any default in the interest should occur. There is an internal debt of about 5,000,000 sucres.

Commerce and Production.—The imports in 1890 amounted to 10,016,352 sucres. The value of the exports was 9,761,634 sucres. The principal exportable product is cacao, the shipments of which amounted to 7,104,140 sucres. The export of coffee was valued at 654,320 sucres; straw hats, 337,250 sucres; hides, 226,874 sucres; India rubber, 153,730 sucres; ivory nuts, 130,800 sucres; and sugar, 87,356 sucres. The export of gold and specie was 1,042,573 sucres. Of the total imports, 2,671,566 sucres came from Great Britain, 2,464,064 sucres from France, 1,607,461 sucres from the United States, 1,318,-932 sucres from Germany, 930,545 sucres from Peru, 365,101 sucres from Chili, 221,944 sucres from Spain, and 107,376 sucres from Colombia. Of the exports, 2,280,218 sucres went to France, 1,842,350 sucres to Spain, 1,729,914 sucres to Great Britain, 1,403,891 sucres to Germany, 930,-530 sucres to the United States, 574,251 sucres to Peru, 459,130 sucres to Chili, and 334,255 sucres to Colombia.

Navigation.—The number of ships entered at the port of Guayaquil in 1890 was 339, of 256,194 tons. There were 108, all sailing vessels, of 5,070 tons, flying the Ecuadorian flag; 111 British vessels, all steamers, of 126,600 tons; 87 other foreign steamers, of 112,612 tons, and 33 foreign sailing vessels, of 11,912 tons. The total number cleared was 317, of 256,412 tons, of which 198, of 239,272 tons, were steamers, and 119, of 17,140 tons, were sailing vessels.

Communications.—The only railroad, running from Duran, opposite Guayaquil, to Chimbo, a distance of 57 miles, is unfinished, and the builders have stopped work because the Government has taken possession of the salt mines, which yield a net profit of 100,000 sucres per annum, because the railroad company, to which the salt monopoly had been handed over, allowed its concession to lapse. The matter is in litigation, and a French company, which agreed in 1891 to continue the railroad to Quito, has not been able to raise sufficient capital.

There are 1,074 miles of telegraph connecting Quito with Guayaquil and with Colombian ports and the ocean cable.

Political Events.—There were rumors in April, 1892, of a revolutionary movement, which were contradicted by the Government. The cause of the ferment was the approaching change of administration. The new President, a Moderate Liberal, was chosen by the National Congress. After assuming the Government in August, he constituted his Cabinet as follows: Minister of the Interior and of Foreign Affairs, Vicente Lucio Salazar; Minister of the Treasury, Antonio Delcaza; Minister of Education, Cavallos Salvador; Minister of War and Marine, José Sevasti.

During the discussion of proposals for reciprocity of commerce between the United States and the Ecuadorian government, the British minister formally protested, in June, 1892, that under the treaty with Great Britain that country would be entitled to any advantage extended to other nations.

EGYPT, a principality in northern Africa, tributary to Turkey. The Government is an absolute hereditary monarchy, under a prince who bears the title of Khedive or Viceroy, under a firman obtained from the Sultan of Turkey. The Khedive Mohammed Tewfik, born Nov. 19, 1852, who succeeded to the throne on the abdication of his father, Ismail Pasha, on June 26, 1879, died Jan. 7, 1892. His son and successor, Abbas, was born on July 14, 1874. Since the occupation of the country by a British army and the abolition of the Anglo-French joint control in 1883, the Khedive has been advised in financial matters by an English financial adviser, who has a seat in the Council of Ministers, and without whose advice no financial measure can be taken.

Finances.—The revenue of Egypt was estimated in 1880 by the international commission of liquidation for 1882 and succeeding years at £ E. 8,411,622, of which £ E. 3,513,734 was assigned to the debt and £ E. 4,897,888 to the expenses of government. The budget for 1892 makes the revenue £ E. 9,950,000, of which £ E. 5,000,000 come from the land-tax, date-tree taxes, etc., £ E. 185,000 from the duty on trade and professions, £ E. 1,400,000 from customs. £ E. 190,000 from *octroi* duties, £ E. 233,000 from salt and natron duties, £ E. 85,000 from fisheries, £ E. 75,000 from navigation dues, £ E. 1,480,000 from railroads, £ E. 36,000 from telegraphs, £ E. 115,000 from the port of Alexandria, £ E. 245,000 from posts, £ E. 100,000 from lighthouses, £ E. 360,000 from the Ministry of Justice, £ E. 80,000 from exemption from military service, £ E. 80,000 from rents of Government property, £ E. 16,000 from the governorship of Suakin, £ E. 55,000 from the pension fund, and £ E. 215,000 from other sources. The total expenditure is estimated at £ E. 9,400,000, of which £ E. 4,015,047 are for the service of the debt, £ E. 665,041 for the tribute to Turkey, £ E. 100,000 for the Khedive's civil list, £ E. 114,127 for the civil lists of Ismail Pasha and his family, £ E. 54,420 for the Khedive's private cabinet, £ E. 499,049 for the Ministry of Public Works, £ E. 385,908 for the Ministry of Justice. £ E. 112,046 for the Ministry of Finance, £ E. 322,027 for the administration of the provinces, £ E. 115,658 for the Ministry of the Interior, £ E. 90,849 for the Ministry of Public Instruction. £ E. 122.263 for other ministries, £ E. 126,870 for administration of the customs, £ E. 38,883 for collection of *octrois*, £ E. 47,240 for collection of the salt and natron taxes, £ E. 8,578 for the fisheries, £ E. 2,979 for navigation, £ E. 700,888 for railroads, £ E. 46,-000 for telegraphs, £ E. 23,000 for the port of Alexandria, £ E. 225,521 for the postal service, £ E. 27,169 for lighthouses, £ E. 707,399 for public security, police, prisons, the Ministry of War, and the British army of occupation, £ E. 119,900 for the administration of Suakin, £ E. 420,000 for pensions, £ E. 250,000 for the suppression of the *corvée*, and £ E. 109,088 for various other purposes.

The public debt at the end of 1891 amounted to £ E. 106,572,400, of which £ E. 9,024,500 represent

payment which will cease in 1894; £ E. 34,871 for the Daira Khassa or commission to administer the Daira Sanieh estate, which is mortgaged for the loan; and £ E. 153,846 for the Moukabala or old internal debt, which was arbitrarily compounded by the debt commissioners for an annuity of this amount payable till 1930.

Military Forces.—The Egyptian army was disbanded in 1892 on the occupation of the country by British troops, and a British general, to whom the title of Sirdar was given, was intrusted with the organization of a new army. This body under the command of the Sirdar F. W.

MOHAMMED TEWFIK, KHEDIVE OF EGYPT, DIED JANUARY 7, 1892.

Grenfell, had a strength of about 13,000 men, officered by 60 Englishmen, in the beginning of 1892. The British army of occupation, which since the rebellion of 1882 has remained in the country, numbered 3,300 men, commanded by Maj.-Gen. Forestier Walker in January, 1891. Sirdar F. W. Grenfell resigned his place as Sirdar, and was succeeded by Col. Kitchener, who for several years had been Governor of Suakin.

Commerce and Production.—The total value of the merchandise imports for 1890 was £ E. 8,081,-297, and of the exports £ E. 11,-876,086. The imports of specie amounted to £ E. 2,971,461, and the exports to £ E. 2,085,455. Of the total imports, 37 per cent. came from Great Britain, 20 per cent. from Turkey, 10 per cent. from France and Algeria, 10 per cent. from Austria, 7 per cent. from the Eastern possessions of England, 4 per cent. from Russia, 3 per cent. from Italy, 1½ per cent. from Greece, 1 per cent. from Malta, and 5½ per cent. from other countries. Of the exports, 65 per cent. went to Great Britain, 9 per cent. to Russia, 8 per cent. to France, 7 per cent. to Austria, 6 per cent. to Italy, 3 per cent. to Turkey, and 2 per cent. to other countries.

The chief imports in 1890 were cotton goods for £ E. 1,674,073, silk, woolen, and linen goods for £ E. 755,469, coal for £ E. 491,495, hosiery

the guaranteed loan paying 3 per cent., £ E. 29,-400,000 the privileged debt bearing interest at 3½ per cent., £ E. 55,986,960 the unified loan on which the rate is 4 per cent., £ E. 7,272,320 the 4-per-cent. Daira Sanieh loan, and £ E. 4,888,-620 the Domains loan, which pays 5 per cent. The expenses for the debt for 1892 include £ E. 2,239,478 for the unified debt, £ E. 1,029,000 for the privileged debt, £ E. 315,000 for the guaranteed loan, £ E. 290,893 for the Daira Sanieh loan, £ E. 258,550 for the Domains loan, £ E. 198,000 for interest on the Suez Canal shares purchased by the British Government, an annual and apparel for £ E. 339,284, timber for £ E. 349,432, coffee for £ E. 243,575, wine, beer, and spirits for £ E. 265,267, tobacco for £ E. 475,- 475, petroleum for £ E. 296,301, machinery for £ E. 187,532, indigo for £ E. 191,379, fruits for £ E. 183,188, rice for £ E. 167,905, animals for £ E. 91,000, and refined sugar for £ E. 84,660.

The chief exports were cotton for £ E. 8,272,- 226, cotton seed for £ E. 1,380,255, beans for £ E. 730,647, sugar for £ E. 338,923, wheat for £ E. 223,906, hides and skins for £ E. 95,- 293, onions for £ E. 72,834, rice for £ E. 70,- 696, wool for £ E. 52,514, Indian corn for £ E. 23,457, and lentils for £ E. 19,627.

Navigation.—The vessels that arrived at the port of Alexandria during 1890 numbered 2,019, of 1,632,220 tons, and the number cleared was 2,020, of 1,613,800 tons. The arrivals and clearances at the other ports numbered 3,942, of 2,- 307,200 tons, of which 930, of 1,342,300 tons, were British. Of the vessels entered at Alexandria, 569, of 756,088 tons, were British; 131, of 263,658 tons, were French; 937, of 239,743 tons, were Turkish; 114, of 157,581 tons, were Austrian; 55, of 82,315 tons, were Russian; 81, of 74,625 tons, were Italian; and 17, of 18,838 tons, were Norwegian and Swedish; the Greek, German, and Danish flags coming next.

Internal Communications.—The length of railroads in operation in 1892 is 1,127 miles, to which 108 miles of new lines under construction were soon to be added. There were 4,696,286 passengers and about 1,900,000 tons of freight carried in 1890. The gross earnings were £ E. 1,408,742, and the total expenditure was £ E. 610,124. The Government telegraph lines in 1891 had a length of 3,168 miles, with 5,430 miles of wire. The number of telegrams sent in 1890 was 819,940. The postal traffic in 1890 comprised 9,356,700 letters and cards sent, and 8,740,000 received, and 3,769,500 papers, samples, etc., carried, and 5,382,940 received. There were 1,630,500 foreign letters forwarded, and 1,499,000 received.

The Suez Canal.—For the year 1890 the number of vessels that passed through the Suez Canal was 3,389, having a gross tonnage of 9,- 749,129 tons. Of the vessels, 2,522, of 7,438,682 tons, were British; 275, of 731,888 tons, were German; 169, of 555,941 tons, were French; 144, of 341,828 tons, were Dutch; 87, of 217,480 tons, were Italian; 55, of 177,941 tons, were Austrian; 34, of 103,111 tons, were Spanish; 43, of 78,107 tons, were Norwegian; 20, of 59,613 tons, were Russian; 21, of 28,303 tons, were Turkish; 4, of 6,300 tons, were Japanese; 7, of 3,814 tons, were Portuguese; 3, of 2,682 tons, were Greek; and 3, of 2,112 tons, were American. The number of passengers who were carried through the canal in 1890 was 161,153. The receipts were £ E. 2,679.340. The canal has a length of 87 miles, including 21 miles of lakes. The share capital amounts to 195,125,000 francs, and the bonds outstanding in 1891 amounted to 121,764,179 francs. Besides the 394,677 shares, of 500 francs each, that were issued to the public, there are 100,000 founders' shares, which have the right to a part of the surplus profits, their share for 1890 having been 2,545,732 francs. Of the other shares, 176,602 formerly belonged to the Khedive and were bought by the British

Government in November, 1875, for £3,976,582. Of the net earnings beyond 5 per cent. interest on the capital stock, the Egyptian Government receives 15 per cent.; the founders' shares, 10 per cent.; the common shares, 71 per cent.; the managing directors, 2 per cent.; and the employees of the company, 2 per cent. In 1890 the net profits were 38,133,384 francs.

The Firman of Investiture.—When Mohammed Tewfik died, on Jan. 7, 1892, his son, Abbas Pasha, was immediately confirmed as Khedive of Egypt by the Sultan of Turkey, according to the existing firman, which gave the right of succession by primogeniture. It was expected that the firman of investiture would be issued shortly, and assurances were given to that effect. When, after a lapse of several weeks, the document was drawn up and signed, a further delay occurred in dispatching the firman. The suspicion of the Khedive and his ministers was thereby aroused, and when Ahmed Eyub Pasha, the Sultan's envoy, arrived in Cairo, on April 4, and refused to disclose the import of the firman before its public reading, the Khedive was prevailed upon not to submit to an investiture before a full knowledge of its contents was obtained. To become a party to any conditions which the Sultan might choose to insert without being made acquainted with them was even considered dangerous to the independence of the Egyptian Government, not to speak of the difficulties it might create with the powers friendly to Egypt. In this the Khedive was strongly supported by Sir Evelyn Baring, the British diplomatic agent. The Sultan's envoy finally consented to disclose the contents of the firman, and a copy was furnished to the Khedive. It appeared from this that the limits of Egypt as described in the new firman were not those set down in the one issued during the reign of Tewfik, following the firman issued to Ismail Pasha, this new firman being based on that issued to Mehemet Ali. This meant a curtailing of the Egyptian eastern frontier, a line being drawn from El Aresh to Suez, at the head of the western branch of the Red Sea, instead of a line drawn from El Aresh to the head of the eastern branch of the Red Sea, the Gulf of El Akaba, whereby Turkey tried to reassert her authority over the Sinai peninsula. Sir Evelyn Baring addressed a note to the Egyptian Minister of Foreign Affairs, calling attention to the departure taken in the new firman, and asking whether a satisfactory explanation from Turkey had been received. The Minister of Foreign Affairs attached a telegram from the Grand Vizier to his answer, which conceded the administrative rights of Egypt over the Sinai peninsula, and also a telegram from the Sultan, stating expressly that the Sinai district was to belong to Egypt. Sir Evelyn Baring answered to this that the Government of Great Britain could not consent to any diminution of Egyptian territory, but that the definition of the boundaries as described in the firman and supplemented by the telegram were satisfactory, and that the Government of Great Britain regarded the telegram as constituting part of the firman, and requested that the two be read together. This was consented to, and the public reading of the firman took place on

April 14, constituting Abbas Pasha legally Khedive of Egypt.

Judicial Reform.—The reforms in the judicial methods, as prepared by Justice Scott in 1891, were to a great extent carried out in 1892; and Justice Scott, in his first report on the native tribunals, gives the scope of the work done since his arrival in the country, in 1890. The system that was in use was the French system, founded on the Code Napoleon, and embodying those rules of equity and good conscience which prevail throughout the civilized world. Apart from their inherent merits, the laws have been in practice in the mixed and native tribunals for a good many years, and the people had become used to them. It was therefore decided not to make a radical change in the existing system, but only to simplify the procedure. It was found that the qualification of the judges was not of a high standard; in almost every tribunal there were numbers who had received no legal training, and who had not been improved by practice. The same drawback to efficiency existed in the Court of Appeal. One by one changes were effected in every tribunal, and those that were clearly unfit were eliminated, and men of good reputation and legal training were put in their places. On account of the difficulty of finding a sufficient number of judges with proper qualifications, the old method of 3 judges sitting together, even in the first instance in all civil and criminal cases, was abolished, and the system of a single judge, sitting in summary civil justice, with a limited criminal jurisdiction, and subject to appeal in all but the smallest matters, was adopted. These summary tribunals were introduced very gradually throughout the country, and numbered 33 on June 1. The introduction of the one-judge system necessitated the establishment of some system of inspection and superintendence, and the Committee of Judicial Surveillance was therefore established. It is composed of the Judicial Adviser Justice Scott, M. Menondo, and M. Le Greele. Under them are 2 inspectors and 1 secretary. Their work consists of inspecting all tribunals, the examination of *dossiers*, chosen weekly at random in every tribunal, on which they have to report to the committee. They also receive and report periodical returns from all tribunals as regards the business done. The judicial adviser has to make periodical visits to the tribunals, so as to see the work of each of them at least once a year. This surveillance is quite independent of the system of appeal; it calls attention immediately to the error, in order to prevent its recurrence, but it does not attempt to set the error right in the particular case. In order to provide a continuous supply of new judges, the Khedivial School of Law was founded some years ago, but it had been without a head for four years; a new director was chosen, and the standard of instruction was raised. Justice Scott proposes to reduce the expense of litigation, reform the bar, and abolish the exceptional tribunals, which under the new organization have lost their usefulness.

Taxation Reforms.—Several taxation reforms were instituted to relieve the burden of the Egyptian people. Salt, of which the Government has a monopoly, was reduced 40 per cent. in price.

The professional tax, which was a grievance, affecting the poorer traders especially, was abolished. About 150,000 acres of uncultivable land, heavily taxed, but of no value, were relieved of taxation. The taxes on the *Mazroof* lands, which were originally sold by the Government against the payment of a quit rent, but which, with the reduced values of produce, could not afford to pay an annual tax fixed in more prosperous times, were reduced so as to equal the taxes levied on other lands in the same localities. In order to carry out the reforms of an equitable reassessment, the rates of taxation, which numbered about 1,400, were reduced to only 220. Liberal fiscal regulations for the purpose of encouraging the reclamation of land and a system of improving the old village land registers were also adopted. A decree prohibiting the importation into the provinces and territory dependent upon Egypt south of 20° of north latitude, or the manufacture in them of distilled liquors, was issued according to the resolution of the Brussels Conference of July, 1890.

Treaty with Germany.—A commercial convention was signed between Egypt and Germany, July 22, 1892, to go into effect April 1, 1893. This treaty differs somewhat from those entered into with Austria, England, and Italy, in that it specifies the procedure to be adopted in case of dispute as to the valuation of goods, a provision as to the admissibility of searching German domiciles for smuggled goods, and in annexing to the treaty a copy of the existing customs regulations and by-laws, which the Egyptian Government is debarred from changing, in certain clauses, without the consent of the German consul-general. A duty of 15 per cent. *ad valorem* is fixed as a maximum which Egypt may impose upon silks, wines, spirits, petroleum, animals, and cereals.

ENGINEERING IN 1892. The past year has still further emphasized the tendency to restore old and create new canal systems. Particularly is this true in Germany, where nearly all the available streams are canalized; in Belgium, where the plan of making Brussels a seaport is well-nigh realized; in Italy, where Rome ere long will complete a canal to salt water; and in France, where the merchandise by canal now amounts to more than one third of that conveyed by rail. In Great Britain many of the old canals were long since acquired by railways and discontinued as canals, the earthwork, of course, being utilized to the new end. The Manchester Ship Canal is the only great work approaching completion. Among the most notable of the works now under way and approaching completion is the Sault Ste. Marie Canal, building by the Canadian Government; the Merwede, connecting Amsterdam with the Rhenish provinces of Germany; the allied Dutch work contemplating the drainage of the Zuyder Zee; and the Manchester Ship Canal, uniting the great cities of Liverpool and Manchester, England. In this country the final collapse of the Panama Canal scheme under French management has been followed by a dramatic exposure of corrupt dealings among its principal officers —dealings, it may be said, which were more than suspected, and were indeed common talk in New York for several years before the final crash. The only other American works of special interest north of the isthmus are in Colorado, where the immense system of irrigating ditches has been greatly extended. During the past twenty years the total tonnage transported on New York canals fell not far short of 110,000,000 tons, with an estimated value of about $3,250,000,000. Such enormous commercial interests naturally suggest the practicability of a ship canal from Lake Erie to the Hudson. This would not far exceed the cost of the Manchester Ship Canal, and there can hardly be a doubt that it would prove largely remunerative.

Improvements in tunneling devices rapidly increase the possibilities of that branch of engineering. No tunnels are sufficiently near completion to merit description at this time, but those under the Thames at London and the Hudson at New York are under way, and will no doubt be pushed forward rapidly. Detailed estimates alike for a bridge across and for a tunnel under the British Channel, from England to France, have been completed to the minutest detail. The cost of a bridge from Cape Blanc Nez to the South Foreland is estimated at $164,000,000, while the smallest revenue is calculated at about $20,000,-000 annually. The only obstacle to the construction of one or both of these works is found in the conservative dread on the part of the British public lest such means of transit should open a weak point in the defensive armor that Nature has provided for Great Britain. On the whole, the year has not been conspicuous for the completion of great engineering projects.

The Viaduct du Loup.—One of the most picturesque and, from an engineering point of

with iron or steel, that the construction of such a work in masonry seems almost a waste of material. It has been done, however, in the present instance, and the effect is described as very beautiful, the curving line of eleven arches, each 63 feet span, sweeping from side to side of the deep valley at a height in the middle sections of 170 feet. The total length of the viaduct is 1,050 feet. It is hardly conceivable that the building of such a structure with stone at this day is really good engineering, considered in the abstract, but it is nevertheless a fine piece of work.

Steel Bridge at Memphis.—The formal opening of the great steel bridge across the Mississippi at Memphis, Tenn., occurred on the 12th of May, when the structure was opened for traffic with appropriate ceremonies and great public rejoicing. Between this bridge and the Gulf of Mexico the Mississippi is not bridged, and above it the nearest bridge is at St. Louis. It is the third largest of its kind in the world. Work was begun in the autumn of 1888, when the first caisson was sunk. There are 5 spans and 6 piers, including the anchorages. The system of construction is the cantilever; the main span, consisting of 2 cantilever arms and 1 intermediate span, is 794 feet. The other spans range from 621 feet to 225 feet. The total length of the bridge is 2,597 feet. An iron viaduct extends the structure westward 2,500 feet, and then changes to timber trestle for 3,000 feet, and nearly a mile of embankment, to a junction with the tracks of the Kansas City, Fort Scott and Memphis Railroad. This junction is near Sibley, Ark. The river piers are sunk to depths varying from 75 to 131 feet below high-water mark; all these were sunk into position by the pneumatic process. They are of masonry from the caissons to the bridge seats. The main posts are 80 feet high, weighing 28 tons each, and many of the single smaller members weigh from 10 to 16 tons. The main pin of the cantilever truss is 14 inches in diameter and weighs 2,200 pounds. The bridge crosses the river, as nearly as can be decided, at the very spot where Ferdinand de Soto

VIADUCT DU LOUP.

view, one of the most difficult regions in southern France, has recently been traversed by a new railway running through Nice, Puget Theniers, and Grasse. Although only 62½ miles long, the road has been very costly, owing to the broken character of the country. The most notable of the bridges, of which there are many, is the viaduct, shown in Fig. 1, crossing the Vallée du Loup, on a curve of 675 feet radius. We are so accustomed to solving problems of this kind

crossed it in 1541. In support of this theory or tradition is the fact that, while excavations were being made for the shore piers on the Tennessee side, several Spanish halberds and sword blades were found, which could hardly have been there legitimately unless left by the early explorers.

Pecos River Bridge.—Owing to difficult grades and numerous bridges the Southern Pacific Railway has undertaken to straighten its line by a cut-off about 800 miles west of New

BRIDGE OVER PECOS RIVER, SOUTHERN PACIFIC RAILWAY.

Orleans. The new work includes a bridge over Pecos river cañon in Texas, a tremendous ravine 400 feet deep and nearly half a mile wide. The bridge, as nearly completed, is shown in Fig. 2. It is surpassed in height by only one other structure of the kind in the world, namely, the Loa Viaduct, in Bolivia, described in the " Annual " for 1889, and falls short of this only by about 8½ feet. Its height above the stream is 328 feet: length, 2,180 feet; width at floor, 20 feet, providing for a single track and footways for employees. The material is steel, the principal tower being 321 feet 6 inches, including the limestone foundation. The viaduct has 48 spans all told, the central or channel span being a cantilever of 185 feet, while the others are plate girders, alternating 35 and 65 feet long. The towers are all 35 × 100 feet at base and 10 × 35 feet at top. The erection of the ironwork was begun in November, 1891, and finished during the summer of 1892, under the supervision of the Southern Pacific engineer corps.

Moving a Bridge Tower.—An interesting engineering feat was accomplished late in December in moving a large drawbridge tower on the Harlem river. The structure is of iron lattice work 126 feet high, 48 feet 6 inches wide, and 34 feet long at the base, tapering upward wedgewise to a horizontal tiebeam at the top of its two vertical main pillars. With its accessory machinery it has for many years done the work of raising and lowering the drawbridge that carries the trains of three great railroad lines, namely, the New York Central, the Harlem, and the New York and New Haven roads. The traffic by river and rail has far outgrown the capacity of the bridge, and a new one is in course of construction. Since no interruption of traffic is ad-

missible, a temporary structure must be erected until the new bridge is ready for use. The most feasible plan seemed to be to move the tower to the line of the temporary bridge. This was accomplished under the management of Mr. Maylan, foreman for Coffrode and Saylor, the original builders of the tower. Two rows of piles were driven, topped with heavy stringers and rails, and the tower, stripped of movables, but still weighing 180 tons, was jacked up 3 feet, rails connected with those on the piling were laid under it, and the tower was lowered into position. Dixon's plumbago lubricator was used on the rails, and with the aid of a powerful hoisting engine and immense sheave blocks the great tower slid easily on its ways and was moved back and forth at the experimental trial at the rate of more than 2 feet a minute. Eventually it was moved without a hitch to its new site, and set to work operating the temporary draw. The new bridge now under construction will carry four tracks in continuation of the present Fourth Avenue system, and will be built to meet the requirements of the United States engineers who have in charge the improvements that will soon change Spuyten Duyvel creek from an insignificant inlet to an important commercial highway.

The Norwegian Ship Canal.—One of the greatest of modern engineering works is undoubtedly the magnificent canal, now completed, which connects the great lake system of Telemarken with the sea near Christiania. It forms a water way of more than 85 miles, traversing half of southern Norway from east to west. It forms, in fact, a beginning of what may be regarded as a main highway between the east and the west coast of the Norwegian peninsula. The work was begun in 1861, when the first of the chain of lakes was connected with the sea. But the engineering difficulties peculiar to the rest of the route postponed further operations until 1886. The Government then decided on its accomplishment, and engineers—mainly Norwegian, we believe—have most successfully overcome the difficulties. By nature the lakes were connected by a considerable river, with frequent rapids and falls, but this, by means of locks and the other appliances familiar to canal builders, has been converted into a navigable channel. The greatest natural obstacle was encountered at Drangfos, a succession of falls and rapids more than a mile long and having a total descent of about 75 feet. Here it was necessary to dam the river at the foot of the incline and raise the water to the height indicated. As the natural foundation was untrustworthy, a massive stone arch was built across the chasm, forming a base for the great dam of masonry which now restrains the rush of water. This canal passes through scenery of great wildness and beauty, and it will no doubt become a favorite route for tourists in this picturesque region.

Drainage Works.—Chicago's long struggle with the question of water supply and drainage has passed several critical periods within a few years, but the coming Columbian Fair has brought matters to a crisis, and it is determined that a large drainage canal shall be opened from Lake Michigan to an affluent of the Mississippi, so that the drainage of the great city will literally be carried into the Gulf of Mexico instead of being emptied, as heretofore, into the source of the city's water supply. It has been held by some geologists that in former ages the lakes found their outlet to the gulf instead of to the Atlantic. However this may be, it is certain that the level of the Mississippi river opposite Chicago is enough lower than the level of the Great Lakes to insure an ample fall for drainage. The beginning of the work has been made at the crest of a ridge known as the Chicago Divide, on what will be the central line of the main channel intersecting the boundaries of Will and Cook Counties. A deal of litigation is unavoidable to decide upon the value of lands taken for the canal, as well as upon consequential damages; this, of course, in cases where the owners and the commissioners can not agree as to terms. Careful estimates give $25,000,000 as a possible minimum, and contracts amounting to about $11,500,000 have been let from Willow Springs to Lockport. This estimate is for actual construction alone, not including the price of land, so that it is extremely probable that the total amount will considerably exceed the sum named above, particularly when the almost uniform tendency of engineers to underestimate is taken into the account. The necessity of the work is imperative, at whatever cost, and no doubt it will be carried out with characteristic energy. The projected canal, saturated as it must be with rich but unsavory fertilizing material, is not without its terrors for suburban residents; but it holds out, at the same time, attractive possibilities for agricultural interests, and will no doubt eventually be utilized for that purpose.

Sewerage is not a particularly savory subject, but it is satisfactory to know that modern scientific ingenuity is reducing its objectionable features, and even rendering it available for purposes that could hardly be anticipated. Recent experiments in the vicinity of Berlin, Germany, are among the most remarkable on record. Two years ago, it is said, a pond having an area of about 1,000 square feet was supplied with water coming directly from the sewerage system of the city after it had been employed for agricultural irrigation. The pond was stocked with trout, which lived through the summer and winter until the following year, when the water was drawn off and 300 trout from 4 to 5 inches long were found. The success of this experiment led to the construction of six new tanks, with an area of more than 40,000 square feet and a depth not exceeding 3 feet. Some of these were stocked with carp and others with trout, and at a banquet lately given to Prof. Virchow about 150 of these "sewer fish" were served in one of the courses. Carp, it is well known, thrive in impure water; but as trout are exceedingly fastidious in the matter of water, the result at Berlin proves that a process of filtration through wide cultivated tracts is highly efficient.

Relief Sewer in Brooklyn, N. Y.—Warned by a startling disaster involving loss of life and considerable damage, the city of Brooklyn has provided a sewer capable of carrying off the surplus water of heavy rainfalls. The dangerous district was about 1,300 acres in extent, and during the first rush of water after a heavy rain the lower streets were flooded, including adjacent cellars, and much damage often resulted. The work just completed is known as the main relief sewer. It is carried across the drainage area through Greene Avenue, Fourth Avenue, and Butler Street to the head of the Gowanus Canal, which falls into the natural cove now mainly occupied by the United States Navy Yard. With this main, the regular street sewers are connected in such a way as to deliver only storm water; thus the regular sewers will only be called upon to do work of which they are amply capable. The tunnel has been made under the Anderson method of construction, using the Beach system of tunneling needles, which is an American invention and was patented as long ago as 1869 by Alfred E. Beach, of the "Scientific American." Recently, however, it has been brought forward as an entirely new thing in Great Britain, where it attracted much attention from engineering authorities. The needles are, in fact, heavy bars of iron or steel. They are driven forward separately into the earth that forms a support for the front part, while the rear end rests on the progressing work of the permanent tunnel. A notable instance of the use of these needles at King's Cross Station in London was described in the "Annual Cyclopædia" for 1890, page 285. The main part of the sewer is circular in section, with a diameter of 10 feet, enlarging successively to 12, 14, and 15 feet as it descends, with walls usually not exceeding 16 inches, except in some places where local features call for a 28-inch side wall. Of this circular portion there are 11,400 linear feet, of which more than 9,000 feet were laid by tunneling, part of it far below the solidly built-up parts of the city. Near the discharge end the section is changed to something nearer a rectangular form, the bottom being an inverted arch of long radius covered by the beam-and-brick arch construction familiar in modern buildings. The discharge is into a silt basin and through 20 pipes of 36 inches diameter each. The silt basin is provided with traps, although the pipes are as much as 8 feet below tide level. It is said that this is the third largest of the working sewers in the world, that of Washington being 20 feet in diameter, while the great sewer of Paris is 18 feet high and 17 feet wide. The Cloaca Maxima of the Romans occupied a total cross area of 30 × 15 feet. It is believed that this sewer will remove a considerable danger which threatened a part of the inhabitants of the city, and the rush of comparatively clean water will no doubt tend to clear out the Gowanus Canal, at present by no means an attractive feature of the Brooklyn water front. L. Russell Clapp and David Brower, assistant city engineers, were in charge of the construction, under Robert Van Buren, chief engineer.

The Water-Power of Niagara Falls.—This vast work is now nearly approaching realization. The enormous forces that go to waste over Niagara have always offered fascinating problems to the utilitarian mind, and as early as 1725 a rude saw mill was erected at the "awful brink"

LOWER TUNNEL, NIAGARA FALLS.

by some pioneer who could not bear to see such a superb water power unemployed. This gave way before the march of tourists as the falls became a center of interest, and although the subject of utilizing the power was often considered, nothing was done until 1873, when the present canal was made, affording about 6,000 horse power and driving several mills. This was a mere trifle compared with the full head of water, and the elaborate plans since perfected are now nearly carried out. Various estimates have been made as to the total power of Niagara Falls, but the lowest places it at several millions of horse power, and it is believed that it is not beyond

proof that its power is twice as great as that of all the combined steam and water power at present employed in the United States. The illustration on page 253 shows the main features of the work. The great tunnel is 7,250 feet long, forming what is known in ordinary works as the tail race. Its outlet is in the river just above the water level, under the cliffs below the town of Niagara. The intake end is on the river bank above the town, where the company own a large tract purchased for the purpose. This is laid out for mill sites and for the required surface canals through which water can be led to the different wheel pits, all of them being connected by lateral tunnels with the main discharge tunnel. The cross section of the tunnel is of the ordinary horseshoe shape, 19 feet wide and 21 feet high inside of the brickwork. The cross-sectional area is 386 square feet, but this does not express the total amount of excavation, the timbering and brickwork calling altogether for a cross-sectional area of 522 square feet. The sill of the tunnel at its discharge opening is 205 feet below the sill of the head gate at the entrance above the falls. Of this about 140 feet is practically available, the difference in perpendicular height being taken up by margin of clearance and for the necessary incline and lateral tunnels, which is generally at a grade of 36 feet to the mile. Abrasion is measurably guarded against by lining the tunnel with heavy cast-iron plates, as it is not believed that brick-work or masonry could stand the wear and tear for any length of time. The illustration shows how the main stream of water is led to the head of the turbine trunk, whence its fall is perpendicular through about 140 feet of pipe. The kind of turbine best for the purpose, and the method of setting the wheel, called for careful investigation, and it was eventually determined that, in order to decrease the wear on the bearings of the wheel shaft, the water should be delivered on the under side of the wheel. A commission was sent to Europe to examine plans for the generation of power by turbines, and prizes were offered for the best devices. The two firms receiving the highest award offered two projects for the utilization of 125,000 horse power and its electrical distribution; these are the adoption of the well-known Girard turbines, with a unit of about 2,500 horse power for each wheel. The company expects to make its contract with the city of Buffalo for lighting the city, about 3,000 horse power being required for the purpose. If this enterprise proves successful, it is difficult to say where the transmission of power by electricity will end. It is by no means unreasonable to anticipate that, with such an enormous power as Niagara available, means for lighting cities hundreds of miles away may be attained.

Masonry Dam, Austin, Texas.—The great Colorado river of the South has been dammed with a view to a water supply for the capital of

METHOD OF UTILIZING THE WATER-POWER OF NIAGARA FALLS.
THE INTAKE.

Texas, and the work has been undertaken on a scale that will probably enable it to furnish water works and electric light, with abundant power for manufacturing. The dam was undertaken by authority of a public election, when the citizens voted bonds to the amount of $1,400,000. It is not by any means the largest masoury dam in the world. At Vrynwy, in Wales, at Bnzey and Grosbois, in France, and at several places in Spain, Belgium, California, and India, are dams that exceed it in size. None of these, however, are built upon rivers nearly as large as the Colorado, and few of them are designed for a continuous flow of water over the crest. They are intended to retain all or nearly all the water of their respective rivers. The Austin dam, on the contrary, crosses the channel of the Colorado where it has 40,-000 square miles of watershed, and where its annual floods reach a volume of 200,000 feet a second. With such a mass of water passing over its crest, it is easy to understand that the highest engineering skill must have been called into service, if the work is well done. It would be difficult, however, for any engineer to devise a dam that would not afford some weak points

MASONRY DAM IN TEXAS.

for the criticism of his professional brethren. The lower face of the dam, on its down-stream side, has a curve of 31 feet radius, tangent at its lowest point to the water surface. The central part of this face has a batter of 4½ inches to the foot. The profile at the top terminates the down-stream face and crest of the dam with a curve of 20 feet radius. To this both the front batter and the surface of the pond at the crest level are tangent. The upper angle of the crest is rounded off with a smaller curve, and the whole front of the masonry becomes a sort of reversed ogee—a form probably as well adapted as any to pass a large volume of water from a great height. The surface curve conforms as closely as possible to that taken by a stream in flood when it passes a low perpendicular fall. At the higher flood stages it is expected that there will be a tendency to a vacuum under the curved stream immediately after it has passed the crest. This, together with the pressure of the atmosphere upon the surface of the water, will keep the full flood stream in close contact with the curved face of the dam, and cause it, even in the heaviest flood, to slide smoothly over the masonry surface to its rock foundation. Such is the theory of the engineers; but only the test of time can decide how successfully they have estimated the forces with which they have to deal. The body of the work is in limestone rock; the two faces, the toe and the crest, where the greatest wear and tear will occur, are of granite, the blocks forming the cap being as large as can be conveniently handled. The entire work is laid in hydraulic cement. It is 1,200 feet long, 60 feet high, and 16 feet wide at the top, increasing downward till its width at the bottom is 50 feet. It is intended to allow a depth of 16 feet of water on the crest, and the abutments at either end rise to more than that

height. At one end of the dam the natural rock rises far higher, and at the other end is an artificial bulkhead, containing the gatehouse and the necessary sluices. The dam is 2 miles above the city of Austin, and when completed will form a lake 25 miles long and from half a mile to a quarter of a mile wide. J. R. Frizzell is chief engineer, with T. J. Fanning assistant.

Masonry Dam in India.—The largest stone dam in the world has lately been finished in India, designed for the supply of water to the city of Bombay. The work stretches across the Tansa valley, about 65 miles north of Bombay. The dam is 2 miles long, 118 feet high, 100 feet thick at its greatest depth, and 15½ feet wide at the top. When filled, the dam will form a lake covering 8 square miles, and the expected water supply will be at the rate of about 100,-000,000 gallons a day throughout the year. More than five years have passed since the work of construction was begun, and from 9,000 to 12,000 men, with 800 carts and animals, have been employed upon it during each working season. Great difficulties of construction were encountered. Sand and cement had to be transported for a long distance; nearly 15,000,000 cubic feet of rubble were used, with 2,200,000 cubic feet of lime and nearly 3,350,000 cubic feet of washed sand. The rock excavations alone amounted to more than 6,700,000 cubic feet, and the completed masonry altogether contains about 11,000,000 cubic feet. The contractors were Glover & Co., of Edinburgh, and the executive engineer was J. B. Clark. From the dam to Bombay the water is led in iron pipes 48 inches in diameter. Fortunately, in this climate the pipes can be laid above ground without danger from frost. Each length of pipe weighs about 4 tons, and their aggregate weight is 50,000 tons.

The Columbia River Jetties.—Since 1884 this great work has been in progress. It has in view the making of a channel over a dangerous bar at the mouth of the river, the contract calling for a depth of 30 feet at low tide. This is to be accomplished in the usual way, by concentrating the current and increasing its power of carrying away sand and other deposit. As the work now stands, it is a low-tide jetty, extending westward from Fort Stephens with a slight curve to the south, the length being about 4½ miles. The ordinary mattress-fascine construction was used, the foundation being about 40 feet wide and from 2½ to 5 feet thick; this, of course, is below water at all times, and upon it is placed the rockwork, extending to a level of 4 feet above mean low water. The latest report of Capt. T. W. Symons, of the United States Engineers, says that before the work was begun the channels over the bar were variable in depth and capricious in location; sometimes there was but one channel, and at other times there were three, varying in depth from 19 to 21 feet. The results already attained are extremely satisfactory. There is one straight-out-and-in channel a quarter of a mile wide and nowhere less than 29 feet deep. About 25,000 tons of rock have been used in securing the jetty and protecting the buildings. The original estimate for the construction was $3,000,710, and it is likely that the work can be finished within those figures.

Government Railways in Sumatra.—Dutch rule in Sumatra has so stimulated commercial interest that a comprehensive railway system has been undertaken, under the direction of Mr. Post, a Dutch engineer. The engineering difficulties have been very great, owing to the mountainous character of the island and the steep gradients and sharp curves that everywhere have to be overcome. In general terms, the line extends across the most densely populated part of the island, its high central plateau touching the principal inland towns and reaching the coast at Port Emma, the terminus. The line ascends to an altitude of 3,785 feet above sea level, and crosses a formidable volcanic range whose Sumatrian name signifies "destroying fire." This section presents gradients as steep as 1 in 12, and these are overcome by means of mechanical appliances on the engines, consisting of 2 coupled axles combining adhesion wheels and cogged wheels, which can be used at the engineer's pleasure according to the steepness of the grade. For connection with the cog wheel, a central, ladderlike rack is bolted to the ties between the ordinary rails. Two types of ties are employed, both being of iron, since wood decays so rapidly in that climate as to be unavailable. The engines are provided with 3 kinds of brakes—spring, air, and a tooth-wheel brake, which is capable of arresting the mechanism. All the machinery has to be of the simplest character possible, because the only engineers available in Sumatra are not accomplished mechanics, and complicated machinery is entirely beyond them. The locomotive is always coupled to the rear of the train, pushing it on the up grades and holding it back during descents. The cars are of the American type, and are arranged for two classes of travelers. One feature, at least, in the construction of this line was very interesting and ingenious: running water was utilized for the purpose of carrying earth and depositing it at the places where it was required. This was effected by means of small canals of steep gradient, sometimes several miles long. The laborers stir up the earth and the water that carries it down steep inclines to places where it is desired to construct an embankment. Here barriers of bamboo are set, which permit water and soluble material to pass, while the solid earth, gravel, and sand settle down and form an embankment. So solid are these deposits that it is perfectly safe to cross them on foot or on horseback while the water is still flowing over the surface. The loss of material is sometimes as high as 30 per cent., but the saving in time and labor largely overbalances this.

Artesian Well.—An interesting but unsuccessful attempt was made at Galveston, Texas, to secure an ample supply of pure water. The city at present draws its water supply from 13 wells ranging from 825 to 1,350 feet deep. It was decided to expend $75,000 for a well at least 3,000 feet deep. The work was done in the usual way, beginning with a section of 15-inch pipe, telescoping smaller sections, and ending with pipe of 9 inches in diameter. No water was reached, but the result of the borings was of interest. They were as follow: Gray sand, 46 feet; red clay and shells, 18 feet: blue clay and wood fragments, 36 feet: sand and seashells, 215 feet; sand and clay, 600 feet; sand, clay, and seashells and wood, 688 feet; and the remainder, to a depth of 3,070 feet, was sand, clay, and large logs. At this point, the contract having been more than fulfilled, the boring ended in a bed of seashells.

Flexible Water-Pipes.—Engineers have repeatedly considered the practicability of laying water mains in the beds of rivers for the purpose of supplying fresh water to cities at the seaboard; but there have been many difficulties to overcome, and it has not been undertaken on a large scale. During the past summer a new plan has been adopted by the authorities of Rotterdam for laying pipes in the bed of the River Maas. A difficulty that had to be surmounted was found in the very large and continuous traffic of the river. Eventually a flexible tube was constructed, consisting of short sections connected with ball joints; each pipe is 23 inches in diameter, made of steel and provided with steel flanges. The ball joints are of cast iron. In sinking the pipes to position, 2 barges were fastened together and an inclined platform about 120 feet long was hung freely between the two. The pipe sections were built up on this platform, and as each joint was completed the barges were hauled astern so that the lowermost section slid off and was deposited on the bottom of the river, leaving room at the top of the incline for the attachment of the next section. The depth of the river averages 36 feet, and work progressed at the rate of about 85 feet a day. The whole length of the tube was about 3,000 feet.

Submarine Borings in Northumberland Straits.—Work has actually begun on the tunnel connecting the mainland of New Brunswick with Prince Edward Island, but it has not progressed far enough to justify description here. The engineer who had charge of the preliminary survey devised a plan of making experimental borings which has the merit of daring and originality. The problem presented was, how to test the character of the earth under the perpetually stormy Straits of Northumberland, often at a

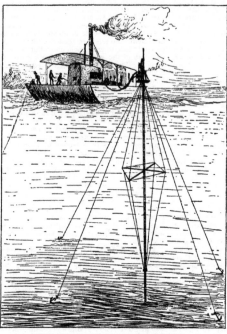

APPARATUS FOR TESTING GEOLOGICAL FORMATION.

depth of more than 100 feet. The apparatus is clearly indicated in the illustration above. A 4-inch wrought-iron pipe, made up in 20-foot lengths, rests upon the bottom of the sea, and at the upper end of the pipe is arranged a platform strong enough to carry an engine capable of developing a high rate of speed. The pipe is braced and anchored so as to secure it in an upright position, and the engine drives a diamond drill within the pipe at the rate of 1,000 revolutions a minute. A scow anchored near carries the boiler and accessory machinery, connections being made with the drill engine by means of flexible tubing. The drill is thus always held in a vertical position, and is not subject to any considerable oscillation, though often subjected to the force of a heavy sea. The inventor of this method is Alfred Palmer, civil engineer, of New York. The tunnel will cross the strait only a few miles from the northern end of the Chignecto ship railway, now approaching completion.

Snow in City Streets.—A problem that confronts all dwellers in northern cities is the speedy removal of snow from city streets. In the far north the work is too great for serious consideration. The snow is merely piled up in the roadways, leveled, and allowed to remain until melted by the advancing season. This at least is the case in Canada. But the large cities of the United States are not content to let nature take its course, and their utmost resources are taxed to clear the streets for traffic after a heavy snowstorm. Various projects have been suggested, and elaborate calculations made, all pointing to the probable economy of melting the snow and causing it to run off through the sewers. Charles E. Emory, one of the best authorities on the use and distributions of steam, has reached this conclusion. The severe winter experience of England during recent years has caused them to investigate the same subject. It has even been estimated that, with the price of gas at 2s. 6d. a thousand cubic feet, snow can be economically melted by burning gas. Mr. Emory has tried a steam-melting process which gave good results and has the merit of simplicity. A tarpaulin 25 feet square was used to cover an area of snow, when spread steam was admitted underneath it, and the snow melted with astonishing rapidity. It was found that in this way large areas could be economically cleared. This method seems more practicable than the gas method, and in streets having steam mains it would seem to be perfectly feasible. The process involves the direct contact of steam and snow, while in the gas process, as described, the heat has to be led through a metal heating plate, undoubtedly a cause of inefficiency and expense. It is believed that none of the engines specially constructed for melting snow have proved practically successful.

EVENTS OF 1892. Europe, although in no way relaxing her warlike preparations, has remained at peace, and actual warfare has been confined to barbarous tribes. The most considerable campaign undertaken by civilized arms was that of the French in the kingdom of Dahomey. The threatened hostilities between the United States and Chili were adjusted, and the Bering Sea dispute with England was again compromised. Cholera was epidemic in many states in Europe, but by dint of extraordinary measures was prevented from gaining a foothold in the United States. The ever-recurrent conflict between labor and capital caused trouble and bloodshed in France, England, and the United

States, the strikes failing in nearly every instance to benefit the strikers. Anarchy has become aggressive in many parts of Europe. In France the year closed with a threatening political crisis resulting from an exposure of the Panama Canal frauds.

January 1. Washington: New Year reception by the President at the White House. New York: Roswell P. Flower inaugurated Governor. Kansas: The Governor appoints the Hon. Bishop W. Perkins United States Senator, *vice* Plumb, deceased.

2. Tennessee: Convict miners, released by violence, are returned under military guard to Coal Creek. Captain Hardie, with a detachment of the Third Cavalry, disperses a band of Mexican outlaws.

4. England: A detachment of the Salvation Army attacked by a mob at Eastbourne. The Pope accepts conciliatory offers on the part of France.

5. Connecticut: The State Supreme Court decides that Morgan G. Bulkley is Governor.

6. Maryland: The Legislature meets at Annapolis and elects Democratic officers.

7. Foreign countries notified by Secretary Blaine that the retaliatory clauses of the United States tariff will go into effect on March 15. Kansas: Four men killed in a fight with outlaws near Springfield. Farmers' Alliance: Secret session of officers at Washington. Massachusetts: Hon. William E. Russell inaugurated Governor. Connecticut: The Legislature meets and adjourns.

8. Memphis, Tenn.: Representative meeting of cotton planters.

9 Washington: First State reception of the year at the White House. Indianapolis: Street railways blocked by a general strike of employees.

11. Ohio: Hon. William McKinley, Jr., inaugurated Governor at Columbus. Formidable revolt in Morocco.

13. Ohio: Senator Sherman re-elected by the Legislature. Maryland: The Hon. Frank Brown inaugurated Governor. Gibraltar: A British squadron sails for Morocco.

14. St. Louis, Mo.: Annual Convention of the Young Men's Hebrew Association. Indianapolis, Ind.: Tramway strike ended by arbitration. England: Death of the heir presumptive to the British throne. Prussia: Opening of the Landtag.

15. Washington: Annual meeting of the Women's Suffrage Association, Susan B. Anthony, president, Elizabeth Cady Stanton and Lucy Stone, honorary presidents.

16. San Francisco: International League of Press Clubs. Washington: Association of American Inventors and Manufacturers of Patented Articles. France: A fight in the Chamber of Deputies. Dahomey: Battle between French and natives, the latter defeated.

20. New York: Meeting of the Society of Civil Engineers. Rio de Janeiro: Successful revolt of prisoners.

21. Maryland: The Hon. Charles H. Gibson chosen United States Senator. Boston: Dedication of Chamber of Commerce building.

22. The Soudan: The French defeat a native force.

23. Washington: The President issues an *ultimatum* regarding the dispute with Chili.

26. Washington: Minister Egan telegraphs that Chili accedes to the demands of the United States.

27. Chicago: National conference of the various "reform" parties, Miss Frances E. Willard, president. Washington: Meeting of the National Board of Trade, Frederick Fraley, president. Spain: Striking miners at Bilbao repel an attack of Government troops. Russian troops called out to suppress bread riots.

Washington: The President announces the satisfactory adjustment of the Chilian trouble. Chicago: Meeting of the National Farmers' Alliance, D. F. Ravens, president. Mexico: A formidable insurrection headed by the outlaw Garza.

VOL. XXXII.—17 A

February 1. Washington: The Supreme Court decides that Boyd is Governor of Nebraska, and that the antilottery law is constitutional. Germany: 20 anarchists arrested in Berlin.

2. Washington: The President proclaims reciprocal trade relations with Germany. Poundridge, N. Y.: A boy kidnaped and $6,000 ransom demanded.

3. Washington: Parcels Post Convention signed between the United States and British Guiana.

5. Washington: The President proclaims reciprocity with the British West Indies.

7. Columbus, Ohio: Meeting of the United Mine Workers of America.

8. Washington: Opening of negotiations concerning free trade between the United States and Canada. France, Italy, and Sweden selected as arbitrators in the Bering Sea question.

9. England: Parliament meets. Mr. Balfour accepts the Conservative leadership.

12. Germany and Spain: Anarchist plots discovered at Berlin and Barcelona.

13. A remarkably brilliant aurora visible in the Eastern States. Kansas: Wolves become troublesome and dangerous in parts of the State.

15. Washington: The Canadian free-trade commissioners return home without having effected a treaty.

16. Baltimore: Annual meeting of the Society of Mining Engineers.

17. Nashville, Tenn.: National Real Estate Congress opens, B. M. Niel, of Milwaukee, president.

18. Washington: A congressional party, numbering about 350, starts for Chicago to inspect the World's Fair site.

21. Indianapolis, Ind.: Strike of tramway employees.

22. Albany, N. Y.: The Democratic State Convention favors Hill for President. Washington: General Congress of the Daughters of the American Revolution, Mrs. Harrison, president.

23. Buffalo, N. Y.: Convention of Electrical Engineers. England: A motion to disestablish the Church in Wales defeated in the House of Commons.

24. Germany: The Emperor makes an extraordinary speech at Brandenburg, much criticism excited. France: Seizures of dynamite by the police in Paris.

25. Washington: Congressional investigation begins of the Pension Office under Commissioner Raum. Philadelphia: Consecration of the Rev. Dr. Ignatius F. Horstman as Bishop of Cleveland (Roman Catholic). Canada: Parliament opened by Gov.-Gen. Lord Stanley. Berlin: Riotous demonstration before the Emperor's palace.

26. Chicago University: John D. Rockefeller gives $1,000,000 in Government bonds. Berlin: Continued disturbances. Indianapolis: The striking tram-car drivers resort to violence. France: A new Cabinet organized by M. Loubet. Germany: More rioting in Berlin.

29. Washington: The Supreme Court renders decisions affirming the constitutionality of the McKinley tariff, of Speaker Reed's method of counting a quorum, and denying a writ of prohibition in the Sayward case. The Bering Sea arbitration treaty signed. Boston: The Grand Jury finds indictments against the Whisky Trust officials. Continued scenes of violence in Indianapolis. New Orleans: Mardi Gras festivities begin.

March 1. Greece: The King dismisses his entire Cabinet. Austria: Much suffering among the poor in Vienna.

2. New York: Mass meeting to celebrate the Pope's birthday. Washington: Lumbermen's Convention, C. W. Goodyear, New York, president.

3. Baltimore: Corner stones laid in connection with the Women's College. Valencia, Spain: Anarchists explode a bomb in a church.

4. Washington, D. C.: Disagreement of experts on the Bering Sea question. Dantzic, Prussia: A mob loots several buildings.

5. Tennessee: Revenue officers and moonshiners killed in an encounter near Ducktown.

6. Dickenson College, Carlisle, Pa.: Dedication of a memorial chapel.

7. Pittsburg, Pa.: Convention of the machinery trades to form a National Union. Guatemala: The President-elect arrested by order of the President. Quebec, Canada: An election results in Conservative victory.

9. Memphis, Tenn.: Three negro convicts taken from jail and shot by a mob. Washington, D. C.: Conference of postmasters at the invitation of the Postmaster-General. By bequest from Gen. George W. Cullom, the Military Academy at West Point receives $250,000 for a memorial chapel, the Geographical Society $100,000, and the Metropolitan Museum $75,000.

10. Announced dissolution of the Standard Oil Trust. Twelve thousand bushels of corn from Bloomington, Ill., and $5,000 from Baltimore, sent to starving peasants in Russia. France and Spain ratify commercial treaties with the United States.

11. Washington, D. C.: An exchange of money orders arranged between the United States and Austria.

12. Great Britain: About 400,000 coal miners strike against a reduction of wages. Paris: Anarchists wreck with dynamite the house of a judge.

13. Washington: The President announces reciprocity with Nicaragua. Vienna: Encounter between the police and starving workmen.

14. Washington: The President proclaims higher duties against Colombia, Hayti, and Venezuela, under the reciprocity act. New York: The steamship Missouri sails for Russia with supplies for starving peasants. Kentucky: Dealing in lottery tickets made a felony by law. Paris: Anarchists explode dynamite near occupied army barracks.

17. England and Denmark appropriate respectively $50,000 and $66,000 for representative exhibits at Chicago. New York gives $300,000 for a State exhibit.

18. Washington: Nine new circuit judges appointed by the President. Two convicted murderers lynched near Gainesville, Va. Paris: Celebration of the Commune anniversary.

20. Albany, N. Y.: Two hundred and fiftieth anniversary of the First Reformed Dutch Church.

21. Chicago: Seven aldermen indicted, and held in $12,000 each, for alleged bribery. Washington: The Interstate Commerce Commission elects William R. Morrison chairman, vice Cooley, resigned.

22. Wisconsin: The State Supreme Court declares the new apportionment unconstitutional. Texas: Roger Q. Mills chosen United States Senator.

23. Washington: Receipt of England's refusal to renew the modus vivendi in Bering Sea. Massachusetts: the Governor's yearly salary fixed at $8,000. Minneapolis: 22,000 barrels of flour sent to the starving Russians.

24. Homestead, Pa.: Andrew Carnegie promises his workmen a library, hall, and gymnasium, worth $100,000. Paris: A new extradition treaty signed with the United States.

27. Washington: An agreement reached with the British Government, renewing the modus vivendi.

30. Boston, Mass.: First State convention of the People's party.

31. Norfolk, Va.: Launch of the United States cruiser Raleigh at the Navy Yard. Findlay, Ohio: a wife murderer taken from jail and lynched by a mob. Germany: The Reichstag prorogued. India: opening of the Bombay water works.

April 2. Mississippi: Adjournment of the State Legislature. Africa: The King of Dahomey attacks the French possessions.

3. Russia: The American relief steamer Missouri reaches Libau with provisions.

5. France and Great Britain agree to continue the modus vivendi as regards the Newfoundland fisheries.

6. Election in Rhode Island (see article on that State). Utah: Completion of the Mormon temple at Salt Lake City.

7. France: Anarchists blow up the police station at Angers.

8. New Orleans: Convention of United Confederate Veterans.

9. Rustlers and cowboys at war in Wyoming and Montana. England: Oxford wins the University Boat Race by two and a quarter lengths.

13. Wyoming: United States troops ordered out to enforce peace between cowboys and "rustlers." Spain: Anarchists explode a bomb in Valencia. Great Britain increases the appropriation for the World's Fair.

14. The United States Government agrees to pay an indemnity of $25,000 for the New Orleans lynching. Wyoming: Cowboys surrender to United States troops. Spain: Two anarchist bombs exploded at Cadiz.

15. Dakota's (North and South) surplus Indian lands, amounting to 547,257 acres, opened to settlement at 12 o'clock, noon.

16. Tennessee: Revolt of convicts at Chickamauga. Revenue steamers Rush and Bear ordered to patrol Bering Sea. Cuba: Anarchist bomb exploded in Havana.

18. Ohio: The State Legislature adjourned to January, 1893. Reading, Pa.: The "First Defenders" of Washington in 1861 hold a reunion.

20. Spain: Anarchists explode bombs in three towns.

21. Fight between cowboys and rustlers at Little Powder River, Mont. Washington: A delegation of colored men call upon the President to protest against alleged Southern outrages. New York: The State Legislature adjourns; 57 Sioux Indians sail for London to recruit Buffalo Bill's troupe. Paris: The Cabinet decides upon war with Dahomey. Rome: Conference of the Red Cross Society.

22. Washington: The President proclaims a renewal of the modus vivendi as between the United States and Great Britain in the Bering Sea.

24. Chicago: Meeting of the International Society of Theosophists, Col. H. S. Olcott, president. Many arrests of anarchists in Europe.

25. Brooklyn, N. Y.: Consecration of Mgr. McDonnell, Roman Catholic Bishop of the diocese. Paris: Anarchists wreck a restaurant with dynamite, killing the proprietor.

26. Baltimore: Dedication of a new Odd Fellows' Hall, seventy-third anniversary of the order. Paris: Anarchists sentenced to penal servitude for life.

27. New York: Corner stone of the Grant monument laid with impressive ceremonies. Washington: Corner stone of the Catholic university laid.

28. Baltimore: Meeting of the Civil Service Reform Association. Atlanta, Ga.: Annual meeting of the Scotch-Irish Society. Four negroes lynched in Tennessee for outraging white women. Anarchists very active in Europe; bombs exploded in France, Belgium, and Italy.

30. New York: Congress and dinner of the Sons of the American Revolution. Elizabethport, N. J.: Launch of the United States practice ship Bancroft.

May 1. Washington: The President announces reciprocity with Honduras. Chicago: Three anarchist flags seized by the police in the May-Day procession. Europe: Several anarchist bombs exploded in different places.

2. Omaha: Methodist General Conference begins its annual session (adjourns May 26). Philadelphia: Conference of the African Methodist Episcopal Church. Labor strikes in several States. The steamer Tynhead sails for Russia with provisions from Washington, D. C. France: Anarchist bombs exploded at Liége.

3. Washington: Annual meeting of Superintendents of Institutions for the Insane. Newfoundland: The Parliament renews tariff discrimination against Canada.

4. Pittsburg, Pa.: Annual conference, African Methodist Episcopal Zion Church (adjourns May 25). Philadelphia: Opening of the graduate department

for women, University of Pennsylvania. Belgium: Many anarchists arrested.

5. The President signs the Chinese Exclusion bill. Wyoming: Two women elected alternate delegates to the State Republican convention. Albany, N. Y.: The Rev. Henry Gabriels, D. D., consecrated as Roman Catholic Bishop of Ogdensburg.

6. England: Conviction of an anarchist editor for inciting to murder. Two explosions of anarchist bombs on the Continent.

7. Ratification of the Bering Sea arbitration agreement between Great Britain and the United States.

8. Hartford, Conn.: Dedication of St. Joseph's Roman Catholic Cathedral. Hungary: Anarchists wreck with dynamite the house of a notary.

9. A number of labor strikes ordered.

10. Memorial Day celebrated throughout the late Confederate States. New York: Convention of the National Order of Hibernians in Tammany Hall.

11. Atlanta, Ga.: Meeting of the Bretherhood of Locomotive Engineers. Chicago: Convention of Women's Clubs. New York: Annual meeting American Tract Society. Cincinnati: Ministerial conference, Church of the New Jerusalem. Bath, Me.: Launch of United States gunboat Castine.

12. Memphis, Tenn.: Opening of the cantilever bridge across the Mississippi (see ENGINEERING). Charleston, S. C.: Meeting of the Supreme Ledge, Knights of Honor. Hermitage, Tenn.: Opening of Confederate Soldiers' Home. Hungary: Anarchists' attempt to blow up a crowded tram car in Buda Pesth.

13. France: Anarchists wreck with dynamite a house at Lens.

14. France: Anarchists wreck another house in Paris.

16. Lakewood, N. J.: Meeting of the American Library Association.

17. Washington: Congress of the National Art Association. Several lynchings, mostly of negroes in the Southern States.

18. Cornell University: Prof. J. G. Schurman elected president, vice Adams, resigned. The French in Tonquin capture a pirate stronghold, losing 58 men and killing 125.

19. Portland, Ore.: One hundred and fourth General Assembly of the Presbyterian Church.

20. Washington: Reciprocity announced between the United States and Guatemala. Baltimore: The city presents a service of plate to the United States cruiser Baltimore. Charlotte, N. C.: Celebration of the one hundred and seventeenth anniversary of the Mecklenburg declaration of independence.

24. Washington: The British minister gives a reception on the seventy-second anniversary of Queen Victoria's birth. Sixty-sixth anniversary of the Congregational Home Missionary Society. Atlanta, Ga.: The Brotherhood of Locomotive Engineers re-elect P. M. Arthur Grand Chief for a term of four years. Boston: Annual meeting of the American Unitarian Association. England: Prince Leopold receives the title of Duke of York.

25. Allegheny, Pa.: General Assembly of the United Presbyterian Church. Nebraska: Twenty-fifth anniversary of admission as a State. Palatka, Fla.: Two train robbers killed by a sheriff's posse. Dallas, Texas: A strong mob of lynchers attacks the jail, but is repulsed by the sheriff and deputies, several wounded. London: Celebration of the Queen's birthday. Denmark: Golden wedding of the King and Queen.

26. Arkansas Hot Springs: General Assembly of the Presbyterian Church, South. Washington: The President receives 700 delegates of the Congregational Home Missionary Society. Reciprocity announced between Austria-Hungary and the United States.

27. Great Britain assumes a protectorate over the Gilbert Islands in the south Pacific. Philadelphia: May anniversaries of the Baptist Church.

28. Newfoundland and Canada agree to remove

the duties recently imposed by their respective Legislatures. Paris: Anarchists formally resolve to continue their warfare against the rest of the world; dynamite explosion at Commentry.

29. Wilmington, Del.: Reunion of railroad men, representing the 6 great orders. Chicago: Dedication of the Bohemian soldiers' monument.

30. Rochester, N. Y.: Soldiers' monument unveiled, the President and other distinguished guests present. Portland, Ore.: the Presbyterian General Assembly remands the Briggs case, and the Union Seminary case, to New York. New Orleans: monument unveiled to Chief-of-Police Hennessy, murdered by the Italian Mafia in 1891.

31. Columbia, S. C.: Meeting of negroes to protest against lynch law and the crimes that provoke its action.

June 1. United States Military Academy graduation exercises. Asbury Park, N. J.: Annual meeting of the Reformed Church. Kentucky: One hundredth anniversary of admission as a State, celebrated at Lexington.

2. Gettysburg, Pa.: "High-water-Mark" monument dedicated on the battle-field.

3. Cedar Rapids, Iowa: Annual convention of the German Baptist Brethren (Dunkards).

4. Mr. Blaine resigns the Secretaryship of State. Chicago: Formation of a national protective league among colored men.

7. Minneapolis: Opening of the Republican National Convention. Germany: The Emperor receives the Czar of Russia at Kiel.

10. Milwaukee: Benjamin Harrison and Whitelaw Reid receive the Republican nominations for President and Vice-President. Spain: Troops called out to quell riots.

13. Washington: Meeting of the American Institute of Homœopathy. Philadelphia: Meeting of the International Typographical Union.

15. Scranton, Pa.: Meeting of the Society of the Army of the Potomac, Gen. Horace Porter chosen president.

17. Ireland: Ulster convention in opposition to home rule at Belfast, 10,000 delegates present.

21. Chicago: Meeting of the Democratic National Convention.

23. Chicago: Grover Cleveland and Adlai Stevenson nominated as President and Vice-President by the Democratic National Convention. India: revolt in Afghanistan.

24. Bethlehem, Pa.: Sesquicentennial anniversary celebrated.

25. England: Mr. Gladstone slightly injured by a missile thrown at him in Chester.

28. Norfolk, Va.: Launch of United States battle ship Texas at the Navy Yard. Jersey City: Thirteen ballot-box stuffers convicted and sent to the State Prison, 7 sent to the Penitentiary. Great Britain: Parliament dissolved.

29. Washington: John W. Foster, of Indiana, appointed Secretary of State, vice Blaine, resigned; the President appoints Gen. E. M. Scofield acting Secretary of War.

30. Cincinnati: Gen. John Bidwell, of California, nominated for President by the Prohibitionists, Dr. J. B. Cranfill, of Texas, for Vice-President (July 1). Homestead, Pa.: The Carnegie Steel Works close, forestalling a threatened strike by a lockout. Ireland: Numerous election fights in the different districts.

July 1. About 100,000 iron workers idle because of labor troubles with the Amalgamated Association. New London, Conn.: Annual Yale-Harvard boat race, Yale wins. Cholera appears in Paris (see article CHOLERA).

2. Nebraska: The People's party meets in national convention at Omaha.

3. Paterson, N. J., celebrates its centennial anniversary. Ireland: Many persons hurt at political meetings.

4. Omaha: The People's party in convention

nominates Gen. James B. Weaver, of Iowa, and James G. Field, of Virginia, for President and Vice-President. Ireland: A Parnellite excursion train narrowly escapes wreck at the hands of political opponents.

5. Homestead, Pa.: The Carnegie works under guard; strikers resist deputy sheriffs.

6. Homestead, Pa.: An attempted re-enforcement of the Carnegie works by Pinkerton men is resisted, 11 strikers and 9 Pinkertons killed, many wounded. Lynchings and attempted lynchings in several States; 3 men shot in Jacksonville, Fla. Ireland: Tercentenary of Dublin University.

7. New York: Convention of Christian Endeavor Societies in Madison Square Garden. Buffalo: Strikers resort to violence in the lumber yards.

8. Charlestown, Mass.: Nine convicts escape from the State Prison through a sewer.

10. Homestead, Pa.: A division of the Pennsylvania National Guard ordered out to keep the peace.

11. Idaho: Fighting between union and non-union miners in the Cœur d'Alêne district; several men killed and wounded, and a mill blown up. Paris: Execution of Ravachol, an anarchist bomb-thrower and murderer.

12. Idaho: Federal troops ordered to the scene of the mining disturbances. Paducah, Ky.: Encounter between a sheriff's posse and armed negroes; a deputy sheriff shot. Mexico: President Diaz re-elected without opposition.

13. The Cœur d'Alêne strikers resist the advance of United States troops. Frankfort, Ky.: A white murderer forcibly taken from jail and lynched.

14. Pittsburg, Pa.: About 3,000 men strike in sympathy with the Homestead movement. Martial law proclaimed in the vicinity of Homestead, also in the Cœur d'Alêne region. Detroit: Young People's Union of America (Baptist) meet in convention.

15. Saratoga: Convention of the National Educational Association. Bridges blown up by strikers in Idaho. England: Orme wins the Eclipse stakes at Sandown Park.

16. The President issues a proclamation, ordering all riotous persons in Idaho to return to their homes; about 400 strikers are under military arrest. Profile House, N. H.: Meeting of the American Pharmaceutical Association. Rome: The Pope issues a Columbus encyclical. Thomas H. Carter, of Montana, chosen chairman of the Republican National Committee.

17. Idaho: Martial law more rigidly enforced in the Cœur d'Alêne region.

18. Arrest of Homestead strikers charged with murder. Dresden: Seventh Congress of the German Chess Association.

19. Washington: The Secretary of State announces the satisfactory settlement of all claims against Chili for the attack on United States seamen in Valparaiso. England: Election returns announced, Liberal majority 42.

20. New York: The Democratic candidates formally notified of their honors at a mass meeting.

21. The President designates Oct. 21 as a national holiday—the four hundredth anniversary of the discovery of America; he appoints Andrew D. White, minister to Russia. William F. Harrity, of Pennsylvania, chosen chairman of the Democratic National Committee.

22. Duquesne, Ill.: Seven hundred steel workers strike in sympathy with the Homestead movement. Honduras closed to foreign commerce.

23. Pittsburg: Alexander Bergman, an anarchist, enters the office of H. C. Frick, superintendent of the Carnegie works, and attempts to kill him.

24. Redding, Cal.: Two stage robbers and murderers lynched by a mob.

26. Homestead, Pa.: Part of the State troops withdrawn.

27. New York: The steamer City of Paris arrives from Queenstown in five days, fifteen hours, fifty-eight minutes, being the quickest passage on record.

30. The President issues a proclamation, ordering the Wyoming rioters to disperse.

31. Spain: Celebration at Cadiz of the discovery of America.

August 1. Homestead, Pa.: It is announced that Private Iams will bring suit against his superior officers for cruel treatment. Washington: The President signs the eight-hour act (see LEGISLATION). Russia: Riots in the cholera districts against suspected physicians, troops called out, sixty killed, several hundred wounded. England: Visit of the German Emperor.

2. Indianapolis: Annual convention of the Catholic Total Abstinence Union. California: Monument unveiled at Mare Island Navy Yard in honor of 15 seamen killed by an explosion in April (see DISASTERS). Spain: Four hundredth anniversary of the sailing of Columbus celebrated at Palos.

3. New Hampshire: Bronze statue of John P. Hale unveiled at Concord. Pittsburg: Several officials of the Carnegie company arrested on charge of murder in connection with the recent strikes. The steamship Teutonic makes the longest day's run on record, 528 miles.

4. Duquesne, Iowa: Strikers use violence at the Carnegie works; the Sixteenth Regiment restores order. Wisconsin: Saw-mill hands strike for a ten-hour day.

5. Congress adjourns *sine die*. New York: The State Supreme Court declares the new apportionment unconstitutional. Michigan: Special meeting of the Legislature to reapportion the State. The Mississippi River Commission has $10,000,000 at its disposal.

7. Canada: The Dominion Cabinet removes the canal tolls, favoring Montreal. France: A departmental election shows a Republican gain of 195.

8. Colorado: Conclave of Knights Templar at Denver. Strikes of mill hands in Duquesne, Iowa, and of the building trades in New York declared off. Montana: National encampment of the Sons of Veterans at Helena. St. Louis, Mo.: Convention of the Brotherhood of Carpenters and Joiners. England: The address from the throne read in Parliament.

10. Africa: The French begin their advance against the Kingdom of Dahomey.

11. It is announced that Chili has agreed to the establishment of a claims commission. Boston: Launch of United States cruiser Marblehead (2,000 tons). Great Britain: The ministry resigns as a result of the general election, and Mr. Gladstone becomes Prime-Minister.

12. Helena, Mont.: Meeting of the military order of the Sons of Veterans, Marvin E. Hill, commander in chief.

13. Tracy City, Tenn.: Riot of miners directed against convict labor. Mystic, Conn.: Convention of the Peace Union, Alfred H. Love chosen president. Chickasaw nation: Jonas Wood, a full-blood Indian, elected Governor.

14. Buffalo: Railroad switchmen strike for higher wages and a ten-hour day. Philadelphia: Interment of boatswain's mate Riggin, killed last year at Valparaiso.

15. Two regiments of New York State troops ordered to Buffalo to repress riotous switchmen, $100,-000 damage already done. Tennessee: Convict miners and their guards forcibly expelled from Inman. Rochester, N. Y.: Meeting of the American Association for the Advancement of Science. England: Mr. Gladstone, new Premier, makes his first official visit to the Queen. Canada: The Dominion Cabinet decides to terminate the canal tolls system.

16. Washington: Eighth annual meeting, Society of American Florists. Mount Sterling, Ky.: A noted desperado taken from jail and hanged by a mob.

17. Oliver Springs, Tenn.: Convict miners and their guards forcibly expelled; the Governor calls out State troops. Buffalo, N. Y.: The Fourth Brigade of the National Guard is on duty to preserve order. Albany, N. Y.: Meeting of the Catholic Young Men's National Union. Ellensburg, Wash.: Three highwaymen murderers captured by vigilantes and hanged. England:

First meeting of the new Liberal Cabinet (see GREAT BRITAIN AND IRELAND).

18. Tennessee: Encounter between troops and miners near Coal Creek. Several killed and wounded on both sides.

19. Tennessee: Further skirmishing between troops and miners, the latter being in the end put to flight.

20. The President issues a proclamation, levying retaliatory toll on all freight in transit to the Dominion of Canada through the St. Mary's Canal. Skirmishing continues near Coal Creek, Tenn., 2 killed. England: Queen Victoria's life threatened by an insane man in the street.

21. Buffalo: The striking switchmen's blockade believed to be permanently broken. Russia: A labor riot suppressed by troops and several persons killed. A train held up and robbed near Augusta, Kan.; the robbers were almost immediately captured.

22. Kansas City, Mo.: Annual convention of the German Society of Army Veterans (Deutscher Krieger Bund), 7,000 delegates present. Bern, Switzerland: Opening of the International Peace Congress.

23. Strikes of switchmen on the great New York and Pennsylvania railroads. Kansas City: Meeting of the Knights of Pythias. Gloucester, Mass., celebrates the two hundred and fiftieth anniversary of its settlement.

24. Buffalo: The switchmen's strike declared off. Saratoga, N. Y.: Annual meeting of the American Bar Association.

25. Richmond, Va.: Corner stone of the new Chamber of Commerce laid, with Masonic ceremonies. France: Two anarchist bombs exploded in Trieste.

26. Washington: Meeting of the Association of Official Agricultural Chemists.

28. New York: National Convention of the Socialist Labor party.

29. Homestead, Pa.: Several additional arrests of Union strikers on charges of conspiracy and aggravated riot.

30. Additional labor strikes at Pittsburg and New Orleans.

September 1. The President orders twenty days' quarantine for all vessels from cholera-infected ports. The Chinese expulsion act, and the retaliation commercial measures as regards Canada, go into effect.

2. Homestead, Pa.: Charges of murder and riot preferred against 10 strikers, and several arrests made. New Jersey: 21 persons sentenced to fines and imprisonment for election frauds in 1889. England: Labor troubles at Northwick, troops called out. Italy: Fight between Radicals and Monarchists at Andria. Many cities in the United States adopt strong measures for protection against cholera. Homestead, Pa.: The house of an artisan in the Carnegie works looted by strikers.

6. The President formally accepts the Republican nomination for re-election. Hazelton, Ind.: The Rev. Sam Small shot in his room, presumably by agents of the liquor interest. France: A confidential clerk in the naval office sentenced to twenty years' penal servitude, and twenty years' banishment for breach of trust.

7. Prize fight at New Orleans: John L. Sullivan badly beaten by James J. Corbett. Warsaw: An anarchist explodes a bomb in a church, and is alone killed by it.

9. The cholera: The President gives orders to prepare Sandy Hook for a quarantine station, and Gov. Flower, of New York, takes like steps on Fire Island. Marinette, Wis.: General strike in the lumber mills.

10. Bering Sea: Crews of sealing vessels seized by Russians.

11. The Peary exploring party are brought back safely to St. Johns, N. F., by the relief steamer Kite.

12. The cholera: Forcible resistance by the neighboring inhabitants to the occupation of Fire Island as a quarantine station. The President notifies the great steamship companies that they must not bring passengers from infected ports. Pittsburg, Pa.: General strike of coal miners against a reduction of pay.

13. The cholera: Two regiments of the National Guard and a battalion of the naval reserve sent to Fire Island to protect the quarantine station. Choctaw Nation: Several men killed in a political fight. California: A sheriff's posse near Fresno has 4 men killed and several wounded in an encounter with train robbers.

14. Ireland: Revocation by the Privy Council of all proclamations made under the coercion act.

15. Buffalo: National League of Republican clubs in convention. Baltimore: Annual reunion of naval veterans. Chattanooga Society of the Army of the Cumberland, annual meeting.

16. New York: Parade of the Italian societies; corner stone of Columbus monument laid. Mexico: Opening of Congress by President Diaz.

17. Gen. James B. Weaver and James G. Field formally accept the nomination of the People's party for President and Vice-President. The late postmaster and assistant postmaster found guilty of assessing employees for campaign purposes. Choctaw Nation: The ringleaders of the late armed opponents have surrendered.

18. Buda-Pesth, Hungary: Celebration of Kossuth's ninetieth birthday.

19. Washington: Opening of the Grand Army of the Republic encampment.

20. The Six Companies (Chinese) issue a proclamation advising against the registration law. Arkansas: Several negroes killed and wounded in a political fight in Calhoun County. Ireland: Eviction of tenants resumed by certain landlords.

21. Washington: Beginning of the Grand Army encampment, about 300,000 strangers in the city; meetings also of auxiliary associations, as the Women's Relief Corps, Union Veterans' Union, and Ex-Prisoners of War. The special train arrives, conveying the President and family; Mrs. Harrison is taken to the White House in an army ambulance.

22. Washington: A. G. Weisbart, of Milwaukee, chosen commander in chief of the Grand Army of the Republic, Gen. S. S. Yoder, commander in chief of the Union Veterans. Texas: The Governor proclaims quarantine against New York and other cholera-infected ports. Pittsburg, Pa.: Officials of the Carnegie company arrested at the instance of the labor organizations. France: Centennial celebration of the first French Republic.

23. Washington: Close of the Grand Army encampment. Georgia: Gen. Weaver declines to address a meeting at Atlanta, alleging that free speech is not allowed in the South.

24. Roslyn, Wash.: Brigands enter the town and rob a bank of $10,000, killing 3 citizens and wounding others.

26. Ex-President Cleveland formally accepts the Democratic nomination for the p e . Colorado: The People's party ticket indorsed by the Democrats. Bologna, Spain: 80 alleged anarchists arrested. A squadron of the British Life Guards mutilate their saddles in protest against excessive drills. London: Six men convicted of literary frauds and sentenced to fines and imprisonment.

28. San Diego Bay, Cal.: Three hundred and fiftieth anniversary celebration of its discovery. New York: Anniversary convention of the Sons of Temperance. Davenport, Iowa: Scottish Rite Masonic Consistory Convention. Spain: The Jesuits elect a new general of their order.

29. Cœur d'Alène City, Ida.: Four strikers convicted of conspiracy, 10 acquitted. Harvard University begins its two hundred and fifty-sixth year with 2,970 students. England: Stuart Knill, a Roman Catholic, elected Lord Mayor of London. Mexico: Gen. Diaz declared President for four years.

30. Toronto, Canada: End of the Pan-Presbyterian Council.

31. Cholera: The President issues an order enforcing twenty days' quarantine from all infected ports. Wisconsin: Present State officers renominated by the Democrats. Independence, Iowa: Trotting mare

Nancy Hanks makes a mile in two minutes, five and a quarter seconds.

October 1. Homestead, Pa.: Nine of the late strikers' advisory committee arrested for high treason. Wisconsin: The Apportionment act declared unconstitutional by the Supreme Court. Chicago: The new university opens with 500 students.

2. Minnesota: Defeat of the Faribault school plan. Woburn, Mass.: Two hundred and fiftieth anniversary celebrated. Hungary: Cholera appears at Buda-Pesth.

3. Tennessee: Gov. Buchanan violently assailed while speaking at Blountsville.

4. New York city: National convention of Democratic clubs. England: An assembly of Low Churchmen attacked at Folkestone, England. Samoa: The United States Government secures a coaling station at Pago Pago.

5. Coffeyville, Kan.: Raid upon banks by outlaws, 4 citizens killed, 3 wounded; of the 6 robbers, 4 were killed, 1 badly wounded, 1 escaped. State election (see GEORGIA). Baltimore: Triennial convention of the Protestant Episcopal Church.

7. Washington: Reception by the President to the delegates of the Colored Odd Fellows. Homestead, Pa.: Nonunion men's boarding house blown up with a dynamite bomb. Africa: The French defeat the King of Dahomey. Spain: Congress of Americanists opened at the Convent of La Rabida. Venezuela: The revolution ends with the triumph of the insurgents.

8. New York: Beginning of the Columbian celebration with religious services in Hebrew synagogues.

10. Salt Lake City, Utah: Close of the sixty-second annual conference of the Mormons.

12. Minneapolis: Triennial meeting of the Congregational Church. Lake Mohonk, N. Y.: Tenth annual Indian conference. The Columbian anniversary celebrated in many European cities.

13. New York: The Columbian celebration ends with a banquet at Lenox Lyceum. Homestead, Pa.: State troops withdrawn after ninety-five days' service protecting the Carnegie works against strikers. The Court of Appeals, New York, affirms the constitutionality of the Apportionment law. France: Riotous strikers at Carneaux; troops called out.

14. Twelve Chinamen arrested while concealed on a barge entering United States territory from Canada. The French gain a victory in Dahomey.

15. The President proclaims 1,800,000 acres in the late Crow reservation, Mont., open to settlement.

16. Columbian celebrations held in several cities.

17. Washington: The Supreme Court affirms the constitutionality of the Michigan electoral law. Fight between cowboys and cattle thieves in northern Idaho, 9 thieves killed. Africa: The Wahehe tribe attacks a German station, killing several settlers.

18. Indianapolis: National Conference of the Society of Friends. Great Britain: Mutinous demonstrations among the Life Guards at Windsor, and the Thirteenth Hussars in Ireland.

19. Chicago: Opening dedicatory services of the Columbian Exhibition. New York: The Inman steamer City of Paris arrives from Queenstown in five days, fourteen hours, twenty-four minutes. Washington: Supreme Court sustains Idaho's "Test-oath law" (see article IDAHO). Vermont: Redfield Proctor elected United States Senator vice Edmunds. Turkey: Riots in Crete, 14 soldiers and 4 rioters killed.

20. Homestead, Pa.: Violence resumed by the late strikers.

21. Columbus Day: A national holiday, celebrated in every town in the United States. In Chicago the World's Fair buildings were dedicated.

22. Chicago: Dedication of many State buildings at the World's Fair.

23. Florida: Encounter between negro outlaws and a sheriff's posse near Titusville, several killed and wounded.

24. New Brunswick: Provincial election, Liberal administration sustained.

25. Washington: Death of Mrs. Harrison, the President's wife.

26. Alliance announced between the Philadelphia and Reading and the Boston and Maine Railroad Companies.

27. Mexico: The village of Tomocnic annihilated for rebellion against the Government.

28. Denver: National Convention of the Women's Christian Temperance Union.

29. Political fight in North Carolina: 5 killed, nearly a dozen wounded.

30. Mexico: Twelve brigands attempt to plunder a store in San Juan, but the townspeople rally, kill 3 and capture 3.

31. Turkey: More fighting in Crete between soldiers and natives.

November 1. Washington: A convention announced between the United States and Great Britain regarding the sale of arms and liquor to Pacific Islanders.

2. Hamburg: The cholera epidemic officially declared at an end. (See article on CHOLERA.)

3. Spain: Riot at Granada due to the unpopularity of the Queen-regent. France: End of the strike at Carmeaux. Washington: The President appoints Nov. 24 for Thanksgiving. Canada: Acquittal of ex-Premier Mercier, tried for malfeasance in office.

5. New Orleans: Dangerous strike among the laboring classes. England: General strike among cotton workers. Pittsburg, Pa.: Cols. Hawkins and Streator found not guilty of assaulting Private Iams, who suffered military punishment during the Homestead trouble.

6. Chicago fails to prevent the erection of a monument to the 4 anarchists executed in 1888.

7. Italy: A general election results in a victory for the Government.

8. General election in the United States; Grover Cleveland elected President. Paris: An explosion, supposed to be the work of anarchists, kills 4 men in a police station. Belgium: Riotous demonstration in Brussels favoring universal suffrage.

10. Brooklyn, N. Y.: Launch of the United States armored cruiser Cincinnati at the Navy Yard. New Orleans: Formidable labor strike, almost stopping business.

11. New Orleans: The strikers fail of their purpose and return to work. A British steamship with arms for Dahomey seized by the French.

13. Homestead, Pa.: Strikers resume the offensive. Many shots fired, but no one hurt.

14. Washington: The President appoints William Potter, of Pennsylvania, minister to Italy; David P. Thompson, of Oregon, minister to Turkey; and Edward C. Little, of Kansas, consul general at Cairo. Memphis, Tenn.: National Convention of the Farmers' Alliance. St. Louis, Mo.: Convention of the Knights of Labor.

15. New York: Meeting in council of the Roman Catholic archbishops of the United States.

16. St. Louis: General Master Workman Powderly delivers his annual address before the Knights of Labor. Washington: Meeting of the National Fraternal Congress, representing several societies. Spain: Nine convicts killed while attempting to escape at Tarragona.

17. Homestead, Pa.: Three hundred of the late strikers resume work at the Carnegie mills.

19. Beaver Falls, Pa.: The great strike officially declared off, the strikers having failed to gain their point. Springfield, Mass.: Yale-Harvard football game, Yale wins, score 6 to 0.

21. New York: General meeting of the Salvation Army. France: Amid great excitement the Chamber of Deputies decrees an inquiry into the affairs of the Panama Canal. Africa: French troops enter the King of Dahomey's capital.

22. St. Louis: The Knights of Labor re-elect T. V. Powderly General Master Workman. Belgium: Meeting of the International Monetary Conference at Brussels. Germany: Opening of the Reichstag, the Emperor delivers his speech.

23. Pittsburg: The trial of Sylvester Critchlow for murder, as a leader in the Homestead strike, resulted in acquittal. The Senate committee on the Pinkerton system began its sessions.

24. Thanksgiving Day generally celebrated. Yale-Princeton football game at New York. Yale wins, score 12 to 0.

25. Sir John Thompson succeeds Sir John C. Abbott as Premier.

26. West Point, N. Y.: Football match with a team from Annapolis, the naval cadets win, score 12 to 4.

27. Pittsburg: The Carnegie mills' strikers refuse to yield until their organization is recognized. Ireland: Stubborn fight between political factions at Limerick.

December 1. New Orleans: Adjournment of the Nicaragua Canal Congress. University of Chicago: Bequest of $250,000 from Mrs. Joseph Reynolds. Mexico: Inauguration of President Diaz.

3. Baltimore: Meeting of the Prison Reform Association (adjourns Dec. 7), address by ex-President Hayes. Russia: The death sentence passed upon 23 cholera rioters.

4. Washington: Publication of the departmental report.

5. Washington: Meeting of the Fifty-second Congress (see article Congress). The Supreme Court decides against the Illinois Central Railroad in the Chicago Lake Front case. France: A new Cabinet formed by M. Ribot.

6. Washington: The President's message read in both houses of Congress.

7. Washington: The President receives a delegation of 200 Hebrew rabbis, representing the convention of that sect. Canada: New Cabinet ministers sworn in. Spain: Resignation of the Cabinet.

9. New Orleans: Two murders, supposed to be by the Mafia.

10. New York: Banquet of the Reform Club in honor of Mr. Cleveland and the recent Democratic victory. Fairhaven, Mass., receives a bequest of $100,000 for a library from the heirs of H. H. Rogers.

11. Chicago receives a bequest of $1,500,000 from Philip D. Armour for an industrial institute. Philadelphia: Annual meeting of the American Federation of Labor. Mexico: A band of Garza's revolutionists make a successful raid across the border from

Texas. France: Extraordinary powers granted to the Panama Canal Investigating Committee. Germany: It is announced that the gold monetary standard will be maintained. Homestead, Pa.: Discovery of an alleged plot by union men to poison nonunion workmen.

13. Cincinnati: Presbytery recommends the suspension from the ministry of the Rev. Prof. Henry P. Smith, convicted of heresy. Attempted robbery of a railway train near Huntington, W. Va., the passengers resist and the robbers are driven off, two passengers wounded.

14. An authorized version published of the Roman Catholic Archiepiscopal Convention, indicating a liberal policy as to the public schools. Cincinnati Presbytery pronounces a sentence of suspension for heresy against the Rev. Prof. Henry P. Smith.

15. Hayti: Attempted assassination of President Hippolyte.

16. Paris: Arrest of prominent movers in the Panama Canal scandal, including Charles de Lesseps; seizure of many papers.

17. Georgia: Adjournment of the Legislature after refusing to accept the Home for Confederates.

19. Italian immigration societies decide to book no more steerage passengers for America.

20. Homestead: Two men confess connection with the poisoning conspiracy and are imprisoned. Wyoming: Two United States deputy marshals and 3 desperadoes killed in an encounter.

27. New York: Corner stone laid of the Protestant Episcopal Cathedral of St. John the Divine.

28. Philadelphia: Second national conference on university extension. Milwaukee, Wis.: A bomb, probably exploded by anarchists, wrecks buildings and causes $500,000 loss.

29. Johns Hopkins University receives from Elizabeth Garrett a gift of $306,000. Paris: Explosion of an anarchist bomb.

30. India: A national congress meets at Allahabad, 700 delegates present. Buenos Ayres: Policemen and firemen arrested for plotting to burn the city. New York: The Rev. Dr. Briggs acquitted of the charge of heresy. Paris: issue of anarchist manifesto.

31. France: Royalists take advantage of the Panama scandal to agitate their claims. Madrid: Serious labor riots.

F

FARMERS' CONGRESS. The twelfth annual session of the Farmers' National Congress of the United States met in Lincoln, Neb., Nov. 22, 1892, and adjourned on the 24th after a three-days' session. The Hon. G. D. Purse, of Savannah, Ga., vice-president of the association, presided in place of the Hon. A. W. Smith, of Kansas, president of the body, who was detained by illness.

The congress was held in the new House of Representatives, which was tastefully decorated with flags and bunting, and the delegations of the various States and Territories were welcomed by Gov. Boyd, Mayor Weir, and the Hon. C. A. Atkinson on the part of the Board of Trade. The Rev. G. W. Crofts read an original ode of welcome, and Mrs. L. Culbertson, of Lincoln, read an original poem. The address of welcome was responded to by the Hon. W. Pope Yeaman, of Missouri; by the acting president of the Congress, the Hon. G. D. Purse, of Georgia; and by Col. Daniel Needham, of Boston, President of the New England Agricultural Association. The opening exercises were interspersed with

music by the Lincoln Cornet Band. The Senate Chamber, at the north end of the Capitol, under the direction of ex.-Gov. Furnas, was completely filled with farm and manufactured products of the young State of Nebraska—a display of what seemed to be every conceivable product of the soil in that latitude.

The following subjects were ably presented and vigorously discussed: "Interdependence of Agriculture and Transportation," by W. Pope Yeaman, of Nebraska; "Best Beet-sugar Industry," by Prof. M. A. Lunn, of Nebraska; "Is Farming a Realized Alchemy?" by Mrs. A. J. Sawyer, of Nebraska; "Highway Transportation," by J. M. Stahl, of Illinois; "Transportation on Common Roads," by W. S. Delano, of Nebraska; "Individuality of American Agriculture," by Daniel Needham, of Massachusetts; "Practical Relations of Science to Agriculture," by M. C. Fernald, President of the State Agricultural College, Maine; "Agriculture in Oklahoma," by H. C. St. Clair; "The Science of Money," by L. W. Weller, of Iowa.

The following resolutions with reference to

legislation were passed, and ordered to be sent to the President of the Senate and the Speaker of the House:

Whereas, It is manifest that there are such imperfections in the national statutes creating the Interstate Commerce Commission and defining the duties thereof as to render the commission ineffective in compassing the ends for which it was created, therefore,

Resolved, That this National Farmers' Congress instruct its national board of agriculture, or five of its members, to confer with the Congress of the United States as to the necessity and manner of so amending the interstate commerce law as to remove all obstruction to its full administration, and to enlarge the powers and jurisdiction of the commission so far as the equitable demands of transportation may from time to time require; and that the commission raised by this Farmers' Congress shall confer with the approaching session of the United States Congress and report to the next annual meeting of this body.

Whereas, The universities and experiments in the interest of agriculture conducted by the national Department of Agriculture have demonstrated their very great value to the country; and *Whereas,* The efficiency of trained specialists is enhanced by continuity of service, therefore,

Resolved, That the National Farmers' Congress, in council assembled, respectfully urges the importance of maintaining the scientific work of this department on a purely nonpartisan basis, to the end that the benefits which science may render to the agriculture of this country may be fully realized.

Whereas, There have been made by the Government surveys and estimates of numerous reservoir sites, many of which are feasible and not expensive, therefore.

Resolved, That we request Congress to make sufficient appropriations to build such reservoirs as will hold back the flood waters, which can be used in time of low waters for irrigation and reclaim hundreds of thousands of acres of arid lands, and enable thousands of settlers to make homes on land that is now a desert.

Resolved, That we respectfully call the attention of the Congress of the United States to the great importance of a deep water way connecting the Atlantic Ocean with the lakes of the Northwest, and, if found practicable, so to shape its legislation as to bring about its early consummation.

Resolved, That the National Farmers' Congress respectfully recommend to the Congress of the United States the present and pressing importance of liberal appropriations for the improvement of the navigable water ways and harbors, as a necessary means of lessening the cost of transportation.

Resolved, That we ask, upon the reassembling of the Congress of the United States, that they will reconsider their decision on the closing of the World's Fair on Sundays, and thereby meet the approbation of a large majority of their constituency.

FIELD, CYRUS WEST, financier, born in Stockbridge, Mass., Nov. 30, 1819; died in New York city, July 12, 1892. He was educated in his native town, and when fifteen years old entered the employ of A. T. Stewart, the merchant, in New York. At twenty-one years of age he began, on his own account, the manufacture and sale of paper, and in a few years became the head of so prosperous a business house that he was able partially to retire from active care only fifteen years after its establishment, in 1840. He then spent six months in travel in South America. Mr. Field's brother, Matthew D. Field, was a civil engineer. In 1854, having built railroads and suspension bridges at the South and West, he was visiting New York, when he met Frederick Gisborne, who was there to interest scientists and capitalists in his scheme for building a telegraph across Newfoundland, to be connected with a line of fast steamships that should touch there, and thus should "convey intelligence between England and America in six days or less." Mr. Field heard the project of Mr. Gisborne with so much interest that he promised to bring it to the attention of his brother Cyrus, and this he did; but Cyrus said he had laid aside responsibilities, had enough money for ease and enjoyment, and

CYRUS WEST FIELD.

was disinclined to enter upon any scheme so vague and uncertain. Nevertheless, the enthusiasm of his brother prevailed, and he gave audience to Mr. Gisborne in his home on Gramercy Park. After the guest was gone, Mr. Field pondered the subject, and walking to the globe in his library, turned it to the island and the ocean that were in his thought, and said to himself, "If that telegraph could span the Atlantic, it would be worth while to undertake its construction." The idea was new to him, although Morse and others had conceived it years before. This was its practical beginning. The more Mr. Field dwelt upon the suggestion, the more his imagination was taken captive. He saw that two questions must be answered before the first step could be taken. The first was put by him immediately to Lieut. Maury, of the United States navy, "Can a cable be stretched across the ocean?" The second he as promptly sent to S. F. B. Morse, "If a cable could be laid across the Atlantic Ocean, would it be good for anything?" Lieut. Maury wrote: "Singularly enough, just as I received your letter, I was closing one on the same subject to the Secretary of the Navy." That letter he inclosed. It runs in part: "The United States brig 'Dolphin,' Lieutenant-Commanding O. H. Berryman, was employed last summer upon especial service connected with the researches that are carried on at this office concerning the winds and currents of the sea. Her observations were confined principally to that part of the ocean which the merchantmen, as they pass to and fro upon the business of trade between Europe and the United States, use as their great thoroughfare. Lieut. Berryman availed himself of this opportunity to carry along also a line of deep-sea soundings from the shores of Newfoundland to those of Ireland. The result is highly interesting, in so far as the bottom of the sea is concerned, upon the question of a submarine telegraph across the Atlantic; and I beg leave to make it the subject of a special report. . . . The distance between the nearest points is about 1,600 miles, and the bottom of the sea between the two places is a plateau, which seems to have been placed there especially for the purpose of holding the cables of a submarine telegraph, and of keeping them out of harm's way. It is neither too deep nor too shallow, yet it is so deep that the wires, but once landed, will remain forever beyond the reach of vessels' anchors, icebergs, and drifts of any kind, and so shallow that the wires may be readily lodged upon the bottom. . . . Lieut. Berryman brought up with the Brooke deep-sea-sounding apparatus specimens of the bottom from this plateau. I sent them to Prof. Bailey, of West Point, for examination under his microscope. All those specimens are filled with microscopic shells. These little shells suggest the fact that there are no currents at the bottom of the sea whence they came."

The reply from Mr. Morse was given verbally, and a lifelong friendship thus began. It was equally encouraging, as Mr. Morse had never changed his opinion since 1843, when he had written to the Secretary of the Treasury, "Telegraphic communication on the electro-magnetic plan may with certainty be established across the Atlantic Ocean!"

Mr. Field, with his enthusiasm now wholly roused, addressed himself to the task of forming a company. The first man spoken to was Peter Cooper, his next-door neighbor. His conditional consent being won, Moses Taylor was consulted, then Marshall O. Roberts, and then Chandler White. To this number was added, a year later, Wilson G. Hunt. The articles were drawn by the first five, and the project set on foot. David Dudley Field was legal adviser, and accompanied his brother on the visit to Newfoundland, during which Mr. Gisborne's charter was surrendered, and a new one was granted to the New York, Newfoundland and London Company. The first work was to build not only a telegraph, but a road across the whole island, a part of the way through unexplored forests and mountains. This, after great suffering and expense, was accomplished within two years, and a cable laid across the Gulf of St. Lawrence. Mr. Field had already made many journeys to Newfoundland, and two or three to Europe, as the personal oversight for the company fell almost wholly upon him. When thus much was done, he had invested in the enterprise over $200,000, and the others each a little less. Up to this time the work was an American enterprise, but the time had come when British interest and capital must be secured. Mr. Field took up a temporary residence, with his family, in London, and engineers, scientists, statesmen, and capitalists were in turn consulted and influenced to action. After a year's absence Mr. Field returned to this country, having reserved as the right of his countrymen the ownership of a quarter of the stock in the new company. Here he was plunged into a public controversy, and found that Washington was buzzing with objections and questionings. Some of the trials of the time are hinted at in the following extract from a speech by Mr. Seward, in 1858, after the first successful laying of the cable:

The two great countries are now ringing with the praises of Cyrus W. Field, who chiefly has brought about this great enterprise to its glorious and beneficent consummation. You have never heard his story; let me give you a few points in it, as a lesson that there is no condition of life in which a man endowed with native genius, a benevolent spirit, and a courageous patience, may not become a benefactor of nations and of mankind. . . . It remained to engage the consent and activity of the governments of Great Britain and the United States. That was all that remained. Such consent and activity on the part of some one great nation of Europe was all that remained needful for Columbus, when he stood ready to bring a new continent forward as a theatre of the world's civilization. But in each case that effort was the most difficult of all. Cyrus W. Field, by assiduity and patience, first secured consent and conditional engagement on the part of Great Britain, and then, less than two years ago, he repaired to Washington. The President and Secretary of State individually favored his proposition; but the jealousies of parties and sections in Congress forbade them to lend it their official sanction and patronage. He appealed to me. I drew the necessary bill. With the generous aid of others, Northern Representatives, and the indispensable aid of the late Thomas J. Rusk, a Senator from Texas, that bill, after a severe contest and long delay, was carried through the Senate of the United States by the majority, if I remember rightly, of one vote, and escaped defeat in the House of Representatives with equal difficulty.

President Pierce signed the bill the day before he went out of office, March 3, 1857. Immediately on learning that the bill had become a law, Mr. Field went again to England to make ready for the laying of the cable that had been in process of manufacture there. The lately discovered gutta-percha, and its application to the telegraph as an insulator, were circumstances that assisted the great enterprise. Mr. S. F. B. Morse had watched the progress of the cable construction, and tried many experiments tending to its successful working. The two American vessels tendered by the Government for the work of laying—the "Niagara" and the "Susquehanna"—reached England two months later, the former ship having been altered to suit the demands of a carrier of a thousand miles of cable. A like amount was loaded upon the British vessel "Agamemnon," and with two or three attending vessels the expedition set out on its undertaking. The plan adopted was to begin laying from the Irish coast, splice the cable in midocean, and continue to submerge it until it reached Newfoundland.

On Aug. 5 the squadron sailed. The "Niagara" was to lay the first half of the cable. Before she had gone five miles the shore end caught in the machinery and parted. She put back, and the cable was "underrun" that distance. The next day a new start was made, and all that day the slow-moving ship was watched with quiet excitement as she paid out the cord that disappeared in the ocean. Few eyes were closed when night came and passed, and still all was going well. On the next two days the sea was calm, and all worked smoothly. They had passed the only danger point laid down upon the submarine charts of the American survey and of the English one that had succeeded it—a dip from 550 to 1,750 fathoms within eight miles. They were now over 200 miles off the Irish coast, at a point where the wire began sinking to the deep-sea level—2,000 fathoms—when on Monday evening there came a sudden break in the flow of electricity, which till then had come continuously from the land. The cable looked as usual, but the voice that spoke through it was silent.

Dr. Santy, the electrician, and Prof. Morse gave up all hope, and the engineers were about to cut the cable and try to wind it up, when the spark as suddenly reappeared and the interrupted current resumed its flow. This mystery was never explained; although afterward, when watching anxiously a great whale that just succeeded in clearing one of the later cables, Mr. Field imagined he had a glimpse of the true cause—that the creature had become entangled, and had finally worked itself loose. On the following morning, when they were over 300 miles out, judging that the cable was paying out too rapidly for the speed of the vessel, the engineers applied the brakes firmly, and as the ship's head rose from the trough of the sea the cable parted. So deep had been the interest felt, that tears rolled down more than one weatherbeaten cheek on realizing that the great experiment had failed. The vessels turned about, and when the Irish shore was reached Mr. Field was ready with the following letter, which he had no idea at the time would ever get into print:

The successful laying down of the Atlantic telegraph cable is put off for a short time, but its final triumph has been fully proved by the experience that we have had since we left Valencia. My confidence was never so strong as at the present time, and I feel sure that, with God's blessing, we shall connect Europe and America with the electric cord. . . . I requested Capt. Wainwright, the commander of the English telegraph fleet, to order the "Agamemnon" to remain with the "Niagara" and the "Susquehanna" in this deep part of the Atlantic for a few days, to try certain experiments which will be of great value to us. I further requested Capt. Wainwright to order the "Cyclops" to sound here where the cable parted. . . . In my letter to Dr. Whitehouse I requested him to telegraph to London and have a special meeting of the directors called for twelve o'clock on Saturday, to decide whether we would have more cable made at once and try again this season, or wait until next year. . . . Do not think that I feel discouraged, or am in low spirits, for I am not; and I think I can see how this accident will be of great advantage to the Atlantic Telegraph Company.

The experience gained convinced the directors, including Mr. Field, that more cautious preparation could and should be made, and the plan was put off until the following year. Mr. Field returned home to find the great commercial crisis of that year, 1857, overwhelming business, and new capital was hard to obtain. But the Government again offered ships, and new cable was ordered, this time with the request that Mr. Field would go to England and take personal control of the affairs of the company. Compensation for this was offered by the directors, but was declined by Mr. Field.

In June, 1858, the second expedition sailed. It was agreed to go to midocean and lay toward either shore. After a calm of two days, followed by a dreadful gale that threatened to sink the ships, the second submerging was begun. When the ships were separated but three miles the cable parted, caught in the machinery of the "Niagara." They spliced the ends, and began once more. Forty miles were safely run, when again the electric current ceased. This was a discouragement that could ill be borne, as it seemed to point to some hidden cause that might at any time elude the skill and knowledge of

scientists and engineers, and the energy of the most confident and enthusiastic.

Once more the cable was joined in midocean, and with trepidation the vessels turned their prows toward opposite continents. Two hundred miles were laid safely, when the cable once more parted. Again Mr. Field immediately made use of this fresh and, as it seemed to others, entirely destructive accident to learn by experiment for future use. He had the strength of the broken cable tested, and when the ships reached Queenstown he hastened to London not to give up, or spread discouragement, but to propose that the vessels should again repair to midocean and, as they still had cable enough, once more attempt to lay it. His courage and counsels prevailed, and on July 17 the fleet sailed once more. Not a cheer followed them, and there was more than one suggestion that it was a fool's errand. The same strange and sudden ceasing and recurrence of the electric flow occurred on this voyage, and this time on both vessels at once; but on Wednesday, Aug. 4, Mr. Field's diary recorded: "Depth of water less than 200 fathoms. Weather beautiful, perfectly calm. 'Gorgon' in sight. Sixty-four miles from the telegraph house. Received signal from the 'Agamemnon' at noon that they had paid out from her 940 miles of cable. Passed this morning several icebergs. Made the land off entrance to Trinity Bay at 8 A. M. Entered Trinity Bay at half past twelve. At half past two we stopped sending signals to the 'Agamemnon' for fourteen minutes, for the purpose of making splice. Thursday, Aug. 5: 'Niagara' anchored. Total amount of cable paid out since splice was made, 1,016 miles, 600 fathoms. Total amount of distance, 882 miles. At 5.15 A. M. cable landed. At 6, end of cable carried into telegraph house, and received very strong currents of electricity through the whole cable from the other side of the Atlantic."

The success of the cable was the occasion of great rejoicing in America, and Mr. Field was the recipient of multitudes of messages of congratulation and admiration. No message could pass between the countries until the connection in Newfoundland could be properly made. The projectors desired to keep the line from public use in order to test and decide upon the best and most rapid method of telegraphing; but the public was at first so eager, and then so incredulous, that a message from Queen Victoria to the President, and his reply, were transmitted on Aug. 16. On the morning of Aug. 17 New York city was waked by the pealing of bells and the roaring of cannon in honor of the event, and Mr. Field's name was on every lip, while at night there was a grand illumination. But one message had preceded those of the potentates. It was from the directors in England to those in the United States, and merely recited the message of joy: "Glory to God in the highest, and on earth peace, good will toward men." On Sept. 1 the city officials gave Mr. Field a public reception, in accepting which he had caused the British as well as the American projectors and officers to be included. As he was getting into his carriage an over-ocean telegram was handed him, and he read it to the assembled multitude amid tremendous cheering. Torchlight processions and banquets followed, and for days the man who disclaimed it as "too much honor," was the boast of his country.

That message was the last that ever passed over the cable. The amazement, the distress, the humiliation felt by Mr. Field, are, to use the time-worn but expressive phrase, better imagined than described. Every form of public disappointment, even to suspicion of a hoax, was heaped upon him. People soon forgot that the agent of the Cunard line of steamships had cabled to London the account of a collision at sea, and the statement of the safety of the vessels, which had saved weeks of anxiety, and that other proofs of not only its success, but its value, were not wanting.

The Atlantic Telegraph Company was revived not as a private but as a Government enterprise, the London Board of Trade appointing a committee to investigate the whole subject. At the end of two years they reported, with details that fill a large volume. Their conclusion was, that a proper telegraph could be made successful. Meantime, this country had been plunged into civil war, and throughout its continuance, though able to obtain nothing in the way of practical aid, Mr. Field kept alive here the interest in his own hope and determination that another trial should be made. Eight years after the failure of the cable, after many journeys back and forth and unsparing work, Mr. Field secured the "Great Eastern," and had her hold fitted for reception for an infinitely better cable, under conditions of far greater mechanical perfection. In laying this cable, it was twice discovered that the electric current was stopped by a bit of wire driven into the cable; and long after the messages were flying back and forth the man who was paid to commit the deed confessed. Fortunately, they were discovered with no greater loss than that of time and patience. The officers on board took turns in watching, Mr. Field was on guard, the same gang of men being in the tank that were in when the former "faults" were noted, when a grating sound was heard once more. Mr. Field gave warning, but before it was heeded the faulty piece had gone overboard, and in a moment there came a snap—the cable had parted. The apparently impossible suggestion was made to grapple for the lost cable. Several times they seized it, only to lose it again, and finally were compelled to steam back and leave it on the bottom of the sea. The intrepid projector set himself once more at work. Out of what seemed at first complete disaster he wrested so much suggestion for future prevention of accident, that at the first meeting of the directors in London it was decided to lay two cables—that is, to raise the one then lost, and to have a new one made. Two years later the indefatigable financier was once more ready with fresh material. One important thing provided by science since the last attempts was that of galvanizing the wire to save it from rust or corrosion by the sea. This did away with the need for gutta-percha, to the sticky surface of which slight fragments of wire might adhere. An invention had been made by which the cable could be tested every instant, so that it was not possible to pay out a faulty section. On Friday, July 13, 1866, the "Great Eastern" put to sea

once more with her precious burden. While the last cable was preparing a war had broken out between Austria, Prussia, and Italy. Out on the Atlantic came at intervals, to the "Great Eastern Telegraph Station," news of its progress. Twice a day a bulletin was set up, and to the excitement of the news was added the interest of its reception in such novel circumstances. On Friday, July 27, the cable was safely landed. The last messages received on shipboard read: "It is a great work, a glory to our age and nation, and the men who have achieved it deserve to be honored among the benefactors of our race." "Treaty of peace signed between Prussia and Austria." As the cable across the Gulf of St. Lawrence was out of order, it was Sunday, the 29th before the first message reached the United States:

"We arrived here at nine o'clock this morning. All well. Thank God, the cable is laid, and is in perfect working order! Cyrus W. Field."

Other dispatches followed, giving news of Europe to people who were reading that which was a fortnight old.

Ten years of idleness had wrought havoc with the telegraph across Newfoundland and the gulf, and although Mr. Field had urged the American company to be ready for the coming cable, they preferred to see first if it succeeded. Mr. Field, without a moment's rest, set about repairing the neglect. In a few days he had completed the work, and the communication was opened that has not since been closed. As soon as coal brought from England in 6 vessels could be taken on board the "Great Eastern," she set out on her further mission of securing the lost cable of 1865. After weeks of grappling, with occasional partial triumphs, the cable was secured, and a message was received through it from the operators in Ireland. On Saturday, Sept. 7, the raised cable was safely brought to its landing at Heart's Content, Newfoundland. At a banquet given in his honor by the Chamber of Commerce of New York, Mr. Field said:

It has been a long, hard struggle. Nearly thirteen years of anxious watching and ceaseless toil. Often my heart has been ready to sink. Many times, when wandering in the forests of Newfoundland in the pelting rain, or on the decks of ships on dark, stormy nights, alone, far from home, I have almost accused myself of madness and folly to sacrifice the peace of my family and all the hopes of life for what might prove, after all, but a dream. I have seen my companions one and another falling by my side, and feared that I might not live to see the end. And yet one hope has led me on, and I have prayed that I might not taste of death till this work was accomplished. That prayer is answered; and now, beyond all acknowledgments to men, is the feeling of gratitude to Almighty God.

Mr. Field received from Congress a gold medal with the thanks of the nation. The Paris Exposition of 1867 bestowed upon him its highest honor, the grand medal. In 1869 he attended, as representative of the New York Chamber of Commerce, the opening of the Suez Canal. He became interested in the elevated-railway system of New York, and bestowed upon it much thought and capital. In 1880 he made a tour round the world, and on his return obtained concessions from the Sandwich Islands for the laying of a cable from San Francisco thence, with a view to its ultimate extension across the Pacific Ocean. His closing years were spent quietly in his Gramercy Park home, and were rendered sad by domestic sorrow and financial losses.

FINANCIAL REVIEW OF 1892. The financial condition of this country seemed to attract the attention of European nations during 1892, and the operation of the silver-purchase law of July, 1890, was watched with keen interest, especially after it was seen that the absorption by this Government of 4,500,000 ounces of silver per month did not result in maintaining the price of the metal. Early in the year Austria put in force preparations for resuming gold payments, and began to attract gold from the United States, practically paying a premium therefor in preference to attempting to secure a supply either from London, Paris, or Berlin, for the reason that she was also seeking to float loans in one or more of those markets, and would probably be unsuccessful if the discount rates were deranged by withdrawals of gold. From February to September inclusive about $46,935,000 gold was shipped hence to the Continent of Europe for Austrian account. The movement was renewed in November, and by the end of the year $12,550,000 more had been sent, making a total of $59,485,000. This drain of gold was facilitated by the low rates for money in New York, which prevented the employment of any portion of the vast amounts of capital lying almost idle in London and at other centers, and there was a feeling of distrust abroad regarding the stability of our currency which discouraged purchases and encouraged sales of American securities. This country was therefore supplying the extraordinary demand of Austria for gold, thereby relieving the principal European centers from meeting this inquiry, and at the same time was absorbing securities held in Europe on speculative or investment account, while the redundancy of our currency checked the natural tendency of our market for money automatically to regulate that for exchange. A fall in the price of bar silver in London, Aug. 12, to 37⅞ $d.$ per ounce, the lowest on record, appeared to intensify the feeling of distrust abroad, and it also excited fears that Indian and English commercial and financial interests would suffer from the derangement of Eastern exchanges resulting from the unsettled price of silver. This had much to do with the acceptance by the English Government of the invitation extended by the United States to the principal European nations to send delegates to an international monetary conference. This assembled at Brussels Nov. 22. A proposition by Mr. Rothschild, of the English delegation, that European nations unite in the purchase of $5,000,000 of silver bullion annually with the object of aiding to maintain stability in the price was rejected, as also was a plan for a bimetallic agreement, and after the discussion of other schemes the conference adjourned Dec. 2, to reassemble in May, 1893. This fulfillment of the prediction of the failure of the conference brought about a revival of the uneasy feeling abroad, which was reflected in another decline in bar silver in London to 37⅛ $d.$ per ounce on Dec. 23, and the renewal of exports of gold from New York to the Continent for Aus-

trian account gave rise to fears that unless the operation of the silver-purchase act of 1890 were suspended by Congress, or the law repealed, the Treasury Department would be unable very long to maintain the notes issued in payment for the silver bullion, then amounting to about $124,000,000, on a parity with gold. At the end of the year efforts were being made to induce members of Congress promptly to act in the matter of a suspension or repeal of the law immediately after the reassembling of Congress in January.

The political situation in France was grave at the end of the year. The sudden death of Baron Reinach in November was alleged to have been due to suicide, caused by his connection with the bribery by the managers of the Panama Canal Company of the Paris press and of members of the French Parliament and officials of high rank. The Chamber of Deputies insisted upon a thorough investigation, and the exhumation of the remains of the baron to determine the manner of his death. While consenting to the inquiry, the Cabinet refused to permit the autopsy, and the Chamber of Deputies, Nov. 28, forced the resignation of the Lonbet ministry. On Dec. 7 M. Ribot formed a new Cabinet, retaining many members of the old, and the Government decided promptly to co-operate with the Chamber in the inquiry into the charges of bribery, receding from its position in the matter of Baron Reinach's remains. Arrests of prominent officials of the company and of ex-members of the Chamber speedily followed, and almost daily disclosures of a startling character were made, not the least important of which was the declaration that the movement against high officers of the state was part of a conspiracy to overthrow the republic. A charge of bribery against M. Rouvier, the Minister of Finance, compelled his resignation, and it was alleged that M. Carnot, the President, was indirectly involved in the scandal, but this was promptly denied. The ministry was, on Dec. 23, sustained by a decisive vote of the Chamber and as the year closed there were indications that the republic would survive the attacks of its enemies. There was some political tension in Germany at intervals during the year, resulting from caustic criticisms of the Emperor by Prince Bismarck, and toward the end of the year the bill for increased appropriations for the army met with opposition in Parliament. With the exception of the substitution of the Gladstone for the Salisbury ministry in Great Britain there was no event of political importance in that country. A strike of cotton spinners, brought about by an attempt to reduce wages, tended to paralyze that industry in the closing months of the year. Trade and speculation in England and on the Continent of Europe continued depressed, mainly from causes operating since the Baring failure in 1890 and partly from the decline in silver. On Jan. 25 the President sent a message to Congress reviewing the troubles between this Government and that of Chili growing out of the attack, on Oct. 16, 1891, by Chilians in Valparaiso upon a company of sailors belonging to the United States ship "Baltimore." Reparation was demanded by this Government, through its minister, and refused, and active preparations were made by the Navy Department to enforce the demand. An ultimatum was sent on the 21st, and after a brief delay a satisfactory response was made and the excitement subsided.

The Asiatic cholera made its appearance in eastern Europe early in the summer. It spread through Russia with devastating effect, and by the close of July it reached France, entering Germany in August, and the mortality in Hamburg by the end of that month was appalling. It had a paralyzing effect upon business on the Continent, and when the scourge reached the seaports it caused an embargo upon commerce. Early in September it made its appearance in London, and later in other parts of England, but the further progress of the disease in Europe was then checked, although for the remainder of the year there were occasional outbreaks in Russia, and more or less of the scourge in Hamburg. On Aug. 31 the steamship "Moravia," from Hamburg, arrived at this port with cholera among the immigrant passengers. The quarantine officials promptly adopted preventive measures, and President Harrison issued a proclamation ordering the detention for twenty days of vessels from European ports with immigrants. With the exception of five deaths from cholera in this city, which were reported Sept. 14, the scourge was confined to the quarantine at New York. There was more or less alarm felt until the close of September, when the excitement subsided. After the assembling of Congress an agreement was reached in the Senate to report a bill suspending immigration for one year from March 1, 1893.

The following tabular survey of the economical conditions and results of 1892, contrasted with those of the preceding year, is from the Commercial and Financial Chronicle:

ECONOMICAL CONDITIONS AND RESULTS.	1891.	1892.
Coin and currency in the United States. Dec. 31..........	$1,748,684,894	$1,764,985,928
Bank clearings in the United States	$56,946,841,805	$62,109,062,074
Business failures	$189,868,688	$114,044,167
Imports of merchandise (year)	828,320,948	876,198,179
Exports of merchandise (year)	976,509,646	938,419,898
Gross earnings 215 roads (year)	545,998,964	574,621,979
Railroad construction, miles..	4,500	4,150
Wheat raised, bushels.......	611,780,000	515,949,000
Corn raised, bushels........	2,060,154,000	1,628,464,000
Cotton raised, bales.........	9,088,707	6,575,000
Pig iron produced (tons of 2,000 pounds)...........	9,278,455	10,255,840
Steel rails, Bessemer (tons of 2,000 pounds)...........	1,366,259	....
Anthracite coal (tons of 2,240 pounds)...............	40,448,386	41,898,320
Petroleum (runs) production, barrels.................	34,486,923	32,149,171
Immigration into the United States (year)............	590,666	543,487

The prices of leading staples on or about the 1st of January, 1893, compared with prices at the same date in 1892 and 1891, were as follow:

STAPLES.	1891.	1892.	1893.
Cotton, middling uplands, per pound....................	9$\frac{7}{16}$	7$\frac{7}{8}$	9$\frac{1}{2}$
Standard sheetings, per square yard....................	7$\frac{1}{4}$	6$\frac{1}{4}$	6$\frac{1}{4}$
Wool, Ohio XX, per pound............................	33 to 34	30 to 31	28 to 29
Iron, American pig No. 1, per ton......................	$16 50 to $17 50	$16 to $17	$15 to $15 50
Steel rails at mills, per ton..........................	$29 50	$30 00	$29
Wheat, No. 2 red winter, per bushel...................	$1 03$\frac{1}{4}$	$1 04$\frac{1}{4}$	79$\frac{1}{2}$
Corn, Western mixed No. 2, per bushel.................	59	52$\frac{1}{2}$	49$\frac{1}{2}$
Pork, mess, per barrel	$11 50 to $12	$10 00	$16 25

The Crops.—The crop season of 1892 presented a strong contrast to that of the previous year. The European yield was comparatively abundant, while in 1891 it was largely deficient, and the cereal crop in this country was this year only a little above the average as to quantity, and generally deficient as to quality. Owing to the large visible supply of wheat in all the world's markets prices were low, and soon after the new wheat began to move to market in this country prices declined, reaching almost unprecedentedly low figures in October, and the fall was accelerated by the offerings of large quantities of the crop of 1891, which had been held back by the farmers. The weather was cold in the spring and very unfavorable in some sections, but in July and August it was hot and forcing, and maturing grain made rapid progress, while harvesting was greatly facilitated. The corn crop was sowed late, and the growth was slow in the early stages, but, influenced by the favorable weather above noted, and also by a late fall, the crop matured under good conditions. Much of the deficiency in quality of wheat and corn was due to a period of very dry weather in August, which caused great damage in Kansas and in adjoining States. Less cotton was planted this year than in 1891, and the yield is estimated at about 2,000,000 bales less than that of last year. Consumption was restricted by the depression in

Taking prices in New York, Jan. 1, if the whole of the crops could have been laid down at that point on that date, the values would have been as follow:

ESTIMATES OF CROP VALUES.

PRODUCTS.	CROP OF 1891.			CROP OF 1892.		
	Yield.	Price, Jan. 1, 1892.	Value.	Yield.	Price, Jan. 1, 1893.	Value.
Wheat, bushels.................	611,780,000	$1 04$\frac{1}{2}$	$640,889,550	515,949,000	$0 79$\frac{1}{2}$	$411,169,827
Corn, bushels.................	2,060,154,000	52$\frac{1}{4}$	1,076,480,465	1,628,464,000	49$\frac{1}{4}$	802,018,520
Cotton, bales.................	9,088,707	7$\frac{1}{4}$	344,600,704	6,575,000	9$\frac{7}{8}$	339,458,125
Total values			$2,051,370,719			$1,552,640,972

cotton-manufacturing industries in Europe, owing to the strike of operatives in England and the derangement of trade with the East, caused by the unsettled price of silver. Speculators based their operations upon the falling off in the yield resulting from decreased acreage, unfavorable weather, and the smaller use of fertilizers, and the price of cotton was maintained at comparatively remunerative figures for the planter. The report of the Bureau of Agriculture showed that the yield of wheat in 1892 was 515,949,000 bushels, valued at $322,111,881; corn, 1,628,464,000 bushels, valued at $642,146,630; and oats, 661,035,000 bushels, valued at $209,253,611.

Stocks.—The principal events affecting the stock market this year were the formation of the coal combination by the Reading managers; the change in the ownership of the New York and New England, and its eventual control by the Reading; the collapse of the Western Traffic Association; almost uninterrupted selling of American securities for European account; the death of Mr. Jay Gould; the semipanic in September caused by the cholera cases in New York; and the unsettling fall, Dec. 19, due to excessively high rates for money resulting from large withdrawals of gold for export to Europe. The feature of the market early in January was an advance in New York and New England, due to purchases for control by Mr. Charles Parsons, formerly President of the Rome, Watertown and Ogdensburg, and by Mr. Austin Corbin, of the Long Island, and it was announced on the 6th that the latter would be made President of the New York and New England. The rise in this stock stimulated an improvement in the whole market, and the tone was very strong until the 7th, when a sharp fall in Chicago Gas had an unsettling effect. This was followed by manipulation which resulted in a general distribution of stocks among nonprofessionals, who were led to purchase by reports that the upward movement had only been temporarily checked, and that it would soon be resumed. Bearish attacks were encouraged by evidence of disagreement among some of the members of the Western Traffic Association. At the meeting of the advisory board on the 15th, charges of rate cutting were presented by the Missouri Pacific against the Chicago, Burlington and Quincy, the Atchison, Topeka and Santa Fé, and the Southern Pacific, and instead of promptly acting upon these charges the board postponed their consideration until the next meeting. This led to a threat by the Vice-President of the Missouri Pacific that his road would withdraw from the association, and the bears claimed that the withdrawal of this road would cause a disruption of the association. The bearish demonstrations were vigorously directed against Missouri Pacific, the other Southwesterns, and the Grangers, and rumors of serious trouble with Chili still further aided the decline in the market. One feature was an advance in the Chesapeake and Ohios on the announcement of a plan to fund the first and second preferred stock. Another feature was a rise in Missouri, Kansas and Texas securities on news that interest would be paid on the second mortgage bonds. The coal shares improved, and Reading and New York and New England advanced on a report that these lines,

the Boston and Maine and the Baltimore and Ohio had obtained control of the Poughkeepsie bridge, but it subsequently appeared that the Reading only was interested. American Sugar Refining stock was broken down about the middle of the month by news that an issue of $25,000,000 more stock had been authorized, but later it recovered on reports of preparations to absorb the Spreckels and other refineries in Philadelphia. Distillers and Cattle Feeders, which had been strong early in the month, fell off on a report that the United States authorities would investigate the business of the trust. After the 22d the Grangers were strong, and there was good buying of National Cordage. Toward the close of the month the Southwesterns improved on news that Mr. Jay Gould would not insist upon a special meeting of the Western Traffic Association to consider the charges made by the Missouri Pacific above referred to. Manhattan Elevated was favorably affected by a decision of the Court of Appeals which settled the question of damages to property on the line of the road; and the whole market was strong at the close on the announcement that Chili had made overtures of peace in response to President Harrison's *ultimatum*. The most prominent feature of the market in February was the formation of the Reading combination to control the production of anthracite coal. On the 4th there were large purchases of Reading, Delaware, Lackawanna and Western, and Central New Jersey, which attracted attention from the fact that the buying was apparently so confident and the rise so decided. On the 10th it was announced that the Reading had secured, by purchase of stock, a controlling interest in the Lehigh Valley; that this road and the Central New Jersey would be leased by the Reading, and that capitalists connected with the Central New Jersey had bought enough stock of the Delaware, Lackawanna and Western to entitle them to representation in the board of directors. On the following day it was further announced that the Central New Jersey would be leased to the Port Reading, a New Jersey corporation controlled by the Reading. These details of the plan for a coal combination caused a sharp advance in all the stocks of the roads named, and Erie, Delaware and Hudson, New York, Susquehanna and Western, and New York and New England moved rapidly upward, the latter in the expectation that this road would be benefited by its connection with the Poughkeepsie bridge, which would be used by the Reading for its Eastern traffic. The business in this group of stocks was enormous, amounting on the 11th to over 1,400,000 shares. After the details of the combination were made public realizing sales were liberal, and investment holders of Delaware, Lackawanna and Western and of the other coal stocks and European holders of Reading stock and bonds sold freely. The downward reaction was aided by the news that the State authorities of Pennsylvania and of New Jersey would inquire into the legality of the combination. The tendency was downward for these stocks until the 26th, when there was a sharp recovery, led by Delaware and Hudson, on a rumor that control of this road was sought by the combination, and the market was active and higher for all the coal properties to the end of the month. Among the other features was an advance in Consolidated Gas, caused by an increase in the dividend. While the movement in the coal shares was at its height the Grangers and the Southwesterns were inclined to be heavy, as it was feared that the boom in the coal properties would suddenly collapse and cause general demoralization. Toward the end of the month gold exports began, the large selling of stocks for European account having turned exchange upward, and there was a sharp fall in Chicago Gas, which temporarily unsettled the market, but it promptly recovered. The feature early in March was a further rise in Delaware and Hudson, followed by Erie, the latter being affected by a traffic arrangement with the Reading. There was also a well-sustained improvement in Lake Shore, based upon a report that a stock dividend was in contemplation to represent earnings expended for betterments, and this started buying of the other Vanderbilt stocks. New York and New England moved upward on a report, which, however, was promptly denied, that the Vanderbilts had obtained control of it, and that the presidency of the company had been offered to a friend of this family. The denial of this story brought about a sharp fall in the stock, and later it appeared that the property had been manipulated by a Boston director in such a way as to antagonize the interests of Mr. Corbin, who resigned as president, and was succeeded by Mr. Charles Parsons. On the 9th it was announced that a bill legalizing the Reading combination had been passed by the Legislature of New Jersey. Negotiations for the absorption of the independent refineries in Philadelphia were opened by the American Sugar Refining Company, and this caused a sharp advance in that stock after the middle of the month. On the 10th the St. Paul directors decided not to declare a dividend on the common stock, and this caused a partial decline in that property. Richmond Terminal stocks and bonds were strong on the 11th and 12th, in anticipation of the publication of the plan of reorganization, but on the issue of the scheme there was a decline. During and after the third week in the month the market was unfavorably affected by arbitrage selling for European account, by the debate on the free silver coinage bill in Congress, and by the publication of the Bering Sea correspondence. Reading and the other coal shares were lower, because of the delay in signing the enabling act passed by the New Jersey Legislature and by rumors that the bill would fail to become a law. On the 25th, news of the defeat of the Free Silver Coinage bill in the House of Representatives temporarily stimulated a recovery in the market, but bearish pressure was soon renewed, Atchison, Topeka and Santa Fé and Northern Pacific preferred were raided, and the tone was irregular and generally lower to the close of the month. Early in April there was a recovery led by the Grangers and closely followed by Delaware and Hudson, which stimulated an improvement in the other coal stocks. There was good buying by the arbitrage houses for European account, and toward the middle of the month Reading advanced on news that control had been obtained of the Pennsylvania, Pough-

keepsie and Boston road. The tendency of the whole market was upward until the third week, when the bears took advantage of free selling by the arbitrage houses to force a decline in leading properties, and the fall was aided by exports of gold to France and by the lateness of the season in the wheat belt, which more or less affected the Grangers. Just before the end of the month the market was unsettled by sharp bearish attacks, but there was a prompt recovery, and, although irregular, the tone was generally stronger at the close. One feature was the failure of an effort on the part of foreign holders of Union Pacific to secure a change of management at the annual election. Another feature was an advance in Minneapolis and St. Louis stocks, due to a movement to discharge the receiver. Early in May selling of stocks for European account was liberal, but the offerings were promptly absorbed, and then followed a reaction in nearly everything except Northern Pacific preferred, which was affected by reports that the dividend would be passed. The coal shares were somewhat feverish, because of the declaration that the Pennsylvania was opposed to the policy of the combination, and also for the reason that the enabling act had not been signed by the Governor of New Jersey. During the second week exports of gold had an unfavorable influence upon the market, and the Atchison, Topeka and Santa Fé securities were broken down by news of the contemplated issuing of a second mortgage, but they subsequently recovered on the announcement that the issue was for the purpose of retiring the income bonds and to provide for betterments. One feature was a rise in Buffalo, Rochester and Pittsburg on news of a traffic alliance with the New York Central. During the third week in the month the market was affected by reports of floods in the Mississippi valley and at other points in the West and South, and there were bearish attacks upon Atchison, Topeka and Santa Fé, Northern Pacific preferred, the Grangers, and Louisville and Nashville. Toward the close of the month the market became oversold, and a covering of short contracts brought about an irregular advance, and the tone was generally strong to the close. Early in June the announcement that the Attorney-General of New Jersey had begun proceedings to annul the lease by the Port Reading of the Central New Jersey, caused a fall in the last-named stock. The Grangers declined in anticipation of reduced earnings as the result of the floods. American Sugar Refining, National Lead, and National Cordage advanced, and although the market was irregular there appeared to be a strong undertone, and on the 8th there was a sharp rally due to rebuying to cover short contracts. New York and New England was favorably affected by reports of a new traffic agreement with the Reading, and news of hot, forcing weather in the corn belt and of generally good conditions for all the grain crops encouraged buying of the Grangers, and the tendency was generally upward until the 14th, although New York and New England was temporarily depressed by the announcement that the Housatonic road had been bought for the New York, New Haven and Hartford. On the 14th the bull movement culminated, and there followed an irregular decline, due to realizations and bearish pressure. aided by engagements of gold for shipment to Europe. The Richmond and Danville, the Richmond and West Point Terminal, and the East Tennessee, Virginia and Georgia were placed in the hands of receivers, the original plans for reorganization having been abandoned. Gradually the market recovered, and the tone was strong until the 23d, when there was an irregular decline, in part caused by engagements of gold for export to Europe. Toward the end of the month. Drexel, Morgan & Co. refused to assist in the reorganization of the Richmond and West Point Terminal, whereupon this stock sharply fell off. The Vanderbilt properties were favorably affected by the declaration of the usual dividends, accompanied by a satisfactory exhibit of their financial condition; Reading and the other coal shares improved because of the advance in the schedule price of coal, and the whole market moved upward, closing generally strong. News of the passage, July 2d, by the Senate of the Stewart bill providing for the free coinage of silver, started selling of stocks for European account; and bearish demonstrations were aided by the strike of the Amalgamated Association of Iron Workers employed in the Carnegie mills at Homestead, Pa., which was brought about by a demand by the company for a reduction of about one third on certain classes of work directly affecting only 325 out of the 3,800 men in the works. The strike was accompanied by a lockout, and efforts by the managers of the mill to employ nonunion labor were forcibly resisted, and in the conflict between the strikers and the Pinkerton guard several of the latter were killed. The bears vigorously raided leading stocks, taking advantage of reports that the strike at Homestead would be followed by a general strike of members of the association and their allies elsewhere. The market was weak until the 7th, when there was a rally caused by rebuying of stocks for European account. The action of the Chicago, Burlington and Quincy, in demanding of the advisory board of the Western Traffic Association certain amendments to the rules had only a temporary effect, mainly for the reason that reports from the growing crops were excellent, and this encouraged buying of all the Grangers. On the 13th, the Senate bill providing for the free coinage of silver was defeated in the House of Representatives by a combination of antifree-coinage men of both parties, and soon after a clique of bull speculators began operations in American Sugar Refining stocks and in National Cordage, and, influenced by the well-sustained advance in these specialties, the whole market improved, and the tone was generally strong to the end of the month. Brilliant crop prospects resulting from hot and forcing weather, which prevailed from the 18th of July until near the middle of August, encouraged buying of the Granger stocks during the early part of this month. One feature was the failure of the strikers at Homestead, Pa., to prevent the operation of the Carnegie mills, the State militia protecting the property. Another feature was a revolt of free against convict labor in coal mines in Tennessee, which was suppressed by the militia of that State. Still another feature was a decision by Judge McCormick of the United States circuit court sitting at Dallas, Texas, against the railroad commissioners of that State; and another feature was a decision by Chancellor McGill, of New Jersey, against the lease of the Central New Jersey by the Port Reading. The tendency of the stock market was upward, with American Sugar Refining, National Cordage, National Lead, General Electric, and Cotton-oil leading, until the second week, when there was an irregular fall due to realizations, assisted by the strike of railroad switchmen in the Reading, Buffalo, Rochester and Pittsburg, Erie, New York Central, and Lake Shore yards at Buffalo, by further shipments of gold to Europe, and by reports of drought threatening the destruction of crops in Kansas. In the third week the strike at Buffalo became so formidable that the militia of the State were sent to that point to guard the railroad property, and this had more or less of an unsettling effect until toward the end of the month, when the collapse of this strike brought about a recovery in the market; but this was followed by a decline on news of cholera in England, it having reached there from Hamburg, where the scourge was raging. On the last day of the month there was a panicky fall in the market on the announcement of the arrival at this port of the steamship "Moravia" from Hamburg with cholera on board. Early in September the market was directly affected by the excitement attending the arrival of other infected vessels, but, influenced by the prompt and effective measures taken by the New York quarantine authorities, and by the President's proclamation detaining for twenty days all vessels which left infected European ports after Sept. 1, the excitement gradually subsided and the markets were recovering, when the announcement was made on the 14th that five deaths had occurred from cholera in this city. This caused another panicky decline, and the market was unsettled until the 16th, when there was an irregular recovery, and the tone was generally stronger to the end of the month. One feature was a sharp advance in American Sugar Refining, due to the embargo upon raw sugar from European ports, and to the check to importations of refined sugar from Hamburg. Another feature was the declaration of a dividend of 2 per cent. on St. Paul common stock, and still another feature was a threatened strike of engineers on the Reading system. The weather at the West was excellent for corn throughout the whole month, and early in October it was announced that the entire crop had matured under favorable conditions. During the first week in the month the market was active and higher, and one feature was a sharp advance in New York and New England, due to a report that the Boston and Maine would absorb the road. and there was good buying of it for Philadelphia account. Reading also rose rapidly. There was a decided improvement in Atchison, Topeka and Santa Fé, Erie, the Grangers, Chicago Gas, American Sugar Refining, and all the leading stocks. General Electric was especially affected by news of a decision by the United States Court of Appeals confirming Mr. Edison's patent of the incandescent lamp. The tendency of the market was upward during the first half of the month. Then came a decline in Reading, caused by news of further proceedings by the authorities of New Jersey against the Reading leases, and the market was irregular until the last week in the month, when it was announced that Mr. A. A. McLeod, President of the Reading, had been elected President of the Boston and Maine, that friends of the Reading had obtained a controlling interest in New York and New England, and that the latter would be made part of the Reading-Boston and Maine system. Some disappointment was manifested by holders of New York and New England, because this alliance did not promise immediately beneficial results to this road, and the stock fell off, but it subsequently recovered, and Reading was also strong. Toward the end of the month Distillers and Cattle Feeders' Trust was vigorously raided with more or less unsettling effect upon the whole market, and it was irregular at the close. One feature was a blockade of nearly all the lines of road centering at Chicago, caused by large deliveries of wheat by farmers who, though the price was very low, were induced to sell by the official estimate of a yield of about 550,000,000 bushels, and much of the grain thus sold was of the crop of 1891, which had been held by the farmers, who were influenced to do so by the advice given by the Farmers' Alliance last year to hold back the wheat for better prices. The blockade was not raised until early in the next month. During the first few days of November the market was generally strong, and the industrial stocks were advanced by the aid of reports that increased dividends would soon be declared, while National Cordage was especially influenced by a statement that the common stock would be increased and the new issue divided among the stockholders. On the 9th the market was vigorously raided on the report that the success of the Democratic party in the presidential election meant that there would be a more vigorous prosecution of all industrial corporations under the antitrust law, and that there would also be a more decided movement against the Reading coal combination. Subsequently efforts were made still further to unsettle the market by asserting that an extraordinary session of Congress would be called in March to amend the tariff. The tendency of the market was downward until the 15th, when the decline was checked, and prices were turned upward by a covering of short contracts induced by the semiofficial statement that there would be no extraordinary session of Congress. On the 17th a firmer tone for exchange gave rise to rumors of intended exports of gold, and this caused a renewal of the selling movement. Reading was at this time affected by reports that full interest on the income bonds would not be paid, the Southwestern stocks were disturbed by the unsettled rate situation in that section, and the Grangers fell off in anticipation of decreased earnings resulting from a lighter movement of grain to market. The engagement on the 23d of $600,000 gold for export to Europe made the whole list heavy, and during the remaining days of the month the market was more or less affected by reports of intended shipments of more gold and by the illness of Mr. Jay Gould, and the tone was heavy at the close of the month. Mr. Gould died on the 2d of December, but the event had only a temporary effect upon the market, principally for the reason that it was stated that the stocks of the Missouri Pacific, Western Union,

and Manhattan Elevated companies owned by him had been placed in the hands of trustees in anticipation of his demise. The rebuying of stock speculatively sold during the last illness of Mr. Gould made the market very strong in the early part of December, and one feature was a well-sustained advance in Western Union on the report that important interests were buying for the purpose of securing a larger representation in the company. Another feature was a rise in Reading on news that the Arnot case, in Williamsport, Pa., had been decided in favor of the company by the master appointed to take the testimony. On the 12th, the announcement that $1,500,000 gold had been engaged for export to Europe served to check the advance in the market, and later, when the engagement of $750,000 more gold was reported, the tone grew heavy. On the following day $1,000,000 more gold was taken for shipment, and the market became weak, with a sharp fall in Western Union as the feature on the denial of the report that the previous buying had been other than a speculative movement. On the 15th, $500,000 more gold was taken for export, whereupon there was an advance in the rate of money to 15 per cent., and the selling of stocks was liberal. On the 16th, money was bid up to 25 per cent., encouraging bearish demonstrations, and the market was ragged on the 17th, opening panicky on the 19th on news of the engagement of $3,900,000 gold for shipment on the following day. This large movement of gold caused a calling in of loans, discrimination against Industrial stocks as collateral, and an advance in the rate of money to 40 per cent. The tendency of the market was generally downward all day, with Sugar Refining Company and Distillers and Cattle Feeders' Company stocks and Reading weakest. On the 20th there was a better feeling, due to easier rates for exchange caused by the high figures for money, which induced the making of sterling loans. In the course of the day the market reacted, and although $500,000 more gold was taken for export, making $4,400,000 for the week, the news had little influence, for the reason that this consignment was part of an unfilled order of the previous week, and exchange was at a point which did not permit of further gold exports. The tendency of the market was irregularly downward, with occasional rallies due to rebuying to cover short contracts, until the last week in the month, when there was a recovery due to easy money and the announcement that no more gold would be sent to Europe, and the feature was an advance in Reading on news that the coal business of the company would be turned over to the Finance Company of Philadelphia, and that interest on the preference bonds would be paid. Another feature was a sharp advance in Manhattan Elevated, caused by the rejection of a bid for the Rapid Transit underground franchise in New York. The market closed active and strong, although $500,000 gold was unexpectedly taken on Friday for shipment on Saturday the 31st. Total sales of stocks at the New York Stock Exchange for the year 1892 were 85,875,092 shares, against 69,031,689 in 1891, 71,282,885 in 1890, and 72,014,600 in 1889.

The following table shows prices of leading

stocks at the beginning of the years 1891, 1892, and 1893:

STOCKS.	1891.	1892.	1893.
New York Central.............	101⅛	116¾	109⅜
Erie..........................	19½	34½	24
Lake Shore....................	106½	123½	128¼
Michigan Central..............	91	106	104¼
Rock Island...................	70⅝	89½	82⅞
Northwest, common............	104⅝	116½	112
St. Paul, common	51	82⅝	78¼
Dela., Lackawanna and Western.	131½	139	154
Central New Jersey............	106⅛	113	126

The following shows the highest prices of a few of the speculative stocks in 1891 and the highest and lowest in 1892:

STOCKS.	1891.	1892.	
	Highest.	Highest.	Lowest.
Atchison, Topeka and Sante Fé..	47¼	46⅝	32⅝
Canada Southern	64¼	64⅛	54½
Central New Jersey	122¾	145	111⅛
Chicago Gas....................	71½	99⅝	71½
Chicago, Burlington and Quincy.	110	110⅝	95
Delaware and Hudson	141½	149¼	122¾
Dela., Lackawanna and Western.	145⅝	167½	138⅛
Erie	34¼	34½	23⅛
Illinois Central	109⅝	110	95¼
Lake Shore	127	140¼	120
Louisville and Nashville	88⅞	84¼	64⅜
Michigan Central...............	109¾	117	102
Missouri Pacific................	77¼	65⅜	53⅞
New York Central	119¾	119½	107⅛
New York and New England ...	43	59	30⅝
Northwestern	118⅝	121¾	110⅛
Northern Pacific	30⅞	26⅛	15
Northern Pacific, preferred	78⅝	72½	44⅞
Pacific Mail.....................	41½	40⅝	25
Pullman	196⅛	200½	184
Reading	48½	65	38
Richmond Terminal	19¼	17⅛	6¼
Rock Island.....................	90¼	94½	75⅛
St. Paul.........................	82⅝	84⅝	75⅝
Union Pacific	52¼	50½	35⅝
Western Union......	85¼	100⅝	82

Foreign Exchange.—The imports of merchandise for the year ending Dec. 31, 1892, were $47,877,236 above those for 1891, and the exports of domestic and foreign merchandise were $32,089,753 less. The excess of merchandise exports over imports for the year was $62,221,714, against $142,188,703 for 1891. The excess of exports over imports of merchandise, coin, and bullion for 1892 was $135,516,820, against $185,805,303 for 1891. Gold exports were $59,045,524 in excess of the imports in 1892, against $34,116,471 in 1891. The market for foreign exchange was generally strong in January, influenced by a demand to remit for stocks sold for European account, by investment purchases of long sterling in order to make interest, and by a scarcity of commercial bills. The market opened at $4.82½ for sixty-day and $4.85 for sight, and it closed at $4.85 for the former and $4.87 for the latter. Gold to the amount of $272,800 arrived from Europe during the month. The inquiry for exchange to remit for stocks and the scarcity of commercial drafts continued throughout February. The market opened at $4.85 for sixty-day and $4.87 for sight, and it advanced to $4.86½ for the former and $4.89 for the latter, closing a little easier in tone. On the 20th, $500,000 gold, and on the 27th, $2,250,000, making $2,750,000 in all, was sent to Europe on special order, in response to a demand from Austria, which was then making preparations to resume gold payments. The sharp advance in stocks during March encouraged large sales of securities for European account, and the market was strong at from $4.86 to $4.87 for sixty-day and from $4.88 to $4.89 for sight, and gold to the amount of $3,280,000 was sent to the Continent of Europe. In April, while there was some buying of stocks by Europeans, the selling for this account was large, and exchange advanced to $4.88 for sixty-day and $4.89½ for sight, and the exports of gold to Europe amounted to $7,555,000. During the early part of May $3,000,000 more gold was exported, exchange continuing firm, but after the 15th the gold movement ceased for that month, to be resumed in June, when the shipments were $16,000,000. Exchange opened in June at $4.87½ to $4.88 for long and $4.89 for short; it moved up to $4.88½ for the former and $4.89½ for the latter by the 15th; it fell to the opening figures by the 22d, but it closed firm at the highest point. In July the market was dull and firm, it being affected by the pending antioptions bill in Congress, which checked speculation, and to some extent the movement in staples, and affected exchange by diminishing offerings of bills against future shipments of cotton and grain. Rates were $4.87½ to $4.88 for sixty-day and $4.89 to $4.89½ for sight. Gold to the amount of $6,000,000 was sent to Europe during the month. In August the market was firm at $4.87½ to $4.88 for long and $4.89 to $4.89½ for short, until the 23d, when rates grew easier in consequence of dearer money, but by the close of the month there was a reaction caused by a scarcity of commercial bills, due to a check to exports by the cholera in Europe. Gold to the amount of $5,450,000 went to Europe, and nearly the whole on special order. In September the market opened at $4.87 to $4.87½ for sixty-day and $4.88½ to $4.89 for sight, and $2,000,000 gold was sent to Germany on the 3d, and only $900,000 went forward for the remainder of the month, as the movement *via* Liverpool was too expensive, and Hamburg was practically a closed port by reason of the cholera. On the 13th, exchange declined in consequence of liberal offerings of loan bills, induced by dearer money, and on the 20th there was a fall to $4.86 to $4.86½ for long and $4.87 to $4.87½ for short, and the tone was easier for the remainder of the month. In October the market opened at $4.86½ for sixty-day and $4.88 for sight, but there was an immediate fall, followed by a recovery caused by a demand to cover loan and commercial bills; but when this inquiry was satisfied rates fell off again, and by the 20th they were $4.84 for long and $4.86 for short. Dearer discounts in London caused a decline to $4.83½ for sixty-day on the 27th, but the tone was firm at the close. In November exchange was strong by reason of a demand to cover loan bills, and there was a scarcity of commercial drafts, in part due to the check to exports of cotton, caused by an advance in the price above the parity of Liverpool. The market opened at $4.84½ for long and $4.87½ for short, and it gradually advanced to $4.86 to $4.86½ for the former and $4.88½ to $4.89 for the latter, and $600,000 gold was sent to Paris on the 26th. In December rates opened at $4.86 to $4.86½ for long and $4.88½ to $4.89 for short, and on the 3d $1,300,000 gold was sent to Europe. The market fell to $4.86 for sixty-day and $4.88½ for sight on the 5th; but it subsequently reacted to $4.86½ for the former and $4.89 for the latter, and it was firm until the 16th, when it grew easier in consequence of active money. The exports of gold were $3,750,000 on the 13th, $1,500,000 on the 15th, and $500,000 on the 17th. The tone became heavy on the 19th because of dear money, which induced drawings of loan bills and a renewal of maturing drafts, and rates fell to $4.85½ for long and $4.88 for short; but after money grew easier the exchange market became firmer, and on the 23d there was an advance to $4.86½ for long and $4.88½ for short. Gold to the amount of $3,900,000 was shipped to Europe on the 20th, and $500,000 on the 21st. The market was dull with an easy tone for the remainder of the month, closing a shade firmer, and $500,000 gold was shipped on the 31st, making $11,950,000 for the month and $59,-485,000 for the year.

Manufacturing Industries. — The annual cotton crop report of the "Financial and Commercial Chronicle" showed that the cotton trade was depressed during the greater part of the year ending Aug. 31, by the steadily declining price of the staple, which touched 6¼ cents for low middling, and 6$\frac{11}{16}$ for middling uplands during the first week of April. Manufacturers who bought at high prices lost heavily, but when the price recovered those who were well stocked made large profits. Production of print cloths at Fall River for the year ending Dec. 31, 1892, was 10,045,000 pieces, against 9,985,000 in the previous year, and the stock on hand was 7,000 pieces, against 90,000, Dec. 31, 1891. The dividends paid by mills showed a large increase over the previous year. The wool and woolen-goods trade was large; sales were heavy, and after the early months of the year prices were steady. The fall demand for goods was very active, and there was an encouraging outlook for this industry at the end of 1892. In the first half of the year iron production was unprecedentedly large, stimulated by the demand for structural iron. The output of pig iron for six months to June 30 was 4,769,683 gross tons, against 3,772,280 in the same time in 1891. The production in the last half of the year amounted to but 2,387,317 tons. Anthracite coal production was stimulated by the Reading combination after February, but the increase was largest in regions not under the control of the combination, private mine owners and companies taking advantage of the high prices for the product, and mining more coal than usual. The total production for the year was 41,893,320 tons, against 40,448,336 in 1891. Business failures involved smaller losses than any year since 1882, the total liabilities being $114,044,167, against $189,868,638 in 1891.

Money.—In January, money on call loaned at 4 per cent. for a few days early in the month, and it then gradually fell to 1. Time loans on stock collateral were offered as low as 2 per cent. for thirty days; 2½ for sixty to ninety days; 3½ for four, and 4 for five to six months. Short prime indorsed commercial paper was 3½ to 4½ per cent. The surplus reserve of the New York banks at the end of January was $36,020,900, or larger than at any time in three years. The range for call loans in February was from 1 to 2 per cent., while time contracts were made as low as at any period in January, and there was no change in commercial paper. In March, call loans were 1½ to 2 per cent., short-time contracts were 3, while longer dates were 3½ to 5 per cent., and the best double-name paper was 3¾ to 4 per cent. In April, call loans averaged less than 2 per cent., and lenders on time were offering contracts for thirty to sixty days at 2 to 3½ per cent., and loans repayable in gold could then be made at 4 per cent. for a year. Commercial paper of short date and prime names was 3½ to 4 per cent. In May, call loans averaged not more than 1½ per cent., time contracts were 2 to 2½ per cent. for thirty to sixty days, and short commercial paper was taken at 3 to 3½ per cent. In June, call loans were 1 to 1½ per cent., until toward the close, when there was an advance to 2. Time contracts were 2 per cent. for thirty to sixty days, growing firmer by the end of the month, in consequence of the large movement of gold to Europe. Short commercial paper was quoted at the unprecedentedly low rate of 2¾ to 3 per cent. On the 18th of June the loans of the New York banks reached the maximum of the year, $496,564,000, and the deposits were also at the highest point, $543,663,100. After the first few days of July money was freely offered, and the average for the month on call was not more than 2 per cent. The demand for time contracts was chiefly for long dates, while the offerings were for shorter periods, and consequently little business was done. Quotations were 2 to 2½ per cent. for thirty to sixty days and 3 to 4 for ninety days to six months. Rates for sixty- to ninety-day indorsed commercial paper were 3½ to 3¾ per cent. In August, call loans moved up from an average of 1½ per cent. early in the month to 2, in consequence of the continued drain of gold to Europe and the withdrawals of currency for the interior for crop purposes. Time contracts advanced to 3 per cent. for thirty days, and commercial paper of prime quality and short date was 4 to 4½ per cent. Preparations for the payment of interest and dividends caused money on call to loan at 6 per cent. on the first day of September, but gradually the rate fell to 3, and the average for the month was 3½. There was a good demand for time contracts at 4½ to 5 per cent. for thirty to sixty days, but there was an increase in the supply toward the end of the month, and rates grew easier. Short commercial paper was quoted at 4½ to 5 per cent. Money on call was active in October in consequence of the diminished surplus reserve of the banks, which on the 15th was at the lowest point of the year, $539,050, while the specie reached the minimum, $70,649,300, on the 22d. On Oct. 3, call money loaned at 10 per cent., but then came a gradual decline to 3 by the 24th, and the average for the month was not above 6. Time contracts were firm at 5½ per cent. for thirty days and 6 for longer periods, but after the middle of the month borrowers declined to make engagements at these figures, and the market grew easier. Short commercial paper was quoted at 5¾ to 6 per cent. During the first few days of November money on call loaned at 8 per cent., but after the middle of the mouth loans were frequent at 3, and the average was not above 4. Time contracts were abundantly offered at 5 to 5½ per cent. for thirty to sixty days, but the demand was not urgent. Commercial paper of first class and short date was quoted at 4¾ to 5½ per cent. In December, until the 15th, call loans ranged from 3 to 7 per cent., averaging about 5½, and time contracts were freely offered at 4 to 4½ per cent. for thirty to sixty days, 5 for ninety days to four months, and 5½ for longer dates, while short-date commercial paper was in good demand at 5 per cent. On the 15th, influenced by the comparatively large movement of gold to Europe, and especially by a realization of the fact that the shipments were largely if not wholly the result of the redundant silver currency of the country, money on call advanced to 25 per cent., and on the 19th it was bid up to 40 per cent., immediately falling to 6 in consequence of a good supply, and by the 21st the market had resumed its normal condition. Time loans were 6 per cent., and this was the rate bid for commercial paper of all dates and grades for the remainder of the month. On the 24th deposits were $444,370,100, and on the 31st loans were $437,722,000, the lowest of the year.

The condition of the New York Clearing-House banks, the rates for money, exchange, and silver, and prices for United States bonds on Jan. 7, 1893, compared with the preceding two years, are as follow:

ITEMS.	1891.	1892.	1893.
NEW YORK CITY BANKS:			
Loans and discounts	$385,678,500	$438,616,400	$441,283,700
Specie	78,663,200	95,972,200	76,626,600
Circulation	8,599,900	5,537,400	5,585,000
Net deposits	386,632,100	466,218,200	455,367,800
Legal tenders	26,571,700	37,814,400	46,157,800
Required reserve	96,658,025	116,554,550	113,841,950
Reserve held	105,234,900	133,786,600	122,784,400
Surplus reserve	$8,576,875	$17,232,050	$8,942,450
MONEY, EXCHANGE, SILVER:			
Call loans	2½ to 8	3	5 to 7
Prime paper, 60 days	7	4½ to 5¼	6
Silver in London, per ounce	48 *d.*	43⅝ *d.*	38⅝ *d.*
Prime sterling bills, 60 days	$4 80	$4 82½	$4 87¼ to $4 87½
UNITED STATES BONDS:			
Currency 6s, 1898	118	115½	112½ bid
4½s coupon, 1891	103½	100 *	100 *
4s coupon, 1907	122½	116½	113½

* Extended 2 per cents.

The following is the New York Clearing-House statement of totals at the beginning of each quarter of 1892 and at the end of the year:

DATE.	Loans.	Specie.	Circulation.	Deposits.	Legal tenders.
January 2	$438,616,400	$95,972,200	$5,537,400	$466,218,200	$37,814,400
April 2	489,725,100	101,894,500	5,569,000	528,447,400	48,235,800
July 2	494,464,100	91,936,600	5,588,400	534,608,400	60,102,100
October 1	464,905,500	71,921,000	5,674,600	476,598,800	51,621,100
December 31	437,722,000	75,968,300	5,554,600	444,589,400	42,018,600

Railroads.—The heavy traffic over the grain-carrying roads, which was a noticeable feature at the end of 1891, continued with few interruptions during the first half of 1892; but in the last six months, when the new crops began to move, earnings did not show a very marked increase, mainly for the reason that comparison was made with the heavy traffic in the last six months of 1891. Complaint was general of low rates on competitive business, which kept net earnings down to a small percentage of the gross receipts, and this led to propositions for pooling business in such a way as not to conflict with the interstate law; but as an amendment of that law, to permit pooling, was discussed after Congress assembled, the consideration of the scheme by the railroads was abandoned. The Western Traffic Association was dissolved Oct. 11, in consequence of the withdrawal of the Chicago, Burlington and Quincy. One important event of the year was the decision in August, by Judge McCormick, sitting as a circuit judge in Galveston, Texas, against the power of the State railroad commissioners to fix rates below a reasonable limit. The Reading coal combination was formed in February, embracing the Central New Jersey, the Port Reading, and the Lehigh Valley Railroads. A bill was passed by the New Jersey Legislature in March to legalize the combination, but this bill failed to become a law. In August, Chancellor McGill, of New Jersey, decided against the validity of the lease of the Central New Jersey to the Port Reading, and by the end of the year this road and the Lehigh and Wilkesbarre Coal Company were withdrawn from the Reading combination. Unsuccessful attempts were made to reorganize the Richmond and West Point Terminal Company, and in June this corporation, the Richmond and Danville, and the East Tennessee, Virginia and Georgia Railroads were placed in the hands of receivers. On Oct. 26 the Boston and Maine passed under the control of the Reading, and friends of the latter, having bought control of the New York and New England, proposed that this road be made a link connecting the two systems. Railroad construction was discouraged by the aggressive course pursued by railroad commissioners and Legislatures of several of the Western States, and also by the low rates made compulsory by the operation of the interstate commerce law. The South was depressed during the first half of the year by reason of the low price of cotton, and the railroad situation there did not improve later in the year. In the State of Washington the largest number of miles of track was laid, 351 miles having been built for the Pacific extension of the Great Northern. Other long lines were in Ohio, in the Indian Territory, and in Wyoming. Toward the end of the year all the principal lines of the country were actively engaged increasing their equipment and improving the road in anticipation of a heavy traffic during the Columbian Exposition at Chicago. The table below shows gross and net earnings of the principal trunk lines:

During 1891 Florida expended $564,304.65 for school purposes, while in 1890 the expenditure was $516,532.70. The counties raised $50,578.87 more by taxation for school purposes in 1891 than in 1890. The population of Florida at the last census was 391,422, and the number of schools in operation last year was 2,348, 1 schoolhouse for every 167 people.

State Superintendent Albert J. Russell, the State Teachers' Association, the county superintendents, and the teachers and pupils, have matured plans by which the school exhibit at the Columbian Exhibition will be representative of the best work done in the State.

ROADS.	1886–'87.	1887–'88.	1888–'89.	1889–'90.	1890–'91.	1891–'92.
PENNSYLVANIA:						
Gross earnings	$55,671,313	$58,172,077	$61,514,445	$66,202,260	$67,426,841	$68,841,845
Net earnings	18,584,728	18,840,925	20,417,640	21,221,706	21,479,396	20,022,468
NEW YORK CENTRAL:						
Gross earnings	35,297,055	36,192,920	35,696,286	37,008,403	37,902,114	45,478,625
Net earnings	12,908,482	8,872,299	9,422,858	12,516,274	12,581,262	14,389,512
ERIE:						
Gross earnings	24,210,358	24,882,819	24,505,273	26,454,834	27,503,638	28,638,740
Net earnings	6,819,085	6,929,350	6,740,848	6,948,882	7,259,698	8,202,801
BALTIMORE AND OHIO:						
Gross earnings	20,659,036	20,353,492	21,303,002	24,412,096	24,530,395	26,084,168
Net earnings	6,588,905	6,152,930	6,492,158	7,445,226	7,452,162	7,488,366

FLORIDA, a Southern State, admitted to the Union, March 3, 1845; area, 58,680 square miles. The population, according to each decennial census since admission, was 87,445 in 1850; 140,424 in 1860; 187,748 in 1870; 269,493 in 1880; and 391,422 in 1890. Capital, Tallahassee.

Government.—The following were the State officers during the year: Governor, Francis P. Fleming, Democrat; Secretary of State, John L. Crawford; Comptroller, William D. Bloxham; Treasurer, Frank J. Pons; Attorney-General, William B. Lamar; Superintendent of Public Instruction, Albert J. Russell; Commissioner of Agriculture, Lucius B. Wombwell; State Board of Health. Richard P. Daniel, William B. Henderson, William K. Hyer; Chief Justice of the Supreme Court, George P. Raney; Associate Justices, Milton H. Mabry and R. F. Taylor.

Education.—The number of youth from six to twenty-one years of age, according to the census of 1892, was 144,017; in 1888 it was 113,647, showing an increase of 30,370. The census heretofore has been taken by the assessors of taxes; in this instance it was taken by school supervisors, under the direction of the county superintendents. The number of white youth is 79,669; the number of negro youth is 64,348. In the census of 1884 the number of white youth in excess of that of negro youth was 1,875, while the number in excess in 1892 is 15,321—an increase of white youth over negro youth since 1884 of 13,246. Leon County has the largest number of pupils of any county, aggregating 10,000, white and colored. There are of the blind of school age 42, and deaf mutes 130; for these the State provides an excellent school, in which they are being clothed, fed, and educated during the school year of eight months. There are 19,798 half orphans, and 2,930 orphans.

During the past decade the value of school sites and buildings in Florida has increased $407,381.07. The public schools now require 2,641 teachers, and there are 2,348 schoolhouses.

Taxes.—The value of property, with gross amount of State taxes, assessed for the year 1891, including licenses and amount of auction tax, was as follows: Total value of real estate, personal property, railroads, and telegraphs, $97,547,004.91; general revenue, $414,780.34; general school tax, $97,598.06; Board of Health tax, $24,634.37; State purposes (license tax not included), $537,013.37; license tax, $163,619.25; county revenue, $305,872.44; county school tax, $485,954.68; county road tax, $98,039.62; county special tax, $104,735.27; total taxes for county purposes, $994,602.01.

The taxes for 1891 were assessed under the revenue law in force Jan. 1, 1891, and completed by the warrant prescribed by that law being attached to the assessment roll. That warrant is now modified by those provisions of chapter 4011, Laws of Florida, which became operative on Jan. 1, 1892. These provisions were found in sections 1, 2, 3 of chapter 4011. No lands can be sold for taxes after the first day of January, 1892. Collectors should receive moneys for taxes on lands until the first Monday in April, 1892. On the first Monday in April, 1892, collectors are directed by the law to close their books, and not to receive further moneys that may remain due for taxes on lands. Within thirty days after the first Monday in April, 1892, lists and certificates of all the lands upon which taxes have not been paid have to be forwarded to the Comptroller. Taxes on personal property must be collected in accordance with sections 44 and 45 of chapter 4010, Laws of Florida. Personal property can not be sold for the payment of taxes assessed against lands; nor can the taxes on personal property be included in the certificates of unpaid taxes on lands. Personal property must be responsible for taxes assessed against personal property, and real estate must be responsible for taxes assessed against real estate.

On Feb. 11, Attorney-General Lamar filed with Gov. Fleming an opinion to the effect that soft phosphates were liable to taxation, and subject to the provisions of chapter 3858, Laws of Florida. The grounds for his decision were that phosphates are not, properly speaking, "marls," and that phosphoric acid, an important element in all fertilizers, and present in these, is specially designated for examination and estimates. The wide use of phosphates as fertilizers precludes the idea that the Legislature meant to include them under the word "marl."

The Supreme Court, in June, gave the following decision, materially modifying section 7, chapter 4011, Laws of Florida: Any purchaser at a tax sale made prior to Aug. 5, 1891, or any person who purchased a tax certificate from the State through the Comptroller's office prior to Aug. 5, 1891, or the assignee of said purchaser, is entitled to a tax deed after the expiration of one year from the date of the tax sale, as shown by the date of the certificate. On the presentation, therefore (after one year from its date), of a tax certificate purchased prior to Aug. 5, 1891, the holder, under the decision of the court, is entitled to a tax deed in accordance with section 57, chapter 3681, Laws of Florida; approved June 7, 1887.

As section 7, chapter 4011, Laws of Florida, went into effect on Aug. 5, 1891, all tax certificates sold after that period are subject to its provisions, and no tax deed can issue upon a certificate purchased after that date, for the period of two years from said Aug. 5, 1891.

Valuations.—The assessment rolls for 1891 show the following property as assessed: Acres, 24,721,296; acres improved and cultivated, 913,562; valuation (except town and city lots) of all improvements, $42,881,184; valuation of town and city lots and all improvements, $21,692,111; aggregate value of telegraph lines, $191,618.95; number of horses, asses, and mules, 45,191; neat stocks and cattle, 455,223; sheep and goats, 119,994; swine and hogs, 216,131; cash value of animals, $5,366,145; personal property, except animals, $11,649,290; value of personal property, $17,015,435; value of real estate, $64,573,295; value of railways, railroads, and rolling stock, $15,766,656.06.

Appropriations.—In the new appropriation bill for river and harbor improvement, Florida's share is as follows: Cumberland Sound, $112,000; Appalachicola Bay, $20,000; Pensacola, $75,000; Tampa Bay, $10,000; Key West, $75,000; St. Augustine, $10,000; Choctawhatchee river, $12,500; St. Johns, from Jacksonville to ocean, $150,000; Appalachicola river, $5,000; Caloosahatchee, $1,000; Escambia and Conechin, $8,000; Manatee, $6,000; Suwanee, $3,000; Volusia bar, $10,000; Ocklawaha river, $1,000; Sarasota Bay, $2,500.

The Columbian Exhibition.—The Florida World's Fair Directory met at Pensacola on Jan. 11, 1892, and $32,000 was reported as secured. Six ladies were added to the board, and resolutions passed that the county commissioners of the State be requested to meet in convention at Tallahassee on Feb. 17, 1892; and that Gov. Fleming be asked to issue an official notice of the meeting. On Jan. 18 Gov. Fleming addressed an open letter to the county commissioners of Florida, calling them to the convention at Tallahassee to discuss the best means of promoting the interest of the State at the World's Columbian Exhibition, and 92 county commissioners from 29 out of the 45 counties of the State responded. A committee of 3 from each geographical division of the State, and 2 from the directory, was appointed. The roll of the counties was called, and the commissioners expressed themselves upon the question of taxing their people, in three-minute talks, with the following result: Opposed, 10; in favor, 2; if legal, 5; left to the people, 4; voluntary contributions, 1; if others agree, 2; expression withheld, 3; divided, 2. Various resolutions were offered, that of Capt. Houston being accepted. He proposed that the question of making appropriations be referred to the people themselves at primary elections to be held in March. By April so little money had been raised that the commissioners were compelled to return their subscriptions, it having been provided by the convention that if $50,000 of the authorized $100,000 were not raised by April 1, 1892, the directors should return to the subscribers their subscriptions, less 10 per cent. which they were authorized to spend for expenses. The board not having secured this minimum, a resolution was adopted at Tampa, on March 23, directing that all subscriptions be returned in full, without reserving any percentage, for the members of the directory have themselves paid the expenses incurred in their efforts to secure a creditable exhibit at the World's Fair. The directory, however, retained their organization in order to see what better means for promoting the interests of the State might be adopted. On July 2, Arthur C. Jackson, State World's Fair Commissioner, published an earnest appeal to the people, calling on them for $50,000 to erect the State building at Chicago, and offering each county, as inducement to subscription, space in the 100,000 copies of the official State "Gazetteer" equal to the amount paid for space in the State building, on the basis of $200 per page.

Board of Trade.—The Tallahassee Board of Trade was permanently organized on April 9, its object being to advance the trade, business, and commerce, and promote the general prosperity and material interests of the city of Tallahassee and the county of Leon, Florida. The board has particularly in view the permanent establishment of the tobacco industry in all its branches.

Pension Bill.—In January, Senator Samuel Pasco introduced into Congress a bill, which was finally approved on July 27, for the granting of pensions to the surviving officers and enlisted men who served for thirty days in the Black Hawk War, the Creek War, the Cherokee disturbances, or the Florida war with the Seminole Indians, embracing a period from 1832-'42. Pensions under this act are at the rate of $8 a month, and payable from and after the passage of the act, for and during the natural lives of the persons entitled thereto. This act does not apply to persons already receiving pensions at $8 a month.

Phosphates.—The discovery of large deposits of phosphates in the State has had a stimulating effect upon business, caused emigrations in large numbers from one part of the State to the other, and the investment of much foreign capital.

Political.—The People's party met at Ocala on Feb. 8, perfecting the first organization of its kind in Florida. Delegates were elected to attend the St. Louis Convention on Feb. 22, and the convention adjourned to meet in Ocala on the second Tuesday in March.

The resolutions refer to both the old parties as being in league with Wall Street, and declare that they will never favor the Ocala demands, or adopt laws by which every man in the country can enjoy the fruits of his labor. "Therefore we pledge ourselves not to affiliate with or support the party or men who will not indorse the Ocala platform, or that enacted in May, 1891, at Cincinnati by the People's party, but will await the action of the St. Louis conference on Feb. 22 before further action in the organization is taken."

The Republican State Convention met at Tallahassee on April 13, and 212 delegates were present, half of whom were white. No ticket of any kind was nominated. A platform was adopted which approved the administration of President Harrison, and his renomination was recommended. The McKinley bill and the Reed rules were approved, and the inability of the Fifty-first Congress to enact the Lodge bill, or some other election law that would secure to the people their rights under the Constitution and maintain the integrity and dignity of the nation, was deplored. The Democratic rule in Florida was denounced as "a long-studied plan to rob the majority of its liberty." The Florida election laws, the reckless expenditure of public money, the system of leasing convicts to the highest bidder, the lynch law as an outgrowth of Democratic misrule, were all condemned, and recommendations for the remedy of these several evils were made.

The Democratic State Convention met at Tampa on Wednesday, June 1, and the following ticket was nominated : For Governor, Henry L. Mitchell ; for Justice of the Supreme Court, R. Fenwick Taylor ; for Secretary of State, John L. Crawford ; for Attorney-General, William B. Lamar ; for Comptroller, William D. Bloxham ; for Treasurer, Clarence B. Collins ; for Superintendent of Public Instruction, W. N. Sheats ; for Commissioner of Agriculture, Lucius B. Wombwell.

In the platform adopted the fundamental doctrines of the National Convention of 1888 at Chicago were reaffirmed, a liberal policy on the part of the General Government in the matter of public improvements was advocated, and the right of the South to demand this policy was upheld "until her water ways and harbors are adjusted to the needs of commerce to the same extent as other sections of the country." The party pledged itself to redress the grievances of the agricultural classes of the State, laboring then under heavy burdens, and demanded for their benefit a financial reform which should relieve the existing agricultural depression. Immigration to the State was encouraged. After denouncing the McKinley and Federal elections bills, the following demands were made:

That Congress shall pass such laws as shall effectually prevent the dealing in futures of all agricultural and mechanical productions, providing such stringent system of procedure in trials as shall secure prompt conviction, and imposing such penalties as shall secure the most perfect compliance with the law.

Unlimited coinage of silver.

Abolition of the national banks, and the substitution of legal-tender Treasury notes in lieu of national-bank notes, issued in sufficient volume to do the business of the country on a cash system, regulating the amount needed on a *per capita* basis, as the business interests of the country expand ; and that all money issued by the Government shall be legal tender in payment of all debts, both private and public ; and we also demand the repeal of all laws imposing a tax and other restrictions upon the State banking system.

That the amount of the circulating medium be speedily increased to not less than $50 per capita. A graduated income tax.

The control by the Government of the railroads was recommended, "transportation being a means of exchange and a public necessity."

At the State elections, held Oct. 4, the entire Democratic ticket was successful. The total vote of the State for Governor was 40,078, of which Mr. Mitchell, the Democratic candidate, received 31,887, and Mr. Baskins, the third-party candidate, received 8,191.

The presidential vote at the November elections was as follows: For the Democratic electors, 30,143 ; for the Weaver electors, 4,845.

FRANCE, a republic in western Europe. The republican form of government was established on Sept. 4, 1870, after the overthrow of the third empire. The Constitution, adopted on Feb. 25, 1875, and ratified on June 16, 1875, was revised in parts in June, 1879, August, 1884, June, 1885, and July, 1889. The legislative power is exercised by the Chamber of Deputies and the Senate, which unite in a Congress or National Assembly every seven years for the purpose of electing a President of the Republic. The National Assembly, thus constituted, has power also to amend the organic law, and by the action of the individual Chambers may be convoked for that purpose. In case of a vacancy in the presidency, the two houses meet immediately to elect a new President. The President appoints the Cabinet ministers from the members of the Chambers, nominates all civil and military officers, is charged with the execution of the laws, and has power to conclude treaties, but not to declare war without the consent of both chambers. With the assent of the Senate he can dissolve the Chamber of Deputies. The Deputies are elected for four years by the suffrage of all male citizens who have lived in one commune for six months previous to the election. Each *arrondissement* forms an electoral district and elects one Deputy, except such as have over 100,000 inhabitants, which are divided into two constituencies. Until 1876, and again in 1885–'89, the Deputies for each department were elected on a collective ticket. When the district system was reintroduced in 1889, a provision was enacted also which prohibits a person from being a candidate in more than one constituency in the same election. The right of deciding in cases of contested seats was taken away from the Chamber and vested in local electoral commissions. The Chamber has 584 members, and the Senate 300. The Senators are elected for nine years by delegates chosen by the Municipal Councils of the communes acting with the Deputies and the members of the councils-general and district councils for each department. Deputies receive 9,000 francs a year, Senators 15,000 francs, and the President 600,000 francs, with an equal sum to defray expenses incident to the post.

The President of the French Republic is Marie François Sadi Carnot, born in Limoges in 1837, who was elected Dec. 3, 1887. The ministers in the beginning of 1892 were as follow : President of the Council and Minister of War, Charles de Freycinet ; Minister of Foreign Affairs, M. Ribot ; Minister of Finance, M. Rouvier ; Minister of Public Instruction and Fine Arts, M. Bourgeois ; Minister of Justice and Public Worship, M. Fallières ; Minister of Marine, Vice-Admiral Barbey ; Minister of Public Works, M. Ives Guyot ; Minister of Agriculture, M. Develle ; Minister of Commerce, Jules Roche ; Minister of the Interior, M. Constans.

Area and Population.—The following table gives the area of the 87 departments (including the territory of Belfort) into which France is divided, and their population as ascertained by the census of 1891, compared with the returns of the last preceding census :

DEPARTMENTS.	Square miles.	LEGAL POPULATION.	
		May 31, 1886.	April 12, 1891.
Ain	2,239	364,408	356,907
Aisne	2,839	555,925	545,493
Allier	2,822	424,582	424,382
Alpes (Basses-)	2,685	129,494	124,285
Alpes (Hautes-)	2,153	122,924	115,522
Alpes-Maritimes	1,482	238,057	258,571
Ardèche	2,136	375,472	371,269
Ardennes	2,020	332,759	324,923
Ariège	1,890	237,619	227,491
Aube	2,317	257,374	255,548
Aude	2,438	332,090	317,372
Aveyron	3,376	415,826	400,467
Belfort	235	79,758	83,670
Bouches-du-Rhône	1,971	604,857	630,622
Calvados	2,132	437,627	428,925
Cantal	2,217	241,742	239,601
Charente	2,294	366,408	360,259
Charente-Inférieure	2,635	462,803	456,202
Cher	2,780	355,349	359,276
Corrèze	2,265	326,494	328,119
Corse	3,377	278,501	288,596
Côte-d'Or	3,383	381,574	376,866
Côtes-du-Nord	2,659	628,256	618,652
Creuse	2,150	284,942	284,660
Dordogne	3,546	492,205	478,471
Doubs	2,018	310,083	308,081
Drôme	2,518	314,615	306,419
Eure	2,300	358,529	349,471
Eure-et-Loir	2,268	283,719	284,683
Finistère	2,595	707,820	727,012
Gard	2,253	417,099	419,388
Garonne (Haute-)	2,429	481,169	472,383
Gers	2,425	274,391	261,084
Gironde	3,761	775,845	793,528
Hérault	2,393	489,044	461,651
Ille-et-Vilaine	2,597	621,384	626,875
Indre	2,624	296,147	292,868
Indre-et-Loire	2,361	340,921	337,298
Isère	3,201	581,680	572,145
Jura	1,928	281,292	273,028
Landes	3,599	302,266	297,842
Loir-et-Cher	2,452	279,214	280,358
Loire	1,838	608,384	616,227
Loire (Haute-)	1,916	320,063	316,735
Loire-Inférieure	2,654	643,884	645,263
Loiret	2,614	374,875	377,718
Lot	2,012	271,514	258,885
Lot-et-Garonne	2,067	307,437	295,360
Lozère	1,996	141,264	135,527
Maine-et-Loire	2,749	527,680	518,589
Manche	2,289	520,865	513,815
Marne	3,159	429,494	434,692
Marne (Haute-)	2,402	247,781	243,533
Mayenne	1,996	340,063	332,887
Meurthe-et-Moselle	2,025	481,693	444,150
Meuse	2,405	291,971	292,253

DEPARTMENTS.	Square miles.	LEGAL POPULATION.	
		May 31, 1886.	April 12, 1891.
Morbihan	2,625	535,256	544,470
Nièvre	2,632	347,645	343,581
Nord	2,193	1,670,184	1,786,841
Oise	2,261	403,146	401,835
Orne	2,354	367,248	354,387
Pas-de-Calais	2,551	856,526	874,364
Puy-de-Dôme	3,070	570,964	564,266
Pyrénées (Basses-)	2,943	432,999	425,027
Pyrénées (Hautes-)	1,749	234,825	225,861
Pyrénées-Orientales	1,592	211,187	210,125
Rhône	1,077	772,912	806,737
Saône (Haute-)	2,062	290,954	280,856
Saône-et-Loire	3,302	625,885	619,523
Sarthe	2,396	436,111	429,737
Savoie	2,224	267,428	263,297
Savoie (Haute-)	1,667	275,018	268,267
Seine	180·6	2,961,089	3,141,595
Seine-Inférieure	2,330	832,886	839,876
Seine-et-Marne	2,215	355,136	356,709
Seine-et-Oise	2,164	618,089	628,590
Sèvres (Deux)	2,317	353,766	354,252
Somme	2,379	548,982	546,495
Tarn	2,217	358,757	346,739
Tarn-et-Garonne	1,436	214,046	206,596
Var	2,349	288,689	288,336
Vaucluse	1,370	241,787	235,411
Vendée	2,588	434,808	442,855
Vienne	2,691	342,785	344,355
Vienne (Haute-)	2,130	363,182	372,878
Vosges	2,266	413,707	410,196
Yonne	2,868	355,364	344,688
Total	204,092	38,218,903	38,343,192

The population given comprises the legal residents, whether present or not. The population actually present in 1891 was 38,095,156, and in 1886 it was 37,886,566. There was a decrease of the legal population in 55 departments, and in 32 an increase. The number of marriages in 1890 was 269,332 ; of births, 838,059 ; of deaths, 876,-505 ; excess of deaths, 38,446, compared with an excess of 85,520 births in 1889. The number of arrondissements in 1891 was 362 ; of cantons, 2,881 ; of communes, 36,144. There are only 232 communes with more than 10,000 inhabitants. The aggregate population of the 56 towns having more than 30,000 was 6,862,822 in 1891, an increase of 340,396 in five years. These towns and their population were as follow : Paris, 2,447,957 ; Lyons, 416,029 ; Marseilles, 403,749 ; Bordeaux, 252,415 ; Lille, 201,211 ; Toulouse, 149,791 ; St. Étienne, 133,443 ; Nantes, 122,750 ; Havre. 116,369 ; Roubaix, 114,917 ; Rouen, 112,-352 ; Rheims, 104,186 ; Nice, 88,273 ; Nancy, 87,-110 ; Amiens, 83,654 ; Toulon, 77,747 ; Brest, 75,-854 ; Limoges, 72,697 ; Angers, 72,669 ; Nimes, 71,623 ; Montpellier, 69,258 ; Rennes, 69,232 ; Tourcoing, 65,477 ; Dijon, 65,428 ; Orléans, 63,-705 ; Grenoble, 60,439 ; Tours, 60,335 ; Le Mans, 57,412 ; Calais, 56,867 ; Besançon, 56,055 ; Versailles, 51,679 ; St. Denis, 50,992 ; Troyes, 50,330 ; Clermont-Ferrand, 50,119 ; St. Quentin, 47,551 ; Béziers, 45,475 : Bourges, 45,342 ; Boulogne, 45,-205 ; Caen, 45,201 ; Avignon, 43,453 ; Lorient, 42,116 : Levallois-Perret, 39,857 ; Dunkirk, 39,-498 ; Cherbourg, 38,554 : Poitiers, 37,497 ; Angoulême, 36,690 ; Cette, 36,541 ; Perpignan, 33,878 ; Rochefort, 33,334 ; Boulogne-sur-Seine, 32,569 ; Pau, 32,111 ; Perigueux, 31,439 : Roanne, 31,380 ; St. Nazaire, 30,935 ; Clichy, 30,608 : Laval, 30,-374. The number of foreigners in France in 1891 was 1,101,728, compared with 1,126,531 in 1886. The number of elementary schools in 1889 was 86,030, including 17,006 private schools.

The number of children in attendance was 5,589,-428, exceeding the number of children in the country between the ages of six and thirteen, which in 1890 was 4,729,511. In the secondary schools 90,908 pupils were taught in 1889.

Commerce.—The total value of the general commerce in 1890 was 5,452,000,000 francs for imports and 4,840,000,000 francs for exports. The special imports, comprising goods entered for home consumption, were 4,437,000,000 francs in value, and the special exports, consisting of the products of French industry and agriculture, were 3,753,000,000 francs. Of the special imports, 1,445,000,000 francs represent food products, 2,342,000,000 francs raw materials, and 650,-000,000 francs manufactured articles. Of the special exports, 855,000,000 francs were food products, 899,000,000 francs raw products, and 1,999,000,000 francs manufactured goods. The values of the principal imports in the special trade of 1890 were as follow: Cereals, 364,000,-000 francs; wine, 350,000,000 francs; wool, 337,-000,000 francs; coal, 248,000,000 francs; raw silk, 240,000,000 francs; hides and furs, 211,000,-000 francs; raw cotton, 206,000,000 francs; oil seeds, 192,000,000 francs; timber, 158,000,000 francs; coffee, 156,000,000 francs; fruits, 83,000,-000 francs; cattle, 69,000,000 francs; woolen manufactures, 67,000,000 francs; silk manufactures, 64,000,000 francs; flax, 58,000,000 francs; sugar, 46,000,000 francs; cotton manufactures, 41,000,000 francs. The chief domestic exports and their values were as follow: Woolen manufactures, 361,000,000 francs; silk manufactures, 274,000,000 francs; wine, 269,000,000 francs; fancy articles, 155,000,000 francs; leather manufactures, 146,000,000 francs; raw silk and silk yarn, 125,000,000 francs; linen manufactures, 125,000,000 francs; raw wool and woolen yarn, 121,000,000 francs; cheese and butter, 118,000,-000 francs; leather, 112,000,000 francs; cotton manufactures, 110,000,000 francs; metal manufactures and implements, 89,000,000 francs; skins and furs, 76,000,000 francs; spirits, 71,000,-000 francs; refined sugar, 62,000,000 francs; chemical products, 50,000,000 francs.

The commerce with the principal countries is shown in the following table, which gives the special imports from and the exports of domestic merchandise to each of them for 1890:

COUNTRIES.	Imports.	Exports.
Great Britain	626,000,000	1,026,000,000
Belgium	500,000,000	588,000,000
Germany	351,000,000	342,000,000
United States	317,000,000	329,000,000
Spain	354,000,000	153,000,000
Algeria	208,000,000	195,000,000
Argentine Republic	210,000,000	103,000,000
Italy	122,000,000	150,000,000
Switzerland	....	243,000,000
British India	210,000,000	....
Russia	195,000,000	....

Navigation.—The number of vessels entered at the ports of France during 1890 was 100,238, of 20,291,949 tons, of which 82,251, of 18,690,537 tons, were with cargoes, and 17,987, of 1,601,412 tons, came in ballast. The total number cleared was 101,037, of 20,691,445 tons, of which 76,161, of 14,669,262 tons, sailed with cargoes, and 24,-876, of 6,022,183 tons, in ballast. Of the vessels entered, 21,755, of 9,801,803 tons, were foreign,

8,834, of 4,482,373 tons, were French vessels in the foreign trade, and 69,649, of 6,007,773 tons, were French vessels in the coasting trade. Of those cleared, 22,632, of 9,911,166 tons, were foreign vessels, 9,356, of 4,772,506 tons, were French vessels engaged in foreign commerce, and 69,649, of 6,007,773 tons, were French vessels in the coasting trade.

The commercial navy on Jan. 1, 1891, numbered 14,001 sailing vessels, of 444,092 tons, with 68,625 men in their crews, and 1,110 steam vessels, of 499,921 tons, employing 13,799 men. Of the sailing vessels, 270, of 31,093 tons, were engaged in the European trade, and of the steamers, 243, of 153,317 tons, while 392 sailing vessels, of 163,901 tons, and 189 steamers, of 308,851 tons, were engaged in long-voyage navigation.

Railroads.—The railroads in 1891 had a total length of 33,547 kilometres, not including 3,150 kilometres of local roads. The state owns 2,628 kilometres. The gross receipts in 1890 were 1,127,600,000 francs. In 1889 the gross revenue was 1,144,400,000 francs, and the expenses 588,-800,000 francs, leaving a net revenue of 555,600,-000 francs. The number of passengers carried was 244,164,701 in 1889, and the freight traffic was 87,043,706 tons.

Posts and Telegraphs.—In 1889 there passed through the post office 710,600,000 letters, 22,-000,000 registered letters, 45,300,000 postal cards, 472,400,000 newspapers and periodicals, 34,900,-000 samples, 458,400,000 printed inclosures and manuscripts, and 26,100,000 money orders, of the aggregate amount of 756,500,000 francs. The internal traffic was 588,900,000 ordinary letters, 18,800,000 registered letters, 41,500,000 postal cards, 399,800,000 journals, 27,400,000 samples, 433,500,000 circulars, etc., and 24,500,000 postal orders, of the value of 678,900,000 francs. The telegraph lines in the beginning of 1890 had a total length of 96,632 kilometres, with 305,460 kilometres of wire. In Paris there are 237 kilometres of pneumatic tubes. The messages in 1889 numbered 35,400,000, of which 28,900,000 were domestic and 6,500,000 international.

The Army.—Every Frenchman not found unfit physically is liable to service from the age of twenty to that of forty-five in the active army or the reserves. The term in the active army is three, in the active army reserve six, in the territorial army ten, and the territorial reserve ten years. France is divided into 18 military regions, under the command of generals of division, and the military regions into districts corresponding to the political departments, each under a general of brigade. Paris, the central citadel, and Lyons, secondary principal strong place, are under separate military administrations. The wall of fortifications surrounding Paris has 97 bastions, with 17 old and 38 new forts, so disposed as to form intrenched camps at Versailles and St. Denis. The first-class fortresses of Belfort, Verdun, and Briançon on the German frontier are supplemented by Langres, by the third-class fortresses of Toul and Auxonne, and by 9 fourth-class fortresses. On the Belgian frontier, Lille, Dunkirk, Arras, and Douai are first-class, Cambrai, Valenciennes, Givet, St. Omer, Mézières, Sedan, Longuy, and Soissons are second-class, and Gravelines, Condé, Landrécies, Rocroi, Montmédy, and Peronne third-class fortresses, besides which there are 6 fourth-class forts. The Italian frontier is protected by first-class strong places at Lyons, Grenoble, and Besançon, and by 11 other forts. On the Spanish frontier there are first-class fortresses at Perpignan and Bayonne, third-class fortresses at St. Jean and Pied-de-port, and 10 of the fourth class. The seaboard fortifications are the naval harbor at Toulon, Antibes, and 21 fourth-class forts on the Mediterranean; Rochefort, Brest, and Lorient as first-class fortresses on the Atlantic coast, Oléron, La Rochelle, and Belle Isle of the second-class, Ile de Rhé and Fort Louis of the third-class, and 17 fourth-class forts; and on the Channel a first-class fortress at Cherbourg, second-class fortresses at St. Malo and Havre, and 16 subsidiary forts.

The active army, according to the budget of 1892, consisted of 570,603 men, including 28,107 officers, with 138,990 horses. There was an increase of 7,927 men and 1,229 horses over the figures for the preceding year. The distribution of the forces and the strength of the several arms, including officers and men, is shown in the following table:

DESCRIPTION OF TROOPS.	France.	Algeria.	Tunis.	Total.
General staff.........	4,010	361	68	4,439
Military schools......	3,351	......	......	3,351
Unclassed...........	2,350	810	109	3,269
Army corps.				
Infantry............	293,260	37,130	8,318	338,708
Administrative.......	11,926	3,454	521	15,901
Cavalry............	65,683	8,259	1,847	75,789
Artillery...........	76,110	2,721	703	79,534
Engineers..........	11,021	747	325	12,093
Train..............	7,591	3,134	1,034	11,759
Total army corps...	465,591	55,445	12,748	533,784
Total active army..	475,302	56,616	12,925	544,843
Gendarmerie.........	21,501	1,058	153	22,712
Garde Républicaine...	3,048	......	......	3,048
Grand total......	499,851	57,674	13,078	570,603

The total includes 3,618 officers of the general staff, 659 in the military schools, 2,757 unattached among the troops, 11,971 in the infantry, 3,804 in the cavalry, 3,719 in the artillery, 434 in the engineers, 412 in the train, 651 in the gendarmerie, and 82 in the Garde Républicaine, making 28,107 altogether, of whom 27,374 are in the active army. Deducting the sick and absent, the effective strength of the active army in 1892 was 499,483, and of the gendarmerie and Garde Républicaine 25,501. The territorial army consists of 37,000 officers and 579,000 men. The total war strength of the republic is about 2,500,000 men, counting only the soldiers of the active army and the various classes of reserve. About half as many more untrained able-bodied men could be called out as a last resort.

The Navy.—The effective navy consists of 393 vessels. The seagoing armor-clad vessels number 32, of which 17 are of steel or iron and steel, and the rest mostly of wood plated with iron. They include 14 barbette ships, 7 vessels with a central battery, 4 turret ships, 5 barbette cruisers, and 2 broadside ships. The "Amiral Baudin," "Formidable," and "Amiral Duperré" have from 21 to 22 inches of armor at the water line, engines developing 8,000 horse powers or more, a displacement from 10,900 to 11,380 tons, an average speed of 19 knots, and each has an armament of 3 or 4 guns with a caliber of 14¾ inches and 12 or 14 5½-inch guns. The "Caïman," "Indomptable," and "Terrible" have 19¾ inches of armor, a displacement of 7,100 tons, and carry each 2 16½-inch and 4 4-inch guns. The "Requin" is more heavily armored and armed, carrying 2 heavy guns of 16½-inch, 2 of 10¾-inch, and 4 of 4-inch caliber. The other barbette armor-clads range from 5,780 to 7,650 tons, with 8¾ or 10 inches of armor, and each carries 4 guns of either 10⅝- or 9⅜-inch bore, and from 7 to 12 smaller guns, on the larger vessels of 9⅜ and 5½, and on the smaller 7⅝ and 5½ inches caliber. The central-battery ships range from 8,650 to 9,500 tons, and armor 14 to 15½ inches thick on 3 and 8¾ inches on the others. The 2 heaviest have each 4 13⅜- and 4 10⅝-inch guns, with 6 5½-inch cannon, and the rest carry 8 10⅝-inch guns each, with 6 or 8 of smaller caliber. The turret ships have 18 inches of armor over vulnerable parts, and each has a displacement of 10,580 tons and engines of 7,000 horse powers, with a speed of 16 knots for the slowest and 17 knots for the fastest. One is armed with 2 guns of 13½-inch, 2 of 10½-inch, and 20 of 5½-inch caliber; 1 with 4 guns of 13½-inch and 19 of 5½-inch caliber; and the other 2 carry 4 13½-inch and 17 5½-inch guns each. The barbette cruisers, plated with 6-inch armor, have a displacement of from 3,560 to 4,600 tons, and carry 10 to 14 guns each, of which the lightest have a bore of 4¾ and the heaviest of 9⅜ inches. The armor-clad vessels for coast defense comprise 2 barbette ships, with 17¾ inches of armor, each mounting 2 guns of 13⅜-inch caliber; 8 turret ships, carrying mostly 9⅜- or 10⅝-inch guns; and 2 turret and 4 barbette gun vessels. There are 12 deck-protected cruisers, of which the 5 lightest, armed with 2 guns of 5½-inch caliber, can make 19½ knots; 1, carrying 6 guns of 6½-inch caliber, can make 20 knots; the heaviest, having a displacement of 6,950 tons and engines of 10,330 horse powers, carries 10 6½-inch and 10 5½-inch guns; and the next heaviest, with a displacement of 5,680 tons and a speed of 20 knots, has the same armament. The vessels under construction in 1891 were 11 sea-going armor-clads, 2 armor-clads for coast defense, 2 seagoing deck-protected cruisers, 3 torpedo cruisers, 5 torpedo dispatch vessels, and 54 torpedo boats. The completed torpedo flotilla consisted of 4 torpedo cruisers, 8 torpedo dispatch vessels, 4 seagoing torpedo boats, 12 first-class, 67 second-class, and 43 third-class torpedo boats, 7 small torpedo boats, and 1 submarine boat.

Finances.—The estimated revenue for 1892 was 3,780,077,692 francs, including 107,322,133 francs entered *pour ordre* and 454,351,426 francs from special resources, or, without these, 3,218,404,133 francs; deducting further 12,176,945 francs of exceptional receipts and 60,609,550 francs of *recettes d'ordre*, the total ordinary receipts amount to 3,145,617,638 francs, of which 472,729,708 francs come from direct taxes, 1,928,618,400 francs from indirect taxes, 619,523,820 francs from state monopolies, 44,714,780 francs from domains and forests, and 26,030,930 francs from various sources. The land tax is estimated at 111,658,768 francs; the tax on buildings, 71,-899,800 francs; the tax on personal property, 82,328,960 francs; the tax on doors and windows, 53,781,280 francs; trade licenses, 113,666,-000 francs; the tax for notices, 622,500 francs; taxes on horses and carriages and other special taxes, 29,963,100 francs; direct taxes of Algeria, 8,808,700 francs; registration fees, 538,224,600 francs; stamps, 169,678,300 francs; customs, 415,341,700 francs; sugar duty, 181,000,000 francs; excise duties and other indirect taxes, 590,572,600 francs; indirect taxes of Algeria, 20,067,900 francs.

The rectified budget estimates for 1891 made the total ordinary revenue 3,077,182,185 francs, and the grand total 3,713,385,754 francs. The land tax for 1891 was estimated at 111,657,686 francs; building tax, 71,251,080 francs; personal-property tax, 81,640,800 francs; door and window tax, 53,285,600 francs; trade licenses, 111,-648,000 francs; tax on notices, 628,500 francs; carriage and special taxes, 29,662,700 francs; direct taxes of Algeria, 9,114,300 francs; registration, 505,502,741 francs; stamps, 163,969,011 francs; customs, 375,321,631 francs; excise and other indirect taxes, 617,575,148 francs; sugar, 175,570,000 francs; indirect taxes of Algeria, 9,114,300 francs; state monopolies, 615,059,804 francs; domains and forests, 43,937,449 francs; various revenues, 26,441,597 francs.

The estimated expenditure for 1892 is 3,779,-499,084 francs, including the 107,322,133 francs of expenditure *pour ordre* and 454,351,426 francs of expenditure out of special resources, excluding which the total of the general budget is 3,217,825,525 francs. The items under the various heads are as follow: Public debt, 1,284,191,-374 francs; the President, Senate, and Chamber, 13,094,440 francs; Ministry of Justice, 37,505,-816 francs; Religion, 45,057,157 francs; Ministry of Foreign Affairs, 15,078,800 francs; Ministry of the Interior for France, 69,634,702 francs; Ministry of Finance, 19,967,490 francs; Posts and Telegraphs, 151,673,074 francs; ordinary expenditures of the Ministry of War, 585,118,197 francs; extraordinary expenditures for War, 85,-402,500 francs; Ministry of Marine, 212,903,414 francs; the Colonies, 55,125,467 francs; Public Instruction, 178,512,914 francs; Fine Arts, 8,140,-955 francs; Ministry of Commerce and Industry, 19,599,636 francs; Ministry of Agriculture, 36,-072,650 francs; Ministry of Public Works, 86,-478,000 francs for ordinary and 110,647,000 francs for extraordinary purposes; expenses for the collection of the revenue, 183,154,944 francs; repayments, etc., 13,025,700 francs.

The rectified budget estimates for 1891 make the expenditures of the several departments as follows: Public debt, 1,274,745,358 francs; President, Senate, and Chamber, 13,051,940 francs; Justice, 37,493,250 francs; Religion, 45,067,003 francs; Foreign Affairs, 14,741,800 francs; Interior for France, 69,469,278 francs; Interior for Algeria, 7,254,447 francs; Finance, 19,937,670 francs; Posts and Telegraphs, 146,147,908 francs; War, 557,669,040 francs of ordinary and 108,-060,000 francs of extraordinary expenditure; Marine, 209,563,781 francs; Colonies, 53,550,553 francs; Public Instruction, 173,372,524 francs; Fine Arts. 8,106,455 francs; Commerce and Industry, 19,725,286 francs; Agriculture, 36,048,-

050 francs; Public Works, 167,460,480 francs; expenses of collecting taxes, 183,387,909 francs; repayments, etc., 13,028,700 francs. The payments on account of the public debt for 1892, amounting to 1,284,191,374 francs, consist of 456,135,244 francs of 3-per-cent. perpetual *rente*, 305,540,276 francs of 4½-per-cent. *rente*, 297,126,-924 francs of terminable annuities, and 225,275,-784 francs for pensions and other life interests. The capitalized value of the consolidated debt is about 21,241,621,712 francs, while the floating debt amounts to 908,724,600 francs, on which interest is paid, and 71,476,000 francs bearing no interest. The total public debt was officially estimated in November, 1890, at a nominal sum of 30,300,813,594 francs, on which 3·48 per cent. interest is paid, or 22,824,043,690 francs at its actual value, yielding 4·62 per cent. interest. The debts of the communes in 1886 amounted to 3,020,450,528 francs. The revenue of the communes for 1889 aggregated 486,553,939 francs. The ordinary expenditure of the city of Paris for 1891 was estimated at 264,691,174 francs, not including 106,324,695 francs for interest on the municipal debt.

Fall of the Freycinet Cabinet.—The long discussion on the budget prolonged the autumn session of the Chambers until it was time to organize for the session of 1892, which the Constitution requires to begin on the second Tuesday in January. After agreeing to a compromise with the Senate on the petroleum duties, the Chamber passed the tariff bill introducing high protection on Jan. 7 by 394 votes to 114. On Jan. 11 the session was closed. The new session opened on the following day. M. Floquet was re-elected President of the Chamber, and M. Le Royer of the Senate. On Jan. 17 the Government introduced a bill on associations which abolishes the licenses heretofore necessary, and simply requires that a society shall deliver to the magistrates a copy of its regulations. No distinction is made between secular and monastic societies ostensibly, yet the restrictions placed upon religious associations are the chief features of the bill. Such as are contrary to law, morality, or public order are prohibited, and a police magistrate may dissolve one for infringement of the law. If a society acknowledges a chief living abroad or has a majority of foreign members or foreigners among its directors, or if it is a branch of a foreign society, it may be dissolved by a decree of the Government. Societies can possess no real property not required for the accomplishment of their proper objects, and are not allowed to receive donations or legacies, which may no longer be held even by trustees, but must be made to a member individually. Any member is entitled to withdraw at any time, in which case he can reclaim the sums that he has paid in. The police are entitled to enter the premises of any society to ascertain that nothing unlawful is being committed. Trading companies do not come under the bill. Societies possessing real estate not necessary for carrying out their objects must dispose of it or apply for incorporation. Corporate rights can only be granted by special legislation. On Jan. 19, when an interpellation based on newspaper attacks on M. Constans, Minister of the Interior, was rejected. M. Laur, its mover, declared that the Chamber sacrificed its liberty in order to screen a member of the Government " who was stigmatized by public opinion." M. Constans could not be restrained from striking the Boulangist Deputy, blows were exchanged by others, and the President, unable to restore order, put on his hat and thus closed the sitting. M. Constans declined a tardy challenge from M. Laur to fight a duel.

On Feb. 18 a motion of urgency for the associations bill was offered by the Radicals, who suspected that the Government had framed the bill as a weapon of offense and had agreed to withdraw it in return for the conciliatory attitude of the Vatican, pressed M. de Freycinet to declare whether the Government, since it declined to support a demand for the immediate discussion of its bill, had entered into such a bargain. M. de Freycinet said that the bill was not aimed at the religious confraternities, and was not intended to pave the way for the separation of Church and state, for the Government was opposed to such separation. If the Chamber was not disposed to support a ministry which represented a moderate policy, he and his colleagues would resign, and therefore he called for a vote of confidence. The order of the day was rejected by a majority of 282, consisting of 151 Conservatives, 29 Boulangists, 12 Socialists, and 90 Republicans, against 210 Republicans. The policy of peace with the Church based on the supremacy of the civil element in the state, as avowed by the Prime Minister, was condemned by the Radicals and by the Conservatives, who together made up the hostile majority. M. de Freycinet announced the resignation of the ministry when the vote was declared. M. Carnot tried to persuade the ministers that the Chamber had not clearly declared against the ministry, because in the same sitting it had rejected the motion for urgency. The ministers urged in reply that the question of confidence had been plainly presented and understood.

President Carnot first commissioned M. Rouvier, a Moderate Republican, to form a ministry. M. Bourgeois, the Radical representative in the outgoing Cabinet, refused to join a Cabinet that would signify the surrender of the anticlerical position and a policy of reconciliation with the Pope, whose encyclical enjoining French Catholics to accept and sustain the republic had appeared after the resignation of the ministers. M. Bourgeois was then requested to effect a combination. M. Ribot raised obstacles to the leadership of a man who was identified with the aggressive enemies of the Church, who would abrogate the concordat. M. Carnot then sent for M. Loubet, a Moderate Republican, who, being a Senator, had no part in the discussion of the associations bill, and could therefore form a ministry which would signify a truce in the religious conflict, and could withdraw the associations bill and still leave the parties exactly where they stood in their relations to the religious question.

The Loubet Ministry.—A Cabinet was constituted by M. Loubet, on Feb. 28, consisting of the following members: Premier and Minister of the Interior, M. Loubet; Minister of War, Charles de Freycinet; Minister of Foreign Affairs, A. Félix J. Ribot; Minister of Finance, Maurice Rouvier; Minister of Public Instruction, Léon Bourgeois; Minister of Public Worship and Jus-

tice, Louis Ricard; Minister of Marine, Godefroy Cavaignac; Minister of Agriculture, Jules Develle; Minister of Commerce, Jules Roche; Minister of Public Works, Jules Viette. M. Loubet, born in 1838, at Marsanne, Drôme, was a lawyer, who entered the Chamber in 1876, who voted for the article against the religious orders but against the separation of Church and state, was elected to the Senate in 1885, voted with the Moderate Left, and was Minister of Public Works under Tirard in 1887. M. de Freycinet, born in 1829, an engineer by profession, organized with Gambetta the National Defense in 1870–'71, has been Minister of Public Works and Minister of Foreign Affairs many times, a conspicuous candidate for the presidency after the resignation of Grévy, four times Minister-President, and since 1890 the indispensable Minister of War, the only civilian who has held that post, in which he has unfolded a remarkable business ability and power of organization, which he had indeed displayed during the National Defense, but had since caused people to forget by exhibiting his talents as an orator, politician, and diplomatist. M. Rouvier, born in 1842, who as a young advocate was one of the fiercest journalistic assailants of the empire, entered the Cabinet of Gambetta in 1881 as Minister of Commerce, was Chief of the Cabinet after the fall of the Goblet ministry in 1886, and held the portfolio of Finance, and since 1889 has been at the head of the same ministerial department, and has won fame as a financier of genius by extinguishing the chronic deficit. M. Ribot, born in 1842, has been a leader of the Left Center in the Chamber, and as Minister of Foreign Affairs managed the understanding with Russia to which the Freycinet Cabinet chiefly owed its long tenure of office, and instituted the policy of reconciliation with the Curia which brought about its fall at last. Léon Bourgeois is a rising young statesman, who entered the Chamber in 1888 from the administrative service, and has displayed parliamentary and political ability of a high order. Jules Roche. who retained the portfolio of Commerce, was opposed to M. Méline's high protective tariff. Of the new ministers, M. Cavaignac, a son of Gen. Cavaignac, chief executive of the republic of 1848, was born in 1853, at first an advanced Radical and afterward an Opportunist, a member of the Chamber since 1882, was the first Minister of Marine appointed from civil life. M. Ricard, born in 1839, a lawyer of Rouen, entered the Chamber in 1885, and gained a high reputation for practical ability and industry. Jules Viette. a member of the Chamber since 1876, was Minister of Agriculture in 1887–'89· M. Develle, an advocate, born in 1845, entered the Chamber in 1877, was Minister of Agriculture under Freycinet and Goblet in 1886, and author of the bill that increased the grain duties and inaugurated the protective policy.

In the ministerial declaration, read on March 3 by the new Premier, the defense of all the Republican laws was put forth as the primary object of the policy to be followed, and in the first rank were placed the military law, "a law of equality and of patriotism," and the education laws, "the source of all the developments of the national spirit and a fundamental guarantee of liberty of conscience." The attitude to be observed in the religious question was thus defined:

The relations of state and Church have aroused debates and incidents in which the complexity of the problem has not, perhaps, admitted of sufficient clearness. Here are the principles which will guide us in this matter. We do not believe ourselves commissioned to prepare the separation of the Churches and the state. There is not in the Chambers, and we do not believe there is in the country, a majority to accomplish this. Our duty, therefore, is to maintain firmly the concordat legislation. We shall apply it in its true spirit. The concordat assures to the clergy a special situation and rights, but in return imposes on them, whatever be their ecclesiastical rank, rigorous obligations. Not only do they, like all citizens, owe obedience to the nation's laws, but they are bound, moreover, to confine themselves to their duties as ministers and to hold themselves absolutely aloof from party struggles. We shall not hesitate to exact of all respect for these obligations. We believe that we have sufficient power to secure such respect; if this were not the case we should ask Parliament for the necessary means of solving difficulties upon which it is for the national representatives to pronounce a sovereign decision.

The legislative programme gave priority to the measures under discussion for the amelioration of the lot of workmen, and in particular those which concern the regulation of the labor of children, girls, and women in industrial establishments, the right to compensation of workmen injured in fulfillment of their duties, arbitration between employers and employed, the healthfulness and security of workshops, the regulation of savings banks, the creation of a national superannuation fund for laborers, and the reform of the liquor traffic. The movement which, outside the interested calculations of parties, promised to bring toward the republic the masses of universal suffrage was welcomed, and the ministers would endeavor, in the wise spirit of a broad tolerance, to extend the feeling that the republic was a guarantee of security and liberty to all, but without sacrificing the principle of the absolute independence of civil society, or losing sight of the guiding ideas of the revolution from which the institutions of the republic collectively sprang. Its aim was "the more and more equitable division of the common burdens and advantages, the progressive elevation of all to an increasing degree of moral and material well-being."

The ministers being challenged to explain the supposed negotiations with the Vatican, M. Ribot declared that there had been none, and that the Pope's encyclical had been wholly spontaneous, although, in accordance with the concordat, on Dec. 17, 1891, the French ambassador at the Vatican had called attention to the campaign of a part of the clergy which had retarded the pacification recommended by the Holy See and endangered the concordat, and said that the Government, anxious as it was to achieve religious peace, could not be responsible for the consequences of a conflict thus provoked by the clergy. The Pope had expressed his intention of seeking to avoid such conflicts. M. Loubet expressed approval of the course that M. Ribot had pursued, and on a resolution accepting the declarations of the ministers the Government was sustained by 341 votes to 91.

M. Rouvier's budget provided for the redemption of 130,000,000 francs of treasury bonds, of 160,000,000 francs due in 1893, out of the surplus of 1890-'91, and for a considerable reduction of the duties on wine and cider and a corresponding increase in those on spirits. The repeal of the duty on railroad passenger tickets was followed by a reduction of 10 per cent. in first-, 20 per cent. in second-, and 30 per cent. in third-class fares. In the municipal elections, which occurred in the beginning of May, the Republicans made large gains. New political groups were formed in consequence of the changed attitude of the Church toward the republic and the thrusting aside of the religious question. A considerable section of the Extreme Left organized and formulated a programme as a Radical-Socialist group. As the immediate result of the Pope's encyclical, 38 Deputies of the Right created a Catholic Republican party to contend for liberal ideas, social and religious peace, and the amelioration of the lot of the workingman. The Union of Christian France, organized by M. de Mun, dissolved after the Pope's encyclical appeared, while a Republican Catholic league for the defense of popular rights was founded by Gaston David.

The Constitutional Right, founded after the last general election for the purpose of co-operating with conservative Republicans within the republic, which it acknowledged as the legal Government of the country, gained new accessions. A group, consisting partly of Monarchists, was formed to look after and promote colonial interests. The Royalist Right, presided over by the Duc de la Rochefoucauld, issued in June a manifesto testifying to their fidelity to the cause of the monarchy. The Radical Left was revived as the anticlerical Union of Radical Republicans.

The detachment of the Under Secretaryship of the Colonies from the Ministry of Commerce and the restoration of the control of the Ministry of Marine over this department was the occasion for much grumbling, and a bill was offered for the creation of a separate Ministry of the Colouies. M. Cavaignac presented a programme which contemplated the increase of the *personnel* of the squadrons from 7,500 to 14,000 men, and the building of 6 ironclads of over 14,000 tons, besides improved cruisers. A misunderstanding between the military and civil and the naval authorities in Dahomey afforded ground for an attack on the new Minister of Marine on July 11, and he was overthrown on a resolution in favor of unity of command, and was succeeded by M. Burdeau, a popular young Deputy who began life as a mechanic, had made his mark soon after entering the Chamber in 1885 at the age of thirty-four, was a delegate to the Labor Conference at Berlin, and in 1891 had gained new distinction by the ability that he displayed as reporter of the budget.

In the bill for arbitration between employers and workmen the Conseils des Prudhommes are constituted the arbitrators. A bill for the renewal of the charter of the Bank of France for twenty-three years, from 1898, requires the bank to advance 180,000,000 francs to the Government without interest, instead of 140,000,000 francs with interest, but allows it to increase its note circulation from 3,500,000,000 to 4,000,000,000 francs. A branch must be established in the chief town of every department, and agricultural and other credit societies may have their bills discounted. The Senate, on March 28, agreed to a bill limiting the hours of labor for women as well as for children employed in factories to eleven hours a day.

A proposition to allow women to vote for the Conseil des Prudhommes was carried in the Chamber by a good majority, but a resolution to allow them to be members of the body was defeated.

In the triennial elections of one half the members of the departmental councils in August many Catholic candidates declared their acceptance of the republic. In the place of 1,980 Republicans and 872 Conservatives who retired, there were elected 2,157 Republicans, 26 Constitutionalists or Republican Conservatives, and 667 Monarchists.

Church and State.—On Jan. 21 Cardinals Richard, Desprez, Langenieux, Place, and Foulon, Archbishops of Paris, Toulouse, Rheims, Rennes, and Lyons published a complaint regarding the situation of the Church, in which they said that the state had become atheistic, and had revived obsolete enactments in order to curtail the liberty of the bishops; that ecclesiastical subsidies were cut down, monks dispersed, and the remaining congregations ruined by unjust taxation; renegade priests were allowed to marry; and the teachings and dignity of the Church were violated in the divorce law, the secularization of the schools, the enforced military service of seminarists, the exclusion of religion from charitable institutions, and the control of churches by municipalities. Catholics were enjoined to respect the laws and the authorities, except where they violated conscience or encroached on the spiritual domain, in which case they should offer a firm resistance. This catalogue of the sins of the republic accompanied a reluctant and equivocal declaration that, in accordance with the orders of the Holy See and with Catholic tradition, they would refrain from opposing the form of government that France had chosen for herself. Cardinal Lavigerie, of Algiers, who had taken the lead in the *rapprochement* between the French Church and the republic, announced his adhesion to the letter as an acceptance of the republic, which Catholics not only had no desire to oppose, but were bound to respect. The declaration of the French cardinals, to which all the bishops, except one, gave their adhesion, did not represent the position of the Holy See, which was unfolded at full length in an encyclical of the Pope to the French bishops, published on Feb. 19. After affirming that religion alone can create a true social bond and solidly secure a nation's peace, and denouncing as a calumny the charge often brought against the Church, that it aims to secure a political domination over the state, the encyclical explains the principles of the relation of the Church to civil government, especially in France.

There have been many governments in France during this century, and each has had its distinctive form—imperial, monarchical, and republican. Each of these is good so long only as it makes for the common well-being, and one form may be good at one time and another at another. Catholics, like all citizens, have a perfect right to prefer one form to another, as none of these forms in itself is opposed to Christian teaching. The Church has always in its dealings with states fully recognized this principle. Each state is a special individual result, growing out of and modified by its peculiar surroundings, and thus obligatory upon the members which compose it, who should do nothing to seek to overturn it or change its form. The Church, therefore, guardian of the truest and loftiest conception of political sovereignty, since it derives it from God, has always reproved subversive doctrines and condemned the rebels to legitimate authority, and this, indeed, even when those in authority used their power against the Church. Yet it must not be forgotten that no governmental form is definitive. The Church alone has been able, and will continue, to preserve its form of government. But in human history crisis follows crisis, revolution revolution, and order anarchy, and in these circumstances a new form of government may be needful to satisfy new wants and conditions. The principle of authority never changes, but only the method of its expression or the form of its incarnation. Hence authority is enduring, for in its nature it is imposed for the well-being of all, or, in other terms, is considered, as such, to be derived from God. Consequently, when a new government is founded, acceptance thereof is not only permissible, but a duty. But for some people there is a difficulty here. This republic, they say, is animated by sentiments so antichristian that honorable men, and Catholics in particular, could not conscientiously accept it, and this is a widespread cause of dissension. But all this divergence might have been avoided but for a regrettable confusion of "constituted powers" and "legislation." Indeed, under the most unimpeachable form legislation may be detestable, and likewise under a very imperfect form there may be excellent legislation. History bears ample witness, and the Church has always recognized this fact. Legislation is the work of men invested with power, who, in fact, govern the nation—whence it results that in practice the quality of laws depends more on the quality of these men than on the form of government. Those laws will be good or bad according as legislators have minds imbued with good or bad principles. The respect due to constituted authorities can not involve the respect, much less the obedience, to any legislative measure whatever enacted by these same authorities. Let it not be forgotten that law is a prescription ordained by reason and promulgated for the good of the community by those who have for that ... s been intrusted with power. Never, consequently, on points of legislation be approved which are hostile to religion and to God. The concordat some of the adversaries of the Church wish to abolish so as to give the state every liberty of molesting the Church, while others wish to uphold it in order to fetter the Church, as though the concessions made by the latter could be separated from the engagements made by the state. Catholics should seek not to provoke a schism on a subject which it is for the Holy See to handle. Separation of the state from the Church is tantamount to separating human from Christian and divine legislation. When the state refuses to give God what is God's, it refuses by a necessary consequence to give citizens that to which they are entitled as men, for the true rights of man spring from his duties to God. In certain countries the churches have been reduced to a common-law *status*, and this, if it has serious inconveniences, may have some advantages. But in France, a nation Catholic by its traditions and by the faith of the great majority of its sons, the Church should not be placed in so precarious a position. Catholics can all the less advocate such a separation as their enemies avowedly aim at—entire independence of political toward religious legislation, indifference to the interests of Christian society, and the very negation of the existence of the Church. As soon as the latter, by redoubled activity, had made its work prosperous, the state would intervene and exclude French Catholics from the common law.

M. Ricard, when he became Minister of Justice and of Worship, applied the laws against clerical activity in politics somewhat more rigorously than his predecessor. Priests who participated in the electoral canvass for municipal offices had their stipends stopped. Pamphlets against secular education published by the Bishop of Mendes were suppressed. Conferences or lectures on controversial subjects given by priests in their churches gave rise to riotous disturbances, which M. Ricard ordered the law officers to take measures to stop; and in the same circular he reminded the bishops that their priests were mainly responsible for the tumults and ought to be restrained. Proceedings were begun against the Bishop of Mendes for a pastoral in which he laid down the doctrine that no one is bound to obey laws of which he conscientiously disapproves, and against the Archbishop of Avignon and his suffragans for a similar pronouncement. Political catechisms issued by bishops for the instruction of the laity had been the subject of a complaint made by the French Government to the Vatican. On May 3 the Pope addressed a brief to the French cardinals, in which he enjoined them, and all Catholics, to recognize the republic unreservedly, making unmistakably clear the lesson of the encyclical, which many pretended to misunderstand. Having convinced the republicans that they are not partisans of the deposed dynasties seeking to transform the Government, but have sincerely accepted the legally constituted order, the French Catholics could display their activity and use their effective influence to induce the Government to change for the better iniquitous laws without giving rise to the suspicion that they are hostile to the authorities deputed to govern public affairs. "But the men who would subordinate everything to the previous triumph of their respective parties, even were it on the plea that it was fittest for the defense of religion, would place, by a pernicious perversion of ideas, the politics which divide before the religion that unites. In this second encyclical letter Leo XIII enforced the doctrine that the republican form of government is as divinely sanctioned as the monarchical, and with his benediction to a congress of Catholics held in May, at Paris, he sent an injunction to obey its instructions.

Anarchists.—A violent explosion of dynamite occurred in the Faubourg St. Germain, in Paris, on March 1, in front of the house occupied by the Princess de Sagan. On March 12, a house which had for one of its occupants a judge who had recently presided at a trial of some anarchists was partially destroyed by dynamite. On March 15, a bomb filled with picric acid was exploded on the sill of the Lobau barrack, the principal damage being the destruction of ancient stained-glass windows in the neighboring church of St. Gervaise. The Government submitted a bill to the Chamber to punish with death attempts to blow up edifices, dwellings, bridges, ships, boats, or vehicles of any kind. Before this, mysterious robberies of dynamite had taken place in various parts of France. Arrests were made of persons suspected of stealing dynamite at Soissy-sous-Étoiles, and of five who were supposed to be concerned in the explosions, and cartridges and bombs were discovered in domiciliary searches.

Threatening letters were received by various persons. On March 16, a dynamite cartridge was placed against the door of the President of the Criminal Court, who the same day had passed sentence on three anarchists. The panic that seized Paris after the first explosions had partly subsided, when one more startling occurred in the Rue Clichy, on March 27. Many persons were injured. The outrage was supposed to be directed against M. Bulot, deputy public prosecutor, who had prosecuted many anarchist prisoners in the last few months. Many foreign anarchists were expelled from France by the police. Ravachol, the supposed ringleader of the anarchist band, evaded the police until March 30. He was identified from a published description by a waiter in an eating-house, who informed the police when he came into the place again, and he was taken after a desperate struggle. He had been in the hands of the police before for theft and other offenses. An accomplice of Ravachol, named Chaumartin, had turned state's evidence against Ravachol. The latter had fled from St. Étienne after committing a murder there a year before, by which he obtained 30,000 francs by a robbery, and was devoting this to terroristic dynamite outrages. He was an adept in the chemistry of explosives, and had invented a panclastite of prodigious power. Ravachol, whose real name was François Königstein, was arraigned before the Seine Criminal Court, with Simon, Jao Beala, Chaumartin, and a girl named Soubère. On April 25, two days after, 122 anarchists had been arrested in Paris and other places on the charge of belonging to societies of malefactors. The restaurant of M. Véry, who had been the chief instrument in delivering Ravachol up to justice, was completely wrecked by a dynamite bomb, and M. Véry and four others were badly injured. On April 27 a jury found Ravachol and Simon guilty, and the other three prisoners innocent; but extenuating circumstances reduced the penalty of the two who were convicted to penal servitude for life. Altogether, 167 anarchists were arrested in the provinces, of whom 118 were liberated after a few weeks of detention. In Paris, 71 arrests were made, and of those arrested 7 were convicted, 8 were held for trial for various offenses, and 56 were set free again. Ravachol was tried on the charge of murdering the old man, and was guillotined.

The anarchists of France are divided into four general classes. The Anarchist Federation, composed of advanced Socialists, theoretical anarchists, and ex-soldiers of the commune, pursues no revolutionary or active propaganda, but allies itself with any party opposed to the Government, and aids the movement with its votes and its influence. The members of this organization are strongly opposed to the employment of criminal means or the commission of dynamite outrages. They have a governing committee of 30 members, and collect funds from the adherents, with which they are enabled to play an important part in strikes and in the Socialist agitation. Their headquarters have never been discovered by the police. The league of the Internationalists and Antipatriots is composed of young men, and has some noted anarchists at its head. The Antipatriots are not numerous, but are divided into several secondary groups, which hold communication with each other only when united action is necessary. They are young Frenchmen whose principal object is to foment anarchistic and internationalist agitation in the army. During 1892 several of these agents were arrested in different parts of France and condemned to from four to eight months' imprisonment, for inculcating by word or by printed documents or writings, some secretly and some with rash bravado, the doctrine that the soldiers should mutiny sooner than use their weapons against the people. The Anarchist Federation holds some communication with this league, and makes use of it sometimes to further its own aims. The Internationalist section of the league is composed almost entirely of foreign refugees— Italians, Germans, Belgians, Russians, Spaniards, and others—who are living in France, usually under assumed names, and are under the double surveillance of the French police and the police agents of their own countries. The Cosmopolitan League has no connection with the other league, but is part of a gigantic international organization of revolutionary anarchists and dynamitards who do not recoil from political assassination. The head of this body in France has been an Italian named Pini, who at first was suspected of arranging the dynamite outrages executed by Ravachol and his accomplices. The latter belong to a distinct order of anarchists, who are the most desperate and fanatical, and the most difficult to watch and detect. They call themselves Independents, and are divided into groups of not more than 10 or 12 members which have no connection with each other. Each member preserves the completest liberty of action. The members are bound by no organization or common tie except their hatred for all forms of government, and a belief in a regeneration of society through anarchy. They are the most dangerous of the anarchistic schools, because they are the most active, the most determined, and the most reckless of consequences.

Strike at Carmaux.—The Socialists in the municipal elections of 1892 put forward many candidates, and were successful in several of the centers of population and in manufacturing and mining communes. In the beginning of September a strike broke out at Carmaux in the works of the Tarn Mining Company, which employs 2,000 men, of whom 1,200 belonged to a trade union. The majority of the Municipal Council were Socialists, and for 1892 they elected as mayor the secretary of the Miners' Union, M. Calvignac, an employee of the company. He became a candidate for the office of district councilor also, and when he returned to his work after the canvass was over, and after his recovery from a short sickness, he received notice of dismissal unless he would promise to work constantly. This he declared he could not do, because his public functions demanded a part of his time. He would require to be absent two days a week, but the company refused to release him for that time. His fellow-workmen, assuming that he was discharged because he was a Socialist, and therefore distasteful to his employers as a public official, went on strike in a body, and the Socialists and extreme Radicals throughout France held the managers up

to scorn as oppressors of labor and nullifiers of universal suffrage. The strikers damaged the company's property, and forced the manager, M. Humblot, who had refused to retain M. Calvignac's services for two thirds of the time, to sign a paper resigning his post. For a long time the directors of the company held firmly to their resolve and refused to submit the matter to arbitration. The Government prosecuted the miners who were guilty of rioting, and several were convicted and sentenced to prison. Arbitration was at length agreed to through the intercession of Minister Viette, and a settlement was reached in the beginning of November, after which the convicted rioters were pardoned.

Defeat of the Loubet Cabinet.—The Carmaux strike and the exaggerated rumors of scandals connected with the Panama company gave the Conservative and Radical critics of the Government opportunities enough to barrass M. Loubet and his colleagues after the reassembly of the Chambers on Oct. 20. The Right accused them of laxity in dealing with the strikers, and the Radicals of truckling to the employers. A Government bill to amend the press law so as to give the authorities power to suppress anarchist journals which sowed sedition was carried by the aid of the Right. Several measures introduced by individual ministers were voted down, but none were of a nature to warrant the retirement of the ministers. M. Loubet seemed to court defeat in his attitude in the Chamber. The Government determined to institute criminal proceedings against several directors and other officials of the Panama Canal Company. On Nov. 20 one of the accused persons, Baron Jacques de Reinach, died suddenly. It was generally supposed that he committed suicide because incriminating documents had some time before been stolen from him, and would now be used against him and others in the trial and the investigation that was instituted by the Chamber. Some suspected that he had been murdered to prevent him from revealing the secrets of disgraceful financial and political intrigues. It was charged that 9,000,000 francs had been used to bribe Deputies, and that large sums had been distributed among newspapers. The local authorities, on the doctors' certifying that Baron de Reinach had died from natural causes, allowed the body to be buried. On Nov. 28 a member of the Right asked the Minister of Justice why an autopsy had not been performed. M. Brisson supported the demand of the Marquis de la Ferronays and moved a resolution expressing regret that the authorities had not sealed the papers of the Baron de Reinach. M. Loubet indignantly denied that the Government had been guilty of negligence, and refused to accept an expression of confidence in the Government that M. Monjon proposed to append to M. Brisson's motion, demanding the order of the day pure and simple. This was refused by 304 to 219 votes, and M. Brisson's resolution was passed by 393 to 3 votes. The majority that upset the ministry was composed of 172 Conservatives and Boulangists and 121 Republicans. M. Loubet handed in the resignations of the Cabinet, and President Carnot sent for M. Brisson, who attempted to form a Cabinet, of which the main task should be to sift the Panama scandal to the bottom, but was unsuccessful. Casimir Perrier, of the Republican center, had no better success. While the Cabinet crisis continued, the parliamentary commission, of which M. Brisson was president, pursued its investigation with determination amid difficulties. M. Beaurepaire, the public prosecutor, refused to impart to the commission the evidence and documents on which the case against the company's officers was based.

The Ribot Ministry.—On Dec. 5 a ministry was constituted under the presidency of M. Ribot, MM. Bourgeois, Develle, and Loubet having successively declined after M. Perrier's failure. The new ministry was composed as follows: Premier and Minister of Foreign Affairs, M. Ribot; Minister of War, M. de Freycinet; Minister of Finance, M. Rouvier; Minister of the Interior, M. Loubet; Minister of Public Instruction, Charles Sarrien; Minister of Public Worship and Justice, M. Bourgeois; Minister of Marine, M. Burdeau; Minister of Commerce, M. Sarrien; Minister of Agriculture, M. Develle; Minister of Public Works, M. Viette.

The new ministry decided to communicate to the investigating commission the documents demanded, whereupon M. Beaurepaire resigned. Many checks of Baron Reinach's were traced to Deputies and Senators, most of whom said that the sums represented were repayments of business debts unconnected with the canal enterprise. It came out that on the eve of the banker's death Minister Rouvier and M. Clémenceau had been with him and had interested themselves as friends to persuade Cornelius Herz to have the newspaper attacks on Baron Reinach stopped. When this fact had become known to the chamber M. Rouvier was compelled to resign from the ministry.

A *post-mortem* examination proved that Baron de Reinach had died from poison. The post of Minister of Finance was immediately, on Dec. 13, given to Pierre Emmanuel Tirard, who had held it with credit before, and had twice been Minister-President. A proposal to invest the investigating committee with judicial powers was opposed by the Government and rejected by the Chamber. Charles de Lesseps and the other accused directors of the company were arrested and committed to prison without bail. One of the incidents of the confused and excited situation was a bloodless duel between Georges Clémenceau, leader of the Radicals, and Paul Déroulède. The revelations made by Cornelius Herz implicated 104 members of the Chamber, and the papers of Baron de Reinach which had disappeared, but were remembered by those who had seen them, cast suspicion on ex-ministers and others of the highest standing in the political world.

Commercial Treaties.—Arrangements were made between the French and the United States governments whereby each enjoys favored-nation treatment—that is, the benefit of the reciprocity clauses in their respective tariffs. The minimum tariff was extended to the Netherlands, and, with some restrictions, to the Dutch colonies, as a temporary arrangement which either government could abrogate. Similar provisional reciprocity agreements were arranged with Belgium, Greece, Sweden and Norway, and Switzerland, terminable on twelve months' notice.

Austria-Hungary, Bulgaria, Chili, Denmark, Egypt, Germany, Great Britain, Hayti, Honduras, Liberia, Mexico, Montenegro, Russia, Servia, and Turkey were entitled to the conventional tariff by virtue of treaties not yet denounced and of special laws. To Persia, Santo Domingo, Servia, and the South African Republic were likewise extended the benefits of the minimum tariff. Negotiations with Spain broke down owing to the difficulty of the question of the alcoholization of wines. A treaty was made with Switzerland in spite of the objections of the Protectionists, in which the minimum rates on watches, cheese, embroideries, silks, and other Swiss products were lowered.

Algeria.—The colony of Algeria is administered by a Governor-General, who is directly responsible to the President of the republic. All legislation must be passed by the French Chambers. The colonial budget is voted by a council composed of delegates from the provincial councils. The receipts are derived mainly from customs, licenses, and excise. The revenue was estimated in the budget of 1892 at 46,330,-898 francs, and the expenditure at 44,162,960 francs. The Governor-General is Jules Cambon, appointed in April, 1891.

The area of Algeria is 184,474 square miles, and the population, as ascertained by the census of 1891, is 4,124,732, of which number 3,636,967 are in the civil and 487,765 in the military territory. Of the three departments, Algiers has an area of 65,929 square miles, with a population of 1,275,650 in the civil and 192,477 in the military territory; Oran, with an area of 44,616 square miles, has 817,450 inhabitants in the civil department and 124,616 in the military; and Constantine, 73,929 square miles in extent, has 1,548,867 inhabitants in the civil and 170,672 in the military department. Each sends a Senator and 2 Deputies to the French Assembly. The total population in 1891 included 272,663 French, 47,667 naturalized Algerian Jews, and 3,567,223 natives who are not citizens. The rest were mostly Tunisians, Moors, Spaniards, Italians, Maltese, and Germans.

The Nineteenth Corps of the French army, which constituted the permanent military force of Algeria, is large enough to be divided in war into two corps. It consists of 53 battalions of infantry, 52 squadrons of cavalry, 16 batteries of artillery, and the auxiliary departments, containing altogether 54,000 men, with 15,000 horses. The only troops recruited from the indigenous population are 3 regiments of native *tirailleurs*, often called Turcos. Other local forces are 3 battalions of African light infantry, 2 foreign legions, and 3 regiments of *spahis* or scouts.

About 20,000,000 hectares are under cultivation, and the area is gradually extending. The following are the principal crops: Wheat, of which 5,246,053 metric quintals were grown in 1890 on 1,113,309 hectares; barley, of which 8,263,633 quintals were produced on 1,361,292 hectares; alfa, of which 741,421 quintals were obtained from 1,582,612 hectares; wine, the yield of which was 2,579,639 hectolitres, the vineyards covering 106,351 hectares; minor cereals, of which 661,031 quintals were harvested on 99,-957 hectares; and tobacco, to which 9,841 hectares were devoted, yielding 3,846,757 kilogrammes. The live stock in 1889 consisted of 329,783 horses and mules, 271,547 camels, 1,217,143 cattle, 9,475,287 sheep, and '4,213,922 goats. The product of iron ore in 1889 was 351,800 tons, valued at 2,457,190 francs. The value of blende, galena, silver, and copper mined was 1,426,457 francs.

The special commerce with France in 1890 amounted to 209,165,021 francs for imports and 209,995,965 francs for exports. The total special imports were 237,268,012 francs, and the exports 261,622,241 francs. The chief imports to France were cotton fabrics, leather manufactures, metal manufactures, and haberdashery. The chief exports to France were cereals valued at 58,067,440 francs, wines valued at 58,895,130 francs, animals valued at 44,012,935 francs, and wool valued at 12,084,973 francs. The imports from Morocco were 11,558,938 francs; from Tunis, 10,395,735 francs in value; from Great Britain, 10,367,946 francs; from Spain, 7,442,871 francs; the exports to Great Britain, 18,126,494 francs. From the United States, goods valued at 1,003,795 francs were imported, and the exports to the United States amounted to 1,444.164 francs.

The railroads of Algeria have a length of 1,910 miles, including a junction line of 140 miles running into Tunis. The telegraphs, with the Tunis connections, have a length of 4,310 miles, with 10,000 miles of wire. They are operated by a private company, which receives a subvention from the French Government. Fortified posts with permanent garrisons have been established in the southwest of Algeria, and roads have been constructed between them, along which wells have been sunk. In the southeast a line for a railroad along the frontier of Morocco has been traced. The Sultan of Morocco has shown a disposition to contest the extension of French influence over the nomads of the Sahara, but he is not so situated as to be able to unfold the military power that France is willing to apply to the subjugation of the southern tribes. A military expedition was sent out by the Sultan in the spring of 1892 to punish the people of the That oases that have declared their independence and their sympathy for the French and to collect the religious tribute that the Tuaregs had neglected to pay for five years. The Sultan's cousin Abd-es-Selam, the head of the Wazzan sect, had entered into close relations with the Governor of Algeria and had influenced the populations of Tuat to accept French protection, and the mission of the Emperor failed, as the military force that he sent was insignificant.

Tunis.—The regency of Tunis, though nominally only a protectorate, is practically governed by the French Ministry of Foreign Affairs through a minister resident and a staff of officials in Tunis and a bureau of Tunisian affairs in Paris. The French resident is M. Massicault. The Bey is Sidi Ali, born Oct. 5, 1817, who succeeded his brother, Sidi Mohammet-es-Sadok, Oct. 28, 1882. The cost of the military occupation by about 10,000 troops, as in the case of the military force in Algeria, is borne by the French Government.

The population is estimated at 1,500,000. The number of French people residing in Tunis was 10,030 in 1891, compared with 3,500 in 1886; of these, 2,000 are children of settlers born in the country. The capital city, Tunis, has a mixed population of Arabs, Moors, Jews, and negroes, numbering about 145,000, including 20,000 Europeans. The revenue for the year ending Oct. 12, 1890, was 33,887,986 piasters, and the expenditure 32,495,179 piasters (1 piaster = 12½ cents). For the next twelve months the revenue was estimated at 33,721,500 piasters, and the expenditure at 36,942,433 piasters, and for the remainder of the calendar year, which has been made the financial year, the estimates are 13,906,000 piasters for receipts and 10,684,766 piasters for expenditures. The debt, as converted in 1888, amounts to the nominal sum of 17,440,750 francs, paying 3½ per cent., and extinguishable in ninety-nine years. Wheat and barley cover about 1,000,000 hectares. The total value of the imports for 1890 was 29,134.600 francs, of which 15,807,080 francs came from France, 6,296,930 francs from Malta, and 2,693,050 francs from Italy. The total exports were 30,599,200 francs, of which 11,230,368 francs were exports to France, 8,576,064 francs to Algeria, 4,807,530 francs to Great Britain, and 3,105,690 francs to Italy. The principal imports were cotton and linen goods, flour, colonial goods, wine and spirits, and raw cotton and silk and yarns. The values of the chief exports were as follow: Wheat. 9,416,640 francs; barley, 5,030,680 francs; olive oil, 4,273,300 francs; alfa, 2,064,880 francs. Other export articles are tanning materials, sponges, dried vegetables, woolen goods, and wine. The length of railroads is 260 miles, and of telegraphs 2,000 miles. The main part of the foreign commerce passes through the port of Goletta, which will be connected with the city of Tunis by a canal 7 miles long, 44 metres wide, and 8 metres deep, is expected to be opened before July, 1894. The export of wine has increased from 1,900 to 11,000 hectolitres in two years. A large proportion of the French colonists are wine-growers. The product of olive oil in 1891 was 30,000,000 litres. The wine harvest increased from 15.000 hectolitres in 1888 to 32,600 in 1889, 52,977 in 1890, and 105,142 in 1891. The soil is favorable for grape culture, and the wine is very strong.

The construction of the harbor of Biserta is an important work of engineering, which is advancing rapidly. The main harbor will be the Lake of Biserta. Harbors are to be made also at Sfax and Susa. The construction of the great harbor at Biserta, under the direction of the Ministry of the Marine, at a cost of not less than 15,000,000 francs, is regarded with suspicion by all the Mediterranean powers, especially by Italy, because the intention must be to make it a naval fortress, although the French Government has not been willing to acknowledge that fortifications of importance were being erected there. The Italian Government was impelled, by the action of the French in beginning the fortification of Biserta soon after taking possession of the country, to construct extensive works in Sicily and Sardinia. English and Italian remonstrances against the construction of a war harbor in Tunis as an infraction of the Bardo treaty were seconded by Germany, and the French Cabinet denied at first that it had military purposes in view, but afterward asserted that it was even bound to take any measures that were necessary for the safety of Tunis and the protection of the Bey's dynasty. Slavery is practically abolished in Tunis. The buying or selling of slaves has been completely suppressed since the French occupation. The Bey of Tunis under the pressure that the English Government brought to bear in 1841, prohibited the export of slaves, and in 1843 proclaimed the emancipation of all imported slaves, and in 1846 the abolition of male slavery. These edicts had not the slightest effect, and in 1875 the English Government interfered again, and obtained a treaty whereby the Bey engaged to have the declaration of 1846 observed. It was not till the French came that the slave trade was effectually suppressed. On May 29, 1890, the Bey issued a decree declaring that slavery exists no longer, and that any slave, irrespective of nationality or color, can apply to a magistrate to obtain his freedom at any time. Another decree requires the masters to provide any slave living with them, male or female, with liberation papers, which the slaves must carry with them and produce whenever an official calls for them. An order issued in April, 1891, requires all cadis to require any slave that they see to produce his emancipation papers, or to punish the master if they are not forthcoming. The only slaves still existing are therefore such as remain voluntarily in that condition, which they can abandon at their option.

French West Africa.—The area of Senegal and Rivières du Sud is about 140,000 square miles, and of the French Soudan 54,000 square miles, not including protectorates. By the Anglo-French agreement of Aug. 5, 1890, the French sphere embraces all the territories south of Algeria and Tunis lying to the north of a line drawn from Say, on the middle Niger, to Barrawa, on Lake Chad. Westward of Say and to the northward of Dahomey, Ashanti, and Togoland is a region about 50,000 square miles in extent that has not been parceled out; and to the east of Lake Chad the native empires of Bornu, Bagirmi, and Wadai, the region south of them as far as the Welle, and the desert to the north as far as the bounds of Tripoli and Egypt have not yet been brought into political relations of any kind with European powers. The French Sahara between Algeria and Lake Chad has an area of about 1,000,000 square miles, but it is mostly desert, and is inhabited by warlike and unfriendly tribes. Including Sokoto and other protectorates attached to Senegal and the French Soudan and those on the Bight of Benin that are attached to the Rivières du Sud, the area in West Africa claimed by France has an extent of about 550,000 square miles. The coast line, beginning at Cape Blanco in the north, is only broken by the British settlements of Gambia and Portuguese Guinea until it reaches Sierra Leone. Farther south the French sphere has an outlet in the Gold Coast settlements, and the French are ambitious to connect their settlements on the Bight of Benin with their possessions on the middle and upper Niger by annexing all or a great part of the Hinterland of the British Gold Coast and German Togoland.

The annexed countries dependent on Senegal are Walo, North Cayor, Toro, Dimar, and Damga. The country occupied by the colony of Senegal includes the coast between the Senegal and Gambia and the banks of the Senegal. The chief town and seat of government is St. Louis, which has 20,000 inhabitants. The total population of Senegal, according to a census taken in 1892, is 1,097,000, of which number 39,-000 inhabit self-governing communes, 51,000 territories under direct French administration, 927,000 territories of immediate protectorate, and 80,000 territories of political protectorate. There are 6,000 Europeans, half of them French. The Governor-General of Senegal is assisted by a Colonial Council. The colony has 164 miles of railways on the coast. India rubber, ground nuts, gum, woods, and skins are exported, and food, drinks, and cloths are imported. The imports in 1889 were valued at 29,000,000 francs, and the exports at 16,500,000 francs. The local budget for 1891 was 3,018,646 francs. The expenditure of France is set down at 6,044,999 francs for 1892. The native population is essentially agricultural.

The Rivières du Sud, which was constituted a separate colony in 1890, has a population of 47,551 in the coast settlements. Administratively connected with it are the settlements on the Gold Coast and the Bight of Benin. In the French budget for 1892 the sum of 33,000 francs is appropriated for this colony and its dependencies, called French Guinea. A telegraph cable connects the capital, Conakry, with Senegal. The French settlements on the Gold Coast are Grand Bassam, Assinie, Grand Lahou, and Jackeville. On the Bight of Benin are Grand Popo, Agoué, Porto Novo, and Kotonu, and other points occupied on the coast of Dahomey (see DAHOMEY). A stretch of 100 miles of coast between the Gold Coast settlements and Liberia was occupied in 1891. The imports of the Gold Coast in 1890 were 2,810,000 francs; those of the Bight of Benin settlements, 3,489,894 francs.

The French Soudan embraces the annexed territories and protectorates on the upper and middle Niger and the upper Senegal. The annexed territories, which are mostly situated on the Senegal, have a population of about 360,000. The protectorates have an estimated area of 230,-000 square miles, and a population of 2,500,000. The French Soudan is administered from Kayes, on the Senegal, by a military commandant, who has formerly acted under the direction of the Governor-General of Senegal. A railroad has been built from Kayes to Bafoulaba, 94 miles in the direction of the Niger. The local revenue is about 400,000 francs. In the budget of 1892 the appropriation for the Soudan is 4,502,728 francs.

Lieut. L. Mizon, in 1891, succeeded after serious misadventures in reaching Sokoto by way of the Benue. The officials of the British Royal Niger Company threw obstacles in the way of his ascending, and when he was attacked by the Patanis and was wounded with others of the party, he suspected that representatives of the company were responsible, probably not by direct incitement, but by allowing the savages to understand by various intimations that the Frenchmen were on no good errand and had no friends. Mizon's wounds were dressed by the company's surgeon, and when he was well again, leaving his steamer and cargo, which the company had sequestrated, he pressed on into

Adamawa, with the sultan of which he made a commercial treaty. Sultan Zubir told him that an agent of the English company named Mackintosh had sent word to him that Mizon was coming to supply the Sultan of Amoka, Zubir's enemy, with carbines. Lieut. Mizon made inquiries at Yola and Garua, and obtained evidence that confirmed this statement. Had he proceeded to Yola at the expected time his party would have been assassinated. He found that the Patanis, instead of being punished, were rewarded with gifts after their murderous attack on the French party. On these grounds Lieut. Mizon brought several charges against the Niger Company, which he accused of resorting to treacherous and illegal practices for the circumvention of French and German political and commercial competition. The Niger, which is declared to be an international river by the treaty of Berlin, they close to all vessels except their own, by making regulations preventing foreigners from landing at other than stated points, or from holding intercourse with the natives, or procuring fuel for their steamers from the woods along the banks, which they claim, without justice, to be their private property. The company is accused of forcibly insuring respect for its flag, and allowing it to be understood, in contravention of duties imposed by the treaty of Berlin, that it was indifferent to the respect shown to other flags, which in Africa is an instigation to pillage and assassination. The attack of the Patanis on the river Forcados was the result of this policy, and one of the officers of the company had said that he had brought it on himself by disregarding the company's regulations. On Aug. 9, 1892, Lieut. Mizon left Paris on a new expedition to the central Soudan by the same route on which before he had encountered treachery and danger of assassination only in the regions where the sovereignty and influence of the Niger Company were in operation. He emerged before at Comasa, M. de Brazza's station on a branch of the Sangha; having made the journey of 434 miles from Yola, through an unknown country, with no escort except 8 Pahouins, without firing a shot. The treaties which he arranged with native chiefs encourage the hope that the French have entertained of uniting their great possessions of Algeria, Senegambia, and the Congo, and of making Lake Chad and the Shari basin their own. Commandant Monteil, who explored the region between Say, on the Niger, and Barrua, on Lake Chad, visited Kano and Kouka, the chief towns of Bornu.

Capt. Ménard set out from Grand Bassam, and, after exploring an unknown part of the banks of the Niger, reached Kong, where he spent some time cementing the friendly and commercial relations which had been arranged previously by Capt. Binger. Taking a southwesterly route thence, he reached Sakhala on Dec. 2, 1891, and there fitted out a caravan for Benty. He left Sakhala on Dec. 29, and when he came to the capital of Fakuru Bemba, chief of Kaladian, a vassal of Draookoro, King of the Bambarras, he found him at war with the people of Seguela, who had revolted and called in the aid of Sekuba, one of Samory's generals, who had occupied and fortified the town of Borutu. Samory was aiming at the conquest of the whole

Bambarras country, and Capt. Ménard was compelled to give what aid he could to the Bambarra chief against the principal enemy of the French. He took up a position with his 10 Senegalese soldiers in a fort near Seguela. Fakuru Bemba, being hard pressed, took to flight without giving thought to his ally. Samory's people were determined to kill the Frenchman, who sent away 5 Senegalese who were left, the others having been killed in defending the baggage, and sold his life dearly, shooting 29 of his assailants before he was overpowered. His head was cut off and sent to Samory.

Capt. Ménard's fate was similar to that of M. Crampel, who was killed in April, 1891, in his expedition from the French Congo to the Soudan, not by negroes, but by Mussulman Arabs, led by a certain Snoussi. M. Biscarrat, who had marched to Crampel's aid with some Senegalese, was attacked and slain, on May 25, and here also the guards were spared by the Mussulmans, who said they would kill the whites, but had no quarrel with the negroes. M. Nebout, one of Crampel's lieutenants, retreated with the rear guard to Brazzaville. The Arabs took from the French expedition many breech-loading and repeating rifles, besides 32,000 cartridges, 500 kilogrammes of powder, and revolvers with their ammunition. Another French expedition led by M. Fourneau, who pursued a route parallel to that of M. Crampel, was compelled to return, owing to the hostility of the natives. The French authorities were not ready to attempt punitive operations in so remote a region. They sent out an expedition under M. Dybowsky to find traces of M. Crampel, and recovered some of his papers. M. Dybowsky founded a station in 6° of north latitude, on the upper Kemo, the northern tributary of the Ubangi, and in the summer of 1892 M. Maistre was sent out to continue his work, accompanied by 5 other Europeans and a force of 95 Senegalese and 150 Kroumen. M. Maistre intended to ascend the Kemo in a northwesterly direction and penetrate into the Chad basin. Dybowsky established friendly relations and concluded many treaties with the negroes of the Ubangi region, owing to a victory he achieved over the Mussulmans who had long levied blackmail on the indigenous inhabitants. He had a force of 43 Senegal riflemen and 62 other followers. The chiefs of the Dakuas and of the Mussulman Ngapus received him kindly, and the camp of the Arabs was pointed out, which he surprised at night. The robbers fled, leaving their plunder, including Crampel's documents. He pursued them for a week, and then returned and destroyed their fortifications.

Of all the enemies of France in West Africa, the most important, more formidable than Behanzin, the King of Dahomey, or than Ahmadu, has been Samory, the sultan over a great part of the region of the upper Niger, who threw off his allegiance to Ahmadu and gained by conquest a kingdom which he organized in 10 provinces and 162 districts before the coming of the French, and which he rules with the prestige of a conqueror, while the great empire established by Ahmadu's father, El-Haj-Omar, has shrunk to a fraction of its former dimensions. Samory was a trader before he won fame as a warrior and became commander of the forces of the King of Torongo. He next set up as an independent ruler, and conquered one country after another, until, in 1878, his influence extended over the whole of the upper Niger. But for the arrival of the French in 1882 he would have been master of all the country down to the Senegal river. He came into collision with the French immediately, and, after several encounters, Gen. Faidherbe gained the victory over him, and treaties were made by which he gave up a slice of territory that he claimed, and, so the French say, accepted a protectorate. This he has always denied. The French Government was compelled to encounter the costs of bringing him to submission, for in no other way could its political supremacy be established or commercial relations extended in the Soudan. Samory is described as a monster of cruelty, who owed the rapidity of his conquests to his practice of burning prisoners of war by the hundred in fiery trenches. Through English traders he is said to have supplied himself with 2,000 repeating rifles and abundant ammunition when the French began their campaign against him in the beginning of 1892.

Lieut.-Col. Humbert, commander-in-chief in the Soudan, crossed the Niger with a strong column on Jan. 1, reached Kankan on Jan. 6, and on the following day put to flight Samory's force that held the route of Ombacuela. Leaving Kankan on the 9th, he delivered battle on the 11th against the *marigot* or marabout of Sombeke, killing 150 and wounding 300, and on the same day fought the *marigot* of Biamako. The French losses were an officer, a European gunner, and 8 men killed, and 2 captains and 43 men wounded. Marching straight upon Bissandugu, Samory's capital, the French shelled the place and drove the enemy out. Samory retired to the hilly country south of Bissandugu, where Col. Humbert established his headquarters, sending out detachments, which met with varying success, one being beaten and losing several prisoners. On Jan. 23 Col. Humbert set out for Sanankoro, Samory's principal stronghold, 50 miles south of Bissandugu and near the bank of the river Milo. The country that he traversed was remarkably rich, though it had been devastated by Samory. Samory's *sofas* endeavored to check them twice on the first day, and were repelled with heavy losses. On the 24th, Samory, at the head of a band of 500 men, gave the French a stiff fight for 3 hours back of the village of Forangugu, and killed 4 Senegal *tirailleurs* and wounded 6 men. On the 25th the French drove the enemy out of Sanankoro by a long fusillade, and compelled them to abandon also another fort called Keruan and retire to the opposite bank. The French loss was 2 *spahis* killed and 2 wounded. After remaining here some weeks for the purpose of winning the confidence of the inhabitants, the French commander again advanced against Samory, who had established himself in a fortified position in Tonkore, a country that he had annexed in 1881, with a large force, for after each defeat he had no difficulty in recruiting a fresh army. The rifles that he had lost in the previous engagements were replaced by a fresh supply brought by a caravan from Sierra Leone. The French took the posi-

tion, but Samory escaped with a part of his troops. Col. Humbert's command was in a precarious situation, remote from the base of supplies, and it was only with the aid of the re-enforcements and fresh stores authorized by the Chamber that the French were enabled to hold the positions that they had taken, without venturing on the pursuit of their resourceful enemy into more distant parts.

M. Lamadou and Capt. Kenny, who were selected as French and English commissioners to demarcate the boundary between Sierra Leone and the Rivières du Sud, set out from the starting-point of the disputed boundary, on the Mahila river, on Dec. 15, 1891. When they came to Dakar serious differences arose, the two commissions separated, and each proceeded to survey the line which it considered the true boundary. The French commissioners advanced into Kong and made a treaty with the Deammaras, which secured to France the direct route by the river Isi to the coast. Pushing on toward the Niger through a country desolated by Samory's raids, they heard that a force was advancing to fight them, whereupon they were deserted by their porters, and after many hardships they reached Benty, through the Comor valley, on April 12, 1892, having gone six hundred miles on foot. The English and French chief commissioners returned to Europe and joined the commission at Paris which was endeavoring to work out a diplomatic settlement of the boundary difficulty on the Gold Coast.

In August, 1892, the partial administrative and political autonomy granted to the French Soudan in the previous year was made complete, except that the chief commander is required to send copies of his reports to the Governor of Senegal and keep him informed in regard to matters relating to the general situation of the colony. The chief commander, who receives all instructions direct from the Under Secretary of the Colonies, will not henceforth be required to conduct military operations, but will commit this task to other officers, while he devotes his chief attention to the political organization and pacification of the territories that have been added to the possessions of France during a long period of military action. Lieut.-Col. Archinard was sent out in the summer to take the command of the French Soudan, with instructions to suppress Samory at any cost. When the work of conquest is concluded and civil administration instituted, and after the boundaries of the new possessions are fairly determined, the whole of French Senegambia is to be united in a general government like that of Indo-China.

Gabun and the French Congo. — Separated from the French possessions in northwestern Africa by the British territories of Sierra Leone and the Niger and the German territories of Togo and Cameroons on the coast region, and in the interior by the vast Hinterland, into which each of the three powers is striving to extend its influence by every channel, is the great block of French territory divided from the Congo State on the southeast by the Congo and Mobangi from Brazzaville to the fourth degree of north latitude, where the recognized limit of the Congo State ends. A line running due east from the mouth of the Campo river divides Gabun from

Cameroons as far as the fifteenth degree of east longitude. Farther east in this region the Germans have not attempted to push their protectorate; but farther north, in the Shari basin, they are anxious to extend their commercial and territorial influence through Adamawa, and the English on the Benue are endeavoring to extend their empire over the Chad countries, with which the French have attempted to enter into relations both from Senegambia and the Congo. Farther eastward, the Welle country is disputed by France and the Congo State. The extent of the recognized French territory is about 250,000 square miles. The population is estimated at 6,900,000. Ivory, ebony, rubber, and palm oil are the principal exports. The commerce of 1888 was 6,600,000 francs, the imports from France amounting to 1,317,680 francs, and the exports to France to 173,271 francs. The colonial budget for 1891 was 1,701,079 francs. The expenditure of the French Government in 1892 was set down in the budget as 1,454,397 francs.

While Dybowsky and Maistre were endeavoring to repair the injury sustained by French prestige in the direction of the Shari, M. de Brazza undertook a mission in the Welle region. A French post was established at Wesso, where the Sicoko joins the Sangha river, in 1891. M. de Brazza advanced from there to the upper Sangha, transporting a steamer around the rapids. Another post was established on the Kotto, a tributary of the Mbomu. The French have disputed the right of the Congo State to establish stations on the Ubangi and its affluents, the Welle and the Mbomu, claiming that the territory of the Free State was limited by treaty to the fourth parallel of north latitude. This interpretation of the treaty has been disputed by the Belgians, and districts alleged to lie within the French sphere by international agreement they claim for the Congo State by right of first occupancy and treaties made with native chiefs by Van Gele and Roger in 1890. When the protests of the Free State against the expeditions of De Brazza and others were disregarded, a Belgian expedition was sent to the same region under Capt. Liotard in February, 1892. When the French Cabinet declined to leave the question to arbitration, and demanded simply the evacuation of the disputed territory, the difficulty became acute. While negotiations were going on in Paris, and an arrangement was being considered that would have given to France compensation on the lower Congo in return for the renunciation of French claims in the north, incidents occurred on the frontier toward the end of June that impelled the French minister, M. Ribot, to increase his demands. A new settlement seemed to be in view when negotiations were resumed in the latter part of July, when M. de Poumeyrac, one of M. de Brazza's lieutenants, was shot on the Kotto by a native with a breech-loading rifle, such as were supplied to the Belgian military guards on the Congo. The French Government demanded explanations, and the Free State officials indignantly denied any complicity in the affair, and disclaimed all responsibility for acts done by natives in Yakoma, a country over which they exercised no jurisdiction. The French contention that the act of Berlin fixed the northern limit of the Congo State at the fourth parallel of latitude is rejected by the Congo Administration, which says that no limit was established by that instrument, but that the French Government, on the contrary, bound itself not to go east of the seventeenth meridian by its treaty with the Free State in 1885, and that the events on the Kotto took place therefore in a region to which France has no claim.

French Indo-China. — Cochin-China, Tonquin, Annam, and Cambodia have been united in a customs union and placed under the supervision of a Superior Council. The trade of Indo-China in 1890 amounted to 60,248,460 francs for imports, and 56,995,119 francs for exports. The imports of French products were 11,286,781 francs, and the exports to France 2,022,379 francs. In Annam, which has an area of 27,020 square miles, not including 19,300 square miles of dependent territories, with a population estimated at 5,000,000. The entire internal administration is carried on by native officials. The military force is 23,230, of whom 11,830 are natives. A French company was organized in 1891 to work coal mines at Turane. The exports are cinnamon bark, cotton, sugar, tea, coffee, tobacco, and seeds.

Cambodia has an area of 38,600 square miles, and about 1,800,000 inhabitants. The revenue in 1888 was 3,275,000 francs; the expenditure, 3,059,236. The exports are salt fish, cotton, beans, indigo, cardamom, sugar, and betel.

French Cochin-China has an area of 23,082 square miles, with a population of 1,991,500, of whom 2,537 are French. The military force consists of 1,830 French and 2,800 Annamite soldiers. Rice is exported to China to the amount of 40,000,000 francs a year. Other products are cocoanuts, sugar cane, and tobacco. There are 51 miles of railway, and 1,840 miles of telegraph lines.

Tonquin is 34,740 square miles in extent, and has a population estimated at 9,000,000. Rice, sugar, cotton, fruits, and tobacco are cultivated. The imports for 1890 were valued at 27,734,212 francs, and the exports at 13,324,720 francs. There were 11,475 French troops in the country in 1889, besides 6,500 native troops. In the French budget for 1892 the sum of 10,450,000 francs was set apart for Tonquin, of which 450,000 francs were for a submarine cable.

M. de Lanessan, the Governor-General of Tonquin, whose administration has been much criticised, affirms that he has succeeded in accomplishing the pacification of the Delta and in fairly securing its borders against inroads of the robber bands of the mountains, and there he believes that his task ends, for the uncultivated hilly region between Tonquin and China has been the abode of brigands for ages. To guard against them numerous outposts connected by well-guarded roads are necessary. In the populous low country the people are becoming more peaceful and law-abiding. Their condition is more prosperous than it was, and the revenue is rapidly increasing and is more easily collected than formerly. M. de Lanessan's policy has been to seek the co-operation of the native authorities, and to intrust the administration as far as possible to natives. The receipts of the Government in 1891 were 1,500,000 francs more than in the previous year, and for 1892 a further large increase was anticipated. The court of Annam has agreed to the construction of a railroad from Hué to Phu-Lang-Thuong, of which the court build the 500 kilometres that are in Annamese territory. The Chambers, in March, voted 12,-000,000 francs for clearing off the deficits of the Tonquin administration. M. de Lanessan's policy was regarded with mistrust by many people in France, chiefly for the reason that he used the native authorities and restored the mandarins to official positions, whereas his predecessors had attempted to govern the country with none but French administrative officers. When he had 300 kilometres of roads built to connect the principal towns, by hundreds of thousands of the population who gave their labor on the demand of the authorities, his critics expressed a fear that at a given moment the reinstated mandarins might in the same way summon hundreds of thousands for the purpose of overthrowing French rule. His conciliatory policy had the effect of causing piracy to disappear from the Delta. The military had a series of successes in a vigorous campaign in the spring, and captured forts and broke up bands. The military situation seemed more favorable than it had ever been until the summer of 1892, when Chinese marauders appeared on the borders of the Delta. Plantations near Phu-Lang-Thuong were looted, and a prominent French colonist named Vézin was kidnaped. On July 9 a convoy carrying stores to the posts in the hilly country fell into an ambush near Bac-Le, and Capt. Charpentier, Commandant Bonneau, and ten men were killed. On July 29 the post of Ha Hoa was surprised and captured by Chinese pirates.

Madagascar.—The island of Madagascar, with an area of 228,500 square miles and a population estimated at 3,500,000, is claimed as a French protectorate, although the native Hova Government, which has its seat at Antananarivo, in the center of the island, remains independent except in its foreign relations. Queen Ranavalona III, born about 1861, succeeded to the throne on July 13, 1883. The Hovas, a mixed Malayan race, who dominate the other tribes, number about 1,000,000. There are about 350,000 Protestants and 35,000 Roman Catholics among them. The absolute despotism that formerly prevailed has been considerably modified, and the practical head of governmental affairs is the Prime Minister, who is assisted by subordinate ministers at the head of the several departments. The present Prime Minister, Rainilaiarivony, was married to Queen Ranavalona previous to her coronation. France has a colony at Diego Suarez, a harbor at the north end of the island, where there are 600 French residents, without counting the garrison. The exports of Madagascar are cattle, rubber, hides, horns, coffee, lard, sugar, vanilla, wax, gum copal, and seeds. The trade is with the neighboring islands of Réunion and Mauritius, and with France, England, and the United States. The trade with the United States is increasing.

Diego Suarez is a district situated on a large bay. It was ceded to France by the treaty of Dec. 17, 1885. The local budget for 1890 was 172,365 francs. The French expenditure for 1892 is 2,112,970 francs. The islands of Nossi-Bé and St. Marie, which have long been French possessions, but are inhabited by Malagasies

and negroes, who cultivate sugar cane, coffee, and rice, are administered from Diego Suarez. Réunion, 420 miles east of Madagascar, has an area of 965 square miles and 165,915 inhabitants, most of them creoles, who cultivate sugar cane, coffee, cacao, vanilla, and spices, and distill rum, which finds a market in Madagascar and on the African continent. The exports in 1889 amounted to 13,901,601 francs. Mayotte and the Comoro islands are the other French possessions in this part of the ocean. Mayotte produces rum, sugar, and vanilla, and most of its exports, like those of Réunion, go to France.

French Possessions in Oceanica. — The chief colony of France in the Pacific is the penal settlement of New Caledonia, which has an area of 6,000 square miles and 62,752 inhabitants, of whom 7,477 are convicts, 2,515 free convicts, 3,-476 officials and military, 5,585 colonists. 41,874 natives, and 1,825 imported laborers. The colonial budget for 1890 was 2,746,798 francs; the expenditure of the home Government for 1892, 2,746,798 francs. Nickel, chrome, cobalt, silver ore. and preserved meat are exported. The value of the imports in 1890 was 11,091,500 francs; of the exports, 7,140,550 francs.

The other French islands include several groups dependent on New Caledonia, the Society Islands, Raiatea and Tubuai-Moru, Huahine and Bora-Bora, the Marquesas Islands, Tuamotu, the Gambier and Tubuai Islands, and Rapa. Tahiti, the chief island of the Society group, has an area of 412 square miles and a population of 11,-200. The exports are copra, mother-of-pearl, cotton, and pearls. The imports in 1890 amounted to £134,144, of which £80,105 came from the United States, and the exports to £126,724, of which £52,492 went to the United States.

Raiatea, Tubuai-Moru, Huahine, and Bora-Bora constitute the Leeward Islands, which remained independent by virtue of an Anglo-French agreement until, in return for the withdrawal of the French from the New Hebrides, Great Britain permitted France to establish her dominion over them. Soon after the French occupation the inhabitants of Huahine and Bora-Bora revolted, but they were persuaded to succumb by the British consul. The Raiateans were not willing to submit to French authority, and when the French officials attempted to impose it in 1892 they prepared to resist. One half of the island was in French possession, having been bought from its chief when the islands were first occupied, in 1888. The other part was ruled by Tamitea, who determined to fight for his prerogative, and made depredations on French territory. He gave in when three cruisers appeared, in May, and landed a force of marines. and thus the rebellion was put down without bloodshed.

The joint French and English control over the New Hebrides was too lax to restrain the lawless savagery of the natives, who killed an Englishman and afterward two French settlers. An English cruiser that was sent after the first murder accomplished nothing, and when the Frenchmen were assassinated an English and a French vessel were sent to punish the natives of the island of Mallicolo, where the crime took place.

On Aug. 23, 1892, the French flag was hoisted on the Gloriosa Islands, between the Aldabra group, lately taken possession of by the English, and Madagascar, and on leaving these islands Commandant Richard formally took possession of St. Paul and Amsterdam islands, south of the equator, between Madagascar and Australia and northeast of Kerguelen.

FREE EVANGELICAL (ENGLISH) CHURCHES, CONGRESS OF. The scheme for holding a congress of the free evangelical churches of England originated at the International Congregational Council of 1891, when the wish was expressed by several persons that such a meeting might be held. A committee on the subject was appointed by the Congregational Union of England and Wales at its autumnal meeting in 1891, but its action was anticipated by a meeting for conference of representatives of evangelical free churches held at Manchester in January, 1892, which passed a resolution "that a congress of representatives of the evangelical free churches in the United Kingdom would be a great service to the churches." Upon this invitation a number of members of evangelical churches met in Manchester, Nov. 9, as the Free Church Congress, for the discussion of questions of common interest to their denominations. The members of this congress were not officially or regularly appointed by the bodies from which they came, but were volunteers or men of reputation and influence in those bodies, and such men as were recognized by common consent as suitable persons to represent them. The Congregational, Wesleyan, United Methodist, Baptist, Presbyterian, Methodist New Connection, Primitive Methodist, Bible Christian, Calvinistic Methodist, and Free Church of England Churches were thus represented by 370 delegates. The Rev. Dr. G. Johnston, Moderator of the English Presbyterian Synod, presided at the opening meeting, and dwelt in his address on the prospect of such congresses as this knitting the different denominations closer together. In the discussion of the first topic, "The Idea of the Church held in Common by the Bodies represented," Prof. Marshall Randels, of Didsbury Wesleyan College, held that the organic union of the churches was of much less importance than the cherishing toward one another of the unity of faith, love, and spirit. The things which divided them, he said, were mechanical, organic, external, and those which united them were spiritual, divine, and abiding. This view was concurred in by all of the congress who touched upon the subject. Papers were read on "The Ministry," by Principal Culross, D. D., of Bristol, the Rev. Thomas Allen, the Rev. John Smith, of Luton, and Mr. T. Snape, M. P.; "The Sacraments," by the Rev. Principal Reynolds, D. D., of Cheshunt College; "The Fellowship," by the Rev. Thomas Sherwood, the Rev. Dr. Wood, and the Rev. W. F. Clarkson ; "The Work of the Churches in the Home and Foreign Field," by Mr. Percy Bunting, the Rev. Thomas Law (especially on "Nonconformist Parishes"), the Rev. J. E. Clapham, and the Rev. Charles Williams (whose special subject was "Rural Parishes"), and others; "Foreign Missions," by Mr. Albert Spicer, M. P.; "Missions and the Churches," by the Rev. W. J. Townsend, D. D., the Rev. G. E. Cutting, the Rev. J. Harris, the Rev. John Smith, of Luton, the Rev. W. Wilson, a former missionary to Fiji,

and the Rev. T. Lawson Forfeit; "The Influence of the Churches on the National Life"—in respect to intemperance—by the Rev. John Smith; "Social Morality," by the Rev. Hugh Price Hughes and volunteer speakers; "Peace and Arbitration," by Mr. Thomas Snape, M. P.; and "Industrial Questions," by the Rev. J. G. Rogers. The appointment of a committee was provided for to consider the question of federation and mutual action in villages. While the congress declined to make a direct expression on the question of disestablishment, it adopted a resolution declaring itself gratified that the discussions of its sessions had made plain "the substantial unity of the religious conception that exists in the evangelical free churches of England"; rejoicing "that they can look to one another to oppose the spread of sacerdotal teaching and practice"; deploring "the prevalence of ecclesiastical and territorial persecution of nonconformists in many parts of the country"; and exhorting the various churches "to stand by one another in their common testimony for Christ, and in all such efforts after absolute religious equality before the law as shall commend themselves to the judgment of their several communities."

FRIENDS. American Quinquennial Conference.—An informal general conference of Friends was held in Richmond, Ind., in 1887, the results of which were so satisfactory that movements were begun looking to the making of such meetings a regular feature. A joint committee of the American yearly meetings was proposed in 1890 by the Iowa Yearly Meeting, to meet and devise a plan for a permanent general conference. The plan was matured and submitted in the course of a year to the American yearly meetings (Orthodox) in correspondence, and delegates were appointed by all of them except those of Canada and Philadelphia; Philadelphia Yearly Meeting having ceased to correspond with the others, and Canada Yearly Meeting not having approved of the general conference. London and Dublin Yearly Meetings were not included in the call, on account of their distance. The General Conference—designated the First Quinquennial Conference of Friends—met in Indianapolis, Ind., October 18. Ten yearly meetings—the New England, New York, Baltimore, North Carolina, Ohio, Wilmington (Ohio), Indiana, Western (Indiana), Iowa, and Kansas—were represented by 103 delegates, 40 of whom were women. An address was delivered by the temporary chairman, James Wood, of New York, on "The Society of Friends and the Maintenance of its Doctrines." J. J. Mills was chosen president of the conference. An associated committee, of which other members are to be named by the yearly meetings consenting, was appointed to devise a plan for a board of publication. The operation of the plan will be dependent upon the assent of seven yearly meetings to it. The most important question discussed was concerning the pastorate. The Friends have never recognized regular pastors or approved a paid ministry, but the active prosecution of evangelistic work in some of the fields of the society has developed a class of members who spend their time in preaching and have to be supported in it, and it has become a question what sanction should be given to this system. Papers bearing on the subject were read on " The Conduct of Meetings for Worship, and the Maintenance of the Ministry," " Proper Qualifications for the Ministry, and Mutual Dependence between Ministers and People," and "Church Government, its Relation to the Pastoral Question," and were followed by debate. The following minute was adopted :

This conference desires to urge upon Friends everywhere the importance of diligent exercise of the various spiritual gifts bestowed by the Master, especially those of the ministry of the Word and of pastoral care of the flock of God. In connection with these services the Church is reminded of its duty in making such provision as may be necessary for the support of those who give their time to the work, so that the Gospel may not be hindered nor the shepherding of the flock impaired by the want of pecuniary means.

At the same time that we strongly commend a proper pastoral system, we desire that Friends shall be careful to see that it is not abused by the assumption of undue authority on the part of pastors, by their standing in the way of any service the Lord may lay upon others, or by leading members of the flock to look to and depend upon human agency instead of the divine Shepherd and Bishop of souls himself. We believe that the faithful exercise of pastoral care is an important agency in the Master's hand in establishing and building up the membership of the Church.

A plan was adopted for a board of foreign missions. It comprehends a bureau with a secretary and three other members, together with two correspondents, one a man, the other a woman, appointed by each yearly meeting. The duties of the bureau are to collect and publish statistics and other information about missions, to serve as a channel of communication between missionary societies, and to assist in finding missionaries, judging of their qualifications, and locating them in the fields. It has no responsibility for missions or finances. A proposition contemplating the formation of a home mission board was defeated. A paper on " Uniformity of Discipline for all Yearly Meetings " was followed by a discussion concerning discipline, which was at last dropped for want of unity upon it. A committee was appointed on a

Friends' exhibit in the Congress of Religions at the Columbian Exhibition. Preferences were expressed, without a formal discussion of the subject, concerning a change of name from " Society of Friends " to " Friends' Church." Another subject discussed was " The Duty of the Church toward Cities." A committee was appointed on the time and place of the next General Conference.

British Friends.—The yearly returns of the Society of Friends show that there are now 340 meetings in Great Britain, and that the membership had increased in 1892 to 22,287, a gain of 221 over the number in 1891.

The sessions of London Yearly Meeting were opened May 16, with the examination and discussion of the reports of the yearly meeting on ministry and oversight, the meetings at large beginning May 18. Epistles were read from the Irish and the American Yearly Meetings, of which some of the American epistles, giving details of the work carried on by Friends within the jurisdiction of the several yearly meetings, gave evidence of the existence of a strong temptation among the Friends in the Western States to depart, under the stress of circumstances, from Quaker principles and methods. The members of a new yearly meeting about to be established in Oregon were said to be adopting so many of the ideas and practices common to the churches around them as to seem far more like Methodists than Friends. Colleges for training ministers, pulpits, organs, and other unquakerly methods were spoken of ; and the tendency to adopt such strange practices was represented as being more or less prevalent throughout the West. The condition of the society and the best methods of holding and extending its influence were the chief subjects discussed. The Committee on Home Missions, the operations of which had excited much uneasiness in the minds of Friends, was reappointed for another year. The meeting decided to summon a representative conference in the autumn, to consider how mission work may be effectually pushed forward, and weak meetings helped, by methods in harmony with Quaker principles.

G

GEOGRAPHICAL PROGRESS. A commission for determining the proper spelling of geographical names used in publications of the various departments of the Government was appointed by President Harrison, Sept. 4, 1890, and its first report was issued in December, 1891. The policy of the board has been, in general, to accept the name in common local use at present. Of course difficulties have sometimes arisen in determining what the local usage is. Where it has been found to be divided between different forms, the effort has been made to select the most appropriate and euphonious. There have also been departures from local usage in certain cases in order to effect what the board has looked upon as reforms in nomenclature. A certain development process in the spelling of names is recognized. For instance, the possessive form of names is rapidly disappearing, ex-

cept in rare cases, where good reason exists for its retention. In most cases this is effected by dropping the apostrophe and the final s. In some cases it was necessary to decide between two names which have heretofore been used indifferently. The mountain known both as Tacoma and Rainier will be Rainier, so far as Government publications are concerned, and the Bear river, in Colorado, must receive its proper name, the Yampa. With names of foreign origin the tendency is to adopt a spelling that indicates the sounds in English rather than to retain the original spelling. Thus, Cañon City is to be written Canyon City. It was decided that the vowels should be pronounced as in Italian and on the Continent of Europe generally, and the consonants as in English.

Among other decisions are the following: Akkra (Africa) instead of Accra ; Akun Island

(Alaska) instead of Akhun, Akoun, or Akan; Baluchistan (India) instead of Beloochistan, Belouchistan, or Belutchistan; Barbados (West Indies) instead of Barbadoes; Bering Sea (Alaska) instead of Behring, Behrings, Kamchatka, etc.; Republic of Chile instead of Chili; Coos Bay (Oregon) instead of Koos or Coose; Haiti instead of Hayti; Hudson Bay instead of Hudson's Bay; Port Townsend instead of Port Townshend; Puerto Rico (West Indies) instead of Porto Rico; Saint Croix (West Indies) instead of Santa Cruz; Unolaska Island (Alaska) instead of Ounalashka, Oonalaska, and other forms.

The rules adopted by the board are substantially those drawn up by the Royal Geographical Society a few years ago.

A like effort has been made in Germany to establish uniform spellings for the geographical names in the territory under German protection.

The United States.—Attention has been attracted by the formation of a lake in the Colorado Desert in southern California, on the line of the Southern Pacific Railway. It was formed by the stream called New river, which is fed by the overflow of the Colorado, whose bed is here considerably higher than the land west of it. Mr. J. W. Redway, in the "Proceedings of the Royal Geographical Society," describes the rise of the lake, beginning with July, 1891:

"Owing to a silting of the channel of the Colorado about 15 miles below Yuma, the axis of the current was thrown strongly against the west bank of the river, and with the coming of high water the overflow into New river received an impetus it had never before possessed. Its volume was strengthened and the channel was therefore deepened. With the current of the main river setting directly toward the break, it became a question of time only until the river itself should be diverted, and by the close of another season of high water it is not improbable that its whole volume will be turned into the desert through New river. Early in September a number of Cocoapah Indian scouts, who were sent to find the location of the break, reported that considerably more than half the current was flowing into New river; and since that time the engineers of the Southern Pacific have reported the volume to be perceptibly increasing. From the break to the head of the gulf the fall is about 135 feet; to the site of the new lake it is 400 feet. Under the circumstances, therefore, it is hardly a matter of wonder that the Colorado should choose the steeper gradient at the first opportunity."

Alaska.—In the "Annual Cyclopædia" for 1890 were given the results of the measurements of the height and location of Mount St. Elias, made by Prof. Kerr, who went to Alaska with Prof. Israel C. Russell under the auspices of the Geographical Society at Washington and the Geological Survey. These differed so widely from the results of former measurements that it was thought best to send another commission, which should make the measurement of the mountain its main object. The results of the measurements by the second expedition, which was also under charge of Prof. Russell, are much nearer to the old figures than to those of Prof. Kerr in 1890. Following are the figures of Dr.

W. H. Dall's measurements in 1874, and of those of 1890 and 1891:

	Height.	Longitude.	Latitude.
Dr. Dall.....	19,500 ± 400 ft.	141° 00′ 11·60″	60° 20′ 45″
Prof. Kerr...	15,350 ft.	140° 47′ 56 ′	60° 12′ 9″
Prof. Russell.	18,100 ft.	140° 55′ 30″	60° 17′ 51″

The question regarding the highest peak in North America is left still unsettled. Mount Wrangell, for which a height of 19,400 has been claimed, seems from recent measurements to be not more than 17,500; but Prof. Heilprin's calculations give Mount Orizaba 18,205 feet, instead of the former figures, 17,880, while Mr. Scovell, who measured it in April, 1892, placed the height at 18,312 feet. Prof. Russell also found that the bay that was placed upon the maps about three years ago under the name Disenchantment Bay, on the report of Mr. M. Pracht, of Sitka, and whose existence has been doubted, does really extend from Yakutat Bay inward among the mountains, though in somewhat different form from that heretofore assigned to it.

The great Malaspina glacier, between Mount St. Elias and the Pacific, is described in the report of Prof. Russell:

The extent of the great field of ice is 1,500 square miles, its extreme length being 70 miles, while it varies between 20 and 25 miles in width. The surface of the ice is about 1,500 feet above the sea, and its top, especially near the center of the area, is smooth, but split by tens of thousands of crevasses. The surface of the glacier is gently undulating, like that of a rolling prairie. Mr. Russell describes it as "a dreary and lifeless prairie of ice." In one place a part of the glacier, known as the Guyot lobe, advances boldly, with a perpendicular front, into the ocean, and as the waves undermine it huge icebergs are broken off and float out to sea.

Lieut. Frederick Schwatka, under the patronage of the New York "Ledger," made a trip into the interior of Alaska in the summer of 1891, accompanied by Dr. C. W. Hayes, of the Geological Survey. The most important feature of the whole trip was the success in breaking through the St. Elias ranges. The party left Juneau, Alaska, on June 25. They ascended Taku river 60 miles, consuming two weeks on account of the swiftness of the current, thence across the country 80 miles to a lake of which the natives had told them. The lake is nearly 100 miles long by 15 miles wide, and was named by the party Ahklain, or Aklen, "big lake." This was formerly Lake Teslin. They then descended Teslin river, which flows from this lake to the Lewes river, to Fort Selkirk, at the junction of the Lewes and Pelly. From Fort Selkirk they went southwest 225 miles to what is supposed to be the region in which copper abounds, but none was found. Several weeks were spent in exploring the Copper river. It is described by the lieutenant as one of the most turbulent streams he ever saw in his travels. After ascending to the mountain peaks in the interior, and taking observations of peaks never before seen by white men, they descended Copper river in canvas boats for nearly 100 miles. On the east of the coast range there is a plateau which was crossed at an elevation of 5,000 feet in passing from the Taku to Lake Aklen. The river valleys lie from 2,000 to 3,000 feet below the general level of the plateau, while broad domelike elevations and a low sharp peaks rise from .700 to 1,200 feet above it.

A railroad route to Asia by way of Alaska is talked of. and it appears that such a road could be run through fertile lands in the British possessions to Alaska.

British America.—The Grand Falls, in Labrador, which were discovered in 1839 by John McLean, an officer of the Hudson Bay Company, and were visited twenty years later by another officer of the company, were not seen by any other white men, so far as is known, until the summer of 1891. The Indians were afraid to approach them, believing that no one could look on them and live. Their traditions said the falls were the haunt of evil spirits, who dwelt under the mist canopy enshrouding the dreadful boiling caldron. In the summer of 1891 two parties set out, independently of each other, to reach the falls, one led by H. G. Bryant, of Philadelphia, and Prof. Kenaston, of Washington, the other by Prof. Lee, of Bowdoin College. Both parties reached the falls, though under great difficulties on account of the numerous rapids and the laborious portages, while toward the end of the route they had to leave the river and tramp through the wilderness. The following is from an account of the journey of Mr. Bryant's party:

After struggling through the dark woods, they stood in front of the Grand Falls. The great mass of white, foaming water, leaping into an unfathomable abyss from a height twice as great as that of Niagara, made the solid rocks all around tremble, and sent up a vast column of vapor, which mounted hundreds of feet into the atmosphere, being visible at a distance of 25 miles. The deep, incessant roar reverberating along the rocky walls of the gorge gave an impressive idea of the mighty forces at work within the seething caldron. From the deep pool into which the river hurls itself, the water rushes away in a wild torrent through a narrow chasm, with rocky walls 300 to 400 feet high. Striking against the sides of this tortuous channel, which makes frequent turns, and flowing over a rough, sloping bottom, the water forms whirlpool rapids, which, impinging on the one bank, rush back, eddying and whirling to the opposite side. The appearance below the falls, as far as the eye can reach, is that of a sea in a storm. The length of this narrow chasm is not less than 25 miles. Going back half a mile from the point where the cataract occurs, they found the river there to be from 400 to 500 yards wide. Then it begins to narrow gradually—the banks approach each other, till at the falls the width does not exceed 200 feet. There are three distinct rapids immediately above the falls, the last being 188 feet long, and the angle of the slope 30°. The water, driven by the two rapids behind and compressed into a channel only 200 feet wide, rises into surges, broken and abrupt, and precipitates itself over the rocky edge with great violence. By careful measurements the explorers ascertained that the height of the falls is 316 feet. If the three rapids be included, the entire descent is 500 feet.

The distance of the falls from the mouth of the river is estimated at 250 miles. The average width of the river is 600 feet; its depth, except at the rapids, is from 10 to 12 feet.

Greenland.—The expedition under Lieut. R. E. Peary, which was sent to Greenland in June, 1891, by the Academy of Natural Sciences of Philadelphia, returned in September, 1892, having accomplished good results, and satisfied the expectations of those by whom it was fitted out. The party, which consisted of Lieut. and Mrs. Peary, Dr. F. A. Cook, Messrs. Langdon Gibson, Alvard Astrup, and John M. Verhoeff, and Matthew Henson, was left by the "Kite" at McCormick Bay. Following are extracts from Lieut. Peary's account:

Two days after the "Kite" left, Redcliff House was completed, to afford a somewhat better protection than the tent from the constant rains and heavy winds which prevailed for ten days following her departure. Two weeks later, the house being completed externally, I sent Gibson in the "Faith" with Dr. Cook, Astrup, and Verhoeff to North umberland and Hakluyt Islands to bring back a native hunter and his family, and a supply of birds from the great rookeries on these islands. The party returned in six days, after a successful trip, bringing a large number of birds and my hunter, Ikwa, with his wife, Mane, two children, their dogs, sledge, and kayak or boat. Work then began on the outer stone and turf wall which was to inclose Redcliff House and protect it from the cold and storms of the long arctic night. On the 1st of September the entire party went to the head of McCormick Bay to start the Humboldt Glacier depot. The party, Astrup, Gibson, and Verhoeff, left on Sept. 7 and returned four days later, baffled by bad weather and deep snow. Astrup and Gibson started again on Sept. 22, and returned seven days later, having penetrated an estimated distance of 30 miles toward Humboldt Glacier.

During the absence of these parties I made boat trips to different places for deer and then attempted to explore Inglefield Gulf. I was stopped by young ice, and nearly lost my boat in an attack from a herd of angry walrus, 7 of which we killed. On Oct. 1 the young ice stopped all further boat work, and two weeks later sledge trips were inaugurated. The beginning of the long night found us with 81 reindeer, several seals and walrus, and several hundred birds in our larder, and a warm, snug house to shelter us. More natives came and settled near us, and the winter passed rapidly in the pr ara ns of our deer skins, the making of our fureplothing, sledge skier, and other equipment, and the visits of the natives from all parts of the coast. The return of the sun in the middle of February was marked by a furious storm, accompanied by torrents of rain and a temperature of over 40° F. During forty-eight hours the entire region was swept and washed almost bare of snow, and Redcliff was nearly flooded.

In the middle of April, with Mrs. Peary and my native driver on a sledge drawn by 13 dogs, I started on the Turf island and shores of Whale Sound and Inglefield Gulf. Seven days later I was back at Redcliff, having traveled some 250 miles behind my wild wolves, visiting all the natives in the gulf, and discovering the Leidy, Heilprin, Tracy, Farquhar, Melville, Meehan, Sun, Brinton, Hart, Hubbard, Sharp, and Dahlgren Glaciers, and Mounts Daly, Putnam, and Adams, and the sculptured cliffs of Kanak. Upon my return, Dr. Cook, Astrup, Gibson, 12 dogs, and all the male Eskimos at Redcliff began transporting the inland ice supplies and equipment to and upon the ice at the head of McCormick Bay. I joined them with Matt and 12 dogs on May 3, and after interruptions and delays from storms and the steep grades of the outer portion of the inland ice everything was brought to the rolling surface of the true ice cap at an elevation of 4,000 feet, and the real start may be said to have begun May 15. At this time there were 4 of us and 16 dogs, Matt having been invalided at home. On May 24, on the edge of the great basin of the Humboldt Glacier, about 130 miles from McCormick Bay, Gibson and Dr. Cook, forming the supporting party, turned back with 2 dogs, and Astrup and myself with the remaining dogs went on. At midnight of May 31 we looked down into Petermann Fiord from the edge of its great glacier feeder basin. Eight days later we saw the land at the head of St. George's Fiord, and then for two weeks were baffled and harassed by storms, fogs, crevasses, and steep slopes, while trying to weather the feeder basins of the St. George's and Sherrard Osbourne glacier system, the Hatteras of the Northern island ice sea. On June 26 we were under the eighty-second parallel, when the land which I had been keeping in view to the northwest fronted me to the northeast, and then to the east, deflecting me to the southeast. After marching four days to the southeast, the land still extending southeast and east, I made direct for it toward a large opening in the mountains, visible over the nearer summits, and landed on July 1.

On July 4, after three days' travel overland, I reached the head of a great bay, latitude 81° 37', longitude 34°, opening east and northeast. I named this Independence Bay, in honor of the day, and the great glacier flowing north into it Academy Glacier. I reached the inland ice again on July 7, with foot-gear cut to pieces and ourselves and our dogs exhausted or dead. We were lame from the hard climbing, sharp stones, and frequent falls we had met. This land, red and brown in color, and almost free of snow, is covered with glacial *débris* and sharp stones of all sizes. Flowers, insects, and musk oxen are abundant. We shot 5 musk oxen and a large number of birds. Traces of foxes, hares, ptarmigan, and possibly wolves were seen. The surface of the bay was covered with winter's still unbroken ice, imprisoning the icebergs from the great glacier. On July 9 we started on the return, taking a course more inland. In seven days we were struggling through the soft snow and wrapped in the snow clouds of the great interior plateau, over 800 feet above the sea level. We remained in the clouds some fourteen days, when we descended from the east of the Humboldt Glacier. Then with the dogs and ourselves trained down to hard pan, we covered over 30 miles a day for seven days till our eyes were gladdened by the deep-green, iceberg-dotted waters of McCormick Bay.

A relief expedition under Prof. Angelo Heilprin was sent in the "Kite" to McCormick Bay in June, 1892. When Lieut. Peary and his men returned from their 1,300 miles' journey they found Prof. Heilprin and other members of his party about to set out toward Humboldt Glacier to meet them. One of the party, John M. Verhoeff, who had been left at the station, had gone out on a geological trip, and though the most diligent search was made for seven days, no trace of him was found. It is feared that he perished in one of the crevasses of the glaciers. Provisions were left, however, and a supply of ammunition, and if, as his friends believe, he is still alive, and had only gone farther north to pursue his researches, he will have no difficulty in living comfortably among the Eskimos till an opportunity is afforded for his return. He was the mineralogist of the company.

Among the discoveries made are the convergence of the Greenland coasts above the seventy-seventh parallel, the deflection of the main divide to the northwest above the same parallel, the termination of the continental ice cap below Victoria inlet and the existence of large glaciers in all the great northern fiords. This indicates that Greenland is an island, and does not reach as far north as the pole. Lieut. Peary reached the highest point yet attained on the eastern coast, 82° north latitude, 34° west longitude. The highest point heretofore attained on the east coast is about 75° or 77°, and was made by Holden, a German. The highest point of the west coast was 83° made by Lockwood and Brainard, of the Greely expedition.

The expedition brings back much ethnological

material, including tents, costumes, sledges, kayaks, and dogs of the northern Eskimo, meteorological and tidal observations, and a large number of photographs of natives, dwellings and costumes, and arctic scenery.

The eastern coast of Greenland was visited in the summer of 1891 by Lieut. Ryder in the Norwegian steamer "Hecla," who wintered at Hecla Harbor, 70° 27' north and 26° 12' west. It appears that Scoresby Sound reaches much farther to the west than was shown by Scoresby's explorations in 1882. The inner fiords were examined to a distance of 50 miles from the coast.

Europe.—Neusiedler lake, in Austria-Hungary, which has attracted attention by its variations, is gradually disappearing, and has scarcely a depth of one metre at its deepest points. The Government therefore designs to drain it entirely by means of a canal connecting with the Raab, and open the bed of the lake to cultivation.

India.—In 1888, Mr. Needham, political resident in Assam, attempted to reach the valley of the Hukong, a tributary of the upper Chindwin, with a view to establishing a direct connection between Burmah and Assam. In the winter of 1891–'92 he made a second and successful attempt, taking a route southward from the former one, accompanied by a detachment of the Assam police. He crossed the Mu Bun range by a pass 7,200 feet high. Two weeks later he reached Maingkhwon, where he was met by a small detachment of British troops that had been sent up the valley of the Hukong to join him. The route does not promise to be a feasible highway for trade, on account of the difficulties offered by the ground to be passed over.

East Africa.—A lake hitherto unknown was discovered by Dr. O. Baumann in the course of a recent journey from Tanga, northwest to Kadoto, on Speke Gulf, an arm of the Victoria Nyanza. His object was to establish a connecting route from German East Africa through the Kilimanjaro region to the eastern shore of Victoria lake. He left Tanga Jan. 15. March 2 he arrived at Umbugwe, a district at the southern end of Lake Manyara. This district lies in a basin, is thickly populated, and well cultivated. Dr. Baumann, by refusing to pay tribute, fell into a fight with the warlike inhabitants of Tembes, in which he lost 14 men, but captured 150 head of cattle, which supplied his men with food when later they reached to join him across the arid lands to the westward. Beyond Umbugwe rises the wall of the Fischer Massai range, or rather, he says, the declivity of the second plateau. The Waniaturu live on these heights in the latitude of Umbugwe. A lofty mountain which was described as being in that region and perpetually covered with snow, was afterward seen from a distance, but the summit was enveloped in clouds. Southward from Umbugwe are the mountains Ufiomi and Gurui. The inhabitants of the latter region live in great caves in the earth. None of these regions were visited, the route leading northward along the west shore of Lake Manyara. The water of this lake, which is about 70 by 18 miles in extent, is very salt. On the western side, at the foot of the steep declivity, among volcanic rocks, are a number of hot springs. Passing Mount Simangori, the expedition reached Leilelei, a camping place for caravans, on March 12, and then ascended the Mutiek plateau, an undulating pasture land traversed by two creeks. Having crossed a high wooded mountain, they came into the basin of Ngorongoro. This, apparently an old crater, is circular and surrounded by mountains. It has no outlet, but its streams unite in a little lake. It is inhabited by Mutiek Massai. Having passed to the northwest over the high plateau of Neirobi, the travelers found themselves on the border of a colossal basin stretching away toward the south. At the bottom of it was a large lake whose southern end disappeared at the horizon. This lake is the Eiassi lake or Nyanza ya Nyalaya. According to the Massai, it extends to Iramba. On their predatory excursions they travel along the eastern shore. They told Dr. Baumann that many streams enter it from the west, among them a very large river coming from Usukuma, the district lying southeast of the Victoria Nyanza. This, he thinks, must be the Wembére, or Liwumbe, discovered by Mr. Stanley, who supposed it to be a tributary of the Victoria Nyanza; but Mr. Ravenstein showed that this could not be, if the altitudes of the region had been correctly estimated. Dr. Fischer crossed the Liwumbe in 1885, and was told that it lost itself in the Wembére Steppe, forming a small lake there in the rainy season. Lake Eiassi is like Lake Manyara, having salt water and no great depth, but it never wholly dries up. The shores are of crystalline rock; the plateau of Neirobi is volcanic.

This lake has been heretofore unknown from actual discovery. But Dr. Emin on his march through Ugogo inferred the existence of a large sheet of water from his observations on the birds of the region. In a report from Tabora, Aug. 9, 1890, he wrote: "It is surprising to see great numbers of water-haunting birds in a region so poor in water as this appears to be, and I have become convinced, especially by observing the pelicans on the pools of the Buhu river, that there must be in the vicinity some large body of water, as yet unknown."

Passing on to the northwest over the Serengeti plateau, among the Ndorobbo, and crossing the water divide, Dr. Baumann came to the district inhabited by the Waschaschi (or Shashi), which extends to the lake and is well cultivated. The journey was made in three months. ' Dr. Baumann thinks there are no obstacles to the construction of a road, except perhaps above Leilelei and to the west of Ngorongoro. He does not advise placing a large steamer upon the lake, as it is difficult to obtain fuel. He prefers a steam launch and a number of sailing boats. The steamer H. Wissmann, which was originally intended for the Victoria Nyanza, is to be sent to Lake Tanganyika.

Dr. Emin Pasha and Dr. Stuhlmann set out on a journey from Kahma, March 22, 1891, to explore the country along the German and English boundaries, and in particular to settle the southern extremity, of Lake Albert Edward. The route lay through the unexplored ground south of Stanley's track to the southern end of the lake, which was reached in the beginning of May of the same year. Particulars of the journey are given by Dr. Stuhlmann. On the way Emin received news that the people of the equatorial province had settled the northern extremity of the lake, but this rumor proved false.

They discovered a river named Kifu flowing into the south end of Lake Albert Edward. There is a conjectural Lake Kifu lying between Tanganyika and Albert Edward, and this may be a portion of the river. Possibly this river is the most southerly source of the Nile.

From the south end of the lake Emin moved into the snowclad mountains westward. Starting May 15, Dr. Stuhlmann ascended one of these mountains and ascertained its height to be 12,-000 feet above sea level. In the course of the journey Emin Pasha established communication with some of his former people, who had settled at Kavilli, on Lake Nyanza, and from them received news of the sad state of his former province. Here 182 Soudanese joined him, and the expedition marched north to Stury, the most northerly point reached. The return journey began Sept. 30, and much the same route was followed. On the way, sickness and hunger and the attacks of hostile tribes caused great suffering. Emin Pasha himself fell ill and almost lost his eyesight. An outbreak of smallpox necessitated dividing the caravan into two parts, and Dr. Stuhlmann moved off at first with the healthy men. He waited some time at Kinjawanga for Emin Pasha, but as no news reached him he, in pursuance of orders, resumed his march after Jan. 15, reaching Bukoba, on Lake Victoria, Feb. 1. Dr. Stuhlmann said that the territory of Mfumbiro, which Stanley claims to have secured for England, is in all probability beyond the thirtieth meridian, and therefore belongs to the Congo State.

Emin afterward arrived at Bukoba, having entirely recovered from his illness. In one of his letters from the west shore of the Albert Nyanza he said there were numbers of slave traders between James Gordon Bennett mountain and the Ruwenzori. In a journey of six days he found 51 emaciated corpses and 39 bodies with broken skulls. He estimates that 2,000 persons have been carried away from that district into slavery.

The most recent visitor to the great falls of the upper Zambesi river is M. Décle, a French explorer, who is now carrying out ethnological investigations in the upper Zambesi region. He says his predecessors have spoken so enthusiastically of the falls that he hardly dares to express his own opinion.

I will content myself by saying that they would be very grand if one could only see them. The great river, about a mile wide at this place, suddenly contracts and disappears, apparently into the bowels of the earth, falling from a height which I estimate at about 400 feet, into a gorge which is about 500 feet wide. The water dashes itself with such violence to the bottom of this gorge that much of it rebounds high in the air, and a column of spray and vapor rises at least 300 feet above the level of the river. One can see this column, plainly marking the location of the falls, seven miles away, and the roar can be heard for several miles. I could find no position where I could see the bottom of the gorge, and there was only a single place where it was possible for me to see as much as 600 feet in width of the falls at one time. It is impossible to compare the Victoria Falls with those of Niagara.

The expedition of Lieut. Mizon in western Africa has attracted attention on account of its political significance. The geographical results are also important. At the outset he met with many difficulties with the English Niger Company. He charged that its workmen drilled holes in the boilers which they pretended to rivet for him, and that its agent did his best to prejudice the Sultan up the river against the coming Frenchman. He reached Jola, the capital of Adamawa, in September, 1891. From this point the northward route to Lake Tchad was rendered dangerous, perhaps impossible, by the warlike operations in that region ; and therefore the lieutenant decided to give up the northern journey and turn southeast toward the Congo. The German view seems to be that he gave up the plan originally announced so very willingly as to make it look like a pretext for drawing the attention of the Germans in the Cameroons from the real object of his expedition. His journey has opened a line of connection between the upper Niger and the French Congo. The following extract sums up the geographical results :

Mizon's chief distinction is that he has solved the question of the water parting between the Niger and the Congo basins. He has followed from its source to its mouth the Sanga river, and has proved that it is one of the most important affluents of the Congo. It flows into the Congo not far from the equator, comes from the far north, and its head waters are near those of the Benue, the greatest tributary of the Niger. Mizon has shown that this river is about 1,000 miles in length, and ranks in importance fourth among the Congo tributaries, the Mobangi, the Kassai, and the Lomami alone surpassing it.

Another fact which makes Mizon's journey conspicuous is that he succeeded in pushing his way entirely across the great country of Adamawa. He says it comprises a succession of elevated plateaus, and is certain to have a great future. Its altitude of 4,500 to 7,500 feet makes it a very healthy region, and a large part of it, Mizon says, can be colonized by white people. Its population is largely composed of the great Fula people of the Soudan, who are farmers and cattle raisers. Mizon says Adamawa extends farther toward the south than had been supposed. In this great region Mizon found that the important commercial center of Gaundere, which was known only vaguely, is a large and picturesque town, well fortified, and having from 20,000 to 25,000 inhabitants. Mizon crossed the large territory of the Sultan Tibati, who is a vassal of the Sultan of Adamawa, and whose country had never before been visited by a white man. He also visited the large market of Gaza, whose name was known, although it has never been possible before to place the town on the maps with approximate correctness.

On his return to Paris a banquet in his honor was given to 400 guests, at which each guest had before him a map of the region between the Congo and Lake Tchad, containing the itinerary of the explorer. On Aug. 10, 1892, he set out from France on a new journey of exploration.

Much has been said of Mashonaland, the new British possession in South Africa—its gold fields, its wonderful ruins, its agricultural capabilities. The ruins were discovered thirty years ago by Karl Mauch, a German traveler, and it is probable that no white man has visited them since, until recently. Theodore Bent was sent to examine them by the Royal Geographical Society and the British South Africa Company. His paper describing them is of great interest. Although many of the results of his work belong

rather to archæology than to geography, a few notes from his account will not be out of place.

The ruins of the great Zimbabwe are in south latitude 20° 16' 30" and east longitude 31° 10' 10", at an elevation of 3,800 feet above the sea level. They form the principal of a long series of such ruins stretching up the whole length of the west side of the Sabi river, the southernmost, which we visited, being that on the Lundi, and the northernmost in the Mazoe valley. There are also many other ruins on the Limpopo, in the Transvaal, in Matabeleland, at Tati, the Impakwe, and elsewhere, all of the same type and construction ; but time would not permit our visiting them. Some are equal to the ruins of the Great Zimbabwe in workmanship, others again are very inferior, and point to the occupation of this country having continued over a long period, probably centuries. These all would seem to have been abandoned at one time in the face of some overwhelming calamity, for all the gateways at the Great Zimbabwe and at Matindela, the second ruin in importance, 80 miles northeast of it as the crow flies, have been carefully walled up as for a siege ; a forcible entry had been effected into the Great Zimbabwe by a gap in the weakest part of the large circular building. Doubtless at this capture of the fortresses a wholesale massacre of the inhabitants took place, and a complete destruction of the people and their objects of art. . . . The Great Zimbabwe ruins cover a vast area of ground, and consist of the large circular building on a gentle rise with a network of inferior buildings extending into the valley below, and the labyrinthine fortress on the hill, about 400 feet above, naturally protected by huge granite bowlders and a precipice running round a considerable portion of it. . . . It [the lower building] is built of small blocks of granite broken with the hammer into a uniform size, but bearing no trace of chisel marks whatsoever, and no mortar had been used in the construction ; in parts this encircling wall is 30 feet high and between 16 and 17 feet in thickness, and the courses of small stones are carried out with surprising regularity, arguing an accurate knowledge of leveling and an unlimited command of labor at a time when slave labor was abundant and time no object. There are three entrances on the north side of the circle, carefully rounded off and protected on the inside with buttresses ; that to the north, facing the fortress on the hill, would appear to have been the principal one, the small space inside being floored with strong reddish cement. Five passages led away from this entrance among the labyrinthine buildings inside. The one to the left went down some cement steps, and was carefully protected by a doorway consisting of two buttresses with apertures on either side to receive some form of door, which seems to have been universally employed in the buildings. These doors at the time of the siege had been removed, and their places supplied by walls carefully constructed of the same kind of stones as the outer walls. Then the left passage led into the long narrow passage, which conducted between high walls to the sacred inclosure . . . where stand the two towers ; the largest is now 32 feet high, and had presumably several more courses. A few courses below the summit ran a pattern formed by the stones in one course being placed edgewise. This tower is really a wonderful structure of perfect symmetry and with courses of unvarying regularity. By working underneath it, and by extracting as many stones as we dared from two holes in the side, which we afterward replaced, we satisfactorily demonstrated that it was solid. It was built on no other foundation but the hard clay of the place, and covered nothing ; the foundations only go down about 2 feet below the present level, and one foot below a floor of cement which presumably covered this inclosure. It has been preserved to us simply by its solidity and the way in which the stones have supported one another. Its religious import would seem to be conclusively proved by the numerous finds we made in other parts of the ruins of a kindred nature. . . . That the ancient inhabitants of these ruins were given to the grosser forms of nature worship was evident from our finds. . . . As to the little tower by the side of the larger one, we felt authorized in almost demolishing it for scientific purposes, and found, as we expected, that it was entirely solid.

There are several points of interest connected with this sacred inclosure. The inner wall in front of the tower had been decorated with courses of black slate; a curious conduit, about 1 foot square and regularly constructed, runs right through the thickness of the outer wall at its thickest point. Similar and equally inexplicable conduits we found about the temple on the fortress. Then there is the raised platform, approached by cement steps, and a gateway just in front of the tower, covered itself with a thick cement, into which a monolith had been stuck; this platform must have been for the king or officiating priest. . . . The summit of the wall for this portion only had been decorated with large monoliths placed at equal intervals. The rest of the inclosure would appear to have been occupied by private buildings also inclosed with circular walls.

Evidences were found that the place had been used as one of feast and sacrifice, and Karl Mauch heard traditions of sacrificial feasts that had taken place at intervals of two or three years. The word Zimbabwe, which is of Kaffir and Abantu origin, means "Here is the great kraal," and is applied to the head kraal of any chief. The most interesting part of the ruins is the hill fortress, which is protected on one side by the cliff, on another by great granite bowlders, and on the only naturally accessible side by a wall 13 feet thick at the top, and 30 feet high in parts. The flat causeway in the top was decorated on the outside edge by a succession of seven small round towers, about 3 feet in diameter, alternating with tall monoliths. The care with which the approaches are guarded at every turn indicates that the occupants were in constant dread of attack. On a little decorated plateau near the summit of the mountain many crushing stones of diorite were found, and a curious stone having lines carried around it with great regularity. The outer wall of the temple in the corner of the fortress was decorated with birds carved on the summit of soapstone beams 5 or 6 feet in height, only one of which is perfect, representing a vulture. Other carvings were found showing good workmanship and correct geometric figures, with grotesque animal forms. Fragments of pottery of excellent glaze and workmanship and many implements of war were found, among them an assegai with a heavy plating of gold upon it. No coins were found, and no traces of any cemetery.

Close underneath the temple stood a gold smelting furnace made of very hard cement, with a chimney of the same material. Hard by, in a chasm between two bowlders lay all the rejected quartz casings, from which the gold-bearing quartz had been extracted by exposing them to heat prior to the crushing; proving beyond a doubt that these ruins, though themselves far from any gold reef, are those of the capital of a gold-producing people who had chosen this hill fortress with its granite bowlders owing to its peculiar advantages for strategic purposes. Near the furnace we found many little crucibles of a composition of clay which had been used for smelting the gold, and in nearly all of them exist small specks of gold adhering to the glaze formed by the heat of the process. There are tools also for extracting gold, burnishers, crushers, and so forth, and an ingot mold of soap-

stone of a curious form, which is still in use among the natives much farther north for ingots of iron.

Mr. Bent says that Mashonaland is not the correct name for the country, since all the people from the Lundi to Fort Charter and east to the Sabi call themselves Makalangas. He believes the race that built the great Zimbabwe to have been of Arabian origin.

Great difference of opinion is expressed in reference to the prospects of mineral and agricultural returns from this region. Lord Randolph Churchill traveled through it with a view to examining its resources, and has published a book, "Men, Mines, and Animals in South Africa," giving the results of his journey. His observations led to the belief that the reports concerning gold were greatly exaggerated. Alfred Beit, a mining engineer, who accompanied him, examined the "Eiffel" district. "The reefs discovered there may be described as typical of the whole Mashona region; there is a considerable outcrop, much of which when broken up offers an alluring appearance of visible gold; this, however, when extracted by crushing and panning, is found to be of the finest and thinnest character. Where the gold is of a coarser and better quality, firmly amalgamated with the quartz itself, there the reef is found either to have no appreciable depth, or else at any appreciable depth to yield but little gold."

According to the same report the prospects for successful farming are not much better.

Australia.—Henry Greffrath gave an account in Petermann's for December, 1891, of Mr. Joseph Bradshaw's expedition into the interior of Australia. The following extracts will give an idea of Mr. Bradshaw's work:

It was believed early in this century that the wholly unknown interior of Australia was watered by a great river system reaching the sea in the deep bays of the northwest part of the continent. It was to establish this supposed fact that Capt. Sir Philip King sailed along this coast in 1820, entering all the deep inlets to find some great river mouth. One day he sailed 25 miles up Hanover Bay, discovering a large river. The next year he ascended the river for 50 miles and named it the Prince Regent.

Nearly seventeen years elapsed before another expedition, under the command of Sir George Gray, was sent to Hanover Bay to complete the exploration of the river. The natives fell upon the party and wounded its leader so badly that he hastened back to civilization. From that day until last year no further effort was made to solve the problem of the Prince Regent river. These are the only attempts made to explore this great river previous to 1891. But West Australia was a Crown colony up to Oct. 21, 1890, when it became a constitutional state; and this formed an obstacle to its development. In 1891 Mr. Bradshaw led an expedition, fitted out at his own expense, to examine the fitness of this northwestern territory for pastoral settlement. Landing at Wyndham, on Cambridge gulf, in March, he found that a tornado, only two days before, had nearly destroyed the little town. The party, consisting of 5 white men and 2 natives, crossed King river at the head of tide water, and skirted for two days the foot of Mount Coburn, a great sandstone mass, rising perpendicularly and marked by many deep vertical clefts. Crossing the Pentecost river, they came upon a great horde of savages, who at sight of the white men plunged into the water and swam away. Some days later they reached the Forest, a clear river over 200 feet broad. This and the Drysdale are permanent, but flow through a poor region utterly unsuited for grazing. Westward they crossed an open level woodland with pine and cypress trees, and quite well covered with grass. Beyond was a high and rocky table-land, scantily watered, though kangaroos, emus, and wild turkeys were seen. Nearly all the way to Prince Regent river the party traveled through tall grass. The species known as the black-oat grass was from 9 to 12 feet high, and it was difficult for the little caravan to force its way through it. On March 31 they reached a little river, bordered with palms, flowing northwestward. At one point on this river, where many enormous sandstone blocks were scattered over the plain, they found numerous large holes in the bowlders, in which the natives had stored the bones of their dead. The skeletons were not preserved intact, but the bones were packed closely together and large stones covered them, apparently to prevent wild dingoes from scattering them. From these natural mausoleums Mr. Bradshaw named the stream Sepulchre creek. He also found a hitherto unknown fish of fine flavor, which he was not able to find in any of the other rivers. He proved that the great desert of inner Australia does not extend thus far to the northwest, for the region through which he passed was watered by scores of creeks and rivers, and tropical vegetation luxuriantly flourished.

One day the party came to an unexpected impediment. A wall of high hills rose so precipitously that it was impossible to lead the horses up the slope. After hours of search a narrow valley was discovered, between whose steep, high sides they traveled for about a mile, until they reached the summit of a comparatively level, well-grassed plain. On this plateau they traveled for several days, when they saw at the left a large creek, which they followed till its waters fell in several cataracts into the jagged abyss of a cleft in a sandstone chain. They were surrounded by rocky hills, and for four days they were busy with axes, under the burning sun, cutting a road for the horses. Soon afterward a river was reached, which is one of the most important tributaries of the Prince Regent. At the end of a beautiful valley was a great sheet of water, and near it a large sandstone rock, almost horizontal, in the midst of which the natives had heaped up a pile of great stones, and at its center a structure which, as seemed by the ashes lying about, was used as an oven and perhaps as an altar. A little beyond they ascended a mountain about 1,500 feet high. On all sides were great blocks of black volcanic rock, lying on a thick carpet of grass, while lagoons and water courses could be descried on all sides through the papyrus and palm trees that fringed them thickly, and away toward the north and west terraces of ragged hills cut through by numerous ravines and valleys. Mr. Bradshaw was particularly struck with the work of white ants in the western part of the region he traversed. In one place, for instance, he discovered a perpendicular pillar with a diameter of about 3 feet, and nearly

10 feet in height. It stood in the middle of an enormous rock at least 40 feet from the nearest bit of soil. All the material for the structure must have been carried by these little insects 40 to 50 feet, involving enormous labor.

They traveled for five days along Prince Regent river to mountains through which the river flows, and along the rocky walls that hem in the narrow river they found many caverns on whose walls the natives had made aintings in red, black, white, brown, yellow, and light blue. There were figures of men with profiles well drawn, and kangaroos, wallabies, crocodiles, and other animals were graphically portrayed. A kind of alphabetic characters appeared among them. The noteworthy discovery was made that for 50 miles Prince Regent river flows between two entirely different rock formations. The right shore is composed of basaltic rocks, and the left is sandstone. The territory on the right bank is well wooded and grassed, while on the west there is found mostly only prickly spinifex and black-oat grass, with bowlders strewn over the country. Between the Prince Regent and the Roe is an extensive table-land, mostly basaltic, divided by rocky ravines, traversed by creeks, bordered with papyrus, box, white gum, and mountain ebony. Less annoyance was suffered from mosquitoes and sand flies than was expected, except in swampy regions, but the grass fly was very troublesome. No centipedes or poisonous spiders or snakes were encountered. The crocodiles in the fresh-water ponds seemed harmless. Numerous alligators were seen at the junction of salt and fresh water in the rivers. Dingoes and emus were infrequent, but the basalt regions were full of kangaroos and wallabies, many of unusual size.

An expedition furnished by Sir Thomas Elder, and led by David Lindsay, for exploring central West Australia arrived at Esperance Bay, Oct. 14, 1891. This lies in the southern coast of West Australia, and forms a station of the overland telegraph from South to West Australia. Mr. Lindsay says the region west of the boundary of South Australia is characterized by sand hills, covered with grass and acacia bushes, by sandy stretches overgrown in places with spinifex, by granite and diorite hills, single or in groups, and farther south by sandstone hills and a girdle of desert gums. Nowhere were found open, permanent bodies of water. The natives first encountered were numerous and friendly, though shy, while farther on they evinced hostility. The want of water finally forced the travelers back, and into a southwesterly course. The outcome of the expedition proved so unsatisfactory that Sir Thomas Elder refused further aid to carry it on.

Recent measurements in the region between Lakes Eyre and Amadeus have shown that the greatest elevation in the interior is not Mount Giles, in the Macdonald range, but Mount Woodroffe, of the Musgrave range, which is 4,400 to 4,500 feet high. Mount Morris, in the west, is 4,100 to 4,200 feet high. The valleys here are well covered with grass and bushes, but toward the west, between the Deering hills and the Mann range, the soil is poorer, and scrub and spinifex prevail in the vegetation.

The water discovered in 1875 by E. Giles in

the desert of West Australia, by him called Victoria spring, which later explorers have sought for without success, has been rediscovered by the Swedish explorer F. Neuman, who penetrated into the interior from Fraser range, and found Victoria spring at a distance of 185 miles. The oasis has a luxuriant growth of grass over a surface of 4,000 acres. Neuman describes the water not as a fountain, but a lake fed by surface waters. It seems to be about 50 miles from the position assigned by Mr. Giles.

Some items of interest appear in the report of a marine survey on the coast of West Australia by Commander Moore, in the British ship "Penguin." The Colonial Defense Commission desired to place a lighthouse at the southwestern point of the colony, and Cumberland Rock was found to be best adapted for the purpose, and was recommended. The Baleine Bank, between Roebuck Bay and King's Sound, was mapped out. It was found that Expedition island, which was placed upon the map on the report of the captain of the bark Tien Tsin, is no longer in existence. According to his report, it was 9¼ kilometres long by 3¼ to 4¼ broad, was covered with vegetation, and surrounded by an extensive reef. The "Penguin" anchored in the midst of its supposed situation, where now there was found to be a depth of 35 fathoms. Not even a sand bank was to be seen at the lowest tide. The islands Montalivet, Maret, Prudhoe, and Biggs were surveyed under great difficulties. These islands are inhabited by fierce cannibals, and it is dangerous to land without firearms. The reef laid down on the maps at 13° 35' south latitude and 125° 13' east longitude is no longer there; this was the case also with other reefs noted on the map, while many new reefs and shallows were found along the channel from Port Darwin or Wyndham on the Cambridge Gulf to Derby or to Roebuck Bay. The ocean was so filled with clay and mire to a distance of 30 to 50 miles from the coast that objects could not be seen at a depth of 3 feet.

That part of the Pacific inclosed between Australia and Tasmania on one side, and New Zealand and smaller islands on the other, has heretofore had no distinctive name. The Australian Association for the Advancement of Science proposed the name Tasman Sea, which has been accepted by the English admiralty.

GEORGIA, a Southern State, one of the original thirteen, ratified the Constitution Jan. 2, 1788; area, 59,475 square miles. The population in 1890 was 1,837,353, of whom 858,996 were colored. Capital, Atlanta.

Government.—The following were the State officers during the year: Governor, William J. Northen, Democrat; Secretary of State, Philip Cook; Comptroller-General, William A. Wright; Treasurer, Robert U. Hardeman; Attorney-General, George N. Lester; Commissioner of Agriculture, Robert T. Nesbitt; State School Commissioner, S. D. Bradwell; Railroad Commissioners, Allen Fort, L. N. Trammell, and James W. Robertson; Chief Justice of the Supreme Court, Logan E. Bleckley; Associate Justices, Thomas J. Simmons and Samuel Lumpkin.

Finances.—The balance in the treasury Oct. 1, 1891, was $730,939.96. The receipts for the year ending Sept. 30, 1892, were $3,145,900.08.

The amount paid out on warrants during the year was $3,128,788.41; the balance in the treasury Oct. 1, 1892, was $748,051.63. The amount of the valid bonded debt Oct. 1, 1891, was $8,283,315; the new bonds sold to redeem maturing bonds amounted to $207,000; matured bonds to the amount of $305,315 were paid, leaving the amount of the present bonded debt, $8,185,000.

Under the act of 1891, bids were invited for the purchase of a small issue of new bonds to meet certain bonds maturing in July, 1892. The sale was made in May to the highest bidder at a premium of one and one sixteenth per cent. The amount of bonds deposited with the Treasurer by insurance companies was $1,425,000; and those on deposit from the lessees of the Western and Atlanta Railroad $500,000.

Valuations.—The total amount of property returned for taxation by individuals in 1891 was $402,586,468, and in 1892 it was $421,149,509. The returns by railroad companies, including street railways, was, in 1891, $42,383,287, and in 1892, $42,604,025. Of the amount returned by individuals in 1891, the colored taxpayers returned $14,196,735, and in 1892, $14,869,575.

The Direct Tax.—Georgia received $83,031.03 of the direct tax levied by the Government in 1861, and now refunded to the several States. Of this amount, $53,937.80 had been paid to 1,322 claimants before Oct. 1; the largest claim amounted to $1,140, and the smallest to 2 cents. The taxes all went from the five counties, Bibb, Chatham, Clarke, Monroe, and Richmond. After five years money not claimed by those who paid the tax or their heirs will go to the State.

Widows' Pensions.—The amount appropriated to pay the pensions provided by State law for the widows of Confederate soldiers was $400,000. The payments were begun in February, and continued till 4,000 claims were paid for the year ending Feb. 15, 1892. The entire sum was exhausted before all claims approved were paid, and it is judged that the number of applicants will be greatly increased the coming year by the addition of those who did not know of the law soon enough to get in their claim for the first year, and others who have met with delay in establishing their proofs. The amount prescribed by law is $100 per annum to each widow. This sum was fixed at a time when the number of pensioners was estimated at 600. The present estimate is 4,500.

Education.—No general report of public schools has appeared since that given in the "Annual Cyclopædia" for 1891. The report of the trustees of the State University at Athens shows that the number in attendance for the year ending in June, 1891, was 178, of whom 19 were in the law department, 57 in the State College of Agriculture, and 102 in Franklin College. In 1892 the whole number was 195, of whom 13 were in the law department, 94 in the College of Agriculture, and 88 in Franklin College.

In the branch colleges there are in attendance as follows: In the Technological School at Atlanta, 125; in the North Georgia Agricultural College, 70, of whom 14 are women; in the South Georgia College, 180, of whom 58 are women; in the Middle Georgia College, 300, of whom 148 are women; in the Southwest Georgia College, 79; and in the Georgia Normal and Industrial College, at Milledgeville, 316, all women.

The standard of scholarship required for entrance has been raised, and an increased age required for matriculation, with good results.

The financial statement shows the receipts for the two years ending June 1, 1892, to have been $200,456.41, and the balance in hand at that date $13,137.15. The sums paid to branch colleges amounted to $70,541.83, of which $68,-291.86 was appropriated by the State. The State does not contribute to the support of the university, its income being derived from its own funds, principally the land-scrip fund from the Federal Government and the Morrell appropriation, also from the Federal Government.

The Technological School at Atlanta suffered great loss in April by the burning of the machine shops. The machinery hall, 85 feet wide and 250 feet in depth, in which were a furnace and foundry with the latest improvements in machinery, was a total loss. The loss was estimated at nearly $35,000; insurance, $18,000. The shops have been rebuilt and partially equipped with the insurance money.

The industrial department of the Normal and Industrial College furnishes instruction for girls in bookkeeping, dressmaking, typewriting, stenography, cooking and domestic economy, telegraphy, industrial drawing, designing, and clay modeling, as well as in the ordinary subjects of academic education.

There is a probability that the Negro Normal School at Savannah will receive the bequest, now amounting to about $8,000, made in 1834 by John McLearn to the negroes on the Gowrie plantation, on which Archibald McLearn died. Consul Levi Brown, of Glasgow, intimates that the Scotch court will sanction a plan to apply the bequest to the education of negroes in the vicinity of the Gowrie plantation in the event that the descendants of these particular persons are dispersed to unknown quarters. It is found that the Gowrie plantation was located in Chatham County, on Savannah river, not far from the site of the Negro Normal School, to which the State transferred a year ago the appropriation of $8,000 per annum heretofore given to the Atlanta University. A claim has therefore been made to the bequest, in the name of the School Commissioner, for the Normal School.

The amount of legislative appropriation for the year for schools was $935,611. Besides this, each county retains its own poll tax for school use. This amounts to about $200,000 for the entire State.

The Gammon School of Theology (colored) at Clarke University has received an addition of $750,000 to its resources. Several years ago, after Clarke University had been established, Elijah H. Gammon, a resident of Batavia, Ill., gave the seminary $100,000, with which it was built. Just before he died, last year, he added $250,000, and in his will made the theological seminary one of the legatees of his estate after his wife's death. Mrs. Gammon died in December, and by the terms of the will half of the fortune of $1,500,000 goes to the seminary.

Militia.—Under the act of 1891 a permanent site for a military encampment was established

near Griffin. The citizens of Griffin gave the State 105 acres of land, built mess halls, kitchens, hospitals, bath houses, stables, etc., and fitted up the water-supply and electric-light apparatus free of cost to the State. It is on high ground, and the supply of pure water is ample. It is of easy access from all parts of the State. During May, June, and July the volunteer organizations of the State held their second annual encampment. Four regiments of infantry, 3 battalions of infantry, 1 regiment and 1 battalion of cavalry, and 2 batteries of artillery were in camp, successively, numbering in the aggregate about 1,800 rank and file, and 240 officers. The expense amounted to $19,154.80.

Cities.—The table given below shows the population of cities of over 8,000:

CITIES.	Total.	Male.	Female.	White.	Colored.
Athens	8,689	3,964	4,675	4,505	4,184
Atlanta........	65,533	31,351	34,182	37,416	28,117
Augusta......	33,300	15,315	17,985	17,895	15,905
Brunswick....	8,459	4,342	4,117	4,527	3,932
Columbus	17,303	7,880	9,423	9,276	8,027
Macon........	22,746	11,126	11,620	11,538	11,208
Savannah.....	43,189	20,729	22,460	20,211	22,978

The Okefenokee Swamp.—A canal has been cut from the eastern border of the swamp, which is to lead to St. Mary's river. The river runs from the swamp at the southeastern corner, but turns upward and runs back toward the eastern bank. The canal starts from this point, and is about 6 miles long. It is designed to furnish communication with the ocean, so that timber can be drifted down and easily transported. If the canal be continued so as to drain the swamp, a tract 45 miles long and 25 miles wide will be reclaimed. The swamp is filled with the finest timber in the country, including long-leaf pine, cypress, maple, and mahogany.

The Experiment Station.—An experiment farm established by the State three years ago on land given by the people of Spalding County is supported by an annual appropriation from the United States Treasury. A bulletin is issued bimonthly, giving the results of the experiments. These are mailed free to all farmers who apply for them, and tuition in the methods approved at the farm is given free to those who choose to take it. Recent experiments have been made with a new process of curing tobacco, which consists in plucking the leaves from the stalks of tobacco successively as they ripen, and then curing them, in three to four days, by fire heat. The crop is thus gone over several times, and the stalks are all left in the field.

Experiments have been made also in hybridizing sea-island with upland cotton, and have resulted in the production of a new variety, which gives approximately a sea-island staple on an upland stalk. The production of this hybrid, it is claimed, makes an era in cotton culture.

The Crops.—The first report of the State Commissioner of Agriculture for the year showed a decided decrease in the acreage devoted to cotton and an increase in that of food crops. The acreage of grasses was much larger than that of 1891.

In the last report for the year at the end of October the following statistics of the yield were given: Specially full reports upon the cotton crop this week show a further reduction to be necessary in the estimated yield. The total yield can not be over 66 per cent. of a full crop. The best results have been realized along a belt extending from Savannah river to the southwestern corner of the State. Along this belt the crop is estimated at 71 per cent. of a full yield. The poorest result is in the southeastern counties, where 55 per cent. is the estimate. The corn crop has proved about an average one for the State. Potatoes, both Irish and sweet, have given good crops. The only complaint made is in the eastern section, where, on strong lands, they have been injured by too much rain. The crop of sorghum is light, but there is a good yield in the southern and eastern sections.

Mineral Resources.—From a report of the assistant State geologist are taken some notes in reference to the undeveloped mineral wealth of the State. The principal minerals of value are gold and corundum. North Georgia is very rich in the latter. It ranks next to the diamond in hardness, and is used in emery wheels and for polishing hard surfaces. Its scarcity makes it of double worth. No other deposits are known except a small one in North Carolina, just beyond the Georgia border. In Rabun and Towns Counties are very large deposits. In Towns and Dawson Counties are inexhaustible supplies of pyrites, some of which are auriferous. When these ores are chlorinated they will not only be of great value on account of the sulphur, but the gold contents will pay for working, and the sulphur may be used in the manufacture of acid.

Other minerals in the State, according to this report, are: Manganese, mica, galena, marble, copper, genthite (a nickel ore), beryl, rutile, epidote, tourmaline (for making boracic acid), garnet, talc, graphite, asbestos, kyamite, ochre, amethyst, kaolin. Specimens of natural products and minerals are collected, and a museum is to be established.

New Uses for Cotton-seed Oil.—Preparations are making at Savannah for a plant for the manufacture of cotton-seed oil into a substitute for India rubber, by a process discovered by J. G. Carter. The substitute contains a percentage of rubber varying from 9 to 50, and can not be distinguished, it is claimed, from the pure rubber, while it can be manufactured at less than one third the cost. Mr. Carter has also discovered a process for making cotton-seed oil into a high class of varnish.

Railroad Tax Decision.—A decision rendered by the Supreme Court in April will, it is estimated, give the treasuries of the various counties more than $200,000 a year, and will have an important influence on the policy of the State Government with respect to taxation of railroads. For years efforts have been made to get through the Legislature a bill for the taxation of railroads in the counties by *ad valorem* tax, so as to make this class of property bear the same burdens as all others; but the effort was not successful until the autumn of 1889, when the Glenn bill passed both Houses. The constitutionality of the act was argued in the Supreme Court, and that body asked for a re-argument upon certain points in January. The opinion of the court, which sustains the law, was written by Judge Lumpkin. The act provides

that the roadbed and other located property of a railroad shall be returned for taxation in each county where located, just as private property is returned. These returns are all sent to the Comptroller-General, who sums them up and ascertains the total return for each road, and the exact proportion returned from each county. The whole rolling stock or unlocated property of the road is returned, and proportional parts of it allotted to each county for taxation. The roads returned for taxation last year $40,823,000 of property. The return for county taxation would have been exactly the same. The average rate of county tax for 1890 was 5 mills. It is about the same now, and this on a return of $40,823,000 will give the counties $204,000 a year. The principle involved extends also to the right and manner of municipal taxation of railroad property, and the decision probably settles the legality of the act of 1890, authorizing taxation of such property by municipal corporations.

Charities.—The number of patients in the State Lunatic Asylum for the past two years was as follows: Oct. 1, 1890, there were 1,089 whites and 477 colored; Oct. 1, 1891, there were 1,142 whites and 523 colored: during the year from Oct. 1, 1891, to Oct. 1, 1892, there were received 230 whites and 130 colored; the number discharged, removed, eloped, and died during the year was 455, leaving the whole number 1,570. The average number during the year under treatment was 1,618; the total number treated 2,025. Of those discharged during the year, 136 were regarded as restored and 10 as improved, while 96 were pronounced incurable but harmless. The cost of maintenance *per capita* for the past year was $118.33; the amount received from the State treasury was $189,999.96, and the expenses $191,463.86.

The number of pupils in the State Academy for the Blind, at Macon, for the year closing Sept. 30, 1892, was 103, of whom 20 were colored. The receipts amounted to $17,700, and the expenditures to $17,571.86.

The report of the trustees of the Institution for the Deaf and Dumb shows an itemized statement of expenses amounting to $17.481.37, and an estimate of the needs of the institution amounting to $19,900.

A Soldiers' Home.—A movement to provide a home for needy veterans of the Confederate service was started by Henry W. Grady some years ago, and a building was erected in Atlanta by voluntary subscription and tendered to the State as a free gift, without conditions, but on the understanding that it be maintained as a home for the soldiers as long as such an institution should be needed. The building and grounds have increased rapidly in value, and are now estimated to be worth $250,000. The gift was rejeeled by a former Legislature, and the question of its acceptance came up again before the present General Assembly; but the bill to accept it, providing the action should be ratified by the people at the county elections in January, was indefinitely postponed.

The Registration Laws.—A decision in regard to the validity of the registration laws has been rendered by Judge Speer in connection with cases in Richmond and Wilkinson Countics, where it was desired to set aside Federal supervisors. Quoting the Constitution as to qualifications of voters and registration, he said:

The grave matter for consideration is: Has the State of Georgia required a registration for all voters at elections for presidential electors and representatives in Congress? Are the local registration enactments prescribed for various counties of the State, which are practically as varying as they are numerous, such a registration law as will relate to such elections? Are such registration laws for particular counties, and differing among themselves in a multitude of material features, in consonance with the Constitution of the State of Georgia and the Constitution and laws of the United States?

The court is of the opinion that, as constituting an obstacle to the appointment of supervisors to supervise a general election, the registration enactments of the General Assembly of Georgia are inoperative and void because in conflict with the Constitution of the State.'

The Legislature.—The Legislature met on Oct. 26, pursuant to the provision of the constitutional amendment. Hon. A. S. Clay was elected President of the Senate and Hon. W. Y. Atkinson Speaker of the House. Among the important bills were the following:

To make it unlawful in Georgia to charge more than 7 per cent. interest.

To create a State board of health.

To grant a certain portion of the land around the old State Capitol at Milledgeville to the city of Milledgeville upon which the city council may build barracks for the Middle Georgia Agricultural and Military College.

To reduce the pensions of widows of Confederate soldiers from $100 to $60 per annum.

To withhold pensions from such widows of Confederate soldiers as are owners of more than is defined in the homestead laws.

To increase the number of Supreme Court judges from three to five.

To prevent railroads from being controlled by syndicates and combinations, and to insure the holding of railroad stock, as far as practicable, by individuals in their own right.

To appropriate $200,000 for the purchase of text-books for the school children.

To provide for the establishment of a more thorough system of volunteer soldiery.

Political.—The Democratic State Convention for choosing delegates to the National Convention at Chicago met at Atlanta in May. The majority of the county conventions that had met previously had declared against the candidacy of Mr. Cleveland, and in favor of tariff reform and the free coinage of silver. Mr. Hill was the favorite as presidential candidate. At the State convention, May 18, the Cleveland men secured a victory in the election of their candidate for temporary chairman, who was then made permanent chairman. A resolution was passed complimenting the administration of Mr. Cleveland, but one instructing the delegates to vote as a unit was lost. The platform contained the following declarations:

We are uncompromisingly opposed to the enlargement and concentration of Federal powers; to the usurpation by the Central Government of the functions of State; to bounties and subsidies in every form; to every species of class legislation and Government partnership with private enterprises; to the whole theory and practice of paternalism.

We demand the free and unlimited coinage of both silver and gold on a parity with each other, to the end that the money of the people shall be such in quantity and quality as was originally contemplated by the Constitution.

We demand that the prohibitory 10-per-cent. tax on State bank issues be stricken out of the national bank law, and, when this is done, we desire that a uniform system of banking be provided for by the Legislature of Georgia, with a flexible expansive State bank currency. We further demand that the prohibition in the national bank law against accepting real estate as security for loans shall be stricken therefrom.

We demand that the amount of the circulating medium be speedily increased on a sound basis sufficient to meet the needs of the country.

We regard as the most important issue before the people a reform of the present iniquitous tariff.

We further demand a just and equitable system of graduated tax on income.

The biennial convention of the Democratic party met in Atlanta on Aug. 12, and placed in nomination the following ticket: For Governor, Hon. W. J. Northen; for Secretary, Hon. Philip Cook; for Treasurer, Col. R. U. Hardeman; for Comptroller-General, Hon. W. A. Wright; for Commissioner of Agriculture, Hon. R. T. Nesbitt; for Attorney-General, Hon. J. M. Terrell. All of these except the last named were present incumbents of the offices.

The Republican State Convention met in Atlanta on Aug. 11, and decided not to put a State ticket in the field. Electors for the presidential contest were nominated.

The People's party held a State convention on July 20. The platform approved the one adopted at the national convention at Omaha, condemned the convict-lease system, demanded economy in public affairs and reduction of taxation, and called public attention to the fact that the producing interest in both city and country is bearing more than its fair share of taxation. The nominations were as follow: For Governor, W. L. Peek; for Secretary, W. R. Gorman; for Comptroller, A. W. Ivey; for Treasurer, J. E. H. Ware; for Attorney-General, J. A. B. Mahaffee; for Commissioner of Agriculture, James Barrett.

At the State election, Oct. 5, the entire Democratic ticket was successful. The total vote of the State was 209,482, of which Northen received 140,492, and Peek 58,990. The House stands, 158 Democrats, 14 of the People's party, and 3 Republicans. The Senate has 43 of the Democratic and 1 of the People's party. There are 2 colored members.

The result of the November election was an overwhelming victory for the Democratic party, the popular vote being 129,386 for Cleveland, 48,305 for Harrison, 42,939 for Weaver, and 988 for Bidwell.

Notice has been given by Mr. Watson, candidate of the People's party for member of Congress from the 10th District, that he will contest the seat with Black, whose election was returned. Charges are made of fraud, bribery, corruption, intimidation, and illegal and frequent repeating of votes. One specification is that there are but 6,000 legal voters in Richmond County, and that over 10,000 votes were polled at the election. Notice of contest was also given in regard to the seat for the 6th District by Chapman Turner, nominee of the third party for Congress. He charges that voters were driven from the polls at Culloden by shotguns, and that illegal votes were cast in other sections of the district.

Constitutional Amendments. — Four constitutional amendments were submitted to the people at the October election, and were adopted.

The first amendment restores the annual sessions of the Legislature, which were abolished by the amendments of 1877, when the sessions were made biennial.

The second amendment, which limits the term of session, reads:

No session of the General Assembly shall continue longer than fifty days, provided, that if an impeachment trial be pending at the end of fifty days, the session may be prolonged till the completion of said trial.

The third amendment provides that on the first and second reading of local bills and railroad and bank charters the title only shall be read, unless said bill is ordered to be engrossed.

The fourth amendment provides that charters for banks, insurance companies, railroad companies, etc., shall be issued by the Secretary of State "in such manner as shall be prescribed by law."

Under the new system, the Legislature will convene once a year, on the fourth Wednesday in October.

GERMANY, an empire in central Europe, founded on treaties concluded at the close of the Franco-Prussian War between the North German Confederation, the kingdoms of Bavaria and Würtemberg, and the Grand Duchies of Hesse and Baden. The empire was proclaimed Jan. 18, 1871, in Versailles, in the presence of all the reigning princes of Germany. The title of Deutscher Kaiser was conferred upon the King of Prussia, and made hereditary in the Hohenzollern family. The Constitution, dated April 16, 1871, provides for the union of all the states of Germany for the protection of the empire and the care of the welfare of the German people. The Emperor is the head of the military forces; he can declare war, if defensive, and make peace, as well as enter into treaties. He has the power to appoint and receive ambassadors. A declaration of war, not defensive, must have the consent of the Bundesrath or Federal Council. The legislative functions are vested in the Reichstag and Bundesrath, which latter body frames the measures and submits them to the former. The Emperor has no veto power over measures passed by these bodies, but in order to make them effective he has to sign them, and they have to be countersigned by the Chancellor. The Bundesrath represents the individual states of the empire, and the Reichstag the German nation. The former has 58 members, who are appointed by the governments of the individual states for each session; the latter consists of 397 members, elected by universal suffrage for the term of five years.

Alsace-Lorraine is represented in the Bundesrath by four commissioners, without votes, who are nominated by the Statthalter.

The Bundesrath and the Reichstag are convoked annually by the Emperor, who has also power to prorogue and dissolve the Reichstag with the assent of the Bundesrath. The prorogation of the Reichstag can not exceed thirty days without their consent; while in case of dissolution new elections must be held within thirty days, and the new session must open within ninety days. The Bundesrath is presided over by the Chancellor of the empire, and the President of the Reichstag is elected by the Deputies. The secretaries of state act independently of each other, under the supervision of the Chancellor.

The following is the representation of the various states in Bundesrath and Reichstag respectively:

STATES OF THE EMPIRE.	Bundesrath.	Reichstag.
Kingdom of Prussia	17	236
" Bavaria	6	48
" Würtemberg	4	17
" Saxony	4	23
Grand Duchy of Baden	3	14
" " Mecklenburg-Schwerin	2	6
" " Hesse	3	9
" " Oldenburg	1	3
" " Saxe-Weimar	1	3
" " Mecklenburg-Strelitz	1	1
Duchy of Brunswick	2	8
" Saxe-Meiningen	1	2
" Anhalt	1	2
" Saxe-Coburg-Gotha	1	2
" Saxe-Altenburg	1	1
Principality of Waldeck	1	1
" Lippe	1	1
" Schwarzburg-Rudolstadt	1	1
" Schwarzburg-Sondershausen	1	1
" Reuss-Schleiz	1	1
" Schaumburg-Lippe	1	1
" Reuss-Greiz	1	1
Free town of Hamburg	1	3
" " Lübeck	1	1
" " Bremen	1	1
Reichsland of Alsace-Lorraine	..	15
Total	58	397

The reigning Emperor is Wilhelm II, born Jan. 27, 1859, who succeeded his father, Friederich III, as King of Prussia and German Emperor on June 15, 1888. The Chancellor of the empire is General Count Georg von Caprivi, appointed March 20, 1890. The other Secretaries of State at the beginning of the year 1892 were: Minister for Foreign Affairs, Freiherr Marschall Bieberstein; Imperial Home Office and Representative of the Chancellor, Dr. von Bötticher; Imperial Admiralty, Herr Hollmann; Admiral Commander-in-Chief, Freiherr von der Goltz; Imperial Ministry of Justice, Dr. Bosse; Imperial Treasury, Freiherr von Maltzahn; President of the Imperial Bureau of the Post Office, Dr. von Stephan; of the Bureau of Railways, Herr Thielen; of the Exchequer Bureau, Herr von Stünzner; of the Invalid Fund Bureau, Dr. Roesing; of the Imperial Bank, Dr. Koch; of the Imperial Debt Commission, Herr Meinecke.

Area and Population. — The area of the empire is 208,738 square miles. The population on Dec. 1, 1885, was 46,855,704. The returns of the census taken Dec. 1, 1890, which are partly provisional, show a population of 49,416,476. Prussia has an area of 134,463 square miles, with a population of 29,955,281; Bavaria follows with an area of 29,282 square miles, and 5,589,382 population; Würtemberg, with an extent of 7,528 square miles, contains 2,035,443 people; Baden, with an area of 5,821 square miles, has a population of 1,656,817; and Saxony, with an area of 5,787 square miles, has 3,500,513 inhabitants. The imperial province of Alsace-Lorraine, with an area of 5,608 square miles, has a population of 1,603,987. Then follow the grand duchies, duchies, principalities, and free towns, which have a population as follow: Mecklenburg-

Schwerin, 578,565; Hesse, 993,659; Oldenburg, 354,968; Brunswick, 403,029; Saxe-Weimar, 326,091; Mecklenburg-Strelitz, 97,978; Saxe-Meiningen, 223,832; Anhalt, 271,759; Saxe-Coburg-Gotha, 206,513; Saxe-Altenburg, 170,-864; Lippe, 128,414; Waldeck, 57,283; Schwarzburg-Rudolstadt, 85,863; Schwarzburg-Sondershansen, 75,510; Reuss-Schleiz, 119,811; Schaumburg-Lippe, 39,183; Reuss-Greiz, 62,754; Hamburg, 622,530; Lübeck, 76,485; Bremen, 180,443. The greatest increase in population was in Hamburg, Lübeck, Reuss-Greiz, Saxony, Anhalt, Bremen, Reuss-Schleiz, and Brunswick. A decrease was noted in Mecklenburg-Strelitz. Of the total population, 24,231,832 were males and 25,189,232 females. The emigration in 1891 was much larger than in the preceding years. From German ports, and from Rotterdam, Amsterdam, and Antwerp, there emigrated in all 115,392 persons, against 91,925 in 1890, and 90,-259 in 1889. The greatest proportion came from Prussia, and particularly from West Prussia and Posen.

Religion.—Liberty of conscience and equality of all religious confessions was reserved by the Constitution. The relation between state and church varies in the different states of the empire. The Jesuits are interdicted in all parts of Germany, and convents and religious orders, except those engaged in nursing the sick, have been suppressed. The religious census of 1885 shows that 62·7 per cent. of the population were Protestants; 35·8 per cent. Roman Catholics; 0·27 per cent. other Christians; 1·2 per cent. Jews; and 0·03 per cent. unclassified. For every 1,000 members of religious bodies in 1871 there was an increase in 1880 to 1,099 members of the evangelical Church and 1,113 Catholics. In 1890 the numbers had increased to 1,190 and 1,240. For every 1,000 persons without religion in 1871 there were 4,000 in 1880 and 14,355 in 1890.

Finances.—The revenue of the empire is derived from customs, certain excise duties, stamps, and the post office, telegraphs, and state railroads. For the difference between these receipts and the requirements of the Government the individual states are assessed in proportion to population. For 1891-'92 the estimated ordinary revenue amounted to 1,013,041,000 marks, while the extraordinary revenue was 91,831,000 marks. The ordinary expenditures for the same time were 1,015,561,000 marks, the extraordinary 91,-831,000 marks. The total revenue for 1891-'92 was estimated at 1,104,872,300 marks, of which 578,753,600 marks are derived from customs and excise, 34,506,000 marks from stamp duties, 23,-776,100 marks from posts and telegraphs, 20,-194,900 marks from railroads, 2,691,700 marks from the Imperial Bank, 1,185,300 marks from the Government printing office, 8,830,500 marks from receipts of the various departments, 25,-453,300 marks from interest of the Invalid fund, 441,600 marks from interest of the imperial funds, 609,200 marks from various other resources, 91,830,800 marks from extraordinary sources, and 316,599,300 marks from matricular contributions of the different states of the empire. The total expenditure for 1891-'92 was estimated at 1,107,392,100 marks, of which 422,300 marks were appropriated for the Reichstag, 148,-600 marks for the chancellory, 9,195,900 marks

for foreign affairs, 16,432,200 marks for the Ministry of the Interior, 413,117,900 marks for the army, 42,818,100 marks for the navy, 1,964,-200 marks for the Department of Justice, 336,-222,700 marks for the treasury, 306,600 marks for the Railroad Department, 53,861,500 marks for the debt of the empire, 608,600 marks for the Audit Office, 40,905,600 marks for pensions, 25,453,800 marks for the Invalid fund, 540,-000 marks for increase of salaries, and 165,394,-100 marks for extraordinary expenses. The debt of the empire at the end of 1890 amounted to 1,123,944,700 marks, nominal value, the bulk bearing 4 per cent., and some of it 3½ per cent., interest. A new loan was issued Feb. 9, 1892, amounting to 340,000,000 marks. The imperial portion is 160,000,000 marks; that of Prussia 180,000,000. The unfunded debt, represented by treasury bills, was 122,908,940 marks on March 31, 1890. The Invalid fund, at the end of · February, 1891, amounted to 470,542,900 marks, 3,412,950 Frankfort florins, and 5,296,-235 silver marks. The fund for the erection of the Reichstag building amounted to 12,959,900 marks. The War Treasure fund, which is hoarded in the fortress of Spandau, amounts to 120,000,-000 marks in gold coin.

In the following table the budgets of the different German states and their debts are given in marks, in most cases for the year 1892, in others for 1891:

STATES.	Revenue.	Expenditure.	Debt.
Alsace-Lorraine	49,598,732	47,122,650	25,799,400
Anhalt..............	11,082,000	11,082,000	2,688,187
Baden..............	65,952,000	68,120,000	328,733,363
Bavaria............	280,291,642	280,291,642	1,338,189,690
Bremen............	20,332,820	28,862,548	80,438,800
Brunswick........	12,460,000	12,400,000	28,871,588
Hamburg..........	55,841,500	55,889,600	233,968,656
Hesse..............	27,016,985	26,664,283	85,267,279
Lippe..............	1,076,909	1,066,401	810,898
Lübeck............	8,528,007	8,528,007	18,265,424
Mecklenburg-Schwerin........	4,057,000	4,057,000	49,241,600
Mecklenburg-Strelitz..........			6,000,000
Oldenburg..........	6,177,651	6,989,641	36,719,202
Prussia............	1,720,884,749	1,720,884,749	5,584,782,604
Reuss-Greiz......	1,081,778	1,081,778	168,750
Reuss-Schleiz....	1,771,220	1,754,341	1,049,550
Saxe-Altenburg..	3,322,554	3,322,589	887,450
Saxe-Coburg-Gotha..	1,647,800	2,074,408	3,458,299
Saxe-Meiningen ...	6,893,780	5,716,280	12,580,947
Saxe-Weimar......	7,696,040	7,696,040	5,724,818
Saxony............	46,810,207	46,810,207	681,967,260
Schaumburg-Lippe..	730,145	788,176	510,000
Schwarzburg-Rudolstadt............	2,542,950	2,542,950	4,018,688
Schwarzburg-Sondershausen.......	2,462,449	2,462,449	3,547,860
Waldeck..........	1,186,802	1,186,802	2,217,600
Würtemberg	64,776,280	65,260,673	427,966,737

The Army.—The present peace footing of the German army is 486,983 men, with 20,440 officers and 93,908 horses. There are 173 regiments of infantry, 19 battalions of rifles, 93 regiments of cavalry, 43 regiments of field artillery, 14 regiments and 3 battalions of foot artillery, 20 battalions of pioneers, 2 railway regiments, including 1 balloon detachment, and 21 battalions of train. In time of peace a company consists of about 138 men, 4 companies forming a battalion, 3 battalions a regiment, 2 regiments a brigade, 2 brigades a division; and 2 divisions an army corps. In addition to 2 cavalry regiments attached to the infantry divisions and 6 field batteries, each army corps is further strengthened by a cavalry division of 4 regiments, with 2 batteries of horse artillery and 1 battalion of pioneers and 1 of train. Service in the army is compulsory, and every able-bodied German between the age of nineteen and forty-five belongs to some military body. All are liable to serve three years in the active army, with the exception of the so-called volunteers, who, on passing an examination as to their education, are discharged after one year's service. If they show proficiency during that time and the subsequent yearly practice they have to undergo, they are promoted to officers, thus forming the large body of reserve officers. Every man on having served his time is transferred to the reserve army, in which he remains four years, and is liable to be called out annually for practice service. On quitting the reserve army he has to form part of the Landwehr for five years in the first class, and up to his thirty-ninth year in the second class. Owing to the legal limitation of the peace strength only a limited number of the yearly conscripts can join the army, and they are usually chosen by lot. The rest are transferred to the Ersatztruppen, another kind of reserve, in which the period of service is twelve years, and these are called out to serve ten, six, or four weeks annually. At the end of twelve years those who received training. which is by no means universal, pass into the Landsturm of the first class, the untrained into the Landsturm of the second class. Every man under the age of forty-five and above the age of nineteen, not belonging to any other part of the army, is enrolled in either the first or second class of the Landsturm. In case of war the numerical strength of the battalion is increased to 1,002 by calling in the reserve. The men belonging to the reserve have to report semiannually to their respective district commands, of which there are 277 throughout Germany. A record is kept there of the occupation, address, etc., of the men of the district, and orders are made out for directing the men where to report for duty in case of mobilization. It is estimated that Germany would have in the last extremity, with her present organization, an army of almost 3,000,000 trained men. The rifle used by the infantry is of the Mauser system of 1888. carrying 5 cartridges in the magazine, and having a caliber of 7·874 millimetres.

The Navy.—In 1891 Germany had 77 war ships, of which 12 were ironclads, 16 coast-defense ironclads, 4 frigate cruisers, 10 corvette cruisers, 5 smaller cruisers, 3 gunboats, 8 avisos, 11 school ships, and 8 vessels for miscellaneous purposes. With the exception of the " König Wilhelm," the two most formidable ships of the navy are the ironclads " Kaiser " and " Deutschland," sister ships 280 feet long, which were launched in 1874. They are protected with an armor of 10 inches thickness over the vital parts and 8 inches elsewhere. They each carry 8 23-ton breech-loading Krupp guns and 7 guns of 4 tons' weight on the upper deck. The " König Wilhelm " carries 18 14½-ton, 4 12-ton, and 7 4-ton Krupp hammered-steel guns. She has plates 12 inches thick amidships at the water line and diminishing to 7 inches 7 feet below. The torpedo flotilla is composed of 6 gunboats, 8 dispatch vessels, 1 torpedo ship, 1 tender, 63 torpedo boats of from 75 to 85 tons, 49 torpedo boats of 50 tons, and 4 of smaller tonnage. There were 12 admirals, 921 officers, and 10,-150 men in the German navy in 1891. Kiel, on the Baltic, and Wilhelmshaven, on the North Sea, form the two ports of war. Three additions to the German navy were launched during the year 1892. One armor-clad for coast defense of the Siegfried type, which was christened " Hildebrand," one first-class ironclad, which received the name " Wörth," and one cruis·r, which was built as a substitute for the " Adler," and was named " Kaiseradler."

Agriculture and Industry.—Of the whole area of Germany, 94 per cent. is productive; 26,-311,968 hectares (1 hectare = 2·47 acres) are cropped land, vineyards, and other cultivated lands; 10,944,570 hectares are meadow. permanent pasture, and fallow lands; and 13,908,898 hectares are woods and forests. All other land makes 2,860,149 hectares. The area under cultivation of the principal crops in 1891 was as follows: Wheat, 1,960,276 hectares; rye, 5,820,222; barley, 1,667,188; oats, 3,904,020; potatoes, 2,905,870; hay, 5,909,543; beet root for fodder, 398,896; vines, 120,300; hops, 44,505. The yield in 1891 was: Wheat, 2,831,011 metric tons (1 metric ton =2,200 pounds); rye, 5,867,931; barley, 2,283,432; oats. 4,913,544; potatoes, 23,320,983; hay, 18-859,888; beet root for sugar, 10,023,319; beet root for fodder. 7,726,896; hops, 24,731; wine, 2,974,-593 hectolitres (1 hectolitre = 22 gallons). About one quarter of the empire is covered with forests, which are managed by the state in a very careful and scientific manner. Westphalia, Rhenish Prussia. and Silesia are the chief mining districts for coal and iron, the Harz produces silver and copper, and Silesia zinc. Saxony has coal, iron, and silver mines. The total value of the minerals raised in Germany and Luxemburg in 1890 was over 725,000,000 marks, against 555,000,000 marks in 1889.

Commerce.—The customs territory of the German Zollverein includes the Grand Duchy of Luxemburg and the Austrian commune of Jungholz. but excludes in German territory a small part of the port of Hamburg, parts of the commune of Cuxhaven, Bremerhaven and Geestemunde, the island of Heligoland, and a few districts in Baden. The total value of the general commerce in 1890 was 10,783,391,000 marks, comprising 5,844,690,000 marks of imports and 4,938,701,000 marks of exports. The value of the special imports was 4,272,910,000 marks, and that of the special exports 3,409,584,000 marks. The value of horses imported in 1890 was 72,-005,000 marks; of swine, 75,188,000 marks; of barley, 98,000,000 marks; of wheat, 104,149,000 marks; of rye, 98,093,000 marks; of coffee, 219,-715,000 marks; of raw hides, 94,325,000 marks; of petroleum, 73,089,000 marks; of cotton, 290,-122,000 marks; of wool, 244,366,000 marks; of raw silk, 108,547,000 marks; and of woolen yarn, 92,823,000 marks. The values of the chief exports were: Sugar, 216,107,000 marks; woolen goods, 161,002,000 marks; mixed silk and cotton goods. 149,309,000 marks; coal and coke, 140,-491,000 marks; ribbons and trimmings. 121,344,-000 marks; leather goods, 107,245,000 marks; hosiery, 106,788,000 marks; paper, 57,502,000 marks; cotton cloth, 56,791,000 marks; wood manufactures, 51,130,000 marks; hops, 45,630,000 marks; aniline dyes, 37,854,000 marks.

The accompanying table shows the values, in marks, of the special imports and exports of the various classes of merchandise in 1890:

MERCHANDISE.	Imports.	Exports.
Animals	229,586,000	29,845,000
Animal products	103,748,000	22,069,000
Articles of consumption	1,167,578,000	441,046,000
Seeds and plants	40,560,000	26,797,000
Fuel	101,520,000	146,509,000
Fats and oils	236,050,000	27,554,000
Chemicals, drugs, etc	261,874,000	274,692,000
Stone, clay, and glass	62,157,000	118,069,000
Metals and metal wares	388,038,000	436,704,000
Wood manufactures	217,990,000	120,054,000
Paper manufactures	15,487,000	89,879,000
Leather, etc	190,244,000	287,154,000
Textiles	1,119,040,000	1,072,136,000
India rubber, etc	89,657,000	30,135,000
Machinery, instruments, etc	92,883,000	104,390,000
Hardware, etc	28,604,000	83,312,000
Literature, art, etc	27,520,000	88,682,000
Various articles		1,617,000
Total	4,272,910,000	3,409,584,000

The commerce with the different foreign countries and the German free ports in 1890, in marks, is set forth in the following table:

COUNTRIES.	Imports.	Exports.
German free ports	19,998,000	104,888,000
Great Britain	640,484,000	705,265,000
Austria-Hungary	598,505,000	351,040,000
Russia	541,887,000	206,457,000
Switzerland	174,165,000	179,629,000
Belgium	316,908,000	150,808,000
Netherlands	309,217,000	255,020,000
France	267,065,000	231,159,000
Italy	140,394,000	94,700,000
Norway and Sweden	68,458,000	131,828,000
Denmark	61,899,000	76,888,000
Spain	84,068,000	59,071,000
Balkan Peninsula	48,655,000	97,249,000
Portugal	11,269,000	21,129,000
India	123,704,000	32,165,000
Other Asiatic countries	36,446,000	61,060,000
Africa	51,459,000	21,925,000
North and Central America	418,254,000	445,948,000
South America and West Indies	838,195,000	151,238,000
Australia	59,362,000	21,954,000
All other countries	16,588,000	11,173,000
Total	4,272,910,000	3,409,584,000

A number of treaties of commerce expired on Feb. 1, 1892; in most cases new treaties were entered into before the expiration of the old ones. Austria-Hungary, Italy, Belgium, and Switzerland were the countries with which the new treaties went into effect on Feb. 1; they were made for the space of twelve years, contain reciprocal concessions, fix the limit of certain other tariffs for the duration of the treaty, and contain the favored-nation clause. The countries benefited by the concessions made to these four nations, on account of having treaties with Germany containing the favored-nation clause, were the following: Argentine Republic, Chili, Corea, Costa Rica, Denmark, Ecuador, France, Greece, Great Britain, Guatemala, Hawaii, Honduras, Liberia, Madagascar, Morocco, Mexico, Netherlands, Paraguay, Persia, Portugal, Salvador, Santo Domingo, Sweden and Norway, Servia, Spain, South African Republic, Turkey, including Egypt, Bulgaria and East Roumelia, United States of America, and Zanzibar.

Navigation.—The number of vessels entered at German ports during 1890 was 67,021, of the aggregate tonnage of 13,320,652 tons; and the total number cleared was 66,938, the tonnage 13,349,336. The number entered with cargoes was 56,653, of 12,210,950 tons; cleared with cargoes, 48,219, of 9,277,525 tons; entered in ballast, 10,368, of 1,109,702 tons: cleared in ballast, 18,719, of 4,071,811 tons. Of the total number of vessels cleared with cargoes, 35,941, of 5,312,228 tons, were German ships; 3,099, of 2,060,846 tons, were British; 3,668, of 633,836 tons, Danish; 1,592, of 391,315 tons, Swedish; 995, of 180,140 tons, Dutch; 747, of 275,870 tons, Norwegian; and 234, of 70,862 tons, were Russian. All other foreign vessels numbered 10,571, of 3,780,707 tons. Of the total number entered with cargoes, 38,979 vessels, of 6,206,555 tons, were German; 4,883, of 3,583,399 tons, British; 4,926, of 709,718 tons, Danish; 2,911, of 589,546 tons, Swedish; 1,285, of 194,527 tons, Dutch; 1,060, of 392,835 tons, Norwegian; 508, of 136,572 tons, Russian; and 15,855, of 5,809,325 tons, were other foreign vessels.

The merchant navy, on Jan. 1, 1891, numbered 3,653 vessels, of 1,433,413 tons. There were 896 steamers, of 723,652 tons, and 2,757 sailing vessels, of 709,761 tons. Of the steamers, 378, of 149,130 tons, belonged to the Baltic ports, and 518, of 574,522 tons, to the ports of the North Sea; of the sailing vessels, there were 863, of 186,032 tons, sailing from Baltic ports, while 1,804, of 523,729 tons, sailed from the North Sea ports. Of the total shipping in 1891, 2,227 vessels, of 362,114 tons, belonged to Prussian ports. Of the sailing vessels, 1,585 were under 100 tons, 750 between 100 and 500 tons, 206 between 500 and 1,000 tons, 204 from 1,000 to 2,000 tons, and 12 were 2,000 tons and over. Of the steamers, 175 were under 100 tons, 225 between 100 and 500 tons, 214 between 500 and 1,000 tons, 203 from 1,000 to 2,000 tons, and 79 were 2,000 tons and over. The crews of the merchant navy in 1891 numbered 40,449.

Railroads.—The total length of railroads in operation on May 1, 1891, was 43,008 kilometres. The great majority of the railroads are owned by the state, only 4,765 kilometres belonging to private companies, and of these 325 are worked by the Government. Of the total number owned by the state, 9,158 kilometres are local lines, while 2,108 kilometres are private local lines. Of 43,008 kilometres, 31,489 are principal lines, of which 12,697 kilometres have two or more tracks.

Post Office and Telegraphs.—The imperial post office and the separately administered royal post offices of Bavaria and Würtemberg carried together, in 1890, 1,073,717,290 letters, 351,459,660 postal cards, 437,921,908 printed matter, 25,808,840 samples, and 818,392,050 newspapers, giving a total, including miscellaneous, of 2,925,041,088 pieces. The money remittances amounted to 21,873,168,000 marks. In 1890 there were 129,000 employees in the post and telegraph service, 24,970 post offices, and 17,454 telegraph offices. The receipts of the united postal and telegraph offices in 1889–'90 were 353,941,253 marks, and the expenses 231,886,252 marks. The total length of telegraph lines in 1890 was 52,067 miles; the length of wires, 219,911 miles. 18,779,848 inland and 8,243,125 foreign telegrams were sent.

Foreign Dependencies.—Since 1884 Germany has acquired a protectorate over various areas in Africa and the western Pacific. Togoland, on the Slave Coast, in Upper Guinea, has an estimated area of 16,000 square miles, and an estimated population of 500,000. It is governed by an imperial commissioner, assisted by a secretary, an inspector of customs, and a local council of representatives of the merchants. The capital is Little Popo ; Lome, Porto Seguro, and Bagida are the ports. The only commerce is the barter trade for palm oil and ivory. The vast resources of the forests, consisting of oil palms, caoutchouc, and dye woods, are not made use of. The imports in 1889–'90 were of the value of 1,630,000 marks.

The Cameroons, on the Bight of Biafra, has an estimated area of 130,000 square miles. with a population of 2,600,000. It is placed under an imperial governor. Plantations of cacao and tobacco exist, and a brisk trade in ivory and palm oil is carried on. Cameroons, in the north, and Batanga, in the south, are the principal towns. The revenue, which is derived from an import duty on European goods, amounted, in 1890, to 289.007 marks.

German Southwest Africa extends along the coast for about 930 miles ; the estimated area is 342,000 square miles, with a population of 250,-000. The Deutsche Kolonial Gesellschaft exercises jurisdiction over the coast lands, calling the southern part of its territories Deutsch-Namaland, and the northern part Deutsch-Damaraland. The southern part and much of the eastern territory is barren desert. Damaraland is adapted for cattle raising, and although copper is found, the expense of working it has so far prevented its being made useful. The trade of the whole of German West Africa with Germany in 1890 amounted to 5,189,000 marks for exports, and 3,243.000 marks for imports.

Kaiser Wilhelm's Land, in the western Pacific, is situated on the northern section of southeast New Guinea, and includes Long island, Dampier island, and some other small islands. It has an estimated area of 72,000 square miles, and a population of about 110,000. Areca and sago palms, bamboos, and ebony grow in profusion. Tobacco is the principal agricultural crop. The executive official is the Imperial Commissioner. The official residence was removed from Finschhafen to Astrolabe Bay, in 1891, on account of the unhealthfulness of the former place ; but the number of deaths which occurred among the officials since leads to the conclusion that this territory is useless for European colonization.

The Bismarck Archipelago, in the western Pacific, has an estimated area of 19,000 square miles, and a population of 190,000. Neu-Pommern, Neu-Mecklenburg, Neu-Lauenburg, Vischer, Gerrit, Denys, Admiralty, Anchorite, Commerson, and Hermit are the principal islands. Cocoanut fiber and copra are the chief exports.

The northern islands of the Solomon group belong to Germany. The estimated area is 9,000 square miles, and the population 80,000. Sandalwood and tortoise shell are the main products.

The Marshall Islands consist of two chains of lagoon islands. The area is estimated at 150 square miles, and the population at 10,000. The seat of the German Imperial Commissioner is on the chief island, Ialuit. Copra is the principal article of trade.

The Prussian Landtag.—A bill was introduced into the Prussian Landtag by Count Zedlitz-Trützschler, Minister of Public Worship and Instruction, which proposed a revision and codification of the laws relating to the primary school system. The bill provided that in organizing primary instruction, religious confessions should as far as possible be taken into consideration. As a rule, children should receive instruction from a teacher of their own creed. New primary schools should only be instituted on a confessional basis. If the number of children attending a school not of their confession exceeded 30, the erection of a separate school might be ordered ; if the number exceeded 60, a separate school must be provided. Religious instruction was to be compulsory, and should be under the supervision of the resident clergyman of the confession with which the school is connected. The clergyman should have a right to attend the instruction, to question the pupils, and, after the lesson, to correct and advise the teacher. These privileges, however, were to be rigidly confined to denominations recognized by the state. The children of parents who belong to unrecognized religions should take part in the religious instruction of the school which they attend, unless the parents could satisfy the authorities that they would receive proper religious teaching at home. The right to give private instruction and to erect a private school was to be conferred on any Prussian subject proving his capability. The main object of the bill was to prevent any Prussian child from being brought up as an atheist ; but inasmuch as the state does not recognize the creeds of the Methodists, the Unitarians, the Old Catholics, and the Reformed Jews, to say nothing of the Freethinkers, this section of the bill was regarded by many as an infringement of religious liberty.

The Center or Clerical party were pleased at the introduction of this measure, which they had been trying in vain to introduce for many years. The Conservatives announced their determination to support it, and thereby a majority for the bill was secured. The National Liberals, with the aid of smaller groups, were thus left to fight the measure alone. Their objection was primarily against the compulsion of religious instruction, thus giving the Church a power which it had not held since the Middle Ages. In their opposition to this measure the Liberal party was sustained by all moderate-thinking citizens of the empire. Hundreds of petitions were presented to the Government, asking for the withdrawal of the bill, eminent professors of the universities being among the signers. The Chancellor, Count von Caprivi, in his capacity of President of the Council of Ministers, delivered a speech before the Abgeordnetenhaus, explaining the position of the Government, and bringing his full influence to bear to urge the adoption of the bill. The Liberal party, he said. would learn once again that the Government could swim against the stream. even though the current were stronger than it was now ; and that the question was not one of Protestantism against Catholicism, but one of Christianity against atheism. This declaration brought forth a storm of indignation from the Moderate parties, but it looked as though the bill was to be pushed through in spite of the general opposition. Emperor Wilhelm, who had given a preliminary sanction to the bill, and believed in the fundamental principle that public instruction should have decidedly religious character, wished that the bill should receive a large majority, including the Liberals; but learning of the vigorous protest, and that it would only be carried through by a slender majority, composed of the Center and the Conservatives, decided to drop the measure, and informed his ministers of his determination. As a natural consequence, Count Zedlitz, the framer of the bill, and Chancellor von Caprivi, who had committed himself uncompromisingly in its defense, felt constrained to tender their resignation. The resignation of the Minister of Public Worship and Instruction was accepted, but Count von Caprivi, in deference to the Emperor's wishes, agreed to remain in office as Chancellor and as Prussian Minister of Foreign Affairs, resigning only the presidency of the Prussian Cabinet. Count Botho von Eulenburg was appointed President of the Prussian Ministry, and Dr. Bosse, who was Secretary of State of the Justice Department of the German Empire, was appointed Prussian Minister of Public Instruction and Worship. The separation of the office of President of the Prussian Ministry from that of the Chancellor was regarded as an unsatisfactory solution, inasmuch as the interests of Prussia and those of the German Empire are so closely interwoven that the combination of the chancellorship of Germany and the premiership of Prussia are considered a necessity. When, in 1873, Prince Bismarck tried the experiment of resigning the premiership to Gen. von Roon, all the members of the Cabinet declared, at the end of ten months, that it was impossible to carry on the business of the state under such conditions, and Prince Bismarck was compelled to resume his former position. Dr. Bosse declared in the Diet that the Government withdrew the Education bill. A bill providing for a salary for the newly created office of Minister President without portfolio was passed by the Prussian Diet.

In consequence of the income-tax bill, passed in 1891, one of the last remaining landmarks which had survived the political change of the century was destroyed. By the treaty of Vienna, in 1817, a host of petty princes and counts who had been swept away by the Napoleonic wars secured for themselves and their heirs immunity from personal taxation in the states with which they were incorporated. The new income-tax bill abolished these rights, and provided that a compensation should be paid by the Government. A special law was passed this year, fixing the compensation to be paid at 13½ times the amount of the yearly taxes.

According to the capitulations which were signed after the war of 1866, the private fortune of the King of Hanover was to be restored to him intact. By the treaty of 1867, however, it was provided that the fortune should remain under sequestration until King George renounced all his rights and claims to the throne of Hanover. This the King refused to do, and

the administration of the royal estates remained in the hands of Prussia. It was provided by law that the income of these estates, amounting to about 500,000 marks yearly, was to be used for the administration of the newly acquired province of Hanover, and for the suppression of designs of King George against the Government of Prussia. Thus a secret fund was established not under the control of the Parliament, and free use was supposed to have been made of it under Prince Bismarck's administration in subsidizing the press. The objections to the use of such a fund without control impelled the Government to ask the Parliament for an appropriation of a special secret fund, and to apply the interest of the Guelph fund to the use of public beneficial institutions. Before this was done, however, the Government desired to try to effect a reconciliation with the Duke of Cumberland, the son and heir of King George of Hanover, and for that purpose sent Baron von Hammerstein to Gmunden, the residence of the duke, to confer with him as to the possibility of arriving at some agreement. At first the negotiations seemed to come to naught, as the Duke of Cumberland regarded his word of honor given to his father, never to renounce his rights to the throne of Hanover, as binding upon him; but on the advice of his family he was prevailed upon to address a letter to the German Emperor containing the following declaration:

I gladly take advantage of this opportunity to repeat my former declaration, that I have not any intention of engaging in any undertaking which would threaten the peace of the German Empire or any of the states appertaining to it. As a German prince, I love my German Fatherland truly and sincerely, and I expressly assure your Imperial and Royal Majesty that I will never knowingly cause or approve any unfriendly enterprise against your Majesty or the Prussian state, and that I will not enter upon nor aid such undertaking, either directly or indirectly, with the means at my disposal or with those which will come to me by the execution of the treaty of 1867. I therefore allow myself to hope that your Majesty will no longer see any impediments toward the carrying out of the said treaty.

Upon the receipt of this letter, Emperor Wilhelm issued a rescript to the ministers of state, accompanied with the letter from the Duke of Cumberland, stating his desire of removing the sequestration laid upon the fortune of King George in 1868, and charging them with the preparation of measures accordingly. A bill was introduced into the Diet to annul the law passed in 1869, which vested the power of disposal over the Guelph fund in the Parliament, in derogation of the power vested in the King of Prussia by the law of 1868. Some objection was made to leaving the final arrangements solely in the hands of the Crown, and, with the consent of the Government, the bill was amended so as to vest the power of abolishing the sequestration in the Minister of Finance. In accordance with this bill the allodial fortunes of the late King of Hanover were turned over to his heir, the Duke of Cumberland, while the administration of the entailed estates of the combined houses of Brunswick-Lüneburg remained with the Prussian Government, subject to a special arrangement to be made with the duke, to which the Prussian Diet has to give its consent.

Riots.—The partial failure of crops in many parts of the empire, and the consequent rise of prices of bread, coupled with the discontent of the working classes and the failure of finding work to provide their families with food, led to serious riots of unemployed workmen in the city of Berlin in the latter part of February, 1892. A body of unemployed workmen, numbering from 3,000 to 4,000, met in the suburb of Friederichshain under socialistic auspices. In inflammatory speeches the Government was denounced for not providing work to keep the people from starvation. A resolution was offered to march in a body to the city, and to submit their grievances to the Emperor. This suggestion was taken up amid cheers and cries of "The Kaiser must see us! we need bread!" The crowd marched into the city, shouting, "To the palace! to the palace!" Arrived at the Schlossplatz, the mob was met by a detachment of police, who made a charge upon them, trying to force them back, but their first attack was repelled. They immediately rallied, however, and using their sabers freely managed to check the onward march of the mob, and after a short resistance the crowd was put to flight, the police being contented with arresting those within easy reach, and allowing the remainder to escape. In the evening the riot grew more serious, the rioters being re-enforced by workingmen returning from their work, and the whole body of police was called on duty. The first alarm came from the northern part of the city, where a crowd of about 400 men paraded the streets, plundered the bake shops and smashed the windows along their line of march. On the arrival of a detachment of police the mob was dispersed, many arrests being made. Similar scenes were enacted in other parts of the city. At midnight the police had fairly managed to restore order, but the streets were sharply patroled and gatherings immediately broken up. It was expected that order would be preserved the next day, but spasmodic and unorganized disturbances occurred throughout the day and the two days following, when order was finally restored. A large number of rioters were seriously injured by saber cuts from the police, and several policemen fared badly at the hands of the mob. A great number of persons were arrested, but the majority were liberated after a few days of imprisonment, while the ringleaders were severely punished. Emperor Wilhelm, on the second day of the riots, went out for a ride on horseback, attended only by a single aid-de-camp and preceded by two mounted policemen. This courageous action pleased the people, and he was cheered in passing through the streets filled with the highly excited populace. The Socialists disclaimed any participation in the affair, and attributed the trouble to the rough element in the city. Similar but not quite as serious affairs occurred in Dantzig, Hanover, and Leipsic.

The Reichstag.—The session of the Reichstag which since May 6, 1890, had only been adjourned, was closed March 31, 1892. The regular session was opened on Nov. 22 by a speech of the Emperor, in which he said: "In view of our friendly relations with all the powers, and the consciousness that in pursuing a common end we shall continue to enjoy the effectual support of the allied states, I cherish the hope that Germany will not be disturbed in her peaceful endeavor to promote her ideal economic interests. At the same time, the development of the military power of the other European states imposes on us the serious, nay, imperative, duty of strengthening the defensive capacity of the empire by thoroughgoing measures." He announced the introduction of a new military bill to meet the expenses of an increase in the army; further taxation of beer and brandy, and also of bourse transactions, was proposed.

The Army Bill.—The most important measure of the session of 1892-'93 was the Army bill. By the law of 1887 the peace footing of the German army was fixed at 468,409 men until March 31, 1894. This number was increased to 486,983 by the law of 1890, and it was necessary, therefore, to pass a new legislative enactment before April 1, 1894. The Government prepared a bill which fixes the peace footing of the German army, including corporals, on a yearly average at 492,068 men from Oct. 1, 1893, to March 31, 1899. The infantry will be composed of 711 battalions, the cavalry of 477 squadrons, the field artillery of 494 batteries, the foot artillery of 37 battalions, the pioneers of 24 battalions, the railway troops of 7, and the train of 21 battalions. The average strength is calculated on the principle that the infantry troops in general will go through two years' active service with the colors. The necessary changes in the establishment of commissioned officers, doctors, and officials will be regulated by the budget of the empire. Privates can be promoted to vacant posts as noncommissioned officers conditionally upon the strength of the establishment being otherwise maintained. The one-year volunteers are not included in the above figures. The Government, in setting forth its reasons for this increase, draws attention to the alteration which has taken place, to the disadvantage of the empire, in the politico-military situation.

The strengthening of the army and the shortening of the time of service implies the institution of supplementary organizations. As such are to be counted the extension of the cadet corps and of the preparatory and higher schools for noncommissioned officers. Measures for increased rewards for proficiency in tactics and marksmanship, and for increased supplies of ammunition for rifle practice, must be taken. The training of the Ersatz reserve in its present shape disappears altogether, but the institution is maintained for certain purposes, such as training recruits, who do not quite come up to the physical standard for bearing arms, in ambulance and administrative duties. Reckoning the future annual contingent of recruits to be enrolled in the active army at 235,000 men, including 9,000 one-year volunteers, and taking the total of 24 such annual contingents, with due allowance for the normal increase of population on the one hand and for a normal waste of 25 per cent. on the other, Germany will have, when the new system has been fully developed, a total force of 4,400,000 trained men, thus overtaking France with 4,053,000 men, and remaining slightly behind Russia with nearly 5,000,000.

Foreign Relations.—The Czar, in the beginning of June, 1892, at length returned the

visit paid by the Kaiser in the beginning of his
reign. The Russian monarch, arriving in his
yacht June 8, was met by Wilhelm at Kiel, and
was entertained there till evening, neither of the
Chancellors being present at the meeting. The
Russian press denied that the interview signified
any improvement in the relations with Germany,
and this fact was emphasized by the simultaneous interview of the Grand Duke Constantine
with President Carnot during the French festivities in Nancy. The King and Queen of Italy
paid a visit to the Imperial Majesties in June,
1892. They arrived in Berlin on June 20, and
were accompanied by the Italian Minister of
Foreign Affairs, Brin. A meeting took place
between him and the German Chancellor, in
which it was determined that full conformity
existed between the two governments in relation
to all important political questions.

The Emperor.—At the annual banquet of
the Brandenburg Diet Emperor Wilhelm delivered a speech which has since become famous.
After alluding to the opposition to the Government and the dissatisfaction with the new course,
which, he said, might lead one to the belief that
Germany was the worst-governed country in the
world, the Emperor continued :

Would it not be better for the grumblers to shake
the dust of Germany from their shoes and leave as
soon as possible this miserable and pitiable position ?
The firm conviction of your sympathy in my labors
gives me renewed strength to persist in my work and
to press forward in the path which Heaven has laid
out for me. I am helped thereto by my feeling of
responsibility to the Ruler of all, and the firm conviction that he, our old ally of Rossbach and Denne-
witz, will not now leave me in the lurch. No, Bran-
denburgers, we are called to greatness, and to glorious
days will I lead you. To the unending complaints
about the new course and the men who direct it, I
answer confidently and decidedly, " My course is the
right one, and I shall continue to steer it."

Great dissatisfaction was expressed by the
press at this speech, and it was freely commented
upon. The result was that a large number of
papers were confiscated, including some of the
leading journals of the empire, and proceedings
of lesè-majesté were instituted against the offending editors, but in most cases the proceedings
were dropped.

Prince Bismarck.—On the way to the wedding of his eldest son, Herbert, in Vienna, on
June 21, 1892, the ex-Chancellor was the recipient of great ovations from the German people.
His short sojourn in Dresden was marked by a
tremendous torchlight procession, in which over
15,000 people took part, and more than double
that number took occasion to do homage to the
man of *blood and iron.* In Vienna he was welcomed with great ostentation by the populace,
and was the receiver of many honors. It was his
desire to be received in audience by the Emperor
Franz Joseph, and for that purpose he was about
to apply to the German ambassador at Vienna,
when he was given to understand that, on request of the German Government, an audience
would not be granted to him. Prior to his departure, in a newspaper interview, Prince Bismarck expressed condemnation of the commercial treaty with Austria as being opposed to German agricultural interests, which also applied to
the treaties with Switzerland and Italy. He re-

marked that since his resignation the friendly
feeling with Russia had been destroyed, that he
had enjoyed the confidence and trust of the
Czar, and therefore had influence over the Russian policy, while his successor did not possess
this personal confidence, and that this explained
the change which had taken place in the political situation of Europe since his retirement. In
München, Augsburg, and Kissingen he received
ovations from the people and from delegates of
the whole southern part of Germany. In Jena
he delivered a speech in which he advocated a
strong parliamentary government. This was all
the more remarkable because, during his own
administration, he had tried to keep down the
power of the Parliament as much as possible.

His utterances were the subject of a long and
bitter newspaper war between the Government
organs and those advocating Prince Bismarck's
cause, with no credit to either side. The attacks
against the Government growing fiercer and
stronger, the Government finally saw fit to break
its long silence, and issued two documents in
the "Reichsanzeiger." The first was addressed
to the imperial representatives abroad, and was
dated May 23, 1892 ; it runs as follows :

If his Majesty's Government, in recognition of the
great statesman's immortal services, could without
hesitation maintain silence in the presence of criticisms dealing mainly with personal relations and internal policy, the expediency of maintaining the same
reserve became more questionable when these utterances came to touch upon questions of foreign policy,
since it might involve the risk of regrettable misunderstandings abroad. His Majesty discriminates between the Prince Bismarck of former times and of to-
day, and is anxious that his Government should avoid
everything which might tend to diminish in the eyes
of the German nation the familiar figure of its greatest statesman. In authorizing your Excellency to express yourself as circumstances may require, in accordance with the above, I have only to add the hope
that the Government to which you are accredited will
not attach any practical importance to the press publications claiming to reproduce Prince Bismarck's
Views.

The second document related to the instructions given to the German ambassador at Vienna, dated June 9, 1892, and runs as follows :

The reports of a *rapprochement* of Prince Bismarck
toward his Majesty the Emperor lack the indispensable condition that the former Chancellor intends to
take the first steps in this direction. Even were this
to happen, such a *rapprochement* could never go so
far as to justify public opinion in assuming that
Prince Bismarck would regain any influence upon
the conduct of public affairs.

The Antisemitic Movement. — The agitation against the Jews is rapidly gaining ground
in Germany, and scandals with which Jews have
been connected have been made the most of in
order to place the antisemites in the light of
champions against corruption. In the beginning of March, 1892, Rector Ahlwardt published
a pamphlet accusing the rifle-manufacturing firm
of Loewe & Co., of Spandau, of furnishing the
German Government with rifles not fit for use
in case of war. This accusation was contradicted
by the German Minister of War, and Ahlwardt
was prosecuted for libel and sentenced to five
months' imprisonment. A letter of Loewe, acknowledged by him, was published, in which
Loewe had offered in 1887 to supply the then

French Minister of War, Boulanger, with the plant and machinery necessary for the manufacture of the Lebel rifle. Loewe's action was all the more condemned by patriotic Germans inasmuch as the offer was made at the time of the Schnaebele affair, when everything pointed to a war between Germany and France, and when Loewe & Co. were employed by the German Government to manufacture the Mauser rifle.

How far the antisemites are carried away by their fanaticism was shown by the Buschhoff case. At Xanten, a small place in Westphalia, a child five years old was found dead in a barn with his throat cut. The barn being near the shop of a Jewish butcher, Buschhoff, he was accused of murdering the child in order to provide blood for mysterious rites. No clew of the actual murderer being found, Buschhoff was put on trial, and at the end of two weeks, after all the testimony had been heard, the public prosecutor asked, on behalf of the Crown, for the prisoner's acquittal, claiming that the accused had proved an *alibi* for every minute of the day of the murder. The jury, after a short conference, announced their verdict of "Not guilty."

GREAT BRITAIN AND IRELAND, a constitutional monarchy in western Europe. The legislative authority for the British Empire is vested in the two Houses of Parliament, and is practically exercised by the lower house or House of Commons, consisting of 670 members, of whom 377 sit for rural constituencies, counties, and county divisions, 284 for boroughs, and 9 for universities. Of the English members, 253 represent counties, 237 boroughs, and 5 universities; of the Scotch members, 39 sit for counties, 31 for boroughs, and 2 for universities; of the Irish members, 85 are elected by county districts, 16 by boroughs, and 2 by universities. The number of registered voters in 1891 was 4,838,080 in England and Wales, 593,877 in Scotland, and 741,711 in Ireland : in all, 6,173,668, constituting about one sixth of the total population. In 1882, prior to the last reform act, the total number was 3,152,910. The voting is secret and by ballot. Any man of full age is qualified to sit in Parliament, unless he is a clergyman of the English or Scotch Establishment or of the Roman Catholic Church, a Government contractor or a sheriff or returning officer, an English or Scotch peer, or an Irish representative peer. When a seat in the House of Commons becomes vacant a writ for the election of a new member is issued by the vote of the House, or on the authority of the Speaker if the House is not sitting. The sessions of Parliament have commonly lasted from the middle of February till about the end of August in recent times, except in the last two or three years, when the sessions have been longer and more irregular. Parliament is summoned by royal writ, which is issued at least thirty-five days before the meeting, and is prorogued by proclamation of the sovereign, all unfinished legislation thereupon falling to the ground. Parliament is dissolved by proclamation, which is usually issued after prorogation. If a Parliament has lasted seven years, it expires by lapse of time. During the present century no Parliament has been dissolved by statutory limitation. The last Parliament lasted from Aug. 5, 1886, till July

15, 1892; the one immediately preceding, from Jan. 12 to June 26, 1886; the one before that, from April 29, 1880, till Nov. 18, 1885; the predecessor of that one from March 5, 1874, till March 24, 1880 : and the one previous to that, from Dec. 10, 1868, till Jan. 26, 1874. The authority of Parliament is virtually absolute, being restricted by no written Constitution. Ministers and members are governed by a conservative regard for constitutional precedents; yet these can be, and have been, annulled and new precedents created by the simple vote of the majority. Such action always proceeds from strong popular pressure, the constituents from whom the members receive their mandates being the final arbiters and repositories of supreme and unlimited political power.

The House of Lords is composed of English peers, who have seats by virtue of hereditary right or by creation of the sovereign; of Irish representative peers, elected for life by the Irish nobility; of Scotch peers, elected for each Parliament; and of English bishops, who are lords by virtue of their office. There were 559 peers on the roll of the House in 1891. All bills to become law must receive the vote of the majority of both houses; yet matters of a political and contentious nature are rarely contested in the House of Lords, which gives its attention to social or imperial matters of a minor and nonpolitical character, and to ecclesiastical and legal questions which are decided in the sense indicated by the ecclesiastical and legal members.

The executive authority, nominally vested in the Crown, is exercised by the Cabinet, which is selected and dominated to a great extent by the Prime Minister, the statesman who is the recognized leader of the party, having a majority of votes in the House of Commons. With the assistance of his colleagues he disposes of the patronage, decides all political, foreign, and imperial questions falling within the wide province of executive action, and arranges and controls the business of Parliament. When the Cabinet ceases to control the votes of a majority of the Commons, and finds its policy condemned by a clear expression of the sense of the House, it either resigns, or if, as is often the case, it considers that it still possesses the confidence of a majority of the voters Parliament is dissolved, and writs for a general election are issued. When a Cabinet resigns the retiring Prime Minister advises the sovereign to call on the leader of the new majority, almost invariably the chosen leader of the opposing great party, to form a new Cabinet. The Cabinet at the beginning of 1892 was composed of the following members : Prime Minister and Secretary of State for Foreign Affairs, the Marquis of Salisbury, appointed Aug. 3, 1886, to the premiership, and constituted Foreign Secretary on Jan. 14, 1887; Lord High Chancellor, Lord Halsbury, formerly Sir Hardinge S. Giffard ; Lord President of the Council, Viscount Cranbrook, formerly Gathorne Hardy, appointed Jan. 14, 1887; Chancellor of the Exchequer, George Joachim Goschen, appointed Jan. 14, 1887; Secretary of State for the Home Department, Henry Matthews; Secretary of State for War, Edward Stanhope, appointed Jan. 14, 1887; First Lord of the Treasury, Arthur J. Balfour, appointed in November, 1891;

Secretary of State for the Colonies, Lord Knutsford, formerly Sir Henry Thurstan Holland, appointed Jan. 14, 1887; Secretary of State for India, Viscount Cross, formerly Sir Richard Cross;
First Lord of the Admiralty, Lord George
Hamilton; Chief Secretary to the Lord Lieutenant of Ireland, William Lawies Jackson, appointed in November, 1891; Lord Chancellor
of Ireland, Lord Ashbourne, formerly Edward
Gibson; Chancellor of the Duchy of Lancaster,
the Duke of Rutland, formerly Lord John Manners; President of the Board of Trade, Sir
Michael Hicks-Beach, who succeeded Lord Stanley of Preston in 1888; Lord Privy Seal, Earl
Cadogan, appointed April 19, 1887; President
of the Local Government Board, Charles Thomas
Ritchie, appointed on Aug. 3, 1886, and admitted to a seat in the Cabinet on April 19, 1887;
President of the Board of Agriculture, Henry
Chaplin, appointed Sept. 5, 1889, when the office was created.

Area and Population.—The area of the
United Kingdom is 121,481 square miles. The
last decennial census, taken on April 5, 1891,
makes the total population 37,888,153, showing
an increase in ten years of 8·17 per cent. In
England and Wales the increase was 11·65 per
cent.; in Scotland, 7·96 per cent.; and in the Isle of
Man and the Channel Islands, 4·7 per cent.; while
in Ireland there was a decrease of 9·1 per cent.
The population of England in 1891 was 27,482,-
104; of Wales, 1,518,914; of Scotland, 4,033,103;
of Ireland, 4,706,162; of the Isle of Man, 55,598;
of the Channel Islands, 92,272. In England and
Wales there were 14,050,620 males and 14,950,-
398 females; in Scotland, 1,951,461 males and
2,081,642 females; in Ireland, 2,317,076 males
and 2,389,086 females.

The density of population of England and
Wales, with an area of 58,186 square miles and
29,001,018 inhabitants, is 498 per square mile, as
compared with 446 in 1881, 390 in 1871, 308 in
1851, 139 in 1831, and 175 in 1811. The urban
population of England and Wales constitutes
71·7 per cent. of the total, and the rural population 28·3 per cent. There are 6 towns of upward of 250,000 inhabitants, containing together 22 per cent. of the whole population of
England and Wales; 18 others with over 100,-
000, which contain 9·6 per cent.; 38 others with
between 50,000 and 100,000, which contain 9 per
cent.; and 296 with over 10,000, which contain
20·9 per cent. The population of the metropolis
of London in 1891 was 4,211,056, showing an increase of 10·4 per cent. since the last census. In
the central area, containing 1,022,529 people,
there was a decrease of 7·2 per cent., but in the
rest of the inner ring or registration district the
population increased by 17·5 per cent. The
outer ring contained 1,422,276 inhabitants, making the population of what is called Greater
London, 5,633,332, showing an increase of 18·2
per cent., a less rate than in the preceding decade, when the growth was 22·7 per cent.

In Scotland, which has an area of 30,417 square
miles, the density of population is 132, as compared with 100 in 1861, and 60 in 1811. There
are 4 towns of over 250,000 inhabitants, in which
is found 27·1 per cent. of the total population,
while 16·4 per cent. lives in 25 more towns having upward of 10,000 inhabitants.

Ireland, with an area of 32,531 square miles,
has 144 inhabitants to the square mile, as compared with 159 in 1881, 178 in 1861, and 239 in
1831. In Leinster the population decreased 6·5
per cent. during the last decade; in Munster,
12·2 per cent.; in Ulster, 7·2 per cent.; in Con-
naught, 11·9 per cent. The urban population is
17·9 per cent. of the whole, 10·8 per cent. being
contained in 2 towns of over 100,000 inhabitants,
Dublin and Belfast.

The number of marriages in England and
Wales in 1890 was 223,028; of births, 869,937;
of deaths, 562,248; excess of births over deaths,
327,689. In Scotland the number of marriages
was 27,441; of births, 121,530; of deaths, 78,978;
excess of births, 42,552. In Ireland the marriages were 20,866 in number; births, 105,343;
deaths, 86,165; excess of births, 19,178.

Between 1853 and 1890 the number of emigrants of British or Irish origin was 7,121,966, of
whom 4,739,547 went to the United States. Of
the latter, 2,341,845 were Irish, 2,019,743 English
or Welsh, and 377,959 Scotch. The number of
persons, natives and foreigners, who emigrated
from the United Kingdom in 1891 was 334,451,
of whom 252,171 were bound for the United
States, 33,791 for British America, and 19,714
for Australasian colonies. The number of British and Irish emigrants in 1891 was 218,263, of
whom 137,658 were English, 58,394 Irish, and
22,211 Scotch. In 1890 the total number of emigrants was 315,980, and during the same year
there were 155,910 immigrants, making the net
emigration 160,070. The total emigration of
persons of British nationality was 218,116 in
1890, and the net British emigration, deducting
109,470 immigrants of British origin, was 108,646.

The Army.—The army estimates voted by
Parliament for the year ending March 31, 1892,
provide for 7,453 commissioned officers, 993 warrant officers, 15,886 sergeants, 3,684 musicians,
and 125,680 rank and file, making a total of 153,-
696, which is 213 more than in the previous year.
This is the regular army of the United Kingdom,
and does not include the troops drafted from the
army to serve in India, and forming the British
army in India, which numbered 73,586 in 1892.
During the three years that the British soldiers
are in the Indian service they are paid and kept
by the Indian Government. The hardiest men in
the service, after about two years of training at
home, are sent out to India, usually at the age
of twenty. The home establishment in 1892
was made up as follows: General staff, 317 officers, with 286 orderlies; surgeons. veterinarians,
chaplains, accountants, etc.; 1,482 cavalry, including the Life and Horse Guards, 555 officers,
1,369 noncommissioned officers, trumpeters, etc.,
and 11,392 rank and file; Royal Horse Artillery,
71 officers, 146 noncommissioned officers, etc.,
and 1,694 rank and file; Royal Artillery, 770
officers, 1,673 noncommissioned officers. etc., and
18,635 rank and file; Royal Engineers, 578 officers, 1,165 noncommissioned officers, etc., and
5,301 rank and file; infantry, including Foot
Guards, 2,790 officers, 6,643 noncommissioned
officers, etc., and 78,463 rank and file; Colonial
Corps, 171 officers, 360 noncommissioned officers, etc., and 4,704 rank and file; Departmental
Corps, 123 officers, 839 noncommissioned officers, etc., and 2,653 rank and file; Army Service

Corps, 237 officers, 857 noncommissioned offi-cers, etc., and 2,660 rank and file; staff of yeo-manry, militia, and volunteers, 628 officers, 6,292 noncommissioned officers, etc., and 10 rank and file; Royal Military Academy at Woolwich, Royal Military College at Sandhurst, Staff Col-lege. instructors in gunnery and musketry, regi-mental schools, and other establishments, 229 officers, 479 noncommissioned officers, etc., and 124 rank and file. The total number of horses was 14,531. The number of officers and men maintained in the United Kingdom in 1891 was 104,591, of whom 73,286 were stationed in Eng-land, 27,162 in Ireland, and 4,143 in Scotland. The force was composed of 12,434 cavalry, 17,583 infantry, 5,350 engineers, and 69,274 infantry and special corps, with 282 field guns and 13,-304 horses and mules. In Egypt were stationed 3,240 British troops, with 253 horses and mules. In the colonies there were 28,069 officers and men, with 616 horses and mules. There were 1,803 officers and men on passage, and in India the British forces numbered 72,196, with 318 field guns and 11,345 horses and mules; making the total strength of the active army 210,499, with 25,518 horses and mules and 600 field guns. The reserves and auxiliary forces are of four classes. The first class of the army reserve in 1892 had 59,280 effectives; the second class, 953; the mi-litia, 114,032; the yeomanry, 10,380; and the vol-unteers, 221,048. Adding these numbers to the effectives returned for the home and colonial forces and the Indian establishments, the fight-ing strength of the nation is found to be 616,642 men of all ranks. The regular army on Jan. 1, 1891, was made up of 152,018 Englishmen, 27,786 Irishmen, 16,412 Scotchmen, 5,330 natives of the colonies and India, and 570 others.

The Navy.—There were 285 naval vessels in commission on Nov. 1, 1891, compared with 278 twelve months before. There were 17 first-class battle ships, an addition of 1; 8 second- and 3 third-class battle ships, 1 having gone out of commission; 2 coast-defense ships, 1 more than in the previous year; 10 first-class cruisers, 1 having been added; 41 unarmored or second-and third-class cruisers, an addition of 3; 1 tor-pedo ram; 15 sloops, 2 less; 7 gun vessels, 1 less; 54 gunboats; 17 special-service vessels; 2 dispatch ships; 7 troop and store ships; 4 Indian troop ships; 4 royal yachts; 8 surveying vessels; 15 torpedo boats, an addition of 3; 9 other un-armored steamers; 6 training brigs; 18 coast-guard tenders or revenue cruisers; 2 other sail-ing vessels; and 35 hulks and stationary vessels. The armor-clad fleet in 1889 consisted of 62 ef-fective ships, of which 17 were first- and 15 sec-ond-class battle ships, 6 battle ships unclassified, 12 coast-defense ships, and 12 first-class cruisers. The programme of construction to be completed in 1894 will add 13 great battle ships of the first class and 2 second-class battle ships. The pro-tected vessels in 1889 were 10 second- and 18 third-class cruisers and 1 torpedo ram. These will be re-enforced by 11 first-class deck-armored cruisers, 41 second- and 6 third-class cruisers, and 1 torpedo depot ship. The unprotected vessels in 1889 numbered 282, comprising 10 second-class cruisers, 1 corvette, 17 sloops, 8 gun vessels, 10 torpedo cruisers, 4 torpedo gunboats, 62 gun-boats, 80 first- and 51 second-class torpedo boats,

2 dispatch vessels, 14 special-service ships, 1 tor-pedo depot ship, and 22 miscellaneous vessels. The programme of construction contemplates the addition of 2 steam sloops, 27 torpedo gunboats, 9 gunboats, and 6 first- and 10 second-class tor-pedo boats. The cost of the projected additions to the navy was calculated at £22,669,000, besides £1,546,000 for the completion of vessels under construction. The total number of vessels in the navy will be increased from 873 in 1889 to 501 in 1894, and the addition will amount to more than the difference, because vessels of obsolete type are to be removed from the navy list. The vessels on foreign service in 1891 numbered 140, of which 30 were in the Mediterranean and the Red Sea, 8 comprised the channel squadron, 11 were stationed in North America and the West Indies, 9 were on the East Indian and 20 on the China station, 14 were at the Cape of Good Hope and on the west coast of Africa, 4 on the south-east coast. 8 in the Pacific, 15 on the Australian station, 10 on particular service, 7 surveying, and 4 constituted the training squadron. The new monster ironclads are designed to carry the heavi-est guns and armor used, and at the same time to be very manageable and to have room for sufficient coal for very long cruises. Of the com-pleted vessels of this class the chief till 1891 was the "Inflexible" turret ship, built at Portsmouth in 1876. She is 320 feet long and 75 broad, and carries 3,275 tons of armor. The central citadel is 110 feet long and 15½ feet high, 6½ feet being below the water line. Protected by from 16 to 24 inches of armor, strongly backed with teak, are the engines, boilers, and hydraulic loading gear. and in the center of the rectangular citadel are the two revolving turrets, 28 feet in diameter and 9 feet high, each holding 2 80-ton guns. During 1890 there were launched 7 deck-protect-ed cruisers, 8 cruisers partly deck-protected, 1 torpedo vessel, and 2 coast-defense ships; and in 1891 were launched 2 steel armor-clad barbette ships, of 14,150 tons displacement each, 5 deck-protected cruisers, 8 partially protected cruisers, 8 gun and torpedo vessels, and 10 second-class torpedo boats. The "Trafalgar" and the "Nile," launched in 1887 and 1888, exceed the "Inflexi-ble" in size, weight of armor, and engine power, having a displacement of 11,940 tons. and engines of 15,000 indicated horse power, with side armor 20 inches thick at the water line. These sister ships are armed with 4 67-ton guns each, with a complete auxiliary armament. The "Sans Pa-reil" and "Victoria," launched in 1887, have 18 inches of side armor, a displacement of 10,400 tons, and engines of 12,000 horse power, and carry 2 111-ton guns each, besides 1 29-ton and 12 5-ton guns. The "Royal Sovereign" is an example of the heaviest class of the new guns. She was laid down at Portsmouth on Sept. 30, 1889, and launched on Feb. 26, 1891. She has a displacement of 14,150 tons. Her engines are designed to develop 13,000 horse power and to show a speed of 17¼ knots. Like the others, she has a steel hull. The belt of armor, varying from 18 to 14 inches in thickness, extends 252 feet amidships, and weighs 1,096 tons. The two pear-shaped barbettes, protected by 17-inch ar-mor, are 54 feet in length. In these are mounted 4 67-ton guns, while 4 100-pounder quick-firing guns are carried in as many steel-armored case-

mates. The aggregate armor weighs 4,500 tons. The 6-inch quick-firing guns number 6 in all, besides which there are 16 6-pounders, 4 3-pounders, and 8 Nordenfeldts, and 10 tubes for 18-inch torpedoes. On the same model as the "Royal Sovereign" are being built the "Renown," "Repulse," "Ramillies," "Resolution," "Revenge," and "Royal Oak."

The *personnel* of the British navy, according to the navy estimates for 1891-'92, comprised 44,764 seamen, including 14 flag officers and 2,690 commissioned officers in active service; 7,149 boys, including 1,050 in training; 13,879 marines afloat and ashore; 4,200 coast guards; and 1,038 officers for various services; making a total of 71,000 of all ranks. There were 21,445 officers and men of the royal navy reserves, 3,010 of the marine pensioner reserves, and 2,000 naval artillery volunteers.

Finances.—The revenue of the Government for the year ending March 31, 1891, amounted to £89,489,112, which was £1,879,112 more than the budget estimate; and the expenditure was £87,732,855, exceeding the estimate by £355,855. In the receipts are not included extra receipts for the army and navy or contributions from India to military charges. The expenditure as stated includes £2,009,958 incurred in connection with the conversion of the debt. Nearly five sixths of the revenue are derived from taxation, including excise, customs, and stamp duties, and the income and property taxes, the land tax, and the house duty. The excise receipts were £29,178,468, of which £15,474,288 came from spirits, £9,781,397 from beer, £3,500,187 from licenses, £324,117 from railroads, and £8,479 from other sources. The customs revenue amounted to £19,753,907, of which £9,536,234 were collected on tobacco, £3,418,562 on tea, £2,420,630 on rum, £1,408,103 on brandy, £1,318,162 on wine, £869,537 on spirits other than rum and brandy, £182,006 on coffee, £156,893 on raisins, £118,334 on dried currants, and £325,446 on other articles. The total receipts from stamps, excluding fee stamps, was £15,827,498, of which £4,827,337 represent the probate duty, £2,661,724 stamps on deeds, £2,626,016 the legacy duty, £1,209,227 the succession duty, £1,125,620 the estate duty on personalty, £754,693 stamps on bills of exchange, £225,701 stamps on patent medicines, £147,948 marine-insurance stamps, £162,729 stamps on licenses, £68,758 the estate duty on realty, and £006,117 other stamp duties. The income and property tax produced £13,143,932; the house duty, £1,526,763; the land tax, £1,025,764. The receipts from the post office amounted to £9,843,269; from the telegraph service, £2,394,579; from crown lands, £428,616: from fee stamps, £809,860; from the Bank of England, £163,754; from the post-office savings banks, £36,050; from the civil departments, £1,588,679; from the revenue departments, £139,684; interest on Suez Canal shares, £241,935; receipts from other sources, £251,150; total receipts for the year, £96,343,908, of which £89,489,112 were actually taken in at the exchequer up to March 31.

The expenditure, on account of the consolidated fund services in 1890-'91, amounted to £28,478,103, of which £25,000,000 were for interest and sinking fund of the debt, 501,473 for judicial salaries, £410,000 for the civil list, £349,-

833 for annuities and pensions, £88,377 for salaries and allowances, £1,428,571 for the naval defense fund, £492,789 for various other purposes, and £207,000 on Suez Canal bonds, etc. Of the debt charges, £15,998,486 were for interest on the funded debt, £6,549,871 for terminable annuities, £988,089 for interest on the unfunded debt, £191,912 for management of the debt, and £1,271,642 for the new sinking fund. The expenditure for the army was £17,560,023; on the navy, £14,125,358; on civil services, £16,040,131; on the customs and inland revenue, £2,643,447; on the post office, £5,682,562; on the telegraph service, £2,272,000; on the packet service, £706,230; total expenditure on the supply services, £59,029,751, not including an additional expenditure of £225,000 for military barracks.

The budget estimate of revenue for 1891-'92 was £90,430,000 and the estimated expenditure £90,264,000, including £1,882,000 of additional or extraordinary expenditures, of which £500,000 are for barrack construction, £920,000 for education, and £400,000 for recoining the gold.

Of the total revenue from taxation in 1890-'91, amounting to £73,578,000, England and Wales contributed £58,398,196; Scotland, £8,179,348; and Ireland, £6,660,456 the taxes paid *per capita* being at the rate of $9.80 in England, $9.86 in Scotland, and $6.88 in Ireland. The income tax is collected only on incomes of £150 and above; and when they fall below £400 exemption is allowed for £120 of their amount. One half the probate duty, amounting to £2,413,668 in 1891, as well as £3,359,783 of license money, and additional beer and spirit duties amounting to £1,300,471, making a total of £7,073,876, was assigned by various acts passed between 1888 and 1890 to the relief of local rates. Of this, £6,974,412 were paid over during the year to the local authorities, of which England got £5,947,613, Scotland £700,938, and Ireland £325,861. The balance in the exchequer on March 31, 1891, was £6,370,897.

The receipts of the local governing bodies for 1889 amounted to £67,526,977, of which £40,751,266 were raised by rates, £7,186,096 by tolls, etc., £8,706,040 by loans, £5,488,845 were contributed by the Government, and £5,424,770 came from rents, sales of property, and other sources. Of the total, £55,416,658 were raised in England and Wales, £7,634,648 in Scotland, and £4,475,671 in Ireland. The urban sanitary rates in England alone amounted to £7,631,043, the poor rates to £8,355,973, the school-board rates to £2,631,344. The expenditure for the United Kingdom was £66,589,916, of which £54,741,275 was in England and Wales, £7,371,537 in Scotland, and £4,477,104 in Ireland. The total expenditure in the United Kingdom for poor relief was £10,315,672; for sanitary and other public works, £32,582,947; for board schools, £6,774,896.

The gross liabilities of the state on March 31, 1891, amounted to £685,954,018, from which are to be deducted sundry assets amounting to £5,272,437, leaving the net total indebtedness £680,681,581. The amount of the funded debt was £379,472,082; the capital value of the terminable annuities, £68,458,798; the unfunded debt, £36,140,079; other capital liabilities, including the Russian Dutch loan, deficiency of savings banks and friendly societies, and £797,780 of liabilities created by the imperial defense act of 1888, £1,-883,059. The gross annual value of property and profits assessed to income tax comes within £15,000,000 of the total national liabilities, and the estimated national income is more than double the amount of the debt, which represents an average debt *per capita* of $87.50, and an average annual burden of $3.25.

Agriculture and Industry.—Of the land in the United Kingdom, 58·5 per cent. is suitable for cultivation or pasture, 3·6 per cent. is covered with woods, and 37·9 per cent. is waste mountain or heath land, or covered with water, or otherwise unproductive. The area under grain crops in Great Britain in 1891 was 7,924,823 acres; under green crops, 3,297,569; under flax, 1,801; under hops, 56,148; bare fallow, etc.. 429,040; under clover and rotation grasses, 4,716,582; permanent pasture, 16,433,850. In Ireland, grain crops occupied 1,492,329; green crops, 1,190,943; flax, 74,672; fallows, 21,786; and clover, grass, and permanent pasture, 12,348,921 acres. The live stock of Great Britain in 1891 comprised 1,488,-403 horses, 6,852,821 horned cattle, 28,732,558 sheep, and 2,888,773 pigs. In Ireland there were 592,861 horses, 4,448,477 cattle, 4,722,391 sheep, and 1,367,776 hogs. The wheat crop of Great Britain for 1890 was 73,354,000 bushels; barley, 73,933,000 bushels; oats, 120,188,000 bushels; beans, 11,697,000 bushels; peas, 6,294,000 bushels; potatoes, 2,812,000 tons; turnips, 27,747,000 tons. In Ireland the wheat crop was 2,639,000 bushels; barley, 6,860,000 bushels; oats, 51,107,000 bushels; potatoes, 1,810,000 tons; turnips, 4,256,000 tons. The average yield of wheat per acre was 30½ bushels in Great Britain and 28½ in Ireland; of barley, 35 bushels in Great Britain and 37½ in Ireland; of oats, 41¼ and 41¾ bushels.

The produce of the sea fisheries in 1890 was £6,743,922, including shell fish and excluding salmon, of which the catch in Ireland was £399,000. and in Scotland £222,000 in estimated value. The number of men engaged in the sea fisheries of Great Britain is 124,787, of whom 55,-148 are Scotch and 41,815 English. The number of registered boats is 27,151. The value of the exports of fish in 1889 was £1,766,639, of the imports, £2,588,623.

The quantity of coal raised during 1890 was 181,614,288 tons, valued at £74,953,997; that of the iron ore, 13,780,767. valued at £3,926,445. The total value of metallic minerals raised, including iron, lead, tin, zinc, copper, bog iron, silver and gold ores, copper precipitate, antimony, and iron pyrites, was £5,273,018. The quantity of iron produced in 1890 was 4,848,748 tons, valued at £14,808,884; of tin, 9,602 tons, valued at £937,760; the value of the lead, £449,-826; of the zinc, £203,358; of copper, £57,650; of silver, £58,040. The total value of nonmetallic minerals raised was £87,519,211, the chief kinds, besides coal, being stone for £8,708,691, slate for £1,027,235, salt for £1,100,014, clays, oil shale, gypsum, arsenic, phosphate of lime, and barytes. The number of persons employed in the coal mines in 1890 was 613,233. The export of coal in 1890 was 30,142,839 tons, of the value of £19,-020,269, which went to France, Italy, Germany, Russia, Sweden, Denmark, Spain, and Egypt. The production of pig iron in 1890 was 7,904,000 tons, and the consumption 7,294,000. The num-

ber of furnaces in blast was 414; the number of puddling furnaces in operation, 3,015: of Bessemer steel converters, 82; of open-hearth steel furnaces, 252. The production of manufactured iron was 1,923,000 tons; of Bessemer steel, 2,015,-000 tons; of open-hearth steel, 1,564,000 tons. The imports of iron ore were 4,471,790 tons, of which 4,028,672 tons were Spanish ore; of bar iron, 93,000 tons; of manufactured iron, 223,000 tons. The imports of copper ore were 215,935 tons; of lead, 158,649 tons; of tin. 27,038 tons.

The imports of raw cotton for 1890 were 1,793,-495,200 pounds, of which 1,578,853,360 pounds were retained for home consumption. The total imports of wool were 633,028,131 pounds, of which 292,315,828 pounds were retained for home consumption. There were 7,190 textile factories in the United Kingdom in 1890, having 53,641,062 spindles and 822,489 power looms. They gave employment to 298,828 men, 86,968 boys working full time, 610,608 women and girls over thirteen years old and working full time, and 40,558 boys and 45,941 girls half time.

Commerce.—The total value of the imports in 1890 was £420,691,997, against £427,637,595 in 1889. The value of the exports of British products was £263,530,585, against £248,935,195. The exports of foreign and colonial products was £64,721,533, making the total volume of commerce £748,944,115, against £743,230,274 in 1889. The share of England in the total trade was 90½ per cent.; of Scotland, 8 per cent.; of Ireland, 1½ per cent. The average value of imports per head of population was about $55, and of exports of domestic products $33. Of the total value of imports for 1890, £97,283,349 came from the United States, £44,828,148 from France, £32,668,797 from India, £29,350,844 from Australasia, £26,073,331 from Germany, £25,900,924 from the Netherlands, £23,750,863 from Russia, £17,363,776 from Belgium, £12,508,533 from Spain, £12,444,489 from British America, £8,-473,656 from Sweden, £8,368,851 from Egypt, £7,753,389 from Denmark, £6,095,612 from South Africa, £5,187,801 from the Straits Settlements, £4,830,850 from China, £4,816,883 from Turkey, £4,447,159 from Roumania, £4,350,675 from Brazil, £4,129,802 from the Argentine Republic, £3,473,348 from Chili and Bolivia, £3,432,689 from Norway, £3,411,200 from Ceylon. £3,093,-918 from Brazil, £2,942,194, £1,962,708 from Greece, £1,806,390 from the British West Indies, £1,728,337 from Austria, £1,647,708 from the Philippine Islands, £1,320,305 from Central America, £1,225,064 from Hong-Kong, £1,223,-035 from Java, £1,093,255 from West Africa. exclusive of British possessions, £1,076,666 from British West Africa. £1,053,604 from Peru, £1,-024,993 from Japan, £958,175 from the Channel Islands, £907,897 from British Guiana, £890,612 from Algeria, £668,034 from Morocco, £542,979 from Mexico, £531,293 from Tunis and Tripoli, and smaller amounts from Uruguay, Colombia, Venezuela, East Africa, Siam, Bulgaria. the Spanish West Indies, Mauritius, Malta, Persia, Madagascar, Hayti and Santo Domingo. Cochin China, Tonquin. and other foreign countries and British possessions. Of the total exports of British produce, £33,641,001 went to India, £32,-068,128 to the United States, £23,006,004 to Australasia, £19,293,626 to Germany, £16,567,927 to

France, £10,121,160 to the Netherlands, £9,128,-164 to South Africa, £8,416,112 to the Argentine Republic, £7,638,712 to Belgium, £7,458,628 to Brazil, £7,225,911 to British North America, £6,-772,061 to Turkey, £6,608,982 to China, £5,751,-601 to Russia, £4,999,705 to Spain, £4,081,793 to Japan, £3,381,830 to Egypt, £3,130,072 to Chili and Bolivia, £3,061,976 to Sweden, £2,883,244 to the Straits Settlements, £2,624,472 to the British West Indies, £2,539,467 to Denmark, £2,528,212 to Hong-Kong, £2,157,784 to Portugal, £2,043,-406 to Uruguay, £1,915,808 to Norway, £1,906,-317 to Mexico, £1,876,756 to the Spanish West Indies, £1,602,314 to West Africa, exclusive of British possessions, £1,469,206 to Java, £1,283,-209 to Austria, £1,270,271 to Roumania, £1,157,-572 to Greece, £1,144,246 to Colombia, £1,123,-395 to Peru, £1,024,392 to Malta, £998,412 to the Philippine Islands, £987,168 to Central America, £921,615 to Ceylon, £896,363 to British Guiana, £869,030 to British West Africa, £828,978 to Venezuela, £726,785 to the Channel Islands, £638,387 to Morocco, £528,357 to Hayti and Santo Domingo, and lesser amounts to Persia, East Africa, Mauritius, Algeria, Ecuador, Tunis and Tripoli, Madagascar, Bulgaria, Siam, Cochin China, Tonquin, and other countries.

The imports of gold bullion and specie during 1891 were £30,275,420, against £23,568,049 in 1890; the exports, £24,228,425, against £14,306,-688: the imports of silver bullion and specie, £9,316,200, against £10,385,659; the exports, £13,114,589, against £10,863,384.

The total imports of merchandise in 1891 were £435,691,279 in value.

The imports of living animals for food were valued at £9,246,398, against £11,216,333 in 1890; the imports of nondutiable articles of food and drink, £148,510,208, against £136,422,110; of dutiable articles of food and drink, £27,004,-982, against £26,216,864; of tobacco, £3,415,400, against £3,542,949; of metals, £23,040,124, against £23,710,901; of raw materials for textile manufactures, £89,215,655, against £85,239,289; of chemicals, dye stuffs, and tanning materials, £7,314,337, against £8,190,389; of oils, £7,339,-994, against £6,991,653; of raw materials for various manufactures, £40,035,435, against £41,-626,155; of manufactured articles, £65,082,129, against £63,218,167; of imports by parcel post, £561,069, against £503,209; of miscellaneous articles, £14,935,548, against £14,007,676. The exports of live animals in 1891 were valued at £672,337; of articles of food and drink, £10,687,-139; of raw materials, £21,342,327; of textile manufactures, £106,017,948; of metals and metal manufactures, exclusive of machinery, £39,230,-009; of machinery, £15,820,316; of apparel and articles of personal use, £8,882,059; of all other manufactured and partly manufactured articles, £32,193,728; of exports by parcel post, £1,095,-463; of exports of foreign and colonial produce, £61,796,593; total exports of merchandise, £309,-068,866.

Exclusive of flour, Great Britain imported 13,262,592 quarters of wheat in 1891, compared with 12,094,836 iu 1890, 12,752,800 in 1880, and 7,131,100 in 1872. The total imports of cereals and flour in 1891 were 150,075,176 hundredweight; of rice, 6,200,820; of bacon and hams, 4,715,012; of refined sugar, 11,322,121; of raw sugar, 16,217,-338; of butter, 2,135,607; of margarine, 1,235,-430; of cheese, 2,041,317; of beef, 2,168,089; of preserved meat, 776,961; of fresh mutton, 1,662,-994; of tea, 240,333,327 pounds; of cattle, 440,503 head; of sheep, 344,504; of spirits, 12,221,389 gallons; of wine, 16,782,038 gallons. Of the wheat imported in 1891 the United States furnished 4,838,991 quarters; Russia, 2,910,581 quarters; India, 2,601,157 quarters; Canada, 634,768 quarters; Chili, 423,975 quarters; Australia, 417,134 quarters; Turkey, 301,989 quarters; and Roumania, 217,666 quarters. Of the flour, equivalent to 3,349,600 quarters of wheat, the United States furnished 2,740,607 quarters. Of the tea imports, 45½ per cent. came from India, 33 per cent. from China, 19 per cent. from Ceylon, and 2½ per cent. from other countries.

The values of some of the chief imports in 1891 were as follow: Grain and flour, £61,571,-504; raw cotton, £46,080,719; wool, £27,856,556; meat, £20,148,874; sugar, £19,855,750; butter and margarine, £15,149,384; timber and wood, £14,829,571; silk manufactures, £11,017,157; tea, £10,775,345; flax, hemp, and jute, £10,116,-591; woolen manufactures, £9,275,179; live animals, £9,246,398; oils, £7,339,394; chemicals and dye stuffs, £7,314,337; seeds, £7,165,293; fruits, £6,910,305; leather, £6,632,442; wines, £5,995,-133; cheese, £4,815,369; copper ore, £4,059,528; eggs, £3,520,918; coffee, £3,442,736; tobacco, £3,415,400. Of the total value of the exports of textile manufactures in 1891, £60,249,759 represent cotton fabrics and £12,189,945 cotton yarns, £18,451,931 woolen fabrics and £3,910,288 woolen and worsted yarns, £5,031,666 linen manufactures and £898,212 linen yarns, £2,552,170 jute manufactures and £342,075 jute yarns, and £5,-150,212 apparel and slops. The value of the iron and steel exports was £26,874,784, of which amount £7,172,256 stand for tin plate, £4,805,-881 for cast and wrought iron, £3,560,476 for hoops and plates, £3,844,925 for railroad iron, £2,322,224 for steel, and £2,209,609 for pig and puddled iron. The export of chemicals was £8,-882,059 in value; of copper, £3,851,129; of hardware and cutlery, £2,525,542.

Navigation.—The number of vessels entered from foreign ports in 1890 was 62,835, of which 24,058 were foreign, and the number cleared was 63,176, of which 24,327 were foreign. The total tonnage of vessels engaged in foreign commerce entered at British ports was 36,835,000 tons, of which 26,777,000 tons were British and 10,057,-000 tons foreign. The tonnage cleared was 37,-448,000 tons, of which 27,195,000 tons were British and 10,253,000 tons foreign. The total tonnage entered and cleared was 74,283,000 tons, of which 53,973,000 tons were British and 20,310,-000 foreign. Of the foreign tonnage, 5,000,-000 tons were Norwegian, 4,393,000 German, 1,900,000 Dutch, 1,854,000 Danish, 1,687,000 French, 1,576,000 Swedish, 1,276,000 Spanish, 873,000 Belgian, 551,000 Russian, 444,000 Italian, 292,000 American, and 118,000 Austrian. Of the total tonnage entered and cleared in the foreign trade, the share of London was 13,480,-767 tons; of Liverpool, 10,941,801; of Cardiff, 8,815,210; of Newcastle, 5,481,458; of Hull, 3,653,134; of North and South Shields, 2,929,-856; of Glasgow, 2,819,362; and of Newport, 2,236,990. Sunderland, Dover, Middlesborough,

Swansea, Grimsby, Leith, and Harwich had over 1,000,000 tons each, and Bristol, Dublin, and Belfast under that figure. The tonnage of vessels entered with cargoes in 1890 was 28,979,000 tons, of which 21,139,000 tons were British and 7,839,000 tons foreign; and the tonnage of vessels cleared with cargoes was 33,857,000 tons, of which 25,267,000 tons were British and 8,590,000 tons foreign. The number of vessels entered coastwise was 307,240, of 47,738,000 tons, and the number cleared was 276,270, of 42,317,000 tons. Including these, the total number of steam and sailing vessels entered at the ports of the United Kingdom in 1890 was 370,075, of 84,574,324 tons, and the total number cleared was 339,446, of 79,766,033 tons.

There were 8,894 sailing vessels, of 575,147 tons, employing 37,618 sailors, and 2,004 steamers, of 325,082 tons, employing 22,850 men, engaged in the home trade in 1890. The number of sailing vessels engaged partly in the home and partly in the foreign trade was 381, of 50,991 tons, employing 2,219 men; and the number of steamers was 250, of 133,563 tons, employing 4,386 men. In the foreign trade alone were engaged 2,295 sailing vessels, of 2,267,434 tons, employing 44,381 men, and 3,601 steamers, of 4,563,119 tons, employing 124,654 men. The total number of vessels was 17,425, and the aggregate tonnage was 7,915,336 tons. The total number of sailors was 236,108, of whom 27,227 were foreigners. The total number of vessels registered as belonging to the United Kingdom and the Channel Islands in 1890 was 21,591, of 7,978,538 tons; and of these, 14,181, of 2,936,021 tons, were sailing vessels, and 7,410, of 5,042,517 tons, were steamers. The number of new vessels built and first registered during 1890 was 858, of 652,013 tons, of which number 217, of 122,224 tons, were sailing vessels, and 581, of 528,789 tons, were steamers.

Railroads.—The length of British railways in operation at the end of 1890 was 20,073 miles, of which 14,119 miles were in England and Wales, 3,162 miles in Scotland, and 2,792 miles in Ireland. The total paid-up capital in shares and loans was £897,472,026. The total receipts for the year were £79,948,702, of which £34,327,956 were from passengers, and £42,220,382 from freight. The number of passengers carried was 817,744,046, exclusive of holders of season tickets. The working expenses amounted to £43,188,556, which was 54 per cent. of the gross earnings.

Posts and Telegraphs.—The number of letters delivered in the United Kingdom during 1891 was 1,705,500,000, being 45 per head of population. In England and Wales the number was 1,462,750,000; in Scotland, 143,000,000; in Ireland, 99,750,000. The number *per capita* was 51 in England, 36 in Scotland, and 21 in Ireland. The number of post cards carried in the United Kingdom was 227,700,000; of book packets, 481,200,000; of newspapers, 161,000,000; of parcels, 46,200,000. There were 8,864,483 inland money orders issued, to the total amount of £23,897,767. Including foreign and colonial orders the number issued altogether was 10,260,852, and the total amount was £27,867,887. The postal orders numbered 48,841,765, of the total value of £19,178,367. Exclusive of telegraphs, the revenue of the post office in 1891 was £9,-

851,078, and the working expenses were £6,687,089, leaving a net revenue of £3,173,989. The length of telegraph lines at the beginning of the fiscal year 1891-'92 was 31,824 miles, and the length of wires 194,312 miles, including 17,211 miles of private wires, but excluding the wires of the railroad companies. The number of messages sent in 1891 was 66,409,211, of which 55,658,088 were in England and Wales, 7,077,388 in Scotland, and 3,673,735 in Ireland. The gross receipts for 1891 were £2,416,691, and the working expenses were £2,266,356, leaving a profit of £150,335, which is insufficient to pay the interest on the capital invested by the Government, amounting to about £300,000 per annum.

The Parliamentary Session.—The seventh and last session of the twelfth Parliament of Queen Victoria, and the twenty-fourth of the United Kingdom, was opened on Feb. 9, 1892. In the speech from the throne announcement was made of the agreement concluded with the United States, defining the mode by which disputes concerning the seal fisheries in Bering Sea will be referred to arbitration. The first place in the list of measures recommended was given to the Irish local-government bill, with which was coupled a bill for supplementing the English act. A measure to promote the increase of small holdings came next, and after this bills dealing with Irish education, private bill procedure in Scotland and Ireland, Indian legislative councils, rates on English elementary schools, church discipline, the examination of accused persons in criminal cases, the agreement between the Government and the Bank of England, and employers' liability. Mr. A. J. Balfour succeeded Mr. W. H. Smith as the leader of the House, while Mr. Chamberlain was elected to the position of leader of the Liberal Unionists, previously held by the Duke of Devonshire. The gap caused by the death of Mr. Parnell was filled by Mr. Redmond, while Mr. Sexton was the head of the anti-Parnellites in the absence of Mr. McCarthy. Mr. Sexton's home-rule amendment to the address was rejected by a vote of 179 to 158. But little progress was made before Easter, and discontent and disorganization were apparently prevalent among the ministerialists. The Irish local-government bill, which was based upon the widest popular franchise, and transferred to county councils all the fiscal powers of the Irish grand juries, with many others, was vigorously denounced by the Opposition, who, however, did not challenge a division, and it was announced that the second reading would not be taken till the small-holdings bill had got through committee. The small-holdings bill, which was introduced by Mr. Chaplin, on Feb. 22, empowered county councils to borrow public money, on easy terms, to an amount not involving for any year a charge on the rates of more than one penny in the pound, in order to purchase land by agreement with the owner, and to sell it to small owners in parcels under 50 acres, the occupier paying one fourth of the purchase money in cash, one fourth remaining secured by a perpetual rent charge, and the remainder being repayable, with interest, by installments. Holdings under 10 acres might be let instead of being sold. The measure passed both the first and second readings without a division, and an amendment to place the work under parish councils or other small bodies having been rejected, the House went into committee on the bill before adjourning for Easter. The bill was taken up again in committee, and amendments were made in a few minor points, among them a reduction in the amount of purchase money from one fourth to one fifth, the permission to let holdings up to 15 instead of 10 acres, and the treatment of the new holdings as personalty instead of realty in cases of intestacy. The bill was read a third time without debate or division, and was passed by the Lords, who reversed the decision of the House on the intestate clause, but otherwise made no substantial changes. The Ministerialists, to obtain the passage of the Irish local-government bill, had considered the advisability of prolonging the session into the autumn. A final settlement of this question was not arrived at when the debate on the second reading of the bill was opened by Mr. Sexton, who moved its rejection. The anti-Parnellites, who were occupied with their feuds at home, took little part in the debate, and the second reading was carried by a majority of 92 on May 24. The Scotch equivalent grant bill and the Irish education bill were framed to make provision for the share of the charge of which the state relieved the parents of children in elementary schools when fees were abolished. It was proposed to distribute the Scotch grant partly in aid of secondary education of the universities and of the maintenance of pauper lunatics, and partly for the relief of local rates. The Scotch members were much divided over the latter clause, but the bill passed substantially as introduced. The scheme for the distribution of the Irish grant met with more opposition. The sum of £200,000 annually was to be distributed partly in a capitation grant, and partly in augmenting the salaries of teachers, coupled with a system of modified compulsion in towns, which was to be ultimately extended to the rural districts. After it had been left to the Irish education commissioners to devise rules under which the schools of the Christian Brothers, who had consented to a conscience clause, might share in the grant, the opposition of the Irish members ceased, and the bill was passed. The criminal evidence bill, the Indian councils bill, and the clergy discipline bill were sent down from the Lords before the end of March. The first of these was smothered in committee, owing to a proposition to exclude Ireland from its provisions. The second, which increased the membership and enlarged the right of debate of the legislative councils, while it gave the Viceroy a discretionary power to appoint persons chosen on some elective system, was passed with but little opposition. The clergy discipline bill, which empowered the removal of clergymen convicted of criminal or disgraceful conduct, was met with obstructive tactics at the hands of a few Welsh members, who favored disestablishment. These were overcome by the aid of the *cloture*. To expedite business and secure the adjournment of the session before the end of June, the Irish local-government bill, the private bill procedure bill, and several minor measures, were dropped.

Bills for the prevention of betting and the borrowing of money by persons under age, for laborers' allotments, and for amending the poor laws in Ireland and the Scotch borough police and health bill, were among the minor measures passed during the session.

An eight-hour bill for minors, a woman-suffrage bill, a bill to assimilate the law of divorce in England to that of Scotland, a bill empowering the local authorities not only to purchase land but to earmark it and claim the unearned increment, the "one-man-one-vote" bill, and a tenure-of-lands bill for Wales, were all rejected. Motions for Scotch and Welsh disestablishment, denouncing the common-law doctrine of conspiracy, attacking the septennial act, and looking to the payment of members of Parliament, were also rejected.

General Elections.—Lord Salisbury, in his appeal to the electors just before the dissolution of Parliament, while avowing his sense of the importance of social questions, maintained that there would be no time for their consideration were the next Parliament to be taken up with a struggle over Irish government. He also deprecated the placing of the Protestants of Ulster, and the loyalists of Ireland generally, under an Irish Parliament.

Mr. Gladstone, in his Midlothian speeches and elsewhere, gave no outlines of the home-rule policy he might be expected to follow, but adhered to the broad lines of his bill of 1886 with the exception of the exclusion of the Irish members. The Parnellites declared themselves his allies only for the limited objects of Irish politics, and then only in case his scheme came up to the level of Mr. Parnell's home rule, while the anti-Parnellites were more stalwart in their support. Mr. Chamberlain and the Liberal Unionists, as in the previous election, cast in their lot with the Conservatives, sinking all minor differences in their opposition to home rule. The Unionist majority had been cut down from 118 in 1886 to 66 at the dissolution. The result of the election was a Gladstonian majority of 42, the Gladstonians having 271 members, the anti-Parnellites 72, the Parnellites 9, and the Labor party 4, a total of 356; while the Conservatives had 268, and the Liberal Unionists 46, a total of 314. The Gladstonians have 196 English, 28 Welsh, and 51 Scotch members; the anti-Parnellites, 71 Irish and 1 Eng.ish; the Parnellites, 9 Irish; the Conservatives, 236 English, 2 Welsh, 11 Scotch, and 19 Irish; and the Liberal Unionists, 32 English, 10 Scotch, and 4 Irish. The political complexion of 562 constituencies remained as it was prior to the general election. The total Separatist vote for the United Kingdom was 2,477,856, the Unionist 2,274,842, a majority for the former of 203,014. In Great Britain, the Unionist vote was 2,139,550, the Separatist 2,105,-736, and in Ireland the anti-Parnellite vote was 233,423, the Parnellite 78,618, a total of 308,898, while the Unionist vote was 78,618.

The Session of the New Parliament.—The newly elected Parliament was opened on Aug. 4. Mr. Peel, who has served as Speaker for eight years, was unanimously re-elected to that office. The Queen's speech was brief and colorless. It referred to the fact of the dissolution and the subsequent appeal to the constituencies, and said there was no business to detain members at Westminster. Mr. Asquith moved as an amendment to the address a vote of no confidence in Her Majesty's ministers. In the debate which followed. Mr. Goschen contended that the London, Welsh, and rural programmes were also before the electors, and declared that the Unionist party would continue the struggle against home rule, while the statesman who denounced the "march through rapine to disintegration" was going to place himself, sword in hand, at its head. Mr. McCarthy condemned the Irish policy of the Government, on the ground of perpetual coercion, and wanted the Home-rule bill kept in the foreground of Liberal legislation. Mr. Redmond hoped that the uneasiness felt by the Irish people would be dispelled by the Opposition, and declared as the best settlement a Parliament on the lines of that proposed by Mr. Parnell in his speech of Jan. 25, 1891. They demanded in the home-rule scheme a clause that, while the Irish Parliament existed, the power of the imperial Parliament should never be used, and that the veto of the Crown should be exercised only with the advice of the Irish executive. Both Mr. Redmond and Mr. McCarthy demanded immediate measures for the reinstatement of evicted tenants and the release of political prisoners. Mr. Gladstone, who censured the mode of procedure followed by the Government, declared the Irish question was almost the last link that bound him to public life. Mr. Balfour inquired, if the present Government was in a minority, who was in a majority, as the Opposition was in three sections with different leaders, and held that, if social and domestic legislation were to be dealt with, it must be done by the Unionists.

Colonies.—The expenditure of the Imperial Government in connection with the colonies, exclusive of India, amounts to about £2,000,000, mainly for military and naval purposes. The colonies contributed £252,250 toward military expenditure in 1891–'92, the Straits Settlements giving £100,000; Ceylon, £72,500; Hong-Kong, £40,000; Mauritius, £30,750; Malta, £5,-000; and Natal, £4,000. The British troops in the colonies in 1891–'92 numbered 32,650 men, rank and file. 8,809 being stationed in Malta, 5,214 in Gibraltar, 3,317 in South Africa, 2,234 in Bermuda, 1,465 in Ceylon, 1,337 in the Windward and Leeward Islands, 1,494 in Halifax, 2,998 in Hong-Kong, 1,511 in Jamaica, 1,588 in the Straits Settlements, 880 in Mauritius, 953 in West Africa, 554 in Cyprus, 155 in St. Helena, and 111 in the Bahamas. There were, besides, 72,496 in India and 3,431 in Egypt. Gibraltar had a population, in 1891, of 25,755, including a garrison of 5,896 men. Gen. Sir Lothian Nicholson was Governor in 1891. The local revenue in 1890 was £62,461; the expenditure, £59,045; the military expenditure of the Imperial Government, £243,806. Malta, with an area of 95 square miles, had an estimated population in 1890 of 165,662, including 2,274 English and 1,149 foreigners. Gen. Sir Henry Augustus Smyth is the present Governor. The revenue in 1890 was £261,254, and the expenditure £266,900. Cyprus, with an area of 3,584 square miles, had a population, in 1891, of 209,291, of whom 106,887 were males and 102,404 were females. The Mohammedans number 48,044; the rest belong mostly to the Greek Church. The island is administered by a High Commissioner, an office

held by Sir Henry Ernest Bulwer, who was appointed in 1886. There is a Legislature of 18 members, 6 being officeholders and 12 elected, 3 by Mohammedan and 9 by non-Mohammedan voters. The revenue for 1890–'91 was £194,936, the expenditure £107,589. The exports for the same period, consisting mostly of grain, carobs, cotton, and the products of the vine, were £433,-583, and the imports £371,077.

Aden, an important coaling station on the Suez Canal route to the east, with an area of 70 square miles, and Perim, a small island at the entrance to the Red Sea, had a population, in 1891, of 41,910. The Government is administered by a political resident, who is also commander of the troops, and is subject to the Government of Bombay. Coffee, gums, skins, cloth, and tobacco, the produce of the interior of Arabia, are the chief exports. The Somali Coast Protectorate, with an area of 30,000 square miles and a population of 240,000, the island of Socotra, with an area of 1,382 square miles and a population of 10,000, and the Kuria Muria Islands, are attached to Aden.

The Bahrein Islands, which have a population of over 16,000, and were taken under British protection in 1867, and again in 1870, have as their sovereign Sheikh Esau. The export of pearls, the main industry, amounted to 3,876,000 rupees. A. C. Talbot is the political resident.

Ceylon has an area of 25,364 square miles, and a population, at the census of 1891, of 3,-008,239. Of this, the Singhalese form about two thirds and the Tamils one fourth, and the remainder are Moormen, or descendants of Arabs, Eurasians and Burghers, Malays, British and other Europeans, Veddahs, and others. The Governor is assisted by an Executive Council of 5 members, composed of the commander of the troops and the leading civil officers, and a Legislative Council which includes the members of the Executive Council, 4 other officials, and 8 appointed members. Sir Arthur Elibank Havelock, appointed in 1890, is the present Governor. The revenue for 1891 was 16,228,769 rupees, and the expenditure 15,316,224 rupees. The public debt at the end of 1890 was £2,492,484 and 345,-401 rupees. A little less than one eighth of the total area of the island is under cultivation. In 1890, 660,669 acres were under rice and other grains, 235,794 under tea, 649,869 under cocoanuts, 66,530 under coffee, 39,587 under cinchona, 40,336 under cinnamon, 15,896 under cacao, and 9,515 under tobacco. There were 713 plumbago mines worked in 1890. The value of the exports in 1890 was 63,091,938 rupees, and of the imports 63,091,938 rupees. The export of tea was 22,899,759 rupees; of cocoanut products, 7,832,475 rupees; coffee, 5,741,838 rupees; plumbago, 3,925,776 rupees; cinchona, 1,053,497 rupees; areca nuts, 1,051,083 rupees. The exports of tea show an increase of about one third over those of 1889, and those of coffee also show a slight increase.

The Straits Settlements embrace Singapore, Penang, including Penang Island, Province Wellesley and the Dindings, Malacca, and the Cocos Islands and Christmas Island. The total population in 1891 was 506,577, distributed as follows: Singapore, 182,650; Penang, 232,977; and Malacca, 90,950. The Chinese outnumber the

Malays and carry on the distributing trade. The Governor is assisted by an Executive Council consisting of the commander of the troops and 7 civil officials, and by a Legislative Council of 10 official and 7 unofficial members, 5 nominated by the Crown and 2 elected by the Chambers of Commerce of Singapore and Penang. Sir Cecil Clemente Smith has been Governor since 1887. The native states on the Malay peninsula under British protection and governed by the advice of British residents had a population in 1891 as follows: Perak, 212,997; Selangor, 81,421; Sungei Ujong, 23,602; Pahang, 52,-803; and Negri Sembilan, 41,617. In 1890 the Chinese immigrants numbered 132,674; the Indian immigrants, 18,901.

The revenue of the colony in 1890 was $4,269,-123, and the expenditure $3,757,691. The debt was increased to $1,258,167. Of the native states, Perak had a revenue in 1890 of $2,504,116. and an expenditure of $2,447,929; Selangor a revenue of $1,888,924, and an expenditure of $1,996,-544; Sungei Ujong a revenue of $277,910, and an expenditure of $261,647; Negri Sembilan a revenue of $107,033, and an expenditure of $115,-589; and Pahang a revenue of $62,077, and an expenditure of $297,702. The imports into Singapore in 1890 were valued at $112,633,960, the exports at $94,131,804; the imports into Penang at $43,788,400, and the exports at $41,349,-247; and the imports into Malacca at $2,228,351, and the exports at $2,244,093. The leading exports are tin, spices, sugar, tobacco, cutch and gambier, and gutta-percha. The number of vessels, exclusive of native craft, entered at the ports of the colony was 8,110, with a tonnage of 4,859,720 tons; and the number cleared was 8,068, with a tonnage of 4,818,939 tons.

Much British capital has been invested in Pahang to work large concessions of land said to be rich in tin, gold, and valuable timber. Owing to this fact, the Sultan was compelled, against his will, to receive a British resident in 1888. He has, however, been loyal since that time, though his headmen have not been so compliant. One of these, the Orang Kaya Semantan, or chief headman of Semantan, was deposed, and about Christmas, 1891, fired on a European officer of the Pahang Government and attacked a police station. He afterward built stockades and declared himself against British rule. The Sultan and Mr. Rodger, the British resident, proceeded against him in January, 1892, with a force of Malays and Sikhs, captured most of the stockades on Semantan river, and caused the leader himself to take refuge in the jungle. Yet he continued to give trouble, and captured some important river stations, waylaid escorts, and murdered a number of people, chiefly Chinese. In March, another headman, the Panglima Mada, murdered two European miners, and threatened Pekan, the principal village of Pahang.

Labuan, a small island about 6 miles from the northwest coast of Borneo was placed under the government of the British North Borneo Company in 1889. The population in 1891 was 5,853, mostly Malays from Borneo, with some Chinese traders and 30 Europeans. The imports in 1890 amounted to £56,229, and the exports to £34,315. Sago, gutta-percha, India rubber, wax, and other produce, are exported from Borneo to Singapore.

The territory of British North Borneo is under the jurisdiction of the British North Borneo Company, which was taken under the protection of the British Crown on May 12, 1888. The area is 31,106 square miles, and the population 175,000, mostly Mohammedan settlers on the coast and aboriginal tribes in the interior, with some Chinese traders and artisans. Charles Vandeleur Creagh is Governor, and Leicester Paul Beaufort the acting Governor. The authorized capital of the company is £2,000,000, and of this £500,000 have been actually raised. Mr. Martin has succeeded Sir Rutherford Alcock as the London chairman of the company. The revenue, which depends mainly on the prosperity of the tobacco interest, is precarious and has been largely exceeded by the expenditure. It reached £102,000 in 1890, the amount received from the sales of land for plantations being over £36,000, but fell to £70,000 in 1891. The imports in 1890 were £2,018,289, and the exports £901,290. Tobacco, which is being planted on a large scale, sago, rice, gums, timber, coffee, pepper, gambier, gutta-percha, tapioca, and sweet potatoes, are the chief products. Lord Brassey, in the House of Lords, ineffectually endeavored to have the territory declared a crown colony.

Brunei and Sarawak are adjacent territories placed under British protection in 1888. The area of Brunei, which is ruled over by a native sultan, is about 3,000 square miles. Sarawak has an area of about 45,000 square miles, and a population of about 300,000, and is governed by Sir Charles Johnson Brooke, who succeeded his uncle as Rajah in 1868. The products of both territories are similar to those of North Borneo.

The Crown colony of Hong-Kong, an island off the southeastern coast of China, has an area of about 29 square miles, and is the center for British commerce with Japan, and a naval and military station of the first class. The population in 1891 was 221,411, of whom 8,545 were white and 212,846 colored. Of the colored population, 210,995 were Chinese, one third being British subjects, and 1,901 Indians, and of the white population about one half are Portuguese and one third English. In 1890 the Chinese immigration was 101,147, and the emigration 42,066. The Governor, Sir William Robinson, is assisted by an Executive Council composed of the officer commanding the troops and 4 civil members, and by a Legislative Council composed of 6 official and 5 nonofficial members, of whom 3,000, including a Chinaman, are nominated by the Crown and 1 is nominated by the Chamber of Commerce and 1 by the Justices of the Peace. The revenue in 1890 from ordinary sources was £1,995,220, and from premiums from land £16,638; while the expenditure for ordinary purposes was £1,517,843, and for extraordinary purposes £397,507, including defensive works. The revenue is derived mostly from land taxes and licenses, and an opium monopoly. In December, 1890, the assets of the colony exceeded its liabilities by £399,732. The exports to Great Britain, consisting principally of tea, silk, hemp, and copper, amounted to £1,225,064 in 1890, and the imports to £2,528,-212. The number of vessels entered in 1890 was 4,114, of 4.893,733 tons, and in addition there were 28,512 junks, of 1,795,261 tons.

The Andaman Islands, in the Bay of Bengal, inhabited by a race of small degenerate savages, variously estimated at from 2,000 to 10,000, are used as a penal colony by the Indian Government. The convict population in 1890 was 12,197, of whom 3,209 were self-supporting. The Nicobar Islands, which lie to the south of the Andamans, have an aboriginal population of 6,915, and export cocoanuts, edible birds' nests, tortoise shell, ambergris, and trepang. The Laccadive Islands, off the Malabar coast, attached in part to the collectorate of South Kanara and in part to Malabar, had a population in 1891 of 14,410, all Mohammedans. The fiber coir is the staple product.

Mauritius, an island in the Indian Ocean, 500 miles east of Madagascar, has an area of 705 square miles. The population in 1891 was 377,986, of whom 258,985 were Hindus, and 119,001 were Africans, Chinese, mixed races, and whites. The Governor, Sir Charles Cameron Lees, who was appointed in 1889, is assisted by an Executive Council consisting of the military commander, the Colonial Secretary, the Procureur-General, the Receiver-General, the Auditor-General, and 2 elected members of the Council of Government, which consists of the Governor, 8 official, 9 appointed, and 10 elected members. The revenue of the colony in 1890 was 7,774,774 rupees, and the expenditure 7,705,311. The imports in 1899 amounted to 16,375,377 rupees, the exports to 26,962,930 rupees. Unrefined sugar is the staple article of export, 23,630,809 rupees having been exported in 1890, and rum, vanilla, cocoanut oil, and aloe fiber are the principal other items. On April 29, 1892, a hurricane devastated the island. The loss of life was 1,230, and the number of wounded 3,167. About 1,453 buildings in St. Louis and 16,976 throughout the island were destroyed or damaged. The barometer fell in the course of an hour to 27·95, and the highest velocity of the wind was estimated at 120 miles an hour. All the vessels in the harbor were damaged, and many were driven ashore. Seychelles, Rodrigues, Diego Garcia, and other islands are dependencies of Mauritius. Cocoanut oil is the principal export.

St. Helena, in the South Atlantic, has an area of 47 square miles. The population in 1891 was 4,116. It is largely used as a recruiting station, and is the headquarters of a fleet of American whalers, the produce of which amounted to £13,433 in 1890.

Ascension, 750 miles northwest of St. Helena, has an area of 35 square miles, and a population of about 360.

The Falkland Islands, near the southern extremity of South America, have an area of 6,000 square miles. The population in 1891 was 1,789. In 1890 the revenue was £9,492, the expenditure £9,389, the imports £67,182, and the exports £115,865. The value of the wool exported in 1890 was £102,460.

The Bermudas are a group of small islands, 360 in number, of which 18 or 20 are inhabited, 580 miles east of North Carolina. The population in 1891 was 15,013, of whom 5,690 were white and 9,323 colored. The white immigration exceeded the emigration by about 100 during the past ten years, due mainly to the immigration of Portuguese from the Azores and Ma-

deiras, while there was a loss of about 340 in the colored population by emigration. The value of the imports in 1891 was £325,976, an increase of £17,960 over 1890. The exports, consisting mostly of potatoes, onions, and lily bulbs, shipped to New York during the months of April and May amounted to £129,803, a decrease of £7,723 compared with 1890, owing to a fall in the price of onions. Small quantities of arrowroot, tomatoes, cut flowers, and beets are also exported. Lieut.-Gen. E. Newdigate-Newdigate is Governor. He is assisted by an Executive Council of 6 and by a Legislative Council of 9 members, and by a Representative House of Assembly of 36 members.

British Honduras, with an area of 7,560 square miles, had a population in 1891 of 31,471, of whom 16,268 were males and 15,203 females. The revenue in 1890 was £51,204, and the expenditure £45,249. The imports for the same period were £282,045, and the exports £287,690, consisting chiefly of 5,500,000 cubic feet of mahogany, logwood, fruit, and sugar. The colonists now have a majority of unofficial persons in the Legislative Council, which consists of 5 official and 6 unofficial members.

British Guiana, with an area of 109,000 square miles, had a population in 1891 of 284,887.

The West African colonies are the Gold Coast, Gambia, Sierra Leone, and Lagos. The Gold Coast proper has an estimated area of 15,000 square miles; including the protectorate, 46,600 square miles, with a population of about 1,905,000. The revenue in 1890 was £156,449, the expenditure £117,899. The exports in 1890 were £601,348 in value, the imports £562,102. Palm oil and palm kernels are the principal products. Gambia has an area of 2,700 square miles, and a population of 50,000. The settlement proper had a population in 1891 of 14,266, of whom 64 were whites, 5,300 Mohammedans, and 2,385 Christians. The revenue in 1890 was £30,573, and the expenditure £22,758. The exports amounted to £163,374, and the imports to £149,548 in 1890. A naval brigade of 4 war vessels was sent up the Gambia in January, 1892, against a chief, Fodi Kabba, who had been engaged in marauding expeditions against his neighbors and threatened the town of Bathurst itself. The expedition landed about 280 miles up the river in the neighborhood of Macarthey island, and made a night attack on the chief at Marige. The town was destroyed, but he escaped. In April another expedition landed at the head of Sankria creek and marched against Toniataba, which was captured after a spirited defense. Capt. Roberts, of the First West India Regiment, was killed, and the enemy's loss was heavy. Sierra Leone has an area of 15,000 square miles, and a population of 180,000. The area of Sierra Leone proper is 400 square miles. The population in 1890 was 75,000, including 270 whites. The revenue in 1890 was £73,708, the expenditure £63,056. The exports were valued at £349,319, and the imports at £389,308 in 1890. In March, 1892, a punitive expedition was sent against the native chief Carimos for an attack on Major Moore's party in May, 1891. Tambi, a stockaded town about 100 miles inland, was assailed, but the British force was compelled to fall back. Lagos, an island on the Slave Coast, has an area, including the protectorate on the mainland, of 1,071 square miles, and a population of about 100,000. The revenue in 1890 was £56,341, and the expenditure £63,701. The exports were £595,193, and the imports £500,827 in 1890.

Jebu, one of the interior countries of the colony of Lagos, forms a frontier along the lagoon giving access to the port of Lagos, and the main roads from a large portion of the rich Hinterland of Xorubaland pass through its territory. The inhabitants are a large and powerful tribe, with considerable quantities of arms and ammunition, and have been in the habit of levying toll on all produce passing through their country. The Government for thirty years had ineffectually endeavored to break down this policy. The new Governor, Mr. G. T. Carter, shortly after his arrival, was instructed to send an ultimatum to the King demanding an apology for an insult offered to Capt. Denton, the acting Governor, who visited Jebu on a friendly mission, and insisting that the roads through the country should be free. The Jebu representatives arrived in Lagos on Jan. 14. 1892, and on Jan. 21 a treaty was signed, in which they agreed to keep the roads open without exacting toll, the King receiving in compensation £500 a year from the Government. Within six weeks the roads were again blockaded, and the Governor, failing to effect a settlement, found it necessary to take more stringent measures. Owing to the weakness of the British forces in Lagos, it was not until after the arrival of West India troops that the punitive expedition, under the command of Col. F. C. Scott, embarked at Lagos for Epé, an important town on the north side of the lagoon, peopled partly by Jebus. They left Epé on May 16 for Jebu Ode, the capital, and on that day succeeded in occupying the Village of Pobo after a stubborn resistance. Eridu was taken on the 17th. The Jebus made their final stand on the 19th, at the Limoyi stream near Mogden, with an army of over 7,000 men, but were routed, the Maxim gun working great havoc in their ranks. On May 20 Jehu Ode was occupied and the King and his followers made prisoners. A flying column was dispatched to Oru, a village to the northeast of Jebu Ode, and the Jebus themselves were made to destroy the toll gates, and the roads into the Ibadan and Xoruba countries were opened.

GREECE, a constitutional monarchy in southeastern Europe. The Constitution of 1864 vests the whole legislative power in a single chamber of representatives, called the Boulé, elected for four years by universal suffrage. By a law passed in 1886 the number of Deputies was reduced to 150. Every candidate must have the approval of at least one thirtieth of the voters of his district. The Boulé meets annually for not less than three nor more than six months. Every bill must be discussed and voted, article by article, three times on separate days. The Constitution can not be reviewed by the Boulé with the exception of the electoral laws and certain other provisions, which may be revised after every ten years. The reigning King is Georgios I, born Dec. 24, 1845. He was elected King of the Hellenes by the National Assembly at Athens on March 18, 1863, and accepted the crown through his father, the present King of

Denmark. The heir-apparent is Prince Konstantinos, Duke of Sparta, born Aug. 2, 1868, who married Princess Sophie of Prussia, sister of the German Emperor, on Oct. 27, 1889. The executive is vested in the King and his responsible ministers. At the beginning of the year 1892 the Cabinet was composed of the following members: President of the Council, Minister of War, and Minister of Finance, P. T. Delyannis; Minister of Foreign Affairs, L. Deligeorges; Minister of the Interior and of Justice, A. T. Zaimis; Minister of Worship and Public Instruction, A. Gherokostopoulos; Minister of Marine, C. A. Koumoundouros.

Area and Population.—Greece has an area of 25,041 square miles, and a population, according to the census of 1889, of 2,187,208 people, 1,133,625 of whom are males and 1,053,583 females. The following are the chief occupations of the people and the percentage employed therein in Greece and the Ionian Islands: Agriculture, 40 per cent.; shepherds, 9 per cent.; industries, 6·37 per cent.; servants, 7·75 per cent.; laborers, 8·11 per cent.; commerce, 6·37 per cent.; proprietors, 6·10 per cent.; seafaring, 3·05 per cent.; army and navy, 4·86 per cent.; priests, 1·50 per cent. In the provinces ceded to Greece by Turkey in 1881 the proportion is: Agriculture, 41·95 per cent.; laborers, 12·32 per cent.; industries, 10·21 per cent.; shepherds, 8·18 per cent.; servants, 7·24 per cent.; commerce, 6·47 per cent.; priests, 1·61 per cent.

Finances.—The revenue for 1891 was 96,541,-462 drachmai or francs, and the expenditure 100,-411,479 drachmai. The deficits of 1885 and 1886, 120,000,000 drachmai, made the reissue of a forced paper currency necessary. A loan of 135,-000,000 drachmai was raised to cover the deficits for the years 1887 and 1888, secured by the produce of the Government monopolies of salt, petroleum, matches, and other articles. During the four years 1888–'91 the extraordinary receipts, which are composed of the proceeds of loans, amounted to 159,542,006 drachmai, and the extraordinary expenditures to 187,460,890 drachmai, including 87,548,838 drachmai for redemption and consolidation of debt, 75,183,622 drachmai for construction of railways, and 21,-513.066 drachmai for naval construction. The funded debt amounted in 1891 to 601,392,500 drachmai, while the unfunded or floating debt amounted to 103,000,000 drachmai. The annual interest and sinking fund of the funded debt amounted to 26,849,587 drachmai, and the interest on the floating debt to 2,090,000 drachmai. Other charges of 7,049,000 drachmai brought up the total charge to 35,988,587 drachmai, against 36,979,632 drachmai in 1888. In June, 1890, a loan of 89,875,000 drachmai was raised, bearing 5 per cent. interest. Part of this loan was used for paying off the 1879 independence loan, which had a heavy sinking fund; the remainder is used for the construction of railroads.

After the overthrow of the Delyannis administration the new Premier, Tricoupis, introduced the budget for 1892 on July 7. The estimated receipts amounted to 103,550,792 drachmai, the expenditures to 99,986,128 drachmai, showing a surplus of 3,564,664 drachmai. Tricoupis's budget will not be applicable until the second half of the financial year, as up to that time the Delyannis budget will be in operation. That budget presented a deficit of 17,000,000 drachmai, which Tricoupis proposes to cover by imposing fresh taxes to the amount of 10,000,000 drachmai, and diminishing the expenditure 7,150,000 drachmai by a reduction of the army estimates.

The Army and Navy.—Universal liability to military service of all able-bodied men is the law. The total service is for nineteen years; two years are spent in active service, eight years in the reserve, and the remainder in the militia. The total strength of the Greek army in 1891 was 28,-224 men: 136 employed in the Ministry of War, 1,485 engineers, 3,837 chasseurs, 3,382 artillery, 1,608 cavalry, 12,544 infantry, 3,759 in general service, 1,178 in military schools, 295 gendarmerie. On the war footing 100,000 men could be mobilized. The reserve forces number 104,-500 men, while 146,000 men belong to the territorial army.

The navy consisted at the beginning of 1891 of 2 small armor-clad line-of-battle ships, 1 steel armor-clad, 2 corvettes, 2 cruisers, 12 gun vessels, 4 gunboats, 3 revenue vessels, 1 steel yacht, and 16 smaller craft. There are 27 torpedo boats and launches, and 2 Nordenfeldt submarine torpedo boats. In 1891 the navy was manned by 3,957 officers and seamen.

Commerce.—The total value of the general commerce in 1889 was 162,122,869 drachmai for imports and 115,974,249 drachmai for exports. The special commerce with Great Britain in 1890 amounted to 33.237,000 drachmai for imports and 33,021,000 drachmai for exports; with Russia, 21,408,000 drachmai for imports and 911,-000 drachmai for exports; with France, 10,255,-000 drachmai for imports and 21,440,000 drachmai for exports; with Austria-Hungary, 16,691,-000 drachmai for imports and 8,598,000 drachmai for exports; with Turkey and Egypt, 19,712,000 drachmai for imports and 12,682,000 drachmai for exports; with Belgium, 4,009,000 drachmai for imports and 6,008,000 drachmai for exports; with Italy, 5,109,000 drachmai for imports and 1,518,000 drachmai for exports; with Germany, 5,651,000 drachmai for imports and 2,372,000 drachmai for exports; with Holland, 1,861,000 drachmai for imports and 1,518,000 drachmai for exports; with the United States, 1,667,000 drachmai for imports and 5,702,000 drachmai for exports; with all other countries, 1,186,000 drachmai for imports and 356,000 drachmai for exports. The principal classes of special imports are grain, yarns, metal goods, minerals, timber, fish, chemicals, animals, hides, sugar, coffee, and rice. The exports consisted of: Currants, 48,-193,000 drachmai; ores, 17,040,000 drachmai; tobacco, 3,976,000 drachmai; wine, 3,770,000 drachmai; olive oil, 2,299,000 drachmai; figs, 2,248,000 drachmai; sponges, 1,959,000 drachmai.

Navigation.—The mercantile marine in January, 1891, was composed of 5,794 sailing vessels, of 222,331 tons, and 86 steamers, of 43,131 tons. In 1890, 6,117 ships, of 2,476,862 tons, entered the ports of Greece, of which 2,486, with a tonnage of 329,781 tons, were Greek vessels; 5,312 vessels, of 2,410,081 tons, cleared, of which 1,888, of 324,002 tons, were Greek. The number of sailors employed was 22,445.

Communications.—In 1891 the length of the railroads open for traffic was 374 miles, while 420 miles were under construction, and 226 miles were projected. The telegraphic lines at the end of 1890 had a total length of 4,058 miles, and the length of the wire was 5,538 miles. There were 976,318 messages dispatched. The receipts of the service in 1888 were 1,130,160 drachmai; the expenses, 992,320 drachmai. The receipts of the post office were 2,603,614 drachmai in 1889; the expenses, 2, 882,240 drachmai. There were handled 7,664,000 letters, 236,000 postal cards, and 6,779.000 samples, journals, and printed matter.

Political Crisis.—When, in 1890, Delyannis became Prime Minister, he was met with the same financial difficulties that had caused the fall of his predecessor. He showed, however, by his weak indecision and inability to devise any plan for meeting the obligations of the Government, that he was not the proper person for a matter so grave and important. King George, recognizing his Prime Minister's ineptitude, and fearing national bankruptcy, requested him, on March 1, 1892, to tender his resignation. Instead of complying with the King's request, Delyannis immediately called a meeting of the Cabinet, and sent the following letter to the King, signed by all the members of the Cabinet:

Your Majesty's secretary came to-day to the house of the Prime Minister and requested him, by order of your Majesty, to send in his resignation. Article XXXI of the Constitution confers on the King the right to appoint and dismiss ministers; consequently it is for your Majesty to exercise the right of dismissal with regard to us, because the Cabinet has no reason, and has not the right, to resign, so long as it enjoys the full confidence of the Chamber.

The King's efforts to induce the Cabinet to resign were thus frustrated, and he adopted the alternative of summary dismissal. He charged M. Constantopoulos, a member of the so-called Third party, composed of a little group—only about half a dozen Deputies—to form a new Cabinet, which was composed of the following men: Constantopoulos, Prime Minister, Minister of the Interior, and Minister of Finance; Philaretos, Minister of Foreign Affairs and Minister of Justice; Papamichalopoulos, Minister of Worship and Public Instruction; Sakhtouris, Minister of Marine; and Col. Mastrapas, Minister of War.

As the decree of dismissal could not issue without the countersignature of the new Prime Minister, the old ministers considered themselves still in office until the new Cabinet had been formally constituted. Delyannis therefore met the Chamber, and explained to his adherents how the King had attempted to dismiss a ministry enjoying the full confidence of the constitutional representatives of the nation. In response to his appeal a unanimous vote of confidence was hurriedly passed, no members of the other party being present, and the meeting adjourned. From the Chamber he went to his house, and there made a speech to the noisy crowd that had escorted him, representing himself and his adherents as the valiant, patriotic defenders of the Constitution and of the national interests. The speech evoked enthusiastic shouts and cheers, and the crowd marched off toward the palace for the purpose of creating a disturbance. The police, being still under the orders of the old ministry, had instructions not to prevent the demonstration, but the King, foreseeing that Delyannis would probably appeal to the populace, had, as chief of the army, given orders to the commandant of the city to prevent any popular disturbance. The crowd, on seeing the streets leading to the palace held by soldiers, hesitated, and it was soon dispersed and order restored. As the majority of the Chamber was composed of adherents of Delyannis, a royal decree was issued on March 25, 1892, dissolving the Chamber, and fixing May 15 for the general election. The number of Deputies was increased again by law to 207. Of this number, 177 adherents of Tricoupis were elected, while the Opposition carried only 30 seats. As a result, Tricoupis was charged with the formation of a Cabinet, which was composed of the following members: Premier and Minister of Finance, Tricoupis; Minister of Education and Ecclesiastical Affairs, Kossonakos; Minister of Foreign Affairs, Dragoumis; Minister of the Interior, Theotokis; Minister of Justice, Simopoulos; Minister of Marine, Skouloudis; Minister of War, Colonel Tsamados.

Religious Riot.—On Feb. 14, 1892, there was an outbreak of religious fanaticism directed against the Protestants of the town of Piræus. During the service, the Protestant church, which had but lately been built by subscriptions from the United States and England, was surrounded by a turbulent mob. Forcing their way into the church, the rioters maltreated the officiating ministers and the worshipers. They pillaged the building, carrying off even the marriage and baptismal registers, and started a big bonfire in the street, pouring petroleum on it. On the arrival of the military forces, which were sent for because the police was unable to cope with the mob, the crowd dispersed, leaving nothing but the bare walls of the church. The perpetrators of the disturbance escaped.

GUATEMALA, a republic in Central America. The Constitution, adopted in 1879, and amended in 1885, 1887, and 1889, vests the legislative powers in a National Assembly elected for four years. The President is elected for six years. Gen. Manuel Lisandro Barillas was elected to the presidency on March 15, 1886.

Area and Population.—The area of the republic is estimated at 46,800 square miles. The population on Dec. 31, 1890, was computed from registration returns to be 1,452,003. About three fifths of the people are of pure Indian blood, and the rest are of mixed European and Indian descent, with the exception of a small fraction of pure whites. There were 4,609 marriages, 61,575 births, and 69,589 deaths registered in 1890. The capital is Guatemala la Nueva, which had 65,796 inhabitants in 1890. The number of pupils in average attendance in the public schools in 1890 was 52,288, out of a total population of 143,453 of school age. The Government expenditure on the schools for that year was $475,092, and that of the municipalities $30,553. The army, on which about 10 per cent. of the public revenue is spent, consisted in 1891 of 3,718 officers and men. There is, besides, a militia of 67,300 officers and men.

Finances.—The receipts of the Government for 1890 were $6,638,336, and the expenditures $8,300,778. The customs duties produce nearly one half of the revenue, and internal-revenue taxes on spirits, tobacco, and minor articles more than one third. The consolidated internal debt in January, 1891, amounted to $6,495,062; the floating debt, $5,554,995; the foreign debt, $4,613,500; total, $16,663,557. In 1890 the debt was increased by $3,094,367.

Commerce and Production.—The most valuable commercial product of Guatemala is coffee, of which very choice qualities are grown. The soil is remarkably fertile in most places. Sugar cane, Indian corn, wheat, rice, cacao, tobacco, rubber, bananas, and cocoanuts are other important products. The live stock of the country, consisting of horses and mules, cattle, sheep, pigs, and goats, is valued at $18,623,000; and the real property of 6,157 owners, not including those of parcels of less value than $1,000, was estimated in 1885 to be worth $38,741,000. The total value of the imports in 1890 was $7,639,833, and that of the exports $14,401,534. The chief imports were: Cotton manufactures, $945,614; telegraph and electric-lighting apparatus, $458,266; woolen manufactures, $486,297; silks, $157,463; flour, $189,631; specie, $992,666. The principal exports, were: Coffee, $12,714,981; hides, $106,502; bananas, $113,230; sugar, $84,198. Of the exports, $1,207,546 came from the United States, $1,722,671 from Great Britain, $935,829 from Germany, $804,561 from France, $785,279 from the other countries of Central America, and $521,938 from South American countries.

The number of vessels entered at the ports of the republic during 1890 was 430, of 548,193 tons, of which 336, of 474,835 tons, belonged to the United States; 40, of 47,309 tons, to Germany; and 48, of 24,334 tons, to Great Britain. The number of letters, post cards, parcels, etc., sent through the post office in 1890 was 5,194,301. The telegraphs have a total length of 2,176 miles. The number of messages sent in 1890 was 603,423. There is a railroad, 72 miles in length, connecting San José with Escuintla and Guatemala City, and one of 27 miles from Retalhuleu to Champerico, which is to be extended from Retalhuleu to San Felipe.

Coffee Plantations.—The coffee industry has developed within a short period, and is capable of further extension. Between 1861 and 1870 the exports were not more than 11,000,000 pounds for the whole period. The coffee plant is supposed to have been introduced from Mocha by Jesuits in the last century. The plant was regarded as an ornamental shrub, and no plantations were in existence before 1835. About twenty years later the plant began to be grown on a commercial scale, and in the past thirty years the plantations have multiplied at a rapid rate, and they are still being extended from year to year. Lack of labor has prevented the growth of the industry to much larger dimensions, for it is estimated that four times the quantity now produced could be grown. The export in 1891 amounted to over 52,000,000 pounds, valued at about $10,000,000. The growers reap a profit of about 20 per cent. a year on their capital, and many of them have amassed large fortunes. The fine grades are exported to Hamburg and London, where they have the highest reputation of any that is brought into those markets. The inferior kinds, unwashed coffee and sweepings, are exported to San Francisco, and are consumed in the United States.

Change of Administration.—In the election for a President for the period from 1892 to 1898 Gen. José Maria Reina Barrios received the majority of votes, and was confirmed by the National Assembly on March 15, 1892. The Cabinet of the new President was constituted as follows: Minister of Justice, Manuel Estrada Cabrera; Minister of Foreign Affairs, Ramon A. Salazar; Minister of Finance, Salvadore Herrera; Minister of Education, Manuel Cabral;

Minister of Public Works, Jorge Velez, who was appointed temporarily to the Ministry of War also. Gen. Barrios promised to give his main attention to reducing to order the finances of the country, and declared that his administration would not be purely partisan, like that of his predecessor, but that he would seek the co-operation of the best men of all parties for the purpose of securing good government and general satisfaction and content. His selection of men who had been his political opponents for some of the high posts in the provincial administrations comported with this declaration.

H

HARRISON, CAROLINE LAVINIA SCOTT, mistress of the White House in 1889–'92, born in Oxford, Ohio, Oct. 1, 1832; died in Washington, D. C., Oct. 25, 1892. Dr. John Witherspoon Scott, her father, was of an old Pennsylvania family. Her mother, Mary Neal, was the daughter of a bank cashier in Philadelphia. Mr. Scott studied theology and entered the ministry of the Presbyterian Church, but subsequently adopted teaching as his life work.

CAROLINE LAVINIA SCOTT HARRISON.

Miami University was founded in Oxford, Ohio, in 1826, and a little later the Oxford Female College was established in the same village; Dr. Scott became its president, and his daughter studied under his tuition. Benjamin Harrison entered the junior class of Miami University, and an attachment soon sprang up between him and Miss Scott, who was an exceedingly attractive as well as strong-natured girl. On leaving college, Mr. Harrison read law for two years in Cincinnati, and then, returning to Oxford, was married on Oct. 20, 1853, and carried his bride to his home at North Bend. There he completed his law studies, and the youthful pair removed to Indianapolis, Ind. They boarded for a time, but on the birth of a son, Russell, began housekeeping. The new home was one story high, with three rooms and a lean-to kitchen. Mrs. Harrison sometimes employed "help," but was often her husband's cook and her baby's nurse, while Mr. Harrison filled the water buckets and the wood boxes before leaving for his office. Of those days he says: "They were close times, I tell you. A five-dollar bill was an event." Two years later they had so far prospered

as to be able to remove to a larger and better house. In 1858 a second child, Mary, was born. From 1862 till 1865 Gen. Harrison was with his troops in the field, and his wife was doing her part for the cause with the other women at home. In 1881 Gen. Harrison was elected to the United States Senate, and Mrs. Harrison accompanied him to Washington. During the six years of their residence there she was especially associated with works of benevolence and public interest, while continuing to make the home circle a charming one for friends and for such strangers as had a right to enter it. The Garfield Hospital, of which she became one of the first directors, largely owed its success to her interest and efforts.

In Indianapolis Mrs. Harrison was especially well known for the brightness and pithiness of the social meetings at her home, and her programmes for a literary organization were always marked by originality and strength, while the fair and the charitable meeting were greatly helped by the influence of her sympathetic personality. She kept up her studies and pursued art as a means of recreation and culture. A friend of hers says: "The Harrisons have been noted for their hospitality. They had always a house full of company at their Indianapolis home." During the political canvass that ended in the election of her husband as President of the United States, one little remark of hers suggested the picture of the careful housewife. Looking at the carpets of her substantial and comfortable home after they had been trodden by the multitude of callers, she said: "My dear, if we don't go to the White House, we shall have to go to the poorhouse." They did go to the White House, and among the women who have presided there in republican simplicity there is no more amiable and attractive figure than that of Mrs. Harrison. She took such pride in it as the nation's representative home as few others have taken, and brought from long-hidden corners objects of historic interest or beauty and set them in their proper relations. She not only redecorated interesting rooms that had been closed or little used, but had important sanitary improvements made in the cellars and kitchens. In a conversation between Mrs. Harrison and Secretary Blaine, their views on the inadequacy of the Executive Mansion were exchanged, she pointing out especially the lack of enough family apartments, of privacy for the ladies of the President's family, and of room for guests at state hospitalities. In a subsequent conversation with Col. John M. Wilson, engineer in charge of the public buildings and grounds, she gave her ideas of the way in which the building should be enlarged, and with the assistance of an architect these were put upon paper in the form of proper drawings. It was Mrs. Harrison's idea to preserve the present White House and build extensive wings, which, with a conservatory, will inclose a rectangle, giving ample room for the public offices as well as for accommodation of the family and guests. The southern façade of her plan is shown in the accompanying engraving.

Two tributes from those who had known her long and well are as follow: "The greatest charm in Mrs. Harrison's disposition was her strong common sense, her evenness of temper, her willingness to oblige, and the kindly thought for everybody else which dominated every act. She cultivated the faculty of saying a happy thing

period. In carrying out the hospitalities of the White House she has never been excelled. She presided with easy dignity and grace upon these occasions, and omitted no detail that would add to the pleasure of those attending them. She carried out to the letter the written and unwritten laws of the house, and did as much more as it was possible to do within the limits of each season."

She had luxuriant brown hair, touched with silver of late years, which fell in waves about her shapely head; she had regular features, dark, expressive eyes, a soft, sympathetic voice, an animated and thoughtful manner of conversing, and a winning and subdued gayety. During the first epidemic of the grippe, Mrs. Harrison cared unweariedly for her aged father, whose home was with her, and for whom she was always most tenderly solicitous, and her grandchildren, who were very ill. After their recovery she herself was prostrated with the disease. The next season she was again attacked, and

MRS. HARRISON'S PLAN FOR ENLARGEMENT OF THE EXECUTIVE MANSION.

of everybody, and repressed the strong inclination to say the witty things which always came so easy to her, for fear she might unwittingly offend a sensitive person. Her high position did not change her in the slightest degree, unless it were to make her feel more than ever willing to give up her private inclinations to do that which was expected from her by the public." "Mrs. Harrison was just the same—kind and thoughtful for everybody, great and small—and the friends of her early days in Washington were her friends to the last. She was probably one of the most industrious mistresses the White House has ever had. Her own method of life was so simple that it gave her more time than ordinarily comes to persons in high places to devote to things she liked best. She was a constant reader of the best literature, and was devoted to her brush. She had been a diligent pupil for several years in the studio of a china painter, and her talent was often displayed in the gifts she made her friends at the holiday

from these illnesses she never wholly recovered, and they were followed in the spring of 1892 by throat and lung difficulties that developed into tubercular consumption. During the summer she was carried to Loon lake, in the Adirondacks, but with no improvement. As her weakness and suffering increased, she longed to return to the comfort and brightness of her home in Washington, and thither she was carried a short time before she passed away.

HAWAII, a limited monarchy, occupying the Hawaiian or Sandwich Islands in the Pacific Ocean. The reigning sovereign is Queen Liliuokalani, born Sept. 2, 1838, who succeeded her brother, Kalakaua, Jan. 20, 1891. Her husband, John O. Dominis, was Governor of Oahu until his death, on Aug. 27, 1891. The new Constitution of 1887 makes the ministers removable by a vote of want of confidence. The Legislature is composed of 24 Nobles, elected by citizens having $3,000 worth of property or an income of $600, and the same number of Representatives, who are elected by all citizens possessing certain educational qualifications. The 4 ministers have seats in the Assembly and votes on all questions except one of want of confidence. The Nobles are elected for six years, one third every two years, and the Representatives for each biennial Parliament. Volunteer military organizations are interdicted, and the only armed force maintained by the Government is the household guard of the Queen, numbering 65 men.

Area and Population.—The area of all the islands is 6,640 square miles. The population as ascertained by the census of 1890 was 89,990, consisting of 58,714 males and 31,276 females, compared with 80,578 in 1884, consisting of 51,-539 males and 29,039 females. In 1890 there were 34,436 natives, 6,186 half-castes, 7,495 of American and European descent, 15,301 Chinese, 12,360 Japanese, 8,602 Portuguese, 1,928 Americans, 1,344 British, 1,034 Germans, 588 Polynesians, 227 Norwegians, 70 French, and 419 other foreigners. Since 1884 the native population has decreased 5,578. In 1890 there were 2,484 arrivals and 1,852 departures, or a net immigration of 632. The bulk of the immigration is from China and Japan. The capital is Honolulu, the chief seaport, on the island of Oahu. The people are Christians, and are divided among the principal creeds as follow: Protestants, 29,-685; Roman Catholics, 20,072; Mormons, 3,576; undesignated, 30,821. There were 178 schools, with 10,000 pupils, in 1890. The Government spent $326,922 on education.

Finances.—The revenue for the biennial period of 1888-'90 was $3,632,197, and the expenditure $3,250,510. For 1890-'92 the revenue was estimated at $2,862,502, and expenditure at $2,853,116. The customs receipts for 1888-'90 were $1,082,766, and the internal revenue $901,-803. The expenditure of the Interior Department was $1,180,123. The debt in 1890 was $2,599,502, paying from 5 to 7 per cent. interest.

Commerce and Production.—The soil is volcanic, and exceedingly fertile. The chief products are sugar and rice. The total imports in 1890 were valued at $6,962,000, and the exports at $13,023,000. The sugar exports were $12,159,585; rice, $545,239; bananas, $176,351; hides, $70,949. The imports consist of provisions and groceries, clothing, cereals, timber, machinery, and cotton cloth. Nine tenths of the foreign trade is with the United States.

The number of vessels entered in 1890 was 295, of 230,120 tons. There are 20 steamers and 28 sailing vessels plying between the different islands. The total number of vessels belonging to the islands was 57 in 1889, of 15,403 tons. The principal islands are connected by telegraph cables. The total length of telegraphs is 250 miles. The number of letters, etc., sent through the post office for the two years 1889-'90 was 3,150,034. Honolulu, with 20,487 inhabitants, has a very complete system of telephones, and is lighted by electricity. The legal currency since 1884 is United States gold coin for all sums over $10, and United States and Hawaiian silver for smaller amounts. There is no paper currency except certificates for coin in the treasury.

Political Events.—The biennial elections in February, 1892, resulted in the return of a majority for the Government to the Legislature.

There was much discontent with the ministry, and on March 28 a rising under the lead of Robert Wilcox was expected to take place. The approaches to the palace were fortified with breastworks of sand-bags, but no attack was made, the malcontents being deterred probably by the presence in the harbor of the United States war ships "San Francisco" and "Iroquois." On Aug. 30, in consequence of a vote of want of confidence, the Cabinet resigned, and from the leading members of the Opposition a new one was constituted as follows: Premier and Minister of Finance, Edward Macfarlane; Minister of Foreign Affairs, Mr. Parker: Minister of the Interior, Mr. Gulick; Attorney-General, Mr. Neumann. On Oct. 17 this Cabinet was defeated on a vote of want of confidence by a majority of 81 to 15.

A Revolution.—The hope that Queen Liliuokalani would follow a more enlightened policy than her brother was disappointed when she entered upon a conflict, soon after her accession, with the Cabinet, which, though supported by a large majority, was compelled to retire. The Queen and her party championed the interests of the natives as opposed to those of the foreign-born element, and the new Cabinet that she appointed obtained a majority in the Legislature. The financial and internal policy of this subservient ministry created misgivings among the property-holders and capitalists. Three parties were represented in the Legislature: the Missionary Reform party, as it was called, which had carried out the revolution of 1887; the Liberal party, which represented the natives and the working classes; and the National Reform party, which was elected by a coalition with the Reform party. In the successive changes that were made in the Cabinet, the Queen, through her arbitrary selection, dictated by an unpopular favorite called Bolabola, prevented the regular and constitutional solution of the questions that were before the country. Her last Cabinet was taken mainly from the Reform party, which was in the minority, but which by its influence and power compelled the Queen to turn to its moderate and experienced men for guidance, for fear of losing her throne. Soon she began to listen to other advisers, and conceived the idea of regaining the royal powers that Kalakaua had surrendered with the support of the native race. The Legislature, on Jan. 11, 1893, passed by a bare majority a bill granting the privilege of establishing a lottery on the promise of an annual payment of $500,000 to the Government. The ministers refused to sign this bill, for which only one white man had voted, and on Jan. 12, by the same majority, a vote of want of confidence was carried, only nine days before the date set for the prorogation of Parliament. The Queen signed the lottery bill on Jan. 14, and proposed to promulgate a new Constitution in which she assumed absolute authority. This act the new ministers declined to approve. Yet on Jan. 15, after the prorogation of Parliament, she attempted to proclaim the Constitution, and appealed to the natives and half-castes to sustain her. This instrument deprived foreign-born citizens of the right of suffrage, and suppressed the existing House of Nobles, but empowered the Queen to create a new one. Judges of the

Supreme Court, who now hold office for life, were to be appointed by the Queen for the term of six years and made subject to her dismissal. The draft Constitution was presented to the Queen by the native group called Hui Kalaiaina, with a petition that it be promulgated to the people as the fundamental law of the land, who went to the palace immediately after the prorogation. The Queen summoned the ministers and demanded that they should sign the proposed Constitution, declaring her firm intention of promulgating it at once. The Attorney-General and the Minister of the Interior refused unequivocally, and their colleagues, with some hesitation, joined in the refusal. When the Queen then threatened to go out and tell the excited people that she wished to give them a new Constitution, but was hindered by the ministers, they fled for their lives. They immediately sent word to find how far the citizens would sustain them in the position they had taken, and, on receiving unanimous promises of support from leading men of all shades of politics, they returned to the palace to urge the Queen to go no further in her revolutionary course. While the troops were drawn up waiting her word of command, she hesitated, and finally consented with bitter reluctance to a temporary postponement of the project, addressing the assembled native members of Parliament and officers of the Government in the following language:

Princes, Nobles, and Representatives: I have listened to thousands of the voices of my people that have come to me, and I am prepared to grant their request. The present Constitution is full of defects, as the Chief Justice here will testify, as questions regarding it have so often come before him for settlement. It is so faulty that I think a new one should be granted. I have prepared one in which the rights of all have been regarded—a Constitution suited to the wishes of the people. I was ready and expected to proclaim the new Constitution to-day as a suitable occasion for it, and thus satisfy the wishes of my dear people. But with regret I say I have met with obstacles that prevent it. Return to your homes peaceably and quietly and continue to look toward me, and I will look toward you. Keep me ever in your love. I am obliged to postpone the granting of the Constitution for a few days. I must confer with my Cabinet, and when, after you return home, you may see it, receive it graciously. You have my love, and with sorrow I now dismiss you.

The native leaders, William White and Kamnamano, addressed the crowd outside with incendiary language, one saying that he thirsted for the blood of the ministers, and the other that the people should kill and bury the Queen, who had betrayed them. She was probably withheld from the purpose that she had announced less by the expostulations of the ministers than by the arrival of the United States war vessel "Boston," whose presence strengthened the resolution of the respectable citizens to resist the threatened state stroke. About 4,000 natives gathered in an excited mass meeting to denounce the ministers for refusing to carry out the Queen's wishes.

On the afternoon of the 15th the Reform leaders formed a committee of safety of 13 members, who called a mass meeting. This was attended by 1,200, or 1,500 persons, who passed resolutions condemning the action of the Queen,

and authorizing the committee to take such measures as were necessary for the public safety. On Jan. 16 a Provisional Government was formed, composed of the following men: S. B. Dole, President of the Executive Council in charge of the Department of Foreign Affairs; J. A. King, administering the Department of the Interior; P. C. Jones, administering the Department of Finance; and W. O. Smith, Attorney-General. An advisory council was constituted, consisting of S. M. Damon, L. A. Thurston, J. Emmeluth, J. A. McCandless, F. M. McChesney, W. R. Castle, W. C. Wilder, A. Brown, J. F. Morgan, H. Waterhouse, E. D. Tenney, F. Wilhelm, W. C. Ashley, and C. Bolte.

On Jan. 17 the Provisional Government issued a manifesto proclaiming the deposition of the Queen in the following terms:

Upon the accession of Her Majesty Liliuokalani, for a brief period the hope prevailed that a new policy would be adopted. This hope was soon blasted by her immediately entering into a conflict with the existing Cabinet, who held office with approval of a large majority of the Legislature, resulting in the triumph of the Queen and the removal of the Cabinet. Appointment of a new Cabinet subservient to her wishes and its continuance in office until a recent date gave no opportunity for further indication of the policy which would be pursued by Her Majesty until the opening of the Legislature in May, 1892. The recent history of that session has shown stubborn determination on the part of Her Majesty to follow the tactics of her late brother, and in all possible ways to secure the extension of the royal prerogatives and the abridgment of popular rights. Five uprisings of conspiracies against the Government have occurred within five years and seven months. We firmly believe that the revolutionary attempt of last Saturday will, unless radical measures are taken, wreck our already damaged credit abroad and precipitate to final ruin our already overstrained financial condition, and guarantees of protection to life, liberty, and property will steadily decrease. The political situation is rapidly growing worse. In this belief, and also in the belief that the action hereby taken is and will be for the best personal, political, and property interests of every citizen of the land, we, citizens and residents of the Hawaiian Islands, organized and acting for public safety and common good, hereby proclaim as follows:

The Hawaiian monarchical system of government is hereby abrogated. Provisional government for the control and management of public affairs and the protection of public peace is hereby established, to exist until terms of union with the United States of America have been negotiated and agreed upon.

The new Government then called for volunteers, who assembled, armed, to the number of 500. The old Government surrendered without striking a blow, although it had about 400 men under arms and a battery of Gatling guns. The old ministers were summoned by the new Executive, and, after parley and consultation with Liliuokalani, they turned over the public buildings with her consent, on the plea that resistance was not feasible. The Provisional Government notified the representatives of foreign governments of the change, and asked recognition. This was at once granted by all the powers except England. The Provisional Government promised peace, and requested all parties to continue in the Government service except the following: Queen Liliuokalani; Charles B. Wilson, Marshal; Samuel Parker, Minister of Foreign Affairs; W. H. Cornwall, Minister of Finance;

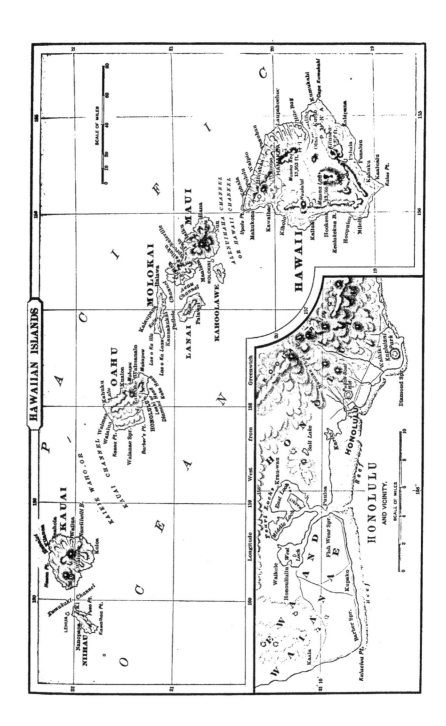

John F. Colburn, Minister of the Interior; and Arthur P. Peterson, Attorney-General.

The Government assumed formal control of the palace and barracks. The ex-Queen retired to her private residence at Washington Place, and the Government granted her an honorary guard. The household guards were paid off and disbanded. A strong force of volunteers took possession of all the Government buildings. The Executive Council issued a proclamation of martial law, and J. H. Soper, in command of all the armed troops on the island, published the following notice:

Under martial law, every person found upon the streets, or in any public place, between the hours of 9.30 P. M. and 5 A. M. will be liable to arrest, unless provided with a pass from the Commander-in-Chief, J. H. Soper. Gathering of crowds is prohibited. Any one disturbing the peace or disobeying orders is liable to summary arrest without warrant. By order of the Executive Committee.

The United States steamer "Boston" arrived in port on Saturday, at the time when the Queen was on the point of promulgating the new Constitution without the sanction of her ministers. On the same day, after the publication of the revolutionary manifesto, 300 marines and sailors were landed to protect American property. The marines, armed with rifles, guarded the American legation, while the sailors, with 2 Gatling guns, took position before the house where the Committee of Safety was in session.

The ex-Queen, after her surrender, issued the following protest, dated Jan. 17, in which she held the United States minister responsible for her downfall:

I, Liliuokalani, by the grace of God and under the Constitution of the Hawaiian Kingdom Queen, do hereby solemnly protest against any and all acts done against myself and the Constitutional Government of the Hawaiian kingdom by certain persons claiming to have established a Provisional Government of and for this kingdom.

That I yield to the superior force of the United States of America, whose minister plenipotentiary, His Excellency John L. Stevens, has caused United States troops to be landed at Honolulu and declared that he would support the said Government.

Now, to avoid any collision of armed forces and perhaps loss of life, I do under this protest, and impelled by said force, yield my authority until such time as the Government of the United States shall, upon facts being presented to it, undo the acts of its representatives, and reinstate me in the authority which I claim as constitutional sovereign of the Hawaiian Islands.

The programme of the Provisional Government was to maintain peace and to carry on the public business until a treaty of annexation to the United States could be negotiated.

The Hawaiian steamer "Claudine" was chartered, which left Honolulu on Jan. 19, with 5 commissioners, who were instructed to go to Washington and negotiate a treaty of annexation. The commissioners were: Lorrin A. Thurston, William C. Wilder, William R. Caset, Charles L. Carter, and Joseph Marsden. The "Claudine" also brought representatives of the deposed Queen to lay her protest before the United States Government.

HAYTI, a republic of the West Indies occupying the western part of the island of Hayti. The legislative powers are vested by the Constitution of 1867 in a National Assembly consisting of a Senate and a House of Representatives. The members of the House are elected directly by the suffrage of all adult males who are engaged in a regular occupation. Their term is five years. The Senators are chosen for six years by the House of Representatives, from two lists made up by the Executive and electoral colleges, and one third go out every two years. Their number is 30. The President, according to the Constitution, is required to be elected for seven years by the popular vote; but most of the recent Presidents have been elected by the National Assembly or by party conventions or have been proclaimed by the troops. Gen. Hippolyte assumed the presidency in October, 1892.

Area and Population.—The Haytians are a negro people, the descendants of slaves who were made free by the French revolution when Hayti was a colony of France. There are very few persons of European descent, and these are mostly resident traders from foreign countries. About nine tenths of the native people are black, and the rest are colored. The population is estimated to number 572,000, living on an area of 10,204 square miles. The common people speak a scarcely intelligible patois called Creole French. The educated class is trained after French methods, a considerable proportion receiving their schooling in France. Elementary education, though free, is not general, except in the towns. There are 400 public schools and 5 lycées. The army has a legal strength of 6,828, besides the guard of the Government, a body of 600 soldiers commanded by 10 generals.

Finances.—The chief sources of revenue are the duties on imports and exports, which amounted to 5,780,404 and 2,820,554 piasters or dollars respectively in 1890. The total revenue in 1888 was $8,047,768. The foreign debt was reported in 1887 to be $4,320,000, and the internal debt $9,180,000. The paper currency in circulation in 1891 amounted to about $5,000,000.

Commerce and Production.—The imports for 1889 amounted to $6,000,000, and the exports to $12,000,000. In 1890 the imports were valued at $19,500,000 and the exports at $15,000,000. The export of coffee was 60,000,000 pounds; of logwood, 200,000,000 pounds; of cacao, 4,900,000 pounds; of cotton, 2,400,000 pounds; of mahogany, 50,000 feet. There were 694 vessels, of 779,676 tons, entered at the three principal ports in 1890. During that year the post office forwarded 479,996 letters and other pieces of mail matter.

Political Situation.—In the latter part of 1892 a restless and unsettled political condition was manifested in the centers remote from the capital, both north and south, but especially in the north, where the leaders were dissatisfied with the President, whom they had fought to place in power, because in the distribution of offices he had preferred his old enemies of the south, and had filled his Cabinet with men who had fought against him under Légitime. The exiled aspirants for the succession—Manigat, Piquant, and Légitime—were said to have sunk their rivalries and formed a compact. They were supposed to be waiting in Jamaica for a favorable opportunity to land in Hayti and organize a revolution, all working in harmony for the overthrow of Hippolyte, on the understanding that the people should freely choose a President from among them, and that the other two should have the most lucrative and important posts under him. Gen. Manigat was the favorite candidate, and a plot to oust Hippolyte in his favor was discovered, in which members of the Cabinet and officers of the navy were supposed to be implicated. On Dec. 2 an attempt was made to kill President Hippolyte by three men, who were caught and immediately shot. Hippolyte's Government had a controversy with the United States because an American citizen, Frederick Mevs, was arrested on a charge of smuggling, and kept in jail without trial for twenty days, though Dr. Terres, the American *chargé d'affaires* demanded his release.

HOLLAND. See NETHERLANDS.

HONDURAS, a republic in Central America. The Constitution, as amended in 1880, vests the legislative authority in a Congress consisting of a single chamber of 37 Deputies. The executive head of the Republic is the President, who is elected by the suffrage of the people, and appoints his ministers independently of Congress. Gen. Ponciano Leiva was elected President on Nov. 10, 1891. There is a regular armed force of about 500 men and 20,000 militia.

Area and Population.—The republic has an area of 46,400 square miles. The population, consisting of aboriginal Indians, except in some of the towns and in the tobacco-growing districts, where there are descendants of the Spanish conquerors, numbered 431,917 in 1889. Tegucigalpa, the capital, has 12,600 inhabitants. It is situated nearly midway between the two coasts, and has very imperfect communications with the sea. The interoceanic railroad which is to be constructed from Puerto Cortez, on the Gulf of Mexico, to Amapala, a port on the Pacific, will pass through the city, and is expected to give a great impulse to agricultural production and commerce and to the development of the neglected mineral resources of the country. The Government does much for education, and the country is provided with two universities, several colleges, and 600 primary schools, with 23,000 pupils in attendance.

Finances.—The strife of factions and wars with the neighboring republics have unsettled the financial condition of the Government, though some improvement was made during the administration of President Bográn. The revenue for the two years 1887–'88 was $2,814,264, compared with $2,596,936 for the preceding biennial period, and the expenditure was $2,826,532. For the year 1889 the receipts were $1,432,522, and the disbursements $1,385,000. For several years fresh loans have been required in order to balance the accounts. The revenue is obtained chiefly from customs and internal-revenue duties. On the foreign debt, consisting of £3,222,000 borrowed in England and £2,176,-570 raised in France, there were arrears of interest amounting to £7,645,518 in 1891, none having been paid since 1872.

Commerce and Production.—The customs revenue is farmed out to private persons, who make no trustworthy reports regarding the imports or exports, because they do not wish to disclose the amount of their receipts. The imports consist mainly of cotton cloth, silks, and hardware. The exports for the year ending July 31, 1888, were valued at $3,350,664, of which $2,790,405 went to the United States, $367,599 to Central American republics, $105,-088 to England, $81,566 to France, and $6,003 to Germany. The exports of vegetable products amounted to $1,122,716; of animal products and manufactures, $376,645; of minerals, exclusive of gold and silver, $1,673,449; of precious metals, $78,853. The largest exports are cattle, bananas, mahogany, hides and deer skins, and India rubber. During 1887 there were 139 vessels, of 59,723 tons, entered at the ports. There are 1,800 miles of telegraph. The only completed railroad is one 37 miles long connecting Puerto Cortez, the starting-point of the projected interoceanic line, with the San Pedro Sula. Another line is planned which will tap the rich fruit-growing districts of the north coast, and put them in communication with the New Orleans steamship lines at Puerto Cortez.

Revolutionary Uprising.—Gen. Luis Bográn retired from his second term as President in November, 1891. He was urged to accept a third term, but believed that the precedents of the United States, after whose Constitution and customs the political system of Honduras is modeled, ought to be followed. His late Secretary of War, Gen. Ponciano Leiva, was elected to succeed him by a majority of the popular votes over Policarpo Bonilla. Gen. Bográn, who was in bad health, abandoned the presidential chair in favor of Leiva a short time before his term had expired. The Cabinet constituted in January, 1892, contained the following members: Minister of Foreign Affairs, Dr. Jeronimo Zelaya; Minister of Home Affairs, Dr. Bendana; Minister of Finance, Col. Vidaureta; Minister of War, Gen. Alvarado; Minister of Public Works, Ponetano Planas; Minister of Justice and Public Instruction, Dr. Zuniga.

There was considerable opposition to the new administration in Choluteca and elsewhere. On May 13 the defeated candidate, Bonilla, attempted a revolution. Gen. Manuel Bonilla, coming from Guatemala, took possession of the customhouse at Puerto Cortez on May 18, and demanded the surrender of the Cuartel. The commander refused to surrender, and when Bonilla attacked the Cuartel he was defeated, with the loss of several officers and men, and fled with his broken force in canoes to Livingston, Guatemala. The plot to seize the Cuartel in the capital was revealed to the Government, and Policarpo Bonilla, Gen. Dionicio Guiteirez, Dr. Enrique Lozano, and others were banished from the country. In Choluteca Gen. Lerencio Sierra raised a force of 1,400 men and proclaimed Bonilla President. Bonilla's friends claimed that the Liberal party had been victorious in the presidential election, but that the officials had suppressed the true returns, and Congress had made a fraudulent canvass. Gov. Domingo Vasquez, at the head of the Government troops, attacked Sierra's forces in the mountains, and drove them into Nicaragua.

Gen. Roque L. Muñoz, who was appointed

administrator of customs on the north coast and Bay of Istanaz, and commander of all the military forces of the department of Colon, began a war against smugglers, and carried out his plans of reform with a rigor and by methods so arbitrary as to incur the enmity of the mercantile and other classes. Col. Leonardo Nuilla, a former partisan of Leiva, who had nevertheless been deposed from his place as lieutenant administrator of customs for the port of Ceiba, took the lead in a conspiracy to oust the Government officials and inaugurate a revolution. On the night of June 23, with 12 men, he overpowered the guard and gained possession of the barracks, customhouse, and telegraph office at Ceiba. A force of 50 insurgents was sent out to seize the towns between Ceiba and Truxillo. The United States steamer "Jos. Otteri, Jr.," then in the port of Ceiba, was boarded by Nuilla, who took away 250 rifles and a quantity of cartridges consigned to the Government, and left a guard. He issued a proclamation, in which he dwelt on complaints made by American citizens against Muñoz for illegalities committed in respect of the American steamers "Professor Morse" and "Rover," of the Central American Pioneer line. At Nuilla's call volunteers flocked in, more than he had arms for, not Hondurians alone, but Salvadorians and citizens of the other Central American republics. He embarked 500 men on the "Jos. Otteri, Jr.," on June 24 for Truxillo. If successful in taking that place, he intended to seize Puerto Cortez, reduce Ruatan, capture the arms that were there, and then march upon the capital. Truxillo was taken by surprise on the night of June 24, and Muñoz was made a prisoner and shot. On the 26th, Nuilla went to capture Ruatan, but the assault was beaten off, and the revolutionists, having lost their boats, returned to Truxillo. Nuilla had possession of the whole north coast, and by his favors won the good will of the merchants. On June 27 he returned with 500 men to Ceiba, on the "Jos. Otteri, Jr.", and on the following day he released the vessel. which departed immediately for New Orleans. Col. Nuilla laid his plans to march secretly into Comayagua on Aug. 4 and capture the city and the Government buildings. Informed of this, the Government took measures to guard the capital, and meanwhile President Leiva chartered the American steamer "Pizatti," converted it into a vessel of war, mounting 2 Krupp guns and 1 Gatling, and sent it with a large body of troops to regain the places in the north. The vessel shelled Ceiba until the insurgents were dislodged, and the Government troops took possession of the town after a short battle on land. The revolutionists fled into the forest, and their friends in Truxillo deserted that town before the "Pizatti" arrived with troops. On Aug. 26 Nuilla was captured and court-martialed.

I

IDAHO, a Northwestern State, admitted to the Union July 3, 1890; area, 84,800 square miles; population, according to the census of 1890, 84,385. Capital, Boisé City.

Government.—The following were the State officers during the year: Governor, Norman B. Willey, Republican; Secretary of State, A. J. Pinkham; Auditor, Silas W. Moody; Treasurer, Frank R. Coffin; Attorney-General, George H. Roberts; Superintendent of Public Instruction, J. E. Harroun; Chief Justice of the Supreme Court, Isaac N. Sullivan; Associate Justices, Joseph W. Huston and John T. Morgan.

Education.—According to the latest school census there were in the State 27,740 children of school age, and under the current apportionment the *per capita* is nearly fifty cents. The school money apportioned in January, 1892, amounted to $1,324.65. In June of the same year the school funds apportioned had increased to $13,674.67, a large advance on that of the preceding year, which then aggregated but $1,942. This increase in the amounts of money apportioned was derived from the interest on the sales of State school lands. The method adopted by the State Board of Land Commissioners of making loans of school money is explained by Attorney-General Roberts as follows:

When there is money in the State treasury, applications for loans are considered in the order of their filing with the secretary. If they are found to be regular on their face, the security offered is ordered appraised. If the security proves to be such as the statute requires, the title is examined and approved,

mortgage and notes executed, and the State Auditor is required to draw his warrant for the amount loaned in favor of the applicant. The whole amount of money received by the board is $74,779.25. There was in May in the treasury $23,009.25. Of this amount $21,300 has been loaned subject to appraisement of the land offered as security.

State Lands.—The General Government granted to Idaho on July 3, 1890, 622,000 acres. Of these, 167,125·34 acres were selected by the State Board of Land Commissioners for public purposes. There were on July 18, 1892, according to a report submitted to the State Board of Land Commissioners, 30,000 acres under inspection for selection.

Under the general grant of the 16th and 36th sections in every township to the State for public-school purposes, there are now surveyed and belonging to the State 558,720 acres. The estimated amount to be surveyed and to inure to the State under this grant is 2,800,000 acres.

Pursuant to the provisions of the act of Feb. 26, 1891, there have been appraised by county commissioners university lands amounting to 5,957 acres, and public-school lands amounting to 40,-899·53 acres. There have been sold at public auction: University lands, 1,797 acres, for $17,-970; and public-school lands, 23,071·58 acres for $570,398.25—a total of 24,868·58 acres for $588,-368.25.

Finances.—The semiannual report of the State Treasurer covering the period between July 1, 1891, and Jan. 1, 1892, is as follows: Balance in the treasury on Jan. 1, 1892, $73,-714.18; indebtedness of the State, $428,111.52;

total receipts during the six months ending Jan. 1, $180,184.97.

On Sept. 23, 1892, the State Auditor, in response to an appeal, published the following in regard to the condition of the State finances: Total fixed appropriations available—State offices, institutions, and departments—$88,460.22. Appropriations for conveying prisoners from county jail to Penitentiary exhausted on July 7, 1892; those for conveying the insane nearly gone. The land department appropriation of $10,000 had been exhausted, and only $72.83 had been thus far presented for audit in excess of appropriation. The amount of claims allowed by the State board then filed (not including riot claims), which under the statute must be certified, was $2,849.12. The claims growing out of the Shoshone County riots amounted to $8,467.26; of that amount $2,-461.75 would be reduced by percentage; the expenses of the regular army being paid by the United States, and the greater part of the expenses chargeable to the State for the subsistence of the State troops having been filed and covered by the amount given, $8,467.26. The State troops are entitled to the same pay while in active service as the regular army, but in many cases there are appreciable offsets for clothing" and other articles. The total may reach $5,000. No railway's claims for transportation of troops have been presented, but the amount that may have to be paid on this account can not be very large.

Irrigation.—The reclaiming of arid lands by irrigation has been a subject of absorbing interest. Various bills relating to the arid-land question have been proposed, and some have been introduced in Congress. Some idea of the extent and uses of irrigation in the State may be obtained from the following statistics: During the year ending May 31, 1890, there were 4,323 irrigated farms in the State, out of a total of 6,654. The total area upon which crops were raised by irrigation was 217,005 acres. The average size of irrigated farms was 50 acres. The average first cost of water right was $4.74 an acre, and the average cost of preparing the land $10.56 an acre. The average value of irrigated land at the time the census was taken was $45.50 an acre. The average value of crops for 1889 was $12.93 an acre, and the average annual cost of maintaining ditches, etc., was 80 cents an acre. Irrigation companies, representing large capitals, have been organized in various parts of the State. An exhibit of an irrigating process has been planned for the World's Fair.

Agricultural.—The agricultural educational appropriation made by the General Government for Idaho amounted to $33,000. Of this sum $15,000 was devoted to the use of the State University at Moscow, and $18,000 to experimental stations in other parts of the State.

Appropriations.—The sum of $20,000 was voted by Congress to the improvement of Snake river. For public-land surveys for the year 1892-'93, $40,000 was appropriated, an excess of $5,000 over the amount appropriated the year before. The Boisé City public building received $100,000.

Suffrage.—State Attorney-General Roberts returned the following opinion to the State Superintendent of Public Instruction: "Women possessing the constitutional and statutory qualifications can vote at all school elections; but to vote upon the proposition as to whether a special tax shall be levied, women must possess, with male suffragists, the additional qualification of being 'an actual resident freeholder or head of a family.'"

Taxation.—In answer to various questions submitted on the subject, the Attorney-General returned the following opinion: "That a license for revenue only is a tax, and that no fees or commissions can be allowed county officers for their services in the collection of the same, except in the case of sheriffs, to a limited extent."

The World's Fair.—Idaho will spend $100,-000 for its World's Fair exhibit. Of this amount $20,000 has already been appropriated by the State, and it is expected that the next Legislature will make up the remainder. In addition to the State appropriations, individual representatives of the greatest industries will devote large sums to the display of their interests. In its exhibit at the World's Fair Idaho will pay special attention to the mining industry. The State has contributed $175,000,-000 of money in gold and silver to increase the wealth and enrich the commerce of the land. It produces half the lead product of the United States. In consideration of these facts, a special effort will be made to have a mining exhibit commensurate with the importance of the State as a mineral producer.

The State's building will be somewhat rustic in appearance, costing $15,000. Here will appear all the more valuable building materials to be found in the State, including marble, brick, and stone. The women of Idaho will assume the responsibility of having it suitably decorated."

The Cœur d'Alêne Riots.—These originated in an attempt of the Mine-Owners' Association to establish a new rate of payment at the Gem and Union mines, discriminating between skilled and unskilled labor as represented by the regular miners and trammers or surface men. The association maintained that theirs was the only camp where such a distinction was not made, and that there was no reason why the Cœur de Alêne mines should be the exception to the rule. The mine owners did not propose to cut the wages of the regular miners. On the contrary, they announced their willingness to enter into an obligation to maintain the scale of prices; but the enforcing by the union of miners' wages for trammers they considered an injustice. They offered, under the new schedule, $3.50 a day for miners; $3 a day for trammers, with an increase in the number of working hours for the latter. These terms the Miners' Union, through its Central Committee, refused, and this decision led to the shutting down of the works at the Gem and Union mines on Jan. 5, 1892.

The next event of importance, and the one that brought the matter for the first time into the courts, occurred on April 29, 1892, when four men attempted to work in the Union mine near Burke. They were forcibly ejected from the mine by a large body of miners, with John Tobin, President of the Miners' Central Union, at its head. They were escorted to the Miners' Union hall at Burke, where two of them were easily induced to join the union, but the other two, William M. Pipkin and George L. Wolf, positively refused to join, although inducements were freely offered. They were then escorted to Tompson's Falls, Mont., by an angry mob, driven out of the country, and cautioned never to return, under penalty of death.

This led to a temporary injunction, issued by the Federal Court, restraining the miners from interfering with work in the mines. The order was issued on Saturday, May 4, and placed in the hands of Marshal Pinkham. The complaint and accompanying affidavits made a bulky document. The mine owners acted through the Cœur d'Alêne Mining and Concentrating Company, which became plaintiff in the action. In the complaint it was set forth that the company owned and operated the Bengal Tiger, the Fraction, the Sherman, and the Union Lode claims in Lelande mining district, Shoshone County, and a concentrating mill run in connection therewith; that the miners' unions were organized for the purpose of controlling the rate of wages paid in the Cœur d'Alêne mines; that the Central Union had general jurisdiction in the county; that the unions claimed the right to prevent any men from working who were not members; that the unions had printed notices in other mining sections advising laboring men not to come to the Cœur d'Alênes; that the unions disclaimed responsibility for particular acts; and that they were not moneyed corporations which might be proceeded against for the recovery of damages. Therefore, a temporary injunction was asked for, restraining the unions and all individuals connected with them from repeating the acts complained of, or in any way interfering with the working of the plaintiffs' property; and that, upon proper hearing, such injunction should be made perpetual.

The temporary restraining order was signed by Judge Beatty, and set the first Monday in June for the defendants to appear before him and show cause why a provisional injunction should not be issued. The bond was fixed at $2,000. In the meantime the defendants were restrained from interfering with the operations of the company or preventing any one from entering into its service. The injunctions were served on the miners on May 12, and were received in good part.

A short time before the injunction was served the Union mine had started up with 135 nonunion men; the Gem was also ready to begin, and other mines signified their readiness to resume work as soon as men could be secured. Three hundred miners left Duluth, in the charge of agents, on May 12, bound for the Cœur d'Alêne mines. The train was met at Bozeman by Joe Warren, a Spokane detective, sworn into service for this occasion by the Mine-Owners' Association, and 53 armed deputies.

On May 21 the Superintendent of the Northern Pacific Railway complained to Gov. Willey that parties of lawless men were boarding the passenger trains and preventing the train men from performing their duties properly, and that

the sheriff was incapable, and asked for an armed force to protect the trains. The Governor visited the scene of the troubles, made a personal investigation, and tried to bring about an amicable settlement, but without success. Therefore, on June 4 he issued a proclamation warning the riotous bands to disperse, and saying that, if order was not soon restored, he would declare Shoshone County in a state of insurrection and order out the troops. The ill feeling between the union and the nonunion miners increased steadily, fights occurred, and mines were barricaded and guarded by armed men. At the Frisco mine there was a serious conflict, and the union miners placed 750 pounds of giant powder on a rail car and sent it down the track, where its explosion demolished the Frisco mill and compelled the surrender of the nonunion defenders. Several men on each side had been killed. There were conflicts also at Wardner and at Wallace, with loss of life.

On the night of Tuesday, July 12, the strikers captured 132 nonunion miners, drove them to the mouth of Fourth-of-July Cañon, near Cataldo, and, after robbing them, fired on them, killing 12 and wounding many others. One hundred and fifty nonunion men left Gem, and 18 box cars, 1 coal car, and 2 coaches loaded with nonunion men, numbering about 200, were sent from Wardner.

The Governor now called out the militia, and at the same time telegraphed to Washington, asking for United States troops. By order of the President troops were sent at once from Fort Sherman, Idaho, and Fort Missoula, Mont., and on July 13 the Governor declared Shoshone County to be in a state of insurrection, and placed it under martial law. Troops were brought also from other posts; and this prompt exhibition of a determination to suppress rioting with an adequate force, put an end to the lawless proceedings, and the miners returned to their homes.

On Sept. 3 the grand jury found indictments against 167 persons for conspiracy to violate the injunction issued by the court.

Political.—The Democratic Convention met at Pocatello on May 25 to choose delegates to the national convention. The 18 counties of Idaho, Owyhee excepted, were represented. The question of silver was vehemently discussed. The platform advocated, "as a matter of right and justice," the adoption at Chicago of a plank devoted to "the free and unlimited coinage of silver as a full legal-tender money, at the present ratio, and the full and unqualified recognition of this idea as a cardinal principle of Democracy." It further commended the organization of the industrial classes for self-protection against trusts, combines, and monopolies. The following demands were made: A constitutional amendment making United States Senators elective by direct vote of the people; the strictest enforcement of the laws excluding Chinese from and prohibiting the importation of foreign contract labor into the United States; the immediate survey of the public domain within this State. The platform denied the right of the Government to levy a protective tariff, except so far as required for purposes of revenue. Resolutions were passed deprecating Federal interference in the labor troubles in northern Idaho.

At the meeting of the convention on Aug. 24 the following State ticket was chosen : For Governor, John M. Burke; Lieutenant-Governor, Frank Harris ; Secretary of State, J. H. Wickersham, Sr.; State Treasurer, Phil Regan ; Auditor, J. W. McClure; Attorney-General, W. T. Reeves ; Superintendent of Instruction, J. W. Farris; Supreme Justice, F. E. Ensign ; for Congressman, E. B. True. The platform adopted included the following propositions :

That whatever of imports are of benefit to the agricultural and laboring masses should be admitted with the lowest duty possible to secure economical government.

We favor enactments, both State and national, for the prevention of trusts and combines, and to insure a free and fair competition in the regulation of prices in all commodities.

We denounce the policy of special governmental protection to gold as a fraud upon labor, and in favor of the nonproducing classes.

We favor the free and unlimited coinage of silver, and that the same be made a full and legal tender for all debts, both private and public.

We denounce the Republican legislation known as the "Sherman act" of 1890 as a cowardly makeshift, fraught with possibilities of danger in the future, which should make all its supporters, as well as its author, anxious for a speedy repeal.

The State Convention of the People's party met on May 26 and chose delegates to the national convention to be held in Omaha, July 4. In the platform adopted the People's party announced itself as the protector of the "toiling masses" against the alleged encroachments of the rich, and against national and State legislation which, it says, for thirty years or more has discriminated in favor of wealthy corporations. Resolutions were passed which made the following demands :

That a national currency, safe, sound, and flexible, issued by the General Government only, a full legal tender for all debts, public and private, and that without the use of banking corporations, a just, equitable, and efficient means of distribution direct to the people, at a rate not to exceed 2 per cent., be provided, as set forth in the subtreasury plan of the Farmers' Alliance, or some better system ; also by payments in discharge of its obligations for public improvements.

Free and unlimited coinage of silver.

An amount of circulating medium not less than $50 per capita.

A graduated income tax.

That postal savings banks be established by the Government.

That all land now held by railroads and other corporations in excess of their actual needs, and all lands now owned by aliens, should be reclaimed by the Government and held for actual settlers only.

That the telegraph and telephone, like the postoffice system, being a necessity for transmission of news, should be owned and operated by the Government.

That the Constitution should be amended to the end that the President, Vice-President, and United States judges be elected by direct vote of the people.

That we condemn the action of the authorities, both State and Federal, in relation to the trouble now existing in Shoshone County between the mine owners and miners, and that we extend our hearty sympathy to the miners' union in their unequal struggle.

That we favor the suppression of Chinese immigration.

In August the party nominated the following ticket: For Governor, A. J. Crook ; Lieutenant-Governor, J. B. Wright; Secretary of State, B.

F. Chaney ; Treasurer, T. J. Sutton; Auditor, J. H. Anderson ; Attorney-General, J. R. Wester; Superintendent of Public Instruction, L. L. Shearer. A platform was put forth which demanded that the veto power should be placed with the people; a board of arbitration to settle difficulties between labor and capital; a repeal of the lien law; legislation for the control of immigration; the holding of water rights to be no longer in the hands of monopolists ; the free and unlimited coinage of silver; and the State Board of Equalization to have its duties defined by law ; and trees, fences, crops, and fruits to be exempt from taxation.

The Republican State Convention met at Pocatello on May 5. In the platform adopted the policy of the Democrats in Congress was held responsible for the crippling of growth and industry in the West, owing to its refusal to provide for the survey of public lands. Reduction of the tariff was opposed, and all legislation that favored one class at the expense of another. "The Republican party to-day," it declared, " is confronted with the alternative of restoring silver to free and unlimited coinage or losing the results of protection." It was therefore resolved that the delegates to Minneapolis be instructed to confer with delegates from other silver States in " order to make a bold, united effort in favor of the white metal," using "their utmost endeavors to secure a plank unequivocally pledging the party to its free and unlimited use."

The ticket chosen in August was as follows : For Governor, W. J. McConnell ; Lieutenant-Governor, Frank B. Willis ; Secretary of State, James F. Curtis ; Attorney-General, George M. Parsons ; Auditor, Frank Ramsay ; Treasurer, W. C. Hill ; Superintendent of Instruction, J. S. Brandon ; Congressman, Willis Sweet.

The platform urged " a free and unlimited coinage of silver." A department of mines and mining, to be created by Congress, was recommended. Republicanism, as in its essence the maintenance of law and the protection of free labor, was pronounced the fundamental principle of the party then assembled. Measures for the protection of labor against capital were urged. " Protection as applied to agriculture, capital, and labor " was pronounced as an unalterable policy of the party. The platform further pledged itself to the most liberal means for advancing the interests of the State at the Columbian Exposition. It called the attention of the National Government to the unnecessary delay in the allotting of lands of the Nez Percé Indian reservation. It promised to furnish the workingmen with facilities for the safe deposit of their earnings. It demanded the amendment of immigration laws, declaring that the naturalization of inadmissible elements " degrades the wages of labor, and endangers our institutions by the debasement and corruption of the suffrage"; and it demanded the amendment of the suffrage laws, limiting the right to vote to those able to read the Constitution and to write their names. Gov. Willey's action in enforcing the laws of the State and restoring a feeling of security was approved, as were the national platform at Minneapolis and the administration of President Harrison. On the Mormon question the following resolutions were adopted :

We congratulate the Mormon Church on its recent declaration abandoning polygamy and in favor of divorce of Church and state in all political affairs; and, accepting this declaration as sincere, we pledge the party that, with continuance of evidences of this sincerity, we will, at the next ensuing session of the Legislature, restore to its members the full political privileges of citizenship secured to all others.

At the convention of the Prohibition party in August but three counties—Ada, Bingham, and Cassia—were represented. Not more than 25 delegates were present. The ticket nominated was as follows: For Governor, Joseph A. Clark; Lieutenant-Governor, Moses F. Fowler; Congressman, E. R. Hedley; Secretary of State, Rev. I. S. Hicks; Auditor, J. W. W. Post; Superintendent of Public Instruction, S. D. Condit; Treasurer, C. W. Ramsay; Supreme Court Justice, T. M. Stewart.

Allegiance to the Declaration of Independence was declared to be the platform adopted. It was also declared that

The traffic in intoxicating beverages is a public nuisance, a producer of crime, poverty, and political corruption; it increases taxes, and diverts over $1,000,000,000 annually from the lines of legitimate business; tax and license laws recognize it as legitimate and increase its power for evil; the traffic, therefore, should be completely suppressed.

Universal suffrage was proposed, and the issue of a circulating medium in gold, silver, and paper sufficient to meet business demands; also the election of President, Vice-President, and Senators by direct vote of the people; the regulation of immigration; the control of railroads, telegraph, express, and telephone lines by the State.

ILLINOIS, a Western State, admitted to the Union Dec. 3, 1818; area, 56,650 square miles. The population, according to each decennial census, was 55,162 in 1820; 157,445 in 1830; 476,183 in 1840; 851,470 in 1850; 1,711,951 in 1860; 2,539,891 in 1870; 3,077,871 in 1880; and 3,826,351 in 1890. Capital, Springfield.

Government.—The following were the State officers during the year: Governor, Joseph W. Fifer, Republican; Lieutenant-Governor, Lyman B. Ray; Secretary of State, Isaac N. Pearson; Auditor, Charles W. Pavey; Treasurer, Edward S. Wilson; Attorney-General, George Hunt; Superintendent of Public Instruction, Henry Raab; Railroad and Warehouse Commissioners, Isaac M. Philips, J. R. Wheeler, and Jonathan C. Willis; Chief Justice of the Supreme Court, Benjamin D. Magruder; Associate Justices, Simeon P. Shope, Alfred M. Craig, John Scholfield, David J. Baker, J. W. Wilkin, and J. M. Bailey.

Finances.—The State is practically free from debt, there being only a few State bonds still unpaid, on which interest has ceased. There is a considerable balance in the State treasury in spite of the low tax rate and generous appropriations for education and charities.

Valuations.—The valuation of property in the State, as assessed and equalized for taxation in 1892, was as follows: Personal property, $143,967,054; lands, $316,659,655; lots, $284,288,202; total railroad property assessed by local assessors, $2,737,803; railroad property assessed by the State Board of Equalization, $77,108,390; capital stock of corporations assessed by the board, $6,549,202; total assessment, $831,310,306. The total assessment of 1891 was $822,109,429. The State board, in the process of equalization, deducted from the land assessment $22,384,265, and added to the city and town lots $23,879,773, and to personal property $167,560. Thus the net gain of the equalized value over the assessed value is $1,663,068.

Included in the total assessment of personal property were 1,181,231 horses, valued at $24,501,154; 2,146,481 cattle, valued at $13,026,538; 91,855 mules, valued at $1,987,999; 833,755 sheep, valued at $887,253; and 1,962,554 swine, valued at $2,482,533. The total equalized valuation of Cook County was $270,637,093.

For 1892 the amount to be raised by taxation upon the total State assessment was $2,500,000, of which $1,000,000 is available for schools.

County Jails and Almshouses.—An inspection made in 1892 showed that the number of prisoners in the county jails was 804—males, 781; females, 23. The number of boys under sixteen years in jail was 51. The jail expenses were $198,054 for the preceding year, of which $131,322 was the cost of feeding prisoners. The number of inmates of the county almshouses when visited was 5,978—males, 3,548; females, 2,430; natives, 2,254; foreigners, 2,857; colored, 108. The pauper expenses for the preceding year were as follow: Maintenance of almshouses, $825,054.26; repairs and improvements, $44,379.80; outdoor relief, $722,288.85; total, $1,591,722.91.

State Banks.—On July 28 there were 108 State banks in operation, with total resources and liabilities of $110,140,081.96. Their loans and discounts amounted to $72,037,983.37; their savings deposits subject to notice to $21,852,906.50; individual deposits subject to check, $43,740,684.60; cash on hand, $8,913,903.70; total capital stock, $17,397,500.

Railroads.—The report of the Railroad and Warehouse Commissioners for the year ending June 30, 1891, shows that the total railroad mileage in the State was 10,179 miles, of which 50 miles had been built during the year. The capital of the railroads doing business in Illinois was as follows: Capital stock, $875,259,455; bonds, $1,001,799,159; current liabilities, $69,605,160; total, $1,946,663,770. The earnings and income in Illinois during the year were: By the passenger department, including mails, express, and extra baggage, $19,654,807.61; by the freight department, $46,131,025.92. There were also other earnings which brought the total income from operation up to $68,095,988.67. The income from property owned but not operated was $5,403,177.77, making the total earnings and income $73,499,166.44. The total expenditures in Illinois during the year were $65,458,260.48, of which $45,135,045.19 went for operating expenses. The number of passengers carried earning revenue was 32,178,183, and the number of tons of freight carried earning revenue was 54,048,837. The number of railroad employees in Illinois during the year was 60,968, and their aggregate salary $36,888,651.07. There was during the year an increase of 3,533 in the number of employees.

Coal.—The statistics of coal production in Illinois for the year ending July 1, 1892, present the following totals: Number of tons mined, 17,949,989; aggregate value at the mines, $19,-688,593; number of employees, 33,625; amount paid in wages, $12,835,512; number of accidental deaths, 57; number of persons injured, 418.

This total product represents an increase over the preceding year of 2,284,291 tons, and is both the largest output and the largest yearly increase in production ever recorded in the State. The aggregate home value of this output is greater by 5,451,519 than that of any other year; and the amount distributed as wages is $1,633,-268 larger than ever before.

Agriculture.—The area devoted to winter wheat this year in the State was 1,895,146 acres, and the total crop raised thereon was 32,831,718 bushels. The area seeded to oats was 2,737,538 acres, of which 1,912,092 acres were in the northern division of the State, 560,520 in the central division, and 264,926 in the southern division. The total yield of the State was 93,314,515 bushels.

For the year 1891, the following report is made by the State Board of Agriculture, showing the total value of the several farm products of the State during that year: Corn, $83,990,210; winter wheat, $26,583,636; spring wheat, $818,926; oats, $32,312,485; rye, $2,541,905; barley, $329,-820; buckwheat, $25,539; hay, $24,202,252; timothy seed, $208,069; clover seed, $303,756; Hungarian and millet seed, $22,904; Irish potatoes, $3,955,879; sweet potatoes, $247,205; turnips and other root crops, $207,780; flax seed, $40,611; broom corn, $532,965; sorghum, $256,-909; beans, $43,826; castor beans, $55,398; tobacco, $50,480; other crops not named, $286,-661; apples, $1,022,036; peaches, $133,713; pears, $8,149; grapes, $68,272; strawberries, $126,250; watermelons, $49,304; other fruits and berries, $116,340; wine, $92,828; honey, $112,934; horses (equalized value), $19,997,119; beef cattle (equalized value), $15,985,158; dairy cows, $17,342,362; hogs (equalized value), $4,-131,570; sheep (equalized value), $680,385; wool, $631,790; milk sold, $12,106,797; cream sold, $1,587,500; butter sold, $4,454,717; cheese sold, $148,488; poultry sold, $1,277,629; eggs sold, $1,142,233. Total, $257,332,190.

Floods.—Early in May, in consequence of the overflow of the Mississippi river and some of its tributaries, notably the Illinois river, a large number of people living in the adjacent lowlands were driven from their homes, their crops injured or destroyed, and their means of livelihood temporarily cut off. Gov. Fifer, after a tour of inspection of the flooded district, being convinced that the burden of this loss should be shared throughout the State, issued, on May 14, a proclamation calling for contributions of money, food, and clothing for the sufferers. The contributions of money were distributed by the State Treasurer, who received and paid out on this account $14,843.52. The money was applied by local relief committees.

Political.—On April 27 a Democratic State Convention assembled at Springfield and selected delegates to the National Democratic Convention, Democratic candidates for presidential electors, and the following ticket for State officers: For Governor, John P. Altgeld; Lieutenant-Governor, Joseph B. Gill; Secretary of State,

William H. Hinrichsen; State Auditor, David Gore; State Treasurer, Rufus N. Ramsey; Attorney-General, Maurice T. Moloney; Trustees of the State University, J. E. Armstrong, J. S. Raymond, and W. B. Morrison; Congressmen-at-Large, Gen. John C. Black and Andrew J. Hunter.

The platform adopted contains the following declarations:

We demand an immediate revision of the tariff, free raw material, a reduction in the duties on all necessaries of life, and such changes in the shipping and navigation law as shall restore the American merchant marine and the supremacy of the American flag upon the high seas. We reiterate our allegiance to the historic policy of the Democratic party in favor of honest money, the gold and silver coinage provided by the Constitution of the United States, and of a currency convertible into such coinage without loss to the holder, and we recommend an invitation by our Government to the commercial powers of the world for an international conference for the purpose of fixing a ratio between the values of gold and silver so that parity may be maintained between the two metals, and all mints thrown open to free coinage.

We denounce the Republican party for enacting a law which tends to bring the cause of popular education into disrepute; a law which takes from the parent the right to educate his child according to the dictates of his conscience; a law which creates a State inquisition over schools toward which the State contributes nothing; a law which gives the absolute power to every local school board, no matter how ignorant or spiteful its actions, to harass and persecute a large class of people who are among our best citizens and who do their full duty both toward the State and their children, and who by their labor, their patriotism and intelligence have contributed very much to our prosperity and greatness.

We favor the election of United States Senators by a direct vote of the people.

We favor all laws that can be enacted under the present Constitution that will prohibit the truck system, enforce weekly payment of wages in cash, and fair weights and measures wherever used in fixing compensation.

The delegates to the National Convention were requested to present the name of Gen. John M. Palmer as the candidate of the Democracy of the State for President.

The Republicans held their State Convention at Springfield on May 4. Gov. Fifer, Lieut.-Gov. Ray, Secretary of State Pearson, and Auditor Pavey were renominated. For State Treasurer the nominee was Henry L. Hertz; for Attorney-General, George W. Prince; and for Trustees of the State University, Solon Philbrick, Emory Cobb, and Robert B. Stinson. George S. Willits and Richard Yates were nominated for Congressmen-at-Large. Delegates to the Republican National Convention and Republican candidates for presidential electors were also selected. A platform was adopted applauding the national policy of the party, instructing the delegates to the National Convention to vote for the renomination of President Harrison, and containing the following:

We heartily approve the emigration laws enacted by the last Congress, and demand such further legislation as shall most effectively exclude paupers, criminals, "contract labor," and other elements hostile to the welfare of the American people and the genius of American institutions.

We indorse the invulnerable administration of Gov. Fifer, and testify our appreciative recognition of its wisdom, its fidelity to the people, and its loyalty to his party and personal pledges. We indorse the official record and faithful services of Senator Cullom and the Republican representatives of Illinois in Congress.

Upon the important subject of education we declare:

(*a*) That since the success of universal suffrage and of popular government requires universal intelligence, therefore the free common schools of Illinois are the chief bulwarks of the Commonwealth and the safeguards of liberty.

(*b*) That the education in elementary branches of each child in the State should be required by law.

(*c*) That all parents and those standing in the parental relation should be left absolutely free to choose in what schools and in what manner they will educate their children.

(*d*) That in no case shall school officers or civil authorities be given authority by law to interfere with private or parochial schools.

(*e*) In pursuance of these principles we pledge ourselves to repeal the present compulsory school act, and in lieu thereof to enact a law in harmony with the view herein stated.

We demand the adoption of a system of uniform rates of appraisement of real estate and personal property, to the end that equal and just corresponding taxation shall prevail and the existing inequalities be removed.

We regard with much gratification the enactment under a Republican administration of a ballot-reform law, and the protection it affords, as demonstrated by experience, of the rights of voters and the purity of our elections.

We denounce the Democratic party for its defiance of existing law in demanding that interest on public funds shall be paid into the State Treasury, and hereby declare in favor of a law which shall provide for the loan of public funds adequately secured, all accretions therefrom to inure to the State.

The People's Party State Convention was held at Danville on May 19. H. E. Taubeneck was nominated for Governor, but refused the honor, and the convention then selected Nathan M. Barnett. For Lieutenant-Governor the nominee was Charles G. Dixon; for Secretary of State, Fred. G. Blood; for Treasurer, Joseph W. McElroy; for Auditor, S. C. Hill; for Attorney-General, Jesse Cox. Delegates to the National Convention of the party and presidential electors were selected. Jesse Harper and Michael McDonough were nominated as Congressmen-at-Large. The platform adopted reaffirms the declarations of the St. Louis platform; declares the constitutional right of free speech, press, and assembly; favors compulsory education and free text-books; opposes convict labor; declares against the appropriation of the interest on the public money by public officers; favors an amendment to the Constitution making a weekly pay-day and a law against truck stores; and advocates an amendment granting equal suffrage.

The nominations of the Prohibitionist party were made at a State Convention in Springfield on May 31, at which delegates to the National Convention of the party and candidates for presidential electors were also chosen. For Governor, Robert R. Link was nominated; for Lieutenant-Governor, James Lamont; for Secretary of State, John T. Killam; for Auditor, Samuel D. Noe; for Treasurer, Thomas S. Marshall; for Attorney-General, Alonzo P. Wright; for Trustees of the State University, Albert G. Gepson, Charles Johan, and Levi T. Regan; for

Congressmen-at-Large, James S. Felter and George W. Gere. In addition to the usual anti-saloon resolutions, the platform contains the following declaration:

We declare in favor of a loyal and steadfast maintenance of our American public-school system as an institution vital to the public well-being and the preservation of our Republican institutions. We denounce all attempts to appropriate any portion of the public funds for sectarian purposes, as well as all plans of partnership or association between our public-school officials and any religious sect in the work of instruction. We denounce the Democratic and Republican parties of Illinois for their cowardly and unpatriotic proposal to surrender our present compulsory education law, and we avow our purpose to maintain the law as it stands with all its provisions intact. We further declare in favor of the State furnishing all school text-books free of cost.

In the canvass following these nominations the local school question played a prominent part. The compulsory school law recently passed by a Republican Legislature had aroused the antagonism of the German Lutherans, and although in their platform the Republicans completely changed front and promised its repeal, yet their original action in passing the law was not forgotten, and the Lutherans generally favored the Democratic candidate.

Another feature of the canvass was the unique course of the Democratic candidate for Governor, who traveled from place to place, visiting all parts of the State and seeking to meet the voters personally by entering their workshops, offices, and other places of business, as well as by holding public receptions. This plan of campaign appears to have been effective, for at the November election the victory of the Democratic ticket was complete. For Governor, Altgeld received 425,497 votes, Fifer 402,659, Link 24,684, Barnett 19,347. The vote for presidential electors was: Democratic, 426.281; Republican, 399,-288; People's party, 22,207; Prohibitionist, 25,-907. Eleven Republican and eleven Democratic Congressmen were chosen. The Legislature of 1892 will be divided politically as follows: Senate, Democrats 28, Republicans 23; House, Democrats 78, Republicans 75.

INDIA, an empire in southern Asia dependent on the British Crown, governed, in accordance with various acts of Parliament, by a Governor-General or Viceroy and subordinate administrators under the general control of the British Parliament exercised through a Cabinet officer, the Secretary of State for India. The Secretary of State is assisted by a Council, consisting of at least 10 members, the majority of whom must have been officials or residents in India for ten years. All expenditures of the public revenues must be subjected to the review of the Council, but in cases involving foreign relations or requiring secrecy the Secretary of State acts without consulting his Council. The Governor-General is assisted by a Council of 5 ordinary members, besides a member representing the Department of Public Works and the commander in chief of the forces. The departments are Home Affairs, Revenue and Agriculture, Military Affairs, Legislation, Finance and Commerce, and Public Works. There is a Legislative Council, which is composed of the members of the Council of the Governor-General, together with from 6 to 12 additional members who are appointed by him, whereas the ordinary members, as well as the Governors of Bombay and Madras, are appointed by the Crown. The Lieutenant-Governors of Bengal and of the Northwest Provinces and Oudh, and the Chief Commissioners of Assam, the Central Provinces, and Burmah, are appointed by the Viceroy, subject to confirmation by the Secretary of State. The Governors of Bombay and Madras have each an executive and legislative council, and a separate civil service and a separate army. The Lieutenant-Governors of Bengal and the Northwest Provinces have legislative councils. The chief commissioners have no legislative powers. The provinces are divided into divisions, administered by commissioners, and these into districts under collector magistrates and deputy commissioners. Each district magistrate has under him usually a joint magistrate, an assistant magistrate, and deputy collectors or other officers. Most of the magistrate collectors exercise judicial as well as administrative functions. The Governor-General is the Marquis of Lansdowne, born Jan. 14, 1845, who succeeded the Marquis of Dufferin and Ava on Dec. 11, 1888. The Secretary of State for India in the beginning of 1892 was Viscount Cross, formerly Sir Richard Cross. On the change of government in the summer he was succeeded by the Earl of Kimberly.

The Indian Councils bill passed by the British Parliament in 1892 gives to the Indian races a slight installment of the additional representation in the Government for which the leaders of the Indian Congresses have clamored. The bill was prepared for the session of 1889, but was not introduced. In 1890 and in 1891 it was passed by the House of Lords, but was not even brought up for discussion in the Commons owing to pressure of other business. The bill permits the Governor-General, and the governors and lieutenant-governors of the great divisions of India to appoint additional nonofficial members of their legislative councils from the native communities. It also enlarges the functions of the councils, gives them a right to examine and criticise financial measures, and allows members a limited right of interpellation. The Legislative Council of the Governor-General, consisting at present of 24 members, is to be increased by not less than 10 and not more than 16 new members, not necessarily to be chosen from the native communities, though a large proportion of them are expected to be, as a certain number in each of the councils are already. A proportional augmentation of the four minor councils was also authorized. Another bill that was discussed in the same session proposes to allow Indian officials, in case of need, to leave India temporarily without vacating their offices.

Area and Population.—The revised returns of the census taken Feb. 26, 1891, make the total population of British India, including the feudatory states, 287,223,431, without counting 870,-000 who were enumerated by houses or tribes. The population of the provinces under direct British rule is 221,172,950, inhabiting an area of 962,070 square miles; that of the feudatory states, covering an area of 595,310 square miles, is 66,050,480. The annexed territories now enumer-

ated for the first time are Upper Burmah, with 2,946,930 inhabitants; North Lushai, with 43,-630; and Cashmere, with 2,543,950. The increase in the population of the whole of India, exclusive of these added territories, averages nearly 11 per cent. since the census of 1881; in that of the provinces directly administered, 9¼ per cent.; in that of the feudatory states, 15¼ per cent. The density of population has risen from 227 to 249 to the square mile in British India proper, and from 107 to 123 in the feudatory states. The density for the whole of India, inclusive of the new provinces and dependencies, is 184 per square mile, 230 for the British provinces, and 111 for the feudatory states. The rate of increase in the two sexes for the whole of British India has been 9·63 per cent. for males and 9·80 per cent. for females; in the feudatory states, 14·81 per cent. for males and 16·29 per cent. for females. The apparent disproportionate growth is explained by a more complete enumeration of the female population, owing to the disappearance of the distrust which impels the Hindu peasant to conceal the number of his female dependents from the census enumerator. The rate of increase in the various British provinces, taking the male returns only, was 23·67 per cent. in Lower Burmah, 19 per cent. in Sindh, 16 per cent. in Ajmir, 15¼ per cent. in Madras, 14 per cent. in Bombay, 11·7 per cent. in Assam, 10·9 per cent. in Oudh, 10·3 per cent. in the Punjab, 8·8 per cent. in the Central Provinces, 8·6 per cent. in Berar, 7·10 per cent. in Bengal, and 4·5 per cent. in the Northwest Provinces, while Coorg has receded 4·5 per cent. Of the feudatory states, those of the Central Provinces show an increase of 25·5 per cent., Mysore 19 per cent., the native states of Bengal 17·75 per cent., Rajputana 17·5 per cent., Hyderabad 17·4 per cent., the native states of Bombay 15·6 per cent., those of Madras 11·5 per cent., the Punjab states 10 per cent., and Baroda 9·9 per cent. The pressure in territories where it is over 200 to the square mile is 522 in Oudh, 471 in Bengal, 385 in the native states of Madras, 204 in Baroda, 252 in the Madras presidency, 207 in Bombay, and 200 in Ajmir. In contrast to these, Upper Burmah has 35, Cashmere 31, Lower Burmah 53, and Sindh 60 inhabitants to the square mile. The urban population of India is small in proportion to most other countries. There are only 2,035 places that can properly be classed as towns, and their inhabitants form but 9·5 per cent. of the total population of India. The small territory of Ajmir-Merwara has 22 per cent. of its population living in towns, Baroda 20 per cent., the presidency of Bombay 19·5 per cent., and the Bombay native states 14·6 per cent. In Assam, the Central Provinces, and the native states of Bengal there are no towns except small local markets, the inhabitants of which constitute 1·86, 1·79, and 0·5 per cent. of their respective total populations. The lieutenant-governorship of Bengal has Calcutta and other populous cities, and yet the ratio of the urban population is only 4·8 per cent., lower than in any of the other provinces. The increase of the urban population, averaging 9·4 per cent. in ten years, was 13·6 per cent. in towns of from 50,000 to 75,000 inhabitants, 11·58 per cent. in those of from 20,000 to 35,000, 10·66 in places of from

10,000 to 20,000, and 10·58 in those of 100,000 and above, while in places below 5,000 there was no increase. Bombay is the largest city, having a population of 821,760 within the corporation limits. Calcutta has a larger aggregation of people if the straggling suburbs are included, containing 978,370 inhabitants; but if only the two immediate suburbs are counted, the number is 741,140. Madras has 452,520 inhabitants; Hyderabad, inclusive of suburbs, 415,000; Lucknow, 273,630; Benares, 219,470. Besides these, there are 22 cities with more than 100,000 inhabitants, and 48 places have between 50,000 and 100,000. Among the instances of rapid growth, that of Karochi, which was 43 per cent. in ten years, and that of Rangoon, which was 34·4 per cent., are notable. Cawnpore increased 24·6 per cent. Some of the large towns, as Patna, Surat, Amritsar, and Merzapur, have declined in population.

The returns according to religions are: Hindus, 207,654,407; Mussulmans, 57,365,204; Christians, 2,284,191; Jains, 1,416,109; Sikhs, 1,907,836; Buddhists, 7,101,057; Parsees, 89,887; Jews, 17,180; animistic worshipers, 9,302,083; atheists, agnostics, etc., 289. Among the Hindus are included 3,401 Brahmos and 39,948 Aryas. The Brahmos are chiefly in Bengal, the Aryas in the northwest and the Punjab. The latter return themselves as Vedic or Aryans by religion, sometimes as Hindu Aryans, while even a few Sikhs describe their sect as Aryan. Some of the tribes that are classed as animistic in one locality have been included by the enumerators among the Hindus in others. A comparison of the results of the censuses of 1872, 1881, and 1891 tends to show that the forest and hill tribes that have followed the low superstitious religions of ghost worship, fetich worship, tree worship, demon worship, and other primitive cults, classed together as animistic or nature worship, are embracing the Hindu religion. Including these semi-Hindus, and all the animistic worshipers and the reformed and theistic Hindus, Hinduism is the faith of 75·5 per cent. of the whole population of India, while Mohammedanism is the religion of 19·96 per cent., 2·48 per cent. are Buddhists, 0·8 per cent. Christians, 0·66 per cent. Sikhs, 0·49 per cent. Jains, 0·03 per cent. Parsees, and 0·09 per cent. Jews, agnostics, and others. Separating the tribes that were formerly classed as nature worshipers from the Hindus, they make 3·23 per cent. of the total population. The increase in the Hindus, including the animistic group, has been for the ten years 10·74 per cent., and that of the Mussulmans 10·7 per cent. The Buddhists, owing to the natural increase in the population of Lower Burmah, have increased 24·5 per cent., and the Christians, owing mainly to conversions among the forest tribes, have increased 22·16 per cent. In Chutra Nagpur, for example, the Roman Catholic missionaries alone have made 40,000 proselytes in ten years. Among the Karens of Lower Burmah the Protestants have gained a large number of adherents, and in Madras and along the west coast of Hindustan the growth of the Christian community has been considerable. The Jews, including the new settlers in Aden, have increased 21 per cent. The Parsees have grown 5·25 per cent. The Jains have recovered some who had embraced Hinduism, and show an increase of 15·89 per cent.

The growth of the Sikhs has been only 2 per cent. Of the children under fifteen years of age, 5·9 per cent. of the boys and 17·02 per cent. of the girls are returned as married, and in every 10,000 of the general population there are 20 boys and 51 girls under fifteen who are returned as widowed, more than one quarter of whom are not yet five years old. The educational statistics for about 262,000,000 people show that 89·1 per cent. of the males and 99·4 per cent. of the females are unable to read and write. According to the census, only 360,000, not including Europeans and Eurasians, are able to read and write English.

The average death rate for British India varied from 20·98 per *mille* in 1880 to 27·98 in 1889. The number of births per *mille* in 1890 was 22·76 in Bengal, 36·98 in the Northwest Provinces and Oudh, 40·28 in the Punjab, 39·30 in the Central Provinces, 21·15 in Lower Burmah, 31·20 in Assam, 30·9 in Madras, 36·49 in Bombay, and 16·36 in Coorg. The ratio of deaths was 25·03 in Bengal, 31·11 in the Northwest, 32 in the Punjab, 43·79 in the Central Provinces, 17·7 in Lower Burmah, 30·7 in Assam, 23·5 in Madras, 31·51 in Bombay, and 22·92 in Coorg.

Pauperism among Europeans and Eurasians, especially in Calcutta, has been a question that has engaged the attention of Anglo-Indian publicists for a long time, and recently the Government of Bengal has been studying the best means of dealing with an evil which has a political as well as an economical aspect, because the sight of so many helpless and degraded Europeans and half-castes tends to lower the opinion entertained by the native races regarding their rulers. Of the Europeans and Eurasians domiciled in Calcutta, nearly one sixth are in actual receipt of charitable relief. Among the Eurasians, 22·3 per cent. of the entire community are dependent wholly or partly on charity. Of the European population of pure descent, 7·9 per cent. are paupers. The East India Company in early times took forcible measures to prevent the growth of a poor white class by expelling every unsatisfactory European from the country. In later times the Indian Government found employment for large numbers of Europeans and men of mixed blood in the departments of opium, finance, customs, and other branches of the uncovenanted civil service. They were in demand also in mercantile establishments on account of their English education. Although favored because of their race, they have been crowded out of private employment by the natives, who are eager to do the same work for less pay, and of whom there are many who are admirably fitted for such occupations since the spread of English education. The Government has deprived them of the monopoly of the minor posts in the civil service by throwing them open to natives. The liberal grants to European and Eurasian schools have not contributed to the improvement of the situation. Excluded from their former occupations, they are unable to enter into competition with the laboring class below them. Their defects of character bring them down to pauperism without a struggle, for of the male paupers among them 76 per cent., and of the female 50 per cent., are reported to be able-bodied. The only remedies proposed, besides a more judicious administration of charitable relief, are the creation of a regiment of Indo-Europeans and a training ship for Eurasians. Sir Charles Elliot, the Lieutenant-Governor of Bengal, dismisses the latter project as impracticable, and regards the other as an expensive and doubtful experiment, as the military authorities regard this class inferior to all except the poorest native fighting material, while the cost of such a regiment would be 80 per cent. greater than that of a native regiment.

Finances.—The revised estimate of revenue for 1890-'91, and the budget estimate for 1891-'92, were, in tens of rupees, as follow:

REVENUE.	1890-'91.	1891-'92.
Land revenue	23,914,600	24,399,300
Opium revenue	7,875,000	7,593,400
Salt revenue	8,458,200	8,343,500
Stamps	4,096,100	4,148,200
Excise	4,928,100	4,953,700
Provincial rates	3,475,400	3,580,900
Customs	1,722,500	1,700,900
Assessed taxes	1,603,500	1,610,300
Forests	1,451,200	1,511,100
Registration	869,100	869,900
Tribute	762,200	765,000
Interest	993,900	808,400
Post office, telegraphs, mint	2,589,500	2,469,700
Civil departments	1,607,600	1,571,300
Miscellaneous	920,600	921,400
Railroads	17,007,600	17,572,400
Irrigation	2,171,200	2,160,600
Buildings and roads	687,700	507,100
Military departments	857,000	800,300
Total	**85,313,500**	**86,025,300**

The expenditure under the various heads for 1890-'91, according to the revised estimates, and for 1891-'92, according to the budget estimates, were as follow, in tens of rupees:

EXPENDITURE.	1890-'91.	1891-'92.
Interest	4,164,700	3,867,200
Refunds, compensation, etc.	1,750,100	1,758,800
Cost of collection	7,871,500	8,281,600
Post office, telegraphs, mint	2,307,500	2,368,100
Civil salaries	13,397,290	13,976,500
Miscellaneous civil charges	4,718,500	4,972,900
Famine relief and insurance	600,000	1,048,000
Railroad construction	9,100	210,500
Railroad revenue account	18,014,400	19,374,100
Irrigation	2,792,800	2,888,100
Buildings and roads	5,892,000	6,109,100
Army	20,897,500	21,951,200
Defense works	523,300	847,700
Total	**82,539,200**	**86,738,100**

Deducting provincial balances coming to the Imperial Government on adjustment of accounts with the local administrations, the expenditure for 1890-'91 is Rx 82,526,400, and for 1891-'92 it amounts to Rx 85,909,700.

The closed account for 1890-'91 makes the gross revenue Rx 85,741,649, and the gross expenditure Rx 82,053,478. The net revenue was Rx 49,354,219, and the net expenditure Rx 45,-666,048, showing a realized surplus of Rx 3,688,-171. This large surplus, which was better by Rx 23,171 than the revised estimate, was attributable to increased receipts and to economies in expenditure in part, but chiefly to American speculations in silver that carried the exchange value of the rupee up to 1s. 9d., giving it an average value of 1s. 6d., whereas it had been taken in the budget at the rate of 1s. 4½d. In the revised estimates for 1891-'92 are Rx 88,-

585,900 for revenue, and Rx 88,665,900 for expenditure, the net revenue being estimated at Rx 49,726,900. and the net expenditure at Rx 49,-806,900, which leaves a deficit of Rx 80,000. The reason for a deficit—which, however, the approximate accounts changed into a surplus—was the difference in the gold value of the rupee, which was estimated in the budget at 1s. 5¼d., but which proved to be only 1s. 4½d. The railroads, owing to the unusual traffic in wheat and seeds for export, had yielded Rx 1,107,900 more than was expected; higher prices had wrought an improvement in the opium revenue, which was Rx 807,500 beyond the estimate; and salt, excise, and stamps had yielded more than was anticipated. The military expenditure had exceeded the estimate by £1,329,000, owing to the expeditions against the tribes on the northwestern frontier, the outbreak in Manipur, and the operations in North Burmah. Notwithstanding this, and disappointments in the land revenue, interest charges, and other heads, the surplus expected to be realized in 1891-'92 was Rx 354,000. The budget estimate of the gross revenue for 1892-'93 is Rx 88,368,000; of the gross revenue, Rx 88,221,000; of the net revenue, Rx 49,583,000; and of the net expenditure, Rx 49,-436,000; showing a surplus of Rx 147,000. In this estimate the price of the rupee was reduced to 1s. 4d., representing an additional exchange for the year of Rx 1,049,000. The loss on exchange has increased year by year until it now amounts to nearly Rx 8,250,000, or about £5,000,000. The amount of the charge on the revenue for exchange was Rx 6,693,000 in 1889-'90, Rx 5,383,-000 in 1890-'91. and Rx 8,224,000 in the budget estimate for 1891-'92. After the publication of the budget for 1892-'93 the price of the rupee fell in India within a few days to 1s. 3d., a penny less than the rate adopted for the budget, which would entail a loss, if it remained at the lower figure, of over Rx 1,700,000. In September, Sir David Barbour, financial secretary to the Government of India, estimated the probable deficit for the current year at from Rx 800,000 to Rx 1,500,000.

The bulk of the revenues of India is collected by the provincial governments. and a large part of the civil expenditure is under their control. Every five years an adjustment of the arrangement by which they receive a certain proportion of the revenues that they collect for their uses is made. The estimate framed in 1887 produced a virtual equilibrium of the receipts and expenditures of the provincial governments. The revenue collected was better than the estimate everywhere except in the Northwest Provinces, and altogether they received as their proportion Rx 6,101,300 more than they expected, of which they gave up Rx 490,000 in 1890-'91 to meet the wants of the General Government. By the new arrangement for the five years the provincial authorities are required to surrender Rx 466,300 annually to the Government of India out of their improved revenues, which in 1891-'92 were Rx 2,042,700 higher than the estimate for 1887-'88, on which the previous agreement was based. The expenditure for the whole of India has increased Rx 2,063,500 a year in the meantime. The surpluses realized in 1890 and 1891, owing to the rise in the selling price of opium and the

Railroads.—The number of miles open to traffic in 1891 was 16,996, compared with 16,092 in the previous year. The total expenditure of capital by the Government up to the end of 1890 was Rx 222,417,543, of which Rx 125,877,000 were expended on lines owned and worked by the state, Rx 26,722,654 on lines owned by the state and leased to companies, Rx 54,065,645 on guaranteed lines, Rx 8,002,514 on lines in the native states, Rx 5,053,660 on subsidies to companies, Rx 1,688,271 on foreign lines, and the rest on surveys, coal mines, interest, etc. The amount of capital raised by companies was £71,958,757. The gross earnings of the railways for 1890 was Rx 20,670,115. The working expenses amounted to Rx 10,308,918, or 49·87 per cent. of the gross earnings, making the net receipts Rx 10,361,197, giving a return of 4·85 per cent., compared with 4·93 per cent. in 1889.

Irrigation.—The area irrigated by major and minor works in all parts of India was 7,984,275 acres in 1891. The value of the crops was Rx 24,554,110. The cost of the works was Rx 25,465,000, not taking into account the old irrigation system in Madras. The canals and reservoirs are made to pay a profit to the Government, which has amounted, up to the end of 1891, to Rx 4,014,502, after deducting 4 per cent. interest on the capital outlay. The aggregate profit from the completed and productive works is Rx 10,735,022. In 1890–'91 the net returns amounted to 4·81 per cent. on the capital, including that expended on large new projects and extensions that are not completed and produce nothing as yet. The income from the productive works averages 5·8 per cent. New works are projected that will irrigate 1,291,260 acres, and are expected to yield a profit of 13·3 per cent. These do not include large extensions in Sindh and a whole system that is contemplated for Upper Burmah, where scientific irrigation has not yet been introduced.

The National Congress.—The seventh annual Indian Congress, held at the close of 1891 in Nagpur, confirmed the predictions of those who said at the beginning of the movement that the demand for representative institutions in India is premature. The interest in the movement did not lag, however, until the Government took quiet but effective measures to repress it, and the participants in the congresses began to see that their meetings were leading to no practical results, and were drawing upon themselves the displeasure of the authorities. The Congress saw its palmiest period in 1887, when 1,248 delegates from every part of the empire, representing every faith, met at Allahabad, and the nationalists among the Indians were encouraged by members of the British Parliament, who came out specially to aid the movement. Since then the numbers of delegates have declined year by year. In 1891 whole provinces, as Bombay, went unrepresented. There were hardly 800 persons present, and of these many had no credentials as elected representatives of their localities. The committee was continued, and a meeting was appointed for December, 1592, but the interest in the Congress was so dead that the chief leader and organizer of the movement, Mr. Hume, resigned, because he had used up his own fortune in the agitation and was unable to induce the large local associations to contribute enough to carry the work forward. Allan Octavian Hume was an Englishman, fifty-three years old, who had an honorable career in the Indian civil service, and resigned his post as Secretary of the Government in order to give himself up to the object of securing representative institutions for the Indian people. The leaders of the Congress had ignored the warning that Lord Dufferin gave them before he retired from the viceroyalty, in 1888, to leave politics alone and confine themselves to social reforms. They paid enough attention to this injunction to organize, in connection with the political, a social congress, which failed to work out any practical projects or agree upon any proposition of the slightest importance. In 1891, when a motion was made to hold a congress in London, the presiding officer, a progressive Brahman, suggested that it would first be necessary to abolish the degrading, costly, and troublesome penance that a Hindu who has made a sea voyage or visited foreign countries, where he can not observe the ordinances of his religion regarding food, drink, and intercourse, must undergo before he is restored to his caste and family. The proposition was submitted to the social congress, and when the native magistrate, Marathe, supported it with a cogent argument, he was howled down, and a motion was carried, with tumult and uproar, condemning any attempt to prescribe to the castes or meddle with religious customs. The congresses have had some influence on the recent action of the Government in providing in the India Councils bill for a larger native representation in the legislative councils, and in throwing open to Hindus a few more posts in the civil service. The election of Mr. Naoraji, a Parsee champion of the Indian national movement, to the English Parliament in July, 1892, was hailed with rejoicing by the vernacular press of India. The new provincial service, to which natives are eligible, was extended and elevated on the recommendation of a commission that studied the public services by having 86 of the higher posts opened to it in 1892 in various provinces. The offices to which they were admitted include the posts of district magistrate and under secretary of state; 21 such appointments were made in the Northwest Provinces, 20 in Bengal, 18 in Bombay, 15 in Madras, and 12 in the Punjab. In the summer of 1892 Mr. Hume published a circular letter calling upon Indian patriots to insist boldly on attention being given to the growing gravity of the situation, and on remedies being found for the "widespread poverty, semistarvation, misery, and discontent" which had brought India to "the verge of a cataclysm," for there were "millions on millions who have nothing to look forward to but death, nothing to hope for but vengeance." The only hope of averting a terrible rising, "when Englishmen will be as men in the desert vainly struggling against the simoom," lies in awakening the British public to a sense of the wrongs of the people by carrying on an English agitation on the lines of the Anti-Corn Law League. In answer to the evidence of misery adduced by him, the Indian officials, while admitting the general poverty of the cultivators, produce statistics to show that the condition of the people everywhere is much better than it was twenty or thirty years ago; that the wages of unskilled labor have increased twofold even in the backward districts, and those of skilled labor in a larger proportion, while domestic servants are paid almost double as much as they were formerly. The people who work with their hands secure enough to supply their needs, although they often voluntarily remain idle half the time. Where 1 or 2 annas per diem were the common wages thirty years ago, as they are still in remote districts, unskilled labor now commands, in Bombay and other presidency towns, 12 annas or 1 rupee. The only classes that are relatively worse off are the inferior land aristocracy and the people who have received a liberal education and must depend on their brains, both of which are the creation of British rule. The main argument against granting a considerable share in the government to natives is that the class to which the nationalist agitation is mainly confined, and from which nearly all the persons qualified by intelligence and training for administrative and legislative work would have to be sought, represents only one of the numerous peoples of India, the Hindus of Bengal, a race that is despised by the sturdy and martial nations which were once its oppressors, and which now furnish the fighting men on whom the English *raj* depends.

Partial Famine.—Scarcity amounting almost to a famine was experienced in various parts of central and southern India in 1891-'92. The Government opened relief works for the employment of 248,000 men, and gave gratuitous relief to many thousands, besides advancing large sums to landholders to enable them to give employment to the poor. The expenditure up to March 31, 1892, had been Rx 233,000 for relief and Rx 233,000 in advances, and Rx 381,000 of taxes had been remitted. There were three principal areas where the agricultural conditions were particularly unfavorable: (1) the districts of Bombay and Madras embraced in the Deccan, with a large part of the states of Mysore and Hyderabad and parts of Madras lying to the south and east of these; (2) Rajputana and some of the parts of the Bombay presidency that lie on its borders; (3) in Bihar. In parts of Bengal also, and in various other parts of India, as well as in Burmah, much distress was felt; but everywhere food was supplied in sufficient quantities to ward off starvation in a way that was impossible before the construction of the railroad system. In Ajmir, where the population had to subsist mainly on imported grain, prices were little higher than in normal seasons; in the affected districts of Bombay and Madras they were hardly more than three fourths as high as in 1876-'77, though the rainfall was less than in that period of scarcity; and in Bihar there was no alarming rise in prices. The monsoon came earlier in 1892 than usual, and this averted famine, and relieved the Government of the charge for relief that taxed its resources severely.

The Opium Question.—The anti-opium resolution passed by the House of Commons in 1891, and the statistics showing the increase in the consumption of opium circulated by the Society for the Suppression of the Opium Trade, placed the Indian officials, who were agreed regarding the impossibility of sacrificing one of the main sources of Indian revenue, on the defensive, and

they took great pains in 1891 and 1892 to collect evidence tending to show that the opium habit was harmless; that it was not practiced to any extent; that a large consumption of opium was beneficial to the natives, because it warded off malaria; that the suppression of the public sale of opium would drive the people to rebellion; that, if the Government should cease to trade in the drug, smuggling and contraband trading would spring up on an enormous scale; that if the natives were deprived of opium they would destroy themselves with bhang and alcohol; that to suppress the cultivation of the poppy would condemn millions to starvation—with other extravagant and contradictory assertions. Sir A. Mackenzie, Chief Commissioner for Burmah, surprised his fellow administrators by recommending that the opium shops should be closed to all men of Burmese race—a proposition to which the Governor-General was unwilling to agree until he could be satisfied that the evil was as great as was depicted, and that its removal would not result in greater evils. In a dispatch in which the members of the Government of India sum up the results of their investigations, they say that nothing in the evidence collected by them affords any foundation for the statement that the consumption of opium in India has increased during recent years, or that there is any cause for apprehending that the opium habit is likely to spread throughout the country. They show that the result of their action has been to restrict the sale of opium, and they believe it to be impossible to enforce complete prohibition. They point out the difficulty of entirely closing the opium dens, but add that orders have been issued to insert in all future licenses a clause forbidding the consumption of opium on the premises.

Conquest of Hunza-Nagar.—The military reasons connected with Anglo-Russian rivalry in Asia, which led to the establishment of a protectorate over Cashmere and the reduction of Gilghit to a British residency, seemed to the Indian authorities to require the incorporation into the Indian Empire of the little Himalayan states of Hunza and Nagar, which lie beyond Gilghit, on the border of the Pamir. They are situated in a valley surrounded by some of the loftiest peaks of the Himalayas. The only practicable gateway to the country for an invading force is the ravine of the Kanjut river, which is closed by the torrent during the summer months. To prevent the construction of a road up this valley as far as Cashmere territory extends, the Hunza-Nagars several years ago seized the outpost of Chalt Fort. In the autumu of 1891 an expedition was sent out from Gilghit, under the command of Col. Durand. Cashmere sepoys holding Chalt Fort and a position further down were re-enforced to prevent attacks that were planned by the Hunzas; but before the expedition could advance to those points it was necessary to build a road along the edge of the cliffs. The Cashmere authorities were not very eager or loyal in providing transport for the commissary stores, and consequently the expeditionary force was not ready to march across the frontier from Chalt. Safdar Ali Khan, the Thum or Rajah of Hunza, expecting Russian aid, answered the proposals of the British commander with insolent defiance.

On Dec. 2, 1891, Col. Durand advanced against the Nagar fortress of Nilt, where the tribesmen were assembled, with a force composed of 230 Goorkhas of the Indian army and 750 Goorkhas and Dogras from the 3 regiments of Cashmere sepoys that constitute a part of the new imperial service troops placed at the disposition of the Indian Government by the larger native states, and trained and officered by Englishmen. In addition to the regulars, the expedition was accompanied by 200 Puniali auxiliaries, armed with Snider carbines, and carrying besides the native shield and sword; several hundred Pathan laborers, a part of whom were armed with rifles, who did the road-making; and 2,000 coolies for the transport service. The only artillery was a Gatling gun and a pair of 7-pounders from the Hazara mule battery. The march of 8 miles was difficult. The stronghold of Nilt is a fortified village, with thick walls and stone houses on which the small shells could make little impression. The whole population was shut up in this fort, and the enemy gave no sign of life until they opened fire on the British, when they approached to 200 yards from the ramparts. The British troops could get no drinking water until they captured the fort. Col. Durand posted his guns within 200 yards of the fort, fully exposed to the fire of the Kanjuts, who had Martinis, Sniders, Winchesters, and Russian Berdan rifles, besides their long home-made matchlocks. Many of them were excellent marksmen, but they were hampered in their fire because the loopholes were too few and too narrow. The Punialis climbed a cliff and fired down upon the fort, while a detachment of the Punjab infantry that accompanied the expedition descended to the other side of the fort and fired into the loopholes. Of those of the garrison who tried to escape many were picked off by the Indian sharpshooters. Col. Durand was disabled by a wound in the groin, and had to turn over the command to Capt. Bradshaw, just after he had given the order to carry the fort by storm. Under cover of a heavy fusillade, Capt. Aylmer, the engineer officer, and 2 other officers and 6 Goorkhas, backed through the abatis of branches and the wooden gate of the outer wall with Kukris, blew open the main gate with guncotton, and were engaged in a hand-to-hand fight with the garrison for many minutes, while one of them (Lieut. Boisragon) went back to bring up his Goorkhas, who had not yet discovered the breach. The Indian forces soon swarmed into the town, and the Kanjuts, who fought desperately for a few minutes, soon lost spirit and broke. They were hunted through the narrow and intricate alleys of the village. The Wazir of Nagar was killed, but the principal leaders and most of the garrison escaped through a secret gate. The British loss was 5 killed and 24 wounded; of the Kanjuts lost, at least 50 were killed. The Kanjuts took up a strong natural position near Nilt, which the British besieged for seventeen days, at the end of which Capt. John M. Smith, with a party of 50 men, supported by 50 more, forced it, leading his men up an almost precipitous cliff, while the defenders at the summit rolled down stones.

Safdar Ali and Azar Khan, the two chiefs, were not willing to give up the struggle yet, but the people had no heart in the work, and were soon thoroughly intimidated by the harsh reprisals taken by the British, who overran the country. By Jan. 6 resistance was at an end, the chiefs of the tribes had made their submission, and the refractory rajahs had fled over the frontier. Safdar Ali was made a prisoner by the Chinese when he entered their territory, but escaped to Yarkand. Azar Khan was arrested, and handed over to the Indian authorities. The chiefs of the Hunza and Nagar tribes met Col. Durand in a *durbar* at Gilghit on March 25, 1892, where it was announced that Mahomed Nazim Khan, half-brother of Safdar Ali Khan, was to be Rajah of Hunza, while Jaffa Khan, a former ruler of Nagar, was reinstated in the chieftainship. Those who had been obliged to leave the country were invited to return, and availed themselves of the permission. The military roads, which had been the occasion of the rebellion, were built to the confines of Hunza-Nagar, giving the British command of the passes of the Hindu-Kush. The Chinese authorities, when they heard of the Hunza-Nagar expedition, sent a letter to Gilghit, saying that the country belonged to China, and calling upon the British to evacuate it as soon as possible.

The Black-Mountain Tribes.—Costly punitive expeditions undertaken in 1888 and 1891 against the tribesmen of the Black mountains, on the Afghan border, have failed to subjugate or dismay the bold Pathan mountaineers, who in their resistance to British authority have received some encouragement from the Ameer of Afghanistan. These tribes engaged to surrender to the British Hashim Ali, ex-chief of the Hassanzais; but when the time arrived for them to fulfill their engagement they refused to do so, and also refused to expel Hashim Ali from their country. Consequently the Indian Government determined to punish them, and early in October, 1892, an expedition, consisting of over 4,000 troops, under command of Col. Sir W. Lockhart, was sent to the valley of the Indus to destroy the town of Baio, in which Hashim Ali had been harbored. This flying column, which was supported by a large reserve force at Darbund, consisted of a European regiment, a battalion of English rifles, 4 battalions of Goorkhas, Sikhs, and Punjabis, 3 British and 1 native mountain battery, 2 companies of sappers, and 2 squadrons of Bengal lancers.

INDIANA, a Western State, admitted to the Union Dec. 11, 1816; area, 36,350 square miles; population, by the census of 1890, 2,192,404. Capital, Indianapolis.

Government.—The following were the State officers during the year: Governor, Ira J. Chase, Republican; Secretary of State, Claude Matthews, Democrat; Auditor, J. O. Henderson, Democrat; Treasurer, Albert Gall, Democrat; Attorney-General, Alonzo G. Smith, Democrat; Superintendent of Public Instruction, Hervey D. Vories, Democrat; Judges of the Supreme Court, Silas D. Coffey, Walter Olds, Byron K. Elliott, Robert W. McBride, and John D. Miller.

Finances.—The receipts from all sources in 1892 were $5,833,431, and the disbursements for all purposes $5,653,586. Under the head of general fund the receipts were $2,758,968, and the disbursements $2,629,663. Of the disbursements, $878,880 was for benevolent institutions, $299,416 for penal, etc., institutions, $29,996 for printing and stationery, $20,394 for custodian State building, $13,575 for engineer State building, $15,644 for the Attorney-General's office.

Valuations.—Under the new tax law, all property is required to be assessed at its actual cash value. Under the old system the total valuation was $852,534,802; under the new it is $1,246,434,777. The new law, besides thus increasing the valuation, increases the levy from 12 to 18 cents on the $100 for general State purposes. The school tax remained 16 cents on the $100 and was therefore made about 46 per cent. greater by the new valuation. As the revenue by the former system was sufficient for school purposes, this leaves a surplus in that fund. The Auditor's report suggests that 5 cents of this 16 cents per $100 devoted to schools be set aside for a sinking fund by which the public debt will be liquidated. The debt now amounts to nearly $9,000,000.

Education.—The number of children of school age, as given in the returns of the enumeration for the apportionment of school moneys, was 776,300, and the amount apportioned $1,340,277.28. The increase of the number of children since the enumeration of 1891 is 13,767. The *per capita* rate is increased from $1.32 to $1.67.

At a meeting of school superintendents in November great dissatisfaction was expressed with the workings of the present law requiring uniform text-books. It was thought impracticable for a central board to select books suitable for use throughout the State, and the only merit of a large proportion of those thus selected seemed to be their cheapness. Teachers were hampered in being compelled to teach pupils of different capabilities and greater and less degrees of intelligence from the same books. A committee appointed to draft a resolution to be presented to the legislative committee reported one recommending that the law be so amended that county superintendents might have the power of indicating what books they desired used in the schools under their jurisdiction; that school superintendents might be allowed to use any books they saw fit intermediating with the course prepared, or supplemental to it, and that the standard of books be raised. It contained nothing radical, but suggested that if no amendments could be obtained a repeal of the entire law would be preferable to letting it stand.

The whole number enrolled in 1891–'92 at the State Normal School at Terre Haute was 1,190, with an average daily attendance of 613. The number in the previous year was 1,086, and in the year before that 1,009. The attendance at the spring term of 1892 was 957. The president says that the full capacity of the school has been exhausted. The total number of students since 1870 is 8,435.

The Northern Indiana Normal School, at Valparaiso, closed in August with 1,248 graduates in all departments, of whom 32 were in the classical course, 597 in the teachers' course, and 402 in the commercial course.

The biennial report of the State University says that the attendance has been doubled during the past four years. The number of graduates in 1893 will be 77, an increase of 7 over last year. The receipts, including the appropriation, were $76,089.46; the expenditures, $73,751.65.

A gift of $30,000 was offered to Wabash College, at Crawfordsville, by Simon Yandes, on condition that $30,000 more be raised, making a total sum of $160,000 given to the college by Mr. Yandes. All but $10,000 having been raised before December, the Montgomery County commissioners granted the remainder on conditions, viz., that $4,000 should be given June 15, 1894, provided the commissioners were allowed to award two perpetual scholarships in the college; and that $6,000 should be given, due June 15, 1896, provided the college should by that time have opened its doors to women.

The agricultural-experiment station at Purdue University, Lafayette, has instituted a special winter course in live-stock husbandry, including dairying and veterinary service, lectures to be given not only by the regular professors, but by practical farmers and stock growers. The courses are open to young men and women over sixteen years of age with fair common-school education. The tuition is $5, and the laboratory and other charges $10. Two scholarships are offered to each county agricultural society or grange, institute, alliance, etc. The annual report for 1891 shows that the Government appropriation of $15,000 has been spent, and that the balance unexpended June 30, 1890, was $413.02, and the receipts from the sale of farm products was $2,311.03.

The Medical College of Indiana graduated in March its largest class, numbering 57, including 2 young women.

Cities.—A special bulletin gives the following statistics of cities having a population of 8,000 or more in 1890: Anderson, 10,741; Elkhart, 11,360; Evansville, 50,756; Fort Wayne, 35,393; Indianapolis, 105,436; Jeffersonville, 10,666; Kokomo, 8,261; Lafayette, 16,243; Logansport, 13,328; Madison, 8,936; Marion, 8,769; Michigan City, 10,776; Muncie, 11,345; New Albany, 21,059; Richmond, 16,608; South Bend, 21,819; Terre Haute, 30,217; Vincennes, 8,853. The growth of Indianapolis and its industries during a decade appears from the table below:

	1880.	1890.
Industries reported............	84	120
Establishments..................	688	1,056
Capital...........................	$10,049,700	$14,510,379
Persons employed...............	10,000	15,967
Wages paid......................	$3,917,114	$7,793,899
Cost of materials...............	$19,198,102	$18,316,065
Value of product...............	$27,458,089	$32,025,851
Population........................	75,056	105,436
Municipal debt..................	$1,914,500	$1,846,672

The number of persons employed increased 59·67 per cent., while the whole amount of wages paid increased 98·98 per cent., and the wages *per capita* from $392 in 1880 to $488 in 1890.

Railroads.—The report on railroads for 1891, given out by the State statistician in May, shows that it was an unusually prosperous year. Reports were received from 33 roads, being 3 less than formerly, owing to consolidations. These consolidations have operated to increase earnings and decrease expenses. The earnings increased

$13,000,000, and the operating expenses only $10,000,000. The following shows the facts in brief:

	1890.	1891.
Total earnings.................	$118,245,292	$128,953,305
Total expenses................	77,083,323	92,748,872
Surplus.......................	35,289,926	36,204,433

The figures as to freight show an upward tendency in cost of moving freight. There are 81,-746 railroad men in the State. A decision was handed down by the Supreme Court in the "blackboard" railroad cases, affirming the one made two years ago. The General Assembly passed an act in 1889 making it compulsory for roads operating in the State to post on a blackboard, at each station, the time of arrival and departure of trains, and how much they were late, if at all. It assessed a fine of $25 for each violation of it. The railroads generally ignored it, and as the result suits were brought in Shelby and Green Counties to collect the fines attached for these violations. There were 186 counts in the Green County bill, each amounting to $25 and nearly a like number in the other. The railroads won the suits in the lower courts. The case was appealed to the Supreme Court, and resulted in a reversal. The railroads petitioned for a rehearing, and the same judge affirmed the previous decision.

The railroads doing business in the State took out injunctions to restrain the county treasurers from collecting taxes from them under the new assessments pending decisions by the courts, claiming that in nearly every case the assessments were too high.

Militia.—The total expenditures for this department for the fiscal year ending in 1891 were $36,850.12; and for 1892, the appropriation being $25,000 instead of $37,000, the expenditures were $24,922.08. The Government aid to Indiana for 1891 was $13,821.45, and for 1892, $13,074. Gen. Ruckle reports 44 organizations in the State's military service. These are divided into 4 regiments. Eight new companies, as yet on probation, have been organized; 7 companies served their three years of enlistment, and were reorganized and mustered in; 7 companies were disbanded.

Prisons.—The Woman's Prison and Reformatory for Girls was destroyed by fire on March 1. The loss was $17,301.42, which was covered by insurance. The insurance money was used in rebuilding. It contained 152 girls in the Reformatory department and about 50 in the prison. The Reformatory keeps its inmates until they reach the age of eighteen years, and then gives them their liberty. The prison contains women sentenced for crime. The *per capita* cost of maintenance at this institution is $164.82, exclusive of clothing. The earnings and receipts were $2,573.37. In the rebuilding of the structure care was taken to provide a more complete separation of the prisoners and the girls, who now only see each other in the chapel on Sundays. During the year, 48 girls were received, 20 discharged, 1 escaped, 4 transferred to the Woman's Prison, 9 returned on ticket-of-leave, 2 died. There are now 144 in the school. The

Woman's Prison has received 25 women, discharged 22, 1 was pardoned, and there is a total of 54. The total expenditure was $40,000, the full amount of the appropriation. The total earnings of the institution were $2,573.37.

The report of the Prison South shows that it has been self-sustaining, having earned $69,-438.05, and expended $69,416.89.

There are 619 prisoners in the Penitentiary, of whom 511 are white and 108 colored, the daily average for the year having been 594.

The secretary of the Board of Charities reported that at the Prison North two new features have been introduced in the government. One is the "free hour," which means that prisoners, in their cells, may do as they please —sing, play instruments, or talk. It is esteemed a safety valve in prison management. The other innovation is a system of private boxes, one at each door, into which the prisoner may drop a note of any complaints he may have, without fear of interference by the guard. The warden alone has a key to the boxes. The plan is said to be working well. The number of prisoners reported at this prison was 763, a falling off of 37. The number received during the year was 378, the number discharged was 415. The earnings were $115,271.78, the expenditures, $100,000.

The semiannual report of the Reform School for Boys, at Plainfield, says the year has been prosperous. The boys have laid up in walks and walls of the new buildings 300,000 brick, and are about completing a kiln of 400,000 more. A printing department has been added for the instruction of the boys. The number of boys in the school at the beginning of the year was 520. The average time of confinement of those who were discharged in 1891 was a little over two years and a half. Nine of those released were returned for bad conduct.

Charities.—The report of the Superintendent of the Central Hospital for the Insane shows that at the close of the year there were 1,503 patients in the institution, a decrease of 38 from the year previous. The number of new patients admitted during the year was 399, of whom 74 were recommittal patients. The number discharged was 337. The board of trustees report that the value of the real estate is $1,472,500; personal, $223,860.83. The total appropriation for the maintenance of the hospital was $260,000, of which all was expended except $8,076.45.

The report of the Eastern Hospital for the Insane gives the highest number of patients during the year as 452, and the average for three months 446. The number admitted was 356; recovered and discharged, 52; convalescent and discharged, 19; deaths, 58. The hospital is reported to be crowded beyond its capacity. The appropriation of $85,000 for the year was not exhausted.

At the Southern Hospital for the Insane, improvements have been made in the grounds as recommended by a landscape gardener. The roads have been macadamized to the extent of 2,014 feet. Wells have been dug, providing an abundance of pure water at a depth of 75 feet. A storehouse, a morgue, a motor house, and a railway station had been built. The value of the land and improvements is $463,489.64, and of the personal property $40,288.56. The total expenditures for two years were $163,111.04, leaving a balance of $6,888.96.

The report for the Northern Hospital for the Insane shows that the total number admitted since the opening of the hospital, in July, 1888, until Oct. 1, is 1,161. The number enrolled Oct. 1 was 433. Fifty per cent. of the patients did some manual work. It was not imposed upon them, but was encouraged. The value of the real estate is $430,268.78, and of the personal property $36,104.81.

The General Assembly of 1891 made a special appropriation of $17,500 for improvements at the Institution for the Education of the Deaf and Dumb. The number admitted during the year was: Boys, 180; girls, 162; total, 342. Number discharged: Boys, 25; girls, 18; total, 43. Number in attendance at end of year: Boys, 141; girls, 127; total, 268. New pupils received during the year: Boys, 15; girls, 20. The school publishes a magazine fortnightly, which has been of great assistance to the pupils in their work. The trades taught, and the number of years occupied in each are as follow: Carpentry and cabinet-making, 6; shoe and leather work, 6; printing—composition, presswork, binding, 4; chair caning, 1; sewing, plain, 2; dressmaking—cutting, fitting, draping, 2; tailoring, 2; sewing—fancy needlework, 1.

The School for Feeble-minded Children, at Fort Wayne, is, according to the report for the year ending Oct. 31, in a most prosperous condition. The appropriation of $33,000 made by the last Legislature has been expended in the erection of a schoolhouse for boys, an industrial building, a fever hospital, and several lesser buildings, all of which are in use. The treasurer closed the year with a balance of $1,000 on hand out of the maintenance fund, the cost of running the institution for the year being $76,949.74. There were 80 new pupils admitted during the year, 17 were discharged, and 9 died. The superintendent says the buildings are filled to their utmost capacity.

A branch of the Children's Home Society was organized in Indianapolis in July. Its purpose is to provide homes for helpless children.

The report of the State Board of Charities, submitted in January, 1893, commended the management of State institutions. The secretary reports that 225 visits to the State and county institutions were made during the year. He shows by statistics that the ratio of insane to population in this State is growing less instead of increasing, as is frequently declared. The rate of increase in the number of insane was 15·6 per cent., while the rate of increase in the population was 25 per cent. for the same period. The Indiana ratio is smaller than that of the whole country.

State Board of Health.—The report of the secretary says the total number of deaths in the State for the year was 16,532, of which 5,011 died from zymotic diseases. A board of health has been organized in every county. The following recommendations to the Legislature were incorporated in the report:

(1) That burial permits be required; (2) that a small fee be authorized for a collection of vitality statistics; (3) that the appointment of health officers be vested in the State board; (4) that an increase in the num-

ber of the reports printed be authorized; (5) that the appropriation be increased from $5,000 to $10,000; (6) that a contingency fund for epidemic emergencies be provided.

The Iron Hall.—Attention was drawn this year to the affairs of this order, which apparently has been one of the most prosperous of the mutual-benefit orders in the West, having had a membership of about 70,000. A complaint was filed, in July, at Indianapolis, asking that a receiver be appointed, and alleging

That the corporation is indebted for maturing benefits for the remainder of the year 1892 over $1,000,000, and for sick and disability benefits over $325,000. For 1893 it is indebted for maturing benefits $4,000,000, and for sick and disability benefits over $650,000. For 1894 it is indebted for maturing benefits $6,000,000; for sick and disability benefits, $650,000. For 1895 it is indebted for maturing benefits over $9,000,000, and for sick and disability benefits over $650,000.

The complaint also charged reckless and extravagant payment of salaries, and the expenditure of large sums of money for traveling expenses and pretended claims, amounting in one year to over $50,000.

A receiver was appointed, the evidence showing gross mismanagement. Over $20,000 had been used ostensibly to influence legislation in the New England and other States. About $720,000 of the funds had been placed in a bank in Philadelphia, of which Somerby, chief justice of the order, was vice-president, and Hayes, a supreme trustee, secretary and treasurer. The books showed only $440,000 of the $720,000. In October the Marion County grand jury found indictments against the supreme officers of the order who voted to transfer money to the Philadelphia bank, the counts charging them with embezzling $200,000 of the order's funds and converting it to their own use by placing it in the bank. In December four of the officers—Messrs. Somerby, Baker, Eckersley, and Gladding—were arrested in Philadelphia on a charge of "conspiring to cheat and defraud, with unlawfully using the money belonging to the order, and with hindering and obstructing the administration of public justice."

The World's Fair.—It was expected that the State building at the fair will be finished in February or March, 1893. It stands between the buildings of California and Illinois, at the side of one of the lakes, and between diverging roadways leading from the main building to most of the other State buildings. It will cover an area of 100 by 170 feet, will be of stone, and will have two stone towers. The Legislature will be asked for an appropriation of $135,000 to carry out the plans of the executive committee.

Road Congress.—The first State Congress in the interest of good roads was held in Indianapolis in December. A permanent organization was made and a report to the Legislature prepared. It asks that body to set aside entirely the present system, abolishing the office of district supervisor, and also the functions now exercised by township trustees in connection with roads. In place of these the commissioners of each county are to appoint a county superintendent of highways, and one supervisor for each township. The supervisors are to have charge of the construction of roads in their respective townships, subject to the control of the county superintendent; and the superintendent and supervisors in each county, in connection with the civil engineer of any city in the county, are to constitute a county board of supervisors of highways, which shall meet once a year to discuss road improvements and fix the rate of taxation for road purposes. Road taxes are to be paid like other taxes, and not worked out, and are to be fairly apportioned between cities and the country. It was the unanimous opinion that no road law can be made effective that does not provide for the payment of the road tax in money and place control of road building in competent hands. Another recommendation asked that it should be made unlawful to haul any loaded wagon over any public highway in the State of Indiana unless said wagon be provided with tires not less than 3 inches wide, after Jan. 1, 1895.

Wabash River Improvement.—The navigation of this river has been limited by shallow rapids near Mount Carmel, Ill., known as Grand Rapids, just above the mouth of White river, no steamboats or barges being able to pass this point. The importance to the two States of the water way is shown by the fact that in 1890 the freight carried on it between Terre Haute and Vincennes amounted to 40,000 tons. In order to render it navigable, the Government has been constructing a lock and dam at the rapids. The lock is on the Indiana side of the river, and is constructed of large sawed blocks of oölitic stone, put together with the most scientific masonry. It is 52 feet wide and 325 feet long. The lift of the dam will be 11¼ feet, which will give slack-water navigation for 11¼ miles.

Disastrous Fire.—On Jan. 21 a fire broke out in the Surgical Institute in Indianapolis, about midnight. A majority of the patients were children rendered helpless by disease and deformity. Nineteen bodies were taken from the ruins, and a large number were badly injured.

Political.—The State Democratic Convention met in Indianapolis on April 21. The platform declared for the autonomy of States and economy in public expenditure, and against the enlargement and concentration of Federal power, bounties and subsidies in any form, class legislation, and Government partnership with private enterprises; and affirmed opposition to the whole theory and practice of " paternalism." The following are extracts from it:

We arraign the administration of Benjamin Harrison for its subserviency to the interests of the money power which created it and its indifference to the welfare of the people; for its brazen violation of its solemn pledges to the country to elevate and purify the public service; for its shameless prostitution of the public patronage to the vilest partisan purposes, as illustrated by the sale of a Cabinet office to John Wanamaker; by the employment of the Pension Bureau as a party machine, and by the promotion of William A. Wood to a higher post in the Federal judiciary as a reward for his services in saving the " blocks-of-five " conspirators from the penitentiary; for its contemptuous repudiation of its promises to the veteran soldiers of the Union; for its wicked attempt to fasten upon the country the odious and un-American Force bill, intended to deprive the people of the right to regulate their own elections; for its weak and demagogical foreign policy, which has exhibited

the American Government to the world as a bully toward the feeble and a truckler to the powerful.

We favor such a radical and comprehensive measure of tariff reform as shall relieve the necessities of the people and crude material of our manufacturers from Federal taxation. We condemn the so-called reciprocity policy.

We favor the election of United States Senators directly by the people, and commend Senator Turpie for his efforts in Congress to secure this great reform.

We most heartily applaud the action of our two last Legislatures in passing the schoolbook laws.

We denounce the infamous conspiracy of the Republican county commissioners, township trustees, and other officials of Indiana, who, for the purpose of creating unfair prejudice against the new tax law, have wantonly and needlessly increased the local taxes in the 46 counties controlled by them more than $1,250,000.

We demand that the Indiana Senators and Representatives in Congress use their influence to secure the passage of laws making greenbacks taxable as other money, and making interstate commerce taxable on the same terms as domestic commerce.

The Democratic party of Indiana expresses its unalterable confidence in and attachment to its gallant leader, Isaac P. Gray, and in the event that the national convention deems the nomination of Mr. Cleveland inexpedient, the delegation is instructed to use every honorable effort to secure the nomination of Gov. Gray for the presidency.

The following were the nominations for State offices: For Governor, Claude Matthews; for Lieutenant-Governor, Mortimer J. Nye; for Secretary of State, William R. Myers; for Attorney-General, Alonzo G. Smith; for Auditor, J. O. Henderson; for Superintendent of Public Instruction, Hervey D. Vories; for Statistician, William A. Peelle; for Treasurer, Albert Gall; for Judges of the Supreme Court, Jeptha D. New, James McCabe, Timothy O. Howard; for Judges of the Appellate Court, George L. Reinhard, Frank E. Gavin, Theodore A. Allen, O. J. Lotz, George W. Ross; for Reporter of the Supreme Court, Sidney R. Moon.

The State Convention of the Prohibition party met at Indianapolis on May 24. The resolutions declared in favor of the issue by the General Government, without the intervention of banks, of a circulating medium of a sufficient volume for the transaction of the business of the country in a manner which will be just to the debtor as well as the creditor class, said circulating medium to consist of gold and silver coin and United States Treasury notes, each to be a full legal tender for all debts, public and private, and each to be taxable; of Government control, and, if necessary to control, ownership of the public means of transportation and communication; of the removal of the tariff from the necessaries of life; of the passage of laws prohibiting alien ownership of land and the reclaiming by the Government of all lands now held by railroads and other corporations in excess of their actual needs; and denounced as infamous the " age of consent " laws. The resolutions also declared that all restrictions on suffrage should apply equally to both sexes, and that the time of residence for naturalization should be extended, and no naturalized person should vote within two years after such naturalization; that public officials should be paid by salary only; that United States Senators should be elected by direct vote of the people; that speculation in margins and the cornering of grain, money, and products should be prohibited; that contract convict labor should be abolished, and that every honorably discharged Union soldier and sailor of the war merits and should have a pension, based upon service and disability, without regard to rank.

The following ticket was put in nomination: For Governor, Rev. Aaron Wirth; for Lieutenant-Governor, C. W. Culbertson; for Secretary, James McCormick; for Auditor, Frank Taggart; for Treasurer, H. H. Moore; for Superintendent of Public Instruction, E. A. Devore; for Attorney-General, C. S. Dobbins; for Statistician, M. E. Shiel; for Supreme Judge, Robert Denny; for Appellate Judges. John Baker, John D. Gouger, and John B. Joyce; for Reporter of the Supreme Court, John W. Bair.

The convention of the People's party met in May. The more important portions of the majority report of the Committee on Resolutions, which was adopted, follow:

We demand the free and unlimited coinage of silver.

We demand that the amount of the circulating medium be speedily increased to not less than $50 *per capita.*

We demand a graduated income tax.

Alien ownership of land should be prohibited; all lands now held by railroads and other corporations in excess of their actual needs, and all lands now owned by aliens, should be reclaimed by the Government and held for actual settlers only.

We demand that the State be redistricted with absolute fairness.

We demand that county superintendents be elected by a vote of the people.

We demand that the office of county assessor be abolished.

We demand such revision of the law for the listing of property for taxation that shall compel all property, both real and personal, to be listed at a fair cash value.

We demand that the Government issue legal-tender notes, and pay the Union soldiers the difference between the price of the depreciated money in which they were paid and gold.

That we favor the enactment of laws under which the people may vote periodically upon doctrine and policies without the intervention of parties or candidates, the results of these elections to be considered as instructions to our legislative servants, and to be enforced by impeachment when such instructions are disregarded.

The right to vote is inherent in citizenship, without regard to sex.

The following was the ticket selected: For Governor, Leroy Templeton; Lieutenant-Governor, J. A. Houser; Secretary of State, Jesse L. Hobson; Auditor, Louis C. Kasten; Treasurer, Townsend Cope; State Statistician, C. H. Bliss; Reporter of Supreme Court, W. H. Dewey; Supreme Judges. Adam Stockington, Silas M. Sheppard, and M. J. Bosart; for Appellate Judges, I. N. Pearce, Joseph Daily, H. C. Barnett, David W. Chambers, and John S. Bender.

The Republicans met in convention at Fort Wayne on June 28. The resolutions approved the nominations of the national convention at Minneapolis, condemned the Democratic management of State affairs as incompetent, wasteful, and in the interest of party managers, and as having burdened the State with a debt of $9,000,000, and said further:

We arraign the Democratic party of Indiana for enacting an unequal and unjust tax law. It imposes upon the farmer, laborer, and householder an excessive and unjust share of the public burden. It creates a great number of unnecessary offices hitherto unknown to law. To the burden of taxation, already too heavy, it adds more than $100,000 for the fees, salaries, and expenses of these offices and officers. We demand its radical revision. We pledge ourselves to enact such amendments to the present tax law as shall relieve the farm and the home from the unjust taxation now borne by them; which shall place a just share of the public burden on capital, and incorporate property and provide a more simple and less expensive method of assessment. We condemn the action of the last Democratic Legislature in largely increasing the fees and salaries of the State and county offices. It made many public offices sinecures by providing for the performance of official duties by deputies paid out of the public funds.

The law passed by the last Democratic Assembly, apportioning the State for legislative and congressional purposes, was designedly and wickedly framed so as to deny to many counties and localities fair and equal representation in the legislative department of the State and nation, to place and retain under Democratic control in this State all its public institutions and affairs, and to give that party an increased and unfair representation in Congress and the Legislature. Such a policy is dangerous, and destructive of all good government, and merits the condemnation of all patriotic people. And we now pledge the Republican party to continue the warfare against this dishonest policy of the Democratic party, until the State shall be honestly apportioned by giving to each county and locality its fair and equitable representation in proportion to its numbers.

We denounce the purpose of the Democratic party, clearly avowed in the national platform, to repeal the law imposing a 10-per-cent. tax on State bank issues, and thus removing the only barrier to a return of the system of "wild cat" money, which once disgraced our State and largely impoverished our people.

We favor amending the law concerning the construction and maintenance of public highways, so as to utilize to the best advantage the large sums yearly expended thereon, and thus put the farmer in close and easy communication with the market at all seasons of the year.

The Democratic party deserves the emphatic condemnation of every citizen of the State for its refusal to place our benevolent institutions upon a nonpartisan basis, when murder, cruelty, debauchery, fraud, and incompetency mark that party's management of many of these institutions, and for still persisting in retaining partisan control of the asylums of the helpless and unfortunate that they may be made the coin in payment for party services.

We favor the enactment by Congress of a law, thrice recommended by President Harrison, compelling the use of standard safety car couplers for the protection of the lives and limbs of employees engaged in interstate commerce.

We also favor a law governing convict labor in the penal institutions of the State that will work the least possible injury to free labor.

We most heartily indorse the generous pension laws enacted by Republicans in Congress, and congratulate the country that during the administration of President Harrison no pension bill has been vetoed.

Following is the ticket nominated: Governor, Ira J. Chase; Lieutenant-Governor, Theodore Shockney; Secretary of State, Aaron Jones; Auditor, John W. Coons; Treasurer, F. J. Scholz; Attorney-General, J. D. Ferrall; Supreme Court Reporter, George P. Haywood; Superintendent of Public Instruction, James H. Henry; State Statistician, Simeon J. Thompson; Judges of the Supreme Court, John D. Miller, Byron K. Elliott, Robert W. McBride; Appellate Judges, A. G. Cavins. C. S. Baker, James B. Black, Henry C. Fox, Edgar C. Crumpacker.

The State Single-Tax League met in June, and adopted resolutions as follow:

The increase of land value prevents the increase of labor value, absorbing the increase of wages to labor and profit to capital; destroys markets; creates idleness, poverty, and vice. Therefore, to restore wages and establish uninterrupted prosperity, we demand the abolition of all taxes except a single tax on land values.

We are opposed to banks of issue.

We are opposed to the giving away of franchises.

It was decided to send delegates to the World's Congress of Single-Taxers, to be held in Chicago during the World's Fair. A committee was appointed to confer with the State convention of the People's party in regard to the land plank of their platform.

At the November election the total vote for first presidential electors was 554,013, of which 262,740 were for Cleveland, 255,615 for Harrison, 13,050 for Bidwell, and 22,208 for Weaver; Cleveland's plurality, 7,125. Republican congressmen were elected in the Sixth and Ninth Districts, and Democratic in the other eleven. The entire State Democratic ticket was successful. Claude Matthews, candidate for Governor, received the largest plurality, 6,976. His total vote was 260,-601; that of Chase, the Republican candidate, 253,625; that of Wirth, Prohibition, was 12,960; and that of Templeton, People's party, 22,017. The General Assembly will be divided as follows: Senate—Democrats 35, Republicans 15; House—Democrats 63, Republicans 37.

INDUSTRIAL LEGION, an organization formed in Memphis, Tenn., Nov. 20, 1892, by leaders of the People's party, who were also active in the Farmers' Alliance. The object of the legion is to carry out politically the measures embodied in the declaration of principles of the Omaha platform of the People's party, together with free speech, a free ballot, and a fair count. The legion is divided into three classes: The first, of male members over twenty-one years of age, known as the senior class; the second, or junior class, of male members under twenty-one and over fourteen years of age, who shall be educated and trained to become voters of the People's party; and the third class, known as the Woman's Aid Corps, intended as an auxiliary to the senior class. The legion is modeled after the Grand Army of the Republic. It partakes of the nature of a secret organization, while the meetings may be secret or open, at the option of the members.

IOWA, a Western State, admitted to the Union Dec. 28, 1846; area, 56,025 square miles. The population, according to each decennial census since admission, was 192,214 in 1850; 674,913 in 1860; 1,194,020 in 1870; 1,624,615 in 1880; and 1,911,896 in 1890. Capital, Des Moines.

Government.—The following were the State officers during the year: Governor, Horace Boies, Democrat; Lieutenant-Governor, S. L. Bestow; Secretary of State, W. M. McFarland; Attorney-General, John Y. Stone; Auditor, James A. Lyons; Treasurer, Byron A. Beeson; Superintendent of Public Instruction, J. B. Knoepfler; Commissioner of Labor Statistics, J. R. Sover-

eign; Railroad Commissioners, Spencer Smith, John W. Luke, Peter A. Dey; Chief Justice of the Supreme Court, Gifford S. Robinson; Associate Justices, Charles T. Granger, Josiah Given, James H. Rothrock, L. G. Kenne.

Appropriations. — The General Assembly made the following appropriations: $7,000 for the College for the Blind; $55,100 for the Hospital for the Insane at Clarinda; $15,750 for that at Independence; $20,500 for that at Mount Pleasant; $20,300 for the Industrial Home for the Blind at Knoxville; $7,150 for the girls' department of the Industrial School, and $25,900 for that of the boys; $16,000 for the Iowa School for the Deaf; $26,600 to the Institution for the Feeble-minded; $23,700 for the Normal School; $19,400 for the Penitentiary at Anamosa; $16,950 for that at Fort Madison; $6,530 for the Soldiers' Home, at Marshalltown; $12,500 for the Soldiers' Orphans' Home, at Davenport; $78,000 for the State University, at Iowa City; $125,000 to the Columbian Exposition.

Education.—The following statistics give the number of inmates admitted to the Industrial School:

Whole number of boys committed to the school since its opening, Sept. 21, 1868, to June 30, 1891 1,655
Number discharged and otherwise released 1,254
Number remaining in school, June 30, 1891 401
Whole number of girls received since opening of school 432
Number discharged or otherwise released 314
Number remaining in institution, June 30, 1891 117

In January, 1892, the new additions to the building having been completed, eligible blind people were admitted.

Taxation.—A tax commission having been created by the last Legislature to prepare a more equitable plan of taxation. the State executive, on July 28, appointed its members. At the meeting held in August it was resolved that no more than two members of the same political party, nor any member of the Twenty-fourth General Assembly, should be a member of the commission. The work. begun in August, 1892, should be finished and filed with the Secretary of State by July 1, 1893.

Valuations.—The assessed valuation of real estate and personal property in Iowa for 1890 amounted to $525,862,858, that for 1880 having been $398,671,251. The assessed valuation *per capita* was $274, that for 1880 having been $245.39.

The Columbian Exposition.—The General Assembly having appropriated but $125,000 of the $339,000 asked for, a complete reorganization of the plans by the committee was deemed necessary. It was decided that no new State building should be erected, but that a remodeling of the "Shelter" should be undertaken, a 1-story structure already existing in Jackson Park, and offered to the Iowa commission.

Agriculture.—The fortieth annual convention of the State Agricultural Society met at Des Moines in January, 1892, 112 delegates being present. According to an estimate submitted. the grand total value of Iowa products of farm. pasture, and dairy is $464,219,308, or over $230 for every man, woman, and child in the State—an average of $1,100 per family. The number of farms in the State being placed at 200,000, this means that the average farmer raised $2,200 worth of products in 1891.

There were sold in the year ending in June, 1890, 121,399 horses. In 1860 there were 178,-088 horses to a population of 674,913; in 1870, 433.642 to a population of 1,624,615; and in 1890, 1,338,867 to a population of 1,911.896. Of milch cows there are in the State 1,278,612; of other cattle, 2,680,247, an increase in the total number of 448,378 over that of 1885.

The amount of butter shipped from the State during the year ending Sept. 30, 1891, was 81,-774,661 pounds. The decrease of practically 10,000,000 pounds over the sales for the year ending Oct. 1, 1890, has been attributed to the uneven crops of 1890, which greatly increased the price of corn and hay. The home consumption of butter is estimated at 100,000,000 pounds. The total make of the State is 168,690,715 pounds.

Road Convention.—Delegates from all parts of the State, met at Des Moines on Aug. 16 and 17, to consider the question of improving the common roads. Gov. Boies, who addressed the meeting, referred to the convention as one of the most important that has been held in the State for years. Various measures were proposed for the best promotion of the object under discussion. Judge Thayer submitted a plan by which 15,000 miles of good road could be built in five or ten years, so that when it was completed no person would be found living more than four miles from a perfect macadamized road, and this without an increase of taxes. In the resolutions finally adopted it was determined that until further legislation a movement should be set on foot in every township looking to the consolidation of the road districts, in order that the permissive provisions of chapter 200 of the acts of 1884 might be taken advantage of. Agitation of the question was suggested in cities and towns, and the propriety of submitting to the people the proposition for a higher levy or the issuance of bonds.

Legislative Session.—The General Assembly sat until March 30. The early meetings of the Senate were disturbed by the question of permanent organization, and the refusal of the Democrats to proceed to business until such an organization was effected. The Republican caucus nominations were disputed, and a deadlock ensued. - This was broken by Lieut.-Gov. Poyneer, who converted a sufficient number of Democrats "present but not voting" to declare a quorum. The permanent officers were then elected, and J. W. Cliff, the Republican nominee, was declared secretary, all the other officers being Democratic.

Mr. Cliff was subsequently deposed (Jan. 21). the Democrats declaring that the minority had no right to foist on the Senate a permanent officer, and disputing the ruling of ex-Gov. Poyneer in declaring a quorum when the Democratic members were present and not voting. The Republicans in turn declined to vote for Samuel N. Parsons, the Democratic nominee. A call of the Senate was made, nearly every one answering "Here," whereupon the 24 votes of the Democrats were decided by the chair to have elected Parsons. The sergeant-at-arms removed Mr. Cliff in spite of protest. This difficulty in regard to the election of the secretary led to the passage of resolutions referring to the Attorney-General for decision the following questions:

Whether the Senate of this State has the power to pass upon and determine the election and qualification of its own secretary. Whether it, as a legislative body, has the power and authority to remove its secretary and elect another. Whether, after the Senate has removed its secretary and elected another, a district court of this State has jurisdiction to try the right of the latter to hold his office. Whether the right of Samuel N. Parsons to act as secretary of the Senate can be inquired into by an injunction proceeding. Whether the Speaker of the House is justified under the law in refusing to concur with the President of the Senate in certifying the election of Samuel N. Parsons as secretary.

Joint resolutions were introduced on high license, to the effect that the Representative in Congress be instructed to secure an amendment to the statute of the United States, changing the amount of tax from $25 to $250 a year, and providing that sales made in violation of the laws of any State where such sales are made shall forfeit such United States special tax license, and subject the offender to the penalties of the statutes of the United States as if no special tax had been paid. The question of allowing licenses or standing by the principles of prohibition absorbed a great part of the disension, the Schmidt bill being again introduced as first on the Senate file. It was argued in opposition that the people of the State had always stood by prohibition; that the claim made by the supporters of the bill to the effect that the traffic in intoxicating liquors was not detrimental to health, morals, or the welfare of the public, was false. Such traffic, they maintained, should be classed with gambling, betting, the vending of obscene literature, and like evils, and made subject to the penalty of the same law. It was claimed further that the passage of this bill would reverse a policy of the State that was adopted by a Democratic General Assembly nearly forty years ago, substituting a system that has never successfully restrained the evils of the liquor traffic. The forcing upon the community of a legalized saloon would be the result. In the protracted discussion that followed it was shown that. according to the "Brewers' Journal," in 1885 there were sold in Iowa 182,524 barrels of beer; in 1886. 197.372; in 1887, 183,-464; in 1888, 174,339; in 1890, 88,266; and in 1891, 105,943—showing under a Democratic rule of eighteen months an increase of 17 per cent. over the amount of the year before. It was shown that under this bill druggists would be allowed to sell without fee or bond, requiring only semi-annual reports and small fines. The bill was before the Senate until March 8, when it passed by a vote of 27 to 22. But on March 22 the bill was killed by the House, it having been argued that it would discriminate against a law-abiding industrious German element, and was a measure giving unequal privileges to certain counties. No other bill absorbed so much attention during the session.

By the Senate and House concurring, the message of President Harrison to Congress on the Chilian question was approved.

A bill providing that fraud or circumvention in obtaining any promissory notes, or other negotiable instruments, can be pleaded in bar to any action for recovery, whether brought by the party obtaining such instrument or an assignee,

popularly spoken of as the " innocent-purchaser"
bill, became the subject of warm debate and frequent amendments, but was finally passed by the
Senate. This bill was vetoed by the Governor.

Among the bills passed were the following:

Forbidding discrimination in regard to color by
restaurant keepers.

Imposing taxes on corporate franchises and shares
of stock.

Exempting passengers getting on or off a car or
train from criminal liability under the act making it
a p c offense for any person not an employee to get
off **on** on a moving train.

Authorizing corporations and persons engaged in
the slaughtering and packing business to issue certificates and warehouse receipts on their own products
while in their custody and control.

Making appropriations for the World's Columbian
Exposition.

Giving local boards of health power to quarantine.

Providing for the collection and tabulation of statistics of crops and live stock.

Authorizing the use of the Australian ballot.

Appropriating $250,000 for the soldiers' monument.

Political.—The State Temperance Alliance
met at Des Moines on March 3. In the resolutions adopted it was determined that the sentiment of Iowa was as strongly for prohibition as
ever, and that the election of a Democratic Governor was not justly attributable to prohibition,
but to the fact that undue importance was given
to other issues during the canvass; that while
the Democratic party made prohibition the chief
issue, the Republicans too often virtually ignored
it. It was also

Resolved, That any government which, for a consideration, licenses a business that debauches all who
engage in it and produces poverty, insanity, and
crime everywhere, not only surrenders its God-ap-
pointed place as the protector of the innocent and
helpless, but becomes a bribed partner of the criminal
classes.

A third resolution was to the effect that, while
the convention fully appreciated the fidelity of
the Republican members of the Legislature, and
expected no backward step, the passage of the
Gatch bill or any bill giving legal sanction to
the outlawed saloon would be conclusive evidence
that the Republican party of Iowa could no
longer be looked to for " the protection of our
homes from the blighting curse of the rum
traffic." In the event of such legislation " we
instruct the officers of the Alliance to issue a
call for a meeting of all the friends of prohibition, to the end that organized action may be
taken that shall stand for the home as against
the saloon, for law as against lawlessness."

Much discussion followed, and an amendment
of the objectionable third clause in the resolutions was suggested, to read as follows : " Legal
sanction to the outlawed saloon will be evidence
that we can no longer look to the two leading
parties for the protection of the home from the
blighting curse of the saloon, and in such event
we recommend that the Alliance call a convention of the friends of prohibition to decide upon
a course of future action."

In the resolutions finally adopted it was agreed
that the question of prohibition in Iowa was
paramount to any political issues now at stake,
and that hereafter no suffrage or influence would
be given to individuals or organizations not true

to prohibition. The proposition to raise money
by the licensed sale of intoxicating liquors at the
Columbian Exposition was denounced, as well as
the Sunday opening of such exposition.

The Republican State Committee met at Des
Moines on March 17 to select four delegates to
the national convention at Minneapolis. Resolutions of confidence in the principles of the
Republican party and in the administration of
President Harrison were passed. It was also
resolved that at the national convention an
appeal should be made to the party to disregard
all local differences in order to accomplish the
following objects: The maintenance of protection ; the full establishment of reciprocity " as a
policy of government which is one of the great
achievements of Republican statesmanship ";
the elevation and prosperity of labor ; the maintenance of a sound currency, " every dollar of
which shall be the equal of every other dollar " ;
and equal legal rights for all citizens, black or
white.

On June 30, the Republicans again met in
convention at Des Moines, and the following
nominations were made: For Secretary of State,
W. M. McFarland ; Treasurer, Byron A. Beeson ;
Attorney-General, John Y. Stone ; Auditor, C.
G. McCarthy ; Railroad Commissioner, George
W. Perkins. A resolution in favor of improving
the highways was adopted, and a platform in
which " special pride " was expressed in the
tariff issue, the silver problem, the temperance
question, and the demands made for an untrammeled ballot by the platform of the Republican National Convention. The attitude of
the Democratic party toward the national tax on
the issue of State banks was denounced.

The Democratic Convention met at Council
Bluffs on May 11, for the selection of delegates
at large to the national convention. By a
unanimous vote the 26 delegates were instructed to vote as a unit for Gov. Horace Boies,
and to use every effort in their power to secure his nomination for the presidency. Mr.
Cleveland's name was omitted, without protest,
from the official declaration of Democratic faith.

In the platform adopted the party's faith in
the principle of all men being born free and
equal was declared to mean more than equal
rights to all men, and an exposition of the principic was made in this manner:

It means the right of every man to put into his own
mouth the bread he earns with his own hands, and
all of it, without having it tolled or taxed for the
private benefit of any of his fellow-men. We denounce all such tolling and taxation as it exists to-day
under the so-called protective tariff system. We declare a citizen is best protected who is insured in the
absolute control and disposition of his own wages
and substance, and that he is most certainly robbed
when deprived of this disposition and control, and
when others exercise it for him, not for his benefit,
but for their own selfish objects and ends. All limitations upon the liberty of the citizen not required in
the earnest of good morals and good government
are odious and tyrannical. We hold it to be self-evi-
dent that the limits imposed by a law which compels
one citizen to his certain loss to trade with designated
classes of citizens for the certain gain of such classes,
is of this odious and tyrannical character. And we
assert our confidence that a free people can not be
permanently deluded into supporting such legislation
upon the pretense that they are thus being protected,

while having their rights invaded and denied for the benefit of monopolies, trusts, and combinations. The conditions which have been brought about by this falsely called protection must be remedied, or we must have, instead of a pure democracy where the voice and liberties and interests of the people are supreme, a government of classes by classes and for classes, in which the masses will be the servitors and subordinates, equally tramped upon and despised. We declare this is the paramount issue in the presidential campaign.

The platform further declared its condemnation of the Republican "policy of a treasury to pay bounties to a favored few." The principles of free trade were declared sound, and the best protection of our citizens against the favoritism shown to monopolies, trusts, and imported wage earners. Unqualified opposition to all legislation calculated to reduce either of the precious metals to a position of a commodity alone, by establishing the other as a single standard for the measurement of value, was declared.

At the Democratic Convention held at Davenport on Aug. 18, in the platform adopted the nomination of Cleveland and Stevenson was upheld. At the same time, the commendation of Gov. Boies as a faithful and wise administrator of the best interests of the State was "renewed with pride and pleasure." The platform further declared that the party hailed the opportunity for a discussion of the radical reforms in the tariff and the maintenance and perpetuity of the doctrine of local self-government, and pledged its earnest and united support to these principles.

A reiteration of the principles enunciated in the platforms of the democracy of Iowa in 1889, and since that time, touching the regulation of the liquor traffic was insisted upon, the party pledging itself to the enactment of laws that shall give the people in their respective localities the management and control of this traffic.

For the management of State institutions it demanded the abolition of the separate boards of trustees and the substitution therefor of a single board of control, nonpartisan in its character, impartial as between the several institutions.

Among the closing paragraphs of the platform was the following:

We declare our purpose to nominate candidates for the United States Senate in general convention, and demand such change in our national Constitution as will permit the election of the same by direct vote of the people.

The ticket chosen reads as follows: For Secretary of State, J. H. McConlogue; Auditor, S. P. Vandyke; Treasurer, Charles Ruwgnitz; Attorney-General, Ezra Willard; Railroad Commissioner, W. G. Kent.

The Third Party Prohibitionists met on the last Wednesday in May. The question of admitting the woman's-suffrage plank in the platform excited some discussion, but it was finally adopted by a unanimous vote. The platform, when completed, demanded "the right of suffrage for all natural born and properly naturalized citizens, without regard to sex." It demanded, further, the protection of the American laborer from "competition with foreign and home criminal labor," an educational and moral qualification to be added to a residence of five years as a condition of naturalization, the Sunday closing of the Columbian Exposition, and prohibition of all intoxicants on the World's Fair grounds. A resolution in favor of placing gold and silver bullion on the ratio of 1 to 16 was passed; and one for the proper supply of full legal tender without corporate intervention.

The People's party of Iowa met at Des Moines in June. The platform adopted contained the following demands:

A national currency, safe, sound, and flexible, issued by the General Government only, a full legal tender for all debts, and without the use of banking corporations, a just, equitable, and efficient means of distribution direct to the people, at a tax not to exceed 2 per cent., be devised, as set forth in the subtreasury plan of the Farmers' Alliance system.

Free and unlimited coinage of silver.

The amount of circulating medium to be speedily increased to not less than $50 per capita.

A graduated income tax.

All State and national revenues to be limited to the necessary expenses of the Government.

Postal savings banks to be established by the Government.

Alien ownership of land to be prohibited. All lands now held by railroads and other corporations in excess of their actual needs, and all lands now owned by aliens, to be reclaimed by the Government and held for actual settlers.

Government control of the railroads, telegraph and telephone, and the postal system.

Resolutions were passed condemning the 9 members of Congress who betrayed their pledges to secure free and unlimited coinage of silver; of President Harrison and his administration for calling an international monetary conference to fix a value on silver.

At the election in November the entire Republican State ticket was elected by majorities of about 23,000. Of the eleven Congressmen chosen. all are Republicans except one. On the Presidential ticket the vote was: Republican, 219,384; Democratic, 196,419; People's, 20,594; Prohibition, 6,317.

ITALY, a constitutional monarchy in southern Europe. The legislative authority is vested by the Constitution in the Parliament, which consists of the Senate and the Chamber of Deputies. The Senate is composed of princes of the royal blood, of persons who fill a high office, of men who have distinguished themselves in science or literature or have in any other pursuit benefited the nation. and of those who pay an annual tax of 3,000 lire. They are appointed by the King for life, and number 335. The Chamber of Deputies is elected by ballot, according to the amended electoral law of 1891, which abolished the *scrutin de liste*. A man to be qualified as a voter must be twenty-one years of age, be able to write and read, and pay an annual tax of 19 lire. Men of the learned professions. or who have served two years in the army, are also qualified to vote. The whole population is divided into 508 electoral districts for the purpose of elections, which number corresponds to that of the Deputies. The legislative period is five years. The King can dissolve the Chamber at any time, but must order new elections within four months. The Parliament meets annually. Money bills must originate in the Chamber. while other measures may be introduced by the Government or members of either house. Senators and Deputies receive no pay except free transportation.

The reigning King is Umberto I, born March 14, 1844, the eldest son of King Vittorio Emanuele II, who died Jan. 9, 1878. The heir-apparent is Vittorio Emanuele, Prince of Naples, born Nov. 11, 1869. The ministry in the beginning of 1892 was composed of the following members: President of the Council and Minister of Foreign Affairs, Starrabara di Rudini, appointed Feb. 9. 1891; Minister of the Interior, Giovanni Nicotera; Minister of Finance, Giuseppe Colombo; Minister of the Treasury. Luigi Luzatti; Minister of Justice and of Ecclesiastical Affairs, Bruno Chimirri, appointed Dec. 31, 1891; Minister of War, Gen. Luigi Pelloux; Minister of Marine, Vice-Admiral Pacoret de Saint Bon; Minister of Commerce, Industry, and Agriculture, Marquis di Rudini, appointed *ad interim*, Dec. 31, 1891; Minister of Public Instruction. Pasquale Villari; Minister of Public Works, Ascanio Branco; Minister of Posts and Telegraphs *ad interim*, Ascanio Branco.

Area and Population.—The area of Italy is 286,588 square kilometres, according to a recent survey, and the population, on Dec. 31, 1890, was 30,158,408. The administrative divisions of Italy are provinces, territories, districts, and communes. There are 69 provinces, of which 60 are divided into 197 territories, and 9 into 87 districts; these are divided again into communes, which numbered 8,253 in 1891. In 1890, 100,259 people emigrated to the different European countries, 48,019 to the United States, 41,-352 to the Argentine Republic, Paraguay, and Uruguay, 20,493 to Brazil and other countries in South and Central America and Mexico, 2,020 to Africa, and 548 to Asia and Australia. The population of the principal cities and towns in the beginning of 1891 was as follows: Naples, 530,872; Rome, 423,217; Milan, 414,551; Turin, 320,808; Palermo, 267,416; Genoa, 206,485; Florence, 191,453; Venice, 158,019; Bologna, 143,607; Messina, 142,000; Catania, 109,687; Leghorn, 104,960.

Finances.—The budget estimate of revenue for the financial year ending June 30, 1892, was 1,775,123,004 lire, and the estimated expenditure was 1,780,942,130 lire, leaving a deficit of 5,819,-126 lire. In the public accounts the receipts and expenditures are divided into four categories: (1) Effective receipts and expenditures; (2) movement of capital; (3) construction of railroads, etc.; (4) receipts *d'ordre*. In the first category the ordinary receipts amounted to 1,543,622,745 lire, and the extraordinary receipts to 12,300,636 lire; the expenditures were figured at 1,550,391,896 lire, thus showing a surplus of 5,531,485 lire. The receipts and expenditures of the second category are classed as extraordinary; the former amounted to 31,867,161 lire, and the latter to 43,217,772 lire, thus leaving a deficit of 11,350,611 lire. In the third category, where receipts and expenditures are also extraordinary, the receipts amounted to 82,944,161 and the expenditures to 82,944,814 lire, showing a deficit of 653 lire. The fourth category embraces the working expenses of the state domains, interest on the funds for securing paper money, treasury deposits, loans for pensions, and other items; receipts balance expenditures in this category, amounting to 104,387,648 lire.

The interest on the consolidated debt for 1890-'91, at 5, and a small part at 3 per cent., amounted to 449,142,335 lire. The interest on debts separately inscribed, paying 3 to 5 per cent., amounted to 20,138,439 lire, and the sinking fund to 1,039,969 lire; while the interest on various other debts at 3 to 6 per cent. amounted to 96,487,707 lire, and the sinking fund to 329,-747 lire. The interest on the floating debt, consisting of treasury bonds, current accounts, and bank advances, was 13,113,635 lire, which, with the permanent annuity to the Holy See of 3,-225,000 lire, brought up the total interest of the public debt to 582,107,116 lire. The capital of the consolidated and redeemable debt amounted to 11,800,454,529 lire in 1891. The property of the state amounted to 6,819,243,094 lire on June 30, 1890, and consisted of financial assets to the value of 617,245,058 lire; loans and real property, etc., 750,456,209 lire; property of an industrial nature, 3,548,791,209 lire; material in use in the army and navy, 185,072,516 lire; and property used in the service of the state, 1,717,-078,102 lire. The revenue from the state property for the year 1889-'90 was 88,267,388 lire, of which 72,235,321 lire were derived from the railroads, 3,974,316 lire from ecclesiastical property, and 12,057,751 lire from other sources.

The Army.—The total aggregate nominal strength of the Italian army in the beginning of 1891 was 2,844,339 men. Of this number, 14,-508 officers and 261,505 men were on active duty in the permanent army, while 11,686 officers and 566,152 men were on unlimited leave of absence; 4,012 officers and 445,004 men belonged to the mobile militia, and 5,250 officers and 1,547,908 men were in the territorial militia. Service in the army is compulsory, and extends over a period of nineteen years. About 200,000 recruits are levied annually, and are divided into three categories; 82,000 men are drafted into the permanent army, and the remainder distributed among the mobile and the territorial militia. By the law of 1891, the annual contingent of the first category is increased to 95,000 men. The time of service in the standing army for the first category is five years for the infantry, four years for the cavalry, and three years for other branches; they are then enrolled in the permanent army under unlimited leave; and after the expiration of four years for the infantry and five years for the cavalry they are transferred to the territorial militia. Those belonging to the other arms are enrolled for five or six years in the permanent army and twelve years in the mobile militia. and are then transferred to the territorial militia. The recruits of the second category are attached for eight years to the permanent army and four years to the mobile militia, and then enter the territorial militia. The men of the third category immediately form part of the territorial militia, but are given unlimited leave of absence.

The Navy.—The Italian navy consisted, on Jan. 1, 1891, of 12 men-of-war of the first class, 14 of the second class, and 21 of the third class; of 16 transport ships, 6 school ships. 5 ships for local defense, and 50 local vessels; 6 lagoon gunboats, 7 torpedo cruisers, and 61 ocean torpedo vessels; 38 torpedo boats of the first class, 21 of the second class, and 12 steam torpedo barges. There were building 1 ironclad of the first class,

6 deck-protected cruisers of the second class, and 5 torpedo cruisers. The total of all ranks for the navy was 70,323, and 689 officers and 48,603 men constituted the reserve.

Commerce.—The special imports in 1890 amounted to 1,319,638,433 lire, and the special exports to 895,945,253 lire. The imports and exports of precious metals were 57,648,000 and 66,-655,100 lire respectively. The values of some of the leading imports in 1890 were as follow: Grain, 128,997,200 lire; raw cotton, 127,169,500 lire; coal, 121,935,716 lire; machinery, 39,414,-280 lire; silk, unbleached, raw, or twisted, 35,-585,800 lire; coffee, 32,160,180 lire; raw sugar, 31,178,035 lire; refined sugar, 984,735 lire; timber for building, 30,854,845 lire; fish, 30,415,630 lire; raw hides, 29,387,935 lire; raw wool, 27,-149,000 lire; animals, 22,169,400 lire; iron, in bars, 17,520,841 lire; leaf tobacco, 15,714,629 lire; refined mineral oil, 14,947,422 lire; cotton prints, 14,176,015 lire; bleached cotton cloth, 6,720,083 lire; colored and dyed cotton cloth, 4,971,238 lire; linen and hemp yarn, 14,030,012 lire; cheese, 13,541,500 lire; manufactures of silk, 11,331,601 lire; cotton yarn, 8,614,311 lire. The values of some of the leading exports in the same year were as follow: Raw and thrown silk, 268,714,900 lire; silk waste, 27,002,805 lire; silk manufactures, 15,568,514 lire; silk cocoons, 4,141,410 lire; fresh fruit, 47,372,022 lire; olive oil, 45,372,022 lire; wine in casks, 34,364,426 lire; sulphur, 26,296,648 lire; hemp and flax, 25,873,180 lire; raw cotton, 22,648,625 lire; eggs, 19,870,760 lire; manufactured coral, 15,227,280 lire; marble, 15,169,676 lire; skins, 14,073,110 lire; fresh and salted meats, 11,262,660 lire; zinc ore, 10,498,670 lire; grain, other than wheat, 10,449,159 lire.

The following table shows the trade with the leading countries, in lire, for the year 1890:

COUNTRIES.	Imports.	Exports.
Great Britain	818,897,000	111,178,000
France	163,506,000	160,620,000
Austria	143,914,000	83,947,000
Germany	140,294,000	118,572,000
Russia	119,852,000	11,255,000
British Asiatic possessions	98,989,000	12,181,000
United States and Canada	81,670,000	78,887,000
Switzerland	55,089,000	168,514,000
Turkey, Servia, and Roumania	37,240,000	18,829,000
Central and South America	87,284,000	46,064,000
Belgium	33,842,000	32,203,000
Egypt	19,873,000	7,271,000
Spain, Gibraltar, and Portugal	11,188,000	13,800,000

Navigation.—On Jan. 1, 1891, the mercantile marine numbered in all 6,732 vessels, of 820,776 tons. Of this number, 6,442 were sailing vessels, with a tonnage of 634,209 tons, and 290 were steamers, of 186,567 tons. In 1890, 121,732 vessels, of 22,459,473 tons, entered Italian ports; 111,586 vessels, of 14,610,961 tons, were Italian, and 10,146 vessels, of 7,848,512 tons, were foreign. There cleared from Italian ports 120,720 vessels, of 22,301,704 tons, of which 110,790, of 14,525,-149 tons, were Italian, and 9,930, of 7,776,555 tons, were foreign.

Posts and Telegraphs.—The number of letters sent through the post office during the year ending June 30, 1890, was 125,155,000, of which 106,751 were registered, with declaration of value; of postal cards, 46,475,000; of circulars and printed matter, 176,839,000; of postal orders, 5,-648,000. The receipts for the year were 45,420,-000 lire, and the expenditures 39,245,000 lire.

On July 1, 1890, the length of the telegraph lines was 36,269 kilometres, and the length of the wires 134,305 kilometres. During the year ending June 30, 1890, there were dispatched 7,342,188 inland telegrams, and there were sent and received from abroad 1,501,053 telegrams.

Cabinet Crises.—The financial question was the cause of the resignation of the Cabinet. The difficulty was as to how the deficit in the new budget was to be covered. Signor Colombo, the Minister of Finance, insisted that the extraordinary expenditures for the War Department should be cut down, and would not hear of new taxes or economies. The Minister of War declared that it was impossible to reduce the expenditures on the army, and, as no agreement could be reached, Prime Minister di Rudini tendered the resignation of the whole Cabinet on April 14, 1892. The King immediately charged him with the reconstruction of the Cabinet, but after long deliberations the ministers were convinced that the deficit should not be covered by retrenchments in the military department, and the old ministry was prevailed upon to stay, with the exception of the Minister of Finance, who resigned, and whose place was filled temporarily by Signor Luzatti, Minister of the Treasury. On the reopening of the Chamber of Deputies, on May 4, 1892, Premier di Rudini explained the ministerial crisis, and announced that the deficit would be partially covered by slight economies in the estimates for the War Department, and that bills would be introduced for selling national property, for establishment of a credit for the railroad treasury, and for establishing a monopoly on matches. After two days of hot and exciting debates a motion of confidence in the Cabinet regarding these statements was put, and was defeated by a vote of 193 to 185. Premier di Rudini then tendered the resignation of the members of his Cabinet, which was accepted by the King on May 6, and Signor Giolitti was charged with the formation of a new Cabinet. After a long delay the new ministers were announced to be the following: Premier, Minister of the Interior, and Secretary of the Treasury *ad interim*, Signor Giolitti; Minister for Foreign Affairs, Signor Brin; Minister of Justice, Signor Bonacci; Minister of Finance, Signor Ellena; Minister of War, Gen. Pelloux; Minister of Marine, Admiral Racoret de St. Bon; Minister of Public Works, Signor Genala; Minister of Agriculture, Signor Lacava; Minister of Public Instruction, Signor Martini; Minister of Posts and Telegraphs, Signor Finocchiaro Aprile.

The Chamber, which had been adjourned during the crisis, met again on May 25, and the new Premier laid before it the programme of the Government, which he said was intended to reduce the finances to order without imposing fresh burdens, if it was possible. On a motion of confidence in the new Cabinet being asked, the Government was sustained by a vote of 169 to 160. Signor Giolitti informed the Chamber the next day that the action of the Chamber did not indicate such support as would be needed to carry the ministry safely through the existing difficulties, and that the ministers had offered their resignations, which the King had refused to accept. He therefore asked the Chamber to pass the most urgent bills now before it, and to grant to the Government a vote on account for the next six months. On June 11 a preliminary budget for six months was voted by the Chamber, 451 deputies being present—a number larger than any since 1878. The Chamber adjourned *sine die* on June 15.

The Elections.—The action of the Government in asking for a preliminary budget indicated the dissolution of the Chamber; it became evident that under the present combination of the Parliament important reforms of the finances could not be carried through, and that a strong Cabinet, which could place the country on a sound financial basis, could only be obtained by an appeal to the country. The Chamber was dissolved on Oct. 10, 1892, and new elections were ordered for Nov. 6. The decree dissolving the Chamber was preceded by a report of the ministers, setting forth the policy of the Government and the measures proposed for the solution of the financial difficulty. Extensive retrenchments are to be made in the War Department, in the distribution of the expenses for building canals and roads, and in pensions. By economizing in these departments it is estimated that the deficit of the budget for 1892-'93, which is estimated to be about 37,700,000 lire, will not only be covered, but that there will be a surplus of 6,000,000 lire; while the budget for 1893-'94, with a deficit of 50,800,000 lire, will close in equilibrium. In order to prepare the way for taxation reforms, the report proposes a Government monopoly on petroleum.

The Government was decidedly victorious in the elections. Out of a total of 508 Deputies, the Left carried 236 seats; the Right, 69 seats; the Left Center, 59 seats; the Right Center, 36 seats; the Center, 45 seats; the Advanced Radicals, 16 seats; the Egalitarian Radicals, 35 seats; the Socialists, 6 seats; and 6 seats were carried by members whose politics were doubtful.

Opening of the Chamber.—The new Chamber of Deputies was opened by King Umberto on Nov. 23, 1892. In referring to the Columbus festivities at Genoa, the King said that the honor in which the navigator was held by representatives of civilized nations was calculated to inspire Italy with legitimate pride. With regard to the financial situation, the speech urged the necessity of balancing revenue and expenditure without recourse to fresh taxation. Several reform bills would be laid before the Chamber, the sole object of which was to distribute more equitably the pecuniary burdens borne by the Italian people. The speech announced reforms of the universities and the public schools, as well as judicial reforms; it also proposed the regulation and termination of canal and railroad works, and the introduction of social reforms. In conclusion the King said:

King Vittorio Emanuele could cherish with predilection the ambition of giving to the Italians a fatherland and realize his desires. I cherish the ambition of seeing my name linked with the economical and intellectual regeneration of the country, and of seeing Italy stong, prosperous, and great, as she hovered before the eyes of those of her children who suffered and died for their country.

Difficulty with the United States.—The difficulty which had arisen between Italy and the United States from the lynching of Italian subjects at New Orleans on March 14, 1891, was brought to a close. After an exchange of notes between the Marquis Imperiali, the Secretary of the Italian Legation at Washington, and Mr. Blaine, the United States Secretary of State, the United States Government tendered the Marquis Imperiali the sum of $25,000 for distribution among the families of the victims, accompanied by a note from Mr. Blaine declaring that, although the wrong was not committed directly by the United States, the latter nevertheless regarded it as a solemn duty, which the National Government fulfilled with great pleasure, to pay to Italy a satisfactory indemnity, to be distributed by the Italian Government. He expressed the hope that this arrangement might close an unfortunate incident, and that the good relations formerly existing between Italy and the United States might be firmly re-established, and that nothing might again arise to disturb them. The Marquis Imperiali, in his reply acknowledging Mr. Blaine's declarations, said that the Italian Government, which had already been happy to take note of the terms in which President Harrison referred to the matter in his Message to Congress, now considered the indemnity as sufficient reparation without prejudice to actions at law which might be brought by the aggrieved parties, and was happy to renew cordial relations with the United States. Baron de Fava, Italian minister at Washington, and Mr. Porter, United States minister at Rome, who had left their places at the rupture of diplomatic relations, returned to their respective posts in April.

Sanitary Conference.—An International Sanitary Conference was opened in Venice on Jan. 5, 1892, by the Under Secretary of State for Foreign Affairs, Count Arco, its president. The object of the conference was to ascertain to what extent the European powers were disposed to accept the protocol adopted by Austria and England, permitting English ships, whether clean or infected, to pass through the Suez Canal without detention, subject to certain conditions. The French delegates presented a counter-project, which consisted in the substitution of disinfection for quarantine in regard to commercial vessels which may arrive infected at Suez, ships conveying pilgrims to be specially treated in accordance with their condition. Passage of everything to which cholera can not be imputed is to be permitted without question. The cargo and ship, as incapable of contracting disease, go free, only those parts of the ship which may have been in actual contact with the disease being subject to disinfection, which, with ships provided with a medical service and disinfecting requisites, is to be effected without external interference. Cases of actual cholera arriving at Suez must undergo treatment at the establishment provided, or to be provided there. The project of the French delegates was adopted by the Conference, with slight alterations, and the protocol was signed by the 33 delegates, presenting 15 different countries, on Jan. 30. As the Government of Egypt maintains its absolute prerogative in the matter, the decision of the conference was only of moral importance, but the agreement of the chief powers will probably determine the decision of Egypt.

Red Cross Convention.—The fifth conference of the Society of the Red Cross was opened in Rome on April 21, 1892, by the president of the Italian association, Count di Somaglia. The conference was attended by delegates from all the European countries except Turkey, from the United States, and Japan. A resolution, expressing the desire of the conference of having the signatories of the Geneva convention extend the activity of the society to naval wars, was adopted. Other resolutions passed, expressing the desire of the conference, were : The transportation, free of charge and duty, of natural products collected by the society and sent to countries at war with each other; the training of nurses and of carriers of the wounded in time of peace ; the study of electric light in the sanitary service. It was further decided that in case of a war beyond the seas, where both countries carrying on war were signatories of the Geneva convention, the aid of the society must be given ; but before giving aid, where only one country has signed, the other country had to bind itself to comply with the rules of the society.

Colonies.—Italian colonies are confined to Africa, where Italy owns several tracts and has established a protectorate over others. Her possessions include the country around Massowah, with Keren and Asmara, the Dahlak archipelago, and the Assab Bay territory.

Italian influence is claimed over the territory of the Habab, Bogos Beni-Amer, and others; over the territory of the Danakil, including the sultanate of Aussa ; over Somali and Gallaland, according to a treaty with England concluded in 1891; and over the Kingdom of Abyssinia, in virtue of a treaty for mutual protection entered into between King Menelek II, of Abyssinia, and King Umberto I, of Italy, in 1889. The total estimated area of the Italian protectorates is 312,000 square miles, and the population 5,400,-000. The total Italian possessions on the Red Sea were constituted as the colony of Evitrea, with an independent administration and management of its own finances. A civil and military governor is the chief executive, and is assisted by three councilors, nominated by the King.

The estimated revenue of the colony for 1890–'91 amounted to 1,313,300 lire, and the expenditures to 2,960,000 lire ; the deficit of 1,646,-700 lire is to be covered by contributions of the Italian Government. Pasturing is the chief occupation of the people, who lead an essentially nomadic life ; but pearl fishing is carried on along the coast and the Dahlak archipelago. The trade of Massowah amounted to 14,980,041 lire in 1890, and in 1889, 2,442 vessels, of 213,955 tons, entered, and 2,519 vessels, of 219,712 tons, cleared that port. In the year 1889–'90 the post office at Massowah handled 258,810 pieces of mail matter.

J

JAPAN, a country in the north Pacific Ocean, east of Siberia, Corea, and China. Geographically, Dai Nippon, as the natives call it, is an archipelago. The empire is a limited constitutional monarchy, governed by the hereditary Emperor, Mutsuhito, born Nov. 3, 1852, the one hundred and twenty-third of the line of mikados, in connection with ministries and the Diet. The Constitution was promulgated Feb. 13, 1889, and the fourth session of the Diet began Nov. 29, 1892.

Area and Population.—With a coast line of 17,575 miles, 4,882 of which belong to Hondo, Japan is well furnished with facilities for sustaining a large population by means of sea food. The area of 155,962 square miles in 1890 was politically divided into 47 prefectures. The average population of a prefecture is 860,712. On Dec. 31, 1890, there were 40,453,461 natives counted in the census, of whom 20,431,097 were males and 20,022,364 were females. These were divided into the three classes of nobles, gentry, and commons—3,768 nobles, 2,008,641 gentry, and 38,441,052 commons. In 1890, 9,062 foreigners, of whom 1,701 were English, 889 Americans, and 4,975 Chinese, lived at the ports opened by treaty, and by special permission in a few other places.

Finances.—The budget for 1891–'92 shows a total revenue of $80,701,473, and a total expenditure of $77,063,748. The receipts are : From taxes on land, $38,771,339 ; saké brewing and sale, $15,588,657; customs, $4,479,096; tobacco, $1,-884,861; internal revenue, $3,673,297; profits on Government industries, $9,262,709, and from taxes on banks and societies, licenses, etc. The

chief items of expense are : Interest on public debts of all sorts and expenses in the nature of debt, $17,829,890; provincial administration, $4,944,836; colonization of Hokkaido, $1,648,-913; extraordinary expenses, $9,278,315; and for the various ministries: War, $12,507,162; navy, $5,712.471; justice, $3,692,537; communications, $4,684,205; finance, $3,041,600; civil list, $3,206,811 ; pensions, $1,027,847; payment of public debt, $3,540,980. The public debt in 1891 was $306,600,727, including $31,370,072 in paper money. In 1890 there were in circulation $1,724,082 in gold yen, $7,226,416 in silver, and $2,100,000 in copper and nickel ; total, $11,050,-498. The total output from the mint sent into circulation from November, 1870, to 1890 was: Gold, $61,379,795 ; silver, $92,391,829 ; copper, $12,289,550 ; nickel, $2,100,000 ; making a grand total of $168,161,174. Of paper money in circulation, April 1, 1891, besides $31,370,072 in national treasury notes, there were $25,461,713 of national bank notes, and $71,948,671 silver certificates of the Bank of Japan, making a total of $128,780,456. In 1882 the national treasury notes aggregated $105,635,228, the reduction in volume being steady until 1891 or the present time. Local taxes in the various prefectures on land, houses, patents, etc., amounted to $15,081,-130 in 1890–'91, and expenditures to $14,965,-757. The chief prefectural expenses were : For public works, $3,759,556; police, $3,688,349 ; prisons, $2,901,109 ; education, $1,193,379 ; subprefectural administration, $1,842,922, etc. Communal or township revenues aggregated $18,-

987,799, and expenditures $17,792,372. In 1889-'90, $21,805,736 were distributed for the relief of various victims of accident, inundation, earthquake, shipwreck, etc., or remitted in taxes to the poor or incapable, the expense being borne out of the national and local treasuries. In the budget for 1893 the revenue is fixed at $85,431,-456, and the expenditure at $83,759,967. The items of revenue are: Taxes, $66,676,136; licenses and fees, $2,173,089; receipts from Government industries, $10,625,659; extraordinary revenues, $4,788,844, etc. In expenses the Crown receives $3,000,000; Foreign Affairs, $689,153; Home Department, $7,875,096; treasury, $28,586,197; war, $12,856,631; navy, $5,915,586; justice, $3,-635,320; education, $1,045,975; agriculture, $1,-062,134; communications, $5,929,617; extraordinary expenditures, $13,164,255.

Army and Navy.—The number of military functionaries in Government pay in 1889 was 247,237, of whom 528 are superior officers, 3,959 officers, 8,294 noncommissioned officers, 1,478 students, 230,632 soldiers and military workers, and 1,716 clerks or office men. Of young men enrolled for conscription there were 360,357, or 7.70 in every 1,000 inhabitants, of whom 5.79 per cent. were selected for active service or the reserve, while 63.52 per cent. were exempted. The actual number of men under arms in the six military districts is nearly 60,000. In 1890 there were 14,039 men in the employ of the Navy Department, of whom 250 were superior officers, 1,048 officers, 1,977 noncommissioned officers, 316 students, 9,083 marines, and 1,365 office employees. Of men-of-war, there were 34, with 198 guns, manned by 5,991 officers and men.

Trade.—The aggregate volume of foreign trade has increased enormously during the past decade, though a marked decrease in imports is noted (we give the figures in silver *yen* or "dollars"). The grand total for 1891 is considerably larger than that of 1890, being $142,454,540 against $138,332,086, but the trade itself shows a wide difference, for whereas in 1890 the imports exceeded the exports by $25,000,000, the conditions were reversed in 1891, when the exports were $16,500,000 larger than the imports, these variations being caused principally by fluctuations in the trade in silk. The imports of 1891, however, being $19,000,000 less than those of 1890, and smaller than those of any year since 1887, show a bad market for foreign goods. In cotton yarns, for example, the imported value in 1888 was $13,662,004; in 1890, $9,928,060; and in 1891, $5,589,289. In gray shirtings, the fall from $2,332,564 in 1888 to $1,656,680 in 1891 is noticeable. On the other hand, raw cotton is in greater demand, making a new trade with the United States, the imports for 1889, 1890, and 1891 being as follow:

COUNTRIES.	1891.	1890.	1889.
British India	$3,881,972	$1,114,164	$47,884
China	2,571,666	2,665,465	3,398,790
United States	1,011,518	351,875	18,489

The cause of this increase in imported raw cotton and of decrease in imported yarn is the establishment of native cotton mills. In 1883 there were but 2 cotton-spinning mills in Japan; in January, 1892, there were 36 in operation, in

29 of which 377,000 spindles employed 4,640 men and 14,012 women, turning out 5,000,000 pounds of yarn a month. The special cause of this improvement, apart from Japan's excellent situation, the low price of coal and labor, with the absence of factory laws permitting the work to be carried on day and night, is the great fall in the price of silver, which has caused an enhancement in the price of English yarns when brought to Japan. In the volume of foreign trade for 1891 Great Britain has lost her leading position, and is now distanced by the United States, which had a total of $36,635,802, or $10,000,000 in excess of 1890, while Great Britain fell behind nearly $6,500,000, and now figures for only $25,629,187. It will also be seen that in the import of raw cotton the Chinese staple has fallen into disfavor, while the demand for American cotton has greatly increased. In raw silk the United States took $17,000,000 in 1891, against $9,000,000 in 1890; and of silk handkerchiefs 750,632 dozen, valued at $1,823,877. The total volume of trade with Great Britain and her colonies is set down at $52,500,000. Of trade at the various ports, Yokohama shows an increase of nearly $6,000,000, Osaka of $1,000,000, while Kobe, Nagasaki, and Hakodate show a falling off, and the minor ports opened to trade slight increase. The trade movement in 1891, from the Japanese point of view, is shown in the official compilation set forth by the Revenue Bureau of the Department of Finance:

VALUE OF EXPORTS AND IMPORTS (IN SILVER YEN).

GOODS.	Exports.	Imports.
Dutiable goods	51,073,752	54,822,791
Duty-free goods	26,841,875	8,104,478
Goods for use of vessels	1,611,645	
Total	79,527,272	62,927,269
Grand total		142,454,540
Excess of exports over imports		16,600,003

VALUE OF EXPORT AND IMPORT OF GOLD AND SILVER.

MOVEMENT.	Gold.	Silver.	Total.
Export	230,446	1,222,518	1,452,964
Import	283,144	18,605,382	13,888,526
Excess of import			12,435,562

COMPARISON OF VALUE.

ACCOUNT.	Exports.	Imports.	Total.
Government		955,085	958,085
Japanese	8,770,765	14,276,880	28,047,145
Foreigners	69,144,862	47,692,804	116,887,666

Totals of trade at the ports: Yokohama, $78,-523,709; Kobe, $47,434,219; Nagasaki, $6,774,-455; Osaka, $5,065,807; Shimonoséki, $1,722,-840; Hakodate, $856,189. Ten other ports are now open to direct foreign trade, though not to foreign residence.

VALUE OF COMMODITIES IMPORTED AND EXPORTED.

COUNTRIES.	Exports.	Imports.	Total.
United States	$29,795,755	$6,840,048	$36,635,803
Great Britain	5,633,137	19,996,051	25,629,188
France	15,120,075	2,884,025	17,954,101
Hong-Kong	12,578,695	5,089,606	17,668,301
China	5,825,851	8,798,428	14,624,280
Germany	1,456,596	5,127,476	6,584,072
Corea	1,466,040	4,032,922	5,498,962
British America	1,342,667	20,835	1,363,502

Adding these columns, after including the values of trade with about 20 other countries, we find the total valuation of imports ($77,915,627) and exports ($62,927,895) (except goods for use of vessels) $140,842,895. In the table of imports of gold and silver Great Britain leads with $6,569,242; China pays $3,495,623; the United States, $1,829,496; and British India, $1,441,000. In exports, 1891, silk figured at $38,558,304, of which $32,175,891 was for raw product and $5,372,413 for manufactured articles; grain, $10,933,467; drugs, $2,506,116; metals, $5,409,773; tea, $7,033,050; coal, $4,749,732; porcelain. etc., $10,070,681. Of imports, the principal articles and values were: Machinery. etc., $4,664,881; drugs, $2,225,767; dyes and paints, $1,218,201; grain and seeds, $6,106,537; metals and metal work, $5,141,892; oil and wax, $4,971,784; sugar, $7,811,307; raw cotton, $8,199,251; textiles, $15,620,732; sundries, $2,248,494. In kerosene oil the import has diminished, chiefly at the expense of the United States, as Russia now supplies one fifth of the whole amount. The import market for two years is thus shown :

SOURCES.	1890.	1891.
	Cases.	Cases.
From America..................	3,611,115	3,250,395
From Russia....................	655,288	769,818
From other countries	10	8
Total.......................	4,266,358	4,048,216

The total bulk, 40,984,206 gallons, was valued at $4,525,615, of which 9,978,180 gallons, valued at $853,385, were Russian. In the iron trade, except nails and a few rails, Great Britain has the monopoly. In spite of the great enterprise shown and the money expended by the Japanese in opening new markets, the tea exported, with the exception of that sent to their old customers, America, China, Corea. and Great Britain, reached a value of less than $3,000 for all grades of leaf, dust, and lump tea.

Agriculture and Industry.—The condition of native industry and the manufacture of articles intended for home consumption is shown in the comparative tables given in the "Résumé Statistique," now annually published in Tokio. In 1887 the land under arable cultivation was nearly 12,000,000 acres, of which 60 per cent. was cultivated by proprietors and 40 per cent. by tenant farmers. Between the years 1880 and 1890 the total cereal product annually varied from 50,000,000 to 80,000,000 bushels, the crop in 1890 being 54,000,000 bushels. The increase of oxen and horses does not keep pace with that of the population, though steam transit by land and sea partly accounts for it. In 1889, 1,021,503 cattle and 1,541,342 horses were owned. Of tea, in 1889 over 55,260,512 pounds were raised, much being consumed beyond the reported figures. Of saké, in 1890, 152,689,040 gallons were brewed, the industry employing 950,763 persons. Textiles to the value of $3,640,667 were reported in 1889; ceramics, $3,208,392; pipes, $1,840,259. In mining, which is under private enterprise, the state having abandoned this industry in 1884, the chief metals brought up and refined are silver, iron, and copper. In 1887, 865,189 persons employed 277,698 fishing boats, the marine prod-

ucts of all sorts being valued in 1889 at $11,015,851, among which sardines to the weight of nearly 240,000,000 pounds are noted. In 1889 20,000,000 bushels of salt were manufactured, chiefly from sea brine, by evaporation on sand meadows covering 19,728 acres, followed by leaching and reduction.

In her foreign exhibits Japan has been represented 14 times, the largest quantity of exhibits, weighing 425 tons, having been sent to the Philadelphia Centennial Exposition. For Chicago, instead of the 1,000 tons expected to be sent, 6,638 tons were forthcoming. For the 50,350 cubic feet allowed for exhibits and 84,000 feet for buildings, selling booths, etc., the authorities have permitted the export of only 1,750 tons, the reduction not being made at a uniform rate, but guided by the articles themselves. Of the World's Fair Commission in Chicago, Mr. S. Tejima is commissioner, who has T. Uchida and Y. Yambei for his secretaries, and 25 workmen, with architect, superintendent of construction, etc. The Japanese building is modeled after the famous Phœnix Palace in Kioto. the three portions being devoted to the art of the Tokugawa (1604–1868), Ashikaga (1333–1573), and the Fujiwara (9th to 14th century) period.

Transportation.—In the development of her railway system and the common roads, Japan is providing not only for her military but also her commercial necessities. On Sept. 30, 1891, there were in the railways owned by the Government $32,760,840 invested, the length projected being 551 miles. But most of the railroads are owned by private corporations, of which 12 are in actual operation, with a total capital of $77,590,000, and an expense of $20,951,112.. The length of finished road in the empire is 1,698 miles, the amount expended being $53,711,952. The rolling stock, consisting of 186 engines, 900 passenger and 2,791 freight cars, conveyed, in 1891, 20,700,327 persons, and about 3,000,000,000 pounds of freight and baggage, 5,303,301 miles. The total receipts were $6,495,850, and expenses $3,629,942. The vehicles drawn or propelled by man, horse. ox, and dog power numbered, in 1889, 934,784. On the water, in 1889, 564 steam vessels, of 88,816 tons and of 88,816 horse power, with 843 vessels in European style, of 52,328 tons, were owned by Japanese, besides 18,796 sailing vessels of native design. with a capacity of 16,380,790 bushels, and 617,900 small boats. Total number of iron ships, 93 ; of iron covered with wood, 14. First class men-of-war and commercial ships are now designed and built by the Japanese. The commercial marine, on ships of European form, comprises 7,988 men, of whom 159 are foreigners. Of shipwrecks, 335, with 114 deaths, are reported for 1889. In the national lighthouse system, Jan. 1, 1891, are 85 lights permanently maintained, an increase of 8 in 1891 being noted, besides 55 local beacons, with sirens, foghorns, meteorological stations, daily weather reports, signals, etc. In 1889, 183,600,105 letters and papers were carried in the mails, 3,332,687 telegraphic dispatches sent and received, of which 38,881 were to or from foreign countries.

Political Administration.—On the pay roll of the National Government in 1890 were the names of 50,360 civil servants, of whom 160 were of the rank of *choku*, appointed directly by the Emperor, 3,496 *sô*, appointed by the Council of State and reported to the Emperor, 25,942 *han*, appointed by the heads of departments, 2,189 police or prison agents, and 18,573 miscellaneous salaried employees. Of the whole, 30,316 serve the national administration directly, and 20,044 the local authorities, the former receiving in salaries $640,473, and the latter $359,674 ; the total public expense for civil service being $1,000,147. In the national election system necessitated by Japan's representative institutions, there were, in 1890. 257 electoral districts, 300 Deputies to be elected to the House of Commons or Representatives, 453.895 electors. or 12 to every 1,000 of the population. The number of electors not voting was 32,689, or 7 out of every 100. The total of ballots cast was 421,206. As yet, the islands of Hokkaido (Yezo) and Okinawa (Riu Kiu) are not organized under the electoral law. In 1890, 2,230 persons sat in the 42 prefectural and 3 imperial city councils. Male citizens aged twenty-five, domiciled three years in their districts, who pay $10 in local taxes, are eligible to these councils, and in 1890 these persons numbered 755.412, while those who had the right to vote numbered 1,409,510. Japan has a total of 136 persons on her foreign consular and legational staff, and she treats on her own soil with 116 foreigners representing the various treaty powers.

The Imperial Diet.—The second session of the Diet opened Nov. 26, 1891. and. after a deadlock between the Government and the Opposition, the lower house was dissolved and the upper house prorogued. During the three months following, after violent agitation, in which more than 40 newspapers were suspended, and election riots, in which 20 persons were killed and 140 wounded, a majority hostile to the Government was returned. Of the 297 members elected to the lower house, 108 are agriculturists, 61 members of prefectural assemblies, 17 barristers, 16 bankers, 13 journalists, and 11 business men. On the whole, there is a decided increase of men who have had practical experience in executive office or in the local assemblies, and the rise of a distinct class of politicians is shadowed forth, with a decrease of barristers and journalists. The results of the election ultimately forced the resignation of the members of the Cabinet, compelled the Government to abandon the attempted prosecution of two Liberals, Counts Okuwa and Itagaki, and to institute an inquiry into governmental interference with the elections. A new coalition Cabinet, consisting mostly of ex-ministers, was formed, and is believed to be one of the strongest in commanding popular confidence organized since 1889. The Diet was convoked May 2, and on the 16th prorogued for one week, on account of its vote of censure passed on the Government. Matters progressed favorably in the Diet on its reassembling. On the 21st the Peace Preservation Regulations were again put in force, and 141 persons, mostly the young ultra-patriotic " fire eaters " called *soshi*, and. as a rule, graduates of the private schools, against which the hostility of the Government is constantly manifest, were expelled from the capital, and ordered not to come within 20 miles of it while the Diet should be in session. On June 15 the ses-

sion closed, after a dispute between the houses, which the Emperor, to whom it was ferred, decided in giving to the upper hous equal right with the lower house to inter with the budget. Of the eleven bills pas eight were Government measures, one was for railway loan of $60,000,000 to be raised in tw years, looking to the purchase of railways owned by private corporations, one for the es lishment of a parcel post, and one postponing new civil and commercial codes until 1896. relegates the question of treaty revision to background, the Japanese not being ready have brought home to their bosoms and busi the Teutonic and Christian ideas that lie at basis of Western law. In Asiatic society unit is the family, and the freedom of the i vidual and the manifold relations growing of it are not practically known, as in Europe America. Five questions of precedent, and vast importance, hitherto unsettled, were deci by this session of the Diet, and the days w Japanese ministers can rule without taking count of the press and of Parliament are pr bly forever over. During August the new co tion ministry, being formed, proceeded to w the local prefectural governors against inter ence in local and national elections, and to miss or change a number of them. Owing the absence of the Portuguese *chargé d'affa* from Japan. the Government, in an impe ordinance dated July 14. denounced its righ extra-territoriality and declared it forfei This means the nullification of the clause the treaty of Aug. 3, 1860, connected with c sular jurisdiction. Portugal has protested. Diet reassembled Nov. 29, being formally ope as usual by the Emperor in person.

Important Events.—Earthquakes, typhoc inundations, smallpox, and fires causing gr loss of life and property were frequent dur 1892. The National Exposition named for 1 has been indefinitely postponed. Dr. Gottfr Wagener, a German inventor, who since 1 had been greatly influential in improving Ja nese artistic and mechanical processes and pr nets, died in Tokio, Nov. 8. and was post mously honored by the Mikado. Dr. J. Hepburn, the American scholar, translator, l cographer, and physician, in active benevol service at Yokohama since 1859, the best kno foreigner in Japan, after many farewell tok of appreciation, sailed for San Francisco, Oct. The death of Gen. Yamada, Minister of Just and hero in the Restoration War in 1868 the Satsuma rebellion of 1877. was made pul Nov. 15. The grotesque mummery of act toward his corpse as if he were a living man. order to invest him, before burial, with sig marks of imperial favor, including confection and a decoration, was kept up in his case. funeral on the 17th was one of gorgeous magn cence and vast expense. The usual milit manœuvres took place at Utsunomiya late October. On Dec. 1, in the Diet, it was nounced by the Minister of State. Watan that a reduction of the land tax to the amou of $3,750,000 was to be made by reassessment taxable values. Thus frankly the Governm has accepted the great fiscal measure long tated by the *jiyu-to* party.

JEWS. The year's record is largely a recital of incidents connected with the Russian persecutions, the continued activity of anti-Semites in Germany, Austria-Hungary, and France; the emigration problem; the founding of colonies in the Argentine; and the slow evolution of form, method, and organization in connection with the settlement of Russian exiles. The picture has its bright colors, however, in the charitable efforts made in England, Germany, France, and elsewhere to aid the immigrants—efforts in which all creeds participated, although the heaviest share of the burden fell upon the Jews themselves. In America, despite the claims made by the newly arrived immigrants, much interest in religious and educational affairs was manifested. A marked development along the lines of commercial activity. The building of new synagogues, orphan asylums, and hospitals, the founding of an American Jewish historical society, and the planting of new colonies for the Russians, are gratifying evidences of growth.

The Russian problem presented a new phase, owing to the outbreak of cholera in Hamburg, with its appearance on incoming steamers from Europe, which produced a partial embargo on immigration from infected ports, and the massing of thousands of intending immigrants in many of the capitals abroad or on the Russian frontiers. Happily the pestilence was checked. In Russia it decimated whole districts, but the pale occupied by the Jews was almost wholly free from the disease—a striking similarity to the biblical account of the Egyptian plagues, which spared the Jewish province of Goshen. United States commissioners of immigration were sent to Europe in 1891 to investigate the causes that incite immigration to the United States, and their report was published in 1892. Col. Weber and Dr. Kempster gave the history of their experiences in Russia— a long, painful record of facts, described without passion or prejudice, but abundantly convincing as to the cruelties practiced in the land of the Czar. The story of the Americans' visit to the Jewish pale, the incidents of their journey, the yearning expressed for America on the part of the people, Jews and others, the sufferers' hope in America as the land of their salvation, forms material for a spirit-stirring epic. The publication in book form of Harold Frederic's letters from Russia to the New York "Times" was also a confirmation of the stories of persecution. Early in the year Col. Goldsmid, of London, became director of the Hirsch colonies in the Argentine, whose condition had grown unsatisfactory. Under his management a more effective organization was established, idlers and malcontents were weeded out, and a gratifying change took place in the character of the colonists and their work. The American colonies in charge of the Hirsch fund in New Jersey and Connecticut, numbering about 2,500 souls, engaged in farming, dairying, and light industries, make a satisfactory exhibit. During the year, according to the latest statistics, from November, 1891, to November, 1892, the Jewish steerage immigration to this country reached 52,134, of whom 18,815 were children; 38,504 remained in New York, and 32,000 claimed attention from the United Hebrew Charities. Of the total number arrived, 41,456 were Russians. The arrival at other ports did not exceed 6,000 for the period named. Only 79 were returned by the Government as coming within the list of barred cases.

Among incidents of note in the record of the Jews abroad may be mentioned the fiftieth anniversary of the Reform Synagogue of London; the four hundredth anniversary of the settlement of the Jews in Turkey; the trial and acquittal of a Jewish butcher of Xanten, Germany, on the mediæval charge of murdering a Christian child for ritualistic purposes; the spirited words of the Pope against anti-Semitism, which had revived in France owing to M. Drumont's writings, and in Germany owing to Rector Ahlwardt's accusation against a Jewish gun-manufacturing firm. The charge of supplying defective guns was not proved, and the rector was sentenced to several months' imprisonment. The production of a genuine letter from Herr Lowe, of the firm, to Boulanger, written many years before, offering to supply France with machinery for the production of guns, has strengthened the anti-Semites, whose cause, however, has been rigorously censured by the Emperor. The opening of the Jaffa-Jerusalem Railroad is chronicled. Rev. Dr. Adler, of London, summoned a conference of ministers to consider modifications in the ritual, but little of any moment was effected. The proposed settlement of Midian by a Jewish colony proved a dismal failure at the start. The death of Capt. A. Mayer, of Paris, at the hands of the Marquis de Mores, in a duel, caused much excitement in France, which extended to the Chamber of Deputies. The marquis was tried for murder, but acquitted. Capt. Cremieux-Foa, who challenged the marquis in his turn, was sent to Dahomey by the Government, where he died in battle as a French soldier. The late David Lewis left £350,000 to the city of Liverpool for workingpeople's homes, without distinction of creed. Prospero Moise Loria, of Milan, bequeathed £600,000 for the erection of a home of employment for artisans out of work, irrespective of creed. The list of deaths included Lady Salomons, of London: Solomon Sehag, of London, who wrote a Hebrew grammar; Lady Julian Goldsmid at Cannes; Miss Frances Barnett, a communal worker of London, in her eighty-third year; Felix Joseph, art specialist, at Southsea, Wales; Baron Weisweiller, Paris; Rabbi E. Loeb, of Altona, Germany; Rabbi Terracini, of Asti, Italy; Rabbi J. Wolf, of Kalocsa, Hungary; Rabbi Jacob Levy, of Breslau, the lexicographer; Rabbi Tobia Foa, of Fiorenzusta, Italy; Rabbi Igel, of Czernowitz; Rabbi M. Wasserman, of Stuttgart; Rabbi Mosse, of Avignon, France; Rabbi B. Lichtenstein. New Zealand; Isidore Loeb, secretary of the Alliance Israelite Universelle; Dr. Elie Roshi Bey; Baron G. A. Gedalia, of Copenhagen; Baroness Hannah de Rothschild; Baroness Albert de Rothschild, of Vienna; Signor Isaac Pesaro Maurogonato, of Rome; Anton von Freistadler, Hungarian philanthropist; Prof. Jacob Lichel, of Prague: Baroness Joseph de Gunzbourgh, at Paris; Dr. A. Symons, at Rotterdam; Frau E. Henle, authoress, at Frankfort; Moritz Wahrmann, Hungarian statesman; Gerson Wolf, historian, at Vienna; Dr. Moritz Steinthal, physician, at Berlin; Albert Wolff and Millaud, French critics; Baron

Michael Erlanger, at Paris; Leon J. Gordon, Hebrew poet and journalist; Senior Sachs, Hebraist, at Paris; Hon. Michael Solomon, of Jamaica. New chief rabbis were elected in Denmark (David Simonsen), Belgium (Hermann Bloch), Milan (Alessandro da Fano), Cairo (Aaron ben Simeon).

In the United States the charitable activity can best be exhibited by a glance at the year's workings of the United Hebrew Charities of New York city. During the year ending Oct. 1, 1892, 8,295 new applications, representing a total of 31,978 persons, were received and acted upon, and 4,284 cases were investigated more than once. In addition, there were 1,368 persons who received help at the office who were homeless or wayfarers. Supplies were given to 4,900 cases, 5,047 persons were supplied with transportation, and 5,385 found employment, making a total of 48,678 persons assisted. Of those who found work, 80 per cent. were Russians, in 130 different branches of industry.

In the special employment bureau for Russian immigrants, for whose aid about $100,000 was raised by a general appeal, there were registered as seeking employment 3,237 workers, representing 5,831 persons to be supported. Employment was found in the various States for 2,733 persons, 218 were recommended to relief agencies in other cities, and 2,803 declined or were averse to accepting the places that were offered by reason of their unwillingness to leave New York.

The Central Conference of American Rabbis held two sessions, one in New York and one in Washington. In the former, special interest attached to the report of the Committee on Proselytes, which presented the following abstract of its report:

The committee maintains: 1. That there are known in history 3 initiatory rites for the proselyte to Judaism—the sacrificial, the ritual bath, and circumcision. 2. Neither of these rites is ordained or otherwise suggested in the Torah, Prophets, and Hagiographa. 3. They appear not in history and literature prior to the conquest of Judea by John Hyrcan, who decreed circumcision on the Edomites contrary to law and custom. 4. From that time initiatory rites became customary, but never became canon law, nor ever rabbinical law proper. 5. In the time of the Amoraim, without any lawful enactment, two rites—the sacrifice having been abolished—were considered necessary, but this never did and never could become canon law.

To this was joined a resolution that "a proselyte shall be lawfully accepted by any officiating rabbi and two associates upon signing a document containing a confession of faith and without any initiatory rites." After a heated debate, the following resolution was adopted by a vote of 21 to 6:

That the Central Conference of American Rabbis, assembled this day in this city of New York, considers it lawful and proper for any officiating rabbi, assisted by two or more associates, in the name and with the consent of the representatives of his congregation, to accept into the sacred covenant of Israel and declare fully affiliated any honorable and intelligent person who desires such affiliation, without any initiatory rite, ceremony, or observance whatever.

Further work done was in reference to a new prayer book and hymnal. At the Washington session both subjects were discussed, and addresses were given or papers read by Rev. A. Kaiser, Baltimore; Rev. Dr. I. M. Wise, Cincinnati; Rev. Dr. J. Silverman, New York; Rev. I. S. Moses, Chicago. At the thirteenth council of the Union of American Hebrew Congregations, held in Washington, action was taken in reference to participating in the religious congress at the World's Fair. During the session the senate and house were opened with prayer by Rev. Drs. Wise and Silverman.

The American Jewish Publication Society issued I. Zangwill's "Children of the Ghetto" and Dr. H. Zirndorf's "Some Jewish Women." No special part was taken in the Columbian anniversary save as American citizens, but the opportunity was utilized for forming an American Jewish Historical Society, with the Hon. Oscar S. Straus as president. At its first session, held in Philadelphia on Dec. 16, the following papers were presented: Dr. Cyrus Adler, "Jews in the American Plantations between 1600 and 1700," "Americana at the Anglo-Jewish Exhibition," "A Political Document of the Year 1800"; Rev. Henry Cohen, "Historical Notes on the Jews of Jamaica"; Dr. S. Solis-Cohen, "Note on David Hays, a Patriot of the Revolution"; Moses A. Dropsie, "Reminiscences concerning the Jews of Philadelphia"; Herbert Friedenwald, "Notes on Jews mentioned in the Journals of the Continental Congress"; J. H. Hollander, "Dr. Jacob Lumbrozo, of Maryland"; Prof. Morris Jastrow, Jr., "Notes on Jews of Philadelphia, from Published Annals"; Col. Charles C. Jones, Jr., "Settlement of the Jews in Georgia"; Max J. Kohler, "Beginnings of New York Jewish History"; Prof. J. B. McMaster, "On Methods of Historical Research"; Rev. Dr. S. Morais, "The First Jewish Congregation in Philadelphia"; Lucien Moss, "John Moss"; Barnet Phillips, "Note on Jews in the United States Navy"; N. Taylor Phillips, "A Landmark"; Hon. Simon W. Rosendale, "A Pennsylvania Document concerning the Franks Family"; David Sulzberger, "Notes on the Jewish Burial Grounds of Philadelphia."

A new hospital was dedicated in Denver, Col., and new orphan asylums in Philadelphia and Brooklyn, N. Y. Synagogues were dedicated in Chesterfield, Conn., Seattle, Wash., Fort Smith, Texas, New York city, Philadelphia, Kingston, N. Y., and Montreal.

Among the deaths were those of Rev. Liebman Adler, Chicago; David Hoffman, Mason Hirsch, Miss S. C. Peixotto, Philadelphia: Seligman Adler, J. Judelsohn, Miss Sophia Tobias, New York.

Rev. Dr. Kohut completed his new edition of a dictionary of the Talmud. Congregations in New York, Baltimore, Chicago, and Easton, Pa., celebrated their fiftieth anniversaries. The District Grand Lodge No. 3 of the B'nai B'rith order began a movement to establish a technical schoo .

K

KANSAS, a Western State, admitted to the Union Jan. 29, 1861; area, 82,080 square miles. The population, according to each decennial census, was 107,206 in 1860; 364,399 in 1870; 996,096 in 1880; and 1,427,096 in 1890. Capital, Topeka.

Government.—The following were the State officers during the year: Governor, Lyman U. Humphrey, Republican; Lieutenant-Governor, Andrew J. Felt; Secretary of State, William Higgins; Auditor, Charles M. Hovey; Treasurer, S. G. Stover; Attorney-General, John N. Ives; Superintendent of Public Instruction, George W. Winans; Superintendent of Insurance, William H. McBride; Railroad Commissioners, George T. Anthony, Albert R. Greene, and William M. Mitchell: Chief Justice of the Supreme Court, Albert H. Horton; Associate Justices, William A. Johnston and Daniel M. Valentine: Supreme Court Commissioners, Benjamin F. Simpson, J. C. Strang, and George S. Green. Attorney-General Ives was elected on the Democratic and Farmers' Alliance tickets; the other elective State officers are Republicans.

Finances.—The total bonded State debt at the close of 1892 was $801,000, of which $9,000 is held by the State University fund, and $536,-000, by the permanent school fund, leaving only $256,000 in the hands of individuals. The total municipal indebtedness is $37,817,755. Wyandotte County leads with a total debt of $2,624,-654. Leavenworth County is next, with $1,823,-510, while Atchison and Sedgwick Counties have the same amount, $1,117,000.

Valuation.—The assessed valuation of the State for 1892 was $342,580,471.82, against $342,-631,307.85 for 1891. In the assessment of 1891 were included 44,700,020 acres of land valued at $170,160,308.68; 1,231,143 town lots valued at $74,203,946.58; personal property valued at $47,401,227.25; and railroad property valued at $50,865,825.34. The rate of State taxation for 1892 was 3·5 mills for current State expenses and 0·2 mill for interest on the State debt.

Education.—The number of children of school age in the State in 1892 was ascertained to be 497,-022. There was apportioned among the several counties from the State school funds the sum of $263,421.66 for support of public schools, or an average of 53 cents for each pupil. At the State Agricultural College more than 500 students were enrolled in February, and at the State University the enrollment for the year was over 600.

Charities.—The Legislature of 1891 made an appropriation for a new building at the Ossawattomie Insane Asylum calculated to accommodate 300 patients. While this addition will afford some relief, yet after it is filled there will still remain in the homes, poorhouses, and private asylums of the State from 300 to 400 insane people. For the biennial period ending June 30, 1892, the average number of patients at the Topeka Asylum was 748, and at the Ossawattomie Asylum 510. The average *per capita* cost of maintaining the former institution was $154.43, and $159.19 for the latter. At the Asylum for Idiotic and Imbecile Youth the average number

of inmates for the same period was 101, and the average *per capita* cost $179.65. The Institution for the Deaf and Dumb had an average of 228 pupils, the average *per capita* cost being $166.50. At the School for the Blind the average number of pupils was 82, and the average *per capita* cost $251.15. The Soldiers' Orphans' Home during the period cared for 120 children on an average, at an average *per capita* cost of $155.32. The amounts appropriated by the Legislature and expended at these institutions for the biennial period are shown in the following table:

INSTITUTION.	Amount appropriated.	Amount expended.
Insane asylum at Topeka.........	$284,872 00	$256,606 26
Insane asylum at Ossawattomie...	183,518 00	170,896 52
Reform school...................	61,018 00	55,896 96
Institution for the deaf and dumb.	88,200 00	74,167 24
Institution for the blind.........	39,200 00	36,257 01
Institution for feeble-minded.....	39,262 96	84,619 13
Soldiers' Orphans' Home........	38,560 00	37,211 06
Industrial School for Girls.......	27,350 00	25,447 82
Total.	$711,975 96	$650,042 00

Prisons.—The appropriations for the State Penitentiary were $373,200.27 for the two years ending June 30, 1892. For the same period the expenditures were $297,409.47, leaving a balance of $75,790.89. The coal mine still furnishes profitable employment for many convicts and is in good condition. The output of coal during the two years was 3,350,411 bushels. In 1891 the sales of coal amounted to $67,639.45, and in 1892 to $54,379.66. The value of coal furnished to State institutions was $42,533.68. At the State Reform School there was an average of 214 inmates for the biennial period, who were supported at an average *per capita* cost of $143.50. At the Industrial School for Girls the average number of pupils was 85, and the average *per capita* cost $180.40.

State Banks.—The total resources on Sept. 1 of the 286 State banks doing business in the State were $24,431,081.97. Their liabilities included the following items: Capital stock, $8,150,588.19; surplus, $723,896.31; undivided profits, $361,649.58; individual deposits, $9,860,-354.13; bank and bankers' deposits, $148,261.50; demand certificates, $1,613,995.50; time certificates, $2,535,013.71.

Railroads.—For the year ending June 30, 1891, the total income of Kansas railroads was $136,038,151, and the total expenses $126,882,-092—net income, $9,156,059. There were paid out in dividends $7,623,864, leaving a surplus of $1,532,195 from the year's operations. The dividend was but 1·46 per cent. of the total capital stock. The railroad mileage of the State is about 8,900 miles.

Coal.—The coal output of Kansas for 1891, the largest ever recorded, amounted to 68,843,-114 bushels, the estimated value being $3,946,-920. Crawford County was the largest producer, putting out over 23,000,000 bushels.

Lead and Zinc.—The total product of lead in the State for 1891 was 7,204,420 pounds, valued at $180,100, and the zinc product 40,527,391 pounds, valued at $405,273. The product of zinc is more than one fourth of the total production of the United States. Lead and zinc are found only in Cherokee and Crawford Counties.

Agriculture.—The following table shows the acreage, amount, and value of several farm products in Kansas in 1891:

PRODUCTS.	Acres.	Product.	Value.
Winter wheat, bu...	3,582,006	56,170,694	$40,997,417 02
Spring wheat, bu...	151,922	2,879,959	1,599,342 07
Corn, bu...........	5,209,234	130,363,991	48,057,978 93
Oats, bu...........	1,298,745	39,904,443	10,594,457 48
Rye, bu...........	332,673	5,449,030	3,528,680 23
Barley, bu........	36,484	1,606,380	411,909 72
Irish potatoes, bu...	69,542	5,483,900	2,689,637 39
Castor beans, bu....	16,428	114,644	143,305 00
Sorghum...........	195,758	....	* 2,060,423 00
Flax, bu..	388,184	2,049,055	1,689,244 00
Millet and Hungarian, tons	308,093	693,405	2,583,620 00
Wool, lbs..........	....	1,578,093	284,218 74
Butter, lbs........	....	29,084,817	4,862,725 55

* Sirup and forage.

Political.—The People's Party State Convention met at Wichita on June 16, and nominated L. D. Lewelling for Governor, Percy Daniels for Lieutenant - Governor, R. S. Osborn for Secretary of State, Van Buren Prather for Auditor, W. H. Biddle for Treasurer, J. T. Little for Attorney-General, H. N. Gaines for Superintendent of Public Instruction, S. H. Allen for Associate Justice of the Supreme Court, and W. A. Harris for Congressman-at-large. The resolutions adopted approve the St. Louis platform and somewhat amplify its demands. They declare that government only is good where injury to one is the concern of all; that public news should be supplied by public agencies; that among other things the Government should provide are public telephones and telegraph lines, and a postal currency for convenience in transmitting small sums of money, and that, as nearly as practicable, the mail of all the people should be delivered at their homes free. They denounce the nonaction of the Republican State Senators regarding the Australian ballot bill, the maximum freight bill, and the bill for election of railroad commissioners by the people, and favor pensions for railroad employees injured in the company's service, to be paid by the companies and to be a first lien on their property.

On June 30 the Republican State Convention met at Topeka, and nominated Abram W. Smith for Governor on the fifth ballot. His competitors were E. N. Morrill and M. M. Murdock. For Lieutenant-Governor, Robert F. Moore was nominated; for Secretary of State, William C. Edwards; for Auditor, Blanche K. Bruce, Jr.; for Treasurer, John Bruce Lynch; for Attorney-General, Theodore F. Garver; for Superintendent of Public Instruction, James C. Davis; for Justice of the Supreme Court, Daniel M. Valentine. The declaration of principles included the following:

We are earnestly in favor of such legislation, State and national, as shall prevent gambling in food products and other necessaries of life.

We indorse the recommendation of the Postmaster-General for the Government control of the telegraph and telephone service, and we favor the free delivery of mail in the country as well as in towns and cities.

As the transportation of agricultural products begins at the farm, we favor such change in the road laws as will insure the better construction and supervision of all highways.

We favor the complete revision of the laws relating to assessment and taxation, and we believe that sound business principles demand that all property be assessed at its actual value.

We demand the enactment of a law making liberal provision for the representation of the State and a display of its resources at the World's Columbian Exposition.

We demand an amendment to the mortgage law so as to provide for a liberal right of redemption of all real property after sale under foreclosure of mortgage.

We demand the strictest legislation for preserving the purity of the ballot and prohibiting the corrupt use of money.

We favor the submission to a vote of the people of an amendment to the Constitution eliminating the disqualification of sex in the enjoyment of the elective franchise.

We favor the nonemployment of children under fourteen years of age in mines, workshops, and factories.

We disapprove the policy of blacklisting employees by railways or other corporations.

We insist that the great transportation companies, which derive their corporate existence from Kansas laws and their financial existence from Kansas trade and commerce, owe to the people of Kansas fair, equitable, and honest treatment in the matter of freight rates.

We also demand of Congress such amendments of the interstate commerce law as will give the people of Kansas and the West the benefits that would accrue to them from their location, and will prevent the railroads from rendering valueless the vast sums of money expended in improving the harbors of the Southwest, by charging the people of Kansas practically the same freight tariffs from the Gulf of Mexico, a distance of 700 miles, that they do from New York, 1,500 miles.

On July 6 the Democratic State Convention at Topeka, after a heated discussion, voted to adopt all the nominations made by the People's party three weeks before, both for the State offices and for presidential electors. The Democratic national ticket was approved, and resolutions were adopted, including the following:

That in our judgment the prohibitory amendment and the laws passed in pursuance thereof have not reduced the evils of intemperance, but have been the fruitful source of perjury, bribery, and injustice of every form. This constitutional amendment, and the laws passed to carry the same into effect, should be repealed, and a reasonable license law be substituted in their stead.

That we are in favor of liberal appropriations for the World's Columbian Exposition.

We demand that the next Legislature of this State enact a law which shall provide that railroad companies shall be liable for damages suffered by their employees by reason of injuries sustained by such employees in consequence of defects in road, tracks, or rolling stock or other negligence of a railroad company, whether such defect was known to such injured employees or not.

That it is the duty of the Legislature to enact such legislation as will provide for a just and equitable system of freight rates which shall extend to every locality in the State.

That the Democrats of Kansas favor the election of the Railroad Commissioners by the people.

On July 13 the Prohibitionists met in State convention, and nominated the following ticket:

For Governor, I. O. Pickering; for Lieutenant-Governor, H. F. Douthart; for Secretary of State, H. W. Stone; for Auditor, Gabriel Burdette; for Treasurer, Joel Miller; for Attorney-General, R. H. Nichols; for Superintendent of Public Instruction, Miss Ida Hodgdon; for Associate Justice of the Supreme Court, C. P. Stevens; for Congressman-at-Large, Rev. J. M. Monroe. Before election, the names of C. N. Howlett for Auditor, Robert L. Davidson for Attorney-General, and Alice M. Henderson for Superintendent of Public Instruction, were substituted for the first nominees.

The platform accuses the Republicans of acting in bad faith in regard to prohibition, and includes the following:

We deplore the number of pardons granted to persons convicted of violating the prohibitory law, both by the present and past administrations, and declare that the absolute power to grant pardons is as dangerous in a republican government as is absolute power to condemn and punish, and should not exist. All power of the executive to pardon should be limited and regulated by law.

We are opposed to the calling of a State constitutional convention as unnecessary expense, and an attempt to sugar-coat resubmission and force it unwittingly upon the people.

Our interstate commerce law should be amended so as to prohibit the introduction of intoxicants into prohibition territory.

No citizen should be denied the right to vote on account of sex, and we denounce the double dealing of the Republican party on this question, as shown by their legislative record.

To the action of the Democratic Convention in surrendering itself to the People's party exception was taken by a large number of Democrats, who refused to be bound by the judgment of the convention, and called a new State convention. At this convention, held in Topeka on Oct. 7, more than 500 delegates, representing about 50 counties, were present. It was deemed inadvisable to nominate candidates for State officers so late in the canvass, but an address to the democracy of the State was issued, advising the voters to defeat the ticket of the People's party, and a platform was adopted, of which the following is a portion:

The action of the State convention of July 6 in attempting to bind Democrats to the support of the so-called People's party State ticket was a crime without a parallel in the political history of our country.

We are opposed to legislation which will unnecessarily disturb the harmonious relations now existing between employer and employee, or which will deprive faithful and honest labor of its just reward.

We are in favor of a convention to revise our State Constitution.

We are opposed to the subtreasury and land-loan schemes, and to the governmental ownership of railroads.

The People's party ticket secured a plurality of the votes cast at the November election. For Governor, Lewelling received 163,507 votes; Smith, 158,075; and Pickering, 4,178. All the other People's party candidates, including Congressman-at-Large, were elected by small pluralities. The vote for presidential electors was as follows: People's party, 163,195; Republican, 157,241; Prohibitionist, 4,553. Of the 7 congressional districts, the Republicans carried 2 and the People's party 5.

In the State Senate of 1893 the People's party have a large majority; but in the House, 64 Republicans, 58 People's party men, 2 Democrats, and 1 Independent Republican were elected. Several seats in each House are contested.

The proposition to call a convention for the purpose of revising the State Constitution, which was submitted to the people at this election, was defeated by a vote of 118,491 in favor of, and 118,957 against it.

KENTUCKY, a Southern State, admitted to the Union June 1, 1792; area, 40,400 square miles; population in 1890, 1,858,635. Capital, Frankfort.

Government.—The following were the State officers during the year: Governor, John Young Brown, Democrat; Lieutenant-Governor, Mitchell C. Alford; Secretary of State, John W. Headley; Auditor, L. C. Norman; Treasurer, Henry S. Hale; Attorney-General, William J. Hendrick; Superintendent of Public Instruction, Edward P. Thompson; Insurance Commissioner, Henry T. Duncan; Register of the Land Office, G. B. Swango; Commissioner of Agriculture, C. Y. Wilson; Railroad Commissioners, C. C. McChord, C. B. Poyntz, and Urey Woodson; Chief Justice of the Court of Appeals, William H. Holt; Associate Justices, William S. Pryor, Joseph H. Lewis, and Caswell Bennett; Clerk of the Court of Appeals, Abram Addams.

Finances.—The Treasurer suspended payment of claims against the State June 30, the end of the fiscal year, in order to recuperate the funds to pay the $700,000 due the school fund on Oct. 1. There was $218,000 in the treasury, but a deficit of $300,000 in the general expenditure fund. The depletion of the treasury was due to the reduction of taxation by the last Legislature, followed by the long session of the Constitutional Convention and this year's session of the Legislature. It was expected that the suspension would last till October or November.

The deficit reported by the Auditor, May 17, was $79,891.77, and he estimated that it would be $200,000 at the close of the fiscal year.

The direct tax paid from the treasury to defray the expenses of the Government during the year was refunded in February. It amounted to $600,000. It was decided last year to have the sum placed to the credit of the common-school fund. It was turned in to meet the general expenses of the State, and the school fund will be paid 6 per cent. per annum on the amount.

Education.—The report of the Superintendent of Public Instruction for the year ending June 30, 1891, was issued in April. The number of white children of school age was 584,073; the aggregate of the school fund apportioned to them was $1,314,164.25, and the *per capita* allowance was $2.25. The number of colored school children was 114,139, the amount apportioned for distribution was $256,792.50, and the *per capita* allowance was $2.25.

The number of white children enrolled was 339,550; the highest number in attendance was 285,891, and the lowest number 90,814. The number of colored children enrolled was 47,998; the highest number in attendance was 38,994, and the lowest number 12,247.

The great deficiency is the lack of local aid to the schools. The schools. as a rule, are taught as long as the school fund will pay for, and no longer.

Geological Survey.—The Senate committee on the geological survey found that of $30,000 appropriated by the last Legislature, $29,952.20 had been expended, leaving unexpended $137.80, to which is to be added $910, making $1,047.80. The field work of the State in the eastern and western mineral fields, where it was richest from a mineral point of view, is mostly completed, excepting a few counties. The committee did not believe the advantage to be derived from the work to the State to justify any great extension of the survey, and recommended that $12,000 be appropriated for the completion of the work in eastern and western fields, authorizing the Governor to appoint a director for two years to carry out the provisions of the report, and making him curator of the bureau.

The entire amount expended from March, 1873, to May, 1890, is $268,300, including an annual appropriation of $5,000 from 1882–'87 for a bureau of immigration conducted in connection with the geological survey.

Railroads.—At the close of a session of several weeks, held in Frankfort, the Railroad Commission published a report. Dec. 2, of which the following are some of the items:

ASSESSMENT, 1892.

Total valuation by the commissioners..........	$52,316,088
Total valuation, as made to the commissioners by the railroads...........................	31,814,855
Increase.................................	$20,501,183

Average valuation per mile of all railroads, $17,316.44.

Assessment, 1892.............................	$52,316,088
Assessment, 1891.............................	50,048,741
Increase.................................	$2,267,297

The mileage reported by the commission in 1891 was 3,020, and in 1890 3,000. No new roads were made in 1892 previous to July 1, when the reports were made to the commission, except one that replaced a track since abandoned. Since July 1 lines have been extended to the amount of about 30 miles, and 40 miles more are in process of construction.

Whisky.—Reports of the Commissioner of Internal Revenue show that Kentucky is still the second State in the Union in production of whisky and payment of internal revenue tax. The amount of this tax paid by Kentucky during the last fiscal year was $21,813,851, which is about one seventh of all internal revenues paid in the United States. The Sixth District paid about half of this.

The total number of stills seized and destroyed in the State during the year was 44, of which 42 were in the Eighth District. Manufacturers and dealers are anxiously discussing the question of restricting each distiller to the use of his firm name in the manufacture of whisky. One distillery is said to be run under 73 distinct names, another 45, another 39.

Intermount.—A company has been formed to found and build a new town at the Cumberland Gap, and has bought several thousand acres of rich mineral and timber land. A large hotel

and sanitarium of 800 rooms is to be built, and to be called the Four Seasons House. The new town is designed to be a resort for invalids.

New Bridge over the Ohio.—It is probable that a sixth bridge will soon be built over the Ohio at Covington. After the necessary charters were secured from Ohio and Kentucky, some difficulties were met in the attempt to secure a permit from the Secretary of War. Opposition was made on the ground that it would be a great obstruction to navigation. The Secretary of War accordingly appointed a committee of expert engineers to examine and report on the proposition. The commission reported favorably to the plan proposed by the projectors with the change of placing the pier on the Kentucky side 100 feet farther south, making the southern span nearly 900 feet long and the building of the new bridge 12 feet higher than either of the two nearest bridges already completed. As this would greatly increase the cost of the structure, those interested drew up a bill, which was presented to Congress, authorizing the construction of the new bridge at the same height above low-water mark as the old suspension bridge. The bill passed in the face of vehement opposition, and it is expected that the work will be vigorously carried on.

Legislative Session.—The Legislature convened in December, 1891, and adjourned on Aug. 16. The Governor then called an extra session, which began on Aug. 25 and ended Nov. 1. Several important bills, upon which much of the time of the session had been spent, were vetoed by the Governor, and the extra session was called for reconsideration of the subjects of those bills, as well as some others which the executive had approved. The subjects were:

Revenue and taxation; corporations; suffrage and elections; World's Columbian Exposition; attorneys at law, Attorney General, attorneys for the Commonwealth, and attorneys for counties; redistricting the State into circuit-court districts; classification of cities; fiscal courts.

In the proclamation calling the Legislature to this extra session the Governor gave his reason for including in the list as given above .some bills that he had approved. He said:

It has been suggested that probably some of them are of doubtful constitutionality by reason of the methods of their adoption by the Legislature. If there be such valid objections to any of these bills, I must say that they were approved by me under the belief that the General Assembly had in their adoption followed the plain requirements of the Constitution. I was astonished when I heard that in the passage of some bills containing an emergency clause or an appropriation the Constitution had not been complied with in giving to such measures, on their final passage, the votes of a majority of all elected to each House of the General Assembly. When I found this had not been done in some instances, I at once consulted the journals of each House relating to every bill thereafter submitted to me in each case. Where the required vote had not been cast for it I returned it with my objections. The General Assembly may now change the date for the assessment of property this year, and pass a revenue and taxation bill under which every individual and corporation be required to pay proper taxation for the year 1892. There is ample time for this to be done; and if any of the bills enumerated require re-enactment, that may be speedily done, if it shall be the pleasure of your honorable body so to do.

The revenue bill was introduced early in the session. It was reported to the House by the Revisory Commission, Jan. 7, and was under consideration by the Committee on Revenue and Taxation, and in Committee of the Whole until May 24, when it passed by a vote of 67 to 0. It was sent to the Senate, where it was reported July 8, by the Committee on Revenue and Taxation with about 100 amendments. The greater part of these were adopted by the Senate, and the bill as thus amended was passed and returned to the House. The House concurred in a few of the amendments, and reported back to the Senate. A conference committee reported in favor of the important part of the Senate amendments.

The cause of the long contention over the bill was its bearing upon the taxation of railroads and other corporations. The bill in its original form, as it passed the House, exempted railroads, fire, life, and accident insurance companies, and foreign building and loan associations from paying a tax upon their franchise as other corporations were required to pay. The Senate adopted an amendment compelling these to pay a tax on their franchise the same as other corporations. It is said that this change made by the Senate would increase the taxes of one railroad more than $300,000 annually. The bill as it passed the House changed the law for the valuation of railroads, which was that they shall be valued for taxation at what they are worth as carriers of freight and passengers, while the bill provided that they should be valued for taxation at the price they would bring at a voluntary sale. The Senate amendment struck out this provision of the bill, and readopted the existing method. The Conference Committee recommended the adoption of the amendments of the Senate, and the bill was sent to the Governor, who vetoed it. The friends of the bill in the Legislature issued an address to the people, setting forth the history of the bill and their answers to the Governor's objections.

The bill as introduced at the extra session differed in some important particulars from the original bill. By it all money was to be paid into the State treasury, not to the Auditor. Besides a tax on their tangible property, all banks, telephone, gas, water, and electric-light and other corporations shall also pay a tax on what has been termed their franchise. This tax is to be paid on the value of the franchise, based on the net earnings.

In the case of railroads the net earnings are ascertained. Assuming that $12 to $16, as the assessors may choose to determine, represent $100 of capital stock, the division of the amount of net earnings in the State by the sum representing $100 of capital stock gives the number of shares proportioned to the miles of road within the State. This quotient multiplied by $100, the value of each share, gives the capital stock fairly assumed to be employed in the State. The Railroad Commissioners' assessment is taken as the value of the road's real property in the State, and the difference between the assumed capital stock and the assessment gives the franchise upon which the regular tax rate is levied.

The separate-coach bill, providing for the carrying of white and colored passengers in separate coaches, caused a great deal of excitement and called out many remonstrances from the colored people; but it was finally passed, with an amendment designed to secure the same kind of coaches for both white and colored passengers. A proposed amendment to make the provisions of the bill apply to street cars was rejected. Among the important bills passed was one abolishing the office of public printer, and providing that the public printing is to be let by contract to the lowest responsible bidder.

The Legal Classification bill divided the cities and towns of the Commonwealth into six classes, of which the first includes Louisville only; the second, Lexington, Covington, and Newport; and the third, Paducah, Owensboro, Henderson, Frankfort, and Bowling Green.

A bill was passed amending section 636 of the Civil Code, and allowing the wife to testify in cases of suit on account when she alone can be apprised of the facts in the case or the correctness of the account; also an antilottery bill, and one creating the office of Inspector of Mines. An important bill was one regulating the sale of tobacco.

A joint resolution was passed and approved by the Governor creating a committee to solicit sites for a new Capitol, and make recommendation thereon after investigating the amount of indebtedness, the rate of taxation, and whether or not the competing cities will be able to make good such bid as they may offer.

Both Houses passed a resolution extending sympathy to the strikers at Homestead, and denouncing the use of Pinkertons. The resolution caused considerable discussion in the House, a minority holding that the State had no official knowledge of the causes that led up to the unfortunate condition of affairs at Homestead, and could not intermeddle with the affairs of Pennsylvania.

On the occasion of the centenary of Kentucky's admission to the Union, June 1, an oil painting of Independence Hall, and some others, were presented to the State by the Philadelphia bar. They were sent by a committee of 40 members, and received at Lexington.

The New Constitution.—The validity of this instrument was called in question on the ground that it is not the same one adopted by vote of the people in 1891. The convention met in September, 1890, and having in April, 1891, completed a draft of a constitution, it by ordinance submitted it to a popular vote, and then adjourned until September. During the recess the work was approved by a majority of nearly 140,000, the total vote cast being 288,360. When the convention reassembled the delegates made numerous changes in the instrument, some of which are claimed to be material, while others were but a change of language or the correction of grammatical errors, and as thus amended it was promulgated by the convention on Sept. 28, 1891, as the Constitution of the State.

Suit was brought by 2 citizens of Louisville against the Public Printer and the Secretary of State, to enjoin the one from printing at the public expense the instrument so promulgated, and the other from preserving it in the State archives as the Constitution of the State, and also asking that it be adjudged not to be such, but spurious and invalid. The suit was dismissed by the lower court, and on appeal the action was sustained by Chief-Justice Holt, Judges Pryor and Lewis concurring. Judge Bennett dissented and brought in a minority opinion. Justice Holt, in conclusion, said:

If through error of opinion the convention exceeded its power, and the people are dissatisfied, they have ample remedy without the j ar being asked to overstep the proper limits of its power. The instrument provides for amendment and change. If a wrong has been done, it can, and the proper way in which it should, be remedied is by the people acting as a body politic. A new constitution has been formed and promulgated according to the forms of law. Great interests have already arisen under it; important rights exist by virtue of it; persons have been convicted of the highest crimes known to law according to its provisions; the political p r of the Government has in many ways recognized it, and under such circumstances it is our duty to treat and regard it as a valid Constitution, and now the organic law of our Commonwealth.

Political.—The Democratic State Convention met at Louisville on May 25 to elect delegates to the National Convention. The party opposed to the nomination of Mr. Cleveland gained a victory in the choice of temporary chairman by a vote of 427 to 290. The platform approved the principles of the Democratic national platform of 1888; condemned the principles of the Republican party as exemplified in its iniquitous tariff legislation, its advocacy of the "force bill," and its wastefulness of the public funds; called for tariff reform and an economical administration of the Government; demanded a sound and stable currency composed of or redeemable in gold and silver, and declared it to be the mission of the Democratic party to preserve the parity in value of gold and silver dollars, and to provide the means by appropriate legislation for the free coinage of silver without detriment to any business interest and to the great relief of overtaxed and debt-ridden people.

The platform further denounced the Republican party for the demonetization of silver; condemned its subsequent legislation in regard to silver coinage; heartily approved the Democratic administration of Grover Cleveland, and sent the Kentucky delegation to Chicago uninstructed for any candidate.

The Republican State Convention met in April. The resolutions affirmed its "full admiration of and adherence to the past history and to the present principles and policy of the Republican party," approved the McKinley tariff bill and the system of reciprocity as now inaugurated by the party, and the earnest maintenance of the honor and dignity of this republic in its relations to and with foreign nations, and opposed the free and unlimited coinage of silver, and recommended its delegates to vote for the renomination of President Harrison.

The total vote for President in November was 340,732, a falling off of 4,068 from the number in 1888. It was divided as follows: Cleveland, 175,424; Harrison, 135,420; Weaver, 23,503; Bidwell, 6,385; total, 340,732; Cleveland's plurality, 40,004.

Of the 11 Congressmen, 10 are Democrats.

KNIGHTS OF INDUSTRY, an organization formed in New York city in January, 1892, not as a rival to the Knights of Labor, but to supplement the work of that organization by political action. The rules of the Knights of Labor and other labor unions prevent the members from using the influence of the unions in political work. The new body is intended mainly for political purposes. Its aim is to protect American labor, and capital as well, from the competition of foreign and domestic cheap goods and cheap labor, and also from prison or convict labor. Efforts are made to reconcile the ideas of the capitalist with those of the laborer, and the laborers favor those manufacturers who agree to employ members of American workingmen's unions. It is proposed to establish a labor bureau, where will be printed and published many documents written by union men belonging to the various trades. The documents will be forwarded to all parts of the country, and will be circulated in factories and shops by delegates. The central council will establish branches in all large cities of the United States, hold meetings, distribute documents, and organize the workingmen for political action. Delegates will be sent to conventions of the Republican and Democratic parties, and requests will be made that certain planks shall be put into the platforms. These will include protection to American labor and capital, reduction of the hours of labor, demands for legislation in favor of factory-inspection bills, against child, prison, and convict labor, and in favor of a system of arbitration and profit sharing that will tend to unite capital and labor and do away with strikes.

L

LIBERIA, a republic on the west coast of Africa. It was originally founded by the efforts of the American Colonization Society, which purchased a tract near Cape Montserrado from the native chiefs in 1820, for the purpose of giving an opportunity to liberated slaves from the United States to settle under conditions of equality that were denied to them in America. (For a general description, see "Annual Cyclopædia" for 1887.)

Finances.—The revenue for 1888 was officially estimated at £35,000, and expenditure at £33,000. The chief expenses of the Government are for civil administration. In 1885 a revenue of £40,000 was collected, and the expenditure was £32,500. The chief source of revenue is the customs. The debt contracted in 1891, including arrears of interest, amounts to £200,000.

Commerce.—The chief exports are coffee, palm oil, palm nuts, cacao, sugar, camwood, gold dust, arrowroot, ivory, and hides. The Liberian coffee is much esteemed. In 1889 the quantity exported exceeded 1,000,000 pounds, of which half went to Germany. The exports and imports together are supposed to amount to about £500,000. The trade is increasing with the increase of the commerce of West Africa. The numerous rivers that descend from the elevated region known as the Kong mountains form excellent water-ways. These mountains are supposed to be very rich in gold.

LITERATURE, AMERICAN, IN 1892. The copyright law was, no doubt, a chief cause of the activity in the book-producing and book-publishing world observed during the year, which exceeded any other previously known. While many of the 4,862 volumes recorded by the " Publishers' Weekly " are to be credited to foreign sources, and many proved old friends in a new dress, yet the proportion of new work from Americans was unusually high ; and, be it remarked, not a small portion, and that of the best, came from the West. Only in the lighter departments of literature were importations from England numerous, and these were offered in a far more attractive form than has prevailed for years. Two new novels were written for every day in the year. not excepting Sundays (735 in all) ; a marked increase was shown in books of poetry, of voyages and travels, of medicine and surgery, of history, of political and social science, of physical science and the useful arts, of biography and of law, while a few additional titles are noted among educational and juvenile books. The decrease in the number of books devoted to the fine arts was more than compensated by the improvement in the character of those offered. Contributions were less numerous to theology and religion, to sports, domestic and rural economy, and mental and moral philosophy.

Biography.—Naturally, in the Columbian year several volumes were devoted to the discoverer of this continent. The "Writings of Christopher Columbus descriptive of the Discovery and Occupation of the New World" were edited, with an introduction, by Paul Leicester Ford ; "Columbus and his Discovery of America" formed the theme of two orations by Prof. Herbert B. Adams and Prof. Henry Wood, of Johns Hopkins University, which were published in the "Studies" of that institution ; Edward Eggleston edited, with an introduction, "The Story of Columbus," written by his daughter Elizabeth Eggleston Seelye, and illustrated by another daughter. Allegra Eggleston, which opened the new "Delights of History" series ; President Charles Kendall Adams, of Cornell University, contributed "Columbus. his Life and Work," to the "Makers of America" series ; "The True Story of Christopher Columbus, called the Great Admiral," was told for youngest readers by Elbridge S. Brooks, and "The Story of the Discovery of the New World by Columbus" by Frederick Saunders ; Franc B. Willie (Poliuto) wrote a "Life of Christopher Columbus" ; Alexander Innes, "The Life and Adventures of Christopher Columbus"; while "Christopher Columbus and his Monument, Columbia," was a concordance of choice tributes to the great Genoese, compiled from upward of six hundred writers, by J. M. Dickey. Vols. XI and XII of the "Writings of George Washington," collected and edited by Worthington C. Ford, were issued ; William S. Baker compiled an "Itinerary of General Washington from June 15, 1775, to December 23, 1783 "; and Washington's "Journal of my Journey over the Mountains while sur-

veying for Lord Thomas Fairfax, Baron of Cameron, in the Northern Neck of Virginia, beyond the Blue Ridge, in 1747-'58," was copied from the original with literal exactness, and edited with notes by J. M. Toner, M. D. "The Story of Mary Washington," by Marion Harland (Mrs. Mary Virginia H. Terhune), contained new and interesting information about the mother of the hero. Vol. I of a new compilation by Paul Leicester Ford of "The Writings of Thomas Jefferson," which will fill ten volumes, opened a rich field of study and delight to the student ; and Vol. III of "Patrick Henry : Life, Correspondence, and Speeches," by William Wirt Henry, the grandson of the great orator, completed a work of rare interest and value. To Henry Hall we are indebted for "Ethan Allen, the Robin Hood of Vermont"; while "Robert Morris," in the "Makers of America" series, by William Graham Sumner, is a condensation of his two volumes on "The Financier and the Finances of the American Revolution," published last year. The "Life of George Mason, 1725-1792," including his speeches, public papers, and correspondence, in two volumes, by Kate Mason Rowland, had an introduction by Gen. Fitzhugh Lee, and three volumes (in one edition, limited to 250 copies) contained the "Letters of William Lee, of Virginia, Sheriff and Alderman of London, Commercial Agent of the Continental Congress in France, and Minister to the Courts of Vienna and Berlin," collected and edited by Worthington C. Ford. To a later period belong "Abraham Lincoln and Men of War Times," by A. K. McClure ; "Abraham Lincoln," by Charles Carleton Coffin ; "The Children's Life of Abraham Lincoln," by M. Louise Putnam ; "In the Boyhood of Lincoln," by Hezekiah Butterworth ; half biography, half romance ; "The Assassination of Lincoln : The Great Conspiracy," by Gen. T. M. Harris ; "Life on the Circuit with Lincoln," a superficial work, by Henry C. Whitney ; and a new revised and enlarged edition of "Abraham Lincoln : The True Story of a Great Life," by William H. Herndon and Jesse W. Weik. The "Autobiography and Personal Reminiscences" of Maj.-Gen. Benjamin F. Butler reviewed his legal, military, and political career ; and in the "Great Commanders" series, edited by James Grant Wilson, "Admiral Farragut" was from the pen of A. T. Mahon, as was "General Taylor" from that of Gen. O. O. Howard. "I married a Soldier ; or, Old Days in the Old Army." by Lydia Spencer Lane, covered the period from 1855 to the close of the war for the Union, and narrated many of the hardships of life on the frontier to the softer sex. "The Adventures of a Blockade Runner" were related by William Watson, author of "Life in the Confederate Army"; and a new edition was published of "Down in Dixie : Life in a Cavalry Regiment in the War Days, from the Wilderness to Appomattox," by Stanton P. Allen, which first appeared in 1888. "Memorials of Sarah Childress Polk. Wife of the Eleventh President of the United States," were written by Anson and Fanny Nelson. A volume upon "Robert Toombs" was contributed by Pleasant A. Stovall ; and from Sarah Ellen Blackwell we have "A Military Genius : Life of Anna Ella Carroll, of Maryland " (" The Great Unrecognized Member of Lincoln's Cabinet "), compiled from family records and congressional documents. George W. Julian attempted to fix "The Rank of Charles Osborn as an Antislavery Pioneer," and wrote also a "Life of Joshua R. Giddings." "The Moral Crusader, William Lloyd Garrison," was a biographical essay, by Goldwin Smith, founded on the story of Garrison's life told by his children. The "Life of Charles Sumner, the Scholar in Politics," in the "American Reformers" series, was by Archibald H. Grimke; and in the "Makers of America" series we had "Charles Sumner," by Anna Laurens Dawes. "Horace Greeley and other Pioneers of American Socialism," by Charles Sothcran, partakes at once of the nature of biography and sociology; while a new revised edition of the "Life and Times of Frederick Douglass, written by himself," with 100 pages of additional matter, may not inaptly be mentioned here. "James Russell Lowell" was the theme of an address delivered by George W. Curtis at Brooklyn Institute, Feb. 22, 1892; and "John G. Whittier, the Poet of Freedom," was commemorated by William Sloane Kennedy, in the "American Reformers" series. "Autobiographia; or, The Story of a Life" selected from the prose writings of Walt Whitman, were edited by Arthur Stedman; and the South Carolinian, "William Gilmore Simms," was the subject of a volume by William P. Trent. "The Life and Letters of Washington Allston," with reproductions from Allston's pictures, we owe to Jared B. Flagg. Vols. III, IV, VI, and VII of "Chronicles of the Builders of the Commonwealth," by Hubert Howe Bancroft, were issued, with an index covering Vols. I to VII inclusive. George F. Parker selected and edited, by permission, the "Writings and Speeches of Grover Cleveland," writing also "A Life of Grover Cleveland, with a Sketch of Adlai E. Stephenson"; and "Speeches of Benjamin Harrison," were compiled by Charles Hedges. Katharine Prescott Wormley, the translator of the great French novelist, contributed "A Memoir of Honoré de Balzac": Poultney Bigelow described, largely from personal acquaintance in early life, "The German Emperor and his Eastern Neighbors"; and the "Life of Christian Daniel Rauch, of Berlin, Germany, Sculptor," was drawn from German authorities by Ednah D. Cheney. "A Memorial Volume to Charles Stewart Parnell," by Robert F. Walsh, contained also the "Life and Public Services of Daniel O'Connell," with an outline of important events in Irish history, by Thomas Clarke Luby. Mrs. Sarah K. Bolton's latest volume was entitled "Famous Types of Womanhood," and the first series also appeared of "Women Writers, their Works and Ways," by Catherine J. Hamilton. Susan Dallas edited the "Diary of George Mifflin Dallas while United States Minister to Russia, 1837 to 1839, and to England, 1856 to 1861"; and "Orations and Addresses on Various Occasions, Civil and Military," by Charles Devens, were edited by his nephew, Arthur L. Devens, with a memoir by John Codman Ropes. "Memoirs of Elias Loomis and William Kitchen Parker," from the "Smithsonian Report for 1890," found readers, as did "Lyman Copeland Draper," a memoir by Reuben Gold Thwaites, reprinted from Vol. XII of "Wisconsin Historical Collections." "John Hancock,"

a memoir with selections from Hancock's writings, by W. H. Venable, commemorated the Ohio educator; while "Men and Events of Forty Years: Autobiographical Reminiscences of an Active Career," by Josiah B. Grinnell, told of pioneer days in Iowa. "A Knight that smote the Dragon: or, The Young People's Gough," by Edward A. Rand, was the story of the famous temperance advocate. Rev. Abijah P. Marvin treated "The Life and Times of Cotton Mather, D. D.; or, A Boston Minister of Two Centuries Ago, 1663–1728"; Rev. Richard S. Storrs, in eight lectures, presented "Bernard of Clairvaux," the great abbot of the twelfth century, against a striking historic background; "Our Birthdays toward Sunset: Seventy-one to One Hundred," by A. C. Thompson, told illustrative anecdotes of more than 300 distinguished persons who outlived the allotted span and continued to labor in their several lines; and "Seventy Years in Dixie," by F. D. Srygley, in addition to recollections, sermons, and sayings of T. W. McCaskey, presented typical scenes of Southern life. "Leaders of Thought in the Modern Church," by Reuben Thomas, and "Some American Churchmen," by Frederick Cook Moorehouse, may be classed together, as may "Representative Women of Methodism," by Charles W. Buoy, D. D., and "Some Christian Endeavor Saints," by Francis E. Clark. "Mark Hopkins," by Franklin Carter, and "Henry Boynton Smith," by Louis F. Stearns, D. D., were the contributions to the "American Religious Leaders" series, as were "The Life and Times of Bishop White," by Julius H. Ward, with an introduction by Bishop Potter, "Most Reverend John Hughes, First Archbishop of New York," by Henry Brann, D. D., and "Jean Baptiste Le Moyne. Sieur de Bienville" (and the first Governor of Louisiana), by Grace King, to the "Makers of America" series. To religious biography belong "Preacher and Teacher: A Sketch of the Life of Thomas Rambaut, D. D.," by Norman Fox, D. D.; "The Early Days of my Episcopate," by Bishop W. Ingraham Kip, of California; "Henry Jackson Van Dyke," a memorial volume; "A Sketch of the Lives and Missionary Work of Rev. Cephas Bennett and his Wife, Stella Kneeland Bennett, 1829–1891," by Ruth Whitaker Ranney; the "Journal of the Life and Religious Labors of Sarah Hunt," published by the Friends; "Caspar Wistar Hodge," a memorial address by Prof. Francis L. Patton; "William Carey: A Sketch of Beginnings in Modern Missions," by Rev. Arthur C. Chute; and the numerous biographies, by Americans of the great English evangelist, among which may be mentioned: "From the Usher's Desk to the Tabernacle Pulpit," by Rev. Robert Shindler; followed by "From the Pulpit to the Palm Branch," by Dr. A. T. Pierson; "Charles H. Spurgeon, Our Ally," by Dr. Justin D. Fulton; "Spurgeon," a collection of anecdotes and reminiscences from the pen of Thomas W. Handford; G. Holden Pike's "Charles Haddon Spurgeon, Preacher, Author, Philanthropist"; "Charles H. Spurgeon, his Faith and Works," by H. L. Wayland; and a monograph by G. C. Lorimer, entitled "Charles Haddon Spurgeon, the Puritan Preacher of the Nineteenth Century." "A Christian Business Man" was the biography of Deacon C. F. Gates, by his son,

Caleb Frank Gates; "Ireland and St. Patrick," by Rev. W. B. Morris, presented a study of the saint's character and of the results of his apostolate; while "My Mother: An Appreciation," was tenderly offered by Bishop John H. Vincent. A book that aroused much attention was "The Life of Thomas Paine," in two volumes, by Moncure D. Conway, including an unpublished sketch of Paine by William Cobbett. An autograph edition of "An American Statesman: The Works and Words of James G. Blaine," was issued a few months prior to the death of its illustrious subject. The first of two volumes of a "Life of Colonel Paul Revere," by Elbridge H. Goss, appeared; and the labors of John Alfred Poor for "The First International Railway and the Colonization of New England" were traced through his life and writings, edited by Laura Elizabeth Poor. "Memories of the Professional and Social Life of John E. Owens" were published by the wife of the actor; and "Peter Henderson, Gardener, Author, Merchant," was the subject of a memoir by Alfred Henderson, his son, somewhat in line with which was L. Menaud's "Autobiography and Recollections of Incidents conuected with Horticultural Affairs, etc., from 1807 to 1892." In the "Great Captains" series "Cæsar" was handled by Captain Theodore Ayrault Dodge. W. E. Fish supplied a "Biography of Ignatius Donnelly," reprinted from "Donnelliana"; "Mark Twain: His Life and Work," was a biographical sketch by William M. Clemens; the "Life and Death of Jay Gould, and how he made his Millions," was anonymous; while from John L. Sullivan came the "Life and Reminiscences of a Nineteenth-Century Gladiator." A second edition was made of the "Autobiography" of Dr. Samuel D. Gross, edited by his sons. Vol. I of the "National Cyclopædia of American Biography," edited by distinguished biographers selected from each State, was issued, the whole to be complete in twelve volumes; John O. Austin edited an "Ancestral Dictionary"; in line with which were a "History of the Putnam Family in England and America," two parts of which were issued, to be followed by eight more; "Descendants of George Wheeler," of Concord, Mass., 1638," compiled by Henry Warren Wheeler; the genealogical, biographical and statistical record of the "Stanton Family," by W. A. Stanton; and the "Jones Genealogy," compiled by L. H. Jones. "Andersonville: An Object Lesson on Protection," was the peculiar title of a critical sketch of Captain Henry Wirtz; "First Days amongst the Contrabands" set forth the results of thirty years work of Elizabeth Hyde Botume; and Mrs. Harriot S. Caswell detailed "Our Life among the Iroquois Indians" of western New York. "Darkness and Daylight; or, Lights and Shadows of New York Life," was by Mrs. Helen Campbell, Rev. Lyman Abbott, and others.

Criticism and General Literature.—Several volumes in this department merit careful perusal. Among these are the lectures of Edmund Clarence Stedman on "The Nature and Elements of Poetry," delivered at Johns Hopkins University, initiating the Percy Trumbull Memorial Lectureship of Poetry, and collected into a volume: "The Art of Poetry," by Prof. A. S. Cook; "The Desire of Beauty: Being In-

dications for Æsthetic Culture," by Theodore Child; "The Golden Guess: Essays on Poetry and the Poets," by John Vance Cheney; "Under the Evening Lamp," biographical and critical papers concerning some of the "unfortunates" of literature, by Richard Henry Stoddard; "The Development of Literature and Language," by Prof. A. H. Welsh, in two volumes; "Social and Literary Papers," by the late C. Chauncey Shackford; "The Real and Ideal in Literature," by Frank Preston Stearns; "Essays in Miniature," welcomed from Agnes Repplier; "Essays in Literary Interpretation," by Hamilton Wright Mabie; "Intellectual Pursuits," by Robert Waters, which supplied hints for culture by self-help; "Quest and Vision: Essays in Life and Literature," by W. J. Dawson, and a second series of "Studies, Literary and Social," by Richard Malcolm Johnston. P. F. Mullany published "Phases of Thought and Criticism," under the pseudonym of Brother Azarias. John Albee contributed "Prose Idyls," which fell little short of poetry, and Thomas Wentworth Higginson was heard from once more "Concerning all of us," in 29 short papers. "Americanisms and Britticisms, with Other Essays on Other Isms," was, of course, by James Brander Matthews; Edward Waterman Evans, Jr., made a critical study of "Walter Savage Landor"; Charles Eliot Norton, in addition to revising his translation of Dante's "Vita Nuova," edited the lectures of James Russell Lowell on "The Old English Dramatists," delivered in 1887, and published in Harper's Magazine; Lucy Allen Paton's essay on "The Personal Character of Dante," first published by the Dante Society, was reprinted, by permission; W. F. C. Wigston stood up for "Francis Bacon, Poet, Prophet, Philosopher, versus Phantom Captain Shakespeare, the Rosicrucian Mask," and also dubbed the great Verulam "The Columbus of Literature." "Tributes to Shakespeare" were collected and arranged by Mary R. Silsby, and a new edition was made of "Typical Tales of Fancy, Romance, and History, from Shakespeare's Plays in Narrative Form," by Prof. Robert R. Raymond. Delicate delineation of nature was found in "Field-Farings: A Vagrant Chronicle of Earth and Sky," by Martha McCulloch Williams; "The Foot-Path Way," by Bradford Torrey; and "Recent Rambles," by Charles C. Abbott, M. D., continuing "A Naturalist's Rambles about Home." "Wood Notes Wild: Notations of Bird Music," by Simeon Pease Cheney, were collected and arranged by his son, John Vance Cheney, and "Autumn" was edited from the Journal of Henry D. Thoreau by H. G. O. Blake. "A Tour around New York and my Summer Acre," by the late John Flavel Mines (Felix Oldboy), gave delightful personal reminiscences of fifty years ago; "The New England Country" was studied con amore by Clifton Johnson; Dr. W. C. Prime traveled "Along New England Roads"; and J. L. Allen wrote "The Blue Grass Region of Kentucky, and Other Kentucky Articles." "Witchcraft in Salem Village in 1692," by Winfield S. Nevins, and "Barbara Frietchie," by Mrs. Caroline Healey Dall, were special studies: another was "The Graves of Myles Standish and Other Pilgrims," by Rev. E. J. V. Huiginn. In an oration before the Phi Beta Kappa Fraternity of Harvard University William Jewett Tucker discussed "The New Movement in Humanity: From Liberty to Unity"; Caroline F. Corbin found a solution for many problems of life in "A Woman's Philosophy of Love," and Julia Duhring propounded theories of her own in "Amor in Society," bearing on the same subject. Robert Grant vouchsafed "Reflections of a Married Man," and Oscar Fay Adams collected his strictures on women from the North American Review into a volume entitled "The Presumption of Sex, and Other Papers." "Old Shrines and Ivy," by William Winter, contains more of the delightful impressions of the wanderer and dreamer, while his "Shadows of the Stage" gives, in 38 brief letters, a permanent record of the theatrical world of this generation. "Social Ethics and Society Duties," by Mrs. H. O. Ward (Mrs. Bloomfield Moore), plead for the thorough education of girls for wives and mothers and for professions; G. T. Howerton gave "Short Talks on Character Building"; W. Taylor, D. D., spoke a word to young men on "Good Character," and "Looking out on Life," by F. E. Clark, D. D., was intended for young girls. Grace H. Dodge edited "Thoughts of Busy Girls"; Eliza Chester, the author of "Chats with Girls," was this time eloquent on "The Unmarried Woman"; "Women of the World: With a Search Light of Epigram," was compiled by Mrs. Alethe Lowber Craig; Rose Porter chose and arranged "Men's Thoughts for Men" in a tasteful manner; and Mrs. Alice L. Williams selected a "Handful of Letters, Old and New." Definitions and opinions from various sources as to "What makes a Friend," were put together by Volney Streamer; "The Schoolmaster in Literature" was another compilation, with an introduction by Edward Eggleston; "Plantation Life before Emancipation" was treated by R. Q. Mallard, D. D.; "Philadelphia Magazines and their Contributors, 1741–1850," by Albert H. Smyth; and "Quakers in Pennsylvania," by Albert C. Applegarth, the last in the "Johns Hopkins University Studies." "Famous Pets of Famous People" were described by Eleanor Lewis; Hamilton B. Tompkins prepared a "Burr Bibliography," the edition of which was limited to 250 copies; 6 charming essays were constructed "From the Books of Laurence Hutton" by their owner; "Martyrdoms of Literature," by Robert H. Vickers, deplored the destruction of famous libraries; Daniel M. Tredwell contributed "A Monograph on privately Illustrated Books: A Plea for Bibliomania"; "Four Private Libraries of New York," by Henri Péne Du Bois, was a contribution to the history of bibliophism in America; "Public Support of Public Libraries" was the subject of a paper read before the American Library Association at San Francisco, Cal., by W. E. Foster; an "Index to the Subject Catalogue of Harvard College Library" was given to the public; and "Indexing: A Manual for Librarians, Authors, and Publishers," came from J. B. Nichols. "Studies and Notes in Philology and Literature" were made by various writers in the "Harvard University Studies," and Vol. III of "Harvard Studies in Classical Philology" was edited by a committee of the classical instructors of the same institution. In line with these is a "Syllabus on the History of Classical Philology," by

Alfred Gudeman; "Germanic Origins: A Study in Primitive Culture," from the pen of Francis B. Gummere; and from Hjalmar Hjorth Boyesen we have "Essays on German Literature." A series of tabular studies of "The Hebrew Verb" was made by Augustus S. Carrier, F. Horace Teall contributed a valuable aid to writers in "English Compound Words and Phrases," and Samuel Ramsey proved exhaustive on "The English Language and English Grammar." Hiram Corson drew up a "Primer of English Verse: Chiefly in its Æsthetic and Organic Character"; Henry Matson prepared "References for Literary Workers"; Prof. George H. Howieson revised and enlarged "Soule's Synonyms"; "To Write or not to Write," hints and suggestions concerning all sorts of literary and journalistic work personally contributed by leading authors of the day, was a useful compilation made by Alice R. Mylene; and for a "Handy Book of Literary Curiosities" we were indebted to W. S. Walsh. "Echoes of the Sunset Club," of Chicago, were collected by W. W. Catlin, to form a readable volume, and a new revised edition was published of "Sea Phantoms; or, Legends and Superstitions of the Sea and of Sailors in all Lands and all Times," by Lieut. Fletcher S. Bassett, U. S. N.; and "Legends of the Pike's Peak Region: Sacred Myths of the Manitou," by Ernest Whitney and W. S. Alexander, were illustrated by Thomas C. Parrish. "Lyre, Pen, and Pencil: Essays, Studies, and Sketches," of Fannie Raymond Ritter, were edited by Millie W. Carpenter; the fourth series was issued of "The Best Reading," edited by Lynds E. Jones; and George E. Hardy selected and classified "Five Hundred Books for the Young."

Educational.—"The History of Modern Education" was written by Samuel G. Williams, in the "School Bulletin" publications, and Louisa Parsons Hopkins treated of "The Spirit of the New Education." In the "International Education Series" "Psychology applied to the Art of Teaching," by Joseph Baldwin, contained the observation and experience of many years, and "English Education in the Elementary and Secondary Schools" was handled by Prof. John Sharpless. "Let him first be a Man, and Other Essays," by W. H. Venable, related chiefly to education and culture, and "Literature for Children" was the title of a paper read before the National Educational Association at Saratoga, July 14, 1892, by George E. Hardy. "Circulars of Information of the United States Bureau of Education," published in 1892, were histories of higher education, respectively, in Ohio, by George W. Knight and John R. Commons; in Massachusetts, by George Gary Bush; and in Michigan, by Andrew C. McLaughlin; also "Southern Women in the Recent Educational Movement in the South," by Rev. A. D. Mayo. "Handbook of University Extension, No. 1," edited by George F. James, was a reprint of about fifty signed articles by prominent writers and educators in the monthly journal of the University Extension Society. "College Requirements" in English entrance examinations, by Rev. Arthur Wentworth Eaton, and in algebra (a final review), by George Parsons Tibbets, met special needs. "Methods of Instruction and Organization of the Schools of Germany" were set forth for

American teachers and normal schools by John T. Prince; and "French Schools through American Eyes" was the report of James Russell Parsons, Jr., to the New York State Department of Public Instruction. In the new series of "Great Educators" " Alcuin and the Rise of the Christian Schools" was by Prof. Andrew Fleming West; "Aristotle and Ancient Educational Ideals," by Thomas Davidson; and "Loyola and the Educational System of the Jesuits," by Rev. Thomas Hughes. "The Place of Comenius in the History of Education" was decided by Nicholas Murray Butler in "The Schoolroom Classics," and "Indian Education" formed the theme of Frank W. Blackmar in "Publications of the American Academy of Political and Social Science." "Physical Education in the Public Schools" was an eclectic system of exercises prepared by R. Anna Morris; Hartvig Nissen drew up the "A B C of the Swedish System of Gymnastics"; a "Handbook of School Gymnastics of the Swedish System" was anonymous; and B. B. Hoffman wrote "The Sloyd System of Woodworking; With a Brief Description of the Eva Rohde Model Series and an Historical Sketch of the Growth of the Manual Training Idea." "Hygienic Requirements of School Furniture" were looked into by G. A. Bobrick. Helen Keller, herself deaf and blind, was the author of the "Souvenir of the First Summer Meeting of the American Association to promote the Teaching of Speech to the Deaf." "The Moral Instruction of Children," a series of lectures by Dr. Felix Adler, formed a volume in the "International Education Series"; "Children's Rights" were vigorously asserted by Mrs. Kate Douglass Wiggin, who has written so charmingly for the amusement of children; and "Children: Their Models and Critics," were reviewed by Mrs. Auretta Roys Aldrich. "The Place of the Story in Early Education, and other Essays," by Sara E. Wiltse, leads naturally to "Stories for Children, containing Simple Lessons in Morals," by Lucretia P. Hale. "A Literary Guide for Home and School" was prepared by Mary Alice Caller, "A Text-book of Elocution," by Maria Porter Brace, and "The Foundations of Rhetoric" were laid by Adams Sherman Hill. Books of practical value were "English Composition by Practice," by Edward R. Shaw; "Plain English," anonymous; "An English Grammar for the Higher Grades in Grammar Schools," adapted by Mrs. Sara E. H. Lockwood from "Essentials of English Grammar," by W. D. Whitney: "Hints for Grammar Lessons," by John A. MacCabe; "Outlines of English Grammar," by Harriet Matthews; "Selections for memorizing for Primary, Intermediate, and High-School Grades," compiled by L. C. Foster and Sherman Williams; familiar talks on "Reading and Speaking" with young men in colleges and higher schools; No. 3 of "The Information Readers," covering "Man and Materials"; several parts of "The Picturesque Geographical Readers," by Charles F. King; Vol. II of "How to teach and study Geography by the Brace System," covering North America, by J. F. Wicks and J. M. Boyer; "The Multiplication Chant and Gesture Drill," by Lizzie Stanley Martyn; J. K. Ellwood's "Table-book and Test Problems in Mathematics"; an "Ele-

mentary Synthetic Geometry," by George Bruce Halsted; "Drawing simplified," for schools and self-instruction, by D. R. Augsburg; "How to teach Writing," a manual of penmanship designed to accompany Appletons' standard copy books, by Lyman D. Smith; a "Manual of the Natural Movement Method in Writing," an original self-instructing system, by Charles R. Wells; and "How to teach Paper Folding and Cutting: A Practical Manual Training Aid," by "MacLeod" in the "Manual Training Series." "An Illustrated Dictionary to Xenophon's Anabasis" was made from the "Anabasis" itself, not compiled from other dictionaries, by John Williams White and Morris H. Morgan; and Prof. Isaac Flagg revised the "Homeric Dictionary for Schools and Colleges," translated from the German by Dr. George Autenrieth. "The Glory of the Imperfect" was the title of an address given at the first commencement of the Woman's College of Western Reserve University, Cleveland, Ohio, in 1891, by George Palmer Herbert. Two papers of interest were "Education as related to Citizenship, by Rev. John W. Chadwick, in the "Evolution Series," and "School Savings Banks" considered by Sara Louisa Oberholtzer in "Publications of the American Academy of Political and Social Science."

Fiction.—No novel of 1892 attained a distinctive reputation, though writers of note were not idle. F. Marion Crawford produced two volumes: "The Three Fates," a story of New York life, and "Don Orsino," a sequel to "Saracinesca" and "Sant' Ilario." William Dean Howells analyzed "The Quality of Mercy," and Mrs. Margaret Deland told in her own charming way "The Story of a Child." Robert Louis Stevenson, with Lloyd Osbourne, recounted the mysterious and amusing adventures of "The Wrecker." Mrs. Burton Harrison (Mrs. Constance Cary Harrison) published "Belhaven Tales," "An Edelweiss of the Sierras," and "A Daughter of the South, and Shorter Stories"; and Mrs. Amelia E. Barr had three volumes, "Love for an Hour is Love Forever," "The Preacher's Daughter: A Domestic Romance," and "Michael and Theodora," a Russian story. The worship of "The Golden Calf" was inveighed against by Hjalmar Hjorth Boyesen; and "Marionettes" was the title of Julien Gordon's (Mrs. Van Rennselaer Cruger) latest. "The Clocks of Rondaine, and Other Stories," was all that Frank R. Stockton vouchsafed; while Edgar Fawcett was prolific as usual, "Women must weep," "The Adopted Daughter," and "An Heir to Millions" having emanated from his pen during the year. "Barbara Dering," by Amélie Rives (Mrs. J. Armstrong Chanler), carried to a conclusion the career of the heroine of "The Quick or the Dead": Mary E. Wilkins wrote her first novel, "Jane Field"; also two volumes of short stories, in which she has proved a proficient—"Young Lucretia, and Other Stories," and "The Pot of Gold, and Other Stories." "Roweny in Boston," by Maria Louise Pool, was followed by a sequel, "Mrs. Keats Bradford"; "Zachary Phips," by Edwin Lasseter Bynner, was executed with the same fidelity to historic detail which characterized that author's previous work; Dr. Weir Mitchell found time for two contributions to the world of romance, "Roland Blake" and "Characteristics"; "A First Family of Tasajara" and "Colonel Starbottle's Client and Some Other People" proved that Francis Bret Harte had lost none of his power; "The Average Woman," by the late gifted Wolcott. Balestier, had a preface by Henry James, and the same author wrote in collaboration with Rudyard Kipling, "The Naulahka: A Story of West and East." "Life and Sylvia" was from the pen of Josephine Balestier; James Brander Matthews wrote alone "In the Vestibule Limited," and with George H. Jessop "A Tale of Twenty-five Hours"; Francis M. Peard told a Dutch story entitled "The Baroness"; Annie Trumbull Slosson rehearsed "The Heresy of Mehetable Clark," and wrote also "Aunt Liefy"; Blanche Willis Howard (now Baroness von Teuffel) collaborated with the well-known English author William Sharp to produce "A Fellowe and his Wife"; and wrote alone "A Battle and a Boy," for children. "Lorelei, and Other Stories," was by Mary J. Safford; Harold Frederic described "The Return of the O'Mahony"; and a new revised edition was published of "The Hoosier Schoolmaster," by Edward Eggleston, in commemoration of the publication of 100,000 copies of the book. Ignatius Donnelly, under his pseudonym of Edmund Boisgilbert, painted Utopian pictures of life in "The Golden Bottle: or, The Story of Ephraim Benezet of Kansas"; and Mrs. Katharine Pearson Woods, the author of "Metzerott, Shoemaker," advanced ethical theories in "From Dusk to Dawn." "His Great Self," by Marion Harland (Mrs. M. V. H. Terhune), and "Miss Bagg's Secretary," a West Point romance, by Mrs. Clara Louise Burnham, represented two popular authors. "An Earthly Paragon" was portrayed by Eva Wilder McGlasson; Sarah P. McLean, author of "Cape Cod Folks," was again heard from in "Vesty of the Basins"; and Mary Hallock Foote was at home in "The Chosen Valley." Capt. Charles King told "A Soldier's Secret," a story of the Sioux war of 1890, and "An Army Portia" was written by him also. Richard Harding Davis described New York life in "Van Bibber and Others"; while genial John Habberton narrated the adventures of "A Lucky Lover," and showed how an ex-teacher was "Well out of it." "San Salvador," by Mary Agnes Tincker, pictured life as it might be. Novels which had a basis in history or dealt with historical characters were: "Columbus and Beatriz," who were both vindicated by Constance Goddard Du Bois; "Saint Augustine," a story of the Huguenots in America, by John R. Musick, who continued his series of "Columbian Historical Novels" with "Estevan," a story of the Spanish conquests, and "Pocahontas," of course a story of Virginia. Elise L. Lathrop adapted from the German of C. Falkenhorst "With Columbus in America," "With Pizarro in Peru," and "With Cortez in Mexico." "David Alden's Daughter, and Other Stories of Colonial Times," twelve in number, were from the pen of Mrs. Jane G. Austin; and Augusta Campbell Watson described "The Old Harbor Town" as visited by Benedict Arnold. "Fergus M. Tavish; or, Portage and Prairie," was a story of the Hud-

son Bay Company, by J. Macdonald Oxley; and a tale of old Pennsylvania, by Olivia L. Wilson, was entitled "At the Sign of the White Swan." Henry W. French, as Abd el Ardavan, told the story of "The Lance of Kanana," the Bedouin boy who delivered Arabia; and "Ben-Beor" was a story of the Antimessiah, in two divisions, by Rabbi H. M. Bien, intended as a companion romance to Eugene Sue's "Wandering Jew." "Thrilling Scenes in the Persian Kingdom" purported to be the story of a scribe, by Edwin MacMinn; A. D. Hall and Robert L. Downing discovered "A True Knight" in the days of Dionysius of Syracuse; "A Highland Chronicle" was written by S. Bayard Dod; and "In the Vulture's Nest," by Mildred Fairfax, depicted the Huguenots at the court of France in 1572. "Virginia Dare," the first white child born in the colony of Virginia, gave her name to a romance by E. A. B. S.; "A Golden Gossip," by Mrs. A. D. T. Whitney, was "Neighborhood Story Number Two," and made a pleasant addition to her wholesome, cheery books; "Silhouettes of American Life," by Mrs. Rebecca Harding Davis, was the first collection made of her shorter stories; and she was also the author of "Kent Hampden." From Eliza Orne White, author of "Miss Brooks," came "Winterborough," another typical New England story: "Quabbin," by Francis H. Underwood, was the story of a small town, with outlooks upon Puritan life; "Walter Graham, Statesman," an American romance, by "An American," dealt with the political situation prior to the war for the Union and until 1887; New York life formed the theme of "Gramercy Park," by John Seymour Wood (who wrote also "A Daughter of Venice"), and of "Some Children of Adam," by R. M. Manley; the scene of "From Schoolroom to Bar," by W. H. W. Moran, was laid in Virginia; while from the author of "Drew Drake and his Nets" we had "Far out on the Prairies." "Early Times in Texas" were described by J. C. Duval, who continued the adventures of Jack Dobell in "The Young Explorers." "Monica, the Mesa Maiden," became the heroine of Mrs. Evelyn Raymond. Southern life was portrayed by Jeanie Drake in a striking novel, "In Old St. Stephen's," the historic church of Charleston, S. C.; while Joel Chandler Harris in "Uncle Remus and his Friends"—which, to the regret of many, concludes the series of Uncle Remus stories—and in his story of a Georgia boy's adventures during the civil war, entitled, "On the Plantation." Richard Malcolm Johnston published "Mr. Billy Downs and his Likes" in the "Fiction, Fact, and Fancy Series," edited by Arthur Stedman; "Mr. Fortner's Marital Claims, and Other Stories"; and six of his original "Dukesborough Tales," being "The Chronicles of Mr. Bill Williams," in "Appletons' Town and Country Library." "Winona," by Ella M. Powell, "A Blonde Creole," by Alice Howard Hilton, "A Modern Quixote," by S. C. McCay, "The Modern Pariah," by Francis Fontaine, and "Buffeting," by Jeannette Pemberton, deal also with life south of Mason and Dixon's line; while "People at Pisgah" (in Vermont) were seen by Edwin W. Sanborn, and "The Down-East Master's First School" was described by

Edward A. Rand. "East and West" was a story of newborn Ohio, by Edward Everett Hale, who wrote also "Sybil Knox; or, Home Again," and, with Lucretia Peabody, "The New Harry and Lucy: A Story of Boston in the Summer of 1891." "Moonlight and 'Six Feet of Romance,'" by Daniel Beard, involves in its intricacies social reforms and the problems of capital and labor. "That Dakota Girl," by Stella Gilman (pseudonym); "Nakoma," a story of frontier life, by Rev. George Huntingdon; "The Jonah of Lucky Valley, and Other Stories," by Howard Seely; "Billow Prairie," by Joy Alleson; "Manuelita," the story of San Xavier Del Bac, the old Catholic mission in California, by Marian Calvert Wilson; and "Green Tea," a love story, the scene of which is also laid in California, by V. Schallenberger, belong to the West, as does "A Little Norsk; or, Ol' Pap's Flaxen," by Hamlin Garland, who wrote, in addition to this pretty, pathetic tale, "Jason Edwards, an Average Man," "A Spoil of Office," and "A Member of the Third House." Other stories of local color were: "An American Nobleman," by William Armstrong; "A Princess of Fiji," by William Churchill; "Don Finimondone," Calabrian sketches by Elizabeth Cavazza, who, despite her Italian name, never set foot upon the soil of the people whom she portrays with such graphic force; "Daughters of Men," by Hannah Lynch, which carries us to Greece; "The Colonel by Brevet," who figures at the Austrian court under the guidance of St. George Rathbone; "Squaw Elouise," by Marah Ellis Ryan, "Onoqua," by Frances C. Sparhawk, and "Manulito; or, A Strange Friendship," by William Bruce Leffingwell (Horace), all three about Indians; and "Kin-da-shon's Wife," an Alaskan story, by Mrs. Eugene S. Willard. "Roger Hunt," Celia Parker Wooley's third novel, aroused comment, as did Anna Fuller's "Pratt Portraits." "Calmire," which appeared anonymously, but is believed to have been written by an American, was serious in tone, attempting to reconcile agnosticism and orthodoxy. "That Angelic Woman," by James M. Ludlow, the author of "The Captain of the Janizaries," proved to be a trained nurse, and Graham Travers delighted to describe "Mona Maclean, Medical Student." "Tatters," by Fanny D. Bates; "Gold or Pleasure," by George Parsons Lathrop; "Other Things Being Equal," by Emma Wolf; "An Artist in Crime," by Rodrigues Ottolengui; "Muriel Howe," by Angelina Teal; "Courtland Laster, Capitalist," by Harley Deene; "The Other House," a study of human nature, by Kate Jordan; "A Son of Esau" and "The Woman who stood between," by Minnie Gilmore; "Miserere," a musical story, by Mabel Wagnalls; "Morris Julian's Wife," by Elizabeth Olmis; "The Primrose Path of Dalliance," by Andrew C. Wheeler (Nym Crinkle); "Sylvester Romaine," by Charles Pelletreau; "Imperia," by Octavia Hensel; and "A Close Shave; or, How Major Flagg won his Bet," by Thomas W. Knox, deserve mention: as do "A Daughter of the Druids," by A. K. Hopkins; "Neva's Three Lovers," "Beatrix Rohan," and "Cecil Rosse," by Mrs. Harriet Lewis; "Sherburne House," by Amanda M. Douglas; "Cynthia Wakeham's Money," by Anna Katharine Green (now Mrs.

Roblfs); "A Soul from Pudge's Corners," by Jessie F. O'Donnell; "John Thorndyke's Prejudice," a novel by Joanna H. Mathews, the author of the "Bessie Books" for children; "A Fellowship of Hearts," by Mary Fenton Bigelow; "The Las' Day," an old-fashioned love story by Imogen Clark; "A Rosebud Garden of Girls," by Nora Perry; "A Colony of Girls," by Kate Livingston Willard; and "A Study in Girls," by Edmund S. Middleton. "Adam's Daughters," by Julia McNair Wright, "Neighbors in Burton Square," by Alice Eddy Curtiss. and "Christine's Inspiration," by Barbara Yechton, were written with a purpose, as were "My Lady" and "Dorothy's Islands," by Mrs. Nathaniel Conklin (formerly Jennie M. Drinkwater). "The Rescue of an Old Place," by Mrs. Mary C. Robbins: "A Gentle Benefactress," by Mrs. J. J. Colter; "Polly Button's New Year," by Mrs. C. F. Wilder; "Sara, a Princess," and "Brian's Home," by Fannie E. Newberry; "The Conways," by Effie W. Merriman; "Miss Wilton," by Cornelia Warren; "Theo Waddington," by Julian Wyndham; "Where Duty lies," by Silas K. Hocking; "By Subtle Fragrance held," by Mary Fletcher Stevens; "The Face in the Rock," by W. J. Pierson; "A Seeming Trifle," by Mrs. M. J. Mallary; "The Opal Queen," by Eliza B. Swan; "Sybil Trevyllian," by Mrs. Reginald Hughes (Lyndon); "Majoribanks," by Elvirton Wright; "In Mother's Place; or, The Jay Family," by Kate Neely Festetits; and "Is it Possible?" by Helen Van Anderson, devoted to woman's rights and individual expansion. "Hermine's Triumphs" were chronicled by Mme. C. Colomb, and "Aurore" was from the pen of Elizabeth Boynton Harbert. "Chickamauga," by F. A. Mitchel, was, as its name indicates, a romance of the American civil war; as was "What it cost; or, Debtor and Creditor," by F. and I. E. Sullivan. "Congressman Swanson," by C. C. Post, and "Roland Graeme, Knight," by Agnes M. Machar, had their origin in the difficulties between capital and labor. Society was satirized in "Mrs. Harry St. John," by Robert Appleton (pseudonym), and other books which had their origin in existing social conditions were "A Survival of the Fittest," by Lewis B. Mason and Norman Elliot, and "A Common Mistake," by Jeanne M. Howell. "Manitou Island,' by M. G. McClelland. hardly presented that author at her best, while from Henry B. Fuller, the author of "The Chevalier of Il Pensiéri Vani," came another volume, "The Chatelaine of la Trinité," somewhat in the same vein. More exciting scenes are portrayed in "Scarabœus: The Story of an African Beetle," by Marquise Clara Lanza and James Clarence Harvey. "A Golden Pilgrimage" was by the first author alone. Ambrose Bierce and Gustav Adolph Danziger adapted from the German version of an old MS. "The Monk and the Hangman's Daughter," and the first told "Tales of Soldiers and Civilians." Mary R. P. Hatch made search for "The Missing Man"; "Sweet Danger" was suggested by Mrs. Ella Wheeler Wilcox, who wrote also "An Erring Woman's Love"; and William C. Hudson was heard from "On the Rack." "The Blue Scarab" was searched for by David G. Adee; "Why I'm Single" was explained by Albert Ross (Linn Boyd Porter); and "The Master of Silence," a phenomenal youth, with preternatural surroundings, was outlined by Irving Bacheller. Other novels of a sensational character were "Gold Dust," by Emeline Daggett Harvey; "Wedded Unwooed," by Julia H. Gatewood; "His Angel," by Henry Herman; "Her Mistake," anonymous; and "The Other Bond," by Dora Russell. "Slaves of the Sawdust" was written by Amye Reade to expose the cruelties of trainers for the circus ring, and "The Mysterious Beggar,' by Albert A. Day, to perform a similar service for professional beggars. Tales of the marvelous were "Messages from Mars by the Aid of the Telescope Plant," by Robert D. Braine; "Born of Flame," a Rosicrucian story, by Mrs. Mary B. Peeke; "The Devil's Gold," by Oscar F. G. Day; "The Goddess of Atvatbar," by William R. Bradshaw; "A Maiden of Mars," by F. M. Clarke; "A Bargain in Souls: An Impossible Story," by Ernest de Lancey Pierson; "Poseidon's Paradise," by Elizabeth G. Birkmaier; "The Austral Globe," by Milton W. Ramsey; "Lost in the Wilderness," by R. H. Jayne; "Two Men and a Girl," by Franklyn Lee; and "Linked with Fate," by J. L. Berry.

Capital volumes of short stories, in addition to those already mentioned, are "In Sunflower Land," by Roswell Martin Field (a brother of Eugene Field); "A New England Cactus, and Other Tales," by Frank Pope Humphrey; "Tales of a Time and Place," by Grace King, the author of "Monsieur Motte"; "My Friend Pasquale, and Other Stories," by James Selwin Tait; "The Lesson of the Master," by Henry James; "The Governor, and Other Stories," by George A. Hibbard; "In Beaver Cove and Elsewhere," by Matt Crim; "Far from To-day," by Gertrude Hall; 'The History of a Failure, and Other Tales," by E. Chilton; "A Capillary Crime, and Other Stories," by F. D. Millet; "A Charge for France, and Other Stories," by John Heard, Jr.; "A Christmas at Sea," edited by E. Shippen; "Old Ways and New," by Viola Roseboro; "Improbable Tales," by Clinton Ross; "A Millbrook Romance, and Other Tales," by A. L. Donaldson; "Merry Tales," by Mark Twain (Samuel L. Clemens); "The Bull Calf, and Other Tales," by A. B. Frost; and "In a Steamer Chair, and Other Shipboard Stories," by Robert Barr (Luke Sharp). "Truth in Fiction," by Paul Carus, consisted of twelve tales with a moral. Katharine Jenkins wrote "Was it a Lost Day, and Other Stories"; Helen M. Gardiner, "Pushed by Unseen Hands"; and Fanny Purdy Palmer, "A Dead Level, and Other Episodes." "Stories from Indian Wigwams and Northern Camp Fires," by Egerton Ryerson Young, portrayed the North American Indian from the experience of a missionary. "O'er Railroad Cross-Ties with Gripsack," by George L. Marshall, was a compilation of stories by and about drummers; "The Story-Teller, No. 1," was the first bound volume of "Two Tales," and No. 6 was issued of "Tales from Town Topics." The recent death of Herman Melville led to a new issue of his four novels, "Typee," "Omoo," "White Jacket," and "Moby Dick; or, The White Whale"; and George W. Curtis's "Prue and I" was beautifully illustrated by Albert E. Sterner. "Tales from the Dramatists," in four volumes, by Charles Morris, and "Tales from Ten Poets" (of the Victorian reign), by Harrison S. Morris, in three volumes, made a success. "The Fate of Fenella" was unique in that it was decided by twenty-four different authors, American and English, in as many chapters. Useful "Descriptive Lists" of novels dealing with life in Germany, France, Italy, and Russia were compiled by William M. Griswold.

Juvenile Books.—The young people of this generation are exceptionally favored. Many of the books provided for their entertainment are now written by authors who have earned their fame in a wider field, and find so many grown-up readers that it is almost impossible to draw the dividing line between adult and adolescent literature. William Dean Howells was the author of "Christmas Every Day, and Other Stories told for Children"; Mrs. Frances Hodgson Burnett published but one book during the year, "Giovanni and the Other: Children who have made Stories"; and "The End of a Rainbow, an American Story," bright and breezy, came from Rossiter Johnson. Hjalmar Hjorth Boyesen described "Boyhood in Norway," "The Fortunes of Toby Trafford" were traced by John T. Trowbridge, and "Gulf and Glacier; or, The Percivals in Alaska," by Willis Boyd Allen, appeared in the "Pine Cone Series." Familiar writers were well represented: Charles F. Holder, by "Along the Florida Reef"; Horatio Alger, Jr., by "Digging for Gold," a story of California, and "The Young Boatman of Pine Point"; Oliver Optic (W. T. Adams) by "A Millionaire at Sixteen," "Fighting for the Right," and "A Young Knight Errant; or, Cruising in the West Indies"; Harry Castlemon (Charles A. Fosdick) by "Marcy the Refugee"; W. O. Stoddard by "The Battle of New York"; Kirk Munroe by "Cab and Caboose," the story of a railroad boy, and "Canoemates"; Edward S. Ellis by "From the Throttle to the President's Chair" and "On the Trail of the Moose"; and Ingersoll Lockwood by "Baron Trump's Marvelous Underground Journey," illustrated by C. Howard Johnson. "Diego Pinzon" was commemorated in "Harper's Young People," new series, by John Russell Coryell; W. E. Meyer narrated the thrilling adventures of three boys "Wrecked on the Bermudas"; and Henry W. French carried two others "Through Arctics and Tropics around the World." "Five Little Peppers Grown-Up," by Margaret Sidney (Mrs. H. M. Lothrop); "In Blue Creek Cañon" and "The Cadets of Flemming Hall," by Anna Chapin Ray; "Tom Clifton; or, Western Boys in Grant and Sherman's Army, 1861-'65," by Warren Lee Goss"; "In Camp with a Tin Soldier," by John Kendrick Bangs, a sequel to the "Tiddledywink Tales"; "Marjorie's Canadian Winter," by Agnes Maule Machar; "Elsie at Viamede," by Martha F. Finley (Martha Farquharson); "Wytch Winnie's Studio," by Mrs. Elizabeth W. Champney; "Miss Malcolm's Ten," by Margaret E. Winslow (both stories for the King's Daughters); "What Girls can do," by Mrs. H. K. Potwin; "Hildegarde's Home," by Mrs. Laura E. Richards; "Flying Hill Farm," by Sophie Swett; "Santos' Brother" and "A Crown of Thorns," by Flora Haines Loughhead; "At the End of a Rainbow," by Julia A. Sabine; "The Rovings of a Restless Boy," by Katharine B. Foot; "Englishman's Haven," by W. J. Gordon; "More Good Times at Hackmatack," by Mary P.

Wells Smith; "The Captain of the 'Kittiewink,'" by Herbert D. Ward; "Miss Millie's trying," by Mary E. Bamford; "The Little Sister," by A. G. Plympton; "Maggie Bradford's Fair," the fourth of a series of sequels to the "Bessie Books," by Joanna H. Mathews; "Little Queenie," a story of child life sixty years ago, by Mrs. Emma Marshall; "Dr. Dodd's School," by James L. Ford; "Dr. Lincoln's Children," by Kate W. Hamilton; "The Moon Prince, and Other Nabobs," by R. K. Munkittrick; "Under the Water Oaks," by Marian Brewster; "The Little Twin Roses" and "Dan: A Story for Boys," by Mary D. Brine; "The Pony-Expressman," by J. F. Cowan; "The Midnight Warning," by E. H. Ilouse; and "The Story of Juliette," by Beatrice Washington, found eager and delighted readers, as did "The Pansy," edited by Isabella M. and G. R. Alden; "A Book of Cheerful Cats and Other Animated Animals," by J. G. Francis; "On Wheels, and how I came there," by W. B. Smith; "Tom Paulding," by James Brander Matthews, the story of a search for buried treasure in the streets of New York; "The Riverpark Rebellion," by Homer Green; "Through the Wilds: A Record of Sport and Adventure in the Forests of New Hampshire and Maine," by C. A. J. Farrar; "In his Own Way," by Carlisle B. Holding; "Jack Brereton's Three Months' Service," by Maria McIntosh Cox; "Roy's Opportunity," by Annie L. Hannah; and "Miss Matilda Archambeau Van Dorn," by Elizabeth Cummings. "Ruby and Ruthy," by Minnie E. Paull, was illustrated by Jessie McDermott; and Marietta Ambrosi described "Italian Child Life; or, Marietta's Good Times." "Miss Ashton's New Pupil" was a story of college life for young girls, by Mrs. S. S. Robbins; and from Marion J. Brunowe came "The Ghost at Our School, and Other Stories," reprinted from "The Ave Maria," and "The Sealed Packet." "A Slumber Song," by Nina Lilian Morgan, practically completes the list; "The Bunny Stories," by John H. Jewett, "The Wild Pigs," by Gerald Young, "The Beautiful Land of Nod," by Mrs. Ella Wheeler Wilcox, and "Maud Humphrey's Book of Fairy Tales" being for little children.

Fine Arts.—"The Grammar of the Lotus: A New History of Classic Ornament as a Symbol of Sun Worship," by William H. Goodyear, Curator of the Department of Fine Arts in the Brooklyn Institute of Arts and Sciences, was a volume of the first importance on the subject of ancient art, which was, moreover, sumptuously illustrated. James M. Hoppin wrote "The Early Renaissance, and Other Essays on Art Subjects," and Montgomery Schuyler made studies of "American Architecture." Two parts were published of "Architectural Rendering in Pen and Ink," by D. A. Gregg, to be followed by two more; and "The Colonial Architecture of Maryland, Pennsylvania, and Virginia" was photographed and arranged under the direction of Joseph Everett Chandler. "English Cathedrals," by Mrs. Schuyler Van Rensselaer, illustrated by Joseph Pennell, which first saw the light in 1887, was brought out anew in 1892, and "American Etchings," by S. R. Koehler and others, were also republished. An *édition de luxe* was issued of "American Illustrators," by F. Hopkinson Smith. "Imaginative Sketches," by Henry P. Kirby, were made from

pen drawings of cathedrals, chateaux, hotels, etc. "Old Italian Masters," engraved by Timothy Cole, with historical notes by W. J. Stillman, and brief comments by the engraver, made one of the handsomest gift books of the year, other exquisite volumes being "The Hours of Raphael in Outline," by Mary E. Williams, and "Recent International Art," by Walter Rowlands. "The Masters of Wood Engraving" received royal treatment at the hands of W. J. Linton; and "Sketches for Wrought-Iron Art Work, chiefly in the Styles of the Sixteenth, Seventeenth, and Eighteenth Centuries," were made by F. Moser. "Masterpieces by Fra Angelico" and "Parisian Photogravures." "In Gold and Silver," four short stories by George H. Ellwanger, illustrated by W. Hamilton Gibson and A. B. Wenzel, and "Poems by Dobson, Locker, and Praed," with facsimiles of water-color paintings, were fine specimens in their several lines. "China Collecting in America" formed the theme of Mrs. Alice Morse Earle, and Frederick Litchfield published an "Illustrated History of Furniture from the Earliest to the Present Time," the edition being limited to 200 copies. The Grolier Club issued a "Catalogue of an Exhibition of Illuminated and Printed Manuscripts, together with a Few Early Printed Books with Illuminations," and "Some Examples of Persian Manuscripts, with Plates in Facsimile and an Introductory Essay." "Pagan and Christian Rome," by Prof. Rodolfo Lanciani, formed a companion volume to "Ancient Rome in the Light of Modern Discoveries," by the same author, and was profusely illustrated. "The Great Streets of the World," illustrated by A. B. Frost, W. Douglas Almond, G. Jeanniot, and others, had the text contributed by Richard Harding Davis, Andrew Lang, and other writers, American and English; while choice collections were "Shepp's Photographs of the World," with "Direct Copies of Famous Paintings and Statuary by the World's Old and Modern Masters," by James W. and Daniel B. Shepp, and "Glimpses of the World: A Portfolio of Photographs, with Descriptive Text," prepared under the supervision of John L. Stoddard. Volume III, new series, of "Amateur Work, Illustrated," was issued, and two dainty books were "Sun Prints in Sky Tints," original designs by Irene E. Jerome, with appropriate selections, and "Gleams and Echoes," with wood engravings from drawings by eminent artists, to which we are indebted to A. R. G. In music we have the ninth volume of "The Musical Year-Book of the United States" for the season of 1891-'92, by G. H. Wilson, and "Rhythmical Gymnastics, Vocal and Physical," by Mary S. Thomson, containing the latest theories as to vocal development. Adolph Kielblock described "The Stage Fright," and told how to face an audience. Florence A. Fowle Adams contributed "Gesture and Pantomimic Action," in fine with which was "Americanized Delsarte Culture," by Emily M. Bishop. "Daisy Miller," by Henry James, was illustrated in an *édition de luxe* limited to 250 copies, and Charles Dudley Warner's "In the Levant" was brought out in a holiday edition; as were Curtis's "Prue and I"; "Marse Chan," by Thomas Nelson Page; "Hyperion," by Longfellow; "Zenobia," by

Ware; Sheridan's "School for Scandal"; and Irving's "Conquest of Granada," the illustrations being mostly in photogravure.

General Science.—The paucity of works of standard value in this department observed for many years is found in 1892. "Evolution in Science, Philosophy, and Art," popular lectures and discussions by eminent authorities before the Brooklyn Ethical Association, were collected into a volume, and Robert Grimshaw published the "Record of Scientific Progress for the Year 1891." "The Three Circuits: A Study of the Primary Forces," by Taylor Flick, was an attempt to prove electricity the direct cause of physical fact, and "Matter, Ether, and Motion," by A. E. Dolbear, reviewed the factors and relations of physical science. "Biological Teaching in the Colleges of the United States," by John P. Campbell, was issued as one of the "Circulars of Information of the United States Bureau of Education"; Arabella M. Buckley (Mrs. Fisher) reviewed "The Moral Teachings of Science," in six chapters, originally written for "The Chautauquan," while "The Doctrine of Evolution, its Scope and Influence," in the "Evolution Series," was from the pen of John Fiske. Volumes III and IV were issued of "The Silva of North America," by Charles Sprague Sargent. "Trees of the Northern United States" were treated by Prof. Austin C. Apgar, for the use of schools and private students; "Our Trees" was a popular account of the trees in the streets and gardens of Salem, and of the native trees of Essex County, Mass., by John Robinson; and J. T. Edwards, D. D., described "The Silva of Chautauqua Lake." Part XII of the third series of "The Butterflies of North America," by W. H. Edwards, was issued. A. A. Crozier supplied "A Dictionary of Botanical Terms," and Harriet C. Cooper made "Short Studies in Botany for Children." "Leaves and Flowers; or, Plant Studies for Young Readers," by Mary A. Spear; "The Making of Flowers," by Rev George Henslow, in the "Romance of Science Series"; "The Vacation Club," by Adah J. Todd; "A Song of Life," by Margaret Warner Morley; and No. 4 of "Nature Readers; Seaside and Wayside," by Julia McNair Wright, were all calculated to simplify and awaken a popular interest in scientific pursuits. Rev. J. A. Zahm enlarged into a volume a course of lectures delivered by him on "Sound and Music" before the Catholic University of America, at Washington, D. C. George Frederick Wright, D. D., contributed "Man and the Glacial Period" (with an appendix on "Tertiary Man," by Henry W. Haynes) to the "International Scientific Series"; "Har-Moad; or, The Mountain of the Assembly," by O. D. Miller, D. D., was a series of archæological studies, chiefly from the standpoint of the cuneiform inscriptions; "Technology and Civilization," by F. Reuleaux, was reprinted from the "Smithsonian Report for 1890," as was "Primitive Urn Burial," by J. F. Snyder, M. D.; "Primitive Man in Ohio," by Warren K. Moorehead, contained an elaborate presentation of recent explorations made among the prehistoric mounds in the valley of the Ohio river; while "Recent Archæological Explorations in the Valley of the Delaware" were chronicled by Charles C. Abbott in the "University of Pennsylvania Series in Philology, Literature, and Archæology." "Tracts for Archæologists," by T. H. Lewis, were reprinted from various periodicals. "Humanity in its Origin and Early Growth," by E. Colbert, traced man's progress through the lowest stages of evolution to his first conceptions of civilization and government; while "The Speech of Monkeys," by R. L. Garner, contained the results of novel experiments made in pursuance of an interesting theory. "Little Brothers of the Air" were lovingly dealt with by Olive Thorne Miller, and Richard Avis gave brief directions for "Bird Preserving, Bird Mounting, and the Preservation of Birds' Eggs." "A Laboratory Course in Invertebrate Zoölogy," by Hermon C. Bumpus; "An Introduction to Qualitative Chemical Analysis by the Inductive Method," by Delos Fall; "A Manual of Chemistry, Inorganic and Organic," with an introduction to the study of chemistry, by Arthur P. Luff, M. D.; "A Manual of Physics," by William Peddie, for university students; a "Manual of Plane Geometry on the Heuristic Plan," by G. Irving Hopkins, for advance work, and "The Theory of Errors and Method of Least Squares," by William Woolsey Johnson, are educational or theoretical; while to science practically applied belong: "Some Observations upon the Conductivity of a Copper Wire in Various Dielectries," by Fernando Sanford, in "Publications of Leland Stanford, Junior, University Studies in Electricity"; the "Standard Electrical Dictionary," by T. O'Connor Sloane, who published also "Electric Toy Making, Dynamo Building, and Electric Motor Construction"; "The Practical Management of Dynamos and Motors," by Francis B. Cracker and Schuyler S. Wheeler; "Electric Motor Construction for Amateurs," by C. D. Parkhurst; "Electricity up to Date for Light, Power, and Traction," by John B. Verity; "Transformers: Their Theory, Construction, and Application simplified," by Caryl D. Haskins; "Dynamometers and the Measurement of Power," by J. J. Flather; "Practical Directions for Winding Magnets for Dynamos," by Charles Hering; Edward Trevert's three books, "Practical Directions for Armature and Field-Magnet Winding," "Practical Directions for Electric Gas Lighting and Bell Fitting for Amateurs," and "How to make and use Induction Coils"; "Telegraphic Connections: Embracing Recent Methods in Quadruplex Telegraphy," by Charles Thom and Willis H. Jones, the first work of the kind in which colors are employed in showing the different lines; "The Mechanical and Other Properties of Iron and Steel in Connection with their Chemical Composition," by Augustus Vosmaer; "The Metallurgy of Lead and the Desilverization of Base Bullion," by H. O. Hofman; and a "Manual of Qualitative Blow-Pipe Analysis and Determinative Mineralogy," by F. M. Endlich.

Works on intellectual science were few, viz.: "A History of Modern Philosophy," from the Renaissance to the present, by B. C. Burt; "The Philosophy of Reid, as contained in the 'Inquiry into the Human Mind on the Principles of Common Sense,'" with an introduction and selected notes by E. Hershey Sneath, in the "Series of Modern Philosophers"; an abridgment by William James of his larger work on "Psychology," in the "American Science Series"; "A Syllabus of Psychology," by William M. Bryant, the author of "The World Energy"; and "The Elements of Logic, Theoretical and Practical," by James II. Hyslop.

History.—"The Discovery of America," with which our history properly begins, was narrated for us, with some account of ancient America and the Spanish conquest, by John Fiske. "The Memorial Story of America," comprising the important events, episodes, and incidents which make up the record of four hundred years, from 1492 to 1892, by Hamilton W. Mabie and Marshal H. Bright, had special chapters contributed by Senators Sherman and Dawes, Hon. Henry L. Dawes, Bishop Vincent, Miss Willard, and others; while "Four Hundred Years of American History," by Jacob Harris Patton, was a new revised and enlarged edition of that author's "Concise History of the American People" brought down to the present time. "America: Its Geographical History, 1492–1892," was the subject of six lectures delivered to graduate students of Johns Hopkins University by Walter B. Scaife, published as an extra of the "Johns Hopkins University Studies," with a supplement entitled "Was the Rio del Espiritu Santo of the Spanish Geographers the Mississippi?" Robert Reid Howison wrote a "History of the United States of America"; James Ford Rhodes, a "History of the United States from the Compromise of 1850," in two volumes, covering the eleven years to the opening of the war for the Union; and the long-expected third volume of John Bach McMaster's "History of the People of the United States, from the Revolution to the Civil War," also saw the light; beginning with the purchase of Louisiana, it closed with the surrender of Detroit by Hull in the War of 1812. A large-paper edition of Bancroft's "History of the United States" was brought out. "Studies in American History" was a teachers' manual drawn up by Mary Sheldon Barnes; D. H. Montgomery contributed "The Beginner's American History"; and the "American Republic" was an anonymous memorial volume of American history from 1492 to 1892. A study of "The Puritan in Holland, England, and America," by Douglas Campbell, in two volumes, was intended as an introduction to American history: while "The Pilgrims, Puritans, and Roger Williams vindicated: and his Sentence of Banishment ought to be revoked," was the rather slovenly title of a volume by Rev. T. M. Merriman. "A Half Century of Conflict," by Francis Parkman, formed Part VI of the series entitled "France and England in North America," filling the gap between Parts V and VII, previously issued, and covering the period between Count Frontenac and Montcalm and Wolfe. "The Colonial Era," in the "American History Series," by Rev. George Parke Fisher, ended with the declaration of war between England and France in 1756; and "Maryland's Attitude in the Struggle for Canada" was defined by J. W. Black in the "Johns Hopkins University Studies." "Fort Pitt and Letters from the Frontier" were published at Pittsburg, Pa., with a life of Gen. James O'Hara, the journal of Calderon, 1749, and the journal and letters of Capt. S. Ecuyer, commandant at Fort Pitt in 1763.

VOL. XXXII.—25 A

Vol. XX of "Early State Papers of New Hampshire" was edited and compiled by Albert Stillman Batchellor, and William L. Saunders performed a similar work (by order of the General Assembly) for "The Colonial Records of North Carolina" in ten volumes. An edition, limited to 500 copies, was issued of "Fragments of Revolutionary History: Being Hitherto Unpublished Writings of the Men of the Revolution," edited by Gaillard Hunt, under authority of the District of Columbia Society; and Clarence Winthrop Bowen edited a "History of the Centennial Celebration of the Inauguration of George Washington as First President of the United States," in an edition limited to 1,000 copies. "Essays on the Constitution of the United States published during its Discussion by the People, 1787–1788," were edited by Paul Leicester Ford. A "Financial History of Massachusetts, from the Organization of the Massachusetts Bay Company to the American Revolution," was written by Charles H. J. Douglas in "Studies in History, Economics, and Public Law," edited by Prof. Edwin R. A. Seligman, another issue of which was a "History of Municipal Ownership of Land on Manhattan Island to the Beginning of Sales by the Commissioners of the Sinking Fund in 1844," by George Ashton Black. Charles Francis Adams chronicled "Three Episodes of Massachusetts History: The Settlement of Boston Bay, The Antinomian Controversy, A Study of Church and Town Government," in two volumes; and "Stories of Massachusetts" were told by Mara L. Pratt, M. D., and Anna Temple Lovering, in the "Young Folks' Library of American History." In the "Story of the States" series, "The Story of Massachusetts" was from the pen of Edward Everett Hale, and "The Story of New Mexico" from that of Horatio O. Ladd. "Vermont: A Study of Independence," fell into line in the "American Commonwealths" series; it was by Rowland E. Robinson. Charles Robinson, the war Governor of the State, presented his views of "The Kansas Conflict"; and "The Story of the Black Hawk War," by Reuben Gold Thwaites, was reprinted from Vol. XII of "Wisconsin's Historical Collections," as was "The Planting of the Swiss Colony at New Glarus, Wisconsin," by John Luchsinger. Part I of Vol. II, "Publications of the Historical Society of Southern California," consisted of "Documents from the Sutro Collection," translated, annotated, and edited by George Butler Griffin. "The Centenary of Kentucky," published by the Filson Club, contained the record of proceedings at the celebration of the hundredth anniversary of the admission of the State into the Union. Vol. II of "The Memorial History of the City of New York," edited by James Grant Wilson, was issued. The "Early Grants and Incorporation of the Town of Ware" were collected into a volume by Edward II. Gilbert, and a "History of the Town of Oxford, Mass., with Genealogies and Notes of Persons and Estates," was published by G. F. Daniels with the co-operation of the town. Canon Brigstocke edited a "History of Trinity Church, St. John, New Brunswick, 1791–1891." Three historical essays by Oliver T. Morton were entitled "The Southern Empire." To war history belong "A Few Acts and Actors in the Tragedy of the Civil War in the United States," by William

Bender Wilson; "Slavery in the District of Columbia: The Policy of Congress and the Struggle for Abolition," by Mary Tremain, in the "University of Nebraska Seminary Papers"; "The Army of Northern Virginia in 1862," by Col. William Allan, C. S. A.; "Personal Recollections of the War of the Rebellion," addresses delivered before the New York Commandery of the Military Order of the Loyal Legion of the United States; "A Famous Battery and its Campaigns, 1861–1864" (Varian's battery of light artillery, formerly Company I of the Eighth New York State Militia), by James E. Smith, including "The Career of Corporal Tanner in War and in Peace"; a "History of the Tenth New York Cavalry"; "Early Days in the Black Hills," and "Some Account of Capt. Jack Crawford, the Poet Scout." The "History of Battery E, First Regiment Rhode Island Light Artillery, in the War of 1861 and 1865 to preserve the Union," was written by George Lewis, and the "History of the First Regiment of Massachusetts Cavalry Volunteers" by B. W. Crowninshield. W. F. Tiemann compiled "The One Hundred and Fifty-ninth Regiment Infantry, New York State Volunteers, in the War of the Rebellion, 1862–1865," and Louis F. Emilio was the author of a "History of the Fifty-fourth Regiment of Massachusetts Infantry, 1863–1865," one of the first black regiments put into the field. Benn Pitman edited "The Trials for Treason at Indianapolis." Leaving our own country, though not our continent, we have "A History of Peru," by Clements R. Markham, an authority, inaugurating the "Latin-American Republics Series," and "Mexico in Transition from the Power of Political Romanism to Civil and Religious Liberty," by William Butler, D. D. "Stories from English History for Young Americans" were collected anonymously, and H. Pomeroy Brewster and George H. Brewster drew up a concise compendium of the history of England and its people under the title of "England and its Rulers"; while several periods of French history were treated in a masterly manner by more than one American author, "France under the Regency, with a Review of the Administration of Louis XIV" being by James Breck Perkins; "The Eve of the French Revolution," by Edward J. Lowell, who took, for an American, a conservative view of the situation in France at the time preceding the great cataclysm; and "Monsieur Henri: A Footnote to French History," by Louise Imogen Guiney, the story of La Rochejaquelin and La Vendée. "France in the Nineteenth Century, 1830–1890," was treated by Mrs. Elizabeth Wormeley Latimer, and "The Rise of the Swiss Republic" by W. D. McCrackan. "A Footnote to History: Eight Years of Trouble in Samoa," came from Robert Louis Stevenson, while Edgar Saltus selected a remoter time and theme, recording in "Imperial Purple" the crimes of the Cæsars, from Julius to Heliogabalus. "Select Mediæval Documents, and Other Material illustrating the History of Church and Empire," 754–1254 A. D.," fell into the hands of Shailer Matthews. "Bibliotheca Americana" is a dictionary of books relating to America from its discovery to the present time, for which we are indebted to Joseph Sabin; Parts CXV and CXVI were published during the year.

Phœbe Elizabeth Thoms compiled "Important Events in the World's History," and a third edition, revised and brought down to 1892, was issued of the "Historical Reference Book," by Louis Heilprin.

Housekeeping.—Two æsthetic volumes contrived in this most prosaic of departments were: "The Art of Entertaining," by Mrs. M. E. W. Sherwood, which contained much entertaining reading matter of a varied literary character as well as valuable practical instruction, and "Three Hundred and Sixty-six Dinners suggested by M. E. N.," the compiler of which was Mary E. Nichol. Mrs. Marie H. Taylor, widow of Bayard Taylor, published for general benefit the "Letters to a Young Housekeeper," originally addressed to her daughter, while Miss Anna B. Warner (Amy Lathrop) was "Up and Down the House" in 19 papers, and Miss Elizabeth F. Holt went "From Attic to Cellar," showing how housekeeping could be made easy. "The Little Dinner" achieved by Christine Terhune Herrick was a success, and the "majority edition" was issued of "Common Sense in the Household," by Marion Harland (Mrs. Terbune). Agnes Bailey showed how to make "The House Comfortable"; Mary Lampson Clarke compiled "Cooking for the Sick and Convalescent." William Schmidt (The Only William), in "The Flowing Bowl," gave full instructions what and when to drink, and how to prepare, mix, and serve drinks; also recipes. Evelyn H. Raymond was an authority on "Mixed Pickles." Edward Atkinson wrote a "Treatise upon the Science of Nutrition," and Annie E. Myers furnished in "Home Dressmaking" a complete guide to household sewing.

Jurisprudence.—Two volumes were devoted to "Modern Equity" by Charles Fisk Beach, Jr., whose "Counter Negligence: A Treatise on the Law of Contributory Negligence," went through a second edition during the year and Joel Prentiss Bishop was heard from in two volumes of a new work based on former editions of "New Commentaries on the Criminal Law upon a New System of Legal Exposition," bearing the same title, Vol. I being "General and Elementary," and Vol. II covering "The Specific Offenses," each volume being complete in itself. Vol. VI was issued of "The Adjudged Cases on Defenses to Crime," by John D. Lawson, being the first supplementary volume to the original series, and Irving Browne drew up "The Elements of Criminal Law, Principles, Pleading, and Procedure," for the use of law schools and students. Louis Hochheimer prepared a "Digest of the Law of Crimes and Criminal Procedure in Maryland," and Vol. VIII of "American Criminal Reports" was issued, with notes and references by John Gibbons; "Rights, Duties, Remedies, and Incidents belonging to and growing out of the Relation of Landlord and Tenant," were defined by David McAdam and Wayland E. Benjamin; and a fourth edition, revised and greatly enlarged, was made of "A Treatise on the Law of Judgments," by A. C. Freeman, in two volumes. Samuel Maxwell wrote a "Treatise on the Law of Pleading under the Code of Civil Procedure, designed for all the Code States," with forms and directions; Frank S. Rice, "General Principles of the Law of Evidence," in 2 volumes; James

Bradley Thayer prepared "Select Cases on Evidence at the Common Law," with notes; while Vol. I of the fifteenth revised edition of "A Treatise on the Law of Evidence," by Simon Greenleaf, was published with large additions by Simon Greenleaf Croswell. "A Treatise on the Law of Malicious Prosecution, False Imprisonment, and the Abuse of Legal Process," was by Martin L. Newell; G. Chase compiled "Leading Cases upon the Law of Torts "; John Chipman Gray's "Select Cases and Other Authorities on the Law of Property," reached Vol. VI; a second edition was published of "An Elementary Treatise on the American Law of Real Property," by Christopher G. Tiedeman ; Richard M. Venable treated "The Law of Real Property and Leasehold Estates," abridged from lectures delivered to the Law School of the University of Maryland; Vol. I of "The Annual of the Law of Real Property," edited by Tilghman Ballard and E. Emerson, appeared; and J. B. Moyle wrote on "The Contract of Sale in the Civil Law," with references to the laws of England, Scotland, and France. Leonard A. Jones published a third revised edition of "Forms in Conveyancing," and general legal forms. "Contractual Limitations," by Charles A. Ray, included trade strikes and conspiracies and corporate trusts and corporations. Louis Boisot laid down "The Law of By-Laws of Private Corporations," and Conrad Reno drew up "A Treatise on the Law of Nonresidents and Foreign Corporations." "A Treatise on the Negligence of Municipal Corporations," by Dwight Arven Jones, was in line with a "Treatise on the Law of Damages by Corporations, including Cases *Damnum Absque Injuria*," in 2 volumes, by George E. Harris, who was also responsible for "A Treatise on Sunday Laws." T. C. Spelling wrote a "Treatise on the Law of Private Corporations," in 2 volumes, which exhausted the subject. "Military Government and Martial Law," much discussed during the year, formed the subject of a volume by W. E. Birkhimer. "A Treatise on the Law relating to Public Officers and Sureties in Official Bonds " was written by Montgomery H. Throop, and S. S. Merrill confined himself to the "Law of Mandamus." Edward N. Darrow sent out a "Treatise on Mortgage Investments"; Stewart Chaplin, "Principles of the Law of Wills, with Selected Cases"; Moses A. Dropsie, "The Roman Law of Testaments, Codicils, and Gifts in the Event of Death"; and D. L. Rhone published Vol. III of "Supplement to Rhone's Orphans' Court Practice in Pennsylvania." "A Treatise on Building Associations," adapted to the use of lawyers and officers, with a complete set of forms, was by Charles N. Thompson ; "The Law of Fire Insurance," with an analytical discussion of recent cases, by D. Ostrander; and a "Treatise on the Law of Insurance, Fire, Life, Accident, Marine," with a selection of leading illustrative cases, by G. Richards. John A. Finch drew up a "Digest of Insurance Cases"; "The Law relating to the Mining of Coal " was set forth by Albert B. Weimar; "The Law of Public Health and Safety, and the Powers and Duties of Boards of Health," by Leroy Parker and Robert H. Worthington; and "The Law of Railroad Fences and Private Crossings," including injuries to animals on right of way caused by negligence, by Claude Tillier. H. C. Chapman, M. D., prepared "A Manual of Medical Jurisprudence and Toxicology," and William F. Rehfuss "A Treatise on Dental Jurisprudence," for dentists and lawyers. "The Law of the Theatre " was a treatise upon the legal relations of actors, managers, and audiences, by Samuel H. Wandell. "Economic Legislation of all the States," in 2 volumes, one of which was published in 1892, edited by Allen Ripley Foote and Charles E. Everett, stated the law of incorporated companies operating under municipal franchises, such as illuminating and fuel gas, electric central station companies, etc. Henry Campbell Black prepared "A Treatise on the Laws regulating the Manufacture and Sale of Intoxicating Liquors "; a second revised edition of Rowland Cox's "Manual of Trade-mark Cases " was brought down to the present time; and "Decisions on the Law of Patents for Inventions rendered by the United States Supreme Court from the Beginning " (from 128 United States, 1888, to 132 United States, 1889), edited by Woodbury Lowery, formed Vol. XIX of Brodix's "American and English Patent Cases." Vols. XVII, XVIII, XIX, and XX of the "American and English Encyclopædia of Law," edited by John Houston Merrill, were published; also Vols. XXXIV, XXXV, XXXVI, and XXXVII of "American and English Corporation Cases," and Vols. XLVII to L, inclusive, of "American and English Railroad Cases." Vol. V was reached of "American Railroad and Corporation Reports," edited and annotated by John Lewis; and Vol. I was issued of "A Digest of all Railroad and Corporation Decisions of the Federal Courts," by Stewart Rapaljé, covering January to June, 1892. H. D. Clarke was the author of a "Handbook of all the Decisions of the Supreme Court of the United States " from its organization to the October term, 1891, Part I being an index by subjects, and Part II an index by cases. Vols. X, XI, and XII of "The United States Supreme Court Reporter" (permanent edition) were sent out ; also the sixth (annual) volume of a "General Digest of the Decisions of the Principal Courts in the United States"; Vols. XXII to XXVII, inclusive, of "American State Reports," by A. C. Freeman; together with a "Digest of the Decisions of the Courts of Last Resort, 1887 to 1892," contained in Vols. I to XXIV, inclusive, of the same; Vol. VII of "American Probate Reports," by Charles Fisk Beach, Jr.; Vols. XXVII and XXVIII of "New Cases," selected by Austin Abbott chiefly from decisions of the courts of the State of New York, with notes; and the "Digest of New York State Reports from Jan. 1, 1891 to Jan. 1, 1892," also by Austin Abbott. "The Pension Attorney's Guide " was due to the joint labors of T. P. Randolph and E. P. Hall; and among the numerous works relating to law in the several States may be enumerated: "The Land Laws of Tennessee," compiled and edited by H. D. Whitney; a "Treatise on the Laws of Texas relating to Real Estate," by John and Henry Sayles; "Precedents and Notes of Practice in Civil Cases in the Higher Courts of Law of the State of New Jersey," by Oscar Jeffery; and Vols. XXVIII and XXIX of "Weekly Notes " of cases argued and determined in the various courts of the eastern district of Pennsylvania. " Lectures on Law for Women," delivered by Isaac Franklin Russell at the University of the City of New York, 1892–'93, were collected into a volume; St. George T. Brooks made " Notes on Common-Law Pleading and Practice," for students in the University of West Virginia; " Contracts," by Clarence D. Ashley, consisted of extracts, citations, condensed cases, and statements prepared for the use of students, and " Experience at the Office Desk " was compiled to the same end by S. Vos. Eugene Wambaugh gave instructions for the " Study of Cases." " Law Language for the Use of Stenographers and Typewriters " proved a useful little manual of its kind, as did the " Instructor in Practical Court Reporting," of H. W. Thorne. " Skill in Trials," by J. W. Donovan, revived famous cases won by famous men. " Martindale's American Law Directory " made its biennial appearance for 1892–'93 ; " Sharp and Alleman's Lawyers' and Bankers' Directory for 1892 " contained over 7,000 names of attorneys in the United States and Canada; and " Hubbell's Legal Directory for Lawyers and Business Men " was issued, revised and brought down to Oct. 1, 1891. A " Legal and Mercantile Handbook of Mexico " was produced by A. K. Coney and J. F. Codoy in collaboration.

Medicine and Surgery.—In medicine we have two volumes on " Modern Therapeutics," by George H. Napheys, M. D. ; " Notes on the Newer Remedies," by David Cerna, M. D., giving the therapeutic applications and modes of administration of comparatively unknown medicinal remedies; " Principles and Practice of Medicine," designed for practitioners and students, by William Osler, M. D. ; a " Text-Book of the Practice of Medicine," by R. C. M. Page, M. D. ; " Essentials of Diagnosis," arranged in the form of questions and answers for students of medicine, by S. S. Cohen, M. D., and A. Eshner, M. D. ; and a " Primer of Materia Medica," for practitioners of homœopathy, by Timothy Field Allen, M. D. ; while " How to feel the Pulse and what to feel in it," by William Ewart, M. D., contained valuable practical hints for beginners. From the same author we had " Cardiac Outlines." N. S. Davis, Jr., M. D., treated " Diseases of the Lungs, Heart, and Liver " in the " Physicians' and Students' Ready Reference Series," and also wrote on " Consumption: How to prevent it and how to live with it " ; Sidney Coupland, M. D., edited a " Treatise on Diseases of the Lungs and Pleura," by Wilson Fox, M. D. ; M. L. Holbrook, M. D., suggested " The Hygienic Treatment of Consumption " ; and J. M. Buckley described " A Hereditary Consumptive's Successful Battle for Life." " Materialism and Modern Physiology of the Nervous System " was the title of an address made before the faculty of Columbia College, Feb. 16, 1892, by Prof. William H. Thomson; Christian A. Herter, M. D., wrote on " The Diagnosis of Diseases of the Nervous System " ; J. A. Ornurod, M. D., on " Diseases of the Nervous System " ; Herbert W. Page on " Railway Injuries, with Special Reference to those of the Back and Nervous System, in their Medico-Legal and Clinical Aspects " (reprinted from " Wood's Medical and Surgical Monographs ");

and a second edition was made of " Nerve Prostration and Other Functional Disorders of Daily Life," by Robson Roose, M. D. George H. Rohé, M. D., and J. Williams Lord contributed a " Practical Manual of Diseases of the Skin " to the " Physicians' and Students' Ready Reference Series " ; " Tuberculosis of Bones and Joints " was discussed by N. Senn, M. D. Vol. II of " Diseases of the Nose and Throat," by Franke Huntington Bosworth, M. D., was issued, devoted to the diseases of the throat; Samuel Sexton, M. D., and Alexander Duane, M. D., wrote, in collaboration, on " Deafness, and Discharge from the Ear " ; G. E. de Schweinitz, M. D., published " Diseases of the Eye," a handbook of ophthalmic practice; A. B. Norton, M. D., " Ophthalmic Diseases and Therapeutics " ; and Henry D. Noyes, M. D., a " Text-Book on Diseases of the Eye." A " Treatise on Diseases of the Rectum, Anus, and Sigmoid Flexure " was by Joseph M. Mathers, M. D. ; " Diabetes: A Post-graduate Course of Lectures, with Microscopic Illustrations," by Robert Saundby, M. D., and " Indigestion," by George Herschell, M. D., were valuable manuals. Allard Memminger, M. D., made a " Diagnosis of the Urine " ; John W. S. Gouley, M. D., described " Diseases of the Urinary Apparatus ; Phlegmasie Affections," in a series of twelve lectures delivered during the autumn of 1891: " Ringworm : Its Constitutional Nature and Cure," was exhaustively treated by J. Compton Burnett ; a " Text-Book of the Eruptive and Continued Fevers " called forth all the ability of George W. Moore, M. D. ; and C. Sihler advocated enthusiastically the " Hydriatic Treatment of Typhoid Fever according to Brand, Tripier, Bouveret, and Vogel." " The Hydropathic Establishment and its Baths " formed the theme of Robert Owen Allsop; and James Graham, M. D., considered " Hydatid Disease in its Clinical Aspeets." Geo. H. F. Nuttall, M. D., condensed information as to " Hygienic Measures in Relation to Infectious Diseases " ; and a similar work, anonymous, was " Safety in Cholera Times: Homœopathic Treatment." " Geographical Pathology," by Andrew Davidson, M. D., in two volumes, made an inquiry into the geographical distribution of infective and climatic diseases. George M. Sternberg drew up " A Manual of Bacteriology " ; Eli F. Brown, M. D., made a study of " Sex and Life " ; S. Pozzi wrote a " Treatise on Gynæcology, Medical and Surgical," in two volumes; George Sedgwick Minot, of " Human Embryology " ; and J. Clarence Webster, of " Tuboperitoneal Ectopic Gestation." " Practical Midwifery " was a handbook of treatment by Edward Reynolds, M. D. ; G. Ernest Herman wrote " First Lines in Midwifery " ; and " The Wife and Mother " formed the theme of Albert Westland. " Marriage and Disease," by S. A. K. Strahan, M. D., made a study of heredity and the more important family degenerations. " Practical Pathology," by G. Sims Woodhead, passed through a third edition, enlarged and revised ; F. J. Brockway arranged " Essentials of Physics," in the form of questions and answers, especially for students of medicine; and Charles E. Pellew published a " Manual of Practical Medical and Physiological Chemistry." " Unsoundness of Mind in its Legal and Medical Considerations," by J. W. Hume Williams, was reprinted from "Wood's Medical and Surgical Monographs." In surgery we had the "American Text-Book of Surgery for Practitioners and Students," by William W. Keen, M. D., and J. W. White, M. D.; "The Mastoid Operation," by S. Ellsworth Allen, giving its history, anatomy, and pathology; "General Orthopedics, including Surgical Operations," by Augustus Schreiber, M. D.; "The Anatomy and Surgical Treatment of Hernia," by Henry O. Marcy, M. D.; and "The Mütter Lectures on Select Topics: Surgical Pathology, for 1890–'91," by Roswell Park, M. D. Franklin Dexter, M. D., made a study of "The Anatomy of the Peritonæum"; George McClellan, M. D., of "Regional Anatomy in its Relation to Medicine and Surgery"; while J. Clarence Webster gave the result of "Researches in Female Pelvic Anatomy." A "Manual of Autopsies" was designed by T. W. Blackburn, M. D., for the use of hospitals for the insane and other public institutions. "Essentials of Medical Electricity" were set forth in short compass by D. D. Stewart, M. D.; Carrie Goldsmith wrote on "Massage for Nurses"; and "Nurses and Nursing" came from the pen of Lisbeth D. Price. Arvid Kellgren, M. D., set forth the "Technic of Ling's System of Manual Treatment as Applicable to Surgery and Medicine." "Hydrotherapy at Saratoga," by J. A. Irwin, M. D., was a treatise on natural mineral waters. Two useful volumes were "Every-day Ailments and Accidents and their Treatment at Home," edited by George Black, and the "First Aid in Illness and Injury," by James E. Pilcher, M. D. "The Microscopical Examination of Potable Water" was made by George W. Rafter. A "New Pronouncing Dictionary of Medicine," a voluminous and exhaustive handbook of medicine and scientific terminology, was produced by John M. Keating, M. D., Henry Hamilton, J. Chalmers Da Costa, and Frederick A. Packard. Vol. XIII of the "Index Catalogue" of the Library of the Surgeon-General's Office at Washington, D. C., was issued, covering Sialagogues–Sutugin; and No. 2 of Vol. XII of "Wood's Medical and Surgical Monographs" was reached. J. Aulde, M. D., constructed a "Pocket Pharmacy," with Therapeutic Index," a résumé of the clinical applications of remedies adapted to the pocket case for the treatment of emergencies and acute diseases; J. J. Taylor, M. D., gave novel advice to "The Physician as a Business Man"; and Thomas Lindsley Bradford. M. D., was the author of a "Homœopathic Bibliography of the United States from 1825–'91, inclusive," in two parts. "Temperament, Disease, and Health" were discussed by F. E. Chadwick. Mrs. Weeks-Shaw revised her "Text-Book of Nursing."

Poetry.—The last we shall ever hear of Whittier came to us "At Sundown," in a memorial volume containing all the poems he wrote after 1886, when he gave to us "St. Gregory's Guest"; and another poet, whose loss was mourned during the year, was recalled in "Selected Poems" of Walt Whitman, edited in the "Fiction, Fact, and Fancy Series" by Arthur Stedman. Maurice Thompson had a volume of "Poems," and Edna Dean Proctor sang in a noble and lofty strain "The Song of the Ancient People" (the Pueblo Indians), which had a preface and notes by John Fiske and a commentary by F. H. Cushing.

Will Carleton's "City Festivals" completed the "Farm and City Series." "Christmas once is Christmas still," a hymn by Bishop Phillips Brooks, was richly illustrated in colors; "The Dead Nymph, and Other Poems" of the late Charles Henry Lüders were selected by his friend Frank Dempster Sherman, who published on his own account "Little Folks Lyrics"; and 2 other books for children from those who have delighted maturer years were "With Trumpet and Drum," 50 poems by Eugene Field, and "Rhymes and Ballads for Girls and Boys," by the familiar Sarah C. Woolsey (Susan Coolidge). Another volume of posthumous verse was the "Poems" of George Pellew, edited, with an introduction, by William Dean Howells. "The Forging of the Sword, and Other Poems," by Juan Lewis, was illustrated by Charles Bradford Hudson; Francis S. Saltus was represented by 2 volumes, "Flasks and Flagons, Pastels and Profiles, Vistas and Landscapes" and "Dreams After Sunset, and Other Poems"; Dr. S. Weir-Mitchell, by 2 also, "The Mother, and Other Poems" and "Francis Drake: A Tragedy of the Sea"; from Clinton Scollard came "Songs of Sunrise Lands"; from Madison J. Cawein, "Moods and Memories" and "Giovio and Giulia," the last a dainty little booklet; and from Anne Reeve Aldrich, whose early death is to be lamented, "Songs about Life, Love, and Death." Oriental stories were "Told in the Gate," by Arlo Bates, in blank verse; and "With the 'Pousse Café'" was a collection of post-prandial verses, medical and humorous, written on occasions, by William Tod Helmuth, M. D. "Songs and Saunterings of a Poet and Naturalist" were chronicled by W. G. Barton and George W. Breed; "The Merrimack River, Hellenics, and Other Poems" of Benjamin W. Ball, were edited, with an introduction, by Frederick F. Ayer: "Songs of the White Mountains," by Alvin L. Snow, "Connecticut River Reeds," by Josiah D. Canning, and "Alaskana; or, Alaska in Descriptive and Legendary Poems," by Bushrod W. James, M. D., belong to what may be called poems of place; while narrative poetry was represented by "Atlina, Queen of the Floating Isle," by Mrs. M. B. M. Toland; "Zululu: The Maid of Anahuac," by Hanna A. Foster, the scene of which is laid among the ancient tribes of Mexico; "Edalaine: A Metrical Romance," by F. Roena Medini; "The Vagrant of Lover's Leap," by John T. Broderick; and "In the City by-the Lake," by Blanche Fearing. "The Song of America and Columbus" emanated from Kinahan Cornwallis; "Columbus" was again the subject of an epic poem by Samuel Jefferson; and "The Voyage of Columbus," by E. Nesbitt, was illustrated in colors by Will and Frances Brundage and J. Pauline Sunter. "Fort Sumter and its Defenders," an illustrated poem in 11 cantos. was from the pen of Samuel T. Baker. "Rowen: Second Crop Songs" were hailed from H. C. Bunner, as was "A Letter of Introduction," a farce by William D. Howells. in Harpers' "Black and White Series." Harriet Monroe published "Valeria," a tragedy, with other poems. No particular merit can be ascribed to "Songs and Sonnets," by Maurice F. Egan; "Thought Throbs," by Creedmore Fleenor; "At the Gate of Dreams," by James B. Kenyon; "The Flaming Meteor." by W. Hubbard Kernan; "A Dream of Other

Days," by J. C. Fife Cookson; "From Heart's Content," by Clara Doty Bates; "Parnassian Riches," by Julius L. Hempstead; "Eleusis, and Lesser Poems," by William Rufus Perkins; "Rings and Love Knots," by S. Minturn Peck; "Quiet Music," by Charles Eugene Banks, with an introduction by Opie Read; "By the Atlantic: Later Poems," of I. D. Van Duzee; "Night Etchings," by A. K. G.; "A Volume of Poems," by Mrs. M. A. B. Kelly; "Dreams and Days," by George Parsons Lathrop; "Souvenirs of Occasions," by Sarah Louisa Oberholtzer; "Losing Ground: A Series of Sonnets," by Henry Wolcott Bowen; "Poems," of Eleanor C. Donnelly; "Lyrics," of Cora Fabbri; "The Wings of Icarus," by Susan Marr Spalding; "Summer-Fallow," by Charles Buxton Going; "The Dream of Art," by Espy Williams; "Links from Broken Chains," by Donizetti Muller; "Poems," by Edith Willis Linn; "Clytie, and Other Poems," by Marguerite E. Easter; and "The Pilgrim's Vision," by Minnie Willis Baines. "The End of Time," by L. G. Barbour, D. D.; "The Story of the Crucifixion," by William Mitchell; "The Feast of the Virgins, and Other Poems," by H. L. Gordon; and "The Tempting of the King," by William Vincent Byars, were all solemn or religious in tone. "Bessie Gray" and "Our Stepmother," by Martha Perry Lowe, were gotten up in holiday style, with pictures by well-known artists. A new complete edition was issued of "Poems," by Mrs. Julia C. R. Dorr; "Some Rhymes of Ironquill of Kansas" saw the light, and "Poems of Gun and Rod," by Earnest McGaffey, were illustrated by Herbert E. Butler. "The Dragon of Wantley," by Owen Wister, offered a new version of the old ballad. "By Mill and Stream" was a collection of poetical selections, compiled by Helen Marion Burnside, whose "Man the Lifeboat" was illustrated in colors; Vol. II was issued of the "Lover's Year-Book of Poetry," collected by Horace Parker Chandler; "A Book of Famous Verse" was selected by Agnes Repplier; Clinton Collins put together "All Poetry: A Selection of English Verse"; M. H. compiled "Poetry of the Gathered Years," as did Katharine Paine Sutton "Leaves of Healing"; and C. M. T. prepared a "Browning Year-Book." "As told by the Butterfly" were stories in verse, told by Mary Kennard, illustrated in color. "Watchwords from John Boyle O'Reilly" was edited, with an estimate of the poet, by Katherine E. Conway.

Political, Social, and Moral Science.—To political science belong "An Introduction to the Study of the Constitution," by Morris M. Cohn, in "Johns Hopkins University Studies," showing the play of physical and social factors in the creation of institutional law; "Man and the State," seventeen popular lectures and discussions of various political subjects before the Brooklyn Ethical Association; "Direct Legislation by the People," advocated by Nathan Cree; "Direct Legislation by the Citizenship through the Initiative and Referendum," stating concisely the methods in vogue in Switzerland, by James W. Sullivan; and "Historical and Political Essays," by Henry Cabot Lodge. "The Old South: Essays, Social, and Political," were written with a purpose by Thomas Nelson Page. The "Theory of Dynamic Economics" was set forth by Simon N. Pat-

ten in "Publications of the University of Pennsylvania, Political Economy and Public Law Series"; and the "Economic Causes of Moral Progress" in "Publications of the American Academy of Political and Social Science." "Patten's Dynamic Economics" were reviewed in the same "Publications," by John B. Clark. Edwin R. A. Seligman wrote "On the Shifting and Incidence of Taxation" in the "Publications of the American Economic Association," another issue of which was "Sinking Funds," by E. A. Ross; "Equitable Taxation" was the theme of six essays by Walter E. Weyl, Robert Luce, Bolton Hall, and others. "The Free-Trade Struggle in England," by M. M. Trumbull (Wheelbarrow), was revised and enlarged in a second edition. William M. Springer touched upon "Tariff Reform: The Paramount Issue"; "State Papers and Speeches on the Tariff," by eminent authorities on both sides of the protective controversy, had an introduction by F. W. Taussig; "The Tariff Controversy in the United States, 1789–1833," with a summary of the period before the adoption of the Constitution, was by Orrin Leslie Elliott, making No. 1 of "History and Economics Monographs of Leland Stanford, Junior, University"; Edward Atkinson collected a series of treatises on the tariff and the currency written by him for various daily newspapers, under the title of "Taxation and Work"; Fletcher W. Hewes and William McKinley, Jr., were jointly responsible for the Republican campaign handbook for 1892, "What are the Facts? Protection and Reciprocity illustrated"; while "Who pays your Taxes?" a consideration of the question of taxation by David A. Wells, George H. Andrews, Thomas G. Shearman, and others, in the "Questions of the Day Series," was edited by Bolton Hall. The "Basis of the Demand for Public Regulation of Industries" was investigated by W. D. Dabney in the "Publications of the American Academy of Political and Social Science"; "The Economy of High Wages," by J. Schoenhof, late United States Consul, had an introduction by Hon. Thomas F. Bayard; Augustus Jacobson prescribed "An Ounce of Prevention to save America from having a Government of the Few, by the Few, and for the Few," and he also published two *brochures*, "The Crisis of a Party" and "The Next Step forward," advocating similar theories. "Samson and Shylock" was a preacher's plea for the workingmen, himself a day laborer, by Rev. J. M. Driver; "Socialism," a chapter of Rev. Victor Cathrein's moral philosophy, edited by Rev. James Conway; and "The American Peasant: A Timely Allegory," by T. H. Tibbles and "Another." "Socialism, from Genesis to Revelation" was traced by Rev. F. M. Sprague. Daniel Strange wrote "The Farmer's Tariff Manual, by a Farmer," and Wilbur Aldrich proposed a project for "Farming Corporations." "The Geometrical Theory of the Determination of Prices" was defined by Léon Walras, and "A Third Revolution" was prophesied by Edward P. Cheyney, in "Publications of the American Academy of Political and Social Science," other issues of which were "Political Organization of a Modern Municipality," by W. D. Lewis; "Sir William Temple on the Origin and Nature of Government," by Frank I. Herriott; "The Influence on Business of the Independent Treasury," by David Kinley; "The Merits and Defects of the Pennsylvania Ballot Law of 1891," by C. C. Binney; "The Practical Working of the Australian System of Voting in Massachusetts," by Richard H. Dana; "River and Harbor Bills," by Emory R. Johnson; and "Cabinet Government in the United States," a pamphlet by Freeman Snow. "Political Economy for American Youth" was written from an American standpoint by Jacob Harris Patten; Thomas Hudson McKee was the author of "A Manual of Congressional Practice" (the United States Red Book); Edward McPherson published the "Handbook of Politics for 1892"; "Principles and Purposes of Our Form of Government as set forth in the Public Papers of Grover Cleveland" were compiled by Francis Gottsberger, while "The Republican Party and its Leaders" were chronicled by Thomas W. Knox. Chandos Fulton wrote the "History of the Democratic Party from Thomas Jefferson to Grover Cleveland," and revised editions were issued of "A Dictionary of American Politics," by Everit Brown and A. Strauss, and Stanwood's "History of Presidential Elections." "Railway Rates and Government Control," by Marshall M. Kirkman, and "State Railroad Commissions," by Frederick C. Clark (the last in "Publications of the American Association"), deserve careful perusal. Henry George was heard from in "A Perplexed-Philosopher: Being an Examination of Mr. Herbert Spencer's Various Utterances on the Land Question, with Some Incidental Reference to his Synthetic Philosophy." "The Sunny Side of Politics," or wit and humor from convention, canvass, and Congress, was compiled by Henry F. Reddall. "Money, Silver, and Finance," by J. Howard Cowperthwait, and "The Question of Silver," by Louis R. Ehrich, in the "Questions of the Day Series"; "The Silver Situation in the United States," by F. W. Taussig, in "Publications of the American Economic Association," and "Silver from 1849 to 1892," by George M. Coffin, with "Cheap Money Experiments," reprinted from "Topics of the Time" in the "Century Magazine," cover the silver question. "The Behring Sea Controversy" was explained by Stephen Berren Stanton. "The New Empire" of Canada was the subject of reflections by O. A. Howard as to its origin and constitution, and its relation to the great republic; and I. Garland Penn wrote upon "The Afro-American Press and its Editors." "The Children of the Poor," by Jacob A. Riis, supplemented his former volume telling "How the Other Half Lives." Frederick J. Brown in "Streets and Slums" made a study in local municipal geography specially applicable in his own city of Baltimore, Md., and George W. Hale supplied a "Police and Prison Cyclopædia." In the "Johns Hopkins University Studies," "The Old English Manor" was a study by Charles McLean Andrews in English economic history. Paul E. Lauer gave his attention to "Church and State in New England," and George Petrie to "Church and State in Early Maryland." "The Bishop Hill Colony: A Religious Communistic Settlement in Henry County, Illinois," was the theme selected by Michael A. Mikkelsen. "The Jew at Home" was described by Joseph Pennell from

personal observation, and "The New Exodus: A Study of Israel in Russia," by Harold Frederic, was called forth by the recent persecution of the race by that country. In the "Evolution Series" of short papers, numerous questions were discussed, among which may be mentioned: "The Race Problem in the South," by Joseph Le Conte; "The Land Problem," by Otis T. Mason; "The Independent in Politics," by John A. Taylor; "The Republican Party," by Roswell G. Horr; "The Democratic Party," by Edward M. Shepard; "The Duty of a Public Spirit," by E. B. Andrews; "Moral Questions in Politics as related to the Other Methods of their Treatment," by John C. Kimball; the "Study of Applied Sociology," by Robert G. Eccles, M. D.; "The Problem of City Government," by Louis G. Janes; "Suffrage and the Ballot," by Daniel S. Remsen; "Representative Government," by Edwin D. Mead; and "The Evolution of the Afric-American," by Samuel J. Barrows. "Our Moral Nature," by James McCosh, D. D., set forth a brief system of ethics; Prof. Borden P. Brown wrote upon "The Principles of Ethics"; and "The Concept of Law in Ethics," by Ferdinand Courtney French, was the thesis accepted by the faculty of Cornell University for the Ph. D. degree.

Sports and Pastimes.—"American Game Fishes: Their Habits, Habitat, and Peculiarities, how, when, and where to angle for them," was a handsome volume to which W. A. Perry (Sillalicum), A. A. Mosher, W. H. H. Murray, and other authorities contributed, while the "Practical Angler," by Kit Clarke, was a less pretentious work covering the same ground. "Favorite Flies and their Histories," by Mary E. Orvis Marbury, contained replies from experienced anglers to inquiries concerning how, when, and where to use them. Of value to sportsmen was "The Dog in Health and in Disease," by Dr. Wesley Mills (Mount Royal), including the origin, history, varieties, breeding, education, and general management of the animal in health, and his treatment in disease; the same writer also told "How to keep a Dog in the City." "Wheels and Wheeling," by Luther H. Porter, proved an indispensable handbook for cyclists. William B. McClellan compiled the "Official Register of American Yachting," and Jerome Flannery "The American Cricket Annual, 1892." "A Bibliography of Card Games, and of the History of Playing Cards," compiled by T. Norton Horr, in a limited edition of 250 copies, and "The Gentleman's Handbook on Poker," by the comedian W. J. Florence, written, as the result of a wager, in one month, complete the short list of books falling under this head.

Theology.—Foremost among works of this class may be mentioned "The Evolution of Christianity," by Rev. Lyman Abbott, the chapters of which were originally delivered as lectures before the Lowell Institute of Boston. "Evolution in Religion" was traced by Rev. William W. McLane, and "The Human and its Relation to the Divine" was thoughtfully studied by Theodore F. Wright, with a view to satisfying the doubts of inquiring minds. "The Soteriology of the New Testament" was examined anew by Prof. William Porcher Du Bose, and Emory Miller, D. D., in his "Evolution of Love," pointed the way toward the highest authority. John Miley, D. D., proposed to set forth "Systematic Theology," in two volumes, one of which was published during the year; and Prof. George B. Stevens, of Yale, inquired into the origin of "The Pauline Theology." Rev. C. H. Waller, Rev. Edward Hoare, Rev. R. B. Girdlestone, and others, labored jointly on "The Church and her Doctrine"; S. W. Pratt wrote on "The Gospel of the Holy Spirit" from an unsectarian standpoint; while George Hodges's "Christianity between Sundays," and "The Every Day of Life," by J. R. Miller, D. D., were somewhat akin in theme. "Elements of Theology, Natural and Revealed," by James H. Fairchild; "Studies in Ethics and Religion," by Alvah Hovey, D. D.; "Natural Religion," by Theodore W. Haven; "God's Image in Man: Some Intuitive Perceptions of Truth," by Henry Wood, author of "Natural Law in the Business World"; "Natural Religion in Sermons," by James Vila Blake; "Religion for the Times," by Lucien Clark, D. D.; and "The Church of To-morrow," eleven addresses delivered in the United States and Canada in the autumn of 1891, by W. J. Dawson, and published in book form, met the requirements of numerous readers. From Philip Schaff, D. D., we had Vol. I of a "Theological Propædeutic: An Introduction to the Study of Theology," and Vol. VII of his "History of the Christian Church," devoted to "Modern Christianity, the Swiss Reformation," and forming the second volume of the "History of the Reformation." He also edited Vols. III and IV of the second series of "A Select Library of Nicene and Post-Nicene Fathers of the Christian Church." Newman Smyth, D. D., contributed his exposition of "Christian Ethics to the International Theological Library." How much there is of "Paganism surviving in Christianity" was shown by Abram Herbert Lewis, D. D., and to Amory H. Bradford, D. D., we owe "Old Wine: New Bottles," some elemental doctrines in modern form. "West Roxbury Sermons, 1837-1848," of Theodore Parker, were brought to light from unpublished manuscripts, and furnished with an introduction and a biographical sketch; and Rufus Leighton selected "Lessons from the World of Matter and the World of Man," from notes of unpublished sermons of the same divine for the ten years from 1849–'59. Another great Unitarian divine had his sermons posthumously collected, "The Lord's Prayer" having been the theme of James Freeman Clarke's eight last discourses. "The Bible, the Church, and the Reason: The Three Great Fountains of Divine Authority," were treated in seven lectures by Charles A. Briggs, D. D., five of which set forth at length the views expressed by him in his inaugural address on the "Authority of Holy Scripture," and from himself we have also stated "The Case against Prof. Briggs." The "Response of Henry Preserved Smith to the Charges presented to the Presbytery of Cincinnati by the Committee of Prosecution" was also printed, as was "An Open Letter to the Rt. Rev. William C. Doane (Bishop of Albany) in reference to the consecration of the Rt. Rev. Dr. Brooks (Bishop of Massachusetts)," by Bishop George Franklin Seymour, of Illinois. "Indications of the Sec-

ond Book of Moses, called Exodus," by Edward B. Latch, carried on that writer's system of interpretation; and from Rev. M. C. Horine we have "Practical Reflections on the Book of Ruth." Two short character studies were "Jeremiah" and "Ezekiel," by President William G. Ballantine, of Oberlin College, Ohio, and from Rev. T. DeWitt Talmage came "Ready! ay, Ready! and Other Addresses." John M. Armour offered his theory as to "Mercy: Its Place in the Divine Government"; William Rounseville Alger discovered "The Sources of Consolation in Human Life"; G. Hepworth heralded "The Life Beyond"; while a religious meditation on affliction, entitled "The Thorn in the Flesh," by J. W. Etter, D. D., had an introduction by Bishop J. F. Hurst. "The Symmetry of Life" was an address to young men by Bishop Phillips Brooks, reprinted from the second series of his sermons; twenty sermons of Charles Cuthbert Hall, D. D., were entitled "Into his Marvelous Light: Studies in Life and Belief"; "Stirring the Eagle's Nest, and Other Practical Discourses," came from Theodore L. Cuyler, D. D.; and other volumes of sermons were, respectively: "Lead me to the Rock," by Rev. T. W. Hooper; "Personality," by Samuel R. Fuller; "Updike's Sermons," delivered in the Christian Tabernacle at Emporia, Kan., and edited by George F. Hall; "A Plea for the Gospel," by Rev. G. D. Herron; and "The Making of a Man," by J. W. Lee, D. D. "Arrows for the King's Archers," were tipped by Rev. H. W. Little; "The Adversary, his Person, Power, and Purpose," was a study in Satanology, by William A. Matson, D. D.; Mary Emily Case was the author of "The Love of the World," a book of religious meditation; Bishop James W. Hott spent "Sacred Hours with Young Christians"; "The Unseen Friend," gentle and spiritual, was from the pen of Lucy Larcom; Elizabeth P. Channing gave utterance to "Kindling Thoughts"; "The Floral Apostles; or, What the Flowers say to Thinking Man," were derived by Rev. Andrew Ambauen largely from the utterances of some of the wisest men of all ages; and among compilations we have "A Book of Prayer from the Public Ministrations of Henry Ward Beecher," by T. J. Ellinwood, from unpublished reports; "Small Helps for To-day," selected by Imogen Clark; and "Comforting Thoughts" in prose and poetry, by Mrs. Alice L. Williams. "Prayer-Meeting Theology" was discussed in a dialogue by E. J. Morris, and "The Revival Quiver" was filled for active use by Louis Albert Banks, D. D. "Young Men's Christian Associations" had a handbook of their history, organization, and methods of work, edited by H. S. Ninde, J. T. Bowne, and Erskine Uhl; and "The Church at Work in the Sunday School" was reviewed by A. R. Taylor. "Notes of Lessons on the Church in the New Testament" were made by Edward L. Cutts, D. D.; "Golden Rules for directing Religious Communities, Seminaries, Colleges, Schools, Families, etc." were drawn up by Rev. Michael Müller; "The Model Sunday School" was outlined by George M. Boynton; "The Highway to Heaven: Its Hindrances and Helps" was intended for Bible classes by Austin Clare. The Monday Club published its eighteenth series of "Sermons on the International Sunday-school Lessons for 1893," and the same lessons were also the subject of "A Standard Eclectic Commentary," by E. B. Wakefield, J. W. McGarvey, and H. K. Taylor. David D. Burrell, D. D., and Rev. Joseph Dunn Burrell were joint authors of "Hints and Helps on the Sunday-school Lessons for 1893," and Jesse L. Hurlbut, D. D., and Robert 'R. Dougherty prepared "Illustrative Notes" on the same. A manual of "Open-Air Preaching" was the work of Edwin Hallock Byington. Bishop John Weaver wrote a "Practical Comment on the Confession of Faith of the Church of the United Brethren in Christ"; A. B. Miller, D. D., on the "Doctrines and Genius of the Cumberland Presbyterian Church"; H. C. Vedder, "A Short History of the Baptists"; R. S. Foster on "Union of Episcopal Methodisms," and James McGee traced "The March of Methodism from Epworth around the Globe." Bishop S. M. Merrill treated "The Organic Union of American Methodism." "Credo and Credulity" was an exposition of the Apostles' Creed by an anonymous "believer," and James Morris White gave talks about the Trinity for thoughtful laymen under the title of "Gloria Patri." "The Democracy of Christianity" was asserted by Rev. Lorenzo White; "Christ enthroned in the Industrial World" was a discussion of Christianity in property and labor by Charles Roads; and "Socialism from Genesis to Revelation" was argued by Rev. F. M. Sprague. An essay in the form of 4 lectures by Josiah Royce investigated the "Spirit of Modern Philosophy"; Thomas Elwood Longshore, of the Society of Friends. touched upon "The Higher Criticism in Theology and Religion contrasted with Ancient Myths and Miracles as Factors in Human Evolution," with other essays on reforms; "The Genesis of Genesis," by Benjamin Wisner Bacon, was a study of the documentary sources of the first book of Moses in accordance with the results of critical science, which had an introduction by George F. Moore. "Genesis I and Modern Science"; "Homilies of Science," by Paul Carus; "Rational Philosophy," by William Poland; "The Irresistible Conflict between Two World Theories," by Rev. Minot J. Savage; "The Creation of the Bible," by Myron Adams: and "Bible Difficulties and how to meet them," a symposium edited by Frederick A. Atkins, presented both sides of the controversy between religion and modern science. Rev. J. Q. Bittinger made "A Plea for the Sabbath and for Man," while "Two Republics; or, Rome and the United States of America," by Alonzo T. Jones, was opposed to Sunday legislation. "Early Bibles of America" were described by John Wright, D. D., and "Ethical Teachings in Old English Literature" were traced by Prof. T. W. Hunt. "The Story of the Token," by Robert Shiells, gave the origin and history of a quaint custom of the Scotch Presbyterian Church. Two volumes contained Rev. Samuel W. Whitney's critical examination of "The Revisers' Greek Text," a work which occupied him during more than ten years. Part I was published of "The Documents of the Hexateuch." the oldest book of Hebrew history, edited by W. E. Addis; and Rev. John Thein wrote upon "Christian Anthropology." Vol. III of Bartlett and Pe-

ters's "Scriptures, Hebrew and Christian," was issued; Sarah Geraldine Stock told "The Story of Uganda and the Victoria Nyanza Mission," and Ellen Blackmar Maxwell described "The Bishop's Conversion" on the subject of missions. "The Divine Art of Preaching" was the theme of sermons preached by Rev. Arthur T. Pierson at the Pastor's College connected with the Metropolitan Tabernacle, London, during the illness and after the death of Spurgeon. "Anglo-Israel and the Jewish Problem," by Rev. Thomas R. Howlett, argued the identity of the Anglo-Saxon race with the ten lost tribes of Israel. "The Spiritual Athlete, and how he Trains," formed the theme of the W. A. Bodell; and W. De Witt Hyde, D. D., explained "Practical Ethics." A new edition was issued of "The Life of our Lord upon the Earth," first published in 1862; also a new, cheaper edition of the lectures upon the "Post-Restoration Period of the Church in the British Isles," delivered in 1890 under the auspices of the Church Club of New York. "Oriental Religions and Christianity" were the theme of the course of lectures delivered by Frank F. Ellinwood, D. D., on the Ely Foundation at Union Theological Seminary. N. Y.; "The Chalcedonian Decree; or, Historical Christianity misrepresented by Modern Theology, confirmed by Modern Science, and untouched by Modern Criticism," of the Charlotte Wood Slocum Lectures, by John Fulton, D. D.; while the Oberlin lectures of 1892 were given by David O. Mears, D. D.. upon "The Pulpit and the Pews." "The Religious Development in the Province of North Carolina" received attention from Stephen Beauregard Weeks in the "Johns Hopkins University Studies." Rev. J. M. Hubbert was the author of "The Preacher's Complete Register."

Unclassified.—Books falling under none of the departments into which this article is divided are: "Florida, South Carolina, and Canadian Phosphates," by C. C. Hoyer Millar; "Coals and Cokes in West Virginia," by William Seymour Edwards; "Old Cashmere Shawls; How they are made and why the Art is lost," by Margaret R. King; "Stereotyping: The Papier Maché Process," by C. S. Partridge; "Mechanical Drawing," by Charles W. MacCord; "Elements of Machine Design, for the Use of Draughtsmen and Students of Engineering," by J. F. Klein; "Machinery Pattern Making," by Peter S. Dingey; "Screws and Screw Making, with a Chapter on the Milling Machine," anonymous; two volumes on "Practical Carriage Building," by M. T. Richardson; "The Construction of Pump Details," by Philip R. Bjorling; "How to make Common Things for Boys," by John A. Bower; a "Manual of Instruction in Hard Soldering," by Harvey Rowell; a "Manual of American Water Works," edited by M. N. Baker; "A Practical Treatise upon warming Buildings by Hot Water," by Charles Hood; "Brick for Street Pavements," by M. D. Burke; a "Treatise on Highway Construction." by Austin T. Byrne; "The Iron and Steel Maker," edited by F. Jaynson; "The Iron Founder," by Simpson Bolland; "The Electric Railway in Theory and Practice," by Oscar T. Crosby and L. Bell; "Electric-Lighting Specifications, for the Use of Engineers and Architeets," by E. A. Merrill; "Photography: Its History, Processes. Apparatus, and Materials," by A. Brothers; "Photo-Engraving," a practical treatise on the production of printing blocks by modern photographic methods, by Charles Schraubstadter, Jr., who supplied also a small "Copy for Photo-Engraving"; "The Practical Polish and Varnish Maker," by H. C. Standage; a "Manual of Mining," by M. C. Ihlseng, based on the course of lectures on mining delivered at the State School of Mines, Colorado; "Experiments with Sugar Beets in 1891," by Harvey W. Wiley, Walter Maxwell, and W. A. Henry, as well as various reports on "Food and Food Adulterants" in bulletins of the United States Department of Agriculture, Division of Chemistry. Bulletins of the Bureau of American Republics (United States State Department) covered "Guatemala," "Colombia," "Venezuela," "Costa Rica," and "Breadstuffs in Latin America." "Engineers' Surveying Instruments: Their Construction, Adjustment, and Use," were described by Ira O. Baker ; "The Breechloader, and how to use it," by W. W. Greener; while Cyrus S. Radford compiled a "Handbook on Naval Gunnery," for the use of the United States Navy and the State Naval Reserves. "The Armies of To-day," an international volume composed of 9 articles, first published in "Harper's Magazine," opened with the army of the United States, by Brig.-Gen. Wesley Merritt, U.S.A. Part II of Robert H. Thurston's "Manual of the Steam Engine" covered "Design, Construction, and Operation," and J. G. A. Meyer published "Modern Locomotive Construction." A "General History of the Music Trades of America" was anonymous; William T. Brannt wrote "The Practical Scourer and Garment Dyer"; G. W. Atkinson, on "Perfumes and their Preparation," "Road, Track, and Stable," by H. C. Merwin, "My Horse: My Love," by Dinah Sharpe, and a complete treatise on determining the "Age of the Domestic Animals," by Rush Shippen Huidekoper, M. D., had their uses; and "The Perfect Keely Cure" was described by C. S. Clark as carried on at Dwight, Ill. "Earth Burial and Cremation" were discussed by Augustus G. Cobb. Henry T. King, as "The Idealist," condemned 150 wrongs daily perpetrated in every-day life. H. L. R. and M. L. R. gave "Talks on Graphology," "Modern Punctuation" was arranged by William Bradford Dickson for stenographers and typewriters, and O. R. Palmer drew up a manual of instruction in "Typewriting and Business Correspondence." "The Test Pronouncer," by William H. P. Phyfe, formed a companion volume to "7,000 Words often mispronounced." "The Technique of Rest" was explained by Anna C. Brackett; and three books which may be classed together were "Beauty of Form and Grace of Vesture," by Frances Mary Steele and Elizabeth L. S. Adams; "The Truth about Beauty," by Annie Wolf; and "Physical Beauty: How to obtain and to preserve it," by Mrs. Annie Jenness Miller. "The Farm and the Fireside," by C. H. Smith (Bill Arp); "The Good Things of Life," ninth series; "Life Fairy Tales," by J. A. Mitchell; "Hans Von Pelter's Trip to Gotham," in pen and pencil, by Palmer Cox ; "The Gilded Fly," a political satire, by Harold Payne; and

"Politics among the Animals," by A. J. Philpott and H. P. Whitmarsh, represent the best of the wit and humor of the year; while "Hospitality in Town and County," anonymous; "Etiquette," by Agnes H. Morton; and "What to do: A Companion to 'Don't,'" by Mrs. Oliver Bell Bunce, answered the many questions which arise in the course of social life. "Poor's Manual of the Railroads of the United States for 1892," by H. V. Poor, saw its twenty-fifth annual issue; Worthington's and Oliver Optic's (W. T. Adams) annuals were published; a "History of the Friendly Sons of St. Patrick, and of the Hibernian Society for the Relief of Emigrants from Ireland," was written by John H. Campbell; and the proceedings of "The Scotch-Irish in America," at their third congress at Louisville, Ky., May 14-17, 1891, were published by that society. "The Rationale of Mesmerism" was set forth by A. P. Sinnett. Alfred T. Schofield, M. D., made "A Study of Faith Healing"; "How to Heal," by George E. Burnell. set forth a system of mental therapeutics; George H. Pember was responsible for "Earth's Earliest Ages and their Connection with Modern Spiritualism and Theosophy," and "Theosophy, Buddhism, and the Signs of the End"; while "Angels' Visits to my Farm in Florida" were welcomed by "Golden Light." "Card Tricks and Puzzles" were contrived by "Berkeley" and T. B. Rowland. John J. Flinn prepared from official sources a "Handbook of the World's Columbian Exposition." Thomas E. Hill wrote "Hill's Souvenir Guide to Chicago and the World's Fair," and Julian Ralph was again heard from in "Harper's Chicago and the World's Fair." The "Columbus Memorial—1492-400-1892" was devoted to the fair's buildings. "A Bookseller's Library, and how to use it," by A. Growoll; Part IV of the "American Catalogue," compiled under the editorial direction of R. R. Bowker, A. I. Appleton, and others, with its second supplement, the "Annual American Catalogue, 1891"; "The Co-operative Index to Periodicals for 1891," edited by William I. Fletcher. with co-operation of members of the American Library Association; and the "English Catalogue of Books for 1891," issued by the office of the "Publishers' Weekly," with the "Publishers' Trade-List Annual, 1892" (in its twentieth year), met the requirements of the book trade; while books of universal value were the "New Cabinet Cyclopædia and Treasury of Knowledge," a concise work of reference on all subjects and for all readers, by Ainsworth R. Spofford, the Librarian of Congress, and Charles Annandale; the "Cyclopædia of the Manufactures and Products of the United States, anonymous; "Everybody's Pocket Cyclopædia of Things worth knowing, Things difficult to remember, and Tables of References"; "Barker's Facts and Figures for 1892," edited by Thomas P. Whitaker; No. 4 of "Information Readers," by Robert Lewis; "The Gast Paul Directory of Bankers and Attorneys, edited by Solon W. Paul; and "Appleton's Annual Cyclopædia and Register of Important Events of the Year 1891," being Volume XVI of the new series. Vol. III of Foster's "Medical Dictionary" came from the press, and the "New Drill Regulations," for infantry, cavalry, and artillery.

Voyages and Travels.—"In Arctic Seas," by Robert N. Keely, Jr., M. D., and G. G. Davis, M. D., chronicled the voyage of the "Kite" with the successful Peary expedition, and was one of the most eagerly welcomed books of the year. Mrs. Alice W. Rollins went " From Palm to Glacier, with an Interlude : Brazil, Bermuda, and Alaska." Our own country was not neglected, as is shown by "The West from a Car Window," by Richard Harding Davis; "Some Strange Corners of our Country: The Wonderland of the Southwest," by Charles F. Lummis, who also took "A Tramp across the Continent of more than 3,000 Miles, from Cincinnati to San Francisco"; and by Robert Louis Stevenson's "Across the Plains." "A Family Canoe Trip," by Florena Watters Snedecker, described a pleasant summer outing on Lake George and Lake Champlain; while "Zigzag Journeys on the Mississippi, from Chicago to the Islands of the Discovery," were made by Hezekiah Butterworth. Julian Ralph was in his element "On Canada's Frontier," and Ernest Ingersoll published Part II of "The Canadian Guide Book." A new edition of "The Oregon Trail," by Francis Parkman, was illustrated by Frederic Remington. Frederick A. Ober conducted "The Knockabout Club in Search of Treasure" through the mountains of Mexico; P. C. Remondino, M. D., described "The Mediterranean Shores of America"—viz., those of Southern California as health resorts; while "Under the Southern Cross," by William F. Hutchinson, M. D., was a guide to the sanitarinus and other charming places in the West Indies and Spanish main, illustrated from sketches and photographs made by the author. Maturin M. Ballou's "Equatorial America" told of a visit to St. Thomas, Martinique, Barbadoes, and the principal capitals of South America ; and James H. Stark wrote "Stark's History and Guide to the Bahama Islands." Crossing to Europe, we can find nothing more delightful than "A Little Swiss Sojourn " of William Dean Howells, or the eloquence of Theodore Child in "The Praise of Paris." "As we saw it in '90 " was the narrative of Grace Carew Sheldon, and Lucy Langdon Williams and Emma V. McLoughlin took " A too Short Vacation " of three months in Europe without a chaperon. Anna Bowman Dodd led her interested readers " In and Out of Three Normandy Inns," to their great satisfaction ; the late Henry W. Hilliard published "Politics and Pen Pictures, at Home and Abroad," as seen by him in a long life; and Poultney Bigelow gave us "Paddles and Politics Down the Danube." "The Danube, from the Black Forest to the Black Sea," was explored by F. D. Millet, and illustrated by the author and Alfred Parsons, who accompanied him on his canoe voyage of 1.775 miles. "A Day at Laguerre's, and Other Days," was a collection of 9 sketches by F. Hopkinson Smith, first published in the "Century Magazine "; and the genial Lee Meriwether was at his best "Afloat and Ashore on the Mediterranean." Goldwin Smith took "A Trip to England," and Henry W. French chronicled the excursions of " Our Boys in Ireland." Canon J. H. Knowles (of one of Trinity parishes, New York city) spent a winter vacation going "To England and Back"; Charles A. Stoddard portrayed "Spanish Cities, with Glimpses of Gibraltar and Tangier";

Louis C. Elson recounted "European Reminiscences "; Joseph and Elizabeth Robins Pennell told of their " Play in Provence"; while "Genoa, the Superb," described by Virginia W. Johnson in a companion volume to "The Lily of the Arno," was again commemorated in "The Cradle of the Colombos," by Rev. Hugh Flattery. "Sweden and the Swedes" were described by W. W. Thomas, Jr. "The Boy Travelers in Central Europe," of Thomas W. Knox, were matched by the "Three Vassar Girls in the Holy Land " of Mrs. Elizabeth W. Champney. "Under Summer Skies," by Clinton Scollard, was illustrated by Margaret Landers Randolph; "To Nuremberg and Back : A Girl's Holiday," by Amy Neally, gave a graphic view of the Continent; and Barbara N. Sulpin was at home in "Foreign Lands." Mary Thorn Carpenter described "A Girl's Winter in India "; Rev. George W. Gilmore saw "Korea from its Capital"; Rev. M. L. Gordon, M. D., recorded his work and impressions as "An American Missionary in Japan"; and William Elliot Griffis gave us "Japan in History, Folklore, and Art." "Peeps into China" revealed much to Rev. Gilbert Reid. "From the Pyramids to the Acropolis" Rev. T. De Witt Talmage was at home. Sullivan H. McCollester saw "Babylon and Nineveh through American Eyes," and Morton W. Easton made "Observations on the Platform at Persepolis." Amos Perry, formerly U. S. Consul at Tunis, and author of "Carthage and Tunis, Past and Present," was heard from in a new volume, "An Official Tour along the Eastern Coast of the Regency of Tunis." "Sultan to Sultan," by Mrs. French-Sheldon, chronicled her adventures among the Masai and other tribes of East Africa, and James Johnston outlined "Missionary Landscapes in the Dark Continent." "South Sea Idyls," of Charles Warren Stoddard, first published in 1873, which have been long out of print, were revived in a new edition, prefaced with a letter from William Dean Howells: "Abroad and at Home," by Morris Phillips, gave practical hints for tourists, and had an introduction by A. Oakley Hall; and "The World we live in," anonymous, gave a pictorial survey of the universe in its various aspects. Useful books of reference were the four volumes compiled by William M. Griswold entitled "France," "Germany," "Italy," and "Switzerland," a series of narratives of personal visits to places therein famous for natural beauty or historical association, extracted from books of travel and magazine articles. Various localities in our own country were the subject of publications such as "Asheville" (North Carolina), by Mrs. Harriet A. Sawyer; "Washington illustrated," by George G. Evans; "Manhattan : Historic and Artistic," by Carolyn Faville Ober and Cynthia M. Westover, a six-days' tour of New York city; "Newburgh" (N. Y.), by John J. Nutt; and a new revised and enlarged edition of "Old Concord : Her Highways and Byways," by Margaret Sydney (Mrs. H. M. Lothrop). "The Universal Atlas" was published, including county and railroad maps of the United States, with carefully prepared maps of all other countries from latest surveys. "The Cruise of a Land Yacht," by Sylvester Baxter, and "By Boat and Rail," a series of travel sketches by J. R. Ever-hart, M. D., conclude the summary of books in this department.

Summary.—The figures of book production in the United States during 1892 are arranged as follow by the "Publishers' Weekly" for comparison with those of 1891:

CLASSIFICATION.	1891. New books and new editions.	1892. New books.	New editions.
Fiction............................	1,105	785	367
Theology and religion..............	528	464	88
Juvenile..........................	460	448	18
Law..............................	343	334	40
Education and language............	355	330	86
Poetry and the drama..............	193	172	87
Political and social science........	197	222	14
Biography, memoirs................	211	224	10
Fine-art and illustrated books......	228	181	20
Description, travel................	189	173	19
Literary history and miscellany.....	251	165	27
History...........................	124	149	16
Medical science, hygiene...........	108	128	27
Useful arts.......................	106	106	23
Physical and mathematical science...	97	91	80
Domestic and rural................	79	57	4
Sports and amusements............	71	87	7
Mental and moral philosophy........	39	29	4
Humor and satire..................	26	29	2
Total..........................	4,665	4,074	788
			4,074
			4,862

LITERATURE, BRITISH, IN 1892. The record of book production in England far exceeded that in our country during the year, the number of new books (4,915) being in excess of new works and new editions issued by American publishing houses. The total of 6,254 books of both classes exceeds the 5,706 books of 1891 by 548, and the excess of entirely new books over the previous year was 486. Of this number, 1,147 were new novels (against 896 in 1891), and 390 works of fiction passed through new editions. A large increase was shown in miscellaneous books, in those devoted to the arts and sciences, and illustrated works, and more poetry and more political economy was served to the British public. Fewer juvenile books are noted (perhaps for the reason that many of them were ranked among works of fiction, for older readers), and there was a falling off in history and biography, in *belles-lettres*, essays, and law, while in theology and medicine and surgery there was but slight variation. Educational, classical, and philological literature showed a difference of but eight books, in favor of 1891.

Biography.—While fewer biographies were published, those that saw the light were deeply interesting, not only to English readers, but to a large majority on this side of the water, who when they threw off the government of the mother country did not renounce the heritage of her literature. Delightful "Gossip of the Century," by the anonymous author of "Flemish Interiors" and "De Omnibus Rebus" filled two volumes, as did the "Diplomatic Reminiscences: 1837–1862" of Lord Augustus Loftus, whose diplomatic career ran almost exactly parallel with the fifty years of the Queen to her Jubilee, and the notes and recollections of "An English-

man in Paris,"·who withheld his name but gave full and brilliant pictures of life in the gay city in the reign of Louis Philippe and under the Empire. "Roundabout Recollections" of John Augustus O'Shea proved exceedingly entertaining and amusing, and Mrs. George Augustus Sala was equally happy in her portraits of "Famous People I have met." The tenth and last volume of "The Speeches and Public Addresses of the Right Hon. W. E. Gladstone, M. P.," edited, with notes and introductions, by A. W. Hutton and H. J. Cohen, was issued in advance of the others, on account of the relevancy of the subjects treated therein to the present time. Vol. I of "Modern English Biography," memoirs of persons who have died since 1850, by F. Boase, covered the names from A to H, and "Our Great Military Commanders" were sketched by Prof. Charles D. Yonge. Literary biography was particularly rich; an important new addition was "Thomas Carlyle," by John Nichol, in the "English Men of Letters Series," and Sir Charles Gavan Duffy also published "Conversations and Correspondence with Carlyle," which go far to relieve the unpleasant impression of the differences between the distinguished author and his wife. "Selections from the Letters of Geraldine Ensor Jewsbury to Jane Welsh Carlyle" were edited, it might be called unscrupulously, by Mrs. Alexander Ireland, as nothing would have been more repellent to the feelings of the writer than such a betrayal of the confidence of friendship. "The Life of William Cowper" was written by T. Wright. "Memoirs of Charles Lamb," by Percy Fitzgerald, and "John Leech, his Life and Work," came from W. P. Frith. The "Life and Letters of Joseph Severn," the friend of Keats, we owe to the poet William Sharp; and "The Life and Letters of Charles Samuel Keene, of 'Punch,'" to George Somers Layard. "Student and Singer" contained the reminiscences of Charles Santley, and "Autobiographical Notes of the Life of William Bell Scott," in two volumes, were edited by W. Minto, a distinguishing feature of the book being the illustrations from the work of the artist and art teacher. Malcolm Bell's record and review of "Edward Burne-Jones" was a beautiful and costly volume. "The Life and Letters of Samuel Palmer," another artist, were edited by A. H. Palmer. "Angelica Kauffmann: A Biography," was from the pen of Frances A. Gerard. "The Life and Works of John Arbuthnot, M. D.," by George A. Aitken, was the first biography ever written of the literary physician, and attempted to settle the many perplexing questions as to the authorship of works attributed to him: and "Letters of Samuel Johnson, LL. D.," selected and edited by George Birkbeck Hill, in two volumes, was exceptionally interesting in that it contained between 90 and 100 letters not previously published. "The Life of Michaelangelo Buonarotti," in two sumptuous volumes, with etched portrait and 50 reproductions of the works of the master, was the contribution of John Addington Symonds. T. Bonner published a "Biographical Sketch of George Meikle Kemp, Architect of the Scott Monument, Edinburgh," Blanchard Jerrold's "Life of Gustave Doré" was published seven years after it had been written, and J. F.

Rowbotham told of "The Private Life of the Great Composers." "Frederic Chopin" was commemorated by Charles Willeby, and Ferdinand Praeger described "Wagner as I knew him." "The Childhood and Youth of Charles Dickens," by R. Langton, possessed interest for all lovers of the great novelist, and not a few were gratified that the "Literary Remains" of Charles Stuart Calverley were prefaced with a sympathetic memoir by Sir Walter J. Sendall. Calverley's translation of "Theocritus" was also published, be it remarked, and contained some of his best and most earnest work. Gerald P. Moriarty devoted himself to "Dean Swift and his Writings," and the late laureate was the subject of two volumes, "Alfred Lord Tennyson," a study of his life and work by A. Waugh, and "Alfred Lord Tennyson, Poet Laureate," by Rev. A. Jenkinson. "Homes and Haunts of Alfred, Lord Tennyson, Poet Laureate," by G. G. Napier, was beautifully illustrated. "Records of Tennyson, Ruskin, and Browning," by Mrs. Anne Thackeray Ritchie, was an opportune volume of surpassing interest. "Letters of Jane Austen," selected by Sarah C. Woolsey, were published for the first time (as was her posthumous novel, "The Watsons") in an American edition of her works. "An Edinburgh Eleven," by J. M. Barrie, supplied pencil portraits from his college life of fellow-students who have attained distinction; "Recollections of a Happy Life" was the title of the autobiography of Marianne North, edited by her sister, Mrs. John Addington Symonds; Cornelia A. H. Crosse filled two volumes with the record of "Red-Letter Days of my Life," and Mrs. F. Hughes told for her children of "My Childhood in Australia." "Sir Henry Sumner Maine" was the subject of a brief memoir by Right Hon. M. E. Grant-Duff. Charles Lowe published an historical biography of "Prince Bismark," reduced and reconstructed from his larger work of five years since. "Ten Years' Captivity in the Mahdi's Camp" was translated from the original manuscripts of Father J. Ohrwalder by Major F. R. Wingate. "Dorothy Wallis," the autobiography of a poor but ambitious girl, had a preface by Walter Besant. Catherine J. Hamilton published the first series of "Women Writers, their Works and Ways," and Mrs. L. B. Walford chronicled "Twelve English Authoresses." "Harvey and his Successors" was the theme of the Harveian Oration, October, 1892, by J. H. Bridges. In the several series which have proved so successful, "Lord Lawrence," by Sir C. Aitchison, "Albuquerque," by H. M. Stephens, "Madhava Rao Sindhia, otherwise called Madhoji," by H. G. Keene, "Earl Canning," by Sir H. S. Cunningham, "Mountstuart Elphinstone," by J. S. Cotton, "Lord William Bentinck," by D. C. Boulger, and "Ranjit Singh," by Sir Lepel Griffin, continued the "Rulers of India;" "Viscount Palmerston, K. G.," by the Marquis of Lorne, "The Marquis of Salisbury," by H. D. Traill, and the "Earl of Derby," by George Saintsbury, "The Queen's Prime Ministers"; "Pitt," by Lord Rosebery, and "Queen Elizabeth," by Edward S. Beasly, were the additions to the "Twelve English Statesmen," while the "English Men of Action" received but one contribution, "Montrose," from the pen of Mowbray Morris. "Heroes of the Nations" were represented by "John Wycklif," from the pen of Louis Sergeant, and "Julius Cæsar," by W. W. Fowler. Arthur Wollaston Hutton wrote "Cardinal Manning" for the "Religious Leaders" series, and from Edwin A. Abbott we have "The Anglican Career of Cardinal Newman," in two volumes. J. J. Ellis added "David Livingston" to "Men with a Mission" and "Charles Haddon Spurgeon" to "Lives that Speak." "Florence Nightingale," by Eliza F. Pollard, and "Michael Faraday," by W. Jerrold, appeared among "The World's Benefactors." "Four Heroes of India," portrayed by F. M. Holmes, were Clive, Warren Hastings, Havelock, and Lawrence; H. de B. Gibbins devoted himself to "English Social Reformers" in the "University Extension Series," and "Famous British Explorers and Navigators from Drake to Franklin" received attention from R. Rowe. "Robert Browning's Prose Life of Strafford" was accredited to the real author for the first time, the poet having written it for John Forster during an illness of that writer, under whose name it originally appeared. J. J. Jusserand outlined "A French Embassador at the Court of Charles II, le Comte de Cominges," from his unpublished correspondence; Violet Fane translated the "Memoirs of Marguerite de Valois, Queen of Navarre"; while another volume of great interest was the "Recollections of Marshal Macdonald, Duke of Tarentum." W. H. Davenport Adams supplied lives of "Warriors of the Crescent"; Grace Johnstone of "Leading Women of the Restoration"; "In Ladies' Company," by Mrs. Fenwick Miller, presented sketches of six interesting women; W. J. Linton furnished recollections of Mazzini and his friends under the title of "European Republicans." "Queen Joanna I of Naples," by St. Clair Baddeley, "Elisabeth Farnese, the Termagant of Spain," by E. Armstrong, and "The Story of Gaspar Hauser," by Elizabeth E. Evans, belong to history; "Bramwelliana, or Wit and Wisdom of Lord Bramwell," we owe to Edward Manson; and Sidney L. Lee supplied notes, appendices, etc., to the "Autobiography of Edward Lord Herbert of Cherbury." "The Life of Lieut.-Gen. Sir Henry Evelyn Wood came opportunely from Charles Williams, and "Admiral of the Fleet Sir Provo W. P. Wallis" was the subject of a memoir by J. G. Brighton. "Letters of James Smetham were edited by Sarah Smetham and William Davies, and "George Gilfillan's Letters and Journals" received similar service at the hands of R. A. and Elizabeth S. Watson. "Letters of Archbishop Ullathorne" formed a valuable supplement to his "Autobiography" published last year. W. L. and L. Rees wrote together the "Life and Times of Sir George Grey," which was eagerly welcomed. Walter Stebbing, M. A., produced a new biography of "Sir Walter Raleigh." The "Autobiography of an English Gamekeeper," edited by Arthur H. Byngs and Stephen M. Stephens, may be mentioned with the "Racing Life of Lord George Bentinck, M. P.," by John Kent, edited by Hon. Francis Lawley; while photographers were especially interested in "Vernon Heath's Recollections." "Twenty-five Years of St. Andrews," by Rev. A. K. H. Boyd, the genial author of "Recreations of a Country Parson," and "Memories of Dean Hole" are deserving of special mention; and in religious biography we have also "John William Burgon, late Dean of Chichester," by E. Meyrick Goulburn, D. D.; "Henry Martyn, Saint and Scholar," by George Smith: "The Story of Bishop Colenso, the Friend of the Zulus," by Florence Gregg: "James Gilmour of Mongolia," by Richard Lovett, " ' Shepherd ' Smith, the Universalist: The Story of a Mind," by Rev. James E. Smith; "Memorials of James Chapman, First Bishop of Colombo"; "Charles Kingsley, Christian Socialist and Social Reformer," by Rev. M. Kaufmann; and "The Life of Catherine Booth, the Mother of the Salvation Army," by F. de L. Booth-Tucker, in two volumes. Spurgeon was commemorated as "The Prince of Preachers" by James Douglas, and from Mrs. Elizabeth Charles we have reminiscences of "Lady Augusta Stanley." the widow of the late dean. "A Protestant Poor Friar," by Brooke Herford, told the work of Travers Madge among the poor of Manchester. "Sixty years of an Agitator's Life," as told by Jacob Holyoake in his autobiography, filled two volumes, and "Heroes of our Day; or, Recent Winners of the Victoria Cross," by W. Richards, illustrated by Harry Payne, had an interest for boys and men. "The Career of Columbus' was traced by Charles Elton, M. P., in a manner that secured it a welcome in our country amid all that was published on the subject during the year. "The Dictionary of Australasian Biography," by P. Mennell, comprised notices of eminent colonists from 1855 to 1892, and four volumes were added to the "Dictionary of National Biography," edited by Sidney Lee, making so far thirty-two in all. "Half Hours with the Millionaires" were edited by B. B. West, showing how much easier it is to make a million than to spend it; and "Serampore Letters," the unfinished correspondence of William Cary and others with John Williams, 1800–'16, edited by Leighton and Mornay Williams, threw much light on missionary work of the period. "Madagascar, its Missionaries and Martyrs," by W. J. Townsend, and "A Galaxy in the Burman Sky," by W. N. Wyeth, belong also to missionary biography.

Fine Arts.—"Man in Art" was a magnificent volume by Philip Gilbert Hamilton, consisting of studies in religious and historical art, portrait and *genre* generally conceded to be the most important contribution to this department of the year's literature. "English Pen Artists of To-day," by Charles G. Harper, added criticisms and appreciations to examples of their work, and was a sort of companion volume to Joseph Pennell's "Pen Drawing," which was published in 1889. "When Art begins" was shown by Hume Nisbet; Walter Crane set forth "The Claims of Decorative Art," with deviations into the domain of socialism; and William Zander supplied designs in color for "Modern Decorative Painting." James Ward wrote on "The Elementary Principles of Ornament." Henry Blackburn edited "Academy Sketches, including Various Exhibitions," with 250 sketches of paintings, water colors, etc., and C. Lowe gave "Four National Exhibitions in London, and their Organizer," with portrait and illustrations. Hubert Herkomer's lectures on "Etching and Mezzotint Engraving," delivered at Oxford, were collected into a volume. Percy Fitzgerald

expatiated upon "The Art of Acting," and A. B. Walkley imparted his "Playhouse Impressions." W. C. Brownell made a study of "French Art: Classic and Contemporary Painting and Sculpture." "Studies in Modern Music," by W. H. Hadow, covered Hector Berlioz, Robert Schumann, and Richard Wagner; W. Spark proffered "Musical Reminiscences: Past and Present," and "Wagner Sketches, 1849," was "a vindication" by W. A. Ellis. "Architecture, Mysticism, and Myth" were studied by W. R. Lethaby, and A. Heales devoted himself specifically to "The Architecture of the Churches of Denmark." "The Poetry of Architecture," as traced by John Ruskin in articles for "Loudon's Magazine," appeared in book form for the first time during the year. "The Cathedral Churches of England and Wales" had their history, architecture, and monuments explored by W. J. Loftie, and the monumental inscriptions and heraldry of "Wells Cathedral" were reproduced by A. J. Jewers. Two volumes contained "The Remains of Ancient Rome," by Prof. J. Henry Middleton, who gave this title to his revised and much enlarged edition of two former works, "Ancient Rome in 1885" and "Ancient Rome ih 1888." A. S. Murray supplied a "Handbook of Greek Archæology," devoted to vases, bronzes, gems, sculpture, terra cottas, mural paintings, architecture, etc.; Jane E. Harrison added "Introductory Studies in Greek Art" to her numerous works on the art and literature of Greece; and J. L. Bowes made notes on "Japanese Pottery." "Historic Bindings in the Bodleian Library, Oxford," described by W. Salt Brassington, was furnished with reproductions of 24 of the finest. "Deer Stalking in the Highlands of Scotland," by H. Hope Crealock, was edited by his brother, Maj.-Gen. J. North Crealock; Richard Lovett edited "Welsh Pictures," with 72 illustrations; and "Views of the Old Halls of Lancashire and Cheshire," by N. G. Philips, were prefaced with a memoir of the author. "The Copper Coins of Europe" was a contribution to "The Young Collector's Series" from Frank C. Higgins; "Coins and Medals" (giving their place in history and art), by the authors of the "British Museum Official Catalogues," was edited by Stanley Lane-Poole, who traced on his own account "The History of the Moghul Emperors of Hindustan Illustrated by their Coins." Reginald Blomfield and F. Inigo Thomas wrote on "The Formal Garden in England," and E. Scott on "Dancing as an Art and Pastime."

Essays.—This title necessarily includes much of criticism and general literary miscellany. Two volumes of "Essays on Literature and Philosophy" came from Edward Caird, the distinguished author of "The Critical Philosophy of Immanuel Kant," and two more of "Essays and Criticisms" from St. George Mivart, the able and accomplished Roman Catholic scientist. George Saintsbury published twelve "Miscellaneous Essays," and Harry Quilter "Preferences in Art, Life, and Literature," including essays on the history of pre-Raphaelitism and on contemporary English art, exquisitely bound, and with 64 full-page plates. "Lectures on the History of Literature," delivered by Thomas Carlyle, April to July, 1838, were printed for the first time during the year, with preface and editorial notes by Prof. J. Reay Greene, and "The Last Words of Thomas Carlyle" also saw the light for the first time, including "Wotton Reinfred" (the only essay in fiction ever made by the sage of Chelsea) his "Excursion (Futile Enough) to Paris," and letters from himself and Mrs. Carlyle. "The History of Early English Literature" was traced by Rev. Stopford A. Brooke in two volumes, uniform with Bryce's "American Commonwealth," and "The Literature of France," by H. G. Keene, formed one of the "University Extension Manuals." William Watson contributed "Epigrams of Art, Life, and Nature"; Edmund Gosse, "Gossip in a Library"; and Joseph Hatton, "Cigarette Papers for Afternoon Smoking." "Meridiana: Noontide Essays," by Sir Herbert Maxwell, were reprinted in book form from Blackwood's Magazine. "Res Judicatæ," by Augustine Birrell, was another delightful collection of short studies after the manner of "Obiter Dicta." W. T. Stead was heard from as "A Journalist on Journalism"; Vols. VIII and IX of Henry Morley's "English Writers" covered respectively "From Surrey to Spenser" and "Spenser and his Times"; and W. H. Low wrote a "History of English Literature from 1620 to 1670." A concise introduction to "English Literature" was supplied by H. W. Dulcken. "Eighteenth Century Vignettes," by Austin Dobson, were at once gossipy, picturesque, vivacious, and brief; W. A. Clouston noted "Literary Coincidences"; W. L. Courtney made "Studies at Leisure"; Sir Arthur Helps offered "Essays and Aphorisms"; Malcolm C. Salaman saw "Woman—through a Man's Eyeglass"; and Barry Pain published "Playthings and Parodies." "The Silver Domino; or, Side Whispers, Social and Literary," was anonymous. Bernard Bosanquet wrote "The History of Æsthetics," and also upon "Knowledge and Reality"; "The Beauties of Nature and the Wonders of the World we Live in" were lovingly portrayed by Sir John Lubbock in a companion volume to "The Pleasures of Life"; "The Toilers of the Field," by Richard Jefferies, contained much that proved new to the majority of his readers. "Echoes of Old County Life," by J. K. Fowler; "More about Wild Nature," by Mrs. Brightwen, who illustrated her own book; "Nature and Woodcraft," by John Watson; "The Birds of Wordsworth," by Mrs. W. H. Wintringham; and "Within an Hour of London Town: Among Wild Birds and their Haunts," by "A Son of the Marshes," edited by J. A. Owen, proved each delightful and characteristic; while bibliophiles found especial charms in "Books condemned to be burnt," by James Anson Farrer, and "Books in Chains, and Other Bibliographical Papers," by William Blades. The fifth series of "The Bookworm" also was issued. J. B. Johnston devoted his energies to "Place Names of Scotland"; Hubert Hall explored "The Antiquities and Curiosities of the Exchequer." T. F. Thiselton Dyer's "Church-Lore Glennings" and Croake James's "Curiosities of Christian History prior to the Reformation" may be classed together, and N. Dickson portrayed "The Auld Scotch Minister" from anecdote and story. "Four Lectures on Henrik Ibsen, dealing chiefly with his Metrical Works," by Philip H. Wick-

steed, were collected into a volume; W. F. Revell expounded "Browning's Criticism of Life"; Edward Berdoe was the author of a "Browning Cyclopædia"; H. S. Salt argued as to "Shelley's Principles: Has Time refuted or confirmed them?"; and William Clark gave a critical exposition of the poetry of "Walt Whitman." "Our English Homer" was Shakespeare historically considered by Thomas W. While; Mrs. Henry Pott was heard from anent "Francis Bacon and his Secret Society"; "A Cabinet of Gems cut and polished by Sir Philip Sidney" were presented without their setting by George MacDonald, "for the more radiance": and F. S. Ellis gave to the world a "Lexical Concordance to the Poetical Works of Percy Bysshe Shelley" in the centenary year of the poet. "The Art of Teaching of John Ruskin" was set forth by W. G. Collingwood, and Mary E. Cardwill selected "Cameos from Ruskin." I. Bassett Choate drew from "Wells of English," reviewing the work of the minor writers of England during the sixteenth and seventeenth centuries; John Marshall made a popular presentation of the "History of Greek Philosophy"; J. P. Mahaffy discovered "Problems in Greek History," and also published the first volume of a "History of Classical Greek Literature"; John Burnet, M. A., presented "Early Greek Philosophy"; as did Prof. S. H. Butcher "Some Aspects of the Greek Genius." Agnes M. Clerke, who has won distinction in astronomical science, offered "Familiar Studies in Homer"; Prof. Lewis Campbell drew up "A Guide to Greek Tragedy for English Readers"; Richard Garnett compiled "A Chaplet from the Greek Anthology"; while Charles Godfrey Leland illustrated his own work on "Etruscan Roman Remains in Popular Tradition." The third and last volume of Prof. W. Y. Sellar's work on "The Roman Poets of the Augustan Age" was devoted to Horace and the elegiac poets. For "The History, Principles, and Practice of Heraldry" we are indebted to F. E. Hulme; and to Rev. J. Woodward and the late G. Burnett, Lyon King at Arms, we owe "A Treatise on Heraldry, British and Foreign," with beautiful colored plates. W. Carew Hazlitt drew up "A Manual for the Collector and Amateur of Old English Plays," and also supplied a volume of "Tales and Legends of National Origin," with a critical introduction to each. C. J. Abbey traced "Religious Thought in Old English Verse"; J. A. E. Stuart visited "The Literary Shrines of Yorkshire"; "Smuggling Days and Smuggling Ways" were the theme of Hon. Commander H. N. Shore, who had many opportunities to make a study of what he terms a "lost art": and similar experience led to "Some Records of Crime," by Gen. Charles Hervey, C. B., "some time General Superintendent of the Operations for the Suppression of Thuggee and Dacoitie in India." W. S. Lilly was entertaining on "Shibboleths.". "Bygone England," by William Andrews, and "Bygone Kent," by R. Stead; "Edinburgh Sketches and Memories," by David Masson, and a second series of "Lancashire Sketches" of Edwin Waugh, edited by George Milner; "The Brighton Road," by C. G. Harper; "London," by Walter Besant, giving pictures of the city and its citizens from early times to the days of George II; and "A High-land Memory," by "An Old Colonial," entertained many readers, as did "Rixae Oxonienses," by Samuel F. Hutton; Part VI of Vol. I of "Ancedota Oxoniensia," by F. C. Conybeare; "Faces and Places," by Henry W. Lucy, and "Number Twenty," by H. D. Traill, both in the "White-friars Library of Wit and Humor"; and the anonymous "In the Temple." Theodore Compton's "A Mendip Valley" was beautifully illustrated. "The Inns of Court and Chancery," visited by W. J. Loftie, were illustrated by Herbert Railton. "Ethnology in Folklore" came from G. L. Gomme in the "Modern Science Series"; G. F. Northall collected "English Folk Rhymes, and M. Tait "Stories from Northumbria," while to J. Jacobs we owe "Fairy Tales of India." "Lectures on the English Poets," by William Hazlitt, appeared in the "Giunta Series," and "Best Letters of Charles Lamb" in the "Laurel Crowned Letters." "Selections from Isaac Pennington" were made by Mary W. Tileston.

Fiction.—Among the numerous English novels of 1892 are to be found several displaying marked ability, though not one claims especial prominence. Mrs. Humphrey Ward published "The History of David Grieve," while Thomas Hardy did some of his best work in his faithful presentation of that pure woman, "Tess of the D'Urbervilles." Mrs. W. K. Clifford created some sensation by her "Aunt Anne," and two other products of her facile pen are to be noted, "Love Letters of a Worldly Woman" and "The Last Touches," with which other shorter stories are included. Walter Besant was represented by one novel, "The Ivory Gate," and "Verbena Camellia Stephanotis, and Other Stories"; Matilda Betham Edwards by "The Romance of a French Parsonage" and "A North-Country Comedy." "Esther Vanhomrigh" was the sad heroine of Margaret L. Woods (the author of "A Village Tragedy"), who founded her story on facts in the life of Dean Swift, Miss Van Homrigh being Dean Swift's "Vanessa," and Maarten Maartens (J. Van der Poorsen Schwartz) told the powerful and touching story of "God's Fool," which enters deep into the study of character and psychology; he also published "A Question of Taste," in another and lighter vein. "The Last Confession" and "Capt'n Davy's Honeymoon" were by Hall Caine; I. Zangwill described the Jews of the East End of London in his "Children of the Ghetto, being Pictures of a Peculiar People," which filled two volumes, while he also chronicled "The Old Maids' Club" in a bright and humorous fashion. Hon. Emily Lawless, the author of "Hurrish," found an entirely new scene for her story of "Grania"; from James Payn came "A Stumble on the Threshold" and "A Modern Dick Whittington"; from Adeline Sergeant, "Sir Anthony's Secret" and "The Story of a Penitent Soul." Frank Barrett wrote "Out of the Jaws of Death"; Mrs. Alexander was at her best in "Mammon," "For his Sake," and "The Snare of the Fowler"; W. E. Norris had but one book, "His Grace"; and Paul Cushing also published but one, "The Blacksmith of Voe." Hamilton Aïdé made "A Voyage of Discovery" through American society; "A Queen of Curds and Cream," by Dorothea

Gerard, was followed by "Etelka's Vow"; Miss M. E. Braddon (Mrs. J. Maxwell) shifted the scene of "The Venetians" to England and back again; H. Merriman Seaton portrayed the London journalist as "The Slave of the Lamp"; Richard Dowling made a happy hit with "Catmur's Cares"; Mrs. Oliphant proved that she still retains her hold on the public heart by the reception of her "Diana" and "The Cuckoo in the Nest"; Robert Buchanan portrayed a charming "Squire Kate"; art and France in the sixteenth century formed the theme of "The Secret of Narcisse," by Edmund Gosse; "Nada, the Lily" of H. Rider Haggard, grew in Africa; and "An Idle Exile" found himself at home and particularly entertaining "By a Himalayan Lake" and "In Tent and Bungalow," in India; he also collected "Indian Idyls." A. Conan Doyle had three books, "The Great Shadow," "The Adventures of Sherlock Holmes," and "The Doings of Raffles Haw." "The Naulahka," in the writing of which Rudyard Kipling was assisted by Wolcott Balestier, the American, had its scene laid in Colorado and India; that of "The Duchess of Powysland," by Grant Allen, lay between England and America; and "The Princess Mazaroff," by Joseph Hatton, found many admirers. F. Anstey Guthrie's latest, "The Talking Horse," was humorous, with the indispensable dash of pathos; "In the Roar of the Sea," a tale of the Cornish coast in the days of the Georges, and "Margery of Quether, and Other Stories," came from Sabine Baring-Gould; W. Clark Russell was unusually prolific, with four books, all about the sea, viz., "A Strange Elopement," "Mrs. Dine's Jewels," "A Marriage at Sea," and "Alone on a Wide, Wide Sea." J. M. Barrie, whose successful novel of last year, "The Little Minister," went through a handsome American edition, limited to 260 copies, with illustrations from etchings by G. W. H. Ritchie, spent "A Holiday in Bed"; and "I saw Three Ships, and Other Winter Tales," were from the fascinating pen of Arthur T. Quiller-Couch. "The One Good Guest," by Mrs. L. B. Walford, received a hearty welcome; as did "T'Other Dear Charmer," by Helen Mathers. Florence Marryat (Mrs. Francis Lean) was the author of "The Nobler Sex," "A Fatal Silence," and "The Little Marine and the Japanese Lily," the last a book for boys; Mrs. Otto Booth (Rita) wrote "Asenath of the Ford" and "The Man in Possession"; Mrs. E. Lovett Cameron "A Loyal Lover," "A Sister's Sin," and "A Daughter's Heart"; Mrs. Frances Eleanor Trollope, "That Wild Wheel"; Christabel R. Coleridge, "Amethyst"; Rosa N. Carey, "Sir Godfrey's Granddaughters": W. Westall, "The Princes of Peele"; Mrs. Campbell Praed, "December Roses"; and Mrs. Louisa Parr, "The Squire." Violet Paget (Lee Vernon) aimed some home thrusts at the woman of fashion in "Vanitas"; E. Chilton narrated "The History of a Failure"; Morley Roberts was responsible for "The Reputation of George Saxon" and "The Mate of the 'Vancouver'"; and Florence Warden (Mrs. G. E. James) published two dissimilar books, "Sea Mew Abbey," which tells of Yorkshire smugglers and their doings, and "Ralph Ryder of Brent," a story of mistaken identity. Fergus Hume was mysterious, by necessity, in "The Fever of Life," "Aladdin in London," "A Creature of the Night," "The Island of Fantasy," and "When I lived in Bohemia," not one of which, however, came up to the mark of "The Mystery of a Hansom Cab." Miss Charlotte M. Yonge was represented by "That Stick"; Ada Cambridge by "Not all in Vain" and "My Guardian"; Hawley Smart by "A Member of Tattersall's"; Rhoda Broughton by "Mrs. Bligh"; Alan St. Aubyn by "The Old Maid's Sweetheart"; George Manville Fenn by "The King of the Castle" and "Nurse Elisia"; Hume Nisbet by "The Bushranger's Sweetheart"; Sarah Doudney by "Through Pain to Peace"; James Baker by "Mark Tillotson," about which Tennyson wrote the last letter that he is believed to have penned; The Duchess (Mrs. Hungerford) by four novels, "The O'Connors of Ballinahinch," "A Conquering Heroine," "Nor Wife nor Maid," and "Lady Patty"; and John Strange Winter (Mrs. H. E. V. Stannard) by as many more, "Experiences of a Lady Help," "Confessions of a Publisher," "Only Human," and "Those Girls." "The Tower of Taddeo" was another Italian story by Ouida (Louise de la Rame); Tasma published "The White Feather" and "The Penance of Portia James"; Mrs. J. H. Needell, "The Story of Philip Methuen" and "Passing the Love of Woman"; and Marchesa Lily Theodoli, "Under Pressure." "Treason Felony," by J. Hill, a new writer, achieved success, as did the anonymous author of "Through To-day." "A Tiger's Club" was by Eden Philpotts; "The Story of Chris," by Rowland Grey; "Miss Merewether's Money," by T. Cobb; "A Son of the Fens," by P. H. Emerson: "The Medicine Lady," by Mrs. Toulmin Smith; and "The March of Fate," by B. L. Farjeon. The younger Charles Dickens carried on his edition of his father's works, a handsome new library edition of Bulwer and Scott were initiated, Charles Reade's "Cloister and the Hearth" filled four exquisite volumes, and Anthony Trollope's "Chronicles of Barsetshire" thirteen. Two editions were offered of Jane Austen's works, and that of William Black's progressed to completion.

History.—Vol. III of Edward A. Freeman's "History of Sicily from the Earliest Times" covered the Athenian and Carthaginian invasions, and, with his "Story of Sicily, Phœnician, Greek, and Roman," in the "Story of the Nations Series," possesses a sad interest, the latter having been one of the last works upon which the historian was engaged; a fourth series of his "Historical Essays" was also published. "The Spanish Story of the Armada, and Other Essays," came from James Anthony Froude, who received his appointment to the chair of Modern History at Oxford during the year; Samuel Rawson Gardiner wrote "A Student's History of England from the Earliest Times to 1885," in one volume; William Connor Sydney, the author of "England and the English in the Eighteenth Century," "Social Life in England from the Restoration to the Revolution, 1660–1690"; C. S. Fearenside, "A History of England, 1640–1670"; H. F. Wright, "The Intermediate History of England from B.C. 55 to 1887"; E. A. W., sketches of English history under the title of "Old England"; T. Dunbar Ingram, "England and Rome: A History of the Relations between the

Papacy and the English State and Church" from the Norman Conquest to the revolution of 1688; J. Waylen, "The House of Cromwell and the Story of Dunkirk"; F. A. Inderwick, "The Story of King Edward and New Winchelsea: The Edification of a Mediæval Town"; and P. W. Clayden, "England under the Coalition," a political history of Great Britain and Ireland from the general election of 1885 to May, 1892. "Ireland under the Land League" was a narrative of personal experiences by C. Lloyd. George Barnett's "History of the English Parliament" filled two volumes, and was "the first complete, consecutive record of the English Parliament as a legislative institution from the earliest times to the present day." It contained also an account of the Parliaments of Scotland and Ireland, and was illustrated with facsimiles of numerous valuable historical documents connected with constitutional history. The first volume of a new illustrated edition of J. R. Green's "Short History of the English People," edited by Mrs. Green and Miss Kate Norgate, appeared; Macmillan's "History Readers" covered "The Tudor Period, 1485–1603," and "The Stuart Period, 1603–1714," with biographies of leading persons; Richard Garnett edited the "Accession of Queen Mary: Being the Contemporary Narrative of Antonio de Guaras"; and George Saintsbury performed a similar service for "Elizabethan and Jacobean Pamphlets." "Mediæval Scotland" occupied the attention of R. W. Cochran-Patrick; Mrs. T. Fielding Johnson published "Glimpses of Ancient Leicester in Six Periods"; and Sir James H. Ramsey, of Banff, Bart., "Lancaster and York: A Century of English History, A.D. 1399–1485," in two volumes. T. W. Shore wrote "A History of the County of Hampshire," including the Isle of Wight; Alfred Beaver, "Memorials of Old Chelsea: A New History of the Village of Palaces," illustrated; John Hobson Matthews, "A History of the Parishes of St. Ives, Lelant, Towednack, and Zennor, in the County of Cornwall"; and G. Crabbe's "History of the Parish of Thompson (Norfolk)" was edited by Jessopp, with drawings of the church by H. G. Green. C. Taylor wrote on "The Huguenots in the Seventeenth Century," including the history of the Edict of Nantes from its enactment, in 1598, to its revocation, in 1685; G. L. Dickinson, on "Revolution and Reaction in Modern France"; and H. Morse Stephens edited, with an introduction and notes, "The Principal Speeches of the Statesmen and Orators of the French Revolution, 1789–1795," in two volumes. Matilda Betham-Edwards took a comparative and retrospective survey of "France of To-day," and Col. G. B. Malleson described "The Refounding of the German Empire, 1848–1871." "The Battles of Frederick the Great" were edited by Cyril Ransome from Carlyle's biography of the Prussian monarch. In the "Story of the Nations Series," "The Story of the Byzantine Empire" was written by C. W. C. Oman. "Studies by a Recluse in Cloister, Town, and Country" was a collection of lectures and essays on historical subjects by A. Jessopp; and from Oscar Browning we have "The Flight to Varennes, and other Historical Essays." "England's Sea Victories" were commemorated by C. R. Low. Evelyn Abbott, in Part II of "A History of Greece," covered the period from the Ionian revolt to the thirty years' peace, 500–445 B. C.; "New Chapters in Greek History" were written by Percy Gardner; "Rome under the Oligarchs," by A. H. Allcroft, covering 202–133 B. C.; and Rev. A. J. Church drew "Pictures from Roman Life and Story," for which the Cæsars furnished the central figures. Several volumes were devoted to England in India. "Bombay, 1885 to 1890," by Sir W. W. Hunter, was a study in Indian administration; Sir John Strachey, in "Hastings and the Rohilla War," reversed the judgment of history, and proved the great oratorical efforts of Burke to have been founded on inaccuracy; H. Compton gave "A Particular Account of the European Military Adventurers of Hindustan from 1784 to 1803"; and W. Pimblett told "How the British won India," "Arakan: Past and Present," by J. O. Hay, was a *résumé* of two campaigns for its development. "Events in the Taeping Rebellion" was from manuscripts copied by Gen. Gordon in his own handwriting, edited by A. Egmont Hake, the author of "The Story of Chinese Gordon." "Fifty Years in the making of Australian History" were traced by Sir Henry Parkes, Prime Minister of New South Wales, 1872–'75, 1877, 1878–'79. Edward J. Payne published Vol. I of a "History of the New World called America," which promises to be a valuable contribution; and W. Kingsford, Vol. V of "The History of Canada." To Church history belong "The Faith and Life of the Early Church," by W. J. Slater; a "History of the Church in England from the Beginning of the Christian Era to the Ascension of Henry VIII," by Mary H. Allies; "The Public Worship of Presbyterian Scotland historically treated," by C. G. M'Crie, in the "Fourteenth Series of the Cunningham Lectures"; "Studies in Scottish History, chiefly Ecclesiastical," by A. T. Innes; "The Church in Spain," by Rev. Frederick Meyrick; "The Church of Ireland," by Thomas Olden; "The Somerset Religious Houses," by W. A. J. Archbold; a "History of the Church in Eastern Canada and Newfoundland," by J. Langtry; and a "History of the Church of St. Mary the Virgin, Oxford, which was the University Church from Domesday to the Installation of the late Duke of Wellington, Chancellor of the University," by Rev. E. S. Ffoulkes. "Annals of Winchester College from its Foundation in the Year 1382 to the Present Time" were the work of T. F. Kirby.

Physical, Moral, and Intellectual Science. —"The Realm of Nature," by Hugh Robert Mill, giving an outline of physiography, will properly open the first division; it appeared in the series of "University Extension Manuals," and next in order comes "The Great World's Farm," by Selina Gaye, showing that almost all the labor that produces its crops is performed by natural agencies. "The Horse," by William H. Flower, formed No. 2 of the "Modern Science Series," edited by Sir John Lubbock, who made "A Contribution to our Knowledge of Seedlings" in two volumes. "The Oak" was a popular introduction to forest botany by H. Marshall Ward; J. W. Tutt published Vol. II of "The British Noctuæ and the Varieties" and "Melanism and Melanochroism in British Lepidoptera"; Alexander Johnstone, a concise manual

of "Botany" for students of medicine and science; G. Schneider, Vol. I of "The Book of Choice Ferns," illustrated with colored plates and wood engravings; M. C. Cooke, "Vegetable Wasps and Plant Worms"; and A. C. Seward, "Fossil Plants as Tests of Climate," the Sidgwick prize essay for 1892. C. Dixon, in "The Migration of Birds," made an attempt to reduce avian season flight to law; R. B. Sharpe published Part I of his "Monograph of the Paradiseidæ, or Birds of Paradise, and Ptilonorhynchidæ, or Bower Birds"; W. J. Gordon illustrated in color his guide to all the birds of Great Britain entitled "Our Country's Birds, and how to know them"; "The Story of the Hills" was a book about mountains, for general readers, by Rev. H. N. Hutchinson, who wrote also on "Extinct Monsters"; "The Visible University," by J. Ellard Gore, consisted of chapters on the origin and construction of the heavens, with stellar photographs and other illustrations; Sir Robert Ball published "In Starry Realms" and "An Atlas of Astronomy," a series of 72 plates: and O. Boeddicker, "The Milky Way from the North Pole to Ten Degrees of the South Declination," drawn at the Earl of Rosse's Observatory, at Birr Castle. In the "Contemporary Science Series," edited by Havelock Ellis, "The Grammar of Science" was by Karl Pearson; "Volcanoes, Ancient and Modern," by Prof. Edward Hull; and "The Man of Genius," by Prof. C. Lomborso. John Gray McKendrick delivered six lectures on "Life in Motion; or, Muscle and Nerve"; G. Allen wrote on "The Colour Sense"; and Sir George Gabriel Stokes's Burnett Lectures were "On Light." "Human Origins" were traced by S. Laing; A. W. Buckland made "Anthropological Studies"; Rev. John Batchelor, a study of the hairy aborigine termed "The Ainu of Japan"; and Sir Daniel Wilson published "The Lost Atlantis, and Other Ethnographic Studies." "Darwin and After Darwin," by G. J. Romanes, "Essays upon Some Controverted Questions," by Prof. Thomas H. Huxley, and "New Fragments" of Prof. John Tyndall (whose "Fragments of Science" went through a revised and enlarged edition), were hailed by the scientific world, and Vol. I of "The Principles of Ethics" appeared, making Vol. IX of Herbert Spencer's "System of Synthetic Philosophy"; it was issued in this country, and he also secured an American copyright for an abridged and revised edition of his "Social Statics," first published in 1850. Henry De Varigny handled "Experimental Evolution," C. M. Williams made "A Review of the Systems of Ethics founded on the Theory of Evolution," while "Elements of Ethics," by J. H. Muirhead, were intended as an introduction to moral philosophy. J. A. Stewart published two volumes of "Notes on the Nicomachean Ethics of Aristotle"; James Sully wrote a text-book of psychology entitled "The Human Mind"; and E. Belfort Bax offered outline suggestions for a philosophical reconstruction in "The Problem of Reality." In the "Social Science Series," "Illegitimacy: A Study in Morals and the Influence of Climate on Conduct" was by Albert Leffingwell, M. D.; "Distributing Co-operative Societies," by Louis Pizzamiglio; "The Destitute Alien in Great Britain," by Arnold White and others; "The

Dawn of Radicalism," by J. Bowles Daly; "The Trade Policy of Imperial Federation," by M. H. Hervey; "The Impossibility of Social Democracy," by A. Schaffle; "Commercial Crises of the Nineteenth Century" were treated with clearness and ability by Henry M. Hyndman; and "The State and Pensions in Old Age," by J. A. Spender, with an Introduction by Arthur H. D. Acland, M. P. Charles Booth, who has devoted so much time to "The Life and Labor of the People in London," wrote "Pauperism: A Picture; and The Endowment of Old Age: An Argument"; "The Fallacy of Saving" was a study in economics by J. M. Robertson; Henry Jephson issued two volumes on "The Platform"; H. D. Traill wrote on "Central Government" in the "English Citizen Series"; Sir Charles W. Dilke and Spenser Wilkinson, on the "Imperial Defense" of Great Britain, preparation for which they urge, after reviewing her army and navy, and their work recalls Chesney's "Battle of Dorking"; G. R. Parkin pronounced "Imperial Federation the Problem of National Unity"; B. R. Wise treated "Industrial Reform"; D. F. Schloss, "Methods of Industrial Remuneration"; and Herbert M. Thompson, "The Theory of Wages and its Application to the Eight Hours' Question and Other Labor Problems." G. V. Pick drew up a "Digest of Political Economy and Some of its Applications to Social Philosophy," and R. H. Inglis Palgrave edited Part III of a "Dictionary of Political Economy." Russell M. Garnier wrote an exhaustive "History of the English Landed Interest"; J. C. Smith had ideas of his own as to "The Distribution of the Produce"; and Earl Grey expressed himself on "The Commercial Policy of the British Colonies and the McKinley Tariff." "A Study in Municipal Government: The Corporation of Berlin," came from J. Pollard. "England in Egypt," by A. Milner; "Egypt To-day: The First to the Third Khedive," by W. Fraser Rae; and "The Egyptian State Debt and its Relation to International Law," by W. Kaufmann, were all timely. A. Rogers published a history of the administration, rise, and progress of "The Land Revenue of Bombay," in two volumes; W. Griffith, "Commentaries on the Indian Transfer of Property Acts, 1892," as well as "International Law: History, Principles, Rules, and Treaties"; while R. Wallace's "Indian Agriculture" was furnished with maps, plates, and illustrations. "The Ruin of the Soudan; Cause, Effect, and Remedy," a résumé of events from 1883 to 1891, came from H. Russell and W. Gattie, and "The Late Battles in the Soudan and Modern Tactics" was "A Reply" by Capt. C. B. Mayne. "Dark Africa and the Way out," by W. Hughes, suggested a scheme for civilizing and evangelizing the Dark Continent. Part II of "The Law and Custom of the Constitution," by Sir W. R. Anson, was devoted to "The Crown"; J. A. Neale compiled an "Exposition of English Law by English Judges"; R. Giffen was the author of "The Case against Bimetallism"; and John Henry Norman of a "Complete Guide to the World's Twenty-nine Metal Monetary Systems." "Special Aspects of the Irish Question," a series of reflections of Hon. W. E. Gladstone in and since 1886, were collected from various sources and reprinted, and "The Irish Peasant"

was an anonymous sociological study. "The Member for Wrottenborough: Passages from his Life in Parliament, edited by his 'Alter Ego,' Arthur A'Becket," proved a bright and readable brochure, by the author of "Papers from Pump-Handle Court." "The Livery Companies of the City of London" had their origin, character, development, and social and political importance traced by William Carew Hazlitt, and Rev. J. Malet Lambert chronicled "Two Thousand Years of Guild Life." "Villeinage in England" in mediæval times was exhaustively treated by Paul Vinogradoff, and "Old Touraine: The Life and History of the Famous Châteaux of France," by Theodore Andrea Cook, filled two volumes. C. F. Bastable wrote on "The Commerce of Nations" in "Social Questions of the Day"; Rev. W. Cunningham traced "The Growth of English Industry and Commerce in Modern Times." "English Trade and Finance, chiefly in the Seventeenth Century," in the "University Extension Manuals," came from W. A. S. Hewins, and P. L. Simmonds prepared "A Handbook of British Commerce." "The Romanes Lecture, 1892," was delivered by Hon. W. E. Gladstone. F. Max Müller delivered the Gifford Lectures before the University of Glasgow in 1891 upon "Anthropological Religion," and also lectured before the University of Cambridge upon "India, what can it teach us?" in addition to editing two volumes and two parts of volumes of "The Sacred Books of the East." "The Faiths of the Peoples," by J. Fitzgerald Molloy, in two volumes; "The Great Indian Religions," by G. T. Bettany, in "The World's Religions Series"; "Buddhism, Primitive and Present, in Magadha and in Ceylon," by R. S. Copleston; "Studies in Mohammedanism, Historical and Doctrinal," by J. J. Pool; and "Imitation of Buddha," compiled by Ernest M. Bowden, with a preface by Sir Edwin Arnold, possessed interest for many readers; and in the "International Theological Library," "Apologetics; or, Christianity defensively stated" came from Dr. Alexander Balmain Bruce. Recently discovered "Meditations on the Life of Christ," by Thomas à Kempis, were translated and edited by Archdeacon Wright and Rev. S. Kettlewell, with a preface by the latter, the leading authority in Europe on all matters relating to Thomas à Kempis. "The Early Religion of Israel as set forth by Biblical Writers and by Modern Critical Historians" was the theme of the Baird Lectures for 1889, by James Robertson, D. D., put into book form during the year; T. G. Bonney delivered the Boyle Lectures for 1891, upon "Christian Doctrines and Modern Thought"; Rev. John Laidlaw wrote upon "The Miracles of Our Lord"; Rev. Charles Gore, the Principal of Pusey House, upon "The Mission of the Church," George MacDonald published twelve sermons on "The Hope of the Gospel"; and Canon Farrar fifteen, upon "The Voice from Sinai," as heard in the Commandments. "The Face of the Deep" was a commentary on the Apocalypse by Christina G. Rossetti. "The Canon of the Old Testament" as examined by Prof. H. E. Ryle attracted some attention, and T. D. Bernard, Canon of Wells, the author of "The Progress of Doctrine in the New Testament," wrote upon "The Central Teaching of Christ." Vols. XVI and XVII of "The People's

Bible," by Joseph Parker, were issued,.devoted
to the prophets Jeremiah, Daniel, Hosea-Mala-
chi; two additions to "The Sermon Bible" covered "John IV to Acts VI," and "Acts VII to I Corinthians XVI"; and in the "Expositor's Bible
Series" we have "Epistles to the Thessalonians,"
by Rev. J. Denney; "Epistles to the Ephesians,"
by Rev. G. G. Findlay; the second volume of
"The Gospel of St. John," by Rev. M. Dods;
the second volume of "The Acts of the Apostles," by Rev. G. T. Stokes; and "The Book
of Job," by Rev. R. A. Watson. "The Dictionary of Hymnology," edited by John J.
Julian, set forth the origin and history of not
less than 400,000 Christian hymns in 200 or
more languages and dialects. "Breaking the
Long Silence" was the title of two brief addresses delivered on the last evening of 1891
and the first morning of 1892 by the late Rev.
C. H. Spurgeon, and his "Scarlet Threads and
Bits of Blue" had a preface by Mrs. Spurgeon.
In the "Preachers of the Age Series," we have
"Verbum Crucis, with Other Sermons," by
Bishop W. Alexander, of Derby; "The Con-
quering Christ," by Rev. Alexander Maclaren;
"Living Theology," by the Archbishop of Can-
terbury; and "Ethical Christianity," by Rev.
Hugh Price Hughes. "Short Sermons," by Rev.
Stopford A. Brooke: "Dissertations on the Apostolic Age," by Bishop J. D. Lightfoot; "The
Natural History of Immortality," by Rev. Joseph
W. Reynolds; "Christ, the Light of all Scripture," and "Growth in Grace and Other Sermons," by Archbishop W. Magee; "Sermons," by
H. Scott Holland; and "From Advent to Advent," by Aubrey L. Moore, deserve mention, as
do "Cathedral and University Sermons" of the
late Rev. R. W. Church, Dean of St. Paul. Works
which possess general or individual interest
which it is impossible to place under any of our
other classifications may as well find a place
here. They are: "The Printing Arts," by J.
W. Howland; "The Romance of Engineering,"
by H. Frith; "The Steam Navy of England,"
by Harry Williams; "The Atlantic Ferry," by
A. J. Maginnis; "The Industrial Arts of the
Anglo-Saxons," by Baron J. De Baye; "Coal
Pits and Pitmen," by R. Nelson Boyd; "The
Metropolitan Water Supply," by H. C. Richards
and W. H. C. Payne; "Lightning Guards," by
Oliver J. Lodge, the author of "Modern Views
of Electricity"; "The Encyclopædia of Photog-
raphy," by W. E. Woodbury; "The Optics of
Photography and Photographic Lenses," by J.
T. Taylor; "The Mechanics of Architecture," a
treatise on applied mechanics especially adapted
to the use of architects, by E. W. Tarn; and J.
B. Lee's useful work "On Indigo Manufacture."
J. T. Arlidge made an interesting study of
"The Hygiene, Diseases, and Mortality of Occupations"; H. C. Burdette gave the origin, history, etc., of "Hospitals and Asylums of the
World"; and S. Wilks and G. T. Bettany wrote
"A Biographical History of Guy's Hospital."
"Suffering London," by A. Egmont Hake, traced
the hygienic, moral, social, and political relation
of our voluntary hospitals to society; and Have-
lock Ellis wrote on "The Nationalism of
Health." The Croonian Lectures before the
Royal College of Physicians in London. June,
1889, were by T. Lauder Brunton, entitled "An

Introduction to Modern Therapeutics." "The
London Daily Press" was an interesting record,
by H. W. Massingham. "Rod and River," by
A. T. Fisher; a second series of "Letters to
Young Shooters," by Sir Ralph Payne Gallwey;
a "Batch of Golfing Papers," by Andrew Lang
and others, edited by R. Barclay; "On Seats
and Saddles, Bits and Bitting," by Francis
Dwyer; and "Mountaineering," by C. T. Dent, in
the Badminton Library; with "Card Tricks and
Puzzles," by "Berkeley" and T. B. Rowland,
met the requirements of the sporting world.
F. Anstey Guthrie reprinted a second series of
"Voces Populi" from "Punch," and J. Scott
Keltie sent out the twenty-ninth annual issue
of "The Statesman's Year Book," a most valuable work of reference.

Poetry.—"The Death of Œnone, Akbar's
Dream, and Other Poems," and "The Forester,
Robin Hood, and Maid Marian," a drama of the
greenwood, were the last utterances of Tennyson
to the world, which he continued to charm to the
last; "Marah" was a volume of posthumous
poems by Owen Meredith (Lord Lytton); and
from poets still with us we have "Potiphar's
Wife, and Other Poems," by Sir Edwin Arnold;
"The Sisters," a tragedy, by Algernon C. Swin-
burne, which disappointed some of his admirers;
and "Poems by the Way," by William Morris.
W. E. Henley sang "The Song of the Sword"
alone, and with Robert Louis Stevenson wrote
"Three Plays," which were reckoned a "brilliant
exception to the usual failure of literary collaboration." "Barrack-Room Ballads, and Other
Verses," proclaim Rudyard Kipling by their
title, as "Flowers o' the Vine" suggest at once
William Sharp. "The Collected Poems of Philip
Bourke Marston" were given to the world with
a sympathetic biographical sketch by Mrs. Louise
Chandler Moulton. Austin Dobson wrote "The
Ballad of Beau Brocade," and Alfred Austin,
"Fortunatus, the Pessimist"; John Davidson,
the author of "Scaramouch in Naxos," "In a
Music Hall, and Other Poems"; William Watson, "Poems," and "Lachrymæ Musarum" (for
the dead laureate); Richard Le Gallienne, "English Poems"; and F. W. Bourdillon, "A Lost
God." Hugh Haliburton's "Ochil Idylls" had
all his old charm, and from Miss Jessie Barlow
we had "Bogland Studies," humorous and pathetic." "The Violet Crown" and "Songs of
England" came from Rennell Rodd; "Granite
Dust: Fifty Poems," from R. C. Macfie; E. Carpenter leaned "Toward Democracy" in imitation of Walt Whitman; and other volumes possessing merit were "Love's Victory: Lyrical
Poems," by J. A. Blaikie; "A Country Muse,"
by Norman R. Gale; "The Ballad of Pity, by
Gascoigne Mackie; "Lays and Legends," by
E. Nisbet; "Poems," by Oscar Wilde; "Sight
and Song," by Michael Field; "Quo Musa
Tendis," a slight volume of humorous verse by
J. K. Stephen; "Occasional Rhymes and Re-
flections upon Subjects Literary and Political,"
by G. H. Powell; "Poems," by William Cald-
well Roscoe; "Bernard and Constantio, and
Other Poems," by C. J. Blake; "Lyrical Stud-
ies," by S. C. Rickards: "Songs of an Exile," by
V. E. Marsden; "Meditative Poems," by J. T.
Chapman; and "Pilgrim Songs, and Other
Poems, written during Forty Years," by Rev.

J. Page Hopps. C. Amy Dawson wrote "Idylls of Womanhood"; A. Dillon, "Gods and Men," dramatic poems; "The Secrets of the South," by S. Jephcott, were Australian poems; Philip Dale and Cyril Haviland published "Voices from Australia"; and W. H. H. Yarrington, "Australian Verses." Mathilde Blind sent out "Dramas in Miniature," and George Meredith, "Poems: The Empty Purse; with Odes to the Comic Spirit, to Youth in Memory, and Verses." In "Poets and Poetry of the Century," edited by Alfred H. Miles, we had "Frederick Tennyson to Arthur Hugh Clough" and "Charles Kingsley to James Thomson." "Love Songs of English Poets, 1500–1800," were compiled, with notes by Ralph Caine, and William Watsou edited "Lyric Love." "A Paradise of English Poetry," selected by H. C. Beeching, filled two volumes. Graham R. Thomson compiled a book "Concerning Cats," and George Eyre Todd edited "Mediæval Scottish Poetry," in the "Abbotsford Series of Scottish Poetry." A centenary edition of Shelley's works was issued by an American publishing house, edited by Prof. George E. Woodberry, and George Meredith's "Modern Love" came from another, in an édition de luxe with a "Foreword" by Mrs. E. Cavazza.

Voyages and Travels. — British travelers were as numerous and adventurous in 1892 as ever, and wrote more voluminous if not more entertaining records of where they wandered and what befell them. In "America and the Americans" A. Craib gave his narrative of a tour through the United States and Canada, not venturing out of the beaten track, and Irving Montagu illustrated "The Land of the Almighty Dollar" as seen by H. P. Gordon. "By Track and Trail" was the account of a journey through Canada by Edward Roper, and "The Barren Ground of Northern Canada," by Warburton Pike, told the story of two years of sport and adventure; while Edward Whymper's "Travels amongst the Great Andes of the Equator," with its "Supplementary Appendix," with contributions by numerous authors, was reckoned by many the best book of travels of the year. An anonymous "Gringo" went "Through the Land of the Aztecs"; Villiers Stuart chronicled "Adventures amidst the Equatorial Forests and Rivers of South America; also in the West Indies and the Wilds of Florida," and told of "Jamaica revisited"; Thomas A. Turner gave his notes and impressions of "Argentina and the Argentines" acquired during a five years' sojourn, 1885–'90; W. H. Hudson visited "The Amazon in La Plata"; G. C. Morant, "Chili and the River Plate in 1891"; while "A Ride through Wonderland," by Georgina M. Synge, described the Yellowstone region. Edward Carpenter entitled his sketches in Ceylon and India "From Adam's Peak to Elephanta"; Sir Joseph Dalton Hooker published "Himalayan Journals," the notes of a naturalist; J. D. Rees, "Lord Connemara's Tours in India, 1886–1890"; W. R. Winston, "Four years in Upper Burmah"; Mrs. C. F. Gordon-Cumming, "Two Happy Years in Ceylon," in two volumes; Walter J. Clutterbuck told "About Ceylon and Borneo"; Maj.-Gen. A. Ruxton MacMahon, of "Far Cathay and Farther India"; Gen. D. Hamilton's

"Records of Sport in Southern India" were edited by his brother, Edward Hamilton; and "Myamma: A Retrospect of Life and Travel in Lower Burmah," by C. F. Paske, was edited by F. G. Aflalo. J. J. Aubertin's "Wanderings and Wonderings" extended over India, Burmah, Cashmere. Ceylon, Singapore, Java, Siam, Japan, Manila, Formosa, etc., while two volumes contained the stray papers, maps, and plans of J. Douglas in "Bombay and Western India." Mrs. Howard Vincent went from "Newfoundland to Cochin-China, by the Golden Wave. New Nippon, and the Forbidden City"; A. E. Pratt, "To the Snows of Thibet through China"; and Julius M. Price, "From the Arctic Ocean to the Yellow Sea." "Siberia as it is," by II. de Windt, had an introduction by Madame Olga de Norikoff. J. Dyer Ball saw "Things Chinese"; Henry Norman devoted his best energies to portraying "The Real Japan," with happy results; A. Tracy described "Rambles through Japan without a Guide"; and Douglas Slader kodaked with a camera and pen "The Japs at Home." "Japanese Letters," giving Eastern impressions of Western men and manners, by Tokiwari and Yashiri, were edited by Commander Hastings Berkeley, and possess value as the earnest and philosophic study of the civilization which the Japanese are accepting, by two cultivated natives of different minds. E. J. Glave's "In Savage Africa; or, Six Years of Adventure in Congo-Land," had an introduction by Henry M. Stanley, and "Stories told in an African Forest," by A. J. Mounteney Jephson, impress us strongly, coming from the pen of one of the heroes of the Emin Relief Expedition. Rev. William Parr Greswell outlined the "Geography of Africa South of the Zambesi," with notes on the industries, wealth, and social progress of the states and peoples, and Stephen Bonsal, Jr., pictured "Morocco as it is." J. E. Ritchie pictured life at the Cape and Natal in "Brighter South Africa"; A. F. M. Ferryman's "Up the Niger" contained the narrative of Major Claude Macdonald's mission to the Niger and Benin rivers, West Africa; Lord Randolph Churchill wrote up "Men, Mines, and Animals in South Africa," in line with which is Lockwood Kipling's "Beast and Man in India"; J. A. Nicolls was "The Sportsman in South Africa"; W. L. Distant, "A Naturalist in the Transvaal"; while A. Groser's "South African Experiences" were illustrated with forty engravings and maps. Reunert's "Diamond Mines of South Africa" contained much interesting information. "The Ruined Cities of Mashonaland" was a record of excavation and exploration in 1891 by J. Theodore Bent, and "Tanganyika: Eleven Years in Central Africa," came from Capt. E. C. Hore. Romolo Gessi's "Seven Years in the Soudan" was edited by his son Felix. Hon. George N. Curzon filled two volumes with "Persia and the Persian Question"; "Homeward Bound after Thirty Years," by Edward Reeves, gave a colonist's impressions of New Zealand, Australia, Tangier, and Spain; J. P. Thompson wrote on "British New Guinea," and W. E. Swanton "Notes on New Zealand." B. F. S. Baden-Powell gave his personal experiences "In Savage Isles and Settled Lands." "Shall I try Australia? or, Health, Business and Pleasure in New South Wales," by G. L. James, and "'Round the Compass in Australia," by Gilbert Parker, with "Hard Life in the Colonies, and Other Experiences by Sea and Land," now first printed, compiled by C. Carlyon Jenkins in the "Adventure Series," exhaust this part of the globe, and we turn to "A Ride across Iceland in the Summer of 1891," by W. T. McCormick for novelty. On the Continent, John Addington Symonds and his daughter Margaret were delightful in "Our Life in the Swiss Highlands"; E. J. Goodman recommended "The Best Tour in Norway"; C. F. Keary described "Norway and the Norwegians"; M. Stokes spent "Six Months in the Apennines"; "The Land of Flowers," by Clement Scott, described the Riviera; W. M. Conway and W. A. B. Coolidge were joint authors of a "Climber's Guide" to the Lepantine Alps; "The Realm of the Hapsburgs," by S. Whitman, gave a descriptive account of the present condition of Austria and Hungary, and Margaret Fletcher contributed "Sketches of Life and Character in Hungary." Miss Margaret Thomas illustrated her own book of "A Scamper through Spain and Tangier"; Mrs. E. R. Whitwell described "Spain as we found it in 1891"; and from Henry Blackburn we had a record of "Artistic Travel" in Normandy, Brittany, the Pyrenees, Spain, and Algeria, with 130 illustrations. H. M. Doughty carried "Our Wherry in Wendish Lands: From Friesland through the Mecklenburg Lakes to Bohemia"; and John Wallace illustrated "Across France in a Caravan," by the author of "A Day of my Life at Eton." A volume on "Russian Characteristics" came out under the collective signature of E. B. Lanin, reprinted from the "Fortnightly Review"; W. Barnes Steveni, the special correspondent of the "Daily Chronicle," went "Through Famine-Stricken Russia," and E. A. B. Hodgetts followed "In the Track of the Russian Famine." A. E. W. Marsh chronicled his "Holiday Wanderings in Madeira"; W. M. F. Petrie, "Ten Years' Digging in Egypt, 1881–1891" (for archæologists); from Stanley Lane-Poole we have sketches of the history, monuments, and social life of "Cairo"; and from Martin Brimmer, "Egypt." "New Light on the Bible and the Holy Land," by B. T. A. Evetts, was an account of some recent discoveries in the East, and Hardwicke D. Rawnsley drew up "Notes for the Nile." "Capitals of the World," in two volumes, were edited by Nancy Bell (N. D'Anvers) and H. D. Traill, and Rev. G. E. Mason went "Round the World on a Church Mission." "Flying Visits" of Harry Furniss to various cities of the British Isles were decidedly entertaining, and had 192 illustrations, by the author; C. W. Methven furnished "Sketches of Durban and its Harbour in 1891"; J. Leyland was at home on "The Yorkshire Coast and the Cleveland Hills and Dales"; Leo H. Grindon described "Lancashire, England"; as did C. R. B. Barrett, "Essex Highways, Byways, and Water Ways"; while "Swin, Swale, and Swatchway; or, Cruises Down the Thames, the Medway, and the Essex Rivers," was by H. L. Jones and C. B. Lockwood. "Round London: Down East and up West," by M. Williams, was reprinted from "Household Words," and Part I of Frank Cowper's "Sailing Tours" was devoted to "The Coasts of Essex and Suffolk." "Sketches in Sunshine

and Storm." by W. J. Knox Little, and "Camping Sketches," by G. R. Lowndes, found readers; and Hew Ainslie's "Pilgrimage to the Land of Burns" was printed in the first complete collection of that author's writings that has been made since 1822.

The following are the figures of book-production in England in 1892, compared with those of 1891, as given by the "Publishers' Circular" (London):

CLASSIFICATION.	1891.		1892.	
	New books.	New editions.	New books.	New editions.
Theology, sermons, biblical, etc.	520	107	528	145
Educational, classical, and philological....................	587	107	579	115
Juvenile works and tales.......	348	99	292	58
Novels, tales, and other fiction..	896	320	1,147	390
Law, jurisprudence, etc.........	61	48	86	29
Political and social economy, trade, and commerce	105	31	151	24
Arts, sciences, and illustrated works	85	31	147	62
Voyages, travels, geographical research......................	208	68	250	86
History, biography, etc.........	328	85	293	75
Poetry and the drama..........	146	55	185	49
Year books and serials in vols...	310	6	360	13
Medicine, surgery, etc..........	120	55	127	50
Belles-lettres, essays, monographs, etc	181	123	107	32
Miscellaneous, including pamphlets, not sermons..........	589	142	713	228
	4,429	1,277 4,429	4,915	1,389 4,915
		5,706		6,254

LITERATURE, CONTINENTAL.

The prodigious and ever-increasing number of volumes now published annually makes even an enumeration of simply all that have been well received by critics and the public almost an impossibility here. Still, we believe that the following *résumé* of the year's doings in literary circles (arranged, as usual, by countries placed in alphabetical order) will be found to make mention of those publications which are of most importance, or which specially illustrate the drift of literary taste in the various countries, or which show specially interesting by-paths entered into in notable individual cases.

Belgium.—History, especially national history, is, as ever, assiduously cultivated in Belgium. The publication of *documents inédits* on the history of the country is diligently continued, the works of this kind including an edition, by M. H. Pirenne, of the famous Latin chronicle of Galbertus of Bruges, in which is related the story of the murder of Charles the Good, Count of Flanders (1127–'28), and the memoirs of Martin del Rio, a Spaniard, dealing with the Netherlands in the sixteenth century, and brought out by Canon Delvigne. Of continuations, there are the tenth volume of the late Baron Kervyn de Lettenhove's "Relations Politiques des Pays-Bas et de l'Angleterre sous le Règne de Philippe II"; the third volume of Marneffe's documents relating to "La Principauté de Liège et les Pays-Bays au XVIᵉ Siècle"; the second part of Abbé Cauchie's learned work, "La Querelle des Investitures dans les Diocèses de Liège et de Cambrai (1092–1107)"; Vol. II of the late E. Poullet's "Histoire

Politique Nationale," completed by the son of the author; as well as the works of Mgr. Namèche and Canon Daris. Poullet's book, we are told, presents an excellent review of the development of the institutions of the Low Countries previous to the French annexation of 1794. A. Henri has written a fairly impartial account of "the secular feud between two races and two languages in Belgium," while Ch. Woeste, the Minister of State, is said to have produced a veritable sensation by his "Neutralité Belge, la Belgique et la France," in which Belgian policy is valiantly defended. Special periods and localities have been treated by J. Frederichs, who has thrown light on a dark subject in his "Le Grand Conseil Ambulatoire des Ducs de Bourgogne et des Archiducs d'Autriche (1446–1504)"; H. Vander Linden, said to be a young writer of promise ("Histoire de la Constitution de la Ville de Louvain au Moyen Âge"); Prosper Claeys, with a three-volume "Histoire du Théâtre à Gand"; and A. Vlaminck, in his "Origines de la Ville de Gand." Monographs on Jean le Maire (by J. Stecher) and Jacques Le Roy (by De Raadt) should also be noted. A number of learned contributions to the history of other lands are likewise to be recorded. An important production is Martin Philippson's "Histoire du Règne de Marie Stuart," a very impartial work by one who formerly held a professorship in the Brussels University. Gen. Wauwermans has issued a volume on "Henri le Navigateur et l'Académie Portugaise de Sagres," and special aspects of French history have been elucidated notably in three works; these are: "Théories Politiques et le Droit International en France jusqu'au XVIIIᵉ Siècle," by E. Nys; L. Leclère's "Les Rapports de la Papauté et de la France sous Philippe III (1270–'85)"; and Frederich's monograph on "Robert le Bougre," Pope Gregory IX's first inquisitor in France. "Élémens de Paleographie et de Diplomatique du Moyen Âge" has been brought out by Canon Reusens. And, finally, touching on the two extremes of ancient and contemporary history, we have *résumés* of the progress of Assyriology during the last eleven years, and of Latin epigraphy during the last fifty, by Father Delattre and M. Waltzing, respectively, and a volume of recollections of the war in the Balkans, by P. F. Levaux, entitled "Ghazi Osman Pacha."

In the field of political and social science, the most notable publication, to which the Government awarded the prize of 5,000 francs founded for books of this character, has been Émile de Laveleye's "Le Gouvernement dans la Démocratic." The book was brought out just before the death of the noted publicist, who was engaged upon a treatise on political economy at the time of his decease. Other new works in this department are "Associations Professionelles d'Artisans et d'Ouvriers" (two volumes), socialistic in tendency, by É. Vander Velde; "Études sur les Questions Ouvrières," by De Quéker; and two works on Belgian affairs: "Les Masuirs" (researches into ancient forms of collective property), by P. Errera, and "Les Finances Communales en Belgique," by Louis Richald. S. Deploige's *brochure*, "Le Referendum en Suisse," is on a subject which seems to have received increased attention in recent years. Furthermore,

we have X. Francotte's "Anthropologie criminelle" (concerned with the theories of Lombroso and Bertillon), L. Franck's "Essai sur la Condition Politique de la Femme" ("crowned" by the Paris Faculty of Law), and a volume on "Les Civilizations animales," by P. Combes. The principal contributions in the domain of theology have been "Les Religions de la Chine," by Mgr. de Harlez, and "L'Idée de Dieu d'après l'Anthropologie et l'Histoire" (Hibbert Lectures), by Count Goblet d'Alviella.

The history of the arts in Belgium has been contributed to in the following works: "Les Peintres Verriers d'Anvers," by C. van Cauwenbergs: "La Sculpture et les Arts Plastiques au Pays de Liège et sur les Bords de la Meuse," by J. Helbig; "Les Tapisseries de Tournai," by E. Soil; and "L'Hôtel de Ville de Léau (1526–'30)," by A. Goovaerts. Here may be named also Countess Marie de Villermont's curious and profusely illustrated "Histoire de la Coiffure." In literary history and criticism, there have been F. Nautet's "Histoire des Lettres Belges d'Expression Française," P. Bergmans's "Étude sur l'Éloquence Parlementaire Belge sous le Régime Hollandais (1815–'30)," Abbé Stiernet's "Histoire de la Littérature Française au Moyen Âge et au XVIᵉ Siècle," an essay on "Le Labeur de la Prose" by Gustave Abel, and a monograph on Ibsen by Ch. Saroléa.

A prodigious number of works of fiction in the French language have been issued during the year, and yet, queerly enough, we are told that the Belgians distrust their French *littérateurs*. Beginning with the old school of novelists, we have notably Xavier de Reul's "Le Chevalier Forelle." "Cycle. Patibulaire" and "Dames de Volupté" are the two latest novels of Georges Eckhoud and C. Lemonnier, probably the two strongest men in the realistic camp, and both books have been characterized as "decidedly crude." "La Jeune Belgique," the new school of "younger men," is attracting much attention. The founder of the movement, Maurice Warlomont ("Max Waller"), who died a few years ago, left a delightful tale, "Daisy," which has been published. Maurice Maeterlinck, of the production of whose strange plays in Paris, London, Copenhagen, and Brussels the press has brought us word, has refused the quinquennial prize for dramatic literature which had been won by his "Princesse Maleine," and has also brought out two new dramas, "Les sept Princesses" and "Pelléas et Mélisande," which appear to have been accorded a more favorable reception than his former works. As to the poetry that has been published, it is characterized as generally exceedingly careful in form but lacking in originality.

In Flemish literature the year's publication of books also includes works of importance. Here, too, we find an active interest in historical studies. Paul Fredericq has issued the first volume of a "Geschiedenis der Inquisitie in de Nederlanden"; Frans de Potter has continued his great work on Ghent, and has also made researches concerning the manners and customs of the Flemings in the thirteenth and fourteenth centuries; J. Frederichs, who, as we have seen, writes also in French, describes a singular sect of Antwerpian libertines in his "De Secte der

Loïsten of Antwerpsche Libertijen (1525-'45)";
the pedagogues Erasmus, Luther, Sturm, and
Melanchthon are dealt with in Stinissen's " Een
Blik in de School der 16ᵈᵉ Eeuw"; Diest in
1789 forms the theme of Di Martinelli; and G.
Bergmann has published his reminiscences of
his friend Jan Franz Willems (founder of the
Flemish movement), King William I, and the
Belgian revolution of 1830. A new edition has
been published of the late Dean De Bo's curious
glossary of the West Flanders *patois*, " West-
Vlaamsch Idioticon," and Abbé A. Joos has issued Part I of a similar work, dealing with the
Pays de Waas. Among the many novels published, Moortgat's has been criticised as ultra-
realistic, while much praise has been accorded to
the plain and graphic descriptions of workaday
life in those of Mlle. Virginie Loveling, " Idonia "
and " Een dure Eed." The latter was highly
successful, especially in Holland, where it first
appeared in the magazine " De Gids." Nap. de
Pauw and L. Gailliard's edition of the " Istory
van Troyen " of Jacob van Maerlant, the thir-
teenth-century poet, is being continued, and
" De bervoete Broeders," a *vaudeville* of the sixteenth century, has been unearthed and published by Stallaert. The few productions by
contemporary poets, like van Droogenbroek
(" Jan Ferguut "), appear to be rather poor in
quality. In dramatic literature, N. de Tiere has
been awarded the triennial prize for his " Een
Spiegel."

Bohemia.—Two causes, we are told, have
given a special impetus to literary productiveness in this country during the past two years:
the Bohemian jubilee exhibition, celebrating the
one hundredth anniversary of the first European
exhibition (held in Prague in 1791), and the foundation of a Bohemian academy for art, science,
and literature. The publication of a new magazine " Cesky lid," devoted to folklore, would seem
to be one of the indications of the increased interest in all that influences the national feeling
of the people.

In " Motley Traveling through Bohemia," in
which the peregrinations of a Bohemian *bourgeois* and his friends, *à la* Pickwick, are described, Sv. Cech takes occasion to expose, with
a mercilessly mordant pen, the foibles of contemporary Bohemian society, which, in his
" M. Broucek's Excursion into the Fifteenth
Century," he places in glaring contrast to the
Hussites of old who fought so valiantly under
Zizka. In " Recollections of the East " he gives
fine descriptions of a journey to the Caucasus.
In the department of fiction the historical novel
has been successfully cultivated by A. Jirásek
and Z. Winter. The latter, in works like " Two
Stories of Rakovnik " and " From the Life of
Yore," the scene of which is laid in Bohemia in
the fifteenth and sixteenth centuries, is said to
combine profound historical research with an
easy style. On the other hand, the novels devoted to social questions appear, as a rule, to suffer from too energetic attempts to point a moral.
Among the better ones of the class are named
" Sychra's Era," by J. Laichter, a new but promising man; " A Father " and " Bliss," both by
M. A. Simácek; and the collections of sketches,
" All Sorts of Grand People," by B. Kaminský,
and " Publicans and Sinners," by G. Jaros. V.

Kosmák, in Moravia, and F. Sláma, in Silesia, have
again turned out a number of stories depicting
types of rural character. Vrchlický has brought
out " New Colored Potsherds," a collection of
sketches, and Julius Zeyer a novel, " Jan Maria
Plojhar," and a georgeous Oriental tale, " Fra-
granee "; while Ig. Hermann has begun the publication of the collected works of Jan Neruda,
the famous poet, who died two summers ago,
the first part of the collection being " Small-
talk," a number of racy *feuilletons*. Among the
poetical productions of the year we note a number by the prolific J. Vrchlický, who is known
also in the fields of dramatic literature and prose
fiction, in which latter he is not so successful,
however. His " Modern Man's Breviary " is described as a sort of confession of faith, in which
characteristic expression is given to the yearning of humanity for the solution of the ever-
present problems of life and death, and for
ideals that seem still to be far from a realization. " Frescoes and Tapestries " and " New
Sonnets of a Recluse " are further new volumes
of poetry from his pen. Julius Zeyer, besides
furnishing the third part of his " Annals of
Love," has issued a romance, " The Four Sons
of Aymon. Special mention should be made
also of " An Old Comedy," by F. Taborský, said
to show the influence of Lermontov, and G. Jaros's " Glory," the latter describing the lives of
Bohemian writers during the revival of the national literature in the first part of this century.
In lyrical poetry there are A. Klásterský, whose
" Through Fields and Forests " and " Songs of
Labor " have won approbation; J. V. Sládek
(" Songs of Yore " and " Mixture," collections of
ballads); and Jar. Kvapil, whose " Quiet Love "
is said to be replete with feeling. Noteworthy
among the newer men are J. S. Machar, with his
thoughtful and pessimistic " Winter Sonnets "
and " Summer Sonnets," and B. Kaminský, who
in his " Zprikopu " makes somewhat melancholy
observations upon life in Prague. In the field
of dramatic literature there are no striking successes to record. J. Vrchlický, already mentioned, has revived the Greek tragedy in his
trilogy, " Hippodamia," and has brought out
also a comedy, " Pietro Aretino." The naturalistic tendencies rampant at present are shown in
M. A. Simácek's picture of factory life, " The
World of Small People "; while Jirásek describes
Bohemian country life in his " Vojnarka," and
takes us back to mediæval Bohemia in his " Cradle." Finally, there are " Velkostatkár," a drama
by F. A. Subert (director of the National Theatre); " Vojtech Zák, výtecnik " and " Degenerated
Blood " (praised as an excellent psychological
study), both by L. Stroupeznicky; and a comedy
by Stolba, " Crooked Ways," which seems to
have been well received.

Denmark.—Limiting ourselves here to a list
of important books, we find the following:
In history: M. Rubin's " Studier til Kjöben-
havns og Danmarks historie "; C. A Hoffmann's
" Erindringer fra Krigen 1864 "; C. Tschudi's
" Keiserinde Auguste: Skildringer fra Hoflivet i
Berlin "; Vol. III of " Danmarks Historie. 1536-
1670," by F. Barfod; S. K. Kabell's " America
för Columbus . . . " (Parts III-VII); H. Weite-
meyer's " Aëmner og Kuriositeter fra Columbus-
tiden og Columbusliteraturen."; and continua-

tions of the large work on Denmark, edited by M. Galschiöt; C. F. Bricka's "Dansk biografisk Lexikon"; the "Corpus Constitutionum Daniae" (a selection of royal ordinances, etc.), edited by V. A. Secher; "Kong Christian den Fjerdes egenhaendige Breve" (1889–'91); and F. Nielsen's "Haandbog i Kirkens Historie."

J. Bondesen's "Jorden rundt," D. Bruun's "Algier og Sahara," and H. Scharling's "Reisestudier fra Aegypten og Palaestina " are among the books of travel; "Daekningsadgang eller Fordringsret," by E. Möller, and V. Richter's "Juridisk Stat" are among the legal tomes of the year; and H. Trier's "Paedagogiske Streiflys" belongs to the literature of education; while Vols. II–IV of "Det videnskabelige Udbytte af Kanonbaaden 'Hauchs' Togter i de danske have og indenfor Skagen in aarene 1883–'86," edited by G. C. Joh. Petersen, contain important contributions to the science of natural history.

In literary history there have appeared: A. Hansen's "En engelsk Forfattergruppe"; T. Bierfreund's "Kulturbaerere: Studier i Middelalderens Digtning"; J. Clausen's "Kulturhistoriske Studier over Heiberg's Vaudeviller"; H. Rasmussen's "Studier over Háfiz . . ."; P. Hansen's "Den Skueplads" (continued); and monographs on Dante by H. Vedel, on Carl Joakim Brandt by F. Rönning, on Peter Andreas Heiberg by H. Schwanenflügel, and on Samuel Richardson by J. Magnussen. "Bibliotheca Danica," covering Danish literature from 1482–1830, is continued under the editorship of Chr. V. Brunn, and A. Hammerich's "Musiken ved Christian den Fjerdes Hof"; H. R. Baumann's "Frans Hals"; Vols. I and II of H. V. Schytte's "Nordisk Musik Lexikon" are contributions to the history of the arts.

Finally, among the newest productions in prose fiction, poetry, and the drama, we have: H. Bang's "Teatret"; L. Budde's "Historier"; C. Dalsgaard's "Tre Fortællinger"; H.F. Ewald's "Clara Bille"; C. Ewald's "Fru Johanne"; H. Jensen's "Pastor Dahlberg"; O. Madsen's "Glade Ungdom"; A. Prydz's "Arnak"; J. Schjörring's "En Krise"; F. Suenssen's "Han er Jöde"; I. C. H. R. Steenstrup's "Fra Fortid og Nutid"; K. A. Tavastjerna's "Unga ar"; V. C. S. Topsöe's "Stagne Folk," etc.

France.—There has been a marked increase in literary productiveness in this country, and that, it seems, in all branches of literature. Contemporary history has received a number of additions. The Comte d'Hérisson, in his "Les Responsabilités de l'Année Terrible," attempts a defense of Marshal Bazaine, whom he regards as a sort of scapegoat, while the "Souvenirs du Général Jarras" form incontrovertible evidence for the other side of the question. Georges Bastard, a thorough and erudite historian, has described another episode of the Franco-Prussian War in a work on the heroic cavalry charges made on the terrible 1st of September; and the Abbó Lanusee recalls the splendid stand made by 62 men of the Foreign Legion against 2,000 Mexicans at the ruins of Camaron, in his "Héros de Camaron." An interesting composite monograph on the "Palais de Justice de Paris," furnished with a preface by Alexandre Dumas, is the joint work of a number of writers. François Bour-

naud's "La Terreur à Paris " is one of the many monographs which, we are told, were called forth by Sardou's "Thermidor"; "Les Rapports du Lieutenant de Police d'Argenson" (1697–1715) form a chronicle of crimes and scandals in the reign of Louis XIV; and in the memoirs of Gen. de Ricard, a fervent Bonapartist, published by L. Xavier de Ricard under the title "Autour de Bonaparte," we find a most unflattering portrait of the King of Westphalia, old Jérome. The exhuming of all sorts of memoirs and recollections is a characteristic illustration of the exactitude and thoroughness exercised by those engaged in historical research. In many of these private papers and diaries, which were, of course, not written for publication, contemporary persons and events are described without the least reserve. Thus the memoirs of Madame du Hausset, a lady-in-waiting of Madame de Pompadour, which have been carefully re-edited by Hippolyte Fournier, are replete with details concerning the villainous scandals in the court of Louis XV. Again, in the "Mémoires d'un Conscrit de 1808," edited by Philippe Gille, the dark side of the Spanish campaign is described with the most unrestrained frankness by a humble baker. To the innumerable personal recollections of the revolution and the wars under the first empire which have already been published, have been added the "Mémoires du Général de Marbot." A. Mézières has published an excellent and exceedingly impartial though sympathetic "Vie de Mirabeau," and the great Tribune is also described from the political standpoint by Rousse, in the important set, "Grands Écrivains Français." In literary biography there is also much new material. Léon Chasles has published in the "Revue Encyclopédique" the biographical notes on Victor Hugo found in some notebooks left by Alexandre Dumas to the father of Chasles. They deal mostly with the poet's infancy, and many of the details were already known through the "Témoin de la Vie de Victor Hugo," but Dumas's version (taken down in 1833) sometimes varies from the other (dictated in 1863) in a perplexing manner, though both were obtained directly from Hugo. News comes to us also of a very interesting trouvaille, a hitherto quite unknown MS. journal of the early years (1852–'56) of Hugo's exile, discovered by Octave Uzanne and published by him in parts. The memoirs of an almost forgotten littérateur, Hippolyte Auger, have been published by Paul Cottin; André Monselet has written a critical biography of his father, Charles Monselet (M. de Cupidon), a volume of whose fragmentary "essais" he has also issued: "Souvenirs littéraires," by Maxime du Camp, has appeared; and Édouard Rod is the author of a monograph on Stendhal (Henri Beyle). Here may be mentioned also the correspondence of Madame Ackerman ("The Sappho of Atheism"). edited by the Comte d'Haussonville. Louis Gallet has republished, in one volume, the sketches, which came out in the "Ménéstrel." dealing with various musicians whom he has furnished with librettos: L. Henry Lecomte has devoted a monograph to Virginie Déjazet, the actress; and Grand-Carteret has added to his caricature histories of Bismarck and Crispi an exceedingly interesting one on Richard Wagner. Hugues Le Roux's vivid portrait sketches of celebrities of the hour in Paris have been collected under the title "Figures de Cire," while Émile Fage has revived the past in his "Portraits du Vieux Temps," a series of able essays on forgotten literary celebrities; and Paul Bourget, well known through his studies in psychology, has issued another series of *pastelles*, bitter sketches of certain literary characters. In the field of literary history and criticism there are De Varigny's historical sketches on the origin of journalism in America and "Enquête sur l'Evolution Littéraire," by Jules Huret, who interviewed prominent authors on the present state of literature in France. Lemercier de Neuville has prepared a full "Histoire Anecdotique des Marionettes Modernes," in which he chronicles the history of a form of amusement which has enjoyed general popularity and has enlisted the services of various writers of note. The literature of art has likewise been enriched by various new works. Arsène Alexandre has written a "Histoire de l'Art Décoratif" and "L'Art du Rire et de la Caricature"; Lefort, a volume of clever papers on "Murillo et ses Élèves"; Maxime Collignon, a "Histoire de la Sculpture Grecque"; and Armand Dayot, H. Beraldi have used the pages of the "Revue Nocturne" for reviving in detail the memory of Raffet, whose admirers have proposed the erection of a monument to his memory. Vol. I of "La France Artistique et Monumentale," by Henry Havard, has appeared, and in the set of "Artistes Célèbres," published in the collection "Bibliothèque d'Art," Fragonard is treated by Félix Naquet, Abraham Bosse by Antony Valabrègue, Watteau by Dargenty, and Corot by Roger Milès. Æsthetic considerations have no doubt influenced also "Japon Pratique," in which the artist Félix Régamey enlightens us in regard to disillusioning accounts by badly informed and unobserving writers. His admiration for Japan is shared by Edmond de Goncourt, who has in hand a series of studies on that land of enchantment. André Chévillon's "Dans l'Inde" is described as a contribution to the literature of Buddhism, which seems to have come into favor in France; Paul Bourget, in "Sensations d'Italie" (impressions of a journey), evokes the art life of the Italy of the past with most exquisite delicacy of feeling; and Georges Rodenbach's "Bruges-la-Morte," though ostensibly a "romance," is of paramount interest in its masterly description of the quaint old town. A. Robida writes of old "Touraine"; "Diverses Curiosités" is the last work of the late X. Marmier; Armand Sylvestre has given us a volume of delightful impressions of a trip to Russia; "En Wherry," anonymous, is an account of the Norfolk "Broads"; and Africa forms the theme of Vigné d'Octon's "Au Pays des Fétiches" (an interesting account of explorations in the Soudan), Chaudoin's "Trois Mois de Captivité au Dahomey," and "A la Conquête du Tchad," in which Harry Alis describes the work of Paul Crampel, and which was published just as the news of the young explorer's tragic end reached France. Ernest Renan, who died during the year, published his "Feuilles détachées," with an interesting preface, as charmingly vague and beguilingly contradictory as ever. Édouard Rod has reprinted a number of essays, from

various periodicals, under the title "Idées Morales du Temps Présent" (dealing chiefly with literary schools); Léon Daudet discusses the human passions and death with much ingeniousness and subtlety of definition in his "Germe et Poussière"; and Charles Richet, in "Dans cent Ans," gives us one of those visions into the future now so much in vogue. Maurice Barrès (who has published also "L'Ennemi des Lois," a *fantaisie socialiste*) explains his worship of the "ego" by the aid of subtle distinctions and cleverly stated propositions in new works such as "Toute Licence sauf contre l'Amour" and "Examen de Trois Idéologies."

A large number of successful novels have seen the light. Such are "Ukko' Till," by Rodolphe Darzens; Jean Rameau's touching "Simple"; Louis de Gramont's amusing "Locataire de Madame Brou"; "La Femme Enfant," by Catulle Mendès; Aurélien Scholl's "L'Amour appris sans Maitre"; three psychological novels by Abel Hermant: "Serge," "Ermeline," and "L'Amant Érotique"; "Faux Départ," by Alfred Capus; Jean Reibrach's "La Gamelle" (military stories); "Le Cuirassier Blanc" and "Sur le Retour," by Paul Marguéritte; a powerful book by Alexandre Hepp, "Le Lait d'un Autre"; and "Les vrais Riches," by François Coppée. Alphonse Daudet's "Rose et Ninette" is a sad and painful story concerned with the disposition made of children in a case of divorce. Lieut. Pierre Loti's "Le Livre de la Pitié et de la Mort" was published just before his election to the Academy; his "Fantôme d'Orient" appeared after that event. The latter is the story of his pilgrimage to the place where Aziyadé, the Turkish maiden, lies buried; it contains many sad and touching passages, but the author has been accused by some of parading his sentiments rather obtrusively. André Theuriet is a most prolific novelist, although the effect of haste is said to be apparent in some of his work, like the "Mari de Jacqueline." More successful is his "Mademoiselle Roche," the scene of which delightful pastoral is laid in the land of the Savoyards, which people long ago expressed their gratitude to the author for his exquisite descriptions which have attracted so much attention to their beautiful country. Ferdinand Fabre is, as always, fine in his descriptions of life in the Cevennes in "Sylviane"; Jules Claretie has published "L'Américaine," a sentimental novel; Henri Lavedan (*Manchecourt*) describes the extravagances of the *fin de siècle* Parisian in his "Nouveau Jeu." Édouard Rod has gone over from naturalism to mysticism in his "Sacrifiée"; Armand Sylvestre's fanciful romance "Floréal" furnishes a picturesque reconstruction of society under the Directoire; the late Xavier Marmier's "Les Contes des Grand'mères" is a collection of northern popular tales; and J. H. Rosny shows a thorough knowledge of archæology in his "Vamireh," which takes us back to the troglodytes; and Madame Jane Dieulafoy, who had been led by a similar enthusiasm for ancient times to the production of "Parysatis," now comes down to the time of the republic in her "Volontaire." Émile Zola's "Débâcle," that graphic description of the deteriorated and demoralized army at Sédan, seems to have excited even more than the usual stir which his works produced. His "Rougeou-Macquart" series is now brought to a close. Paul Bourget's "La Terre promise," has won high praise as a "welcome relief from the gross realism that has pervaded French literature during the last twenty years." Of the usual large number of poetical works may be named "Les Pages," by Stéphane Mallarmé, who has published also "Vers et Prose," etc., and whose writing has given rise to much passionate discussion *pro* and *con*, although his purity of motive seems to be generally respected ; a volume by Albert Mockel, described as a "symbolist"; Verlaine's two last volumes, "Chansons pour Elle" and "Mes Hôpitaux"; Appleton's dramatic adaptation of Longfellow's "Évangeline"; and the fanciful production, "Chats et Chattes." Auguste Vacquerie and Paul Meurice have issued another one of Victor Hugo's unpublished works, "Dieu," a quasi-philosophical poem in which Hugo aims to arrive at a conception of the Godhead, and concludes that through death alone can we get to know Him as He is, thus tending to demonstrate the immortality of the soul. The dramatic literature published during the year includes the "Théâtre" of Octave Feuillet, François Coppée, Ferdinand Dugué, Gondinet, and Jean Jullien ; and Maurice Bouchor's fine "Michel Lando." Translations seem to have come into vogue on the stage, Ibsen, among others, having been brought before the Parisian public in his "Wild Duck," "Ghosts," and "Rosmersholm."

Germany.—This country is ever productive in the fields of history and antiquarian research. Here, too, national history receives a fair share of attention. Ditmar's scholarly "Deutsche Geschichte" and Bruno Gebhardt's "Handbuch der deutschen Geschichte," more popular in style ; Karl Lamprecht's "Deutsche Geschichte" (Vols. II and III), in which the author continues to bring the past vividly before us; and "Deutsches Leben im 14. und 15. Jahrhundert," which Prof. Alwin Schultz has begun issuing, have been favorably criticised. The very important work, "Regesta imperii . . ., nach . . . dem Nachlasse J. F. Böhmer's hrsg. und ergänzt von Julius Ficker und Ed. Winkelmann," has been completed. Other contributions to German history are Horst Kohl's "Bismarck-Gedenkbuch" (a selection of utterances by the ex-chancellor, whose speeches already fill fourteen volumes); Moltke's writings ("Gesammelte Schriften und Denkwürdigkeiten," in seven volumes); and Moltke's "Taktische Aufgaben, 1858-'82," issued by the *Grosse Generalstab*. F. Krones has drawn on the Archduke Johann's letters and other papers for information regarding the history of Austria, with especial reference to the Tyrolese rebellion against the French ; F. Gregorovius's "Kleine Schriften zur Geschichte der Cultur" is completed with the third volume ; W. Müller has prepared a political history of 1891 ; Vol. II of the "Quellen zur Geschichte der Juden in Deutschland" has appeared ; Moritz Brosch has brought out Vol. VII (1603-'88) of the "Geschichte Englands" (begun by Lappenberg and Pauli, both now deceased); and G. Wendt, a book on the history and Constitution of the same country ; Vol. IV of Alfons Huber's history of Austria has appeared ; and a monograph on "Die Entscheidungskämpfe im Chi-

lenischen Bürgerkriege" is of interest on account of the German element in Chili and its army. German historians have naturally contributed their quota to the literature called forth by the quadricentenary of the discovery of America. Js. Rein and Rch. Schillmann have written monographs on Columbus; the committee on the "America Celebration" in Hamburg has issued "Hamburgische Festschrift zur Erinnerung an die Entdeckung Amerika's" (two volumes); Konrad Kretschmar's "Die Entdeckung Amerika's" forms the "Festschrift der Gesellschaft für Erdkunde zu Berlin. Zur 400-jährigen Feier der Entdeckung Amerika's"; while a private "Festschrift" appears in "Amerika," a profusely illustrated compilation in two volumes by Rudolf Cronau, the artist. Of books of travel, we mention Theod. Nöldeke's "Orientalische Skizzen," and Wilh. Junker's "Reisen in Afrika" (1891); and it need hardly be added that Germany's movements in the "Dark Continent" have called forth a number of publications mainly of ethnographical or political interest. There seems to be no end to the making of books of a biographical or quasi-biographical character. Of political memoirs there are the "Denkwürdigkeiten aus dem Leben des General-Feldmarschalls Kriegsministers Grafen von Roon" (two volumes); and the "Denkwürdigkeiten" of Leopold von Gerlach, a general of infantry under Friedrich Wilhelm IV, dealing principally with the period of the Crimean War. Monographs on historical personages of past centuries are furnished by Adolf Hausrath ("Arnold von Brescia, 1891), Heinrich Ulmann (Emperor "Maximilian I," 1891, two volumes), Richard Hirsch ("Louis VII of France"), and Alexander Baumgartner ("Gallus Jakob Baumgartner," dealing with the development of Switzerland, 1797-1869). Autobiographies of Julius Fröbel (1891, two volumes), the late Heinrich Schliemann (the one included in "Ilios" completed by Sophie Schliemann), Georg Ebers, the late Werner von Siemens ("Lebenserinnerungen") and the late Anton Springer, the well-known authority on art, have appeared. Friedrich von Flotow's widow has written the composer's life; J. E. Kuntze gives a sympathetic account of the versatile and clever physicist Gustav Theodor Fechner; R. Haym is the author of a life of the learned historian Max Duncker; C. v. Fabriczy has furnished a volume on "Filippo Brunelleschi." A number of biographies are devoted to theologians : George Evers has published the sixth and last volume of his life of Luther; the life of Karl Gerok—who had much influence as a preacher and Christian poet in Swabia—has been written by Gustav Gerok: Vol. I of Otto Ritschl's life of Albert Ritschl is out; Em.¹l Michael's "Ignaz von Döllinger (second edition) is a Roman Catholic view of the famous theologian ; and the memoirs of the late Karl Hase (the "Protestant Pope"), "Annalen meines Lebens," have been published. The contributions to literary biography are likewise plentiful. Jacob Minor has continued his life of Schiller, and Erich Schmidt's comprehensive one of Lessing is completed.

Heine's nephew, Baron Ludwig von Embden, has published "Heinrich Heine's Familienle-

412 LITERATURE, CONTINENTAL.

ben," a collection of letters written by the poet during 1820–'55. These letters, nearly all to his mother and sister, are written in an incomparably graceful and simple style, and the tender love which they breathe seems to refute Goethe's saying that he "had every gift, but wanted love." The relations of the unfortunate Nicolaus Lenau, who died in a madhouse, to Sophie Löwenthal, are illustrated in his letters to her, edited by his friend L. A. Frankl; while the *brochure* issued in honor of the centenary (occurring Sept. 23, 1891) of the birth of Karl Theodor Körner, the soldier poet, affords an attractive picture of his inamorata, the actress Antonie Adamberger, who subsequently married, and became the mother of the famous historian, Alfred von Arneth. The literature on Goethe and Lessing is ever increasing, and Grillparzer is now coming in for his share. Among the new books concerned with Goethe is a life of his mother, by Heinemann. The "Goethe Annual," published by the Goethe Society at Weimar, has found a counterpart in the "Grillparzer Annual," published by the Grillparzer Society at Vienna. Among the contributions to general literary history we note Wilh. Cloetta's "Beiträge zur Litteraturgeschichte des Mittelalters und der Renaissance" (Vol. II); a history of journalism in Vienna by E. V. Zenker; and one of German literature to the middle of the eleventh century by J. Kelle. In art history there are A. von Warsberg's posthumous essays on the museums of Athens, and on Gaudenzio Ferrari, and "Geschichte der Deutschen Kunst," edited by noted authorities—Dohme, Falke, Lützow, Bode, and Janitschek; and pamphlets on naturalism in art (1891) by Veit Valentin and Aug. Reissmann. Max Lautner, in his "Wer ist Rembrandt?" advances the theory that most of the works ascribed to the famous Dutch master were executed by his pupil Ferdinand Bol. The book has aroused much discussion, but the author's "proofs" want confirmation as yet. "Die Weltanschauung Fr. Nietzsche's" and "Psychopathia Spiritualis," by Hugo Kaatz and Kurt Eisner, are directed against the "Philosophy of the Future," which the followers of the brilliant and original Fr. Nietzsche (whose mental powers have unfortunately become deranged) declare his doctrine to be. "Introductions" to philosophy have been published by J. Volkelt and Friedr. Paulsen, while Jul. Bergmann has issued Vol. I of his "Geschichte der Philosophie." Materialism, so much in vogue, is combated by H. Schmidkunz, M. Carriere, and others, in "Gegen den Materialismus." W. Wundt's "Hypnotismus und Suggestion," and H. Schmidkunz's rather optimistic "Psychologie des Suggestionismus," treat on a subject of current interest. Emil Gregorovius's "Himmel auf Erden" is a humorous anti-Socialistic production. The essay on "Rembrandt als Erzieher" has called forth a torrent of opposition. Among others, Felix Dahn, in his "Moltke als Erzieher," opposes the theory of the untrammeled freedom of the individual by that of the sternest discipline of self, as illustrated in the life of the great commander, whose "History of the Franco-German War" comes in for special praise. In the department of theology we would name Heinrich Brugsch's "Steininschrift und Bibelwort"

(1891); Friedr. Aug. Berth. Nitzsch's "Lehrbuch der evangelischen Dogmatik"; Karl v. Hase's "Reformation und Gegenreformation" (gives a sympathetic and impartial characterization of Luther); A. Kuenen's "Historisch-kritische Einleitung in die Bücher des alten Testaments" (Part II). In philology there are: Richard Simon's edition of the Amaruçataka; F. E. Peiser's "Die Hetitischen Inschriften," and the first parts of Alfred Holder's exceedingly complete "Alt-Celtischer Sprachschatz" and Karl Bohnenberger's "Zur Geschichte der Schwäbischen Mundart im XV. Jahrhundert." Questions of interest are treated by F. Marcinowski, who in "Das Lotteriewesen im Königreich Preussen," desires to prove that the state lottery is beneficial in setting limits to the passion for games of chance; and H. Settegast ("Die Deutsche Freimaurerei"), who shows that masonry in Prussia has lost influence by departing from its noble principles. Continuations innumerable of well-known and important collections in various departments of history and science are going on. New editions also form no small part of the annual product of the press, and of such we should mention the fourteenth edition of the famous "Konversationslexikon" of Brockhaus, of which four volumes have appeared.

In the domain of prose fiction Germany has a number of clever writers. Adolf Wilbrandt's novel "Hermann Ifinger" has won high praise. Though educational in purpose, it is entirely without pedantry, and the composition, delineation of character, and beauty of its ethical teaching combine to make it a notable and representative book. Wilhelm Jensen and Wilhelm Raabe support their reputation in two new books, "Im Zwing und Bann" and "Gutmann's Reisen." Gottschall, Spielhagen ("Sonntagskind"), Ganghofer, and Lindau ("Hängendes Moos," published in translation by D. Appleton & Co.) have also produced new novels. Hermann Heiberg has published "Todsünden" and "Höchste Liebe schweigt"; and the Austrian Lola Kirschner (*Ossip Schubin*), "Gräfin Erika's Lehr- und Wanderjahre" and "Thorschlusspanik." The latter's countrywoman Bertha von Suttner has attracted widespread attention by her "Die Waffen nieder," an impassioned appeal for peace. Conrad Ferdinand Meyer, who was over forty-five when he began to make a stir in literature, and then speedily attained a most enviable reputation, died toward the end of the year. His last book, "Angela Borgia," is remarkable for its truthful rendering of the Renaissance spirit, the scene of the plot being Ferrara in the sixteenth century. Theodor Fontane, on the other hand, describes the Berlin of to-day with photographic fidelity in his "Frau Jenny Treibel" (or, "Gleich und Gleich gesellt sich gern"). And, again, old Hamburg is shown to us, with the most accurate local color, by Ilse Frapan (the biographer of F. Vischer), who has issued a collection of stories under the title "Bittersüss." The Austrian element makes itself strongly felt in the stories of Frau von Ebner-Eschenbach, Ferdinand von Saar, and J. J. David. The first-named author moves in the highest circles of Viennese society, and reproduces its types with unsparing fidelity; but the heroine of her "Magarethe" belongs to another class, the *demi-monde*, and the character is not so successfully portrayed. Of Saar's stories ("Zwei Frauenbilder"), one, "Geschichte eines Wiener Kindes," is an interesting psychological study, but verges at times on the impossible; while J. J. David, a young writer, who appears to have been influenced somewhat by C. F. Meyer, touches on the theory of heredity in his "Blut." Felix Dabu's delightful fancy is shown in his "Odhin's Rache"; and a fine vein of humor runs through H. Hoffmann's "Geschichten aus Hinterpommern"; while the "nervous element" in most modern fiction (of which Hermann Bahr is one of the latest exponents) predominates in "Ich," a collection of "nervous stories" by the talented and eccentric Heinz Tovote, whose "Frühlingsturm" is concerned especially with life in the *cafés* of Berlin. In poetry, we find the influence of socialistic ideas in new works of Maurice Reinhold von Stern (a Livonian living in South America, best in his descriptions of scenery); Karl Henkell (a talented writer of somewhat revolutionary verse); and F. Geyer, who appeals to his Emperor in the cry which once assailed the ears of Louis XVI—"Gib uns Brot, Kaiser!" John Henry Mackay, the Scoto-German, has renounced socialism and adopted anarchism in his newest work, "Sturm." In striking contrast to these is Felix Dahn's lovely and sad romance "Rolandin," filled with a spirit of love and chivalry that seems strange at this day. Two other new volumes bear the names of old favorites—R. Baumbach's "Lieder aus Thüringen," and the selection of posthumous poems by Joseph Viktor von Scheffel, edited by his son. The poems of Josefine Scheffel, the poet's mother, have also been published, and are marked by the same smoothness and melody as her son's, affording proof of the hereditary power of his poetic talent. Two novelists, the late Conrad Ferdinand Meyer and J. J. David, have produced poetry that shows the same notable qualities which characterize their prose writing. On the other hand, three other well-known authors—Spielhagen, the novelist; Petri K. Rosegger, who writes so characteristically of life in the Alps; and Ferd. Gregorovius, the famous historian—have, it seems, added nothing to their fame by venturing into poetry. In dramatic literature there is an interesting play by Richard Voss to record, "Die Neue Zeit," in which the conflict between an orthodox old pastor and his liberal son is described with much dramatic force and excellent characterization. Paul Heyse, famous as a writer of short stories, does not seem to be quite as satisfactory in his newest dramatic productions, "Die Schlimmen Brüder" and "Wahrheit?" Ernst von Wildenbruch, who appeared as a patriotic courtier in "Der Neue Herr," has produced a *Märchenschwank*, "Das Heilige Lachen," which was most graciously received in court circles, but not so well by the critics. The play points a moral too markedly, and at the expense of character delineation, but it contains some beautifully poetic passages. The new school of realists has not been idle. The conflict between laborer and employer, between rich and poor—so well emphasized by Hauptmann and Sudermann—has formed the theme of a number of new productions, notably the versatile Wildenbruch's "Haubenlerche" and Ludwig Fulda's "Das Verlorene Paradies," both of which have been produced in New York city. The former has introduced a decidedly *risqué* scene in his play, while Fulda has been even more frank in his "Die Sklavin."

Greece.—Here, as in Belgium, a notable percentage of authors of repute are historians. Two of them have begun histories of contemporary periods: Epaminondas Kyriakides, with his "History of Contemporary Greece," which is brought down to 1858 in Vol. I; and P. Karolides, with a "History of the Nineteenth Century," to which he has published an introduction. The history of the city of Cos has been written by Tryphon Evangelides, while J. Kophiniotis has begun to perform a like service for Argos, where he has been carrying on important excavations. Valuable material for the history of modern Greece is stored away, we are told, in the documents relating to the death of the martyred Rhigas Velestinlis and his companions in 1798. They have been published at the expense of the Historico-Ethnological Society of Athens, a Greek version being furnished by Spyr. Lambros, who has also published a separate work on the death of Rhigas. The seminary for priests which the brothers Rhizaris established at Athens has found a historian in Nicolas Rhados; Col. Iphikrates Kokkides has written a work on the military geography of the country; Peloponnesian inscriptions, golden bulls from Mistra, etc., form the theme of Constantine Zeziu's "Symmikta," and J. Lambros has begun the publication of a finely illustrated work on Greek coins. Finally, Sakellarios's great monograph on Cyprus, based on forty years' study, has been completed with the publication of the second volume, the third having been previously issued. In the departments of philology and literary history several works of importance to the specialist have appeared. The University of Athens has had the hitherto unpublished twelfth part of the physician Aëtios's treatise printed in Paris, under the able editorship of G. Kostomiris, and a third part of the "Alexandrinos Diakosmos" of Œkonomopulos (giving the literary history of Alexandria from B. C. 331 to A. D. 645) has also been issued. The imperial Palestine Society of St. Petersburg has begun the publication of a five-volume catalogue of the Greek manuscripts in the library of the Jerusalem Patriarchate. About 1,550 of these manuscripts, we are told, are preserved at Jerusalem; the rest—some 850—are in Constantinople. Learned descriptions are furnished by the editor of the catalogue, Athanasios Papadopulos Kerameus. It is proper to mention also Anastasios Zakos's "Critical and Exegetical Observations on Sophocles."

The best fiction still appears in the periodical press, Xenopulos, Krystallis, Papadiamantis, Moraitidis, and Karkavitsas being among those especially prominent in this department. J. Polylas, of Corfu, known as a Shakespeare translator, and J. Psycharis (Renan's son-in-law), who is engaged in the French capital as Professor of Modern Greek, have also entered the field of light literature. We have also to record a new edition of Bikelas's "Loukis Laras," which has been embellished by the pencil of Rhallis, a Greek painter resident in Paris. Something analogous to the "dialect-story" movement in the United States seems to be going on in Greece, though actuated, perhaps, by different motives. Psycharis and Polylas are especially zealous in promoting the tendency to use the popular dialect in works of fiction, and Polylas's "Our Literary Speech" is an interesting contribution to the literature of this question, which is still a matter of dispute. Meanwhile, Alexandros Pallis (who brought out an excellent edition of the "Antigone" of Sophocles) has given practical expression to his preferences by translating six books of the Iliad into the popular language.

Among the few notable productions of the year in poetry we have "Thalassa," said to show much beautifully expressed poetic sympathy with the sea, written by Nicolas Damianos, one of the younger men, and a posthumous collection of poems, "The Pearls," by Demetrios Kokkos (whose dramatic writings have attracted most attention in recent years), edited by his widow. Quite different in style is the third volume ("Phasulis as a Philosopher") of the poems of Georg Souris. This "modern Aristophanes," who is known as the editor of a weekly paper—"The Modern Greek"—(which is a curiosity, inasmuch as it is entirely written in verse, including advertisements), has become exceedingly popular by his witty attacks on social and political weaknesses, and the humor and power of observation displayed in his work.

Holland.—While last year's literary activity in this country has perhaps not fully satisfied all wishes, yet several noteworthy publications are recorded. Some of the most excellent books of the year are found in the department of history. Dutch history especially has received valuable additions in H. Brugman's "Engeland en de Nederlanden in de eerste Jaaren van Elizabeth's Regeering (1558-1567)"; J. de Jong's "Geschiedenis van het Vaderland," Part III (1713-1891); P. J. Blok's voluminous history of Holland, "Geschiedenis van het Nederlandsche Volk" in which are included the results of his extensive researches in foreign archives, undertaken by order of the Government; another history of Holland, by Nyhoff, which has somewhat displeased the Roman Catholic public; the late Prof. Jorissen's "Historische en literarische Studien," "Historische Karakters," and "Historische Bladen," in which essays the author, in well-proved statements, ascribes the misfortunes of the Dutch in the last century to the weak character of the last princes of Orange and the haughty oppression of the patricians; Baron Renger's sketch of parliamentary history since 1849; Vols. VII and VIII of Ter Gouw's exhaustive "Geschiedenis van Amsterdam"; a volume on the manners and customs of the country in past ages, by De Roever; another on the condition of Roman Catholics under the Dutch Republic, by the learned W. P. C. Knuttel, of the Royal Library; and a comprehensive geographical work, "Nederland en zijne Bewoners," by Dr. H. Blink. It should be mentioned, also, that the study of genealogy is pursued with an activity quite American, and is productive of an ever-increasing number of monographs.

Prof. Quack's "De Socialisten Personen en

Stelsels" is praised as rather a summary of facts than an attempt at solving the social problem. The new publications in the field of theology and ecclesiastical history include a life of Ignatius de Loyola by W. van Nieuwenhoff; an important and voluminous work (in English) on the religion of China, by De Groot, Professor of Malay at Leyden; "De Vrouw in den Bijbel," written by the venerable C. E. van Koetsreld, the Queen's chaplain; another series (the third) of studies on Calvin, by the noted scholar Allard Pierson; a new and almost rewritten edition of C. P. Tiele's famous "Geschiedenis van den Godsdienst in de Oudheid tot op Alexander den Groote"; and Hooykaas's edition of various studies by Kuenen on the history of Israel, in which the author's construction of various misunderstood passages in Scripture is laid down. Mention should also be made of Dr. W. G. C. Bijvanck's articles on French literary history, selected for translation by a French publisher, and Karel Alberdingk Thym's well-written life of his father, late Professor of Æsthetics at Amsterdam.

Some valuable contributions to Dutch literary history have appeared. Dr. R. A. Kollewijn has written an important and comprehensive monograph on Bilderdijk, containing much hitherto unpublished material concerning this prominent figure in literature; two critical works on Pieter Langendyk, a writer of comedies, by C. A. Ph. Meyer and F. Z. Mehler, have been brought out; Dr. I. A. Worp is the author of an essay dealing with the influence of Seneca on the Dutch drama, and has also brought out Vol. I of a critical edition of the works of the poet Huygens, of whose poetry H. J. Eymael has likewise proved a critical commentator. Henri Logemen's "Elckerlijk, a Fifteenth-Century Dutch Morality, and Everyman, a nearly Contemporary Translation," is a contribution to the history of the literary relations of Holland and England. Prof. Ten Brink's "De Oude Garde en de Jongste School" is directed against the new school of writers of fiction, but all such attempts can not stop the literary revolution, which began in Holland a dozen years ago, and which is bound to run its course. The work of the younger men—whose official organ is "De Nieuwe Gids"—has been characterized as overloaded with descriptive passages, wanting in analysis of character, affected and strained in style, and not infrequently obscene despite its sentimentality.

One of the most noteworthy of the newer novelists is L. Couperus, author of "Extaze" and "Noodlot," which latter, like his "Eline Vere" (a good description of social life in the Hague), has been translated into English by Grein. His forte seems to lie in the psychological analysis of character, but his style inclines to $_v{}^ag{}_ue{}^ness$. Less talented than he, but still giving signs of promise, are Wagenvoort (*Vosmeer de Spie*) whose "Eene Passie" has some vivid description and displays want of observation; Dr. Alettrino, said to imitate Goncourt in his "Zuster Bertha"; and two *soi-disant* realists, Van Bergen and Kleefstra, who in "Slachtoffers onzer Huwelijkswetten" and "Burgersmenschen," respectively, evince a strong discontent with the present condition of affairs. Th. van

Meerendonk's "Otto Altendorf" has also some merit. Lastly, we name Maarten Maartens, who has attracted much attention in England and America by his "Joost Avelingh" and "God's Fool," written in English, and both published in this country by D. Appleton & Co. Power of conception, caustic satire, originality, and nobility of sentiment characterize his writings. The female contingent among novel writers is a notable one, and includes Mme. la Chapelle-Roobol, who has been before the public half a dozen years, but has just now attracted special attention by the sound realism and character delineation in her novel "Een Gelukskind"; Miss Cornelia Huygens, a bright and able translator, who has reprinted some of her tales from high life under the title "Een Huwelijk"; and V. Loveling, noticed under BELGIUM. Others who ought to be mentioned are Mme. van Wermeskerken-Junius (*Johanna van Woude*), the famous story-teller, who continues to publish tales on the emotional lines laid out in her "Oud Hollandsch Binnenhuisje"; Miss Reynvaan, author of "Züster Clara"; Miss Sloot (*Melati van Java*), whose "Rosa Marina," dealing with modern painters, first appeared in the excellent illustrated monthly, "Elzevier's Maandschrift"; and Mrs. Bakker-Korff Hoogeboom's novel "Meta."

Of poetry there is next to nothing. Dr. M. G. L. van Loghem (*Fiore della Neve*) shows much dramatic force in certain parts of his new romantic epic, "Walter," in which the aping of French manners at a petty German court, toward the end of the last century, is described; and Miss Helene Swarth, long a resident of Belgium, continues to write expressive sonnets in French and Dutch. Nor is there much to say of the drama, although the outlook is not without promise. "Eerloss" and "Goudvischje," both by Nouhuys, have been enthusiastically received; Mrs. Snyders van Wissekerke's "Droomleven" and "Lotos" have had success, as has also the late Maaldrink's "Cleopatra." Emants and Dr. Van Eden are regarded as "coming men."

Hungary.—In this country, again, history holds a prominent place, national history especially having occupied many authors. Jenö Csudai has brought out a new "History of Hungary"; L. Abafi, a comprehensive "History of Freemasonry in Austria-Hungary" (in German); Kálmán Demkó, "The History and Customs of Upper Hungarian Towns in the Fifteenth and Sixteenth Centuries"; and Edward Wertheimer, the second volume of his "Austria and Hungary in the First Decade of the Nineteenth Century." "Memorials of the Hungarian Diets" is edited by W. Fraknói (the noted historian) and A. Károlyi, and a sensation has been created, we are told, by "History of Civilization in Hungary" and "The Time of Joseph II," both by Henrik Marczali, who has prepared also a "History of our Times" (1825-'80) and a "History of Maria Theresia." Other new works selected for commendation are László Kövúry's "Archæological and Historical Memorials of Transylvania," György Rákosi's "Luther in Worms," J. Asbóth's "Essays and Studies in the History of our own Times," and Paul Király's "Dácia Fövárosa, a mai Várhely Hunyadmegyében," which is described as an attractively written scientific monograph on the "Ulpia Trajana Augusta Colonia

Dacica." Continuations have been published of some important books, like Imre Nagy's "Codex Diplomaticus Andegavensis" (Vol. VI), and the comprehensive "History of the Russian People" (Vol. IV), by Gyula Lázár. The first installments of the last-named author's "History of England" and of Theodore Ortvay's "History of the Town of Pressburg" have also been issued. Many of the historical works, and also Jenö Rónai's new edition of the "Strategic Works of Count Nicolas Zrinyi," the poet and soldier, are published by the Hungarian Academy of Science, which society plays an important part in promoting the cause of national literature. A "Life of Shakespeare" (which won an Academy prize), by August Greguss, one of Colbert, by A. Ballagi, and a bulky but excellent volume on András Fáj, the celebrated Hungarian poet, by F. Badies, form the principal contributions to biography.

The translators appear to have been busy enough during the last twelvemonth, but there seems to have been no such activity in the field of original thought, for the report comes to us of the complete absence of any noteworthy efforts in the department of philosophy. Practical considerations, rather than theoretical, seem to have influenced the writers in the field of political and social economy. The Academy of Science, already mentioned, has begun the publication of an exceedingly useful series of translations of standard works by foreigners, books by Adam Smith ("Wealth of Nations"). Malthus, Ricardo, and Holyoake ("Rochdale Pioneers"), having already been issued in the collection. The following may be named as commendable works of more or less practical utility in this department: A monograph of the Buda-Pesth Commercial Bank, by Polza; comprehensive "Statistics of the Hungarian Water Ways," by A. Zawodski; treatises on mortgage (Rath), railway questions (Lipthay), and monetary standard (Count Wickenburg, Armin Neumann, Karl Mandello), and a *brochure* by Földes on "The English Universities and the Labor Question, with Special Regard to Toynbee Hall."

The dictionary makers have also been busy. Ignatius Halász has brought out a "South Laplandish Dictionary," and B. Munkácsy has begun the publication of his "Vojtak Dictionary," said to be important both philologically and ethnographically, while the great "Philological Dictionary" of the Academy is nearing completion. Another very important philological publication is J. Balassa's "Idiotikon of the Magyar Dialects," the first good and comprehensive work of its kind. A similarly epoch-making book is "The Magyar Population of the District of Kalotaszeg," in which the noted geographer János Jankó furnishes what is perhaps the first really scientific introduction to a knowledge of the ethnography of the various nationalities in Hungary. In this connection might be mentioned also three collections of popular songs and ballads: "Szeged Vidéke Népköltése," edited by L. Kálmán; "Bolgár Népköltési Gyüjtemény," translated by Adolf Strauss, and "Vogul Népköltési Gyüjtemény," brought out by B. Munkácsy. They deal with the folk songs of the district of Szegedin (Hungary), Bulgaria, and the Voguls, respectively. Lastly, we have yet to name B. Reiner's "Pictures of Hungarian Life,"

and various publications on Persian and Cha-
gattai philology and ethnography by Vámbéry.
The death of two noted philologists is here to be
recorded—Joseph Budenz, whose specialty was
Altaic languages, and Paul Hunfalvy, who also
established an enviable reputation among eth-
nographers. Literary history and cognate subjects have received interesting contributions in
the shape of Albert Kardos's " History of Hungarian Literature," G. Éle's " Hungarian Printing House in the Eighteenth Century," and the
continuation of G. Petrik's " Hungarian Bibliography, 1712 to 1860."

In the department of fiction the outlook is decidedly cheering, for Hungary harbors not a few
novelists of ability. Jókai, the most renowned
of all, has again added several titles (" There's
no Devil," " The Son of Rákocy ") to the list of
his novels. " Our Comrades" and " Useless
Work" are novels by the late Gregor Csiky, a
dramatist of much renown ; and another noted
writer, Károly Vadnai, has published a volume
of short stories, " Eve's Daughters." Antál Váradi has written a novelette, " Festett Világ " ;
Kálmán Mikszáth (whose collected works are in
course of publication, Vol. VII having already
appeared), a volume of " Sketches of Life in Parliament," in which he has occupied a seat; and
Robert Tábori a couple of novels, " In the Land
of the Crooked Mountains" and " Transforma-
tions." The novelette and the short story seem
to have been cultivated by preference and with
success by the younger authors. Among collee-
tions of stories and sketches are " The Hidden
Nest," by Victor Rákosi (Si palusz), who is described as possessing a vein of delightful humor;
" Mutamur," by Ferencz Herczeg, whose style has
been found to resemble the unfortunate De Mau-
passant's; an interesting " Book of the Hungarian
Lowland," by Zsigmond Justh; and productions
of promising and talented young men like Joseph
Hevesi, Sándor Bródy, Zóltán Ambrus, and Béla
Tóth. And then there is Hungaria's noted
humorist, Dr. Adolf Agai (Porzó), the popular
writer of feuilletons, whose " Dust and Ashes"
has entered upon a second edition, and whose
sparkling humor always shows an undercurrent
of serious thought. In lyric poetry, high praise
has been accorded to the productions of Michael
Szabolcska and A. Kosma, who have been compared to Petöfi and János Arany, respectively.
Noteworthy additions to dramatic literature are
" Countess Vera," a tragedy, by L. Dóczy, and
" Demon," a drama by A. Váradi, and a collected
edition of the dramatic works of Jenö Rákosi has
also been issued. Altogether, we may echo the
opinion of a noted critic, that the literary publications for the past year in Hungary include
very good works, while there is nothing that
rises, by absolute excellence, above the general
satisfactory average.

Italy.—Beginning with history, we note
among numerous recent publications the following : Two important works brought out by
the Italian Historic Institute, i. e., G. Monti-
colo's " La Cronaca del Diacono Giovanni" and
Vol. I of the letters of Coluccio Salutati, collected by F. Novati; " Autobiografia di P.
Giannone " ; Salvatore Lupia's monograph on
Arnoldo da Brescia ; A. Marchesan's " L'Univer-
sità di Treviso nei Secoli XIII. e XIV." ; E. Co-

stantini's " Il Cardinale di Ravenna " ; B. Felici-
angeli's " Caterina Cibo da Varano " ; " I Teatri
di Napoli," by B. Croce ; A. Oriani's " Lotta
Politica in Italia " ; A. V. Vecchi's " Storia della
Marina Italia " ; " La Reazione in Toscana nel
1799," by Apollo Lumini ; L. A. Ferrai's " Studi
Storici " ; D. Berti's " Scritti Vari " ; " Studi Stori-
cie Critici," by P. Villari ; O. Tommasini's " Scritti di Critica e Storia " ; Giuseppe Stocchi's "Aulo
Gabinio e i suoi Processi " ; L. Chiala's " Pagine
di Storia Contemporanea " (1858–'92) ; A. Bianchi's volume on Garibaldi; L. Pianiani's " La
Roma dei Papi," Vol. I, etc. " Toscanelli " is a
new periodical (in French) devoted to historical
research. The four hundredth anniversary of
the discovery of America has naturally called
forth a number of publications, like the works
on Columbus by V. Prinzivalli, M. A. Lazzaroni
(two vols.), de Lollis, and Monsignor Rocco Coc-
chia, or those dealing with later discoverers,
such as Tarducci's " Di Giovanni e Sebastiano
Caboto; " besides which, the Italian Government
is bringing out a great memorial publication of
Columbian documents. Among the contributions to various departments of science are E.
Morselli's " Carlo Darwin e il Darwinismo . . . ."
and Q. Bianchi's " L'Ipnotismo e la Giustizia
Penale," while we note also a number of publications on legal topics, and two new books by P.
Mantegazza, " Dizionario delle cose Belle," and
" L'Arte di prender Moglie." There are two
books of travel that deserve special mention :
Adolfo Rossi's " Un Italiano in America," in
which the checkered career of the author (now a
noted journalist) in the New World and his observations on men and manners there are described, and Ferdinando Martini's " Nell' Africa
Italiana," a work for which he was peculiarly
fitted by his observations made as member of a
Government commission of inquiry to Massowah.
The latter author has also reprinted some of the
best of his articles in the Fanfulla della Do-
menica under the title " Di Palo in Frasca." It
seems that Martini has done much to inaugurate
the specialty of literary journalism in Italy, resulting in a popularizing of culture.

In the department of literary history. the contributions to Dante literature always hold a prom-
incut place. First of all, there is the Frate
Giovanni da Serravalle's Latin commentary on
Dante, written early in the fifteenth century,
from the Guelph point of view, and now edited,
by order of Pope Leo XIII, by Father Marcellino
da Civezza and Father Teofilo Domenichelli,
two Franciscan scholars. Other works concerned
with the great Italian are L. Agnelli's " Topo-
cronografia del Viaggio Dantesco," C. Cipolla's
" Il Trattato De Monarchia di Dante Alighieri,"
A. Buscaino Campo's " Studi danteschi," Corrado Ricci's " L'Ultimo Rifugio di Dante Alighieri," Dr. G. A. Sartazzini's " Dante Handbuch " (written in German and published in Germany), and " Beatrichi nella Vita e nella Poesia
del Secolo XIII," by Isidoro del Lungo, who
shows that Beatrice was the daughter of Folco
Portinari. Other contributions to literary history are the following. placed in chronological
order according to the periods covered : " La
Patria di Guido Colonna " and " Aneddoti per
la Storia dei Laudesi," both by E. Monaci ; Pe-
trarch's " Trionfi," first edition in facsimile;

studies on the "Canzoniere," by G. Mestica; G. Verga's "Bernardo Bellincioni, Poeta di Lodovico il Moro"; Erasmo Percopo's "Le Rime del Chariteo"; "Nuovi Contributi per la Storia dell' Umanesimo," by Ferdinando Gabotto; F. Flamini's "La Lirica Toscana del Rinascimiento"; A. Solerti's "Appendici alle Opere di T. Tasso"; A. Mabellini's edition of the "Rime" of Benvenuto Cellini; Pietro Aretino's "Pasquinate," edited by Vittorio Rossi; A. Borgognoni's "Studi di Letteratura storica"; "Carteggio di Vittoria Colonna," by D. Tordi; Domenico Gnoli's "Un Delitto di lesa Romanità ai Tempi di Leone X"; Mario Menghini's monograph on "Tomaso Stigliani"; Vol. I of "Storia d'Arcadia," by Monsignor Isidoro Carini, librarian of the Vatican Library; Ernesto Masi's "Storia del Teatro Italiano nel Secolo XVIII"; and Giuseppe Chiarini's two-volume "Gli Amoridi Ugo Foscolo," intended to show the noted poet's relation to women, and their influence on his work. To these we may add: Cantu's "Letteratura Italiana," Masotti's "Conferenze letterarie," E. Gorra's "Studi di Critica letteraria," and Manuale della Letteratura italiana" (Vols. I and II), by A. d'Ancona and O. Bacci.

It is claimed by some that the novelist's art is possessed by few Italians, and, in truth, not many novels among the large number published seem to come up to high artistic standards. Two novels of the year seem especially worthy of attention: "Il Paese di Cuccagna," in which Matilde Serao, a noted authoress, vividly pictures the evil passion for the lottery common among the middle classes in Naples, and "L'Innocente," a quite different book, in which Gabriele d'Annunzio studies the most depraved types of humanity. A. Butti's "L'Automa" and A. Lauria's "Donna Candida," both works by beginners; Emma Perodi's study of clerical society, "Il Principe della Marsigliana"; "L'Innamorata," by the Countess Lara, who has published also "Una Famiglia di Topi," a good children's story of the kind combining instruction and amusement, and "La Bocca del Lupo," by Remigio Zena, a pseudonym of the Marchese Gaspare d'Invrea, are referred to as very readable fiction. Of the few good collections of short stories and sketches, the best is "Fra Scuola e Case," a volume of vivid pictures of school life in Italy by that acute observer Edmondo de Amicis, who has also been working on a new book, "Primo Maggio," and who, we hear, has become a Socialist. Corrado Ricci, a young savant, shows a most decided talent for short-story writing in his "Promessa Mortale," while Antonio Morosi discloses a fine vein of humor in his "Novelle Ridanciane Oneste e Liete" (for which volume P. Mascagni furnished a musical motif). He is said to stand somewhat under the influence of Lorenzini, a witty journalist, better known as C. Collodi, a number of whose excellent articles Giuseppe Rigutini, the Florentine philologist, has reprinted from various periodicals, in two volumes, "Divagiazioni" and "Note gaie." F. de Roberto's "La Morte dell' Amore" is composed of three stories on the "wane of passion," and F. Pometti's "Rendenzione" is praised for the sweetness and purity of its ideals, while "Troppo Fiera" and "Realtà," two very clever volumes by Rachele Saporiti

(Fulvia), suffer somewhat through artificiality and sentimentality.

The poetical productions of the year include a volume of poems each by Guido Mazzoni, G. Aurelio Costanzo, and Giovanni Marradi, and a couple of volumes by Angelina de Leva. Severino Ferrari's "Versi"; "Erato," lyrics by Count Giuseppi Campitelli (whose devotion to politics has limited his poetical power); and "Fatalità," by Ada Negri, a young lady of extraordinary promise, have all won praise from the critics; as have also Ugo Ojetti's "Paesaggi"; Alfredo Baccelli's "Diva Natura"; the "Lyric and Satiric" poems of Marino Morelli (1870-'91); the "Versi" of G. Ragusa Moleti, a Sicilian; Eliodoro Lambardi's patriotic glorification of Garibaldi, "Calatafini"; and Gabriele d'Annunzio's "Elegie Romane"; although in the case of these latter names a certain immaturity makes itself felt, for they are nearly all of them young writers. Mario Rapisardi, a Sicilian poet, appears to be increasing in fame. His recent publications include a poem, "Empedocle," some examples of his translations of Shelley, and a third edition of his "Giustizia," a collection of bitter and quasi-socialistic poems. Giosué Carducci, on the other hand, has been very severely criticised of late. Guido Fortebracci (Pietro Bracci), among others, has, in the Rassegna Nazionale, subjected Carducci's recent rather mediocre odes, "Piemonte," "La Bicocca di S. Giacomo," and "La Guerra," to a calmly critical estimate. It might be added, too, that new editions of the late Pietro Ceretti's works continue to appear; here, again, fame comes posthumously. When Italian critics lament the decadence of dramatic literature, they echo a complaint made in many countries. The dearth of dramatic subjects in Italian life, and a perverted popular taste for anything French, are cited by some as the principal causes of the neglect of this branch of literary art in Italy. However, a few plays have won deserved success. "Alleluia," by Marco Praga (a young author of repute), and "La Figlia di Ninotta," by the Duca d'Andria, both favor the theories of atavism and heredity: in both the daughter falls as the mother did before her, in spite of all precautionary efforts. Luigi Capuana's "Malia" and "Disciplina," by F. Calandra and S. Lopez, have both won commendation. But the most successful production was that of Prof. Camillo Antona-Traversi's "Le Rozeno," which was pronounced the best drama produced during the last decade in Italy. On the whole, the proportion of works of real merit in the mass of literature produced during the year is not very large.

Norway.—Here, as under "Belgium," we have to record an interesting contribution to the literature concerned with the ill-fated Mary, Queen of Scots. It is a monograph (1891) by the well-known Gustav Storm, written in popular style, and in a manner at once critical and sympathetic. There are five noteworthy new works relating to Norway: Prof. L. Dietrichson's "De Norske Stavkirker," Part I; the first part of "Norge's Indskrifter med de ældre Runer" (1891), by Sophus Bugge, the renowned philologist; Prof. A. Helland's "Norge's Bergret med Udsigt over andre Landes Bergværkslovgivning"; Ange Skavlan's "Kulturbilleder fra Norges nyere Historie"; and Sten Konow's "Norsk Lommekonversationsleksikon," which contains much information concerning Norway. Descriptions of various parts of Norway and more northern lands are furnished in " Kring om Peisen, jagtminden fra det Sundenfjeldske Norge," stories of the hunt, by T. O. Guldberg, a well-known sportsman ; Alexander Kielland's interesting " Dyr og Mennesker" (relating to the Stavanger district) ; Friis's " Skildringer fra Finmarken" ; a new volume by Frithjof Nansen, noted for his explorations in Greenland, entitled " Eskimoliv"; and " Billeder og Text," in which we get more of artist Kittelsen's impressions " Fra Lofoten." In biography we have a volume of memoirs (" Paa Forpost, Billeder fra sytti aarene ") by Kristofer Kristofersen, and a monograph on the Empress Augusta by Clara Tschudi. Henrik Jaeger's contribution to literary history, " En Gammel Kjærlighedshistorie," is concerned with P. A. Heiberg, the Danish author. Jaeger has also published " Henrik Ibsen og hans Værker." Furthermore, there have appeared Dr. G. Fasting's " Læsekunsten," " Grundtræk of Metafysik," by Halvorsen, a newly fledged doctor of philosophy, and the first part of the voluminous and important " Samlade Skrifter " (collected works) of Camilla Collett, the famous advocate of women's rights.

In the department of fiction some new names have appeared, and the influence of France has made itself felt to a certain degree. Several of the authors of established reputation seem to have devoted themselves in the past year to the short story rather than the novel. Jacob B. Bull has published a collection of " Sketser," mainly of life in eastern Norway, while a similar service is performed for the fisherfolk about Bergen in " Ravenekrokbilleder," a somewhat satirical production by Kristofer Kristofersen (already mentioned) ; and Skeibrok, a sculptor, has collected his popular stories about southwestern Norway under the title " Sandfærdige Skröner." Two new men have likewise drawn direct inspiration from the life of their people : Thomas P. Krag (brother of Vilhelm), in whose " John Græff " and " Fra den Gamle by og andre Skildringer," the sailors and fishermen of northwestern Norway, and their field of action, the sea, are p   r   forth ; and Hans Aanrud, who has made his début with bright and cleverly written sketches of Norwegian life. Per Sivle, who is said to be best in his descriptions of peasant life, treats a theme much utilized of late —the relations between capital and labor—in his romance " Streik," which strongly favors the workingman. Kristofer Janson's " Sara," Johan Vibe's " Fantastiske Fortællinger," and Alvilde Prydtz's " Arnak," are also worthy of note. Amalie Skram (" Forraadt," a strong novel) and Gabriel Finne (" To Söstre ") are described as the most prominent naturalists among Norway's authors. Gallic fin-de-siècle " décadence " has not been without its influence in this country. Gabriel Gram, the free-thinking hero of Arne Garborg's " Trætte Mend," having failed to obtain satisfactory and complete explanations of existence from science, finally turns to Christianity. The book has run through several editions, and has given rise to much discussion. On the other hand, Arne Dybfest's stories (" Fra " and " To Noveller ") are said to be characterized by an excess of glittering verbiage and an abnormal penchant for character analysis of a displeasing nature.

The report comes to us of a gratifying increase in lyric poetry. Engebret Haugen's posthumous works have been published, Haugen being a schoolmaster from whom, in 1842, Asbjörnsen heard the legend of Peter Gynt, which name, together with parts of the story, were subsequently utilized by Ibsen. The same character, by the way, is made to pose as the supposed author of Theodor Caspari's " Digte af Per Gynt ved Theodor Caspari," which seem to show a most decided improvement on Caspari's former work, and are much more Norwegian in feeling. Rosenkrants Johnsen, one of the younger men, shows warmth of feeling and vigor of style in his poems, and Vilhelm Krag, though his work is sometimes burdened by rather meaningless verbosity, is not without much promise. J. B. Bull's " Alvarsmænd," the author's second play, is a very interesting piece of work, despite grave faults in construction, and Hjalmer Christensen also shows talent in his " Loth's Ilustru." There is nothing else to record in dramatic literature, except, perhaps, Otto Valseth's " En Befrielse " and Erik Vullum's " Himlene Aabne," neither of which is especially remarkable, however.

Poland.—The centenary of the Constitution of May 3 naturally gave rise to some literature on the subject, to which K. Bartoszewicz, P. Popiel, L. Finkel, A. Sokolowski, and others have contributed. A résumé of the important new publications in the various branches of literature includes " From the History of the Eighteenth Century," by K. Waliszewski ; Korytkowski's five-volume work on " The Archbishops of Gnezno " ; G. Olizar's " Memoirs " ; Chelmicki's " From Brazil," the result of a Brazilian journey made in the interests of Poland's emigrants ; a " History of the Bulgarian Language," by A. Kalina ; K. Morawski's " Andreas Nidecki " ; A. Jelowicki's " Reminiscences "; and Vol. I of a work on " Lemberg " by A. Czolowski. The first volume of the collected works of Spasowicz, the critic, has been issued. The records enumerate also some scientific publications, among which may be mentioned, without comment, Vol. I of Fr. D. P. Zoll's " Pandekta czyli nauka Rzymskiego prawa prywatnego," a treatise on Roman civil law ; Th. D. Ziemba's " Estelyka praktyczna," Part I (architecture) ; a history of painting in Italy, by W. Dzieduszycki ; a work on æsthetics by H. Struve ; and contributions to philosophical literature by A. Trznadel, Przyborowski, etc.

Among the novelists we note two women : Esteja (Ostoja ?), who inclines to pessimism and superficiality, and who has done good descriptive writing in her " In the Spider's Web" and " Behind the Ocean," and F. Orzeszko, whose " twenty-five years' jubilee " has been celebrated in literary circles, and whose " Beni Nati " is directed against the spirit of caste. J. Zacharyasiewicz shows a masterly power of defining character in " My Happiness "; T. Jeske-Choinski's " Search for the Golden Fleece " is a fine psychological study ; M. Gawalewicz's " Night Butterfly " has a pessimistic flavor ; " The Counselor," by W. Zagorski and A. Zaleski, is said to be best in its satire ; while " Kaleidoscopé," by J. Rogosz, and

" Unhorsed," by Sygietynski, are directed against the moral shortcomings of the nobility in Galicia and other parts of Poland. The popular writer of historical novels, A. Krechowiecki, leaves past ages for the present time in " The Youngest," while K. Rojan, like Esteja (in the two stories mentioned above), lays the scene of his " Tymko Medier" in North America. Z. Cwirko's " When Happiness is gone," A. Konar's " The Bankrupt," " Mis," by G. Myriel, Frau Marrené's " January," and " The Club of Mice," by Abgar-Sottan, should also be noted ; while decided ability is shown by A. Nossig in his " John the Prophet," as also by W. Los, who has published " Aristocracy and Plutocracy," " The Secret of the Hussars," and " The Nocturne of Chopin." As in Hungary, the novelette and short story are very much in vogue, and cultivated with decided success, notably by the younger element. We note a considerable number who have made a reputation in this field: Gawalewicz. who has issued " From my Album " and " The Wife " ; M. Pawlikowski (*Marck Polnicz*), characterized as " thoughtful and patriotic " ; Ostoja, an authoress with a very masculine style ; G. J. Lentowski ; and B. Prus, noted for his wit. Among those whose literary *début* is of more recent occurrence, we have the late M. Czerneda, whose clever and sympathetic sketches of low life have been published posthumously ; C. Walewska ; W. Los; Nagoda, with realistic tendencies ; Z. Niedzwiecki, who has been much influenced by French realism ; S. Rossowski ; and J. Rutkowski, whose " delicacy of touch " has won commendation.

Poetical literature has been enriched by the posthumous publication of two poems written half a century ago by the late Bohdan Zaleski. a Polish author of great renown. One of these, " The Campaign of Zbaraz," has been called a veritable masterpiece. In this department, too, a number of young authors have made their first appearance, with work of much promise : S. Rossowski, whose verses are marked, like his stories, by truth and delicacy of feeling ; A. Fredro, a keen satirist ; K. Tetmajer, who is happiest in his expressions of patriotism ; and J. Styka, who had already gained a reputation in the sister art of painting. There have been a few noteworthy additions to dramatic literature. " The Cradle of the Nation," by Adam Belcikowski, and " The Fatherland," by Orsza, were " crowned " by the competition committee of the Diet of Galicia. E. Lubowski's " A Plaything "—dealing with the career of a young woman who, though educated by rich friends, becomes utterly degraded under the influence of heredity—was exceedingly successful on the stage; the performance of W. Motty's " The Demon of Love " was not so well received.

Russia.—Valuable researches into various aspects of Russian history have been made. Vols. LXXVIII-LXXX of the Historical Society's *Transactions* contain diplomatic correspondence of French and English ambassadors and other documents of last century. Paul Milyoukoff has issued " The National Economy of Russia during the First Quarter of the Eighteenth Century, and the Reforms of Peter the Great " ; Masloffski, his " Notes on the History of the Art of War in Russia (1683–1762) " ; N. Kaptercff, " The Relations of Dositheus, the Pa-

triarch of Jersualem, with the Russian Governments (1660–1707) " ; Prof. Korsakoff, " Out of the Lives of the Russian Men of Action of the Eighteenth Century " ; A. Golubtzoff, an account of the " Debates on Faith." to which the wooing of the Czarevna Irene (daughter of the Czar Michael Feodorovitch) by Prince Waldemar of Denmark (1640–'45) gave rise; and P. Bezobrazoff, a volume on " The Relations between Russia and France " (down to the " Napoleonic Era "). Special periods have also been treated in Barbasheff's " Sketches of Lithuano-Russian History of the Fifteenth Century," Dovnar Zapolski's " History of the Lands of Krivitchski and Dregovitchski," and Grustchevski's " History of the Land of Kieff," as also in two contributions to the history of the nineteenth century, " Minutes of the Committee of Ministers " (1802–'12) and Djanshieff's " The Epoch of Great Reforms," a volume of articles on the reign of Alexander II. Besides all these, there have appeared biographies of Prince Potemkin, by Brückner ; of the Empress Maria Feodorovna (wife of the Emperor Paul), by E. Shumitchorski ; and that of Arsenius Sukhanoff (" one of the authors of the corrections of the Orthodox Greek Psalter which brought about the split in the seventeenth century "), by S. Belokuroff. Other historical works of importance are Schwarz's on the Ἀθηναίων πολίτεια, Scheffer's on Athenian citizenship, two Korelin's volumes on " The Early Italian Humanism and its Historiography " (in which the author has drawn from scarce manuscripts), and Vinogradoff's excellent " Villainage in England." Here may be mentioned also the fourth volume of the " Russian Antiquities " of Count I. Tolstoi and Kondakoff, and N. Pokroffski's valuable work on Christian iconography, which forms the first volume of the *Transactions* of the Archæological Congress at Moscow ; a work on the strategy of the Franco-Prussian War, by N. Michnievitch ; W. Ikonnikoff's " Russian Historiography," Vol. I ; and G. Utin's " William I and Bismarck." A handbook on the Russian laws relating to the Jews, by M. Mysch, seems timely. There have appeared a volume on " Socialism," by K. Golovin, and one on " Darwinism," by I. Tshemen ; while among the new philosophical works that deserve notice are A. Kasanki's elaborate " Teaching of Aristotle on the Value of Experiment with Reference to Knowledge " ; L. Lopatine's dissertation on " The Positive Problems of Philosophy ; Part III : The Law of the Connection of Causes the Basis of an Intelligent Knowledge of the Real " ; " The Sources of the Sophists: Plato as an Historical Witness," a not very strong production by A. Guilyaroff; " Actual Progress and Economic Materialism." by P. Nikolayeff (described as a devoted disciple of Leicester Ward); and. best of all, " Positive Philosophy on the Unity of Science," an able criticism of Kant, by B. Tchetchérin, a follower of Hegel. A storm of controversy has been aroused by the newest teachings of Vladimir Solovieff, who has been said to consider the history of society to be simply the story of its gradual assimilation of Christian ideals, and who has now gone further by announcing that the materialistic and socialistic tendencies of to-day must inevitably lead to true Christianity. As the orthodox spirit of religion in Russia is firmly opposed to compromises with modern feeling, the opposition to Solovieff has produced a voluminous literature of its own. The enthusiastic young Archimandrite Antonius quite scandalized his brother clergy when, in his "Pastoral Letters," he affirmed his belief in the intimate connection between the salvation of the individual and an active and altruistic laboring for the good of others (as opposed to the "red-tape" methods of the clergy), thus in a measure supporting the much-attacked Solovieff. Late as they come, these acrimonious discussions at least show that a more modern spirit is beginning to gain admission where it is greatly needed. It appears also that the tone of social life is undergoing a change. One of the reasons for this new departure, we are told, is to be found in "the negative result obtained from a criticism of the programme of the men of the eighties." But there was also an external stimulus—the terrible famine which fell so heavily upon the poor of Russia, and which aroused the educated class to well-defined and extraordinary efforts in a field which, under ordinary circumstances, would hardly have enlisted their thoughts and sympathies to any great extent. Count Leo Tolstoi, especially, was so impressed by this dreadful calamity that he wrote an article on the subject, which the Government suppressed, but parts of which were published in English papers, calling forth most violent attacks in Russian conservative circles. More than that, however, Tolstoi labored energetically to relieve the wants of his suffering countrymen. However, though he was temporarily drawn away from his ponderings on the subject of passive suffering and nonresistance to evil, he has again enlarged on his favorite theory of self-improvement in one of his latest articles ("The First Step"). It should be added here, that not only were numerous publications issued and lectures delivered for the benefit of the famine-stricken districts, but the famine itself, and the accompanying diseases, formed the theme of a number of works. Some interesting contributions to Russian literary history have appeared. The brilliant "Sketches of the Gogol Period of Russian Literature," which were written in 1850 for the "Contemporary," a Russian periodical, by the late Tchernishevsky, have been reprinted in a separate volume by his son; while in the interesting book, "P. V. Aneukoff and his Friends," are collected that deceased literary critic's reminiscences and correspondence, dating back to 1830. A. Puipin's "History of Russian Ethnography," now complete in four volumes, is also said to contain much information regarding the literary movements of the nineteenth century in Russia; while older periods of literature are treated in Batyushkoff's "Conflict between the Soul and the Body in the Literature of the Middle Ages," and V. Th. Miller's "Excursions in the Regions of the Russian Popular Epos," a work on the "builins" or folklore, which the author believes were originally brought into southern Russia by the Turks.

In the domain of prose fiction we have the collected works, in three volumes, of Madame Khvosttchinski (V. Krestovski), who died in 1891, and whose unfortunate career is sympathetically described by her sister. Potapenko, a very pro-

lific author, who, as recorded last year, has already made an enviable reputation, appears to be less successful in longer novels, like his "No Hero" and "Love," than in his short stories, such as "The General's Daughter," "Six," etc. Mochtet's "New Studies" (some of the tales in which deal with life in Siberia and America) are marked by the passionate emotion we are wont to find in this author's works; and P. Boboruikin describes certain regenerative processes in the moral and intellectual existence of the heroine and hero, respectively, in his "Wedded," and a new novel of merchant life. A similar theme is worked out less ably in "The Duel," by Tchekhoff, who is gifted with much power of observation, however. Finally, Karpoff and Garin seem to be following in the path of the late Karonin. A refreshing change from the depressing motives pervading much of this literature is found in Korolenko's strong and breezy sketches of life in the desolate country watered by the Vetluga, a branch of the Volga, and in Garin's "Childhood of Temy," a charming story of the force of innate purity and moral strength over demoralizing influences. In 1892, just fifty years after Lermontoff's death, the copyright in his writings expired, and numerous editions of his works have begun to appear, among them Vvedensk's, Boldakoff's, the one published by Kushneneff (illustrated by prominent Russian artists), and the fine critical one by Prof. Viskovatoff (who furnishes also an interesting biographical sketch), none of them, it is averred, being as yet altogether satisfactory. Kotlyarevski's biography of the poet has been described as an able though somewhat partial account. There has also appeared a collected edition of the works of A. M. Zhemtchuzhnikoff, whose seventy years seem to have abated neither his graceful style nor the warmth and optimism of his feelings.

Spain.—Literary activity, it appears, is gradually increasing in this country. In the department of history, the Columbian celebration, as was to be expected, continued to call forth a large number of books, pamphlets, and articles: essays on the location of San Salvador, on Pinzon, etc., and other special topics, by Emilio Castelar (Historia del descubrimiento de América) J. M. Asensio, P. M. Angleria, J. E. Campe, Victor Balaguer (Cristóbal Colón), Martin Ferreiro, E. Ibarra y Rodriguez, Miguel Mir, besides the more important larger works, such as José Maria Asensios's sumptuously illustrated work on Columbus, in two folio volumes, and the life by Ferdinand Columbus, which, it is conjectured, is a translation from the Italian version by Alfonso de Ulloa, published in 1571, at Venice. The "Centenario," an illustrated review published by the organizing committee of the Spanish celebration, contains much information of interest and value on the occurrence which called it into existence. Much interest was aroused also by the accidental discovery of three quarto volumes in the handwriting of Las Casas, which proved, however, to contain only his well-known "Historia Apologética de las Indias." In this connection F. Rivas Puigcerver's monograph on the part played by the Spanish Jews and Moriscoes in the discovery of the Western Hempishere should be mentioned. Much information has also been published concerning Spain's former possessions in America. We cite: Cobo's "Historia del Nuevo Mundo" (1645); Andrés Rocha's "Origen de los Indios del Peru, Mexico, Santa Fé y Chile"; "De las Gentes de Peru," which forms part of the "Historia Apologética" of Bartolomé de las Casas; "Noticias Autenticas del Famoso Rio Marañon" (in the "Boletin de la Sociedad Geografia"); the second edition of Father José Coll's "Colon y la Ravida"; and three works on the Philippines, D. J. Rajal y Larré's "Exploracion del Territorio de Davao in Mindanao," D. F. Blumentritt's "Los Moros de Filipinas," and Father Gaspar de San Augustin's "Conquista de las Islas Filipinas." To these we add: E. de la Viñaza's "Bibliografia Española de Lenguas Indigenas de America." There is the usual large number of reprints and of hitherto unpublished documents relating to Spanish affairs. In the series entitled "Libros Raros y Curiosos," there has appeared "Pio IV y Felipe II," a volume of the official dispatches of Luis de Requesens, Spanish ambassador at the court of Rome (1563–'64), and in the well-known collection, "Documentos Inéditos para la Historia de España," has been published the "Correspondencia de Felipe II con los Hermanos D. Luis de Requesens y Don Juan de Zuñiga." These two brothers (Luis having adopted his mother's family name, Juan the father's) were both ambassadors at Rome. The correspondence of Philip II with the princes of the house of Austria (1556–'98) has also been published in these "Documentos Inéditos," as well as a volume of miscellaneous papers (a "fragment of the chronicle of John II, of Castile, by Alvar Garcia de Santa Maria [1428–'34], a narrative of the wars in Barbary, by Fr. Luis Nieto, and another of Mechoacan in 1605"). An abridgment of the history of Charles IV and his son, Ferdinand VII, has also seen the light, as well as a volume of interesting correspondence selected by the Duchess of Alva from the archives of her family. Other reprints issued are: "Loor de Claras mugeres" (fifteenth century); "Amenidades de la Vera de Plasencia": "Opusculos Literarios de los Séglos XIV. á XVI."; "Historia de las Malucas" (Zaragoza, 1609); and Martin Navarrete's essay on the Spaniards in the Crusades. The Royal Academy of History, whose interestingly illustrated "Boletin" increases in scholarly value and importance, has not issued much during the year. Of Fabré's "Documentos Inéditos Relativos á las Antiguas Posesiones Españoles en Ultramar," the fifth and sixth volumes have appeared, while the publication of the chronicle of Catalonia during 1644–'53 had to be suspended after the fourth volume was issued, on account of the death of its editor, the academician Pujol y Camps, on Dec. 28, 1891. The Academia Española, displayed its usual activity. Here, too, the demise of a distinguished member—Manuel Cañete—interfered with the issuing of an intended publication, "Cancionere de Juan de la Encina." Cañete had also been engaged in editing "Propaladia de Torres Naharro." The publication of the complete edition of Lope de Vega's works has been begun by bringing out Vols. I and II, containing his "Autos y Coloquios." It should be mentioned here, also, that an attempt is being made to sift the evidence and prove the facts in the various,

often quite contradictory, chronicles of Spain in a "Historia General de España," which some twenty academicians have begun to compile under the editorship of Antonio Cánovas del Castillo. The most successful historical work has been Antonio Rodriguez Villa's "Juana la Loca," in which his theories regarding Joanna are based on extensive and careful research. José Gestoso y Perez, in his graphic description of an old and beautifully embroidered banner, discovered in Seville and belonging to the Guild of Merchant Tailors, speaks of 143 artists in embroidery who were working from the fourteenth to the end of the seventeenth century in Seville alone, being just eight times as many as were mentioned one hundred years ago for the whole of Spain (18), by Cean Bermudez. In the matter of local Spanish history, a favorite subject, there seems to be almost an overproduction. The ancient monarchies of Leon and Galicia, the province of Castellon de la Plana, the Ciudad Real, in La Mancha, and Toledo, all have found their annalists and historians, and this excessive *penchant* for provincial history extends even to insignificant places like Jarandilla, in Estremadura, and Arcos de la Frontera, in Andalusia. Whatever spirit of sectionalism may be evinced by such efforts is perhaps furthered by the publication of various works bearing on the dialects and literatures of the various races in the p n n-sula. Among such is a dictionary of the dialect in which the works of the famous poet Ausias March were written, with an essay on the Limousin-Valencian dialect, by José Escrig y Martinez. But the spirit is fostered most, probably, by the various modern literary productions in dialect, among which the past year has brought us: Rubé y Fontanet's "Lo Trovador Catalá" and J. M. del Bosch Gelabert's "Lo Segador," in Catalan; "Los Pirineos" and "Trilogia," by Victor Balaguer, an influential and versatile statesman and author, of whose "Tragedies" (in Catalan) a sixth edition has appeared; as well as others, brought out in Valencia, the Balearic Islands, the Basque Provinces, Navarre, etc. To the literature relating to much-discussed Africa, Spain has made a considerable number of contributions, the most important being "Estado Independiente del Congo" and José Valero y Belenguer's "La Guinea Española y la Isla de Fernando Pó," which two appeared in Vols. XXXI and XXXII of the Geographical Society's "Bulletin"; "España y Africa," by Reparaz; Perez del Toro's "España en el Nordeste de Africa"; and "La Cuestion del Golfo de Guinea." by the late A. Cañamaque. An essay on the Spanish Jews, with special reference to those of Majorca; another one on Jubudá Cersquet, who executed a map of the world for John I of Aragon in 1391; a "Mitologia Popular," by M. Cubas; a manual of prehistorical archæology by Manuel Peña y Fernandez; a "Catalogo de Monedas Arabigo-Españolas en el Museo Arqueológico Nacional," by J. de D. de la Rada y Delegado; a "Manual de Numismatico," by Campaner; M. Pardo de Andrade's "Los Gue^ri̯lle^r̯o̯s Gallegos de 1809," Vol. I; and Vols. VIII and IX of J. de Moret's "Investigaciones Históricas de las Antigüedades del Reino de Navarra," complete the list of historical works. In biography there have appeared "Memorias de Gayarre" (the tenor), Doña Sabina de Alvear y Ward's life of her father (Don Diego de Alvear, a noted naval officer), and some provincial biographical dictionaries, among which A. E. de Molins's "Diccionario Biográfico y Bibliográfica de Escritores y Artistas Catalanes del Siglo XIX."

In the political sciences and philosophy there are Arcarate's "Regimen Parlamentario"; Vol. II of the learned Count Torreánaz's work on the "magistracy and councils of Castile during the Middle Ages"; Cánovas del Castillo's "Problemas Sociales"; "La Cuestion Social," by the Bishop of Madrid; U. González Serrano's "Estudios Psicológicos; and the third volume of Pedro Estasen's important "Instituciones de Derecho Mercantil."

Z. Vélez de Aragón has brought out a small "Historia de las Bellas Artes"; and "La Imprenta en Seville," by Hazañas, "La Imprenta de Madrid en el Siglo XVI," by Perez Pastor, "Catalogo de los Libros incunables que se conservan en la Biblioteca de Mahon," and "Biblioteca Colombina" (a catalogue of the books bequeathed to the Cathedral of Seville by Ferdinand Columbus), are among the additions to the already considerable number of works on national bibliography; while Juan P. Oriado y Dominguez has issued an important volume on the "Periodismo Español," originally published in the "Revista Contemporanea."

In the year's list of important books, works of a serious character preponderate largely, there being little of note to record in the department of fiction and poetry, although translations are plentiful (among them works by Daudet, Ibsen, Tolstoi, Turgenief, and Carlyle's "Heroes"). Millam's novel "Menudencias" is notable, chiefly because it is directed against the Jesuit Father Luis Coloma's clever "Pequeñeces," which ran through eight editions, and which was more directly attacked in a lampoon entitled "Caresses of a Layman for Father Luis Coloma, of the Society of Jesus, for his book 'Pequeñeces,' and for the Society to which he himself belongs." Dr. Emilia Pardo Bazan now publishes her work in "Teatro Critico," a fortnightly of which she is owner, editor, and exclusive contributor. "Doña Berta," by Leop. Alas Clarin, has won praise from French critics. New books by Victor Balaguer and Manuel Matoses have also been commended. In poetry, the interminable epics once in vogue are beginning to give way to shorter similar compositions, like Campoamor's "El Licenciado Torralba," in eight cantos; while in the mass of lyrical poetry nothing remarkable has been accomplished. Here, too, there is a dearth of notable dramatic productions, though there are theatres enough. Excepting a three-act comedy by the younger Echegaray (Miguel), and "En Casa de la Modista," a one-act affair, there is nothing that deserves special mention.

Sweden.—The noteworthy literary productiveness of Sweden is all the more remarkable when we consider the limited market which this literary ware must find, notwithstanding the general culture in Sweden and Finland, by virtue of which, it is said, the reading public forms a considerable proportion of the inhabitants. The complaint has been made that the publishing season is practically limited to the holiday period at the end of the year, the only time at which considerable book buying is done by the public; and, in fact, attempts have been made to publish also in the spring. Before passing on to fiction and poetry, in which departments we find most to record, we give an account of the important new publications in other branches of literature. In literary history we have G. Ljunggren's excellent "Swedish Literary Annals after the Death of Gustavus III," and a volume by O. Sylvan, "Sveriges Periodiska Literatur under Frihetstidens förra del." L. Looström, in "The Swedish Academy of Arts during the First Century of its Existence, 1735–1835," gives the history of Swedish art during that period in a full and impartial manner; while G. Nordensvan, a well-known *littérateur*, is furnishing a clever chronicle of Swedish art matters of the present century in his "Svensk Konst och Svenska Konstnärer i 19de århundrated," of which over a dozen parts have already been issued. L. De Geer, the famous old statesman, began to publish an edition of his complete works, the first volume of which contains chiefly writings on æsthetic subjects, marked by elegance and refinement of thought. A. Fryxell's "Berättelser ur Svenska Historien," continued by O. Sjögren (Part XLVIII), and E. Aspelin's "Werner Holmberg, hans Lefnad och Verk," are noted among the contributions to historical literature; and some interesting books of travel have appeared, such as G. Retzius's vivid description of his travels in Sicily and Egypt; a volume from the pen of S. Hedin, who accompanied the embassy sent to the Shah of Persia by King Oscar; and two works on the "Slave Trade" and "Mohammedanism" in Africa, the result of H. H. V. Schwerin's extensive travels in that continent, especially on the Congo. C. A. Cornelius, in his "Krestna Kijrkans Historia" (1889–'91), covers the history of the Christian Church to the nineteenth century, to which latter he has devoted a former work.

Prose fiction has probably been second only to poetry in abundance of new publications. V. Rydberg's "Armorer" ("Vapensmeden") is characterized by the author himself as "mirages from the time of the Reformation," and serves as an interesting medium for conveying the thoughts and opinions of this prominent writer. "En Man öfner Bord" and "Genom Hvirflande" (giving an interesting picture of certain aspects of Swedish life), which have been published by a prominent Government official under the pseudonym *Horatio*, seem to show power of observation rather than proficiency in literary art. The tendencies of the hour are reflected in "Komministeren i Qvislinge," by A. Hedenstierna (*Sigurd*), whose fine humor and sound opinions have made him exceedingly popular; "Genom Skuggor," by Mathilda Roos; and "Sådan var Vägen," by W. H. Wickström. On the other hand, we are told romance has again gained a hearing, in Levertin's "Legends and Ballads," and in Selma Lagerlöf's "Ur Gösta Berlinga Saga," although the latter, the author's first work, does not in its present completed state wholly make good its original promise. Various other novels and shorter stories selected from the year's publications are E. Lundqvist's "Vid Aftonlampan"; Vilma Lindhé's "Motvind"; "Brottsjöar," by A. Jäderin; "Nya Berättelser och Skizzer," by Tor Hedberg, a young author who delights in psychological studies; "Lifsmål," by Elin Ameen; a new volume on certain aspects of student life, by N. P. Oedman, in which, as usual, kindly humor and a lively style are displayed on a background of thoughtful seriousness; "Med Sordin," by Rust Roest; and Anna Wahlenberg's "Stora Barn och Små." It might be added that, while truth to nature has become a recognized desideratum here in prose fiction, the Swedish novel, redeemed from the extreme of idealism by the wholesome influence of the realistic tendencies of the last twenty years, does not err on the side of ultra-realism, but seems to preserve a happy medium. Sweden has lost one of her greatest novelists, whose works were translated into all the principal languages of Europe, and whose fame was world-wide—Emilie Flygare-Carlén. Among the works of this authoress, who lived to a green old age, but had long ago ceased all literary activity, are "Enslingen på Johannesskäret," "Tistelön," and "Ett Köpmanshusi Skärgården."

In lyric poetry, as already indicated, productiveness seems to have been most marked. Both nature and man, in all their varieties of mood, feeling, and thought, have formed themes for these northern singers. V. Rydberg, mentioned before, has published a new collection of poems, in which the realities of modern life are depicted with deep feeling. Thus, "Grubblaren" deals with various questions in the domain of moral and mental science; "Grottesången," a lengthy poem founded on an old myth of the north, is directed especially against what we in America would call the "race for the dollar," etc. Similarly, Ernst Beckman has also occupied himself with questions of the day in his "Skilda Toner." O. Levertin's "Legender och Visor" (already mentioned) displays an exuberant fancy, which is no doubt to be traced to the author's Oriental descent. W. von Heidenstamm's "Hans Alienus," which is partly written in prose, abounds in fine description and charming poetry, but it also gives evidence of a rather extravagant fancy, and must be received mainly as a protest against "materialistic" tendencies of the day and the desire to apply the principle of analysis to every manifestation of thought and feeling. Gustaf Fröding, on the other hand, takes a humorous view of things, and has won favor especially by the sketches of life in a remote province, in his "Guitarre och Dragharmonika." K. A. Melin, a well-known and clever writer, Wirsén, Bååth, and Snoilsky are among those who have helped, by their contributions, to foster the love for p r in these eminently practical times. Of dramatic literature there is little to say, and, in fact, this nation does not seem to have a special bent for the drama. "Himmelrikets Nycklar," a legendary play by Aug. Strindberg, and "En Tvekamp," a play, by Tor Hedberg—these, together with a few comedies and dialogues, make up the list of the year in this branch of literary art.

The Apocryphal Gospel and Apocalypse of St. Peter.—A manuscript on parchment found in the winter of 1886–'87 in a tomb at Akhmin, in Upper Egypt, and published in 1892 by the French archæological mission, contains three documents, two of which are of much value in their bearing on our knowledge of the history of early Christian thought. The writing of the manuscript fixes its probable date as between the eighth and the twelfth centuries. The most important of the documents is a part of the apocryphal "Gospel according to St. Peter," and, with the "Revelation or Apocalypse of St. Peter," which accompanies it, is supposed to have been composed in the early part of the second century. Both of these works, bearing the name of Peter, though not in fact his, are referred to by Eusebius and other early Christian authors. The fragment of the Gospel of Peter which is preserved contains an account of the passion, the crucifixion, and the ascension. The narrative is founded directly upon the accounts given in the four gospels, and the simple diction of the New Testament is preserved with more fidelity than is usual in apocryphal works. Variances appear in it of two kinds—those which have no particular value, but are employed to give greater similitude to the story, and those which are incorporated to further the particular purpose of the writer. He belonged to the sect of the Docitæ, who denied that the Godhead, though incarnated in Jesus, suffered on the cross, and maintained that the divine nature of the Saviour descended upon him in his baptism by John, and reascended when he came to the cross. Accordingly, the expressions relative to suffering are omitted or changed, and the statement is added that when our Lord was crucified he "held his peace, as having no pain." The relation is further marked by animosity against the Jews, which appears in the statement that Herod did not, like Pilate, wash his hands. Another peculiar characteristic of the work is the emphasis that is put upon our Lord's descent into hades and his preaching to the dead. The feature in this "Gospel" of most interest to modern biblical critics is the fact that while the writer formally quotes none of the gospels, he uses them all, including John's, as when he speaks of the nails of the crucifixion, which are mentioned only by John. In this is seen confirmatory proof, in addition to the new evidence afforded by Tatian's "Harmony," that the fourth gospel was in canonical honor as early as the middle of the second century, and an additional argument against the theories prevalent several years ago that it was of later composition. "The Apocryphal Revelation or Apocalypse of St. Peter," or that portion of it which is now recovered, describes the author's vision of the rewards of the blest and the torments of the damned, and furnishes an explanation of the probable origin of some of the beliefs concerning the future state which have prevailed in the Christian Church, and particularly of some of the descriptions imagined by Dante. A third work contained in the manuscript is a part of the Greek text of the apocryphal "Book of Enoch," a writing hitherto known only in seven Ethiopic manuscripts and the Syriac version.

LOUISIANA, a Southern State, admitted to the Union April 30, 1812; area, 48,720 square miles. The population, according to each decennial census since admission, was 152,923 in 1820; 215,739 in 1830; 352,411 in 1840; 517,726 in 1850; 708,002 in 1860; 726,915 in 1870; 939,-946 in 1880; and 1,118,587 in 1890. Capital, Baton Rouge.

Government.—The following were the State officers during the year: Governor, Murphy J. Foster, Democrat; Lieutenant-Governor, Charles Parlange; Secretary of State, Thomas S. Adams; Treasurer, John Pickett; Auditor, W. W. Heard; Superintendent of Public Instruction, A. D. Lafargue; Attorney-General, M. S. Cunningham; Commissioner of Agriculture, Henry C. Newsom; Chief Justice of the Supreme Court, F. T. Nichols; Associate Justices, Charles E. Fenner.

Finances.—In the report of the State Treasurer the following statements were made relative to the general fund warrants:

The outstanding general fund warrants on June 1, 1888, were distributed as follow:

General fund of 1884............................	$94,079 83
General fund of 1885............................	160,409 27
General fund of 1886............................	205,913 74
General fund of 1887............................	81,010 60
General fund of 1888..	20,327 50
Making a total of..........................	$512,240 90

Up to May 9 the above amounts had been paid and reduced as follow:

General fund of 1884...........................	$55,429 05
General fund of 1884, *pro rata* declared in May.	19,575 40
General fund of 1885...........................	890 08
General fund of 1886...........................	8,854 29
General fund of 1887...........................	81,010 60
General fund of 1888...........................	20,327 60
Making a total of..........................	$185,086 97

Thus reducing these outstanding warrants to the following:

General fund of 1884...........................	$19,575 43
General fund of 1885..........................	160,019 24
General fund of 1886..........................	197,559 45
Making a total now outstanding of....... .	$377,154 12

Against $512,240.99 outstanding June 1, 1888.

Education.—According to the school report of 1891, there were 75,688 white children in the schools of Louisiana under 2,116 teachers. There were in the colored schools 55,021 pupils and 887 teachers, or 62 pupils to every teacher.

It was decided at a meeting of the Board of Administrators of the State University, held at Baton Rouge, July 2, to admit young women to the institution.

Agriculture.—During the year ending Aug. 31, 1892, there were 4 cotton mills in operation in the State, with 1,505 looms and 50,700 spindles, 15,322 bales of cotton having been used by them. In 1891 but 13,660 bales were consumed. During the fiscal year ending June 30, $6,882,-589.83 were paid in bounty to the producers of sugar in the State. The total amount paid to all sugar producers was $7,342,077.79, Louisiana having had the largest proportion. This bounty was, according to the United States Commissioner of Internal Revenue, divided among 619 persons, though it was actually paid to a larger number of small planters, selling their cane to the central factories. The bounty, therefore, is estimated to have been of benefit to as many as 400,000 people, that being the number engaged in the sugar industry of the State.

Floods.—The floods in the spring proved disastrous in many respects. Railways suffered to the amount of $200,000, agriculture to $400,-000, and other property to $100,000.

Supreme Court Decisions.—The constitutionality of the law requiring railroad companies to provide separate but equal accommodations for passengers of both races was affirmed by the court in December. A case was tried in which a man had been brought into court on a charge of having violated the separate-car law in refusing to sit in a car assigned to passengers of the colored race. He denied the constitutionality of the law, and the Supreme Court maintained it.

Levees.—The cost of levee work in the State, according to the Governor's statement made in May, 1892, had been, for the two years prior to that time $3,353,890.98 for 17,027,127 cubic yards. The work of this time has involved the construction of 170·11 miles of new levees, and the raising and enlargement of 317·45 miles of old levees. Nearly all the work has been built to grade intended to stand when settled from 2½ to 3 feet above the highest known flood of the river, with crown from 4 to 10 feet wide, according to the exposure. More new levees have been built with a width of base between 6 and 7 times their height, with banquettes 20 feet wide added to the land side across all sloughs, a considerable depression.

Legislative Session.—The General Assembly began its session at Baton Rouge on May 9. The Republicans at once entered a protest against the declared results of the election, claiming that Albert H. Leonard and H. Dudley Coleman received the greatest number of votes cast for Governor and Lieutenant-Governor, and that any other reading of returns was false and fraudulent. An investigation was demanded by Leonard and Coleman.

The contest over the appointment of a successor to Randall L. Gibson as a member of the United States Senate from Louisiana was long, ballots being taken on several successive occasions with no definite result. On June 27 a Democratic caucus decided to postpone the election of Senator till next year, but to ballot daily till adjournment. Senator Gibson died on Dec. 15. Gov. Foster appointed Donaldson Caffery to fill out the unexpired term.

Gov. Foster approved 110 acts passed by the General Assembly. Among them were the following:

Prohibiting the placing of rice flumes, dahls, pipes, or other foreign substances in the levees of the State for purposes of irrigation or otherwise.

Transferring $10,000 from the levee or drainage fund to the Fifth Louisiana Levee District fund.

Prohibiting the gambling game of craps.

Prohibiting the holding of sessions of the peace courts in buildings in which barrooms are kept or spirituous liquors sold.

Repealing all that portion of act 33 of 1879 creating the Third Levee District, and creating a new district, to be styled the Lafourche Basin District Levee, making the Board of Commissioners which govern it a corporate body.

Repealing all that portion of act 33 of 1879 creating the First Levee District, and creating a new district, styled the Lake Borgne Basin Levee District, making the Board of Commissioners a body politic.

Making the destruction of levees a punishable offense.

Prohibiting the sale of lottery tickets and lottery drawings or schemes in the State of Louisiana after Dec. 31, 1893.

Providing a penalty for the willful violation of labor contracts or interference therein by persons not parties to the contract.

Making women eligible to any office of control or management under the school laws of the State.

Preventing the employment of children in places dangerous to their bodies or their morals.

Providing against unsafe flooding or irrigation of Mississippi lands.

Political.—The Farmers' State Union convened at Monroe on Aug. 2, with President T. S. Adams in the chair. In his address the president declared that class legislation had forced the farmer into organization. He said that four decades since the farmers owned 50 per cent. of the wealth, and, notwithstanding much larger crops have been made, they only own 25 per cent. of the national wealth, and pay 80 per cent. of its taxes. He recommended the appointment of 2 standing committees for the future, to wit: 1 on education and 1 on legislation. He suggested that to do good work in their ranks they must "try to capture the next State Democratic Convention in that party's ranks." He recommended that no political resolutions be passed.

The Republican party was divided for some time into the Warmouth and the Leonard factions. Not until Oct. 3 was harmony finally restored, the Warmouth faction then withdrawing and leaving the Leonard faction free to run the campaign. This action was the result of an earnest appeal made by the State Executive Commission, a summary of which is given below:

It has been the purpose and effort of this committee to effect a union of all the different factions and elements of the people inclined to support the Republican presidential and congressional tickets. Recognizing the necessity for such a combination, this committee has striven to secure a representation of the various elements and factions in a single State committee. To this end it proposed to create a new State committee, claiming only a small representation in it for this committee. Failing in that, it proposed a campaign committee, whose authority should be limited to this campaign and for only one third of the representation on it. These propositions were rejected by the Cage committee. In order, therefore, that the best efforts of the party may be put forth under existing circumstances, and in order to show the good will of this committee and its desire to make every and all sacrifices necessary to secure Republican success, it has been determined to withdraw the electoral ticket named by the Republican Convention on the 19th of February last, and to recommend that all Republicans shall vote for the electors named by the Cage committee. It has also been determined to recommend to all Republicans to vote for those candidates for Congress chosen, or to be chosen, by the congressional organization recognized by the National Republican Convention at Minneapolis. Having withdrawn our electoral and congressional tickets, we urge all Republicans to vote for the candidates named as a means necessary to the triumph of Republican principles. We urge all Republicans to forget and forgive any wrongs or insults, real or fancied, which they have sustained, and to remember that they are voting for Benjamin Harrison for President and Whitelaw Reid for Vice-President when they vote for the electoral ticket.

The harmony of the Democratic campaign was marred by certain controversies in the Fifth Congressional District of the State over the basis of representation for the congressional nominating convention for that district. The difficulty grew out of the action of the district executive committee, which met at Monroe on Aug. 6. Then arose a discussion as to the basis of representation for that convention. The committee, by a large majority (15 to 4) resolved to adopt as a basis the total population of the district at the rate of 1 vote for each 500 of people and fraction of 250 or more. Four members of the committee bolted the body, claiming that the representation should be based on the vote cast for Democratic candidates for Governor in the last election, which would practically confine it to the white population. This was the view held by the minority, who proceeded to call a separate convention to nominate a congressional candidate, this convention to be held on Sept. 10. A white basis would have made a great change in the representative strength of the several parishes, cutting down that of the river parishes, where the negro population is large and the white population small, while the hill parishes, which are largely white, would have had a vastly preponderating influence in the convention.

After much exertion in the way of harmonizing, it was determined to reconvene the committee, securing the presence of the members who had been absent at the previous session, and have the matter of the basis of representation passed on. This was done, the committee having been reassembled on Monday, Sept. 5. The subject of the basis of representation was then taken up, and by a vote of 12 to 3, 4 members being absent, the action of the committee at its former meeting was ratified and the basis of representation for each parish fixed on the figures of the total population.

For platforms, etc., adopted by the conventions held late in 1891 or early in 1892, see "Annual Cyclopædia" for 1891, page 445. The State election was held en April 19, 1892, and the following tickets were in the field:

1. A Democratic ticket, with Judge S. D. McEnery for Governor and Robert C. Wickliff for Lieutenant-Governor. A majority of the delegates elected to the State Convention favored McEnery.

2. The Antilottery ticket, headed by Murphy J. Foster, ex-State Senator, with Charles Parlange, ex-United States District Attorney, for Lieutenant-Governor, and Thomas Scott Ames, of the Farmers' Alliance, for Secretary of State.

3. A Republican ticket, headed by A. H. Leonard, who was formerly United States Attorney, and H. Dudley Coleman, ex-Congressman from the Second Louisiana District. Both these gentlemen were ex-Confederates. Ex-Gov. Kellogg has made a vigorous canvass in favor of the Leonard ticket.

4. A Republican ticket, headed by John Ebreaux for Governor and James C. Weeks for Lieutenant-Governor. This ticket was supported by ex-Gov. Warmouth.

5. The People's party ticket for Governor, R. L. Tannehill, for Lieutenant-Governor, I. J. Kills.

These tickets received the following vote: the McEnery ticket, 40,006; the Foster ticket, 79,176; the Leonard ticket, 20,062; the Ebreaux ticket, 12,012; the Tannehill ticket, 8,479.

At the presidential election in November, the Democratic electors received 87,922 votes, the Republican 25,332.

LUTHERANS. The statistics of the Evangelical Lutheran Church in the United States, as gathered by the writer for the "Church Almanac," present the following results: Synods, 61; ministers, 5,219; congregations, 8,908; communicant members, 1,267,984; baptized membership, 6,700,000; parochial schools, 3,020; parochial-school teachers, 3,217; parochial-school scholars, 177,844; Sunday schools, 4,423; Sunday-school scholars, 415,048; benevolent contributions of churches, $829,560.75; theological seminaries, 24; colleges, 30; academies, 35; ladies' seminaries, 12; benevolent institutions, 75; value of property of institutions, $7,102,-200; amount of endowment of these institutions, $1,421,400.

The summary of statistics given above is for the entire Church in the United States. Following are brief reports of the operations of the 4 general bodies and independent synods:

General Council.—This general body, embracing a communicant membership of 291,234, held no convention in 1892. Its missionary, educational, and benevolent operations are carried on by boards. Foreign missionary operations are carried on in India, with Rajahmundry as its central station, with 5 American missionaries, 2 native pastors, and 2 woman missionaries. Home missionary operations are carried on by the district synods in their respective territories, and by the general board of the body in the New England States, Ohio, Illinois, Indiana, Wisconsin, Minnesota, the 2 Dakotas, Montana, Oregon, and Washington. An event of more than ordinary importance to the membership of this body was the quarter-centennial celebration of Muhlenberg College, at Allentown, Pa. This college was founded in 1867, and named in honor of Henry Melchior Muhlenberg, patriarch of the Lutheran Church in Pennsylvania. The college was established in order to meet the wants of the Church in eastern Pennsylvania, especially to increase the supply of ministers for the rapidly increasing number of its congregations. The college had for its first president the now venerable Frederick Augustus Muhlenberg, D. D., LL. D., a grandson of patriarch Muhlenberg, and a distinguished Greek scholar. He managed the affairs of the institution for ten years, when he resigned to accept the professorship of Greek in the University of Pennsylvania. He was succeeded at Muhlenberg by the Rev. Benjamin Sadtler, D. D., who served the college for nine years, and was succeeded by the present incumbent, the Rev. Theodore L. Seip, D. D., who has had charge of the institution since 1886. During the twenty-five years of its existence Muhlenberg College has acquired property worth $100,000, and endowment amounting to $134,000, has graduated 311 young men, and afforded educational advantages to nearly 1,500 students. The quarter-centennial celebration helped materially to present the institution in its true light to its patrons and friends, and to make known to the outside world the results accomplished. As a suitable memorial of the event, a book of 584 pages was published, under the title "Muhlenberg College," a quarter-centennial memorial volume, being a history of the college and a record of its men, edited by the Rev. S. E. Ochsenford, A. M., class of 1876.

General Synod.—This body, which embraces a communicant membership of 159,207, held no convention during the year. Its missionary and other operations are also carried on by boards elected by the body and responsible to it. Foreign missions are maintained in India and Africa, and are in successful operation. Their reports are published biennially; for the latest, see "Annual Cyclopædia" for 1891. Home missions are carried on in many of the United States, as follows: California, 5; Colorado, 4; Connecticut, 1; District of Columbia. 2; Illinois, 9; Indiana, 5; Iowa, 7; Kansas, 17; Maryland, 9; Missouri, 1; Nebraska, 19; New Jersey. 1; New Mexico, 1; New York, 8; Ohio, 15; Pennsylvania, 28; Tennessee, 1; and Wisconsin. 2; employing 151 missionaries, who serve 200 congregations, and for whose support were expended, during two years, $61,106.85.

United Synod (South).—This general body, which embraces a communicant membership of 37,793, held its biennial convention in 1892, at Staunton, Va. Representatives were present from the 8 synods connected with the general body, and legislated in the interest of the affairs of the Church throughout its territory, which covers all the Southern States. This body has recently established a mission in Japan, and is maintaining numerous missions on its own territory. Plans were adopted with reference to the extension of these operations and the improvement of its theological seminary at Newberry, S. C. This institution was established in 1840, and is maintained in connection with Newberry College. Although lacking in endowment and proper support, it is doing an important work for the Church in the South. Two professors give instruction to 6 students.

Synodical Conference.—This general body, embracing 424,497 communicant members, mostly Germans, held its fourteenth convention in New York city, Aug. 10-16, 1892. Much of the time of the convention was devoted to the discussion of theological subjects. The representatives from its 4 large district synods numbered over 1,400 clergymen. The chief items of business were home and foreign missions, education, and the parochial-school question. One new district synod was received at this convention, the Michigan Synod, which several years since left the General Council. The home missionary operations of this body are carried on chiefly by the district synods, for which the Missouri Synod alone (reports from other synods are not accessible) expended $60,000. Foreign mission work is confined to missions among the Indians and the freedmen of the South. This is the only Lutheran general body that is extensively carrying on mission work among the colored people. Missionaries are stationed in Arkansas, Louisiana, North Carolina, Virginia, and Illinois. The following was reported as the condition of the various stations: 7 missionaries. 3 colored pastors, 1 colored teacher, 11 stations, 9 schools with 705 pupils, 13 Sunday schools with 935 pupils, and 437 communicant and 777 baptized members. This work is being prosecuted at an annual expense of about $8,000. The 5 theological seminaries, 5 colleges, and 6 academies of this body, with more than 1,000 students, are exerting a powerful influence in the education of those German immigrants who have settled in our western territory. The next convention will be held in Milwaukee, Wis., in 1894.

Following are the statistics of the Lutheran Church in the great divisions of the world: In

Europe, 23,322 ministers, 30,207 churches, and 43,357,688 baptized members; Asia, 205 ministers, 144 churches, and 90,969 members; Africa, 248 ministers, 642 churches, and 134,437 members; Oceanica, 134 ministers, 304 churches, and 125,094 members; North America, 5,237 ministers, 8,924 churches, and 6,711,500 members; South America, 48 ministers, 72 churches, and 98,250 members; Jewish missions, 20 ministers and 23 churches. The Lutheran is a church of many languages. The latest statistics show that of her baptized membership 32,000,000 speak German, 5,300,000 Swedish, 2,500,000 Norwegian, 2,300,000 Danish, 2,048,000 Finnish, 1,250,000 English, 1,113,000 Hungarian, 624,000 Livonian, 480,000 Courlandish, 272,000 Esthonian, 80,000 French, 70,000 Icelandic, 48,000 Bohemian, and that in every other civilized tongue she is well represented. In the United States she is doing Christian work in 12 different languages, and her membership supports 147 Church periodicals, of which 49 are in English, 54 in German, 17 in Swedish, 14 in Norwegian, 4 in Danish, 3 in Finnish, 3 in Icelandic, 2 in French, and 1 in Slavonic. Twenty-six foreign missionary societies report 357 stations, 728 foreign and 3,390 native workers, 188,020 baptized members, 1,437 schools, and 66,742 pupils, with a total income of $881,839.39.

In Germany, the Lutheran Church has 15,550 ministers, 20,450 churches, 28,369,000 baptized members, 19 city home missionary societies, 40 provincial home missionary societies, with one central society at Berlin, 11 foreign missionary societies, with 400 European ordained missionaries in active service: the Gustavus Adolphus Society, which annually aids 1,500 churches in Roman Catholic countries with 957,656 marks; the Lutheran Lord's Treasury, which does a similar work for the German diaspora at an annual expense of 74,883 marks; 14 institutions for training home missionaries; 18 schools and agencies which have sent more than 1,700 missionary pastors to America; 6 Jewish missionary societies; 17 universities; 25 Bible societies, which annually circulate over 200,000 copies of the Bible; 24 religious publication houses; 1,446 Sunday schools with 137,502 pupils, besides the children's services in most of the churches, which take the place of Sunday schools; 528 Young Men's Christian Associations; 33 women's societies; 148 Christian inns for the traveling public; 330 Christian homes of correction; 31 Christian societies to care for prisoners; 23 societies and homes for the poor; 18 Magdalene institutes; besides the numerous societies and funds for Christian work in various departments. Similar evangelistic agencies have been organized and are being successfully prosecuted by the Lutheran Churches of Denmark, Norway, Sweden, and Finland. In the great cities of German and Scandinavian countries there are many Lutheran churches; and the Lutherans have in Paris 21 pastors, 16 churches, and 30,000 members; in London, 16 pastors, 6 churches, 6 mission stations, and 15,000 members; in St. Petersburg, 30 pastors, 13 parishes, and 79,000 members; and in Chicago, 75 churches, some of which have each over 1,000 communicant members.

M

MAINE, a New England State, admitted to the Union March 15, 1820; area, 33,040 square miles; population in 1890, 661,086.

Government.—The following were the State officers during the year: Governor, Edwin C. Burleigh, Republican; Secretary of State, Nicholas Fessenden; Treasurer, George L. Beal; Attorney-General, Charles E. Littlefield; Commissioner of Industrial and Labor Statistics, Samuel W. Matthews; Superintendent of Common Schools, Nelson A. Luce; Railroad Commissioners, David N. Mortland, Asa W. Wildes, and Roscoe L. Bowers, who died in July and was succeeded by B. F. Chadbourne; State Assessors, Benj. F. Chadbourne, Hall C. Burleigh, Otis Hayford; Adjutant-General, Henry M. Sprague; Insurance Commissioner, Joseph O. Smith; Bank Examiner, Geo. D. Bisbee, who resigned, and was succeeded in August by Charles R. Whitten; State Librarian, Leonard D. Carver; Chief Justice of the Supreme Court, John A. Peters; Associate Justices, Charles W. Walton, William W. Virgin, Artemus Libbey, Lucilius A. Emery, Enoch Foster, Thomas H. Haskell, William P. Whitehouse.

Finances.—The total net bonded debt Jan. 1, 1892, was $2,858,500. The State tax for the year was $850,014.11. The receipts during 1891 were $1,737,090.77, and the expenditures $1,712,953.24. The balance at the beginning of the year was $175,466.17, and at the end, $199,603.60.

The suit brought by the State of Maine against the Grand Trunk Railway of Canada in 1882, to recover taxes claimed to be due, was decided by the United States Supreme Court in favor of the State, the total amount assessed against this company to date being $122,792.44.

The amount of the direct tax refunded to the State by the United States Government was $357,702.10. It was placed in the State treasury April 6, 1891, accounted for in the receipts of the year, and applied to the general expenses of the government.

The total amount of tax paid by the savings banks to the State treasury for the six months ending April 30 was $181,103.80. The tax paid by the savings banks one year ago for the six months ending April 25, 1891, was $171,188.36. The tax for the six months ending Oct. 31, 1891, was $176,380.05. From these figures it is seen that this semiannual savings-bank tax increased for the first half of this year over that of 1891 by $9,515.53.

Valuations.—The new valuation of the State, as taken by the Valuation Commission in 1890, amounts to $309,096,041, making an increase of $73,117,325 over the valuation of 1880. The Legislature of 1891 made the rate of taxation

2·75 mills, which restores it to where it was previous to 1890, it being found that the rate of 2·25 mills, which prevailed during that year, was insufficient to meet the ordinary expenses. The increase in valuation and rate caused an advance in the State tax of $320,044.73, of which amount $73,117.32 was returned direct to the various towns for the benefit of the common schools, as the amount of mill tax to be apportioned is figured at one mill on each dollar of valuation.

Insurance.—The twenty-fourth annual report of the Insurance Commissioner shows that there are 116 companies authorized to do a fire and marine business in the State. Of these, 29 are Maine companies—2 stock, and the other 27 mutual; 61 are stock companies of other States; 4 are mutual companies of other States; and 22 are companies of foreign countries.

The amount written by the Maine mutual fire insurance companies is a trifle smaller than in 1890. The year 1891 was the hardest on insurance companies in Maine of any since 1886, and the losses paid reached $1,099,574.25, which exceeded the premiums received for that year by $21,608.33.

The fire risks written by foreign licensed companies amounted to $95,961,085.57, the premiums to $1,291,798.98, and the losses paid to $795,-533.07. The fire risks written by Maine mutual companies amounted to $2,680,896.

The whole amount of life business in force at the end of the years 1890 and 1891 that appears of record is as follows:

COMPANIES.	1890.	1891.
Level premium companies .	$29,159,412 74	$31,726,486 05
Industrial policies	1,763,849 00	1,783,974 00
Co-operative companies....	36,406,125 00	43,027,875 00
Total	$67,329,386 74	$76,538,285 05

The taxes paid the State by insurance companies doing business in Maine for the years 1887–'91· and the fees for the several years, appear in the following table:

YEAR.	Fire companies.	Life and accident companies.	Total tax.	Fees.
1887.......	$15,316 23	$7,567 31	$22,883 54	$4,656
1888.......	16,409 13	8,416 04	24,825 17	4,556
1889.......	16,010 20	8,450 97	24,511 17	5,742
1890.......	15,573 06	11,774 05	27,347 11	6,891
1891.......	14,904 02	17,070 80	31,974 82	9,276

Railroads.—The thirty-fourth report of Railroad Commissioners, December, 1892, shows little change in the mileage of the steam railroads in Maine over 1891, the total number of miles now being 1,385 miles, or 208 more miles than in 1891. The gross transportation earnings show a marked and gratifying increase, it being $118,-703.53 over that of 1891.

The number of passengers carried in 1891 was 5,502,646. In 1892 the whole number carried was 6,178,076, being an increase during the year of 675,430.

The freight traffic shows a corresponding increase. The total number of tons of freight carried in 1891 was 3,294,000. The total number of tons carried in 1892 was 3,694,934.

The total passenger-train mileage for the year ending June 30, 1892, was 2,650,062 miles. The number of passengers carried one mile was 126,-267,845, and the number of tons of freight carried one mile was 271,319,359.

The street railroads have gained only 6·62 miles, but the returns show a marked increase of travel over that of 1891.

During the past year the extension of the Portland and Rumford Falls Railway from the village of Gilbertville, in Canton, to Rumford Falls has been completed.

The capital stock of the Georges Valley Railroad has been increased, and the gauge changed to conform to the standard.

The location of 200 miles of the Bangor and Aroostook Railroad was approved by the board in May, and the entire line has been put under contract. This road will extend from Brownville, in Piscataquis County, into and through the county of Aroostook *via* Houlton and Presque Isle and Caribou, with branches from Dyer Brook Plantation or vicinity to Masardis and Ashland; and from Easton to Fort Fairfield—in all about 200 miles.

Steam Vessels.—The report of the steamboat inspectors gives the number of steam vessels on the inland waters of Maine, subject to its control, as 100, of which 83, with an aggregate tonnage of 1,548·14 tons, have been inspected and granted certificates. Licenses have been granted to 98 masters and pilots, and 102 engineers.

Education.—The statistics of the common schools for 1890–'91 include the following: Whole number of children of school age, 210,-997, a decrease of 550 from the number reported the previous year; whole number attending school, 141,433, an increase of 1,757; average registered attendance per term for the year, 122,-766, an increase of 3,622; average daily attendance, 103,062, an increase of 4,698. The average school year was twenty-one weeks, less by seven days than that of the year before; the number of teachers employed was 7,314, of whom 782 were graduates of normal schools; the average wages of male teachers, excluding board, $39.90; and of female teachers, $17.56. The whole number of schools was 4,621. a decrease of 214 since the previous report; 839 of these were graded schools, and 3,782 ungraded; 1,160 of the ungraded schools had classes in studies other than those prescribed by law; 504 towns received free text-books, at a cost to the State of $170.-014. The total current resources were $1,211,-252, and the total current expenditures, $1,163,-968, leaving a balance of $47,284. The total expenditures, of which $109,728 was for new schoolhouses, were $1,485,593, and the amount voted by towns for the ensuing year, $720,661.

The decrease in the number of schools is due to the consolidation of small schools. The number of towns and plantations that have either abolished school districts or organized without district divisions increased during the year from 127 to 142, and 111 school districts were done away with. Free high schools are supported in 228 towns, at a total cost of $147,575, with an aggregate attendance of 15,739. The Farmington Normal School had 120 pupils at the spring term and 28 graduates; that at Castine, 106 pupils and 23 graduates; that at Gorham, 134 pupils and 52 graduates. The Madawaska Training School was continued for thirty-two weeks, with 50 pupils the first term and 59 the second.

The regular annual appropriation for the normal schools is $24,000, and for the training school $1,300; the latter had a special appropriation of $5,000 for a building.

Bowdoin College has been especially fortunate of late. Mrs. Catherine Garcelon, of California, who died near the close of 1891, left it a bequest of $400,000; the Fayerweather bequest amounted to $100,000; the Walker art building is under way; and last June the college received from Mr. Searles, of New York, a laboratory which will be, it is said, superior to any other building of the kind in the country.

Rev. B. L. Whitman, in May, was elected President of Colby University, at Waterville, to succeed Dr. A. W. Small, resigned. A chair of Biblical Literature was created at the last commencement meeting of trustees, and Rev. Dr. G. D. B. Pepper, an ex-president of the university, was elected to the professorship.

Fryeburg Academy celebrated its hundredth anniversary on Aug. 17, in the presence of an immense gathering. The academy was founded by Rev. William Fessenden, a graduate of Harvard College. The first teacher of the school was Paul Langdon, also a Harvard graduate, a son of President Langdon, of Harvard University. In 1792 the Massachusetts Legislature—Maine being then a part of the old Bay State—granted a charter to the academy.

Charities.—During the year ending Nov. 30, 1891, the number of patients under treatment at the State Insane Hospital was 871. Of this number, 128 recovered or were discharged for other reasons, and 70 died. The total amount of expenditures was $187,387.21. The farm and garden earned during the year $3,352.51, and the profits from the board of patients and other sources were $11,561.50. The total net profits were $14,913.01. This amount increases the surplus of the capital stock of the hospital.

The report rendered in 1892 gives the following statistics:

At the beginning of the year, Dec. 1. 1891, there were resident in the hospital 673 patients—355 men, 318 women. Two hundred and sixty-nine have been admitted since—167 men, 102 women; making the whole number under treatment 942, of which 522 are men and 420 women. Of these, there have been discharged 257—165 men and 92 women; leaving at close of year 685—327 men and 328 women.

There has been expended the past year, on repairs and sanitary outlays, $16,510.29.

Prisons.—The number of convicts at the State Prison, Dec. 1, 1890, was 174; during the following year 50 were committed, 47 discharged by expiration of sentence, 7 pardoned, and 2 died, leaving 168 in custody Dec. 1, 1891. Special appropriations to the amount of $11,500 were made for buildings and repairs, steam heating, and sewerage.

The average number of convicts in 1892 was 16 fewer than in 1891. The total expense for the year ending Dec. 1, 1892, was $22,524.11, of which $8,836.97 was for officers' salaries, and $5,188.79 for subsistence. In regard to the labor of the convicts the report of inspectors says:

After a careful study of the existing law restricting the employment of convict labor to 20 per cent. of the convicts in any given industry, we are fully prepared to recommend its repeal. With our present small number of convicts it is impossible to obtain the best results in employing them in so many diversified industries with so large a number of instructors and disciplinarians. No man, however great he may be, can be found for a warden who can attain that degree of proficiency that will enable him to so successfully manage 5 different kinds of business as to obtain the maximum results in each; and in these times of close competition maximum results are necessary in order to run a business without loss. If our manufacturing could be reduced to 2 good industries, they to be selected by the inspectors and warden, far better results would be obtained and at far less expense to the State.

The average number of inmates at the Industrial School for Girls, at Hallowell, was 65, who were maintained at a cost of $9,433.30. The report for 1892 gives the following figures:

The average number during the year has been 62; returned, 75; sent to homes, 15; married, 7; died, 3; positively bad record since leaving school, 35. The whole number received since January, 1875, has been 359. Of these, the number married before majority is 56; after majority, 43; now in home, 85; returned to friends, 25; dismissed as incorrigible, 8; unsuitable, 6; escaped and recovered, 4. The present number in the school is 62.

An inspection of the Boys' Reform School, at Cape Elizabeth, in October, furnished the following information:

There were 96 boys belonging to the school, all in good health and apparently enjoying themselves. At present there are 3 schoolrooms, well equipped with books, maps, charts, blackboards, and all theother paraphernalia of a modern schoolroom. In the mechanical school 12 boys are taught at one time. Their skill in the use of tools and machinery is shown in the repairs on the buildings they have assisted in making, and in the construction of many useful articles needed about the buildings. The library contains 2,000 volumes. The boys are also taught to be farmers as well as mechanics. The farm contains 184 acres.

State Board of Health.—The seventh annual report of this board contains a treatise by the secretary on school hygiene and the construction of schoolhouses. During the year 134 analyses of water have been made, 75 of them samples from wells, 32 from springs, 18 from public water supplies, 6 from proposed water supplies, and 3 from other sources. The circulars published by the board have been issued again and again in editions of from 10,000 to 20,000.

With the beginning of the year 1892, an act to provide for the registration of vital statistics went into effect.

Board of Trade.—At the meeting of the State Board of Trade, in October, it was reported that the State has 37 organized boards of trade, with an aggregate of 2,664 members, and 19 of these organizations belong to the State board. The total resources of the savings banks amounted, in December, 1891, to $53,550,871.47: of this, only $22,471,445.27 was invested in Maine securities and loaned upon Maine collaterals and mortgages; and it is probable that a still larger proportion of private investments are placed outside the State.

Fisheries.—The report of Dr. E. W. Gould, Commissioners of Sea and Shore Fisheries, gives a history of the Lapham bill in Congress, to which so great opposition was developed in Maine. The object of the bill was to transfer the fisheries from State to national control. The principal difficulties the commissioner has found in enforcing the law are: Extent of coast to be protected, lack of marine police boat, lack of funds, and skillful evasions of the law.

The commissioner devotes considerable space in his report to a description of the many devices employed by the fishermen, transportation companies, and others in evading the laws relating to short lobsters. "Some idea of the amount of this contraband shipment may be gained from the fact that there is a record at this office of nearly 54,000 lobsters less than the prescribed length detected during the last two years in transit in the city of Portland and vicinity."

Textile Industries.—From a census bulletin issued in November, it appears that Maine in 1890 had only 106 establishments, compared with 122 in 1880. But with 16 fewer mills than in 1880, the returns for the census year of 1890 show an increase of over $1,000,000 in capital invested, upward of 4,000 more hands employed, more than $2,000,000 increase in wages paid, and an increase of about $4,000,000 in the value of product.

The Lumber Product.—The operations along the Penobscot river are the heaviest in the State, and here 198,000,000 feet of long lumber have been manufactured. This is about two thirds of the output of Maine. From the Penobscot river have been sent 72,000,000 cedar shingles, about 75,000 cedar posts used in foundations, fencing. etc., and 40,000 knees for buildings and piers and for the construction of vessels. The heaviest production of a water mill is 20,000,000 feet, and from a steam mill 28,000,-000 feet. Maine has lost the hemlock trade of New England to Pennsylvania, due to lower rates given by the railroads.

The Columbian Exposition.—The last Legislature appropriated $10,000 for the erection of a State building at the World's Columbian Exposition at Chicago. Early in 1891 Maine secured a fine site for a State building. The plans were approved by the chief of construction, but then it was found that a building such as they represented could not be built for the sum appropriated. Business men took hold of the matter earnestly, and advised that the appropriation be supplemented by subscriptions from people residing in the cities and larger towns of the State, and that the next Legislature be asked to refund such amounts as might be subscribed. Subscriptions were rapidly raised, and the building was well advanced at the time of the opening.

The Passamaquoddy Indians.—Claims have been made in the courts of Maine by the Passamaquoddy Indians, a tribe living on Lewey's Island, that certain rights have been taken from them, and they ask a restoration. The courts have decided against them, and they have appealed to the Governor and Council of Massachusetts, as Maine was a part of that State when the Indian treaty was declared. The tribe desires to have the case taken before the United States Supreme Court and there tried. The rights which they claim have been abridged are the privileges to hunt and fish at all seasons.

The Granite-Workers' Strike.—This began at Hallowell at the close of April, with the quarrymen, and soon extended to the cutters. It resulted not only from disagreements about wages, but also from an order of the New England Granite Manufacturers' Association, to which the Hallowell Granite Works belong, that the members should sign only such bills of prices as should expire on Dec. 31, instead of April 30, as formerly. This was understood to be the principal grievance. The change of dates was insisted upon by the company, but they were understood to be willing to compromise the other matters in dispute, namely, increased pay, change from piece work to day work, and a new classification of their employees. As to the change from May 1 to Jan. 1 as the time for the bills to go into effect, the manufacturers said they believed it would be better for both manufacturers and men to have bills end with the calendar year. The large building jobs always came in about the first of the year, and it handicaps contractors to figure on work with an increase in wages pending and the possibility of a strike in the busiest season.

On the other hand, the men claimed that the proposed change would place them absolutely in the hands of the companies. Under the former arrangement the men were practically masters of the situation, as the busy season begins by the first of May, and the companies must have help. They said that if the bills should begin in January it would be during the dull time, when the companies would as soon as not shut down for several months and when the men most need the work. They claimed that the companies could afford to give better wages, and the old arrangement of dates had proved satisfactory to all concerned for several years.

The Granite Manufacturers' Association of New England is composed of all the firms of any importance in the six States, and its decisions are supreme. The New England Granite Cutters', Paving Cutters' and Quarrymen's Unions are affiliated, and together control over 12,000 men. The Hallowell company employed over 300 men, and had a pay roll of $20,000 a month. A settlement was effected in October. Like those made at other New England quarries, it was on the basis of the Westerly, R. I., agreement, the provisions of which were as follow:

Article I provides that the bill of prices existing before the lockout shall continue until March, 1895, and that three months' notice shall be given before that by either party that shall want a change; and (Article V) that if such notice is not given, the same agreement shall run three years longer. Article II, III, and IV provide a method of arbitration as follows: It is also agreed that any contention which may arise shall be referred to a local board of conciliation, consisting of three referees appointed by each par. Pending such arbitration it is mutually agreed that there shall be no strike, lockout, or suspension of work. Articles VI and VII read as follow: It is hereby mutually agreed that every man shall be allowed to earn his livelihood under the conditions guaranteed him by the Constitution of the United States, and the employers agree not to make any unjust distinction among any of the men who have been in their former employ. It is further agreed that the number of apprentices employed shall not be more than one to every five journeymen. Article VIII gives workmen the right to strike without arbitration, or other formalities, in case the employer fails to pay off at the regular pay days without giving satisfactory reasons.

Prohibition.—The second annual meeting of the People's Prohibitory Enforcement League met at Augusta in February. The address of the president, which had been prepared in consultation with the executive committee, was adopted by the League, and 3,000 copies were ordered to be printed and circulated.

Political.—The People's party held its first State Convention at Gardiner on May 3. The statement of principles included the following:

We demand a safe, sound, and flexible currency which shall be a full legal tender for all debts, public and private, to be controlled exclusively by the National Government without the intervention of private corporations, and issued to the extent of $50 *per capita.*

As a step in the right direction, we demand the free and unlimited coinage of silver.

We demand that all revenues shall be limited to the necessary expenses of the Government.

We demand a graduated income tax.

We demand that Congress shall enact a law that any person, firm, or corporation who employs the labor of foreigners not naturalized, shall pay into the United States Treasury one dollar per day for every day such foreign labor is thus employed, or such sum as shall be equal to the highest average protection given to capital employed in the various industries of this country.

We demand that the Government shall at once take charge of the railroad, telegraph, and telephone systems and manage the same in the interest of the people.

We demand equal suffrage regardless of sex.

We recognize the saloon as the mortal enemy of all the above-named reforms, and therefore demand the strict enforcement of our statute laws, and the enactment of such national laws as may be necessary for its complete and universal overthrow.

Luther C. Bateman was nominated for Governor. Delegates were chosen to the national convention at Omaha, and a State committee.

The Prohibition Party's State Convention met at Bangor on May 4, with 152 delegates present. Delegates to the national convention were selected, and Timothy B. Hussey was nominated for Governor.

The Democrats met in convention on June 6 at Bangor. The subcommittee on platform was in favor of instructing the delegates to vote for the nomination of Mr. Cleveland; but after considerable debate the resolution was modified so as only to recommend his nomination. The general feeling was decidedly against instructing the delegates. The subcommittee's report also declared that bimetallism, the free and unlimited coinage of gold and silver under an international compact to which the commercial nations of the world are parties, is the true monetary system for this country, which properly aspires to be the leading commercial nation of the world; and said, in reference to the prohibitory law:

The pretense at the execution of the prohibitory law in the cities and larger towns is but a criminal farce, debauching the officials, degrading the public morals, and increasing the tippling habits of the people, and its principal uses seem to be to fill the Republican exchequer with enforced contributions and the ballot boxes with coerced Republican votes. As the proper execution of all laws depend upon the support of public opinion, which seems wanting in

this case, we demand that the constitutional provision pertaining to the subject he again submitted to the people, to the end that they may become informed of the present disgraceful condition of the matter, and provide some more efficacious mode to stay the increase of the evil of intemperance.

The platform as finally adopted first recommended the nomination of Grover Cleveland; second, opposed the McKinley tariff law; third, declared for free raw material; fourth, denounced the prohibitory law and called for the resubmission of the constitutional amendment; fifth, opposed the adoption of the proposed constitutional amendment regarding the qualifications of electors; sixth, recommended that election day be made a public holiday; seventh, favored abolishing State constables; eighth, favored repeal of the law making hotels and druggists common nuisances. Charles F. Johnson was nominated for Governor.

The Republican convention, which met at Bangor, on April 27, to choose delegates to the Minneapolis convention, recommended the renomination of President Harrison, but left delegates uninstructed. The convention for nomination of State officers was held in Portland on June 21. Following are extracts from the platform:

In matters touching the affairs of the State, it [the Republican party of Maine] is pledged to a prudent and economical administration; a gradual reduction of the State debt; such adjustment of burdens of taxation as shall impose equal tax upon all property; a pure and carefully guarded elective system; a legislative and executive policy which shall improve the condition and maintain the rights of all people who labor, and by constant effort, both by legislative act and individual example, to develop and improve the natural resources of the State, and to keep the men and money of Maine at home for the benefit of all its people. It sees plainly the great benefit which has come to the people of Maine from their firm belief in the cause of temperance and prohibition, and it will continue unfaltering in its fidelity to this cause.

Henry B. Cleaves was nominated for Governor.

At the State election, Sept. 12, the following vote was cast for Governor: Henry B. Cleaves, 67,585; Charles F. Johnson, 55,073; Timothy B. Hussey, 3,731; Edgar F. Knowlton (Union Labor), 166; Luther C. Bateman, 3,005; Scattering, 17. The two proposed amendments to the Constitution were carried. The one providing that the adjutant-general and the quartermaster-general shall be appointed by the Governor was passed by a vote of 9,721 for, to 9,509 against. The other, providing that "no person shall have the right to vote or be eligible to office, under the Constitution of this State, who shall not be able to read the Constitution in the English language and write his name; provided, however, that the provisions of this amendment shall not apply to any person prevented by a physical disability from complying with its requisitions, nor to any person who now has the right to vote, nor to any person who shall be sixty years of age or upwards at the time this amendment shall take effect," was passed by a vote of 25,775 to 18,061.

The number of Senators elected was 30 Republicans, 1 Democrat; the number of Representatives, 107 Republicans, 44 Democrats.

At the November election the total number of votes cast for Harrison was 62,871; for Cleveland, 48,044; for Weaver, 2,045; for Bidwell, 3,062; Union Labor, 336. Four congressmen were elected, all Republicans.

The working of the new ballot law gave general satisfaction. The cost to the State of the official ballots was about $11,000; the amount estimated by the Secretary and appropriated by the Legislature for the purpose was $7,500.

MANITOBA AND THE NORTHWEST TERRITORIES. The progress of these Territories in accessions of population and in development of industries has been so rapid that it is difficult to waylay the statistics. According to the census returns of 1891, Manitoba had increased her population during the previous decade at the rate of 144·95 per cent.; the Territories, at the rate of 75·33. During the same period British Columbia's increase was at the rate of 97·36 per cent. But since the census was taken, or assumed to have been taken, in the spring of 1891, there has been a rapid and continuous influx of population into Manitoba and the Territories. These new arrivals are almost invariably agriculturists. A large proportion of them are from Europe and the eastern provinces of the Dominion; but it is an indubitable fact that the largest proportion are from the adjacent States. All are making for the vast cereal region of the "Great Fertile Belt" of Canada. It is not possible to say even yet, with anything approaching accuracy, what is the real available extent of that fertile belt; but it is certain that cereal crops, and even good sound wheat, can be successfully grown in the Peace river and Mackenzie river regions, as far north even as the arctic circle. Wheat is the prime demand of the host of immigrants pouring into the Canadian Northwest Territories, but it is not the only crop that receives attention. Other cereals produce good results, as do also root crops, which in quality and productiveness can not be surpassed. Cattle ranching has become a prominent industry, especially in the Territory of Alberta, where flocks and herds have already attained large proportions. The resources of this region are not confined to agricultural products. Its mineral wealth abounds especially in the article of coal, a matter of great moment in a country in which fuel wood is rare. Bituminous coal abounds near the eastern flank of the Rocky mountains, from the United States boundary to the Arctic Sea. Deposits of it are being worked at Sethbridge, and rich deposits of anthracite have been exposed near Banff and elsewhere.

The Northwest Mounted Police comprise a force which has no parallel in America. In one sense they comprise a thoroughly and rigidly drilled body of light cavalry; but they are also the equivalents of mounted infantry. They are in the truest sense policemen, and are an exceedingly active and efficient force, which probably will grow to much larger proportions. The cavalry equipment was essential in such an immense plain and prairie country. where the very people who had especially to be kept in order—the numerous tribes of aborigines, that is—were already skillful horsemen. The Mounted Police force has proved a signal success.

The Canadian Pacific Railway, with its many ramifications, must also, so far as can be judged from appearances, be counted a success; and it seems more especially to pertain to the great Northwest. Its published returns of traffic from week to week indicate a steady increase, although it is unequal to the traffic of certain rival lines so far as the eastern provinces are concerned. The projected line from Winnipeg to Churchill, on Hudson's Bay, seems to be in a state of suspension.

MARYLAND, a Middle Atlantic State, one of the original thirteen, ratified the Constitution April 28, 1788; area, 12,210 square miles. The population, according to each decennial census, was 319,728 in 1790; 341,548 in 1800; 380,546 in 1810; 407,350 in 1820; 447,040 in 1830; 470,-019 in 1840; 583,034 in 1850; 687,049 in 1860; 780,894 in 1870; 934,945 in 1880; and 1,042,390 in 1890. Capital, Annapolis.

Government.—The following were the State officers during the year: Governor, Frank Brown, Democrat; Secretary of State, E. W. Le Compte; Attorney-General, John P. Poe; Comptroller, Marion D. Smith; Treasurer, Spencer C. Jones; Insurance Commissioner, J. F. C. Talbott; State Tax Commissioner, Frank T. Shaw; Adjutant-General, H. Kyd Douglas; Chief Justice, Richard H. Alvey; Superintendent of Public Instruction, E. B. Prettyman.

Finances.—The State debt amounts to $10,-721,642.52. As an offset to this, the State holds bonds and stocks to the amount of $6,845,676.-85, on which the interest or dividends are promptly paid. The net debt therefore is $3,875,965.67.

Valuations.—The following comparative table gives the taxable basis in each county of Maryland and the city of Baltimore for the years 1891 and 1892. This is the assessed value of real and personal property. The total increase of 1892 over 1891 is $5,134,451, of which Baltimore County alone contributes $1,079,179, and Baltimore city, $763,560.

COUNTIES.	1891.	1892.
Allegany	$16,082,934	$16,151,558
Anne Arundel	10,725,814	10,874,049
Baltimore city	276,408,052	277,171,612
Baltimore	39,650,654	41,359,723
Calvert	2,087,800	2,033,209
Caroline	4,381,469	4,351,415
Carroll	15,885,655	15,817,537
Cecil	13,389,101	13,271,949
Charles	3,322,016	3,410,140
Dorchester	6,183,618	6,193,888
Frederick	23,189,041	23,613,030
Garrett	4,124,187	4,261,610
Harford	12,137,015	12,444,109
Howard	7,486,312	7,514,064
Kent	7,759,640	7,788,728
Montgomery	9,951,605	10,425,220
Prince George's	9,005,217	9,188,888
Queen Anne's	7,230,844	7,544,416
St. Mary's	2,881,924	2,718,126
Somerset	4,088,342	4,193,568
Talbot	8,634,056	8,698,294
Washington	17,035,413	17,351,775
Wicomico	4,065,605	4,149,119
Worcester	4,477,273	4,605,481
Total	$510,003,077	$515,187,528

The reassessment bills passed by the Legislature were vetoed by Gov. Brown. In November he issued to the people a call for their views upon the best methods for framing a new measure, declaring that it was clearly the duty of the next Assembly to enact a law upon the subject. This proposition met with much opposition, and the Federation of Labor of Baltimore passed the following:

Resolved, That, inasmuch as Gov. Brown totally ignored organized labor in his appointment of State Labor Statistician, and inasmuch as organized labor was the agency which brought the office into existence, we, the delegates composing organized labor in this federation of all the skilled trades of Baltimore and vicinity, hereby express our disapproval of the action of Gov. Brown by refusing to recognize any document coming from said statistician's office, until Gov. Brown or some other Governor recognizes organized labor by the appointment of one of the labor representatives to occupy the office.

Legislative Session.—In the early days of the session the bill for the repeal of what is known as the Eastern Shore law, in reference to the election of a United States Senator, was the subject of interesting debates. Action on it was somewhat retarded by an attempt to complicate with it the election of Treasurer and police commissioner. Western Shore members were reminded that there were two State officers to be voted for, and that there would be no guarantee as to where the Eastern Shore votes would go if the Western Shore insisted on forcing their position too far. The law now on the statute books has been in force since 1809, and was only broken once, in 1867, when Gov. Swann was elected Senator, and the law was immediately re-enacted. At the time of its passage it was urged, in support of the bill, that the Eastern Shore had one third of the population and 8 of the 19 counties in the State, and the facilities for travel were exceedingly limited. Now the Eastern Shore has but 9 counties and about one sixth of the population of the State, comprising, in fact, but one congressional district, while the Western Shore, in addition to Baltimore City, has 14 counties.

No one questioned that the United States Senate would seat a Senator from Maryland elected regardless of the law, yet, so the advocates of the measure said, as long as it is on the statute book no member of the Legislature would seriously vote for a Western Shore Senator, after taking an oath to support the laws and Constitution of the State. After several readings of the bill it was finally killed, but not until March.

The assessment bill was the most important question under discussion during the sittings of the General Assembly. As no assessments had been made since 1876, the political parties in their resolutions had laid stress upon the necessity for new valuations. Gov. Jackson had vetoed last year the bill then under discussion. The bill introduced early in the session was passed by the House of Delegates almost unanimously at the session of January, 1892, after considerable debate, but it was not acceptable to the Senate. That body adopted a far more stringent bill. When this was presented to the House it was, for some reason, not fully discussed or debated. The exigency of other business, and the unwillingness of the House to adjourn without passing an assessment bill, probably inclined that body to defer to the judgment of the Senate, and it therefore passed the Senate bill. It became at once apparent that the bill thus passed whatever may have been its actual merits, was

not satisfactory to the people, and it was vetoed by the Governor. In announcing his decision the Governor said:

I earnestly hoped that the difficulties in the way of the passage of an acceptable bill would be largely removed by the adoption at our last election of the fifteenth article of our bill of rights. Unfortunately, that amendment was rejected, and the General Assembly was left to deal with the subject. Under the controlling restrictions of that article of the Constitution, on the one hand, it was their duty to obey the constitutional mandate "that every person in this State, or person holding property therein, ought to contribute his portion of public taxes for the support of the Government, according to his actual worth in real and personal property." On the other hand, it was incumbent upon them to pass a bill which, while complying with the imperative provision of the Constitution, would at the same time be reasonably practicable in its operation, fairly free from objectionable details, and likely to remedy existing evils and inconveniences.

A bill to place in the hands of the Governor the right to appoint county school boards with the consent and approval of the Senate was introduced. These boards, to consist of 3 members each, were to be elected for two years. The State Board of Education, represented by 5 members before the Senate and House Committees on Education, made no objection to the measure. While before the committee, the State board also urged additions to the Normal School; provision for the annual holdings of State institutes for teachers; the establishment of school libraries; and the distribution of free books for children, proposing, as a means to procure these books, an addition of 2 cents on the $100 of the school tax fund, all of the direct tax fund to be set aside for the maintenance and improvement of the public schools. The Pearre school bill was disapproved of by them. The discussion of the Toadvin bill in the Senate some weeks later led to one of the most spirited debates of the season. When the two bills, calling for $204,000 to provide free books for the schools, were presented to the Governor, he vetoed them, declaring that the treasury of the State does not admit of such large appropriations at this time, when some provision should be made for creating a sinking fund to extinguish the $4,500,000 of loans that mature within the next ten years.

A measure known as the oyster-planting bill was introduced into the House of Delegates. This contained a proposition to cultivate the barren lands at the bottom of the bay. There were 200,-000 acres of natural bars and 400,000 of barren bottoms, which, under cultivation, would yield 40,000,000 bushels of oysters. It was said that in Connecticut the yield of the cultivated beds was 9 times that of the others. Although there was much favorable comment on this bill, it was finally killed. The experiments being made in the same direction in Virginia would, it was said, destroy the value of those in Maryland. Various other bills relative to the cultivation, protection, and sale of oysters were introduced, and a final compromise was made, by which the two measures were united, the other bills being withdrawn. This measure, known as the general oyster bill, provides for the culling of oysters on their natural beds, and makes it a misdemeanor to have in possession oysters more than 5 per cent. of shells, or small oysters less than 2½ inches in length from hinge to mouth. If the percentage is below that amount the cargo shall be taken by the purchaser, without deducting the percentage of culls. The bill makes it unlawful for any packer, commission merchant, or other person to purchase or receive an improperly culled cargo.

Among the 6 amendments proposed to the election law, and 1 to the legislation law, the most important had for its object the surrounding of the mode of nomination prescribed by the Australian ballot law with greater restrictions than at present exist. The law requires that the signers of nomination papers shall be residents of the ward, county, precinct, or district. but not registered voters. Under this provision there has been much carelessness, minors and nonresidents frequently making up the signatures to nomination papers. In the counties all nomination papers shall be signed by registered voters and accompanied by an affidavit made before a justice of the peace, by some one or more persons known personally to the justice and so certified by him, and signed by the affiant, to the effect that the signers are known to him to be registered voters of the district or precinct in which they reside, and that the affiant personally sign the nomination papers.

In the Senate an unfavorable report of the Finance Committee on a bill to appropriate $2,000 for a State weather service. in conjunction with the United States Weather Bureau and the Johns Hopkins University, was substituted for the bill. The Governor withheld his signature, but finally agreed to compromise. The commissioners agreed to sign a paper, in which they pledged themselves to return half the amount, the Governor consenting to give $2,000, but no more.

Two bills disappeared from the engrossing room. One was the bill providing for the taxation of liquor in bond, and the other was that incorporating the Baltimore, East Baltimore, and North Point Railway Company.

A bill that was passed in the Senate. legislating out of office county collectors, led to the first political division of the session. At the last election Republican county commissioners were chosen, and, according to promise made, Fusion Democratic collectors were appointed. The bill. which was passed, provides that the Treasurer. a regular Democrat, shall hereafter do the collecting.

Other acts of the session were as follow:

The telephone bill.

The law fixing not more than ten hours a day's work for children.

Amending the law relating to the draining of lands.

To provide for the appointment of arbitrators to settle the dispute between Maryland and West Virginia in reference to the boundary line.

Amending the act incorporating the "Baltimore College of Dental Surgery" and increasing its powers.

To cede to the United States jurisdiction over certain lands at or near Antietam battle fields.

To authorize the employment of jail prisoners on the streets and roads in Talbot County.

Repealing the local-option law of Calverton, Baltimore city, and providing for the extension of the high-license laws of Baltimore city to that place.

Appropriating $60,000 for the World's Fair and providing for the appointment of a commission, and for the collection, arrangement, and display of the products of the State of Maryland at the Exposition.

To appropriate the direct tax refunded by Congress to the payment of the outstanding debt of the State.

To authorize the city of Baltimore to issue bonds to the amount of $6,000,000.

To provide for the examination of trust, loan, and fidelity companies' business; to add a section to Article LXVI, in relation to mortgages.

To punish malicious destruction of property.

To protect birds and game in Somerset County.

Punishing minors who get whisky by misrepresentation.

Creating a commission to inquire into the distribution of State school tax.

Appropriation for Destitute Mothers and Infants' Asylum.

Providing punishment for keeping bawdy houses.

Amending the revenue laws of the State.

Providing for the destruction of fruit trees affected with yellows.

Amending the registration laws.

Amending the electric laws.

Regulating the prosecution for cruelty to animals.

To protect game in St. Mary's County.

Regulating the catching of terrapin in Charles, Calvert, and St. Mary's Counties; protecting wild fowl in Anne Arundel County; to protect crabs in the Great Choptank river; to protect fish, crabs, and terrapin in Anne Arundel County.

Agricultural Society appropriation bill.

To close Severn river from oyster taking for two years.

Empowering school commissioners of Frederick County to grant free scholarships to the Normal School.

Amending the primary elections law for Queen Anne's County, making the Australian law apply to them.

Amending the fish law of Queen Anne's County; that of Howard County relating to wild fowl; amending the game laws of Cecil County; also, the Anne Arundel County fish laws; providing for the better protection of fish and wild fowl in Harford County; a Washington County game law; amending the trout-fishing laws in Frederick County; also the game laws of Baltimore County; to amend the law relating to gunning and trespass; to protect brook trout in Baltimore County.

Amending the general election laws in reference to registration.

Reducing the Governor's staff to five generals and ten colonels. Under the new law the adjutant-general is the only one of these appointments that must be confirmed by the Senate.

Protecting a wife's property against the debts of her husband.

Education.—The following distribution of the school tax was made by the Comptroller in June, the distribution being made upon the census of 1890, $118,480.72 to the white and $49,-500 to the colored schools. The White State Normal School received $2,625, the colored $500. In October, distribution being again made upon the census of 1890, $100,000 was given to the white school and $24,500 to the colored. To the white normal school, $2,600.25; colored, $500.

The Association of the State School Commissioners met in November, and discussed "The Apportionment of the State School Tax and the Free School Fund." Every year, it was urged, $125,000 is appropriated for the education of the colored children. When the appropriation is made for the school children of the State, the colored children again get an equal share with the white. Within twenty years some counties have had more than they could use, and now have a surplus. Regrets were expressed at the fact that no appropriation had been made by the World's Fair Commission for the school exhibit at Chicago. A committee to confer with Gov. Brown, asking for $1,000 or $500, was appointed, the counties having no other means of making a school exhibit.

Decision. — Judge Morris, of the United States District Court, handed down an important decision in the case of the United States against Henry F. Buckley, one of the judges of election at the last general State election, touching the right of the United States supervisors to accompany illiterate, blind, or otherwise physically disabled voters into the space provided for the preparation or marking the ballot to be cast by the voter, to assist or overlook such marking. Buckley was charged with obstructing United States Supervisor Henry G. Mohr in the performance of his duty, in refusing to allow the latter to inspect the ballots. Judge Morris decided that the supervisor may, if requested by the voter, accompany the ballot clerks to the booth and scrutinize the marking of the ballot, as to the candidate for representative in Congress, to ascertain if it is properly marked, as the voter has desired; that the supervisor may explain to the illiterate voter that it is his privilege to have their scrutiny, or not, as he chooses; and if the voter is content with the ballot clerks, and does not request the presence of the supervisors, then they shall not interfere, and shall not go to the booth.

The Oyster Industry. — According to the report submitted by the commander of the State fishery force to the State Board of Public Works, the supply of oysters in the State for several years has been decreasing. In 1890 the Legislature passed an act (chapter 602), popularly known as the Culling law, requiring the return of all shells and all small oysters less than two and a half inches in length to the bars when taken. This act, which was intended to secure an annual seed supply, was in force last season for the first time. The present season's supply shows not only that the heretofore steady decrease has been stopped, but at least 30 per cent. to last season's catch has been added.

The World's Fair. — The bill appropriating $50,000 absolutely, and $10,000 contingently, for representation of the State at Chicago in 1893, passed the Senate without trouble, but met with much opposition from the Ways and Means Committee. When the Governor signed it, the appropriation was for $60,000 only. The faculty of Johns Hopkins University prepared for the fair an elaborate handbook giving the history and resources of the State.

Agriculture. — At a meeting of the trustees of the Maryland Agricultural College the following appropriations, aggregating $48,200, were voted: For the Agricultural Experiment Station, $15,000; for support of agricultural and horticultural departments of the college, $2,500; expenses of executing the Fertilizer law, $1,100; for disbursement under the Committee on Education, salaries, etc., of the college, $14,000; Sunday services and special instruction, $2,000; mechanical arts department, $1,500; purchases of equipment to be made for the several college departments, under the supervision of the Committee on Facilities for Instruction, $3,000; instruction of colored youth at the branch of the

college, Princess Anne, one fifth of the Morrill annuity, this share amounting to $3,600; reduction of college debt, cost of repairs and improvements and refurnishing of buildings, and for insurance, taxes, and other administrative expenses, to be applied under the supervision of the Finance Committee, $5,500. The State Farmers' Association in February agreed to petition the Legislature for aid, asking for $5,000 a year, to be divided among all agricultural associations in the State having a paid-up capital stock of $10,000. There are now 7 such organizations in the State. A committee was appointed to draft a bill asking for the appropriation.

Prisons. — According to the annual report of the Penitentiary Board, there were, on Dec. 1, 674 inmates in the institution—white men, 265; white women, 7; colored men, 351; colored women, 51; which was an increase of 41 white men and 17 colored women, and a decrease of 3 white women and 13 colored men from the same time of the preceding year. At the end of last year there were 632 inmates in the institution; 302 were received during the year, and 260 were discharged. The largest number in the institution at one time during the year was 681, and the smallest 609. The cost *per capita* for the year was $119.08. The inmates earned for themselves $10,208.51 from overwork. The expenses of the institution amounted to $77,663.84, of which $35,788.04 was for salaries, and $17,245.20 for provisions.

Political. — The Prohibition party of Maryland, meeting at Baltimore in March, was the first to choose delegates to a national convention, although that convention was the last to be held. Nothing of importance marked the meeting, which was characterized by much unanimity of feeling and general satisfaction. There was discussion as to the mode to be pursued in selection of congressional delegates, but it was decided that each district should name its own.

The Republican State Convention met at Frederick on May 4, electing its delegates to the national convention. In the resolutions firm adhesion to the protection policy was declared, "whereby the American workman is everywhere in his own country a sovereign, with the possibility of owning his own home." Attention was called to the fact that "the misrepresentations of the McKinley bill, by which the Democratic party was enabled to obtain control of the Lower House of Congress, have already been corrected by actual demonstration of its practical workings, and the late elections show that the inevitable reaction of truth against falsehood has set in."

Reciprocity as defined by James G. Blaine, and inaugurated under the administration of President Harrison, was recommended, and the duty of Congress to give the people of the United States an American dollar, whether gold or silver or paper, worth 100 cents, was declared.

A convention of the People's party met at Baltimore in August, to select congressional candidates and presidential electors. Three of the congressional districts—the First, Second, and Fifth—were represented. No nominations were made for the Third, Fourth, and Sixth Districts. In October the chairman of the State committee issued an address to the third-party followers, announcing that the People's party had put up a full electoral ticket for Weaver and Field, and had candidates for Congress in the First, Second, and Fifth Districts. The address laid stress upon the grievances suffered by the farmer at the hands of the Democratic Government, and urged some action for redress against the oppressions of Maryland, since no State in the Union has suffered more from political misrule and unfair legislation. The farmers, having had no voice in the government, had now become tribute bearers to the Commonwealth, farm lands having so depreciated in value that the sheriff is the only man who can make a sale. The present assessment of agricultural property was upon a valuation made nearly twenty years ago—a condition of affairs for which the Democratic party are responsible. Attention was also called to the election laws, whereby at least 5,000 people in the Third, Fourth, and Sixth Congressional Districts were disfranchised.

At the election in November the Democrats carried the State by a plurality of 21,130. The vote was: Cleveland, 113,866; Harrison, 92,736; Bidwell, 5,877.

MASSACHUSETTS, a New England State, one of the original thirteen, ratified the Constitution Feb. 6, 1788; area, 8,315 square miles. The population, according to each decennial census, was 378,787 in 1790; 422,845 in 1800; 472,040 in 1810; 523,159 in 1820; 610,408 in 1830; 737,699 in 1840; 994,514 in 1850; 1,231,066 in 1860; 1,457,-351 in 1870; 1,783,085 in 1880; and 2,238,943 in 1890. Capital, Boston.

Government.—The following were the State officers during the year: Governor, William E. Russell, Democrat; Lieutenant-Governor, William H. Haile, Republican; Secretary of State, William M. Olin, Republican; Treasurer. George A. Marden, Republican; Auditor, John W. Kimball, Republican; Attorney-General, Albert E. Pillsbury, Republican; Railroad Commissioners, Everett A. Stevens, William J. Dale, Jr., appointed on Jan. 6, and John E. Sanford, appointed on Jan. 20, in place of George G. Crocker, resigned; Chief Justice of the Supreme Court, Walbridge A. Field; Associate Justices, John Lathrop, James M. Barker, Charles Allen, Oliver Wendell Holmes, Jr., Marcus P. Knowlton, and James M. Morton.

Finances.—The receipts and payments on account of revenue for 1892 were as follow: Cash in the treasury, Jan. 1, 1892, $5,867,760.97; cash received during the year, $21,204,470.93; payments during the year, $20,634,984.85; cash in the treasury, Jan. 1, 1893, $6,437,247.05.

The nominal funded debt on Dec. 31, 1892, was $29,277,415.55. The actual funded indebtedness on that date, however, was only $23,876,415.55. The difference between the two sums is the amount of the Metropolitan Sewerage loan thus far issued ($4,421,000), and the Armory loan ($980,000), these bonds not being properly a part of the State debt, since the interest and sinking-fund requirements of both are annually taxed on the cities and towns benefited by the loans. To meet the indebtedness, as above stated, there are in the sinking fund $20,077,844.81.

During 1893, $1,150,000 of the Troy and Greenfield loan becomes due, and will be paid from the sinking fund established for that purpose. In 1894 the entire Bounty fund loan, amounting to $8,402,148.90, together with $900,000 of the Danvers Hospital loan, and $300,000 of the Troy and Greenfield loan, will mature, making a total of $9,602,148.90 to be paid during that year.

Valuation.—The total assessed valuation of property in the State for 1892 was $2,333,025,-090, personal estate being assessed at $579,369,-392, and real estate at $1,753,655,698. Included in the assessment were 4,054,273 acres of land, 372,545 dwellings, 185.113 horses, 249,817 neat cattle, 47,092 sheep, and 30,866 swine. Personal estate in Suffolk County, which includes the city of Boston, was valued at $216,570,569, and real estate at $708,920,605. For 1892 a total State tax of $1,750,000 was levied.

Legislative Session.—The regular annual session of the General Court began on Jan. 6, and adjourned on June 17.

Early in the session an act was passed prohibiting railroads from issuing free passes to the Governor. Lieutenant-Governor, any member of the Governor's council, any judge, and any member of the General Court. Such persons were forbidden to solicit, accept, or use passes in any form. By the same act the mileage of each legislator was increased to $2 for every mile of traveling distance from his home to the State House. An act to prevent corrupt practices in elections defines strictly the purposes for which candidates may expend money to secure election, requires every political committee to choose a treasurer who shall keep a true account of all receipts and expenses, forbids such committees to solicit money of candidates, and candidates to pay when solicited, although the latter may make voluntary contributions; and requires all such treasurers, and all persons receiving money for campaign purposes, to file a full sworn statement of receipts and payments with the city or town clerk or Secretary of the Commonwealth, as the case may be, such statements being open to public inspection.

In the interest of labor, it was provided that any person or corporation who shall compel any person to enter into an agreement not to join or become a member of any labor organization, as a condition of such person securing employment or continuing in employment, shall be punished by a fine of not over $100. By another act, no minor under eighteen years, and no woman, shall be employed in any manufacturing or mechanical establishment more than fifty-eight hours a week. The act of 1891 forbidding the imposition of fines for imperfect weaving, which was declared unconstitutional by the State Supreme Court, was repealed, and a substitute was enacted which provides that "the system now or at any time hereafter employed by manufacturers of grading their work shall in no way affect or lessen the wages of a weaver except for imperfections in his own work; and in no case shall the wages of those engaged in weaving be affected by fines or otherwise, unless the imperfections complained of are first exhibited and pointed out to the person or persons whose wages are to be affected; and no fine or fines shall be imposed upon any person for imperfect weaving unless the provisions of this section are first complied with, and the amount of the fines are agreed upon by both parties."

The appointment of persons not residents of the State as special police officers was prohibited. Lotteries were forbidden, and persons in any way connected with or representing them in the State were made liable to a heavy fine or imprisonment.

The registration law was amended and codified, and a commission was appointed to arrange and consolidate the laws relating to elections and to report to the next general court. An elaborate law regulating the construction, maintenance, and inspection of buildings in Boston was adopted.

The towns of Medford and Everett were incorporated under special charters. A general law was also enacted, under which any town of 12,000 inhabitants may become incorporated as a city.

An amendment to the State Constitution, abolishing the property qualification for the office of Governor, which was proposed by the Legislature of 1891, was again approved, and provision was made for its submission to the people at the November election. Another amendment was proposed for the first time, striking out the provision that members of the Legislature shall be paid the expense of traveling to and returning home from its meetings once in every session and no more.

A State tax of $1,750,000 for the year was apportioned among the towns.

The sum of $500,000 was appropriated to build an asylum for the chronic insane at Medfield, and the sum of $75,000 to continue the work of exterminating the gypsy moth.

In aid of the State exhibit for the World's Columbian Exposition, a further sum of $75,000 was granted, making the total appropriation for this purpose $150,000.

Near the close of the session sensational charges of attempted bribery were made by Representatives Morse and Simonds against one Horace K. Osborn, alleged to be a lobbyist. An investigation was ordered and a committee appointed from the House. Mr. Osborn refused to testify before this committee, as he had already been arrested on a criminal charge of bribery, and the committee therefore heard only one side of the case. It rendered a report unfavorable to Osborn, and the latter was debarred from acting as legislative counsel or agent for a limited period. Later in the year, on a trial in the State court and a full hearing, Osborn was acquitted of the charges of bribery.

Other acts of the session were as follow:

Allowing fraternal beneficiary associations of other States paying only disability and death benefits to do business in the State under certain restrictions.

Relating to the packing and branding of nails.

Increasing the salary of the Governor from $5,000 to $8,000.

Authorizing steam railroads to use electricity as a motive power.

Making the marriage of any person act as a revocation of any will theretofore made by such person.

To punish the fraudulent conversion of money or securities deposited with any broker or other person for a specific purpose.

Appropriating $10,000 annually to the Massachusetts State Fireman's Association, for relief of firemen and their widows and families.

To prevent the spread of tuberculosis.

Setting off the town of West Tisbury from the town of Tisbury.

Increasing the bounty for the destruction of seals from $1 to $3.

Authorizing the furnishing of books to the value of $100 to the free libraries of towns whose valuation does not exceed $600,000.

Making the record of instruments affecting the title to land conclusive evidence of delivery.

Amending the employers' liability law.

To provide for the licensing and regulating of boarding houses for infants.

Establishing a commission to improve the highways of the Commonwealth.

To establish a naval brigade to be added to the volunteer militia.

To prevent the fraudulent marking of ballots during and subsequent to elections.

To provide for the removal of obstructions in buildings resorted to for the purpose of unlawful gaming.

Requiring railroad corporations to provide mileage tickets which shall be accepted for passage upon all lines in the Commonwealth.

Dissolving the Rapid Transit Commission.

Education.—The following public-school statistics cover the school year 1891–'92: Number of children between five and fifteen years, 382,956; number of all ages in the schools during the year, 383,217; average attendance, 283,648; teachers employed—men 992, women 9,973; average monthly wages of male teachers, $134.22, female teachers, $46.52; number of public schools, 7,336; average length of school year in months, 8·11. During the year 245 high schools were maintained, with 27,482 pupils in attendance, an increase of 1 school and 1,188 pupils. Evening schools to the number of 255 were supported in 55 cities and towns. The number of teachers employed therein were 1,048; the total number of pupils enrolled, 29,221; and the average attendance, 15,287. The whole amount of money raised by taxation for the support of public schools, including only wages of teachers, fuel, and care of fires and schoolrooms, was $5,578,950.29, a decrease of $128,564.08 for the year. The amount expended for new schoolhouses was $1,916,064.99. The expenditures for schools, exclusive of the sum paid for repairing and erecting schoolhouses, was $6,668,690.93. The total expenditures, including repairs and new schoolhouses, aggregated $9,315,556.55.

The Industrial School for Girls, at Lancaster, on Sept. 30, contained 82 pupils; the Lyman School for Boys, 219; and the Primary School, at Monson (at which neglected and dependent children and those convicted of light offenses are cared for), 271, of whom 206 were boys, 51 girls, and 14 women.

Charities.—The following is a summarized statement of the condition of the State charitable institutions: Danvers Lunatic Hospital, patients on Oct. 1, 1891, 817; admitted during the year ensuing, 387; discharged, 341: remaining Sept. 30, 1892, 863; total expenses, $150,538.07. Northampton Lunatic Hospital, patients on Oct. 1, 1891, 453; admitted, 177; discharged, 141; remaining Sept. 30, 1892, 489: total expenses, $94,249.67. Westborough Insane Hospital, patients on Oct. 1, 1891, 493; admitted, 362; discharged, 311; remaining Sept. 20, 1892, 544; total expenses, $103,135.57. Taunton Lunatic Hospital, patients on Oct. 1, 1891, 680; admitted, 341; discharged, 323; remaining Sept. 30, 1892, 698; total expenses, $121,685.63. Worcester Lunatic Hospital, patients on Oct. 1, 1891, 825; admitted, 630; discharged, 564; remaining Sept. 30, 1892, 891; total expenses, $158,591.62. Worcester Insane Asylum, patients on Oct. 1, 1891, 411; admitted, 88; discharged, 50; remaining Sept. 30, 1892, 449; total expenses, $72,006.35. State Almshouse at Tewksbury, insane department, patients on Oct. 1, 1891, 364; admitted, 83; discharged, 67; remaining Sept. 30, 1892, 380; almshouse department proper, inmates on Oct. 1, 1891, 845; admitted, 2,973; discharged, 2,993; remaining Sept. 30, 1892, 825. State Farm at Bridgewater, inmates on Oct. 1, 1891, 612; admitted, 1,015; discharged, 839; remaining Sept. 30, 1892, 788 (of the latter number 230 are insane persons); total expenses, $80,962.62.

Prisons.—The number of convicts at the State Prison on Oct. 1, 1891, was 615; during the year following 215 convicts were received and 174 discharged, leaving 656 remaining on Sept. 30, 1892. The net cost of supporting the prison during the year was $162,014.19, an increase of $13,526.93 over the previous year. The result of employing the prisoners on industries upon the State account was a loss of $8,724.82 for the year, as against a profit of $10,079.65 for 1891. The total cost of the institution to the State for the year was therefore $170,739.05. At the State Reformatory at Concord there were 812 prisoners on Oct. 1, 1891, 811 were received during the year ensuing, and 736 were discharged, leaving 887 remaining on Sept. 30, 1892. The current expenses of the institution were $171,275.56, from which should be deducted $20,971.33, the profit made upon the labor of prisoners, leaving $150,304.23 as the net cost for the year. The Reformatory Prison for Women contained 248 inmates on Oct. 1, 1891, 267 were received during the year following, and 223 discharged, leaving 292 remaining on Sept. 30, 1892. The expenditures for the year were $69,656.07, and the receipts from labor of prisoners and other sources $13,635.11, making the net cost of the reformatory $56,020.96.

In all the penal institutions of the State, including county prisons and houses of correction, there were 6,068 prisoners on Oct. 1, 1891; 26,256 prisoners were committed during the year following; and 25,916 discharged, leaving 6,408 remaining on Sept. 30, 1892.

Militia.—The maximum strength of the militia allowed by law is 448 officers and 6,007 men. Of this total, there are now on the rolls 412 officers and 5,487 enlisted men. The cost of supporting the militia for the year was $163,372.85.

Political.—A State convention of the Prohibition party met at Worcester on June 2, and nominated Walcott Hamlin for Governor, Edward Kendall for Lieutenant-Governor, Samuel B. Shapleigh for Secretary of State, W. D. Farnham for Treasurer, Alonzo H. Evans for Auditor, and Robert F. Raymond for Attorney-General. In addition to the usual resolutions upon the liquor traffic, the platform contains the following:

We believe the perpetuation of our free American institutions depends largely upon the maintenance of our free public-school system. We denounce all attacks on our public schools, from whatever source, as emanating from a spirit un-American, unpatriotic, and hostile to our institutions and our liberties. We are unalterably opposed to the appropriation of a single dollar from the public treasury for the support of any sectarian schools or other sectarian institutions.

The welfare of our country demands greater restriction upon foreign immigration. We believe it inconsistent to tax goods for the protection of our laborers from the competition of labor abroad, and then to allow this labor free entrance to compete with us at home. We also believe that the priceless boon of American citizenship should be more carefully bestowed on those of foreign birth than heretofore.

The Republicans met in State convention on Sept. 14 at Boston, and nominated Lieut.-Gov. William H. Haile for Governor, and Roger Wolcott for Lieutenant-Governor. Secretary of State Olin, Treasurer Marden, Auditor Kimball, and Attorney-General Pillsbury were renomi-

nated. The platform includes the following declarations:

We oppose the inflation of the currency, either by the use of inconvertible paper money or the free coinage of silver. We take the vote of 3 to 1 by the Democrats in the last Congress in favor of free coinage to be an indication of their party policy, and we believe that policy to be a menace to stability and honesty in national finance. We demand a national currency and a national bankruptcy law. We believe a paper dollar should be as good, an honest debt as collectable, a loan as safe in Alabama as in Massachusetts and throughout the Union. We believe the Democratic policy, as announced in the national party platform, of restoring State bank currency, from which we suffered before the war, and which caused the contents of a man's pocketbook to change in value every time he crossed a State line, to be absurd and dangerous. We believe in the extension and maintenance of the civil-service law, and commend the work of the commission appointed by President Harrison in enforcing that law without fear or favor. We believe in a protective tariff, in levying customs duties not only for revenue but for the encouragement of American industries, and the protection of American wages. We believe the present prosperity of the nation is largely due to the joint operation of the system of protection and reciprocity. To further complete the system, to better protect the wage earners, and preserve the quality of American citizenship, we demand that legal barriers be raised against indiscriminate immigration. We believe in the sanctity of individual franchise; that the hand that holds a legal ballot, whether that hand be black or white, is entitled to all the protection which the law of the nation or the State can afford.

In the State we believe in free public schools, free public libraries, and good public roads. That inasmuch as the State is benefited over and above the advantage accruing to particular municipalities by the establishment and maintenance of these institutions, the assistance of the Commonwealth should be extended to those towns and communities unable to maintain them without burdensome local taxation. We approve existing laws to regulate and repress the legislative lobby, and to insure the conviction and punishment of those who attempt to corrupt the people's representatives; but let us not forget that the best guarantee against the influence of the lobby is to be found in the high character of the men sent to the Legislature. We believe in the maintenance of law and order. We believe in liberal appropriations for the State militia. We believe in the advancement of temperance and the enactment and enforcement of practical temperance legislation.

The Democratic State Convention, held at Boston on Sept. 27, renominated Gov. Russell, and completed the ticket by nominating for Lieutenant-Governor, James B. Carroll; for Secretary of State, Charles S. Hamlin; for Treasurer, James S. Grinnell; for Auditor, Irving B. Sayles; and for Attorney-General. Charles S. Lillery. The following is a part of the platform adopted:

We heartily indorse the tariff plank of the national Democratic platform. Tariff taxation, like all other taxation, should be levied for public purposes only. We demand for the true development of our great industries that raw material shall be admitted free of duty, and we particularly emphasize the necessity of free wool, coal, iron, lumber, and all drugs, dyes, and chemicals used in our manufacturing enterprises.

We believe that public office is a public trust, and we urge the extension of the civil-service rules either by executive action or by legislation, so that the people's employees whose duties are not affected by a change of po   cn   policy can be displaced for cause only and ntitfoá political opinion.

We repeat with renewed emphasis our declaration of last year in favor of the repeal of the dangerous Republican silver act of 1890, and we again denounce this measure as "a menace to the maintenance of a sound and stable currency, threatening to derange values, impair the obligation of contracts, and bring the currency of the country to a purely silver basis."

We believe that, as the circulating note features of the national banking system are becoming obsolete in consequence of the contraction of the basis of circulation, it is necessary that some expedient should be found for the issuance and withdrawal, as the needs of trade may demand, of credit notes, under such form of Federal supervision as may be thought desirable.

Believing in a government of the people, and in the local control of local affairs, we insist that each municipality shall have the entire control of its own concerns without the interference of State officials.

The People's party nominated the following ticket: For Governor, Henry Winn; for Lieutenant-Governor, William J. Shields; for Secretary of State, George Kempton; for Treasurer, Thomas A. Watson; for Auditor, Maurice W. Landers; for Attorney-General, Herbert McIntosh. There was also a Socialist Labor ticket in the field, headed by Squire E. Putney as the candidate for Governor.

At the November election the result was largely in favor of the Republicans, but the great personal popularity of Gov. Russell again won for him a re-election. The Republican electoral ticket was successful, receiving 202,-814 votes to 176,813 votes for the Democratic ticket, 7,539 for the Prohibition ticket, and 3,210 for the People's party. For Governor, Russell received 186,377 votes; Haile, 183,843; Hamlin, 7,067; Winn, 1,976; and Putney, 871. For Lieutenant-Governor the vote was as follows: Wolcott, 180,358 votes; Carroll, 170,121; Kendall, 9,162; Shields, 2,732; Wentworth, 1,351. All the Republican candidates on the State ticket, except the candidate for Governor, were elected by substantial pluralities. Seven of the 8 members chosen to the Executive Council are Republicans. In the congressional districts, 10 Republicans, 2 Democrats, and 1 Independent Democrat were elected, a gain of 4 seats by the Republicans. For members of the Legislature of 1893 the result of the election was as follows: Senate—Republicans 30, Democrats 10; House—Republicans 165, Democrats 74, and 1 tie. The constitutional amendment abolishing the property qualification for the office of Governor was submitted to the people at this election, and was adopted by a vote of 141,321 yeas to 68,045 nays.

METALLURGY. Iron and Steel.—Notwithstanding the study that has been given to the conditions under which carbon combines with iron, it is still doubtful, according to Mr. John Parry, whether true chemical combinations of carbon and iron are formed. It has been alternatively assumed that carbon is with difficulty soluble in iron, and that at low temperatures solution may proceed very slowly. In other words, carbon is not easily dissolved except at high temperatures, and it follows that if highly heated iron fully charged with carbon is cooled, a portion of the carbon must be precipitated in this state, existing simply as foreign matter in the metal, but, on reheating, it may again enter into solution. Low-carbon steels may be regarded as dilute solutions of carbon in iron; pig or cast iron as saturated; and intermediate grades may be termed moderately concentrated solutions. Against this, however, there is a mass of evidence which deserves attention, and can not be ignored. After reviewing a number of facts and statements bearing on this matter, Mr. Parry continues by saying that so far there can be no difficulty in assuming at least the probability of the solution of carbon in iron, and that the physical qualities of the metal are determined by the quantity of carbon in solution, i. e., Akerman's hardening carbon. The facts, on the contrary, appear mainly to indicate that carbon is merely sparingly soluble in iron at temperatures below its fusion point. A more serious objection is that carbon is practically infusible, more especially in the graphite form. How this intractable body so readily interpenetrates iron is a problem not easily solved. The ordinary chemical theory of solution as usually understood does not, however, seem applicable on the whole; but some of the results accruing from the recent development of the gaseous, or rather physical, theory of solution, may be made available for this purpose. The application of the law of osmose renders the conception of the transfer of carbon to iron very easy. This force, exerting probably almost illimitable power in Nature, seems the only one capable of overcoming the inertia of bodies, such, for instance, as that of iron and carbon. The physical theory of solution has hitherto only presumptively herein been applied to the solution of solids in liquids; and it may be asked, Is it applicable to the case of the solution of solids in solids, such as carbon and iron, when heated? To this one can reply with confidence that the absolute solid has no existence. Unless we reject the atomic theory, it is evident that no tangible mass of matter can be termed a solid; it is an agglomeration of atoms. Further, accepting the definition of what is termed an atomic volume—the space occupied or kept free from the access of other matter by the material particle itself, together with its investing sphere of heat—it follows that the atoms must be apart from each other in the so-called solid mass, and the distances between the atoms are probably considerable as compared with the actual volume or size of the atoms themselves. Therefore there can be no difficulty in conceiving that osmotic pressure plays a part in the case of a mass of matter "conventionally termed a solid." It is only a question of degree; the quantity of matter dissolved in a given time is simply a function of the temperature, and, at a low temperature, the effective osmotic pressure in the case of solids seems comparable to that of a liquid evaporating under pressure of its own vapor.

Discussing some features in the properties and behavior of fused alloys of iron which the received theories do not adequately explain, Nature agrees with Prof. Roberts-Austen in suggesting that iron is a compound body, the relations between the constituents of which are so close that they have not been isolated. We have evidence, it says, of the possibility of one element merging into another, as has been supposed by Mr. Crookes, and any one who has studied the periodic law can not fail to see at least the probability that minute variations in the composition of elementary bodies may occur, which, however, can not well be differentiated by our present comparatively coarse analytical methods. Admitting this, or, more correctly, that, as urged by Crookes, an element may have more than one atomic weight, the accepted atomic weight being the mean of these, with the periodic law for our guidance, and also attaching due weight to the relations existing betwixt the weight and volume of the atoms, it would seem that the theory of the formation of homogeneous bodies by fusion is in accordance with the periodic law, etc., governing the genesis of the elements. This is equivalent to saying that a fourth state of combination may be imagined which is not solution of one metal in another, or chemical combination of bodies, or intermixture of bodies. We may even assume that the fourth state indicates a species of combination even more intimate than the chemical combination of the chemists. Many of our most eminent metallurgists and men of science have, "by different modes of investigation," come to the conclusion that iron itself is a very complex compound body. It is true that we have merely indirect proof of this, but it only remains to find methods of isolating these bodies from one another.

Several forges of the Catalan type are still operated in Mexico. Four of them, according to Mr. E. V. Wilkes, are at Oajaca—forges of the most primitive Catalan type, using a water blast and hammers of a crude form. The master workmen are brought from Catalonia, Spain. The forges are each equipped with 2 or 3 fires and from 1 to 3 hammers, and have an annual capacity of from 300 to 400 tons of bar iron. The ore used at 2 of the forges is a 55 per cent. hematite, with which about 250 bushels of charcoal are used in producing a ton of iron. At the other 2 forges, magnetic ore containing about 70 per cent. of iron and hematite ore containing 50 per cent. are used, with a consumption of 200 bushels of charcoal to the ton of iron.

In the Lebedieff direct process for producing iron and other metals from their ores the metallic oxides are brought in contact with a strong base (potash, soda, lime, or dolomite), by either melting the two in a finely divided state, or by roasting such mixture in furnaces, provided with a powerful air blast, with frequent stirring of the mass. To hasten the process, common salt or niter may be added to the roasted mixture. Some combinations of metallic oxides with alkalies may be produced by the wet process—for example, alkaline aluminates. Abstracting the pure metals may then proceed in cupolas, open hearths, or in crucibles in reverberatory furnaces. To the mixture prepared as above are added charcoal, coke, etc., as well as a proper amount of siliceous materials to produce slag upon the reduction of the metals. In the reduction of iron and other metals easily separated by coal, etc., gas, under proper pressure, containing a sufficient amount of CO_2, H. or C_4H_4. may be used instead of coal, etc. After properly heating the furnace, the carefully mixed oxides and bases, or the oxides treated with bases, are introduced and heated until thoroughly melted, when the reducing gases are allowed to penetrate the mass. In proportion to the relative reduction of the metal and separation of the bases, a further thin layer

of oxides is added. These latter combine readily with the free base and melt, and the gas then again reduces the metal, the base is again separated, and thus the process continues.

The Ehrenwerth process for producing fluid iron direct from the ore depends upon the fact that carboniferous iron reacts in the highly heated liquid condition on liquid ferriferous slag and melted iron in such a manner that by the carbon contained in the metal iron is reduced from the slag and then unites with the metal already obtained. The process continues till the carbon of the reducing metal is exhausted. On the other hand. fluid iron readily takes up carbon again, and is saturated therewith, according to the temperature, up to nearly 5 per cent. It is thus possible to render decarbonized metal immediately rich again in carbon. As this carboniferous metal is now capable of extracting iron from the ores. it is clear that by repetition of the process of the reaction of liquid carboniferous metal on fluid ores and the recarbonizing of the decarbonized metal, any desired quantity of iron in the liquid condition, as ingot iron or ingot steel, can be obtained direct. In order to carry out this process there is necessary, however, a preliminary—if possible, highly carbonized—metal bath. To promote the rapid issue of the process, very high temperatures are necessary.

In the Middlesborough district, England, according to Thomas Turner, about 63 hundredweight of raw stone are needed to yield a ton of iron. The stone being calcined before it is put into the furnace, is reduced to about 48 hundredweight. In addition to this roasted iron ore, about 12 hundredweight of limestone is added to act as a flux, while about a ton of coke is used as fuel. No less than 5 tons of atmospheric air are required to burn this fuel. and this has to be previously heated to redness. The product of the action of the blast furnace, in addition to the ton of iron, is about 1½ ton of slag and 6½ tons of waste gases. The blast furnace is the most economical apparatus, from a thermal point of view, that we possess. It was formerly thought that the ore was reduced by the direct action of the fuel; but a more careful investigation has shown the great importance of the furnace gases, and it is recognized that, in order to get complete reduction of the ore in a coke furnace, the proportion of carbonic dioxide in the waste gases should not exceed about 12 per cent. When charcoal is used as the fuel a large proportion of carbonic dioxide may be permitted.

Investigation as to the cause of the production of colors in tempering iron shows it to be due to the formation of thin films of oxide on the surface of the metal when it is heated in the presence of air. It also appears from recent researches that the oxide so produced is practically transparent, first, because the sequence of colors is what would be expected in films of a transparent substance when the thickness of the films gradually increases; also, because of observations on the reflected light, the color of which varies somewhat at different angles; but chiefly because it is found that on increasing the temperature a little above the point necessary to produce a dark blue color gradually disappears, and the surface, though covered with more oxide, becomes almost colorless again. The colors being the result of oxidation, it is probable that the nature of the surface to be heated, its freedom from any soiling, and the length of time during which it is heated, must exert a considerable influence on the shade produced.

The apparatus of Henry II. Eames for the extraction of iron consists of an endless belt or band which has along its surface a series of conducting strips, and which is made by means of a series of rollers above and below it to assume an undulating, corrugated, or serpentine form. This band is placed in an inclined position, so that the ores dropped upon it travel naturally upon an inclined corrugated plane. Means are provided for imparting to the strips upon the band, or passing through it, an electric current. The ores or gangues are dropped upon this corrugated band. The current passing through the conducting strips crossing the same causes the particles of iron on the band to attach themselves to the conducting strips. At the same time a stream of water is directed upon the band, which, being inclined, flows in the direction opposite to that in which the band is traveling, and washes back the particles of gold or copper or other metal composing the gangue or sponges, which do not adhere to the metal strips, and continue to flow back until they are washed off from the lower end of the band into a receptacle placed there to catch them. The iron particles adhere to the strips and travel with them to the other end of the apparatus, when the circuit passing through them is broken, and the iron particles fall.

Under the title of special steels, M. Louis Campredon includes all castings obtained from steels that derive their special characteristic properties, ofter, very remarkable, from the presence of an additional foreign substance. Among those best known and which have been found highly serviceable are manganese steel, chrome steel, aluminum steel, tungsten steel, copper steel, silicon steel, nickel steel, etc. Manganese steel is very fluid, and yields excellent castings without blowholes. While the resistance is not very high in the simply cast metal, it is imparted in a very high degree by forging. When cold, this steel is very hard, and can be worked only in the mill, a quality which has stood in the way of its introduction for many uses for which it would be valuable—as in agricultural machines, wagon wheels, horseshoes, rotary axles, and generally for all pieces exposed to wear by friction or to rupture by impact. Aluminum steel is sound, resisting, and elastic. It only requires flame annealing, when ordinary steel would require an oxide annealing. Chrome steels are employed in the manufacture of the hardest projectiles intended to penetrate the thickest armor plates. Nickel promotes the casting of special steels which resist well the impact of projectiles, even chrome-steel projectiles. Among the improvements that have been made and difficulties overcome during the past forty years in the manufacture of cast steel, the author mentions the adoption of a sufficiently refractory and plastic mixture, answering the double purpose of obtaining clean castings with an easily formed mold; production of a fluid metal yielding castings free from blow-holes; obtaining an annealing sufficient to assure to the steel

castings perfect homogeneity of grain; bettering the quality of the metal until it becomes equal to that of forged steel; preparation of alloys or special combinations to meet certain specified requirements. With crucible-steel apparatus light castings are generally obtained for the manufacture of pieces which must possess great resistance. The bulk of pieces of considerable or average weight are cast with Martin-Siemens steel, the manufacture of which has become regular and reliable. In casting marine propellers in one piece, serious difficulties are met with from the unevenness of the contraction, which is liable to cause rupture during cooling. To obviate this inconvenience, the mold which contains the pattern of the propeller is placed in a furnace maintained at the same temperature, and the screw is cast in the same furnace in which it is annealed. The small converter is an intermediary apparatus between the crucible and the Martin furnace, suitable for casting pieces too heavy for the former and rather too light for the latter. In brief, the studies of engineers and chemists, as also the researches of steel manufacturers, have resulted in the production of steel castings capable of advantageously replacing the iron castings hitherto employed.

An examination of manganese steel (10·6 to 12·3 per cent. manganese), made by Mr. Tetskichi Mukan, with a view to discovering the reason of the remarkable toughening which sudden cooling produces in the metal, enabled him to determine the following properties of the substance: The specific gravity of manganese steel in the suddenly cooled state is apparently greater than that of the slowly cooled steel, while the opposite, in general, holds good of other metals; the hardness of the suddenly cooled specimen is greater than that of the slowly cooled, just as in the case of common steel. The hardness is, according to the author, apparently conferred by the hardening carbon; the content of cement or nonhardening carbon is rather large in manganese steel. This, perhaps, is partly due to the large proportion of manganese present. It is the function of manganese to increase the proportion of the so-called chemically combined carbon. Manganese, however, besides doing this, favors the retention of the carbon in the condition of cement or nonhardening carbon. The characteristic features of the structure of manganese steel are the parallel dark plates on its surfaces, which are surrounded by the mother mass. These appearances are often observed in iron rich in manganese. It is clearly seen under the microscope that the grains of the suddenly cooled manganese are larger than those of the slowly cooled. The ductility and malleability of suddenly cooled manganese steel can not be attributed to the condition of carbon, for the carbon behaves as in common steel.

In the discussion of a paper on chrome steel, by Mr. Hadfield, at the Iron and Steel Institute, Prof. Roberts-Austen pointed out that the author's researches supported the views taken by himself and Osmonds as to the dual form in which iron exists. This appeared in the diagrams showing the rate of cooling, which accompanied the report. In these, when the cooling was from a high temperature, 1,320° C., the curve was continuous throughout; but when the cooling was from about 1,000°, a point of recovery was observed, indicating recalescence. The speaker said he had arrived at the same results, working independently. Mr Vickers remarked upon the difficulty of deciding whether the effects noted were due to carbon or chromium, as it seemed impossible to separate the one from the other, the chromium invariably disappearing with the carbon. Mr. F. W. Webb, engineer of the London and Northwestern Railway, gave high praise to chromium steel, saying he used it entirely for springs, and also with advantage for tires. He also found it an excellent material for tool steel.

The high-carbon nickelized-steel armor plate, which has been commended by the United States naval authorities in the highest terms, and has been adopted as the special protection for American ships of war, has endured the tests to which it was subjected by the British Admiralty with great success. The accuracy of the American reports was completely verified by the results of the firing. The most remarkable feature of the trial was the fact that the plate withstood the punishment so well that not a crack was produced.

Bessemer steel for being drawn into wire should not be too highly charged with carbon, and should contain a sufficiency of manganese. The rods are dipped for a half hour in sulphuric-acid solution, and then kept wet till a dark-green, slimy coating, turning brown, is formed on them. They are then dipped quickly in lime water, after which, the ends being pointed, they are ready to be drawn. Reducing the wire too much before annealing causes crystallization, and the wire continues brittle and hard after annealing. In the liquor-bright process for making fine wire the rods are dipped twice in sulphuric acid heated to not more than 130°, and dried between the dippings in the baking oven till a red oxide is formed upon them. Animal fat or grease is employed as a lubricant.

A new steel-hardening process by G. H. Blake has stood the severest tests at the Washington Navy Yard. Cutting tools made of steel hardened by it showed a keenness and tenacity of edge in cutting iron that left nothing to be desired. The most important test was made with a low-priced steel which had been rejected as useless, because it would not stand continuous use. Tools of it hardened by Mr. Blake, subjected to the same conditions, worked nearly nine hours without grinding.

Aluminum.—By means of the electrolytic methods of preparation, an enormous reduction has been achieved in the cost of producing aluminum, particularly at the works in Neuhausen, Switzerland, which are run by water power, so that a metal of 99 per cent. guaranteed purity is obtainable there, according to G. L. Addenbrooke, at 2 shillings, or about 50 cents, or even less, per pound. Alfred E. Hunt, of the Pittsburg Reduction Company, which has made a good many tons of the metal of 99·80 per cent. purity, asserts that by the Hall process it will be possible within the next few years to produce aluminum at a cost of between 18 and 20 cents per pound. In this process there is practically no waste. Most of the aluminum now manufactured is made by

the process of Mr. Hall, of Pittsburg, or by that of M. Heroult, which is employed at Neuhausen. In both cases the reduction is made from the oxide. This is dissolved in a fused flux, consisting of fluorides of aluminum and sodium, and is heated in electric furnaces with carbon anodes. Decomposition takes place at a full red heat, the alumina is resolved into its elements, the oxygen partly uniting with the carbon to form carbonic oxide, and partly escaping free, while the aluminum sinks to the bottom and gradually accumulates. The working quality of the metal manufactured has greatly improved within the last ten years by the reduction of the proportions of iron and silicon, the chief impurities contained in it. The pure metal is rather softer than copper, and behaves in the same way, showing a tendency to pull and tear and clog the tools; it does not cast quite so well, and is not so hard and strong as when it contains from 2 to 3 per cent. of silicon, though then its malleability is decreased, and it has a scratchy, sandy feel. The addition of iron is detrimental. Copper hardens the metal when added up to 5 or 6 per cent., beyond which brittleness is produced; but Mr. Addenbrooke's experiments in remelting the alloy have not given favorable results. According to Mr. Addenbrooke, zinc hardens aluminum and toughens it when added to the extent of 3 or 4 per cent., but the alloy is not clean, is difficult to turn, and does not stand remelting well. Tin, up to 3 or 4 per cent., makes the aluminum short, but improves its turning qualities; if 10 per cent is added, the bar is at first as pliable as the pure metal, and of about the same strength; but if this metal is once or twice remelted it soon becomes crystalline. Nickel has much the same effect, but when added to copper it produces a closer grain, though still leaving a bad surface under the tool. The chief difficulty in casting aluminum, and many of its alloys, arises from the brittleness it acquires by frequent remelting. An alloy of aluminum (23 per cent.) and gold discovered by Prof. Roberts-Austen has a crystalline structure and a very beautiful rose-pink color, very different from anything that has been observed in metal before. Of alloys of aluminum in general, it may be said that they decrease its malleability. The purer the metal the better for rolling or drawing. Sheets of aluminum cold rolled become very hard and quite springy, with a rigidity greater than that of ordinary brass sheets, will still stand a fair amount of bending, and can quickly be made soft by annealing. Aluminum lends itself readily to stamping and spinning. It is very little affected by sea water.

Herr G. Rupp, in his experiments to determine the adaptability of aluminum to the manufacture of domestic utensils, used both drawn vessels of aluminum and aluminum plate 1 millimetre in thickness. The vessels, having been carefully cleaned, dried, and weighed, were supplied with the aliments experimented upon, and left for periods of from four to twenty-eight days, with daily stirrings and shakings. Then the contents of the vessels were examined for the amount of aluminum that had gone into solution, and cleaned, dried, and weighed again. The experiments were conducted with white wine and red wine, beer, cherry-water, cognac, coffee. tea, milk, butter, honey, prepared fruits, potable water, 1 per cent. tartaric acid, acetic acid, 5 per cent. boracic acid, carbolic acid and salicylic acid, and 1 per cent. soda solution. According to the collected results, the action of the substances on the aluminum articles was so very insignificant as to leave hardly any question as to the insolubility of aluminum in contact with alimentary substances. The experiments of Herren Lubbert and Roscher, which led to opposite results, were conducted with leaf aluminum, which has some different qualities from solid aluminum. While the metal in a finely divided condition—leaf aluminum—oxidizes in boiling under development of hydrogen, solid aluminum under the same conditions remains unaltered. But aluminum vessels are not adapted to contact with alkaline fluids.

The use of aluminum tokens as a substitute for the £1 Bank of England notes which it is proposed to issue is suggested by Sir Henry Bessemer. After mentioning the advantages of a hard. permanent substance over a perishable material for such purpose, the author speaks of its extreme lightness as a recommendation, making it possible to distinguish it from any other coin, even in the dark, and as effectually preventing its imitation in plated base metal like lead and pewter alloys.

Mr. Alfred E. Hunt names as among the properties of aluminum which will probably give it the most availability in the arts its relative lightness, its nontarnishing quality as compared with many other metals, its extreme malleability, its easy casting qualities, its influence in various alloys, its high tensile strength and elasticity when weight for weight of it is compared with other metals, and its high specific heat and heat conductivity. He regards the experiments on the ground of which it has been declared not suitable for certain domestic uses not satisfactory, because the tests to which it has been subjected in them never occur in practical housekeeping, while other metals that have been long in domestic use without suspicion suffer as badly, or worse, than it, under such tests; and however much it may be acted upon, it never forms a poisonous compound.

Gold and Silver.—The principal distinction of the matte-smelting process for the extraction of gold and silver from their ores is, according to Herbert Lang, of Mineral, Idaho, that it is pre-eminently suited for the treatment of base ore, particularly sulphureted varieties, and, generally speaking, all such ores as are, or were, classified as refractory or rebellious. Nothing is too difficult for matte smelting, and such substances as sulphur, antimony, arsenic, etc., which give great trouble in other modes of treatment, are of no detriment, and sometimes of great use, in the process. The valuable metals that can be extracted by matte smelting are gold, silver, platinum, copper, nickel, cobalt, and, less perfectly, lead. A large number of the "rare" metals also come down. The percentage saved is rarely less than 90, and is usually somewhat more. Two substances, the slag and the matte, are formed in matting. The latter contains the valuable metals united in a homogeneous mass, with sulphur and with more or less iron. lead, etc.. according to the composition of the ore. The slag

contains silica united with various oxides of the ore, or flux, principally oxide of iron or manganese, which we do not want to save. The simplest ore or mixture of ores that we could treat in a blast furnace would have to contain, besides the valuable metal to be extracted, sulphur, oxide of iron, and silica. Some of the iron would be reduced in the furnace, and would then join the sulphur and form the matte, taking down the values. The remaining oxide of iron would combine with the silica and form slag. Arsenic and antimony serve the same purpose as sulphur, and manganese acts the same as iron ; so neither iron nor sulphur is indispensable, though practically they are both present and perform, with silica, the most important part in the reactions. It is evident that the matting process has a great range of adaptability. Almost every combustible can be used in it. No ore or complication of ores is too difficult for it; and, furthermore, we are not obliged to expend any time or money to find out how to work any proposed combination; a simple chemical analysis of the ore will tell us. Leaching, while it is a failure as applied to raw silver ore, is a useful auxiliary in matte smelting.

The Bartlett zinc-lead process of treating silver ores is based on the fact that when ores containing silver and zinc are burned in the presence of sulphur, the zinc is volatilized, and takes out a small part of the silver with it. Two methods of treating the ores are adopted, according to the amount of zinc and gangue they contain. In the first method, the ores containing stronger proportions of zinc are mixed with hydrocarbon, sulphur is added till a proper proportion is obtained, and the whole is burned in the presence of an air blast and with free air above to prevent with the hydrocarbon flame the formation of sulphuric acid. The zinc and lead are volatilized, and pass off as a fume, leaving the silver and nonvolatile metals. In the second method, for ores less rich in zinc, the ore is continuously charged, without previous burning, in a thin layer, into a special furnace.

An electrolytic process for the decomposition of common salt and its conversion into chlorine gas and caustic soda, applied by Mr. James Greenwood to the manufacture of soda and bleaching powder, is also capable of application to the production of sodium amalgam and chlorine for the extraction of gold and other metals.

The new process of Arcas silver plating is performed with an alloy of silver and cadmium. The preparatory steps are the same as for ordinary silver plating, and the only essential differences in the process are in the alloy and the use of certain chemicals which are employed in the baths. The new alloy is said by those who have used it to wear well. to show greater resistance than ordinary silver-plating material to abrasion, and to resist tarnishing better. It is, moreover, said to be 10 per cent. cheaper than the old process. The superiority of cadmium over copper in an alloy with silver suggests a wider application of it than in this process. The alloy appears to be suitable for use in manufacturing processes requiring stamping, rolling, easting, or engraving, and in coining.

Copper.—As shown by Mr. G. C. V. Holmes, the manufacture of copper goods by electrical methods is beginning to excite considerable attention in the engineering world, because of the extraordinary facility with which such articles as sheets, tubes, rollers, wire, and tape for electric-lighting and telegraphic purposes can be produced in one operation, and of qualities hitherto unattainable. When an anode is composed of a mixture or an alloy of several metals, and the electric current is passed through, the various compound metals are not, as a rule, oxidized and dissolved simultaneously. They are attacked in a certain order, depending upon the energy which they develop when combining with oxygen, and dissolved in the acid of the solution. The metal which is attacked first is that which by its oxidation creates the greatest energy, or which, if used as one of the elements of a primary battery, would develop the highest electromotive force; and so on in regular order. In deposition the reverse order prevails, and the metal is first deposited, the separation of which from the solution requires the least amount of energy. The list of the principal metals found in combination with copper includes, in the order in which they would be dissolved in the electrolytic process, manganese, zinc, iron, tin, cadmium, cobalt, nickel, lead, arsenic, bismuth, antimony (copper), silver, gold; copper having only silver and gold below it. The order in which they are deposited may be found by reading the list backward. The facility with which copper can be refined is due to its low place in the list; for under the ordinary circumstances of deposition the silver and gold do not oxidize and dissolve in the electrolyte, but fall to the bottom of the bath. The copper, though chemically pure, is of a crystalline character, and possesses but little cohesive strength. It is therefore, in its deposited condition, unsuitable for the manufacture of goods. Numerous experiments have been made for securing the deposition of copper in a tough, dense, and reguline condition at the same time that it is being refined. Practical success has been attained by the process of the Messrs. Elmore of continuously burnishing the copper while it is being deposited without removing the cathode from the bath. A mandrel of iron, or preferably of copper, is mounted on insulated bearings in the tank or bath, and a burnisher consisting of a small prism of agate is caused to travel, like the cutting tool in a lathe, along the surface of the mandrel in a direction parallel to its axis. While the current is passing the mandrel is caused to revolve. As the copper is deposited on the revolving mandrel the burnisher presses with even but gentle force on the surface, and breaks down the crystalline formation, converting the deposit into a dense reguline metal of greater specific gravity than ordinary sheet copper. Although the copper is deposited in this process in the form of a tube, the product is applicable for a considerable variety of purposes. Besides articles of a circular section, sheet copper, tape for electric lighting, pots and pans of circular section and with flat or curved bottoms, cartridge cases for heavy and quick-firing guns, and high-conductivity wire, can be produced by simply cutting and drawing without melting the metal. The ingenious device of severing the continuity of the metal at different thicknesses of the deposit,

either by oxidizing the surface or by interrupting or reversing the current, makes it possible to produce several sheets upon a single mandrel from the tank.

Considerable advances have been made during the past three years in reverberatory practice for smelting copper. Furnaces have been enlarged, better methods have been adopted for the removal of the slag, and decided improvements have been made in other directions. The greatest obligations for such service are due, according to E. D. Peters, in his "Modern Copper Smelting," to Mr. Richard Peters, of the Boston and Colorado Works, at Argo, Colorado. By means of them the capacity of the reverberators has been increased from 10 tons to more than 28 tons a day. The improvements involve the consumption of more fuel than was used in the old furnaces, but the increase is considerably less in proportion than the gain in capacity.

Ferdinand Allard's method of tempering copper has borne well the tests to which it has been subjected by the British Admiralty. Officers of the Canadian militia, including Major-General Herbert, having examined cutting tools made by it, have expressed surprise at the fine edge and hardness attained in them. The Lords of the Admiralty in England manifested great satisfaction at the results of the experiments conducted with the trial sheets which the inventor sent over to them. At the Canadian rifle ranges a bullet fired from a distance of 40 yards was shattered into fragments by its impact with the hardened copper. Another bullet was flattened and remained imbedded in the sheet, 1¾ lines in thickness, which it merely indented a trifle, without causing any cracking.

An electrolytic direct process for the reduction of copper and silver ores, introduced by Dr. Höpfner, is highly spoken of. The fundamental principle of it is the use of chlorine. A solution of protochloride of copper, mixed with chloride of calcium or chloride of sodium, is subjected to the action of the electric current. Besides obtaining the metal electrolytically, a lixivium is produced which is capable of lixiviating copper, silver, bismuth, etc., from sulphur ores, and, on its return to the precipitation apparatus, is again ready to precipitate metal and produce lixiviations.

The characteristic feature of the Siemens and Halske copper process is the use of a liquid which dissolves the copper contained in the ore, and gives it up when subjected to the electric current, whereby its solvent capacity is restored, so that the same liquid may be used indefinitely. The solvent agent employed is ferric sulphate, which is partially reduced to the ferrous salt, with an equivalent production of cupric sulphate. By electrolyzing the copper, salt alone is decomposed, and the ferric sulphate is renewed.

T. D. Bottome's process for producing refined-copper castings, having all the properties of tough fibrous copper of high specific gravity and free from blowholes or other defects inherent in ordinary cast copper, depends on the introduction of metallic sodium or other alkali metal into molten copper. By this the dissolved gases are eliminated, and the copper has a certain degree of hardness imparted to it.

Alloys.—Manganine is the name of a new alloy, consisting of copper, nickel, and manganese, which has been put upon the markets as a medium of great resisting power, its specific resistance being higher than that of nickeline, which has hitherto passed as the best resisting metal. It has another advantage in its behavior under variations of temperature, its resistance, it is claimed, being affected only in a minute degree by high temperatures. It is therefore adapted for the manufacture of measuring instruments and electrical apparatus in general, which are required to vary their resistance as little as possible under different degrees of heat.

Specimens of brass made by Prof. W. Spring by compression of the constituents at ordinary temperature, were recently exhibited by Herr Behrens at the Amsterdam Royal Academy of Science. A reddish specimen had been produced by compressing nine parts of copper and one of zinc; a pale-yellow one by compressing a mixture of seven parts copper and three parts zinc. Both had been filed up twice, and again consolidated by pressure. The reddish metal was a little softer than common cast brass: it could be somewhat flattened under the hammer. The yellow metal was harder than common brass, and brittle. Both varieties contained much of a yellow alloy, amorphous, finely granular, and without the crystallites characteristic of copper alloys obtained by fusion; angular fragments of red copper, with yellow threads between the red lumps and strands; and some zinc, angular fragments, and threads, trending outward and uniting near the curved surface of the cylindrical specimens. The metal is nearly, but not wholly, compact. Much evidence exists of a flow in the yellow alloy in the zinc, but nothing points to a truly liquid state in the alloy or one of its components.

The Société de Ferro-Nickel, of France, has succeeded in obtaining a nickel iron and steel containing a large percentage of nickel, and having the remarkable properties in nonoxidizability, brightness, etc., of that metal, and susceptible of being substituted for it in a large number of ores. A category of metals is formed below 25 per cent. of nickel which possess new properties, constituting them a special class of peculiar interest. We have no longer alloys of a somewhat high price, capable, on account of their richness in nickel, of replacing the pure metal, but metals comparable to iron and steel, in which the intervention of even a small proportion of nickel modifies the constitution without materially increasing the cost, and gives the iron and steel remarkable improvement of quality. In the process, manganese and aluminum are simultaneously employed with or without the addition of carbon, and the nickel is introduced either pure or as malleableized metal, or as crude metal more or less rich in nickel. The resultant alloys possess a more perfect homogeneity than iron or steel, and consequently have the qualities of malleability, ductility, tenacity, and elasticity to a superior degree. The tempering qualities improve as the nickel diminishes, till at 7·5 and 8 per cent., and below, alloys are obtained capable of being tempered according to laws analogous to those that govern the tempering of ordinary kinds of steel.

In the method described by M. Mouchel for alloying pure copper with magnesium, the copper is melted with magnesium or with materials capable of producing it by chemical reaction—the main point being that at the end the copper shall contain magnesium—and the resultant metal is treated by the usual methods according to the application proposed. The addition of magnesium to copper imparts to it considerable tenacity and a certain hardness without altering its other properties, and makes it especially suitable for telegraph or telephone wires.

Magnesium has been found to have great value for blending with other metals, when it cleanses the metal with which it is blended from impurities. It has been added to copper for this purpose with very satisfactory results, and is now used by a German establishment for addition to German silver, brass, and nickel.

Processes.—The discovery is reported from Westphalia, Germany, of a process of manufacturing pig iron by the simultaneous application of the electric current and the use of an easily made acid for the extraction of the iron from the ore. The process is said to be 80 per cent. cheaper than the present blast-furnace method.

A process is described by E. Saniter for removing sulphur from iron by means of calcium chloride and lime. The experiments went to prove that lime alone removes a considerable quantity of sulphur from iron if the contact is sufficiently prolonged; and, further, that a mixture of calcium chloride and lime eliminates the sulphur in half an hour.

In M. Faure's new method of decorating cast iron the entire surface of the piece is enameled with any required shade; the casting is then passed to the file wheel, which removes the enamel from the relief portions, and afterward to the burnisher, which polishes the reliefs. The article is then taken to the nickel, copper, or other metallic bath, from which the metallic deposit adheres only to the burnished surfaces. A casting is thus obtained with the indentations enameled and the reliefs metal plated, or simply polished. Other decorative effects may be obtained by bronzing the article after enameling, or by enameling and glazing the object, repassing it through the furnace, and then applying a second coating of transparent enamel of different shade from that of the primary layer.

The process of manufacture of seamless tubes at Taylor & Wiggins's works, Birmingham, England, consists in progressively drawing the tubes down cold, in successive stages, from a disk of steel of varying thickness and diameter into the completed tube. The steel used is of different qualities, according to the purpose for which the tubes are intended, and is supplied to the works in strips of various length and width. The circular blanks are first punched from the strips, and are then passed through the first of a series of vertical presses, in which they are slightly dished. They are then passed successively through dies of gradually increasing depth and decreasing diameter, until the flat disk has assumed the form of a tube ten or twelve inches long and two or three inches in diameter, and closed at one end. Between every pass the embryo tube is subjected to a slight annealing. Having reached a given length in the vertical presses, the work of further elongation and development is carried forward in horizontal drawing tubes. Here the metal tube is drawn through successively decreasing dies, over correspondingly decreasing mandrels, the metal being at the same time evenly and uniformly thinned down by the mechanical operation, the particles following a gradual and regular flow. After each pass the tubes are submitted to the annealing process, as in the case of the vertical presses.

The principal feature of the nonoxidizing process for annealing steel of H. K. Jones, of Hartford, Conn., consists in keeping the retort in communication with the gas holder or gas main during the entire process of heating and cooling, the gas thus being allowed to expand back into the main, and being therefore kept at a practically constant pressure. The process has been in constant use for two or three years, while several tons of metal have been annealed and turned from the retorts daily, bright, and at a very slight expense. The gas was taken directly from the mains supplying the city with illuminating gas. It has been the practice also to reanneal by this process all of the tool steel used in a large machine shop, although it had already been annealed at the steel works where it was made, and the slight additional expense was more than compensated for by the ease with which the steel was worked, and by the saving in the wear of cutting tools. It was also noticed that if metal that had been blued or slightly oxidized was subjected to the annealing process, it came out bright, the oxide having been reduced by the action of the gas.

A process devised by MM. Walrand and Legénisel for the manufacture in converters of small dimensions of steel suitable for castings and ingots is intended to remedy the final failure of temperature, rendering casting difficult, that occurs in ordinary attempts to produce steel in small masses. Its principal feature is the addition of a small quantity of smelted ferro-silicon containing 10 per cent. of silicon at the moment when the Bessemer operation is completed; after which the blast is continued up to the moment determined by the operator. The addition is followed by a great rise of temperature.

In the aluminum process, partly chemical and partly electrical, of William Frishnuth, the aluminum oxide is extracted from clay and dissolved. The solution is then exposed to the electric current, which causes the pure metal to be thrown down on brass plates. From these it is removed by a simple but ingenious chemical process in a state of almost perfect purity, and in the form of a silvery impalpable powder. It only remains to smelt it into ingots. It is claimed that by this process aluminum can be extracted at a price much below the present market value, and in any desired quantity. The by-product or residue of the treatment is a valuable fertilizer.

The chief feature in an improved apparatus for smelting and casting by Herr Eduard Tauss sig is the conducting of the operation in a partial vacuum. The smelting furnace is connected with the casting apparatus and the mold so that they form an air-tight inclosed whole, the separate parts of which are easy of access. The smelting is effected by electricity. The current is conducted through the metal to be melted, which is used in a granular state, by means of electrodes made of the same metal, or of a more refractory one.

Miscellaneous.—In cleaning mercury at the Physikalischtechnische Reichsanstalt, in Berlin, the raw material is filtered and dried, and twice distilled in a vacuum to get rid of the heavy metals. The electro-positive metals, such as zinc and the alkali metals, are separated by electrolysis. The mercury is precipitated from a solution of mercurous nitrate obtained by the action of nitric acid on excess of mercury. The solution, together with the impure mercury acting as an anode, is contained in an outside glass vessel, into which a current from a Gülcher thermopile is conducted by an insulated platinum rod. The cathode rod dips into an interior shallow glass vessel, in which the pure mercury is collected. The mercury thus obtained is fit for use in standard barometers and resistances.

M. Placet has succeeded in preparing considerable quantities of chromium by electrolysis, under such conditions as make commercial production possible. His chromium contains 99 per cent. of the metal, and is therefore of greater purity than that prepared by reduction with carbon, which contains a considerable proportion of that element. The industrial use of chromium is, according to M. Moissan, susceptible of becoming very extensive on account of the unalterable character which it communicates to the surfaces on which it is deposited. It is much superior to nickel for this purpose.

Titanium is found, often in large quantities, in many iron ores. It is difficult to reduce, and the largest part of it in the ore goes to the cinder in the blast furnace, and gives the slag a dark and sometimes black color, while it is very difficult to find even a trace of it in the iron produced. Titanates being difficult to reduce, metallic titanium renders the smelting of the iron difficult. It is believed, however, that the presence of titaniferous ores is favorable to the formation of spiegeleisen. Certain tests made by Clason with pig iron indicate that titanium favors the tendency of iron to combine with carbon. If this is really a case of cause and effect, the action of the titanium must be very strong, because in the different samples of pig iron produced by this method no traces of titanium were found. By the fusion of 99 per cent. of steel and 1 per cent. of metallic titanium, Karsten obtained an exceedingly good steel, of which the tenure in titanium varied greatly, and he discovered in this circumstance another proof that iron and titanium in the metallic state do not enter into a combination, but are only mechanically mixed. From these and other facts mentioned by Mr. J. B. Nau in his paper on the subject, the conclusion may be drawn that if titanium has any notable advantage in the production of steel, its influence on the qualities of iron must be so powerful that even small amounts hardly detected by analysis make themselves felt; or that the influence of titanium is indirect, consisting in the elimination of some obnoxious elements from the steel.

In estimating the temperature developed in various industrial processes, M. Chatelier takes as points of comparison the melting points determined by M. Violle, viz., sulphur, 448° C.; gold, 1,045° C.; palladium, 1,500° C.; platinum, 1,-

775° C. He finds the melting heat of white cast iron 1,135° C., and that of gray cast iron 1.220° C. Mild steel melts at 1,475° C., semi-mild at 1,455° C., and hard steel at 1,410° C. The furnace for hard porcelain at the end of the baking has a heat of 1,370° C. The heat of a normal incandescent lamp is 1,800° C., but it may be pushed to beyond 2,100° C. Previous determinations have been falsified by using for comparison the melting points of palladium and platinum. Thus the temperature of the Bessemer process was fixed by Langley at 2,000° C., because platinum seemed to melt rapidly in the flame. It does not really melt, but it merely dissolves in the minute drops of melted steel carried along by the gaseous current.

According to Cailletet, glass and porcelain tubes can be soldered on to metals by furnishing first the end of the glass tube which is to be joined with a very thin deposit of platinum, and then by electrolysis with a copper ring. The glass tube can thus be handled as if it were a metal tube, and can be soldered by means of tin on to iron, copper, bronze, platinum, etc.

A new paint for preserving metals from rust consists chiefly of a silicate of iron which is found in the neighborhood of natural deposits of iron ores, and which also occurs in veins in deposits of granite that have become decomposed by contact with the air. It is mixed in a finely divided state with oxidized linseed oil and varnish to form a paste. When required as a paint it is thinned down with good linseed oil, to which may be added, if wanted, a drier, such as litharge, and whatever colors may be desired. When applied to sheet iron the coating of this paint was unaffected by warm water or steam, acid and alkaline liquids, ammonia gas, hydrochloric-acid gas, and sulphureted-hydrogen gas.

METEOROLOGY. An account of the earliest meteorological observations and instruments has been published recently by Dr. G. Hellmann. He divides the history of observations into three periods: The first period ends in the middle of the fifteenth century, and represents an epoch when observations were only partial and without precise objects. In the second period, of about two hundred years, observations were made at least once a day. The third period, in which observations have been made systematically and with instruments, dates from about the middle of the seventeenth century. It is not known who was the first person that kept a regular meteorological journal. Humboldt thinks it was Columbus, on his first American voyage. The Italians, however, seem to have made daily observations from the middle of the fifteenth century. The weathercreock is by far the most ancient meteorological instrument. Exact attention was given to the direction of the wind in the time of Homer and Hesiod, eight hundred or nine hundred years before Christ. The first special provision for such observations was given in the Temple of the Winds, at Athens, which was built about one hundred years before Christ. In Charlemagne's time, Eginhard described the winds by the four points of the compass, and noted their variations. The first instrument for measuring the force of the wind is attributed to Robert Hooke, 1667, and is the same as the one used now as Wild's pendulum anemometer. The absorption or organic hygrometer was invented about the middle of the fifteenth century by N. de Cusa, but it is usually credited to Leonardo da Vinci. The first condensation hygrometer was the device of Grand Duke Ferdinand II, of Tuscany. The first continuous hygrometric observations were made by R. Boyle, at Oxford, in June, 1666. The first thermometer is attributed to Galileo, toward the end of the sixteenth century. The instrument was improved some years later, when the graduation was marked by ridges in the glass, every tenth ridge being enameled. The first pluviometer was employed by B. Caselli, in 1639, but a later date is generally assigned to him. The discovery of the Torricellian tube in 1643 is too well known to need more than a mention. Many other points are discussed by Herr Hellmann in his interesting work.

The principal results of the deliberations of the International Meteorological Congress, which met at Munich in August, 1891, are summarized as follow: All temperatures published after 1901 are to be referred to the readings of the air thermometer. Actinometrical observations are not held to be sufficiently certain to justify their general introduction. The application of a ventilating arrangement to wet-bulb thermometers was recommended. It was decided to count as days of rain those on which 0·005 inch (or 0·1 millimetre) of rain was measured, and to print monthly the days on which 0·05 inch (or 1 millimetre) fell. A note is to be made in monthly schedules of the number of days in which about half the country surrounding the station is under snow. A new classification of clouds, proposed by Dr. Hildebrandsson and the Hon. Ralph Abercromby, was adopted by a large majority, England and the United States voting against it. A committee was appointed to consider the general question of typical cloud pictures, taking this classification more or less as a basis of arrangement. A report was adopted on the observation of the motion, etc., of cirrus and other high-level clouds. It was decided that no instrumental results of wind observation should be published, unless the instrument had been previously compared, directly or indirectly, with a standard. A proposal to recommend the adoption of universal or zone time was rejected, on the ground that climatological time alone can be used for climatological inquiry; and it was decided to insist in all publications on beginning the day with midnight as 0 hour. The conference determined to introduce the practice of correcting barometrical readings for the force of gravity at latitude 45° after the beginning of the year 1901. An international meteorological committee was constituted to prepare for a possible congress in Paris in 1896. Questions relating to terrestrial magnetism were referred to a special committee.

Temperature.—It appears from Mr. A. L. Rotch's observations of temperature and atmospheric pressure at Blue Hill Observatory, Massachusetts, that the wind velocity is two thirds greater there than at Boston, about 500 feet lower, but the difference changes for various hours of the day. At low levels the wind force generally increases from the early morning until the afternoon, but the conditions are reversed at higher levels. This fact was pointed out by

Prof. Hellmann in 1875, when studying the Mount Washington observations, and the same fact has since been remarked at Ben Nevis and other observatories. The wind has also a vertical as well as a horizontal motion, which has amounted to 7 miles an hour in a storm. The normal temperature at the summit of Blue Hill is 2° lower than at the base, giving a difference of 1° for each 220 feet of ascent; but inversions frequently occur when the temperature at the base is lower than at the summit.

A study of the influence of forests on the daily variation of air temperature has been made by Prof. Müttrich from data collected at stations in Germany and Austria. The influence seems to be greater between May and September or October than in the other months. In pine and fir woods it rises gradually from January to a maximum in August or September, then falls more quickly to a minimum in December; but in beech woods a minimum occurs in April, then there is a quick rise, till the maximum is reached in July. The daily variation itself is greatest in June, both in forest and open country. The influence of the forest is to lower the maxima and raise the minima, and the former influence is greater in most months than the latter; in December and January, and occasionally in neighboring months, it is less. The influence on the maxima in summer is greatest in beech woods, less in pine, and least in fir. The absolute value of the influence of woods of a given kind of tree is affected by the degree of density of the growth, being higher the denser the forest. The character of the climate (oceanic or continental) also affects the results. From daily observations in forest and open country, every two hours in the second half of June, it appears that, soon after 5 A. M. and 8 P. M. the air temperature in the wood was equal to that in the open; that the maximum was about 0·9° lower in the wood, and the minimum 0·6° higher; that from May to September the difference sometimes reached 2·7°; that the maximum in the wood occurred about half an hour later, and the minimum a quarter of an hour later, than in the open; and that the daily mean temperature was about ¼° less in the wood.

The influence exercised by the mixture of strata of air of different temperatures and nearly saturated with vapor on the formation of fogs and clouds, has been investigated by Herr von Bezold. Thermodynamic considerations derived by graphic methods seem to the author to demonstrate that the mixture of warm air saturated with vapor with nonsaturated cold air, more readily causes condensations than a current of saturated cold air with a stratum of nonsaturated warm air. The quantities of water condensed in this way are very small, for the action of adiabatic expansions and direct cooling removes much. If the air contains suspended particles of water, evaporation and depression of temperature may be produced under the influence of a current of warm air. If the air is mechanically but not hydroscopically saturated, depression may be produced, even if the warm air that comes in is saturated with vapor. But if the cold air is also saturated, the air that comes in should be dry. It is concluded that mixtures of liquid water and nonsaturated air will cool, and

that the cooling will be more sensible according as the air is further removed from its point of saturation and the quantity of water is larger.

It appears from a map constructed by M. Lancaster to show divergences from normal temperature in Europe during the five years 1886–'90, that the center of the "island of cold" lies over the north of France, the south of Belgium, and the most western parts of Germany. From this center the cold decreases with an approach to regularity outward on all sides to a nearly circular line of *nil* divergence, which, embracing the whole of Great Britain, crosses the south of Sweden, then goes along the German-Russian frontier, through Hungary, the south of Italy, the north of Africa, and across Spain. Throughout this inclosed region abnormally low temperatures have prevailed. Siberia, too, shows thermal depression, which M. Lancaster thinks may be connected with that in western Europe.

The details of the process by which all the heat our planet receives from the sun is eventually lost by radiation—evident according to Prof. Cleveland Abbe—has not been completely worked out. Such studies of it as have been made enforce the necessity of carefully distinguishing the influence of the absorption and radiation by the soil, the vegetation, the snow, and the ocean, respectively; and in the atmosphere itself, between the absorbing and radiating powers of the dry air, of the clouds or haze, and of the dust, respectively. Besides what is conducted and conveyed to the atmosphere from the immediate surface of continents and oceans, the radiant heat from those surfaces is in part directly absorbed in the atmosphere, and in part transmitted to outer space. All of this heat must be ultimately lost through a process of radiation from the atmosphere, as distinguished from radiation through the atmosphere. A part of it may even escape from the inner layers through the overlying layers, without being taken up by them, into ethereal space. The researches of Ferrel, Helmholtz, and others show that areas of high pressure and horizontal or inclined or vertical whirls in the atmosphere are kinetic movements, not dependent on conditions of heat or density. The factors that principally affect temperature in extensive areas of high pressure are: 1, the direct absorption by the air of the solar radiation; 2, the direct radiation by the air of its own heat; and, 3, the thermal changes due to changes of barometric pressure on the radiating mass, which are themselves due to its descent in the atmosphere. The cooling by radiation is to only a very slight extent offset by the direct absorption of solar heat, and on the average it is largely compensated for by the warming from compression. The general tenor of observation is that under a cloudy sky the diminution of temperature with ascent is slight and uniform; within a cloud it is given by the laws of evolution of heat; above all clouds and in all clear air, as in areas of high pressure, the temperature depends upon the radiation of heat and the thermo-dynamic changes of a compressible atmosphere. Having reviewed the deductions of various authors relative to these points, Prof. Abbe mentions as among other important problems in the mechanics of the atmosphere that are elucidated by the study of radiation:

The general circulation of the atmosphere from the equator to the pole can only take place by virtue of the fact that the air which overflows from the equator and from the tropical heights actually loses its heat (not merely diminishes in temperature) and contracts as it cools. Radiation is the only efficient process capable of accounting for the great loss of heat that the atmosphere experiences. Although we are not yet able to state the average amount and law of radiation as dependent on temperature and pressure, yet it is easy to see that this must be known, and must enter into our equations of condition, before we can fully account for the phenomena observed in the general circulation of the atmosphere. The passage of a steady atmospheric current over a mountain range, depositing rain and snow on the windward side, but descending as dry air on the leeward side, gives rise to a standing wave, such as may be seen above any obstacle in a rapid river. Thus kinetic energy is converted into static pressure; and therefore on the leeward side, under the summit of the wave, down to the earth's surface, there is a somewhat higher pressure than there would be in case no such current existed. The clear, descending air by its dryness has also a slightly greater density than before at the same temperature and pressure, which adds somewhat to the barometric excess. The coolness by radiation annuls approximately the warming by compression, and again gives increased density. These three factors, therefore, conspire to increase the pressure at the earth's surface, and this is again further increased largely by the influence of the earth's rotation and the southward flow, as explained by Ferrel and Helmholtz. This is the best explanation I have yet been able to frame of the formation of the high areas and cold waves that move southeastward over Canada and the United States. I believe that I first stated my conclusion as to this mechanism when, in 1876, I had occasion to urge the importance of maintaining meteorological stations in Alaska. The reports from these stations as subsequently established, as well as the international maps of the Signal Service, served to confirm that view. The original current on the Pacific side of the Rocky mountains may be due either to a special cyclone, or to the general circulation of the atmosphere, resulting in a standing wave whose summit is over the Mackenzie river. When the current temporarily ceases, the summit and the high area die away; and when it is strongest, the pressure is the greatest. Generally the original current may be considered as a temporary overflow from northern Siberia along the arctic circle to Alaska.

Among the points to which the attention of meteorological observers is called by a pamphlet on "Meteorological Work for Agricultural Institutions," are problems of temperature, such as the differences that occur in quiescent air between places that are close together, and the subject of protection from frosts; moisture in the air, especially measurements of evaporation and the transpiration of plants; condensation and precipitation of moisture, including an accurate record of the amount of dew, and the density of fog which should be recorded on some uniform plan, such as the distance at which a slender pole can be seen, and local weather predictions independent of the daily weather charts.

M. Angot's report on temperature observations made during 1890, at three different heights on the Eiffel Tower, shows that during the night the temperature increases up to a mean height of about 500 feet, then decreases, slowly at first, and afterward more rapidly; at about 1,000 feet the mean decrease of temperature is about 1·4° per 328 feet (100 metres). During the day the temperature decreases constantly from the ground upward; in the lower strata the decrease

VOL. XXXII.—29 A

is slower in winter than in summer. In the later season it amounts to 2·5° per 328 feet; but above 500 feet the rate of decrease does not show a decided annual variation; the amount is about 1·6° per 328 feet. It is worthy of remark that at a height of 984 feet (300 metres) in open air the decrease of temperature is extremely rapid both during the night and during the day, and nearly approaches the theoretical value of the law of the adiabatic expansion of gases.

From an examination of the statistics of the frosts of the present century M. A. Lancaster finds that a cold winter has never been followed by a very hot summer, and that in the great majority of cases the summer following a severe winter has been cold. The same opinion has been expressed by Humboldt, in his "Cosmos," and by other writers.

Clouds.—The average heights of some of the principal clouds at Mr. A. L. Rotch's Blue Hill Observatory were found by H. H. Clayton to be: Nimbus, 412 metres; cumulus (base), 1,512 metres; false cirrus, 6,500 metres; cirro-stratus, 9,652 metres; cirrus, 10,135 metres. The cumulus was highest during the middle of the day. Observations at Upsala, Sweden, show that the base of the cumulus increases in height until evening, but neither of these conclusions applies to the observations at Blue Hill. The average velocity found for the cirrus (82 miles an hour) is twice as great as that found at Upsala. The extreme velocity was 133 miles an hour. A comparison between wind and cloud velocity shows that below 500 metres the wind velocity is less than the cloud velocity. Above that the excess of the cloud velocity increases up to 1,000 metres, and then decreases again till about 1,700 metres, after which it steadily increases. This decrease between 1,000 and 1,700 metres is probably due to the fact that the clouds between 700 and 1,000 metres were mostly observed during the morning, when the cumulus moves most rapidly, and that the clouds between 1,000 and 1,700 metres were mostly observed during the afternoon, when the cumulus moves slowest.

Observations of the phenomena of the "luminous clouds" were again made by Herr O. Jesse, of the Royal Observatory, Berlin, in the summer of 1890. They were visible between May 26 and the beginning of August, or for about four weeks before and four weeks after the summer solstice. The statement that the time when the phenomenon appears in the southern hemisphere has a corresponding relation to the summer solstice there, is confirmed. One hundred and eighty photographs of them were obtained of the clouds at German stations. of which 75, having been secured at the same time in at least two different places, were suitable for the determination of height. Thirty of them, having been taken at proper intervals at the same place, may be used for determining the speed and direction of the movements of the clouds. The phenomenon was again less bright than it had been in the preceding year. Only when the atmosphere was exceptionally transparent was there an approach to the former brilliancy. The aggregations of the masses of particles seem to be becoming thinner, as is also to be perceived from the more distinct appearance of certain relations of structure. It has now been proved more successfully than before that the ridges or longitudinal strips lie parallel to the direction of movement of the entire cloud, while the ridges or cross strips are almost at right angles to it. The measurements of heights, so far as they were definitely calculated, gave a mean value of 82 kilometres, which agrees closely with the value of nearly 83 kilometres deduced from the photographs of 1889. It was again found that the chief component of the movement was directed from east to west, and amounted to nearly 100 metres in the second, while the speed of the revolution of the zone of the earth above which the clouds were placed is about 240 metres in the second from west to east. There was also a smaller and variable component in the direction of the meridian, or from north to south. While the points of view from which the phenomena may be regarded on the ground of the observations already made are numerous, there is still a wide field for research in connection with the questions: What are the forces that make the phenomenon appear chiefly in the morning hours? What is the nature of those forces that cause the movement of the clouds to be mainly from the northeast, and drive them from the northern to the southern hemisphere and back again? The luminous clouds were again visible in 1891 on June 25-26 at Steglitz and Nauen, and were photographed 8 times simultaneously at those two places. They were also seen by Mr. T. W. Backhouse at Sunderland, England, and Mr. D. J. Rowan at Kingstown, Ireland, on the night of June 30. At Sunderland their motion was, "as usual, from a northeasterly direction," and at Kingstown they "appeared well-developed on a polar arc of 30° and at a mean altitude of 5°." They had been faintly visible at Kingstown early in June. Observations of them for 1892 are mentioned by W. Clement Ley, at Lutterworth, England, on the night of June 24; and they were seen from the summit of Ben Nevis all through the night of June 24-25. A special appeal is made by W. Foerster and O. Jesse to astronomers and geophysicists in different countries to make observations of these phenomena. The clouds have been more rarely seen in recent years than in the earlier years of observation, beginning with 1885. Their appearance is subject to great changes. While they frequently exist only in a few little luminous stripes or patches, they appear at times in greater accumulations and with a more intense light. Frequent observations of the movements of the clouds render it probable that they are caused principally by the resisting medium of the mundane space. In accordance with this is the fact that in the half year after its appearance in Berlin the phenomenon has been observed repeatedly in the southern latitude of 53° by the meteorological observer, Mr. Stubenrauch, in Punta Arenas, as well as several times by ship captains; and other observations are cited in confirmation of an annual wandering of this kind. Persons interested in furthering the solution of the questions suggested in these phenomena are therefore invited to co-operate in the study of them.

An envelope of vapor is supposed by Herr von Frank, of Grätz, to explain the floating of particles of cloud or fog. The lengthening of shadows when clouds pass over the sun is attributed to refraction by the vapor envelopes. It is difficult to see how water droplets in the form of cloud or fog could exist at such various temperatures did not the vapor envelopes, as bad conductors of heat, guard them to some extent from evaporating and freezing. The minute particles must soon be dissipated by the sun's rays if they were not in a kind of spheroidal state. This heating expands the envelopes, so that the cloud tends to rise, and various phenomena in nature may be thus explained, such, for instance, as the rise of mist in Alpine valleys. Liquid droplets have been observed by Arsmann floating in an air of -10° C. On meeting a solid body, these froze to ice lumps without crystalline structure. Here, according to Herr von Frank, the vapor envelopes prevent freezing, till they are ruptured by the solid; the droplet thus loses the bad conductor of heat that protected it, and solidifies so quickly that no crystals can form. The author supposes that with much aqueous vapor in the air larger drops form, the clouds floating lower; with less aqueous vapor, the drops are smaller and the clouds higher; the thickness of the envelope, however, being the same for large and small drops under like conditions of the temperature and pressure.

One of the most notable facts brought out by A. L. Rotch's measurements of cloud heights and velocities at the Blue Hill Observatory, is the difference in height between the same clouds in summer and winter; the clouds, with few exceptions, being lowest in winter. The bases of the cumulo-nimbus clouds, however, are generally lower in summer, while their tops are higher than in winter. The heights of the different clouds were found to maintain an almost constant ratio to each other. The mean velocities recorded showed that the entire atmosphere moves twice as fast in winter as in summer. The mean velocity of the highest clouds in winter was about 100 miles an hour; the extreme velocity amounted to 230 miles an hour, from which it appears that the upper currents are much more rapid over America than over Europe; and this possibly explains the greater velocity of the storms in America. The tables show, as to the directions of cloud movement, that from the highest clouds to the earth's surface the prevailing wind is west; above 4,000 metres, more than 90 per cent. of the observations show the clouds moving from some point between south and west and northwest inclusive. In the cirrus and the cumulus regions, and near the earth's surface, the prevailing direction is from a little north of west, but in the intermediate levels from a little south of west, the excess of the southerly component in those regions being possibly due to the influence of cyclones.

Pressure.—In a report of researches into the daily oscillations of the barometer, Dr. J. Hann, of Vienna, deals with a thorough analysis of the barometric oscillations on mountain summits and in valleys, for different seasons, for which he has calculated the daily harmonic constituents, and has given a full description of the phenomenon, showing how the amplitude of the single daily oscillation first decreases with increasing altitude, and then increases again to a higher elevation. The epochs of the phases are reversed at about 6,000 feet above sea level as compared with those on the plains. The minimum on the summits occurs about six o'clock in the morning, and in the valleys between three and four o'clock in the afternoon. The double daily amplitude shows, in relation to its amplitude on the summits nearly the normal decrease, in proportion to the decreasing pressure, but the epochs of the phases exhibit a retardation on the summits of as much as one or two hours. In the tropics, however, this retardation is very small. The author then endeavors to show that these modifications of the daily barometric range on mountain summits are generally explained by the differences of temperature in the lower strata of air.

A close coincidence has been shown, by Prof. Hellmann, from observations taken at different British, Continental, and American stations where barographs are used, to exist between the daily range of the monthly extremes and that of the hourly values of the barometer. The author finds that the hours of occurrence of the highest and lowest readings of the barometer during a month agree almost completely with the times in which the normal daily range has its maxima and minima, both curves being so similar in shape that it may be possible to judge of the general character of the daily range of the barometer from knowing only the hours at which the monthly extremes mostly occur. Hence, as the lowest readings of the barometer are accompanied by cloudy and stormy weather, during which the effect of the solar radiation upon the surface of the earth and the heating of the lower strata of the atmosphere are insignificant. Prof. Hellmann concludes that Prof. Hann and others are right in assuming that the normal daily range of the barometer is chiefly an effect of the absorption of the solar rays in the upper strata of our atmosphere. Prof. Hann has applied the harmonic analysis to the numbers furnished by Prof. Hellmann, and, by combining several stations in a group, has found the coefficients of the periodic formula to be practically the same as those for the normal daily range.

In a paper on the typical weather conditions of winter, Dr. W. J. Van Bebber shows by means of charts how the disposition of barometric pressure over the Atlantic and the continent of Asia regulates the weather over western Europe. Nearly twenty years ago the synoptic charts issued by Capt. Hoffmeyer, of the Danish Meteorological Institute, showed that there were three large areas of very low barometric pressure in the Atlantic, the most important being southwest of Iceland, and two smaller areas, one on the eastern side toward the northern Arctic Ocean, and another on the west side toward Davis Straits. These areas cause the westerly and southwesterly winds which carry the damp and warm air over Europe. The shifting of their positions causes the variations in the western European wind system. M. L. Teisserenc de Bort has pointed out the important part also played by areas of high barometer, which has given greater significance to the Danish synoptic charts. The most important area of high pressure for western Europe is that stretching east-

ward over the Azores and Madeira. If this area shifts northeastwardly toward France, it blocks the way of the air over the ocean, and the weather becomes foggy and cold. Another important barometric maximum persists over central Asia. This maximum is subject to frequent modifications; sometimes it splits up into two parts, one of which often shifts as far westward as Scandinavia, and produces a persistence of cold easterly winds over western Europe—especially when the pressure over southern Europe is low.

Storms.—The view has been propounded by Dr. Hann that the storms of the temperate zone originate not in the convectional ascent of warm air, but in great vortical movements of the upper air currents, which begin over the equator as antitrades, and set continuously toward the poles, being gradually diverted eastward in consequence of the earth's rotation. Owing to the spherical form of the earth's surface these currents become irregularly congested as they necessarily converge on reaching higher latitudes, and thus give rise to anticyclones, or tracts of excessive accumulation and pressure, and to cyclonic vortices in the intervals. Admitting the probability of this view for higher latitudes, H. F. Blanford observes that in low latitudes those causes which impede the even flow of upper currents are at a minimum, for the tendency to congestion must vary as the contraction of the degrees of longitude in successive parallels of latitude, and can only be insignificant in the tropics. On the other hand, the supposed alternative cause of storms—the production and condensation of vapor—is at a maximum in low latitudes; and the facts recorded by Eliot, Pedler, and others who have traced out the early history of cyclones in the Bay of Bengal, go to show that their formation is determined by the inrush of a saturated current from the equatorial sea, which is preceded by a day or two of disturbed squally weather in the birthplace of the storm. The relation of these storms to the features of the terrestrial surface indicates that they are primarily, at least, phenomena of the lower atmospheric strata, even though at a later period the vortical movement may be imparted to the greatly elevated antitrade, and so be carried forward into high latitudes. The temperature test, also, as applied to tropical cyclones, is in favor of this view. After an elaborate discussion of these questions, Mr. Blanford decides that "from every point of view, whether we regard the place and circumstances of their origin, their behavior after formation, their physical constitution, or the relative activity of the causes supposed to be concerned in their production, the conclusion seems irresistible that tropical cyclones originate in a manner quite different from that ascribed to the storms of the temperate zone; that they are in their early stages a disturbance of the lower atmosphere; and that the primary impulse is given by the ascent and condensation of vapor." These remarks apply only to the cyclones of the beginning and end of the summer monsoon, and the cyclonic storms of the summer months; while the storms that traverse northern India in the winter and early spring are of different character, and may originate in the manner suggested by Prof. Hann.

The motions of storms on the earth and those of the spots on the sun have been compared by Camille Flammarion. He brings together in his paper sufficient observations to trace out the paths of many of the most violent storms that have from time to time visited Europe generally. The first storms which he gives are those which occur in the Atlantic; their general direction of motion seems to be from southwest to northeast, pursuing generally the path of the Gulf Stream. Their centers, when traced on a map, seem just to graze the shores of the British Isles, while France is rarely reached by them. From observations made on land, and more especially from those at Paris, M. Flammarion remarks that certain curves with regard to these storms seem to offer many analogies to solar spots. This is so not only for the regular displacements, but even to those which at first sight seem to be void of all regularity. The diagrams which he gives, showing both the paths of the storms and those of sun spots, afford most interesting comparisons and seem to confirm the view suggested by M. Faye that the constitution of spots resembles somewhat that of the cyclones with which we are familiar.

Winds.—In reviewing the history of the development of the theory of the general circulation of the atmosphere, Dr. J. M. Pernter notices Dove's theory of a circulation between the equator and the poles, with his law of wind gyration: Ferrel's theory, accepting three great zones of calm belts, in which Dove's fundamental idea is preserved; Sprung's system, based on the same principles as Ferrel's; and that of Werner Siemens, in which the origin of the general circulation of the atmosphere is deduced from the great principle of the conservation of energy; pointing out to what extent they have been severally verified, and wherein they have failed. Siemens's theory received an apparent support from the rapid westwardly drift of the dust arising from the eruption of Krakatao in 1883, and from observations by Abercromby of the motion of cirrus clouds in the equatorial region, which were, however, apparently contradicted by a subsequent observation. From this analysis the author sketches the outline of the general circulation of the atmosphere which corresponds to the present state of the science, as follows: In consequence of the unequal heating by the sun and of the rotation of the earth, air currents occur in all quarters of the globe. These currents are easterly between 35° north and 35° south latitude, and westerly outside this zone. In the former zone the easterly currents on the earth's surface (in the northern hemisphere) are more northeasterly and northerly the nearer we approach latitude 35°, while in the higher strata they constantly become more southerly as we approach latitude 35°. This explains the circulation between the equator and latitude 35°. At or nearer the equator a calm zone must be found at the earth's surface where the meridional components of the northeast and southeast trades ascend, but the height of this calm zone can not be considerable. Exactly over the calm zone a pure east wind and the strongest of the whole zone will blow, and the higher the strata under consideration the stronger it will be. In latitude 35° north and south, calms exist at the earth's

surface. The air, which has an ascending motion in the equatorial calm, has here a descending movement; but above, the current directed poleward continues to exist. Outside this great region, to the north and south, west winds will prevail; while above, the southwest trade winds blow, which in higher latitudes will become more and more westerly. At the earth's surface, air in southwesterly or northwesterly motion flows from the zone of high pressure at latitude 35°, which becomes more westerly with increasing latitude. At a mean altitude, however, air flows again from the pole toward latitude 35° as a northwest wind. This is the picture of the general circulation of the atmosphere according to the latest researches.

From observations on the motions of dust in various parts of the world, the Hon. Ralph Abercromby has found that the wind sometimes blows dust into streaks or lines, which are analogous to fibrous or hairy cirrus clouds; sometimes into transverse ridges and furrows, like solid waves, which are analogous to certain kinds of fleecy cirrus cloud; sometimes into crescent-shaped heaps with their convex side to the wind, which are perhaps analogous to a rare cloud form called "mackerel scales"; sometimes into whirlwinds, of at least two if not three varieties, all of which present some analogies to atmospheric cyclones; sometimes into simple rising clouds, without any rotation, which are analogous to simple cumulus-topped squalls; and sometimes into forms intermediate between the whirlwind and simple rising clouds, some of which reproduce in a remarkable manner the combination of rounded, flat, and hairy clouds that are built up over certain types of squalls and showers. Excessive heating of the soil alone does not generate whirlwinds; they require a certain amount of wind from other causes to be moving at the time. The general conclusion is, that when the air is in more or less rapid motion from cyclonic or other causes, small eddies of various kinds form themselves, and that they develop the different sorts of gusts, showers, squalls, and whirlwinds.

METHODISTS. I. Methodist Episcopal Church.—The following is a summary of the statistics of this Church as given in the "Methodist Year Book" for 1893. In the cases of those annual conferences held late in the fall, the returns from which had not been made up when the "Year Book" went to press, the statistics for 1891 are included: Number of annual conferences (including mission conferences and missions), 139; of traveling preachers (11,044 effective, 1,113 supernumerary, 1,860 superannuated, and 1,850 on trial), 15,867; of local preachers, 14,542; of members (including 242,789 on probation), 2,442,750; of Sunday schools, 27,989, with 310,000 officers and teachers and 2,369,005 pupils; of churches, 23,866, having a probable value of $101,507,085; of parsonages, 9,050, the probable value of which is $15,405,446; of adults baptized during the year, 107,324; of children baptized, 84,563. Increase in full members during 1892, 58,866. Amount of benevolent contributions: For the Missionary Society, $1,282,676; for the Board of Church Extension, $170,876; for the Freedmen's, Aid and Southern Education Society, $116,796; for the Sunday School Union. $25,375; for the Tract Society, $23,269; for the Board of Education, including interest, loans returned, etc., $80,665; for the American Bible Society, $35,047; for the Woman's Foreign Missionary Society, $265,342; for the Woman's Home Missionary Society, $104,631; total benevolent contributions for the year, $2,-105,037; besides which were paid for ministerial support, including bishops, presiding elders, etc., $10,081,152; for superannuated preachers, $250,-937; for church buildings and improvements, $5,148,201; for indebtedness on church property, $1,653,738; leaving $9,134,644 as the present indebtedness; for current expenses, $2,-615,355.

Book Concern.—The Book Committee reported to the General Conference that the total assets of the Book Concern were $2,378,181, of which $908,047 were in real estate, $791,573 in merchandise, and the rest in notes and accounts and cash; and that its liabilities were $286,841; leaving it a net capital of $2,091,340. The amount of the sales from the Concern during the past four years was $4,235,204, on which the profits were $549,955. Dividends had been paid out to the annual conferences during the four years as follow: 1889, $100,000; 1890, $100,000; 1891, $110,000; 1892, $125,000. These payments had met with great favor, and did not appear to have diminished the local collections for church beneficiaries. The building at the corner of Fifth Avenue and Twentieth Street, New York city, the joint property of the Book Concern (two thirds) and the Missionary Society (one third), had been completed, and was presented to the Church free from incumbrance.

Church Extension.—The General Committee of Church Extension met in Philadelphia, Pa., Nov. 3. The report showed that the year had been the best in the history of the society. The receipts had been $319,981, of which $206,372 had been received on general account, $37,684 had been added to the loan fund, and $75,925 represented the amount of loans returned. Six hundred and three churches had been aided during the year, and the new year found the board granting aid conditionally to 390 churches in the amount of $174,625, and 34 applications on file asking for aid to the extent of $32,620. The board required, for work in hand the sum of $207,245, toward which it had $82,934. Apportionments and estimates were made for the ensuing year to the amount of $316,825.

Freedmen's Aid and Southern Education Society.—The General Committee of the Freedmen's Aid and Southern Education Society met in Harrisburg, Pa., Nov. 7. The society had received during the year $367,751, and had expended $363,614. The sum of $280,471 had been expended in school work. The list of schools included institutions for theological, collegiate, and academic instruction among both white and colored people, in which were 548 teachers and 9,665 students, including in the collegiate classes 66 colored and 100 white students, in the collegiate preparatory courses 371 students among the colored people and 733 among the whites, 277 students preparing for the ministry, 273 studying to be teachers, 3,400 studying music, and 1,829 students in the manual, drawing, and trade schools. All the institutions of the society together formed a

system of federal schools, with the same courses of study as other institutions of similar grade.

Missionary Society.—The annual meeting of the General Missionary Committee was held in Baltimore, Md., Nov. 9 to 15. The total receipts of the treasurer of the society for the year ending Oct. 31 had been $1,282,676, and the expenditures $1,238,302.

The following appropriations were made for the work of 1893:

I. FOREIGN MISSIONS:

Africa	$6,420
South America	58,180
China (four missions)	127,500
Germany	32,100
Switzerland	10,000
Scandinavia	52,424
India	127,729
Malaysia	10,000
Bulgaria	20,888
Italy	44,389
Mexico	60,050
Japan	66,665
Corea	18,555
Lower California	1,000
Total for foreign missions	$665,800

II. DOMESTIC MISSIONS:

Welsh	$2,000
Scandinavian	62,900
German	52,750
French	7,700
Spanish	15,500
Chinese	11,800
Japanese	6,400
Bohemian and Hungarian	9,550
Italian	5,900
Portuguese	800
Hebrew	600
Pennsylvania Dutch	1,000
American Indian	18,550
English-speaking	333,800
Miscellaneous appropriations	119,000
Total for foreign and domestic missions and miscellaneous	$1,279,050

In addition to which, special appropriations were made for payment for property, certain incidental expenses, etc., to the amount of $28,-545.

Three hundred and forty-three missionaries, assistants, teachers, and woman missionaries from the United States, and 3,687 native preachers and other native agents, were employed in the foreign fields. The missions returned, in all, 58,753 members, 32,572 probationers, 73,566 adherents, and an average attendance on Sunday worship of 103,066 persons, 26,771 conversions, and 11,733 adults and 8,282 children baptized during the year; 18 theological schools, with 59 teachers and 434 students; 48 high schools, with 338 teachers and 3,983 pupils; 1,082 day schools, with 32,150 pupils; 2,225 Sunday schools, with 111,365 pupils; 475 orphans cared for; 623 churches and chapels, of the estimated value of $2,027,284; 850 halls and places of worship; 301 parsonages and homes, valued at $700.457; orphanages, schools, hospitals, and book rooms, valued at $763,804; and $338,418 collected for missions, benevolent societies, self-support, and church building and repairs. The domestic missions returned 3,372 missionaries, 249,089 members, 40,306 probationers, 15,767 adults and 12,-454 children baptized, 5,477 Sunday schools, with 279,342 pupils, 4,631 churches and chapels, valued at $8,176,010, and 1,487 parsonages and homes, valued at $1,172,180.

Woman's Missionary Societies.—The eleventh

annual meeting of the Woman's Home Missionary Society was held at Grand Rapids, Mich., Oct. 27. The total receipts in money and supplies had been $127,133. Industrial homes had been erected at Morristown, Tenn., and Ocala, Fla.; mission buildings at Speedwell, near Savannah, Ga., for the Indian work among the Navajos and for the Apaches in New Mexico. Deaconesses' homes had been secured by co-operating conference societies at Baltimore, Md., Brooklyn, N. Y., Des Moines, Iowa, Philadelphia, Pa., and Grand Rapids, Mich.; and through the influence of the society in Cincinnati, Ohio, industrial training and instruction in cooking had been introduced into the schools of that city. The Lucy Webb Training School for Missionaries in Washington had achieved a remarkable success. The society had 50 missions in the South and West, owned property in industrial schools and buildings worth $250,000, and employed, not including those engaged in local work, 150 missionaries. From its organization in 1880 till October, 1892, it had raised and expended $605,363, and had distributed supplies valued at $405,659 in aid of frontier work and missions. The society decided to discontinue receiving aid from the general treasury of the United States for religious and educational work.

General Conference.—The General Conference met in Omaha, Neb., May 2. A motion was passed at the beginning that the lay delegates be permitted to sit separately from the ministerial delegates, and a considerable proportion of the lay members seated themselves thus, while others continued to sit with the ministerial delegates of their several annual conferences. A question arose, on the appointment of the Committee of the Judiciary, as to whether its members should be named by the bishops, as had usually been done, or by the General Conference. It was decided that the bishops should nominate the members of the committee, and the General Conference should confirm them. A committee appointed by the previous General Conference to determine and define the constitution of the Church—that is, to mark the distinction between those parts of the Discipline which are constitutional and can not be changed except in the method prescribed for constitutional amendment, and those parts which are only statutory and can be changed by vote of the General Conference—presented a report designating certain sections of the Discipline as organic law, including the Articles of Religion and the "General Rules," which the General Conference is prohibited from changing, and the constitution of the General Conference, which consists of the six restrictive rules, limiting the power of the General Conference, and certain other sections of the Discipline, which provide for that body itself. New chapters or sections were proposed for adoption, subject to the approval of the annual conferences, for bringing into an orderly arrangement all portions of the organic law. Instead of this report, a substitute was adopted declaring that the section on the General Conference in the Discipline of 1808, as adopted by the General Conference of 1808, has the nature and force of a constitution, and that it, together with such modifications as have been adopted since that time in accordance with the provisions for amendment in that section, is the present constitution of the Church, excepting (1) the change of the provisions for calling an extra session of the General Conference from a unanimous to a two-third vote of the annual conferences; and (2) that which is known as the plan of lay delegation as recommended by the General Conference of 1868 and passed by the General Conference of 1872. A report was made by the Committee on the Itinerancy favorable to the removal of the "time limit" in the pastorate, or the rule under which a minister can not serve as pastor in the same charge more than five years in any ten; but the Conference disapproved the proposition, and declared that, as it did not appear that the people desired a removal, the present time limit of five years should be allowed to stand until the Church has had time to give it a fair and reasonable trial." A proposition was submitted to the annual conferences for approval making the number of lay delegates in the General Conference equal to the number of ministerial delegates, and providing for the election by the several annual conferences of equal numbers of both orders. The Epworth League was adopted as a connectional society of the Church, and provision was made for its recognition in the local churches through their quarterly conferences. The minute embodying this action sets forth that the Epworth League was formed at Cleveland, Ohio, during the preceding quadrennium at a conference of delegates from five already existing societies, all of which had been formed since 1883; that its purpose was to seek to promote among the young people the most earnest piety, loyalty to the Church, and active works of usefulness; and that it had grown in only three years to the number of 1,000 local chapters, embracing a membership of more than 400,000 young people. A note added to the minute explained that it was not intended by this action concerning the Epworth League to disturb the present status of other young people's societies now organized in the Church, which are under the control of the pastor and quarterly conference.

In relation to the admission of women as lay delegates in the General Conference, the conference directed that a proposition be submitted to the annual conferences and the people of the Church,

To amend the second restrictive rule by adding the words, " and said delegates must be male members," after the words " 2 lay delegates for an annual conference," so that it will read, " nor of more than 2 lay delegates for an annual conference, and said delegates must be male members"; and that if the amendment so submitted did not receive the votes of three fourths of the members of the annual conferences and two thirds of the General Conference, the second restrictive rule shall be so construed that the words "lay delegates" shall include men and women, and thus be in harmony with the legislation of previous General Conferences.

In view of the action of the Œcumenical Conference at Washington, D. C., in 1891, in favor of the organic union of Methodist bodies in the United States, of a similar recommendation by the bishops in their quadrennial address, and of the widely expressed evidence of the desire of the Church for union, the bishops were requested to appoint a commission consisting of 3 bishops, 3 ministers, and 3 laymen, to have power to confer with similar commissions from other Methodist bodies upon the desirability of fraternal co-operation and organic union. The bishops were requested to invite other Methodist bodies to appoint similar commissions of conference. A city evangelization union was provided for, to be composed of local organizations doing evangelistic work in cities, the purpose of which is to promote harmony in their operations. On the question of the course that should be pursued toward converts in the foreign mission fields who have contracted polygamous marriages previous to their conversion, the Conference resolved,

That the Christian Church can in no case, directly or indirectly, make any compromise by tolerating the vile practice of polygamy [and that while missionaries are to seek a peaceful and equitable adjustment of the complications of plural marriages], yet they are never to preach any other gospel than that which casts out every vice and implants every virtue, and therefore should never receive into our communion any persons holding polygamous relations.

The Conference advised all members of the Church so to vote as to promote the rescue of the country from the results of complicity with the liquor traffic; recorded its judgment that no political party has a right to expect, or ought to receive, the support of Christian men,

"So long as it stands committed to the license policy, or refuses to be put on record in an attitude of open hostility to the saloon." While using this plain language, the Conference resolved that its report should not be construed as an indorsement of any political party.

Provision was made for the formation of a permanent Committee on Temperance and Prohibition, and the organization of Christian Temperance Leagues in the several churches. The provisions of the Chinese Exclusion act were condemned

as inconsistent with international comity, in violation of the spirit, if not of the letter, of treaties between China and the United States; unnecessary, if not cruel; contrary to the spirit of the genius of free government; at variance with the privileges accorded to American citizens in China; and setting a precedent that might prove inconvenient.

A committee was appointed relative to participation in the contemplated religious exhibit at the Columbian Exposition; and Congress was urged to make any grant of money to the Exposition conditional on its being agreed in writing that the same should be closed on Sunday.

II. Methodist Episcopal Church, South.—
The collections for the Board of Missions of this Church, as reported at the annual meeting in May, 1892, amounted to $129,507 for domestic missions and $304,745 for foreign missions; adding to these sums the collections for the Woman's Board, the whole amount would be brought up to about $525,000. The obligations of the board had been reduced by about $30,000, but it was still embarrassed by its debt. The year had been one of unusual success in all the mission fields. Five new men had been sent to China, 5 to Japan, 3 to Brazil, and 2 to Mexico. The number of missionaries and their wives in the foreign field had increased in six years from 22 to 99.

The Woman's Board of Missions, at its fourteenth annual meeting, June 3, received reports from 3,404 auxiliary and young people's and juvenile societies, having 35,119 members. It had received, in contributions made through the Conference societies, $66,488, and had a balance of $93,992. It supported 29 missionaries—9 in China, 12 in Mexico, 8 in Brazil; 3 teachers in the Indian missions among the wild tribes, 16 assistant missionaries, and 7 native teachers in Mexico; and 39 native missionaries and assistants' and 2 Bible women in China. Nine hundred and thirty-five women and children were under instruction in Mexico, 689 children in China, and 215 pupils in 3 boarding schools in Brazil. Many Chinese women had received medical treatment in the hospital at Foo-Chau.

The year's business in the Publishing House at Nashville, Tenn., amounted to $339,884; $51,007 were added to the assets of the establishment, while its total liabilities were $16,446, with cash resources of $28,799. The assessments for the support of the bishops and the wives of deceased bishops amounted to $35,400, and $17,500 were appropriated for Conference claimants.

The number of Epworth Leagues returned in May as connected with this Church was 524, 1 of which was in Mexico and 1 in Japan.

III. African Methodist Episcopal Church.
—The nineteenth General Conference of the African Methodist Episcopal Church met in Philadelphia, Pa., May 3, and was opened with an address by Bishop Turner. The features in the proceeding presenting the most interest were those concerning the negotiations for union with the African Methodist Episcopal Zion Church. A preliminary consultation on the subject had already been had at a meeting of the bishops of the two churches held in Washington, D. C., in the fall of 1891. A joint commission, composed of twelve members of each of the two bodies, met in Harrisburg, Pa., during the session of the Conference (May 20), and agreed upon a basis of union. The chief point of difference related to the name to be given to the united body. The names "United Methodist Episcopal Church," "African and Zion Methodist Episcopal Church," "African Methodist Episcopal Church United," "United African Zion Methodist Episcopal Church," "Methodist Episcopal Church, United," "African Zion Episcopal Methodist Church," and "Negro Methodist Episcopal Church" were proposed. The name "African Zion Methodist Episcopal Church" was agreed upon, and incorporated in the plan adopted by the commission to be presented to the two General Conferences. This name was rejected by the African Methodist Episcopal General Conference. The Conference, however, in communicating its action to the General Conference of the African Methodist Episcopal Zion Church, intimated that it would accept either the name "African Methodist Episcopal and Zion Church," or "African Methodist Episcopal and Methodist Episcopal Zion Church." The bishops and General Conference of the Zion Church replied, that while they preferred the name proposed by the commission, they would accept that of "African and Zion Methodist Episcopal Church." This name was agreed to by a nearly unanimous vote. Three new bishops were elected, viz., the Rev. B. F. Lee, editor of

the " Christian Recorder," the official newspaper of the denomination : the Rev. M. B. Salters, of Georgetown, S. C.; and the Rev. J. A. Handy, of Washington, D. C., financial secretary during the past four years. Nine new conferences were established. The bishops were requested to see that papers were prepared to represent the Church in the World's Parliament of Religions in Chicago, and to appoint representatives to that assemblage. Resolutions were adopted acknowledging the action of the General Conference of the Methodist Episcopal Church, denouncing barbarities in the treatment of colored Christians in the South, and declaring that when

the white professed Christians of our land exert their influence against a wild and savage disregard of law and an evil which to-day dominates the South, in our opinion, the end of a brutality overshadowing the worst offenses of the King of Dahomey will have been reached.

A memorial was presented from the Haytian Conference, with reference to the distribution by President Hippolyte of $20,000 among the Protestant missions in the republic for church building and repairs, of which the African mission would receive a share : expressing thanks for it ; urging that in view of it the Church make still stronger efforts to establish itself on a firm foundation ; and particularly asking assistance in the conduct of the educational work of the Conference, and in the establishment of a high school at Port au Prince.

The Missionary Board reported the whole amount of the collections for the four years 1889 to 1892 as $27,450. The expenditures—$16,465 —included $14,291 for home work, and $2,175 (special) for African work. The missions are in Africa, Hayti and San Domingo, Demarara, and certain places in the twelfth episcopal district.

IV. African Methodist Episcopal Zion Church.—The General Conference of the African Methodist Episcopal Zion Church met in Pittsburg, Pa., May 4. The financial report showed that more money had been collected during the past quadrennium than in previous years. The collections for the General fund had been $69,181, showing an increase of $11,695. A report was made of the organization of a Sunday school department in accordance with the action of the General Conference of 1888, with a chief office at Montgomery, Ala. The receipts on its account had been $5,506, and the expenditures $5,158. The income of Livingstone College, Salisbury, N. C., during the four years had been $56,000. Its property was valued at $100,000. Gifts had been received by the college of 60 acres of land near Gainesville, Fla., $2,500 for the industrial education of girls, and $500 for the library, with $800 worth of new books. Commissioners were appointed to meet commissioners of the African Methodist Episcopal Church at Harrisburg, Pa., on the subject of organic union. The work of this commission was reported to the Conference before it adjourned, and approved by it (see above, African Methodist Episcopal Church). The report embodied a declaration that in all constitutional elements the two Churches are virtually one, and that all statutory provisions should be referred to the United General Conference for adjustment. Bishop Hood presented

his history, in the course of preparation, entitled "One Hundred Years of the African Methodist Episcopal Zion Church ; or, Centennial of African Methodism." An encyclopædia of the African Methodist Episcopal Zion Church was approved. The Rev. I. C. Clinton, D. D., and the Rev. A. Walters, D. D., were elected bishops. A board of education and the office of educational secretary were instituted. Prof S. G. Atkins was elected to the office. A " correspondence school " which had been established by the Board of Bishops was approved, and regulations were adopted for its management. A report on Church extension called attention to the need of the Church's following the rapid flow of emigration toward the West, especially into Oklahoma Territory, and of the zealous prosecution of work in the South, Southwest, extreme West, and Africa ; and recommended the establishment of a general board for that enterprise. This was approved. The report on the state of the Church committed the Church to uncompromising hostility to the liquor traffic, and to an advanced position on all humanitarian and ethical reforms ; mentioned the increasing importance of city evangelization ; recommended the enlistment of women in the work of the Church ; deprecated Sabbath desecration ; and recognized the growth and usefulness of the Young People's societies. Provision was made for the celebration of the one hundredth anniversary of the organization of the Church at a general conference to be held in Mobile, Ala., in 1896, and for the collection of commemorative funds ; also for a grand central celebration to be held in New York city. Direcetions were given for the preparation of a liturgy for Sunday morning services.

The Board of Education held its first meeting for organization in Washington, D. C., Aug. 30.

Union of African Methodist Churches.— A joint meeting of the bishops of the two Churches was held in Washington, D. C., July 27, which agreed on a plan of organic union to be sent down to the several annual and quarterly conferences for their approval. Finding that the two Churches have the same form of government, and the same ordinances, articles of religion, and doctrines, it provides for a complete union on the proposition receiving the affirmative vote of a majority of all the annual conferenees and of three fourths of all the quarterly conferences and churches or worshiping congregations. On its being approved in both bodies, a joint board or council of bishops is to be called to provide and arrange for a meeting of a united general conference of the " African and Zion Methodist Episcopal Church."

V. Colored Methodist Episcopal Church. —The Colored Methodist Episcopal Church in America has 4 bishops (one, Bishop Miles, has died since the return was made out), 22 annual conferences, 1,111 traveling preachers, 3,219 churches, 2,409 local preachers, 126,893 members, and 2,061 Sunday schools, with 9,731 officers and teachers and 78,928 pupils. Its four institutions of learning are Payne Institute, Augusta, Ga. ; Lane Institute, Jackson, Tenn. ; Haygood Seminary, Washington, Ark. ; and Beebee Institute, New Orleans, La.

VI. Methodist Protestant Church.—The statistical reports of 36 out of the 47 annual conferences of this Church which made returns of their members to the General Conference, give the following footings: Number of itinerant ministers, 1,307; of unstationed ministers and preachers, 987; of members, 131,184; of probationers, 3,882; of churches, 2,083.

The sixteenth General Conference met in Westminster, Md., May 20. Dr. J. W. Hering was chosen president. A question arose on the admission of 3 women who had been chosen as lay delegates by the Iowa, Indiana, and West Virginia Conferences, respectively, and of Mrs. E. F. St. John, who appeared as a ministerial delegate from the Kansas Conference. Two reports were brought in on the question by the Committee on Certificates. The majority report recognized the credentials of Mrs. St. John as a ministerial delegate as regular in form, but, regarding it as contrary to the constitution and laws of the Church to recognize the validity of the ordination of women, recommended that she should not be recognized as entitled to membership. It also recognized the credentials of the women elected as lay delegates as regular in form, but regarded their election as null, because in violation of the constitution and laws of the Church. The minority report found that the credentials of the woman delegates were regular, that the elections had all been constitutionally held and returned, and that the applicants were entitled to seats. The friends of the admission of the women held that by the constitution of the Church the matter of suffrage and eligibility was left to each annual conference to define for itself, and the conferences, having acted according to their wisdom, the General Conference should not interfere. This view prevailed, and the women were admitted. Subsequently, two overtures were submitted to the annual conferences calling for constitutional determinations whether a woman can be elected to the office of elder, and whether a woman can be elected as a representative to the General Conference. Reports were made by the Board of Ministerial Education, which had received $16,420 during the past four years, with $3,628 returned by beneficiaries, had a permanent fund of $5,479, and had aided 98 students; and reported that $8,000 had been subscribed toward a memorial fund of $10,000 of the Rev. J. B. Walker; from the Committee on Sunday Schools, which declared union schools impracticable, and advised that each pastor be required to organize all schools under his charge into Methodist Protestant schools; from the Board of Foreign Missions, showing that its receipts for the past four years had been $52,029, being an average of 32½ cents per member; and from the Woman's Foreign Missionary Society, which had received more than $20,000 in four years. The question of union with the Primitive Methodist Church was informally brought up, and provision was made for sending a fraternal delegate to the next general meeting of that body. A committee was appointed to receive any propositions for union coming from other denominations. The article in the Discipline concerning the control of churches by the trustees was amended by adding a provision that the use of the Church should not be forbidden to any branch of Christian work recognized by the General Conference. The temperance reso-lution insisted upon total abstinence for the individual and the entire suppression of the liquor traffic for the State, and defined the signing of petitions for license and participation in the use of spirituous or malt liquors by a minister to be immorality. Measures were taken for the incorporation of the General Conference under the laws of Maryland. The word "obey" was stricken from the marriage service. Reports were received from Western Maryland College, Westminster, and Adrian College, Mich. The offer of a gift of 150 acres of land for the establishment of a college in Kansas City, Kan., provided a building is erected costing not less than $25,000, and an offer of land for the establishment of a college at West Lafayette, Ohio, were approved and accepted. A proposition for the establishment of a college in Texas was favorably considered, and recognition was given to the proposed Lipscomb College, Waco, Ga.

The receipts of the Board of Missions for the year were $14,296, besides a number of contributions sent directly to the missionaries, and the disbursements amounted to $12,038.

The Board of Home Missions elected by the General Conference met in Pittsburg, Pa., and organized June 15. A conference of 5 preachers and 1,200 members (colored) had been organized in South Carolina, and sent up an appeal for help in education. Arrangements were made for a visitation of the Southern colored conferences and the establishment of an institution of learning among them.

The Board of Foreign Missions returned its receipts for the year, not including contributions sent directly to the missionaries, at $14,296, and its expenditures at $12,038.

VII. Primitive Methodist Church in the United States.—The reports of the meetings for 1892 of the three annual conferences of this denomination were hopeful as to its prospects. Action was taken to promote the interests of the Book Room. The missionary collections were unusually large. Woman's Missionary Societies were formed, and sanction was given to the organization of "Young People's Wesley Leagues."

VIII. American Wesleyan Church.—The Missionary Society of this Church returned an income for the year ending in June, 1892, of $2,407. The work in the recently established foreign mission in Africa had made an encouraging advance. The Superannuated Ministers' Aid Society returned its receipts at $4,921, and the Education Society at $1,450. The Publishing Association, with assets of $64,150, and a year's receipts of $23,939, reported a gain from the year's business of $2,434.

IX. Methodist Church in Canada.—The receipts of the Missionary Society for the year, as returned to the annual meeting in October, 1892, were $249,385, showing an increase of $6,000 over the previous year; the expenditures were $233,624. From the mission in Japan were returned 35 ministers at work, with 1,928 members. Cities and towns were reached by the mission having a total population of at least 4,000,000. The evangelistic work was developing rapidly, and the educational work was being more and more turned to the training of young men for the ministry. A mission had been started in the previous year in east China, to which 4 missionaries, with their wives, were appointed. The Chinese work in British Columbia returned 190 members. The missions to the Indians in British Columbia, Manitoba, and the Northwest, and in the central conferences, were supplied by 46 missionaries, and had 4,330 members. The French mission work included 7 missions, with 7 missionaries and 278 members. The home or domestic mission work returned 393 missionaries, with 35,083 members. An important feature of the French mission work was the Institute, which was attended by the French Catholic and Protestant children.

X. Wesleyan Methodist Church.—The following is a summary of the statistics of this Church in the British and affiliated conferences as they were returned to the British Conference in July:

CONFERENCES.	Members.	On trial.	Ministers.	Ministers on probation.	Super-numeraries.
Great Britain	424,959	27,540	1,581	198	297
Ireland and Irish Missions	25,553	640	176	21	84
Foreign Missions	86,395	6,208	235	106	14
French Conference	1,473	117	33	....	....
South African Conference	33,523	12,231	183	....	....
West Indian Conference	47,817	3,284	104	....	....
Total	569,720	50,020	2,222	384	871

Missionary and other Benevolent Societies. —The annual meeting of the Wesleyan Missionary Society was held in London, May 2. Mr. John R. Hill, of York, presided. The financial statement showed that the receipts for the year had been £125,129, and the disbursements £129,197. Moneys accruing to the society would probably cancel the adverse balance, but the deficit of £19,000 at the opening of the year 1891 had been reduced by only £2,014. The reports from the mission fields showed that while the number of missionaries abroad had slightly decreased, there had been an increase upon the previous year of 70 paid agents—evangelists, teachers, etc.—325 unpaid agents, 1,500 full and accredited members, 1,000 persons on trial for membership, and 2,400 pupils in Sunday and day schools. While the work of the society lay principally in Africa, India, and China, work had also been done by the European missions in Italy, Germany, and France. A special instance of rapid advance was pointed to in a mission in the Transvaal. It was declared to be the constant endeavor of the missionaries to raise up a native Christian agency.

The Chapel Fund Committee had spent £378,-139 during the year on new erections and the reduction of debt, £232,950 of which sum had been raised by voluntary contributions.

Wesleyan Conference.—The one hundred and ninth annual Conference met in Bradford, July 19. The Rev. Dr. J. H. Rigg was chosen president. A discussion of the subject of the extension of the term during which a minister may serve continuously as pastor in the same station, was concluded by appointing a committee to consider during the year the whole question of the term of ministerial appointments in relation to the needs both of special cases and of our circuits generally, with a view to inquiry especially whether any of the suggestions for extending the time, with the necessity of application to Parliament, are practicable or desirable, and to report to the next Conference.

A proposed form of service for the recognition of new members reported for insertion in the ritual of the connection, was remitted for revision, with the expectation of presenting it to the district meetings in May, 1893, for their consideration. A proposition intended to encourage religious study especially among young pupils, for the appointment of an examining board to confer certificates of proficiency in religious knowledge, was approved, and referred to a committee appointed to consider the details of the measure and report to the next Conference. In contemplation of the holding of a third Œcumenical Methodist Conference in England in 1901, ten members, representing the quota of the connection, were appointed to serve on the eastern section of the executive committee for that meeting. Questions having been proposed, "merely to draw attention to the matter," whether the Theological Institutions Committee takes the necessary precautions to ascertain the precise teaching given in the colleges, and whether such teaching is in accordance with the doctrinal standards of Methodism; and, if not, what security Methodist people can have that their students are trained in the fundamental doctrines of Methodism, and not in views that contravene its doctrinal standards, the answer was given, without any resolution, that the appointment of the staff of the colleges is in the hands of the conference, and the members of the staff are subject to the same kind of test by the district committees as all the other ministers are. A proposition for enlarging the district meetings by the special election to them of one or two laymen from each circuit, was approved. A question concerning the enforcement of the rule of baptism as a condition of communicant membership was brought up in the case of the Rev. Mr. Scott, of Luton, who had refused tickets of membership to two members who had not been baptized and did not intend to be baptized. Upon this, the Conference decided:

1. That, in insisting on the divine authority and abiding obligation of Christian baptism as the sacrament of initiation into the visible Church, Mr. Scott was right, and is to be commended, as well as for the high sense of duty under which he acted. 2. That Mr. Scott, however, erred in the following respects: (*a*) In depriving of full membership those who had already been recognized as members of the Church, even though he did not anticipate from them any final objection to being baptized. (*b*) In doing this, in cases in which there was no necessity for immediate decision, without any conversation with the parents of the young people, although the parents were members of the Church, and without taking counsel with his superintendent, and subsequently in not deferring to his superintendent when he urged him to give the tickets. 3. That though Mr. Scott was not constitutionally bound to refer the matter to the leaders' meeting before withholding the tickets of membership, yet Mr. Scott was bound, when a protest had afterward arisen, to instruct the parties that the first court of appeal is the leaders' meeting.

The Conference, while it urged the young men to submit themselves to the "divinely ordained ordinance" of baptism, ordered them to be restored at once to full membership.

XI. Primitive Methodist Church.

The annual meeting of the Primitive Methodist Missionary Society was held in London, May 17. The income of the General fund had been £11,-990, against £11,999 in 1891; and the expenditures had been £11,468. The net income for the African fund had been £3,777. The 54 missions in the United Kingdom were served by 72 missionaries. The returns of the colonial stations (in Australia) were not yet at hand. On the foreign stations (at Fernando Po and Aliwal North, Africa) an increase of nearly 17 per cent. had been realized. The party which had been sent out in 1890 to open a mission in the Zambesi country were still, when last heard from, in January, 1892, awaiting the permission of the Barotse king to settle in some part of his kingdom.

The Conference met in Norwich, June 8. The Rev. J. Travis was chosen president. The report of the Committee on Statistics showed that there had been a decrease of 552 in the number of members, and the fact was made a subject of discussion in the Conference. The African Mission fund returned a total income of £3,777, with a balance in hand of more than £1,000. The report of missionary work showed that the 6 missions in London returned an increase of 15 per cent., the colonies of more than 350 members, and the African mission of 17 per cent. all around. As the next year would be the jubilee year of the society, the preparation of a history of its work was advised. It was decided to start a home missionary van to travel in the country districts and hold temperance and evangelistic meetings. A scheme was approved for raising a missionary jubilee fund in commemoration of the jubilee of the Missionary Society, and £18,-000 were contributed to that object during the sessions of the Conference.

XII. United Methodist Free Churches.

The statistical tables of this body, prepared for the Annual Assembly in July, showed that the number of members at home and abroad was 78,152, with 8,653 persons on trial; of teachers in Sunday schools, 26,598; and of pupils in Sunday schools, 206,039. The trust property of the connection was valued at about £2,000,000, and the liabilities on it at £700,000.

The total income of the United Methodist Free Church missions was returned at the annual meeting of the society, April 25, as £26,-284, showing an increase of £864 over the previous year, while the expenditure had been £25,997. A little more than £6,000 had been promised to the Wesley Memorial fund. The reports from the field showed that the denomination had abroad 68 missionaries and 10,510 members, being an increase of 375 members; and at home and abroad 378 ministers and 77,-710 members. The report affirmed that the society had had considerable success at home and abroad, but principally abroad. "Cheering accounts" had been sent home from Australia, New Zealand, Jamaica, Central America, East and West Africa, and China, "perhaps the most cheering being from China."

The Annual Assembly met in the City Road Chapel of the Wesleyan Connection, London, July 12. The Rev. J. Truscott was chosen president. A report was made of the Wesleyan Memorial fund, which was instituted by the preceding Annual Assembly for aggressive work at home and abroad, that the contributions had not been so large as had been anticipated. Of the £15,000 sought to be raised, only £7,050 had been obtained. The income for home and foreign missions, including foreign local receipts, had been £22,771. The Assembly recommended the observance of a "self-denial week," in which certain sums intended to be expended upon pleasures and upon things that could be done without should be laid aside for this purpose, each year, in aid of the General Mission funds. A case was brought before the Assembly which involved a question of the limits between the principles of circuit independence and connectional control. A dispute in one of the circuits had led to the intervention of the Connectional Committee. This action was protested against as in contravention of the principle of circuit independence. The Assembly, reviewing the whole case, defined its position on this question by declaring

That circuit independence is not absolute, as in our constitution it is limited by the Connectional principle. And as the Foundation Deed gives to the Annual Assembly the right to withdraw itself from any church or circuit which does not act in accordance with the teaching of the New Testament, this right, in the opinion of this Assembly, necessarily carries with it the right of investigation and inquiry; and when there is a *prima facie* case, the circuit is constitutionally bound to admit the investigation, that the Annual Assembly may exercise an intelligent judgment.

That, as the Annual Assembly has, by the provisions of the Foundation Deed, full control over connectional ministers, the principle of circuit independence is not a bar to the proper exercise of that right by the Annual Assembly.

A proposition to recommend a series of suitable books for students for the local ministry, and to recommend a line of study for local ministers fully engaged in their work, was referred to the consideration of the circuits.

XIII. Methodist New Connection.

The numerical summary of this body, reported to the Conference in June, showed that it had 546 chapels, 486 churches, 201 circuit preachers, 1,191 local preachers, 31,288 members, and 4,767 probationers. The Connection had also in England and Ireland 455 Sunday schools, with 11,-196 officers and teachers.

The aggregate amount of money sent to the Conference for the Connectional funds was £16,670. The Beneficent fund for aged ministers and widows returned an income of £3,537, and an invested capital of £25,059. The income for home missions had been £1,153, and showed an increase. The income for foreign missions had been £6,854.

The Conference met at Ashton-under-Lyne, June 13. The Rev. J. C. Milburn was chosen president. A report was made that a small number of circuits had sent resolutions to the Annual Committee, complaining that the last Conference had closed the negotiations for union with the United Methodist Free Churches without consulting the circuits. The resolutions had been duly acknowledged, but, considering the relatively small number of the circuits supporting them, and their comparatively small aggregate membership, and the decision of the Conference, the committee had not seen the way to reopen the question. It had been agreed at the Œcumenical Conference that an attempt should be made on each side of the Atlantic to secure greater mutual co-operation, and President Stevenson, of the Wesleyan Conference, had undertaken to call together all the representatives of English Methodism for this purpose. An executive committee had been formed, with two representatives of the New Connection upon it, whose nomination was confirmed by the Conference. A former resolution of the Conference, disapproving the reading of sermons, was reaffirmed. The Conference accepted the address of the Nonconformist Council in Westminster House Hotel on the subject of the general election and public morals, and authorized the president to sign it. Resolutions were passed on the relations of politics and politicians to public morals, in favor of local option in the suppression of the liquor traffic and the Sunday closing of public houses, and condemning the opium traffic, gambling, and the publication of betting news in the journals. Provision was made for the establishment of a league of the young people on the basis of the Christian Endeavor Society or the Epworth League.

XIV. Bible Christians.—The following is a summary of the statistics of this Church, as they were reported to the Conference in August: Number of chapels, 854; of preaching stations, 138; of ordained ministers, 285; of lay preachers, 1,910; of church members, 31,258, with 733 on trial; of teachers in Sunday schools, 8,950; of pupils, 53,649.

The report of the Bible Christian Missionary Society, made at the annual meeting, May 3, showed that the income for the year had been £7,651, and the expenditure £8,924; and that the debt was £1,272. The society had 139 missionaries, 768 local preachers, and 2,869 teachers, with 402 chapels. Resolutions were passed recognizing the success of the colonial work, and expressing a determination to assist to the utmost in evangelizing China.

The seventy-fourth annual Conference met at Newport, Isle of Wight, July 27. The Rev. William Lee was chosen president. The business transacted related chiefly to the internal affairs of the Connection and its institutions. Members were appointed to represent the Connection on the Permanent Œcumenical Methodist Committee of Eighty, with reference to holding a third Œcumenical Conference in 1901. The Connectional Committee was authorized to confer with other Methodist bodies, as opportunity occurs, with reference to union.

XV. South African Wesleyan Methodist Church.—The statistics of this body for 1892 show that it has 493 churches, 274 ministers or evangelists, 2,057 local preachers, 33,523 members of church, with 12,231 on trial for membership, 357 day schools with 20,845 pupils, and 380 Sunday schools with 24,959 pupils.

MEXICO, a federative republic in North America. The legislative power is vested in a Congress consisting of a Senate of 56 members, 2 from each State, and a House of Representatives, 1 for every 40,000 inhabitants. Members of both houses are elected by the suffrage of all respectable adult male citizens. The President is elected for four years. There are 27 States, with 2 Territories and a Federal District. Gen. Porfirio Diaz was inaugurated as President on Dec. 1, 1884, succeeding Gen. Manuel Gonzalez. The Constitution was amended to enable him to succeed himself, and he was re-elected in 1888. In July, 1892, he was returned for a third term by a large majority. He received the electoral votes of 23 of the States and the 2 Territories. Each State has its government, which is independent of the Federal authorities, and is organized on the same model as the General Government. Each has its governor and legislature, elected by popular suffrage. Except in the States of Vera Cruz and Mexico, all have adopted both the civil and the criminal code of laws enacted by the Federal Congress.

Area and Population.—The area of the republic is 751,664 square miles. The population at the census of 1879 was 9,908,801. In 1890 it was estimated at 11,395,712. The city of Mexico has a population of 329,535; Guadalajara, 95,000; Puebla, 78,530; San Luis Potosi, 62,573; Guanajuato, 52,112; Leon, 47,739; Monterey, 41,700.

Finances.—The revenue for the year 1890–'91 was $39,970,000, and the expenditure was $38,-452,803. For 1891–'92 the revenue was estimated in the budget at $41,550,000, viz., $26,-500,000 from customs, $1,500,000 from internal revenue duties, $9,700,000 from stamps, $1,400,-000 from direct taxes, $1,350,000 from posts and telegraphs, $300,000 from the mint, $300,000 from lotteries, and $500,000 from other sources. The total expenditure was estimated at $38,-377,365, of which $14,432,995 are for the Finance Department, $12,658,101 for the War and Navy Department, $2,480,897 for the Department of Home Affairs, $5,071,453 for the Department of Public Works, $1.639,636 for the Department of Justice and Public Instruction, $558,483 for the Department of Foreign Affairs, $476,785 for the judicial branch, $1,009,036 for the legislative power, and $49,977 for the Executive. The partial failure of the Indian-corn crop and the low price of silver interfered with the calculation, and the actual receipts fell below those of 1891, amounting only to a little more than $37,000,-000. Savings were made in expenditures, and in order to meet the deficiency that would occur before these retrenchments and the new taxes that were decided on could make themselves felt, a temporary loan of $3,000,000, payable in two years, was obtained.

The old English debt, amounting to £22,341,-000, was scaled down and converted into new bonds of the total amount of £13,991,775, in accordance with a compromise effected in 1886. A second operation, effected by means of a 6-per cent. loan of £10,500,000, raised in London and Berlin in 1888 and 1889, enabled the Government to make a new conversion and pay off the floating debt. In September, 1890, another 6-per-cent. loan was raised in London, Berlin, and Amsterdam, amounting to £6,000,000, the proceeds of which were applied to paying off arrears due on railroad subventions, which amounted to $40,000,000. A conversion of the internal debts has also been effected, the amount of the converted bonds being $38,900,000. Very little remains unpaid, and on that the interest is reduced to 3 per cent. from 1890. The total foreign debt is £16,500,000, and the total funded debt amounts to $111,000,000. In the sales of public lands the Government hopes to liquidate a large part of the debt by receiving one third of the price in bonds.

The Army and Navy.—The military forces in 1891 numbered 17,307 infantry, 5,484 cavalry, 1,604 artillery, 655 engineers, 1,950 rural guards, and 244 gendarmes, making a total of 27,244. The number of officers on the army list exceeds 3,000. The reserves bring the war strength of the republic up to 131,523 infantry, 25,790 cavalry, and 3,650 artillery. The military laws make every able-bodied Mexican citizen between the ages of twenty and fifty liable for service. The regular army is largely armed with Remington rifles. The guns for the artillery and the gunpowder are made in the Government arsenal at Mexico city. Most of the officers are educated in the military academy at Chapultepec.

The Mexican war fleet comprises 2 unarmored gunboats of 450 tons, 2 dispatch vessels, 1 transport, 1 small gunboat, and 1 training ship.

Commerce and Production.—The value of the imports in 1890 was $47,000,000, and of the exports $62,499,388. In 1891 the exports were valued at $63,276,395, of which $27,020,023 represent merchandise and $36,256,372 precious metals. The values of the principal individual exports in 1890 were as follow: Henequen, $7,392,244; silver ore, $7,259,958; coffee, $4,811,-000; hides and skins, $1,913,129; woods, $1,739,-138; tobacco, $948,332; vanilla, $917,409; ixtle fiber, $327,980; copper, $735,183; gum, $719,-746; lead, $607,329; live animals, $500,217. The exports to the United States in 1890–'91 amounted to $44,983,086, against $43,022,440 in 1889–'90; to Great Britain, $10,822,728, against $13,722,-122; to France, $3,653,551, against $3,159,258; to Germany, $2,785,875, against $1,693,773; to Spain, $515,194, against $534,057; to other countries, $455,853, against $367,738. Of the imports in 1889–'90, $22,669,000 came from the United States, $6,338,000 from England, $4,957,-000 from France, $2,843,000 from Germany, $1,921,000 from Spain, and $1,297,000 from other countries.

A law was passed in 1863 to facilitate the sale and development of the public lands. Between 1881 and 1888 there were 36,578,780 hectares taken up, mainly by companies. There were 18 colonies, comprising 6,524 settlers in 1891. The main food crops are Indian corn, barley, wheat, and beans. There are 5,000 tons of tobacco of fine quality raised annually in the State of Vera Cruz alone. The value of the tobacco crop is $2,500,-000 a year; of the cotton crop, $10,857,000; of sugar-cane, $8,735,000; of coffee, $3,200,000; of henequen, $3,718,750. Rice, cacao, vanilla, and wine are some of the other products. Great numbers of cattle are raised in the northern States and exported to the United States. The country is exceedingly rich in minerals, and rapid progress is being made in the development of the mines, in which $500,000,000 are invested. There are about 1,000 companies and firms engaged in mining, employing upward of 200,000 men. The annual product of the mines is about $70,-000,000. In 1892 a new mining law was enacted which varies in important regards from the mining code previously in force. Titles of ownership now depend on payment of the new Federal tax, in place of on the mines being worked. Formal documents of title are now obtained from the Department of Public Works. Formerly only a limited number of claims could be owned by any single individual or company, while the new law places no restriction on the number of claims that may be owned. Claims are now subject to no alteration, whatever the lay of the vein may be; while under the former code the size of claims varied with the lay of the vein and the nature of the mineral. The organization of mining companies is now subject to no special rules, but is governed wholly by the commercial code: contracts for lending money to miners to carry on their work will in future be treated as agreements of partnership, or as mortgages, subject to the codes applicable to both. The old law giving the several States the right to tax mines up to 2 per cent. of the gross earnings remains in force, and a Federal tax of $10 on each 100 metres of land is made a condition of title. The smaller miners object to the taxes, and complain further that those who had claims under the old law have to pay the cost of taking out a new title, as well as a tax that was not contemplated when they made their claims.

Communications.—In 1891 there were 6,266 miles of railroad, 360 miles having been constructed during the last three quarters of the previous year. About $245,000,000 is invested in Mexican railroads by United States citizens, and $70,000,000 by Englishmen. The number of passengers carried in 1889 was 12,977,952, from whom the receipts were $2,090,505; the number of tons of freight was 875,894, paying $4,822,690. The Mexican Central trunk line, 1,294 miles, has a branch from San Luis Potosí to the Gulf of Mexico at Tampico, and one running westward to Guadalajara which will be extended to the Pacific coast. A railway is being pushed southward from the city of Mexico toward Guatemala. A narrow-gauge road from Mexico city to Vera Cruz will be extended to the Pacific. The telegraphs in 1891 had a total length of 27,861 miles, of which 14,841 miles belonged to the Federal Government, while the States owned about one third of the rest, and the remainder was divided between the railroad and telegraph companies. The post office in 1891 carried about 125,000,000 letters and other pieces of mail matter. The receipts were $1,097,435.

The merchant marine consists of 16 steamers, of 6,952 tons, and 16 sailing vessels, of 3,302 tons, besides which there are a large number of vessels of less than 100 tons engaged in the coasting trade. In 1890 the number of vessels entered and cleared at the various ports was 1,448. A great artificial harbor is being constructed at Tampico by means of a system of jetties.

MICHIGAN, a Western State, admitted to the Union Jan. 26, 1837; area, 58,915 square miles. The population in 1890 was 2,093,889. Capital, Lansing.

Government.—The following were the State officers during the year: Governor, Edwin B. Winans, Democrat; Lieutenant-Governor, John Strong; Secretary of State, R. R. Blacker; Treasurer, Frederick Braastad; Auditor, George

W. Stone; Commissioner of State Land Office,
George J. Shaffer; Attorney-General, Adolphus
A. Ellis; Superintendent of Public Instruction,
Ferris S. Fitch; Commissioner of Insurance,
William E. Magill; Commissioner of Railroads,
Charles R. Whitman; Commissioner of Labor,
Henry A. Robinson; Commissioner of Mineral
Statistics, Charles D. Lawton; Chief Justice of
the Supreme Court, Allen B. Morse, who re-
signed to accept the nomination of the Demo-
cratic party for Governor; Associate Justices,
John W. McGrath, Charles D. Long, Claudius
B. Grant, R. M. Montgomery.

Finances.—The Treasurer's report for the
year ending June 30, 1892, shows the ensuing
figures: Balance, June 30, 1891, $1,224,644.32;
receipts during the year, $3,210,832.90; expendi-
tures, $3,193,505.40; balance, $1,241,971.82. The
outstanding bonds of the State now are: Past-
due part-paid Five-million Loan Bonds, $19,000;
adjustable at $558.57 per $1,000 (not bearing
interest), $10,992.83.

Following is the condition of the several
funds: General fund, $1,027,656.92; agricul-
tural college interest fund, $27,673.23; normal
school interest fund, $1,027.06; primary school
interest fund, $94,373.98; university interest
fund, $10,813.51; sundry deposits account, $11,-
220; St. Mary's Canal fund, $68,927.12; war
fund, $280.

The trust fund debt, composed of balances
upon which the State, as trustee, pays interest
for educational purposes, now stands: Agricultural college fund, $400,234.63; normal school
fund, $64,742.62; primary school fund, 7 per
cent. $3,650,775.82, and 5-per-cent. $807,215.58;
total school fund, $4,457,991.40; university
fund, $522,211.93; aggregate balance of trust
funds, $5,445,180.58.

Insurance.—The reports for the year 1891,
published in April, 1892, show a large increase
in the insurance business over that of 1890.
There were 34 life-insurance companies doing
business in the State, two of which are Michigan
companies—the Michigan Mutual and the Imperial of Detroit. The total admitted assets of
these companies was $823,851,948.34, an increase
over 1890 of $68,456,486.98, of which amount
$472,783.91 was of the 2 home companies. The
total liabilities of the same companies was
$706,967,536.02, an increase over 1890 of $61,-
048,656.41, of which $57,604,052.79 was increase
in the reinsurance reserve. The increase of
net surplus as to policy holders over that of
1890 is $7,407,830.57. The increase in the total
income compared with that of the previous year
was $15,541,079.76, and of disbursements $9,562,-
985.71. The total increase in premium receipts
was $14,015,269.25, of which amount $17,646.48
is credited to the two State companies. The increase in the amount paid for losses and matured endowments is $4,495,851.69, of which $37,-
133.51 was by Michigan companies. The increase in the number of policies in force was
192,576, and in amount at risk $325,683,542.65.
There were 20,837 policies issued during the
year by the life companies, aggregating an insurance of $23,288,995.04. The Vermont Life
and the Provident Life and Trust companies
were authorized early in 1892 to do business in
the State.

There were 6 co-operative or assessment associations at the beginning of 1891, one of which
transferred its membership to the Massachusetts
Mutual Benefit Association of Boston. The
Michigan M. B. A. of Hillsdale, organized in
1879, was obliged to ask for a receiver in 1892 on
account of heavy losses and decreased membership. The commissioner's report says: "It is
understood that arrangements have been made
for a transfer of its membership to an association of another State, and that its assets will not
be sufficient to pay over 50 per cent. of its liabilities." One new State association and 8 of other
States were admitted during the year, making
the number authorized of other States 41. The
gross assets of this class of companies were $10,-
786 654.91, and the total liabilities $673,273.02.
The total paid to members was $10,426,124.38.
The total number of certificates in force Dec. 31,
1891, was 519,361, and the surplus $10,113,-
381.89.

The year 1891 was one of unusually heavy
losses by fire, the amount of indemnity paid by
companies reporting, on fire business alone,
aggregating $2,479,525.57, as against $2,189,-
462.94 the preceding year. The premiums received were $4,048,219.83 for 1891, and $3,769,-
590 for 1890, the ratio of losses to premiums increasing from 58·1 per cent. in 1890 to 61·2 per
cent. in 1891. The risks written amounted to
$279,173,561. The number of companies report-
ing in fire and inland business was 106.

Railroads.—The net income of the roads of
the State in 1891 was given at $36,165,108; they
paid a tax of $812,999. The total mileage 7,274.-
94, an increase of 339·65 miles.

The total indebtedness of the railroad corporations as reported for the year 1891 amounts to
$435,781,670.32, which is classified as follows:
Funded debt, 91·42 per cent., $398,409,755.20;
unfunded debt, 8·58 per cent., $37,371,915.12.
The above statement shows an apparent increase
in debt over the previous year of $19,396,141.45.
The traffic earnings aggregated $95,777,886.57,
an increase over 1890 of $3,427,093.30, or 3·72
per cent. The total operating expenses and
taxes were $66,030,872.72, being an increase of
$2,105,781.18, or 3·29 per cent. The total
tonnage of freight moved was 57,852,628 tons.

In a suit involving the validity of the 2-cent-
fare law passed by the Legislature of 1889, the
decision of the Michigan Supreme Court was
affirmed by the United States Supreme Court,
and the law declared constitutional.

It is found that one of the laws passed by the
last Legislature relating to railroad taxation is
invalid—the one making the special charter
roads subject to the provisions of the general
railroad tax law. All the other railroad laws
refer with gr a particularity to the railroad act
of 1873 and acts amendatory thereof. This act
does not. It says that all these special charter
roads shall "for all purposes of taxation be subject in all respects to the provisions of chapter
75 of the compiled laws of 1871 and the acts
amendatory thereof, the same as if every such
company had organized under the provisions of
said chapter."

But chapter 75 of the compiled laws of 1871
was repealed *in toto* by an act passed in 1873.
This new act, therefore, attempts to revive an

obsolete law. It attempts to bring the special charter roads under the operation of a statute no longer in existence, and is consequently invalid.

In December an advance in wages was granted by the Lake Shore and Michigan Southern Railroad Company to their engineers and firemen, as the result of many conferences between the company officials and committees of the two brotherhoods. The advance for freight engineers is from 3·07 cents per mile to 4 cents, and for passenger engineers from 3·5 cents per mile to 3·8 cents. The company was ready to grant the advance in view of the promise of the engineers and firemen that they will have nothing to do with the strike of the switchmen, brakemen, and conductors which is expected during the World's Fair next year.

A decision of the Supreme Court in a suit for damages against a street railroad company is of great importance to such companies. The court held that the plaintiff had the same right to travel upon the track as the railway company had, save that it was her duty when she met a car to get off and give the car precedence. She was not a trespasser upon the track in any sense. The right of the railway in the street is only an easement to use the highway in common with the public. It has no exclusive right to travel upon its track, and it is bound to use the same care in preventing a collision as the driver of a wagon or other vehicle. Street cars have precedence necessarily in the portion of the way designated for their use. This superior right must be exercised, however, with proper caution and due regard for the rights of others, and the fact that it has a prescribed route does not alter the duty of the company to the public, who have a right to travel upon its track until met or overtaken by its cars.

The court says further that the contention of the company that a street car is a vehicle, the same as a wagon or omnibus, and is no more bound than is any other vehicle to carry a headlight or to give signals or warnings of its approach, is not law. A street car, it says, can neither turn to the right nor to the left; it runs with greater rapidity and with greater momentum than an omnibus or wagon; therefore, greater precaution must be taken in its running to avoid collisions.

Education.—The following statistics are quoted from the report issued in April by the Superintendent of Public Instruction: Number of school districts, 7,220; number of children of school age, 666,391; number enrolled in graded and ungraded schools, 446,024; percentage of attendance, 66·9; number of private schools, 320, with 302 men and 520 women teachers; whole number of teachers at one time, 11,093; total amount of wages paid to 3,488 male teachers, $941,636.43; to 12,621 women, $2,489,343.54; average monthly wages of men, $47.23; of women, $33.27. There were 7,616 schoolhouses, with sittings for 564,556 pupils, valued at $14,534,203; and 1,621 school libraries, with 534,780 volumes. The net school receipts were $5,509,167.14, and expenditures, $5,458,841.44.

The State Convention of Grangers protested against the movement to change the present system of district schools to the unit system—a system which they thought was practically taking the control of these schools from the hands of the many and giving it into the hands of the few.

State Institutions.—The total appropriations for the asylums for the insane, the institutions for the deaf and dumb and for the blind, and the Soldiers' Home, amounted to $253,203.13; those for prisons and reformatories amounted to $159,615.

The average number of inmates in these institutions was as follows: Michigan Asylum, 1,047; Eastern Asylum, 893; Northern Asylum, 810; Asylum for Dangerous Insane, 164; School for the Deaf, 287; School for the Blind, 70; State Public School, 198; State Prison, 785; House of Correction, 300; Upper Peninsula Prison, 111; Reform School, 433; Industrial Home, 207; Soldiers' Home, 372; total average, 5,677.

The following is the *per capita* cost of food per day: Michigan Asylum, 13·6 cents; Eastern Asylum, 15·5; Northern Asylum, 18·5; Asylum for Dangerous Insane, 14·1; School for Deaf, 15; School for Blind, 13·7; State Public School, 10; State Prison, 8·5; House of Correction, 15·3; Upper Peninsula Prison, 16·2; Reform School, 7; Industrial Home, 8·7; Soldiers' Home, 13·2; total average, 13·5.

The asylum at Pontiac took fire Dec. 24. There were 945 patients in the institution, some of them, of course, being in the cottages and hospitals. About 200 were turned out of their accustomed quarters by the fire. The loss was estimated at $150,000. There was no insurance. The entire building and grounds of 440 acres are valued at 795,000.

Legislative Investigation.—Secretary of State Daniel E. Soper was accused, in 1891, of irregularities in office; he resigned, and the Governor appointed R. R. Blacker to succeed him. The charges against him were made the subject of investigation by a committee, whose report was unfavorable to the ex-secretary. They found that he had given away books without authority and contrary to law, some of which were to be kept as State property and not to be disposed of at any price; also, that pay was received for many of them which should have gone to the State. They found evidence that supplies for the State had been ordered from firms who consented to throw in articles not to be used by the State. They also found, by comparison of letters filed with the cash book of the chief clerk, that money had been received in several instances and none of the amounts entered upon the cash book or turned into the State treasury in the proper way; and "inasmuch as Mr. Soper occupied his office several days and nights after the committee asked him to vacate, and he busied himself in going through his bills and letters, taking away several hundred of the same, it is inferred that much money was taken that was not turned over to the State and properly accounted for." They cited damaging testimony from a letter in regard to the purchase of manual paper.

The committee showed from their findings a shortage of $1,197.50, but avowed their belief that there were other shortages which their limited authority would not permit them to unearth, and recommended that the Governor pursue the matter further.

Nothing more was done about the matter until July, when the Auditor-General applied to the Governor for a statement of the ex-Secretary's indebtedness to the treasury, which he needed in order to balance the account in his office. The Governor sent the figures, and the Auditor made a demand on Mr. Soper for the money, and there the case seems to have rested.

The Mortgage Tax Law.—The movement to test the validity of this law, enacted in 1891, resulted in a decision in its favor. The main opinion was written by Justice Montgomery, and concurred in by Justice McGrath and Chief Justice Morse, Justices Grant and Long dissenting. The main opinion sustains the propositions that the act was properly passed; that it applied to mortgages in existence at the time of its passage; that it applied to mortgages owned by nonresidents and to savings banks and insurance companies, mortgages held by them being taxed as real estate and deducted from the capital stock; and that neither the tax law nor usury law prohibited persons from contracting as to who should pay the tax, even though tax and interest combined exceeded 8 per cent., which is the limit of interest that may be contracted under usury law.

Concerning the objection that so much of the statute as provides for the taxation of the mortgage interest in lands, and points out the method of collection, is unconstitutional, the justice says:

The first criticism passed upon these provisions is that the law requires the mortgageor to pay the mortgagee's tax. It should not be overlooked that the statute contemplates an assessment of the entire interests of the land, both that of the mortgageor and mortgagee, by separate assessments, it is true, but still an assessment of the entire interest. It can not be doubted that it is entirely competent for the Legislature to cause this entire value to be assessed to the mortgageor. This has been the law of Michigan for many years. This act is, then, for the relief of the mortgageor, and it can not be held invalid, because it relieves him only on condition that the owner of the mortgage interest shall within a stated time pay the tax. It is said that the mortgageor would have no right under the law to appear before the Board of Review to ask for a correction of the assessment of the mortgage interest, but I do not so read the statute.

Regarding the claim that the provisions that the mortgageor may pay the tax assessed against the mortgage interest in case of the mortgagee's default, and deduct the same from the amount owing on the mortgage impairs the obligations of contract, he says the view is untenable, and that the contract between the mortgageor and mortgagee remains the same. Regarding the claim of the unconstitutionality of the provision making the mortgageor liable, he says that the relation of the owner of the fee to the property is such that the right to assess the whole to him is undoubted, and that it would be an unsound doctrine which would deny the power of the Legislature to relieve him conditionally.

With reference to the claim that the law is unconstitutional so far as it attempts to tax mortgages owned by nonresidents for the reason that the mortgage is personal property and a mere security for debt, Justice Montgomery says it was competent for the Legislature to treat real-estate mortgages as an interest in lands for the purpose of taxation, and that, even though held by nonresidents, they may be given a *situs* in the place where the mortgage property is located; that this is what the act purports to do, and that it should be sustained. As to the provisions of the act relating to mortgages held by banks and insurance companies, he thought the intent was clear to treat mortgages as real estate, and that the interest in real estate, so taxed to banks and insurance companies, might be deducted from the shares of stock as assessed. If the banks hold property subject to taxation in excess of their actual capital, the case was no harder for them than it is in the case of an individual taxed for the value of property owned by him, though he may be indebted to the amount of nearly or quite its full value.

That it was not the purpose of the Legislature to limit the power of parties to contract as they may choose in regard to the payment of interest, was shown by the fact that a clause prohibiting such contracts was struck out of the bill before its final passage. Such an agreement did not amount to a reservation of interest, but was in the nature of an agreement to preserve the estate which constitutes the security, and was more unlawful than an agreement to keep the property insured for a similar purpose.

The dissenting opinion holds the law to be unconstitutional for several reasons: The entire tax upon the lands and upon the mortgage interest is made a lien upon the land for which it can be sold, and thus the land of the mortgageor is sold to pay the debt of the mortgagee. The mortgage tax may also be collected from the personal property of the mortgageor by seizure and sale, although the tax upon the mortgage interest is against the mortgagee. Although the principal and interest may not be due for five years, yet the collecting officer may seize the last piece of personal property of the mortgageor to satisfy the tax under this act. The opinion says further that an attempt is made to impair the obligation of existing contracts, as applied to mortgages in force at the time of the passage of the law; that the act destroys the uniformity of taxation under Article XIV of section 21 of the Constitution, and that the whole scheme of taxation under the act was so defective that the whole act should fail. In the matter of review, if the mortgagee does not appear before the board he will be barred from contesting the amount of the tax in any court, as the opportunity to appear will be regarded as his day in court upon the question of assessment. He must therefore be upon the watch in every assessment district where property upon which he holds a mortgage is situated.

The Miner Electoral Law.—For the purpose of testing the validity of this law, passed by the last Legislature, which provides that presidential electors should be chosen by congressional districts, instead of on a general ticket, an application was made to the Supreme Court for a mandamus compelling the Secretary of State to notify the sheriff in each county between July 1 and Sept. 1 next that at the time of the next general election electors for President and Vice-President will be chosen. Following were the reasons given for the charge that the law was void:

1. It contains no provision for notice of election.
2. It contains no provision, nor is there provision elsewhere, for the canvass of votes cast in the electoral districts and parts of districts into which Wayne County is divided; nor is there provision for the transmission to any officer of a statement of the votes cast in such districts or parts of districts.
3. The provision for alternate electors is not covered by the title.
4. It contains no provision for the filling of vacancies in the contingency of death or disability of both elector and alternate.
5. It is in conflict with Article II, paragraph 2, of the Federal Constitution.
6. It is repugnant to the fourteenth amendment to the Federal Constitution.
7. It is in conflict with the act of Congress fixing a date for the meetings of the electoral colleges and relating to the certification of election.

In reference to the sixth point noted above, it was said that the ratification of the fourteenth amendment to the Constitution of the United States, while it conferred no new rights upon citizens, guaranteed those already possessed forever, and the most important among them was the right of every male inhabitant of the age of twenty-one years to vote for every presidential elector of his State. This the Miner act denied. If it were declared valid, it would sustain the right of a Legislature to inflict a punishment upon the people of the State by depriving them of rights guaranteed by the Constitution of the United States.

The Supreme Court decided that the law was constitutional. It was held that the use of the district system to a greater or less extent for the first forty years of the history of the country recognizes in the State Legislatures plenary power to control the method of appointing the electors.

The case was appealed to the United States Supreme Court, and the judgment of the Michigan court was affirmed. The court held that the fourteenth amendment does not limit the right of a State to fix a mode of choosing electors.

In the announcement of the decision, the court said that the Supreme Court of Michigan had ruled adversely to the plaintiff in error upon the validity of the local law. In so deciding, the Federal question was necessary to be passed upon, and the validity of the Constitution and laws of the United States had been drawn into the matter because of this Federal question.

The court ruled that in view of the language of the clause of the Constitution giving to the State Legislatures the right to determine the method of choosing presidential electors and of the contemporaneous instruction, it can not now be held invalid for want of power in State Legislatures to pass such a law. "We are clear that the clause of the first section of Article II of the Constitution has not been changed by the fourteenth amendment, and that the law is not obnoxious to that amendment."

Legislative Session.—Important decisions were rendered by the Supreme Court in cases involving the constitutionality of the apportionment acts of the Legislatures of 1891 and 1885. The decision in the case of the senatorial apportionment was given in the suit of a citizen and elector of the Seventh District, which has a population of 91,420. He asked for the writ of man-

damus to restrain the respondent, the Secretary of State, from giving notice of the election of Senators under the act of 1891, and to compel him to give notice under the act of 1885. The petition also contained a prayer for general relief on the basis that the power delegated by the provisions of the Constitution to rearrange the senatorial districts is limited; that the limitation was wholly disregarded by the act in question, and the act is therefore unconstitutional and void. The opinion says:

"The unconstitutionality of the act is clear. The county of Saginaw, with only 16,839 inhabitants in excess of the ratio, is divided into 2 senatorial districts, one having 24,189 and the other 23,334 less than the ratio. There is no basis, constitutional or otherwise, for such an apportionment. A county having an excess of only about one fourth of the ratio is not, in the language of the Constitution, 'equitably entitled to 2 or more Senators,' while 1 district, composed of 8 counties and containing nearly 2½ times the population of each district into which the former county is divided, receives but 1 Senator. Equity has no definition applicable to such a case. The State can not be divided into senatorial districts with mathematical exactness, nor does the Constitution require it. It requires the exercise on the part of the Legislature of an honest and fair discretion in apportioning the districts, so as to preserve, as near as may be, the equality of representation. This constitutional discretion was not exercised in the apportionment act of 1891. The facts themselves demonstrate this beyond any controversy, and no language can make demonstration plainer.

"The petition prays that the respondent be directed to give notice of the election under the apportionment act of 1885. The constitutionality of this act is directly involved in the controversy. It is unnecessary to determine whether such infirmity exists to an equal or a greater or less degree. It is sufficient to say that it is not in accord with the Constitution, and for the same reasons which apply to the act of 1891. It is therefore insisted with great force by the Attorney-General that no election should be ordered under the former act, and he also urges in consequence that no relief can be granted. He also says that all other apportionment acts are subject to the same objection. Under his reasoning it would follow that, if the act of 1891 is held invalid, there is no remedy except the Executive of the State decides to call a special session of the Legislature. In such case there would be no apportionment law under which the people might elect a Legislature. While the Constitution requires the Legislature to rearrange the districts at the next session after each enumeration, yet we are of the opinion that each apportionment act remains in force until it is supplanted by a subsequent valid act. It was my opinion that the respondent should be directed to give notice under the act of 1885, inasmuch as the people have acquiesced in its validity by so long acting under it; but I yield my opinion to that of my brethren, who are of the opinion that the notice should be given under the law of 1881, the validity of which is not here brought into controversy, unless the Executive should call a special session of the Legislature.

"Our conclusions, therefore, are: First, the petition is properly brought into court by the relator; second, the court has jurisdiction in the matter; third, the apportionment acts of 1891 and 1885 are unconstitutional and void; fourth, the writ of mandamus must issue restraining the respondent from issuing the notice of election under the act of 1891, and directing him to issue the notice under the act of 1881, unless the Executive of the State shall call a special session of the Legislature to make a new apportionment before the time expires for giving such notice. No costs will be allowed."

. A similar decision was given in the case brought to test the constitutionality of the reapportionment of representative districts. The acts of 1891 and 1885 were held to be unconstitutional and void, and the conclusion was: "An examination of the apportionment act of 1881 shows it to have been within the constitutional discretion of the Legislature, and therefore the Secretary of State must give his notices under that law, unless a new and valid apportionment shall be made by the Legislature."

In view of these decisions, rendered July 28, the Governor convened the Legislature in special session Aug. 5, for the purpose of making a new apportionment, and transacting such other business as might come before it. The business was concluded Aug. 6, and adjournment taken Aug. 8. New apportionment bills were passed, giving the same number of districts as did the act of the previous session, namely, 32 senatorial and 100 representative districts. The Governor sent a message submitting the question of the appointment of a commission to investigate and report at the next session of the Legislature as to the best plan of legislation looking to the improvement of the highways of the State, and also as to the advisability of employing convict labor in the construction of country roads. A resolution was passed authorizing the Governor to appoint such a commission, which should serve without pay except for necessary expenses.

In the report of this commission, made later in the year, the opinion was expressed that no valid legislation can be enacted under the present Constitution which would result in good roads; and an amendment to the Constitution was suggested in order to enable the Legislature to put in operation a general system of road improvement.

Political.—The People's party of the State was organized at a conference for the political federations of the labor organizations, held at Lansing, Dec. 29, 1891. The platform approved the following propositions: That national banks as banks of issue should be abolished; that the Government should issue a full legal tender currency direct to the people based upon land or its products, and at a tax not to exceed 2 per cent. per annum; that the amount of the circulating medium should be increased to not less than $50 per capita. It advocated the free and unlimited coinage of silver; the abolition of all monopolies, trusts, and combines, and the most rigid State and national control of all corporations in the interests of the people, and Government ownership of all railroads, express, telephone, and telegraph companies that can not be so controlled, and the repurchase of lands held by foreign syndicates. It declared that all lands held by grant to railroads and other corporations in excess of such as is actually used and needed by them, be reclaimed by the Government and held for actual settlers only; that one industry should not be built up at the expense of another, and that all revenues should be limited to the necessary expenses of the State or nation, honestly and economically administered, and that all duties on the necessaries of life should be abolished. It called for the suppression of the liquor traffic for beverage purposes; a graduated income tax; a demand for universal suffrage and equal pay for equal service, and demanded that all under the age of sixteen be removed from the treadmill to the schoolroom; and all old soldiers and sailors receive a per diem pension. The resolution on the liquor traffic, which was adopted by a vote of 109 to 47, was due to the Prohibition delegates. Their party was expected to act with the People's party, but afterward refused to be committed until after the action of the St. Louis convention.

The Prohibitionists met in convention at Owosso, Aug. 10, and nominated a State ticket as follows: For Governor, Rev. John Russell; Lieutenant-Governor, E. L. Brewer; Secretary of State, George R. Malone.

The People's party met in Lansing, June 16, to elect delegates to the Omaha convention. The resolutions declared strongly against fusion, and demanded that the delegates sent to Omaha be only such as had fully severed their connection with any other party.

The State ticket was nominated at a convention held at Jackson, Aug. 2. The resolutions demanded the absolute and continued separation of church and state; that there shall be no appropriation of either State or municipal funds or property to any religious, sectarian, or religio-politico institutions; that all schools for the general education of the young shall be under the supervision and inspection of the State; they denounced that "band of mercenaries known as the Pinkertons, and the system of employing convicts in our penal institutions in any industry that enters into competition with free labor, believing that our convict labor should be employed in improving our public highways; that all manufactured articles should bear the name of the manufacturer and the destroying, defacing, or covering up in any way of the name of the manufacturer should be deemed a misdemeanor."

Other resolutions were, that all election days be made legal holidays; that mine inspectors should be elected by the people, instead of by the board of supervisors, who now are controlled by the mining corporations; that all lands sold for delinquent taxes should be purchased by the State, the title after a reasonable time, if not redeemed, to become absolute, and be held for actual settlers in limited quantities; that the people should have the right to propose laws and to vote upon all legislative measures of importance; in favor of equal suffrage within educational qualifications, and opposed to all monopolistic trusts and combines of whatever nature they may be; and in all cases of difficulty between employers and employees in favor of submission to arbitration.

The ticket was: For Governor, John W. Ewing; Lieutenant-Governor, George H. Sherman; Secretary of State, Frank M. Vandercook; State Treasurer, Joseph W. Welton; Auditor-General, Carrollton Peck; Attorney-General, A. A. Ellis; Superintendent of Public Instruction, O. M. Graves; Commissioner State Land Office, William L. Hayden.

The State Democratic Convention, which met at Muskegon in May, declared tariff reform to be the great issue of the coming campaign, made a demand on the Government for a clear water way from the Great Lakes to the ocean, and instructed the delegates chosen to go to Chicago to vote for the nomination of Mr. Cleveland. The State ticket was nominated in convention at Grand Rapids, Aug. 17. The most significant resolution was the one on silver coinage:

Resolved, That we condemn the Republican party for demonetizing and degrading silver, and thus bringing upon the country the train of evils resulting therefrom; and we would commend to our representatives in Congress the fact that a large majority of the people of this State are in favor of restoring silver to its time-honored and rightful place as the coin of the nation, coequal with gold. We demand that henceforth the issuing of all circulating medium be made under acts of Congress through the National Treasury in such amounts as the business wants of the country require.

Following is the ticket: For Governor, Allen B. Morse; Lieutenant-Governor, James P. Edwards; Secretary of State, Charles F. Marskey; Treasurer, Frederick Marvin; Auditor General, Joseph Vannier; Attorney-General, Adolphus A. Ellis; Commissioner of State Land Office, George F. Shaffer; Superintendent of Public Instruction, Ferris S. Fitch.

Later in the year, William Newton was made the nominee for the office of Justice of the Supreme Court by both the Democratic and People's parties.

The Republican convention met at Saginaw on July 20. The resolutions approved the platform and nominees of the national convention, and condemned long sessions of the Legislature, as follow:

Long sessions of the Legislature are an unnecessary expense to the public, and we condemn the practice, and pledge the people that if the Republican party has control of the next Legislature the business will be done with fidelity and promptness.

That the next Legislature should submit to the people a constitutional amendment providing that all compensation to legislators should cease at the expiration of one hundred days from the date such Legislature shall convene.

That we condemn the practice of railroad companies in giving passes to, and the same being accepted by, legislators and other public officials, and demand that such laws shall be enacted as will effectually put a stop to this evil.

On the subject of the existing Democratic administration the resolutions read as follow:

We condemn the present State Democratic administration for its subserviency to the exactions of political demagogues who have forced upon the intelligent people of Michigan the nefarious Miner law, a measure which every fair-minded citizen condemns, and which Democratic leaders favor only in States where there is a Republican majority. As illustrating the methods and practices of the Democratic party, we call attention to the brazen theft of the Senate of the State during its last session, by unlawfully and corruptly seating two usurpers in that body by the action of less than a constitutional quorum thereof, making it possible to enact the infamous Miner law; the unscrupulous gerrymander of the congressional, senatorial, and representative districts, and much other legislation which is a disgrace to any civilized people, prominent among which is the law lowering the test of illuminating oils at the dictation of the Standard Oil Company.

While pretending to reform the executive and other departments, it has been an example of incapacity and nepotism, and has so mismanaged State institutions in securing parties in control of them, and subsequent inefficient management, as to seriously impair their usefulness and imperil their future.

Michigan Republicans, briefly recalling a few of the more salient features of Democrat rule in this State, refer to the whole record, and ask the co-operation of all good citizens in redeeming the State from such misrule, in order to restore it to its former proud place as one of the best and most economically governed States of the Union.

Following is the ticket: For Governor, John T. Rich; Lieutenant-Governor, J. Wight Giddings; Secretary of State, John W. Jochim; State Treasurer, Joseph F. Hambitzer; Auditor-General, Stanley W. Turner; Commissioner of Land Office, John G. Berry; Attorney-General, Gerritt J. Diekema; Superintendent of Public Instruction, Henry R. Pattengill.

Frank E. Hooker was nominated, in September, for Justice of the Supreme Court.

The municipal elections in April were generally favorable to the Republicans. In the November election the whole State Republican ticket was successful, excepting in the office of Attorney-General. A. A. Ellis, whose name was on the tickets of both the Democratic and the People's parties, receiving 223,741 votes to his opponent's 222,149. The vote for Governor stood: John T. Rich, 221,228; A. B. Morse, 205,138; J. W. Ewing, 21,417; John Russell, 20,777; errors, 76; total, 468,637.

The vote on a proposed convention for the revision of the Constitution gave: Yeas, 16,948; nays, 16,245.

The result of the State canvass on presidential electors gave Mr. Harrison a plurality of 20,412 on a total vote of 465,355, distributed as follows: Harrison, 222,708; Cleveland, 201,296; Weaver, 19,782; Bidwell, 20,596.

The State Legislature will have 88 Republicans and 44 Democrats.

MINNESOTA, a Western State, admitted to the Union May 11, 1858; area, 83,365 square miles. The population, according to each decennial census since admission, was 172,023 in 1860; 439,706 in 1870; 780,773 in 1880; and 1,301,826 in 1890. Capital, St. Paul.

Government.—The following were the State officers during the year: Governor, William R. Merriam, Republican; Lieutenant-Governor, Gideon S. Ives; Secretary of State, F. P. Brown; Auditor, Adolph Bierman; Treasurer, Joseph Bobleter; Attorney-General, Moses E. Clapp; Superintendent of Public Instruction, D. L. Kiehle; Insurance Commissioner, C. P. Bailey; Railroad and Warehouse Commissioners, John P. Williams, John L. Gibbs, George L. Becker; Chief Justice of the Supreme Court, James Gilfillan; Associate Justices, Loren W. Collins,

William Mitchell, Daniel A. Dickenson, and Charles E. Vanderburgh.

Finances.—The financial affairs of the State are in a sound and prosperous condition. With a population of 1,400,000, and assessed valuation of $600,000,000, there is an outstanding indebtedness of only $2,154,000, subject to an annual interest charge of $77,390; and on the last day of November, 1892, there was a balance in the State treasury to the credit of the different funds of $1,688,946.54. The satisfactory result attained in the funding of the public debt has been brought about by the act authorizing the 3½-per-cent. bonds, and the purchase and cancellation of the railroad adjustment bonds. The State debt, which is now comparatively small, will be paid off within a few years by the operation of the sinking fund authorized by law.

In accordance with the law of 1885, a transfer of $50,000 was made from the revenue fund to the school text-book fund. Of this fund, there were on July 1, 1892, $38,753.08 in cash; unpaid drafts for collection to the amount of $8,672.32; making a total of $47,423.40. Loan and trust companies had on deposit in the Auditor's office securities amounting to $1,260,211.34. The permanent school fund amounts to $10,132,-867.43, having increased $1,176,946.97 during the fiscal years of 1891 and 1892. The average price per acre of school lands sold, for all years, is a little less than $6. The grant embraces sections 16 and 36 in every township, or a total of about 3,000,000 acres. In addition to the regular grant for school purposes, this fund will be increased by half of the proceeds of such swamp lands as shall remain to the State after the various grants to railroad companies and State institutions shall have been filled. This fund will eventually amount to about $20,000,000. The income is apportioned for the support of the common schools. The permanent university fund now amounts to $1,000,445.73, and is derived from the sale of university lands. The various grants amount to 169,353 acres. The fund will eventually amount to $1,500,000. The internal improvement land fund is derived from the sale of lands. The original grant amounted to 500,000 acres, and the total accumulations are $2,612,366.92. The accumulations for the State institutions land fund amount to $30,281.28. The Reform School land sales amount to $365,590.50.

Education.—The State University within the past ten years has grown beyond all precedent. In 1882 the total attendance of students was 253; in 1892 it reached 1,374. Departments of law and medicine have been established. There were 453 law and medical students in attendance in 1892. The fees charged in these departments are nearly sufficient to pay the salaries of all the instructors. Nothing pertaining to the progress and growth of the university has been more marked and original than the establishment of a school of practical agriculture, giving special instruction in all that pertains to the theory and practice of agriculture. In connection with this school is a dairy hall, ample and well equipped. In 1891 the attendance was 104; in 1892 it was 115. The library and assembly room are in the old main building, which was so injured by fire in April, 1892, that the assembly room has since been unfit for use.

Prisons.—On Oct. 31, 1892, the number of State convicts was smaller than on Oct. 31, 1891. It was hoped and expected that the problem of keeping the convicts of the Reformatory at St. Cloud employed was solved, and that ample work for many years to come would be found in the quarries; but, under the provisions of chapter 112 of the general laws of 1891, only 33 per cent. of the convicts can be employed in quarrying and preparing granite for sale. The remainder of the convicts, if engaged in granite work at all, can only be employed in quarrying and cutting stone for public buildings of the State, and for walls and improvements on the grounds of the Reformatory. The manufacture of twine has been successfully established at the State Prison, and has met with much favor among the agricultural population.

The Soldiers' Home.—This institution is supported by the Soldiers' Relief Fund, which is derived from a tax of one tenth of a mill on all the property of the State. At the beginning of the fiscal year there was a balance from the preceding year of $24,407.84, and there will be derived from the tax levy of 1893 the sum of $59,558.85, thus giving a total available fund of $83,966.69 for the current fiscal year. During the fiscal year ending July 31, 1892, only $39,-370.42 out of this fund was expended.

Constitutional Amendment.—A constitutional amendment prohibiting special legislation was adopted.

Grain Elevators and Inspection.—In 1885 the Legislature enacted a law for the purpose of regulating and controlling the weighing, grading, and inspection of grain at the terminal points of St. Paul, Minneapolis, and Duluth, and for regulating and controlling grain elevators and warehouses at those places. That portion of the law relating to weighing, grading, and inspection has been utilized and put into successful operation. All that handle grain at these terminal points avail themselves of this feature of the law. Although the fees for the service are small, yet the department is more than self-sustaining, and has a large surplus on hand, as appears from the following comparative statement, showing earnings, expenses, and balances for the several years since its establishment.

YEARS.	Earnings.	Expenses.	Balance on hand.
1886................	$68,471 29	$62,184 90	$287 20
1887................	84,401 51	64,731 80	20,597 41
1888................	90,781 96	81,496 98	30,192 41
1889................	69,661 57	78,947 99	20,905 99
1890................	108,204 07	91,961 08	82,148 98
1891................	109,652 20	98,321 66	48,479 52
1892................	173,701 75	182,428 22	84,753 05

Building and Loan Associations.—There are in the State fifteen building and loan associations, with resources amounting to $8,466,812.-58. The increase in the assets and liabilities since June 30, 1890, has amounted to $2,443,-867.43.

Banks.—A large increase in the number of banks organized under the State law during the past two years is seen. On July 31, 1890, there were 76, and on July 31, 1892, 117. A summary of 93 State banks, July 9, 1891, showed resources amounting to $35,817,493.92. A summary of 117 State banks on July 12, 1892, showed resources amounting to $41,863,107.75.

There are 70 national banks in the State, with resources amounting, on July 12, 1892, to $67,194,071.72. There are 13 savings associations, 7 of them operating under the law of 1867, and 6 under the law of 1889. The total amount of resources and liabilities in December, 1889, was $6,352,533.59. This had increased to $9,409,239.48 in December, 1891.

There are 9 loan and trust companies doing business under the laws relating to annuity, safe deposit, and trust companies. The resources and liabilities increased from $4,295,209.31 on July 31, 1890, to $7,456,743,82 on July 31, 1892.

Taxes.—The tax receipts from all sources for the two years ending July 31, 1892, exclusive of balances, aggregate $31,119,314.99. The amount collected yearly in the Forestry fund tax is about $58,000. The amount to be paid in any one year for bounties given to encourage timber culture is limited to $20,000.

Insurance.—Ten joint-stock fire insurance companies were admitted during the year ending Feb. 29, 1892, their total capital being $2,600,000. The fire losses incurred by all companies authorized to do business in the State amounted to $2,933,587.94 in 1891, an increase in losses over the previous year of $1.163,408.46, while the premium receipts were only increased $249,351.60. Owing to this increase in the ratio of losses to premiums received, many companies retired from the State, and a large number reinsured their risks and retired from business permanently.

Corporations.—During the year, 562 new corporations were created under the laws of the State, of which 120 were for religious, charitable, and social purposes, 442 for business and profit. The recording and other official fees paid into the State treasury by this department were $1,349.80. Within three years the number of new corporations formed has increased thus: In 1890, 415; in 1891, 491; in 1892, 562.

Political.—A Democratic State convention met at St. Paul in April. In the resolutions passed the party "once more dedicated its first and best energies to the accomplishment of a single end—the complete but the intelligent and gradual reform of a system of tariff duties which is both corrupting and unjust." Protection, which "creates burdens affecting different classes and sections of our country disproportionately and inequably," was condemned as "stimulating monopolies, sapping the strength of industrial energies," and "polluting the springs of political action." It demanded the repeal of the Sherman Silver-coinage act, and renewed its pledge of loyalty to ex-President Cleveland.

At a Democratic State convention in August the following ticket was chosen:

For Governor, D. W. Lawler; Lieutenant-Governor, Harry Hawkins; Secretary of State, Peter Nelson; State Treasurer, Joseph Leicht; Attorney-General, J. C. Nethaway; Justices of the Supreme Court, William Mitchell, Daniel Buck,.Thomas Canty.

A Republican State Convention for selecting delegates to the national convention and for nominating presidential electors met at St. Paul on May 5. In the same city another Republican convention met in August for the nomination of State officers. In the platform, allegiance to the principles of the Republican party as set forth in the platform of the Republican National Convention was declared, and the "wise, pure, firm, and intensely American administration of President Harrison" was approved.

From its very infancy, and for upward of a third of a century, our State has been managed and guided by men and principles of the Republican party. During that period the State has grown from a mere outpost of scattered settlements to a commonwealth of 1,500,000 souls, prosperous and aggressive, and equal in moral, intellectual, and commercial vigor to the best of the older States. Such a people, so prosperous and so growing, have not been badly governed. Our State administrations have been clean, able, and always loyal to the best interests of the people.

The necessity of securing a free ballot and a fair count was urged; trusts and combinations to control and unduly enhance the price of commodities were vigorously condemned, and legislation against the evil was demanded. In this connection reference was made "with pride to the establishment and maintenance at the State Prison at Stillwater of the manufacture of binding twine, which has been the means of protecting and defending our farmers against one of the great trusts and monopolies."

In regard to the protection of the workingman the following four suggestions were made: The enactment of suitable laws for the protection of health, life, and limb of all employees of transportation and mining companies; the establishment of boards or tribunals of conciliation and arbitration for the peaceful settlement of all disputes between capital and labor touching wages, hours of labor, and such questions as pertain to the safety and physical and moral well-being of the laborer; the exclusion from our shores, by suitable laws and regulations, of all paupers, criminals, contract labor, and other dangerous classes; the preservation of the public domain for actual and *bona fide* settlers under the homestead law.

For the farmers of the State such laws were favored as would give them cheap, safe, and easily obtainable elevator and warehouse facilities, and proper transportation facilities to all accessible markets. Anti-option legislation by Congress was urged.

The protection of the forest as far as consistent with the general interests of the State was recommended. The following ticket was chosen: For Governor, Knute Nelson; Lieutenant-Governor. David M. Clough; Secretary of State, Fred P. Brown; State Treasurer, Joseph Bobleter; Attorney-General, H. W. Childs; Associate Justices of the Supreme Court, D. A. Dickenson, William Mitchell, C. E. Vanderburgh.

The People's party, at its convention in July, nominated the following ticket: For Governor, Ignatius Donnelly; Lieutenant-Governor. Kittel Halvorsen; Secretary of State, H. B. Martin; State Treasurer, P. M. Ringdal; Attorney-General, J. L. McDonald; Supreme Court Justices, Daniel E. Buck, Thomas Canty, W. N. Davidson. The platform adopted demanded an immediate and radical change in the State control of corporations and transportation facilities, with direct reference to the grain traffic and State taxation, and resolved that the Constitution should be so amended that the people shall have the right to have all laws referred back to themselves for approval or disapproval. The following resolutions were passed:

We demand that the transportation companies shall provide suitable shipping and warehousing facilities at every station on their lines; also, that the State shall erect terminal elevators at Minneapolis, St. Paul, and Duluth, for public storage of grain.

We extend our sympathies to the oppressed workmen at Homestead and all over the United States, in their fight against the oppressions of monopolistic employers, and we urge them to join with us in an attempt to overthrow at the polls our common enemy, the monopolistic millionaires who are now, through their control of the Government and the industries of the country, rapidly and surely reducing the people to a condition of political and industrial slavery.

The State Convention of the Farmers' Alliance met at St. Paul in July. In the platform adopted, hostility to every species of class legislation was declared.

The protective tariff was denounced, and a radical reduction of duties insisted upon.

A gradual increase of the national money to the minimum of $50 *per capita* was demanded, and as a part of this increase the issuance of legal tender treasury notes in sufficient volume to transact the growing business of the country on a cash basis, without damage or advantage to any class; such notes to be a legal tender.

The wheat question was declared to be the paramount issue in the State. Therefore the power of the State is invoked, and the next Legislature asked to make sufficient appropriation for the erection of elevators at deep water on Lake Superior where grain can be stored, unmixed, at a nominal cost, by individual producers awaiting sale and shipment to the markets of the world.

Free passes on railroads were vigorously denounced; and a material reduction of interest, with severe penalties for usury, was demanded.

Congress was appealed to for the passage of laws prohibiting alien ownership of lands, and, if possible, to reclaim all so held by alien and foreign syndicates, and all held by railroad companies in excess of that absolutely necessary, and that these and all other lands be held for actual settlers only.

At the election in November the Republican State ticket was successful by pluralities of about 14,000. The vote on the presidential ticket was: Harrison, 122,736; Cleveland, 100,579; Weaver, 30,398; Bidwell, 14,017. Of the 7 Congressmen, the Republicans elected 4, the Democrats 2, and the People's party 1.

MISSISSIPPI, a Southern State, admitted to the Union Dec. 10, 1817; area, 46,810 square miles. The population, according to each decennial census since admission, was 75,448 in 1820; 136,621 in 1830; 375,651 in 1840; 606,526 in 1850; 791,305 in 1860; 827,922 in 1870; 1,131,597 in 1880; and 1,289,600 in 1890. Capital, Jackson.

Government.—The following were the State officers during the year: Governor, John M. Stone, Democrat; Lieutenant-Governor, M. M. Evans; Secretary of State, George M. Govan; Treasurer, J. J. Evans; Auditor, W. W. Stone; Attorney-General, T. Marshall Miller; Superintendent of Public Instruction, J. R. Preston; Railroad Commissioners, J. F. Sessions, Walter

McLaurin, and J. H. Askew; Chief Justice of the Supreme Court, Thomas H. Woods; Associate Justices, J. A. P. Campbell and Timothy E. Cooper.

Finances.—The total State debt on Jan. 1, 1892, was $3,375,583.59, of which the State will probably never be called upon to pay more than $1,000,000. On a large portion of the debt it is pledged to pay the interest, but not the principal.

Under the new Constitution the expenses for public schools will be largely increased, and the rate of State taxation was therefore increased for 1892 from 4 to 5 mills on the dollar.

Legislative Session.—The first regular session of the Legislature under the new State Constitution began at Jackson on Jan. 5 and ended on April 2. On Jan. 19, United States Senator J. Z. George was re-elected for the term of six years beginning March 4, 1893, by the following vote: Senate—George 24, E. Barksdale 18; House—George 77, Barksdale 40, Ex-Gov. Alcorn 1. On the same day United States Senator E. C. Walthall was accorded a re-election for the term beginning March 4, 1895, the vote being: Senate—Walthall 36, Clarke Lewis 3, C. E. Hooker 1; House—Walthall 99, Lewis 18, Hooker 3. The most important legislative work of the session was the adoption of a new annotated code of laws for the State, based upon the provisions of the new Constitution of 1890. The code adopted is, with a few modifications, substantially the same as that reported to the session by a committee appointed by the constitutional convention. For each of the years 1892 and 1893 a State tax of 5 mills on the dollar was levied for support of the State government and for public schools. In each county the limit of taxation for all purposes, including the State tax, was fixed at 12½ mills, except that counties having a debt may tax themselves to the extent of not over 17½ mills. The amount that each Confederate pensioner may receive under the law was limited to $50 per annum, and the total sum available for pensions in any year was fixed at $64,200, each pensioner being compelled to receive a proportionately reduced amount, if the number of claimants under the law should exceed 1,284. On Feb. 16, immediately after the fire at the State Insane Asylum, an act was passed appropriating $25,000 for repairs, and authorizing the removal of part of the inmates to the East Mississippi Insane Asylum, at Meriden. Later a commission was appointed to rebuild the burned structure, and $87,000 were appropriated for that purpose. For the support of public schools the sum of $920,000 was appropriated for each of the years 1892 and 1893.

Other acts of the session were as follow:

To provide for the appointment of commissioners on the uniformity of State laws.

Accepting the provisions of the act of Congress for the more complete endowment and support of colleges for the benefit of agriculture and the mechanic arts.

To secure to the heirs of deceased persons the proceeds of any life-insurance policy.

Accepting the act of Congress authorizing the refunding of the direct tax of 1861 to the several States.

On March 15, by special invitation of the Legislature, United States Senator David B. Hill, of New York, addressed the members on national political topics.

Education.—The following table presents the public-school statistics of the State for the years 1889-'90 and 1890-'91:

ITEMS.	1889-'90.	1890-'91.
Educable children	455,683	497,622
Enrolled, white................	150,868	154,447
Enrolled, colored..............	183,290	173,378
Enrolled, total.................	324,158	327,702
Average attendance, white......	96,077	93,282
Average attendance, colored	111,627	104.298
Average attendance, total........	207,704	197,580
Schools, White................	3,430	3,528
Schools, colored	2,469	2,543
White teachers.................	4,269	4,584
Colored teachers...............	3,222	3,212
Average monthly salary, white ...	$33 87	$31 32
Average monthly salary, colored..	$23 20	$24 25
Paid in salaries, White...........	$608,859	$620,829
Paid in salaries, colored..........	$346,774	$342,858
Collected for schools.............	$1,333,151	$1,304,014
Expended for schools.............	$1,109,295	$1,160,058
Expended for each pupil enrolled.	$3 32	$3 54

By comparing the year 1888-'89 with the year 1890-'91, there will be found an increase in enrollment of 5,775 pupils, the whites gaining 6,012 pupils and the colored people losing 174. There was an increase of 5,155 in average attendance, about equally divided between the races, an increase of 316 in white teachers and 115 in colored teachers, an increase of 710 in schoolhouses, of 294 in schools of all grades, of 70 in high schools, of $11,741 in the receipts for schools, and of $51,978 in disbursements therefor.

There are 43 towns in the State having graded schools, which are maintained from eight to ten months annually. They have erected 28 new buildings, costing from $10,000 to $40,000 each. The aggregate value of school pr   r   in these 43 towns is $537,050. The enrollment in 1890-'91 was 22,046, and the salaries of teachers $162,675.

By the terms of the new Constitution, the State has assumed the duty of maintaining all the public schools for four months of each year. In order to maintain them at their present efficiency, $850,000 will be required annually. It is estimated that the income from poll taxes will be $250,000, leaving $600,000 to be raised by a tax on property.

Charities.—On Feb. 16 the State suffered a loss of about $200,000 by the burning of the State Insane Asylum at Jackson. There were 601 inmates, all but one of whom were rescued. There was no insurance. The Legislature promptly made provision for rebuilding, and at the end of the year the work was well advanced.

Floods.—The people of the State suffered severely this year from the overflow of streams swollen by the spring rains. From the first freshet, early in April, the counties of Warren, Carroll, Grenada, Clay, Monroe, and Montgomery were severe sufferers. The Tombigbee river rose higher than ever before known, flooding the adjacent country for miles. Many smaller streams in the central portion of the State overflowed their banks, railroad and other bridges were swept away, and farms and farmhouses were submerged. In May the Mississippi river overflowed at many places, causing much loss and suffering, especially in Warren County, where it was claimed that 1,600 people were made destitute.

State Constitution.—Early this year, in the case of Sproule *vs.* Fredericks, the State Supreme Court rendered an important decision upon the validity of the work of the constitutional convention of 1890. The court says:

The validity of the Constitution of 1890 is called in question by appellee. In support of this invalidity of the Constitution two propositions are asserted:

1. A constitutional convention has power only to prepare and frame the body of a Constitution, and that when prepared or framed, the instrument is of no force or effect until ratified by a popular vote of the people; and the Constitution of 1890 having never been submitted to or ratified by the people is invalid; and

2. The changes made by the Constitution in the basis of suffrage are violative of an act of Congress readmitting the State of Mississippi into the Union in the year 1870, and invalidate that instrument.

With confidence we reject both propositions as unsound. The court holds that the constitutional convention was a sovereign body with power to frame a new Constitution and put it into effect without referring it to the people, as the Legislature which called it into existence did not seek to impose on its will by providing that the instrument should be submitted to the people. It wields the power of sovereignty, and the only restriction placed upon its power is that the spirit of republicanism should breathe through its work.

There is little ground for the second branch of the contention. The regulation of the right of suffrage belongs to the State, and the only limitation thereon to be found in the Constitution of the United States, or the latest amendments thereto, will be found in the prohibition of discrimination against persons on account of race or color. It is an idle consumption of time to talk of this as at all doubtful. The Supreme Court of the United States has more than once affirmed it.

Despite the act of Congress referred to when the State was readmitted to her place in the Federal Union, she was restored to all her rights, dignities, and powers. She was admitted as the equal of any other State, with the same power to regulate the right of suffrage in her borders as enjoyed by other States. But the contention is so manifestly untenable, and has been so effectually disposed of by the utterances of the Supreme Court of the United States, that we decline to say more.

Cotton-growers' Convention.—On Feb. 18 a convention of the cotton growers of the State met at Jackson for the purpose of discussing their common interests. The sentiment of the convention was embodied in the following resolutions:

That it is the opinion of this convention that if the amount of cotton produced be reduced one fourth, the aggregate amount of money received in the South will be largely increased; that a reduction in acreage in cotton will result in the raising of an increased amount of provisions and live stock, and thus benefit us by bringing in more money and sending out less.

We recommend that there be a local organization of the Cotton Growers and Merchants' Association in every town and supervisor's district in the cotton-growing region.

We further recommend that every planter and farmer within the cotton-growing States plant more diversified crops.

Political.—In February a State Republican Convention met at Jackson for the purpose of selecting delegates to the national Republican nominating convention. The two factions of the party failed to agree, and opposing delegations were chosen. Later in the year a Republican electoral ticket was placed in the field. The Democrats held their State convention at Jackson on June 8. Delegates to the National Democratic Convention were selected, and presidential electors nominated. The platform contained the following:

We favor reformation of the tariff laws consisting in a reduction of duties to the lowest rate consistent with the needs of an economical administration of the Government. As far as practicable the burdens of taxation should be borne by the luxuries of life, and the necessities relieved of duty as far as possible.

We condemn the so-called reciprocity policy of the Republican party as a fraud invented in the name of commercial freedom to perpetuate the present unjust system of licensed spoliation, for the benefit of monopolies in the interest of the Republican party.

There should be kept in constant circulation a full and sufficient supply of money, consisting of gold and silver and legal-tender paper currency at par with each other.

We believe that every legitimate power of the Government should be exerted to provide the people with cheaper facilities for transportation, inasmuch as a large portion of their earning is now taken from them to pay the cost of marketing their products; we therefore demand liberal appropriations by Congress for the improvement of our rivers and harbors.

The People's party and the Prohibitionists also placed electoral tickets in the field.

As the national election in November was the first election occurring under the new State Constitution, there was considerable curiosity to ascertain the practical effect of the clauses of that instrument relating to registration. Out of a total of 76,742 voters registered, 68,127 were whites and only 8,615 colored. We are told that under the famous "understanding" clause of the Constitution, 1,037 white and 1,085 colored people were registered. No statement is made showing how many of each race were rejected under that clause. The vote at the November election was very light, being as follows: Democratic electors, 38,301; People's party, 9,770; Republican, 1,444; Prohibitionist, 1,079. In the 7 congressional districts the Democratic candidates prevailed by large majorities.

MISSOURI, a Western State, admitted to the Union Aug. 10, 1821; area, 69,415 square miles. The population, according to each decennial census since admission, was 140,455 in 1830; 383,702 in 1840; 682,044 in 1850; 1,182,012 in 1860; 1,721,295 in 1870; 2,168,380 in 1880; and 2,679,184 in 1890. Capital, Jefferson City.

Government.—The following were the State officers during the year: Governor, David R. Francis. Democrat; Lieutenant-Governor, Stephen H. Claycomb; Secretary of State, Alexander A. Lesueur; Auditor, James M. Seibert; Treasurer, Lon V. Stephens; Attorney-General, John M. Wood, all Democrats; Chief Justice of the Supreme Court, Thomas A. Sherwood; Associate Judges, Francis M. Black, Theodore Brace, Shepard Barclay, James B. Gantt, J. L. Thomas, and George B. MacFarlane; Clerk, Jacob D. Conner, all Democrats; Superintendent of Public Schools, Lloyd E. Wolfe.

Finances.—The bonded indebtedness of the State has during the last four years been reduced $2,845,000, and in January, 1893, was but $6,680,000, of which $1,380,000 bears 6 per cent. and $5,300,000 3½ per cent. interest. The annual interest on the present bonded debt is $268,300,

a reduction of $138,220. In the State revenue fund there was on Jan. 1, 1891, a balance of $180,997.73, and on Jan. 1, 1893, a balance of $87,620.95. The balance in the treasury on Jan. 1, 1893, amounted to $562,277.48.

The total receipts from the State interest fund during 1891 and 1892 amounted to $892,732.63 and $921,299.31 respectively. There was for the State sinking fund, on Jan. 1, 1891, a balance of $453,168.49, and on Jan. 1, 1893, a balance of $52,172.17.

For the State school fund, on Jan. 1, 1891, there was a balance of $853, and on Jan. 1, 1893, a balance of 1,538.77. This fund was created by the act of the General Assembly, Feb. 6, 1837, the moneys to be derived from the proceeds of the sales of lands and the net proceeds of the State tobacco warehouse; the moneys so received, by act of March 31, 1883, to be invested in State certificates of indebtedness. The State Seminary funds are derived from sales of land granted by Congress, Feb. 17, 1818, and March 6, 1820; such moneys, when amounting to $1,000, to be issued in 5-per-cent. State certificate as required by act of March 31, 1883, the money so received to be transferred to the State sinking fund and used for the reduction of the bonded debt of the State. Of this State Seminary fund there was, on Jan. 1, 1893, a balance of $95.08. Of the State school moneys derived from the interest on the State certificates of indebtedness, and from the transfer in 1891 and 1892 of one third of the ordinary receipts into the State revenue fund appropriated by the thirty-sixth General Assembly, there was, on Jan. 1, 1891, a balance of $185,528.21, and on Jan. 1, 1893, a balance of $186,274.16, the disbursements for public schools in 1891 and 1892 having been $876,518.89 and $900,306.14.

For the road and canal fund, the receipts in 1892 were $375.51. The executors' and administrators' fund, consisting of unclaimed balances paid in by executors and administrators on the final settlement of estates, showed a balance on Jan. 1, 1891, of $34,856.79, and on Jan. 1, 1893, of $18,634.42. The receipts from fees collected in 1891 and 1892 respectively were $28,858.95 and $27,312.45. The disbursements in 1891 and 1892 respectively were for maintaining State insurance department $15,930.16 and $16,463.16. Of this fund there was transferred to the university building fund, in 1892, $40,000.

The earnings of the Missouri Penitentiary arising from the hire of convict labor, and for work done and materials furnished, were $194,-547.17 in 1891, and $192,902.76 in 1892.

The Colored Institute fund is derived from tuition fees paid in by colored teachers. The thirty-sixth General Assembly failed to make an appropriation of these moneys, so that no warrants could be drawn, and the balance on Jan. 1, 1893, was $1,738.80.

The disbursements for 1892 of the unversity building fund amounted to $86,083.66.

From the swamp land indemnity fund the disbursements in 1891-'92 amounted to $763.42.

The thirty-sixth General Assembly, at its regular session, appropriated for the years 1891-'92 the sum of $3,159,771.42, out of the revenue fund for the expenses of the Government during that period. At its extra session in 1892 it appropriated for the same purpose $70,000.

Taxes.—The assessed valuation of property in the State on June 1, 1890, was $877,722,770, on which the State revenue tax for 1891 was at the rate of 20 cents on the $100 valuation, amounting to $1,755,445.55. The total valuation on June 1, 1891, was $911,794,179, on which the 1892 State revenue tax (15 cents on the $100) amounted to $1,367,686.78.

Legislative Session.—The thirty-sixth General Assembly was convened in extra session Feb. 17, 1892. The session lasted thirty-six days. The subjects for legislation enumerated in the call were: The re-forming of the congressional and State representative districts; the re-forming of the judicial circuits and the adjusting of the salaries of the judges thereof; the cession of Jefferson Barracks reservation to the Federal Government; the re-erection of the buildings of the State University destroyed by fire, and the expenses of the extra session. The bills relating to these subjects were all passed.

During the continuance of the extra session the Governor informed the Legislature that the State Board of Equalization had determined that the assessed value of the taxable property of the State exceeded $900,000,000, and recommended that the tax levy for revenue purposes be reduced from 20 cents to 15 cents on the $100, in compliance with the requirements of the Constitution. Action to that effect was taken, and the State revenue levy for the taxes of 1892 was 25 per cent. less than it had been since 1876.

Prisons.—According to statistics specially compiled at the request of the Governor, the record made by this institution under its present management has not been equaled. The General Assembly appropriated, in addition to the earnings, $175,000 for maintenance during the years 1891 and 1892. Of that fund nothing has been drawn since Feb. 1, 1892, the Penitentiary having been self-supporting during the eleven months that intervened between that time and the making of the report. Of the maintenance fund, $66,724.04 had been drawn previous to Feb. 1. The remainder, $108,275.96, will revert to the general revenue fund.

A fire occurred at the Penitentiary on May 23, 1891. The new building cost $36,995.78 in money, exclusive of the convict labor employed. Had this fire not occurred the Penitentiary would have been self-sustaining during the entire biennial period. The cost exceeded the earnings by about $286,000 during the four years ending Dec. 31, 1888, and by about $112,000 during the past few years.

About 1,100 convicts are employed by the prison contractors, at an average compensation to the State of 50 cents a day; 327 convicts were employed by the State in the work of the institution, 13 were in solitary confinement, the remainder were idle. The receipts from convict labor, etc., in 1891, were $194,547.17; in 1892 they were $192,202.76. The expenditures for support in 1891 were $182,600.00, in 1892 they were $192,902.76; the balance on Jan. 1, 1893, was $11,947.11.

Veterinary Service.—Under the veterinary act of 1889 the Governor is authorized to send a veterinary surgeon to any State or Territory to investigate such dangerous or infectious diseases as may exist there. The thirty-fifth and thirty-

sixth General Assemblies made appropriations for payments for animals with contagious diseases slaughtered by order of the State veterinarian. The Legislature of 1889 appropriated $30,000 for this purpose, and fixed $100 as the maximum value of an animal slaughtered by order of the State veterinarian; the thirty-sixth General Assembly reduced the maximum value to $50, and the appropriation to $10,000.

Natural Products.—The coal production for the year ending June 30, 1891, according to the State mine inspector's figures, was 2,550,028 tons, valued at $3,480,867. This places Missouri second among the coal-producing States west of the Mississippi, and ninth among the coal-producing States of the Union. It is an increase of about 8 per cent. over the preceding year.

The production of iron ore in the State during the year ending June 30, 1891, was 138,356 tons, valued at $331,665. This is a decrease of nearly 40 per cent. from the production of the preceding year.

The surplus products of the State (not including manufactures, but confined to commodities originating in the State) amounted in 1891 and 1892 to $106,903,183 and $126,027,611, an increase of nearly 20 per cent. in one year.

Education.—For the year ending June 30, 1889, the people of Missouri expended $4,898,660.61 for support of the public schools, and for the year ending June 30, 1890, $5,291,956.27. About four fifths of this money was raised by taxes imposed by the taxpayers themselves, at their annual school meetings.

The Constitution requires that at least 25 per cent. of the general revenue of the State shall be set aside for the benefit of the public schools. The General Assemblies of 1887, 1889, and 1891 increased the apportionment to one third of the general revenue. In 1888 one third of the revenue amounted to $772,125.57, and in 1892 it aggregated $900,306.14.

The main buildings of the State University were destroyed by fire on the night of Jan. 9, 1892. The $147,500 insurance was, with the exception of a few hundred dollars, promptly paid. The called session of the Legislature in 1892 authorized the use of the money collected from the insurance companies, together with $40,000 transferred from the State insurance fund, for the re-erection of the buildings, provided the city of Columbia would contribute $50,000 to the same object. The citizens of Columbia, by private subscription, procured the amount required and paid it into the State treasury. In this manner $236,577 was obtained for the re-erection of the buildings. The General Assembly appropriated $88,983 for the support of the State University during the years 1891-'92.

State Banks.—There are in the State 96 private banks and 452 State banks, with an aggregate capital of $21,352,905, and total deposits of $80,910,442. These do not include the national banks in Missouri, which number 81, with a capital of $24,185,000. The national banks are examined at least once annually by a United States bank examiner. The State law does not provide for an examination of State banks.

Insurance Laws.—The laws of 1889 increased the taxes of insurance companies, and require companies incorporated by other States and countries and doing business in Missouri to pay a tax of 2 per cent. on their gross premiums. The companies are given credit for the local taxes on premiums, if they are imposed, and it is made the duty of the Superintendent of Insurance to collect the remainder and pay it into the State treasury. The insurance companies think the tax a great burden, and show that in many instances foreign companies doing business in Missouri pay more in losses than they receive in premiums. In three years $260,657.84 was paid into the General Revenue fund of the State from this source.

Agriculture.—The Legislature of 1891 revised the law creating the State Board of Agriculture, so as to provide that the board should consist of one member from each Congressional district, in addition to the three *ex-officio* members. The General Assembly appropriated $5,200 for the expenses of the board, $10,500 for holding farmers' institutes, and $8,500 for publishing reports. The board has taken great interest in the improvement of country roads; has held one State road congress; and is now making roads the subject of discussion at their meetings.

The World's Fair.—The General Assembly passed an act creating a State Board of World's Fair Commissioners, and appropriating $150,000 for the preparation of a State exhibit and the erection of a building on the exposition grounds; of this, $40,000 was set aside by the commission for the erection of a State building, which is constructed of Missouri material, from the design of a Missouri architect.

Charities.—The General Assembly appropriated $591,200 for eleemosynary institutions for 1891 and 1892. The law provides that each institution shall have five managers, which shall meet once each month, and shall be given an annual salary of $100 each, in addition to their traveling expenses. The Penitentiary is under control of a board of inspectors, composed of the Treasurer, Auditor, and Attorney-General, who receive for that service a yearly salary of $250 each.

The State has three lunatic asylums. The appropriations for 1891–'92 were $369,400. At the State School for the Blind there are 114 pupils in attendance. The most expensive charity maintained by the State is the School for the Deaf and Dumb. The last General Assembly appropriated $118,701.70 for the years 1891–'92. The attendance in January, 1893, was 285. The Industrial Home for Girls has 33 inmates, and $7,500 was appropriated by the last General Assembly for the support of the institution.

Insurance Department.—This department has not only been self-sustaining, but a source of revenue to the State. During the four years of 1889 to 1892 inclusive, its net earnings amounted to $43,788.40. The amount remaining to the credit of the fund on Jan. 1, 1893, was $17,-894.99.

Costs in Criminal Cases.—The largest item of expenditure by the State government for several years past has been for costs in criminal cases, and these are growing, although the number of convicts in the Penitentiary shows no appreciable increase. The appropriation by the thirty-sixth General Assembly for this object

was $585,000. It has all been drawn, and there is a deficit of about $35,000.

Biweekly Payment Law.—The thirty-sixth General Assembly amended the biweekly payment law so as to require all operators of mines to pay their employees at least once in every fifteen days, and to pay them the full amount of their earnings to date of payment.

Political.—The Republicans met in State convention at Jefferson City on April 28, and nominated the following ticket: For Governor, William Warner; Lieutenant-Governor, Rudolph Mueller; Secretary of State, H. T. Alkire; Auditor, John M. Weeks; Treasurer, F. J. Wilson; Attorney-General, David Murphy; Railroad Commissioner, W. S. Hathaway; Judges of the Supreme Court, W. S. Shirk, Chas. Nagel, W. W. Edwards.

The platform congratulated the people of the State upon their material prosperity shown by the Auditor's report, and upon a reduction of taxation for State purposes from 20 cents to 15 cents on the $100 valuation. The Democratic party was condemned as being at the old game of trying to hoodwink the voters of the State in claiming credit for a reduction of taxation, when such reduction was only made in compliance with the plain requirements of the Constitution of the State.

We denounce the Democratic Legislature of Missouri for its gerrymander of the Congressional districts of this State so as to disfranchise 236,000 Republican voters, and the infamous gerrymander of the judicial circuits of the State, thereby identifying the judiciary with party politics.

We are in favor of a fair ballot and a fair count, condemning in unmeasured terms that feature of the present election laws of the State of Missouri whereby the recorders of voters are empowered to appoint not only the judges and clerks of election for the Democratic party, but for the Republican party also.

In order to maintain the purity of elections, immediate steps should be taken before the next State and national elections take place, to purge the registration books now in use of the hundreds and thousands of names of dead men and nonresident voters that are carried thereon purposely year after year.

That our State Legislature be requested to take such action in reference to this matter as will make it possible for the voters of the State of Missouri, irrespective of party, to keep inviolate the most sacred right they have.

The Democratic State Convention met in May, at Sedalia, for the selection of delegates to the national convention. The delegates were instructed to vote for Mr. Cleveland. In July the Democrats again met in convention for the nomination of State officers, and the following was the ticket chosen: Governor, William J. Stone; Lieutenant-Governor, John B. O'Meara: Secretary of State, A. A. Lesueur; State Auditor, Jas. M. Seibert; Treasurer, Lon V. Stephens; Attorney-General, R. F. Walker; Railway Commissioner, James Cowgill. The platform included the following:

We congratulate the people of Missouri on the progress of the State, on its increase of wealth, and on the wisdom of its Democratic Constitution, through the operation of which, with the Democratic party continuously in administration n the State since its adoption, liberty, life, and property have been protected, the increased demand for schools and eleemosynary institutions complied with, while at the same time the rate of taxation has been steadily reduced. We point to the record of the Democratic party under that Constitution as a conclusive reason for its continuance in power through the approving suffrages of the voters. When the Democratic party assumed the administration of the State government, in 1873, the bonded debt of the State was $20,868,000; on July 1, 1892, it had been reduced to $6,830,000. At the beginning of that period the rate of interest on the State debt was 6 and 7 per cent.; it is now but 3½ per cent. on five-sixths of the outstanding debt. During the last year of Republican control the rate of taxation for State purposes was 50 cents on the $100 valuation of property. It has now been reduced to 25 cents on the $100, or one half, 15 cents of which reduction has taken place during the incumbency of the present State administration, which reduction alone will save to the taxpayers of the State $1,500,000 this year.

The State Democratic Convention called to nominate Supreme Court judges to succeed those whose terms were to expire on Jan. 1, 1893, met in July, at St. Louis, and Judges Sherwood, Burgess, and McFarlane were declared the nominees. At the elections in November the Democratic State ticket was successful by a plurality of 29,790. The vote for presidential electors was: Cleveland, 267,353; Harrison, 226,-349: Weaver, 40,925; Bidwell, 4,314.

MONTANA, a Western State, admitted to the Union Nov. 8, 1889; area, 146,080 square miles; population, according to the census of 1890, 132,159. Capital, Helena.

Government.—The following were the State officers during the year: Governor, Joseph K. Toole; Lieutenant-Governor, John E. Rickards; Secretary of State, Louis Rotwitt; Treasurer, Richard O. Hickman; Auditor, E. A. Kenney; Attorney-General, Henri J. Haskell; Superintendent of Public Instruction, John Gannon; Chief Justice of the Supreme Court, Henry N. Blake; Associate Justices, William H. De Witt and E. N. Harwood. All these officers are Republicans except the Governor.

Finances.—The cash balance in all funds of the State treasury on Dec. 1, 1891, was $68,-759.20, and on Dec. 1, 1892, $162,510.61. The total revenue proper for the year was $433,-351.21, and the warrants drawn against the same were $379,357.90, leaving a balance of $53,993.31. The total receipts of the general fund were $508,-106.46, which, added to the balance on hand at the beginning of the year, $63,356.38, give a total of $571,462.84. The total of warrants paid and bonds bought was $418,576.12, leaving a balance of cash on hand of $152,886.72. The revenues from every county in the State have materially increased over those of the previous year, aggregating a net increase of $176,804.83. For the first time, all the several stock funds have a balance to their credit after paying all warrants for the year. The sheep inspector and idemnity fund is credited with a balance of $8,-165.77. It will not be necessary to levy the tax for this fund for some years to come, unless a serious epidemic should attack that class of stock. Only about $21,000 of the school fund has been invested.

Valuations.—The total valuation of property, real and personal, in the State for 1891, as returned by the county commissioners, is $142,-205,428. The values are divided in part as follow: Town and city lots, $30,975,421; railroads,

$7,781,390; money, $4,295,505; other personal property, $59,974,546.

Militia.—The State Constitution compels the maintenance of a State militia, and the code provides for an annual encampment, but none has been held since 1889, owing to the failure of the Legislature to make an appropriation. Under an act of Congress providing for the disposition of the abandoned Fort Ellis reservation the State Board of Land Commissioners has filed on 640 acres for a permanent military camp ground.

Land Grants.—Seventy-two sections of public land were given to the Territory of Montana for university purposes by the United States in 1881, of which 45,226 acres were selected in 1882-'83. Another grant of 622,000 acres was made by the Federal Government in the act providing for the admission of Montana into the Union. The report of the State Board of Land Commissioners for 1892 shows a total selection of 128,823.51 acres.

Industrial.—In 1891 there were 7,646 farms and ranches in the State, containing 1,383,826 acres of fenced land and 2,202,105 unfenced. The acreage cultivated and the crop produced included the following: Wheat, 655,273 bushels; rye, 14,920 bushels; barley, 244,766 bushels; corn, 35,809 bushels; oats, 2,524,507 bushels: peas, 22,000 bushels. Of butter and cheese there were 700,458 pounds, produced from the milk of 13,336 cows. The wool clip was 8,344,830 pounds, and the number of sheep 1,211,746.

The number of quartz mills in the State was 34, the gross receipts of which for 1891 were $30,260,729. Eighty-six reduction furnaces produced 185,294,225 pounds of bullion and matte, the value of which was $30,124,165.

The product of placer mines was $174,667.

Mining Congress.—On July 12 the second session of the National Mining Congress was opened at Helena. Delegates were present from nearly every State and Territory west of the Mississippi. After sessions lasting through three days, during which the silver question was exhaustively discussed, the following resolutions among others were passed:

The National Mining Congress, now in session at Helena, Mont., composed of delegates from 19 States and 2 Territories, having in mind the interests of the cotton planters of the South and the grain growers of the West, of labor and property in all their forms, as well as the interests of the miners in the mountain States and Territories, denounce the act of 1873 by which silver was demonetized as a great national calamity, and we hold it to be the imperative duty of the Representatives of the people, now in Congress assembled, to pass without delay the bill for the remonetization of silver that has already passed the Senate.

We denounce as maliciously and designedly false the charge that the silver men of the country are in favor of a 70-cent dollar, or of any dollar that is of less intrinsic value than any other dollar coined and circulated in the United States. We also declare that the responsibility for the bullion in the silver dollars now coined being of less intrinsic value than the bullion in the gold dollars rests solely with those who demonetized silver and forced the people to accept the laws of 1878 and 1890, by which free coinage for silver has been denied and the purchase of bullion by the Government in the lowest markets of the world substituted in its stead.

The industry of mining for gold, silver, copper,

lead, coal, iron, stone, and all other metals and minerals, has assumed such magnitude and importance that it should be placed on a plane with that of agriculture; and we urge that Congress shall by law create a bureau of mines and mining, and that its head shall be made a member of the President's Cabinet.

Political.—During May and June the Republican, Democratic, and Prohibition parties each held a State convention for choosing delegates to their national conventions. The selection of a ticket for State officers was in each case deferred to a later convention. The first State ticket in the field was nominated by the People's party, whose convention was held at Butte on June 15. This convention selected delegates to the national convention of the party, and nominated William Kennedy for Governor; Harvey H. Cullum for Lieutenant-Governor; Joseph W. Allen for Secretary of State; James D. McKay for Auditor; J. R. Latimer for Treasurer; Miss Ella L. Knowles for Attorney-General; Abram Hall for Superintendent of Public Instruction; William Y. Pemberton for Chief Justice of the Supreme Court; Campton H. Coates for Clerk of the Supreme Court; and Caldwell Edwards for Congressman. Presidential electors were also nominated, and a platform adopted which favored free coinage of silver, an eight-hour law, the election of President and United States Senators by direct vote of the people, and the restriction of immigration. Declarations urging that the land grant of the Northern Pacific Railway in Montana be declared forfeited, and that the National Government should maintain reservoirs for the irrigation of arid land, were also a part of the platform. The name of William D. Lear for Treasurer was later substituted for that of J. R. Latimer, and the name of Abram Hall was withdrawn.

On Sept. 6 the Republicans, in State convention at Great Falls, nominated Lieut.-Gov. Rickards for Governor, and renominated Secretary of State Rotwitt, Attorney-General Halkell, and Chief-Justice Blake. For Lieutenant-Governor the convention selected Alexander C. Botkin; for Treasurer, Frederic W. Wright; for Auditor, Andrew B. Cook; for Superintendent of Public Instruction, Eugene A. Steere; for Clerk of the Supreme Court, Benjamin Webster, and for Congressman, Charles S. Hartman. Presidential electors were also nominated. The following is a portion of the platform adopted:

We demand that the present duty on wool be maintained, and condemn the action of the Democrats in the House of Representatives by which they sought to deny to the wool growers of the West the protection which they conceded to the wool manufacturers of the East.

We regard with bitter indignation the effort of the Democratic majority in the House to admit lead ores, when found in combination with silver, free of duty—a measure which, if it had not been defeated by the Republican Senate or vetoed by a Republican President, would have exposed the miners of Montana to competition with the peons of Mexico, and visited disaster and ruin upon the great industry which is so large a factor in affording employment to working-men, in the creation of wealth, and in promoting the prosperity of our State.

We demand the full recognition of silver as a money metal by the opening of the mints of the United States to its free and unlimited coinage; the use of both gold and silver at their present ratio as legal tenders; that all paper money shall be redeemable in gold or silver, and that thus every dollar, whether gold, silver, or paper, shall be of equal paying and purchasing power.

We recognize without hesitation or qualification the right of labor to organize for its own benefit and protection, and fully approve of such organizations. We believe that they should be conducted in subordination to the laws of the land and in the spirit of American institutions.

We denounce the employment of private and irresponsible bodies of armed men for any purpose whatsoever, and pledge the efforts of the Republican party for the enforcement by appropriate legislation of the provision in our State Constitution to restrain such invasions of the authority of the States and the rights of citizens. We condemn the Democratic House of Representatives for its neglect to pass the anti-Pinkerton bill.

We recommend the passage by Congress of a law making post offices savings banks of deposit and exchange.

The Democratic State ticket was nominated at a convention which met at Great Falls on Sept. 13. For Governor, Timothy E. Collins was named; for Lieutenant-Governor, Henry R. Melton; for Secretary of State, Benjamin W. S. Folk; for Treasurer, Jesse Haston; for Auditor, William C. Whaley; for Attorney-General, Edward C. Day; for Superintendent of Public Instruction, John C. Mahoney; for Chief Justice of the Supreme Court, William Y. Pemberton; for Clerk of the Supreme Court, John Sloane; for Congressman, William W. Dixon. Presidential electors were nominated. The platform denounces the McKinley tariff law, recognizes the proposed reinstatement of silver as the great issue of the day, instructs the representatives of the State in Congress to work for a free-coinage bill, and demands a change in the boundaries of the National Park.

There was a Prohibition ticket in the field, headed by J. M. Waters for Governor, J. C. Templeton for Lieutenant-Governor, and Benjamin R. Atkins for Congressman.

At the November election the total vote cast was 44,315, out of a total registration of 50,909. For presidential electors the Republican ticket received 18,851 votes, the Democratic ticket 17,581, People's party 7,334, and Prohibitionist 549. The vote for Governor was: Rickards, 18,187; Collins, 17,650; Kennedy, 7,794; Waters, 543. For Congressman—Hartman, 17,934; Dixon, 17,762; Edwards, 6,927; Atkins, 601. All the Republican candidates on the State ticket were elected except Judge Blake, the candidate for Chief Justice of the Supreme Court. His opponent, William Y. Pemberton, was the only candidate who received a nomination from both the Democrats and the People's party, and their combined vote elected him. At this election the people were required by the Constitution to express their choice for the permanent State capital. The cities and towns desiring the honor, and the vote for each, were as follow: Helena, 14,010; Anaconda, 10,183; Butte, 7,752; Bozeman, 7,685; Great Falls, 5,045; Deer Lodge, 983; Boulder, 295. At the next general election the people will choose between Helena and Anaconda, the two places having the largest number of votes. A portion of the State Senate of 1893, and all the members of the House, were chosen at this election. The Senate will contain 9 Democrats and 7 Republicans; the House must eventually contain 26 Democrats, 26 Republicans, and 3 People's party men. But the political complexion of the latter body was not fully determined at the close of the year, by reason of a dispute over the returns from Choteau County. The canvassing board of that county refused to count the returns of Box Elder precinct, although they appeared regular on their face, on the ground that the election in that precinct was tainted with fraud. By throwing out these returns, a Democratic majority was obtained, and a certificate was issued to the Democratic candidate. By this action, if it were legal, the Democrats would obtain a majority of both Houses on joint ballot and would easily elect a United States Senator. The Republican candidate, E. E. Leach, who would have been elected if the Box Elder precinct had been counted, applied to the State Supreme Court for a writ of mandate to compel the board to reassemble and complete its work. A demurrer was filed to this petition and overruled by the court, and an answer was filed, after which the case was heard on its merits. On Dec. 24 the court decided in favor of the petitioner, and issued a mandate ordering the board to count the Box Elder returns and issue a certificate accordingly. The court held that the canvassing board had no other authority than to foot up the returns; it could not sit as a judicial body and pass upon the validity of the election. The mandate was served upon the members of the board, but up to the close of the year they had not obeyed.

MOROCCO, a monarchy in northwestern Africa. The Government is an absolute despotism, not restricted by any laws. The Sultan is the chief of the state as well as head of the religion. He is chosen from the family of the Sherifs of Tafilet, and is selected by each Sultan before his death, subject to an election in which all the members of the family are eligible. Owing to the fact that the Sultan's appointee has possession of the imperial treasury and the control of the black body guard, which furnishes a large majority of the court officials, it very rarely occurs that any other than the Sultan's nominee is elected. The reigning Sultan is Muley Hassan, born in 1831, who succeeded his father, Sidi Mohammed, on Sept. 17, 1873. The Sultan has six ministers, who execute his orders, and whom he can consult, if he wishes, on important questions of state. They are the Vizier, the Minister of Foreign Affairs, the Minister of the Interior, the Chief Chamberlain, the Chief Treasurer, and the Chief Administrator of Customs. The Sultan's army consists of 10,000 disciplined infantry, 400 disciplined cavalry, a few batteries of field guns, and 2,000 irregular cavalry. Several of the governors of the provinces are ordered to collect their forces to accompany the Sultan in his annual progresses between Fez and Morocco. English, French, Italian, Spanish, and German officers are detailed by their respective governments for duty in the Sultan's army.

Commerce and Navigation.—About half of the whole trade is in the hands of Great Britain, and France formerly controlled the remainder, but of late years commerce with Germany has been on the increase. The total imports in 1890 amounted to £1,793,689, and the exports to £1,632,626. The principal imports in 1890 were: Cotton goods, £695,308; sugar, £317,138; tea, £74,604; woolen cloth, £58,150; raw silk, £46,320; candles, £35,149; hardware, £24,950; iron and iron goods, £24,063; glass and earthenware, £18,361; spices, £14,340; manufactured silk, £12,325; wines and spirits, £11,061; matches, £8,431; coffee, £6,881; hides, £5,051; linen goods, £4,475. The principal exports for the same period were: Beans, £281,331; wool, £218,280; chick peas, £200,755; olive oil, £174,740; maize, £137,459; goat skins, £118,237; almonds, £92,711; oxen, £65,001; eggs, £40,422; gums, £32,475; beeswax, £23,572; slippers, £19,342; woolen stuffs, £12,732; dates, £8,382; canary seed, £5,712. In the same year, 2,646 vessels, of 933,417 tons, entered, and 2,472 vessels, of 921,571 tons, cleared the ports of Morocco.

The British Mission to Fez.—The trade with Morocco is carried on partly under an old commercial treaty concluded with Great Britain in 1856 by the present Sultan's father, and partly under a treaty concluded with Germany in 1890 by the present Sultan. Although these treaties mitigated the restrictions on commerce to some extent, yet regulations still existed which made profitable trade difficult. To remedy these shortcomings, the Government of Great Britain decided to send a mission to the Sultan to endeavor to negotiate a commercial treaty by which all nations alike would profit. The commercial reforms sought to be obtained were the reduction of import duties on certain articles, the reduction of export duties on the produce of the land, and sanction for the exportation of wheat, horses, and other produce which had heretofore been prohibited. The restrictions put upon Europeans which forbade their owning real property without the permission of the Sultan were to be abolished, and the gradual if not immediate abolition of the *protégé* system as sanctioned by the European powers at the convention of Madrid in 1880 was to be obtained. Its original purpose was to protect European subjects from the cruelties and exactions of the Moorish authorities. It was settled that all Europeans, and Moorish subjects employed in trade in partnership with Europeans, and all Moors actually employed by European legations and consulates, should be protected by the flag of the European power with whom they were connected. As the abuse of this system permitted Moors to commit crimes and then elude justice by buying the protection of some European power, it was thought desirable to effect a change. Sir Charles Bean Euan-Smith, minister plenipotentiary to Morocco, was the head of the mission. The start was made from Tangier on April 27, 1892, and after a journey of about two weeks the mission entered the city of Fez on May 12, where great preparations had been made for its reception. At first it seemed as though the mission would accomplish its purpose, the time up till June 13 being spent in the discussion of the new treaty between the commissioners appointed by the Sultan and Sir C. Euan-Smith and his associates. On that date the commissioners informed the mission that they were authorized by the Sultan to say that he accepted the treaty unreservedly, with the exception of four of the articles, as to which further discussion was necessary. This statement was verified by the Sultan the next day in an audience which Sir C. Euan-Smith had with him, when he expressed his desire to arrive at a satisfactory conclusion. On June 16 an attempt was made to intimidate the mission. At a late hour in the night the Governor of Fez warned Sir C. Euan-Smith that an attack would be made on the members of the mission by the populace, who were highly excited by the demands of commercial reforms, and that their lives were threatened, asking the British minister for his approval for having a special guard placed at his door. Sir C. Euan-Smith, who was aware that no such attempt was contemplated, requested him to have the extra guard withdrawn, and this was done and no disturbance took place. On June 28, while the objectionable articles were still under consideration, the Moorish Minister of Foreign Affairs requested an audience with Sir C. Euan-Smith, and, after everybody except one interpreter had been excluded, offered him a bribe of $100,000 if he would sign the treaty without the clauses distasteful to the Sultan. He said that such steps had been resorted to frequently in cases of various missions of foreign ministers to the Moorish court where difficulties had arisen between them and the Sultan, and he hoped that by this means all difficulties regarding the treaty under consideration might be removed. Moreover, he said that the Sultan desired to make this offer to him personally the next day. When, on the following day, Sir C. Euan-Smith had an audience with the Sultan, the latter repeated the offer made by his minister, and admitted that it was done by his order, adding that if ministers who came to his court went away satisfied it was because they removed difficulties from his way, explaining that he made presents to them, and that they were satisfied and he was also content. Sir C. Euan-Smith declined to discuss these proposals, requesting the Sultan to continue the discussion of the treaty, and urging him not to persist in the rejection of the clauses in question, which had been modified to the utmost possible extent in compliance with his Majesty's wishes. Discussions went on until July 5, when a disturbance took place. It was the first day of the Baïram festival, and large crowds of fanatical tribesmen thronged the city. When the chief interpreter of the British mission, with several Americans and Europeans, accompanied by servants of the Legation, was passing through the crowd, they were met by a mob of about 500, which had gathered near the quarters of the mission, and were hooted and abused, and some stones were thrown at them. It appeared that the Governor of Fez was at the bottom of the disturbance, and that the Deputy-Governor was the leader of the mob. Sir C. Euan-Smith immediately sought an interview with the Sultan, informing him that, if necessary, and if this line of conduct was persisted in, he would hoist the British flag personally, and that he would look to him, under his treaty engagements, to take all necessary measures for due protection and honor being paid to the flag on that occasion. The Sultan requested him not to have the flag hoisted, and promised that

full reparation should be made to the insulted foreigners; accordingly, the Governor was ordered to make official apologies personally to all the persons insulted, and to pay a fine of $10,000, which Sir C. Euan-Smith distributed among the blind and the poor. The Deputy-Governor was sentenced to be imprisoned in chains for one year. On the evening of the same day a deputation of the six principal personages of the Sultan's court waited on Sir C. Euan-Smith, requesting him to come to the Sultan immediately. On his arrival at the palace the Sultan informed him that he thought the negotiations regarding the treaty had gone on long enough, that useful discussion had been exhausted, and that he would give orders for the treaty to be signed and concluded on the following day. After asking for one or two more slight concessions, to which Sir C. Euan-Smith objected, the Sultan declared that the treaty should be concluded as he (Sir C. Euan-Smith) wished. The Foreign Minister was sent for, and orders for its execution were given him in explicit terms, the Sultan remarking that he did this because he was anxious to have it known to all men how great was the friendship between the two governments.

The scribes arrived on the following morning, to make duplicate copies of the treaty, at the same time asking for an extension of time of twenty-four hours for the completion of clerical work. During the two days following the commissioners kept coming to the British envoy and informing him that the Sultan could not keep his promise, and asking for further alterations and concessions. Sir C. Euan-Smith replied that the Sultan's solemn and unsolicited promise barred all further discussion, and begged for the speedy execution of the document. On July 9 he received an Arabic document from his interpreter, which had been handed to the latter by the Foreign Minister with the remark that this was the only treaty which the Sultan was likely to accept; it was unaccompanied by any letter, nor was it sent to Sir C. Euan-Smith direct. Upon examination, it proved to be a travestied copy of the treaty agreed upon on July 5, with every single concession obtained from the Sultan during the subsequent negotiations erased and canceled, and the treaty altered absolutely, in the interests of the Sultan. Sir C. Euan-Smith tore the copy up and returned it to the Foreign Minister, who excused himself for what had occurred, but explained that he had acted under the Sultan's orders. After this last incident Sir C. Euan-Smith arrived at the conclusion that the Sultan was acting on principles or under influences which rendered any attempt at further negotiation hopeless, and that he could not, with due regard to the legitimate demands of British prestige and influence, continue the discussion. He therefore addressed a letter to the Sultan, setting forth the reasons that compelled him to take his departure from Fez without delay, and asked for a farewell audience. The Sultan at this last interview expressed his regret at the prospect of the departure of the mission, and also attempted to apologize for the incident of the treaty referred to above. He acknowledged that he had made many promises regarding the treaty which he had not fulfilled, but that other people had advised him that the promises he had made would have evil results for himself, and therefore he could not act up to them. Just as Sir C. Euan-Smith was on the point of leaving, the Sultan remarked that if he, Sir C. Euan-Smith, would give way and consent to take the article of flour out of the export tariff list, and not insist upon certain other articles being admitted at a duty less than 10 per cent., he would at once accept the treaty. After some reflection Sir C. Euan-Smith consented to this; whereupon the Sultan thanked him warmly, but immediately remarked that there were 16 or 17 other changes which he wished made in the treaty. Seeing that further discussion was useless, the British minister took his departure, leaving Fez at once for his camp, which was pitched about 10 miles from the city. That same night two new special commissioners arrived in the camp with a letter from the Sultan, saying that they were sent out by him to conclude the treaty finally. The next morning Minister Gharnit came out, confirming the statement that the commissioners had full powers, and that he was to sign the treaty. The commissioners themselves declared that they had the fullest powers from the Sultan, that no further reference to Fez was necessary, and that their business would not occupy more than fifteen minutes. Instead of fifteen minutes, the whole day was spent in discussing further modifications, until in the evening they expressed themselves fully satisfied, and declared that the treaty was now finally concluded. Fresh duplicate copies were made out for Minister Gharnit's signature, but when these were finished the commissioners all at once said they must ride into Fez and show the amended treaty to the Sultan as a mere matter of form; that nothing could be changed now, as they had full powers, and that they would return in five hours. After waiting all next day for their return, Sir C. Euan-Smith decided to break camp next day and return to Tangier, considering that to remain in camp under these circumstances would be detrimental to British prestige, and likely to diminish rather than augment his chances of success. Before his departure he was informed that the commissioners had returned, but without the treaty, which the Sultan wished to have changed in some respects, and that he had, moreover, canceled the powers of the commissioners; and so there was nothing left for Sir C. Euan-Smith but to return to Tangier without a treaty. In his official report to the Marquis of Salisbury Sir C. Euan-Smith assigns as the cause of the failure of his mission the innate dislike, if not, indeed, actual loathing, which is felt by the Sultan, as a Mohammedan ruler, to any concession whatever to the demands of a Christian power. He continues in his report:

Arising out of the religious fanaticism of the Moors springs the next most important influence upon the Sultan's mind, his knowledge of the inherent weakness of his position; and the feeble tenure by which he maintains his authority over his people makes him morbidly sensitive to the possible reproach that he may too readily, and save in the face of irresistible pressure, concede privileges and reforms to European demands.

He dreads beyond measure the possibility of the influence of the religious world being excited against him, and of their raising the cry that the interests of Islam are being sacrificed to the requirements of an abhorred civilization; and on the occasion of my stay in Fez he was especially nervous in regard to this matter, because the first appeal for supports that he made to the Ulema did not meet with success.

The Marquis of Salisbury, in his reply to the report, reminds Sir C. Euan-Smith of the false reports that had been given out regarding the intentions of Great Britain in Morocco, which, he says, had gained extended currency throughout Morocco, and in the face of those facts he considers it inexpedient, for the present at least, to make any renewed attempt to induce the Sultan to accept Great Britain's advice upon this subject.

Insurrections of the Tribes.—In the beginning of January, 1892, a revolt took place of the native tribes of the Anghera district, in the vicinity of Tangier. The revolt was not aimed against the Sultan, but against the Governor of Tangier, Hadji Mohammed Ben Abdisadak, who, on the death of his father, about a year ago, had been invested by the Sultan with the governorship. He immediately began to recover the large gift of money which he had been obliged to offer the Sultan on the occasion of his nomination, by a system of exaction which the poor natives were unable to bear. Their complaints remained unanswered, and they finally resorted to arms, driving out the sheiks from the different villages and killing the chief of the district of Gharbia. They formed an army and marched toward Tangier, where they encamped close to the city, and compelled the villagers to supply them with provisions, burning and pillaging the houses of those who refused. The proximity of a large body of bold and determined insurgents created considerable excitement among the Europeans in the town, and fears were entertained as to their safety. The European powers therefore dispatched some war vessels to that port for the protection of their subjects, but as the Sultan acceded to the demands of the insurgents and deposed the Governor, quiet was restored, making the presence of the men-of-war unnecessary. The insurgent tribes accepted the nomination of the new Governor, and order was restored. It was not long, however, before the new Governor followed the same line that had been disastrous to his predecessor, with the result that the people refused to pay the taxes levied, and drove the collectors of the Governor out of their towns and villages. They then proceeded to set up their own Governor, electing Cid Il'mam Said, who was known for his sense of justice. They demanded the recall of the Governor of Tangier, and threatened to repel with arms any attempt to subject them, but they expressed their complete loyalty to the Sultan, and declared that they were only at war with the Governor. The district of Anghera is inhabited by a sturdy half-Berber race of independent character, who live among the heights surrounding Jebel Moosa, and whose homes are almost inaccessible on account of the steep paths and the many passes, which, in the hands of hostile people, are impregnable. The Angherites began hostilities by burning and pillaging several villages friendly to the Governor. The situation becoming critical, the Sultan ordered an army to proceed to Tangier and protect that city from the attacks of the Augherites. A large force of imperial troops was soon collected around Tangier, and Cid Abbas Jamai was appointed chief of the expedition. On Aug. 7, 1892, an encounter took place. The Sultan's troops, numbering about 1,500 men, advanced into the territory of the Angherites. After setting fire to a small village, they were attacked by the enemy, and after a short combat were obliged to retreat. The Moorish cavalry eventually reformed, and charging their foes were again driven back. The Sultan's army retreated to Tangier; their loss was said to be about 30 men killed and wounded, and that of the insurgents 3 killed. After receiving re-enforcements from among the Mesmoda tribes, the Moorish troops again advanced to the scene of the recent fighting; but, not encountering the insurgents, they contented themselves with plundering the villages in their course, not being at all particular as to whether the inhabitants were friends or foes. Having received further re-enforcements, the expedition set out from

Tangier on Aug. 29, and, traversing the country of the Angherites without meeting the enemy, set fire to several villages. Suddenly, when about 8 miles east of Tangier, they encountered the main body of the insurgents. Some sharp fighting ensued, which ended in the retreat of the imperial army. The losses of the Moors were heavy, the number of killed being stated as amounting to 260; while only a comparatively small number of the insurgents were killed. The insurgents captured 54 cavalry and 17 infantry soldiers, among them a kaid of the imperial cavalry. H'mam, the chief of the insurgents, offered to give up his prisoners if the 9 Angherá captives were also released, which was accordingly done. The Sultan, seeing that the submission of the tribe could only be effected by great bloodshed, considered it wiser to resort to negotiations, which finally resulted in the dismissal of the obnoxious Governor and the appointment of Ould Kauja, a native of Anghera and son of a former governor of that district. Full pardon being granted to the insurgent tribes, the war was proclaimed at an end.

N

NATIONAL ACADEMY OF SCIENCES.
Officers: President, Othniel C. Marsh; Vice-President, Francis A. Walker; Foreign Secretary, Wolcott Gibbs; Home Secretary, Asaph Hall; Treasurer, John S. Billings. Two meetings were held during 1892. The first or stated meeting was held in Washington on April 19–22, when the following papers were read: "The Astronomical, Geodetic, and Electric Consequences of Tidal Strains within an Elastic Terrestrial Spheroid" and "On Atmospheric Radiation of Heat in Meteorology," by Cleveland Abbe; "On the Laws of the Variation of Latitude" and "On the Causes of Variations of Period in the Variable Stars," by Seth C. Chandler; "On the Homologies of the Cranial Arches of the Reptilia" and "On the Osteology of the Genus Anniella," by Edward D. Cope; "An American Maar," by Grove K. Gilbert; "The Partition of the North American Realm," by Theodore Gill; "Exhibition of Chladni's Acoustic Figures transferred to Paper without Distortion" and "On the Acoustic Properties of Aluminum, with Experimental Illustrations," by Alfred M. Mayer; "On the Force of Gravity at Washington" and "On the Recent Variations of Latitude at Washington," by Thomas C. Mendenhall; "Asiatic Influences in Europe," by Edward S. Morse; "On the Anatomy and Systematic Position of the Mecoptera," by Alpheus S. Packard; "A Definition of Institutions," by John W. Powell; "Exhibition of Teeth of a Gigantic Bear, probably an Extinct Species, found in Ancient Mounds in Ohio," by Frederick W. Putnam; "Abstract of Results from the United States Coast and Geodetic Survey Magnetic Observatory at Los Angeles, Cal., 1882–'89, Part III, Differential Measures of the Horizontal Component of the Magnetic Force," by Charles A. Schott; "A Means of measuring the Difference between the Tidal Change in the direction of the Plumb Line and the Tidal Deflection of the Earth's Crust," a posthumous paper by J. Homer Lane, also read by Cleveland Abbe, who likewise read a biographical memoir of J. Homer Lane and William Ferrel. The following papers were by nonmembers: "On, the Deflecting Forces that produce the Diurnal Variation of the Normal Terrestrial Magnetic Field," by Frank H. Bigelow, introduced by Cleveland Abbe; "Disruption of the Silver Haloid Molecule by Mechanical Force," M. Carey Lea, introduced by George F. Barker; "On Electrical Discharges through Poor Vacua, and on Coronoidal Discharges," by Michael I. Pupin, introduced by Thomas C. Mendenhall; and "The Form and Efficiency of the Iced Bar Base Apparatus of the United States Coast and Geodetic Survey," by Robert S. Woodward, introduced by Thomas C. Mendenhall. At the meeting held on April 21 the following new members were elected: Carl Barus, physicist, connected with the United States Geological Survey; Samuel Franklin Emmons, geologist, also a member of the United States Geological Survey: and Matthew Carey Lea, chemist, of Philadelphia, whose researches on the salts of silver have become famous. At the same time the Academy elected the following four foreign associates: Prof. Hugo Gylden, Upsala. Sweden; Prof. Carl Weierstross, Berlin, Germany; Prof. August Kekule, Bonn, Germany; and Prof. E. Du Bois-Reymond, Berlin, Germany. An important event connected with this meeting was the acceptance by the Academy of $2,650, a fund collected by the chemists of this country and presented to Wolcott Gibbs on Feb. 21—the anniversary of his seventieth birthday—for the encouragement of chemical research, to be known by his name. In acknowledging the gift Dr. Gibbs wrote: "I therefore propose that the fund raised for endowment shall be given to the National Academy of Sciences, to hold the same

in trust." A resolution was passed accepting this sum of money, and expressing the high appreciation shown by Dr. Gibbs in intrusting this fund to the Academy. The scientific session was held in Baltimore, on Nov. 1-3, when the following papers were read: "On Isothermals and Isometrics of Viscosity," by Carl Barus; "Significance of the Follicle of Salpa" and "Biological Relations of the Oldest Fossils," by William K. Brooks; "On the Motion of the Earth's Pole," by Seth C. Chandler; "On the Vertebrate Fauna of the Blanco Epoch," by Edward D. Cope; "The Evolution of the Moon," by Grove K. Gilbert; "Recent Improvements in Astronomical Telescopes," by Charles S. Hastings; "The Use of Planes and Knife Edges in Pendulums," "On the Observations for Latitude at Rockville, Md.," and "On the Latitude Observations at Honolulu," by Thomas C. Mendenhall; "On Some Curious Double Halides" and "Study of the Action of Light on Acids in Solutions containing a Salt of Uranium," by Ira Remsen: "A Spectroscopic Analysis of the Rare Earths," "A Table of Standard Wave Lengths." and "On the Motion of a Sphere in a Viscous Fluid," by Henry A. Rowland. The following papers were by non-members: "Exhibition of Photographs illustrating New Methods and Results in Solar Physics," by George E. Hale, introduced by Charles S. Hastings; "Crystallized Vegetable Proteids" and "Proteids of the Flaxseed," by Thomas B. Osborne, introduced by S. W. Johnson; "Some Effects of Magnetism on Chemical Action," by George A. Squier and Frank A. Wolff, Jr., introduced by Henry A. Rowland; and "Volcanic Rocks of South Mountain in Pennsylvania and Maryland," by George H. Williams, introduced by Ira Remsen. During the year the Academy has met with severe loss by the deaths of Thomas Sterry Hunt, a member since 1873; Joseph Lovering, a member since 1873; Montgomery Cunningham Meigs, a member since 1865; John Strong Newberry, an original member; Lewis Morris Rutherfurd, an original member; William Petit Trowbridge, a member since 1878; and Sereno Watson, a member since 1889. Biographical memoirs of these scientists have been assigned as follows: T. Sterry Hunt to J. P. Lesley; Joseph Lovering to Josiah P. Cooke; Montgomery C. Meigs to Henry J. Abbot; Lewis M. Rutherfurd to Benjamin A. Gould; William P. Trowbridge to Cyrus B. Comstock; and Sereno Watson to George L. Goodale. Brief notices of their careers also appear among the OBITUARIES, AMERICAN, in the present volume.

NAVY OF THE UNITED STATES. A full account of the development of the new navy, from the ordering of the first advisory board in 1881 to January, 1892, will be found in the "Annual Cyclopædia" for 1888, 1889, 1890, and 1891, especially in the first and last of these. During 1892 the progress in all directions was continuous and satisfactory, and it is especially marked in the manufacture of armor, gun-steel, projectiles, and smokeless powder.

Ships.—Of the vessels given in the tables on pages 544 to 547 of the "Annual Cyclopædia" for 1891, the following, then on the stocks, have been launched: the "Columbia" (cruiser No. 12), the "Olympia" (cruiser No. 6), the "Cin-

VOL. XXXII.—31 A

cinnati," the "Raleigh," the "Marblehead" (cruiser No. 11), the "Castine" (gunboat No. 6), the "Bancroft" (practice vessel), the "Texas," and the "Katahdin" (ram No. 1). "The "Minneapolis" (cruiser No. 13) is still on the stocks, as are the armored battle ships "Indiana," "Massachusetts," and "Oregon." The "Monterey" is the only vessel completed and commissioned within the year. Two new ships, the armored seagoing battle ship "Iowa" and the armored cruiser "Brooklyn," have been authorized by Congress, designed, contracted for, and are about to be laid down.

The "Iowa" is about 1,000 tons larger, but is very similar in design to the "Indiana," "Massachusetts," and "Oregon." The chief difference in the hull is in the raising of the forward part, from the bow to the central superstructure, bringing the forecastle on a level with the latter. This will improve the seagoing qualities very materially. The length is increased 12 feet and the beam 3 feet. The heavy guns are reduced in caliber from 13 to 12 inches, but are arranged in barbette turrets as before, as are also the 8 8-inch guns. The armor belt is reduced in thickness, but extended in length and width. The turret armor is likewise reduced, but in view of the improved quality of the plates produced by the Harvey process, the resistance to penetration of the armor on both belt and turrets is about equal to untreated steel plates of the thickness of those on the "Indiana" class. The speed, coal, and ammunition supply are increased. The dimensions and other details of the "Iowa" are as follow: Length on water line, 360 feet; beam, 72 feet 2¼ inches; mean draught, 24 feet; displacement, 11,296 tons; freeboard (height of side above water) forward, 19 feet; sustained sea speed, 16 knots; coal supply at load draught, 625 tons; total coal supply, 2,000 tons; the armor belt, 7½ feet wide, is not to be less than 14 inches thick amidships; the transverse armor at ends of belt not less than 12 inches; the barbettes and turrets for the 12-inch guns will be not less than 15 inches; the side armor above the belt not less than 5 inches; the armored deck will be at least 3 inches thick forward and abaft the belt, and 2¾ inches over it; a cellulose belt will be fitted above the protective deck forward and abaft the belt and side armor; the conning tower is to be not less than 10 inches, and the communication tube 7 inches; the barbettes for the 8-inch guns will be not less than 8 inches on the exposed side and 6 inches elsewhere; the 8-inch gun turrets will be at least 6 inches, with 3-inch loading tubes; the 4-inch guns will be protected by fixed semicircular shields 4 inches thick and 1½ inch splinter bulkheads; the smaller guns will have shields and extra thick plating on the side abreast them. The battery of the "Iowa" will consist of 4 12-inch and 8 8-inch breech-loading rifled guns, 6 4-inch, 20 6-pounder, and 4 1-pounder rapid-fire guns, 4 machine guns, and 1 field gun. The axes of the forward 12-inch guns will be 25 feet above the water and 6 feet above the deck; the axes of the after 12-inch guns will be 17 feet 8 inches above the water, and the same height above the deck as the forward guns; the guns of both turrets will be capable of firing through an arc of 270 degrees. The contract for the construction of the "Iowa" was awarded on Jan. 11, 1893, to the William Cramp Shipbuilding and Engine Company, at their bid of $3,010,000, on the plans furnished by the Navy Department.

The armored cruiser "Brooklyn," while similar in a general way to the "New York," differs in several respects. She is about 1,000 tons larger; the freeboard at the bow has been increased about 8 feet by raising the deck forward to the level of the superstructure, as in the "Iowa"; the armor has been slightly diminished in thickness and increased in extent; the battery has been heavily increased, as has the coal supply at load draught. The dimensions and other details are as follow: Displacement, 9,150 tons; length on load water line, 400 feet 6 inches; beam, 64 feet; mean draught at load displacement, 24 feet; freeboard at bow, 29 feet 10 inches; at stern, 21 feet 4 inches; total coal capacity, 1,650 tons, at load draught 900 tons; speed to average not less than 20 knots during a four-hour run, with the usual premiums for excess. The engines are triple expansion, of about 16,000 maximum horse power. The protective deck will be 6 inches thick on the slopes amidships; an armor belt, 8 feet wide and 3 inches thick, will extend along the water line abreast the machinery and boilers; behind this armor belt, extending forward and aft the whole length of the ship, will be a thick belt of cellulose, and behind this, still amidships, will be the upper coal-bunkers; the armor on the conning tower will be not less than 7½ inches, and on its communication tube not less than 5 inches; the armor on the 8-inch gun barbettes will be not less than 8 inches, and on the turrets 5½ inches; on fixed shields of 5-inch guns, 4 inches; and on splinter bulkheads 1½ inch. The battery of the "Brooklyn" consists of 8 8-inch breech-loading rifled guns, 12 5-inch rapid-fire guns, 12 6-pounder rapid-fire guns, 4 1-pounder rapid-fire guns, 4 machine guns, and 2 light field pieces. The 8-inch guns will be mounted in pairs in 4 barbette turrets—one forward and one aft, and one on each side amidships; the 5-inch guns will be mounted in sponsons. There will be 5 torpedo tubes.

The bid of the William Cramp Shipbuilding and Engine Company of $2,986,000 for the construction of the vessel on the plans approved and furnished by the Navy Department, was accepted on Jan. 11, 1893, and the work will be undertaken at once.

Guns.—There has been no change in the system of constructing heavy guns, but the increased length of the pieces, and the use of smokeless powders in which the pressure is longer sustained, have caused modifications of the design in the way of increasing the strength and stiffness along the chase, particularly in the larger calibers. The capacity of the gun factory is such that all the guns needed for the new ships will be ready some time before the ships are far enough advanced to receive them. Eighty-three guns of the following calibers were completed in the year ending Nov. 1, 1892: 28 4-inch, 11 5-inch, 18 6-inch, 4 8-inch, 17 10-inch, and 5 12-inch. There were in hand at that date, partly completed: 32 4-inch, 31 5-inch, 12 8-inch, 1 12-inch, and 1 13-inch.

The very excellent qualities of nickel-steel have caused attention to be drawn to its probable value for gun construction, and it is likely that it will be adopted by the Ordnance Bureau for all future work. Nickel-steel forgings for guns have already been ordered.

Smokeless Powder.—The results of the experiments with the new Navy smokeless powder are particularly gratifying. This powder has a gun-cotton base, and the tests show it to be superior to any powder so far produced either at home or abroad. The facts that it was unaffected by long-continued exposure to heat or cold (within ranges considerably beyond any possible atmospheric temperatures), that it was uninjured by moisture, even by boiling in water, and that it was exceedingly safe to handle, were mentioned in the article on the Navy in the "Annual Cyclopædia" for 1891. Further tests and experiments confirm these conclusions. It is now manufactured for calibers up to 6 inches, and the use will be extended to the larger calibers as soon as practicable. The latest results of firing tests are: With a 6-inch gun, charge 26 pounds, muzzle velocity 2,469 feet a second, pressure in gun 13·9 tons to the square inch; in a 5-inch gun, charge 13·4 pounds, muzzle velocity 2,578 feet a second, pressure in gun 15·6 tons. The ordinary service charge of brown powder gives a muzzle velocity of only 2,100 feet a second, with a pressure in the gun of 14 tons to the square inch. In referring to the tabulated report of these tests, Commodore Folger, chief of ordnance of the navy, says: "A comparison of these results with those published abroad (giving due weight to the different lengths of bore and weight of projectile) shows the marked superiority of the American smokeless powder, which gives higher and more regular velocities with much lower and more uniform pressures."

Torpedoes.—A few each of Whitehead and Howell torpedoes have been delivered and tested. The latter are not quite satisfactory in point of speed, but experiments now being made indicate that this difficulty will soon be overcome.

Submarine Gun.—A gun of this type, mounted on board the "Destroyer," was tested in the spring of 1892, and the excellent results show the great importance of this weapon.

Submarine Boat.—No satisfactory submarine boat has yet been constructed. The most promising of recent efforts is that of Mr. Baker, of Detroit. Several fairly successful trials have been made, and, after some changes have been completed, further experiments will be had.

High Explosives.—Recent experiments with gun-cotton and emmensite have demonstrated the value of these high explosives for naval use. Their employment as bursting charges in armor-piercing and certain other forms of shell is expected in the near future.

Armor.—The greatest advance of the year has, perhaps, been in the development of armor. All armor for our naval vessels—except the first few deliveries—will be of nickel steel, supercarbonized and surface-hardened by the Harvey process. The decisive victory of the nickel-steel plate at Annapolis over its rivals has been repeated this year by the Harvey nickel-steel plate tested in Russia in competition with English and French plates of the most recent make, nickel steel and compound. The foreign plates were either perforated or broken up by the projectiles from a 6-inch gun. The same projectiles were broken into fragments against the hard face of the Harvey plate, scarcely indenting it. A 9-inch gun was then employed, and, although the plate was cracked through, the projectiles failed to perforate it, and the backing was uninjured. All the plates were 10 inches thick. The results of this and other recent trials have had a marked influence upon naval ordnance policy. The tendency for the past two or three years has been in favor of limiting the size of guns to a caliber of about 10 inches. But the resisting power of the Harveyized armor is so great, that it is now seen that any large armor-clad can readily carry armor invulnerable to a 10-inch gun at any range, and with any velocity that is likely to be obtained in the immediate future. Upward of 7,000 tons of armor for vessels now building will shortly be contracted for. The requirements will be more severe than those formerly specified, and much more so than the requirements abroad. The latest reports indicate that all foreign governments are ordering plates made by the American process.

Armor-piercing Projectiles.—Recent tests at the proving-ground have shown that the American shells manufactured by the Carpenter Steel Company are superior to the last shells received from abroad. The patents, secrets, etc., of the Holtzer process, with the right to manufacture, have been acquired by an American company, and it has begun production. The Sterling Steel Company, of Delmar, Pa., have begun the manufacture of armor-piercing projectiles by a process of their own, and the shells offered for test have given excellent results. They are now furnishing a considerable number under contract.

Small Arms.—No effort has been made to obtain a suitable rifle for the navy, though all available information of existing arms has been collected. The authorities are awaiting the final action of the Army Board. This board has provisionally approved the Krag-Jorgensen, but definite decision is delayed until some recent American inventions have been examined. It is not expected that the same gun will be selected for use in the navy, but the caliber of both services will be the same, and the ammunition interchangeable.

Naval Stations.—A naval station has been established at Point Turner, Puget Sound, and a dry dock is under construction there. It is the intention to fit this station with tools and appliances sufficient for all necessary repairs to ships and engines. A dry dock is also building at the naval station near Port Royal, S. C. A small outfit of tools, sufficient for ordinary repairs, will doubtless be kept there. A new dry dock of large dimensions (650 feet long) will be built at the Brooklyn Navy Yard. Work will be begun as soon as possible.

Auxiliary Naval Vessels.—Under the contracts made by the Post Office Department, as provided in the postal subsidy bill, a large number of fine seagoing mail steamers have been built or are under construction. On condition that the company would build several fast ships of approximately equal tonnage in American ship-

yards, and comply with existing statutes in other respects, the two Inman Line steamers "City of New York" and "City of Paris" have been admitted to registry by special act of Congress. The new line thus formed will be called the American Line, and the two steamers above mentioned will hereafter be known as the "New York" and the "Paris." The contracts for building the new ships of the line have been let to the Cramps.

The value of the auxiliary navy thus being built up by the operation of the postal subsidy act, and of the recent act referred to above, will be very great in time of war.

NEBRASKA, a Western State, admitted to the Union March 1, 1867; area, 77,510 square miles. The population, according to each decennial census since admission, was 122,993 in 1870; 452,402 in 1880; and 1,058,910 in 1890. Capital, Lincoln.

Government.—The following were the State officers during the year: Governor, John M. Thayer, Republican, succeeded, on Feb. 8, by James E. Boyd, Democrat; Lieutenant-Governor, Thomas J. Majors; Secretary of State, John C. Allen; Auditor of Public Accounts, Thomas H. Benton; Treasurer, John E. Hill; Attorney-General, George H. Hastings; Superintendent of Public Instruction, Alexander K. Goudy; Commissioner of Public Lands and Buildings, A. R. Humphrey; Chief Justice of the Supreme Court, Samuel Maxwell; Associate Justices, T. L. Norval and A. M. Post.

The Governorship.—At the beginning of the year the case of John M. Thayer vs. James E. Boyd, in which the eligibility of the latter to the office of Governor was the question at issue, was pending before the United States Supreme Court on appeal from the State Supreme Court. The latter tribunal had decided that Gov. Boyd was ineligible on the ground that he never had been naturalized, and had awarded the office to ex-Gov. Thayer. Arguments in the case were heard by the Federal Court at Washington on Dec. 8, 1891, but no decision was rendered till Feb. 1, 1892. The court then reversed the decision of the State Supreme Court, and declared Mr. Boyd entitled to the office. It appeared from the records of the case that the father of Gov. Boyd, an alien, though he had duly declared his intention of becoming a citizen during his son's minority, had never taken out his final naturalization papers according to law. But he had exercised all the rights of a citizen for many years without question, and the son had exercised the same rights from the date of his majority, and had held public offices. The court were of the opinion that such evidence, showing that a person otherwise qualified had in fact for a long time voted and held office and exercised the rights belonging to a citizen, would be sufficient to warrant a jury in finding that he was duly naturalized, although he could not produce his naturalization papers, and that, accordingly, both the father and the son must in this case be considered as fully naturalized. By another course of reasoning, leading to the same result, a portion of the court decided that the act of Congress admitting Nebraska to the Union by its term had naturalized all persons then in the State who had declared their intention of becoming citizens, and that as Mr. Boyd was then a resident of the State, he must be considered to have been in the same position that his father would have been if then a resident of the State, and must have been fully naturalized by that act.

Although this decision was rendered on Feb. 1, no order to enforce it could be issued, under the practice of the court, till Feb. 29. Meanwhile Gov. Thayer was disposed to claim all his legal rights, and at first refused to surrender the office till legally notified by the court, but he finally allowed Mr. Boyd to take possession on Feb. 8.

Finances.—For the two years ending Nov. 30, 1892, the State treasury statement is as follows: Balance in all funds, Nov. 30, 1890, $1,592,-248.20; total receipts, $3,982,876.11; total payments, $4,401,038.38; balance on Nov. 30, 1892, $1,181,085.93. The general fund statement for the same period is as follows: Balance on Nov. 30, 1890, $404,367.88; total receipts, $1,886,-881.48; total payments, $2,274,616.31; balance on Nov. 30, 1892, $16,633.05. The marked reduction in the general fund balance is due to the action of the last Legislature in increasing the appropriations without making a corresponding increase in the tax levy. The total appropriations from the general fund authorized for the years 1891 and 1892 were $2,693,750.63, while the estimated revenues for that period were only $1,800,000. As a result, the State Treasurer was obliged, in August, 1891, to begin the registration of warrants. The effect of this action was to make the State liable for interest on these warrants until such time as there should be money in the general fund to pay them. From Aug. 1, 1891, to Nov. 30, 1892, there were registered for payment, in regular order as presented, warrants on the general fund to the amount of $1,718,256.62. Of this amount, the sum of $1,-080,872.79 was paid during the period, leaving a registered indebtedness against the general fund of $637,383.83 on Nov. 30, 1892, drawing 7 per cent. interest per annum. In addition to this constantly accruing obligation there was paid during the period, as interest on general fund warrants redeemed, the sum of $88,817.15.

The Auditor, in his report to the Governor, says:

One of three things must be done to maintain the credit of the State: Compel assessors to list all property at full value, or raise the levy to be made by the State Board of Equalization, or curtail the expenses of the State government.

The following statement shows the different sources of State revenue for the biennial period: State taxes received, $2,234,973.25; from counties, for care of insane, $122,898.11; principal on school lands sold, $255,952.27; interest and rental on school lands, $598,889.93; principal on university lands sold, $3,150; principal on agricultural college lands sold, $16,983.27; interest and rental on university lands, $21,239.97; interest and rental on agricultural college lands, $56,412.92; principal on normal school lands sold, $5,260; interest and rental on normal school lands, $8,299.41; principal on saline lands sold, $2,644.95; interest charged county treasurers, $608.84; interest on United States and county bonds, $322,644.31; miscellaneous sources, including transfers, $352,918.88; total receipts, $3,982,876.11.

Education.—The following is a statement of the condition of the public schools for the year ending July 31, 1891: Children of school age, 333,115; total number enrolled in public schools, 247,320; teachers employed, 8,801; salaries paid teachers, $2,217,316.78; number of schoolhouses, 5,885; total value of school property, $6,959,-607.72; number of school districts, 6,417; average school year in days, 139; total receipts for school purposes during the year, including balance on hand, July 31, 1890, $4,123,799.54; total expenditures for school purposes during the year, $3,390,517.14; balance on hand, $733,-282.40.

There were granted to the State by the Federal Government a total of 2,869,415 acres of land for educational purposes, of which 2,784,-804 acres were given for the support of common schools. The State still holds title to 2,482,704 acres of this area, of which 573,389 acres are under contract of sale, 1,462,707 acres are leased, and 446,607 acres are still undisposed of. The permanent school fund now consists of national, State and county securities to the value of $2,525,872.35, and cash in the State treasury amounting to $490,398.39, making a total of $3,016,270.74, and being an increase during the past two years of $270,963.93.

The State University is in a flourishing condition. There are about 950 pupils enrolled, an increase of nearly 100 per cent. in two years. This enrollment represents 20 States and 64 Nebraska counties.

Charities.—At the State Insane Asylum, at Hastings, there were 366 inmates on Nov. 30, and at the Lincoln Insane Hospital 373. Investigations made this year tend to show that these institutions have not been economically managed, and new officers have been put in control. At the State Industrial Home, at Milford, there were 21 inmates on Nov. 30, 1890; 83 were admitted during the two years following, and 63 discharged.

Railroads.—The number of miles of railroad assessed in 1892 by the State Board of Equalization was 5,456, against 5,418 for the year preceding. The total valuation of railroad property was fixed at $29,339,731, against $29,265,917 for 1891. In his message to the Legislature of 1891, Gov. Thayer said:

Two years ago I made recommendations regarding the matter of regulating freight rates by statute, which, if they had been carried out, I am still of the opinion, would have been of much benefit to our agriculturists, and would not have been unjust to the railroads. That Legislature took a more radical view of the matter than my own, and passed a law which was not only unconstitutional, but so defective that it contained no prop r provisions to give the Supreme Court jurisdiction over the subject matter, and, in a sense of duty, I was compelled to veto it. A year later I secured by correspondence the views of every member of that body, with the purpose of calling an extra session if I found a majority disposed to less radical action. From replies received I became convinced that a moderate measure of reduction, such as I could approve, could not be enacted.

Irrigation.—There are 34 companies in the State engaged in irrigation, operating in 13 counties and having a combined capital stock of about $1,964,200. There have been 882 miles of ditches completed, and 386 miles are under

...truction. The area under ditch is 851,960 ... the average cost of the water supply being ... an acre.

...tical.—On Aug. 4 a Republican Con... met at Lincoln, and nominated Lorenzo ... for Governor; J. G. Tate for Lieuten... Governor; Eugene Moore for Auditor; Jo... & Bartley for Treasurer; John C. Allen for ...tary of State; George H. Hastings for At... General; A. K. Goudy for Superintend... of Public Instruction; and A. R. Hum... for Commissioner of Public Lands. Can... for presidential electors were also chosen. ...platform adopted contains the following deo...ns:

We believe in protecting the laboring man by all ...essary and judicious legislation, and to this end ... favor the enactment of suitable laws to protect ...th, life, and limb of all employees of transporta...on, mining, and manufacturing companies while en...ed in the service of such companies.

The farmers of the State, who constitute the chief ...ment of our productive, wealth-creating population, ... entitled to the cheapest and best facilities for stor...ing, shipping, and marketing their products; and to ... end we favor such laws as will give them a ...cheap, safe, and easily obtainable elevator and ware...house facilities, and will furnish them promptly and ...without discrimination of just and equitable rates, ...per transportation facilities for all accessible mar...ets.

We demand the enactment of laws regulating the ...rates charged by express companies within this State. ...We favor the adoption of the amendment to the ...Constitution providing for an elective railroad com...mission empowered to fix local, passenger, and freight ...rates.

We are in favor of postal telegraph and postal sav...ings banks systems and rural free delivery.

The revenue laws of this State should be carefully ...revised by a commission of competent persons repre...senting the principal industries of the State, to the ...end that all property rightfully subject to taxation ...may be made to pay its just proportion of the public ...revenue.

On the day of the Republican Convention the ...Independent party held a similar convention at ...Kearney, and nominated the following State ...ticket: For Governor, ex-United States Senator ...Charles H. Van Wyck; Lieutenant-Governor, ...Charles D. Shrader; Secretary of State, James ...M. Easterling; Treasurer, Jacob V. Wolfe; Audi...tor, Logan McReynolds; Attorney-General, Vir...gil O. Strickler; Superintendent of Public In...struction, Harmon H. Hiatt; Commissioner of ...Public Lands, Jacob M. Gunnett. Presidential ...electors were nominated. The platform adopted ...included the following:

We demand that such laws be enacted by our ...Legislature as will reduce the rates in Nebraska to a ...level with the rates for like service in the State of ...Iowa; and in the enactment of such law, and in the ...regulation of freights, railways shall be classified and ...the rates adjusted in proportion to the traffic.

We are opposed to the restoration of the sugar ...bounty in any form by the State of Nebraska.

We demand of our next Legislature the passage of ...an act to prescribe the mode of payment of obliga...tions of debt contracted to be paid in money, as fol...lows: Be it enacted, etc., that from and after the ...passage of this act all obligations contracted to be ...payable in any money shall be payable in any money ...authorized by the United States Government, and ...any stipulations to the contrary in said contract or ...obligations are hereby declared to be void.

We demand the submission of an amendment to

the Constitution of this State, providing that the permanent school fund may be loaned to citizens of Nebraska on first mortgage on productive real estate at an interest of not more than 5 per cent., as is now done in many States of the Union.

We are opposed to a system of government that allows corporations or individuals of the United States to employ Pinkertons or any other force to intimidate and coerce organized labor.

We demand the election of President, Vice-President, and United States Senators by a direct vote of the people.

We favor equal pay for equal work for both men and women.

We denounce the convict labor system as practiced in the State of Nebraska.

The Prohibitionists met in convention at Hastings on Aug. 17, and nominated the following candidates: For Governor, C. E. Bentley; Lieutenant-Governor, James Stephen; Secretary of State, Isaac Boostrom; Treasurer, Jerry Denslow; Auditor, J. C. Thomas; Attorney-General, Martin I. Brower; Superintendent of Public Instruction. Mrs. Belle G. Bigelow; Commissioner of Public Lands, Charles E. Smith.

Late in August the Democrats held a State Convention at Lincoln, and placed a ticket in the field, containing the following names: For Governor, J. Sterling Morton; Lieutenant-Governor, Samuel N. Wolbach; Secretary of State, Frank M. Crow; Treasurer, Andrew Beckman; Auditor, P. F. O'Sullivan; Attorney-General, Matthew Gering; Superintendent of Public Instruction, J. A. Hornberger; Commissioner of Public Lands, Jacob Wiggins. Presidential electors were nominated, and a platform adopted, of which the following is a portion:

We recommend the adoption of the constitutional amendment now pending, creating a board of railway commissioners elected by the people.

We believe that Senators of the United States should be chosen by direct vote of the people, and we favor the election of presidential electors by congressional districts.

We denounce the Republican party for its system of contract convict labor, whereby it has given to a single individual the monopoly of all the cheap convict labor of this State, and brought it into direct competition with the honest toilers of the State; and, not content with fastening it upon the people for ten years, have leased it for another ten years before the expiration of the first term.

We condemn the giving of bounties and subsidies of every kind as a perversion of the taxing power.

The State of Nebraska has and exercises the right of regulating the sale of intoxicating drinks in the interests of good order throughout the entire Commonwealth; but the prohibition of the manufacture and sale of such drinks within the State is contrary to the fundamental principles of social and moral conduct.

Soon after the nomination of J. G. Tate by the Republicans as their candidate for Lieutenant-Governor, it was discovered that he had not completed his naturalization as a citizen of the United States, and was therefore not eligible. His name was accordingly withdrawn, and that of Lieut.-Gov. Thomas J. Majors substituted therefor.

At the November election the entire Republican ticket was successful. For presidential electors the following vote was cast: Republican, 87,213; Democratic, 24,943; People's party, 83,256; Prohibitionist, 4,902. For Governor, Crounse received 78,426 votes, Morton 44,195,

Van Wyck 68,617, Bentley 6,235. The Republicans elected their candidates in the Second, Third, and Fourth Congressional Districts; the Democrats were successful in the First District, and the Independents in the Fifth and Sixth Districts. Members of the Legislature were chosen as follow: Senate—Republicans 15, Independents 14, Democrats 5; House—Republicans 47, Independents 40, Democrats 12.

At the same election two constitutional amendments were submitted to the people, and both were adopted. The amendment providing for the election of a board of railroad commissioners by the people received 80,032 affirmative and 14,185 negative votes. The amendment authorizing the investment of the permanent school fund in registered school district bonds received 84,426 affirmative and 11,258 negative votes.

NETHERLANDS, a constitutional monarchy in western Europe. The legislative authority rests conjointly in the sovereign and the Parliament. The latter is called the States-General, and consists of 2 Chambers. The Upper or First Chamber is composed of 50 members, elected by the citizens most highly assessed by the provincial governments. The Second Chamber numbers 100 Deputies, and is elected by male citizens twenty-three years old who pay a ground tax of at least 10 guilders or a personal tax of a higher amount than the limit of partial exemption from taxation, or who are lodgers as defined by the law. The period of election is four years for the Second Chamber and nine years for the First Chamber, the former retiring in a body, and of the latter one third is replaced every three years. The King has the power of dissolving either Chamber or both, new elections to be held within forty days, and the new Chambers to be convoked within two months. The First Chamber can not introduce new bills; it can only approve or reject those introduced by the Government or the Second Chamber, and can not even amend such bills. Constitutional amendments can only be made by a bill explaining the reasons for the change, which must be confirmed by the Chambers, and then, after their dissolution, must be ratified by the new Chambers by a two-third majority.

The reigning sovereign is Wilhelmina Helena Pauline Maria, born Aug. 31, 1880, daughter of the late King Willem III by his second wife, Princess Emma of Waldeck, who acts as Regent during the infancy of the Queen.

The ministry in the beginning of 1892 was composed of the following members: Minister of Foreign Affairs and President of the Ministerial Council, Dr. G. van Tienhoven, appointed Aug. 20, 1891; Minister of the Interior, Dr. I. P. Tak van Poortvliet; Minister of Finance, Dr. H. G. Pierson; Minister of Justice, Dr. H. I. Smidt; Minister of the Colonies, Dr. W. K. Baron van Dedem; Minister of Marine, J. C. Jansen; Minister of War, A. L. W. Seyffardt; Minister of Public Works, C. Lely.

Area and Population.—The area of the kingdom is 12,648 square miles. The estimated population on Dec. 31, 1890, was 4,564,565, of whom 2,255,681 were males and 2,308,884 were females. The number of marriages in 1890 was 32,304; the number of births, 149,329; and the number of deaths, 93,246; thus leaving a surplus of births over deaths of 56,083. Of 17,136 people who emigrated in 1890, 3,526 were Dutch, the remainder foreigners; 3,282 Dutchmen emigrated to the United States, 167 to South America, and 77 to Africa. The principal cities of the kingdom are Amsterdam, with a population of 417,539 in 1890; Rotterdam, with 209,136 inhabitants: the Hague, containing 160,531 people; Utrecht, with 86,116 inhabitants; and Groningen, with 56,413.

Finances.—The budget for 1892 estimates the revenue at 127,600,150 guilders, of which 12,502,000 guilders are derived from land taxes, 11,498,000 guilders from personal taxes, 4,528,000 guilders from patents, 44,720,000 guilders from excise duties, 23,638,000 guilders from indirect taxes, 5,710,800 guilders from import duties, 235,900 guilders from tax on gold and silver, 2,330,000 guilders from domains, 7,100,000 guilders from the post office, 1,368,000 guilders from the telegraph service, 661,500 guilders from state lottery, 140,000 guilders from shooting and fishing licenses, 1,350,000 guilders from pilot dues, 7,250 guilders from dues on mines, 4,345,000 guilders from state railroads, and 7,465,700 guilders from miscellaneous receipts. The expenditure is estimated at 129,959,036 guilders, of which 811,000 guilders are for the civil list, 653,555 guilders for the legislative body and royal Cabinet, 756,173 guilders for the Department of Foreign Affairs, 5,232,774 guilders for the Department of Justice, 11,644,604 guilders for the Department of the Interior, 14,080,420 guilders for the Marine, 18,959,546 guilders for the Department of Finance, 21,299,268 guilders for the Department of War, 20,272,812 guilders for the Department of Public Works, 1,200,071 guilders for the Department of Colonies, 34,998,813 guilders for public debt, and 50,000 guilders for contingencies.

The total funded debt in 1892 amounted to 1,091,447,073 guilders, of which 630,567,200 guilders pay 2½ per cent. interest, 94,642,800 guilders 3 per cent., and the bulk of the remainder 3½ per cent. interest. The interest charge on the funded debt amounted to 31,592,955 guilders, the sinking fund to 2,645,800 guilders, the floating debt to 500,000 guilders, and annuities to 260,057 guilders. The paper money in circulation amounted to 15,000,000 guilders.

(For statistics of the army and navy, see the "Annual Cyclopædia" for 1890.)

Commerce and Production.—The value of trade with the leading countries in 1890 is set forth in the following table, in guilders:

COUNTRY.	Imports.	Exports.
Prussia	247,100,000	498,500,000
Great Britain	283,600,000	270,500,000
Belgium	195,200,000	148,000,000
Dutch East Indies	159,500,000	58,200,000
United States	98,400,000	28,700,000
Hamburg	21,200,000	17,300,000
France	24,200,000	10,800,000
Italy	....	10,800,000
Russia	112,100,000	5,500,000
British India	88,000,000	....

The total estimated value of the imports for home consumption in 1890 amounted to 1,299,750,000 guilders, and the estimates of the exports of home produce for the same year were 1,087,532,000 guilders. The imports of iron and steel in 1890 were valued at 125,552,000 guilders, and the exports at 86,249,000 guilders; imports of textiles at 101,423,000, and exports at 114,-612,000 guilders; imports of cereals at 192,127,-000, and exports at 102,452,000 guilders; imports of coal at 38,833,000, and exports at 2,366,-000 guilders; imports of rice at 39,873,000, and exports at 11,634,000 guilders; imports of mineral oil at 25,954,000, and exports at 428,000 guilders; imports of coffee at 31,980,000, and exports at 24,007,000 guilders; imports of butter at 3,206,000, and exports at 31,644,000 guilders; imports of cheese at 88,000, and exports at 10,610,000 guilders; imports of drugs at 174,-694,000 guilders; imports of coffee at 116,120,000 guilders; imports of vegetables at 981,000, and exports at 19,662,000 guilders; imports of wood at 24,031,-000, and exports at 12,783,000 guilders; imports of skins at 19,178,000, and exports at 20,505,000 guilders; imports of copper at 37,922,000, and exports at 18,652,000 guilders; imports of soot, grease, and tallow at 48,995,000, and exports at 27,114,000 guilders; imports of saltpeter at 13,-958,000, and exports at 13,383,000 guilders; imports of zinc at 10,930,000, and exports at 9,171,-000 guilders; imports of tobacco at 7,612,000, and exports at 3,731,000 guilders; imports of tin at 9,276,000, and exports at 10,498,000 guilders; imports of colors at 12,016,000, and exports at 10,699,000 guilders; imports of seeds at 26,-306,000, and exports at 9,072,000 guilders. The imports of bulbs, shrubs, and trees were valued for 1890 at 217,000, and the exports at 5,012,000 guilders. Very little coal is mined in the kingdom, only 298,585 guilders' worth of coal being extracted in 1890. In the same year 4,326 vessels, with crews numbering about 15,250, were engaged in the fisheries, the herring catch alone amounting to 5,909,495 guilders, and the production of oysters numbering 51,237,506. There were, in 1890, 544 distilleries, 12 sugar refineries, 30 beet-sugar manufactories, 53 salt works, 543 breweries, 96 vinegar manufactories, 91 soap manufactories, and 3 wine manufactories.

Navigation.—In 1890 the Dutch mercantile navy consisted of 500 sailing vessels, of 360,-000 M³ (2·83 cubic metres = 1 ton), and of 118 steamers of 364,000 M³. There entered the ports of the Netherlands 8,711 vessels, of 14,878,000 M³, with cargoes, and 764 vessels, of 535,000 M², in ballast; there cleared from the ports 5,931 vessels, of 8,511,000 M³, with cargoes, and 3,272 vessels, of 6,745,000 M³, in ballast. Of the total number of vessels entered, 2,623, of a tonnage of 4,425,000 M³, and of the vessels cleared, 2,613, of 4,411,000 M³, were Dutch.

Session of the Parliament.—The session of the States-General was opened by the Queen-Regent on Sept. 20, 1892. The speech from the throne stated that the general condition of the country was good, although trade, navigation, and manufactures were only fairly prosperous. Bills were announced dealing with electoral reforms applicable to the States-General and Provincial Assemblies, and measures for professional and trade taxation, for reforming the army and strengthening the navy, and for effectual social reforms, would be introduced. In regard to the Dutch Indies, bills would be proposed dealing with the army, finance, coffee culture, and the working of mines. In the budget for 1893, as presented to the States-General, the revenue is estimated at 128,000,000 guilders, and the expenditure at 131,800,000 guilders. The expenditure includes a sum of 5,000,000 guilders for railroads and canals and a naval credit of 1,500,000 guilders. The deficit of 3,800,000 guilders will be covered by an addition to the floating debt.

Taxation Reforms.—An important measure was passed by the States-General on July 22, 1892, namely, the law dealing with reforms of the finances and taxation. Nine times within forty years have attempts been made to abolish the old system of taxation and to introduce measures juster and more applicable to modern requirements, but every time such measures were defeated by the combined efforts of the Anti-Revolutionists and the Clericals, who were opposed to any bill originated by a Liberal ministry. Minister of Finance Pierson finally succeeded in molding a series of reforms which were passed by the States-General. The main reform was that of imposing a tax on capital consisting of either real or personal property. Any capital below 13,000 guilders is exempt from taxation; properties between 13,000 and 14,000 guilders pay a fixed tax of 2 to 4 guilders, and those from 15,000 to 200,000 guilders pay 1·25 guilders per *mille*. A capital of 200,000 guilders and upward pay a fixed tax of 237·50 guilders, and in addition 2 guilders for every thousand above the sum of 200,000 guilders. Every capital of 13,000 guilders and upward is entitled to an exemption from taxation of the first 10,000 guilders. A second reform was the total abolition of the excise duty on soap, and a reduction of the import duty, which was fixed at 4 guilders per 100 kilogrammes on perfumed and transparent soaps, 2 guilders on all other dry soaps, and 1 guilder on soft soap. The tax on the transfer of real property was reduced from 6·27 per cent. to 2·15 per cent. of the value of the transfer, and the excise duty on salt was reduced from 9 to 4 guilders per 100 kilogrammes. The deficit occasioned by the reductions of the indirect taxes, which are partially covered by the impost on individual capitals, will be made up by higher taxation on distilled liquors, which excise duty is raised from 60 to 63 guilders per hectolitre. Other reforms to be carried through are the reduction of the ground tax, the abolition of the street and road fees, and the substitution of a professional and trade tax for the taxation of patents.

The Election Bill.—The elections in 1891 were fought and won by the Liberal party mainly on their programme calling for a revision of the election laws and the extension of the right of suffrage to the limits fixed by the Constitution as amended in 1887. The election law, as introduced into the States-General, regulates the general and provincial elections and fixes the qualifications of the voters. To be qualified to vote, a person must be able to read and write, and must prove his ability by doing some writing in the presence of a functionary, who in turn submits the document to a municipal commission for examination. A voter must be able to support himself and his family independently of aid from the community or any benevolent society, with the exception of medical assistance, which he may receive gratuitously. Disqualified are persons who have lost their right of administering their own affairs, who are deprived of the right to vote by a sentence of the court, who have not paid their direct taxes, who are serving in the army, who are sentenced to more than four years' imprisonment, or who have been excluded from the army. Of about 1,000,000 adults, 200,000 are disqualified for some of the reasons stated above, so that by the new law about 80 per cent. of the adult male population will be qualified to vote.

The Army Bill.—A reorganization of the Dutch army had long been the desire of the Government, and the Minister of War, A. Seyffardt, presented a bill to the States-General on Nov. 17, 1892, which it is supposed will satisfy the present demands. Those liable to do service are divided by lot into two categories. The first category, which will have a longer period of service in time of peace, forms the active army; the second category, which besides serving a shorter period, has also a considerably smaller sphere of activity, will compose the territorial army, which will be trained by local drills. Besides a reserve in the depots and a small supplemental reserve, the formation of a Landsturm in case of extreme necessity has been provided for. The period of service is to be nine years. The mobile active army will be composed of 3 divisions of 12 battalions each, with cavalry, artillery, and pioneers; the immobile army will number 48 companies of infantry and 46 companies of fortress artillery; both mobile and immobile armies making a total of 68,115 soldiers. The conscriptions for the territorial army are figured at 19,000 men annually, and its duties will be mainly confined to internal defense. The additional expense of this reorganization is estimated at 86,120 guilders annually.

The Merwede Canal.—The new canal connecting Amsterdam with the Rhenish provinces of Germany was completed in 1892, and opened for traffic as far as Vreeswijk. It had long been the aim of the city of Amsterdam to have a more direct route to the upper Waal, so as to be on an equal footing with Rotterdam, which has a free water highway to Germany by way of Dordrecht. The new canal runs from Amsterdam to Utrecht, and thence by way of Vreeswijk, on the Leck, to Gorinchem. It is 65½ feet broad at the bottom, and has a minimum depth of 10¼ feet. At places where an accumulation of vessels is expected it reaches a breadth of 131¼ feet. The locks are 394 feet long and 82 feet wide, the gates 39·4 feet wide. The railroad bridges are fixed, with a minimum height of 21¼ feet from the water line to the under part of the bridge. The total length of the canal from Amsterdam to Gorinchem is 44·7 miles, and the distance opened for traffic in 1892 is 30·3 miles. The new canal will permit the passage of vessels of four times the size of those which can safely pass the older route. The passage is free of tolls, and the time of transit, formerly from sixteen to eighteen hours, is reduced to seven hours.

East Indian Colonies.—These include (1) Java and the neighboring island of Madura;

(2) the outposts, embracing the islands of Sumatra, Borneo, Riau-Lingga archipelago, Banca, Billeton, Celebes, Molucca archipelago, the smallest Sunda Islands, and a part of New Guinea. Java and Madura are divided into provinces, which are administered by a president; the outposts are governed by functionaries with the titles of governor, resident, assistant resident or controleur, who exercise almost absolute control over the provinces in their charge. The executive power over Dutch East India rests in the Governor-General, who is assisted in his administrative duties by a council of five members. He has a right of passing laws and regulations for the administration of the colonies, subject, however, to the power reserved to the Legislature of the mother country, and the constitutional principles as laid down in the "Regulations for the government of Netherlands India, passed in 1854.

.The budget estimates for Dutch India for the year 1892 placed the revenue at 119,599,713 guilders, and the expenditures at 137,451,954 guilders, leaving a deficit of 17,952,241 guilders. The receipts in Holland, from the sales of Government coffee, according to the estimates, amounted to 13,222,523 guilders; from sales of cinchona, 196,020 guilders; from those of tin, 6,-217,340 guilders; from railroads, 855,000 guilders; from various other sources, 1,260,385 guilders. The receipts in India from sales of opium amounted to 18,420,000 guilders; from import, export, and excise duties, 11,264,000 guilders; land revenues, 16,671,000 guilders; sales of coffee, 9,087,500 guilders; sales of salt, 8,047,000 guilders; and other revenues, 34,358,945 guilders; making the total receipts in India 97,848,445 guilders, and those in the mother country 21,-751,268 guilders. Of the expenditures, about one third goes to the army and navy, and another third is used for the general administration. The budget for 1893 estimates the revenues at 139,000,000 guilders, leaving an estimated deficit of 9,000,000 guilders. The coffee crop is estimated in the budget at 395,000 piculs (1 picul = 135·8 pounds), but an actual harvest of about 100,000 piculs more is expected which will be kept in reserve for next year. The Colonial Minister demands a credit of 1,500,000 guilders for the development of the coffee plantations, which are to be inspected and supervised by a technically educated commission. A sum of 9,000,000 guilders has been assigned for irrigation works and the construction of harbors and railroads, including the Tarik-Soerabaya Kalimas line. It is further proposed to impose a tax on the sugar industries, based on the average amount of the export duties which these industries would have paid within the past three years had the duties not been suspended.

The army, which is purely colonial, consisted at the end of 1890 of 1,384 officers and 32,547 subofficers and soldiers, of whom 13,663 were Europeans, 57 Africans, 2,290 Amboinese, and 16,537 natives. The navy, which is partly colonial and partly royal, consisted in the beginning of 1890 of 27 royal vessels manned by 2,380 Europeans and 913 natives, and 36 colonial vessels manned by 117 Europeans and 1,353 natives.

The long-pending difficulties with England regarding the frontier dispute in Borneo were brought to a close by a treaty between the two countries in March, 1892, whereby the protectorate over Sarawak, Brunei, and North Borneo was conceded to the English.

Eruptions.—On June 7, 1892, the island of Great Sangir was visited by a volcanic eruption. The disaster came unexpectedly, without subterranean rumblings or other seismic warnings usual in such cases. The eruption began suddenly from the great volcano Gunona Awa, which is near Tarvena, the capital of the island. Immense masses of ashes and stones began to fall on the unfortunate natives, who were engaged in the fields gathering in the paddy crop, killing hundreds; those who reached their homes were met by a similar fate, as the light wooden houses collapsed under the weight of the stones and ashes, burying whole families in their ruins. The numerous farms and villages on the slope of the mountain were destroyed by great streams of lava, which flowed with astonishing rapidity into the surrounding valleys, carrying with it the houses and burying their occupants. The loss of human life was estimated from 1,000 to 1,500. The crops were completely destroyed, and a famine was averted by the prompt action of the Government, which placed a steamer at the disposal of the local controller for the purpose of bringing relief to those parts of the island which suffered most. Large quantities of rice were furnished by the Government. No Europeans or Chinese were reported to be killed or injured.

Colonies in the West Indies.—These consist of Dutch Guiana or Surinam and the island of Curaçoa. The area of Dutch Guiana is 46,060 square miles, and the population in 1889 was 55,968, of which number 28,526 were inhabitants of Paramaribo, the capital. The executive power is vested in a Governor, who is assisted by a council, of which he is the president, and the Attorney-General the vice-president, and which consists of three other members, all appointed by the Crown. The representative body of the colony is the Colonial States, to which the Governor appoints four members every year, while the others are elected. The revenue for 1891 was estimated at 1,439,000 guilders, and the expenditures at 1,670,000 guilders. In 1889 the production of sugar amounted to 7,507,647 kilogrammes; of cacao, 2,166,930 kilogrammes; of bananas, 569,200 bunches; of coffee, 6,090 kilogrammes; of rice, 17,201 kilogrammes: of fruits, 201,127 kilogrammes; of rum, 469,090 litres; and of molasses, 704,060 litres. In 1889, 625 concessions were granted for gold mining. The output amounted to 894,333 grammes, of the value of 1,125,236 guilders.

Curaçoa and the small surrounding islands belonging to the Netherlands have an area of 403 square miles and a population of 45,162. The chief executive is the Governor, who is assisted by a council of 3 appointed members and the Attorney-General. The budget for 1891 estimated the revenues at 681,211 guilders, and the expenditures at 681,211 guilders. The imports in 1889 amounted to 3,441,508 guilders. The exports, exclusive of those of Curaçoa, were 669,573 guilders.

NEVADA, a Pacific coast State, admitted to the Union Oct. 31, 1864; area, 110,700 square miles. The population, according to each decennial census since admission, was 42,491 in 1870; 62,266 in 1880; 45,761 in 1890. Capital, Carson City.

Government.—The following were the State officers during the year: Governor, Roswell K. Colcord, Republican; Lieutenant-Governor, J. Poujade; Secretary of State, Olin H. Grey; Comptroller, R. L. Horton; Treasurer, John F. Egan; Attorney-General, J. D. Torreyson: Superintendent of Public Instruction, Orvis Ring; Surveyor General, John E. Jones; Justices of the Supreme Court, R. R. Bigelow, M. A. Murphy, C. H. Belknap; Clerk, J. Josephs; Regents of the State University, E. T. George, J. W. Haines.

Finances.—On Dec. 31 the State debt amounted to $218,282.39, of which $183,000 was represented by 4-per-cent. State bonds; $13,160 was accrued interest thereon; $20,174.40 was represented by outstanding warrants, and the balance of $1,947.99 by deficiency claims. At the same date the cash in the State treasury applicable to payment of the debt was $210,655.13. leaving an actual indebtedness of $7,627.26. There is also a nominal State debt of $380,000 held by the State school fund, represented by an irredeemable bond bearing 5 per cent. interest.

The following is a statement of the receipts and expenses of the State treasury for the last biennial period: Balance on Jan. 1, 1891, $366,825.28; receipts during 1891, $453,891.54; receipts during 1892, $437,420.43; disbursements during 1891, $503,414.05; disbursements during 1892, $354,561.17; balance on Dec. 31, 1892, $400,162.03. The State holds in its school fund securities to the amount of $975,000, and in its University fund securities to the amount of $88,000.

Education.—The number of children of school age in the State is 9,755, a large proportion of whom are enrolled in the public schools. The State is fortunate in having a large school fund derived from the sale and rental of public lands. The National Government has been generous in its land grants, and the Legislatures have guarded the funds arising therefrom with wisdom, so that in the near future it will be possible to maintain the public schools without the aid of local taxation. The State University is flourishing, and is supported by liberal appropriations.

Charities.—On Sept. 1 there were 179 inmates of the Insane Asylum at Reno, 139 men and 40 women. The State has recently expended over $12,000 in repairs and additions to the buildings.

Irrigation.—On this subject the Governor says: "Millions of acres are awaiting the coming of the waters that shall turn them into waving fields and blooming meadows. The Legislatures have been considerate and painstaking in trying to find out the best means of assisting. encouraging,and carrying on irrigation, but there everything ceases. No successful effort has been made to organize under the 1891 law and prove its practicability or impracticability. The 1889 law was declared not suitable to our wants, and the $100,000 appropriation was returned into the treasury unused. Nevada's arid lands can not be reclaimed until the question is determined as to ownership of water. The courts and Congress can lend a helping hand by giving the State complete control of its waters and overthrowing the old common law 'riparian rights doctrine' that obstructs our way and hangs like a millstone round our necks."

Agriculture.—Nevada has over 70,000 acres under cultivation, and over 750,000 acres capable of cultivation by individual effort. The Governor reports that the live-stock and sheep-raising industries have made rapid strides since the winter of 1889-'90. Dairying has sprung up within the past year and a half and has become a valuable industry, not only supplying the home market, but also leaving a handsome surplus for exportation.

Political.—On any question affecting the silver-mining industry the people of Nevada are naturally a unit. Without regard to party they demand the free coinage of silver. Accordingly, when the Republican State Convention met at Virginia City in May to select delegates to the national nominating convention, it instructed them to contend for a plank in the national platform for the coinage of silver on the same basis as gold, and to oppose any candidate for President or Vice-President not favoring free coinage of silver. The resolutions of the convention set forth that the people of Nevada universally favor free coinage of silver.

At the Democratic State Convention, held at Winnemucca on May 26, the following resolutions were passed:

That our delegates to the Democratic National Convention are hereby instructed to use all honorable means to secure the adoption of a plank in the national platform declaring in favor of free coinage of silver at a ratio of 16 to 1 of gold, and under no circumstances to vote for any man for nomination to the office of President or Vice-President unless he shall stand upon the free-coinage platform.

That in event of the Chicago National Convention failing to nominate a candidate who is unequivocally in favor of the free coinage of silver and upon the free-coinage platform, the Democrats of Nevada are hereby absolved from all obligations to support nominees of the National Democratic party.

This convention also nominated George W. Cassidy for Congressman and C. H. Belknap for Justice of the Supreme Court. In addition to the resolutions quoted above, declarations were adopted in favor of revenue reform, urging the construction of a competing line of railroad through the State, and favoring the election of a Democrat to the United States Senate—a man who is an actual resident and *bona fide* inhabitant of Nevada.

As a means of asserting their views more effectively, the people of the State early in the year began to form themselves into local associations called silver clubs. This movement extended to every part of the State, and resulted in a State organization, which was formed at a convention of the clubs held at Reno on June 24, which was styled the Silver party of Nevada. The following resolutions were adopted at this convention:

The citizens of Nevada, representatives of the various silver leagues, irrespective of past party affiliations, in convention assembled, do set forth the following declaration of principles:

1. We demand the full remonetization of silver and the free and unlimited coinage thereof at the present ratio of 16 to 1.

2. We are radically and unalterably opposed to the National Republican and Democratic parties on the question of the free coinage of silver, and we denounce the action of their recent national conventions as inimical to the material interests of the people of the United States, and especially to those of Nevada and all the other mining States and Territories; and we hereby repudiate the nominees of their conventions.

We pledge the nominees of this convention for presidential electors to support no man for President or Vice-President of the United States who is not unqualifiedly in favor of free coinage as defined by this convention. We reserve to the silver leagues of Nevada, in convention assembled, the right of directing said presidential electors for whom to cast their votes should contingencies require.

Thomas Wren, M. S. Bonnifield, and C. C. Powning were nominated as presidential electors upon this platform. The sentiment of the convention was largely in favor of the principles of the People's party, and 12 delegates were chosen to attend the national convention of that party at Omaha.

A second Republican State Convention met at Reno on Aug. 30 for the purpose of nominating presidential electors and a State ticket. At a preliminary caucus it became evident that the independent free-silver men would control the convention, and a division in the party was the result. Forty-nine of the delegates, headed by Enoch Strother, chairman of the Republican State Committee, met and selected presidential electors pledged to vote for President Harrison. The congressional nomination was tendered to F. G. Newlands in case he would approve the platform adopted. This he refused to do, and William Woodburn was chosen in his place. The anti-Harrison majority of the delegates, 85 in number, met and adopted the nominations of the Silver party for presidential electors and Justice of the Supreme Court. They nominated Francis G. Newlands for Congress, and H. L. Fish and C. E. Mack for Regents of the State University.

On Sept. 15 a second convention of the Silver party met at Winnemucca. At the prior convention the right to instruct the electors then chosen was reserved to any subsequent convention of the party that might be called. Accordingly, this convention instructed the Silver electors to vote for Weaver and Field, and approved the platform of the Reno convention. Before the election the name of J. C. Hagerman as candidate for Congress was substituted on the Democratic ticket for that of George W. Cassidy, who had died on June 24.

The result of the balloting in November was a victory for the Silver ticket. The Silver party electors received 7,264 votes, the Republican electors 2,811, the Democrats 714, and the Prohibitionists 86. For Congressman, Newlands received 7,171 votes, Woodburn 2,295, Hagerman 345, Gardner, Prohibitionist, 67. For Justice of the Supreme Court, Belknap, who was the nominee of both the Silver party and the Democrats, received all the votes. The State Legislature that was chosen at the same time will be composed almost entirely of men belonging to the Free-Silver party.

NEW BRUNSWICK. The Hon. Sir S. L. Tilley, C. B., K. C. M. G., in November, completed his seventh year as Lieutenant-Governor of the province. The Executive Council at present consists of Hon. A. G. Blair, Attorney-General and Premier; Hon. James Mitchell, Provincial Secretary and Receiver-General; Hon. H. R. Emmerson, Chief Commissioner of Public Works; Hon. Lemuel J. Tweedie, Surveyor-General; Hon. Ambrose D. Richard, Solicitor-General *; Hon. Charles H. La Billois and Hon. H. A. Connell, without offices.

An event of considerable importance in the constitutional history of the province occurred in September, when the Lieutenant-Governor by proclamation dissolved the House of Assembly, by which, under the provisions of the act passed by the Legislature in the session of 1891, the Legislative Council, or second branch of the Legislature, ceased to exist. The legislative powers hereafter will be vested in the Lieutenant-Governor and Legislative Assembly. A general election was held in October, and the constituencies returned a large majority in favor of the Administration, notwithstanding the Government sustained a serious reverse in the defeat of the Attorney-General, with 3 of his colleagues and supporters in the County of York. The Solicitor-General was also defeated. Within a month the Attorney-General was elected for another constituency (Queens), the member elect having resigned to create a vacancy.

Finances. — The statement of the Receiver-General shows that the receipts of the year, closed Dec. 31, 1892, were $834,602.73, and the payments $828,482.97. The balance at debit of the account, $90,338.56 in 1891, is reduced to $84,218.80 in 1892. The receipts were obtained from the following sources of revenue: Dominion subsidies, $483,581.68; Crown lands, $123,-319.60; taxes, $22,410.82; interest, $4,756.26; proceeds of bonds floated for public works, $147,-690; claim against the Maritime Bank, in liquidation, $34,243.74; other sources, $13,600.63. The payments were made for the following services: Administration of justice, $13,292.85; encouragement of agriculture, $16,670.89; education, $175,918.13; interest on the provincial debt, $106,910.84; invested in sinking funds, $8,500; care of the insane, $48,000; Legislature and administration of the Government, $94,844.55; public health, $6,367.91; construction and repairs of public works, $347,749.78; miscellaneous, 10,228.02. The gross debt of the province was $2,728,716.79; the assets, $561,288.03. Of the gross debt, $2,583,500 is represented by provincial bonds afloat at an average interest of 4·65 per cent.; and there were issued to provide for subsidies to provincial railways $1,903,500; construction of public bridges, $400,000; importation of horses for breeding, $30,000; over-expenditure on current revenue account, $250,000. The balance of the debt represents: Interest coupons not presented for payment at close of year, $18,316.25; guarantee deposit, Independent Order of Foresters, $20,000; balance at debit of current revenue account, $84,218.80; balance

* Since the close of 1892 the Hon. A. D. Richard, having been defeated in the election in October, has resigned the office of Solicitor-General, and Hon. N. S. White has been appointed thereto.

due to provincial departments at close of year, $22,681.74. The assets are made up of—amount due from the Dominion Government, $531,185.72, yielding 5 per cent. interest, sinking funds, yielding 4 per cent. interest, $27,595.84; agricultural department for sales of stock, $2,506.47. The province owns over 7,000,000 acres of land.

Legislature. — The local Legislature was convened for its twenty-ninth session since the confederation of the British North American provinces, this being the third session of the House of Assembly elected in March, 1890. The session was one of unusual interest, through the action of the Lieutenant-Governor on a question of responsible government, and important legislation affecting the fiscal policy of the province. The leader of the Opposition, with 11 of his followers, presented to the Lieutenant-Governor a memorial containing 18 specific charges of corruption and fraudulent administration against the Attorney-General and other members of the Executive Council, and requesting the appointment of a court of royal commission, composed of one or more of the judges of the Supreme Court of the province, to investigate and report upon the charges; the commission to have full power and authority to compel the attendance of witnesses and the production of papers and books, and to examine witnesses on oath. The memorialists alleged their full belief in the truth of the charges, and their opinion that an impartial investigation could not be obtained before a committee of the Assembly, of whom a majority were supporters of the Government. The Lieutenant-Governor submitted the memorial, with the following reply, to the Legislature:

SIR: The Lieutenant-Governor was on Thursday last, the 31st ult., at noon, handed a communication from you, accompanied by a memorial, bearing the signatures of yourself and other members of the Legislature reflecting upon the conduct of his Government and members thereof, and requesting that a royal commission be appointed to investigate the matters therein alleged.

The Lieutenant-Governor would remind the memorialists that the usual parliamentary course in such cases is for a member of Parliament, in his place in the House, to formulate his charges, stating at the same time that he is credibly informed and believes he can establish the same by satisfactory evidence, and to ask for the appointment of a special committee to investigate the same, or its reference to a standing committee for that purpose.

The Lieutenant-Governor can not recall to memory a single case where a commission such as has been asked for was granted when these preliminary steps were not taken, or where evidence warranting such a course had not been submitted to, or brought out before a parliamentary committee.

In the present case 16 of the 18 charges made by the memorialists have not been formulated by any member in the Legislature, and the memorial is unaccompanied by any statement of the nature of the evidence upon which the memorialists rely in support of their accusations.

In addition to the specific charges made, it is requested "that any other charges that may be duly submitted to said commission for investigation, and the facts and circumstances preceding, accompanying, causing, and following the payments, contracts, and agreements and arrangements that may be therein alleged respectively, and into all the facts and circumstances which are of a nature to make known by what system, proceeding, or method, by what intermediaries and conditions, contracts, subsidies, practices, advances of public money, leases or grants of lands, and generally the patronage of the Government or of the departments have been retained, granted, or paid from the 3d day of March, A. D. 1883, to the 3d day of March, A. D. 1892."

It appears to the Lieutenant-Governor that the granting of the request of the memorialists, including the general reference asked for, would be not only at variance with the well-established usages of Parliament, but with the principles of British justice. The humblest subject of Her Majesty can only be tried upon the counts in his indictment, and is thus enabled to prepare his defense. While the Lieutenant-Governor is most anxious to guard the public interests in every way possible consistent with and within his constitutional authority, he desires to guard against the breaking down of the parliamentary bulwarks, erected after great experience, with which members of Parliament and governments are wisely surrounded. Under these circumstances the Lieutenant-Governor does not feel warranted in granting the request of the memorialists. He has arrived at this conclusion the more readily, as he has the assurance of his Government that they will afford every facility for the fullest investigation of any charges which may be preferred in the usual manner against them before the Legislature, and have already, as they inform him, invited members who in the House referred to some of the matters contained in the memorial to formulate their charges and call for a committee of investigation in the usual way.

(Signed)   S. L. TILLEY.

A. A. STOCKTON, Esq., M. P. P., and Leader of the Opposition.

The Attorney-General moved the following resolution:

Whereas, It appears by papers laid upon the table of this House by the authority of His Honor the Lieutenant-Governor, that Messrs. Stockton, M'Keown, and 10 other members of this House did, on Thursday, the 31st day of March last, forward a memorial to His Honor containing certain charges and allegations reflecting upon the conduct of his Government and certain members thereof, which charges are numbered from 1 to 18 inclusive, and asking that His Honor would cause a commission to be appointed consisting of one or more judges of the Supreme Court of this province to investigate the said charges;

And whereas, It further appears by the said papers that His Honor has declined to accede to the application of the memorialists, and has indicated that if the said members have any charges against the Government which they believe they can establish, the proper course is to prefer such charges before this House, and call for an investigation by and before a committee thereof in the usual manner;

Therefore Resolved, That in the opinion of this House it is the duty of those members who have subscribed the said memorial, and thereby impeached the integrity and official conduct of the Executive Government and its members, to forthwith demand that a committee of this House be at once appointed for the purpose of an investigation into the charges made, and notwithstanding that the business of the present session is about concluded and the memorialists have not availed themselves of the abundant opportunity open to them during the session of taking action in respect to these charges in the usual manner:

This House hereby declares and affirms its willingness to continue the present session for such length of time as may be necessary for a full, proper, and sufficient inquiry into each and all of the said charges.

The resolution was carried—yeas 22, nays 7. The memorialists did not move for the appointment of a committee of the Legislature, and consideration of the charges was here dropped.

The Legislature passed 64 laws, the most important being:

To impose taxes on certain incorporated companies and associations.

To impose taxes on certain life-insurance agents.

To provide for the payment of succession duties in certain cases.

Under the provisions of these laws all fire-insurance companies doing business in New Brunswick are required to pay a tax of 1 per cent. of the net premiums annually received, and where the principal office or organization is not within the province an additional sum of $100 per annum. Accident and guarantee companies are required to pay a tax of one half of 1 per cent. of the premiums annually received, with an additional tax of $25 per annum. All companies or associations doing the business of endowment or life insurance are required to pay annually $250, except where the company or association has its principal office within the province, in which case the tax is $100. All agents traveling for and soliciting risks for either life or endowment assurance, not being residents of the province, are required to pay a tax or license fee of $100 a year. Express companies operating over a railway mileage of 500 miles and upward within the province will pay a tax of $250 per annum. Similar companies operating over a mileage of 250 and less than 500 miles will pay $125, and where the mileage is not less than 100 nor greater than 250 miles, $50. Telephone companies are required to pay a tax equivalent to 25 cents on each telephone under rental; passenger or street railway companies, $50 to $100 on each mile in operation, at the discretion of the Lieutenant-Governor in Council; building, trust, or loan societies not exceeding $250, at discretion of the Lieutenant-Governor in Council; telegraph companies operating 100 miles or more of wire, $500; operating less than 100 miles, $100. Upon all banks doing business in the city of St. John, having their organization within the province and head office in that city, with a capital of $500,000 and upward, a tax of $1,000, and an additional tax of $100 for each agency, including the principal office, not exceeding 4; upon banks having their organization without the province and having an office in the city of St. John, with a capital of $1,000,000 and upward, a tax of $1,000, and an additional tax of $100 for each agency, not exceeding 4; upon all banks having their organization without the province and an office in St. John, with a capital of $500,000 and less than $1,000,000, a tax of $750, and an additional tax for each agency not exceeding 4, $100; upon all banks having their organization without the province and not having an agency in St. John, with a capital of $500,000 and less than $1,000,000, a tax of $500, and an additional tax of $100 for each agency not exceeding 4; upon all banks having their organization within the province and not having an agency in St. John, with a capital not exceeding $250,000, a tax of $200, and an additional tax of $100 for each agency not exceeding 4.

The " succession duties," or taxes imposed upon estates of deceased persons, were revised by the new law.

Education.—The total cost of education under the free-school system (not including buildings) amounted to $424,619.38. Of this amount $144,068.71 was borne by the Provincial Government and $280,550.67 was raised by assessment. The average cost per pupil was $6.98. The average salaries of teachers, as shown in the report of the chief superintendent, are as follow:

First-class male teacher........	$536 75
Second-class male teacher	302 94
Third-class male teacher....................	225 84
First-class female teacher..................	335 81
Second-class female teacher.................	233 54
Third-class female teacher..................	190 79

The chief superintendent also furnishes the following statistics in reference to school attendance during the two terms embraced in the report:

CLASSIFICATION.	Half year to Dec. 31, 1891.	Half year to June 30, 1892.
Proportion of population at school....	1 in 5·71	1 in 5·28
Number of pupils under five years of age...............................	293	333
Number between five and fifteen.....	58,788	56,612
Number over fifteen	2,136	3,541
Average number of pupils daily present during the time schools were in session...........................	35,203	35,220

Agriculture.—A lively interest in the industry of butter and cheese making has been awakened in the province during the past year. The Government, through the employment of skilled lecturers, has encouraged the formation of dairy associations throughout the farming districts, and about 80 of these societies have been organized. A creamery at Kingsclear, in the immediate vicinity of Fredericton, recently equipped, has manufactured 20 tons of butter, 11 tons of which have been profitably shipped to England. The Secretary for Agriculture says, in his report of the crops, that hay was a full crop, summer wheat about 60 per cent., oats 75 per cent., barley 80 per cent., potatoes 75 per cent., rotting after storing in many districts, other roots about 75 per cent., apples 75 per cent., and small fruits 75 per cent.

Trade.—The volume of trade in 1892 amounted to $11,450,991, being: Goods exported, $6,-183,056; imported, $5.267,935. The duty collected amounted to $1,010,179. Of the exports, goods to the value of $2,623,132 went to the British Empire, $3,112,637 to the United States, $447,287 to other countries. These are classified as follow: Product of the mine, $74,200; fisheries, $661,000; forest, $4,582,500; animals and their produce, $154,600; agricultural products, $161,000; manufactures, $542,000; miscellaneous, $7,700. Of the imports, goods to the value of $1,977,715 came from the British Empire, $2,712,846 from the United States, and $577,374 from other countries. The trade of the province in 1892, compared with the two preceding years, shows a decline.

NEWFOUNDLAND. During the legislative session of 1892 several useful acts were passed. The following is a summary of the more important of these:

The Revenue act continues that of 1891, with certain exceptions. It provides that the duty on Spanish wines in Newfoundland shall be reduced when Spain reduces the duty on codfish to five shillings and sixpence sterling. It indemnifies the Government for duties exacted under section 13 of 54 Victoria, cap. iii, and also for license money collected under the Bait act, subject to the allowance of these provisions by the Imperial Government; and it makes provision for the salary of an inspector of outport customs.

The Act respecting the Labrador fishery provides that the owners of vessels conveying fishermen to Labrador shall take them back to the port from which they sailed, and, failing in this, that they shall be responsible to the owners of such vessels as may take them home for their passage money. The charterer or hirer of a vessel shall, for the purpose of this act, be deemed the owner. In case of a vessel being lost, the owner shall be liable for the passage home of the crew, to the extent of twenty-five cents per quintal upon the fish, four dollars per ton upon the oil, and twenty-five cents per barrel upon the herring of such crew.

The Act to regulate the prosecution of the seal fishery directs that no steamer shall leave port for the seal fishery before 6 o'clock A. M. of March 12, and that no seals shall be killed before March 14 or after April 20 in any year. It prohibits a steamer making second trips unless compelled to return to port for repairs, when she shall not be deemed to have gone on a second trip if she leaves port before March 25. The penalty for a breach of this law is a fine of $4,000, and the sealing master violating the law shall not be competent for two years to take charge of a steamer.

The Act to consolidate and amend the acts for the encouragement of education appropriates $20,000 for the augmentation of the salaries of teachers who have received certificates of qualification, and also provides for the establishment of a teachers' pension fund.

The Act to amend the law for the solemnization of marriage enables commissioners and staff officers of the Salvation Army, when duly licensed by the Governor, to celebrate marriage.

The Act respecting hawkers and peddlers provides that no foreign peddler or hawker shall do business in the colony without having secured a license, the fee for which is to be $50.

The destruction of a large portion of the city of St. John's, by fire, on July 8, 1892, necessitated a special session of the Legislature, during which four acts were passed. The first of these related to the rebuilding of the city, the plan to be adopted, the straightening of streets in the burned district and giving them a uniform width, and also the provision for compensation to be awarded by arbitrators. The second act provides that where a building lease shall be for less than ninety-nine years the tenant shall be compensated for improvements he may make, the amount to be determined by arbitration, the award to be the value to the incoming tenant of the improvements made. The third act provides for the formation of jury lists as if the fire of July 8 had not occurred. The last act amends the Revenue act by admitting iron and steel buildings, iron and steel beams, joists, pillars, columns, doors, sashes, shutters of iron, steel, or composition and cement, plaster and brick, and also sewing and knitting machines, at 10 per cent. ad valorem.

The Fisheries.—The staple industry of Newfoundland is the cod fishery, which is carried on upon the banks, the shores of the island, and the Atlantic coast of Labrador, which is under the jurisdiction of the colony. In 1891 (the latest date for which returns are available) the total export of dried codfish was 1,244,834 quintals, the value of which was $4,864,525. Of this quantity, 297,259 quintals, value $832,324, were exported from Labrador. In addition, boneless codfish to the value of $20,000 was exported. Of cod oil, 3,069 tons, at $76 a ton, were exported; and of refined cod-liver oil, 7,597 gallons, at 50 cents a gallon. The value of the exported products of the cod fishery in 1891 was $5,121,567.

In 1892, 20 steamers were engaged in the seal fishery, their tonnage being 6,278 tons. Their crews numbered 4,548. The number of seals taken was 348,624, their average value being about $2.

The export of herrings in 1891 was 59,568 barrels; value, $201,058. The salmon export was: Pickled, 5,423 tierces, value $91,587; tinned, 463 cases, value $1,758. The export of lobsters in 1891 was 57,291 cases, value $429,681.

In 1892, at the Dildo Hatchery, there were hatched and planted 165,560,000 young codfish. A salt-water pond has been constructed, 48 feet long, 23 feet wide, and 11 feet deep, holding 96,000 gallons. In this the cod are placed and allowed to spawn in the natural way, without being handled or "stripped." The ova are then collected and placed in the hatching jars. This is found to be a great improvement on the former method of stripping the fish by hand, and the results are a larger percentage of hatched ova and much less labor.

The number of lobsters hatched and planted in the floating incubators in 1892 was 429,785,000. A successful experiment was made in transporting live lobsters to England in the autumn of 1892. The loss on the passage was only 9 per cent. The apparatus for their transportation was the invention of Mr. A. Nielsen, Superintendent of Fisheries. The Fisheries Commission have now a protective service for exercising a guardianship over the salmon rivers and enforcing the rules and regulations of the various salt-water fisheries. They also maintain a Bait Intelligence Service. They publish widely instructions for the proper cure and packing of herrings and codfish.

The total value of the Newfoundland fisheries in 1891 was $6,679,574. The value of the imports in the same year was $6,869,458; the value of the exports was $7,437,158; the revenue amounted to $1,820,293. The public debt at the close of 1891 was $5,223,363.

The Census.—The census of 1891 showed the total population to be 202,040. Of these, 4,100 are residents of the Labrador coast. According to religious denomination the population stood as follows: Adherents of the Church of England, 69,834; of the Roman Catholic Church, 72,696; of the Wesleyan Church, 53,276; of the Presbyterian Church, 1,449; other denominations, 4,895. Of the last named, the Salvation Army number 2,092; the Congregationalists, 782; and the Baptists, 37.

In regard to occupations, the census shows that 53,502 are engaged in catching and curing fish; 625 in lumbering; 1,258 in mining; 1,545 in farming; in mechanics and handicrafts, 2,681; in office and shop work, 1,948; clergymen, 181; teachers, 601; lawyers, 48; doctors, 62; merchants and traders, 767. Of the whole population, 193,353 were born in Newfoundland.

A census was taken in 1884. The increase of population in the following seven years was 4,810, or at the rate of 3·4 per cent. for ten years. In the ten years preceding 1884 the increase was at the rate of 22¼ per cent. The fall-

ing off in the increase of population is mainly owing to emigration, which of late has greatly increased.

The late census presents the following facts in regard to agricultural stock and produce: There are 64,494 acres of improved land in the island, and 20,524 acres in pasture. Of oats, 12,900 bushels are produced annually; 36,032 tons of hay; 481,024 barrels of potatoes; and 60,235 barrels of turnips. The number of milch cows is 10,863; of horses, 6,138; of horned cattle, 12,958; of sheep, 60,840; of swine, 32,011.

There are 53 sawmills, 3 tanneries, 2 breweries, 2 iron foundries, 4 furniture factories.

Mining.—The exports of minerals in 1891 were as follow: Copper ore, 7,060 tons, value $63,540; regulus (copper), 3,626 tons, and ingots, 1,139 tons, value $502,510; total value of copper ores, etc., exported, $565,850; iron pyrites, 19,150 tons, value $57,900; antimony, value $1,000; total value of ores, etc., exported in 1891, $624,750. From 1854 to 1891 the total value of copper ore exported was $9,193,790: and the total value of all ores exported in that period was $9,594,717.

Shipping.—The registered shipping at the end of 1891 was 2,207 vessels; tonnage, 98,619.

Railways.—The Hall's Bay Railway, now in course of construction, made good progress in 1892, over 70 miles having been built. It now reaches Gambo.

The Great Fire.—The year 1892 will long be memorable for the great fire, which broke out on July 8, in St. John's, and destroyed between half and two thirds of the city. In 1846 a similar calamity laid waste nearly two thirds of the city; but the value of the property destroyed in the fire of 1892 was five times greater than that of 1846. The fire broke out at 5 o'clock in the afternoon, in a western suburb known as Fresh Water Road and Long's Hill, which stood on elevated ground overlooking the city. For six weeks previously hardly a shower had fallen, so that the wooden houses and buildings were dry as tinder. A furious wind was blowing when the fire began in a stable filled with hay. The water supply was deficient, and the flames spread so rapidly that in half an hour they were beyond control, and advanced, pouring an ever-widening torrent of fire into the heart of the doomed city, wrapping its streets, squares, dwellings, and churches in sheets of flame, and in twelve hours destroying the labors of fifty years, and converting a scene of industry, activity, and prosperity into a mass of ruins. Next morning, of the homes of 12,000 people, nothing was left but overthrown or tottering walls and a forest of chimneys. Thousands who had been driven in terror from their dwellings by the flames were in the morning lying on the ground keeping watch over the poor remains of household goods which they had managed to drag out of their houses. A roaring wind drove the blazing brands far and wide over a large area of wooden dwellings, which were speedily fired in all directions. The heat increased the violence of the wind, and speedily great flakes of burning material rose in the air, and, floating away, created fresh fire centers. The intense heat, the suffocating smoke, the fiery particles that filled the air, the roaring of the wind, the hissing sound as the fire advanced, the crackling of the woodwork as the

ST. JOHN'S, NEWFOUNDLAND.

flames seized it, the crash of the falling roofs, the terror depicted in every face, women dragging away their children, men making frantic but useless efforts to arrest the flames—all combined to form an appalling scene. Stone and brick buildings were consumed almost as rapidly as the wooden structures. The beautiful cathedral of the Church of England, which had cost nearly half a million dollars and was supposed to be invulnerable to any fire from outside, was soon a blazing mass. St. Andrew's Presbyterian Church, a massive stone and brick structure, shared the same fate. The fine Athenæum building, the courthouse, the Commercial Bank, the Atlantic Hotel, St. Patrick's Hall, and all the other halls, went down. It was found that 1,622 buildings had been destroyed, and about 300 stores, stables, and outhouses. The massive stores, filled with valuable goods, the fine shops in the business part of the city, the schools, colleges, halls, and hotels constituted the heaviest losses. The value of the property destroyed is estimated from $15,000,000 to $20,000,000, of which a fourth was covered by insurances. Temporary huts and tents were erected, and a large committee was named by the Governor to take charge of and distribute the relief which was forthcoming, for a stream of charitable donations flowed in from all quarters. Food, clothing, and money were forwarded with a degree of liberality that was marvelous. The contributions exceeded $400,000 in value. At the close of 1892, 1,000 houses were either erected on the burned area or were in course of erection. Plans are made for rebuilding the public edifices and churches, as well as the large mercantile houses.

Political.—The settlement of the French shore question seems as distant as ever. The Legislature passed an act legalizing the provisions of the *modus vivendi* till the end of 1893, but declined to pass a permanent measure that would enable the British Government to enforce the treaties on the French shore. This will necessitate the passing of such an act by the Imperial Parliament, to enable the British Government to keep faith with the French in regard to the observance of the treaties. Meantime the proposed arbitration regarding lobsters is in abeyance.

Newfoundland and Canada held a conference composed of delegates of their respective governments, in Halifax, in the autumn of 1892. The result of its deliberations was a satisfactory settlement of all outstanding difficulties regarding bait supplies and tariffs, and a return to former peaceful relations.

NEW HAMPSHIRE, a New England State, one of the original thirteen, ratified the Constitution June 21, 1788; area, 9,305 square miles. The population, according to each decennial census, was 141,885 in 1790; 183,858 in 1800; 214,460 in 1810; 244,022 in 1820; 269,328 in 1830; 284,574 in 1840; 317,976 in 1850; 326,073 in 1860; 318,300 in 1870; 346,991 in 1880; and 376,530 in 1890. Capital, Concord.

Government.—The following were the State officers during the year: Governor, Hiram A. Tuttle, Republican; Secretary of State, Ezra S. Stearns; Treasurer, Solon A. Carter; Attorney-General, Ed. C. Eastman, whose term began in April, 1892; Superintendent of Public Instruction, James W. Patterson; Insurance Commissioner, John C. Linehan; Railroad Commissioners, Henry M. Pultney, Benjamin F. Prescott, and Thomas Cogswell. Chief Justice of the Supreme Court, Charles Doe; Associate Justices, Isaac W. Smith, William H. H. Allen, Lewis W. Clark, Isaac N. Blodgett, Alonzo P. Carpenter, and William M. Chase.

Finances.—According to the reports of the State Treasurer, submitted June 1, 1892, the liabilities of the State on that date were $2,859,033.86, while the assets were $707,129.97. The net indebtedness was $2,151,903.80. The reduction of the debt during the year was $108,136.75. The total revenue, amounting to $715,242.29, was derived from the following sources: From the State tax, $500,000; from the railroad tax, $122,583.23; from the insurance tax, $14,618.19; from interest on deposits, $5,061.07; from license fees (peddlers), $1,050; from license fees (fertilizers), $1,050; from the telegraph tax, $2,697.33; from the telephone tax, $2,697.33; from fees of insurance department, $6,529.60. The rest of the tax was from miscellaneous sources, the Benjamin Thompson estate, the income for two years to Jan. 30, 1892, amounting to $38,547.50, registration fees, etc. The total expenses of the State amounted to $607,105.84; the ordinary expenses being $220,628.91, and the extraordinary expenses $203,629.49, the excess of revenue over expenses being $108,136.75. The total interest charges on the several trust funds during the year amounted to $182,847.14; the net interest being $139,238,57.

There was paid during the year of the principal of the State debt, State bonds, series 1872, $197,000; series of 1879, $100,000; State note (temporary loan), $100,000; total, $397,000.

Education.—The number of public schools in the State in 1892 was, according to the report of the Superintendent of Public Instruction, 2,226, a decrease of 9 since 1891; number of graded schools, 648, an increase of 21; town and district high schools, 57, a decrease of 3; schools averaging 12 pupils or less, 660, a decrease of 16; average length of schools in weeks of five days, 24·32, a gain of ·58. The number of boys attending school two weeks or more was 31,223, an increase of 200; girls, 30,048, an increase of 876; average attendance of all pupils, 43,508, an increase of 1,412; ratio of average attendance to the whole number, 7·16, a gain of ·01; number of pupils not absent during the year, 4,719, a decrease over 1891 of 590; number pursuing higher branches, 7,321, a decrease of 480.

The number of male teachers employed during the year was 290, a decrease of 15; number of female teachers, 2,814, a decrease of 15; average wages of male teachers per month including board, $48.02, a decrease of 97 cents; of female teachers, $26.09, an increase of 20 cents.

The number of schoolhouses in the State is 2,073, which is 2 fewer than reported a year ago. Those unfit for use is 240, an increase of 16. Thirty-two were built during the year, which is 10 more than were built in 1891.

The teaching of physiology and hygiene, with special reference to the effect of stimulants and narcotics upon the human system, has been made compulsory in all schools except the primary.

Savings Banks.—Including the savings deposits of the trust companies of the State, the deposits of the savings institutions aggregate nearly $75,000,000. The tax on these deposits for 1892 was $730,984.76, of which $652,314.42 was distributed to the towns, and $78,670.34 was carried to the literary fund. Of the unclaimed savings-bank deposits there was on June 1, 1892, a balance of $1,604.68. The law passed by the last Legislature restricting the investments of savings banks has had a year's trial, and under its operation the amount of Western mortgages held by the savings banks has decreased to the extent of $1,785,607.29, while there has been an increase of $2,496,680.39 in the amount of municipal bonds held by these institutions.

State Library.—The Legislature of 1891 passed an act for the erection of a State library building; $175,000 was appropriated for the purpose, and the Governor and Council appointed 4 commissioners to superintend the work. By the terms of the contract it was to be completed in September, 1892, but a labor disturbance caused a cessation of the work in May. During the year ending Oct. 1, 1892, 6,630 volumes, pamphlets, and papers were received. According to the report submitted by the librarian to the Legislature, "from New Hampshire came the earliest legislation authorizing towns to establish free public libraries. To the Legislature of 1849 this distinction belongs. The earliest libraries in the State, however, were known as social libraries. The first of these was incorporated one hundred years ago, and out of the large number established in succeeding years a few still survive."

The World's Fair.—The board of managers was appointed under the act of April 11, 1891. An appropriation of $25,000 was made to carry out the provision of the act, $10,000 of which was for a State building, if the committee deemed such expenditure advisable. The New Hampshire commissioners voted to erect such a building, which will be completed within the amount designated. At a meeting of the commissioners in May, it was resolved that a committee be appointed to collect from railroad corporations and hotel proprietors the sum of $15,000, in order to prepare a map of the State, drawing attention in it to the beauty of its views and the attractiveness of the State as a summer resort.

Cattle Commission. — The Legislature of 1891 created a State Board of Cattle Commissioners. The work of the commission has been directed mainly toward eradicating tuberculosis from the herds of the State. Quarantine orders were established against Massachusetts in January, 1892.

Insurance.—The number of authorized fire-insurance companies at work in the State on Dec. 31, 1892, was 86. Forty-seven of these are from other States and countries. The withdrawal of the foreign companies in 1885 and 1886 consequent upon the enactment of the so-called valued policy law, left the property of the State without adequate protection, and though prompt efforts were made to supply the defect by the organization of new companies, there was for a long time a feeling of insecurity. A comparison of the six years immediately preceding 1885 with the six years immediately following shows

that in the former period the ratio of losses paid to premiums received was 63·6. In the latter period the ratio was 38·4. The act of Aug. 10, 1889, relating to returns and statistics of fires has materially assisted in the good work. Under this law the engineer or the selectmen of towns, within two days of their occurrence, must investigate the causes of fires and make a report to the city or town clerk, who in turn must forward the reports in January and July of each year to the fire commissioner.

Twelve fidelity and casualty and 21 life insurance companies are in business in the State. The Legislature of 1891 enacted a law placing certain corporations, associations, societies, and orders under the jurisdiction of the insurance commissioner. In these would be included certain so-called bond, indemnity, trust, and endowment companies. At the time of the passage of this act 155 of these associations had been incorporated under the laws of the State, and these, in addition to 56 organized under the laws of Massachusetts and 44 under the laws of other States, were already at work or intending to work in New Hampshire. All these, not being able to comply with the provisions of the law, were refused license by the commissioner, and ceased to do business in the State.

Penal and Charitable Institutions.—On Oct. 1, 1892, the whole number of inmates in the Industrial School was 93 (boys 80, girls 13); whole number during the year, 132. From the opening of the institution to the present time the whole number admitted is 1,492.

There were in the State Prison 157 prisoners (153 men and 4 women), a considerable increase over last year. The general health at the prison is good. The sanitary conditions are excellent.

Into the Asylum for the Insane there have been received since its opening, Oct. 28, 1842, 5,943 persons, about equally divided as to sex. The number of inmates in January, 1892, was 359.

Agriculture.—A potent influence in the advancement of the agricultural interests in the State is the Grange. Of this order there are 159 subordinate groups in the State, with a total membership of about 12,000. The act of April 10, 1891, provided for the removal of the Agricultural College from Hanover to Durham, the will of the late Benjamin Thompson having provided for this. All agreements with Dartmouth College have terminated, and all real estate at Hanover owned by the college has been sold. The work of erecting buildings at Durham has been pushed forward as rapidly as the magnitude of the work and circumstances would permit. Five buildings are substantially completed on the outside. The appropriation by the last Legislature was found insufficient to finish and furnish the buildings and for work on the grounds, in order to put the institution in condition for the admission of students at the beginning of the college year in September.

At the annual meeting of the State Board of Agriculture, in August, resolutions were passed inviting the Grange to appoint a committee of three to co-operate with a like committee of the board to take into consideration some means for bettering the public roads of the State.

Fish and Game Commission.—There are 7 hatcheries in the State, and the distribution of fishes, annually increasing, amounted in 1892 to several million of the various species of trout.

The law for the better protection of deer and moose, passed by the Legislature in 1891, coupled with the act authorizing the employment of detectives by the Fish and Game Commissioners, has borne good results, there being a great increase of those animals.

Political.—The Republican State Convention met at Concord, on April 27, to choose delegates to the national convention, and in September the State convention for the nomination of the State ticket was held. John B. Smith was then nominated for Governor. In the platform adopted it was declared that the main issue before the people was the maintenance of the Republican principles of protection and reciprocity on the lines laid down by the Fifty-first Congress. Especial call was made upon those throughout the State whose means of livelihood as wage earners, or whose business prosperity as employers, has been founded upon the principle of the protection of American labor and manufactures, and is dependent upon its perpetuation, to unite in support of the Republican party regardless of their former political association with a party which in its national platform declares against the constitutionality of such legislation. The influence of the party against intemperance and immorality was promised.

The Democratic State Convention chose its delegates to the national convention in May. In September the convention again met for the naming of a State ticket. The resolutions expressed disapproval of the McKinley bill and of all legislation to advance the interests of monopolies. It was also declared that tariff laws should be adjusted with reference to the interests of the manufacturer, the laborer, and the consumer, alike. "Free elections for a free people" were demanded, and the "attempt of the Republicans in the Fifty-first Congress to take from the people their inalienable right to hold their elections in the manner guaranteed by the Constitution" was condemned. The financial policy of the Harrison administration was declared dangerous and insidious. It was resolved

To call upon the people of this State, at the coming election, to aid in righting the flagrant wrong committed at the assembling of the last Legislature, when a subservient clerk nullified the election of Representatives throughout the State, and an armed mob, at the command of a revolutionary Governor, filled the Capitol and insulted the people's representatives, while the larceny of the State government was accomplished.

Prohibition as a means of suppressing the sale of intoxicants was declared to be a failure, and to have fostered the growth of the liquor traffic and increased drunkenness and crime; and reasonable, practicable, and seasonable laws, such as public sentiment will sustain and enforce, were asked for.

Luther F. McKinney was made the nominee for Governor, having received 500 of the 713 votes cast, 357 only having been necessary for nomination.

The Prohibition State Convention met in June. In the resolutions passed it was declared that the Prohibition party of New Hampshire is a living protest against parties that ignore moral principles while claiming patronage through motives of mere expediency, and is the party making the strongest claims upon all who believe that morality should dominate in public and political life just as truly as in private and social life.

The manufacture of and traffic in intoxicating beverages was declared a public nuisance, a producer of crime, poverty, and political corruption.

To the liquor traffic was ascribed the increase of extreme poverty, the accumulation of more than one half the nation's wealth by a little over a two thousandth part of the inhabitants, the oppression of the poor, the lowering of wages, and the depression of agricultural and industrial interests have become matters of great moral and political importance.

Edward L. Carr was unanimously nominated for Governor.

At the elections in November the Republican candidate for Governor was successful by a plurality of 2,175. The total vote was 87,042, of which the Democratic nominee received 41,501, and the Prohibitionist 1,546. The total presidential vote was 90,819, of which Harrison received 45,728, Cleveland 43.456, and Fisk 1,593.

NEW JERSEY, a Middle Atlantic State, one of the original thirteen, ratified the Constitution Dec. 18, 1787. Area, 7,815 square miles; population in 1890, 1,444,933. Capital, Trenton.

Government.—The following were the State officers during the year: Governor, Leon Abbett, Democrat; Secretary of State, Henry C. Kelsey; Treasurer, George R. Gray; Comptroller, William C. Heppenheimer; Attorney-General, John P. Stockton; Superintendent of Public Instruction, Addison B. Poland; Commissioner of Banking and Insurance, George S. Duryee; Adjutant-General, William S. Stryker; Chief Justice of the Supreme Court, Mercer Beasley (reappointed for a fifth term of seven years); Associate Justices, Bennet Van Syckel, Jonathan Dixon, David A. Depue, Alfred Reed, William J. Magie, Edward W. Scudder, Charles G. Garrison, George J. Werts. Judge Manning M. Knapp died early in the year. Chancellor, Alexander T. McGill; Vice-Chancellors, Abraham V. Van Fliet, John T. Bird, Henry C. Pitney, and Robert S. Green.

Finances.—Following are items from the Treasurer's report for the year ending Oct. 31, 1892; Receipts for the year, $1,915,937.89; expenditures, $1,698,405.70. The balance in bank Nov. 1, 1891, was $402,168,96, and on Oct. 31, 1892, it was $619,701.15.

The receipts of the school fund were $262,-230.31, and the disbursements, including investments, $421,091.09; the balance in bank, $321,-974. The receipts from the State school tax were $2,052,560, and the disbursements the same; receipts from the Agricultural College fund, $6,960; local tax on railroad corporations, $358,188.07.

The securities of the State are: 1,887 shares of stock of the joint companies, $188,700; centennial stock, $74,116.67; bonds of the several counties for surplus revenue of the United States loaned, $764,670.44; riparian leases, $13,-694.70.

The amount of war debt Oct. 31, 1891, was $997,300, and on Oct. 31, 1892, it was $934,700.

The sinking fund owed the State fund at the close of the fiscal year $66,746, which sum was borrowed from the State treasury by the late Commissioners of the Sinking Fund, prior to April 10, 1891, when the State Treasurer assumed control of this fund, as directed by law.

Corporation Assessments.—There are 2,377 corporations assessed for taxation in the State, the capital stock of which ranges from $10,000 to $50,000,000. Thirty corporations have a capitalization of more than $3,000,000. Before the passage of the law of 1891 these companies were taxed one tenth of 1 per cent. on their capital, which would make the tax in some instances $40,000 to $50,000. Since the passage of the act of 1891 a tax of one tenth of 1 per cent. is imposed on the capital stock up to and including $3,000,000: on all above that and not exceeding $5,000,000 the rate is one twentieth of 1 per cent., and for every million in excess of that $50 additional tax is assessed.

Railroads.—The aggregate assessed valuation of railroads in 1892 was $216,249,782, an increase of $7,547.314 over the valuation of the previous year. The total tax for State uses was $1,081,248.91, and for local uses $388,529.30.

Banks.—The total resources of savings banks increased during 1891 by the sum of $1,293,252.42. On Jan. 1, 1892, they were $36,875,745.54; the amount of deposits was $33,807,634.16; the surplus, $2,977,239.80; and the other liabilities, $90,871.38. With the exception of $350,785 in bonds of cities and counties of other States, the total resources of the banks are invested in real estate and bonds and mortgages in New Jersey, bonds of the Federal Government, first mortgage railroad bonds, bonds of this State, and of cities and counties of the State. Savings banks are allowed to loan 15 per cent. of their total deposits on certain prescribed collaterals. On Jan. 1, 1892, $1,743,338 was invested in this way, a decrease of $382,085 since the preceding year.

Insurance and Loan Associations.—The paid-up capital of the 10 domestic insurance companies, as given in April, 1892, is $2,555,730; the admitted assets are $7,598,703.73; the liabilities, excluding capital, are $2,136,161.01: the surplus as to policy holders is $5,462,542.72; the liabilities, including capital, $4,691,891.01; the surplus over all liabilities, which includes the capital stock, is $2,906,812.72. Seventy companies doing business in this State are organized under the laws of other States. There are 23 mutual companies operating in this State, which have $2,419,721.48 premium notes in force. The cash assets of these companies amount to $471,348.86, and the liabilities to $86,605.02; the premiums and assessments received, $132,909 09; total cash income, $210,534.83; losses paid, $92,487.77.

The building and loan associations show the following statistics: Number of associations reporting, 271; shareholders, 78,635; shares, 518,777; shares pledged, 131,620; borrowers, 19,205. The aggregate net worth of these associations, which represents substantially the total value of all outstanding shares, is $25,006,373, of which $20,484,172 is to be credited to the installments paid in. The receipts during the year, exclusive of money borrowed from banks and dues

paid in advance, were $12,418,704; disbursements, $11,841,248; the current expenses were $119,680; the salaries, $88,680.

Education.—The number of children of school age was 402,702 by the latest report; 89,546 children were reported as not attending any school; 1,911 over ten years of age were not able to read; 4,610 were employed in factories, mines, stores, and other workshops, who were under fifteen years of age.

The amount of State school tax for the year beginning Sept. 1, 1892, was $2,151,700, and the amount of State appropriation $100,000. The State Normal School sent out this year the largest class it has ever graduated, 118. An appropriation of $48,000 has been expended in the erection of an addition containing a laboratory, a gymnasium, and a large auditorium, besides rooms for a library and a museum.

The dedication of the new halls of the Whig and Cliosophic Societies took place at Princeton in June. They are built of white marble, at a cost of $60,000 each, and reproduce almost exactly on a larger scale the old halls. The corner stone of a student's hospital was laid the same day. The hospital is to be called the Isabella McCosh Infirmary, and is to cost $30,000.

Charities.—At the close of the year there were 120 pupils at the school for deaf mutes at Trenton. Industrial training is given at this school, as well as instruction in elementary English subjects. At the printing office a daily and a monthly paper are published.

The State paid for State lunatic asylums $119,982.06, and for the county asylums $110,096.21.

Under the act of Congress to provide State or Territorial homes for the support of disabled soldiers and sailors of the United States, the Treasurer received $35,935.11 for the Soldiers' Home, and disbursed $23,755.45.

Prisons.—The whole number of inmates of the State Prison at the close of the year was 916, of whom 27 were women. This is the lowest number at the institution for some time. The cost of maintenance for the year was $83,077.91, and the amount of salaries $82,327.55; for repairs, $5,042.49 was expended. The receipts for labor were $75,608.04.

Thirty-one of the prisoners known as the Hudson County ballot-box stuffers were paroled in December, and one was unconditionally pardoned. These prisoners were, with others, convicted of conspiracy to violate the election laws at the general election held in November, 1889. The report of the Committee of the Court of Pardons, to which the cases were referred, concludes:

After a careful examination of the records of these prisoners, which shows that but one of these confined in the State Prison was ever before indicted for any offense, your committee has decided that it will be consistent with the proper and merciful administration of justice to parole the following prisoners on Dec. 24. The paroling of these prisoners does not restore them to citizenship, and their retention of liberty is entirely dependent upon their conducting themselves as good citizens, the State retaining the right to compel a service of the balance of the sentence if any of the prisoners should prove unworthy of the mercy recommended by your committee.

The cost of the Reform School to the State was $54,792.24, and of the Industrial School for Girls $38,549.84.

At the Industrial School an appropriation of $25,000 was used for the building of a new wing to accommodate inmates who had been temporarily housed. There were 81 girls in the institution in June.

Industries.—The State Commission for the World's Fair exhibit have begun the issue of circulars furnishing statistics of the resources and industries of the State. One of these calls attention to the prominence of New Jersey in the cast-iron-pipe industry. In this manufacture the State surpasses in amount of capital invested, wages paid, cost of materials, and value of products not only every other State, but all the New England States, New York, Pennsylvania, and Ohio combined. The tabulated statement shows that the amount of capital exceeds the aggregate of that of the States named by over $613,000; the average number of persons employed in its pipe foundries was 2,208, which is 155 more than the total number employed in all the States above enumerated, and nearly one third of the entire number in the United States. There are 36 cast-iron-pipe manufacturing establishments in the United States, of which 6 are in New Jersey.

A census of the wool industry shows that this State has 55 establishments that manufacture woolen goods, an increase of 10 over the number in 1880. The value of the buildings and machinery is $4,500,494. The other assets of the companies thus engaged are estimated at $3,770,203. The average number of persons employed is 7,243. Five of the establishments are idle, representing a capital of $255,000.

State Survey.—The work of the geological survey has been carried forward in the study of the surface formations of the northern part of the State, in an examination of the oak-land and pine-land belts of the southern parts of the State, in the continued study of the stream flows and the watersheds for the report on water supply and water power, and in the study of the crystalline rocks of the highlands of the northern section of the State.

A portion of the assistant geologist's time was devoted to an examination of the oak and pine belts in the southern part of the State, with a view to determining their adaptation to agricultural improvement. It is a comparatively recent discovery that under modern systems of farming such lands can be profitably tilled. It is estimated that nearly a million acres of land heretofore considered as worthless, or nearly so, may be made available for agricultural purposes. The report shows that even in the driest weather the Delaware alone would furnish a volume of water sufficient every 10 miles to drive the machinery of a Lowell. The fact is pointed out that the use of water power in the State has apparently declined within the last half century, because of the change in the location of the iron-making industry; but inquiries recently made upon the subject show that attention is again being turned toward it.

Water Ways.—Among the appropriations for rivers and harbors made by the House Committee were the following to New Jersey: Raritan Bay, $40,000; Keyport harbor, $5,000; the Delaware river, from Trenton to its mouth, $50,000; the Passaic, below Newark, $30,000; the Raritan,

$40,000; the Shrewsbury, $10,000; Matawan creek, $9,620; South river, $7,000; Alloway's creek, $3,000; Elizabeth river, $5,000; Goshen creek, $3,000; and Salem river, $25,000. Total, $227,620.

The project of a ship canal across New Jersey from Philadelphia to New York is so far advanced as the introduction of a bill to appropriate $25,000 for a survey of the route.

Legislative Session.—The Legislature adjourned on March 11. One of the most important bills passed was the act to tax gifts, legacies, and collateral inheritance. It imposes a tax of $5 on every $100 worth of property that passes by will or by the interstate laws to any person or body politic or corporation other than to or for the use of a father, mother, husband, wife, children, brother and sister and lineal descendants, and the wife and widow of the son and husband of the daughter. All other property which passes by will or through the Orphans' Court will hereafter pay 5 per cent. tax to the Treasurer of the State for the use of the State fund. In order to insure its collection administrators and executors are made liable for it, and estates valued at less than $500 are excepted. The tax becomes due immediately upon the death of the decedent, and if it is not paid within one year 10 per cent. interest is, to be added; if paid within six months, a discount of 5 per cent. will be allowed.

Another important bill was that to establish a Board of Public Works in certain cities of the second class.

Among other acts of the session were the following:

Fixing the terms of mayors of cities of the first class hereafter elected at five years.

Providing for an election in municipalities governed by commissioners to decide whether street improvements shall be made.

Providing that fifty-five hours shall constitute a week's work.

Providing that $50,000 additional be appropriated to the New Jersey World's Fair Commission.

Making it unlawful to imitate trade marks and labels under penalty of $100 fine or ninety days' imprisonment, or both. Passed to protect cigarmakers' unions.

Giving mayors in second-class cities power to veto any resolution involving the expenditure of $50 or over, and requiring a three-fourths vote to pass it over the veto.

Providing that a deed from a married woman for premises shall be legal, and convey complete title without the consent of the husband, if the husband has joined in signing and acknowledging the agreement to sell.

Providing that no public roads shall be more than 2 rods wide hereafter.

Giving the Governor power to appoint police justices in second-class cities.

Amending the public-instruction act by requiring enforcement of the compulsory-education law.

Authorizing boards of freeholders to issue bonds not exceeding $25,000 for the erection of armories.

Compelling insolvent insurance companies to pay the expenses of an investigation by the State Commissioner of Banking and Insurance.

Giving the mayors of second-class cities power to appoint a board of education of 8 members, 4 from each party.

Taking the licensing power from boroughs and placing it in the courts.

Amending the clam and oyster act by providing that none but actual residents of the State for twelve months shall be permitted in the waters of the State fishing for clams and oysters.

Providing that any person carrying a concealed weapon shall be deemed disorderly.

The State Board of Education was empowered by an act of the Legislature to appoint a superintendent of the school census.

A concurrent resolution was adopted requesting those having the matter in charge to have the State exhibit at the World's Fair closed on Sundays, numerous petitions having been sent to the Legislature asking for such action.

A bill was introduced requiring constables to take prisoners before the nearest justice of the peace. This would obviate much of the present trouble at the Guttenburg track caused by the arrest of the bookmakers. Under this law they could be taken before a justice on the grounds and immediately bailed out. Public sentiment was strongly aroused on the subject of this and other anticipated efforts to enable gamblers to evade the law, and protesting petitions and deputations were sent to the Legislature. The bill was lost.

The legality of some of the acts passed by the Legislature was attacked on the ground that the bills were signed by the Governor after the adjournment. The question came up in the case of the Newark Board of Public Works, and the constitutionality of the law giving the Governor thirty days after adjournment to sign bills was denied. The Supreme Court held the law constitutional, and the acts in question consequently legal.

Judicial Decisions.—Decisions were rendered by the Supreme Court in November, maintaining the constitutionality of the bill creating boards of public works, the Police Justice act, and the Commission of Public Institution act.

A decision involving the construction of the election law was given in the Court of Errors and Appeals in the case of the petition of 25 voters of Newark against the Mayor of that city. The petition was framed upon the idea that for the purpose of electing city officers the city of Newark, while comprising many voting precincts, yet constituted but a single election district within the meaning of the Werts law, and the only question in the case was, whether the terms "election district" and "voting precinct" were synonymous. The Supreme Court held that they were, and this court affirms that decision, dismissing the petition.

Railroad Combination.—A bill was introduced into the Legislature legalizing the lease of the New Jersey Central road to the Port Reading. It provided that in all cases in which a lease has been executed between the railroad corporations chartered under the laws of another State "such lease shall be intended by its terms to assign to the lessee the right to use any railroad operated or controlled, whether by means of the ownership of all or any part of the stock of the corporation owning such railroads by the lessor in such lease, and to exercise the franchise of such railroads, it shall be lawful for the lessees in such lease to operate said railroads, and to exercise all the franchises and enjoy the privileges and immunities connected therewith, as fully to all intents and purposes as the same shall be assigned." And that

" if any railroad corporation of this State has or hereafter shall lease its road and franchises to any other railroad corporation of this State the lease shall not be invalid because the capital stock of the lessee in such lease may be owned, in whole or in part, by a foreign corporation or by a resident or residents of any other State." Another section provided for the purchase of the stock of any dissatisfied stockholders by the roads which are parties to the lease and make appraisement by disinterested commissioners legal and binding in case of any disagreement touching the value of such stock, and all conflicting legislation was to be repealed. The bill passed the Legislature and was sent to the Governor on the day of adjournment. It was believed that the object of the bill was to increase the cost of coal to retail dealers, while at the same time it reduced the cost of transportation to the companies. It was vetoed.

In June the matter came before the Court of Chancery. At the same time an injunction was asked against the lease on behalf of a large stockholder of New Jersey Central Railroad, on the ground that it was made without any consultation with or assent of the stockholders, and was destructive of their rights and property. An order was granted by the court enjoining the Port Reading company from operating the Jersey Central. Another order commanded the Port Reading company to desist and refrain from obliterating the marks identifying the property of the Central, and from turning over to the Philadelphia and Reading any of the tools, machinery, or other personal property delivered to the Port Reading under the lease.

The answer of the companies was served in June. As regarded the allegation that the acts in question were tending to a monopoly in the mining and selling of anthracite coal, and that they controlled at least 60 per cent. of the anthracite coal field, it was alleged "that none of the said corporations own any coal lands or sell any coal, and they can not act, either separately or conjointly, in fixing or increasing the price of anthracite coal, or creating any monopoly in the business."

After the hearing of the arguments the Chancellor continued in force the order restraining the companies from carrying out the lease and the tripartite agreement, and ordered the Port Reading road to give up the control of the Central, and cease from intermeddling in any wise with its corporate franchises. The suit that followed had not been decided at the close of the year.

Political.—The nominating convention of Republicans met at Trenton, Sept. 13. On State affairs the platform had the following paragraphs:

We denounce as utterly vicious and contrary to public policy the passage by the last Democratic Legislature, the direction of a Democratic Executive, with the co-operation of members of the Democratic State Executive Committee, of a bill to legalize an unconstitutional and pernicious combination of corporations engaged in the production and carrying of coal, as the result of which the prices of this necessary commodity have been increased, and the burdens of consumers have been vastly augmented. We remind the people that this legislation affects not only men of wealth and the great industries of the

State, but increases the cost of living to that more numerous class who are compelled to meet the increased burden out of the proceeds of their daily toil.

Resolved, That labor and capital should be allies, not enemies. We favor arbitration and profit sharing as remedies for idleness, want, and suffering, and tending to secure peace, plenty, and prosperity to our people. We favor reduction in the hours of labor. We favor tenement-house and factory inspection in the interest of health and morals.

We favor the passage of an act restoring the proceeds of the sale of riparian lands to the school fund of the State.

We are opposed to an administration of the State government for personal uses; to the subserviency of the Legislature and the courts to Executive dictation; to the abolition by the Legislature, under executive orders, of local home government; to the multiplication of public offices and the increase of salaries for the furtherance of personal and political ends; to the appointment of public officers for a stated consideration to be paid to the par campaign fund; to the indiscriminate and wholesale pardon of convicts in the State Prison; to the unheard-of extravagance of the present State administration in the expenditure of public money; to clothing the Governor with dictatorial powers by acts of a Legislature obsequiously subject to executive control; to the creation of unnecessary boards and commissions for partisan purposes, investing them with arbitrary powers, and placing them beyond the control of the people by making their term of office subject to the will of the Governor; to evasions and misconstructions of the Constitution by the chief Executive to secure political and personal support; to the countenance and support by State officers and party leaders of race-track gambling, with all its attendant evils; to the destruction of the right of suffrage by false registry, ballot-box stuffing, and fraudulent count of votes; and to the general maladministration of public affairs, which in these and other matters during the current administration, have brought shame and disgrace upon the State.

John Kean, Jr., was chosen as candidate for Governor.

The Democratic State Convention met at Trenton, Sept. 14. As an answer to criticisms on the management of State affairs by the party, the statement below was introduced into the resolutions:

We call the attention of the people to the following facts: That the only permanent State officers to whom any salary or compensation is allowed, created by the Democratic party during the past three years, are as follow: Commissioner of banking and insurance, a chief of State police, a State board of taxation, a State board for the arbitration of differences between employers and employees, a board of commissioners of electrical subways, a commissioner of mines, a resident physician at the State Prison, and a superintendent of the school census. The acts creating the offices of the commissioner of banking and insurance and commissioners of electric subways provide that the expenses of these departments shall be paid respectively by the insurance and telegraph companies doing business in this State. The total of all salaries to be paid by the State to permanent officers created by Democratic Legislatures during the present administration is less than $15,000. The pledge made in our State platform of 1889, that there should not be any general State tax imposed upon the people, has been faithfully kept, and we renew the promise then made, that there shall not be any general State tax imposed while the affairs of the State are intrusted to the Democratic party. On Jan. 1, 1889, the floating debt of the State amounted to $400,000. Every dollar of this has been paid, and over $250,000 expended for the improvement of public buildings and

the purchase of a camp ground at Sea Girt. That these expenses have been met without the imposition of a single dollar of direct State tax upon the property of private owners, and without an increase in the rate imposed upon the property of corporations, supports our claim that the State government of New Jersey is the most economical in the Union.

That in pursuance of its pledge made in its platform of 1889, to legislate in the interest of labor, the Democratic party has during the present administration, through its legislative representatives, enacted the following measures, all of which have received the approval of a Democratic Governor, to wit: Acts which secure beyond the reach of fraud the payment of wages to mechanics and others engaged in the erection of buildings; an act providing for 60 free scholarships in the State Agricultural College; acts to authorize the establishment of free public libraries and reading rooms in cities and towns; an act giving a lien for wages due for work and labor performed and materials furnished in finishing silk and goods of which silk is a component part; acts for the improvement of the State agricultural experiment station; an act making Saturday a half holiday; an act extending the provisions of the Mechanics' Lien law to money due for labor or materials furnished in the erection of public buildings; an act prohibiting corporations from forcing their employees to contribute to relief funds; an act creating a State board of arbitration for the amicable adjustment of grievances and disputes that may arise between employers and employees; acts providing for absolute secrecy in the exercise of the elective franchise; an act providing for a commissioner of mines to inspect all mines in this State, and to secure proper safeguards for the protection of the lives of men employed therein; an act making wages due workmen and laborers a first lien upon the assets of insolvent corporations; an act providing for the incorporation of trades unions and labor organizations, and other acts. In dealing with the municipal governments of the State, the Democratic party has adopted the plan of vesting in the mayors of large cities the power of appointment of municipal boards and officers, and we submit to the people of the State that this plan of municipal government is entitled to a thorough test in lights other than those afforded by mere political partisanship. Under this system there is a concentration of personal and political responsibility in a single office, the occupant of which is chosen by the votes of the entire city. The plan is in no wise antagonistic to local self-government, but, on the contrary, affords an incentive to citizens to participate in municipal elections. Under it the grievous evil of sectional strife for municipal patronage can be avoided and economy enforced. While the plan is necessarily imperfect, it is subject to amendment and should be given a fair trial and receive impartial judgment before a return is made to a system under which responsibility is distributed and elusive. We denounce all frauds perpetrated upon the elective franchise, and we call the attention of the people to the fact that prosecution and punishment of those crimes have been the work of a Democratic court and prosecutor and Democratic jurors. We ask from fair-minded citizens a comparison of this fact with the action of a Republican Senate which voted to seat, as Senator from Hudson, a man who every one knew was not entitled to the office. The action of that Senate was protected by constitutional privilege, but it was none the less a crime.

The necessity for a diversion of the proceeds from the sale of riparian lands from the school fund to funds necessary to pay the expense of rebuilding the State House and other extraordinary expenses having ceased, we favor a repeal of the act allowing such diversion.

George J. Werts was made the nominee for Governor.

The People's party held a State convention at

Trenton, Sept. 6. passed characteristic resolutions, and nominated Benjamin Bird as their candidate for Governor.

A State convention of Prohibitionists met at Trenton, Aug. 9, and named Thomas J. Kennedy as candidate for Governor. Resolutions were adopted, favoring woman suffrage and a change in the election laws so that "all organizations may have the right of the legal ballot," condemning pool selling, horse-racing, and the county excise law, and denouncing the liquor traffic.

The fourteenth congress of the New Jersey Federation of Trades and Labor Unions was held in Trenton, Aug. 15. The report of the Executive Committee made among others the following recommendations:

The introduction of a bill at the next session of the Legislature making eight hours a legal day's work for all State, county, and city employees.

A declaration by this congress against all kinds of scab labor and in favor of union-made work and union labels.

The formation of State unions of the building trades, printers, cigarmakers, and other trades having five or more unions in the State.

An investigation of the sweating system by the new Executive Committee, with a view to legislative action.

The preparation of a lien bill for the special protection of the wage workers.

The preparation and introduction in the Legislature of a bill providing for the creation of a State printing office.

A declaration by this congress exempting homesteads valued at less than $1,000 from taxation, and in favor of public works for the unemployed.

The introduction of a bill requiring district attorneys to sue upon demand of any persons to recover money due for wages without costs to the plaintiff.

George B. Keim was the Labor candidate for Governor.

At the November election the vote for presidential electors stood: Democratic, 171,042; Republican, 156,068; Prohibition, 8,131; Labor, 1,337; People's 969; total vote, 337,547. The vote for Governor gave Werts 167,257, Kean 159,632, Kennedy 7,750, Keim 1,338, and Bird 894. Six Democrats and 2 Republicans were elected members of Congress. The Legislature will have 16 Democrats in the Senate and 39 in the Assembly, and 5 Republicans in the Senate and 21 in the Assembly.

NEW MEXICO, a Territory of the United States, organized Sept. 9, 1850; area, 122,580 square miles. The population, according to each decennial census, was 61,547 in 1850; 93,516 in 1860; 91,874 in 1870; 119,565 in 1880; and 153,-593 in 1890. Capital, Santa Fé.

Government.—The following were the Territorial officers during the year: Governor, L. Bradford Prince, Republican; Secretary, Benjamin M. Thomas, who died on Oct. 2 and was succeeded by Silas Alexander; Auditor, Demetrio Perez; Treasurer, Rufus J. Palen; Solicitor-General, Edward L. Bartlett; Superintendent of Public Instruction, Amado Chavez; Secretary of the Bureau of Immigration, Max Frost; Chief Justice of the Supreme Court, James O'Brien; Associate Justices, William D. Lee, Edward P Seeds, John R. McFie, and Alfred A. Freeman.

Finances.—The Territorial indebtedness on March 6, 1892, the close of the fiscal year, was as follows: Capitol-building bonds, $200,000; Penitentiary bonds, $100,000; current expense bonds, $150,000; provisional indebtedness bonds, $200,000; Capitol contingent bonds, $50,000; Insane Asylum bonds, $25,000; outstanding warrants, $130,806.12; total, $864,806.12. At the close of the previous year the total debt was $866,433.03.

For the year ending March 6, 1892, the Territorial expenditures were as follow: Penitentiary, $34,749.90; Capitol, current expense, $3,722.66; salaries, $28,713.92; court expenses, $57,119.64; Territorial institutions, $74,444.25; interest on warrants, $5,936.92; deficit of 1889-'90, $36,-392.27; miscellaneous, $29,843.84; total, $270,-923.40. Not only have the expenditures exceeded the revenues for several years, but it has been impossible to collect all the taxes levied. The tax of 1889 should have produced $395,853, but only $280,483 reached the treasury. In 1890, $371,758 was called for and $285,807 was received; and in 1891 the amount due was $404,-608, and only $273,673 has been paid. Here is an average loss of more than one quarter of the taxes, or $322,000 in three years. Certain counties have paid nearly every dollar due, while others are largely in arrears. In one county the loss in three years has been but 2 per cent., and in another 4; while in several the deficit reaches 35 or 40 per cent., and in one 60 per cent. is due.

Valuations.—The total assessed valuation of property in the Territory for 1891 was $45,329,-563.61, an increase of $129,716 over 1890. The valuation of lands, outside of town lots, was $8,957,448.90; of town lots, including improvements, $6,851,354.63; and of railroads, $8,289,-747.74. Included in the assessment were 76,042 horses, valued at $1,502,891; 4,139 mules, valued at $182,920; 1,041,237 cattle, valued at $8,597,-867.50; 1,378,151 sheep, valued at $1,850,962.75; 90,337 goats, valued at $101,687.25; 8,259 swine, valued at $20,412.27; and 7,407 burros, valued at $34,958.

Education.—The last Legislative Assembly of the Territory passed a law establishing a common-school system and creating the office of Superintendent of Public Instruction. This law was approved on Feb. 12, 1891, and went into effect immediately. By its provisions a Territorial board of education was created, consisting of the Governor of the Territory, the Superintendent of Public Instruction, and the presidents of the State University, of the Agricultural College, and of St. Michael's College. Prior to that time there had been no system to govern the common schools, if common schools they were, and the money collected for school purposes was used in various ways without being of any benefit to the school children. The law has not been in operation long enough to show its effects fully, but great progress is being made in every county. New and substantial schoolhouses have been erected, better teachers have been employed, and the adoption of a uniform series of books has improved the work. No opposition has been encountered in any part of the Territory to the introduction of English-speaking teachers in districts where heretofore Spanish alone had been taught. According to the reports of county superintendents made on Oct. 1, 1891, there were then 523 school districts in the Territory, employing 308 male and 179 female teachers. The total enrollment was 14,011 males and 8,588 females, and the average attendance 9,062 males and 5,373 females. The total school population was 44,775, and the total revenue for school purposes for the year preceding $147,830.05. There are about 5,000 pupils in the private schools of the Territory.

Penitentiary.—In the Penitentiary at Santa Fé there were 143 Territorial prisoners on July 1, 1891; 85 were received during the year following, and 91 discharged, leaving 137 remaining on July 1, 1892. At the former date there were 21 United States prisoners in the Penitentiary; 28 were received during the year, and 33 discharged, leaving 16.

Capitol.—On the evening of May 12 the greater part of the Capitol building at Santa Fé was destroyed by a fire which was undoubtedly of incendiary origin. Nearly all the furniture, public documents, and archives were saved. The building was erected in 1885 at a cost of $250,000, and the loss to the Territory will be over $200,000, there being no insurance.

Territorial Institutions.—The Territorial University, at Albuquerque, was opened in the summer for a short session of normal instruction, and is now entering upon its more regular work. The cost of the building, improvement of grounds, etc., was $32,672.

The School of Mines, at Socorro, has completed its laboratory building. To secure its erection the directors were compelled not only to use all the funds on hand, but to pledge the future receipts from the annual appropriations for some time in advance. The institution receives only one fifth of a mill of Territorial taxation, yielding about $7,500 a year.

The Legislature of 1891 authorized the issue of $25,000 in Territorial bonds to aid in the construction of an insane asylum. The proceeds of these bonds were $25,244, and to this was added $16,906 received from taxes. The cost of the building, including fencing, well, etc., was $38,378. It is now ready for use.

The Agricultural College was the first of the Territorial institutions to begin operations, and is in a flourishing condition. The passage of the Morrill act in 1890 brought to it $15,000 for the fiscal year ending June 30, 1890, $16,000 for the next year, $17,000 for the next, and so on until the sum shall reach $25,000 a year. This is to be in addition to the $15,000 that is regularly received for the experiment station, and smaller sums for specific work. Thus the amount of United States money received this year was over $33,000.

Coal.—Coal-mining is carried on extensively at Blossburg, near Raton; at Amargo, in Rio Arriba County; at Gallup; at Cerrillos; and to a smaller extent in other localities. The mines at Carthage, extensively worked for many years, are almost entirely closed, and many buildings have been moved to Cerrillos. The latter has become the most important point in this business in the Southwest. The owners of the great coal tracts in the vicinity have combined all interests, and in connection with the

Atchison, Topeka and Santa Fé Railroad Company are building many miles of branch railroad to connect the various mines with the main line.

Metals.—Since 1890 the production of silver in the Territory has decreased 23·7 per cent., and the production of lead 17·9 per cent. During the same period there has been an increase of 28 per cent. in the gold production. Tin has been identified in Grant County, and the deposits of alumina on the Gila, in the same county, are being explored. While silver has reached the lowest price in its annals, frequent discoveries of silver-ore bodies have been made during the year, as well as of copper, zinc, and lead.

Land Court.—This court, established by act of Congress for passing upon disputed land titles in New Mexico, Arizona, and adjacent States, was organized at Denver, July 1, 1891, and its first session for the transaction of business in the Territory was opened at Santa Fé, Dec. 1, 1891. Subsequent sessions have been held, beginning March 1, 1892, and Aug. 15, 1892. The members of the court are as follow: Hon. Joseph R. Reed, Chief Justice, Iowa. Associate Justices: Hon. Thomas C. Fuller, North Carolina; Hon. Wilbur S. Stone, Colorado; Hon. William W. Murray, Tennessee; Hon. Henry C. Sluss, Kansas. Up to Sept. 1, 1892, a total of 34 claims to land in the Territory had been filed in this court.

Statehood.—At the opening of the last session of Congress in December, 1891, Delegate Joseph introduced an enabling act for the Territory, which was generally satisfactory to the people. This passed the House of Representatives on June 6, 1892. On arriving in the Senate it was referred to the Committee on Territories, and it remained in that committee almost to the end of the session. Finally it was reported with several amendments, which were considered illiberal and unfair. No action has yet been taken by the Senate.

World's Fair.—On account of the small sum available, the World's Fair commissioners representing the Territory have united with the commissioners from Arizona and Oklahoma in erecting a building at Chicago to be used by the three Territories jointly. Under the Territorial law, not more than $12,000 will be raised for the use of the commissioners.

Political.—On April 14, the Republicans, in convention at Silver City, selected delegates to the national nominating convention at Minneapolis, and a few weeks later a Democratic convention made choice of delegates to the Chicago convention. On Aug. 25 a second convention of Republicans was held at Las Vegas, at which Thomas B. Catron was nominated for Delegate to Congress, and a platform was adopted which included the following:

We favor an honest dollar, and unqualifiedly favor the full remonetization of silver; and we also refer with satisfaction to the effort of President Harrison to secure the same through an international conference.

We condemn in the most unmeasured terms the action of the Democratic Administration, in 1887, in the driving away, by the passage of the anti-alien law, from this and other Territories, all investments of foreign capital.

The people of this Territory possess the intelligence,

wealth, and capacity to entitle them to State government, and we insist that they should not longer be deprived of this sacred right guaranteed to them by the Constitution and the treaty with Mexico.

We favor the unqualified protection of all honest labor and capital through the means of local government, and condemn all efforts or attempts to control the same, or the relations of the one to the other, by means of any armed body of men imported into this Territory through private sources, under the name of Pinkertons, or however else designated, believing it to be un-American, and subversive of the rights of the people.

The second Democratic convention met at Santa Fé on Sept. 10, and renominated Delegate Joseph as the party candidate for Congress. A platform was adopted which demands the admission of New Mexico as a State. It favors the repeal of that portion of the public-school law providing for the payment of poll taxes, and declares that it enables unscrupulous politicians to destroy the fundamental principle of the elective system. It declares for a reduction in the existing fee system, demands a law providing for a new Territorial board of equalization, and favors the reconstruction of the financial system of the Territory. It says: "We favor the restoration of silver to its place as a money metal, and demand its free and unlimited coinage at a ratio of 16 grains of silver to 1 of gold."

At the November election the Democrats carried the Territory by a slight majority. For Delegate, Joseph received 15,799 votes, and Catron 15.220. The Legislature elected at the same time will be divided politically as follows: Council—Democrats 5, Republicans 7; House—Democrats 15, Republicans 8, Independent Republican 1.

NEW YORK, a Middle State, one of the original thirteen, ratified the Constitution July 26, 1788; area, 49,170 square miles. The population, according to each national decennial census, was 340,120 in 1790; 589,051 in 1800; 959,049 in 1810; 1,372,111 in 1820; 1,918,608 in 1830; 2,428,921 in 1840; 3,097,394 in 1850; 3,880,735 in 1860; 4,382,759 in 1870; 5,082,871 in 1880; and 5,997,853 in 1890. Capital, Albany.

Government.—The following were the State officers during the year: Governor, Roswell P. Flower; Lieutenant-Governor, William F. Sheehan; Secretary of State, Frank Rice: Comptroller, Frank Campbell; Treasurer, Elliot Danforth; Attorney-General, Simon W. Rosendale; State Engineer and Surveyor, Martin Schenck; Superintendent of Public Instruction, James F. Crooker; Superintendent of Prisons, Austin Lathrop; Superintendent of Insurance, James F. Pierce; Superintendent of Public Works, Edward Hannan; Commissioner of Statistics of Labor, Charles F. Peck; Railroad Commissioners, Michael Rickard, S. A. Beardsley, and Alfred C. Chapin; Chief Judge of the Court of Appeals, Robert Earl; Associate Judges, Charles Andrews, John C. Gray, Rufus W. Peckham, Denis O'Brien, Francis M. Finch, and Isaac H. Maynard.

Finances.—The important officers in the management of the State funds are the Treasurer, Elliot Danforth (salary, $5,000), and the Comptroller, Frank Campbell (salary, $6,000).

The financial condition of the State is shown as follows: Cash in treasury to credit of general fund, Oct. 1, 1891, $5,231,270.46; receipts from all sources during the fiscal year ending Sept. 30, 1892, $6,553,993.16; total. $11,785,263.62. Payments from general fund during fiscal year ending Sept. 30, 1892, $10,083,776.60; balance in treasury, Oct. 1, 1892, $1,701,487.02. Besides which there is a fund balance of $1,746,441.72, distributed as follows: United States deposit fund. $45,397.11; Collegiate land scrip fund, $91,072.60; military record fund, $19,496.36; free-school fund, $378,400.32; canal fund, $1,161,341.31; common-school fund, $47,530.05; literature fund, $3,161.97; Woman's Monument fund, $42; thus making a total balance of $2,447,928.74. Hence there is practically no State debt. The outstanding obligations are already provided for. They consist of $150,000 balance of canal debt, which matures in October, 1893, and for the liquidation of which there is now sufficient money in the canal fund, and of $300,000 Niagara reservation bonds, the last of which do not mature until 1895, but all of which can be paid at any time from surplus moneys now in the treasury, with the proper legislative authority. According to the Comptroller, the receipts from all sources during the year ending Sept. 30 were $15,221,796, and the payments during the year were $19,323,494.

The principal sources of indirect revenue were from the inheritance tax and the franchise and organization taxes on corporations. The former yielded $1,786,218.47, as compared with $890,267.54 for 1891. This increase is owing to the act passed by the Legislature. which placed in the Comptroller's hands $25,000 for examining records of surrogates' offices for the collection of delinquent taxes. The increase from the franchise and organization tax on corporations reached $1,696,960.99, or $161,085.88 in excess of those received in 1891.

The Comptroller in his annual report suggests that the Inheritance Tax law be so amended that the rate be fixed at 1 per cent. upon estates over $10,000 and up to $100,000; 2 per cent. on all sums over $100,000 up to $500,000; 3 per cent. upon sums in excess of $500,000 up to $1,000,000; and 5 per cent. upon all sums in excess of $1,000,000. By adopting such a scale of rates the great accumulations of personal wealth would be required to contribute once in a generation in a substantial way to the expenses of the Government, and would be most satisfactory to the great body of taxpayers of the State.

The State tax for the year ending Oct. 1, 1893, will be 1·98 mill on each dollar of valuation of real and personal property, distributed as follows: Canal tax, ·24 mill; free-school fund, 1 mill; and general fund, ·72 mill. Appropriations were made by the Legislature for general purposes of $8,059,644. There was raised for free-school purposes $3,934.700, and for canal purposes $141,500. The total raised by State taxation was $12,135,844.

Wealth of the State.—The State assessors are William H. Wood, Henry D. Brewster, and John A. Mason, each of whom receives a salary of $2,500. Their annual report presented to the Senate shows that the total assessed value of real and personal property in the State as made by the local assessors in 1891 was $3,779,394,-

746, of which $3,397,234,679 was real estate and $382,159,067 personal property. The general average of assessed value of real estate was 65 per cent. The full value of the realty was $5,202,503,337. The value of personal property owned in the State liable to taxation is estimated to equal the assessed valuation of real estate in 1891. The increase of assessed valuation of realty from 1890 was $98,910,746, and the full increase of valuation in that year was $151,-471,893. The assessed valuation of personal property decreased, in 1891, $3,170.064. Twenty-four counties increased their real-estate valuation $111,046,331, and 31 decreased $12,135.585. Thirty counties increased their personal property valuations $3,204,557, and thirty counties decreased $6,374,623. The increase of real estate value outside of New York County was $44,334,615. The decrease of personal values outside of New York County was $3,670,644.

The following cities increased their real-estate valuations: New York, $66,711,716; Brooklyn, $25,689,471; Buffalo, $4,620,049; Syracuse, $2,101,263; Rochester, $4,272,696; total, $103,-395,195.

In personal property New York city lost $2,703,979; Brooklyn lost $628,469; Buffalo increased $747,115; Rochester, $369,317; and Syracuse, $101,544.

Legislative Session.—The one hundred and fifteenth regular session of the Legislature began Jan. 5 and ended April 21—a period of seventeen weeks—making the shortest session since 1867. An extra session was held April 25–26, for the purpose of reapportioning the State into Senate and Assembly districts. The tax rate was the lowest since 1857, with the exception of 1891. The whole number of laws passed was 715, about 200 more than the average for many years past.

The Legislature assembled under peculiar circumstances. The long contest over the election of November, 1891, had ended by a decision of the Court of Appeals that 15 Republicans and 15 Democrats were elected. The seats of 2 other Senators were in doubt. The State Board of Canvassers, a few days before the Legislature met, awarded one of these seats to a Democrat. The Democrats, being thus in a majority of 1, voted that the other seat should be filled by a Democrat. This made the Senate stand 17 Democrats to 15 Republicans. The seats of 3 Republicans were contested, but not one of the three was removed. The seats of 2 Republicans and 1 Democrat were contested in the Assembly, but none of these were removed.

The first important law enacted appropriated $205,000 for an enumeration of the inhabitants of the State. The enumeration was made between Feb. 18 and Feb. 28. For refusing to vote upon this bill, 3 Republican Senators were placed in contempt and were disfranchised for one week. The apportionment of the Senate and Assembly, based upon this census, gave an increased representation to the cities of New York, Brooklyn, and Buffalo, at the expense of the smaller counties. This increases the probability of the Legislature being Democratic in the future. The Congressional Apportionment bill was passed, based upon the Federal cen-

sus of 1890, which also gives an advantage to the larger cities, and makes the congressional delegation in Congress about equally divided between the two great parties, instead of the advantage being with the Republicans, as hitherto.

The work of the commission on statutory revision was perfected by amendments made to the general railroad law, to the general corporation law, to the stock corporation law, and to the business corporation law. The new laws from the commission were these: Constructing the general statutes relating to the boundaries and the sovereignty of the State; relating to Indians; codifying the election laws; relating to public offices; relating to legislation; relating to executive officers; relating to salt springs; relating to municipal corporations; relating to counties; relating to banks; relating to insurance companies, and amending the penal code generally. The work of the commissioners to promote uniformity of legislation in the United States was extended. The powers of the Comptroller over funds paid into courts were enlarged. The issues to a trial by jury must be more distinctly stated. An unsuccessful attempt was made to exempt bank officials and veterans in the late war from jury duty. Persons from outside the State who take an oath before a notary public must be identified. More notice must be given in reference to *lis pendens*. Judgments for the prevention of waste or injury to property may be obtained against corporations. Stenographers' fees are made a part of the costs. Indictments against corporations must be more strictly drawn. The minimum punishment for all kinds of crimes has been stricken from the penal code, thus allowing very short sentences at the discretion of the court. Corporations may be fined not more than $5,000 if convicted of an offense for which a natural person might be imprisoned. The term of imprisonment in a penitentiary for a felony has been increased from three years to five years. The validity of a will can be contested in the Supreme Court, even after it has been probated in the surrogate's court. The code of evidence failed to become a law, but a law was enacted allowing a subscribing lawyer to a will to testify. Every document bearing upon it a printed scroll or the word "seal," or the letters "L. S.," is made a legal document.

Another of the bills from the statutory revision commission that became a law was the insurance code. This gave more privileges than are now enjoyed to fraternal societies for doing an endowment business. Aside from this, insurance laws were enacted as follow: Authorizing the formation of corporations by benevolent orders for the acquisition of real property and the erection and maintenance of buildings for the use of such orders; giving the fire commissioner of Brooklyn power to enter any building where he has reason to believe combustibles are stored; for the protection of policy holders in fire insurance companies by providing that no such companies shall add any fees or charges to the premiums on policies; allowing the transaction of both fire and marine insurance in this State by any one company.

A new law establishes a State park within the

counties of Hamilton, Herkimer, St. Lawrence, Franklin, Essex, and Warren, to be known as the Adirondack Park, and to be reserved for the free use of the people of the State. The Forest Commission is empowered to purchase land within these counties, but timber may be removed from the same under certain restrictions. Leases may be made within the Adirondack Park not to exceed the term of five years. The Adirondack Park shall be deemed a part of the forest preserve, and the authorities of the fish and game protectors is extended over the same. No appropriation was made for buying the land.

A general law was passed in relation to taxable transfers of property. Another law provides that no deduction from taxable personal property shall be made on account of any debt for the purchase of nontaxable property; but the " listing bill" failed to pass. The bill taxing

evidence of witnesses under oath concerning the value of property bequeathed; also exempting church property held in trust.

The money raised from the tax on racing associations was ordered distributed to county fairs. Parachute ascensions at county fairs are forbidden. The extension of highways through the several counties has been allowed. Trees infected with the " black knot" shall be destroyed. Commission merchants receiving farm produce for sale shall immediately send to the consignor a statement showing what has been received. The adulteration of maple sugar, maple sirup, or honey with glucose or beet sugar is forbidden. The State Board of Health shall stamp out the disease of cattle known as tuberculosis. The law relating to societies for the prevention of cruelty to animals was amended so that no such organizations shall be formed unless they are approved by the American Society, thus doing away with

THE STATE HOUSE AT ALBANY.

corporations for the purpose of organizing was amended so that, if two corporations consolidate, the new corporation shall pay a tax only on the excess of its capital stock over that of the two corporations consolidated. The exemption of American built vessels from State taxation was extended from fifteen to thirty years; but the bill to exempt farm lands from such taxation failed, as did also a bill allowing local option in taxation. The collateral inheritance law was amended so that the cost for a decree from the surrogate shall not exceed $100 where there has been no contest, or $250 where there has been a contest; also allowing an appraiser to take the

many societies that have been organized for purposes of blackmail.

A new banking code was enacted, requiring, among other provisions, that a director must hold at least $1,000 of stock, and that banks of discount in New York and Brooklyn must have a reserve of 15 per cent., and all other banks a reserve of 10 per cent. Another law requires that lists of stockholders in banks must be open for inspection by tax officials. The four hundredth anniversary of the discovery of America, Oct. 1, 1892, was made a legal holiday. A new law requires that commission merchants shall immediately send statements in writing to the consignor; another forbids the appointment of a receiver unless he is a resident of this State; still another grants a charter to the Commercial Travelers' Home Association of America. Corporations are allowed to mortgage their property by consent of two thirds of the stockholders, and they must make reports to the Secretary of State by Feb. 1 in each year. No stock corporation shall combine with any corporation or person to secure a monopoly in the necessaries of life.

Honorably discharged soldiers or sailors of the late civil war who may hereafter be appointed shall not be removed from places of trust under city or county governments except for cause. The law heretofore applied only to soldiers already holding places. The trustees of the Grant Monument Association, in New York city, were given additional powers, but an appropriation of $500,000 for the monument itself did not pass. A new law allows the several cities and towns of the State which have not already refunded to drafted men the money expended in furnishing substitutes in the civil war to refund if they choose. A charter was given to the Sons of Veterans, U. S. Army, Division of New York. The Governor vetoed a repeal of the law exempting from taxation all real estate bought with pension money.

The National Guard was allowed $427,000, and the military code was amended so as to allow the addition of signal and telegraph corps. Pensions were provided for members of the National Guard who have been disabled in the service. An effort was made, without success, to adopt the tactics of the U. S. Army for the National Guard. The Naval Militia, or reserve, was given $25,000, but all of the former acts relating to it were repealed, and a new law was passed which governs the Naval Militia after the manner in which the National Guard is now governed by the military code.

A law was passed codifying the laws regarding the practice of dentistry, and providing that examinations of students to practice the same shall be controlled by the State Dental Society. The medical schools tried, without success, to have the same privileges as to the securing of corpses that are now allowed to medical colleges. An unsuccessful effort was made to establish a State board to control the business of undertaking; and another to prohibit the public exhibition of hypnotic experiments or treatment by any one except duly licensed physicians.

Several important labor bills became laws. One of them regulates the employment of women and children in manufacturing and mercantile establishments, by requiring that there shall be posted in such establishments a notice of the number of hours of labor required from employees therein and the hours of beginning and ending of such labor, and no one shall be required to work longer hours or to begin earlier or work later than the notice stipulates. The hours of labor shall not be changed after the beginning of any week unless by permission of factory inspectors. No child under sixteen years of age shall be employed where its life, limb, or health is endangered. No child under fifteen shall be employed to run an elevator, and no person under eighteen years shall be employed for an elevator running more than 200 feet a minute. No person

shall be employed in any tenement house or building in rear of tenement house in making clothing, feathers, cigars, etc., unless with the consent of the factory inspector, which permit may be revoked at any time. Not less than 250 cubic feet of air shall be allowed for each person in a workroom in the daytime, and 400 cubic feet at night. Another law, requiring special peace officers to be residents of the county in which they are to protect property, was passed to meet the complaints against the Pinkerton detectives. A third law prevents the manufacture and sale of clothing made in unhealthful places. This does away with what is known as the "sweating system." A fourth law extends the mechanics' lien law to municipal corporations. A fifth law limits the hours of service on steam railroads, by providing: First, that no engineer, fireman, conductor, or trainman who has rendered twenty-four hours' continuous service shall thereafter—under ordinary circumstances—continue service, or resume service, without first having had at least eight hours' rest; second, that the working day of every engineer, fireman, conductor, and trainman shall not exceed ten hours of service rendered within twelve consecutive hours; and third, that if any such engineer, fireman, conductor, or trainman shall render more than ten hours' service, he shall receive comparative compensation for the excess in addition to his daily compensation.

About $4,000,000 was appropriated for the ordinary expenses of the canals and claims upon the same for damages. The usual appropriation of about $500,000, to lengthen additional locks on the Erie Canal, was vetoed; but certain of the locks on the Oswego Canal will be lengthened, and a new law appropriates money to restore the water power on the Black river. The bills providing for grain elevators to be erected by the State at New York and Buffalo met with their usual fate. The appropriation for dredging the upper Hudson was only $41,000, there being a disposition to secure aid for this work from the Federal Government. New York and Brooklyn are to be connected by several new bridges. A charter was granted to the Manhattan and Long Island Bridge Company for the purpose of constructing, maintaining, and operating bridges over the East river and Harlem river between the city of New York and Long Island. An amendment was made to the charter of the New York and Long Island Bridge Company, whose bridge will connect with the Grand Central Depot. A charter was granted to the East River Bridge Company, and in connection with it the Rapid Transit act was amended so that connection may be made with the elevated railroad system. The Long Island and New York Terminal Railroad Company was authorized to construct, maintain, and operate a bridge over the East river between the cities of New York and Long Island City. The drawbridge over the Harlem river at Third Avenue was ordered to be raised, and a new bridge was provided to span the Harlem Ship Canal. Three bridge bills failed, as follow: Providing for a commission of bridges over the waters of the East river; incorporating the New York and Nassau Island Bridge Company for the purpose of constructing, maintaining, and operating bridges over the East river and Harlem river between the city of New York and Long Island. Charters were granted for a new bridge at Albany and for a bridge across the St. Lawrence river at Wolfe Island. The Brooklyn Bridge bonds were exempted from taxation.

The general railroad law was amended in many respects, but chiefly to allow any railroad company to build tunnels. Amendments were made to the stock corporation law prohibiting combinations and the issuing of stock at less than par. The Cantor act, incorporated into the General Railroad act, was amended so that if consent for a surface railroad is given it shall be provided that only one fare shall be charged. The number of hours of labor on steam surface railroads is limited to ten. The Railroad Commission act was amended so that the Secretary has larger powers. The commission sent four bills to the Legislature, which were not passed. The first related to the transportation of explosives; the second forbade the use of "center-bearing" rails on surface railroads, but this was incorporated into the amendment to the general law; the third provided that no new railroad should be constructed unless by the approval of the Board of Railroad Commissioners, but allowing an appeal to the courts; this was also incorporated in the amendment to the general law; the fourth provided for grade crossings. Another bill on grade crossings (copying the law of Massachusetts) failed to pass; but the city of Buffalo was given further powers in regard to grade crossings in that vicinity. In New York city the Rapid Transit act was amended so that connection may be made with the new East river bridge; also to allow the rapid transit commissioners to abandon a part of their route without abandoning the whole. Brooklyn has been exempted from the law requiring sand upon the tracks of surface railroads. Bills failed to pass preventing extortion or discrimination in freight or passenger rates; prohibiting the running of hand cars or the changing of brakes by unauthorized persons, and regulating the number of men to manage all kinds of trains.

A so-called "freedom of worship" law was passed, requiring all institutions in the State that receive public money to allow religious services on Sunday and private ministrations to the inmates in such manner as may best carry into effect the free exercise and enjoyment of religious profession and worship without discrimination. A charter was granted to the State Executive Committee of the Young Women's Christian Association of the State of New York. Dwelling houses owned by religious corporations, and the land upon which they stand, were exempted from taxation to an amount not exceeding $2,000 while actually used by an officiating clergyman. The Brooklyn Tabernacle was exempted from the taxes of 1889, and the estate of the late Bishop Loughlin, of Brooklyn, by a general bill, was exempted from the law taxing collateral inheritances.

After many attempts, lasting through a series of years, the excise laws were finally codified. The new law provides a general license at $250; beer and ale from $30 to $75; the hotel license remains as now; no saloon shall hereafter be licensed, except in the country, within 200 feet of a church or school; gives towns and cities local option; prohibits druggists from selling liquor, except on the written prescription of a physician, and each time a new prescription must be written; prohibits the granting of a license to any person who is engaged in the grocery business, where it is intended to carry on a liquor business in connection with or in the same place as the grocery business; allows hotels to sell on Sunday; and provides for the granting of licenses for all-night sales. Supplementary laws were passed allowing druggists licenses, and also allowing a recovery in a civil action for damages suffered by reason of liquor selling. The hiring of barmaids was prohibited. Another law makes it mandatory upon the Excise Board to render a decision upon any verified complaint of a violation of the excise laws within thirty days, or to be guilty of a misdemeanor; but a bill, providing that the excise commissioners can not act in a case until they have the testimony of the complainant under oath failed, as did also a bill seeking to restrict licenses to one in every 500 of the population of the State, and another allowing all town meetings to vote for or against license.

A charter was granted to the General Electric Company, with a capital of $100,000, to do a general electric business, and to combine all electrical companies in the State. Additional powers were given to the Buffalo and Niagara Falls Electric Power Company so that electricity may be furnished to the city of Buffalo. The term of office of the Board of Electrical Control in the city of New York was extended. Town boards may contract for electric lighting, not to exceed a term of three years; but a bill increasing the rate of taxation for electric lighting in villages was vetoed. Attempts were made, without success, to require the written consent of owners of three fifths of the property in cities and villages before electric-light poles can be placed, and also allowing villages to expend not to exceed 50 cents per capita per annum for electric lighting. The tampering with gas meters or pipes, whether used for illuminating, fuel, or natural gas, was made a misdemeanor.

New laws were enacted for the preservation of human life. One of them provides for the safety of workmen in mines by requiring more openings between the shafts. Another provides for a thorough examination of scaffolding, ropes, blocks, pulleys, and tackle used in the construction, repairing, or painting of buildings. The building laws of New York city were codified, and all buildings erected must be passed upon by the fire department. The Governor has appointed a commission of 3 experts to draft suitable laws for the construction, regulation, and inspection of buildings, and the better protection of life and property therein, applicable to the various cities in this State. The fire department of New York city must compel additional safeguards in hotels, lodging houses, and other buildings to facilitate escape in case of fire; and hotels, factories, etc., must be provided with fire-extinguishing apparatus, and must maintain all-night watches.

The health of the public will be better preserved by a number of laws providing as follows: Allowing any city of less than 50,000 inhabitants to establish free public baths; amending the village sewer act so that villages may have more scientific sewer systems; making it unlawful for any one to engage in or carry on the business of fat rendering, bone boiling, or the manufacture of fertilizers, or any business as a public nuisance within the corporate limits of 3 miles of any incorporated city of this State; providing for the registration of plumbers and the supervision of plumbing and drainage in the cities of the State; providing that any incorporated city or Village which has made such provision for the disposal of its sewage as not to pollute or contaminate therewith any river, stream, lake, or other body of water, may have and maintain an action in the Supreme Court to prevent the discharge of any sewage or substance deleterious to health, or which shall injure the potable qualities of the water in any river, stream, lake, or other body of water from which such incorporated city or village shall take or receive its water supply. Several bills increasing the prohibition of cigarettes failed to pass.

Before any child under the age of sixteen shall be licensed to appear in a theatrical exhibition, the mayor of the city or the president of the board of trustees of the village must give his consent; but such consent shall not be given unless notice has been given forty-eight hours before to some society for the prevention of cruelty to children, if such society exists in that locality.

It was enacted that no prisoner in any of the State prisons, penitentiaries, or reformatories shall be employed in making or finishing fur or wool hats, or in making or laundering shirts, collars, or cuffs. A State reformatory for women is to be built within the counties of New York or Kings, and $100,000 was appropriated to begin the same. The sum of $115,000 was re-appropriated to finish the House of Refuge for Women in western New York. The Eastern New York Reformatory, to be erected in Ulster County, was established, and $100,000 was appropriated for the same. The act of 1881 establishing a house of refuge for women was amended as to commitments, and $150,000 was appropriated. A State institution for epileptics was ordered to be established by commission. A small amount was appropriated for the maintenance of pauper insane who do not reside in this State. New York city is allowed to expend $500,000 for new buildings for the insane. The salaries of officers in the insane hospitals was raised. The Governor vetoed a bill prohibiting the opening of certain letters written or received by the inmates of the insane hospitals.

The laws in relation to elections were codified, and the penal code was amended so as to define more clearly the crimes against the elective franchise, like false registration, repeating, bribery, and the mutilation of ballots. Town meetings, by a majority vote of the town board, may use automatic ballot cabinets which register the vote by electricity. The inspectors of election in New York city hereafter will be 2 Democrats and 1 Republican in each election district, instead of 2 from each political party; and in that city all registers of voters and other useless election records shall be destroyed not less than two years after each election. A law was passed providing that all persons, without regard to sex, who are eligible to the office of school commissioner, and have the other qualifications now required by law, shall have the right to vote for school commissioners in the various commissioner districts.

Appropriations were made for the normal schools in Cortland and Geneseo. The boards of education in Troy and Albany were legislated out of office, and new boards were ordered. New York city is allowed to make further appropriations to enlarge or maintain the Metropolitan Museum of Art and the American Museum of Natural History, the latter on condition that it shall be opened on Sunday. Library companies in the city are allowed to consolidate. Brooklyn is authorized to issue $650,000 in bonds for new schoolhouses, and Long Island City about $200,000. Brooklyn may establish and maintain a public reading room at its own expense. The Dudley Observatory in Albany was allowed to sell its real estate and to change its location. The laws relating to the University of the State of New York were codified. Union College is allowed to be a trustee for its allied institutions. A law was passed for the encouragement of common-school libraries; another, providing for the endowment of public libraries; and a third, amending the law of 1890 relative to gifts and bequests so as to provide for and include public libraries.

For the World's Fair, or Columbian Exposition, at Chicago, $300,000 was appropriated. The Mayor of New York city was authorized to appoint a committee of 100 citizens to celebrate the four hundredth anniversary of the discovery of America on the 12th of October, 1892, and $50,000 was appropriated for that purpose. The day was made a legal holiday.

The Legislature passed a concurrent resolution, passed also by the last Legislature, amending the Constitution so that contested elections will be settled by the courts instead of by the two Houses of the Legislature. This amendment was voted on in November, 1892. An amendment increasing the number of judges in the Supreme Court was also voted upon at the same election. A convention to revise and amend the Constitution was ordered to assemble in Albany in June, 1893. One hundred and twenty-eight delegates will be elected by Assembly districts and 32 will be elected at large. In addition to the 160, the Governor shall appoint 3 representatives of the labor interests, 3 of the prohibitionists, and 3 representatives of woman suffrage.

Charters were granted to two new cities, Niagara Falls and Mount Vernon. The first has 10,000 and the second 12,000 inhabitants. This makes the whole number of incorporated cities in the State 34. A general code was enacted in relation to municipal corporations, more particularly to bonded indebtedness. The area of Rochester and Syracuse was enlarged, and the number of wards in each city was increased.

Other acts of the session were as follow:

Allowing a married woman to contract with her husband, or with any other person, to the same extent as if unmarried.

Enabling a divorced woman to convey her inchoate right of dower.

Making it a misdemeanor to cut, break, tap, or make

connection with any telegraph or telephone line, or to read or copy any message passing over the same.

Appropriating $800,000 to continue work on the new Capitol.

Appropriating $25,000 to make improvements at the Executive Mansion.

Codifying the laws in regard to Indians.

Codifying the laws relating to salt springs.

Census.—During February a State census was taken, with the following results:

COUNTIES.	Inhabitants.	Citizens.	Aliens.
Albany.....................	167,380	156,778	10,547
Allegany.................	43,131	42,644	487
Broome...................	62,791	61,589	1,202
Cattaraugus.............	61,776	59,702	2,074
Cayuga...................	62,919	60,691	2,228
Chautauqua.............	78,900	73,884	5,016
Chemung.................	47,223	45,845	1,378
Chenango................	37,601	37,120	481
Clinton..................	46,600	44,519	2,081
Columbia................	45,205	43,990	1,215
Cortland.................	28,289	27,951	818
Delaware.................	45,470	44,976	504
Dutchess.................	78,292	75,047	3,245
Erie......................	347,320	304,718	42,615
Essex....................	33,110	32,092	1,018
Franklin.................	39,848	37,054	2,794
Fulton...................	38,479	37,285	1,194
Genesee..................	33,434	32,327	1,107
Green....................	31,142	30,844	298
Hamilton................	5,216	4,754	462
Herkimer................	47,489	45,768	1,721
Jefferson................	70,358	66,245	4,113
Kings....................	995,276	868,983	126,293
Lewis....................	30,244	29,408	886
Livingston..............	37,009	35,448	1,561
Madison	42,203	41,671	582
Monroe..................	200,059	181,282	18,827
Montgomery.............	46,078	43,827	2,251
New York................	1,801,739	1,423,984	377,755
Niagara..................	64,207	59,043	5,164
Oneida...................	123,756	117,205	6,551
Onondaga................	150,208	142,058	8,150
Ontario..................	48,718	46,894	1,744
Orange...................	97,591	93,085	4,484
Orleans..................	30,763	28,733	2,030
Oswego...................	70,969	69,022	1,947
Otsego...................	50,324	49,825	499
Putnam...................	14,280	13,825	905
Queens...................	141,805	123,974	17,831
Rensselaer...............	128,000	120,756	7,244
Richmond................	53,452	46,592	6,860
Rockland................	33,725	31,324	2,401
St. Lawrence............	85,254	79,679	5,575
Saratoga.................	57,291	54,909	2,382
Schenectady.............	34,194	31,630	2,564
Schoharie................	27,873	27,737	136
Schuyler.................	16,861	16,826	585
Seneca...................	26,542	25,928	614
Steuben..................	82,468	81,400	1,068
Suffolk..................	63,572	58,872	4,700
Sullivan.................	31,914	31,481	433
Tioga....................	29,675	29,365	310
Tompkins................	33,612	33,159	453
Ulster...................	87,652	85,392	2,260
Warren..................	28,616	28,157	461
Washington..............	46,458	45,144	1,314
Wayne...................	48,259	46,538	1,721
Westchester.............	145,106	129,224	15,882
Wyoming.................	31,218	30,253	965
Yates....................	20,801	20,316	485
Total..........	6,510,162	5,787,773	722,389

The following is the population of cities: New York, 1,801,739; Brooklyn, 930,633; Buffalo, 278,796; Rochester, 144,834; Albany, 97,120; Syracuse, 91,944; Troy, 64,986; Utica, 46,608; Long Island City, 35,745; Binghamton, 34,514; Yonkers, 31,419; Elmira, 29,911; Auburn, 24,-737; Newburg, 24,536; Cohoes, 23,234; Poughkeepsie, 23,196; Schnectady, 22,858; Oswego, 21,966; Kingston, 21,495; Jamestown, 18,617; Amsterdam, 18,542; Watertown, 16,982; Lockport, 16,088; Gloversville, 14,694; Rome, 13,-638; Ithaca, 13,450; Ogdensburg, 11,955; Hornellsville, 11,898; Middletown, 11,612; Dunkirk, 10,040; and Corning, 10,025.

Apportionment.—In the execution of the new apportionment law, the deprivation of representatives to strong Republican districts, with the increasing representation accorded to Democratic cities, led to various appeals to the courts. Thus St. Lawrence county, which has had 3 Assemblymen constantly from 1846, was given but 1; the effect of this re luction would naturally tend to lessen the influence of the voters of that county. In similar fashion, Cattaraugus, Jefferson, Washington, Chautauqua, and half a dozen other counties which have had 2 members each since 1846, were to have 1; and Ulster County, which has had 3 members since 1857, was to have but 2.

Several decisions in the general term of the Supreme Court were given, and the matter carried to the Supreme Court of Appeals, where, on Oct. 16, the apportionment act of 1892 was declared constitutional. Judge Rufus W. Peckham wrote the prevailing opinion and Judge Gray a supplemental opinion upholding the law. A dissenting opinion was written by Judge Charles Andrews and concurred in by Judge Finch, excepting to the stand taken by the other five judges as to the question of inequality in the apportionment. In the People ex rel. Pond, appellant, against the Board of Supervisors of Monroe County, and the People ex rel. Horn, appellant, against the Board of Supervisors of Oneida County, order reversed in both cases and motions for a mandamus were granted with costs in all courts. These were cases in which the court was asked to issue orders for writs of mandamus compelling the boards of supervisors of Monroe and Oneida counties to redistrict the Assembly districts in those counties, in compliance with the apportionment law passed by the last Legislature. The order of the lower court was affirmed with costs in all courts in the case of the People ex rel. George E. Carter, of Utica, appellant, against Frank Rice, Secretary of State. In this case the court was asked to grant an injunction order restraining the Secretary of State from recognizing the new apportionment law, or sending out notices of election of members of Assembly to county clerks except under the apportionment law of 1879, the lower court having refused to grant such an order.

The World's Fair.—Under the authority conferred by the World's Fair act, Gov. Flower, in April, appointed as general managers of the New York exhibit at the World's Columbian Exposition Louis M. Howland, of New York, Walter L. Sessions, of Jamestown, and Charles A. Sweet, of Buffalo, who will act with the commissioners appointed by the President of the United States, namely, Chauncey M. Depew, of New York, John Boyd Thacher, of Albany, and Gorton W. Allen, of Auburn. John Foord, of New York, was appointed secretary of the Board of General Managers. Likewise Gov. Flower appointed three commissioners from each judicial district to manage the exhibits from the territory comprised in their districts.

Organization was promptly effected on April 20, when Chauncey M. Depew was made president and Gorton W. Allen vice-president. At a meeting held on May 8 plans for a State building prepared by McKim, Mead & White, of New York city, were accepted. It will be a handsome structure two stories in height, 193 feet long and 97 feet wide, with open terraces on either end. It will be built of staff, a building material made of gravel, cement, etc., and having the appearance of white marble. There will be a terra-cotta roof, and the general style of architecture will be the Italian renaissance. On the ground floor of the building there will be an information bureau, post office, and parcel departments, and on the second floor will be an auditorium and reception rooms, with an apartment equipped for the newspaper fraternity. The auditorium will be 42 by 82 feet. The entire left half of the building will be devoted to the uses of the women's department. The building alone is to cost $77,600, and the furnishings and interior and exterior decorations will cost, approximately, $50,000, outside of $60,000 provided for that purpose.

On Oct. 22 the formal assignment of this building to exposition uses was effected by Chauncey M. Depew as president of the Board of Managers, its acceptance by Director-General Davis, and addresses by Gov. Flower, Archbishop Corrigan, with a dedicatory poem by William H. McElroy followed.

Holidays.—According to the laws of this State, the public holidays are as follow: New Year's Day, Washington's Birthday, Decoration Day, the Fourth of July, Labor Day, Christmas Day, every general election day, and "any day appointed or recommended by the Governor of this State or the President of the United States as a day of thanksgiving or fasting and prayer or other religious observance."

In accordance with the public wishes, an act was passed by the Legislature, and approved by the Governor, designating April 27, 1892, from 12 o'clock at noon. a half holiday in and for the counties of New York, Kings, and Westchester, in order that the celebration of the laying of the corner stone of the memorial of Gen. Grant might be observed. Also, an act of the Legislature was signed making Oct. 12 a legal holiday; and in accordance with a proclamation of the President of the United States, Oct. 21 was observed as a national holiday.

Education.—This department is under the charge of a superintendent, whose salary is $5,000. The present incumbent is James F. Crooker. According to his report, the number of children of school age during the year 1892 was 1,845,519. The number attending the public schools was 1,073,093, leaving 772,426 children to be educated in private or parochial schools, or without instruction in any schools. The amount expended for public schools during 1892 was $21,134,516, an increase of $865,398 over that of 1891.

The Governor, in his message, says: "If the ratio of public-school children to the whole number of children of school age continues to decrease, it will not be long before half the latter are educated at private expense or are not educated at all. It is well known that thousands of children in the State are growing up without any school education whatever, and I renew my

recommendation of last year for a carefully guarded compulsory education law."

The regents of the University of the State of New York met with severe losses in the death of George William Curtis, a regent since 1864, and Francis Kernan, a regent since 1870, and by the resignation of Leslie W. Russell, a regent since 1878. To the last vacancy Bishop William Croswell Doane was chosen, who subsequently became vice-chancellor on the advancement of Anson J. Upson to the chancellorship made vacant by the death of Mr. Curtis.

Charities.—The annual report of the New York State Board of Charities shows that the total expenditures for charitable, correctional, and reformatory purposes during the year ended Oct. 1, 1892, was $18,228,712. The number of beneficiaries of the various charitable, correctional, and reformatory institutions on Oct. 1, 1892, was 76,807. Of these, 17,457 were insane, 24,074 dependent children, 7,875 aged and friendless persons, and 10,539 ordinary poorhouse inmates, the remainder being in blind and deaf-and-dumb asylums and in various reformatory institutions. Concerning the crowded condition of the State Reformatory at Elmira, and the fact that the managers of the institution purpose to ask for an appropriation for additional buildings, the board advises against the granting of such appropriation, and recommends the establishment of an eastern reformatory on the same plan, to be near New York and Brooklyn. The House of Refuge for Women at Hudson is greatly overcrowded, the institution is mismanaged, and good discipline is not maintained. The Houses of Refuge on Randall's Island and at Rochester are in a satisfactory condition, and the management of both in good hands. Gross abuses in the management of the Oswego County Poorhouse have been found, the responsibility for which is placed upon the county superintendent of the poor. The board asks for an appropriation of $40,000 for 1893, in order to carry out the law directing the return to their homes of paupers from other States and counties, and reports favorably upon the workings of that law during the year just closed. The board refers to the necessity for a more decided restriction of foreign immigration, and believes Congress at its present session will enact laws obviously necessary for the protection of the country against burdensome immigrants.

Lunacy.—The State Commission in Lunacy consists of Carlos F. McDonald, Goodwin Brown, and Henry A. Reeves. According to their annual report, on Oct. 1, 1892, the number of committed insane in the State was as follows: State hospitals, 7,832; licensed private asylums, 902; asylums of New York and Kings Counties, 7,887; in county poorhouses awaiting removal, 802; total, 17,423. The policy inaugurated in 1890 of assuming care and custody of dependent insane, with the exception of those in New York and Kings counties, will go into final effect before Oct. 1, 1893. The work of preparation is nearly finished; 9 State hospitals, costing upward of $10,000,000, have been put in readiness; about 7,900 patients from the county poorhouses have been placed in the State hospitals, and the remainder (about 700) are expected to be transferred before May 1, 1893. In order to provide for the maintenance and support of these nearly 9,000 patients the Legislature will be obliged to increase the tax rate by one third of a mill. It has been computed that the cost to be provided for, including salaries, transportation, etc., will be about $1,300,000. The State has been in the habit of providing for $200,000, so that the actual increase of taxation will be about $1,100,-000. In addition, the Commission in Lunacy estimates that provision will have to be made for an increase of 440 patients for the year ending Oct. 1, 1894. These additional accommodations, it is hoped, can be supplied by judicious enlargement of existing hospitals rather than by the construction of new institutions.

A most important reform instituted has been the separation of the criminal from the non-criminal insane. Nearly all of the former have been transferred to the new asylum at Matteawan, near Fishkill on the Hudson. By an official decision of the Attorney-General, the Matteawan asylum has been entirely substituted for the old institution, which has ceased to exist legally, and commitments and transfers on "criminal orders" now apply to the new asylum.

Vital Statistics.—The State Board of Health is composed of the following officials: Thomas Newbold, President; Lewis Balch, Secretary; W. E. Milbank; Thomas S. Dawes; Joseph D. Bryant; Maurice Perkins; John W. Whitbeck; Simon W. Rosendale, Attorney-General *ex officio;* and William T. Jenkins, Health Officer, of New York city, *ex officio.* It has issued the following summary of the mortality of the State for 1892: The total number of deaths during the year was 130,750. This makes the death rate 20·78 to each 1,000 inhabitants; in 1891 it was estimated at 21·43; in 1890 and 1889 at 19·65. The infant mortality (under five years) was 33·5 per cent. The zymotic death rate was 182·87 to the 1,000 deaths from all causes; for the first six months, 132·57; for the last six months, 236·34. In 1891 it was 178, and for the five years preceding, 191. Typhoid fever caused 300 fewer deaths than last year. From diphtheria there were 5,918 deaths, or 850 more than in 1891. Scarlet fever caused 2,177 deaths (2,254 in 1891). Measles caused 1,350 deaths (1,200 in 1891). Whooping cough caused 921 deaths (825 in 1891). There is little variation from last year in the deaths from malarial diseases and cerebro-spinal fever. Smallpox prevailed throughout the year in the maritime district. Of 143 deaths, all but 1 occurred there. Typhus fever has been limited to New York city through the year. From epidemic influenza (grippe), the third appearance of which began in December, 1891, and did not pass entirely away until early summer, 6,000 deaths were estimated to have occurred, and 8,000 including December. It seems to have reappeared in very mild form toward the close of the year. From all local diseases there was a large increase in mortality during the influenza epidemic. The death rate from old age was especially large in January. From consumption there were 13,471 deaths. There was 1 death in every 475·57 of the population, which is about the average for the five years preceding.

Crime.—The statistics for the year ending Oct. 31, 1891, submitted to the Legislature show that the whole number of convictions reported

VOL. XXXII.—33 A

by county clerks in courts of record were 3,607; increase over last year, 243. The convictions thus reported were as follow: Offenses against the person, 617; increase over last year, 67; offenses against property with violence, 959; increase, 65; offenses against property, without violence, 1,540; increase, 188; offenses against the currency, 92; increase, 11; offenses not included in the foregoing, 399; decrease, 88; convictions in courts of record reported by county clerks, 3,607; convictions in courts of record reported by sheriffs, 3,258; excess reported by county clerks, 349; females convicted in courts of record, 162; increase, 6. Special sessions: Convictions reported by county clerks, 61,610; decrease, 2,114. Males convicted in courts of special sessions as reported by county clerks, 54,891; females convicted in courts of special sessions as reported by county clerks, 6,719. Special sessions in cities reported by sheriffs: Convictions, 76,634; decrease, 4,894. Females convicted, special sessions, sheriffs' reports, 20,-635; decrease, 1,595. Aggregate number of convictions: Convictions in courts of record, from county clerks' reports, 3,607; convictions in courts of special sessions, from county clerks' reports, 61,610; total convictions, 65,217.

The State prisons during 1892 came within $140,498.90 of being self-supporting. Prisoners were employed on 22 different industries, and the earnings were $81,707.72 greater than those of the preceding year. At Auburn Prison the earnings exceeded the cost of care and maintenance. Gov. Flower in his message calls attention to the fact that there is now standing unused at Auburn the State building formerly occupied as a prison for insane criminals. He recommends its conversion into a prison for female felons. It was the policy of the State prior to 1877 to maintain a separate prison for females, but since that year they have been sent to county penitentiaries, the State paying a daily amount for their board and keeping. There are now 155 female felons thus confined. The unoccupied building at Auburn is admirably adapted for such inmates. It would easily accommodate 200 prisoners, and is ready for use immediately.

Insurance.—This department is under the direction of Superintendent James F. Pierce (salary, $7,000) and Deputy Michael Shannon (salary, $4,500). The annual report for 1891 was issued in May, from which we find that in 1891 there were 31 life companies, with assets of $819,-402,851.92. Of this, New York State companies have $489,018,671.66; companies of other States, $330,384,180.26. The liabilities, excepting $6,-040,500 of capital stock, were $723,045,944.52. The reserve aggregates $711,281,782. The liabilities of New York State companies as reported are $431,217,618.18; companies of other States, $291,828,326.34. The surplus as regards policy holders is: New York State companies, $57,801,053.48; companies of other States, $38,-555,853.92; aggregate, $96,356,907.40. The aggregate income of New York State companies was $134,266,532.28; other States' companies, $67,664,892.70; making the gross income $201,-931,424.98. The total premium receipts for 1891 were $162,624,444.28.

The expenditures of 1891 were $135,792,048.09.

Of this, $62,731,496.63 was paid for claims; $16,-230,890.96 for lapsed and surrendered policies; $13,991,225.64 in dividends to p icy holders; $488,062.60 in dividends to stockbblders: $21,-379,690.66 for commissions; $8,246,316.59 for salaries and medical examiners' fees; and $72,-724,365.01 for. miscellaneous purposes. This shows that $92,953,613.23 was paid to policy holders. while the cost of management. including dividends, was $42,838,434.86.

In 1891 the New York State companies issued 210,480 policies, insuring $645,246,751. and terminated 126,730 policies, insuring $432,439,788. The companies of other States issued 112,953 policies, insuring $283,009,587, and terminated 65,960 policies, insuring $164,694,115. Total, 323,433 policies issued, insuring $928,256,338, and 192,690 policies terminated, insuring $597,-133,903.

In regard to the insurance code, prepared by the Statutory Revision Commission, the Superintendent says: " No sweeping or serious amendments to the present laws have been made, and the revision is virtually the existing statutes in more presentable garb. There has been enacted in this revision under the requirements relating to 'fraternal beneficiary societies, orders, or associations,' a provision which permits these associations to make a ' payment of money upon the expiration of a fixed period,' and without reference to death or disability." The adoption of this clause was opposed, but without success.

All organizations that promise to pay any definite amount to a member during his lifetime, without regard to his physical condition, are frauds.

Mr. Pierce devoted much space to the recent investigation of the New York Life, and says: " There can be no doubt but that under the new *régime* evils and irregularities will not be tolerated, and that this company's affairs are now to be conducted in the best interests of its policy holders, who are to be congratulated in having made such a judicious selection in choosing an executive officer."

National Guard.—The special charge of the State militia is under the control of the adjutant-general on the Governor's staff. The present incumbent is Maj.-Gen. Josiah Porter. According to the annual report, the National Guard comprises 13 regiments, 1 battalion, and 46 separate companies of infantry, 5 batteries of artillery, 1 troop of cavalry, and 3 signal corps. The strength of the Guard is: First Brigade, 5,062 officers and men; Second, 3,004 officers and men; Third, 2,690 officers and men; Fourth, 2,119 officers and men; general headquarters, 31 officers and men; aggregate strength, 12,906 officers and men. The Second Battery is now fully equipped with the new 3·2-inch steel breech-loading guns, caissons, and harness of the latest regulation pattern, and a combination battery wagon and forge.

Concerning the camp at Peekskill, Gen. Porter says: " The highest attendance at the camp during 1892 was 5,350 officers and men." He renews his recommendation looking to the proper maintenance of the camp as a permanent institution for military instruction. Of this he adds: " Placed on an established foundation, systematized as a school, with a staff of competent in-structors, it will accomplish much more for the military forces of the State than has been or can be done in any other manner or under any other system."

The naval militia is reported in good condition. Uniforms will be issued to it as soon as the pattern and material are prescribed.

The great value of the services of the National Guard at the strike (see " Labor Troubles ") in Buffalo are mentioned. Concerning the expenses incurred, paid by the State up to Nov. 30, in this movement of troops of the First, Second, and Third Brigades, including the pay, and pay only, of the separate companies and Fifth Battery of the Fourth Brigade, paid by the State, up to Nov. 30, was $192,647.30, as follow: Subsistence, $51,175.67; transportation; $48,072.51; pay, $84,-260.85; clothing, camp and garrison equipage, $6,711.11; quartermaster's stores, $2,427.16; total, $192,647.30. The number of men in attendance by brigades was as follow: First, 2,237; Second, 1,410; Third, 1,586; Fourth, 1,963. The Third Brigade, commanded by Gen. Robert Shaw Oliver, had the highest percentage (93·20) of men in the field.

Labor Troubles.—The most important event during the year was the strike at Buffalo of the railroad switchmen. It began on Aug. 13 by the men leaving their work. The railroads chiefly affected were the Lehigh Valley, the Erie, and the Buffalo creek. The demands of the men were for a day of ten hours, and for increase in wages ranging from 2 to 4 cents an hour. As the freight yard at Buffalo is the place where the transfer of freight between the Eastern and Western roads is made, its strategic importance is manifest, and at once a blockade occurred, preventing traffic and causing inconvenience to shippers over a large area of country. The strikers continued quiet until after sunset on Aug. 14, when disorder and rioting began. Freight trains and passenger trains were thrown from the track, buildings were burned, coal trains were sent running down high trestles, crashing into cars at the bottom and causing great destruction; and, worst of all, hundreds of cars were burned. These acts of violence were publicly deplored by Grand Master Frank Sweeney, of the Switchmen's Mutual Aid Association of North America, and by the strikers themselves; but as they continued, the sheriff of Erie County tried to protect the property of the railroads by means of special deputies sworn in for the occasion, but as many of these were induced to desert, an appeal was made to the Governor, as follows:

We have become satisfied that the situation here in Buffalo under the pending strike has become so serious, that we ask that the National Guard of the State be called out to protect the lives and property of citizens of this city and county.

August Beox, *Sheriff.*
Charles F. Bishop, *Mayor.*

Orders were at once issued by the Governor to the adjutant-general, and portions of the First, Second, and Third Brigades, mustering in all 5,233 men, were sent to Buffalo, reaching there within forty-eight hours from the issuance of the orders. The Forty-seventh Separate Company, of Hornellsville, joined the other troops on Aug. 21, making the entire force of militia on the ground, including those of the Fourth Brigade, called out upon request of the sheriff and judge of the Supreme Court, to number 7,196 men. The presence of this large military force prevented further violence and restored civil order. On Aug. 25, 26, and 27 the troops were withdrawn.

Canals.—The tonnage of the canals during the season of 1892 was 281,477 tons less than for the season of 1891. The total tonnage was 4,281,-995 tons, comprising the following classes of freight: Products of the forest, 1,249,381 tons; products of agriculture, 1,038,851 tons; products of manufactures, 125,781 tons; merchandise, 292,-468 tons; all other articles, 1,575,514 tons. The decrease in tonnage is attributed to the fact that the railways have advanced their equipment to such a degree that they are able to transport freight as cheaply as the canals. The only canal boatmen who can now compete with the railroads are the few who have steam canal boats and tow from 3 to 5 boats with them each trip.

To increase the efficiency of the canals, it is urged that means for the propulsion of canal boats by electricity be devised, and that the power from the waste water at the locks be used for its generation. Also certain improvements are needed to increase the usefulness of the canal system. Careful examination by the Governor with the State Engineer and Superintendent of Public Works of the repairs now needed showed that a large appropriation would not be necessary to maintain the canal system in a proper state of efficiency and make necessary improvements. The required dredging of the Champlain Canal will not demand a larger expenditure than $50,000 for the present year. The expense of repairing the Schoharie creek aqueduct should not exceed $25,000, that of the upper Mohawk aqueduct $20,000, and that of the lower Mohawk aqueduct $25,000. These improvements are, however, imperatively needed, and should not be delayed. The Erie basin at Buffalo should be deepened so as to give the canals the same facilities at this terminal point that the railroads have.

Fisheries.—The Commissioners of Fisheries are Robert Hamilton, William H. Bowman, D. G. Hackney, A. S. Joline, and Lawrence D. Huntington. According to their annual report, issued during July, more fish were distributed than in any year since the creation of the commission, and more valuable food fish were turned into the waters of the State than in any previous year. The following is a list of the food fish deposited last year: Pike, 4,000,000; ciscoes, 3,000,000; whitefish, 9,000,000; channel pickerel, 2,000,000; shad, 2,424,000; tom cods, 3,200,000; smelts, 7,400,000; lobsters, 27,700; frost fish, 7,400,000; total, 38,451,700.

The Governor, in his message, says: " A personal investigation during the summer into the work of the Commissioners of Fisheries, including visits to some of the existing hatcheries, persuaded me that only 3 out of the 5 hatcheries are located properly for the successful propagation of fish. I suggest that hereafter, when new hatcheries are needed, the location of the same be left to the discretion of the Commissioners of Fisheries. They are presumably better qualified by reason of their expert knowledge to judge of the comparative merits of dif-

ferent localities as places for fish culture, and such a transfer of responsibility would check a tendency recently observable in the Legislature to make the creation of one new hatchery depend upon the creation of one or more others."

The United States Fish Commission last year caused 9,500,000 shad fry to be deposited in the Hudson between Newburg and Troy.

New Game Laws.—In May the Governor signed the bill for the codification of the game laws, which was the result of many months of work on the part of the special commission appointed in 1890. The provisions of the code are: The Governor to appoint five commissioners of fisheries for one, two, three, four, and five years respectively; but the term of office of each shall be five years, thus retiring one every year. One of the commissioners shall have charge of shell-fish work. They shall have an office in the Capitol at Albany, and hold meetings on the first Friday of January, and every alternate month thereafter. There may be a branch office in the city of New York. The secretary shall have a salary of $2,000. The board shall appoint 20 game and fish protectors, to hold office at pleasure; the chief protector shall have $2,000 a year and his expenses, and each of the other protectors $500 a year and his expenses; the chief protector shall have rooms in the Capitol at Albany.

The new laws prohibit the following:

Game.—Deer, between Nov. 1 and Aug. 15. No person shall take more than 2 deer in a season. Protected in Ulster, Greene, Sullivan, and Delaware Counties for five years. Venison may be possessed between Aug. 15 and Nov. 15. Hounding deer forbidden between Oct. 21 and Sept. 10. Forbidden at all times in St. Lawrence, Delaware, Greene, and Ulster Counties, and between Dec. 1 and Oct. 1 in Sullivan County. Black and gray squirrels, between Jan. 1 and Sept. 1. Hares and rabbits not protected. Wildfowl (except geese and brant), between May 1 and Sept. 1. Quail, between Jan. 1 and Nov. 1. If lawfully killed, or from out the State, may be possessed to Feb. 1. Protected for five years in Orleans, Livingston, Monroe, Cayuga, Seneca, Wayne, Tompkins, Tioga, Onondaga, Steuben, and Cortland Counties. Woodcock and grouse, between Jan. 1 and Aug. 15. If lawfully killed, or from out the State, may be possessed to Feb. 1. Wilson's or English snipe, plover, rail, mudhen, gallinule, grebe, bittern, surf birds, curlew, water chicken, bay snipe, shore birds, between Jan. 1 and Sept. 1. No protection in Onondaga, Wayne, Oneida, Cayuga, Wyoming, Genesee, Niagara, Monroe, Erie, Chautauqua, Cattaraugus, and Orleans Counties. Meadow larks, between Jan. 1 and Nov. 1. All other wild birds (except English sparrow, crane, hawk, crow, raven, crow blackbird, common blackbird, kingfisher) protected always.

Fish.—Trout, between Sept. 1 and April 15. (In Spring Brook creek, Sept. 1 to April 1. In Lake George, Sept. 1 to May 1.) Lawful length, 6 inches. Salmon trout, landlocked salmon, between Oct. 1 and May 1. Lawful length, 6 inches. Black bass, Oswego bass, between Jan. 1 and May 30. (In Lake George, Jan. 1 to Aug. 1. Black Lake, Jan. 1 to May 5.) Lawful length, 8 inches. Muskallonge, between Jan. 1 and May 30. Salmon, between Aug. 15 and March 1.

Lawful length, 18 inches. Wall-eyed pike, yellow bass, pike in Susquehanna river and tributaries, between Nov. 1 and May 30.

Long Island.—Wildfowl (except geese and brant), May 1 to Oct. 1. Plover, etc., Jan. 1 to July 1. Woodcock and grouse, Jan. 1 to Nov. 1. Trout, Sept. 1 to April 1. Salmon trout, landlocked salmon, Oct. 1 to April 1. Black bass, Jan. 1 to May 30. Hares, rabbits, Jan. 1 to Nov. 1. Deer, except from Nov. 10 to 16 inclusive. Black and gray squirrels, Jan. 1 to Nov. 1.

Oyster Culture.—During 1887 an act to encourage oyster planting in Long Island Sound was passed. Very little had been done in the deep-sea cultivation of oysters before that time, and the planters who supply the markets relied almost entirely upon Virginia for sea oysters for cultivation. Since then the industry has made such rapid progress that now conservative estimates place the value of the oysters lying on the beds of Long Island Sound at $1,500,000, and the number of men employed in the industry at 10,000. During the past year 116,000 barrels of oysters, valued at $580,000, were shipped to Europe from New York city. There are about 400,000 acres of water area in the sound which are available for oyster culture under the provisions of the act of 1887. Of this number, upward of 17,000 have been leased. The law provides that plots may be granted to the highest bidder for a perpetual lease. So little has been known about the industry that the greater number of these grants has not brought to the State more than $1 or $2 an acre. It has been demonstrated, however, that while the business is attended by considerable risk, there is an extraordinary percentage of profit when it is at all successful. For this reason recent bids for grants have been somewhat higher.

Political.—On Feb. 24 a Democratic State Convention met in Albany. Edward Murphy, Jr., called the meeting to order, and subsequently Daniel E. Sickles was made permanent chairman. A platform containing the following clauses was adopted:

We are against the coinage of any silver dollar which is not of the intrinsic value of every other dollar of the United States.

We therefore denounce the new Sherman silver law, under which one tenth of our gold stock has been exported, and all our silver output is dammed up at home, as a false pretense, but actual hindrance of return to free bimetallic coinage, and as tending only to produce a change from one kind of monometallism to another.

We therefore unite with the friends of honest money everywhere in stigmatizing the Sherman progressive-silver-basis law as no solution of the gold and silver question, and as a fit appendix to the subsidy and bounty swindle, the McKinley worse-than-war tariff, the Blaine reciprocity humbug, the squandered surplus, the advancing deficit, the defective census and falsified representation, and there volutionary procedures of the billion congress—all justly condemned by the people's great uprising last November (1890); a verdict which, renewed next year (1892), will empower Democratic statesmen to guide the people's councils and to execute the people's will.

In obedience to the mandate of the Democratic voters of New York, the delegates selected by this convention were instructed to present to the National Democratic Convention the name of David B. Hill as their candidate for President of the United States—"a Democrat who has led his party from victory to victory for seven successive years, and who has never known defeat."

The said delegates were further instructed to act as a unit in all matters intrusted to their charge, said action to be determined by the vote of a majority of the delegates.

Delegates to the national convention were chosen, including Roswell P. Flower, Edward Murphy, Jr., Daniel E. Sickles, and Henry W. Slocum, as delegates-at-large; also 36 presidential electors were chosen.

At the same time a gathering of anti-Hill Democrats met in Albany and chose William D. Locke as chairman. After issuing a protest against the action of the Democratic State Convention, they adjourned, to meet in Syracuse on May 31, when, under the permanent chairmanship of John D. Kernan, a platform was adopted containing the following clause:

The Democratic party retains unshaken confidence in the ability and lofty integrity of Grover Cleveland and in his devotion to public duty. He is the choice of an overwhelming majority of the Democrats of New York, and the country may rely with confidence on his ability to carry the State triumphantly in November. We believe that by nominating him to lead the party in the approaching contest for the presidency, the national convention will carry out the almost unanimous wish of the party, and best consult the welfare of the country. We pledge ourselves to support the candidates nominated in Chicago. The delegation chosen by this convention is instructed to act as a unit according to the determination of a majority of its members.

Delegates were then chosen to represent this convention at the national convention.

Meanwhile a Republican State convention was held in Albany on April 28. William A. Sutherland called the convention to order, and Whitelaw Reid was made permanent chairman. In the platform adopted the following clauses appear:

In the success of this administration we recognize the consummate ability of President Harrison and the wisdom and sagacity of his Cabinet, and especially of his chief Cabinet officer, James G. Blaine, whose strong hold upon and intimate relationship with the management of public affairs have been of lasting benefit to the American people.

Concerning local matters the following was adopted:

We denounce the Legislature thus feloniously constituted for its violation of the principles of genuine home rule in enacting notoriously partisan charter amendments; for granting valuable franchises to political favorites without recompense to the people; for the attempted invasion of Central Park; for its removal of wholesome restrictions upon the liquor traffic; for its wasteful expenditure of the people's money, which has increased the tax rate 44 per cent. over that of last year; for its utter failure to keep its ante-election pledges in behalf of ballot reform and tax reform; for its broken promises to the workingmen; for its whitewashing of a guilty judge of the Court of Appeals; for its return to the methods of Tweed in its iniquitous measure conferring upon Tammany officials absolute control of the boards of election inspectors in the city of New York; for constantly legislating for its partisan aggrandizement against the rural districts; for its unconstitutional and fraudulent midwinter enumeration, by which the population of the rural districts was diminished and that of the cities enormously increased, as the basis of an apportionment by which the representation of Republican portions of the State in the Legislature and in Congrees was reduced and all the increase given to Democratic cities, as is signally illustrated by the fact that Republican Monroe, with 181,000 population, receives only 3 Assemblymen, while Democratic Albany, with 156,000 population, is awarded 4.

Subsequently, in October, Charles Andrews was named for the chief justiceship of the Court of Appeals by the Republican State Committee, which nomination was accepted by the Democrats. For the same office, Joseph A. Bogardus was named by the Prohibitionists, Alexander Jonas by the Socialists, and Henry A. Hicks by the People's party.

At the election held on Nov. 8 the electoral tickets received votes as follow: Democratic, 654,868; Republican, 609,350; Prohibition, 38,190; People's, 16,429; and Socialist Labor, 17,656; thus indicating a plurality of 45,518 votes for the Democratic. On the same occasion constitutional amendments were voted for as follow: To transfer legislative contested cases to courts: For, 174,678; against, 180,030. To increase Supreme Court justices: For, 161,759; against, 198,110. To sell salt springs at Onondaga: For, 170,765; against, 171,442. To the State Legislature, 74 Democratic and 54 Republican Assemblymen were elected; also, 20 Democratic and 14 Republican Congressmen were chosen.

NEW YORK CITY. Government.—The city officials who held office during the year were: Mayor, Hugh J. Grant; President of the Board of Aldermen, John H.V. Arnold; Register, Frank T. Fitzgerald; and Sheriff, John J. Gorman, all of whom are Tammany Democrats, and entered on the duties of their offices on Jan. 1, 1891.

Finances.—The condition of the city debt on Jan. 1, 1893, is shown in the accompanying table:

During the year bonds were issued for public improvements amounting to $9,689,919.30; still the public debt, in lieu of diminishing, as was the case last year, was increased by $1,116,309.85.

The interest on the city debt for 1892 amounted to $6,764,300.42. The outstanding bonds were issued when the city was forced to pay 5, 6, and 7 per cent. in order to secure a market for its obligations. The bonds bearing the highest rate of interest will fall due in 1904.

On Oct. 3 the tax books were opened for the receipt of taxes. The total tax for 1892 was $33,725,555.84, and the tax rate 1·85 per cent. on real property, while the rate on personal estate of corporations was 1·7135 per cent. All taxpayers who paid their taxes before Nov. 1 received a discount at the rate of 6 per cent. from date of payment to Dec. 1, 1892; after which 1 per cent. was added to the sum due.

The Sinking Fund Commissioners authorized the payment and canceling on Oct. 28 of city bonds to the amount of $4,286,315.13 due Nov. 1. Of the amount, the Sinking Fund Commissioners held $352,215.13, which was canceled. The balance of $3,934,100 held by private persons and corporations was redeemed. These payments, which formerly were made by taxation, are now made from the accumulations of the sinking fund under the provisions of section 191 of the Consolidation act, which permits such action when it will not impair the preferred claims on the fund. This is by far the largest payment that has ever been made under the provisions referred to. The transaction included the payment of $3,929,400 7-per-cent. city improvement bonds and $4,700 6-per-cent. county courthouse stock. The amount canceled in-

FUNDED DEBT.	Outstanding Dec. 31, 1891.	Issued during 1891.	Redeemed during 1891.	Outstanding Dec. 31, 1891.
1. Payable from the sinking fund, under ordinances of the Common Council	$4,267,200 00			$4,267,200 00
2. Payable from the sinking fund, under provisions of chapter 383, section 6, Laws of 1878, and section 176, New York City Consolidation act of 1882	9,700,000 00			9,700,000 00
3. Payable from the sinking fund, under provisions of chapter 383, section 8, Laws of 1878, and section 192, New York City Consolidation act of 1882, as amended by chapter 178, Laws of 1889	37,633,927 38	$6,399,116 40	$190,018 88	43,843,024 95
4. Payable from the sinking fund, under provisions of chapter 79, Laws of 1889	9,782,000 00	21,000 00		9,803,000 00
5. Payable from the sinking fund, under provisions of the constitutional amendment adopted Nov. 4, 1884	26,600,000 00	1,650,000 00		28,250,000 00
6. Payable from taxation, under provisions of chapter 490, Laws of 1883	445,000 00			445,000 00
7. Payable from taxation, under the several statutes authorizing their issue	56,503,742 85		4,008,796 30	52,494,946 05
8. Bonds issued for local improvements after June 9, 1850	4,798,000 00	1,619,802 90	600,000 00	5,817,802 90
9. Debt of the annexed territory of Westchester County	569,000 00		28,000 00	541,000 00
Total funded debt	$150,298,869 73	$9,689,919 30	$4,826,815 18	$155,161,978 90
TEMPORARY DEBT.—*Revenue Bonds.*				
1. Issued under special laws	27,000 00	331,488 92		358,488 92
2. Issued in anticipation of taxes of 1891	7,600 00		7,600 00	
3. Issued in anticipation of taxes of 1892		17,643,650 00	17,636,050 00	7,600 00
Total amount	$150,333,469 73	$27,665,058 22	$22,470,465 18	$155,528,057 82

Total funded debt $155,161,978 90
Less amount held by commissioners of the
  sinking fund as investments 53,337,606 81
Cash 8,194,799 77
  Total $56,582,406 58

Net funded debt, Dec. 31, 1892 .... $98,629,587 32
Revenue bonds 366,063 92

Debt, including revenue bonds $98,995,651 24

cludes $60,896.30 7-per-cent. improvement bonds, $95,300 6-per-cent. courthouse stock, and $190,018.83 5-per-cent. improvement bonds.

Board of Estimate and Apportionment.—This body, consisting of the Mayor, the Comptroller, and the President of the Department of Taxes and Assessments, allowed the following amounts for 1892: Mayoralty, $28,000; Common Council, $88,000; Finance Department, $301,700; interest on the city debt, $4,948,582; redemption of principal of city debt, $1,499,021; State taxes, $3,554,458; rents, $113,550; armories and drill rooms—rents, $39,050; armories and drill rooms—wages, $58,568; Department of Public Works, $3,014,020; Department of Public Parks, $1,096,455; Department of Street Improvements, Twenty-third and Twenty-fourth Wards, $350,472; Department of Public Charities and Correction, $2,225,425; Health Department, $470,236; Police Department, $5,309,886; Department of Street Cleaning, $2,200,000; Eire Department, $2,223,133; Department of Buildings, $214,250; Department of Taxes and Assessments, $128,220; Board of Education, $4,480,448; College of the City of New York, $150,000; Normal College, $125,000; printing, stationery, and blank books, $268,000; municipal service examining boards, $25,000; coroners, $54,700; commissioners of accounts, $32,500; sheriff, $121,378; register, $130,000; judgments, $375,000; Law departments, $202,000; Bureau of Elections, $370,400; preservation of public records, $45,460; fund for street and park openings, $154,644; jurors' fees, $60,000; salaries—city courts, $383,300; salaries—judiciary, $1,139,890; miscellaneous, $120,228; libraries, $40,000; charitable institutions, $1,305,177; total, $37,444,154. Deduct general fund, $3,000,000; grand total, $34,444,154.

This statement shows that the amount allowed for 1893 is $37,444,154, which is reduced by deducting the general fund made up by receipts from various sources during the year, including the unexpended balances of previous years amounting to $3,000,000. The total amount to be raised by taxation is $34,444,154, which, as compared with the allowance made for 1892, shows an increase of $1,562,949.

In obedience to a mandamus of the Supreme Court, the board at its final session ordered the payment of $21,255 for the expenses of the Washington Bridge Commission. This payment was compelled because the bridge officials succeeded in getting a mandatory act through the Legislature. The board put on record a resolution demanding that hereafter no law be enacted by the Legislature requiring the execution of public work, acquiring of lands, increasing of appropriations, issuing of bonds, or payment of claims, or in any manner compelling the increasing of appropriations, until the local authorities shall have first determined whether such appropriations should be increased, bonds issued, or claims paid, believing that such course of action will result in economy.

Wealth of the City.—According to law, the first Monday in July is fixed for the Common Council to receive the tax rolls. It was found that the assessed value in 1892 of the city's real estate was $1,506,579,703, an increase of $42,331,883 over that of 1891. The total personal estate was estimated at $321,684,572, an increase of $85,054. The total of the real and personal estate of the city was found to be $1,828,264,275, which shows an increase of $42,406,937.

Judiciary.—The Supreme Court consists of the following judges: Charles H. Van Brunt, Presiding Justice, and George P. Andrews, George C. Barrett, Edward Patterson, Morgan

J. O'Brien, Abraham R. Lawrence, and George L. Ingraham, Associate Justices, each of whom is elected for fourteen years and receives a salary of $17,500. In this court litigation has increased to such an extent that it has been impossible for the judges to keep pace with it. Over 1,500 jury cases were disposed of, and nearly 3,200 cases still remain on the calendar. The new system for the regulation and trial of jury cases which was adopted a year ago has met with general satisfaction and approval by the bar. Some 1,107 cases were disposed of at the two Special Terms, and 1,190 new issues were added to the calendar during the year.

The Superior Court consists of the following judges: John Sedgwick, Chief Judge, Charles H. Truax, P. Henry Dugro, John J. Freedman, David McAdam, and Henry A. Gildersleeve, Associate Judges, each of whom is elected for fourteen years and receives a salary of $15,000. In this court 157 cases were disposed of during the year, 390 were disposed of in the Equity and Special Terms, and 1,267 cases were tried before juries. There were 19,116 motions heard and decisions rendered during the year, and 17,280 orders filed. The judges naturalized 9,875 aliens, and 5,552 more declared their intentions of becoming citizens.

The Court of Common Pleas consists of Joseph F. Daly, Chief Judge, and Miles Beach, Roger A. Pryor, H. W. Bookstaver, Henry Bischoff, Jr., and L. A. Giegerich, Associate Judges, each of whom is elected for a term of fourteen years and receives a salary of $15,000. During the year, in this court, 394 appeals were decided and 318 opinions written. There were 679 cases disposed of by juries, and 1,042 notes of issue filed. Over 20,678 orders were granted in chambers, and 3,362 motions heard and decided. Divorces were granted to the number of 58, while 47 persons had their names changed, and 29 people adopted children of other parents. There were 7,781 certificates of naturalization issued during the year, and declarations of intentions of 4,572 Germans and 1,723 citizens of Great Britain issued. Schedules in 127 assignments were filed by assignees, showing aggregated liabilities of $4,689,963.12, nominal assets of $4,487,652.12, and actual assets of $1,519,751.58. The penalty of the bonds filed amounted to $1,344,950.

The City Court consists of Simon M. Ehrlich, Chief Judge, and Henry P. McGown. James T. Fitzsimons, Joseph E. Newberger, Robert A. Van Wyck, and John H. McCarthy, Associate Judges, each of whom is elected for a term of six years and receives a salary of $10,000. In this court litigation likewise increased to an enormous extent during the year. Judgment rolls were filed aggregating $8,570,110.15, as against $5,550,000 for the previous year. The jury calendar was increased by 2,427 cases, and 121 appeals were taken to the Court of Common Pleas from judgments of the General Term of the City Court. There were 1,818 calendar cases disposed of during the year, including 795 by jury and 571 inquests. The appellate branch of the City Court heard 205 appeals and filed 170 opinions.

District Attorney's Office.—The present incumbent is De Lancey Nicoll (salary $12,000), and his office is at 32 Chambers Street.

The total number of criminal cases that were handled during 1892 was 8,518, against 4,172 cases in 1891. Of this number, 5,203 were disposed of in the Court of General Sessions, against 2,990 disposed of in 1891.

The Grand Juries during 1892 acted upon 7,415 cases. Hence for the first time in fifteen years there is no accumulation of complaints in the District Attorney's office which have not been presented to the Grand Jury.

Public Works.—This department is under the charge of a commissioner appointed by the Mayor, independent of the Board of Aldermen. He holds his office for four years, and receives a salary of $8,000. The commissioner during the year was Thomas F. Gilroy, whose office was at 31 Chambers Street. There are nine sub-bureaus, as follow: 1, for laying water pipes, constructing sewers, walls, and hydrants, paving streets, etc. (William H. Burke, water purveyor); 2, for the collection of revenue from the sale and use of water (Joseph Riley, water registrar); 3, for the care of all property connected with the supply of Croton water (George W. Birdsall, chief engineer); 4, for grading, flagging, curbing, and guttering the streets (William M. Dean, superintendent); 5, for lamps and gas (Stephen McCormick, superintendent); 6, for streets and roads (John J. Ryan, superintendent); 7, for repairs of and supplies to, etc. (William G. Bergen, superintendent); 8, for the removal of incumbrances (Michael F. Cummings, superintendent); 9, for the care of sewers (Horace Loomis, engineer).

The annual report of the department shows that in regulating and grading new streets, 123,-000 cubic yards of earth and rock were excavated, and 403,000 square feet of new flagging was laid in building and repairing sidewalks, while 8½ miles of new sewers were built, and considerable progress has been made in the reconstruction of the old sewerage system in the lower part of the city by the building of marginal sewers and outlets along the water front.

The new Criminal Court building is reported as completed, except the interior work of plastering and wood trimming. It contains 201 rooms, and will furnish ample accommodations for the criminal courts, the District Attorney and his staff, and other public officers. The 155th Street viaduct is completed to Eighth Avenue, and the people now have a commodious and convenient footway from Washington Heights to Eighth Avenue.

The report shows that the department collected for Croton water rents $2,982,356.32, while the additional sum of $441,679.69 was assessed as liens upon property where the rental was not paid.

From various other sources the department collected for the city $227,045.09, making its total revenue $3,651,081.

Over 15 miles of additional water mains were laid during the year, and over 66 miles during the past four years. The average daily water supply distributed is 171,000,000 gallons, or about 100 gallons a day for each person. There is sufficient storage capacity in the Croton watershed, and conduit capacity in the two aqueducts, to keep up this rate of supply until the population of the city reaches 4,000,000. The cost of the aqueduct to Dec. 31, 1892, amounted to $26,779,739. Of the receipts, $26,145,000 came from the sale of bonds, $607,168 from premium on bonds, and $8,212 from miscellaneous sales.

The work of laying new pavements made good progress during the year, and 284,549 square yards of granite-block pavement were laid, and 178,547 square yards of asphalt pavement. The total length of new pavements laid in the past four years is 70 miles of granite blocks and 41½ miles of asphalt.

The public lamp service was extended into 10½ miles of new streets. and the city now lights 539 miles of streets. docks, and bridges with 26,-545 gas lamps, 1,535 electric lamps, and 152 naphtha lamps.

The Bureau of Incumbrances made 2,918 seizures and removals of street obstructions, and removed from the streets 1,142 cartloads of abandoned material, 705 decayed shade trees, 731 telegraph poles, and 1,194 miles of telegraph wire. On April 12 the department tried to sell the building material which composes the ruins of the old arsenal at White and Elm Streets. The terms of the sale were that the building should be torn down to the street level and entirely removed within thirty days. But no one wanted it. The city will remove the material. The arsenal was built about fifty years ago by the State, and was considered the finest in New York. The first story is of stone, and the other two of brick. It is of Gothic architecture, and was battlemented and turreted like an old castle. The windows are narrow slits in the wall. During the civil war the First New York Volunteers were recruited in the building. Other regiments were recruited there, and it was the headquarters in war times of the Sixty-ninth Regiment and the Third New York Calvary. When the arsenal at 35th Street and Seventh Avenue was built the State presented the old arsenal to the city.

Public Parks.—This department is under the direction of a board of four commissioners, consisting of Paul Dana, president, who receives a salary of $5,000, and A. B. Tappan, Nathan Strauss, and Henry Winthrop Gray. A bill was passed by the Legislature authorizing the Board of Estimate and Apportionment to appropriate an additional $50,000 for the maintenance of the American Museum of Natural History in Central Park, thus permitting the opening of the new wing of the museum during May. The bill also made possible the opening of the museum on Sundays and two evenings of each week free of charge. The additional appropriation will allow the opening of a space nearly as large as the original building.

Likewise a bill authorizing New York city to spend $150,000 in improving and establishing a public aquarium at Castle Garden and Battery Park was passed by the Legislature. Contracts were signed as follow: Improving the entrance to Central Park at Eighth Avenue and 106th Street; mason and granite work in four small parks on Park Avenue; iron railing for two parks on Park Avenue; repairing the asphalt paved walks in the parks other than Central Park. In April, John W. Smith was appointed superintendent of the menagerie, to succeed William A. Conklin.

Building Department.—The measure known as the Connolly codification of the building laws, which makes a separate department of the Building Bureau and provides for the appointment of a building commissioner, was duly signed by the Governor on April 11. By the terms of the measure the new department will include the Building Bureau, heretofore under the Fire Department, the Bureau of Plumbing and Ventilation, which has been under the Health Department, and the Bureau for Building Vaults, which has been under the Department of Public Works. Mayor Grant promptly appointed Thomas J. Brady to the new commissionership, at a salary of $5,000.

Vital Statistics.—The Board of Health consists of the President of the Board of Police, the health officer of the port, and two commissioners, one of whom must have been for five years a practicing physician. The commissioner who is not a physician is president of the board. The commissioners are as follow: President Charles G. Wilson, Dr. Joseph D. Bryant, Health Officer William T. Jenkins, and President of the Board of Police James J. Martin. The headquarters of the Board of Health is at 301 Mott Street. During 1892 the vital statistics were as follow:

ITEMS.	1892.	1891.
Deaths under one year................	11,944	11,241
Deaths under five years..............	18,589	18,224
Total deaths.........................	44,317	43,659
Total reported births	49,487	46,804
Total reported marriages.............	16,001	15,764
Total reported still-births...........	3,573	3,414
Death rate per 1,000 living	24·25	25·96

The principal causes of death were as follow: Pneumonia, 5,704; phthisis, 5,005; diarrhœal diseases, 3,597; under five years, 3,158; Bright's disease and nephritis, 2,383; heart disease, 2,313; bronchitis, 1,746; accidents, 1,591; diphtheria, 1,425; scarlet fever, 975; influenza, 495; measles, 863; croup, 667; typhoid fever, 399; whooping cough, 369; cerebro-spinal meningitis, 230; malarial fever, 161; smallpox, 81; and typhus fever, 44. Besides the foregoing there were 320 fatal sun-strokes, 240 suicides, and 38 homicides. The special features of the year have been the epidemic of typhus fever and the arrival of the cholera, of which there were several fatal cases. On July 1 the estimated population of New York city was 1,827,396 persons.

Insane.—A board of five commissioners, including Elbridge T. Gerry, Franklin Edson, Oscar S. Straus, Edward P. Barker, and William Lummis, was appointed by Mayor Grant to consider whether New York County should continue to take care of its insane, or whether it should hand them over to State care, submitted a report on March 22. Their recommendation was that the care of these insane should not be transferred to the State. According to the report, there were 5,483 insane persons in the care of the county—namely, on Blackwell's Island, 1,813; Ward's Island, 1,919; Hart's Island, 1,319; Central Islip, 432. They found that it cost $700,000 a year to maintain the insane, which is $2.45 each a week, and the city, besides this, pays 45 per cent. of the cost of caring for the State insane, or about $500,000 more.

Education.—The board having control of this subject consists of 21 commissioners, who are appointed by the Mayor and receive no salary. The president of the board during 1892 was John L. N. Hunt, and the city superintendent John Jasper (salary, $7,500). There are 94 grammar schools and 47 primary schools. During the winter months sessions are held at night in 4 evening high schools, 14 evening schools for males, and 11 evening schools for females. For the support of these institutions there is received from the State school fund the amount of $691,-935.31. Of this, $367,700 is paid on the basis of $100 for each one of New York's 3,677 teachers, $299,303.31 on the basis of a population of 1,515,-301, as returned by the national census, $12,632 for the library fund, and $12,300 for the supervision fund. This is for the fiscal year ending July 31, 1892. It is a noteworthy fact that while New York city receives only $691,935.31, it paid into the State school fund for the same period $1,735,-264.97. Hence the city gets back only about one third of what it contributed.

The autumn sessions began on Sept. 12, and it was then estimated that 275,000 children entered the schools. At that time new schools were opened—one at the corner of Ridge and Broome Streets, and one at the corner of Amsterdam Avenue and 68th Street.

New wings were added to the school at 25 Norfolk Street and the school at 121 East 51st Street. Five other schools are in process of construction, 3 of which were to be ready for use before the close of the year. These are a grammar school at 85th Street and Madison Avenue, with accommodations for 2,350 children; a primary school at 51st Street and First Avenue, with 1,472 sittings; and a primary school at Woodlawn, with seating capacity for 336 pupils. In addition to these 3 new schools, Grammar School No. 62, at 157th Street and Cortlandt Avenue, with accommodations for 2,722 pupils, was ready for use, except that there is no sewer in the street. Other new school buildings—1 at Mulberry and Bayard Streets, with sittings for 1,736 pupils, and 1 at Hester and Chrystie Streets, with a seating capacity of 2,520—will be completed early in 1893.

Police.—This department is controlled by a board of 4 commissioners appointed by the Mayor, and who receive a salary of $5,000 each. The commission during 1892 was composed as follow: James J. Martin, president, John C. Sheehan, Charles F. McLean, and John McClave. On April 12, William Murray, who had been superintendent since Jan. 9, 1885, was retired with a pension of $3,000 a year, and Thomas Byrnes appointed his successor, with a salary of $6,000. Headquarters, 300 Mulberry Street.

Fire.—This department is under the control of a board of 3 commissioners, as follow: Henry D. Purroy, president, S. Howland Robbins, and Anthony Eickhoff, each of whom receives a salary of $5,000. The headquarters of the department is at 157 East 67th Street, and the chief is Hugh Bonner (salary, $5,000).

The department numbers 1,069 officers and men in the service, with 57 engine companies, including the crews of the 3 fire boats, and 22 hook and ladder companies. They have 83 engines, 4 water towers, 29 hook and ladder trucks, and 3 fire boats—the "Zophar Mills," the "Havemeyer," and the "New Yorker." There are 385 fire horses for the companies. During the year there were 3,999 fires, and 17 buildings were completely destroyed. The estimated loss by fires was $4,891,557 : the insurance was $83,246,-935 ; the average loss to the fire was $1,223.19. The fire department caused 21 arrests for arson, of which 9 resulted in conviction.

Rapid Transit.—In the "Annual Cyclopædia" for 1891 a full synopsis of the report of the commission appointed to consider this subject was given. Concerning its feasibility, the Mayor, in his message for 1893, said :

When the nature of the plan finally adopted was at length made public, a feeling of doubt as to its feasibility was generally entertained. But when a commission, selected with special reference to the capacity of its members to deal with the subject, had, after two years' deliberation, decided upon a plan of rapid transit, it was felt that it should have possessed some merits which would commend it to private enterprise as a feasible project and a profitable investment. Judged by the test of an open sale of the franchise, it has, however, been found a total failure, any further consideration of which would only result in vexatious and profitless delay. The whole subject of rapid transit is thus thrown back upon the attention of the commissioners and the municipal authorities, and however much we may deplore the loss of time and money which has already occurred, we must none the less address ourselves energetically to a solution of the question. To say that the growth of the city has been seriously impeded by the failure to provide ampler and more expeditious means of transit, is to treat the subject with moderation. As our population is a constantly increasing one, the necessity for relief in this respect grows every day more urgent. As the question in its present aspect has been forced upon public attention only within a few days, it is not now feasible to make any definite suggestions upon the subject for the consideration of your honorable body, but it is confidently believed that in a very short time a plan will be devised which will bring the means of relief within sight of the people of the city.

Ellis and Ward Islands.—In response to an inquiry, the Secretary of the Health Department of New York city was informed that the Treasury Department in Washington regarded Ellis Island, on which the immigrant station is located, as within the State of New York. This statement was made owing to the controversy between the States of New York and New Jersey concerning their boundary line.

In accordance with the act passed by the State Legislature, by which the city was permitted to purchase the State's share of Ward's Island, the corporation counsel received in June from the Attorney-General the deed by which the State lands on Ward's Island were to be transferred to the city. The city pays the State about $1,000,-000, but this sum will be reduced by discounts, rebates, and set-offs to about $650,000.

Immigration.—The reception of immigrants in New York is under national supervision. Ellis Island has been set apart for this purpose, and is under the direction of Superintendent John B. Weber. On Jan. 1, 1892, the buildings constructed on Ellis Island were formally taken possession of by the Government officials. During 1891 buildings costing $500,000 were erected and arranged with wharves, so that the immigrants from two vessels may be landed at the same time. As soon as disembarked the passengers are shown up a broad stairway on the southern side of the building. Turning to the left, they pass through ten aisles, where are stationed as many registry clerks. After being registered, those of the immigrants who have to be detained are placed in a wire-screened inclosure. The more fortunate ones pass on to a similar compartment, where those going to the West are separated from those bound for New England or local points. By this means as many as 7,000 immigrants can be handled in a single day.

There is an information bureau in the building for the benefit of those seeking friends or relatives among the immigrants. There are also telegraph and railroad ticket offices and a money changer's office.

During 1892, 957 steamships brought to this port 120,991 cabin passengers and 358,486 steerage passengers, of whom 374,000 were aliens, as compared with 430,884 in 1891.

At the close of August, 1892, when the cholera-infected steamship "Moravia" arrived in port with that disease, the immigration had exceeded the immigration of the eight months of the previous year by 17,816. The immigration was then stopped for a while, but has since recommenced.

Post Office.—This department is a Federal office, under the jurisdiction of the Post Office Department in Washington. The postmaster is Cornelius Van Cott. The post-office building is at the junction of Broadway and Park Row, opposite Barclay Street. During the year the total number of pieces of mail matter of all kinds handled was 1,268,066,971, a daily average of 3,854,-307. The increase over the previous year was 118,039,965. There were delivered through lock boxes and by carriers 417,826,923 pieces of mail matter. Of these, 69,237,385 letters were delivered through boxes, and 205,843,629 letters by carriers. In the registered-letter department 1,552,644 pieces were delivered, and 1,544,201 of domestic and 888,361 of foreign pieces were recorded and distributed to other offices. In the distributing department a total of 846,254,842 pieces were handled. The volume of money-order business was as follows : At the general post office, 1,301,623 money orders were issued and paid, amounting to $10,153,027.45, and 865,960 postal notes, amounting to $1,303,707.43. At the 39 branch post offices and substations the number of orders issued and paid was 308,665, amounting to $4,322,360.13, and the number of postal notes 152,629, amounting to $286,545.47. The aggregate business of the money-order department for the year amounted to $111,424,652.60, an increase over the previous year of $4,555,605.-57. The total receipts of the office were $7,059,-525.83, and the total expenditures $2,616,849.48, including $1,155,303.21 expended for free-delivery service, giving a net revenue of $4,442,676.-35. There were sold during the year 245,598,035 postage stamps, 49,608,182 Government-stamped envelopes, and 62,771,725 postal cards. The total weight of mails received and dispatched daily during 1892 was 378 tons. Foreign mails dispatched averaged 34 a week. Foreign mails, both inward and outward, frequently included as many as 1,000 bags, and required from 1 to 12 two-horse trucks for their transportation. The total number of employees was 3,100, of whom 1,300 are letter carriers.

Exchanges.—During 1892, at the Stock Exchange, 86,726,410 shares were bought and sold. Bonds, both State and railroad, valued at $500,-845,200, exchanged hands, while the transactions in Government bonds amounted to $1,662,400. At the Consolidated Stock and Petroleum Exchange the transactions were as follow: Railroad stock clearances, shares, 74,940,000; mining stocks, shares, 1,412,180; bonds, $36,552,000; petroleum, barrels, 21,604,000; wheat, bushels, 21,144,000; corn, bushels, 2,118,000.

The transactions on the Produce Exchange were as follow: Flour, 4,414,200 barrels; wheat, 1,151,448,000 bushels; corn, 295,413,000 bushels; oats, 104,641,000 bushels.

On the Cotton Exchange the transactions by bales were as follow: Sales of spot cotton, 345,-855; sales for forward delivery, 44,414,700; actual cotton received, 1,277,836.

The year's sales on the Coffee Exchange were 6,926,000 bags, as against 7,738,000 bags sold in 1891.

The receipts at the Customhouse during 1892 were $129,552,006.53, as against $123,542,630.97 for 1891. At the U. S. Subtreasury during 1892 the receipts were $1,124,783,218, and the payments $1,223,623,675. The more important items were as follow: Receipts for customs, $134,-212,344; currency received from Washington, $112,441,000; interest payments, $181,538; pension payments, $95,245,968; currency shipped to Washington, $119,373,099; deposits for currency shipments, $67,746,090; purchase of silver bullion, $46,819,373; pension checks paid, 1892, $2,216,016.

Memorial Arch.—On April 5 the last block of marble in the Washington Memorial Arch was placed in position by William R. Stewart, who then reported that the fund had grown to $124,765.20, leaving but $3,234.80 to complete the structure. The scaffolding that surrounded the arch has been taken down, and it is virtually completed. The following was accomplished during the year: 2 stone eagles were carved after designs by Martini, and 4 trophy panels and 4 spandrels were also carved. For this work about $3,000 was required. The stairs to the top of the arch were also completed, 110 in number.

On the large panel of the north front the following has been inscribed:

"To Commemorate the One Hundredth Anniversary of the Inauguration of George Washington as First President of the United States.
"Erected by the People of the City of New York."

On the large attic panel of the south front is a quotation from Washington's address in the Constitutional Convention:

"Let us Raise a Standard to Which the Wise and the Honest Can Repair. The Event Is in the Hands of God."

The arch will not be turned over to the city until the four groups of figures of heroic size are finished and in place on the north and south sides of the two piers of the arch. When this last detail is completed the formal presentation will take place with appropriate ceremonies.

Ultimately, on June 16, all the necessary funds were obtained, or, in all, $128,000. The treasurer then reported that there had been expended in the actual construction of the arch to date $114,966.20, and its total cost would be $124,000. This includes $1,160 paid for granite posts set around the structure to protect it from the street traffic. This item did not enter into the estimates, as at the time they were made it was hoped and believed that the city authorities would see the propriety of protecting a public monument given to it through the public spirit of private citizens, and would not compel the Arch fund to bear the expense. The sum of $4,000 was expended in collecting the funds and other necessary expenses.

Grant's Tomb.—Shortly after the death of Gen. Ulysses S. Grant, and subsequent to the announcement of his decision that his remains were to be interred in the city where his home had been during the last years of his life, a Grant Monument Association was organized. A fund of $155,000 was collected, and designs for an elaborate memorial accepted. Early in the spring Gen. Horace Porter was called to the presidency of the association, and at once inaugurated an active canvass for the collection of the necessary amount to complete the fund of $500,000. Under his systematic direction within a month over $200,000 was collected, and it was decided to lay the corner stone of the monument on April 27, the anniversary of the birthday of the great hero. Legislation making the afternoon of that day a half-holiday was promptly enacted, and at the appointed time the President of the United States, with members of his Cabinet, the Vice-President, and high officials in the army and navy, were driven to Riverside, under the escort of Troop A, where they were met by more than 1,500 veterans of the Grand Army of the Republic, and several hundred members of the Loyal Legion. On the main platform, erected near the temporary tomb, were members of the Grant family, and many citizens of prominence. Promptly on the arrival of the President he was escorted to the stand, and the dedicatory exercises began with a prayer by Rev. John Hall. An address by Gen. Porter followed, in which he announced the amount already subscribed, and the desire of the association "to complete its labor (of collecting the funds) before Decoration Day." President Harrison then laid the corner stone by spreading the mortar prepared for him with a gold trowel designed for the occasion, and made a very brief address. An oration on "Grant as he was," by Chauncey M. Depew, followed, after which Rev. John Hall pronounced the benediction. The crowds dispersed while the bands played in unison the "Army Prayer," and the guns of the "Miantonomoh" in the river boomed a solemn accompaniment. Subsequently the desire of Gen. Porter was realized, and on Memorial Day he announced that funds exceeding the desired $500,-000 were in the hands of the committee.

Centennial of the Stock Exchange.—On May 17 the Stock Exchange celebrated its one hundredth anniversary. In 1792, 25 residents met under an old buttonwood tree, standing at about where No. 60 Wall Street is to-day, and there agreed as follows: "We . . . do hereby solemnly promise and pledge ourselves to each other that we will not buy or sell from this day, for any person whatsoever, any kinds of public stocks at less than one quarter per cent. commission on the specie value, and that we will give a preference to each other in our negotiations." Originally the meetings of the Exchange were held variously, frequently at 47 Wall Street, prior to the adoption of its constitution in 1817. Later it had a room in the building of the "Courier and Enquirer," but finally settled down in the Merchants' Exchange, at the corner of William and Wall Streets. The fire of 1835 drove it from these quarters, and at that time the records were completely destroyed. In 1842 it found quarters in the Merchants' Exchange, now the United States Customhouse, whence in 1853 it removed to the Commercial Exchange Bank Building, at the corner of William and Beaver Streets. Here it remained until its removal to the present building, in Broad near Wall Streets. Its membership has increased to 1,100, the number to which it is limited. There are always several hundred applicants waiting for election, and the seats, as the memberships are called, have increased in value from $25 in 1823 to $3,000 in 1863, and now are worth $23,- 000. As high as $35,000 has been paid for seats. The present officers are F. K. Sturgis, President; Dewitt C. Hays, Treasurer; and George W. Ely, Secretary.

The Columbus Celebration.—Late in April, in accordance with the act of the Legislature, Mayor Grant named a committee of one hundred representative citizens to take charge of the preparations for celebrating the four hundredth anniversary of the discovery of America in New York city on Oct. 12. The first meeting was held in the City Hall on May 2, when a preliminary organization was effected, and a resolution offered authorizing the selection of an executive committee of 25 members, to include the Mayor and the President of the Board of Aldermen, and report the list to the next meeting. At a meeting held on May 3 the following permanent officers were named: President, Hugh J. Grant; Vice-Presidents, Horace Porter, Cornelius Vanderbilt, Samuel D. Babcock, Charles Barsotti, Martin T. McMahon, and Abraham Mead; Secretary, Charles G. F. Wahle; Treasurer, J. Edward Simmons; Auditing Committee, George J. Gould, John H. Starin, David Banks: with the following executive committee: Morris K. Jessup, John D. Crimmins, Arthur Leary, Robert B. Roosevelt, Charles S. Smith, Juan M. Ceballos, William Sulzer, Howard Carroll, Isidor Strauss, Louis Fitzgerald, Ferdinand P. Earle, David McClure, William H. Wickham, J. Schuyler Crosby, William Lyall, Frank Earle Haywood, Charles A. Barratoni, Charles V. Fornes, Henry S. Cram, Edward V. Skinner, Abram J. Dittenhoefer, Charles A. Moore, Edmund C. Stanton, the Mayor, and the President of the Common Council.

Under the management of this organization active preparations were at once begun and the arrangement of the programme effected.

The actual celebration of the quadricentennial of the discovery of America began in New York city on Oct. 8, when religious services were held in the Jewish synagogues. Special programmes were prepared, with patriotic addresses at Temple Emanu-El, where the subject was "America, the Land of Promise," and at Temple Ahavath Chesed, "The Importance of Columbus's Discovery for the Jews." On Sunday, Oct. 9, suitable religious services were held in the Christian churches, many of which were artistically decorated. At St. Patrick's Cathedral the archbishop celebrated a solemn high pontifical mass, after which an appropriate sermon was preached, and at Trinity Church also the preacher did honor to the memory of Columbus. Elsewhere, such sermons as "Columbus's Life," by Rev. W. S. Rainsford; "Columbus, the World's Benefactor," by Rev. E. S. Holloway; "The Santa Maria and the Mayflower," by Rev. C. W. Millard; "Finding a Country," by Rev. James Chambers; "An Epoch in Christian History," by Rev. Ensign McChesney, and others were preached. For the subsequent events the city was elaborately and profusely decorated. Along the leading thoroughfares the buildings were brilliant with masses of color. The national red, white, and blue mingling with the yellow of Spain was the predominating decoration.

At 22d Street was a trellis arch, designed by Stanford White. It spanned the avenue, and was 40 feet wide and 40 feet high. It was of classic design, supported on 12 columns 20 feet high, and bisected at 22d Street by a small arch. The trellis was decorated with laurel and flags wound around the arches and with shields. At night the dome of the arch was filled with lighted lanterns.

Over the stretch of city decoration along Fifth Avenue, from 22d Street to 34th Street, 100 standards were placed, from which were suspended pointed gonfalons and Venetian flags bearing the arms of Ferdinand and Isabella. The standards were surmounted with gilt eagles and decorated at the base with civic shields. Stretched across the avenue between standards were networks of lines, from which were hung flags and Chinese lanterns, forming arches, while at Fifth Avenue and 58th Street was an arch painted to represent white marble, with fountains, polished monolithic columns of red marble, mosaic, and gold inlaying bas-relief work. It was 160 feet high and 120 feet wide. The opening was 80 feet high and 40 feet wide. Figures representing Victory and Immortality stood above the fountains in the piers, and above the figures were panels representing Columbus at the court of Spain and the navigator at the Convent of Rabida on the eve of his voyage. On top of the arch was an elaborate colossal group. The excroises on Oct. 10 included the school and college parade, participated in by 25,000 persons, under Col. David S. Brown, grand marshal. It consisted of a public-school division, of which John D. Robinson was marshal; a Catholic school and college division, of which James R. O'Beirne was marshal; a private-school division, of which Max Reece was marshal; and a college division, of which Franklin Bartlett was marshal. The line of march began at Fifth Avenue and 57th Street, thence down the avenue to 17th Street, to Fourth Avenue, to 14th Street, to Fifth Avenue, to Washington Square, to University Place, to 4th Street, where the parade disbanded. The reviewing stand was on Fifth Avenue, in front of Madison Square, and, in the absence of President Harrison, Vice-President Morton with Gov. Flower reviewed the procession. An interesting feature of the parade was contributed by the school girls on the stand at 44th Street and Fifth Avenue, who wore colored caps and capes, and were arranged in groups so as to represent the American flag. Seven such groups were formed, and at intervals during the passing of the boys sang patriotic choruses.

In the evening a musical allegory entitled "The Triumph of Columbus," by Silas G. Pratt, was given in Carnegie Music Hall. The cantata was divided into six parts: "Columbus's Dream," "The Council of Salamanca," "Columbus and his Boy Diego in Want," "Queen Isabella at her Court," "The Voyage," and "Grand Triumphal March and Reception," and was performed by a chorus of 500 voices, aided by the Symphony Chorus. Also, in the evening, there was an elaborate display of fireworks from Brooklyn Bridge, given at the expense of the trustees of the bridge.

The naval parade took place on Oct. 11. At 12.30 P. M. the U. S. cruiser and foreign war vessels passed through the Narrows amid booming guns from the forts and answering salutes from the war vessels. They entered in the following order; First, the U. S. flagship "Philadelphia" with the U. S. monitor "Miantonomoh," while in the center was the French flagship "L'Arethuse"; then followed the U. S. steamer "Atlanta," the U. S. steamer "Dolphin," with the French gunboat "Hussard" in the center; the U. S. Coast-Survey steamer "Blake," the U. S. steamer "Vesuvius," with the Italian cruiser "Bausan" in the center; the U. S. ship "St. Mary's," the U. S. revenue steamer "Grant," with the Spanish cruiser "Infauta Ysabel" in the center; the lighthouse steamer "America," U. S. revenue steamer "Dexter," and the U. S. steamer "Cushing." The latter had on board S. Nicholson Kane, the director of the parade. The procession then passed up the Hudson river in the following order: Patrolling flotilla, manned by naval militia of the State of New York; director of the naval parade (on board U. S. torpedo boat "Cushing"), with vidette boats; the Committee on Naval Parade and official guests; the ships of war and other Government vessels, led by the U. S. flagship "Philadelphia"; the Committee of One Hundred; the escorting fleet; starboard column, municipal and special boats; port column, steam yachts; eight divisions of steamers, all of which had assembled in the upper bay and joined in the procession after the war vessels had passed up between the two columns. The naval vessels continued up the Hudson river until off Riverside Park, where they anchored to allow the escorting fleet to pass up to Fort Washington, where they turned down stream and then disbanded as they passed the rear of the war ships. Appropriate salutes of 21 guns were fired on passing Forts Wadsworth and Lafayette, Battery Park, and on anchoring at Riverside. In the evening a parade of some 30,000 men belonging to more than 200 Roman Catholic societies in New York and Brooklyn, included in four divisions, under the direction of John A. Sullivan as grand marshal, marched from 59th Street and Eighth Avenue to Fifth Avenue, and thence by similar route as the school children to Washington Square. Simultaneously the literary and musical entertainment of the Catholic clubs and

the U. S. Catholic Historical Society occurred at Carnegie Music Hall. The programme included two orations, one by Frederick R. Coudert, of New York city, and the other by Charles Lee Carroll, of Maryland. A poem written for the event was read by George Parsons Lathrop, and an ode by Miss Eliza Allen Starr, of Chicago, sung by the Palestrina Society and the chancel chorus of the Jesuit Church of New York and Jersey City. Beginning at 8.30 P. M., and continuing for half an hour, was a second display of fireworks from the Brooklyn Bridge, given by the municipal authorities. The great feature of the display was an attempted facsimile of Niagara Falls that occupied the whole length of the bridge, from tower to tower, and represented over 500,000 square feet of waterfall in fire.

By act of Legislature Oct. 12 was made a legal holiday, and the great military parade was assigned to this date. More than 50,000 persons marched in the procession, which was made up as follows: First Division, U. S. Army, including the battalion of cadets from the U. S. Military Academy; Second Division, U. S. Naval Brigade; Third Division, State militia, including contingents from Pennsylvania, New Jersey, and Connecticut, led by their respective governors; Fourth Division, the Grand Army of the Republic; Fifth Division, the U. S. Letter-Carriers' Association; Sixth Division, New York Fire Department; Seventh Division, Exempt Volunteer and Veteran Firemen; Eighth Division, Italian military organizations and French military organizations; Ninth Division, German American societies; and Tenth Division, independent organizations. On this occasion the starting point was the Battery; thence to Broadway, to 4th Street, west around Washington Square, to Fifth Avenue, to 14th Street, to Fourth Avenue, to 17th Street, to Fifth Avenue, to 59th Street, where they disbanded. The grand marshal was Gen. Martin T. McMahon. On the grand reviewing stand, besides Vice-President Morton and Gov. Flower, Gen. Schofield, Gen. Howard, ex-President Hayes, and ex-President Cleveland were present, with numerous other distinguished guests. In the afternoon a marble statue of Columbus, 13 feet high, costing upward of $25,000, and the gift of Italian American citizens, was unveiled at the circle, 59th Street and Eighth Avenue. In the presence of a large gathering, including the Italian military organizations, the monument was unveiled by Miss Annie Barsotti. As the drapery descended, Archbishop Corrigan, in his purple robes, rose and blessed and consecrated the work of art. Carlo Barsotti, as President of the Columbus Monument Executive Committee, presented the monument to the city, and it was then formally so accepted by Gen. James Grant Wilson, in the absence of Gov. Flower and Mayor Grant. Baron Fava, the Italian minister, and Dupuy de Lome, the Spanish minister, spoke, and Jeremiah M. Rusk, representing the President, accepted the statue in behalf of the United States. Gen. Luigo P. di Cesnola delivered an oration, while at appropriate times during the ceremony the Italian bands played Italian and American hymns, and the artillery fired a national salute. The final event of the day was the night parade, with John J. Garnett as grand marshal. The route followed was identical with that of the morning, and in addition to the bunting, Chinese lanterns and illuminations of gas and electricity made the line of march brilliant almost beyond description. The procession included a lantern parade of nearly 5,000 bicyclists, among whom were several hundred women, and 15 floats, as follows: Car of Fame, car of stone age, car of sun worshipers, statue of Columbus, car of the Capitol, car of Liberty, car of the press, car of music, car of science, car of poetry and romance, car of the American women, car of the oceans, Columbus's ship of state, and car of Electra; while between the floats were various groups dressed to represent historical characters, as Indians, Spanish knights, Continentals, etc. The week's celebrations were brought to a close on the evening of Oct. 13, by a banquet at Lenox Lyceum, tendered to the many distinguished visitors by the Committee of One Hundred, at which nearly 700 persons participated. The banquet was opened with a grace said by Bishop Potter, and later was called to order by Mayor Grant, who announced the toasts as follow: "The President of the United States," responded to by Vice-President Morton; "The United States," responded to by Baron Fava and John W. Foster; "The State of New York," by Gov. Flower; "The City of New York," by John H. V. Arnold; "American Patriotism," by Horace Porter; "America and its Discoverer," by Charles G. F. Wahle; "The New York Legislature," by William Sulzer; and "The Congress of the United States," by Amos J. Cummings.

Political.—The election of 1892 was held on Nov. 8, when the following were voted for:

Tammany.—Mayor, Thomas F. Gilroy; Register, Ferdinand Levy; County Clerk, Henry D. Purroy; Judge of the Court of Common Pleas, Leonard A. Giegerich; City Judge, Rufus B. Cowing; Additional Surrogate, Frank T. Fitzgerald; President of the Board of Aldermen, George B. McClellan; Justice of the First District Court, Wauhope Lynn. Also 30 Aldermen and 30 Assemblymen, and members of Congress as follow: Seventh District. Franklin Bartlett; Eighth District, Edward J. Dunphy; Ninth District, Timothy J. Campbell; Tenth District, Daniel G. Sickles; Eleventh District, Amos J. Cummings: Twelfth District, William B. Cockran; Thirteenth District, John D. Warner; Fourteenth District. John R. Fellows; Fifteenth District, Ashbel P. Fitch; and Sixteenth District, William Ryan.

County Democracy.—This organization placed in nomination Justice of the First District Court William J. A. Caffrey, 19 Aldermen, and 15 Assemblymen; also for Congress in the Twelfth District Arthur Dennie, and in the Fourteenth District Francis Hunt.

The *New York Democracy* nominated its candidates in 15 aldermanic districts and in 3 Assembly districts.

Republican.—Mayor, Edward Einstein; Register, Hugh Coleman: County Clerk, Henry C. Botty; Judge of the Court of Common Pleas, Leonard A. Giegerich; City Judge, Rufus B. Cowing; Additional Surrogate, John S. Smith; President of the Board of Aldermen, C. Volney King; Justice of the First District Court, William J. A. Caffrey; also 30 aldermen and 30 Assemblymen, and members of Congress as fol-

low: Seventh District, Samuel A. Brown; Eighth District, Austin E. Ford; Ninth District, John P. Phelan; Tenth District, Charles E. Coon; Eleventh District, Abraham H. Savasohn; Twelfth District, Daniel Butterfield; Thirteenth District, William C. Roberts; Fourteenth District, H. Charles Ulman; Fifteenth District, Henry Robinson; and Sixteenth District, George A. Brandreth.

Socialist.—Mayor, Alexander Jones; Register, August Waldinger; County Clerk, Theodore Birk; Judge of the Court of Common Pleas, Henry Glyn: City Judge, Henry Foth; Additional Surrogate, Charles Franz; President of the Board of Aldermen, Charles F. Wilson; Justice of the First District Court, Lazarus Abelson; also 25 aldermen and 25 Assemblymen, and members of Congress as follow: Eighth District, Joseph K. Newmayer; Ninth District, Aaron Henry; Tenth District, Philip Schaettgen; Eleventh District, George Silburg; Twelfth District, William Klingerberg; Thirteenth District, John J. Flick; Fourteenth District, John N. Bauman; Fifteenth District, Enoch K. Thomas; and Sixteenth District, Howard Balkaus.

Prohibition.—Mayor, Joseph J. Bogardus; Register, Karl Grimskold; County Clerk, Louis E. Van Norman; Judge of the Court of Common Pleas, Charles E. Manierre; City Judge, Harvey P. Hinman: Additional Surrogate, James H. Laird; President of the Board of Aldermen, James H. Hardy; also 30 aldermen and 30 Assemblymen, and members of Congress as follow: Seventh District, Stephen D. Riddle; Eighth District, William A. Crane; Ninth District, Timothy N. Holden; Tenth District, George G. Gethin; Eleventh District, Brown C. C. Hammond; Twelfth District, Richard W. Turner; Thirteenth District, James M. Orr; Fourteenth District, Benjamin T. Rogers, Jr.; Fifteenth District, George B. Hillard; and Sixteenth District, Francis Crawford.

People's Party.—Mayor, Henry A. Hicks; Register, Joseph H. Steinmetz; County Clerk, Edwin G. Bean; Judge of the Court of Common Pleas, Clarence T. Davis; City Judge, Thomas J. Sandford: Additional Surrogate, Stephen W. Linington; President of the Board of Aldermen, Wilbur Aldrich; also 9 aldermen and 12 Assemblymen, and members of Congress as follow: Eighth District, H. Alden Spencer; Tenth District, George W. Reid; Eleventh District, James Bahan; Twelfth District, John J. Daly; Thirteenth District, David Rousseau; Fourteenth District, George A. Hunter; and Fifteenth District, William W. Glenson.

Of the foregoing, the Tammany candidates were elected by handsome majorities, except in the Eighteenth Assembly District, where the regular Democratic candidate was chosen, as was also the case in the Seventh and Sixteenth Congressional Districts. In the voting for members of the electoral college the Democratic ticket received in the County of New York an average of 175,266 votes: the Republican, 98,969: the Labor, 5,945; the Prohibition, 2,439; and the People's, 2,360.

Events.—On Feb. 7 the Hotel Royal, at Sixth Avenue and 40th Street, was burned, with loss of life. On July 9 the New York Society of the Sons of the Revolution celebrated the reading of the Declaration of Independence at White Plains, N. Y. On Aug. 27 the Metropolitan Opera House was almost entirely destroyed by fire. On Nov. 19 a conference of Roman Catholic bishops was held in New York city. On Dec. 27 the corner stone of the Protestant Episcopal Cathedral of St. John the Divine was laid by Bishop Potter, with appropriate ceremonies.

NICARAGUA, a republic in Central America. The legislative power is vested in a Congress consisting of a Senate of 18 members, elected for six years, and a House of Representatives containing 21 members, elected for four years, all by universal suffrage. The President holds office for four years. Dr. Roberto Sacaza was elected President in January, 1891.

Area and Population.—The area of the republic is estimated at 49,500 square miles. The population in 1889 numbered 282,845, of whom 136,249 were males and 146,596 females. There are, besides, about 30,000 uncivilized Indians. The population is made up of aborigines, mulattoes, negroes, mixed races, and a small number of pure whites. Leon, the former capital, has 25,000 inhabitants, and the new capital, Managua, has 18,000.

Finances.—The revenue for 1888 was $3,814,-140, and the expenditure $4,024,602. Government monopolies of spirits, tobacco, and gunpowder produce two thirds of the revenue, and the rest is derived from import duties and a tax on slaughtered cattle. The maintenance of an army of 2,000 men, and the interest on the public debt, consume most of the revenue.

The debt amounts to $1,592,000, in addition to an English loan of £285,000 which was raised in 1886, the interest on which, at 6 per cent., is guaranteed by the hypothecation of the customs and by a mortgage on the railroad owned by the Government.

Commerce and Production.—The raising of cattle is the chief occupation of the people, and there is an export trade in hides, and of late years in bananas. The coffee industry has grown to considerable dimensions, and is extending. About 28,000 acres are planted to coffee. In 1890 nearly 49,000 acres were preempted mainly for coffee and banana plantations. In 1890 there were 19,786,000 pounds of coffee exported. The imports in 1888 amounted to the total of $2,146,000, and the exports to $1,-522,000. In 1889 there were $2,738,500 of imports and $2,376,500 of exports. The exports from Greytown to the United States in 1890 were valued at $985,480. The telegraph lines have a total length of 1,700 miles. The length of railroads in operation is 99 miles, and 274 miles are projected.

NORTH CAROLINA, a Southern State, one of the original thirteen, ratified the Constitution Nov. 21, 1789; area, 52,250 square miles. The population, according to each decennial census, was 393,751 in 1790; 478,103 in 1800; 555,500 in 1810; 638,829 in 1820; 737,987 in 1830; 753,419 in 1840; 869,039 in 1850; 992,622 in 1860; 1,071,-361 in 1870; 1,399,750 in 1880; and 1,617,947 in 1890. Capital, Raleigh.

Government.—The following were the State officers during the year: Lieutenant-Governor and acting Governor, Thomas M. Holt, Democrat; Secretary of State, Octavius Coke; Treas-

urer, Donald W. Bain, who died on Nov. 16 and was succeeded by Samuel McD. Tate, appointed by the Governor; Auditor, George W. Sanderlin; Attorney-General, Theodore F. Davidson; Superintendent of Public Instruction, Sidney M. Finger; Commissioner of Agriculture, John Robinson; Railroad Commissioners, J. W. Wilson, T. W. Mason, and E. C. Biddingfield; Chief Justice of the Supreme Court, Augustus S. Merrimon, who died on Nov. 14 and was succeeded by James E. Shepherd; Associate Justices, Joseph J. Davis, who died on Aug. 8 and was succeeded by James C. MacRae by appointment of the Governor; James E. Shepherd, promoted to be Chief Justice Nov. 16, and succeeded by Armistead Burwell by appointment of the Governor, Walter Clark, and Alphonso C. Avery.

Finances.—By an act of the General Assembly of 1891 the time within which holders of State bonds other than construction bonds might exchange them for new 4-per-cent. bonds under the provisions of the funding law of 1879, was extended to July 1, 1892. Up to that date the amount surrendered to the State was $11,405,-545, in exchange for which 4-per-cent. bonds were issued to the value of $3,298,950. There are bonds still outstanding, which might have been funded under this act, to the amount of $1,221,500, for which the State would have issued new 4-per-cent. bonds to the amount of $316,820. The bonds known as construction bonds, bearing 6 per cent. interest, have been, by act of March, 1879, exchanged for new 6-per-cent. bonds to the amount of $2,720,000, and $36,000 is the remainder of the issue which has not been presented for exchange. The dividends arising from the State stock in the North Carolina Railroad Company are applicable to the payment of interest upon these 6-per-cent. bonds. As the railroad stock yields $180,000 in annual dividends, there is, after paying interest on the 6-per-cent. debt, an excess of $16,800 annually, which remains in the treasury. The State debt, therefore, consists of 4-per-cent. bonds amounting to $3,298,950, and 6-per-cent. bonds amounting to $2,720,000. This may be increased by the refunding of the outstanding $36,000 of construction bonds. The Governor recommends that the funding act of 1879 be still further extended to January, 1895, in which case, if the outstanding bonds subject to this act should be refunded, the debt would be still further increased by the amount of $316,820.

For the fiscal year ending Nov. 30, 1892, the statement of the public or general fund of the State treasury is as follows: Balance on Nov. 30, 1892, $146,006.27; total receipts for the year, $1,217,023.90; total disbursements, $1,053,229.-24; balance on Nov. 30, 1892, $310,400.93. The educational fund statement is as follows: Balance on Nov. 30, 1892, $15,723.67; total receipts for the year, $15,500.24; total disbursements, $2,655.08; balance on Nov. 30, 1892, $28,568.83. There is due from the public fund, for various appropriations, the sum of $225,198.30, leaving an available balance of $85,202.63. The State treasury also holds, as an investment, in 4-per-cent. bonds $146,750, and in Alexander County bonds $13,750, making a total of $160,500.

The Board of Education has, as an investment, in 4-per-cent. bonds $99,250, in bonds recently bought $30,000, and in cash and bonds in the State treasury $28,568.83, or a total of bonds and cash and bonds of $157,818.83. The total assessed valuation of property in the State for 1892 was $262,176,551, of which $19,726,760 was the valuation of railroad property. The State tax for general purposes is 25 cents on each $100 and 15 cents for school purposes.

Education.—For the year ending June 30, 1892, the public-school statistics are as follow: Children of school age, white 386,560, colored 211,696, total 598,256; children enrolled in the public schools, white 215,919, colored 119,441, total 335,358; average attendance, white 132,001, colored 66,746, total 198,747; public schools, white 4,603, colored 2,376, total 6,979; school districts, white 5,168, colored 2,387, total 7,555; value of public-school property, $892,364; total receipts for school purposes, $775,449.63; total expenditures, $760,991.04.

At the State University there were 300 students at the close of this year. By an act of the General Assembly of 1891 a normal and industrial school for girls was established at Greensboro. Buildings have been erected at the expense of the local authorities, and the first term began on Sept. 28, with 176 pupils. The State has heretofore made no attempt to foster the higher education of women.

Charities.—At the Raleigh Insane Asylum there were 294 patients on Nov. 30, 1890; 181 patients were admitted during the two years following, and 175 were discharged, leaving 300 remaining on Nov. 30, 1892. The expenditures for the two years were $120,636.07. The buildings are overcrowded. At the Morganton Insane Asylum there were about 500 patients on Nov. 30, 1892.

By an act of the General Assembly of 1891 the sum of $3,000 per annum was appropriated for the support of a soldiers' home, and the property known as Camp Russell was given to the institution. This property consisted of 5 acres of land and some old buildings of undressed pine, which were reconstructed with funds obtained by private subscription, so as to be tenantable. There are fair accommodations for 40 inmates, but at the close of this year 54 disabled veterans were living in the buildings, and applications for admission are increasing.

Penitentiary.—The biennial report of the directors of the State Penitentiary shows that if credit is given for the value of the permanent improvements made on the farms, and for crops, stock, and other valuable property purchased and now on hand, the institution has been more than self-sustaining during the past two years. Heretofore a large number of convicts have been employed in railroad building, but unless there should be an early revival of that branch of labor in the State the authorities will be obliged to provide some new employment for about 500 prisoners now under railroad contracts that will soon expire.

Railroads.—The Railroad Commissioners in their first report say:

We can briefly state that on all roads making actual expenses the charges for fares and freights have been reduced; and all unjust discriminations originating within the State under our control and brought to our attention have been corrected. The commissioners' standard rates now in effect are lower than in any other Southern State. Until our population becomes more dense, and manufactories more numerous, such rates can not be established as now exist in States north of us without bankrupting the corporations. There are 67 railroads in North Carolina, with a total mileage of 3,432 miles.

Militia.—The National Guard of the State consists of 31 companies of infantry, organized into 4 regiments, 1 troop of cavalry, 2 batteries of naval artillery, and 1 company of colored infantry, with a total of 1,586 officers and men.

Pensions.—During 1892 the sum of $96,951 was paid from the State Treasury under the law pensioning Confederate soldiers and their widows. The number of soldiers receiving aid was 1,893, and the number of widows 2,818.

Political.—On May 18 a Democratic State Convention met at Raleigh, and on the sixth ballot nominated Elias Carr for Governor over three competitors—Lieut.-Gov. Holt, George W. Sanderlin, and Julian S. Carr; for Lieutenant-Governor, Richard A. Doughton was nominated; for Secretary of State, Octavius Coke; for Treasurer, Donald W. Bain; for Auditor, Robert M. Furman; for Attorney-General, Frank I. Osborne; for Superintendent of Public Instruction, John C. Scarborough. Delegates to the National Democratic Convention and candidates for presidential electors were also chosen. The platform denounces the McKinley tariff and the so-called Force bill, demands financial reform, the abolition of national banks, and the substitution of legal-tender Treasury notes for national bank notes, and contains the following declarations:

We demand that Congress shall pass such laws as shall effectually prevent the dealing in futures of all agricultural and mechanical productions.
We demand the free and unlimited coinage of silver.
We demand the passage of laws prohibiting the alien ownership of land.
We demand that Congress issue a sufficient amount of fractional paper currency to facilitate the exchange through the medium of the United States mail.
We favor a graduated tax on incomes.

The Prohibitionists met in State convention at Greensboro' on Aug. 3, and nominated the following ticket: For Governor, J. McP. Templeton; for Lieutenant-Governor, W. G. Candler; for Secretary of State, J. W. Long; for Treasurer, J. B. Bonner; for Auditor, D. R. Nelson; for Superintendent of Public Instruction, R. C. Root. Presidential electors were nominated and a platform adopted.

On Aug. 16 the People's party, which was organized in the State this year for the first time, held a convention at Raleigh for the purpose of placing a State ticket in the field. The nomination for Governor was tendered to Harry Skinner, but as the terms on which he would accept were not satisfactory to the convention, he withdrew, and Wyatt P. Exum was selected for that office. For Lieutenant-Governor the nominee was R. A. Cobb; for Secretary of State, L. N. Durham; for Treasurer, W. H. Worth; for Auditor, T. B. Long (succeeded later on the ticket by E. G. Butler); for Attorney-General, R. H. Lyon; for Superintendent of Public Education, J. W. Woody. Presidential electors were nominated, and the following declarations, among others, were adopted:

We demand of our General Assembly at its next session to pass a bill reducing the legal rate of interest to 6 per cent.

We demand of our General Assembly at its next session the passage of a secret ballot law, with a provision in said law that will secure to voters who can not read an opportunity to vote.

We demand of the General Assembly of North Carolina to force, as far as is in its power, all railroad property and interests that are now escaping taxation, in whole or in part, to pay its full and equal share of taxes for support of the Government of North Carolina, as the property of farmers, laborers, and other citizens are now taxed.

On Sept. 7 a Republican State convention at Raleigh placed in the field a fourth ticket for State officers, containing the following names: David M. Furches, for Governor; James M. Moody for Lieutenant-Governor; Rufus Amis for Secretary of State; Henry C. Dockery for Treasurer; Hiram L. Grant for Auditor; T. R. Purnell for Attorney-General; Edward C. Perissho for Superintendent of Public Instruction; and W. S. Ball for Justice of the Supreme Court.

The platform contained the following:

We denounce the arbitrary system of county government as subversive of the rights of the people.

We denounce the election laws now in force in North Carolina, enacted to prevent fair elections, and so framed as to allow the minority to rule by fraud and trickery and oppress the people.

We denounce the fraudulent pretenses of the Democrats in claiming an economical administration of the State finances, while year after year an increased and fictitious valuation has been placed upon property as a basis of taxation, so that within a few years the burdens of the people have been nearly doubled to meet the extravagant expenditures of the State Government.

We denounce the Democrats for placing convict labor in competition with free labor.

We favor an increase of the national circulating medium in this country and the establishment of postal savings banks for the purpose of securing a better distribution of money.

At the November election the following vote was cast for presidential electors: Democratic, 132,951; Republican, 100,746; People's party, 44,732; Prohibition, 2,636. For Governor, Carr received 135,519 votes; Furches, 94,684; Exum, 47,840; Templeton, 2,457. All the other Democratic candidates on the State ticket were elected by about the same vote as that cast for Governor. Members of the General Assembly of 1893 were chosen as follow: Senate—Democrats 47, People's party 3; House—Democrats 93, Republicans 16, People's party 11. The Democrats elected their candidates for Congress in 8 of the 9 congressional districts, the Republicaus being successful in the 5th District.

A proposed amendment to the State Constitution providing for the election of solicitors in the same manner as judges of the Superior Court was defeated by a vote of 120,476 in its favor and 135,968 against it.

NORTH DAKOTA, a Northwestern State, admitted to the Union Nov. 3, 1889; area, 70,-795 square miles; population, according to the census of 1890, 182,719. Capital, Bismarck.

Government.—The following were the State officers during the year: Governor, Andrew H.

Burke, Republican; Lieutenant-Governor, Roger Allin; Secretary of State, John Flittie; Treasurer, L. E. Booker; Auditor, John P. Bray, who resigned in September and was succeeded by A. Currie, Jr.; Attorney-General, C. A. M. Spencer; Commissioner of Agriculture and Labor, H. T. Helgeson; Commissioner of Insurance, A. L. Carey; Superintendent of Public Instruction, John Ogden; Railroad Commissioners, George W. Harmon, George H. Walsh, Andrew Slotton; Justices of the Supreme Court, Guy C. H. Corliss, Alfred Wallin, J. M. Bartholomew.

Finances.—On Nov. 1, 1891, the balance in the State Treasury was $104,791.51; the receipts for the year ensuing were $2,234,981.36, and the expenditures $1,941,203.27, leaving a balance of $398,569.00 on Oct. 31, 1892. Included in the receipts were $504,536.12 from sale and lease of school lands, $764,823.19 from State taxes levied, $440,153.30 from the 2-mill tax and the poll tax, $171,460.75 from the gross-earnings tax on railroads, $106,000 from sale of refunding bonds, and $80,000 from sale of funding warrants. The largest items of expenditure were as follow: Apportionment of school funds, $607,070.28; school-fund investments, $239,-750.09; gross-earnings tax apportioned to counties, $78,476; funding warrants, $80,000; interest on State debt, $72,847.60; expenses of Legislature, $58,882.80; State University, $58,-343.29; State Penitentiary, $54,945.47; Hospital for the Insane, $157,433.64; School for the Deaf, $23,020.26; Agricultural College, $56,324.90; salaries of State officers, $120,893.62; State militia, $21,923.86; public printing, $28,087.19.

Valuations.—For 1892, the assessed valuation of real property in the State was $60,776,516, of which the valuation of city and town lots and improvements was $9,686,575, and of other lands and improvements $51,089,941. The number of acres of land assessed was 13,786,412, valued at $48,527,809. In the assessment of personal property were included 155,401 horses, valued at $7,280,973; 269,607 cattle, valued at $3,342,328; and 317,647 sheep, valued at $560,085.

The rate of State taxation for 1892 was 3·5 mills for general purposes, and ·5 mill for interest on the State debt.

Legislative Session.—On May 11 Gov. Burke issued his proclamation calling the Legislature together in extra session on June 1 following. It had been discovered that there were no provisions of law for the election of presidential electors, or for canvassing the votes for such electors, or for canvassing the votes for State officers. Moreover, public sentiment in the State appeared to be in favor of an increase of the State appropriation for the World's Fair. The proclamation therefore mentioned these as matters requiring immediate action. The session lasted only three days and resulted in the passage of a bill appropriating an additional sum of $12,500 for the fair, making $37,500 in all, and in the enactment of the following laws:

Providing for the election of presidential electors, State, district, and county officers, and the manner of calling and giving notice of the same.

For the final determination of contests concerning the election of presidential electors.

Fixing the compensation and mileage of presidential electors.

Making an appropriation for the pay and mileage of presidential electors.

Providing for a board of State canvassers.

Requiring railroads to build platforms for the transfer of live stock, grain, and other commodities at their stations.

Education.—At the close of the year 1891 there were in the State 975 public-school districts, with 58 graded schools of 202 rooms, and 1,505 ungraded schools, making a total of 1,707 schools or departments. The number of schoolhouses was 1,584, and their value, including sites, furniture, and apparatus, was $2,423,286. The amount of money paid to school officers for services and expenses was $44,629.78, while the teachers drew in salaries $377,945.65. The enumeration returns showed 47,075 children of school age, with an average daily attendance of 21,413, and a total enrollment of 37,916.

At the normal school, Mayville, there were 126 pupils in the normal department and 144 in the model school, for the year ending Nov. 15, 1892. A new building for this school is in process of erection. For the same period there were 123 pupils at the Valley City Normal School.

Charities.—The appropriation made by the last Legislature for the erection of buildings at the deaf and dumb asylum at Devil's Lake has been expended, and that institution has suitable accommodations for its work. A building for the Soldiers' Home, at Lisbon, has also been completed.

Prisons.—On Dec. 31 there were 95 persons confined in the State Penitentiary. No adequate provision for the employment of prisoners at this institution has been made by law, but during the year a workshop was fitted up, with the intention of employing a limited number in the manufacture of harness. As the State has not yet established a reform school, its refractory youth are sent to the reform school at Plankinton, South Dakota.

Agriculture.—The following table shows the area devoted to the various farm products of the State in 1891 and 1892:

PRODUCTS.	1891.	1892.
	Acres.	Acres.
Wheat	2,847,885	2,898,540
Oats	418,886	405,625
Barley	139,710	189,040
Flax	98,753	24,887
Rye	9,901	25,788
Corn	30,602	11,247
Potatoes	18,681	16,596
Millet and Hungarian	....	79,767
Other tame grasses	....	17,986

The total product for 1891 and 1892 was as follows:

PRODUCTS.	1891.	1892.
Wheat, bu	56,821,804	35,896,886
Oats, bu	12,926,896	18,949,825
Barley, bu	4,567,258	4,950,910
Flax, bu	814,835	286,899
Rye, bu	205,111	498,715
Corn, bu	600,547	272,180
Potatoes, bu	2,554,818	1,804,958
Millet and Hungarian, tons	127,816	154,715
Other tame grasses, tons	16,851	27,191

Banks.—On Oct. 29 there were 74 banks organized under the State law. The statement of

their business is as follows: Total loans and discounts, $2,713,468.63; stock securities, etc., $53,-905.81; due from other banks, $734,903.20; banking-house furniture and fixtures, $179,042.99; other real estate, $50,014.28; current expenses and taxes paid, $90,099.65; cash and cash items, $530,582.50; capital stock paid in, $970,500; surplus and undivided profits, $293,700.35; individual deposits subject to check, $1,895,001.75; demand and time certificates of deposit, $1,108,-308.05; due other banks, $38,239.03; bills payable, $68,287; notes and bills rediscounted, $38,-333.82; total resources, $4,412,370.

Political.—On June 16 a State convention of the Independent or Farmers' Alliance party was held at Valley City for the purpose of nominating an electoral, State, and congressional ticket. It selected the following candidates for State offices: For Governor, Elmer C. D. Shortridge; Lieutenant-Governor, Elmer D. Wallace; Secretary of State, Kemper Peabody; Auditor, Arthur W. Porter; Treasurer, Knud J. Nomland; Superintendent of Public Instruction, Laura J. Eisenhuth; Commissioner of Insurance, James Cudhié; Attorney-General, William H. Standish; Commissioner of Agriculture and Labor, George E. Adams; Justice of the Supreme Court, Guy C. H. Corliss; Railroad Commissioners, Peter Cameron, Nels P. Rasmussen, and Benjamin B. Stevens. The platform adopted reiterates the well-known principles of the Farmers' Alliance.

On Aug. 2 a Republican State Convention met at Fargo and renominated Gov. Burke, on the first ballot, by a vote of 212 to 112 for Lieut.-Gov. Allin. Chief-Justice Corlis and Treasurer Booker were also renominated. Attorney-General Spencer was nominated for Lieutenant-Governor, C. M. Dahl for Secretary of State, C. S. Walker for Auditor, J. M. Devine for Superintendent of Public Instruction, P. H. Rourke for Attorney-General, F. B. Fancher for Commissioner of Insurance, D. H. McMillan for Commissioner of Agriculture and Labor, W. G. Lockhart. N. C. Lawrence, and C. F. Wilbur for Railroad Commissioners. The platform contained the following:

We heartily approve of the administration and favor the re-election of Benjamin Harrison as President of the United States; and especially do we recommend the President to the people as one who has largely retrieved the disaster brought upon us by the action of Grover Cleveland's land commissioner, W. A. J. Sparks, whose administration was so oppressive to our pioneer settlers.

We also bespeak for Mr. Harrison the consideration and support of the old soldiers, who were so grossly insulted by Grover Cleveland in his message, and by his repeated vetoing of pension bills.

The course of our Congressman, Hon. M. N. Johnson, has been worthy of the highest esteem.

We point with pride to the record made by the present State administration, which has been characterized by ability and economy; and by the re-election of Andrew H. Burke for Governor, and the success of our State ticket, we will have an assurance of a continuation of everything that tends to good government.

We consider it of vital importance that a proper exhibit of the products and resources of North Dakota should be made at the Columbian World's Exposition, and earnestly recommend that our State make the necessary appropriation to assure the same.

The Democratic State Convention met at Fargo on Sept. 6. After considerable discussion it was voted to adopt all the nominations of the Independent party (the electoral ticket included) except the nominee for Congressman. For the latter office the convention selected James F. O'Brien as its candidate.

The Prohibition State Convention met at Fargo on the day following the Democratic Convention. It made choice of candidates for presidential electors, and nominated Lieut.-Gov. Allin for Governor, but he declined the nomination. The Republican nominations for Congressman and Secretary of State, and the Independent candidates for Lieutenant-Governor, Treasurer, Attorney - General, and Railroad Commissioners were adopted, and the remaining places on the ticket left unfilled.

At the November election the contest was very close. The Republicans elected their candidates for Secretary of State and for Congressman, while the Independent-Democratic fusionists elected their candidates for all the other State offices and for presidential electors. Chief-Justice Corliss was the nominee of each of the three leading parties, and was elected without opposition. For presidential electors the fusion ticket received 17,700 votes, and the Republican ticket 17,508. For Governor the vote was: Shortridge, 18,995; Burke, 17.236. For Congressman, Johnson, 17,727; O'Brien, 11,-040; Foss, 7,468. Members of the Legislature of 1893 were elected at the same time. That body will be divided politically as follows: Senate—Republicans 19, Democrats 6, Independents, 6; House—Republicans 31, Democrats 15, Independents 15.

An amendment to the State Constitution, increasing the debt limit to 5 mills on the dollar of assessed valuation, was submitted to the people, and was rejected by a vote of 3,848 yeas to 10,600 nays.

NOVA SCOTIA. Prominent among the industries of Nova Scotia are the agricultural, the fisheries (for which see the DOMINION OF CANADA), and the mines, which are under provincial control. The following summary shows in brief the mineral production of Nova Scotia during the year 1891 compared with that of the previous year:

PRODUCTS.	1890.	1891.
Gold, oz.	24,858	23,891
Iron ore, tons	55,191	57,811
Manganese ore, tons	266	41
Coal raised, tons	1,984,001	2,044,784
Coke made, tons	86,738	84,148
Gypsum, tons	146,008	161,934
Grindstones, etc., tons	8,885	19,800
Molding sand, tons	170	280
Antimony ore, tons	26	10
Limestone, tons	85,000	18,000
Copper ore, tons	1,000	900

It is declared by those who profess to be scientific experts in such matters, that this province is still in its infancy so far as relates to gold, silver, copper, iron, and even coal mining, and that there are undeveloped fields in them all, which promise great returns. In 1892 the attention of English capitalists was attracted by this fact as it never was before, and there seems to be a promise of large developments in the near future.

Meanwhile local enterprise and energy are active. This is more especially noticeable in the way of iron mining. The iron deposits of Annapolis County, of Londonderry, Brookfield, Pictou, and Cape Breton are immense, and the ore is of the highest class. At Torbrook, in Annapolis County, at Londonderry, and at East Pictou iron making and iron works are being pushed forward with energy. The construction of iron ships has already been begun. Nova Scotia is, per head of population, a larger owner of ship tonnage than any other country in the world. Timber ships are going out of date, but, judging from present indications, Nova Scotia will, in a very few years, be possessed of an iron mercantile fleet far surpassing in tonnage her present wooden one. All indications favor such a conclusion. Here follow some extracts from official reports:

The past season has exhibited a general increased interest in iron smelting, etc. The Londonderry Iron Company have rebuilt one of their furnaces and raised it to a height of 75 feet, instead of 63 feet. Two new kilns for roasting the spathic ores found so abundantly on the company's property, having a capacity of 100 tons daily, have been erected.

The New Glasgow Iron, Coal and Railway Company expect to have their furnace in blast next June. Their railway to Bridgeville is about completed, and their development work secures them an abundant supply of good ore. The furnace is 65 feet high; bosh, 25 feet 6 inches; hearth, 9 feet 9 inches. Three hot-blast stoves. Two blowing engines of 1,000 horse power each. Capacity, 15,000 feet of air per minute. Anticipated yield, 100 tons per day. The coke ovens are of the Coppee pattern, and are likely to be the first of their kind to go into operation in America. Capacity of each oven, about 6 tons, making 70 to 80 tons of coke per day. The coke is all to be crushed and washed before coking, and the ash reduced to about 4 or 5 per cent. in the coal.

The Pictou Charcoal Iron Company have located themselves at Bridgeville, on the line of the New Glasgow Company's Railway, and the object of their work may be gathered from the following remarks of the manager: " Our object is to establish a charcoal iron plant, to use the brown ores principally, and to produce a charcoal iron specially adapted for car-wheel making, and also for especially strong machine castings. With this object in view we have purchased mining rights of iron ore, limestone and manganese ore, and 6,000 acres of hardwood land. The size of our furnace will be 11 feet bosh and 50 feet in height, and the estimated output for the first few years, 5,000 tons per annum."

About the beginning of March last active operations were begun at Torbrook, Annapolis County, on the bed of red hematite ore discovered there during the previous year. The ore extends along the base of the South mountain, the strike being about N. 60° E., and has been traced on the surface from Nictaux Falls eastward to the Kings County line, 4 miles. The bed has an average thickness of 5¼ feet clear ore, and is so tilted up as to dip at an angle varying from 70° to 80°. Both the hanging and foot walls are of a variegated talcose slate, very light in color, and between 18 and 24 inches thick. The country rock is of a dark-bluish slate, probably of upper Devonian age. A fair sample of the ore yields about 60 per cent. metallic iron.

It is alleged that during 1892 there was a notable increase in mineral products, especially in the fields of metalliferous ores, gypsum, and manganese ; but official returns are not procurable.

O

OBITUARIES, AMERICAN. Adee, Daniel, publisher, born in Pleasant Valley, Dutchess County, N. Y., in 1819; died in East Williamsburg, N. Y., April 25, 1892. He ran away from home when seventeen years old, and, coming to New York city, apprenticed himself to Harper & Brothers, where he learned the printer's trade, and then established himself as a printer and publisher, first in Fulton Street, and afterward, as his business increased, in three buildings in Centre Street. He was the first publisher in America of Braithwaite's "Retrospect" and of Newton's "Principia," and subsequently published "The New York Press" and "The Merchants' Record." About 1840 he removed to Frankfort Street, and in 1843 he was credited with having the largest printing establishment in New York. Soon afterward he was burned out, and he then abandoned printing and publishing and engaged in the manufacture of cast steel. He established the New York Cast Steel Works on Second Avenue, above Forty-sixth Street, in 1845, and was the first manufacturer of that commodity in America. Some of his productions won medals at the Crystal Palace Exhibition in London. He afterward removed his steel works to Furman's island, on Newtown Creek, changed the name to the Continental Steel and Iron Company's Works, and engaged in manufacturing till 1870, when shrinkage in values caused failure. He then returned to the printing and publishing business, and followed it till within a few years of his death.

Agnew, David Hayes, surgeon, born in Lancaster County, Pa., Nov. 24, 1818; died in Philadelphia, Pa., March 22, 1892. He was educated at Jefferson College, Canonsburg, Pa., and at Newark College, Delaware, and was graduated in medicine and surgery at the University of Pennsylvania in 1838. After spending two years attempting to build up a practice in the country, he removed to Philadelphia, and soon afterward was invited to deliver a course of lectures in the Philadelphia School of Anatomy. His success here was so marked that he became regularly connected with the school, and at one time his class numbered 265 students. In 1854 he was appointed a surgeon of the Philadelphia Hospital, where he founded the Pathological Museum, and used unavailing efforts to have the hospital opened to clinical surgery. In 1862 he ceased lecturing in the School of Anatomy, which closed soon afterward in consequence; in 1863 he became demonstrator of anatomy and assistant lecturer in clinical surgery in the medical department of the University of Pennsylvania; and in 1865 he was appointed Professor of Diseases of the Eye at the Wills Ophthalmic Hospital and surgeon at the Pennsylvania and the Orthopædic Hospitals. During the civil war, while attending closely to the duties of his various offices, he was consulting surgeon in the great Mower Army Hospital, on Chestnut Hill, where he paid particular attention to operations made necessary by gunshot wounds, and became widely known as a during and successful operator. In 1870 he was elected Professor of Operative Surgery at the University of Pennsylvania, and in the following year Professor of the Principles and Practice of Surgery. He continued active as professor, operator, and writer till 1884, when he resigned his office of surgeon at the Pennsylvania Hospital. In April, 1888, the jubilee anniversary of his entrance into the profession in Philadelphia was celebrated by a dinner, which was attended by 200 physicians and surgeons, and in October following he resigned his chair in the university. Dr. Agnew was the consulting and operating surgeon in the case of President Garfield in 1881. His publications include "Practical Anatomy," "Lacerations of the Female Perinæum and Vesicovaginal Fistula," a series of 60 papers on "Anatomy and its Relation to Medicine and Surgery," and a work in three volumes, "The Principles and Practice of Surgery." He bequeathed his medical books and instruments to Dr. Hulbert Agnew; all right and title in his books on "The Principles and Practice of Surgery" to the trustees of the University of Pennsylvania, the profits to be used for the benefit of the Pathological Museum; his anatomical and surgical specimens and illustrations to the medical department of the university; and the following money gifts: Trustees University of Pennsylvania, for use of hospital, $50,000; Board of Home Missions of the Presbyterian Church, $4,000; Board of Foreign Missions of the Presbyterian Church, $4,000; to the Pennsylvania Society for the Prevention of Cruelty to Animals, $1,000; Pennsylvania Orphanage, at Kingsessing Avenue and Forty-eighth Street, $2,000; Presbyterian Home for Widows and Single Women, $2,000; Presbyterian Board of Relief for Disabled Ministers and Widows and Orphans of Deceased Ministers, $2,000; University of Pennsylvania, for benefit of Maternity Hospital, $1,000; Kensington Hospital for Diseases of Women, $1,000; and the College of Physicians, $1,000. His biography is being prepared by Dr. J. H. Adams.

Aiken, Charles Augustus, educator, born in Manchester, Vt., Oct. 30, 1827; died in Princeton, N. J., Jan. 14, 1892. He was graduated at Dartmouth College in 1846, and at Andover Theological Seminary in 1853, spending three of the intervening years in teaching in Groton and Andover, Mass., and two years in study at the Universities of Halle and Berlin. He developed a fondness for the study of languages at an early age, and while he was teaching in Phillips Academy, Andover, his linguistic knowledge attracted the attention of many educators, who sought to induce him to engage in educational work. The year following his graduation at the theological seminary he was ordained pastor of the Congregational Church in Yarmouth, Me.; but in 1859 he accepted a call to the chair of Latin in Dartmouth College, where he remained seven years. He then filled the similar chair at Princeton till 1869, when he was elected President of Union College, Schenectady. In 1871 he resigned, to accept the professorship of Christian Ethics and Apologetics at Princeton Theological Seminary; in 1882 he took the professorship of Oriental and Old-Testament Literature there; and in 1888 he took also the Stuart professorship of the Relation of Philosophy and Science to the Christian Religion, and held the two last-named chairs till his death.

Aldrich, Anne Reeve, author, born in New York city, April 25, 1866; died there June 29, 1892. She developed a fondness for writing while a child, and when fifteen years old began composing verses. Subsequently she had several poems and short stories published in "Scribner's Magazine," the "Century," and "Lippincott's Magazine." Her larger works comprised a volume of poems, "The Rose of Flame," and a novel, "The Feet of Love," and she left a third volume in the hands of her publisher. Her writings were unconventional and realistic.

Anderson, John A., clergyman, born in Washington County, Pa., June 26, 1834; died in Liverpool, England, May 18, 1892. He was graduated at Miami University in 1853; was ordained to the ministry of the Presbyterian Church in San Francisco in 1857; was elected a trustee of the State Insane Asylum in 1860; served as chaplain of the 3d Regiment California Volunteer Infantry in 1862; and was California correspondent and agent of the United States Sanitary Commission in 1863–'67. During 1873–'79 he was President of the Kansas State Agricultural College, and was also one of the judges (Group XXI) of the United States Centennial Commission. In 1878 he was elected to Congress from the 5th Kansas District as a Republican, and he was 5 times re-elected. In his last term he was a member of the committees on Alcoholic Liquor Traffic and on Commerce; and soon after its close he was appointed United States consul-general at Cairo, Egypt, where he remained till within a few weeks of his death.

Anderson, Joseph R., manufacturer, born in Walnut Hill, Va., Feb. 6, 1813; died on the Isles of Shoals, N. H., Sept. 7, 1892. He was graduated at the United States Military Academy, second in a class of 68, and was assigned to the Engineer Corps. His first service was at Fort Monroe, whence he was sent to Charleston, S. C., returning to Fort Monroe in 1837, and was detailed to assist Col. Crozet in important internal improvements authorized by the State of Virginia in 1838. He surveyed and superintended the general construction of the great turnpike which was for many years the only highway between Staunton and the lower valley, and which remains an evidence of high engineering skill. After completing this work, he resigned his commission in the army; was engaged for a short time in the commission business in Richmond, and in 1843 leased the noted Tredegar Iron Works in that city for five years, beginning in 1843. Soon afterward he purchased the entire interest of the former firm in the works, and entered into the manufacture of general foundry products and rolled iron. A large portion of the machinery for the sugar mills in Louisiana was manufactured by him, besides ordnance, projectiles, and cable iron for the Federal Government. At the beginning of the civil war he was commissioned a brigadier-general in the Confederate army, with the understanding that he should be recalled from the field whenever the interests of the Confederacy required his supervision over material being manufactured for it at the Tredegar Works. He was several times thus recalled from the field to take charge of the works. At the close of the war the Federal Government took possession of the works as Government property, but soon afterward released them, and in 1867 a new company was formed, with Gen. Anderson as president. From that time till 1873 all kinds of railroad materials were manufactured there; but in that year the company became involved by the crippled condition of railroads dealing with it, and in 1876 it was placed in the hands of a receiver, Gen. Anderson being appointed to that office. The original company was restored to possession of the works in 1878, and Gen. Anderson was active in the management till within a short time of his death.

Astor, William, capitalist, born in New York city, July 12, 1830; died in Paris, France, April 25, 1892. He was the second son of William B. Astor, and a grandson of the first John Jacob Astor. He was graduated at Columbia College in 1849, spent several years in Egypt and the East, became manager of his father's estate in 1853, and applied himself to the care of his own property after his father's death in 1875. Mr. Astor never held a public office, belonged to but one club (the New York), and was a liberal promoter of the interests of the Protestant Episcopal Church. He gave largely to charity, but always with his own hand and under an injunction of secrecy. He had a great love for blooded horses, and for several years kept a breeding farm and stables at Ferncliffe, on the Hudson, where his most noted horse, "Baden-Baden," was foaled. He preferred breeding to racing, though for a time he was active on the turf. His other recreation was yachting, not in speed tests, but for pleasurable outing, and at different times he owned the yacht "Ambassadress" and the steam yacht "Nourmahal." He bequeathed $145,000 to public institutions, including $50,000 to the Astor Library, and left an estate variously estimated at from $30,-000,000 to $40,000,000.

Ayres, Daniel, physician, born in Jamaica, Long Island, N. Y., Oct. 22, 1822; died in Brooklyn, N. Y., Jan. 18, 1892. He began his collegiate education at Wesleyan University, and was graduated at Princeton in 1842 and at the Medical School of the University of the City of New York in 1844. His entire professional life was passed in Brooklyn, with whose medical institutions he was connected for many years. He had long been identified with the Brooklyn City Hospital and the Long Island Hospital and College, and was a professor emeritus at the latter at the time of his death. Throughout his life he was an earnest promoter of the interests of Wesleyan University, and at various times made gifts to it which aggregated $275,000. He also gave $10,000 toward the endowment of the Hoagland Laboratory in Brooklyn. Dr. Ayres was a frequent contributor to medical journals.

Backus, William Woodbridge, born at Yantic (Norwich), Conn., Oct. 22, 1803; died there, July 13, 1892. He was a descendant of the Backus who came from Norwich, England, and settled and named the present town of Norwich in 1659. He became wealthy through real estate, was never married, and during his lifetime gave much to charity, his most important gift being $75,000 with which to build the Backus Hospital in Norwich, which has since been endowed with $250,000 by William A. Slater, of that town. Mr. Backus bequeathed the following sums to Norwich public institutions: Free Academy, $25,000; United Workers, $20,000; Young Men's Christian Association, $20,000; Otis Library, $15,000; First Congregational Church, 1,000; Bean Hill Methodist Church, $500; Grace Chapel at Yantic, $500. He also liberally remembered the Connecticut Home Missionary Society and the State Society for the Prevention of Cruelty to Animals. The residue of his estate was left to the Backus Hospital.

Baldwin, Henry P., merchant, born in Coventry, R. I., Feb. 22, 1814; died in Detroit, Mich., Dec. 31, 1892. He received a common-school education, engaged in mercantile business in his native State in 1834, removed to Detroit in 1838, and was engaged there in mercantile business for many years. He was a member of the convention that organized the Republican party at Jackson, Mich., in 1854; State Senator in 1861 and 1862; Governor of Michigan in 1868-'70; member of the National Republican Convention in 1876; and United States Senator from November, 1879, till March 3, 1881, being appointed to succeed Zachariah Chandler. Gov. Baldwin was for many years a director and President of the Young Men's Literary Society of Detroit. He had been active in political life since 1860, and was identified with the improvements of the Sault Ste. Marie ship canal.

Barbour, John S., lawyer, born in Culpeper County, Va., Dec. 29, 1820; died in Washington, D. C., May 14, 1892. He took a collegiate course at the University of Virginia, was graduated at its law school in 1842, and began practice in his native county. In 1847 he was elected to the Legislature, and by re-elections he served through 4 consecutive sessions. In 1852 he was elected President of the Orange and Alexandria Railroad Company, subsequently known as the Virginia Midland, and he held the office till 1883, when he resigned on account of the pressure of his congressional duties. In 1880 he was elected to Congress from the 8th District of Virginia as a Democrat; in 1882, 1884, and 1886 he was re-elected, and on March 4, 1889, he succeeded Harrison H. Riddleberger as United States Senator. At the time of his death he was a member of the committees on District of Columbia, Education and Labor, Interstate Commerce, Potomac River Front, and on that to establish the University of the United States.

Barnard, Daniel, lawyer, born in Orange, N. H., Jan. 23, 1827; died in Franklin, N. H., Jan. 10, 1892. He was brought up on a farm, and when seventeen years old he began attending the Union Academy at Canaan and teaching in the district schools in winter. He was a supporter of the Free-Soil party, and soon after reaching his majority he was elected to the Legislature, being the youngest member ever elected to that body, and was re-elected 3 times consecutively. While serving in the Legislature he began studying law, and in 1856 he was admitted to the bar. In 1860-'62 he was again elected to the Legislature; in

1865-'66 was a State Senator, and presiding officer in the latter year; in 1870-'71 was a member of the Governor's Council; and in 1872 a delegate to the Republican National Convention. At the time of his death he was Attorney-General of New Hampshire.

Barnum, Henry A., military officer, born in Jamesville, N. Y., Sept. 24, 1833; died in New York city, Jan. 29, 1892. He removed to Syracuse in boyhood, received a common-school education, taught, studied law, and was admitted to the bar, but never practiced. At the beginning of the civil war he enlisted as a private in the 12th New York Volunteers, was chosen captain of Company I, and went to the front with his regiment, which was the first body of troops under fire in the fighting preliminary to the first battle of Bull Run. He was promoted major Oct. 25, 1861, served on the staff of Gen. James S. Wadsworth, and rejoined his regiment in time to take part in McClellan's Peninsula campaign. He was engaged in the siege of Yorktown, and in the battles of Hanover Courthouse, Gaines's Mills, Savage Station, White Oak Swamp, and Malvern Hill, and in the latter battle, July 1, 1862, he was shot through the body with a musket ball, from the effects of which he never recovered. Contrary to many reports of this incident, he was not abandoned on the field as dead, but was conveyed by a special detail of his own men to the Malvern House and put under care of surgeons. After the National forces had withdrawn to Harrison's Landing, and while a sufferer at the Malvern House, he, with many others of the wounded under treatment there, was captured by the Confederates and taken to Libby Prison, where he was confined till July 18 following, when he was exchanged. He was then granted leave till December, and while at home recruited the 149th New York Volunteers, and on Sept. 18, 1862, this regiment was mustered into the service with him as its colonel. He accompanied his new command to Fairfax Station, Va., but a few months afterward he was forced by his wounds into temporary retirement. He was enabled to rejoin his regiment at Edward's Ferry, Md., and to lead it on the bloody field of Gettysburg, being obliged by his wounds to ride his horse man fashion. He rendered distinguished service during the Gettysburg fights, was obliged to retire again for surgical treatment in the following month, and in November resumed command of his regiment. While leading a charge in the battle on Lookout mountain, where his regiment captured 11 Confederate battle flags, he was shot through the sword arm. He was again wounded by a fragment of shell in his right side at Peachtree Creek, Ga., July 20, 1864. In consideration of his distinguished bravery, Gen. Sherman placed his brigade in the extreme advance on the approach to Savannah, and Col. Barnum led it into the captured city. He was brevetted brigadier-general of United States Volunteers while at Savannah, promoted to the full rank May 31, 1865, and brevetted major-general to date from March 13, 1865. He declined a colonel's commission in the regular army, and resigned his volunteer commission Jan. 9, 1866. He then served three years as an inspector of New York State prisons, was deputy tax commissioner of New York in 1869-'72, was elected a member of the Legislature 1885, served as harbor master of the port of New York for one term of five years, and was appointed for a second term in 1889. Gen. Barnum received one of the medals of honor awarded by the War Department, was voted a special gold medal by Congress for general bravery during the war, and received numerous other testimonials. In 1890, Congress, by a special order, voted him a pension of $100 a month, the largest ever granted to an officer in his own right.

Beach, Moses Sperry, publisher, born in Springfield, Mass., Oct. 5, 1822; died in Peekskill, N. Y., July 25, 1892. He was a son of Moses Y. Beach, and an elder brother of Alfred E. Beach, present proprietor of the "Scientific American." His father was inventor of a rag-cutting machine, and after being engaged in the manufacture of paper in Saugerties, N. Y., he began supplying the paper on which his brother-in-law, Benjamin H. Day, a job printer in New York city, printed a little penny paper as an advertisement for his business. This paper, called "The Sun," grew to be an important newspaper. Subsequently, through reverses in the paper-making business, Mr. Beach was obliged to seek employment, and entered Mr. Day's office as a clerk. In 1838 Mr. Beach bought the newspaper for $40,000; in 1845 he admitted Moses S. and Alfred E. Beach to partnership with him; in 1848 they bought him out; and in April, 1852, Moses Sperry Beach became sole proprietor of the paper. Excepting during a short period in the early part of the war till "The Sun" was purchased by the present corporation, it remained in the possession of Mr. Beach. A striking illustration of the improvement in metropolitan journalism is found in the fact that in Mr. Beach's early career as proprietor and publisher he kept carrier pigeons to bring him news from the suburbs. For several years he had occupied himself wholly with the management of a large estate at Peekskill, N. Y.

Beatty, Henry Oscar, jurist, born in Washington, Ky., in 1812; died in Sacramento, Cal., Feb. 14, 1892. At an early age he removed to Ohio, where he studied law, was admitted to the bar, and engaged in practice. In 1851 he settled in Sacramento and practiced there till 1863, when he went to Virginia City, Nev., and in 1864 was elected Chief Justice of the Nevada Supreme Court. In 1868 he resigned his office and returned to Sacramento, where he resumed practice till about ten years ago, when increasing deafness caused him to retire. He was father of the present Chief-Justice Beatty, of California.

Becher, Albrecht, mechanical engineer, born in Stuttgart, Germany, Aug. 8, 1821; died in New York city, Dec. 22, 1892. He was the son of Dr. Frederick Becher, who at one time was physician to the King of Würtemberg. He came to the United States in 1849, distinguishing himself on the voyage by contributing largely to saving the ship when it was imperiled by a leak. Mr. Becher was the projector of many large public works in the United States, was for seventeen years connected with the Morgan Iron Works in New York city, was a member of the United States Navy Advisory Board, and was in the employ of John Roach when he was building the United States vessels "Dolphin" and "Chicago." During the past eight years he had lived in retirement in New York city. His notable works included the water works of Chicago and St. Louis and the great Bessemer Steel Works, at Steelton, Pa.

Beck, William E., jurist, born in Venango County, Pa., in 1832; died in Denver, Col., Sept. 2, 1892. He was brought up on a farm, taught school for several years while studying law, and was admitted to the bar of the Supreme Court of Illinois in 1861. He practiced at Mendota and Ottawa, Ill., till 1871, when he removed to Boulder, Col., where he resumed practice till the autumn of 1876. In October of that year he was elected judge of the 1st Judicial District of Colorado, where he served three years, and was then elected Chief Justice of the Supreme Court. He held this office till January, 1889. On his retirement from the bench he was appointed reporter of the decisions of the Supreme Court and of the Court of Appeals of Colorado, and he held the place till the time of his death.

Bedell, Gregory Thurston, Protestant Episcopal bishop, born in Hudson, N. Y., Aug. 27, 1817; died in New York city, March 11, 1892. When nine years old he entered the Rev. Dr. Muhlenberg's school at Flushing, L. I.; subsequently studied for eight years at Flushing Institute; and was graduated at Bristol College, Pa., in 1836, and at the Virginia Theological Seminary in 1840. He was ordained deacon in the Protestant Episcopal Church, July 19, 1840, and priest, Aug. 29, 1841; was rector of Holy Trinity Church, Westchester, Pa., in 1841-'43, and of the Church of the Ascension, New York city, 1843-'59; was consecrated assistant Bishop of Ohio, Oct. 13, 1859; be-

534   OBITUARIES, AMERICAN. (BENTON—BOOTH.)

came third bishop of that diocese and successor to
Bishop McIlvaine in 1873, and resigned the office on
account of long-continued illness, April 29, 1889.
Bishop Bedell published numerous sermons, addresses, and pastoral letters, and "Canterbury Pilgrimage to and from the Lambeth Conference and
Sheffield Congress" (New York, 1878); and "The
Pastor: a Text-Book on Pastoral Theology" (Philadelphia, 1880).

Benton, Jacob, lawyer, born in Waterford, Vt., Aug.
14, 1819; died in Lancaster, N. H., Sept. 29, 1892. He
received an academic education, taught for several
years, removed to Lancaster, in 1842, and was admitted to the bar there in the following year. He was
elected to the Legislature in 1854, 1855, and 1856; was
a delegate to the National Republican Convention in
1860; was elected to Congress as a Republican from
the Third New Hampshire District in 1867, and was
re-elected in 1869. During his career in Congress he
served on the committees on Land Claims, on Retrenchment, on Pensions, and on Agriculture. After
retiring from Congress he applied himself wholly to
his law practice, in which he was very successful.

Bermudez, Edward Edmond, jurist, born in New Orleans, La., Jan. 19, 1832; died there, Aug. 22, 1892.
He was graduated at Spring Hill College, Alabama,
in 1851; studied law in Frankfort, Ky., and was admitted to the bar there; was graduated at the Law
School of the Louisiana University in 1852, and was
sworn in as an attorney in January, 1853. In 1860-'61
he was a member of the State Convention, and after
the civil war he became assistant City Attorney of
New Orleans, President of the Board of School Directors of that city, and counsel to several large corporations and commercial firms, especially those having
direct business with France. On the reorganization
of the Supreme Court of Louisiana, under Gov.
Wiltz's administration in 1880, he was appointed
chief justice of that court, and he held the office till
the expiration of his term in April, 1892.

Blaine, Emmons, railroad officer, born in Augusta,
Me., in August, 1857; died in Chicago, Ill., June 18,
1892. He was the eldest living son of James G.
Blaine, ex-Secretary of State; was graduated at Har-
vard in 1878, and at its law school in 1880; removed
to Chicago and became a clerk in the freight depart-
ment of the Chicago and Northwestern Railroad
Company, and continued in railroad work till his
death. At various times he was connected with the
West Virginia Central, the Atchison, Topeka and
Santa Fé, the Baltimore and Ohio, the Chicago, Santa
Fé and California, and the Baltimore and Ohio
Southwestern Railroads, becoming general freight
and passenger agent of the Chicago, Santa Fé and
California Railroad Company in 1887, and subsequently Vice-President of the Baltimore and Ohio
Southwestern Company, with headquarters first in
Baltimore and afterward in Chicago, where he had
charge of the Western interests of the company. He
married Anita, daughter of Cyrus H. McCormick, the
inventor, in 1889.

Blanchard, Jonathan, educator, born in Rockingham,
Vt., Jan. 19, 1811; died in Wheaton, Ill., May 14,
1892. He was graduated at Lane Theological Seminary in 1832; was ordained a minister of the Presbyterian Church in 1838; was American Vice-President
of the World's Antislavery Convention in London
in 1843, and accepted the presidency of Knox College
in Galesburg, Ill., in 1846. His administration here
was one of more than usual success, and on resigning
he left the college stronger financially than it had
ever been. In 1860-'82 he was President of Wheaton
College, and on resigning was chosen president
emeritus, subsequently applying his time mainly to
editorial work on the "Christian Cynosure."

Bliss, Edwin Elisha, missionary, born in Putney,
Vt., April 12, 1817; died in Constantinople, Turkey,
Dec. 20, 1892. He was graduated at Amherst College
in 1837, and at the Andover Theological Seminary in
1842; was ordained to the ministry, Feb. 8, 1843, and
in the same month married and sailed as a missionary

for Turkey. He was stationed at Trebizond in 1843-
'52; at Marsovau, Armenia, in 1852-'56; and at Constantinople from 1856 till his death. In addition to
his missionary labors he had edited since 1865 "The
Messenger," p   s   at Constantinople in the
Armenian and Turkish languages, and had compiled
text-books to aid him in his work, notably the "Bible
Handbook" in Armenian.

Blunt, Charles E., military officer, born in New
Hampshire; died in Boston, Mass., July 10, 1892. He
was graduated at the United States Military Academy,
and appointed a brevet 2d lieutenant of engineers in
1846; was promoted 2d lieutenant, Feb. 28, 1848; 1st
lieutenant, Feb. 2, 1854; captain, July 1, 1860; major,
March 3, 1863; lieutenant-colonel, March 7, 1867; and
colonel, June 30, 1882; and was retired, at his own
request, after forty years of consecutive service, Jan.
10, 1887. He was brevetted lieutenant-colonel for
long and faithful service, and colonel for meritorious
service during the civil war, both on June 30, 1866.
Col. Blunt was assistant engineer in the construction
of Fort Winthrop, Boston harbor; during the civil
war was engineer in charge of the construction of the
various defenses in Boston harbor and on the Massachusetts coast; and after the war was engaged in the
construction of defensive works on Lake Erie and
the coasts of Maine and New Hampshire.

Bolles, Timothy Dix, naval officer, born in Boston,
Mass., Oct. 31, 1847; died in San Francisco, Cal.,
Aug. 23, 1892. He was graduated at the United States
Naval Academy in 1869; promoted ensign, July 12,
1870; master, May 24, 1872; lieutenant, June 27, 1875;
and was assigned to the charge of the Hydrographic
Office in San Francisco, April 25, 1891. He was attached to the United States Naval Observatory in
1878-'81; to the United States Coast Survey in
1881-'83; to the Smithsonian Institution in 1885-'87;
and to the storeship "Monongahela" in 1889-'90.
Under this last appointment he arrived with his ship
at Samoa immediately after the terrible disaster to the
American and German men-of-war at Apia, and was
instrumental in saving much of the Government property redeemed from the wrecks. He was a nephew
of Gen. John A. Dix.

Bomford, James V., military officer, born on Govern-
or's Island, New York harbor, Oct. 5, 1811; died in
Elizabeth, N. J., Jan. 6, 1892. He was a son of Col.
George Bomford, United States Army; was graduated
at the Military Academy in 1832; was a lieutenant in
the military occupation at Texas in 1845; captain in
the Mexican War, where he distinguished himself in
the battles of Palo Alto, Resaca de la Palma, Monterey, Vera Cruz, Cerro Gordo, and San Antonio,
the storming of Chapultepec, and the capture of the
city of Mexico, where he was the first man to plant
the American flag on the ramparts. He was brevetted
major for gallantry at Contreras and Churubusco, and
lieutenant-colonel after Molino del Rey, and was
promoted major while on frontier duty in Texas, Oct.
17, 1860. He was surrendered with the rest of the
force by Gen. Twiggs, but, refusing to give his parole
not to fight against the Confederacy, he was held a
prisoner from April, 1861, till May, 1862, receiving in
the meantime promotion to lieutenant-colonel. After
his release he returned to the army, and for distinguished gallantry in the battle of Perryville, Ky.,
where he was chief of staff to Major-Gen. McCook,
and was twice severely wounded, he was brevetted
colonel. At the close of the war he was brevetted
brigadier-general, and served for several years on
Western frontier posts. He was retired with the full
rank of brigadier-general, June 8, 1874.

Booth, Newton, lawyer, born in Salem, Ind., Dec. 25,
1825; died in Sacramento, Cal., July 14, 1892. He
was graduated at Asbury University in 1846, received
his legal education at Terre Haute, Ind., and was admitted to the bar in 1850. Soon afterward he removed
to California, and engaged in mercantile pursuits in
Sacramento till 1857, when he returned to Terre
Haute and practiced law. In 1860 he went again to
California; in 1863 was elected to the State Senate,

and in 1871 was chosen Governor of the State. He resigned this office in March, 1874, having been elected United States Senator as an Antimonopolist. He took his seat March 9, 1875, and served till March 3, 1881. While in the Senate he was a member of the committees on Public Lands, Patents, Mines and Mining, and on Civil Service and Retrenchment. Senator Booth had spent a large part of recent years in foreign travel, and had visited, as he said, all parts of the world that he wished to see excepting Alaska.

Boteler, Alexander R., congressman, born in Shepherdstown, Jefferson County, Va. (now W. Va.), May 16, 1815; died there, May 8, 1892. He was graduated at Princeton in 1835, and for many years was engaged in agriculture and literary work. In 1852 he was a Whig presidential elector; in 1856, an American elector; and in 1859 was elected to Congress, where he served on the Committee on Military Affairs till his resignation, early in 1861. He entered the Confederate army immediately after leaving Congress, was for some time a member of Gen. "Stonewall" Jackson's staff, and resigned from the army on being elected to the Confederate Congress. After the war he was appointed by President Arthur a member of the Tariff Commission, and subsequently was made pardon clerk in the Department of Justice by Attorney-General Brewster.

Bowditch, Henry Ingersoll, physician, born in Salem, Mass., Aug. 9, 1808; died in Boston, Mass., Jan. 14, 1892. He was graduated at Harvard in 1828, and at its medical school in 1832, and afterward spent two years in medical study in Paris. On his return he began practice in Boston; was Professor of Clinical Medicine at Harvard Medical School in 1859–'67; Chairman of the State Board of Health, 1869–'79; was appointed member of the National Board of Health in the latter year; was surgeon of enrollment during the civil war; physician at the Massachusetts General Hospital and the Boston City Hospital in 1868–'72; and President of the American Medical Association in 1877. Dr. Bowditch became an active abolitionist immediately after the mobbing of William Lloyd Garrison in 1835. His discovery of the law of soil moisture as a cause of consumption in New England gave him wide fame and excited large interest in scientific circles. His numerous publications include translations of "Louis on Typhoid" (2 vols., Boston, 1836); "Louis on Phthisis" (1836); "Mannoir on Cataract" (1837); "Life of Nathaniel Bowditch" (1841); "The Young Stethoscopist" (1846; 2d ed., 1848); "Life of Lieutenant Nathaniel Bowditch" (1865); "Soil Moisture as a Cause of Consumption"; "Public Hygiene in America," a centennial address (1876); "Thoracentesis"; "Unwise Treatment of Homœopathy"; and "Eclecticism."

Boyle, Charles Barry, scientist, born in St. Johns, Newfoundland, July 27, 1827; died in New York, Nov. 21, 1892. His father, an officer of the British army and a veteran of the Peninsular War, stationed at St. Johns at the time of his birth, was a descendant of the Irish Boyles. When he was about six years of age his father retired from the military service, and the family removed to Canada. He remained there until his early manhood, when he came to the United States, and shortly afterward returned to Canada as civil engineer on the Grand Trunk Railroad. Some years later, while an established architect in Albany, N. Y., he remodeled the State Geological Hall there. He was the first successful inventor of photographing on wood, and, though the invention literally made modern engraving, he met with the proverbial ill success of inventors, and gained neither money nor credit for his discovery. Being appointed as civil engineer in the United States Lighthouse Board, he went to New York and among other works in that service, he superintended the building of Penfield Reef Light, on Long Island Sound. He was an arduous student even in his boyhood, and early developed the scientific traits that distinguished his ancestors in a marked degree. He became known as a scientific writer and an authority on optics. His

writings include: "The Origin of Worlds" (Appletons' Journal, 1870); "The Scenery of the Moon" (Appletons' Journal, 1871); "Binocular Vision in Telescopes" ("Scientific American," 1880); and articles in the "Annual Cyclopædia," including "Observations on the Moon," "Discoveries on the Planet Mars," and "Binocular Telescopes." His original researches in astronomy, geology, chemistry, and optics resulted in the writing of three scientific works. The labor involved in their preparation extended over the greater part of the author's life, and they were completed about three years before his death. He was the inventor of the binocular telescope, of a binocular comet seeker, and of a remarkable microscopic telescope. At the time of his death he had perfected an unpublished invention that would have revolutionized the science of telescope making. In 1869 he completed a model of the moon, which was exhibited in the American Institute Fair of that year, and received the highest medal awarded by the society. Plaster casts of this model are now in some of the colleges and museums of the United States. He was also the inventor of several astronomical instruments besides the telescopes, the most remarkable of which, styled the cosmoscope, shows the entire series of phenomena that occur in the system of the earth, including the precession of the equinoxes and the earth's great year, it being the only instrument in existence that accomplishes this. It also displays many of the phenomena of the solar system in connection with the other planets. He was at one time president of the old American Optical Company, and was a life member of the American Institute, before which society many of his inventions and discoveries were first presented. He made the first practical demonstration of the true cause of the phenomenon of mirage, proving the correctness of his explanation by a simple optical instrument which renders it possible for a child to produce a mirage at will. Among many other results of his optical studies were a new system of combined search and signal lights for railroad and naval use, and an exceedingly valuable "battery of lights" for coast defenses; also a special system for "high lighting" from towers and other elevated points, and a "flash-light" instrument intended to replace the Fresnel lens in lighthouses. He was an artist of ability, and formulated a new system of perspective which is less complicated than former ones.

Bradford, William, painter, born in New Bedford, Mass., in 1827; died in New York city, April 25, 1892. He was of Quaker parentage, and was brought up in mercantile business, spending much of his leisure in sketching and painting familiar scenes among the shipping in New Bedford harbor and along the New England coast. About 1857 he retired from mercantile life and applied himself wholly to painting, making special studies of the coast scenery along British North America as far as Labrador. His extreme northern trips created a desire to penetrate the arctic regions, and he chartered a vessel for this purpose, and took with him the arctic explorer Dr. Hayes. He explored and sketched the ice fields of the north Atlantic, and the floes, bergs, and coast scenery of the arctic regions. Two photographers who accompanied him were constantly engaged in taking views. He also made an extensive and unique collection of the flora of the arctic zone. His paintings of these scenes attracted much attention in the United States and in England, and some of them were publicly exhibited in both countries. His "Steamer Panther among Icebergs and Field Ice in Melville Bay, under the Light of the Midnight Sun" was purchased by Queen Victoria, and exhibited in the Royal Academy in 1875. Other English purchasers of his works were the Marchioness of Lorne, the Baroness Burdett-Coutts, and the Duke of Westminster. Mr. Bradford entered the lecture field and made a notable success, illustrating his narratives of arctic life by his photographs; and the favor with which his paintings and his lectures were received led him to make

seven trips to that distant region. Among the best
known of his paintings were "Fishing Boats in the
Bay of Fundy," "Shipwreck off Nantucket," "Lighthouse in St. John Harbor," "The Coast of Labrador,"
"Crushed by Icebergs," "Arctic Wreckers," a group
of polar bears, "The Land of the Midnight Sun,"
"Sunset in the North," "Arctic Scene," exhibited at
the National Academy in New York, 1866, "Three
Sealers crushed by Icebergs," and, his last, a summer sketch of the coast of Greenland. Nearly one
hundred of his paintings were exhibited in New York
in November, 1892.

Bradley, Joseph P., jurist, born in Berne, Albany
County, N. Y., March 14, 1813; died in Washington,
D. C., Jan. 22, 1892. With very limited advantages,
his education was sufficient to enable him to support
himself by teaching when he was sixteen years old,
and to provide the means for going to college. He
was graduated with high honors, especially in mathematics, at Rutgers College in 1836, and began preparing for the ministry; but while principal of the
Millstone Academy, New Jersey, he changed his
plans, studied law in Newark, and was admitted to
the bar in 1839. During the ensuing thirty years he
followed his profession closely, was engaged in many
of the important causes tried in the New Jersey courts
and the United States courts of that district, and
achieved large success. For a long time he was a
director in and counsel to the Camden and Amboy
Railroad Company, and was also counsel to the Delaware and Raritan Canal Company. His standing as a
lawyer was further attested by his employment in
causes that attracted more than usual attention, among
them the Passaic Bridge case, which he argued before
the United States Supreme Court in 1860; the Meeker
will case, which occupied the State courts from 1852
till 1860; the Belvidere land controversy; and the
trials for murder of Harden, the Methodist Episcopal
minister who was hanged for poisoning his wife, and
of Donelly, who assassinated his bosom friend at Long
Branch. Besides attending to his law practice, he was
mathematician of the Mutual Benefit Life Insurance
Company in 1851–'63, and President of the New Jersey Mutual Life Insurance Company in 1865–'69. He
delivered the first of several addresses before the
literary societies of Rutgers College in 1849, the
annual address before the New Jersey Historical Society in 1851, many patriotic ones during the civil
war, and the oration at the centennial of Rutgers
College in 1870. He married a daughter of Chief-
Justice Hornblower, of New Jersey, in 1844. Politically, he was a Whig in the days of that party, and
afterward was an ardent Republican. In 1868 he
headed the Republican electoral ticket in his State.
In 1870 President Grant nominated him and William
Strong to fill two vacancies in the United States Supreme Court, and he was assigned to the 5th circuit,
and subsequently transferred to the 3d. Some of
his decisions attracted much attention, notably those
in the Texas slaughter-house cases, and that in the
Grant Parish trials in Louisiana. These trials were
based upon indictments charging certain persons with
murder and a conspiracy to take away the rights of
American citizens of African descent, under the 13th
amendment to the Federal Constitution, and after a
thorough analysis of the evidence, Judge Bradley declared the indictments invalid. For none of his decisions, which fill more than 40 volumes of the United
States Supreme Court "Reports," did he receive adverse criticism excepting from persons whose interests
or political prejudices they antagonized. In 1877, by
the choice of four of his associates on the Supreme
Court bench, he became the fifth member of the electoral commission created by Congress. His appointment gave the Republican party a majority on the commission. He concurred in the Judgment of the Republican members of the commission, and, as if aware
that he was the object of grave suspicion to hosts of
excited politicians, he supplemented his votes by arguments remarkable for their clearness, independence,
and force. Judge Bradley continued to be an inde-

fatigable student to the close of his life. He was fond
of working out intricate mathematical problems, devised a perpetual calendar, and when at his home in
Newark spent his leisure in historical and genealogical research.

Brannan, John Milton, military officer, born in Washington, D. C., in 1819; died in New York city, Dec.
17, 1892. He was graduated at the United States
Military Academy, and appointed brevet 2d lieutenant 1st United States Artillery, July 1, 1841; was
promoted 2d lieutenant, May 16, 1842; 1st lieutenant,
March 3, 1847; captain, March 4, 1854; major, Aug.
1, 1863; lieutenant-colonel 22d Infantry (which he
declined), July 28, 1866; lieutenant-colonel 4th Artillery, July 18, 1877; colonel 4th Artillery, March
15, 1881; and was retired April 19, 1882. In the volunteer service he was commissioned brigadier-general,
Sept. 28, 1861; brevetted major-general, Jan. 23, 1865;
and was mustered out of service, May 31, 1866. During his military career he was brevetted captain, Aug.
20, 1847; lieutenant-colonel, Sept. 25, 1862, for gallantry at Contreras and Churubusco; colonel, Sept.
20, 1863, for Jacksonville, Fla.; brigadier-general,
March 13, 1865, for Chickamauga, and major-general
the same day for the campaign against Atlanta; and
major-general of volunteers, Jan. 23, 1865, for meritorious services in the field during the civil war. In
1870 he was in command of the United States troops
at Ogdensburg at the time of the threatened Fenian
raids into Canada, and in 1877 he commanded the
Federal force that was sent to Philadelphia during
the railroad riots.

Brewer, Francis B., manufacturer, born in Keene,
N. H., Oct. 8, 1820; died in Westfield, N. Y., July 30,
1892. In 1851 he removed to Titusville, Pa., and he
was engaged there ten years in extensive lumber
dealings. During this period he gave much study to
the old Indian traditions that the land in that neighborhood contained veins of oil, which he believed to
be petroleum. The firm of which he was a member
took out the first lease on record in the oil fields,
July 4, 1853, and Mr. Brewer was an incorporator and
director in the first petroleum-oil company ever
formed. After spending several years in the oil fields,
he removed to Westfield, N. Y., was elected to the
Assembly in 1873–'74, was a Government director of
the Union Pacific Railroad in 1874–'78, manager
of the State Insane Asylum at Buffalo in 1881–'82,
and was elected to Congress from the 33d New York
District as a Republican in 1882. While in Congress
he served as a member of the select committees on
the Payment of Pensions, Bounty, and Back Pay,
and on Ventilation and Acoustics.

Brice, Benjamin W., military officer, born in Virginia
in 1809; died in Washington, D. C., Dec. 4, 1892. He
was graduated at the United States Military Academy,
and appointed a brevet 2d lieutenant in the 3d United
States Infantry in 1829, served in the expedition against
the Sac Indians in 1831, and resigned from the army
in 1832. Establishing himself in Ohio, he studied
law, and was admitted to the bar; was brigade major
in the State militia in 1835–'39; became associate judge
of the Court of Common Pleas of Licking County in
1845; and was appointed adjutant-general of the State
in 1846. He re-entered the army as major and paymaster, March 3, 1847, and, after serving through the
Mexican War, was discharged March 4, 1849. On Feb.
9, 1852, he was reappointed major and paymaster; Nov.
29, 1864, was promoted colonel and paymaster-general;
July 28, 1866, brigadier-general and paymaster-general; and Jan. 1, 1872, was retired. He was brevetted
lieutenant-colonel, colonel, and brigadier-general, Dec.
2, 1864, and major-general, March 13, 1865, for faithful and distinguished services in the pay department
during the war.

Brisbin, James S., military officer, born in Boalsburg,
Center County, Pa., May 23, 1837; died in Philadelphia, Pa., Jan. 14, 1892. Prior to the civil war he
taught school, edited the "Center Democrat," and became widely known as an antislavery speaker. He
enlisted as a private in a Pennsylvania regiment in

April, 1861; was appointed 2d lieutenant in the 1st United States Dragoons on the 26th of the same month; was promoted captain 6th United States Cavalry Aug. 5; transferred to the 9th Cavalry Sept. 8, 1846; promoted major 2d Cavalry Jan. 1, .1868, lieutenant-colonel 9th Cavalry June 6, 1885, and colonel 1st Cavalry, Aug. 20, 1889; and was transferred to the 8th Cavalry, April 22, 1891. In the volunteer army he was commissioned colonel of the 5th United States Colored Cavalry, March 1, 1864; was brevetted major-general for meritorious services during the war, March 13, 1865; was promoted brigadier-general May 1, 1865; and was mustered out of the volunteer service Jan. 15, 1866. During the war he was brevetted major for gallantry at Beverly Ford, Va., June 9, 1863: lieutenant-colonel for Marion, Tenn., Dec. 19, 1864; brigadier-general of volunteers, Dec. 12, 1864; and colonel United States army, March 13, 1865. For several years before his death he was a frequent contributor of far Western letters to newspapers and magazines.

Browne, Thomas Haynes Bayly, lawyer, born at Accomack Courthouse, Va., in 1844; died there, Aug. 19, 1892. He was educated at Hanover and Bloomfield Academies in Virginia, and left the latter institution in May, 1861, to enter the Confederate service as a private in the 39th Virginia Infantry. Subsequently he served in Chew's Battery of the Stewart Horse Artillery, and was surrendered with the Army of Northern Virginia in April, 1865. In 1867 he was graduated at the law department of the University of Virginia; in 1873 was elected commonwealth attorney for Accomack County; in 1884 was a Republican presidential elector; in 1886 was elected to Congress from the 1st Virginia District as a Republican; in 1888 was re-elected; and in 1890 .was defeated. During his last term in Congress he served on the committees on Commerce, on Pensions, and on Expenditures in the Navy Department.

Bruce, David, inventor, born in Scotland, in 1802; died in Brooklyn, N. Y., Sept. 13, 1892. When he was six years old he came to the United States with his parents and settled in New York city, where his father established a press room in 1815. Mr. Bruce received a private-school education, and was apprenticed to the printer's trade. At that time the making of type was done wholly by hand, and the most rapid workman could not produce more than 15 a minute. Mr. Bruce conceived the idea of making type by machinery, and applied all his leisure to experimenting. In 1838 he secured several patents, covering a type-casting machine he had made, which by hand power would make 80 or 90 type a minute. He sold his patent rights in Boston, after fully demonstrating the practical working of his machine. While this machine was far in advance of the usual method of making type, it was not wholly satisfactory to him, and he accordingly resumed experimenting till he had perfected a machine to be run by steam power, which turned out about 140 type a minute. Mr. Bruce always claimed that he had been defrauded of his rights in his steam type-casting invention. About 1850, he established a typ foundry in Brooklyn, and he was engaged in the business during the remainder of his active life.

Brush, Christine Chaplin, author, born in Providence, R. I., in May, 1842; died in Brooklyn, N. Y., Feb. 3, 1892. She was a daughter of the Rev. Jeremiah Chaplin, D. D., a writer of religious works, and of Jane Dunbar, a writer of numerous Sunday-school books, and the wife of the Rev. Alfred H. Brush. For several years prior to 1867 she taught drawing in the State Normal School at Framingham, Mass., and afterward she applied herself to water-color painting, chiefly of wild flowers, in which she attained large success, many of her flower pictures, including a well-known one of nasturtiums, having been reproduced and published by L. Prang & Co. In 1877 she studied painting in Paris, and in 1878 she was married. In 1879 she published in the " No Name Series " the " Colonel's Opera Cloak," which has since been republished under her own name. Afterward she published the stories " Inside Our Gate " and " One Summer's Lessons in Perspective," and the poems " The Inland Country " in the "Atlantic Monthly" and " My June Boy " in " Harper's Magazine."

Bryson, Andrew, naval officer, born in New York city, July 22, 1822; died in Washington, D. C., Feb. 7, 1892. He was appointed a midshipman in the United States navy, Dec. 1, 1837; was promoted passed midshipman, June 29, 1843; master, Jan. 30, 1851; lieutenant, Aug. 30, 1851; commander, July 16, 1862; captain, July 25, 1866; commodore, Feb. 14, 1873; and rear-admiral, March 25, 1880; and was retired Jan. 30, 1883. During his naval career he was on sea service twenty-four years, seven months; on shore or other duty, twelve years; and was unemployed eighteen years. During the civil war he commanded the steamer "Chippewa" on special service, 1862-'63; the ironclad "Lehigh" of the South Atlantic Blockading Squadron, 1863; and the ironclad "Essex" in the Mississippi Squadron, 1864-'65. He took part in the reduction of Fort Macon and the principal actions off Charleston, 1863-'64, during which he received a severe wound from a shell. His last service prior to retirement was as commander of the South Atlantic Squadron.

Buchtel, John Richards, philanthropist, born in Greene Township, Summit County, Ohio, Jan. 18, 1822; died in Akron, Ohio, May 23, 1892. The early part of his life was spent in farming, and he acquired the old Thornton farm, on which a portion of the city of Akron was built. On withdrawing from farming he entered the employment of a firm in Canton, Ohio, manufacturing reapers and mowers. In 1856, when the firm's manufactory was burned and an assignment was made in consequence, his personal enterprise restored the firm's prosperity, and he induced it to establish a branch factory in Akron, of which he was for many years president. Having given much time and study to the material development of that city, he undertook the development of the coal and iron resources of the Hocking valley, and among the successes of this enterprise was a thrifty village bearing his name. He continued in the active management of his various interests till 1887, when he was stricken with paralysis, from which he never recovered. Mr. Buchtel will long be remembered for his munificence in the cause of education. In 1870 he made possible the organization of a college by giving $6,000 toward a building fund and $25,000 toward an endowment fund. To secure the location of the institution, citizens of Akron raised a further sum of $60,000, and on July 4, 1871, Horace Greeley laid the corner stone of the institution, then known as "The Universalist Centenary School of Ohio." In 1874 he founded the chair of Physics and Chemistry in the name of his wife, with a gift of $20,000; between 1874 and 1879 he added about $25,000; in 1879 he gave $25,112 toward the extinction of a debt of the institution; between 1879 and 1881 he contributed $24,716 in various sums; in 1881 he gave the college property valued at about $64,000; in 1883 he celebrated founder's day by a gift of $100,000, supplementing this the same year with a gift of lands valued at $2,000; and on commencement day, 1887, he gave $100,000 and all his life-insurance policies, amounting to $74,400. In his will he made the college, to which his own name had been given, his sole legatee. One of the most interesting incidents in his career occurred on June 23, 1887, in connection with the fifteenth annual commencement of the college. Three months previously he had been stricken with paralysis. So eager was he to attend the commencement exercises that he offered the students $1,000 in cash, to be applied to the construction of their gymnasium, if they would take him to the college chapel, in the fifth story of the building, on commencement day. The offer was accepted, and the college corps of cadets, in uniform, marched to his house, carried him in an invalid's chair to a vehicle expressly prepared for the occasion, drove him to the college building, and then took turns in carrying him up the long flights of stairs.

Buck, Hiram, clergyman, born in Steuben County, N. Y., in 1818; died in Decatur, Ill., Aug. 22, 1892. He was one of the pioneers of Methodism in Illinois, having joined the State conference in 1843; had held the office of presiding elder for fifty years; gave a large sum of money toward the endowment fund of the Wesleyan University and Illinois College; and was one of the most widely known clergymen of the Methodist Episcopal Church in the West.

Buckland, Ralph Pomroy, lawyer, born in Leyden, Mass., Jan. 20, 1812; died in Fremont, Ohio, May 28, 1892. His parents removed to Ohio while he was an infant. He was graduated at Kenyon College, studied law, was admitted to the bar in 1837, and settled in Fremont. In 1848 he was a delegate to the Whig National convention, and in 1855–'59 was a State Senator. At the beginning of the civil war he organized the 72d Regiment of Ohio Volunteers, and became its colonel, and was afterward assigned by Gen. Sherman to the command of the 4th Brigade of his division. He served with distinction at Shiloh; was promoted brigadier-general Nov. 9, 1862; and was engaged with the 15th Army Corps at Vicksburg and about Memphis in 1864. In 1865 he was elected to Congress from the 9th Ohio District as a Republican, and, resigning his commission in the army, he was brevetted major-general of Volunteers. He was re-elected to Congress, and was a delegate to the Philadelphia Loyalists' Convention in 1866; was a delegate to the Pittsburg Soldiers' Convention and the Republican National Convention in 1876; served as president of the board of managers of the Ohio Soldiers' and Sailors' Orphans' Home at Xenia in 1867–'73; and was a Government director of the Union Pacific Railroad in 1877–'80.

Buel, Samuel, educator, born in Troy, N. Y., June 11, 1815; died in New York city, Dec. 30, 1892. He was a son of the late Judge David Buel, and was graduated at Williams College in 1833. In 1837 he was stationed in St. Peter's Church, Albany, N. Y.; in 1837–'39 was rector of Trinity Church, Marshall, Mich.; in 1840–'41 was missionary at Minersville and Llewellyn, Pa.; in 1841–'47 was rector of Emanuel parish, Cumberland, Md.; and in 1847–'56 of Christ Church, Poughkeepsie, N. Y. From 1867 till 1871 he was Professor of Ecclesiastical History and Divinity at Seabury Hall, Faribault, Minn., and from 1871 till 1888 Professor of Systematic Divinity and Dogmatic Theology in the General Theological Seminary of the Protestant Episcopal Church in New York city. He resigned on account of failing health in 1888, and was made professor emeritus. He received the degree of S. T. D. from Columbia College in 1862; *ad eundem* from the General Theological Seminary in 1884. Dr. Buel's writings were numerous, and included an essay on "The Apostolical System of the Church," defended in a reply to Dr. Whately on the Kingdom of Christ" (Philadelphia, 1844); "Eucharistic Presence, Sacrifice, and Adoration" (New York, 1874); and a volume of lectures entitled "A Treatise of Dogmatic Theology."

Bull, Richard H., mathematician, born in New York city in 1817; died there, Feb. 1, 1892. He was graduated at the University of the City of New York in 1837, studied one year in Union Theological Seminary, and was then appointed tutor in mathematics in the University of the City of New York. A few years afterward he was made senior Professor of Mathematics, and held the chair till 1885, when he was retired as professor emeritus. He co-operated with Prof. Morse in many of his early experiments with the magnetic telegraph, and was the first mathematician to put into practice for business purposes the idea of obtaining the true time by the sun. For many years he supplied the principal railroads terminating in New York city with correct time, by which the trains were run. He was President of the New York Savings Bank from 1860 till 1882, and during the past ten years had been engaged in the preparation of a treatise on the first book of Genesis, in which he attempted to prove, by the application of mathematical and astronomical reasoning, that the world was created in six days; that Moses was cognizant of the laws of mathematics and astronomy when he wrote the Pentateuch; and that the writing was in harmony with those laws.

Bungay, George Washington, journalist, born in Walsingham, Suffolk, England, July 22, 1818; died in Bloomfield, N. J., July 10, 1892. He came to this country when nine years old, and received a public-school education in New York city. He became editor of the "Metropolitan," a monthly journal; founded the "Independent" in Ilion, N. Y.; was a reporter and editorial writer on the New York "Tribune"; was a strong abolitionist, and an intimate friend of Wendell Phillips, Charles Sumner, John G. Whittier, Frederick Douglass, and other antislavery workers; and was also a strong temperance advocate and lecturer. In the early part of President Lincoln's administration he was appointed to an office in the New York custom house, at the solicitation of Mr. Sumner, where he remained till 1887. Besides his general work in journalism, he wrote an "Abraham Lincoln Songster," "The Poets of Queen Elizabeth's Time," "Offhand Takings," "Crayon Sketches," and "Pen Portraits of Illustrious Abstainers." His principal lecture topics were "Wit and Humor," "The Comic Side of Life," and "The Old Boys." Among his poems, "The Creed of the Bells" was the most popular.

Bunker, Robert, naturalist, born in Ghent, Columbia County, N. Y., Nov. 20, 1820; died in Rochester, N. Y., March 6, 1892. At an early age he removed with his parents to Rochester, where he learned a trade and became a very skillful mechanic. At the same time he cultivated a love for natural history, and finally devoted himself especially to entomology. He was president of the entomological section of the Rochester Academy of Science, and gave it his large collection, one of the finest in the country. In the number and variety of its moths, this collection is said to be the best in existence. It is now in the library building of the University of Rochester. Mr. Bunker contributed to periodicals many articles on subjects connected with his favorite science. He was also the inventor of several mechanical devices.

Burgess, Walter Snow, jurist, born in Rochester, Plymouth County, Mass., Sept. 10, 1808; died in Providence, R. I., July 26, 1892. He was graduated at Brown University in 1831; became principal of Thaxter Academy at Edgartown, Mass., and was admitted to the Rhode Island bar in 1835. President Polk appointed him United States district attorney for Rhode Island in 1845, and after serving in both branches of the Legislature he was Attorney-General for several years. From 1868 to June 1, 1881, when he resigned, he was Associate Judge of the Supreme Court of Rhode Island.

Burns, William Wallace, military officer, born in Coshocton, Ohio, Sept. 3, 1825; died in Beaufort, S. C., April 19, 1892. He was graduated at the United States Military Academy, and entered the army as brevet 2d lieutenant 3d United States Infantry in 1847; was promoted 2d lieutenant, 5th Infantry, Sept. 8 following; 1st lieutenant, Aug. 12, 1850; captain and commissary of subsistence, Nov. 3, 1858; major, Aug. 3, 1861; lieutenant-colonel and assistant commissary-general, June 23, 1874; and colonel, Nov. 9, 1884; and was retired Sept. 3, 1889. In the volunteer army he was commissioned brigadier-general Sept. 28, 1861, and resigned March 20, 1863. During the war he was brevetted lieutenant-colonel for gallantry in the battle of Savage Station, Va., where he was wounded, June 29, 1862; colonel for the battle of Glendale, on the following day; and brigadier-general for services during the war, March 13, 1865.

Burroughs, John Curtis, educator, born in Stamford, Delaware County, N. Y., Dec. 7, 1818; died in Chicago, Ill., April 21, 1892. He was graduated at Yale College in 1842, and at Madison Theological Seminary in 1846; was pastor of Baptist churches in Waterford and West Troy, N. Y., in 1847–'52; accepted a call to the First Baptist Church in Chicago in 1852; and while preaching there began an educational movement which resulted in the establishment of the University of Chicago in 1857. In 1856 he accepted the presidency of the University of Chicago, which he held till 1874, and soon after resigning he was appointed a member of the Board of Education of Chicago. Since 1884 he had been assistant superintendent of public schools in that city.

Canning, Josiah D., author, born in Gill, Mass., in 1817; died there, March 25, 1892. He began writing verses in early life; published his first volume, dedicated to "Every True New Englander, especially the Men of Massachusetts," at Greenfield, in 1838, and a second volume a few years afterward, and had a third volume, entitled "Connecticut River Reeds, blown by the Pleasant Bard," in the hands of a Boston publisher at the time of his death. He was known throughout New England as the "Pleasant Bard," and owned the heavy-clasped Bible that Gov. Moses Gill gave to the church of Gill together with a communion service, in acknowledgment of the naming of the town in his honor.

Carle, James, military officer, born in Windsor, N. Y., Sept. 8, 1835; died in New York city, April 26, 1892. He received a public-school education, and when twenty years old enlisted as a private in the regular army. He served for five years on the plains, and was mustered out of the service immediately before the breaking out of the civil war. When he heard of the firing on Fort Sumter, he re-entered the army as a private in the 6th Pennsylvania Volunteers; was promoted captain, Oct. 25, 1861; was provost-marshal during the Chancellorsville campaign in 1863; was commissioned colonel of the 191st United States Infantry on June 6, 1864; was recommended for appointment as brevet brigadier-general for gallantry at the crossing of James river, where he was in command of a brigade, on June 17 following, and received the appointment in March, 1865. Gen. Carle distinguished himself in the battle of White Oak Swamp, at Gettysburg, where his regiment captured the only gun taken from the enemy on the first day, at Spottsylvania Courthouse, at Bethesda Church, and at the battle for the Weldon Road, where he was captured. He was confined in Libby, Salisbury, and Danville prisons, and contracted rheumatism, from which he never recovered. Since 1870 he had been inspector of cigars in the United States customhouse, New York.

Cassidy, George William, journalist, born in Bourbon County, Ky., April 25, 1836; died in Reno, Nev., June 24, 1892. He was educated in the public schools and by private tutors; made the overland trip to California, and engaged in mining in 1857; and, after settling in Nevada, became editor of the Eureka "Sentinel." In 1872 and 1876 he was elected to the State Senate, and during the session of 1879 he was its presiding officer. In 1880 and 1882 he was elected representative-at-large to Congress as a Democrat, and during his last term he served on the committees on Mines and Mining and on the Pacific Railroad. Shortly before his death he again received the Democratic nomination for Congress. He was a delegate to the Silver Convention in Reno, and died suddenly after delivering an address.

Castle, Orlando Lane, educator, born in Jericho, Vt., July 20, 1822; died in Alton, Ohio, Jan. 31, 1892. He was graduated at Denison University, Ohio, in 1846, spent one year as tutor there, and for several years afterward had charge of the public schools in Zanesville. In 1858 he accepted the call to the chair of Rhetoric, Oratory, and Belles-lettres in Shurtleff College, Upper Alton, Ill., and he retained this office till his death. The patent-office reports show that the Rev. Thomas Hill, D. D., then President of Harvard University, and Prof. Castle on the same day obtained letters patent for an invention under the selfsame title, viz., "An instrument called an Arithmometer, designed to facilitate the addition of long columns." Prof. Castle received the degree of LL. D. from Denison University in 1877. President Kendrick, of Shurtleff College, says of him: "He possessed talent without vanity, learning without pedant-

ry, taste without fastidiousness, and in his department of study was master of all social, scientific, and practical questions."

Chamberlin, Edwin M., journalist and reformer, born in West Cambridge, Mass., in 1835; died in Cambridge, Mass., Feb. 23, 1892. He was heir to valuable property in Boston, and had unusual financial prospects in other directions, but, becoming interested at an early age in the general movement for labor reform, he sacrificed his personal interests to that cause. Believing that the laboring people could gain more from political action than through strikes, he ardently supported every ticket in his State and in the country that was nominated by the Labor party. He was also a stanch friend of the temperance and womansuffrage movements, and for many years was editor and proprietor of "The Echo," a journal for the promotion of radical economic ideas. He served in the national army through the civil war, and was mustered out of the service with the rank of lieutenant. In 1866 he assisted in forming "The Industrial Order of the People," and in 1869 and 1870 was Labor candidate for Governor of Massachusetts, and polled each time from 13,500 to 15,000 votes. Joseph Arch, the famous English agricultural reformer, first came to the United States on the invitation of Mr. Chamberlin. For many years he was a member of the Workingmen's Institute, and conducted the debates and the classes in social economics. The last notable act of his life was his appearance, a few days before his death, before the legislative Committee on Constitutional Amendments to explain his petition for referring to the people all legislative acts, orders, or resolves; also for the purpose of advocating for submission to the popular vote any proposed law that 5,000 citizens might unite in petitioning for. These propositions were based on the Swiss referendum.

Chapin, Aaron Lucius, educator, born in Hartford, Conn., Feb. 4, 1817; died in Beloit, Wis., July 22, 1892. He was graduated at Yale in 1837; was professor at the New York Institute for the Deaf and Dumb in 1838-'43; was graduated at Union Theological Seminary in 1842; and was pastor of the 1st Presbyterian Church in Milwaukee from 1844 till 1850. In February of the latter year he was elected the first President of Beloit College, and he held the office till 1886, when he resigned because of impaired health, and was chosen president emeritus and Professor of Civil Polity. Dr. Chapin was for many years a corporate member of the American Board of Commissioners for Foreign Missions, a life director of the American Home Missionary Society, Vice-President of the American Missionary Association, and president of the board of trustees of the State Institute for Deaf Mutes at Delavan. He was also a member of the board of examiners of the United States Naval Academy in 1872, and of the United States Military Academy in 1873, and was President of the Wisconsin Academy of Arts and Sciences.

Chapin, John Henry, clergyman, born in Leavenworth, Ind., in 1832; died in Norwalk, Conn., March 14, 1892. He was pastor of the 1st Universalist Church in Meriden, Conn., from 1873 till 1885, when he retired from pulpit labor; was elected to the State Legislature as a Republican in 1888; and was the father of the present State antiscreen law. Dr. Chapin was for several years Professor of Mineralogy and Geology in St. Lawrence University, Canton, N. Y., president for twelve years of the Connecticut Universalist Association, chairman for many years of the committee on missions of the Universalist Church, and was an active member of the American Association for the Advancement of Science. During the last two years of his life he was employed on the new topographical survey of Connecticut.

Chase, Thomas, educator, born in Worcester, Mass., June 16, 1827; died in Providence, R. I., Oct. 5, 1892. He was graduated at Harvard University in 1848; was tutor there in 1850-'53; studied in the University of Berlin in 1854, and in the College de France in 1855; was called to the chair of Greek and Latin at

Haverford College, Pa., in 1855; and was president there from 1875 till 1886, when he resigned on account of failing health. He then spent more than a year in visiting the universities and other educational institutions in Europe, and during the last few years applied himself to literary work, and acted at times as professor in the classical course at Brown University. Dr. Chase was a member of the American Committee for the revision of the New Testament, and was also a member of the Philological Congress held in Stockholm in 1889. His publications include an edition of "Cicero on Immortality" (Cambridge, 1881); "Virgil's Æneid" (Philadelphia, 1868); "Hellas: Her Monuments and Scenery" (1863); "Horace" (1869); "First Six Books of the Æneid" (1870); "Four Books of Livy" (1872); "Juvenal and Perseus" (1876); and "A Latin Grammar" (Philadelphia, 1882). He also published Latin text-books, numerous essays, including "Wordsworth," the "Homeric Question," "Curtius's History of Greece," "Goethe and Schiller," "Orations on Abraham Lincoln," and "The Poetry of Whittier," and a memorable address delivered at the opening of Bryn Mawr College on "Liberal Education: Its Aims and Methods."

Chester, Albert Tracy, educator, born in Norwich, Conn., June 16, 1812; died in Buffalo, N. Y., Aug. 7, 1892. He was graduated at Union College in 1833, studied theology with Eliphalet Nott, and was ordained a clergyman of the Presbyterian Church in 1836. During the next thirteen years he was pastor of Presbyterian churches at Ballston Spa and Saratoga, N. Y., and from 1860 till 1886 was principal of the Buffalo Female Academy. Dr. Chester remained active in pulpit work till his final sickness. He was president of the Historical Society, the Natural Science Association, and the Academy of Fine Arts of Buffalo.

Chester, T. Morris, lawyer, died in Harrisburg, Pa., Sept. 30, 1892. He was born of colored parents; was graduated at Thetford Academy, Vermont, in 1856, and then went to Liberia, where he became superintendent of the colony of Africans recaptured from American slavers, with whom he remained as a teacher till the outbreak of the civil war, when he returned to the United States and assisted in raising the 54th and 55th regiments of Massachusetts colored troops. He entered the field himself as war correspondent of the Philadelphia "Express," serving with the armies of the James and of the Potomac till after Lee's surrender, and it is said that his letter on the capture of Richmond was received a day in advance of that of any other correspondent. In 1866 he visited Europe and passed the winter in Russia, where he was a special guest of the Emperor Alexander II at a review of 40,000 troops in St. Petersburg. He then visited the courts of Denmark, Sweden, Saxony, and England, and was well received by many of the literary men of Paris. After spending four years in European travel, he studied law at Middle Temple Inn, London, and was admitted to the English bar in 1870, being the first colored lawyer in England. In 1871 he settled in Louisiana, where he practiced law, and was active in establishing schools for the education of the colored people. He also was appointed commander of the 1st Brigade of the State militia. Mr. Chester was United States commissioner from 1873 till 1879, and became President of the Wilmington, Wrightsville and Onslow Railroad Company in 1884.

Chidlaw, Benjamin W., missionary, born in North Wales, July 14, 1811; died there, July 13, 1892. He came to the United States when ten years old, settled in Ohio, and was graduated at Miami University in 1833. Soon afterward he was ordained a minister of the Presbyterian Church, and for fifty-seven years he was connected with the American Sunday-school Union as missionary or superintendent. In this field he had remarkable success, and it is believed he organized more Sunday schools than any other person.

Clark, Myron Holley, politician, born in Naples, Ontario County, N. Y., Oct. 23, 1806; died in Canandaigua, N. Y., Aug. 23, 1892. He received a common-school education, was apprenticed to the cabinet-

making trade, and followed it for several years. Entering public life at an early age, he was elected to nearly all the town offices successively, and when thirty years old was chosen sheriff. He removed to Canandaigua before the expiration of his term as sheriff; was president of the town in 1850-'51, State Senator in 1852-'54, and was elected Governor in 1854. He had for opponents Horatio Seymour, Greene C. Bronson, and Daniel Ullman; and, although he was the Whig candidate, his nomination was accepted by the State Temperance and the Free-Soil Democratic conventions. He was elected by a small plurality. From 1862 till 1868 he was collector of internal revenue, and on retiring from this office withdrew from public life. Gov. Clark was active in all temperance legislation, and while chairman of the Senate committee on that subject he carried to adoption a prohibitory law, which was vetoed by Gov. Seymour. A new one was passed during his term as Governor, and he signed it.

Colahan, John B., lawyer, born in Ballinasloe, Ireland, in 1815; died in Philadelphia, Pa., March 24, 1892. He came to the United States in early youth, first settling at Alexandria, Va.; was one of the engineers and the astronomer employed by the United States Government in the survey of the boundary line between Louisiana and Texas when the latter was admitted into the Union; and was engaged in the construction of the Eastern Shore and the Northern Central Railroads. During the riots in Philadelphia in 1844, as captain of the Montgomery Guards, with but 19 men, he held the Roman Catholic Church of St. Philip de Neri against a large mob. In later years he was a member of the Philadelphia bar.

Cole, Joseph Foxcroft, painter, born in Jay, Me., Nov. 9, 1837; died in Boston, Mass., May 2, 1892. For several years after leaving school he was employed in Boston as a lithographer. In 1860-'63 he studied painting with Lambinet and Jacque in Paris, and afterward he resided alternately in Paris and Boston. Mr. Cole was a frequent contributor to the Paris *Salon* and to the Royal Academy in London. Many of his most notable paintings are in private galleries and in the Union and Somerset Clubs of Boston. His chief works are: "A Pastoral Scene in Normandy," exhibited in the Paris *Salon* in 1875; "Twilight, Melrose Highlands," "Cows ruminating," and a "Coast Scene in Normandy," shown at the United States Centennial Exhibition, 1876; "A Norman Farm" and "Sheep-Washing in Normandy," at the Royal Academy in London in 1877; "Willow Brook," owned by the Boston Somerset Club; "Weakest goes to the Wall," now in a private gallery in Boston; and the well-known etching, "A Village Street in France, with a Flock of Sheep."

Collins, Frederic, p an r s , born in Philadelphia, Pa., in 1823; died in Chestnut Hill, Pa., Nov. 27, 1892. He was a son of Isaac Collins, the well-known philanthropist of a generation ago. Isaac Collins, among his numerous benevolent occupations, had charge of the Philadelphia House of Refuge, and to this model institution his son Frederic gave many of the best years of his life, succeeding his father as president. To him, in large measure, Pennsylvania owes the abolition of lotteries and much other reformatory work of lasting importance.

Collins, Rebecca, philanthropist, born in Philadelphia, Pa., Oct. 13, 1804; died in New York city, April 30, 1892. She was of German-Lutheran parentage, and when nineteen years old united with the Society of Friends, and began preaching in their meetings and engaging in their religious and philanthropic work. In this labor she passed the remainder of her life, being ably assisted for twenty-five years by her husband, Isaac Collins, who died in 1863. She then removed to New York city, and subsequently made long journeys in England, Scotland, Ireland, France, Germany, and Norway, attending the meetings of the Friends in those countries. She also had visited almost every meeting of the Friends in the United States. While in New York city she extended her philanthropic work to all classes of people; was deeply interested in the House of Refuge, Home for the Friendless, Convalescent Home, Woman's Christian Temperance Union, and kindred institutions; and in recent years had been particularly active in promoting the various enterprises of the New York Bible and Tract Mission, such as its coffee house, lodging house, mission chapel, and broom factory. She continued preaching in the meetings of the society till her final illness.

Colvis, Joseph, physician, born in New Orleans, La., in 1831; died in Paris, France, Aug. 20, 1892. He was born of Creole parents, was taken to France when eight years old, and was educated at the Lycée Bonaparte, subsequently studying medicine and receiving his diploma with the degrees of B. A. and B. S. He acquired a large and lucrative practice, and received several decorations from the French Government for special professional services, and for his aid during the Franco-Prussian War he was awarded the Cross of the Legion of Honor.

Comins, Linus B., merchant, born in Charlton, Mass., Nov. 29, 1817; died in Jamaica Plain, Mass., Oct. 14, 1892. He was graduated at the Worcester County Manual-labor High School, and was engaged in manufacturing and mercantile business through life. In 1846 he was elected to the Roxbury city council; in 1847–'48 was president of the council, and in 1854 was mayor. While holding the latter office he was elected to Congress, where he served in 1855–'58, being a member of the Committee on Commerce. During his service in Congress he was mainly instrumental in securing the appropriation for the erection of the Minot's Ledge Lighthouse, and he delivered the address at the laying of its corner stone. He was a delegate to the National Republican Convention in 1860. His interest in and benefaction to a school in Roxbury led to its being named for him.

Comstock, George Francis, jurist, born in Williamstown, Oswego County, N. Y., Aug. 24, 1811; died in Syracuse, N. Y., Sept. 27, 1892. He was graduated at Union College in 1834, admitted to the bar in 1837, appointed reporter of the Court of Appeals by Gov. Young in 1847, solicitor-general of the United States in 1852–'53 under President Filmore's administration, chief justice of the Court of Appeals of New York in 1856–'62, and was delegate-at-large to the constitutional convention of 1868, where he and the late Judge Folger framed the judiciary article in the present Constitution. In 1865, by request of the heirs of Chancellor Kent, he edited the eleventh edition of "Kent's Commentaries." Judge Comstock was very successful at the bar, and was engaged in several cases of more than usual interest, including the contest of Commodore Vanderbilt's will, where he represented the proponents by prior arrangement with Mr. Vanderbilt; the Cornell University suit over Mrs. Jennie McGraw Fisk's bequest to that institution; and the trial of Jacob Sharp in the Broadway Railway case, in which he was one of the counsel for the people. He was one of the founders of Syracuse University, toward whose establishment he gave $50,000; was the founder of St. John's School for Boys at Manlius, Onondaga County, N. Y., to which he gave $60,000; and for many years was a trustee of the State Institute for Feeble-minded Children in Syracuse.

Conway, Elias, politician, born in Tennessee, May 17, 1812; died in Little Rock, Ark., Feb. 28, 1892. He removed to Little Rock in 1833, and resided there till his death. From July, 1834, till June, 1836, when Arkansas was admitted into the Union, he was Territorial Auditor, and afterward was State Auditor for several years. He was elected Governor on the Democratic ticket in 1852, and re-elected in 1854, and at the close of his administration he left every department of the State in a flourishing condition, especially the treasury. Of late years he had led a very secluded life, and dressed in the old-fashioned garb. He was burned to death in a fire at his residence.

Cooke, Rose Terry, author, born in West Hartford, Conn., Feb. 17, 1827; died in Pittsfield, Mass., July 18, 1892. She was graduated at Hartford Female Seminary in 1843. She was married at New Haven, Conn., April 12, 1873, to Rollin H. Cooke, an iron manufacturer of Winsted, Conn., in which latter town she lived until she removed with her husband to Pittsfield, in 1887. She began to write when she was still a girl, and "The Mormon's Wife" appeared in "Graham's Magazine" when the author was but eighteen. She was one of the earliest contributors to the "Atlantic Monthly," and furnished the story "Sally Parson's Duty" to the first number of that periodical. Her published works include "Poems by Rose Terry" (Boston, 1860); "Happy Dodd" (Boston, 1879); "Somebody's Neighbors" (Boston, 1881); "The Deacon's Week" (New York, 1885); "Root-bound and other Sketches" (Boston, 1885); "No: A Story for Boys" (New York, 1886); "The Sphinx's Children and Other People's" (Boston, 1886); "Poems by Rose Terry Cooke, Complete" (New York, 1888); "Steadfast: A Novel" (Boston, 1889); "Huckleberries" (Boston, 1892). Among the many writers on New England rural life none have shown a clearer insight, or depicted it more faithfully or sympathetically, than Mrs. Cooke has done in her short stories written during the past thirty-five years. Two of the most characteristic of these are "Miss Lucinda" and "Freedom Wheeler's Controversy with Providence." Her verse is thoughtful in its cast, and sometimes reaches a distinctly high level of inspiration. "The Two Villages" is her most quoted poem, but others, like "Segovia and Madrid," "Rêve du Midi," and "Bluebeard's Chamber," are notably good. Her home at Winsted was an old-fashioned structure, which she had filled with antique furniture, and was surrounded by attractive grounds, where she spent the most of her time.

Cooley, Dennis Nelson, jurist, born in Vermont in 1825; died in New York city, Nov. 13, 1892. He was a cousin of Thomas M. Cooley, ex-chairman of the Interstate Commerce Commission, studied law with Judge Barrett, of Brattleboro, and was admitted to the bar there, and when thirty years old removed to Washington, D. C., and engaged in practice, but subsequently made his permanent residence in Dubuque, Iowa. In 1864 he was appointed by President Lincoln a special commissioner to South Carolina; in 1865 was appointed Commissioner of Indian Affairs, and in 1869 was reappointed. In 1873 he was elected State Senator in Iowa, and was appointed commissioner to the Vienna Exposition. In 1873–'82 he owned the Dubuque "Times." At the time of his death he was a judge of the Supreme Court of Iowa.

Corbit, William Pitt, clergyman, born in Philadelphia, Pa., Oct. 12, 1818; died in Brooklyn, N. Y., Dec. 11, 1892. He received a limited education, became a truckman, was converted in 1836, began exhorting in meetings of the Methodist Episcopal Church, and was encouraged to study for the ministry in 1840. In 1841 he was admitted on trial to the New Jersey Conference; in 1842 attracted much attention by preaching before the Philadelphia Conference; in 1847 went to New Jersey, and for several years held pastorates in Newark and Hackensack; in 1854 was transferred to New York city, and till 1885 held charges there, and in Newark, Jersey City, Baltimore, Brooklyn, and New Haven. He was very tall and straight, with long, straight, jet-black hair, high cheek-bones, and swarthy complexion. He was a natural orator, an exceedingly forcible speaker, and much given to startling dramatic effects.

Coxe, Brinton, lawyer, born in Philadelphia, Aug. 3, 1833; died in Drifton, Pa., Sept. 15, 1892. He was a son of Judge Charles S. Coxe, of Philadelphia, and a grandson of Tench Coxe, the writer on political economy. He was graduated at the University of Pennsylvania in 1852, studied law, and was admitted to the bar in 1855. He then spent a year abroad studying law. While actively engaged in his profession he gave much time to literary pursuits, and made special researches into the principles of jurisprudence, history, and political economy. He was President of the Pennsylvania Historical Society from 1884 till his death. Mr. Coxe published a translation, with original notes, of Güterbock's "Bracton in his Relation to the Roman Law" (1866), and at the time of his death was putting through the press a study of the American Constitution, on which he had been at work for many years. He had just completed "An Essay on Judicial Decisions and Unconstitutional Legislation."

Crain, Peter Wood, jurist, born in Charles County, Md., Jan. 9, 1806; died in Baltimore, Md., March 30, 1892. He was admitted to the bar in 1827, was elected to the Legislature in 1841, was first appointed judge of the 1st Judicial Circuit in 1846, and held the office by reappointment till 1851, when the new State Constitution made the judiciary elective. He was elected to the office for a term of ten years, being nominated by both political parties. From this court he was promoted to the Court of Appeals, where he served till 1867, when he resumed practice till his retirement, in 1878. Throughout his public career he was actively identified with State affairs, and he became widely known by his opposition to the scheme of Gov. Thomas for the repudiation of the State debt.

Cranch, Christopher Pearse, artist and poet, born in Alexandria, Va., March 8, 1813; died in Cambridge, Mass., Jan. 20, 1892. He was the son of Chief-Justice Cranch, a noted jurist. He was graduated at Columbian College, Washington, D. C., in 1831, and at the Harvard Divinity School, Cambridge, in 1835, and preached for a few years in Unitarian pulpits, but retired from the ministry in 1842, and turned his attention to landscape painting. In 1846 he went to Italy to study for two years, and in 1853 returned to Europe and lived there for ten years, in which time he painted many Swiss and Italian landscapes. Returning to America in 1863, he was chosen a member of the National Academy the next year, but ceased to contribute to its exhibitions after 1871. The latest years of his life were passed mainly in Cambridge, and he numbered among his intimate friends there both Lowell and Longfellow. He was a man of many gifts, but his personality was more to his friends than anything that he ever did in poetry or painting. His nature was generous and serene, and he attached his friends strongly to him. Among strangers he was reserved even to coldness, but to those whose privilege it was to know him well he revealed himself as one of the most delightful of men. He failed to gain popular applause for his work, and this he seems to have been conscious of; but although this may have intensified his native reserve, it did not make him bitter. After a long illness, he died, leaving behind him the memory of a very sweet and tender soul. Some of his more noted paintings are: "October Afternoon" (1867); "Val de Moline, Amalfi, Italy" (1869); "Venice" (1870); Venetian Fishing Boats" (1871). He published "Poems" (Philadelphia, 1844); "The Last of the Huggermuggers" (1856) and "Kobboltzo" (1857), prose tales for children, illustrated by himself; a blank-verse translation of the "Æneid" (1872); "Satan: A Libretto" (Boston, 1874); "The Bird and the Bell, with Other Poems" (Boston, 1875; 2d ed., 1890); "Ariel and Caliban" (Boston, 1887). "Thought," his best-known poem, was one of his earliest, being contributed to "The Dial" in 1840.

Crawford, Samuel Wylie, military officer, born in Franklin County, Pa., Nov. 8, 1829; died in Philadelphia, Pa., Nov. 3, 1892. He was graduated at the University of Pennsylvania in 1846, studied medicine, and entered the United States army as assistant surgeon in 1851. He served in various forts in the Southwest, chiefly in Texas, till 1860, when he was stationed first at Fort Moultrie and afterward at Fort Sumter, where he commanded one of the batteries during the memorable bombardment in April, 1861. After the surrender of Major Anderson's garrison he was stationed at Fort Columbus, New York harbor, till August, 1861, and then, resigning his commission of assistant surgeon, he accepted the appointment of major in the 13th United States Infantry. In the following year he was commissioned brigadier-general

of volunteers. He served with distinction in the Shenandoah campaign, was present at the battles of Winchester and Cedar Mountain, losing half of his brigade in the last-named action, and succeeded Gen. Mansfield in command of his division at the battle of Antietam, where he was severely wounded. Early in 1863 he was placed in command of the Pennsylvania Reserves, then stationed in the vicinity of Washington, which troops comprised the 3d division of the 5th Army Corps. He again distinguished himself during the battles at Gettysburg, and afterward took part in all the operations of the Army of the Potomac till the close of the war. During 1863-'65 he was brevetted colonel, brigadier-general, and major-general, for gallantry at Gettysburg, the Wilderness, Spottsylvania, Petersburg, Five Forks, and other battles. In 1866 he was mustered out of the volunteer service. He served with his regiment in the South till February, 1869, when he was appointed colonel of the 16th Infantry, was subsequently transferred to the 2d Infantry, and was retired on account of disability resulting from wounds, with the rank of brigadier-general, United States Army, in February, 1873.

Crosby, William Henry, educator, born in New York city, June 28, 1808; died there, May 21, 1892. He was a son of William Bedlow Crosby, and the eldest brother of Howard Crosby. He was graduated at Columbia College in the same class with Hamilton Fish in 1827; studied law, and was admitted to the bar in New York; but, preferring the field of literature and the classics, he accepted a call to the professorship of Latin and Greek at Rutgers College in 1841, where he remained for eight years. In 1849 he removed to Poughkeepsie, and was there engaged in literary pursuits for ten years. During 1859-'60 he occupied temporarily the chair of Latin Language and Literature in Columbia College, and since then he had lived in retirement, the greater part of the time in Poughkeepsie. He was the Vice-President of the New York Bible Society.

Crowninshield, Benjamin William, military officer, born in Boston, Mass., March 12, 1837; died in Rome, Italy, Jan. 17, 1892. He was graduated at Harvard University in 1858. He entered the national army as 1st lieutenant in the 1st Massachusetts Cavalry, Dec. 19, 1861; served through several of the campaigns in Virginia; was an aid on the staff of Gen. Sheridan in 1864; and resigned from the army with the rank of colonel in June, 1865. He was long identified with the Massachusetts Humane Society, and he published a history of the 1st Massachusetts Cavalry in 1890.

Cullis, Charles, p y , born in Boston, Mass., March 7, 1833; died there, June 17, 1892. He suffered from ill health in boyhood; was induced to take up the study of medicine; and about the time of receiving his diploma he became deeply interested in religious matters, and was confirmed in the Protestant Episcopal Church. About 1862 he became such a strong believer in the power of feeling in answer to prayer, that he inaugurated what has since been known as the Faith-cure movement. He wore his life away in this work, and during his career, by prayer alone, he raised several hundred thousand dollars with which to carry on his various enterprises, claiming that he had never asked any one but the Lord to supply a cent. Among the institutions established and managed by him were the Consumptives' Home at Grove Hall; the Faith-cure College at Boston; the Children's Home, the Boynton Orphanage and Institute for Colored Children in Virginia; the Chinese Mission in California; two schools in India; the Cancer Home at Walpole; the Spinal Home; and the Deaconess House. These institutions cost more than $500,000. In 1890 he spent $46,000 for a tract of land on which to erect a church edifice, parsonage, and business house, and $70,000 for an estate of 150 acres at Wellesley Hills, where he intended building a larger consumptives' home.

Cullum, George Washington, military officer, born in New York city, Feb. 25, 1809; died there, Feb. 28, 1892. He was graduated at the United States Military Academy, and entered the army as brevet 2d lieutenant of United States engineers in 1833; was promoted 2d lieutenant 1836, captain 1838, major 1861, lieutenant-colonel 1863, and colonel 1867; and was retired Jan. 13, 1874. In the volunteer service he was commissioned colonel and aid-de-camp Aug. 6, 1861, and brigadier-general Nov. 1 following; was brevetted major-general March 13, 1865; and was mustered out of the service Sept. 1, 1866. He was engaged in the construction of Fort Adams and other fortifications at Newport, R. I., New London, Conn., and in Boston harbor in 1833-'38; was instructor in practical engineering at the United States Military Academy in 1848-'55, excepting for two years which he spent in studying the principal fortifications in Europe; and was in charge of the Atlantic coast defenses, and superintended the construction of fortifications and improvements at Charleston, S. C., New Bedford, Mass., Newport, R. I., New London, Conn., and the eastern entrance to New York harbor, in 1855-'61. After serving as aid-de-camp to Gen. Scott and as chief engineer of the Department of Missouri in 1861, he was chief of staff to Gen. Henry W. Halleck while the latter was in command of the Department of Missouri, and also while he was general in chief of the national armies. He was a member of the United States Sanitary Commission in 1861-'64, directed engineering operations on the Western rivers, projected fortifications for Nashville, and was chief engineer during the siege of Corinth. He was Superintendent of the United States Military Academy from 1864 till 1866. From 1867 till his retirement he was a member of the board for the construction and improvement of the defenses of New York, and of the river and harbor commission of the army. He was a delegate to the conference of the Association for the Reform and Codification of the Laws of Nations, at Cologne, and to the International Geographical Congress at Venice in 1881; Vice-President of the American Geographical Society from 1874, and of the Geographical Library Association of New York from 1880. Gen. Cullum married the widow of Gen. Halleck. Among his notable bequests were $250,000 to the Federal Government for the erection on the grounds of the United States Military Academy of a military "Memorial Hall," and $40,000 with which to purchase busts, portraits, and paintings of military men, and subjects for the Hall, as well as to publish decennially his "Register"; more than $100,000 to the Geographical Library Association for a fireproof building; $20,000 to the Metropolitan Museum of Art; and his books relating to the United States Military Academy and military education to the United States Engineering School at Willett's Point, New York. Besides numerous memoirs, reports, and miscellaneous papers, Gen. Cullum published "Military Bridges with India-rubber Pontoons" (1849); "Register of Officers and Graduates of the United States Military Academy from 1802 to 1850" (1850); translation of Duparcq's "Elements of Military Art and History" (1863); "Systems of Military Bridges" (1863); "Biographical Register of the Officers and Graduates of the United States Military Academy" (1st ed., 1868; 2d ed., 1879; 3d ed., revised and extended, 1891); and "Campaigns of the War of 1812 criticised" (1880).

Dalrimple, Van Cleve, jurist, born in Morris County, N. J., in 1821; died in Morristown, N. J., Nov. 27, 1892. He was educated at Morristown Academy, was admitted to the bar in 1843, and settled in Morristown. He was appointed prosecutor of the pleas in 1852, and held the office five years, and in 1866 was appointed an associate justice of the Supreme Court of New Jersey. He held the latter office for two successive terms, and then retired from public life. In early life he was a Democrat in politics, but at the time of the excitement over the repeal of the Missouri Compromise he joined the Free-Soil party, and subsequently the Republican.

Danforth, Peter Swart, jurist, born in Middleburg, N. Y., June 19, 1816; died there, July 17, 1892. He was graduated at Union College in 1837; studied law, and was admitted to the bar in 1840; was appointed district attorney for Schoharie County in 1845; elected State Senator from Delaware and Schoharie Counties in 1858; and was appointed a justice of the Supreme Court of New York in 1872. Judge Danforth had been connected with the Reformed Dutch Church for more than half a century, and had been frequently a member of its General Synod and of important committees under it.

Davis, Alexander Jackson, architect, born in New York city, July 24, 1803; died in West Orange, N. J., Jan. 14, 1892. He was a son of Cornelius Davis, editor and publisher of the "New York Theological Magazine," which is said to have been the first religious periodical issued in this country. In 1823 he began studying architecture in the Antique School. One of his best known designs was that for the Customhouse in New York, which was approved by the Treasury Department, but, as he claimed, was altered and vulgarized by the commissioners and builders. Mr. Davis was the founder of the American Institute of Architects, and secretary of the American Academy of Fine Arts, which was afterward known as the National Academy of Design.

Davis, Joseph J., jurist, born in Franklin County, N. C., April 13, 1828; died in Louisburg, N. C., Aug. 7, 1892. He received an academical education, was admitted to the bar in 1850; served in the Confederate army during the civil war; was elected to the State Legislature in 1866, and was a member of Congress from 1875 till 1880. During his last term in Congress he was a member of the committees on Banking and Currency and Public Expenditures. In 1886 he was appointed an associate justice of the Supreme Court of North Carolina.

Decker, John, fireman, born in New York city, May 15, 1823; died in Port Richmond, Staten Island, N. Y., Nov. 18, 1892. He was brought up in the oyster business, and for many years was one of the largest wholesalers in the city. In October, 1844, he entered the volunteer fire department of New York city, joining engine company N°° 14; in 1847 was elected assistant foreman; in 1850, foreman; in 1852, assistant engineer; and in 1860 and 1863, chief of the department. He was the last chief of the old volunteer department, serving till the organization of the present paid system. He displayed rare heroism during the draft riots in 1863, at one time was about to be hanged by the mob, and by his personal courage saved several public and private buildings from destruction by fire at the hands of drunken incendiaries. He aided in recruiting the 1st Regiment of Fire Zouaves and in raising $31,000 for its equipment, and personally recruited and maintained the 2d Regiment of fire zouaves. On the organization of the paid fire department the commissioners endeavored to retain his services, but he declined to hold office longer. He organized the Volunteer Fire Department Association in 1865, and was its president till 1889. Mr. Decker served in the Legislature for five terms.

Delevan, Charles H., insurance broker, born in Sing Sing, N. Y., in 1810; died in New York city, April 9, 1892. He was a son of Gen. Daniel Delevan, one of eleven brothers, who served in the Continental army during the Revolutionary War, and was the last representative of the direct branch of the old Huguenot family of that name. In early life he was engaged in the hardware business in New York city with two of his brothers. During the administration of President Pierce he was United States consul at Halifax, and subsequently he held the same office at St. Thomas, West Indies. On returning to New York, he engaged in the fire-insurance business, and retired from active work about 1882. He was personally acquainted with the principal statesmen of his early life, and was well known in New York city and the principal watering places and summer resorts for his idiosyncrasies. He dressed peculiarly, creating his own fashions, and after reaching his sixtieth year he purchased four coal-black horses and a large brake, decorated in flaming colors, with which he drove about the city and its vicinity. His horses, with either the brake or a huge, old-fashioned laudau, were seen regularly for years at Saratoga, and his shirt bosom always exhibited a mass of diamonds. Mr. Delevan spent more than $50,000 in erecting a massive memorial, in the form of a series of monuments, in the cemetery at Sleepy Hollow, where his father and ten brothers were buried.

Dent, Frederick Tracey, military officer, born in White Haven, Mo., Dec. 17, 1820; died in Denver, Col., Dec. 24, 1892. He was a classmate and brother-in-law of Gen. U. S. Grant; was graduated at the United States Military Academy and appointed brevet 2d lieutenant 6th United States Infantry in 1843; was promoted 2d lieutenant 5th Infantry in 1846, 1st lieutenant in 1847, captain 9th Infantry in 1855, major 4th Infantry in 1863, lieutenant-colonel 32d Infantry in 1867, colonel 1st Artillery in 1881, and was retired Dec. 1, 1883. In the volunteer service he was commissioned brigadier-general April 5, 1865, and was mustered out April 30, 1866. During his military career he was brevetted 1st lieutenant for gallantry in the battles of Contreras and Churubusco, captain for Molino del Rey, lieutenant-colonel for the Wilderness campaign, colonel for bravery before Petersburg, and brigadier-general for services in the field during the civil war. On March 29, 1864, he was appointed aid on the staff of Gen. Grant. He was present in the battles and operations of the Richmond campaign of 1864, and in 1865 was military commander of Richmond. After the war he continued on staff duty till Gen. Grant's election to the presidency, when he became his private secretary.

Denver, James W., lawyer, born in Winchester, Va., in 1818; died in Washington, D. C., Aug. 9, 1892. He accompanied his parents to Ohio when thirteen years old, received a public-school education, and removed to Missouri in 1841, where he studied law, and was admitted to the bar. He served through the Mexican War as a captain in the 12th United States Infantry, He removed to California in 1850, and was appointed a member of a special relief committee to protect emigrants, and was chosen a State Senator in 1852. In the latter year he fought a duel with Edward Gilbert, a former member of Congress, in consequence of a controversy over some legislation, and killed his opponent. In 1853 he was appointed Secretary of State of California; in 1855–'57 was a member of Congress; in 1857 was appointed Commissioner of Indian Affairs, but resigned soon afterward to accept the governorship of the Territory of Kansas, which included the present States of Kansas, Colorado, and Nebraska. He resigned as Governor in 1858; was reappointed Indian Commissioner, and held this office till March, 1859. He entered the national army in 1861; was commissioned brigadier-general of volunteers; served in the Western States, and resigned in March, 1863. After the war he practiced law in Washington, D. C., and resisted all appeals to become a candidate for public office till 1870, when, as a candidate for Congress, he met the first defeat of his life. While Governor of Kansas Territory Gen. Denver suggested the name of Colorado for the new Territory formed out of Kansas, and sent a full set of officers to Arapahoe County, where the pioneers and officers named the settlement Denver, in his honor.

Derby, James Cephas, publisher, born in Little Falls, N. Y., July 20, 1818; died in Brooklyn, N. Y., Sept. 22, 1892. He was apprenticed to the book-publishing business in Auburn, N. Y., in 1833, and organized the publishing firm of J. C. Derby & Co. in 1840, the style of which was changed to Derby & Miller in 1848; sold his interest, and went to San Francisco in 1852; and permanently settled in New York city in 1853, forming, two years afterward, the firm of Derby & Jackson. In 1861 the name was again changed to J. C. Derby & Co., and subsequently to Derby & Miller. The first firm to which he belonged published the first hymnal with tunes and words, compiled by the Rev. Josiah Hopkins, D. D., in 1844, and also published the first detailed biographies of George

Washington's mother and wife. In 1848 he brought out a "Life of General Zachary Taylor," and during each of the next ten presidential campaigns he produced biographies of at least one of the candidates. Mr. Derby was the first publisher of "Fanny Fern's" works, and of William II. Seward's "Life of John Quincy Adams," and for many years made a specialty of the works of Addison, Defoe, Fielding, Smollett, Goldsmith, Charles Lamb, and their contemporaries, and of law books, among which were Blatchford's "United States Reports." He was also connected for several years with the subscription-book department of D. Appleton & Co., and published a large volume entitled "Fifty Years among Authors, Books, and Publishers" (New York, 1884).

Dillon, Sidney, railroad builder, born in Northampton, Montgomery County, N. Y., May 7, 1812; died in New York city, June 9, 1892. He received a common-school education, and became an errand boy for the men engaged in building the railroad from Albany to Schenectady, the first in New York State. He then was similarly employed on the Rensselaer and Saratoga Railroad, and when that was completed became a foreman in the building of the Boston and Providence road. From this he went as foreman and manager to the Stonington road; and in 1848 secured his first personal contract for a section of the Western Railroad of Massachusetts. Subsequently he was engaged in the construction of parts or the whole of about thirty roads, including the Troy and Schenectady, the Hartford and Springfield, the Cheshire of Vermont, the Vermont and Massachusetts, the Rutland and Burlington, the Central of New Jersey, the Boston and New York Central, the Philadelphia and Erie, the Erie and Cleveland, and the Morris and Essex Railroads. In 1865 he became interested in the construction and management of the Union Pacific Railroad, with which he remained connected through life. He completed the Union Pacific Railroad in four years, and drove a silver spike on Promontory Point for the last rail that connected the Union Pacific with the Central Pacific road in the spring of 1869. After finishing this work, he built fifty miles of the New Orleans, Mobile and Chattanooga road, and subsequently was concerned in the building of the Connecticut Valley, the Chillicothe, Council Bluffs and Omaha, the Canada Southern, and the Paterson branch of the Morris and Essex Railroad. He also had the contract for lowering the tracks of the New York Central Railroad, and built the Fourth Avenue Tunnel in New York city. Mr. Dillon was a director of the Union Pacific Railroad Company for nearly thirty years; was its president several times, and at the time of his death was chairman of its board of directors. He was also a president or director in many of the largest railroad companies in the country, and for many years had been actively identified with the railroad operations of Jay Gould.

Dougherty, Daniel, lawyer, born in Philadelphia, Oct. 15, 1826; died there, Sept. 5, 1892. He was the son of a poor Irishman, who had been a land surveyor in his own country. He received a common-school education, left home early in life, began studying law in 1844, and was admitted to the bar in 1849. His rapid advance in his profession was caused by his oratorical ability. He identified himself with the Democratic party early in life, and remained in it till his death, excepting during the civil war. In 1861 he gave hearty support to the Union cause. The next year he was one of the founders of the Union League Club in Philadelphia, and in 1864 his speeches in advocacy of President Lincoln's re-election were among the most noteworthy in the campaign. After the war he resumed his connection with the Democratic party, and also became a popular lecturer. Among his best-known efforts in this line were those on "The Stage," on "Orators and Oratory," and on "American Politics." On Nov. 11, 1889, he made what has been considered the greatest public address of his life, at the opening of the Roman Catholic Lay Congress in Baltimore.

Douglas, John Hancock, physician, born in Waterford, N. Y., in 1824; died in Washington, D. C., Oct. 2, 1892. He was graduated at Williams College in 1843, and at the medical department of the University of Pennsylvania in 1847; spent two years in travel and study in Europe, settled in New York city, and became widely known as a specialist in the treatment of lung and throat diseases. From 1856 till 1862 he was editor of "The American Medical Monthly," and in 1865-'66 edited three volumes of "The New York Medical Journal." During the civil war he served in the United States Sanitary Commission, and in 1863, while stationed in the Division of the Mississippi, he became intimate with Gen. Grant. After the war he resumed his practice in New York. In 1884, when Gen. Grant's illness assumed a serious turn, Dr. Fordyce Barker, who was then Gen. Grant's family physician, and was about going to Europe, transferred the patient to Dr. Douglas. During the nine months of the general's illness Dr. Douglas was seldom absent from his patient, having wholly abandoned his own large practice. For his services he was paid $12,000, but the constant care of his patient broke down his own constitution. He sought restoration to health in foreign travel, had two strokes of paralysis, and for some time suffered from the same kind of cancer that caused Gen. Grant's death.

Douglass, Henry, military officer, born in West Point, N. Y., March 9, 1827; died in Barnegat Park, N. J., June 19, 1892. He was a son of Major David Bates Douglass, Professor of Engineering at the United States Military Academy, and was graduated there in 1852. He was commissioned brevet 2d lieutenant, 7th United States Infantry, on graduation; was promoted 2d lieutenant 8th Infantry, Dec. 31, 1853; transferred to 9th Infantry, March 3, 1855; 1st lieutenant, Sept. 10, 1856; captain 18th Infantry, May 14, 1861; major 3d Infantry. July 28, 1866; transferred to 11th Infantry, Jan. 1, 1871; lieutenant-colonel 14th Infantry, Jan. 10, 1876, and colonel 10th Infantry, July 1, 1885; and was retired March 9, 1891. He was assistant Professor of Drawing at the Military Academy from Jan. 16, 1858, till July 2, 1861. He took part in the battle of Bull Run and in the Tennessee and Mississippi campaigns, was wounded at the battle of Stone River, and soon after that battle was taken ill with typhoid fever and had to retire from the army. Before his complete recovery Gov. Tod appointed him army paymaster at Columbus, Ohio. After the war he returned to frontier duty, and subsequently he had charge of the military arrangement of the commission for settling the boundary between the United States and the Canadian Northwest. He was brevetted major United States army for gallant and meritorious service in the battle of Stone River, Dec. 31, 1862, and he performed his last active duty at Fort Marcy, New Mexico.

Dow, John Melmoth, naturalist, born in New York city in 1827; died there, Nov. 4, 1892. He began studying law early in life, but owing to poor health he was induced to make a whaling voyage, and this proved so beneficial that he determined to follow the sea as a business. When twenty-one years old he became captain of a clipper ship, with which he made several successful trips to China and Japan. In 1849 he became General Superintendent of the Pacific Mail Steamship Company on the Isthmus of Panama, and had since made his residence there, visiting his family in New York city once in two years. For nearly thirty years he had cruised along the western coast of Central and South America, in command of various vessels, and during that time he made a thorough exploration of that coast, giving much attention to the study of marine fauna. Through his labors about 200 new fishes were discovered and named, and. he also discovered in the highlands of Guatemala a new species of tapir. A remarkable member of the orchid family, found in Costa Rica, 4,000 feet above the sea, is named *Cattleya Dowiana* in his honor. Capt. Dow received the degree of Ph. D. from the University of Göttingen.

Dowling, John William, physician, born in New York city, Aug. 11, 1837; died in Goshen, N. Y., Jan. 14, 1892. He was a son of the Rev. John Dowling, D. D., author of the well-known "History of Romanism," was educated at Lewisburg College, Pennsylvania, and was graduated at the Hahnemann Medical College in Philadelphia in 1857. In the following year he was associated with Abraham D. Wilson, M. D., of New York, one of the pioneers of the new school of homœopathy; in 1870 he was appointed Professor of Theory and Practice in the New York Homœopathic Medical College, in 1871 was elected registrar, and from 1872 till 1884 was dean of the college. In 1879, on the establishment of the special chair of Physical Diagnosis and Diseases of the Heart and Lungs in the college, he was appointed to fill it. He was elected President of the American Institute of Homœopathy in 1880. The founding of the New York Surgical College was due in a large measure to his work with the Legislature to secure a charter.

Drake, Charles Daniel, jurist, born in Cincinnati, Ohio, April 11, 1811; died in Washington, D. C., March 31, 1892. He studied in St. Joseph's College, Kentucky, and at Partridge's Military Academy in Connecticut. In 1827 he was appointed a midshipman in the United States navy, where he served three years, beginning the study of law while so employed. He was admitted to the bar in Cincinnati in May, 1833; practiced in St. Louis, Mo., in 1834-'47, and in Cincinnati 1847-'50, and then returned to St. Louis. In 1859 he was elected to the Legislature, where he subsequently opposed the secession movement; in 1863 he was a member of the State Convention, and in 1864 Vice-President of the State Constitutional Convention. He was elected a United States Senator in January, 1867, but resigned his seat in December, 1870, on being appointed Chief Justice of the United States Court of Claims, which office he held until January, 1885. He was a conspicuous member of the Presbyterian Church in the West, was a member of the General Assembly (O. S.), 1869, served on the Committee of Conference on Reunion, and was chairman of the committee by which the long-standing controversy regarding the Theological Seminary in the Northwest was settled. In 1854 he published "A Treatise on the Law of Suits by Attachment in the United States," and in 1880 presented a paper on "Christianity the Friend of the Working Classes" before the second General Council of the Presbyterian Alliance.

Dunn, Michael, reformer, born in Manchester, England, Sept. 15, 1826; died in Brooklyn, N. Y., Feb. 22, 1892. He was brought up in ignorance, began a thieving career while a boy, and continued it until late in life. His criminal experiences included tilltapping, pocket picking, burglary, garroting, and dealing in counterfeit money. Before he was twelve years old he had served five terms in prison, and during his life he had been a prisoner in Van Diemen's Land, London, Manchester, Western Australia, Gibraltar, Montreal, Philadelphia, Boston, and Sing Sing. He once escaped from the Penitentiary on Blackwell's Island by swimming to the Long Island shore. While serving his last term in Sing Sing for burglary he was converted to religion, and on his release, in 1879, he established an industrial home for convicts in Water Street, New York, and afterward supplemented it with similar institutions in Chicago, San Francisco, Philadelphia, and other cities. At the time of his death he was preparing his largest enterprise in this direction, in Brooklyn, and expected soon to open a larger home in New York city. In all the Dunn homes the manufacture of brooms was carried on, to aid in supporting them.

Dwight, Theodore William, educator, born in Catskill, N. Y., July 18, 1822; died in Clinton. N. Y., June 29, 1892. He was graduated at Hamilton College in 1840, studied law at Yale in 1841-'42; was tutor in Hamilton College in 1842-'46, and professor there of Law, History, Civil Polity, and Political Economy in 1846-'58. In the latter year he was elected Professor of Municipal Law in Columbia College, and he held this chair, together with the office of warden of the law school, till June, 1891, when he resigned and was made professor emeritus. Prof. Dwight was a member of the State Constitutional Convention, and of its judiciary committee in 1867; was elected nonresident Professor of Constitutional Law at Cornell University, and lecturer on law at Amherst College in 1868; Vice-President of the State Board of Public Charities, and member of the Commission of Appeals in 1873; President of the State Prison Association in 1874; member of the Committee of Seventy which dealt with the Tweed ring in New York city; State Commissioner to the International Prison Congress at Stockholm in 1878; and counsel for the five professors of Andover Theological Seminary against whom complaints of heterodoxy were made in 1886. He was also for many years an associate editor of the "American Law Register," and author of a large number of articles on legal subjects. He was widely known as an eminent authority on the common and civil laws and the laws regulating public charities, and also on the methods of legal teaching.

Earle, Pliny, p s an, born in Leicester, Mass., Dec. 31, 1809; died in Northampton, Mass., May 18, 1892. He was graduated at the Pennsylvania University; spent several years abroad studying the treatment of the insane; was appointed Superintendent of the Friends' Hospital for the Insane at Frankford, Pa., in 1840; was physician in Bloomingdale Asylum in 1844-'49; was appointed Professor of Psychology in Berkshire Medical Institution at Pittsfield, Mass., in 1852; and was Superintendent of the Massachusetts State Hospital for the Insane from 1864 till 1885, when he retired because of advanced age. Dr. Earle was a founder of the American Medical Association. He is said to have been the first person that ever addressed an insane audience on any subject that was not wholly religious, and his policy of combining instruction and amusement as a remedial agency has been adopted in all modern insane institutions. He wrote numerous works on the general subject of mental disorders. He bequeathed $60,000 to the city of Northampton as a fund, the interest of which is to be used toward maintaining the Forbes Library in that city.

Elliott, Charles, educator, born in Castleton, Scotland, March 18, 1815; died in Easton, Pa., Feb. 14, 1892. He was graduated at Lafayette College in 1840; spent a year at Princeton Theological Seminary; taught at Xenia, Ohio, in 1843-'45; was appointed Professor of Belles-lettres in the Western University, Pennsylvania, in 1847; of Greek in Miami University, Ohio, in 1849; of Biblical Literature and Exegesis in the Presbyterian Theological Seminary of the Northwest in 1863; and of Hebrew in Lafayette College in 1882. He was a member of the American Oriental Society, the Philosophical Society of Great Britain, and the American Society of Biblical Literature and Exegesis, and a personal friend of many eminent German scholars. Besides translations of Kleinert's "Commentaries" and the introduction to the prophetic writings in the American Lange Series, he published "The Sabbath" (Philadelphia, 1866); "Inspiration of the Scriptures" (Edinburgh, 1877); in co-operation with the Rev. W. J. Harsha, "Biblical Hermeneutics" (New York, 1879) and "Mosaic Authorship of the Pentateuch" (Cincinnati, 1884).

Ely, Alfred, lawyer, born in Lyme, Conn., Feb. 18, 1815; died in Rochester, N. Y., May 18, 1892. He removed to Rochester in 1835, was appointed clerk of the Recorder's court in 1840, and admitted to the bar in 1841. He was elected to Congress as a Republican in 1858 and 1860, and served as chairman of the Committee on Invalid Pensions. In July, 1861, while visiting the Bull Run battle field, he was captured by the Confederates, and, notwithstanding his claims for exemption on account of being a member of Congress, he was taken to Richmond and confined six months in Libby Prison. He was exchanged for Charles J. Faulkner, the American minister to France, who had been imprisoned through suspicion of disloyalty. He published "Journal of Alfred Ely, a Prisoner of War in Richmond" (New York, 1862).

Faran, James J., lawyer, born in Cincinnati, Ohio, in 1799; died there, Dec. 12, 1892. He was graduated at Miami University in 1831, was admitted to the bar in 1833; elected to the Legislature in 1835, 1837, and 1838, and to the State Senate in 1839, 1841, and 1842, serving the last two terms as Speaker. He was elected to Congress as a Democrat in 1844 and 1846, subsequently was mayor and postmaster of Cincinnati, and was one of the proprietors of the Cincinnati "Enquirer" from 1844 till 1881, and for much of the time its editor-in-chief.

Farley, Frederick A., clergyman, born in Boston, Mass., June 25, 1800; died in Brooklyn, N. Y., March 24, 1892. He was graduated at Harvard in 1818, and was the oldest living alumnus of the institution. In 1821 he was admitted to the bar, and after practicing for several years he was graduated at Cambridge Divinity School in 1827 and was ordained pastor of a new Unitarian Church in Providence, R. I. He preached in Providence till 1841, when he began ministering to the Second Unitarian Church in Brooklyn, with which he remained for nineteen years; then resigned his charge, and was chosen pastor emeritus. He was a Unitarian of the conservative type, and was active in the intellectual and charitable life of Brooklyn.

Fayerweather, Lucy, died in Rutland, Vt., July 16, 1892. She was the widow of Daniel B. Fayerweather, who died in New York city, Nov. 15, 1890, and bequeathed $2,000,000 to charitable and educational institutions, and directed that a further sum, then estimated at $3,000,000, should be placed in the hands of executors for distribution among public institutions according to specific, private instructions (see sketch in "Annual Cyclopædia" for 1890, page 645). Mrs. Fayerweather bequeathed all of her property to her relatives. Shortly before her death an action was begun in her name in the Supreme Court of New York to set aside the compromise which she had previously made with her husband's executors, and since her death some of her heirs have taken steps to continue her action.

Fitch, Graham Newell, p s an, born in Le Roy, N. Y., Dec. 7, 1810; died at Logansport, Ind., Nov. 29, 1892. He was educated at Middlebury and Geneva, N. Y., studied medicine, and removed to Logansport to practice in 1834. He was elected to the Legislature in 1836 and 1839; was a presidential elector in 1844, 1848, and 1856; professor in the Rush Medical College at Chicago in 1844-'49; member of Congress in 1849-'53; and United States Senator in 1857-'61. In the latter body he served as a member of the committees on Post Offices and Post Roads and on Indian Affairs. In the autumn of 1861 he raised the 46th Regiment of Indiana Volunteers, was commissioned its colonel, and served till the following year, when he was obliged to resign on account of injuries. He was a delegate to the National Democratic Convention in New York in 1868.

Fox-Jencken, Catharine, spiritualist, born in Bath, near Lake Ontario, Canada, in 1839; died in New York city, July 2, 1892. She was the second of the three Fox sisters, who attracted wide attention by their alleged *séances* while living at Hydeville, 30 miles from Rochester, in 1848. Catharine and Margaret made a voluntary confession in 1888, in which they asserted that the peculiar sounds which accompanied these *séances* were produced by the manipulation of certain muscles of their toes and fingers, which they had carefully studied in secret. After the *séances* had begun to attract attention, Leah, the eldest sister, took the others to her home in Rochester, where she encouraged the development of their trickery. Owing to the peculiarity of these *séances* the name of the ' Rochester rappings " was given to them, the application of the title being due to the allegation that the communications between the living and the dead, through the mediumship of the sisters, was indicated by means of successive raps. The home of the sisters was visited by Spiritualists from all parts of the country, and by many from Europe, and both scientists and honest seekers after truth visited them. The sisters subsequently went to Philadelphia and New York city, where Margaret and Dr. Elisha Kent Kane, the arctic explorer, became intimately acquainted and (she subsequently declared) were privately married. Catharine kept up the *séances* after Margaret's withdrawal, and was married to Henry D. Jencken, an English barrister, in 1873. He died in Spain about 1882. In 1888, while living in New York city, she was arrested by the Society for the Prevention of Cruelty to Children on a charge of having neglected her two children. The boys were inmates for some time of the Juvenile Asylum, and when they were restored to her she went to England, returning to New York city after a short sojourn, where he lived in retirement till her death.

Francis, James B., hydraulic engineer, born in South Leigh, Oxfordshire, England, May 18, 1815; died in Boston, Mass., Sept. 18, 1892. He came to New York city in April, 1833, and was at once employed on the survey of the New York, Providence and Boston Railroad. In 1837 he was appointed chief engineer by the directors of the Locks and Canal Company of Lowell, Mass., and he remained in charge of their important interests for fifty years. He was then, on retiring from active service, appointed consulting engineer of the company, his son James Francis succeeding him as engineer. There are in Lowell 2 monuments of his engineering skill: one, the northern canal, a mile long, 100 feet wide, and 15 feet deep, which cost $530,000; the other, known as the guard lock, which saved the city from destruction during the memorable freshet of 1852. The citizens were so grateful for their escape through the protective strength of this lock that they presented Mr. Francis with a massive silver pitcher and salver. Mr. Francis had been President of the American Society of Civil Engineering, was a member of the commission to examine into the causes of the Johnstown, Pa., disaster, and compiled a work on the hydraulic experiments at Lowell.

Fry, Benjamin St. James, editor, born in Rutledge, Tenn., June 16, 1824; died in St. Louis, Mo., Feb. 5, 1892. He was educated at Woodward College, Cincinnati; entered the ministry of the Methodist Episcopal Church in 1847; was President of the Worthington Female College, Ohio, in 1856–'60; chaplain of the 63d Ohio Volunteers in 1861–'64; St. Louis agent of the Western Methodist Book Concern in 1865–'72; and from the latter year was editor of The Central Christian Advocate." He published " Property Consecrated," a prize essay (New York, 1856; revised 1884), and biographies of Bishops Whatcoat, McKendree, George, and Roberts.

Frye, Speed Smith, military officer, born near Danville, Ky., in 1817; died in Louisville, Ky., Aug. 1, 1892. He was educated at Center and Wabash Colleges, and was admitted to the bar. He served through the Mexican War, distinguishing himself particularly on the battle field of Buena Vista. After the war he engaged in law practice, and was for several years judge of the county court of Boyle county, Ky. Just before the outbreak of the civil war he opposed the secession movement with great vigor, and after the attack on Fort Sumter he recruited 2 regiments for the National army, took the field as colonel of the 4th Kentucky Regiment, and on March 21, 1862, was promoted brigadier-general of

Volunteers. From 1869 till 1872 he was supervisor of internal revenue in Kentucky, and at the time of his death he was Superintendent of the Soldiers' Home in Louisville.

Gamage, Henry Ten Brook, recluse, born in New York city about 1814; died there, Feb. 12, 1892. He was graduated at Yale in 1837. His father was an enthusiastic collector of paintings and art curios, who died about 1860, leaving his collection to his son and a daughter. The father hired Room 59 on the top floor of the University Building, on Washington Square, several years prior to his death, and the son occupied the room continuously till his lonely death. Here he secluded himself from all society. He had an income suitable to his wants, derived from some investments made in early life, and seemed to the few people who in late years caught glimpses of him to have spent his time in the enjoyment of works of art. He visited the art galleries several times a week, retained the collection of paintings left him by his father through life, and added largely to it at various periods. His room was plainly furnished; had a valuable mahogany case filled with books on science, theology, natural history, and general literature, mostly of the time of Queen Anne; old chairs and sofas, once costly, were numerous; and about the walls and piled on the floor, or laid several deep on sofas and tables, were about 300 oil paintings and works of art, many of which he had claimed were originals by Reynolds, Rubens, Titian, Guido, and Velasquez; one of the latter was valued by him at $40,000. Mr. Gamage had the sole charge of his curious abode, seldom spoke to any one, prepared his own meals, retired early, paid his rent promptly, and was clocklike in all his movements. He left a will making J. Alden Weir, the artist, his executor, and, besides his paintings, left $15,000 in money, bequeathing small sums to several of the enterprises connected with the University Place Presbyterian Church and to several relatives and friends, and the residue of his estate in equal parts to the American Bible Society, the Board of Home Missions of the Presbyterian Church, and the Society for the Employment and Relief of Poor Women. He was found dead in his room. A contest of his will was begun in October.

Gardner, Henry Joseph, merchant, born in Dorchester, Mass., in 1819; died in Milton, Mass., July 21, 1892. He was graduated at Bowdoin College in 1838, was engaged in the dry-goods business till 1876, and from that time till his death in the life-insurance business. In 1850–'53 he was a member of the Common Council of Boston, in 1852–'53 was its president, in 1851–'52 was a member of the Legislature, in 1853 member of the State Constitutional Convention, and in 1855, 1856, and 1857 was elected Governor of Massachusetts. During his terms as Governor much important legislation was accomplished through his efforts, including the Homestead act, the Alien Pauper act, the act regulating appropriations of school money, the act regulating the membership of the General Court, the act reforming the special election laws, and that inserting the "reading and writing" clause in the naturalization laws.

Gayler, Charles, playwright, born in New York city, April 1, 1820; died in Brooklyn, N. Y., May 28, 1892. He received a limited education; taught for two years in Dayton, Ohio; became a newspaper writer; studied law with Abraham Lincoln; was admitted to the bar, and engaged in the political movements of that day. For nearly fifty years he had been a writer for the American stage, and he was credited with having written nearly 400 plays. His first piece, " The Heir of Glen Avon," was produced in 1839. In the early days of the California gold fever he produced the drama " The Buckeye Gold Hunters," which had a successful run in Cincinnati. This was followed by " The Frightened Fiend," an operetta, and " The Clement County Snake," a burlesque. In 1850 he returned to New York, and for some years was employed in journalism. His other dramatic writings include: "A Leaf from the Black Book"; "Taking the Chances" (1856); "Olympiana," written for Frank S. Chanfrau; "The Love of a Prince," in which Laura Keene, Mrs. John Wood, and Maggie Mitchell appeared at different times; "The Son of the Night," an adaptation from the French; "The Robbers of the Rhine"; "The Romance of a (Very) Poor Young Man"; "The Female American Cousin"; "The American Cousin at Home," written for Mr. Sothern; "Bull Run" (1861); "The Wizard's Tempest"; "Aurora Floyd"; "The Connie Soogah," written for Mr. and Mrs. Barney Williams; "Inflation" (1876); "Lord Tatters, Irish"; "The Bohemians," produced in 1885; "98"; "Master of Arts"; "Lights and Shadows of New York," produced in 1888; and "Fritz, our Cousin-German"; the last two being his latest and most successful compositions. Mr. Gayler was almost a giant in stature.

Geddes, George W., jurist, born in Mount Vernon, Ohio, July 16, 1824; died in Mansfield, Ohio, in November, 1892. He received a common-school education, studied law with Columbus Delano, was admitted to the bar in 1845, was elected judge of the Court of Common Pleas of the 6th Judicial District of Ohio in 1856, 1861, and 1862, serving fifteen years in all; and was elected to Congress from the 10th Ohio District, as a Democrat, in 1878, 1880, 1882, and 1884. During his last term he was chairman of the Committee on War Claims.

Gibbons, James Sloane, banker and author, born in Wilmington, Del., July 1, 1810; died in New York city, Oct. 17, 1892. He received a private-school education, engaged in mercantile business in Philadelphia, and in 1835 came to New York city and entered the banking business. He was identified with the abolition movement from its inception, and he and his father-in-law, Isaac T. Hopper, were expelled from the Society of Friends for editing and publishing the antislavery "Standard." In 1863 he illuminated his residence in honor of President Lincoln's emancipation proclamation, for which it was sacked by the mob during the draft riots. During his banking career he was a founder and cashier of the Ocean Bank, a founder of the Broadway Bank, a frequent contributor to the "Banker's Magazine," author of "The Banks of New York: their Dealers, the Clearing-house, and the Panic of 1857," and "The Public Debt of the United States: Its Organization, its Liquidation, and the Financial System"; and of the famous war song, "We are coming, Father Abraham, Three Hundred Thousand more."

Gibson, Randall Lee, lawyer, born in Spring Hill, Ky., Sept. 10, 1832; died in Hot Springs, Ark., Dec. 15, 1892. He was a grandson of Randall Gibson, a Revolutionary soldier of note, and son of Tobias Gibson, a sugar planter in Louisiana. He was graduated at Yale in 1853, and studied law in the University of Louisiana and in Berlin. While abroad he was an attaché of the American legation in Madrid, and, refusing the secretaryship of that legation in 1855, returned to Louisiana and was engaged in sugar growing till the beginning of the civil war. He entered the Confederate army as a private, was soon commissioned captain, and, after serving at Fort Jackson, below New Orleans, was elected colonel of the 13th Louisiana Infantry. At Shiloh he commanded a brigade which attacked the "hornet's nest" in front and was four times repelled; and for his services at Perryville, during Bragg's Kentucky campaign, he was recommended for promotion. In that battle, as well as at Murfreesboro and Chickamauga, his command lost heavily. During Johnston's retreat from Dalton to Atlanta, Gen. Gibson took part in all the engagements, and at Jonesboro he lost half of his command during the fight. He covered the retreat after Gen. Hood's defeat at Nashville, and in Gen. Canby's campaign against Mobile he was charged with the defense of Spanish Fort, where he held the national forces at bay for two weeks, and then withdrew his entire command. He attained the rank of major-general before the close of the war. After the war,

having been financially ruined by it, he engaged in the practice of law and entered public life. In 1872 he was elected to Congress as a Democrat, but was not admitted, and in 1874, 1876, 1878, and 1880 he was re-elected. During his last term he was elected United States Senator, taking his seat March 4, 1883, and in 1888 was re-elected. During his last term in the Senate he was a member of the committees on Agriculture and Forestry, Commerce, Naval Affairs, Transportation Routes to the Seaboard, and University of the United States.

Gilmore, Patrick Sarsfield, musical director, born near Dublin, Ireland, Dec. 25, 1830; died in St. Louis, Mo., Sept. 24, 1892. His parents placed him in a mercantile house in Athlone, where his apprenticeship was cut short by his employer, who, noticing his remarkable taste for music, agreed to give him his time if he would instruct his son in music. Young Gilmore had become a favorite of the master of the military band in Athlone, which, besides its military duties, played the instrumental parts of the mass in the Catholic church, and he not only received special instruction from the bandmaster, but became conversant with the works of the best composers. In 1849 he came to the United States, settled in Boston, and was almost immediately chosen leader of a band. His fame as a cornet player spread through the State, and led to his being engaged as leader successively of the Charlestown, Suffolk, and old Boston Brigade bands. From Boston he went to Salem, where he remained four years, and, returning to Boston after having established a reputation as a bandmaster by nearly 1,000 concerts, he organized in 1858 what has since been known as Gilmore's Band, the one with which he subsequently gave concerts throughout the United States and over half of Europe. At the beginning of the civil war he and his band volunteered with the 24th Massachusetts Regiment. He accompanied Gen. Burnside to North Carolina, and while he was in New Orleans, in 1864, Gen. Banks placed him in charge of all the bands of music in the Department of the Gulf. On March 4, 1864, at the inauguration of Michael Hahn as Governor of Louisiana, Mr. Gilmore gave the first great jubilee of peace, a national concert in which 500 musicians, 10,000 school children, and adequate artillery took part in rendering national airs. At the close of the war he returned to Boston and resumed his musical vocation. He organized the mammoth peace jubilees held in that city in 1869 and 1872, in which more than 20,000 people and 2,000 musicians, together with the best military bands of Europe, participated. For these festivals, buildings holding 30,000 and 50,000 people respectively were erected, and for his services Mr. Gilmore received presents amounting in value to over $50,000. In 1873 he removed to New York, and became bandmaster of the 22d Regiment, and during the next three years he gave more than 600 popular concerts in what was then known as Gilmore's Garden. During the Centennial Exhibition in Philadelphia, in 1876, his band played daily in the main building. The next two years were spent in giving concerts in the principal cities of the United States, and at its close he took his band to Europe, gave concerts in the principal cities there, and won honors at the World's Exposition in Paris in 1878. From 1878 till his death his band played daily during the summer seasons at Manhattan Beach, and from 1884 he gave annual concerts in autumn and winter at the expositions at Louisville, Ky., Kansas City, Mo., and St. Louis. His band of 100 pieces welcomed the opening of the four hundredth anniversary year of the discovery of America in front of the City Hall, New York, playing at midnight to an audience of 30,000 people. Two days before his death he was appointed musical director of the World's Columbian Exhibition, of which he said: "It is the highest honor ever bestowed on a musician in the world's history. I wish to round out my fame with the grandest musical season ever known, and the World's Fair will give me the opportunity." Mr. Gilmore was the author of numerous musical compositions, of which probably the most popular were "Good News from Home," "When Johnny comes marching Home," "The Voice of the Departing Soul," or, Death's at the Door," which was performed at his funeral, the anthems "Columbia" and "Ireland to England," and a national air for the Republic of Brazil.

Goldie, Matthew, college proctor, born in Edinburgh, Scotland, in 1843; died in Philadelphia, Pa., Nov. 25, 1892. In early life he entered the service of the East India Company, and served with the Madras Artillery through the great mutiny. Removing to the United States, he entered the navy at the beginning of the civil war and served till the close. In 1870 he was appointed proctor of the College of New Jersey at Princeton, and when the growth of the college necessitated the employment of other proctors he was elected proctor-in-chief.

Gould, Jay, capitalist, born in Roxbury, Delaware County, N. Y., May 27, 1836; died in New York city, Dec. 2, 1892. He was brought up on his father's farm, studied in Hobart Academy, became bookkeeper for a village blacksmith, acquiring a taste for mathematics and surveying, and found employment in making surveys for a map of Ulster County. In 1853 he completed a survey of Albany County, in 1854 made a survey and map of Delaware County, and afterward organized parties to make county surveys in Ohio and Michigan. Subsequently he was employed by Zadock Pratt to select a site in the western part of New York for a tannery, and afterward he superintended the erection of buildings and was associated with Mr. Pratt in the lumbering business. He bought out Mr. Pratt's interest and conducted the business till shortly before the panic of 1857, when he sold his plant, removed to Stroudsburg, Pa., and became connected with the bank there. While engaged in banking he began his railroad career by buying bonds of the Rutland and Washington Railroad at the rate of 10 cents on the dollar. He soon afterward became president, treasurer, and superintendent of the road, subsequently consolidated it with the Rensselaer and Saratoga Railroad, and, after a brief experience as manager, withdrew his capital and removed to New York city, where he engaged in brokerage, dealing at first in the stocks and bonds of the Erie Railway. In association with James. Fisk, Jr., he entered the directory of the company in 1868, was elected president, with Fisk as vice-president and treasurer, and held the office till the reorganization of the company in 1872. A long litigation ensued between the company and the English bondholders, which resulted in Mr. Gould's being compelled to restore securities representing $7,550,000, a part of the amount which he was charged with having misappropriated while president of the company. After becoming president of the Erie company he made large purchases of stocks of various railroad companies, mainly in the Southwest; invested largely in telegraph stock; and after being forced out of the company he gave his attention chiefly to the Pacific railroad lines that he had become interested in, to the Western Union Telegraph Company, and to the elevated railroad system in New York. He took several railroad companies out of the hands of receivers, built many branch lines, and effected combinations that resulted in the establishment of what was known as the "Gould system." In March, 1882, by reason of the pending financial excitement and a doubt of his financial standing, he summoned several financiers to his private office and exhibited to them certificates of stocks, all registered in his own name, to the face value of $53,000,000, and said he could produce $20,000,000 more if they still doubted his financial ability. His name was intimately connected with many of the largest railroad and financial operations of the past twenty years, as well as with the "Black Friday" and other great financial sensations. In his will he gave small amounts of money and real estate to various relatives, and after disposing of his domestic property among his children, gave to his son, George J. Gould, $5,000,000 as special compensa-

tion for his services during the last five years in taking charge of his father's varied interests, and directed that the rest of his estate be divided into 6 equal shares, to be held in trust and invested for the benefit of his children. He prohibited his children from bequeathing any part of their shares to any but their own issue, and from marrying without the consent of a majority of them. In all cases of controversy among his children affecting the various properties, he declared that the judgment of his son George J. Gould should be authoritative. On Dec. 12 his will was offered for probate, when the executors swore to real property in the State valued at $2,000,000 and personal property aggregating $70,000,000. There was nothing in the abstract of his will which was published by the executors to indicate that he had left a dollar to any servant, friend, or charitable, religious, or educational institution.

Green, George Fleming, inventor, born in Montreal, Canada, March 26, 1832; died in Kalamazoo, Mich., June 7, 1892. He accompanied his parents to the site of the present city of Chicago when seven weeks old, and before he was ten years old was taught by his father the cabinet-making trade. While chafing under the restraints of an uncongenial occupation he found relief in secretly studying electricity. When fourteen years old he entered a machine shop in Chicago, where he attracted attention as a draughtsman, and two years afterward began teaching mechanical drawing. About 1852 he went to Kalamazoo to attend college, and finding his expenses larger than he anticipated, he began his career as an inventor, to raise funds to enable him to continue his special studies. Among the results of his inventive skill were the first wire and cord binder ever used for harvesting in the United States; a complete outfit of dental instruments to be operated by electricity; the cash cars now in general use in large stores for conveying cash from the clerks to the cashier and back; and an application of electric motors to sewing machines. The expenses of his various experiments were heavy, and he struggled bravely to support his family, earning small sums by doing Patent-Office drawing and preparing specifications and patent claims for other inventors. With very modest tastes and habits of strict economy, he succeeded in perfecting a motor for running street cars by electricity supplied by current through the medium of the rails as conductors. His first application of this invention was in 1875, and four years afterward he built another and larger motor, with which he expected to displace steam by electricity on the great railroads. He desired to use the dynamo for obtaining his current, but was too poor either to buy one or the materials to make one. His invention for the electrical propulsion of street cars was fought with great persistency by opponents, and after a long series of obstacles in the Patent Office his application for a patent was rejected. Through the aid of acquaintances who became interested in his struggles, he carried his case to the Circuit Court of the District of Columbia, and on the decisions of that court he received two patents on Dec. 15, 1891. Mr. Green did not live to reap the fruits of his long-contested claims, and during the last few years of his life he supported his family and carried on the struggle by manufacturing a large variety of photographic shutters which he had invented.

Hall, John W., shipmaster, born in Frederica, Kent County, Del., Jan. 1, 1817; died there, Jan. 23, 1892. He passed his early life as a mercantile clerk then engaged in business for himself, and in 1847 became a shipbuilder. In this business he was very successful, and at the time of his death was owner of a large fleet, which he himself had built and which were employed in the Southern coasting trade. In 1866 he was elected a State Senator, and he served for four years, the last two as presiding officer. In 1876 he was a delegate to the Democratic National Convention; in 1878 was elected Governor of Delaware; and in 1890 was re-elected to the State Senate for the term ending in 1893.

Hall, Louisa Jane Park, poet, born in Newburyport, Mass., Feb. 7, 1802; died in Cambridge, Mass., Sept. 8, 1892. She was the daughter of James Park, a physician of Newburyport, who removed to Boston in 1804 to edit a Federalist journal called the "Repertory." In 1811 he opened a school for young ladies, at which his daughter was educated. In 1831 the family removed to Worcester. For some years she was nearly blind, at which time her father read to her and helped her in writing her books. In 1840 she became the wife of the Rev. Edward B. Hall, a Unitarian clergyman of Providence, R. I. "Miriam, a Dramatic Poem," her most noted work, was written in 1825, but was not published until 1837. It describes the struggles of the early Christian Church, and was highly commended in its day. Other works of hers are a "Life of Elizabeth Carter" and "Joanna of Naples" (Boston, 1828), a historical prose romance. At the time of her death she was the oldest American author. Her son, the Rev. Edward H. Hall, is pastor of the Unitarian Church at Cambridge, Mass.

Hardin, Charles Henry, lawyer, born in Boone County, Ky., in 1820; died in Mexico, Mo., July 29, 1892. His parents removed while he was an infant to Missouri, where he was educated at the State University, subsequently being graduated at Miami University, Ohio. He was admitted to the bar, and began practice at Fulton, Mo., in 1843; was elected circuit attorney of the 3d Judicial Circuit of Missouri in 1848; was a member of the Legislature for 2 terms; appointed member of the commission to revise the laws of the State in 1855; again elected to the Legislature in 1858, and to the Senate in 1860; re-elected State Senator in 1872; and was Governor in 1872–'74. He was an active promoter of educational movements, and founded the college named after him with a gift of $37,000 in money and lands.

Hare, George Emlen, clergyman, born in Philadelphia, Sept. 4, 1808; died there, Feb. 15, 1892. He was graduated at Union College in 1826; was ordained to the ministry of the Protestant Episcopal Church, Dec. 20, 1829, and became rector of St. John's Church in Carlisle, Pa., in 1830, of Trinity Church, Princeton, N. J., in 1834, and of St. Matthew's Church, Philadelphia, in 1845. He was head master of the Protestant Episcopal Divinity School in Philadelphia from 1845 till 1857; opened a training school for young men for holy orders in 1857, which was merged in the Divinity School in 1862; and was Professor of Biblical Learning and Exegesis there from 1862 till 1889, when he was made professor emeritus. He was a member of the American Committee on Old Testament Revision.

Harnett, William H., painter, born in Ireland in 1850; died in New York city, Oct. 29, 1892. He was brought to the United States when an infant; was educated in Philadelphia, where he studied in the Academy of Fine Arts, became a skilled designer and engraver on silver, and continued his art studies in the National Academy of Design, where he abandoned the antique for life studies. His designs and engravings on silver for Tiffany and other houses yielded him ample means with which to study abroad. He studied painting in Munich and other art centers, and returning to New York city established himself as a still-life painter. He was a member of the National Academy of Design, and of the Philadelphia Society of Artists. Among his paintings are: "Confusion," for which he received $5,000; "The Old Cupboard," which was sold for $5,000; "After the Hunt," which was exhibited in the Paris Salon in 1855, and sold in New York city for $4,000; "The Old Violin"; "The Bachelor's Friend," exhibited in the National Academy in 1891; "For Sunday's Dinner"; "Recreation"; "Still Life"; and a remarkable reproduction in oil of the face of a $5 bill, which was once seized by United States Secret Service officers as a dangerous counterfeit.

Harrington, George, financier, born in Boston, Mass., in 1815; died at sea, Dec. 5, 1892. He was appointed a clerk in the United States Treasury Department during President Polk's administration, and had continued in that department through all changes of administration till 1865, holding at that time the office of assistant secretary under Secretary Chase. In the latter year he was appointed United States minister to Switzerland, where he remained till 1869. After his retirement from office he engaged in literary work, and published a treatise on the financial policy of the United States during the civil war.

Hayes, Augustus Allen, author, born in Boston, Mass., about 1842; died in Paris, France, April 18, 1892. He was a son of the Boston chemist and scientist of the same name, was graduated at Harvard, and spent many years in China. On his return to the United States he became secretary and acting vice-president of an electric lighting company; subsequently he was one of the founders of the comic weekly "Life," to which he contributed frequently, and he also wrote short stories, including the "Denver Express," "The Jesuit's Ring," and "The Ranch of the Holy Cross," for periodicals. His last publication was an article on "British Opinion of America," in the April number of the "Westminster Review."

Henrici, Jacob, reformer, born in Gross Karlenbach, Bavaria, Jan. 1, 1803; died in Economy, Pa., Dec. 25, 1892. He came to the United States in 1823, and shortly afterward united with the Harmonist Society, founded by George Rapp, then established in the village of Harmony, near Zelionople, Butler County, Pa. In 1824 the society sold its property there and removed to Beaver County, where it founded the village of Economy. On the death of Father Rapp, in 1868, Father Henrici succeeded him as head of the society under the title of first trustee, and he was its director till his death.

Hilliard, Henry Washington, lawyer, born in Fayetteville, N. C., Aug. 4, 1808; died in Atlanta, Ga., Dec. 17, 1892. He was graduated at South Carolina College in 1826, studied law in Athens, Ga., and was admitted to the bar in 1829; was a professor in the University of Alabama in 1831–'34; and then settled in Montgomery to practice. In 1838 he was elected to the Legislature; in 1840 was a Whig presidential elector; in 1842 was appointed United States minister to Belgium, where he served two years; in 1845, 1847, and 1849 was elected to Congress; in 1856 was a Fillmore candidate for presidential elector, and in 1860 a Bell and Everett elector. He was appointed by Jefferson Davis the Confederate commissioner to Tennessee, and in the provisional army of the Confederacy he held the rank of brigadier-general and raised 3,000 troops. Soon after the war he resumed practice in Augusta, Ga., subsequently removing to Atlanta. In 1876 he was defeated for Congress; in 1877 was appointed by President Hayes United States minister to Brazil, where he served till 1881. He had since lived in retirement in Atlanta. He was author of "Roman Nights" (1848); "Speeches and Addresses" (1855); "De Vane," a novel (1865; republished 1886); and "Politics and Pen Pictures" (1892).

Hitchcock, Roswell Dwight, naval officer, born in Massachusetts in 1845; died in New York city, Dec. 3, 1892. He was a son of the late Rev. Roswell Dwight Hitchcock, D. D., President of Union Theological Seminary; was graduated at the United States Naval Academy in 1865; was promoted ensign Dec. 1, 1866; master, March 12, 1868; lieutenant, March 26, 1869; lieutenant-commander, March 26, 1880; and commander, Oct. 15, 1890. During his naval career he was on sea service seventeen years and seven months, on shore or other duty ten years and four months, and was unemployed two years and one month. He had served on the European and the West India stations; was flag lieutenant to Admiral S. H. Stringham at New York; was navigator on Commodore Selfridge's first Darien expedition; twice commanded parties in cutting lines and running levels for a ship-canal route across the Isthmus of Panama; was executive officer of the United States steamship sent to open diplomatic relations with Corea, and of the "Guard" at the Vienna Exposition;

commanded the steamers "Endeavor" and "Gedney," of the United States Coast Survey; was executive officer of the "Supply" at the Paris Exposition in 1878; lighthouse inspector in 1888–'90; and during the summer of 1891 was on duty in Bering Sea.

Hodgkins, Thomas G., philanthropist, born in England in 1804; died in Setauket, Long Island, N. Y., Dec. 1, 1892. He came to the United States in 1833, engaged in the manufacture of candy in New York city, and retired from business wealthy in 1859. He had since lived in strict retirement on a farm at Setauket, spending his time studying science. In 1891 he made a cash gift of $200,000 to the Smithsonian Institution, half of which was to be used in the general maintenance of the institution, and the other half for the diffusion of more exact knowledge in regard to the properties of air and its relation to the physical and intellectual welfare of mankind. In October, 1892, he gave $100,000 to the Royal Institute of Great Britain, to promote scientific research. At other times he had established a free library in Setauket, given $100,000 each to the American Society for the Prevention of Cruelty to Animals and the Society for the Prevention of Cruelty to Children, and personally disposed of more than $500,000 in cash. His will originally gave all his personal estate to the United States Government, but a codicil gave it to the Smithsonian Institution. For many years it was his habit to give to the poor all the products of his large farm, excepting the little he required for himself.

Hoey, John, expressman, born in Drogheda, Ireland, in 1824; died in New York city, Nov. 14, 1892. He tended his father's sheep till ten years old, then ran away from home and came to the United States, and for some years was a newsboy in New York city. He made many friends while selling papers in the office of the express company then recently established by Alvin Adams, and invested his savings in a boat, and used to row out to incoming steamers and sell his papers before the newsboys on shore had a chance to get at the passengers. Mr. Adams, noting the boy's enterprise, engaged him at a salary of $1.50 a week as porter in the New York office. The success of the extension of the line to Boston led Mr. Adams to extend it further, first to Philadelphia, and then to Washington, and this suggested to young Hoey to establish a branch line on his own account extending from Washington to various cities in the South, which became known as Hoey's Charleston Express. In 1854 the Adams, Harnden, Western, and Hoey's express lines were consolidated, and Mr. Hoey was made general manager of the company. He held his office for thirty-four years continuously, and on the death of William H. Dinsmore, President of the Adams Express Company, in 1888, Mr. Hoey was unanimously elected his successor. In the autumn of 1891 Mr. Hoey retired from the presidency of the company in consequence of charges of official misconduct. The investigation conducted by the company resulted in Mr. Hoey's turning over to the company money and securities to the extent of about $500,000. He maintained during the investigation, in all the proceedings in court, and otherwise till his death, that he had been grossly misrepresented in the matter of the transactions leading to his withdrawal from the presidency, and claimed that his conduct had been entirely proper and in the interest of the company. Mr. Hoey had established an elegant estate, called Hollywood Park, near Long Branch, which he always open to the public.

Holden, William Worth, journalist, born in Raleigh, N. C., in 1818; died there, March 1, 1892. He was apprenticed to the printing trade, and at an early age established the "Raleigh Standard," which for twenty-five years was one of the most influential newspapers in the South. Prior to the civil war he advocated secession, and after the fate of the Confederacy became evident he urged the acceptance of peace on any terms. A Georgia regiment mobbed and sacked his office and burned him in effigy, when he fled to the residence of Gov. Vance. In 1865 he was appointed by President Johnson provisional Governor of North Carolina, and in 1868 he was elected to the office as Republican-Reconstruction candidate by a large majority. During his latter term he declared several counties in a state of insurrection because of Kuklux outrages. He raised a considerable military force to suppress the disturbances, and his life was frequently threatened in consequence. In 1871 he was impeached by the Legislature for high crimes and misdemeanors, and after trial was removed from office and forever debarred from holding any office in the State. He then removed to Washington, and became editor of the "Chronicle." While there he was offered by President Grant the mission to Peru, but declined it, and he afterward held the office of postmaster at Raleigh. He made ineffectual attempts to have the Legislature remove his political disabilities.

Holly, Henry Hudson, architect, born in New York city in 1834; died there, Sept. 5, 1892. He studied architecture at home and in England, and was a member of the American Institute of Architects almost from its foundation, in 1857. His designs were principally confined to churches and country houses. He designed the buildings of the Virginia Military Institute, and those of the University of the South at Sewanee, Tenn. He published "Country Seats, containing Designs for Cottages, Villas, and Mansions" (New York, 1864); Church Architecture (Hartford, 1872); Modern Dwellings in Town and Country" (New York, 1878).

Hope, James, painter, born near Abbotsford, Scotland, Nov. 29, 1818; died in Watkins, N. Y., Oct. 20, 1892. He removed to Canada in youth, was brought up on a farm there, subsequently went to Fair Haven, Vt., and became a student and tutor in Castleton Seminary. In 1848 he began studying painting, and in 1853 opened a studio in New York city. He was elected an associate of the National Academy of Design in 1865, and since 1872 had lived in Watkins. His paintings include: "Army of the Potomac," "Rainbow Falls," "The Gem of the Forest," and "The Forest Glen."

Hopkins, Stephen T., merchant, born in New York city, March 25, 1849; died near Atlantic City, N. J., 1892. He was a descendant of Stephen Hopkins, of Rhode Island, one of the signers of the Declaration of Independence, was educated at the Authon Grammar School, and became an iron merchant. In 1885–'86 he was a member of the Legislature of New York and chairman of the committees on Appropriations and on Banks; and in 1886 he was elected to Congress as a Republican from the 17th New York District, where he served on the committees on Manufactures and on Indian Depredation Claims. In the early part of his official life he was very painstaking and laborious, but toward the close he became the victim of an ungovernable appetite. Shortly before his death he became a voluntary patient at the Keeley Institute at White Plains, N. Y., where his genial manners led his associates to elect him President of the Bichloride-of-Gold Club. He was found dead in a ditch near Atlantic City, N. J., on March 3.

Howell, John Cumming, naval officer, born in Philadelphia, Pa., Nov. 24, 1819; died at Folkestone, England, Sept. 12, 1892. After studying at Washington College, Pa., he was appointed a midshipman in the United States navy, June 9, 1836; was promoted passed midshipman, July 1, 1842; master, Feb. 21, 1849; lieutenant, Aug. 2 following; commander, July 16, 1862; captain, July 25, 1866; commodore, Jan. 29, 1872; and rear-admiral, April 26, 1877; and was retired, Nov. 24, 1881. During his naval career he had been on sea service twenty-four years, three months; on shore or other duty, eighteen years, one month; and was unemployed thirteen years, three months. He commanded the steamer "Tahomo," of the Eastern Gulf Blockading Squadron, in 1862–'63, and the "Nevus," of the North Atlantic Squadron, in 1864–'65; was highly commended by Admiral Porter for gallantry in the two attacks on Fort Fisher in 1864–'65; was fleet captain and chief of staff of the European squadron in 1869–'70; and was commandant of the League Island Navy Yard at Philadelphia in 1871–'73. In 1873–'75 he was commandant of the Portsmouth Navy Yard; in 1875–'79 was chief of the Bureau of Yards and Docks, and several times was acting Secretary of the Navy; and in 1879–'81 he commanded the European Squadron.

Howland, William Ware, missionary, born in West Brookfield, Mass., in 1817; died in Jaffna, Ceylon, Aug. 28, 1892. He was graduated at Amherst College in 1841, and at Union Theological Seminary in 1845; had been a missionary of the American Board since the latter year, and had not visited his native country since 1861. He was the oldest missionary in that field, which, at his death, had 9 self-supporting churches, with 2,700 members, and 135 mission schools, with 8,500 pupils. Three of his children also became missionaries.

Hoyt, Henry Martin, lawyer, born in Kingston, Luzerne County, Pa., June 8, 1830; died in Wilkesbarre, Pa., Dec. 1, 1892. He was graduated at Williams College in 1849, was Professor of Mathematics in Wyoming Seminary in 1851–'53, was admitted to the bar in 1853, and practiced at Wilkesbarre till the beginning of the civil war. He aided in raising the 52d Pennsylvania Volunteers, went into service as its lieutenant-colonel, took part in the Peninsular campaign in 1862, was captured in a night attack during the siege of Morris Island by Gen. Gillmore, capturing the fort but being unable to hold it, and was confined at Macon and Charleston. He escaped at the latter place, but was recaptured and held till exchanged, and was mustered out of the service at the close of the war with the rank of brevet brigadier-general. He then resumed law practice till 1867, when he was appointed additional law judge of the courts of Luzerne County. In 1878 he was elected Governor of Pennsylvania as a Republican. During his term the State debt was reduced to $10,000,000 and refunded. After practicing for five years in Philadelphia he returned to Wilkesbarre and retired to private life. He was the author of " Controversy between Connecticut and Pennsylvania " (1879) and " Protection vs. Free Trade " (1885).

Humes, Thomas William, educator, born in Knoxville, Tenn., April 22, 1815; died there, Jan. 16, 1892. He was graduated at East Tennessee College (now the University of Tennessee) in 1830, was ordained to the ministry of the Protestant Episcopal Church in 1843; was rector of St. John's Church, Knoxville, in 1846–'61 and 1863–'69; and was President of the University of Tennessee in 1865–'83. Dr. Humes was from early youth an ardent abolitionist, and, when a young man, was so widely known for his eloquence that he was selected to deliver the principal address at the Knoxville Semicentennial in 1842. He published " Loyal Mountaineers " (Knoxville, 1889), which had a large sale at the North.

Hunt, Thomas Sterry, chemist, born in Norwich, Conn., Sept. 5, 1826; died in New York city, Feb. 12, 1892. He became a special student with Prof. Benjamin Silliman, Sr., in Yale College; studied for two years, spending a part of that time as assistant in the laboratory, and was then offered, but declined, the appointment of chemical assistant to the newly established School of Agricultural Chemistry in Edinburgh. In 1847 he was appointed chemist and mineralogist to the Geological Survey of Canada, and he held this office till 1872, when he resigned. Meanwhile he was Professor of Chemistry in Laval University, Quebec, for six years, lecturing there in the French language, and held a similar appointment in McGill University, Montreal, for six years. Returning to the United States, he was appointed Professor of Geology in the Massachusetts Institute of Technology, where he remained till 1878, since which time he had busied himself with expert and literary work. He was a member of the National Academy of Sciences, and a former President of the American Association for the Advancement of Science, of the American Institute of Mining Engineers, the American Chemical Society, and the Royal Society of Canada. He was also a member of the international juries at the Paris Exposition in 1855 and 1867, and of the Centennial Exhibition in 1876; an officer of the Legion of Honor of France; and an officer of the Order of St. Mauritius and St. Lazarus of Italy. Dr. Hunt developed a system of organic chemistry that was essentially his own, in which all chemical compounds were shown to be formed on simple types represented by one or more molecules of water or hydrogen, and was credited with being the first to apply the theory to the so-called oxygen acid and to the anhydrids. This theory he elaborated in his paper on " A Century's Progress in Chemical Theory," read at the Centennial of Chemistry in 1874. He had previously published (1852) an introduction to organic chemistry, and " Object and Methods of Mineralogy." In geology he originated the names that are now universally accepted of the Laurentian and Huronian, the two subdivisions of the Azoic period, or the earliest known rocks on this continent, and also the designations of Norian, Montalban, Taconian, and Keweenian. In 1869 his attempt to harmonize the facts of dynamical geology with the theory of a solid globe was detailed in an essay on " The Chemistry of the Earth," published by the Smithsonian Institution; and in 1886 he set forth his theories of the origin, development, and decay of crystalline rocks in his " Mineral Physiology and Physiography." Dr. Hunt invented the green ink with which the national paper money known as " Greenback currency " was printed. His latest publications were a second edition of " Mineral Physiology and Physiography " (1890); a third edition of " A New Basis for Chemistry " (1880); a fourth edition of " Chemical and Geological Essays " (New York, 1891); and " Systematic Mineralogy, according to a Natural System " (New York, 1891).

Husted, James William, legislator, born in Bedford, Westchester County, N. Y., Oct. 31, 1833; died in Peekskill, N. Y., Sept. 25, 1892. He was graduated at Yale in 1854, and admitted to the bar in 1857. Immediately after this he entered political life as a member of the " American " party, and was elected county school commissioner. In 1859 he became a Republican. In 1860 he became deputy superintendent of the State Insurance Department; in 1863, harbor master of the city of New York; and afterward deputy captain of the port, which two offices he held for eight years. In 1867 he made his first canvass for the State Legislature, and was defeated; but in the following year he was elected, and, with the exception of one term, he had been a member of the Assembly ever since. In 1874, while serving his sixth term in the Assembly, he was elected Speaker, receiving the unanimous vote of its Republican members, and he was re-elected to the office in 1876, 1878, 1886, 1887, and 1890, being defeated in 1877, 1879, 1880, and 1881. His only absent year from the Assembly after his first election was in 1882. The only State office for which he was ever a candidate was that of State Treasurer, in 1881, when he was defeated. He was a delegate to the National Republican Conventions of 1876, 1880, 1884, 1888, and 1892, and it was at the latter that he contracted his fatal illness. He was Judge-Advocate of the 7th Division of the National Guard of the State of New York for several years, and from 1873 was Major-General of the 5th Division. Gen. Husted was popularly called " the Bald Eagle of Westchester."

Ingalls, Francis T., educator, born in Haverhill, Mass., in 1845; died in Springfield, Mo., Aug. 5, 1892. He was graduated at Williams College in 1864, and subsequently studied at Princeton and Andover Theological Seminary. He held pastorates for nine years at Olathe, Atchison, and Emporia, Kan.; became a regent of the Kansas State University and a trustee of Washburn College, and from 1887 was President of Drury College at Springfield, Mo. He was a brother of ex-United States Senator Ingalls.

Irving, Levin, T. H., jurist, born April 8, 1828; died in Princess Anne, Md., Aug. 24, 1892. He was graduated at Princeton, in 1846; was admitted to the bar in 1849, and practiced in Salisbury for seven years; then spent one year in Cincinnati, returning to his former home in 1857. In 1867 he was elected associate judge of the Court of Appeals of Maryland; in April, 1879, was appointed chief judge to fill a vacancy; and in November, following, he was elected to the office for a term of fifteen years.

Jackson, A. Reeves, physician, born in Philadelphia in 1827; died in Chicago, Ill., Nov. 12, 1892. He received a public-school education, was graduated in medicine at Pennsylvania College in 1848, and practiced in Stroudsburg, Pa., till the beginning of the civil war, when he entered the national army as a surgeon. During his service he was for some time medical director of the forces in Virginia. After the war he resumed practice in Stroudsburg till 1870, when he removed to Chicago. His first year there was spent in organizing the Woman's Hospital of Illinois, which was incorporated in September, 1871, and of which he became surgeon-general. He subsequently was appointed lecturer on gynæcology in the Rush Medical College. During his residence in Chicago, notwithstanding his extensive hospital duties and his large private practice, he wrote considerably for publication, and was editor of the "Medical Register." At the time of his death he was President of the American Association of Gynæcologists. Dr. Jackson was the original "My Friend, the doctor," in Mark Twain's "Innocents Abroad."

Jackson, Richard H., military officer, born in Ireland, July 14, 1830; died in Atlanta, Ga., Nov. 28, 1892. He entered the United States army as a private, Dec. 12, 1851, and received several promotions prior to Sept. 13, 1859, when he was brevetted 2d lieutenant 4th United States Artillery. He was promoted 2d lieutenant 1st Artillery, July 15, 1860; 1st lieutenant, May 14, 1861; captain, Feb. 20, 1862; major, 5th Artillery, July 1, 1880; and lieutenant-colonel 4th Artillery, Dec. 4, 1888. In the volunteer service he was lieutenant-colonel and assistant inspector-general from April 15, 1863, till May 23, 1865; was promoted brigadier-general May 19, and brevetted major-general Nov. 24, 1865; and was mustered out of the volunteer service Nov. 1, 1866. During the civil war he received brevets of major, May 15, 1864, for gallant and meritorious services in the battle of Drury's Bluff; lieutenant-colonel, Oct. 7, for the action at Newmarket Heights; brigadier-general of volunteers, Jan. 1, 1865, for service in the campaign of 1864; colonel and brigadier-general, March 13, for services in the field during the war; and major-general of volunteers, Nov. 24, for gallantry through the war. He took part in the defense of Fort Pickens, Fla., in 1861, and in the operations against Fort Sumter in 1862 and 1863; and was acting chief of artillery in the Army of the James in 1865. In the campaign closing with the surrender at Appomattox Courthouse he commanded the 3d division of the 25th Army Corps. After the war he was stationed at various forts in the vicinity of New York city, had command of the detachment of the 5th Artillery at Mount McGregor at the time of Gen. Grant's death, and several times was detailed as inspector of the New York State Military Camp of Instruction. While at Mount McGregor, he, with another officer, was struck by lightning, from the effects of which he never recovered. At the time of his death he was stationed at Fort McPherson.

Jardine, David, architect, born near Whithorn, Scotland, July 25, 1830; died in Larchmont, N. Y., May 31, 1892. His father was an architect and builder, with whom he learned the building trade. In 1850 he came to New York, and opened an architectural office with Edward G. Thompson, with whom he remained till the beginning of the civil war. After the war he formed a partnership with his brother, John Jardine, and subsequently admitted to it George E. Jardine and John H. Van Norden. Among the buildings erected after the plans of this firm are the Westminster Presbyterian Church, in Brooklyn; the original Fifth Avenue Theatre in New York city; the Harlem Presbyterian Church, the Memorial Presbyterian, and the Fourth Presbyterian Churches, and the Synagogue Anshi Chesed, New York city; a Baptist home for the aged, the Hebrew Home, the Methodist Home, the Ophthalmic Hospital, the University Medical College, the Training Schools for Nurses, the Home for the Aged of the Little Sisters of the Poor, the American Horse Exchange, the Town Hall at Stamford, Conn., and the "Walbraham," in New York.

Johnson, Bradish, sugar planter, born on Woodlawn Plantation, La., April 22, 1811; died in Bay Shore, Long Island, N. Y., Nov. 3, 1892. He was graduated at Columbia College, became connected with his father in the distillery business, subsequently engaged in sugar planting and refining, and at the time of his death owned three large sugar plantations near New Orleans, besides the building of the Lotos Club and much other property in New York city. In the early part of the civil war, and before President Lincoln issued his emancipation proclamation, he freed all his slaves; and when the United States vessels first went up the Mississippi river he raised the American flag on Woodlawn Plantation, and kept it flying there during the remainder of the war.

Jones, Samuel, jurist, born in New York city in 1825; died in Poughkeepsie, N. Y., Aug. 11, 1892. He was a grandson of Samuel Jones, a member of the convention that framed the Federal Constitution, and a son of Samuel Jones, who became Chancellor of the State in 1826, first chief justice of the Superior Court of New York city in 1828, and presiding justice of the Supreme Court in the district of New York city in 1848. The third Samuel Jones studied law with his father, was admitted to the bar soon after reaching his majority, and was Judge of the Superior Court of New York from January, 1866, till January, 1872. In August, 1889, he succeeded Nathaniel Jarvis, Jr., as Clerk of the Court of Common Pleas of New York city, and, owing to the exactness with which he conducted the business of his office, his resignation was sought by Tammany leaders and was tendered in June, 1892. He was a brother-in-law of Judges Joseph F. Barnard and George G. Barnard. Though he was contemporary on the Superior Court bench with Judge McCue, who was impeached for participation in the frauds of the Tweed ring, and on terms of intimacy with the Tammany leaders of that day, no suspicion ever attached to his integrity. On his retirement from the bench he co-operated with ex-Judge Spencer in publishing "Jones and Spencer's Law Reports of the Common Pleas."

Joy, Edmund Lewis, merchant, born in Albany, N. Y., Oct. 1, 1835; died in Newark, N. J., Feb. 14, 1892. He was a descendant of Thomas Joy, who came to the United States with Winthrop in 1630, and, on his mother's side, of Anthony Stoddard, who came to America in 1639. In 1850 he accompanied his parents to Newark. He was graduated at the University of Rochester in 1856, was admitted to the bar in New York city in 1857, and practiced in Ottumwa, Iowa, till the breaking out of the civil war. During his residence in Ottumwa he served a term as city attorney, and became active as a Republican speaker. In the early par of the war he was engaged in raising troops for the national army; in 1862 he was commissioned colonel of the 26th Iowa Infantry, with which he took part in many battles up to the capture of Vicksburg; and in 1864 he was appointed a judge advocate and assigned to duty in the 7th Army Corps, with headquarters at Little Rock, Ark. He had much to do in the administration of justice in Arkansas and in Indian Territory, and later in the work of reconstruction in Arkansas. After the war, owing to the impairment of his health, he abandoned his profession and became a partner in his father's mercantile business. He was a member of the New Jersey Legislature in 1871–'72, for several years President of the Board of Education, and of the Board of Trade of Newark, a delegate to the National Republican Convention in 1880, and a Government director of the Union Pacific Railroad in 1884.

Judd, Orange, agriculturist, born near Niagara Falls, N. Y., July 26, 1822; died in Chicago, Ill., Dec. 27, 1892. He was graduated at Wesleyan University in 1847, spent three years in teaching, and took a course in analytical and agricultural chemistry at Yale. In 1853 he removed to New York city, and was appointed editor of the "American Agriculturist," of which he became owner and publisher in 1856. He was also agricultural editor of the New York "Times" from 1855 till 1863. He organized the Orange Judd Company, and was its president till 1883, when, through personal business reverses, he was obliged to retire from the office and make a personal assignment. He then removed to Chicago and established an agricultural journal, which subsequently became widely known as the "Orange Judd Farmer," and which he published till his death. Mr. Judd was a public-spirited citizen, and engaged in numerous enterprises outside of his publishing business. In 1857 he imported from Europe a quantity of sorghum seed, which he distributed free throughout the country, and thus laid the foundation of the present sorghum industry. In 1863 he served with the United States Sanitary Commission at Gettysburg, and afterward with the Army of the Potomac in all its movements from the Rapidan to Petersburg. After the war he became a large stockholder in Long Island railroads, and was one of the projectors of the network of lines now covering the island. Mr. Judd also completed a series of Sunday-school lessons, on which the Berean and International lessons were subsequently modeled. Through life he retained a warm interest in Wesleyan University, and one of the causes of his financial trouble was his erection of the Orange Judd Hall of Natural Science, at a cost of $100,000, which he presented to Yale University as a memorial of a deceased son. He was president of the alumni association and a trustee of the university for many years.

Judd, Orrin Bishop, clergyman, born in Southington, Conn., Nov. 25, 1816; died in Brooklyn, N. Y., Jan. 12, 1892. He was graduated at Madison (now Colgate) University in 1843, and at Hamilton Theological Seminary in 1845, and was ordained to the ministry of the Baptist Church in the latter year. He held pastorates in New Haven and New York city from 1845 till 1849, was one of the editors of "The Examiner and Chronicle" from 1849 till 1856, and was engaged in translating the Gospel of Matthew from 1852 till 1856. On May 27, 1850, he, with 23 others, met in New York city to consider the question "What the cause of religion demanded of them," and the result of their deliberations was the organization of the American Bible Union on June 10 following, "to procure and circulate the most faithful version of the sacred Scriptures in all languages throughout the world." It was to inaugurate the work of the Union that he translated anew the Gospel of St. Matthew, and he also prepared the constitution of the union. Dr. Judd engaged in literary work from 1856 till 1864, resumed pastoral relations in New Haven in 1864, and from 1878 had been engaged in educational and literary work. He published numerous works, including "Waymarks to Apostolic Baptism," "Baptism in Plain English," "Review of the American Bible Union," "Memoirs of the Rev. William Judd," and at the time of his death was finishing a book entitled "Notes and Observations of Baptist History."

Kargé, Joseph, military officer, born in Posen, Germany, July 3, 1823; died in New York city, Dec. 27, 1892. He was educated at the Gymnasium of Posen and the University of Breslau, where he was distinguished for his proficiency in history and languages. After graduation he took a course of lectures on Slavic literature in the College of France, and afterward continued his study of languages in Berlin. The movement for the independence of Poland in 1849 enlisted his sympathies, and he took an active part in it, for doing which he was obliged to flee the country. He sought refuge first in France and then in England, and in 1851 came to New York city, where he began supporting himself by teaching, eventually becoming the head of a popular classical school. On President Lincoln's first call for volunteers he offered his services to the Governor of New Jersey, and in August, 1861, was acting colonel of the 1st New Jersey Cavalry without commission. In February, 1862, he was commissioned lieutenant-colonel of the regiment, and in August was wounded near Rappahannock Bridge, while aiding in covering the retreat of the Army of Virginia. He was absent from the army on leave about three months; returned to his command before his wound had healed, and took part in the battle of Fredericksburg, Dec. 13. His exposure in this battle so aggravated his wound that he was compelled to resign his commission on Dec. 22. Early in 1863, however, he received authority to raise the 2d New Jersey Cavalry. In June of that year, while engaged in organizing this regiment at Trenton, he was appointed chief of cavalry of New Jersey, with the rank of colonel, for the purpose of taking charge of the New Jersey troops that Secretary Stanton and Gov. Curtin, of Pennsylvania, had asked to have sent into that State to aid in repelling the Confederate invasion. The decisive action at Gettysburg put an end to the emergency. In October he took his regiment to Washington, and in November to Eastport, Miss., under assignment to the cavalry division of the 1st brigade, 16th Army Corps, Army of the Tennessee. His command was in constant service till the close of the war, and he won wide distinction as a cavalry officer. On April 9, 1866, he was brevetted brigadier-general, to rank from March 13, 1865. He was mustered out of the volunteer service in November, 1865. In 1867 he accepted a commission in the regular army and served as commander of military reservations in Nevada till 1870, when, while on a leave of absence, he was chosen Professor of Continental Languages and Literature at Princeton. He resigned from the army, accepted this chair, and held it till his death, which occurred on a ferry boat while crossing from Jersey City to New York.

Kendall, Henry, clergyman, born in Volney, N. Y., Aug. 24, 1815; died in East Bloomfield, N. Y., Sept. 10, 1892. He was graduated at Hamilton College in 1840, and at Auburn Theological Seminary in 1844; held pastorates at Verona, N. Y., for four years; East Bloomfield, N. Y., ten years; and at Pittsburg, Pa., three years. In 1861, on the determination of the General Assembly of the Presbyterian Church to resume its own home missionary work, he was elected secretary of the new Board of Home Missions, and he held the office till his death. He had remarkable administrative ability, and at the meeting of the General Assembly in Portland, Ore., in May, 1892, he was given a special and affectionate reception.

Kennedy, Anthony, legislator, born in Baltimore, Md., Dec. 21, 1810; died in Annapolis, Md., July 31, 1892. He was educated at Charlestown Academy, Jefferson County, Va., studied law, but abandoned it, and subsequently was engaged in the manufacture of cotton in New Orleans and in planting in Virginia. He was a member of the Legislature in 1839–'43, was a Taylor presidential elector, removed to Baltimore in 1850, and was elected to the Legislature of Maryland in 1856, and by that body was elected United States Senator, taking his seat March 4, 1857. He remained in the Senate till 1862, and served as a member of the committees on Private Land Claims and on the District of Columbia. After retiring from the Senate he withdrew from political life, but was a delegate to the convention which framed the Constitution of Maryland.

Kernan, Francis, lawyer, born in Wayne, Steuben County, N. Y., Jan. 14, 1816; died in Utica, N. Y.,

Sept. 7, 1892. He received an academic education in Georgetown, D. C., was admitted to the bar in Utica in 1840, becoming a partner of his preceptor, Joshua A. Spencer; was reporter of the Court of Appeals of New York in 1854–'57, member of the Legislature in 1861, elected member of Congress in 1862, defeating Roscoe Conkling, his Republican opponent; was defeated by Mr. Conkling when candidate for re-election in 1864, and was a member of the State Constitutional Convention in 1857, where, though a member of the Roman Catholic Church, he advocated the policy of excluding sectarian schools from State aid. In 1872 he was defeated as Democratic candidate for Governor of New York by Gen. John A. Dix, and in January, 1875, he was elected United States Senator to succeed Reuben E. Fenton, being the only Democrat so honored in New York State from 1848 till 1891. He was defeated for re-election by Thomas C. Platt. Mr. Kernan was a regent of the University of the State of New York from 1870 till his death, and showed his great interest in the public-school system by serving for more than twenty years as a school commissioner in Utica.

Kimball, Richard Burleigh, author, born in Lebanon, N. H., Oct. 11, 1816; died in New York city, Dec. 28, 1892. When eleven years old he passed the examination for admission to Dartmouth College, but the

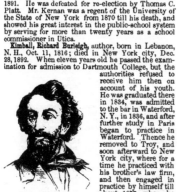

authorities refused to receive him then on account of his youth. He was graduated there in 1834, was admitted to the bar in Waterford, N. Y., in 1836, and after further study in Paris began to practice in Waterford. Thence he removed to Troy, and soon afterward to New York city, where for a time he practiced with his brother's law firm, and then engaged in practice by himself till about 1877, when he retired, and applied himself wholly to literature. He founded the town of Kimball, Texas, built part of the first railroad constructed in that State, running from Galveston to Houston, and was its president in 1854–'60, retiring at the beginning of the civil war. For many years he made a practice of crossing the ocean annually. His publications included: "St. Leger; or, The Threads of Life," a metaphysical novel, which was translated into various foreign languages (1850); "Cuba and the Cubans" (1850); "Romance of Student Life Abroad" (1852); "Undercurrents of Wall Street" (1861); "Was she successful?" (1863); "Henry Powers, Banker" (1868); and "Stories of Exceptional Life" (1887). At the time of his death he had completed "Half a Century of Recollections," in which he wrote of the personal characteristics of many of the eminent people with whom he had been acquainted.

Knapp, Manning M., jurist, born in Newton, N. J., in 1823; died in Jersey City, N. J., Jan. 26, 1892. He was admitted to the bar in 1846, removed to Hackensack to practice the same year, was made a counselor in 1850, was appointed prosecutor of the pleas to fill a vacancy in the latter year, and held the office by reappointments till 1861. In 1875, when Judge Bedle was elected Governor, he appointed Mr. Knapp to fill the vacancy on the Supreme Court bench occasioned by his own election; and Judge Knapp was reappointed by Gov. Ludlow in 1882, and by Gov. Green in 1889. On his first appointment he was assigned by his associates to the Hudson County circuit. As a judge he was noted for his independence and his aggressive opposition to criminals. For several years he had demanded of successive grand juries that they should investigate the frauds perpetrated

by what was known as the "Hudson County Ring." He became indignant that the grand jurors paid little or no attention to his charges, and the failure of the one in session at the time of his death to indict a notorious dive keeper in Hoboken aroused his indignation to the highest pitch. On the day of his death, as the grand jurors were ranged before him in the court room, he denounced them in severe language for their refusal to take cognizance of the proofs in that particular case. While delivering this charge he was suddenly seized with apoplexy, fell back in his chair unconscious, and died within a few minutes. Judge Knapp was an expert on lenses for astronomical instruments, and in his own study of astronomy had from early life been in the habit of making his own lenses, through failure to find any that suited him. At his home in Hackensack he had a workshop, where he found relaxation from judicial worry in making lenses. He frequently presented them to scientific societies, but never would sell any.

Knight, Edward Collings, manufacturer, born in Gloucester, N. J., Dec. 8, 1813; died in Cape May, N. J., July 21, 1892. He was of Quaker descent, served five years as a clerk in a country store, established himself in the grocery business in Philadelphia in 1836, and had carried on a wholesale grocery, commission, importing, and sugar-refining business since 1846. He was the pioneer in importing molasses and sugar from Cuba, and his refineries had a capacity of from 1,000 to 1,500 barrels of sugar a day. Mr. Knight was a director of the Pennsylvania Railroad Company, President of the American Steamship Line, in 1876–'80 President of the Central Railroad Company of New Jersey, and at the time of his death Vice-President of the Guarantee Safe-Deposit Company of Philadelphia. In 1856 he was an unsuccessful candidate for Congress from the old 1st District of Pennsylvania on the American Whig and Reform ticket, and in 1860 he was a Republican presidential elector. Mr. Knight was credited with being the originator of the modern sleeping car, having designed what is believed to have been the first sleeping car ever built in the world. He organized a company to build such cars from his designs, but afterward sold all the rights to the Pullman company.

Knox, John Jay, financier, born in Knoxborough, Oneida County, N. Y., March 19, 1828; died in New York city, Feb. 9, 1892. He was graduated at Hamilton college in 1849, began his business career as a clerk in the bank at Vernon, N. Y., in 1849, and remained in financial business till his death. He came into prominence as a financier in the discussions that preceded the establishment of the national banking system, and particularly by an article that he wrote for "Hunt's Merchants' Magazine" in January, 1862, in which he advocated the passage by Congress of an act similar to the present national banking law. This article attracted the attention of Secretary Chase and Comptroller McColloch, and led to close advisory relations between the three. In 1866 he was sent by the Treasury Department to San Francisco to examine the branch mint in that city, and his report contained so many valuable suggestions that the Secretary of the Treasury deemed it advisable to report it in full to Congress as a part of the official reports. He was next commissioned to go to New Orleans, where he made a special report on a large deficiency in the accounts of the assistant treasury there, and where he remained for some time, acting as assistant Treasurer of the United States. In 1866 he was placed in charge of the mint and coinage correspondence in the Treasury Department at Washington; in 1867 he was appointed deputy comptroller of the currency; in 1870 he made an elaborate report to Congress, including a codification of the mint and coinage laws, with important amendments; and in 1873 he prepared a bill, which was passed with a few modifications, under the title of "the Coinage act of 1873." His terms of office in the Treasury Department were 1867–'72, deputy comptroller; 1872–'77, comptroller, by appointment by President Grant; 1877–'82, comptroller, by appointment by President Hayes; and 1882–'84, comptroller, by appointment by President Arthur. During this period he negotiated many important financial transactions preceding and following the resumption of specie payments, and was especially active in securing the issue and sale of the 3½-per-cent. bonds. Since 1884 Mr. Knox had been President of the National Bank of the Republic in New York city. He published " United States Notes," which was republished in London; and at the time of his death had nearly completed a " History of Banking in the United States," which has been finished by his widow.

Labre, Alexander, hero, born in Montreal, Canada, in 1846; died in New York city, Aug. 12, 1892. He was the son of a French-Canadian shipbuilder, and came to New York city in 1851. When nine years old he was an expert swimmer, and he passed the greater part of his life along the water front of New York, much of the time being employed on ferry boats. Altogether he saved 21 persons from drowning. Twice, unaided, he saved three persons from wrecks of skiffs, and once he dived into a slip and rescued a bridal couple who were on their wedding journey. This latter rescue, on Feb. 28, 1875, excited much interest, and led the Life-saving Benevolent Association of New York to present him with its large silver medal, on which his feat was inscribed. In 1879 a gold medal was presented to him by act of Congress.

Leaming, James Roasbrugh, physician, born in Groveland, Livingston County, N. Y., Feb. 25, 1820; died in New York city, Dec. 5, 1892. He received an academic education, was graduated at the medical department of the University of the City of New York in 1849, and spent his life in practicing in New York city. In 1852–'62 he was attending physician at the Northern Dispensary; in 1859–'69 was associate physician in chest diseases in the Demilt Dispensary; in 1867–'77 was visiting physician in St. Luke's Hospital; and subsequently was special consulting physician in chest diseases there, an office which was created especially for him. He held the latter office till his death, and in addition to it was consulting physician for the Orphans' Home of the Protestant Episcopal Church, and for the Home of Rest for Consumptives before that institution was merged into St. Luke's Hospital. In 1871 he was elected Professor of the Practice and Principles of Medicine in the Woman's Medical College; and was the first President and Professor of Chest Diseases of the New York Polyclinic. Dr. Leaming was one of the most famous specialists on chest diseases. He was a contributor to American, foreign, and international medical publications, and was author of numerous mongraphs and essays, including "Diseases of the Chest," "Thuja Occidentalis in Malignant Diseases," "Cardiac Murmurs," "Plastic Exudation within the Pleura," "Physical Signs of Interpleural Pathology," and "Cough."

Lee, Stephen States, civil engineer, born in South Carolina in 1812; died in Catonsville, Md., Aug. 22, 1892. He was educated as a civil engineer, and engaged in railroad construction at an early age. In 1835 he superintended the building of the Providence division of the New York, Providence and Boston Railroad. In the following year, as agent of Eastern capitalists, he examined and reported unfavorably on a project to construct a large railroad mileage in Illinois for the State government, the capitalists to complete the roads and take State bonds in payment. The panic of 1837 added weight to the value of his judgment on this project. In 1842 he was major and engineer on the staff of Gen. McNeil, commander of the State militia of Rhode Island during the "Dorr rebellion " in that State. In 1843 he began the development of the great Cumberland coal fields, subsequently became agent for the Mount Savage Coal and Iron Company, owned by English capitalists, and in 1869 placed the business, which had grown to large proportions, in the hands of two sons and went to Tours, France, for a period of rest. At the beginning of the Franco-Prussian War he accepted an urgent appeal by the English National society for

Aid for the Sick and Wounded in War to represent that society in the neighborhood of Tours. He accepted the office of honorary secretary of the society, and during the war had entire management of its work in that part of France. After the close of the war he received from the French republic the decoration of the Legion of Honor, from the Prussian Government that of the Royal Crown of Prussia, and from the Bavarian Government that of the Cross of Merit.

Lewis, Edward Parke Custis, diplomatist, born in Audley, Clarke County, Va., Feb. 7, 1837; died in Hoboken, N. J., Sept. 3, 1892. He was a grandson of Lawrence Lewis, whose father married Elizabeth Washington, sister of the general, and of Eleanor Parke Custis, a granddaughter of Martha Washington. He was graduated at the University of Virginia in 1859; studied law in Baltimore, and was admitted to the bar, but never practiced. Though he strongly opposed secession, he went with the Confederacy after the withdrawal of Virginia from the Union. He served for some time in Stuart's "Black Horse Cavalry "; became an aid on that commander's staff; was wounded several times in action; and was twice a prisoner of war, once at Camp Chase, in Ohio, and afterward at Fort Delaware. In 1869 he married, for his second wife, the widow of Gen. Garnett, of the Confederate army, a daughter of the late Edward A. Stevens, of Hoboken, and after this marriage he made his home on the Stevens estate. In 1877 he was elected to the New Jersey Legislature, and during President Cleveland's administration was United States minister to Portugal.

Littlejohn, DeWitt Clinton, manufacturer, born in Bridgewater, Oneida County, N. Y., Feb. 7, 1818; died in Oswego, N. Y., Oct. 27, 1892. He received a thorough preparatory education for college, but changed his mind, and became a member of a firm engaged in transportation and milling. In 1847 he was elected president of Oswego village, and in 1849 and 1855 was mayor. His notable career in the New York Assembly began with his first election in 1853. He was re-elected in 1854, 1855, 1857, 1859, 1860, and 1861, and during his last five terms was Speaker. In 1862 he raised and became a colonel of the 110th New York Volunteers, which he accompanied on the Red River expedition. While in camp in New Orleans he was elected to Congress from the 22d New York District as a Republican, and he resigned his commission to enter that body, in which, however, he served only five months, failing health, resulting from camp exposure, leading him to resign. He was nominated by President Lincoln to be United States consul at Liverpool, but declined, and in 1866, 1867, 1870, 1871, and 1884 was returned to the Assembly, being defeated in 1883. In 1872 he united with the Democrats in the support of Horace Greeley for the presidency, and in 1874 was an unsuccessful candidate for the Democratic nomination for Lieutenant-Governor on the ticket with Samuel J. Tilden. He subsequently returned to the Republican party and remained in it till his death. At different periods he was connected with railroad interests in New York, and was engaged in the forwarding business in Buffalo, and in the manufacture of lumber, with mills at Oswego and Redfield. Mr. Littlejohn had a wide reputation as a parliamentarian, and was a popular presiding officer.

Locke, John Henry, shoemaker, born in North Charlestown, N. H., in 1817; died there, Feb. 9, 1892. He was of English ancestry, tracing his lineage in an unbroken line from John Locke, the philosopher, and was widely known as the "learned shoemaker," being, in his way, nearly as remarkable a character as Elihu Burritt, "the learned blacksmith." He had acquired a thorough knowledge of geology and kindred scientific studies while working at his trade. For many years he was engaged in collecting a rare and valuable cabinet of geological specimens and curios from all parts of the world, the greater part of which he presented to the Farwell High School, in his native town, shortly before his death. He also left a large collection of rare books and manuscripts.

Longfellow, Samuel, clergyman, born in Portland, Me., June 18, 1819; died there, Oct. 3, 1892. He was graduated at Harvard University in 1839, and at the Howard Divinity School in 1846. After two years spent in travel he became pastor of a Unitarian Church in Fall River, Mass., in 1848. He resigned this charge in 1853 to accept a call to a Unitarian church in Brooklyn, N. Y., where he remained until 1860. He then traveled extensively in Europe, making his home in Cambridge, Mass., on his return. In 1878 he became pastor of the Unitarian church in Germantown, Pa., resigning this place in 1882, and once more returning to Cambridge and living in Craigie House after the death of his brother Henry. The last ten years of his life were spent in partial retirement, though he preached occasionally, appeared at social gatherings now and then, took a keen interest in all reforms, and in the summer of 1888 passed some months in Europe. Although he was an advanced religious thinker, he was not aggressive, and never antagonized those who differed with him. He took great pleasure in the company of younger authors, and of young men in general, and in return was much beloved by them. His manner was so gentle and his temperament so sweet and equable, that the real force of his character was not always apprehended by chance acquaintances. His health had long been delicate, and toward the end of summer he was taken ill, and, though he rallied occasionally, failed steadily till the end. His death was as calm and peaceful as his life had always been. He was the author of a number of essays published in "The Radical," and of many very beautiful hymns. His published works include: "A Book of Hymns," with Samuel Johnson (1846); revised edition, "Hymns of the Spirit" (1864); "A Book of Hymns and Tunes for Congregational Use" (1859); a small volume for use at his vesper service; "Thalatta: a Book for the Seaside," with Thomas W. Higginson; a collection of poetry, partly original (1853); "The Life of Henry Wadsworth Longfellow," (2 vols., 1886); "Final Memorials of Henry Wadsworth Longfellow" (1887). A small volume of his poems was printed for private circulation a year or two later.

Lothrop, Daniel, publisher, born in Rochester, N. H., Aug. 11, 1831; died in Boston, Mass., March 19, 1892. When fourteen years old he took charge of his brother's drug store in Newmarket, N. H., and three years afterward he established himself in the same business. Subsequently he established another drug store at Meredith Bridge, and formed a partnership with his two brothers, which was continued for forty years. In 1850 he purchased the stock of a book store in Dover, N. H.; eularged the business, built up a jobbing trade, and made a few ventures in publishing. While supervising these interests he made a trip to St. Peter, Minn., where he opened another drug store, and subsequently established there a banking house. He was a heavy loser during the financial panic of 1857 by the failure of other business houses and the transfer of the State capital to St. Paul; but he paid his debts in full, and then returned to his book store in Dover. In 1868 he established himself in Boston as a publisher. His first venture was a Sunday-school book entitled "Andy Luttrell," which proved successful. Later he published the periodicals "Wide Awake," "Babyland," "The Pansy," "Our Little Men and Women," and "Chautauqua Young Folks' Journal." In the great fire in Boston, in 1872, he sustained heavy losses and costly business delays, and after relocating himself met with reverses from a similar cause. After this he went to the Riverside Press, where his well-known $1,000-prize books were printed. In 1875 he moved from Cornhill to larger quarters at Franklin and Hawley Streets. In 1879 he took a younger brother into partnership, and in 1890 they opened a business house in Washington Street.

Lovering, Joseph, physicist, born in Charlestown, near Boston, Mass., Dec. 25, 1813; died in Cambridge, Mass., Jan. 18, 1892. He was graduated at Harvard in 1830. For a year after graduation he taught in

Charlestown, and then spent two years in the Harvard Divinity School. An early fondness for mathematics led to his pursuing studies in that science during his leisure, and in 1836 he became tutor in mathematics and physics, and two years later succeeded to the

Hollis chair of Mathematics and Natural Philosophy, which he then held continuously until 1888, when he retired, and was made professor emeritus. Prof. Lovering was the first member of the faculty at Harvard to serve his alma mater for fifty years, and the second in the length of his service to the university. He was in 1853–'54 regent of Harvard, and subsequently held that office until 1870; also in 1884 he became director of the Jefferson Physical Laboratory, which place he held until 1888. He contributed largely to the development of the Harvard Astronomical Observatory, and was associated with Prof. William C. Bond in 1840 in the first astronomical work made in the Dana House. The aid of the United States was sought by the Royal Society of London in making simultaneous observations in terrestrial magnetism in Great Britain and the colonies, Cambridge was chosen as one of the American stations, and the observations were made under the direction of Profs. Bond and Lovering. He was also associated with Benjamin Peirce in the publication of the "Cambridge Miscellany of Mathematics and Physics," to which he contributed "The Internal Equilibrium of Bodies," "The Application of Mathematical Analysis to Physical Research," "The Divisibility of Matter," and similar papers. Later, in 1867, when Prof. Peirce became Superintendent of the United States Const and Geodetic Survey, he intrusted the computations for determining transatlantic longitudes from telegraphic observations on cable lines to Prof. Lovering, who continued in charge of this work until 1876. He gave 9 courses, each of 12 lectures, on astronomy and physics before the Lowell Institute in Boston. He delivered shorter courses of lectures at the Smithsonian Institution in Washington, D. C., at the Peabody Institute in Baltimore. Md., and at the Charitable Mechanics' Institution of Boston, as well as occasional lectures elsewhere in New England. In 1839 he was elected to the American Academy of Arts and Sciences, of which he was corresponding secretary in 1869–'73, vice-president in 1873–'80, and president in 1880–'88. He became a member of the American Association for the Advancement of Science in 1849, and from 1854 till 1873 was its permanent secretary, editing 15 volumes of its proceedings. These services were requited by his election to its presidency, and in 1874 he delivered a retiring address, in which he reviewed the progress and development of the physical sciences. Besides membership in other scientific societies, he was in 1873 elected to the National Academy of Sciences. The degree of LL. D. was conferred on him by Harvard in 1879. His papers, more than 100 in number, may be found in the files of the "Proceedings of the American Academy of Arts and Sciences," the "Proceedings of the American Association for the Advancement of Science," the "American Journal of Science," the "Journal of the Franklin Institute," the "American Almanac," the "North American Review," "The Old and New," and "The Popular Science Monthly." His most important researches are included in several papers on the aurora, terrestrial magnetism, and the determination of transatlantic longitudes, which appeared in vols. ii and ix of the "Memoirs of the American Academy of Arts and Sciences," also in vol. x, which consists of his results on "Aurora Borealis" (Boston, 1873). Besides the foregoing, he edited an improved edition of John Farrar's "Electricity and Magnetism" (1842). A biographical memoir of his career, by Josiah P. Cooke, will appear in the forthcoming volume of "Biographical Memoirs of the National Academy of Sciences."

McCarroll, James, journalist, born in Lanesboro, County Longford, Ireland, in 1815; died in New York city, April 10, 1892. He went to Canada while a youth, and was there educated and engaged in literary work. He was a contributor to the "Morning Chronicle" of Quebec, and for a long time was musical critic of the "Leader" and the "Colonist" of Toronto. During his residence in Canada he held important offices under the Government, and became widely known for his classical, scientific, and musical knowledge. From Canada he removed to New York city, and resumed work in journalism, contributing poems, musical and dramatic criticisms, scientific articles, essays, and reviews to the newspapers and magazines. He was author of several dramas and novels, a popular lecturer, a musician, and a musical composer. He invented several useful articles, including a safety elevator for hotels and offices.

McCrady, Edward, lawyer, born in Charleston, S. C., March 16, 1802; died there, Nov. 17, 1892. He was graduated at Yale in 1820, and was admitted to the bar in 1824. In 1832 he took the side of the Unionists in the nullification struggle, and was chairman of the committee of correspondence of the Union party in Charleston. From 1832 till 1850 he was United States District Attorney, and, after resigning, he joined the Southern Rights Association, which was opposed to secession, but favored the maintenance of Southern institutions through co-operation of the States. He believed in the right of secession. In 1852 he was elected to the Legislature, where he served several terms, and in 1860, as a member of the State convention, he voted for and signed the ordinance of secession. During the civil war he continued in practice, and was chiefly engaged in causes arising from the Sequestration act. For fifty years he represented St. Philip's Church in the Protestant Episcopal diocesan convention, and for thirty years was a delegate to the General Convention. He was the oldest living graduate of Yale, the oldest member of the South Carolina bar, and the last prominent participant in the nullification movement.

McKinley, David Allison, merchant, born in Canton, Ohio, in 1829; died in San Francisco, Cal., Sept. 18, 1892. He was a brother of Gov. William McKinley, of Ohio, was educated at Alleghany College, Pennsylvania, and became a clerk in his father's store in Canton. He went to California during the gold excitement in 1852, was engaged in mining and lumbering till 1864, and then established himself in the coal and wood business in San Francisco. He was active in Republican politics, a presidential elector in 1876, United States consul at the Sandwich Islands in 1880–'85, and on his retirement from that office was appointed consul-general of Hawaii at San Francisco, which office he held continuously till his death.

McRae, John E., engraver, born in Edinburgh, Scotland, in 1816; died in Bayonne, N. J., Aug. 23, 1892.

He learned the art of steel-plate engraving and printing in his native city; came to New York in 1857; was in business for himself for more than twenty-five years; and afterward entered into partnership with J. C. Lang, printer and publisher, with whom he remained six years. He executed many steel-plate engravings, including "The Marriage of Pocahontas," "First in Peace," "The Landing of Columbus," "Signing the Declaration of Independence," and "The Perils of our Forefathers." The best collection of his engravings, from the original plates, is that in the national Capitol at Washington, D. C.

Maeder, Gaspard, scenic painter, born in New York city about 1840; died there, Jan. 18, 1892. He was employed in youth at Wallack's Theatre, where he studied scenic painting under Isherwood, the artist of that house. From Wallack's he went to the Globe Theatre, in Boston, and, after several years there, returned to New York, and with Lafayette Seavey opened a studio in Lafayette Place, where the firm made a specialty of painting scenery for traveling companies till the partners separated. Mr. Maeder then went into a partnership with Schaffer, which lasted till the death of the former. Mr. Maeder was equally facile in painting interiors, exteriors, and landscapes. His scenic work included the scenery for Sarah Bernhardt's first production of "Theodora" in this country; that for the several spectacular productions at Niblo's by the Kiralfys; the large battle scene in "Shenandoah"; the scenery in the "Club Fiend"; a large part of that in the "Queen of Sheba," at the Metropolitan Opera House; and some of the best pieces in the Lyceum Theatre.

Manly, Basil, educator, born near Dangerfield, S. C., Dec. 19, 1825; died in Louisville, Ky., Jan. 31, 1892. He was a son of the Rev. Basil Manly, D. D., President of the University of Alabama from 1837 to 1855, was graduated at that institution in 1843, and at Princeton Theological Seminary in 1847, and was ordained a minister of the Baptist Church in 1848. He held pastorates at Providence and Tuscaloosa, Ala.; became pastor of the First Baptist Church in Richmond, Va., in 1850; President of the Richmond Female Institute in 1854; and on the organization of the Southern Baptist Theological Seminary at Greenville, S. C., he was chosen one of the original professors, taking the chair of Old Testament Interpretation and Biblical Introduction, which he held at the time of his death. In 1871 he was elected President of Georgetown College, Kentucky, but in 1879 he resumed his old chair in the Southern Baptist Seminary, which had been removed to Louisville. With his father he compiled the "Baptist Psalmody" (Charleston, 1850), and independently he published "A Call to the Ministry" (Philadelphia, 1857).

Mann, William Julius, theologian, born in Stuttgart, Germany, May 29, 1819; died in Boston, Mass., June 20, 1892. He received a classical training in his native place, studied theology at Tübingen, and was ordained to the ministry of the Lutheran Church in 1841. He served as assistant pastor in Würtemberg until 1845, when he came to this country with his intimate friend and former classmate, the Rev. Philip Schaff, with whom he remained at Mercersburg, Pa., until his removal to Philadelphia, which was his home until his death. In 1850 he was called as the colleague of Dr. Demme and Rev. G. A. Reichert to the pastorate of St. Michael's and Zion Lutheran Church, Philadelphia, and from 1863 until 1884 he was pastor of this congregation, retiring in the latter year as pastor emeritus. He was editor of the "Kirchenfreund" from 1854 to 1860, a monthly theological journal. During his pastorate in Philadelphia the Lutheran interests in the German language were concentrated in one strong organization, reporting 2,500 communicant members, scattered all over the city, and having services for many years in three churches, where the pastors took their turns in officiating, until the erection of the present Zion Church, since which time services have been held in one church. With systematic arrangement of his time, he was enabled to attend to his numerous pastoral duties, and yet devote a great deal of time to theological study. In 1864, when the theological seminary was established in Philadelphia, he was elected as one of the professors, which place he held until his death, having under his special charge Hebrew, ethics, symbolics, and German homiletics. In 1856 came the opportunity for a most valuable service to the Lutheran Church in America. The so-called "Definite Platform" had appeared, the purpose of which was to revise the Augsburg Confession in such a way as to erase from it all distinctively Lutheran doctrines, and teach pure and simple "undenominationalism." As a reply to it he published "A Plea for the Augsburg Confession," which was soon followed by his "Lutheranism in America." These two books were important agencies to check infidelity to the principles of the Church, and to aid in preparing the way for the higher confessional position of the ministerium of Pennsylvania, and afterward of the general council. They were followed by "Luther's Small Catechism explained" with Dr. Krotel (1863); "System of Christian Ethics" (1872); "Vergangene Tagen, aus den Zeiten Mühlenberg's" (1879); "The Lutheran Church and its Confessions" (1880); "Heilsbotschaft," a volume of sermons (1881); "Das Buch der Bücher und seine Geschichte" (1885); "Life and Times of Henry Melchior Muhlenberg" (1887); "Hallesche Nachrichten" (1886); "Muhlenberg's Leben und Wirken" (1892). He also wrote biographies of William Penn and Columbus, besides numerous contributions to German and English periodicals of the Church. But his greatest literary achievements were in connection with the publication of the new edition of the "Hallesche Nachrichten" and the "Life and Times of Muhlenberg." Few books have been edited with the minute care of the former. The plan is carried out of explaining every historical, biographical, and geographical allusion, thus furnishing a rich storehouse for all time concerning the historical foundations of the Lutheran Church along the Atlantic coast. It is a permanent and well-arranged record of the character of the men, the doctrines, and Church life of the first period of the Church's history in this country. He spoke with fluency and earnestness. He esteemed it the highest privilege to preach, and never declined an invitation, whether for German or English services, unless absolutely prevented.

Marvin, Richard Pratt, jurist, born in New York about 1815; died in Jamestown, N. Y., Jan. 11, 1892. He entered political life immediately after reaching his majority; was a member of the Legislature from Chautauqua in 1836, and member of Congress from 1837 till 1841; was a delegate to the State Constitutional Convention in 1846; and was elected a justice of the Supreme Court of New York for the 8th Judicial District in 1847. In January, 1855, he was appointed a justice of the Supreme Court sitting in the Court of Appeals; in January, 1863, was reappointed; and in November following was again elected Supreme Court justice. Since 1872 Judge Marvin had lived in retirement at Jamestown.

Mears, Frederick, military officer, born in New York city, Jan. 1, 1835; died in Fort Spokane, Wash., Jan. 2, 1892. Prior to the civil war he was a sergeant in the 7th Regiment of New York, and in the early days of the war he was employed in drilling recruits in Washington, D. C. He was appointed 2d lieutenant 9th United States Infantry, April 26, 1861; was promoted 1st lieutenant May 17 following; captain, Aug. 27, 1863; major 25th Infantry, April 2, 1883; and lieutenant-colonel 4th Infantry, April 24, 1888. In the volunteer army he was appointed lieutenant-colonel of the 1st United States Sharpshooters, Oct. 1, 1861, and was mustered out of the service Nov. 30 following. He was brevetted major United States army March 13, 1865, for faithful and meritorious services during the war. After the war he was engaged chiefly in Indian campaigns, and in the disastrous campaign of 1876 he was one of the officers who were to co-operate with Gen. Custer on the Little

Big Horn. In 1886-'88 he was in command of the recruiting station at David's Island, New York, and at the time of his death was commandant at Fort Spokane, Wash.

Meigs, Montgomery Cunningham, military officer, born in Augusta, Ga., May 3, 1816; died in Washington, D. C., Jan. 2, 1892. He was graduated at the United States Military Academy, July 1, 1836, but resigned July 31, 1837. He was appointed brevet 2d lieutenant of engineers (to rank from July 1, 1836) in August, 1837; promoted 1st lieutenant, July 7, 1838; captain, March 3, 1853; colonel 11th United States Infantry, May 14, 1861; and brigadier-general and quartermaster-general on the following day; and was retired Feb. 6, 1882, on account of age. He was brevetted major-general

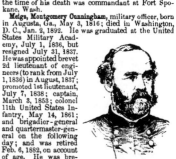

United States army, July 5, 1864, for distinguished and meritorious services during the war. Gen. Meigs was considered the foremost scientific soldier in the United States army, and was practically its quartermaster-general during the entire civil war. While serving in the engineer corps he was engaged in the construction of Forts Delaware, Wayne, Porter, Niagara, Ontario, and Madison, and superintended the construction of the Potomac Aqueduct, of the new wings and iron dome of the extension of the national Capitol, and of the extension of the post-office department. In 1875-'76 he was sent to Europe to study the organization and government of the principal European armies, and was made a member of the commission to reform and reorganize the United States army. Subsequently he was employed in preparing the plans for the new State, War, and Navy Department Building, and the National Museum in Washington, D. C., and after his retirement he was the architect of the new Pension Building in Washington. He was a regent of the Smithsonian Institution and a member of numerous scientific societies. He bequeathed to the United States Government, to be deposited in the National Museum, the following articles of historic interest: A seal ring with intaglio portrait of Julius Cæsar; an antique stone, a large signet of bronze, with stone engraved in intaglio antique of Chiron and Achilles or Æneas; cabinet and collection of coins and medals, some of them antiques, including Alexander the Great, Philip of Macedon, Julius Cæsar, Augustus, and other Roman and Greek heads, and Napoleon, Washington, and other medals; a large silver tureen or vase, given by the citizens of Baltimore to Commodore Rodgers after his defense of Baltimore from the attack of the British fleet, and a silver tea-kettle and lamp, presented to him by the city of Washington on the occasion of the adoption of his project and report upon which the Washington Aqueduct was built.

Mendenhall, James W., clergyman, born in Ohio, Nov. 1, 1844; died in Colorado Springs, Col., June 18, 1892. He was graduated at Ohio Wesleyan University, and studied and practiced medicine some years before entering the ministry. He was author of "Echoes of Palestine" and "Plato and Paul; or, Philosophy and Christianity," and since 1888 had been editor of the "Methodist Review." At the General Conference of the Methodist Episcopal Church in 1892 he was re-elected editor by a practically unanimous vote.

Mendenhall, John, military officer, born in Indiana, July 12, 1829; died in Newport, R. I., July 1, 1892. He was graduated at the United States Military Academy, and brevetted 2d lieutenant 1st United States Dragoons, July 1, 1851; was transferred to 4th Artillery, Feb. 20, 1852; promoted 2d lieutenant, Oct.

8, 1853; 1st lieutenant, March 12, 1856; captain, July 3, 1861; major 1st Artillery, Jan. 10, 1877; lieutenant-colonel 4th Artillery, Oct. 2, 1883; and colonel 2d Artillery, Dec. 4, 1888. In the volunteer army he was commissioned major and judge-advocate, March 17, 1863; promoted lieutenant-colonel, Feb. 27, 1864; and was mustered out of the service Oct. 23, 1865. He was brevetted major United States army, April 7, 1862, for gallantry in the battle of Shiloh, Tenn.; lieutenant-colonel, Sept. 20, 1863, for Chickamauga, Ga.; and colonel, March 13, 1865, for services during the civil war. Prior to the war he served in Florida, Texas, and Kansas; during the war was attached to the Army of the Cumberland; and after the war was on duty in Michigan, California, Alaska, and Rhode Island, where he was commandant of Fort Adam at the time of his death.

Merriman, Truman Adams, journalist, born in Auburn, N. Y., Sept. 5, 1839; died in New York city, April 16, 1892. He was graduated at Hobart College in 1861; entered the national army as captain of an infantry company he had organized, which was mustered as a part of the 92d New York Volunteers in January, 1863; was promoted major in December following, and lieutenant-colonel June 1, 1864; and after taking part in the battle of Fair Oaks, in the Seven Days' battles, and in the trenches before Petersburg, where he commanded his regiment and was severely wounded, he was mustered out of the service, Jan. 7, 1865. After the war he studied law, was admitted to the bar in 1867, and from 1871 till 1884 was a reporter on "The Sun" newspaper in New York. In the latter year he was elected to Congress from the 11th New York District as a Democrat, and in 1886 was re-elected. At the close of his congressional service he engaged in editorial work in New York city. He was three times President of the Press Club.

Merrimon, Augustus Summerfield, jurist, born in Buncombe County, N. C., Sept. 15, 1830; died in Raleigh, N. C., Nov. 14, 1892. He received a common-school education, studied law, and was admitted to the bar in 1852. In 1860 he was a member of the Legislature, and opposed the secession movement till President Lincoln issued his first call for volunteers, when he went into the Confederate army. In 1866 he was elected judge of the Superior Court of North Carolina, and held sessions frequently, under police protection, till Gen. Edward R. S. Canby began issuing military orders to the State judiciary, when he resigned. He was defeated as Democratic candidate for Governor in 1872, and was elected United States Senator for a full term in 1873. On his retirement from the Senate he was elected Associate Justice of the Supreme Court of North Carolina, and on the death of Chief-Justice Smith in 1889 he was appointed to fill the vacancy. In 1890 he was elected Chief Justice.

Miller, Samuel Freeman, farmer, born in Franklin, N. Y., May 27, 1827; died there, March 16, 1892. He was graduated at Hamilton College in 1852, and was admitted to the bar in the following year, but engaged in farming and lumbering. He was elected to the Legislature in 1854 as a Republican, and to Congress in 1862 and 1874; was a member of the State Constitutional Convention in 1867; was collector of internal revenue for his district in 1869–'73; and was a member of the State Board of Charities in 1869–'77.

Mindeleff, Dmetri, chemist, born in Russia, about 1810; died in San Francisco, Cal., Feb. 14, 1892. When about fifty years old he was obliged to leave his native country on account of his republican principles, and settled on a farm near Washington, D. C., where he resided till his home was destroyed by the military operations made necessary for the defense of the national capital. Being unable to obtain any compensation for the loss of his home and its contents, he sold his farm and removed to Washington, where he lived till 1875, when he removed to San Francisco. He had a wide reputation as a chemist. Among his inventions were new methods for reducing cobalt and nickel ores and for destroying phylloxera by means of pyroligneous acid. His most important invention was the new high explosive, which he named "terrorite," a compound said to be more powerful than dynamite, with which the United States Government was experimenting at the time of his death.

Moak, Nathaniel Cleveland, lawyer, born in Sharon, N. Y., Oct. 3, 1833; died in Albany, N. Y., Sept. 17, 1892. He was brought up on a farm; was educated in the academies of Cherry Valley and Cooperstown; and was admitted to the bar in 1856. In 1867 he removed to Albany, and became a partner in the firm of Smith, Bancroft & Moak. He laid the foundation of his reputation as a trial lawyer after settling in Albany, and in the long struggle between Joseph H. Ramsay and Messrs. Fisk & Gould for the possession of the Susquehanna Railroad, he was Mr. Ramsay's counsel. In 1871 he was elected district-attorney of Albany County, serving for two years, prosecuting the celebrated Lowenstein murder case, and that of Phelps, the defaulting State Treasurer clerk. Subsequently he added to his reputation by his participation in the Jesse Billings murder trial. Mr. Moak made numerous contributions to legal literature, and published "Clark's Chancery Reports"; "Moak's English Reports," in 35 volumes; "Moak's English Digest"; "Moak's Edition of Van Santvoord's Pleadings." His private law library was one of the largest in the country, containing all the English, Scotch, Irish, and Canadian reports, all the State and Federal reports, a complete set of all the legal periodicals and of the Australian and New Zealand reports, besides numerous text-books. It is believed to have cost him $75,000. After his death the library was purchased by the wife and daughter of the late Judge Boardman, for presentation to the School of Law of Cornell University.

Moore, Daniel David Tompkins, journalist, born in Marcellus, Onondaga County, N. Y., Feb. 2, 1820; died in New York city, June 3, 1892. When fifteen years old he was apprenticed to the printer's trade in the office of the Rochester, N. Y., "Advertiser," where he not only learned to set type but to do occasional writing for the paper. He was for two years a clerk in the Rochester post-office, and then he began studying law. The death of a brother who had been publishing the "Gazette," a weekly newspaper at Jackson, Mich., caused him to abandon the study of law and to take charge of the newspaper property. He made a success of the "Gazette," sold it, and established the "Michigan Farmer," the first paper devoted to agricultural matters in that State. This in turn he sold, and, returning to New York, purchased and edited for three years the "Genesee Farmer," which at the close of 1849 had a circulation of nearly 20,000 copies. On Jan. 1, 1850, he published in Rochester the first number of "Moore's Rural New-Yorker." This paper proved attractive from the start, and soon obtained a large circulation. In 1869 Mr. Moore moved the publication office from Rochester to New York city, where the expenses were increased without any corresponding increase of income, and in a few years the paper passed from his hands. After this he began a magazine called "Moore's Rural Life." This and other ventures proved failures, and the remainder of his life was spent in conducting agricultural departments in the "Christian at Work," the "Christian Advocate," and the "Independent." While he lived in Rochester he was elected to several public offices, including that of mayor.

Moore, George Henry, librarian, born in Concord, N. H., April 20, 1823; died in New York city, May 5, 1892. He was a son of Dr. Jacob Bailey Moore, at one time librarian of the New York Historical Society, and a brother of Henry Eaton Moore, the author and composer. George Henry was educated at Dartmouth College and at the university of the City of New York, where he was graduated in 1845. While a student at the university he was appointed assistant librarian of the New York Historical Society. In 1849 he succeeded his father as librarian there, and from 1872 till his death was superintendent of the

Lenox Library. He was widely known through his writings, which included "The Treason of Charles Lee," "The Employment of Negroes in the Revolutionary Army," "Notes on the History of Slavery in Massachusetts," "History of the Jurisprudence of New York," "Early History of Columbia College," "Washington as an Angler," and "Witchcraft in Massachusetts."

Moore, James Solomon, merchant, born in Königsberg, Germany, in 1821; died in New York city, March 5, 1892. He received a common-school education, went to Manchester, England, as a clerk for an uncle in 1838, made a thorough study of the principles and methods of foreign and domestic trade, and came to the United States soon after attaining his majority. In 1849 he went to California, and spent two years in San Francisco in general mercantile business; returned to England and entered a mercantile firm; engaged in the Australian and China trade, and within a few weeks went to Melbourne to establish a branch office. As in California, he was highly successful in Australia, and after three years' absence he returned to England and established the firm of J. S. Moore & Co., of London and Bombay, with connections in China. The interests of this firm induced him to make a journey to India, and subsequently to the Cape of Good Hope, stopping at all intermediate ports of importance. In 1866, Mr. Moore settled permanently in New York city and engaged in financial operations. In 1869 he began the publication in the New York "World" of letters on the tariff, under the pen name of the "Parsee Merchant." He favored through life a reduced tariff, and his letters caused him to be called the "Father of Free Trade in America." He had such a grasp of commercial economy and of statistics bearing on it, that, though a strong Democrat politically, he was induced by a Republican administration to enter the New York Customhouse, where his unique experience might be turned to public advantage, and where he remained for many years. During the administration of President Cleveland Mr. Moore spent much of his time in Washington in conference with the Ways and Means Committee of the House of Representatives. He was an accomplished linguist and a man of wide reading.

Morgan, George Washburne, organist, born in Gloucester, England, April 9, 1822; died in Tacoma, Wash., July 10, 1892. When eight years old he began playing the organ in public, performing the entire service in St. Nicholas's Church, Gloucester; and when twelve years old he was appointed assistant organist of the cathedral there. Two years afterward he had charge of the boy choir. In 1851 he held two appointments as organist in London, and in a competitive performance with Sir Henry Smart, then considered the best organist in England, he won the appointment of organist to the Harmonic Union of Exeter Hall, and a year afterward composed an anthem, which the Harmonic Society of 800 members sang. In 1853 he removed to New York city, where he was at different times organist of St. Thomas's, St. Stephen's, St. Ann's, the Reformed Dutch, and Grace Churches; then removed to Brooklyn, and was organist of Dr. Talmage's Tabernacle for fourteen years. He was also organist for many years of the Grand Lodge of Masons of New York. He wrote more than 80 compositions, besides numerous songs, and conducted for many years Lenten recitals in Chickering Hall, New York.

Morgan, Maria, live-stock reporter, born in County Cork, Ireland, Nov. 22, 1828; died in Jersey City, N. J., May 31, 1892. Her father was a landed proprietor of considerable wealth, who gave his children a thorough education, and Maria supplemented the usual course with a special one in languages. From early youth she had a marked fondness for animal life, and a special liking for the chase. The death of the father broke up the home, and soon afterward Maria took her younger sister, Jane, to Rome, to give her an opportunity to study art. While in Rome Maria made many friends among American residents,

artists, and those of the nobility who kept large stables of horses. The sisters remained there nearly two years, when Jane returned to Ireland and Maria removed to Florence, where she was kindly received, and where her intimate knowledge of animals attracted the attention of King Victor Emanuel, who became one of her firmest friends. The King, a great horse fancier and rider, was anxious to acquire some of the noted blooded stock of Ireland, and commissioned Maria to select saddle horses for his own use in her native country. She accordingly returned to Ireland in the spring of 1867, and a few months afterward accompanied a string of Irish hunting mares to Florence. The King showed his appreciation of her fidelity and good judgment by presenting her with a diamond star pendant from which was a double-cased hunting watch bearing his monogram in brilliants. During the remainder of her residence in Italy the knowledge that she possessed the King's friendship secured for her a welcome in the highest social circles. In June, 1869, she came to the United States, bearing letters of introduction to various people, among them Henry J. Raymond and Horace Greeley. She at once sought employment as a live-stock and agricultural-fair reporter, and her first engagement was on the New York "World." Her first assignment was as a special correspondent at the Saratoga race track. At the close of her first season, in September, she presented the letter intended for Mr. Raymond, who had died just before she landed, to John Bigelow, then editor-in-chief of the New York "Times." She at once began reporting on that paper, and continued it to the close of her life, besides writing for the "Herald," "Turf, Field, and Farm," "American Agriculturalist," "Country Gentleman," "Spirit of the Times," and "The Horseman's and Breeder's Gazette." She was one of the most familiar figures at the great cattle yards around New York city, at the horse shows and races, and at the exhibitions of dogs. For several years she lived in Metuchen, N. J., but within a few years of her death she removed to Staten Island, where her sister Jane had settled, and there erected a residence after a plan unique and original. She gathered a large quantity of curious furniture and other household articles. Her death resulted indirectly from an accident in the Jersey City stock yard in 1891. Miss Morgan, who was familiarly spoken of as Middy Morgan, was very tall and slender, thoroughly unconventional in attire and manners, dressed suitably to her occupation, and was a most entertaining talker. She bequeathed her most valuable mementoes to the Metropolitan Museum of Art.

Moss, John Calvin, inventor, born in Washington County, Pa., Jan. 5, 1838; died in New York city, April 8, 1892. He was apprenticed to the printer's trade, and while learning it applied much of his time to the study of art. Finding painting uncongenial, he became a photographer, and in 1856, reading of the experiments, by Niepce and Prof. Grove, to etch on a Daguerrean plate by means of electricity, he made a galvanic battery and attempted to accomplish the result they were aiming at. His wife aided him in his experiments, and completed their first order for a printing plate after he had been compelled by extreme fatigue to abandon it. Encouraged by this success, Mr. Moss and his wife removed to New York city in 1863, and for eight years struggled for a livelihood, through the opposition of wood engravers to their invention; but in 1871 he succeeded in forming a company to develop his invention of photo-engraving, and this venture proving unsuccessful, he established in the following year the Photo-engraving Company, which was successful from the start. In 1880 he established the Moss Engraving Company, of which he remained the head until his death, and spent his last years in improving the art he had made practicable. His processes were not patented.

Mountpleasant, Caroline, Indian queen, born in the Seneca Nation, N. Y., about 1832; died on the Tonawanda Reservation, N. Y., March 18, 1892. She was a sister of Gen. Ely S. Parker, who became noted as a civil engineer, and served in the civil war on the staff of Gen. Grant. She was the widow of John Mountpleasant, head chief of the Six Nations. She received an academic education, and was well informed, particularly in Indian history. She was married in early life, and greatly aided her husband in his attempts to educate the tribes under his chieftainship. After his death she retained her residence with the Tuscaroras, though dividing her time between her own and her husband's tribes. She was a Christian in belief and practice, was active in promoting the interests of the reservation schools, made her home a museum of Indian relics, and to the close of her life opposed the division in severalty of the Indian lands in New York State. Her home was visited every season by large numbers of American and foreign tourists, to whom she accorded a gracious reception.

Mussey, Reuben Dimond, lawyer, born in Hanover, N. H., May 30, 1833; died in Washington, D. C., May 29, 1892. At the time of his birth his father was a professor in the medical department of Dartmouth College, and after graduation there he removed to Cincinnati, where he was engaged for a time on the "Gazette," and in 1859–'60 was its correspondent in Washington, D. C. In 1861 he was commissioned captain in the 19th Ohio Infantry; was brevetted colonel in 1865, and resigned in 1866, with the rank of colonel. He was one of the first officers to volunteer for service with colored troops, and spent much time at Nashville organizing such troops, and mustered in 10 such regiments. He received 3 brevets and 3 promotions for special bravery and for meritorious services during the war. After the war he was private secretary to President Johnson, studied law, was admitted to the bar, and practiced in Washington till within a short time of his death.

Mussey, Artemas Bowers, clergyman, born in Lexington, Mass., Sept. 21, 1802; died in Cambridge, Mass., April 21, 1892. He was graduated from Harvard University in 1824, and from the Harvard Divinity School in 1828. He was ordained as pastor of the Unitarian Society at Framingham, Mass., June 10, 1830, but resigned his pastorate three years later. He was pastor of the Unitarian churches in Cambridgeport for a number of years, and in March, 1854, became pastor of the Unitarian church in Concord, N. H. From Sept. 3, 1857, to May, 1865, he was in charge of the Unitarian church at Newburyport. After the latter date he resided in Cambridge, but supplied the pulpit of the Unitarian church at Chestnut Hill, Brookline, Mass., for some ten or twelve years. He was twice married, his first wife being Hepsibeth Patterson, of Boston, who died in 1859; the second being Lucy J. Moseley, of Newburyport, who died a few months before her husband. He published over two hundred books, sermons, and essays, among which are the following: "The Young Man's Friend" (Boston, 1836); "Sunday-school Guide" (1837); "Moral Teacher" (1839); "The Young Maiden" (1840); "Man a Soul" (1842); "The Fireside: An Aid to Parents" (1849); "Sabbath-school Hymn and Tune Book" (1855); "Christ in the Will, the Heart, and the Life" (Boston 1861); "The Blade and the Ear: Thoughts for a Young Man" (Boston, 1864); "The Value of the Study of Intellectual Philosophy to the Minister" (1869); "Leaves from an Autobiography" (1870–'72); "The Higher Education" (1871); "Personal Recollections of Rev. Dr. Channing" (1874–'75); "Immortality in the Light of Scripture and Science" (1876); "Personal Recollections of Men in the Battle of Lexington" (1877); "Truths Consequent upon Belief in a God" (1879); "Prime Movers of the Revolution known to the Writer" (1890), being "Reminiscences and Memorials of the Men of the Revolution" (Boston, 1883); "Education of Old Age" (1884). He was greatly interested in educational matters, and for some years was connected with the State Board of Education. He also took a keen interest in politics and all the topics of the time throughout his long life.

Neafie, Andrew Jackson, actor, born in New York city in 1815; died there, May 1, 1892. He was apprenticed to the carpenter's trade; made his first appearance on the stage in the old Park Theatre, New York, where he paid the manager $200 for the privilege, and played "Othello," in 1839. Afterward he played at Niblo's, where he won the friendship of Edwin Forrest, and through the influence of that tragedian secured an engagement at the National Theatre, Philadelphia, where he appeared as Falkland in the "Rivals." In 1861 he made a professional visit to England, and subsequently he appeared in various American theatres till 1867, when he retired.

Nevin, William Marvel, educator, born near Shippensburg, Franklin County, Pa., Feb. 7, 1806; died in Lancaster, Pa., Feb. 11, 1892. He was educated at Princeton and at Dickinson College, being graduated at the latter in 1827; studied law, and was admitted to the bar of Cumberland County, Pa., but never engaged in practice. He then began the study of medicine, but as this, too, proved uncongenial, he decided to apply himself to teaching. After being employed in various educational institutions in Ohio, Pennsylvania, and Michigan, he was elected Professor of Latin, Greek, and Belles-lettres in Marshall College, Mercersburg, Pa., in 1840. In 1853, when the college was removed to Lancaster, Pa., and united with Franklin College, he was re-elected to the chair which he had previously filled, and remained there till 1872, when he was elected the first professor of the newly established professorship of English Literature and Belle-lettres. In 1888 he was made professor emeritus, and continued to direct his former department and to lecture twice a week till within a few weeks of his death. He received the degree of LL. D. from Dickinson College in 1881, and at the time of his death was the oldest active college professor in the country. He wrote much in verse and prose, and contributed to religious publications.

Newberry, John Strong, geologist, born in Windsor, Conn., Dec. 22, 1822; died in New Haven, Conn., Dec. 7, 1892. He was descended from early American ancestry, and as a boy accompanied his parents to Ohio. Determining upon a professional career, he was graduated at Western Reserve College in 1846, and at the Cleveland Medical College in 1848, after which for two years he followed special studies in Europe. Returning to the United States, he settled in Cleveland, Ohio, and early in 1851 began the practice of medicine. For four years he continued the active pursuit of his profession, but a fondness for natural history led to his accepting, in May, 1855, the appointment of assistant surgeon in the United States army, in which capacity and that of geologist he accompanied the exploring party sent under Lieut. Robert S. Williamson to examine the country between San Francisco and the Columbia river. Dr. Newberry gathered information on the botany, geology, and zoölogy of this territory, and his reports appear in the "Reports of Explorations and Surveys to ascertain the most Practical and Economical Route for a Railroad from the Mississippi River to the Pacific Ocean, made in 1853–'56," vol. vi (Washington, 1857). While working up the material, he held, during 1856–'57, the chair of Chemistry and Natural History in Columbian University, Washington, D. C. On the completion of his report he was assigned to the expedition under Lieut. Joseph C. Ives, for exploration and navigation of Colorado river. He entered the river at its mouth and ascended the stream by steamer

five hundred miles, until the entrance of the Grand Cañon was reached, where he spent nearly a year in making researches in geology and natural history. His observations formed the most interesting material gathered by the expedition, and more than one half of the "Report upon the Colorado River of the West, explored in 1857-'58" (Washington, 1861), was written by him. Subsequently he was appointed on the expedition sent out for the exploration of the San Juan and upper Colorado rivers, under Capt. John N. Macomb. The greater portion of the summer of 1859 he spent in examining portions of what are now southern Colorado, Utah, northern Arizona, and New Mexico, studying the natural history of a large area of country then unknown, which since has proved to be rich in mineral wealth, and of special interest owing to the remains of an ancient civilization which he examined. The information collected by him was issued in a "Report of the Exploring Expedition from Santa Fé to the Junction of the Grand and Green Rivers" (Washington, 1876). At the beginning of the civil war he was on duty in Washington, where, on June 14, 1861, he was chosen a member of the United States Sanitary Commission. His immediate plan "was to become a medium through which the Sanitary Commission should extend its organization and benefits over the great West." For this purpose he went to Ohio, and early in July made with the Rev. Henry W. Bellows and Dr. William H. Mussey the first sanitary inspection of troops in the West, at Cairo, Ill. On Sept. 1 he resigned his commission in the army and was made Secretary of the Western Department of the United States Sanitary Commission, having supervision of all the work of that body in the valley of the Mississippi. At first he made his headquarters in Cleveland, Ohio, but in order to be nearer the army he removed, on Oct. 1, 1862, to Louisville, Ky., where he remained until his resignation. Dr. Newberry organized the whole of the comprehensive machinery of the commission in the large section that was committed to his care, and by his practical suggestions and enthusiasm stimulated the formation of the tributary societies, including those at Chicago and Cleveland. The first distributing depot of supplies was established at Wheeling, W. Va., on Oct. 8, 1861, and was the source from which the hospitals at Wheeling, Clarksburg, Parkersburg, Grafton, and elsewhere obtained their equipment. Early in 1862 soldiers' homes were established at Louisville and Cairo, being the first of those organized under the Sanitary Commission of the West. A full account of his great work is contained in the report of "The United States Sanitary Commission in the Valley of the Mississippi" (Cleveland, 1871). In this he tells how, between Sept. 1, 1861, and July 1, 1866, he expended more than $800,000 in money, and distributed hospital stores that were valued at more than $5,000,000. During this time the names of more than 850,000 soldiers were collected and recorded in the hospital directory in Louisville, Ky., and food and shelter were given in the various homes of the commission to more than 1,000,000 soldiers, for whom no other adequate provision was made. With the return of peace came the development of economical institutions, and Dr. Newberry was called to the chair of Geology in the recently created School of Mines of Columbia College. He took charge of his department in the autumn of 1866, and, with the same genius for organization shown in his connection with the Sanitary Commission, began the formation of the courses of study. Alone he gave instruction in botany, zoölogy, geology, lithology, palæontology, and economic geology. In 1867 the title of his chair was extended to include palæontology, and he continued in the active charge of the department until December, 1890, when a sudden stroke of paralysis compelled him to give up work. A year's leave of absence was granted him, but at the expiration of that term he was unable to return, and he was made professor emeritus. During his connection with Columbia College he formed a museum of more than 100,000 specimens, principally collected by himself, which serve to illustrate the lectures on palæontology and economic geology. It contains the best representations of the mineral resources of the United States to be found anywhere, as well as many unique and remarkable fossils. In 1869 Dr. Newberry was appointed State Geologist of Ohio by Gov. Rutherford B. Hayes, which place he filled during the continuation of the survey, and made reports on all the counties of the State. The results of his work are given in nine volumes, of which six are on the geology, two on the palæontology, and one on the zoölogy of the State, with a large number of geological maps. He was appointed palæontologist to the United States Geological Survey in 1884, and assigned to the charge of certain portions of fossil botany and fishes, in which branches he was a specialist, and concerning which he reported on the "Fossil Fishes and Fossil Plants of the Triassic Rocks of New Jersey and Connecticut Valley" (Washington, 1888) and on "The Palæozoic Fishes of North America" (1889). Material on the fossil plants of the cretaceous and tertiary rocks of the far West had been for some time in his possession, but was not sufficiently completed for publication at the time of his death. Dr. Newberry's opinion as an expert in mining property was highly valued, and he was frequently consulted, and in consequence he traveled extensively through the mining districts of the United States. He served as one of the judges at the World's Fair held in Philadelphia in 1876, and prepared for the reports of the commission a valuable paper on the "Building and Ornamental Stones" exhibited. In 1867 he received the degree of LL. D. from Western Reserve College, and in 1888 the Geological Society of London conferred upon him its Murchison medal, which was the first time this honor had been bestowed upon an American geologist. Dr. Newberry was a member of scientific societies both in the United States and Europe. In 1863 he was named by Congress as one of the corporate members of the National Academy of Sciences, and in 1867 he was President of the American Association for the Advancement of Science, delivering a retiring address entitled "Modern Scientific Investigation; Its Methods and Tendencies." He was President of the New York Academy of Sciences from 1867 until his death, and also was long President of the Torrey Botanical Club. In the organization of the American Geological Society he was active, and served as its president in 1891; also he was a member of the International Congress of Geologists. Dr. Newberry was a large contributor to the literature of science, and besides the volumes mentioned he was the author of more than 200 papers, chiefly in the departments of geology and palæontology, but also in zoölogy and botany.

Newcomb, Wesley, conchologist, born in 1808; died in Ithaca, N. Y., Jan. 27, 1892. He was one of the most noted conchologists in the world. In his younger days he resided in Albany and Troy, N. Y., California, Florida, Central America, and the Sandwich Islands for five years; and he accompanied President Grant's commission to Santo Domingo. His famous collection of shells was the work of an ordinary lifetime. It was bought by Ezra Cornell for Cornell University in 1869, and occupies the top floor of the university museum in the McGraw building. After its purchase Prof. Newcomb was appointed curator of the collection, and he spent his last twenty-three years in its arrangement, and in collecting and classifying the additions to the original collection.

Nutt, Henry Clay, civil engineer, born in Montpelier, Vt., June 28, 1833; died in Boston, Mass., Aug. 15, 1892. He received a grammar-school education, became a newsboy on the Vermont Central Railroad, and subsequently studied civil engineering. He was successively roadman, assistant engineer, and conductor on the Plattsburg and Montreal Railroad; then became chief engineer of the construction of the Peoria and Oquawka Railroad (now part of the Chicago, Burlington and Quincy); and in 1860 was chief engineer of the Council Bluffs and St. Joseph Railroad. He was employed as contractor for transferring freight over the Missouri river between Council Bluffs and Omaha from 1867 till 1873, and was engaged in the elevator-insurance business in Chicago from 1873 till 1881. In the latter year he removed to Boston, and became President of the Atlantic and Pacific Railroad Company, which office he held till 1889, when, on account of failing health, he was obliged to retire. Mr. Nutt served on the staff of Gov. Kirkwood, of Iowa, with the rank of colonel, during the greater part of the civil war.

O'Neill, John A., expert steel-plate engraver, died in Washington, D. C., June 17, 1892. He was a member of the Board of Freeholders of Hudson County, N. J., in 1869, 1870, and 1873, and subsequently director of the board, and member of the Legislature in 1872; was appointed by the Legislature commissioner of wharves and piers for Passaic river, and was elected Mayor of Hoboken in 1880, after a bitter contest with the local ring, which expected to make much money and political capital out of the erection of the new City Hall, which was to be begun during that mayoralty term. He had much trouble with the ring contractors, but thwarted them, and was sustained in his action by the leading lawyers in his State. In April, 1885, he was appointed chief of the engraving division of the Government Bureau of Engraving and Printing, and because of his ability as an expert steel engraver and as an executive he was retained in the office by the Harrison administration. He selected the picture of Martha Washington for the one-dollar silver certificates, against a protest based on the fact that she would be the first woman that ever graced the face of a paper note.

O'Reilly, Patrick Thomas, clergyman, born in Kill, County Cavan, Ireland, Dec. 25, 1833; died in Springfield, Mass., May 28, 1892. He received his early education in his native town, came to the United States in 1847, studied at St. Charles College, Ellicott City, and St. Mary's Seminary, Baltimore, Md., and was ordained a priest in the Roman Catholic Church in Boston, Aug. 15, 1857. After serving two parishes in that city he held a pastorate in Worcester from 1864 till 1870, when he was chosen the first Roman Catholic bishop of the diocese of Springfield, and was consecrated Sept. 25. In 1890 the twentieth anniversary of his episcopate was celebrated at his cathedral, when he received many and costly presents. Under his administration the new diocese increased from 43 priests to 178; from 2 parochial schools to 26, including 3 high schools; and from a Roman Catholic population of 80,000 to 170,000. Bishop O'Reilly consecrated 4 churches, dedicated 40 others, and confirmed 70,000 people.

Osgood, James Ripley, publisher, born in Fryeburg, Me., in 1836; died in London, England, May 18, 1892. He was graduated at Bowdoin College, and soon afterward became a clerk in the Boston publishing house of Ticknor & Fields, where he rapidly advanced till he became a partner. In 1869 the firm of Ticknor & Fields was succeeded by that of Fields, Osgood & Co., and that in 1871 by James R. Osgood & Co. In 1878 the business was consolidated with the house of Hurd & Houghton, under the title Houghton, Osgood & Co. In 1880 Mr. Osgood retired, and re-established the old firm of James R. Osgood & Co., which continued to do business in Boston till 1885, when Mr. Osgood retired. He then accepted an offer from Harper & Brothers to become their London agent, and represented them in that city till 1890, when he established the London house of Osgood, McIlvaine & Co., which continued the Harpers' agency, and engaged in publication on its own account. The different firms of which Mr. Osgood had been a member were widely known as publishers of "The Atlantic Monthly" and "Every Saturday," and the works of Lowell, Longfellow, Emerson, Hawthorne, Holmes, Whittier, Mrs. Stowe, and other American authors. A memoir of Mr. Osgood, by Mrs. A. V. S. Anthony, is announced.

Overheiser, John C., educator, born in New York city in 1834; died there, May 1, 1892. He was graduated at Rochester University in 1854, and became an instructor in Latin in the Polytechnic Institute of Brooklyn, which he left to establish a private school for preparing young men for college. He was considered one of the most accomplished Latin and Greek scholars in the United States, and for more than thirty years was a member of the Greek Club of New York. He was a trustee of the Baptist City Missions and Tract Society, chairman of its building committee, Vice-President of the New York State Baptist Convention, and trustee of the Leland University for Colored People in Louisiana, and of the Rutgers Female College in New York city.

Packer, Harriet L., philanthropist, born in Vermont, in 1820; died in Brooklyn, N. Y., Jan. 26, 1892. She was the daughter of Rev. Benjamin Putnam, a well-known Baptist clergyman, and widow of William S. Packer, of Brooklyn, to whom she was married in 1842, and who died in 1850. Mr. Packer was one of the founders and original trustees of the Brooklyn Female Academy, in which his wife became deeply interested. The academy was destroyed by fire in January, 1853, and Mrs. Packer contributed $65,000, the entire cost of its rebuilding, and also founded many free scholarships in the institution. In recognition of her generosity, the name of the academy was changed to Packer Institute, and as such it has become one of the most noted institutions for the higher education of women in the United States, having on its rolls at the time of its founder's death the names of 900 students. Mrs. Packer was closely connected with a large number of charitable institutions. She was one of the incorporators, and for some years President, of the Brooklyn Society for the Aid of Friendless Women and Children.

Page, George Shepard, capitalist, born in Readfield, Me., in 1838; died in Morris Plains, N. J., March 26, 1892. He began his business career in Chelsea, Mass., where he was associated with his father in the coal-tar trade. In 1862 he removed to New York city, and afterward made a large fortune by various investments. He was one of the best known men in field sports and fishing circles in the country; was President of the Chatham, N. J., Fish and Game Protective Association, which controlled over 10,000 acres of land along Passaic river; had an estate of several hundred acres at Stanley, N. J., and was the founder of the Quassac Sportsman's Club, whose headquarters are on Rangeley Lakes, in Maine. Mr. Page was also a founder of the American Fish Culturists' Association, which was organized Dec. 20, 1870, and it was through his personal exertions and the influence of this association that Congress created the United States Fish Commission.

Pardee, Ario, manufacturer, born in Nassau, N. Y., Nov. 15, 1810; died on Indian river, Florida, March 26, 1892. In early life he became acquainted with Asa Packer, and with him was engaged in the development of the coal-mining, manufacturing, and railroad interests of the Lehigh valley. He became a practical civil engineer, laid out and superintended the construction of some of the first railroads in Pennsylvania, founded the present city of Hazelton on the Buck mountain in 1836, and began operating the great anthracite coal mines in that section in 1839. He further secured control of seven or eight other valuable mines, and the output of all under his control was about 1,250,000 tons a year. From coal mining he extended his financial operations till he acquired control of the Stanhope, N. J., furnaces. He laid out the town of Hazelton, Ohio, in the richest camnel-coal field in that State; invested heavily in North Carolina timber property; operated mills of various kinds in different places, and established a prosperous banking house. He was, till within a few years, the largest individual operator in the Lehigh coal fields, and his wealth was estimated at from $30,000,000 to $60,000,000. He gave more than $500,000 to Lafayette College for the erection of Pardee Hall; was the principal supporter of the Presbyterian church at Hazelton; and gave freely to the various charities.

Parker, Henry G., journalist, born in Plymouth, Mass., in 1836; died in Boston, Mass., May 13, 1892. He was educated in his native town, and on removing to Boston became confidential clerk in a mercantile establishment in 1869. For several years previously he wrote frequently for newspapers, and on May 7, 1870, he purchased the "Saturday Evening Gazette," of which he was editor and publisher till his death. In 1869 and 1872 he was general secretary of the executive committees of the National Peace Jubilees, and in 1876 he served on the staff of Gov. Talbot.

Parsons, Thomas William, poet, born in Boston, Mass., Aug. 18, 1819; died at Scituate, Mass., Sept. 3, 1892. He was the son of a physician, and was educated at the Boston Latin School. At seventeen he went to Europe, and lived for several years in Italy, where he translated the first ten cantos of the "Inferno," which he published in Boston on his return in 1843. He studied at the Harvard Medical School, and practiced dentistry for several years in his native city; but, abandoning this profession, he went again to Europe, remaining there from 1847 till 1853. In 1854 he published a volume of his collected poems in Boston, with the title of "Ghetto di Roma." In this collection is the famous poem "On a Bust of Dante," which has won enduring fame. His verse was never popular, although he possessed the lyric faculty in no small measure. But his range of thought was too elevated, his fancy too delicate, and even, at times, too involved to catch the popular ear, and he is likely therefore to remain a poet of the few. His scholarship within its lines was most profound and thorough, and his translation of Dante is characterized by a sympathetic fidelity to the original, which some critics have considered unsurpassed. After "Ghetto di Roma," his published works include a completed translation of the "Inferno" (Boston, 1867); "The Magnolia, and other Poems" (printed privately, 1867); "The Old House at Sudbury" (1870); "The Shadow of the Obelisk, and other Poems" (1872). His latest volume, a rendering in verse of the collects of the Protestant Episcopal Church, appeared in 1892, with the title "Circum Præcordia" (Boston).

Patton, Abby Hutchinson, singer, born in New Hampshire, Aug. 29, 1829; died in New York city, Nov. 24, 1892. She was the youngest of the Hutchinson family of singers, which comprised the quartette, Judson, John, Asa, and Abby, and is survived only by her brother John. She joined her brothers on a concert tour when twelve years old, and when she was fourteen the quartette gave their first concert in New York city, and excited an interest still remembered. The family was in sympathy with the antislavery movement, and the singers naturally gave patriotic songs a large share on their programmes. Among their most popular songs at this time were those composed by one of the brothers, Jesse, entitled: "The Old Granite State," "The Slave Mother," "Get off the Track," "Uncle Sam is rich enough," "Pity, Kind Gentlemen," and "The Slave's Appeal." The family made their first trip to Great Britain in 1845, and were cordially received, both in the concert hall and in the highest social circles. In 1849 Abby married Ludlow Patton of New York city, and after marriage sang only occasionally with her brothers, but always responded to calls to sing for charity. Mrs. Patton had set to music the well-known songs, "Kind words can never die" and "Ring out, Wild Bells," and had recently issued a volume entitled "A Handful of Pebbles."

Paull, Richard, painter, born in Chicago, Ill., in 1855; died in Morris Plains, N. J., July 31, 1892. He studied landscape painting with Daubigny and François, and showed much talent and promise. He exhibited at the National Academy in 1886, 1887, 1888, 1889, and 1892, and at the American Water-Color Society exhibition in 1890. His principal paintings were "Evening," "A Glimpse from Weehawken," "Springtime on the Hackensack," "A Breezy Day," "Morning—Valley of the Hackensack," "A Spring Pastoral," "Twilight," and "Evening," and the water colors "Springtime" and "Pont d'Auteuil, Paris."

Peck, William Guy, educator, born in Litchfield, Conn., Oct. 16, 1820; died in Greenwich, Conn., Feb. 7, 1892. He was graduated at the United States Military Academy and brevetted 2d lieutenant of Topographical Engineers in 1844; served with John C. Frémont in his third expedition to the Rocky mountains; was on duty with the army of the West under Gen. Stephen W. Kearny, in the Mexican War; and after the war was Professor of Natural Philosophy and Mathematics at the Military Academy till Oct. 2, 1855, when he resigned his military commission. On leaving West Point he was Professor of Physics and Civil Engineering in the University of Michigan till June 29, 1857, when he was appointed adjunct Professor of Pure Mathematics at Columbia College. Two years afterward he was made full professor. In 1861 his title was changed to that of Professor of Mathematics and Astronomy in the School of Arts; in 1865 he was made Professor of Mechanics in the School of Mines, and in 1890 Professor of Higher Mathematics and Astronomy in both departments of the College. Prof. Peck's publications include "The Mathematical Dictionary" and the "Cyclopædia of Mathematical Science," both of which were edited in conjunction with his father-in-law, Prof. Charles Davies (1855); "Elementary Mechanics" (1859); an edition of Ganot's "Natural Philosophy" (1860; last revised edition, 1881); and a work on "Popular Astronomy" (1883).

Pellew, George, journalist, born in the Isle of Wight in 1861; died in New York city, Feb. 18–19, 1892. He came to the United States while living a boy; was graduated at Harvard in 1880, and at the Cambridge Law School in 1883; was admitted to the bar in Boston and in New York city, but preferred literary work to law practice. While at Harvard he edited the "Harvard Advocate," wrote the Hasty Pudding Club's poem, and the graduating-class ode, and won the Bowdoin prize with an essay on "Jane Austen." In 1887 he traveled through Ireland, and in 1888 removed to New York city, where he was employed on the editorial staff of "The Sun" and in writing for periodicals. He contributed to the "American Statesmen Series" a "Life of Chief-Justice Jay," his maternal grandfather, and published his impressions of Ireland in "Castle and Cabin." He was found dead in an areaway.

Perkins, Charles Allen, diplomatist, born in Salisbury, Conn., in 1832; died in Syracuse, N. Y., Aug. 22, 1892. He was educated in Auburn, N. Y., and in Paris, and was appointed United States consul and Secretary of Legation at Stockholm, with Gen. Joseph J. Bartlett as United States minister. During the administration of Gen. Grant, Mr. Perkins returned to Washington and was appointed United States consul at Barcelona, Spain, where he remained during the revolution. Subsequently he was appointed United States minister to Portugal, and while living in Lisbon he fell in love with the Countess Marie Isabella Françoise, daughter of Count Ignace Gurowsky and of her royal highness Isabella de Bourbon, Infanta of Spain. They were married Nov. 12, 1870, ex-King Don Francisco and ex-Queen Isabella standing as god-parents of the bride; Admiral Glisson, U. S. A., the United States minister, the United States consul, and the Count de Mesquitella as groomsmen; and Pope Pius granting them a special dispensation. Mr. Perkins, who was the only American citizen that had ever contracted a marriage with a person of royal blood, lived happily with his wife and her family till the Carlist uprising in Spain in 1874. At that time he wrote numerous letters to London and Paris newspapers in opposition to the political interests of Alfonso; and when Alfonso became King, Dec. 29, 1874, Mr. Perkins was promptly banished from Spain by royal command. His wife removed to Madrid, while he went to Paris, and after a while she succeeded in inducing her cousin, the King, to allow her husband to re-enter Spain, but he was there subjected to such general annoyance that he returned to the United States, where for three years he was Professor of Languages in Johns Hopkins University. Two children were born of his marriage, both sons, one of whom is now studying law at Madrid, and the other is in the Royal Military School there.

Pettis, George William, journalist, born in Providence, R. I., about 1822; died in Brookline, Mass., March 18, 1892. He was a graduate of Brown University, and for many years was insurance editor and stock-market reporter on the Boston "Advertiser." He was probably best known as an expert whist player, and as an authority on the rules and intricacies of the game. The last few years of his life were devoted almost exclusively to writing on matters pertaining to whist. At the Whist Congress held in Milwaukee in April, 1891, he was regarded as one of the three authorities of the world, the others being Nicholas B. Trist, of New Orleans, and Henry Jones, of London. These players were all agreed on the principles on which a system of play should be based. Mr. Pettis was author of "Whist Universal," "American Whist illustrated," and "Whist in Diagrams."

Pierrepont, Edwards, diplomat, born in North Haven, Conn., March 4, 1817; died in New York city, March 6, 1892. He was graduated at Yale in the same class with William M. Evarts and Morrison R. Waite, in 1837, and was admitted to the bar in 1840. He immediately went to Columbus, Ohio, where he formed a partnership with P. B. Wilcox, then Ohio State reporter, and rose rapidly in his profession. In 1846 he removed to New York city, where he resided till his death. He entered political life with the Democratic party, but declined all offers of public office till 1857, when he gave up a lucrative practice and accepted election to the office of judge of the Superior Court of New York, to fill a vacancy. He resigned this office in 1860. At the outbreak of the civil war, although an opponent of Mr. Lincoln in the presidential campaign, he became a stanch Unionist, and declared in favor of coercive measures toward the States in rebellion. On the organization of the Union Defense Committee he promptly accepted a place on it, and personally assisted in equipping every one of the first regiments that left New York city for the field. In 1862 he and Gen. John A. Dix were appointed by President Lincoln to conduct the trials of the prisoners of state, then confined in various forts and prisons. In 1864 he was conspicuous in organizing the war Democrats and in urging the re-election of President Lincoln; and after the assassination of the President he was appointed the prosecutor of John H. Surratt, one of the conspirators. He was a member of the convention for forming the new Constitution of the State of New York, and was one of its judiciary committee in 1867; was active in the support of Gen. Grant for President in 1868; was appointed United States attorney for the Southern District of New York in 1869; and was a member of the famous Committee of Seventy which fought the Tweed ring in

1870. Three years afterward he was appointed United States minister to Russia, but declined the office. In April, 1875, he was appointed Attorney-General of the United States, and in 1876 he resigned to become United States minister to England. He retired from this mission and resumed law practice in 1878, and was retained by the United States Government as special counsel in several important actions. Judge Pierrepont was a founder and for many years a governor of the Manhattan Club, but withdrew from it at the beginning of the civil war.

Pike, Maria Louisa, naturalist, born in England; died in Brooklyn, N. Y., March 23, 1892. She was a daughter of Benjamin Hadley; accompanied him as British commissioner to South Africa, where she was his official secretary for several years, and employed her leisure in studying, sketching, and painting the flora of that region. In 1870 she went to the island of Mauritius, in the Indian Ocean, and there became acquainted with Nicholas Pike, United States consul, who was studying the scientific features of the island and making collections of natural-history specimens, especially of the fish of the Indian Ocean, for Prof. Agassiz's museum at Cambridge, Mass. Miss Hadley assisted Mr. Pike in classifying more than 800 different species, and made colored drawings of them representing the peculiar hues of the fish of that locality. About 1875 she came to the United States and was married to Mr. Pike; and since then she had written voluminously on various subjects in science and natural history for the "Scientific American," "American Agriculturist," "American Garden," and other publications. Among her most notable works, besides her drawings and descriptions of the Indian Ocean fish, were colored illustrations of a very complete collection of spiders which her husband had made, and pen-and-ink drawings of nearly every snake found in the United States. She was a member of the Brooklyn Institute of Arts and Sciences, and, while an enthusiastic student in many departments of science, in the last few years she took special interest in the department of botany.

Pitcher, John, jurist, born in Watertown, Conn., Aug. 22, 1794; died in Mount Vernon, Ind., Aug. 2, 1892. He was brought up in his native State and admitted to the bar in 1815; went West in the following year and settled in St. Louis, after walking nearly the entire distance; and removed to Indiana in 1820. In 1835 he went to Posey County, where he practiced for more than forty years. He had represented Spencer and Perry Counties in the Legislature, and was also for many years judge of the Court of Common Pleas in Gibson, Posey, Vanderburg, and Warrick Counties. One of his sons was Gen. Thomas Pitcher, of Washington, D. C.

Polk, Leonidas L., agriculturist, born in Anson County, N. C., in 1837; died in Washington, D. C., June 11, 1892. He was brought up on a farm, and continued in association with agricultural life till his death. When twenty-two years old he was elected to the State Legislature. During the civil war he served in the Confederate army, and after the war he was for several years Commissioner of Agriculture in North Carolina. In 1886 he began publishing "The Progressive Farmer," and he was one of the first practical farmers to engage in organizing farmers' clubs for political purposes. In the following year, when he joined the Farmers' Alliance, he had organized nearly 500 clubs in his State. He was soon afterward elected State secretary of the Alliance, and was twice re-elected. In the National Alliance Convention of the same year he was unanimously elected vice-president of the organization; in 1890 and 1891 he was elected its president, and he held the office till his death. He, with other members of reform organizations, formed the Confederation of Industrial Organizations, which met in conference at St. Louis, Mo., in February, 1892, and formally launched the national People's party.

Pollard, Josephine, author, born in New York city about 1842; died there, Aug. 15, 1892. She engaged

In literary work early in life; was editorial writer for the "Sunday-school Times" from its first number; was connected with the Methodist Book Concern for about twenty years, during which time she had charge of a publication issued by it for the benefit of the negroes in the South; and was best known as a writer on religious topics and for children. Her published works include "The Gypsy Books" (1873–'74); "A Piece of Silver" (1876); "Decorative Sisters" (1881); "Elfin Land," poems (1882); "Gullivŏr" (1882); "The Boston Tea Party" (1882); "Vagrant Verses" (1887); and "Favorite Birds, and what Poets sing of them" (1888). She was also the author of numerous fugitive poems and of several hymns, the best known of which is "Outside the Gate."

Pope, John, military officer, born in Louisville, Ky., March 16, 1822; died in Sandusky, Ohio, Sept. 23, 1892. He was graduated at the United States Military Academy and appointed a brevet 2d lieutenant  of topographical engineers in 1842; was promoted 2d lieutenant May 9, 1846, 1st lieutenant March 3, 1853, captain July 1, 1856, brigadier-general July 14, 1862, major-general Oct. 26, 1882, and was retired March 16, 1886. In the volunteer service he was commissioned brigadier-general May 17, 1861, promoted major-general March 21, 1862, and was mustered out Sept. 1, 1866. During his military career he was brevetted 1st lieutenant Sept. 23, 1846, for gallant conduct in the several conflicts at Mouterey; captain, Feb. 23, 1847, for the battle of Buena Vista; and major-general, March 13, 1865, for services at the capture of Island No. 10. His early service included duty in Florida in 1842–'44, in the survey of the boundary between the United States and the British provinces, and in the Mexican War. He was in charge of an exploring expedition in Minnesota in 1849, and proved that the Red River of the North could be navigated by steamers; on engineering service in New Mexico in 1851–'53; and had charge of the survey of the route for the Pacific Railroad near the thirty-second parallel in 1853–'59. In 1860 he was court-martialed for criticising the policy of President Buchanan in the political canvass, but proceedings against him were dropped, and in 1861 he was one of the officers detailed by the War Department to escort President-elect Lincoln to Washington. His first service in the civil war was as commander of the District of Northern Missouri, from which he was transferred successively to the southwestern and the central districts. Here his duty was chiefly in keeping railroad communication open and dispersing guerrillas; but on Dec. 18, 1861, he gained a victory over Gen. Sterling Price at Blackwater, where he captured 1,300 prisoners, 1,000 stand of arms, 1,000 horses, 65 wagons, 2 tons of gunpowder, and a large quantity of army supplies, and forced the Confederates to retreat below the Osage river. His next detail was as commander of the land forces that co-operated with Admiral Foote in the operations against New Madrid and Island No. 10, on the Mississippi. He occupied New Madrid, March 14, 1862, and on the surrender of Island No. 10, on April 8, he received 6,500 prisoners, 125 cannon, and 7,000 stand of arms. After the occupation of Corinth he was transferred from the command of the Army of the Mississippi to that of the Army of Virginia, comprising the corps of Gens. Frémont, Banks, and McDowell. For fifteen days, in August, 1862, he fought a greatly superior force of Confederates, under Gen. Lee, at Bristow Station, Groveton, Manassas Junction, Gainesville, and Germantown, all on the line of the Rappahannock river;

then fell back, first to a position behind Difficult creek, near the Warrenton turnpike, and afterward to within the fortifications of the national capital. On Sept. 3 he asked to be relieved of his command, and soon afterward was appointed to the command of the Department of the Northwest. He charged the failure of his operations in Virginia to the misconduct of Gen. Fitzjohn Porter at the second battle of Manassas or Bull Run. On his charges, Gen. Porter was arraigned before a court-martial in Washington, and on Jan. 21, 1863, was cashiered and forever disqualified from holding any office of trust or profit under the Government of the United States for violation of the 9th and 52d articles of war. Gen. Porter at once began working for a vindication of his conduct, claiming that Gen. Pope's order to him to attack the enemy was not delivered till it was too late for him to obey, and, further, that he had positive knowledge that the opposing Confederate force was much larger than Gen. Pope believed it to be, and that, even if the order had been received in time it would have been sheer folly for him to attack. After a constant agitation for twenty-three years, Congress passed a bill authorizing the President to restore him to the army with the rank of colonel, to date from May 14, 1861, without pay for the interval, and he was so restored by President Cleveland, Aug. 5, 1886, and two days afterward was retired. Gen. Pope, after his assignment to the Department of the Northwest, proved efficient in checking the hostility of the Indians in Minnesota, and held that command till 1865, when he was transferred to the military division of the Missouri, subsequently the Department of Missouri. In January, 1866, he was relieved of this command; in 1867–'68 commanded the 3d Military District, organized under the Reconstruction act of Congress, comprising the States of Alabama, Florida, and Georgia; in 1868–'70 the Department of the Lakes; in 1870–'84 the Department of the Missouri; and from 1884 till his retirement the Department of the Pacific. He published "Explorations from the Red River to the Rio Grande" (in vol. iii, "Pacific Railroad Reports") and the "Campaign of Virginia, of July and August, 1862" (Washington, 1865).

Porter, John K., jurist, born in Waterford, N. Y., Jan. 12, 1819; died there, April 11, 1892. He was graduated at Union College in 1837, and soon afterward was admitted to the bar. He was a natural orator, and delivered a notable address at the Whig National Convention in Baltimore in 1844. In 1848 he removed to Albany and became associated with Nicholas Hill, Jr., and Peter Cagger in law practice, and in 1859, on the death of Mr. Hill, he succeeded him in charge of the firm's cases in the Court of Appeals. He was associated with Charles O'Conor in the noted Parish will case; successfully defended Horace Greeley in the libel suit brought against him by De Witt C. Littlejohn in 1862; and in 1863, in association with William C. Noyes, he won the case of the Metropolitan Bank against the superintendent of the State Bank Department, in which the constitutionality of the Legal-tender act of 1862 was involved. In 1864 he was appointed judge of the Court of Appeals to fill a vacancy, and in the following year was elected to the office as a Republican, for eight years. After serving three years on the bench, he resigned, and removed to New York city. On the disclosure of the Tweed ring infamy he refused retainers from Tweed and his associates to defend them, and was one of a committee appointed to examine the accounts of Comptroller Connolly. He was counsel for the Erie Railroad Company in its long series of litigations; made a memorable argument before the State Senate committee in the Trinity Church case; successfully defended Gen. O. E. Babcock, President Grant's private secretary; was one of the counsel in the Beecher-Tilton trial; and was the senior counsel for the people in the trial of President Garfield's assassin.

Porter, Noah, educator, born in Farmington, Conn., Dec. 14, 1811; died in New Haven, Conn., March 4,

1892. He was a son of the Rev. Noah Porter, for fifty years a clergyman in Farmington; was graduated at Yale in 1831; master of Hopkins Grammar  School 1831-'33; tutor at Yale in 1833-'35; pastor of the Congregational church in New Milford, Conn., in 1836-'43, and at Springfield, Mass., in 1843-'46; and was Professor of Mathematics and Moral Philosophy at Yale in 1846-'71. In the latter year he was elected president of the university, and he held the office till 1886, succeeding the Rev. Theodore Dwight Woolsey, and being succeeded, on his resignation because of age, by the Rev. Timothy Dwight. Dr. Porter was author of many standard works, and was the principal editor of the editions of Webster's "Unabridged Dictionary" in 1864 and 1880. His most widely known publications were: "Historical Discourse at Farmington, Nov. 4, 1840" (Hartford, 1841); "The Educational Systems of the Puritans and Jesuits Compared" (New York, 1851); "The Human Intellect" (1868; 3d ed., 1876); "Books and Reading" (1870; 6th ed., 1881); "American Colleges and the American Public" (1870; 2d ed., 1878); "Elements of Intellectual Science" (1871; 2d ed., 1876); "Sciences of Nature *versus* the Sciences of Man" (1871); "Evangeline: The Place, the Story, and the Poem" (1882); "The Elements of Moral Science, Theoretical and Practical" (1885); "Bishop Berkeley" (1885); and "Kant's Ethics: a Critical Exposition" (Chicago, 1886). Under his presidency the number of instructors at Yale increased from 71 to 114, and the funds from $1,227,305 to $2,155,705; and on his retirement he left also contingent inchoate rights to property estimated at more than $2,000,000.

Potter, Joseph Haydn, military officer, born in Concord, N. H., Oct. 12, 1822; died in Columbus, Ohio, Dec. 1, 1892. He was graduated at the United States Military Academy and appointed brevet 2d lieutenant 1st Infantry in 1843; was promoted 2d lieutenant 7th Infantry Oct. 21, 1845, 1st lieutenant Oct. 30, 1847, captain Jan. 9, 1856, major 19th Infantry July 4, 1863, lieutenant-colonel 30th Infantry July 28, 1866, transferred to the 4th Infantry March 15, 1869, colonel 24th Infantry Dec. 11, 1873, brigadier-general April 1, 1886, and was retired Oct. 12. He took part in the Mexican War, distinguishing himself in the expedition to the Rio Grande, at the bombardment of Fort Brown, Texas, at the battle of Monterey, and at the storming of Fort Soldado, on Federation Hill, where he was wounded; and accompanied the expedition to Utah. In the civil war he was in the Maryland and Rappahannock campaigns with the Army of the Potomac, and was present at the battles of Fredericksburg and Chancellorsville, and was wounded and captured during the latter. He was governor of the Soldiers' Home at Washington, D. C., from July, 1877, till July, 1881, and at the time of his retirement was in command of the Department of the Missouri.

Prince, Henry, military officer, born in Maine in 1811; died in London, England, Aug. 19, 1892. He was graduated at the United States Military Academy in 1835, served through the Seminole and other Indian wars; reached the rank of major during the Mexican War, and was brevetted brigadier-general in the regular army in 1865, for distinguished service during the civil war. He served as paymaster in Boston till 1869; chief paymaster of the Department of the East till 1871; paymaster in New York city till 1875; was on duty on the Pacific coast till his retirement in 1879. He committed suicide while despondent on account of old age and loneliness.

Prince, William Edgar, military officer, born in Boston, Mass., in 1815; died in New York city, Jan. 21, 1892. He was appointed from civil life 2d lieutenant of the 1st United States Infantry, Aug. 1, 1838; was promoted 1st lieutenant, Nov. 8, 1839; captain, Aug. 31, 1849; major of the 3d Infantry, Nov. 23, 1861; and was retired, March 30, 1864, on account of disability incurred in line of duty. He was brevetted captain, March 16, 1848, for gallant and meritorious conduct in the battle of Santa Cruz de los Rosales, Mexico, and lieutenant-colonel, March 13, 1865, for faithful and meritorious service during the civil war. He served through the Seminole War in Florida in 1838-'42; was on Northwestern frontier duty in 1842-'46; was assistant adjutant-general on the staff of Gen. Price in Mexico; and after the Mexican War spent ten years on duty in Texas, where he commanded at different times Forts Arbuckle and Wichita. While actively engaged in the operations in Missouri and Kansas, in the early part of the civil war, he was commissioned a brigadier-general by the Governor of Kansas. After his retirement he lived alternately at Newport and New York city.

Prouty, David, philanthropist, born in Spencer, Mass., Oct. 18, 1813; died there, Sept. 13, 1892. He was brought up on a farm, was apprenticed to the wire-making trade, and after working at it four years purchased the business, and conducted it till 1846, when he sold it to give his time to the farm inherited from his father. In 1852 he entered into partnership with a manufacturer of boots and shoes, and he continued in that business through various changes in the firm name till 1876, when he retired from active life. He presented the high-school building to his native town, April 2, 1888, and bequeathed the following sums to public institutions: Wesleyan Academy at Wilbraham, $15,000; Home Missionary Society, $5,000; First Congregational Society, Methodist Episcopal Society, Universalist Society, and Baptist Society, of Spencer, $4,000 each; Pine Grove Cemetery, at Spencer, $5,000; Amherst College, $15,000; Wellesley College, $15,-000; Baldwinville Hospital Cottages, $6,000; Drury College, Green County, Mo., $15,000; and to trustees for the relief of indigent citizens of Spencer, $5,000.

Prudhomme, John F. E., engraver, born in Santo Domingo in 1801; died in Washington, D. C., June 28, 1892. He was one of the oldest engravers in the United States, if not in the world; had been in the Government service as an engraver for nearly thirty years; became celebrated by engraving on steel Trumbull's painting "The Signing of the Declaration of Independence," and did a good deal of book illustration for George P. Morris, Nathaniel P. Willis, and other authors of their time. He was curator of the National Academy of Design, and for a considerable period was an instructor of the life class there.

Pryer, James, manufacturer, born in New York city in 1816; died there, July 28, 1892. When quite young he became a clerk in a Water Street flour house, where he remained till he established, with his brothers Jasper and George, the firm of J. & J. Pryer & Co., dealers in sperm and whale oil. This firm continued in the business under various titles till 1869. Mr. Pryer was the first person to introduce the method of bleaching whale oil by steam instead of by solar heat; was one of the first to press or manufacture lard oil, and was also one of the first to handle menhaden oil, and up to his retirement from business he controlled the market in the latter commodity. He was a member of the old Volunteer Fire Department, a charter member of the American Institute, a director of several financial institutions, and a member of the New York Historical Society.

Randall, John Witt, naturalist, born in Boston, Mass., Nov. 6, 1813; died there, Jan. 27, 1892. He was graduated at Harvard in 1834, and at its medical school in 1839, and made a special study of entomology. He was appointed zoölogist in the South Sea Exploring Expedition under Capt. Charles Wilkes, but resigned the appointment because of delays and jealousies. He wrote valuable scientific papers, and furnished Dr.

Charles T. Jackson, of Maine, a volume in manuscript on the animals and plants of that State, to accompany Dr. Jackon's zoölogical survey, but the manuscript was lost before it reached the printer. He made large and valuable acquisitions as a naturalist; published one of a series of six volumes of poetical works; and for many years had applied himself almost wholly to gathering engravings, of which he had one of the most rare and original collections in the country.

Ray, Ossian, lawyer, born in Hinesburg, Vt., Dec. 13, 1835; died in Lancaster, N. H., Jan. 28, 1892. He removed in early youth to Irasburg, Vt., where and at Derby he received an academic education, and began studying law. In 1854 he removed to Lancaster, and in 1857 was admitted to the bar. He was a member of the Legislature in 1868–'69; solicitor for Coos County in 1862–'73; delegate at large to the Republican National Convention in 1872; and United States Attorney for the district of New Hampshire in 1879–'80. He was elected to Congress to fill a vacancy from the 2d New Hampshire district, in 1880, as a Republican, and was re-elected in 1881 and 1883. While in Congress he served on the Committee on Invalid Pensions. In his legal practice he made a specialty of railroad cases.

Redding, John R., journalist, born in Portsmouth, N. H., Oct. 18, 1805; died there, Oct. 8, 1892. He received a common-school education, and was apprenticed to the printer's trade in the office of the New Hampshire "Patriot" in Concord. In 1826 he went to Boston, where he was employed on the "Statesman" and the "Post," and subsequently he removed to Haverhill, Mass., where he established the "Democratic Republican," of which he was sole editor and proprietor till 1841. He was postmaster of Haverhill in 1831–'41, was elected to Congress as a Democrat in 1841 and 1843, and was appointed naval storekeeper at the Portsmouth Navy Yard in 1853. Mr. Redding served several terms in the State Legislature, and was elected Mayor of Portsmouth in 1850. Next to Robert C. Winthrop, of Massachusetts, he was the oldest ex-Congressman living, and was the last survivor of the first Congress to which he was elected.

Reed, Henry, journalist, born in Sharon, Conn., Nov. 25, 1809; died in San Francisco, Cal., Aug. 21, 1892. He was one of the best-known journalists in Ohio more than fifty years ago, as well as one of the most forcible and witty writers in the West. He had been employed on newspapers in Toledo and elsewhere before he became connected with the Ohio "State Journal," and was best known through his editorial connection with the Cincinnati "Commercial" under its founder and proprietor, M. D. Potter. When Murat Halstead became editor in chief of that paper, Mr. Reed, with his brother, Samuel R. Reed, founded the Cincinnati "Penny Press," which was the first of the one- and two-cent newspapers in the West. This venture was not successful financially, and he became an editorial writer on the Cincinnati "Enquirer," while his brother took a similar place on the "Commercial Gazette." Of late years he had lived in retirement in San Francisco.

Reese, John J., toxicologist, born in Philadelphia, Pa., in 1818; died in Atlantic City, N. J., Sept. 4, 1892. He was graduated at the University of Pennsylvania in 1836, and at its medical school in 1839, rose rapidly in his profession, and acquired a national reputation by his revelations in toxicology. He served in the United States army as an assistant surgeon through the civil war, and for many years afterward was connected with a firm of analytical chemists in Philadelphia. He was a frequent contributor to medical literature, and by many was believed to stand at the head of the medical profession in this country in toxicology and medical jurisprudence. He was frequently called on to give expert testimony, and his evidence in the celebrated trial of Mrs. Wharton, of Philadelphia, accused of poisoning Gen. Ketchum, of Baltimore, produced a great sensation. Dr. Reese edited the seventh American edition of Taylor's "Medical Jurisprudence," and published "Analysis of Physiology," "American Medical Formulary," "Manual of Toxicology," and a text-book on medical jurisprudence and toxicology.

Renville, Gabriel, Indian chief, born about 1822; died at the Sisseton Agency, South Dakota, Aug. 26, 1892. He had been chief of the Sisseton and Wahpeton tribes of Indians for a number of years, and was widely known because of his services in protecting the whites from raids of hostile Sioux, and for his frequent trips to Washington in the interest of his people. In 1862 he owned a farm of 3,000 acres near the present city of Graceville, on Minnesota river, and during the great Indian massacre of that year he organized and commanded a formidable Indian force for the defense of the white settlers against further outrages, and it was mainly through his efforts that 250 white captives were surrendered at Camp Rivas at the close of the uprising.

Richards, Sarah J., philanthropist, born in Germantown, Pa., in 1820; died in Philadelphia, April 18, 1892. She was among the first to answer Gov. Curtin's call for nurses to go to the battle fields in 1862, and remained with the army till the close of the war, being for a long time connected with the field hospitals of the 2d Army Corps. She served with much effectiveness at the battles of Antietam, Chancellorsville, Gettysburg, and Fredericksburg; and on one occasion, while on the Rappahannock, she prevented the capture of an ambulance full of wounded soldiers, which she was driving in person, by putting a revolver to the head of a Confederate officer who attempted to make them prisoners. To thousands of officers and soldiers she was known as "Mother" Richards. The 2d Army Corps presented her a gold corps badge containing the inscription, "Presented to Mrs. Sallie Richards by the soldiers of the 2d Army Corps, in loving memory of her motherly care of and tender ministrations to them while in hospital under her charge." She was specially commended for her bravery and assiduous attentions by Gens. Grant, Meade, Burnside, Hooker, and Slocum.

Richardson, Ithian Silsby, inventor, born in 1806; died in Woodlawn, Ill., Feb. 1, 1892. He had a natural fondness for mechanics, and during much of his life busied himself inventing new devices and improvements for others already in use. Among his most noted inventions were an apparatus to roll and sugar pills, the machine now employed for placing pins on strips of paper ready for sale, another machine for similarly attaching hooks and eyes, and the pneumatic tube.

Roberts, James, painter, born about 1827; died in New York city, March 21, 1892. He came of a family of scene painters, his father and grandfather having been especially well known, and had been in the service of Daly's Theatre in New York for nearly twenty-three years. For more than twenty years the elaborate stage pictures presented in Mr. Daly's theatres were designed by him, and painted and set under his immediate supervision.

Robinson, James S., military officer, born in Richland County, Ohio, Oct. 14, 1827; died in Toledo, Ohio, Jan. 14, 1892. He was brought up on a farm, was apprenticed to the printer's trade in Mansfield, and, after working in various offices, established the Canton "Weekly Republican" in 1847. In 1856 he was elected clerk of the General Assembly of Ohio as a Republican. At the outbreak of the civil war he enlisted as a private in the 4th Ohio Volunteers. He was appointed a captain a few days afterward, and served in the Rich mountain campaign till commissioned major of the 82d Ohio Regiment, when he accompanied it into the West Virginia campaign. In April, 1862, he was promoted lieutenant-colonel of this regiment and, at the battles of Chancellorsville and Gettysburg he served with distinction, receiving in the latter battle a shot through his lung, and lying helpless for two days and nights between the opposing lines. Recovering from his wound, he rejoined his regiment and served in all the battles of the

Georgia campaign and in the sieges of Atlanta and Savannah. He was promoted brigadier-general of Volunteers in 1864, and was mustered out of the service with the rank of brevet major-general in 1865. After the war he engaged in railroad building; was chairman of the Republican State Executive Committee in the campaigns of 1877, 1878, and 1879; was appointed State Commissioner of Railroads and Telegraphs in 1880; elected to Congress in 1881 and 1883; and was Secretary of State of Ohio in 1884–'88.

Robinson, William Erigena, journalist, born in Unagh, County Tyrone, Ireland, May 6, 1814; died in Brooklyn, N. Y., Jan. 23, 1892. He landed in New York Aug. 30, 1836, possessed of only one sovereign; took out his naturalization papers on March 7, 1837; entered Yale the same year, and was graduated in 1841. He delivered numerous speeches advocating Gen. William Henry Harrison's election to the presidency, and in the same cause wrote prose and poetry for Horace Greeley's campaign paper, the "Log Cabin." He established the "Yale Banner" and founded Beta Chapter of the Psi Upsilon Society in Yale. He partly paid for his education by writing for the New Haven "Herald" and lecturing throughout the country. In 1842 he had charge of the arrangements for Charles Dickens's reception in New Haven, and Mr. Dickens presented him with an autograph description of little Nell's death, written from memory. In 1844 he supported Henry Clay for President, delivering one to two speeches daily during the canvass, and became associate editor of the New York "Tribune." From 1844 to 1848 he was its Washington correspondent, writing under the name of "Richelieu." He also wrote during that period for the Richmond "Whig," the Boston "Atlas," the Louisville "Courier," and the New Orleans "Picayune." His account in the "Tribune" of an Ohio Representative's sausage luncheon in the House led to Mr. Robinson's expulsion; but this action was so ridiculed by the press that he was restored to his seat at the next session by an almost unanimous vote. Mr. Greeley offered him one eighth of the "Tribune" stock for $7,500, but he could not raise the money. In 1846 he was editor of the Buffalo, N. Y., "Express." During the great Irish famine of 1847 he secured the passage of the bill sending the United States war ship "Macedonian," loaded with provisions, to Ireland, and at his suggestion a monster relief meeting was held in Washington, at which Vice-President Dallas presided and Daniel Webster introduced the resolutions. In 1848 he was a member of the Irish Directory to aid the Young Ireland revolutionary party. In 1849, with Thomas Devin Reilly, he established a weekly paper, "The People," of which Horace Greeley was the Washington correspondent. In 1850 Daniel Webster offered him the consulate to Belfast. From 1850 to 1853 he was editor of the Newark, N. J., "Mercury." On July 30, 1851, before representatives of thirteen colleges assembled at Hamilton College, he delivered an oration on the Celt and the Saxon, to which the "Tribune" devoted eight columns. In the presidential canvass of 1852 he stumped the country for Gen. Scott. In 1853 he married Miss Helen A. Dougherty, of Newark, N. J. He was admitted to the New York bar in 1854, and, although a Presbyterian, was in 1856 a member of the Friends of Civil and Religious Liberty organized to oppose Know-Nothingism. In 1859 he revisited Ireland. In August, 1862, President Lincoln appointed him assessor of internal revenue for the 3d New York District, which office he held till March 4, 1867. In 1865 he was defeated by 600 in a vote of nearly 40,000 for collector of taxes. In 1866, 1880, and 1882 he was elected to Congress from the 3d and 4th New York Districts. His most important work in Congress was the passage of the bill which protects abroad the rights of naturalized as well as native-born citizens. He effected this in the face of great opposition and most violent abuse. It finally became a law on July 27, 1868. He was also the author of the East River Bridge bill, passed March 2, 1869; delivered a powerful speech on reconstruction;

advocated penny postage, and the independence and annexation of Cuba; and devoted his utmost energy to secure the passage of a bill for the relief of Mrs. Septimia R. Meikleham, the sole surviving grandchild of Thomas Jefferson. In 1871 he was editor of the "Irish World." From time to time, almost until his last illness, he wrote under his old signature of "Richelieu" for various papers.

Rodgers, Christopher Raymond Perry, naval officer, born in Brooklyn, N. Y., Nov. 14, 1819; died in Washington, D. C., Jan. 8, 1892. He came of a family of naval officers, and was a nephew of Commodore Oliver H. Perry, and son of Commodore George W. Rodgers. He entered the United States navy as a midshipman, Oct. 5, 1833; was promoted passed midshipman, July 8, 1839; lieutenant, Sept. 4, 1844; commander, Nov. 15, 1861; captain, July 25, 1866; commodore, Aug. 28, 1870; and rear-admiral, June 14, 1874; and was retired, Nov. 14, 1881. During his naval career he was on sea service twenty-eight years and nine months; on shore or other duty, fourteen years and ten months; and

was unemployed fifteen years and eleven months. He served on the "Flirt" and commanded the schooner "Phoenix" in the Seminole War in 1839–'41; was on blockading duty off the coast of Mexico in 1847; and distinguished himself in the trenches at the siege of Vera Cruz and at the capture of Tuxpan and Tabasco. For some time prior to the civil war he was on coast-survey duty as commander of the "Bibb" and of the "Gallatin." His first notable service in the civil war was as fleet captain of Admiral Du Pont's fleet during the battle of Port Royal, where he served on the "Wabash." At the capture of Port Pulaski he commanded the naval force that operated in the trenches. After the battle of Port Royal he had the direction of a gunboat fleet organized to occupy important points along the coast farther south, and in 1862 he commanded an expedition to St. Augustine and up St. Mary's river. Early in 1863 he was assigned to the "New Ironsides," and during the attack on the Confederate defenses of Charleston, on April 7, he was fleet captain. He held this appointment till late in 1863, participating meanwhile in the operations of the South Atlantic Blockading Squadron. He was then assigned to the command of the steam sloop "Iroquois," in which he rendered two years of special service. In 1868–'70 he commanded the frigate "Franklin" in the Mediterranean Squadron; in 1871 was on special duty in Europe; in 1871–'74 was chief of the Bureau of Yards and Docks; in 1874–'77 was Superintendent of the United States Naval Academy; in 1877–'80 commanded the Pacific Squadron; and from the spring of 1881 till his retirement was again superintendent of the Naval Academy. In 1885 he was president of the international conference held in Washington to fix a prime meridian and universal day.

Roemer, Jean, educator born in England, about 1806; died in Lenox, Mass., Aug. 30–31, 1892. It is said that he was an illegitimate son of William I, King of Holland; that he was taken to Hanover in infancy, and afterward to Holland, where his early education was conducted by private tutors under the guardianship of King William I and Frederica, Princess of Orange. He was destined for the army and was educated accordingly, and in the war of secession between Holland and Belgium he served in the Dutch army. Afterward he visited the principal military establishments of France, Prussia, and Austria, completing his military education in Lombardy, under the guidance of Field-Marshal Count Radetzky. He spent some time in Naples, and through his friendship with the Prince of Syracuse, ex-Viceroy of Sicily, gave offense to King Ferdinand II, and was recalled from Italy early in 1845. He came to the United States in the following year, became Professor of French in the New York Free Academy in 1848; was appointed Vice-President of the College of the City of New York and Professor of French in 1869, and held these offices till his death. As early as 1843, after the death of King William I of the Netherlands, the pretensions of Prof. Roemer, as son and heir of the King began to take definite shape. He set forth claims to titles and estates, which were never officially recognized. His case was brought before a congress of German sovereigns, held in Frankfort in 1863, and an attempt at conciliation was without satisfactory results. Prof. Roemer, as he was known in this country, in addition to articles and pamphlets on agriculture and education, published a "Dictionary of English-French Idioms," "Polyglot Readers" in French, German, Italian, Spanish, and English, "Cavalry: Its History, Management, and Uses in War," "Principles of General Grammar," and "Origins of the English People and of the English Language." He was very popular with the students, and attended his classes with great regularity, despite his advanced age and infirmities. He was found dead in the hotel at Lenox, where he had been in the habit of spending his summers.

Rogers, Randolph, sculptor, born in Waterloo, N. Y., July 6, 1825; died in Rome, Italy, Jan. 15, 1892. He was engaged in mercantile business till 1848, when he attracted the attention of his employer by exhibiting several statues and a bust of Byron, which he had modeled without instruction. His employer urged him to study sculpture, and provided the means for him to go abroad for that pur s. From 1848 till 1850 he studied in Rome with Lorenzo Bartolini; then opened a studio in New York city, where he remained till 1855, and afterward made his permanent residence in Rome. Among his best-known works are the bas-reliefs on the doors of the Capitol at Washington, D. C., representing scenes in the life of Columbus, which were designed in 1858, and cast in bronze in Munich; the Washington monument at Richmond, Va., which he completed in 1861 from the unfinished material of Thomas Crawford, adding statues of Marshall, Mason, and Nelson, as well as some allegorical figures; "The Angel of the Resurrection," on the Samuel Colt monument at Hartford, Conn. (1861-'62); memorial monuments for Cincinnati (1863-'64), Providence (1871), Detroit (1872), and Worcester, Mass. (1874); "The Lost Pleiad" (1875); "The Genius of Connecticut," on the Capitol at Hartford (1877); an equestrian group of Indians in bronze (1881); the ideal figures of "Ruth" (1851); "Nydia, the Blind Girl of Pompeii" (1856); "Boys Skating"; and the portrait statues of Abraham Lincoln, for Philadelphia, and William H. Seward, for New York (1876).

Rondel, Frederic, painter, born in Paris, France, in 1826; died in New York city, Nov. 22, 1892. He studied painting in Paris with Auguste Jugelet and Theodore Gudin; came to the United States in early life, and exhibited at the National Academy of Design, in 1857, four landscapes, a "Waterfall," and "A Hunting Party in the Woods." In the following year he exhibited "Connecticut Scenery." In 1860 he was elected an associate of the Academy, and in the same year he exhibited "View on Racquette River, New York," and "View from the Palisades, opposite Hastings." In the exhibition of 1892 he showed "Roosting away from Home—Thanksgiving Time," and "Tank Vessels at Point Breeze, Philadelphia, Pa." He passed the greater part of his life in Philadelphia and vicinity, and for many years conducted an art school that was widely known.

Ross, M. Denman, philanthropist, born in Boston, Mass., in October, 1819; died in Jamaica Plain, Mass., Sept. 14, 1892. He was the founder of the Boston Thread and Twine Company, and acquired much wealth in business enterprises. He was considered the father of the Massachusetts Institute of Technology, for it was he who hired the room where the institute met before it had a building of its own, and was connected with its government till his death. He was also an active member of the Massachusetts Historical Society, and had much to do in bringing about the establishment of the present park system of Boston, the kindergartens, the Museum of Fine Arts, Columbus Avenue and its corresponding system of streets, with the projected aquarium, the Eliot School, and other public institutions. His last months were spent in studying the rapid-transit problem of Boston and in elaborating a scheme for the better drainage and water supply of Chicago.

Ruger, William Crawford, jurist, born in Bridgewater, Oneida County, N. Y., Jan. 30, 1824; died in Syracuse, N. Y., Jan. 14, 1892. He received an academic education, was admitted to the bar in Utica, N. Y., in 1845; practiced in Bridgewater till 1853, and subsequently in Syracuse. He was counsel in several important cases, including the Canal ring prosecutions instituted by Gov. Tilden, where he acted for the defendants. Politically he was always a Democrat, and he was a delegate to the "Hunker" convention in 1849; to the State Judicial Convention in 1870; to the Democratic National Convention in 1872; and to the Democratic State Convention in 1877. He was defeated for Congress in 1862 and 1864; was the first President of the Onondaga Bar Association in 1875-'79; and was President of the State Bar Association in 1876 and 1882. In the latter year he was elected Chief Judge of the Court of Appeals of New York.

Rushforth, William Henry, inventor, born in Leeds, England, July 11, 1844; died in Rutherford, N. J., Aug. 21, 1892. When twelve years old he went to work in a railroad repair shop; when seventeen, became a locomotive fireman; when nineteen, a locomotive engineer; and when thirty was chief engineer in charge of thirteen stationary engines. He came to the United States in 1878, and was appointed engineer in a silk factory in Camden, N. J. Mr. Rushforth patented a fire-escape ladder, a jeweler's show window, a combination parlor and ice skate, an extension skate blade, a combination cane and music stand, a ticket box for railroad offices, and a series of automatic safety car signals, to be attached to railroad cars so that the signals might be displayed by the application of the brakes. At the time of his death he was perfecting his last invention, a feed-water heater, to utilize the heat wasted in the smoke boxes of locomotives. This invention received a silver medal and diploma at the Paris Exhibition in 1887.

Rutherfurd, Lewis Morris, physicist, born in Morrisania, N. Y., Nov. 25, 1816; died in Tranquillity, N. J., May 30, 1892. He was graduated at Williams in 1834, where he served as assistant in chemistry and physics, and was admitted to the bar in 1837, after which he entered on the practice of his profession in New York city with Peter A. Jay, and, on his death, with Hamilton Fish. Studies in chemistry and mechanics in their application to astronomy continued to interest him, and led to his retirement from practice in 1849. Thereafter until 1852 he studied and traveled abroad, and on his return to New York erected in the rear of his home on the corner of Second Avenue and Eleventh Street a small but excellent observatory. Spectroscopic investigations claimed his first attention, and during 1862-'63 he contributed papers to the "American Journal of Science," giving the results of his examinations of the spectra of stars, moon, and planets. It was the first published work on star spectra, and in it was made the first attempt to classify the stars according to their spectra. While engaged on this work he discovered the use of the star spectroscope to show the exact state of achromatic correction in an object glass, particularly for the rays that are used in photography. In 1864, after many experiments in other directions but for the same end, he constructed an object glass of 11¼ inches diameter and about 15 feet focal length, corrected for photography alone, which he described in the " American Journal of Science." It proved a great success, and was used constantly in making negatives of sun, moon, and star groups. His photographs of the moon were the finest ever made up to that time, and have only been equaled in very recent years. In 1868 he finished

his 13-inch object glass, which had a focal length of about 15 feet. This glass was an ordinary achromatic, such as is used for vision, and was converted into a photographic objective by the addition of a third lens of flint glass, which made the proper correction and could be affixed in a few minutes. Mr. Rutherfurd constructed a micrometer for the measurement of astronomical photographs, for use upon pictures of solar eclipses or transits and upon groups of stars, of which he measured several hundred, showing, as he claimed, that the photographic method was at least equal in accuracy to that of the heliometer or filar micrometer and far more convenient. With this instrument he photographed the sun, and the series of that orb taken in 1870 showed beautifully the details of spots, the faculæ, and the mottled surface of the photosphere, and exhibited clearly the rotation of the sun and the changes in the forms and groupings of the spots. Indirect doubt having been expressed upon photographs made with the collodion film, he investigated the subject, and in 1872 published a series of measurements which demonstrated conclusively the fixity of the film when used upon a plate treated with dilute albumen. In 1864 he presented to the National Academy of Sciences a photograph of the solar spectrum that he had obtained by means of carbon-disulphide prisms. It contained more than three times the number of lines that had been laid down within similar limits by Bunsen and Kirchhoff. He constructed a ruling engine in 1870, with which he produced interference gratings on glass and speculum metal that were superior to all others until the recent productions of Henry A. Rowland. With one of these gratings, containing about 17,000 lines to the inch, he produced a photograph of the solar spectrum which was for a long time unequaled. Mr. Rutherfurd was appointed a trustee of Columbia College in 1858, and continued as such until 1884, when (December, 1883) he presented to the observatory his 13-inch telescope with its photographic correcting lens, his transit instrument, and other valuable apparatus, worth more than $12,000. Later, in November, 1890, he gave all his negatives of sun, moon, and star groups, nearly 1,500 in number, with funds for their measurement, and already there has been published " The Rutherfurd Photographic Measures of the Group of the Pleiades." Mr. Rutherfurd was one of the original members of the National Academy of Sciences named by act of Congress in 1863.

Saulsbury, Willard, jurist, born in Mispillion Hundred, Kent County, Del., June 2, 1820; died in Dover, Del., April 6, 1892. He was graduated at Dickinson College, studied law, and was appointed Attorney-General of Delaware in 1850. He was a delegate to the Democratic National Convention in 1856, and in 1859 was elected to the United States Senate, where he was active in the exciting period of the civil war, serving two terms, and being succeeded, in 1871, by his brother Eli. In 1874 he was appointed Chancellor of the State, and he occupied the office till his sudden death from apoplexy. With his brothers, Gove and Eli, he formed the famous Saulsbury combination, which ruled Delaware's politics for thirty years. In the contest for the United States Senate in 1871, all three brothers were candidates.

Schaus, William, art importer, born in Selters, Nassau, Germany, July 4, 1820; died in New York city, Dec. 29, 1892. He was educated at Schlangenbad, and after graduation entered the employ of the art firm of Rittner, Goupil & Co., by whom he was sent to New York city in 1847 to establish a branch house. After he had done this he withdrew from the employ of the firm and went into the same business for himself, and continued in it on Broadway and Fifth Avenue till 1886, when he retired, and was succeeded by a nephew and son-in-law. After withdrawing from the firm, he opened the International Art Gallery opposite the Windsor Hotel, but in 1891 sold his pictures, withdrawing and presenting to the French Government the "Joan of Arc" by Jacquet. At the time of his death he retained individual ownership in several noted paintings. Mr. Schaus brought to the United States Rembrandt's famous " Gilder," and it was he who caused the return to Spain, in 1879, of Murillo's "Vision of St. Anthony," which had been cut from its frame in a cathedral at Seville and brought to New York. For this service he received from the Spanish Government the decoration of the Order of Charles III. He was made an officer of the Legion of Honor of France in 1888. Mr. Schaus was considered one of the best judges of the genuineness of works of art, and left an estate supposed to be worth nearly $1,000,000.

Schreiber, George Francis, photographer, born in Frankfort-on-the-Main, Germany, Jan. 10, 1803; died in Philadelphia, Pa., Jan. 3, 1892. He came to the United States in 1834, and founded and conducted for some time the " Alte und Neue Welt." He was one of the first to engage in the business of making daguerreotypes, and he so improved the art that he was enabled to take a view of Niagara Falls by means of a large sectional camera that he designed, for which he received numerous medals. While building up a thriving business, he was constantly experimenting and improving his art. In 1848 he read in a foreign paper that pictures had been taken with plates of glass as a negative from which prints could be made, and he applied himself with earnestness to accomplishing this alleged feat, and succeeded in printing through glass the first photographs ever made in America. These early pictures were called "talbotypes on glass." Next he began using ground glass, and produced what he called the "hyalotype," from which were evolved the first photographic stereopticon views in the world. During the past few years Mr. Schreiber had confined himself to photographing animal and bird life, and in his "Studies from Nature" he left a lasting monument of inventive skill, patient application, and high artistic taste.

Schwatka, Frederick, explorer, born in Galena, Ill., Sept. 29, 1849; died in Portland, Ore., Nov. 2, 1892. He was gr u at the United States Military Academy and commissioned 2d lieutenant in the 3d Cavalry in 1871, and served on frontier and garrison duty till 1877, in the meantime studying both law and medicine, being admitted to the bar in Nebraska in 1875, and graduated in medicine at Bellevue Hospital Medical College in 1876. While on duty with his regiment he took part in several skirmishes with the Indians. In 1878 he obtained leave of absence from the army in order to command an expedition to search for traces of Sir John Franklin. This expedition sailed in the "Eothen" from New York, on June 19, 1878, and returned Sept. 22, 1880. The party found and buried many skeletons of the Franklin party, discovered various relics of Sir John's expedition, and otherwise cleared up much of the mystery that for many years had surrounded the fate of that expedition. He then returned to army duty on the frontier till 1883, when he made an exploring expedition to Alaska for the special purpose of tracing the course of the Yukon river. He again returned to frontier duty, and resigned his commission in the army Jan. 31, 1885. In the following year he commanded a special expedition to Alaska under the auspices of the New York "Times," and subsequently made another voyage to that region for the purpose of exploration, and to attempt the establishment of a large commercial enterprise among the Aleutian Islands. In 1889 he conducted an expedition to the northern part of Mexico, of which little was known on account of the danger of exploring there in consequence of the raids of Apache Indians. He found many interesting relics of Aztec civilization, and made numerous studies and drawings of the cliff and cave dwellers. He received the Roquette Arctic Medal from the Geographical Society of Paris, and a medal from the Imperial Geographical Society of Russia. He published "Along Alaska's Great River," "The Franklin Search under Lieut. Schwatka," "Nimrod of the North," and "Children of the Cold," and wrote many short stories and sketches, and contributed to geographical publications.

Scott, John Witherspoon, educator, born in Hookstown, Beaver County, Pa., Jan. 22, 1800; died in Washington, D. C., Nov. 29, 1892. He was a son of the Rev. George McElroy Scott, a well-known Presbyterian clergyman of his day; was graduated at Washington University, Washington, Pa., in 1823, took a postgraduate course at Yale, and afterward completed his theological studies p   . In 1825 he was appointed Professor of Mathematics and Natural Sciences in Washington College, where he remained four years, resigning to take the similar chair in Miami University, which he occupied for seventeen years. He then removed to College Hill, near Cincinnati, where he founded Belmont College, and soon after its establishment he returned to Oxford, Ohio, where he founded Oxford Female College, of which he was president for ten years. While he was connected with Miami University, Benjamin Harrison, then a student there, became acquainted with his daughter, Caroline, whom he subsequently married (see HARRISON, CAROLINE SCOTT). After leaving Oxford he became a professor in Hanover College, near Madison, Ind., and on retiring from educational labor, after an almost uninterrupted career of fifty-seven years, he applied himself to private teaching and preaching till 1881, when he was appointed to a clerkship in the Pension Office in Washington. After the election of Benjamin Harrison to the presidency Dr. Scott gave up his clerkship and made his residence in the White House, at the request of his daughter. Dr. Scott was ordained a minister of the Presbyterian Church in 1830, and during the whole period of his educational work made it a custom to preach every Sunday.

Searle, Henry, architect, born in Springfield, Mass., in 1809; died in Washington, D. C., Jan. 11, 1892. When seventeen years old he was apprenticed to the cabinetmaker's trade, and after serving his time he became an architect. His first professional work was in connection with the Vermont State Capitol, and afterward he designed and erected several buildings in Burlington, the principal one being a classic Ionic structure for the Congregational church. In 1844 he removed to Rochester, N. Y., where he remodeled the Reynolds Arcade, and planned the post office in that building. His arrangement of this office was so satisfactory to the postmaster-general, that he contracted with Mr. Searle to duplicate it for a post office in Mobile. He

also planned and built Corinthian Hall, which was widely known for its remarkable acoustic properties. In 1868 Mr. Searle took up his permanent residence in Washington, D. C., and for many years he was employed in the office of the supervising architect of the United States Treasury. Among other buildings of note in Rochester which he planned were the Western House of Refuge, the City Hospital, the Third and Central Presbyterian Churches, the Gothic tower of St. Luke's Church, Mount Hope Chapel, the Morgan tomb in Mount Hope Cemetery, and the Rochester Savings Bank. He also superintended the building of Howard University and the Congregational church in Washington, D. C.

Seeley, Charles A., chemist, born in Ballston, N. Y., Nov. 28, 1825; died in Mount Vernon, N. Y., Nov. 4, 1892. He was graduated at Union College in 1847, was Professor of Chemistry and Toxicology in New York Medical College in 1859-'62, and became Professor of Chemistry and Metallurgy in the New York College of Dentistry in 1867. From 1865 till 1886 he was employed as chemical expert in patent litigations, and for many years was a member of the editorial staff of the "Scientific American." Dr. Seeley was one of the pioneers in electric lighting in the United States. He formed an electric-light company in 1861, and in the early days of the dynamo spent much time in endeavoring to obviate the loss of energy in the iron core of the armature. His experiments resulted in the construction of an electric-lighting machine with a coreless armature in disk form, which was exhibited at the Paris Exposition, and received high praise and a bronze medal. In 1882, in London, the machine was exhibited in a competitive trial and gained the gold medal. The principal features of this machine were afterward adopted by Sir William Thomson in a generator of his own. Dr. Seeley invented numerous devices, for which patents were granted in the United States, Great Britain, France, Germany, and Russia, and many valuable processes, including those for making carbolic soap, for preserving wood, for making grape sugar, and for making hop extract.

Sewall, Mary A., philanthropist, died in Medfield, Mass., Aug. 26, 1892. She was a daughter of the late Rev. Charles E. Sewall. She entered the national service as an army nurse in March, 1863, and remained there till March, 1865. She was stationed at Point Lookout Hospital, Maryland, till it became a Confederate camp, and was then attached to the Chester Hospital, Pennsylvania, where she labored till her retirement.

Seymour, Edward Woodruff, jurist, born in Litchfield, Conn., Aug. 30, 1832; died there, Oct. 16, 1892. He was graduated at Yale in 1853, was admitted to the bar at Litchfield in 1856, and practiced there till 1875, when he removed to Bridgeport, and was in law partnership with his brother, Morris W. Seymour, till his death. He was elected to the State Legislature in 1859, 1860, 1870, and 1871, and to Congress as a Democrat in 1884 and 1888, being defeated for re-election in 1886. In 1880 he was appointed judge of the Supreme Court of Connecticut.

Seymour, Norman, historian, born in Rome, N. Y., in 1822; died in Mount Morris, Livingston county, N. Y., Feb. 21, 1892. He had made a special study of the history of the Genesee valley, of the Indian treaties and warfares in western New York, and of the historic places in Livingston and adjacent counties, and had gathered a rare collection of pamphlets, prints, and original manuscripts of the eighteenth century. He wrote numerous papers concerning Mary Jemison, "The White Woman," Red Jacket, and the Six Nations, and at the time of his death had nearly completed a voluminous history of Livingston County. He was secretary for many years of the Livingston County Historical Society, and for twenty-five years had been in the habit of attending the annual meetings of that society and similar ones, and presenting valuable papers on the early history of the towns in which the meetings were held.

Shafter, James McMillin, jurist, born in Athens, Windham County, Vt., May 27, 1816; died in San Francisco, Cal., Aug. 29, 1892. He was graduated at Wesleyan University, Middletown, in 1837; studied law in the Cambridge Law School, and was admitted to the bar in 1840. In 1850 he removed to California, where, till 1889, he was engaged in practice. He was elected State Senator in 1862, presided over the High Court of Impeachment that removed Judge James H. Hardy from the bench, and was a member of the convention that framed the present Constitution of California. On June 12, 1892, he was appointed judge of the Superior Court of the City and County of San Francisco. He was a regent of Leland Stanford, Jr., University from its incorporation, and left an estate valued at $1,000,000.

Sharp, Jacob, military officer, born in Kingston, N. Y., in 1835; died in Detroit, Mich., April 27, 1892. He studied two years at the United States Military Academy, and was graduated at the Chandler School of Science and Arts of Dartmouth College in 1856. On May 11, 1861, he entered the national service as 1st lieutenant in the 20th New York Volunteers; Sept. 13, 1862, was commissioned major of the 56th New York Infantry, and the same day promoted lieutenant-colonel; March 28, 1863, was commissioned colonel of the 156th New York Infantry; and Nov. 6, 1865, was mustered out of the service with the rank of brevet brigadier-general of volunteers. He took part in the battles of Williamsburg, Fair Oaks, the Peninsula, Port Hudson, La., the Red River campaign, the Shenandoah Valley, Cedar Creek, and Winchester, and during the last two years of the war commanded the 2d brigade, 3d division, 19th Army Corps. For several years before his death he was Governor of the Soldiers' Home at Milwaukee, Wis. His death was caused by paralysis resulting from a wound received at Winchester.

Sharpstein, John R., jurist, born in Richmond, N. Y., May 23, 1823; died in San Francisco, Cal., Dec. 28, 1892. He was admitted to the bar in 1847, began practice in Sheboygan, Wis., and in 1853 was appointed District Attorney for Wisconsin. From the expiration of his term till 1862 he owned and edited the Milwaukee "News." During this period he served two terms in the State Legislature. In 1864 he removed to California, and after serving two years on the bench of the 12th District court he was elected justice of the Supreme Court (1866), and at the end of his term was re-elected, and held the office at the time of his death, being the only Democratic justice in that court.

Shea, John Dawson Gilmary, historian, born in New York city, July 22, 1824; died in Elizabeth, N. J., Feb. 22, 1892. He was a son of James Shea, principal of the grammar school of Columbia College, was baptized John Dawson, and added the name Gilmary ("servant of Mary") while a youth. At an early age he became a clerk in the office of a Spanish merchant, where he learned to write and speak Spanish fluently; subsequently he studied law, and was admitted to the bar in 1846. A brief experience in practice, combined with a natural taste for literary work and research, led him to abandon the profession of law for that of letters, and in this occupation, to him the most delightful of all employments, he passed the remainder of his life. His attention was called to the early Catholic missions among the American Indians while he was studying Spanish, and his first endeavor, after deciding to follow literature, was to collect the fullest possible material for a general history of the Catholic Church in the United States. He was a most industrious author and translator, an active member of the New York Historical Society from 1845, an honorary member of nearly every historical society in the United States and of many in Europe, and was the first President of the Catholic Historical Society of the United States. As an evidence of the esteem in which he was generally held it is noted that, while on his death-bed and still conscious, he received by telegraph a special blessing from Pope Leo XIII. In 1883

the University of Notre Dame, Indiana, gave him the Lœtare medal, as being the most distinguished Catholic layman in the United States. For many years prior to 1858 he held an editorial place in Frank Leslie's publishing house, and latterly he was editor of the New York "Catholic News." His publications include: "The Discovery and Exploration of the Mississippi Valley" (New York, 1853); "History of the French and Spanish Missions among the Indian Tribes of the United States" (1854); "Early Voyages up and down the Mississippi" (1862); "Novum Belgium: An Account of New Netherland in 1643-'44" (1862); "The Operations of the French Fleet under Count de Grasse" (1864); a translation of Charlevoix's "History and General Description of New France," with numerous notes (6 vols., 1866-'72); Hennepin's "Description of Louisiana"; Le Clercq's "Establishment of the Faith"; Penalosa's "Expedition to Quivira"; editions of the Cramoisy series of "Relations" and documents in French bearing on the early history of the French-American colonies (24 vols., 1857-'68); "Washington's Private Diary" (1861); Colden's "History of the Five Indian Nations," 1727 edition (1866); and Alsop's "Maryland" (1869). His latest works included "The Catholic Church in Colonial Days" (1883); "The Story of a Great Nation"; the "Life of Father Isaac Jogues" (1885); "The Hierarchy of the Catholic Church in the United States" (1886); "Life and Times of Archbishop Carroll" (1888); and three volumes out of five projected on "The History of the Catholic Church in the United States." Of the last work, which he regarded as the crowning effort of his life, and for which he had been preparing since early youth, he saw the fourth volume in press, and had the material for the last one nearly completed. Besides these works, Dr. Shea had compiled many school histories and text-books, had published a series of grammars and dictionaries of the Indian language, entitled "Library of American Linguistics," and had written the articles on the various Indian tribes in the "American Cyclopædia." He was a man of marvelous memory, ready wit, and strong friendships; and after an intimate association of more than twenty years, it is a gratification to testify here to the unselfishness, the helpfulness, and the uninterrupted cordiality of his nature.

Shufeldt, Mason Abercrombie, naval officer, born in New York city, Nov. 8, 1852; died in Cape Town, Africa, in February, 1892. He was graduated at the United States Naval Academy, May 31, 1872; was promoted ensign in 1874, master in 1880, lieutenant, junior grade, in 1885, and lieutenant in 1886, and resigned on June 30, 1890. While attached to the "Enterprise," in 1881-'84, he received permission to land on Madagascar for the purpose of exploring that island. He was received with distinction by the Queen and the Prime Minister at the capital, and furnished with an escort with which he crossed the island, encountering many hardships in a journey of several months. From Morandava, on the western coast, he made a journey of 700 miles in an open boat to Delagoa Bay. In 1889-'90, while attached to the "Yantic," of the North Atlantic squadron, he experienced his second severe cyclone. The vessel was cast on her beam ends by the force of the wind, and Lieut. Shufeldt risked his life in cutting away her mast. His conduct during this emergency was so gallant that on the arrival of the ship in port both the officers and the crew united in commending him, and a letter commemorating the event was signed by every officer and enlisted man on board ship. After resigning from the navy he was appointed a World's Fair commissioner to Africa. After visiting Zanzibar he went to Cape Town, South Africa, thence made journeys to the diamond mines at Kimberly, to the Orange Free State, and to the copper mines at Port Nolloth, on the western coast, and, returning to Cape Town, was prostrated with diseases incidental to Africa. He had a passion for travel and adventure, and one of his motives in seeking his last official appointment was to enable him to continue his early explorations in that region. Lieut. Shufeldt was a son of Rear-Admiral Robert W. Shufeldt, United States navy, retired.

Small, Michael P., military officer, born in York, Pa., Aug. 9, 1831; died on Governor's Island, N. Y., Aug. 1, 1892. He was graduated at the United States Military Academy, July 1, 1851; was brevetted 2d lieutenant, 3d Artillery, July 1, 1855; promoted 2d lieutenant 2d Artillery, Sept. 21 following; 1st lieutenant, April 27, 1861; captain and commissary of subsistence Aug. 3 following; major, June 23, 1874; and lieutenant-colonel, Oct. 4, 1889. In the volunteer army he was lieutenant-colonel and commissary of subsistence from Aug. 14, 1863, till Jan. 25, 1865, and was colonel from May 25 till Dec. 29 following. He was brevetted major, lieutenant-colonel, and colonel, March 13, 1865, for meritorious services in the subsistence department during the war; colonel of volunteers, Jan. 1, 1865, for distinguished services in the campaign of 1863–'64; and brigadier-general United States army, April 9, 1865, for faithful services in his department during the war. At the time of his death he was assistant commissary-general of subsistence, and was stationed at Governor's Island.

Smith, John Ambler, lawyer, born in Village View, Va., Sept. 23, 1847; died in Washington, D. C., Jan. 6, 1892. He was educated in Richmond, Va., and was admitted to the bar there in 1867. In 1868 he was appointed a commissioner in chancery for the courts of that city, and Attorney of Charles City and New Kent Counties, and was elected State Senator in 1869. In 1872 he was elected to Congress from the 3d Virginia District as a Republican, and there served on the Committee on Railways and Canals. At the close of his term he settled in Washington, and practiced there till his death.

Smith, Roswell, publisher, born in Lebanon, Conn., March 30, 1829; died in New York city, April 19, 1892. He was a nephew of Roswell J. Smith, compiler of several schoolbooks of note in his day, including "Smith's Grammar" and "Smith's Arithmetic." When fourteen years old he became a clerk in the office of his uncle's publishers in New York city. Three years afterward he entered Brown University, where he took the English and scientific courses; then studied law in Hartford, Conn.; and removed to Lafayette, Ind., to begin practice. By 1868 he had acquired large means by law practice and fortunate investments. In that year he disposed of all his business interests in Indiana and took his family to Europe, intending to engage in some branch of publishing on his return. While abroad he met the late Dr. Josiah G. Holland, who had matured plans for an illustrated magazine to be devoted chiefly to promoting American art and literature. Mr. Smith agreed to join Dr. Holland in establishing the magazine, and on their return the two formed a partnership with Scribner, Armstrong & Co., and brought out the first number of "Scribner's Monthly" in November, 1870, with Dr. Holland as editor. In 1873 the firm established "St. Nicholas," and bought and merged into it several juvenile publications. In 1881 Mr. Smith bought Dr. Holland's interest in the publications, and afterward the whole interest of Charles Scribner's Sons, and changed the name of the magazine to the "Century Magazine." As soon as the success of the new venture seemed assured Mr. Smith turned his attention to the publication of a dictionary. This grew far beyond his original plan, and, under the name of the "Century Dictionary," was completed in 6 royal 8vo volumes before his death.

Sproull, Thomas, clergyman, born near Freeport, Pa., in 1803; died in Pittsburg, Pa., March 20, 1892. He was graduated at the Western University of Pennsylvania, and was pastor of the Reformed Presbyterian congregation of Alleghany and Pittsburg from 1834 till 1868. In 1847 he was moderator of the Synod of the Reformed Presbyterian Church, and subsequently he was editor of several religious periodicals and a professor in the Presbyterian College. He was author of pamphlets on theological and de-

nominational topics, and published "Prelections on Theology."

Stackhouse, Eli Thomas, agriculturist, born in Marion, S. C., March 27, 1824; died in Washington, D. C., June 14, 1892. He received a public-school education, was brought up on his father's farm, taught for four years, and was three times elected to the State Legislature. He served through the civil war in the Confederate army, becoming colonel; after the war returned to his farm, and applied himself chiefly to the improvement of agriculture in the Southern States. He was President of the Farmers' State Alliance of South Carolina, was a leader in the councils of the National Alliance, and was elected to Congress from the 6th South Carolina District as a Democrat in 1891, where he was a member of the committees on Militia and on Expenditures in the Department of Agriculture.

Stark, George, civil engineer, born in Manchester, N. H., April 9, 1823; died in Nashua, N. H., April 13, 1892. He was a grandson of Maj.-Gen. John Stark; studied civil engineering, and in early life became connected with railroad building. In 1852 he was made Superintendent of the Hudson River Railroad, which he left to take a similar office on the Nashua and Lowell Railroad and its branches, and from 1857 till 1875 he was manager of the latter road. Resigning in 1875, he was appointed one of a committee of six to reorganize the Northern Pacific Railroad Company, and in the same year he established a banking house in partnership with his son. He was appointed brigadier-general of the 3d Brigade of New Hampshire Militia in 1857, colonel of the Governor's Horse Guards in 1860, and brigadier-general in 1861, and under the latter commission made his headquarters at Portsmouth, and had charge of the organization of State troops for the civil war. He was Democratic candidate for Governor in 1860 and 1861.

Steiner, Lewis Henry, physician, born in Frederick City, Md., May 4, 1827; died in Baltimore, Md., Feb. 18, 1892. He was graduated at Marshall College, Pennsylvania, in 1846, and at the medical department of the University of Pennsylvania in 1849, and settled in Baltimore in 1852. From 1855 he was for many years connected with the management of the "American Medical Monthly"; he contributed frequently to the Mercersburg "Quarterly Review," "Southern Quarterly," and other periodicals; and between 1852 and 1861 he held the chairs of Chemistry and Natural History in Columbia College, of Chemistry and Pharmacy in the National Medical College, Washington, D. C., and was lecturer on applied chemistry at the Baltimore Medical Institute, and on chemistry and natural philosophy in the College of St. James. He was an active Unionist at the beginning of the civil war; assisted in raising troops, and was Chief Medical Inspector of the United States Sanitary Commission in the Army of the Potomac till the close of the war. The abolition of slavery opened to him a new field of labor, and he interested himself in the establishment of schools for colored children throughout Maryland. In 1871, 1875, and 1879 he was elected a State Senator, in 1876 was a delegate to the National Republican Convention, and in 1882, on the establishment of the Pratt Free Library in Baltimore, he was selected for librarian, which office he held until his death. His publications, besides special reports, include "Physical Science" (1851); "The Marvelous in Modern Thought"; and "Abraham Lincoln," an address.

Stewart, William A., jurist, born in Baltimore, Md., Dec. 29, 1825; died there, Aug. 26, 1892. He was graduated at the Maryland University, admitted to the bar in 1847, elected to the Legislature several times, and in the session of 1868 was Speaker. In the judiciary reform movement of 1882 he was elected Judge of the Supreme Court of Maryland, and he held the office till within a few weeks of his death.

Stockton, Thomas Hewlings, clergyman, born in Philadelphia, Pa., in 1839; died in Buenos Ayres, Argentine Republic, Aug. 3, 1892. He received a collegiate education; joined the New Jersey Conference of the Methodist Episcopal Church in 1871, and held pastorates in Newark, Jersey City, and Plainfield till 1880. He was then appointed a missionary to South America, and, settling in Buenos Ayres, became pastor of the first Methodist Episcopal church in that city, the mother church of South American Methodism. While ministering to this congregation he planned the organization of a high-grade educational institution, modeled after those in the United States, for Buenos Ayres, and in that interest he made a tour of the United States in the winter of 1891–'92. He received large encouragement on this tour, and returned with ample moral and financial support for his projected college.

Stout, Francis Aquila, civil engineer, born in New York city, Oct. 21, 1833; died at the Thousand Islands, N. Y., July 18, 1892. He completed his education in Paris, making a specialty of civil engineering. Returning to New York city, he studied law, and became private secretary to Hiram Birney, when the latter was collector of the port. Possessing an ample fortune, he applied himself to scientific study and to charitable works, and became identified officially with many charitable associations. Mr. Stout was the senior vice-president of the American Geographical Society, one of the founders and commissioners of the New York State Survey, a former President of the Nicaragua Canal Company, a trustee of the New York Society Library, and a director or manager of the New York Orthopædic Hospital, the New York Asylum for the Blind, the Cancer Hospital, and the Samaritan Home for the Aged. He was also for many years chairman of the Charities Aid Association of New York. In 1889 he was a commissioner to the Paris Exposition, and in 1891 one of the American delegates to and a vice-president of the International Geographical Congress at Berne, Switzerland. Mr. Stout will be known long and favorably as the father of the New York State Survey.

Strakosch, Max, impresario, born in Selowitz, Austria, Sept. 27, 1835; died in New York city, March 17, 1892. He received a musical education with his brother Maurice in Germany, came to the United States in 1855 as agent for Bernard Ullmann, then managing the New York Academy of Music, and afterward joined his brother in organizing a company for operatic performances. During the partnership of the brothers they introduced to the American public many of the most noted singers on the lyric stage, including Christine Nilsson, Carlotta, Amelia, and Adelina Patti, Pauline Lucca, Parepa, Clara Louise Kellogg, Annie Louise Cary, Marie Rose, and Capaul, Campanini, Maurel, Vieuxtemps, Brignoli, and Karl Formes. In 1876 he surrendered the management of the Academy of Music to Col. Mapleson, and organized a traveling opera company, in which Marie Rose, Clara Louise Kellogg, and Annie Louise Cary were the principal female singers. Under his direction the operas "Aïda" and "Carmen" were first produced in the United States.

Streight, Abdel D., manufacturer, born in Wheeler, N. Y., June 17, 1829; died near Indianapolis, Ind., May 27, 1892. In early life he was apprenticed to the carpenter's trade, which he followed for several years, subsequently engaging in book publishing. He removed to Cincinnati in 1858, and thence to Indianapolis. At the beginning of the civil war he recruited the 51st Regiment of Indiana Volunteers at the request of Gov. Oliver P. Morton, was commissioned its colonel, and in December, 1861, reported to Gen. Don Carlos Buell at Louisville, when his regiment was attached to the Army of the Cumberland. Soon afterward he led a raid into the enemy's country, creating considerable consternation, and subsequently his command was captured, and he and all his officers were sent to Libby Prison, where, because of this raid, they were treated with unusual severity. Col. Streight himself was ironed, confined in a dungeon, and forced to live on corn bread and water for thirty days for attempting to escape. On being released from the

dungeon, he, with Col. Thomas E. Rose, of the 77th Pennsylvania Volunteers, Major Hamilton, of the 12th Kentucky Cavalry, and other officers, planned the memorable escape from Libby, and superintended the excavation of the tunnel through which 108 officers secured their freedom. After a short retirement, Col. Streight resumed command of his regiment, was promoted brigadier-general after the battle of Nashville, and held important commands till the close of the war. Returning to Indianapolis, he resumed the publishing business, afterward engaging in the wholesale lumber trade, and in the manufacture of chairs. Gen. Streight was a Republican, and was defeated for Governor of Indiana by Albert G. Porter in 1876.

Sweeny, Thomas William, military officer, born in Cork, Ireland, Dec. 25, 1820; died in Astoria, L. I., April 10, 1892. He came to the United States in 1832, learned the printer's trade in New York city, and served in the 1st New York Volunteers in the Mexican War, receiving a wound at the battle of Churubusco which made it necessary to amputate his right arm. On returning to New York he was brevetted captain, and was presented with a silver medal by the city government. He was commissioned 2d lieutenant United States Infantry, March 3, 1848; promoted 1st lieutenant, June 11, 1851; captain, Jan. 19, 1861; major 16th Infantry, Oct. 20, 1863; unassigned, March 15, 1869; and was retired as brigadier-general United States army, May 11, 1870. After entering the regular army he was ordered to California, where for a time he was commandant at Fort Yuma, and afterward he distinguished himself in campaigns with the Indians. At the beginning of the civil war he was placed in charge of the United States arsenal at St. Louis, Mo., which he saved by threatening to explode the 40 tons of gunpowder stored there, in case the secessionists attacked him. He was second in command of the national troops at the surrender of the Missouri State forces at Camp Jackson; was commissioned a brigadier-general of volunteers, May 20, 1861, and at the battles of Wilson's Creek he was severely wounded. After this he was given command of the 52d Illinois Volunteers, was attached to Gen. Grant's army, took part in the capture of Fort Donelson, and at the battle of Shiloh successfully defended a gap in the line, for which Gen. Sherman afterward said: "I attach more importance to that event than to any of the hundred events that I have since heard saved the day." In December, 1862, he was given command of a division of the 16th Army Corps, and was engaged in protecting the Memphis and Charleston Railroad. In the Atlanta campaign he commanded the 2d division of the 16th Corps in the Army of the Tennessee, with which he took possession of the Snake Creek Gap twenty-four hours before the arrival of supporting cavalry, and held it against several assaults. Subsequently he took part in the battle of Resaca, forced a passage across Oostenaula river, and fought a successful battle. He also distinguished himself in the battles of Kenesaw mountain, and in the battle before Atlanta, on July 22, 1864, his division repelled an assault and captured four Confederate flags and 900 prisoners. After the occupation at Atlanta he held the post of commandant at Nashville till July, 1865, and was mustered out of the volunteer service on Aug. 24 following. Gen. Sweeny was active in the Fenian invasion of Canada in 1866, during a virtual retirement from the army, and after that event was reinstated in the army and assigned to duty in the southern military district. He was presented by the city of Brooklyn with a costly sword for his services during the civil war.

Swinton, William, author, born in Haddingtonshire, Scotland, April 23, 1833; died in New York city, Oct. 24, 1892. His father was a Scotch farmer, whose ancestors resided in the Lothians; his mother, Jean Currie, belonged to a family of Scotch divines. In 1836 his father emigrated to Illinois, and the family followed about 1843, but upon reaching Montreal they received intelligence of the father's death, and remained in that city. William was educated at

Knox College, Toronto, and at Amherst, Mass. He married Miss Kate Linton, of Montreal, and was first appointed Professor of Languages in Edgeworth Seminary, Greensboro, N. C., and afterward in Mount Washington Institute, New York. During this period he contributed to "Putnam's Magazine" articles entitled "Rambles over the Realms of Verbs and Substantives," which were embodied in "Rambles among Words" (1859). Subsequently he became a member of the editorial staff of the New York "Times," and in 1862 he was sent to the front as a war correspondent. There he incurred the displeasure of the military authorities, and Gen. Burnside's personal encounter with him, Gen. Meade's action (July 6, 1864) in ordering him to leave the lines, and the caustic mention of him in Gen. Grant's "Memoirs," have been much discussed. At the expiration of the war Mr. Swinton visited the Confederate generals and obtained a vast amount of information that was not attainable elsewhere. His principal works on the civil war are: "Campaigns of the Army of the Potomac" (1866), "The Twelve Decisive Battles of the War" (1867), and "The History of the New York Seventh Regiment during the Rebellion" (1870). On July 6, 1869, he was elected Professor of English in the University of California. He was very popular with the students, and was universally recognized by the schoolmen of that State as a man of genius; but he differed with President Gilman in respect to the prominence due to the colleges of mining and agriculture, Swinton wishing the University of California to rank with Cornell and the College of Agriculture at Amherst. He resigned his professorship March 3, 1874, and removed to Brooklyn, N. Y. Here he composed text-books of such excellence that he may be said to have created a new era in school literature, for which he was awarded a gold medal at the Paris Exposition. Personally, he was tall and well formed, with blonde complexion and regular features; eyes large and luminous, voice well modulated, articulation deliberate, without Scotch accent. When engaged upon any literary work he toiled day and night till it was completed, but when his work was done he enjoyed his hours of idleness like an Oriental. Among his unpublished manuscripts have been found a *brochure* on Columbus, materials for an encyclopædia of language, and a brief history of the United States. He also left valuable papers pertaining to the civil war.

Talmage, John Van Nest, clergyman, born in Somerville, N. J., Aug. 18, 1819; died in Bound Brook, N. J., Aug. 19, 1892. He was a brother of the Rev. T. De Witt Talmage; was graduated at Rutgers College in 1842, and at the New Brunswick Theological Seminary in 1845; and was licensed as a missionary by the Philadelphia Classis of the Dutch Reformed Church in 1846. In the same year he began missionary work in China, and he remained there forty years. Dr. Talmage translated several books of the Bible into the colloquial dialect of Amoy, and published a "Chinese-English Dictionary" (1888).

Tanner, Edward Allen, educator, born in Waverly, Ill., Nov. 29, 1837; died in Jacksonville, Ill., Feb. 8, 1892. He was graduated at Illinois College in 1857, taught school for four years, was then appointed Professor of Latin in a college on the Pacific coast, was elected Professor of Latin and Rhetoric in Illinois College in 1865, appointed financial agent of the college in 1881, and elected its president in 1882. He added land, buildings, and endowments, increased the number of professors, raised the standard of scholarship, and brought the institution from a moribund condition to one of prosperity. President Tanner was a clergyman of the Congregational Church.

Taylor, Lathrop Miner, pioneer, born in Clinton, Oneida County, N. Y., Feb. 4, 1805; died in South Bend, Ind., Aug. 29, 1892. His father, Israel Taylor, with his family, removed to Detroit in 1811, and when Gen. Hull surrendered the entire family became prisoners and subsequently were paroled. They removed to Montgomery County, Ohio, in 1814, and thence to

Fort Wayne, Ind., in 1820. Lathrop Taylor went from Fort Wayne to what is now South Bend in 1827, and was the first white man to settle there in the wilderness among the Pottawattamie Indians. He soon mastered their language, and was an Indian trader and an extensive fur dealer, shipping his fur direct to Europe, and for many years afterward was the leading merchant in South Bend. He was an adviser whom the Indians trusted implicitly, and through his efforts they received fair terms in the treaty at Chicago in 1833. He secured for them a large reservation in Michigan, and a large sum of money which otherwise they would not have obtained. He founded the town of South Bend, and he was the first man to bring goods up the St. Joseph river by boat from Lake Michigan. Owing to his efforts the county seat was located at South Bend. He was the first postmaster, the first clerk of the circuit court, and the first county auditor. He was colonel of the 79th Indiana Militia from 1832 to 1837. He retired from active business in 1860.

Ten Broeck, Richard, turfman, born in Albany, N. Y., in 1810; died in San Mateo, Cal., Aug. 1, 1892. He took a partial course at the United States Military Academy in 1829-'30, and subsequently studied law in New York city; but forming a partnership with Col. William Johnson, of Virginia, he abandoned law practice and engaged in horse racing and breeding. He raced horses for several years with uniform success, established racing stables in Havana and Canada, and in 1853 became a part owner of "Darley," afterward famous under the name of "Lexington." The success of this horse was phenomenal, and his victories over "Sally Waters," "Lecompt," "Highlander," "Arrow," and other noted racers of that day, are matters of turf history. In 1856 Mr. Ten Broeck made the first shipment of American racing horses to England, sending "Lexington," "Prioress," "Prior," and "Lecompt." In October, 1857, he won the Czarewitch stakes on the Newmarket course with "Prioress." In 1858 "Lecompt" and "Prior" died, and in 1859, 1860, and 1861 he won several of England's richest stake races with "Starke," "Umpire," and "Optimist," driven by the celebrated English jockey Fordham. Mr. Ten Broeck remained in England with his racing stable ten years, and his winnings aggregated $197,756. On his return to the United States he settled on the Hurstbourne farm, near Louisville, Ky., where he remained till 1887, and then removed to San Mateo, Cal., where, in 1889, he built the Hermitage, in which he died.

Throop, Montgomery Hunt, lawyer, born in Auburn, N. Y., Jan. 26, 1827; died there, Sept. 11, 1892. He was a nephew of Enos T. Throop, who was twice Governor of New York; was educated in Geneva, Switzerland, in Naples, and at Hobart College; and was admitted to the bar in 1848. He practiced in Utica from 1851 till 1864, first with his uncle, Ward Hunt, and afterward with Roscoe Conkling, and in New York city from 1870 till 1878. He was appointed a commissioner to revise the statutes of the State in 1870, was chairman of the commission that prepared the "Code of Civil Procedure," and, after returning to Albany in 1878, applied himself to legal writing. His publications include "The Future" (New York, 1864); "Treatise on the Validity of Verbal Agreements" (Albany, 1870); "Annotated Code of Civil Procedure" (1880); "The New York Justices' Manual" (1880); "Digest of the Decisions of the Supreme Judicial Court of Massachusetts" (1887); and "Revised Statutes of New York" (1888).

Torsey, Henry P., educator, born in Monmouth, Me., Aug. 7, 1819; died at Kent's Hill, Me., Sept. 10, 1892. He was educated in the Maine Wesleyan Seminary at Kent's Hill; became a teacher in the normal department of the East Greenwich, R. I., Seminary in 1841, and assistant in Maine Wesleyan Seminary in 1843; and was principal of that institution from 1844 till 1882, when from failing health he resigned. Dr. Torsey was licensed to preach in 1845, was received into the Maine Conference of the Methodist Episcopal Church in 1848, was a delegate to the General Conference of his Church several times, served in the State Senate two years, and after his resignation was financial agent and professor emeritus of Maine Wesleyan Seminary.

Trotter, Frederick E., military officer, born in Brooklyn, N. Y., April 25, 1838; died in Tacoma, Wash., June 27, 1892. He was graduated at Trinity College, Hartford; enlisted as a private soldier in the 7th Regiment, N. G. S. N. Y., April 26, 1861; entered the national army as captain in the 102d New York Infantry, Dec. 18 following; was promoted major, July 16, 1862; mustered out of volunteer service, March 18, 1863; commissioned captain in the United States Veteran Reserve Corps, June 18, 1863; promoted major, Oct. 15 following, and lieutenant-colonel, March 30, 1864; brevetted brigadier-general of Volunteers, March 13, 1865; and was mustered out of the service, Oct. 11, 1866. In the regular army he was commissioned captain 45th United States Infantry, July 28, 1866; transferred to 14th Infantry, July 22, 1869; and brevetted major and lieutenant-colonel, March 2, 1867, for faithful and meritorious services during the war. He was engaged in the defense of Washington, and was in the actions at Bolivar, Maryland Heights, Cedar mountain, where he was wounded, and in those of Gen. Banks's Shenandoah valley campaign; was connected with the Freedmen's Bureau, with headquarters at Chattanooga, Tenn., where he had charge of the work in 32 counties; and at the time of his death was stationed at Vancouver Barracks, Wash., but was attending the encampment of the State militia at Tacoma.

Trowbridge, William Petit, engineer, born near Birmingham, Oakland County, Mich., May 25, 1828; died in New Haven, Conn., Aug. 12, 1892. He was graduated at the United States Military Academy in 1848, standing first in his class, and entered the army

as 2d lieutenant in the Corps of Engineers. During the last year of his course at the academy he served as assistant Professor of Chemistry, as the war with Mexico had compelled the field services of the available graduates, and on entering the army he was ordered back to West Point as assistant in the Astronomical Observatory under Prof. William H. C. Bartlett, remaining there for two years. In 1851 he entered the service of the United States Coast Survey, and was assigned to duty over the primary triangulation of the coast of Maine under Alexander D. Bache, succeeding in 1852 to the immediate charge of this work. Later he executed surveys of Appomattox river, in Virginia, below Petersburg, with a view to the improvement of its navigation, and also similar surveys of James river near Richmond. At this time

he surveyed the Dutch Gap and recommended the "cut off" or canal, which was subsequently constructed, shortening the distance for vessels by seven miles. In 1853 he was sent to the Pacific coast, where during the subsequent three years he conducted a series of tidal and magnetic observations from San Diego to Puget Sound, a distance of over 1,300 miles. He became 1st lieutenant on Dec. 18, 1854, and resigned from the army on Dec. 1, 1856, to accept the professorship of Mathematics in the University of Michigan in Ann Arbor. A year later, at the solicitation of Superintendent Bache, he accepted the permanent appointment of assistant on the United States Coast Survey, and was assigned to the preparation for publication of the results of the Gulf Stream exploration. In 1860 he was sent to Key West to superintend the erection of a permanent self-registering magnetic observatory, the first in the United States. At the breaking out of the civil war he was called to the service of the engineers, and during 1861 was assigned the duty of preparing minute descriptions of the harbors, inlets, and rivers of the Southern coast from Delaware Bay to Galveston. In 1862 he was ordered to make a hydrographic survey of Narragansett Bay, R. I., in order to determine its availability for a navy yard. The results showed that it was unsuited to that purpose. Thereafter he was placed in charge of the branch office of the War Department in New York city, where his duties included the supply of material for use in the field, involving a responsibility to contractors aggregating several million dollars. He also had charge of the construction of local fortifications, including the fort at Willett's Point, that on Governor's Island, and the repairs of Fort Schuyler. Of the difficulties of the undertaking at Willett's Point, Gen. Henry L. Abbot has written: "By special devices showing much skill and ingenuity, Prof. Trowbridge overcame these difficulties, and not only made astonishing progress with the work, but left it one of the finest specimens of granite masonry to be seen in any of our fortifications." In 1865 he became Vice-President of the Novelty Iron Works in New York city with direction of their shops, where he remained for four years. He was then called to the professorship of Dynamical Engineering in the Sheffield Scientific School of Yale College, which chair he held until May, 1877. During these six years he was active in the development of this new department, and also in the planning and construction of the new Sheffield Hall, in which the engineering instruction was given. Prof. Trowbridge was then called to the charge of the engineering department in the Columbia College School of Mines. This department was at that time in a somewhat chaotic condition and he at once began its reorganization. Courses in thermo-dynamics, dynamics of machinery, and water-supply engineering were successively added, while the existing courses in hydraulics, braced structures, motors and machines, were developed, subdivided, and extended. Later, courses in sanitary engineering and electrical engineering were added to the department. Other plans tending to increase the efficiency of the instruction in engineering were submitted to the trustees, but were held in abeyance until greater facilities could be afforded. While in New Haven, Prof. Trowbridge held various State offices, including that of adjutant-general, with the rank of brigadier-general on the Governor's staff in 1872–'76; also during 1873–'78 he was a commissioner for building the Capitol at Hartford, while during 1870–'76 he was a commissioner for building a bridge across the Quinnipiac river, and during 1872–'78 commissioner for establishing harbor lines in New Haven Bay. Subsequently he was commissioned to examine the State Capitol in Albany, N. Y. Special recognition is his due for his design of the first cantilever bridge. This system he recommended for the spanning of the East river, and in 1869 a company was organized, but the novelty of the plan and the financial crisis of 1873 deprived him of the honor of constructing the first cantilever bridge. In 1880 Prof. Trowbridge was called to the charge of the department of power and machinery employed in manufactures for the tenth census. He organized the collection of statistics for that purpose, and under his direction several important monographs pertaining to the subject were written and appear in the census reports. Prof. Trowbridge likewise invented a coil boiler incorporating the latest knowledge in forced circulation of water, automatic supply of feed water from a magazine, and the self-feeding of the fuel. The degree of A. M. was conferred on him by Rochester in 1856, and by Yale in 1870; that of Ph. D. by Princeton in 1879; and that of LL.D., by Trinity in 1880, and the University of Michigan in 1887. He was a member of numerous scientific societies, having served as Vice-President of the American Society of Mechanical Engineers, of the New York Academy of Sciences, of the American Association for the Advancement of Science in 1882, when he presided over the section of mechanical sciences, and in 1878 he was elected to the National Academy of Sciences. Besides public lectures, he contributed to scientific journals and to the transactions of societies of which he was a member; also he was an associate editor of Johnson's "New Universal Cyclopædia," with charge of the subjects on mechanics, mechanical engineering, etc., and was the author of "Proposed Plan for building a Bridge across the East River at Blackwell's Island" (New York, 1869); "Heat as a Source of Power" (1874); and "Turbine Wheels" (1879).

Tuttle, James M., military officer, born in Summerfield, Ohio, Sept. 24, 1823; died in Casa Grande, Arizona, Oct. 24, 1892. He received a public-school education, removed to Farmington, Iowa, and engaged in agricultural and mercantile business in 1846, and was elected sheriff in 1855, county treasurer in 1857, and recorder in 1859. At the outbreak of the civil war he was commissioned lieutenant-colonel of the 2d Iowa Infantry, and on May 17, 1861, was promoted colonel. In February, 1862, he led the charge of his regiment on Fort Donelson, and his troops were the first to enter the Confederate works. In this charge he was wounded in his sword arm, but he continued in command of his regiment. At the battle of Shiloh he commanded a brigade, with which he fought at the sunken road afterward known as the "Hornet's Nest" because of the resistance offered the Confederates by his troops. For gallantry in this engagement he was promoted brigadier-general, June 9, 1862. After the surrender of Corinth he commanded for some time a division in that vicinity. During the siege of Vicksburg he had command of a division in the 15th Army Corps under Gen. Sherman, and at the first capture of Jackson, May 14, 1863, he executed a flank movement, which compelled the Confederates under Gen. Johnston to retreat across Pearl river, leaving their artillery, which he captured. In the same year, while at home on a short furlough, he received the Democratic nomination for Governor of Iowa, but was defeated. He resigned his commission in the army in June, 1864; was a second time defeated for Governor; served several terms in the Legislature; engaged in farming, real-estate operations, and pork packing till 1877; and was subsequently engaged in mining operations.

Ullman, Daniel, military officer, born in Wilmington, Del., April 28, 1810; died in Nyack, N. Y., Sept. 20, 1892. He was graduated at Yale, studied law, and was admitted to the bar in New York city, where, besides building up a large practice, he was for many years a master in the old Court of Chancery. In 1851 he was the Whig candidate for Attorney-General, and in 1854 the American (or "Know-Nothing") candidate for Governor. After the firing on Fort Sumter he raised and led to the field, as colonel, the 77th Regiment of New York Volunteers, which served at Harper's Ferry, and in many of the early movements in the Shenandoah and Piedmont regions. After the battle of Cedar Mountain, and while the Army of Virginia was retreating, he was prostrated with typhoid fever, and, being left behind, was captured and

confined in Libby Prison. On his liberation he wrote a long letter to President Lincoln, recommending the emancipation of slaves and the arming of the freedmen as soldiers. He was commissioned brigadier-general of volunteers Jan. 13, 1863, and was specially ordered to establish headquarters in New Orleans, and to select and appoint the necessary white officers for 4 regiments of colored troops and 1 regiment of mounted scouts for duty in Louisiana. He rapidly raised and equipped 5 regiments of colored troops, which subsequently grew into a corps of 17,000 men, and in April following he raised and organized in New Orleans the Ullman Brigade, Corps d'Afrique, which in July was engaged in the siege and capture of Port Hudson. In the following year he was placed in command of Port Hudson and all the troops in that district, and he was in chief command at the battle of Atchafalaya. In March, 1865, he was ordered to Cairo, and then to New York city, where he was promoted major-general of volunteers, and mustered out of service. After retiring from the army, Gen. Ullman also retired from active life, and made his home at Grand View, near Nyack, where he passed his time in scientific and literary studies, interrupting them by several trips to Europe. He had been engaged for some time in the preparation of a work on "The Philosophy of History as developed by the American Rebellion," but had been obliged by an almost entire loss of sight to abandon the work.

Van Anden, William, inventor, born near Poughkeepsie, N. Y., in 1815; died in New York city, May 21, 1892. He was apprenticed to the printer's trade in the office of the Poughkeepsie "Telegraph," and subsequently became known as the inventor of laborsaving machines, including the railroad chair to hold the ends of rails in place on the track, and the first machines for making files and spiral springs for beds. For several years he was interested in factories that he established in Poughkeepsie, Montreal, Jersey City, and Trenton, for the manufacture of bolts and rivets and a variety of railroad appliances, many of which were of his own invention.

Van Depoele, Charles J., electrician, born in Lichtervelde, Belgium, April 27, 1846; died in Lynn, Mass., March 18, 1892. He first became interested in telegraphy when a mere boy by seeing a line erected in the neighborhood of his home, and applied his first earnings, gained by running errands, to the purchase of battery cells and instruments with which he experimented. Owing to the opposition of his father, he was compelled to study secretly in the garret. When fifteen years old he was apprenticed to a carver of church furniture and fancy wood in Paris, and he followed this business till 1871, though never abandoning his electrical investigations. In 1871 he came to the United States, and established a woodcarving shop of his own in Detroit, Mich. When, at the height of his success, his father and several friends undertook to force him to abandon his experiments and what they called his waste of money, he declared that he would devote the whole of his time and money to the study of electricity. He placed his father at the head of his shop, and erected a building near by to continue his favorite study. In 1880 he removed to Chicago and formed an electric-lighting company, using a dynamo of his own construction, and in the following year began lighting the streets of that city. As soon as this branch of work began to be remunerative he conceived the idea of attempting to run street-railway cars by electricity, and in 1883 erected a short exhibition road in Chicago. In 1884 he constructed a conduit road at the Toronto Exhibition, Ontario, and in 1885 made the first exhibition of the overhead trolley system at the same place, and completed the first commercial application of his plan for propelling cars by electricity at South Bend, Ind. During the next three years he took out numerous patents, further developed his electric railway plans, and equipped 13 roads with the overhead-wire system. In 1888 he sold out his patents and business to the Thomson-Houston Company of Lynn,

Mass., and in March of that year he became connected with that company as electrician. To Mr. Van Depoele is also due the present electric percussion drill used in mining, on which he began experimenting in 1882. At the time of his death he was improving some of his inventions in the line of electric reciprocating devices, but he will be remembered longest as the "father" of the trolley system of electric railway propulsion.

Vanderbilt, William Henry, student, born in New York city, Dec. 21, 1870; died there, May 23, 1892. He was the eldest son of Cornelius Vanderbilt, and the favorite grandson of William H. Vanderbilt, who bequeathed to him $1,000,000, the income to be paid when he reached his majority, and the disposal of the principal to pass to him when he reached his thirtieth year. Besides this he had a large allowance from his father. After studying at Cutler's School in New York city and at St. Paul's School, Concord, N. H., he entered Yale University in 1889, becoming a member of the class of '93. In his sophomore year he contributed $5,000 to the building fund of the new Yale gymnasium. He was an excellent horseman; the owner of the 46 foot sloop yacht "Ilderim"; and a member of the Knickerbocker, New York Yacht, Seawanhaka Corinthian, Racket and Tennis, Country, Westchester Polo, and Riding Clubs.

Van Nest, Abraham Rynier, clergyman, born in New York city, Feb. 1, 1823; died there, June 2, 1892. He was graduated at Rutgers College in 1841, and at the New Brunswick (N. J.) Theological Seminary in 1847, and was licensed to preach in the Dutch Reformed Church. After holding a pastorate at Newburgh, N. Y., for several years he was stationed at the Dutch Reformed Church in 20th Street, New York city, from 1850 till 1862, and was in charge of the American chapels in Paris, Rome, and Florence from 1863 till 1875. While at Florence he was a founder of an orphan asylum for children of Italian Protestants, and President of the Evangelization Committee of the Free Church in Italy, and before returning he organized the Dutch Reformed Church in Geneva, Switzerland. On his return to the United States he became pastor of a church in Philadelphia, where he remained from 1878 till 1889. He was President of the General Synod of the Dutch Reformed Church in 1870. He published, among other books, "Signs of the Times," and editions of James S. Cannon's "Pastoral Theology" and of George W. Bethune's "Lectures on the Heidelberg Catechism."

Vedder, Nicholas, military officer, born in New York in 1819; died in Washington, D. C., April 15, 1892. He was appointed an additional paymaster in the United States Volunteer Army, Sept. 5, 1861; brevetted lieutenant-colonel, March 13, 1865; appointed major and paymaster United States Army, Jan. 17, 1867; and was retired, Sept. 2, 1882. He was brevetted lieutenant-colonel of volunteers, March 13, 1865, for faithful and meritorious services during the war. During Gen. Sherman's march to the sea he was his chief paymaster, and as such disbursed more than $52,000,000 without making a mistake of a dollar.

Voegtlin, William, scene painter, born in Basel, Switzerland, in 1826; died in Boston, Mass., May 29, 1892. He was the son of a theatrical scene painter, whom he accompanied to the United States about 1852, and had since been employed at scene painting in the theatres and opera houses of New Orleans, San Francisco, New York, Philadelphia, Boston, and other cities. His most noted works were the scenery for the original production of the "Black Crook" at Niblo's Garden, New York; that for the Brocken scene in "Faust"; settings for the Grand Opera House, Booth's Theatre, and the Union Square Theatre, in New York city; and special scenery for many of the theatrical and operatic traveling companies. He was an extremely rapid painter, and in the case of the Brocken scene his canvas was scarcely more than half finished when the curtain rose for the first act, but was completed in time for its proper display, though still wet.

Warren, Orsamus George, publisher, born in Clarence, Erie County, N. Y., July 21, 1846; died in Buffalo, N. Y., May 6, 1892. He was a son of James D. Warren, one of the founders of the "Commercial Advertiser" of Buffalo, and a widely known politician. In 1856, when his father was elected county treasurer, he removed with him to Buffalo, where he received a public-school education, and, after making an extended tour of Europe and studying in Paris, returned to Buffalo and entered the publishing house of Matthews & Warren as a bookkeeper. When his father became sole proprietor of the establishment Orsamus was appointed business manager, and on the death of the elder Warren, in 1886, Orsamus and his brother William formed the firm of James D. Warren's Sons. Orsamus retained the active management of the newspaper till his death, succeeded his father in various political associations, was a member of the State Republican Committee, a delegate to the National Republican Convention in 1888, a member for eight years of the executive committee of the State Associated Press and its President in 1891, and at the time of his death was a delegate-elect to the National Republican Convention.

Watkins, Albert Barnes, educator, born in Naples, N. Y., in 1838; died in Albany, N. Y., March 18, 1892. He educated himself, and while teaching in Fairfield Seminary, Herkimer County, N. Y., studied bookkeeping, mathematics, French, and Latin. He was graduated at Amherst College in 1863, was instructor in Greek in Fairfield Seminary several years, and was principal of the Collegiate Institute in Adams, N. Y., from 1870 till 1882. During this period he was a member of a committee of fifteen educators appointed to secure legislative aid for academies. In 1882 he was elected President of the New York State Teachers' Association, and was appointed by the regents of the university State Inspector of Teachers' Classes, and in 1884 he was elected assistant secretary of the university. He prepared a history of the teachers' training classes for the regents' historical and statistical record, edited the "Regents' Academic syllabus" (1888; revised edition, 1891), and presented at the university convocations notable papers, including those on "The State and Higher Education" and "The Teaching of Literature in Secondary Schools."

Watson, Sereno, botanist, born in East Windsor Hill, Conn., Dec. 1, 1826; died in Cambridge, Mass., March

9, 1892. He was graduated at Yale in 1847, and thereafter taught in various places in New England, in

Pennsylvania, and in New York, and at intervals studied medicine at home and in the medical department of theUniversity of the City New of York. Also he served as a tutor in Iowa College, Grinnell, Iowa, but relinquished teaching to complete his medical studies under his brother, Dr. Louis Watson, in Quincy, Ill., where he spent the years 1853–'55. For a short time he practiced medicine, but in January, 1856, he accepted the appointment of Secretary of the Planters' Insurance Company in Greensboro, Ala., which place he held until April, 1861. The breaking out of the civil war led to his return to the North, where he engaged in various literary pursuits, and for several years was associated with Dr. Henry Barnard in the publication of the "Journal of Education" in Hartford, Conn. During his appointment in Alabama he became interested in botany, and in 1867 went to California, where he met Clarence King, who, when the United States Geological Exploration of the Fortieth Parallel was organized, appointed Dr. Watson as a volunteer aid to the exploration, and in March, 1868, he succeeded Prof. William W. Bailey in the office of botanist. He continued in the field until 1869, when he settled in New Haven and began the examination of the material which he had accumulated in the herbarium of Prof. Daniel C. Eaton, but a year later removed to Cambridge, where, in the herbarium of Prof. Asa Gray, he completed his work, the results of which were published as vol. v, on "Botany," in the "Reports of the Geological Exploration of the Fortieth Parallel" (Washington, 1871). Subsequently much of the botanical work of the "Geographical and Geological Explorations and Surveys West of the One Hundredth Meridian" was sent to him by Prof. Ferdinand V. Hayden, and in 1880 his services were again sought by the Government, and he was assigned to the procuring of special information for the forest department of the United States census of that year. The results of these labors were published in various Government reports and in specially reprinted monographs. Meanwhile, in 1874, when the work of Prof. Gray was divided among his assistants, the office of curator of the herbarium was given to Dr. Watson, which place he then held until his death. During 1881–'84 he was instructor of phytography, and subsequent to the death of Prof. Gray, in 1888, the systematic work at the herbarium was conducted by Dr. Watson. He also took up the editing of the unpublished "Synoptical Flora of North America," and with Prof. John M. Coulter he prepared a revised edition of Dr. Gray's "Manual of the Botany of the Northern United States." His own work included a "Bibliographical Index to North American Botany; Part I, Polypetala" (Washington, 1878), and with William H. Brewer and Asa Gray he prepared the "Botany of California" (2 vols., Cambridge, 1876, 1880), forming part of the series of the geological survey of California. The revising and editing of the "Manual of the Mosses of North America" (Boston, 1880), originally prepared by Leo Lesquereux and Thomas P. James, was intrusted to him. Also, under the title of "Contributions to American Botany," he published the results of special studies made by him, perhaps the most important of which was that on the plants collected by Dr. Edward Palmer in southwestern Texas and northern Mexico. These appeared chiefly in the "Proceedings of the American Academy of Arts and Sciences," and he also contributed to the "American Naturalist," as well as to other scientific periodicals. He was an assistant editor of the "Century Dictionary," in charge of the botany. In 1878 Iowa College conferred on him the degree of Ph. D., and in 1889 he was chosen to the National Academy of Sciences. He was a member of scientific societies, and a fellow of the American Association for the Advancement of Science, and of the American Academy of Arts and Sciences.

Watts, Thomas H., lawyer, born in Montgomery, Ala., in 1820; died there, Sept. 16, 1892. He was graduated at the University of Virginia in 1840, and ad-

mitted to the bar in his native city. He was elected to the Legislature in 1842, and to the State Senate in 1853, and represented Montgomery County in the secession convention. He entered the Confederate army as colonel of the 17th Alabama Regiment. In 1862 he was appointed Attorney-General in the Confederate Cabinet, and in 1863 was elected Governor of Alabama.

Wells, William, military officer, born in Waterbury, Vt., Dec. 14, 1837; died in New York city, April 29, 1892. He received an academical education in Vermont and New Hampshire, and engaged in commercial business. In September, 1861, he enlisted in the 1st Vermont Cavalry as a private, and was chosen 1st lieutenant Oct. 14, and captain Nov. 18, of the same year. On Oct. 30, 1862, he was promoted major, and he took part in the Shenandoah campaign with Gen. Banks, and in the Virginia campaign with Gen. Pope, after which he served in the cavalry corps of the Army of the Potomac till August, 1864, when he was detailed to duty in the Shenandoah valley under Gen. Sheridan, whence he returned to the Army of the Potomac in March, 1865. During his connection with the latter army he commanded the 2d brigade of the 3d Cavalry Division, and for some time the division itself. From June, 1865, till he was mustered out of the service, on Jan. 15, 1866, he commanded the 1st Separate Brigade of the 2d Army Corps at Fairfax Courthouse. He was promoted colonel of his regiment June 4, 1864, brevetted brigadier-general of Volunteers Feb. 22, 1865, and major-general March 30 following, and was promoted full brigadier-general May 14, of the same year. He was Adjutant-General of Vermont in 1866–'72, collector of internal revenue 1872–'85, and State Senator 1886–'87.

West, Mary Allen, philanthropist, born in Galesburg, Ill., in 1837; died in Tokio, Japan, Dec. 1, 1892. She received a common-school education, prepared herself for teaching, and prior to the civil war was superintendent of schools in Knox County, Ill., for nine years. During the war she was Secretary of the Soldiers' Aid Society, and accomplished great good by providing support for the widows and children of soldiers. In the early part of the temperance crusade in the West she became actively interested in the cause and was elected President of the Illinois Woman's Christian Temperance Union. In 1885 she succeeded Mrs. Mary B. Willard as editor in chief of the "Union Signal." Soon after this she removed to Chicago, and was elected President of the Illinois Woman's Press Association. At the time of her death Miss West was taking a trip to recuperate her health, and was spending a few months in Japan, working in the temperance cause, lecturing, and establishing temperance organizations. She was engaged as special correspondent of the "Inter-Ocean" of Chicago, and the first of her letters was published after her death.

Wheildon, William Wilder, journalist, born in Boston, Oct. 17, 1800; died in Concord, Mass., Jan. 7, 1892. In 1825 he became a legislative reporter on the Boston "Statesman," and in 1827 established the "Bunker Hill Aurora" in Charlestown, which he published for forty-four years. In 1828–'29 he studied law, but he never sought admission to the bar, and in 1846 removed to Concord. His publications include: "Curiosities of History," "Siege and Evacuation of Boston and Charlestown, with a Brief Account of Pre-Revolutionary Buildings," "Sentry or Beacon Hill, its Beacon and Monument," "Paul Revere's Signal Lanterns," and a "New History of the Battle of Bunker Hill," in which he undertook to correct several alleged errors in Frothingham's and Lewis's accounts.

White, Charles A., song writer, born in Taunton, Mass., in 1830; died in Boston, Mass., Jan. 18, 1892. He was brought up on a farm, had a natural liking for music, and made his first violin out of a cigar box, when he was twelve years old. When sixteen years old he became acquainted with an English teacher of dancing, who taught him both to dance and to play the violin, and when the United States Naval Academy was removed to Newport he became professor of dancing there. Up to this time he had composed songs, but had never published any. About 1858 he formed a partnership with a friend, at that time clerk in the music-publishing house of Oliver Ditson & Co., and engaged in the same business in Boston. The first success of the friends was with the old and well-known melody "Shoo Fly," and Mr. White's first original composition was "Put me in my Little Bed," of which he wrote both melody and words. This was followed by "Come, Birdie, come," "The Old Home ain't what it used to be," "Moonlight on the Lake," "When 'tis Moonlight," "When 'tis Starlight," "O Restless Sea," "Only tired," his latest composition, and the widely known "Marguerite." Mr. White's songs have been translated into many languages.

Whitefield, Edwin, artist, born in England in 1816; died in Boston, Mass., Dec. 26, 1892. He came to the United States in early youth, spent several years along the banks of the Hudson river, went to Minnesota when the Territory was but little more than a wooded wilderness, and subsequently, crossing into Canada, began his life work of making illustrations of all cities and towns possessing historical interest or picturesque elements. From Canada he returned to the United States, and, till within a few days of his death, was constantly at work in the one line. He was author and publisher of very many pictures of cities and towns in the United States, in Canada, and in England, those in the latter country being selected because of their relations to New England. One of his most widely known drawings was a large view of Boston and the inner harbor, published in 1848; and at the time of his death he was superintending the printing of his last work, "The Homes of Our Ancestors in Massachusetts." He had sketched all the noted old buildings in the United States, and left unpublished a large mass of colored sketches and descriptive manuscript.

Whiting, Daniel P., military officer, born in Troy, N. Y., in 1808; died in Washington, D. C., Aug. 2, 1892. He was graduated at the United States Military Academy, and appointed 2d lieutenant 7th United States Infantry in 1832; was promoted captain in 1845, major 10th Infantry in 1862; was retired on account of disability from long service and exposure in the line of duty in November, 1863, but was in command of Fort Mifflin, Pa., during the greater part of 1864. His army service included frontier and garrison duty, participation in the defense of Fort Brown, the battles of Monterey and Cerro Gordo, and the siege of Vera Cruz, in the Mexican War, service in the Seminole War in Florida, and duty on the examining board. He published the "Army Portfolio," a series of views illustrating the Mexican War.

Wilkie, Francis Bangs, journalist, born in West Charlton, Saratoga County, N. Y., in 1832; died in Chicago, Ill., April 12, 1892. He was graduated at Union College in 1857, removed to Davenport, Iowa, and engaged in journalism in 1859, and subsequently was connected with the "Herald" in Dubuque till the beginning of the civil war, when he went South as a war correspondent. In Macon City, Mo., he established a paper called "Our Whole Nation," in a deserted newspaper office, which he conducted only a short time, and then became one of the war correspondents of the New York "Times," which he served in the field for four years. After the war he was for seventeen years a leading writer on the Chicago "Times," using the pen name of "Poliuto," and was the organizer and first President of the Chicago Press Club. Mr. Wilkie was author of a "History of Davenport," "Walks about Chicago," "The History of Great Inventions," "Sketches beyond the Sea," "A Year among the Cockneys," "Pen and Powder," "The Gambler," and "The Waif."

Williamson, Benjamin, jurist, born in Elizabeth, N. J., in 1808; died there, Dec. 2, 1892. He was a son of Isaac Halsted Williamson, a former judge, Governor; and Chancellor of New Jersey, and president of the convention that revised the State Constitution. He was graduated at Princeton in 1827, was admitted to the bar in 1830, was soon afterward appointed prosecutor of the pleas of Essex County, was appointed Chancellor of the State in 1852, and held the office till 1860. In the latter year he was a delegate-at-large to the Democratic National Convention, in 1861 was a commissioner from New Jersey to the Peace Congress, and in 1863 lacked but a few votes of being elected United States Senator. He had been the counsel for the Central Railroad of New Jersey for many years.

Wilson, Matthew, painter, born in London, England, July 17, 1814; died in Brooklyn, N. Y., Feb. 23, 1892. He was a nephew of Samuel Wilson, once Lord Mayor of London. He came to the United States in 1832, studied painting, and made a specialty of portraiture. Among the persons of whom he painted portraits were Presidents William Henry Harrison, Lincoln, and Arthur, and several members of their Cabinets, Albert Gallatin, Attorney-General Brewster, and three generations of the family of Gov. Fairbanks, of Vermont. He resided alternately in Brooklyn and Philadelphia.

Winslow, John Flack, manufacturer, born in Bennington, Vt., Nov. 5, 1810; died in Poughkeepsie, N. Y., March 10, 1892. He received a private-school education, engaged in commercial business in New York city, and in 1837 formed a partnership with Erastus Corning, at Albany, N. Y., which was continued under various firm names for thirty years, and which controlled the Albany and Rensselaer Iron Works. This firm introduced the manufacture of Bessemer steel into the United States, and made the first steel rails in America. Besides large contracts for railroads and the United States Government, the firm contracted for the construction of Capt. Ericsson's famous "Monitor," which, by dividing the labor of turning out the plate work with another firm, was begun in October, 1861, and delivered to the Government on March 5, 1862, at a cost of $250,000. Mr. Winslow was President of the Rensselaer Polytechnic Institute in 1863–'67, retired from active business in the latter year, and was a presidential elector in 1888.

Withers, David Dunham, turfman, born in New York city, Jan. 22, 1822; died there, Feb. 18, 1892. He was educated in the public schools, was associated for some time with his father in the banking business, represented the business of Howland & Aspinwall in the South, and in 1846 went into business for himself as a cotton planter near Natchez. He met with success, and had so many interests, North and South, at the breaking out of the civil war that he resided in Paris through the struggle to avoid taking sides with either party. Mr. Withers first became known on the turf in 1866, when he bought out the runner "Vespucius," and since 1870 he had been one of the best-known breeders in the United States, his stock farm at Brookdale, N. J., being a model in size, arrangement, and management, and the home of one of the best collections of high-bred horses in any country. He was an original director of the American Jockey Club, chairman of the Board of Control of Racing, a member of the New York and Coney Island Jockey Clubs, and an honorary member of the Jockey Club of Paris. Because of his thorough knowledge of racing matters and the widespread confidence in his integrity, he was frequently in demand for judge at race meetings of more than usual interest. At his Brookdale farm he possessed an extensive library on horse racing and breeding. He made a large fortune out of his cotton plantation and his stock farm.

Wood, James, military officer, born in New York in 1812; died in Dansville, N. Y., Feb. 24, 1892. He was graduated at Union College, was admitted to the bar, and settled in Geneseo to practice, where he had since resided, in 1844. He was district-attorney of Livingston County for several years, and State Senator for two terms. He entered the national army as colonel of the 136th New York Volunteers, and after distinguishing himself in various engagements, was mustered out of the service at the close of the war with the rank of brevet-major-general of Volunteers.

Wood, Walter Abbott, manufacturer, born in Mason, N. H., Oct. 23, 1815; died in Hoosick Falls, N. Y., Jan. 15, 1892. He received a common-school education, served an apprenticeship in his father's plow and wagon manufactory, removed to Hoosick Falls in 1835, and, after working for some time as a machinist, established himself as a manufacturer of reapers, mowers, and binders. He devised many improvements in agricultural implements, and was so successful that in 1858 he established an office in London and began supplying implements for the European market. He received first prizes for exhibits at the World's Fairs in London, Paris, Vienna, and Philadelphia, and was honored by Queen Victoria, Napoleon III, and Francis Joseph of Austria. He never held public office till 1878, when he was elected to Congress from the 17th New York District as a Republican. He was re-elected in 1880, and served on the committees on Public Expenditures and on Expenditures in the Interior Department.

Wray, Mary Retan, actress, born in Ridgefield, Conn., in 1804; died in Newtown village, Long Island, N. Y., Oct. 5, 1892. She married Mr. Wray in 1826, and soon afterward made her first appearance on the stage in the Chatham Street Theatre, New York city, as a dancer. Subsequently she made an engagement at the Old Bowery Theatre, which lasted for six years, and during this time she frequently played with Junius Brutus Booth. She supported Edwin Forrest in " Macbeth " in the Walnut Street Theatre, Philadelphia : made a Southern tour in a company in which Joseph Jefferson and John Ellsler were engaged ; in 1848 was a member of the Seguin Opera Company ; and in 1864 retired from the stage. She was for more than thirty-five years a member of the American Dramatic Fund, and was said to be the oldest representative of the American stage.

Wyant, Alexander H., landscape painter, born in Port Washington, Ohio, Jan. 11, 1836; died in New York city, Nov. 29, 1892. In early youth he showed a strong taste for drawing and painting, and was enabled to study in Carlsruhe, Dusseldorf, and London. In 1864 he opened a studio in New York city ; in 1865 exhibited his first painting at the National Academy of Design, in 1868 was elected an associate of the academy, and in 1869 an academician. He was one of the earliest members of the American Society of Painters in Water Colors, and a member of the Society of American Artists. Among his pictures in oil were : " Staten Island from the Jersey Meadows " (1867) ; " Scene on the Upper Susquehanna " (1869) ; " The Bird's Nest " and " A Changeful Day " (1870) ; " Shore of Lake Champlain " and " A Fool on the Ausable " (1871) ; " Fort at New Bedford " (1874) ; " A View on Lake George " and " A Midsummer Retreat " (1875) ; " Macgillicuddy's Reeks " and " The Wilds of the Adirondacks " (1876) ; " An Old Clearing " (1877) ; " An Old Road—Evening," and " Pool in the North Woods." To the water-color exhibition he contributed : " Scene on the Upper Little Miami " (1867) ; " A Reminiscence of West Virginia " and " Trees and Stuff in New Jersey " (1869) ; " New Jersey Meadows " (1870) ; " Gathering Shells " (1872) ; " Late Autumn, Ausable River " (1876) ; " Scene in Massachusetts " and " An Irish Lake Scene " (1877 ; " Reminiscences of the Connecticut." " Mountains in Kerry," and others (1878). His " Sunset on the Prairie " was in the Centennial Exhibition (1876) ; and his " Reminiscences of the Connecticut," in water color, and " New England Landscape," in oil, were in the Paris Exhibition (1878).

Young, Van Buren, jurist, born in Flat Creek, Bath County, Ky., Jan. 28, 1837; died in South Frankfort, Ky., Feb. 27, 1892. He received a common-school education, studied law in Frankfort, and at the university in Lexington, received a diploma from Transylvania College, and took a further course of private instruction. In 1856 he removed to Leavenworth, Kan., and was engaged in real-estate business till

1860, when he returned to his native county to practice law. Soon afterward he was nominated for presidential elector on the Douglas ticket, and the same year was elected to the Legislature. Before the close of his term he resigned, and was elected clerk of the circuit court and appointed master in chancery. While serving as clerk he was appointed Commonwealth attorney. About 1883 he removed to Mount Sterling, and was elected judge of the Supreme Court of Kentucky; removed to Frankfort, and was chief justice of the court at the time of his death.

OBITUARIES, FOREIGN.

Adams, John Couch, an English astronomer, born in Lidcot, Cornwall, June 5, 1819 ; died in Cambridge, June 21, 1892. He was graduated from St. John's College, Cambridge, in 1843, as senior wrangler, was elected a fellow, and became a mathematical tutor. For several years he was engaged in difficult and delicate observations for the solution of the problem of the irregularities in the motions of Uranus, and was the joint discoverer with Leverrier of the planet Neptune that caused the perturbations, the existence and position of which he also predicted from his calculations. For many years he was Lowndean Professor of Astronomy at Cambridge University and director of the observatory.

Airy, Sir George Biddell, an English astronomer, born at Alnwick, Northumberland, June 27, 1801 ; died at Greenwich, Jan. 2, 1892. He was educated at Celebester Grammar School and Trinity College, Cambridge, graduating from the latter in 1823 as senior wrangler. In 1825 he discovered the optical malady since called astigmatism, and suggested its remedy. In 1826 he became Lucasian professor at Trinity, and from 1827 to 1836 delivered lectures on experimental philosophy, in the course of which he advocated the undulatory theory of light. In 1828 he was elected Plumian professor, and took entire charge of the Cambridge Observatory. In 1835 he became Astronomer Royal, and introduced at Greenwich the altazimuth, the water telescope, transit circle, and other improvements. For fifty years he was recognized as the adviser of the Government on scientific topics of general interest. He investigated the disturbance of the compass in iron ships, and provided a method for correcting the irregularities. From experiments by him were obtained data for weighing the earth and determining the theory of gravity, as well as rendering more exact ancient chronologies. He received from the Universities of Oxford, Cambridge, and Edinburgh the degrees of D. C. L. and LL. D., and was a Fellow of the Royal Astronomical Society and a member of many home and foreign scientific institutes and societies. In 1872 he was created a Knight Commander of the Bath, and in 1881 resigned his post as Astronomer Royal, which he had held for forty-six years. On this occasion he was awarded a pension of £1,100 per annum by the Treasury. He published " Gravitation," originally written for the " Penny Cyclopædia " ; " Mathematical Lectures " ; " Ipswich Lectures on Astronomy " ; ' Treatise on Errors of Observation " (1861) ; " The Invasion of Britain by Julius Cæsar" (1865) ; " Treatise on Sound" (1869) ; " Treatise on Magnetism " (1870) ; " Trigonometry " ; " Figure of the Earth " ; " Tides and Waves "; " Algebraical and Numerical Theory of Errors "; " Lunar Distance " (London, 1881) ; " Terrestrial Magnetic Force in the Horizontal Plane at Greenwich " (London, 1886). He also contributed many technical papers to scientific journals.

Albert Victor Christian Edward, Prince, Duke of Clarence, eldest son of the Prince and Princess of Wales, and next in succession after his father to the British throne, born at Frogmore House, Jan. 8, 1864 : died in Sandringham House, Jan. 14, 1892. He was a seven-months' child, but not a weakly one. When he was thirteen years old he was sent, with his brother George, who was his junior by seventeen months, on board the " Britannica." where the boys underwent the training of midshipmen, while still receiving instruction from their governor, Rev. John Neale Dalton. When they had served two years they were sent with Mr. Dalton on a cruise round the world in the naval steamer "Bacchante," which lasted nearly three years, during which they visited many lands, and while on shipboard continued their studies and their naval exercises. In 1883, still accompanied by Mr. Dalton as tutor, he entered Trinity College, Cambridge. When he left the university and had passed his twenty-first birthday, he went to Aldershot to learn the duties of a military officer, being attached to the 10th Hussars. In 1889 he visited India, and on his return, in May, 1890, he was admitted to the peerage under the title of Duke of Clarence and Avondale and Earl of Athlone. He was entered as a bencher of the Middle Temple, and became an active Free Mason, like his father. In the last three years of his life he appeared many times in public, and made short moral speeches at the laying of corner stones, the opening of benevolent institutions, and the like ceremonial occasions. Only six weeks before his death the announcement was made of his betrothal to his cousin, Princess Victoria Mary of Teck.

Alexandrine, Grand Duchess Dowager of **Mecklenburg,** born Feb. 23, 1803; died in Rostock, April 21, 1892. She was a Princess of Prussia, daughter of King Friedrich Wilhelm III and a sister of Kaiser Wilhelm I. On May 25, 1822, she was married to the heir to the Grand Duke of Mecklenburg, Paul Friedrich, who succeeded to the throne on the death of his grandfather, in 1837, and died in 1842, being succeeded by their son Friedrich Franz, born in 1823, who married a Princess of Reuss in 1849. The second child, the Duchess Luise, married Prince Hugo Windischgrätz in the same year, and the youngest, Duke Wilhelm, married his cousin Alexandrine, daughter of Prince Albrecht of Prussia, in 1865.

Allen, Henry, an English Congregational minister, born in Welton, near Hull, Yorkshire, Oct. 13, 1818; died in London, Oct. 16, 1892. He was educated for the ministry in Cheshunt College, and in 1848 became associate minister, and, on the death of the Rev. T. Lewis, pastor of Union Chapel, Islington. Originally founded in 1801 by a union of evangelical Churchmen and nonconformists, the church increased steadily in numbers and importance during Dr. Allon's ministry of forty-six years. The large building erected in 1877 accommodated 1,800 persons, and its missions many hundred more. He gave much study to the improvement of the musical part of the service of his denomination, editing the "Congregational Psalmist," which advanced the movement considerably. From 1865 to 1886, in addition to his pastoral labors, he edited the "British Quarterly Review." He published biographies of Rev. Thomas Binney and Rev. J. Sherman, besides a great number of magazine articles. He received the degree of D.D. from Yale in 1871, and in 1885 from St. Andrew's.

Anderledy, Anton, General of the Jesuit order, born in Brieg, canton of Valais, Switzerland, in 1819; died in Fiesole, Italy, Jan. 18, 1892. He entered the Society of Jesus at the age of nineteen, became Professor of Theology at Freiburg, and was there in 1847 when the Jesuits were driven out of Switzerland. Taking refuge first in Savoy and then in America, he was the head of a mission on Lake Erie, and returned to Europe in 1850 to teach theology in Belgium, whence he went to Cologne, and then to Paderborn. He took a very prominent part in the missionary work that was carried on there among the German people. In 1863 he became Professor of Moral Theology in the college at Maria Laach, of which he was made rector. He was elected provincial of the German branch of the Jesuit society. In 1870 he became the assistant of Father Beckx, General of the Jesuits; in 1883 was made his coadjutor or vicar-general; and on his retirement, in 1887, was elected to succeed him. He lived retired from the world in the old convent in which he died, where he had his official residence. When he was made head of the society there was a strong opposition to him among the members of the order belonging to the Latin nations. His sagacity and activity are shown by the extraordinary successes and development of the order during the past twenty years.

Annibale, Cardinal **Giuseppi,** an Italian prelate, born in Borbona in 1815; died in Rome, July 19, 1892. He was created a cardinal priest on Feb. 11, 1889, and filled the office of prefect of the Congregation of Indulgences and Holy Relics.

Anselme, Dom, a French monk, born near Cambrai in 1822; died in Grenoble, Oct. 7, 1892. His family name was Bruniaux. He joined the Carthusian order in early life, became prior of the monastery at Valbonne, and in 1879 was elected Superior-General and assumed charge of the Grande Chartreuse.

Arago, Étienne, a French dramatist and politician, born in Perpignan, Feb. 9, 1802; died in Paris, March 6, 1892. He was a brother of the illustrious astronomer, a pupil of Sorèze, and was demonstrator of chemistry in Ecole Polytechnique, where he assisted Balzac in his early works, after which he became a dramatic author. More than a hundred pieces were produced under his name, and he collaborated with the principal *vaudevillistes* of his time. In 1847 his republican drama "Les Aristocrates" was brought out at the Théâtre Français. He was a Republican journalist and an enemy of the restored dynasty, an aid-de-camp of Lafayette in 1830, a member of the Constituante in 1848, and director-general of the post office, and as a participator in the affair of June 13, 1849, was sentenced to deportation, but escaped to Belgium. Returning to France in 1859, he became dramatic critic of the "Avenir National." He was Mayor of Paris in 1870, and was elected after his resignation, on Oct. 31, a member of the National Assembly, but refused the seat. In 1878 he was nominated archivist of the École des Beaux Arts; and from 1879 till his death he was the keeper of the Museum of the Luxembourg.

Archibald, Sir Adams George, a Canadian statesman, born in Truro, Nova Scotia, in 1814; died in Halifax, Dec. 14, 1892. He filled many important public offices in Nova Scotia and Canada. In 1867 he was appointed a member of the Canadian Privy Council. In 1870–'72 he was Lieutenant-Governor of Manitoba and the Northwest Territories. He was twice Lieutenant-Governor of Nova Scotia. He was also the author of some historical works.

Argles, Marsham, an English clergyman, born in Hampshire, July 7, 1814; died at Southsea, Nov. 19, 1892. He was educated at Merton College, Oxford, and was ordained deacon in 1837, and priest in 1838. After serving as curate at Bolton, St. Martin-in-the-Fields, and Cranford, he became vicar of Gretton, and in 1842 was made chancellor of the diocese of Peterborough. In 1849 he was appointed canon residentiary of Peterborough Cathedral, and in 1890 succeeded Dr. Perowne as Dean of Peterborough. At this period the cathedral was undergoing extensive restoration and refitting, a labor in which he was greatly interested. Before he became dean he had subscribed generously toward the rebuilding of the lantern, and since 1890 had given to the cathedral a new pulpit, bishop's throne, and the beautiful and costly marble pavement of the choir. He gave also large sums for other cathedral improvements and for educational purposes. He was buried at Barnack, of which he was rector for almost forty years, and which owes the restoration of its famous Norman church to his munificence. In 1839 he was married to Margaret Davys, daughter of the late Bishop Davys. His wife and one son (Canon Argles of York) and four daughters survive him. The present fine condition of the interior of Peterborough Cathedral is due in great measure to Dean Argles.

Atkinson, Sir Harry Albert, a New Zealand statesman, born in Great Britain about 1830; died in Auckland, June 28, 1892. He emigrated to New Zealand in 1855, and rendered important services in the Maori war as captain of a band of volunteers, for which he was advanced to the rank of major, and on Nov. 24, 1864, having been elected to Parliament in the previous year, was made Minister of Defense in the

Cabinet of Sir Frederick Weld. It fell to him to organize a militia system which should supply the protection previously afforded by British troops, for the British Government had decided to leave the colony to its own military resources. In 1874 he took office under Sir Julius Vogel, whom in 1876 he replaced as Premier and Colonial Treasurer. In 1879 he again occupied the post of Colonial Treasurer, and in 1883 became Premier. In 1884 he retired on Aug. 18, and on Aug. 28 came back when the Vogel ministry had received a rebuff, but two days later was defeated, in turn, on a vote of confidence. In 1887 he took office again as Premier and Colonial Treasurer. In 1890 he retired from active work on account of bad health, but did not resign the premiership until his party sustained a defeat in the elections of January, 1891, having previously nominated himself President of the Legislative Council.

Bailly, Antoine Nicolas, a French architect, born in Paris, June 6, 1810; died there, Jan. 1, 1892. His tastes manifesting themselves early, he entered the École des Beaux Arts, and in 1829 became the pupil of Duban. He was made architect surveyor of Paris in 1834, and Government architect in 1844. He was decorated with the Legion of Honor in 1853, and in 1868 was made officer of the Legion of Honor, and in 1881 commander. In 1875 he was elected a member of the Academy des Beaux Arts in place of Labrouste, and on the occasion of the Vienna Exposition of 1878 the Austrian Government conferred on him the order of the Iron Crown. After his becoming Government architect he was placed in charge of the works in the dioceses of Bourges, Valence, and Digne. At Bourges he completely restored the cathedral and the house of Jacques Cœur, now the Palais de Justice; at Valence he rebuilt the tower of the cathedral in 1862; at Digne he almost rebuilt the cathedral, remodeling the façade and directing the interior decorations. While some of these works were in progress he was made architect in chief of the third and sixth divisions of public works of the city of Paris, and in this capacity he built the Tribunal of Commerce, his most noted work, the *mairie* of the Fourth Arrondissement, and reconstructed the Lycée St. Louis. Among other works of note by him are the Hôtel Schneider, the chateau of M. Lagoretto at Choisy-le-Roi, and the restoration of the chateaux of Cany and Theuville in the Department of Loire Inférieure. He was one of the foremost architects of his time.

Baragnon, Louis Numa, a French politician, born in Nîmes in 1835; died there, May 19, 1892. He was educated as a lawyer and practiced his profession, becoming also a journalist. In September, 1870, he signed an address as municipal councilor welcoming the republic, and a month afterward entered the Chamber as a Royalist, becoming a zealous supporter of the Comte de Chambord. He helped to overthrow Thiers in 1873, and was made Under Secretary of the Interior, and subsequently of Justice. He lost his seat in 1876, and when he was returned in 1877 the election was annulled on the ground of undue influence. Baragnon was notoriously impetuous and passionate in his manner of debating, and constantly interrupted the Republican speakers in the Chamber. In 1878 he was elected a life Senator.

Barbedienne, Ferdinand, a French bronze founder, born in Saint-Martin de Fresnoy, Calvados, in 1810; died in Paris, March 22, 1892. He founded the great establishment for the commercial production of artistic bronzes in 1838, in company with Achille Collas, and from the beginning he gave employment to not less than 300 artists and workmen. In 1874, after the Vienna Exposition, he was made a commander of the Legion of Honor.

Baron, Vincent Alfred, a French sculptor and actor, born in Meximieux, Ain, in 1820; died in Paris, May 7, 1892. He was the son of a painter of panoramas, and at the age of fifteen he went up to Paris, where he attended the Conservatoire and the École des Beaux Arts simultaneously. He played at the Odéon, the Ambigu, the Gaieté, and the Porte-St.-Martin

theatres, creating the *rôles* of Courriol, in the "Courrier de Lyon," Ascanio, in "Benvenuto Cellini," and others. At the same time he exhibited portraits and medallions that were highly esteemed, among them portraits of Rachel and Deburau.

Baross de Bellus, Gabriel von, a Hungarian statesman, born in Pruszina, June 6, 1848; died in Buda-Pesth, May 9, 1892. He was a scion of a family belonging to the small nobility, and was educated for the civil service, studying law in the university at Buda-Pesth. While a court officer in his native county of Trencsin he founded a newspaper for the advocacy of the Magyarization of Transylvania, and in 1875 was elected a member of Parliament. He took an active part in the debates, was reporter in 1877 of the committee which considered the tariff union with Austria, which he had at first opposed, and was for several years a member of the Hungarian Delegation, in which he was reporter of the army budget. Becoming Secretary of the Ministry of Communications in 1883, he labored for the development of the system of State railroads, and in 1886 was selected by Tisza to succeed Baron Kemenyi as Minister of Communications, Industry, and Commerce. Count Szapary, who succeeded Tisza as Prime Minister in March, 1890, retained him in this post.

Battaglini, Francesco, an Italian prelate, born in 1823; died July 8, 1892. He was Archbishop of Bologna, and in 1885 was made a cardinal.

Behnke, Emil, a German voice culturist, born in Stettin in 1836; died in Ostend, Sept. 17, 1892. He went to England when a young man, began to lecture on the mechanism of the voice at the age of thirty, and applied scientific principles to the practical work of the teaching of singing and the restoration of voices impaired by false training with such successful results, that he was accepted as the leading specialist in all matters relating to the voice. He wrote, with Mr. Lenox, "Voice, Song, and Speech" (London, 1883), which went through a dozen editions, and was translated into French and Spanish. His "Vocal Training Exercises" was still more successful.

Bleibtreu, Georg, a German painter, born in Xanten, March 27, 1828; died in Berlin, Oct. 16, 1892. He began to study painting in Düsseldorf at the age of fifteen, and afterward was a pupil of Theodor Hildebrandt. He accompanied the staff of the Crown Prince in the campaign of 1870–'71, and at Versailles he painted a series of pictures representing battles that had taken place, and other scenes of the war, among them one representing the entry of the Crown Prince into Freschweiler after the battle of Wörth, and one representing Count Reille presenting King Wilhelm with the sword of Napoleon III.

Bodenstedt, Friedrich Martin von, a German author, born in Hanover, April 22, 1819; died in Wiesbaden, April 19, 1892. At the age of twenty-one he became tutor to the Prince of Galitzin, at Moscow, and later traveled through Armenia, Caucasia, the Crimea, Turkey, Asia Minor, and the Ionian Islands. It was by these travels that he gained such exceptional knowledge of the Slav and Oriental poetry. During this period he wrote "One Thousand and One Days in the Orient," which first established his fame. In 1853 he took up his residence with the Duke of Gotha, and in 1858 was appointed to the chair of Slav Language and Literature at the University of Munich. The most brilliant of his numerous poetical works is "Lieder des Mirza Schaffy," which has been translated into almost every European language. He devoted much attention to English literature of the Elizabethan period, which is evidenced by his "Shakespeare's Contemporaries and their Works," while his "Shakespeare's Diary" and "Shakespeare's Female Characters" show his intimate knowledge of the English poet's works, his translation of Shakespeare into German being regarded as the best Germany ever had. At various periods he was connected with the political press as managing editor and writer, and in 1850 he represented Schleswig-Holstein at the Peace Congress in Frankfurt.

Bojanowski, Victor von, President of the German Imperial Patent Office, born June 4, 1831; died March 29, 1892. He was descended from a Polish noble family long settled in Germany, and was the son of a Prussian general. He studied law in Berlin and Halle, entered the civil service, and in 1865 went as Prussian consul to Moscow, whence he was called to St. Petersburg as Secretary of Legation, and in 1869 was appointed consul there. In 1873 he went as consul-general to England. He was distinguished for a minute technical knowledge of commercial and industrial matters of all kinds. In 1883 he was appointed Director in the Ministry of Foreign Affairs, but broke down under the load of work, and in 1885–'88 was consul-general at Buda-Pesth, returning to Berlin in 1888 to take charge of the Patent Office, in which he was instrumental in bringing about a reform of the patent laws and a reorganization of the department satisfactory to practical industrialists.

Bouvier, Alexis, a French novelist, born in Paris, Jan. 15, 1836; died there, May 13, 1892. He was the son of a working bronze founder, and while he learned the trade of a chaser he wrote songs and *vaudevilles.* The democratic song of "La Canaille" made him famous. Soon afterward he wrote or helped to write a number of operettas that were given in the theatres of the *faubourgs.* Later he turned his attention to novels, and in this field he won his chief success. The most popular were "La Femme du Mort"; "Les Pauvres"; "La Grande Iza," with its sequels, "Iza la Ruine" and "La Mort d'Iza"; "Le Fils d'Antony"; and "La Rousse."

Bramwell, Lord, an English jurist, born in London, 1808; died in Edenbridge, May 9, 1892. He was the eldest son of a London banker, and after leaving the private school in which he was educated entered his father's bank, studied law, was called to the bar in 1838, and won a high reputation as a special pleader and a learned lawyer. He served on a commission to study reforms of common-law procedure in 1847, was made a Queen's counsel in 1851, and in 1856 was appointed a baron of the Exchequer. The disfavor with which suitors looked upon this court disappeared, owing in a large measure to his plain and sensible methods. In 1876 he was made a Lord Justice of Appeal. He had an important share in the framing of the limited-liability law and several judicature acts. Of all the English judges he was the most popular. In 1881 he retired from the bench, and in 1882 was raised to the peerage as Baron Bramwell of Hever.

Brand, Sir Henry B. W., Viscount Hampden, ex-Speaker of the British House of Commons, born in 1815; died in Pau, March 15, 1892. He held a number privy of official posts, among them that of keeper of the seal of the Prince of Wales, and had acquitted himself as a useful member of the Liberal party when he was chosen Speaker. He retained that post amid all the changes of government until he retired, in 1884, and was advanced to the House of Lords. In the memorable period of Irish obstruction he presided over the House with a degree of tact, decision, and impartiality that commanded general admiration.

Bratiano, Demeter, a Roumanian statesman, born in 1818; died June 21, 1892. He was one of the leaders of the revolutionary movement of 1848, which was frustrated by the interference of Russian and Turkish troops. Banished during the long period of reaction, with his brother Joan and many others of like principles, he joined the band of exiles from all countries which gathered about Mazzini, in London, and sought by writings to make the people of London and Paris acquainted with the situation of the Danubian principalities. With other Roumanian refugees he undertook the publication in Paris of "L'Étoile du Danube," in which he opposed a Russian protectorate and advocated the union of Moldavia and Wallachia. As chief of the Roumanian colony, he laid the cause of his country before Napoleon III and before the English statesmen. When permitted, after the peace of Paris, to return to his own country, he took the most active part in the struggle for the union of the prin-

cipalities, which was carried through in spite of enormous external and internal hindrances, and was one of the principal champions of the Liberal cause and a leader in the overthrow of the Boyar oligarchy, although he was cast into the shade by the genius of his brother, who gradually assumed the leadership of the Liberal party. After he had served as minister in various Liberal governments and had taken an important part in the momentous developments that followed the fall of Cusa, he was sent, after the Berlin Treaty, as the first minister representing Roumania as an independent state at the Porte. When Joan Bratiano, for reasons that have never been historically explained, resigned the prime ministry in 1881, he was succeeded by Demeter, and while he was in office Roumania was declared a kingdom, and Prince Carol crowned King. He was compelled, after three months, to resign the helm of state again into the hands of his brother, who was recalled by the National Liberal party. On account of this a coolness arose between the brothers, which led in time to an open breach. Demeter placed himself at the head of the party of Dissidents, which welcomed all the dissatisfied Liberals, assailed Joan Bratiano with bitter animosity, and went to the length of forming an alliance with the Boyar party, led by Lascar Catargi. The United Opposition thus formed brought about the fall of Joan Bratiano's Cabinet in 1888, the harm done by disrupting the party came home to those who had fomented the feud, and the restoration of unity was brought about, together with a complete reconciliation between the two brothers in the spring of 1890. Demeter Bratiano became president of the central committee of the party, and held that position till the close of his life.

Bruce, John Collingwood, an English archæologist, born in Newcastle, 1805; died in London, April 5, 1892. He was educated at Glasgow University, intending to become a Presbyterian minister, but he afterward left that calling, and was for some years at the head of a school, in which occupation he succeeded his father. In 1858 he retired to private life. A third and revised edition of his most noted work, "The Roman Wall: A Description of the Mural Barrier of the North of England," appeared in 1867. It is a most elaborate and careful work and of undoubted authority. Other books by him are: "Handbook of English History" (1848); "The Bayeux Tapestry elucidated" (London, 1856); "Handbook to Newcastle-on-Tyne" (London, 1863); "The Wallet-Book of the Roman Wall" (London, 1868); "Incised Markings on Stone found in Northumberland, Argyleshire, and Other Places" (London, 1869); "Lapidarium Septentrionale" (edited) (Newcastle, 1875); "Descriptive Catalogue of Antiquities, Chiefly British, at Alnwick Castle" (Newcastle, 1880).

Bucher, Adolf Lothar, a German statesman, born in Neu-Stettin, in 1817; died in Geneva, Switzerland, Oct. 12, 1892. He prepared himself in the University of Berlin for the law, and became a court officer in Pomerania. In 1848 he was elected to the Diet as Deputy for Stolp. He took a prominent part in the legislation that was passed, and in the abolition of the state of siege in Berlin, which resulted in the dissolution of the Chamber. On account of his stand in the taxation conflict in 1850 he was arraigned, and, after his flight to London, was sentenced *in contumaciam* to imprisonment. From London he wrote brilliant political articles for the Berlin "National-Zeitung" and other publications. After the amnesty he returned, and again entered politics as a Radical of socialistic tendencies. Count Bismarck, who knew him and recognized his abilities, induced him to accept office in 1864 in the Foreign Office, and from that time he was the confidential adviser and right-hand man of the Minister-President and Chancellor of the Empire, rising to high posts in the public service.

Burke, Sir J. Bernard, an English genealogist, born in London in 1815; died in Dublin, Dec. 13, 1892. He was educated in the college at Caen, Normandy; was called to the bar at the Middle Temple in 1839,

He edited for many years, at first in conjunction with his father, and alone after his father's death, the "Peerage" and "Baronetage." He was author of "The Commoners of Great Britain and Ireland," afterward republished under the title of "History of the Landed Gentry," "General Armory," "Visitation of Seats," "Family Romance," "Anecdotes of the Aristocracy," "The Historic Lands of England," "Vicissitudes of Families," and "Reminiscences, Ancestral and Anecdotal," besides other books on heraldic, historical and antiquarian subjects. He was appointed Ulster King of Arms in 1853, was knighted in the following year, and had the charge of the arrangements and procedure connected with the ceremonies and pageants of Dublin Castle. He became also keeper of the Irish state papers in 1874.

Butt, Sir **Charles Parker,** an English jurist, born in Gloucester in 1830; died in Wiesbaden, Germany, May 24, 1892. He was called to the bar in 1854, became a Queen's counsel in 1868, entered Parliament in 1880, and in 1883 was appointed to succeed Sir Robert Phillimore as a judge of the Probate, Divorce, and Admiralty Division of the High Court, to the presidency of which he succeeded a year or two before his death. He was particularly strong in admiralty law, and in divorce cases made several decisions in which he created new precedents to fit cases of peculiar hardship.

Caird, Sir **James,** a Scottish economist and agriculturist, born in Stranraer, Wigtownshire, in 1816; died in London, Feb. 10, 1892. He was educated at the high school and University of Edinburgh, and early began the study of agricultural and economic questions. He was an ardent Free Trader, and in 1849 published a treatise on "High Farming as the Best Substitute for Protection." In the autumn of the same year he visited the west and south of Ireland, then suffering from the effects of the famine, and reported on measures for the revival of agricultural enterprise in that country. In 1850 he was appointed commissioner by the "Times" to ascertain the causes of the agricultural depression in England. He described in detail examples of good farming, discussed the condition of the laborer and the relations between landlord and tenants, and called attention to the waste of fertilizing matter from the large towns in his letters, which were afterward published in a volume entitled "English Agriculture in 1850–'51," which was translated into French, German, and Swedish, and was also republished in the United States. In 1858 he published an account of the fertility and possibilities of the Mississippi prairies, which was also translated. In 1852 he was defeated for Parliament in his own district by a majority of one, but was elected in 1857 as the Liberal member for Dartmouth, for which he sat until 1859, when he was elected for Stirling without opposition. He continued to sit for that constituency until 1865. In the session of 1859 he carried a motion that the Scotch census should include inquiry into the housing of the people, from which it was learned that two thirds of the families lived in houses of one or two rooms. On the outbreak of the civil war in the United States he called attention to the possibility of extending the cultivation of cotton to other countries, and visited Algeria and Sicily for that purpose. In 1869 he published a pamphlet on the Irish land question, and articles on "Food for the People." Ten years later he prepared an account of English agriculture, for the French Exposition. He also served on the Indian famine commission, and published an account of its visit to India. In 1889 he became a member of the Board of Agriculture, with the rank of privy councilor. He was knighted in 1865.

Campbell, Sir **Alexander,** a Canadian statesman, born in Yorkshire, England, in 1822; died May 22, 1892. Going to Canada very early in life, he was educated first at Lachine, near Montreal, and afterward at Kingston, Ontario. When of age he was called to the bar of Upper Canada, and in 1856 was created Queen's counsel. In 1858 he entered the Legislative Council of Canada, and was elected Speaker in 1862. He rose to Cabinet rank in 1864, and was Commissioner of Crown Lands for the following three years. As a member of the Quebec Conference he contributed largely to the repeal of the legislative union between the two Canadas by confederation, and was appointed to the Dominion Senate. He was sworn in as a member of the Queen's Privy Council on the original "Dominion Day," July 1, 1867, and took the portfolio of Postmaster-General of Sir John Macdonald's first Federal Cabinet. In 1873 he became Minister of the Interior, but had to resign with the rest of the Cabinet in consequence of the Pacific Railroad scandal later in the same year. On the return of Sir John to power he took up again his first portfolio for a few months, and after a brief tenure of office as Minister of Militia and Defense he was appointed a third time Postmaster-General in 1880. The following year he became Minister of Justice, and in 1887 was appointed Lieutenant-Governor of Ontario. He received his title in 1879, being one of the birthday honors conferred by the Queen.

Campbell, Sir **George,** a Scotch author and Indian administrator, born in 1824; died in Cairo, Egypt, Feb. 18, 1892. He was educated at Edinburgh, St. Andrew's, and Haileybury, entered the service of the East India Company at the age of eighteen, was advanced rapidly, having attracted the attention of Lord Dalhousie, but returned to England on furlough in 1851, and while there published "Modern India" and "India as it may be." Returning to India in 1854, after being called to the bar at the Inner Temple, he held various administrative posts in the Northwest Provinces, was selected as personal assistant by the Governor-General, Lord Canning, and was afterward Judicial and Financial Commissioner of Oudh, Judge of the High Court at Calcutta, and Chief Commissioner of the Central Provinces. Returning to England again in 1868, he wrote a book on land tenures in Ireland. In 1871 he went out to India as Lieutenant-Governor of Bengal. He administered that office with distinguished ability, but resigned it at the end of three years, and went back to England as a member of the India Council. This appointment he gave up in 1875 in order to represent the Kirkcaldy district in Parliament, of which he was a member till his death. He was a laborious legislator and a frequent speaker, yet never gained an influence in Parliament that was at all commensurate with the great reputation he had achieved in India. In 1876 he was an active supporter of Mr. Gladstone's policy in the Eastern question, and published a book on the subject. He interested himself also in colonial and various foreign questions. He visited America twice, and published "White and Black in the United States." On Indian questions as they arose in Parliament he spoke with the weight and authority that his knowledge and experience justified. On the Irish question he was a consistent supporter of Mr. Gladstone. His last published work was "The British Empire," written with special reference to India and the colonies of Great Britain, and issued in 1889.

Carlen, **Emilie Flygare,** a Swedish novelist, born in 1807; died in Stockholm, Feb. 5, 1892. She first began to write in order to help her parents, who were poor. Her first marriage was with the musician Flygare. It proved unhappy, and she obtained a divorce. Her second husband, Carlen, a lawyer and a poet of some merit, died in 1875. She was one of the most prolific of modern writers of fiction, and her works were esteemed by critics, and not only were they very popular in Scandinavia, but many of them were translated into German, and several into English or French, among them "The Confidential Clerk," "The Rose of Tistelen," "A Year of Marriage," "Alma," "A Heroine of Romance," "The Representative," "In Six Weeks," "A Night on Lake Bullar," and "A Name."

Caspari, **Karl Paul,** a Norwegian biblical scholar, born at Dessau, in 1814; died at Christiania about April 11, 1892. Since 1847 he was engaged as docent at the University of Christiania, and since 1857 as professor. The most important of his literary works are: "A Commentary on the Prophet Obadiah," "Contributions to the Introduction into the Book of Isaiah," "Sources to the History of the Symbol of Baptism and of the Rule of Belief," and his "Grammatica Arabica."

Chazal, Baron Emmanuel, a Belgian statesman, born in Tarbes, Department of Hautes-Pyrénées, in 1808; died in Pau, Jan. 26, 1892. He was a son of a member of the French convention who helped Napoleon to escape from Elba, was condemned to death at the restoration, and escaped with his family to Brussels. Young Chazal was one of the foremost champions of Belgian independence in 1830, and after its accomplishment he entered the army, and was rapidly promoted, becoming a general officer in 1842. In 1847 he was made Minister of War in the ministry of Rogier and Frère-Orban, and with short intermissions he remained in this post till 1860. In 1848 he saved the country from revolution by persuading King Leopold to abdicate. In 1859 he carried through the project for the fortification of Antwerp against the opposition of the Clericals, who resisted all his schemes for military reform. He was one of the earliest advocates of universal military service for Belgium. His influence was always great until the Clericals came into power in 1884.

Christophe, Ernest, a French sculptor, died in Paris, Jan. 17, 1892. He was a pupil of Rude. He produced some remarkable allegorical figures, notably the "Comédie Humaine," for which he received a medal in 1876. In this a woman is represented wearing an expression that appears serene and happy; but under this mask is another face drawn with pain, and in the folds of her dress is a viper gnawing her heart. His bronze figure of "Fatality," exhibited in 1885, has a similar subject. His last work was the "Éternelle Enigme," exhibited in 1889.

Child, Theodore, an English writer, born in Liverpool, in 1846; died in Ispahan, Persia, Nov. 2, 1892. He was graduated at Oxford in 1877, and went to Paris as correspondent of the London "Telegraph," and made that city his home, writing anecdotical articles and essays and news budgets on art and literature for American and English magazines and for the London "World" and the New York "Sun." For several years before his death he was the European literary agent for the New York publishing house of Harper Bros. He traveled in Asia and other distant regions, and published a history of the South American republics after visiting them. He had gone to Persia to make studies for a book on India and the Afghan question, and died of cholera.

Cialdini, Enrico, Duke of Gaeta, an Italian soldier, born in Modena, Aug. 8, 1811; died in Leghorn, Sept. 8, 1892. He was educated in a Jesuit school, studied philosophy and medicine in the University of Parma, and in 1831 fought in the insurrection of the Romagna, under Gen. Zucchi. When the rising was suppressed he fled to Paris and resumed there his medical and chemical studies, and translated works of Voltaire and Rousseau into Italian, to earn money for his support. He joined the army of Dom Pedro in 1832, and when the latter was established on the throne of Portugal he remained with his regiment, having been promoted from the ranks to a lieutenancy. In the war against the Carlists, he was made Gen. Durando's adjutant, and afterward he entered the service of the Queen of Spain, as lieutenant-colonel of gendarmes. In 1848 he left this service to take part in the revolution of Lombardy under his old commander, Gen. Durando. He was severely wounded in the battle of Vicenza, and taken prisoner by the Austrians. His next service was in the Crimean War, whither he was sent by the Sardinian Government with the rank of general, and took a prominent part in the battle of Tchernaya. In the war of Italian independence in 1859 he commanded a division, with which he forced the passage of the Sesia, driving the Austrians from their position. For this feat he was made a lieuten-

ant-general. In 1860 he defeated the Papal army under Gen. Lamoricière, at the battle of Castelfidardo. In 1861 he captured Gaeta, which he bombarded for seventeen days, and two weeks after this engagement he took the citadel of Messina, and subsequently he reduced Ancona. He was made a field marshal at the same time as Garibaldi and Fanti, and was placed in charge of the Government of Naples as Viceroy when the war was ended. Intrusted with extraordinary powers, he successfully suppressed brigandage, and after a creditable administration he entered the Italian Senate in 1864. In 1867 he was appointed Minister Plenipotentiary to Vienna, after having taken a prominent part as a commander in the war of 1866 against Austria. Before he started for his post he resigned, in January, 1868, having been selected to form a cabinet to take the place of the retiring Ratazzi ministry. He was not able to get together a ministry to carry out the programme of adherence to the arrangement with France regarding the inviolability of the Papal dominions. Vittorio Emmanuele appointed him commander-in-chief of the forces, and in 1870 he conducted the invasion of the Papal states and inaugurated the arrangements for incorporating it in the Italian kingdom. When the Duke of Aosta was crowned King of Spain he was envoy extraordinary at that court. In 1876 he was sent to Paris as ambassador, and when the Clericals in the French Chamber raised a protest, Gambetta dispelled their misgivings by pointing out that Cialdini was the only member of the Italian Parliament who spoke in favor of intervention on behalf of the French in 1870. After smoothing over many difficulties existing between France and Italy, he took his leave in 1881, at the time when the diplomatic relations between the two countries became strained on account of Tunis, and his attitude in this question made him very unpopular among his countrymen.

Cladel, Léon, a French author, born in Montauban, March 13, 1835; died in Sevres, July 29, 1892. He began life as a lawyer's clerk, and made his *début* as an author under the auspices of Charles Baudelaire with "Les Martyrs Ridicules" (1862). At the same time he began to write Republican articles for the newspapers that were marked with particular vivacity of style and picturesque effects. A novel of his entitled "Pierre Patient," caused the Imperial Government to interdict the circulation in France of "L'Europe," the Frankfort ,o rns, in which it appeared. For "Une Maudite, "which appeared in the "Événement," he had to spend a month in prison as an immoral writer. With "Le Bouscassie," "Va-Nu-Pieds," "L'Homme de la Croix aux Bœufs," and "Ompdrailles," he achieved a less sensational and more literary success.

Claughton, Thomas Legh, an English Churchman, born in Winwick, Lancashire, in 1808; died near Chelmsford, July 25, 1892. His father was Member of Parliament for Newton in 1818–'25. The son was educated at Rugby and at Oxford, where he was a scholar, fellow, and tutor of Trinity College in succession, winning prizes for Latin verse and a Latin essay in 1828 and 1829. In 1841 he was presented to the important benefice of Kidderminster, and there he was a pioneer in the organization of parish work among the poor on energetic High-Church methods. He became known as a preacher throughout England, and his earnest appeals to the heart and conscience of his hearers were effective, though devoid of oratorical art and polish. In 1852–'57 he was Matthew Arnold's predecessor as Professor of Poetry at Oxford. In 1867, after twenty-six years of parochial work at Kidderminster, he was promoted to the vacant bishopric of Rochester. In 1877, when the See of St. Albans was created by separation from that of Rochester, he elected to become its first bishop.

Clough, Anne Jemima, an English educator, born in Liverpool, in 1819; died in Cambridge, Feb. 27, 1892. She was the elder sister of the poet Arthur Hugh Clough. Her early life was spent in Charleston, S. C., and in the Northern States and Canada. Returning to Liverpool at the age of twenty, she opened a school for children. Ten years later she went to the Westmoreland village of Ambleside to live, and there taught the children of the neighborhood till after her mother died, in 1860, and her brother, in 1861. During all the time she was foremost in the movement for promoting the higher education for women, starting lectures for ladies in Liverpool and Manchester, out of which sprang a council for the North of England, which secured the help of men from the universities, and instituted courses of lectures in various towns. In 1871, Miss Clough was invited to take charge of a hall in Cambridge for the accommodation of 5 girls who wanted to attend the university lectures. This developed into Newnham College, at the head of which she remained until she died. In 1875 the 5 students had grown to 50, and the first building was erected, to which a second had to be added in 1881, and in 1888 another annex. The late Principal of Newnham advocated complete university coeducation, and when one of her students won the first place in mathematics and philosophy, she protested vigorously against the regulation which deprived her of the customary honors.

Constantine Nikolaievich, Grand Duke, uncle of the Czar, born in St. Petersburg, Sept. 21, 1827; died there, Jan. 24, 1892. He married Princess Alexandra of Sachse-Altenburg in 1848, was made admiral of the navy in 1853, and his intellectual endowments and liberal views led the progressive parties to set great hopes in him, and bade fair to win for him a permanent place in the annals of Russian history. In 1863 he was appointed Governor-General of Poland, and his administration enhanced his reputation. Later he was made President of the Council of the Empire. The death of his brother, Alexander II, cut short his career, for his nephew, the new Czar, had an antipathy for him and his opinions. In 1882 he was stripped of all his appointments. He was suspected of Radical or nihilistic principles and passed the remainder of his life in retirement, and toward the end tormented by bodily ailments. The eldest of his children, Nikolas, was banished from court in disgrace on account of his wild escapades; the second, Olga, is Queen of Greece; the third, Vera, is widow of the Duke Eugen of Würtemberg; and the two youngest, Constantin and Dimitri, are army officers.

Coode, Sir John, an English civil engineer, born in Bodmin, Cornwall, in 1816; died in Brighton, March 2, 1892. He was educated in the grammar school of his native town, studied engineering under Rendell, became resident engineer at Portland harbor and breakwater in 1847, and on Rendell's death, in 1856, was made engineer-in-chief. He continued in charge till the work was completed, in 1872, when he was knighted. His most important other works were the breakwater and docks at Cape Town, the Colombo breakwater, the improvement of the river Bar in Ireland, and harbor works for the Isle of Man. He drew the plans for a great number of the harbor improvements of Great Britain and the British colonies. In 1884-'85 he was one of the consultative commission of the Suez Canal.

Cook, Thomas, the founder of Cook's excursions, born in Melbourne, Derbyshire, Nov. 22, 1808; died in Leicestershire, July 18, 1892. He was left fatherless at the age of four, and began to earn his living at ten, working in a village garden for 1d. a day. Shortly afterward he began to learn wood turning, and then entered a publishing house at Loughborough in connection with the General Baptist Association. In 1828 he was appointed Bible reader and village missionary for the county of Rutland. In 1832 he married Miss Mason, a farmer's daughter, and moved to Market Harborough, where he carried on the business of wood turning. In 1836 he became a total abstainer, and subsequently published two temperance papers. While walking from Market Harborough to Leicester to attend a temperance meeting, he read a report of the opening of a part of the Midland Railway, and the idea occurred to him that the new mode of travel

might be used for the benefit of the temperance cause. He accordingly made arrangements with the railway company for a special train from Leicester to Loughborough on July 5, 1841. The success of the initial venture caused him to combine the management of excursions with his book and printing business in Leicester, and in 1844 he made permanent arrangements with the Midland company to place trains at his disposal when required. The following year he extended the system to Liverpool, the Isle of Man, and Dublin, and afterward to Scotland, which was the first place in which he provided hotel coupons for his patrons. In 1851 he conveyed many thousands to the Exhibition in Hyde Park. The business began to spread rapidly in England and on the Continent, and in 1872 the first of the annual tours round the world was made by Mr. Cook with nine companions. He retired in 1878, leaving the business to his son.

Cooper, Thomas, an English political agitator, born in Leicester in March, 1805; died in Lincoln, July 15, 1892. He was the son of a poor widow, and learned the shoemaking trade after having had several years of schooling. He acquired knowledge with wonderful facility, and while pursuing his trade gave every spare moment to his books, until overstudy and insufficient nourishment brought on a serious illness. At the age of twenty-three he opened a school in Lincoln, and a year later joined the Wesleyan Methodists and became a local preacher, at the same time writing for newspapers. He removed to London in 1839 to engage in journalism as a profession, but had little success. Returning to his natal town, he joined the Chartists, and conducted their organ, the "Midland Counties' Illuminator." He soon came to be recognized as their leader, and was nominated for Parliament. On his way to a convention in Manchester in 1842 he addressed large meetings of workingmen. A riot occurred at Hanley, after he had gone away. At Manchester military guards were placed in the streets, and the Chartist orators in their convention denounced bayonet rule and advocated armed resistance. He was arrested and taken back to Staffordshire to answer for a charge of arson in connection with the Hanley riot, but was acquitted on his proving that he was not there when the offense was committed. Upon that he was arraigned on the charge of conspiracy and sedition. The Chartist movement was in its last stages when he was brought up for trial before Sir Thomas Erskine, in March, 1843. He defended himself eloquently, but was convicted, and underwent two years of imprisonment in Stafford jail, during which he composed the greater part of an epic poem called the "Purgatory of Suicides," dealing with the great social and religious questions of the age. Douglass Jerrold found a publisher for this poem, which appeared in 1845, and was followed by "The Baron's Yule Feast." In the same year appeared also a volume of simple tales entitled "Wise Saws and Modern Instances." In 1847 he published "Triumphs of Perseverance" and "Triumphs of Enterprise." He became a member of Mazzini's International League, but took no part in the Chartist agitation in 1848, differing totally from Fergus O'Connor. He lectured on political and historical subjects, and in 1853 brought out the novel of "Alderman Ralph." For ten years he was a skeptic and a follower of Strauss, but in 1855 his views underwent another change, and for two years he combated the opinions of atheists in public discussions and lectures in London. In 1859 he became a Baptist preacher. When his health broke down shortly afterward, W. E. Forster, Samuel Morley, and other friends raised a sum sufficient to purchase an annuity of £100 for the lives of himself and his wife. He was able to lecture again from 1867 till 1872. In 1878 a collected edition of his poems was published, and shortly afterward appeared "The Bridge of History over the Gulf of Time." In 1882 he published his "Autobiography."

Cotton, Sir Henry, an English jurist, born in Leytonstone, May 20, 1821; died in Liphook, Feb. 22, 1891.

His father was high sheriff of Essex, and at one time a governor of the Bank of England. The son won a scholarship at Eton, and took high honors at Oxford in Christ Church College. He was called to the bar in 1846, soon acquired a good practice, became a Queen's counsel in 1866, was made standing counsel to the Bank of England, conducted important cases in the Court of Chancery, and in 1877 was made a lord justice of the Court of Appeal, in which he dealt with equity cases. He retired in October, 1890.

Crémieux, Hector, a French dramatist, born Nov. 10, 1828; died in Paris, Sept. 30, 1892. His first dramatic work was a five-act tragedy, written in conjunction with his brother, Emile Crémieux, in 1852. His libretto for Offenbach's "Orphée aux Enfers," produced in 1856, established his reputation, and from that time he wrote a succession of light comedies and operettas, varied in his earlier years by two or three serious dramas. The "Orphée aux Enfers" and "La Jolie Parfumeuse" were his most famous works. He made a successful dramatization of Halevy's "L'Abbé Constantin" with Pierre Decourcelle not long before his death, though latterly he wrote little for the stage, as he acted as secretary for a financial company, which failed. He committed suicide, having been made melancholy by the loss of his wife.

Caillag, Rosa, a Hungarian singer, born in 1835; died in Vienna, Feb. 20, 1892. She began a brilliant career at the age of fourteen in the Berlin Opera House. For ten years she was a prima donna of the Vienna, drawing a salary of 17,000 florins, and sang in the capitals of Europe with the highest success, until her voice gave out, in 1863. A marriage with the magician Hermann was speedily dissolved. She essayed teaching music when she could sing no more, but could earn but little, and in her last days she sank into a condition of wretched poverty.

Decourcelle, Adrien, a French dramatist, born in Paris in 1824; died there, Aug. 12, 1892. He made a hit in 1845 with his first piece, a dramatic sketch entitled "Une Soirée à la Bastille." In collaboration with Thiboust, Barrière, Marc Fournier, and others, he produced many popular plays, such as "Le Joie de la Maison," "Le Bal des Prisoniers," "Diviser pour Regner," "Je dine chez ma Mère," "Un Monsieur qui suit les Bonnes," "Tambour Vattant," "La Bête du bon Dieu," and "Jenny l'Ouvrière." He was also a contributor to the "Figaro," and was reader of new plays for the Comédie Française.

De Kock, Paul Henri, a French dramatist and novelist, born in Paris, in 1821; died in Limay, near Mantes, April 18, 1892. He was the son of Paul De Kock, and a feuilletonist of note, and the author or joint author of many successful plays.

De Vit, an Italian philologist, born in 1810; died at the end of August, 1892. He was educated at the Seminary, Padua, where he afterward became professor. Between 1858 and 1879 he published his great Latin dictionary, and for thirty-six years before his death he had been compiling his "Onomasticon," a work embracing all proper names down to the end of the fifth century, which he had completed as far as the letter P. He was likewise the author of the enlarged edition of Forcellini's "Lexicon Totius Latinitatis" and other works in history, archæology, and philology. In 1888, on the occasion of the jubilee of his literary labors, he received from Pope Leo XIII a large gold medal in recognition of his services to philology.

Dubray, Vital Gabriel, a French sculptor, born in 1818; died in Paris, Oct. 5, 1892. He studied under Ramey, the younger, was employed on the memorial of Joan of Arc at Orleans, and executed statues of numerous celebrated Frenchmen, including Sully, Lannes, and Napoleon Bonaparte.

Duprato, Jules, a French composer, born in Nîmes in 1827; died in Paris, May 19, 1892. He won the Roman prize in 1848, composed the opera of "Les Trovatelles Pâquerette," which was brought out in 1856, and was followed by "Salvator Rosa," in three acts, which was played at the Opéra Comique. His one-act piece called "La Fiancée de Corinthé" was produced at the

Opera. He became Professor of Harmony at the Conservatoire in 1866.

Duveyrier, Henri, a French explorer, born in Paris in 1840; died in Sèvres, April 25, 1892. He was the son of Charles Duveyrier, the dramatic author. Before he was twenty he undertook a series of expeditions in Algeria by which he gained considerable renown. In 1859 he penetrated as far as El Goleah, where no European had been before him. A little later he made a reconnoissance of the south of the province of Constantine and the adjacent Sahara. In 1860 the Government charged him with a mission to the Tuareg country, and by his treaty with Ikhenoukhen, the head of the Ardjer Tuareg confederation, the routes of the Soudan were opened to French commerce. In 1874 he explored the *chotts* of southern Tunis, and in 1876 he went on a mission to Morocco. After that he confined himself to geographical studies at home. He was President of the Geographical Society of France and an officer of the Legion of Honor. For a long time before his decease he was afflicted with some nervous malady that made him despondent, and at last impelled him to take his own life.

Edwards, Amelia Blandford, an English novelist, born in 1831; died in London, April 15, 1892. Her father was an officer who fought in the Peninsular War. She began to compose stories and poems almost as soon as she learned to write, and one of her poems, entitled "The Knights of Old," appeared in print when she was only seven years old. She showed such talent for drawing also, that George Cruikshank, on seeing caricatures that she had scribbled on the back of the leaves of a manuscript sent to him as editor of a magazine, offered to take her as an articled pupil when she was fourteen years old. For some years after this she applied herself to music, becoming an expert performer. Devoting herself subsequently to literature and to archæological studies, she produced novels that were read as much for their learning as for their romantic interest. "Lord Brackenbury," first published as an illustrated serial in the London "Graphic," went through 20 editions, and was translated into German, French, and Russian. "Barbara's History," one of her early works, was especially popular. Others are "Debenham's Vow," "Half a Million of Money," "My Brother's Wife," "Miss Carew," "In the Days of my Youth," "Monsieur Maurice," and "Hand in Glove." Her descriptions of travel were not less successful, particularly "A Thousand Miles up the Nile," which was illustrated from her own sketches, and embodies a large amount of digested knowledge of the antiquities of Egypt. Miss Edwards lectured in the United States in 1889 and subsequent years.

Ekert, Gustav, a German penologist, born in 1824; died in Freiburg, Baden, in June, 1892. He entered the public service in 1849, and after spending eighteen years in the police department was made governor of the cellular prison at Bruchsal, whence he was called to take charge of the larger one at Freiburg. He took a leading part in the establishment in 1864 of a German union of prison officials, and became editor of its organ, the "Journal of Prison Information." He aided in the preparation of the "Handbook of Prison Science," and contributed to the investigation and comparison of facts relating to crime and punishment.

Ellena, Vittorio, an Italian statesman, died in Rome, July 19, 1892. He enjoyed a high reputation as a politician of sincere convictions and of knowledge and sound judgment, especially on all questions connected with commercial relations and finance. He was Minister of Finance for a short time.

Erdmann, Johann Eduard, a German philosopher, born in Wolmar, Livonia, in 1805; died in Halle, in June, 1892. He studied theology, and was pastor in his native parish for some time, resigning for the purpose of devoting himself altogether to philosophy. In 1831 he began to lecture in the University of Berlin, and was one of the most brilliant of the disciples of Hegel. He was called to Halle as extraordinary professor, and in time was made regular professor. His lecture room was always filled with students. Erdmann was almost the last surviving representative of the Hegelian philosophy. His principal works treated of " Faith and Science," " Nature or Creation," " The Body and the Soul," " Psychology," and " Logic and Metaphysics." The principal one was a " History of Modern Philosophy," in three volumes.

Fabre, l'éro Joseph, a French monk, born in 1825; died in Paris, Oct. 25, 1892. He joined the Oblate Missionary order soon after it came into existence, and was the superior-general of the order, being chosen in succession to its founder, Bishop Mazenod, of Marseilles.

Fonseca, Manoel Deodoro da, a Brazilian soldier, and first President of the Republic, born in 1827; died Aug. 23, 1892. He was a soldier all his life, and in the war against Paraguay distinguished himself, and was made a general and afterward marshal of the empire. The members of the Military Club of Rio Janeiro, of which Gen. Fonseca was the leading spirit, conceived the idea that they were the guardians of Brazilian liberties. Fonseca was a personal friend of Dom Pedro, but toward the court of the Regency he showed distrust and antipathy, in consequence of which he was deprived of his command and banished to Matto-Grosso. The Republican agitators chose him for their leader, and when the bloodless revolution of Nov. 15, 1889, was accomplished, and a republican form of government proclaimed, he was made Dictator and Provisional President. The Constituent Assembly, in February, 1891, formally elected him President, not because he was popular with the people, but because of his influence over the army. For a time he professed to act as the constitutional head of a free state, but in order to maintain his position and perpetuate his power he gathered about him a clique of politicians and financial adventurers, whose acts made him much more unpopular, and began to construe his powers under the Constitution in a sense that was not understood by the people and their representatives. Ministers who would not hold themselves responsible to him, instead of to the Parliament, were dismissed, and he assumed that he was alone responsible for the conduct of the Government, declaring that the Constitution was modeled after that of the United States, and not after the parliamentary institutions of Europe. When he supposed that he had consolidated his position, he began to veto the acts of Congress that displeased him; and when Congress attempted to override his veto by a two-thirds vote, he declared himself Dictator on Nov. 3, 1891, and placed the capital under martial law, on the pretext that there was danger of the restoration of monarchical government. On Nov. 23, 1891, when the army and navy had declared against the Dictator, he in turn was compelled to abdicate, and since then he had taken no part in political affairs beyond issuing a manifesto in which he sought to justify his course in dissolving Congress and assuming a dictatorship.

Forckenbeck, Max von, a German statesman, born in Prussia about 1825; died in 1892. He took part in the Liberal movement of 1848, but during the reactionary period that followed practiced law quietly in Elbing till 1858, when he entered the Prussian Diet, where he became a leader of the Fortschrittlers or Progressists, and was a prominent upholder of popular rights in the long struggle with Bismarck and the King, who were determined to reorganize the army against the will of the Parliament. After the war of 1866 his influence contributed to the re-establishment of harmonious relations between Crown and people's representatives, and he was elected President of the lower house. As a member of the North German and afterward of the Imperial German Parliament, he did much to promote the cause of German unity, and was one of the chief founders of the National Liberal party. In 1874 he was elected the second President of the Reichstag, succeeding Herr Simson, and in 1878 he was re-elected, notwithstanding the defeat of the Liberal party in the general elections. In the following year he resigned, for the purpose of reorganizing

the party in order to combat the protectionist and reactionary policy of the Government; but the majority of the National Liberals followed the Chancellor, and in 1884 Forckenbeck consequently left them and joined the Freisinnige party, of which he remained a member for the rest of his life, though in his last years he took little part in the parliamentary warfare against the Government. He was elected head Bürgermeister of Berlin in 1878, and through his energy and good taste in a large measure the dingy old city was transformed into one of the finest capitals in Europe.

Forge, Anatole de la, a French historian, born in 1821; died in Paris, June 6, 1892. He was educated for a diplomatic career, and in 1846 went on a mission to Spain, for which he was decorated with the cross of the Legion of Honor. In 1848 he became a journalist, and wrote political articles for the " Siècle." After the fall of the empire he was Prefect of the Aisne, and took a prominent part in organizing the defense of St. Quentin, where he was wounded. He was then appointed Prefect of the Basses-Pyrénées, retiring after the conclusion of peace in 1871. He was appointed director of the press in the Ministry of the Interior in 1877, and was elected to the Chamber of Deputies in 1881, and sat till 1889. Among his numerous published works the chief is a " History of the Republic of Venice." He wrote a useful account of " Public Instruction in Spain," a study of " Certain Political Vicissitudes of Italy in its Relations with France," and a critical work on " Painting in France."

Franz, Robert, a German composer, born in Halle, June 28, 1815; died there, Oct. 24, 1892. He was educated in the gymnasium of his native place, and did not begin the study of music till 1835, because his family were opposed to his following it as a profession. After studying for two years with Friedrich Schneider, of Dessau, he published a set of 12 songs, which drew forth praises from Schumann and other eminent masters. He was organist and director of the singing academy and of the winter concerts at Halle, and was also lecturer on music in the university, but was compelled by deafness to resign his musical posts. He gave his whole attention to composition, and to editing the works of Bach, Handel, and other old composers. He composed more than 300 songs, besides a Kyrie, and quartets, psalms, etc. As a writer of music for songs of every kind of form and sentiment he stood at the head of contemporary composers.

Freeman, Edward Augustus, an English historian, born at Harborne, a suburb of Birmingham, in 1823; died at Alicante, Spain, March 16, 1892. He was the only son of John Freeman, of Pedmore Hall, Worcestershire, but, both his parents having died when he was quiet young, he was brought up by his grandmother in Northamptonshire. Hannah More, whom he was taken to see as a boy, prophesied for him a distinguished future, a forecast which he always liked to recall. He was educated at a small private school at Ewell, in Surrey, and at Trinity College, Oxford, from which he was graduated in 1845, but remained three two years longer as a fellow till his marriage, in 1847. In 1846 he contended for the English prize essay, the subject being " The Effects of the Conquest of England by the Normans." He failed to win the prize, but one result of the trial was to turn his attention to the epoch of history which he afterward made peculiarly his own. One of his friends at this time was John Henry Parker, the well-known writer on architecture, and Freeman's own tastes in this direction were no doubt stimulated by those of his friend. In 1884 he was made Regius Professor of Modern History at Oxford, succeeding Dr. Stubbs, the present Bishop of Oxford. His whole life was a marvel of activity, and books, pamphlets, lectures, and magazine articles on historical, architectural, and literary topics proceeded in unwearied succession from his pen. His facts were never obtained at second hand, and his conclusions were always thought out for himself. More to him than to any other man is the present generation indebted for the revival of interest in history as a serious study. He was utterly opposed to any arbitrary separation between ancient and modern history, and upheld with all the vigor of profound conviction the continuity of European history from the earliest time to the present moment. An almost equally strong passion with him was the belief that archæology and

geography are of inestimable value to the historian. He placed little value upon theories and conjectures, and in their stead insisted upon the importance of minute accuracy. As a controversialist he was unrelenting when truth was in question, although he hated controversy, but his sympathetic instincts led him to make large allowances for honest and devoted efforts. Somewhat brusque in manner, he was nevertheless warm-hearted and affectionate, keeping his friendships unimpaired through the years. At the time of his death he was traveling in Spain with his wife and daughters, visiting the sites of the Carthaginian colonies. On reaching Alicante, on March 10, he was taken ill with smallpox, of which malady, complicated with bronchitis, he died six days later, and was buried in the Protestant cemetery there. His greatest work is "The History of the Norman Conquest of England: Its Causes and Results," the first volume of which appeared in 1867, and the sixth and last in 1879. His other published works are "Church Restoration" (1846); "A History of Architecture" (1849); "An Essay on Window Tracery" (1850); "A History of Llandaff Cathedral" (1852); "Architectural Antiquities of Gower" (1850); "Poems: Legendary and Historical, by E. A. F. and G. W. Cox" (1850); "The History and Conquests of the Saracens" (London, 1856); "History of Federal Government, from the formation of the Achæan League to the Disruption of the United States" (1st vol. only, London, 1863); "Old English History for Children" (London, 1869); "History of the Cathedral Church of Wells" (London, 1870); "Historical Essays" (London, 1871); "General Sketch of European History" (London, 1872); "Growth of the English Constitution, from the Earliest Times" (London, 1872); "The Unity of History" (London, 1872); "Comparative Politics" (London, 1873); "Historical Essays" (2d series, London, 1873); "Disestablishment and Disendowment: What are they?" (London, 1874); "History of Europe" ("History Primers") (London, 1876); "Historical and Architectural Sketches, chiefly Italian" (London, 1876); "The Turks in Europe" (London, 1877); "The Ottoman Power in Europe: Its Nature, its Growth, and its Decline" (London, 1877); "How the Study of History is let and hindered" (London, 1879); "Historical Essays" (3d series, London, 1879);

"A Short History of the Norman Conquest in England" (Oxford, 1880); "The Historical Geography of Europe" (2 vols., London, 1881); "Sketches from the Subject and Neighbor Lands of Venice" (London 1881); "An Introduction to American Institution History" (Baltimore, 1882); "The Reign of William Rufus and the Accession of Henry the First" (vols., Oxford, 1882); "Lectures to American Audiences" (Philadelphia, 1882; London, 1883); "English Towns and Districts" (London, 1883); "Some Impressions of the United States" (London, 1883); "The Office of the Historical Professor" (London, 1884); "Greater Greece and Greater Britain and George Washington, the Expander of England" (London, 1886); "The Methods of Historical Study" (Oxford, 1886); "The Chief Periods of European History (London, 1887); "Exeter" in "Historic Towns" (London, 1887); "Four Oxford Lectures" (1887); "Fifty Years of European History: Teutonic Conquest in Gaul and Britain" (London, 1888); "William the Conqueror" in "Twelve English Statesmen" (London, 1888); "The History of Sicily, from the Earliest Times" (3 vols., London, 1891–'92); left unfinished; "Historical Essays" (4th series, 1892).

Freyer, Alfred, an English inventor and statistician born in Rastrick, near Huddersfield, 1830; died Wilmslow, near Manchester, Dec. 13, 1892. He showed inventive genius at an early age, became a member of a firm of sugar refiners, and in 1865 perfected the concretor, which enables the West Indian planters send their sugar to the refineries in solid cakes and thus save waste and loss on shipboard. His paper on "Some Peculiarities of the Vital Statistics of the Society of Friends" excited widespread interest, and on "A New Form of Floating Lightship, and a Mode of estimating the Distance of Lights" resulted in the erection of one or more lighthouses. In 1872 a series of papers on "The Influence of Forests on Rainfall led the people of the West Indies to give more attention to the preservation of their forests. He invented a destructor for the treatment of town refuse, which in extensive use. He wrote also on the balance trade, the silver question, vital statistics, the cost living in various countries, and allied subjects.

Furstenberg, Cardinal Landgrave Friedrich, a Bohemian prelate, born in Vienna, Oct. 8, 1812; died Hochwald, Moravia, Aug. 19, 1892. He was created Prince Archbishop of Olmütz in 1853, and during the conflict between the Czechs and the Germanizing Liberal ministry of Schmerling he was a strenuous champion of the Czech nationality, treating the all powerful Prime Minister with a degree of haute that went beyond the limits of civility. He was the most intolerant of ecclesiastics in regard to spiritual questions. He demanded the Papal excommunication of all Catholics who became converted to Protestantism. In refusing burial in consecrated ground to persons not orthodox Catholics, and in other exhibitions of intolerance, he came into frequent conflicts with the civil authorities and public opinion. After receiving the cardinal's hat, on May 12, 1879, his zeal and rigor in religious matters abated, and on political questions he took a less uncompromising attitude. He was the richest of all the opulent Church dignitaries of Austria-Hungary, and the bulk of his immense fortune was left to charitable and religious institutions.

Fyffe, Charles Alan, an English historian, born Blackheath, Kent, December, 1845; died Feb. 1892. He was graduated from Balliol College, Oxford, in 1868. His tastes inclined strongly in the direction of politics, and especially toward European affairs and land reform. He was on the Continent 1870, and is said to have sent to the "Daily News" the first account that appeared in print of the battle of Sedan. He was called to the bar in 1876, but did not practice his profession regularly. His first published work was a "History of Greece" (1875) for Macmillan's "History Primers." The first volume of his elaborate work, "A History of Modern Europe," was published in 1880 (2d edition, 1884). It covers the time from the beginning of the revolutionary war to the accession of Louis XVIII. The second volume was issued in 1886, and the third, which brings the narrative down to the year 1878, appeared in 1890. He was a clear and vigorous writer, of distinct opinions and great abilities. In manner he was reserved and somewhat shy, and in the last year of his life an infamous and wholly false charge being brought against him, he became greatly depressed in consequence. At last the burden became too great for his sensitive nature to withstand, and he died by his own hand.

Galland, Pierre, a French decorative artist, born in Geneva in 1822; died in Paris, Dec. 1, 1892. He was the son of an artistic workman in gold, and he learned the same craft, then studied architectural decoration with Labrouste, and painting with Drolling, and by 1848 was known as one of the most accomplished decorative painters of his time. His first important work was the decoration of a palace belonging to an Armenian millionaire in Constantinople. On returning to Paris in 1853, he opened an *atelier*. He has executed the interior decorations of some of the finest modern houses from Constantinople to New York. He was not a mere copyist of the work of the Italian or the French Renaissance, but developed a style and ideas of his own that were formed and chastened by a knowledge of the styles of all ages and countries. In 1873 he became Professor of Decorative Art in the École des Beaux Arts, and in 1877 director of the Gobelins.

Gindely, Anton, a Bohemian historian, born in Prague in 1829; died Oct. 24, 1892. He was educated in the University of Prague, and, after holding academical posts in various places in Bohemia and Moravia, was made Professor of Austrian History in the university. He won a name as a historian by his "Geschichte der Böhmischen Brüder" (1856–'57), but his reputation chiefly rests on his "History of the Thirty Years' War," which was published between 1869 and 1882.

Gasparis, Annibale de, an Italian astronomer, born in Bugnara, Nov. 9, 1819; died in Naples, March 21, 1892. He went to Naples to study mathematics and astronomy in 1838; became assistant at the observatory of Capodimonte in 1842, and in 1864 succeeded Prof. Capocci as director. He was the discoverer of the planetoid Hygieia in 1849, and discovered, in all, 9 of the earlier known of the small planets, ending with Beatrix, in 1865. Afterward he gave much attention to the determination of the orbits of binary stars.

Gisborne, F. M., a Canadian electrician, born in 1822; died in Ottawa, Aug. 29, 1892. He was employed by the Government in 1850 to make surveys for a telegraph line, and while at St. John's he conceived the idea of laying a submarine cable from the coast of Newfoundland to the east coast of Ireland. This scheme he laid before the authorities of Newfoundland and Nova Scotia and various capitalists in Halifax and Canada, and he went to New York to propose it to moneyed men there, but all considered it chimerical. He became superintendent of the Government telegraphs of the Dominion in later life.

Gonon, Eugène, a French sculptor, born in Paris, Oct. 17, 1814; died there in September, 1892. He was a son of the bronze founder Honoré Gonon, who had rediscovered the process of founding à *cire perdue* practiced by the ancients. He studied under his father, trained himself also in chasing and sculpture, and learned chemistry and metallurgy. He worked under the sculptors Pradier and Blondel, and went through a course at the École des Beaux Arts. He improved upon his father's methods, and with him reproduced groups by Barye, and copied many works, both of modern and ancient sculpture. He also modeled groups of birds and small animals.

Grant, James Augustus, a Scottish explorer, born in Nairn, in 1827; died there, Feb. 11, 1892. He was a son of the parish minister of Nairn; was educated in Marischal College, Aberdeen, and in 1846 obtained a commission in the Indian army. He saw much severe service; was at the two sieges of Multan, the battle of Gujerat, and the relief of Lucknow, and was several times wounded. When Speke, the discoverer of Vic-

toria Nyanza, which he rightly conjectured to be the main source of the Nile, was commissioned, in 1860, by the Royal Geographical Society to take out an expedition to explore the lake, Capt. Grant, who had championed Speke in his controversy with Burton, was glad to accompany his friend. The explorers reached the west shore of the lake from Zanzibar by way of Unyanyembe. They made a friend of King Rumanika, penetrated into Uganda, and in July, 1862, reached the point where the Nile issues from the lake, the discovery of which was the main object of the expedition. They were so long absent that Samuel Baker was sent in search of them. They followed the Nile for 120 miles, when they were obliged to leave it, but 70 miles further down they struck it again; and in February, 1863, they reached Gondokoro, where they were met and relieved by Baker. In 1868 Capt. Grant served in the Abyssinian expedition, and after his return he remained in England, retiring from the army with the rank of lieutenant-colonel. He contributed papers on the African expedition to the "Journal" of the Geographical Society, wrote an account of the botany of the expedition which fills a volume of the "Transactions" of the Linnæan Society, and published "A Walk across Africa" (1864).

Grant, Robert, a Scottish astronomer, born in Grantown-on-Spey, near Glasgow, in 1814; died there, Nov. 1, 1892. He was educated in London, Aberdeen, and Paris; became proficient in the ancient languages and in French and Italian, as well as in astronomy and pure mathematics; and after his return to England, in 1847, he spent five years in writing his "History of Physical Astronomy." He translated, with Admiral Smith, the "Popular Astronomy" of his former instructor, Arago; became editor of the "Monthly Notices" of the Astronomical Society; and in 1859 was appointed Professor of Astronomy in the University of Glasgow. In 1883 he published a catalogue of 6,415 stars, the mean places of which had been determined under his direction in the observatory at Glasgow.

Gravière, J. B. E. Jurien de la, a French naval officer and author, born in Brest, in 1813; died in Paris, March 5, 1892. He was the son of a vice-admiral, and after studying in the naval school he made a voyage to Senegal, from which he returned at the end of two years to enter the service as orderly officer on a vessel stationed in the Levant. His voyages and his travels for four years in China he described in articles published in the "Journal des Deux Mondes." He was on the staff of Admiral Bruat in the Black Sea campaign, and performed brilliant services in the Kertch expedition. On the death of Admiral Bruat, from cholera, he took command, and on his return he was appointed a rear-admiral in December, 1855. During the Italian war he was in command of a division that blockaded Venice. As commander of the expedition against Mexico he arranged with Great Britain and Spain, in December, 1861, the treaty of Soledad, which the French Government refused to ratify. Upon this he gave up the command of the land forces to Gen. Lorencez, but retained that of the naval division. He was promoted vice-admiral in 1862, and returned to France, where he served as aid-de-camp to the Emperor. Afterward he was commander of the Mediterranean, became a Senator, and was appointed a member of the Admiralty Board. In 1870 he took part in the defense of Paris, and subsequently commanded the Levant division, with which he aided in stamping out the separatist movement in Nice. After the war was over he was appointed director of the department of maps and charts in the naval office. In 1866 he was made a member of the Academy of Sciences, and in 1888 he was chosen one of the 70 members of the French Academy. He was president of various societies interested in maritime matters. At the time of his death he was engaged in issuing a series of articles in the "Revue des Deux Mondes" on the liberation of Holland. Admiral Gravière wrote a large number of books that are highly regarded, among them the following: "Souvenir d'un Amiral" (1860); "Guerres Maritimes sous la République et sous l'Empire" (1860); "La Marine d'Autrefois" (1865); "La Marine d'Aujourd'hui" (1872); "Les Marins du Quinzième et du Seizième Siècle" (1879); "La Marine des Anciens" (1880); "Les Campagnes d'Alexandre" (1883); "La Marine des Ptolemées et la Marine des Romains" (1884); "Les derniers Jours de la Marine à Voiles" (1885); "Doria et Barberousse" (1886); "Les Chevaliers de Malte et la Marine de Philippe II" (1887); "Les Corsaires Barbaresques et la Marine de Soliman le Grand" (1888); and "L'Amiral Roussin" (1889).

Gregory, Sir William Henry, an English politician, born in County Galway, Ireland, in 1817; died in London, March 6, 1892. He was educated at Harrow and at Christ Church College, Oxford, and in 1842 he entered Parliament as a Conservative member for Dublin city. He sat till 1847, and was not again elected till 1857, when he went back to Parliament as a Liberal Conservative for Galway, which he continued to represent till 1872. He was much liked as a speaker, and often opened important debates, especially in reference to the civil war in the United States and the Eastern question. He endeavored to get Parliament to recognize the Southern Confederacy and forcibly raise the blockade, and was supported by Lord Robert Cecil, while W. E. Forster made one of his first important speeches against the motion. Later he was the eloquent advocate of the claims of the Servians for protection against Turkish rule and interference. When the Egyptian army under Arabi Pasha rose against the Khedive and the British Government interfered in order to crush the new Government, Sir William Gregory again came out in his character of champion of the weak against the strong. On the home-rule question, on the other hand, he declared against the claims of his countrymen for self-government, deserting the Liberal party in 1866, for which he was rewarded in 1872 with the post of Governor of Ceylon, where he remained five years, proving an excellent administrator and making himself very popular. After his return he made himself useful as a trustee of the National Gallery.

Gresser, Peter Apollonowitsh, a Russian soldier, born in St. Petersburg, in 1833; died May 11, 1892. Educated in the cadet corps he entered the army in 1850, and took part in the Crimean War. Subsequently he attracted the attention of Prince Dondoukoff-Korsakoff, and when the latter was appointed Imperial Commissary in Bulgaria, after the Russo-Turkish War of 1877-'78, he filled the post of the Minister of the Interior under his administration for two years. Returned from Bulgaria, he occupied several important administrative posts in Russia, and, having distinguished himself as a Master of Police in Kieff, he was appointed Master of Police and Prefect in St. Petersburg, in 1883. His position here was one of great responsibility, as he was directly responsible to the Czar for the safety and tranquillity of the capital. He did not confine himself to police duties in the narrow sense of the term, but, by untiring energy, rendered St. Petersburg a tolerably clean and orderly city.

Grévin, Alfred, a French caricaturist, born in Épineuil, Yonne, in January, 1827; died in St. Maur, in May, 1892. He was employed as a draughtsman in the office of the Paris, Lyons, and Mediterranean Railroad, when he began to send designs to the "Journal Amusant" which were soon remarked. He was the most original and happy of the delineators of Parisian types and traits, and was an indefatigable producer. Besides an incalculable number of drawings that appeared in the "Journal Amusant" and "Petit Journal pour Riri," "Charivari," and other comic journals, the costumes and grouping in many famous *féeries* were designed by him, and he planned the theatrical dresses for Judic and other actresses. The most striking of his theatrical creations were reproduced in wax for the museum named after him. With Ernest d'Hervilly, he made a drama, "Le Bonhomme Misère," in 1877.

Guiraud, Ernest, a Franco-American composer, born in New Orleans, June 23, 1837; died in Paris, May 7, 1892. His father was established in New Orleans as a professor of music. The son when only fifteen years old composed "Le Roi David," and a little later went to Paris to follow Halévy's course of composition, supporting himself while studying by playing the kettledrum in an orchestra. He won the first prize of Rome in 1859, and sent from Italy several pieces that were admired. His "Sylvie," performed at the Opéra Comique in 1864, was well received. His other principal productions were: "En Prison," an operetta in one act (1869); "Le Kobold," in one act, given at the Opéra Comique in 1870 just as the war broke out; an orchestral suite executed in 1872; "Le Forgeron de Gretna Green," a ballet (1873); and "Piccolino" (1876). This last had the greatest success. The last work that he completed was "Galante Aventure," which was played in 1882, but was damned in spite of excellent musical qualities. He completed Offenbach's "Contes d'Hoffmann," and wrote the last part of the score of "Kassia," which was left incomplete by his friend Léo Delibes. He worked a long time on a grand opera, "Le Feu," the subject of which was taken from the myths of the Persian fire worshipers.

Hachette, Jean George, a French publisher, born in Paris in 1838; died there, Dec. 16, 1892. He became a partner in the publishing house of which his father was the head, and gave his special attention to the publication of geographical works and atlases.

Henriquel, Nyphen Dupont, best known as Henriquel, a French engraver, born in Paris, in 1798; died there, Feb. 1, 1892. He studied under Guerin and Berwick, and achieved such a reputation at once that he opened a school at the age of twenty. He engraved many of the portraits painted by Ingres and Delaroche, reproduced with remarkable feeling and fidelity Raphael's madonnas, and engraved numerous works of Correggio, Paolo Veronese, and Gerard. He did not drop the burin till he had passed his eighty-sixth year. For many years he was Professor of Engraving in the Central School of Art in Paris.

Herbst, Eduard, an Austrian statesman, born in Vienna, Dec. 9, 1820; died there, June 26, 1892. He studied law in the Vienna University, and, after serving for some time in a public office, began to lecture at the university, and in 1847 became ordinary professor in Lemberg. In 1858 he went to Prague, where he had the reputation of being one of the best instructors in criminal law of all Austria. His "Handbuch des österreichischen Strafrechts" (1855) and "Einleitung in das österreichische Strafprocessrecht" are regarded as standard works on the subject. In 1861, after the Constitution had entered into operation, he was elected to the Bohemian Diet, and was delegated by the Diet and afterward chosen by direct election to sit in the Austrian House of Deputies. His oratorical talent and keen, critical mind, and his astonishing fund of information on all subjects connected with public affairs, placed him at once at the head of the German party in Bohemia, whose leader he was till 1867, during all the period when Bohemian affairs engrossed a great part of the attention of the Austrian Government and were the pivot of its policy. His electoral addresses were the oracles of his party. After the suspension of the imperial Constitution he led the attack against the Belcredi ministry, and when the war of 1866 had proved a deathblow to reaction, he entered the Cabinet of the so-called Bürger ministry on Dec. 30, 1867, as Minister of Justice, resigning control of party matters in Bohemia into the hands of Dr. Schmeykal. He held this post till the ministry was ousted, on April 12, 1870, and during this period he accomplished the abolition of imprisonment for debt, the introduction of trial by jury for press offenses, the organization of district courts, the suppression of public executions, the reform of the laws of bankruptcy, and he took the lead of the Opposition against the Potocki, and then against the Hohenwart ministry, and at that period reached the zenith of his political renown. But the very powers that made him dominant in his party and the most conspicuous figure in Austrian politics, the vigorous, incisive, theoretical criticism of which he was a master, drew the party away from the ground of practical politics, and made compromises, which are necessary in Austria more than elsewhere for an acceptable governmental policy, quite impossible. His opposition against the occupation of Bosnia and against the Berlin treaty, in which the greater part of the party followed him, destroyed the prospects of German Liberalism in Austria and brought about the Taaffe *régime*. He was rejected in his old Bohemian constituency, which chose a representative of more nationalistic tendencies, and in 1885 obtained a mandate from one of the Vienna districts. His high character and spotless record preserved for him the respect of all, and his tireless energy enabled him to take an important share up to the very last in the legislation of a noncontentious character, in which his knowledge of law, finance, and railroads could be turned to account.

Hofmann, August Wilhelm, a German chemist, born about 1820; died in Berlin, May 5, 1892. He studied chemistry under Liebig at Giessen, and devoted himself there to studying the bases of coal tar and metamorphoses of indigo. After spending three years at Bonn, he was, on Prof. Liebig's recommendation, appointed superintendent at the Royal College of Chemistry in London in 1848. In 1853 this institution, which made rapid progress under his direction, became the chemical section of the Royal School of Mines. In 1855 he was appointed a warden of the British Mint. In 1864 he went to Bonn as Professor of Chemistry, and from there he was called to Berlin in the year following, where he occupied the chair of Chemistry till his death. Continuing his early investigation into the organic bases found in cold tar, he made practical discoveries regarding the composition and chemical character of aniline red that have been of immense industrial value. He contributed frequently to the "Annalen der Chemie," the "Transactions of the British Chemical Society," and the "Philosophical Transactions of the Royal Society."

Holstein-Holsteinborg, Count, a Danish rural economist, born in 1816; died on May 1, 1892. At the age of twenty-one he succeeded to a large feudal estate, and devoted himself to agriculture and stock breeding. The remarkable improvement in the Danish cattle industry and the growth of the export trade in butter, live cattle, and bacon was in a measure the result of his activity and example. For a long period he was President of the Danish Royal Agricultural Society. He sat for many years in the Rigsdag, where he was a leading member of the Moderate Liberals. He was Prime Minister in 1870–'74.

Howard, Cardinal **Edward,** an English ecclesiastic, born in Nottingham, Feb. 13, 1829; died in Brighton, Sept. 18, 1892. He was descended from the famous old ducal family of Norfolk, was educated at Oscott College, and served for some years in the Life Guards. At the age of twenty-six he quitted the army to enter the Catholic priesthood. He took holy orders in Rome, and gained the affection and confidence of Pius IX, who sent him on a mission to India to compose the religious conflict that had broken out at Goa. He was vicar to the archpriest of St. Peter's for some years, and in 1872 was consecrated Bishop of Neo-Cæsarea *in partibus*. On March 12, 1877, Monsignor Howard was advanced to the cardinalate, and appointed *camerlingo* of the Sacred College. In 1881 he was appointed archpriest of the patriarchal basilica of St. Peter's, and prefect of the congregation, having charge of the edifice, as successor to Cardinal Borromeo. On March 24, 1884, the Pope raised him from the rank of cardinal priest to that of cardinal bishop, appointing him to the suburban see of Frascati. Cardinal Howard was a famous linguist, speaking with fluency not only all the languages of western Europe, but also Armenian, Arabic, and Russian.

Hubner, Baron J. A., an Austrian diplomat, born in Vienna, in 1811; died there, July 30, 1892. He entered the public service at an early age, holding an appointment in the Foreign Office under Prince Metternich in 1833. In 1849 he was sent to Paris as minister plenipotentiary to the President of the republic. He was a member of the Congress of Paris in 1856, and one of the signers of the treaty of March 30. He was replaced at Paris in 1859 by Prince Metternich, and in 1866 held the post of Minister of Justice in the Austrian Cabinet. In 1868, resigning the Italian ambassadorship, he abandoned the diplomatic career, and devoted himself henceforth to explorations in Asia and America. He has published interesting accounts of his various scientific journeys.

Isidor, Archbishop, Metropolitan of St. Petersburg, Novgorod, and Finland, born in 1799; died in St. Petersburg, Sept. 19, 1892. He was born in the province of Tula, and was educated in the seminary of that district and in the Ecclesiastical Academy of St. Petersburg. He entered the monastic order at the age of twenty-six, became Professor of Theology, and was appointed bishop, first of Plotsk, and subsequently of Moghileff. In 1841 he was appointed Archbishop of the Province of Moghileff, and in this capacity took an active part in the conversion of the Uniates of Poland to the orthodox belief. In 1844 he was appointed Archbishop of Kakhetia in the Caucasus, and Exarch of Georgia, where his energies for missionary work found ample scope. In 1858 he was transferred to the most ancient metropolitan see in Russia, that of St. Sofia, in Kieff, and in 1860 was made metropolitan archbishop of the capital and adjoining provinces. He was President of the Holy Synod. For his benevolence and charity he was universally esteemed by the Russians of all classes.

Jovellar y Soler, Joaquin, a Spanish soldier, born in Mallorca, in 1819; died in Madrid, April 16, 1892. He entered the army at an early age, and first saw active service in the seven years' Carlist war. In 1837 he was present as a sublieutenant at six important engagements, and in the last of them he was severely wounded. Going to Cubas as soon as the war was ended, he saw much active service there for some years. In 1859 he accompanied O'Donnell's army to Morocco, and distinguished himself in the battle of Tetuan and at Wad Ras, where he received a grave wound. On returning to Spain, O'Donnell, who was made Minister of War, chose him for undersecretary. He afterward filled many important civil and military posts, and in 1873 went out to Cuba as captain-general. While he was there the "Virginius" affair occurred, and he had various other delicate questions to deal with. He was recalled to Spain in 1874, to take command of the army of the center against the Carlist insurgents. On the restoration of King Alfonso, in 1875, he was made Minister of War in the first Cabinet formed by Canovas, and on his return from the journey in which he accompanied the King through the northern provinces, he again assumed command of the army of the center, and co-operated with Martinez Campos against the Carlists, who were finally crushed. Gen. Jovellar was an able military organizer and administrator, and many of the reforms that have been introduced into the Spanish military service were originated by him. He was three times Minister of War, and once was Prime Minister for a short time, besides filling various offices of less importance. He was the President of the Supreme Council of War and Marine, and a Senator, and held the rank of captain-general in the army.

Junker, Wilhelm, a German explorer, born about 1845; died in St. Petersburg, Feb. 14, 1892. He went out to the Soudan in 1875 as a naturalist and ethnologist, for the purpose of collecting notes and specimens of plants and animals, and objects connected with anthropology. From Khartoum he made excursions into the countries watered by the western feeders of the Nile, penetrating into the Congo basin. In many of his journeys he accompanied slave-raiding and plundering expeditions of Arabs and Egyptians. He visited the Welle three times, and when he last struck it, in 1883, as far west as 22° 41' east longitude, in 4° north latitude, and found it to be a broad river with many islands, he was ready to abandon the theory of Schweinfurth, that it flowed northwestward into Lake Chad and was identical with the Shari. He was still pursuing his work when the Mahdist rising occurred, and he took refuge with Emin Pasha, whom he left in 1886, managing to reach Zanzibar by way of Victoria Nyanza. The volumes describing his travels were passing through the press in German and English editions at the time of his death.

Kerkapoly, Karl, a Hungarian statesman, born in 1825; died in Buda-Pesth, Jan. 1, 1892. He took part in the revolution of 1848, entered the Hungarian Diet in 1865, became Minister of Finance, and negotiated in Vienna a loan with the Rothschilds, called the Schatzbond loan, at the extraordinary rate of interest of 10½ per cent., an error that sent him into permanent retirement.

Klapka, Georg, a Hungarian patriot and soldier, born in Temesvar, in 1820; died in Buda-Pesth, May 16, 1892. He was a lieutenant in the imperial army, where he placed himself in 1848 at the disposition of the Revolutionary Government of Hungary, and was made chief of staff of the corps operating in the Banat. The plan of campaign that secured the brilliant successes of the insurrectionary troops in the first part of 1849 was his. When Gen. Meszaros was defeated at Kaschau, on Jan. 4, 1849, Klapka was appointed to succeed him. After the victory of Isaszegh; Louis Kossuth raised him to the rank of general on the battlefield. He was Minister of War for the space of a month, and then, in June, was appointed to the command of Komorn and of the forces operating on the right bank of the Danube. Falling back upon Komorn, he defended the fortress from Aug. 13 till Sept. 27, and then surrendered under the most honorable conditions. He lived in exile after the revolution in Switzerland, Italy, London, and Constantinople, and after his return to Hungary, in 1867, made his home in Buda-Pest. He was elected to the Chamber of Deputies, but gave his attention chiefly to industrial enterprises and railroading. He wrote several works on politics and military history, including "La Guerre d'Orient en 1853 et 1854" (Geneva); "La Guerre Nationale en Hongrie et en Transylvanie" (Leipsic); and "Souvenirs" (Zürich, 1887).

Kleist-Retzow, a German statesman, born in 1814; died in Berlin, May 19, 1892. He was the most aggressive and extreme representative of the Junker party, and contended against constitutionalism and liberalism in every form. His eminent abilities and political prominence caused him to be placed at the head of the administration of the Rhenish provinces in 1851. During the reactionary period called the "white terror" he went beyond all his confrères in repressive severity, and political thought was stifled until the Prince-Regent recalled him, in 1858, as soon as he assumed the Government. He abandoned Bismarck when the latter showed signs of departing from strict conservative principles. He was the leader of his party to the end, and although the most uncompromising of them, he was the only one who commanded the general respect of his adversaries.

Klenze, Hippolyt von, a German painter, born in Munich, Aug. 12, 1849; died in Mittelberg, April 30, 1892. He studied under Roth and Schmitzberger, his best works being those representing animals and hunting scenes. He was also a student of chemistry, his specialty being chemistry of milk, which science he applied practically at the estates of Prince Ludwig of Bavaria, whose service he entered in 1877.

Lalo, Edouard, a French composer, born in Lille, in 1831; died in Paris, April 23, 1892. He was of Spanish parentage. His musical talent made itself remarked at an early part of his life. He was a performer on the violin, and prod ced first the opera "Fiesque," which possessed merit of a high order. His first popular success was with " Namouns," on the score of which he labored so intently for eight months that he brought on congestion of the brain. This work delighted the Parisians, and his

"Roi d'Ys" was an equally brilliant and lasting success. Lalo composed a number of symphonies and concerted pieces that are counted among the gems of modern French music.

Lambert, Sir John, an English statesman, born in Wiltshire, Feb. 4, 1815; died in London, Jan. 27, 1892. He was educated at the Roman Catholic college at Downside, near Bath, and became a solicitor. Interesting himself, after the outbreak of cholera, in 1853, in the public health of Salisbury, where he practiced his profession, he was elected mayor in 1854, being the first Roman Catholic to hold that office in any cathedral city of England. He was called to the aid of the Government to prepare schemes for the relief of the famine in Lancashire caused by the stoppage of the supply of cotton from the United States in 1863. He planned the relief works, and the distress was in a great measure removed by the expenditure on public improvements under his superintendence of £1,200,000 advanced as a loan to the local authorities by act of Parliament. In 1865 Lord Russell's Government called upon him to prepare the statistics on which the bill for extending the franchise was based, and he was consulted again when Mr. Disraeli framed his reform bill, in 1867. Mr. Gladstone employed him to go to Ireland in connection with the Irish Church act and the first Irish land bill. In 1867 he also drew up the scheme for the metropolitan poor act, and was made receiver of the poor fund after the act was passed. In 1869 he prepared the scheme for the metropolitan valuation act. He was a member of the commission on parliamentary boundaries under the act of 1867, and of the sanitary commission that made a report which led to the creation of the Local Government Board in 1871, of which he was made the first secretary. He resigned this post in 1882. In 1883 he prepared the scheme on which the parliamentary reform bill of 1884 was based, and in the following year drew up the plans for the redistribution of seats. He acted as chairman of the commissions on the boundaries of the new electoral areas in England and Wales, Scotland, and Ireland. Sir John Lambert, in addition to the enormous amount of official work that he performed, gave considerable attention to floriculture as an amateur, and was deeply interested in music, writing several essays on the subject, and publishing organ accompaniments for the psalms and antiphons of parts of the Roman Catholic liturgy and for the whole of the vesper hymns.

Lamperti, Francesco, an Italian teacher of singing, born in Savone, March 11, 1813; died at his villa on Lake Como, May 6, 1892. He became professor at the Conservatory of Milan in 1850, and from that time his fame spread rapidly through the civilized world. He was held to be the last representative of the great school of Italian singing. A great number of singers who became famous were formed by him, among them Cruvelli, Désirée Artot, Waldmann, Lagrange, Teresina Stolz, Emma Albani, the tenor Campanini, and Collini. Lamperti wrote several books on the principles of the vocal art.

Launay, Count, an Italian diplomatist, born in 1820; died in Berlin, Feb. 7, 1892. He was appointed representative at the Prussian court of the King of Sardinia on June 16, 1853, having previously been attaché. In 1865 he was replaced by Count Barral, but returned in 1867, and remained there as minister and afterward ambassador of the united Kingdom of Italy. He took a prominent part in the conclusion of the triple alliance, was one of the delegates to the Congress of Berlin, and was long the doyen of the diplomatic body in the German capital.

Lavigerie, Charles Allemand, a French ecclesiastic and missionary, born in Bayonne in 1825; died in Algiers, Nov. 26, 1892. He was the son of an officer of the customs service. Showing great promise in the school at Bayonne, he was sent to the Sulpice, in Paris, took his doctor's degree, and became Professor of Ecclesiastical History at the Sorbonne. After the massacre of Christians at Damascus he went to Syria as a missionary, where he conceived the idea of establishing Christian schools as the best means of propagating Christianity in Mohammedan countries. He was afterward French auditor at the Vatican, and was one of the private prelates of the Pope. In 1863 he was consecrated bishop, succeeding Monsignor Darboy at Nancy. In 1867 he became Archbishop of Algeria. His missionary propaganda displeased Marshal MacMahon, the Governor, who feared that it would incense the Arabs, whose religion had been adopted as one of the state churches for Algeria, and therefore ought to be protected against proselytism. Lavigerie supported papal infallibility in 1870 with zeal. In 1871 he offered himself as a candidate for the chamber in the Department of the Pyrénées and in the Landes, and was defeated in both places. He founded the Sahara and Soudan Mission in 1874, sending out missionaries to Tunis, Tripoli, East Africa, and the Congo. On the establishment of a French protectorate over Tunis he revived the bishopric of Carthage, and founded there a college in which Greeks, Protestants, Jews, and Mohammedans, as well as Catholics, are educated. In 1882 he was made a cardinal. His income he spent entirely on his missionary enterprises, and when the French Chamber withdrew the extra stipend allowed to cardinals and the 100,000 francs for Algerian missions, he went over to France and raised the amount by private subscription. He addressed the British and Foreign Antislavery Society in London, in 1888, on the subject of the suppression of the slave trade, and created there, and on the Continent, an interest in the matter which resulted in the Brussels Antislavery Congress of 1889. He also organized a lay order which had for its object to spread Christianity and restore the Sahara to fertility. This society was not successful, and in 1892 it was dissolved. Cardinal Lavigerie was a favorite of the Empress Eugénie under the empire, and under the republic an adherent of the Comte de Chambord, whom he endeavored to rouse to vigorous action. After the death of the Legitimist pretender, he saw little hope for the restoration of the monarchy by the Orleanists, and in 1890 he publicly renounced royalism, and visited Rome to advise the Pope in regard to the reconciliation of the Church with the republic and the reformation of the republic on a Christian basis.

Lemoinne, John, a French journalist, born in London, England, of French parents, Oct. 17, 1815; died in Paris, Dec. 14, 1892. His education, begun at an English school, was completed in France. In 1840 he began his contributions to the "Journal des Débats," and remained on the staff of that paper for fifty-two years, up to 1871 writing articles on English and other foreign questions. Few Frenchmen have understood English affairs better than he, and under the empire he often contrasted English institutions with French, directing the keenest and most polished sarcasms against the imperial rule. Under the republic foreign affairs became of less importance to French readers, and his criticism of England was marked by the same sarcasm that had distinguished his former judgments of French affairs. His nature was essentially critical and demanded a target, and when he was no longer in the ranks of the Opposition in France, he was obliged to look elsewhere for a mark for his shafts. In politics he was a moderate Republican, and as such became, in 1880, a life member of the Senate. His eminence as a journalist secured his entrance into the Academy in 1875, upon the death of Jules Janin. He was at all times a brilliant writer, but his latest work was tinged with a bitterness of tone not apparent in earlier life. He was a frequent contributor to the "Révue des Deux Mondes," and was the author of several historical and political works published in the early portion of his career.

Limnander de Nieuwenhove, Baron **Armand Marie Ghislain,** a Belgian composer, born in Ghent, May 23, 1814; died in Paris, Aug. 19, 1892. He was a pupil of Père Lambilotte, his preceptor at the college of Freiburg, but was considered at first only an amateur, although he devoted himself entirely to music and displayed

marked talent. He wrote "Le Bolero" and other choruses in correct counterpoint, and also religious pieces and chamber music. When fairly launched in his profession he went to Paris. In 1845 parts of his "Druides" were executed at the Conservatoire. In 1849 his "Montenegrins" was produced at the Opéra Comique with a success that was repeated in all the opera houses of Europe. His "Château de la Barbe Bleu" was produced in Dec. 1, 1851, the night of the *coup d'état,* and was not listened to amid the political preoccupations of the audience, whose thoughts were concentrated on the Comte de Morny sitting with an affected air of careless dandyism till the curtain fell. His "Maximilian ou le Maître Chanteur," given in 1856, had no great success, and it was remodeled and presented again in 1877 at the Monnaie in Brussels. "Yvonne" was produced in 1859, and was well received. His conventional music of the old school was already out of date, and as he had not the desire to break with the traditions, he attempted no new original work, spending the remainder of his life on his estate at Moignanville and in the capital.

Lorences, Charles Latrille, Comte de, a French soldier, born in Paris, in 1814; died in Béarn, April 25, 1892. He was on his mother's side a grandson of Marshal Oudinot, Duc de Reggio. He entered St. Cyr in 1830, and in the war in Africa, and especially the siege of Zaatcha, had early opportunities to win distinction, becoming chief of battalion in 1847 and colonel in 1852. For his gallant conduct in the assault of the Malakoff tower in the Crimea he was made general of brigade in 1855. He was military commander of the expeditionary force that was sent to Mexico, and was advanced to general of division. He conducted his troops to Cordova during the *pourparlers,* and, when they failed, marched upon Mexico, gaining some successes, notably at Orizaba. When the attack on Puebla failed he was compelled to retreat. He was an ardent Bonapartist. In the war of 1870 he was commandant of the garrison of Toulouse at first, and afterward led the 3d division of the 4th Corps in the operations at Metz. After his return from captivity he retired into private life, living in his chateau of Laus, near Béarn.

Lowe, Robert, Viscount **Sherbrooke,** an English statesman, born in Bingham, Nottinghamshire, in 1811; died in London, July 27, 1892. He was a son of the rector of Bingham, was educated at Winchester, graduated at Oxford with high honors in 1833, and was made a fellow in 1835. He gave up the fellowship in order to marry in the following year, but remained in Oxford as a tutor, and gained a high reputation as a classical scholar. Afterward he studied law, was called to the bar in Lincoln's Inn in 1842, and went out to New South Wales, where he practiced his profession with great success, was nominated a member of the Legislative Council, and was the author or the furtherer of various reforms of the land laws, legal procedure, and education. He returned to England in 1851, plunged into politics, joining the Liberal party, was elected to Parliament in 1852 from Kidderminster, and at once took high rank as a debater by his vigorous onslaught upon Mr. Disraeli's financial policy. Lord Aberdeen made him one of the secretaries of the Board of Control. Under Lord Palmerston he was Vice-President of the Board of Trade, and afterward Paymaster-General. In 1859 he became President of the Board of Health, and later he was appointed Vice-President of the Education Department, and drew up a scheme of reforms which the House of Commons condemned in 1864 as too liberal. He abandoned Mr. Gladstone in 1865, and became the leader of the "Adullamites," who joined the Tories in opposing the parliamentary reform bill intended to enfranchise a class characterized by Robert Lowe as "residuum" and "dregs of society." His bitterness against the "lower classes" had its origin, perhaps, in his rejection by the voters of Kidderminster in 1859. When his "cave of Adullam" succeeded in defeating Mr. Gladstone's electoral bill, he did not venture to offer himself again to a popular constituency, but got himself elected by the London University, of whose Senate he was a member, and which could not refuse to honor him for his services on behalf of education. Mr. Disraeli's sweeping reform bill was carried, in spite of Lowe's opposition and his admonition to "educate our future masters" before giving them political control. Mr. Gladstone was induced to make Lowe Chancellor of the Exchequer in 1868. His proposition to put a tax on matches roused much popular opposition, and had to be withdrawn. He resigned in 1873, and became Home Secretary, till his party went out in 1874. When they returned, in 1880, he was elevated to the peerage. A volume of poems that he had written in former years, many of them in early life, was published in 1884.

Luce, Auguste Siméon, a French historian, born in Bretteville, Manche, in 1833; died in Paris, Dec. 15, 1892. He was one of the highest living authorities on French mediæval history, and a professor in the École des Chartes, where he had been a pupil. He published a biography of "Jeanne d'Arc" and one of "Duguesclin."

Ludwig IV, Grand Duke of Hesse, born in Bessungen, near Darmstadt, Sept. 12, 1837; died March 13, 1892. He was the son of Prince Karl of Hesse and Elisabeth, a princess of Prussia. On the death of his uncle, Ludwig III, he succeeded to the throne, in June, 1877. He was general of infantry in the Prussian army, with the rank of field marshal and inspector general of the 3d Army Inspection. He married, at Osborne, on July 1, 1862, the Princess Alice, of Great Britain, Duchess of Saxony, who died in December, 1878, having borne him four children, the hereditary Prince Ernst Ludwig, born Nov. 25, 1868, and three daughters. Subsequently he contracted a morganatic marriage with Madame de Kolomine, from whom he was divorced soon afterward.

MacBain, Sir James, an Australian statesman, born in Invergordon, Scotland, in 1828; died in Melbourne, Victoria, Nov. 4. 1892. He entered political life in Australia in 1864, when he was elected to the Legislative Assembly for the district of Winmera, which he represented till 1880. In 1881–'83 he was a member of Sir Bryan O'Loghlen's Cabinet, without a portfolio, and from 1884 till his death he was President of the Legislative Council. He took a prominent part in commercial affairs, and was one of the organizers of the Melbourne Exhibition of 1888.

Mackenzie, Alexander, a Canadian statesman, born in Logierait, England, Jan. 28, 1822; died at Toronto, April 17, 1892. He was the third son of Alexander Mackenzie, an architect and contractor. He went to a private school at Perth for two years, and for two more years to the parish school at Moulin, and spent a few months at the grammar school of Dunkeld. His father died when he was fourteen years old, leaving a widow and seven sons, and the boy went to work as a builder and stone mason. He emigrated to Upper Canada in 1842, and worked first as a Journeyman builder at Kingston. In 1843 he was joined by his brother Hope, and for four years they worked together, making steady progress in business, but even then taking a keen interest in the struggle of the Reform party with Lord Metcalfe, for the completion of responsible government. In 1848 their mother and five other brothers followed them to Canada, and the whole family then settled at Sarnia, in Western Ontario. When the Lambton "Shield" was started to represent the Liberals in that district, Alexander Mackenzie added the editorial duties to his ordinary business for two years. In 1862 he succeeded his brother Hope to the Legislative Assembly of the United Canadas. In Parliament he at once came to the front; his untiring energy, his businesslike accuracy, his keen perception and reliable judgment, and, above all, his inflexible integrity, soon won him the esteem of his fellow-legislators. After the defeat of the Liberal leader at the first Federal election, he became leader first of Ontario Liberal members, and then of the whole Opposition. In 1871 he entered the Ontario Legislative Assembly, as well as the Federal

House, and, after helping Mr. Edward Blake to turn out the provincial ministry, he took office in the new Cabinet, first as Secretary and then as Minister of Finance. In 1872, however, he resigned this position and gave himself up to Federal politics. When, on Nov. 5, 1873, Sir John Macdonald and his ministry had to resign on account of the Pacific Railroad scandal, he was charged with the formation of a new Cabinet. He dissolved Parliament in 1874 and won a sweeping victory, and, backed up by a large majority, he was enabled to carry a remarkable number of important measures. He declared himself an earnest advocate and upholder of the present connection with the mother country, but was in favor of unrestricted reciprocity with the United States, in so far as it could be obtained without discrimination against the mother country. On two occasions the Liberal Premier took ground in opposition to the Imperial Government. In his royal instructions to Lord Dufferin Lord Kimberley had advised the Governor-General to use the prerogative of pardon according to his own discretion, whether the Privy Council for Canada concurred or otherwise. Mackenzie insisted that the prerogative should be exercised only according to the advice of the responsible ministry. The Government gave way to his claim, and he insisted, with a similar result, on the appointment of Canadian diplomats to deal with foreign countries when Canadian interests were involved. At the general election in 1878 he was defeated by an overwhelming majority, the country declaring for Sir John Macdonald's "National Policy," which was to remedy the depression of trade by a protective tariff. He remained a member of Parliament until his death.

Mackenzie, Sir Morell, an English physician, born at Leytonstone, in 1837; died Feb. 3, 1892. He received his medical education at the London Hospital, and at Paris and Vienna. Quite early in his career, in 1863, he founded the Hospital for Diseases of the Throat in London, and in the same year he obtained the Jacksonian prize for an essay on "The Pathology and Treatment of Diseases of the Larynx." Shortly afterward he was appointed, first, assistant physician, and subsequently physician of the London Hospital, in which institution he was also lecturer on diseases of the throat. His contributions to professional literature were numerous, laryngology being his almost invariable subject; and, in particular, his book on "Diseases of the Throat and Nose," which has been translated into French and German, is regarded as a standard work. The treatment of the Emperor Frederick, his most illustrious patient, brought him very prominently before the public, in his own country as well as in Germany. The Emperor's fatal illness was the occasion of a violent dispute between Sir Morell Mackenzie and the German physicians, and by his reply, entitled "The Fatal Illness of Frederick the Noble," to the semiofficial pamphlet of the German doctors, it is obvious that jealousy was on both sides more conspicuous than generosity. He was knighted in 1887 for his services to the Emperor Frederick during the early stages of his illness.

McLaren, A. A., an English missionary, born in Hampshire, in 1854; died in New Guinea about Jan. 1, 1892. He received his early education in a national school, was a clerk in a Government office for three years, entered St. Augustine's College, Canterbury, where he began mission work, which he continued with zeal and success in Queensland, whither he was sent in 1877. Returning to England ten years later to obtain his degree from Durham College, he volunteered for the mission which the Australian Church, aided by the Society for the Propagation of the Gospel, established in 1889 in New Guinea on Bentley Island. He and his assistants entered into friendly relations with several of the native tribes, but their useful activity was arrested by fever, which prostrated the whole party, and was fatal to the head of the mission.

Madier de Montjau, Alfred, a French statesman, born at Nîmes on Aug. 1, 1814; died at Chatou, May 25,

1892. He studied for the bar, and, being an adherent of the revolution in 1848, defended his brother and other socialist prisoners in 1849, and on entering the Assembly joined the Mountain. Being wounded on the barricades in resisting the *coup d'état* in 1851, he was banished, taking refuge in Belgium, where he remained until the fall of the empire. In 1874 he was again a Deputy, sitting with the Extreme Left, being for a time an opponent of Gambetta, but eventually became reconciled to him.

Manning, Henry Edward, an English Roman Catholic prelate, born at Totteridge, Hertfordshire, July 15, 1808; died in London, Jan. 14, 1892. He was educated at Harrow and Balliol College, Oxford, being

graduated in 1830. He was appointed rector of Lavington and Graffham, Sussex, four years later, and became Archdeacon of Chichester in 1840. He was an ardent supporter of the Tractarian movement, and, becoming dissatisfied with the position of the Anglican Church in relation to important doctrines, he resigned his preferments and became a Roman Catholic in 1851. He then entered the priesthood of that Church, and founded an ecclesiastical congregation at Bayswater styled the Oblates of St. Charles Borromeo. On the death of Cardinal Wiseman, in 1865, he succeeded that prelate as Archbishop of Westminster. Pope Pius IX made him a cardinal priest of SS. Andrew and Gregory on the Cœlian Hill in 1875, and in 1877 he received the cardinal's hat. He took a deep interest in questions of social reform, and was a sincere friend of the working classes. He strongly upheld total abstinence, and exerted himself actively in the matter of temperance. Although by temperament an ascetic, he was also a man of the world, and was many-sided enough to win the regard and approbation of men of all ranks and creeds. As a theologian he was not an extremist, and was never a bitter controversialist. His published works include: "The Unity of the Church" (London, 1842); "Sermons" (3 vols., London, 1842-'46); "The Grounds of Faith" (London, 1852); "The Temporal Sovereignty of the Popes" (London, 1860); "The Last Glories of the Holy See Greater than the First" (London, 1861); "The Present Crisis of the Holy See tested by Prophecy" (London, 1861); "The Temporal Power of the Vicar of Jesus Christ" (London, 1862); "Sermons on Ecclesiastical Subjects" (London, 1863-'73); "The Crownin Council on the 'Essays and Reviews'" (London, 1864); "The Blessed Sacrament the Centre of Immutable Truth" (London, 1864); "The Workings of the Holy Spirit" (London, 1864); "The Temporal Mission of the Holy Ghost" (London, 1865); "The Temporal Power of the Pope in its Political Aspect" (London, 1866); "The Reunion of Christendom" (London, 1866); "The Cen-

tenary of St. Peter and the General Council" (London, 1867); "England and Christendom" (London, 1867); "Ireland: A Letter to Earl Grey" (London, 1868); "Rome and the Revolution" (London, 1867); "Devotional Readings" (London, 1868); "The Œcumenical Council and the Infallibility of the Roman Pontiff" (London, 1869); "The Vatican Council and its Definitions" (London, 1870); "Petri Privilegium" (London, 1871); "The Four Great Evils of the Day" (London, 1871); "The Fourfold Sovereignty of God" (London, 1871); "The Dæmon of Socrates" (London, 1872); "Cæsarism and Ultramontanism" (London, 1874); "The Internal Mission of the Holy Ghost" (London, 1875); "The Vatican Decrees in their Bearing on Civil Allegiance" (London, 1875); "The True Story of the Vatican Council" (London, 1877); "Miscellanies" (3 vols., London, 1877-'88); "In Memory of the Prince Imperial" (London, 1879); "The Catholic Church and Modern Society" (London, 1880); "A Letter on the Land Question" (London, 1881); "The Eternal Priesthood" (London, 1883); "Characteristics from the Writings of Cardinal Manning, arranged by W. S. Lilly" (London, 1885); "The Independence of the Holy See," "Religio Viatoris" (London, 1887).

Marchal, Jean Joseph, a French prelate, born April 22, 1822; died May 27, 1892. He was consecrated Bishop of Belley in 1873, and in April, 1880, was made Archbishop of Bourges.

Marlborough, George Charles Spencer Churchill, Duke of, an English nobleman, born May 13, 1844; died in Blenheim Palace, Nov. 9, 1892. He acquired notoriety as Marquis of Blandford by his reckless extravagance and profligate life, and his first wife, Lady Alberta Hamilton, obtained a divorce on the ground of his immoralities in 1883, a few months before he succeeded as eighth duke to the title won by his ancestor, the great Duke of Marlborough. To satisfy his creditors, he sold the famous gallery of paintings and library of his ancestral seat of Blenheim. By his second marriage, in 1888, to the widow of Louis C. Hamersley, of New York, a daughter of Commodore Price, of the United States navy, he obtained an income that enabled him to live again in the style of a nobleman. The Duke of Marlborough was a Liberal, and sometimes he expressed his opinions with considerable force of style in letters to the newspapers; but he never took any part in politics, except to oppose, in the bitter spirit of a family feud, the election of his brother, Lord Randolph Churchill, a Conservative, as representative in Parliament from the family borough of Woodstock.

Martel, Louis Joseph, a French statesman, born in St. Omer, in 1813; died near Evreux, March 6, 1892. He was a Republican under the monarchy, was sent as a Deputy for the Pas de Calais to the Assembly of 1849, and took his seat on the Right, but held himself aloof from the Bonapartists, and after the *coup d'état* he returned to private life till 1863, when his native town chose him as its representative in the Corps Législatif. He associated himself with Thiers, Favre, and Picard, and was one of the founders of what was known as the Third party. In 1870, while supporting the empire, he refused to approve the war. In 1871 he was returned for Pas de Calais, and was one of the supporters of Thiers in the Left Center. He was elected Vice-President of the Assembly, and held that post until he was elected a life Senator on the formation of the Senate. He was the second one chosen, and was made Vice-President of the Senate. In 1876 he was called into the Cabinet of Jules Simon as Minister of Public Worship and Justice. He succeeded the Duc d'Audriffet-Pasquier as President of the Senate in 1879, and in that year presided over the Congress that elected Jules Grévy President of the republic. After presiding over the Congress that in 1880 voted for the return of the Chambers to Paris, he retired for reasons of health, and after that lived quietly on his estate in Navarre.

Matta, Manuel Antonio, a Chilian statesman, born in Copiapo, in 1826; died in Santiago, June 25, 1892. He was educated in the college of his native town and in the German universities, traveled through Europe and America, and after his return to Chili was elected Deputy from Copiapo to the National Congress. Founding the daily paper "La Vox de Chile," he became the leader of the Radical party, and, except while in Colombia as envoy in 1865, sat for his native district in Congress up to 1874, being recognized as one of the strongest speakers in that body. In 1874 he was appointed a member of the Council of State, and in 1876 was elected a Senator for six years. He was chosen President of the Senate, and was twice a candidate for the presidency of the nation. As a prominent member of the Congressional party during the civil war he was made Minister of Foreign Affairs in the Provisional Government, and conducted the controversy with the United States Department of State regarding the murder of sailors of the "Baltimore." In a circular letter sent to the Chilian legations in Europe and America, he declared about the report of the United States Secretary of the Navy and the message of President Harrison upon the occurrence, "that the information on which they are grounded is erroneous or deliberately incorrect," and charged the American authorities with "a want of frankness and exactness in their statements." This letter was formally withdrawn after a long discussion and a final peremptory demand. Señor Matta published translations of German poetry and several political pamphlets.

Mayne, Richard Charles, an English naval officer, born in 1835; died May 26, 1892. He was educated at Eton, and entered the navy in 1847. He served in the Baltic and Black Seas and in the Sea of Azof in 1854-'55, and was wounded in New Zealand in 1863. He commanded the survey expedition to the Straits of Magellan in 1866-'69, and retired with the rank of rear-admiral in 1879.

Medley, John, clergyman, born in London, England, Dec. 19, 1804; died at Fredericton, N. B., Sept. 9, 1892. He was graduated at Wadham College, Oxford, in 1826, was ordained priest in 1828, and was vicar of St. Thomas's, Exeter, 1838-'45, and prebendary of Exeter Cathedral, 1842-'45. In the latter year he was consecrated first Bishop of Fredericton, a diocese which includes the entire province of New Brunswick. He received the degree of D. D. in 1864, and in 1879 became Metropolitan of Canada. He published "The Episcopal Form of Church Government" (London, 1835); "Translation of the Homilies of St. John Chrysostom on Corinthians" (Oxford 1839-'40); "Sermons" (London, 1845); "Translation of the Book of Job, and Commentary" (Fredericton, 1879); "The Reformation" and charges to clergy (Fredericton and Oxford).

Mermillod, Gaspard, a Swiss prelate, born in Carouge, near Geneva, Sept. 22, 1824; died in Bern, Feb. 23, 1892. He studied for the priesthood, took orders in 1846, and displayed such energy and powers of oratory that the Abbé Dunoyer sent him abroad to solicit contributions for the projected cathedral in Geneva, which was built with the money that he obtained, in the grandest style of modern ecclesiastical architecture. The Pope named him Bishop of Hebron *in partibus* and Coadjutor of Lausanne and Geneva, against the desire of Bishop Marilley, who foresaw that the fiery young prelate would probably provoke a conflict. The Protestants and the Federal authorities did not wait for a challenge, but began to harass the Catholics on account of the wild enthusiasm with which they welcomed the promotion of the popular priest. He entered on the contest as fiercely as his opponents, and the climax was reached on his formal deposition by the city authorities of Geneva in 1872. When the Pope detached Geneva from the See of Lausanne in order to make the champion of the rights of the Church vicar apostolic, the Federal Council on Feb. 23, 1873, issued an order for the expulsion of the new dignitary. Mermillod preached in all the cathedrals of Europe, and was landed as a modern confessor, while his country was

torn with the religious war waged over him, and many priests were imprisoned. Leo XIII, when he succeeded to the papacy, sought an opportunity to put an end to the strife, and the Protestants were also weary of the barren struggle. The new Pope restored peace at last by making Mermillod Bishop of Lausanne, to which Geneva was reunited on March 14, 1883, after the death of Bishop Marilley, and suppressing the vicariate apostolic. During his exile Bishop Mermillod lived in Rome a life of monastic austerity, while mingling socially with the aristocracy. He was pardoned by the Federal Council upon making a written declaration of his intention to be faithful to the laws, and his course was entirely pacific after he returned, and was welcomed by his flock.

Millaud, Albert, a French journalist, born in 1844; died in Paris, Oct. 28, 1892. He was the son of Polydore Millaud, the founder of the "Petit Journal." He began by writing humorous articles, and afterward printed satirical verses, signed "Petite Nemesis." He was the principal satirist of "Figaro," and was a master of good-natured ridicule, who could raise a laugh at any public man in France, in which the objects of his satire always joined.

Müller, Carl Louis, a French painter, born in Paris, in 1815; died there, Jan. 22, 1892. He studied in the École des Beaux Arts, and exhibited in 1834 the "Promenade," which was followed by "Christ's Entry into Jerusalem," "Haydée," "Lady Macbeth," "Marie Antoinette," "Proscription of Young Irishmen," "Play," and "A Mass under the Terror." His "Appeal of the Last Victims of the Terror," painted in 1850, is in the Louvre. He decorated the Salle des États and the cupola of the Pavillon Denon in the Louvre. In 1850 he became the director of the Artistic School of the Gobelins. He was elected a member of the Institute in 1864.

Murray, John, an English publisher, born in London in 1809; died there, April 2, 1892. His grandfather was the publisher of the last century, the founder of the house, and the first of the three successive John Murrays. His father was the celebrated publisher of Byron, Scott, and all the great writers of the beginning of the century, and the son was heir to the business. He was educated in Charterhouse School and in the University of Edinburgh, and in 1829 he set out on long and leisurely travels through the Continent, during which he made the notes for the first of Murray's "Handbooks," those for "Holland, Belgium, and the Rhine," for "France," and for "Switzerland." When he had written the first edition of these he engaged the services of distinguished specialists, such as Layard, Ford, and Sir Gardner Wilkinson. On his father's death, in 1843, he settled down to business and managed the publishing house with energy and success. He brought out Layard's account of his archæological discoveries, became the publisher of Dr. William Smith's compilations of classical and biblical information, published Grote's "Greece," Lord Campbell's "Lives of the Chancellors," Livingstone's "Travels," Schliemann's "Archæological Researches," Kugler's books on art, Yule's "Marco Polo," Julian's "Hymnology," Du Chaillu's "Viking Age," and other expensive publications, and was the publisher of Darwin, Sir Henry Maine, Dean Milman, Dean Stanley, and many other authors of the first rank.

Narrey, Charles, a French dramatist, born in 1825 in Bergues, Nord; died in Paris, Nov. 28, 1892. He was of Irish extraction, and followed a literary career in Paris, writing many novels and plays. The most successful of his dramas was "Comme elles sont toutes," which ran for two hundred nights at the Gymnase. In his later life he wrote nothing but articles for the newspapers, mostly humorous.

Natter, Heinrich, an Austrian sculptor, born in Graun, Tyrol, March 16, 1844; died in Vienna, April 13, 1892. He began his career with a bust of the Mayor of Augsburg, Forndrau, and closed it with the Hofer monument in Innsbruck. His tremendous statue of Wotan created a sensation at the Vienna Exhibition in 1873. Among his public monuments are the monument of the heroes of the independence of Tyrol, the Zwingli monument at Zürich, the Haydn statue in Vienna, and a statue of Walther von der Vogelweide for the fountain at Bozen. The busts of Bismarck at Frankfort-on-Main, of the Archduke Franz Karl, of the Austrian Emperor, of the Mayor of Vienna, Uhl, and of the actors Laroche and Meixner, are his best known works of that type.

Nettleship, Richard Lewis, an English educator, born about 1850; died on the Dome du Gouter, Switzerland, Aug. 25, 1892. He was elected a scholar of Balliol College, Oxford, and gained a remarkable number of academic distinctions; became a fellow of his college, and as a classical tutor was one of the most stimulating and helpful of the instructors connected with the university. He took a lively interest in the sports of the undergraduates, and was himself an athlete and a mountain climber. His death was the result of exposure to an Alpine storm that overtook him while he was ascending Mont Blanc.

Nieuwerkerke, Comte Alfred Émilien de, a French artist, born in Paris, April 16, 1821; died near Lucca, Italy, Jan. 18, 1892. He came from a Dutch family; studied sculpture, and in 1843 exhibited a bronze statue of William the Silent, executed for the King of Holland, and shortly afterward made one of Descartes for the city of the Hague, which was duplicated in marble for the city of Tours. In 1849 he was appointed director of the national museums, to which the post of superintendent of the school of fine arts was added directly. He reorganized the Ecole des Beaux Arts in 1863, and kept the post until the advent of the republic, in 1870.

Olphert, Wybrants, an Irish landowner, born in County Donegal, in 1810; died there, Sept. 21, 1892. He was graduated at Trinity College, Dublin, in 1832, and in the following year was commissioned a justice of the peace in the county where his father, the Rev. John Olphert, had a large estate, on which a great number of small tenants resided. To this property he succeeded in 1851. He resided constantly on the estate, and never had serious trouble with his tenants, though he evicted 32 of them in 1884, till 1887, when he refused to make the reductions demanded, and the *plan of campaign* was put in force against him under the lead of Father McFadden, of Gweedore. He carried out evictions in spite of threats and abuse, and forced the tenants at last, in the beginning of 1892, to come to his terms.

Opzoomer, Professor, a Dutch philosopher, born in Rotterdam, Sept. 20, 1821; died in Oosterbeek, near Arnhem, in August, 1892. He was called to the University of Utrecht as Professor of Philosophy at the age of twenty-six. His brilliant powers of presentation and sharp intellect were employed in contesting the speculative philosophy of Van Scholten, which was universally accepted in Holland. He created a new school, the experimental, for which experience forms the only source and marks the final limits of human knowledge. The theories of his system he applied to jurisprudence and theology in several comprehensive works, in which he discussed the fundamental principles of those sciences as well as of metaphysics.

Owen, Sir Richard, an English anatomist, born in Lancaster, July 20, 1804; died at Richmond Park, Surrey, Dec. 18, 1892. At the age of twenty he entered the University of Edinburgh, and while in Edinburgh helped to found the Hunterian Society, and was its first president. In 1825 he removed to London, studied in the Medical School of St. Bartholomew's Hospital, and was graduated there the next year. His first scientific paper was written at this period and published in 1830, and from that time his authorship of scientific monographs and books was almost continuous. By 1878, indeed, the number of scientific papers read and published by him had amounted to 368. He very early became assistant curator of the museum of the Royal College of Surgeons, with the Hunterian department of which his name is indissolu-

bly associated. In 1856 he was transferred from this post to that of superintendent of the natural history department of the British Museum. His life of active work extended over sixty years, and in that space he elaborated and extended the careful system of investigation begun by Cuvier, made the department of palæontological anatomy especially his own, and rose to be the greatest anatomist of modern times. In his old age he linked the old and new in science, and while he received new theories with caution, he was always prepared for changes in scientific thought. His labors for the broadening of human knowledge have been everywhere recognized, and he was made a fellow of nearly every learned body in Europe and America. From the Geological Society he received its highest award, the Wollaston medal, the Linnæan Society granted him its first gold medal for zoölogy, and the Royal Society gave him first its royal medal, and later the "Copley" or olive crown. He was a Knight of the Legion of Honor, and the King of Prussia gave him the Order of Merit. In 1883 he retired from his post at the British Museum, and lived for the remainder of his life at Sheen Lodge, Richmond Park, a residence granted him by the Queen. He was a most exact observer, an extremely clear writer, and as a lecturer to scientific and to popular audiences was equally successful. In 1836 he married Miss Clift, the daughter of William Clift, whose successor he was at the Hunterian Museum. A complete list of his scientific papers and books would number over 400, but his most important works include: "Odontography" (1840); "Lectures on Comparative Anatomy" (1843–'69); "Archetype and Homologies of the Vertebrate Skeleton" (1848); "Nature of Limbs" (1849); "Principles of Comparative Osteology" (1855); "Palæontology" (1860); "British Fossil Mammalia and Birds"; "Fossil Reptiles" (1884).

Oxenden, Ashton, an English bishop and baronet, born at Broome Park, near Canterbury, Sept. 28, 1808; died at Biarritz, France, Feb. 22, 1892. He was graduated from University College, Oxford, in 1831, and was ordained priest in 1834. From 1848 to 1869 he was rector of Pluckley-with-Pevington, Kent, and in 1864 became an honorary canon of Canterbury Cathedral. In 1869 he was consecrated bishop of Montreal, at the same time becoming primate and Metropolitan of Canada. In April, 1878, he resigned his bishopric, feeling himself unequal to its cares, and in May, 1879, was instituted vicar of St. Stephen's, Hackington, near Canterbury, and held that position until 1885. He published "Portraits from the Bible" (London, 1860–'65); "Words of Peace: With Meditations" (London, 1863); "Prayers for Private Use" (London, 1863); "The Parables of Our Lord" (London, 1864); "Our Church and its Services" (London, 1866); "Decision" (London, 1868); "Short Lectures on the Gospels, from Advent to Easter" (2 vols., London, 1868–'69); "My First Year in Canada" (London, 1871); "Thoughts for Lent" (London, 1872); "Thoughts for Advent" (London, 1872); "Simple Exposition of the Psalms" (2 vols., London, 1873); "The Earnest Churchman" (London, 1878); "Counsels to the Confirmed" (London, 1878); "My Father" (London, 1884); "Touchstones: Christian Graces and Characters tested" (London, 1884); "Short Comments on St. Matthew and St. Mark" (London, 1885); "Thoughts for Holy Week, with Meditations and Prayers" (London, 1886).

Peel, Paul, a Canadian artist, born in London, Ontario, in 1860; died in Paris, Oct. 25, 1892. He was the son of a marble cutter. He studied for three years in the Philadelphia Academy of Fine Arts, went in 1880 to England to continue his studies, and ended his preparation with five years of study in Paris, where he was a pupil of Gérôme. His style was entirely French, and he made the French capital his home. He obtained honorable mention in the salon of 1889 for his "Life is bitter," and in 1890 received a gold medal for "After the Bath."

Pelly, Sir Lewis, an English soldier, born in 1825; died in Falmouth, April 22, 1892. He entered the army in 1841, took part in the expedition against Persia in 1857 as aid-de-camp to Gen. Jacob, and in 1860 was *chargé d'affaires* in Persia. In the following year he was sent to Zanzibar in the character of political agent. He had risen in the army to the rank of lieutenant-general before his death. He entered Parliament in 1885, representing North Hackney. Gen. Pelly was an author as well as a soldier, diplomat, and Conservative politician.

Pianell, Count Giuseppe, an Italian general, born in Palermo, Nov. 9, 1818; died in Verona, April 5, 1892. Entering the Sicilian army as captain at the age of nineteen, he soon advanced to the rank of brigadier-general. In 1860 he accepted the portfolio of Minister of War under the new Liberal Cabinet. Being convinced that the Kingdom of Sicily would soon lose its independence and form a part of united Italy, he tendered his resignation, and went to Paris to await developments. From there he offered his services to Count Cavour, and was appointed lieutenant-general in the Italian army. He took part in the campaign of 1866, and distinguished himself in the battle of Custozza. From 1867 to 1870 he was a member of the Italian Chamber, and since Nov. 15, 1871, has belonged to the Senate. He was commander of an army corps until December, 1891, when he retired from the public service.

Poise, Ferdinand, a French composer, born in Nimes, in 1828; died in Paris, May 26, 1892. He was a pupil of Adolphe Adam at the Conservatoire, and took the second prize of Rome in 1852. He produced more than a dozen operas, of which the most liked were: "Bonsoir Voisin!" in one act, given in 1853, his first production; "Les Charmeurs," in one act, produced in 1855; "La Surprise d'Amour," for which Charles Mouselet wrote the libretto after Marivaux, which was presented in 1877; "L'Amour Médecin," after Molière, by the same librettist; and, chief of all, "Joli Gilles." Poise was a composer of comic operas of the traditional French school, who developed, without pretentiousness and with easy grace, an airy vein of light melody not remarkable for originality.

Popelin, Claudius, a French artist and author, born in Paris, in 1825; died there, May 27, 1892. He studied painting under Ary Scheffer, exhibited "Dante reading his Poems" in 1852, a "St. Jerome" in the following year, "Stephanus among the Wise Men who aided him" in 1854, "Guillaume Budé learning Greek" in 1859, and "Dante returning to Florence after Campaldino" in 1861. Turning to the art of enameling, he produced heads of Julius Cæsar, Napoleon III, and Henri de Mertemart, and allegorical pictures of "The Renaissance," "France," and "Truth and its Zealots." In 1866 he published "L'Émail des Peintres," in 1868 "L'Art de l'Émail," and in 1869 "Les vieux Arts de Feu," all illustrated by himself. He also translated from the Italian Picolpassi's work on the potter's art, and from the Latin of Alberti an essay on statuary and painting, and wrote an essay on the Italian Renaissance. Abandoning art except as a pastime, he devoted himself to writing sonnets, which were as admirable as his enamels, illustrations, and oil paintings. He published "Cinq Octaves de Sonnets" in 1875, and in 1888 "Livre de Sonnets."

Protich, Kosta S., a Servian statesman and soldier, born in 1831; died in Brestovacka Banja, June 16, 1892. After passing through the Belgrade gymnasium, he entered the Servian army in 1848, and two years later was one of the first cadets in the new Servian Military Academy. In 1855, after he had become a lieutenant, he was sent to Berlin to take the course of engineering in the Prussian Artillery and Engineer School, after which he was attached to a battalion of pioneers in Dantzic, and to the inspection of engineers in Coblenz, and completed his higher military training in the Belgian engineer corps in Liége. His return to Servia occurred at a period that was favorable for the advancement of capable officers. The year 1858 saw the restoration of the Obrenovich dynasty to the throne. Like Ristich and Belimarkovich, he was a stanch adherent of that family. Less

of a politician, but a better soldier than the other two, his advancement was less rapid. He became a major in 1869, and lieutenant-colonel in 1873, when he was called into the Cabinet of Marinovich as Minister of War. This post he filled till 1875, in which year he was made a colonel. In the war with Turkey in 1876 he was promoted to general for brilliant services in the battle of Shumatovatz, and in the campaign of 1877 he was chief of the general staff. After the war he occupied an important office at court for a time. He retired from active service in 1882. In 1888, when King Milan was preparing for his abdication, he called Protich into the Cabinet of Nikala Cristich as Minister of War. It devolved upon him to go to Wiesbaden to bring the young prince, because the Prussian Government desired that the task should be intrusted to an active minister who held a high rank in the army, although Queen Natalie regarded him as her enemy, and looked upon his selection as a personal insult. In 1889 Milan chose Protich, Jovan Ristich, and Belimarkovich as the three who should administer the supreme power as regents during the minority of the young King. Protich did not take a prominent part in the regency. He devoted himself chiefly in keeping up the standard of the military service. In political affairs he exercised a steadying and conciliatory influence.

Rangabé, Alexander Rizos, a Greek statesman and author, born in Constantinople, in 1810; died Jan. 28, 1892. He was educated in the Military School at Munich. In 1852 he became Greek Minister of Education, and afterward was Professor of Archæology. In 1856–'59 he held the post of Minister of Foreign Affairs. In 1867 he was appointed minister at Washington, and in the next twenty years he represented his Government in the principal capitals, going to Paris after his recall from the United States, and thence to Constantinople, and finally to Berlin. He translated Shakespeare, Lessing, and Goethe into Greek, and published a Greek grammar, a Franco-Greek dictionary, and a "History of Romaic Literature."

Robertson, George Croom, a Scotch educator and metaphysician, born in Aberdeen, in 1842; died in London, Sept. 21, 1892. He was educated at the University of Aberdeen, graduating M. A. in 1861, studied afterward in London, Berlin, Göttingen, and Paris, became assistant Professor of Greek at Aberdeen in 1864, and in 1866 was made Professor of Philosophy of Mind and Logic in University College, London. He acted as philosophical examiner for the universities of London and Aberdeen for many years. He was the editor of "Mind," for which he wrote many papers. He assisted Prof. Bain in editing Grote's "Aristotle," wrote a biographical study of Hobbes, and contributed to the ninth edition of the "Encyclopædia Britannica."

Rochholz, Ernst Ludwig, a Swiss archæologist and Germanist, born in Anspach, in 1808; died in Aarau, Oct. 29, 1892. He studied jurisprudence in the University of Munich, was a friend of Rückert and Döllinger, and of Grimm, under whose direction he devoted himself to the investigation of folklore. He went to Hofwyl in 1833 to assist Fellenberg, and remained in Switzerland. In 1856 he published two volumes of "Schweizersagen," and in the following year "Allemanisches Kinderlied und Kinderspiel." His "Bruder Klaus von Flüe" appeared in 1870, and "Tell und Gessler" in 1876.

Rousset, Camille, a French historian, born in Paris, in 1820; died in Gobain, Oct. 20, 1892. He was Professor of History at Grenoble, and afterward in Paris from 1845 till 1864, when he became librarian and historiographer of the War Office, a post that was abolished in 1876. In 1871 he was made a member of the French Academy, succeeding to the *fanteuil* of Prévost-Paradol. He sought election to the Chamber in 1877 as an Orleanist. He wrote a life of Louvois, edited the correspondence of Louis XV and Marshal Noailles, and published, under the title of "Volontaires de 1771-'94," a book in which he endeavored to prove that the victories of the first republic were mainly achieved by soldiers trained under the monarchy. He wrote also a history of the Crimean War. His principal work was his last, an elaborate history of the French conquests in Algeria.

Saint-Bon, Pacoret de, an Italian naval officer, died in Rome, Nov. 26, 1892. In 1866 he had charge of the "Formidabile." In the attack on the works of Lissa, on July 19, he led the way up the channel, steamed up to within 300 yards of the batteries, and then stern on with anchor down, till the vessel was able to enfilade them. Suddenly deserted by her consorts, the "Formidabile" was badly battered before she could get out to sea again, and during the action 50 of her men were killed. Admiral Saint-Bon in after years performed important services as a naval administrator, first as President of the Council of Marine, then as commander-in-chief at Naples, and for the last two years of his life as chief of the Admiralty. He was a Senator, and at one time Minister of Marine.

Saint-Denis, Marquis Hervey de, a French sinologist, born in Paris, in 1823; died there in November, 1892. He studied Oriental languages, made himself a master of Chinese, and published translations of Chinese tales, poems, and history, and works on the agriculture, poetry, and historical records of China.

Schmitz, Isidore Pierre, a French soldier, born in Neuilly-sur-Marne, July 21, 1820; died in Paris, Feb. 3, 1892. He entered the school of St. Cyr at the age of eighteen; was commissioned as lieutenant in 1845 while serving with the army in Africa, became a captain in 1847, returned to France in 1849, was aid-de-camp to Gen. Forey at Strasburg and in the Crimea, and distinguished himself at Sebastopol. In 1859 he fought in the Italian campaign, and was promoted colonel in 1860. In the war with China he planted the French flag on the parapet at Eangho. He became a general of brigade in 1868. In the Franco-Prussian War he acted as chief of staff to Gen. Trochu at Paris. He was promoted general of division in 1875, and in 1880 was decorated with the grand cross of the Legion of Honor, having served in 14 campaigns.

Sidel-Hadj'-Abd-es-Salaam, Sherif of Wuzzan-Mulai, died in Tangier, in September, 1892. He was a cousin of the reigning Sultan of Morocco, and the chief of the religious brotherhood of the Taïbya or Wazzani, who are scattered throughout Morocco and are numerous in Algeria in the department of Oran. The Sherif had a powerful influence over the Moors and Arabs on account of his reputed sanctity, and was likely to succeed to the throne of Morocco. Though his first wife was an Englishwoman, he was more friendly to the French.

Siemens, Werner von, a German electrical engineer, born at Louthe, in Hanover, in 1816; died at Berlin, Dec. 6, 1892. He entered the Prussian Artillery as a volunteer in 1834, but soon left the service, and some years later joined his younger brother, the late Sir Carl Wilhelm Werner, in England, where the two were associated in various undertakings under the name of "Siemens Brothers." His life, however, was passed mainly in Prussia, where, under governmental encouragement, he invented methods of gold and silver plating, and devoted much attention to the development of electric telegraphy. The telegraph line between Berlin and Frankfort-on-Main, the first great Continental line, was established by him in 1849. Six Atlantic cables, as well as other submarine systems, were laid by the Siemens Brothers. Dr. Werner Siemens invented the pneumatic-tube system and a number of important improvements in dynamos for electric lighting, and was an honorary member of most of the European electrical and scientific societies.

Signol, Émile, a French painter, born about 1810; died in Paris, Oct. 17, 1892. He obtained the *prix de Rome* in 1830, a second medal in 1834, and a first-class medal in the following year. His "Femme Adultère" was the most remarked of any painting exhibited in 1840, and was purchased for the Luxembourg. In that year he was employed in the decora-

tion of the Madeleine, and subsequently he worked in other churches of Paris. In the Universal Exhibition of 1855 he had a large number of paintings. There was a conflict over his election in 1860 to the Académie des Beaux Arts. He was made an officer of the Legion of Honor in 1865.

Simeoni, Giovanni, an Italian ecclesiastic, born in Paliano, July 23, 1816; died in Rome, Jan. 14, 1892. He was distinguished for intellectual ability and knowledge as a young priest, and was appointed auditor of the Nunciature of Madrid in 1847, then prefect of studies in the Pontifical Lyceum of the seminary at Rome, and in 1857 was made domestic chaplain of the Pope and sent on a mission to Spain. He was secretary to the Congregation of the Propaganda for the affairs of the Oriental rite for eight years, and in 1868 became secretary for the Latin rite. In 1875 he went to Spain as nuncio after being created Archbishop of Chalcedonia. On March 15 of the same year he was raised to the cardinalate. Pope Pius IX made him his Secretary of State in 1876, and in March, 1878, when he was succeeded in that office by Cardinal Franchi on the accession of Leo XIII, he was made Prefect of the Propaganda. As Pontifical Secretary of State he was the foremost advocate of the claims of the Vatican to the restoration of the temporal power in Italy, and the upholder of the clergy in their struggles against the civil government in France and other countries. As Prefect of the Propaganda he was responsible for the circular to the bishops in Ireland, which was generally interpreted as prohibiting the priests from contributing or raising money for the Irish party.

Solntseff, Fedor Gregorivich, a Russian artist, born in 1800; died in St. Petersburg, March 20, 1892. He began his artistic career in 1825 and gave much attention to the early art and archæology of his own country. The great work entitled "Antiquités de l'Etat Russe," p   s   by order of the Czar Nicholas, was prepared by him. He made the designs after which the Kremlin was restored, and was the discoverer of the ancient frescoes in the Church of St. Sofia at Kieff and the mural paintings of Kievo-Petchersky.

Stephen, James Kenneth, an English poet, born in 1860; died in London, Feb. 2, 1892. He was educated at Eton and Kings College, Cambridge, where his career was very brilliant. He became a fellow of his college, and acted for a time as tutor to Prince Albert Victor. Going to London, he started a paper called the "Reflector," which was a failure, although he filled it with clever and original satirical articles. His two books of humorous poems "Lapsus Calami" and "Quo, Musa, tendis?" had more success.

Stevens, Joseph, a Belgian painter, born in Brussels, in 1819; died in Ixelles, Aug. 3, 1892. He was the elder brother of Alfred Stevens, and in his special branch, which was the painting of animals, he was almost his equal in technique and as a colorist and a true descendant of the Flemish masters. By not only studying the anatomy and expressive movements and attitudes of animals, especially dogs, but the principles of composition and light and shade, he lifted animal painting to the level of real art. Among his numerous works some of the best known are "Bruxelles le Matin," "Un Métier de Chien," "La Lice et sa Compagne," and "Vielle Lice."

Sutherland, George Granville Leveson Gower, a Scotch nobleman, born in 1828; died in Dunrobin castle, Sept. 22, 1892. He owned nearly 1,000,000 acres in Sutherland County, and had estates in Cromartie and in Staffordshire, England, and was interested in English and Scottish railroads, in the Suez Canal, and other financial enterprises. He was the eldest son of the second duke and a daughter of the Earl of Carlisle, and succeeded to the title and estates in 1861. He was one of the most liberal and enterprising of land owners, spending great sums on the improvement of his estates in the north of Scotland and on the reclamation of waste lands, the building of Highland railroads, and the development of coal mines and the establishment of brick works, steam saw mills, and other local industries. The title descends to his son, the Earl of Stafford, born in 1851.

Tewfik Pasha, Mohammed, Khedive of Egypt, born Nov. 15, 1852; died in the Helouan Palace, near Cairo, Jan. 7, 1892. He was a son of Ismail Pasha by a fellah woman, and was plainly brought up in Egypt, while his brothers were educated in Paris, Oxford, and Woolwich. When Ismail, in 1866, in order to disinherit his uncle, Halim Pasha, had the order of succession changed from the Mohammedan to the European system, he hoped to choose his heir from among his sons, but the powers insisted on the order of primogeniture. Tewfik married, in 1873, Emineh Hanem, a daughter of El Hamy Pasha, who, like himself, was a great-grandson of Mehemet Ali. He was called away from his estate, where he occupied himself with his tenants and with farming, to the head of the ministry in 1878, but he soon resigned. On June 26, 1879, Ismail Pasha was deposed as khedive by the Sultan, and Tewfik succeeded to the throne. For several months there was nothing but confusion in the administration, anarchy in the army, and general disorder. On Nov. 10, 1879, the Anglo-French control was established, and for two years M. de Blignières and Major Baring or Auckland Colvin governed the country. Tewfik bravely remained in Alexandria when it was bombarded. After the suppression of Arabi's revolt he returned to Cairo, and at the dictation of his British advisers he reluctantly consented to the abandonment of the Soudan in 1884. He followed the directions of Sir Evelyn Baring in all important matters, perceiving that it was useless to rebel merely in the hope of re-establishing the dual control, which was no more acceptable to the country, and under which he was no freer. (See portrait on page 246 of this volume.) He was succeeded by his eldest son, Abbas Pasha, who is familiar with European countries and speaks several languages.

Thomas, Arthur Goring, an English composer, born in 1851; died in London, March 20, 1892. He studied music in Paris in 1875-'77, and afterward in London in the Royal Academy of Music and under Arthur Sullivan and Prout. His opera, "Esmeralda," characterized by some of the grace and finish of the French school, attained an exceptional success. His "Light of the Harem" has never been produced, although it was the earliest opera that he composed. "Nadeschda" was brought out in 1885, two years after "Esmeralda." He composed a cantata, "The Sun Worshipers," a *suite de ballet*, a number of orchestral pieces, others for voices and instruments, and a large number of songs which have made him famous. He was mentally deranged after an accident that occurred some months before his death, and in this condition threw himself from a railroad train.

Tong King Sing, director of railways and mines in north China, born in 1832; died in Tientsin, Oct. 7, 1892. He was well known for his progressive ideas and his friendly disposition toward Europeans. He visited Europe in 1882, and was an efficient co-operator of Li-Hung-Chang in the movement to introduce railroads and other technical improvements into China.

Trapani, Prince Francois de Paule de Bourbon, Comte de, born in Naples, Aug. 13, 1827; died in Paris, Sept. 24, 1892. He was the youngest brother of King Ferdinand of the Two Sicilies and the uncle of the ex-King François II. He married, in 1850, the Princess Maria Isabel, Archduchess of Austria-Tuscany, and had two daughters, one of whom married her cousin the Count of Caserta, and the other the Count Zamoyski. The Comte de Trapani lived in very modest style in Paris, as he had no fortune.

Trebelli, Zella, a French singer, born in Paris, in 1838; died in Etretat, Seine-Inférieure, Aug. 18, 1892. Her family name was Gilbert, which she transformed into Trebelli when she went upon the stage. She played the piano with skill and understanding before her training for the lyric stage began, at the age of ten. Her first appearance was in Madrid at the age of twenty, as Rosina in "Il Barbiere," and it was a complete success. This, and Orsini, Ormacc, Urbano, and other contralto parts, she rendered with triumphant success in German cities, and in 1862 she sang Fatima in "Oberon" in London, and became a favorite of the English public. Latterly she gained celebrity in the character of the heroine in "Carmen," and in 1889 made a tour in the United States.

Trollope, Thomas Adolphus, an English novelist and historian, born in 1810; died at Clifton, England, Nov. 11, 1892. His father was a barrister, and his mother the well-known novelist, Mrs. Frances Trollope. He was educated at Winchester and Alban Hall, Oxford, and published his first work, "Britanny," in 1840. The next year he went to live in Florence, Italy, and remained there till shortly before his death. He was twice married, his first wife having been a Miss Garrow, who wrote some works on Italy, and the second Mrs. Frances Eleanor Trollope, whom he married in 1865, a novelist of considerable repute. His knowledge of Italian history and literature was extensive, and he wrote easily and entertainingly in both history and fiction. His most important work is a "History of the Commonwealth of Florence, from the Earliest Independence of the Commune to the Fall of the Republic in 1531," which was published in 1865 in four volumes. Other works by him are: "Western France" (1841); "Impressions of a Wanderer in Italy" (1850); "The Girlhood of Catharine de' Medici" (1856); "A Decade of Italian Women" (1859); "Tuscany in 1849" (1859); "Filippo Strozzi: A History of the Last Days of the Old Italian Liberty" (1860); "Paul the Pope and Paul the Friar" (1860); "La Beata" (1861); "Marietta," a novel (1862); "A Lenten Journey in Umbria and the Marches" (1862); "Giulio Malatesta" (1862); "Beppo, the Conscript" (1864); "Lindisfarn Chase," a novel (1864); "Gemma," a novel (1866); "Artingale Castle" (1867); "The Dream Numbers" (1868); "Leonora Casaloni" (1868); "The Garstangs of Garstang Grange" (1869); "A Siren" (1870); "Durnton Abbey," a novel (1871); "The Stillwinches of Comba Mavis" (1872); "Diamond cut Diamond" (1875); "The Papal Conclaves as they were and as they are" (1876); "A Family Party at the Piazza of St. Peter's" (1877); "Life of Pope Pius the Ninth" (2 vols., 1877); "A Peep behind the Scenes at Rome" (1877); "Sketches from French History" (1878); "What I remember," a book of recollections (1887). As a novelist he never attained to the popularity of his brother Anthony, but his contributions to Italian history have a recognized value, by no means inconsiderable.

Wallis, Sir Provo William Parry, an English naval officer, born April 12, 1791, in Halifax, Nova Scotia; died near Chichester, Feb. 13, 1892. He was listed as a midshipman on the "Cleopatra" for eighteen months before the signing of the treaty of Amiens, on March 25, 1802, and for many years he remained the sole surviving flag officer who had fought in the Napoleonic wars and in the American War of 1812. He was taken prisoner on the "Cleopatra" in 1805, assisted in the capture of the French batteries in Guadeloupe in 1809, and in 1813 was second lieutenant of the "Shannon," and after her fight with the "Chesapeake" took her and the prize into Halifax harbor. For this he was promoted to commander. In 1838-'39 he was present at some of the actions of the French war in Mexico, and also off Tangier when the French fleet bombarded that city and Mogador. He saw service in 1845 in the civil war in Syria. He was aid-de-camp to the Queen in 1847-'51, became a flag officer in the latter year, was made admiral of the white by order of seniority in 1863, rear-admiral in 1869, Vice-admiral in 1870, and admiral of the fleet in 1877. He was knighted in 1860.

Walshe, Walter Hayle, an English physician, born about 1810; died in London, Dec. 14, 1892. He entered Trinity College, Dublin, in 1827, went to Paris in 1830 to study Oriental languages, began the study of medicine in 1832, under Louis, at La Pitié, was graduated M. D. at Edinburgh in 1835, and in 1841 was elected Professor of Pathological Anatomy in University College Hospital, London, where he entered on the practice of medicine. He became Professor of Clinical and Systematic Medicine afterward, and physician to Brompton Hospital for diseases of the chest. He published valuable works on philology, as well as important treatises on medical subjects, including a translation of the work of Louis on "Phthisis," a treatise on "Cancer," others on diseases of the lungs and of the heart, and two theoretical works written after his retirement from practice, entitled "Dramatic Singing physiologically considered" and "The Colloquial Faculty for Language and the Nature of Genius."

Wilder, Jerome A. Victor, a French musical critic, born in Belgium, in 1834; died in Paris, Sept. 9, 1892. He received the doctorate in philosophy and law in the university of Ghent, and in 1860 went to Paris, and became a musical critic, writing for the "Evénement," the "Menéstrel," and other journals. He soon became known as an able translator from the German and Italian, and wrote the French words to which most of the lyrical works of Handel, Weber, Schumann, Mendelssohn, Chopin, Grieg, and Rubinstein are sung. He also wrote a "Life of Mozart" and a "Life of Beethoven." He came conspicuously into public view as the translator of Wagner's operas, and the valiant champion of the composer's fame in France. For some time before his death he was musical critic for the "Gil Blas."

Williams, Montagu, an English magistrate and Queen's counsel, born in Freshford, Somerset, in 1834; died at Ramsgate, Dec. 23, 1892. He was educated at Eton, became at twenty a classical master in the grammar school at Ipswich, and at the outbreak of the Crimean War entered the army and served in the Crimea. After the fall of Sebastopol he left the army, became an actor, and wrote a number of clever farces in collaboration with F. C. Burnand. "B. B." was the most successful of these. While in the theatrical profession he married Miss Keeley, a daughter of the famous actress Mrs. Keeley. Leaving the stage after a few years, he took up the study of law, became a barrister, and one of the most successful criminal lawyers of his time. For a quarter of a century he was engaged as counsel in most of the celebrated cases at the Old Bailey and Clerkenwell. In later life he sat as police magistrate at Greenwich, Woolwich, and Marylebone courts. His position gave him an insight into the life of the very p r, who found in him a staunch friend. He founded the Montagu Williams Relief Fund, and established places in the East End of London for the distribution of bedding and clothes. He contributed many articles to "Household Words," which were very popular, and published the following works which are autobiographical in their nature: "Leaves of a Life," "Later Leaves," "Round London: Down East and up West," 1892. The latter book appeared but a week before the author's death.

Wilson, Sir Daniel, a Canadian educator and author, born in Edinburgh, Scotland, in 1816; died in Toronto, Aug. 7, 1892. He was a nephew of Christopher North and a brother of Dr. George Wilson, Professor of Technology in the University of Edinburgh. Daniel was educated in the high school and University of Edinburgh, and engaged in literary work in London for a few years, then returned to Scotland, won a reputation as an archaeologist, acted as secretary to the Scottish Society of Antiquaries, and through Lord Elgin, who was at one time president of this society, he was called to the University of Toronto, in 1853, as Professor of History. He had published "Memorials of Edinburgh in the Olden Time," illustrated by his own hand (1847); "Oliver Cromwell and the Protectorate" (1848); and "The Archæology and Prehistoric Annals of Scotland" (1851). In Canada he sustained his reputation as a scientific man, and also took a leading part in educational affairs. He became President of Toronto University in 1881, succeeding Dr. McCaul. He was the foremost advocate for a national system of university education in Canada freed from the auspices of denominations or churches and controlled and directed by the state, and his efforts for thirty-five years were finally crowned with success. His greatest book is "Prehistoric Man: Researches into the Origin of Civilization in the Old and the New Worlds" (1862). He published also "Chatterton: A Biographical Study" (1869), and "Caliban, the Missing Link" (1873), and contributed articles on archæology, Canada, confederation, Chatterton, Edinburgh, and Toronto to the "Encyclopædia Britannica." He was the author also of a volume of poems called "Spring Wild Flowers." He was knighted in 1888.

Wolf, Gerson, an Austrian historian, born in Moravia, in 1823; died in Vienna, about Nov. 1, 1892. He was educated for a Jewish rabbi, but took up journalism and literature. For his political writings he was tried by court-martial and sentenced to imprisonment in 1852. He wrote works on the Jews in Vienna, on the history of Vienna University, on Maria Theresa, and on the modern political history of Austria and Hungary.

Woolner, Thomas, an English sculptor and poet, born at Hadleigh, Suffolk, Dec. 17, 1825; died in London, Oct. 7, 1892. In 1842 he exhibited at Westminster Hall a life-size group, "The Death of Boadicea," which attracted much favorable attention. In 1848 he exhibited statues of "Puck," "Titania," and "Eros and Euphrosyne," which added to his fame, already considerable. He was an ardent disciple of the pre-Raphaelite school, and was instrumental with Millais, Holman Hunt, and Dante Rossetti in founding "The Genu," a preraphaelite periodical, begun in 1850. His poetical contributions to that journal were collected in a volume in 1863 with the title "My Beautiful Lady." His other volumes of poems are "Pygmalion" (1881); "Silenus" (1884); "Tiresias" (1886); "Nelly Dale" (1887). He was elected an associate of the Royal Academy in 1871, and a few years later became an academician. For two years from 1877 he was Professor of Sculpture. His most celebrated sculptures include "Constance and Arthur," "Elaine," "Ophelia," "Achilles and Pallas shouting from the Trenches," statues of Macaulay, Lord Laurence, Lord Palmerston, Lord Frederick Cavendish (a recumbent figure); busts of Carlyle, Tennyson, Darwin, Gladstone, Kingsley, Maurice, and others. His verse appeals to the most cultivated intellectual tastes, and has few of the elements of popularity. His best work is undoubtedly included in "My Beautiful Lady." His later poems, though finely conceived, are somewhat cold in treatment.

Wordsworth, Charles, an English clergyman, born in Lambeth Palace, London, Aug. 22, 1806; died at Kilrymont, St. Andrew's, Scotland, Dec. 4, 1892. His father was the younger brother of the poet Wordsworth. His education was gained at Braintree, Harrow, and Christ Church, Oxford, and he was graduated from the university in 1830. He remained at Oxford for some years as a private tutor, and among his pupils were Mr. Gladstone and Cardinal Manning. He was ordained in 1834, and the next year became a master at Winchester College, and filled that position till his resignation, in 1846. A few months later he accepted, at the request of Mr. Gladstone, the wardenship of Trinity College, Glenalmond, Scotland, which office he held until 1854. In 1852 he was elected bishop of the united sees of St. Andrew's, Dunkeld, and Dunblane, and from that time devoted his entire energies to the duties of his office. His consecration took place in 1853, and at the outset he assumed the leading position in the Scottish Episcopal Church. He labored strenuously to effect a reconciliation between Presbyterians and Episcopalians, conceding the validity of Presbyterian orders, but requiring the return of the Presbyterians to the protection of the historic episcopate. His views on this point, however, were distasteful to large numbers of Scottish Episcopalians, and by no means satisfactory to the members of the Kirk of Scotland.

He was but slightly affected by the Oxford movement, although he knew many of its leaders, but his nature was too robustly practical to have much sympathy with the idealism of that school of religious thought. As a young man he was a noted athlete, having achieved distinction in rowing, skating, and on the cricket field, and he carried the athletic temper into all the discussions and controversies of his long life. His beliefs were held with entire confidence, without a shadow of indefiniteness, and the breadth of his views offered at times a strong contrast to the narrowness exhibited by some of his own party. He received many honorary degrees, including a D. C. L. from Oxford, and D. D. from Edinburgh and St. Andrew's. He was a profound scholar, and was one of the company of revisers for the New Testament. In the Scottish Church he held a place which can not readily be filled, and as a large-minded, liberal man he ranks among the notables of his generation of Englishmen. He married, in 1835, Miss Charlotte Day, the daughter of the Rev. George Day, and on her death, in 1839, he remained a widower until 1846, when he married Katharine Mary, the oldest daughter of the Rev. William Barter, rector of Burghcleve, Hants. He was a voluminous writer on ecclesiastical and secular subjects, and among his works are the noted "Graecae Grammaticae Rudimenta" (1849); "Christian Boyhood at a Public School" (1846); "The College of St. Mary, Winton" (1849); "A Greek Primer"; "Shakespeare's Knowledge and Use of the Bible" (1854); "Letter to the Right Hon. W. E. Gladstone on Religious Liberty" (1852); "A United Church for the United Kingdom, etc."; "A Manual of Reformation Facts and Principles"; "The Outlines of the Christian Ministry delineated and brought to the Test of Reason"; "Holy Scripture, Reason, and Experience" (1872); "Catechesis, or Christian Instruction"; "Public Appeals in Behalf of Christian Unity" (1886); "Collects and Select Psalms and Hymns in Latin Verse" (1890); "Annals of my Early Life, 1806-1846" (1891). A promised second volume, entitled "Annals of my Later Life from my Settlement in Scotland, 1847, to the Present Time," was left in manuscript by the bishop at his death. Among works edited by him are "Shakespeare's Historical Plays, Roman and English" (1883).

Yamada, Count Akiosseri, a Japanese soldier and statesman, died in Tokio, Nov. 13, 1892. He took a prominent part on the side of the Mikado in the war of 1867 for the restoration of the ancient monarchy, and after the revolution was a prominent public man, holding the portfolio of the Ministry of Justice for some time, but resigning it a few months before his death on account of ill health.

OHIO. A central Western State, admitted to the Union in 1803; area, 39,964 square miles; population, according to last census (1890), 3,666,719, it being the fourth in rank of the States. Capital, Columbus.

Government.—The government of the State during 1892 was as follows: Governor, William McKinley, Jr.; Lieutenant-Governor. Andrew L. Harris; Secretary of State, Daniel J. Ryan (resigned during term and Christian L. Poorman appointed); Auditor of State. Ebenezer W. Poe; Treasurer of State, William T. Cope; Attorney-General, John K. Richards; Board of Public Works, Frank J. McCulloch, William M. Hahn, Charles E. Groce; Commissioner of Common Schools, Oscar T. Corson; Judges of Supreme Court, William T. Spear. Joseph P. Bradbury, Franklin J. Dickman, Thaddeus A. Minshall, Marshall J. Williams; Clerk of Supreme Court, Urban H. Hester.

Finances.—During the fiscal year ending Nov. 15, 1892, the total receipts were $6,915,- 082.87, being $5,544,491.07 of revenues received from all sources during the year, and a balance of $1,370,591.80 on hand at the close of business hours on Nov. 15, 1891. The total expenditure during the year ending Nov. 15, 1892, from all funds was $6,158,671.24. Of the sum on hand on Nov. 15, 1891, $1,065,705.52 belonged to the sinking fund, and the remainder to the credit of the general revenue fund. The receipts for the year ending Nov. 15, 1892, for the general revenue fund were $3,707,675.88, including the donation of $85,000 from Wayne County for the experiment station, and $74,729.30 accumulated fees from the Secretary of State's office of a preceding year, which were withheld from the treasury because of pending litigation. The total amount paid out during the year from this fund upon the Auditor of State's warrants was $3,- 777,564.20, or $69,888.32 in excess of the receipts for the year.

The funded debt of the State on Nov. 16, 1892, was $2,045,665, bearing 3 per cent. interest, with an annual payment of $250,000 for the years 1893, 1894, 1895, 1896, 1897, 1898, and of $240,000 in 1899 and $300,000 in 1900.

Taxing Incorporated Companies.—Under the so-called Massie law of 1889 the Secretary of State was directed to retain as fees for the State one tenth of 1 per cent. of capital stock of corporations for issuing certificates of incorporation or consolidation. The charge was resisted by several railway corporations as unconstitutional. In June the Supreme Court decided one of the disputed cases in favor of the State, and released to the State the money that had been paid to the Secretary of State and stopped by injunction from being paid by him into the treasury.

State Institutions.—The total number of inmates of the State benevolent and punitory establishments was 11,432; 8,653 were in the benevolent institutions (of which 5,344 were in the insane asylums), 1.053 in the reformatories, and 1,726 in the penal institution.

Legislative.—The seventieth General Assembly organized on Jan. 4. The political character of the two branches was: Senate—Republicans, 21, Democrats 10; House—Republicans 72, Democrats 35; on joint ballot. Republicans 93, Democrats 45. The interest at the opening centered in the election of a United States Senator for the term following that of Senator John Sherman, which expires in 1893. The contest for the Republican nomination was between Senator Sherman and ex-Gov. Joseph B. Foraker, and resulted in the nomination of Mr. Sherman by 53 to 38 for Mr. Foraker, and 1 vote each for William McKinley, Jr., and Charles Foster. The Democrats nominated James E. Neal. Mr. Sherman was elected United States Senator for the sixth time by the following vote: Senate—Sherman 18, Neal 8; House—Sherman 93. Neal 29. The contest for the Republican nomination was so bitter between the supporters of the rival candidates that charges of bribery were freely made. The grand jury of Franklin County investigated the charges, but failed to present an indictment, and after discussion in the Legislature the matter was dropped. An attempt to impeach the title of Mr. Brice, elected to the United States Senate, was finally reduced to a resolution referring the matter to Senator Sherman, and nothing came of that matter either. The chief political legislation of the session was the passage of a congressional apportionment act designed to reverse the political complexion of the delegation elected under the apportionment act passed by the previous (Democratic) General Assembly. A large number of local laws were enacted. Of those of a general nature the following were the principal :

To apportion the State of Ohio into congressional districts under the eleventh census of the United States, and to repeal an act of the General Assembly of the State of Ohio passed 1890.

To amend the act relating to the imprisonment of convicts in the Ohio Penitentiary, and the employment, government, and release of such convicts by the Board of Managers.

To amend the election laws.

To prohibit barbering on Sunday.

To provide for the contest of elections of State and judicial officers.

To provide against accidents in the stairways of buildings.

To afford better protection to life and limb of employees.

To amend the laws governing the militia organizations.

To provide for more efficient organization of the common schools in township districts.

For the better protection of animals in transit.

Amending the laws relating to catching certain fish in spa n ng season.

To provide an additional asylum for care of the insane.

To amend the act for the better protection of skilled labor, and for the registration of labels, marks, names, or devices covering the products of such labor of associations of working men or women.

To amend the act to provide for the better care and protection to the property of imbecile or insane persons.

To regulate the branding of cheese in the State of Ohio, and to prevent fraud in its manufacture and sale.

Political.—The Prohibition party was the first to bring its ticket into the field. Its State Convention was held at Columbus, May 26, and the following ticket nominated : For Secretary of State, George L. Case ; Judges of Supreme Court, Thomas D. Crow, John D. Moore ; Clerk of Supreme Court, Z. C. Paine ; Member of Board of Public Works, Joseph J. Ware. The platform declared that " the manufacture and sale of intoxicating liquors for beverage purposes should be completely suppressed, and the Government should control the manufacture and sale of alcoholic liquors for medicinal, mechanical, and other legitimate purposes ; and that taxation or license of this criminal business in any form is an alliance of government with criminals for felonious purposes, a fraud upon the victims, and an abrogation of the ordained use of civil government " ; opposed any citizen's being denied the right to vote on account of sex ; protested against the right of nonresident aliens to acquire land ; favored the control by the people of railroads, telegraphs, and other natural monopolies, and contained other declarations. There was a controversy in the convention on the tariff declaration reported, and a substitute was adopted, which declared that

Tariff should be levied only as a defense against foreign governments which levy tariff upon or bar out our products from their markets, revenue being incidental. The residue of means necessary to an economical administration of the Government should be raised by a graduated income tax.

The Republican Convention was held at Cleveland, on April 28. The following ticket was nominated : For Secretary of State, Samuel H. Taylor ; Judges of the Supreme Court, William T. Spear, Jacob F. Burket ; Clerk of the Supreme Court, Josiah B. Allen ; Member of Board of Public Works, E. L. Lybarger. The platform approved the administrations of President Harrison and Gov. McKinley, and on the prominent issues of the campaign made the following declarations :

The best exemplification of the principle of protection, a cardinal one with the Republican party, that has found expression in the statutes, is the McKinley bill ; and we cordially declare our adhesion to the doctrines of that great measure, including, as worthy of particular mention, its reciprocity features.

We are opposed to the free coinage of silver by the United States under existing circumstances ; and we would not favor it except under conditions that would reasonably insure the maintenance of the substantial parity between the bullion and the mint or money value of its coin. Every coined dollar should have the intrinsic as well as the monetary value of every other coined dollar.

We favor just and liberal pensions to every soldier and sailor who fought in behalf of the Union.

And we heartily indorse the disability pension bill, as an act of Justice too long delayed because of the opposition to all just pension legislation by a Democratic President and a Democratic Congress.

We believe in a free ballot and a fair count, and affirm that unless intelligent and patriotic sentiment accord these rights to the humblest citizen in every section of the country it becomes the duty of the Federal Government to secure them by Federal enactment under the authority conferred by the Constitution.

While inviting to our shores the worthy poor and oppressed of other nations, we demand the enactment of laws that will protect our country and our people against the influx of the vicious and criminal classes of foreign nations, and the importation of laborers under contract to compete with our own citizens.

The Democratic Convention met at Cleveland, on June 15, and nominated the following ticket : For Secretary of State, William A. Taylor ; Judges of the Supreme Court, John B. Driggs, Thomas Beer ; Clerk of Supreme Court, William H. Wolfe ; Member of Board of Public Works, John Myers. The platform asserted that " the seventieth General Assembly of Ohio, with its Republican majority of two thirds in both branches, will go down in the history of the State as the most inefficient, incompetent, and profligate of any Legislature ever chosen in Ohio," and proceeded to specify the charges. On the general issues it said :

We are opposed to all class legislation, and believe in a tariff levied for the sole purpose of producing a revenue sufficient to defray the legitimate expenses of the Government economically administered, and we protest against the policy of so-called protection illustrated by the McKinley bill, as championed by the Republican party ; and in the interests of agriculture and labor we demand a reform of the present tariff and a reduction of unnecessary and burdensome taxation. That in the high tariff recently imposed by certain European nations on American grain and American meat we recognize an effort on the part of these governments to strike a blow at American agriculture in retaliation for the high duties imposed by the McKinley law, and that on behalf of American agriculture we demand of Congress an immediate modification of our tariff law such as will secure the admission of these agricultural products into the markets of those countries free from duty.

The hypocrisy of the Republican party in the demand in the recent national convention for the right of every citizen of the United States to cast one free and unrestricted ballot and to have it counted, is made most manifest by its almost uniform opposition to the Australian method of voting recently adopted in Ohio and most of the Northern States; and on the other hand its advocacy, as an administrative measure, of the infamous Force bill, designed to suppress by violence the elective franchise in nearly one half of the country.

We favor liberal and just pensions to deserving and disabled soldiers and sailors who fought for the maintenance of the Government, and like pensions to their widows and orphan children.

The People's Party Convention was held at Massillon, Aug. 17. The following ticket was nominated: For Secretary of State, S. C. Thayer; Judges of the Supreme Court, E. D. Stark and J. D. Payne; Clerk of Supreme Court, W. R. Beeles; Member of Board of Public Works, James Houser. The platform demanded the manufacture and sale of intoxicating liquors by the General Government; that the right of suffrage shall depend upon qualified citizenship; proportional representation in all legislative bodies; absolute power for all municipal governments to regulate their own affairs; opposed convict labor; demanded 2 cents a mile for passenger fares on railroads; that all taxes on mortgages shall properly be paid by the mortgagee, and to the extent of his interest in the country and township where the property is located; that all property be listed at its true value; a reduction of all fees and salaries of public officers to correspond with the shrinkage in the value of property; the abolition of capital punishment; that the General Government create and issue $500,000,000 of Treasury notes, making them a full legal tender for all debts both public and private, for the improvement of our public roads, apportioned to each State and Territory *pro rata* with the number of miles of roads in each State and Territory at the rate of $20,000,-000 a month.

Congressional tickets were placed in the field by the four parties. The election resulted in the success of the Republican State ticket. The vote for Secretary of State being: Samuel H. Taylor (Republican), 402,540; William A. Taylor (Democratic), 401,451; George L. Case (Prohibition), 25,885; Solon C. Thayer (People's), 14,494. The average vote on the other offices was 402,-856 Republican and 400,951 Democratic, the variations in the Prohibition and People's candidates being trifling. The Democrats elected 11 congressmen and the Republicans 10. The election for presidental electors held at the same time resulted in the choice of 22 Republicans and 1 Democrat, it being the first time since 1852 that a Democratic presidential elector had been chosen in Ohio. The vote for the Republican electoral ticket was 405,187; for the Democratic, 404,115.

OKLAHOMA, a Territory of the United States, organized by act of Congress approved May 2, 1890; area (including the Cherokee country and No Man's Land), 39,030 square miles; population (including Greer County, claimed by Texas), according to the census of 1890, 61,834. Capital, Guthrie.

Government.—The following were the Territorial officers during the year: Governor, Abraham J. Seay, Republican, appointed in January; Secretary and acting Governor until the appointment of Gov. Seay, Robert Martin; Treasurer, W. T. Higgie; Auditor and Superintendent of Public Instruction, J. H. Lawhead; Attorney-General, Charles Brown; Chief Justice of the Supreme Court, Edward B. Green; Associate Justices, John G. Clark and John H. Burford. The latter was appointed early in the year to fill the vacancy caused by the appointment of Judge Seay to be Governor.

Population.—On this subject the Governor, in his report for this year, says:

No official and reliable census of the inhabitants of the Territory having been taken since 1890, the population on June 30 of this year can only be approximated, but the commission appointed by Congress to make an enumeration visited all the counties and exercised great care in arriving at the approximate results, and I am of the opinion that the figures given are nearly correct.

COUNTIES.	POPULATION.	
	1890.	1892.
A...........................	None.	10,500
B...........................	None.	10,000
C...........................	None.	8,000
D...........................	None.	1,000
E...........................	None.	800
F...........................	None.	700
G...........................	None.	1,000
H...........................	None.	1,600
Beaver......................	2,982	8,000
Canadian....................	7,703	13,500
Cleveland...................	7,011	14,000
Logan.......................	14,254	22,000
Payne.......................	6,835	18,000
Oklahoma....................	12,794	21,000
Kingfisher..................	8,837	16,500
Total......................	60,416	183,100

Total increase, 72,684.

The foregoing figures do not include the Indians, who still maintain their tribal relations.

The population of Oklahoma, as herein enumerated, is approximated as follows: Eighty-five per cent. white, 10 per cent. colored, and 5 per cent. Indians. About 5 per cent. of the whites are foreign born. Nearly every State and Territory in the Union is represented in Oklahoma, but the great majority of our white population is from the adjoining States.

Valuations.—The taxable property of the Territory, as a whole, can not be given, for the reason that no assessment was made for taxes in counties C, D, E, F, G, and H, embracing the Cheyenne and Arapahoe country. None of these lands nor the persons residing in those counties are subject to taxation for the year 1892. The taxable property of the Territory, exclusive of the last-named counties, as shown by the assessor's returns, is $11,485,162.45. The taxable property of the Territory being assessed, on an average, at about two thirds of its actual value, its true value is about $17,150,000. This includes town lots, valued at $3,848,500, and only 85,400 acres of land subject to taxation. Its average assessed value is $6.65 an acre, aggregating $571,000. There are 21,865 homesteads, or 3,500,000 acres, in these last-mentioned counties not included in the list of taxable property, the average value and improvements of which are equal to the lands assessed, and aggregate at the same rate about $23,300,000. Deducting 190,-000 acres for school lands and 160,000 acres for Indian allotments, we have 3,150,000 acres, worth in round numbers $21,600,000, and four fifths of it will be subject to taxation in 1893-'94.

Education.—The school population of the Territory, so far as returns have been made, is as follows: County A, 3,557; County B, 1,626; Beaver County, 810; Canadian County, 3,119; Cleveland County, 2,709; Kingfisher County, 4,573; Logan County, 6,536; Oklahoma County, 5,367; Payne County, 3,623; total, exclusive of C, D, E, F, G, and H Counties, 31,920. This embraces all children between the ages of six and twenty-one years, that are reported.

In addition to what has been raised by direct taxation, and as proceeds from fines in criminal cases, there has been apportioned to the several school districts in proportion to their school population moneys arising from the rental of school lands in the Territory to the amount of $21,346.13. The schools of the Territory, considering the unsettled condition of affairs incident to the development of a new country, are in a very prosperous condition.

There has been established, in pursuance of the act of the first Legislative Assembly, a Territorial university, for the purpose of giving instruction in the higher branches of learning. This institution has been built at the city of Norman, in Cleveland County, and a faculty and a complete corps of instructors have been engaged, and the institution is ready for the reception of students.

A normal school has been established at Edmund, in Oklahoma County, and the board of regents have nearly completed the necessary buildings therefor.

The first Legislative Assembly of the Territory availed itself of the encouragement offered by Congress for the establishment of institutions for the diffusion of knowledge in agriculture and the mechanic arts, and passed a law providing for the erection of an agricultural and mechanical college at Stillwater, in Payne County. The board of regents of that institution have during the past year prepared the land for a farm and erected buildings thereon, and are making rapid progress with the work.

Agriculture.—During the year the climatic conditions have been very favorable to successful agriculture, and the soil of Oklahoma has demonstrated its capability of producing large crops of all the staple cereals, vegetables, and fruits. There have been grown as much as 44 bushels of wheat and 118 bushels of oats to the acre on a few choice farms. Owing to the low prices for cotton, but little was planted; but a large acreage of corn was planted, and in some localities a large crop was raised. In other localities drought cut it short. The 160-acre farms will average 50 acres each in cultivation.

Stock Raising.—For 1892 there were assessed in the Territory for taxation 52,896 horses, mules, and asses, 145,077 cattle, 15,559 sheep, and 30,168 swine. These figures do not include Counties C, D, E, F, G, and H, in which no assessment was made.

VOL. XXXII.—39 A

Railroads.—The Atchison, Topeka and Santa Fé Railroad, running south from Arkansas City, Kan., and crossing the Cherokee Strip, enters the Territory on the north line of Logan County and extends through the Territory in a southerly direction through Logan, Cleveland, and Oklahoma Counties, 80·32 miles, its terminus being at Galveston, Tex.

The Chicago, Rock Island and Pacific Railroad extends south from Caldwell, Kan., and, crossing the Cherokee Strip, enters Oklahoma at the north line of Kingfisher County and runs thence in a southerly direction through the counties of Kingfisher and Canadian into the Chickasaw country, through which it is now being constructed to its ultimate destination, at some point on the Gulf of Mexico.

The Choctaw Coal and Railway Company has built, equipped, and put in running operation a line of road from El Reno, in Canadian County, to Oklahoma City, in Oklahoma County, about 30 miles, during the past year. Work is now progressing on the extension of the line to the coal fields of South McAllister, in the Choctaw Nation.

Banks.—There are 5 national banks in the Territory, of $50,000 capital stock each, with an average of $150,000 deposit account each, and 4 incorporated banks, 2 of $50,000 capital stock each and 2 of $30,000 capital stock each.

Settlement of Lands.—In the reservations that have been opened to settlement, exclusive of the Cheyenne and Arapahoe country, all of the land that is susceptible of cultivation has been entered under the homestead laws and is occupied by settlers and their families. Homes have been established, and the land is being put into cultivation as fast as the time and means of the settlers will permit. In the Cheyenne and Arapahoe country nearly all of the land in the eastern portion has been entered and settled upon, and is fast being converted into an agricultural country. In the western half of the last-named country, while many homesteads have been taken and are being improved, yet there is still a large amount of land unsettled.

There are belonging to the Territory and still unopened to settlement the following areas occupied by Indian tribes: Osages, 2,296 square miles; Kansas, 150 square miles; Tonkawas, 150 square miles; Poncas, 150 square miles; Otoes and Missourias, 200 square miles; Pawnees, 442 square miles; Kickapoos, 270 square miles; Wichitas, 1,161 square miles; Kiowas, Comanches, and Apaches, 4,750 square miles; and the Cherokee Outlet, 9,110 square miles; total, 18,669 square miles.

Political.—As five sixths of the session of the first Territorial Legislature was spent in quarreling over the capital location, but little time was afforded for the work of preparing a code of laws, and many grave defects and omissions in the statutes necessarily resulted. Among other things, the Legislature failed to provide for the division of the Territory into legislative districts, or for holding an election this year for members of the Legislature or for any other officers. These defects were remedied by act of Congress passed in July as a rider to the Deficiency-Appropriation bill, which appointed Gov. Seay and two others as commissioners to apportion the Territory into 13 council and 26 representative districts, provided for the holding of an election on the first Tuesday after the first Monday of November and for canvassing the returns thereof, and prohibited the Legislature so chosen from considering any proposition or passing any bill to remove the capital from its existing location. The clause last mentioned was designed to prevent a repetition of the scenes that disgraced the first Territorial Legislature.

Early in the year each political party held a Territorial convention and selected delegates to the national convention of the party. Subsequently conventions were held for the purpose of nominating candidates for Delegate to Congress. The Republican Convention met at Guthrie on July 14 and nominated Dennis T. Flynn.

At a Democratic convention, held in August, Oliver H. Travers was made the party candidate for Delegate ; and at a convention of the People's party at Oklahoma City, on Aug. 16, N. H. Ward was nominated for the same office. The November election resulted in a complete victory for the Republican candidate, the vote being : Flynn, 9,478 ; Travers, 7,390 ; Ward, 4,348. The second Territorial Legislature, which was chosen at the same election, will be divided politically as follows : Council, Republicans 7, Democrats 5, People's party 1 ; House, Republicans 12, Democrats 10, People's party 4.

At this election the people of County A voted to adopt Lincoln as the permanent county name. In like manner the people of County B adopted the name Pottawattomie ; of County E, the name Day ; of County C. the name Blaine ; and of County H, the name Washita. In counties D and G no names were voted for.

ONTARIO, PROVINCE OF. His Honor Sir Alexander Campbell, Lieutenant-Governor, having become seriously and, as it proved, hopelessly ill, Chief-Justice Hagerty was appointed temporarily as Administrator of the Government, and as such he, on Feb. 11, opened the legislative session with the customary speech. Therein he said : " A commission has been appointed to report upon the desirability of establishing a forest reservation and park in part of the Nipissing district, south of the river Mattawa, and upon the methods and expense of maintaining and managing the same, thus following the wise example set by the United States in several recent instances." Higher-class educational expansion is commented upon in the same speech ; and among others in preparation is announced "a bill for the assessment of collateral or remote inheritances in certain cases" suggestive of a Quebec contemporaneous act enjoining direct taxation (which see) ; and "a bill adopting in substance the recent modifications by the British Parliament of the laws relating to mortmain." This act, providing "for the payment of succession duties," was duly passed ; and important and radical changes were made in the provincial mining laws, necessitated by the recent discoveries of immense deposits of valuable minerals in the Laurentides mountains, especially in silver, nickel, plumbago, apatite (mineral fertilizer), iron, and others. Indeed, the hitherto rather rare mineral asbestos has there

ceased to be a rarity, and it is found in such quantity and such tenuity of fiber as to render it readily available even to be spun and woven into fireproof dresses. Of more than a hundred acts passed by the provincial Legislature during that session, by far the most were private or local.

Ontario claims somehow to be the " Premier Province of Canada." It has undoubtedly the largest population. According to the official census returns of 1891 (which nobody seems to rely upon, however), the total population of Ontario province is 2,114,321, showing an increase of 9·93 per cent. within the decade. This is out of a total assumed population of 4,832,679 for the whole Dominion. The figures for Ontario are probably not wide of the mark. Meanwhile Toronto, the provincial capital of Ontario, claims a population by last census of 181,220, making her the second city of the Dominion, and next to Montreal.

On May 30, 1892, Hon. George A. Kirkpatrick, M. P., was appointed Lieutenant-Governor of Ontario, *vice* Sir Alexander Campbell, deceased. Hon. Oliver Mowatt still holds the office of Premier of the provincial administration, with no noteworthy changes in his Cabinet within the year.

OREGON, a Pacific coast State, admitted to the Union Feb. 14, 1859 ; area, 96,030 square miles. The population was 13,294 in 1850 ; 52,-465 in 1860 ; 90,923 in 1870 ; 174,768 in 1880 ; and 313,767 in 1890. Capital, Salem.

Government.—The following were the State officers during the year : Governor, Sylvester Pennoyer, Democrat : Secretary of State, Auditor, and Insurance Commissioner, George W. McBride, Republican ; Treasurer, Philip Metschau ; Attorney-General, George E. Chamberlain ; Superintendent of Public Instruction. E. B. McElroy ; Railroad Commissioners, J. H. Faull, George W. Colvig, and Robert Clow ; Chief Justice of the Supreme Court, Reuben S. Strahan ; Associates, William P. Lord, Robert S. Bean.

Finances.—The following is from the Treasurer's report for the biennial term ending Dec. 31, 1892 : The total amount of taxable property for 1890 from which the revenue of the State for 1891 was derived was $114,077,988. Upon this was levied a tax of 4 mills to meet the current expenses of the State for 1891, and in addition thereto there was levied a special tax of one seventh of a mill for the support of the State University at Eugene, and one fifth of a mill for the support of the National Guard. There is also a 5-mill tax for the support of the common schools, the latter being collected and distributed by the several counties. Under this levy the following sums were assessed. viz. :

Current expenses, 4 mills	$456,811 15
Support of National Guard, ¼ mill	22,815 55
Support of State University, ⅐ mill	16,296 89
Total	$595,423 59

Under the assessment as returned by the county officers for 1891, from which the State revenue for 1892 was to be derived, the total amount of taxable property was fixed at $128,-132,560. As the result of its labors and findings, however, the State Board of Equalization increased this amount to $151,700,206, upon, which figures the board made its levy as follows:

Current expense tax, 4⅜ mills $706,489 51
Support of Oregon National Guard, ⅛ mill 30,340 03
Support of State University, ⅛ mill............. 21,671 45

Total................................... $758,500 99

Under a decision of the Supreme Court, rendered July 28, 1892, in the case of the Oregon and California Railroad *vs.* E. M. Croisan, Sheriff of Marion County, a portion of the rulings of the Board of Equalization were declared null and void, and by reason of that decision the total amount of taxable property in the State was reduced to $149,884,243, necessitating a new adjustment of State taxes as between the State and the several counties.

Owing to the ruling of the State Board of Equalization as to the assessment of mortgages at their full face value, exceptions have been taken by one or more counties of the State, and the courts thereof have refused to pay the amounts thus levied against them. The matter is now pending in the higher courts. There remains due the State on account of taxes for 1891 about $130,000.

Including $223,144.29 turned over by ex-State Treasurer Webb, Jan. 12, 1891, the receipts during the two years were $2,561,457.14, and the disbursements $2,220,328.39.

The State has no indebtedness, bonded or otherwise, with the exception of a few outstanding warrants, which are being redeemed as rapidly as remittances are received from counties that are behind in the payment of their taxes.

Education.—The biennial report of the schools closes with March 7, 1892. The number of districts in 1892 was 1,826; the number of persons between four and twenty years of age, 111,770; the number enrolled. 75,526; the average daily attendance, 52,724; the number of teachers, 2.694; average number of days taught, 112·80; number of schoolhouses, 1,701; average monthly salary of male teachers, $50.04; of female teachers, $41.49; number of private schools, 121; value of schoolhouses and sites, $2,220,-780.08; total value of school property, $2,494,-233.89; paid for teachers' salaries, $676.973.93.

The interest arising from the irreducible school fund is, under the laws of the State, distributed annually among the several counties for the benefit and support of the common schools, in proportion to the number of persons of school age reported by the county school superintendents. The distribution of 1891 amounted to $153,151.90, and the number of school children was 105,622, the *per capita* being $1.45 each. The amount distributed in 1892 was $162,066.50, the *per capita* being the same as the year previous, among 111,770 children.

The enrollment for the year at the State Normal School was 376. The senior class numbered 40, the largest number graduated at one time in the history of the school.

The total number of students at the Agricultural college in November was 246, of whom 174 were in the regular course and 72 in the preparatory department. The number holding scholarships was 70. Each senatorial and representative district is entitled to as many scholarships as the number of its members in the Legislature.

The register of students at Portland University reached 240 in the spring term. The proceeds of sales of lands in University Park are devoted to retiring the bonds of the institution, and when that is done they will form a permanent endowment fund. The first building, West Hall, was finished during the year, and subscriptions are being received for East Hall, which will be for the young ladies.

Railroads.—The assessment of railroads of the first class ranges from $3,059 a mile in Pierce County, to $9,470 in Whitman, and averages about $6,000. The uniform equalized assessment of roads of this class last year was $5,-300 a mile. The Portland and Astoria road is building rapidly. The sale of the Oregon Pacific was ordered to take place on Jan. 15, 1893, the minimum price being set at $1,250,000.

A bill was introduced by Representative Hermann declaring forfeited " the lands within what is called the quadrant, northwest of Forest Grove, in Oregon. The grant of the Oregon Central Railroad Company, by the act of May 4, 1870, was declared forfeited by the act of Jan. 31, 1885, as to that portion between Forest Grove and Astoria, and the lands forfeited were restored to entry." The railroad company brought suit to set aside a patent issued to a settler for land within the quadrant, and the United States has intervened for the purpose of sustaining the patent and the action of the department in restoring the lands to settlement. About 90,000 acres are involved. Representative Hermann's bill is in the interest of the settlers.

Suit was brought by the Southern Pacific to enjoin the sheriff from attempting to collect $1,600 taxes claimed as due from the railroad. The State Board of Equalization raised the assessment of all railroad lines in Marion County from $3,500 to $5,000 a mile, increasing the company's taxes $1,600. The Supreme Court held that the State Board, being a board of equalization and not of assessment, has no authority to change individual assessments or classify property into any class other than such as are authorized by law and appear upon the county assessment roll.

Penal and Charitable Institutions.—Nearly all these are overcrowded, and increased accommodations will soon become necessary. There were 416 convicts in the State prison in July, a larger number than had ever before been there at one time.

The Reform School, though but recently instituted, is already crowded. It was designed to accommodate 50, but had 62 inmates in August and 79 in November. It is near Salem, on a site comprising 370 acres.

Industries and Products.—The salmon-pack this year amounted to 465,550 cases. There has been a great decline in this industry in recent years, but the present report shows a slight advance. Among the measures recommended by the Fish Commission are an appropriation by the Legislature of $6,000 for a fishway to be blasted in the rock at the Oregon City falls, to permit food fish to ascend the Willamette, where there are good spawning grounds; a law requiring the owners of water ditches to place a wire screen at the inlet to prevent fish from entering the ditch; to prevent fishing by means of spears or poles with hooks; a special law for Clatsop, Columbia, Wasco, and Multnomah Counties for a reward for scalps of seals or sea lions, and a change in the fish commission law to the effect that there be but one commissioner. They also recommend the establishment by the State of hatcheries in the Coquille and Umpqua rivers. Four steamers, 10 sloops, and 949 fishing boats are employed in the industry, and the apparatus used in fishing is valued at $521,570. On the Columbia river are 14 canneries, employing a capital of $640,000, with buildings and machinery valued at $482,055. In the State are 23 factories, valued at $557.055, and employing cash capital of $815,000. There are 3,829 men, including Chinamen, employed as fishermen, who were paid $794,830.

The entire crop of hops harvested was from 24,000 to 25,000 bales, the average yield per acre being from 700 to 800 pounds. The output of wool is estimated at 16,000,000 pounds.

On the basis of returns from circulars sent out by the Secretary of the Board of Horticulture, it is estimated that there are upward of 100,000 acres of fruit lands in the State at the present time, of which half is planted in prunes, one quarter in apples, one tenth in pears, and the remainder in other fruits. The total number of fruit trees is estimated approximately at 10,000,000. This estimate is for orchards only. There are 36 nurseries in the State, covering about 1,576 acres, and capitalized at $236,658. The fruit crop for the past season was the smallest ever known in Oregon. The partial failure is accounted for by the unusually cold rains during the latter part of April.

Since the year 1886, Oregon's production of flour has been greatly increasing. During that year, her exports amounted to $1,688,000, showing an improvement this year of over $420,000 in the amount exported.

Tobacco has been raised on the bottom lands of John Day river, in Grant County, with leaves 33 inches long and 17 inches wide. The soil is light, warm, and quick, and the summer climate is well adapted to the cultivation of tobacco. In the Yaquina country, where the conditions are substantially the same as along the John Day, an excellent quality of tobacco is produced.

Commerce.—From the report of the Collector of Customs for the fiscal year ending June 30, the following items are taken: Number of vessels entered from foreign ports, 106; number of vessels cleared for foreign ports, 141; number of vessels cleared for domestic ports, 135; entries of merchandise for duty, 857; entries of merchandise free of duty, 285; entries for warehouse, 100; entries for warehouse and transportation, 1; entries for rewarehouse, 6; entries from warehouse for consumption, 255; entries for transportation and export to Canada, 69; entries from warehouse for exportation to adjacent British provinces, 11; entries for immediate transportation without appraisement, 205; entries for consumption liquidated, 1,149; entries for warehouse liquidated, 93; certificates of registry granted, 8; licenses for coasting trade granted, 95; licenses to vessels under 20 tons granted, 9. Value of exports: domestic, $6,640,240; foreign, $6,350.18.

Irrigation.—A Government bulletin shows that in Oregon there are 3,150 farms that are irrigated out of 25,885 in the State. The total area of land upon which crops were raised by irrigation in the census year ending May 31, 1890, was 177,944 acres, in addition to which there were approximately 72,000 acres irrigated for grazing.

The Giletz Reservation.—The work of the commissioners on the Giletz Indian reservation is completed, and 180,000 acres will be opened to settlers under the land laws. The lands were allotted to the 532 Indians in severalty, each one receiving 80 acres. There are 178 adults, among them being Indians from nearly all the tribes of western Oregon. There are no longer any tribal chiefs, and, to secure the contract, signatures of a majority of the male adults had to be secured. It was for this purpose and to make an agreement satisfactory to the Indians that the commission was sent out. After the allotments were made, the commissioners negotiated the purchase of the remaining 180,000 acres for $142,600. A great deal of this is fine timber land, the farming land of this reservation having all been allotted. The Government pays for this land $75,000 cash, and the balance is on interest for the benefit of the Indians. The reservation is near Yaquina Bay, and is surrounded by settlements of whites.

Immigration.—The number of immigrants registered during the year ending April 2 was somewhat smaller than that of the preceding year, but it is estimated that a much larger number came for permanent settlement, and brought means to provide themselves with homes. The whole number was estimated at 108,140. The Immigration Board sent out a car, "Oregon on Wheels," which was transported free of charge over many railroads in the Middle and Eastern States. The car was gone twenty-nine weeks: it visited 24 States, traveled 11,625 miles on 30 lines of railway, and had more than 250,000 visitors. The Board of Immigration report that "it has been a most satisfactory mode of advertising the resources of our great State."

Judicial Decisions.—A decision affecting the interpretation of the term "timber land" was rendered by Judge Hanford, and confirmed by the Supreme Court of the United States. The timber-land act was passed in 1878, and provided that lands chiefly valuable for timber could be sold in Oregon, Washington, California, and Nevada for $2.50 an acre. In 1885, Sparks, Land Commissioner, held that land that could grow grass or anything after the timber was off was agricultural land, notwithstanding that the timber was worth much more than the land ever would be, and that it cost more to clear the land than it was worth. Sparks's successor, Groff, held the same view, and the uncertainty has led to much trouble and litigation. The decision is, that land heavily covered with timber is timber land.

In the case of the United States *vs.* the Willamette Valley and Cascade Mountain Wagon Road Company, a suit brought to forfeit the land grant of the company on the ground that the road was not completed within the proper time, Judge Gilbert, in the United States Circuit Court, rendered a decision dismissing the bill, on the ground that it was inequitable, and that the United States should not, at this late date and after such long nonaction and acquiescence, assert title to the lands or claim a forfeiture of the same.

Mount Hood.—A petition was sent to Washington by the Alpine Club in June, asking that the entire Caseade range from Columbia river south be withdrawn from settlement and made a reservation; or, in the event of that being impossible, a tract embracing Mount Hood and vicinity, and extending to the limits of Bitter Lake reservation, or, at least, Mount Hood and vicinity. The main object is to establish a national park and to protect the game and fish.

Improvement of Water Ways.—A commission was created by the Legislature, and authority given to it to issue bonds to the amount of $500,000 for the purpose of making permanent improvements in the channels of the Willamette and Columbia rivers from Portland to the sea. The work has been performed, and the commission has closed its office and disbanded its engineer corps, after expending $366,537.78. There have been built 43,000 feet of dikes for contracting the channel, and 159,500 cubic yards of material have been dredged. The benefit of this work is already apparent in the fact that during the last three months of 1892 42 grain vessels were dispatched from Portland docks, and but 3,600 tons were lightered, while during the same period in 1891 8,200 tons were lightered for only 25 vessels.

Orders have been given by the Government for work for which the following appropriations have been made:

Entrance and harbor at Coos Bay, continuing	$210,000
Harbor at Yaquina Bay, continuing	$5,000
Tillamook bay	15,000
Upper Columbia river, including Snake river, as far up as Asotin, continuing	15,000
Coquille river, continuing	25,000
Mouth of Siuslaw river, continuing	20,000
Upper Coquille river, between Coquille City and Myrtle Point, to be used in deepening channel to 4 feet at mean low water	5,000
Upper Snake river, between Hunting bridge and Seven Devils' mining district	20,000
Nasel river, completing improvement	1,500
Willapa river and harbor, of which $8,000 may be used for closing Mailboat slough	18,000

Political.—The State election was held on June 6. A Supreme Judge and Representatives in Congress were to be chosen, and also State Senators and Representatives. The question arose whether there would be a vacancy in the office of Attorney-General. The last Legislature created that office, and the Governor appointed George E. Chamberlain. One section of the act provided that an Attorney-General should be chosen at the election in June, 1894, and another that the Governor should appoint a suitable person to fill the office until the next general election. The question arose whether the regular biennial election of this year came within the meaning of the act, or whether Mr. Chamberlain should hold over until 1894. It was decided that the intent of the act was that the Governor's appointment was to hold until the people should have an opportunity to choose, and that that opportunity was afforded by the election of this year. Only the Republican and Democratic parties made nominations for the office.

The State Convention of Republicans was held on April 6. Following are the more significant declarations of the platform:

We reaffirm our devotion to the Republican doctrine of protection for our home industries against injurious foreign competition, and recognize the McKinley bill as the ablest expression of that principle, enacted in fulfillment of Republican promises, and as affording equal protection to the manufacturers, the mechanics, and workingmen of America from an unjust and degrading competition with the pauperized and poverty-stricken labor of European countries, and as preserving American markets for the products of American labor.

We denounce the Democratic doctrine of free trade in so-called "raw materials," while insisting upon a high protective tariff on goods manufactured therefrom, as calculated to benefit entirely the foreign at the expense and to the great injury of the American producer. We regard the reciprocity clause of the McKinley law as a wise and masterly stroke of Republican statesmanship, under the operation of which protection guards the home market, while reciprocity reaches out to the foreign market. While protection establishes, builds up, and maintains American industries, reciprocity opens a new outlet for the surplus products of our farms, workshops, and factories.

We demand protection for the wool industry equal to that accorded the most favored manufacturer of wool, so that in due time American wool-growers will supply all wool of every kind required for consumption in the United States.

Thoroughly believing that gold and silver should form the basis of all circulating medium, we indorse the amended coinage act of the last Republican Congress, by which the entire production of the silver mines of the United States is added to the currency of the people.

We are heartily, in favor of the passage by Congress of the bill providing for a boat railway at the Dalles of the Columbia river, which has been twice passed through the Senate by the efforts of Senators Mitchell and Dolph.

We demand the appropriation by Congress of a sum sufficient to complete the work at the cascade locks, and that the work of completing the same be let by contract.

We are opposed to the immigration of Chinese laborers to the United States, and demand such an extension of existing laws as shall effectually and forever exclude Chinese laborers from American soil.

We are in favor of an amendment to the Constitution of the United States providing for the election of United States Senators by a direct vote of the people.

Following were the nominations: For Supreme Judge, Frank A. Moore; Attorney-General, Lionel R. Webster; members of Congress, Binger Hermann, W. R. Ellis.

The convention of Democrats, held in Portland, April 21, left its delegation to the national convention uninstructed, though declaring in favor of Mr. Cleveland's nomination. The platform reaffirmed the doctrine of the Democratic national conventions of 1884 and 1888, pointed with pride to the administration of Grover Cleveland, and condemned the extravagance of the "billion-dollar Congress" and the McKinley bill. On the subject of the tariff it foreshadowed the platform of the national convention by denying the "right of the Government to levy a protective tariff except as incidental to the raising of revenue to defray the expenses of the Government economically administered, or for any consideration save those of public welfare." It demanded that "all money coined or issued by the United States should be of equal monetary value, and of equal purchasing power for the rich and the poor, and that all paper currency issued by the Government should be redeemable in either gold or silver coin at the option of the holder, and not at the discretion of the Secretary of the Treasury."

It declared opposition to all measures in pension legislation which " draw no distinction between the veteran in the field and the camp followers in the rear, as involving a cruel wrong to the soldier and wanton waste of the people's money."

Other resolutions favored the election of Senators by direct vote of the people, the making of eight hours a legal day's labor on all public works, and " laws giving the laborer in all fields of labor a first lien on the product of his labor," demanded the immediate survey of the public lands in the State, and the "immediate and specific forfeiture of the grants of all lands unearned by railroads and wagon roads in the State. The platform further declared in favor of the Geary Chinese exclusion bill, and contained the following on river improvements:

We urge the passage of such appropriations and the adoption of such measures as will tend most speedily and effectively to open the Columbia and Willamette rivers to free navigation, and for such further appropriations as will speedily and fully complete the improvements at the mouth of the Columbia. We condemn the policy of the Republican party in urging upon Congress the feasibility of the boat railway at the Dalles, and denounce the measure as a subterfuge whereby the people of the inland empire must remain in bondage for years; and we condemn the policy of the Republican party, whereby the improvement of the cascades has been delayed unnecessarily by plans and expedients which give no assurance that the obstructions to navigation in the Columbia will be released from the grasp of a grinding monopoly which now holds the people of eastern Oregon in fetters.

Following is the ticket: For Supreme Judge, A. S. Bennett; Attorney-General, George Chamberlain; Representatives in Congress, T. K. Slater, R. M. Veatch.

Gov. Pennoyer deserted the Democratic party after the convention, because it rejected the free-coinage plank on which he was elected in 1890, and gave in his adherence to the People's party.

The People's party held its State convention at Oregon City, March 16. Resolutions were adopted as follow:

All laws shall be submitted to the people for rejection or approval, and that the people shall have an equal right with the Legislatures and Congress to initiate measures for enactment into law, and that they shall have the right to recall their legislators and Congressmen for cause.

Our 9,000,000 farm mortgages, the condition of the thousands of unemployed, and of the world's starving millions, shall be to us both a warning and a spur to untiring, united action.

We recognize in the money power of the world the common enemy of all wealth-producers, regardless of nationality; we recognize the universal brotherhood of humanity, and extend our hearty sympathy to the downtrodden masses of every nation in their struggle for better conditions.

We demand a law prohibiting the confirmation of a mortgage sale, unless such sale shall equal 66 per cent. of the assessed value.

The platform demanded a direct loan by the Government at 2 per cent.; the free and unlimited coinage of silver; the increase of circulating medium to $50 per capita; postal savings banks; no alien landowners; corporation ownership restricted to the actual land used; the Government ownership of railroads; the abolishment of the railroad commission and a maximum rate reducing rates one third; the Government ownership of telegraph and telephone lines; the improvement of Columbia river by building a parallel railroad, to be operated by the Government; the only taxes for the support of the Government, the 2 per cent. on loans by the Government and the graduated land tax; no exemption for indebtedness without a corresponding rendering of taxable credit; equal suffrage; no Chinese immigration; State publication of school books; restriction of county officers to salary; eight hours a day's labor in factories, mines, and shops; declared against Pinkerton detectives; against the Nicaragua Canal, unless owned by the Government and operated at cost; for the direct vote for all officers; the issue of legal-tender notes, and the payment of Union soldiers for loss occasioned by depreciated currency.

Following are the nominations: For Supreme Judge, D. Wright; for member of Congress, Second district, J. C. Luce.

The Prohibitionists met on April 6, in Portland. After reaffirming their own distinctive principles and declaring in favor of national control of all railroad, express, telegraph, and telephone lines, and for the prohibition of all trusts and combinations of capital for the purpose of controlling the price of articles of necessity or popular consumption, the platform made the following declarations:

The adjustment of the duties on imports should be fixed in a businesslike way by a national commission of experts, and not made the football of political acrobats; the amount of duties levied should not exceed the necessary expenses of the Government economically administered, and wealth and luxuries, and not food, clothing, and necessities, should bear the burdens.

The prohibition sentiment that allows itself to be officially misrepresented is impotent against the liquor traffic, and the ballot cast for the candidates of any political party which does not openly antagonize the liquor traffic is a vote for the continued sustenance of such traffic, and the voter casting such ballot is morally responsible for any injury arising from such traffic.

We deplore the rapid increase of landed estates, and favor   limitation of alien and corporate ownership of land he

We favor the election of President, Vice-President, and United States Senators by direct vote of the people.

The required time of residence for naturalization should be extended, and no naturalized person should vote within one year after naturalization papers are issued.

The ticket nominated was: For Supreme Judge, Benjamin P. Welch; members of Congress, W. J. Rigdon, Cornelius J. Bright.

The results of the June election gave to the Republicans the two seats in Congress and the Supreme Judge, and to the Democrats the Attorney-General. The vote for Judge stood:

Moore, 29,805; Bennet, 26,929; Walker, 10,734; Weleh, 2,418.

The Legislature stands: Senate—Republicans, 16; Democrats, 11; People's, 1; Independent Democrat, 1; People's Democrat, 1. House—Republicans, 38; Democrats, 17; People's, 3; Independent Democrats, 2. Republican majority on joint ballot, 18.

At the November election the greatest number of votes cast for any one elector were given to Nathan Pierce, the Populist candidate who was adopted by the Democratic State Central Committee. He received 35,811. The next highest vote was for Caples, Republican, who received 35,002. The electoral vote was therefore divided—3 Republicans, 1 Populist. The highest vote for a Democratic elector was 14,243, and for a Prohibitionist 2,281.

ORIENTAL CHURCHES. In the Coptic Church of Egypt the counsel of influential laymen has been recognized for many years as an advisory element in the administration; and several matters pertaining to the management and welfare of the Church have been referred to laymen's committees for adjustment, or at least for consultation. The patriarch in office in 1892 was appointed partly on the recommendation of the Laymen's Committee, and co-operated with them for a short time after his accession in promoting the reforms they sought. Under the active influence of the Laymen's Committee a strong party grew up in the Church in favor of several important reforms. First, it sought to establish accountability and business responsibility in the management of the large properties and the financial interests of the Church. Second, it insisted upon the provision of Church schools equal in educational standard and efficiency to the Government schools and the missionary schools; this measure was regarded as essential to the continued existence and usefulness of the Church; for while Coptic children could learn nothing in the Church schools, and had to resort to the other schools to obtain any education worthy the name, they became alienated from the Church, and in a large measure from Christianity if they attended the Government Mohammedan schools; and were equally alienated from their Church often to become Protestants, if they attended the mission schools. A third demand was for an educated and salaried ministry, in order that the priests might be at least the equals in position and knowledge and intelligence of their parishioners. The patriarch gradually became weaned from his early sympathy with the progressive party and from his confidential relations with the Laymen's Committee, and fell at last under the influence of the party among the clergy opposed to the projected reforms.

After repeated unsuccessful attempts to bring about an agreement of parties on the matters in issue, the Laymen's Committee addressed an ultimatum to the patriarch, informing him of their determination to act in accordance with the plans they had formulated. The patriarch, although he had committed himself by previous acts to a recognition of the functions of the committee, replied to these demands that it had no precedent or authority in the Church, and its decisions were therefore not binding. The Khedive was appealed to, and declared that the committee's authority to act in the matters for which it was appointed would be sustained. The patriarch sought the support of the Russian consulate; this was regarded by the Khedive as an affront, and when the patriarch sought an audience with him he was not received. On receiving the reply of the patriarch to its demands, the committee deposed him from the presidency of itself, which he held *ex officio*, and chose Athanasius, Bishop of Sanaho, to fill the place as vicar. The patriarch issued a sentence of excommunication against the vicar, ordered the bishops to unite with him in confirming the sentence, and directed that Athanasius be excluded from the patriarchate. The new vicar, on his arrival at Cairo, was escorted by his friends of the reform party, an officer of the Government, and police to the patriarchate, where entrance was three times refused him. The committee then met under the presidency of the vicar, and ordered the patriarch to be banished to the convent of Barmoos — the monastery whence he was called to enter upon the office of patriarch. A similar order was issued against the Metropolitan of Alexandria, directing his banishment to the convent whence he came. Both orders were ratified by the Government and were carried into effect.

P

PARAGUAY, a republic in South America. The country is situated in the heart of the continent, and is bounded on the south and east by the river Paraná, which divides it from the Argentine province of Corrientes and the Republic of Brazil; on the north the twenty-first parallel of south latitude forms the border next to Brazil; and on the west the river Paraguay separates it from Bolivia and the river Pilcomayo from the Argentine Republic. The present Constitution was proclaimed on Nov. 25, 1870, and is modeled on that of the United States. The Congress is composed of the Senate and the House of Representatives, the Senators numbering 13 and the Deputies 26, all elected by districts, each district being allowed one Senator for every 12,000 inhabitants and one Deputy for every 6,000 inhabitants. The Senators and Deputies receive a salary of $250 a month. The President is elected for four years, and has 5 ministers. The present incumbent is Juan G. Gonzalez, who holds office until 1894. The Cabinet is composed of the following members: Minister of the Interior, J. Sosa; Minister of Foreign Affairs, Dr. V. Lopez; Minister of Finance, J. Decoud; Minister of Justice, Public Worship, and Instruction, Dr. F. Insfran; Minister of War, J. Egusguiza.

Area and Population.—The area of the republic is 88,700 square miles. The population, at the census of 1886, was 263,751, of whom 110,280 were males and 153,471 females. The census of 1857 gave the population at 1,337,449, but this was undoubtedly incorrect; the correct figure would probably be nearer 800,000 inhabitants, as estimated in 1860. It was supposed that the population was reduced by three fourths in the war against the triple alliance, thus reducing the number to 200,000 in 1870. The population in 1880 was estimated at 255,860. Since then, owing to the progress made, the annual increase is stated to be 3 per cent., thus placing the population in 1890 at about 400,000. These figures do not include the Indians of the Gran Chaco, who are estimated at 150,000.

The foreign population numbered 13,145 in 1890, of whom 8,350 were Argentines, 1,028 Italians, 904 Brazilians, 875 Germans, 547 Spaniards, 389 French, 337 Orientals, 197 Portuguese, 195 Swiss, 94 Austrians, 68 English, 49 Greeks, 34 Chilians, 27 Bolivians, 25 Belgians, 22 Americans, and 7 Russians. The capital of the republic and the center of commerce is the city of Asuncion, so called because it was founded on the feast of the Assumption of the Blessed Virgin, on Aug. 15, 1536, by Commander Ayola. It has a population of 24,038. The other principal cities are: Villa Rica, with a population of 10,-773 in 1886; Villa Concepcion, with 10,902 inhabitants; Caazapa, with 12,144; and Carapegná, with 10,883.

Finances.—The receipts of the treasury in 1891 amounted to 1,647,717 pesos (1 peso=about 66 cents). Of this amount, 1,196,315 pesos were derived from customs, 190,328 pesos from leases and sales of land, and 261,074 pesos from other sources. The expenses amounted to 2,485,203 pesos, of which 515,232 pesos were expended for the interior, 23,847 pesos for foreign affairs, 187,415 pesos for financial administration, 310,-955 pesos for justice, public worship, and instruction, 842,810 pesos for war and the navy, and 604,944 pesos for extraordinary purposes. The public debt on Jan. 1, 1892, amounted to 26,448,795 pesos, of which 24,981,006 pesos represented the foreign debt and 1,367,689 pesos the internal debt. An additional paper issue of 1,000,000 pesos was authorized by the Congress in May, 1892. In the same month gold reached a premium of 700.

Commerce and Agriculture.—The imports in 1891 were valued at 1,802,000 pesos, and the exports at 3,166,000 pesos. The principal articles for exportation were yerba or maté to the amount of 1,352,000 pesos; tobacco, 626,000 pesos; hides and skins, 379,000 pesos; bark, 295,-000 pesos; woods, 270,000 pesos; and oranges, 75,000 pesos. All foreign merchandise pays an *ad valorem* duty of 25 per cent., but firearms, powder, shot, fine wines and liquors, perfumery, tobacco, cigars, and matches pay a duty of 50 per cent.; clothing, hosiery, saddlery, harness, and carriages, a duty of 40 per cent.; articles made of silk, ordinary table wines, and beer, a duty of 30 per cent.; and jewelry and precious stones a duty of 10 per cent. *ad valorem*. Horses, cattle, fresh fish, cement, effects of immigrants, gold and silver, empty bottles, printed books' globes, maps, scientific instruments, printing presses and type, coal, iron, resin, soda, oil, animal black, and all agricultural implements are exempt from duty. The soil of Paraguay is fertile and well watered, and there are extensive forests, but owing to the financial crisis recent immigration

has been small. The Government holds out great inducements to immigrants, and forms so-called colonies. Each family that establishes itself receives a farm, implements of agriculture, a pair of oxen, a cow, and $50 in money. There are at present 7 flourishing colonies, besides 2 that have been formed later and are in good running order. The country produces cotton, rice, beans, lucern, tobacco, maize, peanuts, wheat, coffee, sugar cane, mandioca, potatoes, and vegetables, besides large quantities of yerba or Paraguayan tea. The cultivation of fruits has been wholly neglected, although the soil is well adapted for that purpose. Oranges are grown in abundance, but owing to the want of a market or facilities of transport, many millions fall to the ground and rot. Cattle thrive well. In 1890 there were 861,954 cattle, 99,693 horses, 2,433 mules, 77,576 sheep and goats, 2,188 asses, and 10,778 hogs.

Industries.—There were, in the beginning of 1892, 30 factories in the country, making bricks, matches, tiles, furniture, leather, liquor, flour, soap, macaroni, beer, artificial ice, and lumber. The natives make intricate puzzle rings of gold, silver, and copper, and the women produce large quantities of handkerchiefs and embroidery of the famous Nanduty lace. Clay articles, towels, hammocks, rope, and other articles of native material find a ready sale. A factory for the production of essence from oranges has been established, and has proved successful.

PATENTS. The statement of receipts and expenditures in the Patent Office, as reported by Commissioner Simonds, are as follow : Receipts, $1,286,331.83; expenditures, $1,110,739.24; receipts over expenditures, $175,592.59. According to the Treasury statement, the amount to the credit of the fund, Jan. 1, 1892, was $4,004,317.67; amount of receipts during the year 1892, $1,286,-331.83; total, $5,290,649.50; deduct expenditures for the year 1892, $1,110,739.24; balance Jan. 1, 1893, $4,179,910.26. The business of the year included the following: Applications for patents for inventions, 39,514; applications for patents for designs, 1,130; applications for reissues of patents, 109; total number of applications, 40,753. Caveats filed, 2,290; applications for registration of trade-marks, 2,179; applications for registration of labels, 458; disclaimers filed, 7: appeals on the merits, 1,025; total, 5,959. Total number of applications, requiring investigation and action, 46,712. Patents issued, including designs, 23,478; patents reissued, 81; trade-marks registered, 1,737; labels registered, 6; total, 25,302.

The total number of patents and designs issued to citizens of the United States during the year was 21,427. The last patent, issued Dec. 31, was numbered 498.932. In the distribution of patents by States and according to population, Connecticut heads the list, as she has for many years, with one patent for each 955 of her inhabitants—a considerable increase over the average of last year. Other States, notably those of New England and the District of Columbia, are not far behind, averaging something more than 1,000 inhabitants for each patent. Mississippi shows the lowest inventive average of any State, having taken out only 55 patents in all, or one to each 23,447 inhabitants. North and South Carolina,

Georgia, Alabama, and the Territory of Oklahoma are among the lowest averages.

In all, 2,051 patents were granted to citizens of foreign countries. England leads, with 653; Germany comes next, with 507. Then the preponderance crosses the Atlantic again to Canada, whose citizens took out 296 United States patents. After Austria-Hungary, which is represented by 66 patents, the average falls rapidly through the less progressive states.

The report of W. E. Simonds, Commissioner of Patents, appears in the "Patent Office Gazette" for Feb. 7, 1893. It opens with the inevitable prayer for increased room in the Patent Office. Substantially the same petition has been repeated by successive Secretaries of the Interior and Commissioners of Patents for several years. The weight of records already stored, and constantly increasing through the necessities of the office, is actually threatening to crush the buildings themselves, and the commissioner pathetically observes that portentous cracks have appeared in the ceiling of his own room.

During 1891 10 persons were added to the examining corps of the Patent Office, and 4 to the clerical force. Prior to that time the work had been falling behindhand, in spite of all efforts to keep it up. With the additions named it has been possible practically to keep up with the demands of the office, although the list is still about 100 cases behindhand. This, however, does not show the real deficiencies in the office, for a large part of the examining corps have been working overtime since the autumn of 1892. There are about 200 of these examiners, and, in round numbers, 40,000 applications for patents come before them every year. This gives each examiner 200 cases, but this does not by any means give an adequate idea of the number of separate actions falling to the share of each. The commissioner estimates that each examiner has an average of about 730 actions on application every year; besides this, they hear and decide upon a great variety of motions, largely petitions for the dissolution of interferences, which are often argued by counsel, and demand the same kind of study and thought that falls to the share of judges in a court of law. Of course this enormous mass of work necessitates elaborate classification, and the patents are all divided into classes. These so overlap each other that each ought properly to be classified by itself, so that each examiner, in deciding upon the novelty of an invention, need go over the ground but once. It is most desirable, in fact, that these classes should all be printed at the public expense and bound in separate volumes. This has been done as a matter of private enterprise in the ease of bicycles and velocipedes, the list filling 2 volumes, or 1,503 pages altogether. Under the official classification these improvements are found in the subclasses of velocipedes and tires, which in turn belong to the general division of carriages and wagons. In the preparation of this digest the examiner had actually to read nearly 200,000 patents, comprised in 150 subclasses, and in almost every one of these were found inventions which had to be included in the final list. The commissioner recommends the appointment of 32 new assistant examiners, at a salary of $1,200

each, to devote all their time for the present to index work of this character. In addition, he would have 16 more assistant examiners, to be employed in bringing current work up to date.

The Columbian Exposition.—The office has been subjected to an extraordinary strain in preparing for the World's Columbian Exposition at Chicago. This has demanded a vast amount of care and labor, and since no addition could be made to the clerical force the end had to be accomplished with the means at hand. The result is most satisfactory, the exhibit comprising about 2,500 working models. These are divided into many groups or classes, the models in each class ranging from more than 200, in the case of steam engines, down to 3 or 4, as in the case of fire escapes, chain making, and wood sawing. The models in each group are carefully arranged in chronological order, exemplifying the universal theory of development. A large proportion of these models have been selected from those in the Patent Office, but many had to be made, and many have been supplied by inventors and manufacturers. The whole exhibit forms a collection which has probably never been equaled in point of cost, value, and perfection of arrangement. Among the most notable and important of the group are the harvesters, the exhibit beginning with a model representing a grain header used in Gaul in the first century of the Christian era, and ending with the machines that are used in gathering the crops of the present year.

Legislation.—The treaty of 1883, designed for the protection of industrial property, was concluded at Paris, and was subsequently joined by the United States in 1887. But no legislation has been enacted to carry out the provisions of the treaty, and there is some fair ground for difference of opinion as to what laws ought to be made. The next conference of the International Union will convene at Brussels in 1894. Our patent laws are exceptionally liberal toward foreigners; but this liberality is not, as a rule, extended to American inventors by foreign countries. The latest German law contains a provision seemingly designed to modify the adverse rulings that have subsisted against American inventors, but no modification of the statute has yet been secured.

Inventions.—Herewith are briefly described, and in many cases illustrated, a number of the inventions that have been patented during the year. The selection is made from a vast number of devices covering upward of 5,000 pages in the "Patent-Office Gazette" and elsewhere, and the omissions of meritorious designs must necessarily be largely in excess of those for which space is available in the "Annual."

Life-Saving Devices.—Early in the year the proprietors of the London "Daily Graphic" offered a prize of $500 to the inventor of the best means of establishing communication between a stranded ship and the shore. Between February and March, when the competition closed, no fewer than 1,899 devices were offered, and soon afterward 300 more which were ruled out on account of limitation of time, making in all 2,200; of this number all but 100 came from Great Britain, and of the remaining 100 Germany and Austria sent the larger part. Singularly enough, considering American fecundity of invention, only a very few came from the United States. The committee of award consisted of Rear-Admiral Seymour, C. B., Capt. Vyvyan, of the royal navy, and Capt. Wyatt. The devices submitted embraced a most extraordinary variety of boats, buoys, kites, balloons, rockets, guns, rafts, mortars, birds and dogs, harpoons, parachutes, anchors, etc. After long and careful deliberation the judges decided in favor of a

the possibility of housing screw propellers within the midship section of seagoing vessels. The advantage of thus placing the screw is that it is not liable to be thrown out of water when the vessel pitches in a heavy sea, and it is effectually protected against fracture by collision with floating substances. The illustrations sufficiently show the general principle. The tunnels in which the screws revolve are open downward, so that the circulation of the water is not perceptibly interfered with. Another advantage resulting from this system of construction is that the draft of the vessel may be comparatively light, because, as the midship section is almost always certain to be submerged, the general draft need not be so deep. One steamer, the "Louvre of Paris," was built and put on service between Paris and London. She made a very good record for herself for nearly a year, but was unfortunately wrecked, through no fault, however, of her peculiar construction. The year closes with similar vessels in course of construction.

Jet Propulsion of Ships.—This problem continues to attract the attention of marine engineers who do not appear to be discouraged from the signal failures that have attended the many experiments in this direction. The latest development is the device of Mr. Vogelsang, who uses two or more jets, and in order that they shall act constantly upon undisturbed water he arranges the nozzles through which the jets are discharged in such a way that they continually revolve around an axis. This is sufficiently shown in the illustration (see next page), which gives a sectional side elevation at the point of discharge. The principle involved commends itself to common sense, for it is evident that a single jet must of necessity blow the water away just where solid resist-

LIFE-SAVING ROCKET.

rocket as affording the best means of communication with the shore. Among the 165 rockets that were submitted many were of considerable merit, but the prize was eventually awarded to Messrs. Thompson & Noble, of Southampton. Their invention, as illustrated herewith, is a grapnel that can be readily fitted to the Board of Trade Life-Saving Apparatus Rocket. The grapnel has arms fitted to it, which shut tight against its sides during flight, but on touching the ground they open out and become firmly fixed in the earth when the line is hauled upon. While there seems to be nothing especially original in this device, it certainly combines efficiency, simplicity, portability and economy, and probably represents the best conclusion at which it was possible for the board to arrive.

Central Screw Propellers.—The attention of marine engineers has lately been attracted to

CENTRAL SCREW PROPELLER. CROSS-SECTION.

CENTRAL SCREW PROPELLER. SIDE VIEW.

ance is most needed. The revolving jet shaft, on the contrary, will, it is thought, constantly

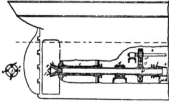

JET PROPULSION.

deliver its strokes against comparatively solid water.

Wreck Buoy.—Among new maritime appliances is one that should commend itself at least to all shipping merchants and insurance companies, if not to mariners. It is, in brief, a properly marked float attached to a long, fine wire or line, and covered by a box, which may serve as a deck seat or other piece of ship furniture. This box is a fixture so long as the ship is afloat, but it is held together with glue, which dissolves after a short period of submergence and liberates the float, which rises to the surface and remains anchored by its line, giving notice to passing vessels that a disaster has occurred, and locating the position of the wreck. Such a device, if it had been in general use, would no doubt have cleared up many mysteries of the sea that must now remain forever unsolved.

Marine Sentry.—This useful invention consists of a trough-shaped float so attached to a wire or line that it will dive to any depth not exceeding forty-five fathoms when towed through the water. (See lower illustration. At its forward end is a trigger, which on touching bottom disengages the forward sling of the towing line, suffering the float to rise to the surface. The diminished pressure strikes a gong on board the ship, announcing whatever depth of water the sentry has been set to report. The upper

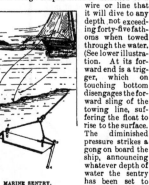

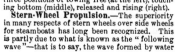

MARINE SENTRY.

part of the engraving shows the sentry in the three positions of towing free (at the left), touching bottom (middle), released and rising (right).

Stern-Wheel Propulsion.—The superiority in many respects of stern wheels over side wheels for steamboats has long been recognized. This is partly due to what is known as the "following wave"—that is to say, the wave formed by water

rising up just after it has passed under the moving vessel. In the case of a stern-wheeler the best results are attained when the paddles revolve just in the crest of this wave, the fluid particles of which are actually in motion in the same direction as that in which the vessel is moving. Mr. Yarrow, the distinguished English builder, has made some interesting experiments in this direction. The principal fault of the stern wheel is that it is difficult to steer the boat. In American waters this has been overcome to some considerable extent by using what is known as a recessed wheel, double rudders being employed, one on each side of the wheel. Boats of this character are extensively used in our Southern rivers, but they do not appear to be known abroad. To meet the difficulties mentioned, Mr. Kincaid, of Glasgow, has devised an engine and paddle-wheel which are made to revolve in trunnions, and by means of proper gear the paddle-wheel can be immersed to a depth representing the greatest efficiency. The whole bed plate, engine, wheel and all, revolves on a pivot in a horizontal direction, so that the wheel can be moved through an angle of 15° on each side of the center line of the vessel; thus are the rudders done away with altogether, and the steering is effected by means of the propulsive apparatus. The attention of English engineers has been drawn to this type of vessel from the necessity of employing shallow-draft boats in navigating the rivers of Africa.

Screw Propellers.—At least two patents have been taken out during the year which bear a

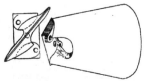

PERFORATED PROPELLER.

striking resemblance to one another. Neither the general shape of the propeller blades nor their pitch is essentially different from those that have long been in use, but, instead of being solid, the part of the blade nearest the hub is cut away so that what is known to engineers as the "dead water" escapes through openings in the blades, and is liberated, instead of acting as a drag as in the case of the ordinary propeller. It is also claimed that less power will be required to drive this than the ordinary type of propeller, and that there will be decidedly less vibration of hull and machinery. Daniel H. Welch, of Astoria, Oregon, and Charles Myers, of Manchester, England, are the patentees.

Hydrophone.—Such is the name given by its inventor, Capt. McEvoy, late of the Confederate service, to a device for detecting the approach of hostile vessels. The idea is to sink electrically connected instruments off shore, each being provided with a sensitive vibrator. No screw-driven vessel can pass within a mile of this without giving notice of its presence. A series of successful experiments has lately been conducted at Stokes Bay in the presence of a committee of English engineer officers. Capt. McEvoy believes that his device is applicable for danger signals near exposed coasts.

Clothes-line Pulley.—An improvement has been patented by John J. Leuzinger, of West New Brighton, N. Y. The pulley, as shown in section and in perspective, is deeply grooved

CLOTHES-LINE PULLEY.

and pivoted in a block which has a semicircular recess in its under face. When in position for use the block revolves in a horizontal plane, and the line, which is continuous or endless, carries clamps fixed at convenient distances and fitted so that they will hold the clothes hung out to dry and permit at the same time the free revolution of the line throughout its entire length. It would seem to be a device eminently adapted to the convenience of dwellers in city blocks.

Improved Wheel-Tires.—The march of improvement in the construction of bicycles and velocipedes of all kinds is so rapid that it is almost impossible to keep up with them from year to year. In construction it would seem that the bicycle frame has reached almost the limit of combined lightness and strength, and yet not a year passes that does not see some decided advance in both these particulars. The most noteworthy improvement of late years has certainly been the pneumatic tire. It is fresh in the recollection of every one how very clumsy this device seemed at first—the bulky rubber tire looking excessively awkward and heavy by comparison with the light cushioned tires to which the public had become accustomed. The pneumatic tire is in effect simply a circular section of rubber hose, made exceedingly strong either by metallic or canvas linings and successive coatings of the toughest rubber. This is stretched around the periphery of the wheel, and the effect of it is to render smooth even a comparatively rough road. The main difficulty lies in providing a practically tight valve wherewith the wheel-tire can be inflated. There is always some leakage, and continual pressure will force the air through several thicknesses of India rubber no matter how carefully they are put together. The pneumatic tire was originally an English

invention, but it has been perfected in this country, and the best valves, it is now admitted, are of American construction. With these tires it is possible to use roads which were heretofore impracticable to wheelmen; and there are cases on record where a good rate of speed has been maintained over railroad ties, the pneumatic tires so far reducing the shock as to render progress comparatively comfortable. Not only has the pneumatic tire been applied to bicycle wheels, but it is rapidly making its way to the trotting race track, and some of the most surprising results have been attained by applying the tire to ordinary wagon wheels. It was thought, when bicycles first made their appearance, that their introduction would result in great improvement on the ordinary country roads; this has already come to pass, as instanced by measures taken in many of the States. The mission of the bicycle is evidently not altogether athletic, if it can extend its influence so as to improve our public roads and the vehicles driven over them.

The vast number of ingenious devices that have been brought to bear upon this problem of elastic wheel-tires is simply amazing. A mere list of them would be too long to be printed here. Suffice it to say that coiled tubes inside the larger tube, springs of metal arranged around the circumference of the wheel, small inflated balls of rubber, and scores of other similar devices, have been patented.

Carpenter's Square.—An improvement in this familiar implement is shown in the illustration. The two arms are pivotally secured at the angle, so that one of them may be swung through an arc of 90°. The pivots and bearings are such that there is a minimum of strain and small liability of wear to the point of inaccuracy. The longer arm of the square has a shallow recess in which is pivoted an extension of the shorter arm, and the adjustment is maintained by a set screw whereby the arms may be locked at any desired angle. As shown in the illustration, the two

CARPENTER'S SQUARE.

arms lock automatically when brought into the ordinary position for use as a square. One obvious advantage of this tool is that it can be folded together so as to go into an ordinary tool box. The inventor is F. W. Palmer, of New York.

Electrical Canal Boats.—The Governor of the State of New York has interested himself in a device intended to introduce electricity as the motive power on State canals, instead of the slower-going and more expensive horses and

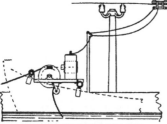

ELECTRICAL TRACTION FOR CANAL BOATS.

mules hitherto employed. The device is in effect the familiar one of the trolley wire set up along the towpath, the contact being made on the upper side of the wires, and the traction performed by a submerged cable lying along the bottom of the canal and taken up and passed over a pulley or drum attached to the bow of the canal boat and actuated by electricity. This has already been practically accomplished in an experimental way by a German engineer, but so far as we know actual experiments are as yet wanting in this country.

Rope-Holder.—A very simple device for shortening and firmly adjusting the length of

a rope has been made by Ephraim T. Rugg, of Alexandria, Ohio. As shown in the illustration, it is simply a metal plate with three perforations loosely fitting the rope on which it is to be

ROPE-HOLDER.

used. It is obvious that when the rope is adjusted as shown, no slip is possible.

Package-carrier for Velocipedes.—The simple device of a small net or hammock suspended between the handles of a crossbar has been patented. This, or something so very like it, has been in use so long among wheelmen that it is incredible that it should be capable of efficient protection under the patent laws. (Patent No. 479,069.)

Ice Velocipedes.—Stimulated by the growing interest in ice yachting, inventors have taken up the subject of mechanical propulsion. Several patents have been issued in this direction, but, so far as known, no very surprising speed has as yet been attained. The propelling force is furnished in most cases either by toothed wheels or by what may be termed a kicking or thrust motion delivered by mechanical connection with treadles. There seems to be no reason why, with proper multiplying gear, very high rates of speed should not be attained with machines of this kind. The speed of the ice yacht is due

merely to a constantly applied but not necessarily powerful wind impulse, and mechanical appliances should at least approximate the same result.

Protection against Frost.—A Californian planter, Everest by name, is credited with having invented an effective method of mitigating the cold that is so destructive to fruit, etc., in semitropical climates. An iron tank, of about 100 gallons capacity, is provided, and oil is allowed to drip slowly from distributing pans into pans set at 20 feet intervals among the trees. The oil is fired in the pans, and the drip is so regulated that the blaze is constant, creating a dense smoke—in itself a potent shield against frost. Besides this, the direct heat of the blaze works to the same end. The cost of plant per acre is about $25, and the expenditure per night of frost about $7 worth of oil.

Coffee-Strainer.—A very simple and scientific coffee-pot attachment, the invention of Robert S. Randall, of Newark, N. Y. The direction of currents in boiling water is indicated by the arrows in the illustration. There is a just prejudice against boiled coffee, but with this inven-

COFFEE-STRAINER.

tion the coffee is properly percolated or strained, the water passing repeatedly through it, and yet the coffee itself is not subjected to the direct boiling action of water. The device can be used in any ordinary coffee-pot or other similar utensil.

Bedbug-Trap.—As described in the patent claim, this invention is "a block of wood, triangular, or approximately so, in shape, sawed

BEDBUG-TRAP.

across the grain, and having parallel saw-kerfs therein extending in the same direction, the corners of said block being left uncut." The evident design is to place the blocks at the bed corners, where the saw-slits will afford a tempting retreat for bedbugs during their hours of idleness. Immersion in scalding water, or burning the block bodily, will effectually destroy the catch. The inventor is F. F. Baggesen, of Brooklyn, N. Y.

Rubber Heel-Cushion.—This invention is designed to relieve the shock that results from walking on hard pavements or from constant standing in moving vehicles. In effect, the device is a small rubber mat, backed with light leather, which is fixed in the heel of the shoe.

RUBBER HEEL-CUSHION.

This mat or cushion, about one quarter the actual size, is shown at the right. The rubber structure magnified is at the left. Railroad men, and others who are subjected to the constant jarring of travel, are liable to spinal complaints, which some such contrivance as this might wholly prevent. C. J. Bailey, of Newton, Mass., is the patentee.

Cyclone Refuge.—In what is known as "the cyclone belt" it has become common to construct subterranean retreats near dwelling-houses, wherein the family may take refuge when the dreaded tornado cloud appears in the circular seat surrounds the central area. Sufficient ventilation is afforded by small holes near the apex of the structure, and a ventilating pipe opens through the floor passing under the exterior wall. The structure, it is believed, will afford perfect security against any storm however violent, and although it might be crushed by the impact of a sufficiently heavy body, the chances are largely in its favor. The structure has been patented by its inventor.

Electric Reading-Lamps.—The question of lighting railway carriages is rather complicated, some passengers preferring just enough light to enable them to enter and leave the train, and others demanding enough to read by while the train is in motion. Of course, the railway companies naturally lean to the side of economy. The Metropolitan District Railway of London has adopted a system which seems to give the public just what it wants, and at the same time permits a satisfactory profit. The invention is neither more nor less than a penny-in-the-slot light. A Mr. Tourtel is the inventor, and preliminary experiments are said to have given satisfaction. The mechanism of the lamp is very simple, being contained in a box three inches by five inches. A penny is dropped into the slot at the top of the box, and on subsequently pressing a knob an electric light is turned on, ample for all purposes of reading, which burns brightly for half an hour. At the end of that time it is automatically extinguished, but can be relighted at the expenditure of another penny. The light is about three-candle power, and is

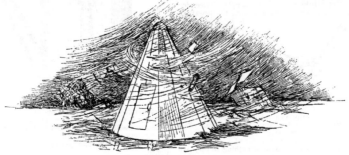

CYCLONE REFUGE.

vicinity. Such hiding-places, however, are apt to be damp and uncomfortable, and an improvement has been attempted by Reuben Quatermass, of Moline, Kan. Several heavy posts are sunk in the earth and securely anchored to beams laid horizontally several feet below the surface of the ground. The posts incline together, forming a conical framework, which is covered with heavy planking securely bolted and with the lower ends sunk a few inches below the surface. An outside sheathing of sheet metal forms an earth connection for electrical currents, and conductors lead still farther into the earth. A heavy door affords access to the interior, where a concentrated by a shaded reflector, so that only he who is entitled to its benefits can receive the direct rays. A most remarkable and commendable feature of the device is its honesty, for if the supply of electricity fails, the penny drops out into the hands of the customer. Should these lamps prove as successful in practice as the preliminary experiments indicate, their use will not be confined to railways.

Improved Dam or Levee.—The country has had such terrible warnings regarding the insecurity of earthen embankments, whether used as dams proper or for levees to confine rivers to their courses, that an invention which promises to afford reasonable security should be welcome. This device, the invention of Charles E. Wright, of Vicksburg, Miss., consists of a bulkhead formed of timbers or heavy planking laid crosswise in two or three layers, and built into the embankment longitudinally with its axis. Similar devices for strengthening embankments have long been in use, and this invention seems to de-

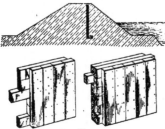

IMPROVED DAM.

·rive its merit mainly from the great coherency resulting from the combination of several thicknesses of plank crossing at right angles in alternate layers. If such a bulkhead had been concealed within the fatal dam near Johnstown, Pa., the terrible disaster of 1889 might probably have been averted. With properly adjusted spillways and wasteweirs such an embankment would yield, if at all, so slowly that the destructive rush of water would be largely mitigated.

Improved Water-Gate.—An ingenious contrivance has been patented by G. W. Norton, of Mohawk, Ariz., designed to open and close automatically the wasteweir of a dam. The engraving

shows the device in vertical section closed. As the water rises above the dam, the receptacle A becomes filled with water until its weight over-balances that at the end of the lever,

AUTOMATIC WATER-GATE.

when it drops, opening the gate and suffering the accumulated water to run off. A small hole in A empties it slowly, in a few minutes the lever-weight raises the empty receptacle, the gate closes, and the water level is maintained within any desired limits. Of course, it may be made of any suitable size, or any number of gates may be adjusted on as many wasteweirs, thus rendering it available for streams of any size.

Voting Devices.—Among the curiosities of the year's inventions are a number hearing upon improved methods of voting. There are, for instance, numerous folding or portable booths for the use of voters while preparing their ballots for the Australian or secret method. There should be a considerable demand for inventions of this character, since, if the system comes gen-

erally into use, the preparation of such booths must necessarily be a considerable item of expense. In this connection the invention of a Mr. Myers, of Rochester, N. Y., may properly be referred to. It is a mechanical electrical device for recording votes. The machine includes a booth made of sheet steel 5 feet square and 7 feet high; at one side of this are a number of knobs numbered, or perhaps colored, to indicate the particular party to which each belongs. All that the voter has to do is to enter the booth and push the knobs which he recognizes as those of his own party. This would seem to require a degree of intelligence at least commensurate with a very moderate political standard. A practical trial of this machine is said to have been made at Lockport, N. Y., and the result is reported as highly satisfactory.

PENNSYLVANIA, a Middle State, one of the original thirteen, ratified the Constitution Dec. 12, 1787; area, 45,215 square miles; population, according to the census of 1890, 5,258,014. Capital, Harrisburg.

Government.—The following were the State officers during the year: Governor, Robert E. Pattison, Democrat; Lieutenant-Governor, Louis A. Watres, Republican; Secretary of the Commonwealth, William F. Harrity; Treasurer, John W. Morrison, Republican; Auditor-General, D. McM. Gregg, Republican; Secretary of Internal Affairs, Thomas J. Stewart, Republican; Superintendent of Public Instruction, D. J. Waller, Jr.; Secretary of Agriculture, Thomas J. Edge, Republican; Adjutant-General, W. W. Greenland, succeeding Gen. Wm. McClelland, who died Feb. 7; Attorney-General, William U. Hensel, Democrat; Insurance Commissioner, G. B. Luper; Superintendent of Banking, C. H. Krumbhaar; Chief Justice of the Supreme Court, Edward M. Paxson; Associate Justices, James P. Sterrett, Henry Green, Henry W. Williams, James T. Mitchell, J. B. McCollum, Christopher Heydrick.

Education.—The Superintendent of Public Instruction reports the year ending June 6, 1892, 977,528 pupils in the schools, an increase of 8,022; the number of schools, 23,436, an increase of 322; the number of teachers, 25,339, an increase of 414. The total expenditures, including that upon buildings, are $14,329,140.46, an increase of $810,431.48. The estimated value of school property is $40,242,664, an increase of $4,404,077. The State appropriation for 1891-'92 was $2,000,000. The appropriation of $5,-000,000 made at the session of the Legislature of 1891 was not available until the first Monday of June, 1892. The effect of this liberal appropriation does not therefore appear in the results of this year.

Charities.—The State insane asylums are overcrowded, averaging about 25 per cent. more inmates than would fill their recognized capacity. Relief will be afforded when the State Asylum for the Chronic Insane is completed. An appropriation was made by the last Legislature, and a commission was appointed. The site selected is near Wernersville. Berks County, on the line of the Lebanon Valley Railway. The buildings will be finished within the coming year. When completed they will have the best approved modern conveniences, and accommodations for 800 patients. Their total cost will be kept within the legislative appropriation.

The Pennsylvania Institution for the Deaf and Dumb, which for more than sixty years has occupied the site at the corner of Broad and Pine Streets, Philadelphia, has been removed to Mount Airy, one of the most elevated and attractive suburbs. The grounds comprise 63 acres. Three buildings are already erected. The plan of the board contemplates the further erection of a building for the industrial department, which is assured by the gift of $50,000 by a friend of the school, who withholds his name, of a gymnasium, and of an additional building for dormitory and schoolroom purposes.

The Soldiers' Orphans' Schools, of which there are 3, contained 527 children at the end of the year. The children are maintained and educated at a cost of $140 *per capita*. In 1883 the Legislature enacted a law providing that " no admission shall be granted to any of the soldiers' orphans' schools or homes after June 1, 1887, and all schools or homes shall close, and all children shall be discharged from said institutions on June 1, 1890." When the commission under the act of 1889 reorganized the schools, assuming control, there were under the charge of the State 1,788 children. By graduation and withdrawal these have been reduced to 527, and it is estimated by Sept. 1, 1893, the number will not exceed 400.

An investigation into the management of the soldiers' orphans' schools by the syndicate that had charge of them before they were organized under the care of the State commission has been dragging for more than a year. There were 4 schools under the charge of the syndicate. The State paid $150 annually for each child ten years of age or over, and $115 for each one under that age. Charges were made that the children were badly fed and had insufficient care, in order to yield a large profit to the syndicate.

Reformatory.—The brush factory and the carpenter shop at the Huntingdon Reformatory were destroyed by fire on Aug. 14, supposed to have been intentionally set on fire by some inmate. The loss was estimated at $40,000. There were about 450 inmates.

An investigation was made during the year into charges of cruelty and excessive punishments at the Reformatory, and the charges were not sustained,

The Fisheries.—The report of the State Fish Commission shows a great increase in the output of shad from the Delaware river during the years 1890 and 1891. In 1881 the value of the shad caught in this river was $80,000. In 1890 it was seven or eight times that amount. There has been also a very large increase in the output of trout fry, from 300,000 in 1885 to 2,500,000 in 1881 : and yet, with all this increase, the supply is largely exceeded by the demand. Last year applications were received for 4,000,000 fry, and this year bids fair to reach 5,000,000, or double the output.

The National Guard.—The year 1892 presented the first occasion when the entire force of the National Guard has been called out for the suppression of strife and violence in the State since it was reorganized in 1878. It was in service in connection with the Homestead troubles ninety-five days. The local military companies were placed in charge of Oil City and Titusville at the time of the flood and fire, in order to protect the inhabitants and their property, and restore order.

The Adjutant-General's report says the aggregate strength of the Guard, Nov. 30, was 8,493, a gain of 65 during the year.

Applications for permission to raise companies of infantry, cavalry, and artillery are constantly received. If all were accepted the strength of the Guard could easily be doubled.

The division now contains 6,507 qualified marksmen, an increase over last year of 753.

The World's Fair Exhibit.—A report of the Executive Committee, in December, showed the total number of applications for space so far made to be 1,088. A statement of all expenditures made thus far was presented, together with an itemized estimate of the probable cost of Pennsylvania's exhibit, which shows there will be a balance of $24,800 of the original $300,000 appropriated.

The following is from a statement made by the chairman in reference to the building:

We can get through and make a highly creditable exhibit on the $100,000 appropriated to collecting, transporting, and installing the work of these various departments ; at the same time we could spend more to advantage and with credit to the State. There will be a great many valuable treasures and articles belonging to the State at the close of the exposition, which it is my earnest wish to use as a nucleus for a museum, which should be built here at the capital of the State.

Among the institutions to which space has been allotted are the University of Pennsylvania, Bryn Mawr College, the Manual Training School, the Drexel Institute, the Philadelphia School of Design for Women, the School of Industrial Art, Girard College, and the Woman's School of Art Needlework.

Girard College has in preparation a model of the original building, surrounded by those of more recent date, in addition to other valuable exhibits.

Railroads.—The latest report at hand of the Secretary of Internal Affairs gives the following summaries of statistics of railroads : Total length of roads reported was 11,784·78 miles, an increase of 903·33 since the last report. The actual combined length of lines within the State boundaries is not far from 9,000 miles. The capital stock paid in for the year ending June 30, 1890, was $799,987,217.65, and for the following year $859,535,920.82, an increase of $59,548,703.17. For the year previous the capital stock per mile of road was $73,559. Returns this year have reduced this amount to $72,936.10 per mile. The funded debt now amounts to $918,771,209.62, or $77,906.25 per mile of road. Last year the funded indebtedness was shown to be $880,589,509.72, or $80,976.31 per mile. To ascertain the entire capitalization of the roads the funded debt and capital stock are added together, and the sum is $1,778,307,130.44, or a capitalization of $150,-898.71 per mile. As shown by the reports of railway interests in the United States to the Interstate Commerce Commission, the capitalization is $60,340 per mile, making the capitalization in Pennsylvania $90,558.71 more per mile than the average in the United States. During the year just closed, $31,000,000 were expended for permanent improvements by the railroads of the State.

The average cost of transportation per mile per ton is less than ·95 of a cent, and the passenger rate is 2·167 of a cent per mile. During the year returns show that the lines in Pennsylvania carried 138,070,156 passengers, an increase of 12,173,097 over the last year.

The number of street railways reporting was 207. The stock capitalization of these corporations is reported at $34,622,120.26, an increase of $7,956,541.67 during the year.

The "Coal Combine."—The following account of the notorious "coal combine" is taken from the Governor's message to the Legislature of 1893:

During the past year an illustration of the especially flagrant manner in which the Constitution is defied has been furnished by the lease or attempted lease and consolidation of the Lehigh and Susquehanna and the Lehigh Valley Railroad Companies by the Philadelphia and Reading. The first intimation which came to the executive officers of the State of any such scheme was the publication in the newspapers that an arrangement had been consummated between the various parties to what is now known as the "Reading Combine," by which the Lehigh Valley Railroad was leased to the Philadelphia and Reading Railroad and the Central Railroad Company of New Jersey, whose system was represented in Pennsylvania by the Lehigh and Susquehanna, passed under the control of the Port Reading Railroad Company, a New Jersey corporation, the creature of and controlled entirely by the Philadelphia and Reading Railroad Company. By the terms of this arrangement it was manifested that three of the great coal-transporting companies of the Commonwealth, practically controlling three or more of the great coal-producing companies, were united into one system, destroying competition, which had previously existed between them to the advantage of the people of this and other Commonwealths, and erecting a consolidated monopoly at once violative of the Constitution and threatening the interests of the public. Immediately, the character of this transaction and its effect upon the public interest and the welfare of the Commonwealth, and the application of the fourth section of the seventeenth article of the Constitution to the facts of the case, became the subject of my attention and of my conference with the Attorney-General. Shortly afterward the complaints of private citizens touching this matter were received by me and were referred to the Attorney-General, at whose instance the representatives of the offending corporations were notified that they would be given a hearing and opportunity to show cause why the Commonwealth should not intervene in the courts to have full discovery made of all the leases, contracts, and agreements involved in or collateral with the consummated railroad "combine," and to have the same declared null and void, as being in violation of the Constitution, injurious to the public interest, against public policy, illegal, and void. At the hearing thus fixed representatives of the corporations complained against appeared and argued that no occasion for such intervention had arisen or existed. After a consideration of the answers thus made, and an examination of the leases submitted to him, it was the opinion of the law officer of the Commonwealth that the combination effected was in violation of the Constitution and against public policy, and he accordingly filed bills in equity in the Court of Common Pleas of Dauphin County on March 14 for a perpetual injunction restraining the lessee and controlling power of the combined companies from operating the corporations of which it had secured control, and asking for a decree

VOL. XXXII.—40 A

to declare the agreements and leases null and void, and for a restoration of the railroads, works, and other property of the different corporations included in the combination, each to its original owner, for separate operation by it, and for a restoration of the conditions which had theretofore existed. Answers were duly filed and examiners appointed to inquire into and report the facts of the case to the court.

Two suits brought by private individuals in other courts of the Commonwealth, touching the same matters, have progressed so far that in the one case a preliminary injunction was refused, and in the other the finding of the masters was adverse to the complaint and in favor of the legality of the "combine." The case of the Commonwealth, which is believed to be stronger than either of these elsewhere instituted, and which seeks to secure a permanent dissolution of the combination, is about ready to be argued in the Dauphin County Court of Common Pleas, and can be readily disposed of in time for final adjudication at the next term of the Supreme Court. It need only be stated, in addition, that, by reason of the legal proceedings in this and other Commonwealths, the Central Railroad Company of New Jersey, upon the 31st day of August, 1891, re-entered upon and resumed possession of the lines of railroad owned, leased, and operated by it in this State, including the Lehigh and Susquehanna, and is now alleged to be in exclusive possession and operation of the same. This step was not taken before the Chancellor of New Jersey had made a decree that the agreement and leases between these railroad companies should be set aside, and from this decree the Port Reading and Philadelphia and Reading Railroad Companies have entered an appeal, which has not yet been finally disposed of.

State Suits.—The report of the Attorney-General for 1891 and 1892 gives the following summary: Besides a half dozen suits instituted of his own motion, and about a score of *quo warranto* proceedings, 254 cases arose in the department upon appeals by corporations, officials, and others from settlements made in the Auditor-General's office, and 112 other claims, not appealed from, were placed in his hands for collection. He has collected and paid into the State treasury $874,506.70, and has suits ready for trial involving nearly a million more.

In the capital stock cases about $325,000 was recovered for the State of taxes due many years ago but not claimed at the time.

The Mercantile Taxes.—These are imposed by the State law upon merchants, brokers, billiard tables, and the like, and special officers are appointed for assessing and collecting them. Under an act of April 20, 1887, five mercantile appraisers were appointed for Philadelphia, and one for each of the other counties in the State, with lavish allowances for advertising. Exposures made during the year showed that in Philadelphia the office of mercantile appraiser was made the means of shameful barter and corruption. "The assessments," says the Governor, in his message, "were a burlesque; exemptions and reductions were made for corrupt consideration; lists were swelled with improper names for improper purposes; thousands of delinquents were reported to the police magistrates, and the proceedings against them for the recovery of taxes due the Commonwealth were farcical, resulting only in mulcting the Commonwealth in hundreds of thousands of dollars of costs without any return; the public advertising was let to newspapers for the consideration of 40 per cent. divided among the officials intrusted by the State with its allotment; until the entire board of mercantile appraisers was taken into the criminal courts, indicted, and dismissed in disgrace." In the suits. the Commonwealth claims the recovery of $50,000 rebates paid by the newspaper publishers. A saving of $60,000 a year to the State is effected by the reforms instituted in the practices of the mercantile appraiser's office.

As to the cases growing out of the Bardsley defalcation, the report of the Attorney-General says judgment for unpaid license taxes has been obtained against Bardsley to the amount of $394,-010.40. From his bondsmen $120,000 has been recovered, and from his depositories, into which State moneys were traced, $37,230.25. Of $1,-004,640 judgment recovered by Bardsley's assignee against the Keystone National Bank, over one fourth has been transferred to the Commonwealth.

Fire and Flood.—The oil regions were visited, on June 5, by a disaster only surpassed in the history of the State by the flood at Johnstown, in 1889. For nearly a month the rains had been almost incessant in western and northwestern Pennsylvania. The small streams were turned into torrents. A cloud-burst a mile above Titusville on the morning of the 5th brought on a flood and turned the creeks into rivers. An immense body of water swept down Oil Creek to Titusville, which is 18 miles south of its source. The lower part of the town was soon flooded. During the confusion a covering of oil appeared on the water, and then three explosions occurred in quick succession, followed by a flood of burning oil. This was caused by three tanks of gasoline, which were probably fired by lightning. The flames communicated to the city, and scores of buildings were soon on fire. The burning flood swept down the creek to Oil City, damaging more or less all the small towns along the distance of 18 miles. Hundreds of people were swept away by the flood or burned in the fire. If they left the burning buildings, they could only plunge into the surrounding water. Rescuing parties went out in boats as soon as the circumstances permitted and saved many lives. The number of the dead has been estimated at 196, but an accurate count was impossible. The damage to property was placed from $1,000,000 to $2,000,000. Bridges were swept away by the flood or burned, and the fire consumed dwellings, factories, refineries, cars, warehouses—all kinds of business buildings that are naturally placed about the water ways and railroads. About one third of Titusville, which is a town of 10,000 inhabitants, was destroyed. Oil City has a population of about 12,000.

The Homestead Strike.—The most serious labor disturbance ever known in the country broke out in the Carnegie Company's mills at Homestead, 8 miles east of Pittsburg, on July 6. The riot, which began on that day, was in consequence of disagreements between the management and the workmen, which had been going on for a month or more. Notice had been given that certain apparent reductions of wages would be made in the steel works; the time of signing the agreement on wages was changed from the summer to January; and the company had refused to recognize the "Amalgamated Association of Steel and Iron Workers" as an organization, or to hold any conference with the workmen for discussing the terms offered. The men, on their part, refused to work at the reduced rate, and at the same time announced their determination to resist all attempts on the part of the company to fill their places with nonunion workmen. The contest was precipitated by the workmen at Homestead hanging H. C. Frick, president of the company, in effigy, after which the company ordered an immediate shut-down of the works two days before the time provided by the contract under which the men were working. The employees at once proceeded to organize for the defensive. On July 5 the company announced its intention to make repairs, and the officials asked the sheriff to appoint deputies to protect their property. The sheriff sent a small squad of men to the works, but the strikers assembled in force and notified them to get out of town, as no disorder was intended and no damage would be done to any property. They even offered to be sworn in as deputies and to give bonds for the faithful performance of their duties as conservators of the peace. When this offer was declined, the advisory committee, which had been directing the action of the workmen, and which had held the turbulent spirits in check, was immediately dissolved, and all the records of the committee were destroyed.

Meanwhile the company had secured the services of a body of Pinkerton detectives, who were gathered in two barges on the Ohio river, some miles below. This became known to the workmen, and they assembled on the banks in great numbers to watch for the barges. When they arrived the workmen broke through the fence surrounding the mill, and, intrenching themselves behind piled-up steel billets, prepared to resist the landing. By 4 o'clock in the morning an effort was made to land the detectives, but the strikers met them, and a fierce battle was precipitated by a heavy volley of shots. The detectives were all armed with Winchester rifles, but at the point where the attempt to land was made there was a steep embankment and they were compelled to go in single file, and were soon driven back to the boats by the steady fire from the shore. They made continued efforts to land, but the strikers took a position behind a breastwork of steel rails and billets, and from this place of safe refuge were able to pick off the detectives as soon as they appeared on the decks of the boats. The great preponderance of evidence goes to show that the firing was begun by the strikers.

The fight was renewed the following day. The strikers secured a brass 10-pounder cannon and planted it within the steel-built embrasure, so as to command the barges moored at the river bank. At the same time the force of 1,000 men took up a position on the opposite side of the river, and planted a cannon, which they protected with a breastwork of railroad ties. Shortly before 9 o'clock the cannon were turned on the boats, and a bombardment was kept up for several hours. The stout oaken timbers forming the sides of the boat were splintered, but the heavy steel plates on the inside prevented the balls from penetrating the interior. When it was found that little impression could be made by the cannon on the boats, an effort was made to fire the barges. Hose was procured and oil sprayed on the decks and sides. While this was being done, barrel after barrel of oil was emptied into the river above the mooring place, the object being to allow it to float against the boats and thus ignite them.

The detectives, thus besieged three times, ran up a flag of truce, and each time it was shot down by the strikers. But later the officers of the Amalgamated Association interfered, and the next offer of surrender was responded to by a committee of strikers sent on board to prepare terms. They guaranteed safe conduct for the Pinkertons, provided they left their arms and ammunition behind and agreed to leave the place under guard. The detectives had no alternative, and accepted the terms. Seven had been killed and 20 or 30 wounded. As they passed through the streets in charge of an escort appointed by the strikers they were attacked by the mob, shot, clubbed, and stoned. The barges were looted and fired. Eleven workmen and spectators had been killed in the fight.

In the emergency the sheriff telegraphed to the Governor for aid at 10 o'clock on the morning of July 6. The Governor answered that the civil authorities must exhaust every means at their command for the preservation of peace, and, in response to further dispatches, that the sheriff must call upon the citizens for an adequate number of deputies. The next day the sheriff sent word that he had 32 deputies, and that they were to report on the morning of the 8th. The same day (the 7th) the Governor was requested to meet a committee of citizens of Homestead, and the meeting took place at Harrisburg. They promised to do all in their power to restore peace, but were apparently unable to accomplish anything. On the 10th the sheriff again called on the Governor for assistance, and the entire force of militia was ordered to Homestead, where they arrived on the 12th. The town was placed under martial law, and order was finally restored, though in many cases non-union men who came to work for the company were assaulted by union workmen.

A committee of Congress was appointed to investigate the affair. The testimony went to show that the apparent reduction proposed in wages was about 18 per cent. From a statement issued by the Executive Committee of the Federation of Labor is taken the following statement of the wages the men were receiving: "We have made a careful investigation, and find that just before the lockout there were 3,421 employed in the mills. Of this number there were 13 whose wages averaged about $7.50 a day, 46 averaged between $5 and $7 per day, 54 averaged from $4 to $5 per day, 1,177 averaged from $1.68 to $2.50 per day, and 1,625 received 14 cents per hour, or less."

The United States Senate adopted a resolution, Aug. 2, which was reported from the Committee on Education and Labor, providing for a select committee of 7 Senators to investigate, and report the facts in relation to the employment for private purposes of armed bodies of men or detectives in connection with differences between workmen and employers; the reasons for the creation of such organized bodies of armed men, their character and uses; where, when, how, and by whom they have been employed and paid, and under what authority.

On July 21, H. C. Frick, manager of the Carnegie Works, was shot and stabbed in his office by an anarchist from New York. Arrests were made on July 18 of some of the leaders of the workmen, on a charge of murder. On Aug. 3 retaliatory suits were begun against the Carnegie officials, the Pinkerton brothers, and 5 of their men, likewise on a charge of murder. Mr. Frick was arrested as soon as he recovered sufficiently to be out. Later, a charge of high treason was brought against the Homestead Advisory Board. On Oct. 11 the Grand Jury returned true bills in the treason cases against the strikers, and also in the murder, conspiracy, and aggravated riot cases against the Carnegie officials and the Pinkerton detectives. The indictments for treason involve 31 defendants. In his instructions to the jury the Chief Justice said:

It is alleged that the Advisory Committee did more than to induce others not to accept employment from the company; that it allowed no person to enter the mill of the Carnegie Steel Company, and even permitted no strangers to enter the town of Homestead without its consent; that it arranged an organization of a military character, consisting of three divisions, with commanders, captains, etc., the captains to report to the division commanders, and the latter to report to the Advisory Committee. Every member of such asserted government, whether it be an advisory committee or by whatever name it is called, who has participated in such usurpation, who has joined in a common purpose of resistance to the law and a denial of the rights to other citizens, has committed treason against the State.

The mills were gradually supplied with new workmen, and the strike was not declared off till Nov. 20. At that time it was stated by the superintendent that not more than 800 of the total number of old employees would be able to secure employment.

In December, a report was published of an alleged conspiracy to poison the nonunion workmen at the works in the summer, said to have been revealed by the confession of a cook employed by the company to furnish meals to the workmen within the inclosure—to the effect that he had been hired to put poison into the food, and promised $5,000 if the works should be shut down in consequence. It was charged that the design was not to kill men, but to use some drug that would make them sick and weak and unable to work, and that such a drug was supplied by a chemist; that 32 died, and 2,000 were made ill. True bills were found Dec. 21 against a district master workman of the Knights of Labor and 3 cooks. In behalf of the men accused, it is said that the situation of Homestead is unwholesome and the water bad, and that strangers, such as the new workmen were, are apt to suffer until they become acclimated.

The cost to the State of the military service will be more than $400,000.

Political.—The Republican State Convention met in Harrisburg, April 20, with 270 delegates, and made the following nominations: For Judge of the Supreme Court, John Dean; for Congressmen-at-large, William Lilly, Alexander McDowell.

The resolutions commended the policy of the Harrison administration, giving enthusiastic praise to Secretary Blaine for his course in the disputes with Italy and Chili, and the threatened complications with Great Britain; reaffirmed the principle of protection, and commended the McKinley act; favored liberal but well-guarded appropriations for internal improvements, and especially the construction of a ship canal to unite the waters of Lake Erie with the Mississippi system; favored liberal pension legislation; called for more stringent immigration laws; approved the general policy of the last Republican Congress in dealing with the silver question, and said further:

We are opposed to the free coinage of silver, but favor the purchase of American silver at its market value, and the issue by the Government of treasury notes in payment thereof.

We believe in a free ballot and a fair count, and affirm that, unless intelligent and patriotic sentiment accord these rights to the humblest citizen in every section of the country, it becomes the duty of the Federal Government to secure them by congressional enactment, under the authority conferred by the Constitution.

We heartily commend the action of the Legislature of 1891 for the decided progress made by it in the direction of the relief of local taxation by the appropriation of $5,000,000 annually for the support of our public schools, the surrender to the local treasuries of the entire revenues derived from retail liquor licenses, and the return to the several counties of three fourths of the revenues derived from the taxation of personal property.

The Democratic State Convention met at Harrisburg, April 13, with 463 delegates. The party in the State was divided between the friends and opponents of the Administration. In the matter of disputed delegations, the credentials of the Governor's faction were accepted; his party also carried its point in the rejection of a resolution instructing the delegates to the National Convention to vote for the nomination of Mr. Cleveland. The delegates were instructed to vote as a unit. A resolution was introduced commending the Governor's action during his former administration, by which a combination of competing railroads was defeated in the courts, and approving of his course in instituting proceedings to suppress and overthrow the present railroad combination and coal monopoly; it approved his expressed confidence in the trial by jury for that purpose, and suggested that the same measures be applied as before. The resolution was referred to the committee and not by them reported. The platform declared "for honest and economical administration; for local self-government; for honest money, the gold and silver coinage of the Constitution, and for a currency convertible into such coinage without loss; for that genuine civil-service reform which recognizes public office as a public trust; for liberal but not reckless pensions; and for the speedy abatement of all forms of needless and oppressive taxation," called for tariff reform, the repeal of the McKinley act, and the placing of essential raw materials of American manufactures on the free list; favored the nomination of Mr. Cleveland; approved the administration of Gov. Pattison; and pronounced the action of the Republican State Senate in evading the duty of pronouncing judgment upon faithless State officials a cowardly subterfuge and a disgraceful violation of public duty. The nominees of the convention were: For Judge of the Supreme Court, Christopher Heydrick: for Congressmen-at-large, George A. Allen, Thomas P. Merritt.

The official returns of the election gave the Harrison electors 516,011; Cleveland, 452,264; Bidwell, 25,123; Weaver, 8,714; Wing, 898. For Judge of the Supreme Court, John Dean received 510,292; Christopher Heydrick, 446,001; Amos Briggs (Prohibition), 22,302; R. B. McCombs (People's), 7,031; N. L. Criest (Socialistic Labor), 540. For Congressman-at-large, William Lilly received the highest number of votes cast, 512,557; Alexander McDowell, 511,433; George A. Allen, 448,714; T. P. Merritt, 447,456; Simeon B. Chase (Prohibition). 23,667; James T. McCrory (Prohibition), 22,930; G. P. Chase (People's), 7,466; G. W. Dawson (People's), 7,313; J. Mahlon Barnes (Labor), 674; Thomas Grundy (Labor), 685.

The Legislature stands: Senate, 33 Republicans and 17 Democrats: House, 134 Republicans and 70 Democrats; Republican majority on joint ballot, 80.

The congressional delegation will consist of 22 Republicans and 8 Democrats.

PERSIA, an empire in central Asia. The Shah is absolute ruler of the country, but he has to conform to the doctrines of the Mohammedan religion as laid down in the sacred book of the Prophet and the interpretation of his oral comments and sayings as adopted by his successors and the high priesthood. The Shah is regarded as vicegerent of the Prophet, and as such claims obedience, although a great many of the priesthood and of the *syeds* deny this power. The present Shah is Nasreddin, born July 18, 1831, who succeeded his father, Mohammed, on Sept. 10, 1848. The Shah has the power to leave the crown at his death to any member of his family. The executive Government is carried on by the aid of a body of ministers, consisting at the end of 1892 of the following: The Grand Vizier, who unites the functions of Minister of the Interior, of the Court, and of the Treasury and Customs, Mirza Ali Asghar Khan; Minister of Posts and President of the Council of State, Emin ed-Daouleh; Minister of War, Kamran Mirza; Minister of Foreign Affairs, Kavam ed-Daouleh; Minister of Finance, Emin el Moulk: Minister of Justice and Commerce, Mohsin Khan; Minister of Instruction, Mines, and Telegraphs, Ali Kouli Khan; Minister of the Press, Mohammed Hassan Khan.

Area and Population.—The area of Persia is about 628,000 square miles, with a population in 1881 of 7,653,000. The population in 1891 was estimated at 9,000,000. The whole country is divided into 22 large and 10 small provinces. Each province has a governor-general or *hâkim*, who is responsible to the Central Government, and who can appoint his own lieutenant-governor or *naib el hukumah*. Every town has a mayor or chief magistrate, called *kalantar*, and every parish and every village has a chief or *kedkoda*. The officers are usually appointed by the *naib el hukumah*, and their duty is to collect the revenues. The chiefs of nomad tribes go under the name of *ilkhani* or sheik, and are responsible for the collection of the revenues to the *hâkim* of the province in which their tribe resides. About 8,000,000 of the population are of the Shiah faith, 800,000 are Sunnis, 9,000 Parsees, 20,000 Jews, 43,000 Armenians, and 23,-000 Nestorians. Only about 800 Europeans reside in Persia. (For finances, see " Annual Cyclopædia" of 1891.)

Army.—The army is raised by tribal levies, although a decree was issued in 1875, but never enforced, ordering that the army should be raised by conscription, and that the term of service should be twelve years. The organization of the army is by provinces, tribes, and districts; each province contributes several regiments, each tribe one, or sometimes two, and each district one regiment, the commanding officer being a chief of the tribe or district from which the regiment is raised. The Christians, Jews, and Parsees, and the Mussulmans of the Kashan and Yezd districts, are exempt from military service. According to the official report of the Minister of War, the army numbers 105,500 men, of whom 20 batteries, comprising 5,000 men form the artillery ; 78 battalions, numbering 54,700 men, the infantry ; 25,200 men the regular and irregular cavalry ; and 24 battalions, containing 7,200 men, the militia. Only half this number is liable to be called for service, while the standing army numbers about 24,500. (For commerce and communications, see the "Annual Cyclopædia" for 1891, page 718.)

Agitation against the Tobacco Monopoly. —Tobacco is one of the most important articles in Persia, the people valuing it higher than food or clothing, and would rather go without the necessaries of life than dispense with their *tumbeki* or *tutun.* When, in 1891, the Shah granted a monopoly on tobacco to the Imperial Tobacco Corporation, an English syndicate, a strong protest was entered by the people, who objected to having their rights of buying and selling tobacco to whom they pleased curtailed. The discontent of the Persian people has been smoldering for long years. The system of farming out every lucrative post to the highest bidder, who reimburses himself at the expense of the people, had become unbearable. The governors of the provinces have to pay a large price for their office to the Shah, besides bribing the ministers in order to obtain the appointment, and then they farm out the offices that they have the power to bestow, to the highest bidders, who in turn make the populace pay their expenses, and endeavor to lay by a fortune in anticipation of their removal from office. Concessions granted to foreigners are in the eyes of the people only another way of robbing them, and they decided to have the principal one, the tobacco monopoly, repealed. Numerous riots took place in the provinces as well as the cities, and the *mollahs*, always ready to sympathize with the people and to oppose the Shah, urged them on to rebellion. Large forces were required to quell the disturbances, but another difficulty arose : the priests issued an order prohibiting the use of tobacco among their adherents. In view of the serious aspect of the case, the Government decided to make concessions, and abolished the projected institution of the tobacco monopoly in the interior of Persia, limiting the concession to export only. The people, however, were not satisfied with this, but demanded the abrogation of the whole measure. This also was finally promised by the Government, but the people distrusted the promises of the Shah, and hesitated to resume smoking before permission was received from the *mollahs.* When, finally, the negotiations with the Régie were concluded, the interdict against the use of tobacco was withdrawn and the people resumed smoking. The Government of Persia undertook to pay to the Imperial Tobacco Corporation an indemnity of £500,000, which is to be secured by the custom duties of South Persia and the Persian Gulf.

PERU, a republic in South America. Until July 28, 1821, it was a Spanish viceroyalty, when it declared its independence, but not until 1824 did it gain its actual freedom from Spanish rule. The present Constitution was proclaimed Oct. 16, 1856, and revised on Nov. 25, 1860. The republic is divided into departments, and the departments are subdivided into provinces. The Senate consists of 40 members, in the proportion of 1 to every 2 provinces of each department : the House of Representatives consists of 80 members, in the proportion of either 1 to every 30,000 inhabitants or 1 to every province. Both houses are elected by indirect suffrage of the departments. The executive power vests in a President, who, as well as the 2 Vice-Presidents, is elected for the term of four years. The present incumbent of the presidential chair is Col. Remigio Morales Bermudez ; the 2 Vice-Presidents are Pedro Solar and Col. Bergoño. The President exercises his executive functions through a Cabinet composed of 5 ministers, which at the beginning of the year consisted of the following members : Prime Minister and Minister of War and of Marine, Justiniano Bergoño ; Minister of Foreign Affairs, Dr. J. Federico ; Minister of Finance and of Commerce, Senor Carbajal ; Minister of the Interior, Dr. F. Herrera ; Minister of Justice, Dr. C. Serpa. (For area and population, see the "Annual Cyclopædia" for 1891.)

Finance.—The revenues were estimated in the budget for 1892 at 7,103,888 silver soles or dollars, of which 5,359,350 soles were derived from customs, 1,218,281 soles from direct taxes, 23,000 soles from telegraphs, 183,500 soles from posts, and 319,757 soles from various other sources. The expenditures were estimated at 7,105,132 soles, of which 306,047 soles were for Congress, 998,988 soles for the Government, 211,-921 soles for foreign affairs, 736,769 soles for the Ministry of Justice, 1,469,211 soles for the financial administration. 3,381,487 soles for the army and navy, and 709 soles for extraordinary expenses.

The public debt is divided into internal and external ; the former was estimated in 1888 at 100,287,000 soles, not including 83,747,000 soles of paper money. The internal debt bears 1 per cent. interest, and the market value of the bonds in 1892 was 5¼ per cent. of their nominal value. The external debt, which was contracted in England in 1870 and 1872, and amounted to £31,579,080, with interest since 1876, was extinguished by the Grace-Donoughmore contract in 1890. (For particulars, see "Annual Cyclopædia " for 1891.)

Commerce.—The foreign trade is largely carried on with Great Britain and France, although of recent years the trade with Germany and the United States has increased to some extent. The imports from Great Britain in 1888 amounted to 5,350,000 soles; from Germany, 1,121,000 soles; from France, 987,000 soles; from China, 704,000 soles; from Italy, 238,000 soles; from Belgium, 133,000 soles; from Chili, 81,000 soles; from other countries besides the United States, 166,000 soles. The total imports were 9,461,000 soles. The exports to Great Britain amounted for the same year to 933,000 soles; to Chili, 570,000 soles; to France, 156,000 soles; to Germany, 15,000 soles; to other countries besides the United States, 353,000 soles. The values of silver, gold, and other minerals are not included in the exports. The commerce with the United States for the years ending June 30, 1890, 1891, and 1892, was as follows: Imports from the United States in 1890, $1,427,301; exports to, $351,695; showing an excess of imports of $1,075,606; imports in 1891, $1,399,991; exports, $386,518; excess of imports, $1,013,473; imports in 1892, $1,007,035; exports, $591,300; excess of imports, $415,735. Of the total amount of the imports from the United States in 1890, merchandise to the value of $1,418,561 was of products of the United States. Of the total exports to the United States, merchandise to the amount of $325,853 entered free, while goods valued at $25,842 were dutiable. The imports of United States products for 1891 were $1,396,207; the exports to the United States free of duty were $369,405, and dutiable exports $17,113. For 1892, the imports of United States products were $1,002,977. Peruvian exports entered free of duty, $555,959; dutiable, $35,341. The imports from the United States vary more in character than those of any other country, the leading imports consisting of provisions, cotton goods, manufactures of steel and iron and furniture; the chief exports are sugar, hides, and skins, cotton, and a small amount of cubic niter.

Political and Financial Affairs.—Owing to differences between the ministers the Cabinet resigned, and a new one was formed on July 2, 1892, composed of the following members: Premier and Minister of the Interior, Carlos M. Elias; Minister of Foreign Affairs, Eugenio Larraburo y Unánue; Minister of Finance and Commerce, Rafael Quiroz; Minister of Justice and of Public Worship, Dr. Ismail Puirredon; Minister of War and Marine, Col. Bruno Morales Bermudez.

The complications which had arisen between Peru and Chili over the distribution of the Peruvian guano money in the hands of Chili were brought to a satisfactory close. According to the treaty of 1883, signed at Ancon, Chili received the income from the Peruvian guano beds, which was to be distributed among the Peruvian creditors, inasmuch as the loans raised by Peru in 1870 and 1872 were secured by the guano deposits. Half of this money was placed in the Bank of England, and the other half was invested in 4½-per-cent. Chilian bonds. In 1890 an arrangement was made with Chili by which the bondholders were to receive certain guano deposits; and by the Grace-Donoughmore contract of the same year Peru ceded, among other things, the guano deposits in question for sixty-

six years in extinguishment of the creditors' claims. In order to work these concessions properly the foreign creditors organized the Peruvian Corporation, and as such demanded the money held by Chili and the Bank of England, which amounted to nearly £1,000,000. But the distribution was opposed by France, which protested that the claims of her citizens should be recognized, although Peru has always maintained that the French claims had no legal standing, and that they should be decided by a Peruvian tribunal. The French minister, M. Bacourt, finally succeeded in arranging a protocol with Chili for the settlement of the French claims against Peru, whereby one half of the amount of £500,000 deposited in the Bank of England was to be reserved pending arbitration, and the balance to be handed over at once to the Peruvian Corporation. Of the £500,000 invested in Chilian bonds, the Peruvian Corporation was to receive 80 per cent., amounting to £400,000, while the remaining 20 per cent. was to be distributed among the French claimants, who are also to share equally in the money in the Bank of England, subject, however, to the decision of the President of the Supreme Court of Justice of the Swiss Republic at Bern, who was appointed arbitrator. The Peruvian Corporation objected to this protocol, but without avail, as it was signed by the French minister and the Chilian Government, and approved by the Congress of the latter country. In pursuance of the convention of 1890 between Peru and Chili, the Chilian Minister of Foreign Affairs, Señor Errázuriz, handed over to the Peruvian *chargé d'affaires* on Dec. 8, 1892, an order for the delivery to the Peruvian Government of the guano deposits on the islands of Huanillos, Punta de Lobos, Pabellon, Pica, and Labos de Afuera, accompanied by an order from the Government making over the concessions held by Chili. The documents were immediately turned over to the Peruvian Corporation.

PHARMACY. This art continues to manifest steady progress in its different branches. Higher education, better laws with their strict enforcement, purer drugs with improved dispensing, and a greater knowledge of commercial practices are the lines on which pharmacy is developing. The proposed recognition of the claims of pharmacists by physicians has met with success. At the meeting of the American Medical Association held in Newport during July, 1890, a committee was appointed to invite the American Pharmaceutical Association to meet with them hereafter. The establishment of the proposed section of pharmacy was, however, postponed till next meeting. At the same time a committee from the American Pharmaceutical Association, led by Joseph P. Remington, presented the "National Formulary" to their attention and requested its indorsement. This section of pharmacy and materia medica came into existence at the forty-second annual meeting of the American Medical Association held in Washington during May, 1891. A number of pharmacists were present, and Dr. F. Woodbury was chosen chairman of the section. Fifteen papers of pharmaceutical interest were presented. A committee of three members of the American Medical Association was appointed to attend the next gathering of the American Pharmaceutical Association. The desirability of interchangeable registration has been discussed at several of the meetings of State associations. That such a reform would be desirable seems undoubted, but the difficulty to overcome is the lack of uniformity in the requirements of the laws of different States, hence the first necessity would be the amending of the laws making the examinations and qualifications of a registered pharmacist the same throughout the United States. .

Colleges.—The department of pharmacy of the Denver University, Col., came into successful existence, and began its second term in the autumn of 1889. A School of Pharmacy was established in 1889 as a department of the Ohio State University in Columbus, Ohio. Its faculty includes members of the university, and the laboratory facilities offered are unusually good. A College of Pharmacy was organized during 1889, in Portland, Ore., under the auspices of the Willamette University. It began with an attendance of 20 students. and, with the exception of the college in San Francisco, is the only pharmaceutical school on the Pacific coast. The New York College of Pharmacy inaugurated a series of lectures on subjects connected with the practice of the art, to be delivered by accepted authorities on the topics considered. These were begun in December, 1889. An appropriation of $21,000 was made by the Legislature of Michigan in 1889 for the enlargement of the building for the School of Pharmacy and the Chemical Laboratory of the University of Michigan, $16,000 of which will be appropriated for building, and $5,000 for heating, ventilation, cases, tables, and fixtures. Student tables for 125 will be furnished in the department of pharmacy. A School of Pharmacy was established by the Legislature of Minnesota in 1890 as a department of the State University, in St. Paul. A department of pharmacy of the Detroit College of Medicine in Detroit, Mich., began its first session on Jan. 5, 1891. The Brooklyn College of Pharmacy was organized in July, 1891, and began its first course in Oct. 5, 1891. The Atlanta Medical College of Atlanta, Ga., inaugurated a department of pharmacy on Oct. 7, 1891. The School of Pharmacy connected with Cornell University proved unsuccessful. and it was discontinued on the opening of the university in the autumn of 1891.

Legislation.—The great value of pharmaceutical legislation has made itself apparent by the efforts in various States to evade its fulfillment, and it is gratifying to record that in nearly every instance where prosecution was resorted to the law was sustained. In New York a case was carried to the Court of Appeals, where the judge, in rendering his opinion, stated that "public safety must be regarded as superior to private rights." Action had been brought to prevent the conducting of a drug store by a person not licensed by the Board of Pharmacy. Early in 1889 Texas and New Mexico passed full laws restricting the practice of pharmacy; Florida followed with a new law in May, 1889; and in October, 1889, the Georgia Legislature passed a series of amendments recommended by the legislative committee of the Georgia Pharmaceutical Association and the Board of Phar-

macy. Its most important features were a series of sections against the adulterations of drugs and chemicals, making it a penal offense to manufacture or sell any adulterated drug. chemical, or pharmaceutical preparation, and defining adulteration. An ordinance prohibiting druggists from selling morphine, cocaine, etc., except when ordered by a prescription from a physician, went into effect in San Francisco, Cal., in 1889. In New York amendments to the law were enacted during 1889, as follow: 1. That an applicant for a license as a pharmacist or assistant must be a resident of the place where he proposes to practice or, if a non-resident, must present an affidavit that he intends to make such a place his residence, and that he has not been refused a license elsewhere in the State during the six months previous. 2. That the widow or legal representative of a deceased pharmacist who was registered may continue the business pr   the actual retailing, dispensing, and compounding of medicines be done only by a legally qualified pharmacist. 3. The phrase "usual domestic remedies" in said act is hereby defined as follows, namely: Medicines that from common use a knowledge of their properties and dose has been acquired, and includes only such remedies as may be safely employed without the advice of a physician, such as Epsom salts, Rochelle salts, salts of tartar, borax, sulphur, magnesia, camphor, aloes, myrrh, guaiac, arnica, rhubarb, senna, squills, ipecac, and preparations of above ; also castor oil, olive oil, origanum, spike, amber, winter-green, peppermint and wormwood, glycerin, spirits of niter, and other like remedies, but does not include opium, morphine, laudanum, strychnine, arsenic, belladonna, aconite, and other poisons requiring knowledge and pharmaceutical skill to safely dispense. unless they be sold in original packages or packages bearing the label of a licensed pharmacist. The phrase "rural districts" used in said act is hereby declared to apply only to small villages and country districts having less than two stores where pharmacy is practiced. The phrase "practice of pharmacy" used in said act is hereby defined as follows, namely: The compounding of prescriptions or of any United States pharmacopœial preparation, or of any substance to be used as medicine, or the retailing of any drug or poison for medicinal purposes. The law in Nebraska in 1889 was amended so as to require three years' practical experience in pharmacy before being eligible for examination for the granting of temporary certificates of registration to the licentiates of such other boards of pharmacy and graduates of colleges of pharmacy as may be deemed proper, which shall be good only until the first regular meeting of the board thereafter. Assistants who have held certificates of registration in the State for two consecutive years and had two years' practical experience in pharmacy previous to registration may register as pharmacists. Every pharmacist must register annually, otherwise his right to act ceases, and he is barred from the practice until he shall pass a new examination. During the session in 1889 of the Illinois Legislature its law was amended so that any person is entitled to registration as a pharmacist "who has had five years' practical experience in compounding drugs in a drug store or pharmacy where the prescriptions of medical practitioners are compounded." The Board of Pharmacy has the right to refuse registration to applicants under this provision whose "credentials are not satisfactory evidence of their competency." Any person who has served three years under a registered pharmacist and who is eighteen years of age is entitled to registration as an assistant pharmacist. The pharmacy law of New Hampshire was amended in 1889 so that the commissioners must examine applicants over sixteen years of age who have served two years under a registered pharmacist, and if found competent, grant a certificate as assistant. It is also made their duty to bring complaints before the authorities against all persons violating the act. The payment of the commissioners is likewise specified in the new law. During 1890 a full pharmacy law was passed by the Legislature of Washington, and during 1891 bills were passed regulating the practice of pharmacy in the States of Arkansas and Oregon. Also a bill was passed in California during 1891, announced to go into effect on Jan. 1, 1892. During 1891 a pharmacy law was passed by Oklahoma Territory. There is still lacking proper legislation on this subject in Alaska, Arizona, Indiana. Indian Territory, Maryland (except Baltimore), Mississippi, Montana, Nevada, Tennessee, Utah, and Vermont.

Pharmacopœial Revision.—The United States Pharmacopœia, which is the accepted authority for the compounding of all articles prepared by druggists, and known as official, is issued once in ten years by a committee, chosen at a convention, where delegates from all incorporated medical or pharmaceutical colleges, associations, or societies may be represented. A call was issued by the president, Dr. Robert Amory, of the revision of 1880, "for a general convention to assemble in Washington, D. C., at noon of May 7, 1890, for the purpose of providing for a revision and publication of the Pharmacopœia of the United States of America." The committee on revision of the last Pharmacopœia very wisely gathered the criticisms that appeared on their work and published a digest of them for the use of their successors. This book was edited by the chairman of the committee, Dr. Charles Rice, of New York city. The journals, both medical and pharmaceutical, devoted much space toward the consideration of possible changes in the work. The issuing of the book at a lower price ($4.00) than the last has been called for; also a more complete and comprehensive description of the drugs and their constituents is urged, although such information finds its proper place in the different commentaries of the Pharmacopœia, such as the Dispensatories; and more exact information on the therapeutic value of drugs has been suggested. Information generally is sought for, although the discussion is chiefly confined to the following items: (1) Articles now official that seem unnecessary; (2) Articles desirable to be made official; (3) Defective formula in the present volume; (4) Improved formula for any present preparation; (5) Formulas for desirable preparations not now official; (6) Working formulas of chemical and pharmaceutical preparations; (7) Shall doses of official articles be appended? The convention met as called for, and the following officers were elected: President, Horatio C. Wood, of Philadelphia, Pa.; Vice-Presidents, William S. Thompson, Washington, D. C.; D. W. Prentiss, Washington, D. C., J. M. Flint, U. S. N., A. E. Ebert, Chicago, Ill., and William M. Searly, San Francisco. Cal.; Secretary, Hobart A. Hare; Assistant Secretary, G. H. C. Klie, St. Louis, Mo. Subsequently the following committee of revision was chosen: Charles Rice, Chairman; Joseph P. Remington, Frederick B. Power, Peter W. Bedford, Dr. W. M. Mew, Dr. John Godfrey, Dr. J. M. Flint, John M. Maisch, Dr. Roberts Bartholow, Dr. Charles O. Curtman, Dr. Frederick A. Castle, Dr. N. S. Davis, Jr., C. Lewis Diehl, Dr. Robert G. Eccles, Dr. Willis G. Gregory. Charles Mohr, George F. H. Markoe, Oscar Oldberg, Lucius G. Sayre, Otto A. Wall, Dr. Thomas F. Wood, Dr. H. H. Rushy, Alfred B. Taylor. Dr. R. T. Edes, and C. S. N. Hallberg. The following topics were discussed at the convention, and the committee instructed in accordance with the wishes of the majority: 1. General directions; 2. Assay processes for drugs; 3. Assay processes for galenical preparations; 4. Assay processes for opium and cinchona; 5. Descriptions of chemicals and tests; 6. Chemical formulas; 7. Proprietary or patented articles; 8. Nomenclature; 9. Specific gravity; 10. Weights and measures; 11. General formulæ; 12. Lists of reagents, tables, etc.; 13. Publication of the Pharmacopœia; 14. Date for the Pharmacopœia to go into effect; and 15. Compensation of experts.

New pharmacopœias for Austria and Germany were announced to appear in 1890. That for Austria was issued in 1890 and that for Russia in 1891, while the Military Pharmacopœia of Austria will be issued in 1892.

Associations.—The thirty-seventh annual meeting of the American Pharmaceutical Association was held in San Francisco, Cal., during June 24–28, under the presidency of Maurice W. Alexander. The opening session was devoted to the reports of officers and committees. A report from the treasurer showed his receipts during 1889 to have been $12,067.37; disbursements, $9,120.92; balance, $2,946.45, being a gain of $1,700 over the balance of 1888. Since the last meeting 106 applications for membership had been accepted, and with the 49 chosen at the present meeting, the total membership was brought up to 1,264. Numerous papers were read and discussed at the scientific session, which was presided over by Emlen Painter. The section on pharmaceutical education was presided over by Peter W. Bedford, and, besides the papers read at its sessions, an important report of the Committee on Preliminary Examinations was considered. Its conclusions were:

1. That this association recommend its members and all others in the retail drug business to refuse to take into their employ as apprentices any boys or young men who have not graduated from a grammar school, or who have not received an education equal to that required for such graduation.

2. That colleges of pharmacy demand as a condition to entrance a certificate of graduation from a State grammar school, or from an institution whose course of instruction is equal to that of the State grammar schools.

3. That irrespective of the possession of a diploma from a grammar school, all applicants be examined in the following branches: English composition, percentage, proportion, and rudimentary Latin.

4. In the absence of such grammar-school diploma the preliminary examinations should embrace:

(a) A thorough examination in the English language, including orthography (chirography), use of capital letters, punctuation, grammatical construction.

(b) Mathematics, common and decimal fractions, percentage, proportion, involution, and evolution, and denominate numbers.

(c) Geography and rudimentary Latin.

5. That all colleges announce that in the year 1891 they will require the candidates to pass an examination in algebra in addition to the foregoing.

Prof. Remington's paper on this subject was also of special interest, and his conclusions referring to training before entering a school of pharmacy were that "it is better for the student to have practical experience before entering college, better for the professors (because of the greater intelligence of the student), better for the college (because it makes better students), and better for the community (for the same reason)." The sections of commercial interests and of pharmaceutical legislation held meetings and discussed pertinent topics. The Ebert prize was awarded to Joseph F. Geisler, of New York city, for his paper, read at the Detroit meeting in 1888, on the "Morphiometric Assay of Opium." The thirty-eighth annual meeting of the American Pharmaceutical Association was held at Old Point Comfort, Va., during Sept. 8-12. Emlen Painter, of New York city, had been chosen president, but, owing to his death, Karl Simmon, of St. Paul, Minn., the first vice-president, filled the chair. The treasurer's report showed that the receipts during the year were $10,511.39, and disbursement $6,370.-82, giving a balance of $4,140.57. Some 97 new members were admitted, bringing the total membership up to 1,367. The scientific section was presided over by H. M. Whelpley, of St. Louis, Mo., and numerous papers were presented and discussed at its sessions. The section on commercial interests was presided over by Henry Canning, of Boston, Mass., and topics of trade interest were considered at its meeting. William Simon, of Baltimore, Md., was chairman of the section on legislation and education, and papers on these subjects were received and discussed. The Ebert prize of 1890 was awarded to W. T. Wenzell, of San Francisco, Cal., for his paper "On the Coloring Matter of Flowers." The thirty-ninth annual meeting of the American Pharmaceutical Association was held in New Orleans, La., from April 27 to May 1, with Albert B. Taylor, of Philadelphia, Pa., as president. According to the secretary of the membership committee there were 1,274 members in good standing, 95 of whom had been elected since the last report, and 13 delegates had been received, making a total membership of 1,382. The association had lost from various causes 196 members. The invested funds were reported as amounting to $12,230.88. A communication from Chicago asking the co-operation of the association in holding a p a r ac a congress in 1893 was read and discussed; a committee to co-operate with the World's Congress Auxiliary was subsequently appointed. Numerous

papers were read before the section on scientific papers, over which Edgar L. Patch presided. The section on commercial interest chose Willard H. Torbert as their presiding officer, and the usual subject of the relations between the wholesale and retail druggists was discussed from the report presented by Henry Canning. Proper papers dealing with subjects pertinent to legislation and education were read before that section, which was presided over by A. B. Stevens. The meeting in 1892 will be held in the Crawford House, White Mountains, N. H., during the first week in September.

A Washington State Pharmaceutical Association was organized on Jan. 28, 1890, and held its first regular meeting in Tacoma in March of that year. On Sept. 16, 1890, a Colorado Pharmaceutical Association was organized in Denver, and on Aug. 24, 1891, a Montana Pharmaceutical Association was organized in Helena.

Trade Associations.—The fifteenth annual meeting of the National Wholesale Druggists' Association was held in Indianapolis, Ind., during Oct. 22-25, under the presidency of George A. Kelly. Over 200 firms were represented, and the meeting was the largest ever held. From the report of the secretary it appears that at the organization of the association only 62 firms were represented, while at the present meeting the membership was increased by 32 who had joined. The treasurer reported a balance from 1888 of $1,639, collections of $3,600, expenditures of $3,370, and a present balance of $1,871. The business of the meeting consisted essentially of the reading of reports of committees appointed to consider various trade interests, which were then discussed and acted on.

The sixteenth annual meeting of the National Wholesale Druggists' Association was held in Washington, D. C., during Sept. 29-Oct. 3, 1890, under the presidency of Peter Van Shaack. The reports of the president and the various committees were received and acted on. No special subjects of unusual importance presented themselves, and the meeting was a quiet one.

The seventeenth annual meeting of the National Wholesale Druggists' Association was held in Louisville, Ky., during Oct. 19-22, 1891, under the presidency of Daniel Stewart. The treasurer's report showed a balance of $1,217.99. The various committees on commercial interests made their reports and they were discussed. The subject of a means to prevent cutting prices by retailers was considered at length. The next meeting will be held in Montreal, Canada, during September, 1892.

The Association of Manufacturers of and Dealers in Proprietary Articles of the United States held their seventh meeting in New York city, on March 21st. The attendance was large, and in the absence of President R. V. Pierce, W. H. Hall presided over the meeting. The principal topics of discussion were the best methods of carrying out the rebate plan so as to exclude the cutter, the freight classifications, and the breakage allowance. A plan was proposed for the establishment of distributing agencies, through which alone the members of the association would sell their goods, and suggested that each of these agencies should be held responsible for the manner in which the sales were conducted in its especial field, and should be given full power to enforce such regulations as could with propriety be imposed in its particular section.

The eighth annual meeting of the Association of Manufacturers of and Dealers in Proprietary Articles was held in Washington during Sept. 30-Oct. 1, 1890, under the presidency of R. V. Pierce. Five new members were elected and subjects of trade interest were discussed.

The ninth annual meeting of the Association of Manufacturers of and Dealers in Proprietary Articles was held in Louisville, Ky., simultaneously with the National Wholesale Druggists' Association. The cutting of prices was the leading question under discussion, and they adopted the conditions proposed by the larger organization. R. V. Pierce, of Buffalo, N. Y., was again chosen president.

The first annual meeting of the National Paint, Oil, and Varnish Association was held in Cleveland, Ohio, on Jan. 22 and 23, 1889. The sessions were devoted chiefly to the working of completing the organization begun in Saratoga Springs, N. Y., during September, 1888. The officers elected were Charles Richardson, of Boston, Mass., as president, and G. H. Vrooman, of Chicago, Ill., as secretary. The second annual convention of this body was held in Cincinnati, Ohio, on Nov. 18, 19, and 20, 1890, at which O. L. Whitelaw was chosen president. The third annual convention was held in St. Louis, Mo., on Nov. 17, 18, and 19, 1891. A membership of 434 was then reported, consisting of members from 13 clubs in different sections of the country. The treasurer's report showed a balance of $547.80 to the credit of the association. New York was chosen as the next place of meeting, and M. D. Egan, of New York city, as president, with F. Beal, of Philadelphia, Pa., as secretary.

Besides the formation of numerous local trade organizations, it is worthy of special note to report the formation, on Jan. 27, 1891, of the New York Drug Exchange, of which John McKesson was chosen chairman.

Literature.—Among the books recently published may be noted: "Practical Hand-book of Toilet Preparations," by Joseph Begg (New York, 1890); "Hand-book of Materia Medica, Pharmacy, and Therapeutics," by Cuthbert Bowen (Philadelphia and London, 1889); "The Pocket Materia Medica and Therapeutics," by C. Henri Leonard (Detroit, 1891); "Tables for Doctor and Druggist," by Eli H. Long (Detroit, 1891); "An Elementary Text-book of Chemistry," by William G. Mixter (New York, 1889); "The American Homœopathie Pharmacopœia," by Joseph T. O'Connor (Philadelphia, 1890); "A Course of Home Study for Pharmacists," by Oscar Oldberg (Chicago, 1891); "Secret Nostrums and Systems of Medicine," a book of formulas by Charles W. Oleson (Chicago, 1890); "The Latin Grammar of Pharmacy," by D. H. Robinson (Philadelphia, 1890); "Essentials of the Practice of Pharmacy," by Lucius E. Sayre (Philadelphia, 1890); "Manual of Chemistry for the Use of Medical Students," by Brandreth Symonds (Philadelphia, 1889); "The Student's Course in Pharmacy," by W. H. Watson (Nashville, Tenn., 1890); "Text-book of General Therapeutics," by W. Hale White (New York,

1889); "International Pocket Medical Formulary," by C. Sumner Witherstone (Philadelphia, 1889); "Nearly Three Hundred Ways to dress Show Windows, also Suggestions and Ideas for Store Decoration, and Novel Ideas for Special Advertising" (Baltimore, 1889); also new editions of "Chemistry: General, Medical, and Pharmaceutical, including the Chemistry of the United States Pharmacopœia," by John Attfield (Philadelphia, 1889); "College Botany, including Organography, Vegetable Physiology, etc.," by Edson S. Bastian (Chicago, 1889); "Lessons in Qualitative and Volumetric Chemical Analysis," by Charles O. Curtman (St. Louis, 1889); "Manual of Pharmacy and Pharmaceutical Chemistry," by Charles F. Heebner (New York, 1889); "Chemistry of Medicine," by John U. Lloyd (Cincinnati, 1889); "Elixirs, their History, Formulæ, and Methods of Preparation," by John U. Lloyd (Cincinnati, 1889); "Dose and Price Labels of all the Drugs and Preparations of the United States Pharmacopœia," by D. L. Lochman (Bethlehem, 1889); "A Laboratory Guide in Chemical Analysis," by David O'Brine (New York, 1889); "A Manual of Organic Materia Medica," by John M. Maisch (Philadelphia, 1890); "A Laboratory Manual of Chemistry, Medical and Pharmaceutical," by Oscar Oldberg (Chicago, 1891); "A Manual of Weights and Measures," by Oscar Oldberg (Chicago, 1890); "Ointments and Oleates," by John V. Shoemaker (Philadelphia, 1890); "The Practice of Pharmacy," by Joseph P. Remington (Philadelphia); and "Lessons on the Life and Growth of Plants," by Alphonso Wood (New York). Pharmaceutical journals have increased in numbers and in quality. The older journals have improved as they have advanced, and several of the larger ones now issue editions for the different sections of the Union containing local news for each department. Thus, the Northeastern edition of the "Druggists' Circular" is distributed in the North Atlantic States. The "American Drug Clerk's Journal," of Chicago, Ill., has changed its name to the "Registered Pharmacist." J. W. Colcord, who formerly edited the "New England Druggist," has been succeeded by J. H. Churchill. In April, 1889, the initial number of the "Pacific Drug Review" appeared. It is the first distinctive drug paper published on the Pacific coast. The "Canadian Druggist," a sixteen-page monthly journal, edited by William S. Dyas, of Strathroy, Ontario, is a new journal that began its publication in 1889. George S. Davis began in November, 1889, the publication, in Detroit, Mich., of a monthly entitled "Pharmacology of the Newer Materia Medica." "The Apothecary" is the title of a quarterly issued for the first time in the autumn of 1891, under the auspices of the Illinois College of Pharmacy. "The Prescription" is likewise a journal of pharmaceutical interest that came into existence during 1891.

PHYSICS, PROGRESS OF, IN 1892.

Constitution of Matter. *The Ether.*—Prof. Oliver Lodge (London Royal Society, March 31) discusses exhaustively the present state of knowledge as to the motion or "drag" of ether close to moving bodies. He concludes that "the law of reflection is not really obeyed in a relatively moving medium, though to an observer stationary with respect to the mirror it appears to be obeyed." The discrepancy is small, but might be detected by very delicate observation. In general the shape of the incident wave is not precisely the same after reflection in a moving medium. To a parallel beam the mirror acts as if slightly tilted; to a conical one as if slightly curved. Experiments hitherto made will not allow of a definite conclusion. Most of them are indecisive; a few show contradictory results.

Molecules. — C. V. Burton (" Philosophical Magazine," February) elaborates the hypothesis that atoms are strain figures in the ether. He supposes that "a given portion of matter consists not of any individual portion of ethereal or other substance, but of modifications in the structure, or energy, or other qualities of the ether, and when matter moves it is merely these modifications which are transferred from one portion of the ether to another." From this hypothesis he succeeds fairly well in deducing most of the known properties of matter. G. Jäger (" Beiblätter der Physik," xvi, p. 345) supposes that molecules may be droplets, formed by impact from larger masses, which ultimately acquire a definite mean size for a given temperature. If the droplets are all of the same size, the drops from which they are formed must be at least twice as large. Since the division is possible only when the *vis viva* of impact is greater than the work of division, it is possible, by determining the increase of surface when a sphere is split in two, to arrive at some idea of the ultimate size of the droplets. The results are in harmony with received ideas as to molecular magnitudes. The calculated diameters, in 10^{-9} centimetres, are: Water, 51; ether, 76; alcohol, 52; methyl alcohol, 37; carbon disulphide, 73; chloroform, 80; acetone, 31. W. Sutherland (" Philosophical Magazine," May), in developing an elaborate kinetic theory of solids, finds it necessary to assume that molecules shrink with rising and expand with falling temperature. This makes melting comprehensible, it being hard to understand otherwise why so small a rise in temperature at a particular point should transform a solid into a liquid. Ladislas Natanson (" Philosophical Magazine," July) thinks that as a general principle atoms and molecules tend—unless they are subjected to mutual or external forces—to assume that kind of ultimate arrangement the (pure) probability of which is greatest. He states Newton's first law thus: " Every time a point does not move in a straight line with a constant velocity, we say that a force is acting on it"; and he gives his principle in analogous form, thus: " Every time molecules or atoms assume some steady state, the probability of which is not the greatest, we say that force is acting on them."

Standard Gauge for Inappreciable Magnitudes.—G. J. Stoney (Dublin Royal Society, March 16) supposes that Angstrom's normal map of the solar spectrum be extended in both directions, so that the numbers read from zero to 10,000, and that an ordinate of 10^{-4} metre be erected on the 1,000 point. From the summit to the further extremity an inclined plane 10 metres long with a grade of 1 in 10,000,000 would thus extend, the distance of which from any ray in the scale would be its wave length. The ordinate at three fourths of a metre from the tip would be the average distance to which molecules of air dart; that at 1 centimetre from the apex is the average interval between gas molecules at the usual temperature and pressure of the air; that at 1 millimetre from the tip is the diameter of a molecule of gas. In this way a step may be taken toward mentally appreciating these infinitesimal magnitudes.

Mechanics. *Elasticity.*—J. O. Thompson (" American Journal of Science," January) has measured the elastic lengthening of wires of brass, silver, and copper 3 metres long by direct observation with two fixed cathetometers. He finds Hooke's law only approximately true, the lengthening (x) being nearly expressed by the equation $x = a\,P + \beta\,P^2 + \gamma\,P^3$, where P is the stretching weight. The moduli of elasticity thus calculated may be 10 per cent. larger than the ones generally received, necessitating a recalculation of many physical constants.

Liquids. *Solution.* — W. Ostwald, perhaps the chief apostle of the physical theory of solution (" Annual Cyclopædia," 1891, p. 726), has published his views in a volume. In reply to a criticism by J. W. Rodger (Nature," Dec. 31. 1891), Prof. Ostwald says that he " can not at all admit the existence of a contrast between the two theories," and that the question as to whether solution is a physical or a chemical process is " unclear, and therefore very harmful." In a subsequent letter (ibid., Feb. 16, 1892) he asserts again that the whole matter may be treated entirely independently of the question of possible chemical interaction between dissolved substance and solvent. Messrs. Wanklyn, Johnstone, and Cooper (" Philosophical Magazine," November, 1891) examine a function which they name the *condensate*. This equals $i - i_1$, where i is the increment of weight due to the entrance of one gramme of substance into 100 cubic centimetres of solvent, and $i_1 = 1 - \dfrac{1}{\text{specific gravity}}$. They show that the condensate bears always an atomic relation to the gramme of the salt in question, while in sugar, for instance, it is zero, since $i = i_1$. They argue that in this last case, and in all similar cases, there is true physical solution; otherwise not. Georges Charpy (Paris Academy of Sciences, March 7) concludes that the variation of the density of a solution as a function of the concentration is a complex phenomenon and can not be used to study the state of the body, and that there is no reason why a solution of maximum density should be regarded as a hydrate. S. U. Pickering (" Philosophical Magazine." July) shows that the solution of gas always evolves heat, and concludes that it is a chemical phenomenon. He thinks that the only bar to the complete acknowledgment of the chemical theory is the question of how chemical union could produce such a state of the dissolved matter as is shown to exist by the facts brought up by adherents of the physical or osmotic theory. He considers, however, that he has already overcome this difficulty in a communication to the German Chemical Society, maintaining that this very quasi-independence of the dissolved substance is a direct consequence of the formation of highly complex hydrates. Picton (" Journal of the Chemical Society,"

February) concludes that there seems to be no satisfactory reason for imagining the existence of any sharp boundary between solution and pseudo-solution. In a continuation of his research he studied colloidal solution from the state where the dissolved, or rather suspended, particles were large enough to be visible, to that where they were so fine as to diffuse; and he found complete continuity from suspension through colloidal solution to non-electrolytic crystallizable solution. He concludes that there is a certain degree of molecular attraction throughout, and that it would be but a step farther to electrolytic solution. On the other hand, C. E. Lincharger (" American Journal of Science," March) finds that colloidal solutions of tungstic acid diffuse at a definite rate and have a definite osmotic pressure, and concludes that colloidal solutions are not emulsions, though only a step removed from them. The phenomena are explained by supposing the colloid molecule to be very large. The lowering of the freezing point in a solution of alcohol, according to the experiments of L. de Coffet (Paris Academy of Sciences, Oct. 31), is sensibly proportional to the quantity of alcohol, but the lowering of the temperature of maximum density is not proportional. For weak solutions there is no lowering at all, but rather an elevation.

Capillarity.—Lord Rayleigh (" Philosophical Magazine," February) proves mathematically the existence of a capillary force connected with the suddenness of transition from one surface to another, which may disappear when such transition is gradual. On the walls of a tube above the point where the liquid seems to end there is yet a thin layer gradually diminishing in thickness and reaching to an immense beight. At every point the fluid must be in equilibrium with the vapor at the same level. Later (ibid., May) he establishes the law that the lowering of tension due to thin films is proportional not to their thickness but to its square. In August (ibid.), in treating of the instability of a cylinder of viscous liquid under capillary forces, he shows that long threads of such liquid do not tend to divide into drops at a distance comparable to the diameter of the thread, but at few and distant places. Albert Colson (Paris Academy of Sciences, Nov. 23), by experiments on the flow of liquids in capillary tubes, has proved that ethers and aldehydes are perfectly mobile, and obey Graham's law that duration of flow is inversely as the square root of the density, but that alcohols and benzines, being imperfectly mobile, give irregular results. His figures for glycerin at different temperatures are as follow:

| Temperature..... | 21° | 100° | 150° | 250° | 265° |
| Duration of flow.. | 8 hrs. | 360 sec. | 114 sec. | 40 sec. | 53 sec. |

Mr. Blakesley, in a discussion at the London Physical Society (Nov. 6), said that when water evaporates from a glass a furrow is formed at the original boundary, as if the glass had been torn there by molecular action, showing the increased energy at the surface. Gossart (" Journal of the Chemical Society," February) has utilized the fact that a liquid may be made to roll on itself in drops, to detect impurities. The rolling is made possible by the formation of a film of vapor, which in pure liquids is absorbed at once.

These, therefore, never roll, and the life of the drops depends directly on the amount of impurity present. By comparison with a standard solution, the per cent. of impurity may be found within $\frac{1}{100}$. Each impurity behaves as if it alone were present. Lord Rayleigh (" Philosophical Magazine," April) shows that water will spread on a clean surface of mercury as theory requires. To obtain a clean surface, it is sufficient to draw the mercury by a faucet from beneath the free surface of the reservoir. He has also observed that lycopodium dusted on a water surface recedes from the edge and leaves a perfectly clear ring. This is not due to grease, but purely to gravity, for when the vessel is filled to overflowing, so that the surface is convex at the edge, the lycopodium moves outward.

Osmotic Pressure.—Tamman (" Zeitschrift für Physikalische Chemie," February) has observed that the osmotic pressure of a salt solution, calculated by the formula of Arrehenius, is always smaller than that observed by the usual method, and shows that this is due to the fact that the membrane is not perfectly impermeable to the salt employed. He therefore makes his measurements by employing external pressure to balance the osmotic pressure.

Viscosity.—R. Cohen (Wiedemann's " Annalen," No. 4, 1892) shows that the viscosity of water is diminished by pressure up to 40°, no minimum being observed at a temperature of 25° up to a pressure of 900 atmospheres. The change of viscosity increases more slowly than the pressure. The viscosity of water varies greatly with the temperature. In concentrated solutions of common salt and ammonium chloride the viscosity increases with pressure, and its change is nearly proportional to the pressure. The more dilute the solution is, the more does the anomalous behavior of the water influence it. The viscosity of oil of turpentine alters with pressure 20 times as rapidly as that of a saturated salt solution.

Density.—Paul Galopin (Paris Academy of Sciences, June 2) finds that increase of pressure lowers the temperature of maximum density of water for that particular pressure, and that under high pressures it corresponds nearly to the freezing point.

Compressibility.—E. H. Amagat (Paris Academy of Sciences, Oct. 31) has found that in ether, alcohol, carbon disulphide, acetone, etc., the coefficient of compressibility decreases regularly as the pressure increases. At 3,000 atmospheres that of water is reduced by one half, and that of ether by two thirds. This diminution is greater the higher the temperature.

Extensibility.—A. M. Worthington (London Royal Society, Feb. 4) has observed the volume extensibility of ethyl alcohol by sealing it in a strong glass vessel, which it nearly fills, the remaining space containing only its own vapor. On being heated it expands and fills the vessel, but on cooling it sticks and does not shrink at once, and thus is for a time under tension. He finds that stress and strain are proportional up to the highest tension used—that of 17 atmospheres—and that the apparent compressibility is the same as the apparent extensibility.

Bubbles in Water.—F. T. Trouton (British Association) finds that the speed of ascent of air bubbles in a tube of water is a periodic function of their size. As the size increases, the speed at first diminishes; then, after reaching a minimum, it increases, and so on, depending on the diameter of the tube. The shape of the bubbles changes at each maximum and minimum, similarly to the breaking up of a liquid column through surface tension.

Stability of Viscous Liquids.—A. B. Basset (London Royal Society, Nov. 1) has further investigated a phenomenon studied by Prof. Osborn Reynolds in 1883: When water flows from a cistern through a long tube, and a stream of colored liquid is made to flow within the water, the colored stream shows no tendency to mix with the water till the velocity attains a certain critical value, when it breaks at a certain point. As the velocity continues to increase, the breaking point moves up toward the point at which the fluid enters the tube. Mr. Basset finds that (1) the tendency to instability increases as the velocity of the liquid, the radius of the tube, and the coefficient of sliding friction increase, but diminishes as the velocity increases, and that (2) the tendency to instability increases as the wave length of the disturbance increases. Mr. Basset investigated also the influence of oil films in calming waves. Since the viscosity of olive oil in C. G. S. units is about 3·25, and that of water 0·014, the case is practically that of a highly viscous liquid in contact with a frictionless one. The result of a mathematical investigation is that the motion will be stable unless the wave length of the disturbance lies between $\frac{9}{11}$ and $\frac{6}{7}$ of a centimetre, which explains the effect satisfactorily.

Gases. *Resistance.*—Cailletet and Colardeau (Paris Academy of Sciences, July 4), in experiments carried on from the Eiffel Tower, find that the resistance of the air to a falling body is proportional to the area of the resisting surface, and independent of its form. The resistance increases rather more rapidly than the square of the velocity.

Barometry.—J. Joly (Dublin Royal Society) has constructed a barometer of mercury and glycerin, a column of the latter 250 centimetres long being weighted by 67 of the heavier liquid, kept from descending to the bottom by a disk that just fills the tube.

Breath Figures.—Papers on this subject were read before the London Physical Society (June 24) by W. B. Cuft and Rev. F. J. Smith. The best figures are to be obtained by alternating two coins with two sheets of glass and then connecting the coins to the poles of an electric machine. After sparks have passed for two minutes the breath will bring out a perfect figure of the coin on the glass. The microscope shows that moisture is deposited over the whole surface, but in drops of different sizes, thus producing the effect. H. F. Croft has brought out the figures by sifting red lead on the glass as well as by breathing on it, and has thus preserved a figure for two years.

Sound. *Phonics of Auditoriums.*— Dr. Ephraim Cutter ("American Journal of Science," December) recommends that the keynote of every auditorium be ascertained experimentally, and posted where speakers can see it. This can be done simply by singing the scale and observ-

ing what note is most strongly re-enforced. The keynote of the Saratoga City Hall was thus found in 1890 to be F.

Vibrations of Strings. — Menzel and Raps (Wiedemann's "Annalen," No. 12, 1891) have studied these by the new method of photographing them by electric light on a revolving cylinder.

Velocity.—L. Melde (ibid., No. 12, 1891) has measured the velocity of sound in membranes by observing the vibration of strips fastened at the ends and rubbed in the middle. His results, in metres per second, were:

Waxed paper	8,040	Cotton string	1,280
Drawing paper	1,955	Silk grosgrain ribbon	980
Satin ribbon	1,950	Waxed cloth	570
Hemp string	1,720		

N. Hesebius ("Journal de Physique," December, 1891) has found that the velocity of sound in porous and fibrous substances is less than that in free air. For cotton, for wave lengths of 24 to 60 millimetres, it was 261 to 146 metres per second. A hemisphere of 25 centimetres diameter made of metal gauze filled with ebonite shavings, acted like a plano-convex lens, concentrating the sound of a Galton's whistle accurately.

Heat. *Calorimetry.* — Harker and Hartog (British Association) have constructed a calorimeter on the principle of the Bunsen ice calorimeter, but using solid acetic acid. It is more delicate than the Bunsen, and can be used at ordinary temperatures.

Thermometry.—H. L. Callender (London Royal Society, Dec. 10) constructs a compensated air thermometer by using an ordinary differential thermometer, one of whose bulbs is kept in melting ice. An auxiliary bulb with taps allows the introduction of known weights of mercury to equalize the pressure, and the weight of this mercury thus measures the dilatation of the air at constant pressure. Prof. Wiborgh (Inst. of Engineers of Scotland, Dec. 22, 1891) has constructed an air pyrometer on a somewhat similar principle, measuring the temperature by increase of pressure, keeping the volume constant. His instrument is made in two forms, resembling the mercury and aneroid barometers respectively. H. Le Chatelier (Paris Academy of Sciences, Feb. 1) measures high temperatures by the intensity of the radiations from a pyrometer of platinum or clay compared with those from a standard lamp.

Thermodynamics. — H. M. Elder (London Physical Society, March 11) treats the action of light on silver chloride in photography as a problem in thermodynamics, regarding the pressure of the liberated chlorine as a function of the intensity of the light, just as the pressure of a saturated vapor is a function of the temperature. Chlorine in the presence of silver chloride and protoxide is thus the working substance in a "light engine." He enunciates a law analogous to the second law of thermodynamics, as follows: "Energy can not of itself pass from a less bright to a brighter body." Peter Lebeden (Wiedemann's "Annalen," No. 2), starting with Maxwell's law of the pressure exerted by incident rays on absorptive bodies, calculates that between two bodies at temperature 0°, with radii of 2 millimetres and density $= 10$, the repulsion due to this cause would exactly balance the attraction of gravity, and that in smaller bodies the repulsion exceeds, so that two particles of dust with radii of $\frac{1}{1000}$ millimetre repel each other at 0° with a force a million times greater than their attraction. This fact evidently must not be neglected in treating of molecular forces, complex though they may be. Sydney Young ("Philosophical Magazine," February) finds as the result of four years' work on the vapor pressure of various benzenes and alcohols that Van der Waals's generalizations concerning vapor pressure do not hold strictly true. Van der Waals showed, as he supposed, that if the absolute temperatures of various substances be proportional to their absolute critical temperatures, their vapor pressures will be proportional to their critical pressures, and their volumes (both as liquid and as saturated vapor) to their critical volumes. This was found nearly true for chloro-, bromo-, and iodo-benzene when compared with fluorbenzene; only approximately for benzene, carbon tetrachloride, stannic chloride, and ether; and not true at all for the alcohols and acetic acid. Sir William Thomson ("Philosophical Magazine," March) states that if the motion of every particle of matter in the universe could once be exactly reversed, the course of Nature would thenceforward be reversed forever. The foam bubble about to break at the foot of a waterfall would reunite and glide upward with the water to the top; bowlders would be again transported to the ledge whence they were torn, and be again resolved into the mud from which they were formed. All these astounding results would proceed from simple thermodynamic principles. In the same article Sir William says that though it is very improbable that in the course of a thousand years one half of a bar of iron will of itself become warmer by a degree than the other, this certainly would happen in a very long time if the bar were covered with a varnish impenetrable by heat; but if it be not so covered, and the number of molecules in the universe can be considered as infinite, then this would never happen. In a subsequent article (ibid., May) he shows by a test case the failure of the so-called law that in the ultimate state of a system the average kinetic energy of two given portions must be in the ratio of the number of degrees of freedom of those portions respectively. This would be true only for a perfect gas, in which the molecules move for comparatively long times in apparently straight lines.

Radiation.—Angstrom has studied the heat radiation of rarefied gases under the electric discharge by means of the bolometer. With a given pressure the radiation varies as the intensity of the current. With a constant current, the radiation does not vary while the pressure increases from 0·1 to 1·5 millimetre, but at higher pressures it increases somewhat. The ratio of the intensity of the radiation of shorter wave length to the whole decreases with increase of pressure. J. T. Bottomley (London Royal Society) finds that the loss of heat by convection and radiation from a surface of soot is $3\cdot42 \times 10^{-4}$ C. G. S. units per square centimetre, per second, per 1° C. difference of temperature, with a difference of 100° and the surface at 14°. In a vacuum of one half millionth atmosphere, it was only $1\cdot40 \times 10^{-4}$. C. C. Hutchins ("American Journal of Science,"

May) has shown that the radiation of air increases with the humidity and with accidental impurities, as carbon dioxide and gases from the decomposition of dust. The absolute radiation was $2,562 \times 10^{-9}$ for a humidity of 90, and only 1,513 for a humidity of 47. The waves from heated air must be very long, for he found that they can not penetrate quartz. Ayrton and Kilgour (London Royal Society, Nov. 19) have measured the emissivity of thin wires in air, each wire being stretched along the axis of a horizontal water-jacketed cylinder 32·5 centimetres long, whose inner surface was black and kept at a constant temperature. They arrived at the following results: 1. Given the temperature, the emissivity is higher the finer the wire. 2. For each wire the emissivity increases with the temperature, the rate increasing with the fineness of the wire. 3. Hence, the effect of the surface on the total loss of heat per second, per square centimetre, per 1° C. excess of temperature, increases as the temperature rises.

Absorption.—Some discussion has arisen as to the efficacy of a solution of alum as an absorber of heat rays. Its power has been taken for granted in numberless experiments, but C. C. Hutchins, of Bowdoin College, finds that it is only a slightly better absorber than pure water, and that even sheets of pure alum are little better. Raoul Pictet ("Comptes Rendus," May 30) gives additional proof of his recent discovery that heat waves of low temperature meet with little resistance ("Annual Cyclopædia," 1891, p. 728). A tube of chloroform is placed in a refrigerator at −120° C. with a thermometer which indicates only −68·5°, while crystals form in the chloroform. But in a refrigerator at −80° the thermometer falls to −80°, and the crystals disappear. The reason is that the latent heat of crystallization prevents the thermometer from falling in the first case. The thermometers used employed alcohol and sulphuric ether, and were checked by hydrogen thermometers.

Conductivity.—Alphonse Berget (Paris Academy of Sciences, June 7) has measured the conductivity of bars of rare metals by observing the Newton's rings formed by the pressure of the end against glass disks as they elongate. C. Barus ("American Journal of Science," July) has measured the change of conductivity in thymol on passing from the solid to the liquid state. The substance being placed between two horizontal copper plates, the lower one was suddenly cooled, and the time rate at which the heat traveled across was measured by a thermo-couple. His results were as follow:

$$k = \text{absolute heat conductivity in } \frac{g}{cs}.$$

Solid (12°) .... $10^6 \times k = 359$
Liquid (18°) .... $10^6 \times k = 313$

$$x = \text{thermometric conductivity in } \frac{c^2}{s}.$$

Solid (12°) .... $10^6 \times x = 1,077$
Liquid (18°) .... $10^6 \times x = 691$

Increment on passing from liquid to solid—
  Respectively ·13 and ·36 with reference to solid.
      "   ·15 and ·56   "   "   " liquid.

Regelation.—H. Le Chatelier (Paris Academy of Sciences, Jan. 11) has developed formulæ from which it appears that compressed pulverized ice in contact with a liquid or vapor that is less compressed increases in solubility, so that fusion or vaporization takes place, bringing about an unstable condition of supersaturation, which disappears by crystallization in the interspaces. Thus solidification by regelation is similar to that which takes place in cements.

Hygrometry.—Henri Gilbault (Paris Academy of Sciences, Jan. 11) has devised a condensation hygrometer in which the dew forms on a thin sheet of platinized glass, whose temperature can be measured very accurately by observing the electrical resistance of the metal. The dew point can thus be found to within $\frac{1}{70}$ of a degree.

Constant Temperature.—Henry Clew (" Philosophical Magazine," January) obtains a very constant temperature by passing an electric current through fine wire coiled about a glass vessel in a calorimeter. He has thus been enabled to maintain a temperature within $\frac{1}{100}°$ for forty minutes.

Light. *Spectroscopy.*—Prof. Michelson has added greatly to the possibilities of spectroscopy by the invention of what he calls the " wave compiler," by which he observes spectra from direct interference of two beams of light. The instrument is essentially a piece of plane glass placed so as to bisect a right angle made by two mirrors. The rays so fall that they are partly reflected and partly transmitted, and movement of one of the mirrors parallel to itself causes interference of the reflected with the transmitted beam with any desired difference of phase. By means of this device many lines never heretofore resolved have been found to be close doublets—notably the two components of the sodium line—and it has been discovered that the widths of the component lines in the hydrogen spectrum decrease as the pressure increases, but not without limit. G. J. Stoney (" Nature," Sept. 29) explains the doubling and multiplying of the gaseous lines by calling attention to the fact that the gases are usually observed in Geissler's tubes, where the motions of the molecules must preponderate in some directions, instead of being indefinitely in all directions, as they would be in open space. The employment of Geissler's tubes to obtain gaseous spectra is commented upon also by E. Pringsheim (Wiedemann's " Annalen," No. 3), who says that owing to this fact there is no direct evidence that mere increase in temperature makes gases glow. Siemens has shown that oxygen, carbon dioxide, nitrogen, and hydrogen do not glow even at 1,500° C. He concludes: (1) No gaseous source of light obeys Kirchhof's law. (2) Glowing gases at a temperature below 150° (cold flames) can be obtained. (3) Salts of sodium glow only by chemical action. (4) There is no experimental or theoretical evidence that gases glow luminously by rise of temperature. Schütze (" Zeitschrift für Physikalische Chemie," February) has found that with a displacement of absorption from the violet to the red color changes take place in substances (as viewed with the naked eye) as follows : Greenish yellow, yellow, orange, red, reddish violet, violet, blue violet, blue, blue green. This he calls lowering the tint. Atoms or atomic groups that lower the tint he terms *bathochromic ;* those that raise it, *hypsochromic.* Hydrocarbon radicals are always bathochromic. The influence of an atom or group increases with increased atomic mass. The addition of hydrogen to a group always raises the tint. C. Runge (" Nature," April 28)

notes, in relation to the line spectra of the elements, that doublets and triplets can be arranged in series which appear to be very regular, the oscillation-frequency of a series being represented by the formula, $A - Bn^{-2} - Cn^{-4}$. For two elements chemically related the series are distinctly homologous in the appearance of the lines and in the values of A, B, and C. With increase of atomic weight the lines shift to the less refrangible end of the spectrum. The doublets and triplets in each group broaden as the atomic weight increases. The absorption spectra of copper sulphate, chloride, and nitrate have been found by T. Ewan (" Philosophical Magazine," April) to change on dilution. The spectra tend toward identity in dilute solutions. The experimenter concludes that the acid and the base are associated in producing absorption in a strong solution, but not in a dilute solution. This accords with the hypothesis of electrolytic dissociation, not with that of hydrolytic dissociation, or that of molecular aggregation. Liveing and Dewar (" Philosophical Magazine ") have examined the spectrum of liquid oxygen in larger quantities than ever before, observing it in tubes 3 to 6 inches long. They find bands at A and B that are related as are the solar groups. The refractive index at the boiling point ($-182°$ C.) is found to be 1·2236 for the D line. König and Ritter (Wiedemann's " Annalen," No. 3) find that the brightness of spectrum colors varies with their absolute intensities. For all observers, even the color blind, the curve for the values of brightness was of almost the same form for the darkest shades, having a maximum at 535 $\mu\mu$ (thallium green). As the brightness increased the maximum increased with trichromatic persons, first slowly, then rapidly, then slowly again. At the brightest shade it was at about 610 $\mu\mu$. Green-blind persons gave the same results as the normal, but with red-blind persons the maximum moved at first toward the long wave lengths, remaining stationary at 570. C. Fery (Paris Academy of Sciences, Dec. 28, 1891) has devised a spectrometer on the principle of annulling by a solid prism of variable angle and constant refractive index the deviation caused by a hollow prism of constant angle, filled with the liquid to be experimented upon. This is effected by a prism-shaped cavity in a double convex lens. The angle of the lens considered as a prism is varied by shifting it in a plane perpendicular to the axis, and the amount of the shifting necessary to correct the deviation of the ray measures the index. B. W. Snow (Wiedemann's " Annalen," No. 10) has investigated the red emission spectra of the alkali metals by a modified bolometer and a delicate galvanometer with one of Boys's quartz fibers. He examined sodium, potassium, rubidium, lithium, and cæsium, and found that the two rarest are specially rich in infra-red lines.

Polarization.—Lord Rayleigh (" Philosophical Magazine," January) finds that the deviations from Fresnel's law as to the disappearance of the reflected polarized ray at the polarizing angle are due to impurities. Jamin's results were thus vitiated ; the deviation in the ease of reflection from clean water was found to be not much more than $\frac{1}{1000}$ of that given by him. Possibly if a perfectly clean surface could be obtained there would be no ellipticity at all.

Phosphorescence.—M. Lenard has invented a phosphoroscope for the observation of bodies illuminated by the electric spark. The results in most cases are similar to those obtained in Becquerel's instrument, but arragonite, which is there invisible, gives a faint reddish phosphorescence by electric spark. Asaron, which is bright in a Crookes tube and glows in the ultraviolet spectrum, is absolutely dark. (See also *Color*, under "Light," below.)

Fluorescence.—G. Salet (Paris Academy of Sciences, Aug. 1) has observed the diagonal spectrum of Stokes's experiment by receiving the spectrum from a quartz prism on a soret eyepiece and projecting it thence transversally on the slit of a second spectroscope.

Photometry.—Charles Henry (Paris Academy of Sciences, Oct. 24) has invented a photoptometric photometer for very feeble light. It uses phosphorescent sulphide of zinc. The law of loss of brilliancy being determined, it is illuminated for a given time by a standard magnesium light, and then the time is observed which elapses before its brilliancy has fallen to that of the light to be measured.

Refraction.—Jaques Chappuis (Paris Academy of Sciences, February) finds that the indices of refraction of sulphurous acid and methyl chloride at 0° C. and under maximum vapor pressure are respectively 1·3518 and 1·3533 for the D line. Rubens and Snow (Wiedemann's "Annalen," No. 8) find by the bolometer that fluorspar has a less dispersion than rock salt in the violet, but enormously greater in the infra-red, and hence is specially adapted for the production of prismatic heat spectra. D. Shea (ibid., No. 10) has measured the refraction and dispersion of several metals by Kundt's method ("Annual Cyclopædia," 1889, p. 697). His platinum prism was made by the disintegration of foil. His results were as follow:

METALS.	Ll. a.	D.	F.	G.
Gold	0·29	0·66	0·82	0·98
Silver	0·25	0·27	0·20	0·27
Copper	0·85	0·60	1·12	1·13
Platinum	2·02	1·76	1·63	1·41

Reflection.—H. E. J. G. Du Bois (Wiedemann's "Annalen," No. 8), in a paper on reflection and transmission in æolotropic media, describes experiments with gratings of bright silver wire, platinum film, scratched metal, and scratched glass, and with crystals of cobaltine and pyrites. In the silver-wire gratings, light polarized in a plane normal to the direction of the wires was transmitted in greater proportion than that polarized in the direction at right angles. The contrary was true with the scratched glass and metal.

Interference.—Dr. Zehnder (Berlin Physical Society, Nov. 6) has devised a simple differential refractor in which the two rays which are ultimately to be made to interfere are kept 50 to 100 centimetres apart, so that they can be subjected to varying experimental conditions.

Magnesium as a Source of Light.—Frederick J. Rogers ("American Journal of Science, April) concludes (1) that the spectrum of incandescent magnesium approaches nearer than any other artificial light to that of sunlight, and (2) that its

temperature is about 1,340° C., lying between that of the Bunsen burner and the air-blast lamp, though its spectrum corresponds to a temperature of 5,000° C. The radiant energy emitted is 4,630 calories per grain, or 75 per cent. of the total heat, while that of gas is only 20 per cent.

Color.—Nichols and White (" Philosophical Magazine," November, 1891) find that the color of a pigment arises from light reflected (1) from the surface and (2) from interior faces. The surface light is nearly white. Heating diminishes the reflective power, especially in the regions of greatest refrangibility with the result of shifting the color toward the red. In chromic oxide and zinc oxide, however, it is shifted toward violet. Later (January, 1892), from further experiments on zinc oxide they conclude that it is highly luminous above 880°, probably from phosphorescence. A. Noble (" Nature," March 24) states that the first visible color of a thin iron sleeve gradually heated by a bar within appeared as described by different observers, to be " gray-white," " white like phosphorus in the dark," or " white with a dark shade." T. C. Porter (ibid. April 14) reports a similar experiment on the carbon filament of an Edison incandescent lamp. There were 25 observers, to all of whom the first visible light appeared very pale. To 13 it was " yellow "; to 7 " faint pink "; to 2 "bluish white." All agreed that it passed through orange before reaching crimson. Prof. S. P. Thompson (London Physical Society, Feb. 12) finds that any non-monochromatic color can be split into two tints, which he calls supplementary. Of these, one may always be grayish, thus verifying Abney's law that any color may be produced by diluting a spectrum color with white. W. Ostwald (Royal Society of Saxony, xviii, 281) finds that the absorption spectrum of a dilute solution of a salt is the sum of the spectra of its ions. In the cases where one ion is more absorbent, the spectra of all salts formed from such ions and the same colored ion are precisely the same.

Iridescent Colors.—Alexander Hodgkinson (" Proceedings of the Manchester [Eng.] Literary and Philosophical Society ") states that long experience in the examination of iridescent objects has shown him that almost without exception their colors are due to interference produced by thin plates, and vary with the inclination of the plate to the light. He proposes that, to secure uniformity in the description of such objects, a particular incidence be always chosen : 90° being the best, because then the trouble of measuring an angle is obviated, it being only necessary to be sure that the reflected ray coincides with the incident. This is easily done by employing a perforated mirror, which Mr. Hodgkinson finds appears to change iridescent bodies wonderfully in appearance. For instance, the crest of a humming bird, which to the naked eye is resplendent with all the colors of the rainbow, appears through the mirror of an unvarying red tint, and hence is described as " iridescent red." Other objects, similarly, are iridescent blue or green. A piece of iridescent iron ore displays different colors in its different parts, but these remain unchanged when the specimen is moved and do not shift as they do when viewed with the naked eye.

Absorption.—W. Peddie (British Association) finds that the coefficient of absorption is not affected by density of illumination. He experimented with intensities varying in the ratio 1 : 1,000 and could have detected a change of 1 per cent.

Velocity.—Charles H. Lees (London Royal Society, Feb. 4) has found that Kundt's law that metals follow the same order as regards both conduction of heat and propagation of light does not hold good for crystals. He employed the divided-bar method, measuring the distribution of temperature. The conductivity of various substances in C. G. S. units was found to be as follow:

Crown glass	·0024	Shellac	·00060
Flint glass	·0020	Pure rubber	·00088
Rock salt	·014	Paper	·00081
Quartz (along axis)	·030	Cork	·00013
Quartz (transverse)	·016	Silk and flannel	·0002

Electricity. *Conductivity and Resistance.*— Reinold and Rucker (British Association) have measured the conductivity of films of soap, glycerin, and metallic salts. When the salts were present the specific conductivity was the same in a film $\frac{1}{20000}$ inch thick as in a mass of the solution; with soap alone, however, the conductivity increased with thinness to 7 times the original amount. This seems due to some breaking down of molecular equilibrium in the film. Ayrton and Mather ("Philosophical Magazine," February) have constructed a noninductive resistance of 12 platinoid strips doubled over upon themselves, with shellacked silk between the folds. The inductance of the arrangement is so small that it can not be measured. Dewar and Fleming (ibid., October) have ascertained the electrical resistance of several substances at the boiling point of oxygen. The mean coefficient of change of resistance between 0° and — 100° C. was found to be as follow:

Silver	·00884	Platinum	·00854
Aluminum	·00890	Tin	·00509
Copper	·00410	Nickel	·00500
Iron	·00531		

At ordinary temperatures the resistance of iron is 7 times that of copper, and that of nickel 10 times that of copper; but at the boiling point of oxygen that of iron is only two thirds, and that of nickel four thirds that of copper. Dr. Dawson Turner (British Association) finds that the electric spark reduces the resistance of powdered aluminum, copper, annealed selenium, and iron, and that of small shot, but that shaking or jarring restores the primary condition.

Cells.—Markovsky (Wiedemann's "Annalen," No. 11) in experiments on gas batteries finds that by adding a solution of platinum sulphate the E. M. F. of an oxygen element is diminished and that of a hydrogen element increased, so that that of an oxygen-hydrogen element is not affected. The E. M. F. is independent of change of the density and temperature of the gas. E. F. Herroun ("Philosophical Magazine," June) notes that though in the text-books platinum is said to be negative to gold, the heat of formation of auric chloride is only half that of platinic chloride, which would indicate the opposite. He finds that the average E. M. F. of a zinc-platinum cell is 1·5, and that of a zinc-gold cell 1·8. If a gold-platinum couple be immersed in water or dilute hydrochloric acid, the gold has the higher potential; in strong hydrochloric acid it

is doubtful which is the higher; in hydro-nitrochloric acid the platinum is the higher. Prof. Schuster has constructed cells in which the electrolyte is a gas, and finds that polarization is absent with an elementary gas, but present in a compound, being marked in a hydrocarbon. The magnitude depends on the electrodes, being small with copper and iron, large with aluminum or magnesium.

Thermo-electricity. — Henri Bagard (Paris Academy of Sciences, Dec. 14) has made a thermo-electric couple with zinc amalgam and a solution of zinc sulphide. He finds that it is absolutely constant between two given temperatures, and varies only ·0001 volt at 0° and 100° when the proportion of zinc varied from ·00025 to ·00075 the mass of mercury.

Electrolysis.—L. Arons (Berlin Physical Society, No. 3) finds that if a cell with sulphuric acid, through which the current passes by platinized electrodes, be halved by a partition of platinum, gold, or silver, so that all the lines of flow traverse the metal, the current is enfeebled, polarization taking place on both sides of the partition, while the resistance was not much altered. He succeeded in making the partition so thin that the polarization on one side quite neutralized that on the other, and the deflection of the galvanometer was unchanged. C. Ludeking ("Philosophical Magazine," June) finds that the decomposition of a gas by an electric current is due partly to true electrolysis, partly to thermolysis, in which heat dissociates the vapor and then the atoms act similarly to charged pith balls. Lagrange and Hoho (Brussels Academy of Sciences, Oct. 10) have observed the following phenomena accompanying the electrolysis of dilute sulphuric acid, the positive electrode being a plate with area of 180 square centimetres and the negative a wire of ·25 millimetre diameter placed half a millimetre below the surface. As the E. M. F. increased a fizzing was heard at the negative electrode and the liquid there boiled. The phenomenon increased with the difference of potential between the electrodes. When this reached 16 volts and the electrodes were 3 millimetres apart a number of luminous points appeared between them and the surface. The phenomenon took place at the same E. M. F. for all electrolytes, for equal acidity. J. Vanni (Wiedemann's "Annalen," No. 10) shows that former results as to change in the electro-chemical equivalent of copper with density of current were due to acidity of the bath, and that the deposition of copper measures currents very exactly if care be taken to form a normal solution.

Electro-magnetic Waves. — Techer (Wiedemann's "Annalen," No. 3) finds that when a Geissler tube is placed between parallel wires connected with the condenser plates of a Hertz apparatus, the nodal points in the tube appear dark, while the other portions glow. L. Arons incloses portions of the parallel wires in a long vacuum tube, which at 10 millimetres pressure is filled with light and dark spaces. Prof. Klemencic (Vienna "Berichte," Feb. 18) determines electro-magnetic radiation by hanging a thermo element near a fine platinum wire heated by the vibration. He thus found ·000155 and ·000088 for the number of calories received per second, where C. V. Boys with an air thermometer had found ·000685. Lucas and Garret ("Philosophical Magazine," March) detect the spark in a Hertz apparatus by causing it to ignite an explosive mixture of gases generated by electrolysis. Arons and Rubens (Wiedemann's "Annalen," No. 10) by a bolometric method of measuring electric waves find that Maxwell's law connecting the dielectric constant with the index of refraction is very well satisfied. By it the index (n) should equal the square root of the constant (μ). The following are his experimental results :

SUBSTANCES.	$\sqrt{\mu}$	n ($\lambda = 6$ in.)	n $\lambda = 6 \times 10^{-7}$ in.
Fluid paraffin.........	1·41	1·47	1·48
Cooling paraffin.......	1·44	1·48	1·48
Solid paraffin.........	1·40	1·43	1·58
Glass (1)...............	2·82	2·33	1·51
Glass (2)...............	2·43	2·49	1·58
Castor oil.............	2·16	2·05	1·48
Olive oil..............	1·75	1·77	1·47
Xylol	1·53	1·50	1·49
Petroleum.............	1·44	1·40	1·45

M. R. Blondlot (Paris Academy of Sciences, Nov. 9) finds that between wave lengths of 8·94 and 35·36 metres electric waves have a velocity of 297,600 kilometres per second. V. Bjerknes (Wiedemann's "Annalen," No. 9) shows that the so-called "multiple resonance" of Sarasin and De la Rive ("Annual Cyclopædia," 1890, p. 715) may be explained mathematically as a phenomenon of damping in accord with the theories of Hertz. Sarasin and De la Rive (Paris Academy of Sciences, Sept. 19) have produced a spark by a Hertz oscillator in liquid dielectrics. In olive oil sparks of 1 centimetre in length were most loud and brilliant. Prof. G. F. Fitzgerald (London Physical Society, Jan. 22) has experimented on the driving of an electro-magnetic engine by electro-magnetic radiation. The method that seems to promise most is one in which collectors are joined to the ends of a vibrating circuit, and inductors and brushes are so arranged that an insulating cylinder turning between them has positive and negative changes distributed alternately on its periphery. By suitable adjustment these could be so collected as to keep up the vibration. Bedell and Crehore ("American Journal of Science," November) show mathematically that when potential and current are propagated in a conductor in harmonic waves whose amplitude decreases with the distance from the origin by logarithmic decrement, the current wave is propagated in advance of the potential wave. The wave of higher frequency goes faster and decays most rapidly, the phenomenon being most marked in the absence of self-induction. Thus there is a limit to the distance at which a telephone can be used, as the components of a complex tone, as they advance, keep shifting their relative phases and change their relative intensities.

The Induction Coil. — Tom Moll (Wiedemann's "Annalen," No. 2) finds by photography that the duration of the spark from a coil is less as the spark becomes longer, and greater as the electrode is more pointed. In the latter case the number of partial sparks increases, but the mean interval between them is less. By rotating a disk of paper between the electrodes he finds that the partial sparks are all in the same direction. He explains the discharge by assuming that the electricity can not flow fast enough to the electrodes, and that the partial sparks occur as soon as the difference of potential reaches the necessary value.

Glow and Vacuum Discharges.—The electrostatic attraction experienced by a plane cathode in a glow discharge has been found (Wiedemann's "Annalen," No. 1) to be measurable by the balance, and to be proportional to the density of the air. In negative glow there is an excess of free positive electricity proportional to this density. The surface of the anode is more feebly attracted and is less charged by reason of this excess. The charge decreases with decrease of pressure. It probably produces eddy currents, which may account for the observed transfer of matter in the positive direction. E. Goldstein (Prussian Academy, vol. xl) concludes that the term "stratification of the cathode" is a misnomer, at least two of the strata pervading the entire luminous region. He finds that the second layer is emitted from the electrode normally to its surface, and is best shown by concave poles. M. J. Pupin ("American Journal of Science," April), in seeking to explain the solar coronal phenomena, has studied the action of vacuum-discharge streamers in the same bulb on each other. He finds that they sometimes repel where one would expect attraction. As streamers in different bulbs do not affect each other, he attributes the movements to a strain caused by a distribution of gas pressure due to disturbance of temperature, rather than to electrostatic action. It increases with increased pressure. In another paper (National Academy of Science, April 27), Pupin states that his experiments support Prof. J. J. Thomson's dissociation theory, and indicate also a translational movement of the gas. An air blast introduced into the bulb deflected the streamers.

Dielectrics.—E. Bouty (Paris Academy of Sciences, June 13) has made a condenser whose dielectric is an electrolyte by dipping two rigidly connected iron disks in a fluid mixture of sodium and potassium nitrates which solidified when the disks were withdrawn. The constant k was found equal to about 4. Dr. W. L. Robb ("Philosophical Magazine," November) finds that oscillations in the charge of a condenser occur during the charging. Their amplitude diminishes rapidly with the time, and may be increased either by diminishing the resistance or by increasing the E. M. F., self-induction, or capacity. F. T. Trouton and W. E. Lilly (ibid., June) measure specific inductive capacity by the force with which a sheet of the dielectric is drawn in between the plates of a condenser. Prof. E. B. Rosa (ibid., October), in experiments on the specific inductive capacity of electrolytes, finds that for water and alcohol it has a genuine value much greater than in other liquids. His results are as follow :

	k		k
Water (at 16·5° C.)....	70	Turpentine............	2·39
Alcohol (98 per cent)...	80·9	Petroleum (300° test)...	2·04
Ether..................	8·4	Petroleum (illuminating)	1·97

D. Negreano (Paris Academy of Sciences, Feb. 15), in experiments on benzene, toluene, and xylene between 5° and 45° C., finds that the dielectric constant diminishes with increase of temperature. E. Bouty ("Comptes Rendus," March 7) finds that the dielectric constant changes but slightly under conditions which vary the conductivity greatly. Thus water and ice have sensibly the same dielectric constant, while the conductivity varies from 1 to 10^5 or 10^6.

The Ratio v.—H. Abraham ("Comptes Rendus," June 7) has measured v, the ratio between the electrostatic and electro-magnetic units, by finding the capacity of a plane guard-ring condenser in both systems. His result was 290.2×10^8.

Current Measures. — Wien (Wiedemann's "Annalen," Nov. 12, 1801) uses for this purpose a telephone with a stylus and mirror. The telephone diaphragm is attuned to the alternating current to be measured and the stylus touches the mirror, which is fastened to a flexible arm clamped to an adjustable support. The device shows readily 3×10^7 ampères.

Point Discharges. — The British Association committee on this subject report that they have found that disturbing influences which have little or no effect on the cathode powerfully affect the anode.

Electricity and Gravity.—G. Gore ("Philosophical Magazine," September) argues that since the mean E. M. F. of an amalgam or solution and its diluent is always increased by further dilution. the E. M. F. varies directly as the degree of molecular freedom, and depends on the velocity of the molecule, and hence on the law of gravity.

The Electric Spark.—Toepler (Wiedemann's "Annalen," Nos. 7 and 8), with the aid of a Toepler-Holtz statical induction machine whose oscillations were much more rapid than those of a coil, has shown that a spark between a conductor and a water surface is not oscillating. He concludes, therefore, that the lightning is probably not oscillatory, and that the production of noise and light does not in general prove the existence of oscillations.

The Voltaic Arc.—Dr. Arons exhibited to the Berlin Physical Society (Oct. 21) an arc light between mercurial electrodes in a vacuum. A dazzling white light was produced, steady at the anode but flickering and jumping at the cathode. The temperature was highest at the cathode, but the tube was not at any time too hot to be held in the hand. The current was found by means of the telephone to be discontinuous. The spectroscope showed a lime spectrum with brilliant yellow. green, and blue lines. It was attempted to obtain the light also with amalgams, but without success except in the one instance of sodium amalgam.

Electricity by Gaseous Friction.—Prof. Wesendruck, of Berlin ("Naturwissenschaft Rundschau"), finds that dustless air in friction with metals does not generate electricity, but that carbon dioxide does, and that this is due to the cloud formation that takes place with the latter.

Electro-Capillary Phenomena.—Gouy (Paris Academy, Jan. 4) has measured the surface tension of more or less polarized liquid amalgams as compared with mercury. The amalgams tested contained $\frac{1}{1000}$ respectively of zinc, cadmium, lead, tin, bismuth, silver, and gold. In a system of nonpolarized mercury, acidulated water, and more or less polarized amalgam the surface ten-

sion of the amalgam was found to be a function of the apparent difference of potential between the amalgam and the mercury.

Magnetism. *Terrestrial Magnetism.*—Henry Wilde has propounded a theory of the earth's magnetism which he illustrates by a remarkable model. According to his view, there have been three stages in the development of terrestrial magnetism: (1) the electro-dynamic stage, where the whole globe, being at a high temperature, was nonmagnetic; (2) the stage where the outer crust had cooled sufficiently ,to be permanently magnetized, and rotated at a different rate and with different poles from the interior; and (3) the present stage, where the crust magnetism is unsymmetrical, owing to irregular configuration of land and water. His model reproduces the interior electro-dynamic globe and the outer unsymmetrical, permanently magnetized crust, and by adjusting the inclination of the two axes and the rates of rotation he gets a close imitation of observed phenomena. So close is the correspondence that it has been thought definitely to prove the existence of a liquid interior of the earth, and so to settle a vexed question in geology. But L. A. Bauer (Washington Philosophical Society, Feb. 27) asserts that Wilde's theory involves (1) a secular change every nine hundred and sixty years throughout the entire globe; (2) the passage through zero of the declination at every point during some time in the cycle; and (3) the approximate equality of the total easterly and westerly declination. These results are all at variance with facts. Bauer therefore concludes. that though Wilde's theory gives a secular variation it does not explain the one that actually exists. E. Marchaud (Paris Academy of Sciences, Jan. 4), by observations made at Lyons Observatory since 1887, has established a connection between lightning discharges and disturbances of terrestrial magnetism. There were noted 73 discharges, of which 40 were accompanied by well-marked disturbances of the declination curve. There was no simple relation, however, between the distance of the discharge and the amplitude of the magnetic oscillation. William Ellis ("Proceedings of the Royal Society, London," 313) concludes from a comparison of records of magnetic disturbances that in the movement preceding a disturbance all the magnets at any one place are affected simultaneously, and in places far distant the movement generally occurs at the same time, though there are small differences which may or may not be accidental.

Propagation of Magnetism in a Metal.—Prof. John Trowbridge ("Philosophical Magazine," April) has made further experiments with a view to detecting whether or not this takes place by wave motion, using his phasemeter—an arrangement by which the vibrations of two telephone diaphragms are compounded and exhibited by means of Lissajous's curves. He finds no true nodes in a bar which is being magnetized, and concludes that, as in the case of heat conduction, magnetization does not proceed in a wave, its propagation being expressed by the equations of motion of molecular magnets in a resisting medium. Julius and Huffel, however, in "Nature" (Aug. 25), assert that the telephone is not a suitable instrument to be used in investigations of this nature, since the variation of magnetic intensity may be too gradual to affect it, as shown in Van Rysselberghe's device for using the same circuit for telegraph and telephone.

Change of Volume by Magnetization.—Knott and Shaud (Edinburgh Royal Society, May 16) find that when an iron tube is magnetized its internal volume is slightly increased in weak fields, but as the field grows stronger it passes through a maximum, then decreases, vanishes, and then changes sign. This cycle is several times repeated, implying a transverse linear dilatation, in general opposite in sign to the well-known longitudinal dilatation. Shelford Bidwell (London Royal Society, May 19) finds that in an iron wire carrying a current the maximum magnetic elongation is greater, and the retraction in strong fields is less, when no current passes. The effect of a current is opposite to that of tension. The magnetic retraction of nickel and cobalt, however, is not sensibly affected by the passage of a current, though it is modified by tension.

Magnetization by Passage of a Current.—Prof. C. G. Knott (Edinburgh Royal Society, Jan. 18) uses iron tubes for experiments on this phenomenon, and measures the circular magnetization produced by the induction current in a wire coil wound longitudinally. When the tube was magnetized by an axial current through a copper wire threading it, or by a sectional current from end to end of the tube itself, the induction was found to be 7 per cent. greater than that required by theory, which, since a current through iron does not increase its permeability to inductive forces perpendicular to the current, shows that the theory must be faulty.

Increase of Current in a Circuit having Large Electro-magnetic Inertia.—Thomas Grey (London Royal Society, May 19) finds that to produce any given percentage of the maximum strength in such a circuit there is always a particular E. M. F. which takes the maximum time. By successive reversals of E. M. F. it can be shown that several minutes may be required for the magnetism to be lost.

Permanent Magnet.—W. Hibbert ("Philosophical Magazine," March) has constructed a strong bar magnet, one end of which is hemispherical, with a pole piece of soft iron, while on the other is a soft iron disk forming the cover of this hemispherical cup. The cover is separated from the edges of the hemisphere by a space $\frac{1}{16}$ inch wide, within which is a helix. This magnet showed no evidence of decay in seven months.

Lamellar Magnet.—Regnier and Parrot (Paris Academy of Sciences, Aug. 8) have constructed a magnet of alternate transverse lamellæ of a conducting metal and a magnetic metal, and find that it has a high inductive efficiency.

Magnetic Curve Tracer.—Prof. Ewing, in a lecture before the British Association at Edinburgh, exhibited a machine of this name, consisting essentially of two wires, which move a mirror, one proportionally to the magnetizing current and the other proportionally to the acquired magnetism, thus causing a spot of reflected light to describe a complex characteristic curve.

Schiseophone.—De Place (Paris Academy, Oct. 24) has given this name to a magnetic device for detecting flaws in steel. The steel being tapped regularly by a rod attached to a microphone produces characteristic sounds in a telephone in an adjoining room. The variation of sound when a flaw is present enables it to be detected at once.

Displacements of a Floating Magnet by a Current.—C. Decharme (Paris Academy of Sciences, Oct. 31) finds that if a light magnetic needle be floated on a bath of pure mercury into which electrodes are dipped in different places, the needle, striving to take up its equilibrium position, and being prevented from doing so at once by the difficulty of motion sidewise, will go through a curious series of movements. If, for instance, the current cross the mercury perpendicularly to the needle, the negative current pole being to the left of the south-seeking magnetic pole, the needle will move away parallel to itself, turn round, and come back to its normal position.

Electro-magnetic Induction.—G. T. Walker (London Royal Society, Dec. 10) finds that when a sheet of copper is so placed as to half cover an alternating magnetic pole, and on this, near the pole, is laid a hollow copper sphere, the electro-magnetic action produces a couple which spins the sphere rapidly. Mr. Walker has succeeded in explaining the phenomenon mathematically.

PHYSIOLOGY. Respiration.—The experiments of H. C. Wood and David Cerna, of the University of Pennsylvania, on the effects of drugs and other agencies upon the respiratory movements, were based on the principle that not rapid breathing—which may coexist with very little movement of air—but the increase of the amount of air breathed in and out of the lungs affords the criterion of a respiratory stimulant. The experiments were performed by connecting the trachea of the animal with a tube, which in turn was connected with two ordinary mercurial valves, one of which allowed the air to enter, the other to escape, the mercurial valve of expiration being in turn connected with an India-rubber bag or reservoir, from which the air was drawn by means of a suction pump. The record of experiments upon the dog, which usually cools itself by rapidly breathing, shows that heat has an enormous effect upon the respiration in narcotism. During narcotism the rectal temperature of the subject had fallen 1·03° C. below the norm; when by means of external heat the rectal temperature was raised about 1° above the norm, the respiratory rate was more than doubled, and the movement of air in the chest increased from 0·15 cubic foot per minute to 0·38 cubic foot. In another case, when the rectal temperature was put up 10° above the norm, the air movement rose to nearly 5° above the normal amount. It is thus demonstrated that the stimulating effect of heat upon the respiratory centers is as great in the narcotized as in the normal animal; and the experiments explain the way in which heat protracts or even saves life during narcotism, and enforce the necessity, by means of the hot-water bath or bed, of overheating the human body when respiratory paralysis from some narcotic agent is threatened. Chloral was proved to be a respiratory depressant, producing a marked reduction in the respiratory movement of the air. Morphine also acted as a depressant, producing very violent effects on the first injection, after which even larger amounts could be tolerated with comparatively light effect. The effects of atropine, strychnine, and curare as respiratory stimulants were studied. The first effect of atropine was enormously to excite the respiratory function; this primary excitement was followed, if the dose had not been very great, by a distinct fall in the air movement, not sufficient, however, to overcome the first rise, and the air movements remained for a long time distinctly above the norm. Atropine failed to increase the respiratory movements of a dog under the influence of opium; but this result is held for further investigation. The antagonism between the action of chloral and atropine was very plain. The air movement in chloralized dogs was increased 250 per cent. by the use of atropine, and it was found possible in one experiment by a reinjection of chloral to reduce for a second time the air movement. As a whole, the experiments with atropine, both in the normal and the chloralized dog, showed that its salts greatly increase the respiratory movement of air, and led to the conclusion that it is a direct and powerful stimulant. The injection with strychnine produced an extraordinary increase in the respiratory air movement, and it was proved to be a true respiratory stimulant. In a single experiment an increase of 60 per cent. produced by strychnine was almost completely overcome by the injection of a solution of morphine. Cocaine was found to act as a powerful respiratory stimulant, the influence of which, however, failed in the presence of an overwhelming dose of a respiratory depressant. In endeavoring to formulate from the experiments a conclusion as to the comparative value of the respiratory stimulants, an almost insuperable difficulty appeared in the lack of uniformity of result. Cocaine and strychnine have so much similarity of action upon the nerve centers that the use of one will probably increase the danger that may have been incurred by the administration of large doses of the other. The relations of atropine to cocaine and strychnine, however, are different, and it would seem that by the combined use of atropine and strychnine, or of atropine and cocaine, the advantages of what Dr. Wood calls "cross action" may be obtained, the two drugs touching and re-enforcing one another in their influence upon the respiratory functions, and spreading wide apart from each other in their unwished-for and deleterious actions.

Prof. Loewy has described experiments on respiration under reduced atmospheric pressure, carried out in a confined space which admitted of very rapid reductions of pressure (to half an atmosphere), with constant composition of the inclosed air. The amount of reduction which was borne without ill effects differed in the case of the three persons on whom the experiments were made, in accordance with the magnitude of their respiratory activities; the greater the latter, the greater was the reduced pressure which could be withstood. For any one person it appeared that a greater reduction could be borne while fasting or during work than after a meal or during repose. Both oxygen and carbon dioxide were found to do away with the discom-

fort resulting from over-rarefaction of the air. Slightly reduced pressure had no effect on respiratory interchange, while, if the reduction was considerable, more carbon dioxide was expired, notwithstanding the diminished supply of oxygen. The reduced pressure of the latter gas was found to act on the respiratory mechanism in such a way as to lead to deeper and hence compensatory respiratory movements.

By introducing a manometer tube into the trachea in cases where tracheotomy had been performed, Dr. Aron has been able to note the intratracheal pressure under various circumstances. He found that inspiration is frequently divided into two portions, but that expiration is always continuous. In quiet breathing the manometer marked in inspiration from -2.08 millimetres to -6.65 millimetres of mercury; in expiration, from $+1.23$ millimetres to $+6.29$ millimetres. In coughing, the inspiration pressure was -6 millimetres, and the expiration pressure as much as $+46$ millimetres.

Circulation.—Prof. Roy and J. G. Adami have spent several years in attempting to give the study of the intact mammalian heart the accuracy which has been attained in the study of the heart of cold-blooded animals. In a paper to the Royal Society they point out the ease with which cardial tracings may be misinterpreted if certain elements of the mechanics of the heart be not constantly kept in mind. Thus, if, when the chambers of the heart become expanded, there is a lessening of the extent to which at each systole the muscular fibers contract, this does not mean that the contractile force is weakened; for with increase in the contents of the cavities of the heart there is increased strain thrown upon the walls, and a comparatively slight diminution in the circumference of the expanded ventricle suffices to expel the same amount of blood whose expulsion when the ventricle is but little expanded is accompanied by a greater diminution in circumference. Thus, in considering the action of the vagus upon the heart, it was shown that stimulation of this nerve does *not* cause loss of ventricular force of contraction. Moderate stimulation induces weakening or paralysis of the auricles, accompanied by ventricular dilatation. This dilatation is due to the increased venous and intraventricular pressure accompanying the slowed rate of beat. And though there is now lessened systolic contraction of the ventricular wall, and also lessened output in a given time, each individual contraction leads to the expulsion of an increased quantity of blood. The only direct action of the vagus upon the ventricle, according to the authors, is a diminution of the excitability of the ventricular muscle. Upon continued fairly strong vagus excitation the auricular rhythm is weakened or inhibited, and does not suffice to set up the normal "sinus," or post-auricular rhythm of the ventricles; so for a time the ventricles usually cease to beat, but soon the independent, idioventricular rhythm manifests itself. The same is to be seen when, after the methods of Woodbridge or Tigerstedt, the mammalian ventricles and auricles are cut off from one another; or, again, shows itself after muscarin poisoning. With a certain degree of vagus excitation, irregularity of the ventricles results in consequence of the sinus and idio-ventricular rhythms interfering with one another. The authors prefer the term augmentor nerves to that of accelerating nerves. Excitation of these nerves in the dog leads more often to augmentation in the force than in the frequence of contraction. The two effects do not go hand in hand. Vagus excitation relieves the heart of work, and therefore of waste, to as great an extent as is compatible with a continuance of the circulation; the vagus may therefore be looked upon as primarily the protective nerve of the heart; secondarily, it acts in the interests of the central nervous system; while the presence in the sciatic and other mixed nerves of fibers which cause reflex vagus excitation seems to indicate that the nerve may be used by other parts of the body to diminish the output of the heart, and so to reduce the activity of the circulation as a whole. The idio-ventricular mechanism must be looked upon as a means whereby arrest of the circulation—and death—is prevented when the vagus action exceeds a certain limit. The augmentor nerves, on the other hand, increase the work and tissue of the heart, and this organ is sacrificed for the needs of the economy until the vagus is called into play by cardiac reflex. The output is increased, and the ventricles are enabled to pump out their contents against heightened arterial blood pressure. Other considerations dealt with by the authors are the mode of interaction of the vagi and augmentors, and factors other than nervous affecting the heart's contractions.

The cause of a difference in the radial pulse of the two sides in certain heart affections has been studied by Prof. L. V. Popoff. The phenomenon is frequently observed with mitral stenosis, associated with mitral incompetence, especially where there is considerable disturbance of the compensation, the pulse being small and irregular, and the dilatation of the heart, and especially of the left ventricle, very marked. Under these conditions the pulse in the left radial artery is found to be decidedly weaker than that in the right—sometimes, indeed, the latter may be easily counted, while the former is hardly perceptible. Sometimes the pulse is so small and weak that it will not give a sphygmographic tracing, and the difference can be detected only by the feel. As the heart's action improves the difference gradually becomes less and less marked. The author says, in explanation of this, that he found in the cases described a pressure of the enlarged auricle and its appendix, and even of enlarged pulmonary vessels, against the arch of the aorta, and especially against the part from which the left subclavian arises. Of course, if the heart's action is feeble, such a pressure must diminish the circulation through the left arm in comparison with that through the right; but if the aorta is well filled out, this pressure may have but little effect. Again, probably the greater length of the arterial course on the left side, and the more acute angle which the left subclavian makes with the arch of the aorta, as compared with that made by the right subclavian with the innominate, must be borne in mind, as it probably has some influence on the question. The differential pulse is more frequently observed in young or

middle-aged subjects than in elderly people, as in the latter the heart, owing to the loss of elasticity and consequent elongation of the great vessels, lies lower, and therefore farther away from the arch of the aorta.

The properties possessed by the serum of blood of killing disease germs and of dissolving and destroying the red blood-corpuscles of other animals, have been studied by Herr Buchner. These powers are gradually lost when the liquid has been removed from the animal, and are destroyed by heating half an hour to from 52° to 55° C. Light also stops both actions, and diffuse daylight more than direct sunlight. It is apparently albumens in the serum that are operative; but whether all the albuminoid constituents, or certain specific albumens, was not determined. It is remarkable that solution of the serum with a 0·7-per-cent solution of common salt does not spoil the action, whereas a similar dilution with pure water makes the serum nearly inactive. But serum made inactive with water recovers its properties if salt solution is added, and this is the case even when the serum has been kept in the active state for from four to twenty-four hours in ice. Serum may also receive a 0·7-per-cent. solution of potassium or lithium chloride, or various other salts of the fixed alkalies, without losing its germicide properties. Ammonium salts even stimulate these. Herr Buchner calls the albumens in question alexines (or protective matters); he supposes they have a like action on foreign cells generally. The serum of dogs and rabbits having been mixed, the power of both alexines was weakened, but those of the rabbit more than those of the dog (for typhus bacilli). After acting some time on each other the globulicide power was extinguished. The author finds in these facts an explanation of the antitoxical action of the serum of animals protected against disease.

Having studied by the aid of original preparations the origin of hæmoglobin of the fusiform corpuscles and of the hæmatoblasts in the blood of amphibia, Dr. A. B. Macallum concludes that the hæmatoglobin of the blood corpuscles is derived from the abundant nuclear chromatin of the hæmatoblasts. This chromatin, he considers, is an iron compound, the constant oxidation and reduction of which constitutes the chemical process underlying life. The fusiform cells of amphibian blood, he maintains, are derived from the blood corpuscles—are, in fact, the remains of the broken-up or destroyed red cells, the latter in this conversion losing the cell membrane and the greater portion of the discoplasma. The hæmatoblasts in amblystoma are probably the direct descendants of cells split off from the extreme ventral portions of the visceral mesoblast. An interesting contribution to our knowledge of the adaptation of structure to function in the human body is afforded by the investigation by Signor Minervini, of Naples, of the blood vessels of the skin in different parts. Portions of skin were prepared so as to show the exact structure of the chief arteries in them. The results are as follow: 1. The artery walls of the skin in men are generally thicker than those of other organs; 2. This greater thickness is due generally, and during most of life, to the thickening of the middle layer; but in childhood the outer, and in advanced years the innermost, layer is most developed; 3. The artery walls in the hollow of the hand, the finger tips, and the sole are, other things being equal, thicker than those in the back of the hand, the forehead, the arm, etc. This greater thickness is due to a greater development of the middle layer in all ages of life. The arteries in the hollow of the hand in the case of occupations involving hard manual labor show a greater increase of thickness than in the case of those with little or no such work. In these cases all three layers of the artery are thickened, but the middle layer most; 4. In women all the chief arteries of the hollow of the hand and of the back of the hand are somewhat less thick than those of men.

The method of fractional heat coagulation has been employed by Prof. Halliburton in the examination of many animal fluids, especially of serum, which he believes in some of the higher vertebrates contains a mixture of 3 albumens. Corin and Berard, using this method, came to a somewhat similar conclusion respecting the white of egg. In 1890 Messrs. Haycraft and Duggan published a criticism on this method, in which they asserted that the coagulation point of a proteid is considerably raised by diluting its solution, and a very dilute solution may not coagulate, even on boiling. Without doubting the possibility of fractionating some proteids this factor in determining the temperature of coagulation has been neglected by Corin and Berard, and by Halliburton, and therefore, the critics say, a doubt is cast upon the results they have obtained by fractional heat coagulation. In order that the proteids separated may be considered distinct from one another, it is necessary that other differences besides that of mere heat coagulation should be demonstrated to exist. It is possible that serum albumen and egg albumen may be single proteids, and the fact that various precipitates at different temperatures are obtainable, can be explained in one of two ways: either that the heat, when applied for a long time, alters the character of the proteid in solution so that its temperature of coagulation is heightened, or that the result is simply a dilution. Even if it be admitted that serum albumen is a single substance, the question arises, What explanation can be given of the fact that various precipitates are obtainable at different temperatures? Haycraft has suggested three possible explanations, viz., that the coagulation point rises in virtue of the solution becoming continually more dilute; its becoming less acid—which may be disregarded, because the acidity can be kept constant; and changes which are being produced in the proteid itself, by the action of the high temperature to which it is subjected. The most stress is laid on the first explanation. The experiments of R. T. Hewlett with the white of egg give no support to the views of these critics, but emphasize the point that it is not necessary to make a distinction between the temperature of opalescence and the temperature of coagulation (formation of flocculi). Both take place at the same temperature, if the rate of heating be sufficiently slow; that the differences observed in coagulation temperatures with slow and rapid heating are only apparent; that a slow rate of heating is essential for obtaining correct coagulation temperatures,

especially when a solution is dilute; that prolonged heating probably does not alter the coagulation temperature of a proteid; that very dilute solutions of a proteid may be prevented from coagulating by a comparatively small excess of either acid or alkali; that the phenomena of fractional heat coagulation are not due to the effects of dilution, for (a) dilution, if the rate of heating be sufficiently slow, does not raise the coagulation temperature; (b) in fractionation the rise in the coagulation temperature is out of all proportion to the dilution; there can be little doubt that white of egg is a mixture of at least three proteids; and it would be advisable to decide upon some standard conditions under which to determine coagulation temperatures.

A report has been made by Dr. Carl Sadler of observations on the conditions of the blood in a wide range of diseases. In acute diseases the author finds a constant but mostly not very marked decrease of red corpuscles. In chronic diseases the diminution is greater, especially in such as exhibit cachexia, and there is a proportionate diminution in the amount of hæmoglobin. An exception to this is met with in tuberculosis so long as nutrition is fairly well preserved. The number of corpuscles is also not affected in valvular disease of the heart. In chlorosis the corpuscles may long remain at the normal standard, while the hæmoglobin falls. In other cases of anæmia, in the essential form and in forms due to losses of blood, atrophy of stomach, and other causes, the decline in corpuscular richness takes place at an even pace with that of hæmoglobin. Acute and profuse diarrhœa produces a notable increase in the proportion of corpuscles and hæmoglobin, attributable to inspissation of the blood, and this may account for the maintenance of a fairly normal standard in some cases of typhoid fever. The author found a diminution in the number of white blood-corpuscles in malaria, apart from the administration of quinine. Leucocytosis is proved to occur during digestion, and also during the puerperal period and the first days of lactation. Pathological leucocytosis is found in all diseases accompanied by exudation, but not invariably. Leucocytosis does not occur in uncomplicated typhoid fever, or in tuberculosis (except during the reaction produced by injections of tuberculin). It was present in only one half the cases of carcinoma examined, and had relation rather to the supervention of ulceration than to infection of lymphatic glands. Singularly, in contrast with carcinoma, leucocytosis is invariably present in cases of sarcoma.

It has been shown by Surgeon-Major Laurie, of India, that the fall of blood pressure in animals made insensible by chloroform is due to the action of the anæsthetic on the brain, and not on the heart. When blood containing chloroform is allowed to reach the brain only, all the ordinary phenomena of anæsthesia are observed; but when such blood is conveyed to every other part of the body except the brain, while that is supplied with pure blood, the anæsthetic effects of chloroform and its depressing effects on the circulation are not observed.

Digestion.—In the case of a patient in whom an operation gave an opportunity to study the process of digestion in the stomach and small intestine, MacFayden, Nencki, and Sieber found that the duration of the passage of food from the mouth to the ileo-cæcal valve was·two hours at the earliest, and the food of one meal continued to pass for from nine to fourteen hours. The food consisted of bread, meat, peptones, oatmeal, milk, eggs, sugar, and beef tea. The chyme as obtained from the end of the small intestine contained dissolved coagulable albumens, mucin, peptones, dextrin, sugar, inactive fermentescible and optically active paralactic acid, volatile fatty acids, especially acetic acid, the biliary acids, and bilirubin. The acid reaction of the chyme was always due to the presence of organic acids. Neither indol, skatol, phenol, leucin, nor tyrosin was present, the fact showing that in this case at least the albumen was hardly touched by microbes in the small intestine, while the carbohydrates were decomposed with formations of acid.

In a research on ferment actions of the pancreas in different animals, Vincent D. Harris and William J. Gow sought to obtain information upon the following points: 1. Whether the ferments with the possession of which the pancreas is usually credited are present in the pancreas of animals of different classes, and, if so, whether there is any marked difference to be discovered in the activity (or amount) of each ferment in each class. 2. Whether the activity or amount of the ferment bears any relation to the food of the animal. 3. Whether the ferments of the human pancreas are markedly affected in activity or amount in morbid conditions of the body; and whether, in addition to the generally accepted pancreatic ferments, the gland possesses any additional ferment action (a) in inverting cane sugar, or (b) in producing any chemical action upon dry or unboiled starch. It had been established from previous observations that very definite ferments exist in pancreatic juice, and may be extracted from the gland by means of glycerin and other vehicles; that these ferments have special relations to the different classes of food stuffs; and that during secretion the ferments which had been previously deposited within the pancreatic cells in granular and undeveloped form are discharged into the lumen of the tubes. The purpose of the authors in their investigation was to inquire whether the ferments, four in number, which the pancreas is said to possess, appear in the gland of all animals. It appears from the researches under the first head, that of the four ferments dealt with the tryptic ferment is by far the most universal and hardy; next to it is put the rennet ferment; next the diastatic; and, lastly, as being that which is, if present universally in the pancreas of animals (which the authors are strongly inclined to doubt), most easily destroyed by preserving the pancreas in spirit, the fat-splitting ferment. No proof was found of any special fat-emulsifying ferment. Concerning the second question, the experiments show that the pancreases of the carnivorous animals—the lion, leopard, serval, and ocelot—have little or no power of converting starch into sugar, do not possess any rennet ferment, and that their tryptic power was unusually active. In the extracts of the pancreases of several other carnivorous animals the diastatic power was slight, while the

horse's pancreas gave an irregular result, was inactive in amylolytic power, and was very active in regard to its tryptic or proteolytic ferment. The tryptic ferments of several carnivorous animals was only slightly active. The fat-splitting ferment was not present in pancreatic extracts. The rennet ferment was more often present than not, and in some pancreases was extremely powerful. The pig, the ox, man, and the sea eagle appear in the first class as regards the activity of all their ferments. The cases experimented upon under the third of the queries were too few to justify definite conclusions; but three of them indicated that the activity of the human pancreatic ferments may be considerably diminished in wasting disease. Under the fourth question, it appeared that neither active brine extracts of pancreas nor fresh pig's pancreas have the power of inverting cane sugar in an active medium, and that fresh pig's pancreas has the power of converting raw starch into dextrin. Experiments with reference to different ferments proved that antiseptics do not interfere with the action of the unorganized ferments, and confirm the results of former experiments by Harris and Tooth.

Experiments were recently made by Herr Roseuberg with a dog, in the inquiry whether the process of digestion is promoted or hindered by bodily exertion. The animal was fed daily with a fixed average ration, and the amount of nitrogen and fat daily absorbed was duly determined. Five series of experiments were made, each including a rest period followed by a working period, in which the dog was made to work on a treadmill. In some cases the efforts were made during stomachic, in others during intestinal digestion. In both series of experiments the differences observed lay within the limits of physiological variations, and the inference was drawn that, in a healthy dog, the utilization of food is independent of the condition whether the dog rests or is energetically at work during digestion.

Nervous System.—In whatever way, says Richard E. Edes, we may picture to ourselves the process going on in a nerve fiber while transmitting an impulse, it must come under one of two heads: It must be either a "chemical" process, comparable to a train of gunpowder, in which we may suppose the decomposition in one part to start decomposition in the neighboring part, and so on; or a physical process, comparable to the vibration of a stretched wire, or the propagation of sound waves in a flexible tube. On the first hypothesis three things must take place: (a) Change in the chemical composition of the transmitting matter, as revealed by chemical tests; (b) production of heat; (c) using up of potentially energetic material with production of waste or unenergetic material, causing phenomena of fatigue. The experiments of Mr. Edes with reference to the determination of these points, performed in the laboratory of the Harvard Medical School, as reviewed by him, are to be divided into two parts: First, those on exhaustibility, which depend for their value on the positive proof of activity after long periods of stimulation, and thus offer positive evidence; and, second, those on heat production and chemical changes recognized by chemical methods, of which the logical value is that of negative evidence, although in this case very strong. In regard to heat, probably nothing further can be brought forward. As to chemical change, however, it is possible that new and more delicate methods may bring out interesting results. Something also might be looked for from the histological comparison of exhausted and nonexhausted fibers. Assuming, then, the practical inexhaustibility of medullated nerve fibers, and the slight, if any, chemical change during activity, it remains to suggest a mode of transmission of energy which shall be to a very slight extent indeed, if at all, other than a physical one. Of such hypotheses the most fascinating one seems that of Engelmann, who supposes the phenomena of the nervous impulse to be an electrical one, having a velocity in the internodal segments far greater than the average velocity in the nerve, the delay taking place at the nodes of Ranvier. In support of this he maintains that the axis cylinder is histologically discontinuous at the nodes. This latter view is opposed by many histologists, and Demoor maintains that the axis cylinder, while continuous throughout, is of a different constitution at the nodes. He considers that such a structure would fulfill the requirements of the hypothesis of Engelmann. This hypothesis Engelmann also holds to account for the interruption of conductivity of the impulse in a ligatured nerve.

Although a large amount of work has been done in the study of the nerves acting on the mammalian heart, the method of direct registration of the movements of auricles and ventricles has been used in only a few cases. To this fact are probably largely owing the numerous gaps in our knowledge of the subject, as compared with the exact knowledge we have of the actions of the nerves in the cold-blooded animals. Having shown in a former paper that the electrical events accompanying the contraction of the mammalian heart are exactly analogous to those occurring in the frog and tortoise, W. M. Bayliss and Ernest H. Starling instituted a new research with a view to determining how far this analogy extends to the innervation of the heart in those two classes of animals, and especially with regard to the influence of the two sets of cardiac nerves on conduction between auricles and ventricles. In their work the authors chiefly concerned themselves with studying the conditions affecting conduction from auricles to ventricles. Their conclusion is that there is no essential difference between the hearts of the mammals and of the cold-blooded animals, and that each is subject to the same varieties of nerve influence.

The results of investigations undertaken by Dr. Risien Russell to ascertain whether it is possible to separate the adductor fibers from the abductor fibers of the recurrent laryngeal nerve, show that these fibers are collected into several separate bundles, each preserving an independent course through the nerve trunk to its termination in the muscle or muscles which it supplies. It was also found that whereas in the adult animal simultaneous excitation of all the nerve fibers in the recurrent laryngeal nerve results in adduction of the vocal cord on the same side, in the young animal the opposite effect — viz., abduction—is that produced by an exactly similar procedure. When the abductor and adductor fibers are exposed to the air the abductor nerves are found to lose their power of electrical excitability much sooner than the adductors, and this is true of both young and adult animals, although in the former the adductor fibers retain their excitability longer. It was further found possible to separate the adductor fibers from the abductor through the whole length of the recurrent laryngeal nerve to their termination in the muscles, and also so accurately to separate the two sets of fibers as to be able to produce abduction or adduction, as the case might be, without evoking any contraction in the muscles of opposite function. The complete separation of the two functions was also shown by the degeneration of the muscles related to one function which followed the division of the corresponding nerve fibers, while the muscles subserving the other function remained unaffected.

Experiments are described by Dr. Boruttau, of Berlin, which were made to determine the cause of the difference in latent period observed during the direct and indirect stimulation of muscles, it being greater in indirect stimulation. The author had satisfied himself by a careful repetition of the experiments under many varying conditions that the difference is due solely to the resistance of the end plates. In connection with this paper, Prof. Gad pointed out the possible bearing of the results obtained on the processes which go on in other organs. Thus, recent anatomical research has shown that in the central nervous system there is no complete continuity between the axis cylinders and ganglia, and hence the existence of some intermediate structure must be assumed, and a portion at least of the slowing which impulses experience in the central nervous system may be due to the resistance offered by this structure.

Some observations have been contributed and an attempt has been made by Messrs. Jaffray and Achard to reconcile the different theories which have been held with reference to the occurrence of atrophy after hemiplegia. This condition, according to Charcot and Leyden and their followers, is a result of an affection of the anterior horns in the spinal cord. Déjérine, on the other hand, ascribes the condition to an affection of the peripheral nerves, while Quincke, Eisenlohr, Babinski, and others hold that there is no discoverable anatomical condition underlying the change, but that it is the result of a functional disturbance in the cells. In two cases examined by the authors, changes were found in the anterior horn cells, so far confirming Charcot's views. To explain the different conditions and reconcile the different theories, the authors suppose that in the first place, on account of the lesion of the pyramidal tracts, there is stimulation of the cells of the anterior horns, giving rise to contracture. If this stimulation is succeeded by exhaustion, then atrophy results, but in this there are several changes. At first there is simple muscular atrophy, the nerves not yet being appreciably altered, and the anterior horns and intramuscular endings being anatomically intact. But later degeneration in the motor nerves sets in, and in the peripheral endings, and, last of all, the cells in the anterior horns undergo visible atrophy.

Special Senses.—The cause of the dilatation of the pupil which is produced by stimulating the cervical sympathetic has been the subject of much controversy. The various theories upon it suppose that the dilatation is due to the action of the sympathetic vaso-constrictor nerves, by decreasing the quantity of blood in the iris so that it shrinks, or by a longitudinal contraction of the radial arteries of the iris, dragging the sphincter outward; that it is caused by the contraction of radially arranged muscular fibers; or by inhibition of the sphincter muscle; or, in certain circumstances, to a certain degree, by a relaxation of the ciliary muscle; or, finally, by the simultaneous action of more than one of these causes. The evidence which has been brought forward in favor of one or other of these theories has not been found by J. N. Langley and H. K. Anderson in any case conclusive. Reviewing the observations, these authors think they show a probability that the sympathetic causes a dilatation of the pupil, not by producing a contraction of the blood vessels, but partly by causing a contraction of the dilator muscle and partly by causing an inhibition of the sphincter muscle. A direct examination of the iris during the stimulation of the cervical sympathetic shows that the pupil dilates before the vessels contract; and assuming that the longitudinal muscular coat of the arteries contracts simultaneously with the circular coat, the experiment shows that the sympathetic dilatation of the pupil is not due to a contraction of the blood vessels. It can be shown also that some radially arranged contractile substance exists in the iris, for when local dilatation of the pupil passes a certain limit the opposite side of the iris is dragged toward the stimulated side. This local dilatation is not produced by an inhibition of the sphincter muscle, for the sphincter muscle can be made to contract at the same time, its contraction being greatest at the most dilated portion of the pupil. Further, stimulation of the sympathetic causes shortening of a radial strip of the iris, isolated from the iris on either side of it, and this shortening may be obtained before or without any contraction of the blood vessels in it; and on examining the posterior surface of the iris, small waves of contraction may be seen on its posterior surface when the sympathetic is stimulated.

From careful studies of the subject Steinach has reached the conclusion that the contraction of the iris when detached from the retina is due to the direct action of light upon its structure. He found that no effect was produced by illuminating the peripheral zone of the iris (ciliary region); but it was necessary that the light should fall upon the pupillary margin, of which, if only a segment be acted upon, contraction occurs. The contraction still took place when the nervous apparatus of the iris was excluded by the action of atropine. The author demonstrates that the contraction is not due to the influence of the chromatophores, and entertains no doubt that it is really the muscular fibers of the sphincter that are acted upon directly. He has made numerous examinations of these, and finds that in amphibia and fishes they are strongly pigmented. In eyes that have been exposed to the light they are short, thick, and not very well defined; while in animals that have been kept in the dark they are slender and sharply contoured. The author regards the presence of pigment in these muscular fibers as the determining cause of their sensibility to light. The several rays of the spectrum are not all of equal power in causing contraction in the isolated iris. In a comment upon Steinach's paper, Langendorff remarks that other muscle cells besides those of the sphincter pupillæ possess pigment granules in their interior—as, for example, those of the tensor choroideæ in mammals.

It is observed by M. A. Chaveau that if one goes to sleep on a seat placed obliquely in front of a window which allows the light from white clouds to fall equally on both eyes, the colored objects in the room appear illuminated by a bright-green light during a very short interval when the eyelids are opened at the moment of awakening. The phenomenon is not observed except at the moment of awakening from a profound sleep. From this it is concluded that there are distinct perceptive centers for the green, and probably also for the violet and the red. Of these the green centers are those which first regain their activity on awakening.

A report was made at a recent meeting of the Vienna Society of Physicians by Dr. Kreidl, an assistant of Prof. Exner, on experiments he had made on deaf mutes concerning the physiology of the labyrinth. Touching the experiments made on this subject by Flourens, Goltz, Mach, and Breur, he pointed out that the membranous canals of the external ear should be regarded as the peripheral part of the mechanism of the sense of equilibrium, the sensations of the disturbance which he takes to be produced by the flow of the fluid of the ampulla and in the membranous canals. If the views of physiologists on the function of the otoliths and the membranous canals be true, it would have been expected that anomalies of the sense of equilibrium should be found in deaf mutes. Purkinje had previously observed that if a person is made to rotate on his own axis, the eyeballs were moved to the side, as in nystagmus. This, in Dr. Kreidl's experiments, was not observed in deaf mutes to any large extent. From other experiments the author was led to regard the otolithic organs as a statical sense.

From observations made upon a student, twenty-one years of age, suffering from complete anosmia—a defect evidently congenital, and inherited from the patient's mother—but in whom taste and common and thermal sensibility were undisturbed, Prof. Jastrow found that the greater number of taste perceptions, as they are commouly understood, are really to be referred to smell. No distinction could be made by the subject between tea, coffee, and hot water, so that he took the hot water, with sugar and milk, as his ordinary breakfast beverage. He confounded bitter-almond water and water three times in five trials, while he correctly discriminated ether and water, the former, he said, producing in his throat the sensation of peppermint. With ammonia and ether he was right six times in eight trials; and Prof. Jastrow ascribes the two errors to fatigue. The various fruit sirups he could not distinguish, merely recognizing them as sweet. Mustard produced a sharp sensation on the tongue, but was not recognized any more than pepper, while cloves and cinnamon were distinguished. Differences of 1° of temperature were easily recognized.

It has been discovered that after chewing the leaves of *Gymnema sylvestre*, an asclepiad plant of India and Africa, sugar no longer excites a sweet taste. L. E. Shore has found that the bitter taste is also easily prevented by this substance, but not so readily as the sweet taste of glycerin. An analysis of the dried leaves of this plant by Hooper showed that an organic acid was present, which, baving obtained it in a crude state, he considered allied to chrysophanic acid and named gymnemic acid. It occurs to the extent of 6 per cent. of dried leaves. •Hooper found that the action of the leaves of the plant on taste was due to this body; and Berthold obtained similar results. From studies of the action of gymnema and other substances on taste, Dr. Shore finds an explanation of it in supposing that the nerve fibers or nerve endings capable of being stimulated by pure sweet and bitter substances are different from those which are excited only by acid and salt. The selective action of cocaine not only on the nerve centers connected with taste, but on others associated with more general sensory impressions, points also to the multiplicity of the kinds of endings of sensory nerves in the tongue. The more powerful action of cocaine on bitter taste than on sweet, and of gymnema on sweet taste than on bitter, may also be an indication that the nerve fibers or nerve endings concerned with those tastes are also distinct. The selective action of drugs between these two tastes is, however, much less marked, and the constant grouping of these together gives some support to the view that they may be due to different molecular activities of the same end organs.

Examining the gustatory sensations excited in 125 fungiform papillæ, Öhnall has found that 21 per cent. are not sensitive at all, while 48 per cent. are sensitive to sweet, bitter, and acid tastes. Some are sensitive to only two, and a few to sweet only, or to acid only, but no papilla was found which was sensitive to bitter only.

In a paper of contributions to the study of the muscular sense before the American Neurological Association, Dr. G. F. Preston thought that it might be considered definitely proved that the muscular sense, or at least one part, is composed of afferent impulses which are independent of general sensibility. The next step that suggested itself was the starting point of these afferent impulses. Clearly, as several observers had noted, the muscles alone—that is, sensations coming from them—could not give us the information we required as to the position of our limbs. Undoubtedly the tendons, the joints and their coverings, and perhaps the bones, all aided in producing the posture sense, or rather from these proceeded nerve fibers conveying posture-sense impressions. The loss or impairment of posture sense was an almost constant symptom 'in sclerosis of the posterior columns of the cord. It seemed probable that the fibers conveying posture-sense impressions passed into the retiform body, thence to the cerebellum, and on to the great brain. In 3 cases of tumor of the cerebellum in which necropsies had been made he had

observed loss of posture sense without impairment of general sensibility.

Muscular System.—A physical theory for the explanation of muscle currents was propounded in 1878, and matured in 1889, by M. D'Arsonval, who supposed them to be due to changes in surface tension, occurring at the planes of separation of the bright and dim disks of the muscle fiber; and he adduced several phenomena of the currents that were explained by it. The principal objections brought against it referred to the absence of disks such as are spoken of in the muscle fibers, and the failure of the theory to explain nerve currents. The results of experiments made by J. Herbert Parsons with a view to testing the theory indicate that D'Arsonval is correct in attributing such muscular currents to a physical cause, although his explanation rested on an erroneous anatomical basis. It would now, says the author, appear probable that muscle and nerve currents are caused by the movements of fluid in capillary tubes; and since it has been indicated by Prof. Burdon Sanderson that the electrical change of contracting muscle does not precede but actually coincides with the mechanical effect, the hypothesis that the electrical variation is produced by chemical changes which precede the actual shortening is no longer necessary.

The physiological action of various pure organic nitrites of the paraffin series upon striated muscular tissue has been studied by J. T. Cash and W. R. Dunstan. When the vapors of these nitrites came into contact with the muscle a paralysing effect was observed. Several series of concordant results were obtained, which lead to two different orders of activity, viz., with reference to the extent to which equal quantities of nitrites shorten the resting muscle, and with reference to the rapidity with which the shortening is produced. The order of activity of the nitrites as regards the extent of the shortening they induce is as follows: Iso-butyl, tertiary amyl, secondary butyl, secondary propyl, propyl, tertiary butyl, butyl, α amyl, β amyl, ethyl, methyl. The order representing the speed with which shortening occurs is: Methyl, ethyl, secondary propyl, tertiary propyl, primary propyl, tertiary butyl, secondary butyl, α amyl, β amyl, primary butyl, isobutyl. In very minute doses, insufficient to cause passive contraction, these nitrites interfere in a marked degree with the active contraction, and cause the muscle to fail in responding to stimulation; while the companion muscle, contained in a closed chamber free from nitrite vapor, still responded to stimulation. The physiological action of these nitrites did not appear to be solely, and in some cases not even mainly, dependent on the amount of nitroxyl they contained. In respect of all phases of physiological activity, the secondary and tertiary nitrites are more powerful than the corresponding primary compounds. A large proportion of an organic nitrite is changed into nitrate in its passage through the organism, and is excreted as an alkali nitrate in the urine.

Kauffmann, experimenting on the masseter and levator labii superioris muscles, has found that the quantity of blood traversing a physiologically active muscle is enormously increased, being in some instances as much as fivefold the ordinary quantity at rest. The capillaries become greatly enlarged, and the tension in the arteries falls, while it rises in the veins.

Action of Poisons.—Some interesting results are derived by Dr. E. Maurel from his experimental researches on the action of poisons on leucocytes. He finds that the toxic action of strychnine on the alkaloids of the animal economy is in the ratio of its destructive action on the leucocytes. The immediate effect of the poison on the white corpuscles is to arrest their spontaneous activity and fix the elements in the spherical state. A similar concordance was found with atropine between the quantity of toxic material necessary to kill the animal and that necessary to kill the corpuscles. As both the hare and its leucocytes enjoy a comparative immunity against this same alkaloid—the immunity of the animal seeming to be closely associated with the immunity of its leucocytes—the author is led to the conclusion that the leucocytes probably have a principal part to perform in poisoning by it. From a similar investigation, Dr. Maurel concludes that death by cocaine is the consequence of the death of the leucocytes or of modifications which they sustain under the action of that agent. Thirty times as much cocaine is required to kill an animal when the salt is taken by the mouth as when it is injected into a vein. In death by intravenous injections of toxic solutions, the death may be caused by the leucocytes suddenly killed being swept along the blood stream and acting as emboli. These elements, in fact, after death take the form of rigid disks, the long diameter of which exceeds by one third at least the caliber of certain capillaries.

The systematic investigation of the albumose which is the active material of cobra poison has been made by A. A. Kanthack, of Cambridge University. The study of the reactions showed that only one, a primary albumose, is present. Tests for the presence of an alkaloid led to a negative result. The action of the poison is cumulative, and experiments show that a more toxic action is produced by injecting at intervals smaller doses. Heat lessens the action of the albumose, but it requires prolonged boiling to destroy it when pure and concentrated. Diffused light has no influence on the solution of albumose or the natural poison. The effect of bright sunlight was not tried—on account of the time of year. Of chemical agents, caustic potash and caustic soda destroyed the toxic power rapidly, but it was restored on the addition of acetic acid. Chlorine water destroyed it if allowed to act long enough; trichloride of iodine, if used strong enough; permanganate of potash, if allowed to act twenty-four hours. Carbolic acid destroys the toxic power of weak solutions; pancreatin destroys the toxic power or delays the toxic effect considerably; nitrate of silver, corrosive sublimate, tannic acid, and alcohol destroy it by precipitating the albumose; ammonia lessens it if allowed to act long enough; and citric acid and pepsin lessen it somewhat. Animals may be accustomed to withstand large doses of the poison; but it is necessary, in the experiments, to allow a sufficiently long interval to elapse between successive doses, as the cumulative effect of the albumose is well marked. Injections of cobra

blood and serum, which were said to give immunity, and injections of the poison itself, boiled till its toxic power was destroyed, gave only negative results. All the substances which outside of the body lessened or destroyed the activity of the albumose, were tried as protective and curative agents, with no success. Strychnine was proved to be neither a chemical nor a physiological antidote. The result of experiments made with reference to that especial point was to satisfy the author that the observations of S. Weir Mitchell and Reichert and Wolfenden, indicating the presence of a globulin in the poison, are not conclusive, but that the body called a globulin is nothing but a mixture of heteroalbumose and dysalbumose.

In publishing his tracings, or graphic records, of the action of chloroform and ether on the vascular system, John A. MacWilliam marks as the chief points to be noticed in them the evidences of enfeeblement and dilatation manifested in the heart under the influence of chloroform, these changes frequently beginning even before the conjunctival reflex was abolished and when the fall of blood pressure was not greater, and often not so great, as during chloroform anæsthesia brought about by inhalation in the usual way; and the contrast between the effects of ether and chloroform upon the heart when the respective anæsthetics are administered, freely diluted with air, in such an amount as to cause abolition of the conjunctival reflex. The dilatation of the heart caused by chloroform is due to a direct action of the anæsthetic upon the cardiac mechanism. It is not obviated by section of the vagus nerves. It does not depend upon the fall of systemic arterial pressure; and it is not produced by obstruction of the pulmonary circulation.

Much, says a writer in the "Boston Medical and Surgical Journal," remains to be discovered relative to the kinds of ptomaines that may develop in animal and vegetable substances out of the body, as well as of the toxines that may form in food after its ingestion. Doubtless the possibilities of ptomaine formation are very great, and under unusual conditions of insalubrity—hot, damp weather, sewage emanations, etc.—the work of decomposition may go on with extraordinary rapidity, and, under the influence of microbes, toxalbumens of great power may form in food that to the eye and taste is still wholesome. There is accumulative evidence to show that this is so. At the same time every investigator of the subject is confronted by the fact that meats that have undergone partial decomposition are not necessarily unwholesome or toxic, for some savage tribes, as the Patagonians and Fiji Islanders, habitually eat putrid meat that is swarming with bacteria. From our present standpoint of enlightenment as to the development of toxines during processes of putrefaction we can not well understand such facts. It must, however, be borne in mind that robust, healthy stomachs are very tolerant of foods which under circumstances of enfeeblement of the digestive tract would cause sickness; that the digestive fluids are more or less destructive to microbes; and that the liver when in a healthy state is capable of destroying considerable quantities of poisonous substances.

Cases of poisoning by food of a relatively innocuous character are not uncommon. Some portion of the ingesta becomes an irritant poison, a fit of indigestion ensues, and often the offending substance is speedily expelled by vomiting. Idiosyncrasies play a part here; it is known that certain articles of diet, such as cheese and shell fish, are toxic to some persons. Generally the state of the alimentary canal at the time is responsible. The most common and best known of the various forms of indigestion is that in which, from the absence or the deficiency of gastric juice and other digestive fluids, the alimentary bolus becomes a gastrointestinal irritant, provoking vomiting, purging, and a catarrhal condition of the digestive tract. A second stage in the process of acute indigestion arises from the presence of abnormal fermentations and decompositions in the alimentary canal. The food substances, under the influence of bacteria unrestrained by the antiseptic digestive fluids, break up into organic acids and alkaloidal products of a lower order, which are in part absorbed and produce constitutional disturbances. This stage borders very closely on that of ptomaine formation. There is good reason to regard cholera nostras and the gastrointestinal catarrh of infants as kinds of ptomaine poisoning due to multiple causes, of which weakening of the alimentary canal and consequent p r of digestive fluids, the ingestion of food of any indigestible character, the putrefactive decomposition of the latter under the influence of microbes, and the formation of toxines, are the principal factors.

Miscellaneous.—The remarkable absence of parasitic growths on the carapaces of crustaceans has struck B. W. Hardy as a notable fact; and the more so as there appears to be no mechanism obviously able to produce this cleanliness. Every animal that inhabits the water, or has a habitually moist external skin, is liable to have larvæ and spores continually settling on its surface to develop into embarrassing growths, unless some method of removing or destroying them is present. In many animals the way in which the surface is kept clean is partly obvious. Commensal forms feeding on matter adherent to the skin contribute to the result. The periodical shedding of an external cuticle is a radical means of ridding the animal of growths that may have obtained a hold in spite of other preventive devices, and the continuous desquamation which is characteristic of the stratified epithelium of the higher vertebrates is a more subtle device of the same nature. The appendages of some animals are used for removing the larger forms of adherent bodies. In the mammalia multitudes of phagocytic wander cells are poured on to the surface to ingest foreign particles. Rubbing and scratching the body are of great service in removing foreign matters. The conspicuous cleanliness of crustaceans is not accounted for by any of these provisions. Even the periodical shedding of their cells is not sufficient, for that does not occur often enough to prevent the growth of parasites. Mr. Hardy's investigations lead him to the conclusion that the source of protection is to be found in the action of the surface slime of animals and of phagocytes. The surface slime may have a mechanical action; for the author thinks it may be taken for granted that the presence of a film of soluble slime on the surface of an animal immersed in water would, like the copper sheathing of ships, mechanically prevent the occurrence of parasitic growths by continually forming a fresh surface; or the slime may have a specific poisonous power directed mainly perhaps against the more minute and subtle forms of vegetable parasites. It has been observed that exposure to the poisons produced by anthrax causes an increased elimination of a rose-staining substance on to the external surface and into the blood plasma, and Hankin has shown that the blood serum of animals contains a substance which has a bactericidal action, and to which the name alexine has been applied. This alexine, he believes, has its origin in the blood corpuscles. Fresh force is thus given to the conception of Ranvier, who long ago styled the wander cells unicellular glands. Possibly the rose-reacting substance of *Daphnia* has a specific bactericidal action, and contains an alexine. It is always produced in increased quantities when the animal is infected with pathogenic growths, and it can not be regarded as the product of the microbes in or on the body of the animal.

The preference shown by tuberculosis for the apices of the lungs has been often explained by the assumption that the apex is not participating fully in the respiratory movements, and that the diminished ventilation of that locality is the cause of its predisposition for the disease. But under the theory that an invasion of tubercle bacilli into the lungs is at the bottom of the disease, we should rather expect that if the apex breathes less the bacilli will have fewer chances of getting in there, and in consequence this part of the lungs, instead of being predisposed for the disease, should rather show a certain immunity against it. To meet this argument, A. Hanau assumed that the expiration is indeed less, whereas, the inspiration is rather better in the apex than in the other parts of the lungs, and that therefore all corpuscular elements of microscopical dimensions, like the bacilli, dust, etc., have a greater chance to get in the alveoli of the apex, while their chances to get out of them by the expiration is reduced. This hypothesis would indeed cover the pathological phenomenon satisfactorily, if it were not that the normal breathing also has to be taken into consideration. Physiology can not afford to ignore this problem, or to solve it with mere theoretical speculations. As it is very difficult to find an exact method of ascertaining directly the degree of distentions of the apex, as compared with those of other parts of the lungs during normal breathing, Dr. S. J. Meltzer first turned his attention to the steadily attending phenomenon of the change of the intrathoracic pressure coeeident with the inspiration and expiration. The purpose of his investigation was to infer the amount of respiration in different localities from the accompanying changes in the intrathoracic pressure. It was found, from his experiments on the mediastinum, to be probable that the apices and the back part of the upper third of the lungs do not participate in the breathing so largely as the other parts of the lungs do; yet, in consideration of the importance of this conclusion, he would not regard it as proved until it has been tested by experiments made on the pleural cavity directly or within the lungs themselves. Besides the relations to the breathing of the upper parts of the lungs, the condition discovered to prevail in the upper part of the mediastinum has an important bearing on the question of the respiratory undulations of the blood pressure. During the inspiration both venæ cavæ and right auricle are, so it is generally assumed, under a considerably lower pressure than the veins outside of the thorax, which difference of pressure causes greater inrush of blood into the great thoracic veins and the right auricle, and thus more blood comes into the ventricle, etc.; the expiration, on the other hand, by the diminished intrathoracic negative pressure diminishes the influx of the blood into the 'ventricle. The same conditions have, it is calculated, an opposite but a smaller effect on the aorta. It appeared in the experiments that the inspiratory changes in the intrathoracic pressure are very small in the upper part of the mediastinum, the main change in the pressure occurring in the lower part of it. As the upper part reaches as far down as the fifth or sixth rib, so this part contains the entire superior vena cava, the arcus aortæ, the auricles, and a considerable part of the inferior venæ cavæ, and the descending aorta. In short, the main circulatory parts which are expected to be influenced by the considerable change in the intrathoracic pressure are located in that part of the mediastinum where, according to the author's experiments, very little change occurs. Dr. Meltzer contents himself with a short paper referring to the subject, awaiting a confirmation of the facts he has stated.

Experiments to determine the effects of ablation of the thyroid gland in the dog are described by M. E. Gley. Hitherto all who have performed this operation on the dog, cat, and ape have found that the result was almost invariably fatal; and in the few cases where it is reported that life has been preserved, the author considers that the successful issue has been due to the presence of accessory thyroid glands which have acted vicariously, and that where the animals have survived for a considerable time death has been really due to the operation, although the connection with it has been overlooked. The experiments of M. Gley, who describes the symptoms in detail, confirm this view; and although they do not afford any clew to the function of the thyroid gland, they seem to demonstrate the remarkable influence that the removal of the organ exercises on the nervo-muscular apparatus.

It has long been a disputed question whether light, by direct action on animal tissue, can influence the carbonic acid excretion as it influences the oxygen excretion of a plant by direct action on the chlorophyll of the leaf. The experiments that have been relied upon in support of the hypothesis of such action are shown by Carl A. Ewald to be liable to some objection that prevents their being regarded as conclusive. Mr. Ewald, by using frogs which had been curarized, avoided errors from any indirect effect of light on the muscles, and from the possibility of post-mortem changes, and was able to deal with typical animal tissue which can be directly

exposed to the light. He then made seventeen series of three observations each, the average of which showed a ratio of carbonic acid excreted in the light to that produced in the dark of 100 to $98\frac{1}{2}$; throwing out two of the series in which an apparent explanation was found for the increased excretion in the light, the ratio became 100 to 99—that is, a difference of only 1 per cent., which is less than the probable error of the experiment. From this it may fairly be concluded, he says, that in the case of a curarized frog, when the possibility of muscular action is eliminated, light does not in any appreciable way affect the carbonic-acid excretion.

With regard to the revival of animals after exposure to great cold, Herr Kochs points out two things which retard formation of ice in the natural body. First, the body does not contain pure water, but salt and albumen solutions which freeze only under zero C. Herr Kochs says that water in a glass tube of from 0·3 to 0·4 millimetres diameter may be cooled to −7° C., and even −10° C., without freezing. With a diameter of from only 0·1 to 0·2 millimetres the water is not frozen, even though the end of the tube be put in freezing liquid. The liquid sheets between two glass plates behave in the same way. If a salt solution freezes, the salts are excluded; and pure water, in freezing, gets rid of its absorbed gas. Fresh blood, according to the author's experiments, freezes only after being strongly cooled to −15° C., and after complete elimination of gases and salts. The blood-corpuscles are dissolved and the blood loses color. The same elimination doubtless occurs in freezing of protoplasm. Experiments cited show that the possibility of "anabiosis" may probably be explained by supposing the decomposition process not to have gone so far as to bring life completely to a standstill. Similar results were obtained in the drying of seeds, and in various animals. It was shown with what tenacity many animals, under most unfavorable circumstances, retain the moisture necessary to life.

In respect to the synthesis by plant cells of the albuminous matter which serves for the formation of protoplasm, O. Loew holds that the living protoplasm is composed of proteids entirely different from the ordinary soluble proteids, as well as from the proteids of dead protoplasm. In other words, if living protoplasm dies, the albuminous constituents change their chemical character. We observe that in the living state a faculty of autoxidation (respiration) exists, which is wanting in the dead condition; and Pflüger, in 1875, drew from this the conclusion that in protoplasm the chemical constitution of the living proteids changes at the moment of death. Among the considerations that induce acceptance of this logical conclusion are the readiness with which chemical changes occur in organic compounds that are of a labile character, and certain experiments cited by the author to show that the albuminous substance formed by synthesis in living plants is different even before it has become protoplasm from ordinary albumen. On treating living plant cells with dilute solutions of ammonia or organic bases or their salts, either numerous minute granules are formed or else little globules are produced, which, flowing together, make relatively large drops of a substance of high refractory power. The former is the action of most bases, and the latter is the result when weak bases, like caffein or antipyrin, are applied. The latter bases in weak solution do not injuriously affect the protoplasm itself; but the cells are soon killed by other bases and their salts. The granules and globules formed in the living cells by the action of caffein have been called by Bokomy and the author *proteosomes*. They give the principal reactions of albuminous bodies, but contain in most cases an admixture of small quantities of lecithin and tannin. These admixtures can, however, be removed by cultivating the objects in solutions rich in tannin. If now by such cultivation the tannin has been removed and the proteosomes are then produced by treatment with caffein, we can observe that these albuminous proteosomes are capable of reducing silver from even highly diluted alkaline solutions. This property is lost after treatment with acids, and after the death of the cells, as when they are treated with ether vapor, etc. In these cases the proteosomes become hollow and turbid, they coagulate and shrink, and they lose their property of being re-

50 cents a barrel at the wells, while the barrels used in carrying it cost $3.50. The charges for teaming were enormous, and became higher as new wells were opened at greater distances from Alleghany river and Oil creek, the only water outlets from the oil district. A lack of water in these streams led to the damming of them until a large number of loaded flatboats had gathered at the dam. The dam was then broken, and the boats were floated to Oil City and other places where the railroads could be reached. The transportation by railroad was first in barrels, then in wooden tank cars, and finally in tank cars made of boiler iron. In 1862 the cost of carrying a barrel to New York was $8, but this had dropped to $6 in 1865. The iron tank cars caused a still further decrease, but not enough to show that transportation by rail would ever make oil as cheap as it should be. Experiments with pipes had already been made on a small scale in 1861; but they were failures. In 1865 a line of four miles of pipe was built from Pithole to the wells of Miller's Farm. The teamsters, realizing the danger to their business, tore up the pipes as fast as they were

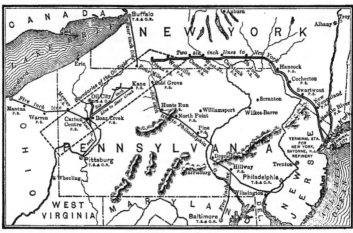

MAP SHOWING THE PIPE-LINES.

soluble in distilled water. There are thus experimental grounds for the conclusion that both the organized albumen of the living protoplasm and the albumen dissolved in the vacuoles—the unorganized albumen—are a different substance from the ordinary albumen, which is present in dead cells.

PIPE-LINES, for conveying crude petroleum or natural gas, have an important place in the transportation of those articles. The original use, for petroleum, was due to the excessive cost of transportation by older methods. In the early days of the oil production in western Pennsylvania, about 1860, the crude oil cost but

laid. They finally yielded, and other short lines were then built, so that by 1877 about ten companies had gridironed the oil district. These companies were consolidated into the United Pipe Line Company, now succeeded by the National Transit Company. This, together with the Tide-Water Pipe Company, is supposed to be controlled by, or to act in unison with, the Standard Oil Company. Of late a rival pipe-line, the United States, is trying to reach the seaboard; and the obstruction offered by the older lines is being fought in the courts. The difficulty lies in the fact that pipe-line companies have the right of eminent domain in Pennsylvania and West Virginia, while in the State of New York they have not that right. The building of the longer lines was begun in 1880 by the United Pipe-Line Company, under a charter granted by Pennsylvania in 1875. The chief lines now built are these: Olean, N. Y., to Saddle river, N. J., 300 miles; Milway to Baltimore, 70 miles; Hilliards, Pa., to Cleveland, 100 miles; Carbon Centre, Pa., to Pittsburg, 60 miles; Four Mile, N. Y., to Buffalo, 70 miles; and Colegrove, Pa., to Philadelphia, 300 miles. The first of these, known as the Seaboard, has a branch line extending under the Hudson and East rivers and across Central Park to Newtown creek and Hunter's Point on Long Island. The termini of all these lines are at refineries, where the crude product is made ready for the market. The pipes are buried under about 2 feet of earth, to escape the variations of temperature. They are laid as nearly in a straight line as possible, and no regard is paid to the topography of the country otherwise. Their diameter is usually 6 inches, and their material, wrought or cast iron, capable of withstanding a pressure of 2,000 pounds to the square inch. Pumping stations are, on an average, about 30 miles apart; but where the pipes are level the oil can be forced with powerful pumps as far as 100 miles. The pumps have a double action—that of forcing and sucking—so that a barrel moves along in about five seconds, an accurate account being kept at each station of all the oil passing through. The pumping goes on by night as well as by day, and the whole length of the line is carefully watched for leaks. Obstructions are removed by automatic scrapers, inserted at one station and removed at the next, which move three or four miles an hour. The tanks of every producer are measured, and an account is kept of the oil he lets into the pipe. He is given a receipt for this amount, which is negotiable paper. The unit of value is a barrel of 43 gallons. In 1865 the range was from $4.62½ to $8.25 a barrel, monthly average; while on the same basis the even dollar a barrel was reached for the first time in 1873; and in November, 1874, the monthly average price fell to 55 cents. In 1891 there was an average monthly production of over 93,000 barrels—the highest since 1882. In 1889, 5,489 new mills were completed; in 1890, 6,358; and in 1891, 3,300.

Oil has not been produced in West Virginia to as great an extent as the supply would warrant. Kentucky and Tennessee will yet produce considerable oil, because the oil-bearing lands underlie portions of those States. Thus far the trials in Texas and Louisiana have not been productive of good results. But, as in salt, whenever the Northern fields give out there will be a chance for the Southern fields to supply the deficiency. The annual exports are decreasing, owing to the increase in home consumption.

Pipe-lines for conveying pulverized coal are said to be feasible, and experiments to that end are now making.

The piping of natural gas is a more simple matter than the piping of oil, less forcing being required, on account of the buoyancy of the article to be transported. The history of natural gas in the United States dates from 1821, when a well was opened at Fredonia, Chautauqua

County, N. Y., and the supply was applied in a small way to illuminating and heating. More than fifty-five years elapsed before its practical utilization for both light and fuel, when in 1878 a large gas well was opened at Murraysville, Pa. The well was on fire for five years, after which the gas was captured and led through pipes to Pittsburg. Since that time new fields of natural gas have been opened in Pennsylvania, West Virginia, Ohio, Indiana, and Illinois; and pipe-lines extend to Buffalo, Cleveland, Chicago, Indianapolis, and many smaller places along the lines. The piping was over 4,600 miles in 1888, and in 1892 it was estimated at nearly 10,000 miles. The annual displacement of coal has averaged about 13,000,000 tons since 1888, with the exception of 1892, when the supply of natural gas showed signs of exhaustion. As the wells become weak, new wells are drawn on, while the old wells have a chance to recuperate. The gas is produced, along with petroleum, in the Devonian slates; but exhausted wells may be drilled deeper into the Trenton limestone, where gas in larger quantities has been found.

PORTUGAL, a monarchy in southern Europe. The Government rests on the Constitutional Charter, which was granted by King Pedro IV, April 29, 1826, and amended on July 5, 1852, Nov. 23, 1859, and July 24, 1884. There are four powers recognized in the state by the Constitution—the legislative, the executive. the judicial, and the moderating authority, which latter is vested in the sovereign. The legislative power is vested in two Chambers, the House of Peers and the House of Deputies. The House of Peers consists at present of 254 members, of whom 52 were hereditary peers, 13 continental bishops, 139 life peers appointed by the King, and 50 elected members. By the law of 1885 hereditary peerages were abolished and the number of life peers reduced to 100, which, however, is to be accomplished gradually, and until the number is reduced to 100 the King can only appoint 1 peer for every 3 vacancies that take place. The hereditary peers and their immediate successors who were living at the time of the passage of the law will continue to enjoy their privileges. The House of Deputies is composed of 180 members, of whom 168 are from the Continent, Madeira, and the Azores, and 12 from the colonies. They are elected by direct suffrage. All persons twenty-one years of age who can read and write, and who have a clear annual income of 100 milreis, or are heads of families, are qualified to vote.

The reigning King is Carlos I, born Sept. 28, 1863, son of Luis I and Pia, daughter of King Vittorio Emmanuele of Italy. He married Marie Amalie, daughter of Philippe, Duc d'Orléans, the Comte de Paris, on May 22, 1886, and succeeded to the throne at the death of his father, Oct. 19, 1889. The executive authority vests, under the sovereign, in a responsible Cabinet, which was composed at the beginning of 1892 of the following members: Prime Minister and Minister of War, J. C. d'Abreu e Sousa; Minister of the Interior, La Vaz de Sampaio e Mello; Minister of Finance, M. C. de Carvalho; Minister of Justice, A. A. de Moraes Carvalho; Minister of Marine and the Colonies, J. Marques de Vilhena; Minister of Foreign Affairs, Count de Valbom; Minister of Public Works, of Commerce, and of Industry, J. Ferreira Franco Pinto Castello Branco.

Area and Population.—The area of continental Portugal, together with the Azores and Madeira, which are regarded as an integral part of the kingdom, is 34,038 square miles. The population, according to the census taken in 1881, was 4,708,178, composed mainly of Portuguese, a strong element of gypsies, and a considerable intermixture of Arabs, Jews, French, English, Dutch, and Frisians, and in the coast towns about 3,000 negroes.

Army and Navy.—By the law of Sept. 12, 1887, military service is made obligatory for every man after he has passed his twentieth year. The duration of service is twelve years, of which three years are spent with the colors, five years in the first reserve, and four years in the second reserve. The contingent raised annually by conscription numbers 10,000 men, and all persons not entering the active service form part of the second reserve for twelve years. By the law of 1884 the peace footing of the army is fixed at 24 regiments of infantry, 12 regiments of chasseurs, 10 regiments of cavalry, 3 regiments of mounted artillery, 1 brigade of mountain artillery, 1 regiment and 4 batteries of garrison artillery, and 1 regiment of engineers. The peace effective of the permanent army for 1892 was 2,089 officers, 25,658 men, and 3,985 horses and mules. The municipal guard was composed of 79 officers, 2,176 men, and 415 horses; and the fiscal guard numbered 178 officers, 4,791 men, and 362 horses. The rifle used by the infantry and cavalry is of the Kropatschek system, a repeater of a caliber of 8 millimetres.

The navy in 1892 consisted of 1 ironclad of 3,200 horse power, carrying 9 guns; 6 corvettes, armed with 48 guns; 14 first-class gunboats, with 53 guns; 7 stationary gunboats, with 16 guns; 9 small gunboats, with 20 guns; 2 armed transports; 5 torpedo boats; and 3 other steamers. In 1892 the navy had 258 officers and 4,360 sailors.

Commerce.—The total value of the special imports of merchandise in 1891 amounted to 39,529,946 milreis, and the exports to 21,378,330 milreis. The imports of precious metals were 8,269,727 milreis, and the exports 29,803,648 milreis. The principal articles of importation and their values were: Cereals, 5,015,000 milreis; cotton goods, 2,663,000 milreis; machinery and instruments, 2,468,000 milreis; iron, 2,244,000 milreis; coal, 2,182,000 milreis; sugar, 1,876,000 milreis; woolens, 1,638,000 milreis; codfish, 1,608,000 milreis; raw cotton, 1,591,000 milreis; railroad material, 1,351,000 milreis; chemicals, 1,264,000 milreis; animals, 1,075,000 milreis; timber, 1,040,000 milreis; wool, 903,000 milreis; hides and skins, 873,000 milreis; silk, 859,000 milreis; rice, 733,000 milreis; coffee, 586,000 milreis; butter and cheese, 542,000 milreis. The chief exports were: Wine, 10,122,000 milreis; cork, 2,951,000 milreis; fish, 1,416,000 milreis; copper, 1,033,000 milreis; animals, 403,000 milreis; onions, 288,000 milreis. The trade with the leading countries in 1888 was as follows: Great Britain, imports 12,088,618 milreis, exports 7,827,923 milreis; France, imports 4,980,-526 milreis, exports 5,207,395 milreis; Germany,

imports 4,712,150 milreis, exports 1,902,589 milreis; United States, imports 4,483,784 milreis, exports 553,606 milreis; Spain, imports 2,550,-674 milreis, exports 939,236 milreis; Brazil, imports 2,148,470 milreis, exports 4,104,622 milreis; Belgium, imports 1,444,882 milreis, exports 376,039 milreis. A commercial treaty between Portugal and Brazil was signed Jan. 15, 1892.

Shipping and Navigation.—The merchant marine of Portugal numbered on Jan. 1, 1891, 553 vessels, of which 67 were steamers and 486 sailing vessels, of an aggregate tonnage of about 35,050 tons. The coasting vessels have a total tonnage of 210,312 cubic metres. In 1891, 8,708 steamers, of 5,181,000 tons, and 2,554 sailing vessels, of 583,000 tons, entered the ports of Portugal, while 3,721 steamers, of 5,187,000 tons, and 2,720 sailing vessels, of 351.000 tons, cleared.

Railroads, Posts, and Telegraphs.—On Jan. 1, 1891, there were 2,149 kilometres of railroads in operation, and 155 kilometres under construction. In 1890 there were transmitted through the post office 21,054,000 domestic letters, 4,317,000 domestic postal cards, and 19,483,-000 domestic printed matter; while the international department handled 6,422,000 letters, 246,000 postal cards, and 5,140,000 pieces of printed matter. Money transmitted by letter or postal order amounted to 28,429,000 francs. The total length of the state telegraph lines in 1888 was 6,090 kilometres, and the length of the wires was 13,894 kilometres. The number of internal dispatches was 547,101, while the number of international dispatches was 512,081. The receipts of the combined postal and telegraph service in 1890 amounted to 5,794,260 francs, and the expenses to 6,629,895 francs.

Finances.—The budget for 1892–'93 estimated the receipts at 46,724,159 milreis, of which 10,-290,500 milreis were derived from direct imposts, 2,139,000 milreis from registration, 1,610,300 milreis from stamped paper, 460,000 milreis from lotteries, 23,342,737 milreis from indirect taxes, 1,994,000 milreis from supplemental duties, 3,848,378 milreis from Government property, and 3,039,244 milreis were *recettes d'ordre*. The expenses were estimated at 48,018,961 milreis, of which 31,234,597 milreis were for the Ministry of Finance, 2,315,977 milreis for the Ministry of the Interior, 1,057,709 milreis for the Ministries of Public Worship and Justice, 5,703,041 milreis for the Ministry of War, 2,854,909 milries for the Ministry of Marine and the Colonies, 458,893 milreis for the Ministry of Foreign Affairs, 4,331,370 milreis for the Ministry of Public Works, and 62,465 milreis for the savings banks.

The funded debt of Portugal in the beginning of 1890–'91 amounted to 533,316,612 milreis, of which 261,989,866 milreis were external bonds bearing interest at 3 per cent., 218,057,466 milreis were internal 3-per-cent. bonds, and 53,-269,280 milreis were 4½- and 5-per-cent. bonds. The extraordinary debt, raised by the treasury in the years 1886–'90, amounted to 45,915,000 milreis; treasury bills issued in 1890 amounted to 16,500,000 milreis; and the floating debt was 23,000,000 milreis. In 1890 a loan of 9,300,000 milreis was brought out in Paris. The revenues of the Government were insufficient to pay the interest on the loans, and the condition of the finances was such that a financial crisis arose in

1891. In order to save the country from bankruptcy, stringent measures had to be adopted. According to the report of the Minister of Finance, Oliveira Martins, who was a member of the new cabinet appointed Jan. 16, 1892, the budget of 1890-'91 had closed with a deficit of 11,550,000 milreis, which was equal to nearly 29 per cent. of the receipts, and he calculated a deficit of 10,000,000 milreis for the budget of 1891-'92, equal to 25 per cent. of the public receipts. The floating debt, at the time of his entering office, he stated to be 23,012,000 milreis, which, however, might be reduced by half if the assets of the Government, consisting of money advances to various commercial undertakings, such as banks, railroads, and an opera company, could be realized. He estimated the sacrifices to be made by the creditors, officials, and taxpayers at 8,500,000 milreis, and administrative economies, together with taxes on the manufacture of matches and alcohol at 1,500,000 milreis, thus covering the deficit of 10,000,000 milreis. The following economics were proposed by the Government and passed by the Cortes : (1) To levy from public functionaries 5 per cent. on annual incomes of from 400 to 600 milreis, 10 per cent. on those from 600 to 900 milreis, 15 per cent. on incomes of 900 to 1,500 milreis, and 20 per cent. on incomes of and above 1,500 milreis. Ministers of the Crown, bishops, diplomatists, and consuls are exempted from this charge, but no public official will be allowed to receive an annual salary exceeding 2,000 milreis after March, 1, 1892. (2) The supplementary tax of 6 per cent. created in July, 1890, on the amount of every kind of taxes paid is increased on taxes exceeding 10 milreis to 10 per cent., on those exceeding 100 milreis, to 12 per cent., and on every 100 milreis 2 per cent. more, until it reaches 20 per cent. on taxes of and above 500 milreis. (3) The income tax on all lands, including the internal public debt, and also the external when the interest on the latter is paid in Portugal, is increased to 30 per cent., the internal and external bondholders to have the option of being exempt from this tax if they agree to join the convention entered into with the exterior debt bondholders. (4) To negotiate a convention with the holders of the foreign debt by which, payment in gold being guaranteed and the bonds included in one series or maintained in the existing series, holders could convert them into a maximum of half their capital value, or accept a payment of half their interest in treasury cedulas with their interest amortizable with or without premiums, the nonconventioned bondholders to be subject to the *régime* of the interior debt. In order to assure to the national foreign creditors the regular and complete payment of interest and amortization, the Government is to assign such state revenues as it considers necessary for this purpose. The above-mentioned taxes to be enforced from the date of the publication of these proposals until the expiration of the economical year 1892-'93, and the Cortes to fix annually new taxes reduced in accordance with the necessities of preserving an equilibrium in the budget for future economical years. While thus serious sacrifices were imposed upon the people, the King, immediately after the passage of the measure, voluntarily relinquished one fifth of his civil list, as a contribution to the general effort. As a further measure of economy, the suppression of the Ministry of Public Instruction was adopted. On Sept. 16, 1892, a decree was issued announcing that Deputies would in future receive no pecuniary indemnity from the treasury. According to the power granted to the Government, a convention of the foreign bondholders was called at Paris, and an agreement was reached between Señor Serpa Pimentel, who acted as commissioner for the Portuguese Government, and the bondholders' committees who represented the creditors, who were mostly French, English, Dutch, and German subjects. By this agreement the payment of the coupons would be reduced 50 per cent. for five years, after which time the payments should gradually be increased until 1926, when payment in full was to be resumed. The Portuguese Government, however, refused to ratify this agreement, and issued a decree on June 13, 1892, reducing the payments on the coupons to one third of their nominal value, until the next meeting of the Cortes, which would regulate the future payments. The report of the ministers, which was published together with the decree, explained that the agreement as reached by the convention in Paris would at best only defer the crisis for a few years, but that it was not even probable that Portugal could live up to its promises under the existing condition of the finances, and that bankruptcy would have been the inevitable result had the Government ratified the agreement. The holders of the exterior debt were treated exactly like those of the internal, and that to foreign creditors even facilities were offered to exchange their bonds for those of the internal debt.

The German Government, through its ambassador at Lisbon, Count Bray, protested against the action of the Portuguese Government, as violating the rights of the German creditors. In reply, the Portuguese Government stated that it was with sincere regret that it was compelled to take action in regard to the debt, but that it was imperative to do so.

Cabinet Changes.—On Jan. 1, 1892, the Royal Portuguese Railroad neglected to pay its coupons, and at a meeting held by the bondholders it was decided to investigate the management of the company. The Minister of Finance, Marianho de Carvalho, who before his appointment to office had been superintendent of the company, had advanced to the railroad company 13,000,000 francs as Minister of Finance, without informing the Government of his action. When the investigation was started his action was discovered, and he was obliged to resign. He was accused of it openly in the Cortes, and set up as a defense that without this advance to the railroad company, which was thereby enabled to pay its coupons, the capital for the payment of the interest on the public debt could not have been procured; that he could have saved himself by sacrificing the country, but that he had preferred to follow the course he had taken, and sacrifice himself in order to save the country. Owing to the difficulties connected with the Ministry of Finance, none of the ministers could be induced to undertake that burden, and consequently the whole Cabinet tendered its resignation on Jan. 15, 1892. Count Valbom was called upon to form a new Cabinet, but was unsuccessful. On Jan. 16 the King summoned Señor Dias Ferreira, and charged him with the organization of a Cabinet. His attempts proved successful, and the new Cabinet was approved of by the King on Jan. 17. It was composed of the following members: Premier and Minister of the Interior, José Dias Ferreira; Minister of Finance, Oliveira Martins; Minister of Foreign Affairs, Costa Lobo; Minister of Public Works, Viscount Chancelleiros; Minister of Justice, Antonio Ayres de Gouveia; Minister of War, General Pinheiro Furtado Coelho; Minister of Marine, Captain Ferreira do Amaral. The ministry went before the Cortes with the programme of economical and financial reconstruction, as explained above. In presenting the new ministers, Señor Ferreira remarked that the country required a Government of concord and conciliation, that for this reason it had not been formed directly from the members of either of the two great political parties, and that the Government understood its mission to be to maintain perfect neutrality as regarded politics.

On May 27, 1892, Minister of Finance Oliveira Martins, Minister of Public Works Chancelleiros, and Minister of Foreign Affairs Costa Lobo tendered their resignation. No reason was given, but it was stated that owing to differences in the Cabinet connected with the agreement entered into with the foreign bondholders those ministers were obliged to take this step. The Cabinet as composed after the reconstruction was as follows: Prime Minister and Minister of Finance, Dias Ferreira, who also took the Ministry of the Interior *ad interim ;* Minister of Justice, Telles Pereira de Vasconcellas; Minister of War, Pinheiro Furtado; Minister of Foreign Affairs, the Bishop of Bethsaida; Minister of Marine, Ferreira do Amaral; Minister of Public Works, Pedro Victor. On Dec. 23, 1892, the Minister of Foreign Affairs, the Bishop of Bethsaida, resigned, and his place was filled by Ferreira do Amaral, the Minister of Marine.

Elections.—General elections for the Chamber of Deputies were held Oct. 23, 1892. The result was favorable to the Government. Of the 149 Deputies elected, 62 were Regeneradores, 43 Progressists, 29 Conservative Regeneradores, 11 Independents, and 4 Republicans. Some surprise was created by the defeat of the Premier, Dias Ferreira, as he had been returned as Deputy from the District of Aveiro for twenty years.

Colonial Possessions.—The Portuguese colonies are situated in Africa and Asia. Those in Africa include the Cape Verd Islands, Portuguese Guinea, Prince's and St. Thomas Islands, Angola, Ambriz, Benguela, Mossamedes, Portuguese Congo, and East Africa, with an aggregate area of 916,100 square miles and a population of 11,781,970. The possessions in Asia comprise Goa, Damao, and Diu in India, Macao in the China Sea, and the Archipelago of Timor and Kambing, with an aggregate area of 7,900 square miles and a population of 868,570.

According to a decree issued on Sept. 30, 1891, the colony of Mozambique was constituted as the Free State of East Africa. It was divided into two provinces, Mozambique, north of the river Zambesi, and Lourenço Marques, south of that river. The province of Mozambique includes the district of that name, and that of Quilimane and 3 intendencies in the region conceded to the Cape Delgado Company. The province of Lourenço Marques embraces, besides the district of that name, 3 intendencies in the region granted to the Inhambane Company and 3 in the region conceded to the Mozambique Company. A royal commissioner is appointed for three years, who administers the government but hopes are entertained that the state will become self-governing.

POSTAL CARDS were first suggested by the postal authorities of Prussia, in 1865, but the plan was abandoned. In 1869 Austria began to issue "correspondence cards." Prussia then adopted the plan, and during the Franco-Prussian War of 1870 the cards were given to the German soldiers without charge. The United States adopted the postal card in May, 1873. The factory for postal cards was first at Springfield, Mass., and then at Castleton, N. Y., on the Hudson river, 7 miles below Albany. They have been made in Shelton, Conn., since 1890.

The contract, advertised for by the Postmaster-General, covers a space of four years, but it may be taken away if the product is not up to the standard shown by the samples given to each bidder. Every card must be of an even size, thickness, and weight. Until very lately only three sizes and weights were offered to the bidders. A recent contract was made as follows:

SIZES.	Size in inches.	Color.	Weight per 1,000.	Price for making and printing per 1,000.
Size 1....	$2\frac{18}{} \times 4\frac{8}{}$	Pearl gray.	5 lbs. 12 oz.	37 cents.
Size 2....	$3 \times 5\frac{1}{}$	Buff.	5 lbs. 5 oz.	35 cents.
Size 3....	$3\frac{1}{4} \times 6\frac{1}{4}$	Buff.	9 lbs. 1 oz.	50 cents.

This contract did not call for the "International card," as there were on hand, belonging to the Government, about 3,000,000 such cards, or more than enough for four years. The size of the international card is the same as that of size 2. Of late another card, the "Paid reply," has been issued. It is rather larger than size 2, and it is folded double at the top, so that the part for the reply can be separated from the original card. By far the largest product, about 400,000,000 yearly, is that of size 2, while the total of all cards issued by the United States Government reaches nearly 1,000,000,000 annually. Although they belong to the Government, they are in the custody of the contractor, and are boxed and issued by him without expense to the Government. Several shipments are made from the factory every week to the Grand Central Depot in New York city, where the cases and pouches are transferred and shipped to their respective destinations. From the beginning of the manufacture to the final delivery every postal card is under the direct eye of the Government. The factory is in the especial charge of the third Assistant Postmaster-General, who appoints an agent to represent him, and this agent is allowed several clerks. He had 7 before the establishing of the subagencies, but now he has only 3. There are subagencies in Chicago, Washington, and St. Louis for the distribution of cards. Requisitions are made every day from the Post-Office Department in Washington. The subagencies order large quantities at intervals, the order from Chicago being from 20,000,000 to 25,000,000, and from St. Louis 10,000,000 to 15,000,000. New York, Boston, Philadelphia, and Cincinnati have 4,000,-000 to 5,000,000 at each shipment. No post office is allowed to take fewer than 500 cards, and any order for fewer than 3,000 is carried in mail bags or pouches. The wooden cases containing larger quantities are carried as fast freight.

In drawing the contract, the Postmaster-General reserves the right to change the printed design, the color or quality of the ink, and even the weight of the cards. If the contractor is at expense for any of these changes, the difference is made up to him; and if he is the gainer, some of his pay is deducted. The former contracts specified explicitly the formula for manufacturing the postal-card paper. It was "75 per cent. of number 2 country rags, and 25 per cent. of chemical wood pulp." The present contract was awarded upon the samples noted above, the bidders being allowed to offer such qualities "as they shall consider suitable for postal-card use." Nothing was said about the formula. It is therefore allowable to use wood or other paper having no rags in its composition, but showing a tensile strength beyond the requirements of the contract. Whatever the material, the paper must be well "calendered"—that is, it must be pressed to a uniform weight and thickness, and finished upon both sides so that it will take equally well the printer's ink, the writer's ink, and the lead pencil. Without calendering, both kinds of ink would spread, and make the card useless.

If rags are used they are first sorted. All the stray money is taken out of old pockets, and buttons and other hard substances are removed. A chipping machine cuts even the largest rags into small bits, and a blower drives out the dust. Then come a succession of baths, and a cleaning process by means of chloride of lime and other chemicals. By this time the old rags are not recognizable in the clean, pasty product, that feels pleasant and has an odor not unlike the mushroom. Wood pulp and rag pulp meet in one of the vats, which has a kind of steamboat wheel to mix the two kinds of mash and keep them moving. If wood pulp alone is used, the corded pulp is picked to pieces and mixed in the vat until it becomes of the same pasty consistency as the rag pulp. The pulp is lifted from the vat and placed upon a strainer so that it may lose as much as possible of its water. The edge of the mass finds itself drawn into one end of a paper or card making machine about 60 feet long. Soon it begins to hang together, and then it passes under and over numerous rollers heated by steam from within. It grows thinner and harder at every step, until it reaches the other end in the shape of a long roll of cardboard, ready for the printer after it has been calendered and cut into sheets 21 by 30¼ inches (the size of 40 postal cards), or larger sheets containing 100 cards. A former contractor cut some of his cards into rolls 4 cards wide, and fed them into a printing machine. The present contractor has adopted machines that feed from a continuous roll at the rate of 300 cards a minute. The Government furnishes the plates for printing. They are of the hardest steel, and their life is about two years. The contractor, who is under bonds

of $300,000, is held responsible for their safety, as much as he is held for the safety of the cards that are printed. All spoiled cards are destroyed in the presence of a Government official, and the contractor has no pay for them. An attachment to some of the presses cuts and counts the cards. It also straps them in packages of 25, and the cost of the little paper strap is $1,200 a year. The former contractor cut the printed sheets lengthwise on a "slitter," and crosswise on a rotary "cutter." The machines were operated by girls, who counted, sorted, and bound; and their expertness was remarkable. They would count the 25 cards in a package while the visitor had difficulty in counting 5. Counting by hand has been abandoned for the most part. Twenty packages, or 500 cards, fill a pasteboard box; but quantities of 2,000, 4,000, 6,000, 8,000, 12,000, 16,000, and 25,000 are packed in wooden cases.

PRESBYTERIANS. I. The Presbyterian Church in the United States of America.— The following is the summary of the statistics of this Church for 1892: Number of synods, 30; of presbyteries, 217; of candidates, 1,280; of licentiates, 431; of ministers, 6,331; of elders, 24,790; of deacons, 8,099; of churches, 7,208; of churches organized during the year, 196; of communicants, 830,179; added during the year on examination, 57,478; of adult baptisms, 20,-859; of infant baptisms, 25,762; of members of Sabbath schools, 894,628. Amount of contributions: For home missions, $998,111; for foreign missions, $812,793; for education, $141,661; for Sunday-school work, $129,806; for church erection, $309,022; for the Relief fund, $102,414; for the freedmen, $131,822; for sustentation, $71,-192; for the General Assembly, $80,908;* for aid for colleges, $159,915; for congregational purposes, $10,033,128; miscellaneous contributions, $1,314,790; total contributions, $14,-285,562.

Benevolent Societies.—The receipts of the Freedmen's Board had amounted to more than $172,000, while its expenditures had been about the same. It had employed 371 missionaries, had aided 300 churches and missions, and maintained 80 parochial and 14 boarding schools, with a total of 9,229 pupils. It had also under its charge 276 schools, with 18,221 pupils. Two new school buildings had been erected at a cost of $24,000. Property for church and school purposes had been bought at Richmond, Asheville, and Little Rock. Ten new churches had been organized during the year.

The total receipts of the Board of Home Missions for the year ending in May were $925,949, and the total income available for its current work was $843,353. The debt had been reduced by $31,253 during the year, and was now $67,-092. Fourteen hundred and seventy-nine missionaries and 360 missionary teachers had been employed, and returned 8,808 additions on profession of faith during the year, a total membership of 93,504, with 132,651 persons in congregations, 3,368 adult baptisms, 4,680 infant baptisms, 360 Sunday schools organized, and a total of 2,190 Sunday schools, with a membership of 141,236. One hundred and seven new churches had been organized, and 52 churches had become self-sus-

* Includes synodical and presbyterial expenses.

taining during the year, and 111 church buildings had been erected.

The Board of Foreign Missions had received during the year $931,292. The missions—among the Seneca, Nez Perces, and Dakota Indians in Mexico, Guatemala, United States of Colombia, Brazil, Chili, West Africa, India, Laos, China, Japan, Corea, Persia, Syria, and among the Chinese and Japanese in the United States—returned 210 American and 420 native ministers, 386 American and 1,108 native lay missionaries, 384 churches, with 30,479 communicants and 3,430 added during the year, 771 schools, with 29,011 pupils, 26,393 pupils in Sabbath schools, 167 students for the ministry, and $38,731 contributed by the native churches.

General Assembly.—The General Assembly met at Portland, Ore., May 19. The Rev. William C. Young, D. D., of Danville, Ky., was chosen moderator. The Committee on a Consensus Creed reported that, since its last report, action looking to the formation of such a creed had been taken by several churches, among which were the Free Church of Scotland, the Presbyterian Church in England, the Reformed Church of England, the Reformed Church in America, the Presbyterian Church in Canada, the Cumberland Presbyterian Church, the Reformed Church of Hanover, the Presbyterian Church in New South Wales, the Christian Missionary Church of Belgium, and the Evangelical Syriac Church of Persia. The committee had prepared a creed consisting of twenty-two articles. This creed was not submitted to the General Assembly for action, because it was the desire of the committee first to arrive at an understanding with the committees appointed on the same subject by sister churches. In reply to overtures asking for the preparation of a shorter creed, the Assembly replied that as the subjects of the Consensus Creed and of the Revision of the Confession of Faith would necessarily occupy the attention of the Church for a considerable time to come, it was inexpedient to introduce another kindred question at this time. The committee appointed to confer with the Board of Directors of Union Theological Seminary concerning its relation to the General Assembly, reported concerning the discussions it had held with that body, the result of which was that it was found impossible to harmonize the conflicting views as to the meaning of the Theological Seminary compact of 1870. The board adhered strenuously to the opinion that the General Assembly had no right under the compact to veto the transfer of a professor, and the committee under its instructions could do nothing more than to report the results of its work to the General Assembly. It was believed, however, that the joint conference prepared the way, in a large degree, for a better understanding between the Assembly and the seminary, and, in the hope that an adjustment might be reached in the near future, a paper was prepared by both bodies, and signed jointly by their respective representatives, recognizing the fact that there was a wide difference of opinion between the parties in the matter of the interpretation of the agreement or compact of 1870, and suggesting that something like the following might be done:

1. Each party may fully respect the opinions of the other, and conclude for the present that the difference is irreconcilable.

2. The seminary might report to the next General Assembly substantially that their understanding of the compact differed from that of the General Assembly as applied to transfers, and that, although the Assembly had disapproved the appointment of Dr. Briggs, the directors had not seen their way clear, in view of their obligations, to do other than continue him in the active duties of his office.

3. The committee, on the other hand, might report the facts to the General Assembly, and in view of the relations of the parties, and in recognition of their honest difference, recommend that the *status quo* be recognized, in the hope that some action may be taken which may lead to a harmonious adjustment of all the matters at issue.

The trustees of the seminary submitted a supplementary report defining their position in the matter. They regarded themselves solemnly bound by their interpretation of the agreement, and must discharge their duties as directors accordingly. They saw no reason to modify their understanding of the agreement. The board's concessions to the General Assembly included only one thing—viz., the right to disapprove the election or appointment of a professor. If Dr. Briggs had been elected or appointed to the chair of Biblical Theology, the disapproval of the Assembly would have been decisive with them. But a professor could be elected only according to the laws of the institution, and according to those laws Dr. Briggs was not elected. The report was accompanied by a memorial setting forth more explicitly the points of difference. In its final action the Assembly approved the interpretation of the compact of 1870, as expressed by the action of the Assembly of 1891; declined to be a party to the breaking of the compact with Union Theological Seminary; expressed the persuasion that the Church should have direct connection with its theological seminaries and control over them; appointed a committee to take into consideration the whole subject of the relation of the Assembly to its theological seminaries; to confer with the directors of those seminaries, and to report to the next General Assembly such action as may result in a still closer relation between the Assembly and its seminaries than that which at the time existed; recognized the *status quo* as to the different interpretations given by the directors of Union Seminary from that given by the Assembly's Committee of Conference, and, in accordance with the proposition suggested by the Committee of Conference, agreed to submit the difference of interpretation of the compact as to transfers to a committee of arbitration; and made provisions for the selection of arbitrators. A minute was adopted reminding all under the care of the General Assembly

That it is a fundamental doctrine that the Old and New Testaments are the inspired and infallible Word of God. Our Church holds that the inspired Word, as it came from God, is without error. The assertion of the contrary can not but shake the confidence of the people in the sacred books. All who enter office in our Church solemnly profess to receive them as the only infallible rule of faith and practice.

If they change their belief on this point, Christian honor demands that they should withdraw from our ministry. They have no right to use the pulpit or the chair of the professor for the dissemination of their errors until they are dealt out by the slow process of discipline. But if any do so act, their presbyteries should speedily interpose and deal with them for a violation of ordination vows. The vow taken at the beginning is obligatory until the party taking it is honorably and properly released.

Majority and minority reports were presented from the Judicial Committee on the matter of the appeal from the judgment of the Presbytery of New York dismissing the case of the prosecution against Prof. Briggs. The question was as to the régularity of the appeal to the General Assembly over the head of the Synod. The majority report found the appeal in order, and recommended proceeding under it. The minority report recommended that the appeal be not entertained, that the papers be returned to the appellants, and that they be advised to bring their appeal or complaint before the Synod of New York. The Assembly decided, by a vote of 429 to 87, that the appeal be sustained, and ordered the case removed to the Presbytery of New York for a new trial,

With directions to said Presbytery to proceed to pass upon and determine the sufficiency of the charges and specifications in form and legal effect, and permit the Prosecuting Committee to amend the specifications of charges, not changing the general nature of the same, if, in the furtherance of justice, it be necessary to amend, so that the case may be brought to issue and tried on the merits thereof as speedily as may be practicable.

The Special Committee on the Co-operation of Churches reported that it had carried on an extensive correspondence, within and without the Church, on the subject, and had conferred with the Secretary of the (Congregational) American Missionary Association. The results of the conference and correspondence could be stated only in the most general terms, but they furnished an intelligent basis for the recommendations which the committee had to make. Facts had been developed in correspondence with respect to the excessive multiplication of feeble churches, the continuance for many years of churches that give no sign of achieving self-support, and the rivalry of allied denominations in the same mission field, that abundantly justified the action of the Assembly in appointing a committee to inquire into the matter. The committee recommended certain measures intended to make missionaries, synods, and presbyteries more careful in starting new enterprises and in maintaining unproductive ones, and advised the holding of a joint conference of allied denominations on the subject.

The judgment of the Assembly was expressed by resolution, that "all public moneys expended upon the education of the Indian ought to be expended exclusively by the Government officers upon Government schools," and that "the practice of appropriating public money for the support of sectarian schools among the Indians, as is now done in the contract schools, ought at once to cease"; and it approved "all efforts to secure the constitutional prohibition of all appropriations of public moneys to sectarian schools either by States or by the General Government." It further gave its adhesion to a proposed sixteenth amendment to the Constitution of the United States forbidding the States to aid sectarian schools.

The Committee on Revision of the Confession of Faith reported upon the meetings which it had held for the examination of the expressions of the presbyteries upon the proposed revised confession which had been sent down to them by the preceding General Assembly. It had been found impossible to meet the individual preferences of every presbytery without setting aside what were known to be the views of a large majority of the Church. Nor was it practicable to take up and act upon the thirty-five requests for a new creed, because the committee felt that it should prosecute its work in the line marked out and within the restrictions imposed upon it by the General Assembly. The report contained 28 overtures, each covering a change proposed to the Confession. This report was sent down to the presbyteries for their action upon it, each of the overtures to be considered separately.

Union Theological Seminary.—The General Assembly having refused the request of the Directors of Union Theological Seminary that it consent to annulling the compact of 1870, by which the Assembly was given a veto power in the election of professors, the Board of Directors met Oct. 13, and, fortified by the opinion of counsel that the entering into the compact was outside the powers conferred by the charter, decided, by a vote of 19 to 1, to break the connection between the seminary and the General Assembly. The minute adopted as embodying this action recites that

There is no provision whatever in our charter or constitution for " the principle of synodical or Assembly supervision." The Committees on Reunion and both Assemblies in 1869 recognized this important fact, and advised the introduction of that principle into our Constitution. Upon this advice no action was taken. The Constitution was not changed; therefore the seminary could not rightfully give, and the Assembly could not rightfully receive or exercise, the veto power under our existing charter and Constitution.

Since the action of the General Assembly at Portland, our board has obtained the best legal advice as to the points at issue between the seminary and the Assembly. This advice leaves us no room to doubt that, under the laws of the State of New York, the attempted agreement of 1870 was beyond the powers of the Board of Directors of the seminary. We " can not abdicate any of our official duties in whole or in part."

Therefore, as the sole directors of Union Theological Seminary, we are compelled by the practical considerations presented in our memorial, and by constitutional and legal considerations, to maintain our rights and to fulfill our chartered obligations, which can be neither surrendered nor shared. In this action we regret deeply that we have been refused that concurrence of the Assembly which we respectfully asked, and which would have done much toward softening the past and relieving the present. Obliged to act alone for the protection of the institution committed to our care, and actuated by sincere regard for the highest interests both of Union Seminary and of the Church we love, we do now

Resolve, That the resolution passed May 16, 1870, adopting the memorial to the General Assembly of the Presbyterian Church in the United States of America, which provided that all appointments of professors "shall be reported to the General Assembly, and no such appointment of professor shall be considered as a complete election if disapproved by a majority vote of the Assembly," be, and the same hereby is, rescinded.

And that the said arrangement between the Union Theological Seminary in the city of New York and the General Assembly of the Presbyterian Church in the United States of America be, and the same is hereby, terminated; thus reinstating the relations between the seminary and the General Assembly as they existed prior to May, 1870.

The Case of Prof. Briggs.—At the meeting of the Synod of New York, held in Albany, Oct. 18, complaints were presented concerning the action of the Presbytery of New York in dismissing the case of Prof. Briggs. Of these, decisive action was taken upon the complaint of Rev. Dr. Francis Brown against the rulings of the moderator of the presbytery, that the committee which had preferred the charges against Prof. Briggs was a committee of prosecution as provided for in the Book of Discipline, and as such was an original party, and virtually and practically independent of the presbytery. The complaint argued that the committee was not thus constituted, but was the creature of the presbytery, and that its appeal against the decision of the presbytery in dismissing the case was virtually an appeal of the presbytery against itself. The synod refused, by a vote of 122 to 40, to sustain the complaint, and adopted the following minute:

In the matter of the Briggs case the committee find the complaint to be in order, but recommend that it is inexpedient to take action at the present time, because the case, through the action of the General Assembly and of the Presbyter of New York, is again before the presbytery, and the complainants will there have their remedy in their own hands. And in case the remedy there be found insufficient, they will afterward have opportunity by appeal or complaint to bring the case again before the synod.

The new trial of Prof. Charles A. Briggs was begun in the Presbytery of New York, obediently to the directions of the General Assembly, Nov. 9. A new indictment had been prepared, including some new charges and variant readings of the old charges, making the whole number of charges 8. The amended charges, without the specifications by which they were supported, are as follow:

1. The Presbyterian Church in the United States of America charges the Rev. Charles A. Briggs, D.D., being a minister of the said Church and a member of the Presbytery of New York, with teaching that the reason is a fountain of divine authority which may and does savingly enlighten men, even such men as reject the Scriptures as the authoritative proclamation of the will of God and reject also the way of salvation through the mediation and sacrifice of the Son of God as revealed therein; which is contrary to the essential doctrine of the Holy Scripture and of the standards of the said Church, that the Holy Scripture is most necessary and the rule of faith and practice.

2. With teaching that the Church is a fountain of divine authority which, apart from the Holy Scripture, may and does savingly enlighten men; which is contrary to the essential doctrine of the Holy Scripture and of the standards of the said Church, that the Holy Scripture is most necessary and the rule of faith and practice.

3. With teaching that errors may have existed in the original text of the Holy Scripture as it came from its authors; which is contrary to the essential doctrine taught in the Holy Scripture and in the standards of the said Church, that the Holy Scripture

is the Word of God written, immediately inspired, and the rule of faith and practice.

4. With teaching that many of the Old Testament predictions have been reversed by history, and that the great body of Messianic prediction has not been and can not be fulfilled; which is contrary to the essential doctrine of Holy Scripture and of the standards of the said Church, that God is true, omniscient, and unchangeable.

5. With teaching that Moses is not the author of the Pentateuch; which is contrary to direct statements of Holy Scripture and to the essential doctrines of the standards of the said Church, that the Holy Scripture evidences itself to be the Word of God by the consent of all the parts, and that the infallible rule of interpretation of Scripture is the Scripture itself.

6. With teaching that Isaiah is not the author of half of the book that bears his name; which is contrary to direct statements of Holy Scripture and to the essential doctrines of the standards of the said Church, that the Holy Scripture evidences itself to be the Word of God by the consent of all the par s, and that the infallible rule of interpretation of Scripture is the Scripture itself.

7. With teaching that the processes of redemption extend to the world to come in the case of many who die in sin; which is contrary to the essential doctrine of Holy Scripture and the standards of the said Church, that the processes of redemption are limited to this world.

8. With teaching that sanctification is not complete at death; which is contrary to the essential doctrine of Holy Scripture and of the standards of the said Church, that the souls of believers are at their death at once made perfect in holiness.

Besides presenting a demurrer to the validity of the indictment, Prof. Briggs offered objections to the fourth and seventh charges as consisting of new matter. The trial then proceeded on the other six charges. The vote of the presbytery was taken Dec. 30, and resulted in a verdict of "Not sustained" on all the charges, as follows: First charge, 59 to sustain and 69 not to sustain; second charge, 55 to 72; third charge, 61 to 72; fourth charge (numbered 5 in the indictment given above), 54 to 72; fifth charge (numbered 6), 48 to 76; sixth charge (numbered 8), 57 to 69. In the minute recording its verdict, adopted Jan. 9, 1893, the presbytery explained:

The presbytery have kept in mind these established principles of our polity, "that no man can rightly be convicted of heresy by inference or implication"; that in the interpretation of ambiguous expressions "candor requires that a court should favor the accused by putting upon his words the more favorable rather than the less favorable construction"; and that "there are truths and forms with respect to which men of good character may differ."

Giving due consideration to the defendant's explanations of the language used in his inaugural address, accepting his frank and full disclaimer of the interpretation which has been put upon some of its phrases and illustrations, crediting his affirmations of loyalty to the standards of the Church and to the Holy Scriptures as the only infallible rule of faith and practice, the presbytery do not find that he has transgressed the limits of liberty allowed under our Constitution to scholarship and opinion.

Therefore, without expressing approval of the critical or theological views embodied in the inaugural address, or the manner in which they have been expressed and illustrated, the presbytery pronounces the Rev. Charles A. Briggs, D.D., fully acquitted of the offenses alleged against him—the several charges and specifications accepted for probation having been "not sustained." . . .

Accordingly, the presbytery, making full recognition of the ability, sincerity and patience with which the Committee of Prosecution have performed the onerous duty imposed upon them, do now, to the extent of their constitutional power, relieve said committee from further responsibility in connection with this case. In so doing the presbytery are not undertaking to decide how far that committee is subject to the authority of the body appointing them, but they intend by this action to express their earnest conviction that the grave issues involved in this case will be more wisely and justly determined by calm investigation and fraternal discussion than by judicial arraignment and process.

In view of the present disquietude in the Presbyterian Church, and of the obligation resting upon all Christians to walk in charity and to have tender concern for the consciences of their brethren, the presbytery earnestly counsels its members to avoid, on the one hand, hasty or overconfident statement of private opinion on points concerning which the profound and reverent students of God's Word are not yet agreed, and, on the other hand, suspicions and charges of false teaching which are not clearly capable of proof.

Moreover, the presbytery advises and exhorts all subject to its authority to regard the many and great things in which we agree rather than the few minor things in which we differ, and, turning from the paths of controversy, to devote their energies to the great and urgent work of the Church, which is the proclamation of the gospel and the edifying of the body of Christ.

The Prosecuting Committee in January, 1893, filed notice of an appeal to the General Assembly.

The Trial of Prof. Smith.—The Rev. Henry Preserved Smith, D. D., Professor of Hebrew in Lane Theological Seminary, was tried before the Presbytery of Cincinnati in November for heresy, on charges based upon articles which he had published in the "New York Evangelist," and on the teachings contained in a pamphlet written by him entitled "Biblical Scholarship and Inspiration." The charges, which were supported by specifications consisting of citations from the article and from the pamphlet, were three in number, and as follow:

CHARGE I.—The Presbyterian Church charges the Rev. Henry Preserved Smith, D. D., with teaching, contrary to the regulations and practice of the Church founded on the Holy Scriptures and set forth in the Constitution of said Church, that a minister in said Church may abandon the essential features of the system of doctrine held by said Church, and which he received and adopted at his ordination, and rightfully retain his position as a minister.

CHARGE II.—The Rev. Henry Preserved Smith is charged with teaching, in a pamphlet entitled "Bible Scholarship and Inspiration," contrary to a fundamental doctrine of the Word of God and the Confession of Faith, that the Holy Spirit did not so control the inspired writers in their composition of the Holy Scriptures as to make their utterances absolutely truthful—viz., free from error when interpreted in their natural and intended sense.

CHARGE III.—The Presbyterian Church in the United States of America charge that the Rev. Henry Preserved Smith, D. D., a minister in said Church, a member of the Presbytery of Cincinnati, in a pamphlet entitled "Biblical Scholarship and Inspiration," while alleging that the Holy Scriptures are inspired, and an infallible rule of faith and practice, with denying, in fact, their inspiration in the sense in which inspiration is attributed to the Holy Scriptures, by the Holy Scriptures themselves, and by the Confession of Faith.

Prof. Smith's demurrer and objections to the charges and specifications were overruled, and the presbytery found, Dec. 9 and 12, that the first charge was not sustained (vote 28 affirmative, 31 negative); while the second charge was sustained (vote 38 to 20), and the third charge was sustained (vote 32 to 26). The presbytery, therefore, sitting as a court, gave its judgment that Prof. Smith be suspended from the ministry of the Presbyterian Church,

Until such time as he shall make manifest to the satisfaction of the presbytery his renunciation of the errors he has been found to hold, and his solemn purpose no longer to teach or propagate them. At the same time the presbytery expresses the kindest feelings toward Prof. Smith, and it makes this disposition of the case because the interests of truth imperatively demand it.

The vote on this sentence was 31 affirmative and 26 negative. The Executive Committee of the Board of Trustees of Lane Seminary afterward requested Prof. Smith to continue his work at the seminary till a meeting of the Board of Trustees should be held.

II. Presbyterian Church in the United States.—The following is a summary of the statistics of this Church as they were reported to the General Assembly in May, 1892: Number of synods, 13; of presbyteries, 72; of ministers, 1,239: of candidates, 409; of licentiates, 64; of churches, 2,572; of churches organized during the year, 92; of ruling elders, 7,859; of deacons, 6,128; of communicants, 182,516; added on examination during the year, 11,224; of adults baptized, 3,835; of infants baptized, 5,025; of baptized noncommunicants, 35,905; of teachers in Sabbath schools, 16,271; of pupils in Sabbath schools, 118,852. Amounts of contributions: For sustentation, $47,011; for evangelization, $90,189; for the Invalid fund, $15,485; for foreign missions, $118,442; for education, $47,937; for publication, $9,264; for colored evangelization, $8,855; for church erection, $40,829; for the Bible cause. $5,459; presbyterial contributions, $16,201; for pastors' salaries, $776,592; for congregational purposes, $627,876; miscellaneous contributions, $117,490. Total contributions, $1,921,630.

The Executive Committee on Colored Evangelization reported that its receipts for the year had been $10,438, and that its beneficiaries had received an average of $85.40 each. The secretary had traveled extensively within the Church, and some in the North, where he had delivered three addresses at important meetings, on "The Evangelization of the Negro." The Executive Committee of Education had expended $30,000, and had 261 candidates for the ministry enrolled. The sum of $10,359 had been contributed in aid of the publishing interests of the Church. The sales from the depository had amounted to nearly $37,000; the net assets had increased $8,857 during the year, making the total net assets $93,055. The receipts of the Executive Committee of Home Missions for Sustentation, Church Extension, and the Evangelistic and Invalid funds, had been $81,730, or $12,119 more than those of the preceding year. Two hundred and thirty-four ministers serving weak congregations had been aided from the Sustentation fund, and 29 infirm ministers, 104 widows of ministers, and 9 children of ministers had been assisted from the Invalid fund.

The total receipts of the Executive Committee of Foreign Missions for the year had been $130,-276, or $17,325 in excess of the receipts of any previous year. One hundred and two missionaries were at work, as follow: 33 in China, 28 in Brazil, 6 in Mexico, 4 to the Greeks, 2 in Italy, 23 in Japan, 4 in the Congo Free State, and 2 in Cuba. One hundred and twenty-three native helpers had been employed, and the number of communicants was 2,702, 301 of whom had been received by baptism during the year. An autonomous church, with a local synod, has been formed in Greece, with which the older churches established under the mission have been incorporated.

The General Assembly met at Hot Springs, Ark., May 19. The report of the Standing Committee on Colored Evangelization commended the work that was already accomplished in behalf of that cause, and advised an increase of financial support to it of $200,000. The committee was empowered by the Assembly to confer with the Freedmen's Board of the Presbyterian Church of the United States of America " to ascertain whether there is not some basis of co-operation or united effort in the religious culture of the negro." A commissioner who had been appointed to assist in the organization of a synod of colored Presbyterians reported that that object had not yet been effected. A committee appointed to consider the subject reported in favor of the organization of a colored synod, which for the present should be in connection with the General Assembly. An *ad interim* committee was appointed, with power, if it should deem it advisable, to call a conference of all the colored ministers connected with the Church, " to confer with them about organizing an independent Presbyterian Church, and any other matter pertaining to the best interests of Presbyterianism among the colored people."

The Executive Committee of Foreign Missions was authorized to confer with the Board of Foreign Missions of the Northern Church with reference to co-operation in the foreign mission field. A proposition for the observation of "a week of self-denial" in behalf of foreign missions was not favored, the feeling of the Assembly appearing to be that such an expedient should not be adopted except on the occasion of an emergency. The Assembly refused to approve the appointment of financial agents in the synods for the purpose of visiting the churches and raising money for foreign missions. An effort was made in favor of the institution of more stringent regulations concerning the furnishing of aid to students for the ministry; but the Assembly decided to make no change in its system of beneficiary education. On the consideration of the report of the Executive Committee of Home Missions, the Assembly recorded its disapproval of the employment of paid financial agents to solicit contributions. An *ad interim* committee was appointed to consider the relations of the home mission work of the General Assembly and the home mission work of the synods and presbyteries, and the means of bringing them into harmony. The work of revision of the Directory of Worship, which has

been going on for several years in the Assembly's committee, was continued by referring it to a new committee, to which the presbyteries are invited to send their views. to be incorporated in the work if the committee deem it desirable. On the question of the proper kind of wine to be used in the sacrament of the Lord's Supper, diverse reports were made by the committee to which the subject was referred. The Assembly decided that the ordinary fermented wine was the scriptural wine, but that the validity of the sacrament was not affected by the use of unfermented grape juice.

On an invitation of the Northern General Assembly to petition Congress against the opening of the Columbian Fair on Sunday, and against permitting the sale of liquor within its gates, the Assembly decided that, while it was opposed to any mingling of the affairs of Church and state, this was a matter in which the interests of religion and the Church are vitally concerned, and the particular occasion was a critical one, and to join in the petition.

III. United Presbyterian Church in North America.—The following is the summary of the statistics of this Church as they were reported to the General Assembly in May, 1892 : Number of synods, 10 ; of presbyteries, 60 ; of ministers, 791 ; of licentiates, 61 ; of students of theology, 92 ; of ruling elders, 3,619 ; of congregations, 920 ; of pastoral charges, 158 ; of mission stations, 169 ; of new mission stations during the year, 11 ; of members, 109,018 ; of members received on profession, 6,975 ; of baptisms, 1,661 of adults and 4,149 of infants ; of Sabbath schools, 1,090, with 11,415 officers and teachers, and 98,859 pupils ; of young people's societies, 589, with 23,094 members. Amounts of contributions : For salaries of ministers, $543,400 ; for congregational purposes, $401,-690 ; for the boards, $267,023 ; for general purposes, $74,175 ; total, $1,286,288 ; average per member, $13.38 ; average salary of pastors, $1,025.

The thirty-fourth General Assembly met in Allegheny, Pa., May 26. The Rev. David McGill, D. D., was chosen moderator. The Committee on Federation of Churches, appointed by the preceding General Assembly, reported that it had called a conference which only a few delegates attended, some of the churches having apparently overlooked the matter. Those who met submitted a statement to the churches interested, and requested the appointment of delegates to another conference. The report explained that this was not a movement for a consensus creed, but for such a federation as would provide for a General Council to take action in relation to subjects common to all, and to unite the moral forces of the Church against prevailing evils. The Woman's Board reported that its receipts for the year had been $35,869, and its expenditures $39,552. It had during the year separated the work of church extension from that of home missions, and appointed a secretary for it. Its work in the home mission department had increased. The work of the board was approved by the Assembly, and its zeal and efficiency were commended. In consonance with the recommendation of a committee which had been appointed to consider

PRESBYTERIANS.

the relations of the board to the other boards of the Church, the Assembly declared the relation to be that of an auxiliary, and it adopted a minute more closely setting forth the fact. The board was given the right, which was already enjoyed by the other boards, of appearing and speaking in the General Assembly through its representatives. The Permanent Committee on Theological Seminaries having recommended action relative to the Assembly having a veto power in the election of professors, and control of the seminaries in other points, the Judiciary Committee reported that, as now constituted, the Assembly had no power so to interfere in the affairs and work of the existing seminaries. This report was adopted, and a committee was appointed to prepare and submit to the next General Assembly a form of overture on the powers of the Assembly over the seminaries. Memorials were received from the Presbytery of Sealkote, India, asking for the organization of three new presbyteries and of the Synod of Punjaub; from members of the same presbytery requesting the General Assembly to define the relation between the foreign missionaries and the native ministers; and from the session, asking for a deliverance on the duties and powers of the presbytery and its members. These requests brought up the question of the amount of authority to be given to the native ministers, and of the extent to which they shall be allowed to participate in the control of the funds and in the general management of the mission. They were referred to the Board of Missions, to be reported upon at the next General Assembly. The lower courts of the Church were admonished to enforce the law of the Church on the subject of psalmody, "as prohibiting the use of uninspired songs in the worship of God under any or all circumstances." The proper committee was instructed to bring in an overture amending the Book of Government so as to limit the right of appeal to the Assembly to matters of doctrine, and the interpretation and rules and regulations in discipline and the order of worship. The report on reform reiterated and emphasized the previous declarations of the General Assembly concerning prison and divorce reform, secret oath-bound societies, temperance, and the observance of the Sabbath; condemned the Chinese exclusion act; and declared it not within the province of the Assembly to give a deliverance on the question of giving women the right to vote for members of Congress. The work of the American Sabbath Union was commended.

The negotiations for union with the Associate Reformed Synod of the South have suffered a delay in consequence of difference of views concerning the position to be given in the new standards to the fourteenth, fifteenth, and sixteenth articles in the "Testimony" of the United Presbyterian Church (concerning secret societies and slavery).

IV. Cumberland Presbyterian Church.— The following is a summary of the statistics of this Church as they were reported to the General Assembly in May: Number of presbyteries, 124; of congregations, 2,916; of ordained ministers, 1,670; of additions to the Church, 14,862; of communicants, 171,009. *Contributions:* For church erection, $9,428; for ministerial relief, $9,868; for ministerial education, $10,525; for home missions, $22,499; for foreign missions, $20,431. Total contributions, $794,576.

The sixty-second General Assembly met in Memphis, Tenn., May 19. The Rev. W. S. Danley, D. D., of Missouri, was chosen moderator. The Board of Education had received $10,665, and had aided 90 students during the year. The Board of Missions and Church Erection had received $42,885, of which $20,431 were for foreign missions and $22,498 for home missions, while a small sum was described as "other receipts." Of the total sum, $12,305 had been received through the Woman's Boards. Favorable reports were received from the mission in Japan, which is connected with the United Church of Christ in that country; in Mexico, where there are stations at Aguas Calientes and Guanajuato; and in the Cherokee, Chickasaw, and Choctaw Nations of Indians. In the Home Mission department missions are maintained in 30 cities. The total resources of the Church Erection fund were $9,428, and $4,485 had been expended on its account. The total contributions to the Ministerial Relief fund had been $9,868, and the total income $10,-392, while $5,897 had been paid to beneficiaries. A woman's department had been found helpful by the board. The Board of Publication reported the completion of the new building at a cost, for building and land, of $81,603. The profits of the year had been $7,405. The question having been asked the Assembly by a presbytery, whether a woman can be ordained as an elder, it was referred to a committee, from which a majority report denying the legality of such ordination, and a minority report affirming it, were presented. The minority report was adopted. It finds that there is no prohibitory law against the ordination and installation of women as ruling elders, and recommended that the Assembly declare that the same may be done where it shall appear needful. A protest was entered against this action. The Assembly decided that the presbyteries have authority to license exhorters or lay preachers; but it denied that any presbytery could set up a standard of scholarship for an ordained minister. A motion that the mission in Japan be withdrawn from its connection with the United Church and its work be made strictly denominational, was defeated, and the Assembly decided that the existing relations should not be disturbed. The Young People's Society of Christian Endeavor was commended, and a separate denominational organization was decided against as hurtful and unwise. The Assembly declared that while unwilling to commit the Church to the advocacy of any political platform, it was not willing that the danger of so doing should deter it from an unqualified declaration in favor of the prohibition, by legislative enactment, of the manufacture and sale of intoxicating liquors. Positive prohibition was the only consistent position for the Church to take on that question. Action was taken on several points pertaining to the constitution and work of the Boards of Publication and Education.

Cumberland Presbyterian Church (Colored).— This Church was organized in May, 1869, at Murfreesborough, Tenn., under the direction of the General Assembly of the Cumberland Presbyterian Church, and was constituted of colored ministers and members who had been connected with that Church. Its first presbytery was formed in 1870, its first synod in 1871, and its General Assembly in 1874. It has the same doctrinal symbol as the parent body and the same system of government and discipline. According to the report of the United States census, it has 23 presbyteries, and is represented in 9 States and 1 Territory, and has 238 congregations, all but 37 of which worship in their own buildings: 13,439 communicants, and church property (192 edifices) valued at $202,961, or an average value of $1,053 to each edifice.

V. Presbyterian Church in Canada.—The following is a summary of the statistics of this Church for the year ending April 30, 1892: Number of synods, 5; of presbyteries, 43; of persons belonging to the Church, 525,236 (the Dominion statistics give 765,189); of families, 92,483; of single persons not connected with families in the Church, 16,580; of communicants, 173,904; net increase of communicants during the year, 6,637; number of ministers, 1,000; of elders, 6,106; of other office-bearers, 10,045; of baptisms during the year, 11,762; of members of Sabbath schools and Bible classes, 138,059; of persons engaged in Sabbath-school work, 16,051; of missionaries, catechists and teachers in foreign fields, 257.

Contributions.—For the College fund, $40,105; for the Home Mission fund, $57,027; for augmentation, $32,057; for French evangelization, $29,749; for foreign missions, $93,273; for the Ancient and Infirm Ministers' fund, $26,632; for the Widows' and Orphans' fund, $6,096; for the Assembly fund, $4,492; Sabbath-school and Bible-class contributions, $27,865; amount received for foreign missions by the Woman's Foreign Missionary Society, $39,432; synodal and presbyterial funds, $8,591; contributions for general religious purposes, $108,269.

The eighteenth General Assembly met in Montreal, June 8. The Rev. William Caven, D. D., Principal of Knox College, Toronto, was chosen moderator. The report of the Committee on Statistics showed that there were connected with the Church 850 pastoral charges, 559 mission stations or groups of stations, and 119 vacancies, 919 enrolled ministers and 72 ministers residing in bounds whose names were not enrolled, and 56 licensed students for the ministry. The total income for all purposes was $2,003,239, besides $63,996 contributed from the mission stations. The receipts for home missions had been $78,741, of which $8,000 had been transferred to the Augmentation fund, and appear in its financial statement. The whole number of missionaries was 309, of which 97 were in the Eastern section (including the Maritime provinces and Newfoundland), and 272 in the Western section (including the rest of the Dominion). The widest field for this work was opened in the Northwest and British Columbia. More than 60 missionary stations were supplied by the five college societies. Missions to lumbermen were carried on in the regions of the upper Ottawa and its tributaries. Thirty-one depots and 113 shanties had been visited during the previous winter, with a total expenditure of $403. The total receipts of the Augmentation fund had been $35,621. In ten years 150 congregations, or half the whole number on the fund, had become self-sustaining, and 55 congregations had been put off because unwilling to help themselves vigorously. The following receipts were reported of the several relief funds: Aged and Infirm Ministers' fund (Eastern division), $5,509; Maritime Widows' and Orphans' fund, $5,629; Widows' and Orphans' fund (western section), $59,124. This fund now amounted to $138,650; Ministers' Widows' and Orphans' fund of the Synod of the Presbyterian Church in Canada in connection with the Church of Scotland, $24,785; while the whole amount of the fund was $116,389. The total receipts for foreign missions had been $115,766. Six missions were cared for by the Eastern and Western sections in the New Hebrides, Trinidad (the East Indian coolie population), Central India, Formosa, and Honan in China, and the Indians of the Northwest, to which have recently been added a mission to the Jews in Palestine and a mission to the Chinese in British Columbia. The report of the Board of French Evangelization showed that there were now 20,000 French Protestants in the Province of Quebec, and 15,000 in New England—the latter mostly converts from Quebec or persons who had been converted under the preaching of missionaries trained in Canada. In respect to the theological department of Queen's College, the election of the Board of Trustees and of the professors in which is now outside of the General Assembly, a resolution was adopted calling the attention of the governing body of the institution to the desirability of bringing the theological department into closer relations with the Church, and requesting the board to consider the subject with the view of suggesting some modification by which, if possible, this end may be secured. In order to obviate the disadvantages suffered by the home missionary fields from the fact that the students on whom they largely depend for pastoral supply have to leave them vacant during the winter in order to attend their colleges, the previous General Assembly had referred to the presbyteries the question of establishing a summer session of a theological school. A large majority of the presbyteries had voted in favor of the overture, and the Assembly decided to open the summer session at Manitoba College. The report on Sabbath Observance represented that the advices from the maritime provinces were especially encouraging, particularly with reference to the diminution of Sunday traffic and mechanical labor on the Intercolonial Railway. From other parts of the Dominion the reports were less encouraging, or of an opposite character. Resolutions were adopted reiterating previous declarations of the Assembly on the subject, and disapproving of the opening of post offices on the Lord's Day. A committee was appointed to consider and report to the next General Assembly how the young people of the Church may be organized, under the sanction of the General Assembly, for the cultivation of their spiritual lives and their training for Christian work. The Hymnal Committee was instructed to correspond with committees in Scotland respecting the preparation of a common hymnal.

VI. Church of Scotland.—The General Assembly of the Church of Scotland met in Edinburgh, in May. Prof. A. H. Charteris was chosen moderator. The Committee on Statistics reported that the whole number of members was 597,077, or 3,684 more than in 1890; and that the total contributions for 1891 amounted to £376,000, or £13,416 more than in 1890. The income for the Jewish missions had been £6,541, and the expenditure £5,581. Favorable accounts were received from most of the schools of this mission—which are established at Alexandria, Beyrout, Constantinople, Salonica, and Smyrna, in the Turkish Empire. On the presentation of the report of the Committee on Church Interests reviewing the conditions of the agitation for disestablishment, a resolution was adopted approving the report; instructing the committee to do their utmost to complete the organization of the Committee on Church Defense; approving the action of the committee regarding the reconstruction proposal of the Laymen's League; and recording the readiness of the Assembly to enter into any reasonable arrangement which would make it possible for those now separated from the Church of Scotland to share in the enjoyment of the privilege and heritages of a national Church if they desire to do so. The report on the proper conduct of public worship, which was adopted, recommended that the Lord's Prayer be used at every service; that a table of systematic readings in the Old and New Testaments be drawn up; that the Psalms in prose or metre should occupy a prominent part of the service of praise; that reverence of demeanor should be observed at prayer; and that the Psalmody Committee be directed to print the Apostles' Creed and the Nicene Creed at the end of the Hymnal. The committee appointed by the previous General Assembly to consider the subject of competitive preaching by ministerial candidates, presented a report recommending the institution of an advising committee to assist the congregation in selecting a minister.

VII. Free Church of Scotland.—The General Assembly of the Free Church of Scotland met in Edinburgh, in May. Prof. W. G. Blackie, was chosen moderator. The report on the Declaratory Act, which is intended to remove difficulties and scruples in the way of signing the Confession of Faith (see "Annual Cyclopædia" for 1891), was presented. A resolution was passed declaring that "the Assembly, finding that the overture of a declaratory act anent the Confession of Faith has obtained the requisite approbation from the presbyteries of the Church, pass the same as a declaratory act with the consent of the presbyteries." The vote on this resolution stood 346 in favor of it to 195 against it. The report of the Committee on Church and State, referring to the memorandum of the Laymen's League, said that "the proposal seemed to have awakened no interest in the press or in the country, and it was needless to dwell on the futility of issuing schemes of this kind now." A motion recommending favorable consideration for all practical suggestions directed to the reconstruction of the national Church of Scotland was defeated by a majority of 250. The vote is interpreted as substantially a declaration by the Assembly that with it disestablishment is an indis-

pensable prerequisite to union. The Assembly was informed that the sum of $100,000 had been given it in trust from the estate of Mr. George R. Mackenzie, of New York, the income to be devoted to certain church purposes, viz., half of it to the general sustentation fund, and half to poor congregations in the Highlands.

VIII. United Presbyterian Church in Scotland.—The Synod of the United Presbyterian Church in Scotland met in Edinburgh, May 2. The Rev. Dr. Black, of Glasgow, was chosen moderator. The statistical report showed that 1 congregation and 3 stations had been added during the year, and that the number of communicants was 185,298, showing an increase of 478. The total income for all purposes from congregational sources had been £335,733, or £5,502 more than in the previous year. The missionary and benevolent contributions had increased by £3,270. The whole amount raised for missions, at home and in the mission fields, was £60,713. The Committee on the Disestablishment and Disendowment of the Established Churches of England and Scotland reported concerning measures of defense that had been taken in behalf of the Church of Scotland, by the circulation of leaflets, tracts, and pamphlets, the starting of two newspapers, and speaking by political candidates; but notwithstanding these efforts, it said, public opinion, where it had been tested, had shown itself steadily set in the direction of disestablishment. The synod testified by resolution

Its adherence to the voluntary principle, and its disapproval of civil establishments of religion; rejoiced in the prospect of a speedy termination to the state church system in Scotland and Wales; instructed the committee to continue to oppose grants of public money to denominational training colleges, and enjoined it to watch ever, in the line of previous decisions of the synod, measures designed to confirm and extend the privileges of the Established Church; to use diligence in maintaining and diffusing a knowledge of the synod's distinctive principles; and to support by all suitable means the resolution of Dr. Cameron for the disestablishment and disendowment of the Church of Scotland.

The synod declined to approve an overture sent up by the Greenock Presbytery asking it to declare elders as well as ministers eligible to the office of moderator of the presbytery. An overture asking for the abolition of trials for ordination was approved generally and sent down to the presbyteries. It was held by the movers of the overture that the appointment of the minister and his approval by the congregation showed that he was an approved person; and that the trials were useless, because no minister had ever been kept back from ordination by failure to pass them.

IX. Presbyterian Church in England.—The Synod of the Presbyterian Church in England met in Birmingham, April 25. The statistical report showed that, with 290 congregations, the number of members of the Church had increased during the year from 65,841 to 66,744. The total income had been £235,650. The increase for foreign missions had been £16,016, besides which £8,000 had been raised to clear off liabilities. The staff, etc., in China included 20 ordained European missionaries, 10 medical missionaries, 10 native pastors supported by their congregations, 108 evangelists, 43 theological students, 43 organized congregations, 92 preaching stations, and 3,800 communicants. The Woman's Missionary Association supported about 20 woman missionaries, who labored among the women in China, conducting schools for women and girls, visiting from house to house, and attending in hospitals. The Committee on the Confession made its final report, and was discharged. The clause "Whatever respect some may pay to other days of commemoration, yet do these lack scriptural authority, and may not be enforced as binding on the Christian conscience," was retained, against a motion to strike it out because it might be interpreted as giving an implied sanction to "other days of commemoration." A clause was ordered inserted in the formulas for ordination and licensure recognizing the Articles of Faith as embodying the doctrine set forth in the Confession of Faith.

X. Welsh Calvinistic Methodists.—The General Assembly of the Welsh Calvinistic Methodist Church met at Machynlleth, Montgomeryshire, June 7. The Rev. William James presided as moderator. The report of the statisticians was invested with unusual interest, because of the discussions that had been provoked by the assertion of the Bishop of St. Asaph that dissent, and particularly this denomination, was declining in Wales. The statisticians found that they were able to make a most satisfactory report. The increase in contributions for the year had been £35,000, against £15,000, the largest increase returned in any year previously—in 1872. This was mostly in the additions (£26,000) to the collections for foreign missions: but apart from this, there was an addition of nearly £9,000 to the other collections. The total amount of the collections was £266,718, showed an increase of 1,364 in membership, notwithstanding all the emigration that had taken place. During twenty-four years since statistics had first been collected, there had been no falling off in membership except in 1869, and the collections had fallen off in only four years. A table was published showing that the increase in the connection had been continuous.

XI. General Council of the Presbyterian Alliance. —The fifth General Council of the Alliance of the Reformed Churches holding the Presbyterian system met in Toronto, Ont., Sept. 21. The Rev. W. Garden Blaikie, D. D., of Edinburgh, presided. The Eastern section of the Executive Committee reported concerning the adoption of the plan for raising funds for future meetings by annual contributions according to representation in the Council; concerning visits paid to churches in Bohemia and Moravia, Hanover, Belgium, Holland, France, Spain, Russia, Italy, and Switzerland; concerning efforts to remove obstacles raised by the Turkish Government to the work of missionaries; concerning the visit of a deputation to the International Conference at Brussels; and concerning the visit of Dr. Blaikie to the United States in 1889. The receipts of the treasurer had been £2,706, and he held a balance of £154. A report was presented of the statistics of all the Presbyterian Churches, of which about 90 distinct branches were represented in the Alliance. Many of these

are small, consisting in some cases of a single presbytery, and they are scattered over continental Europe and in the mission fields. The following table presents a condensed statement of the different bodies:

CHURCHES OF—	Churches.	Presbyteries.	Synods.	Ministers.	Communicants.
European continent.	81	221	63	5,602	752,901
United Kingdom...	12	176	54	4,642	1,436,152
Asia	6	14	2	122	16,964
Africa	10	18	6	174	105,872
North America.....	17	658	108	12,782	1,708,543
South America.....	82	5	1	87	8,425
Western islands....	25	6	1	41	10,869
Australia	8	43	4	405	89,590
New Zealand.......	2	14	2	166	19,149
Total..........	...	1,249	236	23,951	4,092,965

Total of licentiates.........................	2,594
" " theological students........	4,169
" " number of Sabbath schools	25,708
" " teachers and officers........................	405,985
" " pupils in attendance........	3,020,765

Papers were read upon "The Protestant Reformation: In its Spiritual Character and its Fruits on the Individual Life," by Prof. Thomas Lindsay, D. D. ; "Its Influence in Communities and Nations on their Moral and Religious Condition," by Prof. H. Bavinck, D. D., of Hampden, Holland; "Upon the Intellectual State and Progress of the Nations at the Time," by Prof. M. Leitch, of Belfast, Ireland; and "Upon its Influence upon the Civic and Political Institutions of the Nations of the Sixteenth Century," by Prof. Henry M. Baird; Upon the General Subject of "Our Reformed and Presbyterian Churches: Their Characteristics and Mission," by the Rev. D. E. Van Horne, D. D.; "Their Strength and Weakness," by Rev. Dr. Monro Gibson; "Their Unsolved Problems and Resources," by the Rev. Evart Van Syke, D. D., and the Rev. E. R. Eschbach, D. D. The reports on foreign mission work included notices of the Union of Presbyterian and Reformed Missions into single ecclesiastical organizations in Japan, Mookhden in north China, Korea, Syria, and Brazil. In this department papers were read on "Native Agents and their Training," "Native Churches and Self-Support," "Relation of Native Churches to the Home Church," "Cultivation of a Missionary Spirit at Home," "A Century of Missions," "The Gospel in the Dark Continent," "Mission Work in the South Seas," "Among the Hindoos," and "The Celestial Empire." Papers under the head of "Training of the Ministry" included those on "The Minister as an Organizer," by the Rev. Ross Taylor, D. D. ; "Training in View of the Drifts of Theological Thought in Apologetics and Criticism," by Principal G. H. Hutton; and "Short Courses of Study," by President W. II. Black. Under the general topic of "Christianity in Relation to Social Problems" were discussed: "The Wage Question," "The Opium Question in India," "The Recreation Question," and "The Drink Question." A sitting was given to the discussion of "Aspects of Romanism" in Europe, Great Britain, Canada, North and South America, and the Foreign Mission Field. A paper by the Rev. James McCosh, D. D., LL. D., on "What Philosophy can do for Religion," was read in his absence. Other papers were read on "The Doctrinal Agreement of the Reformed and Presbyterian Churches," by the Rev. T. W. Chambers, D. D., LL. D.; "The Biblical Idea of the Ministry," by Principal McVicar; and "The Minister as a Teacher," by the Rev. Alexander Oliver, D. D., of Glasgow, Scotland. Reports were made of the work of the American churches among the negro race, the Indian aborigines, the European immigrants, and the Asiatics; of work in the British colonies—in Canada and the Northwest, and in Australia; of work on the European Continent, including the Reformed Church in Germany, missionary work in Belgium, the Waldensian Church in India, and English services on the Continent; and conferences were held on Spiritual Life and the Relation and Duty of the Church to Outside Societies doing Christian work. A Woman's Missionary Conference of the Churches represented in the Alliance was held during the week of the meeting.

PROFIT-SHARING, a term applied to any arrangement whereby labor is rewarded in addition to its ordinary wages, or, in place of wages, by a participation in the profits of the business. The term is somewhat synonymous with the word co-operation. The latter is divided into distributive and productive. Distributive co-operation (known more properly as co-operation) aims to save money to consumers by dispensing with middlemen. A notable instance of success is shown by the Beverly Co-operative Association, organized in Massachusetts in 1875. It began with a capital of $102, which has grown to $7,000. It sells goods nearly at cost, and only a single share can be owned by one person. It pays no dividends and it sells everything. College co-operative societies are represented at Harvard and Yale and the University of Michigan. Some of them sell books, crockery, and tennis goods, and they have direct connections with town tradesmen.

Profit-sharing is the productive or participative branch of co-operation. It should always be known by that term, and not be confounded with distributive co-operation. Of foreign works on the subject, those of Dr. Böhmert, of Dresden, and M. Fougerousse, of Paris, are the most valuable. The latter declares that the simplest system is that which distributes this share in ready money at the close of each year's account without making any conditions as to the disposal of the sums so paid over. This mode is adopted by but a limited group of firms, the most important among which is the piano-forte-making establishment of M. Bord, in Paris. Participation was introduced in 1865, in consequence of a strike, on the following basis: After deduction from the net profits of interest at 10 per cent. on M. Bord's capital embarked in the business, the remainder is divided into two parts. One of these parts is proportional to the amount of interest on capital drawn by M. Bord; the other is proportional to the whole sum paid during the year in wages to the workmen. The former of these two parts goes to M. Bord; the latter is divided among all his employés who can show six months' continuous presence in the house up to the day of the annual distribution. The share obtained by each workman is proportional to the sum that he has

earned in wages, paid at the full market rate during the year in which the division of profits is made. The number of M. Bord's employés is a little over 400, and the sums he has paid in labor dividends average about 14 per cent. on the men's earnings in wages. Profit-sharing was introduced nearly forty years ago, under the auspices of M. Alfred de Courcy, into one of the most important insurance companies of Paris. Five per cent. on the yearly profits is allotted to its staff, which numbers about 250 employés of all grades, whose fixed salaries are at least equal to those paid in non-participating insurance offices at Paris. No part of this share in profits is handed over in annual dividends. Each successive payment is capitalized, and accumulates at 4 per cent. compound interest until the beneficiary has completed twenty-five years of work in the house or is sixty-five years of age. At the expiration of this period he is at liberty either to sink the value of his account in the purchase of a life annuity in the office, or to invest it in French Government or railway securities. Should he decide on the investment, he is allowed to draw only the annual dividends arising from it, as the company retain the stock certificates, and not till after his death abandon their hold on the principal in favor of such persons as he may designate by will to receive it. Leclaire, a house-painter, tried the system among his employés. He finally had his establishment incorporated as a co-operative house, and as such it still exists. The two heads of the firm each receive $1,200 as the compensation for his work as manager; the capital is allowed an interest of 5 per cent; then, one fourth of the profits goes to the two managers, one fourth to a mutual benefit society and insurance fund, and one half to the laborers, who receive shares proportionate to their wages. Not only is the system a financial success, but the painters of the establishment are among the best workmen and most thrifty men in Paris. It is said that more than 100 continental firms are now working on a participatory basis. The principle has been introduced with good results into agriculture; into the administration of railways, banks, and insurance offices; into iron-smelting, type-founding, and cotton-spinning; into the manufacture of tools, paper, chemicals, lucifer matches, soap, cardboard, and cigarette papers; into printing, engraving, cabinet-making, house-painting, and plumbing; into stock-broking, book-selling, the wine trade, and haberdashery. The establishments differ in size and importance as much as in the character of the industry they pursue, from the paper mills of M. Laroche-Joubert, at Angoulême, with their 1,500 workmen, to the establishment of M. Lenoir, in Paris, with its 40 house-painters.

In the United States, profit-sharing dates from the time when the whaling-ships of New England first went out "on shares" to all in any way concerned in the capture. But the form of profit-sharing whereby the worker has somewhat to do with the capital is of more recent years. Perhaps the oldest example of productive co-operation is the Somerset Co-operative Foundry Company of 1867, which has been fairly successful. The origin of all our co-operative concerns shows that they are born from a strike, when men are left to shift for themselves. There are many boot and shoe co-operative companies which have met with great success. Co-operative creameries were established because farmers were bled by middlemen, and in self-defense they pooled their dairy products and turned out butter and cheese. They have that special advantage which a limited production gives. So far the companies give no share of profits in proportion to wages. When profit-sharing and wages are considered together the matter is more complex. The Lynn Knight of Labor Co-operative Boot and Shoe Company, now three years old, marks the newer movement. In 1887 it had a capital of $9,000. It sells its goods in part to the Knights of Labor, but as it makes excellent goods, its wares are in fair demand. Profits are divided in this way: Ten per cent. goes to a sinking fund; 5 per cent. interest is paid on capital stock; 10 per cent. of the remainder goes to the Knights of Labor Association for a co-operative fund to be used in assisting co-operative enterprises; 45 per cent. is to go to capital; and 45 per cent. to labor in proportion to wages. The Cushman Shoe Factory, at Auburn, Me., has recently distributed 4 per cent. upon wages earned. The business was larger by $150,000 under the profit-sharing system than ever before. This was the result of the interest taken by the workers, as is best described in the report of their committee:

How much could you contribute to the profits of the business? You had provided for the firm, now what was to be done to insure you a good profit? Every cent's worth of waste lessened your profit, every cent saved increased it. Every mite of poor work returned (and there has been a good deal the past year) has been the diminishing of your dividend. The dividend might have been 1 per cent. more if we had all realized just how much rested with us. We have seen, time and again, 10 cents wasted by one person in a day. "Oh, that is nothing," you say. Well, if every one of the 700 or 800 wastes that amount in a day, is that anything? Of course this does not happen, but you can see how a mite from all would count up big at the end of the year.

One of the largest granite quarries in the United States, at Westerly, has made a profitable arrangement of this sort: It was agreed that at the end of the year the net income should be divided into three equal parts—one for the laborers, one for the company, and one for a reserve fund. The labor dividend should be paid annually, and before the dividend to capital. No officer, overseer, clerk, or subcontractor should share in the dividend. The true value of all labor contributed should be determined by the amounts earned and credited to each workman as wages for labor performed during the year. Accounts should be examined by auditors mutually agreed upon, and laborers arbitrarily discharged or necessarily deprived of work should not be debarred from receiving their share of the dividend. Disagreements should be settled by arbitration, and a bill of prices should be agreed upon on or before Jan. 1 of each year. No reduction of wages should be made to affect any contract on hand; and in case of an increase of rates on any contract, the difference might be adjusted in making up the dividend. A firm of clothiers in New York city explained its plan to its employés in this way:

The purpose is to set aside a certain percentage of our net gain as ascertained at the end of the year, and with that sum declare a dividend upon the total amount of wages paid to those who work under our own roof. Whoever has earned even so much as a week's wages, will participate, provided he or she was not discharged for cause. Upon the basis of our last year's business you would have received nearly 5 per cent. upon the total of your year's earnings. In other words, the man who drew $20 a week, or $1,040 during the year, would have had a check for nearly $50.

John Wanamaker, of Philadelphia, recently issued a circular declaring that all who have been in the employ of the house for seven years, and those whose term of service shall hereafter reach that length of time, are to participate in the profits of the business. All employés who do not come in the seven year class are to have added to their regular salaries a sum each week graded by their sales. In the clerical, packing, invoice, and various offices, a civil-service system is to be strictly followed in making promotions and advancements. The record of each person in the employ of the house will be carefully kept, and will govern all changes. There will also be a special honor list, "for the more rapid perferment of those showing marked business ability, rapid improvement, diligence, economy, and usefulness." The distribution for the first year was $109,439.68. The employés of the store were called together at the expiration of the second year in May, 1889. At that time $46,082.29 was paid, which, added to $58,263.29 already paid, made a total of $104,345.68. The following statement was made by the proprietor:

In two years we have paid the usual salaries, and exactly $213,785.39 more by this free-will distribution. Not one person, to the best of my knowledge and belief, would have had any larger salary had this plan of distribution not been in force. So that it is out of our pockets into yours, and without any obligation on our part except good will and interest in the welfare of our good people. Under a system of monthly examinations of individual records, all our clerks have had proper consideration according to merit, and perhaps a few salaries have been reduced as above value of services, while many have been advanced without solicitation. This is the present and future policy of the house. The checks given out to-night might all have been larger, and it is a disappointment to me that they are not. You have it in your power, by your enthusiastic and earnest efforts, to increase or diminish what the firm has set aside for this distribution. I wish to do two things by this plan: 1st, to give actual pr f of heartfelt interest to our people; 2d, to solidify the people into one mighty and perfect force, to increase the business for the benefit of themselves and their employers.

In May, 1889, the Bourne Mills corporation of Fall River, Mass., adopted a plan to provide sharing with its employés. It was proposed that every man, woman, and child continuing in the employ of the company from July, 1889, to January, 1890, should receive some share of the profits, to be paid in cash on Feb. 10, 1890, in proportion to the wages earned for the whole six months; and that the total amount divided shall not be less than 6 per cent. of the amount of cash dividends declared and paid to the stockholders during the same time. The only condition was faithful and continuous service, except on account of sickness or any other sufficient reason.

A publishing house in Chicago has tried the profit-sharing system for several years. About twelve years ago, when the capital stock of the firm was $200,000, it induced its foreman and heads of departments to buy 5 shares of stock at par, to be paid for at the rate of not less than $1 a week. Notes bearing 6 per cent. interest were accepted when the employé did not wish to pay in cash. A block of 5 shares more could be purchased at par whenever the first block had been paid for. As the stock advanced in value, all availed themselves of the option. Eight years ago, when the capital stock of this house was increased to $1,000,000, the oldest and most faithful workmen were taken in as partners—that is, allowed to buy stock to the aggregate amount of 1,000 shares. Out of a total force of 600 men, about 50 have already become partners. The results to the firm are great prosperity, largely due to increased zeal and activity among stockholding employés, greater permanency, and a more watchful care to prevent waste of material and of time on the part of non-shareholders. The results to the employés are increased thrift, economy, and sobriety, and a greatly increased self-respect ; also profits to the original 10-share stockholders amounting to 60 per cent. per annum, so that many of them have become property-owners worth from $20,000 to $50,000 ; and 12 per cent. annual profit to the later shareholders, so that many of these are now worth from $10,-000 to $20,000. Their co-operative stock is above par ; but, of course, after they had made the first thousand dollars, other profitable investments helped to swell their fortunes.

An enterprise similar to the old whaling system of profit-sharing was entered into by the menhaden fishermen of New Jersey in 1889. A firm of tin makers in Chicago has declared a dividend of 7·7 per cent. upon earnings, and a manufacturing company of St. Louis 5 per cent. The stockholders of the Toledo, Ann Arbor and Northern Railroad have informed their men that in any dividend year each of them (except the president) who has been five years employed shall receive a dividend upon his wages just as though his total year's earnings were so much stock. The workmen of Proctor & Gamble, soap-makers, of Cincinnati, have accepted a proposal that profits above interest on capital shall form a surplus fund, to be divided between employers and employed in the proportion of capital invested to wages earned. Pillsbury & Co., of Minneapolis, the largest milling firm in the West, have made a division of $40,000 among their employés, in pursuance of a profit-sharing plan adopted four years ago. For two years no money has been divided, but the past year has been profitable and the firm kept its promises. Profit-sharing in Minneapolis has raised the cooper from a wandering mechanic to an important factor in that busy community,

Of course, failure has attended many experiments in profit-sharing. A notable instance was that of a maker of furniture in Albany, N. Y. The profits were to be divided at the end of six months, one fourth going to the proprietor and the remainder to be apportioned among the men. But before the division was made the proprietor deducted from the profits the running expenses of the factory and the interest on the capital in-

vested, leaving only the net profits. During the six months the men received 90 per cent. of their former pay, the remaining 10 per cent. being held back. No account was taken of this deduction, and it did not appear again until the end of the six months, when it appeared in the net profits. This plan differed from the usual co-operative system in that the latter deducts nothing from the wages of the men, but gives them only 25 per cent. of the profits, while the manufacturer receives 75 per cent. By this plan the proprietor received 25 per cent. of the deduction from the men's wages, while they received 75 per cent. of the profits of his business.

It is evident, from the instances given above, that there are three general types of co-operation, or profit-sharing, in manufacturing. The first of these is strictly co-operative, no wages being paid, the gross profits being divided upon some agreed plan between proprietors and employés. The result of this plan has almost invariably been failure. Employés like to share in the profits, but they want a certainty of weekly or monthly wages as a basis. The second plan is to have the employés hold stock, and receive the same wages that are paid in non-co-operative institutions for the same work. This plan has obvious advantages over the first, and has been successfully carried out in numerous instances. The stock owned by the employés was in some cases purchased outright ; in others, paid for gradually out of weekly earnings ; and in others, acquired by the application of profits voluntarily assigned to them by employers. The third plan is to divide among employés a certain percentage of the profits in proportion to the wages earned. This is the simplest plan, and the one generally adopted. It enables employers to retain full and unquestioned control of their business, and when carried out in good faith assures a division of actual profits between the labor and the capital employed. Substantially this plan is in operation in many establishments in this country and Europe, although no two of them, perhaps, are precisely alike. As such an agreement would necessarily be terminated if a strike occurred, strikes are rarely indulged in ; and as the employés are vitally interested in making the profits as large as possible, they work with greater care and cheerfulness. Some employers who have adopted this plan claim that their profits are increased instead of diminished by the division of profits, owing to the better quality and amount of work secured. No one plan, however, can be successfully applied to all kinds of manufacturing business. An unprofitable year is the test of profit-sharing, because it shows whether the worker is willing to be debited for the losses. An instance is known of a concern where a large number of the workmen were small holders of stock. A bad season made it necessary to make an outlay of about $25,000 for improved machinery in order to meet competitors. There was only one way to provide for it, and this was by assessment of the stockholders. The small holders could not see that the investment of further money was for their benefit. Some of them raised the cry of robbery ; and the result was that, in order to save the business, many of them were bought out. They would have made money if they had remained in, but there was no reasoning with them. The moment there was a bad showing for business, the proprietors lost the sympathy of the men. The latter would not permit a reduction of wages, and they even declared that they preferred to go back to the old method of employment in which they had no share of the profits.

To generalize from all these facts, it appears that the great army of the employed desire fixed wages in some shape as a basis upon which profit-sharing may be built afterward; and that the employers who make profit-sharing a success are those who succeeded as small employers a generation ago, before the advent of the great corporations. Co-operation as known in its old form, though proved fairly applicable to distribution, has usually failed when applied to production. In profit-sharing, the element of weakness which was fatal to co-operation—the impossibility of finding men of sufficient ability to manage great producing operations on the terms which co-operation offered—is successfully met by a limited and carefully adjusted proportionate interest of the workmen in the business of their employer, with just so much voice in the management of affairs as their interest entitles them to, and no more. A most valuable work upon profit-sharing has recently been published by Nicholas Paine Gilman. Mr. Gilman believes that the time has come to identify more completely the interests of the wage-earner and the wage-payer, and that, so far as change of method can go, profit-sharing has greater promise of good than anything else that has been suggested.

PROTESTANT EPISCOPAL CHURCH IN THE UNITED STATES. The year 1892, being that of the meeting of the General Convention, was full of interest and importance for Episcopalians. During the last three years efforts have been continued in order to bring about a satisfactory reunion among Protestant Christians, and the proposal made by this Church has been much discussed on the part of the chief denominations in the United States. As was pointed out three years ago, the question as to the "historic episcopate," and in how far that is necessary to constitute and perpetuate a valid ministry, after the pattern of the early Church, is the crucial question. Until this is agreed upon and decided, there appears to be little ground for hope of accomplishing an actual, working reunion. The matter remains in much the same condition in which it has been during past years. Between 1889 and 1892 there has been time for a fair and much needed trial of the proposed changes in the Book of Common Prayer. The convention of the Church, held in Baltimore, in October, 1892, as was expressly required, gave the whole subject most careful consideration, and the revised and amended Prayer Book was finally adopted and published. The Hymnal of the Church, not being quite satisfactory, had been placed in the hands of a commission of experts, in 1889, for further enlargement and enrichment. This commission reported in favor of adopting the Hymnal submitted by them: but, owing to some dissatisfaction in the Church in regard to the omission of a considerable number of old favorites in the existing Hymnal, the matter was not definitely settled by this convention. It

was ordered that the present book be continued as authorized for use until further action be had in the premises. The sources of information in preparing this article are the Journal of the General Convention of 1892, Pott's "Church Almanac," and Whittaker's "Protestant Episcopal Almanac." The following table presents a summary of statistics of Church progress from 1889 to 1892:

PROGRESS BY DIOCESES.

DIOCESES.	Clergy.	Parishes.	Baptisms.	Confirmations.	Communicants.
Alabama	85	59	1,363	1,210	6,196
Albany	184	116	5,768	4,155	17,662
Arkansas	16	20	688	563	2,200
California	105	43	3,597	2,552	9,901
Central New York	109	110	4,790	3,240	16,055
Central Pennsylvania	115	94	4,574	3,279	10,021
Chicago	92	50	1,905	1,188	14,107
Colorado	36	65	1,560	955	4,386
Connecticut	201	150	6,640	4,155	27,874
Delaware	38	37	1,440	719	2,948
East Carolina	27	37	1,046	696	8,474
Easton	38	88	1,152	629	8,169
Florida	50	22	1,716	1,352	4,409
Fond du Lac	29	17	1,331	1,210	8,494
Georgia	89	23	1,477	1,196	5,975
Indiana	49	40	1,642	1,371	6,126
Iowa	56	48	1,859	1,482	6,526
Kansas	85	81	888	1,005	3,100
Kentucky	50	39	1,852	1,615	7,079
Long Island	121	115	8,156	5,498	25,812
Louisiana	29	44	1,786	1,409	5,256
Maine	28	24	989	562	3,060
Maryland	188	127	8,043	5,438	27,787
Massachusetts	208	125	9,680	5,665	29,487
Michigan	81	67	4,696	3,218	13,953
Milwaukee	60	45	2,180	1,865	7,115
Minnesota	108	178	8,430	2,852	8,379
Mississippi	28	44	951	891	8,251
Missouri	45	36	2,811	1,788	4,852
Nebraska	84	19	1,649	1,033	8,844
Newark	102	68	5,586	3,850	16,570
New Hampshire	39	22	960	666	3,015
New Jersey	107	102	4,699	2,820	18,251
New York	868	170	19,952	12,950	54,057
North Carolina	65	45	1,461	1,287	4,986
Ohio	76	77	3,487	2,685	10,227
Oregon	25	14	856	515	2,265
Pennsylvania	240	125	13,705	7,368	38,400
Pittsburg	65	125	4,043	3,040	10,474
Quincy	26	30	649	556	2,423
Rhode Island	62	50	3,558	1,823	10,888
South Carolina	55	68	1,266	1,020	5,179
Southern Ohio	62	48	1,668	1,674	7,830
Springfield	51	24	1,008	790	8,510
Tennessee	41	38	1,588	1,145	6,800
Texas	82	81	1,800	660	8,500
Vermont	38	42	1,166	864	4,244
Virginia	157	148	4,509	4,204	19,042
Western Michigan	25	26	1,510	1,048	4,529
Western New York	105	105	5,252	8,918	16,090
West Missouri	81	26	1,197	807	8,958
West Virginia	27	27	719	569	8,124
MISSIONARY JURISDICTIONS.					
Montana	15	2	680	854	1,514
Nevada and Utah	16	1	676	848	1,848
New Mexico and Arizona	6	17	258	168	696
North Dakota	19	51	562	275	828
Northern California	15	14	631	837	1,162
Northern Texas	14	12	427	407	2,000
South Dakota	27	8	2,886	1,104	2,857
Washington	30	49	1,089	658	2,500
Western Texas	22	15	645	489	1,900
Wyoming and Idaho	84	54	825	172	1,788
The Platte	10	4	878	228	
Cape Palmas	15	9	704	281	1,288
Yedo	18		846	617	1,459
Shanghai and Yangtse Valley	86		1,283	1,285	851
Total	**4,250**	**3,327**	**188,810**	**125,788**	**565,805**

Number of dioceses...............................	52
Number of missionary jurisdictions..................	18
Bishops..	76
Candidates for orders...........................	592
Priests...	3,365
Deacons..	313
Whole number of clergy.........................	4,250
Lay readers.....................................	1,806
Number of parishes.............................	3,327
Church edifices (2,281 being free churches and chapels)...................................	4,581
Rectories......................................	1,521
Baptisms (infants, 147,287; adults, 36,023)........	183,310
Confirmations..................................	125,738
Communicants..................................	505,305
Marriages......................................	49,193
Funerals......................................	96,243
Number of families.............................	209,967
Sunday-school teachers.........................	42,828
Sunday-school scholars.........................	398,378
Pupils in parish schools........................	10,246
Church hospitals...............................	73
Orphanages....................................	49
Homes...	62
Academic institutions..........................	129
Collegiate institutions..........................	19
Theological institutions.........................	20
Other institutions..............................	73

Contributions and offerings:

Diocesan................................	$3,205,884 49
Parochial...............................	33,680,256 56
Beyond the diocese......................	3,780,853 74
Aggregate, or total....................	$40,566,529 79

The General Convention.—This body, which under the constitution of the Protestant Episcopal Church is the supreme legislature of that church, meets triennially, in the place appointed from time to time. In 1886 it met in Chicago, and in 1889 in New York city. In 1892 it assembled in Baltimore, Md., Oct. 5, and continued in session until October 25, inclusive. There were 58 of the bishops present, and clerical and lay deputies from all the dioceses, and delegates from 12 missionary jurisdictions. The convention consists (as it has from the beginning) of two houses, which hold sessions as distinct bodies, viz., the House of Bishops and the House of Clerical and Lay Deputies; but concurrent action is necessary to any complete, valid legislation. In addition to regular business which requires attention, such as amendments to the constitution and canons, reports of standing and special committees, the state of the Church, education and progress, etc., the chief features of interest to Episcopalians in general this year were, the final adoption of the new, revised Prayer Book, with some discussion as to the new Hymnal (referred to above), the largely increased work of the Church at home and abroad, and the like (noted at the beginning of this article).

Domestic and Foreign Missionary Society.—The society which has this as its legal title comprehends all persons who are members of the Protestant Episcopal Church. Its work is conducted by the Board of Missions, which consists of the bishops of the Church, of the members of the House of Deputies, of the delegates from the missionary jurisdictions, and of the Board of Managers. For facilitating business, and securing as full attendance as possible, the board holds its sessions at the same time and place with the General Convention. A Missionary Council is appointed at every triennial meeting of the General Convention, consisting of all the bishops, an equal number of presbyters, and an equal number of laymen. Its meetings are held annually (except in the years when the Board of Missions assembles), and it is charged with taking all necessary action in regard to the missionary work of the Church. The Board of Managers is selected from the Missionary Council, comprising the presiding bishop as president, and 15 other bishops, 15 presbyters, and 15 laymen. This board is charged with the management of the general missions of the Church, and, when the Board of Missions is not in session, it exercises all the corporate powers of the Domestic and Foreign Missionary Society. All other bishops of the Church, together with the secretary and the treasurer of the society and of the Board of Managers, are *ex officio* members of the Board of Missions, but have not the right to vote. The board divides its work between a domestic and a foreign committee, with headquarters, mission rooms, etc., in New York city. The triennial meeting of the Board of Missions was held in Emmanuel Church, Baltimore, Oct. 7, and by adjournment there were held sessions on six other days. The meetings were largely attended, and ardent zeal in the good cause was manifested. Eloquent addresses were made by clergymen and laymen, and high hopes were expressed of being able, by God's help, to increase the efficiency of the society's work both at home and abroad.

Domestic Missions.—Sept. 1, 1891, to Sept. 1, 1892: Missionaries (13 missionary jurisdictions and 34 dioceses): Bishops, 12; other clergy (white, colored, Indian), 535; teachers, other helpers, etc., 60; total, 595. The financial condition was as follows: Cash in hand (September 1891), $33,215.63; offerings, etc., $215,192.35; legacies, $43,961.38; special, $44,671.48; legacies for investment, $27,250. Total, $364,290.74. Expenditures (15 missionary jurisdictions and 36 dioceses), $119,669.16; missions among Indians and colored people, $96,317.42; specials, $44,645.20; office expenses, salaries, printing, etc., $19,613.55; legacies on deposit, etc., $27,492.36; return of trust fund, etc., $29,500; balance in hand, $27,058.05. Total. $364,290.74.

Foreign Missions.—Sept. 1, 1891, to Sept. 1, 1892: Number of missionary bishops, 3; number of clergy (white and native), 65; teachers, physicians, helpers, etc., 237; total, 302. The financial condition was as follows: Cash on hand (September, 1891), $12,841.86; offerings, general fund, legacies, etc., $218,177.43; specials for Africa. China, Japan, Haitian Church, etc., with other specials, $30,173.32; legacies for investment, $27,250; personal loan of the treasurer, etc., $22,189.48. Total, $310,632.09. Expenditures on account of missions, etc. (including Haiti and Mexico), $174,285.96; specials for China, Africa, Japan, with other specials, $27,377.69; salaries, rent, office expenses, etc., with printing, $19,705.91; legacies for investment, $27,400; return of trust funds. loan, etc., $42,689.48; balance in hand, $19,173.05. Total, $310,632.09. The mission property at foreign stations is estimated to be worth in Africa, at Monrovia. Cape Palmas, and other localities, some $42,600; in China, at Shanghai, Wuchang, Hankow, Pekin, etc., fully $170,000; and in Japan, at Tokio, Osaka, and Nara, over $80,500. Total, about $300,000.

Church in Hayti.—This Episcopal Church, though independent, is not strong enough as yet to be self-supporting; consequently it seeks aid from the Episcopal Church in the United States. A commission of the House of Bishops has it in charge, and it receives help from the Domestic and Foreign Missionary Society. Aid was extended during the year to the amount of $8,959.-33. Statistics: Bishop, 1; other clergy, 13: teachers, lay readers, etc., 39. The estimated value of mission property at Port au Prince is $6,480; at Jérémie, $7,500: at Aux Cayes, $3,-300; and at four smaller places, $2,450. Total, $19,730.

Protestant Episcopal Churches in Europe, under the charge of a bishop of the American Church: In France, 2; in Germany, 1; in Italy, 2; in Switzerland, 3; clergy, 7; churches, 6; rectories, 2; hospital, 1. The baptisms numbered 34: confirmations, 56; communicants, 973; marriages. 11: burials, 27; Sabbath-school teachers, 8; Sabbath-school pupils, 91; contributions, $26,605; estimated value of church property, about $25,000.

The Woman's Auxiliary to the Board of Missions renders important and efficient aid in all departments, by means of parochial, city, county, and diocesan associations of ladies, formed for the purpose of raising money, preparing and forwarding boxes to missionaries and mission stations, and in various other ways giving help to the missions of the Church. Money raised for domestic, foreign, Indian, freedmen, and other missions, 1891–'92, $154,-323.72; boxes for the same (4,255), value, $197.-724.21; total in money and boxes, $352,047.93. Entire work of the Woman's Auxiliary in money and boxes for twenty-one years (1871–'92), $3,623,505.60.

The American Church Missionary Society (also auxiliary to the Board of Missions) employs missionaries in both the domestic and foreign departments. It has 47 missionaries laboring in 22 dioceses and missionary jurisdictions. Since 1889 this society has been actively engaged in forwarding missionary work in Brazil and Cuba. In the former are 16 laborers and 10 stations. In the latter, natives of the island do the work, 2 being in orders received in the United States. Several schools have been opened and are well attended. Altogether, the prospect is very encouraging. The financial condition, Sept. 1, 1892, was as follows: Balance, September, 1891, $10,007.40; received for domestic missions, $17,274.43; received for foreign missions, $10,757.47; specials, $708.23; balance, September, 1892, $22,402.43; total, $61,149.96. This society has also in securities, property, etc., $135,500.

Church Work in Mexico.—This is placed under the direct supervision and control of the presiding Bishop of the Protestant Episcopal Church, the constitution of the Mexican Episcopal Church being temporarily in abeyance. There is an advisory committee in the United States to the presiding bishop, consisting of 3 bishops, 7 presbyters, and 9 laymen. The Rev. W. B. Gordon, superintendent, has been succeeded by Rev. Henry Forrester, who is now the priest in charge. Clergy. 6; churches and organized missions, 32; baptisms, 126; communicants, 1,200; in mission schools, 400; value of church property, $46,500.

The American Church Building Fund Commission, established in 1880, continues to do good and efficient work. The trustees in charge keep steadily in view the raising the fund to $1,000,000, as was proposed at the first. In their report (September, 1892) the trustees say as to this point: "While the accumulation of the fund has been much less rapid than was hoped in the beginning, yet we feel that we can thank God and take courage. The great amount of good which has been accomplished by the means at command shows what could be done by a fund of adequate extent, and should be an incentive to generous donations." The fund has increased to date to $225,960.89; in 1889 it stood at a little less than $177,000. More than 200 loans have been made during the year (mostly in small sums from $300 to $500), amounting to $121,701.54.

The Society for promoting Christianity among the Jews (also auxiliary to the Board of Missions) reports fair progress during 1892. The attitude of the Jews toward the work in hand is more encouraging. The society has missionaries diligently occupied in the good cause in six of the large cities. There are 4 missionary day schools, and 8 or 10 other schools. New publications have been added to those formerly issued, and these, with the Holy Scriptures and the Prayer Book, have been put into circulation in English, Hebrew, German, and other languages. Financial condition: Balance in hand Sept. 1, 1891, $1,669.11; total receipts for fiscal year (September, 1891, to September, 1892), $12,978.70 = $14,647.81. Disbursements for the fiscal year, $11,638.51; balance in hand, $3,009.30; total, $14,647.81.

General Condition of the Church's Affairs.—Since the General Convention of 1889, 5 of the bishops have died, viz.: Bishop B. H. Paddock, of Massachusetts; Bishop C. F. Knight, of Milwaukee; Bishop W. J. Boone, of Shanghai; Bishop J. N. Galleher, of Louisiana; and Bishop G. T. Bedell, of Ohio. Eleven out of the ranks of the presbyters have been consecrated bishops, viz.: W. A. Leonard, D. D., Bishop of Ohio; T. F. Davies, D. D., Bishop of Michigan; A. R. Graves, D. D., Missionary Bishop of the Platte; W. F. Nichols, D. D., Assistant Bishop of California; E. R. Atwell, D. D., Bishop of West Missouri; H. M. Jackson, D. D., Assistant Bishop of Alabama; Davis Sessums, D. D., Assistant Bishop of Louisiana; Phillips Brooks, D. D., Bishop of Massachusetts; I. L. Nicholson, D. D., Bishop of Milwaukee; C. K. Nelson, D. D., Bishop of Georgia; and C. R. Hale, D. D., Assistant Bishop of Springfield. The Committee of the House of Deputies on the State of the Church opens its report with gratulations on the final adoption and publication of the new, revised, amended, and enriched Prayer Book, and urges upon both clergy and laity freely and faithfully to use it, not only for personal advantage in spiritual things, but also as an admirable means of spreading abroad the truth of God as this Church holds it. As to Christian unity, no marked results have been reached as yet of efforts in this direction; but in the Pastoral Letter of the Bishops it is urged upon all to be patient, to continue in steadfastness, and to hold out loving hands to all men, so that the

Lord's last prayer shall find its answer. Higher and fuller training is urged in the matter of the ministry, and the power of the living voice is earnestly presented. Parents are affectionately urged anew to the importance of consecrating some one or more of their sons to the sacred ministry, as well as to yield up beloved daughters to the solemn service of ministering in the Lord's behalf where alone they can do the imperatively needed work. Noting, in conclusion, that the Church sends forth this year 7 mission-ary bishops, the Fathers of the Protestant Episcopal Church thus bring their letter to an end: "So, brethren, we are set in our high estate and called to our high and holy calling, to prepare the world which He has redeemed for the coming of its Lord and ours; to watch, and wait, and toil; to do our day's work faithfully, looking in unfaltering hope for the hour when the awakening cry shall ring across all earthly nights and days, 'Behold, the King cometh!' and his knock shall shake the gates of mortal life!"

Q

QUEBEC, PROVINCE OF. The most prominent political event of 1891, in this province, was the fall of the local Premier, Count Mercier, and his colleagues, and the advent to power of the De Boucherville administration. The new ministers were at once confronted by the necessity of adopting direct taxation as the only means by which the Government could be carried on. The following preamble, common to three different provincial acts, assented to on June 24, 1892, explains the position in which M. De Boucherville and his colleagues found themselves:

Whereas, The funded debt of this province, on the 30th of January, 1887, was $18,155,013.33, and on the 17th of December, 1891, had been increased to $25,-209,873.33, and the ordinary expenditure had been increased from $3,032,771.45, in the year ending 30th of June, 1886, to the sum of $4,095,520.45 for the year ending 30th of June, 1891, and to an estimated expenditure of $4,436,907.50 for the year ending 30th of June, 1892, and the total expenditure has been increased from $3,532,742.27, in the year ending June 30, 1886, to the sum, for the year ending 30th of June, 1891, of $5,871,394.86, and to an estimated expenditure for the year ending 30th of June, 1892, of the sum of $6,247,997.96; *Whereas,* also, the floating debt of this province, on the 17th of December, 1891, exclusive of claims and petitions of right, and of the loan of 20,-000,000 francs falling due on the 16th of July, 1893, amounted to a sum of over $8,000,000; *Whereas,* although, during the last five years, additional taxes have been levied, yet the ordinary revenue was $2,948,-999.69 for the year ending 30th of June, 1886, and only $3,457,144.32 for the year ending 30th of June, 1891, and an estimated revenue of $3,392,106.71 for the year ending 30th of June, 1892, and is totally inadequate to meet the increased expenditure; *Whereas,* the present revenue is insufficient to meet the increased expenditure and additional burdens put on this province, and it is expedient and necessary to levy new taxes to meet such debts and obligations; Therefore her Majesty, etc., enacts, etc.

Then it is enacted that all members of the liberal professions, which are held to be advocates, notaries, physicians, dentists, land surveyors, civil engineers, and architects, practising within the limits of the province, pay a direct tax, viz., those who reside in incorporated cities and towns, to pay an annual sum of $6; those who reside in other municipalities of the province, an annual sum of $3. All members of the Executive Council of the province, members of the civil service, and public employees and officers receiving a fixed salary, are to pay a direct tax of 2½ per cent. upon their salaries of over $400. The professionals are to pay on or before the first judicial day in October of each year, or incur the penalty of a fine equal to double the tax, recoverable with costs before any court of competent jurisdiction. In the case of executive councilors and public officials the tax is to be retained monthly out of their salaries. Further, on the sale, transfer, assignment, or exchange of immovable property within the province, not exceeding $5,000 in value, there is to be levied a tax of 1½ cent per dollar upon the *bona fide* value of the property sold, etc., payable one half by each of the parties to the transaction; in case of such parties understating such value, the tax is to be doubled. In the case of succession to the property, movable or immovable, of deceased persons, the successor is to pay a tax of from 1 to 10 per cent. upon its value, according to his propinquity of relationship to the deceased. These measures are probably only the insertion of the wedge, since it would be an intensely long task for Quebec to get rid of her pecuniary difficulties by these means alone.

Meanwhile the De Boucherville administration began legal proceedings against Mercier and his principal agent, Pacaud, for virtual malappropriation of the public funds. It was not denied that these two financiers had done what was laid to their charge, yet they were acquitted of that charge by a *Quebecois* jury; and Count Mercier was afterward chaired by his friends, who have probably taken this means of expressing their views of direct taxation.

Late in November a Quebec judge decided, on appeal, that the above-mentioned "act respecting duties on successions and on transfers of real estate" was *ultra vires* of the Provincial Legislature; but there is no probability that such a decision will be sustained.

Among other phenomenal acts of the last Legislature was one that provides for free grants of, in each instance, 100 acres of Crown lands to the father or mother of a family of 12 children living and born in lawful wedlock.

By another such act, widows and spinsters, otherwise qualified as by law provided, are entitled to be entered on the list of electors, and to vote at all municipal elections, in any city, town, village, or rural municipality, and also to vote for school commissioners and trustees. Quebec has thus become the first of the Canadian provinces to confer the franchise, at municipal elections, upon women.

During the latter days of the year, Hon. J. E. Chapleau accepted and assumed the duties of Lieutenant-Governor, *vice* Hon. A. R. Angers, who took a portfolio in Sir John Thompson's Cabinet.

Point Caribou

G U L F

L A W R E N

Riviere a Chaude

e Vallee

Chlorydormes

amqui

Causapacal o

Lake a la Croix

OTTA

R

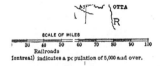

SCALE OF MILES

| 30 | 40 | 50 | 60 | 70 | 80 | 90 | 100 |

Railroads

(ontreal) indicates a population of 5,000 and over.

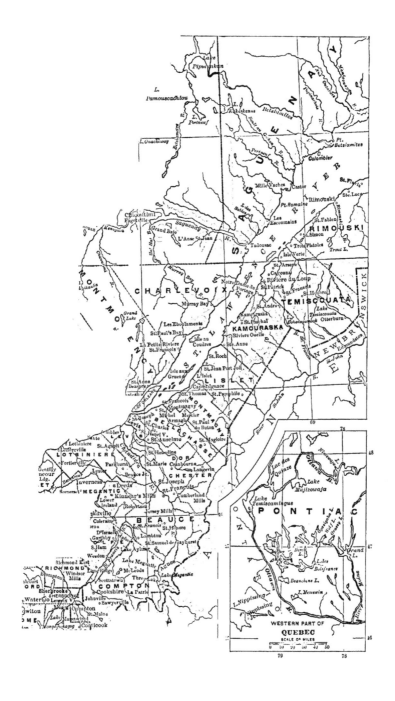

WESTERN PART OF
QUEBEC
SCALE OF MILES

R

RECEIVER, an officer appointed by a court to take charge of the property of an insolvent corporation, and to pay the stockholders or policy-holders, if an insurance company, whatever is due them. The loose laws of the several States relating to bankruptcy brought on a condition of things between 1875 and 1882 that favored the abuse of office by those who held receiverships. So many flagrant instances of abuse were known that the Legislature of New York, in 1882 and 1883, made a thorough investigation of about twenty insolvent insurance companies that had suffered at the hands of receivers. It was found that in a list of eighteen life insurance companies there had passed through the hands of the receivers the sum of $11,531,957.17; that they paid for legal expenses, including their own fees, $737,101.86; that they paid for other expenses, including salaries, clerk-hire, stationery, office-rent, taxes, and repairs of real estate, traveling expenses, auctioneers' fees, appraisers' fees, and miscellaneous expenses not otherwise classified, $598,464.54; that they distributed among the creditors of the corporations, and in accordance with court orders based upon findings of referees, $2,426,692.55 ; that at the date of their last annual reports (Dec. 31, 1881) there remained undistributed, and presumably to the credit of the funds, $3,565,041.37; that there was lost to the creditors from depreciation of the securities, bad debts, and worthless assets, $4,089,800.07 ; and that there appeared to be unaccounted for, $134,856.78. The average percentage of expenses to amount distributed was 235¼ per cent. The statements of the receivers showed marked differences in the methods of administering the various trusts, and wide divergence in the amount of expenses incurred and compensation received. The investigation showed that a certain person (called for convenience Mr. A) kept two accounts with Messrs. B and C, afterward kept two accounts with D and E, stock brokers doing business in Wall Street, and subsequently transferred the accounts to their successors, Messrs. F, G & Co., on the dissolution of the original firm. One of these accounts was for Mr. A individually, the other was in his name as receiver. As receiver he loaned to the firm of D & E large sums of money, ranging from $100,000 to $400,000, upon which D & E deposited securities as collaterals for the loans. These securities never left the possession of Messrs. D & E, but were merely nominally transferred to Mr. A, and held by the firm to his credit as a private customer of the concern. The same course was adopted by the other firms. In his private account he bought and sold stocks for speculation, depositing collaterals with his brokers as margin. But the brokers' books failed to disclose what stocks were thus deposited as collateral security, and the testimony of witnesses under examination was to the effect that if the collaterals which they put up for the loans were used by Mr. A as margin in his stock speculations, precisely the same character of entries would be made in their books that were found in them when ex-

amined by the committees. In other words, it was possible for Mr. A to use the trust funds that he held as receiver for speculative margins as a stock gambler in Wall Street ; and the manner in which the books of his brokers were kept would be explainable equally on the theory that this was a legitimate investment or a dishonest use of trust funds. It was significant in this connection to observe that Mr. B of the firm of D & E was a special partner of Mr. A in his business as a banker and broker. It further appeared that the drafts drawn against the fund by Mr. A failed to disclose from which fund they were drawn, the brokers honoring his drafts either from the loan account as receiver or from balances to his credit from stock transactions indifferently ; that is to say, they were prepared to honor whatever drafts he drew against them up to the amount to his credit, either as loans made by him as receiver or as profit passed to his account from his stock speculations. Moreover, interest was allowed by the brokers to Mr. A on his loan account as receiver at the rate of 4 per cent., and interest was charged against Mr. A on his individual account as stock speculator at the rate of 7 per cent., and yet but one interest account was kept with Mr. A. It was also shown that Mr. A's administration of the insurance company was characterized by all the objectionable features incident to the existing system of receiverships, with this additional objection in his case, that the order appointing him receiver did not contain a direction as to the investment of the funds or designate the trust company in which they should be deposited or the class of securities that should be purchased for investment, as was usual in other orders appointing other receivers. This omission from the order permitted Mr. A to open the call-loan accounts with the several firms of brokers heretofore mentioned. It was further shown that the most prominent evils of the system of receiverships arose from the difference in the *personnel* of the receivers, some being competent, diligent, and honest, others incompetent, slothful, and careless ; from the difference in their compensation, some being grossly excessive, others reasonably fair, and others not sufficiently remunerative : from the enormous expenses incurred in the administration of the fund, these expenses being of two kinds—legal expenses, so called, which included fees to counsel, referees', receiver's, and court fees : and expenses consisting of office rent, clerk hire, traveling expenses, payments to experts, book-keepers, and accountants, maintenance and repairs of real property, and payment of taxes. Another evil was the lack of uniformity in the proportion that the expenses bore to the amount realized and distributed ; in some cases the percentages being higher than 200 per cent., and in other cases as low as 18 per cent. Another evil of the system was the lack of uniformity in the methods of keeping accounts. In some instances were made clear and accurate statements made, showing in items the various amounts received and disbursed. In other instances, the receipts and disbursements were so mingled together, and the assets and income so mixed, that it was found difficult, if not impossible, to analyze the accounts and arrive at correct conclusions. Another evil was that the receiver, ostensibly the officer of the Supreme Court, was practically under the jurisdiction and supervision of that department of the court in which the business of the trust was conducted. Thus there were, in the various judicial departments, conflicting decisions in the receiverships and the questions arising between the receivers and the creditors. These conflicting decisions led to another evil in the form of "interveners" bringing suits to determine the rights of creditors as against their trusts, which suits were variously disposed of without any uniformity or exact determination of the rights of the respective parties.

It was recommended that a department of the State Government should be created to take charge of receiverships. But the Legislature chose rather to pass a law limiting the fees of receivers to 5 per cent. on the first $100,-000 that was received and paid out and 2½ per cent. upon all sums in excess of that sum. Provision was also made for more frequent reports, and for the speedy closing up of all insolvent corporations then in the hands of receivers. It was further provided that the Attorney-General should have the power to appoint or to remove a receiver, and that copies of all the papers should be left with that officer. Two years later the Legislature amended this law so as to require the receiver of any kind of corporation to report once in six months to the Supreme Court as to the progress of his work; and to send duplicates to the Attorney-General and to whatever department of the State Government was interested in his particular corporation. Another provision forbade any receiver to pay counsel until he had reported the amounts to the court as expenses actually incurred; and, even then, the court must give its approval before they were paid. A general law was passed in 1886 for the dissolving of corporations already dissolved by acts of the Legislature. This applied particularly to the charter of the Broadway Street Railway Company in the city of New York. A law was passed in 1887 providing that no receiver shall be appointed for a life insurance company if it can show actual funds invested of a net cash value equal to its liabilities, and a proper reserve fund on unmatured policies and claims. In 1889 the code of civil procedure was amended so that if it shall be made evident to the court that a corporation is insolvent, the court may, at any stage of the proceeding before final order, on motion of the petitioners on notice to the Attorney-General, or on motion of the Attorney-General on notice to the corporation, appoint a temporary receiver of the property of the corporation, which receiver shall have all the powers and be subject to all the duties that are defined as belonging to temporary receivers appointed in an action. The court may also, in its discretion, at any stage in the proceeding after such appointment, on like motion and notice, confer upon such temporary receiver the powers and authority, and subject him to the duties and liabilities of a permanent receiver, or as much thereof as it thinks proper, except that

he shall not make any final distribution among the creditors and stock-holders before final order in the proceedings, unless he is specially directed so to do by the court. If such receiver be appointed, the court may in its discretion, on like motion and notice, with or without security, at any stage of the proceeding before final order, grant an injunction restraining the creditors of the corporation from bringing any action against the corporation for the recovery of a sum of money, or from taking any further proceedings in such an action theretofore begun. Such injunction shall have the same effect and be subject to the same provisions of law as if each creditor upon whom it is served were named therein. It was also enacted, in 1889, that any receiver of an insolvent estate, corporation, or individual might treat as void all transfers made in fraud of the rights of creditors.

REFORMED CHURCHES. I. Reformed Church in America.—The following is a summary of the statistics of this Church as they were reported to the General Synod in June, 1892: Number of classes, 34; of churches, 590; of ministers, 592, with 15 licentiates; of families, 54,132; of communicants, 95,963; of persons received during the year on confession, 5,089; of baptisms, 5,776 of infants and 1,214 of adults; of baptized noncommunicants, 46,646; of catechumens, 33,917; of Sunday schools, 837, with an enrollment of 107,538 members. Amount of contributions: For denominational benevolent objects, $206,634; for other benevolent objects, $85,697; for congregational purposes, $1,-068,083.

The Board of Education had received $59,-341, and had 103 names on its roll of beneficiaries.

The receipts of the Board of Domestic Missions from all sources had been $66,247. It had aided 165 churches and missions, with which 6,804 families and 9,747 communicants were connected, with 12,837 members of Sunday schools, and which returned for the year 728 additions on confession. The total receipts of the Board of Foreign Missions, exclusive of what had been given in response to a recent appeal for contributions toward the payment of the debt, had been $112,163. Of this amount, $2,617 were designated as for sufferers by famine in India, and $10,192 had been derived from legacies. The expenditures had been $116,225. From the mission fields—in China, India, and Japan—were returned 15 stations, 178 out-stations, 24 ordained and 3 unordained missionaries, 39 assistant missionaries, 37 native ordained ministers, 282 native helpers, 53 churches, 5,559 communicants, 498 received on confession during the year, 14 seminaries with 636 pupils, 4 theological schools with 57 students, 128 day schools with 3,848 pupils, and 2 hospitals in which 10,-442 patients had been treated; amount of native contributions, $8,032.

The General Synod met in Asbury Park, N. J., June 1. The Rev. F. S. Schenck, D. D., was chosen president. The most important business transacted related to the question of federal union with the Reformed Church in the United States. The basis of federation agreed upon by the committees, and approved by the General Synods of the two bodies in the previous year (see "Annual Cyclopædia" for 1891), had been submitted to the classes, to be voted upon by them. Two reports were presented from the committee having the consideration of the subject. The majority of the committee reported that official returns of the voting had been received from 26 classes, and unofficial returns from 7 other classes. Of the answers officially returned, 18 were unconditionally affirmative, 2 conditionally affirmative, and 6 negative; including the answers unofficially returned, 21 were unconditionally affirmative, 3 formally conditional, and 9 negative. The measure "having already been approved by the General Synod, and having now received the affirmative votes of much more than a clear majority of the classes, it only remained for this synod to utter a final declaratory resolution announcing its adoption by the Reformed Church in America." The committee therefore recommended immediate action to give effect, so far as this General Synod was concerned, to the plan of federation. The minority report assumed that the analysis of the vote did not show "that necessary unanimity of feeling and consensus of views so useful as the basis of a permanent federation and successful co-operation," and proposed the appointment of a committee to prepare a more acceptable basis, to be submitted to the next General Synod. The majority report was approved, with the exception of the enacting clause, instead of which a substitute was adopted deferring action on the proposed articles of Constitution and Federal Union till the next General Synod, "in order that they may be considered in connection with the report of the committee on the broader plan of federal union [to include all the Reformed Churches in the land holding the Presbyterian system] then to be presented." Resolutions were adopted denouncing the efforts of the Roman Catholics to obtain recognition of their schools in the public system; refusing to take any part in the Columbian Exhibition if it is open on Sunday; and condemning the Chinese exclusion act. The Theological Seminary at Arcot, India, was placed on "exactly the same footing" as the other theological schools of the Church. The Board of Foreign Missions was authorized to open negotiations with the Arabian mission (recently established by voluntary personal effort among Arabs) with a view to receiving it under the care of the Church. The Rev. James F. Riggs, D. D., was elected Professor of Hellenistic Greek and New Testament Exegesis in the Theological Seminary at New Brunswick, N. J. The Board of Direction reported that, following the instructions of the preceding General Synod, it had procured a building for a Church Home in New York city, at 25 E. 22d Street, to be occupied by the different boards, woman's boards, ministers' meetings, etc.

II. Reformed Church in the United States.—A comparison of the statistics of this Church for 1892 with those for the previous year shows that it has enjoyed, above all losses by death and transfer, an increase of 16 ministers, making the whole number 885; of 16 congregations, to a total of 1,558; of 4,753 members, total 212,830; of 306 baptisms, total 14,526; of $28,940 in contributions for benevolent purposes, total $237,-

421; of $50,232 in contributions for congregational purposes, total $1,063,228.

RENAN, ERNEST, a French philosopher, critic, and historian, born in Tréguier, on the coast of Brittany, Feb. 27, 1823; died in Paris, Oct. 2, 1892. He was the son of a master of a coasting vessel, who was lost at sea. The family was impoverished, and he received his earlier

ERNEST RENAN.

education at the municipal college at Tréguier. In 1838 he carried off all the prizes at the college, and attracted the attention of the Abbé Dupanloup, director of the seminary of St. Nicolas du Chardonnet, who saw in him a promising recruit for the priesthood, and sent for him to Paris. He spent three years at this seminary in studying for the priesthood, and then entered the seminary of Issy, near Paris. In 1843 he began the study of theology at St. Sulpice, and while there became acquainted with the writings of the German biblical critics. He lost his faith in Catholicism, and on Oct. 6, 1845, left St. Sulpice. He supported himself in Paris by teaching Oriental languages while continuing his own studies. In 1848 he obtained the Volney prize in an essay on Semitic languages. His sister Henriette came from Poland, where she had been engaged as a governess, and made her home with him. An essay on the "Origin of Language" was the first work to bring him literary renown. In 1849 he went to Italy and collected materials for his doctoral thesis on the Averrhoes. In 1851 he received an appointment in the Paris National Library, and in 1856 he succeeded Augustin Thierry in the Academy of Inscription. In 1860 he went to Syria as director of a scientific expedition for the exploration of ancient Phœnicia with his sister and wife, who was the daughter of the painter Ary Scheffer and a Protestant, and familiarized himself with the scene of the Gospels. His sister, who read and criticised the manuscript of the "Life of Jesus," died of fever at Byblus, on Sept. 24, 1861. In 1863 the "Life of Jesus" appeared, and excited a storm of controversy, and in the same year he was nominated Professor of Hebrew at the College of France. A hostile demonstration was made at his first lecture, and in consequence the Government refused to ratify his appointment. In 1869 he was an independent and unsuccessful candidate for the Chamber. During the War of 1870 he made an ineffectual appeal to Strauss for intervention in behalf of France. The Republic reinstated him in his professorship, which he retained till his death. He was elected a member of the Academy, to succeed Claude Bernard in 1878, and, Vice-Rector of the College of France in 1883, and he was made grand officer of the Legion of Honor in 1888. In his youth he showed prodigious powers of acquiring knowledge, and an insatiable thirst for more. He renounced the priesthood, for which he had been destined from his earliest years, when he found that his intellect no longer permitted him to accept the legendary and the miraculous. A belief in God he always entertained, and, while regarding Christ as nothing more than a divinely inspired philosopher, cherished and preached the moral doctrines of Christianity—charity, love, and pardon. "Jesus is the highest of these pillars which show to man whence he came and whither he should tend. In him is condensed all that is good and lofty in our nature. . . . Whatever may be the surprises of the future, Jesus will never be surpassed. His worship will grow young without ceasing; his legend will call forth tears without end; his sufferings will melt the noblest hearts; all ages will proclaim that among the sons of men there is none born greater than Jesus." His French prose has been regarded as unsurpassed in his generation. He has been criticised as a historian for ignoring meagerness of positive knowledge and supplying details of his own, but his literary gifts are admitted as supreme. He did not concern himself so much with comparison of texts, analysis of documents, exposure of contradiction and omissions, as to lend to his writing a personality and animation which changed abstract dissertations into dramatic recitals. He did not attempt to proselytize, nor to inflict his opinions upon others. "If I had been born head of a school," he said, "I should have had a singular caprice; I should have loved only those of my disciples who would detach themselves from me. For my own part, the day on which any one should convict me of an attempt to imbue with my ideas any one who did not come voluntarily, would cause me most acute pain." Religious development, he contended, would no longer proceed by way of sectarian proselytism, but by way of harmonious internal development. His personal appearance was unprepossessing, and in his private relations he excelled in the brilliance of his conversation, and his simplicity and amiabilty made him one of the most charming of men. He leaves a widow and two children. The son is a painter of the Puvis de Chavanne school; the daughter is married to a Greek, M. Psichaire.

Renan's works embrace: "Vie de Jésus"; "Les Apôtres"; "St. Paul"; "Antichrist"; "Les Évangiles et la Séconde Genération Chrétienne"; "Marc Aurèle et la fin du Monde Antique"; "Le Livre de Job"; "Le Cantique des Cantiques"; "L'Ecclesiaste"; "Histoire Générale du Langues Sémitiques"; "Histoire du Peuple d'Israel"; "Études d'Histoire Réligieuse"; "Nouvelles Études d'Histoire Réligieuse";

"Averroes et l'Averroïsme"; "Essais de Morale et de Critique"; "Mélanges d'Histoire et de Voyages"; "Questions Contemporaines"; "La Réforme Intellectuelle et Morale de l'Origine du Language"; "Dialogues Philosophiques"; "Caliban"; "L'Eau de Jouvence"; "Discours et Conférences"; "L'Avenir de la Science"; "Missions de Phénicie"; and "Conférences d'Angleterre."

REUNION OF THE CHURCHES. A series of conferences on the reunion of the Protestant Churches was held at Grindenwald, Switzerland, in July, and, after a recess, in September. Most of the Protestant Churches, particularly of Great Britain, were represented, and addresses were made from day to day by representative men of the different denominations, presenting various aspects of the subject : The essentials of a true union; suggestions as to means of harmonizing differences; the methods, whether speedy or gradual, by which reunion can be promoted; accounts of methods and results of Christian work in the foreign missionary and the home fields; the office of education, etc. The Rev. C. A. Berry (Congregational) insisted that reunion must come by stages, and that the first stage must be the reunion of the free Churches, which is opposed by no difficulties of dogma, and only a few and minor difficulties of method. Reunion was defined by Bishop Perrowne, of Worcester, as meaning that those who have separated themselves from the communion and fellowship of the Church of England shall by some means and in some way be united to it. Père Hyacinthe (the Rev. M. Loyson) mentioned as the two steps necessary for reunion the establishment of the episcopate, as a fact, not as a dogma, and the acceptance of the Nicene Creed as the only œcumenical creed. The Rev. Dr. T. B. Stephenson, ex-President of the Wesleyan Conference, objected to the Church of England as the nucleus for reunion, and insisted, as two essential preliminaries to reunion, that existing orders must be recognized, and the autonomy of the several Churches must be respected. The Rev. Hugh Price Hughes (Wesleyan) advocated an organic reunion ; thought the Church of England the best nucleus for it ; and was willing to consent to absorption at once, if that was the will of God. No definite conclusions were announced, the meetings having been called only for conference.

RHODE ISLAND, a New England State, one of the original thirteen, ratified the Constitution May 29, 1790 ; area, 1,250 square miles. The population, according to each decennial census, was 68,825 in 1790 ; 69,122 in 1800 ; 76.931 in 1810 ; 83,015 in 1820 ; 97,199 in 1830 ; 108,830 in 1840 ; 147,545 in 1850 ; 174,620 in 1860 ; 217,353 in 1870 ; 276,531 in 1880 ; and 345,506 in 1890. Capitals, Newport and Providence.

Government.—The following were the State officers during the year : Governor, Herbert W. Ladd, Republican, succeeded by D. Russell Brown, Republican; Lieutenant-Governor, Henry A. Stearns, succeeded bv Melville Bull; Secretary of State, George H. Utter ; General Treasurer. Samuel Clark ; State Auditor and Insurance Commissioner, Albert C. Sanders; Attorney-General, Robert W. Burbank; Railroad Commissioner, Edward S. Freeman ; Commissioner of Public Schools, Thomas B. Stockwell; Chief Justice of the Supreme Court, Charles Matteson; Associate Justices, Pardon E. Tillinghast, John H. Stiness, George A. Wilbur, Horatio Rogers, and William W. Douglas.

Finances.—The following is a statement of the State finances at the close of 1892:

Funded debt.................................	$1,288,000 00
Sinking fund.................................	1,145,891 82
State debt less sinking fund...............	$137,108 68
State debt less sinking fund, Jan. 1, 1892......	233,236 82
Decrease past year...........................	96,127 64
Balance in the treasury, Jan. 1, 1892..........	75,940 07
Receipts from Jan. 1, 1892, to Dec. 31, 1892....	1,138,199 40
Total.....................................	$1,214,139 47
Payments from Jan. 1, 1892, to Dec. 31, 1892...	1,114,131 53
Balance in treasury, Dec. 31, 1892.........	$100,007 94

This is the first year in which there has been an excess of receipts over expenditures since 1889, when there was a balance amounting to $116,454.05. At the close of 1890 the excess was upon the expenditure side to the extent of $93,-639.16; and at the close of 1891 the excess in the same direction was $9,588.50, or $97,081.84 if we deduct from the receipts of that year $87,493.34, the amount of direct tax money received from the Federal Government.

On July 1, 1893, a part of the State debt, to the amount of $584,000, will be paid out of the sinking fund.

Legislative Session.—The General Assembly, elected in 1891, convened at Providence on Jan. 19, and adjourned on May 21. Two important amendments to the State Constitution were proposed—one providing for biennial instead of annual elections for State officers and members of the General Assembly; the other, authorizing the General Assembly to pass general laws for the creation and control of all corporations, except those having power to exercise the right of eminent domain or to acquire franchises in streets and highways. Corporations of the latter class shall be created only by special act.

The sum of $120,000 was appropriated for the support of public schools, and a further appropriation of $25,000 was made in aid of the State exhibit at the Columbian Exposition. Provision was also made for submitting to the people at the November election the question whether the General Assembly should be directed to authorize the issue of State bonds not exceeding $1,500,000 in amount, the proceeds to be expended in purchasing a site and erecting a building for a new State House.

Other acts of the session were as follow:

Reapportioning the members of the Lower House among the several towns.

Prohibiting the sale or giving of cigarettes to minors under sixteen years of age, and prohibiting such minor from using tobacco in any form in the streets or public places.

Further regulating the sale of commercial fertilizers.

To prevent blindness in children.

Providing for the establishment and control of free public libraries in towns.

To appoint and regulate railroad and steamboat police.

Accepting the provisions of the act of Congress for the more complete endowment and support of colleges of agriculture in the several States.

The General Assembly chosen at the April election assembled at Newport, on May 31, and declared the election of D. Russell Brown as Governor, Melville Bull as Lieutenant-Governor, and George H. Utter as Secretary of State. There having been no election by the people for General Treasurer and Attorney-General, it proceeded to elect, by a strict party vote, Samuel Clark to the former and Robert W. Burbank to the latter office. On June 14, U. S. Senator Nelson W. Aldrich, Republican, was re-elected for the full term of six years from March 3, 1893, the vote being: Senate—Aldrich 25, David S. Baker, Jr., Democrat, 10; House—Aldrich 39, Baker 28. The two constitutional amendments proposed at the January session received the approval of a majority of this Assembly, and provision was made for submitting them to the people at the November election. An act was passed, prescribing the manner of voting for presidential electors under the Australian ballot law, and another act established Oct. 21, 1892, as a legal holiday. The session ended on July 1. In October the members were called together by Gov. Brown, in special session, for the purpose of amending the laws in relation to municipal elections. Through the differences of local officials in the city of Newport no call was issued and no election held in that city in September on the day set apart by law for such election. It was even claimed by Democratic officials of the city that the law respecting the holding of such election was invalid and should not be obeyed. The session was called to meet on Oct. 4, from which day an adjournment was taken to Oct. 7. An act framed by the Republicans was then passed, which provided for a new election on the fourth Wednesday of October following, and every year thereafter, and which imposed a fine of $1,000 and imprisonment not less than three months nor over one year on every local official who should fail to perform the duty imposed upon him by the election laws. This measure proved effective; the election was held on Oct. 26, and the officials then elected were inaugurated in January, 1893.

Education.—For the school year ending April 30, 1891, the Commissioner of Public Schools reports the following statistics: Pupils enrolled, 81,-482; average attendance, 34,901; average school year, nine months eight days; male teachers, 175; female teachers, 1,280; average monthly wages—male teachers, $89.54; female teachers, $49.11; paid for teachers' wages. $614,923.32: total receipts for school purposes during the year, $1,185,-103.53; total expenditures for school purposes, $1,057,656.22; number of schoolhouses, 491; value of school property, $3,002,123. There were 59 evening schools conducted during the year, for an average of twelve weeks, in which 8,527 pupils were enrolled, the average attendance being 3,408. There were 145 male and 250 female teachers employed in these schools. The annual census of children of school age (between five and fifteen years of age) taken in January, 1891, showed 44,690 attending public schools; 8,663 attending Catholic schools; 1,440 attending select schools; and 11,915 not attending any school. The attendance at the State Normal School for the year ending June 26 was 203, an increase of 3 over the previous year. There were

95 pupils at the Agricultural School at Kingston during the last school year.

Charities.—On Jan. 1, 1892, there were 541 persons confined at the State Insane Asylum, of whom 252 were men and 289 were women. On Dec. 31 of the same year the number had increased to 563, of whom 268 were men and 295 women. At the State Home and School there was an average of 115 children during the year. A new institution, known as the State Institute for the Deaf, was opened at Providence on Jan. 2, and now has about 40 pupils. The cost of the land and buildings was $50,000. The property consists of a mansion house and a dormitory, capable of accommodating about 60 pupils. The Soldiers' Home at Bristol, opened in May, 1891, contained, on Dec. 31, of this year 105 inmates.

Banks.—From reports made to the State Auditor on Nov. 17, 1892, it appears that the deposits in institutions of savings on that date amounted to $69,906,992.57, a gain of $3,630,835.13 for the year; the number of depositors was 142,492, an increase of 5,844 for the year. The deposits in trust companies (participation account) on Nov. 17, 1892, amounted to $7,732,856.62. The number of depositors was 4,503, or an increase of 741 for the year.

Fisheries.—The taking of scallops from Narragansett Bay has become an important industry. Three seasons ago it was estimated that 200,000 bushels of this shell fish were taken from the waters of the bay. In the following season the yield was very small, but during the season of 1892 it probably amounted to 125,000 bushels.

Political.—On March 2 a State Convention of the Democratic party met at Providence, and nominated William T. C. Wardwell for Governor, Charles E. Gorman for Lieutenant-Governor, John J. Heffernan for Secretary of State, Thomas Spencer for General Treasurer, and Ziba O. Slocum for Attorney-General. The platform adopted demands free wool, iron, coal, and lumber; protests against the free coinage of silver; demands honest money, whether gold, silver, or paper; denounces the General Assembly for passing acts interfering with the internal affairs of Newport, Lincoln, and Scituate; scores the Republican party for endeavoring to legislate so as to close the polls at five o'clock, to the injury of the workingmen; calls for plurality elections; and instructs the State delegation to vote for the nomination of ex-President Cleveland.

On March 15 a Republican State Convention at Providence nominated D. Russell Brown for Governor, Melville Bull for Lieutenant-Governor, George H. Utter for Secretary of State, Samuel Clark for General Treasurer, and Robert W. Burbank for Attorney-General. The platform contains the following:

Resolved, That the adoption of the proposition which has the support of a controlling majority of the Democratic party to open the mints of the United States to the free coinage of silver would, in the absence of an international agreement for the monetary restoration of silver, result in a disastrous derangement of our currency; unsettle and destroy business confidence; insidiously but surely depreciate the value of the earnings and savings of labor, and unjustly diminish the purchasing power of money paid by a grateful Government to its pensioners.

That we heartily approve the policy inaugurated by

the enactment of the reciprocity section of the tariff act of 1890.

That the maintenance of the tariff system for the protection of American labor is the cardinal principle of the Republican party. The comfort and prosperity of the great mass of the people of the United States are directly dependent upon the continuance of the present high level of wages in all American industries, and this result can only be obtained by levying such pro e v duties upon competing articles imported from foreign countries as shall give to American workmen an equal chance to secure American markets.

The People's party placed in the field a ticket headed by Franklin E. Burton for Governor, and the Prohibitionists supported the following nominees: For Governor, Alexander Gilbert; for Lieutenant-Governor, Samuel O. Tabor; for Secretary of State, Lewis E. Remington; for General Treasurer, William S. Brownell; and for Attorney-General, Thomas H. Peabody. At the April election the Republican candidates for Governor, Lieutenant-Governor, and Secretary of State each received a majority of all the votes cast, and were elected by the people. There was no election for General Treasurer or Attorney-General, and the choice for these offices fell upon the General Assembly, which on May 31 elected the Republican candidates. The vote for Governor was: Brown, 27,461: Wardwell, 25,433; Gilbert, 1,598; Burton, 187. Members of the General Assembly were voted for at this election, but several by-elections were necessary before the full membership was determined. There were chosen to the Senate 28 Republicans and 9 Democrats; and to the House, 43 Republicans and 29 Democrats.

At the national election in November, Republican presidential electors were chosen by the following vote: Republican, 26,972; Democratic, 24,335; Prohibitionist, 1,654; People's party, 228. There was no choice by the people for Congressman in either of the congressional districts, no candidate having a majority of the votes. Two constitutional amendments were submitted to the people at the same time—one, in favor of biennial elections, receiving 18,749 affirmative and 13,907 negative votes, and being rejected; the other, authorizing the General Assembly to pass a general corporation law, receiving 17,959 affirmative and 10,632 negative votes, and being adopted. A three fifths vote in favor of an amendment is necessary for its adoption. On the question whether bonds to the amount of $1,500,000 should be issued for building a new State House, the vote was 20,997 in favor of such issue, and 12,205 against it.

ROMAN CATHOLIC CHURCH. The Vatican medal for 1892 bears the head of Leo XIII and "Fifteenth Year of Pontificate" on one side, the reverse being descriptive of his encyclical on labor. The design appropriately emphasizes the attitude of the papacy on the social questions. The messages from the Vatican during the year, especially to the bishops of Italy, France, Belgium, Great Britain, Ireland, and America, have all been in keeping with the popular character thus indicated. Conciliatory policies were adopted toward the governments of Russia and France, the negotiations for the restoration of Catholic rights in Germany and Poland being continued, and the opposition to the precedence of civil over religious marriages in Hungary and to the divorce laws in Italy being sustained.

The principal document was a letter to the Italian people against infidelity in the form of the Masonic ramifications. Under this guise, the Pope declares, a war is carried on against religion and civilization. The immediate cause of the pronouncement is the support by the Free Masons of the proposed divorce bills, and the effort to introduce civil marriages and civil funerals. The body, he says, is an egotistic sect, getting its first hold under the specious guise of a philanthropic society, and dominating Italy and Rome and the public powers, with the now avowed purpose of emancipating man from God, the licensing of error and vice, the substitution of a masked conspiracy for the free will of the people, and the interference with the true law of equality and charity by the erection of an artificial barrier against those who refuse to be its tools and instruments. The confiscation of Church property and disregard of religious right of association is traced to Masonic perversity. "The state, instead of holding its high and noble office of recognizing, guarding, aiding in their harmonious universality, divine and human rights, believes itself to be their arbitrator, and discountenances or restricts them at caprice. . . . The religion of our fathers has been made a sign for persecutions of every kind, with the satanic intent of substituting naturalism for Christianity, the worship of Reason for the worship of Faith, and the so-called independent morality for Catholic morality, for progress of spirit, progress of matter." After this arraignment the body is recondemned, and the faithful are exhorted to combat it by founding societies of mutual succor and institutes of credit which shall do not only for members but for all the indigent, showing that true charity is the daughter of Him who makes his sun to rise and the rain to fall on the just and the unjust. In conclusion it is said:

This egotistic sect strives to render the Church subservient, and to place her, a humble handmaid, at the feet of the state! And you, do not cease to beg and, within legal bounds, revindicate her due liberty and independence. . . . The Apostolic See has ever been the inspirer and jealous custodian of Italian grandeur. Be, therefore, Italians and Catholics; free, and not sectaries; faithful to your country and at the same time to Christ and to his visible Vicar, persuaded that an antichristian and antipapal Italy will be opposed to the divine order, and therefore condemned to perish.

The Temporal Power.—The only direct reference made to this subject by the Pope, although in all the documents of the year he spoke of the difficulties which menaced the free administration of his office, was at Christmas. Prince Alteiri, captain of the Noble Guard, in presenting the Vatican forces and wishing the Holy Father the happiness of the season, expressed the hope of his comrades that the pleasure would be theirs soon of escorting him through the streets of Rome. Leo XIII replied: "The day will doubtless come, but the precise time is in God's keeping." Personally, the pontiff is said to be impatient with those who put forward his claim on the old plea of

kingly sovereignty, rejecting as he does the idea that the people have no right to change their form of government. He feels that his position would be better under a republic, and believing Italy the providential land of the papacy, his trust is that eventually its people will see the necessity for its and their own sake of guaranteeing a perfect independence for the conduct of Church affairs.

The Catholic Congress of Ecuador, at Quito, in October, declared on this head:

The Catholic Congress of Ecuador hopes that all the Equatorians, and all the Catholics of Spanish America, will agitate with ardor and perseverance for the re-establishment of the temporal power of the Pope, putting in action the most efficacious means for accomplishing this end—that is to say, the propagation of sound doctrine by word and by means of the press; by prayer, both in their families and in the churches (in imitation of what was done in the primitive Church to obtain the liberty of the Prince of the Apostles); the organization of Catholic congresses, and the formation of a central committee to be put in relations with the committees of other Catholic states, and direct, in accord, the movement already commenced.

The demonstration of Catholic workmen in New York on Pope Leo's birthday, March 2 (organized in the spirit of gratitude for the declarations in the encyclicals on the labor question), presided over by Austin E. Ford and addressed by Archbishop Corrigan and Hon. E. F. Dunne, sent a message of sympathy in resolutions of a like import, as did also the Spanish and German Catholic congresses.

The College of Cardinals at the end of 1892, contained but 49 members—5 cardinal bishops, 38 cardinal priests, and 6 cardinal deacons; 13 deaths occurred between November, 1891, and December, 1892, viz.: Dominico Agostini, Patriarch of Venice, aged sixty-six, created in 1869, like many of his ancestors a distinguished Church writer. Victor Felix Bernardou, Archbishop of Sens, France, seventy-five, created in 1886. Rico Y. Paya, Primate of Spain and Archbishop of Toledo, eighty, founder of the world-famed "El Eco de la Religion," of Valencia, created in 1884. Francesco Battaglini, Archbishop of Boulogne, sixty-nine, created in 1885. Joseph D'Annabale, Titular Bishop of Carystus, seventy-six, for over thirty years holding high office at the Propaganda, created in 1889. Frederick von Furrstenberg, Archbishop of Olmütz, Moravia, eighty, created in 1879. Edward Howard. Charles Martal Allemand Lavigerie, Archbishop of St. Augustine's See of Carthage and Algeria, born in Bayonne, France, 1825, died Nov. 26. Henry Edward Manning, Archbishop of Westminster, who died Jan. 14, was born in England, July 15, 1808. Giovanni Simeoni, died the same day as Cardinal Manning, aged seventy-six. Gaspard Mermillod, died Feb. 23, aged sixty-eight. (For sketches of these Cardinals see OBITUARIES, FOREIGN.) Paul Melchers, Archbishop of Cologne and Church historian, died the same month as Cardinal Mermillod. He was born in Münster, Germany, in 1813.

Angosto Theodoli, who died June 26, was seventy-three years old.

At the close of the year it was announced that at the Consistory, in January, 14 new cardinals (whose names were given) would be created, and

2 reserved *in petto*, the latter supposed to be Mgr. Francis Satolli, Ablegate to the United States, and the other Most Rev. John Ireland, D. D., Archbishop of St. Paul, Minn.

The Reunion of Eastern Churches with the Holy See received a substantial impetus by the conversion of Mgr. Chisnoun, the Nestorian patriarch, and his following, which for fifteen hundred years had refused to accept the leadership of Rome. Pope Leo's plan of conciliating and bringing in all the unattached unorthodox Greek Catholics through allowing existing nonessential customs and privileges, but insisting upon a uniformity of discipline through gradual change, is meeting with deliberate consideration from those most interested, and the Vatican diplomats report wonderful changes as imminent. In accordance with this purpose, representatives of the Eastern and Western churches will meet within the shadow of the Holy Sepulchre in a Congress of the Holy Eucharist at Jerusalem in 1893. At Christmas time 30 patriarchs, bishops, and apostolic delegates had responded favorably to the call. Cardinal Langenieux, Archbishop of Rheims, was appointed to preside as legate of the Holy See.

The Jesuit Generalship became vacant by the death of Father M. A. Anderledy, Jan. 18, and the election of his successor saw a remarkable representation of the 12,000 members of the order at the mother house in Spain. Father Martin, S. J., was the choice for general, and for the first time in half a century "the black Pope," as the incumbent of the office is sometimes designated, undertook a tour of inspection through English-speaking countries.

The beatification causes of Joan of Arc and of the venerable servant of God Francesco Severio Bianchi, of the Barnabites, were progressed.

The Educational Question, especially that phase of it relating to the co-operation of church and state, occupied a large share of attention at the Vatican. A violent agitation in America brought the subject directly to the notice of Leo XIII, under whose direction the Propaganda rendered a decision favorable to the largest latitude in compromise that will secure religious and technical instruction. The year ushered in a vigorous discussion, which eventuated in open and secret opposition to the so-called "Faribault plan," those opposed to state participation and jurisdiction holding that the Most Rev. John Ireland, D. D., Archbishop of St. Paul, Minn., had acted contrary to Catholic doctrine in turning over his parochial schools to the local authorities, notwithstanding his reservation of the right religiously to instruct the pupils before or after the regular hours for secular study. The German clergy, in particular, were hostile to this departure, and although similar arrangements had been entered into previously in ten other dioceses, Archbishop Ireland's innovation was most fiercely attacked. He was finally forced to defend his course at Rome. There the organ of the Jesuits had joined in the antagonism, and all this, with the strictures of some of his brother prelates, made it appear for a time as if some doctrinal error had been committed by Archbishop Ireland and Cardinal Gibbons, who had approved his views. The Commission of Cardinals rendered a famous *tolerari potest*

decision, allowing the Archbishop Ireland plan to be adopted wherever conditions warranted. Not only that, in reply to an effort to twist the definition as adverse by being exceptional in its application, a letter was sent to the American bishops by Cardinal Ledochowski, Prefect of the Propaganda, advising harmonious relations and co-operation with civic authorities in such and all elevating efforts for the people. An amplification of the Church's position was given at a meeting of the archbishops of the United States in New York, Nov. 19, by Mgr. Satolli, papal ablegate, who presented a series of propositions, the ninth of which fully recognized the right of the state as a particular one, and taking a position more extreme than that broached before by Prof. Bouquillon. The hierarchy, with two exceptions, under a misapprehension of Mgr. Satolli's true position as the mouthpiece of the Pope, voted against accepting the propositions. Various phases of the school question arose during the year in Germany, France, Ireland, and Canada. In the Illinois election the Catholics and Lutherans joined, as in Wisconsin, to defeat the Edwards law aimed at private schools, and succeeded. In Minnesota they failed.

The Vatican and the United States.—The year 1892 is in some respects essentially an American year in the history of the Church Universal. The school decision was followed by another on a subject equally disturbing—"Cahenslyism," or the recognition of foreign nationalities in the appointment of bishops and formation of congregations. In refusing such recognition, national distinctions were deprecated, and those advancing such were admonished to desist, as their efforts were calculated to arouse racial animosities prejudicial to religious unity. Rome thus set its face against the perpetuation of foreign languages and customs in the American Church, and set to work in earnest to adapt its organization to the New World surroundings, harmonize its parts, and at the same time to bring its thought and workings directly under the observation of the American people. The Columbian celebration offered favorable opportunity for the next step in this direction. The United States Government, through Hon. John W. Foster, Secretary of State, had requested the co-operation of the Pope in behalf of the World's Fair, and promised special care for the mementoes of Columbus and such of the Vatican treasures as he would send. Secretary Foster's letter said :

> The intimate association of the Holy See with the Columbian enterprise and its results has so linked the memory of Rome and her pontiffs with the vast achievement of Christopher Columbus and his comrades and competitors in the work of discovery and colonization, and exerted so marked an influence on the destinies and progress of the New World they revealed, that an exhibit such as, by the President's direction, I have the honor to suggest could not fail to be among the most noteworthy contributions to this international celebration of the four hundredth anniversary of the discovery. By co-operating to this end, His Holiness will manifest for our country a regard which will be highly appreciated not only by the managers of the exposition, but by the American people at large.

In response, Cardinal Rampolla wrote an acceptance of the invitation, saying :

In the meantime His Holiness, who has so many reasons to entertain special regard for the United States Government, on account of the liberty which is enjoyed in the said States by the Catholic Church, and who justly admires the enterprise and progress of that country, has decided to be represented at the public demonstrations which are to be held there in honor of the Genoese hero on the fourth centenary of his memorable discovery, by a person who is no less distinguished by his personal qualities than by his grade in the ecclesiastical hierarchy. This person is Mgr. Francesco Satolli, Archbishop of Lepanto, a prelate who is highly to be esteemed on account of his virtues as for his profound scholarship, of which he has given many evidences in his writings. His Holiness does not doubt that this decision of his will be received with pleasure by the Government, and feels assured that your Excellency will welcome the prelate with your accustomed courtesy.

Mgr. Satolli was officially received in New York harbor, and by the President and Cabinet at Washington, and was present at Chicago in October at the dedication of the exposition buildings. He brought three letters—one of congratulation to President Harrison, one to Cardinal Gibbons, and one to Archbishop Ireland. The two latter commended him to the care of those dignitaries, and virtually indicated that his conduct of ecclesiastical affairs would be on the lines recommended by them. He was constituted ablegate for the adjustment of pending disputes, but his status being questioned, and an unfriendly disposition being manifested among some of the more rigorous ecclesiastics, the Holy See invested him with extraordinary powers, and indicated that it would still further increase them to that of a full and unappealable delegateship, if necessary.

The case of the Rev. Edward McGlynn, D. D., was the first to be settled. He had been suspended by Archbishop Corrigan six years before for disobedience in advocating the theory of land-values taxation of Henry George, and excommunicated for refusing to recant and go to Rome on the request of Cardinal Simeoni. Mgr. Satolli absolved Dr. McGlynn, on his testimony that he harbored no doctrine contrary to the Church's teaching. Dr. Burtsell, counsel for Dr. McGlynn, submitting a statement of his client's views on the land question, Mgr. Satolli declared that they did not imperil faith or morals, and could consistently be held by Catholics. A series of restorations for disciplinary infractions on the part of priests followed. The right of a priest to publish his views on a question affecting the welfare of the Church or country, arising through the trial of the Rev. Patrick Corrigan for criticising in the New York "Freeman's Journal" his bishop's action in presiding at the German Catholic Congress, Newark, where Cahenslyism was advocated, the priest was practically sustained, the trial being abandoned by Bishop Wigger. Mgr. Satolli took up his quarters at the Catholic University, Washington, and proceeded to adjudicate differences as a supreme arbiter, and his rulings were ratified by Rome in every instance.

United States Summary.—A remarkably large mortality manifested itself among the priests and religious of the United States and Canada, although that among the hierarchy was unusually small. One archbishop, 5 bishops, 230 priests, and 100 religious died within the year.

Official statistics report 14 archbishops, 75 bishops, 9,288 priests, 8,477 churches, 3,485 stations, 1,763 chapels, 38 seminaries, 127 colleges, 654 academics, 3,587 parochial schools, 738,269 parochial-school children, 245 orphan asylums, 26,533 orphans, 463 charitable institutions, and a church membership of 8,806,095 (estimated).

Colored and Indian Missions.—The colored Catholic population is set down at 152,700, with 21 churches, 34 priests, 115 schools, 8,280 pupils, and 14 colleges, orphanages, etc.

The Indian Catholic population is 80,856, with 80 churches, attended by 63 priests. In 1892 about 500 adults were baptized, and 1,056 children. The 78 schools were attended by 4,246 pupils; 36 boarding schools and 15 day schools, in which 3,596 students are cared for, receive Government aid.

The Convent of St. Elizabeth, the mother house of the new Order of the Blessed Sacrament, founded, directed, and endowed by Mother Katherine (Miss Drexel) for mission work among Indians and negroes, was opened near Philadelphia. The building will cost $200,000.

The third Catholic Colored Congress of the United States was held in Philadelphia, the first week in January, the delegates prior to the opening attending the dedication in honor of St. Peter Claver of the first church for colored Catholics in that city.

New Bishops.—Six vacant sees were filled. Dr. Ignatius F. Horstmann was consecrated Bishop of Cleveland, Ohio, as successor to Bishop Gilmour, in Philadelphia, Feb. 25; Rt. Rev. Charles E. McDonnell was consecrated Bishop of Brooklyn vice Rt. Rev. John Loughlin, D. D., deceased, by Archbishop Corrigan, in New York, April 25; Very Rev. Henry Gabriels was consecrated Bishop of Ogdensburg, vice Wadhams, deceased, at Albany, May 5; Rt. Rev. John Stephen Michaud was consecrated auxiliary bishop to Rt. Rev. Louis De Goesbriand, of Burlington, June 29; Rt. Rev. Sebastian G. Messmer was consecrated Bishop of Green Bay, March 27; Rt. Rev. James Schwebach was consecrated Bishop of La Crosse, Feb. 25; Rt. Rev. Thos. D. Beaven was consecrated Bishop of Springfield, in succession to Rt. Rev. P. T. O'Reilly, Oct. 18.

The archbishops, at their meeting in November, resolved to make special provision for the religious instruction of children attending the public schools, and also promote the erection of Catholic schools where possible.

Miscellaneous Events.—The Catholic Summer School, formed on the Chautauqua plan, held its first session in New London, Conn., between July 30 and Aug. 20. It was successful. The corner stone of the Hall of Philosophy of the Catholic University was laid April 27. It is the gift of Father McMahon, whose name it will bear. Cardinal Gibbons, and Charles J. Bonaparte were the speakers. The Catholic ritual for the dead was performed for the first time in the United States Senate Chamber by Rt. Rev. J. J. Keane, D. D., at the funeral of Senator Kenna. Three other distinguished lay Catholics died, in the persons of John Gilmary Shea, Catholic historian: Daniel Doherty, orator and jurist: and Patrick Sarsfield Gilmore, bandmaster. Oct 12 was marked by extraordinary public Catholic demonstrations in honor of Columbus. Archbishop Ireland made the opening address before the World's Fair Association of Auxiliary Congresses, and Archbishop Corrigan dedicated the New York State building.

The Pope and the French Republic.—A continuance of his support of democratic policy in the Government of France characterized Leo XIII. He addressed a letter to prelates and people urging them to freely and fully accept the republic and in answer to the criticisms with which it was received he followed it with a special rescript to the cardinal archbishops, in which he admonished the clergy to recognize and comply with the established order. At the request of the Holy Father, on his way back from Rome Archbishop Ireland delivered a series of discourses in sustenance of this attitude, in one of which he thanked God that "through France and Leo XIII the republic has become canonized at last." The formation of a Catholic republican party to counteract the irreligious elements is projected.

Germany presented a parliamentary situation with the German Catholic center of 107 members controlling the destinies of the empire, and demanding as the price of their support the return of the Jesuits and a religious educational system. The latter was formulated by the Government, but afterward withdrawn.

Ireland.—The agitation for Catholic university rights from the Government found an unexpected accession in the chief directors of Trinity College, Dublin, who publicly recorded themselves on the side of educational equality, and received the thanks of Archbishop Walsh therefor. As a concession to the demands of the Irish hierarchy the schools of the Christian Brothers were included in the grants of the Government, and now come under the rules of the National School Board. In the parliamentary elections the priests sided with the Nationalists led by Justin McCarthy, with the result that but 9 Parnellite Nationalists were returned, the seat of Michael Davitt for Meath being contested on the ground of clerical intimidation, and John Redmond, the Parnellite leader, threatening a penalty bill against clerical interference in elections. The close of the year brought word that Archbishop Logue, primate of all Ireland, had been chosen by the Pope as the Irish representative in the College of Cardinals. The census showed that while there had been a falling off in Catholic Church membership, there had also been a diminution of other denominations, with the exception of the Methodists, whose increase is chiefly by inroads on other Protestant sects. The new order of Sisters of St. Brigid, whose mother house is at Tullow, Carlow, received the Pope's approval.

Scotland and Wales show marked increase in Catholic growth. Rt. Rev. Angus McDonald was translated to the see of St. Andrews and Edinburgh in July, and his place in the Highland diocese of Argyle and the isles, where half a century ago a Catholic dare not proclaim himself, was filled by the elevation of Very Rev. George John Smith, Chaplain to the Marquis of Bute. In twenty-five years the number of Catholic priests has increased in Scotland from 200 to nearly 400.

England saw a Catholic Lord Mayor of London in 1892 for the first time since the Reformation, and an effort was made to prevent Alderman Stuart-Knill, to whom the office went by right of seniority in the board, from taking his seat. The Catholic city of Dublin, whose Lord Mayor is an English Protestant, conferred its freedom on Mayor Knill.

The anticatholic course of Capt. Lugard in Uganda, in the interest of the Protestant missionaries caused an inquiry in Parliament, and the withdrawal of the charter of the British East Africa Company, for whom Lugard was agent, ensued.

Bishop Vaughan, of the diocese of Salford, succeeded to the see of Westminster, made vacant by the death of Cardinal Manning, and he signalized his advent by instituting a movement for the encouragement and revival of Christian art in England. He was called to Rome at the close of the year to receive the red hat from Pope Leo. Cardinal Vaughan is owner of the "London Tablet," and comes of an old and distinguished family in English Catholic annals.

"The Happiness in Hell."—A remarkable article thus entitled appeared in the "Contemporary Review" for December, from the pen of St. George Mivart, the Catholic scientist, bringing on the sharpest religious discussion in England since the day of Dr. Newman and the Puseyites. The criticisms were fierce on all sides, Prof. Mivart finding theological defenders and opponents. Rev. Richard Clarke, S. J., and the Bishop of Nottingham figured most prominently among the latter. The thesis claims to be grounded thoroughly on theology, and the writer fortifies it with the authorities of the Catholic doctors, notably St. Augustine and St. Thomas. On their interpretation of the Church's doctrine he closes the hell of the damned as far as permissible, carrying the theory of evolution into it by insisting upon the most charitable teaching with regard to the destiny of unbaptized children, and of those infants of larger growth, the untutored savages, and by a broad interpretation of the "baptism of desire" he includes among those saved from the exterior darkness vast numbers commonly supposed to be lost. He then interprets the conditions necessary for a hell-deserving sin to be the full knowledge, the free deliberation, and the plenary consent; contending that heredity and environment diminish the malice of grievous sins, and therefore, their punishment, in the order of mercy what *pœna sensus* there may be inflicted—mitigating, until existence will be in a sense tolerable, and certainly more desirable, than annihilation.

Spain and Portugal.—The principal events cluster around the Catholic Congress at Seville, where the discussions took the character of ameliorative recommendations for the wage earners on the lines of Pope Leo's encyclical on the labor question, and the revival of Catholic literature by the publication under the apostolate of the press of popular works bearing upon faith and morals, and their systematic distribution among the people. In this connection several daily and weekly journals were established, and two high-class reviews—one at Madrid, by the Jesuits, styled "Estudios Religiosis," and the other at Valencia, under the auspices of the archbishop, entitled "Soluciones Católicus." In December a great demonstration was held throughout Spain in protest against the proposed opening in Madrid of "The Church of Spain," as the sect which has been recognized by "the Church of Ireland" has styled itself. This body, after repeated failure to receive recognition from the Established Church of England, which deprecated its methods, applied to Lord Plunkett, the Protestant Archbishop of Dublin, and he, selecting Père Hyacinthe (M. Loyson) as his companion, went to Madrid and formally consecrated a church, and g it status by consecrating a bishop for it. He then appealed to the English and Irish public for a proselytizing fund. The Catholic protest was against the use of the title "Church of Spain" as an infringement upon the rights of the state Church; against the appropriation of public moneys which follows Government recognition; and against the insinuation, which the whole proceeding took the character of, that Spain is wanting in loyalty to the see of Peter, or is in any way lacking in the elements of Christian civilization. The protest was so unanimous that the Prime Minister withheld the sanction necessary under the law to the public advertisement of the Church and its programme of propaganda. The census shows that Spain's population is 17,519,858 Catholics, 6,654 Protestants, and 23,732 others. The Queen regent was this year honored with the Golden Rose by His Holiness.

British America.—The bulletin of the ninth census shows the Catholic population of Canada to be 1,990,464, or 41·46 per cent. of the total population. The increase in ten years is 198,483. This showing is much less than the official returns to the ecclesiastical authorities, who place the total number of Catholics at 2,117,538, under 8 archbishops, 22 bishops, and 2,530 priests. There are 2,115 churches and chapels, 11 seminaries, 44 colleges, and 674 charitable institutions.

The school question in Manitoba, caused by legislative denial of the right of Catholics to share the public educational fund as elsewhere, still remains a burning issue in the Northwest.

Two new bishops were consecrated in 1892— Rt. Rev. M. T. Labrecque, as Bishop of Chicoutin, archdiocese of Quebec, May 22; and Rt. Rev. J. M. Emard, Bishop of Valleyfield, archdiocese of Montreal, June 9.

Archbishop Jean Langevin died at St. Germain of Rimouski, Jan. 26. He was born in Quebec, 1821, and stands as one of its most brilliant scholars. He served in that province as priest, and then took charge of its "Normal School," from which, in 1867, he was promoted to the charge (territorially) of the largest diocese in Canada. Rt. Rev. T. O'Mahony, D. D., died in Toronto, Sept. 7. He was born in Ireland, 1825, ordained in Rome, and sent out as first Bishop of Armsdale, Australia. He returned to Rome for his health, and later went to Canada with Archbishop Lynch, becoming pastor of St. Paul's, Toronto, in which charge he died.

ROUMANIA, a monarchy in eastern Europe. The Government rests on the Constitution of 1866, as amended in 1879 and 1884. The legislative power vests in a Senate of 120 members and a Chamber of Deputies having 183 members. The Senators are elected for eight years by two and the Deputies for four years by three electoral colleges in each district. The reigning King is Carol I, born April 20, 1839, son of Prince Karl of Hohenzollern-Sigmaringen. He was elected Domnul or Lord of Roumania on May 22, 1866, and was proclaimed King on March 26, 1881. He was married on Nov. 15, 1869, to Princess Elizabeth von Neuwied, born Dec. 29, 1843. His marriage remaining childless, the succession of the throne was settled upon his elder brother, Prince Leopold of Hohenzollern-Sigmaringen, who renounced his rights in favor of his eldest son, Prince Wilhelm, in October, 1880, who in turn renounced his rights on Nov. 22, 1888, in favor of his brother, Prince Ferdinand, born Aug. 24, 1865, and the latter, by decree of the King, on March 18, 1889, was created Prince of Roumania.

The executive vests in a Council of Ministers, which at the beginning of 1892 was composed of the following members: Prime Minister, I. E. Florescu; Minister of the Interior, L. Catargi; Minister of Finance and Minister of Justice *ad interim*, G. Vernescu; Minister of Foreign Affairs, C. Escarcu; Minister of War, I. Lahovari; Minister of Public Works, C. Olanescu; Minister of Agriculture, Industry, Commerce, and Domains, Ilariu Isvoranu; Minister of Public Instruction and Worship, P. Poui.

Area and Population.—The area of Roumania is 48,307 square miles, with a population in 1889 of 5,038,342. The Roumanians are distributed in large numbers in the neighboring countries—Transylvania, Servia, and Bulgaria—about 4,500,000, or half of the race, living in Roumania proper. The number of marriages in 1891 was 44,267; the number of births, 228,283; the number of deaths, 162,996.

Finances.—The budget for 1891–'92 estimates the receipts and expenses at 169,738,600 lei or francs each. Of the total receipts, 29,335,000 lei were derived from direct taxes, 41,205,000 lei from indirect taxes, 42,950,000 lei from state monopolies, 23,619,600 lei from domains, 13,527,000 lei from public works, 10,877,000 lei from various administrative departments, and 8,225,000 lei from various other sources. Of the total expenditures, 61,441,318 lei were for the public debt, 63,560 lei for the Council of Ministers, 38,355,598 lei for the Ministry of War, 22,335,435 lei for the Ministry of Finance, 17,537,886 lei for the Ministry of Public Instruction and Worship, 12,226,571 lei for the Ministry of the Interior, 6,176,548 lei for the Ministry of Public Works, 5,229,544 lei for the Ministry of Justice, 4,171,068 lei for the Ministry of Domains, 1,508,666 lei for the Ministry of Foreign Affairs, and 692,406 lei for the fund of supplementary and extraordinary credits.

The public debt on April 1, 1893, amounts to 1,109,720,925 lei. The larger part of this debt was contracted for railroad construction and public works, the balance to pay for peasant freeholds, to cover deficits, and to reduce the unfunded debt. (For the army and navy, see "Annual Cyclopædia" for 1891.)

Commerce.—The total value of imports in 1891 was 436,682,685 lei, and the total exports amounted to 274,662,083 lei. Of the imports, 139,608,000 lei came from Germany, 114,705,000 lei from Great Britain, 71,037,000 lei from Austria-Hungary, 41,726,000 lei from France, 15,698,-000 lei from Turkey and Bulgaria, 13,732,000 lei from Russia, 19,396,000 lei from Belgium, 8,592,-000 lei from Switzerland, 6,846,000 lei from Italy, 1,436,000 lei from Greece, and 3,907,000 lei from other countries. Of the total exports, 143,716,-000 lei went to Great Britain, 30,990,000 lei to Germany, 41,215,000 lei to Belgium, 23,195,000 lei to Austria-Hungary, 9,818,000 lei to France, 9,956,000 lei to Turkey and Bulgaria, 3,269,000 lei lei to Russia, 6,242,000 lei to Italy, 385,000 lei to Greece, 407,000 lei to Switzerland, and 5,469,-000 lei to various other countries. The imports of textiles amounted to 184,200,000 lei, and the exports to 4,800,000 lei; the imports of metals and metal manufactures to 82,100,000 lei, and the exports to 1,500,000 lei; the imports of fruits, legumes, etc., to 26,100,000 lei, and the exports to 24,200,000 lei; the imports of hides, skins, and leather to 24,000,000 lei, and the exports to 1,300,-000 lei; the imports of drugs and dyes to 17,500,-000 lei; the imports of minerals, glass, and crockery to 16,200,000 lei; the imports of chemicals to 12,800,000 lei; the imports of paper to 15,800,000 lei; the imports of oil, wax, etc., to 10,300,000 lei; the imports of animals and animal products to 9,700,000 lei, and the exports to 5,800,000 lei; the imports of wood and wood manufactures to 8,600,000 lei, and the exports to 3,500,000 lei. The exports of cereals amounted to 225,000,000 lei.

All the commercial treaties with foreign countries expired on July 1, 1892, and none of them were renewed at the time, so that all imports from all countries stood on an equal footing, and were subject to the general tariff, which had been so modified that the duty on some articles was reduced to a point below that which had been stipulated by the treaties. The Government retained the power, however, to increase the duties, even up to a prohibitive point, for the whole or any part of the imports from countries where large or prohibitive duties are levied on Roumanian goods or produce. On July 4, 1892, a provisional treaty was entered into with Germany, to be in force until Nov. 30, 1892, by which Roumania granted Germany the same advantages she possessed under the old treaty, and Germany accorded to Roumania the most-favored-nation treatment for cereals. A commercial treaty was signed with Italy on Dec. 30, 1892.

Communications. — The railroads in Roumania all belong to the state; in 1892 the total length of railroads open to traffic was 2,557 kilometres, while 544 kilometres were under construction, and 1,094 kilometres were in contemplation.

In 1891 the post office handled 15,289,336 letters, 4,524,277 postal cards, and 7,773,512 pieces of printed matter. The receipts were 3,649,035 lei from the post office and 2,395,699 lei from the telegraph service; the expenses of both were 4,550,745 lei. In 1891 there were 5,571 kilometres of telegraph lines, and 12,008 kilometres of wire. The total number of telegrams sent was 1,574,359, of which 1,086,388 were domestic, 437,171 external, 49,376 in transit, and 1,424 were Government dispatches.

European Commission of the Danube. — The navigation of the Danube is carried on under an agreement of the leading powers made at the Berlin Conference in 1878 and modified in 1883. From its mouth to the Iron Gate the river is regarded as an international highway, and is superintended by a commission, to which Austria, Bulgaria, Roumania, and Servia each appoint one member, while a fifth is appointed for six months by the signatory powers in turn. The International Danubian Commission has its seat at Galatz. The receipts in 1891 amounted to 3,649,578 francs, and the expenses to 2,721,151 francs. The debts of the commission were paid up on June 30, 1887, and the overplus of the receipts has been invested in different funds. There were, in 1891, 1,000,000 francs in the reserve fund, 413,874 francs in the pension fund for employees, and 60,063 francs in the pension fund for pilots. The number of vessels which cleared at the Sulina mouth of the Danube was 1,723, of 1,512,030 tons, of which 1,246, of 1,429,433 tons, were steamers, and 477, of 82,597 tons, were sailing vessels. Of the total number, 773, of 990,935 tons, were English; 106, of 142,187 tons, were Greek; 102, of 78,841 tons, were Austrian; 86, of 35,325 tons, were Russian; 41, of 23,129 tons, were Turkish; 37, of 46,499 tons, were French; 33, of 35,057 tons, were Italian; 29, of 34,455 tons, were Norwegian; 22, of 25,354 tons, were German; 8, of 8,887 tons, were Dutch; and 9 vessels, of 8,764 tons, belonged to different nationalities. There were exported, in 1891, 3,303,-000 quarters of wheat, 583,000 quarters of rye, 3,739,000 quarters of maize, and 1,898,000 quarters of barley.

The Elections. — General elections for the Chamber of Deputies were held in the beginning of February, 1892, which resulted in favor of the Government. Of the 183 deputies elected, 151 were Conservatives, and 32 belonged to the Opposition. Elections for the Senate took place a little later in the same month, when 92 Conservatives, 20 members of the Opposition, and 8 bishops were elected. In former years the parties in the two houses were very much divided, making it extremely difficult for the Government to pass strong and stringent laws. This year, however, the Conservatives and the Junimists joined hands and agreed on a mutual platform, of which the following are the principal planks: Agrarian reforms, consisting of a large creation of peasant proprietorships; a readjustment of the system of national taxation; judicial reforms, the main object being to make judges irremovable; closer relations with the Triple Alliance; and the promotion of trade. The Opposition went to the country with an unpopular programme, one of the leading points being the disparagement of the ministry, on the ground that it was purely the creation of the King.

Session of the Parliament. — The Roumanian Parliament was opened on March 7, 1892, by a speech from the throne, in which the King, in alluding to the recent elections, remarked that they were an eloquent testimony of the will of the people, which desired before all things order and stability. Bills for the reform of internal organizations were announced, and the attention of the Parliament was called to the agrarian reform bill which had been introduced in 1890, and which had so far not been passed upon. A bill was introduced into the Chamber by the Minister of Finance, dealing with the regulation of agrarian credits. The object of the measure is to do away with the private loan institutions, vesting the right of lending money to farmers in the hands of the Government, and, by improving the material condition of the farmer, to raise the intellectual standard of the farming population. The bill calls for a sum of 23,000,000 francs, which is to be divided into two equal parts; one part is to be used to grant the farmers, and the trades closely connected with farming, the necessary credits; the other part will be advanced to the rural population, enabling them to found homes of their own by purchasing some of the salable state domains. The State Loan Institution will lend money on security, give advantages for the purchase of animals, seeds, and agricultural implements, and advance money for the erection of agricultural buildings. Not more than 1,000 francs are to be advanced at one time, and interest is not to exceed 5 per cent.

In opening the second session of the Parliament, on Nov. 27, 1892, the King announced the impending marriage of Prince Ferdinand, the heir apparent, to Princess Marie of Edinburgh, which he pronounced as a happy event, whereby the links between the British and Roumanian dynasties and the two peoples would be strengthened, and a guarantee afforded for the future of the country. In referring to the difficulty with Greece, the King declared that Roumania maintained her rights as a sovereign state, and was resolved to defend them without displaying a spirit of provocation, but at the same time without weakness. In conclusion, he announced that the revenue showed an increase over the estimates, up to Sept. 30, of 22,000,000 francs.

Difficulties with Greece.—A dispute arose between the Roumanian and Greek governments regarding a contested will made by two Greek subjects residing in Roumania, and it led to a rupture of diplomatic relations. The will in dispute was made about twenty-five years before, by two brothers,Zappas, Greek merchants residing in Roumania, and by it a large fortune was bequeathed for agriculture, manufactures, and arts in Greece. The estate was subject to a life interest of a near relative. Early in 1892 this relative died, and the Roumanian Government seized the property on the ground that foreigners were debarred by the Roumanian law from disposing of real estate to foreign institutions. The Greek Government contended that the will was made when Roumania itself formed an integral part of the Ottoman Empire, and that the law subsequently enacted could not apply to this case. As no amicable settlement could be reached, the Greek Government offered to leave the question to arbitration, but to this the Roumanian Government objected, and maintained that the case should be decided by the Roumanian tribunals. The Greek Government would not agree to this, and presented an ultimatum to the Roumanian Government demanding an arbitration; the latter Government declining to do so, Greece recalled her ministers and consuls on Oct. 16, 1892, leaving the Greek interests in the hands of the Russian minister at Bucharest. The Roumanian minister at Athens was also recalled,

VOL. XXXII.—44 A

the Italian minister attending to Roumanian affairs in Greece.

RUSSIA, an empire in northern Europe and Asia. The legislative, executive, and judicial power is vested in the autocratic hereditary monarch of the Romanoff-Holstein-Gottorp family. The rule of succession is that of regular descent, by the right of primogeniture, through the male line, and in default of male descendants through the female line. Every sovereign of Russia, and his consort and children, must belong to the Orthodox Greek Church, and, by a decree of Alexander I, the princes and princesses of the imperial house, to be able to inherit the throne, must have the consent of the Emperor to any marriage they may contract. The reigning Emperor or Czar is Alexander III, born Feb. 26, 1845, the eldest son of Emperor Alexander II and of Princess Maria, daughter of the Grand Duke of Hesse-Darmstadt. He ascended the throne at the death by assassination of his father on March 1, 1881; was crowned at Moscow on May 27, 1883. He married, Nov. 9, 1866, Maria Dagmar, daughter of King Christian IX of Denmark. The Government is carried on by the Czar through the medium of four consultative and administrative bodies: (1) The Council of State, which consists of a president and an unlimited number of members appointed by the Czar. Its chief functions are the examination of proposed laws brought before it by the ministers, and the discussion of the budget and expenditures. (2) The Ruling Senate, which is composed of persons of high rank or station, though each department is presided over by a lawyer of eminence; it promulgates laws, superintends the courts of law, and has power to remonstrate with the Emperor against his decrees. (3) The Holy Synod, which consists of the metropolitan bishops of St. Petersburg, Moscow, and Kieff, the archbishops of the Caucasus, Kholm, and Warsaw, and several bishops; it has the supervision of the religious affairs of the empire. (4) The Committee of Ministers, who are the immediate advisers of the Czar. The following were the ministers in office in 1892: Minister of the Imperial House, Gen. Vorontzoff-Dachkoff; Minister of Foreign Affairs, Nicholas Carlovich de Giers; Minister of War, Gen. Vannovski; Minister of the Navy, Vice-Admiral Tchikhatcheff; Minister of the Interior, Privy Councilor Durnovo; Minister of Public Instruction, Privy Councilor Delianoff; Minister of Finance, Privy Councilor Witte; Minister of Justice, Privy Councilor Manassein; Minister of the State Domains, Privy Councilor Ostrovski; Minister of Public Works and Railroads, Privy Councilor Krivochein; Chief of the Department of General Control, Privy Councilor Filipoff.

Area and Population.—About one seventh of the land surface of the globe belongs to Russia, the area being 8,644,100 square miles. No general census has been taken since 1859, but various enumerations taken in nearly all parts place the population of the empire, in 1887, at 113,354,649. The European provinces of Russia have a total area of 1,902,092 square miles, and a population of 86,594,226. Poland has an area of 49,157 square miles, and a population of 8,385,807. The area of the Grand Duchy of

Finland is 144,255 square miles, and the population 2,305,916. Northern Caucasia, with 86,858 square miles, has 2,673,601 inhabitants; Transcaucasia, with an area of 95,799 square miles, and a population of 4.784,550. The Kirghiz Steppe has an area of 755,793 square miles and a population of 2,000,970; Turkestan, an area of 409,414 square miles and 3,341,913 inhabitants; Transcaspian Territories, an area of 214,237 square miles and a population of 301,476; the Caspian Sea, an area of 169,381 square miles; Western Siberia, an area of 870,818 square miles and a population of 2,023,129; Eastern Siberia, an area of 3,044,512 square miles and a population of 1,680,768; the Amur region, an area of 888,830 square miles and a population of 166,-007; and Sakhalin, an area of 29,336 square miles and a population of 14,645. In the European provinces of Russia the number of marriages in 1888 was 804,084; births, 4,251,473; deaths, 2,749,085. In Poland the figures were: 67,392 marriages, 334,268 births, and 204,031 deaths; in Finland, 16,748 marriages, 80,172 births, and 45,417 deaths; in Siberia, in 1887, 23,481 marriages, 212,148 births. and 150,197 deaths; in the Caucasus, 56,550 marriages, 268,-250 births, and 171,708 deaths; Russians in central Asia in 1885, 8,540 marriages, 52,361 births, and 41,519 deaths.

(For religion, see the "Annual Cyclopædia" for 1891.)

Finances.—The revenues are principally derived from direct and indirect taxes, state domains and salt mines, and the monopolies of salt and tobacco. The ordinary revenue in 1891 amounted to 891,594,000 rubles, and the extraordinary revenue to 37,201,000 rubles, a total of 928,795,000 rubles, showing a surplus over the budget estimates of 14,287,000 rubles. The ordinary expenditures amounted to 875,349,000 rubles, while the extraordinary expenditures amounted to 240,298,000 rubles, a total of 1,115,647,000 rubles, which exceeded the budget estimates by 153,344,000 rubles. The receipts from direct taxes were 87,021,000 rubles; from indirect taxes, 503,256,000 rubles; from monopolies, 35,221,000 rubles; from domains, etc., 94,780,000 rubles; from other sources, 168,611,-000 rubles. Of the ordinary expenditures, 248,-020,000 rubles were for the public debt; 2,648,-000 rubles for the superior governing bodies, 11,340,000 rubles for the Holy Synod, 10,560,000 rubles for the Ministry of the Court. 4,784,000 rubles for the Ministry of Foreign Affairs, 226,-108,000 rubles for the Ministry of War, 45,468,-000 rubles for the Ministry of Marine, 113,427,-000 rubles for the Ministry of Finance, 24,532,-000 rubles for the Ministry of Domains, 80,203,-000 rubles for the Ministry of the Interior, 22,769,000 rubles for the Ministry of Public Instruction, 56,148,000 rubles for the Ministry of Communications, 23,874,000 rubles for the Ministry of Justice, 4,220,000 rubles for the Control Department, and 1,248,000 rubles for the imperial stud. The budget for 1892 estimates the total revenue at 965,303,066 rubles, of which 886,544,325 rubles are ordinary receipts; 4,490,-336 rubles, extraordinary receipts; and 74,268,-375 rubles, the available fund of the Chamber of Finances to cover the deficit. The expenditures are estimated at 965,303,063 rubles, of which 911,668,066 rubles are for ordinary expenses, and 53,635,000 rubles for extraordinary expenditures.

On Jan. 1, 1892, the part of the debt of the empire payable in specie, including the Polish debt, was 1,155,309,650 rubles, £2,489,700, and 543,787,000 francs; the debt payable in paper currency, 3,024,213,178 rubles. The expenditures on the debt in 1892 amounted to 247,824,838 rubles. The debts to the state of railroads, municipalities, and local treasuries, on Jan. 1, 1891, amounted to 1,330,136,754 rubles. On April 10, 1892, a new internal railroad loan of 75,000,000 rubles was issued, bearing 4½ per cent. interest, and redeemable in eighty-one years.

The Army.—Military service is obligatory, and begins for all Russians at the age of twenty years. The term of service is in European Russia five years in the active army, thirteen years in the reserve, and five more years in the first ban of the territorial army. In Turkestan, the Amur region, as well as for the marine troops, the period of service is seven years in the active army, and six years in the reserve; while the troops in northern Caucasia and in the Transcaspian Territories remain three years with the colors and fifteen years with the reserve. The men who are not selected for the permanent army form part of the first ban of the territorial army, from the ages of twenty to forty-three; they, as well as the men belonging to the reserve, are called out twice a year for a six weeks' drill—in the former case, however, only up to the age of twenty-five. All who are incapable of carrying arms are allotted to the second ban of the territorial army, and are only called upon in case of war to complete the territorial army. The total period of service for the Cossacks is twenty years. All Cossacks not serving in the army, or after completing their term, form part of the troops of the national defense, and may only be called out by the Czar under exceptional circumstances. The Christian clergy is entirely exempt, and physicians, veterinarians, and pharmaoists are relieved from duty in time of peace. All men professing the Mohammedan religion can exempt themselves by paying a certain military tax. For men who can prove a certain degree of education, the military service is reduced in proportion to their knowledge.

The Russian army is divided into field troops, fortress troops, local troops. reserve, second reserve, and auxiliary corps. The field troops consisted in 1891 of 193 regiments of infantry, 20 regiments of riflemen, 77 separate battalions, 338 squadrons of cavalry, 350 batteries of artillery, and 34¼ battalions of engineers, giving a total strength of 599,000 men, with 78,500 horses. The fortress troops were composed of 1 regiment of infantry, 26 battalions of infantry, 5 sally batteries, and 51¾ battalions of artillery, making a total of 37,500 men, with 250 horses. The local troops formed 165 detachments, and the number of men was 24,000. The reserve consisted of 18 regiments of infantry, 88 battalions of infantry, and 33 batteries of artillery, making a total of 69,500 men, with 2,250 horses. The second reserve had 18 *cadres* for cavalry, and 2 batteries of artillery, a total of 5,500 men and 5,100 horses. The train consisted of 5 battalions, with 2,000 men and 500 horses; while the auxiliary bodies numbered 43,000 men, with 2,500 horses. The Cossacks formed 49 regiments of cavalry, 6 battalions of infantry, and 20 batteries of artillery, a total of 58,500 men, with 45,500 horses. The militia numbered 3,500 men, with 3,000 horses. The grand total, on the peace footing, was 843,000 men and 137,250 horses. The war effective for 1892, exclusive of the territorial army and the Cossack troops, was officially stated to be 2,532,496 combatants, with 577,796 horses and 5,264 guns.

The Navy.—The Russian navy is organized in two divisions—the fleet of the Baltic and that of the Black Sea. The fleet of the Baltic consisted, in 1892, of 5 turret ships, with 53 guns; 11 armored cruisers, with 330 guns; 13 ironclad monitors; 3 ironclad gunboats; 3 armored cruisers, with pear-shaped redoubts; 8 torpedo cruisers; 2 cruisers; 3 corvettes; 10 torpedo gunboats; 8 yachts; 2 torpedo vessels; 12 torpedo boats of the first class; 8 torpedo boats of the second class; 2 transports; and a large number of smaller boats properly belonging to the revenue marine. In construction are 2 ironclad cruisers and 8 first-class torpedo boats. The fleet of the Black Sea consists of 6 turret ships, 7 cruisers, 7 schooners, 2 steamers, 2 torpedo cruisers, 16 torpedo boats of the first class, 1 transport, and a number of smaller vessels. There are 1 turret ship, 3 torpedo cruisers, 1 torpedo transport, and 9 torpedo boats of the first class under construction. The fleet kept in Siberia numbers 7 vessels and 26 smaller boats, while the fleet in the Caspian Sea is composed of 8 gunboats, 1 schooner, and 18 small boats. The fleet had, in 1892, 1,249 officers, 807 employees, and 25,736 suboflicers and sailors.

The volunteer fleet, which is destined for commerce and transport of exiles in time of peace, numbers 23 vessels, but by a law enacted Feb. 23, 1892, it will receive an annual subsidy of 600,000 rubles for ten years, on condition that the fleet is augmented by 4 new fast-sailing vessels, with a displacement of at least 8,000 tons, and 2 new transports, which shall be specially adopted for commerce.

The biggest ironclad cruiser afloat, the "Rurik," was launched from the yards of the Baltic works, on the Neva, on Nov. 3, 1892. The "Rurik" measures from stem to stern 435 feet, with 67 feet beam, 25 feet 9 inch depth, and 10.933 tons displacement. Her speed is calculated at 18 knots, with triple-expansion engines of 13,250 indicated horse power. She will be armed with 6 8-inch guns in turrets, 14 6-inch guns, 6 2½-inch guns, and 19 47-millimetre and 11 37-millimetre rapid-firing guns; also 2 torpedo dischargers and 2 torpedo boats. The armor down to the water line is 10 inches thick, and below, including the keel, 5 inches.

Commerce.—The value of the imports, in 1891, from European countries, exclusive of precions metals, was 326,300,000 rubles; from Asia, 39,400,000 rubles; from Finland, 12,800,000 rubles; total imports, 378,500,000 rubles. The value of exports to European countries was 627,300,000 rubles; to Asiatic countries, 77,200,000 rubles; to Finland, 16,400,000 rubles; total exports, 720,900,000 rubles.

The following table shows the trade with the different countries in 1891, in rubles:

COUNTRIES.	Imports.	Exports.
Germany	103,260,000	192,982,000
Great Britain	58,060,000	179,905,000
France	16,691,000	48,906,000
Austria-Hungary	15,903,000	84,001,000
Belgium	6,678,000	28,069,000
Netherlands	8,099,000	44,064,000
Turkey	6,365,000	20,616,000
Italy	10,596,000	32,895,000
Sweden and Norway	4,903,000	10,812,000
Denmark	1,291,000	10,111,000
Greece	1,984,000	10,251,000
Roumania	1,544,000	8,599,000
United States	39,781,000	2,019,000
China	28,967,000	4,220,000
Persia	10,854,000	9,957,000
All other countries	44,570,000	89,277,000
Total	378,546,000	720,937,000

The imports and exports through the Russian ports of the Baltic were 145,900,000 and 168,700,000 rubles respectively; across the Finland frontier, 12,800,000 and 16,400,000 rubles; across the European land frontiers of Russia, 119,000,000 and 187,100,000 rubles; by the Black Sea ports, 60,600,000 and 264,700,000 rubles; by the White Sea ports, 800,000 and 6,800,000 rubles; across the Asiatic frontiers, 39,400,000 and 77,200,000 rubles.

The following table shows the imports and exports in 1891, in rubles:

MERCHANDISE.	Imports.	Exports.
By the European frontiers:		
Cereals	845,000	323,082,000
Drinks and alcohol	9,158,000	5,757,000
Tea and coffee	28,228,000	116,000
Tobacco, etc	2,076,000	1,085,000
Fruits, legumes	5,280,000	933,000
Sugar	10,000	28,294,000
Other produce	18,867,000	26,552,000
Oil	12,020,000	52,000
Raw metal	20,865,000	1,985,000
Linseed	....	38,786,000
Hides and skins, etc	8,888,000	14,042,000
Hair, bristles	25,000	9,908,000
Textiles	102,605,000	84,782,000
Lumber	4,425,000	43,306,000
Dyeing materials	12,919,000	168,000
Naphtha and petroleum	82,000	4,056,000
Different materials	41,405,000	12,749,000
Pottery and glassware	2,688,000	860,000
Apparel and trimmings	8,370,000	7,687,000
Machines, etc	84,588,000	2,267,000
Various manufactures	41,405,000	12,749,000
Precious metals	77,463,000	194,000
By way of Finland:		
Articles of food	1,952,000	9,640,000
Raw and half-manufactured articles	5,029,000	2,584,000
Manufactured goods	5,197,000	8,748,000
Animals	615,000	129,000
By way of Asia:		
Tea	14,879,000	10,000
Tissues	2,800,000	5,678,000
Textiles	2,054,000	2,475,000
Furs, skins	1,514,000	1,107,000
Fruits, legumes	2,944,000	164,000
Cereals, etc	2,688,000	24,424,000
Other merchandise	13,017,000	43,898,000
Precious metal	5,877,000	5,774,000

Navigation.—At the ports of the Baltic, in 1890, there were 5,638 vessels entered, of which 3,305 were with cargoes and 2,333 in ballast, while 4,983 vessels with cargoes and 589 in ballast cleared. In the White Sea ports there were 319 vessels entered with cargoes and 277 in ballast, while 581 vessels cleared with cargoes. In the Black Sea and the Sea of Azov 1,441 entered with cargoes and 3,370 in ballast, and 4,292 cleared with cargoes and 468 in ballast. Of the total number of vessels entered, 11,045 at all the ports, 7,966 were steamers; while of 10,913 vessels cleared, 7,822 were steamers. Of the total number of vessels entered, 1,347 were Russian, 3,710 English, 1,603 German, 1,376 Swedish and Norwegian, 608 Turkish, 944 Danish, 229 Austrian, and 127 Dutch, etc.

Railroads, Posts, and Telegraphs.—At the beginning of 1891 the total length of the Russian railroads was 20,085 miles, and 272 miles were in construction.

The post office in 1890 forwarded, in the internal service, 171,686 letters, 22,109 postal cards, 22,485 pieces of printed matter, and 12,457,000 money letters of the declared value of 14,940,-133,000 francs. In the external service, 25,570 letters, 4,072 postal cards, 10,201 pieces of printed matter, and 460,000 money letters of the declared value of 488,248,000 francs, were expedited. The receipts were 81,641,260 francs, and the expenses, including those of the telegraph service, were 95,812,692 francs. The receipts from telegraphs were 41,086,144 francs. The state telegraph lines had a length of 119,046 kilometres, with 229,084 kilometres of wire. The number of domestic telegrams was 8,761,896; of international telegrams, 695,836 were sent and 745,679 received; the number in transit was 153,197, and 624,577 were official messages.

Finland.—The Grand Duchy of Finland is a constitutional monarchy, ceded to the Emperor of Russia by the treaty of Friederichsham, Sept. 17, 1809. Its Constitution of 1722, which was amended in 1789, 1869, and 1883, was acknowledged by a manifesto of Alexander I in 1810, and since by each of his successors. The Constitution provides for a National Assembly, consisting of 4 estates, viz., tho nobility, the clergy, the burghers, and the peasantry, the consent of all four of which is requisite to change the Constitution or impose new taxes. The National Assembly is convoked by the Emperor as grand duke for four months, whenever the country requires legislative enactments. Its duties are to consider laws proposed by the Emperor and elaborated by the Committee for the Affairs of Finland, which consists of the State Secretary and 4 members nominated by the Emperor, and which has its seat in St. Petersburg. The Emperor has the power to veto any measure that is passed. The superior administrative power vests in a senate under the presidency of the Governor-General, and is nominated by the Crown. The Governor-General and chief commander of the military forces is Count T. Heyden. The area of Finland consists of 373,604 square kilometres, of which 47,829 square kilometres are covered with water. The population, on Dec. 31, 1890, was 2,380,140, of whom 1,171,-541 were males and 1,208,599 females. Of the total population, 2,334,547 were Lutherans, 45,-132 Greek Orthodox, and 461 Roman Catholics. Finnish was spoken by 2,048,545 people, Swedish by 322,604, Russian by 5,795, German by 1,074, Laplandish by 1,106 people, etc. The number of marriages was 16,835; births, 79,991; deaths, 48,610; excess of births, 31,381. The receipts of the Government were estimated in the budget for 1892 at 59,908,875 Finnish marks (1 mark = 19·3 cents). Of the receipts, 6,038,088 marks were from State domains, railroads, and canals; 5,496,100 marks from direct taxes; 21,568,000 marks from indirect taxes; 1,000,000 marks from stamps; 480,000 marks from passports, etc.; 1,800,000 marks from posts; 8,131,901 marks from different sources; and 420,020 marks from the surplus of the preceding year. The expenditures are made to balance the receipts. The public debt amounted to 77,736,801 marks on Jan. 1, 1892. The imports from Russia in 1891 amounted to 51,700,000 marks; from Sweden and Norway, to 10,900,000 marks; from Denmark, to 3,700,000 marks; from Germany, to 46,800,000 marks; from Great Britain, to 21,-500,000 marks; from France, to 1,400,000 marks; from the Netherlands, to 500,000 marks; from Belgium, to 2,000,000 marks; from Spain, to 1,600,000 marks; and from other countries, to 6,400,000 marks; total imports, 146,500,000 marks. The exports to Russia were 36,100,000 marks; to Sweden and Norway, 6,200,000 marks; to Denmark, 15,000,000 marks; to Germany, 7,300,000 marks; to Great Britain, 19,000,000 marks; to France, 11,300,000 marks; to the Netherlands, 2,700,000 marks; to Belgium, 1,500,-000 marks; to Spain, 4,700,000 marks; to other countries, 400,000 marks; total exports, 104,200,-000 marks. The chief imports are: Cereals, of the value of 27,800,000 marks; coffee, 12,000,000 marks; iron, 11,000,000 marks; sugar, 6,100,000 marks; machinery, 6,100,000 marks; cotton, 5,700,000 marks. Of the principal exports, lumber was valued at 44,800,000 marks; butter, 14,700,000 marks; paper stock, 8,600,000 marks; cereals, 7,100,000 marks. In 1891 there were 11,633 vessels, of 1,991,539 tons, entered at the ports of Finland, and 12,110 vessels, of 2,043,465 tons, cleared. On Dec. 31, 1891, the total length of railroads was 1,930 kilometres.

Russia and the Pamirs.—The dispute over the boundary line in the Pamirs between Russia and Afghanistan led to a serious encounter between the troops of the two countries. When, in 1873, the boundary of Afghan territory was fixed by Russia and England, the upper Oxus was stated to be the dividing line, but it was omitted to define which of the branches of this great stream was meant. Russia claimed that the most southerly branch had been understood in the agreement, while England maintained that the northerly branch had been intended as the boundary. At the time the matter was allowed to rest. The region which Russia claims is in itself an undesirable acquisition, consisting of bare and storm-swept downs, about 13,000 to 14,000 feet above the sea level, almost arctic in its desolation. The importance attached to the Pamirs depends on the fact that the territories of India, Afghanistan, Russian Turkestan, and China are adjacent to its borders, with very ill-defined boundary lines. Hitherto it had been understood that the passes leading through the mountains were of little or no value for strategic purposes, the country being regarded as almost impassable. It seems, however, that the many Russian explorers sent to this region have discovered some passes which lead into the different countries, and which are of more importance than they had been credited with. Russian diplomatists assert that the strategic importance of the country lies in its relation to China, but it can not be denied that the passes, if they exist, would aid Russia materially in an onward march to India. In the early summer of 1892 an expedition started out under the command of Col. Yanoff, ostensibly with the view of strengthening Russian authority in her own district and securing the evacuation of territory arbitrarily occupied by the Chinese, and to protect the Russian Kirghiz encamped in the Pamirs against the aggression and the exactions of the Afghans. Col. Yanoff, in his report to the Governor of Budukhshan, states that when he arrived in the territory claimed by Russia he found several Chinese outposts established on Russian territory, but that they evacuated their positions on demand. Then, hearing that about 1,000 Afghans were encamped at Somatash, he proceeded thither with 1,000 troops for the purpose of obtaining an explanation from the Afghan leader. Col. Yanoff went in advance with a small force and tried to induce the Afghan in command to meet him amicably; this he refused to do, but approached at the head of his followers, who had their guns cocked, using abusive and threatening language, whereupon Col. Yanoff ordered his men to disarm them. Then the Afghans opened fire, killing 1 Russian and wounding 2; the Russians returned the fire, killing 9, including an officer, and wounding 2, besides capturing 7 prisoners. This encounter created a good deal of excitement in India as well as in Europe, owing to the difficulty of obtaining an accurate report of the number of the Russian forces and their object, but, as a matter of fact, Russia only exercised her authority over territory which she has long claimed as her own, and expelled from it foreign forces which refused to leave Russian soil. The expedition was withdrawn in September, but as the reappearance was feared of Chinese and Afghans in the Pamirs, who might disturb or oppress the inhabitants, a small force of observation was left in cantonment near the tomb of the Shah Djan, on the right bank of the Murghab. Baron Vrevsky, Governor-General of Turkestan, in a general order which he addressed to his troops, expressed full satisfaction with the manner in which the Pamir expedition was carried out.

The Famine.—The famine which visited Russia in 1891-'92 extended over an area of about 475,000 square miles, and afflicted a population of nearly 30,000,000 souls. The reasons for such a frightful calamity are various and many. The area covered by the famine was formerly the most fertile and productive part of Russia, but of late years the crops have been falling off. In 1886 the distressed provinces produced 140,914,948 chetverts (1 chetvert = about 5·9 bushels) of grain, and in 1889 the harvest was 105,914,000 chetverts; but in 1891 the produce had fallen to 71,371,900 chetverts. The exports were not reduced in proportion to the decrease in production, for while the exports in 1888 amounted to 484,891,000 poods, those of 1891, the year of the famine, still amounted to 310,000,000 poods. The total harvest of 1891 of all cereals and potatoes for the European provinces of Russia and Poland, after deducting the exports, was about 14 poods per head; as, however, 14½ poods per head is the required annual amount, there was a deficit of about half a pood per head. The amount on hand, if evenly distributed at the beginning, would probably have sufficed to sustain the population; but a surplus in one part and a large deficit in other parts of the empire, coupled with the limited means of communication, made it impossible to establish an equilibrium. In spite of the strenuous efforts of the Government to mitigate the terrible suffering in the famine districts, there were thousands of unhappy peasants who succumbed to the ravages of hunger; and when, in consequence of the bad nourishment, diseases broke out, the number of deaths increased 50 per cent. in some localities. Up to March 1, 1892, the Government had spent 150,000,000 rubles for the support of the sufferers, and on June 1 the sum was estimated to have reached 200,000,000 rubles. Besides this, taxes were remitted, the forests of the imperial domains were opened to the peasants for fuel, and thousands of men were employed on public works, wherever practicable. Private relief was given by persons in as well as outside of Russia. The large and generous contributions from the United States deserve special attention. Besides money contributions, not including those sent through private channels, four ships were dispatched to the sufferers laden with flour and other bread stuffs, and containing clothing for the half-naked peasants. The total sum received from the United States, including the cargoes, exceeded 1,000,000 rubles, which was equivalent to supporting over 21,000,000 people for a day, or more than 700,000 for a month. Proper arrangements were made at St. Petersburg to apply the American donations judiciously and conscientiously, the knowledge of which had extended even into the remote interior, and the name of America is gratefully cherished there.

S

SALVADOR, a republic in Central America. Its independence dates from 1840; the present Constitution was adopted in 1864, and has been revised and amended several times, the last revision taking place in 1888. The legislative authority is vested in a Chamber of 42 Deputies, elected annually by the suffrage of all the male citizens of the republic. The executive power rests in the hands of a President, who is chosen for four years by the direct vote of the nation. The President in office is Gen. Carlos Ezeta, elected for the term beginning March 1, 1891. The ministry is composed of the following members: Minister of Finance, War, and Marine, D. Angulo; Minister of Foreign Affairs, Justice, and Public Worship, Dr. S. Gallegos; Minister of the Interior and Public Works, Dr. D. Jimenez; Minister of Public Instruction, Dr. D. Castro.

The area of the republic, according to a recent survey, is 21.070 square kilometres. The population on Jan. 1, 1891, was 777,895; the capital, San Salvador, had 20,000 inhabitants. The army numbers 4,000 men, and in case of need the militia, 15,000 men, may be called out.

Commerce.—The imports in 1890 amounted to $2,401,000, against $2,886,050 in 1889; the exports to $7,579,000 and $5,673,786 respectively. The imports from Great Britain amounted in 1889 to $957,359; from France, $312,295; from Germany, $328,650. Of the exports, $940,-154 went to Great Britain, $1,027,980 to Germany, $1,158,806 to France. The trade with the United States has been steadily increasing, the imports in 1892 amounting to $1,294,268, against $1,150,460 in 1891 and $899,546 in 1890; the exports amounting to $2,330,702, $1,783,066, and $1,453,958 respectively for the three years. Of the total exports to the United States in 1892, merchandise to the value of $2,330,697 entered free of duty. The reciprocity treaty with the United States went into effect on Feb. 1, 1892.

SANTO DOMINGO, a republic occupying about two thirds of the island of Hayti. The Constitution dates from Nov. 24, 1844, and was last modified on Nov. 17, 1888. The legislative power vests in a Congress of 22 members, elected, 2 for each province, for four years by the indirect vote of the people. The executive is vested in a President, elected for the term of four years. The present incumbent of the presidential chair is Ulises Heureaux, elected in 1886. The ministry is composed of the following members: Minister of the Interior and Police, Gen. W. Figuereo; Minister of Foreign Affairs, Gen. J. Gonzalez; Minister of War and Marine, Gen. F. Lithgoro; Minister of Finance and Commerce, Gen. J. F. Sanchez; Minister of Justice and Public Instruction, G. Perez; Minister of Public Works, Gen. A. Wos y Gil.

The area of the republic is 18,045 square miles, and the population was estimated in 1888 at 417,-000 inhabitants. Santo Domingo, the capital city, has a population of about 25,000, and Puerto Plato, the principal seaport, has a population of 15,000. (For finances, see "Annual Cyclopædia" for 1891.)

Commerce.—The principal cultivated products are tobacco, coffee, cacao, cotton, and sugar, while the exports consist chiefly of coffee, fustic, tobacco, sugar, cacao, logwood, lignum vitæ, and mahogany. The total imports through the port of Santo Domingo in 1890 amounted to $1,123,-947, while those of 1891 amounted to $1,086,501. The exports for the same years were $922,471 and $638.497 respectively. The chief exports from Puerto Plata in 1890 were: Tobacco, 4,714,-704 pounds, valued at $358,296; coffee, 896,216 pounds, valued at $179,216; mahogany, 841,025 feet, valued at $120,571; cacao, 255,251 pounds, valued at $51,050; logwood, 718 tons, valued at $7,180; sugar, 895,540 pounds, valued at $26,-866; and hides and skins of the value of $38,-985. The United States custom reports gives the value of exports from the United States to Santo Domingo for 1891 as amounting to $1,-023,751, and for 1892 as $1,019,450. The imports into the United States from Santo Domingo amounted in 1891 to $1,610,360, of which merchandise to the value of $1,009,690 was free of duty, while $600,670 was dutiable; for 1892 the total was $2,293,748, of which $2,279,-267 worth was free and $14,481 dutiable. The number of vessels entered and cleared in 1891 was 175, of 104,342 tons.

SERVIA, a monarchy in southeastern Europe. By the treaty of Berlin, July 13, 1878, Servia obtained its independence, and it was proclaimed a kingdom on March 6, 1882. The Constitution, dated June 11, 1869, was modified on Jan. 3, 1889. The executive is vested in the King, and is exercised by a Council of Ministers, who are individually and collectively responsible to the National Assembly, or Skupshtina. On March 6, 1889, King Milan abdicated in favor of his son, and established a regency until the latter should become of age. It consists of 3 members, and was composed in the beginning of 1892 of J. Ristich, Gen. J. Belimarkovich, and Gen. K. S. Protich. The Skupshtina meets annually, and is composed of 134 members, elected indirectly by the people by *scrutin de liste.* Each county is entitled to one Deputy to every 4,500 taxpaying males; when the surplus is more than 3,000 taxpayers, they are at liberty to elect an additional one. The State Council consists of 16 members, of which 8 are chosen by the Skupshtina and 8 are nominated by the King. The Great Skupshtina is called when important business of the state requires it; it has double the number of the Deputies elected for the ordinary Skupshtina. The ministry at the beginning of 1892 was composed of the following members: Premier and Minister of Finance *ad interim,* N. Pachieh; Minister of Public Works, P. Velimirovich; Minister of Justice, G. Guerchich; Minister of Agriculture and Commerce, K. Tauchanovich; Minister of Foreign Affairs, M. K. Gjorgjevich; Minister of the Interior, J. Djaia; Minister of Public Instruction and Worship, A. Nikolieh; Minister of War, Col. Z. D. Praportchetovich.

Area and Population.—The area of the kingdom is 18,855 square miles. The population, according to the census of Jan. 1, 1891, is 2,162,759, of whom 1,110,731 are males and 1,052,028 females. Of the total population, 26·30 per cent. of those living in towns and 97·20 per cent. of the country population are dependent on agriculture. In 1884, 1,693,373 of the population were Servians, 149,727 Roumanians, 34,-066 gypsies, 2,961 Armenians and Turks, 4,127 Jews, 6,749 Bulgarians, and 10,733 other foreigners. The principal towns are Belgrade, the capital, with 54,458 inhabitants; Nisch, with a population of 19,970; Leskovatz, with 12,146 inhabitants; Pozarevatz, with 11,140; and Pirot, with 10,108.

Finances.—The chief revenue is derived from direct taxes on real estate and incomes and from the Government monopolies. The total revenue for 1892 was estimated in the budget at 60,135,-839 dinars or francs, and the expenditures at 60,110,595 dinars. Of the total revenue, 22,186,-469 dinars are derived from direct taxes, 12,426,-000 dinars from monopolies, 3,700,000 dinars from customs, 3,000,000 dinars from excise, 3,230,000 dinars from domains, posts, and telegraphs, 6,000,000 dinars from state railroads, 2,395,000 dinars from judicial fees, 623,370 dinars from state mortgage banks, and 6,575,000 dinars from various sources. Of the total expenditures, 20,466,188 dinars are for the public debt, 1,200,-000 dinars for the civil list, 150,000 dinars for the Skupshtina, 187,910 dinars for the Council of State, 280,782 dinars for general expenses,

1,930,605 dinars for pensions and dotations, 2,023,535 dinars for the Ministry of Justice, 3,818,890 dinars for the Ministry of Public Instruction and Worship, 1,192,563 dinars for the Ministry of Foreign Affairs, 2,683,720 dinars for the Ministry of the Interior, 5,567,818 dinars for the Ministry of Finance, 11,327,483 dinars for the Ministry of War, 4,828,599 dinars for the Ministry of Public Works, 3,252,502 dinars for the Ministry of Agriculture and Commerce, and 1,200,000 dinars for various purposes. The public debt amounted on Jan. 1, 1892, to 328,739,836 dinars. Of this sum, 157,635,000 dinars represent the loans for the construction of railroads; 3,222,836 dinars the Russian loan; 6,473,500 dinars were raised for the purpose of indemnifying Turkish proprietors who emigrated; 67,180,500 dinars represent the lottery loan; 39,682,500 dinars were raised in 1884; 38,653,500 dinars were raised in 1885; for a loan of 6,000,000 dinars the salt monopoly is pledged; and there is a loan of 9,892,000 dinars for which the tobacco monopoly is given as security.

Commerce. — The total imports in 1891 amounted to 42,806,000 dinars, of which 28,903,000 dinars came from Austria, 2,055,000 dinars from Turkey, 1,190,000 dinars from Roumania, 1,314,000 dinars from Russia, 1,798,000 dinars from Germany, 548,000 dinars from Italy, 514,000 dinars from Switzerland, 4,323,000 dinars from Great Britain, 1,447,000 dinars from America, and the remainder from Bosnia, Bulgaria, Greece, France, and Belgium. The total exports amounted to 52,480,000 dinars, of which 45,154,000 dinars went to Austria, 887,000 dinars to Bulgaria, 1,800,000 dinars to Turkey, 1,588,000 dinars to Germany, 2,073,000 dinars to France, 325,000 dinars to America, and the balance to Bosnia, Roumania, Italy, Switzerland, and Great Britain. The principal imports and their values were : Fruits and agricultural produce. 974,000 dinars; colonial produce, 3,651,000 dinars; hides, skins, and India rubber, 4,061,000 dinars; woolens, 3,260,000 dinars; legumes, etc., 2,014,000 dinars; wooden goods, 2,244,000 dinars; metals, 4,848,000 dinars; pottery, glass, etc., 2,212,000 dinars; drugs and chemicals, 1,519,000 dinars; machines and instruments, 1,339,000 dinars; cottons, etc., 8,589,000 dinars; hardware, 1,895,000 dinars; apparel, 3,674,000 dinars. Of the exports, fruits and agricultural produce were valued at 25.104,000 dinars; animals and animal produce at 19,456,000 dinars; leather, skins, etc., 2,564,000 dinars; food and drink, 1,696,000 dinars; wood and wooden ware, 1,374,000 dinars.

Communications.—The total length of railroads in 1891 was 540 kilometres. The telegraph lines in the same year had a length of 2,978 kilometres, with a length of wire of 4,981 kilometres. There were transmitted over the wires 617,071 messages, of which 496,398 were domestic, 95,881 international, 17,866 were in transit, and 6,926 were service despatches. The receipts were 334,214 francs, and the expenses 380,610 francs. The post-office forwarded 5,088,000 letters, 72,000 postal cards, 3,185,000 pieces of printed matter, and 198,000 money letters, of the declared value of 94,904,000 francs, in the internal service; 3,470,000 letters, 215,000 postal cards, 1,326,000 pieces of printed matter, and 98,000 money letters of the declared value of 57,493,000 francs, in the external service; and 530,000 letters, 17,000 p   cards, 204,000 pieces of printed matter, and 484,000 money letters of the declared value of 11,201,000 francs, were expedited in the transit service. The receipts were 898,395 francs, and the expenses 728,924.

Politics.—In the beginning of February, 1892, the Servian Government received a communication from the Austrian Government, in which the latter remonstrated against the harboring of Bulgarian refugees in Servian territory, whose object was the overthrow of the Bulgarian Government. Servia had permitted these refugees to carry on their schemes openly, and had not tried to restrain them in any way. The Austrian Government reminded the Servian Government of the Treaty of Berlin, and furthermore declared that it would hold Servia responsible for any disturbance of the peace in Bulgaria. It was understood that the triple alliance was behind this demand, and Servia was compelled to take measures against the refugees, and actually expelled some and imprisoned others. At a convention held by the Radicals under the leadership of Ranko Taisich, this action of the Radical ministry was strongly condemned, the Premier Pachich being accused of showing a marked degree of weakness in yielding to the demands of the triple alliance; dissatisfaction was also expressed with the manner in which the Government had suppressed the freedom of the press since coming into office, and a discussion in the Skupshtina regarding the banishment of Queen Natalie tended to widen the breach in the Radical party. At a meeting of the Radical Club the actions of the Radical Government were repudiated, and after a stormy debate Prime Minister Pachieh declared that he would resign, thus enabling the Regents to form a Liberal Cabinet. He consequently tendered the resignation of his Cabinet on March 8, 1892. He was well aware, however, that the Radicals still held a majority in the Skupshtina. and that the Regents could not at the time afford to experiment with an untried premier; but he wanted to threaten the Radical Club, that if they persisted in their attacks against the ministry all their hard-earned advantages, together with the offices they held by means of a Radical Government, would be lost should the Liberals get into power. Pachieh had calculated correctly, for the Regents charged him with a reconstruction of the Cabinet, and after considerable difficulty he managed to form a compromise Cabinet, which satisfied the Regents as well as the Radical Club. It was composed as follows : Premier and Minister of Foreign Affairs, as well as Minister of Finance *ad interim*, Pachieh ; Minister of the Interior. Milosavljewich ; Minister of Agriculture and Commerce, Duchmanich ; Minister of War, Col. Gjurich ; Minister of Justice, Gjorgjewich.

The truce thus effected was not of long duration. In June, Gen. Protich, one of the Regents, died, thus leaving a vacancy which each party desired having filled by one of its members. The Regency was composed of members of the old Liberal party, and naturally the latter considered the post as belonging to them. The lack of organization and the dissension in the Radical party worked to the advantage of the

Liberals; the abuse of the power of the state officials and the serious financial condition imbittered the supporters of the Radicals, and a number of Deputies deserted the cause of Premier Pachieh. In the meantime the Liberals and Progressists agitated against the Government in power, under the leadership of the former Prime Minister, Garashanin, and not without success, for when Pachieh, in order to prevent the total dissolution of his party, undertook a tour through the provinces, making speeches in which he advocated his party's cause, he found that the popularity which he had formerly enjoyed had seriously diminished. The question of filling the third place in the Regency not only affected the parties, but was of the greatest importance to the Regents themselves, for in case a Radical obtained the office he could bring the whole business of state to a standstill by refusing his signature to important measures. Premier Pachieh desired to fill the place of a third Regent himself, and to be able to reunite his party he endeavored to have himself elected, and then come before the party convention called for Sept. 1, 1892, with the accomplished fact. For this purpose he demanded 'the immediate convocation of the Skupshtina, grounding his demand on the necessity of ratifying the Austro-Servian commercial treaty. The first Regent, Ristich, declared himself ready to come to a compromise with the Government regarding the election of a Regent, and that no necessity existed for convoking the Skupshtina. Prime-Minister Pachieh insisted that such action of the Regents was unconstitutional, and that he would insist on his demands. The Regent replied that, this being true, he would have to request the ministry to resign, and that he would call in a Liberal ministry, which was constitutional. Consequently the Pachieh Cabinet on Aug. 15 tendered their resignations, which were immediately accepted, and the leader of the Liberals, Avakumovich, was charged with the formation of a new Cabinet. Evidently the fall of the Radicals had been expected, for it did not require any length of time to complete the list of ministers, the new Cabinet being composed of the following members: Premier and Minister of Foreign Affairs, Jovan Avakumovich; Minister of the Interior, Stojan Ribaraz; Minister of Finance, Demeter Stojanovich; Minister of Justice, Witskovich; Minister of Public Instruction and Worship, Jovan Boskowich; Minister of War, Gen. Bogitchevich; Minister of Public Works, Prof. Alkovich; Minister of Agriculture and Commerce, Svetozar Gwozdich. The programme of the new Cabinet embraced friendly relations with all powers, to secure Servia's neutrality; strong administration of all branches of the Government; extension of the means of communication and regulation of the system of taxation, so as to balance the financial budget; and to properly organize the national defense. To prevent the Radicals from electing one of their number to the vacant post in the Regency, the regular meeting of the Skupshtina was postponed two months, and at the expiration of this time the Chamber was dissolved, and new elections ordered to be held in February, 1893.

At a mass meeting of the Radical party held at Alexinatz, Sept. 5, 1892, resolutions were adopted declaring the Radical Government justified in tendering its resignation, and giving it the approval of the Assembly. A second resolution condemned the action of the Regents as being opposed to parliamentary order, in appointing a ministry from among a party which only represented a small minority.

Session of the Skupshtina.—A bill was submitted to the Skupshtina and passed on March 24, 1892, dealing with ex-King Milan's renunciation of his Servian citizenship. By this measure Milan, in consideration of a stipulated sum of money, renounces absolutely all his rights as a Servian citizen and his ties with the Servian royal house; he gives up his influence over the education as well as financial affairs of the King; he agrees never to make any further demands on the Servian Government nor on the royal house; nor can he again become a Servian citizen without the consent of the Skupshtina. He is forbidden ever to return, remain, or settle in Servia, except in the case of a serious sickness of his son, when he may be permitted, with the consent of the Regency, to remain with his son during the duration of such sickness.

The commercial treaty with Austria was prolonged until Jan. 1, 1893, a new treaty being under consideration. A sum of 26,000,000 francs was granted by the Skupshtina to complete the organization of the army.

SEVENTH-DAY BAPTIST CHURCH.

Seventy-three churches of this denomination which reported to the General Conference returned a total of 458 additions, of which 287 were by baptism and 27 by testimony, and a total decrease of 355; a net gain of 103 members.

The ninetieth General Conference met at Nortonville, Kan., Aug. 24. Mr. David E. Titsworth, of Plainfield, N. J., was chosen president. Meetings of the Tract, Education, and Missionary Societies were held in connection with this meeting. The Tract Society reported that its receipts had been $8,708. About 294,000 pages of new tracts had been added during the year, aside from the Reform Library, comprehending 30,000 evangelical tracts and 31,000 Sabbath tracts, some in English and some in German. The Reform Library is a regular monthly publication of tracts, both old and new, distributed through the mails as second-class mail matter. The publishing house returned a net gain in values of $974, its present worth being $13,362. An office had been opened in New York city. At the annual meeting of the society a memorial to Congress was adopted against legislation forbidding the Sunday opening of the World's Columbian Exposition, on the ground, as the position of the body is defined, that Congress should "not thus enter upon the work of legislation concerning religious questions. Your petitioners believe that such a law would be contrary to the principles of religious freedom and the entire separation of Church and state upon which the National Government of the United States is based. We urge our prayer in the name of religious liberty and the noninterference of Congress, directly or indirectly, in religious matters." The Education Society reported concerning the condition of Salem College, West Virginia; Milton College, Wisconsin; and Alfred University, New York. The Missionary

Society had received $13,174, and its expenditures had been $12,556. An attempt was making, in connection with the "Carey Centennial," to raise a thank offering of $5,000. The mission in Shanghai, China, returned 4 foreign workers, 2 native preachers, 1 church, 2 preaching places, 30 members, and 4 schools, with 6 teachers and 71 pupils, and an average Sabbath-school attendance of 50. At the dispensary, 3,752 patients had been treated. From the other foreign mission—at Haarlem, Holland—progress was reported. Home mission work was carried on at many points in the several district associations.

The general conference adopted resolutions declaring the work of Sabbath reform to be the distinctive work of the denomination; deprecating the prevalence of loose views and practices as a serious drawback to the effectiveness of efforts in that direction; recommending, as the only sure means of checking the growing evil of apostasy to the Sabbath, "the cultivation in children of a sensitive conscience, both by precept and example, to exercise a careful discrimination between the right and the wrong not only in Sabbath observance, but also in all matters of thought and action." Special committees were appointed to prepare addresses on the doctrine of the Sabbath (or Seventh day) as of divine obligation upon every man, to be presented before the annual and general conventions, etc., of the different Christian bodies. Provision was made for the establishment of a Seventh-Day Baptist Employment Bureau.

SHIPPING ON THE GREAT LAKES.

According to the best authority, the number and tonnage of all sea-going vessels of 100 tons or more, for all the countries of the world in the year 1889, were as follow:

COUNTRIES.	No. of vessels.	Tonnage.
Argentine Republic	126	43,142
Austria	368	269,643
Belgium	85	110,571
Bolivia	8	2,302
Brazil	506	149,066
Chili	152	102,891
China	41	45,840
Colombia	2	444
Costa Rica	3	816
Denmark	808	280,065
France	1,980	1,045,102
Germany	1,876	1,569,811
Great Britain and colonies	12,071	11,597,106
Greece	971	307,640
Hawaii	27	19,405
Hayti	18	4,890
Italy	1,555	916,567
Japan	289	171,554
Mexico	32	11,041
Montenegro	17	8,282
Netherlands	544	878,784
Norway	3,869	1,584,855
Persia	1	838
Peru	37	11,048
Portugal	216	91,202
Roumania	5	986
Russia	1,181	427,835
Sarawak	7	2,616
Siam	10	4,168
Spain	853	584,811
Sweden	1,470	475,964
Turkey	907	229,777
United States of America	3,272	1,823,852
Uruguay	81	12,014
Venezuela	18	8,758
Zanzibar	6	4,723
Other countries	21	15,762
Total	32,298	22,151,651

For several years there has been a continuous decrease in the number of vessels afloat; and this feature is again apparent, the number being fewer by 364 at the end of 1889 than at the close of the previous year. But while the number of vessels has decreased, the aggregate tonnage has increased by 1,102,947 tons. Evidently larger vessels take the place of those that disappear. Since the end of 1885 the number of vessels has diminished by 3,110; and yet, despite the fact that for two years there was a diminution of tonnage, the extent of tonnage afloat at the close of 1889 was 643,795 tons greater than at the close of 1885. According to the table, the United States continues to be the second ship-owning nation. This is due to the large extent of sailing tonnage owned in the States. But if a steam vessel be considered as equal to three sailing vessels of the same tonnage (which ratio has been accepted frequently), the United States falls to the third position, the relative efficient tonnage of the ship-owning countries next in importance to the United Kingdom being as follows:

	Tons.
Germany	3,247,188
United States of America	2,858,670
France	2,664,298
Norway	2,177,698

The materials of which the steam sea-going vessels existing in the years 1888 and 1889 were built is shown by this table:

MATERIAL.	1888.		1889.	
	No. of vessels.	Tonnage.	No. of vessels.	Tonnage.
Iron	7,721	8,572,692	7,719	8,495,920
Steel	1,522	2,563,612	2,343	4,096,555
Composite	135	42,026	144	42,750
Wood	882	373,771	902	360,147
Total	10,260	11,552,101	11,108	12,985,372

The figures for 1890 show a still further tendency toward the decrease of wood and iron vessels upon salt water. According to the report of the United States Bureau of Navigation, vessels were built during 1889 and 1890 as follows:

GRAND DIVISIONS.	1889.		1890.	
	No.	Tons.	No.	Tons.
Atlantic and Gulf Coasts	657	93,912·24	663	156,755·99
Pacific Coast	112	17,989·43	93	12,334·92
Northern lakes	225	107,080·30	191	108,525·87
Western rivers	83	12,202·86	104	16,505·98
Total	1,077	281,184·83	1,051	294,122·76

A comparison with 1887 and 1888 shows a constantly increasing number of vessels built, and an increased tonnage, in all of the divisions but the Pacific coast, where both the number and the tonnage have fallen off since 1888. The number of vessels built during the year ending June 30, 1890, compared with the gross tonnage of the same, showed the remarkable fact that the average tonnage for each vessel built was as follows: Pacific coast, 133 tons; Western rivers, 159 tons; Atlantic and Gulf coasts, 236 tons; Northern lakes, 577 tons. The iron and steel vessels built in the United States during the fiscal year 1889-'90 amounted to 80,378 tons. During the fiscal year there were built at the lake ports

23 iron and steel vessels, with a tonnage of 38,-602 tons; and, on the Atlantic coast, 41,776 tons. The documented iron tonnage on the lakes was 29,327 tons, and on the sea coast 494,004 tons. The tonnage on the Northern lakes, June 30, 1890, was 1,063,064 tons; on the Western rivers, 204,446 tons; on the Pacific coast, 428,392 tons; and on the Atlantic and Gulf coasts, 2,638,595 tons. La Salle appeared on Lake Huron in 1679 with the "Griffin," but it went down, and for a century nothing but canoes and bateaux were seen on any Northern lake. In 1783 the "Gladwin," a brig of 80 tons, was plying between Detroit and Mackinac. Sometimes it was in the service of the Government, and again it was dealing in furs and supplies for the trappers in the wilderness. It was lost on Lake Erie. Eli Granger, in 1798, three miles below Rochester, built the "Jemina,"* a vessel of 30 tons, which was the first American ship built on Lake Ontario. The first American vessel built on Lake Erie was the "Washington," near Erie, Pa., in 1797. Others followed, but the demand for them was not great, and ship-building as an industry was hardly a recognized interest. During the War of 1812 many of the vessels on the lakes were purchased by the Government, and some of them were used by Commodore Perry in his fight on Lake Erie. The first steamboat on the lakes was the "Ontario," which was made after the pattern of the "Sea-Horse," then running on Long Island Sound. The "Ontario" was launched in 1817. It was 110 feet long and of 237 tons burden. The first Canadian steamer on the lakes was the "Frontenac," of 500 tons. The famed "Walk-in-the-Water" was built on Niagara river, and put into service in 1818. She was the first steamer to navigate Lakes Erie and Michigan. Emigration to the Northwest now filled the upgoing vessels, and the returning vessels were freighted with furs. In 1827 the schooner "Tiger" took a cargo of 410 packs of furs, valued at $62,000, from Detroit to Buffalo. But the shipping interest languished, and from 1816 until 1836 only 41 vessels were built on the lakes. The "Uncle Sam" touched at Chicago in 1834, and thereafter during the season that city was favored with one steamer a week.

The slow development of commerce on the Great Lakes was undoubtedly owing to the fact that the water ways are open but seven months in the year, and all efforts thus far to keep them open through the winter months have failed. Nearly all natural obstructions, like falls and rapids, have been overcome, and other improvements are now in progress, notably the increased lockage at the canal around St. Mary's Falls. The development of lake transportation has, as a rule, followed the development of railroad lines; for, with the exception of the ores of iron and copper on Lake Superior, no loads were at hand on the upper lakes for return cargoes. The building of railroads from the interior to the upper lakes brought to the vessels wheat and other articles that could be carried in bulk.

Even with this advantage, the development of traffic upon the lakes was slow until it was found that coal might be sent from the lower ports to the upper as a return cargo. With this discovery, the real trade of the Great Lakes took a sudden start, and it has been developed to enormous proportions. The passenger traffic of the lakes began soon after the opening of the Erie Canal, in 1825, and continued until about 1855. The closing days of the immense passenger traffic saw the building of such great steamers as the "Plymouth Rock," which ran between Buffalo and Detroit, and the "Western Metropolis," which ran between Cleveland and Buffalo. About 1850 it became evident that the commerce of the lakes would be almost exclusively a freight commerce. The building of wooden sail vessels of large capacity had scarcely begun. Down to that date the 2-masted or 3-masted schooners had an average tonnage of about 400. From 1854 to 1857 3-masted schooners were built. About 10 of them, averaging from 800 to 1,000 tons, formed a fleet that carried grain and lumber from Chicago, Detroit, and Cleveland to Liverpool or London. Return cargoes of sundries were taken. But the broad-bottomed boats, with center boards, did not prove equal to the long voyages across the Atlantic. They were no match for the deep keels of the salt-water vessels, and they were soon withdrawn.

Soon after 1850 there was built a type of screw steamers known as propellers. They were long in body, and strengthened by a beam on either side known as the "hog-back." The bow was high out of water, and the engine was in the stern. But one mast was carried, which could be rigged, on short notice, with a large mainsail and jib. Boats of this kind had lines without beauty, and they were able to make but about 10 miles an hour. This style of vessel was succeeded, two or three years later, by a sternwheeler of more graceful lines, with the same general features as the original propeller, but without the hog-back frames, which made the old style of freight boats so unattractive. The style without the hog-back began to be built about 1860, and what few were built during the civil war were after that pattern. After the war, when the ocean tonnage of the United States had become small, men who had been connected with it went to several points on the Great Lakes and took an interest in their navigation. They had a fair knowledge of naval construction, and also of the methods and requirements of navigation, and their presence and their knowledge had a decided influence upon the commerce of the lakes. Nearly all those who had built vessels upon the lakes down to that time had adapted to the lakes the naval architecture of the canals and the Western rivers. The ungraceful lines of the old propeller were pointed out by the new-comers, and it was soon agreed that the salt-water type of vessel was not only more beautiful but more desirable, built with those changes that would allow a small draft, so that the lake vessels could pass over the several shallow spots along the great routes of trade.

The builders of sailing vessels began to see that steam would soon take the place of wind as a motive power, but they kept bravely at work; and in the last days of their prosperity, just before the civil war, they turned out some remarkable specimens, both in beauty and in sailing power. They still used wood for the hulls, as also did the builders of steam vessels, long after it had been discarded on salt water. Even the makers of engines for the freight boats were a long time in learning the value of the combined and triple marine engine. About 1880 began to be developed a type of vessel that had lines something like the ocean steamer, but with less free-board and with a perfectly flat bottom, the keel being inside, so as to make every inch of the draft available. Such vessels were built in groups of two or three. The first, usually the larger, had an engine too powerful for its own use. The object was to tow the barge or barges, almost as large as itself, on the principle that a steam engine which can not propel a large vessel will tow it and another vessel if the engine is placed on a tug or a launch. That is to say, an extra large steam engine for one boat would carry that boat along, together with another as a tow; while, if the same horse-power were distributed in the two or three vessels, it would not be strong enough to move them independently. Thus far all vessels carried three or four masts, whether provided with engines or not, so that advantage might always be taken of the wind when it was favorable. The first of such steamers and barges were made of wood; but soon it was found that iron was better and more economical, and that even iron frames, covered with wood planking, made a "composite" vessel that was far superior to the wooden one. The change has been so marked that to-day scarcely a vessel of any kind, along the whole length of the lakes, aside from small coasting schooners, is built of wood. Even the side-wheel passenger steamers (which are very few, and for the most part confined to Lake Erie and the route between Detroit and Cleveland) have been so modified that they bear no resemblance to the side-wheelers of twenty years ago. The wheels of large steamers with wheel boxes standing far above the upper decks have been discarded, and in their place much smaller vessels are used, with paddle boxes covered by at least one deck above them. The width of the guards has also been reduced, so that they now overhang but half the distance of the guards formerly built. This type of steamer, with small wheels and increased revolutions, is found to be much more seaworthy than the former. The feature of the paddle-wheel, well aft of the engine, is still retained, after the manner of the steamboats on the Western rivers. The finest steamers of this sort are those running between Cleveland and Detroit, which route is profitable because the railroad milenge between the two cities is so great. The steamers on this line cost about $250,000 each. The latest product in the line of vessels adapted for both passengers and freight is a twin-screw steel passenger steamer, built for the Goodrich Transportation Company, of Milwaukee. The length is 270 feet over all; the accommodations are for 140 passengers, and the cost is over $300,000.

Within the past five years the use of iron has almost wholly given way to the use of mild steel for large vessels of all descriptions on the lakes. The short life of thin steel plates has been lengthened by the use of soapstone, or special compositions of enamel. Only 30·3 per cent. of the tonnage built in 1885 in the world was constructed of steel; in 1886, 45·4 per cent.; in 1887, 72·2 per cent.: in 1888, 84·2 per cent.; and in 1889 and 1890 the percentage in favor of steel

was still more marked. By far the larger part of the increase in the building of steel over iron came from the ship-yards of the lakes. A ship-builder of the Clyde recently gave this complimentary statement regarding the latest styles of naval architecture on the lakes: "The water-bottoms of your steel steamers on the lakes are different from any I have ever seen, and better, too. In all my experience of forty years I never saw anything to equal the 'Mariska' in construction. Her water-bottom is superior to any I ever saw, and I am told that it is similar to the bottom of all your lake steamers. There never was a steamer built on the Clyde that equals her in construction. As proof that I am in earnest, let me add that I have instructed my people across the water to get all the risks they can on steamers constructed like the 'Mariska.' Do you know what would have been the result had a Clyde-built steamer been on the rock where the 'Mariska' was? She would have been there yet. Her entire cargo would have been taken out; and if she had been loaded with anything that would be spoiled by contact with water most of her cargo would have been ruined. She would have been in dry-dock over a month, and most of her water-bottom would have been torn out. I think if European builders were acquainted with this style of water-bottom they would adopt it. It's wonderful to me to think of a boat tearing a hole in her bottom as the 'Mariska' did and not damaging her cargo. If she had been loaded with silk, it would have been the same—her cargo would have been saved."

The real development of modern steel and iron ship-building on the lakes began about 1880, when largely increased railway facilities brought coal in large quantities to Lake Erie ports. After a trial of several years with the motor vessels, and their consorts in tow, it was found that the slow progress resulted in a loss of at least two or three trips during every season. As the season, at its best, is only about seven months, and as the rivalry over freight rates cut them down to a low figure, the loss of two or three trips often meant the absence of any profit for the season. Therefore the motor and tow boats, of large build, gave way to the present type of vessel, each having its own motor and running independently of all others. Then came the development in engines, which, by the use of combined and triple marine, shortened the time of trips so that every season might show a profit. Owing to this latter development, more than to any other, iron and steel ship-building on the lakes has grown rapidly within the past four years. Among the larger boats of this class are the "Susquehanna," launched in Buffalo in 1886, with a length of 323 feet, and the "Owego," also launched at Buffalo in 1887, with a length of 357 feet. A brief description of the "Owego" follows: The depth molded at the lowest point is 25 feet and 6 inches, and the beam, molded, is 41 feet. The whole is of steel, except a few parts of the internal inclosures about the engines and boilers. The vessel has three decks, and it is propelled by a triple-expansion, inverted-vertical, direct-acting, jet-condensing, three-cylinder compound engine. The engines work under a boiler pressure of 160 pounds. They are managed from the lower engine room from the level of the shaft. Steam is supplied by six boilers, each 11½ feet long. The vessel is fitted with a double bottom 3 feet deep, forming a ballast tank of about 800 tons capacity. It is designed to carry 2,800 tons of cargo and fuel on 15 feet 6 inches draft of water, and with this load to steam 14 knots or 16 miles an hour.

Since the building of the "Susquehanna" and the "Owego" the tendency has been to make vessels of a shorter length and standing higher out of water. Of these, the "Tuscarora," built in Cleveland in 1890, is, perhaps, a fair specimen. She is of 290 feet keel, 312 feet over all, 40 feet beam, and 25½ feet depth. Over 1,600 tons of plate were used in her hull, and she is in many respects superior to the modern steel boats of the lakes, as there was no attempt to save money in her construction. She has the usual water capacity—8 compartments of about 800 tons. She has 2 flush steel decks, the top one being covered with 3-inch pine, and an additional tier of deck beams below, or virtually a third deck. Her water-bottom runs clear aft, and she has 3 longitudinal keelsons on either side of the main keelson. The middle one of this third tier of keelsons on either side runs down to the skin of the vessel. It is said that when one of the boats of the fleet, the "Saranac," was driven ashore on the rocks at Buffalo, in the spring of 1890, it was the additional strength of such keelsons that saved her bottom. The "Tuscarora" is very strong in other ways. Her trunk around the engine and boiler, is carried up with quarter-inch boiler plate, and the boiler house is also of quarter-inch boiler plate. She carries 4 spars, the mizzen of steel. Five hoisting engines on the deck operate 7 spar derricks, so that time is saved in handling cargo by having it worked through the hatches as well as the gangways. The engines have 24-, 38-, and 61-inch cylinders, with 42-inch stroke; but they are placed forward about 40 feet farther than in the ordinary lake carrier, and the shaft alley is, of course, very large. She has 3 boilers of 12 x 12½ feet, which are allowed 160 pounds of steam, and her wheel is sectional, 14 x 17. A feature of the "Tuscarora's" power is the Worthington independent condenser, which has greatly increased her speed. It is claimed that she and her sister vessels are the only boats on the lakes to compete with the record of 16·4 miles an hour held by the "Owego." This is a vast improvement over the old line of freighters, which made scarcely 10 miles an hour as late as 1880. But there is a structural weakness in all the large steel boats, arising from the necessities of the carrying trade, which would be fatal to their use in the heavy seas of salt water. The plates of iron and steel are usually much thinner than those of the salt-water vessels, and the frames are much lighter. While there are occasionally heavy storms upon the lakes, yet something may be risked in the way of lighter construction, because none of the lake boats run during the winter months. The chief element of weakness, however, is in the large and frequent openings through all the decks for the purpose of loading and unloading. The hatches of the upper deck are 26 x 8 feet, the greater length being across the vessel. The hatches in the lower decks are 16 x 8 feet. All the hatches are placed at distances of 24 feet, center to cen-

ter. The immense cranes on the docks are also placed 24 feet from center to center.

At Marquette, on Lake Superior, whence hundreds of thousands of tons of ore are shipped annually, the railroad company that brings the mineral down to the lake shore has built a pier more than 1,000 feet long, having a height of about 40 feet above the water level. The freight cars are run out upon this, and their contents are dumped into large bins directly under the tracks. These bins are built to correspond in dimensions with the hatches of the lake vessels. The latter pull alongside of the pier, the legs or chutes of the bins are thrust through the great hatches of the upper deck, the catch that keeps the bin door in place is pulled, and the entire contents of that receptacle fall into the hold of the vessel with a roar that can be heard for miles. Manual labor is reduced to the mere duty of supervision; but in discharging cargoes a different process is adopted. No plan has yet been devised of lifting a vessel up and letting her cargo fall out; neither has it been found possible to unload iron ore and coal as grain is discharged, by means of the endless belt of an elevator. These heavy materials have to be put into tubs and lifted out of the ship's hold, and the merit of the frequent-hatch plan consists in the opportunity it affords for several gangs of men to work simultaneously. Mechanical science has been brought into play in the construction of hoisting and conveying machines to supplement the efforts of the men in the hold. The superintendent of an ore-wharf at Cleveland asserts that with the assistance of three operators and one foreman he has in nine hours discharged a cargo of 1,980 tons of ore, working six hatches with nine men at a hatch, and carrying the ore from 50 to 150 feet from the vessel. During the process the men are all under cover, and are exposed neither to the rain nor to the direct heat of the sun. The cost of putting the ore into the buckets by the men in the hold averages about 15 cents a ton. Instances are on record where a cargo of 2,000 tons of coal has been put on board of a steamer in one hour and twenty minutes, and a similar quantity of iron ore in one hour and thirty minutes. Two thousand tons of coal have been discharged in eleven hours, and a similar quantity of iron ore in six hours. These instances cited are exceptional, but the average does not fall far below them.

At the Lake Erie ports—Cleveland, Ashtabula, Fairport, Buffalo, Erie, Sandusky, Toledo, and Lorain—whence all the coal is shipped, and where by far the larger part of the ore is received, there are nearly 16 miles of dockage, about 56 per cent. of which is occupied by the ore business and the remainder by the coal traffic.

The grain trade is chiefly between Chicago, West Superior, Duluth, and Milwaukee on the west, and Buffalo on the east. In 1889 these four ports shipped 34,887,000 bushels of wheat alone to Buffalo. The total corn tonnage was still greater, while the flour traffic reached a total of over 3,850,000 barrels. In 1890 the grain season opened the second week in April, and the grain fleet on its first trip brought down from Chicago 110,000 tons, distributed as follows: 2,802,000 bushels of corn, 1,194,000 bushels of wheat, 137,000 bushels of rye, 71,000 of oats, and

65,000 of flaxseed. During the first twenty-four days of the season one third as much grain was shipped from Chicago as was exported from New York in the twelve months of 1889. Only a heavy fall in rates prevented the moving of a still greater quantity. The total for the season of 1800 was slightly less than that of 1889, chiefly owing to short crops in the great Western grain belt. The mammoth proportions of the carrying trade for 1889 and 1890 are shown by a comparison with the figures between 1886 and 1889. The year 1886 was the thirtieth in the history of the iron-ore industry of the Lake Superior district. Over 3,500,000 tons were then brought to the furnaces from the ports of that lake. The quantity shipped in 1887 was over 4,000,000 tons; in 1888, over 5,000,000 tons; in 1890, 6,000,000 tons; and in 1891, 6,500,000 tons. In the season of 1888 100,000,000 bushels of grain were shipped eastward from the upper lakes. During two hundred and thirty-four days of navigation in 1889 tonnage was passed through Detroit river to the amount of 10,000,000 tons, which was more than the entries and clearances of all the seaports of the United States, and 3,000,000 tons more than the combined coastwise shipping of Liverpool and London. In 1890 the net capacity of the vessels employed on all the Great Lakes was 826,-360 tons, against 634,652 in 1886: and their value, $58,128,500, against $30,597,450.

Cleveland is the greatest ship-building place on the lakes; Bay City and West Bay City come next, and then follow, in the order given, Detroit and its suburbs, Buffalo, Chicago, Milwaukee, Marine City, and the ports of Gibraltar and Trenton on St. Clair river. At the several ports on the lakes iron and steel steamers for the freight traffic were built as follow: In Cleveland, 1887, 4; 1888, 8; 1889, 11; 1890, 14. In Chicago, 1890, 2. In West Bay City, 1890, 5. In Buffalo, 1882, 1; 1883, 3; 1884, 1; 1885, 1; 1886, 1; 1887, 1; 1888, 1; 1889, 2; 1890, 4. In Toledo, 1890, 3. In Milwaukee, 1890, 2. In Detroit, 1884, 2; 1885, 1; 1886, 1; 1887, 1; 1888, 1; 1889, 1; 1890, 2. In Duluth, 1889, 3; 1890, 5. Thus a total of 35 steel and iron vessels was built upon the lakes during the season of 1890. This work is continued through the winter months, and the output for 1891 was still greater. All the vessels averaged a tonnage of considerably over 2,000. Their average length was nearly 300 feet. A type of freight carrier known as the "whale-back" is built exclusively at Duluth. It is claimed for this model that it will carry larger loads with less expenditure of fuel, and in a shorter time, than any other. The performances of the "Colgate Hoyt," of this type, seem to warrant the claim. One of the whale-backs made a successful voyage to Liverpool with a cargo of grain in the summer of 1891. In the season of 1891, from April 27 to Dec. 7, 10,191 vessels, steam and sail, were looked through from Lake Superior—a number slightly smaller than that for 1890. In 1891 less iron ore and grain other than wheat passed through the St. Mary's Falls Canal; but of wheat there was an excess of 22,599,200 bushels over 1890. This means that about 7 per cent. of the wheat crop of the entire country passed through the canal; and there were also returned through it to West-

ern consumers by Eastern shippers nearly 300,-000,000 tons of merchandise.

With the increase of size and carrying capacity in lake vessels there has come also an increase in speed. Five years ago there was not a 12-mile-an-hour freight boat on the lakes; now there are dozens. Many of the new steel steamers can make 15 miles an hour, and some of them will make a round trip from Cleveland to Escanaba or Marquette at a rate little under 14 miles. The record for speed is held by the steamships "Tioga" and "Owego." The "Owego" has made the round trip from Buffalo to Chicago at the rate of 15 miles an hour, running light going up, and bringing down 85,000 bushels of corn. All the lake ports are so connected by telegraph service that up and down cargoes are easily arranged long before the arrival of the vessels at their destination.

The importance of the St. Mary's Falls Canal is well known to all familiar with the traffic on the lakes. There passed through this canal in the season ending Dec. 3, 1890, a grand total of 9,041,000 tons, against 7,500,000 in 1889. The canal was operated two hundred and twenty-eight days, six fewer than in the year before. The number of vessels increased 10 per cent.; lockage, 6; freight tonnage, 20; coal, 34; flour, 45; manufactured and pig iron, 102; salt, 6; copper, 31; iron ore, 15; and lumber, 3 per cent. In 1881 1,500,000 tons passed through the canal, and in nine years the increase was 480 per cent.

The latest records show that small craft are fast disappearing from the lakes and large vessels are taking their places. The total cost of carrying freight for the year ending in June, 1890, was $8,600,000. The value of the craft engaged in this traffic was $25,500,000. Canadian vessels carried 4 per cent. of the tonnage, against 6 per cent. in 1889.

The statistics for 1891 showed that the lake fleet numbered 3,600 vessels, while the number of vessels engaged in the foreign trade of the Atlantic, Gulf, and Pacific coasts together was only 1,579, and the average size of lake vessels was considerably greater than of the ocean traders. Reckoning ocean coasters with the foreign traders, it was found that the lake fleet was equal to more than one third of the whole salt-water fleet, its tonnage being 1,154,870 against 3,221,-541 tons of the ocean fleet. The lake tonnage was nearly double what it was ten years ago, while during that time the increase in the Atlantic and Gulf coasting fleet had hardly made up for the loss of foreign business. In 1892 the shipment of ores from the upper lakes exceeded that of any previous year. The average profit on the $50,000,000 invested in lake vessels was between 9 and 10 per cent.

The average size of a seaboard sailing vessel is 128 tons, while the lake sailing vessel has of an average of 258 tons. The ocean steamer averages 299 tons; the lake steamer 428 tons. The lakes have 272 steamers measuring over 1,000 tons, while the whole merchant marine of the coasts and the Western rivers has only 207 of that size. To make a still more familiar comparison, the lakes carried about three fifths as much freight per mile in 1891 as ten trunk-line railroads carried.

SOUTH CAROLINA, a Southern State, one of the original thirteen, ratified the Constitution May 23, 1788; area, 3,750 square miles. The population, according to each decennial census, was 249,073 in 1790; 345,591 in 1800; 415,115 in 1810; 502,741 in 1820; 581,185 in 1830; 594,398 in 1840; 668,507 in 1850; 703,708 in 1860; 705,606 in 1870; 995,577 in 1880; and 1,151,149 in 1890. Capital, Columbia.

Government.—The following were the State officers during the year: Governor, Benjamin R. Tillman, Democrat; Lieutenant-Governor, Eugene B. Gary; Secretary of State, J. E. Tindal; Treasurer, W. J. C. Bates; Comptroller-General, W. H. Ellerbe; Attorney-General, T. L. McLaurin until Nov. 30, then D. A. Townsend; Superintendent of Education, W. D. Mayfield; Adjutant-General, H. L. Farley; Railroad Commissioners, D'Arcy P. Duncan, Eugene P. Jervey, H. R. Thomas; after the passage of the new railroad law the legislature elected T. A. Sligh, D. P. Duncan, and H. R. Thomas as Railroad Commissioners; Chief Justice of the Supreme Court, Henry McIver; Associate Justices, Samuel McGowan and Y. J. Pope.

The governor and his cabinet entered upon their second term of office on Nov. 30.

Finances.—Following is a summary of the treasury accounts for the year ending Oct. 31, 1892:

Interest due and not called for, $177,880.73; interest from January 1, 1880, to July 1, 1892, on $268,288.15, $201,216.11; sinking fund commission, $36,861.34; direct tax fund, $60,623.70; Morrill fund, $66,000; balances appropriations unpaid, (about) $70,000; unpaid accounts, $8,808.03; total cash liabilities, $621,389.91.

General account, $29,455.83; sinking fund commission, $36,861.34; privilege tax on fertilizers, $320; department of agriculture, $1,114.52; redemption deficiencies, $998.97; escheated estates, (cash) $2,729.73; Downer fund, $864.95; direct tax fund, $60,623.70; Morrill fund, $66,000; Clemson bequest cash account, $2,779.86; total assets, $201,748.90; net cash liability, Nov. 1, 1892, $419,641.01.

The receipts for the year ended Oct. 31, 1892, including balance on hand, were $1,326,787.46. The expenditures were $1,125,038.56.

The moneys received from the United States on account of the Morrill fund belong to the agricultural colleges at Orangeburg and Fort Hill. An account of the plan for refunding the State debt may be found under the head "Legislative Session."

Valuations.—The total valuation of the property in the State is $168,871,227, about $600,000 more than last year. The constitutional tax of 2 mills for school purposes has a tendency to keep the assessments low and make the levy for State purposes correspondingly high. This was 5 mills, but was raised to 5½ by the last legislature.

Education.—The South Carolina College at Columbia is not in a satisfactory condition. The legislature of 1891 discontinued the institution as a university, and made of it a literary, classical, and scientific college. The attendance, which was 226 in 1889–90, had fallen to 98 in June, 1892, and at the autumn opening was but 70.

Clemson College is not yet opened, but it is expected that it will be ready in May, 1893. The

funds arising from the privilege tax, and those given by the United States Government—known as the Hatch, the Morrill, and the land-script funds—were found not to be sufficient, as it had been hoped they would be, to build, equip, and run the college; and consequently the legislature was called upon for $40,000. The original plan was to provide for about 250 pupils; but so many applications have been made for admission, that accommodations are preparing for 600.

The main building of the Citadel Academy was destroyed by fire on March 14, but has been rebuilt in more modern style and is better adapted to its purpose than before the fire; 137 students were in attendance during the fall term.

The Winthrop School is still conducted in Columbia. The General Assembly of 1891 passed an act founding an institution for the industrial training of girls, in connection with a normal school, to be called the South Carolina Industrial and Winthrop Normal College, to be located in the town making the highest bid for grounds, building, and equipment. The city of Anderson offered the highest bid, $75,000; but before the bonds were issued it was found that this proposed addition to the city's debt would carry it beyond the 8 per cent. limit prescribed by the constitution. A decision given by the Supreme Court in a friendly lawsuit brought for a test of the validity of the proposed bonds, was against it, and bids will be taken again.

Claflin College, at Orangeburg, a branch of the South Carolina University, receives half of the Morrill fund. A large part of it has been devoted to an increase in the force of teachers and the purchase of machinery and other improvements in the equipment. It is for colored youth of both sexes, and over 600 are in attendance.

Charities.—The number of patients under treatment at the State lunatic asylum, Nov. 1, was 764. The income of the institution from all sources was $115,385.57, and the expenditures, $112,371.73. The legislature passed an act to regulate the admission of patients.

Penitentiary.—The number of convicts on Nov. 1 was 900, an increase of 107 over the number last year. The total receipts during the year were $75,081.41, of which $30,681.83 was for convict hire and $19,326.16 from sales of cotton and other farm products; $36,350.36 represents the assets in cash, bills due for convict hire, and unsold farm produce. Among the disbursements were $14,-872.20 for the pay rolls, $17,169.87 for subsistence, $2,995.73 for transportation of new convicts, $3,221.21 for Clemson College pay-rolls, etc., and $5,000 for payment on De Saussure farm.

Railroads.—The General Assembly, at the session of 1891, directed the Attorney-General to investigate the complaints that the Port Royal and Augusta Railroad was controlled by a foreign corporation, to the detriment of the State. He found that it was under the control of the Georgia Central, a competing line, and that in consequence it was operated as part of the Central system, to the disadvantage of the section of the State through which the Port Royal runs, and to the detriment of Port Royal harbor. The Governor therefore sent a special message to the last legislature, recommending that the Attorney-General be authorized to begin proceedings against the railroad to compel it to abide by its charter.

The number of miles of railroad built during the year is 177.32, and the number of miles in operation 2,535.80.

The following roads are given as in the hands of receivers: the Asheville and Spartanburg, Atlanta and Charlotte Air Line, Columbia, Knoxville and Western, Three C's, Charleston, Sumter and Northern, Charlotte, Columbia and Augusta, Cheraw and Chester, Chester and Lenoir, Columbia and Greenville, Laurens Railroad, Port Royal and Augusta, Port Royal and Western Carolina, South Carolina Railway, and the Spartanburg, Union and Columbia. These roads represent more than half of the total railroad mileage of the State, 1,487½ miles.

The new railroad law will be found under "Legislative Session."

Manufactures.—A census bulletin issued in October makes the following exhibit of the growth of Charleston manufactures in ten years:

	1890.	1880.
Number establishments reported............	566	194
Number industries reported..............	67	87
Capital invested.......	$4,730,070	$1,718,300
Number of hands employed	5,283	2,146
Amount paid in wages..	$2,203,970	$639,030
Cost of material used..	$4,800,421	$1,468,375
Value of products.....	$8,892,860	$4,732,590

Percentages of increase for Charleston are given as follows:

Number of establishments reported.....	....121.65
Capital invested.........................	.310.15
Number of hands employed................	.125.35
Wages paid...............................	.226.24
Cost of materials used...................	.223.80
Value of products at works...............	.210.75

Industries dealt with in this bulletin are: For Charleston, men's clothing, 5 establishments; cooperage, 6 establishments; cotton compressing, 4 establishments; fertilizers, 3 establishments; flouring and grist mills, 7 establishments; foundry and machine shops, 4 establishments; lumber manufactories, 10 establishments; printing and publishing, 9 establishments; rice cleaning and polishing, 4 establishments; shipbuilding, 7 establishments.

The Phosphate Industry.—The report of the board of phosphate commissioners says of the condition of that industry:

The present condition of the phosphate trade is very unsettled and the market glutted. There have been previous periods of depression, but from other causes than those which have produced the present low prices. Within the last few years very extensive deposits of phosphate rock, both on land and in rivers, have been discovered in Florida, and a large amount of capital has been invested in developing those mines. The rock is of a higher grade than ours, and, it is said, can be mined much more cheaply, but it has cut a small figure in the markets of the world until within the last twelve months. The Florida miners labor under the disadvantage of having poor shipping facilities, and they are handicapped also by higher freights, but their production of rock has been very large, and this has been thrown upon the market now for almost any price it would bring, and while we have every reason to believe that the Florida miners are selling below the cost of production, nevertheless their rock is displacing ours and forcing the price down until the margin of profits has grown very small, and with some of the companies may have disappeared altogether.

The depression in the cotton market, which has lessened very largely the use of fertilizers, has also entered into the conditions which brought about these low prices.

Rivers and Harbors.—Congress has made the following appropriations for improvements in the State: Charleston harbor, $225,000, and contracts may be entered into for the entire completion of the project of improvement; Georgetown harbor, $12,000; harbor at Winyah Bay, $100,000; Edisto River, $7,385; Great Pee-Dee River, $10,000; Santee River, $30,000, to be used in snagging and in making a new cut between Estherville and Minim Creek; Waccamaw River, $10,000; Wappoo Cut, $10,000; Wateree River, for maintenance, $2,500; Congaree River, $5,000; Mingo Creek, $3,000; Little Pee-Dee River, $5,000; Clark River, $2,500; Beaufort River, $12,500.

Port Royal naval station, completion of dry dock, change of location of naval wharf, erection of office building, necessary dredging, etc., $150,000; officers' quarters, $5,000; telephone line, $1,500; erection of a building for marine barracks, $3,000.

Commerce.—The Bureau of Statistics gives the figures below for the year ending June 30, and the previous year:

Charleston: Imports, 1892, $896,081; 1891, $993,248. Exports, 1892, $16,718,386; 1891, $21,940,886.

Beaufort: Imports,1892,$25,000; 1891, $90,483. Exports, 1892, $544,903; 1891, $982,607.

The total collections of the internal revenue department in the State were $71,812.85.

Legislative Session.—The legislature convened on Nov. 23, and adjourned on Dec. 24. The number of bills and joint resolutions passed was 261. About 50 were continued till the next session. Among the measures introduced was a prohibition bill. An amendment or substitute was placed in its stead and passed. This is to regulate the sale of liquor by placing it in the hands of the government. It provides that the "Governor shall within 30 days from the approval of the Act appoint a commissioner, believed by him to be an abstainer from intoxicants, who shall, under such rules and regulations as may be made by the State Board of Control, purchase all intoxicating liquors for lawful sale in this State, giving preference to manufacturers and brewers in this State and furnish the same to such persons as may be designated as dispensers thereof, to be sold as hereafter prescribed in this Act." The commissioner is to hold office for two years, to reside and have his place of business at Columbia, to receive a salary of $1,800, and to be allowed a bookkeeper at a salary of $1,200, and such other assistants as the board of control may deem necessary.

He shall not sell to the county dispensers any intoxicating or fermented liquors except such as have been tested by the chemist of the South Carolina College and declared to be pure and unadulterated. Said chemist and such assistants as may be appointed to aid him, to be allowed such compensation, if any, as the board of control may determine. He shall not receive from said county dispensers for such liquors sold to them more than 50 per cent. above the net cost thereof, and all amounts so received by him from said sales shall be by him paid over to the Treasurer of the State monthly, under such rules as may be made by the State board of control to insure the faithful return of the same ; and the State Treasurer shall keep a separate account with said fund, from which the commissioner shall draw, from time to time, upon warrants duly approved by the said board, the amounts necessary to pay the expenses incurred in conducting the business of said agency. All rules and regulations governing the said commissioner in the purchase of intoxicating liquors, or in the performance of any of the duties of his office, where the same are not provided for by law, shall be prescribed by a State board of control, composed of the Governor, the Comptroller-General and the Attorney-General.

The State board of control is to appoint in each county a county board of control consisting of three persons, believed not to be addicted to the use of intoxicating liquors, to serve without fees, and to make rules for their respective counties ; any county dispenser or clerk purchasing from any one except the State Commissioner, or convicted of adulterating any liquors, shall be guilty of a misdemeanor and subject to a fine of not less than $200 or imprisonment for not less than six months.

No other person than those thus designated will be allowed to manufacture or sell intoxicating liquors after July 1, 1893, when the law goes into effect, and all licenses shall terminate then.

The county dispenser must require from every person purchasing a dated and printed or ink-written request, stating the age and residence of the one for whose use the liquor is required, with his signature ; and this must be attested by the county dispenser. But he must refuse to sell if he knows the person applying to be a minor, or a drunkard ; and if he does not know him, he must have these facts certified by some trustworthy person whom he does know.

Another important measure passed is entitled :

An Act to amend Title 12, Chapter XL., of railroad corporations and general railroad law, and to provide for the regulation of railroad freight and passenger tariffs in this State ; to prevent unjust discrimination and extortion in the rates charged for transportation of passengers and freights, and to prohibit railroad companies and corporations and lessees in this State from charging other than just and reasonable rates and to punish the same, and prescribe a mode of procedure and rules of evidence in relation thereto ; providing for the election of railroad commissioners and prescribe their powers and duties in relation to the same.

It provides for the election by the present General Assembly of three railroad commissioners for the terms of two, four, and six years respectively. the length of the respective terms of those elected to be determined by lot. Those hereafter elected shall serve each a term of six years.

One of their duties is to make a schedule of rates for every railroad corporation as soon as practicable ; and that "schedule shall, in suits brought against any such railroad corporation wherein is involved the charges of any railroad corporation for the transportation of any passengers or freight or cars or unjust discrimination in relation thereto, be deemed and taken in all courts of this State as sufficient evidence that the rates therein fixed are just and reasonable rates," and as often as circumstances require they may change and revise the schedule.

After its passage the legislature elected the following to be railroad commissioners, according to its provisions : Rev. Jefferson A. Sligh, D'Arcy P. Duncan, H. R. Thomas. The last two are farmers ; the first, pastor of a church in Newberry county and a farmer.

An act to provide for the redemption of that part of the State debt known as the Brown consol bonds and stocks by issue of other bonds and stocks was one of the important measures passed. A former legislature had provided for the issue of four per cent. bonds to take the place of the six per cents. but up to the end of October, 1892, only $33,726 of four per cents had been issued under the act, and efforts to place the new bonds at a satisfactory price had failed.

The act provides for an issue of bonds of the denominations of $500 and $1,000, and certificates of stock, bearing interest at the rate of 4½ per cent., payable semi-annually. The bonds and certificates are to become payable at the end of the term of forty years from Jan. 1, 1893, the State reserving the right to call in and pay the whole or any part of the issue at any time after the expiration of twenty years,—the first called in to be those of the highest numbers, or the last issued, and thereafter the registered bonds or stock in the same order. All coupons of the bonds and all interest orders of the certificates are to be receivable in payment of State taxes, which are payable the same year except for taxes levied for the support of schools. As further security "for the reduction and payment of this debt the revenue to the State arising from royalty on phosphate beds shall be set aside to the amount of $37,500 each half year, beginning with the 1st January, 1894, as a sinking fund for the reduction of said debt." It is further agreed with the holders of the bonds and stocks that if the State shall at any time sell the phosphate interest. there shall be reserved from the proceeds of such sale a sum sufficient to provide for the payment and retirement of the bonds when due or called, and for the continuance of the sinking fund until such time as the whole debt shall be provided for. The bonds and certificates are to be free from all State, county, and municipal taxes.

A joint resolution was passed providing for the calling of a constitutional convention.

A new insurance law increases the license to $100 and requires licenses from building and loan and land loan associations, and to enforce a more rigid system of returning for taxation.

A resolution to submit to a popular vote the question of amending the constitution so as to confer upon women the right to vote and hold office, was lost, but received the votes of two-fifths of the senators.

A bill to establish a home for disabled ex-Confederate soldiers was defeated by a large majority.

Other bills and joint resolutions passed are the following :

To entitle all persons charged with forgery to the benefit of an arraignment and challenge of jurors as other persons charged with felony.

To amend the 8th section of an Act entitled "An Act to provide a more efficient system of working the public roads in Laurens, Anderson, Edgefield, Lexington, Marlboro, Richland, Abbeville and Newberry counties," so far as the same relates to Abbeville County, by enabling hands liable to work on public roads 'in said county to compound for their work by paying two dollars each per annum.

Appropriating $800, if so much be necessary, to complete the Confederate rolls.

Vesting all the right and title of the State in or to Wateree Canal in the owners of lands adjacent thereto severally.

Amending an Act entitled "An Act to prohibit non-residents from hunting, ducking, fishing and gathering oysters and terrapin within the limits of the counties of Georgetown, Charleston, Beaufort, Colleton and Berkeley, except upon certain conditions," so as to embrace other shell fish than oysters, and so as to include the county of Horry in the provisions of said Act and its amendments.

Re-chartering the South Carolina Medical Association and establishing a State board of health.

An Act to prevent cruelty to children.

Political.—The quarrel between the two factions of the Democratic party was very bitter during the first part of the year. The opponents of the State administration—that is, the Cleveland Democrats or Conservative Democracy—held a convention at Columbia on March 24, with 272 delegates. A State ticket was nominated, headed by ex-Gov. John C. Sheppard as candidate for Governor. A platform was adopted of which the following are the more significant declarations :

We submit that the course of the head of our present State Administration, both before and since his election, has been in many respects unwise and unjust. We believe the tendency of his methods and policy is to destroy the credit of the State, to the injury of the people, by making it impossible to refund our State debt at a reasonable rate of interest, such as is given our sister States of the South ; to involve us in long and expensive lawsuits, without proper cause, eating up the substance of the taxpayers for the enrichment of attorneys and court officials; to keep alive discord and strife, which endanger the party, on which the safety of the State, her men, women and children depend, by constantly adding to the number of the disaffected ; to make a servile Legislature and an intimidated judiciary and thereby to pervert what should be the responsible and protecting Government of a free people into an absolute dictatorship, with all power in the hands of one man ; to make the Governor the master and king of the people instead of their servant.

We demand of the next General Assembly such legislation as will give us a reasonable and equitable system of assessment for taxation. We will demand also the continuation of the work of completing and opening of Clemson College.

We denounce the proposition to increase the poll tax to $3 a year, because it would unjustly put a burden on people not able to bear it.

We oppose and will labor to change the present system of management of the Penitentiary, by which convict labor is used to make cotton in competition with honest farmers and agricultural laborers.

We charge that the present constitution of the State Democratic party is unfair and undemocratic and constructed in the interest of machine politics and bossism.

Speeches were made in various parts of the State during the summer by the opposing candidates, calling out large audiences and arousing great enthusiasm and strong factional feeling.

A State convention was held on May 19 for the purpose of electing delegates to the National Convention at Chicago. This convention was entirely in control of the administration party. The resolutions declared in favor of the Ocala platform, which calls for the abolition of national

banks, the establishment of sub-treasuries for lending money at 2 per cent. interest on farm products and real estate, the increase of the circulating medium to not less than $50 *per capita*, laws against dealing in futures, free and unlimited coinage of silver, laws prohibiting alien ownership of land, and government control of railroads. The resolutions gave the following utterance on the coming nomination at Chicago :

We see with displeasure and apprehension that the money changers of Wall street have invaded the sacred temple of Democracy and that they will try and force upon our party a candidate representing not the wishes and well-being of our people, but their own selfish interest. We assert that Grover Cleveland does not represent the principles of Democracy as taught our forefathers and as we understand them.

We therefore enter our solemn protest against the nomination of Grover Cleveland or any other candidate known or believed to be selected in the interest of and at the dictation of Wall street; but we demand as our standard-bearer a man for the people and with the people, and who will serve the people and not any class or faction.

We shall look upon the nomination of Ex-President Cleveland if forced upon the party at the Chicago Convention as a prostitution of the principles of Democracy, as a repudiation of the demands of the Farmers' Alliance, which embody the true principles of Democracy, and a surrender of the rights of the people to the financial kings of the country.

After these declarations it was further resolved :

That we pledge the Democracy of South Carolina to abide by and actively support the nomination of the National Democratic party at the Chicago Convention, and the platform upon which such nominations shall be made.

The primaries held on Aug. 30 were overwhelmingly in favor of the administration party, and made the renomination of the Governor secure.

The convention for nominating State officers and presidential electors met in Columbia, Sept. 21. The existing State officers were all renominated, with the exception of the Attorney-General, for whose office D. A. Townsend was the candidate.

The Republican convention met at Columbia, Sept. 28. The platform affirmed allegiance to the party principles as expressed at Minneapolis, pledged support to the national candidates, and declared that "with a free ballot and a fair count the State of South Carolina would be placed in the column of Republican States by a majority of forty thousand votes," and further,

That the registration and election laws of South Carolina, by means of which the Democratic party of the State is enabled to give to the nominees of that party the electoral vote of the State, deprive us of the benefits of a republican form of government, as declared by the Constitution of the United States, and call for the interposition of the National Government to protect us in the rights and liberties guaranteed to us by the fundamental laws of the land.

That the meager and inadequate educational facilities afforded by the State is a just cause for serious and anxious consideration in view of the large percentage of illiteracy within our borders, and the outlook for the future of the youth who are to be fitted and prepared for the grave and responsible duties of citizenship; that in liberal, progressive education the future weal and prosperity of the Commonwealth is assured, while criminal neglect of a matter supreme in its importance will assuredly tend to demoralization, and result in serious consequences under the changed conditions of society.

It was resolved not to nominate a State ticket. The People's Party had electors in the field, but no State ticket. The Prohibitionists made no nominations. At their convention in May, they resolved to request the various newspapers of the State each to grant them the use of a column during the canvass, which the county committees should fill with appropriate matter.

The vote of the State was as follows : Cleveland, 54,692 ; Harrison, 13,345 ; Weaver, 2,407. Six Democrats were elected representatives in Congress, and one Republican ; G. W. Murray, Rep., receiving a plurality of 40 in the 7th district. The vote for Governor Tillman was 56,673. The State Senate will consist of 36 Democrats ; the House, of 120 Democrats and 4 Republicans.

SOUTH DAKOTA, a Western State, admitted to the Union Nov. 3, 1889 ; area, 77,650 square miles ; population, according to the census of 1890, 328,808. Capital, Pierre.

Government.—The following were the State officers during the year : Governor, Arthur C. Mellette, Republican ; Lieutenant-Governor, G. H. Hoffman ; Secretary of State, A. O. Ringsrud ; Treasurer, W. W. Taylor ; Auditor, L. C. Taylor ; Attorney-General, Robert Dollard ; Superintendent of Public Instruction, Cortez Salmon ; Commissioner of School and Public Lands, Thomas H. Ruth ; Commissioner of Labor, R. A. Smith ; Chief Justice of the Supreme Court, John E. Bennett ; Associate Justices, A. G. Kellam and Dighton Corson.

Finances.—The entire bonded indebtedness of the State on June 30, 1892, was $1,040,200. In the latter part of the year the Treasurer succeeded in refunding $92,500 of this amount from 4½ per cent. to 3½ per cent. bonds, the latter being sold at par. He also refunded $15,-000 of Dakota University 6 per cent. bonds into 4 per cents., which sold at a premium $600.

On Dec. 1, 1890, the total balance in all funds of the treasury was $63,422 ; the total receipts for the 19 months following were $1,396,795 ; the total disbursements $1,151,103, and the balance on June 30, 1892, $309,114. In the general fund alone the balance on Dec. 1, 1890, was $10,052 ; the total receipts for 19 months following were $814,580 ; the total payments were $784,948, and the balance on June 30, 1892, $39,684. On the latter date the balance in the permanent school fund was $148,189.

The receipts from the State ad valorem tax during the period amounted to $424,794.

The assessed valuation of property in the State for 1892 aggregated $127,478,228, against $128,318.244.50 for 1891. The valuation of real and personal property was $118,223,307 ; of railroads, $8,816,698, and of telephone, telegraph, and express companies, $338,283.

Education.—The Governor, in his biennial message, says :

There are within the State, according to the census of 1892, 87,317 persons of school age, with an average enrollment of 73,962 pupils for the past two years. The average number of teachers employed for the same period is 4,298, of whom 1,169 are male and 3,129 female, the latter receiving $966,603, the former $415,238—total, $1,381,841. The total number of school buildings in 1892 is 3,253, showing a marked increase over the previous year. The valuation of school property is $2,704,933. The public school lands belonging to the State at the date of admission amounted to 2,823,320 acres, of which 101,879 acres have been sold and contracted at an average price per acre of $13.64, amounting to $1,387,318.71, leaving 2,721,464.76 acres, which at an average price of $10 per acre, the minimum price at which, under the law of Congress and the State constitution, they can be sold, will realize $27,214,-947.60, and this added to the sum already realized as above stated, fixes the minimum permanent school fund to result from the sale of lands at the enormous sum of $28,602,260.31, yielding upon six per cent. securities $1,716,201.97. The income from present sales and leases enabled the commissioner of school lands to disburse 52 cents for each school child for the year 1891, and for the year 1892 the apportionment will be 86 cents.

The total attendance at the State University for the year ending in June was 251, a decrease of about one-third compared with the previous year. The buildings are in need of repair, and new structures are required for some of the departments. At the Agricultural College the attendance for the year was 279, and at the School of Mines at Rapid City there were 56 pupils. The Normal School at Spearfish enrolled 161 pupils in the normal department and 218 in the training school; and the Madison Normal School, 180 pupils in its single normal department.

Charities.—The School for Deaf Mutes contained only 41 pupils during the last term of 1892, although there are in the State about 120 children who are entitled to the privileges of the institution. The Soldiers' Home was opened on Nov. 25, 1890. From that date to June 30, 1892, 155 persons had been admitted, of whom 80 remained at the latter date.

Prisons.—On Dec. 1, 1890, there were 96 convicts in the State Prison ; during the subsequent nineteen months, 88 were admitted and 102 released, leaving 82 prisoners on June 30, 1892. Of all the State prisoners incarcerated during the nineteen months, exactly half came from the Black Hills. Convict labor is employed entirely in the quarrying of stone, but the product is not thrown upon the market to compete with free labor. It will be used in the construction of such buildings as the State may decide to erect. At the State Reform School there were 68 inmates on June 30—52 boys and 16 girls.

Banks.—There are in the State 50 private banks, 40 State banks organized under the general corporation law, and 70 State banks doing business under the banking law passed at the last session of the Legislature. The private banks are not under supervision, owing to a decision of the State Supreme Court holding that the banking law that sought to subject private banks to examination was unconstitutional. During the last fiscal period 8 private banks have failed, while among the State banks there have been but 2 failures. In all the State banks that failed there were county deposits, which resulted in considerable losses of public funds. According to reports made May 14, 1892, by the 70 banks organized under the banking law, and the 40 banks organized under the general corporation law, their total resources were $5,308,557.

Railroads.—The total railway mileage in the State is 2,708 miles, of which the Chicago, Milwaukee and St. Paul has 1,096; the Chicago and Northwestern. 744: the Fremont, Elkhorn and Missouri Valley, 185; and the Burlington and Missouri River, 169, with the rest divided between thirteen companies.

The railroads paid during the fiscal year ending June 30, 1892, taxes in South Dakota amounting to $220,760.

Decision.—The State Supreme Court this year rendered a decision sustaining the validity of the State prohibitory law. The case came up on appeal from a decision of the Judge of Lawrence County, who had rendered a decision that the law was void because it violated that clause of the State constitution which provides that no law shall embrace more than one subject, and that shall be expressed in its title.

World's Fair.—Early in the year Gov. Mellette sent a communication to each member of the Legislature, asking whether, if an extra session should be called, the member would agree to vote for an appropriation for the World's Fair at Chicago, and would also attend the session without cost to the State. As a majority of the legislators refused to make such an agreement, the Governor refused to call them together. A World's Fair Commission was organized on May 7, without official authority, for the purpose of doing such preliminary work as should be necessary to secure an exhibit from the State at the Fair. It was decided that $25,000 would be needed at the outset, and that sum was apportioned to the several counties according to their wealth. A considerable portion of this sum was paid over to the commission before the end of the year, so that it was able to make provision for the erection of a State building.

Settlement.—On April 15 the lands embraced in the Sisseton and Wahpeton Indian reservation, which had been purchased by the national government, were thrown open to settlement, and the usual wild scenes attending the entrance of settlers were enacted along the border of the reservation. The signal was given at noon, and it is estimated that 3,000 people rushed across the reservation limits, vying with each other in reaching the most eligible locations. The area open to settlement was about 600,000 acres, nearly all excellent agricultural land.

Exports.—During 1891, 601,778 carloads of surplus products were sent out of the State, of which 30,113 carloads were of wheat; 1,264, corn; 2,228. oats; 5,376, flax; 1,734, flour; 1,531, hay; 51 of butter and eggs; 3,075 of stone, almost entirely from Minnehaha County; 169, cement from Yankton County; 7.342 of cattle; 4,065 of hogs; 215 of horses and mules; 337 of sheep; and 175 of mixed stock. The valuation of some of these shipments is as follows: Cattle, $4,405,200: hogs, $3,252,000; horses and mules, $430,000; sheep, $101,000; wheat, $10,840,680; corn, $303,360; oats. $501,300; flax, $2,688,-000; flour, $1,213,800; hay, $61,240.

Political.—At a State convention of the Independent or Farmers' Alliance party, held at Redfield on June 23, A. L. Van Isdel was nominated for Governor. M. Price for Lieutenant-Governor, C. G. Morgan for Secretary of State, P. O. Peterson for Treasurer. G. W. Evarts for Auditor. W. H. Curtiss for Attorney-General. Mrs. R. B. Hassell for Superintendent of Public Instruction. Otto Anderson for Commissioner of Labor and Statistics, and William Cook for Commissioner of Lands. Presidential electors and delegates to the National convention at Omaha were also selected and a platform was adopted.

On July 22 a Republican State convention met at Madison and selected the following ticket: For Governor, Charles H. Sheldon; for Lieutenant-Governor, C. W. Herried; for Secretary of State, Thomas Thorson; for Treasurer. W. W. Taylor; for Auditor, J. E. Hipple; for Attorney-General, Coe I. Crawford; for Superintendent of Public Instruction, Cortez Salmon; for Commissioner of Lands, Thomas H. Ruth; for Commissioner of Labor and Statistics, Walter McKay; for Congressmen, J. A. Pickler and W. V. Lucas. The following is a portion of the platform:

We urge upon the general government such legislation as will secure to the several States for agricultural purposes the arid lands within their borders, and we urge upon our Senators and Representatives in Congress to continue their best efforts to secure from the general government liberal aid for the establishment of a system of irrigation by means of artesian wells.

We demand such legislation by our general and state government as will prevent dealings in options of agricultural products by speculators and the forming of combinations and trusts.

We commend the present administration in its management of the affairs of the General Land Office.

We commend to the thoughtful consideration of our people the adoption of such methods of road improvement as will insure the building of durable and substantial roadways in all sections of the State.

We demand the passage of a registration law to apply only in towns and cities having a population of 1,000 or more.

We are in favor of the postal telegraph and postal savings bank systems, also of rural free delivery.

We favor the enactment of such laws for the regulation of railroads within this State as will insure absolute equality to all classes of patrons and all localities.

The Democratic State convention met at Chamberlain on Sept. 1, and nominated Peter Couchman for Governor, and S. A. Ramsey for Lieutenant-Governor. Candidates for the remaining places on the State ticket and for Congressmen were also selected. The platform demands re-submission of the Prohibition question to the people, denounces "Pinkertonism," approves tariff reform, and contains the following declarations:

We demand that the school funds of our State be loaned to the people of the State upon ample security, at a reasonable rate of interest, and we denounce the action of our Republican legislature and State officers in depriving the mass of the people of the use of such funds under proper safeguards and regulation.

Believing that unnecessary taxation is unjust taxation, we pledge the Democracy if intrusted with power to a rigid and economical administration of the trust reposed in them by the people.

A Prohibition ticket was nominated at Sioux Falls on Sept. 14, but, owing to failure to comply with the provisions of the Australian ballot law, the names of the nominees did·not appear on the official ballot.

At the November election the entire Republican ticket was elected, the vote for Governor being : Sheldon, 33,414 ; Van Isdel, 22,524 ; Couchman, 14,472. For Presidential electors the vote was : Republican, 34,888 ; Independent, 26,644; Democratic, 9,081. Members of the State Legislature were elected at the same time as follows : Senate—Republicans, 33 ; Independents, 6 ; Democrats, 3 ; House—Republicans, 64 ; Independents, 14 ; Democrats, 6.

An amendment to the State constitution, reducing the mileage allowable to legislators to five cents a mile, was submitted to the people at this election and was approved by a vote of 39,634 in its favor and 11,236 in opposition.

SPAIN, a monarchy in southern Europe. The present Constitution was proclaimed June 30, 1876. The legislative power is vested in the Cortes, ·consisting of the Senate and the Congress. The Senate is composed of 100 life senators, nominated by the king ; 80 senators by right of birth or office ; and 180 elected members. The Congress consists of 432 Deputies, chosen for 5 years by the electoral colleges, at the rate of 1 deputy to every 50,000 inhabitants. The executive power vests in the king. At present the royal prerogative is exercised by the Queen-mother, Maria Christina, who acts as Regent for King Alfonso XIII., born May 17, 1886, until he reaches his legal majority at the age of 16. The ministry, in the beginning of 1892, was composed of the following members : Prime Minister, Antonio Canovas del Castillo ; Minister of Foreign Affairs, the Duke of Tetuan ; Minister of Finance. Juan de la Concha Castañeda ; Minister of the Interior, A. Elduayen ; Minister of Justice, F. CosGayon ; Minister of Instruction, Commerce, and Agriculture, A. Linares Rivas ; Minister of War, Gen. de Ascarraga ; Minister of Marine, Admiral F. Montigo ; Minister of the Colonies, F. Romero Robledo.

Area and Population.—The area of Spain, including the Canary and Balearic Isles and 13 square miles on the northwest coast of Africa, is 197.670 square miles. The total population in 1887 was 17,550,246, of whom 8.607,242· were males and 8,943,004 females. Of the total population 17,516,049 were native-born Spaniards, 7,188 naturalized Spaniards, 18,480 French, 6,755 Portuguese, 5,719 English, 3,877 Italians, 1,826 Germans, and 5,738 belonged to other nationalities. Of the principal cities, Madrid had 470,283 inhabitants ; Barcelona, 272,481 ; Valencia, 170,763 ; Sevilla, 143,182 ; Malaga, 134,016.

Finance.—The revenue was estimated, in the budget for 1892–93, at 747,960,550 pesetas or francs, of which 289,007,000 pesetas are derived from direct taxes ; 291,112,000 pesetas from indirect taxes and customs, 126,150,000 pesetas from stamps and régie enterprises, 29,221,550 pesetas from government property, and 12,470,-000 pesetas were in the public treasury. The expenditures were estimated at 741,206,994 pesetas, of which 9,000,000 pesetas are for the civil list ; 1,724,260 pesetas for legislative expenses ; 290,966,415 pesetas for the public debt ; 2,023,205 pesetas for judicial expenses ; 54,751,-200 pesetas for indemnities and pensions ; 2,181,-550 pesetas for the Presidency of the Council of Ministers ; 4,975,237 pesetas for the Ministry of Foreign Affairs ; 56,467,532 pesetas for the Ministry of Justice ; 140,647,247 pesetas for the Ministry of War ; 29,741,572 pesetas for the Ministry of Marine ; 28,386,042 pesetas for the Ministry of the Interior ; 74,716,565 pesetas for the Ministry of Public Works and Instruction ; 16,504,142 pesetas for the Ministry of Finance ; and 29,122,027 pesetas for the cost of collecting the revenue. On Jan. 1, 1890, the public debt amounted to 6,207,027,482 pesetas, on which the interest was 233,312,491 pesetas.

The Army.—Service in the army is obligatory for every male citizen above the age of 19. The term of service is 12 years, of which 3 years are spent in the active army, 3 years in the first reserve, and 6 years in the second reserve. Against the payment of 1,500 pesetas anyone may procure exemption from service. The annual contingent was fixed by the law of Dec. 16, 1891, at 80,000 men. There are 12 military districts in continental Spain, which are divided into 108 recruiting districts and which again form 16 recruiting divisions, thus forming a basis for military organization in time of peace. In 1892 the peace effective was composed of 61 regiments of infantry of the line, 20 battalions of chasseurs, 68 squadrons of infantry reserve, 28 regiments of cavalry, 28 squadrons of cavalry reserve, 13 regiments of artillery, 3 battalions horse artillery, 10 fortress battalions, 7 squadrons of·artillery reserve, 4 companies of workmen, 2 companies attached to the military academy and central shooting school, 4 regiments of engineers, 1 regiment of pontoniers, 1 battalion of telegraphists, 1 battalion of railroad engineers, 1 brigade of topographists, and 4 squadrons engineer reserves. The total force of the peace effective in 1892 numbered 9,442 officers, 91,928 sub-officers and men, and 14,887 horses and mules. In case of war the strength of the army can be increased to 26,005 officers, 311,675 sub-officers and men, and 33,938 horses and mules.

The Navy.—The naval forces in 1892 consisted of 1 turret ship. with 17 guns ; 3 broadside ships ; 3 deck-protected cruisers of the first class and 3 cruisers of the second class ; 2 frigates ; 6 cruisers of the first class ; 7 cruisers of the third class ; 4 gunboats of the first class, 7 of the second class, and 33 of the third class ; 6 torpedo gunboats ; 13 gun launches ; 1 torpedo catcher ; 12 torpedo-boats of the first class and 3 of the second class ; 1 submarine boat ; 4 transports ; and 2 school ships. There are under construction 2 turret ships, 3 armorclad frigates, and 3 armorclad cruisers. The navy was manned in 1892 by 1,138 officers, 661 employés, 180 pilots, 7,715 sailors, and 8,500 marines.

Commerce.—The total imports, in 1890, amounted to 941,138,000 pesetas, and the exports to 937,760,000 pesetas. The following table shows the trade for 1890 with the leading countries, in pesetas :

COUNTRIES.	Imports.	Exports.
France	292,300,000	425,600,000
Great Britain and Gibraltar	107,400,000	220,400,000
Germany	44,500,000	11,800,000
Belgium	40,500,000	21,400,000
Portugal	34,900,000	35,700,000
Sweden and Norway	37,200,000	1,400,000
Russia	26,400,000	400,000
Italy	16,400,000	8,100,000
Turkey	8,400,000	
Netherlands	2,800,000	13,900,000
America	175,300,000	171,400,000
Philippine Islands	24,600,000	9,200,000
Northern Africa	18,000,000	4,400,000
Other countries	22,400,000	14,100,000
Total	941,100,000	937,800,000

The principal imports and their values were as follows : Cotton, 69,773,000 pesetas ; sugar, 45,-791,000 pesetas ; coal, 44,660,000 pesetas ; woods, 44,512,000 pesetas ; machinery, 41,083,000 pesetas ; iron, 33.890,000 pesetas ; tobacco, 33,622,-000 pesetas ; codfish, 29,864,000 pesetas ; wheat, 29,050,000 pesetas ; spirits, 26,084,000 pesetas ; chemicals, 22,776,000 pesetas ; woolen goods, 22,-449,000 pesetas ; hides and skins, 16,721,000 pesetas ; cacao, 14,848,000 pesetas ; linen thread, 13,-697,000 pesetas ; cotton goods, 11,579,000 pesetas ; petroleum, 11,145.000 pesetas ; animals. 10,456,-000 pesetas ; silk manufactures, 9,580,000 pesetas. The values of the principal exports were as follows : Wine, 309,965.000 pesetas ; lead, 66,744,-000 pesetas ; iron, 62,797,000 pesetas ; copper, 55,052,000 pesetas ; dried raisins, 28,457,000 pesetas ; cork, 23,852,000 pesetas ; oranges, 18,265,000 pesetas ; animals, 18,220,000 pesetas ; boots and shoes, 17,379,000 pesetas ; olive oil, 13,154,000 pesetas ; raisins, 11,903,000 pesetas ; flour, 10,-158,000 pesetas ; hides, 9,643,000 pesetas.

Navigation.—The total number .of vessels entered at Spanish ports in 1891 was 19,248, of 11,646,232 tons. Of this number 6,341 vessels, of 4,912,271 tons, were Spanish steamers ; 7,718, of 5,989,442 tons, foreign steamers ; 2,655, of 181,-400 tons, Spanish sailing vessels ; and 2,534, of 563,119 tons, foreign sailing vessels. The total number of vessels cleared was 18,202, of 11,843,-018 tons. Of this number 5,969, of 5,142,795 tons, were Spanish steamers ; 8,071, of 6,069,426 tons, foreign steamers ; 2,134, of 205,554 tons, Spanish sailing vessels ; and 2,028, of 425,243 tons, foreign sailing vessels.

Railroads, Posts, and Telegraphs.—The total length of railroads at the end of 1889 was 9,774 kilometers. The post-office in 1890 forwarded 99,751,000 letters, 918,000 postal cards, 34,728,000 pieces of printed matter, and 91,000 money letters of the declared value of 119.875,-000 francs, through the internal service; 12.522,-000 letters, 221.000 postal cards, 16,088,000 pieces of printed matter, and 25,000 money letters of the declared value of 31,587,000 francs, through the external service ; and 122,000 letters, 2,000 postal cards, and 52,000 pieces of printed matter, through in transit. The receipts were 22,315,773 francs, and the expenses 12,178,588 francs.

The total length of telegraph lines in 1890 was 25,257 kilometers, with a length of wire of 55,920 kilometers. The internal department dispatched 3,191,428 messages. and the international department 1,098,388, while 147,402 were service dispatches. The receipts were 6,190,973 pesetas, and the expenses 6,333,156 pesetas.

Anarchist Disturbances.—On the night of Jan. 8, 1892, a large force of anarchists forced the gates of Xeres, overpowered the police, and put themselves in possession of the town. When the troops arrived on the scene a fierce fight ensued, in which a number of soldiers and revolters were killed, and which ended in the retreat of the anarchists. A large number of persons was arrested and tried ; four anarchists were found guilty of p   in the riots, sentenced to death, and anticipation Feb. 10, 1892.

A plot was discovered on April 4, 1892, which had for its object the destruction of the Congress House as well as the Royal Palace. Two foreigners were arrested while they were entering the former building, and when they were examined at the police station two bombs were found on their persons, which, according to subsequent examination, were sufficient to destroy any building. About the same time a number of explosions took place in Madrid, Bilbao, and other places, with the result that most of the leaders of the anarchists were arrested. Amongst those arrested was a Spaniard named Muñoz, who, on being confronted with Deboche and Ferreira, the two foreigners charged with the intention of blowing up the Chamber of Deputies, admitted that he was the leader of the movement, that their intention was to destroy the Chamber of Deputies, the Senate, and the Royal Palace, and that Deboche and Ferreira had been designated by lot to put the plan into execution. The offenders were sentenced to imprisonment, the law not permitting capital punishment in such cases.

Labor Troubles and Riots.—Ever since the May-day demonstrations of 1891 discontent has prevailed among the miners of the Bilbao district, which finally culminated in a strike of the miners for shorter hours and higher wages in January, 1892. The strikers paraded the streets of the mining villages and forced those unwilling to quit work to join them, and they destroyed the pits, tore up the rails along the railroad lines, and cut the telegraph wires to prevent the authorities from sending for aid. Numerous encounters with the gendarmerie took place, in which the latter were usually overpowered and forced to retreat. All work in the mines was suspended, and general anarchy prevailed. The gendarmerie being unable to cope with the rioters, military forces were sent for, and on Jan. 27 General Loma arrived with three battalions of infantry, several guns, and a detachment of lancers. A state of siege was proclaimed and the whole mining district occupied by troops. The arrival of troops had a quieting effect upon the strikers, and work was resumed in the mines under military protection. Quiet was restored by Feb. 16, and the troops were withdrawn, the miners returning to work at the former terms.

On June 8, 1892, a riot occurred in Barcelona. The conflict originated in a movement among the workingmen for shorter hours and an increase of pay. The refusal of the masters to grant these demands led to a strike which gradually grew in proportion until finally thousands of workingmen were out of employment. A meeting of the

strikers. at which revolutionary speeches were
made, was dispersed by the police, and this was
the signal for the ensuing riots. On June 8,
about 3,000 strikers met at a suburb called Bar-
celoneta, and denounced the Government for interfering with their meetings, and by way of protest, signified their intention of marching to the
Palacio. The authorities, who were informed of
the proceedings. did not wish to wait until the
mob would reach the city, and therefore sent a
large body of police to intercept them on the
way. Attempts to disperse the mob in a quiet
way proved fruitless, and the police charged it
with swords drawn. A fierce fight followed,
in which a number of police and rioters were
wounded, but finally the police succeeded in dispersing the mob. A number of smaller cneoun-
ters took place in which the police were sometimes
worsted, and it was finally found necessary to
call in military assistance. On June 11 the mob,
partially armed with rifles and revolvers, commenced to destroy property and actually pillaged
a number of cotton and woolen factories, before
the police, assisted by troops, appeared on the
scene. A sanguinary fight took place, a number
of the police as well as of the people being killed
and wounded, but at length the police managed
to gain the upper hand, and succeeded in dispersing the rioters. Martial law was declared, and
all public buildings occupied by troops. Re-
enforcements were sent to the Fort of Montjuiz,
which commands the city, and the public was
given to understand that, if necessary, the bombardment of 1842 would be repeated. Encounters
between the troops and the mob continued for
several days, but, owing to the vigorous efforts of
the authorities to maintain order, these were suppressed, and order was established again on June
16. On June 19, 1892, 3,000 telegraph operators
went out on a strike. This move was sudden and
unexpected, and, as it extended over the kingdom,
the Government was unable to replace the striking employés, thus causing great inconvenience
and loss to business people and to the public in
general. The employés demanded higher wages,
more advantageous terms as to pensions, and a
better and more capable form of administration
in their department. This state of things lasted
five days, during which time communication by
wire was stopped completely, but finally the Government agreed to a settlement of the grievances,
on condition that the employés should return to
work at once. This was agreed to, and business
was resumed. A rather unique riot occurred in
Madrid on July 3, where the marketwomen armed
themselves with sticks and brooms, and marched
through the city, breaking the windows along the
line, and compelling the storekeepers to close
their shops. The cause of it was the introduction
of higher municipal market taxes. The governor
of the city immediately expounded the law as not
including the marketwomen, but the mischief had
been done, and their places were filled by a mob
who replaced broomsticks by knives and revolvers,
thus compelling the authorities to disperse the
mob by force of arms, whereby several people
were killed and a large number wounded. Other
riots occurred during the year in Granada, Va-
leucia, Corunna, and other places.

Cabinet Crisis.—The municipal administration
of the city of Madrid had become such a public
scandal that the government saw itself forced to
take some action, and appointed a special committee to investigate matters. The mayor of
the city became so unpopular that he had to
resign before the termination of the investigation.
The Marquis de Cubas stepped into his place,
and the energy with which he commenced the
reforms soon won him the confidence of the
people. The report of the committee was submitted to the Cabinet, and the Minister of the
Interior, Villaverde, urged that the former officials should be prosecuted. This did not meet
with the approval of the Ministers, and Señor
Villaverde resigned, his place being filled by
Señor Dauvila. All the civic authorities followed
Villaverde's example, with the exception of the
Marquis de Cubas. who refused to resign. Immediately after the reopening of the Cortes. the
Government was interpellated as to the action
adopted in the municipal scandals which had
brought about the resignation of the Minister
of the Interior. Señor Canovas. the Prime Minister, defended the action of the Government;
his Conservative adherents, however, did not
bear him out, but approved the course taken by
Señor Villaverde, and when Canovas asked the
Chamber for a vote of confidence, in that the
course adopted in regard to the municipal scandals was the only legal one, the motion of the
Government was defeated, and Premier Canovas
tendered the resignation of the whole Cabinet on
Dec. 7, 1892. The Queen-Regent accepted their
resignation and charged Señor Sagasta with the
formation of a new Cabinet, who on Dec. 11
submitted the following list of Ministers to the
Queen, which was subsequently ratified : President of the Council, without portfolio, Senor
Sagasta ; Minister of Foreign Affairs, Marquis
de la Vega de Armijo; Minister of Justice,
Montero Rios ; Minister of Finance. Señor
Gamazo; Minister of the Interior, Venancio
Gonzalez ; Minister of War, Gen. Lopez Dominguez ; Minister of Marine, Admiral Cervera ;
Minister of Public Works, Moret Prendergast ;
Minister of the Colonies, Señor Maura. The
new Liberal Government adopted the procedure
regarding the scandals which was suggested by
Señor Canovas, and accordingly the inquiries
will be conducted in the first instance before
the Civil Governor of Madrid ; it will then be
laid before the Minister of the Interior, and
lastly before the Council of State.

The Colonies.—The colonies of Spain may be
divided into three classes : (1) Possessions in
America (see CUBA AND PORTO RICO); (2) Possessions in Asia; (3) Possessions in Africa. The
possessions in Asia consist of the Philippine Islands, Sulu Islands, Caroline Islands and Palaos,
and the Marianne Islands, having a total area of
116,256 square miles, with a population of 7,-
121.172. The most important group are the
Philippine Islands, with an area of 114,326 square
miles and a population of about 7,000,000. The
imports in 1889 amounted to 23,450.689 pesos,
against 22,240,295 pesos in 1888. The exports
amounted to 34,547,863 and 26,358,640 pesos for
the two years respectively. The principal exports in 1889 and their values were manilla hemp,
14,789,000 pesos ; sugar, 11,206,000 pesos; tobacco, 3,148,000 pesos; coffee, 2,407,000 pesos ;
rice, 358,000 pesos. In the same year 415 vessels

of 426,589 tons entered the ports, and 401 vessels of 418,418 tons cleared. The difficulty between the United States Government and Spain regarding the American missionaries in the Caroline Islands was settled satisfactorily in April, 1892. The Spanish Government consents to the return of the missionaries to the islands, and undertakes that their propaganda shall not be interfered with, on the condition that the missionaries do not interfere in local government matters or in questions between the island authorities and the natives.

The possessions in Africa embrace Rio de Oro, Adrar, Ifni, Fernando Po, Annabon, Corisco, Elobey, and San Juan. The total area is 243,877 square miles and the population is 136,000.

SPURGEON, CHARLES HADDON, an English Baptist clergyman, born in Kelvedon, Essex, England, June 19, 1834; died in Mentone, France, January 31, 1892. His father, the Rev.

CHARLES H. SPURGEON.

John Spurgeon, who still survives, and his grandfather, the Rev. James Spurgeon, were ministers of the Independent, or Congregational, denomination. Charles received his education at Colchester and Maidstone, and at a very early age his scholarship was conspicuously above the average. In his sixteenth year he was engaged as usher in a school at Newmarket. During his residence there his religious convictions became settled, and, as he had embraced decided views on the subject of immersion as the proper mode of baptism, he united with the Baptist church in Isleham, a village seven miles distant. After spending a year at Newmarket, he removed to the university town of Cambridge, where he again held the place of usher in a well-known private school. He had already begun to speak in religious meetings, and soon developed so marked a capacity for such service that before he was eighteen he became pastor of the Baptist church at Waterbeach, a village five miles north of Cambridge. His ministry there lasted for two years, but the compensation he received was so meager that he was obliged to eke out his support by continuing his duties as usher in the Cambridge school.

In 1853, when he was just turned nineteen, young Spurgeon, to his own great surprise, received a call to the pastorate of the New Park Street Baptist church in Southwark, London. The congregation, which in former years had been large, was greatly run down. The income was no longer sufficient to meet a pastor's salary and pay the ordinary expenses of the place, and no definite pecuniary inducement could be offered to the new preacher. But his success was unmistakably assured from the first Sunday of his preaching in London. The New Park Street chapel, although capable of seating 1,200 persons, soon became intolerably crowded, and plans were promptly made for its enlargement. Meanwhile the congregation moved to Exeter Hall, and that commodious auditory was thronged at every service. When they returned to the remodeled chapel, in spite of all that had been done to increase its accommodations, they found themselves more inconvenienced than before. The project of a great metropolitan tabernacle was then formed. To collect the necessary funds for this enterprise, and to complete the immense building, occupied five years. During that time Mr. Spurgeon preached chiefly in Exeter Hall and in the Surrey Gardens Music Hall. At the latter place, on the evening of his first service there, a false alarm of fire created a panic in which seven persons were killed and many others were seriously injured. Contributions towards the tabernacle were received from all parts of Great Britain, the indefatigable pastor traveling far and wide, preaching and collecting money. In May, 1861, the edifice was completed, paid for, and opened for worship.

The Metropolitan Tabernacle, Newington, which has been one of the sights of London for thirty years, is 146 feet long, 81 feet broad, and 62 feet high. It contains, with its double galleries, 5,500 sittings, and will hold 6,000 persons without excessive crowding. There are also in the building a lecture hall, holding about 900, a schoolroom for 1,000 children, six class-rooms, three vestries for pastor, deacons, and elders, a young men's class-room, and rooms for other purposes connected with the multiform work of which the church is the center. The district in which it is situated is described as including "some of the worst, most degraded, and most dangerous spots in all London." The influence of Spurgeon and his Tabernacle has gone far to transform this neighborhood. Acres of slums have been cleared; drinking-shops have been closed; festering tenements have given way to model dwellings; while outcasts without number have been reclaimed, and the deserving poor have been assisted in earning a decent livelihood. "The whole quarter," says a competent observer, "has been converted from a scene of sordid poverty and the lowest forms of vice to one of healthful peace and comparative prosperity."

As a preacher, Mr. Spurgeon was characterized, first of all, by intense and never-flagging earnestness. His speech was always that of a man who had something to say of supreme importance to himself and to those whom he addressed. He used no set religious phrases; he discarded conventions and formalities; his manner was conversational, not rhetorical. He made no attempt to be eloquent; he was only profoundly and urgently real. By natural gift he had extraordinary fluency of utterance. By study of the English Bible and the religious literature of the 17th century, he acquired an unparalleled mastery of pure and nervous Anglo-Saxon. His voice was of astonishing volume, sonorousness, and power, and singularly sweet in tone. Without apparent effort he made himself easily heard by the great audiences to whom he habitually spoke, and upon occasion by still larger assemblages. In May, 1867, while the Tabernacle was undergoing repairs he preached for five Sundays in the Agricultural Hall, a place "like uninclosed space for vastness," and his congregation numbered not fewer than 12,000 persons; and once, in the Crystal Palace, at Sydenham, he had an audience of more than 20,000. His doctrinal position was emphatically Calvinistic; he had no toleration for what he esteemed the undue laxity of some modern theologians. He even withdrew from the Baptist Union of Great Britain on account of theological tendencies which he disapproved in some of the churches composing that body. He never ceased, however, to command the respect and love of those whom he most strenuously antagonized. His exalted Christian spirit and his heroic life of practical self-devotion, far more than his credal attitude, determined the estimate in which he was held, not only by his fellow Baptists, but by the leading spirits of all communions, including Dean Stanley, Archbishop Tait of Canterbury, and Cardinal Manning.

Mr. Spurgeon's achievement as an author was scarcely less phenomenal than as a preacher. He published, by actual count, more than 2,200 sermons, of which literally millions of copies were sold and eagerly read in all parts of the world. He issued a voluminous commentary on the Psalms, entitled "The Treasury of David," the preparation of which covered a period of twenty years; and he edited a monthly magazine, "The Sword and the Trowel." In addition to the many volumes of his sermons, he published three large books of family devotions, and a number of smaller works, such as "John Ploughman's Talk" and "Pictures," "Feathers for Arrows," "Lectures to My Students," "Commenting and Commentaries." The popularity of these writings is indicated by the fact that "John Ploughman's Talk" has reached a sale of 320,000 copies, while of its sequel, the "Pictures," 100,000 copies have been sold. It is stated on good authority that Spurgeon's printed books, including "The Sword and the Trowel," comprise nearly one hundred volumes. Prof. William C. Wilkinson remarks that, "in the capacity of author alone this fecund genius did enough to give him unchallenged rank among the most successful literary men of his generation."

A third aspect of Mr. Spurgeon's career which challenges admiration was his faculty for organizing and administering important enterprises. Besides directing the affairs of a church of 6,000 members, he was the originator and active head of a Pastors' College, which in 1890 had sent out nearly 1,000 preachers, missionaries, and evangelists. He also founded an Orphanage at Stockwell, where 500 boys and girls are cared for in large separate families, instead of being massed together on the workhouse system. For the benefit of the aged poor connected with his church he built, not far from the Tabernacle, a group of almshouses, in which there are also quarters for a "ragged school" of nearly 400 children, with daily sessions and a resident schoolmaster. He established a Colportage Association, which employs more than fifty men and has sold many thousand pounds' worth of religious books. There is a Tabernacle Building Fund, for lending money without interest to aid poor churches in building houses of worship; a Book Fund, administered by Mrs. Spurgeon, for supplying needy ministers of all denominations with books; a Church Poor Fund, which distributes annually about $5,000; and there are missions to the number of twenty-five or thirty carried on under the auspices of the Tabernacle. Mr. Spurgeon's brother, the Rev. James A. Spurgeon, became his co-pastor in 1867, and remains in charge of the church's affairs. The pulpit is at present supplied by the Rev. A. T. Pierson, D.D., a Presbyterian clergyman of Philadelphia. Two sons of Mr. Spurgeon, his only children, are pastors of Baptist churches, one in Australia and the other in the vicinity of London. Mr. Spurgeon died at Mentone, whither, as often before, he had been driven to retire for rest and possible recuperation, by the painful disease of gout, from which he suffered much in his later years.

STEVENSON, ADLAI EWING, twenty-third Vice-President of the United States, born in Christian county, Ky., Oct. 23, 1835. He was educated in the common schools of that State and afterward at Centre College in Danville, Ky., and at the Illinois Wesleyan University. When he was seventeen years old, his parents removed to Bloomington, Ill. His attention was first attracted to politics in the Know-Nothing campaign in Illinois, and while yet a boy, before he had attained his majority, he endeavored himself to the large Irish and German population of his section by his able and eloquent speeches in denunciation of the proscriptive policy of the Know-Nothings. At Bloomington he began the study of law, and was admitted to the bar in May, 1857. He then removed to Metamora, Woodford county, Ill., where he began the practice of his profession, appearing frequently before the courts of Woodford and McLean counties, especially at Bloomington. His legal abilities attracted the attention of the Circuit Judge, who appointed him Master in Chancery, which office he held from 1860 to 1864. In the latter year he canvassed the State for the Democratic candidates for electors, of whom he was one. He was at the same time a candidate on the Democratic ticket for the office of Prosecuting Attorney for the 23d Judicial district and was elected, serving one term of four years. He then returned to Bloomington, which has ever since been his home. Here he resumed the practice of law, forming a partnership in January, 1868, with James S. Ewing, a relative, as senior member of the firm of Stevenson & Ewing. This partnership still exists. He was one of the earliest advocates of currency reform and was nominated for Congress on that issue in 1874 by the Democrats of the Bloomington district. He drew to his support many Independents, and, although his district had been Republican by 3,000 majority, after a very exciting canvass he defeated his Republican opponent, the sitting member, Gen. John C. McNulta, by 1,232 votes. While in the 44th Congress he served on the Committees of the District of Columbia and Territories. He was renominated by acclamation in 1876, but was defeated, the district giving a majority of 242 votes for his Republican opponent, while Mr. Hayes carried it by a majority of nearly 3,000 for President. In the short session of the 44th Congress he was in his seat during all the exciting scenes that accompanied the

man T. F. Tipton, Republican, and 134 votes for L. M. Bickmore, Prohibitionist. In the 46th Congress he served as Chairman of the Committee on Mines and Mining. At the end of his term, in 1881, he returned again to his law practice at Bloomington, but retained his political connections and was looked upon as the leader of the Democracy in his section of the State.

By the Democrats he was chosen as a delegate in 1884 to the National Convention that nominated Grover Cleveland for President, and after

ADLAI EWING STEVENSON.

counting of the electoral votes in the Tilden-Hayes contest, and was always an earnest and outspoken advocate of a peaceful settlement of the differences in the great controversy. On the expiration of his term he resumed his law practice, and he served in 1877 as a member of the Board of Visitors to West Point. The next year he was nominated for Congress in the Bloomington district by the National Greenback-Labor party. He was accepted by the Democrats, and carried every county in the district, receiving 13,870 votes, against 12,058 votes for Congress.

the latter's election Mr. Stevenson was appointed First Assistant Postmaster-General. This appointment was undoubtedly due to Mr. Vilas, Mr. Cleveland's Postmaster-General, who had been Mr. Stevenson's close personal friend for years. In his capacity of First As had jurisdiction over the appointments of more than 44,000 third-class postmasters. He was outspoken in his belief that, other things being equal, when reputable and efficient Democratic applicants presented themselves as candidates, it was his duty to remove Republican postmasters and appoint Democrats in their places. The celerity that he displayed in this work made him very popular with Democratic partisans, especially throughout the South, and "Adlai's axe" became almost a proverbial expression. His urbanity and courtesy in social life made him exceedingly popular with all classes of people, and he was one of the favorites of Mr. Cleveland's administration at Washington during the four years of Democratic rule. He was nominated by President Cleveland to the bench of the Supreme Court of the District of Columbia, but the Republican Senate refused to confirm him. After Mr. Harrison's inauguration Mr. Stevenson again returned to his law books, but in 1892 he was chosen as a delegate-at-large from Illinois to the National Democratic Convention in Chicago and earnestly worked for the nomination of Mr. Cleveland. He was unanimously elected chairman of the Illinois delegation, and made all the announcements of its vote until his name was entered in the Vice-Presidential contest, when he retired to the gallery. He accepted the nomination in an eloquent speech at the official reception to the candidates in Madison Square Garden, New York, and afterward took a very active part in the canvass, speaking in most of the Western, Central, and Southern States. He is of commanding presence, being over six feet tall and of good build. He has a clean-cut face with Scottish features, sharp blue eyes, gray hair, and a drooping iron-gray mustache. Mr. Stevenson is married and has three daughters and one son. The accompanying portrait is made by permission from a photograph by Sarony.

SUGAR.—It has been the policy of this country to foster the sugar industry by a protective tariff since the foundation of the Government. The first tariff act passed after the adoption of the Constitution, that of July 4, 1789, placed a duty of one cent a pound on raw sugar, and of three cents on refined sugar; and the various tariff acts enacted since have imposed duties on sugar, either *ad valorem* or specific.

The tariff act of October 1, 1890 (26 Stat. 567), commonly known as the McKinley Bill, made a radical change in the mode of affording protection. It provided for the admission of sugar up to and including No. 16 Dutch Standard of color free of duty from April 1, 1891.

Sugar above No. 16 Dutch Standard was made liable to a duty of one cent a pound, and one-tenth of one cent per pound in addition when exported from, or the product of any country which pays, directly or indirectly, a bounty on the exportation of any sugar that may be included in this grade which is greater than is paid on raw sugars of a lower saccharine strength.

Section 3 of the act authorized the President, after January 1, 1892, to suspend the provisions relating to the free introduction of sugar from any country producing and exporting it, when satisfied that the Government of such country imposes duties upon the products of the United States, which, in view of the free introduction of sugar, molasses, coffee, tea, and hides into the United States, might be deemed reciprocally unequal and unreasonable.

Reciprocal commercial arrangements have been made with Germany, Austria-Hungary, Brazil, Spain for Cuba and Puerto Rico, Santo Domingo, Salvador, Great Britain for British Guiana and the British West Indies, Nicaragua, Honduras, and Guatemala. No arrangements having been made with Hayti, Venezuela, and Colombia, the President issued proclamations, March 15, 1892, declaring sugars from those countries subject to the duty fixed by the act. As these countries export little or no sugar to this country the imposition of duties has little effect except to show that the Government intends to carry out this provision of the law.

To compensate sugar producers for the loss sustained by the removal of duties and to encourage the industry, the law provided that for a period of 14 years, from July 1, 1891, to July 1, 1905, there should be paid, from any moneys in the Treasury, not otherwise appropriated, to the producer of sugar, testing not less than ninety degrees by the polariscope, from beets, sorghum, or sugar cane grown within the United States, or from maple sap produced within the United States, a bounty of two cents per pound; and upon such sugar testing less than ninety degrees by the polariscope, and not less than eighty degrees, a bounty of one and three-fourths cents per pound. The sugar producer intending to claim the bounty must file, prior to July 1st of each year, with the Commissioner of Internal Revenue, a notice of the place of production, with a general description of the machinery and methods to be employed by him, with an estimate of the amount of sugar proposed to be produced, including the number of maple trees to be tapped, and make an application for a license, which notice and application must be accompanied by a bond in such an amount as the Commissioner shall prescribe, conditioned that the applicant shall faithfully observe all the rules and regulations which shall be prescribed.

If the application and bond are satisfactory and approved, a license is issued. All the details relating to the supervision of the factories, weighing the sugar, and payment of the bounty, are matters of regulations prescribed by the Commissioner of Internal Revenue with the approval of the Secretary of the Treasury.

The sugar is weighed at the place of production or at designated central places by weighers appointed by Collectors of Internal Revenue. Claims for bounty are first presented to the Collector of Internal Revenue of the district, who certifies them to the Commissioner of Internal Revenue, by whom they are examined and forwarded to the proper accounting officers of the Treasury. After final allowance, drafts upon the Treasury are issued in payment, which are mailed or delivered to the persons entitled thereto.

All sugar must be classified under the law according to the polariscope test. The polariscope that has been adopted by the Internal Revenue Bureau is the "half shadow" apparatus made by Schmidt and Haensch, Berlin. This instrument is adapted for use with white light illumination from coal oil or gas lamps. It is easy to read, requiring no delicate discrimination of colors by the observer, and can be used by a person who is color-blind. It is adjusted to the Ventzke scale—that is, 1 degree of the scale is the $\frac{1}{100}$th part of the rotation produced in the plane of polarization of white light in a column

200 millimeters long by a standard solution of chemically pure sucrose at 17.5° Centigrade; the standard solution of sucrose in distilled water being such as to contain at 17.5° C., in 100 cubic centimeters, 26.048 grams of sucrose. If the scale reads 80 degrees it shows that the sample contains 80 per cent. of sucrose or pure sugar.

The regulations concerning the testing of sugar by the polariscope are based upon various official procedures, such as the one used in the United States Custom Houses, the method prescribed by the German Government, etc. They embody also the result of recent research in regard to sources of error in polarimetric estimation of sugar.

All weights, flasks, polariscopic tubes, and quartz control plates used in the work of testing sugar by the polariscope are standardized, and their accuracy attested by the Office of Weights and Measures, U. S. Coast and Geodetic Survey.

In addition to the national bounty the State of Kansas pays a bounty of ¾ of a cent a pound on sugar made from beets, sorghum, or other sugar-yielding cane or plants grown in the State; the sugar to polarize at least 90°, the amount having been reduced from two cents a pound by Act of March 4, 1891. All property of sugar factories in that State is exempt from taxation until 1895.

In Utah the territorial law (Act of March 12, 1890) provided under certain conditions for a bounty of one cent a pound for the years 1890 and 1891 on sugar made from sorghum, beets, or other sugar-bearing plants grown in Utah.

In Canada, by an act passed September 30, 1891, sugar made from beets, from July 1, 1891, to July 1, 1893, is entitled to a bounty of one dollar per hundred pounds and, in addition thereto, three and one-third cents per one' hundred pounds for each degree or fraction of a degree over seventy degrees shown by the polariscope.

The so-called bounty laws of the continental countries of Europe are quite different from the law in this country. A tax is imposed upon the sugar manufactured or upon the raw material, beets, and when the sugar is exported, a drawback or rebate is allowed, originally intended to be simply a return of the duty. But as the manufacturers, by the method of computation, receive upon exportation a greater amount as rebate than was paid as tax, this premium operates as a bounty on sugar exported. In Germany a new law went into effect on the 1st of August, 1892, which abolished the tax on beets, and increased the tax on sugar entering into consumption, and authorized rebates on sugar exported for a period of five years, after which it is supposed that no rebate in the form of a premium will be paid.

In France the new law in regard to sugar went into effect on Sept. 1, 1891, according to which the Government guaranties to manufacturers of sugar a minimum premium of 4.50 francs per 100 kilograms of sugar. For those manufacturers who work with rich beets the premium will vary from 8 to 9 francs per 100 kilograms, according to the richness of the beets.

In Austria direct premiums are paid on sugar exported according to polariscopic test. The annual maximum of premiums is not to exceed 5,000,000 florins, or 10,750,000 francs. If the premiums exceed this sum, the excess is to be reimbursed by the sugar factories in proportion to their production.

Cane.—Sugar cane is about 10 per cent. fiber and 90 per cent. juice. The juice contains from 15 to 18 per cent. of solids, of which 12 to 14 per cent. on a good average is sucrose, 1¼ per cent. to 2 per cent. glucose, ¼ per cent. albuminoids. There are also small quantities of non-saccharine solids, such as gums, dextrine, etc.

The process of boiling or evaporating the juice into sirup is carried on either in open kettles or in closed vessels in which the vacuum-pan principle of boiling is brought into play. This latter is the modern scientific method. The vessels or pans used for boiling by this process are provided internally with a series of closed pipes through which steam is conveyed for heating, the steam from the boiler of the first passing by a pipe into the worm of the second, and similarly the steam from the second into the worm of the third, when a third vessel is employed. This apparatus is called a "double effect," or "triple effect," according as two or three vessels are used. A quadruple or multiple effect continues the process a step further. The first cost of the apparatus is high, but its use results in great economy of fuel with a marked improvement in the quality and quantity of sugar produced.

A modern factory with the appliances requires large capital. The factory recently erected by the Caffrey Central Sugar Refinery and Railroad Company near Franklin, La., with seven roller mills and every improvement needed to handle 600 tons of cane a day, cost $525,000.

A majority of the sugar producers in this country still use the old-fashioned open kettle process, boiling the juice in open kettles until the sirup has reached a certain density, when it is conveyed to coolers to granulate or crystallize into sugar. The product is put into hogsheads and the molasses allowed to drain off. The chief objection to this method of evaporation arises from the fact that the high temperature required to boil sugar solutions in the open air converts the crystallizable sugar into inverted sugar or glucose. The yield is much less than by the improved methods, and the product of a poorer quality. The central factory system, which is being gradually adopted, tends to lessen the number of small factories. Planters find it more profitable to sell the cane to large factories. The molasses which results from the process of making sugar amounts to about 70 gallons to 1,000 pounds of sugar made by the open kettle process, and about 40 gallons to 1,000 pounds of sugar made by the centrifugals.

The average yield of cane is about 20 tons an acre. The highest yield known in this country is 65 tons per acre, raised on the grounds of the Louisiana Experiment Station. The yield of sugar per ton of cane ranges from 100 to 200 pounds, and exceptional yields have been as high as 230 pounds to the ton.

The quantity of sugar cane under cultivation in the United States is about 250,000 acres. There is sufficient land within the Southern States suited to the production of sugar cane to supply the entire domestic market. A crop of cane properly managed is as certain as any crop grown, and with a yield of 20 tons per acre, a net profit of $30 per acre can be realized.

Sorghum.—Sorghum, or Chinese sugar cane, (*Sorghum vulgare,*) has been in cultivation in China from very early times. It was introduced into this country by the Patent Office, in 1853–4, the seed having been obtained from France. Large sums have been appropriated by Congress for the development of the sorghum industry in this country, in experimenting to determine the territory best adapted for sorghum culture, the varieties best suited to that territory, and to develop by selection of seed the chosen varieties.

Peculiar difficulties have been encountered in making sugar from sorghum, owing to the presence of gummy substances in the juice, which hinder crystallization. But recent experiments have shown that these substances can be separated from the juice by the use of alcohol, and the yield of sugar largely increased. The Act of Congress of March 3, 1891, authorized distilled spirits to be withdrawn from distillery warehouses, free of tax, to be used in the manufacture of sugar from sorghum. With sorghum cane, averaging 13 or 14 per cent. of sugar in the juice, it is possible by using alcohol to obtain 150 pounds of first sugar per ton, and from 20 to 30 pounds of seconds. The yield of sorghum per acre is about 8 or 9 tons, as received at the factory, with the tops of the stalks cut off for seed.

The cultivation of sorghum is much easier and less expensive than the cultivation of sugar cane or of sugar beets, the cost of sorghum cane being $2 to $2.50 a ton, while the cost of sugar cane, and of sugar beets, reaches $4 to $5 a ton for the same percentage of sugar. There were only three factories that claimed bounty on sugar from sorghum during the year 1891—all in Kansas. They were in operation an average of forty-four days and produced 1,113,036 pounds of sugar. The only licensed sorghum-sugar factories for the year 1892 were the Medicine Lodge Sugar Company (Limited), Medicine Lodge, and the Parkinson Sugar Company, Fort Scott, Kansas.

Beet Sugar.—The beet from which sugar is obtained is a variety of the common garden beet (*Beta vulgaris*). By scientific experiments carried on for a long time, selecting for seed those beets having a high percentage of sucrose, a variety of sugar beet has been obtained which contains sufficient saccharine matter to make its use in the manufacture of sugar a profitable industry.

The beet-sugar industry in the continental countries of Europe has grown within recent years to great dimensions, the result of improved methods of manufacture and the system of bounties paid on sugar exported. These countries manufacture enough sugar to supply their own people, and have a large supply for export.

The production of beet sugar in Europe during the year 1891–2, with an estimate of the crop for 1892–3, in metric tons. of 2,204.6 pounds, is given by Mr. Licht, statistician, as follows :

	1892–3.	1891–2.
Germany	1,200,000	1,198,156
Austria	750,000	786,556
France	625,000	650,377
Russia	480,000	560,000
Belgium	200,000	180,377
Holland	75,000	46,815
Other Countries	80,000	78,000
Together	3,410,000	3,500,291

Our soil and climate are as well adapted to the growth of sugar beets as European countries. The Pacific Coast, the plateaus of Utah and Colorado, parts of Nebraska and the Dakotas, Southern Iowa, Minnesota, Winconsin, Northern Indiana, Ohio, and New York are probably the localities best adapted for the purpose. An acre of land will yield from twelve to fifteen tons of beets. The yield of sugar from a ton of beets containing 12 per cent. of sucrose is about 200 pounds. When the percentage of sugar in beets is below 12, they cannot be profitably used in the manufacture of sugar.

For the season of 1890–1, the yield in Austria-Hungary was 9.8 tons an acre; in France, 11.3 tons an acre; and in Germany, 13.8 tons an acre. The per cent. of sugar ·in beets in Austria-Hungary during the season of 1890–1 was 12.9 ; in France, 13.6 ; in Germany, 14.5, on the assumption that 85 per cent. of the total weight of sugar in the beet was obtained. At the Agricultural Experiment Station at Schuyler, Nebraska, during the past year, the yield was 21 tons of beets an acre, with a content of sugar of about 13 per cent.

The process of manufacture of sugar from beets is similar to that employed in the manufacture of sugar from sugar cane, but a more complicated apparatus for purification of the juice is necessary, as beet juice contains more non-saccharine substances, consisting of gums, acid bodies, nitrogenous matter, and various salts. Beet molasses has an extremely disagreeable taste. and can only be utilized for the manufacture of vinegar or converted into alcohol by fermentation and distillation. The pulp after the sugar has been removed makes an excellent food for fattening cattle. The total cost of a complete apparatus for manufacturing sugar from beets varies from $75,000 to $500,000. In 1892 there were manufactured, according to the returns made to the Commissioner of Internal Revenue, 27,000,000 pounds of beet sugar, of which about 21,800,000 pounds were produced in California, 3,800,000 pounds in Nebraska, and 1,400,000 pounds in Utah, against a total product of 12,004,838 pounds in 1891.

The following is a list of beet-sugar factories in this country : Utah Sugar Co., Lehi, Utah ; Alameda Sugar Co., Alvarado, Cal. ; Western Beet Sugar Co., Watsonville, Cal. ; Chino Valley Beet Sugar Co., Chino, Cal. ; Oxnard Beet Sugar Co., Grand Island, Neb. ; Norfolk Beet Sugar Co., Norfolk, Neb.

The following is a summary of operations for the year 1891–2 : Average number of days in operation, 58½ ; number of employés, 847 ; acres of beets used, 7,155 ; tons of beets used, 72,-529.9 ; sugar made per ton of beets, 165.5 pounds ; sugar made per acre of beets, 1,677 pounds.

Maple Sugar.—The annual production of maple sugar in the United States is estimated at 32,000,000 pounds. The following table shows the number of producers of 500 pounds, or upward, of maple sugar according to the Eleventh Census : Connecticut, 5 ; Illinois, 8 ; Indiana, 24 ; Iowa, 23 ; Kentucky, 1 ; Maine, 39 ; Maryland, 78 ; Massachusetts, 415 ; Michigan, 1,135 ; Minnesota, 23 ; Missouri, 5 ; New Hampshire, 1,725 ; New York, 7,884 ; North Carolina, 2 ;

Ohio, 930 ; Pennsylvania, 1,101 ; Tennessee, 2 ; Vermont, 10,099 ; Virginia, 4 ; West Virginia, 26 ; Wisconsin, 4—total, 23,533.

The number of licenses issued to sugar producers by the Commissioner of Internal Revenue for the year ending June 30, 1893, was as follows : Producers of sugar from sugar cane, 727 ; producers of sugar from beets, 7 ; producers of sugar from sorghum, 6 ; producers of sugar from maple sap, 4,240—total, 4,980.

The amount of sugar produced upon which bounty was paid during the year ending June 30, 1892, was as follows :

Cane sugar :	Pounds.	
Louisiana	354,901,053	
Mississippi	9,543	
Florida	929,248	
Texas	8,989,567	Pounds.
		364,829,411
Beet sugar :		
California	8,175,438	
Nebraska	2,734,500	
Utah	1,094,900	
		12,004,838
Sorghum sugar :		
Kansas		1,136,086
Maple sugar		144,882
Total		378,115,217

The sum of $7,342,077.79 was paid as bounty during the fiscal year ending June 30, 1892. The expense of carrying out the provision of the law relating to bounty during the year was $147,831.61, or about two per cent. of the amount paid out.

The amount of sugar imported into this country during the fiscal year ending June 30, 1892, was as follows : beet sugar, free of duty, 293,134,261 pounds ; cane or other sugar, free of duty, 3,-248,494,502 pounds ; sugar not classified, above No. 16, Dutch standard, dutiable, 14,880,402 pounds—total, 3,556,509,165 pounds.

We import cane sugar principally from Cuba, Brazil, British West Indies, British Guiana, Porto Rico, San Domingo, the Hawaiian Islands, the Dutch East Indies, and the Philippine Islands, and beet sugar from Germany, Belgium, and Austria-Hungary ; more than half of the sugar imported comes from Cuba. The amount of duty collected on sugar for the year ending June 30, 1890, was $53,992,107.55 ; for the year ending June 30, 1891, $32,290,773.03 (three months under the present tariff) ; and for the year ending June 30, 1892, $76,795.14.

There were no importations of sugar in 1892 at any port in the United States except New York, Boston, Philadelphia, Baltimore, New Orleans, and San Francisco. Comparatively little sugar is exported from the United States.

The exports of sugar during the year ending June 30, 1892, amounted to 19,414,620 pounds, valued at $830,045 ; most of which was refined, principally to Canada, the West Indies, and the Central and South American States.

The total amount of sugar of all kinds produced in the United States during the year ending June 30, 1892, was 412,893,230 pounds.

The consumption of sugar in the United States during the year ended June 30, 1892, was 4,024,646,975 pounds, which, divided by 64,817,-000 (estimated population Jan. 1, 1892), gives the amount consumed per capita as 62.09

pounds. The consumption of sugar per capita, in pounds, in European countries is as follows, according to the latest estimates : Germany, 23.9 ; Austria, 15.0 ; France, 28.7 ; Russia, 9.9 ; Holland, 27.7 ; Belgium, 21.6 ; Denmark, 41.0 ; Sweden and Norway, 22.5 ; Italy, 7.9 ; Roumania, 3.9 ; Spain, 9.4 ; Portugal, 13.8 ; England, 78.7 ; Bulgaria, 4.1 ; Greece, 10.1 ; Servia, 8.8 ; Turkey, 8.1 ; Switzerland, 32.9—average, Europe, 22.2.

SWEDEN AND NORWAY, two kingdoms in northern Europe, united under a common sovereign. Common diplomacy is directed by a Council of State in which both nations are represented. The reigning king is Oscar II., born Jan. 21, 1829, who succeeded his brother, Carl XV., on Sept. 18, 1872. The heir-apparent is the king's oldest son, Gustaf, Duke of Wermland, born June 16, 1858.

Sweden.—The Constitution of Sweden was proclaimed June 6, 1809, and was modified June 22, 1866. The legislative power vests in a Diet composed of two Chambers. The First Chamber consists of 147 members, elected for 9 years by the communes. The Second Chamber consists of 228 members, elected for 3 years by direct suffrage in the towns, and by direct or indirect suffrage, according to the decision of the people, in the rural districts. The executive is vested in the king, who acts under the advice of a Council of State. The following were the ministers in the beginning of 1892 : Minister of State, Erik Gustaf Bastrom ; Minister of Foreign Affairs, Count Carl Lewenhaupt ; Minister of Justice, August Ostergren ; Minister of War, Baron Nils Axel Hjalmar Palmstierna ; Minister of Marine, Baron Carl Gustaf von Otter ; Minister of the Interior, Victor Lennart Groll ; Minister of Finance, Baron Fredrik von Essen ; Minister of Education and Ecclesiastical Affairs, Gunnar Wennerberg ; Ministers without department, Baron Albert Lars Evert Ackerhielm and Sven Herman Wikblad.

Area and Population.—The area of Sweden is 170,979 square miles, and the population, according to the definite returns of the census taken Dec. 31, 1890, is 4,784,981. Of the total population, 2,317,187 were males, and 2,467,794 females. On Dec. 31, 1891, the population was estimated at 4,802,751, of whom 2,325,978 were males and 2,476,773 females. The marriages in 1890 numbered 28,611 ; births, 137,154 : deaths, 85,381 ; excess of births, 51,773. In the same year 34,212 persons emigrated, and 6,030 persons immigrated. On Dec. 31, 1891, Stockholm had a population of 250,528 ; Göteborg, 106,518 ; Malmö, 49,402 ; Norrköping, 33,431 ; Gefle, 24,337 ; Upsala, 21,441.

Finances.—The budget for 1893 estimates the ordinary revenue at 20,455,000 kronor (the Swedish krona and the Norwegian krone = 27¼ cents). The extraordinary revenue is estimated at 69,000,000 kronor, of which 37,500,000 kronor are derived from customs ; 7,800,000 kronor from posts ; 3,500,000 kronor from stamps ; 13,-700,000 kronor from impost on spirits ; 1,800,000 kronor from impost on beets ; 4,200,000 kronor from income tax ; 500,000 kronor from various sources. The net profit of the State Bank in 1891 amounted to 1,750,000 kronor, and the surplus from previous years amounted to 5,818,-

000 kronor. The total expenditures were estimated at 97,023,000 kronor, of which 1,320,000 kronor was for the civil list ; 3,887,900 kronor for justice ; 606.750 kronor for foreign affairs ; 21,069,700 kronor for the army ; 6,539,090 kronor for the navy ; 4,803,612 kronor for the interior ; 12,559,958 kronor for public worship and instruction ; 2,915,550 kronor for pensions ; 16,-534,966 kronor for finances. The extraordinary expenditures amounted to 15,739,474 kronor, of which 4,028,310 kronor is for the army and navy. The expenses on the public debt amounted to 10,463.300 kronor, while 250,000 kronor represents the reserved fund for the construction of a building for the Legislature and the State Bank ; 100,000 kronor the fund for insurance of workers against accidents ; and 227,700 kronor were carried to the floating capital of the state. The public debt amounted on January 1, 1892, to 258,071,781 kronor.

Commerce.—The total value of imports in 1890 amounted to 377,188,090 krónor and the exports to 304,592,000 kronor. Of the total imports those from Norway amounted to 32,833,000 kronor ; from Finland, 6,981,000 kronor ; from Russia, 22,737,000 kronor ; from Denmark, 44,-084,000 kronor ; from Germany, 118,322,000 kronor ; from the Netherlands, 9,638,000 kronor ; from Belgium, 10,101,000 kronor ; from Great Britain, 108,869,000 kronor ; from France, 7,933,-000 kronor ; from the United States, 8,183,000 kronor ; from all other countries, 7,507,000 kronor. Of the exports 18,093,000 kronor went to Norway ; 7,907,000 kronor to Finland ; 3,940,000 kronor to Russia ; 33,231.000 kronor to Denmark ; 36,677,000 kronor to Germany ; 16.278,000 kronor to the Netherlands ; 11,020,000 kronor to Belgium ; 137,403,000 kronor to great Britain ; 24,-422,000 kronor to France ; 7,430,000 kronor to Spain ; 919,000 kronor to the United States ; and 7,272,000 kronor to all other countries. The imports of articles of consumption amounted to 113,500,000 kronor, consisting of cereals for 30,300,000 kronor ; of spirits for 8,100,000 kronor; of colonial goods for 40,500,000 kronor ; of tobacco for 9,100,000 kronor ; of animals and animal victuals for 17,800,000 kronor ; of fruits and legumes for 5,200,000 kronor ; of salt for 2,500,000 kronor. The exports of articles of consumption amounted to 72,100,000 kronor, of which cereals were of the value of 8,900,-000 kronor ; spirits, 3,300,000 kronor ; colonial goods. 500.000 kronor ; animals and animal victuals, 58,400,000 kronor ; fruits and legumes, 1,000,000 kronor. Imports of raw materials amounted to 90,400,000 kronor, consisting of coal to the value of 30,600,000 kronor ; metals. 7,600,000 kronor ; hides and skins, 12,500,000 kronor ; textiles, 28,200,000 kronor ; wood, 2,-700,000 kronor ; minerals, 8,800,000 kronor. Exports of raw materials amounted to 153,000,000 kronor, including 36,800,000 kronor for metals ; 1,400,000 kronor for hides and skins ; 108,600,-000 kronor for lumber ; and 6,000,000 for minerals. The imports of manufactured goods amounted to 128,800,000 kronor, of which 1,800,000 kronor were for glassware ; 14,600,000 kronor for metal wares ; 74,600,000 kronor for textiles ; 5,300,000 kronor for paper ; 21,100,000 kronor for machines, ships, and wagons ; and 11,400,-000 kronor for other manufactures. The ex-

ports of manufactured goods, of the value of 71,100,000 kronor. consisted of glassware of the value of 1,600,000 kronor ; metal wares, 5,100,000 kronor ; textiles. 8.400,000 kronor ; paper, 23,400,000 kronor ; machines, ships, and wagons, 5,500,000 kronor ; and other manufactures, 27,100,000 kronor. The imports of oils, drugs and chemicals, and other miscellaneous merchandise amounted to 43,000.000 kronor, and the exports to 8,300,000 kronor. The imports of precious metals amounted to 660,000 kronor, and the exports to 100,000 kronor.

Navigation.—The number of vessels entered at Swedish ports during the year 1890 was 31,005 of 5,373,000 tons, of which 14,256 of 1,812,000 tons were Swedish ; 2,430 of 494,000 tons Norwegian, and 14,319 of 3,067,000 tons belonged to other nationalities. Of the total number 11,899 vessels of 2,435,000 tons were with cargoes. Included in the total are 13,343 steamers of 3,845,000 tons. The number of vessels cleared was 29,078 of 5,394,000 tons, of which 12,709 of 1,813,000 tons were Swedish, 2,428 of 508,000 tons Norwegian, and 13,941 of 3,073,000 tons were of other nationality. Of the total number of vessels cleared 13,319 of 3,867,000 tons were steamers ; and 20,067 vessels of 4,030,000 tons cleared with cargoes.

The merchant navy on Jan. 1, 1891, consisted of 3,874 vessels of 510,947 tons, as compared with 3,822 vessels of 504,679 tons in 1890. Of the total number, 2,858 of 369,680 tons were sailing vessels, and 1,016 of 141,267 tons were steamers.

Communications.—The length of the Swedish railroads at the end of 1891 was 8,279 kilometers, of which 2,742 kilometers were owned by the state, and 5,537 kilometers by private companies.

The length of telegraph lines, in 1891, was 12,688 kilometers, with a length of wire of 37-944 kilometers. Of these the Government owns 8,938 kilometers of line and 23,836 kilometers of wire. There were expedited during the year 1,164,167 domestic dispatches ; 635,267 international dispatches ; 202,501 messages were in transit ; and 75,975 were telegrams of the service. The receipts were 2,034,015 and the expenses 1,986,660 francs.

The post-office forwarded 44,044,000 domestic letters, 12,287,000 international letters, and 205,-000 letters in transit ; 4,942,000 domestic postal cards, 754,000 international postal cards, and 17,000 postal cards in transit ; 3,171.000 pieces domestic printed matter, 3,272,000 pieces international printed matter, and 58,000 pieces of printed matter in transit ; 1,666,000 domestic money letters of the declared value of 610,503,000 francs, 220,000 international money letters of the declared value of 50,687,000 francs, and 2,000 money letters of the declared value of 587,000 francs in transit. The receipts amounted to 10,504,301 francs, and the expenditures to 9,843,602 francs.

Extraordinary Session of the Diet.—A special session of the Swedish Diet was called for, Oct. 18, 1892, to discuss a bill, prepared by the Minister of War, for the reorganization of the army. The constant and increasing armaments of the large Powers compel the smaller countries to increase their war effective, if not for the purpose of taking an active part in any European war, yet with the object of presenting a formidable strength and compelling the belligerent countries to respect the neutrality of non-combatants. This applies with great force to Sweden, as her army has hitherto been very weak and inefficient to cope with emergencies such as would occur in case of war. According to the old system the army of Sweden is divided into three different classes. The first class represents the standing army, which is recruited by voluntary enlistment. The second class consists of the *Indelta*, an institution which borders closely on the feudal military tenure. By an agreement entered into between the Government and the landowners some 200 years ago, privileged landowners were relieved from personal military service against the payment of a certain tax on their lands for the support of the *Indelta*, and non-privileged landowners had to raise and maintain, at their own expense, a given number of men. In order to arrive at some equitable distribution, the territory was divided into districts, and each district had to support one soldier. The soldier would bind himself by contract with the landowner, who in turn would not only have to furnish the soldier, besides paying him in money, with a cottage, a small piece of land, and certain supplies, but was responsible for him to the Government. The service of the men of the *Indelta* was 30 years, and their drill amounted to 42 days during the first two years, and afterward occasional musters and maneuvers formed the principal part of their training. The third class was composed of *Landwehr* and *Landstorm*, which were organized on the basis of universal liability to service, but their training and organization were so inefficient that the standing army and the *Indelta* were regarded as the marrow of the Swedish army.

In order to bring the Swedish army up to the proper standard, the Government introduced a bill dealing with its reorganization. The soldiers of the *Indelta*, according to the new law, will henceforth be paid by the state, the raising and maintenance of the men to be accomplished by districts as heretofore, only the costs are refunded to the landowners. The tax placed upon the land of the privileged landowners for the support of the *Indelta* is abolished; thus the whole cost of keeping the same, hitherto borne in specie or in kind by the agricultural population, will be defrayed by the state. The period of regular training for the *Indelta* is extended to 68 days in the first year and 22 days in the second year; a total of 90 days for the first two years, as against 42 days formerly. The term of liability to bear arms in the *Landwehr* and *Landstorm* is raised from 12 to 20 years, viz., 8 years in the first ban of the *Landwehr*, 4 years in the second ban, and 8 years in the *Landstorm*. The men of the first ban of the *Landwehr* are to be called out annually for the same periods of training and at the same time as the *Indelta*, and are to form an integral part of the first fighting line. The second ban of the *Landwehr* forms a reserve for the first fighting line, and the *Landstorm* is to be called out for garrison duty only, and for the defense of the country against foreign invasion. The annual contingent to be enrolled is estimated at 24,000 men. The Swedish army will be divided into 6 military districts; 5 of these are distributed along the entire coast-line of Sweden, and 1 is located inland in the western provinces, serving as a reserve, ready to be directed at any moment to any threatened spot. Each military district will have 12 battalions of infantry, 5 squadrons of cavalry, and 6 batteries of artillery, besides engineers and train. The inland district, however, will have 19 battalions of infantry. The increased annual expenditure is estimated at 3,500,000 kronor, thus bringing up the total expenses of the army to about 10,000,000 kronor. In order to provide this sum, the Government presented bills increasing the taxes on landed property, imposing special taxes on personal incomes and legacies, and increasing the stamp duties. All the measures dealing with the reorganization of the army were passed by the Diet on November 21, 1892, whereupon the special session was closed.

Norway.—The present Constitution of Norway was adopted on Nov. 4, 1814. The legislative power is vested in the Storthing, which is composed of 114 representatives, 38 from towns and 76 from rural constituencies, elected for 3 years by suffrage of chosen electors. The Storthing meets annually in February for two months, and elects one-fourth of its members to form the Lagthing; the remaining three-fourths forming the Odelsthing. All new laws are first laid before the Odelsthing, and then pass to the Lagthing to be accepted or rejected. In case of disagreement of the Houses, a common sitting is held and a two-thirds majority of the members will carry the bill; the same majority is required for alterations in the Constitution. The executive vests in the king, who exercises his authority through a Council of State, which in the beginning of 1892 consisted of the following members: Minister of State, Johannes Vilhelm Christian Steen, appointed March 6, 1891, who also holds the office of Minister of Finance and Customs; Education and Ecclesiastical Affairs, Vilhelm Andreas Wexelsen; Justice, Ole Anton Qvam; Interior, Wollert Konow; Public Works, Hans Hein Theodor Nyson; Defense, Lieut.-Col. Peter T. Holst; Delegation at Stockholm, Otto Albert Blehr, Carl Christian Berner, Jacob Otto Lange.

Area and Population.—The area of Norway is 124,495 square miles, and the population, according to the census of Jan. 1, 1891, is 1,988,664, of which 951,269 are males and 1,037,395 females. The urban population is 463,631, and the rural population 1,525,033. In 1890 there were 12,922 marriages; 60,108 births; 35,492 deaths; excess of births, 24,616. The number of emigrants in 1891 was 13,341, as against 10,991 in 1890. The present population of Christiania at the census of 1891 was 148,231; Bergen, 52,803; Trondhjem, 24,743; Stavanger, 22,483; Drammen, 20,437.

Finances.—The ordinary receipts in the year ending June 30, 1891, amounted to 51,166,200 kroner, of which 22,792,500 kroner are derived from customs, 4,077,900 kroner from the spirit duty, 2,295,100 kroner from the malt duty, 636,-900 kroner from stamps, 1,006,600 kroner from courts of justice, 588,100 kroner from succession duties, 1,435,900 kroner from State domains, 7,676,200 kroner from railroads, 10,627,000 kroner from capital, posts and telegraphs, the university, etc. The extraordinary revenue consisted of local contributions for the construction of railroads, to the amount of 280,300 kroner, making the total receipts 51,446,500 kroner. The total expenditures amounted to 48,261.500 kroner, of which 92,400 kroner were extraordinary expenses for the construction of railroads. The ordinary expenditures amounted to 48,169,100 kroner, of which 484,500 kroner were for the civil list, 498,- 800 kroner for the Storthing, 1,195,700 kroner for the Council of State, 4,717,900 kroner for instruction and ecclesiastical affairs 5,012,700 kroner for justice, police, and sanitary supervision, 6,385,200 kroner for the interior, 9,921,- 800 kroner for public works, 8,344,100 kroner for finances, 7,729,400 kroner for the army, 3,099,- 900 kroner for the navy, 670,300 kroner for foreign affairs, and 108,800 kroner for miscellaneous expenses. The debt, which was contracted for reproductive works, amounted on June 30, 1891, to 116,062,700 kroner; this was offset, however, by railroads and other assets to the amount of 140,348,200 kroner. (For the army and navy, see " Annual Cyclopædia " for 1891.)

Commerce.—The total value of the imports in 1891 amounted to 223,024,000 kroner, as against 208,659,000 kroner in 1890, and 191,609,000 kroner in 1889. Of the total imports, goods of the value of 63,032,000 kroner were from Great Britain, 56,347,000 kroner from Germany, 25,- 397,000 kroner from Sweden, 24,840,000 kroner from Russia and Finland, 12,056,000 kroner from Denmark, 5,746,000 kroner from France, 8,152,000 kroner from the Netherlands, 6,314,- 000 kroner from Belgium, 14,745,000 kroner from the United States, and 6,395,000 kroner from other countries. The total exports amounted to 130,383,000 kroner, of which 43,029,000 kroner went to Great Britain, 16,028,000 kroner to Germany, 19,002,000 kroner to Sweden, 5,129,000 kroner to Denmark, 9,861,000 kroner to France, 5,963,000 kroner to the Netherlands, 4,760,000 kroner to Belgium, 13,460,000 kroner to Spain, 1,687,000 kroner to the United States, and 11,- 462,000 kroner to other countries. The imports of articles of consumption amounted to 93,300,- 000 kroner, consisting of cereals of the value of 48,900,000 kroner ; spirits, 5,000,000 kroner ; colonial goods. 23,000,000 kroner ; fruits and legumes, 2,700,000 kroner ; animals and animal victuals, 13,700,000 kroner. The exports of articles of consumption were of the value of 50,300,- 000 kroner, and included cereals for 1,300,000 kroner, spirits for 300,000 kroner, colonial goods for 1,300,000 kroner, fruits and legumes for 200,- 000 kroner, and animals and animal victuals for 47,200,000 kroner. Imports of raw materials amounted to 45,500,000 kroner, consisting of coal to the amount of 12,800,000 kroner ; metals, 9,600,000 kroner ; hides and skins, 6,800,000 kroner ; textiles, 6,900,000 kroner; lumber, 4,500,000 kroner ; minerals, 4,900,000 kroner. The exports of raw materials were valued at 41,- 900,000 kroner, and were made up of metals to the amount of 1,600,000 kroner ; hides and skins, 7,200,000 kroner ; textiles, 800,000 kroner ; lumber, 30,500,000 kroner ; minerals, 2,300,000 kroner. The imports of manufactures amounted to 42,400,000 kroner. and consisted of metal ware of the value of 8,600,000 kroner ; textiles, 28,- 100,000 kroner; paper and paper products, 1,900,000 kroner ; manufactures of leather,

1,600,000 kroner ; manufactures of wood, 2,200,- 000 kroner. The exports of manufactures, of the value of 25,500,000 kroner. included 3,800,000 kroner for metal ware ; 4,400,000 kroner for textiles ; 2,600,000 kroner for paper ; 300,000 kroner for manufactures of leather ; 14,400,000 kroner for manufactures of wood. The imports of drugs, chemicals. and oils, and other miscellaneous merchandise, amounted to 41,800,000 kroner, and the exports to 12,700,000 kroner.

Navigation.—The total number of vessels which entered Norwegian ports in 1890 was 12,- 386 of 2,654,277 tons. Of these, 3,553 of 962,910 tons were Norwegian which entered with cargoes, 3,118 of 753,096 tons Norwegian which entered in ballast, 2,151 of 645,839 tons foreign which entered with cargoes, and 3,564 of 292,432 tons foreign which entered in ballast. The number of vessels cleared was 12,444 of 2,699,853 tons. Of these, 6,749 of 1,752,375 tons were Norwegian, and 5,695 of 947,478 tons were foreign. Of the Norwegian vessels, 6,216 of 1,533,878 tons cleared with cargoes, and of the foreign vessels, 5,155 of 748,040 tons cleared with cargoes.

The merchant navy numbered on Jan. 1, 1891, 7,432 vessels of 1,705,699 tons, as compared with 7,285 vessels of 1,611,398 tons in 1890. The steam fleet numbered in 1890, 672 vessels of 203,115 tons.

Communications.—The railroads in 1891 had a total length of 1,562 kilometers. The length of telegraph lines belonging to the state was 7,633 kilometers, with a length of wire of 14,880 kilometers. The number of domestic telegrams dispatched was 1,044,100 ; of international messages, 549,533 ; and dispatches of the service, 10,248. The receipts were 1,208,000 kroner ; and the expenses, 1,215,118 kroner.

The post-office forwarded in 1891, 20,721,400 domestic letters, 7,646,200 international letters ; 25,506,500 pieces of domestic printed matter, and 3,452,700 pieces of international printed matter ; 1,474,400 domestic money letters of the declared value of 222,800,000 kroner, and 63,600 international money letters of the declared value of 18,500,000 kroner. The receipts amounted to 2,989,465 kroner, and the expenditures to 2,897,- 526 kroner.

Political Crisis.—The constitutional question between Norway and Sweden about independent diplomatic and consular representatives, which was for a time suspended, broke out with full force again in 1892. In the elections, which followed the formation of the Steen Cabinet, the Government had called upon the voters for support in its vindication of Norwegian rights to full coequality in the union, and the country had decided in its favor, electing 65 Radicals. 36 Conservatives, and 13 Moderates. The Radicals, claiming that under the Constitution Norway had a right to appoint its own consular representatives, had introduced and carried a resolution in the Storthing in 1891, declaring its adhesion to that principle. At that time King Oscar expressed his regret at the action of the Storthing, but remarked that a resolution was not a legislative enactment, and that until such an act was passed by the Legislature, which would tend to undermine the Act of Union, he would abstain from taking any steps in the matter, in his capacity as king of the two kingdoms. Immediately after the opening of the Storthing on Feb. 8, 1892, the Radicals brought their demands to an issue, and the House adopted a resolution by a vote of 64 to 48 that the establishment of separate Norwegian consulates was within the competency of the Norwegian Council of State, as distinct from the Joint Council of State, and granted a sum of 50,000 kroner for the preliminary expenses of severing the consular affairs of Norway from those of Sweden. The king informed the Norwegian Ministers that he would not sanction the vote of the Storthing, and on June 29, 1892, the Ministry resigned, the premier explaining that the step was taken owing to the king's refusal to sanction the resolution of the Storthing in regard to the establishment of separate Norwegian consulates, a decision for which no member of the Cabinet was willing to take the responsibility. When Premier Steen announced the resignation of the Cabinet to the Storthing the next day, that body adjourned until further notice. The president subsequently presented an address to the king expressing the regret of the Chamber at the king's refusal to sanction the resolution of that body regarding the consular question, and thereby causing the resignation of the Ministry. The address furthermore urged the king to give his approval to the resolution, for the sake of the Union and of the Monarchy, and thus obviate the necessity of the retirement of the Ministry, which, the address declares, was the only combination which at the present commanded the confidence of the Storthing. In the answer to this address the king explained that, although, in case of proposals being submitted to him by the Council of State, he could, after hearing its advice, decide according to his own judgment, yet, when he announced his intention of making use of this right, he was prevented from doing so by the resignation of his Ministers, before any legal action in the matter had been taken, and simply on the ground of non-official conferences and private interviews; and that he was thereby prevented from explaining and proving to the Norwegian people what he should decide to do after hearing the advice of his councillors. As regards the question of separate consular representation he would remark that he would abide by his decision of March 14, and would only add that it was by reason of the explanations as to the scope and extent of the resolution, as given to him by the members of the Council of State, that he was obliged to adhere to his decision not to sanction the resolution of the Storthing.

In the meantime the crisis was complete. The efforts of the king to form a new Cabinet proved fruitless. The conservative ex-premier, Stang, was called and consulted as to taking office himself, but he declared himself unwilling to take the responsibility unless the king agreed to confirm the Storthing vote. While the crisis continued, Christiania was the scene of tremendous demonstrations and counter-demonstrations, and even rural districts were affected by the heat of political controversy. At a meeting of the Storthing on July 26, an address to the members of Premier Steen's Cabinet was voted, demanding, for the sake of the welfare of the country, that an end should be put to the situation by the deferring of the settlement of the Consulate question *sine die* and the continuance of the Steen

Ministry in office. This solution was agreeable to King Oscar, and on July 27 he requested Steen to withdraw his resignation, which the latter did on the conditions proposed in the above resolution of the Storthing.

SWITZERLAND, a federal republic in central Europe. The Swiss Confederation was founded on Jan. 1, 1308, by the 3 cantons of Uri, Schwyz, and Unterwald. In 1815 the number of cantons, which had previously been changed and increased, was fixed at 22 ; and in the same year Austria, France, Great Britain, Prussia, and Russia guaranteed the perpetual neutrality of Switzerland. In 1848 Switzerland was transformed from a league of republics into a federal republic. The present Constitution was proclaimed on May 29, 1874, and may be revised either by federal legislation or by direct vote of the people. The Federal Assembly is composed of the Nationalrath, consisting of 147 members, elected by direct suffrage for a term of 3 years ; and a Ständerath, consisting of 44 members, elected two for each canton. The two chambers, also called the Bundes-Versammlung, represent the supreme government of the Republic. The chief executive is vested in a Bundesrath or Federal Council, consisting of 7 members, elected by the Federal Assembly for 3 years. The President and Vice-President of the Federal Council are also elected by the Federal Assembly from among the members of the former, for the term of 1 year, and they are the chief magistrates of the Republic. Laws passed by the Federal Assembly may be vetoed by the people on a demand for a *referendum*, which consists of submitting a petition to the Government, signed by 50,000 voters, demanding the revision or annulment of an obnoxious measure, which must then be left to the direct vote of the people.

The Federal Council for 1891–93 is composed of the following members : President of the Confederation for 1892, Walter Hauser, of Zurich, chief of the Department of Finance and Customs ; Vice-President for 1892, Dr. K. Schenk, of Bern, chief of the Department of the Interior ; L. Ruchonnet, of Vaud, chief of the Department of Justice and Police ; Dr. N. Droz, of Neufchâtel, chief of the Department of Foreign Affairs ; Dr. A. Deucher, of Thurgau, chief of the Department of Industry and Agriculture ; E. Frey, of the rural division of Basel, chief of the Department of Military Affairs ; I. Zemp, of Luzern, chief of the Department of Posts and Telegraphs. On Dec. 15, 1892, the Federal Assembly elected Dr. K. Schenk President, and M. E. Frey Vice-President, of the Federal Council for 1893. M. A. Lachenal, President of the National Council, was elected to succeed Dr. N. Droz, resigned, as chief of the Department of Foreign Affairs.

Area and Population.—The area of Switzerland is 15,976 square miles. The domiciled population, according to the census of 1888, numbered 2,917,754 individuals. of which 1,417,574 were males and 1,500,180 females. Of the total population 2,688,104 were Swiss, and 229,650 foreigners ; of these 112,342 were Germans, 53,627 French, 41,881 Italians, 14,181 Austrians and Hungarians, 3,577 English, 1,354 Russians, 2,153 from other European countries, 1,019 North Americans, and 516 from other countries. The number of marriages in 1890 was 20,836 ; births, 81,620 ; deaths, 64,877 ; excess of births, 16,743. Of 7,516 persons who emigrated in 1891 to transmarine countries, 6,936 went to North America, 8 to Central America, 500 to South America, and 72 went to other parts of the world. On June 1, 1892, Zurich had a population of 96,839 ; Geneva, 78,106 ; Basel, 73,958 ; Bern, 47,270 ; and Lausanne, 35,124.

Finances.—The receipts of the Federal Government for 1891 were 80,563,995 francs, of which 336,358 francs were from real property ; 1,253,115 francs from capital invested, 27,506 francs from the general administration, 226,244 francs from the political department, 1,003 francs from justice and police, 14,660,041 francs from the military arsenals, 34,025,800 francs from finance and customs, 173,082 francs from industry and agriculture, 29,849,052 francs from posts, telegraphs, telephones, and railroads, and 11,794 francs from miscellaneous sources. The total expenditures amounted to 84,534,105 francs, of which 2,651,-572 francs were for interest on the public debt and sinking fund, 908,714 francs for the general administration, 134,179 francs for justice and police, 36,726,542 francs for the military department, 5,775,619 francs for finance and customs, 893,367 francs for the political department, 8,244,323 francs for the interior, 1,742,390 francs for industry and agriculture, 27,421,316 francs for posts, telegraphs, and railroads, and 36,083 francs for miscellaneous expenses.

The Federal debt on Jan. 1, 1892, amounted to 60,964,575 francs, against which the Government holds general assets to the amount of 97,521,894 francs, and 16,096,261 francs in special funds.

Commerce.—The total value of the special imports in 1891 was 932,391,000 francs, and that of the exports 671,867,000 francs. The special commerce with the principal countries in 1891 is given in the following table, in francs:

COUNTRY.	Imports.	Exports.
Germany	293,140,000	164,045,000
France	214,036,000	124,979,000
Italy	135,990,000	46,997,000
Great Britain	46,103,000	113,096,000
Austria-Hungary	87,727,000	36,246,000
Belgium	23,984,000	11,110,000
Russia, Europe and Asia	46,867,000	13,678,000
Netherlands	9,722,000	4,530,000
Rest of Europe	12,452,000	32,483,000
United States	30,563,000	71,700,000
Rest of America	9,893,000	16,650,000
Asia	7,094,000	28,523,000
Africa	13,630,000	4,810,000
Australia and Polynesia	2,190,000	3,011,000
Total	932,391,000	671,867,000

The total imports of grain and flour were valued at 116,813,000 francs ; spun silk, 71,725,-000 francs ; animals, 48,357,000 francs ; raw silk, 45,425,000 francs ; woolen thread and cloth, 42,355,000 francs ; cotton, 34,693,000 francs ; wine, 34,567,000 francs ; apparel, 28,492,000 francs ; iron, 25,881,000 francs ; cottons, 24,-221,000 francs ; chemicals, 21,637,000 francs ; machinery and carriages, 21,076,000 francs ; sugar, 19,090,000 francs ; coffee, 18,980,000 francs ; precious metals, 18,143,000 francs ; manufactures of iron, 17,575,000 francs ; silk manufactures, 13,881,000 francs ; timber, 13,-351,000 francs ; manufactures of wool, 11,352,-

000 francs ; leather, 10,637,000 francs ; leather manufactures, 10,579,000 francs. The chief exports were silk manufactures, to the value of 125,437,000 francs ; cotton goods, 122,261,000 francs ; watches, 100,547,000 francs ; silk yarn, 56,418,000 francs ; cheese, 38,614,000 francs ; machinery and carriages, 21,565,000 francs ; cotton, 21,238,000 francs ; milk, 15,114,000 francs ; animals, 14,830,000 francs ; coloring matters, 11,722,000 francs ; apparel, 11,100,-000 francs ; raw silk, 8,925,000 francs ; wool, 8,907,000 francs ; hides and skins, 7,868,000 francs ; manufactures of straw, 7,335,000 francs. Of the total imports, 27.5 per cent. were articles of consumption ; 7 per cent., animals ; 28.9 per cent., raw materials ; and 36.6 per cent., manufactured articles. Of the exports, 9.4 per cent. were articles of consumption ; 2.6 per cent., animals ; 2.9 per cent., raw materials ; and 85.1 per cent., manufactured articles.

The Army.—By the laws of Nov. 13, 1874, and Feb. 15, 1887, military service was made compulsory on every Swiss citizen, who has to serve in the *Auszug* from his 20th to his 32d year, and from then until his 44th year in the *Landwehr*. The service in the *Auszug* consists of the short space of time necessary for acquiring the rudiments of military tactics, and is followed by annual exercises of a few weeks' duration. Every Swiss citizen between the ages of 17 and 50 belongs to the *Landsturm*, but exemption from service may be bought by an annual tax ranging from 6 to 300 francs. In 1891 the strength of the Swiss army was as follows :

DESCRIPTION OF TROOPS.	Auszug.	Landwehr.	Landsturm.
General staff	49		
Staffs of combined troops.	786	248	
Infantry	97,785	62,830	78,848
Cavalry	3,019	2,880	
Artillery	18,085	10,886	3,481
Engineers	4,991	2,105	
Pioneers			101,889
Auxiliary troops	1,897		84,497
Sanitary troops		1,004	
Administrative troops	1,286	319	
Judicial officers	75		
Total	127,973	80,272	268,715

Communications.—The length of railroads open for traffic on Jan. 1, 1891, was 3,199 kilometers.

The post-office in 1891 forwarded 66,692,000 domestic letters, 13,590,000 domestic postal cards, 22,520,000 pieces of printed matter, and 3,197,000 domestic money letters of the declared value of 365,303,000 francs ; and 27,365,000 international letters, 6,889,000 postal cards, 15,-775,000 pieces of printed matter, and 740,000 international money letters of the declared value of 42,482,000 francs.

The length of telegraph lines in 1891 was 7,245 kilometers, with a length of wire of 19,188 kilometers. There were forwarded, through 1,411 telegraph offices, 3,818,538 dispatches, of which 1,974,048 were domestic, 1,239,490 international, 467,337 in transit, and 137,663 service telegrams. The receipts amounted to 4,387,-796 francs, and the expenses to 4,280,661 francs.

Congress of the Institute of International Law.—A meeting of the Institute of International Law was held in Geneva in the beginning of September, 1892. The countries represented were the United States, England, France, Germany, Italy, Austria, Switzerland, Belgium, Spain, Sweden and Norway, and Japan. Rules relating to the expulsion and exclusion of foreigners were drawn up. The rules regarding exclusion are as follows :

The free entrance of foreigners into a state cannot be prohibited in a general manner or permanently, unless for reasons of public interest or motives of the gravest nature, viz., by reason of fundamental differences in customs or civilizations, or by reason of dangerous organizations or accumulations of foreigners who present themselves *en masse*. The protection of national labor by itself, is not sufficient reason for non-admittance.

Entrance into a state may be forbidden to any individual in a state of vagrancy or beggary, or who is afflicted with a contagious disease, or who is strongly suspected of grave offenses committed in the foreign state against the public security, against the life or health of a person, or against property, or who has been condemned in a foreign country for the above-named offenses.

In order to facilitate the definitions of political offenses to be excepted in extradition treaties, the following rules were adopted :

1. Extradition is not to be granted for political crimes or for misdemeanors of a purely political character.

2. This shall also apply to offenses mixed or connected with political crimes or to misdemeanors called relative political misdemeanors, unless they are crimes of the gravest nature as regarded by common morals or right, such as assassination, murder, poisoning, voluntary and premeditated mutilation and wounding, also attempts on property by fire, explosion or inundation, and grave robberies, especially if the latter have been committed with violence or by force of arms.

3. Persons who have committed acts in the course of an insurrection or a civil war, in the interest of either of the parties to such warfare, shall not be extradited, unless such acts constitute odious barbarism or unnecessary vandalism according to martial law, and in such cases only after the civil war is ended.

4. Under the former sections, such acts as are committed against the fundamental law of society, and not against any government in particular, are not included in these rules.

A further proposal was adopted to establish an international bureau of information at Bern, *i.e.*, a bureau which is to be charged with the centralization and publication of international arrangements and documents particularly, so as to enable the public to ascertain the contents of treaties, which has hitherto been a difficult task.

Session of the Peace Congress.—A meeting of the Peace Congress was held at Bern in the latter part of August, 1892. The Congress decided to establish a permanent international peace bureau at Bern, for the support of which the Government of Switzerland is to approach the constitutional authorities of all civilized states. A further resolution invites all European peace societies to declare as their highest aim the creation of a confederation of European states, based upon the solidarity of interest of the sepa-

rate states. Proposals were discussed touching a future congress of nations, and a request to all European powers to abolish the present preparations for war. The Congress was attended by delegates from almost all nations, Americans and British furnishing a large proportion. Chicago was selected as the place of meeting for 1893.

Session of the Inter-Parliamentary Conference.—The meeting of the Inter-Parliamentary Conference took place at Bern from August 29 to 31, 1892. The countries represented were Switzerland, Great Britain, France, Germany, Denmark, Greece, Italy, the Netherlands, Norway, Austria, Portugal, Roumania, Sweden, Spain, Liberia, Hungary, and Honduras. The following proposals were adopted :

1. The members engaged in the Conference are to ask their respective Governments to help to organize an international conference for the recognition of the rights of private property at sea in time of war.

2. The members pledge themselves to try and induce their Governments to respond to the overtures of the United States with reference to the conclusion of treaties of arbitration with that Republic.

3. The Inter-Parliamentary Conference is the organ of groups of members of Parliament which have been constituted or may yet be constituted for the purpose of obtaining in their respective states recognition for the principle that disputes between states ought to be submitted for final settlement to courts of arbitration.

In order to deal with other international questions of general interest, the conference establishes a permanent central bureau, under the name of the International Arbitration Court, with its seat in Bern.

The director of the bureau will be elected by delegates of the various Parliamentary groups for a term of four years, and will be eligible for re-election.

The duties of the bureau will be as follows : To keep a register of the composition of the national Parliamentary groups ; to enter into communication with the members of all Parliaments for the purpose of bringing about the constitution of national Parliamentary groups in all countries ; to summon inter-Parliamentary conferences and to occupy itself with the execution of their resolutions ; to act as the central organ of the national Parliamentary groups for all questions regarding their mutual relations ; to keep the records and collect all documents having reference to arbitration and the preservation of peace ; and, finally, to take generally all suitable steps for advancing the objects of the Inter-Parliamentary Conference.

The costs of the bureau will be defrayed by the national groups in the ratio of the population of the different states represented by them.

The conference intrusts the execution of the above resolution to a committee of five members of the Swiss Federal Assembly.

The Central Parliamentary Bureau in connection with the conference will consist of the following members : Dr. Baumbach (Germany), Mr. P. Stanhope (England), Herr Pirguet (Austria), Signor Pandolfi (Italy), M. Trarieux (France), M. Rahnsen (Netherlands), Señor Marcoartu (Spain), M. Urecchia (Roumania), and M. Ullman (Norway). The next meeting will be held at Christiania.

T

TENNESSEE, a Southern State, admitted to the Union June 1, 1796 ; area, 42,050 square miles. The population, according to each decennial census since admission, was 105,602 in 1800 ; 261,727 in 1810 ; 422,771 in 1820 ; 681,904 in 1830 ; 829,210 in 1840 ; 1,002,717 in 1850 ; 1,109,801 in 1860 ; 1,258,520 in 1870 ; 1,542,359 in 1880 ; and 1,767,518 in 1890. Capital, Nashville.

Government.—The following were the State officers during the year : Governor, John P. Buchanan, Democrat ; Secretary of State, Charles A. Miller ; Treasurer and Insurance Commissioner, M. F. House ; Comptroller, J. W. Allen ; Attorney-General, G. W. Pickle ; Superintendent of Public Instruction, W. R. Garrett ; Commissioner of Agriculture, Statistics, and Mines, D. G. Godwin ; Chief Justice of the Supreme Court, Peter Turney ; Associate Justices, W. C. Caldwell, B. L. Snodgrass, H. H. Lorton, and Benjamin J. Lea. After Judge Turney became Governor, Judge Lorton was made Chief-Justice and J. S. Wilkes elected to the vacancy.

Finances.—The amount received from the usual sources of revenue for the past two years is $3,493,862.89, an increase of $313,887.55 over the receipts during the two years preceding. The expenses have been raised by the increase in the appropriation for the payment of Confederate soldiers' pensions, in those to the industrial school and the Peabody Normal School, and by the ordinary growth of State institutions. The new appropriations were : Confederate Soldiers' Home, $35,000 ; improvement of waterways, $5,000 ; Capitol improvement, $30,000 ; enumeration of voters, $17,180.79 ; total, $87,180.79.

The following were the expenses incurred on account of the labor troubles at the mines : on account of arresting convicts, for the ultimate payment of which the State looks to the lessees, $14,616.82 ; on account of military in the field,—salaries, transportation, maintenance, $107,205.94. There is claimed to be due to the State from lessees on rental, which has been withheld and is now in litigation, $114,000.

The State owed on borrowed money, Dec. 20, 1890, the sum of $459,797.10, which has all been paid. The State is in debt $59,000, and but for the expenses of the mining insurrections and the loss or delaying of the money due by the lessees of convicts, would have a surplus in the treasury.

An act passed by the Forty-seventh General Assembly authorized the sale of fifteen-year 4 per cent. bonds, and with the proceeds of such sale the retirement of 5 and 6 per cent. bonds issued under act of 1883. The board, acting under this law, sold the bonds, payment being made by installments. When the trade has been fully carried out, the State will save $24,294 annually on interest account.

Under the direction of the Forty-seventh General Assembly, expressed by the act approved March 25, 1891, the direct tax levied by the Federal Government in 1861, and refunded to the several States, has been distributed to all the proper claimants who have made application for it. The amount received from the United States Government was $402,908.58. Of this amount $368,699.49 has been distributed, leaving a residue of $34,209.09.

Education.—The entire school population is 697,662, of whom 172,954 are colored. This is an increase of the white school population over 1890 of 14,119, or 2.7 per cent., and a decrease of the colored 2,767, or a loss of 1.6 per cent. The net gain is 11,352, or 1.7 per cent. The enrollment was,—white, 380,456 ; colored, 107,051 ; total, 487,507. The daily average attendance was : white, 274,482 ; colored, 75,001 ; total, 349,383. This shows a marked increase over the figures of 1890. The increase in enrollment is 67,403, or 16 per cent. The increase in average attendance is 52,718, or 18 per cent. The average time during which the schools were open was 96 days.

Only 2,177 of the 8,612 teachers in the State, or 25 per cent., have remained more than one term in the same school. In 23 counties all the schools are completely graded, in 56 some are graded or partially so, in 11 none are graded, and 6 are not reported in this respect.

The legislature appropriated $1,500 for teachers' institutes, and $2,000 was received from the Peabody fund for the same purpose.

The enrollment in the Peabody Normal College in 1891–92 was 470. The registration is now 500, of whom 275 are residents of Tennessee. The Trustees of the Peabody Education Fund are spending on this school annually in the way of scholarships and salaries about $34,000.

In addition to the college registration proper, there are now enrolled in the Winthrop Model School 75 children. This school represents the work done in the first eight years of the public school course, and employs 2 regular teachers and an assistant.

The biennial report of the trustees of the State University, at Knoxville, shows continued growth in the institution. A new building of brick and stone, four stories high, has been erected for a science hall and gymnasium, and two additional dwellings for professors. No appropriations were made by the legislature, the funds for building having been received from rents, the sale of lands, and savings from current expenses. $149,345 has been thus saved and used in permanent improvements during the last six years.

Confederate Soldiers.—The home has been completed and was formally opened on May 12. It has accommodations for 125. The pension law has been in operation two years.

The amount appropriated by the last General Assembly for the payment of the pension roll was $60,000 per annum.

Charitable Institutions.—The School for the Deaf and Dumb has 142 pupils. A fine building has been constructed with the appropriation made by the Forty-seventh General Assembly. The appropriations for 1891–92 amounted to $69,375.

The School for the Blind has 97 in attendance. By act of 1891 there was appropriated for its maintenance $37,000 ; for building and repairs. $3,000, making a total of $40,000. The report shows the need of an appropriation of $40,000 for 100 pupils, and then an extra appropriation for necessary repairs and purchases.

The Industrial School reports 316 inmates. A girls' department has been added. It has become necessary to rent three additional buildings for the increased work of the school. It cost the State $22,386.81 for the biennial period.

The Watkins Institute, though supported by private benefaction, is under the care of the State. A night-school is maintained for four months in the year, with 5 teachers and 375 pupils.

The Lunatic Asylums received during 1891-2 the amount of $369,521.33.

The State Prison.—This institution is greatly overcrowded. It is small and badly ventilated, and has accommodations for only 320 inmates. There were 340 before the trouble at Tracy City, and when the 350 were sent from that place, some were compelled to sleep on the stone floors of the wings, while two were placed in each cell ; and 290 more were afterward sent on. The leasing of convict labor has enabled the State to get along without more penitentiary room, and left it unprovided for an emergency like that of August last.

The Comptroller's report shows that $24,997.87 was expended for building and repairs at the prison during 1891-2. The amounts received from lessees were $97,020.68, with $114,000 yet due, according to the claim made by the State.

Agriculture.—A "Less-cotton Convention" was held in Memphis, Jan. 8. The low price of cotton caused by the large crop of 9,000,000 bales in 1891 reduced the whole cotton-producing section to the verge of financial ruin. In order to start a movement to induce the farmers of those States to reduce their cotton acreage and increase the quantity of food crops, the Commissioner of Agriculture called the convention, "to be composed of representatives of the Department of Agriculture of the interested states, of planters, of delegates from the Cotton and Merchants' Exchange and from the agricultural societies, and of all others who were interested directly or indirectly in the attainment of the object had in view. The 20 per cent. reduction recommended by this convention as necessary in order to make the cultivation of cotton once more profitable was not reached, but the report of the United States Commissioner of Agriculture shows a reduction of sixteen and five-tenths per cent. in acreage, and a reduction of about 2,000,000 bales in yield, the decrease being attributed, in a large measure, to the small acreage. As a result of this reduced supply of cotton, prices advanced 40 per cent. and the farmers in the cotton section by means of the increased food crops are better prepared for the cultivation of the next year's crop."

The yield of the cotton crop this year was estimated in November at 47.3 per cent. against 72.8 per cent. in 1891. The corn yield, which was 89.6 in 1891, was 78.2 in 1892.

Railroads.—Some progress has been made in the building of the Nashville and Knoxville, or Crawford road. When the contractors reached the gap for which the Nashville, Chattanooga & St. Louis Railway claimed it had a right of way and where some grading was done by it last year,

that road enjoined the Crawfords from taking possession of the pass, but Chancellor Webb dissolved the injunction, the Crawfords entering into a $30,000 bond to reimburse the Nashville, Chattanooga & St. Louis if so decided by a court on final adjudication of the claims of both roads. This road will lead to the oil field, which now bids fair to be one of the most important in the country.

A receiver was appointed in July for the Memphis and Charleston road. Owing to the depression of business, the net earnings of the road fell short of those of the preceding year by $175,000, and in addition the company was compelled to build a drawbridge near Florence at a cost of $80,000, so that it could not meet the interest on its bonds.

River Improvement.—A new organization, to be known as the "Mississippi River Improvement Association," was formed in Memphis, May 13. Its object is to co-operate with the National Mississippi River Commission and urge upon Congress the necessity of carrying out promptly the recommendations of that body. The design is to include in the membership every civil engineer and capitalist of the hundreds of river towns in the Mississippi Valley, and to proceed with method. No improvement will be pressed before Congress until it has stood the test of scientific examination and been approved by this organization.

Convict Labor Troubles.—Another disturbance broke out this year in the mining district northwest of Knoxville, where the Tennessee Coal, Iron and Railroad Company employs convicts leased from the State. The chronic dissatisfaction of the miners at being compelled to compete with convict labor was intensified by the fact that as the work grew slack the free miners were worked on short time, while the convicts were kept at full time. Trouble was feared in July, but apparently no unusual precautions were taken. The miners were perhaps emboldened by the fact that the rioters of 1891 had escaped without punishment, and believed that by a few bold strokes they might succeed in causing a change in the convict-labor law and thus rid themselves forever of the hated competition.

The first attack was made at Tracy City on the morning of Aug. 13. The guards at the stockade were overpowered, the convicts were brought out, and the stockade was burned. The convicts and guards were placed on a train and started for Nashville. Not a shot was fired by either side. Thirteen of the convicts escaped from the train, having disconnected the car they were in. Five of these were recaptured, one killed, one badly wounded, and six made good their escape. There were 362 convicts in all at Tracy City.

The next attack was made on Inman by the mob from Tracy City, and the operations at Tracy City were repeated, except that the stockade was pulled down instead of burned ; 282 convicts and 27 guards were taken to the station at Victoria and sent away. The stockade was not burned, as there is a high trestle of the branch road built above it, which would also have burned, making work in the mines impossible. No free miners were employed at Inman.

On the night of the 16th, a company of miners from Coal Creek, Jellico, and other places, seized three trains and with Winchesters compelled the train men to take them to Oliver Springs. The convicts were taken out and sent away.

Up to this time no serious effort appears to have been made to support the local authorities and restore order. It was expected that the next point of attack would be Coal Creek, where a garrison has been kept for nearly a year, numbering about 150 men. In response to appeals for assistance, the Governor ordered the sheriff to take a posse of 500 men from Knoxville, but they were hard to get, on account of widespread sympathy with the miners. On the 18th, the Governor ordered out all the organized militia. The attack was made the same day the militia were ordered out, the 18th. The garrison, in charge of Col. Anderson, made resistance and repelled the mob, which then sent up a flag of truce and asked for an interview with Col. Anderson. He went out with the flag, and was taken prisoner. He was ordered, under threats of death, to sign a letter to his lieutenant directing the surrender of the stockade and fort. He steadily refused to sign the letter, and was kept all night in the mountains, where the miners discussed the policy of hanging him.

Meantime Gen. Carnes had advanced to Coal Creek with reënforcements from Chattanooga, and on the 19th the miners were routed in a fierce battle. Some were taken prisoners, and the insurgents were notified that unless Col. Anderson was brought back in safety the prisoners would be put to death. He was finally restored unhurt. Three, at least, of the soldiers were killed in the attack, and it was supposed that several miners fell. One of the worst of the leaders, Bud Lindsay, was captured on the 21st by a party of citizens. He begged for his life and offered to give evidence against the other leaders, and on this condition his life was spared. Gen. Carnes proceeded against him and other leaders, under civil warrants, and 200 were under arrest by the 20th. He took a force on that day and went to Briceville, where the houses of the miners were searched and about 60 prisoners taken. By the 22d, 500 men had been arrested.

A dispute arose between the State authorities and the lessees as to the rent for the leased convicts in Nashville after they were sent from the mines. It is quite possible that the system of leasing convicts may be abandoned, as the general sentiment in the State seems to be that, while the law must be enforced so long as it remains on the statute-books, it would be wiser to do away with it.

Political.—A Governor, ten representatives in Congress, and a legislature that would elect a United States Senator in place of W. B. Bate, were to be chosen on Nov. 8.

The Democratic Convention for the selection of delegates to the national convention met, May 26. The delegates were instructed to vote for Cleveland as long as his name should be before the convention. The platform declared for the autonomy of the States, and economy in governmental expenditures; against the enlargement and concentration of Federal powers, bounties, and subsidies in every form, and "the whole theory and practice of paternalism." It declared the party to be the fast friend of the farmer and the laboring man. It denounced the McKinley act, and the reciprocity policy "as a temporizing scheme intended to soothe the people with a measure of partial free trade, delay the downfall of monopoly, and throw a sop to New England." It condemned the "Force bill," and the pension policy, which it characterized as "a part of the general policy of the Government under the Republican rule to drain the South of its wealth and carry it to more favored sections."

On the subject of coinage it said:

We favor a currency of gold, silver, and of paper convertible into coin at the option of the holder, and in such amount as will meet the business necessities of internal trade and commerce among the people; and we further favor a parity of the two metals as a common unit of value and as a legal tender for the payment of all debts, public and private, as existed under the laws of the United States down to the infamous and surreptitious demonetization of silver in 1873 by the Republican party; and we further favor the continued coinage of both silver and gold bullion in such manner as that every dollar so coined shall be equal to every other dollar.

Chief-Justice Peter Turney had been put forward for the gubernatorial nomination. The primary elections were largely in his favor, and on Aug. 4 Gov. Buchanan issued an address withdrawing his name from consideration before the nominating convention. The convention met on Aug. 9, and nominated Turney by acclamation. In reference to State affairs, the resolutions called for the reduction of taxation and the retrenchment of expenses, and declared that labor should not be "under duress from convict labor and its corporate organization"; and therefore favored the abolition of the penitentiary lease system, and the erection of a prison large enough to hold all the convicts and so constructed as to allow of classification, that the young and those convicted of lesser offenses might be separated from old and hardened criminals.

On Aug. 10 the city of Memphis was thrown into a state of great excitement by the announcement that the Governor had commuted the sentence of Col. H. Clay King, who was to have been hanged on the 12th, for the murder of D. H. Poston, and at night a crowd assembled at the most central point in the city and hanged the Governor in effigy.

On Aug. 15 the Governor announced himself an independent candidate for re-election.

The People's party had met in June and adopted resolutions and appointed a delegation to Omaha, but postponed naming a candidate for Governor till Aug. 18. The resolutions demanded free coinage and an increase of the volume of the currency to the extent of $50 per capita. It demanded that United States Senators be elected directly by the people. In State matters, the abrogation of the convict lease system was demanded, and it was declared that salaries of all State and county officials should be reduced, and that a tax on the people to pay the railroad debt was unconstitutional.

At the convention, Aug. 18, the following resolution was adopted:

Whereas, John P. Buchanan has announced himself as an independent candidate for Governor upon a platform of principles which are sound and in accord with the reform movement; therefore,
Resolved, That it is the desire of this convention

J. Stephenson, Sculp^t

Yours ever

A Tennyson

... nomination be made, and that we give them ... hearty support.

The Republicans met in convention May 4, ... nominated George W. Winstead for Go v ... The resolutions commended the policy of the national Republican administration, and in reference to State affairs, denounced the in-competency of the State government, which has been unable to cope with any of the great questions of state policy that have come up from time to time during the long and uninterrupted Democratic rule; which has expended large sums of money and has conferred no benefits on the people of the State; which has tampered with and destroyed the militia system of the State so that its inefficiency is now a by-word; which has by tampering with the convict lease system, dis-graced the State, so that, as a culmination of the outrageous management, to-day the public work of the capital city of the State is performed by penitentiary convicts, and convicts are now em-ployed on the public streets of the capital city, in full view of the State capitol, to the great det-riment and injury of honest laborers, who, with their families, are dependent on such work, and are forced to seek employment elsewhere."

They demanded the abolition of the convict lease system, the repeal of the poll-tax provision in the election laws, and an amendment of the laws so that illiterate voters may have assistance in casting their votes; denounced all intimida-tion and other frauds for depriving voters of their rights under the Constitution. They declared in favor of measures for the punishment of petty offenses without the intervention of grand juries, condemned the refusal of the legislature to secure to the State representation at the World's Fair, and demanded a just and equitable system of assessment and taxation, to the end that all property of the State may be taxed uniformly, and that neither the industrial interests of the State nor the landed property and homes be required to bear unnecessary and unequal burthens.

The State Convention of Prohibitionists met on June 2, and nominated for Governor Judge Edward H. East.

The total vote polled for presidential electors was 267,503—much smaller than in 1888, when it was 303,736. This was in part due to the reduc-tion of the negro vote. There are about 75,000 negro voters in the State, but a large part of them were practically disfranchised by the operation of the poll-tax law, which went into effect in 199 t, and the Australian ballot system, which has been adopted in some counties, including those containing the larger cities. The official returns were as follows: For Cleveland, 138,874; for Harrison, 100,331; for Weaver, 23,447; for Bidwell, 4,851; for Turney. 127,247; for Win-stead, 100,629; for Buchanan, 31,515; for East, 5,427. For members of Congress, 8 Democrats and 2 Republicans were elected. The State legislature is constituted as follows: Senate—Democrats, 26; Republicans, 6; People's or In-dependent, 1; House—Democrats, 68; Repub-licans, 26; People's or Independent, 5. Demo-cratic majority on joint ballot, 56.

Judge Turney did not resign his judgeship till after he became Governor, when he appointed Judge Lorton his successor.

TENNYSON, ALFRED ..., an English poet, born in Somersby Lincolnshire, Aug. 6. 1809; died at Aldworth House, near Haslemere, Surrey, Oct. 6, 1892. His father, the Rev. George Clayton Tennyson, was rector of Som-ersby and Enderby, and vicar of Great Grimsby. He was highly educated, and accomplished in painting, music, and languages, as well as in the art in which his son so far transcended him. He had also a great fondness for nature and the charms of out-of-door living were readily revealed by him to his children, who accompanied him in his rambles and drives.

Mr. Tennyson belonged to the family of D'Eyncourt, Norman Plantagenets, which, at the time of Alfred's birth, was represented in Parlia-ment by the eldest member, Rt. Hon. Charles Tennyson D'Eyncourt. The poet's mother was a daughter of the Rev. Stephen Fytche. Alfred had three brothers—Frederick, Charles, and Sep-timus. Frederick Tennyson took the prize at Trinity College, Cambridge, for a Greek poem and afterward published a volume of poems, en-titled "Days and Hours." Charles Tennyson, who also was graduated at Cambridge, took orders, became vicar of Grasby, and assumed the family name of his father's mother—Turner —on inheriting from her an estate in Lincoln-shire.

Like his brothers, Alfred entered Trinity Col-lege, Cambridge, and, like them, wrote poetry while there. He gained the Chancellor's medal, offered for an English poem, the prize being awarded to his "Timbuctoo." He left college before graduation. Because of his constant ef-forts to maintain strict privacy, and his resent-ment of anything like personal publicity, little more can be said of Alfred Tennyson's life than the bare statement of the facts that he received a pension of £1,000 a year, and lived in and about London till he was forty years of age, when he married Emily Sellwood, and went to live at Twickenham; that on the death of Words-worth in 1850 he succeeded him as Poet-Laure-ate; that soon afterward he removed to the Isle of Wight, where he lived for many years at Farringford, Freshwater; that about 1869 he pur-chased a place at Petersfield, Hampshire, and years afterward Aldworth House, near Hasle-mere, where he died; and that in December, 1883, he was raised to the peerage as Baron Tennyson of D'Eyncourt. Tennyson once wrote to Sir Henry Taylor that he "thanked God Al-mighty with his whole heart and soul that he knew nothing and that the world knew nothing of Shakespeare but his writings, and that he knew nothing of Jane Austen, and that there were no letters preserved either of Shakespeare or of Jane Austen"; that they, in fact, had not been "ripped open like pigs." Years before, in his lines "After Reading a Life and Letters," he had expressed the same sentiment poetically:

> You have miss'd the irreverent doom
>   Of those that wear the Poet's crown:
>   Hereafter, neither knave nor clown
> Shall hold their orgies at your tomb.
>
> For now the poet cannot die
>   Nor leave his music as of old,
>   But round him ere he scarce be cold
> Begins the scandal and the cry ·

J. Stephenson. Sculp^t

Yours ever

A. Tennyson

that no nomination be made, and that we give him our hearty· support.

The Republicans met in convention May 4, and nominated George W. Winstead for Governor. The resolutions commended the policy of the national Republican administration, and in reference to State affairs, denounced the incompeteney of the State government, "which has been unable to cope with any of the great questions of state policy that have come up from time to time during the long and uninterrupted Democratic rule ; which has expended large sums of money and has conferred no benefits on the people of the State ; which has tampered with and destroyed the militia system of the State so that its inefficiency is now a by-word ; which has, by tampering with the convict lease system, disgraced the State, so that, as a culmination of the outrageous management, to-day the public work of the capital city of the State is performed by penitentiary convicts, and convicts are now employed on the public streets of the capital city, in full view of the State capitol, to the great detriment and injury of honest laborers. who, with their families, are dependent on such work, and are forced to seek employment elsewhere."

They demanded the abolition of the convict lease system, the repeal of the poll-tax provision in the election laws, and an amendment of the laws so that illiterate voters may have assistance in casting their votes ; denounced all intimidation and other frauds for depriving voters of their rights under the Constitution. They declared in favor of measures for the punishment of petty offenses without the intervention of grand juries, condemned the refusal of the legislature to secure to the State representation at the World's Fair. and demanded a just and equitable system of assessment and taxation, to the end that all property of the State may be taxed uniformly, and that neither the industrial interests of the State nor the landed property and homes be required to bear unnecessary and unequal burthens.

The State Convention of Prohibitionsts met on June 2, and nominated for Governor Judge Edward H. East.

The total vote polled for presidential electors was 267,503—much smaller than in 1888, when it was 303,736. This was in part due to the reduction of the negro vote. There are about 75,000 negro voters in the State, but a large part of them were practically disfranchised by the operation of the poll-tax law, which went into effect in 1890, and the Australian ballot system, which has been adopted in some counties, including those containing the larger cities. The official returns were as follows : For Cleveland, 138,874 ; for Harrison, 100,331 ; for Weaver, 23,447 ; for Bidwell, 4,851 ; for Turney. 127,247 ; for Winstead, 100,629 ; for Buchanan, 31,515 ; for East, 5,427. For members of Congress, 8 Democrats and 2 Republicans were elected. The State legislature is constituted as follows : Senate— Democrats, 26 ; Republicans, 6 ; People's or Independent, 1 ; House—Democrats, 68 ; Republicans, 26 ; People's or Independent, 5. Democratic majority on joint ballot, 56.

Judge Turney did not resign his judgeship till after he became Governor, when he appointed Judge Lorton his successor.

TENNYSON, ALFRED, Lord, an English poet, born in Somersby, Lincolnshire, Aug. 6, 1809 ; died at Aldworth House, near Haslemere, Surrey, Oct. 6, 1892. His father, the Rev. George Clayton Tennyson, was rector of Somersby and Enderby, and vicar of Great Grimsby. He was highly educated, and accomplished in painting, music, and languages, as well as in the art in which his son so far transcended him. He had also a great fondness for nature, and the charms of out-of-door living were early revealed by him to his children, who accompanied him in his rambles and drives.

Mr. Tennyson belonged to the family of D'Eyncourt, Norman Plantagenets, which, at the time of Alfred's birth, was represented in Parliament by the eldest member, Rt. Hon. Charles Tennyson D'Eyncourt. The poet's mother was a daughter of the Rev. Stephen Fytche. Alfred had three brothers—Frederick, Charles, and Septimus. Frederick Tennyson took the prize at Trinity College, Cambridge, for a Greek poem, and afterward published a volume of poems, entitled "Days and Hours." Charles Tennyson, who also was graduated at Cambridge, took orders, became vicar of Grasby, and assumed the family name of his father's mother—Turner —on inheriting from her an estate in Lincolnshire.

Like his brothers, Alfred entered Trinity College, Cambridge, and, like them, wrote poetry while there. He gained the Chancellor's medal, offered for an English poem, the prize being awarded to his "Timbuctoo." He left college before graduation. Because of his constant efforts to maintain strict privacy, and his resentment of anything like personal publicity, little more can be said of Alfred Tennyson's life than the bare statement of the facts that he received a pension of $1,000 a year, and lived in and about London till he was forty years of age, when he married Emily Sellwood, and went to live at Twickenham; that on the death of Wordsworth in 1850 he succeeded him as Poet-Laureate; that soon afterward he removed to the Isle of Wight. where he lived for many years at Faringford, Freshwater ; that about 1869 he purchased a place at Petersfield, Hampshire, and years afterward Aldworth House, near Haslemere, where he died ; and that in December, 1883, he was raised to the peerage as Baron Tennyson of D'Eyncourt. Tennyson once wrote to Sir Henry Taylor that he "thanked God Almighty with his whole heart and soul that he knew nothing and that the world knew nothing of Shakespeare but his writings, and that he knew nothing of Jane Austen, and that there were no letters preserved either of Shakespeare or of Jane Austen" ; that they, in fact, had not been "ripped open like pigs." Years before, in his lines " After Reading a Life and Letters," he had expressed the same sentiment poetically :

> You have miss'd the irreverent doom
> Of those that wear the Poet's crown;
> Hereafter, neither knave nor clown
> Shall hold their orgies at your tomb.

> For now the poet cannot die
> Nor leave his music as of old,
> But round him ere he scarce be cold
> Begins the scandal and the cry :

" Proclaim the faults he would not show ;
　Break lock and seal : Betray the trust :
　Keep nothing sacred, 'tis but just
The many-headed beast should know."

He gave the people of his best :
　His worst he kept, his best he gave.
　My Shakespeare's curse on clown and knave
Who will not let his ashes rest !

Who make it seem more sweet to be
　The little life of bank and brier,
　The bird that pipes his lone desire
And dies unheard within his tree,

tum of James Russell Lowell, " Style is the man."
And to learn what Tennyson was, as well as what
he said, we must go to his life-work of poetry.

The difference between prying, or even idle
curiosity, and a desire for knowledge of the outward ways and looks of those who are gifted
above their fellows, is world-wide. Browning,
who wrote :

Friends, the good man of the house at least
　Kept house to himself till an earthquake came :
'Tis the fall of its frontage permits you to feast
　On the inside arrangement you praise or blame.

SOMERSBY RECTORY : TENNYSON'S BIRTHPLACE.

Than he that warbles long and loud
　And drops at Glory's temple-gates,
　For whom the carrion vulture waits
To tear his heart before the crowd !

The English press was flooded, after his death,
with anecdotes of the man of whose daily life
during eighty-three years most of his countrymen had known little more than had the world
outside his native land ; but these anecdotes,
even if they could be repeated as authentic, are
nearly all insignificant and unsatisfactory. The
famous saying of Novalis, " Every Englishman
is an island," is truer of him than of any famous
Englishman that ever lived.

In judging of him we must recall, not the
epitaph of Ben Jonson on Sir Charles Cavendish,
" I made my life my monument," but the dic-

Outside should suffice for evidence :
　And whoso desires to penetrate
Deeper, must dive by the spirit-sense—
　No optics like yours, at any rate !

was the most genial of men. He loved them, and
trusted to their memories his daily acts and
words, without a thought that they looked to
criticise or listened to betray ; and the Robert
Browning of biography is the complement of the
Robert Browning of literature. To Tennyson
the social instincts of Browning were incompre-
hensible. To Carlyle's letters to Ralph Waldo
Emerson we are indebted for a description of
Tennyson's appearance in 1844 :

One of the finest-looking men in the world. A
great shock of rough, dusty-dark hair : bright,
laughing, hazel eyes : massive aquiline face—most
massive, yet most delicate : of sallow-brown complexion, almost Indian-looking : clothes cynically
loose, free and easy—smokes infinite tobacco. His

voice is musical-metallic, fit for loud laughter and piercing wail, and all that may lie between: speech and speculation free and plenteous. I do not meet in these late decades such company over a pipe.

Mr. Wemyss Reid, in his life of Lord Hough-

MANOR HOUSE, SOMERSBY: "THE MOATED GRANGE."

ton, gives the following story of the granting of a pension to Tennyson, which Mr. Milnes was expected to secure. He was one day visiting Carlyle, when the latter said: "Richard Milnes, when are you going to get that pension for Alfred Tennyson?" "My dear Carlyle," replied Milnes, "the thing is not so easy as you suppose. What will my constituents say if I do get a pension for Tennyson? They know nothing about him or his poetry, and they will probably think he is some poor relation of my own, and that the whole affair is a job." "Richard Milnes," answered Carlyle, "on the day of judgment, when the Lord asks you why you didn't get that pension for Alfred Tennyson, it will not do to lay the blame on your constituents; it is you that will be damned." Peel was prime minister, and after a time asked Lord Houghton whether he should give a pension of a thousand dollars a year to Tennyson or to Sheridan Knowles, adding, "I don't know either of them." "What," said Milnes, "have you never seen the name of Knowles on a play-bill?" "No." "And never read one poem of Tennyson's?" "No." Milnes sent him "Locksley Hall" and "Ulysses," with a letter in which he gave it as his opinion that if the pension were a charitable bestowment, it should be given to Knowles, but if it were to be used in the interests of English literature, then certainly Tennyson should receive it. Peel gave it to Tennyson.

While in college, in 1820, Tennyson won the Chancellor's medal for a poem entitled "Timbuctoo," and in a college paper, called "The Snob," Thackeray published a parody of it.

Two years previous to the writing of this poem a little volume had appeared bearing the title "Poems by Two Brothers," the work of Charles and Alfred Tennyson. Coleridge preferred the elder brother's productions, and Wordsworth told Emerson that he had been of that impression. In 1845 Wordsworth wrote to Prof. Henry Reed: "I saw Tennyson in London several

times. He is decidedly the first of our living poets, and I hope will give the world still better things. You will be pleased to hear that he expressed, in the strongest terms, his gratitude to my writings."

In 1830 appeared Tennyson's next work, "Poems, Chiefly Lyrical." In later editions he omitted some of these poems, which he once more included in still later issues, with the comment: "The Poems which follow include all those which have been omitted by the author from his latest revised editions, or never acknowledged by him. They are here printed, because, although unsanctioned by Mr. Tennyson, they have recently been collected from various sources, and printed *in America*." In that little volume may be seen the promise of much that is best in the finished work of the great poet. The most notable instance is the suggestion of the "Lotos-Eaters," to be found in the "Sea-Fairies":

Slow sail'd the weary mariners and saw,
Betwixt the green brink and the running foam,
Sweet faces, rounded arms, and bosoms prest
To little harps of gold; and while they mused,
Whispering to each other half in fear,
Shrill music reach'd them on the middle sea.

TENNYSON'S HOUSE AT TWICKENHAM.

Whither away, whither away, whither away? fly no more.
Whither away from the high green field, and the happy blossoming shore?

Day and night to the billow the fountain calls;
Down shower the gambolling waterfalls
From wandering over the lea:
Out of the live-green heart of the dells
They freshen the silvery-crimson shells,
And thick with white bells the clover-hill swells
High over the full-toned sea:
O hither, come hither and furl your sails,
Come hither to me and to me:
Hither, come hither and frolic and play;
Here it is only the mew that wails;
We will sing to you all the day:

FRESHWATER BAY.

Mariner, mariner, furl your sails,
For here are the blissful downs and dales.
And merrily merrily carol the gales,
And the spangle dances in bight and bay,
And the rainbow forms and flies on the land
Over the islands free;
And the rainbow lives in the curve of the sand;
Hither, come hither and see;
And the rainbow hangs on the poising wave,
And sweet is the color of cove and cave,
And sweet shall your welcome
    be:
O hither, come hither, and be
    our lords,
For merry brides are we:
We will kiss sweet kisses, and
    speak sweet words:
O listen, listen, your eyes shall
    glisten
With pleasure and love and
    jubilee:
O listen, listen, your eyes shall
    glisten
When the sharp clear twang
    of the golden chords
Runs up the ridged sea.
Who can light on as happy a
    shore
All the world o'er, all the
    world o'er?
Whither away? listen and stay:
    mariner, mariner, fly no
    more.

"The Deserted House"
and "Love and Death" are
as characteristic of the after-
Tennyson as they are beautiful, while the
opening lines of "The Poet,"

The poet in a golden clime was born,
    With golden stars above;
Dowered with the hate of hate, the scorn of scorn,
    The love of love,

and the one called "The Poet's Mind," beginning,

Vex not thou the poet's mind
    With thy shallow wit;
Vex not thou the poet's mind;
    For thou canst not fathom it,

contain the lofty and supercilious mental attitude which through life he appeared to maintain. One of the omitted poems which appeared
in this later edition is "Hero to Leander," which
seems to come nearer the high-water mark of his
later work than any that he kept. It runs:

O go not yet, my love!
    The night is dark and vast;
The white moon is hid in her heaven above,
    And the waves climb high and fast.
O, kiss me, kiss me, once again,
    Lest thy kiss should be the last!
O kiss me ere we part;
Grow closer to my heart!
My heart is warmer surely than the bosom of the
    main.
O joy! O bliss of blisses!
    My heart of hearts art thou.
Come bathe me with thy kisses,
    My eyelids and my brow.
Hark how the wild rain hisses,
    And the loud sea roars below.

Thy heart beats through thy rosy limbs,
    So gladly doth it stir;
Thine eye in drops of gladness swims.
    I have bathed thee with the pleasant myrrh;
Thy locks are dripping balm;
Thou shalt not wander hence to-night,
    I'll stay thee with my kisses.
To-night the roaring brine
    Will rend thy golden tresses;
The ocean with the morrow light
    Will be both blue and calm;
And the billow will embrace thee with a kiss as soft
    as mine.

FARINGFORD HOUSE, ISLE OF WIGHT.

No Western odors wander
    On the black and moaning sea,
And when thou art dead, Leander,
    My soul must follow thee!

O go not yet, my love!
    Thy voice is sweet and low;
The deep salt wave breaks in above
    Those marble steps below.
The turret-stairs are wet
    That lead into the sea.

Leander ! go not yet.
The pleasant stars have set :
O, go not, go not yet,
Or I will follow thee !

The next volume appeared in 1832. Among
its now thrice-familiar contents are, "The Lady
of Shalott," Tennyson's first study for the versification of the Arthurian legends, now especially
associated with his name. Its series of pictures
in flowing measure made it at once a favorite.
"The Miller's Daughter" was his first story-
poem, of which the beauty lay chiefly in the
songs included in it. The most charming of
these is :

Love that hath us in the net,
Can he pass, and we forget ?
Many suns arise and set.
Many a chance the years be-
    get.
Love the gift is Love the debt.
    Even so.

Love is hurt with jar and fret.
Love is made a vague regret.
Eyes with idle tears are wet.
Idle habit links us yet.
What is love ? for we forget :
    Ah, no ! no !

Out of the expression
"idle tears" grew one of the
loveliest of his lyrics. The
volume contained "Œnone,"
the first of the poems on
classic themes ; "The Palace of Art," "Lady Clara
Vere de Vere," "The May
Queen," "The Lotos-Eat-
ers," "A Dream of Fair
Women," "The Death of
the Old Year," and several
fragments without name.
"The Lotos-Eaters" is the
perfection of melody from
the first line to the last.
It is doubtful if the English
language is capable of being
woven into more exquisite
drapery for thought than that which clothes the
pleasant fancy of the Choric Song in this poem :

There is sweet music here that softer falls
Than petals from blown roses on the grass,
Or night-dews on still waters between walls
Of shadowy granite, in a gleaming pass ;
Music that gentlier on the spirit lies,
Than tir'd eyelids upon tir'd eyes :
Music that brings sweet sleep down from the bliss-
    ful skies.
Here are cool mosses deep,
And thro' the moss the ivies creep,
And in the stream the long-leaved flowers weep,
And   the craggy ledge the poppy hangs in
    sleep.

Why are we weigh'd upon with heaviness,
And utterly consumed with sharp distress,
While all things else have rest from weariness ?
All things have rest : why should we toil alone,
We only toil, who are the first of things,
And make perpetual moan,
Still from one sorrow to another thrown :
Nor ever fold our wings,
And cease from wanderings,
Nor steep our brows in slumber's holy balm :
Nor hearken what the inner spirit sings,

"There is no joy but calm !"
Why should we only toil, the roof and crown of
    things ?

Lo ! in the middle of the wood,
The folded leaf is woo'd from out the bud
With winds upon the branch, and there
Grows green and broad, and takes no care,
Sun-steep'd at noon, and in the moon
Nightly dew-fed ; and turning yellow
Falls, and floats adown the air.
Lo ! sweeten'd with the summer light,
The full-juiced apple, waxing over-mellow,
Drops in a silent autumn night.
All its allotted length of days,
The flower ripens in its place,

TENNYSON'S FAVORITE ARBOR, AT FARINGFORD.

Ripens and fades, and falls, and hath no toil,
Fast-rooted in the fruitful soil.

Hateful is the dark-blue sky,
Vaulted o'er the dark-blue sea.
Death is the end of life ; ah, why
Should life all labor be ?
Let us alone. Time driveth onward fast,
And in a little while our lips are dumb.
Let us alone. What is it that will last ?
All things are taken from us, and become
Portions and parcels of the dreadful Past.
Let us alone. What pleasure can we have
To war with evil ? Is there any peace
In ever climbing up the climbing wave ?
All things have rest, and ripen toward the grave
In silence ; ripen, fall and cease :
Give us long rest or death, dark death, or dream-
    ful ease.

How sweet it were, hearing the downward stream,
With half-shut eyes ever to seem
Falling asleep in a half-dream !
To dream and dream, like yonder amber light,
Which will not leave the myrrh-bush on the height ;
To hear each other's whisper'd speech ;
Eating the Lotos day by day,
To watch the crisping ripples on the beach,
And tender curving lines of creamy spray ;

To lend our hearts and spirits wholly
To the influence of mild-minded melancholy ;
To muse and brood and live again in memory,
With those old faces of our infancy
Heap'd over with a mound of grass,
Two handfuls of white dust, shut in an urn of brass !

We have had enough of action, and of motion we,
Roll'd to starboard, roll'd to larboard, when the
    surge was seething free,
Where the wallowing monster spouted his foam-
    fountains in the sea.

Where   smile in secret, looking over wasted
    landsbey
Blight and famine, plague and earthquake, roaring
    deeps and fiery sands,
Clanging fights, and flaming towns, and sinking
    ships, and praying hands.
But they smile, they find a music centred in a dole-
    ful song
Steaming up, a lamentation and an ancient tale
    of wrong,
Like a tale of little meaning tho' the words are
    strong ;

1 Burlington H.
Brighton
Jany. 25th

Mr Alfred Tennyson begs to present his compliments to Messrs Chapman and Hall and to thank them for their kind gift of the Westminster Review containing one of the very few favourable public notices of his Ode

Let us swear an oath, and keep it with an equal
    mind,
In the hollow Lotos-land to live and lie reclined
On the hills like Gods together, careless of man-
    kind.
For they lie beside their nectar, and the bolts are
    hurl'd
Far below them in the valleys, and the clouds are
    lightly curl'd
Round their golden houses, girdled with the gleam-
    ing world :

Chanted from an ill-used race of men that cleave
    the soil,
Sow the seed, and reap the harvest with enduring
    toil,
Storing yearly little dues of wheat, and wine and
    oil ;
Till they perish and they suffer—some, 'tis whis-
    pered—down in hell
Suffer endless anguish, others in Elysian valleys
    dwell,
Resting weary limbs at last on beds of asphodel.

Surely, surely, slumber is more sweet than toil,
    the shore
Than labor in the deep mid-ocean, wind and wave
    and oar;
O rest ye, brother mariners, we will not wander
    more.

In this volume Tennyson first used the peculiar form of stanza that he afterward made so well known by "In Memoriam," in three short poems, the best of which is this, in some respects one of his finest:

You ask me, why, tho' ill at ease,
    Within this region I subsist,
    Whose spirits falter in the mist,
And languish for the purple seas?

It is the land that freemen till,
    That sober-suited Freedom chose,
    The land, where girt with friends or foes
A man may speak the thing he will;

A land of settled government,
    A land of just and old renown,
    Where Freedom broadens slowly down
From precedent to precedent:

Where faction seldom gathers head,
    But by degrees to fulness wrought,
    The strength of some diffusive thought
Hath time and space to work and spread.

Should banded unions persecute
    Opinion, and induce a time
    When single thought is civil crime,
And individual freedom mute;

Tho' Power should make from land to
    land
    The name of Britain trebly great—
    Tho' every channel of the State
Should almost choke with golden sand—

Yet waft me from the harbor-mouth,
    Wild wind! I seek a warmer sky,
    And I will see before I die
The palms and temples of the South.

In 1842 he published, in two volumes, "English Idyls and Other Poems," which at once made him preëminent among his contemporaries. Among the new pieces in these volumes were: "Morte D'Arthur," "St. Simeon Stylites," "The Talking Oak," "Ulysses," "Locksley Hall," "The Two Voices," and "The Day-Dream." The "Morte D'Arthur" was his first attempt to use the Arthurian legends, and in all his subsequent "Idyls of the King" there is no finer piece of work. In "St. Simeon Stylites" we have a specimen of the most subtle thinking that Tennyson ever put into his poetry—in fact, it is his only poem in which there is real subtilty of thought. In Browning's hand the legend of St. Simeon's pillar would have suggested a crowd of ideas leading to discussions on religious, literary, and mythological themes; in Tennyson's poem the satire and the pathos with which he sets forth the image of the poor saint, half dupe and half deceiver, is greatly strengthened by the smoothness of the unrhymed measure, and the clearness of the expression:

Altho' I be the basest of mankind,
From scalp to sole one slough and crust of sin,
Unfit for earth, unfit for heaven, scarce meet
For troops of devils, mad with blasphemy,

I will not cease to grasp the hope I hold
Of saintdom, and to clamor, mourn, and sob,
Battering the gates of heaven with storms of
    prayer,
Have mercy, Lord, and take away my sin.
    Let this avail, just, dreadful, mighty God,
This not be all in vain, that thrice ten years,
Thrice multiplied by superhuman pangs,
In hungers and in thirsts, fevers and cold,
In coughs, aches, stitches, ulcerous throes and
    cramps,
A sign betwixt the meadow and the cloud,
Patient on this tall pillar I have borne
Rain, wind, frost, heat, hail, damp, and sleet, and
    snow;
And I had hoped that ere this period closed
Thou wouldst have caught me up into thy rest,
Denying not these weather-beaten limbs
The meed of saints, the white robe and the palm.

    O Jesus, if thou wilt not save my soul,
Who may be saved? who is it may be saved?
Who may be made a saint, if I fail here?
Show me the man hath suffered more than I.
For did not all thy martyrs die one death?
For either they were stoned, or crucified,

ALDWORTH HOUSE, WHERE TENNYSON DIED.

Or burn'd in fire, or boiled in oil, or sawn
In twain beneath the ribs; but I die here
To-day, and whole years long, a life of death.
Bear witness, if I could have found a way
(And heedfully I sifted all my thought)
More slowly-painful to subdue this home
Of sin, my flesh, which I despise and hate,
I had not stinted practice, O my God.

And they say then that I work'd miracles,
Whereof my fame is loud amongst mankind,
Cured lameness, palsies, cancers. Thou, O God,
Knowest alone whether this was or no.
Have mercy, mercy; cover all my sin.

Bethink thee, Lord, while thou and all the saints
Enjoy themselves in heaven, and men on earth
House in the shade of comfortable roofs,
Sit with their wives by fires, eat wholesome food,
And wear warm clothes, and even beasts have
    stalls,
I, 'tween the spring and downfall of the light,
Bow down one thousand and two hundred times,
To Christ, the Virgin Mother, and the Saints.

Good people, you do ill to kneel to me.
What is it I can have done to merit this?
I am a sinner viler than you all.
It may be I have wrought some miracles,
And cured some halt and maim'd; but what of
　　that?
It may be, no one, even among the saints,
May match his pains with mine; but what of that?
Yet do not rise: for you may look on me,
And in your looking you may kneel to God.
Speak! is there any of you halt or maim'd?
I think you know I have some power with Heaven
From my long penance: let him speak his wish.
　　Yes, I can heal him. Power goes forth from me.

　　　　　　　Is that the angel there
That holds a crown? Come, blessed brother, come.
I know thy glittering face. I waited long;
My brows are ready. What! deny it now?
Nay, draw, draw, draw nigh. So I clutch it.
　　Christ!
'T is gone: 't is here again; the crown! the
　　crown!
So now 't is fitted on and grows to me,
And from it melt the dews of Paradise,
Sweet! sweet! spikenard, and balm, and frank-
incense.

"Ulysses," a monologue, is one of the noblest
of all poems, both in thought and in expression.
It can hardly be divided without doing it violence; but two passages are all that we have
room for here:

I am a part of all that I have met;
Yet all experience is an arch wherethro'
Gleams that untravell'd world, whose margin fades
Forever and forever when I move.
How dull it is to pause, to make an end,
To rust unburnish'd, not to shine in use!
As tho' to breathe were life. Life piled on life
Were all too little, and of one to me
Little remains: but every hour is saved
From that eternal silence, something more,
A bringer of new things; and vile it were
For some three suns to store and hoard myself,
And this gray spirit yearning in desire
To follow knowledge, like a sinking star,
Beyond the utmost bound of human thought.

　　My mariners,
Souls that have toil'd, and wrought, and thought
　　with me—
That ever with a frolic welcome took
The thunder and the sunshine, and opposed
Free hearts, free foreheads—you and I are old;
Old age hath yet his honor and his toil;

Death closes all: but something ere the end,
Some work of noble note, may yet be done,
Not unbecoming men that strove with Gods.
The lights begin to twinkle from the rocks:
The long day wanes: the slow moon climbs: the
　　deep
Moans round with many voices. Come, my friends,
'T is not too late to seek a newer world.
Push off, and sitting well in order smite
The sounding furrows; for my purpose holds
To sail beyond the sunset, and the baths
Of all the western stars, until I die.

Some of Tennyson's admirers consider "Locksley Hall" his best poem, and it is likely to remain forever one of his most popular. The
spirit of the age, the forces of invention and
civilization, and the poetry of the whole round
world seem to run all through it in a rhythmic
braid, as shown notably in these passages:

Can I but relive in sadness? I will turn that
　　earlier page.
Hide me from my deep emotion, O thou wondrous
　　Mother-Age!

Make me feel the wild pulsation that I felt before
　　the strife,
When I heard my days before me, and the tumult
　　of my life;

Yearning for the large excitement that the coming
　　years would yield,
Eager-hearted as a boy when first he leaves his
　　father's field,

And at night along the dusky highway near and
　　nearer drawn,
Sees in heaven the light of London flaring like a
　　dreary dawn;

And his spirit leaps within him to be gone before
　　him then,
Underneath the light he looks at, in among the
　　throngs of men;

Men, my brothers, men the workers, ever reaping
　　something new;
That which they have done but earnest of the
　　things that they shall do:

For I dipt into the future, far as human eye could
　　see,
Saw the Vision of the world, and all the wonder
　　that would be;

Saw the heavens fill with commerce, argosies of
　　magic sails,
Pilots of the purple twilight, dropping down with
　　costly bales;

Heard the heavens fill with shouting, and there
　　rain'd a ghastly dew
From the nations' airy navies grappling in the
　　central blue;

Far along the world-wide whisper of the south-wind
　　rushing warm,
With the standards of the peoples plunging thro'
　　the thunder-storm;

Till the war-drum throbb'd no longer, and the
　　battle-flags were furl'd
In the Parliament of man, the Federation of the
　　world.

There the common sense of most shall hold a fret-
　　ful realm in awe,
And the kindly earth shall slumber, lapt in univer-
　　sal law.

　　　　　　　　　　Ah, for some retreat
Deep in yonder shining Orient, where my life began
　　to beat;

Where in wild Mahratta-battle fell my father evil-
　　starr'd;—
I was left a trampled orphan, and a selfish uncle's
　　ward.

Or to burst all links of habit—there to wander far
　　away,
On from island unto island at the gateways of the
　　day.

Larger constellations burning, mellow moons and
　　happy skies,
Breadths of tropic shade and palms in cluster,
　　knots of Paradise.

Never comes the trader, never floats an European
　　flag,
Slides the bird o'er lustrous woodland, swings the
　　trailer from the crag;

Droops the heavy-blossom'd bower, hangs the heavy-
fruited tree—
Summer isles of Eden lying in dark-purple spheres
of sea.

There methinks would be enjoyment more than in
this march of mind,
In the steamship, in the railway, in the thoughts
that shake mankind.

There the passions cramp'd no longer shall have
scope and breathing-space ;
I will take some savage woman, she shall rear my
dusky race.

Iron-jointed, supple-sinew'd, they shall dive, and
they shall run,
Catch the wild goat by the hair, and hurl their
lances in the sun ;

Whistle back the parrot's call, and leap the rain-
bows of the brooks,
Not with blinded eyesight poring over miserable
books—

Fool, again the dream, the fancy ! but I *know* my
words are wild,
But I count the gray barbarian lower than the
Christian child.

I, to herd with narrow foreheads, vacant of our
glorious gains,
Like a beast with lower pleasures, like a beast with
lower pains !

Mated with a squalid savage—what to me were sun
or clime ?
I the heir of all the ages, in the foremost files of
time—

I that rather held it better men should perish one
by one,
Than that earth should stand at gaze like Joshua's
moon in Ajalon !

Not in vain the distance beacons. Forward, forward let us range.
Let the great world spin forever down the ringing
grooves of change.

Thro' the shadow of the globe we sweep into the
younger day :
Better fifty years of Europe than a cycle of Cathay.

In " St. Agnes' Eve " Tennyson has embodied
the feeling of religious ecstasy with a wonderful
delicacy of touch :

Deep on the convent-roof the snows
Are sparkling to the moon :
My breath to heaven like vapor goes :
May my soul follow soon !
The shadows of the convent-towers
Slant down the snowy sward,
Still creeping with the creeping hours
That lead me to my Lord :
Make Thou my spirit pure and clear
As are the frosty skies,
Or this first snowdrop of the year
That in my bosom lies.

As these white robes are soiled and dark,
To yonder shining ground ;
As this pale taper's earthly spark,
To yonder argent round ;
So shows my soul before the Lamb,
My spirit before Thee ;
So in mine earthly house I am,
To that I hope to be.

Break up the heavens, O Lord ! and far,
Thro' all yon starlight keen,
Draw me, thy bride, a glittering star,
In raiment white and clean.

He lifts me to the golden doors ;
The flashes come and go ;
All heaven bursts her starry floors,
And strows her lights below,
And deepens on and up ! the gates
Roll back, and far within
For me the Heavenly Bridegroom waits,
To make me pure of sin.
The sabbaths of Eternity,
One sabbath deep and wide—
A light upon the shining sea—
The Bridegroom with his bride !

" The Two Voices " is perhaps his most metaphysical poem, but the metaphysics are much
more strongly as well as more poetically expressed in the " In Memoriam. "

" The Princess : A Medley," was first published
in 1847, and was much improved in later editions. In this poem he treats the question of
woman's rights, or the equality of the sexes. It
is chiefly admired for its songs—" As through
the land," " Tears, idle tears," " The splendor
falls," " Thy voice is heard," " Home they
brought her warrior dead," " Sweet and low,"
" O swallow, swallow," and " Ask me no more."
For pure pathos it is doubtful if the " Tears, idle
tears " has ever been equaled :

Tears, idle tears, I know not what they mean,
Tears from the depth of some divine despair
Rise in the heart, and gather to the eyes,
In looking on the happy Autumn-fields,
And thinking of the days that are no more.

Fresh as the first beam glittering on a sail,
That brings our friends up from the underworld,
Sad as the last which reddens over one
That sinks with all we love below the verge ;
So sad, so fresh, the days that are no more :

Ah, sad and strange as in dark summer dawns
The earliest pipe of half-awaken'd birds
To dying ears, when unto dying eyes
The casement slowly grows a glimmering square ;
So sad, so strange, the days that are no more.

Dear as remember'd kisses after death,
And sweet as those by hopeless fancy feign'd
On lips that are for others ; deep as love,
Deep as first love, and wild with all regret ;
O Death in Life, the days that are no more.

In 1850, the same year in which he succeeded
Wordsworth as Laureate, Tennyson published
(anonymously) his " In Memoriam." an elaborate
elegy for his early friend Arthur Henry Hallam,
son of the historian, who died in 1833. Hallam had shown some ability as a writer, and was
betrothed to Tennyson's sister. This work is
made up of 129 short poems. written at different
times and in various moods through sixteen
years. The form of versification is admirably
chosen for such an elegy, and almost every reader
of poetry has his favorite passages in it. It has
furnished many popular quotations, the foremost
of which is the stanza :

This truth came borne with bier and pall.
I felt it, when I sorrow'd most,
'T is better to have loved and lost,
Than never to have loved at all.

Among the others are :

> Oh, yet we trust that somehow good
> Will be the final goal of ill ;

and,

> There lives more faith in honest doubt,
> Believe me, than in half the creeds ;

and,

> I do but sing, because I must,
> And pipe but as the linnets sing ;

and the passage beginning,

> Ring out, wild bells !

The apology is gracefully set forth in these lines:

> I sometimes hold it half a sin
> To put in words the grief I feel ;
> For words, like Nature, half reveal
> And half conceal the Soul within.

> But, for the unquiet heart and brain,
> A use in measured language lies ;
> The sad mechanic exercise,
> Like dull narcotics, numbing pain.

> In words, like weeds, I'll wrap me o'er,
> Like coarsest clothes against the cold ;
> But that large grief which these enfold
> Is given in outline and no more.

After which the poet is at liberty to discuss any subject that is either directly or remotely connected with the topic, and he produces many picturesque passages—as this :

> Calm is the morn without a sound,
> Calm as to suit a calmer grief,
> And only thro' the faded leaf
> The chestnut pattering to the ground :

> Calm and deep peace on this high wold,
> And on these dews that drench the furze,
> And all the silvery gossamers
> That twinkle into green and gold   :

> Calm and still light on yon great plain
> That sweeps with all its autumn bowers,
> And crowded farms and lessening towers,
> To mingle with the bounding main :

> Calm and deep peace in this wide air,
> These leaves that redden to the fall ;
> And in my heart, if calm at all,
> If any calm, a calm despair :

> Calm on the seas, and silver sleep,
> And waves that sway themselves in rest,
> And dead calm in that noble breast
> Which heaves but with the heaving deep.

The poem was a favorite with President Garfield, who especially admired this passage, which was much quoted in connection with the eulogies upon him :

> Dost thou look back on what hath been,
> As some divinely gifted man,
> Whose life in low estate began
> And on a simple village green ;

> Who breaks his birth's invidious bar,
> And grasps the skirts of happy chance,
> And breasts the blows of circumstance,
> And grapples with his evil star ;

> Who makes by force his merit known,
> And lives to clutch the golden keys,
> To mould a mighty state's decrees,
> And shape the whisper of the throne ;

> And moving up from high to higher,
> Becomes on Fortune's crowning slope
> The pillar of a people's hope,
> The centre of a world's desire ;

> ' Yet feels, as in a pensive dream,
> When all his active powers are still,
> A distant dearness in the hill,
> A secret sweetness in the stream,

> The limit of his narrower fate,
> While yet beside its vocal springs
> He play'd at counsellors and kings,
> With one that was his earliest mate ;

> Who ploughs with pain his native lea
> And reaps the labor of his hands,
> Or in the furrow musing stands :
> " Does my old friend remember me ? "

In 1855 appeared " Maud, and Other Poems." To many lovers of Tennyson's poetry this was a disappointment ; it is hard to say why.   It was interesting as a story, more dramatic and intense in action than any other of his, and more sustained.   It had admirers as vehement as its critics.   On the beauty of one portion—that beginning , " Come into the garden, Maud," there was no dispute.

> Come into the garden, Maud,
> For the black bat, night, has flown ;
> Come into the garden, Maud,
> I am here at the gate alone ;
> And the woodbine spices are wafted abroad,
> And the musk of the roses blown.

> For a breeze of morning moves,
> And the planet of Love is on high,
> Beginning to faint in the light that she loves
> On a bed of daffodil sky,
> To faint in the light of the sun she loves,
> To faint in his light, and to die.

> All night have the roses heard
> The flute, violin, bassoon ;
> All night has the casement jessamine stirr'd
> To the dancers dancing in tune ;
> Till a silence fell with the waking bird,
> And a hush with the setting moon.

> I said to the lily, " There is but one
> With whom she has heart to be gay.
> When will the dancers leave her alone ?
> She is weary of dance and play."
> Now half to the setting moon are gone,
> And half to the rising day ;
> Low on the sand and loud on the stone
> The last wheel echoes away.

> I said to the rose, " The brief night goes
> In babble and revel and wine.
> O young lord-lover, what sighs are those,
> For one that will never be thine ?
> But mine, but mine," so I sware to the rose,
> " Forever and ever, mine."

> And the soul of the rose went into my blood,
> As the music clash'd in the hall ;
> As long by the garden lake I stood,
> For I heard your rivulet fall
> From the lake to the meadow and on to the wood,
> Our wood, that is dearer than all ;

> From the meadow your walks have left so sweet
> That whenever a March-wind sighs
> He sets the jewel-print of your feet
> In violets blue as your eyes,
> To the woody hollows in which we meet
> And the valleys of Paradise. .

The slender acacia would not shake
  One long milk-bloom on the tree ;
The white lake-blossom fell into the lake,
  As the pimpernel dozed on the lea ;
But the rose was awake all night for your sake,
  Knowing your promise to me ;
The lilies and roses were all awake,
  They sigh'd for the dawn and thee.

Queen rose of the rosebud garden of girls,
  Come hither, the dances are done,
In gloss of satin and glimmer of pearls,
  Queen lily and rose in one ;
Shine out, little head, sunning over with curls,
  To the flowers, and be their sun.

There has fallen a splendid tear
  From the passion-flower at the gate.
She is coming, my dove, my dear ;
  She is coming, my life, my fate ;
The red rose cries, "She is near, she is near" ;
  And the white rose weeps, "She is late" ;
The larkspur listens, "I hear, I hear" ;
  And the lily whispers, "I wait."

She is coming, my own, my sweet ;
  Were it ever so airy a tread,
My heart would hear her and beat,
  Were it earth in an earthly bed ;
My dust would hear her and beat,
  Had I lain for a century dead ;
Would start and tremble under her feet,
  And blossom in purple and red.

But the soul of the poem is in the 18th section, which contains these lines :

There is none like her, none.
Nor will be when our summers have deceased.
O, art thou sighing for Lebanon
In the long breeze that streams to thy delicious
  East,
Sighing for Lebanon,
Dark cedar, tho' thy limbs have here increased,
Upon a pastoral slope as fair,
And looking to the South, and fed
With honey'd rain and delicate air,
And haunted by the starry head
Of her whose gentle will has changed my fate,
And made my life a perfumed altar-flame ;
And over whom thy darkness must have spread
With such delight as theirs of old, thy great
Forefathers of the thornless garden, there
Shadowing the snow-limb'd Eve from whom she
  came.

Here will I lie, while these long branches sway,
And you fair stars that crown a happy day
Go in and out as if at merry play,
Who am no more so all forlorn,
As when it seem'd far better to be born
To labor and the mattock-harden'd hand,
Than nursed its ease and brought to understand
A sad astrology, the boundless plan
That makes you tyrants in your iron skies,
Innumerable, pitiless, passionless eyes,
Cold fires, yet with power to burn and brand
His nothingness into man.

But now shine on, and what care I,
Who in this stormy gulf have found a pearl
The countercharm of space and hollow sky,
And do accept my madness and would die
To save from some slight shame one simple girl.

Among the other poems in this volume were "The Brook," a fine specimen of onomatopoetic verse, and the strong "Ode on the Death of the Duke of Wellington," which had been published separately on the morning of the funeral.
In 1859 Mr. Tennyson published four "Idyls

of the King—" "Enid," "Vivien," "Elaine," and "Guinevere—" a rendering into graceful, and in many passages powerful, English blank verse, of four stories from the Arthur myth. Afterward he wrote many more of these idyls, apparently with the purpose of exhausting the material, but none that can compare with the first four.

Next appeared, in 1864, "Enoch Arden," which attained considerable popularity because of its quality as a story, but added nothing to Tennyson's poetical fame. In the same volume, however, were some notable poems. The "Northern Farmer" (Yorkshire) was the Laureate's first attempt at dialect, a vivid and original picture. "Sea Dreams" is remarkable only for the high price paid by an English magazine for its first publication (said to have been £10 a line). "Tithonus" is a monologue to be placed beside "Ulysses."

"The Window; or, Songs of the Wrens," which appeared in 1870, is a little song-cycle, written to be set to music by Arthur Sullivan. His remaining volumes of poetry include "Ballads, and Other Poems" (1880); "Tiresias, and Other Poems" (1885); "Demeter, and Other Poems" (1889); and "Akbar's Dream, and Other Poems" (1892). In 1875 he published his first attempt at drama, "Queen Mary"; and this was followed by the plays "Harold," "The Cup," "The Falcon," "Becket," "Promise of May," and "The Foresters," several of which were put upon the stage. But Mr. Tennyson was not a dramatic poet, and none of these plays can be considered successful in any sense.

As he approached the end of his long life, the Laureate seemed to sing his own elegy. His "Crossing the Bar," written about a year before his death, is one of the best of his short poems, and has been universally admired :

Sunset and evening star,
  And one clear call for me !
And may there be no moaning of the bar
  When I put out to sea,

But such a tide as moving seems asleep,
  Too full for sound and foam,
When that which drew from out the boundless deep
  Turns again home.

Twilight and evening bell,
  And after that the dark !
And may there be no sadness of farewell
  When I embark ;

For tho' from out our bourne of Time and Place
  The flood may bear me far,
I hope to see my Pilot face to face
  When I have crossed the bar.

And when he was still nearer to the close of his career he wrote, in immediate anticipation of his departure, the little poem, "Silent Voices" :

When the dumb hour clothed in black
  Brings the dreams about my bed,
Call me not so often back,
  Silent voices of the dead,
Toward the lowland ways behind me,
  And the sunlight that is gone.
Call me rather, silent voices,
  Forward to the starry track,
Glimmering up the heights beyond me,
  On and always on.

Both of these were sung at his funeral, the later one being set to music by his widow.

Tennyson died of old age, passing away peacefully after several days of painless illness or gradual sinking. In the afternoon of his last day he asked his son to bring him his copy of Shakespeare, of which he turned the leaves till he came to the song in the fourth act of "Cymbeline"—

Fear no more the heat o' the sun.

Placing his hand upon this, and telling his son not to let it be removed, he kept it by him till he died. It was buried in the coffin with him. The end came an hour and a half past midnight. Sir Andrew Clark, the physician, says: "In all my experience I have never witnessed anything more glorious. There were no artificial lights in the chamber, and all was in darkness save for the silvery light of the moon at its full. The soft beams of light fell upon the bed and played upon the features of the dying poet like a halo of Rembrandt."

Tennyson had a horror of hearses, and at his obsequies none was used. The London Times's correspondent wrote: "On the morning of Oct. 11 a heart-of-oak coffin arrived at Aldworth, and in this the remains of the poet were placed. The coffin was then lifted into a car—an ordinary 'country gentleman's shooting-car'—where it was covered, in the first place, by a pall of handwoven Ruskin linen, made at the Keswick School of Industrial Art. This, however, was soon smothered in wreaths. The procession started. In front, at a foot-pace, went the rustic car, led by Lord Tennyson's old coachman. Behind came as chief mourners the Hon. Hallam Tennyson and Mrs. Tennyson, and then Miss Maud Tennyson and Mr. Hitchens, a very old friend of the family. Next came a little pony-carriage drawn by a black pony, heavily laden with wreaths and like tributes, and then a long train of household servants and humble neighbors, headed by the nurses. That was all. The Hon. Hallam Tennyson superintended the removal of the coffin to the train, and the funeral party then started for London, reaching Waterloo between half-past eight and a quarter to nine. A further removal then occurred, the coffin being placed in a van and Mr. and Mrs. Hallam Tennyson entering the carriage that was in waiting. Half way down Stamford Street there was a halt, and the Union Jack, suggested by Lady Tennyson as the most appropriate covering for the coffin, was placed upon it. The temporary resting place was St. Faith's Chapel, in the Abbey."

The burial took place on Oct. 12, in the Poets' Corner, close by the grave of Chaucer.

TEXAS, a Southern State, admitted to the Union Dec. 29, 1845; area, 265,780 square miles; population, according to each decennial census since admission, 212,592 in 1850; 604,215 in 1860; 818,759 in 1870; 1,591,749 in 1880; and 2,235,523 in 1890. Capital, Austin.

Government.—The following were the State officers during the year: Governor, James S. Hogg, Democrat; Lieutenant-Governor, George C. Pendleton; Secretary of State, George W. Smith; Treasurer, W. B. Wortham; Comptroller, John D. McCall; Attorney-General, Charles A. Culberson; Superintendent of Public Instruction, J. M. Carlisle; Commissioner of General Land Office, W. L. McGaughey; Commissioner

of Insurance, John E. Hollingsworth; Railroad Commissioners, John H. Reagan, L. L. Foster, W. P. McLean; Chief Justice of the Supreme Court, John W. Stayton; Associate Justices, Reuben R. Gaines and John L. Henry; Court of Appeals, Presiding Judge, John P. White, who resigned on April 27 and was succeeded by James M. Hurt, Judges W. L. Davidson and E. J. Simkins; Commission of Appeals, Sec. A, Presiding Judge, Edwin Hobby, Judges W. E. Collard and D. P. Marr; Sec. B, Presiding Judge, C. C. Garrett, Judges D. B. Tarlton and H. C. Fisher. By act of the Legislature, passed at the special session held in March, the Court of Appeals and the Commission of Appeals were superseded on Sept. 1 by three Courts of Civil Appeals and one Court of Criminal Appeals. The following members of these courts (with the exception of Judge Hurt who held over under the law) were appointed by the Governor on Sept. 1 and subsequently elected by the people at the November election: Court of Civil Appeals, First district, Presiding Judge, C. C. Garrett, Judges Frank A. Williams and Henry C. Pleasants; Second district, Presiding Judge, H. C. Fisher, Judges William Key and W. E. Collard; Third district, Presiding Judge, D. B. Tarlton, Judges, H. O. Head and I. W. Stephens. Court of Criminal Appeals, Presiding Judge, James M. Hurt, Judges W. L. Davidson and E. J. Simkins.

Finances.—The balance in the State treasury, which was $1,007,193.87 on Aug. 31, 1891, had increased to $1,322,253.21 on Aug. 31, 1892. In the general revenue fund the balance on the latter date was $450,332; in the available school fund, $367,543.76; and in all other funds, $504,377.45. The following bonds were held in the State treasury on Aug. 31, 1892, to the credit of the various permanent State funds: Permanent school fund, $7,821,336.50; permanent university fund, $571,340; Blind Asylum fund, $109,300; Deaf and Dumb Asylum fund, $59,000; Lunatic Asylum fund, $106,400; Agricultural and Mechanical College fund, $209,000; other funds, $90,456.19; total, $8,966,832.69. The income of these bonds is used for the support of schools and public institutions.

The assessed valuation of property in the State for 1891 was $856,200,283, an increase of $74,088,400 in one year. The tax rate for all State purposes was 29½ cents on each $100.

Legislative Session.—On Feb. 18 Gov. Hogg issued his proclamation calling upon the Legislature to meet in special session at Austin on March 14. Among the subjects for legislative action enumerated in the proclamation were the election of a United States Senator, the reapportionment of the State into Congressional, senatorial, judicial, and representative districts, the passage of laws to enforce the constitutional amendments adopted in August, 1891, and the restriction and regulation of the bond and stock issues of railroads, counties, and municipalities. The choice for United States Senator fell upon Congressman Roger Q. Mills, who received the following vote in each house on March 22: Senate—Mills, 29; scattering, 2; House—Mills, 94; scattering, 9. Mr. Mills thereby became the successor of Hon. Horace Chilton, who was appointed by the Governor in 1891 to succeed Hon. John H. Reagan, resigned. His term will expire on March

3, 1893. Acts were passed dividing the State into 13 Congressional districts and establishing new districts for members of the Senate and House of Representatives. The judicial system of the State was changed by the abolition of both the Court of Appeals and the Commission of Appeals and the establishment of courts of appeal having final jurisdiction over many cases heretofore brought into the Supreme Court. The State was divided into three judicial districts, each having a Court of Civil Appeals composed of three judges elected by the people of the district for the term of six years. A single Court of Criminal Appeals for the whole State was also established, the three judges composing it to be elected by the people for the same term. These changes, which took effect on Sept. 1, were for the purpose of relieving the pressure of business before the Supreme Court.

Other acts of the session were as follows :

Appropriating $248,700 to pay that part of the bonded debt of the State held by individuals and falling due March 1 and April 1, 1892.

Amending the laws governing usury. The legal rate of interest is fixed at 6 per cent., but parties may agree to a higher rate not exceeding 10 per cent. Usurious contracts shall be void only as to the interest stipulated. The principal may be recovered.

Forbidding the ownership of land in the State by non-resident aliens, except for a limited period, and providing for the escheat of land held contrary to the provisions of the act.

Providing for the transfer annually of one per cent. of the permanent school fund of the State to the available school fund, to be applied in the support of the public schools for that year.

Authorizing the Governor to collect the money due the State as a refund of the direct tax of 1861 and providing for its disbursement to the people entitled thereto.

The session ended on April 12.

Education.—The total number of children of school age in the State in 1892 was 605,495, divided as follows : white males, 234,070 ; white females, 219,740 ; colored males, 76,765 ; colored females, 74,920. For the education of these children during the year the State appropriated $3,027,475, or $5 *per capita*. The State Constitution requires that public schools shall be supported for six months each year, but there are no statutes to enforce this provision.

The State Agricultural and Mechanical College is in a flourishing condition, 230 students being in attendance at the close of 1892. The various normal schools are also doing good work.

Charities.—At the North Texas Hospital for the Insane there were 606 patients on Oct. 31, 1891 ; 388 patients were admitted during the year following and 265 discharged, leaving 729 remaining on Oct. 31, 1892. The expenses for the year were $123,956.39. The new Asylum of the Insane at San Antonio was opened for patients in the early part of this year, the buildings therefor having been accepted by the State on Feb. 5. At the State-Institute for the Deaf and Dumb the number of attendants enrolled at the close of the year was 235.

Prisons.—At the State Penitentiary there were 3,575 convicts on Oct. 31, 1892, an increase of 376 in two years. Of this number 588 are employed outside of the walls of the Penitentiary upon rail-road building and 1,237 upon farms. The State employs 427 of the latter number on its own farms, and the remaining 810 are leased to individuals for work on private plantations.

Railroad Commission.—On April 30 five suits were begun in the United States Circuit Court of Texas against five of the leading railroads of the State, the Railroad Commissioners, and the Attorney-General, in which the constitutionality of the railroad commission law of 1891 was brought in question. These cases came up before Judge A. P. McCormick in July upon the question whether a preliminary injunction should be issued restraining the railroads from putting in force the rates established by the Railroad Commissioners and restraining the latter and the Attorney-General from bringing suits to enforce such rates. The plaintiffs contended that the Commissioners' rates were unreasonably low and that the entire law was unconstitutional, because it deprived the railroads of their property without due process of law. By a decision rendered on Aug. 22 Judge McCormick supported these contentions and ordered the injunctions to issue. The defendants therefore appealed to the United States Supreme Court, where the case is still pending.

Drouth.—On April 13 an appeal for help was made to the people of the State in behalf of the citizens of Starr and Hidalgo counties, where dry weather for several seasons had prevented the growth of crops and reduced the inhabitants nearly to starvation. In response to this appeal contributions of corn and money were forwarded to the local relief committee, which, according to a report made in July, was assisting no fewer than 4,100 destitute people. The citizens of Cameron county in July made a similar appeal for aid on account of the drouth. Nearly every county in the Southern portion of the State adjacent to the Rio Grande river suffered severely during the year from the same cause.

Political.—The political contest of 1892 was one of the most interesting and important in the history of the State. During its progress the People's party for the first time developed elements of strength, while the Democrats became hopelessly divided over questions connected with Gov. Hogg's administration. Division arose in the Republican ranks also by reason of the attempt of certain leaders to establish a new party organization controlled only by white men. Although a National election was impending, the National issues which held prominence in other States were almost lost sight of, and State questions became the chief theme of platform discussion.

On March 9 a Republican State convention met at Austin and selected delegates to the National convention of the party at Minneapolis. Five weeks later another Republican convention, to which only white men were admitted as delegates, met at Dallas, selected another set of delegates to the Minneapolis convention, and nominated Presidential electors and the following State ticket : For Governor, Andrew J. Houston, son of Gen. Sam Houston ; for Lieutenant-Governor, James W. Newcomb ; for Comptroller, J. S. Schmitz; for Treasurer, R. B. Baer ; for Attorney-General, Waters Davis ; for Superintendent of Public Instruction, D. C. Morgan ; for Land Commissioner, R. W. Thompson. Resolutions were adopted in favor of the McKinley tariff and opposing the so-called "Force bill." An address to the people was issued, of which the following is a portion :

We feel justified in assuming that the Republican party of Texas has no organization such as is recognized as requisite to constitute a political party. That it has degenerated into an unorganized mob, whose biennial gatherings have wrought disgrace and despair to our patriotic people who hold to the tenets of the Republican party. Therefore, the necessity has arisen for the organization of the Republican party of Texas, independent of its past history, and upon the further recognition of the fact that only upon the intelligence and manhood of the white American citizens can any party in this country hope for growth and success. We call upon the white Republicans of the State and those in sympathy with the principles and politics of the Republican party to come to our aid and give us their assistance in building up Republicanism in Texas.

On April 26 a Prohibition State convention met at Waco, and nominated delegates to the National convention, Presidential electors, and a State ticket. This ticket, as voted at the November election, contained the following names: For Governor, D. M. Prendergast ; for Lieutenant-Governor, J. W. Williams; for Comptroller, W. J. Clayton ; for Treasurer, H. G. Damon ; for Attorney-General, J. B. Goff; for Superintendent of Public Instruction, R. Clark ; for Land Commissioner, S. G. Tomlinson.

The Democrats held a State convention at Lampasas on June 7, at which time delegates to the National convention of the party and Presidential electors were selected.

On June 23 the People's party in convention at Dallas nominated the following State ticket : For Governor, T. L. Nugent ; for Lieutenant-Governor, Marion Martin ; for Comptroller, W. J. Moseley ; for Treasurer, W. W. Durham ; for Attorney-General, James H. Davis; for Superintendent of Public Instruction, W. E. Clemmens ; for General Commissioner, S. D. A. Duncan. Before the November election the two candidates last mentioned were succeeded on the ticket by E. C. Chambers and Henry E. McCulloch respectively, and the names of William L. Burkhart and E. L. Dohoney for Judges of the Court of Criminal Appeals were added. Delegates to the Omaha national convention and Presidential electors were nominated at this time. The following declarations upon State issues, among others, were adopted :

All the public lands of Texas remaining and that can be recovered should be reserved as homesteads for actual settlers. All lands heretofore granted to individuals or corporations in which the grantees have not complied with the conditions of the grant should be forfeited to the State for homestead purposes: no alien ownership of lands should be allowed in Texas ; corporations shall not be allowed to own more land than they actually use in the prosecution of their business.

We favor an effective system of public schools for six months in the year for all children between the ages of 6 and 20. We demand the adoption of a uniform series of text-books for the public schools of this State, and that they be published at the expense of the State.

We demand an amendment to our State Constitution authorizing the loaning of our permanent school fund not otherwise invested upon lands of the people of this State at a low rate of interest, with proper limitations upon the quantity of land and the amount of money. .

We demand fair elections and an honest count of the votes, under either the Australian or some similar system of voting.

We favor a railway commission with power to fix and maintain rates that will insure equal and exact justice to the people and the railways.

We demand an efficient lien law, that will protect the artisan, mechanic, laborer, and material men.

We demand that a law be passed declaring eight hours to be a legal day's work, where it is not otherwise provided by contract.

We favor such change in the Constitution as shall prohibit national bankers and members of railway, telegraph, and telephone companies, and their attorneys, or who shall have held such positions within two years prior to an election, from holding any legislative or judicial office within this State.

The Democratic State convention for the nomination of a State ticket met at Houston on Aug. 16. For several months preceding, an active canvass of the State had been made by the two leading candidates for the gubernatorial nomination, Gov. Hogg and Judge George Clark. Two years before, Gov. Hogg had obtained the Democratic nomination upon the issue that the powers of railroad corporations should be restricted by legislation, and after his election the Legislature of 1891, in accordance with his views, enacted a railroad commission law, by which the authority to fix passenger and freight rates, and otherwise to regulate the management of railroads, was delegated to a commission of three members. This law the Governor defended upon the stump, at the same time insisting that further restrictions should be placed on all kinds of corporations, especially such restrictions as should prevent the issue of fictitious stocks and bonds. Judge Clark and his supporters, on the other hand, asserted that the Governor's hostility to corporations was driving capital out of the State, as well as deterring new capital from entering it, and that his course was, therefore, opposed to the best interests of the people. They also complained of the dictatorial conduct of the Governor in the administration of his office. Before the convention met, it was evident that a majority of the delegates elected were supporters of the Governor. So heated had the contest become, however, that neither party felt disposed to yield to the other, and when at the opening of the convention a disagreement arose upon the question of electing a temporary chairman, the Clark delegates withdrew in a body and organized a separate convention. The Hogg men proceeded to renominate Gov. Hogg, Comptroller McCall, Treasurer Wortham, Attorney-General Culberson, Land Commissioner McGaughey, and Superintendent of Public Instruction Carlisle. For Lieutenant-Governor the nomination fell to M. M. Crane, and for Judges of the Court of Criminal Appeals to W. L. Davidson and E. J. Simkins. A platform was adopted demanding free coinage of silver, opposing national banks, favoring a graduated income tax, denouncing bounties and subsidies granted by the Federal Government, and containing also the following declarations:

We demand a law that will effectually prevent the issuance of fictitious and watered bonds and stocks by railway companies in this State, believing that these great enterprises should be conducted upon commercial principles, and not as gambling devices.

We demand the passage of a law that will prevent

the useless and extravagant issuance of bonds by cities, towns, and counties in this State.

We favor an amendment to our State Constitution that will permit the legislature to provide for the indigent ex-Confederate soldiers resident in our State, that were disabled in the military service of the Confederate States, in any manner that may be deemed best.

We demand the constitutional provision requiring the public free school to be maintained and supported for a period of not less than six months each year, shall be fully and faithfully carried out, and the university, its branches, and other public educational institutions be properly endowed and maintained.

The nominees of the Clark convention were George Clark for Governor, C. M. Rogers for Lieutenant-Governor, Thomas J. Goree for Treasurer, C. B. Gillespie for Comptroller, E. A. McDowell for Attorney-General, Jacob Bickler for Superintendent of Public Instruction, W. C. Walsh for Land Commissioner, and W. D. Wood and R. H. Phelps for Judges of the Court of Criminal Appeals. The name of Ethan Allen was later substituted for that of C. B. Gillespie, who declined the nomination. The platform adopted includes the following resolutions :

We favor the election of all officers by the people themselves.

We favor the continuance of the present method of railway regulation.

We condemn all forms of communism and State socialism, and view with alarm the existing war upon the rights of property.

We condemn all secret oath-bound political organizations as un-American and undemocratic, contrary to the genius of our institutions, and destructive of the liberties of the people.

We oppose what is commonly called the Jester amendment and the law enacted thereunder, because the effect of the same will be to ultimately squander the permanent school fund.

We oppose the investments of the school fund in railroad securities. We oppose perpetuities and monopolies, and we oppose the acquisition of lands by corporations except such as may be necessary to enable them to carry on business for which they are created.

We arraign the administration of Governor Hogg because it has driven and is keeping capital from the State, because his administration has been undemocratic and despotic.

On Sept. 14 another Republican State convention was held at Fort Worth, representing the regular party organization as opposed to the white Republican movement. This convention decided to adopt the nomination of Judge Clark for Governor, but made no nomination for other places on the State ticket, or for Presidential electors. The platform demands a State university for the colored people, the employment of penitentiary convicts on the public roads, and protection to every citizen in voting. It condemns the administration of Gov. Hogg for the following, among other, reasons :

It has discouraged immigration, thereby retarding agricultural development, thus robbing the farmer by decreasing values, and the State by restraining production.

It has prevented the organization and upbuilding of new industries that would have employed large capital, given profitable employment to many laborers, and increased the values of farm products.

Its ignorance of the Constitution as evidenced by the approval and attempted enforcement of the alien land law, the usury law, the railway commission law, and other laws, has been a just cause of complaint and imposed vexatious burdens alike on the people and the courts.

It, for selfish purposes, deprived the public treasury of large moneys that should have been placed there to the credit of the State, by refusing to accept the bounty on sugar due Texas from the federal government.

For a selfish if not corrupt purpose it has invaded and begun to destroy the common heritage of the children of Texas, the sacred school fund, bequeathed in trust to them by their forefathers.

At the November election the Democratic electoral ticket received its usual large majority, the vote being as follows : Democratic, 239,148 ; Republican, 81,444 ; People's party, 99,638 ; Prohibitionist, 2,165. For Governor, Hogg received 190,486 votes ; Clark, 133,395 ; Nugent, 108,483 ; Houston, 1,322 ; and Prendergast, 1,605. All the other candidates on the Hogg ticket were elected by nearly the same vote as that cast for Governor. Thirteen Democratic members of Congress were chosen, and the following members of the State Legislature for 1893 : Senate—Democrats, 29 ; People's party, 1 ; Independent, 1 : House—Democrats, 112 ; People's party, 8 ; Republicans, 1 ; politics unknown, 7. Of the 141 Democratic members of the two Houses, 97 are classed as adherents of Gov. Hogg.

Judicial Election.—On Aug. 2 Democratic conventions were held in each of the three judicial districts created this year by the Legislature, and the following candidates for judges of the new Courts of Civil Appeals were nominated : 1st district at Houston, Presiding Judge, C. C. Garrett, Judges Frank A. Williams and Henry C. Pleasants ; 2d district at Austin, Presiding Judge, H. C. Fisher, Judges William Key and W. E. Collard ; 3d district at Dallas, Presiding Judge, D. B. Tarlton, Judges H. O. Head and I. W. Stephens. In each of these districts there was an opposition ticket in the field, but the above-named candidates were elected in November by considerable majorities.

Special Election.—On June 14 a special election was held in the 9th congressional district, for the purpose of choosing a successor to Hon. Roger Q. Mills. elected United States Senator. E. L. Antony, the Democratic nominee, was successful.

TURKEY, an empire in southeastern Europe and western Asia. The fundamental laws of the Empire are based on the Koran. A Constitution adopted Dec. 23, 1876, was never enforced, and no meeting of the Assembly created by it has been held since 1877. The Sultan is the supreme ruler and is represented as such for the affairs of the State by the Sadr-azam or Grand Vizier, and for the ecclesiastical affairs by the Sheïk-ul-Islam. The succession to the throne is to the eldest of the princes of the house of Osman. The reigning Sultan is Abdul Hamid II., born Sept. 22, 1842, who succeeded his elder brother, Sultan Murad V., on Aug. 31, 1876, the latter being deposed on the ground of insanity. The Sheïk-ul-Islam in the beginning of 1892 was Djomalledin Effendi, appointed in September, 1891, and the Grand Vizier, appointed at the same time, was Gen. Djevad Pasha. In the beginning of 1892 the following was the Cabinet of Ministers, which is presided over by the Grand Vizier: Minister of Foreign Affairs, Said Pasha; Minister of War. Riza Pasha; Minister of Marine, Hassan Pasha; Minister of the Interior, H. Rifot Pasha; Minister of Public Works, Commerce, and Agriculture, Suhdi Pasha; Minister of Justice. Riza Pasha; Minister of Finance, Nasif Effendi; Minister of the Civil List, Mikael-Effendi-Portokal; Minister of Public Instruction, Sihni Pasha; Minister of Evkafs, or Ecclesiastical Affairs, Galib Pasha.

Area and Population.—The area of the Ottoman Empire, including Bulgaria, Eastern Roumelia. Bosnia, Herzegovina, Novibazar, Samos, and Egypt, is estimated at 1,609,240 square miles, and the population at 39,212,000. The territory under the immediate rule of the Sultan contains 61,200 square miles, with 4,780,000 inhabitants in Europe; 687,640 square miles, with a population of 21,608,000, in Asia; and 398,738 square miles, with 1,300,000 inhabitants, in Africa. In the European provinces under immediate Turkish rule, Turks, Greeks, and Albanians are about equally numerous, constituting about 70 per cent. of the whole population. Other races represented are Serbs. Bulgarians, Roumanians, Armenians, Magyars, Gipsies, Jews, and Circassians. The population in Asiatic Turkey is largely of Turkish origin, with about 4,000,000 Arabs, and some Greeks, Syrians, Kurds, Circassians, Armenians, Jews, and other races. The principal cities in European Turkey are Constantinople, with 873,565 inhabitants; Salonica, 150,000; Adrianople, 70,886. In Asia, Smyrna has a population of 225,000; Damascus, 150,000; Aleppo, 110,000; Bagdad, 100,000; Beirout, 85,000; Erzerum, 60,000; Broussa, 60,000.

Finances.—An international arrangement was made in 1881 by which the debt was reduced to £106,437,234. The Turkish Government. agreed to transfer all excise revenues to an international commission, to be administered entirely separately from the other government administrations. The total revenue collected by this commission for the year 1889–90 amounted to £T2,336,251 (1 l. Turkish = 100 piasters; 1 piaster = 4.3 cents). and the expenses to £T393,689, leaving a surplus to be applied on the debt of £T1,942,562. Up to March 1, 1887, there were paid on the debt £1,978,528, leaving a debt of £104,458,706.

The Army.—By the laws of 1886 and 1888 military service is obligatory, for a term of 3 years in the infantry, and 4 in other arms of the permanent army. After a service of 5 months, however, conscripts can buy exemption from further active service. They are then enrolled in the reserve for 3 or 2 years respectively, 8 years in the *Redif,* and form then for the space of 6 years part of the *Mustahfiz.* The army is divided into 7 army corps, besides 3 separate divisions, located, one each, in Arabia, Crete, and Africa. Each army corps consists of 2 divisions of infantry, 1 division of cavalry. 1 brigade of field artillery, 2 divisions of the first ban of the *Redif,* and 2 divisions of the second ban of the *Redif.* The sixth army corps lacks the 2 divisions of the second ban of the *Redif,* and the seventh corps lacks the division of cav-

alry as well as the 4 divisions of the *Redif.* The peace effective in 1892 consisted of 246 battalions of infantry, 190 squadrons of cavalry, 208 batteries of field artillery, 92 companies of fortress artillery, 30 companies of garrison artillery, 39 companies of engineers, and 21 companies of train, a total strength of 183,000 officers and men, with about 30,000 horses, 1,248 pieces of field artillery, and 2,300 pieces of fortress artillery. The infantry is equipped with repeating rifles of the Mauser system, having a caliber of 11 mm.

The Navy.—The Turkish navy consisted at the beginning of 1892 of 7 armored frigates, 8 armored corvettes. 1 river monitor, 2 river gunboats, 27 torpedo gunboats, 30 sea-going torpedoboats, 2 submarine boats, 1 torpedo school-ship, 2 frigates, 1 spar-deck corvette, 1 corvette, 11 dispatch gun-vessels, 6 gunboats, 17 dispatch vessels and yachts, 6 dispatch boats, and 5 river transports, besides coal-ships, tugs, etc. The time of service in the navy is 12 years, of which 5 years are spent in active service, 3 years in the reserve, and 4 years in the *Redif.* The nominal strength of the navy in 1892 was 977 officers, 30,000 sailors, and 9,650 marines.

Commerce.—The total imports in 1889–90 amounted to 2,104,152,000 piasters, and the exports to 1,517,243,000 piasters. The following table shows the trade with the principal countries for 1889–90 in piasters:

COUNTRIES.	Imports.	Exports.
Great Britain	914,514,000	583,393,000
France	254,369,000	426,951,000
Austria-Hungary	409,144,000	135,482,000
Russia	173,323,000	52,414,000
Bulgaria	112,420,000	38,119,000
Persia	58,001,000	1,181,000
Italy	42,438,000	68,075,000
Belgium	41,574,000	1,671,000
Roumania	30,451,000	24,619,000
Greece	29,435,000	53,115,000
Netherlands	9,849,000	25,031,000
Servia	6,438,000	3,538,000
United States	6,028,000	15,735,000
Germany	2,649,000	5,358,000
Tunis	2,009,000	298,000
Egypt	1,897,000	98,777,000
Other Countries	5,514,000	2,691,000
Total	2,104,152,000	1,517,243,000

The principal articles of importation and their values were: sugar, 153,785,655 piasters; cotton thread, 117,111,525; cotton prints, 119,284,233; coffee, 84,249,778 piasters; wheat. 83,301,044 piasters; calico, 68,334,140 piasters; petroleum, 59,797,681 piasters; woolen stuffs, 54,674,420 piasters; flour, 43,845,052 piasters; cloth, 37,588,487 piasters; bar iron. 33,170,906 piasters; cotton and linen stuffs, 28,849,144 piasters; cashmere. 27,174,252 piasters; ready-made clothes. 25,737,262 piasters; sheep and goats, 25,636,376 piasters; fezzes, 22,588,869 piasters; coal, 21,767,627 piasters; hardware, 21,675,995 piasters; butter, 21,329,019 piasters; timber, 20,597,455 piasters; chemicals, 19,525,182 piasters; carpets, 17,316,582 piasters; silken goods, 16,306,303 piasters; leather, 15,084,416 piasters; corn. 14,334,426 piasters; spirits, 16,264,472 piasters; indigo-blue, 14,233,353 piasters; raw silk, 13,960,266 piasters; linen stuffs, 13,110,973 piasters; live animals, 12,412,905 piasters; iron tools, 11,549,850 piasters; skins,. 10,831,381 piasters;

maize, 6,784,054 piasters. The principal exports and their values were : raisins, 147,274,497 piasters ; wheat, 136,345,572 piasters ; raw silk, 97,632,138 piasters ; olive oil, 68,014,986 piasters ; mohair, 66,880,777 piasters : coffee, 64,-070,750 piasters ; opium, 62,938,572 piasters ; wool, 56,508,277 piasters ; cocoons, 55,266.001 piasters ; valonia, 51,184,191 piasters ; cotton, 50,081,639 piasters ; corn, 51,201,795 piasters ; figs, 46,822,702 piasters ; skins, 40,037,620 piasters ; minerals, 29,077,555 piasters ; nuts, 27,-196,512 piasters ; sesame, 23,501,097 piasters ; beans and lentils, 23,210,981 piasters ; carpets, 22,227,110 piasters ; chemicals, 21,833,839 piasters ; gall nuts, 14,270,222 piasters : dates, 16,-717,075 piasters ; oranges and lemons, 10,921,-150 piasters.

Navigation.—In 1890–91, 179,317 vessels of 30,509,861 tons entered and cleared the Turkish ports. Of these, 38,591 were steamers and 140,-726 were sailing vessels. Of the total number, 140,257 were Turkish, 14,053 Greek, 13,882 English, 4,041 Austrian, 1,998 French, 1,781 Russian, 1,651 Italian, 511 Swedish and Norwegian, 356 German, 167 Dutch, 155 Danish, 376 Montenegrin, and 139 from other countries. The merchant navy in 1891 was composed of 43 steamers of 26,553 tons, and 541 sailing vessels of 97,895 tons.

Posts and Telegraphs.—The post-office forwarded in 1888–89 through the internal service, 7,284,000 letters, 57,000 postal cards, and 539,-000 pieces of printed matter ; through the external service, 2,562,000 letters, 53,000 postal cards, and 567,000 pieces of printed matter ; in transit, 387,000 letters, 9,000 postal cards, and 180,000 pieces of printed matter. The receipts were 2,615,322 francs, and the expenses 1,571,-135 francs.

In 1889 the telegraph lines had a length of 32,-223 kilometers, with a length of wire of 50,707 kilometers. The cable lines were 597 kilometers long, with 642 kilometers of wire. The receipts amounted to 51,615,526 piasters, and the expenses to 17,669,044 piasters.

Railroads.—For the past few years the Government of Turkey has done much to extend the railroad system in general, and especially in the Syrian part of the Empire. The construction of three new lines has been undertaken, running through the northern and central portions of Asia Minor. The first of these lines starts from Haidar Pasha and runs right through the heart of Asia Minor to the Tigris Valley, and thence down to Bagdad and the Persian Gulf, thus connecting the latter gulf with the waters of the Golden Horn. The second road starts from Samsun, on the Black Sea, and runs southward to Ayas, on the Mediterranean Sea. The third line starts from Acre, on the Mediterranean Sea, and runs through Damascus and the Euphrates Valley to the Persian Gulf. The first line, undertaken by a German company, has already been carried to Angora, 440 miles from Constantinople. The construction of the second line has been granted to a Belgian company, which has completed the survey of the first section. The concession of the third line is held by an English company, which has begun the actual construction of the first portion running from Acre to Damascus. Leaving Acre, this line will run parallel with Acre Bay to the river Kishon, thence to and across the Plain of Esdraelon to Jezreel, through the narrow plain formed by the Galilean hills on the north and the range of Mount Gilboa on the south, passes the Gideon's Spring, along the whole length of the Jezreel Valley to the river Jordan. Crossing this famous river by a bridge 66 feet long, near the old bridge which has formed the highway from Egypt to Damascus from time immemorial, the line will cross the mountains on the southeastern shore of the Sea of Galilee to the Bashan plateau, thence in a northeastern direction to the city of Damascus. The length of this portion of the line will be 135 miles ; it will have a gauge of 4 feet 8½ inches, and is estimated to cost £1,900,000. The new railroad between Moudania, on the Sea of Marmora, and Broussa, a distance of about 42 kilometers, was opened for traffic on June 17, 1892. The total length of railroads in European Turkey in September, 1889, was 963 kilometers : in Asia Minor, 853 kilometers ; and in Syria, 88 kilometers.

Insurrection in Arabia.—The insurrection of the tribes of the Yemen province, which broke out in 1891, had assumed such large proportions, that, on the arrival of the Turkish re-enforcements under the leadership of Ahmed Fehzy Pasha, he found the whole country, with the exception of Sanaa and Amran, and of the plains, in the hands of the rebels. (See the "Annual Cyclopædia" for 1891.) The forces of the Turks had met reverse after reverse at the hands of the Arabs, and owing to bad equipment and lack of nourishment had become disorganized and discouraged, many falling an easy prey to the prevailing cholera. Sanaa was besieged by large forces of the Arabs, who were stationed on the mountains surrounding the city, pouring forth the contents of their guns and rifles and threatening to destroy the place completely. Several sorties were made by the besieged army with varying success. Just before re-enforcements arrived for the relief of the city the Turks had made a sortie and succeeded in driving the Arabs from their commanding position on the ridge of the Gibel Negum, with great slaughter and heavy losses to the Arabs, who retreated to Dar-es-Salem, south of Sanaa. The Turks, following up their success, turned their guns on that village and destroyed it, compelling the rebels to retreat still farther. The small forces of the Turks, however, were insufficient to enable them from preventing the Arabs regaining their former positions, and it was not until the arrival of the re-enforcement that the rebels finally retreated from Sanaa, leaving the plains surrounding the city covered with the corpses of the slain. The re-enforcements, led by Ahmed Fehzy Pasha, numbered about 16,000 men. The road leading from Hodaidah to Sanaa was occupied by the Arabs, and when Ahmed Fehzy Pasha advanced to the relief of the latter city he was met with small detachments of the rebel forces, who tried to stop his progress. The first encounter of any importance took place at Hojeila, a place 50 miles from Hodaidah. The road here leaves the plains and ascends the mountains. As soon as the Pasha heard of the advance of the Arabs he fortified his camp by throwing up earthworks, and received the enemy with an annihilating fire from his guns, doing serious injury to the Arabs, and compelling them to retreat. His onward march was attended with great difficulties, as the field guns had to be dragged up the mountains about 8,000 feet, but by hard labor this was accomplished, and Menakha was retaken a few days after the first encounter. From Menakha onward the Turkish army was constantly beset by bands of Arabs, but in spite of the difficulties of the road the Turks proceeded, using their field guns wherever serious resistance was made, and bombarding the villages along the road, which suffered heavily under the effective fire of the Turks. At Hajarat-ibn-Mehedi the rebels had taken up a strong position under Seyd-el-Sherai, and it took 12 days of fighting before the road was cleared, the chief and a large portion of the Arab forces being killed. The road to Sanaa was now open, and the Turks hastened to the relief of that city without a halt. After Sanaa was relieved, the Turkish army went north to Randah, which was easily taken, and leaving a small force there for its defense, they proceeded to the relief of Amran, which had suffered even greater hardships. On the approach of the Turkish army, the Arabs raised the siege and retired into the mountains. Ahmed Fehzy Pasha then returned to Sanaa and established his headquarters there, declared military law throughout the country, increased the price paid for rebels' heads, and sent expeditions into the southern section of the province, to retake the places then in the hands of the rebels and to punish the inhabitants on the road. The Turkish forces marched from Sanaa to Kataba, the southern frontier town on the road leading from Sanaa to Aden, and there encamped, retaking on the march Maaber, Damar, Yerim, Sedda, and Sobeh, almost without resistance, the inhabitants having taken refuge in the mountains, and leaving their houses to be destroyed by the Turks.

Although the tribes of the southern parts of the province had been brought to submission, the northern tribes were still in open revolt, and owing to their secure positions in the mountains it was difficult to make them submit with the force of Turkish soldiers that were in the field. Slowly, however, these tribes were conquered one after the other. On June 21, 1892, the town of Hafs, which was regarded as the center of the revolution, was taken with little resistance, the inhabitants having fled into the desert. The nomad tribes of Husseinie, led by Mehmed Reched, were dispersed, after a fierce struggle, by two battalions of Turkish troops under the command of Col. Rached Bey. In another direction, the Hachids were conquered and were compelled to give up the prisoners taken at the beginning of the revolt. The last place of refuge of the Arabs was Saade, about 130 miles north of Sanaa, which was taken by assault after a sanguinary fight. In September Ahmed Fehzy Pasha reported to the Ottoman Government that the insurrection was completely crushed, that Hamid-Eddin, the false Imaum, who had headed the rebels and directed their movements, had been killed, together with 20 of the chiefs acting under him, that the whole of Yemen was completely pacified, and that the Imperial troops were returning to Sanaa.

Outrage on American Missionaries.—On Aug. 19, 1892, news was received from the United States Chargé d'Affaires at Constantinople to the effect that the house of Dr. Bartlett, an American missionary at Burdur, in Asia Minor, had been burned, and that the life of the missionaries was in danger. At the time when Dr. Bartlett decided to build a house at that place, he was refused a permit to build unless he gave bonds to the local authorities guaranteeing that he would not instruct children or even hold religious services on the premises, this being based on orders from Constantinople. Remonstrances being made by the United States Legation at Constantinople to the effect that under the treaty rights Americans could not only hold lands but also enjoy the same, the Sultan yielded, and the permit was forwarded to Burdur, but when the house was barely finished, it was burnt down by riotous fanatics. A demand made by the United States Government for the protection of its citizens in Asia Minor and for an indemnity, was acquiesced in by the Turkish Government, and an indemnity of the full value of the unfurnished house burned as well as personal indemnity to Dr. Bartlett was tendered and accepted.

U

UNITED STATES. The Administration.—The only change in the Cabinet that took place in 1892 was occasioned by the sudden resignation of James G. Blaine, Secretary of State, on June 4. John W. Foster, of Indiana, was appointed in his place, and qualified on June 29.

The Judiciary.—The United States Supreme Court on March 1, 1892, affirmed the constitutionality of the McKinley tariff act. The death of Justice Joseph P. Bradley, of the third circuit, on Jan. 22, 1892, left a vacancy on the bench of the Supreme Court, which was filled by the appointment of George Shiras, Jr., of Pennsylvania, as Associate Justice.

The following departmental officers were appointed during the year : William M. Grinnell, of New York, third Assistant Secretary of State ; George M. Lambertson, of Nebraska, and J. H. Grear, of Iowa, Assistant Secretaries of the Treasury ; A. Barton Hepburn, of New York, Comptroller of the Currency ; Ernst G. Timme, of Wisconsin, fifth Auditor of the Treasury ; Charles H. Aldrich, of Illinois, Solicitor-General ; H. Clay Evans, of Tennessee, first Assistant Postmaster-General ; William M. Stone, of Iowa, Commissioner of the General Land Office ; and Mark M. Harrington, of Michigan, Chief of the Weather Bureau.

In the diplomatic service the principal appointments were the following : Frederick H. Grant, of Washington, Minister to Bolivia ; Rowland B. Mahany, of New York, Minister to Ecuador ; T. Jefferson Coolidge, of Massachusetts, Minister to France, in the place of Whitelaw Reid, resigned ; Frank L. Coombs, of California, Minister to Japan ; Andrew D. White, of New York, Minister to St. Petersburg ; A. Loudon Snowdon, of Pennsylvania, Minister to Spain ; David P. Thompson, of Oregon, Minister to Turkey ; William D. McCoy, of Indiana, Minister Resident

John Watson Foster was born in Pike County, Ind., March 2, 1836. He was graduated at the Indiana State University in 1855, studied law at Harvard, and practiced at Evansville, Ind., until the civil war broke out, when he entered the army as a major of volunteers, and served under Grant and Sherman in the West, becoming colonel of an Indiana regiment, and commanding the brigade of cavalry that occupied Knoxville in 1863. He edited the Evansville "Journal" after the war until 1873, when he was appointed United States Minister to Mexico by President Grant. President Hayes reappointed him to that post in 1880, and in March, 1881, transferred him to St. Petersburg. He resigned that mission in the following November, and settled in Washington, where he became counsel for some of the foreign legations in matters that came before commissions or were submitted to arbitration tribunals. In February, 1883, President Arthur appointed him Minister to Spain. After negotiating a commercial treaty, he resigned in March, 1885, and returned to the United States, but was sent over by President Cleveland on a special mission with the object of obtaining modifications in the terms, in which he was unsuccessful.

at Monrovia, Liberia ; and Watson R. Sperry, of Delaware, Minister Resident at Teheran, Persia.

Postal Service.—During 1891–92 the Government effected a saving of $1,000,000 on mail contracts. Free delivery was extended to 50 per cent. more offices, and the distribution of mail by cities on trains was increased in the same proportion. The ocean mail service to Central and South America and to Europe was greatly extended. The new mail contracts are made with 11 different steamship lines. The contractors will have to be provided with 41 ships, of 85,500 tons, and to complete this fleet they must spend $14,000,000. There will be weekly mails to Southampton, Boulogne, and Antwerp, carried by the new American line, which now has two of the fastest and finest ships on the ocean, the "City of Paris" and the "City of New York," naturalized by special act of Congress, and intends to build five more, of 10,000 tons each. The bill granting American registry to these ships provides that they may be used by the Government by charter or by purchase in case of war, as well as the other vessels of the same class and size which the company, formerly called the Inman

Company, undertakes to build in the United States. The contracts made with the lines sailing to South and Central America have increased the frequency and shortened the time of the trips, besides adding new ports of call, and have sustained lines that otherwise would have been withdrawn. There will be a tri-monthly service to La Guayra, both from New York and from Galveston, a weekly service from New York to Tuxpan, one to Cuba weekly, and one every 24 days to Rio. There is also a mail service to Buenos Ayres, the first ever carried under the American flag, once a week with calls or once in 28 days without. The daily free delivery service in villages has proved profitable, and Postmaster-General Wanamaker thinks that it should be introduced in country districts, whether it pays a profit or not. The collection of mail matter from letter boxes at house doors was tested in Washington and St. Louis, and it was found that the carriers lost no time. Accordingly an order was issued on Sept. 9, 1892, directing postmasters of free-delivery cities to have the mail taken up at the houses on any carrier's route where two-thirds of the householders desired it and equipped their houses with boxes of any of the kinds that have been found suitable and safe. The application of the merit system of promotion to departmental officials, to the classified offices, and to the railway mail has proved very satisfactory, and the Postmaster-General advocates making all promotions for merit alone, a permanent staff in the department with the exception of the Postmaster-General and the Fourth Assistant, the appointment of Deputy Postmaster-Generals

George Shiras, Jr., was born in Allegheny County, Pa., in 1832. He was graduated at Yale in 1853, studied for the bar, and became one of the leading lawyers of western Pennsylvania. He was once a candidate for the United States Senate, but was never active in politics. His deep knowledge of law, especially of the commercial branch, was recognized by the bench and bar. Justice Joseph P. Bradley died on Jan. 22, 1892, and President Harrison, after long deliberation, selected Mr. Shiras for the vacant judgeship, announcing the nomination on July 19.

for New York and San Francisco and a Comptroller in Washington, a reduction of hours of labor at almost all points, and the equalization and advance of the pay of employés. A reform that he thinks advisable and urgent. in view of the rapid growth of the service, which will soon have 100,000 offices and 250,000 or 300,000 employés, is the division of the country into postal districts, with a strongly centralized local organization and supervision,which would accomplish in a practical way the purpose of the bill to select fourth-class postmasters without political intervention, relieve members of Congress from departmental drudgery, and bring the department into touch with the employés, and the latter with the people whom they serve. Such an organization would be fit to handle the telegraph and telephone systems if they should be attached to the post-office department. Besides these services, the department should provide postal savings depositories and pneumatic tubes or electric devices for forwarding mail matter between stations in such cities as New York and Chicago. There is a prospect of one-cent letter postage, and that may even be the international rate. The two-cent rate pays double the cost of handling the letters, while heavy p   of advertising circulars and of books and periodicals, which are carried for a cent a pound, actually cost the department seven times more than they receive.

The number of post-offices on June 30, 1892, was 67,119, of which 3,156 were Presidential and 63,963 fourth-class offices. In the previous year the total number was 64,329. The post routes had a total length in 1892 of 447,591 miles. The revenue of the Department for the year was $70,930,475, and the expenditure $76,323,762. The expenses for salaries were $15.249,565 ; for transportation of the mails, $38,837,236.

Patents.—The total number of patents granted up to Oct. 25, 1892, was 485,158. About 25,000 patents are granted annually out of 40,000 applications. The receipts of the Patent Office for the year ending June 30, 1892, were $1,268,727, and the expenses were $1,114,134.   There was a balance in the Treasury to the credit of the Patent fund of $4,102,441. The expenses for salaries are about $650,000 a year, and for printing and lithographing, $400,000. The number of applications for patents in 1892 was 39,987 ; for design patents, 983 ; for reissues, 114 ; for registration of trade marks, 1,919 ; for registration of labels, 541 ; the number of caveats filed, 2,401. The number of patents issued was 23,- 626 ; of trade marks registered, 1,563. There were 3,622 patents withheld for non-payment of dues. During the year 12,427 patents expired.

Public Lands.—The vacant public lands of the United States are estimated at 567,586,783 acres, exclusive of Alaska, which has an area of 369,529,600 acres, and also of Indian reservations and the Indian lands and railroad grants which may hereafter be added to the public domain. The largest aggregate areas of unoccupied land in the individual States and Territories are 74,- 558,143 acres in Montana, 54,720,863 in New Mexico, 54,608,531 in Arizona, 52,055,248 in Wyoming, 50,132.241 in California, 42,385,734 in Nevada, 41,998,871 in Colorado, 38,435,873 in Oregon, 35,231,466 in Utah, and 34,225,449 in Idaho. There have been 36,681,527 acres forfeited by acts of Congress and restored to the public domain.   The public land grants for railroads and other public improvements in the beginning of 1892 comprised 46,317,226 acres.

The receipts from sales of public land in 1892 were $3,261.876. Of the total area vacant and subject to entry on June 30, 1892, the areas surveyed comprised 289,691,953 acres, and the unsurveyed portions 277,894,830 acres. In 1892 7,716,062 acres were entered under the Homestead acts, and under the Timber Culture act, 41,375.

Pensions.—There were on the pension rolls under the general law on June 30, 1892, 889,748 invalid pensioners of the army, a decrease of 23,849 during the year : 108,680 widows of soldiers, an increase of 120 ; 5,046 invalids of the navy, a decrease of 403 ; and 2,600 widows of sailors, an increase of 32. The following numbers were receiving pensions under the act of June 27, 1890 : army invalids, 283,734, an increase of 186,598 : widows of soldiers, 44,696, an increase of 32,487 ; invalids of the navy, 9,334, an increase of 5,858 ; widows of sailors, 9,917, an increase of 1,481. The surviving pensioners of the war of 1812 numbered 165, a decrease of 119, and of widows of soldiers of 1812, 6,651, a decrease of 939. The pensioners of the Mexican war numbered 15,215 veterans, 1,164 having died, and the widows 7,282, an increase of 306. The total number of pensioners on the rolls was 676,160 in 1891 and 876,068 in 1892, showing an increase in twelve months of 199,908. The total for 1892 comprised 703,242 invalid survivors and 172,826 widows. The number of applications filed during 1891–92 was 198,345. The number of claims allowed was 224,041, making a total of 1,236,291 since 1861. The aggregate amount of money paid out in pensions since 1861 was $1,418,348,211. The annual value of the new pensions allowed in 1892 is $25,668,802 ; of increase of pensions and reissued and additional pensions, $6,038,245 ; of renewed and restored pensions, $354,408. The total annual value of pensions paid in 1891 was $116,879,867, and in 1892 it was $139,035,612. For 1893 the sum appropriated is $144,956,000, which is less than the estimated amount required by $10,508,621. For 1894 the estimate is $165,- 000,000. The applicants in 1892 include 131,484 invalids and 31,282 widows under the act of June 27, 1890, and 395 survivors and 759 widows of the Mexican war. The claims allowed in 1892 include 162,896 invalids and 34,974 widows under the act of 1890 and 416 survivors of the war with Mexico.

Indians.—The total number of Indians in the United States, according to the census, is 249,273, exclusive of those of Alaska. This includes 32,- 567 who are taxable and self-sustaining. The number on the Indian reservations or in schools under the control of the Indian Office is 133.382, inclusive of 68,371 Indians and colored people of the five civilized nations who are controlled by the Indian Office, though self-supporting. The Cherokee nation numbers 25,387 Indians and 4,202 colored ; the Chickasaws have 3,464 Indians and 3,718 colored ; the Choctaws, 9,996 Indians and 4,401 colored ; the Creeks, 9,291 Indians and 5,341 colored ; the Seminoles, 2,539 Indians and 22 colored. The New Mexico Pueblos number 8,278 ; the Six Nations, 5,304 ; the eastern Cherokees in North Carolina, 2,885 ; Apaches held as prisoners of war, 384 ; and Indians in penitentiaries, 184. There are, exclusive of the Pueblos, 20.521 Indians in New Mexico, 19,845 in South Dakota, 16,740 in Arizona, 15,283 in California, 10,837 in Washington, 8,892 in Wisconsin, 7,952 in North Dakota, and smaller numbers in Michigan, Oklahoma, Oregon, Utah, Idaho, and elsewhere.

Foreign Relations. — Reciprocity treaties under the tariff act of Oct. 1, 1890, known as the McKinley law, were concluded with the majority of the countries of North and South America and of the commercial powers of Europe under separate arrangements with each of them. The treaty with Brazil was the first, having been proclaimed on Feb. 5, 1891. A treaty with Spain for Cuba and Porto Rico was proclaimed on July 31, and one with Santo Domingo on Aug. 1, 1891. The treaty with Salvador was proclaimed on Dec. 31, 1891. The treaty with Germany, proclaimed on Feb. 1, 1892, provides that American wheat and rye shall pay a duty of 3.50 marks per 100 kilograms, and maize 1.60 marks. A treaty with Great Britain for British Guiana, Trinidad, Tobago, Barbadoes, and the Leeward and Windward Islands, excepting Grenada, was proclaimed on Feb. 1, 1891. A treaty with Nicaragua was proclaimed on March 12, 1891, one with Honduras on April 12, and one with Guatemala on May 18. One with Austria-Hungary, in which American products are subjected to the favorable terms contained in the treaty between Austria and Germany, was proclaimed on May 26. On March 15 the existing reciprocity treaty with Hayti was suspended, no arrangement under the McKinley law having been concluded.

An extradition treaty between France and the United States was signed at Paris on March 26, 1892. The difficulty with Chili regarding the killing and wounding of American sailors by rioters in Valparaiso was settled by the withdrawal of Minister Matta's offensive note, accompanied with an apology for the riots, on Jan. 25, 1892, and the subsequent tender and payment by the Chilian Government of $75,000 as an indemnity to the families of the sailors of the Baltimore who were killed, and to those who were wounded. A convention was signed for the submission to arbitration of the mutual claims of Chilian and United States citizens, many of which have been pending for years and have hitherto been the subject of unfruitful diplomatic correspondence. On April 12, 1892, the United States Government paid over to the Government of Italy $25,000, which was accepted as an indemnity to be distributed among the families of Italian subjects who were lynched in New Orleans, thus closing the affair.

The Senate, altering its previous decision, authorized the President to ratify the general act of the Brussels Anti-Slavery Conference, and on Feb. 2, 1892, the United States Minister at Brussels handed the ratification to the Belgian Minister of Foreign Affairs. The protocol reproduces the resolution passed by the Senate, to the effect that the United States intend to remain neutral as regards territorial questions in Africa which may require international adjustment. To this proposition all the signatory powers have assented.

A treaty providing for the submission to arbitration of the dispute between the United States and Great Britain with regard to the killing of seals in the Bering Sea was concluded on Feb. 29, 1892. The treaty was ratified by the Senate

without opposition on March 29, accompanied by an agreement prohibiting pelagic sealing pending the arbitration. In November, 1891, Mr. Blaine had consented that the matters in dispute should be referred to a tribunal of 7 members, one of whom would represent Canada, one Great Britain, and two the United States, while the remaining members should be selected from other nations. A convention renewing the *modus vivendi* was agreed to after some correspondence. By it the Government of Great Britain agreed to prohibit, so long as the arbitration was pending, all killing of seals in that part of Bering Sea which lies eastward of the line of demarcation laid down in the Russian treaty of cession, and to use its best efforts to insure the observance of the prohibition by British subjects and vessels. The United States Government agreed on its part to prohibit sealing, beyond the killing of 7,500 seals to provide means for the subsistence of the natives, and to use its best efforts to insure the observance of the prohibition by citizens and vessels of the United States. Every vessel offending against the prohibition by hunting seals in Bering Sea could be seized and detained by the naval officers of either contracting power, but should be handed over as soon as practicable to the authorities of the nation to which they respectively belong, who alone should have jurisdiction to try and punish them. The British Government Commissioners should be permitted to visit and remain on the seal islands at any time for the purpose of collecting evidence to present to the the arbitration tribunal. If the result of the arbitration should affirm the right of British sealers to take seals in Bering Sea within the bounds claimed by the United States, then compensation should be made by the United States for the loss to British subjects incurred by abstaining from the exercise of the right pending the arbitration, calculated on the basis of such regulated catch as in the opinion of the arbitrators might be taken without diminution of the seal herds. If, on the other hand, the result of the arbitration should be to deny the right of British sealers to take seals in these waters, then the British Government should pay compensation to the United States on the basis of the difference between 7,500 seals and such catch as the arbitrators judge might have been taken without undue diminution of the herds. The convention runs till Oct. 31, 1893, and may be denounced by either party after that date on two months' notice being given. It was signed by Secretary Blaine and Sir Julian Pauncefote at Washington on April 18, 1892, and was confirmed by the Senate on the following day. Under the instructions issued by Secretary Tracy on May 1, any vessel found sealing in Bering Sea was to be seized without previous warning, and the presence of a vessel in Bering Sea with a sealing outfit was sufficient warrant for her seizure. All persons on board a captured vessel were to be sent as prisoners with the vessel to suffer the penalty provided by law. The American law imposed a penalty of 6 months' imprisonment and a fine of $1,000, and the British law a fine of $500 and imprisonment at hard labor not to exceed 6 months, on all persons killing or abetting the killing of fur seals in Bering Sea.

The ratifications of the treaty of arbitration were exchanged in the beginning of September. The powers which were asked to appoint the three neutral arbitrators were France, Italy, and Sweden. The United States Government selected as its representatives in the arbitration tribunal Justice Harland, of the Supreme Court, and Senator Morgan, of Alabama. The counsel for the United States were Mr. Phelps, ex-Minister to Great Britain ; James C. Carter, of New York ; and Judge Henry Blodgett, of the United States District Court. John Foster was appointed agent to prepare the case and represent the United States Government officially before the Arbitration Board. The French Government selected Baron Alphonse de Courcel to act as the French member of the Arbitration Commission. The Italian member was the Marchese Emilio Visconti-Venosta. The arbitration treaty provided that each of the parties to the controversy should deliver in duplicate to each of the arbitrators and to the agent of the opposite party an original presentation of its case, accompanied by the documents, the official correspondence, and other evidence and statements, within a period not to exceed 4 months from the date of the exchange of ratifications. Each side has then 3 months in which to consider and digest the original case and submit a counter case, but either party may, on giving notice within 30 days after receiving the case of the opposite side, demand an additional period not to exceed 60 days, or 5 months in all, in which to gather further evidence to be presented in its counter case. After the presentation of the counter case 30 days are allowed for the submission of printed arguments which may be supported before the Commission of Arbitration by oral argument.

While the seals were on their way to the breeding grounds, a large number were taken by Canadian and American sealers—probably as many as 35,000 ; and many more were captured in Bering Sea by the unusually large fleet of sealing vessels that were sent out early from British Columbia, and began their operations before the United States revenue and naval vessels were on the ground. The British naval authorities co-operated with the American, and the shooting of seals at sea, which is destructive to the stock, because a large proportion of those killed are gravid females, was effectually stopped in Bering Sea, especially after the capture of the tender of the Canadian sealing fleet with the provisions for the season and several thousand skins aboard, on June 22, by the revenue cutter "Corwin." This vessel, the "Coquillon," was seized for discharging cargo 3 miles off shore at Tonki, in contravention of the United States revenue laws. About 25 sealing vessels were also captured in Alaskan waters for violating the *modus vivendi.*

A conference to discuss reciprocal commercial arrangements with Canada took place, at the suggestion of the Canadian Government at Washington. Secretary Blaine acted for the United States Government, and the British Minister and three members of the Dominion Government, who acted as commissioners of the British Government, represented Canada. The conference came to naught because the Canadian Government was only prepared to offer the admission of natural products in exchange for the concessions asked, being precluded from granting favored rates to the United States as against the mother country. The discussion was therefore

terminated by Mr. Blaine. The conference resulted, however, in signing a convention for the survey of the Alaskan boundary and the waters of Passamaquoddy Bay adjacent to Eastport, Maine, and in an agreement for the protection of fish life in the conterminous and neighboring waters on the northern boundary of the United States. A controversy with Canada regarding discriminative tolls imposed on American vessels in the Welland Canal was presented to Congress, and an act was passed and signed by the President on July 26, 1892, empowering the Administration to apply retaliatory measures. It provided for the imposition of tolls in the St. Mary's Falls, or Sault Ste. Marie, Canal on all Canadian vessels or American vessels bound for Canadian ports. The Canadian Government imposed a toll of 20 cents a ton on all freight passing through the Welland Canal in transit to places in the United States, and a further toll on all United States vessels and on passengers in transit to ports of the United States. On grain shipped to Montreal or ports farther east for export, a rebate of 18 cents was allowed. This discrimination was a violation of the Treaty of Washington, concluded on May 8, 1871, and accordingly the President made use of the authority granted by the act of Congress, and on Aug. 20 issued a proclamation ordering that from Sept. 1, 1892, a toll of 20 cents a ton should be collected on freight passing through the St. Mary's Falls Canal in transit to any Canadian port, whether carried in vessels of the United States or of other nations.

An extradition treaty with Germany, which included embezzlement, obtaining money by false pretenses, perjury, assaults upon females, and mutiny and other crimes committed on the high seas among the extraditable offenses, was proposed by Minister Phelps in Berlin, and was discussed, but was not concluded, chiefly because the United States Government could not see its way to undertaking the police and legal business connected with the extradition of German fugitives from justice.

The Chinese Minister in Washington filed a protest against the Chinese exclusion bill after it was passed, making the following objections : (1) It renewed the Scott act of 1888. (2) It deprived Chinese subjects of the right of bail in *habeas corpus* cases. (3) It required the registration of Chinese laborers under conditions with which it was impossible for them to comply, because a Chinaman who was in the United States previous to the first exclusion act in 1882 would have to produce white witnesses to prove that he was in the country at that time. These features of the bill were in violation of the treaty of 1880, executed in Pekin at the request of the United States Government, which guaranteed to Chinese laborers in the United States the treatment accorded to the subjects of the most favored nations.

A proposal to invite the governments of commercial nations to an international conference on bimetallism was approved by the Senate, and the principal governments of Europe accepted the invitation issued on April 21, 1892, to take part, Great Britain and some others declaring at the same time that they could not be bound by any conclusions reached by the Conference.

The following delegates were selected to represent the United States : Senators William B. Allison, of Iowa, and John P. Jones, of Nevada ; Congressman James B. McCreary, of Kentucky ; E. O.eLeecb, Director of the Mint ; E. Benjamin Andrews, President of Brown University ; Ronald P. Falkner, of the University of Pennsylvania ; H. W. Cannon, President of the Chase National Bank ; and James T. Morgan. Thomas T. Keller, and Thomas W. Cridler. The Conference met at Brussels, Belgium, on Nov. 22. The proposals submitted by the United States delegates and the substitute plan suggested by the British representatives, as well as other suggestions, were not easy to harmonize, and the divergent views and interests of the various countries admitted of no speedy compromise or satisfactory conclusion. For that reason the Conference suspended its sittings on Dec. 17, and adjourned till May 13, 1893.

Republican Convention.— The 10th National Convention of the Republican party met at Minneapolis on June 7, 1892. Three days before, James G. Blaine had resigned the post of Secretary of State in order to compete for the nomination. The contest was chiefly between his supporters and those of President Harrison, though ex-Governor McKinley of Ohio, the author of the new protective tariff, was also a strong candidate. J. Sloat Fassett, of New York, was elected temporary chairman. The Committee on Resolutions, of which Joseph B. Foraker, of Ohio, was chairman, drew up the following platform, which was unanimously adopted by the Convention in the evening session of June 10.

The representatives of the Republicans of the United States, assembled in general convention on the shores of the Mississippi River, the everlasting bond of an indestructible Republic, whose most glorious chapter of history is the record of the Republican party, congratulate their countrymen on the majestic march of the nation under the banners inscribed with the principles of our platform of 1888, vindicated by victory at the polls and prosperity in our fields, workshops, and mines, and make the following declaration of principles :

Protection.—We reaffirm the American doctrine of protection. We call attention to its growth abroad. We maintain that the prosperous condition of our country is largely due to the wise revenue legislation of the Republican Congress. We believe that all articles which cannot be produced in the United States, except luxuries, should be admitted free of duty, and that on all imports coming into competition with the products of American labor there should be levied duties equal to the difference between wages abroad and at home. We assert that the prices of manufactured articles of general consumption have been reduced under the operations of the tariff act of 1890. We denounce the efforts of the Democratic majority of the House of Representatives to destroy our tariff laws piecemeal, as is manifested by their attacks upon wool, lead, and lead ores, the chief products of a number of States, and we ask the people for their judgment thereon.

Reciprocity.—We point to the success of the Republican policy of reciprocity, under which our export trade has vastly increased, and new and enlarged markets have been opened for the products of our farms and workshops. We remind the people of the bitter opposition of the Democratic party to this practical business measure, and claim that, executed by a Republican Administration, our present laws will eventually give us control of the trade of the world.

Silver.—The American people, from tradition and interest, favor bimetallism, and the Republican party demands the use of both gold and silver as standard money, with such restrictions and under such provisions, to be determined by legislation, as will secure the maintenance of the parity of values of the two metals, so that the purchasing and debt-paying power of the dollar, whether of silver, gold, or paper, shall be at all times equal. The interests of the producers of the country, its farmers and its workingmen, demand that every dollar, paper or coin, issued by the Government shall be as good as any other. We commend the wise and patriotic steps already taken by our Government to secure an international conference to adopt such measures as will insure a parity of value between gold and silver for use as money throughout the world.

Free Ballot and Fair Count.— We demand that every citizen of the United States shall be allowed to cast one free and unrestricted ballot in all public elections, and that such ballot shall be counted and returned as cast ; that such laws shall be enacted and enforced as will secure to every citizen, be he rich or poor, native or foreign born, white or black, this sovereign right guaranteed by the Constitution. The free and honest popular ballot, the just and equal representation of all the people, as well as their just and equal protection under the laws, are the foundation of our Republican institutions, and the party will never relax its efforts until the integrity of the ballot and the purity of elections shall be fully guaranteed and protected in every State.

Southern Outrages.— We denounce the continued inhuman outrages perpetrated upon American citizens for political reasons in certain Southern States of the Union.

Foreign Relations.—We favor the extension of our foreign commerce, the restoration of our mercantile marine by home-built ships, and the creation of a Navy for the protection of our National interests and the honor of our flag ; the maintenance of the most friendly relations with all foreign Powers, entangling alliances with none, and the protection of the rights of our fishermen. We reaffirm our approval of the Monroe Doctrine, and believe in the achievement of the manifest destiny of the Republic in its broadest sense. We favor the enactment of more stringent laws and regulations for the restriction of criminal, pauper, and contract immigration.

Miscellaneous.—We favor efficient legislation by Congress to protect the life and limbs of employés of transportation companies engaged in carrying on interstate commerce, and recommend legislation by the respective States that will protect employés engaged in State commerce, and in mining and manufacturing.

The Republican party has always been the champion of the oppressed, and recognizes the dignity of manhood, irrespective of faith, color, or nationality ; it sympathizes with the cause of Home Rule in Ireland, and protests against the persecution of the Jews in Russia.

The ultimate reliance of free popular government is the intelligence of the people and the maintenance of freedom among men. We therefore declare anew our devotion to liberty of thought and conscience, of speech and press, and approve all agencies and instrumentalities which contribute to the education of the children of the land ; but, while insisting upon the fullest measure of religious liberty, we are opposed to any union of Church and State.

Trusts.—We reaffirm our opposition, declared in the Republican platform of 1888, to all combinations of capital organized, in trust or otherwise, to control arbitrarily the condition of trade among our citizens. We heartily indorse the action already taken upon this subject, and ask for such further legislation as may be required to remedy any defects in existing laws and to render their enforcement more complete and effective.

Post-office Reforms.—We approve the policy of extending to towns, villages, and rural communities the advantages of the free delivery service now enjoyed by the larger cities of the country, and reaffirm the declaration contained in the Republican platform of 1888, pledging the reduction of letter postage to one cent at the earliest possible moment consistent with the maintenance of the Post-office Department and the highest class of postal service.

Civil Service Reform.—We commend the spirit and evidence of reform in the civil service and the wise and consistent enforcement by the Republican party of the laws regulating the same.

The Nicaragua Canal.—The construction of the Nicaragua Canal is of the highest importance to the American people, both as a measure of national defense and to build up and maintain American commerce, and it should be controlled by the United States Government.

Admission of the Territories.—We favor the admission of the remaining Territories at the earliest possible date, having due regard to the interests of the people, of the Territories, and of the United States. All the Federal officers appointed for the Territories should be selected from *bona fide* residents thereof, and the right of self-government should be accorded as far as practicable.

Cession of the Arid Public Lands.—We favor the cession, subject to the homestead laws, of the arid public lands, to the States and Territories in which they lie, under such congressional restrictions as to disposition, reclamation, and occupancy by settlers as will secure the maximum benefits to the people.

The World's Fair.—The World's Columbian Exposition is a great national undertaking, and Congress should promptly enact such reasonable legislation in aid thereof as will insure a discharge of the expenses and obligations incident thereto, and the attainment of results commensurate with the dignity and progress of the nation.

The Liquor Traffic.—We sympathize with all wise and legitimate efforts to lessen and prevent the evils of intemperance and promote morality.

Soldiers' Pensions.—Ever mindful of the service and sacrifices of the men who saved the life of the nation, we pledge anew to the veteran soldiers of the Republic a watchful care and recognition of their just claims upon a grateful people.

President Harrison's Administration.—We commend the able, patriotic, and thoroughly American administration of President Harrison. Under it the country has enjoyed remarkable prosperity, and the dignity and honor of the nation, at home and abroad, have been faithfully maintained, and we offer the record of pledges kept, as a guaranty of faithful performance in the future.

On June 11 Senator Edward O. Wolcott, of Colorado, nominated for President James G. Blaine, and ex-Secretary of the Navy R. W. Thompson, of Indiana, nominated Benjamin Harrison. There were 904 delegates present, making the number necessary for a choice 453. President Harrison was renominated on the first ballot, receiving 535 votes, or a clear majority of 166. His plurality over Blaine, who received 182 votes, was 353. McKinley also received 182 votes; while 4 were cast for ex-Speaker Reed, and 1 was given to Robert Lincoln, Minister at London. In the evening Whitelaw Reid, of New York, was nominated for Vice-President by Edmund O'Connor, of New York, and the nomination was made unanimous. Thomas B. Reed, of Maine, was also put in nomination, but he withdrew his name before a ballot was taken.

Democratic Convention.—The National Convention of the Democratic party met in Chicago on June 21, 1892. William C. Owens, of Kentucky, was made temporary chairman, and William L. Wilson, of West Virginia, permanent chairman. The struggle for the nomination was chiefly confined to the friends of ex-President Cleveland and the adherents of Senator Hill, of New York. The latter had called together an early State convention at Albany on Feb. 22, and chosen delegates who were instructed to vote for Hill. On May 31 a rival convention of the Anti-Snapper New York Democrats met in Syracuse, and chose contesting delegates, who went to Chicago, but were not admitted. There were several candidates who were put forward as the second choice, in case the Convention should be so equally divided between Cleveland and Hill that neither could obtain the nomination. The strongest of these was Gov. Boies of Iowa, whose friends worked hard to bring him to the front as one of the principal candidates on the strength of his having won the governorship of a State that had always been Republican.

The platform prepared by the committee on resolutions was adopted, with the exception of the tariff plank, which was altered at the instance of Cleveland's opponents into a demand for a tariff for revenue only. The platform as adopted was as follows:

The representatives of the Democratic party of the United States, in National convention assembled, do reaffirm their allegiance to the principles of the party as formulated by Jefferson and exemplified by the long and illustrious line of his successors in Democratic leadership from Madison to Cleveland; we believe the public welfare demands that these principles be applied to the conduct of the Federal Government through the accession to power of the party that advocates them, and we solemnly declare that the need of a return to these fundamental principles of a free popular government based on home rule and individual liberty was never more urgent than now, when the tendency to centralize all power at the Federal Capital has become a menace to the reserved rights of the States that strikes at the very roots of our Government under the Constitution as framed by the fathers of the Republic.

Elections Bill.—We warn the people of our common country, jealous for the preservation of their free institutions, that the policy of Federal control of elections, to which the Republican party has committed itself, is fraught with the gravest dangers, scarcely less momentous than would result from a revolution practically establishing monarchy on the ruins of the Republic. It strikes at the North as well as the South, and injures the colored citizens even more than the white; it means a horde of deputy marshals at every polling place armed with Federal power, returning boards appointed and controlled by Federal authority, the outrage of the electoral rights of the people in the several States, subjugation of the colored people to the control of the party in power and the reviving of race antagonisms now happily abated, of the utmost peril to the safety and happiness of all, a measure deliberately and justly described by a leading Republican Senator as "the most infamous bill that ever crossed the threshold of the Senate." Such a policy, if sanctioned by law, would mean the dominance of a self-perpetuating oligarchy of office-holders, and the party first intrusted with its machinery could be dislodged from power only by an appeal to the reserved rights of the people to resist oppression which is inherent in all self-governing communities.

Two years ago this revolutionary policy was emphatically condemned by the people at the polls, but in contempt of that verdict the Republican party has defiantly declared in its latest authoritative utterance that its success in the coming elections will mean the enactment of the Force bill, and the usurpation of despotic control over elections in all the States. Believing that the preservation of republican government in the United States is dependent upon the defeat of this policy of legalized force and fraud, we invite the support of all citizens who desire to see the Constitution maintained in its integrity with the laws pursuant thereto which have given our country a hundred years of unexampled prosperity; and we pledge the Democratic party, if it be intrusted with power, not only to the defeat of the Force bill, but also to relentless opposition to the Republican policy of profligate expenditure which, in the short space of two years, has squandered an enormous surplus, emptied an overflowing Treasury, after piling new burdens of taxation upon the already overtaxed labor of the country.

Tariff.—We denounce Republican protection as a fraud, a robbery of the great majority of the American people for the benefit of the few. We declare it to be a fundamental principle of the Democratic party that the Federal Government has no constitutional power to impose and collect tariff duties, except for the purpose of revenue only, and we demand that the collection of such taxes shall be limited to the necessities of the Government when honestly and economically administered. We denounce the McKinley tariff law enacted by the LIst Congress as the culminating atrocity of class legislation; we indorse the efforts made by the Democrats of the present Congress to modify its most oppressive feature in the direction of free raw materials and cheaper manufactured goods that enter into general consumption, and we promise its repeal as one of the beneficent results that will follow the action of the people in intrusting power to the Democratic party. Since the McKinley tariff went into operation there have been ten reductions of the wages of the laboring man to one increase. We deny that there has been any increase of prosperity to the country since that tariff went into operation, and we point to the dullness and distress, the wage reductions and strikes in the iron trade, as the best possible evidence that no such prosperity has resulted under the McKinley act. We call the attention of thoughtful Americans to the fact that after thirty years of restrictive taxes against the importation of foreign wealth, in exchange for our agricultural surplus, the homes and farms of the country have become burdened with a real estate mortgage debt of over $2,500,000,000, exclusive of all other forms of indebtedness; that in one of the chief agricultural States of the West there appears a real estate mortgage debt averaging $165 per capita of the total population, and that similar conditions and tendencies are shown to exist in other agricultural exporting States. We denounce a policy which fosters no industry so much as it does that of the sheriff.

Reciprocity.—Trade interchange on the basis of reciprocal advantages to the countries participating is a time-honored doctrine of the Democratic faith, but we denounce the sham reciprocity which juggles with the people's desire for enlarged foreign markets and freer exchanges by pretending to establish closer trade relations for a country whose articles of export are almost exclusively agricultural products with other countries that are also agricultural, while erecting a custom-house barrier of prohibitive tariff taxes against the rich and the countries of the world that stand ready to take our entire surplus of products and to exchange therefor commodities which are necessaries and comforts of life among our people.

Trusts.—We recognize in the trusts and combinations which are designed to enable capital to secure more than its just share of the joint product of capital and labor, a natural consequence of the prohibitive taxes which prevent the free competition which is the life of honest trade, but believe their worst evils can be abated by law, and we demand the rigid enforcement of the laws made to prevent and control them, together with such further legislation in restraint of their abuses as experience may show to be necessary.

The Republican party, while professing a policy of reserving the public land for small holdings by actual settlers, has given away the people's heritage, until now a few railroads and non-resident aliens, individual and corporate, possess a larger area than that of all our farms between the two seas. The last Democratic administration reversed the improvident and unwise policy of the Republican party touching the public domain, and reclaimed from corporations and syndicates, alien and domestic, and restored to the people nearly one hundred million acres of valuable land to be sacredly held as homesteads for our citizens, and we pledge ourselves to continue this policy until every acre of land so unlawfully held shall be reclaimed and restored to the people.

Silver.—We denounce the Republican legislation known as the Sherman act of 1890 as a cowardly makeshift, fraught with possibilities of danger in the future, which should make all of its supporters, as well as its author, anxious for its speedy repeal. We hold to the use of both gold and silver as the standard money of the country, and to the coinage of both gold and silver without discriminating against either metal or charge for mintage, but the dollar unit of coinage of both metals must be of equal intrinsic and exchangeable value, or be adjusted through international agreement, or by such safeguards of legislation as shall insure the maintenance of the parity of the two metals, and the equal power of every dollar at all times in the markets, and in payment of debt; and we demand that all paper currency shall be kept at par with and redeemable in such coin. We insist upon this policy as especially necessary for the protection of the farmers and laboring classes, the first and most defenseless victims of unstable money and a fluctuating currency.

Tax on State Banks.—We recommend that the prohibitory ten per cent. tax on State bank issues be repealed.

Civil Service Reform.—Public office is a public trust. We reaffirm the declaration of the Democratic National Convention of 1876, for the reform of the civil service, and we call for the honest enforcement of all laws regulating the same. The nomination of a President as in the recent Republican Convention, by delegations composed largely of his appointees, holding office at his pleasure, is a scandalous satire upon free popular institutions, and a startling illustration of the methods by which a President may gratify his ambition. We denounce a policy under which the Federal office-holders usurp control of party conventions in the States, and we pledge the Democratic party to reform these and all other abuses which threaten individual liberty and local self-government.

Our Foreign Policy.—The Democratic party is the only party that has ever given the country a foreign policy consistent and vigorous, compelling respect abroad and inspiring confidence at home. While avoiding entangling alliances, it has aimed to cultivate friendly relations with other nations, and especially with our neighbors on the American continent, whose destiny is closely linked with our own, and we view with alarm the tendency to a policy of irritation and bluster which is liable at any time to confront us with the alternative of humiliation or war. We favor the maintenance of a navy strong enough for all purposes of national defense and to properly maintain the honor and dignity of the country abroad.

Sympathy with the Oppressed.—This country has always been the refuge of the oppressed from every land—exiles for conscience' sake—and in the spirit of the founders of our Government we condemn the oppression practiced by the Russian Government upon its Lutheran and Jewish subjects, and we call upon our National Government, in the interest of justice and humanity, by all just and proper means, to use its prompt and best efforts to bring about a cessation of these cruel persecutions in the dominions of the Czar and to secure to the oppressed equal rights.

Irish Home Rule.—We tender our profound and earnest sympathy to those lovers of freedom who are struggling for home rule and the great cause of local self-government in Ireland.

Immigration.—We heartily approve all legitimate efforts to prevent the United States from being used as the dumping ground for the known criminals and professional paupers of Europe, and we demand the rigid enforcement of the laws against Chinese immigration or the importation of foreign workmen under contract, to degrade American labor and lessen its wages, but we condemn and denounce any and all attempts to restrict the immigration of the industrious and worthy of foreign lands.

Soldiers' Pensions.—This convention hereby renews the expression of appreciation of the patriotism of the soldiers and sailors of the Union in the war for its preservation, and we favor just and liberal pensions for all disabled Union soldiers, their widows and dependents, but we demand that the work of the Pension Office shall be done industriously, impartially, and honestly. We denounce the present administration of that office as incompetent, corrupt, disgraceful, and dishonest.

Improvement of Waterways.—The Federal Government should care for and improve the Mississippi River and other great waterways of the Republic, so as to secure for the interior States easy and cheap transportation to the tidewater. When any waterway of the Republic is of sufficient importance to demand the aid of the Government, such aid should be extended on a definite plan of continuous work until permanent improvement is secured.

The Nicaragua Canal.—For purposes of national defense and the promotion of commerce between the States, we recognize the early construction of the Nicaragua Canal and its protection against foreign control as of great importance to the United States.

The World's Columbian Fair.—Recognizing the World's Columbian Exposition as a national undertaking of vast importance, in which the General Government has invited the co-operation of all the powers of the world, and appreciating the acceptance by many of such powers of the invitation so extended, and the broad and liberal efforts being made by them to contribute to the grandeur of the undertaking, we are of opinion that Congress should make such necessary financial provision as shall be requisite to the maintenance of the national honor and public faith.

Freedom of Education.—Popular education being the only safe basis of popular suffrage, we recommend to the several States most liberal appropriations for the public schools. Free common schools are the nursery of good government, and they have always received the fostering care of the Democratic party, which favors every means of increasing intelligence. Freedom of education, being an essential of civil and religious liberty, as well as a necessity of the development of intelligence, must not be interfered with under any pretext whatever. We are opposed to State interference with parental rights and rights of conscience in the education of children as an infringement of the fundamental Democratic doctrine that the largest individual liberty consistent with the rights of others insures the highest type of American citizenship and the best government.

Admission of Territories.—We approve the action of the present House of Representatives in passing bills for admitting into the Union as States the Territories of New Mexico and Arizona, and we favor the early admission of all the Territories having the necessary population and resources to entitle them to statehood, and while they remain territories we hold that the officials appointed to administer the government of any territory, together with the District of Columbia and Alaska, should be *bona fide* residents of the territory or district in which their duties are to be performed. The Democratic party believes in home rule and the control of their own affairs by the people of the vicinage.

Protection of Railway Employés.—We favor legislation by Congress and State legislatures to protect the lives and limbs of railway employés and those of other hazardous transportation companies, and denounce the inactivity of the Republican party, and particularly the Republican Senate, for causing the defeat of measures beneficial and protective to this class of wage workers.

Labor Evils.—We are in favor of the enactment by the States of laws for abolishing the notorious sweating system, for abolishing contract convict labor, and for prohibiting the employment in factories of children under fifteen years of age.

Sumptuary Laws.—We are opposed to all sumptuary law as an interference with the individual rights of the citizen.

The platform, as reported from the Committee on Resolutions, contained this declaration, as the first paragraph of Sec. 3, with the heading " Revenue Tariffs " :

We reiterate the oft-repeated doctrines of the Democratic party that the necessity of the government is the only justification for taxation, and whenever a tax is unnecessary it is unjustifiable ; that when custom-house taxation is levied upon articles of any kind produced in this country, the difference between the cost of labor here and labor abroad, when such a difference exists, fully measures any possible benefits to labor, and the enormous additional impositions of the existing tariff fall with crushing force upon our farmers and workingmen, and for the mere advantage of the few whom it enriches, exact from labor a grossly unjust share of the expenses of the Government, and we demand such a revision of the tariff laws as will remove their iniquitous inequalities, lighten their oppressions, and put them on a constitutional and equitable basis. But in making reduction in taxes it is not proposed to injure any domestic industries, but rather to promote their healthy growth. From the foundation of this Government taxes collected at the custom house have been the chief source of Federal revenue. Such they must continue to be. Moreover, many industries have come to rely upon legislation for successful continuance, so that any change of law must be at every step regardful of the labor and capital thus involved. The process of reform must be subject in the execution of this plain dictate of justice.

On motion of Lawrence T. Neal, of Ohio, the above paragraph was struck from the platform, and the plank contained in the platform as given above was substituted by a majority of 564 to 342, including 40 negative votes that were counted with the majority under the unit rule. Gov. Leon Abbett of New Jersey presented the name of Grover Cleveland, of New York, for President ; William C. DeWitt, of New York, nominated David B. Hill ; and John F. Duncombe, of Iowa, brought forward the name of Horace Boies. Mr. Cleveland was nominated on the first ballot, receiving 617 out of 909 ballots, 10 more than the two-thirds majority that was necessary for a choice. The vote for Hill was 114 and for Boies 103, while Arthur P. Gorman received 36, Adlai E. Stevenson 16, John G. Carlisle 14, William R. Morrison 3, James E. Campbell 2, Robert E. Pattison 1, William E. Russell 1, and William C. Whitney 1. On June 23, Adlai E. Stevenson, of Illinois, was put forward for Vice-President by Nicholas E. Worthington, of Illinois, and received 402 votes, while Isaac P. Gray received 343, Allen B. Morse 86, John L. Mitchell 45, Henry Watterson 26, Bourke Cockran 5, and Lambert Tree and Horace Boies 1 each. Mr. Stevenson was then nominated unanimously by acclamation.

People's Party Convention. — The People's party held its National Convention at Omaha on July 2. C. H. Eddington, of Georgia, was chosen temporary, and H. L. Loucks, of South Dakota, permanent, chairman. The platform adopted on July 4 consisted of a preamble and a declaration of principles running as follows :

The conditions which surround us best justify our co-operation. We meet in the midst of a nation brought to the verge of moral, political, and material ruin. Corruption dominates the ballot box, the legislatures, the Congress, and touches even the ermine of the Bench. The people are demoralized ; most of the States have been compelled to isolate the voters at the polling places to prevent universal intimidation or bribery. The newspapers are largely subsidized or muzzled, public opinion silenced, business prostrated, our homes covered with mortgages, labor impoverished, and the land concentrating in the hands of the capitalists. The urban workmen are denied the right of organization for self-protection ; imported pauperized labor beats down their wages ; a hireling standing army, unrecognized by our laws, is established to shoot them down, and they are rapidly degenerating into European conditions. The fruits of the toil of millions are boldly stolen to build up colossal fortunes for a few, unprecedented in the history of mankind, and the possessors of these in turn despise the Republic and endanger liberty. From the same prolific womb of governmental injustice we breed the two great classes—tramps and millionaires.

The national power to create money is appropriated to enrich bondholders ; a vast public debt, payable in legal tender currency, has been funded into gold-bearing bonds, thereby adding millions to the burdens of the people. Silver, which has been accepted as coin since the dawn of history, has been demonetized in order to add to the purchasing power of gold by decreasing the value of all forms of property as well as human labor, and the supply of currency is purposely abridged to fatten usurers, bankrupt enterprise, and enslave industry.

A vast conspiracy against mankind has been organized on two continents, and it is rapidly taking possession of the world. If not met and overthrown at once, it forbodes terrible social convulsions, the destruction of civilization, or the establishment of an absolute despotism. We have witnessed, for more than a quarter of a century, the struggles of the two great political parties for power and plunder, while grievous wrongs have been inflicted upon the suffering people. We charge that the controlling influences dominating both these parties have permitted the existing dreadful conditions to develop without serious effort to prevent or restrain them. Neither do they now promise us any substantial reform. They have agreed together to ignore, in the coming campaign, every issue but one. They propose to drown the outcries of a plundered people with the uproar of a sham battle over the tariff, so that capitalists, corporations, national banks, rings, trusts, watered stock, the demonetiza-

tion of silver, and the oppressions of the usurers may all be lost sight of. They propose to sacrifice our homes, lives, and children on the altar of mammon ; to destroy the multitude in order to secure corruption funds from the millionaires.

We declare :

1. That the union of the labor forces of the United States this day consummated shall be permanent and perpetual ; may its spirit enter into all hearts for the salvation of the Republic and the uplifting of mankind.

2. Wealth belongs to him who creates it, and every dollar taken from industry without an equivalent is robbery. "If any will not work, neither shall he eat." The interests of rural and civic labor are the same ; their enemies are identical.

3. We believe that the time has come when the railroad corporations will either own the people or the people must own the railroads ; and should the Government enter upon the work of owning and managing all railroads, we should favor an amendment to the Constitution by which all persons engaged in the Government service shall be placed under a civil service regulation of the most rigid character, so as to prevent the increase of the power of the National Administration by the use of such additional Government employés.

Money.— We demand a national currency, safe, sound and flexible, issued by the General Government only, a full legal tender for all debts, public and private, and that without the use of banking corporations ; a just, equitable, and efficient means of distribution direct to the people at a tax not to exceed 2 per cent. per annum, to be provided as set forth in the Sub-Treasury plan of the Farmers' Alliance, or a better system ; also by payments in discharge of its obligations for public improvements.

1. We demand free and unlimited coinage of silver and gold at the present legal ratio of 16 to 1.

2. We demand that the amount of circulating medium be speedily increased to not less than $50 per capita.

3. We demand a graduated income tax.

4. We believe that the money of the country should be kept as much as possible in the hands of the people, and hence we demand that all State and National revenues shall be limited to the necessary expenses of the Government, economically and honestly administered.

5. We demand that postal savings banks be established by the Government for the safe deposit of the earnings of the people and to facilitate exchange.

Transportation.—Transportation being a means of exchange and a public necessity, the Government should own and operate the railroads in the interest of the people. The telegraph and telephone, like the post-office system, being a necessity for the transmission of news, should be owned and operated by the Government in the interest of the people.

Land.—The land, including all the natural sources of wealth, is the heritage of the people, and should not be monopolized for speculative purposes, and alien ownership of land should be prohibited. All land now held by railroads and other corporations in excess of their actual needs, and all lands now owned by aliens, should be reclaimed by the Government and held for actual settlers only.

James B. Weaver, of Iowa, was nominated on the first ballot for President, receiving 995 votes, against 295 for James H. Kyle, of South Dakota, and 3 scattering. For Vice-President, James G. Field, of Virginia, received the necessary majority of ballots.

Prohibition Conventions. —The National Prohibition party held its convention in Cincinnati, where its delegates assembled on June 29. On June 30 the platform was adopted, In regard to the trade in alcohol it contained the following declaration :

The liquor traffic is a foe to civilization, the arch enemy of popular government, and a public nuisance. It is the citadel of the forces that corrupt politics, promote poverty and crime, degrade the nation's home life, thwart the will of the people, and deliver our country into the hands of rapacious class interests. All laws that under the guise of regulation legalize and protect this traffic or make the Government share in its ill-gotten gains are "vicious in principic and powerless as a remedy." We declare anew for the entire suppression of the manufacture, sale, importation, exportation, and transportation of alcoholic liquors as a beverage by Federal and State legislation, and the full powers of the Government should be exerted to secure this result. Any party that fails to recognize the dominant nature of this issue in American politics is undeserving of the support of the people.

The planks of the platform on other subjects contained declarations in favor of woman suffrage ; a currency issued by the Government only, and consisting of gold, silver, and paper, of a volume fixed at a definite sum per capita ; a tariff for defense against governments that levy duties on American products, with incidental revenue and direct taxes for the support of the Government ; Government control of railroads and telegraphs ; revision of the immigration laws ; and prohibition of alien ownership of land. The platform ended with the following arraignment of the Republicans and Democrats, and invitation to party fellowship :

We arraign the Republican and Democratic parties as false to the standards reared by their founders ; as faithless to the principles of the illustrious leaders of the past to whom they do homage with the lips ; as recreant to the "higher law," which is as inflexible in political affairs as in personal life ; and as no longer embodying the aspirations of the American people, or inviting the confidence of enlightened, progressive patriotism. Their protest against the admission of "moral issues" into politics is a confession of their own moral degeneracy. The declaration of an eminent authority that municipal misrule is "the one conspicuous failure of American politics," follows as a natural consequence of such degeneracy, and it is true alike of cities under Republican and Democratic control. Each accuses the other of extravagance in Congressional appropriations, and both are alike guilty ; each protests when out of power against infraction of the civil service laws, and each when in power violates those laws in letter and in spirit ; each professes fealty to the interests of the toiling masses, but both covertly truckle to the money power in their administration of public affairs. Even the tariff issue, as represented in the Democratic Mills bill and the Republican McKinley bill, is no longer treated by them as an issue between great and divergent principles of government, but is a mere catering to different sectional and class interests. The attempt in many States to wrest the Australian ballot system from its true purpose, and to so deform it as to render it extremely difficult for new parties to exercise the rights of suffrage, is an outrage upon popular government. The competition of both these parties for the vote of the slums, and their assiduous courting of the liquor power and subserviency to the money power, have resulted in placing those powers in the position of practical arbiters of the destinies of the nation. We renew our protest against these perilous tendencies, and invite all citizens to join us in the upbuilding of a party that has shown in five national campaigns that it prefers temporary defeat to abandonment of the

claims of justice, sobriety, personal rights, and the protection of American homes.

Recognizing and declaring that prohibition of the liquor traffic has become the dominant issue in national politics, we invite to full party fellowship all those who on this one dominant issue are with us agreed, in the full belief that this party can and will remove sectional differences, promote national unity, and insure the best welfare of our entire land.

John Bidwell, of California, was nominated for the Presidency on the first ballot, receiving 590 votes, while 179 were given to Gideon L. Stewart, of Ohio, and 139 to W. Jennings Demorest, of New York. James B. Cranfill, of Texas, was nominated for Vice-President over Joshua Levering, of Maryland.

Socialistic Labor Convention.—The Socialistic Labor party met in convention in New York City on August 28, 1892, and nominated for President of the United States Simon Wing, of Massachusetts ; for Vice-President, Charles H. Matchett, of New York. The platform that was adopted was the same one that had been framed for the party in 1889, containing the following demands :

Social Demands : 1. Reduction of the hours of labor in proportion to the progress of production.

2. The United States shall obtain possession of the railroads, canals, telegraphs, telephones, and all other means of public transportation and communication.

3. The municipalities to obtain possession of the local railroads, ferries, water-works, gas-works, electric plants, and all industries requiring municipal franchises.

4. The public lands to be declared inalienable. Revocation of all land grants to corporations or individuals, the conditions of which have not been complied with.

5. Legal incorporation by the States of local Trade Unions which have no national organization.

6. The United States to have the exclusive right to issue money.

7. Congressional legislation providing for the scientific management of forests and waterways, and prohibiting the waste of the natural resources of the country.

8. Inventions to be free to all ; the inventors to be remunerated by the nation.

9. Progressive income tax and tax on inheritances ; the smaller incomes to be exempt.

10. School education of all children under fourteen years of age to be compulsory, gratuitous, and accessible to all by public assistance in meals, clothing, books, etc., where necessary.

11. Repeal of all pauper, tramp, conspiracy, and sumptuary laws. Unabridged right of combination.

12. Official statistics concerning the condition of labor. Prohibition of the employment of children of school age, and of the employment of female labor in occupations detrimental to health or morality. Abolition of the convict labor contract system.

13. All wages to be paid in lawful money of the United States. Equalization of women's wages with those of men where equal service is performed.

14. Laws for the protection of life and limb in all occupations, and an efficient employers' liability law.

Political Demands : 1. The people to have the right to propose laws and to vote upon all measures of importance, according to the Referendum principle.

2. Abolition of the Presidency, Vice-Presidency, and Senate of the United States. An Executive Board to be established, whose members are to be elected, and may at any time be recalled, by the House of Representatives as the only legislative body. The States and Municipalities to adopt corresponding amendments to their constitutions and statutes.

3. Municipal self-government.

4. Direct vote and secret ballots in all elections. Universal and equal right of suffrage, without regard to color, creed, or sex. Election days to be legal holidays. The principle of minority representation to be introduced.

5. All public officers to be subject to recall by their respective constituencies.

6. Uniform civil and criminal law throughout the United States. Administration of justice to be free of charge. Abolition of capital punishment.

The Political Canvass.—On June 27 the Republican National Committee chose W. J. Campbell, of Illinois, to be chairman; but he declined, and finally I. H. Carter, of Montana, was selected. The Secretary was L. E. McComas, of Maryland; treasurer, C. N. Bliss, of New York; vice-chairman, M. H. De Young, of California. Mr. Cleveland's letter of acceptance was given to the public on Sept. 23. The Democratic National Committee had for chairman W. F. Harrity, of Pennsylvania, and for secretary, S. P. Sheerin, of New York. The Democrats named no electoral tickets in Colorado, Idaho, Kansas, North Dakota, and Wyoming, but voted for the people's party electors with the object of taking those States away from the Republicans. They put out an electoral ticket in Nevada, but still voted mostly for the Populist electors. In North Dakota also there was a partial fusion between the Democrats and the People's party, and in Minnesota a part of the Weaver electoral ticket was accepted by the Democrats. In Louisiana there was a fusion of the Republicans and the People's party, each nominating half of the 8 electors. In Alabama there was a fusion of some of the Republicans with the People's party. In Texas a Republican ticket called the Lily White was set up, which differed from the regular ticket. In Michigan a new electoral law, which was declared constitutional by the United States Supreme Court on Oct. 17, 1892, provided for the separate election of a Presidential elector in each Congressional district, and in consequence the electoral vote of the State was divided. In Oregon the name of one of the four electors on the People's ticket was also placed on the Democratic ticket. The Presidential election took place on Tuesday, Nov. 8. The total popular vote cast was reported as 12,154,542. The official popular vote by States and Territories is set forth in the accompanying table:

STATES AND TERRITORIES.	Cleveland.	Harrison.	Weaver.	Bidwell.	Wing.	PLURALITIES.		
						Cleveland.	Harrison.	Weaver.
Alabama	138,138	9,197	85,181	239	...	52,957	...	...
Arkansas	87,834	46,884	11,831	113	...	40,950	...	...
California	117,908	117,618	25,226	8,056	...	290	...	...
Colorado	...	38,620	53,584	1,638	...	...	...	14,964
Connecticut	82,395	77,025	806	4,025	329	5,370	...	...
Delaware	18,581	18,083	...	565	...	498	...	...
Florida	30,143	...	4,843	475	...	25,300	...	...
Georgia	129,361	48,305	42,937	988	...	81,056	...	...
Idaho	...	8,599	10,520	288	...	...	...	1,921
Illinois	426,281	399,288	22,207	25,870	...	26,993	...	...
Indiana	262,740	255,615	22,208	13,050	...	7,125	...	...
Iowa	196,307	219,795	20,595	6,402	...	...	22,965	...
Kansas	...	157,237	163,111	4,539	...	...	...	5,874
Kentucky	175,461	135,441	23,500	6,442	...	40,020	...	...
Louisiana	87,922	13,882	13,281	...	...	61,359	...	...
Maine	48,044	62,923	2,381	3,062	...	...	14,879	...
Maryland	113,866	92,736	796	5,877	...	21,130	...	...
Massachusetts	176,813	202,814	3,210	7,539	676	...	26,001	...
Michigan	202,296	222,708	19,892	14,060	...	...	20,412	...
Minnesota	100,920	122,823	110,256	29,313	...	...	12,367	...
Mississippi	40,237	1,406	10,256	910	...	29,081	...	...
Missouri	268,398	226,918	41,213	4,331	...	40,480	...	...
Montana	17,581	18,851	7,334	549	...	...	1,270	...
Nebraska	24,943	87,227	83,134	4,902	...	...	4,093	...
Nevada	714	2,811	7,264	89	...	...	...	4,003
New Hampshire	42,081	45,658	292	1,297	...	...	3,547	...
New Jersey	171,042	156,068	969	8,131	1,337	14,974	...	...
New York	654,868	609,350	16,429	38,190	17,956	45,518	...	...
North Carolina	132,951	100,342	44,736	2,636	...	32,609	...	...
North Dakota	...	...	17,519	17,700	899	...	...	181
Ohio	404,115	405,187	14,852	26,012	...	...	1,072	...
Oregon	14,243	35,002	26,965	2,281	...	...	8,037	...
Pennsylvania	452,264	516,011	8,714	25,123	808	...	63,767	...
Rhode Island	24,335	26,972	228	1,654	...	...	2,637	...
South Carolina	54,692	13,345	2,407	...	...	41,347	...	...
South Dakota	9,081	34,888	26,544	...	...	...	8,344	...
Tennessee	138,874	100,331	23,477	4,851	...	38,543	...	...
Texas	230,148	81,444	99,688	2,165	...	130,460	...	...
Vermont	16,325	37,992	43	1,415	...	...	21,667	...
Virginia	163,977	113,262	12,275	2,738	...	50,715	...	...
Washington	29,802	36,460	19,165	2,542	...	...	6,658	...
West Virginia	84,467	80,293	4,166	2,145	...	4,174	...	...
Wisconsin	177,335	170,791	9,900	13,132	...	6,544	...	...
Wyoming	...	8,454	7,722	530	...	...	732	...
Total	5,556,533	5,175,577	1,122,045	279,191	21,191	...	...	...

In Oregon, the fusion candidate received the plurality of 811 as above, and cast his vote for Weaver, but the other electors that were chosen were Republicans. In California and Ohio the popular vote was so closely divided between Cleveland and Harrison that the electoral vote was split. In North Dakota one of the two electors on the People's party ticket who received a majority cast his vote in the electoral college for Cleveland, thus causing an equal division of the electoral vote of the State between Harrison, Cleveland, and Weaver. The total p Democratic vote showed an increase of 49,809 since 1888, when it was 5,538,233. In the Republican vote, which was 5,440,216 in 1888, there was a decrease of 264,639. The plurality of Cleveland over Harrison in the popular vote of 1892 was 382,956. Of the total vote of the country Cleveland obtained 46 per cent., Harrison 43 per cent., Weaver 9 per cent., and Bidwell 2 per cent. Wing, the Socialist candidate, received some votes in Maine and Maryland also, and 21,534 votes were cast which were defective, blank, and scattering. The electoral vote of the different States was cast as follows : Alabama, 11 for Cleveland ; Arkansas, 8 for Cleveland ; California. 8 for Cleveland and 1 for Harrison ; Colorado, 4 for Harrison ; Connecticut. 6 for Cleveland ; Delaware, 3 for Cleveland ; Florida, 4 for Cleveland ; Georgia, 13 for Cleveland ; Idaho, 3 for Weaver ; Illinois, 24 for Cleveland ; Indiana, 15 for Cleveland ; Iowa, 13 for Harrison ; Kansas, 10 for Weaver ; Kentucky, 13 for Cleveland : Louisiana, 8 for Cleveland ; Maine, 6 for Harrison ; Maryland, 8 for Cleveland ; Massachusetts, 15 for Harrison ; Michigan, 5 for Cleveland and 9 for Harrison ; Minnesota, 9 for Harrison ; Mississippi, 9 for Cleveland ; Missouri, 17 for Cleveland ; Montana, 3 for Harrison ; Nebraska, 8 for Harrison ; Nevada, 3 for Weaver ; New Hampshire, 4 for Harrison ; New Jersey, 10 for Cleveland ; New York, 36 for Cleveland ; North Carolina, 11 for Cleveland ; North Dakota, 1 for Cleveland, 1 for Harrison, and 1 for Weaver ; Ohio, 1 for Cleveland and 22 for Harrison ; Oregon, 3 for Harrison and 1 for Weaver ; Pennsylvania, 32 for Harrison ; Rhode Island, 4 for Harrison ; South Carolina, 9 for Cleveland ; South Dakota, 4 for Harrison ; Tennessee, 12 for Cleveland ; Texas, 15 for Cleveland ; Vermont, 4 for Harrison ; Virginia, 12 for Cleveland ; Washington, 4 for Harrison ; West Virginia, 6 for Cleveland ; Wisconsin, 12 for Cleveland ; Wyoming, 3 for Harrison. Of the total 444 votes, Cleveland received 277, Harrison 145, and Weaver 22, giving Cleveland a plurality of 132 over Harrison, and a majority of 110 in the electoral college.

UNITED STATES FINANCES.—The effect of the tariff act of 1890 and the extension of pension benefits has been sensibly felt in the financial transactions of the fiscal year ending June 30, 1892. The customs revenue has fallen off $42,-069,241 from that of the previous year, to which should be added $7,342,078 bounties paid for sugar, causing a net depletion of the Treasury through the tariff legislation of $49,411,319. At the same time payments on account of pensions have increased $10,167,102. Meanwhile the expenditures for interest on the public debt have decreased $14,169,019. Exclusive of payments

on account of the principal of the public debt, the excess of receipts over expenditures has been $9,914,453, the details of which appear in the following statement.

The receipts and expenditures of the United States for the year ending June 30, 1892, compared with those of the previous year, were as follow :

RECEIPTS.

SOURCES.	YEAR ENDING JUNE 30.	
	1892.	1891.
Internal revenue..................	$153,971,072	$145,686,249
Postal service....................	70,930,476	65,931,786
Customs..........................	177,452,964	219,522,205
Sales of public land..............	3,261,876	4,029,535
Tax on circulation of national banks...........................	1,261,338	1,236,043
Repayment of interest by Pacific Railways......................	962,438	823,904
Sinking fund for Pacific Railways.	1,828,771	2,326,359
Customs fees, fines, penalties, and forfeitures.....................	909,250	966,122
Fees, consular and lands..........	1,843,828	1,714,526
Proceeds of sales of Government property......................	1,027,454	259,379
Profit on coinage of silver dollars,	2,020,512	6,221,334
Profit on other coinage...........	*	1,480,656
Revenues District of Columbia,...	2,967,045	2,853,898
Proceeds funding bonds Dist. of Columbia, ...	2,412,744	
Tax on seal skins................	46,749	269,674
Fees on letter patents............	1,286,609	1,305,256
Miscellaneous	3,685,134	3,917,305
Total net receipts exclusive of the public debt.............	$425,868,260	$458,544,233
Public debt principal.........	381,463,512	373,208,858
Grand total............	$807,331,772	$831,753,091

* Not separately reported.

EXPENDITURES.

OBJECTS OF EXPENDITURE.	YEAR ENDING JUNE 30.	
	1892.	1891.
Congress....................... ...	$6,725,518	$7,108,470
Executive Department............	12,132,669	12,526,569
Judiciary.......................	4,855,826	5,806,081
Postal service..................	70,930,476	65,931,786
Deficiency in postal revenues....	4,051,490	4,741,772
Foreign intercourse.............	1,742,400	2,028,715
Improving rivers and harbors.....	13,017,208	12,250,027
Other expenses, military establishment......................	33,878,248	36,469,438
Constructing new war vessels.....	13,756,500	10,609,197
Other expenses, naval establishment	15,417,639	15,504,690
Indians.........................	11,150,578	8,527,469
Pensions,.......................	134,583,053	124,415,951
Construction public buildings including sites........	6,319,227	4,811,822
District of Columbia......, ...	6,361,961	5,635,511
District of Columbia funding bonds.......................	2,412,744	
Premiums on bonds purchased....		10,401,221
Interest on public debt..........	23,378,116	37,547,135
Bounty on sugar......	7,342,078	
Miscellaneous	47,928,026	67,992,298
Total net ordinary expenditures............,........	$415,953,807	$431,705,691
Public debt principal.........	338,995,958	365,352,471
Grand total........ ...	$754,949,765	$797,058,162

Public Debt.—Owing to the comparatively small excess of revenue above current expenditures which it seems continued throughout the calendar year, no marked change in the public debt has occurred, the net reduction of principal without an equivalent reserve, for the year ending December 31, 1892, being $9,208,808, mainly in the liability of the Government for the redemption of national bank notes. As during the year in question there was a decrease in the Treasury balance of $5,481,540 as will be seen hereafter, only $3,727,358 could have been used of ordinary receipts, and this amount was the entire surplus of revenues for that period.

The public debt admits of two divisions, one being that having no specific reserve; the other that having a full reserve in cash and used mainly for circulation as money.

The following statement shows the public debt having no specific reserve on the dates named:

CHARACTER.	OUTSTANDING.	
	Dec. 31, 1892.	Dec. 31, 1891.
Four and one-half per cents, continued at two per cent........	$25,364,500	$25,364,500
Four per cent. bonds..........	559,592,400	559,574,000
Four per cent. certificates.......	76,180	88,470
Old demand notes.............	55,647	55,647
Legal tender notes, old issue....	246,681,016	246,681,016
National bank redemption account.............	23,466,502	32,679,299
Fractional notes..............	6,903,462	6,905,673
Total............	$862,139,707	$871,348,605

The following statement shows the public debt having equivalent cash reserve on the dates named:

CHARACTER.	Redeemable in	OUTSTANDING.	
		Dec. 31, 1892.	Dec. 31, 1891.
Old loans matured....	(Coin)	$2,385,045	$4,683,340
Legal tender notes, old issue.............	(Coin)	100,000,000	100,000,000
Legal tender notes of 1890....	(Coin)	124,745,623	77,327,102
Clearing house certificates.............	(Notes)	7,590,000	9,465,000
Gold certificates......	(Gold)	141,347,889	165,578,839
Silver certificates.....	(Silver)	325,783,504	324,772,318
Total..........		$701,852,061	$681,776,599

Of the latter the reserve for old loans matured is not specifically required by law, but in determining the actual available cash on hand the Treasury has usually deducted the amount of such obligations, the loans being liable for payment upon presentation.

Of the amount without reserve $277,106,627 is payable on demand and bears no interest. Of this amount $55,647 is part of the issue of $60,-000,000 demand notes authorized in 1861, and none has been redeemed during the last year. Probably most of the amount outstanding have been lost or destroyed. Of the amount of fractional notes only a little more than $2,000 has been redeemed during the year, and doubtless a considerable portion of the remainder will never be presented for redemption. The amount reported does not, however, represent the entire amount of fractional notes unredeemed. About $8,000,000 has been arbitrarily removed from the monthly debt statement. The true amount of fractional notes outstanding on June 30, 1892, was $15,279,401. nearly all of which will probably never be presented for redemption. It must be also remembered that of the other notes a con-

siderable portion will naturally never be paid, especially those of the earlier issues, subjected as they were to the hard usage of the civil war.

Circulation.—Of the money in circulation in the country there has been an increase during the fourteen months ending December 31, 1892, of paper $44,375,307, and a decrease in that of coin of $6,326,263, a net increase of $38,049,044. The principal items of increase are that of silver dollars, $8,401,617, and that of the legal tender notes of 1890, which was $56,020,353. These notes are issued in payment at market price of silver bullion, of which there are required monthly purchases of 4.500,000 fine ounces. The silver purchased is stored by the Treasury and held as reserve, but the law seems to indicate that the notes may be redeemed in gold or silver at the discretion of the Secretary of the Treasury and as may be necessary to maintain the two metals at a parity of value under the present coinage ratio of about 16 to 1. The principal items showing a decrease during the period are gold coin, $26,752,860 : gold certificates, $15,542,850. The changes in detail are shown in the following table.

The following statement shows the monetary circulation of the country at the dates named :

CLASSIFICATION.	Dec. 31, 1892.	Nov. 1, 1891.
	$	$
Coin :		
Gold coin ...., ...	569,633,412	596,386,272
Silver dollars.....;..........	417,876,985	409,475,368
Silver fractional pieces......	77,898,748	77,301,515
Total coin in country.......	1,065,409.145	1,063,163,155
From which should be deducted the coin held in Treasury as reserve, as follows :		
For redemption of gold certificates	141,347,889	156,890,739
For redemption of silver certificates....................	325,783,504	323,668,401
For redemption of legal tender notes (old issue)............	100,000,000	100,000,000
In all.............	567,131,393	580,559,140
Leaving net coin circulation	498,277,752	502,604,015
Paper :		
Legal tender notes, old issue..	346,681,016	346,681,016
Legal tender notes of 1890....	124,745,623	68,725,270
Fractional notes.............	6,903,403	6,906,692
National bank notes..........	174,404,424	172,184,558
Old demand notes...........	55,647	55,647
Gold certificates.............	141,347,889	156,890,739
Silver certificates............	325,783,504	323,668,401
Clearing-house certificates....	7,590,000	11,095,000
Total paper circulation.....	1,127,511,566	1,086,207,323
From which should be deducted legal tender notes reserved for certificates................	7,500,000	11,095,000
Fund for redemption of Nat. bank notes................	6,215,474	5,781,538
In all.....................	13,805,474	16,876,538
Leaving net paper circulation.....	1,113,706,092	1,069,330,785
Add net coin circulation..........	498,277,752	504,604,015
Total circulation .:..........	1,611,983,844	1,573,934,800

Coinage.—The mandatory coinage of silver dollars ceased on June 30, 1891, and there were coined of such pieces for the fiscal year 1892 only 8,329,467, while during the same period there were coined 2,954,185 gold pieces having a value of $35,506,987 ; also of fractional silver coins

40,689,998 pieces, having a value of $6,659,812, and 61,582,474 minor coins having a value of $1,296,710. The most important operation of the mint has been the purchase of 4,500,000 ounces of silver bullion per month, under the act of July 14, 1890, aggregating 54,355,748 fine ounces, at a cost of $51,106,608, or an average cost of $0.94 per fine ounce. For this purchase legal tender certificates were issued in payment.

Condition of the Treasury.—During the last calendar year the available balance in the Treasury has been reduced $5,481,540. Outside of the general balance the Treasury carries as a public depository a large amount of funds for various public purposes—mainly as a reserve for paper circulation. Of its aggregate holdings there was an increase during the year of $12,480,550. The principal item of increase was that of silver dollars and bullion, $48,611,020 ; of decrease, that of gold coin and bullion, $40,486,949. The balances held by National bank depositories have been reduced $4,145,028, and the fractional silver coins on hand $3,217,844. The items are as follows:

ITEMS.	Dec. 31, 1892.	Dec. 31, 1891.
Assets :		
Gold coin and bullion.......	$238,359,801	$278,846,750
Standard silver dollars and bullion........	451,798,037	403,187,017
United States notes, old issue...	15,747,475	12,913,665
United States notes of 1890.....	2,705,966	2,081,045
National bank notes..........	6,043,050	4,651,152
Balances in National bank depositories........	15,092,654	19,837,682
Gold certificates...............	24,254,750	17,472,720
Silver certificates...........	3,748,403	3,954,750
Bonds and interest checks paid.	13,646	96,665
Currency certificates...........	490,000	200,000
Minor coins and fractional currency....	355,620	319,661
Fractional silver coins........	10,571,481	13,780,325
Total................	$769,780,982	$757,300,432
Liabilities :		
Gold certificates...............	$141,347,889	$165,578,839
Silver certificates............	325,783,504	324,772,318
Note certificates............	7,590,000	9,465,000
U. S. Treasury notes of 1890....	124,745,623	77,327,102
Redemption U. S. notes (old issue)	100,000,000	100,000,000
Redemption National bank notes Public disbursing officers......	6,215,474	5,936,720
Outstanding checks and drafts..	30,796,752	35,368,563
General Treasury available balance...................	29,092,588	34,574,128
Total................	$769,780,982	$757,300,432

National Banks.—There was a net increase of 94 National banks within the last fiscal year, involving a net increase of $9,112,800 capital, and of $11,932,650 bonds deposited for circulation. Of the 163 newly organized banks 22 were located in Texas, 13 in Iowa, 12 in Indiana, 11 in Ohio, 10 in Pennsylvania, and the remainder

distributed throughout the country. The note outstanding on Sept. 30, 1892, were $172,786,760, of which $25,595,167 were secured by lawful money deposited with the Treasurer of the United States to meet their payment on presentation. For the remainder the Treasurer holds United States bonds as collateral security. During the year ending Dec. 31, 1892, there was a net increase of $2,219,966 of notes outstanding. The condition of the banks is as follows:

RESOURCES.	3,773 BANKS. Sept. 30, 1892.	3,567 BANKS. Sept. 25, 1891.
Loans and discounts......	$2,171,041,088.11	$2,005,463,205.
Bonds for circulation.....	163,275,300.00	150,085,600.
Bonds for deposit........	15,382,000.00	20,432,500.
U. S. bonds on hand......	4,882,250.00	4,439,450.
Other stocks and bonds...	154,535,514.54	125,179,076.
Due from reserve agents..	236,484,330.80	198,990,323.
Due from National banks..	140,516,353.09	115,196,682.
Due from State banks....	32,572,735.51	29,471,898.
Real estate, etc..........	87,861,911.86	83,270,122.
Current expenses........	10,317,125.23	9,879,231.
Premiums paid...........	14,029,616.43	14,705,700.
Cash items.............	17,705,981.31	13,272,545.
Clearing-house exchanges.	105,522,711.81	122,039,882.
Bills at other banks......	19,557,474.00	10,991,167.
Fractional currency......	934,648.37	867,462.
Specie.................	209,116,378.69	183,515,075.
Legal tender notes.......	104,267,945.00	97,615,608.
U. S. certificates of deposit	13,905,000.00	15,720,000.
5% fund with Treasurer...	7,139,564.69	6,536,931.
Due from U. S. Treasurer	1,106,987.03	1,457,807.
Total...............	$3,510,004,897.46	$3,213,080,271.

LIABILITIES.	Sept. 30, 1892.	Sept. 25, 1891.
Capital stock............	$686,573,015.00	$677,426,870.
Surplus fund............	238,871,424.84	227,576,485.
Undivided profits........	101,652,754.66	108,284,673.
National bank circulation.	143,423,298.00	131,323,301.
State bank circulation....	75,076.50	74,118.
Dividends unpaid.......	3,888,865.78	1,453,735.
Individual deposits.......	1,765,422,983.08	1,588,318,081.
U. S. deposits...........	9,828,144.24	15,700,672.
Deposits U. S. disbursing officers.......	4,044,734.04	4,566,660.
Due to National banks....	352,046,184.05	288,576,703.
Due to State banks.......	178,607,018.34	142,018,070.
Notes and bills rediscounted..........	17,132,487.71	21,981,952.
Bills payable............	6,540,163.65	10,778,944.
Liabilities other than those above stated............	1,979,746.97	....
Total...............	$3,510,004,897.46	$3,213,080,271.

As the policy of withdrawing the national tax on the circulation of State banks has attracted some attention, the following summary is shown of the number, capital, and deposits of such banks in 1882 and 1892, arranged by geographical divisions. It will be seen that while the number and capital of such banks in the Eastern States have largely diminished, there has been a great increase throughout the South and West.

DIVISION.	NUMBER.		CAPITAL.		DEPOSITS.	
	1882.	1892.	1882.	1892.	1882.	1892.
Eastern....	24	14	$4,323,363	$3,256,675	$4,813,757	$4,946,408
Middle.........	171	306	28,833,815	44,788,610	99,987,167	248,279,260
Western........	92	574	16,857,360	48,934,076	28,002,571	87,450,651
Southern........	324	1,863	21,202,244	81,260,453	95,739,415	240,117,780
Pacific.........	61	434	20,591,431	55,511,357	32,819,393	67,719,611
Total	672	3,191	$91,808,213	$233,751,171	$261,362,303	$648,513,809

UNITED STATES CENSUS.—A full report of preliminary results appeared in the last two issues of the Annual Cyclopædia, and contained in substance the contents of all census bulletins issued up to time of going to press.

Population.—General statistics of population were given in the 1890 issue, with tabular exhibits showing rank in population of States and Territories, with figures giving comparative statistics concerning population of many cities. Under the heading of Population in the last issue of the Annual appeared a tabular exhibit, by States, of cities having a population of 1,000 or over.

This table gave the number of cities in the different classes, and the aggregate population in each class in each State. The population of Alaska in detail was also shown.

From later bulletins now available, the following particulars can be given on the general subject:

Color, Sex, and General Nativity.—The aggregate population of the country, according to the revised returns, was, 1890, 62,622,250. Of this number 32,067,880 were males, and 30,554,-370 females. The native born population numbered 53,372,703; foreign born, 8,249,547. The total number of whites is given as 54,983,890; colored, 7,638,360. The Superintendent of Census says, in his remarks summarizing the tabular exhibits: "The population as a whole has increased, during the decade from 1880 to 1890,

eign born. In 1880 there were 43,475,840 native born and 6,679,943 foreign born. The increase in native born during the decade was 9,896,863, or 22.76 per cent., as against an increase for the decade ending with 1880 of 10,484,698, or 31.78 per cent. The increase in foreign born during the decade from 1880 to 1890 was 2,569,604, or 38.47 per cent., the increase for the decade ending with 1880 being 1,112,714, or 19.99 per cent.

"According to the census of 1890 there are in the United States 54,983,890 white persons and 7,638,360 colored persons, meaning, by 'colored,' persons of African descent, Chinese, Japanese, and civilized Indians. There has been an increase in the white from 1880 to 1890 of 11,580,-920, or 26.68 per cent., and an increase in the colored for the same decade of 885,547, or 13.11 per cent. For the decade from 1870 to 1880 the white increased 29.22 per cent. and the colored, apparently, 35.90 per cent. As has already been explained in previous bulletins, however, the increase from 1870 to 1880 was to a certain extent fictitious, particularly as regards the colored population of the south. As stated in Bulletin No. 16, giving the official count of population by states and territories, 'the census of 1870 was grossly deficient in the southern states, so much so as not only to give an exaggerated rate of increase of the population between 1870 and 1880 in these states, but to affect very materially the rate of increase in the country at large.'

CENSUS YEARS.	AGGREGATE POPULATION.*		MALES.		FEMALES.	
	Total.	Increase: Number.	Total.	Increase: Number	Total.	Increase: Number.
The United States:						
1890....................	62,622,250	12,466,467	32,067,880	6,549,060	30,554,370	5,917,407
1880....................	50,155,783	11,597,412	25,518,820	6,025,255	24,636,963	5,572,157
1870....................	38,558,371	7,115,050	19,493,565	3,408,361	19,064,806	3,706,689
1860........	31,443,321	8,251,445	16,085,204	4,247,544	15,358,117	4,003,901
1850....................	23,191,876	a6,122,423	11,837,660		11,354,216	

CENSUS YEARS.	NATIVE.		FOREIGN.		WHITE.		COLORED.	
	Total.	Increase: Number.	Total.	Increase: Number.	Total.	Increase: Number.	Total.	Increase: Number.
The United States:								
1890...	53,372,703	9,896,863	9,249,547	2,569,604	54,983,890	11,580,920	7,638,360	885,547
1880............ ...	43,475,840	10,484,698	6,679,943	1,112,714	43,402,970	9,813,593	6,752,813	1,783,819
1870........... ...	32,991,142	5,086,518	5,567,229	1,428,532	33,589,377	6,666,840	4,908,904	448,210
1860...............	27,304,624	6,357,350	4,138,697	1,894,095	26,922,537	7,369,469	4,520,784	681,976
1850..............	20,947,274	....	2,244,602	....	19,553,068	5,357,263	3,638,808	765,160

* In the second table the number and per cent. of native and foreign born for the decade ending with 1850 is not shown, as the foreign born population was not separately returned for the census of 1840.

a Including 6,100 persons on public ships in the service of the United States returned in 1840, but not separated according to sex.

12,466,467, or 24.86 per cent., the total population returned in 1890 being 62,622,250 as against a total population in 1880 of 50,155,783. The males have increased from 25,518,820 in 1880 to 32,067,880 in 1890, the numerical increase being 6,549,060, or 25.66 per cent. The whole number of females returned in 1880 was 24,636,963, while in 1890 there were 30,554,370. The females have increased, therefore, 5,917,407, or 24.02 per cent., since 1880.

"Considering the population classified as regards native and foreign born, we find that 53,372,703 are native born and 9,249,547 are for-

CENSUS YEARS.	SEX.		NATIVE AND FOREIGN.		COLOR.	
	Male.	Female.	Native.	Foreign.	White.	Colored.
The United States:	p. c.	p. c.	p. c.	p. c.	p. c.	p. c.
1890............	51.21	48.79	85.23	14.77	87.80	12.20
1880............	50.88	49.12	86.68	13.32	86.54	13.46
1870............	50.56	49.44	85.56	14.44	87.11	12.89
1860............	51.16	48.84	86.84	13.16	85.62	14.38
1850............	51.04	48.96	90.32	9.68	84.31	15.69

"From this table of percentages it is seen that 51.21 per cent. of the total population returned in 1890 are males and 48.79 per cent. are females. In 1880 the males represented 50.88 per cent. and the females 49.12 per cent. The percentages of males and females in 1870 were about the same as those just stated for 1880, or 50.56 per cent. for males and 49.44 per cent. for females, while in 1860 they were very nearly similar to those given for 1890, or 51.16 per cent. for males and 48.84 per cent. for females. The excess of males over females in 1890 is 1,513,510, as against an excess in 1880 of 881,-857. In 1870 the males only exceeded the females by 428,759, whereas in 1860 there were 727,087 more males than females. In 1850 the males exceeded the females by 483,444. The very large excess of males in 1890 is readily accounted for by the greatly increased number of immigrants who have come to this country since 1880, over three-fifths of the entire number of immigrants being males.

"Analyzing the results of the distribution of population according to native and foreign born, it is seen that 14.77 per cent. of the population in 1890 are foreign born, as against 13.32 per cent. in 1880, and 9.68 per cent. in 1850. The native born in 1850 represented 90.32 per cent. of the whole population, while in 1890 they represented 85.23 per cent.

"The colored element of our population, including Chinese, Japanese, and civilized Indians, as well as persons of African descent, represents 12.20 per cent. of the population in 1890, as against 15.69 per cent. in 1850. The relatively decreased per cent. of colored in 1870 as compared with 1860, and also with 1880, is due, as has already been stated, to the deficient census of 1870 in the southern states.

"The following table gives for each state and territory the classification of the population, expressed in percentages, according to native white of native and foreign parents, foreign white, and total colored for 1890, and for native and foreign white and total colored for 1880.

"By native parents is meant all native white persons having both parents native born, or one parent native born and one parent for whom the birthplace was returned as 'unknown,' as well as native white persons for whom the birthplace of both parents was reported as 'unknown.' By foreign parents is meant all native white persons having one or both parents foreign born.

"Analyzing briefly the results for the United States as a whole, we find that out of a total population returned in 1890, 73.24 per cent. are native white, 14.56 per cent. foreign white, and 12.20 per cent., as has already been stated, are colored. In 1880, 73.46 per cent. of the total population were returned as native white, 13.08 per cent. as foreign white, and 13.46 per cent. colored. The native white of native parents in 1890 represent 54.87 per cent., and the native white of foreign parents 18.37 per cent., of the entire population."

The population of each of the States and Territories of the United States, according to the census of 1890, by sex and nativity, is shown in the accompanying table.

Colored Population.—The total colored population, according to the census of 1890, is 7,638,-

STATES AND TERRITORIES.	SEX.		NATIVE AND FOREIGN BORN.	
	Male.	Female.	Native.	Foreign.
United States.	32,067,880	30,554,370	53,372,703	9,249,547
No.Atlantic div .	8,677,798	8,723,747	13,513,368	3,888,177
Maine	332,500	328,496	582,125	78,961
New H'shire..	186,566	189,964	304,190	72,340
Vermont	169,327	163,095	288,334	44,088
Massachusetts.	1,087,709	1,151,234	1,581,806	657,137
Rhode Island .	168,025	177,481	239,201	106,305
Connecticut...	369,538	376,720	562,657	183,601
New York....	2,976,893	3,020,960	4,426,803	1,571,050
New Jersey...	720,819	724,114	1,115,958	328,975
Pennsylvania..	2,666,931	2,591,683	4,412,294	845,720
So. Atlantic div .	4,418,769	4,439,151	8,649,395	208,525
Delaware	85,573	82,920	155,382	13,161
Maryland	515,691	526,699	948,004	94,296
Dist. of Col...	109,584	120,808	211,622	18,770
Virginia	824,278	831,702	1,637,606	18,374
West Virginia.	390,285	372,509	743,911	18,883
No. Carolina..	709,149	818,798	1,614,245	3,702
So. Carolina...	572,337	578,812	1,144,879	6,970
Georgia.......	919,925	917,428	1,825,216	12,137
Florida.......	201,947	189,475	368,490	22,982
No. Central div .	11,594,910	10,767,369	18,302,165	4,060,114
Ohio.........	1,855,736	1,816,580	3,213,023	459,293
Indiana........	1,118,347	1,074,057	2,046,199	146,305
Illinois........	1,972,308	1,854,043	2,984,004	842,347
Michigan.....	1,091,780	1,002,109	1,550,009	543,880
Wisconsin....	874,951	811,929	1,167,681	519,199
Minnesota....	695,321	606,505	834,470	467,356
Iowa	994,453	917,443	1,587,827	324,069
Missouri......	1,385,238	1,293,946	2,444,315	234,869
North Dakota.	101,590	81,129	101,258	81,461
South Dakota.	180,250	148,558	237,753	91,055
Nebraska......	572,824	486,086	856,368	202,542
Kansas........	752,112	674,984	1,379,258	147,838
So. Central div ..	5,598,877	5,379,016	10,651,072	321,821
Kentucky.....	942,758	915,877	1,799,279	50,356
Tennessee....	801,585	875,933	1,747,489	20,029
Alabama......	757,456	755,561	1,498,240	14,777
Mississippi....	649,687	630,913	1,281,648	7,952
Louisiana	559,370	559,237	1,068,840	49,747
Texas	1,172,553	1,062,970	2,082,567	152,956
Oklahoma	34,783	27,101	59,094	2,740
Arkansas.....	585,755	542,424	1,113,915	14,264
Western div ...	1,782,526	1,245,087	2,256,703	770,910
Montana......	87,882	44,277	89,063	43,096
Wyoming.....	39,343	21,392	45,792	14,913
Colorado	245,247	166,951	328,208	83,990
New Mexico ..	83,055	70,538	142,394	11,299
Arizona......	36,571	23,049	40,825	18,795
Utah	110,463	97,442	154,841	53,064
Nevada......	29,214	16,547	31,055	14,706
Idaho	51,290	33,095	66,929	17,456
Washington...	217,562	131,828	259,385	90,005
Oregon.......	181,840	131,927	256,450	57,317
California	700,059	508,071	841,821	366,309

360. Of this number, 7,470,040 are persons of African descent, 107,475 are Chinese, 2,039 Japanese, and 58,806 civilized Indians. Those of African descent include 6,337,980 Blacks, 956,-989 Mulattoes, 105,185 Quadroons, and 69,936 Octoroons. The three States having the largest colored population are Mississippi (744,749), South Carolina (689,141), and Alabama (679,299). The three States having the largest number of Blacks are Georgia (773,682), Mississippi (657,393), and South Carolina (621,781). The three States having the largest number of Mulattoes are Virginia (102,217), Louisiana (76,840), and Mississippi (72,945). The three States having the largest number of Quadroons are Virginia (9,772), Georgia (8,795), and Louisiana (8,597). The

three States having the largest number of Octoroons are South Carolina (5,633), North Carolina (5,617), and Louisiana (5,516). The three States containing the largest number of Chinese are California (72,472), Oregon (9,540), and Washington (3,260). The largest number of Japanese are to be found in California (1,147), Washington (360), and New York (148). California contains more civilized Indians than any other State (11,517), the next in rank being New Mexico (8,554), and Michigan (5,624).

Of the whole number of persons of African descent, 3,262,690, or 43.68 per cent., are in the South Atlantic division, and 3,479,251, or 46.58 per cent., are in the South Central division of States and Territories. The population of persons of African descent in 1850 was 3,638,808; 1860, 4,441,830; 1870, 4,880,009; 1880, 6,580,793; 1890, 7,470,040. This shows an increase since 1850 of 3,831,232. The number of Chinese in the United States in 1860 was, according to the census returns, 34,933; 1870, 63,199; 1880, 105,465; 1890, 107,475. According to these figures, the increase in Chinese population since 1860 has been 72,542. The returns of 1870 show that there were 55 Japanese in the country at that time; in 1880, 148; 1890, 2,039. The whole number of civilized Indians given in the returns for 1860 was 44,021; 1870, 25,731; 1880, 66,407; 1890, 58,806. The per cent. of increase in population of persons of African descent, 1880–1890, was 13.51; Chinese, 1.91.

Dwellings and Families.— A special census bulletin gives some interesting statistics under this heading. It is explained that a dwelling, for census purposes, means any building or place of abode in which any person was living at the time the census was taken, whether a room above a warehouse or factory, a loft above a stable, a wigwam on the outskirts of a settlement, a hotel, a boarding or lodging house, a large tenement house, or a dwelling house as ordinarily considered. The total number of occupied dwellings in the United States in June, 1890, was 11,483,318. In 1880 a total of 8,955,812 dwellings was returned, showing an increase of 2,527,506, or 28.22 per cent., during the decade. The number of persons to a dwelling, 1890, is given as 5.45 as against 5.60 in 1880. The three States having the largest number of dwellings are Pennsylvania, 999,364; New York, 895,593; and Ohio, 720,414.

The word family, for purposes of the census, includes not only the normal family, as generally understood, but also all persons living alone, and all larger aggregations of people having only the tie of a common roof and table, as the inmates of hotels, hospitals, prisons, asylums, etc. The total number of families, as just defined, living in the United States in June, 1890, was 12,690,152, with an aggregate population of 62,622,250, or 4.93 persons, on the average, to each family. In 1880 there were returned 9,945,916 families, the average size of each family at that period being 5.04 for the entire country, with a population of 50,155,783. The States having the largest number of families, 1890, are New York, 1,308,015; Pennsylvania, 1,061,626; and Ohio, 785,291. The per cent. of increase in the number of families in 1880–1890 is shown as 27.59.

From a table of cities in this bulletin, it is gathered that the three cities having the largest number of families, 1890, are New York (312,766); Chicago (220,320); Philadelphia (205,135). The three cities having the largest number of dwellings, 1890, are Philadelphia (187,052); Chicago (127,871); and Brooklyn, N. Y. (82,282). New York stands fourth on the list, with 81,828 dwellings. One of the most useful exhibits in the bulletin reveals the fact that there were, in 1890, 72,558 dwellings each of which contained 21 persons or over; 71,582, 16 to 20 persons; 354,832, 11 to 15 persons; 385,149, 10 persons; 511,069, 9 persons; 762,568, 8 persons; 1,056,289, 7 persons; 1,375,953, 6 persons; 1,712,525, 5 persons; 1,822,092, 4 persons; 1,711,898, 3 persons; 1,276,736, 2 persons; and 370,067 dwellings were reported as containing only 1 person in each.

Juvenile Reformatories.—Additional facts and figures have been furnished concerning the inmates of juvenile reformatories. They include tabular exhibits with classifications by age, sex, and offenses charged. A comparison is made of the total number of offenses by adults as against those committed by juveniles. The number of offenses committed by adults for the year ending June 1, 1890, was 82,329; by juveniles, 14,846. Of the adults, 75,924 offenses were committed by males and 6,405 by females. Details as to juvenile offenses show 11,535 by males and 3,311 by females. Under the heading Offenses against the Government, 1,839 are charged against adults and 18 against juveniles; against society, 18,865 adults, 6,930 juveniles; against the person, 17,281 adults, 308 juvenile; against property, 37,707 adults and 4,515 juvenile. The Superintendent of the Census remarks in his report that the greatest social peril of juvenile crime consists in its irregularity, not in its audacity. It is the promise of future peril to the community rather than any present or immediate danger.

Homicide.—It is reported that of 82,329 prisoners in the United States, June 1, 1890, the number charged with homicide was 7,836, or 8.97 per cent. Omitting 35 who were charged with double crimes, 6,958, or 94.65 per cent., were men, and 393, or 5.35 per cent., were women. Of the total, 4,425 were white, 2,739 negroes, 94 Chinese, 1 Japanese, and 92 Indians. One-sixth of them are reported as under 24 years of age, and more than one-half under 33 years of age. Nearly one-half were unmarried. The percentage of those able to read and write, 61.73; of those who can read only, 4.84; of those who can do neither, 33.43. More than four-fifths have no trade. The habits of 973, in respect to the use of intoxicating liquors, are not stated. The remaining 6,378 are classed as follows: total abstainers, 1,282; occasional or moderate drinkers, 3,829; drunkards, 1,267. Four hundred and sixty-three have served as soldiers in the Civil War. Concerning their physical condition, 6,149 were in good health, 600 ill, 283 insane, 24 blind, 14 deaf and dumb, 18 idiots, and 263 cripples.

Of those convicted, it is reported that, when the returns were made, 158 were awaiting execution, 2,406 had been sentenced to imprisonment for life, 845 for 20 years and over, 1,438 for from 10 to 19 years, and 1,395 for less than 10 years. The tendency to greater severity increases slightly from east to west, and from north to south. The average sentence less than life is .13 years 292 days. The number of cases classed as murder is 5,548, of which nearly one-half received a life sentence. The number classed as manslaughter is 1,704, of which nearly one-half received a sentence of over 10 years. Of the 58 prisoners awaiting execution, 49 were found in the Kansas penitentiaries, no date having been fixed for their execution by any Governor since 1872. The death penalty is practically abolished in Kansas, though not by statute. In 1880, 4,608 prisoners were charged with homicide ; in 1890 the number was 7,351. This is an increase of 59.53 per cent. ; the increase in the total population has been 24.86 per cent. One hundred and fifty-six executions were reported during 1889, of which 94 were in South Atlantic and South Central divisions. Of the 117 lynchings also reported, 94 were in the same divisions.

Education.—Tables summarizing the number of teachers and pupils in public schools have been published in previous census articles. More recent statistics for the year ending July, 1891, give the apparent enrollment in schools. The aggregate is shown as 14,219,571 pupils, 12,728,417 being in the public schools. Out of this latter number, 64,725 are in schools not denominated common schools although public. The number of pupils enrolled in private schools is given as 753,-972 ; parochial schools, 737,182. The three States having the largest enrollment of public school pupils are New York (1,049,952), Pennsylvania (973,232), and Ohio (798,093). The public school enrollment in 1880 was 9,951,608, the total population of the country at that time being 50,155,-783. The per cent. of enrollment to population in 1880 was 19.84 ; 1890, 20.22.

An interesting tabular exhibit .for Southern States, including Delaware, Maryland, District of Columbia, Virginia, West Virginia, North Carolina, South Carolina, Georgia, Florida, Missouri, Kentucky, Tennessee, Alabama, Mississippi, Louisiana, Texas, and Arkansas, shows a population, 1890, of 15,493,323 ; colored, 6,944,-915, and an enrollment of white pupils in these States of 3,358,527, the per cent. of enrollment of population being 21.68. The number of colored pupils enrolled is given as 1,288,229, the per cent. of enrollment to population being 18.55. The increased enrollment of white pupils for the same States is recorded as 1,056,723, or 45.91 per cent. ; increase of colored pupils since 1880, 490,943, or 61.58 per cent.

The total number of parochial schools reported, July 1, 1891, but subject to revision, is 737,182. By denominations the numbers are as follows : Catholics, 567,555 ; Lutheran, 141,388 ; Evangelical, 15,218 ; Protestant Episcopal, 6.964 ; Reformed Episcopal, 241 ; Reformed Church of America, 2,190 ; German Presbyterian, 1,160 ; Holland Christian Reformed, 1,311 ; Mennonite, 610 ; Moravian or United Brethren, 204 ; Dutch Reformed, 341.

The apparent enrollment in schools for the census year, reported to July, 1891, exclusive of special classes, dependents, and Indians, arranged by States grouped in geographical divisions, is shown in the table included in the next column of this article.

STATES AND TERRITORIES.	PUBLIC SCHOOLS: APPARENT TOTAL ENROLLMENT.		Private Schools.	Parochial Schools.
	1880.	1891.		
The United States...	9,951,608	12,728,417	753,972	737,182
North Atlantic Division	2,949,904	3,078,829	195,083	272,890
Maine.................	150,811	140,650	6,521	4,015
New Hampshire......	64,679	59,947	4,134	5,919
Vermont.............	73,237	66,720	4,168	3,071
Massachusetts.......	316,630	373,087	28,183	38,240
Rhode Island (a)...	42,489	52,974	3,050	6,995
Connecticut	118,589	127,308	8,746	15,380
New York...........	1,027,938	1,049,952	76,342	109,322
New Jersey..........	205,240	234,964	15,831	27,327
Pennsylvania........	950,300	973,232	47,899	61,921
South Atlantic Division	1,239,053	1,758,384	151,577	27,534
Delaware.... ..	26,412	31,434	1,126	1,711
Maryland............	149,981	185,058	12,501	14,288
District of Columbia.	26,439	36,906	5,503	3,252
Virginia............	220,733	343,970	17,318	2,240
West Virginia.......	143,796	194,356	3,548	1,519
North Carolina......	256,422	326,895	39,117	1,539
South Carolina......	134,842	203,080	18,796	658
Georgia	237,124	344,062	49,209	934
Florida.............	43,304	91,723	4,369	1,393
North Central Division.	4,089,585	5,022,284	180,258	383,587
Ohio.................	752,442	798,093	39,264	60,552
Indiana.............	512,301	509,355	17,911	26,307
Illinois.............	704,041	781,004	29,555	81,638
Michigan............	362,459	430,665	11,057	37,328
Wisconsin (b).......	290,514	354,675	7,904	65,043
Minnesota...........	186,544	284,308	7,518	33,266
Iowa................	425,665	494,957	20,188	23,099
Missouri............	486,002	623,071	27,740	33,022
North Dakota (c)....	3,746	35,694	509	1,803
South Dakota.......	9,972	67,492	1,432	2,179
Nebraska............	100,871	241,446	5,518	9,567
Kansas..............	246,128	401,464	11,577	9,183
South Central Division.	1,374,035	2,340,614	175,649	36,667
Kentucky............	292,427	408,208	27,301	13,258
Tennessee...........	291,500	456,242	47,342	2,391
Alabama.............	187,550	306,350	23,295	1,150
Mississippi.........	237,065	351,919	21,927	2,337
Louisiana...........	81,012	125,159	18,040	10,339
Texas (d)..........	176,245	477,320	25,404	5,120
Oklahoma (e).......	....	579	1,203	....
Arkansas............	108,236	223,837	11,137	2,172
Western Division......	299,031	519,306	50,805	16,504
Montana (f)........	4,667	16,980	1,119	884
Wyoming............	2,907	7,134	140	191
Colorado............	28,252	66,173	4,735	2,498
New Mexico.........	4,755	18,249	4,413	571
Arizona......	4,212	7,861	469	518
Utah................	25,792	36,730	10,314	665
Nevada.............	8,918	7,524	131	325
Idaho...............	5,834	14,311	1,104	....
Alaska.............	....	908	780	....
Washington.........	14,780	55,705	3,457	914
Oregon.............	37,437	63,987	4,073	616
California...........	161,477	223,749	20,220	9,826

a An apparent loss from original report by rejecting 1,396 duplicates, explained in Bulletin No. 84.

b Column 6 includes 1,381 over and under school age, not in manuscript report of State superintendent.

c Public school enrollment larger than in Bulletin No. 53, by addition of 4,722 city enrollment ; explained in Bulletin No. 84.

d Column 6 includes 65,512 over and under school age, explained in text but not included in table of Bulletin No. 53.

e The public school enrollment of Oklahoma is that of Greer County.

f Increase in public schools of 173 from Bulletin No. 36, explained in Bulletin No. 84.

Of the 12,728,417 pupils ,enrolled in public schools, 45,840 are reported as belonging to superior schools; secondary schools, 277,049; elementary schools, 12,405,528. Of the 1,491,-154 enrolled in private schools, 99,565 are credited to superior schools, 277,241 to secondary schools, 1,034,382 to elementary schools, and 79,966 to commercial schools. Of the total parochial school enrollment (737,182), 567,555 are Catholic pupils and 141,388 Lutheran. It is noted that all figures given in these educational reports are subject to revision in the final volume.

Religion.—In the "Annual Cyclopædia" for 1891 statistics were given showing the membership and property of each sect so far reported. A statement has since been issued with reference to numerous other denominations.

DENOMINATIONS.	Membership.	Property.
Disciples of Christ	641,051	$12,206,088
Christians, or Christian Connection.	90,718	1,637,202
Evangelical Association	133,313	4,785,680
Primitive Methodists	4,764	291,903
Union American Methodist-Episc'p'l	2,279	187,000
Seventh Day Adventists	28,991	644,075
Church of God (7th Day Adventist)	647	1,400
United Zion's Children	525	8,300
Society of Ethical Culture	1,004	
German Methodists:		
Central German	14,391	771,000
Chicago German	7,873	368,400
East German	5,239	589,900
Northern German	4,643	257,950
Northwest German	4,371	180,850
St. Louis German	11,100	491,400
Southern German	2,470	72,700
West German	5,554	265,650
California German Mission	829	121,400
North Pacific German Mission	685	52,750
Spanish Methodists:		
New Mexico Spanish Mission	1,475	38,700
Scandinavian Methodists:		
Northwest Swedish	9,236	397,100
Norwegian and Danish	4,782	173,600
Northwest Norwegian and Danish Mission	548	87,500
Churches and Missions in other countries	3,254	277,300
Methodist Denominations	1,209,976	18,775,362
Congregational	312,771	43,335,437
Protestant Episcopal	532,054	81,066,317

Finance.—In previous articles the finances of States and Cities were shown (Annual for 1890). In the "Annual Cyclopædia" for 1891 figures were given showing the financial condition of the United States as a unit; of the States aggregated; of the counties aggregated; and of important municipalities. The aggregated assessed valuation of real estate and personal property was also given. Since that time reports have been furnished giving a revised summary of National, State, and Local Indebtedness, and also giving the annual Interest Charge on Bonded Indebtedness.

National, State, and Local Indebtedness.—The revised figures, 1890, of the debt of the United States as a unit, less sinking fund, are $891,960,104; decrease since 1880, $1,030,557,-260; revised State debt, separately considered, $68,246,706; revised county debt, separately considered, $145,048,045, an increase of $20,943,-018 since 1880; revised municipal debt, separately considered, $724,463,060, an increase of $40,114,217; school district debt, $36,701,948, an increase of $19,121,266, since 1880. It is noted that the average annual decrease in the national debt of the United States during the decade exceeded $100,000,000; the decrease per capita of combined National, State, and Local debt during the same period was from $60.73 to $32.37, while other statistics show that the value of property assessed for taxation increased meanwhile from $17,000,000,000 to $25,500,000,-000, or 50 per cent., "indicating a reduction of public debt and an increase of wealth for the country unprecedented, at least in modern times."

In the separate tabular statements it is shown that the aggregate debt, less sinking fund, of municipalities having 4,000 or more population, 1890, was $646,507,644 as against $623,784,262. The debt per capita is given as $31.39; 1880, $45.06. The aggregate debt, less sinking fund, of municipalities having less than 4,000 population, 1890, is given as $77,955,416, as compared with $60,564,581 in 1880. The per capita of debt in these latter municipalities, 1890, is $1.87; 1880, $1.68.

Interest Charge on Bonded Indebtedness.—The Annual Interest Charge on the national Bonded Debt, 1890, ($711,313,110,) is shown as $28,997,603, the average rate of interest being 4.08, and the interest charged, per capita, $0.46. The annual interest charged on the combined State and Local bonded debt, 1890, ($1,243,268,-399,) of which $5,333,716 bears no interest, is reported as $65,541,776; the average rate of interest is given as 5.29 per cent., and the interest charged, per capita, $1.05.

Agriculture.—In the Annual for 1891 there appeared statistics on Hops; Truck Farming; Floriculture; Viticulture; Irrigation in Arizona, Idaho, Montana, Nevada, New Mexico, and Utah; Horses, Mules, and Asses on Farms; Live Stock on Ranges; Nurseries, Seed Farms, and Tropic and Semi-tropic Fruits and Nuts. Since the publication of figures under the above headings numerous other bulletins have appeared, with statistics as under:

Irrigation.—For Nevada, 224,403 acres are reported as used for crops raised by irrigation in the Census Year ending May 31, 1890. The number of farms irrigated is given as 1,167 out of 1,341. The figures for other States are as follows: Idaho, 217,005 acres irrigated, on 3,203 farms out of 6,654; Montana, 350,582 acres, on 3,706 farms out of 5,664. In addition to the acreage above given for Montana, 217,000 acres were returned as irrigated, 1890, for grazing purposes; Washington, 48,799 acres on 1,046 farms out of 11,237 farms in 13 counties where irrigation is practiced; Oregon, 177,944 acres on 3,150 farms out of 10,513 in 16 counties.

Now that the irrigation reports are practically all in, it may be useful to include in tabular form the net results of the inquiry on Irrigation in Arizona. New Mexico, Utah, Wyoming, Montana, Nevada, Washington, and Oregon. (See table on page 764.)

Artesian Wells.—The total number of artesian wells on farms in June, 1890, in the States and Territories forming the western half of the United States, was 8,097, representing an estimated aggregate investment of $1,988,461.26. It is reported that complete statistics concerning the depth, cost, discharge, and other features of only 2,971 of such wells, fairly distributed through the various counties and States through which they are reported, have been obtained. From the averages derived from these statistics,

ITEMS.	Arizona.	New Mexico.	Utah.	Wyoming	Montana.	Nevada.	Washington.	Oregon.
Irrigated acreage in crop........................	65,821	91,745	263,473	229,676	350,582	224,403	48,799	177,944
Number of irrigators.............................	1,075	3,085	9,724	1,917	3,706	1,167	1,046	3,150
Av. size of irrigated farms, in acres (crop area only)	61	30	27	119	95	192	47	56
Av. size of irrig. farms of 160 acres and up, in acres	287	312	312	404	307	513	324	300
Per cent. of acreage to total acreage irrigated......	34	21	10	65	50	79	35	43
Av. size of irrigated farms under 160 acres, in acres	43	24	25	50	56	58	32	35
Average first cost of water right per acre..........	$7.07	$5.58	$10.55	$3.62	$4.63	$7.58	$4.08	$4.64
Average annual cost of water per acre	$1.55	$1.54	$0.91	$0.44	$0.95	$0.84	$0.75	$0.94
Av. first cost per acre of preparation for cultivation	$8.60	$11.71	$14.85	$8.23	$8.29	$10.57	$10.27	$12.59
Av. value of irrigated land, including buildings....	$48.68	$50.98	$84.25	$31.40	$49.50	$41.00	$50.00	$57.00
Average annual value of products per acre........	$13.92	$12.80	$18.03	$8.25	$12.96	$12.92	$17.09	$13.90

the number of artesian wells used for the purpose of irrigation is computed at 3,930; average depth per well, 210.41 feet; average cost per well, $245.58; total discharge of water per minute, 440,719.71, or 54.43 gallons per well per minute; average area irrigated per well, 3.21 acres, and average cost of water per acre irrigated, $18.55. More than one-half of these wells are in the State of California, where 88,378 acres of agricultural lands are irrigated by artesian water.

Tobacco.—A special census bulletin on tobacco reports its production in 42 States and Territories, the only non-producing States and Territories being Idaho, Nevada, Rhode Island, Wyoming, Oklahoma, and Utah. The entire crops of the country in 1889 amounted to 488,-255,896 pounds, the number of planters being 205,862, and the area devoted to tobacco culture, exclusive of counties cultivating less than one acre, 692.990 acres, or 1,082.80 sq. miles. The area in cultivation, 1889, was unequally distributed, Kentucky having 39.63 per cent. of the total acreage. producing 45.44 of the entire crop, and the six States next in rank of production, 50.16 per cent. of the acreage, and 42,498 pounds of the crop. while 20 States and Territories having the smallest production had less than 900 acres in tobacco, and yielded an aggregate of only 451,025 pounds, or less than one-tenth of 1 per cent. of the entire crop. The average product per acre of the entire country, 1889, was 705 pounds. The average area cultivated by each planter was 3.17 acres, and the average product of each plantation, 2,372 lbs. The total value of the crop of the producers, estimated on the basis of actual sales, was $34.844.449, an average of 7.01 cents a pound, or $50.28 an acre. The average prices per pound received by the producer in States producing 5,000,000 pounds, ranged from 4.5 cents in Missouri, 4.7 cents in Maryland, and 12.8 cents in Connecticut, to 14.2 cents in North Carolina. The product of Louisiana averaged 25.2 cents a pound to the producer. The following is the product of the six most important tobacco States, 1889: Kentucky, 221,880,303 lbs.; Virginia, 48,522,655 lbs.; Ohio, 37,853,563 lbs.; North Carolina, 36,375,258 lbs.; Tennessee, 36,-363,395 lbs.; and Pennsylvania, 28,956,247 lbs. In 1879 the six highest in rank were Kentucky, 171,120,784 lbs.; Virginia, 79,988,868 lbs.; Pennsylvania, 36,943,272 lbs.; Ohio, 34,735,235 lbs.; Tennessee, 29,365,052 lbs.; and North Carolina, 26,986,213 lbs. In 1869 the six highest States stood: Kentucky, 105,305,869 lbs.; Virginia, 37,086,364 lbs.; Tennessee, 21,465,452 lbs.; Ohio, 18,741,973 lbs.; Maryland, 15,785,-339 lbs.; and Missouri, 12,320,483 lbs. In

1859 the ranking was as follows: Virginia, 121-787.946 lbs.; Kentucky, 108,126,840 lbs.; Tennessee. 43,448,097 lbs.; Maryland, 38,410,965 lbs.; North Carolina, 32,853,250 lbs.; and Ohio, 25,092,581 lbs.

Flax and Hemp.—The total area devoted to the cultivation of flax in 1889 is reported as 1,318,698 acres; product of flax-seed, 10,250,410 bushels; product of fiber, 241,389 lbs.; amount of flax-straw sold or utilized at a determinable value, 207,757 tons; total value of all flax products, $10,436,288.

Flax-seed is reported from 31 States. Of these, Minnesota, Iowa, South Dakota, and Nebraska produce 80.06 per cent. of the total amount, or 1,035,613 bushels in excess of the entire product of 1880. South Dakota, 1880, had the largest acreage devoted to flax, and Minnesota the largest production of seed. Of the States containing 1,000 acres or upward in flax, Wisconsin had the highest average yield of flax-seed per acre, 11.42 bushels, and had the highest average value per acre of all flax products, $13.39.

The total area of land devoted to the cultivation of hemp in 1889 was 25,054 acres, and the product of fiber was 11,511 tons, valued at $1,-102,602 to the producers. This branch of agricultural industry is confined almost exclusively to the State of Kentucky, which produces 93.77 per cent. of the total hemp crop. The average yield per acre for the country is 1,029 lbs., and the average value $41.01, or $95.79 a ton.

Cotton.—The preliminary reports under this heading summarize the results of the inquiry in Texas, Georgia, Mississippi, Alabama, South Carolina, Arkansas, Louisiana, North Carolina, Tennessee, Florida, Missouri, Virginia, Kentucky, Oklahoma, and Kansas. For the purposes of this article, the statistics of States are given according to the number of bales of cotton produced in 1889–1890.

In Texas the total area devoted to the cultivation of cotton in 1889–1890 was 3,932,755 acres, and the production of cotton 1,470,353 bales, as compared with a cultivated area of 2,178,435 acres and a production of 805,284 bales in 1879–1880. There was, therefore, an increase of 1,754,320 acres, or 80.53 per cent., in the area cultivated, and of 665,069 bales, or 82.59 per cent., in the number of bales produced, the yield in 1879–1880 being at the rate of 0,370 of a bale to the acre, or 2.705 acres to the bale, and in 1889–1890 at the rate 0.374 of a bale to the acre, or 2.675 acres to the bale.

In Georgia the total area devoted to the cultivation of cotton in 1889–1890 was 3,345,526 acres, and the production of cotton 1,191,910 bales, as compared with a cultivated area of

2,617,138 acres and a production of 814,441 bales in 1879–1880. This shows an increase of 728,388 acres, or 27.83 per cent., in the area cultivated and of 377,478 bales, or 46.35 per cent., in the number of bales produced, the yield in 1879–1880 being at the rate of 0.31 of a bale to the acre, or 3.21 acres to the bale, and in 1889–1890 at the rate of 0.36 of a bale to the acre, or 2.81 acres to the bale.

In Mississippi the total area devoted to the cultivation of cotton in 1889–1890 was 2,882,499 acres, and the production of cotton 1,154,406 bales, as compared with a cultivated area of 2,106,215 acres and a production of 963,111 bales in 1879–1880. This shows an increase of 776,- 284 acres, or 36.86 per cent., in the area cultivated, and of 191,295 bales, or 19.86 per cent., in the number of bales produced, the yield in 1879–1880 being at the rate of 0.46 of a bale to the acre, or 2.19 acres to the bale, and in 1889–1890 at the rate of 0.40 of a bale to the acre, or 2.50 acres to the bale. The total value of the cotton crop of the State to the producers was $51,484,053, an average of $44.60 per bale, or $17.86 per acre.

In Alabama the total area devoted to the cultivation of cotton in 1889–1890 was 2,761,771 acres, and the production of cotton 915,414 bales, as compared with a cultivated area of 2,330,086 acres and a production of 699,654 bales in 1879–1880. There was, therefore, an increase of 431,685 acres, or 18.53 per cent., in the area cultivated, and of 215,760 bales, or 30.84 per cent., in the number of bales produced, the yield in 1879–1880 being at the rate of 0.30 of a bale to the acre, or 3.33 acres to the bale, and in 1889–1890 at the rate of 0.33 of a bale to the acre, or 3.02 acres to the bale. The total value of the cotton crop of the State to the producers was $42,119,171, an average of $46.01 per bale, or $15.25 per acre.

In South Carolina the total area devoted to the cultivation of cotton in 1889–1890 was 1,987,651 acres, and the production of cotton 746,798 bales, as compared with a cultivated area of 1,364,249 acres and a production of 522,548 bales in 1879–1880. There was, therefore, an increase of 623,- 402 acres, or 45.69 per cent., in the area cultivated and of 224,250 bales, or 42.91 per cent , in the number of bales produced, the yield in 1879–1880 being at the rate of 0.38 of a bale to the acre, or 2.61 acres to the bale, and in 1889–1890 at the rate of 0.38 of a bale to the acre, or 2.66 acres to the bale.

In Arkansas the total area devoted to the cultivation of cotton in 1889–1890 was 1,700,612 acres, and the production of cotton 691,423 bales, as compared with a cultivated area of 1,042,976 acres and a production of 608,256 bales in 1879–1880. This shows an increase of 657,636 acres, or 63.05 per cent, in the area cultivated and of 83,167 bales, or 13.67 per cent., in the number of bales produced, the yield in 1879–1880 being at the rate of 0.58 of a bale to the acre, or 1.71 acres to the bale, and in 1889–1890 at the rate of 0.41 of a bale to the acre, or 2.46 acres to the bale. Every county in the State produced more or less cotton in 1889–1890, only 2 counties having less than 500 acres in that product.

In Louisiana the total area devoted to the cultivation of cotton in 1889–1890 was 1,270,885 acres, and the production of cotton 659,583 bales, as compared with a cultivated area of 864,- 787 acres and a production of 508,569 bales in 1879–1880. There was, therefore, an increase of 406,098 acres, or 46.96 per cent., in the area cultivated and of 151,014 bales, or 29.69 per cent. in the number of bales produced, the yield in 1879–1880 being at the rate of 0.59 of a bale to the acre. or 1.70 acres to the bale, and in 1889–1890 at the rate of 0.52 of a bale to the bale, or 1.93 acres to the bale.

In North Carolina the total area devoted to the cultivation of cotton in the year 1889–1890 was 1,147,206 acres and the production of cotton 336,245 bales, as compared with a cultivated area of 893,153 acres and a production of 389,- 598 bales in 1879–1880. While, therefore, there was an increase of 254.053 acres, or 28.44 per cent., in the area cultivated, there was a decrease of 53,353 bales, or 13.69 per cent., in the number of bales produced, the yield in 1879–1880 being at the rate of 0.44 of a bale to the acre, or 2.29 acres to the bale, and in 1889–1890 at the rate of 0.29 of a bale to the acre, or 3.41 acres to the bale.

In Tennessee the total area devoted to the cultivation of cotton in the year 1889–1890 was 745,176 acres, and the production of cotton 189,- 072 bales, as compared with a cultivated area of 722,562 acres and a production of 330,621 bales in 1879–1880. While, therefore, there was an increase of 22,614 acres, or 3.13 per cent. in the area cultivated, there was a decrease of 141,549 bales, or 42.81 per cent. in the number of bales produced, the yield in 1879–1880 being at the rate of 0.46 of a bale to the acre, or 2.19 acres to the bale, and in 1889–1890 at the rate of 0.25 of a bale to the acre, or 3.94 acres to the bale.

In Florida the total area devoted to the cultivation of cotton in 1889–1890 was 227,370 acres and the production of cotton 57,928 bales, as compared with a cultivated area of 245,595 acres and a production of 54,997 bales in 1879–1880. With a diminished area in cotton to the extent of 18,225 acres, or 7.42 per cent., Florida has increased its production by 2,931 bales, or 5 33 per cent., the yield in 1889–1890 being at the rate of 0.25 of a bale to the acre, or 3.93 acres to the bale, as compared with 0.22 of a bale to the acre, or 4.47 acres to the bale, in 1879–1880.

In Missouri the total area devoted to the cultivation of cotton in 1889–1890 was 54,886 acres and the production of cotton 14,461 bales, as compared with a cultivated area of 32,116 acres and a production of 20.318 bales in 1879–1880. While, therefore, there was an increase of 22,- 770 acres, or 70.90 per cent., in the area cultivated, there was a decrease of 5,857 bales, or 28.83 per cent., in the number of bales produced, the yield in 1879–1880 being at the rate of 0.63 of a bale to the acre, or 1.58 acres to the bale, and in 1889–1890 at the rate of 0.26 of a bale to the acre, or 3.80 acres to the bale.

In Virginia the total area devoted to the cultivation of cotton in 1889–1890 was 39,213 acres, and the production of cotton 5.375 bales, as compared with a cultivated area of 45.040 acres and a production of 19,595 bales in 1879–1880. There was, therefore, a decrease of 5,827 acres, or 12.94 per cent., in the area cultivated, and of 14,220

STATES AND TERRITORIES.	Barley: Bushels.	Buckwheat: Bushels.	Indian Corn: Bushels.	Oats: Bushels.	Rye: Bushels.	Wheat: Bushels.
Alabama	2,002	4,622	30,073,036	3,231,085	14,618	208,591
Arizona	252,992		82,535	33,996	207	100,328
Arkansas	994	5,074	33,982,318	4,180,877	15,181	955,568
California	17,548,386	10,388	2,381,270	1,463,068	243,871	40,809,337
Colorado	331,556	2,081	1,511,907	2,514,480	54,158	2,845,430
Connecticut	5,747	46,104	1,471,979	593,601	214,935	7,482
Delaware	205	3,081	8,097,164	382,900	6,625	1,501,050
District of Columbia		20	10,755	1,371	1,099	600
Florida	128	126	3,701,264	391,321	18,389	290
Georgia	6,053	3,527	29,261,422	4,767,456	87,021	1,096,312
Idaho	296,471	395	24,605	587,407	10,809	1,176,878
Illinois	1,197,266	107,066	289,629,705	137,603,804	2,027,949	37,371,061
Indiana	250,200	99,950	108,843,004	31,491,661	877,532	37,318,706
Iowa	13,406,122	286,746	313,130,782	146,670,289	1,445,283	8,249,786
Kansas	165,715	67,115	250,574,508	44,620,034	2,917,386	30,390,871
Kentucky	165,959	3,804	78,434,847	8,775,814	423,847	10,707,462
Louisiana	598		13,081,954	297,271	374	257
Maine	286,362	466,411	380,662	3,568,909	6,664	79,826
Maryland	18,778	96,747	14,928,142	2,019,658	352,596	8,348,177
Massachusetts	38,715	31,300	1,330,101	388,810	117,091	1,812
Michigan	2,522,376	811,977	28,785,579	30,061,193	2,101,713	24,771,171
Minnesota	9,100,683	281,705	24,696,446	49,958,791	1,252,663	52,300,347
Mississippi	875	345	26,148,144	1,362,290	3,544	16,570
Missouri	34,963	28,440	190,904,915	39,820,149	308,807	30,113,821
Montana	160,902	128	14,225	1,535,615	188	457,607
Nebraska	1,822,111	120,000	215,895,996	43,843,640	1,085,068	10,571,059
Nevada	237,192		6,540	99,126	502	81,486
New Hampshire	112,378	75,048	988,806	802,243	11,962	35,192
New Jersey	1,043	114,026	8,637,011	2,837,293	874,049	1,823,382
New Mexico	35,024	3,124	583,480	206,182	810	341,104
New York	8,220,242	4,675,735	15,109,960	38,896,479	3,065,623	8,304,539
North Carolina	3,521	12,021	25,785,623	4,512,762	276,609	4,292,085
North Dakota	1,560,167	589	183,929	5,769,584	72,195	26,388,455
Ohio	1,050,915	162,833	113,802,318	40,186,782	1,007,156	35,559,208
Oklahoma	112		234,315	76,194	1,052	30,175
Oregon	875,063	2,678	238,203	5,948,504	63,206	9,298,294
Pennsylvania	493,893	3,069,717	42,318,279	36,197,409	3,742,164	21,595,499
Rhode Island	8,009	349	253,810	100,520	9,617	91
South Carolina	9,428	472	13,770,417	2,273,182	17,303	658,351
South Dakota	902,005	11,423	13,152,008	7,460,846	65,183	16,541,138
Tennessee	63,866	7,143	63,685,850	7,855,100	165,621	8,900,789
Texas	47,692	1,263	69,031,493	12,578,880	62,120	4,272,392
Utah	163,328	316	84,760	597,947	33,928	1,515,465
Vermont	430,761	271,216	1,700,688	3,316,141	43,256	164,720
Virginia	40,982	41,199	27,154,633	5,698,875	307,394	7,897,800
Washington	1,269,140	480	156,413	2,273,182	19,188	6,345,426
West Virginia	5,387	120,469	13,730,506	2,946,653	117,118	3,634,197
Wisconsin	15,225,872	1,064,178	34,034,316	60,739,052	4,250,582	11,696,922
Wyoming	11,573	100	25,162	362,162	2,055	73,318

bales, or 72.57 per cent., in the number of bales produced, the yield in 1879–1880 being at the rate of 0.44 of a bale to the acre, or 2.30 acres to the bale, and in 1889–1890 at the rate of 0.14 of a bale to the acre, or 7.30 acres to the bale.

In Kentucky the total area devoted to the cultivation of cotton in 1889–1890 was 2,629 acres, and the production of cotton 873 bales, as compared with a cultivated area of 2,667 acres and a production of 1,367 bales in 1879–1880. There was, therefore, a decrease of 38 acres, or 1.42 per cent., in the area cultivated, and of 494 bales, or 36.14 per cent., in the number of bales produced, the yield in 1879–1880 being at the rate of 0.51 of a bale to the acre, or 1.95 acres to the bale, and in 1889–1890 at the rate of 0.33 of a bale to the acre, or 3.01 acres to the bale.

In Oklahoma the total area devoted to the cultivation of cotton in 1889–1890 was 1,109 acres, and the production of cotton 425 bales, being at the rate of 0.38 of a bale to the acre, or 2.61 acres to the bale. With the exception of Greer county, which is in dispute, being claimed by Texas, and which produced 381 of the 425 bales, this Territory was not created, nor were its lands thrown open to settlement, until 1889.

The six counties in Kansas from which a small production of cotton is reported for 1889–1890 form part of the extreme southern tier bordering on Indian Territory. The total area devoted to the cultivation of cotton in these counties i[n] 1889–1890 was 731 acres, and the production o[f] cotton 212 bales, being at the rate of 0.29 o[f] bale to the acre, or 3.45 acres to the bale. N[o] cotton was reported from Kansas in the yea[r] 1879–1880, but in 1869–1870 2 bales were reporte[d] from Cherokee county and 5 bales from Clou[d] county, and in 1859–1860 60 bales were reporte[d] from Doniphan county and 1 bale from Lin[ ] county.

The product of cereals in the United States i[n] 1889 is shown in the table above.

Manufactures. *Iron and Steel.*—In the la[st] issue of the Annual, results were given from [a] report on the product of iron and steel in th[e] New England States. Since then, figures hav[e] been published having special reference to th[e] Southern States. A comparative statement [is] given in this article, showing the actual co[n]dition of the industries in 1880 and 1890. Th[e] States included are Alabama, Delaware, Georgi[a,] Kentucky, Maryland, North Carolina, Tennesse[e] Texas, Virginia, and West Virginia.

On page 767 is a comparative statement of th[e] iron and steel manufacture, Southern State[s] 1880 and 1890.

Coke.—A special report has been made of th[e] coke product in the Flat Top region of Virgin[ia] and West Virginia, known as the Pocahont[as] district. The report shows that the avera[ge]

BRANCHES.		Number of Establishments.	Capital Invested.	Cost of Materials.	Value of Products.	Tons of Products.
Blast furnaces...................	{ 1880	121	$16,964,207	$4,452,864	$7,769,050	350,436
	{ 1890	92	33,207,370	15,410,082	22,494,870	1,834,586
Rolling mills and steel works......	{ 1880	48	11,665,860	10,252,608	17,092,587	290,324
	{ 1890	49	17,528,096	13,036,029	519,920,952	515,775

b The decline in prices of products accounts for the apparently small increase in value, notwithstanding the great increase in quantity of production.

number of persons employed in the Flat Top coke works during the year 1889 was 533, the total amount of wages paid being $149,727. The number of cars of coke shipped from the Flat Top district by the various railroads increased from 8,665 in 1887 to 20,883 in 1890. Shipments to points south of Bristol, Tennessee, were augmented from 1,275 cars in 1887 to 6,127 cars in 1889 and 9,143 cars in 1890, evidencing the increasing demand made by the furnaces at Chattanooga, Florence, Sheffield, and other points in Tennessee, Alabama, and the South for coke from this region.

The number of coking ovens built and in use in the Flat Top Company's districts increased from 200 in 1888 to 1,833 in 1889, and 631 additional ovens were then under construction. The value of the coke at the ovens increased from $44,345 in 1883 to $542,219 in 1889.

The statistics of production of coke in the Flat Top field of Virginia and West Virginia, in 1889, is shown in the accompanying table :

DISTRICTS.	OVENS.		Coal Used. (Short Tons.)	Coke Produced. (Short Tons.)	Total Value of Coke.
	Built.	Building.			
Pocahontas	400	250	130,080	81,300	$136,584
Bluestone......	578	150	169,460	103,438	177,600
Elkhorn........	855	231	218,073	136,948	228,035
Total.......	1,833	631	517,613	321,686	$542,219

Of the production by districts, almost all of that in the Pocahontas field is produced in Virginia. A small amount comes from Mercer County, West Virginia. All the production of the Bluestone and Elkhorn districts, however, is in West Virginia. The total capital employed in this industry is reported as $1,528,386.

Dyeing and Finishing Textiles.—The following table presents for this industry the percentages of increase or decrease under the principal heads of inquiry during the past decade. The more thorough inquiry employed at the present census may have, in a measure, affected the increase shown in some of the items, especially that of capital. The accompanying table exhibits a comparative statement of the industry of dyeing and finishing textiles :

GENERAL HEADS.	1890.	1880.
Number of establishments reported.....................	248	191
Capital invested................	a$38,450,800	$26,223,981
Number of hands employed......	20,207	16,698
Wages paid....................	$9,717,011	$6,474,364
Miscellaneous expenses.........	$3,154,219	
Cost of materials..............	$12,362,082	$18,664,295
Total value work done...........	$28,900,560	$32,297,420

a Does not include hired property to the value of $1,819,779, which is omitted for comparative purposes, as this item was not reported at the census of 1880.

Combined Textile Industries.—The increase of silk manufacture since 1880 has been 112.75 per cent. in the value of its products ; that of the cotton manufacture ranking second, 39.51 per cent., and that of the wool manufacture 26.39 per cent. The average increase in the entire textile industry is 38.51 per cent. The relative rank in importance of these industries is reversed, wool manufacture in all its branches (including all descriptions of hosiery and knit goods) standing first, with gross products valued at $337,768,524 ; cotton manufacture second, with products valued at $267,981,724 ; and silk manufacture third, with products valued at $87,298,454. The actual increase in the value of products has been $70,515,611 in wool, $75,891,614 in cotton, and $46,265,409 in silk. These combined industries yielded a product in the present census year worth $693,048,702, as compared with a product in 1880 of $500,376,068, an increase in 10 years of $192,672,634.

GENERAL HEADS.	1890.	1880.
Number of establishments........	3,805	3,827
Capital invested.................	$701,522,861	$386,497,515
Number of hands employed (not including officers and clerks in cotton industry).	488,921	365,438
Amount of wages paid (not including wages paid officers and clerks in cotton industry).	$162,365,508	$98,576,302
Miscellaneous expenses..........	$40,910,405	(a)
Cost of materials................	$408,328,226	$289,045,599
Value of product................	$693,048,702	$500,376,068

(a) This item was not reported at the census of 1880.

Silk Industry.—In the preliminary report of the Superintendent of the Census under this heading it is remarked that the classification of silk goods of American manufacture is now practically without limit, embracing every article made in the older silk manufacturing countries, and fully equal to the foreign product in quality of weave, beauty of design, and excellence of finish. The value of the net or finished production of silk goods manufactured during the census year 1890 was $69,154,599, against $34,519,723 for the census year 1880, an increase of $34,634,876, or 100.33 per cent. The accompanying table gives a comparative statement of the silk manufacture :

GENERAL HEADS.	1890.	1880.
Number of establishments reported	472	382
Capital invested (a).............	$51,007,537	$19,125,300
Number of hands employed......	50,913	31,337
Amount of wages paid	$19,680,318	$9,146,705
Miscellaneous expenses.........	$4,315,032	(b)
Cost of materials used..........	$50,919,016	$22,467,701
Value of product...............	$87,298,454	$41,033,045
Number of spindles.............	1,254,768	508,137
Number of looms	22,509	8,474

(a) This does not include the sum of $10,355,160, value of "property hired," as this item was not reported at the census of 1880.

(b) This item was not reported prior to the census of 1890.

The Cotton Industry.—It is pointed out in the Census Bulletin on cotton manufactures that the growth of the cotton manufacturing industry of the United States has been constant. One of the most gratifying features of the situation is the great extension of this industry in the South, where a marked addition is shown in the number of cotton mills established and successfully operated. The magnitude of this movement is demonstrated by the fact that the consumption of raw cotton in the Southern States in 1890 exceeded that of 1880 by 166,308,889 pounds, while in New England, the chief seat of this manufacture, the excess of consumption of 1890 over that of 1880 was only 173,317,834 pounds. Nevertheless, the development of cotton manufacture throughout the country, measured by any test, was large and healthy. Inasmuch as the manufacture of cotton is one of the principal industries to which the factory system is applied, its condition, as herein exhibited, throws much light upon the industrial situation. The following table gives a comparative statement of the cotton manufacture:

GENERAL HEADS.	1890.	1880.
Number of establishments reported....................	904	736
Capital invested	$354,020,843	$208,280,346
Number of hands employed (officers and clerks included)........	221,585	174,659
Amount of wages paid (amount paid officers and clerks not included)..............	$66,024,538	$42,040,510
Amount of wages paid to officers and clerks..................	$3,464,784	....
Miscellaneous expenses	$17,036,135	....
Cost of materials used	$154,503,368	$102,206,347
Value of product..................	$267,981,724	$192,090,110
Number of spindles..............	14,098,103	10,653,435
Number of looms..............	324,866	225,759
Pounds of raw cotton consumed ..	1,117,945,770	750,343,981

Operating Telephone Companies.—The important items of this business for 1890 are exhibited in the following summary: Number of companies, firms, and persons reporting, 53 ; total investment, $72,341,736 ; gross earnings, $16,404,-583 ; gross expenses, $11,143,871 ; net earnings, $5,260,712 ; number of exchanges, 1,241 ; number of telephones and transmitters, 467,350 ; miles of wire, 240,412 ; number of employés, 8,645 ; number of subscribers, 227,357 ; number of conversations, 453,200,000.

Transportation.—Special statistics have been prepared under this heading. Among the numerous totals it is shown that the transportation fleet of the United States at the beginning of 1890, with the exception of craft used on canals, numbered 25,540 steamers, sailing vessels, and unrigged craft, with gross tonnage of 7,633,-676 tons, and estimated commercial value of $215,069,296. During the preceding year the freight movement by the whole operating American mercantile fleet amounted to 172,110,423 tons of all commodities. The number of persons of all classes employed to make up the ordinary or complementary crews of all operating vessels of the United States, exclusive of pleasure craft on the Atlantic coast and Gulf of Mexico, numbered 106,436, and the total amount paid out in wages amounted to $36,867,305. On the Atlantic coast, during the year ending December 31, 1889, were registered and owned, in the ports extending from Eastport in Maine to Key West in Florida, 2,713 steamers, 6,490 sailing vessels, and 3,250 unrigged, a total of 12,453 craft of all descriptions. The gross tonnage of this Atlantic coast fleet was 2,794,440 tons, divided as follows : 793,571 tons as the tonnage of the steamers, 1,383,-108 tons as the tonnage of the sailing vessels, and 617,761 tons as the tonnage of the unrigged. The estimated commercial value of the unrigged was $7,735,730, that of the sailing vessels was $45,545,357, and that of the steamers $70,593,-090, making a total value for the whole Atlantic coast fleet of $123,874,177. The freight movement by the entire mercantile fleet during the year was 77,597,626 tons, of which amount 28,-778,341 tons were carried on steamers and 10,-535,884 tons towed by them on barges, the remaining 38,283,401 tons being carried by the sailing vessels. The number of employés making up the ordinary crews of the entire Atlantic coast fleet, with the exception of pleasure craft, was 54,859 officers and men of all grades, of which number 23,174 formed the complement of the ordinary crews of the steamers and 31,685 the total making up the ordinary crews of the sailing vessels. The wages paid for the operation of the whole Atlantic coast fleet, with the above indicated exception, was $18,862,199, of which amount $10,358,426 was paid to the steamer employés and $8,503,773 to those on the sailing vessels.

In the ports of the Gulf of Mexico, the registered fleet numbered 1,008 craft of all kinds, that total being made up of 220 steamers, 613 sailing vessels, and 175 unrigged, these figures including the craft running from New Orleans seaward and those employed on Lake Pontchartrain. The gross tonnage of the fleet was 77,562 tons, of which amount 45,591 tons were steamer tonnage, 17,249 tons were sailing tonnage, and 14,722 tons belonged to the unrigged. The estimated commercial value of the fleet was $3,851,-270, the steamers being valued at $2,961,450, the sailing vessels at $788,110, and the unrigged at $101,710. The freight movement by the Gulf of Mexico mercantile fleet was 2,864,956 tons, the steamers carrying 1,455,450 tons and the unrigged 49,980 tons, leaving 1,359,526 tons as the movement on board the sailing vessels. The complement of crews, with the same exception as in the case of the Atlantic coast, numbered 3,891, the steamer crews numbering 2,479 and those of the sailing vessels numbering 1,412. The wages paid during 1889 amounted to $1,215,-744, and this sum was allotted as follows : $880,-743 to steamers and $335,001 to sailing vessels.

The Pacific coast fleet for 1889 numbered 1,842 craft of all kinds, 531 of these being steamers, 822 being sailing vessels, and 489 being unrigged. The gross tonnage of the fleet amounted to 441,939 tons, that of the steamers being 170,-503 tons, that of the sailing vessels being 208,-080 tons, and that of the unrigged being 63,356 tons. The estimated commercial value of the fleet was $23,067,370, that of the steamers being $15,526,455, that of the sailing vessels $6,715,570, and that of the unrigged $835,345. The freight movement of the entire mercantile fleet was 8,818,363 tons, the steamers' share in this amount being 5,741,940 tons, that of the sailing vessels 2,761,826 tons, and that of the unrigged 314,597 tons. The number of employés making up the ordinary crews of the Pacific coast fleet was 15,-809, of which number 9,750 constituted the complement of the steamers with their unrigged attachments and 6,059 formed the complement of the sailing vessels. The wages paid during the year amounted to $6,127,701, the amount for working the steamers being $3,682,062, and that paid on board the sailing vessels amounting to $2,445,639.

On the Great Lakes, out of the total fleet of 2,784 craft, 1,489 were steamers, 987 sailing vessels, and 308 unrigged. The gross tonnage of the fleet amounted to 926,355 tons, 599,949 tons forming the tonnage of the steamers, 187,006 tons forming the tonnage of the sailing vessels, and 139,400 tons forming the tonnage list

Iowa were made known in 1891. The showing of mortgage indebtedness in five States is exhibited in the accompanying table. Figures for Nebraska have also been announced. The real estate mortgage business of Nebraska during the 10 years 1880–1889 is represented by 337,872 mortgages made to secure a debt of $274,368,-358. Of this debt 48.44 per cent. remained unpaid January 1, 1890. Nearly one-third (31.90 per cent.) of the existing debt is on village and city lots, and the principal portion of this is in the counties of Douglas and Lancaster, containing, respectively, the cities of Omaha and Lincoln. In Douglas county the existing debt is $27,064,041, of which 87.60 per cent. is on lots, In Lancaster county the existing debt is $9,172,-206, of which 64.97 per cent. is on lots.

MORTGAGES, ACRES, LOTS, AND INTEREST RATES.	Alabama.	Illinois.	Iowa.	Kansas.	Tennessee.
Number of mortgages recorded during 1880–1889.........	93,828	612,249	520,448	654,243	93,282
Amount of mortgages recorded during 1880–1889.........	$91,099,623	$870,699,940	$439,936,354	$498,653,903	$100,212,257
Number of mortgages in force January 1, 1890...........	35,331	297,247	252,539	298,880	39,470
Amount of mortgages in force January 1, 1890...........	$39,027,983	$384,299,150	$199,774,171	$243,146,826	$40,421,396
Number of acres encumbered during 1880–1889...........	16,175,153	21,578,919	33,864,721	58,510,069	7,209,279
Number of lots encumbered during 1880–1889...........	34,649	602,152	303,556	544,934	65,566
Number of acres encumbered January 1, 1890.............	6,008,636	10,751,244	16,312,176	26,590,795	3,085,816
Number of lots encumbered January 1, 1890.............	14,213	287,378	163,712	265,462	32,957
Percentages of debt 1880–1889, January 1, 1890...........	42.84	44.14	45.41	48.76	40.34
Percentages of acres encumbered January 1, 1890........	21.67	31.04	46.96	61.59	11.72
Equated life of mortgages (in years).....................	2.73	4.02	4.92	3.38	2.81
Range of interest rates (per cent.).....................	1–40	1–18	1–20	1–60	1–12
Amount per capita of mortgages January 1, 1890.........	$26	$100	$104	$170	$32

of the unrigged. The value of the unrigged was estimated at $3,472,500, that of the sailing vessels at $4,275.650, that of the steamers at $41,-193,324, and that of the entire fleet at $48,941,-474. The freight movement of the mercantile fleet reached 53,424,432 tons, of which amount the steamers carried 20,181,483 tons, the sailing vessels 19,302,949 tons, and the unrigged 13,-940,000 tons. The wages paid during 1889 amounted to $5,322,799, of which amount $3,-891,601 formed p   of the expense account of the steamers and $it431,198 was an item in the expense account of the sailing vessels.

The fleet operating on the rivers of the Mississippi Valley division numbered 7,453, 6,339 being unrigged and 1,114 being steamers, the peculiarities of the constitution of this fleet (the reason, however, is patent) being the entire absence of sailing vessels and the preponderance of unrigged or towed craft. The tonnage, for instance, of the entire fleet amounted to 3,383,380 tons, of which amount the unrigged figures up to 3,182,608 tons. In the disposition of values, however, there is a shifting of this preponderance, the steamer value being $10,539,-251, while that of the unrigged is $4,795,754. The freight movement for the year was 29,405,-046 tons, divided as follows: 10,345,504 tons carried on the steamers and 19,059,542 tons towed on the unrigged. As there are no sailing vessels in operation on the rivers of the Mississippi Valley, and as the wage account of the unrigged is included in that of the steamers, there is no division of items, the number of employés making up the ordinary crews of the valley fleet being 15,996, and the amount paid in wages being $5,333,862.

Farms, Homes, and Mortgages.—Several State reports have been prepared and published since the preliminary returns from Alabama and

Insurance.—Several extra Census bulletins have been issued giving results in detail of an exhaustive inquiry into the condition of the insurance business of the United States, but a summary of verified totals has not yet been issued.

UPSON, ANSON JUDD, Chancellor of the University of the State of New York, was born in Philadelphia, Nov. 7, 1823. He is the eldest son of Dana Judd Upson, of Connecticut, and soon after his father's death went to Utica,

ANSON JUDD UPSON.

N. Y., where he was brought up in the family of William Clarke, his maternal grandfather. He was graduated at Hamilton College in 1843, with one of the highest honors. For two years he studied law with Joshua A. Spencer and

Francis Kernan, of Utica ; but before admission to the bar he accepted a tutorship in Hamilton College as more congenial. In 1849 he became adjunct professor of rhetoric and moral philosophy ; and in 1853, professor of logic, rhetoric, and elocution. While in the latter office, which he held for seventeen years, Dr. Upson became the leading instructor in oratory in the United States. One of his friends said : "He combines in a rare degree the faculties of acquisition and communication, and is able to impart knowledge and inspire enthusiasm. The high rank of Hamilton College in the matter of preparation for the rostrum and the pulpit, the use of the pen and the use of the tongue, is mainly attributable to the genius and talent of one who could condescend from the professor's chair to give a stammering, awkward student such painstaking drill as that to which Demosthenes owed his oratorical efficiency." Another said : "There is no other living man who can train young men in speaking and writing as he can do it. In his hands, rhetorical training becomes a fine art." Still another wrote : "Taking the system of Mandeville as a basis, he enlarged and improved upon it in many ways, with the result that no institution in the country could compare with Hamilton in its training of speakers. The eloquence this college has contributed to the pulpit and the bar has been due to Prof. Upson's painstaking instruction to an extent that it would be difficult to estimate. Nor was his influence limited by the professions named, but it extended to all callings which those who were under him went out into the world to follow. For he was peculiarly a teacher of, and a sympathizer with, young men outside of as well as in the midst of the class-room routine. His readings, his lectures, and his sermons always found eager listeners and left lasting impressions upon the mind of his hearers." In 1856 Dr. Upson began to study theology ; in 1859 he was licensed to preach by the Presbytery of Utica, and in 1868 he was ordained. His only charge was over the Second Presbyterian Church of Albany, N. Y. where he was the immediate successor of Rev. William B. Sprague, D.D., author of "Annals of the American Pulpit," who had just resigned after a pastorate of forty years. After occupying this place for ten years, from 1870 to 1880, Dr. Upson resigned to take the chair of sacred rhetoric and pastoral theology in Auburn (N. Y.) Theological Seminary. Failing health obliged him to resign in 1887, since which time he has been emeritus professor and has lived in retirement at Glens Falls, N. Y. Hamilton College gave him the degree of D.D. in 1870 ; and Union College, of LL.D. in 1880. Dr. Upson was a trustee of Hamilton College, 1872–1874, resigning in the latter year to become a regent of the University of the State of New York. He was vice-chancellor of the university, 1890–1892. In September, 1892, he was elected chancellor of the university, in place of George William Curtis, deceased.

Dr. Upson was a delegate to the Evangelical Alliance, in Belfast, in 1884; member of the Presbyterian General Assembly in 1871, 1877, and 1884 ; preacher at Cornell University, 1876 ; prize orator, Young Men's Association, Utica, 1845 ; alumni orator at Hamilton College, 1849 ;

orator of literary societies, Rochester University, 1857, and at Vermont University, 1857 ; orator of Phi Beta Kappa at Union College, 1864, and at Hamilton College, 1870 ; orator of Sigma Phi, Williams College, 1869 ; orator of literary societies, Rutgers College, 1865 ; at Vassar College, 1868 ; and at Elmira College, 1881. While still connected with Hamilton College, Dr. Upson delivered over 300 lectures, mostly in the Western and the New England States. He has contributed liberally to reviews. Among his published works are these : "Historical Address at the Laying of the Corner Stone of the Utica Orphan Asylum" (1860) ; "A Defense of Rhetoric" (1864) ; "The Outside of Books" (1865) ; "Notions about Names" (1866) ; "The Bible Imperishable" (1872) ; "Memorial of Rev. W. B. Sprague, D.D." (1876) ; "1817 compared with 1871" (1877) ; "The Imperial State" (1879) ; "Address at the Inauguration of President Darling, Hamilton College" (1881) ; "Memorial of Charles J. Folger, Secretary of the Treasury of the United States" (1884) ; "Rhetorical Training for the Pulpit" (1880) ; and "The University of the State of New York" (1892).

URUGUAY, a republic in South America. The Republic declared its independence from Spain, on Aug. 25, 1825, the Constitution being proclaimed Sept. 10, 1829. The Congress consists of a Senate of 19 members, 1 from each department, elected for six years by an electoral college, and a House of Representatives with 60 members, 1 for each 3,000 inhabitants, elected for three years by direct suffrage. The President is elected for four years ; the present incumbent of the presidential chair being Dr. J. Herrera y Obes, elected President for the term ending March 1, 1894. The following is the Cabinet as composed in the beginning of 1892 : Minister of the Interior and Justice, Gen. L. G. Perez ; Minister of War and Marine, Gen. P. Callorta ; Minister of Agriculture, Industry, Instruction, and Public Works, A. Capurro ; Minister of Finance, Dr. C. M. Ramurez ; Minister of Foreign Affairs, Dr. M. Herrero y Espinosa.

Area and Population.—The area of Uruguay is estimated at 72,110 square miles, with a population in 1890 of 706,524, which estimation is stated to be below the actual population, which is supposed to number 748,915. The number of marriages in 1891 was 3,524 ; births, 28,696 ; deaths, 13,146 ; excess of births, 15,550. The active army in 1892 numbered 223 officers and 3,221 men, the police troops about 3,200 men, and the National Guard 20,000 men. The navy consists of 2 gunboats, 1 steam sloop, and 5 small steamers, manned by 22 officers and 162 men in 1892.

Finances.—The total revenue for the financial year ending June 30, 1891, was 14,954.500 pesos, of which 10,000,000 pesos were derived from customs ; 1,800,000 from direct contributions ; 950,-000 pesos from patent fees ; and 2,204,500 pesos from various sources. The expenditures amounted to 14,589.513 pesos, of which 545,146 pesos were for the legislature ; 64,636 pesos for the President ; 149,758 pesos for foreign affairs ; 2,028,112 pesos for the general administration ; 1,172,707 pesos for finance ; 1,222,885 pesos for justice, worship, and instruction ; 3,397.068 pesos for war and marine ; and 6,009,231 pesos for the public debt. The public debt amounted on Jan. 1, 1891, to 89,848.851 pesos.

Commerce.—The total imports amounted to 18.978.000 pesos in 1891, of which 5.477,000 pesos came from Great Britain, 2,476,000 pesos from France, 1.844,000 pesos from Germany, 1,826,000 pesos from Spain, 1,085,000 pesos from Brazil, 1,956,000 pesos from Italy, 1,578,000 pesos from the Argentine Republic, 928,000 pesos from the United States, 736,000 pesos from Belgium, 200,-000 pesos from Cuba, 127,000 pesos from Chili, 96,000 pesos from Paraguay, 25,000 pesos from Portugal, and 20,000 pesos from other countries. The total exports amounted to 26,998,000 pesos, of which 6,284,000 pesos went to France, 4,961,-000 pesos to Great Britain, 4,712,000 pesos to Brazil, 3,580,000 pesos to Belgium, 2,472,000 pesos to the Argentine Republic, 1,849,000 pesos to the United States, 1,473,000 pesos to Germany, 563,000 pesos to Italy, 348,000 pesos to Cuba, 227,000 pesos to Spain, 184,000 pesos to Portugal, 168,000 pesos to Chili, and 178,000 pesos to other countries. The principal exports were wool of the value of 8,207,000 pesos ; hides and skins. 7,624,000 pesos ; meat, 3,501,000 pesos ; extract of beef, 2,135,000 pesos ; animals, 1,509,-000 pesos ; tallow, 1,504,000 pesos ; hair, 410,000 pesos. There were 1,092 ocean vessels entered in 1891, of 1,429,661 tons, of which 658, of 1,154,-477 tons, were steamers, and 959 vessels. of 1,283,-049 tons, cleared, of which 635. of 1,074,036 tons, were steamers. (For communications, see the "Annual Cyclopædia" for 1891.)

UTAH, a Territory of the United States, organized Sept. 9, 1850 ; area, 84,970 square miles ; population in 1890, 207,905. Capital, Salt Lake City.

Government.—The following were the Territorial officers during the year: Governor, Arthur L. Thomas ; Secretary, Elijah Sells ; Treasurer, Josiah Barnet ; Auditor, Arthur Pratt ; Commissioner of Common Schools, Jacob S. Boreman ; Chief Justice of the Supreme Court, Charles S. Zane ; Associate Justices, Thomas J. Anderson, John W. Blackburn, James A. Miner. Judge Anderson resigned during the year, and President Harrison appointed G. W. Bartch to succeed him, in January, 1893.

United States Marshal Ellis H. Parsons resigned in September, and was succeeded by Irving A. Benton.

Finances.—The receipts of the Territory for 1890–91, the last biennial period reported, were $1,477,140.31, and the expenditures, $1,500,-413.80.

Classification of Population.—A census bulletin recently issued gave statistics of population of the Pacific States and Territories, by which it appears that of the 207.905 of population in 1890, 110,463 were males and 97,442 were females, the excess of males being 13,021. The native born numbered 154.841, against 53,064 foreign born. The total number of colored persons in the Territory was 2,006 ; this includes Chinese, Japanese, and civilized Indians as well as persons of African descent. The proportion of foreign born to native born people in Utah is less than in Montana, Wyoming, Arizona, Nevada, Washington, and California. And her colored population is less in proportion to the whites than that of any of the Pacific States and Territories.

The total number of children in Utah between the ages of five and seventeen was 67,465, of w   62,463 were native born and 5,002 foreign bdrown

The number of males of. militia age in Utah—that is, from eighteen to forty-five years, inclusive—was 45,139, of whom 30,640 were native born and 15,074 foreign born. The total number of males of voting age in Utah was 54.471. The percentage of aliens in Utah who speak the English language is larger than in any other of the Pacific States and Territories.

The Capital.—A preliminary report on the industries of Salt Lake City for the year ending May 31, 1890, gives the following statements : Between 1880 and 1890 the number of industries reported decreased from 52 to 45. and the number of establishments reporting from 166 to 149; the amount of capital increased from $860,415 to $2.658,676 ; the number of persons employed, from 928 to 1,997 ; the amount of wages paid, from $425,537 to $1,276,219 ; the cost of materials used, from $812,736 to $1,665,877 ; the value of the product, from $1,610,133 to $3,864,463.

The population was 20,768 in 1880 and 41,843 in 1890. The assessed valuation rose in the ten years from $7,301,325 to $53,926,924. and the municipal debt from $67,000 to $500,000.

Education.—The average number of children attending the public schools of the capital was 6,686, and the original enrollment, 7,247. The school census shows a total number of school age of 10,519. of whom 6,305 are Mormon children.

A Chautauqua assembly for Utah was inaugurated in August at Calder's Park. In the same line of work the faculty of the Brigham Young College, at Logan, have prepared for a non-resident college course leading to a diploma. Courses of study will be laid down and examinations held in various parts of the Territory.

The Agricultural College, at Logan, advertised in December a free course of lectures on practical agriculture, to open in January, and continue with three lectures a day, for ten weeks.

A suit was brought by the trustees of the Agricultural College to compel the auditor to pay them $16,250 of the $65,000 appropriated by the Assembly in March. The money was also claimed by a board of construction appointed at the time the appropriation was made. The decision of the court was : "That neither the trustees nor the intervenors are entitled to a writ of mandate against the auditor, and the judgment of the district court must be reversed and the case remanded with directions to dismiss the application of the plaintiff and the petition of intervention."

The first Arbor Day in the Territory was observed, April 2, as a legal holiday.

Territorial Institutions.—The repairs in the Lunatic Asylum were completed late in the year, the blacksmith shop finished, and a contract let for putting electric wires into the new apartments.

The expenses for the year of the Women's Industrial Christian Home aggregated $3,995.33. This taken from the annual appropriation of $4,000, leaves a balance in hand of $4.67. The average number of inmates during the year has been 20 ; that is, from 5 to 18 women, and from 12 to 15 children.

Irrigation.—A company are at work on a canal and reservoir, to utilize the waters of Beaver River, for irrigating farm lands. Four miles of the canal were reported completed in the summer, and work on the reservoir was about to begin ; this is to have a capacity of 659,642,000 cubic feet. Beaver River, which rises in the Beaver Mountains, had a flow from the latter part of April to the first of July, of 923,-000,000 cubic feet. The scheme, when perfected, will irrigate 30,000 acres of land, lying in Beaver and Millard counties.

The projectors of the plan will give the farmer a perpetual water right for the consideration of $10 an acre ; or will take their pay in land, requiring a one-half interest in all lands irrigated. The section of country embraced in this irrigation scheme is now intersected by the Union Pacific Railroad, and quite generally under cultivation.

Beet Sugar.—The crop of beets this year was the largest ever grown in the Territory. The product of the Lehi Sugar Works in October amounted to 783,400 pounds. The Government pays a bounty of 2 cents a pound, and the Territory 1 cent. In September the run was not so large, the bounty amounting to only $3,954. The first granulated sugar made in the Territory was turned out this year. The sugar company had 500 acres in beets this season, while last season there were but 200 acres. Next year the company will put 1,000 acres in beets, and will gradually increase their acreage until their yearly minimum acreage is 2,000 acres. This year's beet crop for use at the sugar works was grown under the supervision of the sugar works company.

Minerals.—The year's production is given as below in Wells, Fargo & Co.'s annual statement:

Copper—1,822,616 pounds, at 5 cents per pound..........................	$91,130 80
Unrefined lead—91,117,107 pounds, at $55 per ton........................	2,505,720 42
Fine silver—8,969,656 ounces, at 86½ cents per ounce....................	7,792,388 65
Fine gold—38,182 ounces, at $20 per ounce..............................	763,640 00
Total export value.............$11,152,879 87	

Computing the gold and silver at their mint valuation, and other metals at their value at the seaboard, would increase the value of the product to $16,276,818.

Gold-fields.—The gold-field recently discovered is thus described by Cass Hite, explorer and prospector :

At a point on San Juan river about forty miles from its confluence with Colorado river, enters from the Navajo country on the south (heading for the Sierra Calabasa) the Moonlight canyon. Nearly opposite, coming from the north, enters the clay wash, heading in the Elk mesa. That point, the mouth of Moonlight canyon, is, from the latest reports, the heart of the gold-field. From there to Dandy Crossing on the Colorado, as the raven makes it, is about forty miles, but up White canyon to its head and down the clay wash is about sixty miles. From Bluff City by the San Juan river is about seventy miles, and by the detour made from the Ruicon on the Bluff road around the base of the Elk mountains and down the clay wash, it is 100 miles. With the Arizona and Utah line for a center from north to south, and the mouth of the Moon-

light canyon from east to west, there is an area of 200 miles square that covers that entire country in question. It is the bottom of an old silurian sea. The only eruptive spots in it are the Henry mountains, the Navajo mountains fifty miles south at the junction of the San Juan and Colorado, the Chuck-a-luck mountains on the Navajo reservation, the Blue and Elk mountains on the north. The rest of the entire area is sedimentary. All the mountains named are island mountains and were formed by laccolites, the igneous rocks being invariably trachyte.

At the lower end of this canyon is the mouth of Moonlight. At this point for five to eight miles are large deposits of gravel bars. From thence on the river enters the great San Juan canyon, which is about thirty miles from its mouth. Mighty sluice-boxes cover this entire area. On almost a water level lie the sedimentary strata, and in them a stratum of quartz pebbles and sand many feet in thickness—up to 500. This stratum in many places carries gold and is sometimes rich.

Other reports and estimates are not so favorable. At the close of the year there were about 5,000 men in the new fields.

Carbonate Mines.—Rich carbonate strikes have been made at Eureka, in the Tintic district, 90 miles south of Salt Lake. The discovery is of such magnitude, the bodies of ore so extensive and rich, as to lead many to predict that a new district has been opened in Utah which is equal to Creede, and may even rival Leadville. The formation in which the ore is found is a dolomitic limestone. This is traversed for a considerable distance by dikes of porphyry, and there are mountains of the last-named rock which have been thrown up through the lime.

Onyx.—A valuable deposit of onyx has been found on the west shore of Utah Lake, and a company is being formed to develop and operate the property. It is described by a mining engineer as "one of the most valuable deposits in the world, being finely stratified and lying in such a manner that blocks of any size can be taken out. Many pillars now in view will cut ten and twelve feet in length and almost any width, while the thickness will be fourteen to eighteen inches. The whole structure is incased in a black lime and is perhaps the only regular deposit in existence. All the onyx of the old world and the Eastern States lies principally in bowlders, and comparatively few are of any value whatever." The onyx shows a great variety of color.

Natural Gas and Oil.—A flow of natural gas was struck in January, six miles north of Salt Lake City, at a depth of 200 feet. Other wells have been driven in the vicinity, with good results, the fourth one having been driven to a depth of 700 feet, and a well opened which gives 160 pounds pressure, and is estimated to yield from 12,000,000 to 20,000,000 feet of gas a day. A well within the city limits yielded gas when driven to a depth of 950 feet, and later oil was reported to have been struck at a depth of 1,000 feet.

Gas was found at Ogden in March, at a depth of 200 feet. In boring, the drill passed through shale which is impregnated with oil. The region of country east of Great Salt and Utah lakes has for many years been regarded as rich oil and gas fields.

Salt.—The product of salt from the lake is about 300,000 tons a year. The salt beds or gardens on the eastern shore of the lake the past season covered 3,000 acres, being from 12 to 350 acres each. The largest company engaged in the business has beds covering 273 acres.

World's Fair Exhibit.—The Utah building was to have been finished by Dec. 5. The design, which called for an outlay of $25,000, was modified so as to bring the cost within $12,-000. It is 82 by 46 feet and two stories in height. Plans are preparing for the Great Salt Lake pavilion, to be erected on the southwest corner of the Utah grounds. In this pavilion will be constructed a model of the lake. It will be an exact representation of that body of water in every respect, showing the natural outline of the shore, all the islands, location of bathing resorts, salt works, etc. This lake will be filled with water from the Great Salt Lake, which the Union Pacific company has agreed to haul free of charge.

The most important part of the exhibit will probably be that of minerals.

The Escheated Church Property.—The celebrated case of the United States *vs.* the Church of Jesus Christ of Latter-day Saints *et al.*, in reference to the personal property taken, has been before the Supreme Court, the point in direct issue being consideration of the report of Master in Chancery Loufbourow, to whom the cause was referred in 1891. It appears that when the matter was considered several different parties appeared before the referee and presented schemes for the division of the escheated funds. To the right of any except such as were parties to the record, appearing in the consideration of the case at this stage, the attorneys for plaintiff objected, which position was sustained by the court, and the cause as thus simplified presented but two issues or schemes—one advanced by the attorneys for plaintiff sustaining the report, and the other by the defendants, asking for a diversion of the fund to all the original purposes to which it had been devoted that might not be shown to be unlawful.

The report in question was as follows :

1. That the fund be constituted into a permanent school fund for the perpetual endowment of the public schools of the Territory of Utah ;
2. That a commissioner be appointed under bond to have custody and control of the fund, to loan the same under the direction of the court, etc.;
3. That he report his acts and doings biennially to this court ; and,
4. That the income from said fund, after paying expenses, etc., be apportioned among the several counties ratably according to the children of school age.

The Church, by its counsel, argued that the use of the funds for school purposes would be as far as possible from the use contemplated by the donors. On the side of the master, it was argued that the scheme proposed by the Church was really a suggestion to return the fund into the identical hands from which it had been taken, based no doubt on the theory that conditions have been changed in regard to the practice and teaching of polygamy ; that as it is decreed that the property is not lawfully applicable to the purposes for which it was originally acquired and to which, at the beginning of the suit, it was being devoted, it would not be competent for this court

to make an order which is not consistent with the original decree; that in reference to the claim that the practice and teaching have changed in regard to polygamy, the testimony had shown that there is no change in the belief of the original authenticity of the revelation, and that it is still a doctrine, but has only been modified by the later one suspending its practice, and it is maintained that even this may be changed at any time. Should the people receive such a revelation, there would be nothing to prevent them from re-entering into that practice except the civil law of the land. The word of the head of the Church has changed the practices of this entire people in a day, because of their belief that the Deity so directed. From the books of doctrine, from the lips of every teacher of that creed, there constantly comes the statement that the revelation of polygamy is still a doctrine, but has been only suspended. It was argued also that, under the claim of the defendants, everything would be really administered by the Church heads, though trustees would be nominally created.

The decision, rendered in November, was in favor of the Church.

Notice has been filed of an appeal to the Supreme Court of the United States.

The Question of Statehood.—As will be seen by reference to the platforms of the three political parties, the Liberals protested against immediate Statehood, while the Democrats and Republicans declared in favor of it. A bill conferring it was introduced in Congress on July 30, by the Utah delegate. It provides for a constitutional convention and the submission of the work of that convention to the vote of the people.

Of course, it was not expected that anything would be done about the bill before the next session of Congress.

The annual report of the Utah Commissioners, made to the Secretary of the Interior in September, takes the ground that the sanction of the Church has been withdrawn only temporarily from the practice of polygamy, and will be restored after a political purpose has been served, and affirms that reports indicate that the practice has not entirely ceased. This President Woodruff denies, and says no polygamous marriage has been contracted for two years.

Political.—At the municipal election in the capital, Feb. 8, the first in which national party lines were drawn, the Liberals—the party which had opposed the division—elected the whole city ticket, and a large majority of the councilmen.

The Republican convention, held in September, nominated Frank J. Cannon for delegate to Congress. While expressing allegiance to the general policy of the party, the platform called for free and unrestricted coinage of silver. On matters concerning the Territory it declared opposition to the removal of the Utes to Utah, but favored the giving of sufficient lands of the several reservations to the Indians thereof in severalty, and the opening of the remainder to settlement under the homestead laws, particularly the Uintah reservation ; favored the cession of the arid lands to the several States and Territories, and such an amendment of the land-laws as will allow resident citizens to take from the public lands the necessary timber for all domestic purposes ; called for the employment of Utah workmen on Utah public works, and the use on them of Utah material. and for the eight-hour system of labor ; and contained, further, the resolutions below :

We unqualifiedly denounce the un-American course of the late Democratic Legislative Assembly of this Territory in attempting to strike down the great sheep industry, for its refusal to further encourage the production of Utah sugar, for the open hostility it displayed to the policy of develop-ing the manufacturing industries of the Territory, for its despicable attempt to divert the money appropriated for the use of the Logan Agricultural College to partisan uses and purposes, and for its utter failure to legislate intelligently upon ques-tions of vital interest to the people.

The people of Utah are particularly interested in the maintenance of republican institutions and republican principles. Her principal productions —wool, lead, silver, and farm products—are profita-bly produced here only because of Republican pro-tection. And yet these same productions receive the special, open, and malignant hostility of the Democracy.

We again affirm our opposition to the disfran-chisement of any citizen except for crime of which he shall have been convicted by due process of law, and we favor the free exercise of the power of am-nesty to all citizens disfranchised on account of polygamy or polygamous relations, who will obey and uphold the laws of the United States.

The Democratic convention met in Provo, Oct. 5. and nominated Joseph L. Rawlins for dele-gate to Congress. After denouncing paternalism in government, protection. subsidies, and Federal control of elections, the resolutions declared :

We denounce the action of the Republican con-vention in this Territory in approving the exercise by the Governor of the absolute power of veto. The subsequent withdrawal of that approval when its probable effect upon the citizens was appreciated, was but a subterfuge too flimsy to cover the real sentiment of the party. Its action in reference to statehood was similar in spirit, and a plain indica-tion that Utah need not look to the Republican party for aid in speedy deliverance from territorial vassalage.

We condemn the covert charge of the Utah Commission, signed by all its members except that grand old veteran Democrat, Gen. McClernand, that polygamous marriages are still being con-tracted in Utah, and that a large number of people are living in polygamous cohabitation, as false and designed to deceive the American people and hinder the progress of the Territory to the grand position of statehood.

We announce our complete confidence in the sincerity of the Mormon people in their abandon-ment of polygamy, in submission to the laws of the land, and their division on party lines, and our full

faith in the pledges of their church leaders that the freedom of the members in political affairs shall not be interfered with by them in any particular. We view the attempts of individuals to make it appear that the Mormon presidency secretly desire and work for the success of any party, as a slander upon the church officials and a disgrace to those engaged in such despicable trickery.

The resolutions further declared emphatically in favor of statehood for Utah, and the restora-tion of silver, and expressed the friendship of the party to organized labor and its opposition to the "policy of the Republican party in the inter-est of capital, which results in the reduction of wages, the importation of cheap workmen, the employment of Pinkerton hirelings, and the oppression of the laboring classes."

The convention of Liberals met at Ogden, Oct. 12. The resolutions declared unalterable oppo-sition to statehood, expressing the belief that, with the opportunity which statehood would bring, the priesthood would again assume com-plete control. The reason for that belief is given in the following, from the preamble :

The Liberal party fails to see any such changed conditions as others assert that they see. It looks upon the assurance that conditions have changed as a theory and not an established fact, and it recoils from the prospect of imminent statehood.

Anxious as every Liberal is to see every difference adjusted, as anxious as they are to exercise the utmost privileges accorded to the most favored Americans, they remember what first caused clash-ing here was the presence and control of an un-yielding theocracy and an *imperium in imperio*, and they cannot fail to note that at the last conference of this theocratic organization the old assumptions were all renewed. The bliss which awaits the po-lygamous family in heaven was vividly portrayed, the necessity of paying tithing was eulogized upon, and the declaration was boldly made that they are a distinct people, that their spiritual and temporal affairs are inextricably blended, and that the only remedy for trouble or differences should be an ap-peal to the priesthood.

Clarence E. Allen was chosen candidate for Delegate to Congress.

At the election, Nov. 8, the Democratic candi-date, J. L. Rawlins, received 15,211 votes ; F. J. Cannon, Republican, 12,405 ; and C. E. Allen, Liberal, 6,989. The whole vote was 34,605, while in 1890 it was 23,290.

The vote for Commissioners to locate univer-sity lands was different in each case from the vote for Delegate. The Democratic vote ranged from 15,568 to 15,651 ; the Republican vote, from 11,-502 to 11,516 ; the Liberal vote, from 7,035 to 7,062.

V

VENEZUELA, a republic in South America. It seceded from the Federal Republic of Colombia in 1830, and the Constitution was proclaimed in Sept. 30 of that year. The system was federal, as in the Constitution of the United States, but with a larger degree of State rights and munic-ipal autonomy. José Antonio Paez, Bolivar's chief lieutenant, was the first President, and his influence was predominant until the party of the

landowners, called the Oligarchists. was over-thrown by the Liberals after José Tadeo Mona-gas, who had been made President in 1847 as the nominee of Paez, became the pretended cham-pion of the democracy. Monagas had led an unsuccessful revolt against the Government in 1835, and after he ascended the Presidential chair he called into his Cabinet the revolutionists who were associated with .him, disarmed the

Government troops, and committed other acts that exasperated the party of wealth and respectability which had placed him in power. In Jannary, 1848, the Congress, which had begun impeachment proceedings against Monagas. was broken up by the mob and the Liberal Militia, an organization substituted by the President for the regular army which he had disbanded. Paez led a revolt against the dictator, but could not raise enough men to make a long fight. The hostile political leaders were executed or sent into exile, and for ten years Monagas ruled despotically and corruptly under constitutional forms, the Presideney passing in succession to members of his own family. He was overthrown in 1858 by a rebellion headed by Gen. Tovar Castro, who became President. In the struggle which ensued between the Federalists or Monaguistas, upholders of a loose confederation, and the advocates of a strong centralized union, Castro was deposed because he identified himself with the Monaguistas Gen. Paez was called from his exile in New York to take command of the army, and when Castro's successor, President Gual, feeling strong enough as leader of the Liberal party to stand alone, demanded his resignation, Paez was upheld by the Federal Council, and Gual himself was forced out. Paez was made President with dictatorial powers for the purpose of fighting the rebellion led by Gen. Juan C. Falcon. The rebellion gained ground, and in the spring of 1863, when Gen. Antonio Guzman Blanco lay before the capital with a victorious rebel army, Paez made terms, the result of which was that he retired, and was succeeded by Castro, with Guzman Blanco as Vice-President. The democratic and progressive elements were in the ascendency for the first time since the Liberal administration of Paez in 1843, and Guzman Blanco, the real political leader, had the statesmanlike gifts necessary to guide the movement and direct the intellect and energy of the nation into channels of peace and progress. A new Constitution was proclaimed on March 28, 1864, which established the rights of petition and free assembly, popular suffrage, the inviolability of the mails, and the right of imprisoned persons to speedy examination and release in case the charge fails, guaranteed free elections, and declared the autonomy of the States. In 1867 partisan quarrels brought on a civil war which lasted till December, 1871, when Blanco, as leader of the Federalists. was proclaimed Provisional President or Dictator. Blanco was elected President in 1873, and in 1877 he was re-elected, and also in 1881, after suppressing two uprisings in 1879. He was the controlling spirit behind every administration, including that of Gen. Crespo, who was chosen President in 1884. Under his direction an admirable system of compulsory public instruction was organized, a telegraph and postal system was established, and railroads were built connecting Caracas and Valencia with their seaports. An amended Constitution, adopted on April 27, 1881. consolidated the 20 States which had constituted the Republic from the beginning, into 8 States. 5 Territories, and 1 Colony. Long tenure of power rendered Blanco vain, self-willed, and arbitrary, and his extortionate greed in accumulating a vast fortune out of the public wealth made him so unpopular that he was over-

thrown by a popular revolution in 1888. Dr. Pablo Rojas Paul was elected President for the term ending Feb.20, 1890, and he was succeeded on March 7, 1890, by Dr. Raimundo Andueza Palacio for the term expiring Feb. 20, 1892.

A revised Constitution, adopted on April 16, 1891, divides the country into 9 States, 1 Federal District, 3 Territories, and 2 Colonies. The Senate is composed of 27 members, 3 from each State, who are elected for 4 years by the State Legislatures. The Chamber of Deputies numbers 57 members, 1 for every 35,000 inhabitants, elected also for 4 years by direct suffrage in the individual States. The President holds office for 2 years. He is assisted by a cabinet of 6 Ministers and by the Federal Council, consisting of 19 members who are chosen every 2 years by Congress. The Federal Council has for its President the President of the Republic, who is elected from among its members by the Council after it is constituted in the beginning of each biennial session of Congress, and is not eligible for the next succeeding term, nor can any member of the Council be appointed twice in succession. The National Legislature consists of the two Houses, one of Senators and another of Deputies. These bodies meet every year in the capital, Caracas, on the 20th of February, and their sessions last 70 days and may be prolonged for 20 more. Each house may be organized with two-thirds of its total members, and once they have commenced to hold sessions they can continue them with two-thirds of those who opened them, provided the number of members present be equal at least to one-half their full number. Both houses discharge their functions separately, having, however, the power to meet in joint session in certain cases, or when one of the two deems it necessary. The election of the Federal Council takes place in the first and third year of each term of office of the legislative body and within the first 15 days of its meeting.

Area and Population.—The area of Venezuela was 1,043,900 kilometers before the recent ratification of the Colombian frontier. The population of the different States and Territories, according to the census of 1891, is as follows :

SECTIONS.	Males.	Females.	Total.
States :			
Federal District............	40,650	48,483	89,133
Bermudez...................	149,022	151,575	300,597
Bolivar....................	29,064	27,225	50,289
Carabobo	97,270	100,751	198,021
Falcon	66,717	72,393	139,110
Lara	117,863	128,897	246,760
Los Andes.................	163,937	172,209	336,146
Miranda...................	234,095	250,414	484,509
Zamora	126,248	120,428	246,676
Zulia......	41,077	44,379	85,456
Territories :			
Amazonas.................	23,603	21,494	45,197
Colon (popul. flottante)......	125	4	129
Delta.....................	3,908	3,314	7,222
Goajira...................	30,818	35,142	65,960
Yuruary.......	12,712	9,680	22,392
Total....... :..........	1,137,139	1,186,388	2,323,527

Yuruary has lately been incorporated in the State of Bolivar. The capital city, Caracas, had 70,466 inhabitants in 1891. Valencia. the capital of the State of Carabobo, had in 1888 a population of 38,654 ; Barquisimeto, 31,476 ; Barcelona,

12,785 ; Ciudad de Cura, 12,198 ; Merida, 12,-018 ; Ciudad de Bolivar, 11,686 ; Guanare, 10,-880 ; Capatarida, 3,606. The number of marriages registered in 1889 was 6,705 ; births, 76,187 ; deaths, 55,218 ; surplus of births, 20,969. The number of immigrants in 1890 was 1,555.

Commerce and Communications.—The following values were exported of the principal commercial products of the country in 1889–90 : Coffee, 71,168,000 bolivars ; cacao, 9.329,000 bolivars ; gold, 9,072,000 bolivars ; hides and skins, 4,728,000 bolivars ; copper, 1,972,000 bolivars ; live animals, 1,290,000 bolivars. The total value of the imports was 83,614,411, compared with 81,372,257 bolivars in 1889, and the value of the exports was 100,917,838, compared with 97,271,-306 bolivars.

There were 430 kilometers of railroads in operation in 1891. The state telegraphs had a total length of 5,645 kilometers. The number of dispatches in 1890 was 419,724. The receipts were 326,904 bolivars, and the expenses 949,846 bolivars. The post-office forwarded 1,572,292 letters and cards, and 1,365,576 items of printed matter. The expenses for 1890 were 961,815 bolivars.

Finances.—In the budget for 1890–91 the total receipts of the Government were set down as 35.976,000 bolivars or francs, of which 25,000,000 bolivars were the estimated receipts from customs, 162,000 bolivars represent other duties, 6,060,000 bolivars indirect taxes, and 4,916,000 bolivars rents. The expenditure was made to balance the revenue, 7,340,406 bolivars being allocated to the Interior Department, 2,004,969 bolivars to the Ministry of Foreign Affairs; 2,685,437 bolivars to the Department of Fomento, which includes colonization, posts and telegraphs, and the state printing-office; 3.758,158 bolivars to the Ministry of Public Instruction, 5,790,767 bolivars to the Ministry of Public Works, 4,953,226 bolivars to the Ministry of Finance, 5,445,120 bolivars to the public debt, and 3,997,917 bolivars to the army and navy. Since no budget was passed for the financial year 1891–92, the same one, under the Constitution, was applicable for that year.

The public debt on Dec. 31, 1890, amounted to 110,938,687 bolivars, of which 38,130,077 bolivars constituted the consolidated national or internal debt, 67,388,462 bolivars the foreign consolidated debt, and 5,420,148 bolivars a debt raised in Spain, France, and Germany.

The Army and Navy.—The permanent army consisted in 1891 of 11 battalions, each of 4 companies of 120 men, 2 separate companies of infantry, and 2 companies of artillery with 15 guns, and numbered altogether 5,760 men. For 1892 the effective was fixed by Congress at 5,000 men. The fleet in 1891 was composed of an iron steamer and 3 sailing vessels, and there were 4 gunboats under construction.

Constitutional Dispute.—Amendments to the Constitution adopted by Congress in June, 1891, and approved late in the year by the State Legislatures, provided that Congress should elect the President, instead of the Federal Council, prolonged the Presidential term from 2 to 4 years, restored the original 20 States, and introduced changes tending to enlarge the powers of the central executive and of Congress at the expense of State sovereignty. Under the old Constitution

it was the duty of Congress on assembling in February, 1892, to choose a Federal Council, which should immediately proceed to elect a President to succeed Dr. Andueza Palacio for the term of two years beginning Feb. 20. President Palacio and his Cabinet and supporters in Congress held that Congress should immediately declare the new Constitution in force and elect a President in accordance with its provisions. The Opposition insisted on proceeding under the old law and proclaiming the new Constitution only after the inauguration of a new Administration. They suspected that Dr. Andueza Palacio, prompted by Dr. Casañas, Minister of the Interior, and other members of the party in possession of the offices, was scheming to have himself continued in power by the election of a candidate who would be a mere stalking-horse for his schemes and was accused of attempting to secure the election of a temporary President or be made provisional President himself until a Congress elected under the new Constitution could assemble. They dubbed his party the Continuists, while they called themselves Legalists, as upholding the legal and constitutional mode of procedure. The contending factions both formed part of the great Liberal party. When the time for the assembling of Congress came, the Continuists kept away, as they had been placed in the minority by the action of the State Legislatures in electing Senators opposed to Palacio and his supposed dictatorial projects, and hence the Legalists, who met at the regular date and organized Congress, were unable to elect a Federal Council, not having the necessary two-thirds quorum in the Senate. The Senate therefore closed its doors, and did not afterward meet. The House of Deputies had enough members to proceed to business, and continued in session. The Opposition held that in such an emergency Congress should organize a Provisional Government, but the President's faction asserted that in the absence of a constitutional successor he was the rightful President in the interim. He therefore held over, though he was denounced as a usurper and all his acts were declared to be illegal by the Constitutionalists. Palacio tried to win over the less determined of his opponents, and when persuasion failed, he attempted to intimidate his enemies by arresting some of the most prominent of them. On March 8, 1892, a formal protest was signed by 46 members of Congress, who then withdrew. As soon as it appeared Palacio assumed dictatorial powers, and ordered wholesale arrests. The Rotunda or city prison of Caracas was filled with political prisoners, and all who escaped to Curaçoa or Trinidad were proscribed and prohibited from returning on pain of death. The seats of the imprisoned or exiled Legalist members were filled by Presidential decree with creatures of Palacio and Casañas, in some cases by policemen. While rebellion was breaking out in the provinces, the sympathizers with resistance in the capital appealed to the Federal Supreme Court to decide the question whether Palacio's continuance in office was legal. On March 26 the judges rendered a unanimous decision pronouncing Palacio's retention of office unconstitutional. When Palacio heard this he was so transported with anger that he ordered the judges to be imprisoned. All except those who evaded arrest were thrown into jail, and kept there for weeks. This act and the arbitrary dissolution of Congress that followed it caused those friends of order who had stood by the President to go over in great numbers to the Opposition and greatly strengthened the cause of the revolution. Palacio offered to resign the Presidency as soon as his successor should be elected and the centralized form of government proclaimed under the new Constitution, and when Congress refused these terms he closed it with military force and ordered the arrest of the members who voted against his proposal. While Gen. Crespo was gathering, arming, and drilling an insurgent army in the South, Caracas was placed under martial law by the President. All men suspected of disloyalty were placed behind bars, and when the prisons overflowed private houses were turned into jails. Every member of the Federal Council was imprisoned. A strict censorship was kept over the press, and no news was published except such as the Government gave out. Eventually all the newspapers except the Government organ were suppressed or discontinued. Troops patrolled the city and guarded the outlets to prevent the supporters of the insurgents from getting away. Many of the merchants were imprisoned and trade came to a standstill. The President, in answer to a manifesto of the leader of the revolutionists, issued a proclamation disclaiming any personal motives or ambitious designs, and solemnly declaring that his only purpose was to safeguard the liberties of the people, preserve the independence of the States, and avert the horrors of civil war. The principal passages were as follow :

Fellow Patriots—Complying with a solemn duty as President of the Union, as guardian of the tremendous responsibilities of the future, as leader of the grand revolution toward liberal reform, and as principal and most zealous guardian of the sovereign autonomy of the States and of the rights and privileges of the municipalities, which are the prime source of authority in any democratic government, I announce unto you the imminent danger which menaces the popular cause and the most noble of the aspirations of the Republic, viz., the reform of the Constitution sanctioned by the last Congress and by the Legislatures of the States in past sessions and their declared opinion in favor of its immediate consideration and adoption. My period of constitutional command is now nearing its end. In sight there is the road to happiness, but in a dark corner I see a shadow that threatens to dispel this happiness, and it belongs to me as helmsman of the ship of state to call the necessary forces of the nation to its rescue.

The most terrible catastrophe that can happen to the liberal cause is being quietly prepared, and with it the federation, with all its great conquests and hopes, must perish. Why ? Because a group of men in the body of the National Congress—some because of personal ambition, others for hatred to the great Liberal party—are prompting the immoral combination, which will cover the Republic with blood, with ruin, and with desolation—a sinister group, a most hybrid offspring of the most vicious ambition and of the most unpatriotic of all schemes. The former Congress has already voted upon the reform Constitution, approving it without a single protest or saving vote. The very same people are to-day conspiring for a fresh postponement of its consideration and are conjuring up a farce more in accordance with popular aspirations. It was submitted to the Legislatures of the States, eight of which approved it unanimously, without any alteration whatsoever,

and seven have asked for its immediate enforcement. It is a universal rule of right that the commander has to submit suggestions for instructions to those who give commands, and it is an undeniable principle of the most pure and radical liberalism that the follower is at all times authorized to revoke the powers which he has conferred upon his leader. Congress, then, has in the present case a limited sovereignty by an express and authoritative vote of the States, the municipalities and the people, who reserve unto themselves, as accorded by constitutional mandates, their immediate sovereignty over themselves. From the moment that high body exceeds its powers or debases the nature of this mandate, it exercises an authority usurped from the people and consequently is null and without effect. The constitutional point cannot be clearer, more simple, and more evident in favor of the people, and the Representatives and Senators cannot legally separate themselves from a liberal criticism.

From the eminence of the supreme magistracy, I am and will be principal guardian of the Constitution and the law, of your guaranties, and of your rights. I am and will be the watchful sentinel of peace and ever the patient champion for public liberty. And never shall I permit the Liberal flag, that symbol of glorious conquests, of civilization, and of progress, to be trampled upon, conquered, and humiliated. The ignominious epoch of autocracy has passed forever. I do not aspire to establish a personal government, which I in my strict republican convictions abhor, and I swear that I do not accept nor will I accept, even though force be used toward me, a new constitutional period of power. This would be a stain on the country and an indelible stain upon the liberal cause.

I simply aspire to revindicate the autonomy of the twenty States of the ancient and glorious federation and to give back unto the people a suffrage at once universal, direct, and secret for the election of its magistrates.

The revolts that were begun in various States were fostered and aided greatly from the beginning by the ex-President, Dr. Rojas Paul, whom Palacio has exiled on account of his influence and popularity. His agents and other exiles in the West Indies procured arms and ammunition, which were smuggled in to the troops that Crespo and his lieutenants were drilling.

The Cabinet resigned after Palacio's assumption of the dictatorship, and a new one was appointed on March 28, which was composed as follows: Minister of the Interior, Dr. Benito Guillerte Andueza ; Minister of Foreign Relations, Dr. Manuel Clemente Urbaneza ; Minister of War, Gen. Julio F. Barrio ; Minister of Agriculture, Manuel Antonio Mattas ; Minister of the Treasury, Dr. José Angel Ruiz ; Minister of Posts and Telegraphs, Gen. Dominio A. Carvajol ; Minister of Public Instruction, Dr. Manuel Palacios Rengifo ; Minister of Public Works, Carlos José Monagas.

Civil War.—Ex-President Joaquin Crespo, who had retired from active political life, and was managing his extensive coffee plantations in Zamora, offered his services to the exiled Senators and Deputies in Curaçoa and Trinidad, and they formed a Junta and nominated him commander-in-chief of the Constitutionalist or Congressional forces. The people of his province who had taken part in the rebellion of 1888 had hidden in mountain eaves about 800 rifles, which Crespo had afterward refused to deliver up to Rojas Paul. These weapons served to arm the nucleus of the insurgent army which he now set about raising for the overthrow of Palacio. By the middle of March he had 1,500 men organized in the Apure country, whence he pushed northward after the imprisonment of the Federal judges, fighting unimportant skirmishes with the various Government garrisons in Zamora.

Meanwhile Gen. Eliseo Aranja began collecting a body of revolutionists in the State of Los Andes. Crespo, an experienced fighter, crossing into Miranda, marched on toward Caracas, engaging the scattered forces of the Government. His force was not strong enough or well enough equipped for a descent on the capital, and the other bodies that were recruited in distant parts of the country were unable to cooperate in such a maneuver. Arms and equipments were wanting for all the revolutionary forces, but arrangements were made for introducing them from the West India Islands and from New York and Hamburg. Crespo therefore adopted waiting tactics, and began a series of maneuvers intended to draw the Government troops out upon the plains, where his cavalry, hardy llaneros mounted on strong mustangs and expert with the lance, could deliver their impetuous attacks. The Government forces were much better provided with arms in the beginning of the struggle, but an extravagant administration had left the Treasury empty, the Government being necessitated to obtain an advance of 3,000,-000 bolivars from the Bank of Venezuela at the start, and after a while even the wretched pay of 20 cents a day which was decreed for the common soldier was held back and cut down, while, when food rose to famine prices in the cities held by the Presidential forces, rations were reduced to less than was necessary to sustain the strength and preserve the contentment and loyalty of the soldiers. Palacio's generals pushed out in strong columns, for it was necessary for them to strike quickly and also to occupy the principal towns in force. Crespo's bands did not attempt to stand before them, but disappeared after firing away their scanty supply of ammunition from behind stones and trees, inflicting usually much heavier losses than they received. These skirmishes were chronicled in the Government reports as important victories, and the revolutionary army was stated in the reports sent abroad to have been dispersed and Crespo and his generals to be fugitives, at the time when they were gaining recruits faster than they could arm them and after they had begun to gain battles and were joined by whole battalions of Government soldiers who deserted with their arms, and were drawing their lines constantly closer to Caracas.

Dr. Sebastian Casañas, a politician of force and ability, but inexperienced in military affairs, was made commander-in-chief of the expeditionary force that was sent out against Crespo when hostilities began. He made his headquarters at La Victoria, a town of 10,000 inhabitants, half-way between Caracas and Valencia. A large number of rifles and cartridges were seized by workmen on the railroad near La Victoria, who cut down the escort of 60 soldiers, and went off to the rebels with the six car-loads of munitions. Arms and ammunition were smuggled out of Caracas to the insurgents who swarmed in the neighboring mountains. There was no difficulty in landing arms at Guanta, the port of Barce-

lona or other places on the coast or on the Orinoco or Apure rivers, especially after the capture of a Government war vessel had given them the naval command of the Orinoco. A war steamer was captured carrying military supplies by a party of young revolutionists who surprised the captain and crew on Lake Maracaibo. In the evening of March 24, a dynamite bomb was exploded with terrifying force in the garden of the Casa Amarilla, the President's official mansion in Caracas. It caused all the military and police to rush to the defense of the President, and thus accomplished its object, which was to enable numerous revolutionists who understood the signal to pass through the unguarded streets and make their escape to the mountains.

The first regular engagement was fought near El Totumo, only 3 days' march from Caracas. The insurgents were successful at first, driving back the force which had been sent to occupy Gen. Crespo's cattle ranch at El Totumo, but reenforcements came up, and with 7,500 men, outnumbering the enemy three to one, the Presidential troops made a stand on a hill, which the Crespists tried to storm three times, losing 300 killed, and then retreated, being pursued in their turn, in the direction of Crespo's base in eastern Zamora. Skirmishes took place almost daily for the next two months, but the revolutionists did not again rashly join battle with the troops that Palacio hurried into the field. The next encounter of any importance took place at Ortiz, where Gen. Rodriguez attempted to intercept a force that was marching from the Orinoco to join Crespo. Here the Government troops were compelled to fall back, leaving the town of Ortiz, in the State of Guarico, in the insurgents' hands, and on the heels of this victory for the rebels came the seizure of the National gunboat "Nueve de Julio," which was stationed at Esmerelda on the Orinoco river. Two transports loaded with arms for the Government were captured subsequently. On April 1, three dynamite bombs were exploded in the Plaza Bolivar in front of the Casa Amarilla, and in the midst of the confusion that followed the prisons were broken open by the revolutionists, who released the political prisoners. A large part of a regiment quartered in the Caracas barracks deserted at this time to the enemy, with its commander, Gen. Pulgar.

On April 6 the Governor of Zamora issued a proclamation denouncing Palacio as a tyrant and usurper, and calling for volunteers to expel the dictator from Venezuela. On the same day 600 infantry and 5 troops of cavalry left to form a junction with a body of insurgents from the State of Lara, who were advancing to join Gen. Crespo, who then had his headquarters in the State of Carabobo. Gen. Polanco marched out from Valencia to intercept them, and on the morning of April 7 he overtook the rebels, who had combined under Gen. Manzano, and numbered 5,000. A fierce battle ensued, in which both sides lost heavily, and the Government troops, who were greatly inferior in numbers, but were better armed and trained, forced the rebels to abandon the town of Araure and fall back toward Acaragua, which Manzano had taken possession of a day or two before. In the night, re-enforced by 500 cavalry, the rebels made a stand, and when Gen. Polanco attacked them at noon of the 8th with only half his force of the previous day, Mauzano cut through the Government ranks, retook Aruure, was joined by more cavalry coming from Miranda at Tinaquilla, camped near Valencia, where he received arms and money from sympathizers in the city, and then passed eastward to join Crespo.

On April 14 a large Government force attempted to dislodge Gen. Mora, who was intrenched beyond Polito for the purpose of covering the landing of arms on the coast. After two furious but unsuccessful assaults, Palacio's troops fled in disorder in every direction, and were pursued by the insurgents. Many fell on both sides, but the loss of the Government was the heavier, the official report making it one-third of the force. A considerable proportion of the troops went over to the enemy. On April 18 one of Palacio's most efficient commanders, Gen. Juan Quevedo, was assassinated by the villagers of Los Teques, who hated him for his cruelties. When Gen. Crespo effected a junction with Gen. Mora on the shores of Lake Valencia, he not only threatened La Victoria, which was the key to Caracas, but cut off Gen. Casañas and Gen. Alejandro Ybarra, with 4,000 men, at Calabozo, Valencia, and Puerto Cabello, from the main body of Palacio's army. A son of Gen. Crespo was taken prisoner, and it was reported that Palacio threatened him with death if his father advanced to within a league of Caracas.

A battle was fought at Tompit de Colon. The Government troops, though they repulsed the Federalists, lost 350 killed to 110 on the other side. Gen. Pedro Aranjo, an experienced cavalry officer, who collected a large force from the shores of Lake Maracaibo, attacked Gen. Cipriano Castro at that point on March 29. The battle was suspended after 4 hours of severe fighting, but Aranjo by a diversion held Castro's attention while a detachment intercepted a large quantity of ammunition intended for Castro, after which he retired, joined forces with Gen. Baptista, and defeated Gen. Diego B. Ferrer at Canitos. A commission was sent into Los Andes by Palacio to treat for peace, without being able to effect an arrangement. The President of the State of Los Andes issued a stirring appeal calling on the citizens to rise and expel the troops of the usurper. The Government forces, amounting to 1,500 men, were victorious at Merida and in other engagements, but Gen. Castro was compelled to divide his army to operate against various points, and in the constant fighting his excellent troops melted away. Aranjo cut them off from receiving re-enforcements from Barquisimeto. On April 16 Gen. Castro gained a technical victory at Cuchicuchi, where he attempted to intercept a body of 500 men who were marching to join the insurgent Gen. Cordona. The latter occupied Cuchicuchi first, and repulsed the veteran battalion, which made a stand on the mountain slope until the rebels were out of ammunition, when on the arrival of re-enforcements they drove the insurgents back, and occupied the town. There were 200 killed of the insurgents and 235 on the Government side. The Government force was so reduced that it could do no more than hold the city of Merida, and Gen. Leon Farias was in the same condition at Maracaibo.

Dr. Casañas advanced imprudently to Calabozo in the beginning of the campaign, leaving his rearguard in an unprotected condition. His aim was to get at Crespo and crush his force before it could be trained and armed. In this he was prevented by Gen. Guerra and Gen. E. Rodriguez, who harried his column while Crespo was receiving arms and re-enforcements. He was at length shut in at Calabozo, and in a number of encounters, in which his forces were cut down, he attempted a desperate battle with Crespo's army on the plains, in which his division was used up, after which he escaped, badly wounded, to Caracas, with only 374 men left. His defeat was the turning-point in the war. Fresh dynamite explosions in Caracas on April 30, one alongside of the Federal Palace and one in the military barracks, added to the dictator's alarm, but he was compelled to denude the capital of troops to succor the forces that were in a precarious position in the field. A new army was sent out under Gen. Domingo Monagas and Gen. Francisco Esteban Rangel. The forces of Marcos Rodriguez, Francisco Batalla, Guillermo Esteves, and Eleazar Urdaneta were mostly recruited in the country, and were often successful in coping in guerrilla fashion with the partisans of Crespo, who was not provided with the means of keeping large bodies of men in the field, and after reverses or inaction saw his forces dwindle as well as those of the Government under like conditions. Want of arms and ammunition prevented him from striking a decisive blow, and after pushing forward his line to San Sebastian, where he expected to be joined in the investment of La Victoria by Guerra, who had been harassing Casañas at Calabozo, he was compelled to retreat before the well-equipped troops, greatly superior in numbers, that were advancing. His force was well armed, and consisted at that time of 3,000 infantry and 1,200 horse. The towns that were captured could not be held. The Government were occupying Maracaibo, Trujillo, Merida, Barquisimeto, and Bolivar, as well as Valencia and the seaports of La Guayra and Puerto Cabello in the beginning of May, but the coast and rivers and the mountains were in the hands of the revolutionists, and arms were then coming in for them from abroad. In Curaçoa, with the financial support of Rojas Paul, Gen. Leon Colina raised a force of Venezuelan refugees and sailed for the Venezuelan coast with arms and ammunition sufficient to equip a considerable army that had been raised and was ready to march under his command as soon as he should appear in the Coro district. On May 11 a bomb was exploded in Caracas in front of the residence of Señor Mattos, a relative of Guzman Blanco and president of the Bank of Venezuela, who had assumed the Ministry of Finance. In a fight near Los Teques a Government battalion, commanded by an American, repulsed 350 of Crespo's lancers after a sharp fight, killing one-third of them. Crespo retired to Calabozo, where he concentrated several bodies of troops under revolutionary leaders and received arms enough to supply an army of about 11,000 men. Valencia was closely invested by Gen. Mora, and after a series of skirmishes and sorties, Gen. Ybarra's army was totally defeated. In Los Andes the Legalists were not so successful. At Mocoti Gen. Ferrer was defeated and badly wounded, but at Jajo a force of 1,000 men under Aranjo and Baptista was almost destroyed. After their victory the Congressionalists attempted to join Gen. Monzano on the other side of the mountains, but Gen. Ybarra had provided for the effectual defense of the passes. The Legalists won an important victory at Tichua, and marched upon Barquisimeto with 4,000 men. In Zamora the rebel forces were beaten by the energy and generalship of Eleazar Urdaneta, and a Presidential Commissioner was placed at the head of the State administration in the room of the Governor, who had declared for the revolution. Gen. Colina landed on May 15, captured the towns of La Yela and Coro, and advanced into the State of Falcon. Gen. Mora took the seaport of Tucacas and two Government steamboats, after a desperate resistance in which 150 men and Gen. Garcia were killed. When Crespo began his advance again toward Caracas the tide had turned in his favor. Many of the underfed and unpaid soldiery of the Government were ready to desert to his standard. Palacio was persuaded by his Cabinet to open negotiations with Crespo for a surrender. He offered to turn over the Government to the leader of the revolution if the latter would accept the centralized Constitution, call Congress, and vacate the dictatorship as soon as a constitutional President should be elected, and meanwhile make Dr. Casañas his Minister of War and appoint Palacio Minister to a European court. Crespo replied that he would accept nothing short of unconditional surrender. After this divisions broke out in the Government. Palacio's advisers urged him to resign, and several of them were scheming to take the place of the chieftain whose fall was seen to be near. Mattos insisted on resigning the Ministry of Finance, and Casañas resigned his command.

On May 23 Gen. Urdaneta landed with a large force at La Vela, in order to re-establish the authority of the Government in the States of Falcon and Zulia. With 2,000 well-equipped men he was able to re-occupy the principal places in the Paraguara peninsula. While thus in the west the rebels were held in check, but not defeated, for Gen. Bustillos raised a new congressional army in Los Andes, and new guerrilla forces sprang up in Zulia to aid Colina, some of them led by priests; in the east and center Palacio's cause was waning. Gen. Gonzalez Gil defeated a Government force at Calcara, on the Orinoco, capturing the commander, Gen. Espinosa, with his staff and 200 men. The city of Bolivar, the last place held by Palacio's army on the Orinoco river, at length fell into the hands of the rebels. One of the remarkable features of the war was the use by the insurgents of dynamite, with which they were supplied by the men working on the railroad, that a German company was building. The pickets of the Crespist cavalry were supplied with dynamite petards. Col. Granjos, who had been an engineer on the railroad, laid a mine in the Andes at a spot which a treacherous guide induced Col. Villafane to make his camping-ground, and the entire force was destroyed by the explosive, and by the machetes of the llaneros who fell upon the survivors. In some of the engagements near Valencia, roads and passes were undermined. In the middle of May, with Gen. Diaz Araña and Gen. Matute at Pao, Gen. Manzano intrenched in the valley of the Turen, Gen. Julio Montenegro encamped at Tinaquilla, and Gen. Mora between Nirgua and Barquisimeto, Gen. Colina occupied Salona Alta, and co-operated with Crespo, who was joined by Monzano, and in a series of engagements defeated Palanco and Guede on the Chirgua, drove back the army of Rangel and Monagas, who were intrenched at Calabozo, and in an engagement at Cayman, south of Ortiz, defeated them again. Gen. Pacheco commanded the Government forces, which lost nearly 1,000 men, killed, wounded, and deserters. Gen. Guerra cut off Rangel's retreat, and compelled him to turn toward Valencia. Between Guigue and Valencia, fierce battles were fought on June 1 and 2, in which the Congressionalists were victorious, the Government troops retiring into the city, which was closely invested. Gen. Colina, after winning three victories in the Coro district, was advancing on Puerto Cabello, and Gen. Ybarra had gone to that place with a majority of his command. In a spirited battle fought at Meron, west of the port, 500 men fell on both sides, and Palacio's generals were compelled to retire to Palite. Before the rapid advance of the Crespists a body of 2,000 troops had been sent into the Orinoco country to recapture Ciudad Bolivar, and this Palacio's troops succeeded in doing, while their brothers were being worsted on the plains, before Valencia and Caracas. The rebels were not able to hold the town because their ammunition had given out. They returned a few weeks later, and defeated the national troops in a stubbornly contested fight at Guacipati, on June 15. On June 13 serious riots occurred in Caracas. The friends of Crespo, who attempted to liberate the political prisoners, were fired upon by the soldiers, and a large number, some of whom were young students, were shot down. Gen. Ybarra, returning from Puerto Cabello to succor Valencia, attempted to make a stand against Crespo, and was beaten, retreating with 2,000 men toward Caracas. Gen. Castro, who had marched up from Los Andes to relieve Ybarra, had previously been utterly defeated, and had surrendered with 1,200 men. Gen. Rangel, with the remnant of his army, was in Valencia, but he refused to make any resistance. Gen. Crespo entered Valencia on June 10, and, after dismantling the works, marched upon Caracas, by way of Cura and San Sebastian, while Gen. Guerra advanced simultaneously through Aragua. Both commands encamped within 5 miles of the city. Crespo intrenched his army of 10,000 men at El Valle, and began the siege on June 12. After each defeat of Palacio's generals, prominent men deserted him and went over to the enemy. Town after town rose against the dictator, and the recruits whom he had pressed into the service deserted whenever an opportunity occurred. Even those bodies that had fought loyally and bravely refused to strike another blow for him. Crespo had it in his power to capture the city at any moment. He refrained at the request of the merchants of Caracas, and because he could not trust some of the semi-civilized people who fought under his banner to respect the property of the citizens or the soldiers of the Government to refrain from reprisals, perhaps against his own family, the members of which had been kept in the city by Palacio, virtually as hostages, except his son, who had made his escape some weeks before. Palacio would not yield to Crespo, but could not remain at the head of the Government. Reluctantly and practically under compulsion he resigned his powers into the hands of Domingo Monagas and Julio F. Sarria, who undertook to continue the fight against the Federalists, each of them hoping to succeed to the leadership of the Liberal party and to the Presidency. On June 17 Palacio laid down his office, and was taken on a Government man-of-war to Martinique, whence he sailed for Paris.

Andueza's Administration.—Palacio, on the demand of the men who had stood by him till now, resigned the Presidency in favor of Dr. Guillermo Tell Villegas, who was Vice-President of the Federal Council, and as such the regular successor to the President. The first act of the new Government was to release all the political prisoners. Gen. Monagas and Vice-President Villegas invited Crespo to join with them in the plan that they proposed for the reorganization of the Government and the election of a President. He refused peremptorily to accept any plan except the constitutional procedure as understood by the Legulistas. A ship was sent to Curaçoa to bring Dr. Rojas Paul to Caracas. Gen. Luciano Mendoza, as commander-in-chief, with Gen. Domingo Monagas, Sarria, the Minister of War, and Dr. Casañas reorganized the military forces for the purpose of giving battle to Crespo if peace could not be arranged. A committee of citizens headed by the Archbishop attempted to effect a compromise, but Crespo refused to receive them. On June 29 another committee was sent by Monagas, bringing an offer to call Congress together for the election of a President, and meanwhile to withdraw the Government troops from Caracas, to make Crespo's soldiers the Government army and him chief military commander, and to allow him to name four members of the Cabinet. He rejected the offer, which was sanctioned by Villegas, insisting that those who had broken the law should suffer the penalty of the law or leave the country. On the following morning Gen. Mendoza attacked Crespo's intrenched position at Guayabo, and other attacks were made on the center and the right. The Crespists were entirely destitute of powder, and abandoned the position. A heavy fog and rains favored the retreat, and a detachment of 1,600 men, stripping themselves to the waist in order that they might know one another in the fight, got back into the earthworks and in a hand-to-hand combat with machetes made it a drawn battle, in which the attacking party suffered the heaviest losses owing to numerous desertions. Crespo was attacked while he was awaiting the return of a commissioner that he had sent to Villegas with the terms on which he would make peace.

Dr. Rojas Paul arrived in Caracas on July 19, and hostilities were suspended during negotiations for peace. Gen. Sarria, who was particularly obnoxious to the Crespist party, resigned his place as Minister of War, which was taken by Gen. Ybarra. Congress was convoked, and the Legalist Congressmen who were fighting in the armies of Crespo went to the capital to resume their seats in the Senate and the House. Shortly before Rojas Paul's arrival La Victoria was taken by the revolutionary General Rodriguez, who was proclaimed Governor of the State of Guzman Blanco, as Guerra had been of Carabobo after occupying Valencia. Gen. Casañas, Palacio's Military Governor of the State of Bolivar, joined the revolution. Barcelona was the only city still loyal to the Caracas Government, and Sarria, who attempted to organize a section of the Liberal party in order to get himself elected President, and was suspected of the intention of reviving the unpopular Godo or Guzmancist party, joined Domingo Monagas there after being forced to retire from the Ministry. Gen. Andrew Velutich with 3,000 men lay encamped before that strongly fortified town, while Gen. Leoncio Quintana, with 1,000 men, and Gen. Martin Vega, with a somewhat larger force, held Gen. Luciano Mendoza beleaguered in Cua. They were re-enforced by a detachment from Los Teques, where Crespo's main army was encamped. Gen. Urdaneta, commanding the forces in the State of Zulia, which the regular bodies of Crespists had long since abandoned in order to join the revolutionary chieftain, would not recognize the new Executive at Caracas. The President of the State, at his prompting, gave notice that none of the customs duties of Maracaibo would be forwarded to Caracas until a settled Government should be established. The courts in Caracas, which had been formerly closed by one of the judges of the Court of Cassation after their release, were reopened. Congress met and appointed election committees, but it was soon apparent that no combination would give the two-thirds majority necessary for the election of a President, as the adherents of Palacio and his successors were too strong in Congress and too determined to accept either Rojas Paul or Crespo, although willing to vote for Fonseca or Dr. Villanueva, two Congressmen who had signed the protest of the 46 against Palacio. On July 19 some skirmishing took place between the forces of Quintana and Vegas and Gen. Mendoza at Cua. Crespo, who had retired to Parapara in the mountains, advanced again after receiving ammunition from the Orinoco, taking San Juan, Cura, Cagua, and other strategic points in the line of his march, and then La Victoria, and, on July 28, Los Teques, both of which towns were evacuated by the troops of Monagas, making the latter his base of supplies. Guerra threw up a half-moon of fortifications around the northern and eastern portions of Caracas, connecting with Crespo's works on the other side. The Crespists were not sufficiently provided with ammunition and improved rifles to force the fighting. Dr. Rojas Paul's pecuniary sacrifices were discontinued after his diplomatic efforts had failed to put an end to the civil war, and he had withdrawn from Caracas, Congress having broken up. On Aug. 10 the Legalists recaptured Bolivar City after a sanguinary battle. The revolutionary chiefs Gonzalez, Gallindez, Avendano, and Hernandez united their forces, amounting to 4,000 men, at Palo Grande. Gen. Hernandez made a feint with 300 men which drew the commander of the town, Gen. Carrera, with 1,000 men, into a place where the cavalry of Gonzales could fall upon them, and the whole Legalist army surrounded them on the bank of an impassable lagoon. A corps of sharpshooters, commanded by a German, picked off the Government generals, all of whom were shot. The fight lasted 5 hours, and about 500 fell on each side. The army that captured Bolivar City, and established the Legalists in control of the State of Bolivar, proceeded as rapidly as possible toward Barcelona to co-operate with the forces commanded by Gen. Velutini and Joaquin Crespo, the son of the commander-in-chief. On Aug. 8 Crespo had cut the army of Rangel and Zuloaga to pieces at Cura, capturing Rangel and killing the other general, after first separating them from Mendoza's forces in a desperate battle fought at Cagua. They occupied Cura and intrenched themselves in the plaza. Crespo having surrounded the city with his cavalry, and planted his guns on a neighboring hill, first threw the enemy into confusion by a bombardment and by a well-directed shot which killed Zuloaga and his staff in a church tower, and then carried the intrenchments with the infantry in a combat lasting 2 hours. The fleeing troops, led by Rangel, were overtaken and cut down by the lances and machetes of Crespo's cavalry, and the majority returned to Cura, and went over to the revolutionists. Over 600 were killed on the Government side, while Crespo's loss was 206 killed. Two days later Mendoza was attacked on all sides at La Victoria, and a severe battle took place, in which Crespo was victorious. Re-enforcements sent from Caracas to Mendoza were checked and driven back at Guaya and compelled to intrench themselves at Antimano. Mendoza fell back on Caracas, and Crespo again laid siege to the capital, with an army of 6,000 men. In a battle near Barcelona between the forces of Morales and young Crespo and the troops commanded by Gen. Monagas, a brother of Domingo Monagas, this general was slain.

Urdaneta's Dictatorship.—At this juncture, when Villegas and Ybarra were ready to capitulate to Crespo, and Mendoza and Sarria. in Barcelona, were hard pressed by the Legalist forces, Gen. Eleazer Urdaneta determined to head a counter-revolution and attempt to mount to supreme power by crushing the Crespists. He formed a league of the 5 western States, over which he proclaimed himself dictator. Dr. Villegas called Mendoza and Sarria back to the capital. Monagas, who had been engaging the rebels in Bermudez, was called back by the urgent appeals of Villegas and his friends, who were now willing to follow the lead of Monagas and Sarria again. He returned as far as Carupano and Camano, re-established his authority there, and made an attempt to join Mendoza in the defense of the capital, which had been well fortified when Ybarra held command. In this he was unsuccessful. Urdaneta considered himself strong enough to make his own terms. He arrived at La Guayra with his fleet of 4 steamers and 3 sailing vessels on Aug. 18, and, landing a force of 1,200 men, took possession of the custom-house and the military and police headquarters without a blow or a protest from anybody. Urdaneta believed in Palacio's scheme of wiping out the sovereign States, by restoring the original number of 20 States, which would be reduced in effect to the condition of departments, with Governors who should be subservient to the will of the chief magistrate of the Republic, elected by the direct vote of the people for four years and ineligible for a second term. This last part of the programme accorded with Crespo's ideas, but not the plan which Palacio, before his abdication, and

now Urdaneta, suggested for its execution, which was to call upon the townships and municipalities to send delegates to a National Convention, which should proclaim a new Constitution, order the election of a President by the people, and appoint a new Congress. The official body at La Guayra formally joined the Liberal League of the West and acknowledged Urdaneta Provisional Executive of the Republic. Dr. Sebastian Casañas, Garcia Gomez, and other prominent military and political leaders in Caracas, accepted Urdaneta, and were taken into his counsels. He occupied the forts of San Carlos and El Vijia with his troops, and sent to Dr. Villegas to demand the surrender of the capital into the hands of the League. As 3d Vice-President of the Republic, Urdaneta was in the line of succession to Villegas, but only after Iturbide. On Aug. 19, after an arrangement had been made with President Villegas, Minister Sarria, and Gen. Carbajal, he marched his forces into the capital and quietly took possession. Dr. Villegas was caught and imprisoned. Iturbide had fled. Urdaneta agreed to leave Vice-President Villegas in nominal possession of the Government, provided he would act on the advice of Ministers selected by Urdaneta ; viz., Casañas, Sarria, Carbajal, Garcia Gomez, Ferrel Pulido, Castro, and Adrian. Congress refused to approve the change, and in consequence it was dissolved, and several Senators were arrested. Monagas, in Barcelona, protested in any change in the Government that was not ordered by the Federal Council, and Mendoza from Victoria positively refused to recognize the new Executive and threatened to make terms with Crespo. Under these circumstances, and in consequence of the rebellion against his authority in Zulia and the renewed activity of Leon Colina in Coro, Urdaneta could get the support of only half the Federal Council, and was compelled to leave for the west.

After the abandonment of Maracaibo by Urdaneta it was taken possession of by the Legalists, who were as strong in the west as Urdaneta's followers. The commandant left by Urdaneta in the city, Gen. Arrias, issued a proclamation in favor of Crespo, and Gen. Timoteo Leal, who had been left in command of Fort San Carlos, at the entrance of Lake Maracaibo, also declared for the revolutionists, who were supplied with a large quantity of arms and ammunition just landed by Gen. Pulgar. Ferrer, Palacio's general, who had refused to support the Caracas triumvirate, was equally indisposed to join Urdaneta, and struck no blow after the departure of his old chief. Puerto Cabello surrendered on Aug. 22 to Gen. Mora, the commander of the Legalist forces in the North. The rebel skirmishers carried the intrenchments at sunrise, and an hour later forced the capitulation of the plaza. A part of the Government troops, with the custom-house officials, escaped to the island in the harbor, and from the fort fired shells into the city. Mora's forces landed twice on the island, but were unable to capture the Castillo, 46 of the 300 defenders of which were killed in the two assaults. Gen. Urdaneta, whose plan of forcing himself on the country as dictator, against the wishes of all the other generals and most of the political chiefs, depended on his retaining possession of the custom-houses, which supply nearly the entire revenue of the Venezuelan Government, took command in person of a fleet which was dispatched to recapture Puerto Cabello. Abandoning Caracas, accompanied by Sarria, Casañas, Carbajal, and Adrian, he sailed with his whole force of 1,500 men for the relief of the famished defenders of the Castillo.

Mendoza's Dictatorship.—After Urdaneta's departure, Villegas advised Mendoza to capitulate to Crespo, whose forces on the night of Aug. 24 had crushed the left wing of the Government army at Cua, which was commanded by Natividad Mendoza. Every member of the Cabinet except one voted in favor of an honorable peace —Dr. Renjifro Palacio, Minister of Public Instruction. The commander, determined to fight till the last, deposed Villegas, and proclaimed himself military dictator, appointing Dr. Palacio Provisional President. The actual members of the Government not only protested, but resisted his authority. Giuseppe Monagas was forcibly expelled from the Governor's palace, Dr. Villegas was placed under a strict guard in his private house, Ybarra attempted to hold the Casa Amarilla, Gen. Leopoldo Sarria made efforts to raise troops to upset the dictatorship, and when all failed, the Secretary of State, Urbaneja, of the deposed Cabinet, sent a formal notice to the foreign legations that all legal government had ceased. Crespo took possession of Valencia, and named Mora provisional Governor of Carabobo. The troops of Mendoza were withdrawn from La Victoria, which was occupied by Crespo. Mendoza exacted forced loans from the banks and mercantile houses. All who criticised his conduct were sent to the Rotunda. He banished the archbishop, sent priests to jail, robbed the richest church in Caracas, and compelled the agents of the wealthy planters to pay blackmail. He levied contributions from the merchants of La Guayra also, and arrested those who refused. The consuls of Germany, Belgium, and other countries were arrested, but were released on the demand of American Consul Mr. Hanna, supported by the Spanish, French, and British consul, and the foreign warships in the harbor. After this complication, Gen. Mendoza resigned the dictatorship. He had exiled Dr. Villegas, and could not restore to him the authority, but he transferred it to Villegas Pulido, a nephew of Dr. Villegas.

Pulido's Dictatorship.—On Sept. 9 the "South Portland," a steamer about to leave with a cargo of arms and ammunition for the Crespists, was ordered to be detained in New York harbor by United States officers on complaint of the Venezuelan Minister at Washington. The captain, however, obtained clearance papers, and slipped out to sea at night. Crespo's cause received a setback by the repulse of Vegas at Guetive by Guevarra. Before the flight of Mendoza Gen. Urdaneta and his lieutenant, Sarria, had encountered the forces of Colina at La Vela, and had been utterly routed, leaving 1,500 of their men dead on the field. There were several engagements, in which Colina's men took about 750 rifles and muskets and 850 prisoners. Urdaneta escaped in a sloop to Hayti. Colina and his army of lancers and riflemen marched on to Valencia to support Crespo, who had ordered a final advance on Caracas. Colina's victory was followed

by one achieved by Gen. Manzano over the troops of Gen. Battalla at Ospino. Monagas had been defeated, and nothing remained to hinder the triumph of the revolution save the fortifications of Caracas, which Pulido was determined to hold. On the report of Renjifro Palacio, Acting President Pulido cancelled the *exequatur* of United States Consul Hanna for his course in regard to the arrest of foreign consuls, but in the end Palacio was removed from office and the action was recalled. Macuto, which fell into Crespo's hands on Sept. 18, and was afterward retaken by the Government forces, was again captured by Col. Piñango. On Sept. 27 the Government troops sent to attack this position were repulsed, and Gen. Ramos, the commander, with 40 others, was made prisoner and 100 men were killed. Gen. Ignacio Pulido, uncle of the Acting President, was appointed general-in-chief of the Government troops, and he began to intrench the 3,000 men to which the army was reduced. Pulido's main position was at Los Teques. Gen. Crespo concentrated at that point about 14,000 men. After a number of preliminary skirmishes a decisive battle was fought at the village of San Pedro on Oct. 5. After a short and at first fierce engagement, the Government troops wavered and the line was broken by many refusing to continue the fight, and going over to the enemy. The Crespists followed up their advantage, and inflicted great slaughter with their guns and machetes until the rout was complete. The soldiers of Pulido threw down their arms and scattered in all directions. This fight ended the resistance. Villegas Pulido and his whole Cabinet departed quickly for La Guayra, and took ship for Europe.

Crespo's Administration.—On Oct. 7 the capital was occupied by Gen. Guerra. Gen. Rodriguez, and Gen. Fernandez, with 3,000 troops, in a few hours after the flight of the members of the defeated Government. In the interval the lawless element had held possession and committed many acts of pillage, to which the soldiers put a stop. La Guayra was also filled with rioters and plunderers until a detachment of Crespo's army arrived, though the looting had been arrested to some extent by the United States naval commander, who landed a party of sailors and marines to protect property. On Oct. 9 Gen. Crespo held his triumphal entry into Caracas. The political and military leaders met and formally elected and proclaimed him Provisional President. He issued a pronunciamiento in which he named the following men as members of the Provisional Cabinet : Minister of Foreign Affairs, Pedro Ezequiel Rojas ; Minister of the Interior, Leon Colina ; Minister of Finance, Dr. Juan Pietri ; Minister of War, Guzman Alvarez ; Chief of Police, Gen. Victor Rodriguez ; Chief of Telegraphs, Leopoldo Baptista ; Minister of Public Works, Muñoz Tebar ; General-in-Chief, Ramon Guerra ; Minister of Instruction, Silva Gaudolphy ; Governor of Caracas, Señor Andrade.

Except the garrison of Barcelona, the only Continuistas remaining under arms were scattered bands in Los Andes and a small body in the State of Bermudez. These were easily crushed and dispersed, and Gen. Yaguaracuto, who commanded under the direction of Gen. Monagas at Barcelona, surrendered and was taken prisoner, with his whole army, as soon as Crespo's troops arrived to take possession. A difficulty arose between the United States and the new Government in reference to the refugee Gen. Mijares, Governor of Caracas under the Palacio Government, who was charged of common crimes because, like many other Continuist officers, he seized cattle and other property belonging to Crespo's sympathizers, without paying or accounting for them. The master of the United States steamer "Philadelphia," who had Mijares on board when his ship touched at La Guayra, refused to allow the police to come on board and make an arrest, and the vessel put to sea, under directions from United States Minister Scruggs, without clearance papers, which the port authorities refused to issue. On Oct. 23 the United States Government gave official recognition to the new Government, and recognition by other powers followed. Provisional President Crespo issued a decree declaring confiscate the property of the men who had held official position under Palacio, in accordance with which the estates of M. A. Mattos and others were seized. The plantations of Andueza, Palacio, Sarria, Casañas, and Urdaneta were also confiscated, and Andueza's great mansion in Caracas was converted into a barracks. The obligations undertaken by the successive Executives that came into power during the revolution were repudiated. Elections were ordered for a National Assembly to meet in February, 1893. By the beginning of December the Legalista army was pa off and disbanded.

VERMONT, a New England State, admitted to the Union March 4, 1791 ; area, 9,565 square miles. The population, according to each decennial census since admission, was 154,465 in 1800 ; 217,895 in 1810 ; 235,966 in 1820 ; 280,652 in 1830 ; 291,948 in 1840 ; 314,120 in 1850 ; 315,-098 in 1860 ; 330,551 in 1870 ; 332,286 in 1880 ; and 332,422 in 1890. Capital, Montpelier.

Government.—The following were the State officers during the year : Governor, Carroll S. Page, Republican, succeeded on Oct. 6 by Levi K. Fuller, Republican ; Lieutenant-Governor, Henry A. Fletcher, succeeded on Oct. 6 by F. S. Stranahan : Secretary of State and Insurance Commissioner, Chauncey W. Brownell, Jr. ; Treasurer, Henry F. Field ; Auditor, E. Henry Powell, succeeded on Oct. 6 by Frank D. Hale ; Superintendent of Education, Edwin F. Palmer, succeeded by M. S. Stone ; Inspector of Finance, Savings Banks, and Trust Companies, F. G. Field, succeeded by W. H. Du Bois ; Railroad Commissioners, Samuel E. Pingree, Amory Davison, Leon G. Bagley ; Chief Judge of the Supreme Court, Jonathan Ross ; Assistant Judges, John W. Rowell, Russell S. Taft, James M. Tyler, Loveland Munson, Henry R. Start, and L. H. Thompson.

Finances.—The State treasury statement for the biennial period ending June 30, 1892, is as follows : Cash on July 1, 1890, $117,708.74 ; total receipts for two years ensuing, $2,138,585.-30 ; total disbursements, $2,058.956,89 ; balance on July 1, 1892, $197,337.15. The receipts may be classified as follows : From United States—for Soldiers' Home, $12,018.43 ; for Bennington Monument, $14,000 ; for Agricultural College, $48.000 ; for direct tax refunded, $179,407.80—total from United States, $253,426.23 ; from

State school tax, $174,322.93 ; from State general tax, $272,858.85 ; from corporation taxes, $579,393.20 ; from Probate and County courts, $114,663.14 ; from licenses, $8,470 ; from State institutions, $33,540.77 ; from temporary loans, $620,000 ; from interest on deposits, $2,842.40 ; from miscellaneous sources, $78,967.78. The disbursements were as follows : On Auditor's warrants, $1,108,122 ; temporary loans paid, $620,-000 ; interest on same, $9,447.95 ; State school tax paid to towns, $89.103.22 ; General Assembly, regular session, $55.615.40 ; extra session, $7,672.50 ; interest on State debt. $16,260 ; United States funds distributed to Soldiers' Home, Agricultural College, and Bennington Monument fund, $74,018.43 ; sundry payments, $78,717.39. During the two years the total taxes assessed on corporations were $572,672.96 and the license taxes were $8,537. In addition a direct tax of 18 cents on the dollar (aggregating $312,054.97 on an assessed valuation of $1,733,638.69) was levied during the period, one-half payable on or before Nov. 10, 1891, and one-half on or before June 10, 1892.

The Governor says : "The enactment of the corporation tax law in 1882 was well calculated to raise the hope that a direct State tax would not much longer be needed, but the increasing demands of the times have gone far beyond its ability to supply the money necessary for State expenses, although it has been revised until its revenues to the State have nearly doubled."

The State debt amounts to $135,500, funded into 6 per cent. bonds due in 1910, all of which are held by the Agricultural College fund.

Legislative Session.—The regular biennial session of the State Legislature began on Oct. 5, and ended on Nov. 22. On Oct. 18 Hon. Redfield Proctor was elected United States Senator for the unexpired term of Hon. George F. Edmunds, resigned, and also for the full term of six years beginning March 4, 1893. The vote in each house was as follows : Senate—Proctor, 28 ; House—Proctor, 195 ; Edward J. Phelps, Democrat, 35. An important result of the session was the passage of an act abolishing school districts and establishing the town system of school government throughout the State. The act provides that all property of school districts shall become the property of the respective towns within which the districts are situated, and requires each town to maintain schools for at least 26 weeks each year. A board of school directors, elected by the town, shall have the control of all matters pertaining to public schools. The act is to take effect on April 1, 1893.

By another act, the town offices of surveyor of highways and street commissioner were abolished, and in place thereof the office of road commissioner was established. It was further provided that the selectmen of each town shall annually assess a tax of 20 cents on each $100 of valuation, the proceeds of which shall be paid to the town treasurer and used for the repair of highways. A State tax of 5 cents on each $100 shall be assessed annually throughout the State for the support of highways and paid to the State treasurer by the several towns and cities, according to their assessed valuation. The tax so raised shall then be reapportioned and repaid to the several towns and cities upon the basis of their road mileage, which shall be ascertained in a manner prescribed by the act. Towns and cities are authorized to issue bonds for the purpose of purchasing road-making apparatus and for building permanent highways.

The Australian ballot law of 1890 was re-enacted, with amendments and additions. It is now provided that the names of all the candidates of each political party shall be grouped together in a column on the official ballot under the party designation, and an elector may vote the straight ticket by placing a cross at the head of the column containing the party nominees,

The Governor was authorized to appoint three commissioners whose duty it should be to revise, consolidate, and compile the public statutes of the State, and to report the result of their labors at the next biennial session. The following appropriations were made : $65,000 for expenses of the General Assembly ; $425,000 for the year 1892–3 and $400,000 for 1893–4 for general State expenses; $30,000 for each of the years 1892–3 and 1893–4 for paying interest on State loans ; and $50,000 for each of these years for the expenses of penal institutions. The State treasurer was authorized to borrow not over $500,000 to meet State expenses. The fish and game laws were thoroughly revised.

Other acts of the session were as follows:

Abolishing the Board of Cattle Commissioners. Its duties shall hereafter be performed by the Board of Agriculture.

Encouraging the improvement of unoccupied lands by authorizing towns to exempt from taxation for five years certain real estate, formerly unoccupied, which has been built upon or improved.

Exempting honorably discharged Union soldiers and sailors, having no taxable property, from the payment of a poll tax, if they request such exemption.

Taxing telegraph companies at the rate of 60 cents a mile of poles and one line of wire, and 40 cents a mile for each additional line of wire owned or operated in the State. In lieu thereof, such companies may pay 3 per cent. of their entire gross earnings in the State.

Providing for 30 scholarships at each of the following institutions : Middlebury College, University of Vermont and State Agricultural College, and Norwich University, such scholarships entitling the holders to free tuition. The sum of $2,400 annually is appropriated to each of said institutions to pay for such tuition.

Revising the law so as to expedite legal proceedings.

Abolishing days of grace on notes, bills, checks, and other evidences of indebtedness.

Providing a new general law for the formation of corporations.

Enlarging the list of investments that savings banks and trust companies may make.

Giving the Insurance Commissioner power to revoke licenses issued to foreign insurance companies.

To provide for the improvement of the militia.

To establish a naval battalion to be attached to the National Guard.

To punish persons who carry concealed weapons.

To prevent fraud in horse races at agricultural fairs.

To prevent fraud in the sale of lard.

To prohibit obscene advertisements and shows.

To prohibit smoking in barns, stables, and other outbuildings belonging to another.

Education.—The following is a summary of public school statistics for the nine months ending March 31, 1891, and for the year ending March 31, 1892:

ITEMS.	1891.	1892.
School districts...................	2,211	2,230
Public schools....................	2,424	2,524
Average number of days of school	106.5	138
Pupils enrolled...................	60,000	65,314
Average daily attendance.........	....	45,057
Male teachers.....................	505	538
Female teachers..................	2,933	3,813
Weekly wages, male teachers.....	....	$9.60
Weekly wages, female teachers...	....	$6.20
Schools having not over twelve pupils......................	676	633
Total school revenue.............	$695,214.14	$727,782.25
Total expenditures...............	$574,033.24	$743,543.21
Pupils attending private schools.	4,026	3,552
Pupils attending parochial schools	4,334	4,305

The Legislature of 1890 passed an act providing that the school year should thereafter begin on April 1, instead of July 1 as formerly. The school year 1890–1 was thereby shortened to nine months. According to the census of 1892 the number of children in the State between the age of five and eighteen years is 77,477.

The attendance at the Castleton Normal School for the year 1890–91 was 204, and for 1891–'92, 198.

Charities.—At the Brattleboro Insane Asylum there were 485 patients on June 30, 1890 ; 185 were admitted during the two years following, and 322 discharged, leaving 348 remaining on June 30, 1892. The total expenses for the period were $179,421.05. In August, 1891, the buildings for the new Insane Asylum at Waterbury were so far completed as to admit of the transfer of patients from the Brattleboro Asylum. Before the end of 1891 a total of 185 patients had been received from the Brattleboro institution, and up to June 30, 1892, the total admissions amounted to 224. During the period 31 were discharged, leaving 193 remaining on the last-mentioned date. The total expenses for the period since the opening of the asylum were $26,291.07. At the Soldiers' Home at Bennington, the number of persons admitted during the two years ending June 30, 1892, was 54 ; discharged, 54 ; remaining at the end of the period, 49.

Prisons.—At the State Prison at Windsor there were 93 convicts on June 30, 1890; 85 were received during the two years ensuing, and 90 discharged, leaving 88 remaining on June 30, 1892. The cost of the institution to the State for the period, after deducting the amounts received from convict labor, was only $8,682.45.

At the Reform School at Vergennes on June 30, 1892, there were 13 girls and 71 boys under restraint, and 10 girls and 54 boys were absent from the institution on furlough. The total expenses for the two years preceding were $32,168.65, and the total receipts from the operations of the school, $3,107.92, leaving a net expense to the State of $29,060.73.

At the House of Correction the number of prisoners on June 30, 1890, was 50 ; during the next two years 611 prisoners were received and 578 discharged, leaving 83 remaining on June 30, 1892. The expenses were $18,991.67, and the receipts $5,855.93, leaving $13,136.74 as the net expenses of the State.

Militia.—The National Guard of Vermont, as shown by the annual returns for the year ending June 30, 1892, consists of 74 officers and 762 enlisted men, organized as a three-battalion regiment of infantry, and a four-gun battery of light artillery. The troops are well armed and uniformed, and are supplied with camp equipage, except knapsacks or clothing bags.

Savings Banks.—On June 30, 1892, the deposits in savings banks in the State aggregated $24,674,741.76, an increase of $5,344,176.84 in two years. The number of depositors was 80.740, an increase of 14,981 in the same period. Of these, 71,635 were residents of the State and had deposits aggregating $20,888,054; 9,105 were non-residents and had deposits aggregating $3,786,687. Of the total deposits the banks had $5,042,373.33 invested in Vermont real estate mortgages, $9,007,792.97 in real estate mortgages outside of the State, and $6,687,794.33 in State, municipal, and school bonds. The number of savings banks in the State is 21.

Political.—On April 13 a Republican State convention met at Montpelier and selected delegates to the National Convention at Minneapolis, but made no nominations for State officers. The first State ticket in the field was nominated by the Democrats in State convention at Montpelier on May 5, and contained the following names: For Governor, Bradley B. Smalley; Lieutenant-Governor, William B. Viall; Treasurer, Alexander Cochrane; Secretary of State, John J. Enright; Auditor, Elisha May. Delegates to the Chicago National Convention and candidates for Presidential electors were selected.

The platform declares for tariff reform, deprecates the conversion into money of more silver than is required for circulation, asks for more efficient management of the Pension Department, and hopes that Mr. Cleveland may be again chosen to lead the party. That part of the platform which relates to Vermont affairs is as follows:

We denounce the Republican party of Vermont for its extravagance in its management of the State Government by which the expenses have nearly doubled in the past twelve years, for its creation of commissions and offices not called for by our needs, which offices and commissions it has filled with partisans of its own faith, for its unfair treatment of the minority in appointments to offices, for its unjust and unfair method of taxing mortgaged real property, its refusal to revise or alter these methods, its improper if not illegal use and distribution of the Huntington fund of more than $200,000, the income of which fund is now distributed upon the basis that the richer the town the more of such income it should receive, when it was the intent of the donor that the smaller counties should share equally with the larger. We urge appropriate legislation to give each town non-partisan election boards for town, county, and State offices. We oppose and denounce the unjust sumptuary laws of Vermont. We will do all we can to make Labor Day a legal holiday in Vermont.

The Prohibitionists held a State convention at Rutland, on May 25, at which they selected delegates to the national convention of the party, and nominated Presidential electors, and the following State ticket: For Governor, Edward L. Allen; Lieutenant-Governor, Wendell P. Stafford; Treasurer, Milon Davidson; Secretary of

State, Ernest T. Griswold; Auditor, Homer F. Cornings. A platform was adopted.

A second Republican convention, for the nomination of State officers, was held at Burlington on June 22. Levi K. Fuller was nominated for Governor on the first ballot over Lieut.-Gov. Fletcher. F. S. Stranahan was chosen as the candidate for Lieutenant-Governor and Frank B. Hale for Auditor. Secretary of State Brownell and Treasurer Field were renominated. The platform upholds the principles of protection and reciprocity, demands restriction of immigration, favors a law to secure fair elections in the Southern States, and contains the following declarations upon local issues:

In the administration of our State affairs we favor economy, not parsimony; the careful consideration of our public schools; and the passage of such laws as will tend, so far as possible, to retain at home the accumulations of our own resources, and the building up of our industries.

We demand a continuance of the prohibitory law. We believe that law is on the whole more efficient and better enforced to-day than ever before; and we assert that the attitude of Republicans in the State toward that question is such as to leave the prohibition party of Vermont without an occupation.

At the September election the entire Republican State ticket was elected, but the pluralities were much smaller than those which have been given for the Republican ticket in recent years. The vote for Governor was: Fuller, 38,918; Smalley, 19,216; Allen, 1,525. Members of the State Legislature were chosen as follows: Senate—Republicans, 30; House—Republicans, 199; Democrats, 40; Prohibitionist, 1; Independent, 1. At the November election the following vote for Presidential electors was cast: Republican, 37,992; Democratic, 16,325; Prohibitionist, 1,415; People's party, 42. Two Republican Congressmen were elected.

VIRGINIA, a Southern State, one of the original thirteen, ratified the Constitution June 25, 1788; area, 42,450 square miles. The population, according to each decennial census, was 747,610 in 1790; 880,200 in 1800; 974,600 in 1810; 1,065,116 in 1820; 1,211,405 in 1830; 1,239,797 in 1840; 1,421,661 in 1850; 1,596,318 in 1860; 1,225,163 in 1870; 1,512,565 in 1880; and 1,655,980 in 1890. Capital, Richmond.

Government.—The following were the State officers during the year: Governor, Philip W. McKinney, Democrat; Lieutenant-Governor, J. Hoge Tyler; Secretary of State. H. W. Flournoy; Auditor, Morton Marye; Second Auditor, Josiah Ryland; Treasurer, A. W. Harman; Attorney-General, R. Taylor Scott; Adjutant-General. James McDonald; Superintendent of Public Instruction. John E. Massey; Commissioner of Agriculture, Thomas Whitehead; Railroad Commissioner, James C. Hill; President of the Court of Appeals, L. L. Lewis.

Legislative Session.—The legislature met Dec. 2, 1891, and adjourned on March 4. 1892, having been in session 93 days. One of its earliest acts was the election of John W. Daniel to the United States Senate. Five circuit court judges were named during the session, and county judges were elected, by the legislature, for each of the one hundred counties in the State.

An apportionment was made both for congressional representation, and for members of the Virginia House and Senate. The railroad legislation which was adopted, was important. The Mason bill, framed largely on the lines of the Interstate Commerce law, went into effect June 1. It prohibits the railroads from charging more for a short haul than for a long one ; prohibits the granting of special rights, drawbacks and rebates, and prevents unjust discrimination ; provides the most convenient arrangement for the interchange of passenger and freight traffic at crossing points ; provides for the publication, at the various depots, of the amounts charged for freight and passenger traffic, and forbids any change of price, except after ten days' notice ; prohibits false billing and false classification, and requires duplicate bills of lading and expense bills to be furnished ; requires the establishment of telegraph offices, and fixes regulations with reference to the notification, by the train dispatcher, of the arrival and departure of trains ; requires annual reports from the commissioner, and also the publication of the laws and their posting at stations. The most important section of the law is the fourteenth, which provides that, where any common carrier has been guilty of any violation of the law, either with reference to its freight charges, its train connections, special rates, unjust discriminations, or unreasonable preference, the Railroad Commissioner shall, upon complaint made to him by any one, give notice to the common carrier, and require it to correct the cause of complaint, and if the common carrier fails in ten days to so correct the cause of complaint it is the bounden duty of the Commissioner to proceed, in the name of the Commonwealth, before the circuit court of the county where the cause of action arises, or the judge thereof in vacation, against the company. The case is to be heard without formal pleadings, and is to have precedence over all other business on the docket. The Commonwealth's attorney is required to represent the Commissioner, and the Judge is empowered by mandatory or restraining orders to prevent the common carrier from further violation of the law. In addition to the restraining order provided in this section, the thirteenth section makes the commission of any of the above-named acts a misdemeanor, and subjects the carrier, for each act, to a fine of not less than $100, nor more than $500.

An act was passed for the taxing of the Pullman cars that pass through the State, and also one requiring railroad companies to return for taxation an itemized statement of all bonds, stocks, and other securities held by them.

Two bills affecting the oyster industry were passed. One provides for an accurate survey of the grounds, to be made during the summer. The second provides for the appointing of inspectors for each county where oysters are caught or planted.

The State debt question was the most complex and important subject presented for settlement ; this, however, was disposed of in a manner which met the unanimous approval of the Assembly.

The bill for the distribution of the direct tax money returned by the Federal Government, which amounts to about $470,000, was also passed.

Appropriations for the lunatic asylums, and for the Confederate soldiers, were made, as was a small appropriation for the monument to the private soldiers and sailors.

An appropriation of $25,000 for the Virginia exhibit at the World's Fair was also made.

Among the other acts passed were the following :

To prohibit book-making and pool-selling.
To provide for the treatment of the indigent but curable blind.
To authorize the copying of certain county records prior to 1700.
To provide for the erection of a public fireproof library building within the Capitol square at Richmond, to cost $200,000, in which shall be offices for the State officials and for the Supreme Court of Appeals.
To make Labor Day a State holiday.

Finances.—The report of the Second Auditor for the fiscal year ending Sept. 30, 1892, is especially noteworthy, as it rehearses the particulars of the settlement of the State debt under the act of Feb. 2, 1892. It enumerates the securities presented by the Bondholders' Committee to the Commissioners of the Sinking Fund for verification under the act, as follows : Bonds and certificates issued under act of March 30, 1872 : coupon bonds, having thereon tax-receivable coupons due January 1, 1892, and subsequent, $11,985,200—coupons thereon, $4,488,255 ; registered bonds and fractional certificates, $6,893.- 69—interest thereon, $7,736.43. Bonds and certificates issued under act of March 30, 1871, as amended by act of March 7, 1872 (Peelers) : coupon bonds, $148,900 ; coupons, $146,281 ; fractional certificates, $745.59—interest, $894.68. Bonds and certificates issued under act of March 28, 1879 : coupon bonds (dollar and sterling), having tax-receivable coupons due Jan. 1, 1892, and subsequent, $5,165,500 ; coupons, $1,015,- 219 ; registered bonds, $30,900—interest, $8,- 294.50. Bonds and certificates issued under acts passed prior to April 17, 1861, (old unfunded,) and under act of March 2, 1866 ; also sterling certificates issued under act of March 30, 1871 : coupon bonds, 1866 and 1867, $49,000—interest, $67,952.19 ; registered bonds, 1866 and 1867, $2,811—interest, $4,140.25 ; old coupon bonds, $168,500—interest, $226,253.55 ; old registered bonds, $3,200—interest, $3,882 ; sterling old coupon bonds, $394,000 ; coupons, $350,656.90 ; sterling coupon bonds, 1866–67, $97,000 ; coupons, $86,120.80 ; sterling certificates, issued under act of March 30, 1871, $79.457.50—interest, $74,160.33 ; black scrip (dollar), $31,625 ; black scrip (sterling), $14,356.12. Total presented for verification, $24,658,035.55. Deduct from this West Virginia's portion of old debt : interest-bearing certificates, $264,650.18 ; non-interest-bearing certificates, $287,186.48—total, $551,- 842.66. Amount to be redeemed by Virginia in the proportion of 19 to 28 : $24,106,192.89. Amount of new bonds to be issued therefor, $16,357,- 773.74. Recapitulation : principal presented, $18,163,732.78 ; interest, $6,494,302.77—total, $24,658.035.55. The act of Feb. 20, 1892, made advisable a change in the character of the State securities held by the several institutions of learning, and an act to effect this was passed Feb. 23, and under this act registered certificates were issued to the amount of $2,459,855.85, the annual interest on which is $146,067.32. The total amount of old securities left unfunded is less than $1,000,000.

The Literary Fund exhibit is as follows : Investments in 3 per cent. per annum registered bonds, issued Sept. 27, 1886, in funding bonds standing in the name of the fund, $1,084,227.28 ; purchased out of Literary Fund fines and the proceeds of the payment of bonds of the Richmond and Danville Co., held by the fund, $305,100 ; total investment in Virginia 3 per cent. registered bonds, $1,389,327.28. There is also held by the fund a 6 per cent. registered bond of the City of Richmond, and a 6 per cent. loan to Washington College, $2,000, and West Virginia certificates, $719,022.09.

Assessments and Taxes.—From the railroads the State will receive $204,434.28 taxes, an increase over last year's taxes from this source of $14,317.04. The amount to be paid by the street railways will be $3,083.89, an increase over 1891 of $1,201.47.

The Commonwealth has never collected a tax from property owners at Old Point. Investigation of the matter has led to the conclusion that all private property on the reservation is subject to taxation, and therefore the Hygeia Hotel was this year assessed to the amount of $25,570, for taxes from 1876 to the present year, inclusive. If the State collects this sum other assessments will be made.

Commissioners and distributing agents of the direct tax fund were appointed, who made distribution, to the various counties and cities, of $442,026.72.

Education.—The work of the Peabody Institutes, held during the summer, was highly successful. These are provided for the special benefit of teachers of the public schools. The attendance of teachers at each of the institutes was as follows : White—Bedford City, 410 ; Staunton, 510 ; West Point, 134 ; total, 1,054. Colored—Lynchburg, 265 ; summer session of Virginia Normal and Collegiate Institute, Petersburg, 259 ; total, 524. In addition to the amount contributed by the Peabody Board of Trust to aid the State normal schools and hold teachers' institutes, eighteen scholarships endowed by this board in the Peabody Normal College, Nashville, Tenn., are allotted to Virginia. The scholarships are good for two years and are valued at $100 a year, and the students' traveling expenses to and from Nashville are paid. Applicants must pledge themselves to make teaching their life work, and agree to teach in the public schools of the State for at least two years.

Early in September the Superintendent of Public Instruction apportioned among the counties and cities of the State $202,562.06. This fund consisted of accumulated interest on securities held by the Literary Fund and appropriations made by the General Assembly. It was apportioned on the basis of the school population of the respective counties and cities, the rate being 31 cents per capita. On the 19th the superintendent apportioned, in the same manner, $731,967.80, the amount due the schools from the State revenue assessed for the year. This fund

was apportioned at the rate of $1.0202 per capita. These apportionments aggregate $34,466.89 more than the two similar ones made for the school year 1891–92.

Farmers' Institutes were held at various points in the State, and the attendance was larger than in any previous year.

Charities and Prisons.—In 1883 Lee Camp, No. 1, Confederate Veterans, was organized to take care of needy ex-Confederate soldiers. In November, 1884, the Home property, consisting of thirty-six acres and an old house, was bought for $14,000, and on Jan. 1, 1885, the first inmate was admitted. Soon thereafter the building was enlarged and remodeled and handsome cottages were erected. More recently other buildings have been erected by the board, including a mess-hall, stable, and hospital, which last named cost $35,000. For the first two years the home was supported by voluntary contributions, then the State came to the relief of the institution, and up to Feb. 12, 1892, the board had received from that source $60,000. In March, 1892, the legislature passed a bill the conditions of which were that the State would appropriate to the Home $150 a year for each inmate, for a period not exceeding twenty-two years, no annual appropriation to exceed $30,000, and that at the end of twenty-two years the State was to take possession of the property under a deed from Lee Camp.

Since the establishment of the Home it has cared for 484 veterans. The present roll embraces 166 men.

The number of State convicts on Oct. 1 was 1,202. Of these, 167 were employed on public works, 103 being with the Warm Springs Valley Railroad and 64 with the Roanoke and Southern Railroad. Of the 1,035 convicts within the penitentiary, 209 are white males and 2 are white females ; 729 are colored males and 95 are colored females ; 46 are fifteen years old or under, and 137 are between the ages of fifteen and twenty. The majority of these prisoners are hired to contractors who have leased shops from the State. More than a million pairs of shoes are turned out of the shoe shop annually, and millions of pounds of tobacco are manufactured. The receipts for the fiscal year from the hire of convicts have been more than enough to meet all expenses for the maintenance of convicts, and also for the erection of a fourth story to the penitentiary and for improvements to the office building, a total of $35,681.21.

Under pressure from the Woman's Christian Temperance Union, the General Assembly passed a bill authorizing the appointment of a matron for the female wards, who has been employed this year for the first time.

The expense of keeping 1,252 prisoners (that being the daily average for twelve months) was $78,865.45 ; per capita per year, $63 ; per capita per day, $0.17⅖⁰⁄₁₀.

Agriculture.—The acreage of corn, hay, oats, tobacco, and wheat has been greater than that of 1891 ; the wheat crop was the best for several years. The production of corn, tobacco, hay, Irish and sweet potatoes, and peanuts is hardly as large as in 1891. Throughout the year increased numbers of inquiries in reference to Virginia lands and industries have been received.

The Commissioner strongly approved of the

suggestion of the Superintendent of the Penitentiary, that a State Farm be established. This could be made an experimental station, its object being to make field experiments and test fertilizers, to distribute valuable seeds among the farmers, and to enable agriculturists to procure pedigreed stock at low rates.

At the November meeting of the Board of Agriculture a committee of three was appointed to report on the advisability of suggesting that the legislature should make an appropriation for the purchase and development of an agricultural experimental farm. At the meeting in January, 1893, a partial report was submitted, as a minority report, by Major Gaines, who thought that the board had not the legal power to take the proposed steps, and that the legislature would not look favorably upon the scheme.

Railroads.—The number of miles of roadway assessed is 3,286.56 ; value of roadway, $36,036,-167 ; value of depots, $1,862,341.42 ; value of real estate, $1,498,388.48 ; value of rolling stock, $10,158,730.60 ; value of stores or supplies, $420,470.96 ; value of telegraph lines, $15,995.-70 ; value of stocks and bonds of other companies, etc., $555,731.89 ; value of stocks and bonds owned and held by trustee, $46,650 ; miscellaneous property, $19.800. Total, $50,714,-276.05. The value of rolling stock shows an increase of $4,579,671.18 over the value placed thereon for 1891, and the roadway stock shows an increase in value of $2,917,970 over 1891. There is a decrease in the value of stocks and bonds of $3,560,737.80, due to the fact that last year the Richmond and West Point Terminal Railway and Warehouse Company reported under this head $3,962.794.13, whereas this year it reports only $399,186.85, because a large bulk has been disposed of and others have deteriorated in value. The Chesapeake and Ohio Railway Company, Crany Valley branch, built 26 miles of road ; Hot Springs branch, 25 miles ; Louisville and Nashville Railroad, 65 miles ; Norfolk and Western Railroad Company, Clinch Valley Division, 23 miles ; and Roanoke and Southern Division, 75 miles. Total, 215 miles.

The street-car companies show an increase in mileage of 24 miles, and an increase of $264,995 in the value of property.

Rivers and Harbors.—The bill reported in March by the Federal House Committee on Rivers and Harbors made the following appropriations for Virginia improvements : For Norfolk harbor, $150,000 ; for Onancock harbor (to complete), $6,511. For rivers : Appomattox, $15,000 (to complete) ; Nansemond, $10,000 ; James, $200,000 ; Nomoni Creek, $10,000 ; Rappahannock, $20,000 ; York, $35,000 ; Chickahominy (to complete), $2,500 ; Mattaponi, above Abbott's, $1,500 ; Mattaponi, $4,000 ; Pamunkey (to complete), $3,000 ; Aquia creek, $5,000 ; Occoquan (to complete), $5,000.

Tobacco and Brandy.—During the last fiscal year 153 tobacco factories were in operation. which consumed 48,544,639 pounds of leaf tobacco, 743,832 pounds of seraps, 15,821 pounds of stems. 3,379,621 pounds of licorice, 2,449.362 pounds of sugar, and 2,067,197 pounds of other materials. There were 227 cigar and cigarette factories operated, which consumed for cigars 1,568,000 pounds of tobacco, and for cigarettes 1,655,046 pounds. The number of cigars manufactured was 6,485,415, and of cigarettes, 768,-875,000. There were produced of plug tobacco 38,729,912 pounds, of smoking tobacco 2,910,019 pounds, and of snuff 776,397 pounds.

Virginia produced 138 gallons of apple-brandy, 590 gallons of peach-brandy, and 1,549 gallons of grape-brandy. Eighty-two illicit stills were seized and destroyed, and 41 persons were arrested.

Boundary.—In 1889 some question about the Pocomoke fishery rights arose, and the Governor of Maryland asked for a conference of legislative committees of the two States, asserting that the trouble was due to a misunderstanding relating to the boundary-line. The Virginia joint legislative committee was appointed, but when it assembled it was found that, through misapprehension, the Maryland committee had not been appointed. At the last session of the Virginia Legislature its committee was continued, the Maryland Legislature having in the meantime also appointed a joint legislative committee, the purpose of the two committees being to determine the fishery rights of the two States in Pocomoke Sound. There were three subjects to be considered : 1. To determine what were the headlands of the Potomac, as meant by the Black and Jenkins award of 1877. 2. To make the laws of Virginia conform to those of Maryland with reference to culling oysters in the waters in which the two States have concurrent fishing-rights, and also to make the time for beginning and ending the fishing and oystering season the same in both States. 3. To determine the right of Maryland to fishing and oystering privileges in Pocomoke River. Maryland claiming equal rights with Virginia in the Pocomoke River under the compact of 1785, and declaring that what is now known as the Pocomoke Sound, lying wholly south of the dividing line as drawn by the award of Black and Jenkins in 1877, is the Pocomoke River spoken of in the compact of 1785 and so recognized by the said award.

After several conferences it was found that the two committees could not agree, and that the matter must be carried to the courts and a judicial interpretation of the compact of 1785 and of the award of 1877 must be had in order to determine the question in dispute.

Political.—The State Republican Convention, under the leadership of Gen. William Mahone, met on May 5 at Roanoke. Delegates to the Republican National Convention were chosen, and also candidates for Presidential electors. The platform adopted approves President Harrison's Administration, praises Mr. Blaine, calls for immediate action on the free-silver question, approves the McKinley bill, and demands efficient coast-defenses and a navy that shall inspire due respect for our name and flag throughout the world.

The Democratic State Convention met in Richmond, May 19. and chose delegates to the Democratic National Convention and candidates for Presidential electors. The platform adopted advises the cultivation of a spirit of conciliation, denies that all the barriers of the Constitution have been broken down. that all its limitations of power have been removed, that the Federal character of the Government has been destroyed, and asserts the belief that the Union is to be indissoluble, but that it is to be an indissoluble Union of free and indestructible States ; opposes centralization ; denounces the so-called "Force bill"; favors taxation of the luxuries and not the necessaries of life ; favors the unconditional and immediate abolition of the internal revenue system ; reaffirms the Virginia Democratic platform of 1889 and the National Democratic platforms of 1884 and 1888 ; demands an increase in the volume of currency ; and condemns the extravagance of the Fifty-first Congress.

The first convention of the People's party of Virginia met in Richmond, June 23, selected delegates to the National Convention of the party, and nominated candidates for Presidential electors. The platform recommends and reaffirms the bill of rights of the Industrial Conference held at St. Louis, Feb. 22, 1892 ; declares for the union of labor forces ; demands a national currency, safe, sound, flexible, and issued by the General Government only ; free and unlimited coinage of silver ; that the amount of circulating medium be not less than $50 per capita ; a graduated income tax ; demands that postal savings banks be established by the Government ; asserts that all lands now held by railroads and other corporations in excess of their actual needs, and all lands now owned by aliens, should be reclaimed by the Government and held for actual settlers ; that the telegraph and telephone, like the post-office system, is a necessity for the trans-

mission of news and should be owned and operated by the Government in the interest of the people ; and declares for honest elections.

The State Prohibition Convention met at Lynchburg, June 7, and selected delegates to the National Convention. Candidates for Presidential electors were also named. The platform set forth that the Prohibition party of Virginia has no affiliation with the Democratic or Republican party, but is a distinct political organization and in harmony with the National Prohibition party only. The manufacture or traffic in intoxicating liquors should be suppressed by law ; and no compromise should be accepted. It denounces as a prostitution of government the action of the National Government in attempting, through the Department of State, to foster American breweries by extending the business of "drunkard-making" into our sister republics of South America ; the present tariff is condemned as unjustly discriminating in the interest of capital against labor. It asserts that the circulating medium should consist of gold, silver, and paper, every dollar of which should be equal to every other dollar ; and favors the Australian ballot system, and a more liberal free-school system.

At the election, on Nov. 8, the vote for Presidential electors was as follows : Democratic, 164,058 ; Republican, 113,217 ; People's party, 12,191 ; Prohibition, 2,681. Ten Democratic Congressmen were elected.

W

WASHINGTON, a Pacific Coast State, admitted to the Union Nov. 11, 1889 ; area, 69,180 square miles ; population, according to the census of 1890, 349,390. Capital, Olympia.

Government.—The following were the State officers during the year: Governor, Elisha P. Ferry, Republican; Lieutenant-Governor, Charles E. Laughton ; Secretary of State, Allen Weir ; Treasurer, A. A. Lindsley ; Auditor, T. M. Reed ; Attorney-General, W. C. Jones ; Superintendent of Public Instruction, R. B. Bryan ; Commissioner of Public Lands, W. T. Forrest ; Chief Justice of the Supreme Court, T. J. Anders ; Associate Justices, Elmon Scott, R. O. Dunbar, T. S. Stiles, J. P. Hoyt.

Finances.—The report of the State Auditor shows that the floating debt of the general fund on Oct. 31, 1892, was $434,408.75, and of the military fund, $62,507.77. Adding to these sums the interest due thereon, the total floating debt is found to be $510,166.52 above the cash on hand, against $270,442.82, the amount of the net floating debt on Oct. 31, 1890. There is also a bonded debt of $300,000, making the total liabilities of the State, bonded and floating, $810,-166.52. Referring to the increase of the debt, the Auditor says :

"The rate of taxation for general State purposes, which for 1891 was 3 mills, was reduced for 1892 to 2½ mills, although the assessed value of property in the State was $45,373,242 less in 1892 than in 1891. This reduction in the assessed value of property should not be regarded as an indication that there has been any actual depre-

ciation in value. In 1891 several counties, in their anxiety to be first in point of wealth, returned very high assessments. The consequent increased amount of taxes in those counties prevented a repetition of what was to them a costly mistake."

The State University.—At the State University there were about 250 students during the year 1891-2, a slight decrease from the preceding year, caused by the abolition of the preparatory department.

Charities.—At the Steilacoom Insane Asylum there were 378 patients on Oct. 1, 1890 ; 381 were admitted during the two years ensuing, and 396 discharged, leaving 363 on Sept. 30, 1892. The total expenditures for the period were $165,-482.60. In May and July, 1891, 122 patients were transferred from this institution to the Eastern Washington Asylum at Medical Lake.

State Lands.—In his message to the Legislature of 1893, Gov. Ferry says :

There were granted to the State by the general government, at the time of our admission, 622,000 acres of land for the establishment and maintenance of a scientific school ; of State normal schools ; of public buildings at the State capital ; of agricultural colleges, and of State charitable, educational, penal, and reformatory institutions. These lands were to be selected by the State under the direction of the secretary of the interior from the surveyed unappropriated public lands of the United States. At the first session of the legislature a law was enacted creating the State land commission, composed of the secretary of state, auditor and commissioner of public lands, who, with seven agents, appointed by the governor under an act approved March 10, 1891, were empowered to select and secure for the State the lands thus granted. The act of 1891 expressly provided that it should not take effect until the rules and regulations referred to should be promulgated by the secretary of the interior. The issuance of these regulations was long delayed. When they were received and the land commission organized it was ascertained that no appropriation had been made by the last legislature for the compensation of the agents nor for the payment of the fees which would become due at the United States land offices when application was made to enter the selected lands. By an arrangement made with the agents, payment for their services was postponed until the legislature should convene and make appropriation therefor. The land office fees, amounting to $4,000, have been advanced by two State officers.

On January 7, 1893, there had been selected 316,575 acres, of the appraised value of $3,701,960.

Railroads.—On Jan. 6, 1893, the last spike was driven which completed the connection, by way of the Great Northern Railroad, between St. Paul and Seattle. This road, after entering the State, runs southwesterly by way of Chattaroy to Spokane and passes through that city over the tracks of the Spokane Falls & Northern and Union Pacific roads. Then it starts west parallel with the Seattle, Lake Shore & Eastern across the rolling wheat lands, and runs through the Big Bend of Columbia River along the valley of Crab Creek, where the growing of wheat is rapidly increasing, around the foot of Badger Mountain and the lower end of Moses' Coulee to Columbia River at Rock Island. There a great steel cantilever bridge is to span the river, and is being erected, trains temporarily crossing by a ferry after running a few miles along the bluffs. From Wenatchee it ascends the river of the same name and turns up Nason Creek to the summit of the Cascades, which it crosses by a switchback 10.2 miles long at Stevens pass. This is to be replaced by a tunnel 3.3 miles long. After crossing the mountains the road runs down the Skykomish Valley, where it taps a rich and untouched timber and mineral belt, and down Snohomish River to Everett, where it joins the Coast lines. The number of miles of new railroad constructed in the State in 1892 was 420. No other State or Territory approaches this record.

Political.—At a Republican State Convention, held at Seattle on April 14, delegates to the Minneapolis National Convention were selected, and on May 25, at a similar convention at Vancouver, the Democrats elected delegates to their National Convention at Chicago. The first State ticket in the field was nominated at Ellensburgh on July 25, by a State convention of the People's party. It contained the following names : For Governor, C. W. Young ; Lieutenant-Governor, C. P. Twiss ; Secretary of State, Lyman Wood ; Treasurer, W. P. C. Adams ; Auditor, Charles Rudolph ; Attorney-General, Guvnor Teats : Justices of the Supreme Court, E. W. Carner, Frank P. Reid ; Superintendent of Public Instruction, J. M. Smith ; Commissioner of Public Lands, T. M. Calloway ; State Printer. A. J. Murphy ; Congressmen, J. C. Van Patten. M. Knox. Presidential electors and delegates to the Omaha National Convention were selected. A platform was adopted in harmony with the principles of the National Farmers' Alliance.

On August 10 a second Republican State convention met at Olympia, and nominated John H. McGraw for Governor on the first ballot, by a vote of 252, to 119 for George V. Calhoun. For Lieutenant-Governor, F. H. Luce was nominated ; for Secretary of State, James H. Price ; Treasurer, O. A. Bowen ; Auditor, L. R. Grimes ; Attorney-General, W. C. Jones ; Superintendent of Public Instruction, C. W. Bean ; Commissioner of Public Lands, W. T. Forrest ; State Printer, O. C. White ; Justices of the Supreme Court, T. J. Anders, Elmon Scott ; Congressmen John L. Wilson, William H. Doolittle. Candidates for Presidential electors were nominated, and a platform was adopted, of which the following is a portion :

We favor the remonetization of silver upon a recognized parity with gold, and its restoration to the dignified place it has occupied for forty centuries as money.

We recognize the importance to our people of the improvement of our rivers and harbors, and we especially commend as worthy of the attention of Congress the Columbia River, the harbors of our Pacific coast and of Puget Sound and of the ship canal connecting Puget Sound with Lake Washington ; we condemn the action of the Democratic House of Representatives in refusing an appropriation for the opening of the Columbia River and the Lake Washington ship canal, and we most heartily approve the course of Senators Allen and Squire, and of Representative Wilson, in their advocacy of those measures ; we are heartily in favor of the speedy opening to settlement of the Puyallup and other Indian reservations within this State.

We call for the allotment of lands in severalty to the wards of the Government, and the throwing open thereafter of the Indian reservations in this State to the American farmer and producer.

We demand a prompt settlement of all harbor lines, tidelands, and other questions in which a large portion of our State is so vitally interested, and promise all needed legislation to promote the irrigation of our arid lands and regulate the use of water for irrigation so that the greatest good may be done to the greatest number.

We believe that the betterment of the condition of our industrial and producing classes should be the first care of this State, and promise such legislation as will insure a reasonable reduction in charges made by those engaged in transporting passengers or freight, whenever such rates are proven to be excessive or exorbitant.

We are in favor of a law making eight hours a day's labor on all public works.

The Second Democratic State convention met at Olympia on Aug. 24, and nominated H. J. Snively for Governor ; H. C. Willison for Lieutenant-Governor ; John McReavy for Secretary of State ; Harrison Clothier for Treasurer ; Samuel Bass for Auditor ; R. W. Starr for Attorney-General ; J. B. Morgan for Superintendent of Public Instruction ; F. S. Lewis for Commissioner of Public Lands ; E. H. Borden for State Printer ; W. H. Brinker and Eugene K. Hanna for Justices of the Supreme Court ; Thomas Carroll and James A. Munday for Congressmen. The platform adopted favors free silver coinage, the survey and opening of public lands, the election of President, Vice-President, and United States Senators by direct vote of the people, and the speedy completion of the Nicaragua Canal. It contains also the following resolutions, the first of which was adopted only after prolonged and heated discussions :

We strongly condemn the course of Senators Allen and Squire in advocating the appropriation for the Lake Washington ship canal, to the exclusion of needed appropriations for the necessary improvement of our rivers and harbors.

Upon the present Republican administration in this State we call down the indignation of an outraged people. In its executive branch it has been weak, negligent, profligate, without capacity and without patriotic spirit. In its legislative it has defied the wishes of the people, acted with total disregard to the public good, and squandered the people's money in idle and extravagant schemes, while the State went without a capitol building and the patriotic members of the National Guard went unpaid.

We believe that eight hours should constitute a day's labor on all public works.

We favor the abolition of the poll tax and denounce the present revenue law in regard to the collection of delinquent taxes which confiscates the property of our people.

We pledge ourselves in favor of such legislation in Congress as will at once settle to the so-called lieu lands in Washington, in order that the settlers thereon shall be enabled to complete their title to said lands at once.

We pledge ourselves to favor reasonable legislation reducing freight rates and fares charged by transportation companies in this State.

The Prohibitionists met at Tacoma on Aug. 26, nominated Roger S. Greene for Governor, and selected candidates for the other State offices, for Congressmen, and for Presidential electors. The convention adopted resolutions favoring prohibition ; no distinction of sex in the elective franchise ; that the tariff should be levied as a defense against foreign governments which levy upon or bar out our products, the revenue being incidental ; an increase in the circulating medium ; restriction of foreign immigration : election of President, Vice-President, and United States Senators by the vote of the people ; abolition of the poll tax, and the adoption of a system of public road-making : a law enforcing the Sabbath, and the establishment of State courts of arbitration.

After an interesting canvass, the entire Republican ticket was successful at the November election. For Presidential electors the vote was : Republican, 36,470 ; Democratic, 29,844 ; People's party, 19,105 ; Prohibitionist, 2,553. For Governor, McGraw received 33,228 votes ; Snively, 28,948 ; Young, 23,780 ; Greene, 3,941. Two Republican Congressmen were elected. Members of the Legislature were chosen as follows : Senate —Republicans, 25 ; Democrats, 9 ; House—Republicans, 50 ; Democrats, 19 ; People's party, 8. A proposed constitutional amendment, increasing the State debt limit, was submitted to the people at this election and defeated, the vote being 13,- 625 in its favor and 35,207 against it.

WEST INDIES.—The islands of the West Indies. with the exception of the independent republics (see HAYTI and SANTO DOMINGO) and the Spanish colonies (see CUBA and PUERTO RICO) belong to Great Britain, Denmark, France, and the Netherlands.

The British colonies are Jamaica, the Bahama Islands, Barbadoes, Trinidad, and the Leeward and Windward Islands.

Jamaica.—The colony of Jamaica has representative government. The Legislative Assembly is composed of 18 members, half of whom are elected by the people and half are nominated by the Governor, or official. the latter composing the Governor's privy council. The Governor receives a salary of £6,000. The present incumbent is Sir Henry Arthur Blake. The area of the island is 4,200 square miles. Turk's and Caicos Islands, which are attached to it, besides the small Cayman Islands and Pedro and Movant Cays, have an area of 224 square miles. The population at the census of 1891 was 639,491, divided into 305,948 males and 333,543 females. The white population in 1881 was 14,432. Kingston, the capital, has about 40,000 inhabitants. There were in 1889 in the colony 13,041 coolie immigrants from the East Indies, the importation of whom was stopped in 1886. The number of marriages in 1889 was 3,323 ; of births, 22,044 ; of deaths, 13,874. There were 867 elementary schools in 1890, receiving a government grant of £26,859, and having 75,613 pupils on the rolls.

The chief products of Jamaica are sugar, rum, coffee, fruit, vegetables, cacao, cinchona, cattle, and pimento. The area under cultivation in 1890 was 628,035 acres, an increase of 13,134 acres over the preceding year. Of the individual holdings 84,283 are under 5 acres and 457 exceed 1,000 acres. The railroads have a length of 64 miles, from which the receipts were £60,- 819 in 1889, while the expenses were £32,321. There are about 650 miles of telegraph. The number of messages in 1889 was 86,604. The number of letters sent through the post-office was 1,451,718. The cays called Turk's Islands are the seat of an important salt industry. About 2,000,000 bushels are exported annually to the United States and Newfoundland. From the Cayman Islands cocoanuts and turtles are exported.

The revenue of Jamaica for 1890 was £788,888, and the expenditure, £606,415. In Turk's Islands a revenue of £8,901 was collected, while the expenditure was £8,263. Of the revenue of Jamaica £378,542 were derived from customs, and of that of Turk's Islands, £6,479. The expenses of civil administration in Jamaica amounted to £400,200 in 1889. The public debt of the colony in 1891 was £1,543,120, of which £823,695 were raised for railroads.

The exports of Jamaica in 1890 were valued at £1,902,814, and the imports at £2,188,937. The exports from the Turk's Islands were £42,651, while the imports amounted to £42,108. Of the imports into Jamaica cotton goods were valued at £326,057 ; wheat flour, £188,026 ; salt fish, £122,512 ; rice, £41,916. The export of sugar amounted to £236,188 ; rum, £199,198 ; coffee, £283,800 ; fruit, £444 368. The tonnage entered and cleared in 1890 was 1,230,506 tons.

Barbadoes.—The island of Barbadoes, lying east of the Windward Islands, has an area of 166 square miles, and a population, after the census of 1891, of 182,322. The capital, Bridgetown, has 21,000 inhabitants. The number of births in 1890 was 7,419 ; of deaths, 5,000. Barbadoes has been the headquarters of the British military force in the West Indies. In 1892 the garrison numbered 47 officers and 844 men. The Governor of the colony is Sir Walter J. Sendall. The chief commercial product is sugar. About 30,000 acres are planted to sugar-cane, yielding 85,261 hogsheads in 1890. There are 370 boats and 1.500 persons employed in the fisheries, the annual product of which is £17,000.

The revenue of the colony in 1890 was £186,-179, and the expenditure, £181,635. The expenses for the establishments were £65,206 in 1889. The sum of £9,340 was spent on public schools in 1890, and £33,635 in poor relief. The debt amounts to £30,100. The imports for 1890 were £1,198,723 in value, and the exports, £1,-204,389. The value of the sugar exported was £818,680 ; of molasses, £162,200 ; of salt fish, £34,073; of flour, £25,297. The imports of linen and cotton goods were £198,645 ; of flour, £90,-620 ; of rice, £49,621. The vessels entered and cleared had an aggregate tonnage of 1,246,262 tons. There is a railroad, 24 miles long, which receives an annual subsidy of £6,000.

Trinidad.—Trinidad is an island of the Lesser Antilles, lying off the coast of Venezuela, north of the mouth of the Orinoco River. There is a Legislative Council of 18 members, of whom 8 are official and the rest are appointed by the Governor. The Governor, at present Sir F. Napier Broome, receives a salary of £5,000. Tobago, which since Jan. 1, 1889, has been administratively dependent on Barbadoes, has a commissioner. The area of Trinidad is 1.754 square miles. The population in 1890 was 208,-030. Tobago, with an area of 114 square miles, had a population of 20,727. The capital of Trinidad is Port of Spain, which has 33,782 inhabitants. The number of births in 1890 was 6,057 ; deaths, 5.612 ; marriages, 986. There were 4,921 immigrants in 1890, most of whom were East Indian coolies. About 194,000 acres are under cultivation, of which 52,160 acres are devoted to the sugar-cane, 43,360 to coffee and cacao, 18,053 to ground produce, and 2,767 to cocoanuts. The export of asphaltum is steadily increasing. There is a railroad, 54 miles in length, of which the gross receipts for 1890 amounted to £51,912. The export of sugar in 1890 amounted to £630,815 ; of molasses, £62,-929 ; of cacao, £603.506. The chief imports were: flour, £122,512 ; rice, £125,222 ; cotton and other cloths. £346,517 ; pickled meat, £64,-555. The total imports amounted to £2,248,893, and the exports to £2,179,432. The imports of Tobago were £23,403, and the exports £19,371. The tonnage entered and cleared during 1890 was 1,276,870 tons. The exports of cacao and of cocoanuts have doubled since 1881, and within two cr three years a considerable trade in oranges, bananas, pineapples, and limes has sprung up with the United States.

Leeward Islands.—The group comprises : Antigua, with an area of 108 square miles, and its dependencies, Barbuda and Redonda, 62 square miles, having in all a population of 36,700 ; the Virgin Islands, 58 square miles, with 4,640 inhabitants ; Dominica, 291 square miles, with 29,000 inhabitants ; St. Kitt's, 65 square miles, Nevis, 50 square miles, and Anguilla, 35 square miles, with an aggregate population of 47,660 ; and Montserrat, 32 square miles, with 11,760 inhabitants. The Governor is Sir William Frederick Haynes Smith. Antigua produces sugar and pineapples. The sugar export in 1889 was 16,220 tons, of the value of £180,701. The total exports from the island in 1890 were valued at £218,223, and the imports at £184,591 ; exports

from the Virgin Islands, £5,050, and imports, £4.144 ; exports from St. Kitt's and Nevis, £225,-233, and imports, £181,546 ; exports from Montserrat, £22,755, and imports, £24.096 ; exports from Dominica, £41,009, and imports, £57,-382. The total exports of sugar from the islands were valued at £396,914 ; of molasses, £49,304. The imports of breadstuffs into St. Kitt's and Nevis in 1889 were £33,279 in value ; of textile goods, £36,580. The tonnage entered and cleared was 488,262.

Windward Islands.—The group comprises : Grenada, with an area of 120 square miles and 51,427 inhabitants ; St. Vincent, 132 square miles, with 41.054 inhabitants ; St. Lucia, area 245 square miles, with 41,713 inhabitants ; and the Grenadines, attached a part to St. Vincent and part to Grenada, the largest island being Carriacou, with 6,000 population. The Governor is Sir W. F. Hely-Hutchinson. In Grenada, cacao, cotton, and spices are grown ; the products of St. Vincent, which is owned and cultivated chiefly by three firms, are sugar, rum, spices, arrowroot, cacao, and timber ; and in St. Lucia they are sugar, cacao, and logwood. The exports of St. Lucia for 1890 were £197,452 in value, and the imports, £206,693 ; exports of St. Vincent, £104,744, and imports, £97,808 ; exports of Grenada, £266,302, and imports, £170,-874. The export of cacao from Grenada was £228,889 ; of spice, £15,955 ; of sugar from St. Vincent, £53,062 ; of arrowroot, £31,270 ; of sugar from St. Lucia, £83,578 ; of cacao, £26,-864 ; of logwood, £9,438. The tonnage entered and cleared in 1890 at St. Vincent was 300,222 tons ; at St. Lucia, 878.315 tons ; at Grenada, 477,028 tons. The public revenue of the different islands, each of which has its separate administration, was in 1890 as follows : St. Lucia, £50,232 ; St. Vincent, £27,047 ; Grenada, £47,422. The expenditures were: for St. Lucia, £45,430 ; for St. Vincent, £25,941 ; for Grenada, £53,356. A new coaling station has been established at Castries Bay, St. Lucia, and the troops hitherto stationed at Barbadoes are to be removed to that island. A large sum has been spent in converting the harbor, which is spacious and safe, into a strongly fortified arsenal. The people of St. Vincent have been very indignant over an ordinance from the Colonial Office in London, and in 1892 this difficulty led to the resignation of all the members of the Colonial Council. Every citizen who was applied to declined to serve under the Government in the place of the retiring officials.

The Bahamas.—The Bahama Islands have a total area of 5,450 square miles, and in 1888 had 48,000 inhabitants. The number of births in 1890 was 1,871 ; of deaths, 899. The value of the sponge fishery in 1890 was £63,099. The exports of pineapples were £49,795. The area planted to sisal plants in the beginning of 1891 was over 4,200 acres. The Governor is Sir Ambrose Shea. The revenue for 1890 was £54,826, and the expenditure, £48,688. The total exports amounted to £168,121 and the imports to £222,-512. There were 270,874 tons entered and cleared.

The Danish Antilles.—The West India islands subject to Denmark are: St. Croix or Santa Cruz, having an area of 74 square miles and 18,-430 inhabitants ; St. Thomas, with an area of

23 square miles and 14,380 inhabitants; and St. John, with an area of 21 square miles and 944 inhabitants. The islands are populated with free negroes, who cultivate the sugar-cane. The annual export of sugar amounts to 16,000,000 lbs., besides a large quantity of rum.

The French Islands.—The French colonies are: the island of Guadeloupe with its dependencies, having an area of 720 square miles and 165,154 inhabitants; and Martinique, with an area of 380 square miles and 175,863 inhabitants. The imports of Guadeloupe in 1889 were 10,919,-000 francs from France, 1,192,000 francs from French colonies, and 12,581,000 francs from foreign countries; and the exports were 24,691,000 francs to France, 438,000 francs to French colonies, and 722,000 francs to foreign countries. The imports of Martinique in 1888 were 7,959,000 francs from France, 664,000 francs from French colonies, and 14,293,000 francs from foreign countries; and the exports were 22,249,000 francs to France, 106,000 francs to French colonies, and 1,100,000 francs to foreign countries.

The Dutch Antilles.—The Netherlandish colony of Curaçoa consists of the islands of Curaçoa, Bonaire, Aruba, a part of St. Martin, St. Eustache, and Saba. They lie off the coast of Venezuela. Curaçoa has an area of 210 square miles and 26,245 inhabitants; Bonaire, area 95 square miles, has 3,821 inhabitants; Aruba, area 69 square miles, has 7,743; the southern, or Dutch portion of St. Martin, the rest of which is French, has an area of 17 square miles and 3,882 inhabitants; St. Eustache, 7 square miles in extent, has 1,588; and Saba, area 5 square miles, has 1,883. The Colonial Council consists of 8 nominated members and the 3 members of the Governor's Council. The revenue for 1891 was estimated at 661,000 guilders and the expenditure at 681,000 guilders. The Netherlands Government makes a grant to cover a deficit that occurs in the budget. The value of the imports for 1890 was 3,441,508 guilders. The principal produets are Indian corn, beans, pulse, cattle, salt, and lime. In 1890 there were 2,801 vessels, of 1,327,506 metric tons, entered at the ports of the colony.

WEST VIRGINIA, a Southern State, admitted to the Union June 19, 1863; area, 24,780 square miles. The population, according to each decennial census since admission, was 442,014 in 1870; 618,457 in 1880; and 762,749 in 1890. Capital, Charleston.

Government.—The following were the State officers during the year: Governor, A. B. Fleming, Democrat; Secretary of State, William A. Olney; Treasurer, William G. Thompson; Auditor, Patrick F. Duffey; Attorney-General, Alfred Caldwell; Superintendent of Free Schools, Benjamin S. Morgan; Adjutant-General, B. H. Oxley; President of the Supreme Court, Daniel B. Lucas; Judges—Henry Brannon, J. W. English, H. A. Holt; Clerk, O. S. Young; State Librarian, C. L. Hagan; Bank Examiner, C. W. Young.

Finances.—At the beginning of the fiscal year 1890-1 there was in the treasury the sum of $451,580.83. The receipts from all sources, during the year, amounted to $1,351,722.67, so that the total in the treasury during the year was $1,803,303.50. The amount disbursed for all

purposes was $1,311,328.54, making the balance in the treasury on Oct. 1, 1891, $491,974.96. This balance was made up of the following distinct funds: the State fund, $44,857.66; the General School fund, $320,383.37; and the School fund uninvested, $126,974.96.

At the beginning of the fiscal year 1892-3 there was in the treasury $491,974.96. The receipts from all sources during the year were $1,257,908.03, making the total in the treasury during the year $1,749,882.99. There was disbursed during the year $1,267,278.58, making the balance in the treasury on Oct. 1, 1892, $482,604.41. This balance was made up of the following distinct funds: the State fund, $36,-567.71; General School fund, $291,480.95; School fund uninvested, $154,555.75.

The bonded State debt has been discharged since the beginning of the last fiscal year. This amounted to $101,170, due the irreducible or permanent school fund, the balance of temporary loans negotiated several years ago to meet casual deficits in the treasury. The State debt, amounting to $184,511.48, has been discharged.

Education.—According to the report submitted to the Governor, the whole number of school-houses in the State in 1892 was 5,004; the school population, 276,452; the average daily attendance, 128,044; the teachers employed, 5,747; the average length of term in days, 110; value of school property, $2,746,234.00; invested school fund, $706,025.75; the general school fund, $336,389.64; the total cost of education, $1,436,062.53.

In accordance with the provisions of chapter 65 of the Acts of the Legislature of 1891, the Board of the School Fund purchased 30 acres on Kanawha River eight miles west of Charleston, and constructed thereon buildings for the West Virginia Colored Institute, the total cost of grounds and buildings aggregating $9,546. The institute was opened in the spring, twenty students entering.

The total enrollment for the year ending June, 1890, in West Virginia University was 208. For the year ending June, 1891, the total was 205, and for the year ending June, 1892, it was 224. For the current year the enrollment is 207.

In the six Normal schools of the State the total number of students enrolled for 1891 was 9,241, and the number of graduates was 59. The total number enrolled for 1892 was 1,015, and the number of graduates was 72. The attendance for 1892 shows an increase of 175 over the enrollment of 1890.

Prisons.—Of the 347 male convicts confined in the State Penitentiary, 267 are employed in the manufacture of whips, brooms, and fly-nets, at 42 cents per man per day. The contract was let after repeated advertisements made, as the law directs, and was the only proposal received. This leaves 80 male convicts not under contract, of whom 55 are needed for cooks, etc., 25 being available for contract. On Sept. 30, 1880, there were 260 convicts in the prison. On the same date in 1890 there were 306, making a total increase of but 46 in ten years. On Oct. 1, 1892, there were 352 inmates in the prison. There were at the last report, Oct. 1, 1892, 219 white men, 128 colored men, and 5 colored women in the prison, making a total of 352.

It cost the State daily per capita, to maintain its convicts at the penitentiary in 1889, over forty-two cents, and in 1890 thirty-six and a fraction cents. The average daily cost per capita for the two fiscal years ending Sept. 30, 1892, was a fraction over thirty-four cents. It cost daily per capita, to feed the prisoners in 1889, twelve and a half cents, and in 1890 ten and two-third cents. The average daily cost per capita for the last two years was ten cents. The daily average cost per capita for maintaining convicts includes salaries of all officers and employés, and every other item of expense.

Charities.—In the State Reform School the number of boys admitted in 1891 and 1892 was ninety-nine.

There were present in the school term ending June 11, 1891, 107 inmates in the School for the Deaf and Blind.

In the Hospital for the Insane there were, according to the superintendent's report submitted on Sept. 30, 1892, 944 patients. Of these, 451 were white males, 447 white females, 20 colored males, and 26 colored females.

Natural Products.—According to the Governor's message, the amount of coal produced in the State in 1892 was 8,710,888 tons over the 1,404,008 tons pr   in 1880. The amount of coke produced in 1892 was 1,313,449 tons over the 121,715 tons produced in 1880.

While West Virginia accordingly maintains its rank as fourth among the coal-producing States of the Union and second in the production of coke, the development of its timber interests has so increased that the products of its forests yield more wealth annually than do its mines.

Agriculture.—The State Board was created by act of Legislature, March 13, 1891, and there has not been time for it to accomplish more than a thorough organization of the bureau and map out and satisfactorily begin the work expected to be performed.

Banks.—The report of the Bank Examiner shows that there is invested in banks and banking institutions in the State the sum of $5,017,-486.49, of which $2,563,486.49 is in State banks and $2,454,000 in National banks. There was on deposit in the various banks at the date of their several reports the aggregate sum of $15,161,-541.97, an increase of $1,567,391.77 over the deposits reported the previous year.

Taxes.—By reason of the revaluation of real estate, the taxable values of the State have been increased over $25,000,000. This, at the present rate of 25 cents on the $100, means an increased annual revenue of $62,500 for State purposes. During the past three years, notwithstanding the large appropriations made by the last legislature, every demand upon the treasury was met without borrowing; the so-called State debt, which aggregated $184,511.48, being discharged. The present rate of taxation will yield more revenue than the necessities of the State require.

Political.—The Democratic State Convention, held at Parkersburg in August, nominated the following: For Governor, W. A. McCorkle; Auditor, J. V. Johnson; Superintendent of Schools, Virgil A. Lewis; Treasurer, John M. Rowan; Attorney-General, T. S. Riley; Judge of Supreme Court; Long term, Marmaduke Dent; Short term, Homer A. Holt.

At the Republican State Convention, held in May, for the selection of delegates to the National Convention, resolutions were adopted upholding the principles of the Republican party in all questions referring to the tariff, to protection, to reciprocity, to the equalization in value of all gold, silver, and paper issues, and to liberal pensions. The administration of President Harrison was approved.

The following ticket was chosen when the State Convention met in August: For Governor, Thomas E. Davis; Auditor, Jacob S. Ilyer; Treasurer, William P. Payne; State Superintendent of Schools, Thomas C. Miller; Attorney-General, T. O. Bullock; Judge—Long term, J. M. McWhorter; Short term, Warren Miller.

The platform declared:

As West Virginians, we are in favor of that policy which has developed and made great States of less wealth in natural resources than our own, bringing the workshop class to the farm and gathering about the opened coal seams large communities of wage-earners who make a ready market for the products of agriculture. We denounce the Democratic doctrine that it is unconstitutional to open coal mines and establish factories in West Virginia. We accept as better authority the decision of the Supreme Court of the United States, that the McKinley tariff act is a constitutional measure. Moreover, we believe it to be one of the best measures ever passed by the Congress of the United States.

Restriction of immigration was earnestly advocated. The passage of a law to prevent the further use of hired troops for the settlement of difficulties between miners and their employers was made a subject of special plea. The Democratic administration of the State was characterized as fruitful of disastrous results.

The act of the legislature "in refusing Nathan Goff the office of Governor of West Virginia, to which he was justly and legally elected by the people," was characterized as destructive of free government and disgraceful to Christian civilization.

In November the Democrats elected their whole State ticket, and all four Representatives in Congress. On the Presidential ticket, out of a total vote of 171,048, the vote was, for Harrison, 80,285; for Cleveland, 84,468.

WHITMAN, WALT, an American poet, born at West Hills, Huntington township, Suffolk county, Long Island, N. Y., May 31, 1819; died in Camden, N. J., March 26, 1892. His ancestry dates back with considerable certainty to Zechariah Whitman, who emigrated from England to Milford, Conn., about 1640. The latter's son, Joseph, removed to Huntington, Long Island, as early as 1664, where the burial hill of the Whitmans is still to be found, containing the graves of many generations of the family. Walt, as he was called to distinguish him from his father, Walter Whitman, was born on the ancestral farm. His mother belonged to one of the old Dutch families that settled the western end of Long Island. She was the daughter of Major Cornelius Van Velsor and of Amy Williams, of the Society of Friends. Thus Whitman combined in himself the three most vigorous strains of American descent. He was the second of a family of nine children, most of whom he survived. His father, who had learned the

Walt Whitman

Born in New York state (West Hills, Suffolk Co. L.I.) May 31. 1819. Parentage on the father's side English, on the mother's (Van Velsor) side, Holland Dutch. From early childhood transport'd to in Brooklyn and New York cities — went to the public schools several years — then learn'd (1835-45?) the trade of printer & worked at it as compositor in N.Y. & Brooklyn offices. Also as editor and Magazine-writer. In 1847. '8 and 9 made a leisurely tour through the United States, travelling nearly every section, especially on the Mississippi, Missouri, & Ohio rivers, & Canada. Returning to Brooklyn (1851, '3 '4) went into carpentering & building. In

1855 published the first [installment] of "Leaves of Grass," (to which thereafter [successive] editions gradually [added] five other cumulative issues, making the work in its [present] state, a book of about 380 ordinary [octavo] pages.) During the war of from 1862 to '65, [many] [chapters] of [Leaves] among the armies on the field in Virginia; [spent] the camp hospitals, & [especially] in & the immense army [at] Washington City, as a volunteer aid & nurse to wounded & sick of the [army], both North & South. In 1865 was appointed to a Clerkship in Attorney General's office, Washington, which he held till 1874. Was of remarkable bodily health & [physique] till 1873, when he had a stroke of paralysis, from which he is still [disabled]. His writings, in the [later] [form], & as [completed] [consist] "Leaves of Grass" and another [volume] called of the before-mentioned "Leaves of Grass," "Two Rivulets," a mixed collection of prose & poetry. Of the "Leaves" it has been said & [probably] the whole of these unrhymed songs, [if] not all Whitman's writing, any [sing] the changes [statement] on the [circulation]. Howsoever it [may be] [slight] [a] [human] being [is] [honestly] [on] [record]. Whitman is unmarried & now (1875) in [his] 57th year. [Lives] in seclusion at Camden, New Jersey.

trade of carpenter in New York, removed from West Hills to Brooklyn in 1823. There Whitman remained until about 1836. He studied in the public schools until his twelfth year, when he was employed as a boy in the office of a Brooklyn lawyer, who instructed him in composition and gave him the run of a circulating library. Two years later he was apprenticed to a printer in the same city, and thereafter until the civil war he was chiefly occupied as printer, editor, and miscellaneous writer.

WALT WHITMAN.

He began very early the practice of spending as much time as he could spare on the Long Island beaches, or mingling with the crowds at the ferries and in the streets of Brooklyn and New York, thus gaining his familiarity with nature and men. From eighteen to twenty he taught country schools in Western Long Island, and in 1839 established and published for about a year his first newspaper, the "Long Islander," at Huntington, his native town. Returning to Brooklyn and New York, he was miscellaneously engaged as printer and writer, with occasional activity as a politician, until 1846, when he assumed the editorship of the Brooklyn "Eagle." He was a frequent attendant of the New York theaters during this period, and some interesting reminiscences of the drama and opera of the time are to be found among his prose writings. In 1848 he accepted a place on the "Crescent," at New Orleans, La., and greatly enjoyed his first extended journey down the Ohio and Mississippi Rivers.

Returning after a year's residence in New Orleans, he established and edited for a short time the Brooklyn "Freeman," but soon gave up this and devoted himself to building and selling houses in that city for two or three years. About 1853 he began to formulate his ideas for a new kind of poetry, as developed in the first edition of his "Leaves of Grass" (1855). As he himself expressed it, he "had great trouble in leaving out the stock 'poetical' touches, but succeeded at last." His contributions to literature, up to this time, consisted chiefly of stories and poems of a conventional character, and were printed in the "Democratic Review" and other periodicals of the day. With "Leaves of Grass" he adopted a policy of individuality from which he never afterward swerved. He assumed a workingman's costume, but this should not be taken to mean that he was negligent in dress, for his personal neatness was marked to a degree, and became "one of the roughs," associating more than ever with the common people. From 1855 to the breaking out of the civil war he was a picturesque character on the streets of New York, and made himself aggressively conspicuous.

"Leaves of Grass" was received by the critical

press with widely differing opinions. It may be said, however, that the preponderance of these was in Whitman's favor. The "North American Review," in particular, gave the book a handsome reception. In addition to this a warm letter from Emerson, soon printed in the papers, attracted much attention to the new poet. A second edition of "Leaves of Grass" appeared in 1856, and it was to the use of his name in connection with this edition that Emerson seriously objected, for it contained additional poems on sexual subjects which the Concord writer could not approve of, although he had passed over those in the first edition. Yet the friendship of Emerson and Whitman was not broken by this incident. Whitman visited Boston in 1860, to superintend the publication of the third edition of "Leaves of Grass" (1860–61), and then renewed his friendly relations with the former. With the appearance of the third edition, what has been called the "Whitman cult" had its beginning in a series of articles on the poet in the New York "Saturday Press." From that time Whitman never lacked for a defender, often from imaginary attacks. The most notable episode of his life undoubtedly was his three years' experience as a volunteer nurse in the army hospitals of Washington. In December, 1862, hearing that his brother, Col. George W. Whitman, was wounded at the first Fredericksburg battle, Walt left for the front. Thereafter he was a constant worker in the hospitals until they closed, late in 1865. He established himself in lodgings at Washington and, supporting himself by miscellaneous work, raised funds among friends known and unknown for the purpose of obtaining small luxuries for the wounded soldiers. These he distributed himself, writing letters for the soldiers, attending to their wants, and making their stay in the hospitals more endurable generally. The amount of good he was able to do in this way was very great, and many affecting stories are told of the soldiers' gratitude for his devotion.

He himself has preserved an interesting record of this work in his "Memoranda during the War" (1875), afterward incorporated in the volume of his prose works entitled "Specimen Days and Collect." In the summer of 1864, after a specially trying experience in nursing some badly wounded soldiers, he became saturated with the hospital malaria and was obliged to go north for some months. He never thoroughly recovered from the effects of this attack, which is considered responsible for his final breakdown. Returning to Washington in February, 1865, he obtained a place in the Department of the Interior, and gained more leisure for his hospital work. From this he was dismissed by a new secretary of the department, Hon. James Harlan, in July of the same year. Mr. Harlan had found a copy of "Leaves of Grass," and was unwilling that its author should remain on his staff. For this outrage Mr. Harlan was soon afterward roundly denounced in the now famous pamphlet, "The Good Gray Poet: A Vindication," written by William Douglas O'Connor and published early in 1866. Mr. O'Connor, as the case seemed to demand, came forward on several subsequent occasions in defense of his friend, but never quite so effectively as in this brochure. Shortly after his dismissal Whitman was sent for by Attorney-General Speed, who offered him a clerkship in his own department, which Whitman held until his attack of paralysis in 1873. Whitman's war experiences had modified his personal characteristics to a considerable extent. Always frank and cordial in his address, a touch of graciousness was now added, which, with his whitening hair, fitted him admirably to fill the rôle assigned him by a devoted coterie of friends. The influences of the war developed into the sequence of poems, "Drum-Taps," which was just ready for the press at the time of Lincoln's assassination. Whitman delayed publication until he had written "Sequel to Drum-Taps," containing "When Lilacs Last in the Door-Yard Bloomed" and "O Captain! My Captain!" The whole was published with the title, "Walt Whitman's Drum-Taps," under the date 1865-66. This volume attracted much attention and confirmed the author's reputation as a poet. The ensuing six years were probably the most enjoyable of Whitman's life. He was able to contribute to the support of his mother's family, he saw himself taken up in England, where William Michael Rossetti's eclectic edition of "Poems by Walt Whitman" appeared in 1868, gaining him a new clientage, and he received gratifying letters from Tennyson and other famous authors. In 1866 he busied himself with a rearrangement of "Leaves of Grass" and additional poems, which were bound up with "Drum-Taps" and pages containing the "Songs before Parting," and published in one volume as "Leaves of Grass" (1867). In 1867 also appeared John Burroughs's "Notes on Walt Whitman As Poet and Person" (second edition, enlarged, 1871). Still another revision of "Leaves of Grass" was published in 1871, and the same year were issued "Passage to India," containing both new and old poems, and "After All, Not To Create Only," a poem delivered at the opening of the fortieth annual exhibition of the American Institute in New York. All these were bound up in one volume as "Leaves of Grass" (1872). "Democratic Vistas," Whitman's first prose work, came out in 1871, and contains his views as to the present condition and future of "These States." It contains also some savage reflections on his brother poets, and incidentally may be considered his first response to the plentiful abuse his sexual poetry had received in certain quarters, and to the various criticisms of his metrical methods. "As a Strong Bird on Pinions Free, and Other Poems" (1872) was Whitman's next volume. In January of 1873 he suffered an attack of paralysis, from which he never fully recovered. Partial recovery ensued at once, but the death of his mother in the following May completely prostrated him. He gave up his clerkship in Washington, and removed to the home of his brother, Col. Whitman, in Camden, N. J.

He remained there, boarding with his brother's family, until 1883. A series of articles in the Springfield (Mass.) "Republican" for 1875 called attention to his feeble condition and moderate circumstances, and friends in America and England rallied to his support. Their efforts were continued at intervals through the remainder of his life. In 1875 Whitman published "Memoranda during the War," already noticed. The

next year he prepared the "Centennial edition" of his works in two volumes, "Leaves of Grass" and "Two Rivulets." The former volume is identical with the 1871 edition. The latter contains "Democratic Vistas," "Memoranda during the War," "Passage to India," and new "Centennial Songs," and other poems. The books are unique in appearance and make-up. In fact, no other American poet has so carefully attended to the frequent arrangement and publication of his works. At Camden Whitman endeavored to recover health by resuming an outdoor life. He found a quiet country farmhouse some distance from Camden, and spent much of his time in the woods and along a small creek. His life at this time, and sundry visits to New York, to his birthplace on Long Island, and to the homes of his friends, John Burroughs and Dr. R. M. Bucke, were described in pleasant letters to the New York "Tribune" and "Critic." These journals, with the old "Galaxy," accepted almost every poem and article offered them by Whitman. The "North American Review" and "Lippincott's Magazine" printed much of his work during the last decade of his life, but acceptances by other magazines were scanty. The editors of the latter have declared that they were not prejudiced against Whitman, but that they often found what he sent them unavailable for their constituencies. In 1879 Whitman visited New York for the purpose of delivering a lecture on the death of Abraham Lincoln. This he repeated, publicly or privately, for a number of years, on the anniversary of that occasion. It was delivered, by the arrangements of friends, before large audiences in New York in 1887, in Boston in 1881, and in Philadelphia in 1880 and 1890, bringing Whitman material financial returns. The lecture in Boston was followed by an offer from a firm of that city to publish a new edition of "Leaves of Grass." The offer was accepted, and Whitman spent some weeks in Boston in revising the proofs of what was to be a definitive edition. It appeared as "Leaves of Grass" (1881-82), and gained a large sale through regular trade channels, but in the spring of 1882 the Attorney-General of Massachusetts called upon the publishers to suppress certain passages or withdraw the book. The firm was unwilling to test the matter in court, and Whitman was again an outlaw. The copyright receipts enabled him to purchase the plates, and a new edition was brought out by a Philadelphia publisher. It was followed by "Specimen Days and Collect" (1883), a collection of his prose works to that date. In 1883 also appeared "Walt Whitman," by Richard Maurice Bucke, the only real biography of the poet yet written, although the story of his life as told by himself has been selected from his prose writings, and published as "Autobiographia" (1892). The income from his books and lectures, and contributions from his friends, enabled Whitman to purchase the little house in Mickle Street, Camden, to which he removed in 1883. He remained there until his death, gratified by the attentions of comrades in Philadelphia and New York, who, with the co-operation of a devoted young friend, Horace L. Traubel, of Camden, saw that his comfort was assured. During this period he was able from various sources to gather a considerable sum of money, with which he erected a handsome tomb at Harleigh Cemetery in the outskirts of Camden. It was designed by himself, and some of the granite blocks weigh seven tons or over. His remains were placed there with impressive ceremonies. Additional books and editions to those already named are "November Boughs" (1888) and "Good Bye My Fancy" (1891), containing his latest work in prose and verse; "Complete Poems and Prose" (1889), comprising "Leaves of Grass," "Specimen Days," and "November Boughs" in one quarto volume; "Leaves of Grass" (1892), the final complete edition; and a complete volume of his prose works,

WHITMAN'S HOME IN CAMDEN.

also issued in 1892. "Selected Poems" (1892) and "Autobiographia" (1892) were edited by the writer of this sketch. Mr. Whitman shortly before his death for the first time consented to the publication of the above-named American eclectic edition of his poems. Many such editions had appeared in England, where a full edition was not published until 1880.

The accompanying fac-simile is from a sketch that Mr. Whitman wrote in 1876, when asked to furnish the facts of his life for the "American Cyclopædia." The original is on the back of a blue letter-sheet on which some one had written to ask him for his autograph.

WHITTIER, JOHN GREENLEAF, an American poet, born in Haverhill, Mass., Dec. 7, 1807; died in Hampton Falls, N. H., Sept. 7, 1892. The first ancestor of the name came to this country in 1638, was a member of the Bay Colony, and was of the Puritan faith. In the second generation from him, at a time of the most violent persecution of that body, the head of the family embraced the doctrines of the Friends—or Quakers, as they are called by those outside the sect. The homestead in which Whittier was born was built in 1688. It was a typical New England farmhouse, standing alone, with low walls, great oaken beams, small windows, doors hung on mighty hinges, and a huge central chimney. The family were poor, in the same sense in which most of the farmers of that day were; they had nothing for the luxuries of which they had no thought or care, but the result of cheerful labor gave them sufficient for all needs. Thrifty and strong. the Whittiers asked no odds 'of fortune, although the basket and store never overflowed. In the prelude to his volume entitled "Among the Hills," he says :

A farmer's son,
Proud of field-lore and harvest craft, and feeling
All their fine possibilities, how rich
And restful even poverty and toil
Become when beauty, harmony, and love
Sit at their humble hearth as angels sat
At evening in the patriarch's tent, when man
Makes labor noble, and his farmer's frock
The symbol of a Christian chivalry
Tender and just and generous to her
Who clothes with grace all duty; still, I know
Too well the picture has another side,—
How wearily the grind of toil goes on
Where love is wanting, how the eye and ear
And heart are starved amidst the plenitude
Of nature, and how hard and colorless
Is life without an atmosphere.

When seven years of age, Whittier began to attend the neighborhood school, of which there were two sessions a year, of three months each. Here, until he was sixteen, he continued to gain the rudiments of an education, under constantly changing teachers. Sixty years afterward his memory furnished him with an incident of this time. which he embodied in his poem entitled "In School-Days :"

Still sits the school-house by the road,
 A ragged beggar sunning;
Around it still the sumachs grow,
 And blackberry vines are running.

Within, the master's desk is seen,
 Deep scarred by raps official;
The warping floor, the battered seats,
 The jack-knife's carved initial;

The charcoal frescos on its wall;
 Its door's worn sill, betraying
The feet that, creeping slow to school,
 Went storming out to playing!

Long years ago a winter sun
 Shone over it at setting;
Lit up its western window-panes,
 And low eaves' icy fretting.

It touched the tangled golden curls,
 And brown eyes full of grieving,
Of one who still her steps delayed
 When all the school were leaving.

D. APPLETON & C?

of money, with which he erected a handsome
tomb at Harleigh Cemetery in the outskirts of
Camden. It was designed by himself, and some
of the granite blocks weigh seven tons or over:
His remains were placed there with impressive
ceremonies. Additional books and editions to
those already named are "November Boughs"
(1888) and "Good Bye My Fancy" (1891), containing his latest work in prose and verse;
"Complete Poems and Prose" (1889), comprising "Leaves of Grass," "Specimen Days," and
"November Boughs" in one complete volume;
"Leaves of Grass" (1892), the final complete edition; and a complete volume of his prose works,

WHITMAN'S HOME IN CAMDEN.

also issued in 1892. "Selected Poems" (1892)
and "Autobiographia" (1892) were edited by
the editor with a sketch. Mr. Whitman shortly
before his death for the first time consented to
the publishing of the above named American
eclectic editions of his works. Many such editions had appeared in England, where a full edition was not published until 1868.

The accompanying fac simile is from a sketch
that Mr. Whitman wrote in 1876, when asked to
furnish the facts of his life for the "American
Cyclopædia." The original is on the back of a
blue letter-sheet on which was then had occasion
to ask him for his autograph.

WHITTIER, JOHN GREENLEAF,
American poet, born in Haverhill, Mass., Dec.
1807; died in Hampton Falls, N. H., Sept.
1892. The first ancestor of the name came to
this country in 1638, was a member of the Bay
Colony, and was of the Puritan faith. In the
second generation from him, at a time of the
most violent persecution of that body, the head
of the family embraced the doctrines of the
Friends—or Quakers, as they are called
outside the sect. The homestead in which
Whittier was born was built in 1688. It was a
typical New England farmhouse, standing
alone, with low walls, great oaken beams, small
windows, doors hung on mighty hinges, and a
huge central chimney. The family were poor, in
the same sense in which most of the farmers
of that day were; they had nothing for the
luxuries of which they had no thought or care,
but the result of cheerful labor gave them sufficient for all needs. Thrifty and strong, the
Whittiers asked no odds of fortune, although
the basket and store never overflowed. In the
prelude to his volume entitled "Among the
Hills," he says:

A farmer's son,
Proud of field-lore and harvest craft, and feeling
All their fine possibilities, how rich
And restful even poverty and toil
Become when beauty, harmony, and love
Sit at their humble hearth as angels sat
At evening in the patriarch's tent, when man
Makes labor noble, and his farmer's frock
The symbol of a Christian chivalry
. . . . to her
. . . . still, I know
. . . . side.
. . . . goes on
What . . . . . . how the eye and ear
And . . . . . . carved amidst the plenitude
Of nature, and how hard and colorless
Is life without an atmosphere.

When seven years of age, Whittier began to
attend the neighborhood school, of which there
were two sessions a year, of three months each.
Here, until he was sixteen, he continued to gain
the rudiments of an education, under constantly
changing teachers. Sixty years afterward his
memory furnished him with an incident of this
time, which he embodied in his poem entitled
"In School-Days:"

Still sits the school-house by the road,
    A ragged beggar sunning;
Around it still the sumachs grow,
    And blackberry vines are running.

Within, the master's desk is seen,
    Deep scarred by raps official;
The warping floor, the battered seats;
    The jack-knife's carved initial;

The charcoal frescos on its wall;
    Its door's worn sill, betraying
The feet that, creeping slow to school,
    Went storming out to playing!

Long years ago a winter sun
    Shone over it at setting;
Lit up its western window-panes,
    And low eaves' icy fretting.

It touched the tangled golden curls,
    And brown eyes full of grieving,
Of one who still her steps delayed
    When all the school were leaving.

John G. Whittier

D. APPLETON & C?

For near her stood the little boy
  Her childish favor singled ;
His cap pulled low upon a face
  Where pride and shame were mingled.

Pushing with restless feet the snow
  To right and left, he lingered ;—
As restlessly her tiny hands
  The blue-checked apron fingered.

He saw her lift her eyes ; he felt
  The soft hand's light caressing,
And heard the tremble of her voice,
  As if a fault confessing.

" I'm sorry that I spelt the word :
  I hate to go above you,
Because,"—the brown eyes lower fell,—
  " Because, you see, I love you ! "

Still memory to a gray-haired man
  That sweet child-face is showing.
Dear girl ! the grasses on her grave
  Have forty years been growing !

He lives to learn, in life's hard school,
  How few who pass above him
Lament their triumph and his loss,
  Like her,—because they love him.

The library in his home was large for the
time ; it contained twenty volumes, mostly religious. This was supplemented by that of the
neighborhood
physician, Dr.
Elias Weld,
and many
other friends,
so that, when
Whittier en-
tered Haver-
hill Academy,
he had read
far more than
was usual for
boys of his
age and class.
He was thir-
teen years old

WHITTIER'S HOME.

when one of the itinerant merchants that long
supplied the New England housewife with
everything, from a skein of yarn to a Sunday
dress, came to the farm to display his wares.
At the hospitable hearth he sang the songs of
Robert Burns, a name unknown to Quaker ears.
It was years before a printed line of the original came into Whittier's hands, but meantime
the impression that molded his future had been
formed.

Whittier had been taught shoemaking, as was
the custom, and with the results of his home
work on winter evenings he paid for six months'
schooling in the Academy. He was then considered competent to take a district school himself, and with the proceeds of that he obtained
another course of study, covering six months,
which ended his school training.

Two years later, at the age of twenty-two, he
edited for a few months, in Boston, " The American Manufacturer." In 1830 he became editor
of the " Haverhill Gazette," and six months
later he succeeded George D. Prentice as editor
of " The New England Weekly Review," at Hartford, Conn. His first published volume, " Legends of New England, in Prose and Verse "

(1831), was made up of matter that had been
printed in his papers, much of which had commanded attention. One of these, " The Frost
Spirit," early found its way into school readers,
and was a favorite poem for recitation on Friday
afternoons :

He comes,—he comes,—the Frost Spirit comes !
  You may trace his footsteps now
On the naked woods and the blasted fields and the
  brown hill's withered brow.
He has smitten the leaves of the gray old trees
  where their pleasant green came forth,
And the winds, which follow wherever he goes,
  have shaken them down to earth.

He comes,—he comes,—the Frost Spirit comes!—
  from the frozen Labrador.—
From the icy bridge of the Northern seas, which
  the white bear wanders o'er.—
Where the fisherman's sail is stiff with ice, and the
  luckless forms below
In the sunless cold of the lingering night into marble statues grow !

He comes,—he comes,—the Frost Spirit comes !—
  on the rushing Northern blast,
And the dark Norwegian pines have bowed as his
  fearful breath went past.
With an unscorched wing he has hurried on, where
  the fires of Hecla glow
On the darkly beautiful sky above and the ancient
  ice below.

He comes,—he comes,—the Frost Spirit comes !—
  and the quiet lake shall feel
The torpid touch of his glazing breath, and ring to
  the skater's heel ;
And the streams which danced on the broken rocks,
  or sang to the leaning grass,
Shall bow again to their winter chain, and in mournful silence pass.

He comes,—he comes,—the Frost Spirit comes !—
  let us meet him as we may,
And turn with the light of the parlor-fire his evil
  power away ;
And gather closer the circle round, when that firelight dances high,
And laugh at the shriek of the baffled Fiend as
  his sounding wing goes by !

Whittier was compelled, by the death of his
father, to retire from editorial work, and take
charge of the farm and the family. To that
household—then consisting of mother, two sisters, one brother, and an aunt—his devotion was
absolute. " Snow-Bound," his longest and most
sustained poem, is at once a record of the New
England that is fast becoming only a tradition,
of the household band, and of his undying affection for them. It is also a production that goes
far toward placing him in the front rank of our
poets. The following passages are from it:

What matter how the night behaved ?
What matter how the north-wind raved ?
Blow high, blow low, not all its snow
Could quench our hearth-fire's ruddy glow.
O Time and Change !—with hair as gray
As was my sire's that winter day,
How strange it seems, with so much gone
Of life and love, to still live on !
Ah, brother ! only I and thou
Are left of all that circle now,—
The dear home faces whereupon
That fitful firelight paled and shone.
Henceforward, listen as we will,
The voices of that hearth are still ;

Look where we may, the wide earth o'er,
Those lighted faces smile no more.
We tread the paths their feet have worn,
  We sit beneath their orchard-trees,
  We hear, like them, the hum of bees
And rustle of the bladed corn ;
We turn the pages that they read,
  Their written words we linger o'er,
But in the sun they cast no shade,
No voice is heard, no sign is made,
  No step is on the conscious floor !
Yet Love will dream, and Faith will trust,
(Since He who knows our need is just,)
That somehow, somewhere, meet we must.
Alas for him who never sees
The stars shine through his cypress-trees !
Who, hopeless, lays his dead away,
Nor looks to see the breaking day
Across the mournful marbles play !
Who hath not learned, in hours of faith,
  The truth to flesh and sense unknown,
That Life is ever lord of Death,
  And love can never lose its own !
As one who held herself a part
Of all she saw, and let her heart
Against the household bosom lean,
Upon the motley-braided mat
Our youngest and our dearest sat,
Lifting her large, sweet, asking eyes,
  Now bathed within the fadeless green
And holy peace of Paradise.
O, looking from some heavenly hill,
  Or from the shade of saintly palms,
  Or silver reach of river calms,
Do those large eyes behold me still ?
With me one little year ago :—
The chill weight of the winter snow
  For months upon her grave has lain ;
And now, when summer south-winds blow
  And brier and harebell bloom again,
I tread the pleasant paths we trod,
I see the violet-sprinkled sod
Whereon she leaned, too frail and weak,
The hillside flowers she loved to seek,
Yet following me where'er I went
With dark eyes full of love's content.
The birds are glad ; the brier-rose fills
The air with sweetness ; all the hills
Stretch green to June's unclouded sky ;
But still I wait with ear and eye
For something gone which should be nigh,
A loss in all familiar things,
In flower that blooms, and bird that sings.
And yet, dear heart ! remembering thee,
  Am I not richer than of old ?
Safe in thy immortality,
  What change can reach the wealth I hold ?
What chance can mar the pearl and gold
Thy love hath left in trust with me ?
And while in life's late afternoon,
  Where cool and long the shadows grow,
I walk to meet the night that soon
  Shall shape and shadow overflow,
I cannot feel that thou art far,
Since near at need the angels are ;
And when the sunset gates unbar,
  Shall I not see thee waiting stand,
And, white against the evening star,
  The welcome of thy beckoning hand ?

In 1836 Mr. Whittier became secretary of the American Anti-Slavery Society, and went to Philadelphia, where he edited the "Pennsylvania Freeman." His office was sacked and burned, and he was exposed to the violence of a mob. The cause of the slave had been espoused in no careless moment. Unlike the Puritans, he learned sympathy with the persecuted from the experiences of his own sect. While his writings were impassioned, he was never a fanatic, and he refused to follow Garrison, his first inspirer, in his political vagaries. Peace-loving and shrinking as he was, Whittier was ready to suffer for his opinions, and was more than once subjected to public fury. In Concord, N. H., with George Thompson, he was obliged to flee before a mob. In 1835-6 he was Member of the Massachusetts Legislature from Haverhill. In 1840 he took up his residence in Amesbury, Mass., where he spent his days, except for a brief sojourn in Lowell, where he edited the "Middlesex Standard." From 1847-1859 he contributed editorially to the "National Era," in which "Uncle Tom's Cabin" first appeared, which was published in Washington, D. C. All this while he was devoting much time to writing verse. His beautiful and familiar hymn, beginning :

Blest land of Judea, thrice hallowed in song,
Where the holiest of memories, pilgrim-like,
  throng,

was written in 1837, and several of the legendary and descriptive ballads that came to be distinctive of him appeared in that year.

One thing to be taken into consideration, in reviewing the poetry of Whittier, is the difficulty of the task, from a poetical view-point, which he consciously set himself—to be true at once to the spirit of fancy and the reality of fact. The ease with which he blended them is as marked as it is exceptional. In the nature of the case, such work is limited, genius or no genius ; but, by delicacy of feeling mingled with fervor, he was enabled to make such choice of words as to produce poetic effect, and still detail historic fact with due order and precision. A fine example of this was the legendary poem entitled "Cassandra Southwick," which is also the first instance of his use of the swinging ballad measure that Macaulay used with so much effect.

The poem entitled "Massachusetts to Virginia," written in the same year, 1843, shows again the force that a fine measure can add to a moving theme, and names and facts are woven in with grace and dignity :

The blast from Freedom's Northern hills, upon its
  Southern way,
Bears greeting to Virginia from Massachusetts Bay:—
No word of haughty challenging, nor battle bugle's
  peal,
Nor steady tread of marching files, nor clang of
  horsemen's steel.

No trains of deep-mouthed cannon along our highways go,—
Around our silent arsenals untrodden lies the snow ;
And to the land-breeze of our ports, upon their
  errands far,
A thousand sails of commerce swell, but none are
  spread for war.

We hear thy threats, Virginia ! thy stormy words
  and high,
Swell harshly on the Southern winds which melt
  along our sky ;
Yet, not one brown, hard hand foregoes its honest
  labor here,
No hewer of our mountain oaks suspends his axe in
  fear.

A voice from lips whereon the coal from Freedom's
  shrine hath been,
Thrilled, as but yesterday, the hearts of Berkshire's
  mountain men :

The echoes of that solemn voice are sadly lingering still
In all our sunny valleys, on every wind-swept hill.

And when the prowling man-thief came hunting for his prey
Beneath the very shadow of Bunker's shaft of gray,
How, through the free lips of the son, the father's warning spoke,.
How, from its bonds of trade and sect, the Pilgrim city broke!

Four years later "Barclay of Uri," another characteristic historical ballad, on the wrongs suffered by the Friends, appeared, and became widely popular at once.

In 1847 a new edition of Whittier's poems was brought out. From it he excluded many things that were restored in final collections, not because the author desired to have it so, but because the early work was familiar, and was requested by publishers. The poet always seemed genuinely unconscious of his power, and surprised at the extent of his reputation. In the preface to his last edition he says:

Perhaps a word of explanation may be needed in regard to a class of poems written between 1832 and 1865. Of their defects from an artistic point of view it is not necessary to speak. They were the earnest and often vehement expression of the writer's thought and feeling at critical periods in the great conflict between Freedom and Slavery. They were written with no expectation that they would survive the occasions that called them forth: they were protests, alarm signals, trumpet-calls to action, words wrung from the writer's heart, forged at white heat, and of course lacking the finish and careful word-selection which reflection and patient brooding over them might have given. Such as they are, they belong to the history of the Anti-Slavery movement, and may serve as way-marks of its progress. If their language at times seems severe and harsh, the wrong of slavery which provoked it must be its excuse, if any is needed. In attacking it, we did not measure our words.

In the proem he says:

I love the old melodious lays
Which softly melt the ages through,
The songs of Spenser's golden days,
Arcadian Sidney's silvery phrase,
Sprinkling our noon of time with freshest morning dew.

Yet, vainly in my quiet hours
To breathe their marvellous notes I try;
I feel them, as the leaves and flowers
In silence feel the dewy showers,
And drink with glad still lips the blessing of the sky.

The rigor of a frozen clime,
The harshness of an untaught ear,
The jarring words of one whose rhyme
Beat often Labor's hurried time,
Or Duty's rugged march through storm and strife, are here.

Yet here at least an earnest sense
Of human right and weal is shown;
A hate of tyranny intense,
And hearty in its vehemence,
As if my brother's pain and sorrow were my own.

Thrice familiar is the close of "The Crisis," written on learning the terms of the treaty with Mexico:

The Crisis presses on us; face to face with us it stands,
With solemn lips of question, like the Sphinx in Egypt's sands!
This day we fashion Destiny, our web of Fate we spin;
This day for all hereafter choose we holiness or sin;
Even now from starry Gerizim, or Ebal's cloudy crown,
We call the dews of blessing or the bolts of cursing down!

By all for which the martyrs bore their agony and shame;
By all the warning words of truth with which the prophets came;
By the Future which awaits us; by all the hopes which cast
Their faint and trembling beams across the blackness of the Past;
And by the blessed thought of Him who for Earth's freedom died,
O my people! O my brothers! let us choose the righteous side.

So shall the Northern pioneer go joyful on his way;
To wed Penobscot's waters to San Francisco's bay;
To make the rugged places smooth, and sow the vales with grain;
And bear, with Liberty and Law, the Bible in his train:
The mighty West shall bless the East, and sea shall answer sea,
And mountain unto mountain call, PRAISE GOD, FOR WE ARE FREE!

In "Randolph of Roanoke," Whittier gave one of the best instances of his capacity to be just to men who widely differed with him in nature and conduct. Holmes, in a tribute after Whittier's death, said: "The next poem that I remember as having deeply impressed me was that vigorous and impassioned burst of feeling, 'Randolph of Roanoke.' I can never read it now without an emotion which makes my eyes fill and my voice tremble." Two stanzas characterize Randolph:

Bard, Sage, and Tribune!—in himself
All moods of mind contrasting,—
The tenderest wail of human woe,
The scorn-like lightning blasting;
The pathos which from rival eyes
Unwilling tears could summon,
The stinging taunt, the fiery burst
Of hatred scarcely human!

Mirth, sparkling like a diamond shower
From lips of life-long sadness;
Clear picturings of majestic thought
Upon a ground of madness;
And over all Romance and Song
A classic beauty throwing,
And laurelled Clio at his side
Her storied pages showing.

In "Ichabod" Whittier gave vent to a tremendous burst of feeling on learning that Daniel Webster had spoken in Congress, in favor of the Fugitive Slave Law. The poem also furnishes a noble specimen of many in which he distinguished between the deed and the actor:

So fallen! so lost! the light withdrawn
Which once he wore!
The glory from his gray hairs gone
Forevermore!

Revile him not,—the Tempter hath
A snare for all;
And pitying tears, not scorn and wrath,
Befit his fall!

O, dumb be passion's stormy rage,
    When he who might
Have lighted up and led his age,
    Falls back in night.

Scorn ! would the angels laugh, to mark
    A bright soul driven,
Fiend-goaded, down the endless dark,
    From hope and heaven !

Let not the land once proud of him
    Insult him now,
Nor brand with deeper shame his dim,
    Dishonored brow.

But let its humbled sons, instead,
    From sea to lake,
A long lament, as for the dead,
    In sadness make.

Of all we loved and honored, naught
    Save power remains,—
A fallen angel's pride of thought,
    Still strong in chains.

All else is gone ; from those great eyes
    The soul has fled :
When faith is lost, when honor dies,
    The man is dead!

Then, pay the reverence of old days
    To his dead fame:
Walk backward, with averted gaze,
    And hide the shame !

In 1854 Mr. Whittier received the gift of a
sprig of blooming heather. and the poem suggested by it. a song on Robert Burns, tells the
true story of Whittier's own transformation from
a plow-boy into a poet :

No more these simple flowers belong
    To Scottish maid and lover ;
Sown in the common soil of song,
    They bloom the wide world over.

In smiles and tears, in sun and showers,
    The minstrel and the heather,
The deathless singer and the flowers
    He sang of live together.

I call to mind the summer day,
    The early harvest mowing,
The sky with sun and clouds at play,
    And flowers with breezes blowing.

I hear the blackbird in the corn,
    The locust in the haying ;
And, like the fabled hunter's horn,
    Old tunes my heart is playing.

How oft that day, with fond delay,
    I sought the maple's shadow,
And sang with Burns the hours away,
    Forgetful of the meadow !

Bees hummed, birds twittered, overhead
    I heard the squirrels leaping,
The good dog listened while I read,
    And wagged his tail in keeping.

I watched him while in sportive mood
    I read " The Twa Dogs' " story,
And half believed he understood
    The poet's allegory.

Sweet day, sweet songs !—The golden hours
    Grew brighter for that singing.
From brook and bird and meadow flowers
    A dearer welcome bringing.

I saw through all familiar things
    The romance underlying ;
The joys and griefs that plume the wings
    Of fancy skyward flying.

I saw the same blithe day return,
    The same sweet fall of even,
That rose on wooded Craigie-burn,
    And sauk on crystal Devon.

I matched with Scotland's heathery hills
    The sweet-brier and the clover ;
With Ayr and Doon, my native rills,
    Their wood-hymns chanting over.

O'er rank and pomp, as he had seen,
    I saw the Man uprising ;
No longer common or unclean,
    The child of God's baptizing !

To quote once more from the last of the noble
circle of poets with which the first century of our
national existence has been marked, Dr. Holmes
says of Whittier:

Of late years I have been in close sympathy with
him—not especially as an abolitionist—not merely
through human sympathies, but as belonging with
me to the " Church without a Bishop," which seems
the natural complement of a " State without a
King." I mean the church which lives by no formulæ ; which believes in a loving Father, and trusts
Him for the final well-being of the whole spiritual
universe which He has called into being. All
through Whittier's writings the spirit of trust in a
beneficent order of things and a loving superintendence of the universe shows itself, ever hopeful, ever
cheerful, always looking forward to a happier,
brighter era when the Kingdom of Heaven shall
be established. Nature breeds fanatics, but in due
time supplies their correctives. She will not be
hurried about it, but they come at last. Thomas
Boston, the Scotch Calvinist, was born in 1676.
Robert Burns—objectionable in many respects, like
the royal Psalmist of Israel, but whose singing protest against unwholesome theology was mightier
than the voices of a thousand pulpits—was born in
1759. Jonathan Edwards, whose theological barba-
risms reached a lower depth, if possible, than those
of his Scotch model, Thomas Boston, was born in
1703. John Greenleaf Whittier reached the hearts
of his fellow-countrymen, especially of New Eng-
landers, paralyzed by the teachings of Edwards, as
Burns kindled the souls of Scotchmen palsied by the
dogmas of Thomas Boston and his fellow sectaries.

One of the earliest, as well as one of the most
characteristic expressions of this faith is found
in " My Psalm " :

I mourn no more my vanished years :
    Beneath a tender rain,
An April rain of smiles and tears,
    My heart is young again.

The west-winds blow, and, singing low,
    I hear the glad streams run ;
The windows of my soul I throw
    Wide open to the sun.

No longer forward nor behind
    I look in hope or fear ;
But, grateful, take the good I find,
    The best of now and here.

I plough no more a desert land,
    To harvest weed and tare ;
The manna dropping from God's hand
    Rebukes my painful care.

I break my pilgrim staff,—I lay
    Aside the toiling oar ;
The angel sought so far away
    I welcome at my door.

Enough that blessings undeserved
    Have marked my erring track ;
That whereso'er my feet have swerved,
    His chastening turned me back ;—

That more and more a Providence
Of love is understood,
Making the springs of time and sense
Sweet with eternal good;—

That death seems but a covered way
Which opens into light,
Wherein no blinded child can stray
Beyond the Father's sight;—

That care and trial seem at last,
Through Memory's sunset air,
Like mountain-ranges overpast,
In purple distance fair;—

That all the jarring notes of life
Seem blending in a psalm,
And all the angles of its strife
Slow rounding into calm.

And so the shadows fall apart,
And so the west-winds play;
And all the windows of my heart
I open to the day.

From the hour when his voice could make itself heard effectively, Whittier had used it to portray the sinfulness of slavery and, if not directly the sinfulness of war, at least the blessings and duty of peace. As the struggle that was evoked by slavery approached the necessity for a death-grapple, he was sorely tried. His heroic nature would not permit his pen to be idle, while his life-long principles made it almost impossible to wield it in defense of war even for his country's life and slavery's death. The first stanza that he wrote in that crisis was :

We see not, know not; all our way
Is night,—with Thee alone is day:
From out the torrent's troubled drift,
Above the storm our prayers we lift,
Thy Will be done!

The second poem, entitled " A Word for the Hour," ran :

Let us not weakly weep
Nor rashly threaten. Give us grace to keep
Our faith and patience; wherefore should we leap
On one hand into fratricidal fight,
Or, on the other, yield eternal right,
Frame lies of law, and good and ill confound ?
They break the links of Union; shall we light
The fires of hell to weld anew the chain
On that red anvil where each blow is pain ?

His next poem was the prophetic one entitled " Ein Feste Burg ist unser Gott," which begins:

We wait beneath the furnace-blast
The pangs of transformation ;
Not painlessly doth God recast
And mould anew the nation.
Hot burns the fire
Where wrongs expire ;
Nor spares the hand
That from the land
Uproots the ancient evil.

How the education of our poet proceeded is shown in the dialogue between Peace and Freedom, which he called " The Watcher." Part of it is as follows :

" How long ? "—I knew the voice of Peace,—
" Is there no respite ?—no release ?—
When shall the hopeless quarrel cease ?

" O Lord, how long !—One human soul
Is more than any parchment scroll,
Or any flag thy winds unroll.

" What price was Ellsworth's, young and brave ?
How weigh the gift that Lyon gave,
Or count the cost of Winthrop's grave ?

" O brother ! if thine eye can see,
Tell how and when the end shall be,
What hope remains for thee and me. "

Then Freedom sternly said : " I shun
No strife nor pang beneath the sun,
When human rights are staked and won.

" I knelt with Ziska's hunted flock,
I watched in Toussaint's cell of rock,
I walked with Sidney to the block.

" The moor of Marston felt my tread,
Through Jersey snows the march I led,
My voice Magenta's charges sped.

" But now, through weary day and night,
I watch a vague and aimless fight
For leave to strike one blow aright. "

One of the most melodious of his songs is that which was written for the " Battle Autumn " of 1862, beginning :

The flags of war like storm-birds fly,
The charging trumpets blow ;
Yet rolls no thunder in the sky,
No earthquake strives below.

And, calm and patient, Nature keeps
Her ancient promise well,
Though o'er her bloom and greenness sweeps
The battle's breath of hell.

And still she walks in golden hours
Through harvest-happy farms,
And still she wears her fruits and flowers
Like jewels on her arms.

The rhymes of this peace-lover had by this time become a power. The musical poem, " At Port Royal," at once became a favorite, and " Barbara Frietchie " attained the greatest popularity.

In regard to the origin of " Barbara Frietchie," Whittier said that he was waiting one day for his mail, in the Amesbury post-office, when he overheard a soldier, home on leave, who had been wounded in the battle of Monocacy, describe the scene from his own observation. He did not know the woman's name. Whittier wrote to the postmaster of Frederick, describing the incident, and asking for the name. The reply was : " In all probability the heroine's name is Barbara Frietchie."

The abolition of slavery and the end of the war afforded more grateful themes. A portion of " Laus Deo," written on hearing the bells that announced the passage of the Fifteenth Amendment to the Constitution, runs :

It is done !
Clang of bell and roar of gun
Send the tidings up and down.
How the belfries rock and reel !
How the great guns, peal on peal,
Fling the joy from town to town !

Ring, O bells !
Every stroke exulting tells
Of the burial hour of crime.
Loud and long, that all may hear,
Ring for every listening ear
Of Eternity and Time !

Let us kneel :
God's own voice is in that peal,
And this spot is holy ground.
Lord, forgive us ! What are we,
That our eyes this glory see,
That our ears have heard the sound ?

In regard to the way of dealing with the
questions that arose after the war, he wrote, in a
poem entitled " To the Thirty-ninth Congress ":

Enough of blood the land has seen,
And not by cell or gallows-stair
Shall ye the way of God prepare.

Say to the pardon-seekers,—Keep
Your manhood, bend no suppliant knees,
Nor palter with unworthy pleas.

Above your voices sounds the wail
Of starving men ; we shut in vain
Our eyes to Pillow's ghastly stain.

What words can drown that bitter cry ?
What tears wash out that stain of death ?
What oaths confirm your broken faith ?

From you alone the guaranty
Of union, freedom, peace, we claim ;
We urge no conqueror's terms of shame.

Make all men peers before the law,
Take hands from off the negro's throat,
Give black and white an equal vote.

Keep all your forfeit lives and lands,
But give the common law's redress
To labor's utter nakedness.

Revive the old heroic will ;
Be in the right as brave and strong
As ye have proved yourselves in wrong.

Defeat shall then be victory,
Your loss the wealth of full amends,
And hate be love, and foes be friends.

The poet was once more at liberty to return to
more congenial themes, and the chastening of
his nature showed itself in a succession of fine
devotional poems. One of the most characteristic of these is " The Eternal Goodness."

I see the wrong that round me lies,
I feel the guilt within ;
I hear, with groan and travail-cries,
The world confess its sin.

Yet, in the maddening maze of things,
And tossed by storm and flood,
To one fixed stake my spirit clings ;
I know that God is good!

Not mine to look where cherubim
And seraphs may not see,
But nothing can be good in Him
Which evil is in me.

The wrong that pains my soul below
I dare not throne above :
I know not of His hate,—I know
His goodness and His love.

I know not where His islands lift
Their fronded palms in air ;
I only know I cannot drift
Beyond His love and care.

In 1866 appeared " Snow-Bound," the fame of
which was a continual surprise to its author. A
year later he published "The Tent on the Beach,"
in which were woven several short poems. The

tenters were James T. Fields, Bayard Taylor, and
Whittier himself, who is thus described in it :

And one there was, a dreamer born,
Who, with a mission to fulfil,
Had left the Muses' haunts to turn
The crank of an opinion-mill,
Making his rustic reed of song
A weapon in the war with wrong,
Yoking his fancy to the breaking-plough
That beam-deep turned the soil for truth to spring
   and grow.

Too quiet seemed the man to ride
The winged Hippogriff Reform ;
Was his a voice from side to side
To pierce the tumult of the storm ?
A silent, shy, peace-loving man,
He seemed no fiery partisan
To hold his way against the public frown,
The ban of Church and State, the fierce mob's
   hounding down.

For while he wrought with strenuous will
The work his hands had found to do,
He heard the fitful music still
Of winds that out of dream-land blew.
The din about him could not drown
What the strange voices whispered down ;
Along his task-field weird processions swept,
The visionary pomp of stately phantoms stepped.

Few events of public significance were allowed
by Whittier to pass without the comment of his
muse. "Freedom in Brazil," "Howard at
Atlanta," "Garibaldi,' "Centennial Hymn,"
and "The Emancipation Group," are among
these. One of the most characteristic of his
poems contains the same sort of protest against
publicity that Browning, Tennyson, and Lowell
had each expressed. It was written in 1870 :

O living friends who love me,
O dear ones gone above me,
Careless of other fame,
I leave to you my name.

Hide it from idle praises,
Save it from evil phrases :
Why, when dear lips that spake it
Are dumb, should strangers wake it ?

Let the thick curtain fall ;
I better know than all
How little I have gained,
How vast the unattained.

Not by the page word-painted
Let life be banned or sainted :
Deeper than written scroll
The colors of the soul.

Sweeter than any sung
My songs that found no tongue ;
Nobler than any fact
My wish that failed of act.

The poem " At Last," which has been reprinted since Whittier's death, in connection
with final words from Browning and Tennyson,
was written ten years ago. One of the really
latest, " A Legacy," has a still higher theme :

Friend of my many years !
When the great silence falls, at last, on me,
Let me not leave, to pain and sadden thee,
A memory of tears,

But pleasant thoughts alone,
Of one who was thy friendship's honored guest
And drank the wine of consolation pressed
From sorrows of my own.

I have with thee a sense
Of hands upheld and trials rendered less—
The unselfish joy which is to helpfulness
  Its own great recompense ;

The knowledge that from thine,
As from the garments of the Master, stole
Calmness and strength, the virtue which makes
    whole
And heals without a sign ;

Yea more, the assurance strong
That love, which fails of perfect utterance here,
Lives on to fill the heavenly atmosphere
  With its immortal song.

One cannot close a sketch of Whittier's life and work without a thought of gratitude for his legacy to this young country. His humble birth, his comparatively wide knowledge of books and of events, the unalterable integrity of mind, the large faith, the tender affection, the espousal of unfashionable and unfavored causes, the power to put all these in rhyme at once homely and yet refined, strong and yet not rough, impassioned and yet loving, made John G. Whittier unique among American authors.

A new and carefully revised edition of his poems, in four volumes, appeared during the last year of his life.

WISCONSIN.—A Western State, admitted to the Union May 29, 1848 ; area, 56,040 square miles. The population, according to each decennial census since admission, was : 305,391 in 1850 ; 775,881 in 1860 : 1,054,670 in 1870 ; 1,315,-497 in 1880, and 1,686,880 in 1890. Capital, Madison.

Government.—The following were the State officers during the year : Governor, George W. Peck, Democrat ; Lieutenant-Governor, Charles Jonas ; Secretary of State, T. J. Cunningham ; Treasurer, John Hunner ; Attorney-General, J. L. O'Connor ; Superintendent of Public Instruction, O. E. Wells ; Insurance Commissioner, W. M. Root ; Railroad Commissioner, T. Thompson.

Finances.—The total receipts of the general fund for 1891-2 were $3,224,047.41 ; the disbursements were $2,980,614.82. The heaviest item of increase in the revenue, for the past two years, was in the receipts from railroads, which amounted to $2,360,000, and in the amounts received from counties for the maintenance of State hospitals, which were $402,000. The school fund receipts were $588,640.76. The amount of productive school funds on hand on Sept. 30, 1891, was $3,253,632.55 ; the amount on hand on the same date, 1892, was $3,358,-502.50. The disbursements by departments were as follows, omitting cents : For salaries, $356,497 ; for permanent appropriations, $83,-845 ; for legislative expenses, $157,181 ; for charitable and penal institutions, $775,040 ; for clerk hire, $109,164 ; for labor about capitol, $92,898 ; for sundry expenses, $1,406,006.

Legislative Sessions.—The legislature of 1891 passed a law redistricting the State into Assembly districts. It was asserted that this apportionment was made unfairly, and with the intention of making the State representation Democratic, and that the law was void under the constitution. The Attorney-General therefore began an action in the Supreme Court to determine its validity,' praying that the Secretary of State be restrained from issuing and publishing notices of

the election of members of the legislature under the law of 1891. On March 22 the court announced its decision. The finding was unanimous, and held that the apportionment of the State into Assembly districts, made by the Democratic legislature of 1891, was in violation of the constitution, and therefore was invalid. Section 10 of the court's decision adds : " This decision does not impeach the validity of acts otherwise valid of a legislature elected under an invalid legislative-apportionment statute."

In order that a law for the election of another legislature might be enacted, Gov. Peck called a special session of the legislature, which met on June 28. The appointments made by the Governor since the last session were confirmed, and a new apportionment act was passed by both houses and signed by the Governor, the legislature adjourning July 1. It was again claimed by the Republicans that this new act was unconstitutional, insomuch as that the division and consolidation of counties was unfairly made, and that the apportionment was not " according to the number of inhabitants." The Supreme Court was again required to determine the question, and the opinion of the court, in the second gerrymander suit, was filed Oct. 14. It decided that the apportionment act passed July 1 was unconstitutional and therefore void. The closing portion of the opinion is as follows :

" If, as claimed, there has never been any such equal apportionment in the State, then there certainly has never been any legislative construction of the words quoted [according to the number of inhabitants] ; for in order to give any effect to such construction, the words construed must be ambiguous and capable of two or more meanings, one of which the legislature has adopted. Where, however, the words are unambiguous, and the legislature has never undertaken to construe them, but simply disregarded them, their action, though often repeated, cannot be allowed to have the effect of *pro tanto* repealing the constitution."

On Oct. 10, after the decision of the Supreme Court had been made, Gov. Peck issued a proclamation calling the legislature to convene on Oct. 17. In the message that he read to the legislature after its assembling, he expressed surprise at the necessity of calling the legislators together, asserting that the apportionment of July 1, in his opinion, "appeared to conform to the requirements of the constitution, and to have met every rule of its interpretation so far as had been then declared by the Supreme Court." He further said that, " by the same rules and principles which have now been announced by the court, no apportionment ever made in the State, since the adoption of the constitution, has been constitutional or valid, and therefore no apportionment whatever remains available to the electors of the State." After a three-days' session, a new apportionment act was passed by both houses and signed by the Governor, and the legislature adjourned on Oct. 20.

Education.—The State Superintendent reports that he has made the apportionment, to each town, city, and village, of the school fund arising from the tax of one mill on each dollar of the assessed valuation of the taxable property of the State. He reports that the number of children of school age in the Sate is 623,428 ; the total apportionment from the one mill tax is $652,-116.14. There are 190 high schools in Wisconsin, and 15 normal schools. The sum expended for school purposes is more than $4,000,000, exclusive of the amount paid to the State University.

During the year the State Superintendent issued a pamphlet containing suggestions for securing the best results from the observance of Arbor day. He also issued a new edition of the school laws of Wisconsin for the use of school officers, and a pamphlet relating to school libraries, in which he says: "No money expended for school purposes in this State, during the past year, has done so much good, on the whole, in proportion, as that invested in school libraries."

University Dairy Certificates were issued this year for the first time. To obtain a certificate, the student must complete the twelve-weeks course at the university, pass satisfactory examinations in all the branches, and subsequently have one season's experience either in a cheese-factory or a dairy. If he had no experience previous to his course in the university, he must spend two years in the cheese-factory or dairy; he must likewise be the head of the factory, and not an assistant. The students never have any difficulty in securing places, for the demand is far greater than the supply. One of the students in 1892 was 64 years of age.

The Farm Institutes, meeting at different points in the State, were 94 in number. Bulletin No. 6 of the Wisconsin Farm Institutes was issued in December. In these bulletins every subject relating in any way to farming, stock-raising, and agricultural instruction is taken up, long and exhaustive treatises are written upon each, and they are then discussed.

Prof. Richard T. Ely, late of Johns Hopkins University, was made director and professor of political economy of the new Wisconsin School of History and Economics, founded in the University a year ago, and opened in September. The other members of the faculty are: John B. Parkinson, professor of civil polity and political economy; Frederick J. Turner, professor of American history; Charles H. Haskins, professor of constitutional history; Walter A. Scott, associate professor of political economy; John M. Parkinson, associate professor of civil polity; Albert Shaw, special lecturer on municipal problems; Amos G. Warner, special lecturer on pauperism; F. H. Wines, special lecturer on the criminal; David Kinley, assistant in economics; F. W. Speers, extension lecturer on history. It is claimed that the founding of this school is a fact of national importance, and that it gives "a State institution in the Northwest, the precedence in social and economic science of any other institution in the country." An appropriation of $5,000 was made by the regents of the university for the purchase of a library for the school of economics and history.

The corner-stone of Pearsons' Hall, the new science building of Beloit College, was laid on May 12. Of the $70,000 which it cost, $60,000 was given by Dr. Pearsons. The building has lecture and laboratory rooms, and rooms for a college museum, and an auditorium.

Charitable and Penal Institutions.—From the biennial report of the Board of Control (the first report since the board came into existence), it is learned that at the Mendota Hospital 1,792 patients have been treated during the past two years. The Northern Hospital treated a daily average of 526.

The Delevan School for the Deaf had a daily attendance of 171, and an enrollment of 210.

The Janesville School for the Blind had a daily attendance of 74 pupils. This school is maintained for the education of children of school age whose sight is so defective that they are unable to study in the common schools. All the common-school and high-school branches are taught, and instruction on the piano, organ, and violin, and in vocal music is given. Rag-carpet weaving, chair-caning, broom-making, hammock, fly-net, and fish-net making, plain and fancy sewing, knitting and crocheting are also taught. Board and tuition are free.

The report asks for a new school building for the industrial school for boys, which now has a surplus fund of $24,000. The number of boys committed to the school during the past two years is 354.

The buildings of the State prison are unfavorably commented upon, while its management is commended. The Wisconsin system of contract labor is asserted to be the best.

At the meeting of the Wisconsin department of the Grand Army of the Republic, which began March 9, J. H. Woodnorth submitted the report of the Board of Trustees of the Waupaca Home. The cost of maintaining the home for the year was $25,304. The cost of subsistence was $11,-180, making the per capita cost of subsistence $65. The rations per capita averaged in cost 17½ cents a day. The cost per capita of clothing for the inmates was $5.63. The total cost of maintenance per capita for the year was $144.84, an average per week of $2.78. The number of inmates is 214, of whom 146 are males and 68 females; the average age of the males is 62 years, and of the inmates who are wives, 48; the average age of the widow inmates is 60 years. The number of persons in the home receiving pensions is 110, and the average pension per month is $9.49. During the year there was spent on permanent improvements $25,000 of the $50,000 appropriated by the legislature in 1891. A new building for the old people was completed in May; an office building and addition to the main hospital has also been completed. An electric lighting plant, costing $4,000 and furnishing light for all the buildings, has been put in. A chapel for the home was built by the Woman's Relief Corps.

Labor Statistics.—From the report of the Commissioner of Labor Statistics, we learn that "the artisan classes have manifested great interest in the work of the bureau," and "that the work of the bureau is coming more in touch with, and is more appreciated by the people and manufacturing interests in the State, from year to year; the manufacturers manifest a readiness to furnish all required information asked for." In the first part of the report are given statistics as to the building trades and house-ownership: employers' statistics of wages paid in the building trades; and a comparison of the rate of wages paid in Milwaukee in the building trades with the wages paid in thirty leading cities of the country. This comparison indicates an increase in wages during the past two years in the building trades in Milwaukee, where the lowest amount paid is 26.9 cents an hour, and also in most of the other cities considered. The upward tendency of wages is also shown in the amount paid to the labor in the factories of the State. This will be seen by examination of the following statement: Number of employés at $4 and over, 1,707 in 1889, and 2.271 in 1891; at $3.50 but under $4, 968 in 1889, and 1,278 in 1891; at $3 but under $3.50, 1,987 in 1889, and 5,489 in 1891; at $2.50 but under $3, 4,300 in 1889, and 7,344 in 1891; at $1.50 but under $2, 22,570 in 1889, and 29,212 in 1891; at $1.25 but under $1.50, 18,640 in 1889, and 19,249 in 1891; at $1 but under $1.25, 8,478 in 1889, and 10,447 in 1891; at 75 cents but under $1, 5,406 in 1889, and 6,111 in 1891; at 50 cents but under 75 cents, 5,582 in 1889, and 6,100 in 1891; at less than 50 cents, 2,752 in 1889, and 2,981 in 1891. The commissioner, however, says that "by an examination of the different tables of this report it will be seen that the per capita wages for the last two years in a large number of cases is less than in former years."

Railroads.—The total railroad mileage in the State, on June 30, was 578,507 miles; the total capital stock is $113,187.843.51; funded debt, $150,769,094.39; net earnings for 1892, $11,649,-434.65. The total amount of license fees received from railroad companies for 1892 was $1,220,-674.88, equivalent to $211 per mile. There are 19.369 railway employés in the State, and they received as wages in 1892 $11,999,992.38, an average of $614.38. In 1892 there were 8 passengers killed and 45 injured; 62 employés killed and 400 injured; 90 trespassers killed and 37 injured; and 19 not trespassing killed and 23 injured. The total number of persons killed was 179, and injured 511.

Fisheries.—At the State hatchery 6,500,000 brook trout, 14,000,000 white fish, and 12,000,-000 wall-eyed pike were raised during the past season. The season's hatch of brook-trout fry was the most successful in the history of the fish commission; next year the number of breeders in the Madison trout-pond will be doubled. The experiment of propagating muskellunge is being tried at Phillips. Wisconsin is the first State to attempt the propagation of pike and white bass. The commission has decided to construct a hatchery in the northern part of the State, and also to collect statistics relating to the number of fish caught in the lakes and the number of men engaged in the fishing industry.

Internal Revenue.—The amount of internal revenue collected from all sources was $3,794,-699. The report shows that 9,876 wholesale and retail liquor dealers paid the special tax required by law. During the fiscal year ending on June 30, there were manufactured in the State 91,831,-959 cigars, and 6,822,448 pounds of smoking and chewing tobacco. During the year ending Dec. 31, Milwaukee brewers sold 2,213,078 barrels of beer.

Miscellaneous.—A monument to the soldier dead of Sauk County, erected in the cemetery at Reedsburg, was unveiled on June 4. The shaft is a beautiful piece of sculpture; it is of Barre, Vt.,' granite, and stands 27 feet high from the foundation. The shaft is surmounted by the figure of a soldier in full uniform, erect, but with his musket at rest.

The State Historical Society held its fortieth annual meeting in December. The library contains 152,474 volumes and pamphlets, and is by far the largest reference library west of the Alleghanies. The society has a high reputation for its newspaper-files, and has the largest and most complete set in the country, with the exception of that in the national library at Washington. Its files of papers published during the civil war are exceptionally complete.

The problem of suppressing the tramp received a great deal of attention from the various county boards, and many plans for punishing them and discouraging vagabondage were discussed.

A succession of fires in Milwaukee, resulting in enormous loss of property and the sacrifice of at least five lives, believed to be of incendiary origin, aroused the Common Council to call for a grand jury to investigate the subject. The Chamber of Commerce arranged a mass meeting to take action against the fire-bugs, and insurance companies refused to continue their insurance except at excessive rates. The loss to insurance companies in two months was over $5,000,000.

Political.—The People's party, at its first convention, held March 30, approved the resolutions adopted at the St. Louis conference, demanding free and unlimited coinage of silver, a graduated income tax, postal savings-banks, and Government ownership of railroads and telegraph and telephone lines. It demanded that evidence of indebtedness shall be taxed, and shall not draw interest unless shown to be duly assessed; that board-of-trade gambling be suppressed, and laws enacted to prohibit combinations to control the markets; asks Wisconsin representatives in Congress to support the passage of an anti-option bill, and favors woman suffrage. On May 25 the People's party nominated its State ticket and chose candidates for Presidential electors, and delegates to the National Convention.

The State Democratic Convention met at Milwaukee May 4, and chose delegates to the National Convention of the party. The platform adopted favors tariff for revenue only; opposes the project of unlimited coinage of silver dollars of less commercial value than gold dollars; denounces Republican legislation on this subject, more particularly the Sherman act of 1890, and demands its repeal; opposes State interference with parental rights and rights of conscience in the education of children; opposes sumptuary laws; praises the Democratic State Government; praises Mr. Cleveland, and instructs the delegates to Chicago to act as a unit. A second State Democratic Convention was held at Milwaukee Aug. 31, when the entire State ticket was renominated by acclamation. The platform adopted at this convention dealt mainly with State issues. It asserted that the pledges made by the Democratic Convention in 1890 had been redeemed; that economy and business methods have characterized every branch of the State Government, the result being a great saving to the tax-payers; that more than $60,000 have been saved in administrative and legislative expenses; that the cost of maintaining the State institutions has been economized more than $52,000;

that more than $42,000 of accrued interest on bank deposits has been covered into the treasury ; that the treasurer, at the end of his term, will have a surplus of more than $300,000, instead of the deficiency that existed two years before ; that trust funds have been promptly invested for the benefit of the schools ; that suits have been rigorously prosecuted to establish the right of the people to the interest earned by their money in the treasury : and that right has been adjudged and liability fastened upon the two last State treasurers to the amount of more than $250,000 for interest money misappropriated by them. It asserts that the Democrats of Wisconsin have shown their loyalty to the cause of popular education in a practical form by adding over $100,000 to the school fund and by increasing the appropriations to the State University over $65,000 a year for the next six years. It opposes centralization and paternalism, and all mischievous meddling with rights of conscience and religion, especially in the care and education of children , opposes sumptuary laws, and approves the Democratic nominees and the principles enunciated by the Chicago platform.

The Republicans also held two State conventions, both meeting at Milwaukee. At the first convention, May 5, delegates to the Republican National Convention were selected. The platform adopted at this time approves the administration of President Harrison, and the tariff legislation of the 51st Congress ; denounces the narrow parsimony of the present Democratic House of Representatives, and asserts that, while favoring the use of both gold and silver as money metals, the party is unalterably opposed to the free and unlimited coinage of silver. The movement of the international silver conference is commended, and the modification of the silver act of 1890, to enable the President to regulate silver purchases, is favored ; the educational issue of 1890 is declared permanently settled, and further agitation of the subject is denounced as harmful in tendency ; the "Dodge legacy law" is denounced as a most unjustifiable form of paternal legislation, and satisfaction with the "gerrymander" decision is expressed.

The Republican Convention to nominate State officers met on Aug. 17. The platform approves of the platform promulgated by the National Republican Convention and of the administration of President Harrison. It opposes the proposition, in the Democratic National platform, to repeal the tax on the circulation of State banks. It denounces the statement made by the Democratic press in Wisconsin, that Republican success means a surrender or compromise of any rights of the State upon the bonds of ex-treasurers. It favors the amendment of the law regulating the deposit at interest, in the banks of the State, of surplus moneys belonging to the people. It approves the declaration of the convention of May 5, upon the educational question ; "denounces the outrageous partisanship of the Democratic majority at the late extra session of the legislature in forcing the enactment, without legislative consideration, deliberation, fair opportunity for debate, or amendment, of the present so-called apportionment law, in defiance of the plain provisions of the Constitution ;" and denounces the parsimony of the Democratic party

in its refusal to make adequate appropriation of money for a fit representation of the State at the Columbian Exposition. The following plank was added on motion of William T. Green, colored delegate from Milwaukee :

We denounce and condemn the cruel and barbarous treatment of American citizens in some of the Southern States, as tending to corrupt good government, and as contrary to the spirit of the Constitution of the United States.

The convention of the Prohibition party met on June 1, and nominated a State ticket, chose delegates to the national convention, and adopted a platform which demands that the traffic in intoxicating liquor as a beverage be forever prohibited and suppressed ; that all money be issued directly by the federal government ; that the great lines of transportation and communication, including the telegraph and telephone, be controlled by the government ; that no restriction be placed upon the right to vote other than the requirement of a residence for such time and education to such extent as shall insure intelligent citizenship ; that the laws relating to highways be amended to the end that thoroughly constructed and permanent roads may be given to the people ; that the tariff laws be so changed that no special privileges be granted to one class of citizens at the expense of other classes ; and that the poor be relieved of the unjust taxes they are now compelled to pay. It favors a liberal education, in the English language, enforced and supervised by the State, and invites all voters to join with the Prohibition party in the campaign.

At the election, Nov. 4, the Democratic ticket was successful. The vote for Governor was : Democratic, 178,198 ; Republican, 170,354 ; Prohibition, 12,664 ; People's, 9,513. The vote for Presidential Electors was as follows : Democratic, 177,448 ; Republican, 170,978 ; Prohibition, 13,045 ; People's, 9,870. The legislature of 1893 consists of 27 Democrats and 6 Republicans in the Senate, and 56 Democrats and 45 Republicans in the House. Six Democratic and 4 Republican Congressmen were elected.

WOOD PULP, or Wood Fibre.—It is less than half a century since paper was made wholly from rags or straw ; from the former for writing, printing, drawing, and card stock, and from straw for wrapping paper and common board covers for books. At that time the varieties and qualities of paper were limited, and the varieties in writing and printing paper resulted more from the size and weight of the sheets than from the kind and quality of the material composing the paper. The cost of paper to the consumer was large, compared with present prices, and the cost arose more from the limited supply of the material required (rags) than from the cost of converting the rags into paper. Rags were not a commercial product, but the remains of woven linen and cotton fabrics which had given long service in the form of garments, bed clothing and house linen. At present rags have come to be, to a great extent, only an incident in paper making. Severe economy on the part of consumers of linen and cotton fabrics can no longer keep up the prices of paper, or limit its variety, or restrict its use. The discovery of a great variety of vegetable materials capable of yielding suitable fibre, together with inventions relating to processes and apparatus for treating those substances for their conversion into paper stock, have so greatly enlarged the capabilities of paper-makers that they can produce any desired amount, and in an endless variety of size, weight, and strength.

Poplar, bass, sycamore, pine, spruce, and hemlock are the principal woods now used for paper stock ; while oat, rye, and wheat straws, old rope, jute buts, and a variety of grasses, each contribute valuable fibre for the use of the paper-maker. The process of reducing wood to pulp was invented in Germany, and it is only recently that it has been conducted in this country. The process consists in sawing the sticks to a small size and then putting them, in a wet condition, to a grinding machine, which takes them at the end and reduces them to what would be a fine powder if they were dry. The pulp is allowed to run into vats, where it becomes thoroughly soaked. It is then drawn off upon broad rollers covered with cloth, after the manner of a paper-making machine. A small percentage of some glutinous substance is added ; and the pulp, after becoming of uniform thickness, is run between rollers and the water expressed. In this shape it is rolled into bundles and tied. It is bought and sold wet, for the reason that it will absorb a certain amount of water until saturated, and then will take no more. In bills of sale, about 40 per cent. of the watered pulp is considered the true weight. Another process, known as the sulphite, yields a strong and fine fibre. Recent discoveries have been made, and processes and apparatus have been devised, which have greatly cheapened the cost of converting wood into fibre for paper. The latest processes, known as the "soda," include large boilers or digesters, made of iron or steel, capable of holding two or more cords of wood, and strong enough to stand a pressure of 120 to 150 pounds to the square inch. In these digesters the wood, straw, or other vegetable substances are subjected to the action of a suitable chemical cooking-liquor of a given strength, under pressure varying from 50 to 120 pounds to the inch, according to the material. This is known as the "new process," and is adapted for economical use, for treating any of the woods above-named and straws, grasses, old rope, and other materials. But, because of some differences in the characteristics of each of these materials, the apparatus employed is modified in some of its features, so as to meet the requirements necessary in securing the most economical operations for saving time, labor, fuel, and chemicals in the treatment of the respective materials. Some kinds of wood have as a constituent part a resin or gum, which requires a higher temperature and strength of the chemical cooking-liquor. So also with the different straws and grasses, the nature and peculiar qualities of the substances composing the lignine in them, which are to be dissolved (so as to free the true fibre from the matters that are worthless for making paper fibre), require different degrees of temperature and strength of cooking-liquors, and varying length of times of treatment, for the economical production of the commercial fibre. Again, the different substances permit the use of different kinds of chemicals. The usual chemicals employed are lime, potash, soda-ash, and caustic soda. For the reduction of wood the last-named is generally employed, while for the reduction of straws and grasses lime is used because of its cheapness. Cooking-liquors of all these kinds of alkalies have been employed in open vessels made of wood, for cooking straw and grasses and old rope, jute buts, etc., and, because in such vessels the temperature of the liquor could not be had above boiling heat, these substances were necessarily cooked from forty-eight to sixty hours. By the use of closed vessels with a pressure of two or three atmospheres, the time of cooking is reduced to two or three hours ; but the liquor is kept circulating so as to prevent a packing of the material that is being cooked.

There is one apparatus for the reducing of the various kinds of straw; another for cooking old manilla rope ; a third for reducing straws and grasses to fibre by the use of alkaline cooking-liquors, by which all the lignine will be dissolved, leaving the fibre free. In this complete reduction of the straw and grasses, the mass of material treated will be generally reduced in bulk as the cooking of the material is advancing, and as this reduction of the bulk of the charge progresses, the operator will open the valves of the three upper branch pipes at intervals, one at a time, beginning with the upper one. After the cooking of the material is completed, the product will be blown out and subsequently treated as cooking straws and grasses are generally treated. This form of apparatus is admirably adapted to reducing jute buts. A fourth apparatus is used for reducing poplar and other woods. The wood is reduced to small chips and filled into the chamber of the boiler in the usual manner. The chamber contains central within it a steam heater composed of a series of three-inch pipes running from the top to the bottom, and extending across the chamber from its rear side to its front, so as to divide the chamber proper into two equal compartments, into which the wood chips will fall when introduced from the machine above. The caustic soda is introduced within the boiler up to about five-eighths of its vertical extension, and live steam at about 120 pounds is introduced into the steam heating pipes (dividing the chamber of the boiler), for heating the cooking-liquor while it is being circulated. By means of a pump, a dual circulation of the liquor will be produced, as the pump draws the liquor from an annular strainer, at two-thirds of the height of the boiler, and forces the liquor continuously in two directions. One portion of the liquor, taken from the annular strainer, is forced into a circular sprinkler arranged in the upper end of the boiler, to escape in numerous small streams that fall on the wood chips below and saturate them ; while the other portion is forced into the boiler at a point below its perforated bottom, and is made to move upward through the lower portion of the mass of wood chips. This dual circulation is continued without any change for about five hours for reducing poplar, basswood, or other woods that are free from pitch or resins; and about eight hours for reducing wood of the nature of pine, spruce, and hemlock. With this dual circulation, only about two-thirds of the volume of cooking-liquor heretofore required, and of the same strength as generally used, is employed.

The product resulting from this apparatus is a uniformly reduced material, in which no portion is either over-cooked or under-cooked, and no powder-like particles are formed, to be washed away in subsequent operations. This uniformity of cooking of all portions of the charge enables the manufacturer to produce at least 100 pounds more of a commercial fibre from a cord of wood than is generally produced under the old process; and it also produces a stronger fibre, because of the great reduction of the time of subjection of the wood to the combined action of great heat and strength of the alkaline liquor used in cooking.

A cord of wood will make about 1,650 pounds of ground pulp, 1,000 pounds of sulphite fibre, or 800 pounds of soda pulp. Soda mills use all kinds of mill refuse, thus effecting a great saving of expense and utilizing a vast amount of material that would otherwise go to waste; but sulphite and grinding mills require wood in the log; and in this is found the only serious objection to the pulp business. Ground pulp is worth from $22 to $28 a ton. Domestic sulphite fibre sells at $67.50 to $70 a ton, and the best imported at $67.50 to $100. The Germans have a superior sulphite process, and produce the best fibre in the world. The duty on sulphite fibre is 10 per cent. *ad valorem*, and large quantities of it are imported. This fibre is rather stiff and wiry, and all the ingenuity of men of science and manufacturers is being applied to the problem of softening it. Solution of bisulphite of lime or magnesia removes all organic matter from wood, leaving only the fibre, which is used in conjunction with rags, or even alone, with ground pulp for paper. It is estimated that, by the new process, the cost of production of fibre will be still more reduced, so that the paper-maker can furnish to the book-maker, news publisher, and other users of paper, at less rates than now. As the manufacture of fibre from wood is a specialty, to a large extent, so will the manufactures of fibre from straws, grasses, jute buts, etc., soon become specialties. Wood pulp has brought the price of white paper down to three or four cents a pound, and it provides an article that readily takes ink and is especially adapted to fast presses. Ground pulp constitutes over 80 per cent. of the common white newspaper in use; rags and sulphite fibre making up the remainder. Even the contractor for making postal cards is allowed to use 75 per cent. of wood pulp. Sulphite and soda fibres are largely used in the manufacture of fine grades of paper.

Another use for pulp has been found in the making of water pipes, which are treated by a process that makes them practically indestructible. In this form the product is known as indurated fibre. Pipe is made from a specially prepared pulp which is forced into a rubber bag in the centre of which is a brass strainer or form. The form gives the size to the pipe. If the strainer is two inches in diameter, the pipe made upon it will be of that diameter. When the rubber bag, which is three or four inches larger than the brass strainer, is filled with pulp, several tons of hydraulic pressure is laid about the rubber bag from without. As the strainer and rubber bag are inclosed in a large iron pipe, the hydraulic pressure holds the rubber bag firmly about the pulp and strainer. The strainer being perforated, the water in the pulp escapes freely. In about ten minutes the pulp has been reduced to a pipe three-quarters of an inch thick. The pipe is then saturated with a preparation containing a large percentage of asphaltum. The pipes are baked in kilns, thus rendering them strong, hard, and impervious to acids and moisture. Great care must be taken during this process to prevent the pipes from warping. If the slightest imperfection is detected, the pipe is cast into a vat and turned again to pulp. When thoroughly baked, the pipes are trimmed and shaped in a machine, and finished when the threads are cut in the ends.

WORLD'S COLUMBIAN EXPOSITION.— The last issue of the "Annual Cyclopædia" contained such facts as were available, up to the day of going to press, concerning the World's Columbian Exposition from the time of its inception. The article reviewed briefly the history of similar enterprises during the past forty years, and described the proposed site at Chicago, with dimensions of the buildings then in course of construction, and numerous facts and figures relating to appropriations and estimated expenditures. Many plans, measurements, etc., having been changed during the past twelve months, the figures and statements given in this volume must be considered as canceling those previously published. The area in acres, whenever given, includes floor space and galleries.

In this article will be set forth the present condition of affairs connected with the Exposition; the exact location of important structures, and some details as to the arrangements now in course of development for carrying extensive plans and projects to a successful issue. Rapid progress has been made in every department, more particularly since the dedication ceremonies were held, in October, 1892.

The Reception.—On Wednesday, Oct. 21, a brilliant reception, admirably arranged and managed, was held at the Auditorium. The most distinguished men of every State and nation were invited and took part in the proceedings on this memorable occasion, Hon. Levi P. Morton, Vice-President of the United States, occupying the post of honor as representative of President Harrison, who, owing to the severe illness of Mrs. Harrison, was unable to be present. Fully 3,560 persons responded personally to the invitations of the Directors.

The Civic Parade.—On Thursday, Oct. 22, Vice-President Morton reviewed, from the Government Building within the Exposition grounds, a great Civic Parade, marshaled by Major-General Nelson A. Miles. This procession, principally composed of organizations and societies, took three hours to pass the reviewing stand. This part of the ceremonial programme was in every way a success.

The Dedication.—On Friday, Oct. 23, the dedication ceremonies took place. More than 250,000 people were carried to the parks on the trains, cable lines, and boats. The number who visited the Exposition grounds and vicinity in other vehicles or on foot was enormous. The day's proceedings began promptly at 9 A. M. Many

GENERAL

State governors, with State officials, accompanied the Federal representatives, their presence doing much to inspire the Directors and Managers with enthusiasm. After an imposing military review in Washington Park, the Vice-President, eminent visitors, and Exposition officials proceeded to the Manufacturers' Building, where nearly 100,000 persons had been provided with seats from which to witness the last and most important of the ceremonial exercises. When the dignitaries had taken the places assigned to them, the chorus sang John Knowles Payne's Columbus Hymn.

Bishop Fowler, of the Methodist Episcopal Church, having then formally opened the proceedings with prayer, Director General George R. Davis delivered an appropriate address. This was followed by the reading of Harriet Monroe's Columbian Ode by Mrs. Le Moyne; a presentation of medals to the master artists and architects of the buildings; an impressive speech by Mrs. Potter Palmer; the handing over of the buildings by President Higinbotham, in behalf of the Local Directory, to the National Commission; and a speech of acceptance by President Palmer, who, in his turn, bestowed them upon the nation, through its representative. Vice-President Morton responded briefly. Speeches were made by Henry Watterson and Chauncey M. Depew. The singing of Beethoven's anthem, "In Praise of God." was followed by the benediction by Rev. H. C. McCook, of Philadelphia.

Amid salvos of artillery the conclusion of the ceremonies was announced, and work on the buildings was resumed with more than usual vigor. There was a display of fireworks in the evening of Oct. 23, a striking feature of this entertainment being the releasing of one hundred fire balloons in Washington, Lincoln, and Garfield Parks. Rockets attached to the balloons were discharged in mid-air, producing a novel and most impressive spectacle.

The Opening Ceremonies.—The programme for opening the World's Fair on May 1, 1893, has been completed by the committee having the matter in charge. President Cleveland will deliver the only address and start the machinery. A poem, probably by Oliver Wendell Holmes, will precede the Presidential address. The public cannot attend the opening exercises, as the festival hall seats but 5,000 persons. One thousand of these will be reserved for officials of the Fair, members of Congress, and other notable individuals. The remaining 4,000 seats will be sold at $5 each, tickets being issued on invitation. The exercises will begin at exactly 10 o'clock on the morning of May 1, and close at noon or earlier. From noon to 1.30 lunch will be served to the President and the thousand special guests. The public will be admitted to the grounds upon the payment of the regular price of admission, which has been fixed at 50 cents. The Exposition will remain open until Oct. 30, 1893.

The Exposition.—The site of the World's Columbian Exposition is four times as large as that occupied by the Paris Expositions of 1878 and 1889. The frontage extends two miles on Lake Michigan. Considering the area of the buildings, those of the Chicago World's Fair occupy twice the space devoted to exhibits in the Paris Exposition of 1889. The cost of erection

will be twice as much. "The most delightful, probably, though not the speediest, means by which the visitor may reach the Exposition grounds will be by steamboat on Lake Michigan. When abreast of the site, a grand spectacle of surpassing magnificence will be before him—the vast extent of the beautiful park; the windings of the lagoon; the superb array of scores of great buildings, elegant and imposing in their architecture, and gay with myriads of flags and streamers floating from their pinnacles and towers." For the purposes of this article, it is deemed most practical to reach the grounds by way of Cottage Grove Avenue, at the western limit of Midway Plaisance.

Midway Plaisance.—At the entrance to the covered walk, on each side, there will be a nursery exhibit. Proceeding along the Plaisance toward the 60th St. station of the Illinois Central Railroad, the exhibits on the right hand side, in their order, are:

> The National Hungarian Orpheum.
> Roman House.
> Dahomey Village, 150x195 ft.
> Austrian Village, 195x510 it.
> Chinese Tea House, 55x100 ft.
> French Cider Press, 40x50 ft.
> Model of "St. Peter's."
> Ferris Wheel.
> Ice Railway, 60x400 ft.
> Moorish Palace.
> Turkish Village, 190x450 ft.
> Panorama of the Bernese Alps.
> Natatorium, or Swimming Baths.
> Dutch Settlement.
> Hagenbeck Animal Show.
> Venice Murano Company Exhibit.

Crossing the 60th St. station, still keeping to the right, the next exhibit is of *Irish Industries*. In the center of the Plaisance, at this point, will be the *Circular Railroad Tower*. On the left of this tower will be the Bohemian Glass Company's exhibit. On the opposite side of the Plaisance, to the right of visitors who may have entered at Cottage Grove Avenue mentioned above, the exhibits in the order as they occur are:

> The Libby Glass Co.
> Japanese Bazar.
> Dutch Settlement.
> German Village, 223x780 ft.
> Persian Concession.
> Street in Cairo, 223x391 ft.
> Algeria and Tunis, 165x280 ft.
> Panorama of Volcano Kilauea, 135x225 ft.
> Morocco Exhibits, 150x150 ft.
> Chinese Village and Theatre, 150x22 ft.
> Captive Balloon, 205x225 ft.
> American or Indian Village.
> Indian Village.

The "Sliding Railroad" of the Plaisance will run behind the exhibits on the opposite side to those just mentioned. This will take visitors near the circular tower, or "Tower of Babel." On the inner side of Stony Island Avenue, behind the Elevated Railroad station, there will be a Workingman's Home. Further within the grounds proper, and exactly opposite the inner end of Midway Plaisance, stands one of the principal buildings of the Exposition:

The Woman's Building.—This building, facing the lagoon, was the first to be completed. The size of the structure is 198x398 ft., having an area of 3.3 acres. The approximate cost is given as $138,000. There is a staircase and landing leading to a terrace six feet above the water. A lobby 40 ft. wide leads into the rotunda (70x65 ft.), which is surmounted by an ornamental skylight. Around the rotunda is a two-story open arcade. On the first floor is a model hospital, a model kindergarten, each 80x60 ft., and the whole floor of the south pavilion has been set apart for the reform work and charity organizations. Each floor 80x20 ft. Opposite the main front entrance are the library, bureau of information, records, etc. In the second story are the ladies' dressing-rooms and parlors, and an assembly-room, with an elevated stage for speakers, and club-room. The south pavilion has been provided with model kitchen and refreshment-rooms.

The exterior design was furnished by a woman architect, Miss S. G. Hayden, of Boston. Here the lady managers will have their headquarters. The women of the State of New York have secured permission to equip one of the rooms as a woman's library, containing only works written by women.

To the left still further, and immediately south of the entrance to Jackson Park from the Midway Plaisance will be another of the most important divisions of the Exposition.

The Horticultural Building.—The size of this building is 250.8 by 997.8 ft., the area being 8 acres; and the approximate cost, $287,000.

The groups of statuary on either side of the main entrance, and the Cupid frieze which runs around the building, are the work of Lorado Taft.

The Choral Hall, or Festival Hall, stands to the south of the Horticultural Building. Fronting the lagoon, between the Horticultural and Transportation Buildings, it occupies a prominent position. This structure is intended to seat 6,500 persons, including a chorus of 2,000 and orchestra of 250. Francis M. Whitehouse, of Chicago, designed the interior after the Trocadero of Paris. There will be a large concert organ erected for choral purposes before the Exposition opens. The Festival Hall programme includes four series of oratorio festivals, six series of international concerts, concerts by German, Swedish, and Welsh societies, and popular concerts of orchestral music.

The Transportation Building.—The size of the Transportation Building is 256x960 ft., with an area of 9.4 acres. The size of the annex is 435x850 ft.; its area being 8.5 acres. The approximate cost of both buildings is given as $369,000. The main building lies between the Horticultural and Mines Buildings and faces eastward. It is of the Romanesque style of architecture and is surmounted by a cupola. The interior of the building has broad naves and aisles, and the roof is in three divisions. The cupola is reached by eight elevators. From this extends westward to Stony Island avenue a capacious annex. It is but one story in height.

The scope and plan of this department includes railways, vessels, and vehicles—comprising all known means, methods, and appliances of travel and conveyance on land and water, in ancient and modern times.

Elaborate and costly models of the best trans-

atlantic steamers will be shown. In addition, the department comprises whatever relates to the science of navigation, and to docks, harbor works, wrecking and life-saving apparatus, etc.

The bas-reliefs on the main building, both over the doorways and in the panels on either hand, have been modeled by John J. Boyle of New York. The panel over the central doorway represents the apotheosis of transportation, suggested by the world floating in the ether of space, surmounted by the genii of transportation. The four horses are put in for ornamental effect of movement. On the right corner the figure represents abundance; on the left, force and rapidity of motion. The panels on either side of the entrance portray the evolution of transportation from its rudest to its most modern forms.

Statuary groups will be prepared for the adornment of the main *façade*. These will symbolize the spirit which has animated the inventions that have made possible the great advances in this department of modern industry and typify some of the industries themselves.

Hall of Mines and Mining.—The size of the Mines and Mining Building is 350x700 feet, with an area of 8.5 acres. The approximate cost is estimated at $266,500. This structure is of the Italian Renaissance order of architecture, and is located at the southern extremity of the western lagoon, just between the Electricity and Transportation Structures. On the ground floor are restaurants and toilet rooms. The galleries are 25 feet high and 60 feet wide. The covered promenades are each 25 feet in width by 230 feet in length. Between the main entrance and the pavilions are ornamental arcades, forming a loggia on the ground floor and a recessed promenade on the gallery floor; a great portion of the roof is covered with glass.

The raw material to be exhibited in the Mines and Mining Department will form the basis of every other exhibit except those of Agriculture and Horticulture. The groundwork of all the arts and sciences and the mechanical industries will be grouped in this division. All precious and industrial minerals, precious stones, coals, building stones and marbles, clays and sands, salts and pigments, as well as the machinery, implements and appliances employed in their conversion to the uses of man, will be represented. The coal resources of countries, States, and sections will be shown by geological maps and drawings. An important exhibit of iron will be made. A complete series of metallurgic processes from mineral to metal will be shown; apparatus employed in petroleum and natural gas industries will be displayed; also an accurate reproduction of ancient mining and metallurgical methods, appliances, tools, and processes.

The Electrical Building.—The size of the Electrical Building is 345x690 feet, with an area of 9.3 acres. The approximate cost is said to be $413,500. The Electrical Building is opposite the Manufactures Building, and on the west side faces the Mines Building. The exterior of the building is of the Corinthian order of architecture, and the general plan is that of a longitudinal nave, crossed in the middle by a transept having a pitched roof with skylights; the rest of the building a flat roof with skylights. The area of the galleries in the second story is

THE GATEWAY OF THE TRANSPORTATION BUILDING.

118,546 square feet. The east and west central pavilions are composed of towers 168 feet high. From each upper pilaster is a pedestal bearing a lofty mast for the display of banners by day and electric lights by night. In the center of the attic niche is a colossal statue of Franklin. There will be 40,000 panes of glass in the Electricity Building, and the exhibit, by reason of the brilliancy of its electrical effects, and the extensive glass surface, will be especially conspicuous at might.

Midway between the buildings set apart for Mines and Mining and Electricity, and those devoted to Machinery, in the great court containing three fountains—the McMonnees Fountain and one on either side—stands one of the most important buildings connected with the executive work of the Fair.

Administration Building.—The size of this building is 262x262 ft. Its area is 4.5 acres, and the approximate cost is given as $436,500. It is located at the west side of the great court. The ground floor contains in one pavilion the Fire and Police Departments, with cells for the detention of prisoners; in the second pavilion are the offices of the Ambulance service, the Physician and Pharmacy, the Foreign Departments, and the Information Bureau; in the third pavilion the Post-office and a bank, and in the fourth the offices of Public Comfort and a restaurant. Provision has been made in the second, third, and fourth stories for the Board rooms, the Committee rooms, the rooms of the Director-General, the Department of Publicity and Promotions, and for the United States Columbian Commission.

To the southwest of the Administration Building may be seen the ample railway facilities for arrival and departure of visitors. Six parallel tracks enter the grounds in a circle at the extreme southwest portion, entering and leaving at nearly the same point. Within the bend made by these railway tracks is the machinery annex, containing overflow exhibits from Machinery Hall, with which it is connected by subways. The main power-house, from which power is furnished for several buildings, is located close by.

To the south of the line of buildings, arranged along the south side of the grand avenue, is an open expanse devoted to the live stock exhibit, covering 25 acres, and costing $210,000.

Machinery Hall.—The size of the Machinery Hall is 494x342 ft. The size of the annex is 490x551 ft. The approximate cost of both buildings is said to be $1,050,750. The size of the adjoining machine shop and boiler house is 86x1,103.6, having an area of 2.2 acres, the approximate cost being $75,000. The exhibit which is promised will far excel any previous exposition of methods of labor-saving devices and motive power, and will be participated in by the best representatives of the noted manufacturing countries and cities of the world.

In the vicinity of the main Machinery Building, to the south are the logger's camp, oil exhibit, saw mill, 60x100 ft., and the Stock Pavilion, 265x960 ft., covering an area of 5.8 acres, and costing $35,000.

Agricultural Building.—The size of the Agricultural Building is 500x800 ft., having an area of 15 acres. The size of annex is 312x550.5 ft., having an area of 4 acres. The approximate

cost of both buildings is reported as $691,500. The style of architecture of this building is classic Renaissance. It is surrounded by the lagoons that lead into the park from the lake. It is a single-story building. On either side of the main entrance are Corinthian pillars 50 feet high and 5 feet in diameter. The center pavilion is 144 feet square. The rotunda is 100 feet in diameter. The structure is conveniently near one of the stations of the elevated railway. On the first floor is a Bureau of Information, suitable committee rooms for Live Stock Associations, waiting rooms for ladies, and lounging rooms for gentlemen. The assembly room, upstairs, has a seating capacity of 1,500. Lectures will be delivered upon every topic relative to agriculture, live stock, etc. Adjacent to the Agricultural Building and its annex are buildings for the forestry and dairy exhibits, whose dimensions are 200x500 ft. and 95x200 ft. respectively.

The "Diana" of Augustus St. Gaudens surmounts the main copper dome. The statuary, including groups, is by Philip Martiny. The main pediment is by L. G. Mead. It describes the triumph of Ceres. The subjects in this department embrace natural and prepared products, mineral waters, natural and artificial; machinery, tools, processes, and appliances; farms and farm buildings; literature, and statistics of agriculture, and miscellaneous animal products.

The exhibit of cereals, grasses, and forage plants will be exhibited in the spaces allotted to States and Territories. The exhibit of honey, honey bees, hives, and appliances will be made in the second story. There will be a special display of sugar beets during the two weeks beginning Oct. 29, 1893; a display of potatoes and other tubers for two weeks beginning Sept. 11, 1893; and of dairy products between the 1st and 10th of the months of June, July, September, and October, 1893. The exhibits of wool will be divided into four classes: pure-bred fine wool, pure-bred middle wool, pure-bred long wool, and all cross-bred wool. In connection with the Department of Agriculture, in a building specially designed for the purpose, a model dairy will be in operation; the milk to be obtained from cows furnished by the associations representing the different breeds of cattle in the United States. The purpose of the dairy is to afford a practical test of the relative merits of the various breeds of dairy cattle, and incidentally to illustrate the best methods of handling milk and making butter.

The following is a partial list of allotments of space to foreign countries in the Agricultural Building: Brazil, 7,200; Argentine Republic, 2,976; Chili, 731; Honduras, 999; Nicaragua, 1,180; Colombia, 1,810; Peru, 1,342; Salvador, 1,342; Bolivia, 1,342; San Domingo, 912; Porto Rico, 912; Cuba, 1,444; Ecuador, 1,710; Guatemala, 978; Hayti, 978; Ceylon, 1,684; Mexico, 6,020; Germany, 11,875; Great Britain, 18,346; France, 6,835; Denmark, 1,584; Sweden, 1,760; Japan, 3,038.

To the south of the agricultural annex, and west of what is known as South Pond, is the Agricultural Implement exhibit, including windmills. There is also a colonial exhibit south of the pond, and within this section of the grounds will be Krupp's Gun Works exhibit, the Leather exhibit, Forestry exhibit, Ethnographical exhibit, and an Indian school.

Leather Building.—The size of this building is 150x625 ft., having an area of 4.3 acres. The approximate cost will be $100,000. Everything of interest in connection with the leather industry will be shown in this building.

Forestry Building.—The size of the Forestry Building is 208x528 ft., having an area of 2.6 acres. The approximate cost will be $90,250. The structure is of a rustic order of architecture. There is a veranda supporting the roof, the colonnade of which is composed of tree trunks, each 25 feet in length, all of them in their natural state. The roof is thatched with tan bark and other barks. The various wood finishings of the interior are both unique and attractive. The tree trunks were contributed by different States and Territories and foreign countries, the name of each tree being shown by a placard. The building has on exhibit forest products, logs and sections of trees, dressed lumber, such as flooring, casing, shingles, etc., dye woods and barks, lichens, wood pulp, rattan willow ware, wooden ware and numerous other specimens. Several complete sawmills will be in operation. The sawmill plants occupy a separate building costing about $35,000.

Ethnological Exhibit.—This exhibit, originally intended to be held in the Manufactures and Liberal Arts Building, has been moved to a separate building, thus giving additional space to the Educational Department. Its exact location, size, area, and cost, under the heading of Ethnology are not available at this writing.

The scientific exhibits of the department will furnish a tableau of six months' duration, and so far as they were obtained by special exploration at the expense of the Exposition, will be retained in Chicago as the nucleus of a Museum of Natural History to be established as a permanent memorial of the World's Columbian Exposition.

The section of American Archæology will begin as far back as the existence of man in America can be traced. The conditions under which man lived at that remote age will be shown by diagrammatic paintings representing the terminal portion of the ice sheet, with the deposits of clay, gravel, and boulders at its edge, and the flora and fauna of that time. In this connection will be shown portions of human skeletons and objects of man's handiwork which have been found in the glacial gravel, and which furnish evidence of his existence at that early period.

Collections and models illustrative of the Eskimo and other Northern tribes of the Continent, and of the tribes of Central and South America, will be shown. All the most distinctive earthworks which show the phases of prehistoric life on the Continent will be represented. All the material collected this year by the Peabody Museum Honduras expedition will be loaned to this department.

Pier, Movable Sidewalk, and Greek Pavilion.—The pier, or landing point for visitors who shall arrive on the grounds via Lake Michigan, runs into the lake for 1,500 feet or more, the entrance to this pier from the grounds being east of the Casino. A movable sidewalk, with seats, will traverse the pier from end to end. At the eastern extremity will stand the *Greek Pavil-*

ion, light, airy, and artistic in appearance, yet well secured on firm foundations of masonry. The size of this pavilion will be 200x100 feet. Architecturally, it will combine the Doric and Ionic orders, the decorations being of white and gold.

Casino, Peristyle, and Music Hall.—The composite structure is Roman in character and was designed by Charles B. Atwood. The Peristyle consists of forty-eight columns disposed in four rows on each side of an archway spanning the entrance from Lake Michigan to the great basin. These columns are sixty feet in height, and extend from the Music Hall on the one end to the Casino on the other. The central archway is 80 feet high. Upon the top of this arch will be the Columbian quadriga. As the structure as a whole is one of the most striking features of the Exposition, the description of F. D. Millet will be of interest :

"Names of eminent musicians find a place on the Music Hall, and the composers are duly honored in like manner on the Casino, while the wealth of statuary on the Peristyle will have an echo in female figures representing music, which adorn each of the above mentioned buildings. All these single figures are now being executed by Theodore Baur of New York, a sculptor of great skill and widely recognized ability. The great archway which spans the canal between the basin and the lake, and forms a great central feature dominating the Peristyle, is dedicated to the discoverers who figure in the history of this Continent ; and it might, therefore, more properly bear the name of Discoverer's Gate than the rather absurd title by which it has been known, Columbus Porticus. The great pylon-like pedestal on top of this archway is to support a colossal group, by Mr. D. C. French and Mr. Edward C. Potter, the former modeling the figures and the latter the horses. A Roman chariot with a typical figure of a discoverer is drawn by four horses, each pair of which is led by a female figure, graceful in action and beautiful in proportion, and on either side of the chariot mounted pages accompany the quadriga. The whole composition is exceedingly rich in grouping, joyous and free in movement. Seen from any point of view the Peristyle is marvelously impressive. From the lake it towers like a palace of the Cæsars, with the additional charm of the reflection of its beauties in the mirror of the water which washes its very foundations. From the basin it extends with its bewildering profusion of columns from the huge pavilion of the Manufactures Building on the one side to the stately colonnade of the Agricultural Building on the other. The opening of the archway frames a bewitching expanse of the lake with its ever changing lines, and, seen between the columns, the water often takes a clear turquoise hue by contrast with the pure warm white of the graceful shafts."

The Casino and the Music Hall will each be devoted to the work of the Musical Department. The Music Hall will hold 2,000 persons, exclusive of stage accommodation for a chorus of 300 and an orchestra of 120. A separate room, to seat 500 persons, has been set apart for chamber music and recitals. As many of the choral and orchestral entertainments will be held in these two buildings, this may be the most fitting place to state briefly the plans of the Musical Director, Theodore Thomas. The range of work proposed is thus classified :

Semi-weekly orchestral concerts in Music Hall.
Semi-monthly choral concerts in Music Hall.

THE AGRICULTURAL BUILDING.

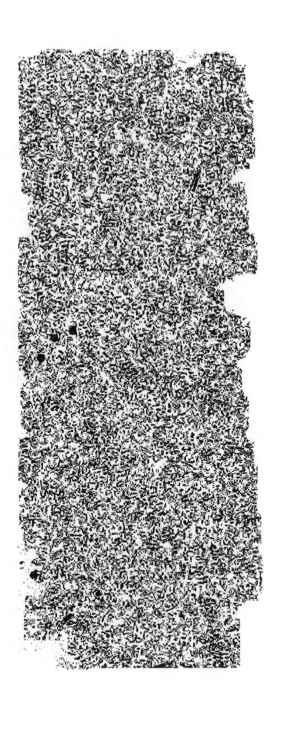

Six series of international concerts, choral and orchestral, each consisting of from four to six, in Festival Hall and in Music Hall.

Four series of oratorio festivals by united American choral societies in Festival Hall.

Concerts in Festival Hall under the auspices of German singing societies.

Concerts in Festival Hall under the auspices of Swedish singing societies.

Concerts in Festival Hall under the auspices of Welsh singing societies.

Six series of popular miscellaneous festival concerts by American singers.

Twelve children's concerts by Sunday school, public school, and especially organized children's choruses.

Chamber-music concerts and organ recitals.

Popular concerts of orchestral music will be given frequently in Festival Hall during the six months of the Exposition.

Provision is being made for the appearance at the Exposition of the representative orchestras of New York City and Boston. Invitations have been sent to the New York Philharmonic Society, Anton Seidl, conductor ; and the Boston Symphony Orchestra, Arthur Nikisch, conductor, to give several concerts each.

Invitations to representative European composers to visit the Exposition as guests, and to conduct programmes of their own compositions, have been sent. Acceptances have been received from Camille Saint-Saens of France, and Dr. A. C. Mackenzie of England, who will visit the Exposition in September. Each will appear as conductor of his own choral and instrumental compositions, and Saint-Saens will take part in several concerts of chamber music, and will appear as interpreter of his own pianoforte concertos, and as organist. Among others invited are Massenet, Grieg, Sgambati, Dvorák, and Dr. Arthur Sullivan. Among the German musicians invited were Dr. Johannes Brahms and Dr. Joseph Joachim, both of whom find it impossible to accept.

Manufactures and Liberal Arts Building. —The size of this structure is 787 x 1,687 ft., having an area of 44 acres. The approximate cost is reported as $1,600,750. This is the largest of all the buildings. The great central hall has a clear space of 1,280 feet by 380 feet, and is surrounded by two galleries. The apex of the roof is 245½ feet, which is supported by steel arches. The length of the gallery is 3,504 feet. The east and west halls of the nave are 1,588 feet long, and the length of the nave, 4,119 feet. The building is three times as large as St. Peter's in Rome. The style of architecture is Corinthian, and it has four great entrances, one in the center of each façade. The Department of Manufactures consists of thirty-four large groups, divided into two hundred or more classes of the leading industries, collectively representing the products of modern machinery and man's handiwork in every form and design. The National Commission has approved the recommendation of the Director-General that a special medal of award be given for the best artistic display or installation of exhibits in each of the groups.

The exhibit of the Liberal Arts Department will include an historical display of the progress of the United States in this direction during the

past, illustrative of the development of American ingenuity and endeavor.

The only attractive sculptural features are the eagles that surmount the columns near the entrance, and the spandrils. The mammoth wings of the eagle of the Manufactures Building are capable of supporting nine men.

The exhibit of the Hygiene and Sanitation Bureau, organized as a section of the Department of Liberal Arts, will deal with sanitary affairs in every phase. Physical development, food supply, preparation of food, cooking and serving, dwellings and buildings, hygiene of the workshop and factory, food inspection, quarantine, reception, care and protection of immigrants, and numerous kindred subjects will be represented.

"Every possible sanitary precaution that tends to prolong life and minimize the dangers from disease will be shown either by actual appliances or models ; the evils of the 'tenement' and 'sweating' systems will be brought out very forcibly by models of old-style tenements and sweat-shops exhibited beside models of the best possible apartment houses and workshops. Heating, lighting, and drainage systems will be shown in contrast with exhibits illustrating the diseases and deformities caused by unwholesome trades and professions, or equally unwholesome quarters for the workingmen.

"A notable exhibit will be that relating to public institutions of charity and their work. This will be made under the auspices and direction of the Bureau of Charities and Corrections, created for this purpose by the Exposition authorities.

"The educational exhibit, principally on the ground floor of the Manufactures and Liberal Arts Building, will be organized both by States and by grades.

"Each State will occupy a definite area, which will be assigned with reference to the elements which the several States will have to represent as nearly as that can be ascertained. These areas will be side by side, in parallel subdivisions extending north and south. The parochial schools will have a definite place in the scheme, conformably to the same system. Each State exhibit will include : A presentation of its public-school system ; its academies, normal schools, colleges and universities ; its special, technical, and professional schools ; except in cases where a specialty in education can be better illustrated by a collective exhibit independent of State lines. Thus there will be a single collective exhibit, showing library organization and management ; one of commercial schools ; of manual-training schools ; of trade schools, etc. This method should probably be adopted, with exhibits of schools for the blind, the deaf, etc. In the presentation of public-school systems the several States and Territories will be the smallest units for which separate provision can be made by the chief of the department.

"The assignment of space to the several States and Territories will be determined by the information secured as to the character of the respective State systems. Each State should present a clear and concise epitome illustrative of its public-school system. As the conditions in the several States vary widely, exact rules of procedure cannot be formulated.

"The organization and administration of educational work in the different States will be presented in detail. A map of the State upon a generous scale will be provided ; by suitable conventions of color the location of every educational institution, from the common school up, will appear, proving by many instances that the schoolhouse crowns every hilltop and nestles in every valley. That the colors may be uniform, special directions and scale will be furnished by the chief of the department."

United States Government Building.—The size of the Government Building is 351x421 ft., having an area of 6.2 acres. The approximate cost is given as $400,000. The exhibit will include contributions from the War, Treasury, Agricultural, Interior, Post-Office, and Naval Departments at Washington ; also from the National Museum, Smithsonian Institute, etc. Details as to the space allotted to each section were given in the last issue of the Annual.

The section from one of the big California redwood trees, which the Government will exhibit in its building, required eleven freight cars to convey it across the Continent. It measures thirty feet long by twenty-three feet in diameter. The section is hollowed out, and when placed on end, divided into two stories and lighted, as it will be, it will form a rustic house large enough for a family to live in.

Naval Exhibit.—An imitation battle-ship occupies a space of 69.25x348 ft. The approximate cost is estimated at $100,000.

This ship, built of brick and coated with cement, is erected on pilings alongside a pier, apparently moored at a wharf on the lake front, in the northeast portion of Jackson Park. The structure is made to represent a full-size first-class battle-ship of the new navy for coast-line defense, designed by the Bureau of Construction and Repairs. It is surrounded by water and has all the guns, turrets, torpedo tubes, torpedo nets, booms, anchors, chain cables, and all other fittings and appliances of a regular battle-ship. During the exhibition, the ship will be manned by a full complement of officers, sailors, and marines ; and all explanations in regard to the mode of life upon a man-of-war will be made, and the method of handling the vessel during an engagement. The dimensions of the structure are : length, 348 feet; width amidships, 69 feet 3 inches; and from the water-line to the top of the main deck, 12 feet—or the exact dimensions in detail of a battle-ship. The battery is mounted as on a regular war vessel. The berth deck will be an open space for the Navy Department's exhibit. Each bureau will exhibit special articles. One of the most interesting exhibits on this vessel will be a naval museum containing relics of naval wars. An exhibit of the Bureau of Ordnance has been arranged for. On the port side of the berth deck the Bureau of Construction and Repair will place on exhibition a number of models of new cruisers now in the Navy Department. Opposite, on the same deck, the Bureau of Steam Engineering will exhibit a fully equipped machine-shop similar to those that will be put on the real battle-ships. The Bureau of Medicine and Surgery will make an exhibit of the Medical Department. The Bureau of Supplies and Accounts will send an exhibit of provisions, clothing, mess gear, cooking utensils, and all articles necessary for a crew's comfort. With this bureau's exhibit will also be a collection of naval uniforms of the patterns in use from the creation of the navy to the present time. The electric lighting arrangements now in use in the navy will be shown by the Bureau of Equipment.

In the main lagoon, to the west of the Government Building, will be a wooded island having an area of twenty to thirty acres. The various animals, trees, plants, and flowers on this island will not be interfered with in any way, the idea being to allow visitors an opportunity to ramble freely through a miniature primeval forest.

Fisheries Buildings.—The size of the main building is 162.1x361.1, having an area of 1.4 acres. The size of annexes will be 135 feet in diameter, the area of annexes being 7 acres. The approximate cost of all buildings is stated to be $224,750.

The location of the Fisheries Building is at a point northwest of the United States Government Building. The aquaria, ten in number, are supplied with gold, tench and other fish, and have a capacity of from 7,000 to 27,000 gallons each. The glass fronts of the aquaria are about 575 feet in length and have 3,000 square feet of surface. The supply of sea water was secured by evaporating the necessary quantities, at the Woods Holl station of the United States Fish Commission, to about one-fifth of its bulk, thus reducing both quantity and weight for transportation about 80 per cent. The fresh water required to restore it to its proper density was supplied from Lake Michigan.

One section of the Fisheries exhibit will be devoted to aquaria, a second to angling, and a third to commercial fisheries. The progress made in the character of fishing vessels will be fully illustrated. Exhibits from England and Newfoundland are expected.

On the grounds northeast of the Government Building, and about midway between it and the Fisheries Buildings, will be found the Heliograph, Light House Exhibit, Weather Bureau and Life Saving Station, with an exhibit of various types of life-boats. To the north of these will be seen the foreign exhibits, including, in their order from west to east, Brazil, Colombia, Nicaragua, Sweden, Turkey, Hayti, Russia, Canada and Great Britain. The group of foreign buildings to the north of those just mentioned, on the eastern side of the grounds, includes Costa Rica, Guatemala, Ecuador, Norway, Ceylon, France, Austria, and Germany. There is also a Japanese exhibit on the wooded island to the west of the Fisheries Buildings.

Foreign Nations.—The following foreign nations and colonies will be represented. The amounts opposite the names in the table show the sum set apart by the several nations and colonies for the purposes of their exhibits, so far as obtainable. (Revised Statements.)

Germany.—The German exhibit will contain an architectural display, including drawings illustrating 200 or more of the most notable buildings in the Empire.

Sweden.—This exhibit is in part designed on the lines of the old Norse stave churches. Most of the work has been done in Sweden, being shipped to Chicago in sections. The Swedish Government has prepared an excellent and comprehensive exhibit.

Chili.—The nitrate industry will be illustrated by an elaborate exhibit. "The prominence this product has attained in the finance of Chili makes the proposed exhibit doubly interesting."

Venezuela.—The Venezuela building will be one story in height, of white marble, in the

Argentine Republic.........	$100,000	Ceylon....................	$65,600	Netherlands................	
Austria-Hungary............	102,300	Fiji......................		Dutch Guiana.............	$10,000
Belgium	57,900	India.....................	17,380	Dutch West Indies........	5,000
Bolivia....................	30,700	Jamaica...................	24,333	Nicaragua.................	30,000
Brazil.....................	600,000	Leeward Islands	6,000	Norway....................	56,290
Bulgaria...................		Malta.....................		Orange Free State.........	7,500
China.....................		Mashonaland		Paraguay..................	100,000
Chili.....................		Mauritius.................		Persia....................	
Colombia..................	100,000	Newfoundland..............		Peru......................	140,000
Corea.....................		New South Wales..........	243,325	Portugal..................	
Costa Rica................	150,000	New Zealand...............	27,500	Madeira...................	
Denmark...................	67,000	Queensland................		Rumania...................	
Danish West Indies.......	1,200	South Australia..........		Russia.	31,860
Ecuador...................	125,000	Straits Settlements		Salvador..................	12,500
Egypt.....................		Tasmania..................	10,000	San Domingo...............	25,000
France....................	733,400	Trinidad..................	15,000	Servia....................	
Algeria...................		Victoria..................		Siam	
French Guiana.............		West Australia............		Spain.....................	14,000
Congo.....................		Greece....................	57,900	Cuba......................	25,000
French India..............		Guatemala.................	200,000	Porto Rico................	
New Caledonia.............		Hawaii....................		Sweden....................	53,600
Tunis.....................		Hayti.....................	25,000	Switzerland...............	23,160
Germany...................	690,200	Honduras..................	20,000	Transvaal.................	
Great Britain.............	291,990	Italy.....................		Turkey....................	17,466
Barbadoes	5,840	Japan.....................	630,765	Uruguay...................	24,000
Bermuda...................	2,920	Liberia...................		Venezuela.................	
British Guiana...........	. 25,000	Madagascar................			
British Honduras	7,500	Mexico....................	50,000	Total............$5,379.505	
Canada	100,000	Morocco...................	150,000	Forty-nine nations. Thirty-seven col-	
Cape Colony..............	50,000			onies and provinces.	

Græco-Roman style, with three handsome towers. On the left tower a life-size statue of Columbus will be placed, and on the right a statue of Bolivar, the South American liberator.

Austria.—The Austrian wood-carving industry will be represented by a number of expert wood-carvers from Vienna, who will exhibit their work in its various branches.

The glassmakers of Bohemia, and the china manufacturers of Carlsbad and the surrounding neighborhood, have agreed to prepare a display of their industries. The manufacturers of stained glass in Tyrol will join in the exhibit.

France.—A large number of silk manufactories at Lyons will make exhibits. This city made an impressive display at the Paris Exposition of 1889.

Japan.—The Japanese building is termed the Hooden (Phœnix Palace). It will consist of three pavilions, connected by as many corridors. Each of the pavilions will represent an era in the architectural and decorative history of the country. The style which was followed from the tenth to the thirteenth centuries, known as Fujinari, will be shown in the left wing. The interior of this pavilion will represent the decoration of the palace of a court noble.

The architecture of the fifteenth century is shown in the right wing. The villa of a Shogun will be reproduced. In the central pavilion will be represented the sitting-room of a Japanese feudal lord of the eighteenth century. The central wall of this pavilion will be decorated with phœnixes and a large pine tree, the Japanese emblem of strength. In the next room to this will be seen a gorgeous fan design, having nearly three hundred panels in colors and gold of phœnixes.

China.—The Chinese exhibit will include models of Chinese sailing craft of all kinds.

Persia.—This exhibit will embrace exquisite specimens of rich and highly wrought fabrics, fine embroideries and elaborately worked gold and silver jewelry, Persian rugs, carpets, hangings, etc. There will be a special department for manufactured articles, such as arms, curios, and richly wrought armor, tiles and tile work,

mosaics, objects of art, antiquities, musical instruments, and wearing apparel.

Hebraic.—The Alliance Israelite Universelle will exhibit specimens of the work performed by pupils in all its schools, photographs of the school buildings, products of the agricultural school at Jaffa and of the technical school at Jerusalem, and of its boy and girl apprentices in workshops. The collective exhibit will give an idea of the results obtained by the society since its foundation in the domain of elementary and technical education. Documents will be exhibited giving an account of the action taken by the Alliance in the interests of the Jews in countries where they are still subjected to persecution.

Canada.—The Provinces of Ontario and Quebec will provide a large exhibit of minerals. Nova Scotia will send specimens of her richest deposits. Asbestos, mica, plumbago, and phosphate deposits will form prominent features in the Quebec exhibit. The nickel ores of Ontario will be a special feature. The Dominion geological survey will make a useful exhibit, affording facilities for studying the mineral resources of the country as a whole.

The special foreign exhibits in Midway Plaisance are mentioned in the first part of this article.

Midway in the upper northern section of the grounds to the west of the foreign buildings, a large building devoted to art has been erected, with annexes.

Art Galleries.—The size of the main art building is 320x500 feet, having an area of 4.6 acres. The size of annexes will be 136x220 feet, having an area of 1.4 acre. The approximate cost of all buildings is estimated at $670,500.

The Art Palace, as it is termed, is oblong and of the classic Grecian-Ionic style of architecture. It is 125 feet in height to the top of the dome. It is intersected by a nave and transept, 100 feet wide and 70 feet high, and the dome, 60 feet in diameter, is surmounted by a colossal statue of Winged Victory. Around the building are galleries 40 feet wide. The interior and exterior are ornamented with wall paintings, sculptures and portraits in bas-relief of the masters of ancient art. The main building is entered by four large portals ornamented with sculptured designs. The wall paintings illustrate the history and progress of the arts. The building is in the northern portion of the park with the south front facing the lagoon.

In the United States section of this department there will be a collection of about 1,200 paintings of a much higher quality than has been shown in any previous American exhibition. A hanging space of 36,000 square feet has been set aside for the artists of this country. In addition to paintings, there will be shown superior collections of sculpture, architectural drawings, engravings, etchings, etc.

One of the galleries in the American section will be devoted to the retrospective collection, comprising the best works produced by Americans. This collection will exhibit the various stages of American art development. About 100 examples will be shown, a number of which already have been secured.

The loan collection will include modern European masterpieces owned in this country.

In the foreign-art sections at the Exposition all the well-known artists will be represented by some of their best productions.

The assignment of space in the Art Building to the different nations is as follows: the United States, 34,636 square feet; France, 33,393; Germany, 20,400; Great Britain, 20,395; Italy, 12,410; Belgium, 12,318; Austria, 11,564; Holland, 9,337; Norway, 8,462; Spain, 7,807; Russia, 7,725; Sweden, 7,005; Denmark, 3,900; Japan, 2,919; Canada, 2,895, and Mexico, 1,500. The exhibits of France and the United States will be connected by a large gallery in which will be placed a collection of French masterpieces owned in this country, which will be loaned for exhibition.

States and Territories Participating.—Each of the States and Territories will take part in the Exposition. The following 31 States and 2 Territories have made appropriations through their legislatures. The figure as to appropriations are revised up to date.

Arizona	$30,000	New Hampshire	$25,000
California	300,000	New Jersey	70,000
Colorado	100,000	New Mexico	25,000
Delaware	10,000	New York	300,000
Idaho	20,000	North Carolina	25,000
Illinois	800,000	North Dakota	25,000
Indiana	75,000	Ohio	125,000
Iowa	130,000	Pennsylvania	300,000
Kentucky	100,000	Rhode Island	50,000
Louisiana	36,000	Vermont	15,000
Maine	40,000	Virginia	25,000
Maryland	60,000	Washington	100,000
Massachusetts	150,000	West Virginia	40,000
Michigan	100,000	Wisconsin	65,000
Minnesota	50,000	Wyoming	30,000
Missouri	150,000		
Montana	50,000	Total	$3,441,000
Nebraska	50,000		

The following States are raising funds by stock subscriptions:

Alabama	$20,000	Oregon	$50,000
Arkansas	40,000	South Dakota	25,000
Florida	50,000	Texas	50,000
Georgia	100,000		
Kansas	100,000	Total	$435,000

Many of the States which have made appropriations are raising additional amounts, aggregating $750,000. The total expenditure by States and Territories will approximate $5,000,000.

State Buildings.—The State buildings are arranged to occupy space to the southwest and north of the Art Galleries, at the extreme northern section of the Exposition grounds. The most southerly and nearest to the Midway Plaisance entrance is the Illinois exhibit. Proceeding thence in a northwesterly direction, the buildings represent the following States and Territories:

Indiana, California, Wisconsin, Ohio, Michigan, Colorado, Washington, South Dakota, Nebraska, North Dakota, Kansas, Texas, Minnesota, Arkansas, Florida, Mississippi, Missouri, Alabama, Louisiana, Kentucky, Virginia, West Virginia, Utah, Montana, Idaho, New Mexico, Arizona, Wyoming, North Carolina, Pennsylvania, New York, Maryland, Delaware, Massachusetts, Vermont, Maine, Rhode Island, Connecticut, New Hampshire, New Jersey, and Iowa.

The State buildings of Colorado, Washington, South Dakota, Nebraska, North Dakota, and Kansas will be almost immediately behind each other in a line running northward near the border of the Northwest Pond on the northwest extremity of the grounds.

The buildings representing the industries of Texas, Utah, Montana, Idaho, New Mexico, Arizona, Wyoming, and Iowa form a line running from west to east along the edge of the extreme northern boundary, the Iowa building occupying the northeast corner. Information concerning certain details connected with several of the State exhibits are now available and may be noted here.

Illinois.—The Illinois building will be one of the most imposing of the State structures. It will cost $350,000, the style of architecture being severely classic, with a central dome and a great porch facing southward.

Ohio.—Cost $30,000. This building will be 100 feet square, colonial style. State contributions will bring its value up to $50,000. In front of the building will be the Ohio monument, erected by authority of the State legislature at a cost of $25,000.

Iowa.—The Iowa exhibit will be in "The Shelter," 112 x 80 feet. The building will be of granite, with slate roof. Conical towers or pavilions will be erected at the corners.

Nebraska.—This building, 60 x 100 feet, will occupy 6,000 square feet of ground space, and 12,000 square feet of floor space. There will be two stories, the height to ridge of roof being 45 feet. Style of architecture, strictly classical of the Corinthian order.

Minnesota.—In the Minnesota Building will be exhibited the old printing-press upon which the first newspaper that was ever printed in the State—the Minnesota Pioneer—was produced in 1849.

Wisconsin.—In the Wisconsin exhibit will be an immense monolith of the finest quality of brown-stone. It is 106 feet in height, exclusive of the base, which would give it a total height of 117 feet. At the base the obelisk is 9 by 9 feet, and tapers to 3 by 2 feet at the top. It will be larger than Cleopatra's Needle or any of the great obelisks of Egypt, and is said to be the largest monolith in the world.

Washington.—More than 200 panels of native woods will be used in the interior decoration of the Washington State Building. Some will be

THE ART BUILDING.

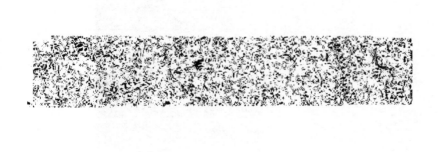

carved and others decorated with paintings of Washington scenery and groupings of flowers, fruits, grains, fish, game, birds, etc.

California.—Among the most interesting exhibits will be a Pampas Plume Palace, consisting of a light wood framework, octagonal, covered partially with blue plumes, the roof being tiled with red plumes, the combination with white pluming thus representing the national colors. An American flag, hanging from a gilded frame, all made of pampas, will surmount the whole. On the inside walls of the palace will be a frieze, four feet wide, which will be made of wire in an artistic design, and the pampas, separated into small pieces, will be tied on. There will also be a dado in the same style of decoration, furnished with mirrors, a fireplace, tea-kettle, Persian rug, etc., all made of pampas plumes.

New Hampshire.—The structure of New Hampshire is fashioned after a Swiss chateau. It is founded upon granite. Within a spacious gallery will be shown raised and topographical maps, portraits of "favorite sons," mineral specimens, etc.

State Commissioners.—*Alabama.*—F. G. Bromberg, O. R. Hundley, G. L. Werth, William S. Hull.
Arkansas.—John D. Adams, J. H. Clendening, J. T. W. Tillar, Thos. H. Leslie.
California.—M. H. de Young, William Forsyth, Geo. Hazleton, Russ D. Stephens.
Colorado.—R. E. Goodell, Jos. H. Smith, H. B. Gillespie, O. C. French.
Connecticut.—L. Brainerd, Thos. M. Waller, Charles F. Brooker, Charles R. Baldwin.
Delaware.—Geo. V. Massey, W. H. Porter, Chas. F. Richards, William Saulsbury.
Florida.—C. F. A. Bielby, Richard Turnbull, Dudley W. Adams, J. T. Bernard.
Georgia.—L. McLaws, C. H. Way, James Longstreet, John W. Clark.
Idaho.—G. A. Manning, J. E. Stearns, A. J. Crook, John M. Burke.
Illinois.—C. H. Deere, A. T. Ewing, Lafayette Funk, De Witt Smith.
Indiana.—T. E. Garvin, E. B. Martindale, Wm. E. McLean, Charles M. Travis.
Iowa.—Jos. Elboeck, W. F. King, C. N. Whiting, John Hayes.
Kansas.—C. K. Holliday, jr., R. E. Price, M. D. Henry, Frank W. Lanyon.
Kentucky.—Commissioners: John Bennett, J. A. McKenzie. Alternates: D. N. Comingore, John S. Morris.
Louisiana.—D. B. Penn, T. J. Woodward, Alphonse Le Duc, P. J. McMahon.
Maine.—A. R. Bixby, W. G. Davis, J. A. Boardman, Clark S. Edwards.
Maryland.—James Hodges, L. Lowndes, George M. Upshur, D. E. Conkling.
Massachusetts.—F. W. Breed, T. E. Proctor, George P. Ladd, C. E. Adams.
Michigan.—M. H. Lane, George H. Barbour, Ernest B. Fisher, L. D. Norris.
Minnesota.—H. B. Moore, O. V. Tousley, T. C. Kurtz, M. N. Leland.
Mississippi.—J. M. Bynum, R. L. Saunders, Fred. W. Collins, J. H. Brinker.
Missouri.—T. B. Bullene, C. H. Jones, O. H. Picher, R. L. McDonald.
Montana.—L. H. Hershfield, A. R. Mitchell, B. F. White, T. E. Collins.
Nebraska.—E. Martin, A. G. Scott, William L. May, John Lauterbach.
Nevada.—J. W. Haines, George Russell, Enoch Strother, Richard Ryland.
New Hampshire.—Walter Aiken, C. D. McDuffie, George Van Dyke, Frank E. Kaley.

New Jersey.—W. J. Sewell, Thomas Smith, Frederick S. Fish, Edwin A. Stevens.
New York.—C. M. Depew, J. B. Thacher, James H. Breslin, James Roosevelt.
North Carolina.—A. B. Andrews, T. B. Keogh, Elias Carr, G. A. Bingham.
North Dakota.—H. P. Rucker, Marlin Ryan, Charles H. Stanley, Peter Cameron.
Ohio.—H. P. Platt, Wm. Ritchie, Lucius C. Cron, Adolph Pluemer.
Oregon.—H. Klippell, M. Wilkins, J. L. Morrow, W. T. Wright.
Pennsylvania.—R. B. Ricketts, J. W. Woodside, G. A. Macbeth, John K. Hallock.
Rhode Island.—Lyman B. Goff, G. C. Sims, Jeffrey Hazard, Lorillard Spencer.
South Carolina.—A. P. Butler, J. R. Cochran, E. L. Roche, J. W. Tindell.
South Dakota.—M. H. Day, W. McIntyre, S. A. Ramsey, L. S. Bullard.
Tennessee.—L. T. Baxter, T. L. Williams, Rush Strong, A. B. Hurt.
Texas.—A. M. Cochran. J. T. Dickinson, Lock McDaniel, Henry B. Andrews.
Wyoming.—A. C. Beckwith, Henry G. Hay, Asa S. Mercer, John J. McCormick.
Territories.—*Alaska.*—Ed. de Groff, Louis L. Williams, Carl Gruhn, N. A. Fuller.
Arizona.—Geo. F. Coats, W. K. Meade, W. L. Van Horn, Herbert H. Logan.
New Mexico.—T. C. Gutierres, R. M. White, L. C. Tetard, Chas. B. Eddy.
Oklahoma.—O. Beeson, F. R. Gammon, John Wallace, Jos. W. McNeal.
Utah.—F. J. Kiesel, P. H. Lannan, William M. Ferry, Charles Crane.
District of Columbia.—A. T. Britton, A. A. Wilson, E. Kurtz Johnson, Dorsey Claggett.

World's Congress Auxiliary.—The World's Congress Auxiliary will comprise a central organization, authorized by the Exposition Directory of the World's Columbian Exposition, and recognized by the Federal Government; a local committee of arrangements for each Congress; an advisory council for each committee; general honorary and corresponding members, and committees of co-operation, appointed by particular organizations, and recognized by the Auxiliary as representatives of societies or institutions. The Woman's Branch of the Auxiliary consists of committees of women appointed to co-operate with the corresponding committees of the men in making arrangements for Congresses appropriate for the participation of women. Mixed committees are not appointed, but the two committees may act as a joint committee, when occasion requires. In case a separate Congress of Women is desirable, it will be in special charge of this branch of the Auxiliary, of which Mrs. Potter Palmer is president and Mrs. Charles Henrotin vice-president.

The work of the Congress will be divided into seventeen departments: Agriculture, Art, Commerce and Finance, Education, Engineering, Government, Literature, Labor, Medicine, Moral and Social Reform, Music, Public Press, Religion, Science and Philosophy, Temperance, Sunday Rest, and a General Department embracing Congresses not otherwise assigned. These general departments have been divided into more than one hundred divisions, in each of which a Congress is to be held. Each division has its own local committee of arrangements. Representative men from all parts of the world will participate in the proceedings.

The Congresses will be held in the permanent Memorial Art Palace, on the Lake Front Park. This building will have two large audience rooms, to seat about 3,000 persons each, and more than twenty smaller rooms, which will accommodate from 300 to 700 persons each. Popular meetings will be held in the main audience rooms. Meetings of chapters and sections of different Congresses for the discussion of subjects of more limited interest will be held in the smaller rooms. It will be possible to have two general Congresses and twenty,special Congresses or Conferences in session at the same time, and, if necessary, to have three times as many meetings within a single day by arranging different programmes for morning, afternoon, and evening.

At least one hundred congresses will be held in Chicago during the Exposition. The proceedings of the Congresses will be subsequently published in permanent form, and a programme is now being arranged for the various departments and their divisions by which the great specialists and advanced thinkers of the age may participate in discussing the important questions of the day.

The officers of the Auxiliary are Charles C. Ronney, *President;* Thomas B. Bryan, *Vice-President;* Lyman J. Gage, *Treasurer;* Benjamin Butterworth, *Secretary.*

Objects.—The objects of the Congress are: "To provide for the proper presentation of the world's intellectual and moral progress, with the assistance of the leaders in all the chief departments of human achievement; to provide places of meeting and other facilities for kindred organizations to unite in Congresses in Chicago during the Exposition season, for the consideration of questions in their respective departments; to conduct popular Congresses in which will be presented summaries of the progress made and the most important results attained in the several departments of civilized life; to provide for the proper publication of the Congress proceedings as the most valuable and enduring memorial of the Exposition; and to bring all the departments of human progress into harmonious relation in the Exposition."

Woman's Progress.—Includes all the fields in which women have achieved success; and will embrace a General Congress of representative women of all countries, beginning May 15, 1893.

Public Press.—Includes the Daily Press, Weeklies and Magazines, the Religious Press, Trade Journals, Scientific and Professional Journals, etc. Congresses will be held during the week beginning May 22, 1893.

Medicine.—Includes General Medicine and Surgery, Homeopathic Medicine and Surgery; Eclectic Medicine and Surgery; Medico-Climatology. Congresses will be held during the week beginning May 29. The Congresses of Dentistry, Pharmacy, and Medical Jurisprudence have been transferred to the week beginning August 14, 1893.

Temperance. — Includes the Woman's Christian Temperance Union; Catholic Temperance Societies, National Temperance Society; Independent Order of Good Templars; Sons of Temperance; Templars of Honor and Temperance; Royal Templars of Temperance; Non-partisan W. C. T. U.; Law and Order Leagues; Vegetarian Societies and similar organizations. Congresses will be held during the week beginning June 5, 1893.

Moral and Social Reform.—Includes Philanthropy, Prevention, Charity, and Reform, as represented by the National Conference of Charities and Correction; Women's Exchanges; Lodging Houses; Newsboys' and Bootblacks' Homes; Humane Societies; Provident Associations; Industrial Schools; Children's Missions; Children's Aid Societies; Day Nurseries; Relief Societies; Orphan Asylums; Homes for Old People; Asylums for Incurables; Hospitals; Little Sisters of the Poor: Fresh Air Work; Soup Houses; Penal Institutions; Woman's Refuges; Houses of the Good Shepherd; Reform Schools; the Salvation Army, and the like. Congresses will be held during the week beginning June 12, 1893.

Commerce and Finance.—Includes the general divisions of Banking and Finance; Boards of Trade; Stocks and Bonds; Water Commerce; Railway Commerce; Commercial Clubs and kindred organizations; Insurance; Building Associations; Mercantile Business, etc. The Insurance Congresses will include Fire Insurance, Marine Insurance, Life and Accident Insurance, Mutual Benefit and Assessment Associations, Fidelity and Employers' Liability Insurance, and Insurance Specialties. Congress will begin on June 19, 1893. The Water Commerce Congress will be held during the first week of August, simultaneously with the Engineering Congress.

Music.—Includes Orchestral, Art, Choral Music and Training, Songs of the People, Organ and Church Music, Musical Art and Literature, Musical Criticism and History, Opera Houses and Music Halls. Congresses will be held during the week beginning July 3, 1893.

Literature.—Includes Libraries, History, Philology, Authors, Folk-lore, and Copyright. Congresses will begin on July 10, 1893.

Education.—Includes Higher Institutions of Learning and University Extension; Public Instruction; the Kindergarten; Manual and Art Training: Business and Commercial Education; Education in Civil Law and Government: Instruction of the Deaf; Education of the Blind; Representative Youth of Public Schools; College and University Students; College Fraternities; Psychology—Experimental and Rational; Physical Culture; Domestic and Economic Education; Agricultural Education; Authors and Publishers. The General Division of Public Instruction in Music is transferred to the Department of Musical Art. Congresses will begin on July 17, 1893, and will be followed by the World's General Educational Congress, in which all Departments of Education will be represented.

Engineering.—Includes Civil Engineering, Mechanical Engineering, Mining Engineering, Metallurgical Engineering, Electrical Engineering, Military Engineering, Marine and Naval Engineering, Aerial Navigation, Engineering Education. Engineering Congresses and Water Commerce Congress will be held during the week beginning July 31, 1893.

Art.—Includes Architecture, Painting, Sculpture, Decorative Art, Photographic Art, Governmental Patronage of Art—Art Museums, Art Education, etc. Congresses will open on July 31, 1893.

Government.—Includes Jurisprudence and Law Reform, Political and Economic Reform, City Government, Executive Administration, Intellectual Property, Arbitration and Peace. Jurisprudence and Law Reform will include the Laws of Nations, Expatriation, Naturalization, and Extradition; International Privileges of Citizenship, the Administration of Justice, etc. Political and Economic Reform will include Political Economy and Economic Science, Profit-sharing, Social Science, the Single Tax and other Theories; Public Revenues, Statistics, Weights and Measures and Coinage, Postal Service, Suffrage in Republics, Kingdoms, and Empires, Civil Service Reform, etc. City Government will include Municipal Order, the Public Service, Public Works, Police Protection, Public Revenues and Expenditures, and other important subjects. Executive Administration will include the nature, office, and application of Executive Power, in Municipal, State, and National Government. Intellectual Property will include Trademarks and Patents, both National and International.

THE WOMAN'S BUILDING.

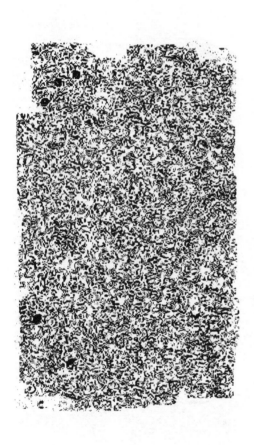

Copyright has been transferred from Government to Literature. Arbitration and Peace will include the establishment of permanent International Courts of Justice, the substitution of Arbitration for War, the establishment of Courts of Conciliation and Arbitration for the voluntary settlement of private controversies, etc. Congresses of this division will begin on August 7, 1893, and may extend into the following week. The Economic Congress will be deferred to the week beginning August 28, and held simultaneously with the Labor Congress.

General Department of Subjects Specially Assigned.— Includes Congresses not properly belonging to any other Department; also Congresses which could not be held in their appropriate places in the other Departments, such as the Dental Congress, Pharmaceutical Congress, Congress of Medical Jurists, Congress of the African Continent and People, Horticultural Congress, and Chess Congress. Congresses will begin on August 14, 1893. The Congress of Pharmacists will be held during the following week in connection with the Congress of Chemists.

Science and Philosophy.—Includes General Physics, Astronomy and Mathematics, Meteorology, Geology, Geography, Chemistry, Electricity, Botany, Zoology, Microscopy, Anthropology, Ethnology, and Archæology, Indian Ethnology, African Ethnology, Psychical Science, Philosophy. Congresses are assigned to the week beginning August 21, 1893. The Congress of African Ethnology will open during the preceding week.

Labor.—Includes Historic Development of Labor, Labor Organizations, Conflicts of Labor and Capital, Labor Economics and Legislation, Woman's Work and Wages, Domestic Economy, Child Labor, Education, Public Opinion and Progress. Congresses will be held in the last days of August and the first days of September, closing on "Labor Day," Sept. 4, 1893.

Religion. — Includes the following General Divisions, subject to additions: Baptist, Catholic, Congregational, Christian, Evangelical Association, Evangelical Church, Friends, Jews, Lutheran General Council, Lutheran General Synod, Lutheran Synodical Conference, Methodist Episcopal, New Jerusalem, Presbyterian, Protestant Episcopal, Reformed Church of North America, Dutch Reformed Church, Reformed Episcopal, Swedish Evangelical, United Brethren, Unitarian, Universalist, Missions, Evangelical Alliance, Young Men's and Young Women's Christian Associations, Society of the Christian Endeavor, Epworth League, Brotherhood of Christian Unity. The Catholic Congress will begin on Sept. 5, the World's Parliament of Religions on Sept. 11, the Denominational Congresses on Sept. 21, and the Missionary Congresses on Sept. 28, to be followed by Congresses of the Evangelical Alliance and other bodies named.

Sunday Rest.—Includes Physiological Relations, Economic and Business Relations, Governmental and Political Relations, Social and Moral Relations, and Religious Relations of the Weekly Rest Day. Congresses will be held in October, immediately after those of the Religious Societies.

Public Health.—Includes Sanitary Legislation, Public Health Authorities, Governmental Administration in relation to Epidemics and Contagious, Food Inspection and other Food Problems. Congresses will follow that of Sunday Rest in October.

Agriculture.—Includes Farm Culture and Cereal Industry, Animal Industry, Agricultural Organizations and Governmental Departments of Agriculture, Agricultural Education and Experiment, Good Roads, Household Economics, and Horticulture. Congresses begin on October 16, 1893.

Awards.—The report of the sub-committee on Awards of the Judiciary Committee, made September 15, 1890, upon the question of the rights, duties, and powers of the Commission under the act of Congress, named, as among the "original and exclusive powers of the Commission," the power "to appoint judges and examiners for the Exposition, and to award all premiums." At a meeting of the Executive Committee of the Commission held October 18, 1890, a resolution was adopted authorizing President Palmer to appoint a committee of four from the Commission to confer with a similar committee from the local directory, and to determine "whether awards shall be granted and what character of awards shall be made, if any."

This committee reported the following among other recommendations:

"That awards be granted upon specific points of excellence or advancement, formulated in words by a board of judges, who shall be competent experts; that the evidence of awards be parchment certificates accompanied by bronze medals."

"That there be but one class or kind of medal, to be made of bronze, and to be works of art selected from competitive tests by the Committee on Fine Arts of the Commission, or, if more desirable, by the Joint Committees on Fine Arts of the Commission and the local directory."

These recommendations were adopted by the commission; and at the meeting of its Executive Committee held Sept. 1, 1891, the following resolution was adopted:

"There shall be a committee on awards, to be appointed by the president, consisting of twelve commissioners, which is authorized to meet at the call of the chairman and shall have charge of the subjects of awards, and who shall, in connection with the Director-General, select and appoint the board of judges, subject to the approval of the Commission."

This committee, it is understood, will be formed by the appointment of one member from each of the committees representing the twelve great departments of the Exposition.

Finance.—The following is a recently published authentic statement concerning the estimated receipts and expenditures:

RECEIPTS.

Capital stock and City of Chicago bonds,		$10,500,000
U. S. Treasury appropriation in souvenir coins.		2,500,000
Premium on same		2,500,000
Debenture bonds (now offered)		4,000,000
Total		$19,500,000
Gate receipts	$10,000,000	
Concessions and privileges	3,500,000	
Salvage	1,500,000	15,000,000
Total estimated receipts		$34,500,000

EXPENDITURES.

Constructing buildings and preparatory expenses to May 1, 1893	$18,750,000
Operating expenses from May 1, 1893	2,500,000
Total estimated expenditures	$21,250,000
Net amount available for payment of bonds	13,250,000
Total	$34,500,000

The cost of the Exposition structures is estimated at $8,000,000. This amount represents less than half of the total estimated expenditure for the enterprise. The Grounds and Buildings

Committee recently issued the following list of necessary expenses: Grading, filling, etc., $450,-400; landscape gardening, $323,490; viaducts and bridges, $125,000; piers, $70,000; waterway improvements, $2?5,000; railways, $500,000; steam plant, $800,000; electricity, $1,500,000; statuary on buildings, $100,000; vases, lamps, and posts, $50,000; seating, $8,000; water supply, sewerage, etc., $600,000; improvement of lake front, $200,000; World's Congress Auxiliary, $200,000; construction department expenses, fuel, etc., $520,000; organization and administration, $3,308,563; operating expenses, $1,550,000; total, $10,530,453.

This sum, added to the amount to be expended in the erection of buildings, makes neces-ary a total expenditure for Exposition purposes of $18,530,453. (In round numbers, allowing a margin for contingencies, $18,750,000.) This does not include any part of the United States Government appropriation, or any part of the appropriations of the several States, or foreign countries. Of this $18,750,000 it is estimated that $17,000,000 will have to be paid out before the opening of the gates of the Exposition on May 1, 1893.

Legislation.—The act of April 6, 1892, provides that no citizen of any other country shall be held liable for the infringement of any patent granted by the United States, or of any trade-mark or label registered in the United States, where the act complained of is or shall be performed in connection with the exhibition of any article or thing at the World's Columbian Exposition at Chicago.

The act of May 12, 1892, provides that any National bank located in Chicago may be designated by the World's Columbian Exposition to conduct a banking office upon the Exposition grounds, and, upon approval by the Controller of the Currency, may open and conduct such office as a branch of the bank, subject to the same restrictions and having the same rights; provided, that the branch shall not be operated for more than two years, between July 1, 1892, and July 1, 1894.

The act of August 4, 1892, changes the date of the dedication of the buildings of the World's Columbian Exposition from October 12 to October 21, 1892.

The act of August 5, 1892, provides that for the purpose of aiding in defraying the cost of completing in a suitable manner the work of preparation for inaugurating the World's Columbian Exposition, there shall be coined at the mints of the United States silver half-dollars of the legal weight and fineness, not to exceed five million pieces, to be known as the Columbian half-dollar, struck in commemoration of the World's Columbian Exposition, the devices and designs upon which shall be prescribed by the Director of the Mint, with the approval of the Secretary of the Treasury; and said silver coins shall be manufactured from uncurrent subsidiary silver coins now in the Treasury. All provisions of law relative to the coinage, legal-tender quality, and redemption of the present subsidiary silver coins are applicable to the coins issued under this act, and when so received there is appropriated from the treasury the said five millions of souvenir half-dollars, and the Secretary of the Treasury is authorized to pay the same to the World's Columbian Exposition, upon estimates and vouchers certified for labor done, materials furnished and services performed in prosecuting the work of preparing the Exposition for opening as provided by the act of April 25, 1890; provided, however, that before the Secretary of the Treasury shall pay to the Exposition any part of the five million silver coins

satisfactory evidence shall be furnished him showing that the sum of at least $10,000,000 has been collected and disbursed as required by said act; and provided, that the Exposition shall furnish a satisfactory guarantee to the Secretary of the Treasury that any further sum actually necessary to complete the work of the Exposition to the opening has been or will be provided by the World's Columbian Exposition.

The appropriation thus provided shall be upon condition that the Exposition maintain and pay all expenses, costs, and charges of the great departments organized for conducting the work of the Exposition out of the Exposition funds. Fifty thousand bronze medals and the necessary dies therefor, with appropriate devices, emblems and inscriptions, celebrating the 400th anniversary of the discovery of America, shall be prepared under the supervision of the Secretary of the Treasury at a cost not to exceed $60,000, and the Bureau of Engraving and Printing shall prepare plates and make therefrom 50,000 vellum impressions for diplomas at a cost not to exceed $43,000. The medals and diplomas shall be delivered to the World's Columbian Commission, to be awarded to exhibitors in accordance with the provisions of the act of Congress approved April 25, 1890, and there is appropriated, from any moneys in the treasury not otherwise appropriated, $103,000, or so much thereof as may be necessary, to pay the expenditures authorized by this section; and authority may be granted by the Secretary of the Treasury to the holder of a medal, properly awarded to him, to have duplicates made at any of the mints of the United States from gold, or silver, or bronze, at the expense of the person desiring the same.

All appropriations herein made for or pertaining to the Exposition are upon the condition that the Exposition shall not be opened to the public on Sunday; and if the appropriations be accepted by the World's Columbian Exposition, upon that condition, it is made the duty of the World's Columbian Commission to make the necessary modification of the rules of the Exposition corporation.

This bill, in its final shape, passed the Senate without discussion. In the House the vote was: Yeas, 131 (Reps. 82, Dems. 49); nays, 83 (Dems. 75, Inds. 8).

Officials.—The revised list of officials is as follows:

President, Thomas W. Palmer, Michigan; First Vice-President, Thomas M. Waller, Connecticut; Second Vice-President, M. H. de Young, California; Third Vice-President, Davidson B. Penn, Louisiana; Fourth Vice-President, Gorton W. Allen, New York; Fifth Vice-President, Alexander B. Andrews, North Carolina; Secretary, John T. Dickinson, Texas; Vice-Chairman Executive Committee, James A. McKenzie, Kentucky.

Commissioners-at-Large.—Commissioners: Aug. G. Bullock, G. W. Allen, P. A. B. Widener, Thos. W. Palmer, R. W. Furnas, Wm. Lindsay, Henry Exall, M. L. McDonald; Alternates: Henry Ingalls, Louis Fitzgerald, John W. Chalfant, James Oliver, Hale G. Parker, Patrick Walsh, H. C. King, Thomas Burke.

Exposition Association of Chicago.—Director-General, George R. Davis; President, Harlow N. Higinbotham; First Vice-President, Ferd. W. Peek; Second Vice-President, Robert A. Waller; Secretary, Howard O. Edmonds; Treasurer, Anthony F. Seeberger; Auditor, William K. Ackerman; Attorney, William K. Carlisle; Chief of Construction, D. H. Burnham; Traffic Manager, E. E. Jaycox; Directors, William T. Baker, C. K. C. Billings, Thomas G. Bryan, Edward B. Butler, Benjamin Butterworth, Isaac N. Camp, William J. Chalmers, Robert C. Clowry, Charles H. Chappell, George R. Davis, Arthur Dixon, James W. Ellsworth, George P. Englebard,

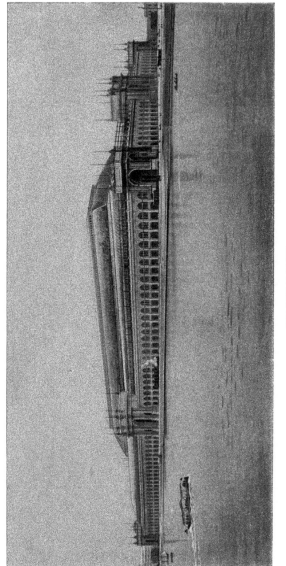

THE MAIN BUILDING.

Lyman J. Gage, Charles Henrotin, H. N. Higinbotham, Charles L. Hutchinson, Elbridge G. Keith, William D. Kerfoot, William P. Ketcham, Milton W. Kirk, Edward F. Lawrence, Theis J. Lefens. Andrew McNally, Addolph Nathan, Robert Nelson, John J. P. Odell, Ferd. W. Peek, Eugene S. Pike, Washington Porter, Alexander H. Revell, Edward P. Ripley, A. M. Rothschild, George Schneider, Charles H. Schwab, Paul O. Stensland, Henry B. Stone, Charles H. Wacker, Edwin Walker, Robert A. Waller, Hempstead Washburne, John C. Weiling, Frederick S. Whinstou, G. H. Wheeler, Charles T. Yerkes.

Regular meetings of the Directory, second Friday of each month.

Directors' Executive Committee.—Harlow N. Higinbotham, President; Ferd. W. Peck, First Vice-President; Robert A. Waller, Second Vice-President; Henry B. Stone, Edwin Walker, William D. Kerfoot, Charles H. Schwab, Alexander H. Revell, Edward P. Ripley, George R. Davis, Charles L. Hutchinson, James W. Ellsworth, Robert C. Clowry, John J. P. Odell, Edward B. Butler, Theis J. Lefens, Lyman J. Gage, William T. Baker.

Chairmen of Standing Committees.—Finance, Ferd. W. Peck; Legislation, Edwin Walker; Agriculture, William D. Kerfoot; Mines, Mining, and Fish, Charles H. Schwab; Press and Printing, Alexander H. Revell; R. J. Murphy, Secretary. Transportation, Edward P. Ripley; Fine Arts, Charles L. Hutchinson; Liberal Arts, James W. Ellsworth; Electricity, Electrical and Pneumatical Appliances, Robert C. Clowry; Manufactures and Machinery, John J. P. Odell; Ways and Means, Edward B. Butler; Samuel A. Crawford, Secretary. Foreign Exhibits, Theis J. Lefeus; R. L. Fern, Secretary. Special Committee on Ceremonies, Edward F. Lawrence; E. C. Culp, Secretary.

Executive Committee.—President, T. W. Palmer, Michigan, Chairman; James A. McKenzie, Kentucky, Vice-Chairman; John T. Dickinson, Texas, Secretary; M. L. McDonald, Commissioner-at-Large; R. W. Furnas, Commissioner-at-Large; Henry Exall, Commissioner-at-Large; P. A. B. Widener, Commissioner-at-Large; John T. Harris, Virginia; William J. Sewell, New Jersey; B. B. Smalley, Vermont; E. B. Martindale, Indiana; John Boyd Thacher, New York; Francis W. Breed, Massachusetts; Euclid Martin, Nebraska; James D. Butt, West Virginia; Adlai T. Ewing, Illinois; William F. King, Iowa; H. P. Platt, Ohio; L. McLaws, Georgia; T. L. Williams, Tennessee; C. F. A. Bielby, Florida; R. L. Saunders, Mississippi; L. H. Hershfield, Montana; R. E. Goodell, Colorado; A. T. Britton, District of Columbia.

Judiciary Rules and Bylaws.—William Lindsay, Kentucky, Commissioner-at-Large, Chairman; G. V. Massey, Delaware, Acting Secretary.

Tariffs and Transportation.—V. D. Groner, Virginia, Chairman; H. P. Rucker, North Dakota, Secretary.

Foreign Affairs.—C. M. Depew, New York, Chairman; G. V. Massey, Delaware, Acting Secretary.

Fine Arts.—A. G. Bullock, Massachusetts, Commissioner-at-Large, Chairman.

Science, History, Literature, and Education—O. V. Tousley, Minnesota, Chairman.

Agriculture.—John D. Adams, Arkansas, Chairman; H. H. McIntyre, Vermont, Secretary.

Live Stock.—George Russell, Nevada, Chairman; H. P. Rucker, North Dakota, Secretary.

Horticulture and Floriculture.—W. Forsyth, California, Chairman; Willard Hall Porter, Delaware, Secretary.

Finance.—Charles H. Jones, Missouri, Chairman; H. H. McIntyre, Vermont, Secretary.

Auditing.—T. E. Garvin, Indiana, Chairman; P. Allen, Jr., Wisconsin, Secretary.

Ceremonies.—P. A. B. Widener, Pennsylvania, Commissioner-at-Large, Chairman; Edward C. Culp, Kansas, Secretary.

Classification.—C. H. Deere, Illinois, Chairman.

Manufacture.—L. Brainard, Connecticut, Chairman; Willard Hall Porter, Delaware, Secretary.

Commerce.—Lloyd Lowndes, Maryland, Chairman.

Mines and Mining.—P. H. Lannon, Utah, Chairman; J. E. Stearns, Idaho, Secretary.

Fisheries and Fish Culture.—A. R. Bixby, Maine, Chairman; R. E. Goodell, Colorado. Secretary.

Electricity, Electrical and Pneumatic Appliances.—G. C. Sims, Rhode Island, Chairman; Martin Ryan, North Dakota, Secretary.

Forestry and Lumber.—J. W. St. Clair, West Virginia, Chairman.

Machinery.—William Ritchie, Ohio, Chairman; Willard Hall Porter, Delaware, Secretary.

World's Congresses.—J. W. Woodside, Pennsylvania, Chairman.

Printing.—C. K. Holliday, Jr., Kansas, Chairman; P. H. Lannan, Utah, Secretary.

Grounds and Buildings. — E. B. Martindale, Indiana, Chairman.

Federal Legislation.—J. W. St. Clair, West Virginia, Chairman.

Awards.—B. B. Smalley, Vermont, Chairman; O. R. Hundley, Alabama, Temporary Secretary.

Department Chiefs.—Agriculture, William I. Buchanan; Horticulture, John M. Samuels; Live Stock, E. W. Cottrell; Fish and Fisheries, John W. Collins; Mines and Mining, Frederick J. V. Skiff; Machinery, Lewis W. Robinson; Transportation, Willard A. Smith; Manufactures, James Allison; Electricity, John P. Barrett; Fine Arts, Halsey C. Ives; Liberal Arts, Selim H. Peabody; Ethnology, Frederick W. Putnam; Forestry, temporarily in charge of Chief Buchanan, of the Department of Agriculture; Publicity and Promotion, Moses P. Handy; Foreign Affairs, Walker Fearn; Secretary of Installation, Joseph Hirst.

Board of Control and Management, United States Government Exhibit.—Edwin Willits, Chairman; Seveloa A. Brown, Chief Clerk Department of State, to represent that department; Allured B. Nettleton, Assistant Secretary of the Treasury, to represent Treasury Department; Major Clifton Comly, U. S. A., to represent the War Department; Captain R. W. Meade, U. S. N., to represent Navy Department; A. D. Hazen, Third Assistant Postmaster-General, to represent Post-office Department; Horace A. Taylor, Commissioner of Railroads, to represent Interior Department; Elijah C. Foster, General Agent Department of Justice, to represent that department; Edwin Willits, Assistant Secretary of Agriculture, to represent Department of Agriculture; Professor G. Brown Goode, Assistant Secretary Smithsonian Institution, to represent that institution and the National Museum; J. W. Collins, Assistant-in-Charge Division of Fisheries, to represent United States Fish Commission.

Board of Reference and Control.—Thomas W. Palmer, Michigan, President; James A. McKenzie, Kentucky Vice-President; George V. Massey, Delaware; William Lindsay, Kentucky; Michael H. de Young, California; Thomas M. Waller. Connecticut; Elijah B. Martindale, Indiana; J. W. St. Clair, West Virginia.

Council of Administration.—H. N. Higinbotham, Chairman, and Chas. H. Schwab, appointed by the World's Columbian Exposition; J. W. St. Clair, of West Virginia, and Geo. V. Massey, of Delaware, appointed by the Board of Control of the World's Columbian Commission.

Lady Managers.—President, Mrs. Potter Palmer, Chicago; Vice-Presidents, Mrs. Ralph Trautman, New York; Mrs. Edwin C. Burleigh, Maine; Mrs. Charles Price, North Carolina; Miss Katherine L. Minor, Louisiana; Mrs. Beriah Wilkins, D. C.; Mrs. Susan R. Ashley, Colorado; Mrs. Flora Beall Ginty, Wisconsin; Mrs. Margaret Blaine, Salisbury, Utah; Vice-President-at-Large, Mrs. Russell B. Harrison, Montana; Secretary, Mrs. Susan Gale Cooke, Tennessee.

The following were appointed by Commissioners-at-Large:

Mrs. D. F. Verdenal, New York; Mrs. Mary Cecil Cantrill, Kentucky; Mrs. Mary S. Lockwood, D. C.; Mrs. John J. Bagley, Michigan; Miss Ellen A. Ford, New York; Mrs. Mary S. Harrison, Montana; Mrs. Ida Elkins Tyler, Pennsylvania; Mrs. Rosine Ryan, Texas.

The following were appointed by Commissioners of the States:

Alabama.—Lady Managers: Miss H. T. Hundley, Mrs. A. M. Fosdick; Lady Alternates: Mrs. S. H. Bush, Mrs. I. W. Semple.

Arkansas.—Lady Manager: Mrs. R. A. Edgerton; Lady Alternates: Mrs. M. G. D. Rogers, Mrs. W. B. Empie.

California.—Lady Managers: Mrs. P. P. Rue, Mrs. J. R. Deane; Lady Alternates; Mrs. I. L. Requa, Mrs. Frona E. Wait.

Colorado.—Lady Managers: Mrs. L. P. Coleman, Mrs. S. R. Ashley; Lady Alternates: Mrs. A. B. Patrick, Mrs. M. D. Thatcher.

Connecticut.—Lady Managers: Miss F. S. Ives, Mrs. I. B. Hooker; Lady Alternates: Mrs. A. B. Hinman, Mrs. V. T. Smith.

Delaware.—Lady Managers: Mrs. M. R. Kinder, Mrs. J. F. Ball; Lady Alternates: Mrs. M. E. Torbert, Mrs. Theo. Armstrong.

Florida.—Lady Managers: Mrs. Mary C. Bell, Miss E. N. Beck; Lady Alternates: Mrs. Chloe M. Reed, Mrs. H. K. Ingram.

Georgia.—Lady Managers: Mrs. W. H. Felton, Mrs. C. H. Olmstead; Lady Alternates: Miss Meta T. McLaws, Mrs. George W. Lamar.

Idaho.—Lady Managers: Mrs. A. E. M. Farnum, Mrs. J. C. Straughan; Lady Alternates: Mrs. L. L. Barton, Mrs, E. R. Miller.

Illinois.—Lady Managers: Mrs. R. J. Oglesby, Mrs. F. W. Shepard; Lady Alternates: Mrs. M. L. Gould, Mrs. I. L. Candee.

Indiana.—Lady Managers: Miss Wilh. Reitz, Mrs. V. C. Meredith; Lady Alternates: Miss Susan W. Ball, Miss M. H. Krout.

Iowa.—Lady Managers: Mrs. W. S. Clark, Miss Ora E. Miller; Lady Alternates: Mrs. Ira F. Hendricks, Miss M. B. Hancock.

Kansas.—Lady Managers: Mrs. J. S. Mitchell, Mrs. H. A. Hanback; Lady Alternates: Mrs. Sara B. Lynch, Mrs. Jane H. Haynes.

Kentucky.—Lady Managers: Miss J. W. Faulkner, Mrs. A. C. Jackson; Lady Alternates: Miss S. F. Holt, Mrs. A. B. Castleman.

Louisiana.—Lady Managers: Miss Kath. L. Minor, Miss Jos. Shakespeare; Lady Alternates: Mrs. B. S. Leathers, Mrs. B. H. Perkins.

Maine.—Lady Managers: Mrs. E. C. Burleigh, Mrs. L. M. N. Stevens; Lady Alternates: Mrs. S. H. Bixby, Miss H. M. Staples.

Maryland.—Lady Managers: Mrs. Wm. Reed, Mrs. Alex. Thomson; Lady Alternates: Mrs. J. W. Patterson, Miss E. Roman.

Massachusetts.—Lady Managers: Mrs. Rufus H. Frost, Mrs. J. H. French; Lady Alternates: Mrs. A. F. Palmer, Miss M. C. Sears.

Michigan.—Lady Managers: Mrs. E. J. P. Howes, Mrs. S. S. C. Angeli; Lady Alternates: Mrs. F. P. Burrows, Miss A. M. Cutcheon.

Minnesota.—Lady Managers: Mrs. F. B. Clarke, Mrs. H. F. Brown; Lady Alternates; Mrs. P. B. Winston, Mrs. M. M. Williams.

Mississippi.—Lady Managers: Mrs. Jas. W. Lee, Mrs. J. M. Stone; Lady Alternates: Mrs. G. M. Buchanan, Miss Varina Davis.

Missouri.—Lady Managers: Miss Ph. Couzins, Miss L. M. Brown; Lady Alternates: Mrs. Patti Moore, Mrs. A. L. Y. Swart.

Montana.—Lady Managers: Mrs. E. Rickards, Mrs. C. L. McAdow; Lady Alternates: Mrs. Laura E. Howey, Mrs. M. D. Cooper.

Nebraska.—Lady Managers: Mrs. J. S. Briggs, Mrs. E. C. Langworthy; Lady Alternates: Mrs. M. A. B. Martin, Mrs. L. A. Bates.

South Carolina.—Lady Managers: Mrs. E. M. Brayton, Miss F. Cunningham; Lady Alternates: Miss C. A. Perry.

South Dakota.—Lady Managers: Mrs. J. R. Wilson, Mrs. H. M. Barker; Lady Alternates: Mrs. M. Daniels, Mrs. M. J. Gaston.

Tennessee.—Lady Managers: Mrs. L. Gillespie, Mrs. S. G. Cooke; Lady Alternates: Mrs. C. Mason, Mrs. B. B. McClung.

Texas.—Lady Managers: Mrs. I. L. Turner, Mrs. M. A. Cochran; Lady Alternates: Miss H. E. Harrison, Mrs. K. C. McDaniel.

Vermont.—Lady Managers: Mrs. E. M. Chandler, Mrs. E. V. Grinnell; Lady Alternates: Mrs. M. G. Hooker, Mrs. T. J. Cochrane.

Virginia.—Lady Managers: Mrs. J. S. Wise, Mrs. K. S. G. Paul; Lady Alternate: Miss M. P. Harris.

Washington.—Lady Managers: Mrs. M. D. Owings, Mrs. A. Houghton; Lady Alternates: Mrs. C. W. Griggs, Miss J. H. Stimson.

West Virginia.—Lady Managers: Mrs. W. N. Linch, Miss L. I. Jackson; Lady Alternates: Mrs. G. W. Z. Black, Miss A. M. Mahan.

Wisconsin.—Lady Managers: Mrs. F. B. Ginty, Mrs. W. P. Lynde; Lady Alternates: Mrs. S. S. Fifield, Mrs. J. Mont. Smith.

Wyoming.—Lady Managers: Mrs. F. H. Harrison, Mrs. F. E. Hale; Lady Alternates: Mrs. E. A. Stoue, Miss G. M. Huntington.

Nevada.—Lady Managers: Miss E. M. Russell, Mrs. M. D. Foley; Lady Alternate: Miss M. E. Davies.

New Hampshire.—Lady Managers: Mrs. M. B. F. Ladd, Mrs. Daniel Hall; Lady Alternates: Mrs. F. H. Daniell, Miss E. J. Coles.

New Jersey.—Lady Managers: Mrs. M. B. Stevens, Miss M. E. Busselle; Lady Alternates: Mrs. A. M. Smith, Mrs. C. W. Compton.

New York.—Lady Managers: Mrs. R. Trautman; Lady Alternates: Mrs. John Pope, Mrs. A. M. Palmer.

North Carolina.—Lady Managers: Mrs. F. H. Kidder, Mrs. Charles Price; Lady Alternates: Mrs. S. S. Cotton, Miss V. S. Divine.

North Dakota.—Lady Managers: Mrs. S. W. McLaughlin, Mrs. W. B. McConnell; Lady Alternates: Mrs. A. V. Brown, Mrs. F. C. Holley.

Ohio.—Lady Managers: Mrs. M. A. Hart, Mrs. W. Hartpence; Lady Alternates: Mrs. H. T. Upton, Mrs. A. S. Bushnell.

Oregon.—Lady Managers: Mrs. E. W. Allen, Mrs. M. Payton; Lady Alternates: Mrs. A. R. Riggs, Mrs. H. E. Sladden.

Pennsylvania.—Lady Managers: Miss M. E. McCandless, Mrs. H. A. Lucas; Lady Alternates: Mrs. Sam Plumer, Mrs. W. S. Elkins.

Rhode Island.—Lady Managers: Mrs. A. M. Starkweather, Miss C. F. Dailey; Lady Alternates: Mrs. G. A. Mumford, Miss L. P. Bucklin.

Alaska.—Lady Managers: Mrs. A. K. Delaney, Mrs. A. E. Austin; Lady Alternates: Miss M. Stevenson, Mrs. L. Vanderbier.

Arizona.—Lady Managers: Mrs. T. J. Butler, Miss L. Lovell; Lady Alternates: Mrs. G. Hoxworth, Mrs. H. J. Peto.

New Mexico.—Lady Managers: Mrs. F. L. Albright, Mrs. E. L. Bartlett; Lady Alternates: Miss Lucia Paria, Mrs. F. G. Campbell.

Oklahoma.—Lady Managers: Mrs. F. H. Harrison, Mrs. Gen. Guthrie; Lady Alternates: Mrs. J. Wallace, Mrs. M. S. McNeal.

Utah.—Lady Managers: Mrs. T. A. Whalen, Mrs. M. B. Salisbury; Lady Alternates: Mrs. S. B. Emery, Miss M. Keogh.

District of Columbia.—Lady Managers: Mrs. J. A. Logan, Mrs. B. Wilkins; Lady Alternates: Mrs. E. D. Powell, Miss E. C. Wimsatt.

By the President of the Commission.—From Chicago—Lady Managers: Mrs. B. M. H. Palmer, Mrs. S. Thatcher, Jr., Mrs. J. A. Mulligan, F. Dickinson, M.D., Mrs. M. R. M. Wallace, Mrs. M. Bradwell, Mrs. J. R. Doolittle, Jr., Mrs. M. B. Carse.

WYOMING.—A Northwestern State, admitted to the Union July 10, 1890; area, 97,890 square miles; population in 1890, 60,705. Capital, Cheyenne.

Government.—The following were the State officers during the year: Governor, Amos W. Barber (former Secretary of State; J. E. Osborne, elected Nov. 8, 1892, to fill vacancy caused by resignation of Francis E. Warren, took office Dec. 2, 1892); Secretary of State, Amos W. Barber; Treasurer, Otto Gramm; Insurance Commissioner, C. W. Burdeck; Attorney-General, C. N. Potter; Adjutant-General, F. A. Stitzer; Chief Justice, H. V. S. Groesbeck; Superintendent of Public Instruction, S. T. Farwell.

Finances.—According to the report of the State Auditor, there was, on Sept. 30, 1891, a balance in the treasury of $53,927.79. Moneys from all sources deposited with the Treasurer during the year ending Sept. 30, 1892, $199,588.28. The total disbursements from the treasury for the year ending Sept. 30, 1892, were $139,427.05. Balance in the treasury Sept. 30, 1892, $115,950.

The amounts received from rentals and interest on the permanent funds are as follows for the year ending Sept. 30, 1892: Common school land income, $9,649.48; university land income, $229.62; buildings at State capital land income, $101.30; Blind, Deaf and Dumb Asylum, land income, $315.69; Uinta County Insane Asylum, land income, $682.73; Fish Hatchery land income, $30.56; total, $11,009.38.

In contrasting the Territorial and State expenditures, the auditor submits the following items:

The actual expenditures for the years 1891 and 1892 were $286,430.47; from which, for comparison with Territorial expense, there should be deducted State fees, not heretofore collected, years 1891 and 1892, $2,712.85; funds from State lands, 1891 and 1892, $27,868.69; the insane asylum expense assumed by the State in 1892, heretofore paid by the counties, was, during year ending Sept. 30, 1892 (9 months), $6,837.71; the items of State expense, additional, and not formerly a Territorial expense: Legislature, biennial session, $23,000; Judicial Department, two years, $36,000; Executive Department (Governor and Secretary), two years, $12,000) $108,419.25; basis for comparison, $178,011.42. The Territorial expense, net, years 1886 and 1887, was $111,575.85; difference for two years, $66,435.57; demand item of interest on State debt, not levied prior to 1887, amounting in two years to $38,400.

Education.—The enrollment of pupils in the schools of the State is as follows: For 1890, 7,875; 1891, 8,726; 1892, 9,426. The amount raised for school buildings throughout the State was, for 1890, $10,583.63; for 1891, $8,931.85; for 1892, $12,220.40. The amount paid teachers during that time was, in 1890, $88,859.59; in 1891, $108,757.66; in 1892, $124,721.42.

Taxes.—The sources of State tax for the year 1892, and assessed valuations, were as follows:

Railroad property, including Pullman cars, etc., $7,466,135.64; telegraph lines (Western Union Telegraph Company), $114,525.90; land and improvements, 6,289,089.95 acres, $6,998,296.19; town lots and improvements thereon, $5,966,424.88; cattle,

428,853 head, $4,654,379; horses, 78,286 head, $2,000,681; mules and asses, 1,858 head, $95,225; sheep and goats, 639,205 head, $1,204,787.50; swine and dogs, $8,247.50; clocks, watches, and jewelry, $45,973.50; musical instruments, $51,858.50; capital in merchandise and manufactures, $1.587,823; carriages and wagons, $180,118; moneys and credits after deducting debts, $663,280.91; stock in corporations, $306,299; insurance premiums, $5,794.95; farming utensils and mechanics' tools, $152,652; private libraries, $19,235; household furniture, not exempt, $126,904.75; other property, not herein enumerated, $608,857.91—total, $32,257,500.13.

There were returned for taxation in 1892, 97,860 head of cattle, and 5,721 head of horses fewer than in 1891, while of sheep the returns indicated a gain of 88,837.

Political.—The Republicans in May met in convention for the purpose of naming delegates to the National Convention. Every county of the State was represented. The delegates were not instructed, but were all for the renomination of President Harrison. In regard to the presence of women it was declared:

We hail with pleasure the presence of ladies in this convention as accredited delegates, and the Republican party cordially and earnestly invites the women of the State to participate in the conventions of the party.

In September a Republican State Convention was again held, for the purpose of nominating candidates for governor, a justice of the Supreme Court, a representative in Congress, and three Presidential electors.

The platform adopted declared:

In the administration of our State affairs we are opposed to all class legislation and are in favor of the equal and exact enforcement of all the laws of the State. The equal and full protection of life and property, and the equal fostering and encouragement of every industry.

We favor the cession of the arid lands to the State, subject to the homestead laws, with such legislation as will secure maximum benefits to the people and prevent the accumulation of such lands in large tracts in the hands of single individuals or corporations, and with power to lease the same in small tracts to actual settlers.

The following was the ticket chosen: For Governor, Edward Ivinson; Justice of the Supreme Court, Carroll H. Parmelee.

The Prohibition party convention, which met in May, nominated William Brown for Governor. The Democratic and People's parties combined, naming as candidate for Governor John E. Osborne. The Democratic platform, adopted April 15, included these passages:

We arraign the National Republican party for its pursuance of a ruinous public policy, detrimental to the general welfare of the great laboring and producing masses of the people of the United States. We denounce the appropriations of the 51st Congress as a reckless and extravagant expenditure of public money, and we demand strict economy in the management of governmental affairs.

At the election in November the Democratic and People's candidate was successful. The vote for Governor was as follows: Republican, 7,509; Democrat and People's, 9,290; Prohibitionist, 4,210. For Judge of the Supreme Court the vote was: Republican, 7,671; Democratic and People's 9,240. On the national ticket, the Republicans cast 8,454 for Harrison electors, while the Democratic and People's party cast 7,722 for Weaver electors.

When the newly-elected Democratic Governor, John E. Osborne, attempted to take office on Dec. 2, 1892, some difficulty was experienced.

He reached the executive office only through a window, which had been forced open by a carpenter. Gov. Barber, meanwhile, former Secretary of State and acting governor, declared that he would not resign until his successor produced his certificate of election and regularly qualified.

Y

YACHTING.—In the " Annual Cyclopædia " for 1885 was published a condensed but comprehensive article on " Yachting," reviewing its development to that time—the immediate occasion being the first of three international races which greatly stimulated popular interest in the sport.

The year 1886 saw a race between the "Galatea" and the "Mayflower," and 1887 one between the "Thistle" and the "Volunteer," the Americans winning handsomely in both instances.

It was certainly remarkable that such noteworthy success should attend first efforts in the direction of designing and building large sloops. The "Puritan" and the "Priscilla" were so evenly matched in the trial race of 1885 that there was room for difference of opinion as to which was the better boat. The "Puritan" was chosen, however, and brought into prominence the name of her designer, the late Edward Burgess, of Boston, whose subsequent work in the "Mayflower" and the "Thistle," as well as in a large fleet of other vessels, placed him easily at the head of American designers.

During all these years American sloops and English cutters had been modifying one another in model and rig. The sloop had grown deeper and narrower, and the cutter had grown broader and shallower, but the sloop retained her distinctive center-board, and, as we have seen, maintained her supremacy in all the international contests. The center-board, too, at first ruled out by British yacht clubs, at last won its way to recognition, and is now acknowledged as a legitimate nautical device by the Royal Yacht Racing Association rules.

A somewhat vexatious experience of challenges and races in three successive years convinced the managers of the New York Yacht Club that further modifications were necessary in the deed of gift. Accordingly, the cup was given back to Mr. Schuyler, and a third deed was drawn with great care, intended to cover all possible points of controversy. It need not here be quoted except in two of its specifications; namely, the "dimension clause" and the "mutual agreement clause." The first of these requires that a challenge must be filed ten months in advance of the intended races, and must give length and beam on load-water line, and extreme draught, the dimensions not to be exceeded, under certain specified penalties. The mutual agreement clause reads : "The club challenging for the cup and the club holding the same may, by mutual consent, make any arrangements satisfactory to both, as to dates, course, number of trials, rules and sailing regulations, and any and all other conditions of the match ; in which case also the ten months' notice may be waived."

The provisions of this deed called out so much denunciation that the New York Yacht Club deemed it best to announce that the conditions under which the cup races of 1885, 1886, and 1887 were sailed were still satisfactory, and that they were open to any challenge, but it must be positively understood that the winner must hold the cup under the new deed.

Obviously, these provisions were intended to be at once liberal and binding : liberal in the "mutual agreement cause," and binding in that no foreign club, having won it, should be permitted to guard the cup with new and possibly prohibitive conditions. At first, English yachting authorities declared that no British club could challenge under such conditions, and six years passed before the true intent of the deed became apparent to them. In November, 1892, however, Lord Dunraven challenged, with the consent of the Royal Yacht Squadron; and the challenge was duly accepted. His new cutter, the "Valkyrie," has not at this writing been authentically described, beyond her general dimensions.

She was designed by G. L. Watson, and is building on the Clyde, by Henderson & Co. Hardly was this news made public when it was announced that the Prince of Wales and A. D. Clark had each ordered large cutters. Lord Dunraven will therefore have at least three new rivals against which to test the merits of the "Valkyrie" before crossing the ocean.

A short time before the Dunraven challenge was made public, Royal Phelps Carroll, of the New York Yacht Club, challenged for an English trophy known as the Victoria Gold Cup, and for the Brenton's Reef Cups, which were captured by the "Genesta" when she was here in 1885. At the same time, he gave his order to the Herreshoffs, of Bristol, R. I., for an 85-foot cutter (the "Navahoe") with which to cross the ocean. These challenges have been ratified in due form. It was at first thought that Mr. Carroll's cutter would perhaps be called upon to serve as a cup defender, and her owner even expressed his willingness to forego his foreign voyage ; but within a very short time orders were placed with the Herreshoffs for two "cup-defenders,"and with Lawley, of Boston, for two more, so that there will be no fewer than four first-class single-stickers to compete for the honor of defending the cup. At this writing few details are known concerning these boats, but center-boards and keels with the latest improvements in outside ballast and the like will certainly be fully represented.

All these conditions point to an activity in yachting circles, on both sides of the ocean, such as has never before been witnessed.

INDEX TO VOLUMES XIII, XIV, XV, XVI, AND XVII.
1888-1892.

844   INDEX.

END OF VOLUME XVII.

Lightning Source UK Ltd.
Milton Keynes UK
UKHW012302171218
334172UK00012B/391/P